W9-CXY-980

PART IV: Enactment of Technology Strategy—Creating and Implementing a Development Strategy

Part IV examines the key stages and tasks involved in new product development, managing the interfaces between key functional groups in the product development process, the role of the project manager, and the link between product and business strategy. This part contains the following new cases: Improving the Product Development Process at Kirkham Instruments Corporation and We've Got Rhythm! Medtronic Corporation's Cardiac Pacemaker Business.

PART V: Conclusion: Innovation Challenges in Established Firms

The final part recapitulates the major theme and unifying thread running through the book, which is how to augment and develop the firm's capabilities for managing technological innovation. This part provides an integrated perspective on four key strategic management challenges in established firms: (1) exploiting opportunities associated with the core business, (2) exploiting new opportunities that often emerge spontaneously, (3) balancing the emphases on the first two challenges, and (4) stimulating strategic renewal. This part contains a new case, Intel Beyond 2003: Looking for Its Third Act.

STRATEGIC MANAGEMENT
OF TECHNOLOGY AND INNOVATION

FOURTH EDITION

STRATEGIC MANAGEMENT
OF TECHNOLOGY AND INNOVATION

FOURTH EDITION

Robert A. Burgelman
Stanford Business School

Clayton M. Christensen
Harvard Business School

Steven C. Wheelwright
Harvard Business School

McGraw-Hill
Irwin

Boston   Burr Ridge, IL   Dubuque, IA   Madison, WI   New York   San Francisco   St. Louis
Bangkok   Bogotá   Caracas   Kuala Lumpur   Lisbon   London   Madrid   Mexico City
Milan   Montreal   New Delhi   Santiago   Seoul   Singapore   Sydney   Taipei   Toronto

STRATEGIC MANAGEMENT OF TECHNOLOGY AND INNOVATION
Published by McGraw-Hill/Irwin, a business unit of The McGraw-Hill Companies, Inc.,
1221 Avenue of the Americas, New York, NY 10020. Copyright © 2004 by The McGraw-Hill
Companies, Inc. All rights reserved. No part of this publication may be reproduced or
distributed in any form or by any means, or stored in a database or retrieval system, without
the prior written consent of The McGraw-Hill Companies, Inc., including, but not limited to,
in any network or other electronic storage or transmission, or broadcast for distance learning.
Some ancillaries, including electronic and print components, may not be available to customers
outside the United States.

This book is printed on acid-free paper.

1 2 3 4 5 6 7 8 9 0 CCI/CCI 0 9 8 7 6 5 4 3

ISBN 0-07-253695-0

Editor in chief: *John E. Biernat*
Sponsoring editor: *Ryan Blankenship*
Editorial coordinator: *Lindsay Harmon*
Marketing manager: *Lisa Nicks*
Executive producer: *Mark Christianson*
Senior project manager: *Pat Frederickson*
Freelance project manager: *Rich Wright, Omega Publishing*
Production supervisor: *Gina Hangos*
Designer: *Kami Carter*
Photo research coordinator: *Kathy Shive*
Senior supplement producer: *Susan Lombardi*
Senior digital content specialist: *Brian Nacik*
Typeface: *10/12 Times Roman*
Compositor: *G & S Typesetters*
Printer: *Courier Kendallville*

Library of Congress Cataloging-in-Publication Data

Burgelman, Robert A.
   Strategic management of technology and innovation / Robert A. Burgelman, Clayton M.
Christensen, Steven C. Wheelwright.— 4th ed.
     p. cm.
   Includes index.
   ISBN 0-07-253695-0 (alk. paper)
   1. Technology innovations—Management.   2. New products—Management.   3. High
technology industries—Management.   I. Christensen, Clayton M.   II. Wheelwright, Steven
C., 1943–   III. Title.
HD45.B799   2004
658.5′14—dc21

                              2003054138

www.mhhe.com

ABOUT THE AUTHORS

ROBERT A. BURGELMAN is the Edmund W. Littlefield Professor of Management and Director of the Stanford Executive Program of the Stanford University Graduate School of Business. Professor Burgelman has taught strategic management at Stanford since 1981. Previously he was on the faculties of Antwerp University (Belgium), New York University, and Harvard Business School (as a Marvin Bower Fellow). He holds a licenciate degree in Applied Economics from Antwerp University and an M.A. in Sociology and a Ph.D. in Management of Organizations from Columbia University, where he studied as a European Doctoral Fellow (Ford Foundation) and ICM Fellow (Belgium). He also received an honorary doctorate from the Copenhagen Business School. Professor Burgelman's research concerns the role of strategy in firm evolution. He has studied, in particular, the strategic processes involved in and the adaptive consequences of internal corporate venturing, strategic business exit, and co-evolutionary lock-in. His current research focuses on complex strategic integration in multibusiness firms. His newest book is entitled *Strategy Is Destiny: How Strategy-Making Shapes a Company's Future* (Free Press, 2002). He is also co-author of *Inside Corporate Innovation* (Free Press, 1986) and has published numerous articles in leading academic and practitioner journals. Since 1989, he has served as co-editor of *Research on Technological Innovation, Management and Policy* (JAI Press). He has taught executive programs and led senior and top management seminars worldwide, for many leading companies. He currently serves on several boards of directors and advisory boards of private companies.

CLAYTON M. CHRISTENSEN is the Robert and Jane Cizik Professor of Business Administration at the Harvard Business School. His research and teaching interests center on the management of technological innovation and finding new markets for new technologies. Prior to joining the HBS faculty, Christensen served as chairman and president of CPS

Corporation, a materials science firm that he co-founded with several MIT professors. He holds a B.A. in economics from Brigham Young University; an M.Phil. in economics from Oxford University, where he studied as a Rhodes Scholar; and M.B.A. and D.B.A. degrees from the Harvard Business School. In various years, he and his co-authors have won awards given for the best articles published in *Harvard Business Review, MIT Sloan Management Review, Business History Review,* and *Production and Operations Management.* His book, *The Innovator's Dilemma,* received the 1997 Global Business Book Award for the best business book published that year. His most recent book is *The Innovator's Solution* (Harvard Business School Press, 2003). He serves as a consultant to the management teams of many of the world's leading corporations. He and his wife Christine are the parents of five children.

STEVEN C. WHEELWRIGHT is Baker Foundation Professor of Management at the Harvard Business School. At HBS, he is also the Senior Associate Dean, Director of Publication Activities, and the Chair of the Executive Committee for the Baker Library Academic Center. His teaching and research are focused on technology and operations management, with a special focus on effective new product development. Prior to his current appointment, Wheelwright served in a full-time volunteer position as the President of the London, England Mission of The Church of Jesus Christ of Latter-Day Saints. In that assignment he was responsible for 200 young men and young women serving as full-time missionaries in London and Southeast England. From 1970 to 2000, Wheelwright held academic appointments at INSEAD, the Stanford Graduate School of Business, and the Harvard Business School. He holds an M.B.A. and a Ph.D. from Stanford University, a B.S. from the University of Utah, and an Honorary Doctorate from Harvard University. His articles have appeared in *HBR, Management Science, ASQ,* and numerous other academic publications, and his books include titles in forecasting, new product development, operations strategy, and technology strategy. His newest book, *Pursuing the Competitive Edge: Strategy, Operations and Technology,* co-authored with Robert Hayes, Gary Pisano, and David Upton, will be published by Free Press in 2004. He serves as a Board Member for a number of significant organizations. He and his wife Margaret are the parents of five children.

CONTENTS

PART ONE

INTEGRATING TECHNOLOGY AND STRATEGY: A GENERAL MANAGEMENT PERSPECTIVE

TECHNOLOGICAL INNOVATION   13

CASE I-1
Elio Engineering, Inc.   13

READING I-1
Profiting from Technological Innovation:
Implications for Integration, Collaboration,
Licensing, and Public Policy   32

CASE I-2
Advent Corporation   49

READING I-2
How to Put Technology into
Corporate Planning   62

TECHNOLOGICAL INNOVATION AND STRATEGY   67

CASE I-3
Electronic Arts in 1995   67

CASE I-4
Electronic Arts in 2002   83

READING I-3
The Core Competence of the Corporation   102

READING I-4
What Is Strategy?   113

READING I-5
The Art of High-Technology Management   130

PART TWO

DESIGN AND IMPLEMENTATION OF TECHNOLOGY STRATEGY: AN EVOLUTIONARY PERSPECTIVE

TECHNOLOGICAL EVOLUTION   157

CASE II-1
Asymetric Digital Subscriber Line:
Prospects in 1997   157

READING II-1
Management Criteria for Effective
Innovation   172

CASE II-2
The Optical Components Industry:
A Perspective   179

CASE II-3
CIENA Corporation   189

READING II-2
Patterns of Industrial Innovation   202

READING II-3A
**Exploring the Limits of the Technology
S-Curve. Part I: Component Technologies**   208

READING II-3B
**Exploring the Limits of the Technology
S-Curve. Part II: Architectural Technologies**   227

CASE II-4
Hewlett-Packard's Merced Decision   233

READING II-4
**Customer Power, Strategic Investment,
and the Failure of Leading Firms**   245

CASE II-5
**Making SMaL Big: SMaL Camera
Technologies**   265

READING II-5
**Disruption, Disintegration and the
Dissipation of Differentiability**   278

INDUSTRY CONTEXT   303

CASE II-6
**The U.S. Telecommunications Industry:
1996–1999**   303

CASE II-7
Slouching Toward Broadband   318

CASE II-8
**The PC-Based Desktop Video-
Conferencing Systems Industry in 1998**   330

CASE II-9
SAP America   348

READING II-6
Crossing the Chasm—and Beyond   362

READING II-7
Competing Technologies: An Overview   368

CASE II-10
**Digital Distribution and the Music
Industry in 2001**   378

READING II-8
**Finding the Balance: Intellectual
Property in the Digital Age**   398

READING II-9
**Note on New Drug Development in the
United States**   410

CASE II-11
**Eli Lilly and Company: Drug
Development Strategy**   415

ORGANIZATIONAL CONTEXT   431

READING II-10
**Gunfire at Sea: A Case Study of
Innovation**   431

READING II-11
**Architectural Innovation: The
Reconfiguration of Existing Product
Technologies and the Failure of
Established Firms**   441

CASE II-12
Intel Corporation: The DRAM Decision   454

READING II-12
Strategic Dissonance   478

CASE II-13
Intel Corporation: Strategy for the 1990s   490

CASE II-14
Managing Innovation at Nypro, Inc.   501

READING II-13
**Intraorganizational Ecology of Strategy
Making and Organizational Adaptation:
Theory and Field Research**   511

CASE II-15
**Hewlett-Packard: The Flight of the
Kittyhawk**   529

READING II-14
**Meeting the Challenge of Disruptive
Change**   541

STRATEGIC ACTION   550

READING II-15
Strategic Intent   550

READING II-16
**Strategy as Vector and the Inertia of
Coevolutionary Lock-In**   562

CASE II-16
**Inside Microsoft: The Untold Story of
How the Internet Forced Bill
Gates to Reverse Course**   587

CASE II-17
Charles Schwab & Co., Inc., in 1999   592

CASE II-18
Amazon.com: Evolution of the E-Tailer   610

CASE II-19
Display Technologies, Inc. (Abridged) 629

CASE II-20
Rambus Inc. 642

PART THREE

ENACTMENT OF TECHNOLOGY STRATEGY—DEVELOPING A FIRM'S INNOVATIVE CAPABILITIES

INTERNAL AND EXTERNAL SOURCES OF TECHNOLOGY 671

READING III-1
The Lab That Ran Away from Xerox 671

CASE III-1
Du Pont Kevlar® Aramid Industrial Fiber 674

READING III-2
Transforming Invention into Innovation: The Conceptualization Stage 682

READING III-3
Technology Markets, Technology Organization, and Appropriating the Returns from Research 690

READING III-4
The Transfer of Technology from Research to Development 708

READING III-5
Absorptive Capacity: A New Perspective on Learning and Innovation 716

CASE III-2
NEC: A New R&D Site in Princeton 732

CASE III-3
Cisco Systems, Inc.: Acquisition Integration for Manufacturing 745

CASE III-4
PlaceWare: Issues in Structuring a Xerox Technology Spinout 762

READING III-6
Making Sense of Corporate Venture Capital 773

LINKING NEW TECHNOLOGY AND NOVEL CUSTOMER NEEDS 781

CASE III-5
Innovation at 3M Corporation 781

READING III-7
Note on Lead User Research 794

CASE III-6
What's the BIG Idea? 801

CASE III-7
Intel Corporation: The Hood River Project 816

READING III-8
Discovery-Driven Planning 838

READING III-9
Living on the Fault Line 846

INTERNAL CORPORATE VENTURING 869

CASE III-8
Cultivating Capabilities to Innovate: Booz Allen & Hamilton 869

CASE III-9
Cisco Systems, Inc.: Implementing ERP 877

CASE III-10
R. R. Donnelley & Sons: The Digital Division 889

CASE III-11
3M Optical Systems: Managing Corporate Entrepreneurship 902

READING III-10
Managing the Internal Corporate Venturing Process: Some Recommendations for Practice 915

READING III-11
Ambidextrous Organizations: Managing Evolutionary and Revolutionary Change 925

PART FOUR

ENACTMENT OF TECHNOLOGY STRATEGY—CREATING AND IMPLEMENTING A DEVELOPMENT STRATEGY

NEW PRODUCT DEVELOPMENT 957

CASE IV-1
Product Development at Dell Computer Corporation 957

READING IV-1
Communication Between Engineering and Production: A Critical Factor 970

READING IV-2
The New Product Learning Cycle 977

CASE IV-2
Eli Lilly: The Evista Project 990

CASE IV-3
Team New Zealand 1005

READING IV-3
Organizing and Leading "Heavyweight" Development Teams 1012

READING IV-4
The Power of Product Integrity 1023

BUILDING COMPETENCES/ CAPABILITIES THROUGH NEW PRODUCT DEVELOPMENT 1035

CASE IV-4
Braun AG: The KF 40 Coffee Machine (Abridged) 1035

READING IV-5
Creating Project Plans to Focus Product Development 1051

CASE IV-5
Improving the Product Development Process at Kirkham Instruments Corporation 1062

CASE IV-6
We've Got Rhythm! Medtronic Corporation's Cardiac Pacemaker Business 1076

READING IV-6
The New Product Development Map 1089

READING IV-7
Accelerating the Design-Build-Test Cycle for Effective New Product Development 1098

PART FIVE

CONCLUSION: INNOVATION CHALLENGES IN ESTABLISHED FIRMS

CASE V-1
Apple Computer, 1999 1110

CASE V-2
Intel Beyond 2003: Looking for Its Third Act 1127

READING V-1
Building a Learning Organization 1162

READING V-2
The Power of Strategic Integration 1174

Index 1183

PREFACE

Technology and innovation must be managed. That much is generally agreed upon by thoughtful management scholars and practitioners. But can the management of technology and innovation be taught and, if so, how? What concepts, techniques, tools, and management processes facilitate successful technological innovations? The answers to these and several related questions are of great interest to those academics and practitioners who concern themselves with organizations in which technology and innovation are vitally important. A quick overview of the evolution of *Strategic Management of Technology and Innovation* serves to underscore this.

In the United States, these concerns were heightened during the late 1970s and 1980s when it became clear that America no longer enjoyed supremacy as the world's technological superpower. Japan, Korea, Germany, and other European and Asian countries had made major inroads in industries once considered unassailable U.S. strongholds. At first it seemed that the challenge was mainly in the traditional, capital-intensive, heavy-manufacturing industries such as steel and automobiles. But during the 1980s and early 1990s, the challenge broadened to include machine tools, consumer electronics, many aspects of semiconductors, computers and telecommunications, aerospace, and some aspects of biotechnology.

Hayes and Abernathy's 1980 *Harvard Business Review* article, "Are We Managing Our Way to Economic Decline?" signaled the growing awareness in the United States that effective management of technological innovation was becoming a high-priority concern of U.S. business. During the 1980s and early 1990s, the importance of technological innovation for competitive advantage, at the level of both the firm and the country, spurred

research and the development of related teaching materials. Literally hundreds of universities, through their schools of engineering or business (or both), introduced or substantially expanded the management of technology and innovation as part of their curriculum and degree programs, as this field became a major topic of broad interest to students, managers, and academics. During the decade of the nineties, the first two editions of *Strategic Management of Technology and Innovation* contributed to the development of courses on this subject in many schools.

In the background of these anxiety-provoking industrial developments and calls-to-arms, however, a new revolution was already in the making: the digital revolution. The first step in the digital revolution was the radical impact of microprocessor technology on computing and communications. The enormous growth of the demand for microprocessor-based personal computers created two new technological giants during the mid-1980s—Microsoft and Intel—that spawned entirely new ecosystems comprising thousands of new high-technology companies providing complementary products.

The second step was the growing importance during the 1990s of digital networks for enterprise data communications, which created yet another new giant—Cisco—and also spawned a new ecosystem of new high-technology companies. These developments, in turn, enabled the emergence and fast growth of still other major information-processing companies such as enterprise software giants Oracle, SAP, Siebel Systems, and BEA Systems among many others.

The third step in the digital revolution was the enormous growth since the mid-1990s of the Internet, which also created new ecosystems and literally thousands of new companies including new types of players such as Netscape, Yahoo!, e-Bay, and Amazon.com. It is no exaggeration to say that the Internet has affected all industrial and commercial activity and is a "mega-change" rivaling the magnitude of the impacts of the introductions of the automobile, electricity, and the telephone.

The digital revolution once again put the United States at the center of technological innovation. But it also increased the strategic importance of technology and innovation for just about every company. Around the time of the publication of the third edition of *Strategic Management of Technology and Innovation,* Intel's Chairman Andy Grove predicted that by 2005 only companies that had adopted the Internet as a mission-critical technology would survive. In 2003, his prediction seems likely to be correct, which means that *all* companies have to address technology as a critical element in their strategic management.

Since 2001, the so-called dot-com meltdown has eliminated myriad Internet-related companies, and its painful aftermath is still being felt throughout the economy in 2003. But it has also had the healthy consequence of reconfirming the relevance of fundamental business principles (e.g., profits matter after all) and the importance of sound strategic management. While this shakeout continues, the digitization of telecommunications equipment, the adoption of digital broadband technologies, and the growth of wireless data and voice telecommunications also continue to unfold.

Another revolution, the long-anticipated biotechnological revolution, seems imminent. Building on the first gene-splicing techniques developed in 1973, practical applications of cloning technologies have dramatically gained in power during the late 1990s. Such developments and the published documentation of the complete human genome promise to revolutionize the pharmaceutical and health-care industries during the first half of the twenty-first century.

The fourth edition of *Strategic Management of Technology and Innovation* continues to reflect and address these revolutionary developments. Like its predecessors, this new edition aims to achieve two important goals. The first is to provide continuity and refinements in terms of conceptual approach. We think this is important because it allows instructors to build further on their intellectual capital investments, and it deepens their ability to consider new developments and strategy questions in a framework of cumulative knowledge development.

The second goal is to provide change in terms of teaching material in order to reflect the evolving reality of technological innovation in leading companies and industries. We think this is important to help instructors maintain their courses up-to-date and to stimulate their own interest as well as that of their students. Consequently, although the fourth edition maintains and enhances the conceptual framework developed for the third edition, much of the teaching material for the fourth edition is new. Many new cases and industry notes that have been developed during 2000–2003 are included in this edition.

OVERVIEW

The fourth edition of *Strategic Management of Technology and Innovation* continues to take the perspective of the general manager at the product line, business unit, and corporate levels. The book not only examines each of these levels in some detail, but also addresses the interaction among the different levels of general management—for example, the fit between product strategy and business unit strategy and the link between business- and corporate-level technology strategy.

The book's structure reflects a conceptual framework rooted in evolutionary theories of technology, strategy, and organization that became prominent during the 1990s and continue to spawn new research findings. Each part of the book starts with an introduction laying out an overall framework and offering a brief discussion of key tools and findings from existing literature. The remainder of each part offers a selected handful of seminar readings and case studies. Almost all of the cases deal with recent events and situations, including several that are concerned with the impact of the Internet. A few "classics" have been retained, however, because they capture a timeless issue or problem in such a definitive way that the historical date of their writing is irrelevant.

Part One, "Integrating Technology and Strategy: A General Management Perspective," discusses what the general manager needs to know to integrate technology with the firm's strategy and to assess the firm's capacity for innovation. It provides tools for examining the links between technology and firm strategy and for auditing the firm's innovative capabilities. The fourth edition strengthens this introductory part. It contains a new case on Elio Engineering, Inc., a fledgling design company trying to enter the automotive industry, and a new case on Electronic Arts in 2002.

Part Two, "Design and Implementation of Technology Strategy: An Evolutionary Perspective," discusses the substance of a technology strategy and the key external and internal forces that determine its evolution. In this part, we bring together new cases and recent advances in the academic literature on technological evolution, industry and competitive dynamics involving technology, interplays between technology and organizational context, and issues of strategic choice and intent. This part contains the following new cases and notes: "The Optical Components Industry: A Perspective," "CIENA Corporation," "Making SMaL Big: SMaL Camera Technologies," "Slouching Toward Broadband," "Digital Distribution and the Music Industry in 2001," "Managing Innovation at Nypro. Inc.," "Amazon.com: Evolution of the E-Tailer," and "Rambus, Inc."

Part Three, "Enactment of Technology Strategy— Developing a Firm's Innovative Capabilities," deals with key issues in implementing a technology strategy: internal and external technology sourcing and managing corporate innovation. The readings and cases in this part examine issues such as managing corporate R&D, strategic alliances, internal corporate venturing, and acquisitions. This part contains the following new cases: "Du Pont Kevlar® Aramid Industrial Fiber" and "What's the BIG Idea?"

Part Four, "Enactment of Technology Strategy— Creating and Implementing a Development Strategy,"

examines the key stages and tasks involved in new product development, managing the interfaces between key functional groups in the product development process, the role of the project manager, and the link between product and business strategy. This part contains the following new cases: "Improving the Product Development Process at Kirkham Instruments Corporation" and "We've Got Rhythm! Medtronic Corporation's Cardiac Pacemaker Business."

Part Five, "Conclusion: Innovation Challenges in Established Firms," recapitulates the major theme and unifying thread running through the book, which is how to augment and develop the firm's capabilities for managing technological innovation. This part provides an integrated perspective on four key strategic management challenges in established firms: (1) exploiting opportunities associated with the core business, (2) exploiting new opportunities that often emerge spontaneously, (3) balancing the emphases on the first two challenges, and (4) stimulating strategic renewal. This part contains a new case on Intel: "Intel Beyond 2003: Looking for Its Third Act."

ACKNOWLEDGMENTS

The fourth edition of *Strategic Management of Technology and Innovation,* like its predecessors, is inspired by the work of the many colleagues who have helped shape this dynamic and important field. We continue to be grateful to all our own teachers and current colleagues that have contributed to the perspective that informs our conceptual framework and choice of materials. We also want to thank the new scholars who have contributed directly to the materials in this fourth edition by letting us use their work, as well as our research associates and collaborators on the cases and industry notes. We are also grateful for the generous help of the anonymous colleagues who have provided insightful and helpful comments on the third edition so as to improve the fourth one.

Ultimately, the test of the value of teaching materials lies in their use in the classroom. Many hundreds of Stanford and Harvard M.B.A. students and executive education participants have helped us with that test. We thank them for their feedback and comments.

Robert Burgelman wants to express special thanks to Dr. Andrew S. Grove, Chairman of Intel Corporation, who has continued to be a valued colleague at Stanford Business School, and to Research Associate Philip Meza, who has co-authored many cases and notes. Clayton Christensen extends his gratitude to Professors Burgelman and Wheelwright, both of whom have been patient mentors who have profoundly influenced his understanding of technology and innovation management. His research associate Scott Anthony, representing the finest of the next generation of innovation scholars, has been consistently helpful and insightful. Steven Wheelwright extends his special thanks to Robert Burgelman and Clayton Christensen and many other colleagues who have carried on this work without his direct help so that he could serve in London in a full-time service role for a three-year period.

The fourth edition of *Strategic Management of Technology and Innovation* would not have been possible without the support of Stanford Business School and Harvard Business School. For Robert Burgelman, this has come through the ongoing support for his research and course development thanks to a large extent to the generous contributions of the school's alumni and friends. Steven Wheelwright and Clayton Christensen are similarly indebted to the students, alumni, and directors of research at the Harvard Business School, who have selflessly shared their ideas and resources.

As anyone who has completed a book-length manuscript knows, the final product is a team effort. This fourth edition would not have been completed without the help of Ryan Blankenship, our senior editor at McGraw-Hill, and the able assistance of Lindsay Harmon; Susan Supnet, Robert Burgelman's Administrative Assistant at Stanford Business School; and Christine Gaze at Harvard Business School.

Finally, a word of thanks to Rita Burgelman, Christine Christensen, and Margaret Wheelwright for their continued patience, understanding, and support.

A SPECIAL NOTE OF THANKS TO MODESTO ("MITCH") A. MAIDIQUE

As President of Florida International University, Mitch Maidique has assumed duties that have made it impossible for him to continue to participate in the development of *Strategic Management of Technology and Innovation.* Consequently, he graciously decided to withdraw as co-author for its fourth edition and welcomed Professor Clayton Christensen of Harvard Business School as a new co-author. In many ways, as a scholar and practitioner, Mitch was part of the founding team of the field of technology and innovation management. He made lasting contributions, as witnessed by the fact that this fourth edition still contains two seminal papers he co-authored. He has always combined the sharply honed mind of a physicist with the practical knowledge of a successful technological entrepreneur and institutional leader and with a real interest in and appreciation of the liberal arts. Mitch has also always been very generous in his recognition of the contributions made by other scholars. This rare combination of course made him the perfect university president. We thank him for getting this book started. We will do our best to keep it going with his high standards in mind.

1

INTEGRATING TECHNOLOGY AND STRATEGY: A GENERAL MANAGEMENT PERSPECTIVE

A key purpose of this book is to help the general manager—someone responsible for the overall strategic management of an organization or autonomous business unit—deal with issues of technology and innovation. Established high-technology companies typically spend at least 5 percent of sales on technology and innovation-related activities; start-up companies may spend significantly more. Although most of the companies studied here are considered high-technology, the issues and problems associated with technology and innovation in the environment of the 1990s are part of the general management task in *all* firms.

One key task of the general manager is to acquire, develop, and allocate an organization's resources. Technology is a resource of paramount importance to many organizations; managing this resource for competitive advantage entails integrating it with the firm's strategy. A second key task of the general manager is to develop and exploit the firm's capacity for innovation. This requires that the general manager be able to assess the firm's innovative capabilities and identify how they may be leveraged or improved. We provide here a set of tools the general manager can use to accomplish both of these major tasks.

Three sections follow. The first defines a set of key concepts concerning technological innovation and then outlines their interrelations. This step is important because strategic management of technology and innovation is a young field, and the domains of different, partly overlapping concepts are still somewhat in flux. Though we do not claim that the definitions and interrelations presented here are definitive, they are generally accepted by scholars and practitioners in the field, and they are useful for organizing the discussion of cases and readings that follows. The second section discusses the integration of technology with business and corporate strategy. The third section presents a framework for auditing and assessing the firm's innovative capabilities. A brief conclusion follows the third section.

KEY CONCEPTS AND THEIR RELATIONSHIPS

Inventions/Discoveries/Technologies

At the origin of the technological innovation process are inventions or discoveries. As Webster points out, "We discover what before existed, though to us unknown; we invent what did not before exist." Inventions and discoveries are the result of creative processes that are often serendipitous and very difficult to predict or plan. For instance, Aspartame, a sweetener used in many food and beverage products, was a chance discovery. Researchers in universities, the government, and industrial labs following the canons of modern science—as well as idiosyncratic tinkerers in a garage—play a role in these processes. *Basic* scientific research refers to activities involved in generating new knowledge about physical, biological, and social phenomena. *Applied* scientific research is geared toward solving particular technical problems. The cumulative body of systematic and codified knowledge resulting from scientific research forms

the substratum for many, but not all, inventions and discoveries (e.g., the wheel was not the result of scientific research).

The criteria for success regarding inventions and discoveries are technical (Is it true/real?) rather than commercial (Does it provide a basis for economic rents?). Through *patents,* inventions and discoveries sometimes allow their originators to establish a potential for economic rents with subsequent innovations (see below), but there may be a significant time lag (ten years or more) between doing scientific research and using the inventions and discoveries to create successful innovations (superconductivity and genetic engineering are examples).

Technology refers to the theoretical and practical knowledge, skills, and artifacts that can be used to develop products and services as well as their production and delivery systems. Technology can be embodied in people, materials, cognitive and physical processes, plant, equipment, and tools. Key elements of technology may be implicit, existing only in an embedded form (e.g., trade secrets based on know-how). Craftsmanship and experience usually have a large tacit component, so that important parts of technology may not be expressed or codified in manuals, routines and procedures, recipes, rules of thumb, or other explicit articulations. The criteria for success regarding technology are also technical (Can it do the job?) rather than commercial (Can it do the job profitably?). Technologies are usually the outcome of development activities to put inventions and discoveries to practical use. The invention of the transistor (1947), integrated circuit (1959), and microprocessor (1971), for example, gave rise to successive generations of new technologies in the semiconductor industry that were, in turn, applied in areas such as data processing and telecommunications.

Technological Innovations

Some innovations are technology based (e.g., disposable diapers, oversized tennis racquets, electronic fuel injection, and personal computers). Other innovations, such as new products or services in retailing and financial services, are facilitated by new technology (e.g., electronic data processing). The criteria for success of technological innovation are commercial rather than technical: A successful innovation is one that returns the original investment in its development plus some additional returns. This requires that a sufficiently large market for the innovation can be developed. Innovations are the outcome of the *innovation process,* which can be defined as the combined activities leading to new, marketable

EXHIBIT 1   The Relationships Among Key Concepts Concerning Technological Innovation

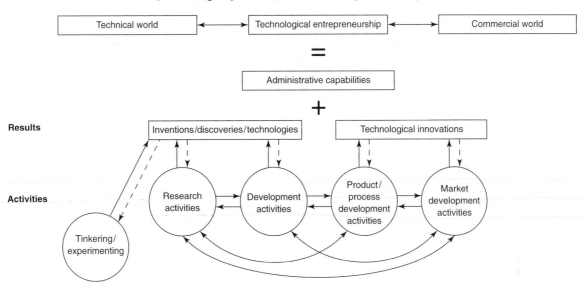

Different types of innovation have been identified in the literature. *Incremental* innovations involve the adaptation, refinement, and enhancement of existing products and services and/or production and delivery systems—for example, the next generation of a microprocessor. *Radical* innovations involve entirely new product and service categories and/or production and delivery systems (e.g., wireless communications). *Architectural* innovations refer to reconfigurations of the system of components that constitute the product (e.g., the effects of miniaturization of key radio components).

Technological Entrepreneurship

Entrepreneurship is a fundamental driver of the technological innovation process. *Technological entrepreneurship* refers to activities that create new resource combinations to make innovation possible, bringing together the technical and commercial worlds in a profitable way. Administrative capabilities must be deployed both effectively and efficiently. Technological entrepreneurship can involve one individual (*individual* entrepreneurship) or the combined activities of multiple participants in an organization (*corporate* entrepreneurship).

Activities and Outcomes

This discussion of key concepts suggests that it is useful to distinguish between activities and outcomes. Inventions, discoveries, and technologies (outcomes) are the result of tinkering and experimenting, as well as of sys-

tematic basic and applied R&D (activities). Technological innovations (outcomes) are the result of product, process, and market development (activities). Technological entrepreneurship involves product, process, and market development (activities) as well as the development of administrative capabilities.

Interrelations Among Key Concepts

Exhibit 1 shows the relationships among key concepts in the technological innovation process. It highlights the activities constituting the process and the outcomes produced. The process depicted in Exhibit 1 can start with market development or technical activities. In reality, the technological innovation process will almost always be iterative and concurrent rather than unidirectional and sequential.

INTEGRATING TECHNOLOGY AND STRATEGY

Perspectives on Strategy

Positive Versus Normative Views   The positive view of strategy is concerned with the firm's actual strategy and how it comes to be. The normative view, on the other hand, is concerned with what the firm's strategy should be.

The positive view of strategy proposes that the firm's strategy reflects top management beliefs about the basis of the firm's past and current success.[1] These beliefs

---

[1] See, for example, R. A. Burgelman, "Corporate Entrepreneurship and Strategic Management: Insights from a Process Study," *Management Science* 29 (1983), pp. 1349–64.

Positive ⇒ fact, what is
Normative ⇒ what it should be.

concern (*a*) core competencies, (*b*) product market areas, (*c*) core values, and (*d*) objectives, as well as associations among these elements and the firm's success. They can be viewed as the result of organizational learning processes. They drive top management's efforts to establish a strategic process that will take advantage of this organizational learning. Not surprisingly, there is likely to be a good deal of inertia associated with this set of beliefs.[2] Hence, to understand a firm's strategy, it is necessary not only to consider top management statements and assertions about the firm's strategy but also to observe what the firm actually does. Quite often, especially in the dynamic environments associated with high-technology firms, there is a divergence between professed strategy and strategic action.[3]

Product-Market Versus Resource-Based Views The product-market view of strategy is primarily concerned with how the firm competes with its products and services. The resource-based view of strategy is concerned primarily with how the firm can secure the factors needed to create the core competencies and capabilities that form the basis for establishing and sustaining competitive advantage. Strategy is inherently a function of the quantity and quality of a firm's capabilities. Strategy without capabilities has no force. On the other hand, capabilities without strategy remain aimless. Strategy asks the question "How do competencies and capabilities help create and sustain competitive advantage?" Strategy thus articulates the ways in which the opportunities that are created by the firm's capabilities can be exploited.

During the 1980s, normative views of product-market strategy received widespread attention. Porter's "five forces" and "generic strategies" frameworks offered tools for explaining why some industries are inherently more attractive than others, for understanding a firm's strategic position relative to that of its rivals, and for devising strategic actions that can affect the overall industry attractiveness and the strategic position of individual firms.[4] Normative statements about core competence and capabilities-based competition during the early 1990s indicate the growing prominence of the resource-based view of strategy.[5] Current normative work in strategy is oriented toward better integrating the product-market and resource-based views.

Connecting Technology and Strategy

During the 1980s, strategic management scholars began to recognize technology as an important element of business definition and competitive strategy. For instance, Abell identifies technology as one of three principal dimensions of business definition, noting "technology adds a dynamic character to the task of business definition, as one technology may more or less rapidly displace another over time."[6] Porter observes that technology is among the most prominent factors that determine the rules of competition.[7] Friar and Horwitch explain the growing prominence of technology as the result of historical forces: disenchantment with strategic planning, the success of high-technology firms in emerging industries, the surge of Japanese competition, a recognition of the competitive significance of manufacturing, and the emergence of an academic interest in technology management.[8]

But what, precisely, does a general manager considering the role of technology in a firm's strategy need to know? According to one school of thought, it is enough to understand the parameters transformed by the technological black box (the computer or instrument in question). That is, it is enough to know *what* the technological device or system does, not *how* it does it. An alternative view argues that unless one understands the functioning of a device and the laws that delineate its limitations, one cannot make effective judgments regarding the shaping of relevant technologies into successful products. The position taken in this book is that general managers need not have backgrounds in science or engineering, but they do need to invest significant effort in learning to understand the technologies important to their business. They must also identify reliable and trustworthy sources of technical advice. Most important, they must be able to frame the key strategic questions in relation to technology. The remainder of this section focuses on these key questions and discusses the tools necessary to examine

[2]R. A. Burgelman, "Intraorganizational Ecology of Strategy Making and Organizational Adaptation: Theory and Field Research," *Organization Science* 2 (1991), pp. 239–62.

[3]R. A. Burgelman, "Fading Memories: A Process Theory of Strategic Business Exit in Dynamic Environments," *Administrative Science Quarterly* 39 (1994), pp. 24–56.

[4]M. E. Porter, *Competitive Advantage* (New York: Free Press, 1985).

[5]C. K. Prahalad and G. Hamel, "The Core Competence of the Corporation," *Harvard Business Review,* May–June 1990; G. Stalk, P. Evans,

and L. E. Shulman, "Competing on Capabilities: The New Rules of Corporate Strategy," *Harvard Business Review,* March–April 1992.

[6]D. Abell, *Defining the Business* (Englewood Cliffs, N.J.: Prentice Hall, 1980).

[7]M. E. Porter, "The Technological Dimension of Competitive Strategy," *Research on Technological Innovation, Management, and Policy* 1 (1983), pp. 1–33.

[8]J. Friar and M. Horwitch, "The Emergence of Technology Strategy: A New Dimension of Strategic Management," *Technology in Society* 7 (1985), pp. 143–78.

how a firm's technology and business strategy can be integrated most effectively.

Technology and Competitive Strategy Porter's "generic strategies" concept is a widely used framework for classifying competitive strategies. The generic strategies are (*a*) industrywide differentiation, (*b*) focused differentiation, (*c*) industrywide cost leadership, and (*d*) focused cost leadership. Companies pursuing industrywide differentiation seek sustainable competitive advantage in a broad range of industry segments through offering products or services that are better than those of competitors in terms of quality, performance, features, delivery, support, and so on. Companies pursuing focused differentiation attempt to achieve similar sustainable competitive advantage in a narrow set of industry segments. One objective indication of having achieved differentiation is customers' willingness to pay a premium price. Companies pursuing industrywide cost leadership seek sustainable competitive advantage in a broad range of industry segments through offering at lower prices products or services that are comparable to those of competitors on the relevant set of dimensions that are of concern to customers. Companies pursuing focused cost leadership attempt to achieve similar sustainable competitive advantage in a narrow set of industry segments. To be viable, a company's cost leadership strategy must be based on possessing a lower delivered cost infrastructure.

Porter points out that technology strategy is a potentially powerful tool for pursuing each of the four generic strategies, but that each one requires a somewhat different technology strategy. Also, strategic decisions about both product and process (manufacturing) technology can serve the purposes of both the differentiation and cost leadership strategies. Process-related technology may be key to product performance and hence differentiation. During the early 1980s, for instance, manufacturing excellence allowed the Japanese DRAM manufacturers to differentiate their products along the quality dimension from those of many of the United States–based manufacturers. On the other hand, product-related technology may be the basis for lower cost. For instance, designing different models of cars in such a way that they can share major structural components (e.g., chassis) will lower the cost of the different models.

The link between technology strategy and generic competitive strategies is captured in Exhibit 2.

focused → narrow set of industry segments.

EXHIBIT 2 Technological Policies and Generic Competitive Strategies

	Generic strategy			
	Overall cost leadership	**Overall differentiation**	**Focus-segment cost leadership**	**Focus-segment differentiation**
	Technological policies			
Product technological change	Product development to reduce product cost by lowering materials content, facilitating ease of manufacture, simplifying logistical requirements, etc.	Product development to enhance product quality, features, deliverability, or switching costs	Product development to design only enough performance for the segment's needs	Product design to meet exactly the needs of the particular business segment application
Process technological change	Learning curve process improvement. Process development to enhance economies of scale	Process development to support high tolerances, greater quality control, more reliable scheduling, faster response time to orders, and other dimensions that improve the ability to perform	Process development to tune production and delivery system to segment needs in order to lower cost	Process development to tune the production and delivery system to segment need in order to improve performance

We are bad at this

Source: M. E. Porter, "The Technological Dimension of Competitive Strategy," *Research on Technological Innovation, Management, and Policy* 1 (1983), pp. 1–33.

EXHIBIT 3   The Product/Technology Matrix

	Product A	Product B	• • •	Product N
Technology 1 Technology 2 • • • Technology ∞	(*)			

Note: Each entry (*) should establish the firm's relative strength vis-à-vis the state of the art.
Source: Adapted from A. Fusfeld, "How to Put Technology into Corporate Planning," *Technology Review,* May 1978. Reprinted with permission from *Technology Review,* MIT Alumni Association, © 1978.

EXHIBIT 4 Developing the Technology Portfolio

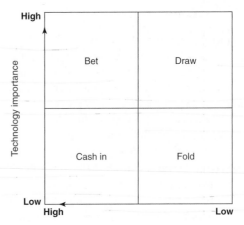

Source: J. M. Harris, R. W. Shaw Jr., and W. P. Somers, *The Strategic Management of Technology* (New York: Booz Allen Hamilton Inc., 1981).

Technology and Product-Market Strategy   A firm's strategy is expressed in the products and services it brings to market. One way to get at the integration of a firm's technology and product-market strategy is to decompose each product or service into its constituting technologies and assess the relative strength—the degree of distinctive competence—the firm has with respect to that technology. Exhibit 3 shows the outline for constructing a technology/product matrix.

Although Exhibit 3 is a first step in analyzing a firm's degree of integration, it is often difficult to specify the various technologies in the matrix at the appropriate level of detail and in their concrete relation to the firm's products. It is obvious that a firm manufacturing and marketing cameras should have competencies in optics, for instance. But it is not enough to determine the strength of the firm's capabilities; it is also necessary to specify how the firm's strengths in the area of optics help the firm's cameras have higher quality or lower cost.

Technology Portfolio   Harris, Shaw, and Somers suggest that once the various technologies have been identified, they can be classified in terms of their importance for competitive advantage.[9] Next, the firm's position relative to its competitors can be assessed. *Technology importance* needs to be expressed in terms of the value it brings to a particular class of products and the value it could potentially bring to other product classes for the customer/user. The importance of a particular technology is strongly affected by where it is situated in the technology life cycle (see p. 7). *Relative technology position* should be expressed in reference to competitors in terms

of, for example, patent position, know-how and trade secrets, learning curve effects, and key talent. Relative technology position is strongly (but not wholly) affected by the firm's historical and future levels of investment.

Exhibit 4 presents a framework based on these two dimensions. Harris, Shaw, and Somers propose that technologies in the "bet" quadrant warrant the firm's full commitment.[10] That is, the firm should be willing in those cases to engage in frontier R&D, push the limits of its product development process, and invest in the newest equipment.

Technologies in the "cash in" quadrant should be examined carefully. These technologies may have been very important at one time, but changes in the basis of competition in the industry may have reduced their relative importance. Understanding these changes and why they came about often leads to insight into the firm's strategic situation.[11] Also, while "cash in" might suggest that no further investment in these technologies is warranted, such a move may be premature or misguided. Sometimes parts of these technologies continue to be linked in subtle ways with other technologies judged to be relatively more important.

Technologies in the "draw" quadrant are also positioned ambiguously. A technology may be placed here because of changes in the basis of industry competition. In this case, the firm must decide whether to invest, prob-

[9] J. M. Harris, R. W. Shaw Jr., and W. P. Somers, *The Strategic Management of Technology* (New York: Booz Allen Hamilton Inc., 1981).

[10] Ibid.
[11] For example, see Burgelman, "Fading Memories," pp. 24–56.

EXHIBIT 5   Matching Business and Technology Portfolios

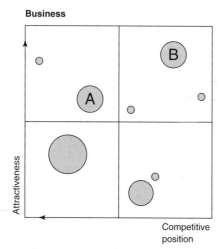
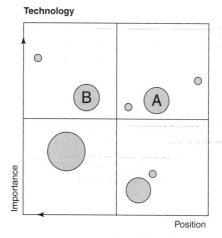

Source: J. M. Harris, R. W. Shaw Jr., and W. P. Somers, *The Strategic Management of Technology* (New York: Booz Allen Hamilton Inc., 1981).

ably heavily, in the technology so as to reach (at least) parity with its competitors or to disengage from a particular product or business. Again, it is extremely important to ask why and how this change came about.

Technologies in the "fold" quadrant require that the firm reconsider its investments in them. Inertial forces often lead to continued investment in R&D beyond the level at which reasonable returns can be expected. Regular reviews of investment patterns may indicate a need to disengage and redeploy resources.

Technology Portfolio and Business Portfolio   Many companies have multiple businesses in their corporate portfolios, each with its own technologies. Corporate strategy development has been enhanced by portfolio planning techniques, but most have failed to pay explicit attention to technology. One such portfolio planning tool is McKinsey's framework based on *industry attractiveness* and *competitive position* dimensions. Harris, Shaw, and Somers suggest examining the relationship between the traditional portfolio planning matrix and the technology portfolio matrix (see Exhibit 3).[12] This is presented in Exhibit 5.

Such analysis offers the possibility of investigating the match (or mismatch) between a firm's business and technology portfolios and its resulting technology investment priorities. For instance, standard strategic analysis may indicate that a particular business is in

a strong competitive position in an attractive industry. However, technological analysis may indicate that the technologies supporting this business, while important for competitive advantage, are actually in a relatively weak position. This would indicate the need to increase investment in technology development.

Technology and the Value Chain

In the broadest sense, the term *technology* encompasses the entire set of technologies employed in the sequence of activities that constitute a firm's value chain.[13] Exhibit 6 shows an example of various technologies in a firm's value chain.

As Porter points out, any of these technologies can affect the industry structure or a firm's differentiation or cost position—and, therefore, its competitive advantage.[14] Hence, it is important for the general manager to track the evolution of all the technologies that affect the firm's value activities. Designing a technology strategy (Part II of this book) requires that the firm decide (*a*) how each technology can be used for competitive advantage and (*b*) whether a given technology should be developed in-house or procured.

Technological Evolution and Forecasting

Technology Life Cycle   Technological change is one of the most important forces affecting a firm's competitive position, and research suggests that firms find it

---

[12] Harris et al., *The Strategic Management of Technology.*

[13] Porter, *Competitive Advantage.*
[14] Ibid.

EXHIBIT 6   Representative Technologies in a Firm's Value Chain

Transportation technology	Basic product technology	Transportation technology	Media technology	Diagnostic and testing technology
Material handling technology	Materials technology	Material handling technology	Audio and video recording technology	Communication system technology
Storage and preservation technology	Machine tool technology	Packaging technology	Communication system technology	Information system technology
Communication system technology	Material handling technology	Communication system technology	Information system technology	
Testing technology	Packaging technology	Information system technology		
Information system technology	Maintenance methods			
	Testing technology			
	Building design operation technology			
	Information system technology			
Inbound logistics	Operations	Outbound logistics	Marketing sales	Service

Source: Adapted with permission of the Free Press, a division of Macmillan, Inc., from M. E. Porter, *Competitive Advantage: Creating and Sustaining Superior Performance* (New York: Free Press, 1985). Copyright © 1985 by Michael E. Porter.

difficult to respond to such changes.[15] Integrating technology and strategy should, therefore, be a dynamic process, and it requires that the firm understand the dynamics of the life cycle of the various technologies it employs. Exhibit 7 shows the link between stages in the technology life cycle and the potential for competitive advantage.

Technology Forecasting   An important element in integrating technology and strategy is the capacity to perform systematic technological forecasting. Several authors have presented useful techniques, such as technological progress functions (S-curves), trend extrapolation, the Delphi method, and scenario development.[16] Underlying the capacity to forecast—and, perhaps more importantly, to see the relationships between technologically significant events—is the effort to gather data systematically and continuously. Maintaining a log book for this purpose is often effective.

ASSESSING INNOVATIVE CAPABILITIES

General managers are responsible for managing the innovation process. They must make difficult decisions about which innovations will receive managerial attention and resources. Insights into the firm's innovative potential and into the barriers to innovation are necessary to make effective proactive strategic choices. But how can general managers assess the innovation potential of their organizations? The remainder of this chapter offers a framework for doing an *innovative capabilities audit.*[17] Such an audit may help the general manager assess the potential of existing innovative capabilities and construct a development plan for the future. An audit must address at least three questions:

1. How has the firm been innovative in the areas of product and service offerings and/or production and delivery systems?
2. How good is the fit between the firm's current business and corporate strategies and its innovative capabilities?

[15]A. C. Cooper and D. Schendel, "Strategic Responses to Technological Threats," Business Horizons, February 1976, pp. 61–63; M. L. Tushman and A. Anderson, "Technological and Organizational Environments," Administrative Science Quarterly 31 (1986), pp. 439–65; R. Henderson and K. B. Clark, "Architectural Innovation: The Reconfiguration of Existing Systems and the Failure of Established Firms," Administrative Science Quarterly 35, no. 1 (1990), pp. 9–30; and Burgelman, "Fading Memories," pp. 24–56.
[16]See, for example, B. Twiss, *Managing Technological Innovation* (London: Longman, 1980); R. N. Foster, *Innovation: The Attacker's Advantage* (New York: Summit, 1986); and S. C. Wheelwright and

S. Makridakis, *Forecasting Methods for Management,* 5th ed. (New York: Wiley-Interscience, 1989).
[17]R. A. Burgelman, T. J. Kosnik, and M. Van den Poel, "Toward an Innovative Capabilities Audit Framework," in R. A. Burgelman and M. A. Maidique, eds., *Strategic Management of Technology and Innovation* (Homewood, Ill.: Richard D. Irwin, 1988).

EXHIBIT 7   Technology Life Cycle and Competitive Advantages

Stages in Technology Life Cycle	Importance of Technologies for Competitive Advantage
I. Emerging technologies	Have not yet demonstrated potential for changing the basis of competition.
II. Packing technologies	Have demonstrated their potential for changing the basis of competition.
III. Key technologies	Are embedded in and enable product/process. Have major impact on value-added stream (cost, performance, quality). Allow proprietary/patented positions.
IV. Base technologies	Have minor impact on value-added stream; common to all competitors; commodity.

Source: Adapted from Arthur D. Little, "The Strategic Management of Technology," *European Management Forum,* 1981.

3. What are the firm's needs in terms of innovative capabilities to support its long-term business and corporate competitive strategies?

Innovative Capabilities Audit Framework

Innovation depends on technological as well as other critical capabilities in areas such as manufacturing, marketing and distribution, and human resource management. For example, a technology strategy designed to achieve superior product performance must be complemented by a technically trained sales force that can educate the customer regarding the product's performance advantages and by a high-quality manufacturing system.

Innovative Capabilities   Innovative capabilities can be defined as *the comprehensive set of characteristics of an organization that facilitate and support innovation strategies.* Innovative capabilities exist at the business unit and corporate (multibusiness) levels.

- Business unit—a unit for which a particular strategy and resource commitment posture can be defined because it has a distinct set of product markets, competitors, and resources is a business unit. An innovative capabilities audit identifies the critical variables that influence the innovation strategies at this level.
- Corporate—an audit at this level identifies the critical variables that influence both the relationships between corporate and business unit levels in terms of innovative capabilities and the formulation and implementation of an overall corporate innovation strategy.

Business Unit Level Audit   In general, the innovative strategies at this level with respect to new products and services and/or new production and delivery systems can be characterized in terms of

- timing of market entry,
- technological leadership or followership,

- scope of innovativeness, and
- rate of innovativeness.

Five important categories of variables influence the innovation strategies of a business:

- Resources available for innovative activity
- Capacity to understand competitors' strategies and industry evolution with respect to innovation
- Capacity to understand technological developments relevant to the business unit
- Structural and cultural context of the business unit affecting internal entrepreneurial behavior
- Strategic management capacity to deal with internal entrepreneurial initiatives

These are represented in Exhibit 8.

EXHIBIT 8   Innovative Capabilities Audit Framework–Business Unit Level

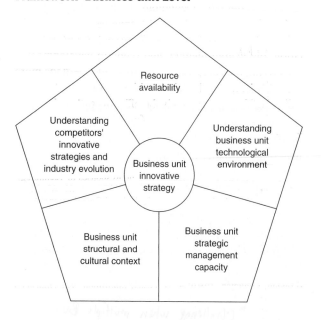

EXHIBIT 9   Innovative Capabilities Audit Framework–Business Unit Level

1. *Resource Availability and Allocation*
   - Level of R&D funding and evolution:
     – In absolute terms
     – As percentage of sales
     – As percentage of total firm R&D funding
     – As compared to main competitors
     – As compared to leading competitor
   - Breadth and depth of skills at business unit level in R&D, engineering, and market research
   - Distinctive competences in areas of technology relevant to business unit
   - Allocation of R&D to
     – Existing product/market combinations
     – New product development for existing product categories
     – Development of new product categories
2. *Understanding Competitors' Innovative Strategies and Industry Evolution*
   - Intelligence systems and data available
   - Capacity to identify, analyze, and predict competitors' innovative strategies
   - Capacity to identify, analyze, and predict industry evolution
   - Capacity to anticipate facilitating/impeding external forces relevant to business unit's innovative strategies
3. *Understanding the Business Unit's Technological Environment*
   - Capacity for technological forecasting relevant to business unit's technologies
   - Capacity to assess technologies relevant to business unit
   - Capacity to identify technological opportunities for business unit
4. *Business Unit Structural and Cultural Context*
   - Mechanisms for managing R&D efforts
   - Mechanisms for transferring technology from research to development
   - Mechanisms for integrating different functional groups (R&D, engineering, marketing, manufacturing) in the new product development process
   - Mechanisms for funding unplanned new product initiatives
   - Mechanisms for eliciting new ideas from employees
   - Evaluation and reward systems for entrepreneurial behavior
   - Dominant values and definition of success
5. *Strategic Management Capacity to Deal with Entrepreneurial Behavior*
   - Business unit level management capacity to define a substantive development strategy
   - Business unit level management capacity to assess strategic importance of entrepreneurial initiatives
   - Business unit level management capacity to assess relatedness of entrepreneurial initiatives to unit's core capabilities
   - Capacity of business unit level management to coach product champions
   - Quality and availability of product champions in the business unit

The first three categories just listed are important inputs for the *formulation* of business unit innovation strategies; the final two are important for the *implementation* of business unit innovation strategies. Exhibit 9 lists some of the critical issues for auditing each of the five categories. This list is not exhaustive; additional items may be added to reflect the particulars of different situations.

The combination of the five categories determines the relative strength of the business unit for formulating and implementing innovation strategies. Thus, the audit should address this as well. For example, a business unit may have ample resources for new product development but lack the strategic management capacity to channel these resources (both within the unit and relative to competitors' moves). Alternatively, the necessary resources and strategic management capacity may bring about new products whose technologies are on the verge of becoming obsolete.

Corporate Level Audit   The raison d'être of multi-business firms is based on corporate management's ability to identify and exploit synergies. An audit at the corporate level thus introduces an additional dimension. Here it is necessary to examine how the corporate innovative capabilities enhance the innovative capabili-

EXHIBIT 10 Innovative Capabilities Audit Framework—Corporate Level

ties at the business unit level. In other words, it is necessary to investigate whether and how the total corporate innovative capabilities are larger than the sum of the business units' innovative capabilities. In general, corporate level innovative capabilities can be characterized in terms of

- the scope and rate of development of new products and services and/or production and delivery systems that are derived from combining innovative capabilities across existing business units,
- the scope and rate of new business development based on corporate R&D and technology development efforts, and
- the timing of entry with respect to the previous two.

Again, five categories of variables are considered for the corporate level audit, each of which corresponds to a category at the business unit level but with a somewhat different emphasis: the capacity to do more than what the business unit could do on its own. Exhibit 10 represents the five categories of variables:

- Resource availability and allocation (e.g., corporate R&D, cash availability for risky projects)
- The capacity to understand multi-industry competitive strategies and evolution (e.g., corporate strategic planning for innovation)

- The capacity to understand technological developments (e.g., multi-industry scanning and technological forecasting)
- Corporate structural and cultural context
- Corporate strategic management capacity (e.g., exploitation of synergies in innovation through "horizontal" strategies; internal corporate venturing and acquisition strategies)

Resource availability and corporate level capacities to understand the competitive and technological environments again serve as inputs for corporate strategy formulation. Corporate structural and cultural context as well as corporate strategic management capacity serve as inputs for corporate strategy implementation. Exhibit 11 lists critical issues to be addressed in each category to carry out the corporate level audit. As for the business level audit, the combinatory effects of the five categories of variables on corporate innovation strategies should be assessed.

Audit Frames of Reference   One frame of reference for interpreting the results of the innovative capabilities audit is historical—how the current situation compares to the past; a second frame of reference concerns the firm's position relative to current competitors. Both allow major variances with respect to positions desired to be identified.

Who Should Do the Audit?   General managers will have to rely on others to collect much of the information necessary for the audit and for some of the interpretation as well. They will have to decide how much to rely on help from insiders and outsiders. Insiders are likely to have an advantage in understanding the firm's resource availability and structural and cultural context. Outsiders may provide a more realistic assessment of the firm's strategic management capacity and its ability to understand the competitive and technological environments. The major disadvantage of using insiders is the possibility of a narrow or biased perspective. Outsiders, on the other hand, are more likely to misunderstand internal realities and deliver impractical recommendations.

   The audit could be undertaken by the firm's strategic planning department. More valuable insights would probably be generated by setting up an ad hoc audit team with representatives from strategic planning, R&D, new product managers, and key functional managers.

EXHIBIT 11   Innovative Capabilities Audit Framework—Corporate Level

1. *Resource Availability and Allocation*
   - Corporate R&D funding level and evolution:
     - In absolute terms
     - As percentage of sales
     - As compared to average of main competitors
     - As compared to leading competitor
   - Breadth and depth of skills of corporate level personnel in R&D, engineering, and market research
   - Distinctive competences in areas of technology relevant to multiple business units
   - Corporate R&D allocation to
     - Exploratory research
     - R&D in support of mainstream business
     - R&D in support of new business definition
     - R&D in support of new business development
2. *Understanding Competitors' Innovative Strategies and Multi-Industry Evolution*
   - Intelligence systems and data available
   - Capacity to identify, analyze, and predict competitors' innovative strategies spanning multiple industries
   - Capacity to develop scenarios concerning evolution of interdependencies among multiple industries
   - Capacity to anticipate facilitating/impeding external forces relevant to firm's innovative strategies
3. *Understanding the Corporate Technological Environment*
   - Capacity for technological forecasting in multiple areas
   - Capacity to forecast cross-impacts among areas of technology
   - Capacity to assess technologies in multiple areas
   - Capacity to identify technological opportunities spanning multiple areas
4. *Corporate Context (Structural and Cultural)*
   - Mechanisms to share technologies across business unit boundaries
   - Mechanisms to define new business opportunities across business unit boundaries
   - Internal and external organization designs for managing new ventures
   - Mechanisms to fund unplanned initiatives
   - Evaluation and reward systems for entrepreneurial behavior
   - Movement of personnel between mainstream activities and new ventures
   - Dominant values and definition of success
5. *Strategic Management Capacity to Deal with Entrepreneurial Behavior*
   - Top management capacity to define a substantive long-term corporate development strategy
   - Top management capacity to assess strategic importance of entrepreneurial initiatives
   - Top management capacity to assess relatedness of entrepreneurial initiatives to the firm's core capabilities
   - Middle-level management capacity to work with top management to obtain/maintain support for new initiatives (organizational championing)
   - Middle-level management capacity to define corporate strategic framework for new initiatives
   - Middle-level management capacity to coach new venture managers
   - New venture managers' capacity to build new organizational capabilities
   - New venture managers' capacity to develop a business strategy for new initiatives
   - Availability of product champions to identify and define new business opportunities outside of mainstream activities

CONCLUSION

A variety of concepts, tools, perspectives, and roles are important and useful to the management of technology, strategy, and innovation. It is the premise of this book, however, that the *leadership* of general managers is critical to the success of these endeavors. Thus, while much can be done to assist general managers in these tasks, nothing can substitute for or replace their leadership. Throughout the subsequent text and cases, we will highlight not only analytical and organizational approaches, but also methods and techniques for asserting and exercising leadership.

TECHNOLOGICAL INNOVATION

Elio Engineering, Inc.

Hari Sankara and Harald Winkmann

ORIGIN OF ELIO ENGINEERING

As Paul Elio pulled into the parking lot of Bostrom Seating on a cold and damp Alabama morning in February 1999, he reflected on the events that had brought him there. Barely a few months back, he had not even heard of Bostrom Seating. At this moment the first meeting with the company was a distant memory.

Since 1996, Paul had been working on a revolutionary bike design for which he had received a patent. He had lined up investors for that venture and pushed the design along for two years, but the venture failed to take off.

Paul wanted to improve his financial position quickly so, in February 1998, he flew from his home in Phoenix to meet with his old employer in Michigan, automotive seat supplier Johnson Controls (JCI), to see if he could work as part of a product design team from his office in

Source: This case was prepared by Hari Sankara and Harald Winkmann, under the supervision of Professor Robert A. Burgelman as a basis for class discussion, rather than to illustrate either effective or ineffective handling of a management situation. Copyright © 1999 by the Board of Trustees of the Leland Stanford University. All rights reserved.

Phoenix. He loved Phoenix and had vowed never to return to the harsh winters of the Midwest. JCI management expressed reservations about his being part of a team in Michigan long distance. On his flight back to Phoenix, Paul drew a crude sketch of a new seat design, which was later named the *NC seat. NC* stood for "No Compromise," because the new seat design made possible simultaneous progress on cost, weight, and performance.

As a co-op student from the General Motors Institute, Paul had not found his stay at the Benchmarking Department of JCI very challenging. The Structural Design and Analysis Department held more appeal for him. There, he had seen computer simulations of automotive crashes and structural tests. These simulations, Paul had observed, would predict actual behavior and performance of the seats before they were even tested. He wanted to be able to do that. *Wanted to simulate*

Hari Sankara became his mentor in Structural Design and Analysis. Hari was impressed with Paul's academic achievement and his engineering talent. They developed a mutual admiration, which turned into a strong friendship. In 1997, after approximately nine years in the Structural Design & Analysis Department, Hari quit his job to pursue an MBA at the Stanford Business School.

Hari later joined the management-consulting firm Booz Allen Hamilton in Los Angeles as a summer associate. In July 1998, after his disappointing meeting at JCI, Paul called Hari about his sketch. Paul explained that his sketch represented a new concept for an automotive seat. They agreed to meet at a friend's place in Venice, California.

13

When Hari saw the aluminum prototype of the concept for the first time, he knew that he was looking at something special. Paul's seat was part of a special class of automotive seats in the industry called *all-belts-to-seat* (ABTS), wherein the shoulder belt and lap belt originate from the seat rather than from the auto body. Because the structural loads[1] on an ABTS seat are much higher than in a conventional seat, such seats had typically been very heavy and expensive. The entire automotive seating industry had been trying for years to find a cost-effective solution to the problem, and in the meantime they installed ABTS seats only in luxury automobiles and high-end sports convertibles. Paul's NC seat, however, utilized a new technology. The resulting structure would be low-cost, lightweight, and strong, thereby potentially permitting penetration of all segments of the auto market.

Paul and Hari entered into a partnership arrangement soon thereafter, founding Elio Engineering. At this point, Paul did not have any external sources of funding and squeaked by with personal resources and help from family. After his summer stint at Booz Allen, Hari worked out of Phoenix for a few weeks helping advance the design before returning to Stanford. Elio Engineering did not have the capital to develop the design using a build-and-test approach. The computers and software needed to simulate the tests were so expensive that only a few Fortune 100 companies could afford them. But in a stroke of fortune, at this very moment the price points came down. In addition, around this time the performance of PCs was enhanced and became comparable to that of expensive work stations, so computer-based testing had become affordable (PCs were priced at around $5,000 compared to $25,000 for work stations).

With a couple of functional prototypes and computer-aided structural analysis to back up their work, Paul and Hari set out to show the concept to the automotive seating industry. At this point Paul had not been working on his bike invention for six months. He had placed all his bets on the seat invention, and he was very anxious to reach an agreement quickly. Nevertheless, he and Hari were well aware of the enormous potential of the invention and were determined to get a fair value in any deal they would strike. While the auto companies greeted the invention with a lot of enthusiasm, Elio was unable to reach a financial deal, primarily due to the fact that a few of the critical items had not yet been patent protected and hence could not be revealed and because of some internal political issues.

Not deterred by the setback, Paul and Hari continued to advance the design and then approached Bostrom Seating. A seat supplier for the heavy truck and bus industry, Bostrom Seating was a wholly owned subsidiary of Johnstown America Industries, Inc. Elio had learned that Bostrom was looking to develop an ABTS seat. In November of 1998, Paul and Hari met with them and presented their seat. Soon thereafter they concluded an option agreement to prototype and test their NC seat.

The team became based at Bostrom's site, packaging and developing the seat to fit their environment. Bostrom signed a letter of intent with respect to a licensing agreement, which would follow successful prototype testing. By early 1999, Elio was able to support three full-time engineers with an advance against future royalties and prototype assistance from Bostrom. Bob Glaspie joined in as the third member of the Elio team after quitting his job at Structural Dynamics Research Corporation (SDRC). Prior to this, he had worked with Hari in the Structural Analysis Department at JCI. By February 1999, prototype tests had proven very promising, and the OEM (original equipment manufacturer) customer's response had also been favorable. In the option agreement, Bostrom had stipulated that the prototypes had to take 130 percent of the FMVSS loads. The first track prototypes withstood 92 percent of the load. In subsequent redesigns, the track and recliner parts of the seat withstood 185 percent and 115 percent of the FMVSS requirement. Based on the prototype performance, Bostrom made a licensing deal with Elio in mid-February.

Bostrom planned to unveil the NC seat at an annual trade show in March of 1999 in Louisville, Kentucky. While they had run into a few design-engineering challenges, the Elio team was confident that the NC seat would come together nicely for the March show. In fact, Bostrom intended to ramp up production very soon. The size of the U.S. truck market in 1999 was expected to be around 500,000 units with Bostrom commanding a market share of 50 percent. The European market was about the same size, but Bostrom had no presence there. Elio expected to be able to get 2 to 5 percent royalties on sales in the truck industry.

As Paul Elio got out of his car at Bostrom one month before the trade show, he was reflecting on his vision of bringing the seat to the entire automotive industry, potentially saving millions of lives around the world. He was wondering if Bostrom would be the right partner for such a gigantic task.

---

[1] Automotive seats have to meet FMVSS (Federal Motor Vehicle Safety Standard) specification 207/210, which calls for the seat to withstand 6,000 pounds without material breakage.

SEAT MECHANISM TECHNOLOGIES

Existing Seat Technologies

The seat system is a key component of a car interior. A typical conventional front seat is priced around $500 to OEMs. The cost of a conventional seat is lower than that of an ABTS seat. A complete seat system consisting of two front seats and a back row is an expensive standard part of a car (on average about $2,500).

Conventional Car Front Seat Technology The seat frame, recliner, and seat tracks (seat adjuster) are major components of a conventional car seat structure (Exhibit 1). Additional seat components are suspension, trim, and foam. These together constitute the seat system (Exhibit 2). The seat mechanism, consisting of recliner and tracks, constitutes the technological core of the seat system as it determines safety, ease of use, comfort, and, with the frame, about 60 percent of the total cost.

While some conventional seat mechanisms are electric, most are manual; that is, the seat is adjusted along the track by hand and reclined manually. Manual seat recliners are not infinitely adjustable and instead rely on interlocking gears. Most seats manufactured by U.S. com-

EXHIBIT 1 Seat Track (Adjuster; Top) and Seat Structure (Bottom)

EXHIBIT 2 Seat System

panies are built with single-sided recliners. The seat shoulder belt is attached directly to the door pillars and the floor, which, in the event of a crash, take much of the load off the seat.

Over the past couple of decades, conventional seat mechanism technology has not experienced any major breakthroughs, and innovation has been primarily incremental. All car seats have had to meet strict minimum safety standards determined in the United States by the National Highway Traffic Safety Administration (NHTSA) and be able to withstand specified minimum crash loads. While the conventional seat mechanisms on the market passed the NHTSA standards, they had a low strength-to-weight ratio, and the failure mode at the ultimate load was characterized by catastrophic failure. In other words, once the force reached the failure level, the stress on the seat system caused the seat material to break, fracture, or buckle, often resulting in fatal injuries to passengers.

The major benefits of conventional car seat technology are that the components and materials are relatively inexpensive, lightweight, and, after decades of accumulated experience with the technology, fairly easy to manufacture and assemble.

All-Belts-to-Seat (ABTS) Seat Mechanisms Over the past twelve to fifteen years, the major seat system and component suppliers, such as Johnson Controls, Lear, and Magna, have attempted to develop all-belts-to-seat seats. An ABTS seat integrates the seat belt directly into the seat (Exhibit 3).

According to feedback from focus groups and thousands of end users, the main, directly observable

EXHIBIT 3 ABTS Seat Frame (Left) and ABTS Seat System (Right)

advantages of existing ABTS designs over conventional seats are ease of use, higher comfort level, more attractive appearance, and better maneuverability of removable seats.[2] They are also potentially safer than conventional seats since the ABTS seat belt "hugs" the occupant in the event of a rear collision. In the case of a traditional belt attached to the pillar, on the other hand, the occupant recedes from the shoulder belt as he or she moves rearward in a rear impact.

However, seat manufacturers are still using fundamentally the same recliner and track concepts as for conventional seats. Since the force is no longer deflected to the pillars and the floor and instead is fully applied to the seat structure, the seat has to be much stronger to meet federal safety regulations.

ABTS designs have only been able to meet government regulations by using existing recliners in tandem and adding more metal to the seat mechanism and structure to scale up the strength. As a result, a typical ABTS seat is about twice as heavy as a conventional seat, and the cost of a typical ABTS seat is estimated to be more than 1.5 times higher than that of a conventional seat. ABTS seats are priced on average around $750 to OEMs.

In all, however, the ABTS system is superior to conventional systems, despite the cost. Bob Velanovich, JCI's V.P. for engineering, offered an additional advantage to ABTS technology:

We have considerable data demonstrating that our [ABTS seat] system passes all automakers and government safety specifications but I'm convinced the Number One reason these seats offer the opportunity for increased safety is because consumers will use seat-integrated safety belts more, since they fit better and feel better.[3]

Elio Engineering ABTS Technology

The Elio Engineering ABTS seat mechanism is a new state-of-the-art technology in the automotive seat industry. The broadly patented mechanism is based on cable and drum elements as opposed to gears.[4] The key benefit of the new technology is that it does not permit catastrophic failure. A special new load-leveling recliner mechanism[5] with a high strength-to-weight ratio ensures that the seat does not fracture or buckle at the failure level. When the force diminishes, the seat structure is still fully functional. This constitutes a major technological breakthrough that had been vigorously pursued for many years. In fact, when Elio met with auto executives, they confirmed that the seating industry had been unsuccessfully trying to design a load-leveling recliner for quite some time.

The design also uses fewer and lighter parts because it is a single-sided recliner. The Elio technology allows for the seat to be at least as light as a conventional seat. The

---

[2] "1996 Seat Quality Report," *J. D. Power and Associates;* David Sedgwick, "Focused on Customers," *Crain's Detroit Business,* March 25, 1996.

[3] James McCoy, "Next Advance: Belts That Are Part of the Seat," *Buffalo News,* March 31, 1996.

[4] The proprietary nature of the technology precludes Elio Engineering from revealing greater detail.

[5] In normal recliners, after the peak load (failure level) is reached, the load-carrying ability of the recliner drops to zero, which results in material fracture.

seat mechanism does not rely on gears and is infinitely adjustable both for manual and electric seats, which improves comfort and ease-of-use. The seat structure is also easy to assemble and does not require expensive high-tolerance parts. The technology improves user comfort by minimizing buzz, squeak, and rattle problems. Finally, the seat-belt retractor (the component containing the belt spool) in the Elio design is located at the bottom of the back frame, not at the top as is the case for other ABTS technologies. The belt is routed from bottom to the top, which reduces the load-carrying requirement of the back frame by approximately 20 percent. The whole design is sturdy enough that the seat structure was upon introduction to the market expected to outperform all other major ABTS technologies on the market. The NC seat is stronger, lighter, and cheaper due to the high strength-to-weight ratio of its mechanisms. Because its mechanisms are nicely packaged, the seat structure strength is not compromised. Additionally, the design simplicity results in fewer parts and connections, which in turn reduces the cost.

The NC seat innovation represents a major change in the technological trajectory of seat system technology. As a result, all follow-on technological improvements are expected to be incremental in nature.

INDUSTRY AND REGULATORY ENVIRONMENT

Customers

The ultimate user of the technology is the buyer of a new (or used) car. However, OEM customers of seat system suppliers make the buying decisions. The seat system not only needs to fit the body of a particular car model, but also is part of the "total interior design" of the car: the door panel, instrument panel, console, and headliner. The OEM provides suppliers with specs as to required type, structure size, and styling. Most OEMs used a sophisticated market segmentation of car purchasers based on demographic parameters, needs, and/or lifestyles and try to match the car interior accordingly. Currently positioned as a high-end seat, the ABTS seat is installed mostly in luxury and sports cars.

The OEM market is highly concentrated, and buyer power is enormous (Exhibit 4). In the North American market, the "Big Three" U.S. auto manufacturers, Ford, GM, and Daimler Chrysler, each has so much power that it has been able to squeeze the operating margins of major U.S. seat system suppliers (themselves often multibillion dollar companies) down to about 2 to 5 percent. With such an unfavorable bargaining position

EXHIBIT 4 U.S. 1998 Light Vehicle Market Share Total U.S. Sales: ~15 million units

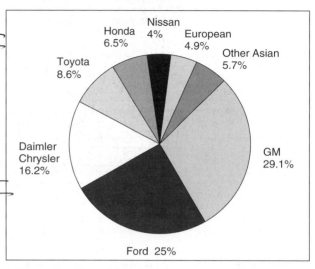

Source: Donaldson, Lufkin, & Jenrette.

for seat suppliers, it was of paramount importance to Elio not to reveal exact cost information to OEMs, such as through an overly simple design that could easily be reverse engineered.

OEMs prefer multiple sources of seat technologies and systems and often dictate that one leading tier-one supplier supply its competitor(s) with its seat technology, components, or systems. In the global market for seat systems, the situation is similar and expected to be reinforced in the future as OEM consolidation in the industry continues.

Although the weighting of the purchase criteria varies, the key criteria are generally safety, cost, reliability, and comfort and ease of use. Some OEMs consider the seat system so crucial that design and manufacturing of high-end seats for some car models are done in-house. OEMs are increasingly putting pressure on the incumbent suppliers to find cost-effective solutions for quality ABTS seat systems.

Potential Market Size for Elio ABTS Seat Technology

A few years ago when ABTS seats went beyond the advanced prototyping stage and first hit the market commercially, many industry experts predicted that the conventional seat would soon "go the way of the carburetor."[6] In 1996, for example, J. D. Power and Associates

---

[6] Michelle Krebs, "Integrated Seat-Belts for Sebring Convertible," *Winnipeg Free Press,* September 6, 1996.

EXHIBIT 5   Benefits of Adopting NC Seat *for who?*

Benefit	Rationale	Implication
OEMs share cost benefits	Reduced ABTS weight	Cost
Reduced R&D expense	NC seat is scaleable and portable across multiple platforms	Cost
Reduced inventory carrying costs	Fewer parts—less variability and less buffer stock to protect against stockout	Cost
Enhanced market position by being low cost producer	Improved business capture (including available conventional seat market in N. A. and Europe and new markets in Asia, Latin America, and Southern Europe); better margins	Cost/revenue
Decreased product liability issues	No catastrophic modes of failure; better energy management; ABTS seat advantages in rear impact	Cost
Decreased warranty issues	Fewer welds, fewer parts, and fewer fatigue problems	Cost
Increased leverage with OEMs	Sustainable competitive advantage with NC seat system—patent protected; OEMs *have* to come to supplier for NC seat	Revenue
Fewer production issues	Lower tolerance requirements; thinner gauge steel than most seats	Cost
Premium pricing	Innovative design features—zero-chuck (no looseness in the system), continuously variable and continuously engaged track and recliner mechanisms; high strength characteristics; enhanced safety	Revenue

called the Johnson Controls ABTS seat, known as the Integrated Structural Seat, "a major innovation that could replace conventional seats and seat belt systems on many future vehicles."[7] Also in 1996 the V.P. of sales and marketing for TRW, a supplier of conventional and ABTS seat-belt components, predicted that "looking out to the year 2000, we see 20 to 25 percent of the vehicles going to integrated seat-belts."[8] Experts anticipate that "in the next ten years, there probably won't be a seat supplier using conventional seat-belt systems except perhaps for specific vehicles like dump trucks. . . ."[9] Similarly, Johnson Controls claimed that belt-integrated seats would be the industry standard worldwide within ten years.[10]

However, the high cost of existing ABTS seats had so far limited the potential market size for ABTS technology to the high-end segments of the passenger car market. The total U.S. luxury segment of brands[11] had hit

unit sales of 2.16 million in 1997 and constituted about 15 percent of the total U.S. light vehicle market.[12]

On the OEM side, there was definite awareness of ABTS' benefits and strong latent demand for the technology. As early as 1994, Ford's executive director of the Automotive Safety and Engineering Standard's office, Robert Munson, predicted that ABTS seat systems would become standard and identified them as the key lever to improve people's safety:

> As an industry, we should pay more attention to seat belts. The next generation we're going to see will be seat belts that are part of the seat. . . . The shoulder-height attachment point automatically moves up and down as the seat is moved forward or back. That requires a much stronger seat and a more secure anchor but provides better fit.[13]

A seat system based on Elio's ABTS technology thus offered several strong benefits over existing models to

---

[7] "Automotive Seats from JCI Rank Highest in Quality, Appeal in J. D. Power and Associates Study," *PR Newswire,* November 11, 1996.
[8] Ron Turner in *ibid.*
[9] Ed Colasanti, product manager of seating systems for Findlay Industries, in *ibid.*
[10] "Automobile of the future," *Newsbytes News Network,* January 16, 1996.

[11] Defined as passenger vehicles with an average base price of more than $30,000 including sport-utility vehicles and luxury passenger cars but excluding several vans and high-price pickups.
[12] Jean Halliday, "Luxury SUVs Steal Some Horsepower from Rival Cars," *Advertising Age,* September 28, 1998.
[13] Jim Henry, "Ford Sees Simple Safety Solutions," *Automotive News,* June 6, 1994.

EXHIBIT 6   Global 1997 Vehicle Unit Sales by Region

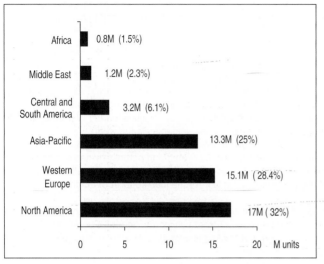

Africa — 0.8M (1.5%)
Middle East — 1.2M (2.3%)
Central and South America — 3.2M (6.1%)
Asia-Pacific — 13.3M (25%)
Western Europe — 15.1M (28.4%)
North America — 17M (32%)

0   5   10   15   20   M units

Source: 1998 Automotive News Data Book Supplement.

EXHIBIT 7   European 1997 Market Share in Automotive Seats
Total European Revenues: ~$7.5 Billion

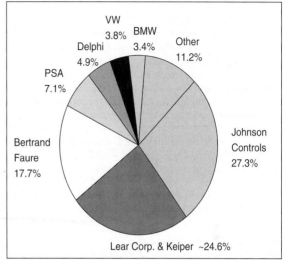

VW 3.8%
BMW 3.4%
Delphi 4.9%
Other 11.2%
PSA 7.1%
Bertrand Faure 17.7%
Johnson Controls 27.3%
Lear Corp. & Keiper ~24.6%

Source: Automotive News, Lear Corp., 1997 Form 10-K.

OEMs and end users (Exhibit 5). Given that it would also significantly reduce unit costs, the technology was expected to be very price competitive, appeal to a much wider share of the market, and, eventually, become the technology of choice for all OEM brands. This would suggest an annual market potential of up to 17 million units in North America or up to 53 million units worldwide (Exhibit 6). The technology could potentially penetrate the sizable heavy truck, aircraft, and passenger train markets.

Competitors

The North American automotive seating market was also highly concentrated. Two tier-one players, Johnson Controls Inc. (JCI) and Lear Corp. almost equally split about 60 percent of the market and had a dominant share worldwide. The number-three player, Magna, achieved about a 10 percent share in the United States (Exhibits 7, 8). With $12.6 billion (approximately $9 billion automotive) and $7.3 billion in sales, respectively, JCI and Lear were fairly large Fortune 500 companies. Exhibit 9 gives in-depth company profiles of the three leading tier-one suppliers, JCI, Lear, and Magna.

Many of the potential competitors already had an ABTS seat in their product portfolio or were currently working on the technology. Many smaller seat component suppliers were also designing or manufacturing ABTS seat mechanisms. However, the designs currently

EXHIBIT 8   U.S. Seat Systems: 1997 Market Share
Total Revenues: ~$8.2 Billion

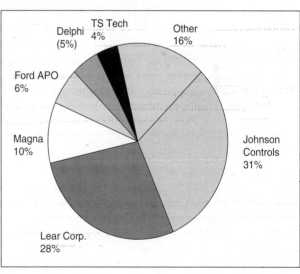

Delphi (5%)
TS Tech 4%
Other 16%
Ford APO 6%
Magna 10%
Johnson Controls 31%
Lear Corp. 28%

Source: Automotive News, Lear Corp., 1997 Form 10-K.

available on the market were not cost-effective solutions. While it was possible for a new technology to emerge at any time, numerous industry experts who had the opportunity to see Elio's design acknowledged that the Elio mechanism was a breakthrough innovation. It

EXHIBIT 9   Company Profiles

JOHNSON CONTROLS, INC.

Johnson Controls, Inc., a Wisconsin-based Fortune 500 company, is a global leader in supplying automotive seating and interior systems.

Automotive Systems Group

The Automotive Systems Group consists of its seating and interior systems business, which designs and manufactures complete automotive seating and interior systems for manufacturers of cars and light trucks, and its battery business, which produces automotive batteries for the replacement and original equipment markets. The business' seating systems products include seats, seating foam pads, mechanisms, metal frames, and trim covers. The business' interior systems products include overhead systems, door systems, floor consoles, and instrument panels; JCI specializes in the integration of electronics into vehicle interiors. Worldwide the business is among the top twenty automotive suppliers, with sales to the top ten automobile companies in the world.

In addition to having domestic operations, the seating and interiors business has operations in the Asia/Pacific region, Canada, Europe, Mexico, South America, South Africa, and Australia through wholly owned, majority-owned and partially owned businesses. JCI operates wholly owned and majority-owned manufacturing and assembly facilities in 137 locations worldwide. The business is the world's largest supplier of automotive seating systems and the largest independent North American supplier of automotive interior systems, subsystems, and components.

JCI's seating and interior systems business has grown significantly during the last several years. While the seating systems operations have expanded through internal growth, the interior systems growth has been fueled by vigorous strategic acquisitions. Seating and interior systems business sales represent approximately 90 percent of total segment sales. The Automotive Systems Group's battery business accounts for the remaining portion of the segment's sales.

Major Customers and Competition

Sales to JCI's major customers, as a percentage of consolidated net sales, were as follows for the most recent three-year period:

Customer	1998	1997	1996
Ford Motor Company	16%	17%	14%
General Motors Corporation	13%	13%	11%
Chrysler Corporation	10%	11%	10%

Source: Johnson Controls 10-K, December 1998.

Approximately 60 percent of the seating and interior systems sales over the last three years were to the three automobile manufacturers listed in the table. In 1998, approximately 75 percent of these sales were domestic, 15 percent were generated in Europe, and 10 percent were attributable to other foreign markets. New vehicle sales of major automotive manufacturers have a major impact on JCI's operations. Therefore, this business segment is affected by general business conditions in the automotive industry.

The business' seating systems operations principally compete in North America with Lear Corporation and Magna International, Inc. In Europe, the seating systems operations primarily compete with Lear Corporation, Faurecia, and automotive manufacturers. In North America, the business' interior systems operations compete with Lear Corporation; Davidson Interior Trim, a division of Textron, Inc.; UT Automotive, a subsidiary of United Technologies, Inc.; and Visteon, a division of Ford Motor Company. In Europe, the primary competitors are Lear Corporation and Sommer Allibert.

Financials

JCI has experienced strong growth in sales as well as operating and net income until end-of-year 1998. In fiscal year 1998, JCI earned $337 million on sales of $12.5 billion. This included a restructuring charge of $48 million, to be incurred in the aftermath of the Becker acquisition (discussed later).

JOHNSON CONTROLS, INC.
Annual income statement ($ millions)

	30-Sep-98	30-Sep-97	30-Sep-96	30-Sep-95	30-Sep-94
Sales—core business	12,586.8	11,145.4	9,210.0	7,400.7	6,870.5
Total sales	**12,586.8**	**11,145.4**	**9,210.0**	**7,400.7**	**6,870.5**
Cost of goods sold	10,776.2	9,485.6	7,878.3	6,236.0	5,762.0
SG&A expense	1,146.6	1,062.7	852.8	769.6	743.3
Unusual income/expense	0.0	70.0	0.0	0.0	0.0
Total expenses	**11,922.8**	**10,618.3**	**8,731.1**	**7,005.6**	**6,505.3**

	30-Sep-98	30-Sep-97	30-Sep-96	30-Sep-95	30-Sep-94
Interest expense, Non-operational	(133.5)	(122.7)	(73.4)	(53.7)	(40.7)
Other—net	86.3	21.2	16.0	(3.1)	1.9
Pre-tax income	**616.8**	**425.6**	**421.5**	**338.3**	**326.4**
Income taxes	256.0	180.9	171.8	143.0	140.3
Income after taxes	**360.8**	**244.7**	**249.7**	**195.3**	**186.1**
Minority interests	(23.1)	(24.1)	(27.0)	(27.3)	(20.9)
Preferred dividends	(9.5)	(9.5)	(9.5)	(9.4)	(9.3)
Net income (excluding E&D)	**328.2**	**211.1**	**213.2**	**158.6**	**155.9**
Discontinued operations	0.0	67.9	12.0	27.8	0.0
Accounting change	0.0	0.0	0.0	0.0	0.0
Net income (including E&D)	**328.2**	**279.0**	**225.2**	**186.4**	**155.9**
Primary EPS excluding E&D	3.88	2.53	2.58	1.93	1.90
Primary EPS including E&D	3.88	3.34	2.73	2.27	1.90
Dividends per common share	0.92	0.86	0.82	0.78	0.72
Shares to calculate primary EPS	84.5	83.5	82.6	82.3	82.0

JOHNSON CONTROLS, INC.
Annual balance sheet ($ millions)

	30-Sep-98	30-Sep-97	30-Sep-96	30-Sep-95	30-Sep-94
Assets					
Cash & equivalents	134.0	111.8	165.2	103.8	132.6
Accounts receivable	1,821.1	1,467.4	1,376.7	1,287.5	1,067.0
Inventory	428.2	373.4	344.7	355.5	304.7
Other current assets	1,020.9	576.7	962.5	317.1	274.2
Total current assets	**3,404.2**	**2,529.3**	**2,849.1**	**2,063.9**	**1,778.5**
Long-term investments	166.2	144.6	128.4	90.8	99.7
Property plant and equipment	3,652.0	3,100.1	2,618.5	3,041.5	2,669.2
Accumulated depreciation and amortization	(1,769.1)	(1,567.1)	(1,298.3)	(1,522.7)	(1,335.8)
Property plant and equipment, net	1,882.9	1,533.0	1,320.2	1,518.8	1,333.4
Goodwill/intangibles	2,084.5	1,560.3	548.2	519.1	493.8
Other long-term assets	404.3	281.4	145.3	128.3	101.5
Total assets	**7,942.1**	**6,048.6**	**4,991.2**	**4,320.9**	**3,806.9**
Liabilities					
Accounts payable	1,625.2	1,341.9	1,178.2	983.5	814.9
Short-term debt	1,289.5	537.8	248.1	130.2	19.2
Current LT debt and CLOs	39.4	118.4	33.2	67.7	24.8
Other current liabilities	1,334.3	974.6	723.1	728.1	657.5
Total current liabilities	**4,288.4**	**2,972.7**	**2,182.6**	**1,909.5**	**1,516.4**
Long-term debt	997.5	806.4	752.2	630.0	670.3
Total long-term debt	**997.5**	**806.4**	**752.2**	**630.0**	**670.3**
Deferred taxes	0.0	0.0	0.0	0.0	0.0
Other long-term liabilities	714.8	581.6	548.6	441.2	417.4
Total liabilities	**6,000.7**	**4,360.7**	**3,483.4**	**2,980.7**	**2,604.1**

EXHIBIT 9 (continued)

JOHNSON CONTROLS, INC.
Annual balance sheet ($ millions)

	30-Sep-98	30-Sep-97	30-Sep-96	30-Sep-95	30-Sep-94
Stockholders' equity					
Preferred stock	140.1	143.4	154.6	160.1	164.1
Common stock	14.5	14.4	7.2	7.1	7.1
Additional paid in capital	569.9	552.6	535.0	520.5	509.9
Retained earnings	1,463.3	1,217.9	1,010.7	853.3	730.7
Treasury stock	(138.6)	(121.0)	(70.0)	(62.1)	(62.4)
ESOP debt guarentee	(107.8)	(119.4)	(129.7)	(138.7)	(146.6)
Total shareholders' equity	**1,941.4**	**1,687.9**	**1,507.8**	**1,340.2**	**1,202.8**
Total liabilities and shareholders' equity	**7,942.1**	**6,048.6**	**4,991.2**	**4,320.9**	**3,806.9**
Shares outstanding	84.8	84.1	82.9	82.2	81.3

LEAR CORPORATION

Lear Corporation is a Fortune 500 company that was founded in 1917 as American Metal Products. Since its inception, it has been a supplier of automotive seat frames to GM and Ford. In 1988, Lear went through a leveraged buyout initiated by the company's management, which eventually accelerated growth and set the stage for an Initial Public Offering in 1994.

Since the LBO, Lear's revenue has experienced impressive growth up from $900 million to $7.34 billion in 1997. Lear moved beyond its expertise in seat frames and is now focusing on the U.S. market and United States–based OEMs through internal growth and acquisitions of various seat system and subsystem suppliers around the world. These acquisitions have boosted Lear's domestic and global market share and enabled the company to secure 28 percent in the United States and 18 percent share in the Western Europe seat system market. Through these acquisitions as well as through twenty-six joint ventures, Lear has also established a local presence in Russia, South Africa, Thailand, and China as well as obtained access to the Latin American market.

Lear now manufactures and supplies OEMs with complete automotive interiors, including floor and acoustic systems, door panels, instrument panels, and headliners. Lear is currently supplying twenty-seven OEMs of which the major customers are Ford, GM, Fiat, Daimler Chrysler, Volvo, Saab, Volkswagen, and BMW. Ford and GM accounted for approximately 29 percent and 27 percent, respectively, of the company's net sales. Over 40 percent of Lear's revenues are attributable to sales in the light truck category (see table).

Light Truck	Midsize	Compact	Luxury/Sport	Full Size
43%	21%	18%	12%	6%

Source: Form 10-K.

Lear's main capability lies in its strong systems integration skills, such as in seat systems and the entire automotive interior. As a result of integrating components from many different sources, the final system design may not always possess the highest conceptual integrity, but Lear may be more inclined to incorporate a brand-new innovative external technology into its seat systems.

Lear also has adequate global expertise in JIT manufacturing and an adequate ability to integrate acquisitions, although it is somewhat behind JCI in both. Strong resources such as good engineering talent and a customer-focused organizational structure contribute to Lear's competitive advantage. The strong customer focus of its organization and long-standing close relationships with OEMs allow Lear quickly to become aware of and address market needs. Its adequate JIT facility network helps the company and its customers achieve low-cost positions and deliver products to OEMs on short notice.

Financials

Lear has experienced strong growth in sales as well as operating and net income until end-of-year 1997 (see table). In December 1998, however, Lear announced a restructuring plan entailing the closure or consolidation of eighteen manufacturing facilities and a cut in the workforce of 2,800 employees, or 4 percent, "to improve Lear's cost structure and competitive positioning."

LEAR CORPORATION
Annual income statement ($ millions)

	31-Dec-97	31-Dec-96	31-Dec-95	31-Dec-94	31-Dec-93
Sales—core business	7,342.9	6,249.1	4,714.4	3,147.5	1,005.2
Total sales	**7,342.9**	**6,249.1**	**4,714.4**	**3,147.5**	**1,005.2**
Cost of goods sold	6,533.5	5,629.4	4,311.3	2,883.9	933.0
SG&A expense	286.9	210.3	139.0	82.6	27.7
Depreciation	41.4	33.6	19.3	11.4	4.8
Other operating expense	0.0	0.0	0.0	0.0	18.0
Total expenses	**6,861.8**	**5,873.3**	**4,469.6**	**2,977.9**	**983.4**
Interest expense, Non-operational	(101.0)	(102.8)	(75.5)	(46.7)	(24.8)
Other—net	(34.3)	(19.6)	(16.4)	(8.3)	(6.3)
Pre-tax income	**345.8**	**253.4**	**152.9**	**114.6**	**(9.3)**
Income taxes	143.1	101.5	63.1	55.0	13.5
Income after taxes	**202.7**	**151.9**	**89.8**	**59.6**	**(22.8)**
Minority interests	(3.3)	(4.0)	1.7	(0.5)	(0.1)
Equity in affiliates	8.8	4.0	2.7	0.7	(0.2)
Net income (excluding E&D)	***208.2***	***151.9***	***94.2***	***59.8***	***(23.0)***
Extraordinary items	(1.0)	0.0	(2.6)	0.0	(11.7)
Net income (including E&D)	***207.2***	***151.9***	***91.6***	***59.8***	***(34.7)***
Primary EPS excluding E&D	3.14	2.51	1.93	1.26	(0.65)
Primary EPS including E&D	3.13	2.51	1.87	1.26	(0.98)
Dividends per common share	0.00	0.00	0.00	0.00	0.00
Shares to calculate primary EPS (millions of shares)	66.3	60.5	48.9	47.4	35.5

LEAR CORPORATION
Annual balance sheet ($ millions)

	31-Dec-97	31-Dec-96	31-Dec-95	31-Dec-94	31-Dec-93
Assets					
Cash & equivalents	12.9	26.0	34.1	32.0	55.0
Accounts receivable	1,065.8	909.6	831.9	579.8	272.4
Inventory	231.4	200.0	196.2	126.6	71.7
Other current assets	304.8	211.8	145.0	79.9	34.4
Total current assets	**1,614.9**	**1,347.4**	**1,207.2**	**818.3**	**433.6**
Long-term investments	0.0	0.0	0.0	30.3	11.7
Property plant and equipment	1,380.6	1,176.7	860.4	504.5	361.5
Accumulated depreciation and amortization	(441.5)	(310.4)	(217.6)	(150.3)	(110.5)
Property plant and equipment, net	939.1	866.3	642.8	354.2	251.0
Goodwill/intangibles	1,692.3	1,448.2	1,098.4	499.5	403.7
Other long-term assets	212.8	154.9	112.9	12.8	14.4
Total assets	**4,459.1**	**3,816.8**	**3,061.3**	**1,715.1**	**1,114.3**

EXHIBIT 9 (continued)

LEAR CORPORATION
Annual balance sheet ($ millions)

	31-Dec-97	31-Dec-96	31-Dec-95	31-Dec-94	31-Dec-93
Liabilities					
Accounts payable	1,186.5	960.5	786.6	656.7	298.3
Short-term debt	37.9	10.3	16.9	84.1	48.2
Current LT debt and CLOs	9.1	8.3	9.9	1.9	1.2
Other current liabilities	620.5	520.2	462.6	238.5	158.1
Total current liabilities	**1,854.0**	**1,499.3**	**1,276.0**	**981.2**	**505.7**
Long-term debt	1,063.1	1,054.8	1,038.0	418.7	498.3
Total long-term debt	**1,063.1**	**1,054.8**	**1,038.0**	**418.7**	**498.3**
Deferred taxes	61.7	49.6	37.3	25.3	15.9
Other long-term liabilities	273.3	194.4	130.0	76.3	38.7
Total liabilities	**3,252.1**	**2,798.1**	**2,481.3**	**1,501.5**	**1,058.6**
Stockholders' equity					
Common stock	0.7	0.7	0.6	0.5	0.4
Additional paid in capital	851.9	834.5	559.1	274.3	156.6
Retained earnings	401.3	194.1	42.2	(49.4)	(109.2)
Treasury stock	(0.1)	(0.1)	0.0	0.0	0.0
Other equity	(46.8)	(10.5)	(21.9)	(11.8)	8.0
Total shareholders' equity	**1,207.0**	**1,018.7**	**580.0**	**213.6**	**55.6**
Total liabilities and shareholders' equity	**4,459.1**	**3,816.8**	**3,061.3**	**1,715.1**	**1,114.3**
Shares outstanding	66.9	65.6	56.2	46.1	34.5

MAGNA INTERNATIONAL, INC.

Magna International, Inc. is a leading global supplier of technologically advanced automotive systems. The company employs more than 49,000 people at 159 manufacturing divisions and 31 product development and engineering centers throughout North America, Europe, and Asia. Magna designs, engineers, and manufactures a complete range of exterior and interior vehicle systems. Magna has a focus on leading-edge technology and processes, with a stated minimum of 7 percent of EBIT invested in Research and Development. This investment paired with engineering, manufacturing, and distribution synergies among Magna's eight automotive business groups have made it one of the largest automotive parts manufacturers in the world.

Magna Interior Systems (MIS)

Magna Interior Systems is one of the world's largest full-service suppliers of integrated interior systems and components. The group's major products include seating, seat tracks, safety restraints, interior door panels, instrument panels, consoles, overhead systems, and package trays.

Financials

Magna has experienced strong growth in sales as well as operating and net income through end-of-year 1998. Consolidated sales increased to $9.2 billion. Net income was $454 million compared to $426 million in the previous year, excluding unusual gains (see table).

MAGNA INTERNATIONAL, INC.
Annual income statement (millions of Canadian dollars)

	31-Jul-98	31-Jul-97	31-Jul-96	31-Jul-95	31-Jul-94
Sales—core business	9,190.8	7,691.8	5,856.2	4,795.4	3,883.9
Total sales	**9,190.8**	**7,691.8**	**5,856.2**	**4,795.4**	**3,883.9**

	31-Jul-98	31-Jul-97	31-Jul-96	31-Jul-95	31-Jul-94
Cost of goods sold	7,582.5	6,366.2	4,811.2	3,855.7	3,085.5
SG&A expense	618.1	481.7	377.8	163.2	137.6
Depreciation	306.2	232.1	190.3	313.7	263.9
Interest expense	(2.9)	(16.5)	(4.3)	2.5	10.1
Other operating expense	(23.2)	(31.6)	(19.6)	(7.8)	(5.6)
Unusual income/expense	0.0	0.0	0.0	0.0	0.0
Total expenses	**8,480.7**	**7,031.9**	**5,355.4**	**4,327.3**	**3,491.5**
Other—net	54.2	189.6	0.0	17.0	0.0
Pre-tax income	**764.3**	**849.5**	**500.8**	**485.1**	**392.4**
Income taxes	245.7	232.5	162.3	156.4	140.1
Income after taxes	**518.6**	**617.0**	**338.5**	**328.7**	**252.3**
Minority interests	(12.4)	(13.6)	(19.3)	(11.7)	(17.9)
Miscellaneous earnings adjustment	(28.4)	(19.4)	(14.4)	0.0	0.0
Net income (excluding E&D)	**477.8**	**584.0**	**304.8**	**317.0**	**234.4**
Net income (including E&D)	**477.8**	**584.0**	**304.8**	**317.0**	**234.4**
Primary EPS excluding E&D	6.64	8.29	4.90	5.20	4.19
Primary EPS including E&D	6.64	8.29	4.90	5.20	4.19
Dividends per common share	1.29	1.14	1.08	1.08	0.81
Shares to calculate primary EPS	71.9	70.4	62.2	61.0	56.0

MAGNA INTERNATIONAL
Annual balance sheet (millions of Canadian dollars)

	31-Jul-98	31-Jul-97	31-Jul-96	31-Jul-95	31-Jul-94
Assets					
Cash & equivalents	1,019.6	878.8	1,089.8	413.9	205.0
Accounts receivable	1,801.9	1,165.0	927.2	670.6	546.7
Inventory	1,094.7	669.3	526.1	446.9	296.6
Prepayments & advances	75.6	34.9	24.3	29.9	15.5
Other current assets	0.0	0.0	0.0	0.0	0.0
Total current assets	**3,991.8**	**2,748.0**	**2,567.4**	**1,561.3**	**1,063.8**
Long-term investments	147.9	99.9	82.6	75.4	183.1
Property plant and equipment, other	3,737.9	2,071.1	1,509.5	1,304.7	940.0
Property plant and equipment, net	3,737.9	2,071.1	1,509.5	1,304.7	940.0
Goodwill/intangibles	464.6	297.8	126.5	89.8	67.5
Other long-term assets	278.5	111.9	91.3	78.6	56.2
Total assets	**8,620.7**	**5,328.7**	**4,377.3**	**3,109.8**	**2,310.6**
Liabilities					
Accounts payable	1,785.4	1,069.2	718.5	611.6	502.3
Short-term debt	301.6	44.5	52.9	92.0	44.1
Other current liabilities	808.7	466.6	286.7	306.5	203.8
Total current liabilities	**2,895.7**	**1,580.3**	**1,058.1**	**1,010.1**	**750.2**
Long-term debt	502.4	248.9	284.0	244.7	43.7
Total long-term debt	**502.4**	**248.9**	**284.0**	**244.7**	**43.7**

EXHIBIT 9 (continued)

MAGNA INTERNATIONAL
Annual balance sheet (millions of Canadian dollars)

	31-Jul-98	31-Jul-97	31-Jul-96	31-Jul-95	31-Jul-94
Other long-term liabilities	277.2	233.5	278.2	263.4	196.9
Total liabilities	**3,675.3**	**2,062.7**	**1,620.3**	**1,518.2**	**990.8**
Stockholders' equity					
Preferred stock	0.0	0.0	0.0	0.0	0.0
Common stock	2,189.5	1,569.3	1,464.4	952.1	942.6
Additional paid in capital	894.7	457.8	430.1	0.0	0.0
Retained earnings	1,697.8	1,302.3	798.3	561.8	325.2
Other equity	163.4	(63.4)	64.2	77.7	52.0
Total shareholders' equity	**4,945.4**	**3,266.0**	**2,757.0**	**1,591.6**	**1,319.8**
Total liabilities and shareholders' equity	**8,620.7**	**5,328.7**	**4,377.3**	**3,109.8**	**2,310.6**
Shares outstanding	77.3	70.1	68.5	60.3	59.7

JOHNSTOWN AMERICA INDUSTRIES, INC.

Johnstown America Industries, Inc. (JAII) is the parent company of Bostrom Seating. Through its subsidiaries, it designs and manufactures components and assemblies for medium and heavy-duty trucks and high-quality, complex iron castings for transportation-related and a variety of other markets. JAII conducts its business through three operating groups within the transportation industry: truck components and assemblies operations, iron casting operations, and freight car operations.

Truck components and assemblies

Gunite Corporation is a leading North American supplier of wheel-end systems and components such as brake drums, disc wheel hubs, spoke wheels, and rotors to OEMs in the heavy-duty truck industry. Gunite is a market leader in the production of automatic slack adjusters (braking devices mandated for all new trucks produced with air brakes since October 1994) and wheel-end components for anti-lock braking systems. In addition to serving OEMs, Gunite has significant sales to the less cyclical aftermarket. Bostrom Seating, Inc. (Bostrom) is a leading manufacturer of air suspension and static seating systems for the medium and heavy-duty truck and bus industries. Fabco Automotive Corporation (Fabco) is a leading supplier of steerable drive axles, gear boxes, and related parts for heavy on-/off-highway trucks and utility vehicles.

Bostrom seating

On January 13, 1995, JAII acquired Bostrom Seating. The total purchase price was approximately $32.4 million. Bostrom Seating designs, manufactures, and markets a full line of air suspension and static seating systems. Bostrom is ISO 9001 certified. Its products are sold primarily to the OEM heavy-duty truck market as well as to the aftermarket. It also supplies its seating systems to the medium-duty truck and bus markets. Bostrom's seats are offered as standard or as an option by all major North American heavy-duty truck manufacturers. Its top five customers accounted for 83 percent of Bostrom's 1997 net sales. Navistar accounted for approximately 30 percent of such sales (including both OEM and aftermarket sales). Bostrom is the leading market supplier for the supply of seating for new trucks, with an estimated market share in excess of 50 percent.

Bostrom sells its products through three distribution channels: direct installation in new vehicles by OEMs, stocking distributors, and truck dealers. It uses a combination of direct salespeople and independent sales representatives to service these market channels. Bostrom also sells directly and, by means of its stocking distributors, to a large number of smaller OEMs who produce specialty vehicles, buses, and construction equipment, among other things.

Bostrom's manufacturing facility is located in Piedmont, Alabama. For a number of its OEM customers, Bostrom ships its seats to line-setting facilities, which it has established near certain OEM plants to provide just-in-time inventory of seats to the assembly line in the order that the seats will be used.

Financials

During 1997, JAII's truck components and assemblies, iron castings, and freight car operations generated net sales of $284.7 million, $130.9 million, and $234.7 million, respectively. During 1996, they generated net sales of $237 million, $125.1 million, and $197.8 million, respectively. The significant decline in demand experienced in 1996 and early 1997 in freight car operations produced significant operating losses that, coupled with JAII's significant debt service requirements, offset strong operating income from its truck components and assemblies and iron castings operations. Although demand for freight cars has improved, the market remains subject to pricing pressures, uneven demand, and production overcapacity. See the table for selected financial data.

JOHNSTOWN AMERICA INDUSTRIES, INC.
Annual income statement ($ millions)

	31-Dec-97	31-Dec-96	31-Dec-95	31-Dec-94	31-Dec-93
Sales—Core Business	650.3	560.0	668.6	468.5	329.1
Total sales	**650.3**	**560.0**	**668.6**	**468.5**	**329.1**
Cost of goods sold	556.4	474.2	609.0	442.2	301.6
SG & A expense	46.2	46.6	28.1	13.1	11.3
Depreciation	8.6	10.2	6.5	3.6	3.7
Unusual income/expense	(15.1)	(1.4)	0.0	0.0	0.0
Total expenses	**596.0**	**529.6**	**643.6**	**458.9**	**316.7**
Interest net, non-operational	(35.4)	(35.8)	(14.7)	(0.3)	(3.0)
Other—net	0.0	0.0	0.0	0.0	0.0
Pre-tax income	**19.0**	**(5.4)**	**10.3**	**9.4**	**9.5**
Income taxes	9.5	(0.1)	4.7	3.7	4.1
Income after taxes	**9.5**	**(5.4)**	**5.6**	**5.7**	**5.4**
Net income (excluding E&D)	**9.5**	**(5.4)**	**5.6**	**5.7**	**5.4**
Extraordinary items	(2.0)	0.0	0.0	0.0	(2.9)
Net income (including E&D)	**7.5**	**(5.4)**	**5.6**	**5.7**	**2.5**
Primary EPS excluding E&D	0.96	(0.55)	0.57	0.58	0.66
Primary EPS including E&D	0.76	(0.55)	0.57	0.58	0.30
Dividends per common share	0.00	0.00	0.00	0.00	0.00
Shares to calculate primary EPS (millions of shares)	9.9	9.8	9.8	9.8	8.2

JOHNSTOWN AMERICA INDUSTRIES, INC.
Annual balance sheet ($ millions)

	31-Dec-97	31-Dec-96	31-Dec-95	31-Dec-94	31-Dec-93
Assets					
Cash & equivalents	30.9	24.5	11.6	1.8	7.1
Accounts receivable	60.5	49.3	60.0	32.5	26.8
Inventory	58.7	49.6	43.9	48.0	17.9
Prepayments & advances	4.0	3.2	8.8	1.0	1.8
Other current assets	13.5	16.1	14.2	0.0	0.0
Total current assets	**167.6**	**142.8**	**138.4**	**83.2**	**53.7**
Property plant and equipment	153.7	145.9	137.8	39.8	32.6
Accumulated depreciation and amortization	(40.3)	(26.5)	(13.2)	(7.3)	(4.6)
Property plant and equipment	4.7	4.5	4.1	0.9	0.9
Property plant and equipment, net	118.1	123.9	128.8	33.5	28.8
Goodwill/intangibles	243.2	251.7	259.5	17.3	21.0
Other long-term assets	50.0	36.9	52.1	9.4	4.4
Total assets	**578.8**	**555.3**	**578.8**	**143.4**	**108.0**
Liabilities					
Accounts payable	55.2	43.3	39.6	44.8	29.0
Current LT debt and CLOs	4.8	17.2	16.8	0.0	0.0
Other current liabilities	58.6	55.0	57.3	13.4	9.1
Total current liabilities	**118.7**	**115.6**	**113.7**	**58.2**	**38.1**

EXHIBIT 9 (continued)

JOHNSTOWN AMERICA INDUSTRIES, INC.
Annual balance sheet ($ millions)

	31-Dec-97	31-Dec-96	31-Dec-95	31-Dec-94	31-Dec-93
Long-term debt	307.5	286.9	313.0	7.6	0.0
Total long-term debt	**307.5**	**286.9**	**313.0**	**7.6**	**0.0**
Deferred taxes	36.4	29.2	28.1	0.0	0.0
Other long-term liabilities	45.3	60.0	55.1	14.3	12.7
Total liabilities	**507.8**	**491.7**	**510.0**	**80.1**	**50.7**
Stockholders' equity					
Common stock	0.1	0.1	0.1	0.1	0.1
Additional paid in capital	55.1	55.0	55.0	55.0	54.0
Retained earnings	15.9	8.4	13.8	8.2	2.5
Other equity	(0.0)	(0.0)	(0.0)	(0.1)	0.6
Total shareholders' equity	71.0	63.5	68.9	63.2	57.2
Total liabilities and shareholders' equity	**578.8**	**555.3**	**578.8**	**143.4**	**108.0**
Shares outstanding	9.8	9.8	9.7	9.7	9.3

was expected to have a cost and functionality advantage over competing technologies for some time to come.

JCI and Lear, however, had significant economies of scale, such as in manufacturing and distribution. In addition, their large global presence allowed them to establish fairly strong relationships with major OEMs, which provided them with fast and easy access to OEMs for new products.

JCI, in particular, was renowned for its design and manufacturing expertise. It had a reputation for being able to handle complex manufacturing challenges on a large scale. Its just-in-time (JIT) capabilities allowed it to become the supplier of choice of Japanese automakers. JCI had excellent seat system and total car interior engineering capabilities and strong expertise in concurrent engineering and software tools. Its ability to manage the seat system development from concept to production for the OEMs also provided it with a competitive advantage.

JCI was strong at effectively integrating strategic acquisitions into its organizational structure. It was thus heavily vertically integrated, whereas Lear was inclined to outsource more of the design and manufacturing work and merely act as a seat "systems integrator." For Lear, strong supplier networks were thus critical success factors. Other smaller suppliers tended to focus on niche markets for seats and/or specialize in certain seat components.

While there were several suppliers with ABTS seats, OEMs preferred to deal with as few as possible (but more than one). Since there was currently no clearly superior ABTS technology on the market, the two large incumbents had the advantage of leveraging their existing relationships and distribution networks for their ABTS products.

Barriers to Entry (BTE)

Incumbents were categorized into tier-one, tier-two, and tier-three suppliers. In general, a new entrant faced fairly low BTE at the tier-three supplier level or below. Hundreds of small to medium component suppliers by and large possessed no significant sustainable competitive advantage over new entrants.

Tier-one suppliers, on the other hand, enjoyed huge scale advantages in manufacturing and distribution. Moreover, they were at the far end of the learning curve in terms of design, development, and, above all, manufacturing processes. At least for standard products and incremental innovations, this provided them with a significantly lower cost position and a shorter time to market. Moreover, their strong ties to the OEMs constituted a positional advantage that was almost impossible to replicate for a new entrant. OEMs strongly preferred dealing directly with only a very limited number of tier-one suppliers, and they emphasized reliability and standardized processes, such as through stringent supplier certification norms.

It was possible, however, for a tier-two supplier with innovative technologies to be rewarded through new contracts directly with an OEM. Meritor Automotive Inc.'s Seat Adjusting Systems, for example, had developed an ABTS seat mechanism that was one of the lightest and most easily packaged of its type in the industry. In 1998, it was selected by General Motors to supply the OEM with 100 percent of the power and manual seat adjusters for a new GM truck program. J. Douglas Lamb, V.P. and general manager of Meritor's Seat Adjusting Systems business, was pleased:

"We're very excited about this business and the opportunity to offer new seat adjuster technology. We're especially optimistic about our new All-Belts-To-Seats (ABTS) design and its potential new application."[14]

Visteon, a subsidiary of Ford Motor Company, was a captive supplier of automotive components (excluding seats). Ford had previously sold Visteon's seating business to a major tier-one. There were talks of an impending divestiture of Visteon, either through a sale to a major tier-one or a spin-off. In the latter case, Visteon with its deep pockets ($17 billion in revenues) might be interested in accessing new technologies to re-enter the seating market.

Nevertheless, it would be extremely difficult for a brand-new entrant to compete with the incumbents, particularly in manufacturing and distribution. In the design and development part of the value chain, however, entry barriers were somewhat lower. Increasingly, sophisti-

cated software applications facilitated the development process. For instance, they dramatically reduced the need for and increased the accuracy of initial prototyping. Recently, hardware and software costs had fallen dramatically. As a result, analysis that was challenging for large teams could now be performed by one or two skilled structural design engineers expert in the simulation and analysis applications.

A broad patent provided an innovator lasting protection. In general, a new entrant had at least two major options. The first was to enter the market as a tier-three or -two supplier of seat mechanisms or seat structures. To avoid major capital investments, manufacturing could be outsourced to one of the many seat components and systems manufacturers. The advantage of this strategy was that the new entrant could supply its technology to all tier-one suppliers. Moreover, the new entrant could keep greater control over its core ABTS technology. However, no capabilities were built in integrating complete seat systems. This could be a disadvantage as the new entrant was likely to receive a relatively small piece of the final product's total value-added compared to a tier-one supplier who in-sourced ABTS technology and integrated it into a complete seat system. Moreover, the lack of manufacturing and marketing expertise of a new entrant significantly increased the technological and market risk.

Alternatively, a new entrant could try to partner with one of the tier-one or tier-two suppliers or with an OEM and develop and market the seat in a joint venture or through a licensing agreement. While this strategy would provide the newcomer with substantial resources and significantly reduce technological and market risks, an exclusive partnership with a tier-one or OEM would limit the size of the total market for the new entrant. Moreover, it could leave the new entrant with less control over its core ABTS technology and, depending on its bargaining position, with a potentially lower margin.

Role of Upstream or Downstream Products or Firms

As discussed, in the United States there was basically an oligopoly of tier-one suppliers with direct access to the OEMs. Tier-two and tier-three suppliers of components and raw materials were numerous and had generally very little market power. There were exceptions, however, such as when OEMs insisted that tier-one suppliers source from certain tier-two suppliers to ensure access to a particular component or technology.

[14]Kevin Jost, "Meritor's Seat Adjusting Systems Allow Standardization," *Automotive Engineering,* May 1, 1998.

Regulatory Issues

Seat suppliers had to fulfill strict federal safety standards set by the NHTSA and codified in the Federal Motor Vehicle Safety Standards. They had to demonstrate the safety of their products by ensuring their seats would pass a multitude of stringent static and dynamic crash tests.

TECHNOLOGICAL BARRIERS AND RISKS

Bottlenecks to Commercializing the Technology

One major potential bottleneck for the Elio seat technology was federal safety requirements. At the prototyping stage, the Elio ABTS seat mechanism had passed the major structural test by a wide margin. Another potential bottleneck had its roots in material science: The Elio ABTS seat mechanism required the use of raw materials such as brake friction materials and some urethanes, and it remained to be seen how the latter would perform under extreme temperature conditions.[15] If there were major problems with the material, the functionality of the Elio mechanism would be jeopardized. Additional bottlenecks were large capital requirements if the seat were to be manufactured in-house, lack of Elio competencies in manufacturing and distribution, and getting access to OEMs. Stringent OEM seat design requirements, certification requirements and supplier preferences, and unknowns regarding end-user taste with respect to ABTS seats and seat styling could also become challenges. In potential partnerships with an incumbent supplier, the "not-developed-here" syndrome and political turf battles in the partner's organization could seriously hamper the joint technology development efforts.

Manufacturing Issues

In general, the manufacturing complexity and cost of a car seat is directly proportional to the number of parts, to the tolerance requirements, and to the strength of the material used. Manufacturing of ABTS components and seats based on existing technology was slightly more complex along these dimensions than was production of conventional seats. By this measure, the Elio ABTS technology compared very favorably, as it required fewer parts and lower strength materials, and it could accommodate lower tolerance requirements.

The major manufacturing issues for Elio Engineering as an independent entrant were that manufacturing was not its core competence and the fairly large capital requirements of building a new plant. The required manufacturing techniques, however, were by no means unusual; they included common processes such as stamping, pressing, welding, casting, and injection molding. A minor uncertainty existed with respect to a potential innovative substitution for the welding. An additional issue was having to quickly implement a JIT delivery system required of tier-one and certain tier-two suppliers. Concurrent engineering resulting in quick and efficient implementation-readiness for manufacturing would pose an additional challenge in the absence of early input of manufacturing expertise.

Relevant Supporting Technologies for Elio's ABTS Seat Mechanism

The main supporting technologies were concurrent engineering and material science. Concurrent engineering allowed the development team to understand technologies and products from a "manufacturability" standpoint during the early design stage and communicate product information to everyone involved in the product development process, including design, manufacturing, marketing, and management. It had become essential to achieve more robust designs, reduce development costs, facilitate implementation readiness, and decrease time-to-market. This required access to and skills in integrated CAD, CAM, and CAE software packages. Highly skilled analysts could achieve over 90 percent accuracy for seat structures designed with computer analysis and simulation.

Materials science was important for the Elio seat mechanism as it relied on somewhat more exotic materials. In practice, materials are often found by trial and error, although the process can be outsourced to material science specialists. The importance of manufacturing technology to ensure quality, remain cost-competitive, and enable JIT deliveries was discussed earlier.

CAPABILITIES REQUIREMENTS FOR PLAYERS IN AUTOMOTIVE SEATS AND COMPARATIVE COMPANY PROFILES

As discussed, companies need a variety of capabilities to compete successfully in automotive seat systems. Some of the key requirements for a leading tier-one supplier

---

[15]FMVSS specs require satisfactory performance at 66°C.

EXHIBIT 10 Comparative Capabilities Profile of Selected Players

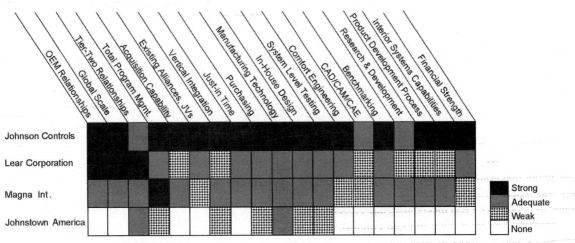

Source: 10-Ks, industry press, authors' analysis.

are strong relationships with OEMs and a large global presence and scale. The ability to manage the seat system development from concept to production for the OEMs as well as strong supplier networks are other critical success factors.

On the engineering side, concurrent engineering and in-house design and interior systems capabilities are crucial to achieve fast time-to-market as well as a low cost and high quality position. For similar reasons, state-of-the-art manufacturing technology as well as JIT capabilities are important. Vertical integration is critical in taking a systems approach to product development. On the other hand, systems integration capability is key for an external sourcing strategy.

Exhibit 9 provides a detailed company profile of Johnstown. Exhibit 10 compares four companies' capabilities with respect to seat systems.

JCI had a strong capability in almost every dimension crucial to success. In the few areas where it was not strong, JCI was in a better position relative to its competitors, with the exception of relationships with tier-two suppliers. While this factor was important for an external sourcing strategy, it was less significant in the vertical integration approach adopted by JCI.

It appeared that Lear could not quite match JCI's engineering and manufacturing capabilities. Nonetheless,

it compensated by executing superbly on systems integration, facilitated by its strong tier-two relationships. Since OEM relationships and global reach were by far the most important determinants of success in the tier-one supplier market, Lear could compete successfully with JCI.

While Magna did not lead in any one area, it exhibited adequate capabilities in most areas. Its relatively strong regional presence in Canada enabled it to carve out a slice of the market. Johnstown America was currently poorly positioned to compete as a tier-one supplier in the automotive market.

DECISION TIME

It was now February of 1999. In the past four months, the NC design had developed substantially. The Bostrom alliance agreement for the truck market had been concluded. The questions about Elio's strategy for entry into automotive still remained. Should Elio joint venture with Bostrom? Should it partner with a tier-one or a tier-two automotive supplier? Was Elio's technology strategy aligned with the requirements for a successful entry into the automotive market? Paul and Hari realized that they needed answers to these questions in the coming days.

READING I-1

Profiting from Technological Innovation: Implications for Integration, Collaboration, Licensing, and Public Policy

David J. Teece*

This paper attempts to explain why innovating firms often fail to obtain significant economic returns from an innovation, while customers, imitators, and other industry participants benefit. Business strategy—particularly as it relates to the firm's decision to integrate and collaborate—is shown to be an important factor. The paper demonstrates that when imitation is easy, markets don't work well, and the profits from innovation may accrue to the owners of certain complementary assets, rather than to the developers of the intellectual property. This speaks to the need, in certain cases, for the innovating firm to establish a prior position in these complementary assets. The paper also indicates that innovators with new products and processes which provide value to consumers may sometimes be so ill positioned in the market that they necessarily will fail. The analysis provides a theoretical foundation for the proposition that manufacturing often matters, particularly to innovating nations. Innovating firms without the requisite manufacturing and related capacities may die, even though they are the best at innovation. Implications for trade policy and domestic economic policy are examined.

INTRODUCTION

It is quite common for innovators—those firms which are first to commercialize a new product or process in the market—to lament the fact that competitors/imitators

*I thank Raphael Amit, Harvey Brooks, Chris Chapin, Therese Flaherty, Richard Gilbert, Heather Haveman, Mel Horwitch, David Hulbert, Carl Jacobsen, Michael Porter, Gary Pisano, Richard Rumelt, Raymond Vernon, and Sidney Winter for helpful discussions relating to the subject matter of this paper. Three anonymous referees also provided valuable criticisms. I gratefully acknowledge the financial support of the National Science Foundation under grant no. SRS-8410556 to the Center for Research in Management, University of California-Berkeley. Earlier versions of this paper were presented at a National Academy of Engineering Symposium titled "World Technologies and National Sovereignty," February 1986, and at a conference on innovation at the University of Venice, March 1986.
Source: Research Policy 15 (1986), pp. 285–305. © 1986 Elsevier Science Publishers B. V. (North-Holland).

EXHIBIT 1 Explaining the Distribution of the Profits from Innovation

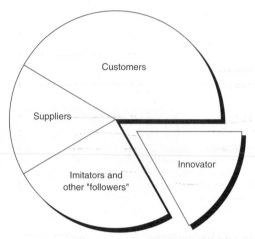

What determines the share of profits captured by the innovator?

have profited more from the innovation than the firm first to commercialize it! Since it is often held that being first to market is a source of strategic advantage, the clear existence and persistence of this phenomenon may appear perplexing if not troubling. The aim of this article is to explain why a fast second or even a slow third might outperform the innovator. The message is particularly pertinent to those science- and engineering-driven companies that harbor the mistaken illusion that developing new products which meet customer needs will ensure fabulous success. It may possibly do so for the product, but not for the innovator.

In this paper, a framework is offered which identifies the factors which determine who wins from innovation: the firm which is first to market, follower firms, or firms that have related capabilities that the innovator needs. The follower firms may or may not be imitators in the narrow sense of the term, although they sometimes are. The framework appears to have utility for explaining the share of the profits from innovation accruing to the innovator compared to its followers and suppliers (see Exhibit 1), as well as for explaining a variety of interfirm activities such as joint ventures, coproduction agreements, cross distribution arrangements, and technology licensing. Implications for strategic management, public policy, and international trade and investment are then discussed.

THE PHENOMENON

Exhibit 2 presents a simplified taxonomy of the possible outcomes from innovation. Quadrant 1 represents posi-

EXHIBIT 2 Taxonomy of Outcomes from the Innovation Process

	Innovator	Follower-Imitator
Win	**1** • Pilkington (Float Glass) • G.D. Searle (NutraSweet) • DuPont (Teflon)	**2** • IBM (personal computer) • Matsushita (VHS video recorders) • Seiko (quartz watch)
Lose	**4** • RC Cola (diet cola) • EMI (scanner) • Bowmar (pocket calculator) • Xerox (office computer) • de Haviland (Comet)	**3** • Kodak (instant photography) • Northrup (F20) • DEC (personal computer)

tive outcomes for the innovator. A first-to-market advantage is translated into a sustained competitive advantage which either creates a new earnings stream or enhances an existing one. Quadrant 4 and its corollary quadrant 2 are the ones which are the focus of this paper.

The EMI CAT scanner is a classic case of the phenomenon to be investigated.[1] By the early 1970s, the U.K. firm Electrical Musical Industries (EMI) Ltd. was in a variety of product lines, including phonographic records, movies, and advanced electronics. EMI had developed high-resolution TVs in the 1930s, pioneered airborne radar during World War II, and developed the United Kingdom's first all-solid-state computers in 1952.

In the late 1960s Godfrey Houndsfield, an EMI senior research engineer, engaged in pattern recognition research which resulted in his displaying a scan of a pig's brain. Subsequent clinical work established that computerized axial tomography (CAT) was viable for generating cross-sectional views of the human body, the greatest advance in radiology since the discovery of X rays in 1895.

While EMI was initially successful with its CAT scanner, within six years of its introduction into the United States in 1973 the company had lost market leadership, and by the eighth year had dropped out of the CAT scanner business. Other companies successfully dominated the market, though they were late entrants, and are still profiting in the business today.

Other examples include RC Cola, a small beverage company that was the first to introduce cola in a can

and the first to introduce diet cola. Both Coca Cola and Pepsi followed almost immediately and deprived RC of any significant advantage from its innovation. Bowmar, which introduced the pocket calculator, was not able to withstand competition from Texas Instruments, Hewlett-Packard, and others and went out of business. Xerox failed to succeed with its entry into the office computer business, even though Apple succeeded with the Macintosh, which contained many of Xerox's key product ideas, such as the mouse and icons. The de Haviland Comet saga has some of the same features. The Comet I jet was introduced into the commercial airline business two years or so before Boeing introduced the 707, but de Haviland failed to capitalize on its substantial early advantage. MITS introduced the first personal computer (the Altair), experienced a burst of sales, then slid quietly into oblivion.

If there are innovators who lose, there must be followers/imitators who win. A classic example is IBM with its PC, a great success since the time it was introduced in 1981. Neither the architecture nor components embedded in the IBM PC were considered advanced when introduced; nor was the way the technology was packaged a significant departure from then-current practice. Yet the IBM PC was fabulously successful and established MS-DOS as the leading operating system for 16-bit PCs. By the end of 1984, IBM had shipped over 500,000 PCs, and many considered that it had irreversibly eclipsed Apple in the PC industry.

PROFITING FROM INNOVATION: BASIC BUILDING BLOCKS

In order to develop a coherent framework within which to explain the distribution of outcomes illustrated in Exhibit 2, three fundamental building blocks must first be put in place: the appropriability regime, complementary assets, and the dominant design paradigm.

Regimes of Appropriability

A regime of appropriability refers to the environmental factors, excluding firm and market structure, that govern an innovator's ability to capture the profits generated by an innovation. The most important dimensions of such a regime are the nature of the technology and the efficacy of legal mechanisms of protection (Exhibit 3).

It has long been known that patents do not work in practice as they do in theory. Rarely, if ever, do patents confer perfect appropriability, although they do afford considerable protection on new chemical products and

[1] The EMI story is summarized in Michael Martin, *Managing Technological Innovation and Entrepreneurship* (Reston, Va.: Reston Publishing Company, 1984).

EXHIBIT 3 Appropriability Regime: Key Dimensions

■ Legal instruments	■ Nature of technology
—Patents	—Product
—Copyrights	—Process
—Trade secrets	—Tacit
	—Codified

rather simple mechanical inventions. Many patents can be "invented around" at modest costs. They are especially ineffective at protecting process innovations. Often patents provide little protection because the legal requirements for upholding their validity or for proving their infringement are high.

In some industries, particularly where the innovation is embedded in processes, trade secrets are a viable alternative to patents. Trade secret protection is possible, however, only if a firm can put its product before the public and still keep the underlying technology secret. Usually only chemical formulas and industrial-commercial processes (e.g., cosmetics and recipes) can be protected as trade secrets after they're out on the market.

The degree to which knowledge is tacit or codified also affects ease of imitation. Codified knowledge is easier to transmit and receive and is more exposed to industrial espionage and the like. Tacit knowledge by definition is difficult to articulate, and so transfer is hard unless those who possess the know-how in question can demonstrate it to others.[2] Survey research indicates that methods of appropriability vary markedly across industries, and probably within industries as well.[3]

The property rights environment within which a firm operates can thus be classified according to the nature of the technology and the efficacy of the legal system to assign and protect intellectual property. While a gross simplification, a dichotomy can be drawn between environments in which the appropriability regime is "tight" (technology is relatively easy to protect) and "weak" (technology is almost impossible to protect). Examples of the former include the formula for Coca Cola syrup; an example of the latter would be the Simplex algorithm in linear programming.

The Dominant Design Paradigm

It is commonly recognized that there are two stages in the evolutionary developments of a given branch of a science: the preparadigmatic stage, when there is no single, generally accepted conceptual treatment of the phenomenon in a field of study, and the paradigmatic stage, which begins when a body of theory appears to have passed the canons of scientific acceptability. The emergence of a dominant paradigm signals scientific maturity and the acceptance of agreed upon standards by which what has been referred to as normal scientific research can proceed. These standards remain in force unless or until the paradigm is overturned. Revolutionary science is what overturns normal science, as when Copernicus's theories of astronomy overturned Ptolemy's in the 17th century.

Abernathy and Utterback[4] and Dosi[5] have provided a treatment of the technological evolution of an industry which appears to parallel Kuhnian notions of scientific evolution.[6] In the early stages of industry development, product designs are fluid, manufacturing processes are loosely and adaptively organized, and generalized capital is used in production. Competition amongst firms manifests itself in competition amongst designs, which are markedly different from each other. This might be called the preparadigmatic stage of an industry.

At some point in time, and after considerable trial and error in the marketplace, one design or a narrow class of designs begins to emerge as the more promising. Such a design must be able to meet a whole set of user needs in a relatively complete fashion. The Model T Ford, the IBM 360, and the Douglas DC-3 are examples of dominant designs in the automobile, computer, and aircraft industry, respectively.

Once a dominant design emerges, competition shifts to price and away from design. Competitive success then shifts to a whole new set of variables. Scale and learning become much more important, and specialized capital gets deployed as incumbents seek to lower unit costs through exploiting economies of scale and learning. Reduced uncertainty over product design provides an opportunity to amortize specialized long-lived investments.

[2]D. J. Teece, "The Market for Know-How and the Efficient International Transfer of Technology," *Annals of the American Academy of Political and Social Science,* November 1981.
[3]R. Levin, A. Klevorick, N. Nelson, and S. Winter, "Survey Research on R&D Appropriability and Technological Opportunity," unpublished manuscript, Yale University, 1984.

[4]W. J. Abernathy and J. M. Utterback, "Patterns of Industrial Innovation," *Technology Review* 80(7) (January/July 1978), pp. 40–47.
[5]G. Dosi, "Technological Paradigms and Technological Trajectories," *Research Policy* 11 (1982), pp. 147–162.
[6]Thomas Kuhn, *The Structure of Scientific Revolutions,* 2d ed. (Chicago: University of Chicago Press, 1970).

EXHIBIT 4 Innovation over the Product/Industry Life Cycle

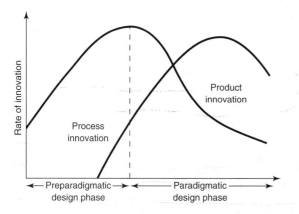

Innovation is not necessarily halted once the dominant design emerges; as Clark[7] points out, it can occur lower down in the design hierarchy. For instance, a "v" cylinder configuration emerged in automobile engine blocks during the 1930s with the emergence of the Ford V-8 engine. Niches were quickly found for it. Moreover, once the product design stabilizes, there is likely to be a surge of process innovation as producers attempt to lower production costs for the new product (see Exhibit 4).

The Abernathy–Utterback framework does not characterize all industries. It seems more suited to mass markets where consumer tastes are relatively homogeneous. It would appear to be less characteristic of small niche markets where the absence of scale and learning economies attaches much less of a penalty to multiple designs. In these instances, generalized equipment will be employed in production.

The existence of a dominant design watershed is of great significance to the distribution of profits between innovator and follower. The innovator may have been responsible for the fundamental scientific breakthroughs as well as the basic design of the new product. However, if imitation is relatively easy, imitators may enter the fray, modifying the product in important ways, yet relying on the fundamental designs pioneered by the innovator. When the game of musical chairs stops and a dominant design emerges, the innovator might well end up positioned disadvantageously relative to a follower. Hence, when imitation is possible and occurs coupled with design modification before the emergence of a dominant design, followers have a good chance of having their modified product anointed as the industry standard, often to the great disadvantage of the innovator.

Complementary Assets

Let the unit of analysis be an innovation. An innovation consists of certain technical knowledge about how to do things better than the existing state of the art. Assume that the know-how in question is partly codified and partly tacit. In order for such know-how to generate profits, it must be sold or utilized in some fashion in the market.

In almost all cases, the successful commercialization of an innovation requires that the know-how in question be utilized in conjunction with other capabilities or assets. Services such as marketing, competitive manufacturing, and after-sales support are almost always needed. These services are often obtained from complementary assets which are specialized. For example, the commercialization of a new drug is likely to require the dissemination of information over a specialized information channel. In some cases, as when the innovation is systemic, the complementary assets may be other parts of a system. For instance, computer hardware typically requires specialized software, both for the operating system and for applications. Even when an innovation is autonomous, as with plug-compatible components, certain complementary capabilities or assets will be needed for successful commercialization. Exhibit 5 summarizes this schematically.

Whether the assets required for least-cost production and distribution are specialized to the innovation turns out to be important in the development presented below. Accordingly, the nature of complementary assets is explained in some detail. Exhibit 6 differentiates between complementary assets which are generic, specialized, and cospecialized.

Generic assets are general-purpose assets which do not need to be tailored to the innovation in question. Specialized assets are those where there is unilateral dependence between the innovation and the complementary asset. Cospecialized assets are those for which there is a bilateral dependence. For instance, specialized repair facilities were needed to support the introduction of the rotary engine by Mazda. These assets are cospecialized because of the mutual dependence of the innovation on the repair facility. Containerization similarly required the deployment of some cospecialized assets in ocean shipping and terminals. However, the dependence of trucking

[7]Kim B. Clark, "The Interaction of Design Hierarchies and Market Concepts in Technological Evolution," *Research Policy* 14 (1985), pp. 235–251.

EXHIBIT 5   Complementary Assets Needed to Commercialize an Innovation

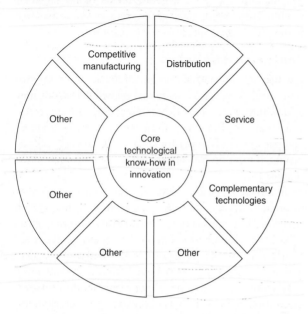

EXHIBIT 6   Complementary Assets: Generic, Specialized, and Cospecialized

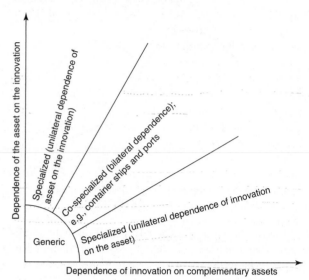

on containerized shipping was less than that of containerized shipping on trucking, as trucks can convert from containers to flat beds at low cost. An example of a generic asset would be the manufacturing facilities needed to make running shoes. Generalized equipment can be employed in the main, exceptions being the molds for the soles.

IMPLICATIONS FOR PROFITABILITY

These three concepts can now be related in a way which will shed light on the imitation process and the distribution of profits between innovator and follower. We begin by examining tight appropriability regimes.

Tight Appropriability Regimes

In those few instances where the innovator has ironclad patent or copyright protection or where the nature of the product is such that trade secrets effectively deny imitators access to the relevant knowledge, the innovator is almost assured of translating its innovation into market value for some period of time. Even if the innovator does not possess the desirable endowment of complementary costs, iron clad protection of intellectual property will afford the innovator the time to access these assets. If these assets are generic, contractual relation may well suffice, and the innovator may simply license its technol-

ogy. Specialized R&D firms are viable in such an environment. Universal Oil Products, an R&D firm developing refining processes for the petroleum industry, was one such case in point. If, however, the complementary assets are specialized or cospecialized, contractual relationships are exposed to hazards, because one or both parties will have to commit capital to certain irreversible investments which will be valueless if the relationship between innovator and licensee breaks down. Accordingly, the innovator may find it prudent to expand its boundaries by integrating into specialized and cospecialized assets. Fortunately, the factors which make for difficult imitation will enable the innovator to build or acquire those complementary assets without competing with innovators for their control.

Competition from imitators is muted in this type of regime, which sometimes characterizes the petrochemical industry. In this industry, the protection offered by patents is fairly easily enforced. One factor assisting the licensee in this regard is that most petrochemical processes are designed around a specific variety of catalysts which can be kept proprietary. An agreement not to analyze the catalyst can be extracted from licensees, affording extra protection. However, even if such requirements are violated by licensees, the innovator is still well positioned, as the most important properties of a catalyst are related to its physical structure, and the process for generating this structure cannot be deduced from structural

Someone will get around the IP.

analysis alone. Every reaction technology a company acquires is thus accompanied by an ongoing dependence on the innovating company for the catalyst appropriate to the plant design. Failure to comply with various elements of the licensing contract can thus result in a cutoff in the supply of the catalyst and possibly facility closure.

Similarly, if the innovator comes to market in the preparadigmatic phase with a sound product concept but the wrong design, a tight appropriability regime will afford the innovator the time needed to perform the trials needed to get the design right. As discussed earlier, the best initial design concepts often turn out to be hopelessly wrong, but if the innovator possesses an impenetrable thicket of patents or has technology which is simply difficult to copy, then the market may well afford the innovator the necessary time to ascertain the right design before being eclipsed by imitators.

Weak Appropriability

Tight appropriability is the exception rather than the rule. Accordingly, innovators must turn to business strategy if they are to keep imitators/followers at bay. The nature of the competitive process will vary according to whether the industry is in the paradigmatic or preparadigmatic phase.

Preparadigmatic Phase In the preparadigmatic phase, the innovator must be careful to let the basic design "float" until sufficient evidence has accumulated that a design has been delivered which is likely to become the industry standard. In some industries there may be little opportunity for product modification. In microelectronics, for example, designs become locked in when the circuitry is chosen. Product modification is limited to "debugging" and software modification. An innovator must begin the design process anew if the product doesn't fit the market well. In some respects, however, selecting designs is dictated by the need to meet certain compatibility standards so that new hardware can interface with existing applications software. In one sense, therefore, the design issue for the microprocessor industry today is relatively straightforward: deliver greater power and speed while meeting the computer industry standards of the existing software base. However, from time to time windows of opportunity emerge for the introduction of entirely new families of microprocessors which will define a new industry and software standard. In these instances, basic design parameters are less well defined and can be permitted to float until market acceptance is apparent.

The early history of the automobile industry exemplifies exceedingly well the importance for subsequent success of selecting the right design in the preparadigmatic stages. None of the early producers of steam cars survived the early shakeout when the closed body internal combustion engine automobile emerged as the dominant design. The steam car, nevertheless, had numerous early virtues, such as reliability, which the internal combustion engine autos could not deliver.

The British fiasco with the Comet I is also instructive. De Haviland had picked an early design with both technical and commercial flaws. By moving into production, significant irreversibilities and loss of reputation hobbled de Haviland to such a degree that it was unable to convert to the Boeing design which subsequently emerged as dominant. It wasn't even able to occupy second place, which went instead to Douglas.

As a general principle, it appears that innovators in weak appropriability regimes need to be intimately coupled to the market so that user needs can fully impact designs. When multiple parallel and sequential prototyping is feasible, it has clear advantages. Generally, such an approach is simply prohibitively costly. When development costs for a large commercial aircraft exceed $1 billion, variations on a theme are all that is possible.

Hence, the probability that an innovator—defined here as a firm that is first to commercialize a new product design concept—will enter the paradigmatic phase possessing the dominant design is problematic. The probabilities will be higher the lower the relative cost of prototyping and the more tightly coupled the firm is to the market. The latter is a function of organizational design and can be influenced by managerial choices. The former is embedded in the technology and cannot be influenced, except in minor ways, by managerial decisions. Hence, in industries with large developmental and prototyping costs—and hence significant irreversibilities—and where innovation of the product concept is easy, then one would expect that the probability that the innovator would emerge as the winner or amongst the winners at the end of the preparadigmatic stage is low.

Paradigmatic Stage In the preparadigmatic phase, complementary assets do not loom large. Rivalry is focused on trying to identify the design which will be dominant. Production volumes are low, and there is little to be gained in deploying specialized assets, as scale economies are unavailable and price is not a principal competitive factor. However, as the leading design or designs begin to be revealed by the market, volumes increase and opportunities for economies of scale will induce firms to begin gearing up for mass production by acquiring specialized tooling and equipment and possibly specialized distribution as well. Since these investments involve significant irreversibilities, producers are likely to proceed with caution. Islands of specialized capital will begin to appear in an industry, which otherwise features a sea of general-purpose manufacturing equipment.

However, as the terms of competition begin to change and prices become increasingly unimportant, access to complementary assets becomes absolutely critical. Since the core technology is easy to imitate, by assumption, commercial success swings upon the terms and conditions upon which the required complementary assets can be accessed.

It is at this point that specialized and cospecialized assets become critically important. Generalized equipment and skills, almost by definition, are always available in an industry, and even if they are not they do not involve significant irreversibilities. Accordingly, firms have easy access to this type of capital, and even if there is insufficient capacity available in the relevant assets, it can easily be put in place as it involves few risks. Specialized assets, on the other hand, involve significant irreversibilities and cannot be easily accessed by contract, as the risks are significant for the party making the dedicated investment. The firms which control the cospecialized assets, such as distribution channels, specialized manufacturing capacity, and so on, are clearly advantageously positioned relative to an innovator. Indeed, in rare instances where incumbent firms possess an airtight monopoly over specialized assets, and the innovator is in a regime of weak appropriability, all of the profits to the innovation could conceivably accrue to the firms possessing the specialized assets, which should be able to get the upper hand.

Even when the innovator is not confronted by situations where competitors or potential competitors control key assets, the innovator may still be disadvantaged. For instance, the technology embedded in cardiac pacemakers was easy to imitate, and so competitive outcomes quickly came to be determined by who had easiest access to the complementary assets, in this case specialized marketing. A similar situation has recently arisen in the United States with respect to personal computers. As an industry participant recently observed,

> There are a huge numbers of computer manufacturers, companies that make peripherals (e.g. printers, hard disk drives,

floppy disk drives), and software companies. They are all trying to get marketing distributors because they cannot afford to call on all of the U.S. companies directly. They need to go through retail distribution channels, such as Businessland, in order to reach the marketplace. The problem today, however, is that many of these companies are not able to get shelf space and thus are having a very difficult time marketing their products. The point of distribution is where the profit and the power are in the marketplace today.[8]

CHANNEL STRATEGY ISSUES

The above analysis indicates how access to complementary assets, such as manufacturing and distribution, on competitive teams is critical if the innovator is to avoid handing over the lion's share of the profits to imitators and/or to the owners of the complementary assets that are specialized or cospecialized to the innovation. It is now necessary to delve deeper into the appropriate control structure that the innovator ideally ought to establish over these critical assets.

There are a myriad of possible channels which could be employed. At one extreme the innovator could integrate into all of the necessary complementary assets, as illustrated in Exhibit 7, or just a few of them, as illustrated in Exhibit 8. Complete integration (Exhibit 7) is likely to be unnecessary as well as prohibitively expensive. It is well to recognize that the variety of assets and competences which need to be accessed is likely to be quite large, even for only modestly complex technologies. To produce a personal computer, for instance, a company needs access to expertise in semiconductor technology, display technology, disk drive technology, networking technology, keyboard technology, and several others. No company can keep pace in all of these areas by itself.

At the other extreme, the innovator could attempt to access these assets through straightforward contractual relationships (e.g., component supply contracts, fabrication contracts, service contracts). In many instances such contracts may suffice, although it sometimes exposes the innovator to various hazards and dependencies that it may well wish to avoid. In between the fully integrated and full contractual extremes, there are a myriad of intermediate forms and channels available. An analysis of

---

[8] David A. Norman, "Impact of Entrepreneurship and Innovations on the Distribution of Personal Computers," in R. Landau and N. Rosenberg, eds., *The Positive Sum Strategy* (Washington, D.C.: National Academy Press, 1986).

EXHIBIT 7 Complementary Assets Internalized for Innovation: Hypothetical Case #1 (Innovation Integrated into All Complementary Assets)

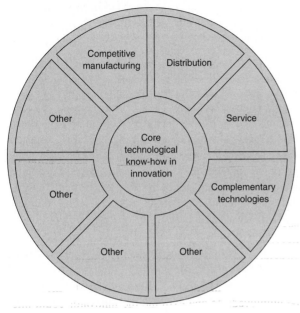

☐ Assets under common (integrated) ownership

EXHIBIT 8 Complementary Assets Internalized for Innovation: Hypothetical Case #2 (Innovation Subcontracts for Manufacturing and Service)

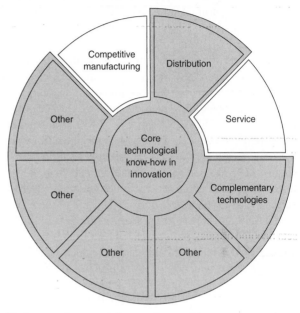

☐ Assets under common (integrated) ownership

the properties of the two extreme forms is presented below. A brief synopsis of mixed modes then follows.

Contractual Modes

The advantages of a contractual solution—whereby the innovator signs a contract, such as a license, with independent suppliers, manufacturers, or distributors—are obvious. The innovator will not have to make the upfront capital expenditures needed to build or buy the assets in question. This reduces risks as well as cash requirements. Contracting rather than integrating is likely to be the optimal strategy when the innovator's appropriability regime is tight and the complementary assets are available in competitive supply (i.e., there is adequate capacity and a choice of sources).

Both conditions apply in petrochemicals for instance, so an innovator doesn't need to be integrated to be successful. Consider, first, the appropriability regime. As discussed earlier, the protection offered by patents is fairly easily enforced, particularly for process technology, in the petrochemical industry. Given the advantageous feedstock prices available in hydrocarbon-rich petrochemical exporters and the appropriability regime characteristic of this industry, there is no incentive or advantage in owning the complementary assets (production

facilities) as they are not typically highly specialized to the innovation. Union Carbide appears to realize this and has recently adjusted its strategy accordingly. Essentially, Carbide is placing its existing technology into a new subsidiary, Engineering and Hydrocarbons Service. The company is engaging in licensing and offers engineering, construction, and management services to customers who want to take their feedstocks and integrate them forward into petrochemicals. But Carbide itself appears to be backing away from an integration strategy.

Chemical and petrochemical product innovations are not quite so easy to protect, which should raise new challenges to innovating firms in the developed nations as they attempt to shift out of commodity petrochemicals. There are already numerous examples of new products that made it to the marketplace, filled a customer need, but never generated competitive returns to the innovator because of imitation. For example, in the 1960s Dow decided to start manufacturing rigid polyurethene foam. However, it was imitated very quickly by numerous small firms which had lower costs.[9] The absence of low-cost manufacturing capability left Dow vulnerable.

---

[9]Executive V. P. of Union Carbide, Robert D. Kennedy, quoted in *Chemical Week,* November 16, 1983, p. 48.

Contractual relationships can bring added credibility to the innovator, especially if the innovator is relatively unknown when the contractual partner is established and viable. Indeed, arm's-length contracting which embodies more than a simple buy-sell agreement is becoming so common and is so multifaceted that the term *strategic partnering* has been devised to describe it. Even large companies such as IBM are now engaging in it. For IBM, partnering buys access to new technologies enabling the company to "learn things we couldn't have learned without many years of trial and error."[10] IBM's arrangement with Microsoft to use the latter's MS-DOS operating system software on the IBM PC facilitated the timely introduction of IBM's personal computer into the market.

Smaller, less-integrated companies are often eager to sign on with established companies because of the name recognition and reputation spillovers. For instance, Cipher Data Products, Inc., contracted with IBM to develop a low-priced version of IBM's 3480 0.5-inch streaming cartridge drive, which is likely to become the industry standard. As Cipher management points out, "One of the biggest advantages to dealing with IBM is that, once you've created a product that meets the high quality standards necessary to sell into the IBM world, you can sell into any arena."[11] Similarly, IBM's contract with Microsoft "meant instant credibility" to Microsoft.[12]

It is most important to recognize, however, that strategic (contractual) partnering, which is currently very fashionable, is exposed to certain hazards, particularly for the innovator, when the innovator is trying to use contracts to access specialized capabilities. First, it may be difficult to induce suppliers to make costly irreversible commitments which depend for their success on the success of the innovation. To expect suppliers, manufacturers, and distributors to do so is to invite them to take risks along with the innovator. The problem which this poses for the innovator is similar to the problems associated with attracting venture capital. The innovator must persuade its prospective partner that the risk is a good one. The situation is one open to opportunistic abuses on both sides. The innovator has incentives to overstate the value of the innovation, while the supplier has incentives to

"run with the technology" should the innovation be a success.

Instances of both parties making irreversible capital commitments nevertheless exist. Apple's Laserwriter—a high-resolution laser printer which allows PC users to produce near–typeset-quality text and art-department graphics—is a case in point. Apple persuaded Canon to participate in the development of the Laserwriter by providing subsystems from its copiers—but only after Apple contracted to pay for a certain number of copier engines and cases. In short, Apple accepted a good deal of the financial risk in order to induce Canon to assist in the development and production of the Laserwriter. The arrangement appears to have been prudent, yet there were clearly hazards for both sides. It is difficult to write, execute, and enforce complex development contracts, particularly when the design of the new product is still floating. Apple was exposed to the risk that its coinnovator Canon would fail to deliver, and Canon was exposed to the risk that the Apple design and marketing effort would not succeed. Still, Apple's alternatives may have been rather limited, inasmuch as it didn't command the requisite technology to go it alone.

In short, the current euphoria over strategic partnering may be partially misplaced. The advantages are being stressed,[13] without a balanced presentation of costs and risks. Briefly, there is the risk that the partner won't perform according to the innovator's perception of what the contract requires; there is the added danger that the partner may imitate the innovator's technology and attempt to compete with the innovator. This latter possibility is particularly acute if the provider of the complementary asset is uniquely situated with respect to the complementary asset in question and has the capacity to imitate the technology, which the innovator is unable to protect. The innovator will then find that it has created a competitor who is better positioned than the innovator to take advantage of the market opportunity at hand. *Business Week* has expressed concerns along these lines in its discussion of the "Hollow Corporation."[14]

It is important to bear in mind, however, that contractual or partnering strategies in certain cases are ideal. If the innovator's technology is well protected, and if what the partner has to provide is a "generic" capacity avail-

[10] Comment attributed to Peter Olson III, IBM's director of business development, as reported in "The Strategy Behind IBM's Strategic Alliances," *Electronic Business,* October 1, 1985, p. 126.

[11] Comment attributed to Norman Farquhar, Cipher's vice president for strategic development, as reported in *Electronic Business,* October 1, 1985, p. 128.

[12] Regis McKenna, "Market Positioning in High Technology," *California Management Review* 27 (3) (Spring 1985), p. 94.

[13] For example, see McKenna, "Marketing Position in High Technology."

[14] See *Business Week,* March 3, 1986, pp. 57–59. *Business Week* uses the term to describe a corporation which lacks in-house manufacturing capability.

able from many potential partners, then the innovator will be able to maintain the upper hand while avoiding the costs of duplicating downstream capacity. Even if the partner fails to perform, adequate alternatives exist (by assumption, the partners' capacities are commonly available), so the innovator's efforts to successfully commercialize its technology ought to proceed profitably.

Integration Modes

Integration, which by definition involves ownership, is distinguished from pure contractual modes in that it typically facilitates incentive alignment and control. If an innovator owns rather than rents the complementary assets needed to commercialize, then it is in a position to capture spillover benefits stemming from increased demand for the complementary assets caused by the innovation.

Indeed, an innovator might be in the position, at least before its innovation is announced, to buy up capacity in the complementary assets, possibly to its great subsequent advantage. If future markets exist, simply taking forward positions in the complementary assets may suffice to capture much of the spillovers.

Even after the innovation is announced, the innovator might still be able to build or buy complementary capacities at competitive prices if the innovation has ironclad legal protection (i.e., if the innovation is in a tight appropriability regime). However, if the innovation is not tightly protected and once out is easy to imitate, then securing control of complementary capacities is likely to be the key success factor, particularly if those capacities are in fixed supply—so called bottlenecks. Distribution and specialized manufacturing competences often become bottlenecks.

As a practical matter, however, an innovator may not have the time to acquire or build the complementary assets that ideally it would like to control. This is particularly true when imitation is easy, so that timing becomes critical. Additionally, the innovator may simply not have the financial resources to proceed. The implications of timing and cash constraints are summarized in Exhibit 9.

Accordingly, in weak appropriability regimes innovators need to rank complementary assets as to their importance. If the complementary assets are critical, ownership is warranted, although if the firm is cash constrained, a minority position may well represent a sensible trade-off.

Needless to say, when imitation is easy, strategic moves to build or buy complementary assets which are specialized must occur with due reference to the moves

EXHIBIT 9 Specialized Complementary Assets and Weak Appropriability: Integration Calculus

Time required to position (relative to competitors)

	Long	Short
Minor	OK if timing not critical	Full steam ahead
Major	Forget it	OK if cost position tolerable

Investment required

Optimum investment for business in question

	Minor	Major
Critical	Internalize (majority ownership)	Internalize (but if cash constrained, take minority position)
Not critical	Discretionary	Do not internalize (contract out)

How critical to success?

of competitors. There is no point moving to build a specialized asset, for instance, if one's imitators can do it faster and cheaper.

It is hopefully self-evident that if the innovator is already a large enterprise with many of the relevant complementary assets under its control, integration is unlikely to be the issue that it might otherwise be, as the innovating firm will already control many of the relevant specialized and cospecialized assets. However, in industries experiencing rapid technological change, technologies advance so rapidly that it is unlikely that a single company has the full range of expertise needed to bring advanced products to market opportunely and cost-effectively. Hence, the integration issue is not just a small-firm issue.

Integration Versus Contract Strategies: An Analytic Summary

Exhibit 10 summarizes some of the relevant considerations in the form of a decision flowchart. It indicates that a profit-seeking innovator, confronted by weak intellectual property protection and the need to access

EXHIBIT 10   Flowchart for Integration versus Contract Decision

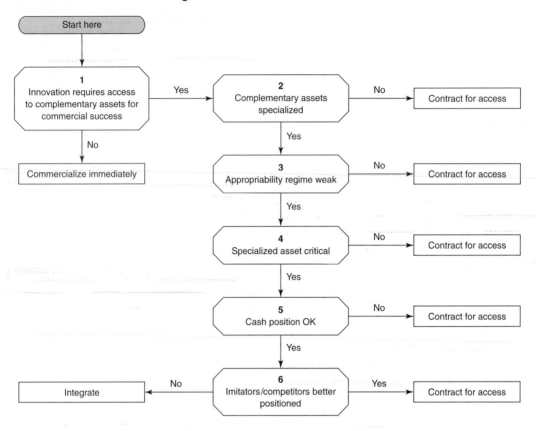

specialized complementary assets and/or capabilities, is forced to expand its activities through integration if it is to prevail over imitators. Put differently, innovators who develop new products that possess poor intellectual property protection but which require specialized complementary capacities are more likely to parlay their technology into a commercial advantage, rather than see it prevail in the hands of imitators.

Exhibit 10 makes it apparent that the difficult strategic decisions arise in situations where the appropriability regime is weak and where specialized assets are critical to profitable commercialization. These situations, which in reality are very common, require that a fine-grained competitor analysis be part of the innovator's strategic assessment of its opportunities and threats. This is carried a step further in Exhibit 11, which looks only at situations where commercialization requires certain specialized capabilities. It indicates the appropriate strategies for the innovators and predicts the outcomes to be expected for the various players.

Three classes of players are of interest: innovators, imitators, and the owners of cospecialized assets (e.g., distributors). All three can potentially benefit or lose from the innovation process. The latter can potentially benefit from the additional business which the innovation may direct in the asset owner's direction. Should the asset turn out to be a bottleneck with respect to commercializing the innovation, the owner of the bottleneck facilities is obviously in a position to extract profits from the innovator and/or imitators.

The vertical axis in Exhibit 11 measures how those who possess the technology (the innovator or possibly its imitators) are positioned vis-à-vis those firms that possess required specialized assets. The horizontal axis measures the *tightness* of the appropriability regime, tight regimes being evidenced by ironclad legal protection coupled with technology that is simply difficult to copy; weak regimes offer little in the way of legal protection and the essence of the technology, once released, is transparent to the imitator. Weak regimes are further

EXHIBIT 11   Contract and Integration Strategies and Outcomes for Innovators: Specialized-Asset Case

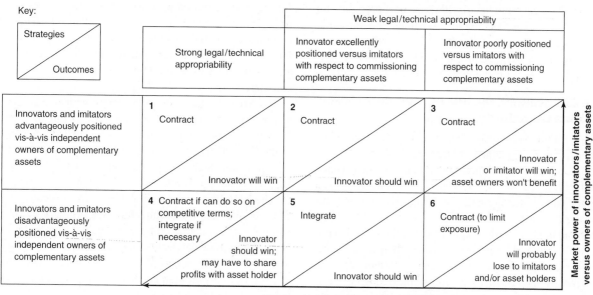

Degree of intellectual property protection

subdivided according to how the innovator and imitators are positioned vis-à-vis each other. This is likely to be a function of factors such as lead time and prior positioning in the requisite complementary assets.

Exhibit 11 makes it apparent that even when firms pursue the optimal strategy, other industry participants may take the jackpot. This possibility is unlikely when the intellectual property in question is tightly protected. The only serious threat to the innovator is where a specialized complementary asset is completely locked up, a possibility recognized in cell 4. This can rarely be done without the cooperation of government. But it frequently occurs, as when a foreign government closes off access to a foreign market, forcing the innovators to license to foreign firms, but with the government effectively cartelizing the potential licensees. With weak intellectual property protection, however, it is quite clear that the innovator will often lose out to imitators and/or asset holders, even when the innovator is pursuing the appropriate strategy (cell 6). Clearly, incorrect strategies can compound problems. For instance, if innovators integrate when they should contract, a heavy commitment of resources will be incurred for little if any strategic benefit, thereby exposing the innovator to even greater losses than would otherwise be the case. On the other hand, if an innovator tries to contract for the supply of a critical capability when it should build the capability itself, it

may well find it has nurtured an imitator better able to serve the market than the innovator itself.

Mixed Modes

The real world rarely provides extreme or pure cases. Decisions to integrate or license involve trade-offs, compromises, and mixed approaches. It is not surprising, therefore, that the real world is characterized by mixed modes of organization, involving judicious blends of integration and contracting. Sometimes mixed modes represent transitional phases. For instance, because of the convergence of computer and telecommunication technology, firms in each industry are discovering that they often lack the requisite technical capabilities in the other. Since the technological interdependence of the two requires collaboration amongst those who design different parts of the system, intense cross-boundary coordination and information flows are required. When separate enterprises are involved, agreement must be reached on complex protocol issues amongst parties who see their interests differently. Contractual difficulties can be anticipated since the selection of common technical protocols amongst the parties will often be followed by transaction-specific investments in hardware and software. There is little doubt that this was the motivation behind IBM's purchase of 15 percent of PBX manufacturer Rolm in 1983, a position that was expanded to

100 percent in 1984. IBM's stake in Intel, which began with a 12 percent purchase in 1982, is most probably not a transitional phase leading to 100 percent purchase, because both companies realized that the two corporate cultures are not very compatible, and IBM may not be as impressed with Intel's technology as it once was.

The CAT Scanner, the IBM PC, and NutraSweet: Insights from the Framework

EMI's failure to reap significant returns from the CAT scanner can be explained in large measure by reference to the concepts developed above. The scanner which EMI developed was of a technical sophistication much higher than would normally be found in a hospital, requiring a high level of training, support, and servicing. EMI had none of these capabilities, could not easily contract for them, and was slow to realize their importance. It most probably could have formed a partnership with a company like Siemens to access the requisite capabilities. Its failure to do so was a strategic error compounded by the very limited intellectual property protection which the law afforded the scanner. Although subsequent court decisions have upheld some of EMI's patent claims, once the product was in the market it could be reverse engineered and its essential features copied. Two competitors, GE and Technicare, already possessed the complementary capabilities that the scanner required, and they were also technologically capable. In addition, both were experienced marketers of medical equipment and had reputations for quality, reliability, and service. GE and Technicare were thus able to commit their R&D resources to developing a competitive scanner, borrowing ideas from EMI's scanner, which they undoubtedly had access to through cooperative hospitals, and improving on it where they could while they rushed to market. GE began taking orders in 1976 and soon after made inroads on EMI. In 1977 concern for rising health care costs caused the Carter Administration to introduce "certificate of need" regulation, which required HEW's approval on expenditures on big ticket items like CAT scanners. This severely cut the size of the available market.

By 1978 EMI had lost market share leadership to Technicare, which was in turn quickly overtaken by GE. In October 1979, Godfrey Houndsfield of EMI shared the Nobel prize for invention of the CT scanner. Despite this honor and the public recognition of its role in bringing this medical breakthrough to the world, the collapse of its scanner business forced EMI in the same year into the arms of a rescuer, Thorn Electrical Industries, Ltd. GE subsequently acquired what was EMI's scanner business from Thorn for what amounted to a pittance.[15] Though royalties continued to flow to EMI, the company had failed to capture the lion's share of the profits generated by the innovation it had pioneered and successfully commercialized.

If EMI illustrates how a company with outstanding technology and an excellent product can fail to profit from innovation while the imitators succeeded, the story of the IBM PC indicates how a new product representing a very modest technological advance can yield remarkable returns to the developer.

The IBM PC, introduced in 1981, was a success despite the fact that the architecture was ordinary and the components standard. Philip Estridge's design team in Boca Raton, Florida, decided to use existing technology to produce a solid, reliable micro rather than state of the art. With a one-year mandate to develop a PC, Estridge's team could do little else.

However, the IBM PC did use what at the time was a new 16-bit microprocessor (the Intel 8088) and a new disk operating system (DOS) adapted for IBM by Microsoft. Other than the microprocessor and the operating system, the IBM PC incorporated existing micro "standards" and used off-the-shelf parts from outside vendors. IBM did write its own BIOS (Basic Input/Output System) which is embedded in ROM, but this was a relatively straightforward programming exercise.

The key to the PC's success was not the technology. It was the set of complementary assets which IBM either had or quickly assembled around the PC. In order to expand the market for PCs, there was a clear need for an expandable, flexible microcomputer system with extensive applications software. IBM could have based its PC system on its own patented hardware and copyrighted software. Such an approach would cause complementary products to be cospecialized, forcing IBM to develop peripherals and a comprehensive library of software in a very short time. Instead, IBM adopted what might be called an "induced contractual" approach. By adopting an open system architecture, as Apple had done, and by making the operating system information publicly available, a spectacular output of third-party software was induced. IBM estimated that by mid-1983, at least 3,000

---

[15] See "GE Gobbles a Rival in CT Scanners," *Business Week,* May 19, 1980.

hardware and software products were available for the PC.[16] Put differently, IBM pulled together the complementary assets, particularly software, which success required, without even using contracts, let alone integration. This was despite the fact that the software developers were creating assets that were in part cospecialized with the IBM PC, at least in the first instance.

A number of special factors made this seem a reasonable risk to the software writers. A critical one was IBM's name and commitment to the project. The reputation behind the letters I.B.M. is perhaps the greatest cospecialized asset the company possesses. The name implied that the product would be marketed and serviced in the IBM tradition. It guaranteed that MS-DOS would become an industry standard, so that the software business would not be solely dependent on IBM, because emulators were sure to enter. It guaranteed access to retail distribution outlets on competitive terms. The consequences were that IBM was able to take a product which represented at best a modest technological accomplishment, and turn it into a fabulous commercial success. The case demonstrates the role that complementary assets play in determining outcomes.

The spectacular success and profitability of G. D. Searle's NutraSweet is an uncommon story which is also consistent with the above framework. In 1982, Searle reported combined sales of $74 million for NutraSweet and its table top version, Equal. In 1983, this surged to $336 million. In 1985, NutraSweet sales exceeded $700 million[17] and Equal had captured 50 percent of the U.S. sugar substitute market and was number one in five other countries.

NutraSweet, which is Searle's tradename for aspartame, has achieved rapid acceptance in each of its FDA-approved categories because of its good taste and ability to substitute directly for sugar in many applications. However, Searle's earnings from NutraSweet and the absence of a strategic challenge can be traced in part to Searle's clever strategy.

It appears that Searle has managed to establish an exceptionally tight appropriability regime around Nutra-Sweet—one that may well continue for some time after the patent has expired. No competitor appears to have successfully "invented around" the Searle patent and commercialized an alternative, no doubt in part because

the FDA approval process would have to begin anew for an imitator who was not violating Searle's patents. A competitor who tried to replicate the aspartame molecule with minor modification to circumvent the patent would probably be forced to replicate the hundreds of tests and experiments which proved aspartame's safety. Without patent protection, FDA approval would provide no shield against imitators coming to market with an identical chemical and who could establish to the FDA that it is the same compound that had already been approved. Without FDA approval, on the other hand, the patent protection would be worthless, for the product would not be sold for human consumption.

Searle has aggressively pushed to strengthen its patent protection. The company was granted U.S. patent protection in 1970. It has also obtained patent protection in Japan, Canada, Australia, the United Kingdom, France, Germany, and a number of other countries. However, most of these patents carry a 17-year life. Since the product was only approved for human consumption in 1982, the 17-year patent life was effectively reduced to five. Recognizing the obvious importance of its patent, Searle pressed for and obtained special legislation in November 1984 extending the patent protection on aspartame for another five years. The United Kingdom provided a similar extension. In almost every other nation, however, 1987 will mark the expiration of the patent.

When the patent expires, however, Searle will still have several valuable assets to help keep imitators at bay. Searle has gone to great lengths to create and promulgate the use of its NutraSweet name and a distinctive "Swirl" logo on all goods licensed to use the ingredient. The company has also developed the "Equal" tradename for a table top version of the sweetener. Trademark law in the United States provides protection against unfair competition in branded products for as long as the owner of the mark continues to use it. Both the NutraSweet and Equal trademarks will become essential assets when the patents on aspartame expire. Searle may well have convinced consumers that the only real form of sweetener is NutraSweet/Equal. Consumers know most other artificial sweeteners by their generic names—saccharin and cyclamates.

Clearly, Searle is trying to build a position in complementary assets to prepare for the competition which will surely arise. Searle's joint venture with Ajinomoto ensures them access to that company's many years of experience in the production of biochemical agents. Much of this knowledge is associated with techniques for

---

[16]F. Gens and C. Christiansen, "Could 1,000,000 IBM PC Users Be Wrong?" *Byte,* November 1983, p. 88.

[17]See *Monsanto Annual Report,* 1985.

distillation and synthesis of the delicate hydrocarbon compounds that are the ingredients of NutraSweet and is therefore more tacit than codified. Searle has begun to put these techniques to use in its own $160 million Georgia production facility. It can be expected that Searle will use trade secrets to the maximum to keep this know-how proprietary.

By the time its patent expires, Searle's extensive research into production techniques for L-phenylalanine and its eight years of experience in the Georgia plant should give it a significant cost advantage over potential aspartame competitors. Trade secret protection, unlike patents, has no fixed lifetime and may well sustain Searle's position for years to come.

Moreover, Searle has wisely avoided renewing contracts with suppliers when they have expired.[18] Had Searle subcontracted manufacturing for NutraSweet, it would have created a manufacturer who would then be in a position to enter the aspartame market itself or to team up with a marketer of artificial sweeteners. But by keeping manufacturing in-house and by developing a valuable trade name, Searle has a good chance of protecting its market position from dramatic inroads once patents expire. Clearly, Searle seems to be astutely aware of the importance of maintaining a "tight appropriability regime" and using cospecialized assets strategically.

IMPLICATIONS FOR R&D STRATEGY, INDUSTRY STRUCTURE, AND TRADE POLICY

Allocating R&D Resources

The analysis so far assumes that the firm has developed an innovation for which a market exists. It indicates the strategies which the firm must follow to maximize its share of industry profits relative to imitators and other competitors. There is no guarantee of success even if optimal strategies are followed.

The innovator can improve its total return to R&D, however, by adjusting its R&D investment portfolio to maximize the probability that technological discoveries will emerge that are either easy to protect with existing intellectual property law or which require for commercialization cospecialized assets already within the firm's repertoire of capabilities. Put differently, if an innovat-

ing firm does not target its R&D resources towards new products and processes which it can commercialize advantageously relative to potential imitators and/or followers, then it is unlikely to profit from its investment in R&D. In this sense, a firm's history—and the assets it already has in place—ought to condition its R&D investment decisions. Clearly, an innovating firm with considerable assets already in place is free to strike out in new directions, so long as in doing so it is cognizant of the kinds of capabilities required to successfully commercialize the innovation. It is therefore rather clear that the R&D investment decision cannot be divorced from the strategic analysis of markets and industries and the firm's position within them.

Small-Firm Versus Large-Firm Comparisons

Business commentators often remark that many small entrepreneurial firms which generate new, commercially valuable technology fail while large multinational firms, often with a less meritorious record with respect to innovation, survive and prosper. One set of reasons for this phenomenon is now clear. Large firms are more likely to possess the relevant specialized and cospecialized assets within their boundaries at the time of new product introduction. They can therefore do a better job of milking their technology, however meager, to maximum advantage. Small domestic firms are less likely to have the relevant specialized and cospecialized assets within their boundaries and so will have to incur the expense either of trying to build them or of trying to develop coalitions with competitors/owners of the specialized assets.

Regimes of Appropriability and Industry Structure

In industries where legal methods of protection are effective or where new products are just hard to copy, the strategic necessity for innovating firms to integrate into cospecialized assets would appear to be less compelling than in industries where legal protection is weak. In cases where legal protection is weak or nonexistent, the control of cospecialized assets will be needed for long-run survival.

In this regard, it is instructive to examine the U.S. drug industry.[19] Beginning in the 1940s, the U.S. Patent Office began, for the first time, to grant patents on certain natural substances that involved difficult extraction pro-

---

[18]Purification Engineering, which had spent $5 million to build a phenylalanine production facility, was told in January 1985 that their contract would not be renewed. In May, Genex, which claimed to have invested $25 million, was given the same message. See "A Bad Aftertaste," *Business Week,* July 15, 1985.

[19]P. Temin, "Technology, Regulation, and Market Structure in the Modern Pharmaceutical Industry," *The Bell Journal of Economics,* Autumn 1979, pp. 429–446.

cedures. Thus, in 1948 Merck received a patent on streptomycin, which was a natural substance. However, it was not the extraction process but the drug itself which received the patent. Hence, patents were important to the drug industry in terms of what could be patented (drugs), but they did not prevent imitation.[20] Sometimes just changing one molecule will enable a company to come up with a different substance which does not violate the patent. Had patents been more all-inclusive—and I am not suggesting they should—licensing would have been an effective mechanism for Merck to extract profits from its innovation. As it turns out, the emergence of close substitutes, coupled with FDA regulation which had the de facto effect of reducing the elasticity of demand for drugs, placed high rewards on a product differentiation strategy. This required extensive marketing, including a sales force that could directly contact doctors, who were the purchasers of drugs through their ability to create prescriptions.[21] The result was exclusive production (i.e., the earlier industry practice of licensing was dropped) and forward integration into marketing (the relevant cospecialized asset).

Generally, if legal protection of the innovator's profits is secure, innovating firms can select their boundaries based simply on their ability to identify user needs and respond to those through research and development. The weaker the legal methods of protection, the greater the incentive to integrate into the relevant cospecialized assets. Hence, as industries in which legal protection is weak begin to mature, integration into innovation-specific cospecialized assets will occur. Often this will take the form of backward, forward, and lateral integration. (Conglomerate integration is not part of this phenomenon.) For example, IBM's purchase of Rolm can be seen as a response to the impact of technological change on the identity of the cospecialized assets relevant to IBM's future growth.

Industry Maturity, New Entry, and History

As technologically progressive industries mature, and a greater proportion of the relevant cospecialized assets are brought in under the corporate umbrellas of incumbents, new entry becomes more difficult. Moreover, when it does occur it is more likely to involve coalition formation very early on. Incumbents will for sure own the cospecialized assets, and new entrants will find it necessary to forge links with them. Here lies the explanation for the sudden surge in strategic partnering now occurring internationally and particularly in the computer and telecommunications industry. Note that it should not be interpreted in anticompetitive terms. Given existing industry structure, coalitions ought to be seen not as attempts to stifle competition, but as mechanisms for lowering entry requirements for innovators.

In industries in which technological change of a particular kind has occurred, which required deployment of specialized and/or cospecialized assets at the time, a configuration of firm boundaries may well have arisen which no longer has compelling efficiencies. Considerations which once dictated integration may no longer hold, yet there may not be strong forces leading to divestiture. Hence existing firm boundaries may in some industries—especially those where the technological trajectory and attendant specialized asset requirements have changed—be rather fragile. In short, history matters in terms of understanding the structure of the modern business enterprise. Existing firm boundaries cannot always be assumed to have obvious rationales in terms of today's requirements.

The Importance of Manufacturing to International Competitiveness

Practically all forms of technological know-how must be embedded in goods and services to yield value to the consumer. An important policy for the innovating nation is whether the identity of the firms and nations performing this function matter.

In a world of tight appropriability and zero transactions cost—the world of neoclassical trade theory—it is a matter of indifference whether an innovating firm has an in-house manufacturing capability, domestic or foreign. It can simply engage in arm's-length contracting (patent licensing, know-how licensing, co-production, etc.) for the sale of the output of the activity in which it has a comparative advantage (in this case R&D) and will maximize returns by specializing in what it does best.

However, in a regime of weak appropriability and especially where the requisite manufacturing assets are specialized to the innovation, which is often the case, participation in manufacturing may be necessary if an innovator is to appropriate the rents from its innovation. Hence, if an innovator's manufacturing costs are higher

---

[20] Ibid., p. 436.
[21] In the period before FDA regulation, all drugs other than narcotics were available over-the-counter. Since the end user could purchase drugs directly, sales were price sensitive. Once prescriptions were required, this price sensitivity collapsed; the doctors not only did not have to pay for the drugs, but in most cases they were unaware of the prices of the drugs they were prescribing.

than those of its imitators, the innovator may well end up ceding the lion's share of profits to the imitator.

In a weak appropriability regime, low-cost imitator-manufacturers may end up capturing all of the profits from innovation. In a weak appropriability regime where specialized manufacturing capabilities are required to produce new products, an innovator with a manufacturing disadvantage may find that its advantage at early stage research and development will have no commercial value. This will eventually cripple the innovator, unless it is assisted by governmental processes. For example, it appears that one of the reasons why U.S. color TV manufacturers did not capture the lion's share of the profits from innovation, for which RCA was primarily responsible, was that RCA and its American licensees were not competitive at manufacturing. In this context, concerns that the decline of manufacturing threatens the entire economy appear to be well founded.

A related implication is that as the technology gap closes, the basis of competition in an industry will shift to the cospecialized assets. This appears to be what is happening in microprocessors. Intel is no longer out ahead technologically. As Gordon Moore, CEO of Intel points out, "Take the top 10 [semiconductor] companies in the world . . . and it is hard to tell at any time who is ahead of whom. . . . It is clear that we have to be pretty damn close to the Japanese from a manufacturing standpoint to compete."[22] It is not just that strength in one area is necessary to compensate for weakness in another. As technology becomes more public and less proprietary through easier imitation, then strength in manufacturing and other capabilities is necessary to derive advantage from whatever technological advantages an innovator may possess.

Put differently, the notion that the United States can adopt a "designer role" in international commerce, while letting independent firms in other countries such as Japan, Korea, Taiwan, or Mexico do the manufacturing, is unlikely to be viable as a long-run strategy. This is because profits will accrue primarily to the low-cost manufacturers (by providing a larger sales base over which they can exploit their special skills). Where imitation is easy, and even where it is not, there are obvious problems in transacting in the market for know-how, problems which are described in more detail elsewhere.[23] In particular, there are difficulties in pricing an intangible asset whose true performance features are difficult to ascertain ex ante.

The trend in international business towards what Miles and Snow[24] call *dynamic networks*—characterized by vertical disintegration and contracting—ought thus be viewed with concern. Dynamic networks may not so much reflect innovative organizational forms, but the disassembly of the modern corporation because of deterioration in national capacities, manufacturing in particular, which are complementary to technological innovation. Dynamic networks may therefore signal not so much the rejuvenation of American enterprise, but its piecemeal demise.

How Trade and Investment Barriers Can Impact Innovators' Profits

In regimes of weak appropriability, governments can move to shift the distribution of the gains from innovation away from foreign innovators and towards domestic firms by denying innovators ownership of specialized assets. The foreign firm, which by assumption is an innovator, will be left with the option of selling its intangible assets in the market for know-how if both trade and investment are foreclosed by government policy. This option may appear better than the alternative (no remuneration at all from the market in question). Licensing may then appear profitable, but only because access to the complementary assets is blocked by government.

Thus when an innovating firm generating profits needs to access complementary assets abroad, host governments, by limiting access, can sometimes milk the innovators for a share of the profits, particularly that portion which originates from sales in the host country. However, the ability of host governments to do so depends importantly on the criticality of the host country's assets to the innovator. If the cost and infrastructure characteristics of the host country are such that it is the world's lowest cost manufacturing site, and if domestic industry is competitive, then by acting as a de facto monopolist, the host country government ought to be able to adjust the terms of access to the complementary assets so as to appropriate a greater share of the profits generated by the innovation.[25]

---

[22] "Institutionalizing the Revolution," *Forbes,* June 16, 1986, p. 35.
[23] Teece, "The Market for Know-How and the Efficient International Transfer of Technology."

[24] R. E. Miles and C. C. Snow, "Network Organizations: New Concepts for New Forms," *California Management Review,* Spring 1986, pp. 62–73.
[25] If the host country market structure is monopolistic in the first instance, private actors might be able to achieve the same benefit. What government can do is to force collusion of domestic enterprises to their mutual benefit.

CASE I-2

✳ Advent Corporation

R. S. Rosenbloom

Early in November 1970, Henry Kloss was reviewing the progress Advent Corporation had made in the preceding months. The September profit and loss statement had registered a net profit of almost $30,000, against a cumulative loss of nearly $165,000 in the preceding 10 months. The new Advent cassette recorder, Model M200, had just completed its third month on the market. The M200 recorder, with its sophisticated circuitry, was felt to represent real potential as a replacement for the phonograph as the central element in any home entertainment system. With the financial turnaround, Mr. Kloss felt confident that a sales level of $40 million to $50 million was achievable by Advent within five years. His problem was how to organize for continuing innovation.

INTRODUCTION

Mr. Kloss was a well-known figure in consumer electronic product design and manufacturing. Prior to Advent, he had participated in the founding and operation of Acoustic Research, Inc. (AR), and later, KLH Corporation. He had been the mind behind the products at KLH, an organization which was renowned for its very high quality, slightly oddball electronic products. He left KLH in 1967 after 10 years as president.

The formation of AR had originated during the Korean crisis. While stationed in New Jersey, Mr. Kloss was able to attend the City College of New York, where he was a student of Edgar Vilchur. He and Vilchur had mutual interests in an acoustic suspension speaker because of its immense reproductive advantages over conventional mechanical speaker systems and its small size. With Mr. Kloss providing some capital and a "garage," Acoustic Research, Inc., was formed. Financial guidance of the business was provided by Anton (Tony) Hofmann, who was later to become a principal of KLH and then treasurer of Advent.

Mr. Kloss and other active management sold their share of AR, Inc., after irreparable disagreements with Vilchur over company policies. KLH was initiated shortly

thereafter with $60,000 in capital and Mr. Kloss as president, Malcolm Low as manager of sales, and Mr. Hofmann as financial manager. After seven years and a series of innovative audio products that were producing a $4 million level of sales, KLH was sold because of sheer tiredness of the managers and uncertainties associated with KLH's growing size. With the sale, Mr. Kloss agreed to remain as president for three years, and he left in 1967.

Advent Corporation was incorporated by Mr. Kloss in May 1967 for the purpose of manufacturing specialized electronic products for home entertainment use. The actual justification for forming the company was to do work in television, especially to create an organization which would support the R&D and marketing of a large screen (4′ × 6′) color television system. Formal development work on the television system had been suspended in 1970.

With the formation of Advent Corporation, Mr. Kloss embarked on a plan to see what a big company could do. He felt that growth was always a primary goal, always desirable, but that one had to think in terms of what was realizable without beating one's head against the wall. Mr. Kloss sought to retain strong financial control of the company, having sold his share of Acoustic Research, Inc., under duress and his share of KLH Corporation with mixed feelings. He had this to say to the case researchers about financial policies:

> The size one desires is really only limited by the dollars available for working capital. There's a firm intention to reach the middle tens of millions of dollars certainly in less than five years; one anticipates a faster accumulation of staff, faster than the 30 percent one might be able to do from profits, so the question becomes how fast does one dribble out equity if you're not staff limited?

Mr. Kloss continued:

> Eighteen months ago, there was a small private offering of 12 percent of the company in which we offered 20 units consisting of $10,000 in 8 percent convertible debentures, and 300 shares of equity common at $7.50 per share, 10 cents par value. I retained 75 percent control; company directors and others have 13 percent. It was simply that circumstances warranted our doing that. In addition, we have a $1.15 million line of credit, of which $600,000 is revolving and $550,000 open, secured by the directors and pegged to 80 percent of the accounts receivable. I will not offer any further equity until a really big push (for which the sales are guaranteed) requires it and when a price several times the $7.50 price per share is attainable. Beyond that, we are working hard to slash overhead and to build profits.

EXHIBIT 1 Advent Corporation Balance Sheet as of September 26, 1970

Assets

Current assets:		
Cash		$ 64,488.34
Accounts receivable		650,226.68
Less: Reserve for bad debts		(10,000.00)
Advance to employees		(650.00)
Inventory:		
Material	$ 375,486.13	
Labor	37,076.97	
Manufacturing overhead	38,189.91	450,753.01
Prepaid insurance and other assets		10,958.21
Total current assets		1,165,770.24
Property, plant, and equipment	221,030.07	
Less: Accumulated depreciation	(57,524.71)	163,505.36
Deferred financing expense		5,450.00
Advent television system		205,085.92
Total assets		$1,539,811.52

Liabilities

Current liabilities:		
Accounts payable		$ 347,449.36
Notes payable, bank		666,714.00
Due officers		0.00
Loans, other		50,000.00
Accrued debenture interest		4,002.65
Accrued payroll		17,441.39
Royalties payable		(2,000.00)
Accrued royalty expense		7,584.80
Accrued audit and legal fees		20,628.38
Accrued taxes and fringe benefits		37,083.67
Accrued promotion and discount allowances		65,312.20
Miscellaneous accounts		17,471.29
Total current liabilities		1,231,687.74
Long-term debt:		
8% convertible debentures		200,000.00
Stockholders' equity:		
Common stock (10¢ par value)	$ 45,925.10	
Additional paid-in capital	821,866.29	
Retained earnings deficit to 10/31/69	(595,130.66)	
Deficit 11/1/69 to date	(164,536.95)	
Total stockholders' equity		108,123.78
Total liabilities and stockholders' equity		$1,539,811.52

Financial data regarding the operations of Advent Corporation are given in Exhibits 1 and 2.

CURRENT OPERATIONS

In the fall of 1970, Advent Corporation manufactured and sold five products for home entertainment use: the Advent loudspeaker; the Advent Frequency Balance Control, which allowed the listener to alter the relative musical balance in any audible octave; two models of the Advent Noise Reduction Unit, which allowed virtually hiss-free tape recording and playback; and the new Advent Tape Deck, which also featured noise-free recording and playback. These products, as well as a special recording tape that Advent sold under license from Du Pont, are described in detail in Exhibit 3, in a piece of Advent promotional literature.

Several specific policies of Advent Corporation served to interlock the company with the consumer electronics market. Most important, perhaps, was product

EXHIBIT 2 Advent Corporation Statement of Profit and Loss as of September 26, 1970

	Current Month		November 1, 1969, to Date Amount
	Units	Amount	
Gross sales:			
Regular speakers	1,561	$115,222.44	$ 685,003.10
Utility speakers	278	17,838.58	46,653.19
F.B.C.	151	23,148.34	182,995.73
M 100	303	50,481.83	260,995.63
M 101	295	24,139.50	68,485.25
M 101 Advocate	146	11,826.00	13,284.00
M200	988	170,718.00	245,960.30
CC-1	6	100.02	363.40
WC-1	138	1,603.12	3,371.03
Parts	—	605.00	2,757.16
Crolyn tape	1,824	3,997.44	11,108.20
Total		419,680.27	1,520,976.99
Less: Provision for promotional and quantity discounts		21,489.78	86,385.59
Net sales		398,190.49 (100%)	1,434,591.40
Cost of sales:			
Material		196,431.82	663,770.07
Labor		41,366.25	199,930.01
Manufacturing overhead		45,908.85	232,392.33
Royalties		3,182.88	13,222.26
Total cost of sales		286,889.80 (72%)	1,109,314.67
Gross profit		111,300.69 (28%)	325,276.73
Operating expenses:			
Sales		47,517.13	242,799.78
General and administrative		13,753.68	91,570.51
Research and development		14,371.13	195,877.20
Total operating expenses		75,641.94 (19.0%)	530,247.49
Operating profit (loss)		35,658.75 (9.0%)	(204,970.76)
Other income (expense)		(6,428.79) (−1.6%)	(34,652.11)
Capitalization of Advent TV system (included in R&D above)			75,085.92
Net profit		$ 29,229.96	$ (164,536.95)

policy. Mr. Kloss felt that there were several repugnant aspects to direct competition with the industry giants such as Zenith, Magnavox, and Motorola. Advent sought to turn to specialized areas of the audio market, the 5 percent or so where no competition existed, where whole new classes of products might be developed. Quality was an important Advent byword: to make the most efficient piece of equipment at the lowest possible price to the consumer was the primary objective. Such product sanctity was not protected by patent but rather by the product itself, which had a real name, which gathered equity as it was seen and became known, and which hopefully represented the perfect low-price product. Even though the entry fee was low, Advent anticipated specializing upon a base product already determined by the major suppliers (e.g., tape decks), which had an appeal to a broad spectrum of the market.

did own manufacturing, Kloss had experience

Production operations of Advent Corporation were closely supervised by Mr. Kloss, although there was a production manager for all but the M200 line. Speakers were manufactured in a separate 12,000-square-foot plant in Cambridge, Massachusetts. Major operations of the company took place in a 20,000-square-foot, three-story building also in Cambridge, which Mr. Kloss leased upon forming the company. A move was being planned to consolidate the operations of the company in the spring of 1971 into a 64,000-square-foot building also in Cambridge, which had already been leased.

Production itself was typical of the small manufacturers in the industry. Approximately 130 production workers formed the products in a specified sequence of assembly steps that was usually determined by Mr. Kloss. He also carried out "time and motion" studies to determine an appropriate production rate. No significant

MBA 520 notes

EXHIBIT 3 Advent Promotional Literature

A Progress Report from Advent on Loudspeakers, Cassette Recorders, a New Kind of Tape, and Other Matters

good quote

After more than a year in business, we (Advent Corporation) think it's time for an accounting of where we are and why.

We began, you may remember, with the intention of making products that would differ significantly from other people's—products that would fill special needs others weren't filling, explore genuinely new ways of doing things, and keep testing accepted limits of performance and value.*

One of the products we had in mind was a new kind of color television set, a high-performance system with a screen size several times the present limit for home use. We are happy to report that it's coming along nicely (and slowly, as such things do), and that the present prospects for prerecorded video material make it look more appealing than ever.

Audio, however, was where we could do the most the quickest, and our first product was:

THE ADVENT LOUDSPEAKER

Anybody who knew us might have predicted that we would make a loudspeaker system pretty early in the game, but few would have predicted that we'd make just *one,* call it simply The Advent Loudspeaker, and say flatly that it was the best we could offer for a long way into the future.

The reason for that was, and is, that it had become possible to design a speaker system as good as anyone would ever need for home listening—one as good in every measurable and audibly useful way as any speaker system of any size or price—at a cost slightly below what most people consider the "medium price" category. Our prior experience in design and manufacturing techniques convinced us that this could be done, and we did it.

We will be happy to send you full particulars on The Advent Loudspeaker, including its reviews. But we believe its sound will tell you quickly enough why it has become, in its first year, one of our industry's all-time best sellers.

(To avoid surprises in a showroom, we should note that our one speaker system comes in two styles of cabinet: the original walnut model, priced at $125†, and a "utility" version that is actually in a rather handsome vinyl finish that looks like walnut, priced at $105.† Both sound the same.)

All of the first year's reviews of The Advent Loudspeaker finished by saying that it was an auspicious beginning for a company. But it represented only one of our immediate directions. The next was:

---

*Having helped found two successful companies previously, and having prior credit for some of audio's most significant products (including something like half of the loudspeakers in use in music systems and serious radios and phonographs in this country), our president, Henry Kloss, had some pretty firm notions about what he wanted to do now.
†Slightly lower in some parts of the country.

THE ADVENT FREQUENCY BALANCE CONTROL

One of the things to be learned in the design of speaker systems is that "flat" frequency response is in the ear of the beholder and virtually nowhere else. True, there are amplifiers and tuners with straight-line frequency response, but practically everything else—recordings, listening rooms, cartridges, loudspeakers—is anything but flat. Different things sound different, not because of basic differences in quality or performance in many instances, but because a recording engineer, or speaker designer, or room plasterer had a slightly special view of the world.

There is nothing wrong with those differences, in our view. And one of the challenges for a speaker designer is to accept and cope with them by designing for an octave-to-octave musical balance that sounds "right" with the wildest variety of present recording techniques. But there is no single perfect balance, and that lack is a source of discomfort to a number of critical listeners. It causes many listeners with really superb (and really expensive) sound equipment to keep trading for new and more expensive equipment in the hope that it will sound "perfect" for everything from Deutsche Grammophon's conception of the Berlin Philharmonic's sound to Columbia's notions about Blood, Sweat, and Tears.

Anyone who keeps pursuing that ideal, and many who don't, would be well advised to investigate our Frequency Balance Control, a unique device that enables listeners to alter the relative musical balance of any octave in the audible frequency spectrum. It is uniquely flexible and uniquely effective in dealing with sonic differences between recordings, equipment, and even the placement of speakers in a room—and in making things sound subjectively "right" more consistently than could be accomplished any other way.

The FBC, designed around our own experience with subjective judging of sound quality, is worth investigation by anyone who can't just sit back and listen, accepting the bad with the wonderful. At $225‡, it is a far better, more pertinent investment than most changes of components.

One of the special abilities of the FBC is the reclaiming of many recordings from an unlistenable state. The need for another kind of recording reclamation led to another kind of product.

THE ADVENT NOISE REDUCTION UNITS
(MODELS 100 AND 101)

Background noise in tape recording—specifically, tape hiss—is a far bigger enemy of sound quality than most listeners realize. One reason it isn't properly identified (and vilified) is that

---

‡Slightly higher in some parts of the country.

few people have heard tape recordings without it. Lacking the standard of blessed silence is something like never having seen a television picture without "snow." If you don't know it isn't supposed to be there, you just look or listen past it and accept it as part of the medium. But once you see—or hear—things free of interference, life is different.

Getting rid of tape noise is a prime function of the now-famous Dolby® System of noise reduction, which in its professional version is in use in virtually every major recording studio in the world.§ We became interested in the Dolby System not only because it helps rid even the best conventional tape recordings of background noise, but because it had even greater possibilities when applied to low-speed home tape recording. Home recording at 3 3/4 and 1 7/8 ips has been plagued by the problem of really excessive tape hiss—which manufacturers have chosen either to tolerate or to "reduce" by giving up frequency and dynamic range in recording at those speeds. The Dolby System makes it possible to remove that problem and get first-class performance at the low speeds best suited, from the standpoint both of economy and convenience, to home recording.

So we designed a product that would make the Dolby System available—in a version designed by Dolby Laboratories exclusively for home recording and prerecorded tapes—for use with any good tape recorder. The product was our Model 100 Noise Reduction Unit, a flexible and effective piece of equipment that can make any recorder sound better and can do wonders in opening up the world of low-speed recording to the home user.

The Model 100 combines the Dolby System with a recording control system that supersedes a recorder's own and provides a recording accuracy and simplicity seldom seen in home tape equipment. One crucial advantage of that control system, which provides separate input level controls (with input-mixing) *and* a master record-level control, is that it gets stereo recording balance right and does so easily. Improper balance, almost guaranteed with many tape recorders, is the chief reason for recordings (on even the best recorders) that don't sound like the original. It is, in other words, the chief reason for many people's dissatisfaction with their recorders.

The Model 100, at $250, is a required investment for anyone who takes recording very seriously and measures the results critically. But since some people won't need its tremendous flexibility, we also decided to offer the Model 101—which, at $125, provides identical performance at half the price. To make that possible, we omitted the input-mixing provided with the Model 100, supplied slightly less flexible recording controls (it takes a bit longer to get stereo balance just right), and provided one Dolby circuit per channel instead of two. (As in the professional studio Dolby System, you switch the Model 101's two circuits to function first for stereo recording and then for stereo playback, but not for both at the same time.) The result, again, was performance identical to the more elaborate unit, at a price that makes sense for serious recordists on tight budgets.

While designing the Noise Reduction Units, we became interested in what the Dolby System and other factors might do for a kind of tape recording that no one was taking seriously enough. The result was:

THE ADVENT TAPE DECK (MODEL 200)

We had known before, and confirmed in our work on the Model 100, that tape hiss was the underlying reason for the compromised, AM-radio kind of sound quality that people had come to associate with cassette recording. Because the hiss was present in a quantity that made wide-range recording unpleasant to listen to on cassettes, it had effectively set an upper limit on quality—giving manufacturers little incentive to optimize *any* aspect of cassette recording, including mechanical performance.

We realized that once you used the Dolby System to get rid of the noise, you would then have reason to go on to improve all the performance areas that nobody was really attending to. So, to show just how good cassette recording could be, we optimized everything we could around a good cassette transport, added our Noise Reduction Unit, and held a demonstration for the press. The reaction, even though we couldn't demonstrate everything we wanted to in a rigged-together unit, was that we had proved that cassette performance could be as good as, and in some ways better than, the standard for records.

In the meantime, we worked on our own cassette recorder—which was to include not only the Dolby System and the necessary improvements in all areas of performance, but also the means, not given to our knowledge with any previous cassette recorder, to make really superb recordings. That meant effective and precise controls for setting balance and recording levels, including a VU meter that read both stereo channels simultaneously and indicated the louder of the two at a given moment.

We felt that calling the resulting tape machine a cassette recorder wouldn't fully indicate our conviction that it was probably the single best choice among *all* kinds of recorders for most serious listeners who want to tape records and broadcasts. So we called it The Advent Tape Deck (Model 200) and let its being a cassette machine speak for itself. At $260, it is a new kind of tape machine that we hope will prove the key, given "Dolbyized" commercial cassette releases, to making cassettes the medium most serious listeners prefer for most listening.

About midway in our development of The Advent Tape Deck, we became convinced that the Dolby System's contribution to performance would become even greater if it were combined with the use of Du Pont's chromium-dioxide tape in cassettes. Lots of people had been talking about Du Pont's "Crolyn," but nobody had hard facts on what it could do in cassette recordings.§ So we got samples, experimented with its characteristics, and were convinced that we had to supply a means to use it on our recorder. That meant a special switch on The Advent Tape Deck to provide the right recording and playback characteristics (a good bit different from those of

§ "Dolby" is a trademark of Dolby Laboratories. "Crolyn" is a trademark of Du Pont.

EXHIBIT 3 (continued)

other tape formulations) for its use. It also meant another product:

ADVOCATE CROLYN TAPE

Although Du Pont's Crolyn tape was being used extensively in critical video recording applications, and justifying its advance press notices, no one had made the leap to marketing it for audio purposes for home use. We decided to do so because we felt that Crolyn was necessary for the very best in potential cassette performance.

We are, then, marketing Crolyn tape under the "Advocate" brand in cassettes. One of our hopes in doing so is to get others to market chromium-dioxide tape as well.

There is no doubt in our mind that it's worth the trouble. Chromium dioxide has the ability to put greater high-frequency energy on tape than other oxide formulations, and is also increasingly sensitive as frequency goes up. Those are ideal characteristics for cassette recording, making possible a still greater signal-to-noise ratio in conjunction with the Dolby System and better overall high-frequency performance than any other tape we know of.

THE ADVENT PACKET

At this writing, we can't predict exactly what product is going to follow Advocate Crolyn tape. As you probably have noted by now, we develop products in what might be thought of as organic style, letting each product stand on its own. We don't sit down and decide to manufacture a "line" of speakers or amplifiers or tape recorders.

We are into other things at this point, and hope that they will be firm enough to talk about soon. In the meantime, we invite you to write us at the address below for any information you would like, including a list of Advent dealers.

If you like, ask for "The Advent Packet." That will bring you everything we have on all of our products, and will also—unless you specify otherwise—put you in jeopardy of getting future informational mailings from us.

So much for the first year.

Advent Corporation, 377 Putnam Ave., Cambridge, Mass. 02139.

---

economies of scale existed in the industry. Mr. Kloss felt very strongly that higher overhead would destroy any advantages to be gained by mechanization. In addition, it seemed that after a quantity order of 100 per week more, no important savings could be gained from higher quantity parts orders. It had been found that direct labor ran about one half of material cost over a wide range of products. With manufacturing overhead being determined as a percent of direct labor, cost of sales could easily be forecast for any given product and a price determined on the basis of a typical margin percentage. Pricing policy, therefore, was also dependent upon the emphasis on making an excellent low-cost product and not on selling products at a what-the-market-may-bear level.

Marketing management at Advent was a relatively autonomous activity. Vice president of sales was Mr. Stan Pressman, who had performed similar duties at KLH before coming to Advent. Nationwide distribution was maintained through 150 dealers across the country, who were carefully selected on their ability to sell and service Advent products intensively. Shelf space was originally attained by contacting each dealer personally and promising a succession of useful and high-quality products, with which it would be valuable for the dealer to be associated. The reputation of Mr. Kloss was also emphasized. Finally, exposure to the trade press and to the pub-

lic had been attained through press conferences designed to place the Advent audio products in sink-or-swim competition with similar offerings then on the market. Response had been overwhelmingly favorable.

Under pressure to reach the marketplace with successful products and to improve profitability, Advent had expanded on a day-to-day functional basis. Emphasis on "continually optimizing its position" rather than responding to a long-range plan had placed substantial importance upon production efficiency and rapid response to daily marketing problems. As a result, current operating managers were expected to monitor the functions of their departments in fine detail.

INNOVATION AT ADVENT

Both Acoustic Research and KLH had demonstrated the ability to recognize changing product and consumer trends and to respond quickly in a dynamic marketplace. Henry Kloss had been able to achieve similar success during the initial life of Advent. Mr. Kloss was unable to explain why Advent had succeeded in accomplishing responses to market needs in advance of other companies in the industry. He discussed this phenomenon at some length during conversations with the case researchers in his president's office, a room that was bewilderingly clut-

[handwritten margin notes: "Stayed close to technology → not just bus side", "Du Pont did what they're good at"]

...tered with all sorts of electronic gear. His desk was laden with trade journals and other papers reporting the current developments in home electronics. Only a few feet from his desk was the door that led to the R&D section, which was never seen closed.

Mr. Kloss

Perhaps a recent example will highlight what I mean. Du Pont Company, which is really not concerned with products at all, I mean, their basic formulations are raw materials or processes to make raw materials, recently developed a way of making a material which is simply a process kind of thing. That was chromium dioxide, which can be used in the manufacture of magnetic tape and which results in a really quite important product. But Du Pont stopped short very early in the process. They'll sell you all the chromium dioxide you want. But their involvement with the resulting product (Crolyn tape) was absolutely nil. A lot of time was lost until Advent recognized the product and did something about it. They (Du Pont) had no market for it at all. And they are extremely grateful to us for it now. I really didn't think a big company could be so pleasant to work with.

Casewriter

Are you suggesting that product innovation is primarily characterized by observation that a need or a market exists for that product and then going after it, after that specific product?

Mr. Kloss

Yes. And from the process innovation, which is a new way of making something, or some new combination of things. Often a new process could have a connection with a new product, but it doesn't tell.

All of *our* working has been backwards from the person. Others work hard to find a physical phenomenon, or to develop a new bearing, and then work hard to find a market. This is to work completely in isolation, with no connection to the product at all.

Nobody asked at Du Pont, "In what way can this new process make a higher quality result?" At the same time, we were asking, "In what way can this be used irrespective of presently established systems of using tape—what are the limitations inherent within this tape on its ability to produce music for the listener at home?" And we found that it had a distinct and strong advantage, and this has not even been done by the Du Pont people. You know, it's really hard to believe! I'm not trying to boost Advent, or knock Du Pont, but their detachment from this thing in terms of people was absolutely complete!

Exemplifying the kind of reasoning that went on at Advent prior to a product decision, Mr. Kloss mentioned the following incident:

Somebody came around the other day with a way of making a very high powered amplifier that requires only a very small size and bulk. Any normal amplifier wastes up to half its power at any one moment in heat loss. There is a way of making an amplifier, which we've known for some time, that is 97 percent efficient—you waste almost no power in the amplifier itself. Now since the size of the amplifier is largely determined by the need to dissipate power, clearly the size here could be reduced. One has known it can be done; it's called Class D circuitry. This size might make possible a whole new class of things; whether we do this in a year or so is uncertain. But it's a possible kind of thing, which we didn't go to invent, and which has been around for years and years and years, but which might become practical to do, if you do the rest of the things to get all the merit out of it, such as creating a small power supply and all, which calls for minor invention on our part. We've had a feeling that exceedingly small kinds of things were worthwhile; when something like this comes up, you notice it more sharply than somebody else, who looks at it only as just a cheaper way of getting a high-power amplifier.

[handwritten margin note: "Innovative"]

Formal market research at Advent Corporation was never mentioned. Mr. Kloss had the following remarks to offer when the case researchers asked him about it:

Mr. Kloss

Oh! One never does market research! The only test of the market that there will ever be is to fully commit to a product itself; one is never going to make any test marketing or any asking of anything. And it will be done whenever it's the product that will most certainly, most quickly, give a certain amount of money here. It's just a matter of priority of products; one could, within a couple of months' time, make a noise reduction unit and turn it into a product and sell it. That had to be done first.

Casewriter

But with all due respect, you must feel that it will go, that when people see it, they're going to buy it?

Mr. Kloss

Well, yes. But there's no way of proving this before you spend the money to produce it, that I know of.

Casewriter

Experience and intuition tell you that it will go?

Mr. Kloss

This is about, yes, all that one has. Experience that my intuition has been right gives me a little more confidence, maybe.

THE DOLBYIZED CASSETTE RECORDER

Critical to Advent's recovery from unprofitable development operations was the successful manufacture and marketing of the Dolbyized cassette recorder (Advent Tape Deck M200), described briefly in Exhibit 3. The way the idea of noise reduction recording became a product for Advent, and at just the right time, is indicative of the whole Advent innovation process.

Mr. Kloss had noted very early in the company's history that it was possible, in theory, to do something like noise reduction. That is, he noted that at any moment in the recording process, the normal recording methods from basic information theory resulted in great waste. He noted that there ought to be some way of continuously optimizing the recording technique. However, his investigation stopped there. He knew it was possible, but he did not embark then and there upon a process of invention. Instead, Mr. Kloss became sensitized to noticing if somebody else had really done it. All of the Advent products began in familiar fashion. Mr. Kloss commented,

> The things that I have done have never started from noticing something was important and then working backwards to the fundamental way to do it. You know, "Gee, it would really be desirable to have instant photographs," and then work hard to do it. I don't know if that's what Land did or not. But that has never been our particular way of doing things. All of the work has been to think about things that would be desirable to do, and then be continuously looking around to see what things are possible to do, perhaps with minor invention on our part, which would satisfy a perceived need in the market and begin to define a product. Only when the need in the marketplace simultaneously matches the knowledge of the technology does one spend more than a few minutes thinking about it.
>
> . . . So any product I think of for longer than a few minutes is already one that I know can be made. . . . You want to constantly have in mind, stored with very short access time, the different technologies. You sort of somehow keep aware of what kind of things can be done. When several of these come together to form a product, that can result in your deciding to make that product. You have to have, at any moment, a moderate-sized number of floating possibilities of things that you can do.

But there's a cost to this floating process of having all these pieces of information available which makes it very hard to expand to a large group of people.

In 1967, Mr. Kloss heard about Ray Dolby, a man who had been making professional noise reduction systems in England and was just starting to sell them in the United States. That was just at the conclusion of Mr. Kloss's presidency at KLH. He negotiated an agreement between Dolby and KLH for KLH to have the rights to incorporate that system in a tape deck. Mr. Kloss agreed to manufacture that tape deck for KLH, to help KLH introduce the Dolby system to the world.

For many reasons, the product, which was envisioned as a $600 reel-to-reel machine with Dolby circuitry, never got made. By May 1969, Mr. Kloss personally had suffered a loss of $265,000, largely through design and production problems. At that time, Advent began manufacturing the Advent loudspeaker to support further development work on the large-screen television. Simultaneously, KLH had renegotiated a manufacturing contract with a Japanese firm, Nakamichi, to build a $250 reel-to-reel machine with Dolby circuitry. Such a product was on-line by the fall of 1969, when Nakamichi offered KLH a similar deal on a cassette recorder with Dolby circuitry. Mr. Kloss described the events that followed:

> Even though KLH had a selling reel-to-reel machine with Dolby, they decided not to make the cassette machine. There were many reasons for this; they were having trouble with the Nakamichi machine they had, they had had gross trouble with my deck, and they had just gotten a new president who was against expansionist moves. So they just backed off the whole thing, just when the right product was there. Advent's contribution to the process was really a floating knowledge of the benefits of chromium dioxide tape, the Dolby circuit, and a manufacturer of heads who knew about Dolby. It was gathering these things together into a product and bringing them to people's attention that Advent accomplished.

Within hours, before the Nakamichi representatives had returned to Japan, Mr. Kloss had negotiated an agreement granting Advent the productive capacity to employ Nakamichi heads in an Advent deck. The Dolby system it uses is described in Exhibit 4. While the new product received numerous adulations in the press, by October 1970 Mr. Kloss felt that the primary shift toward central cassette recording that he had expected with the marketing of the Advent Tape Deck was not occurring as fast as he had hoped. He felt that the primary reason for this deficiency was the inherent difficulty of depending on a dealer organization to push Advent products that incorporated sophisticated innovations, features that had to be understood by the consumer before he made the logical choice of an Advent product. Consequently, he and Mr. Pressman were spending considerable time in attempting to find a solution to this problem, the final step in completing the innovation of the Dolbyized recorder.

Exhibit 4   How the Dolby System Works

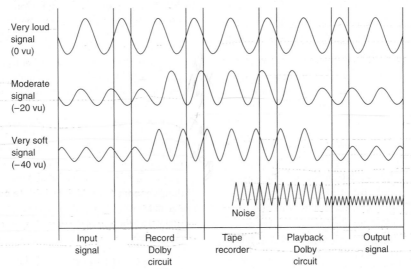

1. The signal being recorded passes through the record Dolby circuit *first*. The Dolby circuit operates on the higher ("hiss") frequencies in a predetermined manner, depending on their loudness level. The loudest signals (0 vu) pass unaffected through the circuit. Signals of moderate intensity (−20 vu) are boosted moderately, while the very soft signals (−40 vu) receive maximum boost.

2. After being thus "Dolbyized," the signal is recorded onto the tape. It is at this point that tape hiss makes its appearance. You can see on the diagram how the record Dolby circuit's action has made the low-level signal louder than usual, relative to the tape hiss.

3. On playback, the signal from the tape is passed through the playback Dolby circuit, which is an exact "mirror-image" of the record Dolby circuit. The playback Dolby *lowers* the previously boosted parts of the signal, by precisely the same amount they had been boosted. The tape hiss—which made its appearance between the record and playback halves of the Dolby System—is automatically lowered at the same time by a very substantial amount, effectively 100 db, or 90 percent. At the same time, because of the precise "mirror-image" playback action, the Dolby System causes no other change in the signal relative to the original source that was recorded.

TELEVISION

Although Mr. Kloss had suspended formal development work on Advent's large-screen color television set, he continued to make minor modifications to it when time was available. Several experimental sets functioned without major problems in the Advent plant and homes of employees, but decisions remained as to the exact design the set would have and the marketing approach to be used. Mr. Kloss estimated that the first production models would be available for sale six to nine months after the "go" decision was made, and that the decision would be made "whenever it's the product that most certainly, most quickly, can give the right amount of money here."

Describing the product's origins, Kloss said:

I was vaguely interested in TV as an important medium. One reads a magazine article that points out a way to make projection television. All you had to do was read that article and see that it could apply to a screen this size [four and one-half feet by six feet]. And then you quickly ask the question, Is this worthwhile? You make a guess that it might be worthwhile at the right price.

In 1964, Kodak announced the development of a screen which could effectively increase the amount of perceived reflected light by a factor of five over ordinary mat screens. This development suggested that it might be possible to diffuse light from a projection tube over a larger screen of this type and still retain satisfactory brightness. However, Mr. Kloss said that he would have built a high-quality television set even if the large screen had not been possible.

If there never was a big screen, we'd be in television anyway because you can do a high-quality small set. So our interest in TV is not restricted to the big screen, though it's much more fun because there's no comparison available.

Mr. Kloss believed he could discern in color TV the typical product life cycle of consumer electronics products working to the advantage of new producers with sufficient marketing skill. During the late 1950s and early 1960s, color TV quality improved as bugs were worked out of it, but by 1966 short-cut production methods were reducing overall quality. Mr. Kloss observed:

NTSC [National Television Standards Committee] standards permit a very high quality to be broadcast which is usually badly degraded by a set at home. What you see on a regular picture is not what you would see on a really high quality set.

Evaluation of demand, though not verbalized, suggested to Mr. Kloss that larger-screen TV was an inherently desirable thing. The evaluation was not, he said, an extrapolation of the popularity of larger screens in ordinary television sets. Nor could he isolate any one other factor which dominated his evaluation except that it was the kind of thing he would like to have in his home. There was no way to extrapolate from sales of expensive large-screen sets. He said:

There is absolutely no experience on large-screen television for consumer use. . . . Yes, I feel that large-screen TV will be popular but there's no way to prove this until you spend the money to produce it, that I know of.

A lot of people go to the flicks. The whole business is to bring things up close, large, and important. . . . This is doing that and there's that kind of rightness about it. That's about the only defense one has. It just doesn't have any connection with television as one thinks about it. Once you say television, somebody brings to mind almost repugnant kinds of images. They don't do it for books though. You talk about books and they think about great books and the University of Chicago, and this kind of thing. They don't think about the kinds of things they sell down on Washington Street.

. . . And for big screens, there's no expressed desire for anybody to want a big screen. . . .

Exactly what's happening out in the store, where people are expressing what they want, sure I get some information on that from somebody else. But this sort of shapes the end features of products. People are not out there expressing a new kind of thing that they would like to have—a compacter for kitchen garbage: I've never heard anybody say that they ever wanted something like this. I think maybe some people do; we'll see. . . . The kinds of products that people might want are not limited to what people have said they want or what people, when you knock on their door, say that they will want. In the first case, it's too late if people express the desire for what they want. In the second case, the answers are invalid when you ask about it.

Development

Shortly after organizing Advent Corporation in May 1967, Mr. Kloss began working on the television set.

Though he was confident that the idea was technically feasible, there were many questions yet to be answered regarding design. For example:

The way of finishing mirrors at a very low cost—it's been used in the eyeglass industry; it's not used in making lenses; it's not used in telescopic work. But the technology to make very low cost kinds of mirrors exists in the trade. And we sort of know that technology is there and go and use it. If it had required our finding a very low cost way of making a lens which hadn't been developed yet, I would have cut out from any of our consideration the making of a low-cost projection television. . . . It maybe would have been a very fruitful investigation, but it would have been the kind of thing for which you couldn't be absolutely certain of finding an answer. We've always avoided the kind of investigation where the answer had some reasonable chance of being negative.

The major cost in operating the Advent large-screen TV was expected to be cathode-ray tube replacement. Phosphor life (and therefore tube life) was expected to lie between 700 to 2,500 playing hours. The projection tube had been used in some of the earliest television sets, but the large screen desired would put new demands on it for maximizing total light output. Thus, an RCA commercial projection system with the mirror and corrector lens outside the tube was rejected as too inefficient and troublesome.

Rights to produce the Kodak screen had been given to Advent with no guarantee of the practicality of doing so in a large size. It was concave toward the audience and leaned forward slightly. These two factors required that the screen extend about a foot out from a normal wall. Brightness fell off rapidly as the viewer moved about 70° off an axis perpendicular to the screen. While satisfactory viewing required the room to be no brighter than would be required to read a newspaper with strain, a bright light could be situated to the side of the screen without seriously degrading the image. Mr. Kloss believed the Kodak screen was the best presently available, but hoped to develop a proprietary flat screen which could be patented. It would be composed of many elements which would each direct light in the optical direction.

In a conventional color receiver, the electronics assembly feeds information to a single picture tube which contains three electron guns. The Advent system was based on similar electronic circuitry, but the video image was projected on the screen by three separate cathode-ray tubes, one each for the red, green, and blue color constituents. The Advent tube is diagramed in Exhibit 5. Within each tube, a stream of electrons of varying inten-

EXHIBIT 5   Projection Television Tube

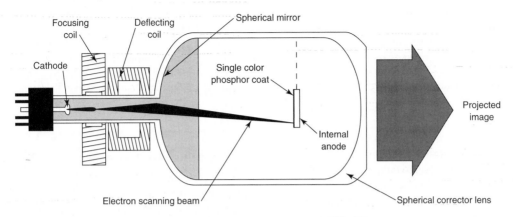

sity was beamed toward the positively charged internal anode, coated with a phosphor that generated one of the three colors to be projected. This beam was accelerated, focused, and deflected in a rapid horizontal scan of 15°, with the U.S. standard 525 sweeps for each vertical transit. This stream of electrons hitting the anode re-created the transmitted picture for that color. The internal spherical mirror reflected this image and focused it through the corrector lens on the external screen where the three colors were superimposed.

Tests of experimental models had shown that this system, based on three projection tubes with internal optics, could produce large images of amazingly high quality. Internal optics (mirror and corrector lens within the tube) were superior to external optics which required exact positioning of mirrors, greater light wastage, and attendant problems in keeping the optics clean. Internal optics had been used by the U.S. Navy many years previously and were not patentable. Mr. Kloss commented, "We may very well have been in error in the past in not getting some nominal patents to make it easier to sit down with somebody and sell some of this technology." He did not feel that protection was the primary value in patents "because the reluctance of manufacturers to get into any new field is really quite surprising. It's unfamiliar, sort of strange; they would like to buy it. We wouldn't mind, but it's always a mess to do manufacturing for someone else."

Competition

There were no large-screen TV sets on the market which would compete directly with the Advent set in the home market. The Eidophore system, developed in Switzerland in the early 1950s, used an electron beam physically to change the surface of an oil film. A light projected through this film and onto a screen provided a much brighter and larger picture. The Eidophore set, however, required an operating technician and cost about $40,000 for a monochrome version and over $100,000 for color. General Electric had produced a modified version which was more easily operated and cost about $29,000 in monochrome and $38,000 in color. People who had seen this set reported to Mr. Kloss that its brightness and resolution were inferior to Advent's, though he felt that improvement might be obtained by using a higher gain screen.

Very little of the current discussion in trade journals about future trends in television centered on large screens. More was aimed at miniaturized TV or at development of a flat screen which could be installed in a wall. Mr. Kloss commented that "there might be a message there. You talk about desirable things of the future; nobody talks about larger screen television at all." During 1968, Sony Corporation demonstrated an experimental set which was flat and large (eight feet diagonally). This set was essentially a board of 26,000 elements of one red, one blue, and one green light each. This compared with 350,000 elements of phosphor in the typical shadow mask tube and resulted in a picture of noticeably poor resolution. The problems to be solved were to decrease the size of individual lights and obtain more rapid switching of the lights. While many years of development work remained before this set could be competitive, Mr. Kloss felt that the ultimate and best TV of the future would in some way generate light on the screen itself.

Although projection television was well recognized in the industry as a means of obtaining both a large and flat screen, the immediate objection was that it could not be made bright enough for viewing in a lighted room. Several large companies had experimented with it, nonetheless. Mr. Kloss described one such effort in explaining why the large manufacturers were unlikely to provide competition soon after he began production. A large military and consumer electronics firm had shown him a cathode-ray tube under development for projection use. A configuration of optics very similar to Advent's had been adopted, but a maximum falloff in brightness at the edges of the screen of 10 percent to 20 percent had been specified by someone. Conventional knowledge of human eye sensitivity would suggest that humans would be insensitive to falloffs of 200 percent to 300 percent. However, this error caused engineers to design an aspherical corrector lens which would disperse light nearly perfectly on the screen and cost many thousands of dollars. Similar mistakes eventually caused the system to reach a height of nearly six feet and to require a sealed refrigeration unit for cooling. RCA had estimated about a year earlier that it could develop a large-screen TV within several years for from $5 million to $50 million (the exact figure was not recalled). Mr. Kloss believed that a radically improved system could not be designed and built within 5 years and more likely 10 years. Competitive projection systems would probably require two years minimum after the Advent set was introduced.

Production and Costs

Production was expected to be carried out in Advent's new 64,000-square-foot plant. Receiver units were the same as those required in ordinary sets except that less deflection power was needed due to the decreased deflection angle. No decision had yet been made whether to make or buy the receiver units. Projection tubes were expected to cost about $50 each produced on a small scale and involved no unusual technology. Some equipment had already been purchased to produce test models. The cost could probably be reduced to $100 for a set of three tubes on an automated line. Production of the screen involved handwork to sketch and mold a thin aluminum foil, apply backing, and construct a frame and stand.

Mr. Kloss did not envision a highly automated line. He believed from experience at KLH and Acoustics Research that cost penalties would be only 10 percent to 20 percent if as few as 100 sets a week were produced. Electronic components were priced the same to all buyers if ordered in quantities over approximately 1,000, and the inflexibility and high fixed costs of an automated line would prevent great economies of scale. Tooling costs for a line adequate for 100 sets per week would be "many tens of thousands of dollars." Production costs were expected to be similar to those for other Advent products, with direct labor costing about one half as much as materials. Mr. Kloss believed that production costs of

shadow mask tubes were about $100 and far outweighed cabinet and receiving equipment costs.

Concessions were made to simplify design, and production of the Advent set included replacement of electrostatic focusing with the less common and more expensive static magnetic focusing. This decision would result in a selling price about $200 higher than it would otherwise be. Similar concessions were expected in screen design.

Distribution and Marketing

Mr. Kloss believed that most of the expected technical problems which could become customer complaints had been effectively ironed out of the TV design. He felt that sales personnel could cause complaints, however, by creating or allowing unreasonable expectations. He said that "the expected kinds of troubles are that we just haven't anticipated somebody's attitude toward this or his expectations. This comes from rather recent learning in noise reduction systems where you have a difficult time explaining to someone."

Although the set would eventually be designed for installation by the customer, the first installations would require a technician:

> It will be exactly equivalent to what the early color sets had with technicians running around. . . . The whole thing was mechanically fragile and fussy. . . . The beginning of any new kind of thing is troublesome. You can't even tell how you finally want to make it until you go through this manufacturing process.

Retail price had originally been estimated at $1,500 to $2,000, but had been revised upward to $2,000 to $2,500 based upon estimated costs and normal margins.

Mr. Kloss expected to engage in enough advertising to identify the product in consumer minds as reasonably priced and to lock in a portion of the market. The only scheme he had which might help lock in the consumer was to give the product a simple name and then not change it. He would "never engage in what might be interpreted as an annual model change." He felt that this strategy had given KLH an advantage over other companies which introduced new products and consequently destroyed their equity in the name.

Mr. Pressman, marketing vice president of Advent, said he had purposely avoided having his attention diverted by the TV, which was still at least several months from introductions. He did feel that video products were exciting and had a greater long-range potential for Advent than audio did. He thought, as well, that 5,000 unit sales a year sounded possible. Though attempts by other video product manufacturers to distribute through audio dealers had proven unsuccessful, he had not eliminated the possibility of trying it again. No opinions regarding advertising and promotional strategies had been formed.

When the Advent large-screen television was conceived, Mr. Kloss envisioned its use in the home as a high-quality display medium and believed that the increasing quantity of broadcast materials would lead to proportionally increased quality programs for which a large screen would be preferred. Video tape recording units being brought out by several manufacturers would permit quality programs to be recorded or purchased, which might encourage more intensive viewing of programs at convenient times on a unit like the Advent TV. However, recorders would have to have sufficient capability to reproduce most of the information content of the signal broadcast so that playback on a large screen would be of adequate quality. Mr. Kloss had no immediate plans to produce complementary products except the improved screen, though he did wish to broaden Advent's product line over the long term.

The possibility of selling the television set to another company was not considered:

> If a product that I developed and sold to somebody else did not succeed, I would be free to blame somebody else. And that's an unsatisfactory position. I have to have the complete responsibility. I really, honestly wouldn't know whether it was their fault or mine; so I have no way of knowing whether I've done anything worthwhile or not if I don't have complete knowledge of the total process. So to me it would be very unsatisfactory to invent things and sell them to somebody. If they continually and regularly were successful, I'd, after a period of time, be satisfied . . . with my contribution. This probably wouldn't happen.

THE FUTURE

Despite several problems with Advent that were apparent in late 1970, the company's future promised to be an exciting one. Mr. Kloss especially looked forward toward making the decisions necessary to reach his stated sales goal, a level of sales which he felt confident of reaching. Specifically, Mr. Kloss felt that a $50 million sales level could be reached within the $2.25 billion audio equipment market and the $2.5 billion television market, without sacrificing Advent's policy of operating within a specialized and protected market niche. Beyond that point, however, it was uncertain whether such a position could be maintained. Mr. Kloss commented:

> If one grows in an established market area, then there can be a succession of products that are based on a careful and sen-

sitive reading of what people in the marketplace express that they want, and what competent engineering can produce, and this may well be an important part of Advent's future. . . . I've no objection to growing in the regular kind of way, and that's the kind of thing that can be happily delegated to somebody else. In fact, to delegate enough of that to make a strong, growing company, and yet continue in the company, would be highly desirable. How strong you have to be before you can have the luxury of doing "me too" kinds of products, though, I don't know.

> I think a perfectly honorable way is to continue to grow making products which, on the strength of the market position, are salable. . . . Up until now one has restricted one's attention to things which are fundamentally better and different than anything else. But there is nothing wrong with growing doing ordinary kinds of products. . . . The idea of making products which continually add to the volume of Advent may well be completely done by someone else. I'd be happy to have that done. That would leave me increasingly free to think longer about things which were different in kind, new kinds of products.

> There's an ideological inclination to want to make broad-spectrum kinds of products. The interest is to get back to where one was at KLH. The cassette recorder with Dolby, I envision that as not nearly as broad-spectrum at the present time as it was planned to be. All the products that would grow out of the fact of the cassette being the primary music listening medium for a lot of people in the home, this isn't happening so fast.

One issue of great concern to Mr. Kloss was the institutionalization of the Advent innovation process. On the one hand, Mr. Kloss felt it would be possible to find a full-time administrator who could work closely with him in handling the company's growing management responsibilities, while he could continue to devote his major efforts to the very enjoyable work of conceiving new products and staying abreast of consumer electronics technology. On the other hand, Mr. Kloss felt that it was possible to institutionalize the product conception function, but he was unsure how best to proceed. In the current situation, he personally perceived market needs, was able to match those needs with the technological state of the art, and was further capable of completing the product conception that fulfilled the market-technology match. As the company grew, Mr. Kloss recognized that some division of these functions would have to take place. Should he separate the more routine R&D functions from the esoteric, or should he attempt to pool the efforts of a large number of people in order to arrive at an effective product conception function? In late 1970, Mr. Kloss could not see how the latter plan might work.

Concerning his role as Advent grew, Mr. Kloss mentioned his admiration for the situation Edwin Land was reputed to have at Polaroid, namely, the situation of ready access to any level of R&D. Mr. Kloss commented: "To contribute to it or direct it without interfering with its normal process. That to me is a really very desirable kind of thing. And it can't frequently be achieved." Mr. Kloss felt that he might be on the way toward such a situation already, toward an Advent that could carry on, increasing a bit in his absence, but to which he could contribute substantially.

READING I·2

How to Put Technology into Corporate Planning

Alan R. Fusfeld

Every executive knows of corporate successes in which technology has played a dominant role. Almost everyone in venture capital and entrepreneurship has a personal list of these successes to emulate. Dreams of technology turned to profit are nurtured by real-life success—Intel Corporation, Minnesota Mining and Manufacturing (3M), Polaroid, Hewlett-Packard, and Digital Equipment Corporation, to name a few of many.

Despite the obvious role of technology in superlatively successful enterprises, technological issues only occasionally are included explicitly in typical corporate strategy reviews, and only rarely are they among the regular inputs to corporate planning and development.

TECHNOLOGY: THE UNDERUTILIZED INPUT TO PLANNING

Most executives have limited management experience with technology. They see research and development as a black box: money and manpower resources are put in, but what should come out? How should these resources be directed and managed? And what should be the characteristic delays, success rates, and managerial control variables? General business management lacks an intuitive feel for strategically directing and positioning research and development investments as compared with

similar investments in marketing, sales, and manufacturing. The result is that technology issues tend to be downgraded in overall importance to the business. Technology is addressed in strategic plans only implicitly, except in the case of special endeavors which are outside the main lines of production—new and joint business ventures, licensing, and acquisitions. In these, technology cannot be overlooked; it is often a major ingredient and even rationale in a purchase or joint venture plan.

In general, key management decision makers have inadequate background and ability to make judgments and forecasts in the area of technology. Without that ability, their options in utilizing technology in corporate strategy are severely limited.

There are many reasons for this blindness to technology and its management in our traditional administration practices:

- Most managers have been trained and have made their successful contributions in marketing, manufacturing, law, accounting, or some other corporate function. Their limited training in science or engineering is not enough to give them confidence in dealing with technological change.

  For similar reasons, corporate economists fail to recognize the process of technological change in their economic forecasts. They either consider all products as homogeneous or see technological change as a wildcat input to their processes—something that comes from heaven or not at all.

  Market research, too, has drawn very little on the technological field. Market researchers typically focus on short-term perspectives. Good, future-oriented market research should provide information that puts together a corporate strategy involving a realistic contribution from technology.
- We know very little about the process of technological change; the knowledge we have is new (accumulated in the last 10 to 15 years) and has yet to be synthesized.
- Partly due to limited experience, we lack adequate frameworks for viewing technological change. There is nothing comparable in this field to the simplifying frameworks for strategic business planning which have become prevalent in the last decade. The management of technology is, in fact, the only functional area which is not represented by a discipline within any management school.
- Technological change proceeds slowly: significant change requires 5 to 10 years. This time span meshes poorly with the planning objectives of most American

corporations. Although most corporations have five-year plans, 90 percent of their research and development activities are designed to be implemented within three years, and the remaining 10 percent within four years. Most corporations outline their strategic objectives on the short time horizon enforced by their need to manage short-term cash flow needs. That's not a time horizon appropriate for significant technological change.

Most research and development objectives are biased toward existing needs—such defensive goals as product improvement and cost reduction. This bias toward the use of technology in the support role to implement strategic objectives planned for three or four years in advance is the obvious result when managers lack an intuitive understanding of any larger goal for their research and development investments.

- Most U.S. corporations are organized around the production process. They are not organized to recognize or to reward the uncertainties, risks, and time constraints of the technological innovation process. Not surprising, then, that most significant technological change originates outside of the firm—or even of the industry—that eventually uses it.

In only three areas of strategic corporate planning has technological change been widely—and, in general, wisely—considered in corporate planning. Acquisition has been a major activity of corporate development and diversification in the last half-century, and expected technological change and the acquisition of new technology has usually been an explicit consideration in this area. Technology has also been addressed explicitly in the licensing area, and it is an implicit part of new venture activities. In all these cases, technology is the essential element of the new opportunity.

PUTTING TECHNOLOGY IN ITS PLACE

Put yourself in the place of an executive assigned to set forth a corporate strategy. You must consider many elements—the broad characteristics of the industry, the qualifications of your firm's competitors in it, and your organization's corporate resources—managerial, financial, organizational, research and development, manufacturing, marketing, and distribution.

Technological issues enter as a result of activities both inside and outside the industry. They can affect the whole range of corporate activities: management, materials procurement, manufacturing, marketing, financial

results, and future growth through new products and into new markets.

As you begin your analysis of corporate strategy, ask yourself such questions as these:

- How are technological issues recognized by your senior management? As a black box? As an input to long-range planning? For meeting short-term objectives? How explicit is the recognition of technology in each of these roles?
- How has management used technology to implement strategic objectives?
- How has technology been monitored? (One of the simplest and most conventional ways is by simply maintaining a research and development department to keep abreast of the state of the art. Other methods include outside technology boards and liaison activities to keep informed on areas where your own technical resources are limited.)
- How are activities relevant to technology recognized and organized in your enterprise? Where are they located, and how are they rewarded? (The typical corporate reward system is biased to short-term, cash flow performance; these criteria are simply not appropriate to the risks that must be taken in a viable technological development system.)

THE FUNDAMENTAL UNITS OF TECHNOLOGY

To improve your understanding of technology in your corporation, you will need first of all an adequate unit of analysis.

When we talk about technologies, we tend to speak of specific techniques and products—internal combustion engines, refrigeration and air conditioning, and machine tools, for example. But technology flows in and out of such products as these, and they do not provide the fundamental basis by which to measure technological change. The analysis must be on the level of generic technologies. A carburetor, for example, is an application of the generic technology of vaporizing a liquid and mixing it with a gas. The same technology applied in the paint industry might become an automatic paint sprayer or in the aerospace industry a jet backpack. This way of focusing on generic technologies and the variety of technical applications of each is necessary if your planning is to be effective at capturing the implications of technological change that's going to affect a company's general product area. Consider, for example, how Raychem and Hewlett-Packard have succeeded by concentrating on a single generic technology, developing and exploiting it in countless products for many different industries.

SEVEN DIMENSIONS OF PRODUCT ACCEPTABILITY

Having defined the unit of technology for analysis, you now need some basic parameters for explicit analysis of how a given technology is to be applied in your company's products and how effective they will be as a result.

After collecting information from many corporations on the characteristics of successful new products, I have found seven qualities which determine the success of any embodiment of any generic technology by any industry:

- *Functional performance*—an evaluation of the basic function that a device is supposed to perform. For example, the functional performance of a household refrigerator is to remove heat, and engineers evaluate a refrigerator's performance of this basic task in terms of what is called pull-down efficiency.
- *Acquisition cost*—in the example of the refrigerator, the price per cubic foot.
- *Ease-of-use characteristics*—the form of the user's interface with the device; in the example of the refrigerator, magnetic door latches and automatic defrosters contribute to the consumer's acceptance of the technology.
- *Operating cost*—in the case of the refrigerator, the number of kilowatt-hours used per unit of service performed.
- *Reliability*—the question of how often the device or process normally requires service, how free it is from abnormal service requirements, and—ultimately—what its expected useful lifetime is.
- *Serviceability*—the question of how long it takes and how expensive it is to restore a failed device to service.
- *Compatibility*—the way the device or product fits with other devices in the context of the larger system.

These are useful categories for analyzing applications of technologies because they are general, applying to everything from refrigerators to jet engines to medical services; they describe technology in a specific application very quickly and very adequately; they describe the goals of most research and development efforts; and they describe most of the emphasis in advertising and marketing strategies. Without such a set of dimensions, you will find yourself talking about the costs and benefits of potential technological change in haphazard, incomplete ways.

TECHNOLOGY DEMAND ELASTICITIES

Economists talk about price elasticity for a product, an indication of the role of price in determining demand. In the same way, each of the different dimensions in which technological change can affect the acceptability of a product is subject to evaluation in a fashion analogous to price elasticity. For example, you can analyze the change in demand for a product when its functional performance has been improved or when its ease of use has been increased or its service requirements lowered. In some cases elasticity will be low, in other cases high. Such data can be measured and used in the same way as the economists obtain and use price elasticity.

Two types of elasticity—absolute and relative—are very important in technology planning. Absolute elasticity represents the responsiveness of total market demand to improvements in function, ease of use, reliability, cost, and the like. Relative elasticity is a similar measure of the tendency for shifts in market share to occur as competitors introduce new products with better performance in one or more of the various dimensions.

To see how these ideas enter into technological planning, consider a piece of medical equipment. In one case the product is destined for emergency room use in a hospital; in another the same functions are to be performed in an individual doctor's office. Some characteristics will be more important in one market than in the other. Cost and ease of use will be relatively unimportant to the hospital; medical insurance will pay most of the bills, and the machine in the emergency room will be operated by a technician. The individual doctor, who must collect from individual patients and use the machine without a technician's help, will put a higher priority on low cost and ease of operation.

Or consider the example of Black and Decker, a company that once concentrated exclusively on commercial and industrial construction tools. The technological demands and price constraints of that market are different from those of the market for home use, and until Black and Decker recognized the differences and developed its technology accordingly, its penetration of the home tool market was very small.

In short, there are significant differences among customers' preference sets and hence different technological market elasticities. Calculation of technology elasticity results from analyzing statistically different market segments according to priorities in purchase decisions which can be established for each individual class of behavior.

PROFILING TECHNOLOGY BY MARKET SEGMENTS

You now have determined a unit of technology on which to concentrate, the dimensions in which it is embodied in the market, and the relative demand for those dimensions. The next step is to apply these analyses to compare your company's technology with the needs by market segments, producing a competitive technological profile. Where do competitors' technologies stand in relation to yours in any particular market? Where did they stand a few years ago? And where are they going? Your goal, of course, will be to answer a question such as this: by the time my company's new technology-based product or service is in operation or online, what will be the competitive situation be?

The competitive profile helps answer that question by answering some simpler ones: what have the rates of change been in the past? And can you project a continuation of those rates into the future? How fast must one company move to gain ground on the others?

ASSESSING THE TECHNOLOGY AND PRODUCT PORTFOLIO

To develop an overall technology strategy around your company's existing technical and business strength, draw a chart (such as Exhibit 1) to show the generic technologies in which your company is engaged and the products in which they are applied. Such a chart provides a profile of the portfolio of technologies and products which may be illuminating to a management whose business has grown and developed in an opportunistic way. A similar chart for competitors in your company's product lines will help reveal what competitors are doing and what has been their strategy.

The company represented in Exhibit 2 may have difficulties in the future because it is trying to manage under the same roof different kinds of technology in which the manufacturer has different roles.

Exhibit 2 reveals that particle separation is a primary driving force of this company's corporate strategy, and there is at least the possibility that the company intends to be a leader in that field. The chart also shows that another part of this company is pursuing strategy that emphasizes a product area, picking up all kinds of technologies because of their common applications. This company may be said to have two parts—one technologically driven and one driving technology. Their technological strengths, their laboratories, their organiza-

EXHIBIT 1 Matching Technology-Imparted Qualities with Customer Needs

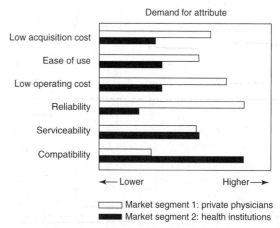

Cost is relatively unimportant to an institutional buyer of medical equipment—but it is a major consideration of the physician in private practice. Reliability is important to both, but the hospital may have a technician to effect repairs promptly. An analysis such as this demonstrates the different technological market elasticities for the same product in different markets—an important concept in any firm's planning for future investment in technology.

tions, their pursuit of joint ventures and acquisitions programs, and their technology strategy in general are different. Indeed, these two parts of the company are so different that the company as a whole may be weakened by having to accommodate two such very different enterprises in its management structure.

A chart of this kind is the first stage in combining all the ideas previously discussed so that you may understand the role of technology in your company and weigh the investment and strategy options that are open to it. To select a particular strategy, begin by considering the generic technological strengths of your enterprise. You may find that you have no adequate strengths: you may find that your strengths in technology are not complemented by strengths in manufacturing or marketing, for example. Or you may find that your organization is fully prepared to drive a particular technology into many different product applications. Or you may see that your best strategy is to capitalize on similar applications of different technologies. Depending on your analysis, you may want to add by merger a new generic technology in order to extend your applications area one step further, or you may want to offer your technology through merger to some firm which is equipped to capitalize on it through manufacturing and marketing.

EXHIBIT 2   Profile of Generic Technologies in Relation to Principal Products of a Hypothetical Company

Principal product applications

Generic technologies	Industrial pollution	Commercial filtration	Medical filtration	Construction	Wall/floor coverings	Automotive engines
Particle separation	○	○	○			
Metal fiber formation				○		
Molded material formation					○	
Noise control						○
Static electricity control					○	
Energy conservation					○	

All six of this company's technological interests are good examples of what the author calls generic technologies, and all are sensible responsibilities of a central research and development laboratory. But only one of them is germane to more than one of the company's products; three of them result from the company's interest in the wall/floor coverings industry. Such a chart could be revealing to a management whose business has grown and developed in an opportunistic way. In this case it reveals that this company is actually two companies—one driving the technology of particle separation and one driven by the several technologies involved in floor coverings of several kinds.

In making these decisions, review the profile of your technologies by your market segments. Which technological dimensions of your products are important? Reliability? Function? Ease of use? Operating cost? How much emphasis will you place on reducing acquisition costs? On increasing ease of use? On reducing operating costs? On improving service?

This evaluation of technology dimensions in relation to market needs and competitive thrusts—the elasticity of technology demand—is the part that's missing from most research and development plans. But it provides answers to the crucial questions: What is your basic competitive advantage relative to other people? Why is your product or service going to sell? Why is it going to work in the marketplace?

Answering such questions succinctly and consistently will help many managements increase the strategic use of technology in their corporate planning.

TECHNOLOGICAL INNOVATION AND STRATEGY

Electronic Arts in 1995

C. C. Oliver

INTRODUCTION

In early 1995, Larry Probst, chief executive officer of Electronic Arts (EA), contemplated the state of the entertainment software industry. The past year had been another good year for EA. Revenues had increased by over 40 percent, and operating margins had remained strong. With its rapid growth, EA had become the largest U.S. provider of entertainment software, with 1994 revenues of over $400 million. Nonetheless, Probst was concerned about imminent changes in the video game industry as computers, consumer electronics, and interactive television converged. To date, EA had derived much of its success from developing software for the 16-bit game car-

tridges of Sega Enterprises and Nintendo. EA had also begun developing 32-bit CD-ROM programs for its affiliate, 3DO. However, in 1995, Sega, Nintendo, and newcomer Sony all planned to introduce new 32-bit or 64-bit hardware platforms. Despite Electronic Arts' considerable resources, Probst wondered whether EA would be able to afford the development costs required to support all of the new platforms, and which standard(s) he should back. To further complicate the situation, the growing popularity of online services, along with the potential explosion of PC games, presented new opportunities for the industry. Probst worried that EA might miss out on the new markets if it did not act quickly.

HISTORY OF THE VIDEO GAME INDUSTRY

Phase 1: The Rise and Fall of Atari

The home video game industry developed in the early 1970s as companies combined emerging electronics and semiconductor technologies to create devices that allowed individuals to play interactive games on the family television or stand-alone machines. Atari Corporation— a Warner Communications subsidiary—introduced in 1975 a home version of its popular arcade game, Pong. These early systems consisted of simple, dedicated consoles that allowed a user to play a single game. By the end of 1976, the industry had generated more than $200 million in retail sales. Participants included semiconductor makers, consumer electronics companies, and toy manufacturers; the top three players—Magnavox,

Source: Copyright © 1999 by The Board of Trustees of the Leland Stanford Junior University. All rights reserved. Stanford University Graduate School of Business Case SM 8 (rev. November 1999). This case was revised by Philip Meza. It was prepared by Carrie C. Oliver, M.B.A. 1995, under the supervision of Professor Robert A. Burgelman, as a basis for class discussion, rather than to illustrate either effective or ineffective handling of a management situation. David Bartenwerfer, Jeff Skoll, Lindsay Van Voorhis, and John Wright, all M.B.A. 1995, and Jeff Maggioncalda, M.B.A. 1996, contributed to the research.

Atari, and Coleco (a large toy company)—accounted for almost two-thirds of industry sales.[1]

The sophistication of home video games leaped forward when microprocessor prices dropped sharply in the mid-1970s. Atari capitalized first on low semiconductor prices, introducing in 1976 the Atari 2600, a programmable video game console with a removable cartridge. This second-generation machine allowed a user to play several different games on a single platform by simply switching cartridges. By the end of 1977, programmable video games had captured almost 40 percent of the market, and industry retail sales increased to $420 million.

The industry's rapid growth between 1975 and 1977 led a number of companies to introduce new platforms for the 1978 holiday season. Apparently confused by the number of incompatible hardware platforms, consumers purchased few systems (almost two-thirds of all toy sales take place during the holidays). Wholesale revenue dropped from $200 million to less than $135 million, and most new entrants abandoned the market.[2] Despite the 1978 Christmas slump and a lull in 1979, the market rebounded. Atari, which had adopted a "razors and blades" strategy to help get its 2600 platform into as many homes as possible, successfully defended itself against two major platform introductions from Mattel and Coleco.

Atari's success was short-lived. In 1981, only one other company manufactured Atari-compatible cartridges—so that Atari was enjoying virtually all of the revenue generated by applications for the 2600.[3] A year later, there were more than 20 companies manufacturing video game software and hardware and reportedly some 1,500 Atari-compatible applications available on the market. As consumers deferred hardware purchases in 1982 and 1983, manufacturers were left with swollen inventories that they then dumped at closeout prices.[4] Depressed prices led to massive losses among all industry participants, including the retail trade, as retail sales declined from $3 billion in 1982 to less than $100 million in 1985.[5] Along with several software developers, most hardware manufacturers pulled out of the market, and Atari, teetering on bankruptcy, was divested by Warner.

Phase 2: Nintendo Emerges

After the "Crash of 1984," many industry analysts believed that the "set-top box" home video game industry was a passing fad in the United States. One company, however, decided that 1985 was the perfect time to enter the U.S. market. Nintendo, a Japanese toy manufacturer, believed that the U.S. market would continue to grow and that Atari and others had simply failed to recognize several lessons from previous slumps.

According to Nintendo, U.S. hardware and software manufacturers had mismanaged their inventories, allowing the market to be flooded with unwanted games. Also, the U.S. industry had failed to realize that it was not the number, but the quality, of software applications that led consumers to adopt one hardware system over another. While there were hundreds of different video games on the market, there was little variety and originality among them. Finally, Nintendo felt that U.S. companies had limited the potential market for video game systems by positioning the products too much as computerized toys, leaving the industry vulnerable to the boom-and-bust cycles of the volatile toy industry.[6]

In 1985, Nintendo entered the U.S. market with the 8-bit Nintendo Entertainment System (NES). Nintendo also followed the "razors and blades" strategy of accepting smaller hardware margins in exchange for larger margins on software. To maintain profitability, the company maintained tight control over the number of games produced for its system. While the company used both in-house software programmers and independent licensees to develop games for the NES platform, Nintendo retained sole manufacturing rights for the cartridges, thus allowing it to control the number of cartridges available on the market at any one time. In addition, Nintendo included in each cartridge a lockout chip that prevented non-Nintendo applications from working on the NES. By managing the inventory level of NES games, Nintendo thus reduced the possibility of discounting.

Nintendo aimed to have a wide selection of the most original, creative, and exciting games on the market. The company sought to attract the best in-house and independent software developers to produce for the NES. With its licensees, the company instituted an exclusivity clause that limited the total number of game titles a developer could produce for the NES each year. Additionally, Nintendo required in-house developers or licensees to submit their games to a rigorous quality review. Fi-

---

[1] *Standard & Poors Industry Surveys,* 1977.
[2] Atari had estimated that industry wholesale sales would be $350–$400 million in 1978 (*Standard & Poors Industry Surveys,* 1979).
[3] *Standard & Poors Industry Surveys,* 1991 (citing *Warner Communications 1983 Annual Report*).
[4] Unit sales of video game hardware fell 26 percent in 1983 to 6.4 million, down from 8.6 million in 1982 (*Standard & Poors Industry Surveys,* 1984).
[5] *Standard & Poors Industry Surveys,* 1989.

[6] David Sheff, *Game Over* (New York: Random House, 1993).

EXHIBIT 1A Nintendo Co., Ltd. Selected Financial Data: Income Statement Data

	U.S. dollars in thousands	
	1993	**1992**
Total net sales	5,626,825	5,050,298
Cost of sales	3,337,179	2,926,885
Gross profit	2,289,646	2,123,413
Selling, general and administrative expenses	577,474	482,115
Net income	763,970	750,898

nally, Nintendo required publishers to purchase a set number of cartridges in advance, thus passing off to the software shops the risk of product failure.

After subjecting the NES to test markets in New York and two other cities, Nintendo launched an aggressive, nationwide marketing campaign to generate excitement and develop the Nintendo brand name. While retailers and distributors were initially reluctant to push another platform so soon after Atari's collapse, Nintendo had the good fortune to have a smash hit product on its hands: *Super Mario Bros.* Because of Nintendo's decision to bundle the software with the NES, children across the country begged their parents for "the machine that plays Mario," and sales took off. Nintendo then established a customer service "hotline" staffed by "game counselors," who gave tips to eager young Nintendo fans, which was combined with elaborate in-store promotions, event marketing, a "Nintendo Power" magazine, and other marketing tactics. Consequently, Nintendo developed a huge installed base: by 1990, one-third of American homes had the Nintendo system plugged into their televisions—an installed base of 30 million units. The company's 1990 worldwide retail sales of $3 billion made Nintendo the largest toy company in the world (see Exhibit 1A).

Phase 3: Say It, Say It, Sega!

Like IBM, Apple, and other computer hardware manufacturers, Nintendo had established a closed architecture platform. The company had built a business model around controlling the underlying hardware, distribution channels, and third-party software development for its systems. But as the decade ended, Nintendo failed to realize several key factors. First, the company appeared to overlook the fact that its independent software develop-

ers were highly, if not solely, dependent upon Nintendo for their livelihood. Nintendo's high royalty fee and requirement that licensees pre-buy cartridges meant that developers had to bear a significant amount of market risk. While the upside for independents was high, Nintendo was not popular with many of its software designers. Also, Nintendo retailers and distributors had also become highly dependent on NES sales. For instance, NES hardware and software accounted for 17 percent of Toys "R" Us sales in 1989 and 22 percent of that company's profits. Nintendo also enforced a "no return" policy and had been accused of rationing cartridges to favored distributors and retailers during peak demand periods.[7] And finally, Nintendo failed to generate the technological change that would lead to a next generation machine. All these factors opened the door for a new industry entrant.

Sega Enterprises, a Japanese arcade manufacturer, in 1989 introduced a 16-bit system called the Genesis. Based on the powerful Motorola 68000 processor, the Genesis offered vastly superior game play—through improved graphics, color, sound, and interactivity—over the Nintendo 8-bit platform. Unable to attract Japanese software designers, the company looked to the United States to find companies to develop 16-bit games for the Genesis. Several U.S. game developers (including Electronic Arts), frustrated with Nintendo's heavy-handed tactics, jumped at the chance to build applications for the Genesis. Sega also moved quickly to establish distribution channels in the United States. Initially wary, retailers were however eager to reduce their dependence on Nintendo.

While the Genesis received positive reviews, software available for the system was slow and thus did not offer challenging game play. But much as *Super Mario Bros.* propelled Nintendo to fame, Sega eventually discovered its own "hit" title: *Sonic the Hedgehog,* billed as the fastest video game on the market. For the 1991 holiday season, Sega lowered the price on the Genesis to $140 and bundled it with Sonic. The games proved popular in particular with older children and young adults, and Genesis hardware sales skyrocketed from a few hundred

---

[7] In the late 1980s, a worldwide semiconductor shortage reportedly left many of the computer chips used in Nintendo cartridges in short supply. Nintendo rationed the number of cartridges available to each of its software licensees, and many retailers were unable to meet customer demand. Several independent licensees and retailers accused Nintendo of creating an even greater shortage than actually existed in order to generate publicity and make its games "status" items among young consumers (see David Sheff, *Game Over*).

EXHIBIT 1B   Sega Enterprises, Ltd. Selected Financial Data: Income Statement Data

	U.S. dollars in thousands
	1994
Total net sales	3,432,206
Cost of sales	2,620,505
Gross profit	811,701
Selling, general and administrative expenses	359,980
Net income	225,138

EXHIBIT 2A   16-Bit U.S. Retail Software Sales (Millions of Units)

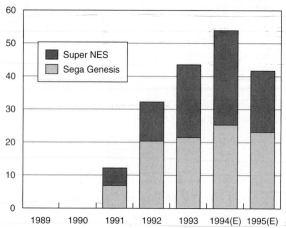

Source: Toy Manufacturers of America: Volpe, Welty & Co. Estimates.

EXHIBIT 2B   16-Bit U.S. Retail Hardware Sales (Millions of Units)

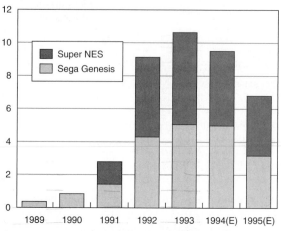

Source: Nintendo and Sega: Volpe, Welty & Co. Estimates.

EXHIBIT 2C   North American Installed 16-Bit Hardware Base (Millions of Units)

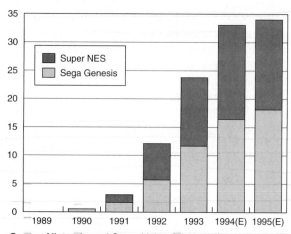

Source: Nintendo and Sega: Volpe, Welty & Co. Estimates.

thousand units in 1990 to 1.5 million in 1991 and almost 5 million units in 1992.

Sega's success (see Exhibit 1B), meanwhile, forced Nintendo to scramble to release its own 16-bit system in time for the 1991 holiday season. The Super Nintendo Entertainment System (Super NES), although incompatible with existing 8-bit NES software, was an instant success and prevented Sega from usurping the entire 16-bit market (see Exhibits 2A, 2B, 2C, 3A and 3B for estimates of 16-bit related sales). With worldwide retail sales of close to $3 billion, Sega revenues were second only to Nintendo's $4.8 billion. In 1993, the Super NES and Genesis platforms accounted for over 75 percent of the $5.3 billion retail U.S. video game market (handheld systems comprised the bulk of the difference).

Phase 4: Convergence

While Sega and Nintendo occupied enviable positions in the home video game market in 1993, the next several years promised to be a time of great turmoil. Because the existence of competing platforms increased hardware manufacturers' needs to differentiate their systems, independent software developers who could generate hit titles were able to extract some of the industry profits. Moreover, in recent years, software sales had increasingly driven industry profits. While competition drove hardware prices down, software remained expensive: a typical game cost $60 and could sell over a million

EXHIBIT 3A Estimated Cumulative Sales of Home-Based Games-Playing Hardware (North America)

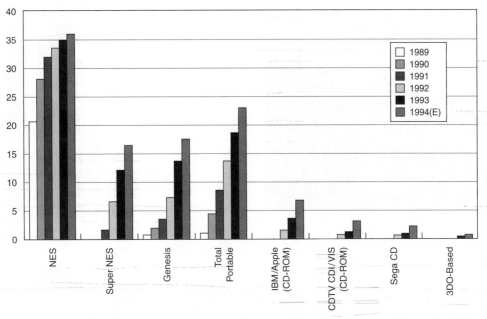

Source: Gerald Klauer Mattison & Co., *Interactive Electronic Entertainment Industry Report,* 28, 1993.

EXHIBIT 3B Estimated Cumulative Sales of Home-Based Game-Playing Hardware (Europe)

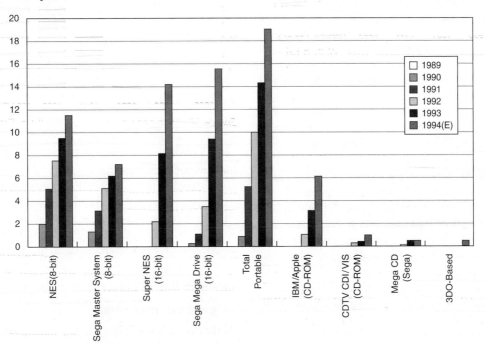

Source: Gerald Klauer Mattison & Co., *Interactive Electronic Entertainment Industry Report,* 28, 1993.

EXHIBIT 4A   16-Bit Transition to 32- and 64-Bit Platforms (Millions of Units, Estimated)

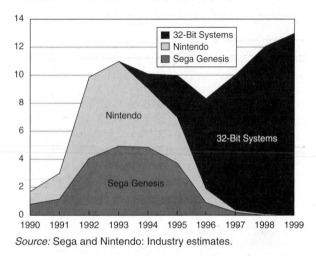

Source: Sega and Nintendo: Industry estimates.

EXHIBIT 4B   32- and 64-Bit Game Platform U.S. Sales (Millions of Units)

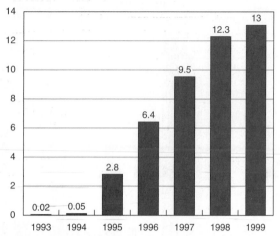

Source: Volpe, Welty & Co. Estimates.

copies. Indeed, software drove the combined profits of Nintendo and Sega to $1 billion worldwide in 1993.[8]

By 1993, a number of platform manufacturers—including several new entrants—had also announced or already launched next-generation machines based on 32- and 64-bit processors. Not only would there be as many as five new platforms available in 1995, but these platforms were expected to be based on incompatible technologies. Most companies were designing hardware based on CD-ROM technology, which offered extra memory for graphics and special effects. Nintendo, however, hinted that it would introduce a 64-bit system based on a cartridge system, arguing that CD-ROM systems would be not only too expensive but also too slow and difficult to program. Recalling the industry collapses of 1978 and 1984 as models, many analysts believed that platform proliferation would lead the market to stagnate as consumers waited for the dominant standard(s) to emerge (see Exhibits 4A and 4B).

Finally, many believed that the home video game industry was positioned squarely at the point of convergence between the computer, communications, and entertainment industries. In addition to traditional consumer electronics companies, who were already desperately searching for the next big product, powerful companies in other industries—such as AT&T, Microsoft, Blockbuster, and Time-Warner—had begun to form alliances to build multimedia systems, which were ex-

pected to eventually supersede demand for stand-alone video game consoles. Coupled with growth in online services, over which video games could be downloaded directly over the wire, these technological changes had the potential to dramatically upset the structure of the video game industry.

ELECTRONIC ARTS

We want EA to be the best place in the industry for producers to work. We have created an environment that is much like the movie business in the 1930s.
—Bing Gordon, Executive Vice President, Entertainment Production

Company Founding

Electronic Arts was formed in 1982 by Trip Hawkins, a 1978 Stanford M.B.A. who had honed his marketing skills at Apple. As spreadsheets and word processing markets began to grow, some believed that personal computers would create a market for interactive entertainment software as well. Hawkins recruited Bing Gordon, a friend and former classmate from Stanford who had been working at a high-technology advertising firm, and secured $2 million in venture capital to form Amazing Software. Later, inspired by the name of movie studio United Artists, he renamed the company "Electronic Arts."

Original Business Plan

At the time EA was founded, most software game developers were individuals or small groups working out of

---

[8] *Fortune,* December 27, 1993.

their garages. Once programmers had designed an interesting application, they would attempt to sell the idea to one of the larger platform manufacturers (personal computer manufacturers and dedicated video game companies) to gain access to hardware specifications. Hawkins believed that video game development was similar to movie development and that a professionally run organization could add a great deal of value to the software development process. (The Appendix provides a characterization of the movie industry.)

In forming EA, Hawkins aimed to strike a balance between administrative and entrepreneurial arrangements. Under the assumption that most programmers—like film producers—preferred to work on their own and be well compensated for their efforts, EA's business model was based on that of the Hollywood movie studios. EA's permanent staff would be positioned within the "studio" to work on financing, marketing, and distributing software, while game designers would be allowed to work outside of the studio organization. EA would pay advances against future royalties to these designers, who would develop interactive software "scripts." If an EA project review committee approved the project at this stage, it would go into production with teams of actors, producers, and technicians. A typical contract with an independent developer would include periodic progress payments based on prespecified milestones. Like in the movie and recording industry, EA would strive to nurture its software designers through intrinsic and extrinsic incentives. Besides collecting royalties on each game sold, software designers would be recognized as creative artists, similar to pop recording stars, and credited directly on EA packaging.

EA built a unique culture that attracted, developed, and retained the best production talent in the industry. Unlike most organizations in which the business and marketing functions fought with the creative functions, artists at EA were recognized as strategically important to the business development plans of the company. More than 50 percent of the executive staff had come from the development domain, and their technical knowledge and appreciation for game playing provided invaluable perspective in determining the technical merits and likely success of new platforms and other innovations. Gordon believed that the balance between marketing, product development, and senior management was held in place largely through cultural mechanisms and that this balance provided EA with a substantial advantage in recognizing and responding to technological change in the industry.

response to tech change

Hawkins made three other important decisions in 1982. First, he decided that EA would design software only for the personal computer (PC) market. Hawkins—along with most other software developers at the time—believed that PCs would provide superior platforms to the Atari, Mattel, and Coleco players and would broaden the entertainment software market beyond the existing target market of 6- to 16-year-old males who comprised the vast majority of video game users. Second, to avoid dependence on any one hardware platform, EA would produce applications for a number of PC systems, including those from Apple, Amiga, Commodore, and IBM. And third, EA would outsource all manufacturing and assembly of its software, producing in-house only the set of master diskettes, documentation, and packaging.

Biz model

Company Evolution

EA's first year brought creative success, but sales were slow because the company lacked clout in software distribution channels. In addition, because home interactive entertainment applications had short lives—typically ranging from 6 to 18 months—the pressure to develop hit titles left EA vulnerable. Developing hit products was as much art as science and depended largely on timing and relative product quality. First-mover advantages, including reduced advertising costs and mindshare, accrued to the first high-quality product to be introduced in a category on a given platform. Once entrenched, a leading title could have a lifespan of almost three times that of a number three or four title in that category. Product quality was a function of: (1) the relative technological superiority of the product, which often depended on the product's ability to exploit the unique advantages of the hardware platform; (2) creative leadership, which depended upon the originality of the game concept and content; (3) "game polish," a superior feel of the game, which required top design and programming talent and was not necessarily tied to the hardware platform lifecycle.

Short life cycles → constant new products

To respond to these challenges, EA made a number of adjustments over the next several years. Hawkins first hired an experienced sales executive, Larry Probst, as vice president of sales. Together, Hawkins and Probst sought to achieve economies of scale and scope in distribution by establishing EA Affiliated Labels, which would act as a distribution arm for products from other entertainment software firms. Combined with EA Studios products—which were created and published by EA—Affiliated Labels was also expected to allow the company to broaden its product line with fewer development risks, to reduce its dependence on studio products alone, and to enhance its power with the trade.

Probst also established a direct sales force. In the early 1980s, most independent interactive software designers relied on distribution companies to move their products. Probst, however, believed that distributors acted primarily as order-takers who had little vested interest in the success of products from any one manufacturer. He felt that a direct sales force would not only work harder to push EA Studios and Affiliated Labels, but also be able to develop stronger relationships with retailers by providing services, such as periodic training sessions, promotional in-store appearances, and other sales materials. The use of a direct sales force resulted in strong retailer relationships, which were important for quick marketing responses such as pricing and promotion as well as inventory management. The sales force also provided EA with market intelligence and was deeply involved in product forecasting and competitive assessments.

From the start, Hawkins invested in leading-edge computer technology, developing hardware tools to help software artists design their products. In particular, EA developed a proprietary tool, the Artist Workstation, which made it easier for programmers to develop across a variety of hardware platforms. In the company's words, the Artist Workstation allowed "cost-effective development, easier portability, and the ability to maximize the full capabilities—weather music, sound, animation, or graphics—of the target platform."[9]

Finally, as part of an overall branding strategy, Hawkins recruited celebrities to help design and market EA Studio products. For instance, EA used football announcer and former NFL coach John Madden to help design and market an interactive football game, and Larry Bird and Michael Jordan were tapped to help design and promote basketball video games. These franchises allowed EA to extend brands in time and across platforms. For instance, the *John Madden Football* franchise represented more than 17 products on eight platforms over seven years and had sold 5.6 million units as of December 1995.

The 1980s: Company Growth and Products   By the late 1980s, Electronic Arts had developed a sound reputation for innovative, high-quality games and was credited with clever marketing and excellent public relations. In 1989, the company was marketing over 100 Studio

---

[9] *Electronic Arts Prospectus*, September 20, 1989.

EXHIBIT 5   1994 Revenues from Top-Selling PC Game Software (in Millions)

Top 5 titles	$ 41.76
Top 10 titles	$ 57.57
Top 20 titles	$ 75.65
Top 50 titles	$108.51
Top 200 titles	$178.29

Source: PC Data, 1994.

titles and distributing an additional 250 through Affiliated Products. More than 40 EA titles had generated at least $1,000,000 in net revenues, but while EA had developed many hits, no one game accounted for more than 6 percent of revenues at any time. This was different from the industry as a whole, in which the top few titles accounted for a large percentage of total industry revenues (Exhibit 5).

EA net revenues in 1989 were $63 million, up 27 percent. In 1988, growth was 67 percent, which the company attributed to the introduction of several unusually successful titles and to the development of new markets overseas. Approximately 45 percent of 1989 net revenues came from Affiliated Labels, up from 30 percent in 1987. About one-third of Affiliated Label revenues were in turn generated by sales from three software publishers: Strategic Simulations, The Software Toolworks, and Arcadia Software. Sales of EA Studios products and Affiliated Label products produced gross margins of about 70 percent and 25 percent, respectively. The company also earned revenue from the licensing of EA Studios products for marketing by third parties, such as home video game systems, and in certain international markets. Gross margins from these licenses averaged about 80 percent.

In 1989, EA products were available in 10,000 retail locations in the United States and Canada. About one-third of domestic net revenues were derived from five specialty retail chains. EA earned about 80 percent of its net revenues from sales in the United States and Canada, another 15 percent came from Europe, and 5 percent from the rest of the world. EA Studios products included simulation (*Chuck Yeager's Advanced Flight Trainer*), sports (*John Madden Football*), and action games, along with some interactive stories and "family activity" products. In 1989, the company was producing games for 10 different PC hardware formats, having supported over 15 formats since 1982. Most EA titles were produced for the 16-bit IBM PC and Commodore Amiga, the fastest growing segments of the home computer market.

(handwritten margin notes at top: "4M PC's", "22m game controllers", "5-6x")

Crisis in 1989   While home entertainment software for floppy disk–based computers had experienced steady growth in the 1980s, by 1989, cartridge-based home video game systems had emerged as the dominant game platform. Approximately four million IBM PCs and compatibles had been sold to the home market, creating an estimated market of $230 million for PC-based games. In comparison, dedicated 8-bit video game consoles were estimated to have penetrated as many as 22 million, or 24 percent, of all U.S. households, generating some $1.6 billion. The software market for a hardware platform depended not only on the installed base, but also on the tie ratio, the number of software titles sold for each new unit sale of hardware, and the tie ratios for dedicated game machines were much higher than for PCs (see Exhibit 6). Nintendo systems alone were thought to have penetrated some 19 million homes. Indeed, the huge NES installed base and high tie ratio meant that games developed for that system could generate sales of 1 million or more units, while a successful floppy-disk game might sell only 50,000 units. Having never developed a single product for the Nintendo platform, EA suffered in 1989 and Hawkins nearly lost control of the company as investors balked. In the face of mounting pressure, Hawkins shifted EA's focus to the stand-alone video game market.

(handwritten margin note at left: "against plans")

The economics of the cartridge-based home video game market, however, were very different from those of the floppy-disk–based PC market. In the PC market, nearly all costs occurred prior to product release, when uncertainty regarding demand and future revenues was high. With Nintendo, lead times were longer and capital commitments more substantial. First, the average cost to produce a floppy disk was less than $3, whereas Nintendo charged an average up-front royalty fee of $12, plus manufacturing fees ranging from $12 to $16, for each cartridge.[10] In addition, Nintendo's tight control over game design meant that independent designers had to spend months working with Nintendo's quality control teams to fine-tune any one game. Then, once a game was approved, the independent was required to submit an order for a specified number of cartridges, well in advance of launch, and wait for several months while Nintendo manufactured the cartridges. Finally, because most distributors and retailers required software publishers to accept returns of all unsold games, inventory risk in the cartridge category was higher than that in the PC market.

---

[10] David Sheff, *Game Over*.

EXHIBIT 6   Historical and Expected Tie Ratios

8-bit	Nintendo	12
16-bit	Super NES	10
	Sega Genesis	10
32-bit	Sega Saturn	15
	Sony Playstation	15
	3DO	15
PC	PC Floppy	1
	PC CD-ROM	2

Note: The tie ratio is the number of software titles sold for each hardware unit sold.
Source: Industry source.

Recognizing the increased importance of capital in the programmable cartridge industry—and in order to pay for its first installment of Nintendo cartridges—Hawkins took Electronic Arts public in 1989 at $8 a share. Its first "buy" of cartridges from Nintendo cost $4 million, equal to the entire finished-goods inventory of all of the company's floppy-disk products.

Electronic Arts in the Early 1990s

As it entered the 1990s, EA made several significant strategic decisions.

Backing Sega   True to the company's historical aversion to dependence on any one hardware platform, EA decided to back a Nintendo competitor, Sega Enterprises, and its 16-bit Genesis machine. Nintendo's huge installed base had rendered the 8-bit NES architecture a de facto industry standard and had given the company a near monopoly position in home video game systems. EA's Bing Gordon argued in 1995 that game developers as a group were, at best, breaking even in the late 1980s. Nintendo's policies effectively delayed the release of new games and left independent publishers vulnerable to high inventory costs. In addition, Nintendo's control over manufacturing made it difficult for independents to meet sudden demand surges, should a product become a big hit.

EA's decision to design games for the Genesis was risky on several fronts. First, since it was a general industry rule that the software development cycle became longer as more complex platforms emerged, designing games for the 16-bit Genesis was expected to be more expensive.[11] Like any new computer platform, it typically took approximately 6–12 months for software

---

[11] Development costs for 16-bit software averaged about $250,000 and ranged as high as $1 million (industry source).

artists to become familiar enough with the nuances of a new hardware architecture to design compelling applications. In addition, small teams of software designers—rather than a single artist—were likely to be needed to produce games for the more sophisticated Genesis architecture. Also, if the Genesis platform failed to capture a significant share of the market, software sales were also likely to be low, making it unlikely that EA would recover its initial investment. NEC, a Japanese consumer electronics company, had recently introduced its own 16-bit console, only to see it fail in the market. At the end of 1989, Sega appeared to be heading for a similar fate: after almost a year on the market, the Genesis had generated software sales of only $77 million. Moreover, Nintendo was continuing to offer exciting games for the NES, arguing that parents who had just bought the system were not likely to purchase another video game console in the near future. And finally, Nintendo had in the past been known to severely punish software publishers or retailers who took actions against Nintendo's wishes. Therefore, there was some risk that Nintendo could refuse to allow EA to produce games for its systems if EA produced games for the Sega Genesis.

Despite these risks, Hawkins believed that 16-bit video game systems would provide the growth engine for the entertainment software industry in the early 1990s and that increased competition between platform manufacturers would provide leverage to independent software publishers. As EA developed titles for new platforms it built its "navigational competence," its ability to recognize platform changes and to develop the platform-specific skills necessary to bring compelling titles to market quickly. The company set up "tiger teams" to explore new operating systems and hardware platforms. It set up special technical task forces to quickly learn and disseminate techniques for developing on new platforms, and it shortened lines of communication to facilitate dispersion of new learning across product development teams and throughout the organization as a whole. EA's ability to assess the likely success of a new platform was unparalleled and arose from its hardware objectivity, intelligence from its direct sales force, and its technologically savvy management teams.

EA's decision to become the first third-party developer for the Sega Genesis paid off. Because Sega needed to attract high quality software developers to its platform to stimulate hardware sales, EA had been able to negotiate a favorable licensing agreement under which Sega charged a maximum royalty per unit (reportedly $8) and offered more creative freedom. EA's earnings increased rapidly when unit sales of the Genesis began to boom in 1991.

Further, by the time Nintendo released its own 16-bit machine in the U.S. market, EA developers were well along the learning curve for producing software that could fully utilize the 16-bit technologies. As such, EA was one of the first to release a game for the Super NES, an updated *John Madden Football* which went on to become the top seller during the 1991 holiday season. Indeed, in 1992, EA had delivered 43 new 16-bit products for the top four 16-bit platforms (Genesis, Super NES, IBM PC and compatibles, and Commodore Amiga), six of which were among the top 15 best-selling games that year. Thus, by 1992, EA had become a clear leader in 16-bit entertainment software, with worldwide net revenues of $175 million, up from $78 million in fiscal year 1990. Net income, meanwhile, increased from $5.3 million to $18.7 million over the same period. (See Exhibits 7A and 7B.)

Founding 3DO Despite EA's success on Sega and other platforms, Trip Hawkins still believed that the business model for the entertainment software segment was biased against independent publishers. While price competition emerged in the hardware category, both Sega and Nintendo continued to charge independent software developers high fees for each game sold, and both maintained significant artistic control over the applications produced for their systems.[12]

Having "bet the company" once on a new hardware platform, Hawkins formed a group within Electronic Arts focused on next-generation hardware. Many industry participants believed that rapid improvements in semiconductor and CD-ROM technologies and the convergence of video, telecommunications, and computing industries would lead to the demise of the stand-alone video game console, perhaps as early as the mid-1990s. Instead, new "multimedia" platforms would emerge that would incorporate interactive software capabilities with a number of other activities, such as movies-on-demand. Others believed that dedicated game players would continue to provide the dominant platform for interactive games for at least the next generation of machines.

In 1991, Electronic Arts spun off the venture as an independent company, later named 3DO, with Hawkins at the helm. Matsushita, Time Warner, Kleiner Perkins Caufield & Byers, MCA (owned by Matsushita), and Electronic Arts were all early investors in 3DO. The company was taken public in May 1993. Unlike others, 3DO would not become an electronics manufacturer. Instead, the company would design an open architecture

---

[12] In 1993, Nintendo was charging as much as $20/cartridge in manufacturing costs and royalties (*Fortune,* December 27, 1993).

EXHIBIT 7A Electronic Arts Selected Financial Data

Income statement data
($000)

	1994	1993	1992	1991	1990
Net revenues	418,289	298,386	175,094	113,098	78,236
Cost of goods sold	224,606	160,578	90,915	61,847	39,652
Gross profit	193,683	137,808	84,179	51,251	38,584
Operating expenses:					
Marketing and sales	44,847	38,465	22,679	15,153	11,753
General and administrative	23,767	20,713	13,962	9,218	8,026
Research and development	62,570	37,451	21,533	12,372	10,987
Total operating expense	131,184	96,629	58,174	36,743	30,766
Operating income	60,499	41,179	26,005	14,508	7,818
Interest and other income, net	3,782	2,537	1,522	1,243	709
Net income	44,737	30,858	18,688	10,837	5,311
Balance sheet at fiscal year-end					
Case and short-term investments	142,249	98,029	59,053	27,579	21,377
Working capital	135,741	85,094	57,375	33,437	23,881
Total assets	273,651	181,257	105,773	65,674	49,069
Total liabilities	97,988	67,687	37,764	22,020	17,540
Minority interest	3,485	2,999	0	0	0
Total stockholders' equity	172,178	110,571	68,009	43,654	31,529

Source: Electronic Arts 1995 Annual Report.

EXHIBIT 7B Electronic Arts Gross Margins by Platform

	1993	1994	1995	1006E	1007E
Sega Genesis	50%	51%	43%	42%	41%
Super Nintendo	31%	32%	31%	26%	25%
PC/MAC	60%	62%	69%	67%	65%
3DO, Saturn, Playstation		75%	62%	62%	62%
Other platforms	40%	40%	42%	40%	40%
License/OEM	80%	89%	79%	84%	80%
Affiliated labels	20%	20%	18%	18%	17%

Source: Alex, Brown report, December 4, 1995.

develop product + license

for an advanced home entertainment machine that would leapfrog existing machines, and then license the operating system to other companies to do the actual manufacturing. Because it would take time to develop software for the new system and to persuade hardware manufacturers to build machines based on the 3DO standard, Hawkins offered to give away the designs for a nominal fee. Then, in order to attract software developers to design games for the new system, 3DO offered technical assistance, free access to the film, publishing, and recording libraries of Time Warner, and a lower royalty fee of $3 to developers. Finally, to assure consumers that the technology would not soon become obsolete, 3DO announced that all future generations—unlike the Genesis,

Super NES, and many 16-bit PC operating systems—would be compatible with existing software.

Panasonic introduced the first machine based upon 3DO's technology—known as the REAL 3DO Interactive Player—in late 1993 at a list price of $699. The system came bundled with three CD-ROM games, including the popular "Crash and Burn," created by Crystal Dynamics. Despite Hawkins's prediction that the installed base would grow quickly, early sales of the REAL 3DO were disappointing, blamed by many on the system's high price, a dearth of compelling software, and lackluster marketing. In an attempt to build the installed base, 3DO announced that it would charge licensees a surcharge on software products to help subsidize the hardware manufacturers and fund an aggressive 3DO marketing campaign.

Just prior to the critical 1994 holiday season, Panasonic cut the price of the system to less than $500, and Goldstar, a Korean firm, introduced its own 3DO multiplayer at a suggested retail price of $399.[13] Finally, despite

---

[13] 3DO's agreements with hardware manufacturers did not give the company any right to dictate the retail price of 3DO systems. However, in 1994, Hawkins began offering 3DO hardware manufacturers equity incentives in the company in exchange for lower prices (*San Francisco Business Times,* December 30, 1994).

earlier assurance that it would not compete directly with hardware or software producers, 3DO established its own in-house software development division in 1994.

By January 1995, Trip Hawkins estimated that the worldwide installed base of 3DO systems had reached 500,000, of which 200,000 were in North America. Independent analysts also predicted an installed base of 500,000, up from 250,000 in August 1994. (See Exhibit 6 for tie ratios of 32- and 64-bit installed base and unit sales.)

Pursuing Educational and Reference Software

EA also decided in the 1990s to broaden its product line. While the company produced interactive software for many game categories, it was truly dominant only in the sports games segment. The EA SPORTS division, with titles such as *John Madden Football '94, FIFA Soccer, NBA Showdown '94,* and *PGA Tour Golf,* had developed a powerful brand image. However, EA was weaker in another important market segment: educational software. In Probst's opinion, interactive educational and reference products were likely to be a high-growth category, particularly when electronic distribution and interactive cable became more common.

In February 1994, EA announced that it would acquire Broderbund Software, the developer that dominated the educational software category with titles like the popular, *"Where in the World Is Carmen Sandiego?"* The deal, a stock swap, valued Broderbund at approximately $440.8 million. Driving the transaction was Probst's desire to "be in a leadership position in as many segments as we can before the business gets re-engineered with electronic distribution and new platforms. Educational product is likely to be one of the most desirable interactive cable products in the future."[14] Upon announcement of the transaction, EA shares fell over 20 percent, driving the acquisition price down to $320 million. At this time, another software maker, Software Toolworks, was acquired by a publisher for $462 million in cash. Believing it was no longer fairly valued, Broderbund backed out of the deal in May 1994.

In November 1994 Electronic Arts formed a fifty-fifty joint venture with Capital Cities/ABC to develop education and reference applications. The joint venture gave EA access to Capital Cities/ABC's news and entertainment intellectual properties and content, as well as capital.

---

[14] *Forbes,* March 28, 1994.

Other Developments

By 1994, Electronic Arts was developing games for 8 hardware platforms, having supported 30 different computer and video game platforms in its 12-year history. Total sales in 1994 topped $400 million, with approximately 53 percent generated from games built for the Sega platform, 22 percent from Nintendo, 3 percent from 3DO titles, 15 percent from PC sales, and 8 percent from Affiliated Labels (see Exhibits 7A and 7B for EA financial data). EA released 85 titles in 1994 and planned to develop 100 products in 1995 at a cost of approximately $120 million. Since 1982, 186 titles had generated revenue of $1 million or more, with 44 titles generating more than $5 million and 10 titles selling more than $20 million. Over the last several years, EA applications regularly appeared on retailers' Top 10 best-seller lists in markets around the world (see Exhibit 8).

In March 1994, EA reorganized to create four divisions to align production, development, and marketing: EA SPORTS, Simulations and Interactive Movies (which marketed titles sold under the brand name Origin), EA Entertainment, and EA*Kids. EA SPORTS was the most recognizable sports video brand in the United States and had a strong reputation for developing high-quality games. Several action games, such as Jungle Strike, Road Rash, and Wing Commander, were also well recognized EA subbrands.

EA continued to invest in hardware development, including enhancements in its Artist Workstation and the creation of the 4-Way Play adapter, a peripheral device that allowed as many as four individuals to play simultaneously on the Sega Genesis.

EA also continued to invest in direct and indirect distribution. By supporting Genesis, the company had capitalized on retailers' and distributors' dependence on Nintendo and built its channel relations early, including with mass merchants and superstores. EA also invested heavily in state-of-the-art distribution systems, including installation of an electronic data interchange (EDI) in 1994. The EDI system connected the company to 20,000 toy stores, department stores, software specialty retailers, consumer electronic chains, and discount retailers in North America. Efficient distribution was expected to become increasingly important as the consumer moved toward these latter channels, which typically stocked only a limited number of top-rated, reasonably priced, and well-backed titles. Further, by 1994, the Affiliated Label Program included 11 independent U.S. publishers, 4 European publishers, and 5 Australian publishers.

EXHIBIT 8   Electronic Arts Geographic Breakdown of Revenues, Fiscal Year 1994

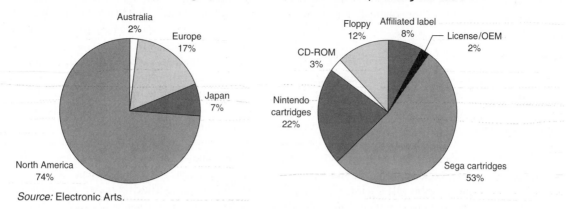

Source: Electronic Arts.

Finally, EA had moved aggressively to expand overseas. Over the past two years, the company had formed a joint venture with JVC in Japan to translate and publish EA applications for the Japanese market and opened offices in the United Kingdom, Germany, and France. EA had also invested in distributorships in Germany and Spain and acquired several software houses, including Bullfrog Productions, Inc., a well-known United Kingdom–based interactive entertainment developer. By 1996, EA expected 40 percent of its overall revenue to be generated outside of the United States.

THE VIDEO GAME INDUSTRY IN 1995: EXPECTED PLATFORM INTRODUCTIONS

By the end of 1994, at least five companies had announced that they would launch 32-bit or 64-bit video game platforms in the United States: 3DO, Atari, Sega, Nintendo, and Sony. The 3DO system is described above.

Atari

Hoping to use the transition to next-generation technology to regain its once leading position in the market, Atari launched a 64-bit CD-ROM stand-alone video game platform in 1993 known as the Jaguar. Offered at a retail price of $250, the Jaguar was manufactured by IBM. While the Jaguar's technology offered superior playability and animation over the 16-bit systems, the system had a limited number of games available and early sales were slow.

Sega

Through 1994, Sega concentrated its marketing and software development on producing games for the 16-bit

Genesis and CD-ROM attachments that allowed players to upgrade the system to 32 bits. However, in 1995 the company was expected to shift much of its effort to the new 32-bit Sega Saturn console, a CD-ROM–based player. Sega described the Saturn as a dedicated game player but said that the system would eventually feature adapters to allow video movies and other interactive elements. To develop the Saturn system, Sega teamed up with Hitachi to build its central processing unit, JVC to build visual processors, and Yamaha to build audio processors. Sega launched the Saturn in Japan in late 1994 and expected to enter the U.S. market in late 1995. While Sega had not yet announced a retail price, the Saturn listed in Japan for about $480.

Nintendo

Nintendo had long argued that the market for 32-bit or 64-bit platforms would not develop prior to 1996. Therefore, the company decided to skip the 32-bit generation. Instead, in August 1993, the company announced that it was teaming up with Silicon Graphics to develop the Ultra 64 (code-named "Project Reality"), hoping to tap that company's expertise in simulation. The Ultra 64 would be based on a chip set consisting of a 64-bit MIPS RISC microprocessor, and software developers would be encouraged to use the Indy desktop computer to create applications for the system. The Ultra 64 would not be based on CD-ROM technology, but instead on a silicon-based cartridge format. Nintendo has stated that the new cartridge system would have an access time 2 million times faster than that of current CD-ROM technology.[15]

---

[15] Nintendo claimed that the Ultra 64 chip set would offer graphic realism "an order of magnitude" above its competitors. The Atari Jaguar,

The machine was expected to be launched in Japan in late 1995 and the United States soon thereafter at a price under $250.

Sony

A new entrant in the home video game industry, Sony introduced a new machine called the PlayStation in the United States by late 1995. This 32-bit CD-ROM player purportedly had superior graphics, video, and sound quality. The machine was powered by a CPU chip, developed exclusively for Sony by LSI Logic Corporation, which comprised three high-performance subsystems on a single chip: a built-in 32-bit MIPS RISC microprocessor for faster processing power, a 3D engine subsystem for advanced geometric graphics, and a decompression subsystem for high-resolution full-motion video.[16]

Sony had strong technical expertise in CD-ROM technology, which most analysts predicted would replace cartridge-based technology in the video game industry. The company also had access to content through its own movie studios, including Columbia Pictures. Finally, Sony had a very strong brand image as a technical leader in consumer electronics and experience in selling to teenagers, with its Walkman, Diskman, and boom boxes.

According to Sony, as many as 164 Japanese game companies signed up to produce titles for the PlayStation. Sony hinted that the system, available in Japan at a street price of about $480, would retail for around $300 in the U.S. Nevertheless, analysts believed it would be difficult for Sony to make a profit at this price, given the PlayStation's high fixed costs and complicated technology.

INDUSTRY TRENDS

Capital Requirements

As the home video game industry evolved in the 1990s, access to capital was expected to play a critical role in a company's ability to produce software. Cash had always been needed to sign licenses and to attract celebrity promoters. However, while development costs for a 16-bit product ranged from $200,000 to $600,000 per product

per platform, 32- and 64-bit titles were expected to cost $1 million or more, due to a longer product development process, higher costs of animation and simulation, and a need for larger product development teams to bring these games to market. A whole production team was required to create a game instead of a single software engineer or small team: at Electronic Arts, for instance, software engineers, artists, staff writers, sound engineers, musicians, and marketers were headed up by project managers, who oversaw the project to keep it on schedule.[17] (Given the importance of the holiday selling season, missing a scheduled launch date could spell financial disaster.) Indeed, Electronic Arts spent nearly $5 million developing *Wing Commander III,* a flight-simulation game for the PC with live action video, starring Mark Hamill of Star Wars fame.[18] According to Larry Probst, porting applications to new platforms was also expensive, costing between $500,000 and $750,000 per port and representing 25–35 percent of total development costs, on average.

According to *Dealerscope Merchandising,* cartridge-based games took an average of 15 months from concept to retail delivery: game development (9 months), game testing (1 month), approval from Sega (1 month), production (4 months or more, depending upon the backlog), and then shipping time to the licensees and then retail customers. Because CD-ROMs had virtually unlimited memory, allowing video footage and other sophisticated features to be included, developing and testing games for this medium may add several more months to the process (although manufacturing lead times for CD-ROMs are shorter).[19]

Marketing and distribution costs were also expected to rise in the future. In the 1980s, Nintendo expanded the home video game sales channels beyond toy and department stores to include specialty software vendors, electronics chains, and mass merchandisers. As shelf space became more difficult to obtain in each channel, companies turned to prelaunch marketing blitzes in an attempt to generate excitement for new games. For example, Acclaim backed up its *Mortal Kombat* release in September 1993 with a $10 million marketing campaign—far more than Acclaim or others had spent marketing a single game in the past. In turn, the game was expected to gen-

---

which was also 64-bits, reportedly did not offer game play significantly superior to some 32-bit machines, such as the Sega Saturn. However, Nintendo argued that its use of a special bus architecture would allow the central processing unit to communicate with memory at an "unprecedented" 500 MHz (Nintendo of America, 1995). The Sega Saturn contained two 32-bit RISC CPUs running at 28.6 MHz and 25 MIPS each, and a double speed CD-ROM drive (Sega of America, 1995).
[16]*Business Wire,* June 15, 1994.

---

[17]According to Electronic Arts, while 2–3 developers might be capable of creating a 16-bit application, as many as 30 individuals might be needed to develop applications for 32- and 64-bit platforms.
[18]*Los Angeles Times,* December 7, 1994.
[19]*Dealerscope Merchandising,* January 1993.

Prod dev
1 Soft Eng → whole team
86.0 → 646A

erate $150 million in revenues, about one-third of Acclaim's total sales.[20] In addition, some believe that video game rentals (through such companies as Blockbuster) could eventually play a role in an application's success by giving consumers the opportunity to "test run" a game.

The PC Market

The strong growth in PC-based CD-ROM players was estimated to have siphoned off as much as 15 percent of cartridge-based home video game sales in 1994, as upgrade kits and sharp price reductions have made it affordable for consumers to buy more powerful PCs with CD-ROM drives. Indeed, with upgrade kit prices typically below $250, over 5 million American households were expected to own "multimedia capable" PCs by the end of 1994.[21] In one sign of the growing popularity of PC-based games, Bing Gordon predicted that CD-ROM games would represent 20–25 percent of EA's total revenue in 1995, up from 2 percent in 1994.[22] Larry Probst, however, expects that the 32-bit and 64-bit PlayStations (non–PC-based) would continue to capture 75 percent of the interactive entertainment software business over the next few years. Personal computers were still expensive relative to the PlayStations, and installation of most PC-based CD-ROM applications had proven difficult for the average personal computer user, whereas the PlayStations were "plug and play." The average PC consumer is older than the average consumer of entertainment software. Sega and Nintendo applications are not available on PC.

Interactive Media and Online

As the communications, computing, and entertainment/media industries converged in the mid-1990s, many companies jostled for position in a world where the personal computer, the telephone, and the television set linked into a full service interactive network.

Many believed that interactive software developers, such as Electronic Arts, would be well-positioned in a multimedia environment, no matter the eventual standard. The introduction of several new dedicated video game platforms was expected to weaken Nintendo's and Sega's control over software licensees. Further, industry participants were betting that video game applications would play a critical role in the success of any new platform or operating system, whether a dedicated console or a multifunctional set-top box or PC-based machine. As platform manufacturers, operating systems designers, and electronic distributors raced to increase their installed base and capture network externalities, many believed that companies that could produce blockbuster software products would gain significant market power.

In the short term, the market for interactive software was expected to flatten as consumers postponed hardware decisions in 1995. In the longer term, since the new CD-ROM–based machines (whether PC or set-top box) could play games with near video quality, Hollywood studios and other content providers could enter the market. In fact, by October 1994, nearly 40 such companies had established interactive divisions targeted toward the multimedia market.[23] Since EA and many other game makers currently licensed characters and other content from these same movie and recording studios, some believed that access to content could become more expensive or limited in the future.

The exploding growth in the online services industry also presented new challenges to the home video game industry. Many believed that it was premature to utilize the Internet and available commercial services, such as America Online and Prodigy, to distribute software applications. Online delivery speed was generally too slow for the most popular "twitch" games, and the networked environment and current infrastructure of online services present complicated design issues for software developers. Nevertheless, several companies, including Electronic Arts, have begun working with infrastructure providers to explore opportunities and to overcome obstacles. In particular, in December 1994, Sega introduced the first online video game service, the Sega Channel, in a joint venture with Time Warner. Priced in the range of most pay-cable subscription services, Sega Channel subscribers could choose from a selection of popular video games and "test drive" soon-to-be-released titles. However, Sega had not provided a technology upgrade path for online delivery from 16-bit cartridges to 32-bit games and had reportedly met with limited success. With the World Wide Web currently boasting over 30 million users, this new form of distribution could play a key role in the new multimedia environment.

[20] *Forbes*, February 28, 1994.
[21] Ibid.
[22] Ibid.

[23] *Los Angeles Business Journal*, October 17, 1994.

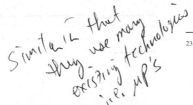
Similar in that they use many existing technologies i.e. µP's

ELECTRONIC ARTS IN 1995

In mid-1995, CEO Probst needed to decide in what direction to take Electronic Arts. Probst and Vice President Gordon believed that EA was in a better position than its rivals to address the coming market hardware proliferation. However, they remained concerned that despite strong resources, EA could not simultaneously back all of the new 32-bit and 64-bit technologies, and it was not clear whether EA could afford to develop for both cartridge and CD-ROM technologies. A key question for Probst was: For which platform(s) should EA develop its applications?

Probst and his staff also discussed the broader corporate strategy issues: What should the company's strategy be relative to hardware? How should EA manage its relationship with 3DO and other hardware providers? How should EA develop its strategic position in the horizontal interactive software market? How can the company develop and leverage intellectual properties in a wide variety of media, such as television, feature and animated films, and merchandising?

APPENDIX

The Entertainment Industry

Harry Cohn, a famously tyrannical studio boss of Columbia, thought that there was nothing in the movie business that "couldn't be learned in six months." He was right. A business school course on the commercial aspects of entertainment would be over in a morning. There are probably only three basic rules: the sunk cost rule, the hit rule, and the nobody-knows-anything rule.

The *sunk cost rule* dictates that nearly all the cost of making entertainment software is fixed and up-front. An average American film takes around two years to complete from script to opening night. Its production cost is around $20 million, with a further $7 million to market in America and $3 million of studio overheads. That $30 million cost is sunk—it will barely change whether the movie makes $10 million, $100 million, or $1 billion. . . .

The *hit rule* is that most of the profit comes from a tiny part of the output. Just 3 percent of the films released in 1988 accounted for close to a third of box office receipts. Because most of the cost is fixed, any revenue above that line is profit. McKinsey has calculated that, assuming costs do not change, a 10 percent increase in an entertainment company's revenues pushes profits up by around 50 percent.

Only 4 of 10 films are ever profitable, but they pay for a string of flops. *Batman* cost Warner $75 million: by the time all the merchandising rights, video, records, and T-shirts are added in, the film will bring in around $1 billion. On a smaller scale, *Sex, Lies, and Videotape* cost $1 million to make; it has earned $24 million at the American box office. . . .

The final rule is based on William Goldman's famous book, *Adventures in the Screen Trade.* **"Nobody knows anything,"** wrote Goldman. Popular taste and creative talent being as fickle as they are, there is no surefire formula for making a hit. . . .

Mr. Christopher Dixon at Kidder, Peabody, an investment bank, points out that the calculation about hit or miss is even harder to make before production has begun. Imagine that you were a mogul and you were offered a script for an expensive comedy/action picture, to be produced by George Lucas or Steven Spielberg and to feature a lovable animal and a lot of expensive gimmickry. The result: either Mr. Spielberg's hit *Who Framed Roger Rabbit,* or Mr. Lucas's flop *Howard the Duck.*

All You Need Is Cash and Talent

From these rules, it follows that two things will always rule the entertainment industry: talent and capital. The first goes without saying. In an industry where nobody knows anything, an established popstar, a director, or even a mogul with a good "hunch" record will always be in demand.

But an entertainment company also needs financial muscle to produce enough software to give itself a decent chance of bringing in a hit, and marketing muscle to make the most of that hit when it happens. The result: consolidation. The big studios produced fewer than a third of the films released in 1988, yet they accounted for 80 percent of the box office take. In the record industry, the same five companies are just as dominant.

Source: The Economist, December 23, 1989.

Electronic Arts in 2002

*"We want to be the number one
entertainment company in the world."*
—John Riccitiello, President and COO, Electronic Arts [1]

Frederic Descamps

INTRODUCTION

Over the past decade, Electronic Arts (EA) negotiated both technological uncertainty and fickle consumer tastes to become a leading maker of video games for consoles and personal computers (PCs). In August 2002, EA's President and COO, John Riccitiello discussed several elements that had contributed to the company's success. He firmly believed that ultimately the company's success derived from EA's team. Riccitiello stressed that the management team—comprised of several executives including himself—formed the strategy and provided the leadership that guided the company. Riccitiello added:

We nailed distribution. Our internal studio model works. We stopped marketing small games and became better at selecting games on which to bet big. Our marketing presence is stronger than anybody else's. We articulated a clear strategy. We focused our efforts on the PlayStation (Sony) and not on Dreamcast (Sega). We redirected our online efforts but did not kill them. We focused on our people. We have made mistakes in the past, but our strength is that we can stop them and learn.

Looking forward, Riccitiello said that EA would try to achieve its vision of becoming the "greatest entertainment company in the world" by focusing on just a few key strategic challenges. EA needed to remain the number one content provider for console, personal computer (PC) and online games. The company also needed to continue its success with attracting and developing talented people. Riccitiello showed a three-page presentation laying out the six areas critical to EA's realization of its vision (Exhibit 1).

In 2002, however, EA had to contend with a series of new threats and opportunities that would affect its ability to realize its vision. Some challenges were technological, such as online gaming, while others stemmed from

[1] All quotes from John Riccitiello are from the authors' interview on August 21, 2002.
Source: Frederic Descamps (M.B.A., 2003) prepared this case under the supervision of Professor Robert A. Burgelman and Philip Meza as the basis for class discussion rather than to illustrate either effective or ineffective handling of an administrative situation. This case can be used in conjunction with "Electronic Arts in 1995," Case I-3. *Copyright © 2002 by the Board of Trustees of the Leland Stanford Junior University. All rights reserved. To order copies or request permission*

to reproduce materials, e-mail the Case Writing Office at cwo@gsb .stanford.edu or write Case Writing Office, Stanford Graduate School of Business, 518 Memorial Way, Stanford University, Stanford, CA 94305-5015. No part of this publication may be reproduced, stored in a retrieval system, used in a spreadsheet, or transmitted in any form or by any means—electronic, mechanical, photocopying, recording, or otherwise—without the permission of the Stanford Graduate School of Business.

EXHIBIT 1 Electronic Arts Goals

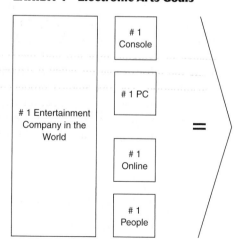

- Drive "Harry Potter" to year-over-year growth.
- Make "FIFA" the undisputed #1 in WW sports.
- Build global recognition of EA's intellectual property—"Medal of Honor," "The Sims," "Sim City."
- Win November . . . flawless global execution on "Harry Potter," "James Bond," and "Lord of the Rings."
- Prove online subscription model with "The Sims Online" and "Earth & Beyond," . . . Drive to #1.
- Drive EA SPORTS to #1 in all major sports.

Source: John Riccitiello, Electronic Arts.

the fast-changing developments among potential collaborators and competitors. Software giant Microsoft entered the market with its Xbox console at the same time that the once dominant, but more recently beleaguered, console and game maker Sega abandoned the console hardware business to focus solely on creating games. Since 1995 Sony had been the undisputed leader of the last generation consoles. Sony would try to extend its dominance in the 128-bit console market with its PlayStation 2, while Microsoft would likely prove to be a fierce competitor. Nintendo seemed relegated to third place yet maintained a stranglehold on the market for younger audiences. Meanwhile, online gaming emerged as the fastest growing trend in the industry, but few companies had managed to generate profits out of it.

To go beyond its current success, EA had to find new sources of growth. Would online gaming ever be profitable for EA? What would it take to lead in this segment? What is the nature of the threat and challenge to EA represented by Microsoft and its Xbox and the new generation of 128-bit consoles? What skills, competencies, and resources did EA need to compete?

GENERAL INDUSTRY TRENDS

Overall, the video game market was thriving. The industry had grown at an average rate of 12 percent per year over the last six years in the U.S. alone.[2] Moreover, the introduction of a new generation of 128-bit consoles initiated a new cycle of growth for the industry.[3] The video game industry generated revenues exceeding Hollywood's ticket sales, reaching $6.35 billion[4] in the United States alone and over $20 billion worldwide[5] in

EXHIBIT 2 Dollar Sales for United States Video Game Industry, PC and Console Software, 1997–2001

Year	Annual Sales
2001	$9.4 billion
2000	$6.6 billion
1999	$6.9 billion
1998	$6.2 billion
1997	$5.1 billion

Source: "First Quarter 2002 Video Games Fact Sheet," NPD Funworld at http://www.npdfunworld.com/funServlet?nextpage=trend_article1.html.

2001 (Exhibit 2). In the same year, over 225 million units of games were sold in the United States; more than 11 times the number of tickets sold to National Basketball Association (NBA) and National Hockey League (NHL) games combined and about 14 times the number of National Football League (NFL) tickets sold in the 2000 season.[6] Some analysts predicted the video game industry would achieve household penetration of over 50 percent in the United States and 35 percent in Europe by 2005.[7] The entire industry experienced a 20 percent increase in sales for the first half of 2002, with analysts forecasting a similar performance for the second half of the year.[8] The industry was expected to grow by 40 percent in the United States by 2006.[9]

Video games had come a long way. No longer the realm of boys playing alone in their rooms, the PC and console game industry had grown into one of the largest and most dynamic segments of the entertainment industry. New gaming techniques such as massive multiplayer online gaming, dynamic content creation, community-driven modification, and persistent-state worlds added to the excitement (see below). Content continued to improve, and titles originally developed for games, such as the popular "Mario Bros." and "Tomb Raiders" franchises, were extended into motion pictures. With more technology advances on the horizon, growing online game revenue opportunities, and increasingly advanced artistry and creativity by developers, the video game industry was likely to gain even more importance in the overall entertainment industry in the coming years.

---

[2] "Fast Facts: Historical U.S. Sales Figures," The Interactive Digital Software Association (IDSA) at http://www.idsa.com/ffbox7.html.

[3] A new generation of more powerful consoles is released approximately every five years. Traditionally, the processing power increases greatly with each new generation. The last generation was based on 32-bit and later 64-bit processors, whereas the current generation is based on 128-bit processors.

[4] "2001 Game Industry Sales Data & Graphs," IDSA at http://www.idsa.com/2001SalesData.html.

[5] "Video Game Market Thriving Despite Economic Slowdown," *Los Angeles Times,* November 11, 2001. N.B.: Other sources estimated that movie box office revenue accounted for 14% ($8.26 billion) of the $59 billion spent on entertainment in 2001. Video and DVD sales and rentals accounted for 28% ($16.52 billion) in 2001. (*Source:* "Numbers," *Business 2.0,* September 2002, p. 38, citing A. C. Nielsen; Kagan; Veronis Suhler.) While the issue of which was larger, video games revenue or box office receipts, may be important for bragging rights, the close content relationship between video games and movies, as well as the fact that movie rentals/sales were double the size of box office receipts, could bode well for the video game industry.

[6] "2001 Game Industry Sales Data & Graphs," IDSA at http://www.idsa.com/2001SalesData.html.

[7] International Development Group, "The Multimedia Markets in North America and Europe," p. 1, Executive Summary, March 2002.

[8] *NPD Funworld Press Release,* August 20, 2002.

[9] "The U.S. Market for Video Games and Interactive Electronic Entertainment," Press Release, DFC Intelligence, February 2002.

EXHIBIT 3   Demographics of PC and Console Game Players by Percent of Total

PC	1997	1998	1999	2000	2001
Male	55%	62%	57%	59%	61%
Female	45%	38%	43%	41%	39%
Under 18	28%	30%	31%	28%	32%
18–35	35%	31%	29%	30%	28%
36+	38%	39%	40%	42%	39%
Console					
Male	73%	70%	65%	70%	74%
Female	27%	30%	35%	30%	26%
Under 18	54%	44%	46%	42%	43%
18–35	34%	36%	35%	37%	36%
36+	13%	20%	19%	21%	21%

Source: Interactive Digital Software Association (IDSA), 2001.

In the 1980s, the core age demographic of gamers was 12 to 18 and overwhelmingly male. At that time, there were around 20 million people falling within that age group in the United States. By 2002, the core age demographic of video game players expanded to 10 to 45 for men and 10 to 35 for women, with a population of around 96 million people in those age ranges in the United States. By 2006, the population of these demographics could reach 120 million people.[10]

The range of game titles expanded to meet the needs of this older demographic. Many games were developed that featured more mature content, advanced gameplay and sports-oriented themes. This in turn attracted new audiences from among adults who previously had not been gamers. By 2000, 60 percent of all Americans, or about 145 million people, played console or PC games on a regular basis. The majority of console game players were 18 and older.[11] Meanwhile, media franchises marketed to children, such as Pokemon, Monsters Inc., and Disney, systematically added video games to their portfolios of intellectual property. The video game industry was now considered by many to be another form of mainstream entertainment—as important as movies and television (Exhibit 3).

THE CONSOLE MARKET: A CYCLICAL BUT PREDICTABLE INDUSTRY

The console market was highly cyclical. The growth cycles were determined by the release of each new genera-

tion of consoles, which had occurred approximately every five years for the last two generations of consoles. Hardware and software cycles were closely intertwined in a relationship described by the "tie ratio," the average number of games sold for each console sold. The video game industry was one of the very few industries that knew in advance about the transitions it was going to experience and could therefore anticipate peaks and troughs in demand for content. The industry experienced well-defined and regular cycles over the life of any given platform (Exhibit 4).

The Transition Years: End of a Cycle and Market Anxiety

A few years into a generation of consoles, manufacturers started announcing work on the next new generation of more powerful consoles. As the release dates of the new generation approached, sales of current generation consoles slowed down. In turn, sales of the then current generation software slowed down dramatically, decreasing revenues for game companies. At the same time, game developers needed to allocate resources to the production of new and updated titles for the next generation of consoles.

The Introduction of the New Generation (1st Year) New platforms, even when introduced simultaneously by competitors, usually commanded premium pricing. This helped companies recoup upfront investment in development, sales, and marketing. In the past, new consoles were usually first introduced in Japan followed by the United States and then other markets such as Europe and elsewhere in Asia up to six months later. Going forward, some believed that consoles would be first introduced in the United States. New platforms were purchased by early adopters: hardcore gamers who often own one or more consoles of the previous generations and are somewhat price insensitive. It was critical for each console manufacturer to feature star titles to help jumpstart console sales. Console makers hoped to develop or attract software that was exclusive or otherwise unique in order to draw audiences to the new platform. Most console makers also acted as game developers, creating game titles for the launch of their consoles and also striking deals with third-party publishers such as EA, Activision, THQ, or Namco.

The Price War (1st and 2nd Years)   After each console maker introduced its new platforms, competition heated up among the manufacturers, prompting them to

[10] "The Online Game Market 2002," Press Release, DFC Intelligence, June 2002.
[11] 2000 Survey by Peter Hart Research for the IDSA, *State of the Industry Report 2000–2001*, p. 7.

EXHIBIT 4   Gaming Console Installed Base: Cumulative Hardware Unit Sales (U.S.)

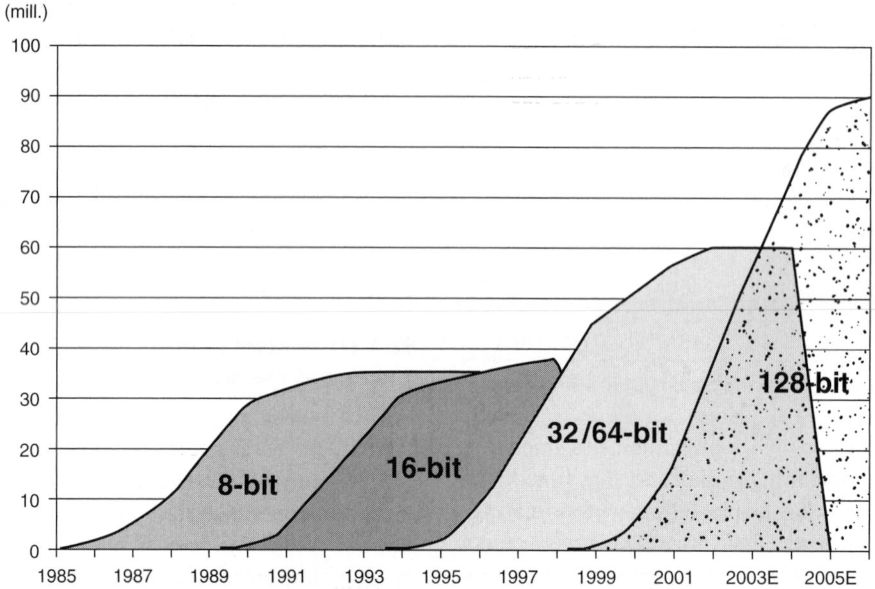

(mill.)

Source: Wedbush Morgan Securities, "Content Is King: An In-Depth Look at Interactive Entertainment Software," p. 18, May 2002.

lower the prices of their hardware. Price cuts were generally initiated by the manufacturer that first introduced its new console in the market. The other console manufacturers followed suit and reduced their prices. Most of them sold the platform hardware at a loss, hoping to make money on the sales of software and licensing fees to third-party publishers. The reduction in console prices attracted a broader wave of gamers, resulting in a surge in hardware and software sales.

Maturity and Mass Market (3rd and 4th Years)   At this stage, console prices were further reduced, making the consoles accessible to more gamers. Games became more sophisticated as developers were now accustomed to the technical specifications of the consoles. In addition, they were able to publish more games due to streamlined development processes and reduced production costs. Game prices decreased. Console manufacturers reduced their first-party publisher activities on the current generation to focus on managing third-party publishers and investing in developing titles for the next generation of consoles.

The End of the Cycle—Market Anxiety (5th Year)
A couple of years before the beginning of a new cycle,

console manufacturers announced their plans for the next generation of consoles. Core gamers refrained from buying games and systems in anticipation of the forthcoming generation. As the release dates for new consoles neared, prices of the current generation machines dropped further, making them a commodity. Soon, a new cycle began, and older-generation consoles were slowly phased out.

The End of the 32-Bit/64-Bit Generations: One Clear Winner by Knock-Out

For Sega and Sony, their 32-bit console cycles began in 1994 with the introduction of the 32-bit Sega Saturn and Sony PlayStation in Japan. In 1995 Sega and Sony launched their 32-bit consoles in the United States. Later in 1995, Nintendo made a false start with its proposed 64-bit console. In 1996 Nintendo finally launched its 64-bit N64. During the 32-bit/64-bit cycle, Sony supplanted Nintendo as the leading console manufacturer and relegated Sega to third place. With double-digit growth, 1999 was a record-breaking year for the game industry. During 2000, the transition year, sales did not plummet but remained flat at $6 billion. Some thought this attested to a new level of durability and maturity for the overall market.

EXHIBIT 5   Selected Financial Data for Sony Corporation (Millions of Yen)

	31-Mar-2002	31-Mar-2001	31-Mar-2000	31-Mar-1999	31-Mar-1998
Sales—core business	7,542,068	7,276,150	6,651,389	6,754,786	6,715,866
Sales—other	36,190	38,674	35,272	49,396	45,138
Total Sales	**7,578,258**	**7,314,824**	**6,686,661**	**6,804,182**	**6,761,004**
Cost of goods sold	5,700,771	5,476,409	4,984,765	4,955,107	4,889,696
Sales, general and administrative expenses	1,742,856	1,613,069	1,478,692	1,500,863	1,345,584
Unusual income/expenses	0	0	0	0	0
Total expenses	**7,443,627**	**7,089,478**	**6,463,457**	**6,455,970**	**6,235,280**
Interest expense	(36,436)	(43,015)	(42,030)	(48,275)	(62,524)
Other expenses	(5,420)	83,537	83,136	77,754	(3,937)
Pre-tax income	**92,775**	**265,868**	**264,310**	**377,691**	**459,263**
Income taxes	65,211	115,534	94,644	176,973	214,868
Income after taxes	**27,564**	**150,334**	**169,666**	**200,718**	**244,395**
Minority interests	16,240	15,348	(10,001)	(12,151)	(16,813)
Misc. earnings adjustments	(34,423)	(44,455)	(37,830)	(9,563)	(5,514)
Net income (excluding extraordinary items and depreciation)	**9,381**	**121,227**	**121,835**	**179,004**	**222,068**
Accounting change	5,978	(104,473)	0	0	0
Net income (including extraordinary items and depreciation)	**15,359**	**16,754**	**121,835**	**179,004**	**222,068**

Note: The U.S. dollar ranged between 116.2 and 127.6 Yen in 2001 and 117.9 and 133.7 Yen in the first nine months of 2002.
Source: OneSource.

Sony emerged as the clear winner of the 32-bit/64-bit console generation battles. The company achieved an installed base of 90 million PlayStation Ones (PS1), compared to 18 million for Nintendo's N64 and a mere 9 million for Sega's Saturn.[12] The PS1 also benefited from a significantly broader software library. Unlike the existing Sega and Nintendo systems, the PlayStation platform (PSX) relied heavily on third-party software to generate hardware sales. Sony managed to appeal to nontraditional gamers, such as young adults and adults, whereas its competitors appealed mainly to younger audiences. PlayStation became a significant line of business for Sony, at times accounting for more than a third of the electronic giant's operating profit (Exhibit 5).

Nintendo took second place with its strong positioning among kids and teenagers. It was also almost at par with Sony in Japan, their home market. Nintendo's strategy was to sell its hardware cheaper than its competitors, marketing its console more like a traditional toy,

targeted toward the 8- to 16-year-old demographic. Sales of Nintendo's games followed the same seasonal pattern as toys, selling the most during holiday seasons. Nintendo managed to develop and perpetuate over the years strong properties such as "Mario Bros.," "Pokemon," and "Zelda" that had been tremendous successes among kids since its first console, the Nintendo Entertainment System (NES), debuted in the 1980s. Some of these properties managed to keep their appeal to gamers as they grew into young adults and adults. In 2001, Nintendo released the GameBoy Advance, a handheld console with the power of 32-bit generation consoles (Exhibit 6).

At the end of 2000, Sega retreated from the console market to focus exclusively on its strong software business. This decision came after several months of heavy losses incurred by its Dreamcast, the first of the 128-bit consoles. After having finished third behind Sony and Nintendo in the 32-bit/64-bit generations, Sega hoped to get a significant market advantage by launching its 128-bit console ahead of its competitors. The platform never achieved the sales needed to make a profit. Dreamcast did not attract the market's attention, which was anticipating the release of the PlayStation 2 (PS2). Sega raised

---

[12] International Development Group, "The Multimedia Markets in North America and Europe," March 2002. Source of installed base for Sega Saturn (as of 1997): http://www.sega-saturn.com/saturn/other/news-jan.htm.

EXHIBIT 6   Selected Financial Data for Nintendo Corporation (Millions of Yen)

	2002	2001	2000
Net sales	554,886	462,502	530,340
Cost of sales	334,620	278,462	289,638
Gross margin	**220,266**	**184,040**	**240,702**
Selling, general and administrative	101,114	99,342	95,361
Operating income	**119,151**	**84,697**	**145,341**
Other income			
Interest income	22,904	39,133	23,119
Foreign exchange gain (loss)	43,419	66,335	(62,486)
Other	2,391	3,600	
Total other income	68,715	109,069	
Other expenses			
Total other expenses	**1,248**	**1,520**	**NA**
Income before income taxes and extraordinary items	**183,023**	**168,651**	**NA**
Provision for income tax and enterprise tax	74,351	93,710	46,675
Income taxes deferred	2,445	(21,358)	
Minority interests income	(218)	(303)	338
Net income	**106,444**	**96,603**	**56,061**

Note: NA indicates data was unavailable for the category. The U.S. dollar ranged between 116.2 and 127.6 Yen in 2001 and 117.9 and 133.7 Yen in the first nine months of 2002.
Source: Company reports.

the bar quite high by integrating a modem and a browser into the Dreamcast to enable multiplayer online gaming. Sega bet heavily on advanced technological features as well as on online gaming. In 1995 Sega was the first console manufacturer to develop and maintain an online gaming infrastructure, years ahead of its competitors. However, the manufacturing and infrastructure costs associated with the Dreamcast proved prohibitive in the end. Sega slowly phased out support for its Dreamcast console and became a third-party publisher like Electronic Arts (Exhibit 7).

Sega hoped to leverage competencies it had developed over the years as both a console manufacturer and software publisher. Sega benefited from popular proprietary intellectual property (IP), with titles such as "Sonic: The Hedgehog" that it had developed for its platforms and was now porting to Sony and Xbox platforms. Sega also decided to focus on professional sports titles, one of the most popular game genres. The pro sports genre had long been dominated by Electronic Arts, which owned the leading titles for most of the major professional sports. Sega also took aim at developing games for wireless devices with its Sega Mobile Division, which rolled out its first wireless games in August 2002.

EXHIBIT 7   Selected Financial Data for Sega Corporation (Millions of Yen)

	31-Mar-2001	31-Mar-2000	31-Mar-1999	31-Mar-1998	31-Mar-1997
Sales	242,913	339,055	266,194	331,605	432,826
Total sales	**242,913**	**339,055**	**266,194**	**331,605**	**432,826**
Cost of goods sold	218,235	290,492	201,819	270,710	347,325
Sales, general and administrative expenses	76,697	88,917	62,287	63,043	72,320
Total expenses	**294,932**	**379,409**	**264,106**	**333,753**	**419,645**
Interest expense	(2,414)	(3,226)	(2,175)	(3,719)	(2,768)
Other expenses	(1,060)	151	(32,563)	(10,628)	4,801
Pre-tax income	**(55,493)**	**(43,429)**	**(32,650)**	**(16,495)**	**15,214**
Income taxes	(792)	1,531	10,573	3,165	9,105
Income after taxes	**(54,701)**	**(44,960)**	**(43,223)**	**(19,660)**	**6,109**
Minority interests	2,971	2,080	342	339	108
Misc. earnings adjustments	0	0	0	(16,314)	(4,185)
Net income (excluding extraordinary items and depreciation)	**(51,730)**	**(42,880)**	**(42,881)**	**(35,635)**	**2,032**
Net income (inxcluding extraordinary items and depreciation)	**(51,730)**	**(42,880)**	**(42,881)**	**(35,635)**	**2,032**

Note: Sega FY 2002 results were unavailable as of September 2002. The U.S. dollar ranged between 116.2 and 127.6 Yen in 2001 and 117.9 and 133.7 Yen in the first nine months of 2002.
Source: OneSource.

The Beginning of a New Cycle:
The 128-Bit Generation

The new generation console cycle was kicked off in October 2000 with the launch of Sony's PS2 in Japan, North America, and Europe. In 2001, the console market turned lukewarm, as gamers awaited the arrival of the Microsoft's Xbox and Nintendo's GameCube. The new generation console was based on 128-bit technology. In an unprecedented move inside the industry, Sony decided to make the PS2 backward compatible with PS1 games. The PS2 was an immediate success and Sony took the lead by establishing a strong position in the market.[13] In December 2001, one year after its inception, the installed base of PS2 was around 20 million in Japan, the United States, and Europe.[14] The PS2 was also an attempt by Sony to reach beyond the game market. The PS2 was meant to be a family entertainment center, capable of playing DVDs and CDs, as well as video games. By being first on the market, Sony managed to get a head start over Microsoft's Xbox and Nintendo's GameCube. In April 2002, 18 months after it introduced the PS2, Sony dropped its console price to $199. Microsoft and Nintendo dropped their prices to $199 and $149, respectively.

Traditionally, each new growth cycle increased technological innovation and sales revenues. In the past, the console market grew by 50 percent or more with each new generation of technology. EA estimated that the 128-bit generation consoles would develop an installed base of between 180–200 million systems worldwide by 2006, compared to the 125 million units of the previous generation console sold by 2002 (Exhibit 8).[15]

By the end of 2002, Sony was expected to reach an installed base of slightly under 30 million PS2s in North America and Europe, trailed by Microsoft and Nintendo with 10 million and 8 million units, respectively. In the battle for second place, Microsoft was ahead of Nintendo, which had a strong market share in Japan and was popular among younger gamers. Sony already leaked its ambitious plans for the PS3, poised for release around

2005. Microsoft was said to be considering launching a mid-generation console, which would be an enhanced version of its Xbox, or even contemplating a leap straight to the next generation.

THE PC MARKET

In 2001, the PC game market reached revenues of $1.5 billion in the United States and $1.2 billion in Europe (Exhibit 9).[16] The market was currently dominated by four publishers: Electronic Arts, Vivendi Universal Games, Infogrames Entertainment, and Microsoft. These publishers represented 64 percent of the retail market.

There were a few important differences between the console and the PC game markets. The PC platform changed more rapidly than did platforms for consoles. New PC processors were put on the market every quarter and 3D accelerating video cards every sixth months or so. Consequently, PC games were usually more advanced than their console counterparts since they took advantage of the more powerful machines. In 2002, top-of-the-line PCs featured over 2GHz processors with 512 MB of RAM and GeoForce 4 video cards, whereas consoles were equipped with processors running around 300 MHz. In addition, PCs were easily networked and connected to the Internet, whereas consoles were not. Online gaming drove the sales of numerous titles. Valve Software's best-selling title "Half-Life," for instance, was still selling well a few years after its inception in 1998 thanks to "Counter-Strike," a free multiplayer modification that was exclusively played online.

PC games could be very attractive to developers since there were often no console-related royalties to pay, leading to greater margins for software producers. In addition, there were no console cycles to deal with, while PCs offered a continuously improving hardware platform. Yet it was still a very difficult business. Over the last four years, PC game sales continued to grow steadily. Another complication to the PC market was the increasing competition from console games. Traditionally, the two markets used to cater to slightly different demographics and gaming genres. As consoles became more technologically advanced, certain genres such as strategy, role-playing, or adventure games that used to be found only on PCs also became available on consoles.

[13] Sony did not have adequate supply of PS2 consoles at launch. In its 10k report issued on 14 August 2001, EA noted that, "At launch, Sony shipped only half of the number of PlayStation 2 units to retailers in North America that it had originally planned, and it shipped significantly fewer units than planned at launch in Europe as well. [Console] shortages were announced as being caused by shortages of components for manufacturing. Due to these shortages, our results of operations for fiscal 2001 were adversely affected."
[14] International Development Group, "The Multimedia Markets in North America and Europe," Executive Summary, PV, March 2002.
[15] Ibid, p. 13.

[16] International Development Group, "The Multimedia Markets in North America and Europe," p. 7, March 2002.

EXHIBIT 8   Console Hardware Market Data

Console hardware unit sales, North America and Europe, 1999–2005 est.

(in 000 units)	1999	2000	2001	2002E	2003E	2004E	2005E
Total North America	**18,315**	**15,273**	**21,060**	**27,261**	**28,146**	**24,609**	**17,465**
Nintendo 64	3,900	2,694	1,053	107	N/A	N/A	N/A
Nintendo GameCube	N/A	N/A	1,290	4,320	5,292	5,076	3,564
Sony PlayStation	6,265	3,410	2,376	1,391	535	N/A	N/A
Sony PlayStation 2	N/A	1,144	6,552	8,000	8,367	6,848	4,415
Microsoft Xbox	N/A	N/A	1,492	5,243	6,527	6,420	4,066
Game Boy/Color	8,150	8,025	2,996	1,540	N/A	N/A	N/A
Game Boy Advance	N/A	N/A	5,301	6,660	7,425	6,265	5,420
Total Europe	**12,163**	**10,475**	**11,981**	**17,205**	**20,794**	**22,435**	**21,365**
Nintendo 64	1,090	612	275	115	N/A	N/A	N/A
Nintendo GameCube	N/A	N/A	N/A	2,335	3,165	3,905	4,510
Sony PlayStation	6,768	3,395	2,054	980	630	355	N/A
Sony PlayStation 2	N/A	658	4,363	6,120	7,810	7,630	6,230
Microsoft Xbox	N/A	N/A	N/A	2,595	3,630	4,485	5,275
Game Boy/Color	4,305	5,810	2,419	650	N/A	N/A	N/A
Game Boy Advance	N/A	N/A	2,870	4,410	5,559	6,060	5,350
Total	**30,478**	**25,748**	**33,041**	**44,466**	**48,940**	**47,044**	**38,830**
Total (in 000s of U.S. $)	**2,122,422**	**1,690,901**	**4,908,515**	**6,772,107**	**6,406,709**	**5,279,600**	**4,195,525**

Source: International Development Group, "The Multimedia Markets in North America and Europe," p. 12, March 2002.

Console hardware installed base, North America and Europe, 1999–2005 est.

(in 000 units)	1999	2000	2001	2002E	2003E	2004E	2005E
Total North America	**64,717**	**79,990**	**101,058**	**128,319**	**98,762**	**92,230**	**109,695**
Nintendo 64	14,578	17,272	18,325	18,432	N/A	N/A	N/A
Nintendo GameCube	N/A	N/A	1,290	5,610	10,902	15,978	19,542
SonyStation	23,429	26,839	29,215	30,606	31,141	N/A	N/A
SonyStation 2	N/A	1,144	7,696	15,696	24,063	30,911	35,326
Microsoft Xbox	N/A	N/A	1,500	6,743	13,270	19,690	23,756
Game Boy/Color	26,710	34,735	37,731	39,271	N/A	N/A	N/A
Game Boy Advance	N/A	N/A	5,301	11,961	19,386	25,651	31,071
Total Europe	**45,915**	**56,390**	**68,471**	**85,676**	**70,224**	**92,659**	**87,070**
Nintendo 64	5,090	5,702	5,987	6,102	N/A	N/A	N/A
Nintendo GameCube	N/A	N/A	N/A	2,335	5,500	9,405	13,915
SonyStation	19,560	22,955	24,989	25,969	26,599	26,954	N/A
SonyStation 2	N/A	658	5,131	11,251	19,061	26,691	32,921
Microsoft Xbox	N/A	N/A	N/A	2,595	6,225	10,710	15,985
Game Boy/Color	21,265	27,075	29,494	30,144	N/A	N/A	N/A
Game Boy Advance	N/A	N/A	2,870	7,280	12,839	18,899	24,249
Total	**110,632**	**136,380**	**169,529**	**213,995**	**168,986**	**184,889**	**196,765**

Source: International Development Group, "The Multimedia Markets in North America and Europe," p. 13, March 2002.

WIRELESS GAMES

Games that traditionally had been played on PCs and consoles were reaching other platforms such as the Internet and wireless devices or personal digital assistants (PDAs). Though still limited in size and scope, these markets were growing quickly and were expected to contribute incremental revenue in the latter end of the current game console cycle and into the next. These channels could constitute a new attractive market for video game companies. As telecom operators deployed next generation 2.5 G and 3 G wireless networks, some looked to games to provide compelling advanced applications to help speed customer adoption. In 2000, there were 7.3 million wireless data subscribers in the United States,

EXHIBIT 8   Console Software Market Data (continued)

Console software unit sales, North America and Europe, 1999–2005 est.

(in 000 units)	1999	2000	2001	2002E	2003E	2004E	2005E
Total North America	**121,400**	**126,441**	**137,803**	**157,199**	**179,896**	**178,919**	**152,284**
Nintendo 64	28,500	29,141	14,605	1,080	N/A	N/A	N/A
Nintendo GameCube	N/A	N/A	3,639	19,476	29,900	36,233	30,294
SonyStation	66,500	60,900	49,118	23,868	6,048	N/A	N/A
SonyStation 2	N/A	2,812	31,665	52,909	74,358	65,664	51,188
Microsoft Xbox	N/A	N/A	4,926	26,068	37,830	46,522	37,902
Game Boy/Color	26,400	33,588	23,759	8,448	1,960	N/A	N/A
Game Boy Advance	N/A	N/A	10,091	25,350	29,800	30,500	32,900
Total Europe	**58,261**	**66,172**	**69,610**	**67,294**	**93,589**	**119,569**	**143,380**
Nintendo 64	7,201	6,173	3,233	1,139	N/A	N/A	N/A
Nintendo GameCube	N/A	N/A	N/A	7,315	13,758	20,795	32,330
SonyStation	41,843	40,926	32,798	11,610	6,420	2,588	N/A
SonyStation 2	N/A	1,390	14,475	26,865	38,940	46,682	47,840
Microsoft Xbox	N/A	N/A	N/A	6,981	15,535	23,149	34,140
Game Boy/Color	9,217	17,683	14,921	2,564	N/A	N/A	N/A
Game Boy Advance	N/A	N/A	4,183	10,820	18,936	26,355	29,070
Total	**179,661**	**192,613**	**207,413**	**224,493**	**273,485**	**298,488**	**295,664**

Source: International Development Group, "The Multimedia Markets in North America and Europe," p. 18, March 2002.

EXHIBIT 9   PC Data

Multimedia home PC installed base, North America and Europe, 1999–2005 est.

(in 000 units)	1999	2000	2001	2002E	2003E	2004E	2005E
Total North America	51,190	58,932	65,023	70,946	76,536	81,671	86,360
Total Europe	36,218	44,648	51,722	58,171	64,874	71,673	78,530
Total	**87,408**	**103,580**	**116,745**	**129,117**	**141,410**	**153,344**	**164,890**

Software sales data

PC CD-ROM software unit sales 1999–2005

(in 000 units)	1999	2000	2001	2002E	2003E	2004E	2005E
Total North America	88,744	91,503	89,210	91,886	94,940	98,596	102,529
Total Europe	48,735	53,492	56,008	59,125	62,563	65,755	68,925
Total	**137,479**	**144,995**	**145,218**	**151,011**	**157,503**	**164,351**	**171,454**

PC CD-ROM software sales 1999–2005*

(in 000 U.S. $)	1999	2000	2001	2002E	2003E	2004E	2005E
Total North America	2,106,157	1,920,642	1,867,924	1,925,866	1,941,295	1,924,581	2,001,876
Total Europe	1,717,955	1,590,300	1,516,343	1,556,605	1,584,043	1,623,130	1,665,496
Total	**3,824,112**	**3,510,942**	**3,384,267**	**3,482,472**	**3,523,140**	**3,545,924**	**3,665,579**

Entertainment PC CD-ROM software unit sales 1999–2005

(in 000 units)	1999	2000	2001	2002E	2003E	2004E	2005E
Total North America	59,199	66,332	68,795	72,095	76,259	80,382	84,896
Total Europe	36,892	41,757	44,512	47,770	51,360	54,790	58,100
Total	**96,091**	**108,089**	**113,307**	**119,865**	**127,619**	**135,172**	**142,996**

Entertainment PC CD-ROM software sales 1999–2005

(in 000 U.S. $)	1999	2000	2001	2002E	2003E	2004E	2005E
Total North America	1,439,849	1,410,438	1,496,641	1,562,549	1,599,514	1,610,024	1,697,285
Total Europe	1,271,584	1,238,909	1,208,915	1,262,653	1,299,610	1,353,972	1,407,413
Total	**2,711,433**	**2,649,347**	**2,705,556**	**2,825,202**	**2,899,124**	**2,963,996**	**3,104,698**

Source: International Development Group, "The Multimedia Markets in North America and Europe," pp. 2, 4–7, March 2002.

but some analysts expected this market to grow dramatically. One report projected the number of wireless data subscribers to increase to 137.5 million by 2005.[17]

There were several barriers to the development of wireless gaming. Wireless handset manufacturers used closed, proprietary operating systems in their phones.[18] Further, most wireless devices were not browser-enabled and could accommodate only very limited services such as text messaging. This constrained the quality and quantity of games available for wireless devices. The small size and poor quality of the video display available on next generation wireless devices further inhibited game attractiveness, and the limited data storing capacity of these devices increased demand on network bandwidth —an expense that the small base of users could not support. In 2002, EA had made only small investments in this market.

THE ONLINE GAMING PHENOMENON

By 2002, three types of online gaming emerged: multiplayer online games; massive multiplayer online games in persistent state worlds; and portal games.

Multiplayer gaming, the first type of online game to appear, was introduced to the mass market in 1991. Early titles such as "Doom" and "Duke Nukem" were among the first games to be published with a multiplayer-option and played over local area networks (LANs) or direct dial-up connections. With the massive adoption of the Internet, online gaming became one of main trends to shape PC games through the 1990s. The most popular genres were first-person shooters, real-time strategy, and, more recently, role-playing games. An increasing number of games were played exclusively online. With hundreds of thousand of gamers playing online at any given moment throughout the world, online games opened a new universe of possibilities both for gamers and game makers. Instead of merely battling their computers, players now tested their skills against human counterparts, who were unpredictable by nature. This constant reservoir of players endlessly expanded the possibilities of games. In addition, these games did not have any specific endings and could be played indefinitely.

A new subset of online games called massive multiplayer online games (MMOG) or persistent-state world games emerged. These games staged persistent worlds, games that subsist independently of the players on a continuous basis and can host simultaneously hundreds of thousands of players. These new types of games featured continuously developing original story lines, and some actually reached out to players in the physical world through cell phones, instant messaging, pagers, or fax machines.

Portal games were different from the two other types of online gaming. They were played almost exclusively on the Web, via portals that offered a wide variety of games. The types of games played were simpler, more traditional games such as backgammon, chess, and card games. They appealed to a much broader audience of casual gamers. This audience was drawn to free, easy-to-play games offered by a range of portals and pure-play online game sites. Yahoo!'s Games and EA's Pogo portals were among the most visited. In 2002, there were between 4,000 and 5,000 online gaming sites worldwide, with more than 30 million people in the United States playing an online game at least once per month.[19] Casual Web gaming represented half of the time spent on broadband entertainment.[20]

By 2006, 114 million people were predicted to play online worldwide, 23 million people playing via consoles.[21]

Opportunities in Online Gaming

For game makers, the development costs of multiplayer online games were higher than for traditional games. Still, online multiplayer features became standard, and the vast majority of PC games shipped in 2002 had this capability. For game publishers, the challenge associated with online games was keeping players interested. One way of doing that was to introduce new content into the game on a regular basis. For instance, they staged events, introduced new quests, and hired players to play roles or trigger events such as natural catastrophes in their virtual worlds. The role of managing content was new to publishers who, like other consumer software vendors, were used to simply releasing their products and then issuing

[17]"Efiles: Games Without Frontiers," Gartner Group Eweek, July 2, 2001.
[18]N.B.: In June 1998, leading mobile phone makers Nokia, Motorola, and Ericsson and handheld computer maker Psion formed a joint venture called Symbian to develop software to run mobile phones and devices. By 2002, Nokia was known to sell its software cheaply to other mobile phone producers.

[19]"Interactive Entertainment—Hitting the Cycle's Sweet Spot," Credit Suisse First Boston, May 15, 2002.
[20]"Can Broadband Save Internet Media?" *McKinsey Quarterly,* 2002, Number 2.
[21]"The Online Game Market 2002," Press Release, DFC Intelligence, June 2002.

add-ons and patches and selling expansion packs. With online multiplayer games, the lifecycle of games was extended beyond purchase and launch.

To finance the development and maintenance costs of online games, game makers adopted subscription-based business models. After purchasing a game, players had to pay a monthly fee to access the corresponding online content. Many online services that were originally free started to require paid subscriptions, typically ranging from $10 to $20 per month for unlimited game time. With hundreds of thousands of paying players, popular online computer games such as "EverQuest" and "Ultima Online" generated steady revenue streams and were envied by other segments of the software and entertainment industry. For instance, Sony's "EverQuest" had attracted about 400,000 subscribers worldwide and generated $5 million in revenue every month with a gross-profit margin of over 40 percent.[22] Yet the majority of online gamers were still reluctant to pay to play. In 2002, pay-based online games attracted only hard-core gamers. As with other media, video game publishers had to educate their customer base about this new model and justify the premium they required by offering attractive content that would keep players coming back and paying. These business models were far from perfect, however; while Sony's "EverQuest" had been a success, Electronic Arts decided to close the doors on its "Majestic" online offering. Some predicted that total United States revenue from online gaming in 2002 would reach approximately $280 million and grow at a rate of 25 percent to 30 percent each year until 2005.[23] Analysts thought advertising could account for one third of these revenues while the bulk would come from subscriptions. With "The Sims Online" coming out in November 2002 and "Star Wars Online" slated for launch in 2003, a real test of the mass market popularity of online gaming may have been at hand.

The Challenges of Online Gaming

Online gaming presented many challenges to developers. Online computer games required higher upfront investments than traditional games. The game engines were more complex because they had to process interactions among players over networks, which increased their development costs. Also, game publishers had to make significant investments in the server infrastructure necessary to host games. Dedicated high-availability servers were needed to insure persistent play and a high quality of service, a prerequisite if companies wanted their players to continue paying subscriptions.

These games also required continued investment after the launch. As opposed to traditional games, online game makers needed to dedicate entire creative teams to support the service after the game's launch. This turned video game companies into service providers, with requisite demands for competencies such as customer relationship management capabilities (24 hours, 7 days per week). Other challenges to surmount included the lower than expected penetration of broadband and the necessary consumer education on pay-for-play gaming.

Online Console Gaming

Microsoft planned to launch its online console gaming service, called "Xbox Live," in Fall 2002. Microsoft announced it would spend over $2 billion over the next few years to build out the Xbox Live network and develop the next generation of its game console. From the start, Microsoft had looked toward online gaming, making its Xbox the only 128-bit console to integrate a cable modem. Microsoft developed a proprietary network infrastructure which favored the "walled-garden" or closed network, with Xbox gamers able to connect to each other only through the Microsoft-maintained Xbox Live system. Microsoft would even control bandwidth used to run titles from third-party publishers. The system would include games from Microsoft and third-party publishers. Microsoft planned to sell a $50 Xbox Live starter kit that included a headset, microphone, a one-year subscription to the service, and software that allowed the Xbox to tap into an existing broadband Internet connection.

Nintendo planned to release its online gaming peripheral in Fall 2002. Selling for around $34, the device would feature both dial-up and broadband adapters. Nintendo's online gaming strategy was the most conservative among the three console manufacturers. Nintendo would leave the management of online gaming to publishers. Game publishers themselves would be responsible for operating the online networks on which their games ran. Neither would Nintendo collect any additional revenue from "GameCube Online" games nor would it charge an access fee.

Sony announced the launch of its online gaming service in August 2002. Unlike Microsoft, Sony left it to individual game publishers to do the back-end work of maintaining servers and other infrastructure, while Sony

[22] Geoff Keighley, "The Sorcerer of Sony," *Business 2.0,* August 2002, http://www.business2.com/articles/mag/0,1640,42210,FF.html.
[23] International Development Group, "The Multimedia Markets in North America and Europe," Executive Summary, PI, March 2002.

would provide the software to make it work. The PS2 was not equipped with online capabilities. Sony sold a $40 adapter that supported both analog and digital Internet connections.

Despite the flurry of activity, the general sense among console makers was that online console gaming would not see a major uptake during this generation of consoles. Many analysts thought that online game investments would not pay off before the next new generation of consoles, expected in 2006, when broadband penetration in households likely would be higher. Also, game consoles had mass-market appeal because they only required a television set, compared to the expensive broadband Internet connections (ranging between $34 and $54 per month in the United States) plus a monthly subscription for game content.

ELECTRONIC ARTS MAINTAINS INDUSTRY LEADERSHIP

In 2002, Electronic Arts was the leading publisher of both PC and third-party console titles (Exhibit 10). In the last quarter of FY2002, EA had three of the top ten titles for both Sony's PS2 and PS1, as well as Microsoft's Xbox consoles. EA produced top-selling games in most of the existing genres. With the 128-bit cycle in full swing worldwide, EA enjoyed double-digit revenue growth in all of its geographic regions during FY2002. At a time when corporate balance sheets were under intense scrutiny, EA offered investors an unlevered company with almost $1 billion in cash. In the fourth quarter of FY2002 alone, EA added over $300 million to its cash reserve (Exhibit 11).

EA Went Long on PlayStation

Since the middle of the 1990s, EA made three strategic decisions that accounted for most of its continued success. According to Frank Gibeau, Vice President of North America Sales and Marketing, "The most important decision EA made over the last years was the single-minded deliberateness with which we bet on Sony's PS1 and then PS2." As it did during the 32/64-bit generation consoles with the PS1, EA bet that Sony's PS2 would become the dominant platform in the next generation. Gibeau said:

> We evaluate the potential of platforms by asking three questions: Does the underlying technology enable us to develop advanced entertainment? What is the probability of success in the three major markets: Asia, the United States, and Eu-

rope? For Microsoft, the answer was negative in Asia and to a lesser extent negative in all markets because of Microsoft's lack of reputation as a console gaming company. The response was neutral for Sega and positive for Nintendo and Sony. Finally, does each manufacturer have the capital and corporate will to support its console business? The answer was negative for Sega so EA decided to support the PS2 over the Dreamcast.[24]

EA concentrated its development efforts on the PS2 and supported its launch aggressively by releasing its bestselling titles on it. Gibeau explained, "From our standpoint, it is like a military battle: the winner is the one who gets there first and with the most numerous forces." EA even passed Sony as the number 1 publisher of titles for the PS2 with 28 percent market share and five of the top ten titles in the United States in fiscal year 2002.[25]

Why EA Learned to Love Transitions

Most game developers dreaded the transition years between two generations of consoles. For the majority of game companies that derive much of their revenues from the console market, it meant plummeting sales and profits. In 2001, the industry had seen rough times. Several companies including Sega, Electronic Arts, and Infogrames eliminated jobs to trim expenses. A number of small game studios shut their doors or looked for buyers because they could not cover development costs.

EA's CFO Stan McKee described how the company handled platform transitions:

> Having lived through several console generations, we have learned to adapt through the difficult console transition period. Actually, we see the transition years between two generations of consoles as an opportunity for us to get fit and lean. One year before the transition starts, EA starts trimming. Last year was the middle of a transition period for us, but we managed to keep operating expenses in the low single digits while revenues were up 30 percent, which levered income up by 100 percent.
>
> We clamp down on "science projects" among studios, i.e., small development efforts that we don't know about that consume an enormous amount of resources when you multiply one or two of these across all of our studios. We'll watch expenses and sometimes make the studios more responsible for sticking to budgets. No area is sacred and immune to this approach. However, the key franchises such as "The Sims" or our sports titles are not going to get starved.

---

[24] All quotes from Frank Gibeau are from the author's interview on August 16, 2002.
[25] *2002 Annual Report.*

EXHIBIT 10   U.S. Market Share per Publisher

Top 10 entertainment PC CD-ROM publishers 2001 (ranked by value)

Publisher	Dollar sales	Unit sales	# of SKUs	Mkt. shr. (by $)	Mkt. shr. (by units)	ARP
Electronic Arts	$ 312,359,172	12,763,748	281	22%	20%	$24
VUG	$ 266,055,440	10,717,601	371	19%	17%	$25
Infogrames	$ 210,249,940	11,773,327	471	15%	18%	$18
Microsoft	$ 121,942,997	3,575,843	75	9%	6%	$34
Activision	$ 73,387,008	3,759,944	252	5%	6%	$20
Ubi Soft	$ 53,456,544	1,617,807	97	4%	2%	$33
Take-Two	$ 49,090,979	2,065,259	181	3%	3%	$24
Disney	$ 33,220,369	2,033,554	76	2%	3%	$16
Valusoft	$ 27,822,531	2,199,364	79	2%	3%	$13
Eidos	$ 22,084,396	895,793	55	2%	1%	$25
Top 10 total	**$1,169,669,337**	**51,402,241**	**1,938**	**83%**	**79%**	**$23**
Ent. CD-Rom Total	**$1,413,026,071**	**64,857,223**	**3,278**	**100%**	**100%**	**$22**

Source: International Development Group, "The Multimedia Markets in North America and Europe," March 2002.

Top 10 console and handheld publishers 2001 (ranked by value)

Publisher	Dollar Sales	Mkt. Share by $	Unit Sales	Mkt. Share by Unit	ARP
1. Electronic Arts	$ 730,376,846	16%	18,394,255	13%s	$40
2. Nintendo	$ 710,479,261	16%	19,843,015	14%	$36
3. Activision	$ 366,792,950	8%	11,295,702	8%	$32
4. Sony	$ 358,021,304	8%	11,878,606	8%	$30
5. THQ	$ 284,058,201	6%	8,819,582	6%	$32
6. Take-Two	$ 204,587,897	4%	6,475,495	5%	$32
7. Konami	$ 173,642,109	4%	4,406,766	3%	$39
8. Infogrames	$ 159,432,835	4%	7,248,952	5%	$22
9. Sega	$ 157,916,167	3%	5,334,590	4%	$30
10. Acclaim	$ 148,959,220	3%	5,466,486	4%	$27
Top 10 Total	**$3,294,266,790**	**72%**	**99,163,449**	**70%**	**$33**
Market Total	**$4,547,095,791**	**100%**	**140,986,669**	**100%**	**$32**

Source: International Development Group, "The Multimedia Markets in North America and Europe," March 2002.

In parallel, EA mitigates the lower console revenues associated with the transition by getting more revenues out of the PC market as well as by beefing up its global distribution capability.

This practice is now deeply ingrained in the company's tactics and will be used again for the next transition. In short, we say that transition is our friend.[26]

Managing Risks and Making Hits

At the heart of EA's hits are hit-making studios. In 2002, EA operated 11 studios in four countries. Stu-

dios were responsible for conceiving and developing games. The studios housed a mix of game developers and programmers.

John Riccitiello described how the role of studios inside EA evolved over the years as they learned to collaborate more with other parts of the organization:

Studios are traditionally at the center of the organization—they are the heroes—however the marketing function is increasingly equally responsible for the success of games. This creates creative friction. For instance, there will be debates concerning the complexity of a game versus the size of the market. It is critical to find the key thing that will make a game a success. Together, the studio and marketing teams partner to ensure we create a great gaming experience

---

[26] All quotes from Stan McKee are from the author's interview on August 7, 2002.

EXHIBIT 11   Selected Financial Data for Electronic Arts

Year Ended March 31, 2001

	EA Core (excl. EA.com)	EA.com	Adjustments and Eliminations	Electronic Arts
Net revenues from unaffiliated customers	$1,280,172	$ 42,101	$ —	$1,322,273
Group sales	2,658	—	(2,658)	—
Total net revenues	1,282,830	42,101	(2,658)	1,322,273
Cost of goods sold from unaffiliated customers	640,239	12,003	—	652,242
Group cost of goods sold	—	2,658	(2,658)	—
Total cost of goods sold	640,239	14,661	(2,658)	652,242
Gross profit	642,591	27,440	—	670,031
Operating expenses:				
Marketing and sales	163,928	12,475	8,933	185,336
General and administrative	93,885	10,156	—	104,041
Research and development	248,534	77,243	63,151	388,928
Network development and support	—	51,794	(51,794)	—
Customer relationship management	—	11,357	(11,357)	—
Carriage fee	—	8,933	(8,933)	—
Amortization of intangibles	12,829	6,494	—	19,323
Charge for acquired in-process technology	—	2,719	—	2,719
Total operating expenses	519,176	181,171	—	700,347
Operating income (loss)	123,415	(153,731)	—	(30,316)
Interest and other income, net	16,659	227	—	16,886
Income (loss) before benefit from income taxes and minority interest	140,074	(153,504)	—	(13,430)
Benefit from income taxes	(4,163)	—	—	(4,163)
Income (loss) before minority interest	144,237	(153,504)	—	(9,267)
Minority interest in consolidated joint venture	(1,815)	—	—	(1,815)
Net income (loss) before retained interest in EA.com	$ 142,422	$(153,504)	$ —	$ (11,082)

BALANCE SHEET DATA AT FISCAL YEAR END	2002	2001	2000	1999	1998
Cash, cash equivalents, and short-term investments	$ 796,936	$ 466,492	$ 339,804	$312,822	$374,560
Marketable securities	6,869	10,022	236	4,884	3,721
Working capital	699,561	478,701	440,021	333,256	408,098
Long-term investments	—	8,400	8,400	18,400	24,200
Total assets	1,699,374	1,378,918	1,192,312	901,873	745,681
Total liabilities	452,982	340,026	265,302	236,209	181,713
Minority interest	3,098	4,545	3,617	2,733	—
Total stockholders' equity	1,243,294	1,034,347	923,393	662,931	563,968

Source: Company reports.

that is well targeted and extremely focused on a specific gameplay experience.

In other cases, the issue is uphill marketing, which is the extra marketing effort that is sometimes necessary to make a game a success. The publishing organization often does not want to do it, so this requires being able to decide which are the truly worthy titles. To be able to do this requires teamwork, which depends on the mutual respect that exists between the key executives heading our studios and the pub-

lishing division. There are many personal bonds between these two groups.

Rusty Rueff, Senior Vice President of Human Resources for EA, outlined the company's studio strategy:

We see our system of studios as a family. You can have siblings with immensely different personalities but still they share the same values stemming from their familial educa-

EXHIBIT 11   (continued)

Net revenues by region for fiscal 2002 and 2001

	2002	2001	Increase	% change
North America	$1,093,244	$ 831,924	$261,320	31.4%
Europe	519,458	386,728	132,730	34.3%
Asia Pacific	53,376	51,039	2,337	4.6%
Japan	58,597	52,582	6,015	11.4%
International	631,431	490,349	141,082	28.8%
Consolidated Net Revenues	$1,724,675	$1,322,273	$402,402	30.4%

Source: Company reports.

Worldwide net revenues by product line for fiscal 2002 and 2001 (in thousands)

	2002	2001	Increase/(Decrease)	% change
EA Studio:				
PlayStation 2	$ 482,882	$ 258,988	$ 223,894	86.4%
PC	456,292	405,256	51,036	12.6%
PlayStation	189,535	309,988	(120,453)	(38.9%)
Xbox	78,363	—	78,363	N/A
Nintendo GameCube	51,740	—	51,740	N/A
Game Boy Advance	43,653	—	43,653	N/A
Game Boy Color	38,026	—	38,026	N/A
Advertising	38,024	6,175	31,849	515.8%
Online Subscriptions	30,940	28,878	2,062	7.1%
License, OEM, and Other	24,762	20,468	4,294	21.0%
N64	18,152	67,044	(48,892)	(72.9%)
Online Packaged Goods	3,296	3,198	98	3.1%
	1,455,665	1,099,995	355,670	32.3%
Affiliated Label:	269,010	222,278	46,732	21.0%
Consolidated Net Revenues	$1,724,675	$1,322,273	$402,402	30.4%

Source: Company reports.

tion. Likewise, when we acquire a new studio, we look for a baseline set of values but then we encourage different personalities to co-exist.

Our pipeline of creativity is one of our top competitive advantages. This stems from three elements. First, EA has the top talents in the industry. Our people have track records of creating hit games and are recognized by their peers in the industry. Many have lived through several technology cycles and transitions and have learned to adapt quickly to new technology.

Second, we are investing significant efforts in training and development to make sure our people are ahead of the curve in terms of technology. The only way to be the number one on current and next generation consoles is to have top mastery of the technology.

Third, today we enjoy a strong culture of knowledge sharing among our studios. This is also key to our success: people share tips, tricks, code, development tools and technical breakthroughs on a regular basis across our studios.

The next challenge is to grow the next generation of creative leaders in our studios. In Hollywood, people who can direct $100 million movie projects are very few. This is because the people who finance such projects only trust a limited number of people with the appropriate skills. The video game industry is becoming similar with production budgets increasing more and more. A few years ago, one person could be responsible for multiple franchises. Now, we assign one creative leader per project, sometimes on multiple platforms. The development cycle of a game is around two years and can require a team of over 60 people. Who do you trust for such projects? It is therefore key for EA to be able to nurture our creative managers and help them grow to handle such responsibilities.[27]

---

[27] All quotes from Russell Rueff are from the author's interview on August 21, 2002.

EA has also learned to better allocate its resources to maximize the market potential of its games. John Riccitiello explained:

> Last year, barely any of the products we launched lost money. This stems from two facts. First, we are not afraid to kill products, even just before their launch if we think they are not going to make it big. We stopped marketing small games. The winning formula for us is to have fewer SKUs (stock keeping units) and invest more per title. We get a better payoff by letting certain products die and by putting twice as much money behind other products. Five years ago, we used to ship between 65 and 70 SKUs a year. This year, we are shipping 58 SKUs. This means we are getting better at what we are doing. It is like a diet. This is easy to understand why it is good for you, but conceptually hard to do.
>
> In turn, we are betting more on big games. We go big on each of our launches. We do not have any stealth launches. In the creative industry, it is important to go big, to get the marketplace to know what you are doing. EA is expert at moving audiences and creating hits.

Feeding and Milking the Video Cash Cow

Electronic Arts developed several lines of successful franchise products including "FIFA Soccer," "Madden NFL," "NHL Hockey," "Triple Play," and "The Sims." In 2002, EA established a dominant position in most of the gaming genres. This was achieved year after year by producing a broad type of "A" titles. For instance, in 2001 "Harry Potter" was EA's most successful title launch ever, with sales of more than 7 million units on four platforms. EA managed to create new genres with games like "The Sims." In March 2002, EA announced that it had shipped over 6.3 million copies of "The Sims" worldwide and over 12 million units including "Sims" expansion packs, making it the best-selling PC game of all time. Still, no title made up more than 10 percent of EA's total revenues, eliminating dependencies on any single brand or release. Unlike many of its competitors, EA could afford to have a portfolio strategy: exploring both strategic and risky avenues. Risky projects were financed by titles that were more predictable, such as sequels to hits. Smaller video game companies did not have this luxury since they relied on fewer titles and had to consider breakeven economics on a title-by-title basis.

EA can afford not to break even quickly on a few titles, or to suffer a few lackluster years developing a title franchise. Stan McKee said, "EA's business is not entirely based on hit picking," adding:

> Actually, I would argue that 80 percent of our revenues are predictable. We have a lot of recurring revenues from iterations of existing licenses. For example sports games, which generate approximately 45 percent of our revenues, are mostly simple iterations over the years. Likewise, Sims' expansion packs sell approximately 2 million units on average.

Over the last ten years, an important trend in games had been licensed brands and sequels. As video games moved into the mass-market, brands and sequels began to dominate. The company's popular franchises in the sports genre and leading non-sports products like "*007*," "The Sims," "Medal of Honor," and others give EA a level of sales predictability found nowhere else in the industry.

Betting on EA Sports

Thanks to top-of-the-line sports games, grassroots marketing techniques, and massive amounts of TV advertising during major sports events, EA Sports was becoming one of the most recognized sports brands in the United States. EA Sports game franchises dominated their respective markets worldwide. EA aspired to become one of the top sports brands, on par with Nike, ESPN, or *Sports Illustrated*.

Since its beginning in the 1990s, EA Sports had been able to fend off serious competition in the sports genre, in particular from Microsoft and Sega. Sega publicly stated that it was aiming for EA Sports. With sports games representing 25 percent of the industry and growing at 25 percent per year, some at EA were unsure why Sega would target the Leviathan of the industry instead of focusing on building its own franchises. Even Microsoft, as yet, failed to make a dent into EA's sports franchises. John Riccitiello said:

> On football, EA enjoys 75 percent market shares against Sony, Sega, and Microsoft, three of the biggest electronic entertainment companies in the world. EA outsells Microsoft nine-to-one on their own platform in sports games. Microsoft said a few years ago that they would knock us off on PC sports games. It got us scared at first, but we continued to focus on producing great games. Microsoft was reducing their prices to compete against us. It didn't work and they exited because they could not build any continuity.

EA Vice President of Marketing and Brand Innovation, Don Transeth, who was part of the original team that launched the EA Sports brand, discussed EA's success in the sports genre:

> From the very beginning, we pinned our ambitions on becoming a major sports brand with benchmarks such as Nike,

ESPN, *Sports Illustrated,* and the like. We have always seen ourselves as a sports company that makes video games. While our competitors focus exclusively on creating sports games, we have managed to make our games part of the sports world. Cyberstrator [a device for using "Madden" graphics to demonstrate plays on TV broadcasts] is a prime example of our strategy. We offered the most prominent TV sports programs, such as Monday Night Football, the use of our Madden NFL game engine to simulate and create views of the games to support their pre- and post-game commentaries. All the while, our brands and our technology are prominently displayed to the large audience.[28]

Grassroots Marketing Strategy: The Example of "Madden NFL 2003"

Aside from creating content, EA's success in the sports genre stemmed from its extensive marketing efforts. To support its sports brands, EA used a variety of approaches to marketing. Those ranged from traditional media advertising, PR events involving big name athletes such as golf pro Tiger Woods and pro basketball player Jason Kidd, co-promotion partnerships with selected top brands, event sponsorship, promotional events around major sports venues like the Super Bowl, syndicated TV programming, and numerous grassroots initiatives.

John Riccitiello pointed to "Madden NFL 2003" as exemplifying EA's approach to marketing:

First, we work hard at generating very positive word-of-mouth from key purchase influencers through grassroots marketing strategies. In the purchase process, most people ask others about what games they should buy. They also look at websites and magazines. The gamer population can be segregated into three groups: at the top of the pyramid, there is the core audience of hard-core gamers. In the case of "Madden," those are NFL (National Football League) players, football players, fraternity guys, football fans. At the bottom of the pyramid is the mass market.

Every other company does a good job at reaching mass-market gamers. Yet, we are second to none at reaching the top of the pyramid. We put a lot of emphasis on grassroots marketing for journalists, websites, beta-testers, EA campus representatives, trade magazines, by being present at football games, by going directly to football players. Our goal is that when one of these core influencers is asked about a game, he has been hit a dozen times by our marketing message and will therefore recommend our game.

EA Campus Reps initiative is a great example of how we excel at reaching key influencers. Every year, EA Sports enlists over 30 campus representatives selected among stu-

dents to promote our games on university campuses all over the United States. We bring them to our headquarters to train them and expose them to our brand. They then become peer marketers, whose mission is to create a buzz about EA Sports on campus. They in turn look for trend setters and taste makers on campus and get our products in their hands.

The second part of our marketing strategy is advertising. We consider that the war starts months before the launch of the game. As such, our advertising efforts start between 6 and 12 months before the actual launch. For instance, we were advertising for "Madden" on the NFL draft five months before the actual launch of the game. We run commercials with rookies during programs that typically get low viewers' ratings but are watched by super hard-core football fans. Sports writers wrote about our commercials and that also helped us spread the word. In the end, we have created this omnipresent presence in the market even before our game has arrived.

Third, we invest a lot in our distribution operations to make sure our games arrive on time at the thousands of stores that carry our products.

EA's Publishing and Distribution Strategy[29]

EA was the first company in the video game industry to develop a direct distribution system. As early as 1984, the company chose to make direct distribution a cornerstone of its strategy. Ted Judson, Director of Channel Marketing and Development, recounts the four historical steps EA took to build its top-notch distribution system[30]:

In 1984, we were the first company to sell direct to Egghead [a national computer products retailer] and the mom-and-pop's [small retailers]. It was controversial for a $25 million company, as we were at that time, but it forced us to create a sales organization. The second turning point was when we entered the console market in 1988 with games for the Nintendo console. This enabled us to develop broader distribution relationship with specialized retailers. The most important breakthrough came at the beginning of the 1990s when sales of our games for the Sega 16-bit system exploded and were even driving hardware sales. This gave us the clout necessary to create relationships with large retailers such as Target, Wal-Mart, and K-Mart.

This boom in the console business had a profound structural impact on our distribution system. It drove the development and re-design of our distribution capacity, our sales force, our back-end system, and our point-of-sale marketing

---

[28] All quotes from Don Transeth are from the author's interview on August 23, 2002.

[29] For information concerning EA's distribution strategy in the mid 1990s, see Burgelman and Meza, "Electronic Arts in 1995," Stanford Graduate School of Business.

[30] All quotes from Ted Judson are from the author's interview on August 28, 2002.

strategy. In 1996, as the game market had become more mature, we started seeing our large accounts having two buyers; for PCs and consoles, respectively. In 1997, we decided to split our sales force to reflect this evolution. Actually, the two markets have quite different dynamics. The console market is TV-driven and based on volume. The PC market is more sophisticated, there is more product selection, and the audience is older.

In 2002, EA had a direct sales force in North America and international subsidiaries in 27 countries. From the warehouse it built in Louisville, Kentucky, in 1996, EA manufactured, packaged, and distributed titles created in its studios, as well as those created by some third-party game developer partners in 75 countries. By distributing its products directly to retailers, EA competed more effectively for shelf-space and deployed better point-of-sale promotions. Direct distribution also enabled EA to better manage inventory levels and to respond to market trends more rapidly. Typically, EA had a worldwide time-to-market of two weeks once a game was finished. In 2001, EA won the prestigious Wal-Mart Vendor of the Year Award, competing against major electronics and entertainment corporations.

Ted Judson outlines how EA's current distribution system constituted a competitive advantage: "Our system is capable of handling massive numbers of orders of all sizes. We have real time reporting capabilities of our sales performance, which allows us to better manage our inventory and track demand. We know exactly how our business is doing and our market shares. [Because of this] retailers have learned to lean on us for their purchasing strategy of our games."

Frank Gibeau said:

The efficiency and extensive international scope of our distribution system has also enabled us to pick up business from video game companies with no publishing and distribution activities such as game development studios. EA's distribution business took one of three forms:

- Distribution only, in which the partnering game companies did their own production and advertising and EA distributed their titles. This earned the least amount of money for EA.
- Co-publishing, where companies produced the games and EA marketed and published them. EA receives 20 to 30 percent in royalties. EA has these relationships with Disney, Fox Interactive, and Lego Interactive.
- Development plus publishing where EA found third-party titles produced by independent studios and did all testing, marketing, and distribution. The margins EA earns depends on the size of the deal and the nature of the companies involved.

Despite being the worldwide leader in its industry, EA still did not enjoy the same dominance in Asia. The main Asian market for EA was Japan, which with the United States and Europe were the world's three main geographical markets in terms of video game sales. While its shares in Australia, New Zealand, South Korea, and Singapore were similar to those attained in the United States, its shares in console markets were lower in Japan. The company was also the number two maker of PC games in Japan, but number one in online gaming in that important Asian country. One of the main barriers to EA's development in Asia was piracy, especially in mainland China and neighboring countries.

Other Avenues for Growth

Beyond extending its franchises, EA looked for growth through licensing relationships and acquisitions. EA sought to license IP with potential for series development (e.g., "James Bond" titles, "Lord of the Rings," "Harry Potter"). The company tried to be very conservative about striking such deals. EA would license only material that had proven popularity and durability. It would not take a chance on licensing an unproven property. The company also prided itself on its discipline in avoiding bidding wars for material.

EA tried to exercise similar fiscal discipline in its acquisitions. EA looked to acquire IP or brands that it could extend into new markets. Any company it considered buying also had to have good management in place and be culturally compatible with Electronic Arts. Further, EA eschewed many of the distractions that acquisitions often entailed. Stan McKee said:

We try to buy only the precise assets we want. For example, we paid significantly more to buy just Westwood Studios, which was a part of Virgin Interactive, than what we were willing to pay for the whole Virgin Interactive property. There was a lot of duplication in distribution and there were studios and titles we did not want. We figured it would cost us $30–$40 million, not including the management distraction, to dispose of the assets we did not want. In the end, it was worth it to us to pay $120 million for only the part [Westwood Studios] that we wanted. We didn't want the distraction of closing studios and dismantling distribution chains across the globe.

While this acquisition was paid with cash, most of EA's acquisitions were paid for with another currency that the company jealously guarded: shares. EA viewed its share price as a strategic asset, allowing the company to fund acquisitions while inoculating itself against unwanted advances from would-be acquirers. Over the past few years there had been speculation that EA would make a good acquisition target for a Hollywood studio. Indeed, games benefit from better economics than movies since they are more profitable. For example, "Madden NFL" cost around $10 million to develop on all platforms and sold 4.5 million units, which generated approximately $190 million in revenues. On average, EA games generated 54 percent gross margins. EA's "Harry Potter" game sold 9 million units which generated approximately $270 million. Some studios tried to enter the video game market but met little success. Viacom and Disney both had prominent failures in games. McKee observed, "The gap between EA and traditional entertainment companies is narrowing."

The Online Challenge for EA

Since 1998, EA made significant investments in developing a solid online infrastructure through its EA.com business unit. EA.com was launched in October 2000 to house all the company's online gaming initiatives, including Web-based gaming as well as multiplayer games. EA.com's business model was to generate revenues from both subscriptions and advertising. With the economic downturn beginning 2001 and the dramatic decrease in Internet advertising, EA.com had been experiencing significant financial losses. Still, in 2002, EA considered its online group to be a major strategic investment (Exhibit 12).

In November 1999, EA.com partnered with AOL in a five-year $85 million marketing agreement to provide the game channel for all of the AOL brands and services. AOL was responsible for ad sales and marketing the site to its users. EA.com's business model included revenue from advertising, sponsorships, and subscriptions.

The objective of the deal was to marry AOL's traffic with EA's content. The deal exposed EA to two expensive challenges. EA had to come out of the gates with both diverse content and infrastructure in place to accommodate, from day one, traffic sent from AOL. The service had to be capable of handling the visitors it attracted from AOL's base of then 25 million subscribers. At the outset, 8 million to 10 million visitors were expected. After some growing pains, the service became the fourth most visited site on the Internet after AOL, Yahoo, and MSN. In May 2002, the service attracted 13 million unique visitors who spent 5 billion minutes there. The site accounted for 44 percent of market share in game sites in May 2002.

EA acquired the casual gaming site Pogo.com early 2001. Pogo.com and EA.com have one of the most recognized brands in the online gaming space, and Pogo.com brought over 15 million subscribers to the EA.com site.

Free Web gaming notwithstanding, EA had not made significant inroads in subscription-based multiplayer gaming. In 2001 and 2002, EA launched "Majestic" and

EXHIBIT 12   U.S. Online Gaming

PC online gaming households in the United States

Data in millions, unless otherwise stated

	1999	2000	2001	2002	2003	2004	2005
Total U.S. household	100.4	103.2	104.3	105.5	106.6	107.7	108.8
U.S. online PC gaming household	20.71	24.8	29.16	34.19	40.33	45.36	48.19
Penetration %	21%	24%	28%	32%	38%	42%	44%
Average number of online PC gamers/households	1.5	1.65	1.7	1.7	1.67	1.65	1.65
Total number of U.S. online PC gamers	31.06	40.91	49.58	58.12	67.35	74.84	79.51

Source: IDC, CSFB Technology Group Estimates.

Console online gaming forecast

	2001	2002	2003	2004	2005
U.S. households with online game consoles (%)	1.10%	4.80%	11.80%	16.70%	18.70%
U.S. households online via consoles (%)	0.00%	1.40%	5.60%	10.30%	13.10%
Annual online console gaming revenue ($ M)	3	293	1,022	1,788	2,322
Average spending for online gaming/household ($)	58	196	167	156	157

Source: GartnerG2, CSFB Technology Group Estimates.

"Motor City Online," two sophisticated pay-for-play initiatives that both folded a few months after their inceptions. In 2002, EA counted on the releases of major online-only massive multiplayer games such as "The Sims Online" and "Earth and Beyond" to start recouping its investments in EA.com. EA looked to "The Sims Online," an online sequel to all-time best-seller "The Sims," to provide a proof of concept for subscription-based online gaming. If "The Sims Online" did not turn out to be profitable, what would work? The success of "The Sims Online" could validate online pay-for-play for mass-market customers, beyond those hard-core gamers who, as yet, comprised the only paying audience for online games.

CONCLUSION

By carefully selecting platforms and dominating the genres in which it decided to compete, Electronic Arts successfully navigated the complex marketplace for game software. The company married creative and technical skills—a competency that eluded many entertainment companies such as Hollywood studios—to produce market-leading content for game consoles and PCs. The conservative management of EA's resources brought the company to its current level of success. However, EA was now exposed to new and powerful forces as it looked for future growth and pursued its mission to be "the number one entertainment company in the world."

COO John Riccitiello was thinking particularly hard about several strategic leadership issues:

> First, the strategic chess game of resource allocation to different technological platforms: Which partners can we trust? Who will be able to execute? Second, the identification of new intellectual properties that could be turned into multi-hundred-million franchises: How many? How to get the right ones? How to make them bigger? Third, capability development: Good ideas are numerous in our organization, but what is important is to be able to select and develop them. We have lots of good people who can deliver, but there are not enough of them to execute all the ideas we have. We need to constantly invest in training programs to develop people, teach them, and cull them. Fourth, our culture: A single-purpose entertainment company has never been developed before.

In addition to the internal challenges EA faced, several external opportunities and threats existed in 2002. Would Internet gaming, which had proved to be an electronic boneyard for many others, be profitable for Electronic Arts? What role would Microsoft play in EA's future?

That company was famous for successful second tries: What if it also picked up on Sega's challenge to "Beat EA"? Could Electronic Arts resist such an onslaught?

READING 1·3

The Core Competence of the Corporation

C. K. Prahalad and Gary Hamel

The most powerful way to prevail in global competition is still invisible to many companies. During the 1980s, top executives were judged on their ability to restructure, declutter, and delayer their corporations. In the 1990s, they'll be judged on their ability to identify, cultivate, and exploit the core competencies that make growth possible—indeed, they'll have to rethink the concept of the corporation itself.

Consider the last 10 years of GTE and NEC. In the early 1980s, GTE was well positioned to become a major player in the evolving information technology industry. It was active in telecommunications. Its operations spanned a variety of businesses, including telephones, switching and transmission systems, digital PABX, semiconductors, packet switching, satellites, defense systems, and lighting products. And GTE's Entertainment Products Groups, which produced Sylvania color TVs, had a position in related display technologies. In 1980, GTE's sales were $9.98 billion, and net cash flow was $1.73 billion. NEC, in contrast, was much smaller, at $3.8 billion in sales. It had a comparable technological base and computer businesses, but it had no experience as an operating telecommunications company.

Yet look at the positions of GTE and NEC in 1988. GTE's 1988 sales were $16.46 billion, and NEC's sales were considerably higher at $21.89 billion. GTE has, in effect, become a telephone operating company with a position in defense and lighting products. GTE's other businesses are small in global terms. GTE has divested Sylvania TV and Telenet, put switching, transmission, and digital PABX into joint ventures, and closed down semiconductors. As a result, the international position of GTE

---

has eroded. Non-U.S. revenue as a percent of total revenue dropped from 20 percent to 15 percent between 1980 and 1988.

NEC has emerged as the world leader in semiconductors and as a first-tier player in telecommunications products and computers. It has consolidated its position in mainframe computers. It has moved beyond public switching and transmission to include such lifestyle products as mobile telephones, facsimile machines, and laptop computers—bridging the gap between telecommunications and office automation. NEC is the only company in the world to be in the top five in revenue in telecommunications, semiconductors, and mainframes. Why did these two companies, starting with comparable business portfolios, perform so differently? Largely because NEC conceived of itself in terms of *core competencies,* and GTE did not.

RETHINKING THE CORPORATION

Once, the diversified corporation could simply point its business units at particular end product markets and admonish them to become world leaders. But with market boundaries changing ever more quickly, targets are elusive and capture is at best temporary. A few companies have proven themselves adept at inventing new markets, quickly entering emerging markets, and dramatically shifting patterns of customer choice in established markets. These are the ones to emulate. The critical task for management is to create an organization capable of infusing products with irresistible functionality or, better yet, creating products that customers need but have not yet even imagined.

This is a deceptively difficult task. Ultimately, it requires radical change in the management of major companies. It means, first of all, that top managements of Western companies must assume responsibility for competitive decline. Everyone knows about high interest rates, Japanese protectionism, outdated antitrust laws, obstreperous unions, and impatient investors. What is harder to see, or harder to acknowledge, is how little added momentum companies actually get from political or macroeconomic relief. Both the theory and practice of Western management have created a drag on our forward motion. It is the principles of management that are in need of reform.

NEC versus GTE, again, is instructive and only one of many such comparative cases we analyzed to understand the changing basis for global leadership. Early in the 1970s, NEC articulated a strategic intent to exploit the convergence of computing and communications, what it called C&C.[1] Success, top management reckoned, would hinge on acquiring *competencies,* particularly in semiconductors. Management adopted an appropriate "strategic architecture," summarized by C&C, and then communicated its intent to the whole organization and the outside world during the mid-1970s.

NEC constituted a C&C Committee of top managers to oversee the development of core products and core competencies. NEC put in place coordination groups and committees that cut across the interests of individual businesses. Consistent with its strategic architecture, NEC shifted enormous resources to strengthen its position in components and central processors. By using collaborative arrangements to multiply internal resources, NEC was able to accumulate a broad array of core competencies.

NEC carefully identified three interrelated streams of technological and market evolution. Top management determined that computing would evolve from large mainframes to distributed processing, components from simple ICs (integrated circuits) to VLSI (very-large-scale integration), and communications from mechanical cross-bar exchange to complex digital systems we now call ISDN (integrated services digital network). As things evolved further, NEC reasoned, the computing, communications, and components businesses would so overlap that it would be very hard to distinguish among them and that there would be enormous opportunities for any company that had built the competencies needed to serve all three markets.

NEC top management determined that semiconductors would be the company's most important *core product.* It entered into myriad strategic alliances—over 100 as of 1987—aimed at building competencies rapidly and at low cost. In mainframe computers, its most noted relationship was with Honeywell and Bull. Almost all the collaborative arrangements in the semiconductor-component field were oriented toward technology access. As they entered collaborative arrangements, NEC's operating managers understood the rationale for these alliances and the goal of internalizing partner skills. NEC's director of research summed up its competence acquisition during the 1970s and 1980s this way: "From an investment standpoint, it was much quicker and cheaper to use foreign technology. There wasn't a need for us to develop new ideas."

---

[1] For a fuller discussion, see our article, "Strategic Intent," *Harvard Business Review,* May–June 1989, p. 63.

No such clarity of strategic intent and strategic architecture appeared to exist at GTE. Although senior executives discussed the implications of the evolving information technology industry, no commonly accepted view of which competencies would be required to compete in that industry were communicated widely. While significant staff work was done to identify key technologies, senior line managers continued to act as if they were managing independent business units. Decentralization made it difficult to focus on core competencies. Instead, individual businesses became increasingly dependent on outsiders for critical skills, and collaboration became a route to staged exits. Today, with a new management team in place, GTE has repositioned itself to apply its competencies to emerging markets in telecommunications services.

THE ROOTS OF COMPETITIVE ADVANTAGE

The distinction we observed in the way NEC and GTE conceived of themselves—a portfolio of competencies versus a portfolio of businesses—was repeated across many industries. From 1980 to 1988, Canon grew by 264 percent, Honda by 200 percent. Compare that with Xerox and Chrysler. And if Western managers were once anxious about the low cost and high quality of Japanese imports, they are now overwhelmed by the pace at which Japanese rivals are inventing new markets, creating new products, and enhancing them. Canon has given us personal copiers; Honda has moved from motorcycles to four-wheel off-road buggies. Sony developed the 8mm camcorder, Yamaha, the digital piano. Komatsu developed an underwater remote-controlled bulldozer, while Casio's latest gambit is a small-screen color LCD television. Who would have anticipated the evolution of these vanguard markets?

In more established markets, the Japanese challenge has been just as disquieting. Japanese companies are generating a blizzard of features and functional enhancements that bring technological sophistication to everyday products. Japanese car producers have been pioneering four-wheel steering, four-valve-per-cylinder engines, in-car navigation systems, and sophisticated electronic engine-management systems. On the strength of its product features, Canon is now a player in facsimile transmissions machines, desktop laser printers, even semiconductor manufacturing equipment.

In the short run, a company's competitiveness derives from the price/performance attributes of current products. But the survivors of the first wave of global competition, Western and Japanese alike, are all converging on similar and formidable standards for product cost and quality—minimum hurdles for continued competition, but less and less important as sources of differential advantage. In the long run, competitiveness derives from an ability to build, at lower cost and more speedily than competitors, the core competencies that spawn unanticipated products. The real sources of advantage are to be found in management's ability to consolidate corporationwide technologies and production skills into competencies that empower individual businesses to adapt quickly to changing opportunities.

Senior executives who claim that they cannot build core competencies either because they feel the autonomy of business units is sacrosanct or because their feet are held to the quarterly budget fire should think again. The problem in many Western companies is not that their senior executives are any less capable than those in Japan or that Japanese companies possess greater technical capabilities. Instead, it is their adherence to a concept of the corporation that unnecessarily limits the ability of individual businesses to fully exploit the deep reservoir of technological capability that many American and European companies possess.

The diversified corporation is a large tree. The trunk and major limbs are core products, the smaller branches are business units; the leaves, flowers, and fruit are end products. The root system that provides nourishment, sustenance, and stability is the core competence. You can miss the strength of competitors by looking only at their end products, in the same way you miss the strength of a tree if you look only at its leaves. (See Exhibit 1, "Competencies: The Roots of Competitiveness.")

Core competencies are the collective learning in the organization, especially how to coordinate diverse production skills and integrate multiple streams of technologies. Consider Sony's capacity to miniaturize or Philips's optical-media expertise. The theoretical knowledge to put a radio on a chip does not in itself assure a company the skill to produce a miniature radio no bigger than a business card. To bring off this feat, Casio must harmonize know-how in miniaturization, microprocessor design, material science, and ultrathin precision casing—the same skills it applies in its miniature card calculators, pocket TVs, and digital watches.

If core competence is about harmonizing streams of technology, it is also about the organization of work and the delivery of value. Among Sony's competencies is miniaturization. To bring miniaturization to its products, Sony must ensure that technologists, engineers, and mar-

EXHIBIT 1 Competencies: The Roots of Competitiveness

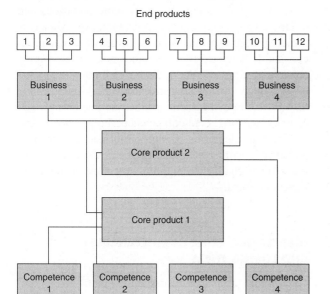

The corporation, like a tree, grows from its roots. Core products are nourished by competencies and engender business units, whose fruits are end products.

keters have a shared understanding of customer needs and of technological possibilities. The force of core competence is felt as decisively in services as in manufacturing. Citicorp was ahead of others investing in an operating system that allowed it to participate in world markets 24 hours a day. Its competence in systems has provided the company the means to differentiate itself from many financial service institutions.

Core competence is communication, involvement, and a deep commitment to working across organizational boundaries. It involves many levels of people and all functions. World-class research in, for example, lasers or ceramics can take place in corporate laboratories without having an impact on any of the businesses of the company. The skills that together constitute core competence must coalesce around individuals whose efforts are not so narrowly focused that they cannot recognize the opportunities for blending their functional expertise with those of others in new and interesting ways.

Core competence does not diminish with use. Unlike physical assets, which do deteriorate over time, competencies are enhanced as they are applied and shared. But competencies still need to be nurtured and protected; knowledge fades if it is not used. Competencies are the glue that binds existing businesses. They are also the engine for new business development. Patterns of diversification and market entry may be guided by them, not just by the attractiveness of markets.

Consider 3M's competence with sticky tape. In dreaming up businesses as diverse as Post-it notes, magnetic tape, photographic film, pressure-sensitive tapes, and coated abrasives, the company has brought to bear widely shared competencies in substrates, coatings, and adhesives and devised various ways to combine them. Indeed, 3M has invested consistently in them. What seems to be an extremely diversified portfolio of businesses belies a few shared core competencies.

In contrast, there are major companies that have had the potential to build core competencies but failed to do so because top management was unable to conceive of the company as anything other than a collection of discrete businesses. GE sold much of its consumer electronics business to Thomson of France, arguing that it was becoming increasingly difficult to maintain its competitiveness in this sector. That was undoubtedly so, but it is ironic that it sold several key businesses to competitors who were already competence leaders—Black & Decker in small electrical motors, and Thomson, which was eager to build its competence in microelectronics and had learned from the Japanese that a position in consumer electronics was vital to this challenge.

Management trapped in the strategic business unit (SBU) mind-set almost inevitably finds its individual businesses dependent on external sources for critical components, such as motors or compressors. But these are not just components. They are core products that contribute to the competitiveness of a wide range of end products. They are the physical embodiments of core competencies.

HOW NOT TO THINK OF COMPETENCE

Since companies are in a race to build the competencies that determine global leadership, successful companies have stopped imagining themselves as bundles of businesses making products. Canon, Honda, Casio, or NEC may seem to preside over portfolios of businesses unrelated in terms of customers, distribution channels, and merchandising strategy. Indeed, they have portfolios that may seem idiosyncratic at times: NEC is the only global company to be among leaders in computing, telecommunications, and semiconductors *and* to have a thriving consumer electronics business.

But looks are deceiving. In NEC, digital technology, especially VLSI and systems integration skills, is fundamental. In the core competencies underlying them, disparate businesses become coherent. It is Honda's core competence in engines and power trains that gives it a distinctive advantage in car, motorcycle, lawn mower, and generator businesses. Canon's core competencies in optics, imaging, and microprocessor controls have enabled it to enter, even dominate, markets as seemingly diverse as copiers, laser printers, cameras, and image scanners. Philips worked for more than 15 years to perfect its optical-media (laser disc) competence, as did JVC in building a leading position in video recording. Other examples of core competencies might include mechantronics (the ability to marry mechanical and electronic engineering), video displays, bioengineering, and microelectronics. In the early stages of its competence building, Philips could not have imagined all the products that would be spawned by its optical-media competence, nor could JVC have anticipated miniature camcorders when it first began exploring videotape technologies.

Unlike the battle for global brand dominance, which is visible in the world's broadcast and print media and is aimed at building global "share of mind," the battle to build world-class competencies is invisible to people who aren't deliberately looking for it. Top management often tracks the cost and quality of competitors' products, yet how many managers untangle the web of alliances their Japanese competitors have constructed to acquire competencies at low cost? In how many Western boardrooms is there an explicit, shared understanding of the competencies the company must build for world leadership? Indeed, how many senior executives discuss the crucial distinction between competitive strategy at the level of a business and competitive strategy at the level of an entire company?

Let us be clear. Cultivating core competence does *not* mean outspending rivals on research and development. In 1983, when Canon surpassed Xerox in worldwide unit market share in the copier business, its R&D budget in reprographics was but a small fraction of Xerox's. Over the past 20 years, NEC has spent less on R&D as a percentage of sales than almost all of its American and European competitors.

Nor does core competence mean shared costs, as when two or more SBUs use a common facility—a plant, service facility, or sales force—or share a common component. The gains of sharing may be substantial, but the search for shared costs is typically a post hoc effort to rationalize production across existing businesses, not a premeditated effort to build the competencies out of which the businesses themselves grow.

Building core competencies is more ambitious and different than integrating vertically, moreover. Managers deciding whether to make or buy will start with end products and look upstream to the efficiencies of the supply chain and downstream toward distribution and customers. They do not take inventory of skills and look forward to applying them in nontraditional ways. (Of course, decisions about competencies *do* provide a logic for vertical integration. Canon is not particularly integrated in its copier business, except in those aspects of the vertical chain that support the competencies it regards as critical.)

IDENTIFYING CORE COMPETENCIES— AND LOSING THEM

At least three tests can be applied to identify core competencies in a company. First, a core competence provides potential access to a wide variety of markets. Competence in display systems, for example, enables a company to participate in such diverse businesses as calculators, miniature TV sets, monitors for laptop computers, and automotive dashboards—which is why Casio's entry into the handheld TV market was predictable. Second, a core competence should make a significant contribution to the perceived customer benefits of the end product. Clearly, Honda's engine expertise fills this bill.

Finally, a core competence should be difficult for competitors to imitate. And it *will* be difficult if it is a complex harmonization of individual technologies and production skills. A rival might acquire some of the technologies that comprise the core competence, but it will find it more difficult to duplicate the more or less comprehensive pattern of internal coordination and learning. JVC's decision in the early 1960s to pursue the development of a videotape competence passed the three tests outlined here. RCA's decision in the late 1970s to develop a stylus-based video turntable system did not.

Few companies are likely to build world leadership in more than five or six fundamental competencies. A company that compiles a list of 20 to 30 capabilities has probably not produced a list of core competencies. Still, it is probably a good discipline to generate a list of this sort and to see aggregate capabilities as building blocks. This tends to prompt the search for licensing deals and alliances through which the company may acquire, at low cost, the missing pieces.

Most Western companies hardly think about competitiveness in these terms at all. It is time to take a tough-minded look at the risks they are running. Companies that judge competitiveness, their own and their competitors', primarily in terms of the price/performance of end products are courting the erosion of core competencies—or making too little effort to enhance them. The embedded skills that give rise to the next generation of competitive products cannot be "rented in" by outsourcing and OEM (original equipment manufacturer) supply relationships. In our view, too many companies have unwittingly surrendered core competencies when they cut internal investment in what they mistakenly thought were just "cost centers" in favor of outside suppliers.

Consider Chrysler. Unlike Honda, it has tended to view engines and power trains as simply one more component. Chrysler is becoming increasingly dependent on Mitsubishi and Hyundai: between 1985 and 1987, the number of outsourced engines went from 252,000 to 382,000. It is difficult to imagine Honda yielding manufacturing responsibility, much less design, of so critical a part of a car's function to an outside company—which is why Honda has made such an enormous commitment to Formula One auto racing. Honda has been able to pool its engine-related technologies; it has parlayed these into a corporationwide competency from which it develops world-beating products, despite R&D budgets smaller than those of GM and Toyota.

Of course, it is perfectly possible for a company to have a competitive product lineup but be a laggard in developing core competencies—at least for a while. If a company wanted to enter the copier business today, it would find a dozen Japanese companies more than willing to supply copiers on the basis of an OEM private label. But when fundamental technologies changed or if its supplier decided to enter the market directly and become a competitor, that company's product line, along with all of its investments in marketing and distribution, could be vulnerable. Outsourcing can provide a shortcut to a more competitive product, but it typically contributes little to building the people-embodied skills that are needed to sustain product leadership.

Nor is it possible for a company to have an intelligent alliance or sourcing strategy if it has not made a choice about where it will build competence leadership. Clearly, Japanese companies have benefited from alliances. They've used them to learn from Western partners who were not fully committed to preserving core competencies of their own. As we've argued in these pages before, learning within an alliance takes a positive commit-

ment of resources—travel, a pool of dedicated people, test-bed facilities, time to internalize and test what has been learned.[2] A company may not make this effort if it doesn't have clear goals for competence building.

Another way of losing is forgoing opportunities to establish competencies that are evolving in existing businesses. In the 1970s and 1980s, many American and European companies—like GE, Motorola, GTE, Thorn, and GEC—chose to exit the color television business, which they regarded as mature. If by "mature" they meant that they had run out of new product ideas at precisely the moment global rivals had targeted the TV business for entry, then yes, the industry was mature. But it certainly wasn't mature in the sense that all opportunities to enhance and apply video-based competencies had been exhausted.

In ridding themselves of their television businesses, these companies failed to distinguish between divesting the business and destroying their video media–based competencies. They not only got out of the TV business but they also closed the door on a whole stream of future opportunities reliant on video-based competencies. The television industry, considered by many U.S. companies in the 1970s to be unattractive, is today the focus of a fierce public policy debate about the inability of U.S. corporations to benefit from the $20-billion-a-year opportunity that HDTV will represent in the mid- to late 1990s. Ironically, the U.S. government is being asked to fund a massive research project—in effect, to compensate U.S. companies for their failure to preserve critical core competencies when they had the chance.

In contrast, one can see a company like Sony reducing its emphasis on VCRs (where it has not been very successful and where Korean companies now threaten), without reducing its commitment to video-related competencies. Sony's Betamax led to a debacle. But it emerged with its videotape recording competencies intact and is currently challenging Matsushita in the 8mm camcorder market.

There are two clear lessons here. First, the costs of losing a core competence can be only partly calculated in advance. The baby may be thrown out with the bath water in divestment decisions. Second, since core competencies are built through a process of continuous improvement and enhancement that may span a decade or longer, a company that has failed to invest in core competence building will find it very difficult to enter an

---

[2] "Collaborate with Your Competitors and Win," *Harvard Business Review,* January–February 1989, p. 133, with Yves L. Doz.

emerging market, unless, of course, it will be content simply to serve as a distribution channel.

American semiconductor companies like Motorola learned this painful lesson when they elected to forgo direct participation in the 256k generation of DRAM chips. Having skipped this round, Motorola, like most of its American competitors, needed a large infusion of technical help from Japanese partners to rejoin the battle in the 1-megabyte generation. When it comes to core competencies, it is difficult to get off the train, walk to the next station, and then reboard.

FROM CORE COMPETENCIES TO CORE PRODUCTS

The tangible link between identified core competencies and end products is what we call the core products—the physical embodiments of one or more core competencies. Honda's engines, for example, are core products, linchpins between design and development skills that ultimately lead to a proliferation of end products. Core products are the components or subassemblies that actually contribute to the value of the end products. Thinking in terms of core products forces a company to distinguish between the brand share it achieves in end product markets (for example, 40 percent of the U.S. refrigerator market) and the manufacturing share it achieves in any particular core product (for example, 5 percent of the world share of compressor output).

Canon is reputed to have an 84 percent world manufacturing share in desktop laser printer "engines," even though its brand share in the laser printer business is minuscule. Similarly, Matsushita has a world manufacturing share of about 45 percent in key VCR components, far in excess of its brand share (Panasonic, JVC, and others) of 20 percent. And Matsushita has a commanding core product share in compressors worldwide, estimated at 40 percent, even though its brand share in both the air-conditioning and refrigerator businesses is quite small.

It is essential to make this distinction between core competencies, core products, and end products because global competition is played out by different rules and for different stakes at each level. To build or defend leadership over the long term, a corporation will probably be a winner at each level. At the level of core competence, the goal is to build world leadership in the design and development of a particular class of product functionality—be it compact data storage and retrieval, as with Philips's optical-media competence, or compactness and

ease of use, as with Sony's micromotors and microprocessor controls.

To sustain leadership in their chosen core competence areas, these companies *seek to maximize their world manufacturing share in core products*. The manufacture of core products for a wide variety of external (and internal) customers yields the revenue and market feedback that, at least partly, determines the pace at which core competencies can be enhanced and extended. This thinking was behind JVC's decision in the mid-1970s to establish VCR supply relationships with leading national consumer electronics companies in Europe and the United States. In supplying Thomson, Thorn, and Telefunken (all independent companies at that time) as well as U.S. partners, JVC was able to gain the cash and the diversity of market experience that ultimately enabled it to outpace Philips and Sony. (Philips developed videotape competencies in parallel with JVC, but it failed to build a worldwide network of OEM relationships that would have allowed it to accelerate the refinement of its videotape competence through the sale of core products.)

JVC's success has not been lost on Korean companies like Goldstar, Sam Sung, Kia, and Daewoo, which are building core product leadership in areas as diverse as displays, semiconductors, and automotive engines through their OEM-supply contracts with Western companies. Their avowed goal is to capture investment initiative away from potential competitors, often U.S. companies. In doing so, they accelerate their competence-building efforts while "hollowing out" their competitors. By focusing on competence and embedding it in core products, Asian competitors have built up advantages in component markets first and have then leveraged off their superior products to move downstream to build brand share. And they are not likely to remain the low-cost suppliers forever. As their reputation for brand leadership is consolidated, they may well gain price leadership. Honda has proven this with its Acura line, and other Japanese car makers are following suit.

Control over core products is critical for other reasons. A dominant position in core products allows a company to shape the evolution of applications and end markets. Such compact audio disc-related core products as data drivers and lasers have enabled Sony and Philips to influence the evolution of the computer-peripheral business in optical-media storage. As a company multiplies the number of application arenas for its core products, it can consistently reduce the cost, time, and risk in new product development. In short, well-targeted core products can lead to economies of scale *and* scope.

THE TYRANNY OF THE SBU

The new terms of competitive engagement cannot be understood using analytical tools devised to manage the diversified corporation of 20 years ago, when competition was primarily domestic (GE versus Westinghouse, General Motors versus Ford) and all the key players were speaking the language of the same business schools and consultancies. Old prescriptions have potentially toxic side effects. The need for new principles is most obvious in companies organized exclusively according to the logic of SBUs. The implications of the two alternative concepts of the corporation are summarized in Exhibit 2, "Two Concepts of the Corporation: SBU or Core Competence."

Obviously, diversified corporations have a portfolio of products and a portfolio of businesses. But we believe in a view of the company as a portfolio of competencies as well. U.S. companies do not lack the technical resources to build competencies, but their top management often lacks the vision to build them and the administrative means for assembling resources spread across multiple businesses. A shift in commitment will inevitably influence patterns of diversification, skill deployment, resource allocation priorities, and approaches to alliances and outsourcing.

We have described the three different planes on which battles for global leadership are waged: core competence, core products, and end products. A corporation has to know whether it is winning or losing on each plane. By sheer weight of investment, a company might be able to beat its rivals to blue-sky technologies yet still lose the race to build core competence leadership. If a company is winning the race to build core competencies (as opposed to building leadership in a few technologies), it will almost certainly outpace rivals in new business development. If a company is winning the race to capture world manufacturing share in core products, it will probably outpace rivals in improving product features and the price/performance ratio.

Determining whether one is winning or losing end product battles is more difficult because measures of product market share do not necessarily reflect various companies' underlying competitiveness. Indeed, companies that attempt to build market share by relying on the competitiveness of others, rather than investing in core competencies and world core-product leadership, may be treading on quicksand. In the race for global brand dominance, companies like 3M, Black & Decker, Canon, Honda, NEC, and Citicorp have built global brand umbrellas by proliferating products out of their core competencies. This has allowed their individual businesses to build image, customer loyalty, and access to distribution channels.

When you think about this reconceptualization of the corporation, the primacy of the SBU—an organizational dogma for a generation—is now clearly an anachronism. Where the SBU is an article of faith, resistance to the seductions of decentralization can seem heretical. In many companies, the SBU prism means that only one plane of the global competitive battle, the battle to put competi-

EXHIBIT 2   Two Concepts of the Corporation: SBU or Core Competence

	SBU	Core Competence
Basis for competition	Competitiveness of today's products	Interfirm competition to build competencies
Corporate structure	Portfolio of businesses related in product-market terms	Portfolio of competencies, core products, and businesses
Status of the business unit	Autonomy is sacrosanct; the SBU "owns" all resources other than cash.	SBU is a potential reservoir of core competencies.
Resource allocation	Discrete businesses are the unit of analysis; capital is allocated business by business.	Businesses and competencies are the unit of analysis: top management allocates capital and talent.
Value added of top management	Optimizing corporate returns through capital allocation trade-offs among businesses	Enunciating strategic architecture and building competencies to secure the future

tive products on the shelf *today*, is visible to top management. What are the costs of this distortion?

Underinvestment in Developing Core Competencies and Core Products

When the organization is conceived of as a multiplicity of SBUs, no single business may feel responsible for maintaining a viable position in core products or be able to justify the investment required to build world leadership in some core competence. In the absence of a more comprehensive view imposed by corporate management, SBU managers will tend to underinvest. Recently, companies such as Kodak and Philips have recognized this as a potential problem and have begun searching for new organizational forms that will allow them to develop and manufacture core products for both internal and external customers.

SBU managers have traditionally conceived of competitors in the same way they've seen themselves. On the whole, they've failed to note the emphasis Asian competitors were placing on building leadership in core products or to understand the critical linkage between world manufacturing leadership and the ability to sustain development pace in core competence. They've failed to pursue OEM-supply opportunities or to look across their various product divisions in an attempt to identify opportunities for coordinated initiatives.

Imprisoned Resources

As an SBU evolves, it often develops unique competencies. Typically, the people who embody this competence are seen as the sole property of the business in which they grew up. The manager of another SBU who asks to borrow talented people is likely to get a cold rebuff. SBU managers are not only unwilling to lend their competence carriers, but they may actually hide talent to prevent its redeployment in the pursuit of new opportunities. This may be compared to residents of an underdeveloped country hiding most of their cash under their mattresses. The benefits of competencies, like the benefits of the money supply, depend on the velocity of their circulation as well as on the size of the stock the company holds.

Western companies have traditionally had an advantage in the stock of skills they possess. But have they been able to reconfigure them quickly to respond to new opportunities? Canon, NEC, and Honda have had a lesser stock of the people and technologies that compose core competencies but could move them much quicker from one business unit to another. Corporate R&D spending at Canon is not fully indicative of the size of Canon's core

competence stock and tells the casual observer nothing about the velocity with which Canon is able to move core competencies to exploit opportunities.

When competencies become imprisoned, the people who carry the competencies do not get assigned to the most exciting opportunities, and their skills begin to atrophy. Only by fully leveraging core competencies can small companies like Canon afford to compete with industry giants like Xerox. How strange that SBU managers, who are perfectly willing to compete for cash in the capital budgeting process, are unwilling to compete for people—the company's most precious asset. We find it ironic that top management devotes so much attention to the capital budgeting process yet typically has no comparable mechanism for allocating the human skills that embody core competencies. Top managers are seldom able to look four or five levels down into the organization, identify the people who embody critical competencies, and move them across organizational boundaries.

Bounded Innovation

If core competencies are not recognized, individual SBUs will pursue only those innovation opportunities that are close at hand—marginal product-line extensions or geographic expansions. Hybrid opportunities like fax machines, laptop computers, hand-held televisions, or portable music keyboards will emerge only when managers take off their SBU blinders. Remember, Canon appeared to be in the camera business at the time it was preparing to become a world leader in copiers. Conceiving of the corporation in terms of core competencies widens the domain of innovation.

DEVELOPING STRATEGIC ARCHITECTURE

The fragmentation of core competencies becomes inevitable when a diversified company's information systems, patterns of communication, career paths, managerial rewards, and processes of strategy development do not transcend SBU lines. We believe that senior management should spend a significant amount of its time developing a corporationwide strategic architecture that establishes objectives for competence building. A strategic architecture is a road map of the future that identifies which core competencies to build and their constituent technologies.

By providing an impetus for learning from alliances and a focus for internal development efforts, a strategic architecture like NEC's C&C can dramatically reduce the investment needed to secure future market leadership. How can a company make partnerships intelligently without a clear understanding of the core competencies it is trying to build and those it is attempting to prevent from being unintentionally transferred?

Of course, all of this begs the question of what a strategic architecture should look like. The answer will be different for every company. But it is helpful to think again of that tree, of the corporation organized around core products and, ultimately, core competencies. To sink sufficiently strong roots, a company must answer some fundamental questions: How long could we preserve our competitiveness in this business if we did not control this particular core competence? How central is this core competence to perceived customer benefits? What future opportunities would be foreclosed if we were to lose this particular competence?

The architecture provides a logic for product and market diversification, moreover. An SBU manager would be asked: Does the new market opportunity add to the overall goal of becoming the best player in the world? Does it exploit or add to the core competence? At Vickers, for example, diversification options have been judged in the context of becoming the best power and motion control company in the world (see the insert "Vickers Learns the Value of Strategic Architecture").

The strategic architecture should make resource allocation priorities transparent to the entire organization. It provides a template for allocation decisions by top management. It helps lower level managers understand the logic of allocation priorities and disciplines senior management to maintain consistency. In short, it yields a definition of the company and the markets it serves. 3M, Vickers, NEC, Canon, and Honda all qualify on this score. Honda *knew* it was exploiting what it had learned from motorcycles—how to make high-revving, smooth-running, lightweight engines—when it entered the car business. The task of creating a strategic architecture

Vickers Learns the Value of Strategic Architecture

The idea that top management should develop a corporate strategy for acquiring and deploying core competencies is relatively new in most U.S. companies. There are a few exceptions. An early convert was Trinova (previously Libbey Owens Ford), a Toledo-based corporation, which enjoys a worldwide position in power and motion controls and engineered plastics. One of its major divisions is Vickers, a premier supplier of hydraulics components like valves, pumps, actuators, and filtration devices to aerospace, marine, defense, automotive, earthmoving, and industrial markets.

Vickers saw the potential for a transformation of its traditional business with the application of electronics disciplines in combination with its traditional technologies. The goal was "to ensure that change in technology does not displace Vickers from its customers." This, to be sure, was initially a defensive move: Vickers recognized that unless it acquired new skills, it could not protect existing markets or capitalize on new growth opportunities. Managers at Vickers attempted to conceptualize the likely evolution of (a) technologies relevant to the power and motion control business, (b) functionalities that would satisfy emerging customer needs, and (c) new competencies needed to creatively manage the marriage of technology and customer needs.

Despite pressure for short-term earnings, top management looked to a 10- to 15-year time horizon in developing a map of emerging customer needs, changing technologies, and the core competencies that would be necessary to bridge the gap between the two. Its slogan was "Into the 21st Century." Vickers is currently in fluid-power components. The architecture identifies two additional competencies, electric-power components and electronic controls. A systems integration capability that would unite hardware, software, and service was also targeted for development.

The strategic architecture, as illustrated by the Vickers example, is not a forecast of specific products or specific technologies but a broad map of the evolving linkages between customer functionality requirements, potential technologies, and core competencies. It assumes that products and systems cannot be defined with certainty for the future but that preempting competitors in the development of new markets requires an early start to building core competencies. The strategic architecture developed by Vickers, while describing the future in competence terms, also provides the basis for making here-and-now decisions about product priorities, acquisitions, alliances, and recruitment.

Since 1986, Vickers has made more than 10 clearly targeted acquisitions, each one focused on a specific component or technology gap identified in the overall architecture. The architecture is also the basis for internal development of new competencies. Vickers has undertaken, in parallel, a reorganization to enable the integration of electronics and electrical capabilities with mechanical-based competencies. We believe that it will take another two to three years before Vickers reaps the total benefits from developing the strategic architecture, communicating it widely to all its employees, customers, and investors, and building administrative systems consistent with the architecture.

forces the organization to identify and commit to the technical and production linkages across SBUs that will provide a distinct competitive advantage.

It is consistency of resource allocation and the development of an administrative infrastructure appropriate to it that breathes life into a strategic architecture and creates a managerial culture, teamwork, a capacity to change, and a willingness to share resources, to protect proprietary skills, and to think long-term. That is also the reason the specific architecture cannot be copied easily or overnight by competitors. Strategic architecture is a tool for communicating with customers and other external constituents. It reveals the broad direction without giving away every step.

REDEPLOYING TO EXPLOIT COMPETENCIES

If the company's core competencies are its critical resource and if top management must ensure that competence carriers are not held hostage by some particular business, then it follows that SBUs should bid for core competencies in the same way they bid for capital. We've made this point glancingly. It is important enough to consider more deeply.

Once top management (with the help of divisional and SBU managers) has identified overarching competencies, it must ask businesses to identify the projects and people closely connected with them. Corporate officers should direct an audit of the location, number, and quality of the people who embody competence.

This sends an important signal to middle managers: core competencies are *corporate* resources and may be reallocated by corporate management. An individual business doesn't own anybody. SBUs are entitled to the services of individual employees so long as SBU management can demonstrate that the opportunity it is pursuing yields the highest possible payoff on the investment in their skills. This message is further underlined if each year in the strategic planning or budgeting process, unit managers must justify their hold on the people who carry the company's core competencies.

Elements of Canon's core competence in optics are spread across businesses as diverse as cameras, copiers, and semiconductor lithographic equipment and are shown in Exhibit 3, "Core Competencies at Canon." When Canon identified an opportunity in digital laser printers, it gave SBU managers the right to raid other SBUs to pull together the required pool of talent. When Canon's reprographics products division undertook to develop microprocessor-controlled copiers, it turned to the

EXHIBIT 3 Core Competencies at Canon

	Precision mechanics	Fine optics	Micro-electronics
Basic camera	■	□	
Compact fashion camera	■	□	
Electronic camera	■	□	
EOS autofocus camera	■	□	■
Video still camera	■	□	■
Laser beam printer	■	□	■
Color video printer	■		■
Bubble jet printer	■		■
Basic fax	■		■
Laser fax	■		■
Calculator			■
Plain paper copier	■	□	■
Battery PPC	■	□	■
Color copier	■	□	■
Laser copier	■	□	■
Color laser copier	■	□	■
NAVI	■	□	■
Still video system	■	□	■
Laser imager	■	□	■
Cell analyzer	■	□	■
Mask aligners	■		■
Stepper aligners	■		■
Excimer laser aligners	■	□	■

Every Canon product is the result of at least one core competency.

photo products group, which had developed the world's first microprocessor-controlled camera.

Also, reward systems that focus only on product-line results and career paths that seldom cross SBU boundaries engender patterns of behavior among unit managers that are destructively competitive. At NEC, divisional managers come together to identify next-generation competencies. Together they decide how much investment needs to be made to build up each future competency and the contribution in capital and staff support that each division will need to make. There is also a sense of equitable exchange. One division may make a disproportionate contribution or may benefit less from the progress made, but such short-term inequalities will balance out over the long term.

Incidentally, the positive contribution of the SBU manager should be made visible across the company. An SBU manager is unlikely to surrender key people if only the other business (or the general manager of that business who may be a competitor for promotion) is going to benefit from the redeployment. Cooperative SBU managers should be celebrated as team players. Where priorities are clear, transfers are less likely to be seen as idiosyncratic and politically motivated.

Transfers for the sake of building core competence must be recorded and appreciated in the corporate memory. It is reasonable to expect a business that has surrendered core skills on behalf of corporate opportunities in other areas to lose, for a time, some of its competitiveness. If these losses in performance bring immediate censure, SBUs will be unlikely to assent to skills transfers next time.

Finally, there are ways to wean key employees off the idea that they belong in perpetuity to any particular business. Early in their careers, people may be exposed to a variety of businesses through a carefully planned rotation program. At Canon, critical people move regularly between the camera business and the copier business and between the copier business and the professional optical-products business. In midcareer, periodic assignments to cross-divisional project teams may be necessary, both for diffusing core competencies and for loosening the bonds that might tie an individual to one business even when brighter opportunities beckon elsewhere. Those who embody critical core competencies should know that their careers are tracked and guided by corporate human resource professionals. In the early 1980s at Canon, all engineers under 30 were invited to apply for membership on a seven-person committee that was to spend two years plotting Canon's future direction, including its strategic architecture.

Competence carriers should be regularly brought together from across the corporation to trade notes and ideas. The goal is to build a strong feeling of community among these people. To a great extent, their loyalty should be to the integrity of the core competence area they represent and not just to particular businesses. In traveling regularly, talking frequently to customers, and meeting with peers, competence carriers may be encouraged to discover new market opportunities.

CONCLUSION

Core competencies are the wellspring of new business development. They should constitute the focus for strategy at the corporate level. Managers have to win manufacturing leadership in core products and capture global share through brand-building programs aimed at exploiting economies of scope. Only if the company is conceived of as a hierarchy of core competencies, core products, and market-focused business units will it be fit to fight.

Nor can top management be just another layer of accounting consolidation, which it often is in a regime of radical decentralization. Top management must add value by enunciating the strategic architecture that guides the competence acquisition process. We believe an obsession with competence building will characterize the global winners of the 1990s. With the decade under way, the time for rethinking the concept of the corporation is already overdue.

READING I-4

What Is Strategy?

Michael E. Porter

I. OPERATIONAL EFFECTIVENESS IS NOT STRATEGY

For almost two decades, managers have been learning to play by a new set of rules. Companies must be flexible to respond rapidly to competitive and market changes. They must benchmark continuously to achieve best practice. They must outsource aggressively to gain efficiencies. And they must nurture a few core competencies in the race to stay ahead of rivals.

Positioning—once the heart of strategy—is rejected as too static for today's dynamic markets and changing technologies. According to the new dogma, rivals can quickly copy any market position, and competitive advantage is, at best, temporary.

But those beliefs are dangerous half-truths, and they are leading more and more companies down the path of mutually destructive competition. True, some barriers to competition are falling as regulation eases and markets become global. True, companies have properly invested

Source: Harvard Business Review, November–December 1996. Copyright © 1996 by the President and Fellows of Harvard College. All rights reserved.
This article has benefited greatly from the assistance of many individuals and companies. The author gives special thanks to Jan Rivkin, the coauthor of a related paper. Substantial research contributions have been made by Nicolaj Siggelkow, Dawn Sylvester, and Lucia Marshall. Tarun Khanna, Roger Martin, and Anita McGahan have provided especially extensive comments.

energy in becoming leaner and more nimble. In many industries, however, what some call *hypercompetition* is a self-inflicted wound, not the inevitable outcome of a changing paradigm of competition.

The root of the problem is the failure to distinguish between operational effectiveness and strategy. The quest for productivity, quality, and speed has spawned a remarkable number of management tools and techniques: total quality management, benchmarking, time-based competition, outsourcing, partnering, reengineering, change management. Although the resulting operational improvements have often been dramatic, many companies have been frustrated by their inability to translate those gains into sustainable profitability. And bit by bit, almost imperceptibly, management tools have taken the place of strategy. As managers push to improve on all fronts, they move farther away from viable competitive positions.

Operational Effectiveness: Necessary but Not Sufficient

Operational effectiveness and strategy are both essential to superior performance, which, after all, is the primary goal of any enterprise. But they work in very different ways.

A company can outperform rivals only if it can establish a difference that it can preserve. It must deliver greater value to customers or create comparable value at a lower cost or do both. The arithmetic of superior profitability then follows: delivering greater value allows a company to charge higher average unit prices; greater efficiency results in lower average unit costs.

Ultimately, all differences between companies in cost or price derive from the hundreds of activities required to create, produce, sell, and deliver their products or services, such as calling on customers, assembling final products, and training employees. Cost is generated by performing activities, and cost advantage arises from performing particular activities more efficiently than competitors. Similarly, differentiation arises from both the choice of activities and how they are performed. Activities, then, are the basic units of competitive advantage. Overall advantage or disadvantage results from all a company's activities, not only a few.[1]

Operational effectiveness (OE) means performing similar activities *better* than rivals perform them. Operational effectiveness includes but is not limited to efficiency. It refers to any number of practices that allow a company to better utilize its inputs by, for example, reducing defects in products or developing better products faster. In contrast, strategic positioning means performing *different* activities from rivals' or performing similar activities in *different ways.*

Differences in operational effectiveness among companies are pervasive. Some companies are able to get more out of their inputs than others because they eliminate wasted effort, employ more advanced technology, motivate employees better, or have greater insight into managing particular activities or sets of activities. Such differences in operational effectiveness are an important source of differences in profitability among competitors because they directly affect relative cost positions and levels of differentiation.

Differences in operational effectiveness were at the heart of the Japanese challenge to Western companies in the 1980s. The Japanese were so far ahead of rivals in operational effectiveness that they could offer lower cost and superior quality at the same time. It is worth dwelling on this point, because so much recent thinking about competition depends on it. Imagine for a moment a *productivity frontier* that constitutes the sum of all existing best practices at any given time. Think of it as the maximum value that a company delivering a particular product or service can create at a given cost, using the best available technologies, skills, management techniques, and purchased inputs. The productivity frontier can apply to individual activities, to groups of linked activities such as order processing and manufacturing, and to an entire company's activities. When a company improves its operational effectiveness, it moves toward the frontier. Doing so may require capital investment, different personnel, or simply new ways of managing.

The productivity frontier is constantly shifting outward as new technologies and management approaches are developed and as new inputs become available. Laptop computers, mobile communications, the Internet, and software such as Lotus Notes, for example, have redefined the productivity frontier for sales-force operations and created rich possibilities for linking sales with such activities as order processing and after-sales support. Similarly, lean production, which involves a family of activities, has allowed substantial improvements in manufacturing productivity and asset utilization.

---

[1] I first described the concept of activities and its use in understanding competitive advantage in *Competitive Advantage* (New York: The Free Press, 1985). The ideas in this article build on and extend that thinking.

For at least the past decade, managers have been preoccupied with improving operational effectiveness. Through programs such as TQM, time-based competition, and benchmarking, they have changed how they perform activities in order to eliminate inefficiencies, improve customer satisfaction, and achieve best practice. Hoping to keep up with shifts in the productivity frontier, managers have embraced continuous improvement, empowerment, change management, and the so-called learning organization. The popularity of outsourcing and the virtual corporation reflects the growing recognition that it is difficult to perform all activities as productively as specialists.

As companies move to the frontier, they can often improve on multiple dimensions of performance at the same time. For example, manufacturers that adopted the Japanese practice of rapid changeovers in the 1980s were able to lower cost and improve differentiation simultaneously. What were once believed to be real trade-offs—between defects and costs, for example—turned out to be illusions created by poor operational effectiveness. Managers have learned to reject such false trade-offs.

Constant improvement in operational effectiveness is necessary to achieve superior profitability. However, it is not usually sufficient. Few companies have competed successfully on the basis of operational effectiveness over an extended period, and staying ahead of rivals gets harder every day. The most obvious reason for that is the rapid diffusion of best practices. Competitors can quickly imitate management techniques, new technologies, input improvements, and superior ways of meeting customers' needs. The most generic solutions—those that can be used in multiple settings—diffuse the fastest. Witness the proliferation of OE techniques accelerated by support from consultants.

OE competition shifts the productivity frontier outward, effectively raising the bar for everyone. But although such competition produces absolute improvement in operational effectiveness, it leads to relative improvement for no one. Consider the $5 billion-plus U.S. commercial-printing industry. The major players—R.R. Donnelley & Sons Company, Quebecor, World Color Press, and Big Flower Press—are competing head to head, serving all types of customers, offering the same array of printing technologies (gravure and web offset), investing heavily in the same new equipment, running their presses faster, and reducing crew sizes. But the resulting major productivity gains are being captured by customers and equipment suppliers, not retained in superior profitability. Even industry-leader Donnelley's profit margin, consistently higher than 7% in the 1980s, fell to less than 4.6% in 1995. This pattern is playing itself out in industry after industry. Even the Japanese, pioneers of the new competition, suffer from persistently low profits. (See the insert "Japanese Companies Rarely Have Strategies.")

The second reason that improved operational effectiveness is insufficient—competitive convergence—is more subtle and insidious. The more benchmarking companies do, the more they look alike. The more that rivals outsource activities to efficient third parties, often the same ones, the more generic those activities become. As rivals imitate one another's improvements in quality, cycle times, or supplier partnerships, strategies converge and competition becomes a series of races down identical paths that no one can win. Competition based on operational effectiveness alone is mutually destructive, leading to wars of attrition that can be arrested only by limiting competition.

The recent wave of industry consolidation through mergers makes sense in the context of OE competition. Driven by performance pressures but lacking strategic vision, company after company has had no better idea than to buy up its rivals. The competitors left standing are often those that outlasted others, not companies with real advantage.

After a decade of impressive gains in operational effectiveness, many companies are facing diminishing returns. Continuous improvement has been etched on managers' brains. But its tools unwittingly draw companies toward imitation and homogeneity. Gradually, managers have let operational effectiveness supplant strategy. The

EXHIBIT 1 **Operational Effectiveness Versus Strategic Positioning**

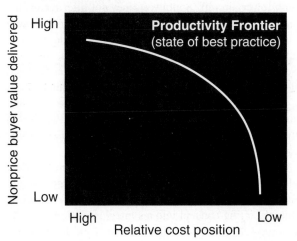

Japanese Companies Rarely Have Strategies

The Japanese triggered a global revolution in operational effectiveness in the 1970s and 1980s, pioneering practices such as total quality management and continuous improvement. As a result, Japanese manufacturers enjoyed substantial cost and quality advantages for many years.

But Japanese companies rarely developed distinct strategic positions of the kind discussed in this article. Those that did—Sony, Canon, and Sega, for example—were the exception rather than the rule. Most Japanese companies imitate and emulate one another. All rivals offer most if not all product varieties, features, and services; they employ all channels and match one anothers' plant configurations.

The dangers of Japanese-style competition are now becoming easier to recognize. In the 1980s, with rivals operating far from the productivity frontier, it seemed possible to win on both cost and quality indefinitely. Japanese companies were all able to grow in an expanding domestic economy and by penetrating global markets. They appeared unstoppable. But as the gap in operational effectiveness narrows, Japanese companies are increasingly caught in a trap of their own making. If they are to escape the mutually destructive battles now ravaging their performance, Japanese companies will have to learn strategy.

To do so, they may have to overcome strong cultural barriers. Japan is notoriously consensus oriented, and companies have a strong tendency to mediate differences among individuals rather than accentuate them. Strategy, on the other hand, requires hard choices. The Japanese also have a deeply ingrained service tradition that predisposes them to go to great lengths to satisfy any need a customer expresses. Companies that compete in that way end up blurring their distinct positioning, becoming all things to all customers.

Source: This discussion of Japan is drawn from the author's research with Hirotaka Takeuchi, with help from Mariko Sakakibara.

---

result is zero-sum competition, static or declining prices, and pressures on costs that compromise companies' ability to invest in the business for the long term.

II. STRATEGY RESTS ON UNIQUE ACTIVITIES

Competitive strategy is about being different. It means deliberately choosing a different set of activities to deliver a unique mix of value.

Southwest Airlines Company, for example, offers short-haul, low-cost, point-to-point service between midsize cities and secondary airports in large cities. Southwest avoids large airports and does not fly great distances. Its customers include business travelers, families, and students. Southwest's frequent departures and low fares attract price-sensitive customers who otherwise would travel by bus or car, and convenience-oriented travelers who would choose a full-service airline on other routes.

Most managers describe strategic positioning in terms of their customers: "Southwest Airlines serves price- and convenience-sensitive travelers," for example. But the essence of strategy is in the activities—choosing to perform activities differently or to perform different activities than rivals. Otherwise, a strategy is nothing more than a marketing slogan that will not withstand competition.

A full-service airline is configured to get passengers from almost any point A to any point B. To reach a large number of destinations and serve passengers with connecting flights, full-service airlines employ a hub-and-spoke system centered on major airports. To attract passengers who desire more comfort, they offer first-class or business-class service. To accommodate passengers who must change planes, they coordinate schedules and check and transfer baggage. Because some passengers will be traveling for many hours, full-service airlines serve meals.

Southwest, in contrast, tailors all its activities to deliver low-cost, convenient service on its particular type of route. Through fast turnarounds at the gate of only 15 minutes, Southwest is able to keep planes flying longer hours than rivals and provide frequent departures with fewer aircraft. Southwest does not offer meals, assigned seats, interline baggage checking, or premium classes of service. Automated ticketing at the gate encourages customers to bypass travel agents, allowing Southwest to avoid their commissions. A standardized fleet of 737 aircraft boosts the efficiency of maintenance.

Southwest has staked out a unique and valuable strategic position based on a tailored set of activities. On the routes served by Southwest, a full-service airline could never be as convenient or as low cost.

Ikea, the global furniture retailer based in Sweden, also has a clear strategic positioning. Ikea targets young furniture buyers who want style at low cost. What turns this marketing concept into a strategic positioning is the tailored set of activities that make it work. Like Southwest, Ikea has chosen to perform activities differently from its rivals.

Consider the typical furniture store. Showrooms display samples of the merchandise. One area might contain 25 sofas; another will display five dining tables. But those items represent only a fraction of the choices available to customers. Dozens of books displaying fabric swatches or wood samples or alternate styles offer customers thousands of product varieties to choose from. Salespeople often escort customers through the store, answering questions and helping them navigate this maze of choices. Once a customer makes a selection, the order is relayed to a third-party manufacturer. With luck, the furniture will be delivered to the customer's home within six to eight weeks. This is a value chain that maximizes customization and service but does so at high cost.

In contrast, Ikea serves customers who are happy to trade off service for cost. Instead of having a sales associate trail customers around the store, Ikea uses a self-service model based on clear, in-store displays. Rather than rely solely on third party manufacturers, Ikea designs its own low-cost, modular, ready-to-assemble furniture to fit its positioning. In huge stores, Ikea displays every product it sells in room-like settings, so customers don't need a decorator to help them imagine how to put the pieces together. Adjacent to the furnished showrooms is a warehouse section with the products in boxes on pallets. Customers are expected to do their own pickup and delivery, and Ikea will even sell you a roof rack for your car that you can return for a refund on your next visit.

Although much of its low-cost position comes from having customers "do it themselves," Ikea offers a number of extra services that its competitors do not. In-store child care is one. Extended hours are another. Those services are uniquely aligned with the needs of its customers, who are young, not wealthy, likely to have children (but no nanny), and, because they work for a living, have a need to shop at odd hours.

The Origins of Strategic Positions

Strategic positions emerge from three distinct sources, which are not mutually exclusive and often overlap. First, positioning can be based on producing a subset of an industry's products or services. I call this *variety-based positioning* because it is based on the choice of product or service varieties rather than customer segments. Variety-based positioning makes economic sense when a company can best produce particular products or services using distinctive sets of activities.

Jiffy Lube International, for instance, specializes in automotive lubricants and does not offer other car repair or maintenance services. Its value chain produces faster service at a lower cost than broader line repair shops, a combination so attractive that many customers subdivide their purchases, buying oil changes from the focused competitor, Jiffy Lube, and going to rivals for other services.

The Vanguard Group, a leader in the mutual fund industry, is another example of variety-based positioning. Vanguard provides an array of common stock, bond, and money market funds that offer predictable performance and rock-bottom expenses. The company's investment approach deliberately sacrifices the possibility of extraordinary performance in any one year for good relative performance in every year. Vanguard is known, for example, for its index funds. It avoids making bets on interest rates and steers clear of narrow stock groups. Fund managers keep trading levels low, which holds expenses down; in addition, the company discourages customers from rapid buying and selling because doing so drives up costs and can force a fund manager to trade in order to deploy new capital and raise cash for redemptions. Vanguard also takes a consistent low-cost approach to managing distribution, customer service, and marketing. Many investors include one or more Vanguard funds in their portfolio, while buying aggressively managed or specialized funds from competitors.

The people who use Vanguard or Jiffy Lube are responding to a superior value chain for a particular type of service. A variety-based positioning can serve a wide array of customers, but for most it will meet only a subset of their needs.

A second basis for positioning is that of serving most or all the needs of a particular group of customers. I call this *needs-based positioning*, which comes closer to traditional thinking about targeting a segment of customers. It arises when there are groups of customers with differing needs, and when a tailored set of activities can serve those needs best. Some groups of customers are more price sensitive than others, demand different product features, and need varying amounts of information, support, and services. Ikea's customers are a good example of such a group. Ikea seeks to meet all the home furnishing needs of its target customers, not just a subset of them.

A variant of needs-based positioning arises when the same customer has different needs on different occasions or for different types of transactions. The same person, for example, may have different needs when traveling on business than when traveling for pleasure with the

Finding New Positions: The Entrepreneurial Edge

Strategic competition can be thought of as the process of perceiving new positions that woo customers from established positions or draw new customers into the market. For example, superstores offering depth of merchandise in a single product category take market share from broad-line department stores offering a more limited selection in many categories. Mail-order catalogs pick off customers who crave convenience. In principle, incumbents and entrepreneurs face the same challenges in finding new strategic positions. In practice, new entrants often have the edge.

Strategic positionings are often not obvious, and finding them requires creativity and insight. New entrants often discover unique positions that have been available but simply overlooked by established competitors. Ikea, for example, recognized a customer group that had been ignored or served poorly. Circuit City Stores' entry into used cars, CarMax, is based on a new way of performing activities—extensive refurbishing of cars, product guarantees, no-haggle pricing, sophisticated use of in-house customer financing—that has long been open to incumbents.

New entrants can prosper by occupying a position that a competitor once held but has ceded through years of imitation and straddling. And entrants coming from other industries can create new positions because of distinctive activities drawn from their other businesses. CarMax borrows heavily from Circuit City's expertise in inventory management, credit, and other activities in consumer electronics retailing.

Most commonly, however, new positions open up because of change. New customer groups or purchase occasions arise; new needs emerge as societies evolve; new distribution channels appear; new technologies are developed; new machinery or information systems become available. When such changes happen, new entrants, unencumbered by a long history in the industry, can often more easily perceive the potential for a new way of competing. Unlike incumbents, newcomers can be more flexible because they face no trade-offs with their existing activities.

family. Buyers of cans—beverage companies, for example—will likely have different needs from their primary supplier than from their secondary source.

It is intuitive for most managers to conceive of their business in terms of the customers' needs they are meeting. But a critical element of needs-based positioning is not at all intuitive and is often overlooked. Differences in needs will not translate into meaningful positions unless the best set of activities to satisfy them *also* differs. If that were not the case, every competitor could meet those same needs, and there would be nothing unique or valuable about the positioning.

In private banking, for example, Bessemer Trust Company targets families with a minimum of $5 million in investable assets who want capital preservation combined with wealth accumulation. By assigning one sophisticated account officer for every 14 families, Bessemer has configured its activities for personalized service. Meetings, for example, are more likely to be held at a client's ranch or yacht than in the office. Bessemer offers a wide array of customized services, including investment management and estate administration, oversight of oil and gas investments, and accounting for racehorses and aircraft. Loans, a staple of most private banks, are rarely needed by Bessemer's clients and make up a tiny fraction of its client balances and income. Despite the most generous compensation of account officers and

the highest personnel cost as a percentage of operating expenses, Bessemer's differentiation with its target families produces a return on equity estimated to be the highest of any private banking competitor.

Citibank's private bank, on the other hand, serves clients with minimum assets of about $250,000 who, in contrast to Bessemer's clients, want convenient access to loans—from jumbo mortgages to deal financing. Citibank's account managers are primarily lenders. When clients need other services, their account manager refers them to other Citibank specialists, each of whom handles prepackaged products. Citibank's system is less customized than Bessemer's and allows it to have a lower manager-to-client ratio of 1:125. Biannual office meetings are offered only for the largest clients. Both Bessemer and Citibank have tailored their activities to meet the needs of a different group of private banking customers. The same value chain cannot profitably meet the needs of both groups.

The third basis for positioning is that of segmenting customers who are accessible in different ways. Although their needs are similar to those of other customers, the best configuration of activities to reach them is different. I call this *access-based positioning.* Access can be a function of customer geography or customer scale—or of anything that requires a different set of activities to reach customers in the best way.

Segmenting by access is less common and less well understood than the other two bases. Carmike Cinemas, for example, operates movie theaters exclusively in cities and towns with populations under 200,000. How does Carmike make money in markets that are not only small but also won't support big-city ticket prices? It does so through a set of activities that result in a lean cost structure. Carmike's small-town customers can be served through standardized, low-cost theater complexes requiring fewer screens and less sophisticated projection technology than big-city theaters. The company's proprietary information system and management process eliminate the need for local administrative staff beyond a single theater manager. Carmike also reaps advantages from centralized purchasing, lower rent and payroll costs (because of its locations), and rock-bottom corporate overhead of 2% (the industry average is 5%). Operating in small communities also allows Carmike to practice a highly personal form of marketing in which the theater manager knows patrons and promotes attendance through personal contacts. By being the dominant if not the only theater in its markets—the main competition is often the high school football team—Carmike is also able to get its pick of films and negotiate better terms with distributors.

Rural versus urban-based customers are one example of access driving differences in activities. Serving small rather than large customers or densely rather than sparsely situated customers are other examples in which the best way to configure marketing, order processing, logistics, and after-sale service activities to meet the similar needs of distinct groups will often differ.

Positioning is not only about carving out a niche. A position emerging from any of the sources can be broad or narrow. A focused competitor, such as Ikea, targets the special needs of a subset of customers and designs its activities accordingly. Focused competitors thrive on groups of customers who are overserved (and hence overpriced) by more broadly targeted competitors, or underserved (and hence underpriced). A broadly targeted competitor—for example, Vanguard or Delta Air Lines—serves a wide array of customers, performing a set of activities designed to meet their common needs. It ignores or meets only partially the more idiosyncratic needs of particular customer groups.

Whatever the basis—variety, needs, access, or some combination of the three—positioning requires a tailored set of activities because it is always a function of differences on the supply side; that is, of differences in activities. However, positioning is not always a function of differences on the demand, or customer, side. Variety and access positionings, in particular, do not rely on any customer differences. In practice, however, variety or access differences often accompany needs differences. The tastes—that is, the needs—of Carmike's small-town customers, for instance, run more toward comedies, Westerns, action films, and family entertainment. Carmike does not run any films rated NC-17.

Having defined positioning, we can now begin to answer the question, "What is strategy?" Strategy is the creation of a unique and valuable position, involving a different set of activities. If there were only one ideal position, there would be no need for strategy. Companies would face a simple imperative—win the race to discover and preempt it. The essence of strategic positioning is to choose activities that are different from rivals'. If the same set of activities were best to produce all varieties, meet all needs, and access all customers, compa-

The Connection with Generic Strategies

In *Competitive Strategy* (The Free Press, 1985), I introduced the concept of generic strategies—cost leadership, differentiation, and focus—to represent the alternative strategic positions in an industry. The generic strategies remain useful to characterize strategic positions at the simplest and broadest level. Vanguard, for instance, is an example of a cost leadership strategy, whereas Ikea, with its narrow customer group, is an example of cost-based focus. Neutrogena is a focused differentiator. The bases for positioning—varieties, needs, and access—carry the understanding of those generic strategies to a greater level of specificity. Ikea and Southwest are both cost-based focusers, for example, but Ikea's focus is based on the needs of a customer group, and Southwest's is based on offering a particular service variety.

The generic strategies framework introduced the need to choose in order to avoid becoming caught between what I then described as the inherent contradictions of different strategies. Trade-offs between the activities of incompatible positions explain those contradictions. Witness Continental Lite, which tried and failed to compete in two ways at once.

Positioning:
1. *variety based – produce subset of industries prod/serv. Based on choice of varieties.*
2. *Needs based – serve most or all of the needs of particular group of cust.*
3. *Access-based – segment customers who are accessible in different ways.*

nies could easily shift among them and operational effectiveness would determine performance.

III. A SUSTAINABLE STRATEGIC POSITION REQUIRES TRADE-OFFS

Choosing a unique position, however, is not enough to guarantee a sustainable advantage. A valuable position will attract imitation by incumbents, who are likely to copy it in one of two ways.

First, a competitor can reposition itself to match the superior performer. J.C. Penney, for instance, has been repositioning itself from a Sears clone to a more upscale, fashion-oriented, soft-goods retailer. A second and far more common type of imitation is straddling. The straddler seeks to match the benefits of a successful position while maintaining its existing position. It grafts new features, services, or technologies onto the activities it already performs.

For those who argue that competitors can copy any market position, the airline industry is a perfect test case. It would seem that nearly any competitor could imitate any other airline's activities. Any airline can buy the same planes, lease the gates, and match the menus and ticketing and baggage handling services offered by other airlines.

Continental Airlines saw how well Southwest was doing and decided to straddle. While maintaining its position as a full-service airline, Continental also set out to match Southwest on a number of point-to-point routes. The airline dubbed the new service Continental Lite. It eliminated meals and first-class service, increased departure frequency, lowered fares, and shortened turnaround time at the gate. Because Continental remained a full-service airline on other routes, it continued to use travel agents and its mixed fleet of planes and to provide baggage checking and seat assignments.

But a strategic position is not sustainable unless there are trade-offs with other positions. Trade-offs occur when activities are incompatible. Simply put, a trade-off means that more of one thing necessitates less of another. An airline can choose to serve meals—adding cost and slowing turnaround time at the gate—or it can choose not to, but it cannot do both without bearing major inefficiencies.

Trade-offs create the need for choice and protect against repositioners and straddlers. Consider Neutrogena soap. Neutrogena Corporation's variety-based positioning is built on a "kind to the skin," residue-free soap formulated for pH balance. With a large detail force calling on dermatologists, Neutrogena's marketing strategy looks more like a drug company's than a soap maker's. It advertises in medical journals, sends direct mail to doctors, attends medical conferences, and performs research at its own Skincare Institute. To reinforce its positioning, Neutrogena originally focused its distribution on drugstores and avoided price promotions. Neutrogena uses a slow, more expensive manufacturing process to mold its fragile soap.

In choosing this position, Neutrogena said no to the deodorants and skin softeners that many customers desire in their soap. It gave up the large-volume potential of selling through supermarkets and using price promotions. It sacrificed manufacturing efficiencies to achieve the soap's desired attributes. In its original positioning, Neutrogena made a whole raft of trade-offs like those, trade-offs that protected the company from imitators.

Trade-offs arise for three reasons. The first is inconsistencies in image or reputation. A company known for delivering one kind of value may lack credibility and confuse customers—or even undermine its reputation—if it delivers another kind of value or attempts to deliver two inconsistent things at the same time. For example, Ivory soap, with its position as a basic, inexpensive everyday soap, would have a hard time reshaping its image to match Neutrogena's premium "medical" reputation. Efforts to create a new image typically cost tens or even hundreds of millions of dollars in a major industry—a powerful barrier to imitation.

Second, and more important, trade-offs arise from activities themselves. Different positions (with their tailored activities) require different product configurations, different equipment, different employee behavior, different skills, and different management systems. Many trade-offs reflect inflexibilities in machinery, people, or systems. The more Ikea has configured its activities to lower costs by having its customers do their own assembly and delivery, the less able it is to satisfy customers who require higher levels of service.

However, trade-offs can be even more basic. In general, value is destroyed if an activity is overdesigned or underdesigned for its use. For example, even if a given salesperson were capable of providing a high level of assistance to one customer and none to another, the salesperson's talent (and some of his or her cost) would be wasted on the second customer. Moreover, productivity can improve when variation of an activity is limited. By providing a high level of assistance all the time, the salesperson and the entire sales activity can often achieve efficiencies of learning and scale.

Finally, trade-offs arise from limits on internal coordination and control. By clearly choosing to compete in one way and not another, senior management makes organizational priorities clear. Companies that try to be all things to all customers, in contrast, risk confusion in the trenches as employees attempt to make day-to-day operating decisions without a clear framework.

Positioning trade-offs are pervasive in competition and essential to strategy. They create the need for choice and purposefully limit what a company offers. They deter straddling or repositioning, because competitors that engage in those approaches undermine their strategies and degrade the value of their existing activities.

Trade-offs ultimately grounded Continental Lite. The airline lost hundreds of millions of dollars, and the CEO lost his job. Its planes were delayed leaving congested hub cities or slowed at the gate by baggage transfers. Late flights and cancellations generated a thousand complaints a day. Continental Lite could not afford to compete on price and still pay standard travel-agent commissions, but neither could it do without agents for its full-service business. The airline compromised by cutting commissions for all Continental flights across the board. Similarly, it could not afford to offer the same frequent-flier benefits to travelers paying the much lower ticket prices for Lite service. It compromised again by lowering the rewards of Continental's entire frequent-flier program. The results: angry travel agents and full-service customers.

Continental tried to compete in two ways at once. In trying to be low cost on some routes and full service on others, Continental paid an enormous straddling penalty. If there were no trade-offs between the two positions, Continental could have succeeded. But the absence of trade-offs is a dangerous half-truth that managers must unlearn. Quality is not always free. Southwest's convenience, one kind of high quality, happens to be consistent with low costs because its frequent departures are facilitated by a number of low-cost practices—fast gate turnarounds and automated ticketing, for example. However, other dimensions of airline quality—an assigned seat, a meal, or baggage transfer—require costs to provide.

In general, false trade-offs between cost and quality occur primarily when there is redundant or wasted effort, poor control or accuracy, or weak coordination. Simultaneous improvement of cost and differentiation is possible only when a company begins far behind the productivity frontier or when the frontier shifts outward. At the frontier, where companies have achieved current best practice, the trade-off between cost and differentiation is very real indeed.

After a decade of enjoying productivity advantages, Honda Motor Company and Toyota Motor Corporation recently bumped up against the frontier. In 1995, faced with increasing customer resistance to higher automobile prices, Honda found that the only way to produce a less-expensive car was to skimp on features. In the United States, it replaced the rear disk brakes on the Civic with lower-cost drum brakes and used cheaper fabric for the back seat, hoping customers would not notice. Toyota tried to sell a version of its best-selling Corolla in Japan with unpainted bumpers and cheaper seats. In Toyota's case, customers rebelled, and the company quickly dropped the new model.

For the past decade, as managers have improved operational effectiveness greatly, they have internalized the idea that eliminating trade-offs is a good thing. But if there are no trade-offs companies will never achieve a sustainable advantage. They will have to run faster and faster just to stay in place.

As we return to the question, What is strategy? we see that trade-offs add a new dimension to the answer. Strategy is making trade-offs in competing. The essence of strategy is choosing what *not* to do. Without trade-offs, there would be no need for choice and thus no need for strategy. Any good idea could and would be quickly imitated. Again, performance would once again depend wholly on operational effectiveness.

IV. FIT DRIVES BOTH COMPETITIVE ADVANTAGE AND SUSTAINABILITY

Positioning choices determine not only which activities a company will perform and how it will configure individual activities but also how activities relate to one another. While operational effectiveness is about achieving excellence in individual activities, or functions, strategy is about *combining* activities.

Southwest's rapid gate turnaround, which allows frequent departures and greater use of aircraft, is essential to its high-convenience, low-cost positioning. But how does Southwest achieve it? Part of the answer lies in the company's well-paid gate and ground crews, whose productivity in turnarounds is enhanced by flexible union rules. But the bigger part of the answer lies in how Southwest performs other activities. With no meals, no seat assignment, and no interline baggage transfers, Southwest avoids having to perform activities that slow down other airlines. It selects airports and routes to avoid congestion that introduces delays. Southwest's strict limits on the type and length of routes make standardized aircraft possible: every aircraft Southwest turns is a Boeing 737.

What is Southwest's core competence? Its key success factors? The correct answer is that everything matters. Southwest's strategy involves a whole system of activities, not a collection of parts. Its competitive advantage comes from the way its activities fit and reinforce one another.

Fit locks out imitators by creating a chain that is as strong as its *strongest* link. As in most companies with good strategies, Southwest's activities complement one another in ways that create real economic value. One activity's cost, for example, is lowered because of the way other activities are performed. Similarly, one activity's value to customers can be enhanced by a company's other activities. That is the way strategic fit creates competitive advantage and superior profitability.

Types of Fit

The importance of fit among functional policies is one of the oldest ideas in strategy. Gradually, however, it has been supplanted on the management agenda. Rather than seeing the company as a whole, managers have turned to "core" competencies, "critical" resources, and "key" success factors. In fact, fit is a far more central component of competitive advantage than most realize.

Fit is important because discrete activities often affect one another. A sophisticated sales force, for example, confers a greater advantage when the company's product embodies premium technology and its marketing approach emphasizes customer assistance and support. A production line with high levels of model variety is more valuable when combined with an inventory and order processing system that minimizes the need for stocking finished goods, a sales process equipped to explain and encourage customization, and an advertising theme that stresses the benefits of product variations that meet a customer's special needs. Such complementarities are pervasive in strategy. Although some fit among activities is generic and applies to many companies, the most valuable fit is strategy-specific because it enhances a position's uniqueness and amplifies trade-offs.[2]

There are three types of fit, although they are not mutually exclusive. First-order fit is *simple consistency* between each activity (function) and the overall strategy. Vanguard, for example, aligns all activities with its low-cost strategy. It minimizes portfolio turnover and does not need highly compensated money managers. The company distributes its funds directly, avoiding commissions to brokers. It also limits advertising, relying instead on public relations and word-of-mouth recommendations. Vanguard ties its employees' bonuses to cost savings.

Consistency ensures that the competitive advantages of activities cumulate and do not erode or cancel themselves out. It makes the strategy easier to communicate to customers, employees, and shareholders and improves implementation through single-mindedness in the corporation.

Second-order fit occurs when *activities are reinforcing.* Neutrogena, for example, markets to upscale hotels eager to offer their guests a soap recommended by dermatologists. Hotels grant Neutrogena the privilege of using its customary packaging while requiring other soaps to feature the hotel's name. Once guests have tried Neutrogena in a luxury hotel, they are more likely to purchase it at the drugstore or ask their doctor about it. Thus Neutrogena's medical and hotel marketing activities reinforce one another, lowering total marketing costs.

In another example, Bic Corporation sells a narrow line of standard, low-priced pens to virtually all major customer markets (retail, commercial, promotional, and giveaway) through virtually all available channels. As with any variety-based positioning serving a broad group of customers, Bic emphasizes a common need (low price for an acceptable pen) and uses marketing approaches with a broad reach (a large sales force and heavy television advertising). Bic gains the benefits of consistency across nearly all activities, including product design that emphasizes ease of manufacturing, plants configured for low cost, aggressive purchasing to minimize material costs, and in-house parts production whenever the economics dictate.

Yet Bic goes beyond simple consistency because its activities are reinforcing. For example, the company uses point-of-sale displays and frequent packaging changes to

---

[2] Paul Milgrom and John Roberts have begun to explore the economics of systems of complementary functions, activities, and functions. Their focus is on the emergence of "modern manufacturing" as a new set of complementary activities, on the tendency of companies to react to external changes with coherent bundles of internal responses, and on the need for central coordination—a strategy—to align functional managers. In the latter case, they model what has long been a bedrock principle of strategy. See Paul Milgrom and John Roberts, "The Economics of Modern Manufacturing: Technology, Strategy, and Organization," *American Economic Review* 80 (1990): 511–528; Paul

Milgrom, Yingyi Qian, and John Roberts, "Complementarities, Momentum, and Evolution of Modern Manufacturing," *American Economic Review* 81 (1991) 84–88; and Paul Milgrom and John Roberts, "Complementarities and Fit: Strategy, Structure, and Organizational Changes in Manufacturing," *Journal of Accounting and Economics,* vol. 19 (March–May 1995): 179–208.

EXHIBIT 2   Mapping Activity Systems

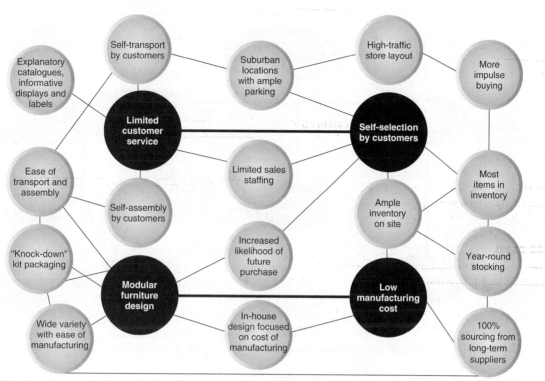

Activity-system maps, such as this one for Ikea, show how a company's strategic position is contained in a set of tailored activities designed to deliver it. In companies with a clear strategic position, a number of higher-order strategic themes (in black) can be identified and implemented through clusters of tightly linked activities (in grey).

stimulate impulse buying. To handle point-of-sale tasks, a company needs a large sales force. Bic's is the largest in its industry, and it handles point-of-sale activities better than its rivals do. Moreover, the combination of point-of-sale activity, heavy television advertising, and packaging changes yields far more impulse buying than any activity in isolation could.

Third-order fit goes beyond activity reinforcement to what I call *optimization of effort*. The Gap, a retailer of casual clothes, considers product availability in its stores a critical element of its strategy. The Gap could keep products either by holding store inventory or by restocking from warehouses. The Gap has optimized its effort across these activities by restocking its selection of basic clothing almost daily out of three warehouses, thereby minimizing the need to carry large in-store inventories. The emphasis is on restocking because the Gap's merchandising strategy sticks to basic items in relatively few

colors. While comparable retailers achieve turns of three to four times per year, the Gap turns its inventory seven and a half times per year. Rapid restocking, moreover, reduces the cost of implementing the Gap's short model cycle, which is six to eight weeks long.[3]

Coordination and information exchange across activities to eliminate redundancy and minimize wasted effort are the most basic types of effort optimization. But there are higher levels as well. Product design choices, for example, can eliminate the need for after-sale service or make it possible for customers to perform service activities themselves. Similarly, coordination with suppliers or distribution channels can eliminate the need for some in-house activities, such as end-user training.

---

[3]Material on retail strategies is drawn in part from Jan Rivkin, "The Rise of Retail Category Killers," unpublished working paper, January 1995. Nicolaj Siggelkow prepared the case study on the Gap.

EXHIBIT 3 **Vanguard's Activity System** *Cost focused*

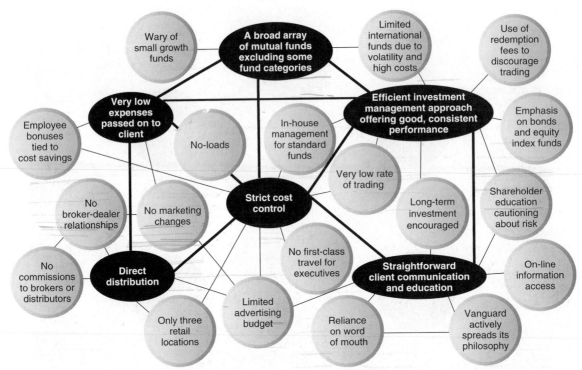

Activity-system maps can be useful for examining and strengthening strategic fit. A set of basic questions should guide the process. First, is each activity consistent with the overall positioning—the varieties produced, the needs served, and the type of customers accessed? Ask those responsible for each activity to identify how other activities within the company improve or detract from their performance. Second, are there ways to strengthen how activities and groups of activities reinforce one another? Finally, could changes in one activity eliminate the need to perform others?

In all three types of fit, the whole matters more than any individual part. Competitive advantage grows out of the *entire system* of activities. The fit among activities substantially reduces cost or increases differentiation. Beyond that, the competitive value of individual activities—or the associated skills, competencies, or resources—cannot be decoupled from the system or the strategy. Thus in competitive companies it can be misleading to explain success by specifying individual strengths, core competencies, or critical resources. The list of strengths cuts across many functions, and one strength blends into others. It is more useful to think in terms of themes that pervade many activities, such as low cost, a particular notion of customer service, or a particular conception of the value delivered. These themes are embodied in nests of tightly linked activities.

Fit and Sustainability

Strategic fit among many activities is fundamental not only to competitive advantage but also to the sustainability of that advantage. It is harder for a rival to match an array of interlocked activities than it is merely to imitate a particular sales-force approach, match a process technology, or replicate a set of product features. Positions built on systems of activities are far more sustainable than those built on individual activities.

Consider this simple exercise. The probability that competitors can match any activity is often less than one. The probabilities then quickly compound to make matching the entire system highly unlikely (.9 × .9 = .81; .9 × .9 × .9 × .9 = .66, and so on). Existing companies that try to reposition or straddle will be forced to reconfigure many activities. And even new entrants,

EXHIBIT 4 Southwest Airlines' Activity System

Cost focused, offer a service variety

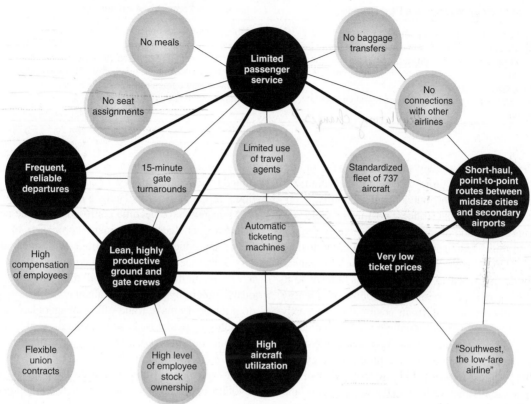

though they do not confront the trade-offs facing established rivals, still face formidable barriers to imitation. The more a company's positioning rests on activity systems with second- and third-order fit, the more sustainable its advantage will be. Such systems, by their very nature, are usually difficult to untangle from outside the company and therefore hard to imitate. And even if rivals can identify the relevant interconnections, they will have difficulty replicating them. Achieving fit is difficult because it requires the integration of decisions and actions across many independent subunits.

A competitor seeking to match an activity system gains little by imitating only some activities and not matching the whole. Performance does not improve; it can decline. Recall Continental Lite's disastrous attempt to imitate Southwest.

Finally, fit among a company's activities creates pressures and incentives to improve operational effectiveness, which makes imitation even harder. Fit means that poor performance in one activity will degrade the performance in others, so that weaknesses are exposed and more prone to get attention. Conversely, improvements in one activity will pay dividends in others. Companies with strong fit among their activities are rarely inviting targets. Their superiority in strategy and in execution only compounds their advantages and raises the hurdle for imitators.

When activities complement one another, rivals will get little benefit from imitation unless they successfully match the whole system. Such situations tend to promote winner-take-all competition. The company that builds the best activity system—Toys "R" Us, for instance—wins, while rivals with similar strategies—Child World and Lionel Leisure—fall behind. Thus finding a new strategic position is often preferable to being the second or third imitator of an occupied position.

The most viable positions are those whose activity systems are incompatible because of trade-offs. Strategic positioning sets the trade-off rules that define how individual activities will be configured and integrated. Seeing strategy in terms of activity systems only makes it clearer why organizational structure, systems, and

EXHIBIT 5 **Alternative Views of Strategy**

The Implicit Strategy Model of the Past Decade	Sustainable Competitive Advantage
• One ideal competitive position in the industry • Benchmarking of all activities and achieving best practice • Aggressive outsourcing and partnering to gain efficiencies • Advantages rest on a few key success factors, critical resources, core competencies • Flexibility and rapid responses to all competitive and market changes	• Unique competitive position for the company • Activities tailored to strategy • Clear trade-offs and choices vis-à-vis competitors • Competitive advantage arises from fit across activities • Sustainability comes from the activity system, not the parts • Operational effectiveness a given

processes need to be strategy-specific. Tailoring organization to strategy, in turn, makes complementarities more achievable and contributes to sustainability.

One implication is that strategic positions should have a horizon of a decade or more, not of a single planning cycle. Continuity fosters improvements in individual activities and the fit across activities, allowing an organization to build unique capabilities and skills tailored to its strategy. Continuity also reinforces a company's identity.

Conversely, frequent shifts in positioning are costly. Not only must a company reconfigure individual activities, but it must also realign entire systems. Some activities may never catch up to the vacillating strategy. The inevitable result of frequent shifts in strategy, or of failure to choose a distinct position in the first place, is "me-too" or hedged activity configurations, inconsistencies across functions, and organizational dissonance.

What is strategy? We can now complete the answer to this question. Strategy is creating fit among a company's activities. The success of a strategy depends on doing many things well—not just a few—and integrating among them. If there is no fit among activities, there is no distinctive strategy and little sustainability. Management reverts to the simpler task of overseeing independent functions, and operational effectiveness determines an organization's relative performance.

V. REDISCOVERING STRATEGY

The Failure to Choose

Why do so many companies fail to have a strategy? Why do managers avoid making strategic choices? Or, having made them in the past, why do managers so often let strategies decay and blur?

Commonly, the threats to strategy are seen to emanate from outside a company because of changes in technology or the behavior of competitors. Although external changes can be the problem, the greater threat to strategy often comes from within. A sound strategy is undermined by a misguided view of competition, by organizational failures, and, especially, by the desire to grow.

Managers have become confused about the necessity of making choices. When many companies operate far from the productivity frontier, trade-offs appear unnecessary. It can seem that a well-run company should be able to beat its ineffective rivals on all dimensions simultaneously. Taught by popular management thinkers that they do not have to make trade-offs, managers have acquired a macho sense that to do so is a sign of weakness.

Unnerved by forecasts of hypercompetition, managers increase its likelihood by imitating everything about their competitors. Exhorted to think in terms of revolution, managers chase every new technology for its own sake.

The pursuit of operational effectiveness is seductive because it is concrete and actionable. Over the past decade, managers have been under increasing pressure to deliver tangible, measurable performance improvements. Programs in operational effectiveness produce reassuring progress, although superior profitability may remain elusive. Business publications and consultants flood the market with information about what other companies are doing, reinforcing the best-practice mentality. Caught up in the race for operational effectiveness, many managers simply do not understand the need to have a strategy.

Companies avoid or blur strategic choices for other reasons as well. Conventional wisdom within an industry is often strong, homogenizing competition. Some managers mistake "customer focus" to mean they must serve all customer needs or respond to every request from distribution channels. Others cite the desire to preserve flexibility.

Organizational realities also work against strategy. Trade-offs are frightening, and making no choice is sometimes preferred to risking blame for a bad choice. Companies imitate one another in a type of herd behavior, each assuming rivals know something they do not. Newly empowered employees, who are urged to seek every possible source of improvement, often lack a vision of the whole and the perspective to recognize trade-offs. The failure to choose sometimes comes down to the reluctance to disappoint valued managers or employees.

The Growth Trap

Among all other influences, the desire to grow has perhaps the most perverse effect on strategy. Trade-offs and limits appear to constrain growth. Serving one group of customers and excluding others, for instance, places a real or imagined limit on revenue growth. Broadly targeted strategies emphasizing low price result in lost sales with customers sensitive to features or service. Differentiators lose sales to price-sensitive customers.

Managers are constantly tempted to take incremental steps that surpass those limits but blur a company's strategic position. Eventually, pressures to grow or apparent saturation of the target market leads managers to broaden the position by extending product lines, adding new features, imitating competitors' popular services, matching processes, and even making acquisitions. For years, Maytag Corporation's success was based on its focus on reliable, durable washers and dryers, later extended to include dishwashers. However, conventional wisdom emerging within the industry supported the notion of selling a full line of products. Concerned with slow industry growth and competition from broad-line appliance makers, Maytag was pressured by dealers and encouraged by customers to extend its line. Maytag expanded into refrigerators and cooking products under the Maytag brand and acquired other brands—Jenn-Air, Hardwick Stove, Hoover, Admiral, and Magic Chef—with disparate positions. Maytag has grown substantially from $684 million in 1985 to a peak of $3.4 billion in 1994, but return on sales has declined from 8% to 12% in the 1970s and 1980s to an average of less than 1% between 1989 and 1995. Cost cutting will improve this performance, but laundry and dishwasher products still anchor Maytag's profitability.

Neutrogena may have fallen into the same trap. In the early 1990s, its U.S. distribution broadened to include mass merchandisers such as Wal-Mart Stores. Under the Neutrogena name, the company expanded into a wide variety of products—eye-makeup remover and shampoo, for example—in which it was not unique and which diluted its image, and it began turning to price promotions.

Compromises and inconsistencies in the pursuit of growth will erode the competitive advantage a company had with its original varieties or target customers. Attempts to compete in several ways at once create confusion and undermine organizational motivation and focus. Profits fall, but more revenue is seen as the answer. Managers are unable to make choices, so the company embarks on a new round of broadening and compromises. Often, rivals continue to match each other until desperation breaks the cycle, resulting in a merger or downsizing to the original positioning.

Profitable Growth

Many companies, after a decade of restructuring and cost-cutting, are turning their attention to growth. Too often, efforts to grow blur uniqueness, create compromises, reduce fit, and ultimately undermine competitive advantage. In fact, the growth imperative is hazardous to strategy.

What approaches to growth preserve and reinforce strategy? Broadly, the prescription is to concentrate on deepening a strategic position rather than broadening and compromising it. One approach is to look for extensions of the strategy that leverage the existing activity system by offering features or services that rivals would find impossible or costly to match on a stand-alone basis. In other words, managers can ask themselves which activities, features, or forms of competition are feasible or less costly to them because of complementary activities that their company performs.

Deepening a position involves making the company's activities more distinctive, strengthening fit, and communicating the strategy better to those customers who should value it. But many companies succumb to the temptation to chase "easy" growth by adding hot features, products, or services without screening them or adapting them to their strategy. Or they target new customers or markets in which the company has little special to offer. A company can often grow faster—and far more profitably—by better penetrating needs and varieties where it is distinctive than by slugging it out in potentially higher growth arenas in which the company lacks uniqueness. Carmike, now the largest theater chain in the United States, owes its rapid growth to its disciplined concentration on small markets. The company quickly sells any big-city theaters that come to it as part of an acquisition.

Globalization often allows growth that is consistent with strategy, opening up larger markets for a focused strategy. Unlike broadening domestically, expanding

Reconnecting with Strategy

Most companies owe their initial success to a unique strategic position involving clear trade-offs. Activities once were aligned with that position. The passage of time and the pressures of growth, however, led to compromises that were, at first, almost imperceptible. Through a succession of incremental changes that each seemed sensible at the time, many established companies have compromised their way to homogeneity with their rivals.

The issue here is not with the companies whose historical position is no longer viable; their challenge is to start over, just as a new entrant would. At issue is a far more common phenomenon: the established company achieving mediocre returns and lacking a clear strategy. Through incremental additions of product varieties, incremental efforts to serve new customer groups, and emulation of rivals' activities, the existing company loses its clear competitive position. Typically, the company has matched many of its competitors' offerings and practices and attempts to sell to most customer groups.

A number of approaches can help a company reconnect with strategy. The first is a careful look at what it already does. Within most well-established companies is a core of uniqueness. It is identified by answering questions such as the following:

- Which of our product or service varieties are the most distinctive?
- Which of our product or service varieties are the most profitable?
- Which of our customers are the most satisfied?
- Which customers, channels, or purchase occasions are the most profitable?
- Which of the activities in our value chain are the most different and effective?

Around this core of uniqueness are encrustations added incrementally over time. Like barnacles, they must be removed to reveal the underlying strategic positioning. A small percentage of varieties or customers may well account for most of a company's sales and especially its profits. The challenge, then, is to refocus on the unique core and realign the company's activities with it. Customers and product varieties at the periphery can be sold or allowed through inattention or price increases to fade away.

A company's history can also be instructive. What was the vision of the founder? What were the products and customers that made the company? Looking backward, one can reexamine the original strategy to see if it is still valid. Can the historical positioning be implemented in a modern way, one consistent with today's technologies and practices? This sort of thinking may lead to a commitment to renew the strategy and may challenge the organization to recover its distinctiveness. Such a challenge can be galvanizing and can instill the confidence to make the needed trade-offs.

---

globally is likely to leverage and reinforce a company's unique position and identity.

Companies seeking growth through broadening within their industry can best contain the risks to strategy by creating stand-alone units, each with its own brand name and tailored activities. Maytag has clearly struggled with this issue. On the one hand, it has organized its premium and value brands into separate units with different strategic positions. On the other, it has created an umbrella appliance company for all its brands to gain critical mass. With shared design, manufacturing, distribution, and customer service, it will be hard to avoid homogenization. If a given business unit attempts to compete with different positions for different products or customers, avoiding compromise is nearly impossible.

The Role of Leadership

The challenge of developing or reestablishing a clear strategy is often primarily an organizational one and depends on leadership. With so many forces at work against making choices and trade-offs in organizations, a clear intellectual framework to guide strategy is a necessary counterweight. Moreover, strong leaders willing to make choices are essential.

In many companies, leadership has degenerated into orchestrating operational improvements and making deals. But the leader's role is broader and far more important. General management is more than the stewardship of individual functions. Its core is strategy: defining and communicating the company's unique position, making trade-offs, and forging fit among activities. The leader must provide the discipline to decide which industry changes and customer needs the company will respond to, while avoiding organizational distractions and maintaining the company's distinctiveness. Managers at lower levels lack the perspective and the confidence to maintain a strategy. There will be constant pressures to compromise, relax trade-offs, and emulate rivals. One of the leader's jobs is to teach others in the organization about strategy—and to say no.

Strategy renders choices about what not to do as important as choices about what to do. Indeed, setting limits is another function of leadership. Deciding which target group of customers, varieties, and needs the company should serve is fundamental to developing a strategy. But so is deciding not to serve other customers or needs and not to offer certain features or services. Thus strategy requires constant discipline and clear communication. Indeed, one of the most important functions of an explicit, communicated strategy is to guide employees in making choices that arise because of trade-offs in their individual activities and in day-to-day decisions.

Improving operational effectiveness is a necessary part of management, but it is *not* strategy. In confusing the two, managers have unintentionally backed into a way of thinking about competition that is driving many industries toward competitive convergence, which is in no one's best interest and is not inevitable.

Managers must clearly distinguish operational effectiveness from strategy. Both are essential, but the two agendas are different.

The operational agenda involves continual improvement everywhere there are no trade-offs. Failure to do this creates vulnerability even for companies with a good strategy. The operational agenda is the proper place for constant change, flexibility, and relentless efforts to achieve best practice. In contrast, the strategic agenda is the right place for defining a unique position, making clear trade-offs, and tightening fit. It involves the continual search for ways to reinforce and extend the company's position. The strategic agenda demands discipline and continuity; its enemies are distraction and compromise.

Strategic continuity does not imply a static view of competition. A company must continually improve its operational effectiveness and actively try to shift the productivity frontier; at the same time, there needs to be ongoing effort to extend its uniqueness while strengthening the fit among its activities. Strategic continuity, in fact, should make an organization's continual improvement more effective.

A company may have to change its strategy if there are major structural changes in its industry. In fact, new strategic positions often arise because of industry changes, and new entrants unencumbered by history often can exploit them more easily. However, a company's choice of a new position must be driven by the ability to find new trade-offs and leverage a new system of complementary activities into a sustainable advantage.

Emerging Industries and Technologies

Developing a strategy in a newly emerging industry or in a business undergoing revolutionary technological changes is a daunting proposition. In such cases, managers face a high level of uncertainty about the needs of customers, the products and services that will prove to be the most desired, and the best configuration of activities and technologies to deliver them. Because of all this uncertainty, imitation and hedging are rampant: unable to risk being wrong or left behind, companies match all features, offer all new services, and explore all technologies.

During such periods in an industry's development, its basic productivity frontier is being established or reestablished. Explosive growth can make such times profitable for many companies, but profits will be temporary because imitation and strategic convergence will ultimately destroy industry profitability. The companies that are enduringly successful will be those that begin as early as possible to define and embody in their activities a unique competitive position. A period of imitation may be inevitable in emerging industries, but that period reflects the level of uncertainty rather than a desired state of affairs.

In high-tech industries, this imitation phase often continues much longer than it should. Enraptured by technological change itself, companies pack more features—most of which are never used—into their products while slashing prices across the board. Rarely are trade-offs even considered. The drive for growth to satisfy market pressures leads companies into every product area. Although a few companies with fundamental advantages prosper, the majority are doomed to a rat race no one can win.

Ironically, the popular business press, focused on hot, emerging industries, is prone to presenting these special cases as proof that we have entered a new era of competition in which none of the old rules are valid. In fact, the opposite is true.

The Art of High-Technology Management

M. A. Maidique and R. H. Hayes

Over the past 15 years, the world's perception of the competence of U.S. companies in managing technology has come full circle. In 1967, a Frenchman, J.-J. Servan-Schreiber, expressed with alarm in his book *The American Challenge* that U.S. technology was far ahead of the rest of the industrialized world.[1] This "technology gap," he argued, was continually widening because of the *superior ability of Americans to organize and manage technological development.*

Today, the situation is perceived to have changed drastically. The concern now is that the gap is reversing: the onslaught of Japanese and/or European challenges is threatening America's technological leadership. Even such informed Americans as Dr. Simon Ramo express great concern. In his book *America's Technology Slip,* Dr. Ramo notes the apparent inability of U.S. companies to compete technologically with their foreign counterparts.[2] Moreover, in the best-seller *The Art of Japanese Management,* the authors use as a basis of comparison two technology-based firms: Matsushita (Japanese) and ITT (American).[3] The Japanese firm is depicted as a model for managers, while the management practices of the U.S. firm are sharply criticized.

Nevertheless, a number of U.S. companies appear to be fending off these foreign challenges successfully. These firms are repeatedly included on lists of "America's best-managed companies." Many of them are competitors in the R&D-intensive industries, a sector of our economy that has come under particular criticism. Ironically, some of them have even served as models for highly successful Japanese and European high-tech firms.

For example, of the 43 companies that Peters and Waterman judged to be excellent in *In Search of Ex-* *cellence,* almost half were classified as high-technology firms, or as containing a substantial high-technology component.[4] Similarly, of the five U.S. organizations that William Ouchi described as best prepared to meet the Japanese challenge, three (IBM, Hewlett-Packard, and Kodak) were high-technology companies.[5] Indeed, high-technology corporations are among the most admired firms in America. In a *Fortune* study that ranked the corporate reputation of the 200 largest U.S. corporations, IBM and Hewlett-Packard (HP) ranked first and second, respectively.[6] And of the top 10 firms, 9 compete in such high-technology fields as pharmaceuticals, precision instruments, communications, office equipment, computers, jet engines, and electronics.

The above studies reinforce our own findings, which have led us to conclude that U.S. high-technology firms that seek to improve their management practices to succeed against foreign competitors need not look overseas. The firms mentioned above are not unique. On the contrary, they are representative of scores of well-managed small and large U.S. technology-based firms. Moreover, the management practices they have adopted are widely applicable. Thus, perhaps the key to stimulating innovation in our country is not to adopt the managerial practices of the Europeans or the Japanese, but to adapt some of the policies of our *own* successful high-technology firms.

THE STUDY

Over the past two decades, we have been privileged to work with a host of small and large high-technology firms as participants, advisors, and researchers. We and our assistants interviewed formally and informally over

Source: Reprinted from *Sloan Management Review* 25 (Winter 1984), pp. 18–31, by permission of the publisher. Copyright © 1984 by the Sloan Management Review Association. All rights reserved.
[1] See J.-J. Servan-Schreiber, *The American Challenge* (New York: Atheneum Publishers, 1968).
[2] See S. Ramo, *America's Technology Slip* (New York: John Wiley & Sons, 1980).
[3] See R. Pascale and A. Athos, *The Art of Japanese Management* (New York: Simon & Schuster, 1981).

[4] See T. J. Peters and R. H. Waterman, Jr., *In Search of Excellence* (New York: Harper and Row, 1982). For purposes of this article, the high-technology industries are defined as those which spend more than 3 percent of sales on R&D. These industries, though otherwise quite different, are all characterized by a rapid rate of change in their products and technologies. Only five U.S. industries meet this criterion: chemicals and pharmaceuticals, machinery (especially computers and office machines), electrical equipment and communications, professional and scientific instruments, and aircraft and missiles. See National Science Foundation, *Science Resources Studies Highlights,* NSF81-331, December 31, 1981, p. 2.
[5] See W. Ouchi, *Theory Z: How American Management Can Meet the Japanese Challenge* (New York: John Wiley & Sons, 1980).
[6] See C. E. Makin, "Ranking Corporate Reputations," *Fortune,* January 10, 1983, pp. 34–44. Corporate reputation was subdivided into eight attributes: quality of management, quality of products and services, innovativeness, long-term investment value, financial soundness, ability to develop and help talented people, community and environmental responsibility, and use of corporate assets.

250 executives, including over 30 CEOs, from a wide cross section of high-tech industries—biotechnology, semiconductors, computers, pharmaceuticals, and aerospace. About 100 of these executives were interviewed in 1983 as part of a large-scale study of product innovation in the electronics industry (which was conducted by one of this article's authors and his colleagues).[7] Our research has been guided by a fundamental question: What strategies, policies, practices, and decisions result in successful management of high-technology enterprises? One of our principal findings was that no company has a monopoly on managerial excellence. Even the best run companies make big mistakes, and many smaller, lesser regarded companies are surprisingly sophisticated about the factors that mediate between success and failure.

It also became apparent from our interviews that the driving force behind the successes of many of these companies was strong leadership. All companies need leaders and visionaries, of course, but leadership is particularly essential when the future is blurry and when the world is changing rapidly. Although few high-tech firms can succeed for long without strong leaders, leadership itself is not the subject of this article. Rather, we accept it as given and seek to understand what strategies and management practices can *reinforce* strong leadership.

The companies we studied were of different sizes ($10 million to $30 billion in sales), their technologies were at different stages of maturity, their industry growth rates and product mixes were different, and their managers ranged widely in age. But they all had the same unifying thread: a rapid rate of change in the technological base of their products. This common thread, rapid technological change, implies novel products and functions and thus usually rapid growth. But even when growth is slow or moderate, the destruction of the old capital base by new technology results in the need for rapid redeployment of resources to cope with new product designs and new manufacturing processes. Thus, the two dominant characteristics of the high-technology organizations that we focused on were growth and change.

In part because of this split focus (growth and change), the companies we studied often appeared to display contradictory behavior over time. Despite these differences,

in important respects, they were remarkably similar because they all confronted the same two-headed dilemma: how to unleash the creativity that promotes growth and change without being fragmented by it, and how to control innovation without stifling it. In dealing with this concern, they tended to adopt strikingly similar managerial approaches.

THE PARADOX: CONTINUITY AND CHAOS

When we grouped our findings into general themes of success, a significant paradox gradually emerged— which is a product of the unique challenge that high-technology firms face. Some of the behavioral patterns that these companies displayed seemed to favor promoting disorder and informality, while others would have us conclude that it was consistency, continuity, integration, and order that were the keys to success. As we grappled with this apparent paradox, we came to realize that continued success in a high-technology environment requires periodic shifts between chaos and continuity.[8] Our originally static framework, therefore, was gradually replaced by a dynamic framework within whose ebbs and flows lay the secrets of success.

SIX THEMES OF SUCCESS

The six themes that we grouped our findings into were (1) business focus, (2) adaptability, (3) organizational cohesion, (4) entrepreneurial culture, (5) sense of integrity, and (6) hands-on top management. No one firm exhibits excellence in every one of these categories at any one time, nor are the less successful firms totally lacking in all. Nonetheless, outstanding high-technology firms tend to score high in most of the six categories, while less successful ones usually score low in several.[9]

1. Business Focus

Even a superficial analysis of the most successful high-technology firms leads one to conclude that they are

---

[7] See: M. A. Maidique and B. J. Zirger, "Stanford Innovation Project: A Study of Successful and Unsuccessful Product Innovation in High-Technology Firms," *IEEE Transactions on Engineering Management,* EM–31, no 4 (1984); M. A. Maidique, "The Stanford Innovation Project: A Comparative Study of Success and Failure in High-Technology Product Innovation," *Management of Technological Innovation Conference Proceedings* (Worcester Polytechnic Institute, 1983).

[8] A similar conclusion was reached by Romanelli and Tushman in their study of leadership in the minicomputer industry, which found that successful companies alternated long periods of continuity and inertia with rapid reorientation. See E. Romanelli and M. Tushman, "Executive Leadership and Organizational Outcomes: An Evolutionary Perspective," *Management of Technological Innovation Conference Proceedings* (Worcester Polytechnic Institute, 1983).

[9] One of the authors in this article has employed this framework as a diagnostic tool in audits of high-technology firms. The firm is evaluated along these six dimensions on a 0–10 scale by members of corporate

highly focused. With few exceptions, the leaders in high-technology fields, such as computers, aerospace, semiconductors, biotechnology, chemicals, pharmaceuticals, electronic instruments, and duplicating machines, realize the great bulk of their sales either from a single product line or from a closely related set of product lines.[10] For example, IBM, Boeing, Intel, and Genentech confine themselves almost entirely to computer products, commercial aircraft, integrated circuits, and genetic engineering, respectively. Similarly, four-fifths of Kodak's and Xerox's sales come from photographic products and duplicating machines, respectively. In general, the smaller the company, the more highly focused it is. Tandon concentrates on disk drives, Tandem on high-reliability computers, Analog Devices on linear integrated circuits, and Cullinet on software products.

Closely Related Products   This extraordinary concentration does not stop with the dominant product line. When the company grows and establishes a secondary product line, it is usually closely related to the first. Hewlett-Packard, for instance, has two product families, each of which accounts for about half of its sales. Both families—electronic instruments and data processors—are focused on the same technical, scientific, and process control markets. IBM also makes two closely related product lines—data processors (approximately 80 percent of sales) and office equipment—both of which emphasize the business market.

Companies that took the opposite path have not fared well. Two of yesterday's technological leaders, ITT and RCA, have paid dearly for diversifying away from their strengths. Today, both firms are trying to divest many of what were once highly touted acquisitions. As David Packard, chairman of the board of Hewlett-Packard, once observed, "No company ever died from starvation, but many have died from indigestion."[11]

A communications firm that became the world's largest conglomerate, ITT began to slip in the early 1970s after an acquisition wave orchestrated by Harold Geneen. When Geneen retired in 1977, his successors attempted to redress ITT's lackluster performance through

a far-reaching divestment program.[12] So far, 40 companies and other assets worth over $1 billion have been sold off—and ITT watchers believe the program is just getting started. Some analysts believe that ITT will ultimately be restructured into three groups, with the communications/electronics group and engineered products (home of ITT semiconductors) forming the core of a new ITT.

RCA experienced a similar fate to ITT's. When General David Sarnoff, RCA's architect and longtime chairman, retired in 1966, RCA was internationally respected for its pioneering work in television, electronic components, communications, and radar. But by 1980, the three CEOs who followed Sarnoff had turned a technological leader into a conglomerate with flat sales, declining earnings, and a $2.9 billion debt. This disappointing performance led RCA's new CEO, Thorton F. Bradshaw, to decide to return RCA to its high-technology origins.[13] Bradshaw's strategy is to concentrate on RCA's traditional strengths—communications and entertainment—by divesting its other businesses.

Focused R&D   Another policy that strengthens the focus of leading high-technology firms is concentrating R&D on one or two areas. Such a strategy enables these businesses to dominate the research, particularly the more risky, leading-edge explorations. By spending a higher proportion of their sales dollars on R&D than their competitors do or through their sheer size (as in the case of IBM, Kodak, and Xerox), such companies maintain their technological leadership. It is not unusual for a leading firm's R&D investment to be one and a half to two times the industry's average as a percent of sales (8 to 15 percent) and several times more than any individual competitor on an absolute basis.[14]

Moreover, their commitment to R&D is both enduring and consistent. It is maintained through slack periods and recessions because it is believed to be in the best, long-term interest of the stockholders. As the CEO of Analog Devices, a leading linear integrated circuit manufacturer, explained in a quarterly report which noted that profits had declined 30 percent, "We are sharply constraining

---

and divisional management, working individually. The results are then used as inputs for conducting a strategic review of the firm.
[10] General Electric evidently has also recognized the value of such concentration. In 1979, Reginald Jones, then GE's CEO, broke up the firm into six independent sectors led by "sector executives." See R. Vancil and P. C. Browne, "General Electric Consumer Products and Services Sector," Harvard Business School Case Services 2-179-070.
[11] Personal communication, March 4, 1982.

---

[12] After only 18 months as Geneen's successor as president, Lyman Hamilton was summarily dismissed by Geneen for reversing Geneen's way of doing business. See G. Colvin, "The Re-Geneening of ITT," *Fortune,* January 11, 1982, pp. 34–39.
[13] See "RCA: Still Another Master," *Business Week,* August 17, 1981, pp. 80–86.
[14] See "R&D Scoreboard," *Business Week,* July 6, 1981, pp. 60–75.

the growth of fixed expenses, but we do not feel it is in the best interest of shareholders to cut back further on product development . . . in order to relieve short-term pressure on earnings."[15] Similarly, when sales, as a result of a recession, flattened and profit margins plummeted at Intel, its management invested a record-breaking $130 million in R&D and another $150 million in plant and equipment.[16]

Consistent Priorities Still another way that a company demonstrates a strong business focus is through a set of priorities and a pattern of behavior that is continually reinforced by top management: for example, planned manufacturing improvement at Texas Instruments (TI), customer service at IBM, the concept of the entrepreneurial product champion at 3M, and the new products at HP. Belief in the competitive effectiveness of their chosen theme runs deep in each of these companies.

A business focus that is maintained over extended periods of time has fundamental consequences. By concentrating on what it does well, a company develops an intimate knowledge of its markets, competitors, technologies, employees, and the future needs and opportunities of its customers.[17] The Stanford Innovation Project recently completed a three-year study of 224 U.S. high-technology products (half were successes, half were failures) and concluded that a continuous, in-depth, informal interaction with leading customers throughout the product development process was the principal factor behind successful new products. In short, this coupling is the cornerstone of effective high-technology progress. Such an interaction is greatly facilitated by the long-standing and close customer relationships that are fostered by concentrating on closely related product-market choices.[18] "Customer needs," explains Tom Jones, chairman of Northrop Corporation, "must be understood *way ahead of time*" (author's emphasis).[19]

[15] See R. Stata, Analog Devices *Quarterly Report,* 1st Quarter, 1981.
[16] See "Why They Are Jumping Ship at Intel," *Business Week,* February 14, 1983, p. 107, and M. Chase, "Problem-Plagued Intel Bets on New Products, IBM's Financial Help," *The Wall Street Journal,* February 4, 1983.
[17] These SAPPHO findings are generally consistent with the results of the Stanford Innovation Project, a major comparative study of U.S. high-technology innovation. See M. A. Maidique, "The Stanford Innovation Project: A Comparative Study of Success and Failure in High-Technology Product Innovation," *Management of Technology Conference Proceedings* (Worcester Polytechnic Institute, 1983).
[18] See Maidique and Zirger, "Stanford Innovation Project." Several other authors have reached similar conclusions. See, for example, Peters and Waterman, *In Search of Excellence.*
[19] Personal communication, May 1982.

2. Adaptability

Successful firms balance a well-defined business focus with the willingness, and the will, to undertake major and rapid change when necessary. Concentration, in short, does not mean stagnation. Immobility is the most dangerous behavioral pattern a high-technology firm can develop: technology can change rapidly, and with it the markets and customers served. Therefore, a high-technology firm must be able to track and exploit the rapid shifts and twists in market boundaries as they are redefined by new technological, market, and competitive developments.

The cost of strategic stagnation can be great, as General Radio (GR) found out. Once the proud leader of the electronic instruments business, GR almost singlehandedly created many sectors of the market. Its engineering excellence and its progressive human relations policies were models for the industry. But when its founder, Melville Eastham, retired in 1950, GR's strategy ossified. In the next two decades, the company failed to take advantage of two major opportunities for growth that were closely related to the company's strengths: microwave instruments and minicomputers. Meanwhile, its traditional product line withered away. Now all that remains of GR's once dominant instruments line, which is less than 10 percent of sales, is a small assembly area where a handful of technicians assemble batches of the old instruments.

It wasn't until William Thurston, in the wake of mounting losses, assumed the presidency at the end of 1972 that GR began to refocus its engineering creativity and couple it to its new marketing strategies. Using the failure of the old policies as his mandate, Thurston deemphasized the aging product lines, focused GR's attention on automated test equipment, balanced its traditional engineering excellence with an increased sensitivity to market needs, and gave the firm a new name—GenRad. Since then, GenRad has resumed rapid growth and has won a leadership position in the automatic test equipment market.[20]

The GenRad story is a classic example of a firm making a strategic change because it perceived that its existing strategy was not working. But even successful high-technology firms sometimes feel the need to be rejuvenated periodically to avoid technological stagnation. In the mid-1960s, for example, IBM appeared to have little reason for major change. The company had a near

[20] See W. R. Thurston, "The Revitalization of GenRad," *Sloan Management Review,* Summer 1981, pp. 53–57.

monopoly in the computer mainframe industry. Its two principal products—the 1401 at the low end of the market and the 7090 at the high end—accounted for over two-thirds of its industry's sales. Yet, in one move, the company obsoleted both product lines (as well as others) and redefined the rules of competition for decades to come by simultaneously introducing six compatible models of the "System 360," based on proprietary hybrid integrated circuits.[21]

During the same period, GM, whose dominance of the U.S. auto industry approached IBM's dominance of the computer mainframe industry, stoutly resisted such a rejuvenation. Instead, it became more and more centralized and inflexible. Yet, GM was also once a high-technology company. In its early days when Alfred P. Sloan ran the company, engines were viewed as high-technology products. One day, Charles F. Kettering told Sloan he believed the high efficiency of the diesel engine could be engineered into a compact power plant. Sloan's response was: "Very well—we are now in the diesel engine business. You tell us how the engine should run, and I will . . . capitalize the program."[22] Two years later, Kettering achieved a major breakthrough in diesel technology. This paved the way for a revolution in the railroad industry and led to GM's preeminence in the diesel locomotive markets.

Organizational Flexibility   To undertake such wrenching shifts in direction requires both agility and daring. Organizational agility seems to be associated with organizational flexibility—frequent realignments of people and responsibilities as the firm attempts to maintain its balance on shifting competitive sands. The daring and the willingness to take "you bet your company" kinds of risks is a product of both the inner confidence of its members and a powerful top management—one that has either effective shareholder control or the full support of its board.

3.   Organizational Cohesion

The key to success for a high-tech firm is not simply periodic renewal. There must also be cooperation in the translation of new ideas into new products and processes. As Ken Fisher, the architect of Prime Computer's extraordinary growth, puts it: "If you have the driving func-

tion, the most important success factor is the ability to integrate. It's also the most difficult part of the task."[23]

To succeed, the energy and creativity of the whole organization must be tapped. Anything that restricts the flow of ideas or undermines the trust, respect, and sense of a commonality of purpose among individuals is a potential danger. This is why high-tech firms fight so vigorously against the usual organizational accoutrements of seniority, rank, and functional specialization. Little attention is given to organizational charts: often they don't exist.

Younger people in a rapidly evolving technological field are often as good a source of new ideas as are older ones—and sometimes even better. In some high-tech firms, in fact, the notion of a "half-life of knowledge" is used; that is, the amount of time that has to elapse before half of what one knows is obsolete. In semiconductor engineering, for example, it is estimated that the half-life of a newly minted Ph.D. is about seven years. Therefore, any practice that relegates younger engineers to secondary, nonpartnership roles is considered counterproductive.

Similarly, product design, marketing, and manufacturing personnel must collaborate in a common cause rather than compete with one another, as happens in many organizations. Any policies that appear to elevate one of these functions above the others—either in prestige or in rewards—can poison the atmosphere for collaboration and cooperation.

A source of division, and one which distracts the attention of people from the needs of the firm to their own aggrandizement, is the executive perks that are found in many mature organizations: pretentious job titles, separate dining rooms and restrooms for executives, larger and more luxurious offices (often separated in some way from the rest of the organization), and even separate or reserved places in the company parking lot all tend to establish distance between managers and doers and substitute artificial goals for the crucial real ones of creating successful new products and customers. The appearance of an executive dining room, in fact, is one of the clearest danger signals.

Good Communication   One way to combat the development of such distance is by making top executives more visible and accessible. IBM, for instance, has an

---

[21] See T. Wise, "IBM's 5 Billion Dollar Gamble," *Fortune,* September 1966; "A Rocky Road to the Marketplace," *Fortune,* October 1966.
[22] See A. P. Sloan, *My Years with General Motors* (New York: Anchor Books, 1972), p. 401.

[23] Personal communication, 1980. Mr. Fisher was president and CEO of Prime Computer from 1975 to 1981.

open-door policy that encourages managers at different levels of the organization to talk to department heads and vice presidents. According to senior IBM executives, it was not unusual for a project manager to drop in and talk to Frank Cary (IBM's chairman) or John Opel (IBM's president) until Cary's recent retirement. Likewise, an office with transparent walls and no door, such as that of John Young, CEO at HP, encourages communication. In fact, open-style offices are common in many high-tech firms.

A regular feature of 3M's management process is the monthly Technical Forum where technical staff members from the firm exchange views on their respective projects. This emphasis on communication is not restricted to internal operations. Such a firm supports and often sponsors industrywide technical conferences, sabbaticals for staff members, and cooperative projects with technical universities.

Technical Forums serve to compensate partially for the loss of visibility that technologists usually experience when an organization becomes more complex and when production, marketing, and finance staffs swell. So does the concept of the dual-career ladder that is used in most of these firms; that is, a job hierarchy through which technical personnel can attain the status, compensation, and recognition that is accorded to a division general manager or a corporate vice president. By using this strategy, companies try to retain the spirit of the early days of the industry when scientists played a dominant role, often even serving as members of the board of directors.[24]

Again, a strategic business focus contributes to organizational cohesion. Managers of firms that have a strong theme/culture and that concentrate on closely related markets and technologies generally display a sophisticated understanding of their businesses. Someone who understands where the firm is going and why is more likely to be willing to subordinate the interests of his or her own unit or function in the interest of promoting the common goal.

Job Rotation   A policy of conscious job rotation also facilitates this sense of community. In the small firm, everyone is involved in everyone else's job: specialization tends to creep in as size increases and boundary

lines between functions appear. If left unchecked, these boundaries can become rigid and impermeable. Rotating managers in temporary assignments across these boundaries helps keep the lines fluid and informal, however. When a new process is developed at TI, for example, the process developers are sent to the production unit where the process will be implemented. They are allowed to return to their usual posts only after that unit's operations manager is convinced that the process is working properly.

Integration of Roles   Other ways that high-tech companies try to prevent organizational, and particularly hierarchical, barriers from rising is through multidisciplinary project teams, special venture groups, and matrix-like organizational structures. Such structures, which require functional specialists and product-market managers to interact in a variety of relatively short-term problem-solving assignments, inject a certain ambiguity into organizational relationships and require each individual to play a variety of organizational roles.

For example, AT&T uses a combination of organizational and physical mechanisms to promote integration. The Advanced Development sections of Bell Labs are physically located on the sites of the Western Electric plants. This location creates an organizational bond between Development and Bell's basic research and an equally important spatial bond between Development and the manufacturing engineering groups at the plants. In this way, communication is encouraged among Development and the other two groups.[25]

Long-Term Employment   Long-term employment and intensive training are also important integrative mechanisms. Managers and technologists are more likely to develop satisfactory working relationships if they know they will be harnessed to each other for a good part of their working lives. Moreover, their loyalty and commitment to the firm is increased if they know the firm is continuously investing in upgrading their capabilities.

At Tandem, technologists regularly train administrators on the performance and function of the firm's products and, in turn, administrators train the technologists on personnel policies and financial operations.[26] Such a

---

[24] At Genentech, Cetus, Biogen, and Collaborative Research, four of the leading biotechnology firms, a top scientist is also a member of the board of directors.

[25] See, for example, J. A. Morton, *Organizing for Innovation* (New York: McGraw-Hill, 1971).

[26] Jimmy Treybig, president of Tandem Computer, Stanford Executive Institute Presentation, August 1982.

firm also tends to select college graduates who have excellent academic records, which suggest self-discipline and stability, and then encourages them to stay with the firm for most, if not all, of their careers.

4. Entrepreneurial Culture

While continuously striving to pull the organization together, successful high-tech firms also display fierce activism in promoting internal agents of change. Indeed, it has long been recognized that one of the most important characteristics of a successful high-technology firm is an entrepreneurial culture.[27]

Indeed, the ease with which small entrepreneurial firms innovate has always inspired a mixture of puzzlement and jealousy in larger firms. When new ventures and small firms fail, they usually do so because of capital shortages and managerial errors.[28] Nonetheless, time and again they develop remarkably innovative products, processes, and services with a speed and efficiency that baffle the managers of large companies. The success of the Apple II, which created a new industry, and Genentech's genetically engineered insulin are of this genre. The explanation for a small entrepreneurial firm's innovativeness is straightforward, yet it is difficult for a large firm to replicate its spirit.

Entrepreneurial Characteristics First, the small firm is typically blessed with excellent communication. Its technical people are in continuous contact (and oftentimes in cramped quarters). They have lunch together, and they call each other outside of working hours. Thus, they come to understand and appreciate the difficulties and challenges facing one another. Sometimes they will change jobs or double up to break a critical bottleneck; often the same person plays multiple roles. This overlapping of responsibilities results in a second blessing: a dissolving of the classic organizational barriers that are major impediments to the innovating process. Third, key decisions can be made immediately by the people who first recognize a problem, not later by top management or by someone who barely understands the issue. Fourth, the concentration of power in the leader/entrepreneurs makes it possible to deploy the firm's resources very rapidly. Lastly, the small firm has access to multiple funding channels, from the family dentist to a formal public

offering. In contrast, the manager of an R&D project in a large firm has effectively only one source, the "corporate bank."

Small Divisions In order to re-create the entrepreneurial climate of the small firm, successful large high-technology firms often employ a variety of organizational devices and personnel policies. First, they divide and subdivide. Hewlett-Packard, for example, is subdivided into 50 divisions: the company has a policy of splitting divisions soon after they exceed 1,000 employees. Texas Instruments is subdivided into over 30 divisions and 250 tactical action programs. Until recently, 3M's business was split into 40 divisions. Although these divisions sometimes reach $100 million or more in sales, by Fortune 500 standards they are still relatively small companies.

Variety of Funding Channels Second, such high-tech firms employ a variety of funding channels to encourage risk taking. At Texas Instruments, managers have three distinct options in funding a new R&D project. If their proposal is rejected by the centralized strategic planning (OST) system because it is not expected to yield acceptable economic gains, they can seek a "Wild Hare Grant." The Wild Hare program was instituted by Patrick Haggerty, while he was TI's chairman, to ensure that good ideas with long-term potential were not systematically turned down. Alternatively, if the project is outside the mainstream of the OST system, managers or engineers can contact one of dozens of individuals who hold "IDEA" grant purse strings and who can authorize up to $25,000 for prototype development. It was an IDEA grant that resulted in TI's highly successful Speak and Spell learning aid.[29]

3M managers also have three choices: they can request funds from (1) their own division, (2) corporate R&D, or (3) the new ventures division. This willingness to allow a variety of funding channels has an important consequence: it encourages the pursuit of alternative technological approaches, particularly during the early stages of a technology's development, when no one can be sure of the best course to follow.

---

[27] See D. A. Schon, *Technology and Change* (New York: Dell Publishing, 1967), and Peters and Waterman, *In Search of Excellence*.

[28] See S. Myers and E. F. Sweezy, "Why Innovations Fail," *Technology Review,* March–April 1978, pp. 40–46.

[29] See *Texas Instruments* (A), Harvard Business School case 9-476-122; *Texas Instruments Shows U.S. Business How to Survive in the 1980s,* Harvard Business School case 3-579-092; *Texas Instruments "Speak and Spell Product,"* Harvard Business School case 9-679-089, revised 7/79.

IBM, for instance, has found that rebellion can be good business. Thomas Watson, Jr., the founder's son and a longtime senior manager, once described the way the disk memory, a core element of modern computers, was developed:

> [It was] not the logical outcome of a decision made by IBM management; [because of budget difficulties] it was developed in one of our laboratories as a bootleg project. A handful of men . . . broke the rules. They risked their jobs to work on a project they believed in.[30]

At Northrop, the head of aircraft design usually has at any one time several projects in progress without the awareness of top management. A lot can happen before the decision reaches even a couple of levels below the chairman. "We like it that way," explains Northrop Chairman Tom Jones.[31]

Tolerance of Failure Moreover, the successful high-technology firms tend to be very tolerant of technological failure. "At HP," Bob Hungate, general manager of the Medical Supplies Division, explains, "it's understood that when you try something new you will sometimes fail."[32] Similarly, at 3M, those who fail to turn their pet project into a commercial success almost always get another chance. Richard Frankel, the president of the Kevex Corporation, a $20 million instrument manufacturer, puts it this way: "You need to encourage people to make mistakes. You have to let them fly in spite of aerodynamic limitations."[33]

Opportunity to Pursue Outside Projects Finally, these firms provide ample time to pursue speculative projects. Typically, as much as 20 percent of a productive scientist's or engineer's time is "unprogrammed," during which he or she is free to pursue interests that may not lie in the mainstream of the firm. IBM Technical Fellows are given up to five years to work on projects of their own choosing, from high-speed memories to astronomy.

5. Sense of Integrity

While committed to individualism and entrepreneurship, at the same time successful high-tech firms tend to exhibit a commitment to long-term relationships. The firms view themselves as part of an enduring community that includes employees, stockholders, customers, suppliers, and local communities: their objective is to maintain stable associations with all of these interest groups.

Although these firms have clear-cut business objectives, such as growth, profits, and market share, they consider them subordinate to higher order ethical values. Honesty, fairness, and openness—that is, integrity—are not to be sacrificed for short-term gain. Such companies don't knowingly promise what they can't deliver to customers, stockholders, or employees. They don't misrepresent company plans and performance. They tend to be tough but forthright competitors. As Herb Dwight— president of Spectra-Physics, one of the world's leading laser manufacturers—says, "The managers that succeed here go *out of their way* to be ethical."[34] And Alexander d'Arbeloff, cofounder and president of Teradyne, states bluntly, "Integrity comes first. If you don't have that, nothing else matters."[35]

These policies may seem utopian, even puritanical, but in a high-tech firm they also make good business sense. Technological change can be dazzlingly rapid; therefore, uncertainty is high, risks are difficult to assess, and market opportunities and profits are hard to predict. It is almost impossible to get a complex product into production, for example, without solid trust between functions, between workers and managers, and between managers and stockholders (who must be willing to see the company through the possible dips in sales growth and earnings that often accompany major technological shifts). Without integrity, the risks multiply and the probability of failure (in an already difficult enterprise) rises unacceptably. In such a context, Ray Stata, president and CEO of Analog Devices and cofounder of the Massachusetts High-Technology Council, states categorically, "You need an environment of mutual trust."[36]

This commitment to ethical values must start at the top; otherwise, it is ineffective. Most of the CEOs we interviewed considered it to be a cardinal dimension of their role. As Bernie Gordon, president of Analogic, explains, "The things that make leaders are their philosophy, ethics, and psychology."[37] Nowhere is this dimension more important than in dealing with the company's employees. Paul Rizzo, IBM's vice chairman, puts it this way: "At IBM we have a fundamental respect for the individual . . . people must be free to disagree and to be

[30] Thomas Watson, Jr., address to the Eighth International Congress of Accountants, New York City, September 24, 1962, as quoted by D. A. Schon, "Champions for Radical New Inventions," *Harvard Business Review,* March–April 1963, p. 85.
[31] Personal communication, May 1982.
[32] Personal communication, 1980.
[33] Personal communication, April 1983.

[34] Personal communication, 1982.
[35] Personal communication, 1983.
[36] Personal communication, 1980.
[37] Personal communication, 1982.

heard. Then, even if they lose, you can still marshal them behind you."[38]

Self-Understanding This sense of integrity manifests itself in a second, not unrelated, way—self-understanding. The pride, almost arrogance, of these firms in their ability to compete in their chosen fields is tempered by a surprising acknowledgment of their limitations. One has only to read Hewlett-Packard's corporate objectives or interview one of its top managers to sense this extraordinary blend of strength and humility. Successful high-tech companies are able to reconcile their dream with what they can realistically achieve. This is one of the reasons why they are extremely reticent to diversify into unknown territories.

6. Hands-On Top Management

Notwithstanding their deep sense of respect and trust for individuals, CEOs of successful high-technology firms are usually actively involved in the innovation process to such an extent that they are sometimes accused of meddling. Tom McAvoy, Corning's president, sifts through hundreds of project proposals each year trying to identify those that can have a "significant strategic impact on the company"—the potential to restructure the company's business. Not surprisingly, most of these projects deal with new technologies. For one or two of the most salient ones, he adopts the role of "field general": he frequently visits the line operations, receives direct updates from those working on the project, and assures himself that the required resources are being provided.[39]

Such direct involvement of the top executive at Corning sounds more characteristic of vibrant entrepreneurial firms, such as Tandon, Activision, and Seagate, but Corning is far from unique. Similar patterns can be identified in many larger high-technology firms. Milt Greenberg, president of GCA, a $180 million semiconductor process equipment manufacturer, stated: "Sometimes you just have to short-circuit the organization to achieve major change."[40] Tom Watson, Jr. (IBM's chairman), and Vince Learson (IBM's president) were doing just that when they met with programmers and designers and other executives in Watson's ski cabin in Vermont to finalize software design concepts for the System

360—at a point in time when IBM was already a $4 billion firm.[41]

Good high-tech managers not only understand how organizations, and in particular engineers, work, they understand the fundamentals of their technology and can interact directly with their people about it. This does not imply that it is necessary for the senior managers of such firms to be technologists (although they usually are in the early stages of growth): neither Watson nor Learson was a technologist. What appears to be more important is the ability to ask lots of questions, even "dumb" questions, and dogged patience in order to understand in-depth such core questions as: (1) how the technology works; (2) its limits, as well as its potential (together with the limits and potential of competitors' technologies); (3) what technical and economic resources these various technologies require; (4) the direction and speed of change; and (5) the available technological options, their cost, probability of failure, and potential benefits if they prove successful.

This depth of understanding is difficult enough to achieve for one set of related technologies and markets; it is virtually impossible for one person to master many different sets. This is another reason why business focus appears to be so important in high-tech firms. It matters little when one or more perceptive scientists or technologists foresee the impact of new technologies on the firm's markets if its top management doesn't internalize these risks and make the major changes in organization and resource allocation that are usually necessitated by a technological transition.

THE PARADOX OF HIGH-TECHNOLOGY MANAGEMENT

The six themes around which we arranged our findings can be organized into two, apparently paradoxical groupings: into one group fall business focus, organizational cohesion, and a sense of integrity; adaptability, entrepreneurial culture, and hands-on management fall into the other group. On the one hand, business focus, organizational cohesion, and integrity imply stability and conservatism. On the other hand, adaptability, entrepreneurial culture, and hands-on top management are synonymous with rapid, sometimes precipitous change. The fundamental tension is between order and disorder. Half of the

[38] Personal communication, 1980.
[39] Personal communication, 1979.
[40] Personal communication, 1980.

[41] See Wise, "IBM's 5 Billion."

success factors pull in one direction, and the other half tug the other way.

This paradox has frustrated many academicians who seek to identify rational processes and stable cause–effect relationships in high-tech firms and managers. Such relationships are not easily observable unless a certain constancy exists. But in most high-tech firms, the only constant is continual change. As one insightful student of the innovation process phrased it: "Advanced technology requires the collaboration of diverse professions and organizations, often with ambiguous or highly interdependent jurisdictions. In such situations, many of our highly touted rational management techniques break down."[42] One recent researcher, however, proposed a new model of the firm that attempts to rationalize the conflict between stability and change by splitting the strategic process into two loops, one that extends the past, the other that periodically attempts to break with it.[43]

By their very nature, established organizations resist innovation. By defining jobs and responsibilities and arranging them in serial reporting relationships, organizations encourage the performance of a restricted set of tasks in a programmed, predictable way. Not only do formal organizations resist innovation, they often act in ways that stamp it out. Overcoming such behavior—which is analogous to the way the human body mobilizes antibodies to attack foreign cells—is, therefore, a core job of high-tech management.

The Paradoxical Challenge

High-tech firms deal with this challenge in different ways. Texas Instruments, long renowned for the complex, interdependent matrix structure it used in managing dozens of product-customer centers (PCCs), recently consolidated groups of PCCs and made them into more autonomous units. "The manager of a PCC controls the resources and operations" for his or her entire family. "In the simplest terms, the PCC manager is to be an entrepreneur," explained Fred Bucy, TI's president.[44]

Meanwhile, a different trend is evident at 3M, where entrepreneurs have been given a free reign for decades. A recent major reorganization was designed to arrest snowballing diversity by concentrating its sprawling structure of autonomous divisions into four market groups. "We were becoming too fragmented," explained Vincent Ruane, vice president of 3M's Electronics Division.[45]

Similarly, HP recently reorganized into five groups, each with its own strategic responsibilities. Although this simply changes some of its reporting relationships, it does give HP, for the first time, a means for integrating product and market development across generally autonomous units.[46]

These reorganizations do not mean that organizational integration is dead at Texas Instruments, or that 3M's and HP's entrepreneurial cultures are being dismantled. They signify, first, that these firms recognize that both (organizational integration and entrepreneurial cultures) are important and, second, that periodic change is required for environmental adaptability. These three firms are demonstrating remarkable adaptability by reorganizing from a position of relative strength—not, as is far more common, in response to financial difficulties. As Lewis Lehr, 3M's president, explained, "We can change now because we're not in trouble."[47]

Such reversals are essentially antibureaucratic, in the same spirit as Mao's admonition to "let a hundred flowers blossom and a hundred schools of thought contend."[48] At IBM, in 1963, Tom Watson, Jr., temporarily abolished the corporate management committee in an attempt to push decisions downward and thus facilitate the changes necessary for IBM's great leap forward to the System 360.[49] Disorder, slack, and ambiguity are necessary for innovation since they provide the porosity that facilitates entrepreneurial behavior—just as do geographically separated, relatively autonomous organizational subunits.

But the corporate management committee is alive and well at IBM today. As it should be. The process of inno-

[42] See L. R. Sayles and M. K. Chandler, *Managing Large Systems: Organizations for the Future* (New York: Harper and Row, 1971).

[43] See R. A. Burgelman, "A Model of the Interaction of Strategic Behavior, Corporate Context, and the Concept of Corporate Strategy," *Academy of Management Review* (1983), pp. 61–70.

[44] See S. Zipper, "TI Unscrambling Matrix Management to Cope with Gridlock in Major Profit Centers," *Electronic News,* April 26, 1982, p. 1.

[45] See M. Barnfather, "Can 3M Find Happiness in the 1980s?" *Forbes,* March 11, 1982, pp. 113–16.

[46] See R. Hill, "Does a 'Hands-Off' Company Now Need a 'Hands-On' Style?" *International Management,* July 1983, p. 35.

[47] See Barnfather, "Can 3M Find Happiness?"

[48] S. R. Schram, ed., *Quotations from Chairman Mao Tse Tung* (Bantam Books, 1967), p. 174.

[49] See: D. G. Marquis, "Ways of Organizing Projects," *Innovation,* August 1969, pp. 26–33; T. Levitt, *Marketing for Business Growth* (New York: McGraw-Hill, 1974), in particular, chap. 7.

vation, once begun, is both self-perpetuating and potentially self-destructive: although the top managers of high-tech firms must sometimes espouse organizational disorder, for the most part they must preserve order.

Winnowing Old Products

Not all new product ideas can be pursued. As Charles Ames, former president of Reliance Electric, states, "An enthusiastic inventor is a menace to practical businessmen."[50] Older products, upon which the current success of the firm was built, at some point have to be abandoned: just as the long-term success of the firm requires the planting and nurturing of new products, it also requires the conscious, even ruthless, pruning of other products so that the resources they consume can be used elsewhere.

This attitude demands hard-nosed managers who are continually managing the functional and divisional interfaces of their firms. They cannot be swayed by nostalgia, or by the fear of disappointing the many committed people who are involved in the development and production of discontinued products. They must also overcome the natural resistance of their subordinates, and even their peers, who often have a vested interest in the products that brought them early personal success in the organization.

Yet, firms also need a certain amount of continuity because major change often emerges from the accretion of a number of smaller, less visible improvements. Studies of petroleum refining, rayon, and rail transportation, for example, show that half or more of the productivity gains ultimately achieved within these technologies were the result of the accumulation of minor improvements.[51] Indeed, most engineers, managers, technologists, and manufacturing and marketing specialists work on what Thomas Kuhn might have called "normal innovations,"[52] the little steps that improve or extend existing product lines and processes.

Managing Ambivalently

The successful high-technology firm, then, must be managed ambivalently. A steady commitment to order and organization will produce one-color Model T Fords. Continuous revolution will bar incremental productivity gains. Many companies have found that alternating periods of relaxation and control appear to meet this dual need. Surprisingly, such ambiguity does not necessarily lead to frustration and discontent.[53] In fact, interspersing periods of tension, action, and excitement with periods of reflection, evaluation, and revitalization is the same sort of irregular rhythm that characterizes many favorite pastimes—including sailing, which has been described as "long periods of total boredom punctuated with moments of stark terror."

Knowing when and where to change from one stance to the other and having the power to make the shift are the core of the art of high-technology management. James E. Webb, administrator of the National Aeronautics and Space Administration during the successful Apollo ("man on the moon") program, recalled that "we were required to fly our administrative machine in a turbulent environment, and . . . a certain level of *organizational instability was essential if NASA was not to lose control*" (authors' emphasis).[54]

In summary, the central dilemma of the high-technology firm is that it must succeed in managing two conflicting trends: continuity and rapid change. There are two ways to resolve this dilemma. One is an old idea: managing different parts of the firm differently—some business units for innovation, others for efficiency.

A second way—a way which we believe is more powerful and pervasive—is to manage differently at different times in the evolutionary cycle of the firm. The successful high-technology firm *alternates* periods of consolidation and continuity with sharp reorientations that can lead to dramatic changes in the firm's strategies, structure, controls, and distribution of power, followed by a period of consolidation.[55] Thomas Jefferson knew this secret when he wrote 200 years ago, "A little revolution now and then is a good thing."[56]

---

[50]Charles Ames, former CEO of Reliance Electric, cited in "Exxon's $600 Million Mistake," *Fortune,* October 19, 1981.

[51]See, for example, W. J. Abernathy and J. M. Utterback, "Patterns of Industrial Innovation," *Technology Review,* June–July 1978, pp. 40–47.

[52]See T. Kuhn, *The Structure of Scientific Revolutions,* 2d ed. (Chicago: University of Chicago Press, 1967).

[53]After reviewing an early draft of this article, Ray Stata, president, Analog Devices, wrote, "The articulation of dynamic balance, of yin and yang, . . . served as a reminder to me that there isn't one way forever, but a constant adaption to the needs and circumstances of the moment." Ray Stata, personal communication, November 29, 1982.

[54]Quoted in "Some Contributions of James E. Webb to the Theory and Practice of Management," a presentation by Elmer B. Staats before the annual meeting of the Academy of Management on August 11, 1978.

[55]See Romanelli and Tushman, "Executive Leadership."

[56]See J. Bartlett, *Bartlett's Familiar Quotations,* 14th ed. (Boston: Little, Brown), p. 471B.

DESIGN AND IMPLEMENTATION OF TECHNOLOGY STRATEGY: AN EVOLUTIONARY PERSPECTIVE

Technology is a resource that, like financial and human resources, is pervasively important in organizations. Managing technology is a basic business function. This implies the need to develop a technology strategy, analogous to financial and human resource strategies. Technology strategy serves as the basis for fundamental business strategy decisions. It helps answer questions such as these:

This section is an elaboration and extension of R. A. Burgelman and R. S. Rosenbloom, "Technology Strategy: An Evolutionary Process Perspective," *Research on Technological Innovation, Management, and Policy* 4 (1989), pp. 1–23.

EXHIBIT 1   A Capabilities-Based Organizational Learning Framework of Technology Strategy

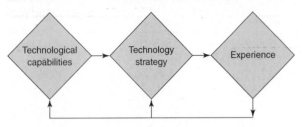

Tech Strategy Questions

1. Which distinctive technological competences and capabilities are necessary to establish and maintain competitive advantage?
2. Which technologies should be used to implement core product design concepts and how should these technologies be embodied in products?
3. What should be the investment level in technology development?
4. How should various technologies be sourced—internally or externally?
5. When and how should new technology be introduced to the market?
6. How should technology and innovation be organized and managed?

Technology strategy encompasses but extends beyond R&D strategy (Mitchell, 1986; Adler, 1989). Strategy making concerning technology can be conceptualized as an evolutionary organizational learning process. This is shown in Exhibit 1.

Exhibit 1 shows the linkages among technical competencies and capabilities, technology strategy, and experience. Technology strategy is a function of the quantity and quality of technical capabilities and competences. Experience obtained from enacting technology strategy feeds back to technical capabilities and technology strategy.

We will now examine the three interrelated elements of technology strategy making. First, we will examine technological competencies and capabilities. Next, we will discuss the substance of technology strategy: the theoretical dimensions in which technology strategy can be expressed. Then, we'll review the internal and external forces that shape the evolution of a firm's technology strategy. Finally, we'll discuss experience through the enactment of technology strategy: the various key tasks

through which the firm's technology strategy is actually implemented and experience accumulated.

TECHNOLOGICAL COMPETENCE AND CAPABILITY

Over time organizations develop distinctive competences that are closely associated with their ability to cope with environmental demands (Selznick, 1957). McKelvey and Aldrich (1983) view distinctive competence as "the combined workplace (technological) and organizational knowledge and skills . . . that together are most salient in determining the ability of an organization to survive" (p. 112). Nelson and Winter (1982), in similar vein, use the concept of "routines," which they consider to play a role similar to genes in biological evolution. It is important to note that research has revealed that distinctive competences can become a competence trap (Levitt and March, 1988) or core rigidity (Leonard-Barton, 1992). Other research has found that there are strong inertial forces associated with distinctive technological competences, but that strong technological competences are also likely to generate innovations (Burgelman, 1994).

In general, a firm's distinctive competence involves the differentiated skills, complementary assets, and routines used to create sustainable competitive advantage (Selznick, 1957; Andrews, 1981; Teece, Pisano and Shuen, 1990). Prahalad and Hamel (1990), building on the work of Selznick and Andrews, define *core competencies* as "the collective learning in the organization, especially how to coordinate diverse production skills and integrate multiple streams of technologies" (p. 82); these authors also provide criteria for identifying a firm's core competence (pp. 83–84): A core competence should (1) provide potential access to a wide variety of markets, (2) make a significant contribution to the perceived customer benefits of the end product, and (3) be difficult for competitors to imitate.

Here we are primarily concerned with the subset of technological competences of the firm, but the interrelationships with competences in other key areas, such as marketing, are always to be considered as well.

Stalk, Evans, and Shulman (1992) distinguish core competence from a firm's strategic capabilities: "whereas core competence emphasizes technological and production expertise at specific points along the value chain, capabilities are more broadly based, encompassing the entire value chain" (p. 66). They define a *capability* as "a set of business processes strategically understood. . . . The key is to connect them to real customer needs" (p. 62). Thus, technological competences and capabilities are complementary concepts, and value chain analysis (e.g., Porter, 1985) provides a useful tool for examining their interrelationships.

SUBSTANCE OF TECHNOLOGY STRATEGY

Technology strategy can be discussed in terms of (1) the deployment of technology in the firm's product-market strategy to position itself in terms of differentiation (perceived value or quality) and delivered cost and to gain technology-based competitive advantage; (2) the use of technology, more broadly, in the various activities comprised by the firm's value chain; (3) the firm's resource commitment to various areas of technology; and (4) the firm's use of organization design and management techniques to manage the technology function. These constitute four substantive dimensions of technology strategy (Burgelman and Rosenbloom, 1989; Hampson, 1993).

Competitive Strategy Stance (Porter)

Technology strategy is an instrument of more comprehensive business and corporate strategies. As part of these broader strategies, a business defines the role that technology should play in increasing the differentiation and/or reducing the costs of its products and services (Porter, 1983, 1985). From a competitive strategy point of view, technology can be used defensively to sustain achieved advantage in product differentiation or cost or offensively as an instrument to create new advantage in established lines of business or to develop new products and markets.

Technology Choice Recent work on the distinction between design concepts and their physical implementation (Clark, 1985) and on the distinction between components and architecture in product design and development (Clark, 1987; Henderson and Clark, 1990) is useful to establish a framework for technology choice. Henderson and Clark (1990) offer the example of a room fan, which is a system for moving air in a room. The major components of a room fan include the blade, the motor that drives it, the blade guard, the control system, and the mechanical housing. A component is defined as "a physically distinct portion of the product that embodies a core design concept and performs a well-defined function"

(p. 2). Core design concepts correspond to the various functions that the product design needs to embody so that the manufactured product will be able to serve the purposes of its user. For instance, the need for the fan to move corresponds to a core design concept. Core design concepts can be implemented in various ways to become components. For instance, movement of the fan could be achieved through using manual power or electrical motors. Each of these implementations, in turn, refers to an underlying technological knowledge base. For instance, designing and building electrical motors requires knowledge of electrical and mechanical engineering. Each of the core concepts of a product thus entails technology choices. A product also has, in addition to components, an architecture that determines how its components fit and work together. For instance, the room fan's overall architecture lays out how its various components will work together. Product architectures usually become stable with the emergence of a "dominant design" (Abernathy and Utterback, 1978) in the industry. Product architecture also affects technology choice.

Technology choices require careful assessments of technical as well as market factors and identify an array of targets for technology development. The relative irreversibility of investments in technology makes technology choice and targets for technology development an especially salient dimension of technology strategy. Targeted technology development may range from minor improvements in a mature process to the employment of an emerging technology in the first new product in a new market (Rosenbloom, 1985).

Technology Leadership The implications of technological leadership have been explored in earlier writings on technology and strategy (e.g., Ansoff and Stewart, 1967; Maidique and Patch, 1978). Discussions of technological leadership are often in terms of the timing (relative to rivals) of commercial use of new technology—that is, in terms of product-market strategy. A broader strategic definition views technological leadership in terms of relative advantage in the command of a body of technological competencies and capabilities. This sort of leadership results from commitment to a "pioneering" role in the development of a technology (Rosenbloom and Cusumano, 1987), as opposed to a more passive "monitoring" role. Technological leaders thus have the capacity to be first movers but may elect not to do so.

A firm's competitive advantage is more likely to arise from the unique aspects of its technology strategy than from characteristics it shares with others. Companies that are successful over long periods of time develop technological competences and capabilities that are distinct from those of their competitors and not easily replicable. Crown Cork and Seal, Marks and Spencer, and Banc One are examples we'll briefly discuss. Canon (Prahalad and Hamel, 1990) and Wal-Mart (Stalk et al., 1992) are other examples. The capabilities-based strategies of such companies cannot easily be classified simply in terms of differentiation or cost leadership; they combine both. The ability to maintain uniqueness that is salient in the marketplace implies continuous alertness to what competitors are doing and should not be confused with insulation and an inward-looking orientation.

 The competencies and capabilities-based view of technological leadership draws attention to the importance of accumulation of capabilities (e.g., Barney, 1986; Itami, 1987). Technological leadership cannot be bought easily in the market or quickly plugged into an organization. A firm must understand the strategic importance of different competencies and capabilities and be willing to build them patiently and persistently, even though it may sometimes seem cheaper or more efficient in the short term to rely on outsiders for their procurement.

Thinking strategically about technology means raising the question of how a particular technical competence or capability may affect a firm's future degrees of freedom and its control over its fate. This involves identifying and tracking key technical parameters, considering the impact on speed and flexibility of product and process development as technologies move through their life cycles. It also requires distinguishing carefully between the technologies that are common to all players in the industry and have little impact on competitive advantage and those that are proprietary and likely to have a major impact on competitive advantage. Furthermore, it requires paying attention to the new technologies that are beginning to manifest their potential for competitive advantage and those that are as yet only beginning to emerge (Arthur D. Little, 1981).

Technology Entry Timing The timing of bringing technology to market, of course, remains a key strategic issue. Porter (1985) identifies conditions under which pioneering is likely to be rewarded in terms of lasting first-mover advantages. While noting the various potential advantages accruing to first movers, Porter also identifies the disadvantages that may ensue, highlighting the significance of managerial choice of timing and the impor-

tance of situational analysis to determine the likely consequences along the path chosen.

Teece (1986) extends the analysis by identifying the importance of appropriability regimes and control of specialized assets. *Appropriability regimes* concern the first mover's ability to protect proprietary technological advantage. This usually depends on patents, proprietary know-how, and/or trade secrets. The legal battle between Intel and Advanced Micro Devices about access to Intel's microcode for microprocessor development is an example of the importance of appropriability regimes (Steere and Burgelman, 1994). An important consideration here is the cost of defending one's proprietary technological position. For instance, the prospect of rapidly escalating legal costs and/or claims on scarce top-management time may sometimes make it difficult for smaller firms to decide to go to court to protect their proprietary position unless violations are very clear. *Control of specialized assets* concerns the fact that in many cases the first mover may need access to complementary specialized assets owned by others. Gaining access to those assets—through acquisitions or strategic alliances—may absorb a large part of the rent stream coming from the innovation. The alliances between start-up and established firms in the biotechnology industry are an example of the importance of complementary assets (e.g., Pisano and Teece, 1989). Unless companies command strong positions in terms of appropriability regimes and complementary assets, their capacity to exploit potential first-mover advantages remains doubtful.

Technology Licensing Sometimes firms need to decide whether they will bring technologies to market by themselves or also offer other firms the opportunity to market them through licensing arrangements (e.g., Shepard, 1987). Ford and Ryan (1981) identify several reasons companies may not be able to fully exploit their technologies through product sales alone. First, not all technologies generated by a firm's R&D efforts fit into its lines of business and corporate strategy (see also Pavitt, Robson, and Townsend, 1989). Second, companies may need to consider licensing their technology to maximize the returns on their R&D investments, because patents provide only limited protection against imitation by competitors. Licensing may be a strategic tool in discouraging imitation by competitors or in preempting competitors with alternative technologies. Third, smaller firms may be unable to exploit their technologies on their own because they lack the necessary cash and/or complementary assets (e.g., manufacturing). Fourth, international market development for the technology may require licensing local firms because of local government regulation. Fifth, antitrust legislation may sometimes prevent a company from fully exploiting its technological advantage on its own (Kodak, Xerox, and IBM are fairly recent examples). Technology-rich companies should therefore consider developing a special capability for marketing their technologies beyond embodiment in their own products.

Value Chain Stance

Technology pervades the value chain. A competencies and capabilities-based view goes beyond the strategic use of technology in products and services and takes a competitive stance toward its use in all the value chain activities (Porter, 1985).

Scope of Technology Strategy   Considering technology strategy in relation to the value chain defines its scope: the set of technological capabilities that the firm decides to develop internally. This set of technologies can be called the *core technology*. Other technologies, then, are peripheral. Of course, in a dynamic world, peripheral technologies today may become core technologies in the future and vice versa. Core technologies are the areas in which the firm needs to assess its distinctive technological competences and to decide whether to be a technological leader or follower and when to bring the technologies to market. The scope of technology strategy is especially important in relation to the threat of new entrants in the firm's industry. All else being equal, firms with a broader set of core technologies would seem to be less vulnerable to attacks from new entrants attempting to gain position through producing and delivering new types of technology-based customer value. However, resource constraints will put a limit on how many technologies the firm can opt to develop internally. Thus, it is important to limit the scope of technology strategy to the set of technologies considered by the firm to have a material impact on its competitive advantage.

The scope of a firm's technology strategy may be determined to a significant extent by its scale and business focus. Businesses built around large, complex systems like aircraft, automobiles, or telecommunication switches demand the ability to apply and integrate numerous distinct types of expertise creating *economies of scale, scope, and learning* (synergies). General Electric, for instance, was reportedly able to bring to bear high-

powered mathematical analysis, used in several divisions concerned with military research on submarine warfare, to the development of computerized tomography (CT) products in its medical equipment division (Rutenberg, 1986). Other fields may actually contain diseconomies of scale, giving rise to the popularity of "skunkworks" (e.g., Rich and Janos, 1994) and discussion of the "mythical man-month" (Brooks, 1975). The emergence of a new technology raises issues concerning the scope of the technology strategy. And this, in turn, may impact the delineation of the set of core technologies of the firm and the boundaries among the business units that it comprises (Prahalad, Doz, and Angelmar, 1989).

Resource Commitment Stance

The third dimension of the substance of technology strategy concerns the intensity of its resource commitment to technology. The variation among manufacturing firms is pronounced: Many firms do not spend on R&D; a few commit as much as 10 percent of revenues to it. While interindustry differences can explain a large share of this variation, substantial differences in R&D intensity still remain between rivals.

Depth of Technology Strategy   Resource commitments determine the *depth* of the firm's technology strategy: its prowess within the various core technologies. Depth of technology strategy can be expressed in terms of the number of technological options that the firm has available. Depth of technology is likely to be correlated with the firm's capacity to anticipate technological developments in particular areas early on. Greater technological depth may offer the benefit of increased flexibility and ability to respond to new demands from customers/users. It provides the basis for acting in a timely way.

Management Stance

Recent research (Hampson, 1993) based on Burgelman's and Rosenbloom's (1989) framework suggests that the substance of technology strategy also encompasses a management stance: the choice of a management approach and organization design that are consistent with the stances taken on the other substantive dimensions.

Organizational Fit   Firms that can organize themselves to meet the organizational requirements flowing from their competitive, value chain, and resource commitment stances are more likely to have an effective technology strategy. For instance, a science-based firm that has decided to be a technology leader for the long run probably needs to create a central R&D organization. One that is satisfied with commercially exploiting existing technologies to the fullest may be able to decentralize all R&D activity to its major businesses. Imai et al. (1985) describe how Japanese firms use multiple layers of contractors and subcontractors in an external network to foster extreme forms of specialization in particular skills; this practice provides them with flexibility, speed in response, and the potential for cost savings since the highly specialized subcontractors operate on an experience curve even at the level of prototypes.

EVOLUTIONARY FORCES SHAPING TECHNOLOGY STRATEGY

An evolutionary process perspective raises the question of how a firm's technology strategy actually comes about and changes over time. Evolutionary theory applied to social systems focuses on variation-selection-retention mechanisms for explaining dynamic behavior over time (e.g., Campbell, 1969; Aldrich, 1979; Weick, 1979; Burgelman, 1983, 1991; Van de Ven and Garud, 1989). It recognizes the importance of history, irreversibilities, invariance, and inertia in explaining the behavior of orga-

nizations. But it also considers the effects of individual and social learning processes (e.g., Burgelman, 1986). An evolutionary perspective is useful for integrating extant literatures on technology. The study of technological development, for instance, contains many elements that seem compatible with the variation-selection-retention structure of evolutionary theory (e.g., Rosenberg, 1982; Kelly and Kranzberg, 1978; Abernathy, 1978; Clark, 1985; Henderson and Clark, 1990; Burgelman, 1994). While cautioning against the fallacy of unwarranted analogy in applying concepts from biological evolution to cultural (organizational) evolution, Gould's (1987) interpretation of the establishment of QWERTY (David, 1985) as the dominant, if inferior, approach to laying out keys on typewriter keyboards shows the power of evolutionary reasoning to identify and elucidate interesting phenomena concerning technological evolution.

The evolutionary factors that shape the creation of technology strategy comprise internal and external generative and integrative forces. In this section, we explore a simple framework to conceptualize these forces, presented in Exhibit 2.

The idea expressed in Exhibit 2 is that technology strategy is shaped by the generative forces of the firm's strategic action and the evolution of technology and by the integrative, or selective, forces of the firm's organizational context and the industry context.

Technology Evolution

A firm's technology strategy is rooted in the evolution of its technical capabilities. However, the dynamics of these capabilities, and hence the technology strategy, are not completely endogenous. A firm's technical capabilities are affected in significant ways by the evolution of the broader areas of technology of which they are part and that evolve largely independently of the firm. Different aspects of technological evolution have been discussed in the literature: (1) the evolution of technologies along S-curve trajectories (e.g., Twiss, 1980; Dosi, 1982); (2) the interplay between product and process technology development within design configurations over the course of a particular technological trajectory (Abernathy, 1978); (3) the emergence of new technologies and their trajectories (S-curves) (Foster, 1986); (4) the competence-enhancing or -destroying consequences of new technologies (Astley, 1985; Abernathy, Clark, and Kantrow, 1983; Tushman and Anderson, 1986); (5) dematurity: renewed technological innovation in the context of well-established markets, high production volumes, and well-established organizational

EXHIBIT 2 Determinants of Technology Strategy

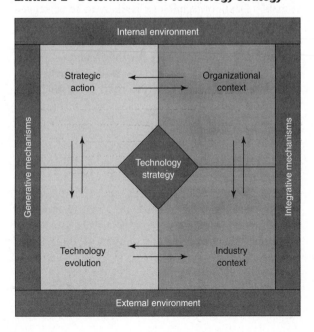

arrangements (Abernathy, Clark, and Kantrow, 1983); and (6) the organizational determinants of technological change (Tushman and Rosenkopf, 1992). These are some of the major evolutionary forces associated with technological development that transcend the strategic actions of any given firm.

Industry Context

One important aspect of industry context is the industry structure, which can be understood in terms of five major forces (Porter, 1980), all of which can be affected in important ways by technology (Porter, 1983), but the interplay of which, in turn, determines the technological competences that can form the basis of competitive advantage (Burgelman, 1994). Other aspects are (2) the appropriability regime associated with a technological innovation (Teece, 1986); (3) the complementary assets needed to commercialize a new technology (Teece, 1986); (4) the emergence of dominant designs (Utterback and Abernathy, 1975; Abernathy, 1978); (5) increasing returns to adoption for particular technologies (Arthur, 1988; David, 1985); (6) the emergence of industry standards (Farrell and Saloner, 1987; Metcalfe and Gibbons, 1989); (7) the social systems aspects of industry development (Van de Ven and Garud, 1989); and (8) the competitive effects of the interplay of social systems characteristics and technological change (Barnett, 1990). These various factors and their interplays affect the likely distribution of profits generated by a technological innovation among the different parties involved as well as the strategic choices concerning the optimal boundaries of the innovating firm. They also affect the expected locus of technological innovations (von Hippel, 1988).

Strategic Action

A firm's strategy captures organizational learning about the basis of its past and current success (Burgelman, 1983, 1991; Donaldson and Lorsch, 1983; Weick, 1979). Strategic action is, to a large extent, induced by the prevailing concept of strategy. Induced strategic action is likely to manifest a degree of inertia relative to the cumulative changes in the external environment (Hannan and Freeman, 1984). Cooper and Schendel (1976) found that established firms, when confronted with the threat of radically new technologies, were likely to increase their efforts to improve existing technology rather than switch to new technology even after the latter had passed the threshold of viability. Abernathy, Clark, and Kantrow (1983, p. 23) point out that "core design concepts" may

emerge that "'lock in' or stabilize the domain of relevant technical effort" (Clark, 1985). Henderson and Clark (1990) found that firms faced with architectural innovations were often unable to adapt their product development efforts. Burgelman (1994) found that inertial forces associated with a firm's distinctive competence impeded adaptation to changes in the basis of competition as a product moved from specialty to commodity.

Firms also exhibit some amount of autonomous strategic action aimed at getting the firm into new areas of business (e.g., Penrose, 1968; Burgelman, 1983, 1991). These initiatives are often rooted in technology development efforts. In the course of their work, for example, technical people may serendipitously discover results that provide the basis for redirection or replacement of major technologies of the firm. The existence of a corporate R&D capability often provides a substratum for the emergence of such new technical possibilities that extend beyond the scope of the firm's corporate strategy (Rosenbloom and Kantrow, 1982; Burgelman and Sayles, 1986; Pavitt, Robson, and Townsend, 1989). Participants engaging in autonomous strategic action explore the boundaries of a firm's capabilities and corresponding opportunities sets (Burgelman, 1983). Itami (1983) has observed that "in reality, many firms do not have . . . complete knowledge and discover the full potential of their ability only after the fact" (p. 15).

Organizational Context

The industry context exerts strong external selection pressures on the incumbent firms and their strategies. However, a key feature of established firms is that they have an organizational context that allows them, to some extent, to substitute internal for external selection. Organizational context thus serves as an internal selection environment (Burgelman, 1991). Continued survival may very well depend on the effectiveness of the firm's internal selection environment. It affects the capacity of the firm to deal with major strategic management challenges: (1) the ability to exploit opportunities associated with the current strategy (induced process), (2) the ability to take advantage of opportunities that emerge spontaneously outside the scope of the current strategy (autonomous process), and (3) the ability to balance challenges (1) and (2) at different times in the firm's development (Burgelman and Sayles, 1986).

Organizational context takes shape over time and reflects the administrative approaches and dominant culture of the firm. The dominant culture as it relates to technology may be different depending on whether the firm's distinctive competencies are rooted in science (e.g., pharmaceutical firms), engineering (e.g., semiconductor firms), or manufacturing (e.g., Japanese firms); whether the product development process has been driven by technology push, need pull, or a more balanced approach; and so on. Some research (e.g., Boeker, 1989) suggests that the background and management approaches of the founders have lasting impact on the firm's organizational context. Other research (Henderson and Clark, 1990) has shown that product architecture becomes reflected in organization structure and culture and greatly affects communication channels and filters. This, in turn, makes it difficult for organizations to adapt to architectural innovations that change the way in which the components of a product are linked together but leave intact the core design concepts (and thus the basic technological knowledge underlying the components). Still other research (Burgelman, Cogan, and Graham, 1997) has found evolving links between a firm's technology strategy and substantive and generic corporate strategies. While, initially, technology strategy drives substantive as well as generic corporate strategies, over time these relationships become reciprocal. Generic corporate strategy, however, may be a more enduring driver than substantive strategy because it becomes embedded in the firm's organizational context (internal selection environment).

Applying the Framework: Research and Practice

Several examples can be offered to indicate how the framework illustrated in Exhibit 2 may help situate new research findings in the field of strategic management of technology as well as provide insight into the practice of firms' strategic management of technology.

Research   Recent empirical work on "disruptive technologies" by Clayton Christensen and his collaborators (e.g., Christensen and Bower, 1996) allows us to illustrate the usefulness of the framework for integrating new research findings as they come along. Disruptive technologies have the potential to cannibalize existing technologies and to undermine the strategic position of incumbent firms in an industry. Christensen's research shows this phenomenon in the magnetic disk drive industry, where the emergence of a new generation of smaller form factors (smaller disks) materially affected the success of the prominent firms in the preceding generation. Other examples of disruptive technologies, among many, are the transistor, electronic fuel injection, and the personal computer. Christensen distinguishes disruptive from sustaining technologies. The latter lever-

age the existing technologies and may reinforce the strategic position of incumbents. (In the terminology of economics, disruptive technologies may be viewed as substitutes, sustaining technologies as complements.)

Christensen's research shows that disruptive technologies often emerge first in incumbent firms where technical people engage in autonomous *strategic action* to champion the newly discovered technological opportunity. The existing *organizational context,* however, is usually not receptive to these initiatives. This is so, in part, because the firm's sales force experiences a lack of interest on the part of existing customers. This, in turn, implies unpromising returns to investment in the foreseeable future. The existing customers are typically interested in improvements of performance along the technology dimensions that are relevant to them and their own current product development efforts and not in the improvement along different technology dimensions promised by the new technology. This is, therefore, very much a rational source of resistance. Hence, initially, the *industry context* represented by existing customers and the organizational context reinforce each other in resisting the new technology.

Often, however, in the face of organizational rejection or recalcitrance, the initiators of the new technology will leave the incumbent firm and start their own to pursue the technological opportunity. The new entrepreneurial firm will have to find and pursue new customers who are interested in the improvements offered by the new technology along the different dimensions. For instance, personal computer makers may be more interested in the size of the disk than in its price/performance ratio. As new users adopt the technology, *technological evolution* is likely to lead to improvements along the technology's other dimensions (e.g., price/performance). As a result, the new technology may become attractive to the customers of the old technology. This may precipitate a major shift in the market (*industry context*) and propel the new companies to prominence in the industry. Note that the performance of the old technology usually continues to advance as well (*technological evolution*) but in ways that exceed performance levels valued by the old customers, thereby becoming irrelevant.

Practice   Crown Cork and Seal (CC&S) was able to do very well over a thirty-year period as a relatively small player in a mature industry. Technology strategy seems to have contributed significantly to Crown's success. When taking over the company in 1957, CEO John Connelly recognized the existence of Crown's strong skills in metal formation and built on these to specialize in "hard-to-hold" applications for tin cans (*competencies/capabilities*). Crown did not have an R&D department, but it developed strong links between a highly competent technical sales force and an applications-oriented engineering group to be able to provide complete technical solutions for customers' "filling needs" (*competencies/capabilities*). In the face of a major external technological innovation—the two-piece can—initiated by an aluminum company (*technology evolution*), Crown was able to mobilize its own capabilities and those of its steel suppliers quickly to adapt the innovation for use with steel. Over several decades, CC&S continued to stick to what it could do best (*strategic action*)—manufacturing and selling metal cans—driven by a strong customer-oriented culture (*organizational context*), while its competitors were directing their attention to diversification and gradually lost interest in the metal can industry (*industry context*). CC&S has continued to refine the skill set (*experience*) that made it the only remaining independent metal can company of the four original major players.

The success of Marks and Spencer (M&S), a British retailer with a worldwide reputation for quality, is based on a consistent strategy founded on an unswerving commitment to giving the customer "good value for money." The genesis of its technology strategy was the transformation, in 1936, of a small textile-testing department into a "Merchandise Development Department," designed to work closely with vendors to bring about improvements in quality. Thirty years later, its technical staff, then numbering more than 200 persons working on food technology as well as textiles and home goods, allowed M&S to control the cost structure of its suppliers. The development of the technical capability itself was driven by the strong value of excellent supplier relationships held and continuously reinforced by top management.

Banc One Corporation is a Midwest banking group that consistently ranks among the most profitable U.S. banking operations. In 1958, the new CEO of City National Bank of Columbus, Ohio (CNB), John G. McCoy, persuaded his board to invest 3 percent of profits each year to support a "research and development" activity. Over the next two decades, CNB, which became the lead bank of Banc One Corporation, developed capabilities that made it a national leader in the application of electronic information processing technologies to retail banking. It was the first bank to install automatic teller machines and a pioneer in the development of bank credit cards, point-of-sale transaction processing, and home banking. While not all of its innovative ventures

succeeded, each contributed to the cumulative development of a deep and powerful technical capability that remains a distinctive element of the bank's highly successful competitive strategy.

The three companies cited are notable for the consistency of their strategic behavior over several decades. The following example illustrates the problems that can arise in a time of changing technology and industry context when a fundamental change in strategy is not matched by corresponding adaptation of the organizational context.

The National Cash Register Company (NCR) built a dominant position in worldwide markets for cash registers and accounting machines on the basis of superior technology and an outstanding sales force created by the legendary John H. Patterson. By 1911, NCR had a 95 percent share in cash register sales. Scale economies in manufacturing, sales, and service presented formidable barriers to entry to its markets (*industry context*), preserving its dominance for another sixty years. Highly developed skills in the design and fabrication of complex low-cost machines (*competencies/capabilities*) not only supported the strategy, but they also shaped the culture of management, centered in Dayton, where a vast complex housed engineering and fabrication for the traditional product line (*organizational context*). In the 1950s, management began to build new capabilities in electronics (*a revolution, not just evolution, in technology*) and entered the emerging market for electronic data processing (EDP). A new strategic concept tried to position traditional products (registers and accounting machines) as "data-entry" terminals in EDP systems (*changing strategic behavior*). But a sales force designed to sell stand-alone products of moderate unit cost proved ineffective at selling high-priced "total systems." At the same time, the microelectronics revolution destroyed the barriers inherent in NCR's scale and experience in fabricating mechanical equipment. A swarm of new entrants found receptive customers for their new electronic registers (*changing industry context*). As market share tumbled and red ink washed over the P&L in 1972, the chief executive was forced out. His successor was an experienced senior NCR manager who had built his career entirely outside of Dayton. He moved swiftly to transform the ranks of top management, decentralize manufacturing (reducing employment in Dayton by 85 percent), and restructure the sales force along new lines. The medicine was bitter, but it worked; within two years, NCR had regained leadership in its main markets and was more profitable in the late 1970s than it had been at any point in the 1960s.

EXPERIENCE THROUGH ENACTMENT OF TECHNOLOGY STRATEGY

A Note on Performance (Enactment) as Experience

The conventional view of performance in the strategy literature is in terms of outcomes such as ROE, P/E, market share, and growth. Typically, strategy researchers have tried to establish statistical associations between such outcomes and strategic variables (e.g., the association between profitability measures and measures of product quality). Establishing such associations is useful, but little insight is usually provided in how exactly outcomes come about (e.g., how quality is achieved and how it influences buyer behavior). In the framework represented in Exhibit 1, experience is viewed in terms of actually performing (enacting) the different tasks involved in carrying out the strategy. This view of performance is akin to that used in sports. For instance, to help a swimmer reach his/her highest possible performance, it is not enough to measure the time needed to swim a certain distance and communicate that outcome to the swimmer or to establish that, on average, a certain swimming style will be associated with better times. Sophisticated analysis of the swimmer's every movement traversing the water is needed to provide clues on how this particular swimmer may be able to achieve a better time. Similarly, experience derived from using technology in strategy provides feedback concerning the quantity and quality of the firm's technical competences and capabilities and the effectiveness of its strategy. The learning and unlearning potentially resulting from this, in turn, serve to leverage, augment, and/or alter the firm's capabilities, the strategy, or both (e.g., Maidique and Zirger, 1984; Imai, Nonaka, and Takeuchi, 1985; Itami, 1987; Burgelman, 1994).

Technology strategy is realized in practice through enactment of several key tasks: (1) internal and external technology sourcing, (2) deploying technology in product and process development, and (3) using technology in technical support activities. Performing these activities, in turn, provides valuable experience that serves to augment and change the firm's technical competencies and capabilities, and it leads the firm to reconsider certain substantive aspects of its technology strategy.

Technology Sourcing

Since the sources of technology are inherently varied, so too must be the mechanisms employed to make it accessible within the firm. It is useful to distinguish between internal R&D activity and acquisitive functions that import technology originating outside the firm.

Internal Sourcing Internal sourcing depends on the firm's R&D capability. Each firm's technology strategy finds partial expression in the way it funds, structures, and directs the R&D activities, whose mission is to create new pathways for technology. Relatively few firms—primarily the largest ones in the R&D-intensive industries—are able to support the kind of science-based R&D that can lead to important new technologies. A recent example is the emergence of high-temperature superconductivity from IBM's research laboratories. Most established technology-based firms emphasize applied R&D in support of existing and emerging businesses. Cohen and Levinthal (1990) found that an internal R&D capability is also an important determinant of the firm's "absorptive capacity"; that is, the firm's "ability to recognize the value of new, external information, assimilate it, and apply it to commercial ends" (p. 128). This indicates a close link between internal sourcing of technology and the capacity to use external sources of technology.

External Sourcing Many important technologies used in the value chain are outside of the technological capabilities of the firm. While internal sourcing seems necessary for most of the firm's core technologies, some may need to be sourced externally through exclusive or preferential licensing contracts or through strategic alliances. Every firm finds that it must structure ways to acquire certain technologies from others. The choices made in carrying out those tasks can tell us a great deal about the underlying technology strategy. To what extent does the firm rely on ongoing alliances, as opposed to discrete transactions for the acquisition of technology (Hamilton, 1985)? Is the acquisition structured to create the capability for future advances to be made internally, or will it merely reinforce dependence (Doz, Hamel, and Prahalad, 1989)?

Continuous concern with improvement in all aspects of the value creation and delivery process may guard the firm against quirky moves in external technology sourcing that could endanger the firm's competitive product-market position. Viewing the issue of external sourcing from this perspective highlights the importance of managing interdependencies with external providers of capabilities. One requirement is a continuous concern for gaining as much learning as possible from the relationship in terms of capabilities and skills, rather than being concerned solely with price. To the extent that a firm engages in strategic alliances, it must establish the requisite capabilities for managing the relationships. For instance, to develop unique and valuable supplier relationships, a company may need a strong technical staff to manage these relationships. If the strategic alliance is necessary because the firm is behind in an important area of technology, it may need to invest in plant and equipment to apply what is learned from the partner and begin building the technological capability in-house. For example, when Japanese electronics firms acquired technology from abroad during the 1950s and 1960s, most of them structured it in ways that allowed them to become the leaders in pushing the frontiers of those same technologies in the 1970s and 1980s (Doz, Hamel, and Prahalad, 1989).

Product and Process Development

Technology strategy is also enacted by deploying technology to develop products and processes. Product and process development activities embody important aspects of the dimensions of technology strategy. An understanding of the strategy can be gained from considering the level of resources committed, the way they are deployed, and how they are directed in product and process development. For instance, how does the organization strike the delicate balance between letting technology drive product development and allowing product development and/or market development to drive technology? The availability of integrated circuit technology drove product development in many areas of consumer electronics. New product development efforts, on the other hand, sometimes stimulate the development of new technologies. Notebook computers, for instance, drove the development of new disk drive technology and semiconductor "Flash" memory. The mammoth personal computer industry was founded when the young engineers of Apple sought to exploit the potential inherent in the microprocessor, at a time when corporate managers in Hewlett-Packard, IBM, and other firms were disdainful of the commercial opportunity. A decade later, however, it was clear that market needs were now the primary force shaping efforts to advance the constituent technologies.

Wheelwright and Clark (1992) suggest three potential benefits associated with product and process development: (1) market position, (2) resource utilization, and (3) organizational renewal and enhancement. They point out that these benefits are seldom fully realized because most firms lack a development strategy framework that helps them consistently integrate technology strategy

with product-market strategy. Recent work on technology integration (Iansiti, 1997) goes one step further, focusing on the role of technology evaluation and selection processes that precede actual product development processes. These technology integration processes are different from the various types of "advanced development projects" identified by Wheelwright and Clark. They are concerned with how choices of new technological possibilities (deriving from fundamental research) in relation to the existing application context (represented by the current product, manufacturing, and customer/user systems) affect the speed and productivity of the product development processes at the project level.

Technical Support

The function commonly termed *field service* creates the interface between the firm's technical function and the users of its products or services. Experience in use provides important feedback to enhance the firm's technological capabilities (Rosenberg, 1982). Airline operations, for example, are an essential source of information about jet engine technology. In some industries, such as electronic instrumentation, important innovations often originate with the users (von Hippel, 1978). The technology strategy of a firm, then, finds important expression in the way it carries out this important link to users. Two-way flows of information are relevant: Expert knowledge from product developers can enhance the effectiveness of field operations, while feedback from the field informs future development.

ENACTMENT REVEALS SUBSTANCE OF TECHNOLOGY STRATEGY

Studying the processes involved in performing the key tasks sheds light on how technology strategy relates technical capabilities to competitive advantage and how organizational learning and unlearning actually come about. In other words, enactment reveals the substance of technology strategy. The matrix illustrated in Exhibit 3 presents a framework for mapping the interactions among the components of substance and enactment in technology strategy making.

Two Conjectures

Implicit in the foregoing discussion are two normative conjectures about technology strategy. The first is that the substance of technology strategy should be comprehensive. That is, technology strategy, as it is enacted

EXHIBIT 3   Substance and Enactment in Technology Strategy

Substance	Enactment (modes of experience)				
	External technology sourcing	Internal technology sourcing	Product development	Process development	Technical support
Competitive strategy stance (choice/leadership/ entry timing/licensing)					
Value chain stance (scope)					
Resource commitment stance (depth)					
Management stance (organizational fit)					

through the various tasks of acquisition, development, and technical support, should address the four substantive dimensions and do so in ways that are consistent across the dimensions. The second is that technology strategy should be integrated. That is, each of the key tasks should be informed by the positions taken on the four substantive dimensions in ways that create consistency across the various tasks.

CONCLUSION

This chapter argues that an evolutionary process perspective provides a useful framework for thinking about technology strategy and about its role in the broader competitive strategy of a firm. The essence of this perspective is that technology strategy is built on technical competencies and capabilities and is tempered by experience. These three main constructs—technical competencies and capabilities, strategy, and experience—are tightly interwoven in reality. Technical competencies and capabilities give technology strategy its force; technology strategy enacted creates experience that modifies technical competencies and capabilities. Central to this idea is the notion that the reality of a strategy lies in its enactment, not in those pronouncements that appear to assert it. In other words, the substance of technology strategy can be found in its enactment of the various modes by which technology is acquired and deployed—sourcing, development, and support activities. The ways in which these tasks are actually performed, and the ways

in which their performance contributes, cumulatively, to the augmentation and deepening of competencies and capabilities, convey the substance of technology strategy in practice.

A second central idea is that the ongoing interactions of technical capabilities—technology strategy—experience occur within a matrix of generative and integrative mechanisms that shape strategy. These mechanisms (sketched in Exhibit 2) are both internal and external to the firm. Anecdotal evidence suggests that successful firms operate within some sort of harmonious equilibrium of these forces. Major change in one, as in the emergence of a technological discontinuity, ordinarily must be matched by adaptation in the others. Which leads to our final conjecture, namely, that it is advantageous to attain a state in which technology strategy is both comprehensive and integrated. By *comprehensive* we mean that it embodies consistent answers to the issues posed by all four substantive dimensions. By *integrated* we mean that each of the various modes of performance is informed by the technology strategy.

REFERENCES

Abernathy, W. J. 1978. *The Productivity Dilemma: Roadblock to Innovation in the Automobile Industry.* Baltimore: Johns Hopkins University Press.

Abernathy, W. J., and J. Utterback. 1978. "Patterns of Industrial Innovation." *Technology Review.*

Abernathy, W. J., K. Clark, and A. M. Kantrow. 1983. *Industrial Renaissance.* New York: Basic Books.

Adler, P. 1989. "Technology Strategy: A Review of the Literatures." In R. S. Rosenbloom and R. A. Burgelman (eds.), *Research on Technological Innovation, Management, and Policy,* vol. 4, pp. 25–152. Greenwich, CT: JAI Press.

Aldrich, H. E. 1979. *Organizations and Environments.* Englewood Cliffs, NJ: Prentice Hall.

Andrews, K. 1981. *The Concept of Corporate Strategy.* Homewood, IL: Irwin.

Ansoff, H. I., and J. M. Stewart. 1967. "Strategies for a Technology-Based Business." *Harvard Business Review,* November–December.

Arthur, W. B. 1988. "Competing Technologies: An Overview." In G. Dosi et al. (eds.), *Technical Change and Economic Theory.* New York: Columbia University Press.

Astley, W. G. 1985. "The Two Ecologies: Population and Community Perspectives on Organizational Evolution." *Administrative Science Quarterly* 30, pp. 224–41.

Barnett, W. P. 1990. "The Organizational Ecology of a Technological System." *Administrative Science Quarterly* 35.

Barney, J. 1986. "Strategic Factor Markets: Expectations, Luck, and Business Strategy." *Management Science* 32.

Boeker, W. 1989. "Strategic Change: The Effects of Founding and History." *Academy of Management Journal* 32, pp. 489–515.

Brooks, F. P. 1975. *The Mythical Man-Month.* Reading, MA: Addison-Wesley.

Burgelman, R. A. 1983. "Corporate Entrepreneurship and Strategic Management: Insights from a Process Study." *Management Science* 29, pp. 1349–64.

Burgelman, R. A. 1986. "Strategy-Making and Evolutionary Theory: Towards a Capabilities-Based Perspective." In M. Tsuchiya (ed.), *Technological Innovation and Business Strategy.* Tokyo: Nihon Keizai Shinbunsha.

Burgelman, R. A. 1988. "Strategy-Making as a Social Learning Process: The Case of Internal Corporate Venturing." *Interfaces* 18, no. 3 (May–June), pp. 74–85.

Burgelman, R. A. 1991. "Intraorganizational Ecology of Strategy Making and Organizational Adaptation: Theory and Field Research." *Organization Science* 2, pp. 239–62.

Burgelman, R. A. 1994. "Fading Memories: A Process Theory of Strategic Business Exit in Dynamic Environments." *Administrative Science Quarterly* 39.

Burgelman, R. A., and L. R. Sayles. 1986. *Inside Corporate Innovation.* New York: Free Press.

Burgelman, R. A., and R. S. Rosenbloom. 1989. "Technology Strategy: An Evolutionary Process Perspective." In R. S. Rosenbloom and R. A. Burgelman (eds.), *Research on Technological Innovation, Management, and Policy,* vol. 4, pp. 1–23. Greenwich, CT: JAI Press.

Burgelman, R. A., G. W. Cogan, and B. K. Graham. 1997. "Strategic Business Exit and Corporate Transformation: Evolving Links of Technology Strategy and Substantive and Generic Corporate Strategies." In R. A. Burgelman and R. S. Rosenbloom (eds.), *Research on Technological Innovation, Management, and Policy,* vol. 6, pp. 89–153.

Campbell, D. T. 1969. "Variation and Selective Retention in Sociocultural Evolution." *General Systems* 14, pp. 69–85.

Christensen, C. M., and J. L. Bower. 1996. "Customer Power, Strategic Investment, and the Failure of Leading Firms." *Strategic Management Journal* 17, pp. 197–218.

Clark, K. B. 1985. "The Interaction of Design Hierarchies and Market Concepts in Technological Evolution." *Research Policy* 14, pp. 235–51.

Clark, K. B. 1987. "Managing Technology in International Competition: The Case of Product Development in Response to Foreign Entry." In M. Spence and H. Hazard (eds.), *International Competitiveness,* pp. 27–74. Cambridge, MA: Ballinger.

Cohen, W. M., and D. A. Levinthal. 1990. "Absorptive Capacity: A New Perspective on Learning and Innovation." *Administrative Science Quarterly* 35, pp. 128–52.

Cooper, A. C., and D. Schendel. 1976. "Strategic Responses to Technological Threats." *Business Horizons* (February), pp. 61–63.

David, P. A. 1985. "Clio and the Economics of QWERTY." *American Economic Review* 75, no. 2 (May), pp. 332–37.

Donaldson, G., and J. W. Lorsch, 1983. *Decision Making at the Top.* New York: Bani Books.

Dosi, G. 1982. "Technological Paradigms and Technological Trajectories: A Suggested Interpretation of the Determinants and Directions of Technical Change." *Research Policy* 11, pp. 147–62.

Doz, I. L., G. Hamel, and C. K. Prahalad. 1989. "Collaborate with Your Competitors—and Win." *Harvard Business Review,* January-February, pp. 133–39.

Farrell, F., and G. Saloner. 1987. "Competition, Compatibility, and Standards: The Economics of Horses, Penguins, and Lemmings." In G. Landis (ed.), *Product Standardization and Competitive Strategy,* pp. 1–21. New York: Elsevier.

Ford, D., and C. Ryan. 1981. "Taking Technology to Market." *Harvard Business Review,* March–April.

Foster, R. N. 1986. *Innovation: The Attacker's Advantage.* New York: Summit.

Gould, S. I. 1987. "The Panda's Thumb of Technology." *Natural History* (January), pp. 14–23.

Hamilton, W. F. 1985. "Corporate Strategies for Managing Emerging Technologies." *Technology in Society* 7, nos. 2/3, pp. 197–212.

Hampson, K. D. 1993. *"Technology Strategy and Competitive Performance: A Study of Bridge Construction."* Doctoral dissertation, Department of Civil Engineering, Stanford University.

Hannan, H. T., and J. H. Freeman. 1984. "Structural Inertia and Organizational Change." *American Sociological Review* 43, pp. 149–64.

Henderson, R. M., and K. B. Clark. 1990. "Architectural Innovation: The Reconfiguration of Existing Product Technologies and the Failure of Established Firms." *Administrative Science Quarterly* 35, pp. 9–30.

Iansiti, M. 1997. *Technology Integration.* Boston: Harvard Business School Press.

Imai, K., I. Nonaka, and H. Takeuchi. 1985. "Managing the New Product Development Process: How Japanese Learn and Unlearn." In K. B. Clark, R. H. Hayes, and C. Lorenz (eds.), *The Uneasy Alliance: Managing the Productivity-Technology Dilemma.* Boston: Harvard Business School Press.

Itami, H. 1983. "The Case for Unbalanced Growth of the Firm." Research Paper Series #681, Graduate School of Business, Stanford University.

Itami, H., 1987. *Mobilizing Invisible Assets.* Cambridge: Harvard University Press.

Kelly, P., and M. Kranzberg (eds). 1978. *Technological Innovation: A Critical Review of Current Knowledge.* San Francisco: San Francisco Press.

Leonard-Barton, D. 1992. "Core Capabilities and Core Rigidities: A Paradox in New Product Development." *Strategic Management Journal* 13 (Special Issue, Summer), pp. 111–26.

Levitt, B., and J. G. March. 1988. "Organizational Learning." *Annual Review of Sociology* 14.

Little, Arthur D. 1981. "The Strategic Management of Technology." *European Management Forum.*

Maidique, M. A., and P. Patch. 1978. "Corporate Strategy and Technological Policy." *Harvard Business School* case 9-679-033, rev. 3/80.

Maidique, M. A., and B. J. Zirger. 1984. "The New Product Learning Cycle." *Research Policy,* pp. 1–40.

McKelvey, B., and H. E. Aldrich, 1983. "Populations, Organizations, and Applied Organizational Science," *Administrative Science Quarterly* 28, pp. 101–28.

Metcalfe, J. S., and M. Gibbons. 1989. "Technology, Variety, and Organization: A Systematic Perspective on the Competitive Process." In R. S. Rosenbloom and R. A. Burgelman (eds.), *Research in Technological Innovation, Management, and Policy,* vol. 4, pp. 153–94. Greenwich, CT: JAI Press.

Mitchell, G. R. 1986. "New Approaches for the Strategic Management of Technology." *Technology in Society* 7, nos. 2/3, pp. 132–44.

Nelson, R. R., and S. G. Winter. 1982. *An Evolutionary Theory of Economic Change.* Cambridge: Harvard University Press.

Pavitt, K. L. R., M. J. Robson, and J. F. Townsend. 1989. "Technological Accumulation, Diversification, and Organization of U.K. Companies, 1945–83." *Management Science* 35, pp. 91–99.

Penrose, E. T., 1968. *The Theory of the Growth of the Firm.* White Plains, NY: M. E. Sharpe.

Pisano, G., and D. J. Teece. 1989. "Collaborative Arrangements and Global Technology Strategy: Some Evidence from the Telecommunications Equipment Industry." In R. S. Rosenbloom and R. A. Burgelman (eds.), *Research on Technological Innovation, Management, and Policy,* vol. 4, pp. 227–56. Greenwich, CT: JAI Press.

Porter, M. E. 1980. *Competitive Strategy.* New York: Free Press.

Porter, M. E. 1983. "The Technological Dimension of Competitive Strategy." In R. S. Rosenbloom (ed.), *Research on Technological Innovation, Management, and Policy,* vol. 1, pp. 1–33.

Porter, M. E. 1985. *Competitive Advantage.* New York: Free Press.

Prahalad, C. K., and G. Hamel. 1990. "The Core Competence of the Corporation." *Harvard Business Review,* May–June, pp. 79–91.

Prahalad, C. K., I. L. Doz, and R. Angelmar. 1989. "Assessing the Scope of Innovation: A Dilemma for Top Management." In R. S. Rosenbloom and R. A. Burgelman (eds.), *Research on Technological Innovation, Management, and Policy,* vol. 4, pp. 257–81. Greenwich, CT: JAI Press.

Rich, B. R., and L. Janos. 1994. *Skunk Works: A Personal Memoir of My Years at Lockheed.* Boston: Little Brown.

Rosenberg, N. 1982. *Inside the Black Box.* Cambridge: Cambridge University Press.

Rosenbloom, R. S. 1978. "Technological Innovation in Firms and Industries: An Assessment of the State of the Art." In P. Kelly and M. Kranzberg (eds.), *Technological Innovation: A Critical Review of Current Knowledge.* San Francisco: San Francisco Press.

Rosenbloom, R. S. 1985. "Managing Technology for the Longer Term: A Managerial Perspective." In K. B. Clark, R. H. Hayes, and C. Lorenz (eds.), *The Uneasy Alliance: Managing the Productivity-Technology Dilemma.* Boston: Harvard Business School Press.

Rosenbloom, R. S., and A. M. Kantrow. 1982. "The Nurturing of Corporate Research." *Harvard Business Review,* January–February, pp. 115–23.

Rosenbloom, R. S., and M. A. Cusumano. 1987. "Technological Pioneering: The Birth of the VCR Industry." *California Management Review* 29, no. 4 (Summer), pp. 51–76.

Rutenberg, D. 1986. "Umbrella Pricing." Working paper, Queens University.

Selznick, P. 1957. *Leadership in Administration.* New York: Harper and Row.

Shepard, A. 1987. "Licensing to Enhance Demand for New Technologies." *The Rand Journal of Economics* 21, pp. 147–60.

Stalk, G., P. Evans, and L. E. Shulman. 1992. "Competing on Capabilities: The New Rules of Corporate Strategy." *Harvard Business Review,* March–April, pp. 57–69.

Steere, D., and R. A. Burgelman. 1994. "Intel Corporation (D): Microprocessors at the Crossroads." Stanford Business School Case BP-256D.

Teece, D. I. 1986. "Profiting from Technological Innovation: Implications for Integration, Collaboration, Licensing and Public Policy." *Research Policy* 15, pp. 285–305.

Teece, D. J., G. Pisano, and A. Shuen. 1990. "Firm Capabilities, Resources, and the Concept of Strategy." Working Paper #90-9, University of California at Berkeley, Center for Research in Management.

Tushman, M. L., and P. Anderson. 1986. "Technological and Organizational Environments." *Administrative Science Quarterly* 31, pp. 439–65.

Tushman, M. L., and L. Rosenkopf. 1992. "Organizational Determinants of Technological Change." In B. Staw and L. Cummings (eds.), *Research in Organizational Behavior,* vol. 14, pp. 311–25. Greenwich, CT: JAI Press.

Twiss, B. 1980. *Managing Technological Innovation.* London: Longman.

Utterback, J., and W. J. Abernathy. 1975. "A Dynamic Model of Product and Process Innovation." *Omega* 3, no. 6, pp. 639–56.

Van de Ven, A. H., and R. Garud. 1989. "A Framework for Understanding the Emergence of New Industries." In R. S. Rosenbloom and R. A. Burgelman (eds.), *Research on Technological Innovation, Management, and Policy,* vol. 4, pp. 195–226. Greenwich, CT: JAI.

von Hippel, E. A. 1978. "Has a Customer Already Developed Your Next Product?" *Sloan Management Review,* Winter.

von Hippel, E. 1988. *The Sources of Innovation.* New York: Oxford University Press.

Weick, K. 1979. *The Social Psychology of Organizing.* Reading, MA: Addison-Wesley.

Wheelwright, S. C., and K. B. Clark. 1992. *Revolutionizing Product Development.* New York: Free Press.

TECHNOLOGICAL EVOLUTION

CASE II·1

Asymmetric Digital Subscriber Line: Prospects in 1997

Tien Tzuo

On October 23, 1996, Pacific Bell reported that one of every six telephone calls in Silicon Valley was not going through on the first try because of people logging on to online services. "The explosion of the Internet is flooding our network," said a Pac Bell marketing manager. Another Pac Bell executive stated that the situation was so dire that California's entire phone system was in danger of breaking down. Pac Bell's critics argued that these claims were simply part of the phone company's efforts to persuade federal regulators to eliminate a 15-year ruling exempting Internet service providers from paying the expensive per minute charges that were levied on long-distance providers. They pointed out that Pac Bell used statistics gathered from a single neighborhood in Silicon Valley and only between the hours of 7 P.M. and 11 P.M. Nevertheless, the public telephone network was designed with the expectation that an average phone call

would last about four minutes. The growing use of online services challenged this assumption. In 1994, more than 20 percent of all online data service connections lasted more than an hour, with the average connection being 30 minutes. In a certain neighborhood in Santa Clara where online usage was high, 2.5 percent of the phone lines accounted for 20 to 36 percent of the total telephone traffic. In the worst-case scenario, emergency 911 calls could be blocked due to the increased traffic caused by long online sessions.

Ironically, as home usage of online services was growing; it was also becoming an increasingly frustrating experience. The graphical nature of Web browsers that made the World Wide Web so compelling as a consumer product also made accessing Web pages very slow, given the existing data transmission speeds available in homes. New multimedia technologies such as RealAudio, 3D graphics, and video further highlighted bandwidth limitations. A 4-minute (10 megabyte) video clip took 46 minutes to download over a 28.8K modem. Pundits began to refer to the online browsing experience as the World Wide Wait.

These vignettes highlight a fundamental shift in the assumptions that were underlying the global communications infrastructure. The rise of the Internet had spawned the vision of a global information highway that delivers interactive, multimedia, data-oriented services to the home. However, the existing public telephone network was built to carry two-way voice traffic and was increasingly inadequate when used to access data-oriented services. First, available bandwidth on the voice network

157

was divided into circuits, where each phone call ties up a specific circuit for the duration of the call. Because the quality and usefulness of voice conversations degrade significantly if transmission delays are introduced, dedicating a circuit per call allowed the network to guarantee timely transmission of the voice signal. In contrast, online connections were characterized by long sessions where repeated periods of inactivity were punctuated by bursts of data transmission. Thus, voice networks were highly inefficient when used to carry data traffic. Also, phone networks and switches were sized with enough circuits to handle the projected demand within the neighborhoods they serve. Because the average length of an online session was an order of magnitude greater than the average length of a phone call, online usage was likely to continue to tax the local phone company's ability to keep up with demand. Finally, existing digital transmission speeds over the copper wires which connected homes to the phone network were insufficient to carry anything but text and basic graphics.

For the Internet to fulfill its promise as a mass-market consumer medium, a new technology was required that could deliver high-speed digital data into the home without compromising the voice network. In the past year, a technology called asymmetrical digital subscriber line (ADSL) had emerged as a promising contender for such a solution. ADSL offered a number of benefits:

- It allowed digital data to be transmitted over existing copper phone lines up to 40 times faster than conventional modems.
- It did not require the phone companies to perform expensive upgrades to their network.
- It could coexist with conventional telephone service on the same copper wire.
- It allowed the phone companies to separate off data from voice traffic, thus freeing up the voice network.

Although these benefits were compelling, ADSL existed in a complex, dynamic environment characterized by rapidly evolving technologies, fierce industry competition, and deregulation. Industry observers wonder what were the prospects for ADSL to become the leading solution to the bandwidth problem.

This paper examines the forces that were likely to shape the adoption of ADSL. It examines the advantages and disadvantages of ADSL against existing and emerging technologies, within the context of the industry dynamics and market forces surrounding the race to deliver high-speed data access to the home.

ADSL

History

Digital subscriber line technology was invented at Bellcore in the 1980s as a high-speed method of transmitting digital data to a local phone company's customers, or subscribers. Several variations of DSL existed, including ADSL (asymmetric DSL), HDSL (high-speed DSL), and VDSL (very high–speed DSL). All DSL technologies used advanced digital signal processing (DSP) technologies to transmit data over copper phone lines, which made up virtually all of the "last mile" of the telephone network between homes and the central office that served their neighborhood.[1] ADSL was asymmetric in the sense that the downstream transmission speed (from central office to the home) is greater than the upstream speed.

ADSL was first used in Bell Atlantic and British Telecom's endeavors to provide interactive TV services to their customers. Foreseeing upcoming deregulation of the telecommunications industry, the phone companies were wary of cable companies entering their core markets. According to the *Wall Street Journal,* "Rushing to enter the television business seemed a strategic way to counter that cable threat—and one-upping cable by offering more-sophisticated interactive fare, letting viewers order movies on demand and other features, promised to give them an edge."[2] In 1994, Bell Atlantic launched Stargazer, a 1,000-user video-on-demand trial in Reston, Virginia, using ADSL to pump digital video streams into the homes of subscribers. British Telecom initiated a similar trial in Ipswich and Colchester, England.

A number of factors, however, prevented the phone companies from rolling out the service to their customer base. First, the phone companies encountered a number of problems with ADSL. Bell Atlantic had hoped that ADSL could be used in 95 percent of the homes in its service area. However, the company found that long distances to the central office, poor quality of copper wire, and electrical interference from external sources such as hair dryers and radio signals prevented ADSL from transmitting digital signals at the speed required to deliver VCR-quality video. Only 50 percent "of the loops were capable of handling ADSL," said Larry Plumb, di-

---

[1] Digital signal processing technology is used to process and manipulate signals in real time after they have been converted from analog to digital form. CD players, electronic music synthesizers, and PC sound cards are examples of devices using DSPs to produce audio effects.
[2] *Wall Street Journal,* September 16, 1996.

EXHIBIT 1 Internet Access Sources

Access location	Nielsen	FIND/SVP	VALS2
Home	62%	69%	42%
Work	54%	47%	33%
School	30%	21%	25%

According to three separate surveys, most people were connecting to the Web using their PCs at home, and at-home accounts are the primary access method for the majority of Internet users. FIND/SVP is a consulting, research, and advisory services firm based in New York City. Nielsen Media Research is a market research firm based in New York City.

rector of communications for Bell Atlantic's Entertainment and Information Services Group.[3]

In addition, the phone companies realized that the revenue from video-on-demand was not in itself sufficient to support the infrastructure investment required to install the networks and deploy the service.[4] Between January and September of 1996, the participants in Bell Atlantic's trial purchased an average of 3.6 videos per month at a cost of $2 to $5. The cost to provide the service, including the implementation of ADSL, the video content management hardware and software, and other infrastructure components, turned out to be more than $2,000 per subscriber. The phone companies had hoped that other new services such as interactive shopping and home banking could bring in additional revenue per subscriber. However, until the infrastructure was in place, there would not be the critical mass of people needed to compel content providers to provide such services. As a result, the phone companies delayed their plans to enter the TV market as they explored alternative technologies such as direct-broadcast satellite and fiber optics. In October 1996, Bell Atlantic formally shut down the Stargazer project.

During 1996, several factors caused a renewed interest in ADSL. The growth of the Internet had begun to fuel demand for high-speed digital access from homes. As Internet content became increasingly consumer oriented, online access had shifted from corporations and universities and into the home (see Exhibit 1). In 1995, there were 12 million home-users connected via modems to the Internet and 7.5 million subscribers to online services such as Compuserve and America Online. This

number was expected to double in 1996. In addition, an estimated 30 million telecommuters accessed corporate networks from home. The Internet, in effect, solved the chicken-and-egg dilemma faced by Bell Atlantic's Stargazer trial by providing both compelling content and a large base of users demanding high-speed access to that content.

In the meantime, ADSL vendors made significant improvements in the technology. New variants of ADSL promised to deliver digital signals at speeds up to 6 Mbps. Other improvements to ADSL also allowed it to be more impervious to noise and to adapt to the quality of the underlying copper wire. PairGain, a leading supplier of DSL equipment, had recently estimated that 85 percent of U.S. copper lines could support ADSL without modification.[5]

Finally, cable TV companies had been aggressively developing high-speed Internet access solutions over their own coaxial cable networks. Increased competitive pressure would force the phone companies to offer similar high-speed data access solutions that do not require expensive and time-consuming upgrades to the existing phone network.

How ADSL Works

A long time ago, it was determined that "the human voice creates sound at a pitch, or frequency, ranging from 0.5 to 10,000 cycles per second (10 kilohertz)."[6] Telephone systems were designed to capture signals below 4 kilohertz (KHz), a range sufficient to allow unique voices to be distinguishable. Telephone switches strip out all signals above 4 KHz to reduce any distortion caused by noise on the telephone line. Modems are used to convert digital data to analog signals for transmission over the telephone network. Existing modems, often referred to as POTS (plain old telephone service) modems, had to work within the 4 KHz analog bandwidth constraint. Because of this constraint, digital transmission speeds in current modems were limited to 33.6 Kbps, with 56 Kbps modems on the horizon.[7]

---

[3]"ADSL Politically Correct?" *America's Network,* November 15, 1996.
[4]"The Telephone's Second Chance," *The Economist,* July 13, 1996.

[5]Ibid.
[6]Christopher J. Crespi, "*xDSL for Poets,*" Montgomery Securities, September 13, 1996.
[7]Kbps stands for Kilobits, or 1 thousand bits, per second. Mbps stands for Megabits, or 1 million bits, per second. In an analog context, *bandwidth* refers to the width of frequency used. In a digital context, *bandwidth* refers to the transmission speed of digital data. Increasing analog bandwidth leads to greater digital bandwidth.

EXHIBIT 2   ADSL Transmission Rates

Data rate	Wire gauge	Distance
1.5 or 2 Mbps	24 AWG	18,000 ft
1.5 or 2 Mbps	26 AWG	15,000 ft
6.1 Mbps	24 AWG	12,000 ft
6.1 Mbps	26 AWG	9,000 ft

ADSL uses a much wider range of frequencies, up to 1.2 MHz (or 1,200 KHz), to create three different channels. The signals below 4 KHz are split off for normal, analog telephone service. ADSL uses the remaining frequency space above 4 KHz to create two digital channels—a high-speed downstream channel and a medium-speed duplex (bidirectional) channel. ADSL incorporates the latest digital signal processing (DSP) technology, called *line coding,* to increase digital transmission speeds to as much as 6.1 Mbps downstream and 640 Kbps bidirectional.[8] The exact speed of the digital channels depends on several factors, including the distance and wire gauge (width) of the copper wire (see Exhibit 2). About two-thirds of all homes in the United States were within 12,000 feet from a central office.

At a minimum, implementing ADSL requires two modems: one at each end of the copper line. In phone company parlance, the modem at the home was called an ATU-R, and the modem at the phone company's central office location was called an ATU-C. A more complete configuration is shown in Exhibit 3. At both the customer's and the phone company's central-office locations, a POTS splitter separates the normal analog telephone signals below 4 KHz from the digital ADSL signals. This guarantees uninterrupted telephone service even if the ADSL service goes down. At the central office, multiple ADSL lines are converged into a single data stream and directed to the appropriate location, such as the Internet backbone. At the customer location, the ADSL modem converts the ADSL connection to a PC-compatible data interface, such as an Ethernet port. In contrast from POTS modems that dial in to a data network on demand, ADSL provides a continuous connection to the network.

Competing ADSL Standards

There were two competing line-coding standards for implementing ADSL: CAP and DMT. The original parties involved in developing ADSL specified CAP (carrierless amplitude phase) as the DSP technology to use for encoding digital data for transmission over copper wires. Globespan Technologies Inc. was the supplier of CAP technology and had produced available chipsets.[9] Globespan licensed its CAP technology to a number of other vendors, including Westell, a leading supplier of equipment used in ADSL trials. In its original form, CAP enabled downstream transmission speeds of 1.5 Mbps. CAP-based technology was used in the initial video-on-demand trials.

DMT (discrete multitone) was an alternative DSP solution created by Dr. John Cioffi, a young faculty member in electrical engineering at Stanford University, who founded Amati Communications. DMT took advantage of the fact that digital transmission speeds were higher at lower analog frequency ranges. DMT divided the frequencies between 4 KHz and 1.2 MHz into 256 distinct subchannels, each 4 KHz in bandwidth, and transmitted digital data at different speeds depending on the carrying capacity of each subchannel. DMT could thus provide a higher bandwidth digital solution, and one that was *rate-adaptive* to the capabilities of the copper wire given varying quality and distances. DMT enabled downstream transmission rates of up to 6.1 Mbps at distances under 12,000 feet and 1.5 Mbps at distances up to 18,000 feet. Using network management software, service providers could specify a base transmission speed or allow the ADSL modem to self-adjust downwards to the maximum speed the connection would support. DMT also introduced advanced noise correction and cancellation technology. A variant of DMT called DWMT (discrete wavelet multitone transmission) was introduced by Aware, Inc.

DMT was selected by both the American National Standards Institute (ANSI) and the European Telecommunications Standards Institute (ETSI) as the line-coding standard for implementing ADSL. In addition, the telephone companies showed a preference for DMT. They estimated that they could serve more than 80 percent of their customers using DMT.[10] However, the stan-

---

[8] According to the National Telecommunications and Information Administration (part of the U.S. Department of Commerce), a *code* is a set of unambiguous rules specifying the manner in which data may be represented in a discrete (binary) form. A *line code* is a code chosen for use within a communications system for transmission purposes. A line code may, for example, reflect a requirement of the transmission medium (e.g., optical fiber versus shielded twisted pair).

[9] Formerly the Advanced Transmission Unit of AT&T Paradyne, which was renamed Globespan in August 1996. Paradyne itself was sold off by Lucent after the AT&T spin-off.

[10] "Powering ADSL," *Telephony,* December 9, 1996.

EXHIBIT 3   Sample ADSL Configuration

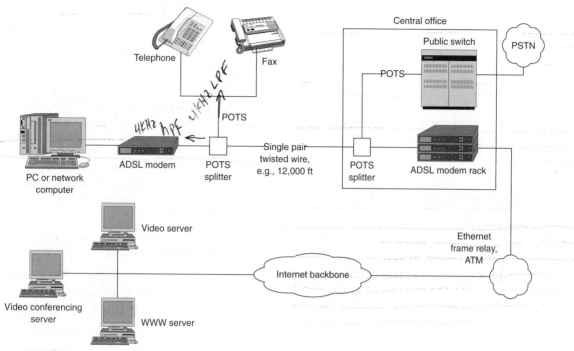

Source: Analog Devices

dards issue was far from resolved. Due to its earlier start, CAP-based solutions had been available and were used in virtually all the existing ADSL trials. Globespan claimed that over 10,000 subscriber lines were using CAP-based ADSL services. In contrast, DMT solutions from Amati or Aware were being used in fewer than four U.S.–based trials. CAP's relative maturity also gave it a lead in both cost and size. Globespan was continuing to improve its CAP-based technology. It had recently introduced rate-adaptive ADSL (RADSL), which could also adjust transmission speeds downwards according to the quality of the wire, and was testing a new version of its technology capable of transmitting downstream data at 7 Mbps.

Over time, both DMT and CAP were likely to trend towards one another, creating more options for vendors. If both performed similarly, cost and manageability were likely to be the deciding factors between the two. It remained to be seen which method would be preferred in carrier networks, and most consumers would not know which was implemented in their modems.

Initial ADSL Trials

In 1996, ADSL was being used in trials around the world. InterAccess, an independent Internet service provider (ISP), was one of the few companies offering ADSL commercially. Based in the Chicago region, InterAccess charged $200/month for the service and $1,600 for the ADSL modem. Although no major telephone company had yet offered ADSL as a commercial service, all seven Baby Bells and GTE were engaged in trials of ADSL for use in Internet access.

In Boston, Nynex had teamed up with Lotus and Westell in a trial to support telecommuting. Nynex was using Westell's FlexCAP ADSL modems to provide a 1.5 Mbps link from its central office (CO) to the homes of 60 Lotus software designers. Nynex then established a link from its CO to Lotus's corporate network.[11] Bell Atlantic, a leading proponent of ADSL for its earlier video-on-demand efforts, began a 100-line trial using ADSL for Internet access. The trial also used Westell's Flex-CAP modems. Bell Atlantic hoped to have the service rolled out to over 20,000 residences by the second quarter of 1997. As part of a joint venture with IBM, Ameritech began a trial late in 1996 involving 200 Chicago-area customers. Ameritech was charging field test customers $200 per line for the duration of the trial.

---

[11] Nynex press release, August 27, 1996.

Pacific Bell began a trial late in 1996 in San Ramon, California, to about 100 subscribers using modems supplied from Alcatel. GTE was trialing both Westell's CAP and Amati's DMT-based chips in Redmond, Washington, and Dallas, Texas. The Redmond trial was part of a joint effort with Microsoft.

Interest in ADSL was also strong in Europe. In May 1996, Telia, Sweden's state-owned national operator, became the first carrier in Europe to commit itself to deploying ADSL to all of its 4 million households by 2002. The services that were being targeted include video-on-demand, online information access, and home shopping.

Obstacles Facing the Adoption of ADSL

ADSL faced several obstacles in gaining wide acceptance. The DSP semiconductor chips that are at the core of ADSL were not widely available. While the CAP-based chips from Globespan used in current trials could be purchased in large quantities, the phone companies appeared to be waiting for DMT or newer CAP chips. Analog Devices and Motorola, two of the leading suppliers of DMT chipsets, expected to have components available by the middle of 1997.

The cost to deploy ADSL was high compared to alternative technologies. It was estimated that the initial cost of deployment would run about $2,000 per line. However, the largest component of this cost was the ADSL chipset. As volume increased, the deployment costs were expected to drop to about $500 per line. Westell, a leading manufacture of CAP-based modems, expected per subscriber costs to fall to below $300.

ADSL's success depended in large part on the actions of its sponsors. The local phone companies needed to aggressively roll out and attractively price the service. Unfortunately, the local phone companies had a spotty history of promoting remote data access technologies. Although it had been available for 20 years, ISDN was only then finding a market. The *Wall Street Journal* reported a story that reflected the difficulty that ADSL faced:

> Andrew Grove, Intel Corp.'s chief executive officer, recalls meeting three Bell company chiefs in Atlanta on the first weekend of the Olympics. He asked each of them about ADSL. "The first one was very enthusiastic," Mr. Grove says. "The second one said, 'No way.' The third one said, 'I'll let No. 1 demo it and wait and see.'" [12]

New competitive forces, however, could force the phone companies to move quicker. Pacific Bell was targeting monthly charges of $75–$125 for an untimed, ADSL-based continuous connection to the Internet, with a $500–$600 installation charge. Bell Atlantic was projecting a $30–$50 per month charge, and US West was projecting $50–$100 per month. Aware's business plan targeted modem prices at $300–$600 to support $50–$75 monthly access charges from the service providers. [13]

Finally, ADSL was constrained by its ability to serve only users within 18,000 feet of a central office. Ironically, however, the need for high-bandwidth data services may be proportional to the distance from a central office, as people in remote locations are often the best candidates for telecommuting.

THE ADSL SUPPLY CHAIN

The ADSL supply chain consists of layers of solutions that made ADSL service to consumers possible. The supply chain is depicted in Exhibit 4.

Digital Signal Processing Technology

At the bottom of the value chain were the companies that design the digital signal processing technology that made ADSL possible. The underlying DSP technology was extremely complex and was difficult to reverse engineer or duplicate. There were only three companies at this stage of the value chain. **Globespan,** a division of Paradyne, which was itself spun off from AT&T during the past year, was the leading supplier of CAP-based ADSL technology. DMT was introduced by **Amati,** a company founded by John Cioffi, a Stanford engineering professor. Finally, a company called **Aware** introduced a variant of DMT called discrete wavelet multitone (DWMT), which involved different software algorithms to enable a DMT solution. While Amati claimed that its patents covered all DMT-based solutions, Aware and its partners claimed to have found a way to circumvent them.

Amati and Aware were too small to compete effectively in the semiconductor market and instead chose to license their technology to larger semiconductor producers. Aware had an exclusive agreement with Analog Devices, and Amati had relationships with several firms, including Texas Instruments and Motorola.

If ADSL had been rolled out at the end of 1996, CAP would probably have become the leading standard, since

[12] *Wall Street Journal,* September 16, 1996.

[13] "Will ADSL Outpace ISDN in the Telecom Race?" *Network Computing,* December 16, 1996.

EXHIBIT 4 The ADSL Supply Chain

Service providers
Access network equipment
Modems and modem boards
Semiconductor chipsets
DSP technology

(value chain)

EXHIBIT 5 ADSL Chipset Suppliers

Analog Devices	Used DMT technology from Aware. AD20msp910 family of chips reduced number of chips needed from 24 to 5.
Motorola	Used DMT technology from Amati. Will have the MC 14560 processor sometime in the middle of 1997. Promising downstream support of 8 Mbps, as well as rate adaptivity in 32 Kbps increments.
Texas Instruments	Licensed DMT technology from Amati.
NEC	Licensed DMT technology from Amati.
Alcatel	DynaMiTe chipset uses DMT technology from Amati.
Westell	Uses CAP technology from Globespan.
Globespan	Uses own technology.

interesting

only CAP-based solutions were available. Amati projected that its partners would have chipsets ready by the fall of 1997. The phone companies had expressed a preference for DMT due to its better handling of signal noise and ability to divide the frequency spectrum into multiple digital channels. DMT was also officially backed by the ANSI standard. The U.S. and European standards bodies were working closely to ensure a common standard internationally.

Semiconductor Suppliers

The DSP companies licensed their technology to semiconductor manufacturers who then designed chipsets to implement the DSP solution. A chipset typically included the chip that implements the DSP technology itself along with other chips that served necessary functions, such as the control logic and transceiver. The major players vying to provide chipsets for the ADSL industry included Motorola, Analog Devices, Texas Instruments, and Alcatel. Westell and Globespan were smaller players. Exhibit 5 summarizes the technologies employed by each chip manufacturer.

Modem Manufacturers

Modems were a necessary component in implementing ADSL. ADSL modem manufacturers made modems or modem boards for use in equipment in both the customer location and the central office. Much more variety existed at this level, as different manufacturers produced modems targeted at different uses. A PC modem had a much different form factor and function set than a modem designed to go into a modem rack at the central office. Modems had little distinguishing features and were quickly becoming a commodity product. The competition in this sector was likely to be based on price and available distribution channels.

Access Network Equipment Suppliers

Access network equipment providers supplied the full system-level solution that service providers purchased and installed in their central offices. Because the stan-

dards were undefined, these suppliers had to offer both the central office equipment and the modems to be used at the customer location. In 1996, two key types of equipment were being offered: *concentrators* and *DSL access multiplexors* (DSLAM). Concentrators grouped multiple ADSL lines into a single pipe that could be fed into a high-speed digital line, such as a T3 or fiber optic OC-3 line. A DSLAM integrated multiple types of modems (ADSL, VDSL, frame relay, IDSL, etc.) into a single rack.

In September 1996, SBC Communications, BellSouth, Pacific Bell, and Ameritech had issued a request for proposal (RFP) for an ADSL DSLAM that would sit in the central office. The RFP included specifications for other infrastructure components such as billing interfaces, test and diagnostic functionality, and network management capability.[14] In December 1996, the companies reached an agreement with Alcatel to use Alcatel's equipment for delivering ADSL-based services to consumers and businesses.[15]

There were many players in this sector, including the large networking companies: Ascend, 3COM, Alcatel, and Nortel. ADSL was an example of how the lines were beginning to blur between a traditional supplier of telephone equipment, such as Nortel and Alcatel, and a supplier of Internet access solutions, such as Cisco and

---

[14] "xDSL for Poets," Montgomery Securities, September 13, 1996.
[15] Alcatel press release, available at http://www.ans.alcatel.com/news/pressrel/96/96-40.html.

large Innovation

3COM. Because ADSL was a new technology and involved a necessary break from traditional approaches to delivering data services, this sector was open to innovation. For instance, 3COM had recently announced a DSLAM solution that allowed a service provider to measure how many bytes were being used by each user. Existing high-speed data access solutions were not "usage" billed but were priced using monthly flat fees. With ADSL, the service providers had an opportunity to change their underlying business model to a usage-based structure.

Service Providers

The service providers actually provisioned ADSL service to end customers. Phone companies and other ADSL service providers purchased access network equipment that fit within their environment and within the services that they wished to offer. Additionally, service providers had to look at issues such as billing, customer service, installation and maintenance, and sales and marketing support. Potential service providers included the local phone companies, as well as the independent Internet service providers.

The local phone companies were the strongest force affecting the adoption of ADSL. If the local phone companies were slow and indecisive, adoption of ADSL could stagnate as ISDN had for the last decade. Two things were different in 1996 with respect to ADSL as compared to the situation with ISDN a decade ago. First, the cable companies were now in competition to be the providers of a high-speed data link to the home. Cable modems were a reality, and field trials of Internet access via cable coaxial lines had proved successful. Second, the Telecommunications Act of 1996 allowed the ISPs to compete with the phone companies on the local copper wire loop itself. According to the Act, an ISP could request from the phone company access to the copper line running from the central office to the home. The access rates for these lines would be regulated. An ISP could then splice the line into its own location and offer high-speed, ADSL-based Internet solutions directly to its customers, completely bypassing the local phone carrier. Ascend had begun to market products specifically enabling this opportunity.

EXISTING DATA ACCESS ALTERNATIVES

Leased Lines

In 1996, a corporation requiring data access would typically request a *leased line* from the phone company. Data

was transmitted over the leased line, which was usually copper, using T1 technology at 1.544 Mbps. T1 technology had its roots in the 1960s when the phone company found digital transmission of voice traffic to be more reliable than analog. The 4 KHz frequency range that makes up a phone call can be digitized and transmitted at 64 Kbps. Twenty-four calls may be aggregated and simultaneously transmitted using T1 connections. With the advent of fiber, T1 was extended into T3 technology that could transmit 44.74 Mbps over a fiber optic line to carry 672 simultaneous voice conversations. T1 is not a DSP solution; rather than using modulating signals, T1 transmits digital information by alternating the voltage on the wire to represent either a 1 or a 0. Because the strength of voltage signals degrades with distance, T1 lines required repeaters every 3,000 to 4,000 feet to amplify and rebroadcast the electrical signal. In Europe, a slight variant of T1 was used; E1 lines transmit digital data at 2.048 Kbps and can carry 30 simultaneous voice calls.

In addition to using T1 lines to transmit voice traffic between central offices, the phone companies also began in the 1980s to offer them to corporations for use in their private networks. In 1996, corporations used leased lines to connect different sites within the company, in a wide area network (WAN) configuration, or to connect the company to the Internet backbone via an Internet service provider (ISP). It was estimated that over 700,000 T1 lines had been installed in the United States and that 80 percent of them were over copper wires.[16] In the early 1990s, the phone companies began to offer Frame Relay services which allowed corporations to share a T1 line.[17] Depending on the amount of traffic, the actual bandwidth could be greater or less than the targeted bandwidth. In California, T1 services were available from Pacific Bell for about $350–$500/month plus a one-time installation charge of $1,267. In contrast, a 56 K frame relay line cost $75/month plus a one time charge of $375.

T1 was primarily a corporate WAN solution and was not suitable for connecting individual residences to data networks. T1's method of transmitting digital signals created enough noise such that telephone companies could not put more than a single T1 circuit in a typical

---

[16] "Copper Cable: A Historical Perspective," PairGain, at http://www.pairgain.com/copperop.htm.

[17] Frame relay technology provides a means for statistically multiplexing many virtual circuits over a single physical transmission link. Frame relay's statistical multiplexing provides more flexible and efficient utilization of available bandwidth. Transmission rates are usually between 56 Kbps and 1.544 Mbps (the T1 rate).

cable that contained 50 copper lines. Because residences did not normally have spare copper wires already laid, offering T1 services to homes required new wire or cabling. High installation costs and monthly charges priced T1 service out of reach of consumers and small businesses.

High-Speed POTS Modems

In 1996, most home and small business computer users connected to data networks using a modem over voice phone lines. Because they transmitted data over analog lines intended for plain old telephone service, these modems were often referred to as POTS modems or analog modems. At the time, 63.5 percent of these modems connected at 14.4 Kbps, while less than 15 percent connected at 28.8 Kbps.[18] Recent improvements had increased transmission speeds of POTS modems to 33.6 Kbps. However, this appeared to be approaching the theoretical maximum bandwidth possible, given the 4 KHz of analog bandwidth constraint of the voice network. Recently, Lucent, Rockwell, and US Robotics had announced a new technology that would allow POTS modems to receive data at 56 Kbps and send data at 33.6 Kbps, provided that the modem on the other side was a digital modem (i.e., the ISP had to be connected to the public phone network via ISDN).

The greatest advantage of POTS modems was their relative maturity, convenience, and low cost. POTS modems could be easily purchased for $100–$200, and the consumer did not have to wait for installation of new lines or activation of service. The ubiquity of telephone lines meant that POTS modems could be used virtually anywhere. It was estimated that about 600 million phone lines currently existed worldwide, growing to 750 million by 2000.[19] About 10 to 20 million households in the United States currently used modems to access online services. Since most home PCs were currently sold with a built-in modem, this number was expected to continue to increase.

The greatest disadvantage of POTS modems was their speed limitation. If 56 Kbps was indeed the maximum throughput possible over POTS modems, then transmission of multimedia content such as VCR-quality video and 3D graphics would not be possible. Another disadvantage of POTS modems was that they worked over a voice network that was never designed for data transmission. Most data networks were *packet switched networks* designed exclusively for data transport. On a packet switched network, data is broken down into smaller units and placed into individual packets which are sent over the network. Each packet is identified with the address of its destination, and the network routes the packet to the appropriate location. In this way, a packet switched network is similar to the postal system. The benefit of a packet switched network was that all users could share the network without a single user tying up an entire line. Inversely, a disadvantage was that as more people used the network, the speed of packet delivery per person slowed down. The phone system, on the other hand, was a *circuit switched network*. The quality and usefulness of voice conversations degrade significantly if transmission delays are introduced. On the voice network, each phone call tied up a specific circuit for the duration of the call, thus enabling the network to guarantee transmission of the voice data. Phone networks were sized and the number of circuits were allocated given projected demand. Because online sessions lasted much longer than a typical phone call, POTS modems tied up the voice network.

The adoption rate of ADSL and other emerging home-based data access technologies was expected to cut directly into the growth of POTS modems. However, because of their ubiquity and large installed base, POTS modems were expected to continue to dominate for a number of years as the technology of choice for remote data access. In the mobile-user market, POTS modems were expected to continue to be used as the only option for anytime, anywhere network access. It was unlikely that hotel rooms would be outfitted with ADSL or other data access technologies anytime soon. Jupiter Communications, a New York City–based consulting and research firm, had recently published a study, "Midband and Broadband to the Home," which focused on the immediate future of access technologies. In the study, Jupiter predicted that 56 K modems would control 50 percent of the access market by 1998, growing to 65 percent by 2000.

ISDN

Aside from POTS modems, the only other affordable option consumers had for remote data access was ISDN. ISDN was invented by Bell Labs in the 1970s with the goal of converting the POTS network into a true end-to-end digital network. Most telephone transmissions were carried digitally between central office locations—it was only in the last mile of copper that analog transmission

---

[18]Punk, Ziegel, and Knoell, "Communications/Networking," April 30, 1996.
[19]*America's Network,* April 1, 1996.

was used. By implementing an end-to-end digital solution, ISDN was able to provide two 64 Kbps channels of digital bandwidth.[20] Either both channels could be combined to create a 128 Kbps data channel, or one channel could be reserved for voice and one for data.

One of the first applications of ISDN was video conferencing. Companies such as PictureTel and Ascend sold equipment that enabled video conferencing over ISDN lines. Using a technique the company called "reverse multiplexing," Ascend was able to offer equipment that combined multiple ISDN lines to provide 512 Kbps of throughput or higher.

Because it used the public telephone network, ISDN was like POTS in that each connection tied up a single circuit in the voice network. Unlike POTS, however, ISDN required the phone companies to make costly software upgrades or replacement of central office voice switching equipment. This had limited the availability of ISDN. In 1994, fewer than half of the homes in the United States had access to ISDN. By 1996, about 80 percent of the U.S. population could order ISDN from their local telephone company.[21] Although ISDN had been around for over two decades, it was only in the most recent two years that the U.S. phone companies had begun to push it heavily as a service offering and priced it accordingly. Demand for high-speed Internet access was behind this push. Between the 3rd quarters of its 1995 and 1996 year, Nynex reported a 74 percent increase in requests for ISDN lines. Bell Atlantic noted a 34 percent increase from the beginning of 1996 to the end of October and was installing 4,000 to 5,000 lines a month towards the end of 1996.[22] At the end of 1995, about 500,000 ISDN lines had been installed in the United States.[23] The Gartner Group predicted the U.S. ISDN market to grow to over 2.5 million installations by the end of 1998.

In Europe and Asia, the adoption rate of ISDN was even greater than in the United States, in large part due to the willingness of overseas phone companies to promote the service. There were more than 2 million ISDN lines in Germany and 1.5 million ISDN lines in France.[24] In the United Kingdom, British Telecom had about 250,000

ISDN connections, and with competitors such as Nynex Cablecomms and CableTel beginning to offer their own ISDN services, the market was expected to continue to increase.[25] In Japan, NTT, the only domestic provider of ISDN service, reported that 206,000 new subscribers signed up for its ISDN service in 1996, up 193 percent from a year ago.[26]

Along with its use for video conferencing, ISDN was used predominantly by small- to medium-sized businesses and high-end consumers who desired faster access to the Internet and by large corporations who needed to support telecommuting. There were a number of costs to the user implementing ISDN. The cost of the service itself varied across regions. Bell Atlantic offered its residential customers a wide range of pricing ranging from $31 a month for 20 hours of access to $110 a month for 500 hours of access, plus an installation fee of up to $200. Pacific Bell's rates included a $125–$160 installation fee and a monthly fee of $25 that did not include usage. Actual phone calls were charged at standard local call rates. If the user wished to use the ISDN line for voice calls, a digital phone costing several hundred dollars was also required. Finally, Internet service providers typically charged a higher rate for high-speed ISDN connections as compared to POTS connections.

Although ISDN's use was growing, it was clearly threatened by newer technologies such as ADSL. ISDN was expected to continue to be used in video conferencing types of applications that required constant throughput speeds. Because it used the circuit switched network, ISDN provided the deterministic bandwidth required by real-time video transmissions. However, as adoption of ADSL increased, the use of ISDN for data access was likely to be squeezed out by high-speed 56 Kbps modems and 1.5 to 6.1 Mbps ADSL. Compared to 56 Kbps modems, ISDN was an expensive alternative that only doubled data throughput speeds. ADSL, on the other hand, offered vastly superior data speeds, could coexist with existing POTS service, and did not require installation of new cabling. VCR-quality video transmission required speeds that only ADSL could deliver. As both ISDN and ADSL were sponsored by the phone companies, there was a possibility that the telcos would limit the rollout of ADSL given their existing investment in ISDN. However, competition from cable and long-distance companies was likely to force the local

---

[20] These 64 Kbps channels are referred to as B channels. An additional 16 Kbps D channel is used for control signals.

[21] Michael Cristinziano, "Mass Market Dial-Up Internet Access," Needham & Company, Inc., April 1996.

[22] *Computer Retail Week*, December 9, 1996.

[23] Punk, Ziegel, Knoell, "Communications/Networking," April 30, 1996.

[24] *Telecom Markets*, October 10, 1996.

[25] *Telecom Markets*, December 5, 1996.

[26] *Wall Street Journal*, November 25, 1996.

providers to offer the faster services that ADSL could provide. In its study of access technologies, Jupiter Communications projected that ISDN would be in only 6 percent of online households by 2000.

EMERGING DATA ACCESS ALTERNATIVES

HDSL

High-speed digital subscriber line (HDSL) was developed at Bellcore as a method of applying DSL concepts to replace noisy T1 lines. Because copper wires tend to distort digital signals, traditional T1 lines leased by corporations often were not capable of delivering the true 1.544 Mbps bandwidth. In addition, the need for repeaters every 3,000 to 4,000 feet for signal amplification made installation and maintenance of T1 lines a labor-intensive and expensive process. Using HDSL, phone companies could deliver T1 equivalent bandwidth without requiring repeaters. PairGain, a leading supplier of HDSL solutions, claimed that HDSL could quadruple the distance a digital signal could travel without the need for amplification and better compensate for signal distortion to allow lower grade copper wires to be used. PairGain believed that HDSL could be deployed in 99 percent of the available, existing copper. Since its introduction, HDSL was being widely used by phone companies when installing or upgrading leased T1 lines.[27]

HDSL was different than ADSL in several ways. First, HDSL offered lower speeds but over greater lengths than ADSL. Second, HDSL was symmetric—available digital bandwidth was the same in both directions. Finally, HDSL could not coexist with POTS on the same copper phone line. Consumers who wished to have both digital HDSL data access and voice service would require installation of new wiring. This effectively limited the mass appeal of HDSL.

VDSL

Very high-speed DSL (VDSL) is a variant of ADSL that allows asymmetric transmission of data at higher speeds but over shorter distances. Downstream rates vary from 12.96 Mbps to 55.2 Mbps, depending on distance (see Exhibit 6). Upstream rates vary from 1.6 Mbps to 2.3 Mbps. VDSL was still in the design stage and was expected to go into trial use sometime during 1996. Production VDSL components were not expected to be

EXHIBIT 6 VDSL Throughput Speeds

Downstream Speeds	Distance
12.96 Mbps–13.8 Mbps	4,500 ft.
25.92 Mbps–27.6 Mbps	3,000 ft.
51.84 Mbps–55.2 Mbps	1,000 ft.

available until 1998, at the earliest. Like ADSL, both CAP and DMT were being proposed as the line code transmission standard. VDSL also split off signals below the 4 KHz frequency threshold so that POTS service was maintained.

VDSL was being considered primarily for hybrid switched digital video (SDV) networks that use both fiber and copper. Fiber is the ideal transmission medium for digital data. However, an all-fiber solution that involves laying fiber to the home (FTTH) was too expensive and time-consuming a proposition. It was estimated that it would cost the phone companies on the order of $1,500 to $2,000 per subscriber to convert from copper to a fiber-optic transmission line. With 172 million subscriber lines in the United States, the total cost for such an endeavor would exceed $250 billion. Unless the government funded such an effort with tax dollars, the phone companies were unlikely to make the investments necessary to wire homes with fiber connections. In addition, the local phone companies could not realistically install new cabling for more than 7 percent of their installed subscriber base in any given year. Factoring in a 3 percent growth rate in new lines, the net annual upgrade rate to the network would be 4 percent. Thus, a complete fiber overhaul would take the telephone companies at least 20 years to complete.[28]

Alternatively, the phone companies were looking at running fiber to the neighborhood (FTTN) to terminate at an optical network unit (ONU). Either coaxial cable or copper could then be used to transmit data from the ONUs to residences. The use of coax, for instance, was $400 cheaper per household than bringing fiber all the way to the home.[29] (Hybrid fiber coax configurations are discussed in the next section.) While coax is preferred over copper as a data transmission medium because of its greater bandwidth capabilities, the phone companies did not already have coax cable in their networks. VDSL would allow a phone company to take advantage of

---

[27]"Copper Cable: A Historical Perspective," PairGain, at http://www.pairgain.com/copperop.htm.

[28]Telecommunications Act of 1996 Web page.
[29]Nicholas Negroponte, "2020: The Fiber-Coax Legacy," *Wired*, October 1, 1995.

existing copper to transmit the signal over the final segment.[30]

VDSL was seen as a long-term solution to be implemented as fiber was deployed on a wider scale. Current bandwidth requirements for multimedia Internet access were within the capabilities of ADSL. However, the greater digital bandwidth provided by hybrid configurations such as switched digital video might be necessary to deliver advanced interactive services such as video conferencing and high-definition video.

Hybrid Fiber Coax and Cable Modems

The technologies examined above all fell within the domain of the local phone companies that own the copper wires over which communications to the home were made possible. But the shift from voice to data communications had opened the door to new entrants to the home-based data access market. The cable companies were the leading challengers to the local phone companies in providing digital transmission into the home. Although only 65 percent of American households subscribed to cable, 90 percent of the homes were already wired for cable service.[31] Cable networks were made up of coaxial cable, a better signal transmission medium than the twisted pairs of copper wire used within the telephone network. Coax provided higher bandwidth and greater signal integrity over longer distances. Theoretically, 735 MHz of bandwidth could be used in a coax cable, compared to the 1.2 MHz that ADSL uses. According to Bell Atlantic, a full hybrid fiber coax (HFC) configuration could deliver all of the following services simultaneously:

- Plain old telephone service (POTS).
- 23 to 37 broadcast analog TV channels.
- 188 broadcast digital TV channels.
- 272 to 464 digital point cast channels (that deliver customer requested programming at a time selected by the customer).
- High speed two-way digital link (in both directions).

In the past 18 months, the cable companies had been testing the use of cable modems to allow users to access the Internet over cable networks at downstream throughput speeds up to 10 Mbps. HFC configurations were also being tested by phone companies, such as Ameritech, who were considering laying down a brand new network

separate from its copper-based infrastructure. However, for this service to be viable, a number of improvements had to be made to the cable companies' networks. Designed to broadcast multiple channels of analog video signals, cable networks were laid out very differently than phone networks. Every telephone outlet was directly connected to the switch that serviced the neighborhood it is in. Dedicated lines allowed each user of the phone network to engage in a private conversation. As a broadcast medium, cable TV sent the same signal to all its subscribers. Rather than providing a point-to-point link to its customers, the cable network was laid out like a tree trunk with offshoot branches. A main trunk delivered the video signal to a neighborhood. The signal was then spliced and sent along various branches to individual homes. Thus, the capacity in a cable TV network was shared by all the users that were downstream of that portion of the trunk or branch. Because a single coax cable was not sufficient to support a neighborhood of Internet users, each making separate throughput demands on the network, the cable companies had to upgrade their coax trunks to fiber. These HFC configurations were very similar to the switched digital video configurations, described above, being considered by the phone companies. A main fiber was laid to a neighborhood to serve between 500 and 2,000 homes, and coax-based branches or rings connected the fiber trunk to subscribers. While an individual coax cable could transmit digital signals at over 10 Mbps, the actual speed available to individual users might be much less.

Fortunately for the cable companies, the upgrade from coax to fiber had already been initiated even before they began to consider offering digital services. Fiber-rich networks greatly reduced the cable companies' maintenance costs and allowed them to offer more channels. In the affluent areas where the companies planned to offer Internet services first, virtually all networks were already a hybrid of fiber and coax.[32]

The upgrade of cable trunks to fiber was not the only change the cable companies had to make. Most of the amplifiers and switches in the cable network were only capable of transmitting signals one way and would have to be upgraded to two-way equipment. Estimates varied on the percentage of the cable network that would have to be upgraded. The *Wall Street Journal* reported that only 7 percent of United States cable systems were equipped to handle two-way communications.[33] In con-

---

[30] ADSL Forum, A VDSL Tutorial.
[31] Frederick D. Ziegel, "The 'Tweeners,'" Punk, Ziegel & Knoell, September 15, 1996.

[32] *The Economist,* July 6, 1996.
[33] *Wall Street Journal,* December 9, 1996.

trast, another analyst reported that 70 percent of the cable networks would have to be upgraded.[34] In any event, the ability for a home user to access the Internet using cable modems would depend on how aggressive their local cable company was in performing the necessary upgrades to the network. Dataquest predicted cable operators would be able to sell broadband service to only 3 percent of their customers by 2000.[35]

Towards the end of 1996, cable modems had been in trial for about a year and were just starting to be used in commercial services. CATV CyberLab, an online directory and news source developed for the cable television industry, estimated that cable modem trials were in about 800 different locations worldwide. CATV Cyber-Lab maintained a list of over 300 trials on its website.[36] About 70 of the trials listed had been upgraded to commercial deployments. Cox began offering service to its customers in Orange County, California, in December 1996, and planned to begin service in San Diego and Phoenix in the first quarter of 1997 and five additional markets in the remainder of 1997.

Cable modems from LANcity and Zenith accounted for over 80 percent of the modems used in the trials. Recently, Motorola had been very aggressive in signing supplier agreements with many major cable companies. In September of 1996, LANcity had shipped over 40,000 and Zenith had shipped about 30,000 modems. Motorola announced in February that they had shipped over 50,000 modems to 80 different locations.

The cost of the service in the initial trials was between $30 and $50 a month, plus installation charges. The @Home service in Fremont, California, charged $35/month for service with a $150 installation fee. Time Warner Cable planned to price its RoadRunner service in Elmira, New York, and Akron, Ohio, at $39.95/month. In Continental Cable's cable modem trial at Boston College, students and teachers who used the service said they would pay between $10 and $20 a month to receive the service commercially.

Wireless and Satellite Data Transmission

Wireless technologies included cellular, PCS, satellite and other methods of transmitting signals that did not depend on wireline cables. Until recently, wireless data transmission involved using a cellular or packet radio modem to transmit data signals over an analog wireless circuit. Data transmission speeds were limited to 9.6 Kbps. Although recent improvements in digital cellular and PCS promised to increase data throughput speeds, high per minute costs and limited wireless capacity were likely to cause data transmission over this medium to remain a niche market.

Digital satellite, also referred to as wireless cable, had traditionally been a broadcast medium targeted towards delivering the same video signals to a broad audience. There were about 900,000 digital satellite subscribers in the United States. Late in 1996, Hughes Network Systems, the maker of DirecTV, began to offer an Internet service, called DirecPC, that used satellite technology as a method of providing downstream data speeds of up to 400 Kbps. Although a digital satellite "channel" was capable of digital transmitting speeds greater than 10 Mbps, this bandwidth had to be divided among all potential users, limiting effective speed available to each subscriber. Installation costs of $999 included the satellite dish and the interface software. Monthly fees started at $15.95/month.[37]

Separately, AT&T had announced a new radio-based technology, code-named Angel, that allowed it to bypass the local carriers to provide local service to homes. The technology involved an 18-inch transmission box that is placed outside of a house and connected to existing telephone wires. Because the service was digital, AT&T could offer Internet connections at 128 Kbps, the same speed as ISDN.[38] (The various data transmission technologies are summarized in Exhibit 7.)

MARKET SEGMENTS *chicken-egg*

While significant demand existed for higher bandwidth, the viability of new technologies such as ADSL and cable modems depended on whether their costs of implementation were sufficiently low enough for the service providers to bundle them within an attractively priced service. Adoption of these technologies was likely to depend on the service provider's ability to identify initial customer segments that placed high value on bandwidth and were less price sensitive. An analogy can be drawn to the cellular phone market, where prices were initially high and service targeted at mobile business people who were willing to pay a premium for the service. As prices decreased, the cellular phone companies attracted more

[34] Ziegel, "The 'Tweeners.'"
[35] *Computer Retail Weekly,* November 25, 1996.
[36] See http://www.catv.org/modem/.

[37] *Wall Street Journal,* December 9, 1996.
[38] *Fortune,* March 17, 1997.

EXHIBIT 7 Comparison of Data Transmission Technologies

Technology	Transmission	Downstream speed	Upstream speed	Medium	Line installation	Customer equipment	POTS	Medias supported	Install/monthly cost	U.S. install base	Applications
POTS modems	Symmetric dial-up	56 Kbps	33.6 Kbps	Copper	Not required	POTS modem	Yes	Text, graphics	Local phone charges	Millions	Voice, low-speed Internet access
ISDN	Symmetric dial-up	128 Kbps	128 Kbps	Copper	Required	ISDN modem, digital phone	Yes	Graphics, low-quality video, speech-graded audio	$150/$25 + usage	500,000	Voice, medium-speed Internet access, low-quality video conferencing
T1	Symmetric continuous	1.5 Mbps	1.5 Mbps	Copper	Required	CSU/DSU	No	Medium-quality video, high-fidelity audio	$1,267/$350–$500	700,000	WAN, high-speed Internet access
HDSL	Symmetric continuous	1.5 Mbps–2.0 Mbps	1.5 Mbps–2.0 Mbps	Dual copper	Required	CSU/DSU	No	Medium-quality video, high-fidelity audio	Same as T1	With T1	T1 replacement
SDSL	Symmetric continuous	1.5 Mbps–2.0 Mbps	1.5 Mbps–2.0 Mbps	Copper	Required	POTS splitter, SDSL modem	Yes	Medium-quality video, high-fidelity audio		Lab tests	Higher bandwidth version of HDSL
ADSL	Asymmetric continuous	1.5 Mbps–6.1 Mbps	16 Kbps–640 Kbps	Copper	Not required	POTS splitter, ADSL modem	Yes	VCR-quality video	$500/$75	Trial	High-speed Internet access, simplex video
HFC	Asymmetric shared	4 Mbps–10 Mbps	600 Kbps	Fiber, coax	Not required	Cable modem	No	High-quality video		Trial	High-speed Internet access, simplex video
VDSL	Asymmetric continuous	13 Mbps–52 Mbps	1.5 Mbps–2.3 Mbps	Fiber, copper	Not yet available	VDSL modem	Yes	High-quality video	n/a	Lab tests	Video on demand, interactive multimedia
Fiber	Continuous	51 Mbps–466 Mbs	51 Mbps–466 Mbs	Fiber	Required		No		n/a		
Digital satellite	Asymmetric dial-up	400 Kbps		Wireless	Not required	Satellite dish	No	Low-quality video, speech-graded audio	$999/$16	n/a	Medium-speed Internet access
Radio	Symmetric dial-up	128 Kbps	128 Kbps	Wireless	Not required	Transmission box	Yes	Low-quality video, speech-graded audio	n/a	Lab tests	Medium-speed Internet accesss

casual users by introducing rate plans that made cellular phone charges comparable to regular phones.

Remote Office/Branch Office

The potential customers of high speed remote access services could be segmented by size into large businesses, small- to medium-sized businesses, and residential users. In the large-business segment, these technologies could be used to support telecommuters and remote offices/branch offices (often referred to as the ROBO market). Support for telecommuters was the basis behind Nynex's ADSL trial with Lotus, described previously. The @Home network had recently introduced its @Work service targeted at this segment. Due to the asymmetric nature of both ADSL and cable modems, neither was appropriate for large corporations building wide area networks (WANs), where a peer-to-peer solution was required to connect geographically dispersed sites. However, it was not cost-effective for a corporation to connect remote users or remote branches with few employees directly into the corporate network. Instead, telecommuters and remote offices connected to corporate networks through a public phone system, using ISDN or POTS modems. New technologies such as ADSL or cable modems would allow corporations to provide remote connectivity that was comparable to being in the office.

Small Office/Home Office

ADSL and cable modems could also be used by small- to medium-sized businesses for accessing the Internet. This group was often described as the small office/home office (SOHO) segment. Because of the asymmetrical nature of the technologies, they were more appropriate for businesses seeking to *access* the Internet, as opposed to businesses placing *content* on the Internet for others to access. Initial target segments included businesses that performed extensive research, such as lawyers or investment advisors, or businesses that exchanged electronic information with other businesses. Growth of ADSL and cable modems in this segment would come at the expense of ISDN.

Residential

The residential market would ultimately be the largest market for the new data access technologies. The demand for high-speed Internet connectivity was the driving force behind this market. In 1996, there were 20 million Internet users worldwide, expected to reach 200 million by the year 2000. As more services were introduced on the Internet and as content became more com-

EXHIBIT 8   Spending of a High-Value Residential Customer

A typical high-value residential customer spends $3,000 to $3,500 a year on information and communications.* A breakdown follows:

Cellular	$625–$675
Local phone service	$475–$525
Long distance	$375–$425
Cable, pay-per-view, video-on-demand	$350–$400
Newspaper, magazine, and fiction	$300–$350
Paging	$225–$275
Online access	$175–$200
Information hardware	
(e.g., PC, phone, answering machine)	$200–$250
Entertainment hardware (e.g., TV, radio)	$375–$425

* Wall Street Journal.
Sources: Andersen Consulting, American Demographics, and the Insight Research Corp., and the Federal Communications Commission.

plex, users would want convenient, easy, and fast access to these services.

Within this segment, most companies would initially target the power user, a residential user who spent between $3,000 to $3,500 a year on information and communication services. Exhibit 8 gives a breakdown of the spending patterns of a typical power user. As online services became more compelling and consumer-oriented, spending on online access was expected to increase at the expense of other services, such as cable TV, magazines, or entertainment hardware. In this context, the ability to deliver video might be a key ingredient for the Internet to compete with other entertainment and information options.

Within the residential segment, phone companies were increasingly looking beyond the value of selling a single service to their customers. With competition eroding customer loyalty, phone companies were hoping to lock in a customer by offering a bundle of services, including local, long distance, paging, cellular, Internet access, and eventually, cable or satellite TV. MCI's MCI One service was the first example of this trend. The value of what was viewed as a lifetime customer could not be judged simply by the short-term revenue potential of the services offered. Some estimates valued a lifetime customer at $5,000 to $8,000 or more.[39] The long-distance carriers were willing to take initial losses to acquire a customer who might buy a bundle of services for life. As the local phone market becomes deregulated, the local phone companies should also follow this trend.

---

[39] Ibid.

READING II-1

Management Criteria for Effective Innovation

George R. White

Early in the corporate era, it may have been easy to believe that technological stability was the normal condition and technological innovation the occasional, fortuitous balm for problems to which we otherwise could have adapted. But since World War II, innovation has been the norm; technology-based innovations, coming in rapid sequence, have been seen as the crucial source of prosperity, the panacea for all business problems.

Now we know that this panacea is not necessarily benign. The U.S. electronics industry was in far better condition in the early 1950s, before the emergence of the transistor, than it is now with the consumer business largely penetrated by Japan. On the other hand, it is also true that a previous modest participant in electronics, the Motorola Corporation, used the transistor to expand its position in consumer electronics and then, by integration backwards, gained a significant new role as a component supplier.

When compared to those available in finance, marketing, and production, the tools available to management for assessing and directing technological innovation are rudimentary. Intrigued by this fact, Margaret B. W. Graham and I determined to study in detail two fully completed, well-documented innovations—the transistor in consumer electronics and the jet engine in subsonic jet transports. We postulated that the criteria for success in these cases could be applied to predicting the future outcomes in two immature innovations—the supersonic transport and computerized automobiles.

We conclude that we can in fact identify management criteria which effectively discriminate between profitable and unprofitable new technologies, and that these criteria have utility in appraising technological innovation in a wide variety of cases.

THE DETERMINANTS OF SUCCESS

We began by predicting that determinants of success could be found in both technology and business con-

texts. In the realm of technology, the determinants would surely depend on some appraisal of the quality and significance of the innovative concept itself: It must be new, and it must also be good. But such an innovative concept alone does not assure technical potency; there must be an embodiment for the new device, a product or system which is waiting for it. The embodiment surrounding an inventive concept has a major effect on how profitable the new technology proves to be.

Even with technical potency, a high rate of adoption and great profitability are not assured. The operational consequences of the new technology on manufacturing, marketing, and distribution must be considered.

Finally, market dynamics are extremely important—and often complex. Many industries have several dependent stages of intermediate demand; for example, transistor manufacturers sell to radio manufacturers, and radio manufacturers in turn sell to consumers. It is not enough to study the transistor market; analysis of final consumer demand is essential to understanding the outcome of transistor technology.

Balancing Old and New Constraints

Three questions turn out to be crucial in determining the technical potential of any inventive concept:

What fundamental technical constraints limiting the prior art are lifted? This is the key technical challenge: Identify the core physical constraints underlying the previous technologies that have been lifted by the new invention and assess the significance of lifting those constraints. Consider an example from the field of aircraft engines. In the piston engine, the upper limit in compression ratio is set by the detonation of the fuel charge in the cylinder. A turbine engine has no such limit; it is possible to have a higher compression ratio in a turbine engine than in a piston engine, and today's successful turbine engines do have those higher compression ratios.

What new technical constraints are inherent in the new art? The first question had to do with the credit side, and this question determines the debit side—that is, what fundamental constraints limit the effectiveness of the innovation? In jet engines, for example, the wake efficiency or the Froude efficiency of an aircraft propulsion system depends on the ratio of the velocity of the rearward stream of air to the forward velocity of the aircraft; the lower that ratio, the more efficient the propulsion. A propeller, moving a large amount of cold air slowly, has a higher wake efficiency than a jet engine moving a small amount of hot air rapidly, so a new constraint exists.

Source: Technology Review, February 1978, pp. 21–28. Reprinted with permission from *Technology Review,* MIT Alumni Association. Copyright © 1978.

How favorable is relief of the former weighed against the stringencies of the latter? The net of the first two questions with respect to any inventive concept is a qualitative technical balance. The comparisons cannot be quantitative because they are not necessarily of similar characteristics; so this is highly judgmental balance, but it can be technically quite meaningful.

Putting Innovations in Context

The second stage of applying these management criteria is to analyze the embodiment in which the new technology will go to market. Here again the analysis takes the form of answering three questions:

Is the end product enhanced by additional technology and components required to make use of the innovation? This question calls for an analysis of the changes which must be made to a product if the innovation is to be used in it. A good example occurs in radios. Every radio must have a power supply, an R-F section, an I-F section, and an audio section. The transistor penetrated the automobile radio as a replacement for the output power tube, but the R-F and I-F sections of the radio were unaffected by the presence of a germanium power transistor instead of an output power pentode; however, because the output stage no longer required 300-volt B+ plate potential, it was possible to eliminate the unreliable vibrator power supplies as soon as R-F and I-F tubes requiring only 12-volt B+ potential were developed. These hybrid radios were much more reliable, but they could not have succeeded without the 12-volt tube development.

Is the inventive concept itself diluted or enhanced by the embodiment required? Now analyze the effect on the innovation itself of the changes required for its use in the product. There are favorable cases where the additional art surrounding the new invention enhances its value; that is a very happy situation. But there are many cases where the embodiment surrounding the new art dilutes it.

Does the additional embodiment offer opportunity for further inventive enhancement? Once more a balance is needed, this time between the value added to a product and that subtracted from it by the requirements of the innovation. Does it add more punch, or does the new innovation on balance decrease the acceptability of the product into which it is incorporated?

A Balance Sheet on Financing Business Operations

The answers to these two sets of questions establish the technical potency of a new innovation, but they offer no criteria in the business context from which to judge such things as profit potential. Three questions are also involved here:

What previously emplaced business operations are displaced or weakened by the new innovation? Assess the potential changes in existing business that will be brought about by the innovation. In the case of the entry of the transistor into electronics, the impact on the dealer service network is a perfect example. All tube sets were guaranteed to have tube failures and to require tube replacement. That phenomenon simply does not exist in transistor devices, and the dealer service network predictably declined in importance as transistors were introduced.

What new business operations are needed or wisely provided to support the new innovation? Assess the nature and cost of new business operations required by adoption of the new technology. The Japanese penetration of the U.S. consumer electronics market provides an example; it was simultaneously an innovation in distribution and retail marketing. Trading companies were now the distributors, and retail sales by stores, department stores, and discount houses replaced the previous pattern of selling which focused on the brand-franchise dealer.

How favorable is cessation of the former practices weighed against provision of the latter? Draw the trial balance again; we claim that this analysis can yield a qualitative business balance stemming from the new invention.

What Will Sell and What Won't

Finally, we determine a set of criteria having to do with market dynamics, on the basis of three questions:

Does the product incorporating the new technology provide enhanced effectiveness in the marketplace serving the final user? The Pilkington Float Glass Process represents a substantially more effective way of making plate glass by casting the glass against molten tin instead of grinding the surfaces; there are dramatic cost savings. But smooth glass is smooth glass, and there is no increased effectiveness resulting from its use in windows. The process is a perfect example of an innovation which made no change at all in the marketplace; it does not, unlike many others, yield economic payback because of market expansion due to enhanced effectiveness.

Does the operation reduce the cost of delivering the product or service? Taken together, this question and the one above are really the scissors of supply and demand, the first dealing with demand, the second with supply.

If the answer to both of these questions is no, we can forget the whole thing; and if it is yes, then there need be little market uncertainty. The challenging case is where one of these is positive and the second is not.

Does latent demand expansion or price elasticity expansion determine the characteristics of the new markets? When the factor driving a market area is lower price per unit, market expansion by hundreds of percent is hard to obtain; major expansion in revenue is much more likely when the change in the market is driven by a dramatic change in product effectiveness. This final question, of course, determines the quantitative business balance.

In these criteria, we have avoided terms such as *return on investment* and *return on assets managed*. Our view is that these issues are overwhelmed whenever a new inventive concept can be placed in a beneficial embodiment which will enhance its value in a major latent market with lowered operational costs. If evaluations of an innovation must be based on assumptions of narrow differences in return on investment, they are quite possibly based on fallacy. What we propose is a logic structure to identify a small class of innovations of great promise whose success will transcend the cash value of any normal investment.

PUTTING THE DETERMINANTS TO THE TEST OF HISTORY

Some examples from our work show how this logic structure might have served as a meaningful discriminant between successful and unsuccessful innovations in the past.

The Japanese Portable Radio Game

Consider first three aspects of the changes in the consumer electronics market wrought by the transistor. Transistor radios made their first strong showing in the U.S. portable radio market in 1956; prior to that time all portables had been tube sets. In 1956, the center of gravity of the U.S. market (according to listings in *Consumer Reports*) was in personal-size transistorized portable radios weighing an average of 20 ounces and costing an average of $57; eight models were available. This was a substantial innovation; the dominant radio in the previous year's market had been a tube-based portable weighing about six pounds. No Japanese sets were in the U.S. market in 1956.

By 1959, the U.S. industry had responded fully to the transistor as it was then applied; there were 25 por-

table models in the 20-ounce size, and prices were down slightly.

But in 1959, there was also a new market never populated before, filled by 11 different Japanese miniature portable sets weighing about 10 ounces (less than half as much as the smallest U.S. radios then available) and costing 10 percent less than the 20-ounce U.S. radios. The Japanese had made a dramatic innovation in the size and weight of personal portable radios and thus had opened up a new market not serviced by the U.S. industry.

The Japanese did not do this by innovating in transistors; they did it by other innovations through which they reduced the sizes of tuning capacitors, loudspeakers, battery supplies, and antennas. It was the transistor innovation supported by these additional innovations that allowed the Japanese to open up this exclusive new pocket-radio market and begin their successful penetration into U.S. consumer electronics. In fact, the U.S. industry's innovation based on the transistor was an incomplete innovation; it had not taken advantage of the embodiment surrounding the transistor as the Japanese had done.

By 1962, the market outcomes were clear. In 1955, the U.S. market for portables was 2 million sets, all tubes and all made in the United States. By 1962, the Japanese had captured 58 percent of the market, and they had in fact captured 68 percent of the market growth made possible by the transistor.

Auto Radios and TV: Who Needs Transistors?

Compare this history with that of the second transistor innovation, which was in auto radios.

In 1955, the only auto radios were tube sets; they used high-voltage R-F, I-F, and output tubes, and of course they required vibrator power supplies.

In 1956 came a new type of auto radio with no vibrator power supply, no step-up transformer, and no high B+ potential. Germanium output transistors allowed low power drain; they were driven directly by the negative-ground 12-volt power supply of the automobile battery. In addition, an embodiment innovation provided 12-volt B+ tubes to handle R-F and I-F.

Only one year later, the first all-transistor auto radio, completely transistorized in R-F and I-F and with low-drain output transistors, all running directly on the battery supply, became available.

On average the tube sets of 1955 cost $45, the hybrid sets cost $8 more (a modest step-up), and the completely transistorized sets of 1957 cost $125, a luxury prestige item in the Cadillac Eldorado but otherwise priced out of the market.

The production of auto radios follows very closely the production of automobiles. In the mid-1950s, 67 percent of new cars went to market with radios. Since then this figure has increased steadily—no sudden changes in auto radio use have been associated with the new technologies—until now it is almost 100 percent. There were 6.86 million auto radios made in 1955 and only 6.43 million in 1960; these figures reflect almost exactly the volume of new-car demand. In this period, the transition from tube sets to the tube-plus-output-transistor hybrid set was essentially completed (fully transistorized radios were still not sold in any meaningful quantity). Yet there was no expansion at all in this market.

Turn now to color television consoles, the last of three transistor substitution innovations we have studied. All consoles marketed from 1955 through 1967 used tubes. The first transistorized console was available in 1968, but only in 1974 (almost two decades after the first transistor portable was sold) did transistorized color sets become the industry standard. Since portability and maintenance cost are dominated by the vacuum cathode-ray tube, transistor penetration was very slow.

Summing a Transistorized Balance

Portable radios, automobile radios, and color television consoles represent three different transistor innovations which were technically very similar in circuit design and in cost. Yet the business outcomes were dramatically different. Our criteria applied to this field reveal the differences in technology and its business context that led to these strikingly different outcomes.

Recall that our criteria reflected first a balancing of constraints removed against new constraints added by an innovation. In the case of portable radios, transistors meant that weight, size, and frequency of repair were all improved dramatically. For auto radios, the vibrator failure mode (which provided 60 to 80 percent of the maintenance engagement) was eliminated and with it the problem of battery drain when the radio was used without the engine running. Frequency of repair was generally reduced. In television, transistors served only to reduce the frequency of repair. As we progress from auto radios to television, the value of constraints lifted by the transistor declines.

New technology always has new problems. The audio fidelity of the little portable radios was poor, and that is a fundamental constraint. Similarly, the capture value of the tiny ferrite antennas was not as good as that of the bigger antennas. There were no particular penalties in auto radios or in television.

Drawing a technical balance on the value of these inventions, we conclude that the portable radios presented a vast increase in portability—from six to eight pounds down to shirt-pocket size. The auto radios offered a major increase in reliability. Transistorized television sets only had a slight increase in reliability going for them. We conclude that the portable radio had dramatic new value, the auto radio had substantial new value in its hybrid mode, and the television set had very little new value.

Next, what additional technology was required in the embodiments in which transistors were placed to realize their full potential? Small tuning capacitors, loudspeakers, antennas, and batteries were crucial to the reduced size of the portable radios. If these had not been included, the value of the transistor innovation would have been diluted, since in fact tubes were not the fundamental limit on the size of portable radios. As the Japanese demonstrated—to the detriment of their American competitors—only if you spent extra money to miniaturize all the other components could you fully capitalize on the transistor invention itself.

The additional innovation required for auto radios were the 12-volt tubes for R-F and I-F sections, and these were rapidly achieved. This allowed elimination of the vibrator; without that, the transistor innovation would have been diluted, and transistorized auto radios might not have been successful.

An interesting situation prevails in television. As far as we can imagine now, a television set requires a cathode-type picture tube. Even after 20 years of looking, we find the prospects dim for a cheap, all-solid-state display. Therefore, we are nailed to the low reliability, high repair cost, and large size of present picture tubes. There is essentially no opportunity for incremental enhancement in the embodiment surrounding the transistors.

As we compare these different applications of the transistor on the basis of these criteria statements, we can understand why the portable radio transition was complete and rapid, why the auto radio transition was quite rapid for one portion (hybrid) and quite slow for the other portion (fully transistorized), and why the color television transition was quite slow. (See Exhibit 1.)

On the operational side, the transistor led to some business innovations. In Japan, a wholly new concept of low-cost mass marketing followed the design of nine-ounce radios.

EXHIBIT 1 **Effects of the Advent of the Transistor**

	Portable radios	Auto radios	Television
Inventive concept			
Constraints lifted	Weight, size, and frequency of repair	Vibrator failure, battery drain, and frequency of repair	Frequency of repair
New constraints	Low sensitivity, low fidelity	None	None
Advantage	Vast increase in portability	Major increase in reliability	Slight increase in reliability
Embodiment merit			
Additional components	Condenser, speaker, antenna, and battery	12-volt R-F/I-F tubes	Cathode-ray tube
Dilution or enhancement	Dilution of size and weight gains	Dilution if vibrator required	Dilution, since no rewards of small size or low weight
Additional opportunity	Enhancement if above are miniaturized	Enhancement if 12-volt tubes eliminate vibrator	No enhancement; elimination of CRT seems impossible.
Operational practice			
Displaced business operations	Dealer service no longer very important	Service less important	Service slightly easier
New business operations	Low transport and inventory cost encourage wide distribution network.	New field of transistor and electronic manufacture opened	None
Advantage	Low-cost mass marketing opens new market to imports.	Radio makers integrate backward to transistors, auto makers to radios.	Slight if any
Market dynamics			
Enhanced effectiveness to final user	Great increase only in portability	Slight	None
Reduced cost	Higher cost in early years	Only slightly higher cost, due to vibrator savings	Much higher cost in early years
Expansion of substitution market	Expansion in miniature size only	Substitution	Substitution

The author proposes that analysis of these 12 aspects of the changes wrought by the transistor demonstrates why its penetration was so instant and its revolution so complete in the portable radio industry, its penetration equally complete but its revolution insignificant in auto radios, and its penetration small and slow in the television industry.

The fundamental change in a key component of auto radios—the output tube became a germanium output transistor—was adopted throughout the industry and led to a new business opportunity. The Motorola Corporation, a radio manufacturer which never made tubes in its life, was effectively able to integrate backwards and started making germanium power output transistors—first for use in its own production of auto radios and also in its military equipment and later as components for sale to others. Thus this change in technology allowed Motorola to expand its role and penetration in the industry. The transistorized television set, having only slight ad-

vantages, offered no new business opportunities; essentially it is a null case.

The application of transistors to the portable radio definitely increased the effectiveness of the product to the final user; it now became a go-with-you-anywhere radio rather than a carry-it-and-set-it-down radio. The combination of the transistor and the further innovation surrounding it led to a new product that claimed a new latent market never populated before, rather than a substitution market. In contrast, the enhanced effectiveness of the transistorized auto radio to the final user was quite slight—a little bit of reliability, a little bit of battery drain. It was a substitution market; in fact, the total demand did not increase at all. There simply was one radio (approximately) for every new car sold. The television case is our null case; nothing happened.

The Battle of the Turbines

Here is a brief review of how our criteria illuminate the different outcomes in the case of turbine aircraft. Here we are dealing with three fundamentally different types of aircraft—the wide-bodied jets (707 and DC-8), the Lockheed Electra, and the Boeing 727. The first jets, as well as the first Electras, entered service in 1958. By 1961, the Big Five U.S. airlines (these firms provided 75 percent of U.S. passenger miles in the late 1950s, and they were historically the airlines which first bought new equipment) had 177 big jets; by 1969 they were using 500 such aircraft. The Lockheed Electra went from an initial 1961 fleet of 72 down to only 28 aircraft in 1969. The 727, which was not even in the first round of purchases, turned out to be the single most effective jet aircraft; by 1969, 400 of them were in service in the United States.

The inventions on which these aircraft were based were largely similar—the substitution of rotating compressors and high-temperature gas turbines for reciprocating pistons. But these aircraft are very different in their ensemble of other elements beyond turbine engines—embodiment merit, according to the terminology of this article. To achieve the full potential for higher speed inherent in the turbine, the 707 and DC-8 used swept wings, at 35° and 30°, respectively. This was possible because Boeing and Douglas engineers solved (each in slightly different fashion) the problem of controlling a phenomenon called Dutch roll, which affected stability. The outcome was that the 707 and DC-8 were fundamentally faster than the British Comet, which was designed with a 20° wing sweep to avoid the stability problem. Thus the opportunity came not in jet engines but in solving aerodynamic problems brought into relevance by jets.

Lockheed engineers were trapped with a dilemma in designing the Electra. They concluded that they were better off moving a large mass of cold air slowly than a small mass of hot air rapidly, because of the runway length requirements of the latter. So they stuck with propellers. But propellers in fact have an ultimate speed limit, since their tips cannot easily go faster than the speed of sound, and this in turn constrains the aircraft to a top speed nearly 200 miles slower than that of a turbo-

jet such as the 707. The Electra designers chose the old, familiar art of propellers, where no risk was entailed but no new enhancement was possible.

The 727, the third member of our jet set, has been successful because of two additional embodiment innovations—fanjet engines and high-wing-lift devices. In order to use the short runways of intermediate-range airports, the 727 had to obtain much more take-off thrust and much more lift from the wing in landing than had been possible before, yet it also required a small wing for cruising at high speed. This was achieved by using fanjet engines (with cold air flow around the hot turbine exhaust) in the rear of the aircraft so that the wing was clean and by using triple-slotted flaps with leading edge slats which provided the equivalent of a variable-configuration wing. The innovation was effective; the 727 ended up with short-field capability that matches that of propeller aircraft, yet it cruises at speeds typical of all jets.

Market dynamics are the next criterion of importance. The 707 and DC-8 presented a great advantage in comfort and speed; they flew higher and faster than any aircraft before, and it was simply more pleasant to travel. In addition, because of their high speed and capacity, they cost less per seat mile to operate than long-range piston planes. So the best of all possible worlds was obtained: Demand was higher and cost was lower. These aircraft led to a strong market expansion for air travel.

The Electra offered only modest improvements. Some of the vibration coming from piston engines had disappeared, but Electras could not fly as high or as fast as the jets. Operating cost per seat mile excluding depreciation was less than that of medium-range piston aircraft, but this meant a market based on substitution (slowly penetrating by doing the same function against depreciated equipment), not one based on expansion (rapidly penetrating on the basis of payback from new customers).

Finally, the 727 had the speed and comfort of the big jets and costs roughly equal to the Electra, and it could fly in and out of the smaller airports. As soon as the 727 was available, all of the intermediate-range traffic, piston or Electra, went to it. (See Exhibit 2.)

FORECASTING FUTURE INNOVATION

Now that we have seen how the innovation criteria apply to the transistor case and to the case of jet aircraft, it is appropriate to make some general statements about their application to two prospective innovations, microprocessors for automobiles and supersonic transport aircraft.

EXHIBIT 2   The Battle of the Turbine-Powered Transports

	707/DC-8	Electra	727
Embodiment merit			
Additional components	Swept wings required	Propellers required	High-lift wing devices needed
Dilution or enhancement	Slight roll control problem	Speed and maintenance constraint	Clean wing with triple-slotted flaps from rear engine
Additional opportunity	Speed advance over Comet due to high sweep angle	None	Short-field capability matches that of propeller aircraft.
Market dynamics			
Final user effectiveness	Great advance in speed and comfort	Only modest gain over piston engine in speed and vibration	Great advance in speed and comfort
Cost reduction	Net cost less than long-range piston	Cost much less than piston planes	Costs roughly equal to Electra
Expansion or substitution market	Strong expansion	Substitution for piston craft	Substitution for Electra and piston craft

Only 6 of the author's 12 criteria are needed to demonstrate the superiority of pure jets in the marketplace—why the 707, DC-8, and 727-type aircraft became the standard for U.S. air travel in the 1970s. He believes the same kind of analysis can be used to show why innovations leading to a supersonic transport aircraft have much less potential in the U.S. market.

Automotive Microprocessors: Everything Up

Microprocessors promise flexibility and precision of control and operation of automotive engines that are simply not available in mechanical control systems, and this is the heart of the technical advantage.

At the level of embodiment, we find that the sensors and actuators, not the computer chips, are the most crucial components requiring further development. An automobile is an analog mechanical environment; a microprocessor is a digital electronic environment. We need either sensors, actuators, and/or analog-to-digital converters, and these are the key embodiment elements. We also know that they represent the dominant portions of system cost and are the dominant determinants of system performance. If these can be made right, there will be regulatory benefits, better driveability (which to the auto industry means desire to buy cars), and long-life, stable performance; automobiles will stay in tune, and their control and performance functions will not deteriorate over the life of the car.

These will be major new design, manufacturing, and marketing opportunities, and our operational practice criteria are useful in seeing how to make a business operation out of these possibilities. Absolutely, one would expect that firms such as Bendix or TRW (with aerospace and electronic skills and a large presence in the auto industry) could take advantage of this opportunity to expand backwards (as Motorola did with auto radios) into special electronic precision sensors and actuators, seiz-

ing a key part of this technical ensemble for a long-term, stable market. We also have the possibility of car manufacturers expanding their domain of technical activities.

The market that is implied by these prospects for computerized automobiles is absolutely unique. It has been decreed by the U.S. government. Microprocessors and related control systems do not have to be evaluated against the cost of today's mechanical alternatives; they offer the most promising way we can yet envision to meet emission and economy standards mandated for motor vehicles in the 1980s. There is a billion-dollar value to manufacturers in avoiding the fines for high fuel consumption or the preemption of marketability if new automobiles fail to meet pollution standards set by federal law. The value to the auto industry hinges not on new revenue gain—because all the industry can hope to do is continue to sell high-value cars—but rather on the avoidance of loss.

The Fundamental Problem of the S.S.T.

To evaluate prospects for a supersonic transport, one can go through the same four-point check sequence on criteria. The key inventive concept, the thing that is fundamentally new on supersonic transports, is supersonic aerodynamics, the increase of aerodynamic drag at supersonic speed. Two different aerodynamic structures to deal with this problem have been examined in the United States. One (which is now a failed concept for transports) is the swing wing; the other, which survived until the entire transport project was shelved, is a wing swept back at an angle sharper than the Mach cone so the wing is subsonic while the airplane is supersonic.

This is a good concept. But it cannot deal with the fact that aircraft flying faster than the speed of sound always leave a sonic boom below, and the energy required to overcome that lost in the sonic boom results in high fuel consumption. So there is a good concept, but it has some debits.

Now we go to the embodiment criteria. The key regulatory decision was that sonic booms would not be allowed over the United States. So American supersonic aircraft must be efficient at subsonic cruise over the United States as well as at supersonic cruise over areas where boom is permitted. This requires what are called variable configuration engines, operating in bypass mode below the speed of sound and as straight jets above—a corollary innovation. The sharply swept wings present some unique control and stability problems; they lack the inherent stability of conventional wings, behaving much like classroom paper airplanes. There must be active controls, called "fly-by-wire." This is not hard, but creating reliable "fly-by-wire" equipment that will last for the 20-year life of an airplane presents a significant challenge.

A supersonic aircraft requires structures that go beyond those we have had before, because supersonic flight causes thermal as well as aerodynamic loads. The required composite materials represent a new art which now must be mastered.

Finally, we have a question about pollution: We absolutely know that oxides of nitrogen behave differently in the meteorological system at 65,000 feet than at 25,000 feet. The problem is that we do not know how they behave. If these oxides lead to depletion of the ozone layer, we will have somehow to change engine combustion.

If we understand all these embodiments surrounding the supersonic wing innovations, we can proceed to the issues of operational practice. The key problem here is that the U.S. domestic market has underwritten the basic costs of all major air transport innovations since the DC-3. It will not do so for the supersonic transport; long-range aircraft earn value only in international travel. Our airlines and our manufacturers need to understand what it means to be primarily international; pooling of traffic and manufacturing consortia are probable.

The market outcome is not clear. Is it an expansion market or a substitution market? We already have very effective long-range aircraft; if the only problem were to fly 4,000 to 5,000 miles, supersonic travel would be a substitution market, and the economics would not be optimistic. On the other hand, if the value of time saved is substantial, it is conceivable that supersonic travel could result in market expansion.

Having followed this procedure of drawing orderly balances in the areas of inventive concepts, embodiment merit, operational practices, and market outcomes, I have concluded that though no single constraint prohibits supersonic transports from being commercially successful, the broad array of concerns says that the mere passage of time will not assure an S.S.T. There must be some urgent national mission to override some of the constraints to their emergence.

We believe our procedure for evaluating the viability and likely outcomes of an innovation can largely account for the differentiated outcomes in high-technology businesses—businesses that are as far removed from each other as transistor radios and jet transports. When these criteria are applied to important potential future innovations, they indicate plausibility for a computerized car, given a reasonable regulatory atmosphere, and they indicate implausibility for many years for a U.S. supersonic transport. We are convinced that a similar analysis can be useful in indicating the likely future course of other projected innovations.

CASE II-2

The Optical Components Industry: A Perspective

I suspect we will see the first trillion-dollar market cap come out of this sector (optical components).
—Vinod Khosla, Kleiner Perkins Caufield & Byers,
January 2001 [1]

---

[1] "Khosla: Optical Markets Still Huge," as reported in *Light Reading,* January 18, 2001.

A couple of years ago, everyone wanted to get into the optical components business. Now vendors can't exit it fast enough.
—Pauline Rigby, *Light Reading,* September 2002[2]

Excluding the few hundred optics and IC start-up casualties, our prediction sees the top 25 optical and comm-IC vendors dwindling to just four or five by 2006.
—James Jungjohaan, CIBC World Markets, September 2002[3]

Q: Do you have a favorite box?
A: No, the downturn enabled everyone to catch up . . . now they are all pretty much the same. The key differences are cost and power.
—Director of Research, Top Five Service Providers, October 2002[4]

Christopher Thomas

INTRODUCTION

Optical networking, or the usage of light as the physical carrier mechanism for the transport of information, is one of the core technologies of the telecommunications ("telecom") industry. The basic building blocks of the optical networking industry are optical components.

In early 2003, components for the optical networking business fell into two major categories: true optical or opto-electronic active or passive components (lasers, filters, photodiodes, arrayed waveguide gratings, variable optical attenuators, optical amplifiers, etc.) and communications integrated circuits, or "comm-ICs." Both were necessary and complementary for use in optical networks. The former dealt in the optical domain and could be semiconductor-based, waveguide-based, or use other technologies. The latter operated almost entirely in the digital domain and performed logic processing to add intelligence in the network. They were generally designed and manufactured with "traditional" silicon CMOS techniques. Common functions performed by comm-ICs in the optical network included network processors (performing operations on Internet Protocol packets, Ethernet frames and ATM cells such as routing, encryption, flow control, and ensuring Quality of Service), Ethernet Media Access Controllers, Synchronous

Optical Network (SONET)/Synchronous Digital Hierarchy (SDH) framers and mappers (format and frame data or voice streams for transport over the SONET/SDH network), transceiver devices (performing analog multiplexing, de-multiplexing, and clock operations), and physical media-dependent devices (to drive, modulate, receive, or convert analog signals from the optical components). Different comm-ICs were also used in non-optical communications such as wireless or copper networks. This paper focuses primarily on the dynamics of the optical networking comm-IC market.

The ISO Open Systems Interconnect reference model for network design (summarized in Exhibit 1) is a useful tool for segmenting the many complex functions performed by networks. Most true optical or optoelectronics components operated primarily at Layer "0" of the protocol stack (i.e., below the network "intelligence")—they enabled simple transmission of data as it was formatted, routed, switched, protected, and checked for errors in the electronic realm by comm-ICs. (There was limited photonic-based switching and bandwidth management in the network, but this was negligible versus the electronic alternatives.) Comm-ICs worked primarily at layers 1–4 of the reference model, performing physical layer, data link, network, and transport layer operations for the network.[5]

Optical components were purchased (or sometimes manufactured internally) by system vendors. System vendors designed these different components onto line and control cards and added internally and externally designed communications and non-communications components (such as control plane processors, copper wire interconnects, field programmable gate arrays) to complete the design. System vendors sometimes relied on third-party subsystem vendors to package, assemble, and integrate these components for them. These complete systems were then bundled with extensive software, tested, qualified, and finally installed in service provider networks. The service providers (often called "carriers") managed these networks and provided a wide variety of bandwidth services either to end customers (ranging from "plain old telephone services" to high-speed international connectivity) or to other service providers who might not own or manage their own networks (see Exhibit 2).

[2]"Components Overboard," *Light Reading,* August 1, 2002, http://www.lightreading.com/document.asp?doc_id=19285.
[3]"Components Darwinism: Embracing the Upcoming Shakeout," CIBC World Markets, September 5, 2002.
[4]Quoted from personal conversation by the author.

[5]More information can be found at http://www.dis.port.ac.uk/~rogerb/nedmm/nedmm02notes.html#ISOmodel).

EXHIBIT 1   Summary of the ISO Open Systems Interconnect Model

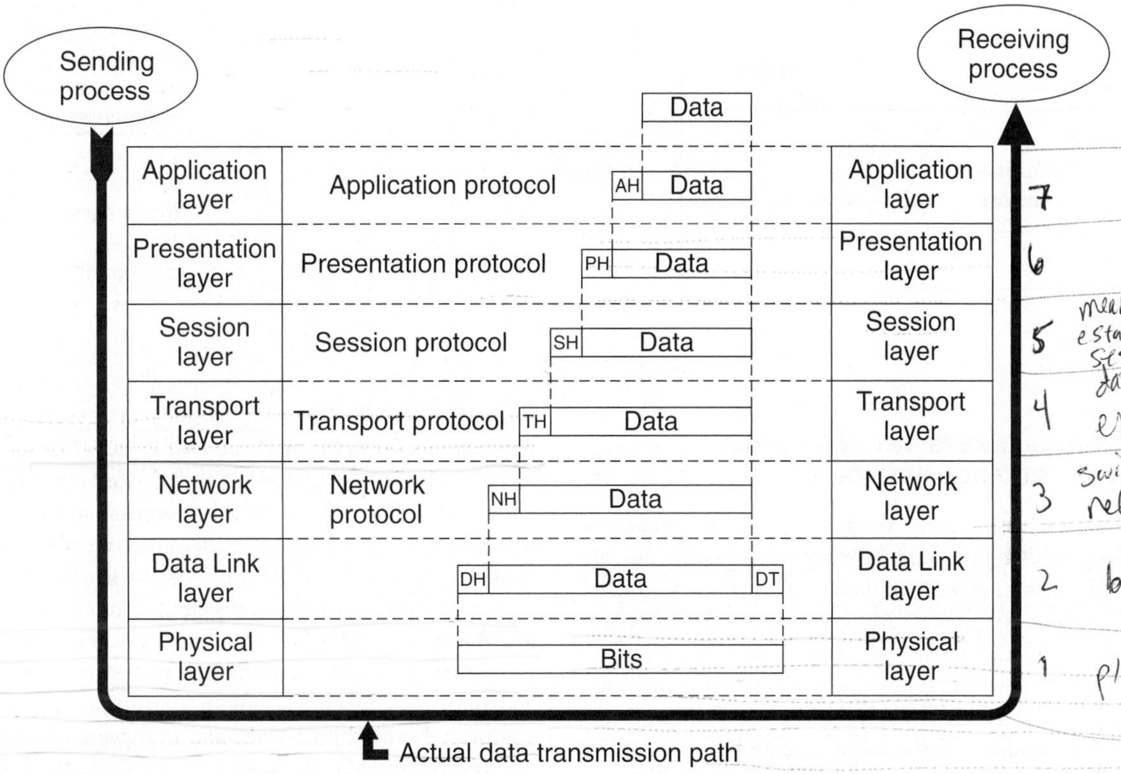

Actual data transmission path

Protocol Layer Overview (Layers 1–5 Only)

1. Physical layer

This layer defines the physical connection between the computer and the network and among the various components of the network. It includes the mechanical and electrical aspects of the connections, the plugs, cables, digital signals, etc. It is sufficiently detailed to permit manufacturers to build hardware that conforms to the standard.

2. Data link layer

This layer is responsible for maintaining the integrity of information sent between two points. It defines the techniques for overcoming a "noisy" channel and for breaking the raw bit stream seen by the physical layer into meaningful sections, or frames. Frames usually have a frame number to permit corrupt frames to be re-transmitted and some form of frame receipt acknowledgment, if needed.

3. Network layer

This layer adds destination switching, routing, and relaying functions and presents these in a manner independent of the actual network in use. This provides interconnection across a variety of interlinked networks and independence from the technologies used.

4. Transport layer

This provides reliable, transparent transfer of data between end points. It provides end-to-end error recovery and flow control. This layer was introduced with the aim of shielding upper layers from the details of specific networks across which information is to be transmitted.

5. Session layer

The purpose of this layer is to provide a means of establishing a communications session between two processes with facilities to police the session and to terminate it in an orderly fashion. It provides support for synchronization and check-points to which a return can be made in case of failure.

Source: Adapted from http://www.dis.port.ac.uk/~rogerb/nedmm/nedmm02notes.html#ISOmodel.

EXHIBIT 2 Simplified Optical Networking Value Chain

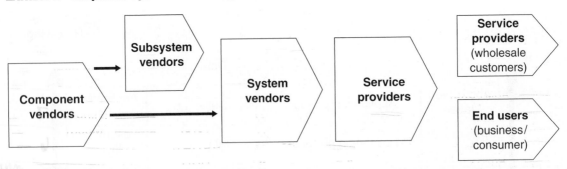

THE END MARKETS: THE WIDE AREA AND METRO AREA NETWORKS

The business of system vendor and service providers could also be segmented by the type of services they offered (even though the boundaries among these segments were often blurry). Wide Area Network ("WAN") competitors offered products or services for long-distance links among states, countries, or even across continents. Metro Area Network ("MAN") competitors offered services in discrete metropolitan locations, connecting network access aggregation points through a defined regional area. Access service providers enabled connectivity between enterprise-based Local Area Networks (LANs) or Storage Area Networks (SANs) and the metro or long-haul network. All of these networks were linked together to enable end-to-end connectivity. The telecommunications network "went optical" first in the WAN (where the greatest capacity was needed), when fiber optics replaced alternative technologies such as microwave transmission or copper wires. Optical technology then migrated to the metro and, to a certain extent, the access network. Optical technologies were only entering the enterprise, data center and storage area networks in early 2003. The WAN and MAN networks were primarily based on the SONET/SDH network hierarchy originally standardized in the 1980s. SONET/SDH networks had an enormous installed base of equipment, and the incumbent carriers were very familiar with the technology.[6]

Each of these market segments experienced different dynamics (even though the optical component or integrated circuit features for the actual end systems could have significant overlaps). This paper focuses on trends for components in the WAN and MAN networks. An abstract view of the technologies, network speeds, and commonly used optical network systems in the WAN and MAN is laid out in Exhibit 3. (Please see Exhibit 4 for an overview of SONET/SDH transmission speeds.)

Vendors addressing the opportunity for Comm-ICs in the MAN and WAN often shared two key characteristics. First, they had often acquired the technology for these end markets via acquisitions of startup companies developing these products. Second, they were often moving towards the MAN and WAN from strengths in other parts of the network. PMC-Sierra Corporation, one market leader, built its business on success in access networks and had a strong position in T1/E1/T3 (plesiochronous digital hierarchy, or PDH) products. Vitesse Corporation and Applied Micro Circuits (AMCC) entered this market via the long-haul WAN market space (the subsegment of the WAN and MAN that had been the most overbuilt during the bubble and was now the weakest overall market). These were now moving to the metro and access markets. Intel Corporation had long been a leader in enterprise (e.g., Ethernet technologies) connectivity and had entered the WAN and MAN markets via several acquisitions. While Intel had a limited product portfolio and was not yet recognized as a top player, competitors and analysts alike believed it had the opportunity, though not the certainty, of becoming a market leader. Broadcom Corporation bought vital DWDM and SONET/SDH technology via acquisition and used its superior CMOS analog design capabilities to address this market. Numerous smaller public companies, such as Transwitch Corporation and Multilink Corporation, also had product lines for these segments. Finally, despite the tremendous slowdown in venture capital funding, several startups such as Galazar, Inc., West Bay Semiconductor,

---

[6]Steven Shepard, *SONET/SDH Demystified,* 2001.

EXHIBIT 3   Simplified View of the Wide Area and Metro Area Networks

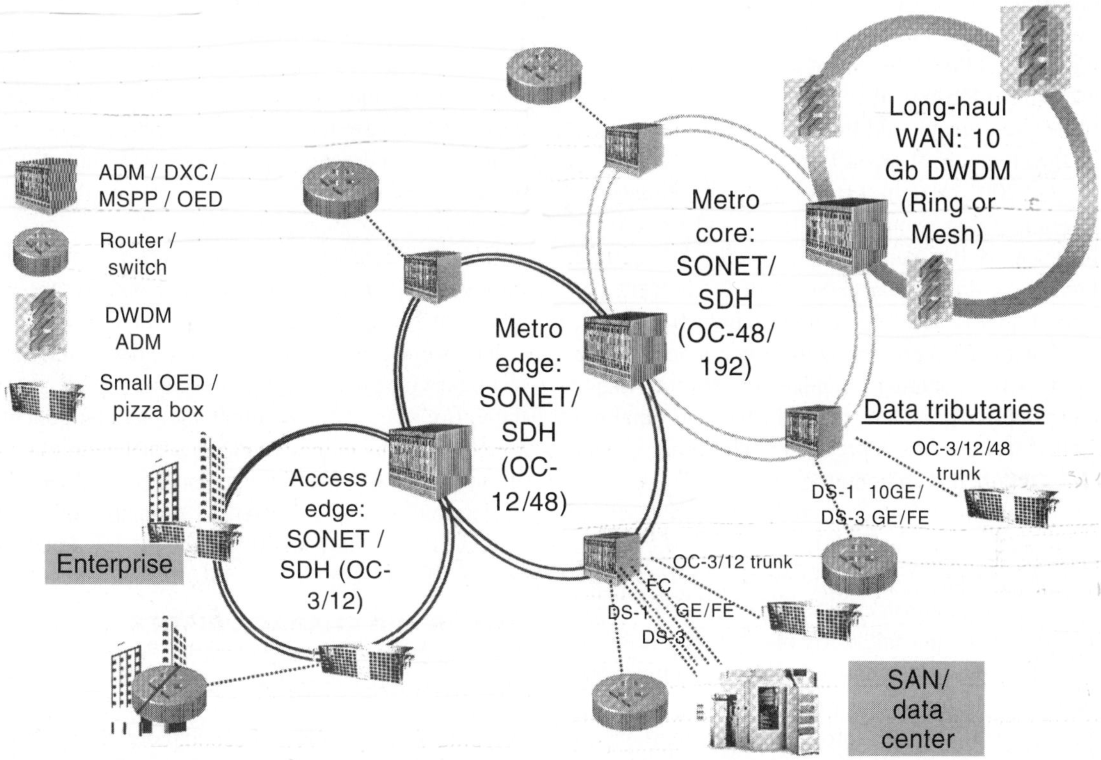

EXHIBIT 4   SONET/SDH Transmission Speeds

Protocol	Transmission speed
OC-3	155 Megabits/second
OC-12	622 Megabits/second
OC-48	2.5 Gigabits/second
OC-192	10.0 Gigabits/second
OC-768	39.8 Gigabits/second

and Ample Corporation had also garnered limited market traction.

IMPACT OF THE GREAT TELECOM BUBBLE

The full causes and effects of the telecommunications industry "bubble" between 1998 and 2000 and the subsequent "popping" of that bubble in 2001 and 2002 are subjects that cannot be fully explored here. But the general characteristics of that bubble and its aftermath are easy to summarize.

In the mid- to late-1990s, investors, corporate leaders, analysts, and others all saw an attractive mix: technological breakthroughs such as dense wavelength division multiplexing (DWDM), new end-user applications

such as the Internet and its associated technologies (e-commerce, etc.), and high stock market returns for early industry entrants. These factors combined to give investors and industry players the impression that very high profits were available in the telecommunications market. With easy access to capital, hundreds of new firms entered the market at nearly every level of the value chain. According to one observer, "Never in the history of the industry have more participants showed up in such a short period of time."[7] Large incumbent firms increased capacity by multiples. By the end of 2000, the market became crowded with competitors, often with little or no product or service differentiation.[8] Overall telecom capacity far outstripped the industry's long-term carrying capacity in nearly every niche and market segment. Too many goods and services were chasing too few buyers. This larger industry trend played out precisely to stereotype in the optical components segment. In late 2000, despite signs of slackening demand from

---

[7] Leo Hindery as quoted in "Telechasm," by Frank Rose, *Wired Magazine,* September 2001.

[8] "Khosla: Optical Markets Still Huge," *Light Reading,* January 18, 2001.

carriers, system vendors began to build inventories of opto-electronic components to unheard-of levels, doubling inventory levels between the end of 1999 and the first quarter of 2000.[9] This inventory buildup artificially inflated demand for optical components and comm-ICs, prompting even greater additions to capacity and larger product development efforts.

2001 and 2002 brought the inevitable shakeout, with intense competition, company failures, and price wars (for instance, dollar per megabit pricing on certain long-haul links dropped an average of 70 percent per year 1999 through 2002[10]). All of these industry factors, combined with a general economic recession and the uncovering of accounting scandals by several major U.S.-based service providers, created what some analysts have called a "telecom depression." The employment statistics support this extreme description. There were 500,000 layoffs in the telecommunications industry in the two years from January 2001 to early 2003.[11] This may be more personnel than were employed *in total* by pure-play Internet companies at their peak in 2000.[12]

All of this "rise and fall" took place in an era when end-user demand for delivered telecommunications bandwidth (the ultimate end product of this industry) continued to grow steadily across all major markets, in some cases at greater than 100 percent annually.[13,14]

All of the major players and segments in the telecommunications market suffered from these industry conditions. Hundreds of carriers, both large and small, declared bankruptcy. Long-time leading vendor Nortel Networks' quarterly revenue fell by 70 percent in just seven quarters from Q1 2001 to Q3 2002, or $23 billion on an annualized basis. Sycamore Networks, a newer

entrant, experienced an 85 percent decline in revenues over that same time period.[15] The optical components vendors did not fare any better than their customers. The total market value of the 28 major publicly traded optical component companies dropped 86 percent between January 2001 and September 2002, with a range of −98 percent to −48 percent.[16] Investors lost over $100 billion dollars in the new millennium by casting their fate with the optical component companies.

These negative economic conditions persisted through 2002 and into 2003. Capital expenditure budgets announced or rumored, especially for U.S. service providers, were generally thought to be below maintenance level. Service provider capital expenditure budgets drove the entire market for communications components, yet there was not enough funding even to maintain overall network capacity. The largest U.S. spender, Verizon Technologies, was expected to drop its 2003 wireline CapEx 30 percent from 2002's already low levels.[17]

TRENDS AND CHARACTERISTICS OF THE COMM-IC MARKET FOR WAN AND MAN MARKETS

While it is impossible to fully explore all of the market dynamics of the comm-IC market for the WAN and MAN, there were several key commercial and technological issues that need to be addressed by vendors in this market.

Budget Constraints for Product Development

The primary pressure that comm-IC vendors faced at the end of 2002 was, not surprisingly, economic. With virtually no funding available from the private or public markets, vendors had to be extremely careful with their product development investment choices. Not only was it difficult to justify any new product development initiatives with the extremely low near-term market opportunities, but also many development efforts were entering their final investment stages and appeared increasingly unattractive. Companies were faced with the unappetizing choice of either completing projects with funding they did not have or telling customers that they would not

[9] "Semiconductors for Communications 4.0," Merrill Lynch, March 2002.

[10] *MANs 2003*, published by TeleGeography.

[11] "Telecom Layoffs Tapering Off," *Light Reading*, October 7, 2002, http://www.lightreading.com/document.asp?doc_id=22238.

[12] *The National Investor*, August 2002, http://www.nationalinvestor.com/telecom_quagmire.htm.

[13] Several sources, including "Internet Traffic Soars, but Revenues Glide," RHK, May 2002, and "Fiber Optic Network Capacity and Utilization," Telecommunications Industry Association, September 2002.

[14] Accurately assessing the growth of total and Internet-related telecommunications traffic has been an issue of great controversy, with incomplete analyses, statements by telecom executives that either intentionally or unintentionally exaggerated traffic growth, countless research papers, and disagreement among experts characterizing the debate. For a good overview of research on the matter, please visit the website of one of the leading researchers in the field, Andrew Odlyzko at the University of Minnesota, http://www.dtc.umn.edu/~odlyzko/doc/networks.html.

[15] Wall Street Journal Telecommunications Sector Overview, http://online.wsj.com/technology/telecommunications?mod=2_0018.

[16] "Components Darwinism: Embracing the Upcoming Shakeout," *CIBC World Markets*, September 5, 2002.

[17] Mary Jander, "Carrier Spending Hopes Dim," September 24, 2002, http://www.lightreading.com/document.asp?doc_id=21652.

receive the devices that were promised. It was very probable that promising but long-term technologies would not be developed due to the lack of resources applied to their development by the component vendors.

This funding shortfall was exacerbated by the increasing expense of designing and manufacturing semiconductors on increasingly advanced processes. Most major chip designers spent millions moving their tools, intellectual property libraries, and design rules to semiconductor manufacturing processes with 130 nm minimum geometry. However, marginal costs for chips developed on 130 nm processes remained high—purchasing a mask set and manufacturing samples for a new device could cost over $1 million with multiples of that required for product research and development. In addition, some manufacturers were moving to the next process with 90 nm minimum geometry. While this new process offered substantial benefits in terms of device size and power consumption, the move required substantial investment to adapt the tools and intellectual property libraries again.

Uncertain Path to Industry Consolidation

Despite the limited dollars available for product development and the bankruptcy/retrenchment of numerous market entrants, the comm-IC market continued to exhibit a high level of competition; at least 12 substantial vendors were still addressing this market.

However, most external analysts (and most internal industry observers) believed that the overall market opportunity for comm-ICs in the MAN and WAN was too small to support more than two to four vendors.[18] With the movement to higher speed and more highly integrated devices on ever smaller semiconductor geometries, product development costs were rising rapidly. It was simply too expensive for five to seven companies to spend the 10 million dollars or more necessary to develop similar components all aimed at the same limited market opportunities.

It was commonly asserted that the "tyranny of the market" would rapidly reduce the number of players and competing products to an economically prudent level. This was so evident in the venture capital market that the conventional wisdom ran, "No investor wants to fund R&D anymore."[19] The budget constraints were also threatening to leave established players with incom-

plete product portfolios. Even they were being reduced to competing in niches and hoping that the return on investment would be improved by competitors exiting from that niche. Competitors might also choose to broaden their portfolios by adding complementary product lines or resources through acquisition or merger. Both of these actions would generally reduce the number of competitors in the MAN and WAN market. See Exhibit 5.

However, by early 2003, very little consolidation had taken place in the MAN and WAN comm-IC market. There had been no major announced mergers of equals or large acquisitions by even larger competitors. Some analysts theorized that corporate management was so focused on near-term budget, customer and capital market pressures that there was no time for the strategic and operational evaluation of large consolidation efforts.[20] A desire to avoid stock purchases at the market's current low level and the need to conserve cash reserves also played into these decisions. Finally, there was still an open debate on the type of combinations that would take place. Would the market move towards vertical integration, whereby comm-IC vendors would combine with opto-electronic or pure optical concerns to be able to provide both solutions for the MAN and WAN, or would it move towards horizontal integration, whereby two players with competing comm-IC portfolios would combine and rationalize their product lines? The consolidation paths chosen (either explicitly due to action or implicitly due to inertia) by senior management at the leading market players would determine long-term structure, level of competition, and thus profitability of the comm-IC market.

Economic Impacts of the Changing Service Provider Mix

The telecom industry meltdown not only impacted the overall market opportunity, but it also radically changed the relative mix of customers for comm-IC products. Much of the system vendor demand during 1999–2001 was driven by emerging, newly funded carriers: Competitive Local Exchange Carriers (CLECs) such as Allegiance Telecom and CTC Communications; MAN Ethernet Service Providers such as Yipes Enterprise Services and Telseon Incorporated; and new entrants to the long-haul service provider market such as Level 3

---

[18]Numerous research reports and personal conversations with the author.

[19]Quoted from personal conversation with the author.

[20]"Components Darwinism: Embracing the Upcoming Shakeout," CIBC World Markets, September 5, 2002, and "Semiconductors for Communications 4.0," Merrill Lynch, March 2002.

EXHIBIT 5   Evolution of the Optical Networking Value Chain in the MAN and WAN

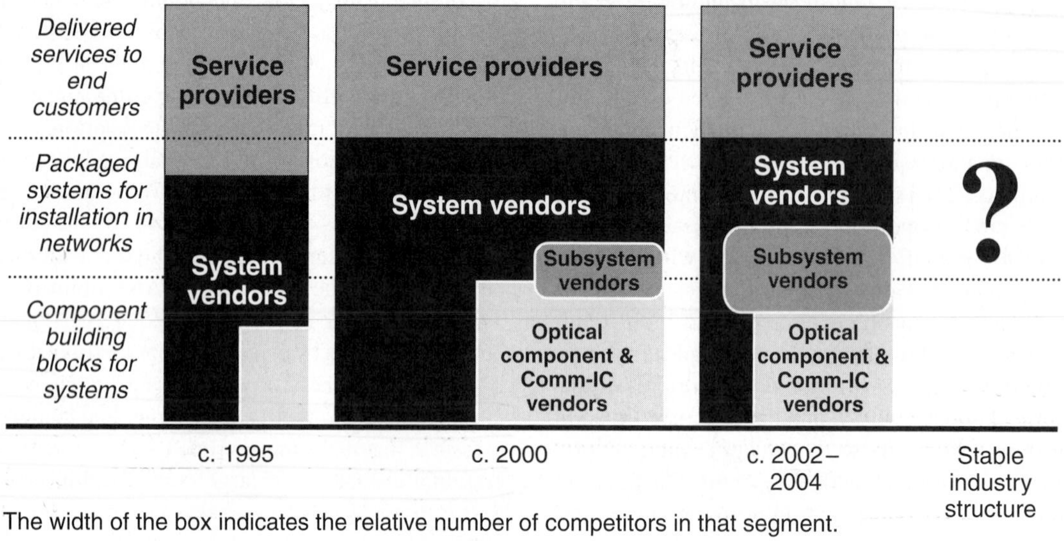

The width of the box indicates the relative number of competitors in that segment.

Networks and Global Crossing, Ltd. However, the downturn in the market in 2002 left these vendors either bankrupt or with reduced funds for capital spending. Service provider spending, especially in the United States and Europe, was now driven by the better-funded incumbent carriers such as Verizon, AT&T Corporation, Deutsche Telekom, SBC Corporation, and others. The percentage of U.S. capital expenditures by emerging carriers was expected to fall from 16 percent of total spending in 2000 to 3 percent in 2002.[21]

Incumbent carriers had different purchasing requirements and customer relationships than the emerging carriers. They had far larger and more complex networks, with equipment from many different eras of the telecom industry. They also tended to be more conservative in technical and business matters and wary of protecting existing revenue streams. Thus, incumbent service providers tended to buy their equipment from more established and "traditional" system vendors than the CLECs, who often purchased equipment from newer, emerging system vendors.

Comm-IC vendors who had built products and developed customer relationships to win business with the emerging system vendors or to support the greenfield networks of new carriers realized they might need to change their business model and product development efforts to "follow the money."

The Outsourcing of Component Development from the System Vendors

Fifteen years ago, the major system vendors were vertically integrated across components, subsystems, and finished products. Over time, merchant market component suppliers such as JDS Uniphase and PMC-Sierra (in the pure optical components and the comm-IC markets, respectively) entered and began to supply components or subsystems to these vendors. This trend has accelerated in the last few years for several reasons, including (1) the emergence of new system players without the "in-house" optical component expertise; (2) the increasing costs to semiconductor development as transistor densities multiplied, giving the advantage to projects that could spread costs out over several customers rather than one in-house project; and (3) reduced engineering capacity at the system vendors due to the massive layoffs discussed earlier.[22]

The most evident outsourcing moves were from major system vendors that had entirely abandoned their internal development of pure optical components. Alcatel Net-

---

[21] "Global Telebits," UBS Warburg, July 10, 2002.

[22] "Components Darwinism: Embracing the Upcoming Shakeout," CIBC World Markets, September 5, 2002, and "Semiconductors for Communications 4.0," Merrill Lynch, March 2002.

works and Nortel Networks substantially abandoned the optical components business in 2002, offering to sell their operations or, absent an adequate bid, to just "shut the doors."[23] They were joined by major component vendor Agere Systems, a company which exited the industry its predecessor essentially founded, when it was a part of AT&T. (Agere will continue to compete in comm-ICs.)[24]

As of early 2003, the final level of vertical integration in the optical system and components industry segments remained to be seen.

Such a development would lead to another industry dynamic and possible dilemma. The system vendors had the greatest repository of optical networking technology, system, and topology knowledge. They had always driven the technology envelope. However, the constant improvement in semiconductor manufacturing techniques had enabled comm-ICs to become ever more powerful. Comm-IC vendors would be able to integrate more and more functions into a single device. In this eventuality, component vendors could become the "drivers" of technological development in the industry: What they built would determine which network capabilities would be enabled. However, these comm-IC vendors generally did not possess the same level of systems expertise as the incumbent system vendors. The ideal business model for transferring that systems expertise from the system vendors to the comm-IC vendors remained unclear.

Technical Choices to Address Multi-Protocol Nature of Metro Access Networks

Systems designed for the access edge of the MAN, where the traditional SONET/SDH network and the SAN, LAN, and traditional telecom access networks met, have had to deal with a dizzying array of complementary and competing technologies and standards. The amount of bandwidth connectivity in the metro access had traditionally been multiples below both that in the LAN on one side and the WAN on the other, making it an area of great opportunity.[25] Service providers attempted, with difficulty, to build low-cost services across these access points for customers to connect enterprise, LAN, and SAN networks through the WAN or MAN. One of

the reasons for this struggle was the wide variety of protocols and technologies that had to be taken into account in system design. In the telecom industry, "a carrier doesn't take out a box that's making money."[26] Thus, emerging and disparate technologies such as 10-Gigabit Ethernet, virtual concatenation, and Generic Framing Protocol have to interoperate and take into account 20-year-old (or older) technologies such as ESCON or Frame Relay. All of these different protocols and their interworking requirements created great complexity in comm-IC and system design.

Enabling the Existing MAN and WAN Network to Efficiently Carry Data

This market dynamic was linked to the one above. The established optical network primarily used the time division multiplexing-based SONET/SDH protocol as the standardized transport mechanism in the WAN and the MAN; subsequently, nearly all optical networking took place on SONET/SDH systems. This protocol was optimized to encapsulate and transport analog voice traffic over optical networks. However, by early 2003, the majority of MAN and WAN traffic was data, generally Ethernet, Internet Protocol (IP), or Fiber Channel (FC) traffic generated by end users in enterprises or residences (and demand for data continued to grow far more rapidly than demand for voice[27]). While each of these data protocols had a native transport layer that enabled it to be utilized *without* the SONET/SDH hierarchy, service providers were reluctant to build entirely new MAN and WAN networks for this data traffic, especially in an uncertain economic environment. Yet system vendors and their component suppliers had been tasked to enable solutions that were amenable and efficient for transporting data and that leveraged the billions invested in SONET/SDH.

The Uncertain Migration Path to DWDM Technologies in the MAN

DWDM technologies, or the ability to "pack" numerous different wavelengths on a single optical fiber, were firmly established in the WAN market and were used primarily as solutions to augment capacity. However, the role of DWDM in metro networks was less clear. DWDM began to migrate to the short-haul MAN in 1997 and 1998. It was not until several years later that

[23] Pauline Rigby, "Opto Units: Red Tag Sale," *Light Reading,* August 23, 2002.
[24] "Moving On: What Agere's Departure Means for the Company and the Industry," *CIR Optical Components Watch,* August 2002.
[25] "Finding Light in Optics' Future," Forrester Research, September 2001.
[26] Quoted from personal conversation with the author.
[27] "Internet Traffic Soars, but Revenues Glide," RHK, May 2002.

these DWDM technologies garnered significant interest from MAN service providers.[28] However, the implementation of these technologies remained unclear, and vendors continued to provide a wide variety of other technologies to offer DWDM services. Some offered protocol-transparent wavelength services that were indifferent to the data being wrapped; others used new DWDM framing protocols such as ITU G.709 optical transport network (OTN) digital wrappers. Still others attempted to switch and route wavelengths entirely in the optical realm (commonly called optical-optical-optical or "OOO" switching), while a few preferred to offer the additional granularity and bandwidth management of switching in the electrical realm.[29] In addition, it was unclear for how long DWDM technologies would remain in stand-alone transport platforms before they would be fully integrated into more "traditional" SONET/SDH add-drop multiplexers and digital crossconnects that provided circuit provisioning and bandwidth management.

Each of these different DWDM system design options required a different underlying comm-IC to perform protocol, bandwidth, and transport management. Comm-IC vendors would need to "place bets" on different views of the DWDM technology migration to the metro.

The Continued Pushout of the "All-Optical" Network

During the peak of the boom years, there was increasing momentum behind the idea of "all-optical networks," transferring those layer 1, 2, and 3 digital activities to the photonic world. This would involve switching, routing, and provisioning at the wavelength level, rather than on the digital bits that were encoded in the analog wavelength. Proponents of this technology believed that it would lower equipment and network management costs and improve network scalability: "Throw in the benefit of staying that price whether you put OC-48, OC-192, or OC-768 through it, since a beam of light looks quite the same no matter how it's modulated."[30] Yet, despite the market penetration of DWDM technologies, the market opportunity for all-optical services such as wavelength routing and switching remained elusive; major system vendors Cisco Systems, Lucent Technologies, and Nortel Networks stopped their primary product development

in this area in 2002.[31] There were many reasons for this, but two primary causes were commonly referred to by industry analysts: (1) that service providers want to provision, manage, and scale their networks at very fine granularities (far below the bandwidth capacity of a lambda), and (2) that the constant improvement in the performance/cost ratio of comm-ICs reduced the economic benefits of operating entirely in the analog optical domain. In the words of one analyst:

> The enthusiasm around transparent optical networks was driven by the belief that the pace of bandwidth demand in a network core would consistently outstrip Moore's law, driving electronics costs through the roof. The only solution seemed to be one that eliminated electronics, replacing them with optics. . . .
> Today, my guess is that the photonic future will forever be out of reach, not because of technology but because of network economics.[32]

However, the continued economic and technological uncertainty that plagued the optical networking industry made predictions about the long-term network structure very difficult; the "all-optical" network seemed a possibility that might become a reality someday.

CONCLUSION

The optical components industry had endured one of the greatest creations and subsequent destructions of "paper wealth" in industrial history. At its peak, the market value of Transwitch Corporation, a medium-sized comm-IC vendor, was greater than the October 2002 combined market value of Nortel Networks and Lucent Technologies. These two long-time system vendors essentially invented, designed, and built optical networking in North America (and most of Asia and South America as well). Market players were only now adjusting their strategies and market perspectives to this new reality of greatly reduced market opportunities and the end of easy money.

In the words of one analyst, "Most vendors have accepted the bad news. There is no 'second wave' coming, but the market is not going down to zero either."[33] Even with this new realistic perspective, component vendors

---

[28] Jack Hunt, Nortel Networks, as quoted in "Metro DWDM," *Light Reading,* September 23, 2002.

[29] "Metro DWDM," *Light Reading,* September 23, 2002.

[30] "Building Optical Networks Digitally," *Light Reading,* August 1, 2002,

[31] "Lucent Terminates the LambdaRouter," http://www.lightreading. com/document.asp?doc_id=19801, and "Cisco Kills Monterey Router," http://www.lightreading.com/document.asp?doc_id=4575.

[32] Scott Clavenna as quoted in "Building Optical Networks Digitally," *Light Reading,* August 1, 2002, http://www.lightreading.com/document.asp?doc_id=19291.

[33] Vladimir Kozlov, "NFOEC and ECOC 2002 Review," RHK, September 26, 2002.

faced innumerable challenges—lack of funding, too much competition, numerous technology choices, industry consolidation, and the unappetizing task of downsizing development teams to deal with empty bank accounts. Perhaps most difficult of all was making decisions despite the lack of information from "stalled" markets exhibiting little commercial activity. Or, as an executive at a major components firm lamented, "It's difficult to understand what customers want when nobody's buying anything. If I sell one of this type of chip and two of that type of chip, does that mean the second chip is attacking twice as big a market?"[34]

CASE II-3

CIENA Corporation

In an environment of carriers facing massive debt and bankruptcies, CIENA's strategy can be summarized as the two "I's": Incumbents and Integration.
—Gary Smith, CEO of CIENA Corporation, May 15, 2002[1]

Ben Shih, Juan Posada, and Yann Ngongang

INTRODUCTION

Of course, it was not just the telecommunications carriers who faced difficulties in the telecom bust that followed the Internet implosion in 2000. The market for telecom equipment suppliers, which had been strong for the latter half of the 1990s, turned down dramatically in

---

[34]Quoted from personal conversation with the author.
Source: Ben Shih (M.B.A. 2002), Juan Posada, (M.B.A. 2002), and Yann Ngongang (M.B.A. 2003) prepared this case under the supervision of Professor Robert A. Burgelman and Philip E. Meza as the basis for class discussion rather than to illustrate either effective or ineffective handling of an administrative situation. The authors wish to thank Francois Locoh-Donou (M.B.A. 2002) for his support during the development of this case. Copyright © 2002 by the Board of Trustees of the Leland Stanford Junior University. All rights reserved. To order copies or request permission to reproduce materials, e-mail the Case Writing Office at cwo@gsb.stanford.edu or write Case Writing Office, Stanford Graduate School of Business, 518 Memorial Way, Stanford University, Stanford, Calif. 94305-5015. No part of this publication may be reproduced, stored in a retrieval system, used in a spreadsheet, or transmitted in any form or by any means—electronic, mechanical, photocopying, recording, or otherwise—without the permission of the Stanford Graduate School of Business.
[1]All quotes from Gary Smith are from the authors' interview unless otherwise indicated.

2000 and continued to weaken. Some equipment suppliers went out of business while others struggled to redefine themselves. In May 2002, Gary Smith, Chief Executive Officer of CIENA, discussed his strategy for the company. Tying his technology vision with economic reality, Smith said, "the two 'I's—Incumbents and Integration—are our new focus." Integration described the company's internal efforts to develop the end-to-end network. Incumbents referred to the company's new strategy of pursuing the top 30 or 35 global telecom carriers that were responsible for 80 percent of the world's spending on optical networking. Smith said, "The effort requires moving quickly [against competitors] to get in and create the right fit."

Smith pointed to three specific challenges CIENA faced. "First, short-term tactics had to be balanced against long-term strategy." New technology development required at least two years to bring to market. However, diminishing profits made spending on research and development difficult. "Second, the shift in customer concentration was also leading CIENA to evolve from a United States–centric company to a global firm," a process that was not yet complete in 2002. "Third, the current environment presented an opportunity for CIENA to capture new customers." Smith observed that carriers were "worried about their existing vendors who exhibited a risk of failure during this time. These carriers became willing to initiate new relationships."

The widespread failures and capital expenditure cuts among CIENA's customer base presented the company with new and fundamental challenges. How could CIENA ensure its viability in this contracting marketplace? Should the company try to find the next winning product or should it focus on its current market position? More broadly, how should CIENA change to meet the challenges presented by the precipitous fall in spending among its customers?

HISTORY AND EVOLUTION OF CIENA

CIENA designs and sells optical networking equipment and services for telecommunication service providers. As a startup, it revolutionized the telecom industry in 1996 by releasing the first commercial product based on the Dense Wavelength Division Multiplexing (DWDM)[2] optical transport technology, helping to create a segment

---

[2]DWDM is a technology that combines data from different sources on an optical fiber, with each signal carried at the same time on its own separate light wavelength.

that generated an estimated $1.6 billion in revenues for CIENA and a 19 percent market share in 2001.[3] From its leadership position in optical transport equipment, the company anticipated the next untapped market in telecom: optical switching.[4] In 1999, CIENA acquired Lightera, a startup developing an intelligent optical switch, and in 2000 the company released the world's first optical switch, the CoreDirector™. With a 12-month lead on its competition, CIENA used the CoreDirector to carve out another billion-dollar category in the telecom equipment market. With these two successful product breakthroughs, CIENA claimed a place among the much larger, established telecom equipment manufacturers.

CIENA was founded in 1992 by Dr. David Huber, a physicist who patented a number of innovations around DWDM technology for multiplexing multiple light signals on a single optical fiber. Huber intended to apply this technology to cable television equipment. This DWDM technology enabled all types of data (voice, video, Internet traffic, etc.) to be pushed through fiber optic cables on up to 16 channels per fiber for 600 km without regeneration. At the time, digital networking companies used SONET (Synchronous Optical Network)[5] technology to transport a single channel per fiber with regeneration at every 30 km.

Voice traffic differs technically from data traffic in the way it is measured (minutes versus bytes); in the impact of latency on the quality of service the end user perceives (delays are virtually unnoticeable in data applications but very significant in voice applications); in the average time a given connection is established (a data connection might last hours or even days; a voice connection rarely lasts this long); and in the ability to deal with network congestion (handled more easily in data networks). Despite these differences, both voice and data networks benefited greatly from the increased capacity provided by CIENA's DWDM technology because of the dramatic decrease in the cost of long-haul transport of data.

CIENA received venture capital funding in 1994 in a round led by Sevin Rosen Funds. After providing the funding, Jon Bayless, a general partner at Sevin Rosen, recommended that Huber consider applying his technology to the voice and data carrier market instead of the cable television market. As a pre-condition to funding

the company, Bayless recommended that Huber hire Dr. Patrick Nettles, a former telecom network equipment executive, as President and CEO instrumental in reformulating the strategy of CIENA. Huber followed both recommendations.

Core DWDM Transport (1996–1998)

Working with $40 million from a second-round venture investment, Huber and Nettles focused the company on designing and manufacturing a DWDM system (eventually the MultiWave Sentry® 1600) that allowed voice and data telecom service providers to increase the channel density and reach of their optical networks. Introduced with a 12-month lead on the competition, the MultiWave Sentry reduced the cost of carrying one gigabit of data per second per kilometer by 70 percent from an estimated $700 in 1994.[6]

Three major forces—deregulation, the Internet, and a tech-enamored capital market—created a strategic inflection point in the industry in the middle of the 1990s.[7] Due to projected exponential growth in data traffic, network operators had to increase their network capacity or lose customers to the new competitors created by the unprecedented influx of capital into the industry. In 1999, there were more than 1,600 Competitive Local Exchange Carriers (CLECs) operating in the country, and during 2000, CLECs received more than $3.4 billion in venture capital funding.[8] These emerging carriers did not have a long history or established relationships with incumbent suppliers and differentiated themselves with better technology. CIENA capitalized on the opportunity to sell to these next-generation carriers, capturing 15 customers by the end of 1998 and generating revenues of over $500 million (Exhibits 1 and 2).

CIENA introduced its product to incumbent long distance providers such as Sprint and WorldCom as well as fast growing startups like Williams and Broadwing, which were flush with capital and wanted the latest telecommunications equipment. In January 1997, CIENA announced that WorldCom had selected CIENA as its exclusive DWDM-system supplier. In fewer than six months, CIENA's revenues from Sprint and WorldCom grew to $60 million, and revenues of $374 million would

---

[3] "Optical Systems," *Merrill Lynch Research,* April 1, 2002, p. 28.
[4] Switching is the optical networking technology that directs individual optical wavelengths to specific network paths. Switches enable packets of data to move to the correct network destination.
[5] SONET is a standard for synchronous data transmission on optical media.

[6] All quotes from Steve Chaddick are from the authors' interview on April 23, 2002.
[7] Coined by Intel co-founder, chairman, and former CEO Andrew S. Grove, a strategic inflection point refers to the point in time at which the forces governing a company or industry fundamentally change, allowing the business to ascend to new heights or fall to new depths.
[8] Bruce Kramer, "Telecommunications in the U.S.: State of the Marketplace," *Faulkner Information Services,* December 2001, pp. 3–4.

EXHIBIT 1 CIENA's SEC Quarterly Cumulative Balance Sheet Report

Currency: USD

Assets	07/31/02	04/30/02	01/31/02	10/31/01	07/31/01	04/30/01	01/31/01	10/31/00
Cash	715.18	514.73	472.53	397.89	869.60	1,144.21	176.73	143.19
Marketable Securities	971.76	853.99	1,051.12	902.59	528.82	357.16	82.96	95.13
Receivables	43.29	61.19	150.22	395.06	370.76	267.01	251.00	248.95
Inventories	65.48	75.57	250.19	254.97	306.57	276.02	207.22	141.28
Raw Materials								
Work In Progress								
Finished Goods								
Notes Receivable								
Other Current Assets	64.80	56.25	107.34	240.57	219.54	199.33	207.29	184.47
Total Current Assets	1,860.51	1,561.74	2,031.41	2,191.09	2,295.30	2,243.73	925.19	813.01
Net Property & Equipment	248.14	214.88	316.04	331.49	314.90	622.49	212.38	189.23
Property, Plant & Equipment	248.14	214.88	316.04	331.49	314.90	622.49	212.38	189.23
Accumulated Depr.								
Interest & Adv to Subsidiaries	566.54	348.94	416.33	494.66	369.60			
Other Non-Current Assets								
Deferred Charges	54.48	52.55						
Intangibles	822.92	223.14	224.95	226.77	2,023.86	2,099.36	8.85	9.05
Deposits & Other Assets	77.46	72.00	230.05	73.30	66.40	64.85	20.74	15.91
Total Assets	**3,630.03**	**2,473.25**	**3,218.78**	**3,317.30**	**5,070.06**	**5,030.42**	**1,167.15**	**1,027.20**

Liabilities	07/31/02	04/30/02	01/31/02	10/31/01	07/31/01	04/30/01	01/31/01	10/31/00
Notes Payable								
Accounts Payable	53.14	48.07	46.96	68.74	95.29	115.41	82.48	70.25
Current Long Term Debt			176.53					
Current Portion Capital Lease								
Accrued Expense	156.31	164.81	125.88	148.52	135.97	128.67	90.41	84.16
Income Taxes	7.27	6.25	6.40	6.65	6.29	7.23	7.27	7.48
Other Current Liabilities	47.37	22.50	22.59	30.48	31.91	19.26	21.01	11.44
Total Current Liabilities	264.09	241.63	378.37	254.38	269.47	270.57	201.16	173.34
Mortgages								
Deferred Charges to Income	73.65	69.33	76.30	64.07	39.15	39.55	39.15	39.15
Convertable Debt	910.59	690.00	690.00	863.88	866.83	864.19		
Long Term Debt								
Non-Current Capital Leases								
Other Long Term Liabilities	111.48	5.61	5.74	5.98			4.99	4.88
Total Liabilities	**1,359.81**	**1,006.57**	**1,150.41**	**1,188.32**	**1,175.44**	**1,174.32**	**245.29**	**217.37**
Minority Interest (Liab)								
Preferred Stock								
Common Stock Net	4.32	3.30	3.29	3.28	3.27	3.27	2.88	2.87
Capital Surplus	4,649.75	3,688.25	3,676.19	3,667.51	3,708.80	3,703.52	615.90	557.26
Retained Earnings	−2,386.15	−2,226.16	−1,614.01	−1,543.42	258.87	253.21	303.89	250.65
Treasury Stock								
Shareholders' Equity	**2,270.22**	**1,466.68**	**2,068.37**	**2,128.98**	**3,894.62**	**3,856.11**	**921.86**	**809.84**
Total Liabilities & Net Worth	**3,630.03**	**2,473.25**	**3,218.78**	**3,317.30**	**5,070.06**	**5,030.42**	**1,167.15**	**1,027.20**
Rate Used to Translate from USD to USD	1.00	1.00	1.00	1.00	1.00	1.00	1.00	1.00

EXHIBIT 2   CIENA's Revenues and Performance

SEC Quarterly Cumulative Income Statement

Currency: USD

Quarterly Income Statement	07/31/02	04/30/02	01/31/02	10/31/01	07/31/01	04/30/01	01/31/01	10/31/00
Net Sales	50.03	87.05	162.16	367.77	458.07	425.40	351.99	287.59
Cost of Goods Sold	92.15	310.80	139.69	221.55	259.65	231.51	191.84	158.01
Gross Profit	−42.12	−223.75	22.47	146.22	198.42	193.89	160.15	129.58
R&D Expenditure	53.95	59.56	64.76	72.19	65.79	100.24	43.51	36.67
Selling General & Admin Expenses	40.39	59.17	51.26	54.05	47.83	55.57	40.78	66.72
Income Before Depreciation & Amortization	−136.46	−342.47	−93.54	19.98	84.80	38.07	75.86	26.19
Depreciation & Amortization	2.34	1.81	1.81	78.80	77.02	26.37		
Non-Operating Income	−9.96	−111.23	−1.10	−1,732.51	−2.41	17.97	4.30	12.06
Interest Expense	10.61	8.64	10.51	12.10	11.28	7.13	0.09	0.08
Income Before Taxes	−159.38	−464.15	−106.96	−1,803.43	−5.91	22.55	80.07	38.17
Provision for Income Taxes	0.61	148.00	−36.37	−1.15	−11.57	73.23	26.82	12.41
Minority Interest (Inc)								
Investment Gain (Loss)								
Other Income								
Net Income Before Extraordinary Items	−159.99	−612.15	−70.59	−1,802.28	5.65	−50.68	53.25	25.76
Extraordinary Items & Disc Ops								
Net Income	−159.99	−612.15	−70.59	−1,802.28	5.65	−50.68	53.25	25.76
Common Shares Outstanding (th):	431,507	329,813	328,578	286,531	286,531	326,454	286,531	286,531
Rate Used to Translate from USD to USD	1.00	1.00	1.00	1.00	1.00	1.00	1.00	1.00

eventually be achieved in FY1997.[9] With its revenue growth, technology leadership, and growing customer base, CIENA completed an initial public offering (IPO) in February 1997 that valued the company at $3.7 billion. Subsequently, secondary offerings raised $400 million in July 1997 and $600 million in February 2001.

Soon after the success of the MultiWave, Huber left CIENA, citing disagreements with other members of the management team and the board of directors. Huber was convinced that CIENA should next focus on the optical-optical (OO) approach to data transmission and switching. Theoretically, compared to the existing optical-electrical-optical (OEO) networks, the OO technology would provide remarkable performance gains. Except for Huber, CIENA senior management was convinced that the technology was far from ready.

In June 1998, CIENA announced that it had agreed to merge with Tellabs, a leader in voice and data communications equipment with FY1998 revenues of $1.6 billion. Minutes before the shareholder vote, AT&T informed CIENA that it had discontinued testing CIENA's trans-

port equipment. Industry speculation was that the timing of AT&T's announcement was not coincidental and that perhaps Lucent, a CIENA rival, pressured AT&T's management into this decision. CIENA postponed the shareholder meeting following the news.[10] In the wake of AT&T's announcement, CIENA's management team felt that a fair price was unobtainable, and the merger talks were cancelled. CIENA's stock price fell from a high of approximately $100 per share to $10 per share after the cancellation.

By the end of 1998, competitive offerings in the DWDM transport category imposed price pressure on CIENA whose margins dropped as a result. At the time, many industry observers believed that the basis for competitive advantage would shift from technology leadership to low-cost and large-scale manufacturing. Believing that it could not survive as a one-product company, CIENA looked for new ways to differentiate itself in new optical telecommunications technologies.

---

[9] Hoovers Online (www.hoovers.com) historical financials on CIENA Corporation.

[10] "Falling Star," *Kiplinger's Personal Finance Magazine*, April 1999, http://media.kiplinger.com/magazine/archives/1999/April/rocket4.htm.

EXHIBIT 2 (continued)

SEC 5-Year Summary Report

Currency: USD

Balance Sheet	10/31/01	10/31/00	10/31/99	10/31/98	10/31/97
Total Current Assets	2,191.09	813.01	455.92	378.65	378.65
Total Current Liabilities	254.38	173.34	105.53	64.62	53.60
Other Assets	240.57	184.47	46.65	39.52	11.23
Total Assets	3,317.30	1,027.20	677.84	602.81	447.23
Total Liabilities	1,188.32	217.37	147.36	101.77	83.64
Total Common Equity	2,128.98	809.84	530.47	501.04	363.58

Income Statement	10/31/01	10/31/00	10/31/99	10/31/98	10/31/97
Sales	1,603.23	858.75	482.09	508.09	413.22
Cost of Goods Sold	904.55	477.39	299.77	256.01	166.47
Net Income	−1,794.06	81.39	−3.92	45.70	115.57

Cash Flow Statement	10/31/01	10/31/00	10/31/99	10/31/98	10/31/97
Net Cash Flow from Operating	156.99	59.04	28.68	48.84	84.70
Net Cash Flow from Investing	−1,490.64	−103.17	−149.74	−106.98	−67.03
Net Cash Flow from Financing	1,588.35	43.88	13.79	35.57	231.58
Rate Used to Translate from USD to USD	1.00	1.00	1.00	1.00	1.00

CIENA Corp Revenue Segmentation

	FY2000	FY2001	FY2002E	FY2003E
Net Sales	$858	$1,603	$354	$260
Long Haul DWDM	$713	$1,203	$102	$29
CoreDirector	$38	$218	$124	$91
Metro DWDM	$62	$92	$46	$56
Cyras (Metro switching)	$0	$3	$27	$41
Services	$63	$85	$54	$42
International Sales	$272	$384	?	?

Source: Lehman Brothers, "It's All Relative" Report, August 2002.

Core Switching (1998–2000)

CIENA began in-house development of an intelligent optical switch.[11] According to Steve Alexander, CIENA's Chief Technology Officer, the company realized from interacting with customers that a next generation switching platform was needed to accommodate the channel growth introduced by DWDM transport.[12] The company started developing an intelligent optical switch internally using OEO technologies, while Steve Chaddick, then the VP of Corporate Development, searched for startups to acquire that had already tackled this problem. According to Alexander, customer relationships enabled CIENA to determine the specific features of a switch that would open this emerging bottleneck.

In early 1999, Steve Chaddick reported to the management team that he had found a startup, Lightera, which was developing the CoreDirector, an intelligent optical switch that met CIENA's requirements. While many other competitors had optical switches on their drawing boards, Lightera's was the closest to deployment.[13] In March, CIENA acquired the 60-person startup

[11] The intelligence in an optical switch refers to technology that allows it to make decisions automatically, without the manual intervention that is required in the first-generation switches, which were simply digital cross-connects.

[12] All quotes from Steve Alexander are from the authors' interview on May 9, 2002.

[13] Including Xros (later acquired by Nortel), Monterey (later acquired by Cisco), Calient, Tellium, Sycamore, Corvis, and several others.

EXHIBIT 3 Summary of Selected CIENA Acquisitions

In an effort to be the premier provider of next generation optical products and services, CIENA has embarked on a path of intense product innovation. In addition, they have continually surveyed the progress of existing early phase companies that, if acquired, would catapult CIENA further ahead than if they were to attempt to develop the product internally. CIENA has acquired several of these promising startups including AstraCom, ATI, Terabit, Lightera, Omnia, Cyras, and ONI.

AstraCom
On December 10, 1997, CIENA announced the first of their acquisitions—that of AstraCom. Valued at approximately $13 million, the acquisition basically provided CIENA with 14 talented engineers.

ATI
On January 26, 1998, CIENA announced the second of their acquisitions—that of ATI Telecom International of Canada. ATI was a service provider in the Engineering, Furnishing, and Installation (EF&I) of telecommunications products. The goal of this acquisition was to not only provide customers with high quality products, but to be able to provide consulting services to design and install systems that utilize that equipment. The deal was valued at approximately $52.5 million.

Terabit
A short time later, on April 22, 1998, CIENA announced their third acquisition. In a transaction valued at $11.7 million, CIENA announced that they had acquired Terabit Technology, Inc., a maker of optical components called photodetectors and optical receivers. This vertical integration would allow CIENA to produce their own components for less than purchasing from suppliers would cost.

Lightera
With the acquisition of Lightera, CIENA entered the optical switching business. Announced on March 15, 1999, and com-

pleted on March 31, 1999, this acquisition was valued at $463 million.

Omnia
Considered by many industry experts to be a failure, the acquisition of Omnia, maker of optical products that service the "last mile," was announced simultaneously with the Lightera acquisition on March 15, 1999. The acquisition was completed on July 6, 1999. CIENA acquired Omnia in exchange for 16 million shares of CIENA stock, valued at approximately $464 million.

Cyras
On December 19, 2000, CIENA announced plans to acquire Cyras for approximately $2.6 billion. Cyras makes a product called K2, which is a data-optimized SONET platform that combines the functions of stand-alone digital cross-connects (DCS), SONET add/drop multiplexers (ADMs), ATM switches, Frame Relay switches, and digital subscriber line access multiplexers (DSLAMs). The K2 also supports WDM.

ONI
On February 18, 2002, CIENA and ONI announced a definitive agreement under which the companies would combine to form a new next-generation optical networking leader. Based on the terms of the agreement and the closing price of CIENA stock on Friday, February 15, 2002, the deal is valued at approximately $900 million.

Source: CIENA Press Releases.

---

for $500 million, and Chaddick moved to Cupertino, California, to head this new switching division (Exhibit 3). Rick Dodd, a former executive at Lightera and CIENA, commented on the "perfect fit" between the two companies—Lightera was founded to solve the bandwidth explosion problem posed by CIENA and other DWDM providers, a problem one of Lightera's co-founders, Charles Chi, had identified while at CIENA.[14]

The CoreDirector performed the same functions as existing ADM-based switching fabrics, the switching systems used by previous SONET-based networks, but with a three-fold reduction in equipment, space, and power requirements. In addition, its intelligence utilized available bandwidth much more efficiently and created new, differentiating optical services for carrier customers, changing the fundamental economics of building

carrier networks. As Steve Chaddick put it, "Technology only exists in our world to provide economic value; it does not stand on its own." After the acquisition, CIENA invested heavily in the switch, quadrupling the size of the organization over a 2-year period. As Dan Klausmeier, CTO and Founder of Lightera, said:

> CIENA was aware they needed switching to survive as an independent company. They shared our motivation to deliver a successful product to market and dedicated many resources to this effort. We effectively inherited a huge fan club and a new pool of resources. Unlike many mergers, where there is a great deal of politics, there was virtually none here. Everyone across CIENA was focused on a common goal—delivering our switch to market as soon as possible.[15]

---

[14] All quotes from Rick Dodd are from the authors' interview on May 22, 2002.

[15] Chuck Seiber, Ali Rowghani, Francois Locoh-Donou, and Kendra Harris, "CIENA Corporation Strategic Audit," *Stanford GSB Class Paper,* January 28, 2002.

In mid-2000, CIENA was the first to ship an intelligent optical switch. The compelling value of the product made it an immediate success with carriers. Furthermore, unlike with its earlier product introduction, CIENA leveraged an existing customer base to market the CoreDirector and sped product adoption. By the end of 2000, CIENA was the clear market leader in optical switching, once again enjoying a lead on its competition. This propelled CIENA's margins on the new product (and the company's market valuation) to its earlier levels.

Metro Transport and Switching (2000–2002)

Hired in 1997 from Intelsat where he was Vice-President of Sales and Marketing, Gary Smith rose through the sales management ranks and was named President and CEO of CIENA in October 2000. Upon taking the helm, Smith and his management team realized that changes were on the horizon. Smith believed the next growth area in networking would be in the transport and switching market for metropolitan area networks (MANs). If this came to pass, the new breed of customers would be the incumbent carriers (Sprint, AT&T, WorldCom), regional bell operating companies (Verizon, BellSouth, etc.), and international carriers (British Telecom, France Telecom, Deutsche Telekom). The massive debt accumulated by emerging carriers (Williams, Broadwing, Level3, Enron, etc.) and the heavily spending incumbents of the late 1990s would prevent them from sustaining this ongoing growth. Smith believed that these new customers would require integrated, end-to-end equipment solutions, which meant that CIENA had to add MAN capabilities. In addition, as DWDM products continued to be commoditized, successful metropolitan solutions could offer differentiation and support profitability.

Up to this period, CIENA's DWDM transport and switching products were focused on carrying and distributing large blocks of bandwidth among major metropolitan network centers over several hundred miles. Typically, DWDM transport equipment from one vendor would be used to build a service provider's network route, which would often girdle the continent. For example, a network could span from a network operation center in New York to one in Los Angeles via an intermediate point, such as Denver. In Denver, an intelligent optical switch would be installed to route traffic to other destinations, such as Dallas. Metropolitan networks, on the other hand, transported and dispatched smaller amounts of bandwidth on shorter distances among network closets within a metropolitan area. As such, it was

estimated that the equipment market for metro area optical networks would grow from $13 billion in 2001 to $23.6 billion in 2005.[16]

Once again, CIENA chose to acquire the desired technology rather than develop it internally. In March 2001, the company paid $1.1 billion for Cyras Systems, a startup developing a switch (called the K2) for MANs. Moving quickly to integrate Cyras, CIENA shipped the product before year-end and began at least one major scale deployment of the K2 switch.

In early 2002, CIENA announced the acquisition of ONI, combining its core optical networking and switching with ONI's metropolitan optical networking capabilities. According to Smith, the acquisition's objective was not only to broaden CIENA's product portfolio, but also to address his company's declining financial performance. Smith said, "Together, we can combine our efforts, consolidate our resources, and target new market opportunities. As a result, we expect to accelerate CIENA's return to profitability."[17]

NEW CHALLENGES

During the first and second quarters of 2002, CIENA reported revenues of $162 million and $87 million, representing a 56 percent and 80 percent drop in revenues from the same quarters in the previous year. With operating losses of $432 million in the first half of 2002, it was clear that CIENA faced a new environment with challenges characterized by increased competition and a changing customer base.

Intense Competitive Environment

CIENA's suite of optical networking products covered the core switching, core transport, metro switching, and metro transport. In each marketplace, CIENA faced different competitors with varying technology strength and customer penetration. CIENA's main competitors were the following companies (Exhibits 4 and 5).

Alcatel This was a leading French industrial company with both wireline and wireless telecom equipment offerings for transport, switching, and access. With FY2001 sales of $22 billion and a staff of 99,000 people in 2001,

[16] Sherry Kercher, "Optical Ethernet in the MAN," Faulkner Information Services, September 2002, p. 3.
[17] "CIENA and ONI Systems Agree to Unite," CIENA Press Release, CIENA Corporation, February 18, 2002.

EXHIBIT 4 Telecommunications Equipment Competitive Landscape

	RBOCS			Emerging IXCs					IXCs				
	BellSouth	SBC	Verizon	360 Network	Broadwing	Global Crossing	Level 3	Williams	AT&T	Genuity	Qwest	Sprint	WorldCom
Core switching	Cisco, Sycamore	CIENA, Fujitsu, Mitsubishi	Fujitsu, Marconi	Sycamore	CIENA, Cisco, Corvis	Cisco, Lucent, Nortel	Alcatel, CIENA, Fujitsu	CIENA, Cisco, Corvis, Nortel, Redback, Sycamore	CIENA, Cisco	CIENA, Nortel, Redback	CIENA, Cisco, Corvis, Fujitsu, Lucent, Redback, Tellium	Tellabs	Cisco, Lucent
Core transport	CIENA		CIENA, Lucent, Nortel	Alcatel, Fujitsu, Nortel	CIENA, Cisco, Corvis, Lucent, Nortel	CIENA, Cisco, Lucent, Nortel	Nortel	CIENA, Corvis, Nortel, Sycamore	CIENA, Lucent, NEC	Nortel	CIENA, Corvis, Nortel, Sycamore	CIENA	CIENA, Fujitsu, Lucent, Nortel
Metro DWDM		Nortel		Nortel		Nortel		CIENA/ONI, Sorrento	CIENA		CIENA/ONI	Nortel	Siemens
IP routing	Cisco	Cisco		Cisco	Cisco	Cisco, Juniper, Pluris	Cisco, Juniper	Avici, Cisco, Juniper	Avici, Cisco	Cisco, Juniper	Avici, Cisco, Juniper	Cisco	Cisco, Juniper
Other	Lucent, Marconi, Riverstone, Sonus	Alcatel, Cisco, Lucent, Marconi	Alcatel, Lucent, Nortel		Alcatel, Cisco	Juniper, Lucent, Sonus	Lucent, Marconi, Nortel, Sonus	Lucent, Nortel	Cisco, Clarent, Lucent, Nortel, Riverstone	Alcatel, Cisco, Lucent, Nortel, Riverstone	Alcatel, Cisco, Lucent, Nortel, Riverstone	Cisco, Lucent, Marconi, NEC, Nortel	Alcatel, Cisco, Lucent, Nortel, Marconi

Source: "Telecom Equipment Industry," SG Cowen Report, February 2002.

EXHIBIT 5 Comparative Financials for Industry Players

	Stock DATA				Income STMT. DATA ($ billions)				Balance SHEET DATA ($ billions)					
	Market Cap ($ billions)	Price 11/21/02	Price High 5-Yr. Avg.	Price Low 5-Yr. Avg.	Sales	COGS	Interest Expense	Net Income	Cash and ST Investment	Total Inventory	Total Cur. Assets	Total Cur. Liabilities	Total LT Debt	Total Liabilities
Alcatel	6.9	16.6	55.0	19.8	22.6	15.8	0.2	(4.5)	4.4	4.3	20.5	13.6	5.2	22.3
CIENA	1.9	14.3	74.9	10.8	1.6	0.9	0.0	(1.8)	1.3	0.2	2.1	0.2	0.8	1.1
Cisco	102.5	18.1	42.9	16.5	22.2	10.0	N/A	N/A	6.9	1.6	12.8	7.3	0.0	6.7
Corvis	0.2	3.2	N/A	N/A	0.1	0.0	N/A	(1.4)	0.6	0.0	0.8	0.0	0.0	0.0
Lucent	4.2	5.2	43.2	15.4	21.2	15.4	0.5	(14.2)	2.3	4.6	16.1	10.1	3.2	18.1
Marconi	0.1	N/A	N/A	N/A	9.8	5.8	0.3	(0.4)	0.7	2.4	6.5	5.6	3.2	10.2
Nortel	8.4	11.9	53.9	18.7	27.1	20.8	0.4	(37.8)	5.5	2.5	18.7	15.0	6.5	21.6
Sycamore	0.7	5.4	N/A	N/A	0.3	0.1	N/A	(0.3)	0.8	0.0	0.9	0.1	0.0	0.1
Tellabs	3.1	15.0	60.1	22.1	2.1	1.0	0.0	(0.2)	1.1	0.3	1.9	0.3	0.0	0.4
Tellium	0.0	6.2	N/A	N/A	0.0	0.0	0.0	(0.3)	0.2	0.0	0.3	0.0	0.0	0.0
AT&T	53.2	168.5	456.2	233.2	52.5	13.9	3.2	(6.9)	11.2	0.0	22.5	25.4	40.5	105.3
Qwest	6.3	14.1	41.9	17.2	19.6	7.1	1.6	(4.0)	0.2	0.3	5.7	9.9	20.1	37.1
Sprint	12.2	20.1	N/A	N/A	16.9	8.2	0.3	(0.2)	0.1	0.2	3.4	6.2	3.2	12.4
Broadwing	0.5	N/A	36.0	17.3	2.3	1.1	0.1	(0.3)	0.0	0.0	0.4	0.9	2.7	3.9
Genuity	0.0	31.6	N/A	N/A	1.2	1.3	0.0	(4.0)	0.9	0.0	1.3	0.6	2.3	3.0
Global Crossing	0.0	N/A	N/A	N/A	N/A	N/A	N/A	N/A	N/A	N/A	N/A	N/A	N/A	N/A
Level 3	1.9	5.0	N/A	N/A	1.5	0.7	0.7	(6.1)	1.6	0.0	2.0	1.3	6.2	9.3
Williams	N/A	N/A	N/A	N/A	N/A	N/A	N/A	N/A	N/A	N/A	N/A	N/A	N/A	N/A
BellSouth	48.3	38.2	46.0	31.4	24.1	12.4	1.3	2.5	0.5	0.3	6.8	10.0	15.0	33.0
SBC COMM	83.7	39.2	53.0	35.0	37.5	19.0	1.5	7.2	0.7	0.0	12.5	23.9	17.1	63.8
Verizon	107.2	47.5	60.0	40.5	67.1	N/A	3.7	0.5	2.9	1.9	23.1	38.0	45.6	116.1
Cable and Wireless	3.1	14.8	50.1	23.3	10.4	6.3	0.4	3.8	10.7	0.4	14.2	5.9	3.3	10.3
Deutsche Telekom	49.4	16.9	53.6	22.1	43.1	22.5	4.1	(3.1)	2.9	1.4	15.1	21.8	48.3	87.3
France Telecom	15.3	40.0	111.8	48.3	38.3	16.0	3.4	(4.5)	3.6	0.8	20.5	31.1	48.6	82.7
KPN	15.7	5.1	38.4	12.7	10.4	6.6	1.3	(6.7)	6.5	0.3	9.6	8.8	14.9	24.6
NTT Docomo	91.9	N/A	N/A	N/A	42.0	28.7	0.2	3.2	0.9	0.9	9.5	13.5	5.2	19.2
Telefonica	48.2	38.5	58.7	30.5	27.6	14.8	1.7	1.8	2.6	0.6	10.9	16.4	20.1	43.9

Source: Authors and Thomson Financials (November 2002).

it was a giant in this market. The company sold networking equipment as well as consulting, integration, design, planning, operation, and maintenance services, mainly for large European clients such as Deutsche Telekom and Orange. In 2001, these European customers represented over half of Alcatel's revenues.[18] As an incumbent in telecommunications equipment, Alcatel traditionally supplied its carrier customers with older generation SONET equipment for voice and data services. However, with the advent of DWDM, the company quickly caught up and led, particularly among European carriers. In the face of growing price pressure and the severe slowdown in the telecom market, Alcatel attempted to merge with Lucent in mid-2000. However, the financial community did not support the plans, and the merger talks were aborted a few weeks after they began.

Corvis Dr. David Huber, CIENA's founder, left the company to start Corvis in 1997 to implement his vision of an all-optical network. Specifically, instead of using the low port count and electronic switching fabric that CIENA used in its CoreDirector, Huber proposed to develop an OO (optical-to-optical)[19] switch that could achieve higher switching speed and fiber port density than existing OEO solutions, even though the product would be limited in functionality since it would not perform electronic-level grooming.[20] Corvis introduced in November 1999 the CorWave, an all-optical intelligent switch with a capacity of 2.4Tb/s, 30 times faster than CIENA's CoreDirector at the time.[21] The CorWave was sold to emerging carriers such as Qwest, Broadwing, and Williams, which desired very high capacity switches to meet the expected Internet traffic explosion.

With $68 million in revenues in FY2000 and 1,400 employees, Corvis went public in July 2000 and quickly reached a market capitalization as high as $40 billion. As of May 2002, Corvis had reduced its workforce to just over 800 as revenues dropped precipitously and its mar-

ket capitalization hovered just over $350 million with a stock price that was below $1 per share.[22]

Lucent Spun off from AT&T in 1996 to focus on designing and selling telecom equipment, Lucent maintained deep relationships with incumbent carriers and RBOCs in North America. Moreover, the company's research division, Bell Laboratories, had been a center for innovation in several technology areas. With FY2001 revenues of $21 billion and 77,000 employees, Lucent was a major force covering wireline, voice, optical, and wireless equipment, serving carriers globally.

At the height of the telecom bubble in 1999, Lucent had $38 billion in revenues and over 150,000 employees. As carrier spending slowed and its revenues dropped, Lucent executed massive layoffs and divestitures. The company spun out its microelectronics division (Agere) and its voice switching and access equipment divisions (Avaya) in 2000. Then the company restructured to focus on optical networking equipment for incumbent carriers, leveraging its existing relationships.

Nortel This Canadian networking equipment company was one of the first traditional voice switching equipment companies to leap into DWDM transport technologies. With FY2001 revenues of $17 billion and 57,000 employees, Nortel was capable of aggressive price-cutting to win or sustain customer relationships in DWDM long-haul transport, according to Mike McCarthy, CIENA's Senior VP of Sales.[23] Yet, as Nortel's revenues dropped 40 percent in 2001, it had to reduce its workforce by a similar percentage. It has focused its energies on optical solutions for metro area networks as well as wireless equipment for carriers.

Cisco This networking behemoth sold data networking and access equipment. Unlike Lucent or Alcatel, Cisco's products were for the CPE (Customer Premise Equipment) or local CO (Central Office) markets with customers ranging from small enterprises to local service providers but not carriers. The company penetrated the metropolitan market from its leadership in access and routing by acquiring Cerent and Monterey Networks in August 1999 for $6.7 billion and $500 million. Through

---

[18] Hoover's Online (www.hoovers.com) capsule on Alcatel.

[19] The OO switch does not transfer data onto an electrical fabric like an OEO switch (such as the CoreDirector). Light particles or photons are faster than electrons, and an OO switch can create much higher data transfer performance than an OEO switch.

[20] Electronic level grooming refers to the segregation and management of data traffic beyond an optical channel or wave but at the electronic level. An all-optical switch can only manipulate light waves while an OEO switch can analyze electronic traffic and provide more granularized switching functions.

[21] "Williams Communications and Corvis Announce Field Trial of Breakthrough Terabit Optical Network," Corvis Press Release, Corvis Corporation, November 11, 1999.

[22] Hoovers Online (www.hoovers.com) capsule on Corvis. Q102 revenues were $8.7 million versus $84.1 million in the same quarter the year prior.

[23] All quotes from Mike McCarthy are from the authors' interview on May 31, 2002.

these acquisitions, it offered SONET-based optical transport and switching for metro area networks.

With 2001 revenues of $22 billion, a workforce of 38,000, and a strong presence in the enterprise and local service provider space, Cisco was looking for next generation networking solutions to attack the core of carriers' networks. It has had a history of adding products and technologies to its portfolio through acquiring small and promising technology startups, having made more than 70 acquisitions from 1993 to 2002.[24]

Changing Customer Base

CIENA faced the new challenges of the depressed economic environment. Its customers were similarly impacted by this downturn.

Incumbents and European Telecom Carriers Having overspent on network capacity, the incumbents faced low utilization rates in the 10–15 percent range. Suffering most severely were carriers that focused on optical networks and ignored other business lines. These entities now depended solely on selling raw data capacity at extreme discounts.[25]

These carriers took on high debt to build and provision their networks and now faced daunting interest payments. This financial picture also made raising new capital difficult. Yet another issue was the heightened accounting scrutiny that resulted from the Enron fiasco. Many carriers utilized aggressive accounting practices and later came under heightened scrutiny by the United States Securities and Exchange Commission. These constraints forced the carriers to restructure and lay off employees.

In the midst of this, carrier network spending was expected to be minimal. Network bottlenecks remained, but the spending to address these problems remained low. Another factor was the distressed network assets that were available for purchase, but it was unclear how much of this equipment would be reusable.

The problem of telecommunication carriers was not limited to North America. The heavy spending on 3G wireless licenses left the major European carriers (or PTTs) with heavy debt and limited their ability to invest in capital expenditures such as CIENA's network equipment. On a global level, the industry was made up of a few concentrated buyers of CIENA's internetwork-ing products. Gary Smith claimed, "There are only 30 or so carriers in the world that represent 70 percent of purchases." He also mentioned some attractiveness of the Chinese market where the government was instituting a "stepped approach" to building its data and voice infrastructure.

The Big Three As prices dropped and competition grew, profit margins for long distance voice services continued to slide. The Big Three—AT&T, WorldCom, and Sprint—were under great financial pressure. Shrinking revenues and profit compelled AT&T and WorldCom to undertake restructuring initiatives to separate their domestic long distance business from other, more profitable businesses. WorldCom revived the MCI brand and provided domestic voice services under it, while the World-Com Group became the provider of business services. AT&T realigned itself along four business lines—AT&T Consumer, AT&T Broadband, AT&T Business, and AT&T Wireless—each individually listed on the New York Stock Exchange. AT&T Wireless was spun off from its parent in July 2001, and the company was taking bids for its broadband cable unit in mid-2002.

Emerging Carriers Five years after the Telecom Act, the RBOCs maintained a 92 percent market share, with the CLECs holding the remaining 8 percent. The ILECs also began to gain approval to provide long distance services within their operating regions. Consequently, the Baby Bells effectively began to become regional monopolies, further eroding the power of the CLECs.[26]

By 2002, many IXCs (interexchange carriers, often referred to as long distance carriers) had filed for bankruptcy or been acquired as distressed assets—including high-profile companies such as Worldcom, Williams Communications, Global Crossing, 360 Networks, Flag Telecom, and Yipes. Those that survived did so tenuously. This environmental change can be seen in the shift in capital expenditure. The ILECs and major long distance carriers, combined, were expected to spend $56.8 billion and $41.5 billion in 2001 and 2002, down 5 percent and 31 percent, respectively, from the $59.8 billion they spent in 2000. The emerging carriers and CLECs were expected to spend $16.3 billion and $4.2 billion in 2001 and 2002, down a dramatic 46 percent and 86 percent, respectively, from the $30.5 billion they spent in 2000.[27]

---

[24]Hoovers Online (www.hoovers.com) capsule on Cisco Systems.
[25]Elizabeth Douglass, "Analysts Keeping Eyes on Fiber Optics Sector," *Los Angeles Times,* April 24, 2002.

[26]Bruce Kramer, "Telecommunications in the U.S.: State of the Marketplace," *Faulkner Information Services,* December 2001, p. 3.
[27]"Global Telebits," UBS Warburg LLC Research, April 2002.

New Basis for Competitive Differentiation

Over the core transport (1996 to 1998) and core switching (1998 to 2000) phases of CIENA's evolution, the main basis of competitive advantage was product and technology leadership, according to Steve Alexander. During the first startup phase for CIENA, the company bet on the emerging DWDM technology to dramatically transform the economics of telecom networks built by service providers. CIENA initially faced an aggressive set of buyers—the newly funded emerging carriers—who focused on the best technology. The product sales cycles for these companies were typically short because they were eager to build out their network to compete in the then-heady market. With its 12-month lead, CIENA needed only to focus on technology to maintain its growth.

As CIENA's competitors caught up and the margins on its long-haul DWDM transport product dropped, the company used its execution and acquisition capabilities to re-create a lead in the switching market. In this phase, according to Alexander, it was execution that enabled CIENA to remain competitive in the switching market. While the emerging carriers were still eager to buy the latest technologies, other equipment providers closed on CIENA with competing solutions. To maintain market leadership, the company institutionalized excellence in its ability to bring new products and technologies to the marketplace. This strategy had two elements—external acquisition of technologies and spotless execution to deliver new products.

In this second phase, CIENA acquired five companies for a total value of $3.6 billion. According to Steve Chaddick, the acquisition route was faster from the perspective of time-to-market than pure internal development, particularly in the tight technology labor market of 1999 to 2000. CIENA targeted small companies with 70 to 100 employees that were pre-revenue or beginning to earn revenue. The companies usually had strong technical teams, incomplete business infrastructures, and product and technology visions similar to those of CIENA.

Moreover, CIENA instituted what it called the "ONTG" philosophy to maintain product leadership in the market and integrate the new organizations and technologies from acquisitions. ONTG, which stands for "One Neck To Grab," was a practice that assigned responsibility for every task or project to a single individual. This developed accountability across the growing organization and helped CIENA meet its aggressive product release schedules and sales targets.

As CIENA faced the 2000 to 2002 period, carriers were straining under heavy debt and had shifted their focus from building new networks to maintaining and optimizing their existing ones. The technology evolution had slowed from its rapid pace in the mid-1990s, and the incumbent carriers were under severe pressure to conserve cash to service debt. Gary Smith summarized the change in CIENA's customers' outlooks as a shift of focus from "capex" (capital expenditure) to "opex" (operating expenditure).

Rather than aggressively pursuing the latest technologies, carriers became focused on solutions that helped reduce the costs of operating their networks. In this new environment, sales cycles to incumbent customers grew longer—up to two years, according to Mike McCarthy. McCarthy's new sales strategy became focused on hiring experienced executives with deep relationships among carriers, to shorten sales cycles and attract new customers.

Customers also began to demand total network solutions that yielded better costs. They required vendors to provide extensive services to integrate new additions to their network. Some in the equipment industry thought that margins would increasingly migrate away from hardware and toward services.

Impact on Telecom Equipment Providers

The IXC industry was in difficulty. They reported exponential growth in terms of access lines, but these carriers continued to amass huge net losses that led many of them to default or drove them out of business altogether (Exhibit 6). Additionally, the venture capital that provided an essential lifeline to competitive carriers dried up. There was $1.6 billion in strategic investments made in the CLEC industry in 2000, down from $7.4 billion in 1999.[28]

Total telecom spending fell to an estimated $53 billion in 2002 from $92 billion in 2000 and affected all equipment providers to some degree.[29] Diversified providers like Lucent and Nortel saw optical equipment revenues fall to a smaller share of overall corporate revenues. But for CIENA and other optical networking pure-plays, this contraction impacted their entire business line (Exhibit 7).

Equipment vendors competed for customers, and existing relationships became an advantage. Because customers were concerned with ongoing upgrades, main-

---

[28] Bruce Kramer, "Telecommunications in the U.S.: State of the Marketplace," *Faulkner Information Services,* December 2001, p. 4.
[29] "The Capex Conundrum," *RHK—STARTRAX2001 Presentation,* October 2001.

EXHIBIT 6 Bankruptcies and Default in the Telecom Industry

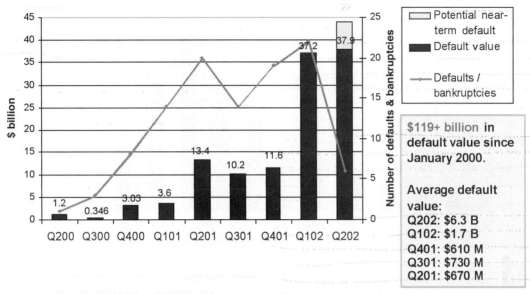

Source: CIENA Presentation at Stanford Graduate School of Business, May 15, 2002.

tenance, and support, they remained with familiar or established vendors. CIENA's marketing and sales efforts had been more focused on the engineers and the technical personnel. As a result, these efforts were less familiar to business decision makers.

THE FUTURE

Stephen Alexander, CTO of CIENA, described the company's future as the third phase in an evolution: "Phase one was DWDM. Phase two was intelligent optical switching. Phase three is the end-to-end network." By this, Alexander was describing a network with the intelligence to "pack wavelengths as early as possible, carry data as far as possible without examining them." Such a network would be highly efficient, dramatically reducing both capital and operating expenses. CIENA pursued this vision with the LightWorks software suite—which provided centralized network management and control—and began to shift its business to the designing and selling of entire networks, as opposed to point solutions. Yet, CIENA was not alone in this thinking; Nortel and Lucent had similar visions.

One area CIENA needed to address was the technological changes in optical networks. Improved optical components continued to multiply fiber speeds (from 10Gb/s to 40Gb/s and more), and Nortel and Lucent had built a lead in this area based on their history in compo-

nent research.[30] Similarly, the all-optical network architecture was coming closer to reality, with Corvis leading. The growth of IP (Internet Protocol) traffic in the network might ultimately lead to a dominant standard, which would alter how carriers evaluated optical systems. The capacity of broadband wireless technologies had also been increasing significantly, which could eventually allow wireless solutions to compete with optical ones. Current wireless technologies could not handle the scale of traffic required at the core of existing networks and therefore would not substitute CIENA's internetworking equipment. New applications in optical networks were also becoming prevalent. For example, ONI itself had added features to its systems that handled storage networking protocols.

CONCLUSION

In its brief history, CIENA led two product revolutions. First, it introduced a DWDM transport product that helped transform the economics of telecommunications services. Next, it introduced the CoreDirector optical switch, which created dramatic operating efficiencies and cost reductions within the network. The company grew by introducing key products that solved pressing

[30] "Long-Haul WDM: RFI Exercise," *Light Reading Report,* www .lightreading.com, March 12, 2002.

EXHIBIT 7 Capital Expenditures in Optical Equipment in the Telecom Sector

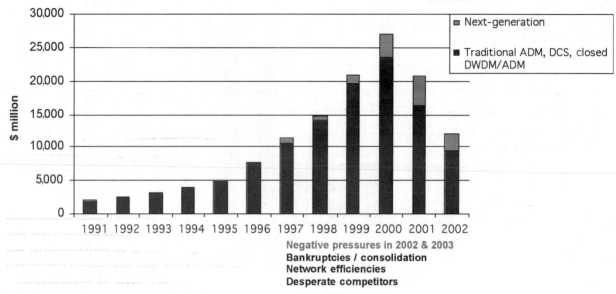

Negative pressures in 2002 & 2003
**Bankruptcies / consolidation
Network efficiencies
Desperate competitors**

Source: CIENA Presentation at Stanford Graduate School of Business, May 15, 2002.

needs in what had been an extraordinarily buoyant market for telecommunications technologies.

However, CIENA now faced a depressed telecommunications marketplace characterized by a shrinking customer set, a dramatic decrease in spending, and fierce competition. The company's acquisitions of ONI and Cyras combined its portfolio of core transport and switching devices with metro transport and switching products. Now CIENA faced the new challenge of delivering integrated services instead of individual systems.

Before CIENA could hope to introduce a third revolution, it had to cope with the fundamental shifts in its clients' needs and, in some cases, abilities to survive. What could Gary Smith do to ensure that CIENA was positioned once again to lead the new revolution?

READING II-2

Patterns of Industrial Innovation

William J. Abernathy and James M. Utterback

How does a company's innovation—and its response to innovative ideas—change as the company grows and matures? Are there circumstances in which a pattern generally associated with successful innovation is in fact more likely to be associated with failure? Under what circumstances will newly available technology, rather than the market, be the critical stimulus for change? When is concentration on incremental innovation and productivity gains likely to be of maximum value to a firm? In what situations does this strategy instead cause instability and potential for crisis in an organization?

Intrigued by questions such as these, we have examined how the kinds of innovations attempted by productive units apparently change as these units evolve. Our goal was a model relating patterns of innovation within a unit to that unit's competitive strategy, production capabilities, and organizational characteristics.

This article summarizes our work and presents the basic characteristics of the model to which it has led us. We conclude that a productive unit's capacity for and methods of innovation depend critically on its stage of evolution from a small technology-based enterprise to a major high-volume producer. Many characteristics of innovation and the innovative process correlate with such a historical analysis, and on the basis of our model we can now attempt answers to questions such as those above.

Source: Reprinted with permission from *Technology Review,* MIT Alumni Association. Copyright © 1978.

A SPECTRUM OF INNOVATORS

Past studies of innovation imply that any innovating unit sees most of its innovations as new products. But that observation masks an essential difference: what constitutes a product innovation by a small, technology-based unit is often the process equipment adopted by a large unit to improve its high-volume production of a standard product. We argue that these two units—the small, entrepreneurial organization and the larger unit producing standard products in high volume—are at opposite ends of a spectrum, in a sense forming boundary conditions in the evolution of a unit and in the character of its innovation of product and process technologies.

One distinctive pattern of technological innovation is evident in the case of established, high-volume products such as incandescent light bulbs, paper, steel, standard chemicals, and internal-combustion engines, for examples.

The markets for such goods are well defined; the product characteristics are well understood and often standardized; unit profit margins are typically low; production technology is efficient, equipment intensive and specialized to a particular product; and competition is primarily on the basis of price. Change is costly in such highly integrated systems because an alteration in any one attribute or process has ramifications for many others.

In this environment innovation is typically incremental in nature, and it has a gradual, cumulative effect on productivity. For example, Samuel Hollander has shown that more than half of the reduction in the cost of producing rayon in plants of E. I. du Pont de Nemours and Company has been the result of gradual process improvements which could not be identified as formal projects or changes. A similar study by John Enos shows that accumulating incremental developments in petroleum refining processes resulted in productivity gains which often eclipsed the gain from the original innovation. Incremental innovations, such as the use of larger railroad cars and unit trains, have resulted in dramatic reductions in the cost of moving large quantities of materials by rail.

In all these examples, major systems innovations have been followed by countless minor product and systems improvements, and the latter account for more than half of the total ultimate economic gain due to their much greater number. While cost reduction seems to have been the major incentive for most of these innovations, major advances in performance have also resulted from such small engineering and production adjustments.

Such incremental innovation typically results in an increasingly specialized system in which economies of scale in production and the development of mass markets are extremely important. The productive unit loses its flexibility, becoming increasingly dependent on high-volume production to cover its fixed costs and increasingly vulnerable to changed demand and technical obsolescence.

Major new products do not seem to be consistent with this pattern of incremental change. New products which require reorientation of corporate goals or production facilities tend to originate outside organizations devoted to a "specific" production system; or, if originated within, to be rejected by them.

A more fluid pattern of product change is associated with the identification of an emerging need or a new way to meet an existing need; it is an entrepreneurial act. Many studies suggest that such new product innovations share common traits. They occur in disproportionate numbers in companies and units located in or near affluent markets with strong science-based universities or other research institutions and entrepreneurially oriented financial institutions. Their competitive advantage over predecessor products is based on superior functional performance rather than lower initial cost, and so these radical innovations tend to offer higher unit profit margins.

When a major product innovation first appears, performance criteria are typically vague and little understood. Because they have a more intimate understanding of performance requirements, users may play a major role in suggesting the ultimate form of the innovation as well as the need. For example, Kenneth Knight shows that three-quarters of the computer models which emerged between 1944 and 1950, usually those produced as one or two of a kind, were developed by users.

It is reasonable that the diversity and uncertainty of performance requirements for new products give an advantage in their innovation to small, adaptable organizations with flexible technical approaches and good external communications, and historical evidence supports that hypothesis. For example, John Tilton argues that new enterprises led in the application of semiconductor technology, often transferring into practice technology from more established firms and laboratories. He argues that economies of scale have not been of prime importance because products have changed so rapidly that production technology designed for a particular product is rapidly made obsolete. And R. O. Schlaifer and S. D. Heron have argued that a diverse and responsive group of enterprises struggling against established units to enter the industry contributed greatly to the early advances in jet aircraft engines.

A TRANSITION FROM RADICAL TO EVOLUTIONARY INNOVATION

These two patterns of innovation may be taken to represent extreme types—in one case involving incremental change to a rigid, efficient production system specifically designed to produce a standardized product, and in the other case involving radical innovation with product characteristics in flux. In fact, they are not rigid, independent categories. Several examples will make it clear that organizations currently considered in the "specific" category—where incremental innovation is now motivated by cost reduction—were at their origin small, "fluid" units intent on new product innovation.

John Tilton's study of developments in the semiconductor industry from 1950 through 1968 indicates that the rate of major innovation has decreased and that the type of innovation shifted. Eight of the 13 product innovations he considers to have been most important during that period occurred within the first 7 years, while the industry was making less than 5 percent of its total 18-year sales. Two types of enterprise can be identified in this early period of the new industry—established units that came into semiconductors from vested positions in vacuum tube markets and new entries such as Fairchild Semiconductor, IBM, and Texas Instruments, Inc. The established units responded to competition from the newcomers by emphasizing process innovations. Meanwhile, the latter sought entry and strength through product innovation. The three very successful new entrants just listed were responsible for half of the major product innovations and only one of the nine process innovations which Dr. Tilton identified in that 18-year period, while three principal established units (divisions of General Electric, Philco, and RCA) made only one-quarter of the product innovations but three of the nine major process innovations in the same period. In this case, process innovation did not prove to be an effective competitive stance; by 1966, the three established units together held only 18 percent of the market while the three new units held 42 percent. Since 1968, however, the basis of competition in the industry has changed; as costs and productivity have become more important, the rate of major product innovation has decreased, and effective process innovation has become an important factor in competitive success. For example, by 1973 Texas Instruments, which had been a flexible, new entrant in the industry two decades earlier and had contributed no major process innovations prior to 1968, was planning a single machine that would produce 4 percent of world requirements for its integrated-circuit unit.

Like the transistor in the electronics industry, the DC-3 stands out as a major change in the aircraft and airlines industries. Almarin Phillips has shown that the DC-3 was in fact a cumulation of prior innovations. It was not the largest, or fastest, or longest-range aircraft; it was the most economical large, fast plane able to fly long distances. All the features which made this design so completely successful had been introduced and proven in prior aircraft. And the DC-3 was essentially the first commercial product of an entering firm (the C-1 and DC-2 were produced by Douglas only in small numbers).

Just as the transistor put the electronics industry on a new plateau, so the DC-3 changed the character of innovation in the aircraft industry for the next 15 years. No major innovations were introduced into commercial aircraft design from 1936 until new jet-powered aircraft appeared in the 1950s. Instead, there were simply many refinements to the DC-3 concept—stretching the design and adding appointments; and during the period of these incremental changes, airline operating cost per passenger-mile dropped an additional 50 percent.

The electric light bulb also has a history of a long series of evolutionary improvements which started with a few major innovations and ended in a highly standardized commoditylike product. By 1909, the initial tungsten filament and vacuum bulb innovations were in place; from then until 1955 there came a series of incremental changes—better metal alloys for the filament, the use of "getters" to assist in exhausting the bulb, coiling the filaments, "frosting" the glass, and many more. In the same period, the price of a 60-watt bulb decreased (even with no inflation adjustment) from $1.60 to 20 cents each, the lumens output increased by 175 percent, the direct labor content was reduced more than an order of magnitude, from 3 to 0.18 minutes per bulb, and the production process evolved from a flexible jobshop configuration, involving more than 11 separate operations and a heavy reliance on the skills of manual labor, to a single machine attended by a few workers.

Product and process evolved in a similar fashion in the automobile industry. During a four-year period before Henry Ford produced the renowned Model T, his company developed, produced, and sold five different engines, ranging from two to six cylinders. These were made in a factory that was flexibly organized much as a job shop, relying on trade craftsmen working with general-purpose machine tools not nearly so advanced as the best then available. Each engine tested a new concept. Out of this experience came a dominant design—the Model T; and within 15 years, 2 million engines of this single basic design were being produced each year (about 15 million all told) in a facility then recognized as the most efficient and highly integrated in the world. During that 15-year period, there were incremental—but no fundamental—innovations in the Ford product.

In yet another case, Robert Buzzell and Robert Nourse, tracing innovations in processed foods, show that new products such as soluble coffees, frozen vegetables, dry pet foods, cold breakfast cereals, canned foods, and precooked rice came first from individuals and small organizations where research was in progress or which relied heavily upon information from users. As each product won acceptance, its productive unit increased in size and concentrated its innovation on improving manufacturing, marketing, and distribution methods which extended rather than replaced the basic technologies. The major source of the latter ideas is now each firm's own research and development organization.

The shift from radical to evolutionary product innovation is a common thread in these examples. It is related to the development of a dominant product design, and it is accompanied by heightened price competition and increased emphasis on process innovation. Small-scale units that are flexible and highly reliant on manual labor and craft skills utilizing general-purpose equipment develop into units that rely on automated, equipment-intensive, high-volume processes. We conclude that changes in innovative pattern, production process, and scale and kind of production capacity all occur together in a consistent, predictable way.

Though many observers emphasize new product innovation, process and incremental innovations may have equal or even greater commercial importance. A high rate of productivity improvement is associated with process improvement in every case we have studied. The cost of incandescent light bulbs, for example, has fallen more than 80 percent since their introduction. Airline operating costs were cut by half through the development and improvement of the DC-3. Semiconductor prices have been falling by 20 to 30 percent with each doubling of cumulative production. The introduction of the Model T Ford resulted in a price reduction from $3,000 to less than $1,000 (in 1958 dollars). Similar dramatic reductions have been achieved in the costs of computer core memory and television picture tubes.

MANAGING TECHNOLOGICAL INNOVATION

If it is true that the nature and goals of an industrial unit's innovations change as that unit matures from pioneering to large-scale producer, what does this imply for the management of technology?

We believe that some significant managerial concepts emerge from our analysis—or model, if you will—of the characteristics of innovation as production processes and primary competitive issues differ. As a unit moves toward large-scale production, the goals of its innovations change from ill-defined and uncertain targets to well-articulated design objectives. In the early stages, there is a proliferation of product performance requirements and design criteria which frequently cannot be stated quantitatively, and their relative importance or ranking may be quite unstable. It is precisely under such conditions, where performance requirements are ambiguous, that users are most likely to produce an innovation and where manufacturers are least likely to do so. One way of viewing regulatory constraints such as those governing auto emissions or safety is that they add new performance dimensions to be resolved by the engineer—and so may lead to more innovative design improvements. They are also likely to open market opportunities for innovative change of the kind characteristic of fluid enterprises in areas such as instrumentation, components, process equipment, and so on.

The stimulus for innovation changes as a unit matures. In the initial fluid stage, market needs are ill-defined and can be stated only with broad uncertainty, and the relevant technologies are as yet little explored. So there are two sources of ambiguity about the relevance of any particular program of research and development—target uncertainty and technical uncertainty. Confronted with both types of uncertainty, the decision maker has little incentive for major investments in formal research and development.

As the enterprise develops, however, uncertainty about markets and appropriate targets is reduced, and larger research and development investments are justified. At some point before the increasing specialization of the unit makes the cost of implementing technological innovations prohibitively high and before increasing cost competition erodes profit with which to fund large indirect expenses, the benefits of research and development efforts would reach a maximum. Technological opportunities for improvements and additions to existing product lines will then be clear, and a strong commitment to research and development will be characteristic of productive units in the middle stages of development. Such firms will be seen as "science based" because they invest heavily in formal research and engineering departments, with emphasis on process innovation and product differentiation through functional improvements.

Although data on research and development expenditures are not readily available on the basis of productive units, divisions, or lines of business, an informal review of the activities of corporations with large investments in research and development shows that they tend to support business lines that fall neither near the fluid nor the specific conditions but are in the technologically active middle range. Such productive units tend to be large, to be integrated, and to have a large share of their markets.

A small, fluid entrepreneurial unit requires general-purpose process equipment which, typically, is purchased. As it develops, such a unit is expected to originate some process-equipment innovations for its own use; and when it is fully matured, its entire processes are likely to be designed as integrated systems specific to particular products. Since the mature firm is now fully specialized, all its major process innovations are likely to originate outside the unit.

But note that the supplier companies will now see themselves as making product—not process—innovations. From a different perspective, George Stigler finds stages of development—similar to those we describe—in firms that supply production-process equipment. They differ in the market structure they face, in the specialization of their production processes, and in the responsibilities they must accept in innovating to satisfy their own needs for process technology and materials.

The organization's methods of coordination and control change with the increasing standardization of its products and production processes. As task uncertainty confronts a productive unit early in its development, the unit must emphasize its capacity to process information by investing in vertical and lateral information systems and in liaison and project groups. Later, these may be extended to the creation of formal planning groups, organizational manifestations of movement from a product-oriented to a transitional state; controls for regulating process functions and management controls such as job procedures, job descriptions, and systems analyses are also extended to become a more pervasive feature of the production network.

As a productive unit achieves standardized products and confronts only incremental change, one would expect it to deal with complexity by reducing the need for information processing. The level at which technological change takes place helps to determine the extent to which organizational dislocations take place. Each of these hypotheses helps to explain the firm's impetus to divide into homogeneous productive units as its products and process technology evolve.

The hypothesized changes in control and coordination imply that the structure of the organization will also change as it matures, becoming more formal and having a greater number of levels of authority. The evidence is strong that such structural change is a characteristic of many enterprises and of units within them.

FOSTERING INNOVATION BY UNDERSTANDING TRANSITION

Assuming the validity of this model for the development of the innovative capacities of a productive unit, how can it be applied to further our capacity for new products and to improve our productivity?

We predict that units in different stages of evolution will respond to differing stimuli and undertake different types of innovation. This idea can readily be extended to the question of barriers to innovation and probably to patterns of success and failure in innovation for units in different situations. The unmet conditions for transition can be viewed as specific barriers which must be overcome if transition is to take place.

We would expect new, fluid units to view as barriers any factors that impede product standardization and market aggregation, while firms in the opposite category tend to rank uncertainty over government regulation or vulnerability of existing investments as more important disruptive factors. Those who would promote innovation and productivity in U.S. industry may find this suggestive.

We believe the most useful insights provided by the model apply to production processes in which features of the products can be varied. The most interesting applications are to situations where product innovation is competitively important and difficult to manage; the model helps to identify the full range of other issues with which the firm is simultaneously confronted in a period of growth and change. (See Exhibit 1.)

CONSISTENCY OF MANAGEMENT ACTION

Many examples of unsuccessful innovations point to a common explanation of failure: certain conditions necessary to support a sought-after technical advance were

EXHIBIT 1 The Changing Character of Innovation and Its Changing Role in Corporate Advance

Seeking to understand the variables that determine successful strategies for innovation, the authors focus on three stages in the evolution of a successful enterprise: its period of flexibility, in which the enterprise seeks to capitalize on its advantages where they offer greatest advantages; its intermediate years, in which major products are used more widely; and its full maturity, when prosperity is assured by leadership in several principal products and technologies.

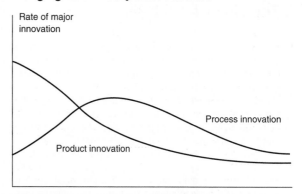

	Fluid pattern	Transitional pattern	Specific pattern
Competitive emphasis on	Functional product performance	Product variation	Cost reduction
Innovation stimulated by	Information on users, needs and users, technical inputs	Opportunities created by expanding internal technical capability	Pressure to reduce cost and improve quality
Predominant type of innovation	Frequent major changes in products	Major process changes required by rising volume	Incremental for product and process, with cumulative improvement in productivity and quality
Product line	Diverse, often including custom designs	Includes at least one product design stable enough to have significant production volume	Mostly undifferentiated standard products
Production processes	Flexible and inefficient; major changes easily accommodated	Becoming more rigid, with changes occurring in major steps	Efficient, capital-intensive, and rigid; cost of change high
Equipment	General-purpose, requiring highly skilled labor	Some subprocesses automated, creating "islands of automation"	Special-purpose, mostly automatic with labor tasks mainly monitoring and control
Materials	Inputs limited to generally available materials	Specialized materials perhaps demanded from some suppliers	Specialized materials demanded; if not available, vertical integration extensive
Plant	Small-scale, located near user or source of technology	General-purpose with specialized sections	Large-scale, highly specific to particular products
Organizational control is	Informal and entrepreneurial	Through liaison relationships, project and task groups	Through emphasis on structure, goals, and rules

not present. In such cases, our model may be helpful because it describes conditions that normally support advances at each stage of development; accordingly, if we can compare existing conditions with those prescribed by the model, we may discover how to increase innovative success. For example, we may ask of the model such questions as these about different, apparently independent, managerial actions:

- Can a firm increase the variety and diversity of its product line while simultaneously realizing the highest possible level of efficiency?
- Is a high rate of product innovation consistent with an effort to substantially reduce costs through extensive backward integration?
- Is government policy to maintain diversified markets for technologically active industries consistent with

The Unit of Analysis

As we show in this article, innovation within an established industry is often limited to incremental improvements of both products and processes. Major product change is often introduced from outside an established industry and is viewed as disruptive; its source is typically the start-up of a new, small firm, invasion of markets by leading firms in other industries, or government sponsorship of change either as an initial purchaser or through direct regulation.

These circumstances mean that the standard units of analysis of industry—firm and product type—are of little use in understanding innovation. Technological change causes these terms to change their meaning, and the very shape of the production process is altered.

Thus the questions raised in this article require that a product line and its associated production process be taken together as the unit of analysis. This we term a *productive unit.* For a simple firm or a firm devoted to a single product, the productive unit and the firm would be one and the same. In the case of a diversified firm, a productive unit would usually report to a single operating manager and normally be a separate operating division. The extreme of a highly fragmented production process might mean that several separate firms taken together would be a productive unit.

For example, analysis of change in the textile industry requires that productive units in the chemical, plastics, paper, and equipment industries be included. Analysis involving the electronics industry requires a review of the changing role of component, circuit, and software producers as they become more crucial to change in the final assembled product. Major change at one level works its way up and down the chain, because of the interdependence of product and process change within and among productive units. Knowledge of the production process as a system of linked productive units is a prerequisite to understanding innovation in an industrial context.

a policy that seeks a high rate of effective product innovation?

- Would a firm's action to restructure its work environment for employees so that tasks are more challenging and less repetitive be compatible with a policy of mechanization designed to reduce the need for labor?
- Can the government stimulate productivity by forcing a young industry to standardize its products before a dominant design has been realized?

The model prompts an answer of no to each of these questions; each question suggests actions which the model tells us are mutually inconsistent. We believe that as these ideas are further developed, they can be equally effective in helping to answer many far more subtle questions about the environment for innovation, productivity, and growth.

Exploring the Limits of the Technology S-Curve. Part I: Component Technologies

Clayton M. Christensen
Harvard University Graduate School of Business Administration, Boston, Massachusetts

The technology S-curve is a useful framework describing the substitution of new for old technologies at the industry level. In this paper I use information from the technological history of the disk drive industry to examine the usefulness of the S-curve framework for managers at the *firm* level in planning for new technology development. Because improvements in over-all disk drive product performance result from the interaction of improved *component* technologies and new architectural technologies, each of these must be monitored and managed. This paper focuses on component technology S-curves, and a subsequent paper . . . examines architectural technology S-curves. Improvement in individual components followed S-curve patterns, but I show that the flattening of S-curves is a firm-specific, rather than uniform industry, phenomenon. Lack of progress in conventional technologies may be the *result,* rather than the stimulus, of a forecast that the conventional technology is maturing, and some firms demonstrated the ability to wring far greater levels of performance from existing component technologies than other firms. Attacking entrant firms evidenced a distinct disadvantage versus incumbent firms in developing and using new component technologies. Firms pursuing aggressive S-curve switching strategies in component technology development gained no strategic advantage over firms whose strategies focused on extending the life of established component technologies.

Source: Reprinted by permission from *Production and Operations Management* 1, no. 4 (Fall 1992). Copyright © 1992, Production and Operations Management Society.

EXHIBIT 1   The Technology S-Curve

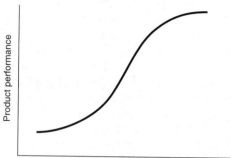

Product performance (vertical axis)

Time or engineering effort

The technology S-curve has become a centerpiece in thinking about technology strategy. It represents an inductively derived theory of the potential for technological improvement, which suggests that the magnitude of improvement in the performance of a product or process occurring in a given period of time or resulting from a given amount of engineering effort differs as technologies become more mature. The theory, depicted in Exhibit 1, states that in a technology's early stages, the rate of progress in performance is relatively slow. As the technology becomes better understood, controlled, and diffused, the rate of technological improvement increases (Sahal 1981). But the theory posits that in its mature stages, the technology will asymptotically approach a natural or physical limit, which requires that ever greater periods of time or inputs of engineering effort be expended to achieve increments of performance improvement.

Foster (1986) used S-curves to explain a general phenomenon of the sort observed by Cooper and Schendel (1976) and Henderson (1988)—that radically new technologies are frequently developed and brought into an industry by *entering* firms, rather than by the incumbent leaders. Foster cites the tendency of leading firms to reinforce and refine maturing technological approaches and their failure to spot new, successor technologies in a timely way as a primary reason why leading firms lose their positions of industry dominance.

The unit of analysis in most published studies of technology maturity and technology S-curves has been at the industry level. For instance, Roussel (1984) looked at foam rubber; Constant (1980) examined aircraft engines; van Wyk, Haour, and Japp (1991) studied permanent magnets; and Foster (1986) used examples from a range

of industries. My purpose in this paper is to summarize a body of theoretical and empirical research, much of it relating to patterns of technological progress in the disk drive industry, to enrich our understanding of the uses and limits of technology S-curve theory *from the point of view of a manager within a single firm.* Given that S-curve phenomena have convincingly been shown to exist at more aggregate levels, I explore in this paper and its companion paper (Christensen 1992b) the strengths and shortcomings of S-curve theory when managers use it within individual firms to plan technology development. I have summarized the data sources and the methodologies employed to collect and analyze it in Appendixes A and B.

Drawing upon analyses of the disk drive industry, I offer four propositions about the usefulness of technology S-curves to managers of technology development and suggest that the insights drawn from studying the disk drive industry may be archetypical of a broader range of industries whose products are complex assemblies of components:

1. At the industry level, using a high-level measure of product performance—the recording density of magnetic disk technology, in the case studied here—S-curves can provide rather convincing explanations of why alternative technologies have made or have failed to make substantial inroads against currently dominant technology.

2. To achieve improvements in the sorts of high-level measures of system performance mentioned in (1) above, managers must conceive and execute a sequence of projects to improve the component technologies used in a product and to refine or revamp the architectural system design within which the components operate. For an engineering or research manager, therefore, technology S-curves will be operationally useful if they aid in planning component and architectural technology development programs.

3. When used to assess component technologies' improvement trajectories, S-curves may be useful in describing an individual firm's experience, but the framework has serious shortcomings if used in a *prescriptive* sense to indicate the direction *future* research programs ought to take. The levels at which individual firms perceived component technologies to have plateaued differed across firms by nearly an order of magnitude. The industry's leading incumbent firms were generally the most aggressive in switching to new component technology S-curves, but there

is no evidence that they gained any sort of strategic advantage over firms that stayed longer with conventional componentry. If anything, a strategy of extending or "riding" the S-curve of conventional technology and of switching component technology S-curves *behind* the industry's component technology leaders seems to have led to greater success.

4. In the disk drive industry, the technological changes in which attackers have demonstrated strategic advantage (Foster 1986) have been *architectural* in nature. Established firms find these technologies difficult to spot because alternative architectures are often initially deployed in historically unimportant commercial applications. Typical S-curve frameworks in which a new technology S-curve rises from beneath and intersects the performance obtainable from mature technologies tend to frame architectural innovation only in *technological* terms. In reality, architectural technology change involves an intense degree of *market* innovation, in addition to technological innovation. I propose an alternative S-curve framework for assessing architectural change, one which embraces both aspects of such technologies.

This paper supports the first three of these propositions; the fourth is discussed in the subsequent paper (Christensen 1992b). This paper is divided into three principal sections. In the first, I summarize key concepts treated in earlier studies of technological innovation and briefly outline the technological history of the disk drive industry. In the second, I evaluate the usefulness of S-curves in assessing the potential for performance improvement of magnetic recording technology versus other technologies at an industry level. In the third section, I examine the value and limits of S-curve frameworks to managers in planning a sequence of projects to develop new component technologies.

CONTEXT OF THIS STUDY

I define technology for the purposes of this study as a process, technique, or methodology—embodied in a product design or in a manufacturing or service process—which transforms inputs of labor, capital, information, material, and energy into outputs of greater value. Building upon the work of Sahal (1981), I define a technological change as a change in one or more of such inputs, processes, techniques, or methodologies that improves the measured levels of performance of a product or process. Technology defined in this way is specific to particular products or processes. As such, it is distinct

from *knowledge,* whose value may not be unique to specific products or processes. Definitions of the technical terms related to disk drives used in the following discussion can be found in Appendix B.

The vertical axis of technology S-curves is constructed to measure an important dimension of product or process performance. Choice of the units measured on the horizontal axis generally reflects the purpose of the author (O'Brien 1962). Scholars whose objective is to measure the relative efficiency or potential productivity of development teams' efforts generally measure engineering effort along the horizontal axis (Foster 1986). Those attempting to assess the impact of differences in technological maturity on product sales or competitive position often measure time on the horizontal axis (Becker and Speltz 1983; Roussel 1983; Thomas 1984).

Although many of the researchers cited herein simply report observations of S-curve phenomena, a few examine processes of technology maturation in considerable depth. For example, Foster (1986) suggests that the leveling of a technology's trajectory of improvement is attributable to limits imposed by fundamental facts of nature. Foster supports this explanation of maturity with examples from several industries—one of which is the substitution of steam for wind-powered ships: he shows that the speed of wind-powered vessels was inherently limited by the physics of wind and water. Constant (1980) explored a single industry and technology at much greater depth, showing how the substitution of turbojet technology for piston engine technology in the aircraft industry proceeded through a series of asynchronous, discontinuous improvements in the performance of individual materials and components. Sahal (1981) essentially offers a *theory* of technology maturity: he posits that the rate of performance improvement achievable within a given technological approach declines because of *scale* phenomena (things either get impossibly large or small) or because of system *complexity.* Because either of these problems makes further progress more difficult, Sahal suggests that the only way to maintain the pace of progress is through radical system redefinition.

Rigid disk drives are an interesting product category to which S-curve analysis might be applied. The industry has been characterized by a high degree of technological turbulence since IBM invented the first disk drive at its San Jose, California, laboratories in 1956. In investigating how new technologies emerged and substituted for maturing ones in this industry, I employ the typologies of technological change proposed by Henderson and Clark (1990). *Architectural change* involves a rearrangement of the way in which components (whose fundamental technological basis remains unchanged) relate to each other within a product's system design. *Modular innovation* is a fundamental change in the technological approach employed in a component, where the product architecture is fundamentally left unchanged. *Incremental change* refers to (1) improvements in component performance that build upon the established technological concept or (2) refinements in system design that involve no significant changes in the technical relationships among components. *Radical innovations* involve both a new architecture *and* a new fundamental technological approach at the component level.

At the architectural level, seven distinctively different architectural technologies captured a double-digit share of market units at some point between 1960 and 1990. And at the component level, there were innumerable incremental technological advances, as well as several modular or "competency-destroying" ones (Tushman and Anderson 1986) in the heads, disks, actuators, motors, and controller software or firmware that constitute the drive. At the architectural and component levels, this has been an industry in which the strategic management of technology seems to have been an extraordinary challenge. Over 130 firms entered the world disk drive industry between 1960 and 1990—firms ranging from such vertically integrated computer giants as IBM and Fujitsu to venture capital–backed start-ups. Leadership in this industry has been tenuous: in the merchant or original equipment manufacturer (OEM) disk drive market, an entrant company emerged to lead five of the seven architecturally defined product generations.

Rigid disk drives are comprised of one or more rotating disks—polished aluminum platters coated with magnetic material—mounted on a central spindle. Data is recorded and read on concentric tracks on the surfaces of these disks. Read/write heads, one each for the top and bottom surfaces of each disk on the spindle, are aerodynamically designed to fly a fraction of a micron over the surface of the disk. They generally rest on the disk's surface when the drive is at rest, "take off" as the drive begins to spin, and "land" again when the disks stop. The heads are positioned over the proper track on the disk by an actuator motor, which moves the heads across the tracks in a fashion similar to the arm on a phonograph. The head is essentially a tiny electromagnet whose polarity changes when the direction of electrical current passing through it changes. Because opposite magnetic poles attract, changes in polarity of the head orient the polarity of the magnetic domain on the disk's surface immediately beneath it, resulting in a sequence of positively and negatively oriented domains. In this manner, data is

written in binary code on the disk. To read data, the drive uses changes in magnetic field on the disk as it spins beneath the head to induce changes in current flow, essentially the reverse process of writing. Disk drives also include electronic circuitry enabling computers to control and communicate with the drive.

As in other magnetic recording products, *areal recording density* (measured in megabits per square inch of disk surface area, or mbpsi) is the pervasive measure of product performance in the disk drive industry. A drive's total capacity is calculated by multiplying the total available square inches on the top and bottom surfaces of the disks mounted on the spindle of the drive by its areal recording density.

AN AGGREGATE, INDUSTRY-LEVEL VIEW OF TECHNOLOGICAL MATURITY IN MAGNETIC RIGID DISK DRIVES

Exhibit 2a charts the average areal density of all disk drive models introduced for sale by all manufacturers in the world between 1970 and 1989. The pace of improvement has been remarkably steady over this period, averaging 34 percent per year; with time as the horizontal metric, no S-curve pattern of progress is yet apparent.

In spite of this progress, radically different technologies such as bubble, optical, and flash memory—which actually or potentially have offered greater recording density, speed, or reliability—have loomed threateningly on the horizon of economic and technological competitiveness for years. The approach employed by S-curve theorists, such as Foster (1986), offers an explanation for why magnetic recording technology has held competing approaches at bay for so long. Foster notes that even though it may be natural to think of technological improvement in terms of an annual rate, it is *engineering effort,* not time, that causes technology to improve. Foster therefore urges that the horizontal axis of S-curves should measure engineering effort. Constructing an areal density S-curve with a proxy for engineering effort on the horizontal axis, rather than time, can indeed help us understand why alternative recording technologies have not yet significantly displaced magnetic disk memory technology in spite of repeated forecasts of its demise (e.g., Drexel, Burnham, and Lambert 1985).

Exhibit 2b shows that what appeared in Exhibit 2a as a relatively constant rate of improvement *over time* in areal density appears instead to be an *increasing* rate of improvement *per unit of engineering effort applied.* (Because accurate measures of industry engineering effort are unavailable in public sources, I have measured total

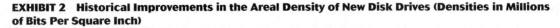

EXHIBIT 2   Historical Improvements in the Areal Density of New Disk Drives (Densities in Millions of Bits Per Square Inch)

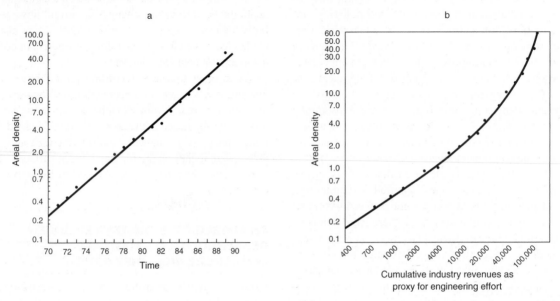

industry revenue on the horizontal axis of Exhibit 2b as a proxy for effort. The percentage of industry revenues devoted to research and engineering has not changed significantly.) Foster (1986) contends that during such periods of increasing returns to technology development effort as are shown in Exhibit 2b, the performance of alternative techniques rarely surpasses that of established technologies. S-curve theory, when used in a descriptive or predictive mode at the industry level, would suggest that it is only after the industry's technological productivity has reached its zenith at the S-curve's point of inflection, that magnetic disk recording technology might begin to be vulnerable to alternative approaches.

As a *descriptive or predictive theory,* S-curves such as these can be helpful in understanding more thoroughly the dynamics of technologically competitive environments, at least at an aggregate, industry level. Similar analyses such as Roussel's (1984) for foam rubber, Tchijov and Norov's (1989) for computer-integrated manufacturing (CIM) technologies, and van Wyk, Haour, and Japp's (1991) for permanent magnets seem to provide useful insights about the potential of alternative technologies at an industry level.

After drawing upon the S-curve's descriptive power at an aggregate industry level, a number of writers have advocated the use of S-curves as a firm-level *prescriptive* guide in the strategic management of technology. Becker and Speltz (1983) and Foster (1986), in particular, seem

to draw strong prescriptive implications for managers from industry-level observations. Exhibit 3 shows the essence of these prescriptions. These authors urge strategists to identify when the S-curve of the technology they currently employ has passed its point of inflection, to identify new approaches that are rising from below at a more productive rate and that may in the future intersect with the current technology, and to launch efforts to acquire or develop the new technology in time to switch to it when its performance surpasses the capabilities of the present technology. In other words, prescriptive S-curve theory would have a firm follow the dotted line in Exhibit 3.

Although this framework seems sensible, studies of technology maturity to date have not empirically addressed how managers at the firm-level might use S-curve analysis as a guide in the strategic management of technology development within their individual firms. As I show in the following analysis, the view from the trenches is more ambiguous than aggregate views.

Questions of whether and when a radically new technological approach such as optical storage or flash memory will intersect with the magnetic recording S-curve are important long-term strategic questions for disk drive company managers. On a month-to-month and year-to-year basis, however, technology managers in disk drive companies are not occupied with such high-level questions. The smooth performance improvement trajectories

EXHIBIT 3   Prescriptive S-Curve Strategy

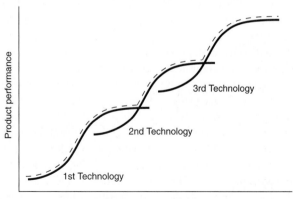

mapped in Exhibit 2 are a summary manifestation of myriad Exhibit 3-type technology extensions and substitutions at lower component and architectural technology levels. Engineers manage improvements in over-all product performance by interactively affecting the capabilities of *components* and by refining or overhauling the product's *architectural design.* These are the sorts of technology planning decisions that dominate the technology manager's planning calendar. To keep up with the industry's relentless pace of improvements in recording density, technology managers must monitor improvement trajectories of present and potential architectural technologies and the extent to which individual component technologies constitute an actual or potential bottleneck to the continued improvement in the recording densities of their disk drives. They then must conceive a set and sequence of architectural and component technology development programs that, when successfully executed and integrated, will keep their firms in the competitive technological race charted in Exhibit 2. When using the firm as a unit of analysis, therefore, one must assess the value of S-curves in planning component and architectural technology development.

As an example of how S-curves might be used as a framework for planning component technology change, consider the role of read-write head technology change in driving disk drive system performance improvement. In the conceptual framework of Exhibit 3, there were numerous incremental improvements to the original ferrite head technology, which enabled manufacturers to grind the heads to smaller, more precise dimensions. Such improvements were the drivers of performance along the first technology curve. Thin film heads represented a second, modularly different technology, which displaced

ferrite heads in most models between 1979 and 1990—analogous to the way in which the second curve intersects with the first in Exhibit 3. Magneto-resistive heads have recently emerged, representing a third, fundamentally different approach to head design, illustrated in concept by the third curve. This sequence of technology substitution is typical of what has occurred with each component and architectural technology over the past 30 years. The driver of the smooth progression of performance at the system level has been extensive technological turmoil at the component and architecture levels.

Analyzing technological maturity at the component *and* architectural levels is important in firm-level analyses such as this not only because both sorts of innovation can be sources of system performance improvement but because *component* and *architecture* are relative, not absolute, concepts. For example, a read-write head can be viewed at one level as a complex *system architecture,* comprising component parts and materials that interact with each other within an architected system. At the next level, the head is a component in a disk drive, which itself is a complex architected system, composed of a variety of components. At a yet higher level, the disk drive is a component in a computer, in which a central processing unit, semiconductor memory, rigid and floppy drives, and input-output peripherals interact within a designed architecture. And finally, such a computer is itself a component in an information processing system architecture, comprised of the computer, software, operators, applications, sources and uses of data, and so forth. These constitute a sort of *nested system of architectures.* System performance at any given level within a nested system such as this is generally driven not only by innovations at that level but by improvements in component performance and architectural design at lower levels in the system.

For these reasons, in this paper and its companion (Christensen 1992b), I focus first on the use of S-curve theory in planning component technology development and then examine the value of S-curve theory in guiding plans for architectural technology development.

USING S-CURVES TO PRESCRIBE DEVELOPMENT OF NEW COMPONENT TECHNOLOGIES

Whether S-curves can be used to guide the planning of component technology development is important because, to borrow bank robber Willie Sutton's phrase, "That's where the money is." In the enterprise of disk drive research and engineering, as shown by Christensen (1992a), component technology development often begins with fundamental research questions, passes through applied research and product design and development, and ends in extensive process engineering. The development of thin film heads at IBM alone took longer than a decade and cost over $300 million, and the industry spent well over $1 billion on thin-film disk development. Development of new product architectures, on the other hand, at most costs developers a few million dollars and often consumes less than a year of calendar time.

Evidence from the substitution patterns of successive waves of new component technologies in disk drives suggests that using S-curve analysis as a basis for prescribing new component technology development programs can be problematic at several levels. In the discussion that follows I describe in detail the substitution of new-technology thin-film read-write heads for ferrite heads and of thin-film disks for particulate oxide-coated disks as an example of the difficulties individual managers may confront when managing the switch from one component technology to another. Similar accounts could be constructed for every other significant component technology in the industry's history. I then present evidence that despite these difficulties, and contrary to Foster's (1986) observation that attacking firms often seize the advantage when new technologies invade a market, the incumbent firms quite capably used new component technologies to preempt competitive attacks into existing markets.

THE EMERGENCE OF THIN-FILM HEAD AND DISK TECHNOLOGIES

The physical size of the head's electromagnet is a critical factor affecting a drive's recording density. Heads were traditionally built by coiling fine copper wire around tiny, precision-ground cores of ferrite. For reasons of cost, reliability, and certainty of supply, engineers generally had strong incentives to continue using conventional ferrite heads as long as possible. As engineers sensed they were approaching the physical limits of how small ferrite cores could be machined, however, they began efforts in the early 1970s to use thin-film photolithography—a process used in integrated circuit manufacturing—to create much smaller, more precise electromagnets on the heads.

Disks historically were coated with microscopic particles of magnetic metal oxide. Efforts to improve density within the particulate oxide approach involved making the particles smaller and more uniform and dispersing them so that the maximum possible surface area on the disk was coated with magnetic media. When disk engineers felt they had reached the limits of fineness, uniformity, and dispersion, they too turned to thin-film deposition technology, attempting to coat substrates with extremely thin, continuous coatings of metal.

There were *great* differences in perceptions—*within* firms and *across* firms—about whether and when thin film heads and disks needed to be substituted for the established ferrite and oxide technologies. Both types of ambiguity are illustrated in Exhibit 4, which charts the experiences of two of the industry's leading competitors, Fujitsu and Control Data Corporation (CDC), as they wrestled with the switch from ferrite to thin-film head technology and from particulate oxide to thin-film disk technology as means for achieving greater areal density. Control Data was the largest American supplier of disk drives to OEM computer manufacturers throughout the 1970s and 1980s, with a market share in several of those years exceeding 60 percent. Fujitsu was the largest Japanese maker of disk drives from 1977 to the present. Exhibit 4 casts both firms' performance with ferrite heads and oxide disks in an S-curve format, where the maximum areal density of models introduced in each year is measured on the vertical axis and time is charted on the horizontal axis. (Since this analysis involves comparing two firms' technical progress over time, rather than assessing the productivity of engineering efforts targeted at two different technologies, I have charted time rather than engineering effort on the horizontal axis.) Note that for each firm there appear to have been *two,* not one, ferrite/oxide S-curves. What accounts for the first plateau of ferrite/oxide technology and its subsequent second wind?

Apparently, according to the industry participants I interviewed for this study, both firms launched development efforts for thin-film heads and/or disks just prior to the onset of the plateau—CDC in about 1977 and Fujitsu in 1980. Both firms' projects encountered a range of unforeseen problems, however, and neither could introduce these components according to their original plans. With no technological alternatives, their only choice was to wring additional performance from the ferrite/oxide approach while they scrambled to get thin-film components ready. Both firms' engineers met this challenge with astounding success, pushing areal densities with ferrite/oxide technology to about *triple* the level at which each seems initially to have planned to abandon ferrite/oxide technology.

The proximate cause of the temporary plateaus in Exhibit 4 seems to have been that engineering resources

EXHIBIT 4 S-Curves for Ferrite/Oxide Technologies at Fujitsu and Control Data Corporation

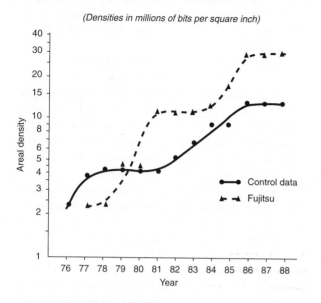

(Densities in millions of bits per square inch)

were reallocated: in both instances, these firms scaled back the engineering effort targeted at ferrite heads and oxide disks, betting that ferrite/oxide technology was nearing its limit and that thin film was a key to future system improvement. The time-measured plateaus in the areal density achieved with ferrite heads may have been "induced" by the appearance of the alternative thin-film approach, which relieved the pressure—and usurped the resources—to push conventional technology further. In other words, the very *forecast* that the conventional technology was approaching its natural limit may in fact have been the proximate *cause* of a leveling in the technology's improvement trajectory, because of the impact the forecast had on the allocation of engineering resources. Whether the 30 mbpsi plateau Fujitsu achieved in 1987 represents the "real" natural limit of recording density achievable with ferrite heads and oxide disks or is simply a self-fulfilling prophecy that the future belongs to thin film we may never know.

Steele (1983) examined this phenomenon, noting that executives and engineers alike often become enamored with radically new technologies—we might call them technological long shots—as solutions to product performance plateaus. Steele shows that these long shots generally require far more time and money to develop than originally believed and that most progress is achieved instead through the incremental, steady advance of conventional technology. The forecast arrivals of such technological long shots as gallium arsenide, op-

tical disk memory, and ceramic engines have been delayed or preempted by the steady cumulation of incremental improvements to conventional technology. The cases presented here support the proposition that there can be far more latent performance potential in a conventional technology than individual firms or industry experts may perceive.

The innovations that enabled the second burst of performance improvement for each of these firms were of the incremental sort defined by Henderson and Clark (1990). For example, three important incremental technologies advanced the performance of ferrite heads. A modified barium-doped ferrite material was developed, which had the strength to be ground to thinner dimensions. Lapping processes capable of making smaller and more precise heads supplanted grinding. And finally, placing a strip of metal in the gap separating the leading and trailing sections of the head proved to strengthen the magnetic field created by the head. Similar incremental improvements were made in the size, uniformity, and dispersion of oxide particles that coated the disks. The cumulation of these developments in ferrite heads and oxide disks pushed performance far beyond what initially had been viewed as limits.

An explanation of why Fujitsu and CDC perceived limits to be at such different levels is that *nobody knows* what the natural, physical performance limit is in complex engineered products, such as disk drives and their components. Since engineers do not know what they may discover or develop in the future, since the physical laws (and the relationships between laws) governing performance are imperfectly understood, and since possibilities for circumventing known physical limits cannot be well foreseen, the natural or physical limits cited by scholars of technological maturity, such as Foster (1986) and Twiss (1979), may in practice be moving targets rather than immovable barriers. Foster (1986) cites sailing ships as an example in which the physics of wind and water imposed a natural limit on the speed of sailing ships. In retrospect, given what we now know, that is probably a true statement. But to the designers of ships in the 1800s (and one might say the 1990s), the interactive physics of wind and water were themselves being explored and defined by those practicing the art of sailing ship design. Such limits are dynamic, relative, changing concepts from the point of view of technology developers.

Even when designers confront an apparently immutable natural limit in a component within a product system as complex as that of a disk drive, there may be several engineering avenues for resolving the system-level performance problem—there is often more than one way to skin the cat. Although one component's performance may be on a plateau—an actual or perceived physical limit—engineers can continue to improve system performance by applying effort to less mature elements of the system design. For example, the discovery of run-length–limited recording codes in the mid-1980s contributed to the resurgence of ferrite-oxide disk drive performance, because it boosted the density of drives by 30 percent independently of which disk and head technologies were employed in a model. In an even more dramatic instance, Henderson (1993) has shown that the line resolution that could be achieved with step-and-repeat photolithographic equipment by 1986 was substantially less than the minimum possible resolution that had been calculated, in the early 1980s, to be constrained by the *wave length of light.*

Because actual or perceived limits can be circumvented through advances in less mature elements of a product's design, when designs differ significantly across firms, perceptions of technological maturity may be highly firm specific. Whether a particular component technology is perceived to be a bottleneck to further improvement and whether viable alternatives exist for circumventing such a bottleneck may depend upon firm-specific characteristics of a product's design. Such firm specificity is apparent in Exhibit 4. Note that CDC's initial "limit" for ferrite/oxide technology was about 4 mbpsi—one third the density at which Fujitsu encountered its initial "limit."

Exhibit 5 illustrates the extent of these across-firm differences in perceptions about the limits of density achievable with ground ferrite heads and particulate oxide-coated disks across a wider range of firms. On the horizontal dimension, it shows that the timing of switching to thin-film technology differed among leading firms by a decade—a *very* long time in such a turbulent industry. On the vertical axis, Exhibit 5 shows that the densities to which the late-moving firms had pushed the conventional technology were an order of magnitude beyond the levels achieved by the first movers. The chart shows that there was a long, close race between the conventional and new technologies before thin film finally triumphed.

The solid S-curve drawn through the black dots in Exhibit 5 tracks the *industry-average* areal density for drives using ferrite heads and oxide disks between 1975 and 1990. The dashed line above the industry S-curve charts the highest density available in ferrite-oxide drives in each year. Note that densities at this upper performance envelope were generally twice that of the industry average. The dotted line which is just slightly above the ferrite-oxide envelope represents the thin-film envelope—the highest density among all models using thin-film technology.

The paired open circles connected by solid lines denote the points at which the industry's leading firms started their switch to the new component technology S-curve by introducing their first product employing either a thin-film head or a thin-film disk. The first open circle in each pair denotes the highest density the company had achieved in a model using ferrite-oxide technology prior to its introduction of thin-film components. The second circle in each pair is placed at the density achieved in its initial thin-film model. The figure depicts each firm moving from its *highest* density conventional model to its *first* thin-film model. As such, it appears that most of the innovators were above the industry average curve to begin with. Each firm, however, had a range of models with a range of densities—some above and some below the industry average. The highest density conventional models of a few of the firms—Rodime, Hewlett-Packard, Quantum, Seagate, and DEC—were actually below the industry average.

Several features in Exhibit 5 merit comment. Only 5 of the 15 firms shown actually leapt above the ferrite-oxide envelope with their first thin-film model. Although most achieved higher density in thin film than they had in ferrite-oxide, they usually ended up within the range achievable with conventional technology when they switched S-curves. Second, thin-film technology eventually triumphed only after a decade-long battle with ferrite-oxide. Key engineering managers involved in this race indicated that the conventional technology progressed *far* further than anyone had anticipated when thin-film technology was first recognized as a technological alternative. Third, different competitors switched S-curves at different points. IBM moved to thin-film technology when its ferrite-oxide capability had reached 3,500,000 bpsi in 1979. Hitachi and Fujitsu rode the conventional S-curve far longer and had achieved 27 and 30 million bpsi, respectively—over eight times the performance IBM seemed to have identified as the limit of the ferrite-oxide approach—by the time they switched to thin film.

Finally and possibly most important, there is little evidence that the firms that switched component S-curves early—in this case IBM, Memorex, Storage Technology, NEC, CDC, and Rodime—enjoyed sustained first-mover advantages. I have shown this ordinally in

EXHIBIT 5   Points at Which Thin-Film Technology Was Adopted by Leading Manufacturers, Relative to the Capabilities of Ferrite-Oxide Technology at the Time of the Switch

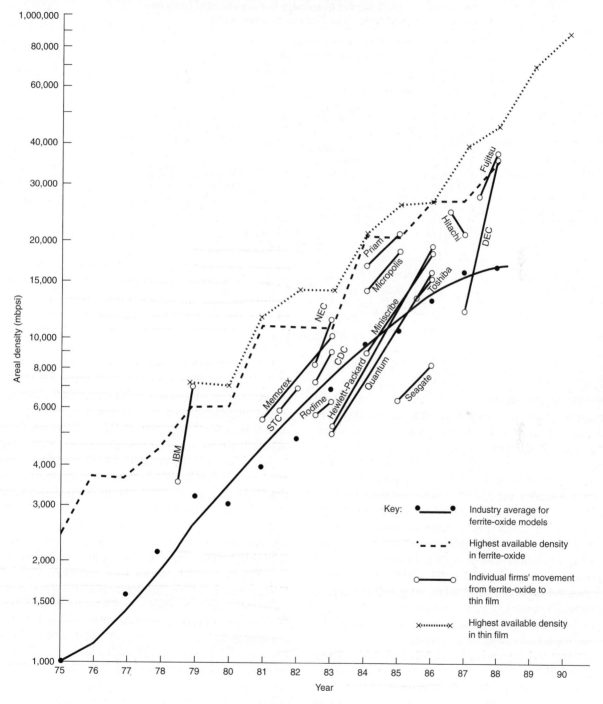

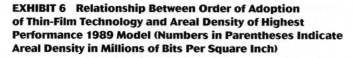

EXHIBIT 6 **Relationship Between Order of Adoption of Thin-Film Technology and Areal Density of Highest Performance 1989 Model (Numbers in Parentheses Indicate Areal Density in Millions of Bits Per Square Inch)**

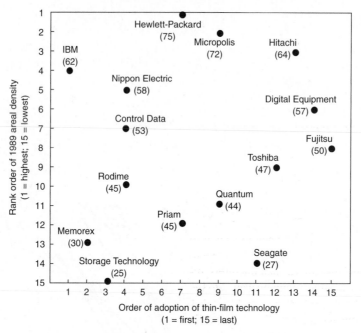

Exhibit 6. The horizontal axis in that chart marks the order in which the leading firms adopted thin-film technology—IBM being 1st, Fujitsu being 15th, and so on. The vertical axis ranks the firms according to the areal density of their most advanced model in 1989. There seems to be no correlation between order of adoption—and presumably the deeper experience with the technology that leadership might entail—and the density each was ultimately able to achieve. In fact, the combined share of the total world market held by the early adopters of thin-film technology fell from 60 percent in 1981 to 37 percent in 1989. The firms that switched curves later—Priam, Micropolis, Miniscribe, Seagate, Hewlett-Packard, Quantum, Toshiba, Hitachi, DEC, and Fujitsu—saw their combined world market share rise from 10 percent in 1981 to 33 percent.

Christensen (1992a) shows that the industry's leading incumbent firms were consistently the leaders in developing and adopting new component technologies. Entrant firms that pioneered the use of new component technologies as a vehicle for achieving improved product performance were rarely successful: entrants enjoyed no attacker's advantage. Many factors affect the success and failure of firms, only one of which is component tech-

nology strategy. The point, however, is that switching to new component technology S-curves early does not seem to have been necessary or sufficient for competitive success in this industry. In contrast, I show in the companion article to this paper (Christensen 1992b) that those firms which led the industry in switching to new *architectural technology* S-curves enjoyed powerful first-mover advantages.

This suggests that the S-curve switching mode of planning for component technology development prescribed in Exhibit 3 may not be the manager's only option. Since industry-level technological maturity curves are aggregates of the performance achieved by many firms and since a product's performance results from the complex interaction of many different components and system design alternatives, individual managers may have substantial leeway for extending the performance of established component technologies before undertaking the risk and expense of developing and employing new componentry based upon fundamentally different technological approaches.

There may not always be such wide differences of opinion about S-curve exhaustion within an industry as are illustrated here. Indeed, in some technical questions, such as whether to switch from one type of material to another, the natural limits of performance may be relatively unambiguous, broadly known, and uniformly understood. In instances such as the one above, however, in which a technology's performance results from exploiting some combination of broadly understood physical laws and firm-specific, experience-based know-how, the shape of perceived technology S-curves may be unique to individual firms rather than driven by absolute laws and physical relationships. Descriptions and predictions based upon industry-level maturity curves, therefore, need not and possibly *should not* be taken as prescriptions of firm-level strategy.

DO SYSTEMATIC DIFFERENCES EXIST IN HOW FIRMS RESPOND TO POTENTIAL MATURITY IN COMPONENT TECHNOLOGY?

Given this ambiguity in whether and when to switch to new component technology S-curves, it is instructive to examine whether leading disk drive manufacturers responded to that ambiguity in any systematic way—to see whether some firms' technology strategies might emphasize switching component technology S-curves, while the strategies of other firms might emphasize extending the S-curves of current component technologies. To do this, I compared data on changes in the component and architectural technologies employed in each firm's disk drive models with changes in the performance of these models over the 1976–1989 period, to trace the means by which each firm achieved performance improvement. Based on this analysis, I found that some firms, such as IBM, tended systematically to rely upon frequent switches to more advanced component technologies as a primary driver of performance improvement. Other firms, such as Hewlett-Packard, tended to rely upon incremental improvements in established component technologies and upon refinements in system design to achieve competitive performance improvements. Most firms' tendencies were consistent over time, essentially reflecting conscious or de facto technology strategies.

These findings emerged from a regression analysis, in which I estimated coefficients to a multivariate equation that describes the log of areal recording density as a function of (1) the year in which a model was first shipped and (2) technologies employed in that model for the components that most directly determine areal density—actuator motors, disks, heads, recording codes, interfaces, and the basic architectural technologies. Data used to estimate these coefficients were the detailed product speci-

fications for every disk drive model announced in the world between 1979 and 1990. I coded the technologies used in these models by dummy variables: use of the early, dominant technology was coded as 0, and use of a new technology was coded as 1. In some components, there was a progression of new technologies over the period studied rather than a single new replacement technology. For example, modified frequency modulation (MEM) recording codes were replaced by the sequence of 2,7 RLL, 1,7 RLL, and partial-response, maximum-likelihood (PRML) codes. The dummy variable technique used here measures the impact on density of each of these technologies relative to the original technology (MFM in the case of code technology), rather than measuring density relative to the immediately prior technology. Exhibit 7 describes the variables included in this exercise, along with the coefficients and t-statistics, which were estimated using multiple least squares.

The interaction between head and disk technologies was captured in an interaction term in this specification. Interviews with industry technical experts suggested that from an engineering perspective, this was the primary interaction that needed to be measured to isolate the impact of changes in individual component technologies on improvements in recording density. To gauge the stability of the measured coefficients over time, I split the sample into two periods, 1979–1986 and 1987–1990. The coefficients of the equation estimated from these two subsets of the population are reported in the right-most columns of Exhibit 7. To better understand possible differences in strategic approaches toward new component technology, I first estimated the coefficients from the entire industry data base and then estimated coefficients using only the models introduced by specific firms.

Note in Exhibit 7 that since the dependent variable is the log of areal density, if the coefficients for each of the explanatory variables are exponentiated and significant interactions are taken into account, the result is the percentage improvement in density associated with the use of each new technology. The improvement in density *not* attributable to modular changes in component technology or system architecture—and presumably due to the combined impact of incremental improvements in established component technologies and refinements in system design—is captured by the coefficient of the *time* variable. Its value in the total-period equation of 0.163 (which exponentiated is 1.18) indicates that of the 34 percent average annual rate of improvement in areal density over this period, slightly more than half—18 percent—is attributable to incremental improvements that

EXHIBIT 7 Measured Impact of New Component Technologies on the Areal Recording Density of Disk Drives

New technology variables, coded by dummy=1			Total period, 1979–1990			1st period, 1979–1986		2nd period, 1987–1990		Original (reference) technology, coded by dummy=0
			Coeffi-cients	t-statistics	% increase in density associated with variable*	Coeffi-cients	t-statistics	Coeffi-cients	t-statistics	
Constant	B_0		1.935			0.601		2.65		
Time	B_1		0.163	26.31	18%	0.179	18.41	0.155	11.96	Continuous variable
Modular component technologies										
Actuator motor	Stepper motor	B_2	−0.437	−14.48	−35%	−0.588	−13.63	−0.295	−7.41	Voice coil motor
	Torque motor	B_3	−0.136	−2.84	−13%	−0.121	−2.02	−0.213	−2.88	Voice coil motor
Disk	Thin film	B_4	0.275	9.88	32%	0.223	5.92	0.248	6.91	Particulate oxide
Head	Thin film	B_5	0.346	6.65	41%	0.436	6.37	0.127	1.70	Ferrite
	MIG	B_6	0.116	2.54	12%	n/a		0.192	4.62	Ferrite
Recording code 2,7 RLL	RLL	B_7	0.206	6.07	23%	0.198	4.18	0.335	7.06	MFM
	1,7 RLL	B_8	0.454	9.38	57%	0.394	2.58	0.635	11.33	MFM
	PRML	B_9	0.390	2.67	48%	n/a		0.507	3.91	MFM
Servo System	Embedded	B_{10}	0.004	0.12	0%	0.006	0.00	0.029	0.91	Dedicated disk
Interface	Embedded SCSI, AT, or ESDI	B_{11}	0.188	5.45	21%	0.176	3.30	0.202	4.49	ST506, ST412, SA1000, ANSI
	SMD	B_{12}	0.306	6.30	36%	0.300	5.19	0.220	2.58	ST506, ST412, SA1000, ANSI
	IPI-2	B_{13}	0.356	3.72	43%	0.267	2.02	0.235	2.18	ST506, ST412, SA1000, ANSI
	Proprietary	B_{14}	0.202	4.48	22%	0.196	3.59	0.205	2.75	ST506, ST412, SA1000, ANSI
Architectural technologies										
	8-inch	B_{15}	0.097	2.19	10%	0.117	2.29	0.057	0.53	14-inch
	5.25-inch	B_{16}	0.185	3.25	20%	0.248	3.42	0.022	0.21	14-inch
	3.5-inch	B_{17}	0.315	4.77	37%	0.663	6.64	0.015	0.98	14-inch
Interaction	Thin-film head×thin-film disk	B_{18}	−0.098	−1.67	−9%	−0.317	−2.40	0.167	2.13	
Goodness of fit	R^2		0.91			0.81		0.81		
Number of observations			1033			544		489		

Dependent variable is the log of areal density.

MIG, metal-in-gap; RLL, run length limited; MFM, modified frequency modulation; PRML, partial response, maximum likelihood.

*This measure quantifies the impact on density of each new technology as if it were "inserted" individually into a new drive model, with all other component and architectural technologies held unchanged. To ascertain the *net* effect on areal density in the case of head and disk technologies, the interaction between the components must also be accounted for.

cannot be traced to specific new component or architectural technologies. The remaining 16 percent of the industry-average 34 percent annual rate of improvement was the summary impact of the modular substitution of new component technologies, made component by component, model by model, year by year, and firm by firm.

A way to visualize these measures of the impact of incremental and modular modes of component technology development on the improvement of industry-average areal density is in the framework of Exhibit 3. On average for the industry, slightly more than half (53 percent) of the total improvement came from progress *along* established component or architectural technology S-curves and slightly less than half came from *switching* S-curves. Note that in the split-sample analysis the B_1 coefficient for the *time* variable, a proxy for the contribution of incremental innovation to over-all improvement, was similar in the two periods.

The middle section of Exhibit 7 presents the coefficients for the sequence of new architectural technologies. When compared to the density of 14-inch drives with equivalent component technology in the total-period sample, the smaller the form factor, the greater the density. This is because smaller drives have more rigid components; the head-disk assembly weighs less, so that it can be positioned more accurately, with less inertia, over more finely spaced tracks; and there is less vibration. The 8-inch architecture enabled a 10 percent density improvement over the 14-inch drives; 5.25-inch drives had 20 percent higher areal density than 14-inch drives with equivalent componentry, and 3.5-inch products enabled a 37 percent density increase over 14-inch products, holding component technology and vintage of models constant. Unlike the coefficients for the *time* variable, however, the coefficients for these architectural technologies declined in magnitude and statistical significance from the first to the second periods in the split-sample analysis. This seems to be the result, according to industry experts, of cross-architecture learning about mechanical and electronic design. Designers of each successively smaller architecture reduced the part count significantly by incorporating more functions that had previously been handled mechanically into the electronics of the drive. Designers of larger-architecture drives were then able to incorporate these design insights into subsequent generations of their 14-, 8-, and 5.25-inch designs.

The bottom section of the table shows the coefficients for the head-disk interaction term. This was included to test the possibility that simultaneous adoption of modular head and disk technologies could contribute synergis-

tically to performance improvement. Note that although the total-period interaction was negative and of marginal statistical significance, the interaction in the first period was significantly negative, while it was significantly *positive* in the latter period. A possible interpretation of this, which is consistent with information I obtained in interviews with company engineers, is that in the early years of a component technology's commercial existence, the systemwide impact of incorporating it into a design is inadequately understood. Designers who used thin-film heads and disks together in the early years therefore suffered a performance penalty—negative synergy—because the systemwide impact of the components was unknown. As designers learned about these technologies, they were able to optimize the design to capture the full benefits, so that use of thin-film heads and disks created positive synergy in the second period. There was not a collinearity problem in measuring the individual contribution of thin-film heads and disks to increases in recording density. Thin-film disks penetrated much more rapidly than disks, so that there were many models using ferrite heads with thin-film disks. Conversely, there were also a number of firms which used thin-film heads with oxide disks.

The R^2 value of 0.91 indicates that the variables included in the equation accounted for 91 percent of the variation in the areal density of the 1,033 models in the total-period data base.

To explore whether firms' technology strategies might differ systematically along the spectrum of relying upon incremental versus modular component technology development as the primary engine of system performance improvement, I estimated the equation specified in Exhibit 7 separately for several of the industry's leading firms. Exhibit 8 presents the results for two technology/performance leaders, IBM and Hewlett-Packard. The average areal density of the product lines of both firms increased at approximately the same rate as the industry average over the period studied, 35 percent. The coefficients for the *time* variable shown in Exhibit 8 indicate, however, that the *sources* of that improvement were different for the two firms. For IBM, the coefficient of the *time* variable, B_1, was 0.14, indicating (when the coefficient is exponentiated) that IBM realized about 15 percent density improvement each year from incremental innovations. Since IBM's total annual improvement in density was 35 percent, this means that the other 20 percent annual improvement came from switching to the new component technologies specified in the equation. In contrast, the B_1 coefficient for the *time* variable

EXHIBIT 8 Measured Impact of Incremental Innovation and New Component Technologies on the Areal Recording Density of Disk Drives: A Comparison of IBM and Hewlett-Packard Products

New technology variables, coded by dummy = 1			IBM		Hewlett-Packard		Original (reference) technology, coded by dummy = 0
			Coefficients	t-statistics	Coefficients	t-statistics	
Constant		B_0	3.86		−3.81		
Time		B_1	0.140	10.47	0.240	6.35	Continuous variable
Modular component technologies							
Actuator motor	Stepper motor	B_2	−0.406	−3.96	—*		Voice coil motor
	Torque motor	B_3			—*		Voice coil motor
Disk	Thin film	B_4	0.191	2.41	1.12	4.88	Particulate oxide
Head	Thin film	B_5	1.070	10.31	0.218	1.41	Ferrite
	MIG	B_6	0.089	0.97			Ferrite
Recording code	2,7 RLL	B_7	0.290	2.86	0.571	3.34	MFM
	1,7 RLL	B_8	0.348	2.83	—*		MFM
	PRML	B_9	0.820	4.43	—*		MFM
Servo system	Embedded	B_{10}	0.006	0.91	−0.279	−3.53	Dedicated disk
Interface	Embedded SCSI, AT, or ESDI	B_{11}	0.199	1.85	—*		ST506, ST412, SA1000, ANSI
	SMD	B_{12}					ST506, ST412, SA1000, ANSI
	IPI-2	B_{13}	0.360	2.09	—*		ST506, ST412, SA1000, ANSI
	Proprietary	B_{14}	−0.189	−1.67			ST506, ST412, SA1000, ANSI
Architectural technologies							
	8-inch	B_{15}	0.373	4.17	−0.097	−0.41	14-inch
	5.25-inch	B_{16}	−0.039	−0.031	0.151	1.20	14-inch
	3.5-inch	B_{17}	0.406	2.61	−0.132	−1.33	14-inch
Interactions	Thin-Film Head × Thin-Film Disk	B_{18}	−0.610	−3.32	0.191	0.03	
Goodness of fit		R^2	0.97		0.97		
Number of observations			126		49		

Dependent variable is the log of area density.

For abbreviations, see Exhibit 7.

* Hewlett-Packard never produced models employing stepper motors, 1,7 RLL and PRML recording codes, and ST506, ST412, SA 1000, or ANSI interfaces, so the contribution of new interface technologies relative to these standards could not be calculated.

in the Hewlett-Packard equation was 0.24. This means, when the coefficient is exponentiated, that Hewlett-Packard achieved a 27 percent annual rate of improvement in density through incremental technological change alone, without relying on the modular adoption of new component technologies. Adoption of new, modular component technologies accounted only for 8 percent annual improvement (27 + 8 = 35 percent overall annual rate of improvement). Indeed, there were a number of component technologies that IBM had adopted which Hewlett-Packard never employed during this period.

In other words, these two firms employed very different means to achieve nearly identical annual rates of density improvement: IBM derived most of its improvement from switching to new component technologies in the "strategic leaps" tradition noted by Hayes (1985), while Hewlett-Packard's performance improvement came largely from extending the efficacy of technological approaches it already employed.

This statistical finding is consistent with the views of IBM and Hewlett-Packard's technological strengths which industry engineering managers expressed in my interviews with them. IBM managers and their competitors uniformly viewed IBM's technological strength as component technology development, while they saw Hewlett-Packard's technical team as masters in system design—as being able to wring more performance from a given set of components than other firms in the industry.

SUMMARY

Although technology S-curves seem to provide useful insights at an aggregate, industry level about the potential for continued improvement of fundamentally different technologies, the application of this framework at a *managerial* level to planning component technology development seems to be very ambiguous. In the disk drive industry, it appears that the perceived flattening of a component's performance trajectory is for practical purposes a firm-specific phenomenon. In fact, it may be that a slowdown in improvement is the *result* of forecasts that improvement potential has been exhausted and the resource allocation decisions that follow from that forecast. Limits to performance improvement, while often clear in retrospect, are changing, dynamic concepts in the world of the operating manager. Since there are many different component and system technology levers to pull in the pursuit of performance improvement (there is

more than one way to skin the cat), even limits imposed by widely understood natural laws have been circumvented. These options seem to have created substantial leeway in the technology strategies chosen by different competitors. Some have gotten most of their performance improvement by extending the performance trajectories of existing component technology, whereas others have followed a technology strategy of switching technology S-curves rather aggressively.

Although S-curve patterns in component technology progress clearly exist, there was no clear evidence of any first mover benefits or "attackers' advantage" (Foster 1986). Firms that switched late to new technology S-curves successfully matched the product performance of the early adopters. In the industry overall, it was the leading, incumbent disk drive manufacturers that consistently led the industry in switching to new component technologies. Would-be attackers, which entered the industry employing new component technologies as a source of product performance advantage, were rarely successful: attackers seem to have been at a decided disadvantage in exploiting new component technologies. The second paper in this series (Christensen 1992b) shows that the opposite case is true at points of architectural technology change. In that study, I show that architectural technologies also follow an S-curve pattern of performance improvement and that first movers and attacking firms enjoyed a decided advantage over late adopters and incumbent firms in architectural technology innovation.[1]

APPENDIX A: DATA SOURCES AND RESEARCH METHODOLOGY

I have taken the data about disk drives reported in this paper from a larger study of that industry (Christensen 1992a). The products upon which I focused that study were rigid disk drives, a product category including drives commonly labeled as Winchester disk drives, which have one or more nonremovable rigid (hard) disks hermetically sealed in the drive housing, as well as drives that employ packs of removable rigid disks. I did not include floppy disk drives in the study. Data in this study

---

[1] I thank Professors Kim B. Clark, Robert H. Hayes, and Steven C. Wheelwright of the Harvard Business School; Professors Rebecca Henderson and James Utterback of the Sloan School of Management, Massachusetts Institute of Technology; and the anonymous referees for invaluable guidance and suggestions for improvement to earlier drafts of this paper. Any remaining shortcomings are my sole responsibility.

essentially drew information from three sources. The first was *Disk/Trend Report,* an industry survey published annually. The editors of *Disk/Trend* collect from each firm participating in the world disk drive industry their revenues and product shipments by "form factor" (disk diameter) and capacity and use that data to calculate the size of each product-market segment, as well as average pricing levels in each segment. They also report the disk drive revenues of each firm and market shares of the principal competitors in each product-market segment. In addition, *Disk/Trend* publishes detailed product performance specifications and a listing of component technologies used in each model currently offered for sale by each of the manufacturers. This listing includes the year and month of first shipment for each disk drive model as well as the list price for a majority of the models. In addition, the editors of *Disk/Trend* allowed me to draw additional data not published in the *Report* from manufacturers' product specification sheets on file in the *Disk/Trend* archives. I used this data to identify the specific models in which each new component and architectural technology was first used in the industry and to trace the patterns of diffusion for each of these new technological approaches. By charting each firm's revenues, by size and capacity of drive over time, I could reconstruct the commercial fortunes of each firm in considerable detail. I gratefully acknowledge the generous assistance of the editors and staff of *Disk/Trend Report* during this project.

The second source of data for the study was trade publications, particularly *Electronic Business Magazine.* I searched each monthly (and more recently, twice-monthly) issue of *Electronic Business* since it was first published in 1976 for notes and articles about disk drive technology, the disk drive industry, and firms participating in it. My purpose was to understand more completely the corporate histories, organizational structures, and competitive strategies pursued by the competitors in the industry, as well as to identify additional disk drive manufacturers that might not have been captured in *Disk/Trend Report* (I found only one such firm). I combined this information with the data from *Disk/Trend* on the sources and patterns of diffusion for each new technology to analyze which *types* of firms tended to pioneer the development and adoption of each new technology. This enabled me to determine the patterns of commercial success and failure among different groups of firms. Comparisons of entrants versus established firms (building on the work of Henderson and Clark 1990) proved particularly fruitful, as did comparisons of firms whose corporate forms were different: venture capital–backed start-ups, vertically integrated computer manufacturers, integrated firms that produced other magnetic recording products, and horizontally diversified firms that produced other computer peripheral products, such as printers and tape drives.

The third category of data used in the study was information from over 60 personal interviews with founders and key engineering and marketing executives associated with eight of the major disk drive manufacturers: IBM, CDC, Digital Equipment, Micropolis, Quantum, Seagate Technology, Miniscribe, and Conner Peripherals. In addition, I interviewed executives at the three largest independent component manufacturing firms: Komag, Read-Rite, and Applied Magnetics. I also interviewed other industry experts and consultants. My purpose in these interviews was to understand and reconstruct as carefully as possible the managerial decision processes that led to these firms' decisions whether or not to develop and deploy particular new technologies, whose importance to the industry was highlighted through work with the data described above.

I gratefully acknowledge the support of the Harvard Business School Division of Research, whose financial assistance made a study of this scope possible.

APPENDIX B: GLOSSARY OF TECHNICAL TERMS

Actuator   The mechanism that positions the head over the proper track on the drive. The class of actuators that has become most commonly used because of its superior positioning ability is called a voice coil motor. This operates on a principle similar to that used in telephones: an arm is moved in and out via electromagnetic forces. Voice coil motors have been made in linear and rotary designs, but the rotary design, which works like the arm on a phonograph, has become the dominant design because it requires less space. A much less expensive actuator mechanism is a stepper motor, in which a shaft rotates in discrete steps to new positions in response to changes in the surrounding magnetic field. Stepper motors are much less expensive than voice coil motors and were used primarily on low-capacity drives targeted to price-sensitive markets. Torque motors and DC motors were also used on a limited number of models in the low-moderate performance range.

Areal Density   The amount of information that can be stored in a square inch of disk surface, measured in megabits per square inch (mbpsi). This is determined by multiplying the number of bits of information storable along a linear inch of track (bit density) by the number of tracks per inch of disk radius (track density).

Disk   The round, rigid platter on which data is magnetically recorded. It is comprised of a substrate, typically made of aluminum polished perfectly flat, coated with particles of magnetic metal oxide or thin metal films. These magnetic coatings are, in turn, coated with lubricating and protecting materials.

Drive   The computer industry's term for the equipment that contains rotating magnetic media—reels of tape, flexible (floppy) disks, or rigid disks—and that controls the flow of electronic information to and from that media.

Embedded Servo System   Mechanical shocks, differential thermal expansion, and a host of other factors can affect the accuracy with which an actuator can position a head over a particular track on a disk. Low-performance drives using stepper motor actuators got around this problem by spacing the tracks far enough apart that such subtle changes and misadjustments rarely caused the head to be mispositioned over the wrong track. High-performance drives, however, require a closed-loop feedback system to the actuator, so that the head can continuously be repositioned precisely over the proper track on the disk. This enables much greater track density. One way of keeping precise head-disk alignment was to dedicate one complete surface of one disk on the spindle to tracking information only. The head reading information off that track and feeding it back to the actuator motor provided such a closed-loop, continuous-adjustment mechanism. In an embedded servo system, track identification markers are written (embedded) on each individual track of each recording surface. This frees up for user information the entire surface that otherwise would have been reserved for tracking information only.

Ferrite   A magnetic compound comprised of iron and oxygen. In disk drives, the primary use of ferrite has been as the core material around which fine copper wires were coiled to form an electromagnet in the head.

Head   A device that contains a tiny electromagnet, positioned on an arm extending over the rotating disk. When the direction of current through the head changes, its polarity switches. Because opposite magnetic poles attract, changes in the polarity of the head cause an opposite change in the polarity of the magnetic material on the disk as it spins immediately beneath the head. The head writes information in binary code in this fashion. Heads read data in the opposite manner—changes in the magnetic flux field over the disk's surface as it spins beneath the head induce changes in the direction of current in the head, reversing the information flow. In rigid disk drives, heads are aerodynamically designed to fly a few millionths of an inch above the surface of the disk; they generally rest on its surface when the drive is at rest, take off as the disk begins spinning, and land when the disk stops again. Heads in floppy disk drives generally do not fly but glide on the disk's surface.

Interface   This refers to the electronic circuitry through which the drive and computer communicate. A description of the differences among interfaces is beyond the scope of this paper. Originally, interfaces were custom-written by each drivemaker for each customer. Although some standard interfaces such as SMD emerged as 8-inch drives were used with minicomputers, the trend toward standardization was accelerated by Seagate Technology's ST412 interface, which required that the rate at which the drive took data off the disk was equal to the rate at which the drive could transfer data to the computer. While low-cost and efficient, this effectively put a ceiling on the bit density of the drive. Subsequent interfaces such as *SCSI* (used primarily with Apple computers); *AT* (used with IBM-compatible computers), and *ESDI* (used primarily with engineering workstations) decoupled these activities. With these interfaces, the drive could take data off the disk as rapidly as its designers wanted, cache it, and then transfer it to the computer as rapidly as the computer could accept it. This enabled much greater bit densities than had been possible under the ST412 interface. Other interfaces used only on a limited number of models were *IPI-1*, *IPI-2*, and *ANSI*.

MFM   An acronym for modified frequency modulation, an early coding technique used in writing data on disks, wherein a magnetic marker was placed on the disk to denote the beginning and ending of each individual piece of information.

MIG Heads   An acronym for metal-in-gap, a version of ferrite head wherein a strip of metal was deposited in the gap between the leading and trailing portions of the head. This strengthened the magnetic flux fields that could be created and sensed by the head, enabling data to be written and read on smaller domains on the disk surface.

Oxide   The term used in the industry for particles made from a compound of oxygen and a magnetic metal, such as iron, cobalt, and chromium. Oxide particles were used to coat mylar substrates to create magnetic tape and floppy disks, and to coat aluminum disks used in rigid, or "hard," disk drives. The oxide particles are the media in which, through changes in the particles' magnetic polarity, data is stored magnetically. The particles are generally of an elongated, needle-like shape.

Photolithography   The manufacturing process through which a desired pattern of one material is applied onto another substrate material. Typically, the substrate is first coated (by plating or sputtering) with the material from which the final pattern is to be made. This is in turn coated with a light-sensitive monomeric material, called a photoresist. A mask of the desired pattern is then held over the photoresist, and the unmasked material is exposed to light, causing the exposed material to cure. The unexposed photoresist is then washed away. Through a subsequent series of etching and washing steps, only the desired material, in the desired pattern, is left on the substrate. Integrated circuits are built on silicon wafers, and thin film heads are built, through photolithographic processes.

PRML   An acronym for partial response, maximum likelihood, a coding technique that has followed RLL and MFM recording codes.

Recording Density   See *areal density*.

RLL   An acronym for run-length–limited recording codes, which enable data to be written more densely than was possible with MFM codes. Two versions of RLL codes have been used: 2,7 and 1,7.

Spin Motor   The electric motor that drives the rotation of the spindle upon which the disks are mounted. In 14- and 8-inch drives the spin motor often was situated in the corner of the drive and drove the stack of disks via a pulley. In the 5.25 and subsequent drive architectures, a flat, direct-drive "pancake" motor was positioned beneath the spindle.

Spindle   The shaft upon which one or more disks was mounted.

Stepper Motors   See *actuators*.

Thin Film   A continuous, very thin film (often only a few angstroms thick) of a material (often a metal) on another substrate material. This is generally applied through a process called sputtering, in which a substrate is placed at the bottom of a vacuum chamber. A target of the film material is then bombarded with electrons,

which dislodge ions of the target material. These ions float like a vapor in the vacuum chamber and then gradually settle in a thin, continuous film on the surface of the substrate. This deposition technique is one of the early production steps in the manufacture of integrated circuits and thin-film heads. It is also the technique used to coat disks with very thin films of magnetic material.

Torque Motors   See *actuators*.

REFERENCES

Becker, R. H., and L. M. Speltz (1983). "Putting the S-Curve Concept to Work." *Research Management* 26, September–October, 31–33.

Christensen, C. M. (1992a). "The Innovator's Challenge: Understanding the Influence of Market Environment on Processes of Technology Development in the Rigid Disk Drive Industry." D.B.A. dissertation, Graduate School of Business Administration, Harvard University, Cambridge, MA.

Christensen, C. M. (1992b). "Exploring the Limits of the Technology S-Curve. Part II: Architectural Technologies." *Production and Operations Management* 1, no. 4, 358–366.

Constant, Edward W. (1980). *The Origins of the Turbojet Revolution*. The Johns Hopkins University Press, Baltimore.

Cooper, A., and D. Schendel (1976). "Strategic Responses to Technological Threats." *Business Horizons* 19, February, 61–69.

Drexel, Burnham, and Lambert (1985). *The Disk Drive Industry*. Drexel, Burnham, and Lambert, New York.

Foster, R. (1986). *Innovation: The Attacker's Advantage*. Summit Books, New York.

Hayes, Robert (1985). "Strategic Planning—Forward in Reverse?" *Harvard Business Review* 63, November–December, 190–197.

Henderson, R. (1988). "The Failure of Established Firms in the Face of Technological Change." Ph.D. dissertation, Harvard University, Cambridge, MA.

Henderson, R. M. (1993). "Of Life Cycles Real and Imaginary: The Unexpected Old Age of Optical Lithography." Mimeo paper, Sloan School of Management, Massachusetts Institute of Technology, Cambridge, MA.

Henderson, R., and K. B. Clark (1990). "Architectural Innovation: The Reconfiguration of Existing Systems and the Failure of Established Firms." *Administrative Science Quarterly* 35, March, 9–32.

O'Brien, M. P. (1962). "Technological Planning & Misplanning." In *Technological Planning at the Corporate Level*, J. R. Bright (ed.). Harvard University Press, Cambridge, MA, 73–97.

Roussel, P. A. (1983). "Cutting Down the Guesswork in R&D." *Harvard Business Review* 61, September–October, 154–160.

Roussel, P. A. (1984). "Technological Maturity Proves a Valid and Important Concept." *Research Management* 27, January–February, 29–34.

Sahal, D. (1981). *Patterns of Technological Innovation.* Addison-Wesley, London.

Steele, L. (1983). "Managers' Misconceptions About Technology." *Harvard Business Review* 61, November–December, 133–140.

Tchijov, I., and E. Norov (1989). "Forecasting Methods for CIM Technologies." *Engineering Costs and Production Economics* 15, August, 323–389.

Thomas, L. J. (1984). "Technology and Business Strategy— The R&D Link." *Research Management* 27, May–June, 15–19.

Tushman, M. L., and P. Anderson (1986). "Technological Discontinuities and Organizational Environments." *Administrative Science Quarterly* 31, no. 3, 439–465.

Twiss, B. (1979). *Management of Technological Innovation.* Longman, London.

Van Wyk, R. J., G. Haour, and S. Japp (1991). "Permanent Magnets: A Technological Analysis." *R&D Management* 34, October, 301–308.

READING II-3B

Exploring the Limits of the Technology S-Curve. Part II: Architectural Technologies

Clayton M. Christensen
Harvard University Graduate School of Business Administration, Boston, Massachusetts

This is the second in a two-paper series in which I use information from the technological history of the disk drive industry to examine the usefulness of the technology S-curve as a framework for managers engaged in planning technology development. The first paper (Christensen 1992b), also published in this text, focused on the challenges and benefits of the S-curve framework in managing the development of new component technologies. In it, I showed that while component technologies follow an S-curve improvement pattern, there are many alternatives to switching to new technologies when a current component technology appears to be maturing. Furthermore, I showed that few, if any, first-mover ad-

Source: Reprinted by permission from *Production and Operations Management* 1, no. 4 (Fall 1992). Copyright © 1992, Production and Operations Management Society.

vantages accrued to firms that aggressively led the industry in adopting new component technologies. I refer the reader to descriptions of the study methodology and to a description of disk drive technology in that paper.

In this paper, I reach the opposite conclusion about architectural technology change. Architectural technologies indeed follow S-curve patterns of improvement. When new architectures emerged in the disk drive industry, entrant firms and first movers that adopted the new technology early enjoyed a decided advantage over the industry's incumbent firms and generally were able to ride the new architectural technology to positions of industry leadership. In the disk drive industry, it was the advent of new *architectural* technologies, not component technologies, that precipitated the downfall of the industry's leading firms. The reason for this is that architectural innovations generally found earliest use in emerging markets. Entrant, attacking firms succeeded with architectural innovations because they were better at attacking these emerging markets, not because they possessed superior capabilities to develop the architectural technology *per se.*

Between 1973 and 1990, five successive architectural technologies emerged in the disk drive industry: 14-, 8-, 5.25-, 3.5-, and 2.5-inch diameter Winchester drives. While these architectures are identified by their reduced sizes, their architectural distinctiveness lies in the reduction of total part count and in changes in how components related to each other within the system design. This is the essence of Henderson and Clark's (1990) definition of architectural technology change. In a classic S-curve sequence such as that modeled in Exhibit 1, the performance of each of these generations (defined by areal density) initially was inferior to that of the prior generation. But as the rate of improvement within each architecture

EXHIBIT 1   Prescriptive S-Curve Strategy

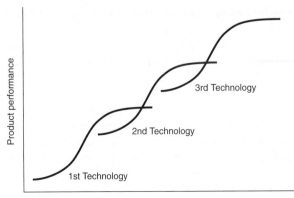

began to slow, the performance of new architectures surpassed the old.

Unlike the cases of component technology described in Christensen (1992b), *entrant* firms were the leaders in developing and shipping each new architectural generation. Control Data, the dominant 14-inch producer in the OEM market, was upstaged by entrants Micropolis, Priam, and Shugart in the 8-inch architecture. Seagate, Miniscribe, and Tandon entered to dominate the 5.25-inch generation, eclipsing the former leaders. And Conner Peripherals and Quantum achieved similarly dominant positions in the market for 3.5-inch drives relative to the leaders in the 5.25-inch architecture. Why were the established drivemakers able to lead the industry in developing component technology, while they were dethroned at points of architectural technology change?

The answer does not appear to be that development of new architectural technology was intrinsically more challenging from a technological standpoint than was new component technology. In terms of timing, the engineering groups within the leading, incumbent firms were typically among the *first* in the industry to develop working prototypes of the new-architecture products. And Christensen (1992a) shows that the quality of the incumbent leaders' architectural designs, defined in terms of cost and performance, was fully competitive with that of entrant firms.

The difference seems to have been in the relative abilities of established versus entrant firms in taking the two types of technologies into the market. New component technologies generally were the drivers of performance improvement along the dimensions of performance most valued in established markets. Taking them to market was straightforward—the leading drivemakers designed them into new product models and sold to their major customers. But new architectural technologies tended to redefine the product's functionality—the parameters by which system performance was assessed. Because of this, new architectural technologies generally were first deployed in *new* market applications. It was failure to innovate in the *market,* rather than failure to innovate in the laboratory, that seems to underlie the failure of established firms at points of architectural technology change in the history of the disk drive industry.

A typical characteristic of architectural innovations is that they employed proven component technologies and *underperformed* the dominant architectural technologies at first—when performance was measured along the dimensions which were most highly valued in established markets. For example, the principal customers for the 14-

and 8-inch architectures were the makers of mainframe and minicomputers, respectively. Performance of these drives was measured primarily along two dimensions: *total capacity* and the *speed* with which information could be stored and retrieved. The 5.25-inch drive architecture that emerged in 1980 was markedly inferior to the 14- and 8-inch architectures along both of these dimensions. It sported a capacity of five megabytes (mb) and access speeds of 160 milliseconds (ms), whereas the larger drives at that time boasted average capacities of 100–500 mb and speeds of 30 ms. Not surprisingly, the established makers of mainframe and minicomputers ignored the new architecture because 5.25-inch drives lacked the needed performance. Because the makers of large-diameter disk drives listened to and understood the needs of their customers, they also ignored the new architectural technology, focusing instead on the component-level improvements that drove performance within the 8- and 14-inch architectural frameworks.

But along *other* dimensions of performance that were irrelevant in the large computer markets—notably capacity per cubic inch and total cost per unit—the 5.25-inch architecture was *superior* to the performance of the larger drives. And there was an emerging market application for disk drives—desktop personal computing—where it was important to measure disk drive performance along these new, unconventional dimensions of functionality. Hence, drives employing the new architectural technology were in heavy demand in the emerging desktop computer market, even while they were being ignored by rational customers and customer-driven disk drive suppliers in the large, mainstream markets of the time. The firms that led in the introduction of the 5.25-inch architecture were therefore entrants to the industry.

This is the first important part of the architectural innovation story, which explains why established firms were late to spot opportunities to exploit attractive, emerging markets. The second part of the story, however, is that missing the new market eventually proved fatal to established firms in their *home* markets. Once the new architectural technology became established in its new market, 5.25-inch drivemakers found they were able to increase the capacity and speed of their drives at much faster annual rates than were demanded in the desktop market. Hence, within a few years 5.25-inch drives became able to compete with earlier-architecture drives in the minicomputer and mainframe markets on the *original* bases of performance in those markets—total capacity and speed. This was because the pace of improvement in density which technologists were able to *supply* within the new architecture exceeded the rate of performance improvement *demanded* in the established mainframe and minicomputer markets. At this point, the entrant firms that had pioneered the 5.25-inch architecture in the desktop market had much larger volumes, deeper technological experience and lower costs in the new architectural technology than did the established makers of larger drives. The entrants invaded the larger-computer markets with these capabilities, and quickly captured these markets as well. Through essentially this same process, new firms dethroned prior industry leaders in five of the seven architecturally defined disk drive product generations.

When applied to situations in which a new technological architecture redefines the functionality of the product and is therefore initially deployed in new applications, Exhibit 1 does not seem to be an accurate conceptualization of the architectural technology substitution process. This is because the curve for the new architectural technology cannot be plotted on the same graph as the curve for the established architecture. The measures of performance for the two technologies in their respective markets may be different.

This situation is depicted in Exhibit 2. The new technology (2) is deployed in a new application (B) wherein performance is defined differently than it had been in the established market, Application A. Technology 2 is in fact the *superior* performer in Application B and achieves a measure of commercial maturity there. At some point in this progression the new architecture becomes capable of addressing the performance demanded

(and defined) in the original market more effectively than the established technology. When this occurs, the new technology invades the original market, swiftly substituting for the old.

The importance of understanding the improvement trajectories of new architectural technologies along the dimensions employed in their initial markets is illustrated in Exhibit 3, where the average densities of drives in each architectural category are listed for each year. At first glance, these seem to map out a neat, Exhibit 1–style pattern of intersecting S-curves—the density of 8-inch drives surpassed that of the 14-inch architecture in 1983, and the density of the 5.25-inch architecture surpassed that of 8-inch drives in 1989. The truth, however, is that the substitution of each new architecture for the prior one began *long* before the new technology was strictly performance-competitive with the old approach on an areal density basis. For example, as noted by the bold 8.26 entry in the 5.25-inch column, shipments of 5.25-inch products in the 30–100 mb range in the total market first surpassed unit shipments of 14- and 8-inch drives in 1984, when areal density of the new architecture was still nearly 40 percent below that of 8-inch products. In the next generation, 3.5-inch unit volume surpassed all earlier architectures in the 30–100 mb category in 1988 and in the 100–300 mb category in 1989, even though their densities were still substantially inferior to those achieved in the prior architectures. This is because 5.25-inch products were first used in desktop computing and 3.5-inch drives in portable computing, where the metrics of performance were very different than the simple areal

EXHIBIT 2 A Different S-Curve Model of Architectural Innovation

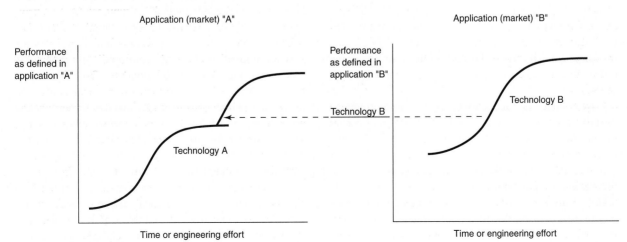

EXHIBIT 3   Intersecting Performance Trajectories of Successive Disk Drive Architectural Technologies

Year	14-inch drives	8-inch drives	5.25-inch drives	3.5-inch drives
1971	.22			
1972				
1973	.48			
1974	.73			
1975	.92			
1976	1.11			
1077	1.64			
1978	2.27	1.15		
1979	2.53			
1980	3.02	2.80	2.02	
1981	5.39	**4.01**	2.49	
1982	6.34	5.01	3.63	
1983	7.91	8.60	5.32	
1984	9.68	<u>13.28</u>	**8.26**	
1985	11.46	15.47	11.28	9.85
1986		19.41	<u>13.88</u>	12.78
1987	15.87	24.72	18.99	17.21
1988		28.94	27.58	**25.55**
1989		33.90	43.03	<u>36.28</u>
1990		50.61	56.15	43.18

Average areal density of all models introduced, in millions of bits per square inch.
Bold entry indicates year in which the architecture captured over 50% of total industry shipments in 30–100 mb drives. *Underlined* entry indicates year in which the architecture captured over 50% of total industry shipments in 100–300 mb.

density measure that had been sufficient when evaluating larger drives used with larger computers. One might argue, in fact, that by the time 5.25-inch drives became performance-competitive with 8-inch drives according to the metric of areal density, the battle between the two architectural technologies was already over.

Because the invading technology in these instances was commercially mature and not nascent, the displacement of the old architecture by the new was *very* rapid. Within two years after a new architecture appeared in a market segment, it generally accounted for over 50 percent of all units sold; and within four years, the old architecture had essentially disappeared from that segment.

The framework for architectural technology change suggested in Exhibit 2 may clarify the findings of earlier important studies of innovation that did not distinguish between component and architectural innovations. For example, Foster (1986) studied the substitution of steam for wind-powered ships—noting that most manufacturers of sailing vessels continued to engineer and manufacture sailing ships through the early 1900s, even though the interactive physics of wind and water were limiting the rate of improvement in wind-powered sailing vessels. Although steam power as an alternative technology was on a trajectory that would soon intersect and surpass the performance of wind power, these firms ignored steam engines and were driven from the shipbuilding industry very rapidly by the builders of steamships.

A more complete version of this story in the context of Exhibit 2 is that in the market where steam-powered boats were first used—inland lakes and rivers—performance was defined very differently than it was in transoceanic trade. Where the direction and force of wind was unreliable, steam power—although slow, expensive, dangerous, and subject to frequent breakdown—outperformed sail power. By the metrics of performance employed in the transoceanic trade (speed, cost per ton, and no midocean breakdowns), steam power underperformed wind power for at least 75 years after Fulton's first steamboat ride up the Hudson. Steam technology was first deployed in markets that were commercially unimportant to the transoceanic shippers. As steam was reaching a significant level of technological and commercial maturity in inland waterways, the business of the transoceanic sailing shipbuilders was not adversely affected. In fact, transoceanic shipping was *helped* by steam power's facilitation of inland commerce. The two technologies were initially complementary. The makers of transoceanic sailing ships, in fact, *could not* introduce steam-powered ships at this stage without entering the market for inland waterway vessels—selling to a completely new customer group. When steam power finally had matured sufficiently in the inland waterway markets to become fully competitive with wind power on the metrics of performance used in transoceanic shipping, the substitution of steamships for sailing ships was stunningly swift and fatal to the makers of sailing ships, because the technology had become well developed in another market context.

Likewise, Utterback and Kim (1984, p. 121) observed that "because performance will initially be unreliable and costs higher, new technology will tend to start in a relatively small market where its unique performance advantages are critical." In the context of the disk drive industry, this would not be a true statement for innovations in *componentry*—they were targeted quite directly at the needs of major customers in established markets. It is a very accurate characterization, however, of some innovations of *architectural* technology in disk drives.

Christensen (1992b) showed that in managing component technology change, the traditional S-curve framework of Exhibit 1, with all the difficulties associated with its use, is at least an accurate conceptualization of a sequence of component technologies. This is because the metric of performance on the vertical axis generally does not change as the industry moves from one component curve to the next. But using the Exhibit 1 framework to think about *architectural* technology change can be a misleading conceptualization of the architectural innovation process, because it frames the issue exclusively in *technological* terms. Since new architectural technologies that change the functionality or definition of performance of a product or process involve *market* innovation as much as technological innovation, Exhibit 2 may be a more useful way for managers to plan for architectural technology change.

Furthermore, in spite of the ambiguity associated with managing technological change at the component level, the evidence from the disk drive industry is that the leading incumbent firms were able consistently to lead entrant firms in the switch to each new component technology S-curve. The fact that entrants had the upper hand in instances in which new architectural technologies were initially deployed in new markets suggests that the primary managerial challenge in switching architectural technology S-curves may not be technological, so much as strategic.

Preliminary evidence suggests that this framework, in which the new architecture (1) redefines the functionality of a product or process, (2) is initially deployed in a new or remote market segment, and (3) invades established markets after reaching a level of commercial scale and maturity in that new market, may be a more accurate description of processes of architectural innovation in a variety of industries. Although a comprehensive review of its value in understanding innovations in other industries is beyond the scope of this paper, I summarize two examples below to suggest that this perspective may be a useful framework for understanding technological change in a broader set of industries.

Roussel (1984) chronicled the substitution of polyurethane foam rubber technology for latex foam technology and showed that *none* of the makers of latex foam successfully made the transition to polyurethane technology. At one level, the latex-to-urethane history provides an example of the attacker's advantage described by Foster (1986). In terms of Exhibit 1, the established latex foam makers stayed too long on a mature S-curve and were driven from the market when entrants rode a new technology past them.

Roussel has subsequently noted in a personal interview that the conquest of latex foam by urethane foam involved not just technological innovation but substantial market innovation as well. Although the principal markets for latex foam were in furniture, bedding, and padding applications, polyurethane foam was not suitable for those markets when it first was developed because it was quite rigid; it did not have the right feel. It was therefore first used for insulation—a market commercially unimportant to the makers of latex foam. The urethane foam makers developed commercial scale and cash flow in that application for several years. After urethane technology improved to the point that it offered competitive feel and flexibility, its substitution for latex foam in the furniture and bedding markets was fatally swift to the prior industry leaders.

This framework may also provide deeper insight about the sluggishness with which integrated steelmakers have responded to important new processing architectures such as minimill and continuous thin-slab steelmaking from 100 percent scrap (Christensen and Bower 1993). Not a single U.S. integrated mill and only one Japanese steelmaker has invested in minimill or continuous thin-slab casting process technologies, even though (1) these approaches now account for over one-third of all steel manufactured in the United States and (2) state-of-the-art minimill technology now requires less than one-third the man-hours per ton required by the most efficient integrated U.S. and Japanese companies.

Integrated steel manufacturers generally employ a manufacturing process architecture in which they procure iron ore, coal, and limestone; make steel; shape it; and then sell it—primarily to automobile, appliance, can, and electrical equipment manufacturers. When minimill and thin-slab casting technologies emerged, they were not capable of providing steel with the surface, structural, and metallurgical integrity required by the mainstream customers of the integrated steel manufacturers. The pioneers of these technologies—which represent new process *architectures* and generally required little new *component* technology—deployed them in markets that were commercially unimportant and technologically irrelevant to the integrated mills. Structural minimills initially made reinforcing bar for concrete construction, and the pioneering thin-slab casting minimills attacked markets for rolled products like corrugated steel culverts and construction decking. In the manner described in Exhibit 2, once minimill and thin-slab processing technologies were established in these segments, the capabilities of their practitioners improved at a much faster rate than was required to remain competitive in those initial markets. The most technologically aggressive minimills such as Nucor and Chaparral have exploited these new process architectures—initially refined in remote markets—to aggressively invade successively more sophisticated, demanding markets.

In a similar way, the framework for architectural technology change in Exhibit 2 is consistent with studies of innovation in industries as diverse as semiconductor photolithographic equipment (Henderson 1988, 1990), and computers, retailing, hydraulic excavators, and footwear (Christensen and Bower 1993).

SUMMARY

Identifying new technologies that may supersede existing approaches—a critical job of technology development managers—is always difficult. In this two-paper series on the use of S-curves in the strategic management of technology development I have attempted to highlight both the usefulness and limitations of this theory when it is used to guide new technology development programs in the firm.

S-curves can provide an important perspective on what is happening to performance trajectories at average,

aggregate levels. When S-curves are used to plan technology development at the level of the firm, however, I discussed in Christensen (1992b) three issues that suggest caution in using S-curves as a prescriptive tool for new component technology development.

1. Substantial differences can exist across firms in the level of performance at which a technology appears to mature. Managers in the disk drive industry who switched technology S-curves seem generally to have been responding to firm-specific, rather than uniform, technological phenomena. This suggests that benchmarking against competitors' performance, in addition to a firm's own-historical performance and perceived natural limits, may provide a clearer view of the potential for improvement within an established technological approach.

2. The observed maturation of a technology may be the *result,* rather than the *cause,* of the launch of an alternative development program within a firm. Indeed, when necessity has demanded it, firms have shown the ability to push conventional technology beyond what had been perceived as the limits of known physical laws—reminding us that we don't know what we do not know about such laws and that they can be moving targets, rather than fixed ceilings.

3. There are *many* alternatives to switching S-curves at the component level. Some firms have demonstrated that improvements in architectural system efficiency coupled with incremental improvements in componentry can be the dominant drivers of system performance over long periods—offering an alternative to the S-curve–hopping strategies pursued by some firms. In particular, no evidence exists that leading the industry in switching to new component technology S-curves led to a strengthening of the leading firms' market positions.

   To these three propositions about component technologies, this paper adds a fourth concerning architectural technology.

4. In contrast to the situation in componentry, timely S-curve switching seems critical when confronting architectural technology change. It is important, however, for managers to evaluate architectural innovation both in its technological and market dimensions. If they assess the performance of a new architectural technology along metrics commonly used by established firms in established market applications, they may dismiss new architectures as irrelevant or too inferior to merit immediate attention. Often they need to assess new architectures along new performance

criteria that are defined in new or remote market applications with which established firms may not be familiar. When the performance of the new architecture improves at a rate that is faster than the rate of improvement demanded in established markets, the new architecture, after reaching commercial scale in a new and different market, can penetrate established markets quickly. This process of technological substitution is somewhat more complex than the process summarized by the standard S-curve theory, which ignores the critical processes of market innovation, and focuses only on the technological dimensions of new architectures.[1]

REFERENCES

Christensen, C. M. (1992a). "The Innovator's Challenge: Understanding the Influence of Market Environment on Processes of Technology Development in the Rigid Disk Drive Industry." D.B.A. dissertation, Graduate School of Business Administration, Harvard University, Cambridge, MA.

Christensen, C. M. (1992b). "Exploring the Limits of the Technology S-Curve. Part I: Component Technologies." *Production and Operations Management* 1, no. 4, 334–357.

Christensen, C. M., and J. L. Bower (1993). "Customer Impetus: A Driver of the Innovative Abilities and Disabilities of Successful, Established Firms." Working paper, Division of Research, Harvard Business School, Cambridge, MA.

Foster, R. (1986). *Innovation: The Attacker's Advantage.* Summit Books, New York.

Henderson, R. (1988). "The Failure of Established Firms in the Face of Technological Change." Ph.D. dissertation, Harvard University, Cambridge, MA.

Henderson, R. (1990). "Keeping Too Close to Your Customers: Architectural Innovation in the Marketplace and the Failure of Established Firms." Working paper, Sloan School of Management, Massachusetts Institute of Technology, Cambridge, MA.

Henderson, R., and K. B. Clark (1990). "Architectural Innovation: The Reconfiguration of Existing Systems and the Failure of Established Firms." *Administrative Science Quarterly* 35, March, 9–32.

Roussel, P. A. (1984). "Technological Maturity Proves a Valid and Important Concept." *Research Management* 27, January–February, 29–34.

Utterback, J., and L.-S. Kim (1984). "Invasion of a Stable Business by Radical Innovation." In *The Management of Productivity and Technology in Manufacturing,* P. R. Kleindorfer (ed.). Plenum Press, New York, 113–151.

[1] I thank Professors Kim B. Clark, Robert H. Hayes, and Steven C. Wheelwright of the Harvard Business School; Professors Rebecca Henderson and James Utterback of the Sloan School of Management, Massachusetts Institute of Technology; and the anonymous referees for invaluable guidance and suggestions for improvement to earlier drafts of this paper. Any remaining shortcomings are my sole responsibility. EDITOR'S NOTE: An earlier combined version of this paper and the preceding paper published in *Production and Operations Management* won the 1991 William Abernathy Award for the best paper in management of technology.

CASE II·4

Hewlett-Packard's Merced Decision

Matthew C. Verlinden

From Jim Davis's Fort Collins, Colorado, office, the serenity of the nearby Rocky Mountains was in sharp relief to the decisions that Davis was faced with making in the summer of 1998. Davis was the general manager of the Hewlett-Packard (HP) IA-64 program office for Enterprise Systems Group (ESG) (see Exhibits 1 and 2). It was his responsibility to recommend a cogent and pragmatic technology strategy for mission-critical enterprise computer systems, including both proprietary and PC-based workstations and servers.

ESG, which was formed in 1997 in response to increasing competitive pressures, was responsible for producing scaleable, high-performance computing systems that made up the backbone of corporate information networks, including powerful network servers and mainframe storage solutions. ESG systems ran the complex, mission-critical applications that their customers depended on to run their businesses and to Web-enable their information technology infrastructures for the future.

The central issue for Davis was to recommend whether HP should continue to allocate a large share of its resources to extending the capability of its *proprietary* UNIX-based performance architecture (PA) based on a *proprietary* HP RISC microprocessor (detailed later) or whether HP should dramatically shift resources to develop workstations and servers based on both a new chip, code named Merced, and its corresponding new architecture called IA-64 (Intel Architecture 64-bit data transfer).

EXHIBIT 1   Hewlett-Packard Corporate Organization

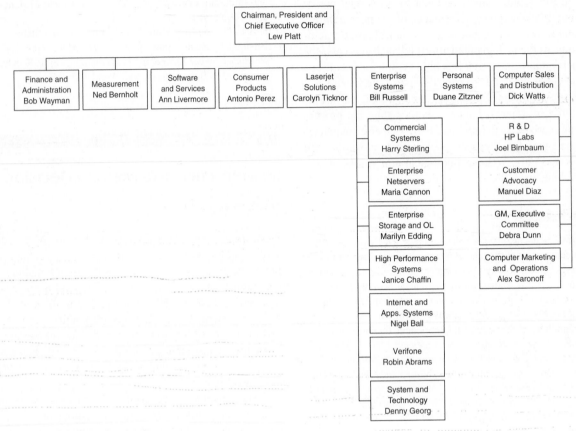

Source: Company documents.

EXHIBIT 2   Organization Chart for Enterprise Systems Group's Systems and Technology

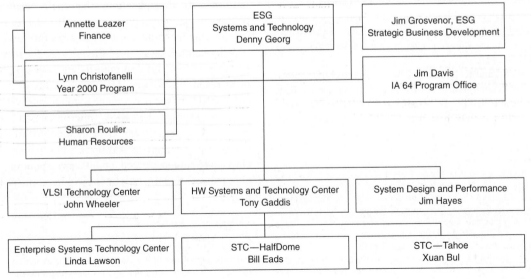

Source: Company documents.

HP had codeveloped Merced and IA-64 with Intel, and it had already committed vast resources to the development of the new chip. Senior management at HP had committed these resources because they believed that Merced would be a growth engine for its future generations of enterprise computing products. Davis also believed in IA-64. He believed that IA-64 would eventually triumph. The problem, however, was knowing when and how HP should change from its proprietary PA to IA-64. Compounding the complexity of this recommendation was the fact that Intel had recently announced that the release of the Merced was going to be delayed by *at least* six months. This was only one year before McKinley, the second-generation IA-64 microprocessor, had been scheduled for its release. McKinley, as a second-generation chip, promised to have significant performance advantages over Merced. Did it make sense for HP to develop a new enterprise computer platform based on Merced when McKinley was around the corner?[1] One industry analyst quipped,

> In fact, some IA-64 system makers are quietly saying, "Wait for McKinley," referring to a second IA-64 processor due to ship in 2001. McKinley, the story goes, will be twice as fast as Merced in the same IC process, showing off the true performance characteristics of the IA-64 instruction set.[2]

While Merced had been delayed, HP's competitors were not standing still. Sun Microsystems (Sun) had already launched a campaign to convert second-tier UNIX-based workstation and server suppliers to their proprietary operating system. Sun, particularly through its CEO Scott McNealy, was publicly questioning HP's commitment to UNIX-based machines. And there were early signs that Sun's campaign was working: it was gaining shares steadily in the market for RISC/Unix computers.

As Davis gazed at the mountain vista, the complexity of this increasingly changing market and technologies struck him as ironic. From this complexity, he would need to define a plan that was acceptable to HP senior management (which was feeling increasing pressure

from financial markets to deliver near-term improvement in earnings growth) and would strengthen HP's long-term position in the high-end market—a business that analysts estimated could generate $12 billion in revenues in 1999.

COMPANY BACKGROUND

HP, an international manufacturer of instrumentation, health care, computer, and communication products, was founded in 1939 by Bill Hewlett and David Packard in a one-car garage in a region in Northern California now called Silicon Valley. From its humble beginnings as a start-up with an initial investment of only $538, HP grew to more than $43 billion in sales and $3.1 billion in net profits in 1997 (see Exhibits 3 and 4). Recognized as an industry leader, HP, over its history, acquired a reputation for its innovative products and management culture, with a particular ability to reinvent itself as markets changed and evolved.

In 1938, one year before the partnership was formalized, Hewlett and Packard had developed an audio oscillator, based on Hewlett's research work at Stanford University. Walt Disney was their first major customer, purchasing eight audio oscillators for its film *Fantasia*. Hewlett and Packard then built upon this technology

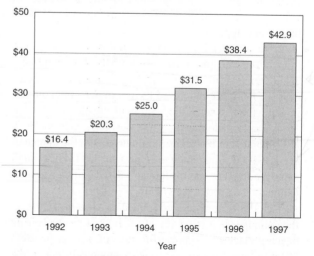

EXHIBIT 3   HP's Net Revenues for the Period 1992 to 1997 (Fiscal Year-End October 31)

Source: HP annual reports.

---

[1] It was unclear whether and to what extent Intel's delay in developing the Merced would impact its McKinley introduction schedule. Within Intel, the development of these two chips had been assigned to different project teams. To some extent, however, the McKinley team was likely to attempt to leverage upon the learning from the predecessor Merced project.

[2] "What's Wrong with Merced?" *Microdesign Resources,* August 3, 1998.

EXHIBIT 4 HP's Net Income for the Period 1992 to 1997 (Earnings Before Effect of Accounting)

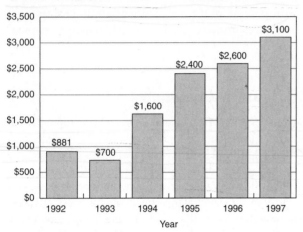

Source: HP annual reports.

a product line of oscilloscopes and related equipment that formed the foundation of their company. From its inception, HP had created a tradition of building testing and measurement instruments used by engineers and scientists.

In 1966, designed as an extension of some of the company's test and measurement instruments, HP's first computer—the HP 2116A—was built. Two years later, HP produced the world's first desktop scientific calculator—the HP 9100A. The 9100A was the forerunner of HP's workstation business, and with its launch, HP had established itself as a leader in computer hardware. In 1969, HP marketed its first time-share operating system on a minicomputer.

In the 1970s, HP continued its tradition of growth and innovation with the introduction of the first hand-held calculator and an expansion of its minicomputer business. In 1972, HP pioneered the era of personal computing with the first scientific hand-held calculator—the HP 35—which made the slide rule obsolete. Also in 1972, HP expanded into business computing with the launch of the HP 3000 minicomputer. One year later, HP's small general computer was the industry's first commercial distributed data processing system.

The 1980s marked a continued expansion for HP in the computer industry with a full range of products from desktop machines to powerful minicomputers. In 1980, HP introduced its first personal computer. In late 1982,

the company introduced the HP 8000 technical computer with 32-bit "superchip" technology—the first "desktop mainframe"—as powerful as room-sized computers of the 1960s. In 1986, HP introduced a broad new family of computer systems based on innovative RISC[3] architecture. To further strengthen its product offerings in this market segment, HP acquired Apollo Computer, a workstation manufacturer in 1989.

In the 1990s, HP continued its expansion in computing and worked to merge many of the technologies it held in its portfolio—measurement, computing, and communication—in order to reinvent itself and capitalize on high-growth markets such as those connected with the Internet. In 1991, the company launched the HP 95LX palmtop PC, which combined advanced calculation features and data-communication capabilities. In 1997, HP acquired VeriFone, the industry leader in electronic-payment systems, strengthening HP's capabilities in information systems, particularly electronic commerce.

HP continued to be a market leader in both proprietary hardware and software. In 1997, HP refocused its efforts on enterprise computing by forming the Enterprise Systems Group. ESG's products were built around proprietary RISC microprocessors and proprietary UNIX operating systems, both of which are described below. HP used these proprietary system components because, by being able to integrate the design of the two in unique ways, they were able to stretch the performance of their computer systems far beyond what could have been achieved by building computers from standard, modular components that were designed and sold by third-party vendors.[4] By 1997, ESG had an installed base of more than 1.3 million UNIX systems (HP-UX) worldwide. In all, the division had sales of nearly $10 billion in 1997. In that year, the total market was estimated to be worth more than $60 billion.[5] In the server segment, HP had

---

[3] The differences between reduced instruction set computing (RISC) and complex instruction set computing (CISC) are explained in the Appendix.

[4] Hewlett-Packard historically had not only designed its own RISC microprocessors, but had manufactured many of them as well—under the belief that in order to achieve maximum performance of the chips, HP needed to control its manufacturing processes as well. Some of its processing requirements were nonstandard, dictated by the unique designs of its chips. Other of HP's competitors, notably Sun Microsystems, had never manufactured its own RISC processors. They also developed proprietary designs, but then had their chips manufactured by contract by independent fabricators.

[5] "Inside Intel, the Future Is Riding on a Chip," *The New York Times,* April 5, 1998.

been the number one UNIX server vendor by revenue since 1993 with its HP-UX product line.

MARKET AND TECHNOLOGY TRAJECTORIES

Enterprise computing had historically been the domain of mainframe and minicomputers, whose logic circuitry was built in complex, multilayered printed circuit or wiring boards. Powerful computers employed such circuitry because all of the required functionality could not be integrated into a single silicon chip, as was the case with less powerful microprocessor-based computers. A number of changes, caused by advances in semiconductor manufacturing, microprocessor design, and operating systems, had changed the industry dramatically, however (see Exhibit 5). During the 1950s, mainframe computer manufacturers, such as IBM and UNIVAC, created the enterprise computing market with their delivery of systems that were able to handle companywide business applications, such as accounting, reliably.

In particular, the mainframe computer manufacturers capitalized on Bell Laboratories' 1947 invention of the first useful solid-state semiconductor—the transistor. The transistor, in contrast to its counterpart, the vacuum tube, had a number of attractive performance parameters, including small size, great durability, low power consumption, low rate of heat output, and eventually ease of manufacture. Although transistors could not initially handle the power required to be useful in existing markets, their set of performance attributes differed significantly from those of vacuum tubes. Transistors enabled the rapid commercialization and proliferation of enterprise computing.

During the 1960s and 1970s, mainframe manufacturers dominated enterprise computing. By 1970, IBM alone had sales which soared to $7 billion and a growth rate of more than 15 percent. By the end of the decade, IBM's dominance of mainframes was so pervasive that 70 percent of the world's computer installations were centered around its equipment.[6] But while mainframe manufacturers dominated enterprise computing in the 1950s, 1960s, and 1970s, a new product architecture appeared on the horizon—minicomputers.

These minicomputers were low-cost, high-performance machines targeted at sophisticated users who did not want or need to pay for extensive software and support services that came bundled with mainframes. In 1964, DEC introduced the PDP-6 with time sharing—a single main computer that could support multiple simultaneous users. DEC followed up with a steady stream of new products, which cost about a fifth of a mainframe. By the late 1970s, DEC introduced its powerful VAX line of minicomputers, which made serious inroads at the low end of the mainframe market because their technology trajectory improved at such a rate that it could satisfy low-end enterprise computing needs.

In the early 1970s, yet another computing device appeared on the horizon—the microprocessor. Microprocessors were essentially a computer on a chip. While mainframes and minicomputers had printed wiring board logic circuits, microprocessors used a combination of general logic circuits, firmware, and software to integrate computing capability onto a single silicon chip.

While the systems built around microprocessors, such as workstations and personal computers (PCs), could not initially fulfill the requirements of mainstream minicomputer users, the computing power of the microprocessor improved at a rate much faster than the needs of minicomputer users, as diagrammed in Exhibit 5. As a result, by the early 1990s systems based on the microprocessor had penetrated the lower tiers of enterprise computing. RISC microprocessors, which were developed by IBM scientists in the 1970s (see Appendix), played a key role in this process. RISC chips were much faster than CISC processors. They represented a dramatic, discontinuous improvement in microprocessor speed. IBM wrestled for years with whether and how it could implement RISC within its existing customer base—but by the time it had adapted the technology to be compatible with its existing customers' installed mainframe and minicomputer hardware and software base, IBM had compromised the RISC chips' performance so significantly that they offered few advantages.

In contrast, a set of new companies in the 1980s—such as Sun Microsystems, MIPS, and Silicon Graphics—adopted RISC as a technology that might help them build small, cost-effective computers that targeted the applications that historically had used minicomputers. They and the products they made (workstations and network servers) were highly successful, as they displaced minicomputers and the companies that made them, such as Digital Equipment, Data General, Prime Computer, Nixdorf, and Wang. Although most RISC chips were fabricated by semiconductor companies such as Fujitsu,

---

[6] Charles H. Ferguson and Charles R. Morris, *Computer Wars* (New York: Time Books, 1993).

EXHIBIT 5   Market Application Tiers and System Solutions

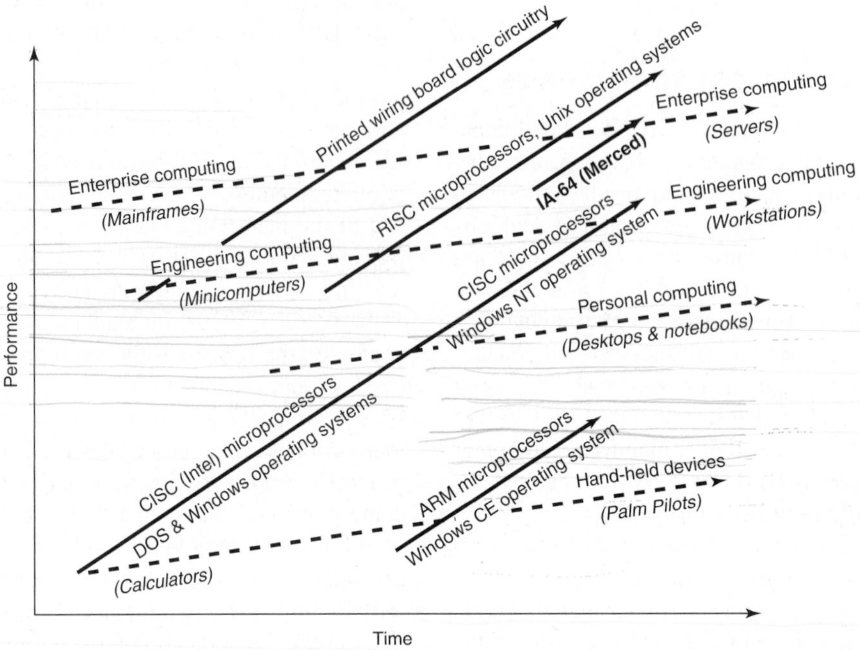

the designs of the chips were often done by the computer makers. Sun Microsystems (with its SPARC chip), Silicon Graphics, and Hewlett-Packard were known for their strong capabilities in RISC microprocessor design.

Almost all RISC-based computers employed Unix operating systems. Unix was an operating system architecture developed by AT&T's Bell Laboratories. Whereas DOS and Windows operating systems sold by Microsoft Corporation were standard products sold to manufacturers and owners of computers that were built around Intel Corporation's microprocessors, most RISC-based computer makers created their own proprietary versions of UNIX, in order to extract as much performance as possible from their particular computer hardware designs. Because each manufacturer's version of UNIX was somewhat different, independent software vendors (ISVs) had to write different versions of their programs to run on each manufacturer's version of UNIX. In the market, RISC microprocessors tended to be bundled with UNIX operating systems, and CISC microprocessors tended to be bundled with Windows operating systems. Hence, two different "worlds" had emerged in the microprocessor-based computer industry: a RISC-UNIX world, and a CISC-Windows (Intel-Microsoft) world.

Companies in these different value networks created two sequential waves of innovation that swept through the enterprise computing market, as shown in Exhibit 5. Workstations and servers in the RISC-UNIX value network were the first to enter this market tier with proprietary designs. These were followed by systems based on standard, commercially available microprocessors and operating systems, principally those of Intel and Microsoft. By the mid-1990s, the combination of Intel Pentium Pro microprocessors and Windows NT had combined into a powerful "WINTEL" system, a new technology in the lower tiers of the enterprise computing market space. Although these systems did not perform as well as the proprietary RISC-UNIX systems above them, they were capturing market share rapidly because of their lower cost. Computer systems based on standard WINTEL building blocks clearly had begun to exert a large influence in enterprise computing. Although the WINTEL combination accounted for only 9.3 percent of the market for servers in 1997, sales of products based on these two technologies grew 66 percent from 1996 to 1997 (see Exhibit 6). This trend was expected to continue as advances were made in both Intel microprocessors and the Windows NT operating system.

EXHIBIT 6   Server Market Forecast: End User Spending of Server Market by Platform, 1995–2001 ($ Millions)

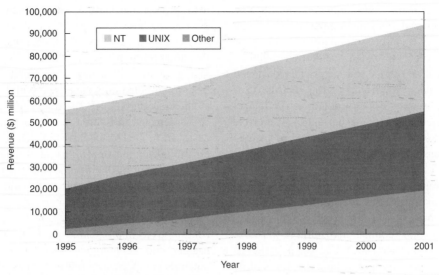

Source: Analysis of Bear, Stearns Co. data.

While the use of standard modular components had enabled PC manufacturers such as Dell, Compaq, and Hewlett-Packard's Personal Computer Systems Group (PSG)[7] to access this upscale market quickly with relatively limited incremental technology investment, modularity had also meant that customers would no longer be captive to a single vendor. The industry's adoption of modular products had lowered entry barriers, and a number of PC manufacturers had successfully moved upmarket to supply their corporate customers with servers, workstations, and full-scale corporate networks using merchant microprocessors from Intel running the standard Windows NT operating system from Microsoft. Consequently, increasing competition drove margins down. While gross margins on proprietary RISC-Unix servers and workstations had typically been at 50–

60 percent, margins on new WINTEL systems were often 40 percent or less. Product modularity was indeed a double-edged sword, and it had altered the basis of competition amongst computer makers in markets where it had become prevalent.

THE UNIX MARKET

While WINTEL systems were clearly an emerging force to be reckoned with in enterprise computing, UNIX-based systems in 1997, such as HP's PA and Sun Microsystems' SPARC, continued to dominate the market with a 37.3 percent share (see Exhibit 6). This dominance, especially at the high end of the market, was expected to continue for several years. The growth rate for UNIX-based machines from 1996 to 1997 was 9.1 percent, with this expected to slow to a CAGR of 5 percent from 1997 to 2001, as systems based on Intel microprocessors and a Windows operating environment became increasingly more powerful and reliable.

Although the growth in market share for proprietary UNIX-based machines was expected to slow, UNIX-based environment still accounted for worldwide revenues of nearly $25 billion in 1997 (see Exhibit 6). By 2002, UNIX was expected to be the mainstream operating system for servers priced at more than $100,000,

[7] Hewlett-Packard, as Exhibit 1 shows, has a highly decentralized structure. Its Enterprise Systems Group (ESG) competed very effectively in the highest-performance tiers of the market, while its Personal Systems Group (PSG) operated autonomously in lower-performance tiers, employing standard Intel (CISC) microprocessors and Microsoft Windows operating systems. PSG was migrating steadily toward higher-price–performance tiers of the market—in essence, striving to compete against the low end of ESG's product line. This was not unusual. HP's laser-jet printer business in Boise, Idaho, competed aggressively against its ink-jet printer business, located in Vancouver, Washington.

accounting for more than 50 percent of spending.[8] UNIX machines offered proven mission-critical solutions with the scalability, resilience, and high availability features to meet high-end entering computing needs that WINTEL-based systems were still unable to offer.

HP, along with other server and workstation manufacturers such as Sun and IBM, had historically designed their systems around a *proprietary* RISC microprocessor. RISC chips, because of their limited instruction set architecture, offered computer makers significant performance advantages over CISC microprocessors such as those made by Intel. These RISC chips enabled manufacturers to offer high-performance machines needed for enterprise computing at attractive prices, particularly when compared to mainframes.

While RISC chips had steadily progressed in performance since their initial commercialization in the early 1980s, many in the industry, including Davis, believed that RISC architecture was approaching the limits of its performance. In addition, as WINTEL systems captured increasing volumes at the low end of the workstation/server market, the economies of scale for producing proprietary RISC chips were increasingly unattractive. Given the rapidly increasing fixed cost of designing chips and building state-of-the-art semiconductor fabrication plants, the specter of diminishing unit volumes of RISC chips portended the need to raise prices—exacerbating the competitive disadvantages of RISC-Unix computers.

For example, it was estimated that the cost of building a semiconductor lab capable of manufacturing a state-of-the-art RISC chip was over $3.5 billion in 1997.[9] RISC chips, which were manufactured in quantities of tens or hundreds of thousands, had huge scale disadvantages to their merchant chip counterparts which, in the case of Intel microprocessors, were manufactured in quantities of millions. In addition, software applications development had become more costly on a per system basis because of the shrinking RISC/UNIX volume base and the need to port software to each UNIX version.

IA-64 AND ITS IMPACT

With these factors in mind, HP decided to jointly develop a new microprocessor with Intel. In 1994, with little fanfare, Intel and HP announced that they were entering into the joint development of a new 64-bit, parallel processing microprocessor architecture.[10] The joint development project married the semiconductor-manufacturing prowess of Intel with the high-end microprocessor design expertise of HP. Merced, code-named for the river that flows through Yosemite Valley, was conceived as the first generation of a new chip architecture—IA-64—that would potentially supersede both the Intel 80 × 86 architecture and the HP-PA architecture.[11]

As depicted in Exhibit 5, the IA-64 architecture was designed to enable an Intel-branded microprocessor to directly attack the very high end of the computer industry, made up of the mainframes that run the operations of large corporations, the exploding world of Internet Web servers, and the supercomputers and workstations used by scientists and engineers. It constituted a dramatic, discontinuous technological leap upmarket. As such, it was fraught with technological uncertainty but offered high potential compensatory rewards. Merced featured 64-bit data transfer, an initial processor speed of nearly 800 MHz, and the ability to perform an explicitly parallel instruction computing, or EPIC (described in the Appendix). Merced was designed to incorporate a gang of 64-bit RISC processors to support EPIC. In addition, Merced was designed with a sector devoted to the stripped-down core of the Pentium to maintain backward compatibility with a Windows operating environment, as well as a sector that would hold PA-RISC circuits to maintain compatibility with HP-UX. Hence, Merced would constitute a bridge between the historically separate worlds of RISC and CISC—hopefully (in the eyes of Intel, at least) eliminating the distinction between the two in the eyes of the customer.

EPIC itself was a major advance in microprocessor design. It allowed the Merced chip the potential to paral-

---

[8] Analysis of Hewlett-Packard documents.

[9] Ibid.

---

[10] The term *64-bit* refers to the length of a "word" that could be processed. One way to understand the impact of progressing from the 32-bit architecture characteristic of Intel's Pentium processor line to the 64-bit architecture is to visualize a pipe carrying fluid. The amount of fluid the pipe can transport over time depends upon its diameter and the speed at which the fluid moves through the pipe. Increasing the word length to 64 bits essentially doubles the diameter of the pipes that carry digital information in the microprocessor. Historically, each doubling of word length—from 4- to 8-, 16-, 32-, and 64-bit architectures—had constituted a significant, difficult step ahead for the computer industry.
[11] Although there was a strong possibility that Intel would ultimately abandon its line of 32-bit microprocessors (branded Pentium, Pentium Pro, Pentium II, etc.) in favor of the IA-64 architecture, Intel had not yet announced whether and when it would do so. In fact, most industry observers believed that Intel would continue to extend this product line beyond the Pentium II, for a number of years in the future.

lel process up to 12 instructions per clock cycle, in contrast to the 6 possible with the most advanced superscalar RISC chips.

While HP signaled to the market its commitment to the IA-64 architecture, its competitors in the RISC-Unix value network did not stand still. In particular, Sun presented itself to customers and independent software vendors such as Oracle and SAP as the vendor of choice for UNIX-based systems. By the time ESG was formed in May 1997, customers and the industry consultants who advised them had voiced their concerns about HP's commitment to UNIX. Independent software vendors were particularly concerned about shouldering the development costs for any new versions of HP's proprietary UNIX (HP-UX) operating system when future volumes of HP's proprietary RISC architecture (HP-PA) were in question, given the commitment HP had made to IA-64.[12]

Sun had gained market momentum and mindshare with the independent software vendor community by achieving performance leadership on several key benchmarks, a dominant position in the Internet market space, and by making an advantage of their focus on UNIX. Industry experts had suspected that HP's plan was to disinvest in UNIX: HP had a major hole in its high-end UNIX product line.

It appeared to many in the industry that ESG had conceded the UNIX market to Sun. In an October 1997 *Fortune* magazine interview, Scott McNealy, chief executive officer of Sun, sought to capitalize on this by stating his position: "HP is pulling out of the UNIX business and becoming an OEM for Intel and Microsoft." By the second quarter of 1998, Sun shipped more UNIX servers than any other vendor, including HP and IBM.

Exacerbating this situation was that the UNIX business had already entered into a phase of rapid consolidation with second-tier systems vendors, such as Silicon Graphics, Unisys, and Hitachi, losing market share to HP, Sun, and IBM. As a result, the second-tier players could no longer get the attention of independent software vendors. The installed base business of these weaker vendors represented about 40 percent of the market in 1997.[13] Most second-tier vendors had decided to align with top-tier vendors for access to future UNIX technol-

ogy. As early as 1995, Sun had launched an initiative to convert its smaller competitors (which historically had maintained their own proprietary UNIX operating systems), into using Sun's proprietary *Solaris* UNIX operating system. This would consolidate volume for scale for the independent software vendors. Although Sun was able to capture Fujitsu, NCR, and Siemens-Nixdorf (adding $2 billion per year of UNIX partner revenues committed to Solaris), HP and IBM had not joined by mid-1998.

THE ARCHITECTURE OF COMPETITIVE ADVANTAGE

For HP, the development of the Merced chip had marked a strategic turning point in its enterprise computing operations. Traditionally, HP had manufactured its proprietary PA RISC chips to run its most powerful machines in a proprietary UNIX-based operating system platform: HP-UX. In contrast, the Merced, which had sectors dedicated to both HP's proprietary RISC circuits and a Pentium core, was able to support both UNIX and Windows NT. Merced was also a merchant chip—it would be sold on the open market and available to all makers of servers, workstations, and PCs. The new HP strategy for successful commercialization of the IA-64 architecture was necessarily a departure from the strategy of commercialization for HP-PA.

ESG had expected that enterprise computing customers would want to deploy their mission-critical applications on IA-64 technology rather than proprietary RISC chips with the availability of a viable and reliable IA-64 platform. ESG believed that IA-64 would be perceived as the first Intel technology capable of broadly supporting enterprise applications. HP believed that customers who had watched Intel technologies become pervasive in commercial desktops, file and print servers, and technical workstations would expect the same to happen in the mission-critical server market. Over time, HP believed that this would result in significant market share changes away from all RISC technologies.

The customers who followed this trend would select the best enterprise-class operating environments available on IA-64 to support new deployments. HP was the only top-tier enterprise vendor committed to selling only IA-64 platforms. While this was perceived to be a strong initial selling point against other vendors, over the longer term it raised the question for HP and its potential competitors using IA-64 chips about how they could differentiate their platforms from one another.

---

[12] The skepticism of the independent software vendors suggests that they were unsure whether future programs written for Hewlett-Packard's HP-UX machines would, in fact, run well on the "hybrid" Merced chip.

[13] Analysis of HP documents.

With Merced, HP was counting on an in-depth knowledge of and early access to the IA-64 architecture as a competitive advantage. HP had hoped that this knowledge and experience would give it an advantage in designing ancillary systems such as the compiler and the complex electronic circuitry surrounding Merced.

Seeking to gain competitive advantage with Merced and the IA-64 architecture, HP had placed particular emphasis on the compiler, and its design was a strategic leverage point for HP. Compilers played a key role in the speed with which an application ran on any piece of hardware and in any operating system. When a software developer wrote an application, it had to be "compiled" before the microprocessor could execute the program. Compilers were responsible for translating software code into "machine language," a binary code that the microprocessor could understand and execute. The efficiency with which the compiler converted the application software had a direct influence on the speed with which the application would execute, and execution speed was a primary measurement of performance for the hardware and operating system.

For the IA-64 architecture and specifically because of EPIC, the compiler was responsible not only for translating the software program into machine language but also for parceling the programs into sequences of independent instruction sets that could be independently parallel processed. These independent instructions could run in any order and be carried out by whatever resources were available at the time. Hence, the compiler was key to enable ISVs to take advantage of Merced with its EPIC capability, and the hardware provider with the best compiler would have a distinct advantage in the marketplace.

THE LOW END GETS RISC-Y AGAIN

As Davis contemplated his recommendations for ESG, he was also concerned by a new microprocessor technology that was actively being out-licensed to chip makers by a British firm, ARM Holdings Ltd. ARM chips were beginning to appear in the very low end of the market. He knew that he needed to understand the impact of this emerging technology for senior management. In particular, Davis was concerned with a new generation of simple and relatively inexpensive RISC microprocessors called ARM. These ARM microprocessors had already made significant market inroads, and all indications were that they had the potential to penetrate larger portions of the marketplace.

Advanced RISC Machines (ARM), which originally had manufactured single-board controllers,[14] had evolved to develop a simple yet powerful RISC chip which had found its way into products such as mobile fax-phones, personal digital assistants, hard disk drives, smart cards, and printers. The entry into these markets was made possible because of unique architecture which combined a powerful low-energy–consuming RISC-based microprocessor, a very small footprint (7 millimeters square), and a price under $50. In 1998, some industry experts thought that ARM microprocessors were staged to become a tidal wave of change in the computer industry.[15]

ARM chips were only a tenth of the price of conventional microprocessors; and, although they were currently limited in their processing power vis-à-vis their traditional counterparts, there was a significant and rapidly growing market that was being satisfied by their performance attributes (see Exhibit 5). ARM chips were also rapidly increasing in processing power while maintaining a very cost-competitive profile. Davis had seen technology such as this (e.g., Intel's CISC microprocessor) emerge at the bottom of the market before, and he knew that it was just such types of technology that had the ability to redefine the competitive landscape.

A number of HP divisions manufactured hand-held computing and scanning devices that utilized ARM-like microprocessors. As one of HP's senior technology strategists, Davis felt he also needed to recommend to HP's senior management what strategic posture they should take relative to ARM-like processors. Should they begin designing and/or manufacturing these chips in-house? Or should they continue to outsource the chips, focusing their resources and competency development efforts in the design and assembly of final, end use products?

THE MERCED DECISION

As Davis considered his recommendations, he realized that the complexity of creating a sound strategy for the future of the ESG products was compounded by the mounting pressure of today's decisions—what were seemingly tactical resource allocation decisions were, in fact, not. Today's decisions defined tomorrow's choices.

---

[14]Began as Acorn Computers Ltd. of Cambridge, England.
[15]"ARM's Way," *Electronic Weekly,* April 29, 1998.

In the enterprise computing arena, new product design did not simply consist of piecing together off-the-shelf modules or components from independent vendors. Rather, it required the parallel development of multiple subsystems, each of which entailed lengthy development times. These subsystems included microprocessor design, system design (including complex electronic circuitry, or CEC), firmware, compilers, and packaging. Hence, what was decided today would have far-reaching consequences for tomorrow. Resources were limited, and HP needed some winners—some big winners. Davis knew this. He also knew that limited resources would make it difficult for ESG to hedge its bets to any significant degree, by pursuing RISC-Unix and Merced platforms simultaneously.

Increasing the pressure on Davis was the fact that HP had disappointed Wall Street analysts for seven consecutive quarters. There was tremendous pressure on management to increase revenues and profits and to increase them quickly.

One option available was to abandon RISC and UNIX in order to focus exclusively on IA-64. With the limited resources currently available, didn't it make sense to concentrate on one project and do that project well? If Davis chose this path, the next decision was whether to develop a platform product on Merced or to use Merced as a development tool and focus energies on McKinley as the basis of a new product platform. McKinley was scheduled to be released only one year after Merced and would have significant performance advantages.

Although Davis found it logically compelling to concentrate on one technology, particularly one that seemed to hold the future of enterprise computing, he could not ignore the impact on current revenues if HP made a committed decision to disinvest UNIX and PA. Was there a way to reach a middle ground? For example, would it make sense for HP to join Sun's Solaris camp, which was emerging as the de facto standard in UNIX? This would help HP continue to have a handsome revenue stream, but with much lower upkeep costs. Or should HP head in the opposite direction and commit fully to continuing their proprietary RISC technology and proprietary UNIX? All industry forecasts and analysis projected that UNIX-based machines would be the loci of attractive margins and revenues for years to come. Why not put IA-64 on the back burner until its schedules and technologies were more certain?

And then there was ARM. The technology was not currently a threat to HP's enterprise computing, but where was the technology heading? As Davis looked to the serenity of the mountain vista, he knew that the decisions he faced would not be easily answered.

APPENDIX: HISTORY OF THE MICROPROCESSOR

The microprocessor was invented in 1971 by a start-up company called Intel whose main product had been memory devices. Ted Hoff, a young Intel engineer, had been working on a contract to build a hand-held calculator for Busicom, a Japanese company. Hoff's assignment was to build a series of integrated circuits that performed each of the calculator's functions. However, Hoff had the vision that he could use Intel's memory technology to store the calculator's operations as software instructions. Then, instead of constructing hard-wired circuits for every operation, he placed enough general-purpose logic circuits on a silicon ship to perform whatever operations the software instructed them to do. Hoff's team had, although it was primitive in nature, created a computer-on-a-chip—the microprocessor.

CISC

The Intel microprocessor evolved on a design philosophy called complex instruction set computing (CISC). CISC used commands that incorporate many instructions to carry out a single operation. There were a number of characteristics that defined this architecture:

1. Built into every CISC microprocessor was a large set of commands, with several subcommands of varying length needed to complete a single operation. This set of commands was called a microcode. Individual commands were called by either the operating system or a software application when the processor needed to perform a task.

2. The CISC commands were not all the same size. This meant that the microprocessor needed to examine each command to determine the required processing space and the correct treatment of each command. This increased execution time.

3. The processor sent the requested commands to a decode unit, which translated the complex command into microcode—a series of smaller instructions directed to the nanoprocessor. The nanoprocessor was a processor within the processor, with corresponding complex circuitry because each instruction it executed might need to pass through several transistors in

order for it to be processed. Consequently, the instructions moved relatively slowly through the CISC circuits.

4. With the possibility that one command might depend on the results of another, all instructions needed to be performed in order, one at a time. This meant that all pending instructions were put on hold until the current instruction was completed.

RISC

In the 1960s, when John Cocke, a senior scientist in IBM's Yorktown Heights Research Center, was focusing on building faster processors, he noticed that the growing complexity of the microcodes was overburdening the processor and reducing the processor's speed and hence computer performance. Cocke, who had always been interested in the relationship between hardware and software, focused on the instruction set as a possible mechanism for increasing processor speed. Cocke discovered that if he reduced the instruction set and constructed the instructions themselves to be executed in one clock cycle of the microprocessor, the computer executed almost any software program much faster. IBM had kept this work secret, attempting to implement RISC in a number of its product lines.[16]

While IBM struggled to find ways to use RISC in its products, by the late 1970s other researchers had begun to experiment with the reduced instruction set, principally David Patterson at Berkeley and John Hennessy at Stanford. In 1980, Patterson designed a new microprocessor, called RISC I. Patterson's work led directly to Sun Microsystems' highly successful SPARC RISC microprocessor. Hennessy left Stanford to cofound MIPS. Both companies dominated the RISC market in the second half of the 1980s, exploiting the booming markets for engineering workstations and network servers.

The RISC chip used fewer operations. This relative simplicity made RISC chips easier to design and manufacture. As a result, RISC chips were inherently cheaper and smaller. The emergence of RISC computing in the mid-1980s represented a new approach to computing, which without any advances in manufacturing or process technologies, resulted in machines that ran two to four

times faster than conventional CISC designs. RISC improved processing speed in the following manner:

1. Each command in a RISC processor consisted of several small, discrete instructions that each performed only a single operation. Application software, which was compiled specifically for a RISC processor, told the processor which combination of its smaller RISC commands to execute to complete an operation.
2. All RISC commands were already microcode of identical size, and there was only one way to load and store them. As a result, RISC commands were ready to execute faster than CISC commands.
3. When software for a RISC processor was compiled, the compiler determined which commands were independent of the results of the other commands. This allowed for the potential of the processor being able to execute more than a single command simultaneously.
4. The RISC processor had simpler circuitry than its CISC counterpart because the RISC processor dealt with simpler commands. For a comparable operation, RISC interpreted and executed instructions at an average of 4 to 10 times faster than it takes to load and decode a complex CISC command and then execute each of its components.

For comparison, CISC microprocessors were only able to execute approximately 0.3 instructions per cycle when RISC microprocessors were commercially introduced in the mid-1980s. Early RISC chips boosted performance to one instruction per clock cycle. Hence, for any given clock speed in a chip—100 megahertz, for example—RISC chips could process three times as many instructions. In later generations of RISC chips, the number of instructions executed per clock cycle was increased further, leading to even more significant performance advantages over CISC circuitry.

Superscalar RISC

In the late 1980s, an additional level of parallel instruction computing was added to RISC chips in order to increase their performance. These new chips were deemed "Superscalar RISC." Superscalar RISC chips were able to execute independent instructions in parallel, doubling processor speed.

In addition to parallel instruction set computing, Superscalar RISC chips often employed branch prediction. Branch prediction was a way to prefetch data in advance of when the application software needed it to execute. Branch prediction was designed to lessen the impact of

---

[16] An account of IBM's discovery of RISC and its attempts to adapt it for use in its existing product lines can be found in Ferguson and Morris, *Computer Wars,* 1993.

memory latency. Memory latency occurred when the microprocessor was left waiting or stalled for information contained in memory. For example, a microprocessor might have had to wait 90 nanoseconds for the information contained in memory to arrive. While that was a very short time on an absolute scale, the microprocessor was cycling at 10 to 15 nanoseconds. Delays incurred if execution of the instruction was halted until the required data arrived from memory. In 1998, superscalar RISC technology was firmly established in the marketplace with chips such as Hewlett Packard's PA RISC, Digital Equipment Corporation's Alpha, Sun Microsystems' UltraSPARC, and the PowerPC, designed jointly by IBM and Apple Computer.

READING II-4

Customer Power, Strategic Investment, and the Failure of Leading Firms

Clayton M. Christensen and Joseph L. Bower

Why might firms be regarded as astutely managed at one point, yet subsequently lose their positions of industry leadership when faced with technological change? We present a model, grounded in a study of the world disk drive industry, that charts the process through which the demands of a firm's customers shape the allocation of resources in technological innovation—a model that links theories of resource dependence and resource allocation. We show that established firms led the industry in developing technologies of every sort—even radical ones—whenever the technologies addressed existing customers' needs. The same firms failed to develop simpler technologies that initially were only useful in emerging markets, because impetus coalesces behind, and resources are allocated to, programs targeting powerful customers. Projects targeted at technologies for which no customers yet exist languish for lack of impetus and resources. Because the rate of technical progress can ex-

ceed the performance demanded in a market, technologies which initially can only be used in emerging markets later can invade mainstream ones, carrying entrant firms to victory over established companies.

Students of management have marveled at how hard it is for firms to repeat their success when technology or markets change, for good reason: there are lots of examples. For instance, no leading computer manufacturer has been able to replicate its initial success when subsequent architectural technologies and their corresponding markets emerged. IBM created and continues to dominate the mainframe segment, but it missed by many years the emergence of the minicomputer architecture and market. The minicomputer was developed, and its market applications exploited, by firms such as Digital Equipment and Data General. While very successful in their initial markets, the minicomputer makers largely missed the advent of the desktop computer: a market which was created by entrants such as Apple, Commodore and Tandy, and only later by IBM. The engineering workstation leaders were Apollo and Sun Microsystems, both entrants to the industry. The pioneers of the portable computing market—Compaq, Zenith, Toshiba, and Sharp—were not the leaders in the desktop segment.

And yet even as these firms were missing this sequence of opportunities, they were *very* aggressively and successfully leading their industries in developing and adopting many strategically important and technologically sophisticated technologies. IBM's leadership across generations of multi-chip IC packaging and Sun Microsystems' embrace of RISC microprocessor technology are two instances. There are many other examples, discussed below, of firms that aggressively stayed at the forefront of technology development for extended periods, but whose industry leadership was later shaken by shifting technologies and markets.

The failure of leading firms can sometimes be ascribed to managerial myopia or organizational lethargy or to insufficient resources or expertise. For example, cotton-spinners simply lacked the human, financial, and technological resources to compete when Du Pont brought synthetic fibers into the apparel industry. But in many instances, the firms that missed important innovations suffered none of these problems. They had their competitive antennae up, aggressively invested in new products and technologies, and listened astutely to their customers. Yet they still lost their positions of leadership. This paper examines why and under what circumstances financially strong, customer-sensitive, technologically

Source: Reprinted from *Strategic Management Journal* 17 (1996), pp. 197–218. Copyright © 1996 by John Wiley & Sons Ltd. Used with permission.

deep, and rationally managed organizations may fail to adopt critical new technologies or enter important markets—failures to innovate which have led to the decline of once-great firms.

Our conclusion is that a primary reason why such firms lose their positions of industry leadership when faced with certain types of technological change has little to do with technology itself—with its degree of newness or difficulty, relative to the skills and experience of the firm. Rather, they fail because they listen too carefully to their customers—and customers place stringent limits on the strategies firms can and cannot pursue.

The term *technology,* as used in this paper, means the processes by which an organization transforms labor, capital, materials, and information into products or services. All firms have technologies. A retailer such as Sears employs a particular technology to procure, present, sell, and deliver products to its customers, while a discount warehouse retailer such as the Price Club employs a different technology. Hence, our concept of technology extends beyond the engineering and manufacturing functions of the firm, encompassing a range of business processes. The term *innovation* herein refers to a change in technology.

A fundamental premise of this paper is that patterns of resource allocation heavily influence the types of innovations at which leading firms will succeed or fail. In every organization, ideas emerge daily about new ways of doing things—new products, new applications for products, new technical approaches, and new customers—in a manner chronicled by Bower (1970) and Burgelman (1983a, 1983b). Most proposals to innovate require human and financial resources. The patterns of innovation evidenced in a company will therefore mirror to a considerable degree the patterns in how its resources are allocated to, and withheld from, competing proposals to innovate.

We observe that because effective resource allocation is market-driven, the resource allocation procedures in successful organizations provide impetus for innovations known to be demanded by current customers in existing markets. We find that established firms in a wide range of industries have tended to lead in developing and adopting such innovations. Conversely, we find that firms possessing the capacity and capability to innovate may fail when the innovation does *not* address the foreseeable needs of their current customers. When the initial price/performance characteristics of emerging technologies render them competitive only in emerging market segments, and not with current customers, resource alloca-

tion mechanisms typically deny resources to such technologies. Our research suggests that the inability of some successful firms to allocate sufficient resources to technologies that initially cannot find application in mainstream markets, but later invade them, lies at the root of the failure of many once-successful firms.

EARLIER VIEWS OF FACTORS INFLUENCING PATTERNS OF RESOURCE ALLOCATION IN THE INNOVATION PROCESS

Our research links two historically independent streams of research, both of which have contributed significantly to our understanding of innovation. The first stream is what Pfeffer and Salancik (1978) call *resource dependence:* an approach which essentially looks *outside* the firm for explanations of the patterns through which firms allocate resources to innovative activities. Scholars in this tradition contend that firms' strategic options are constrained because managerial discretion is largely a myth. In order to ensure the survival of their organizations, managers lack the power to do anything other than to allocate resources to innovative programs that are required of the firm by external customers and investors: the entities that provide the resources the firm needs to survive. Support for this view comes from the work of historians of technological innovation such as Cooper and Schendel (1976) and Foster (1986). The firms they studied generally responded to the emergence of competitively threatening technologies by intensifying their investments to improve the conventional technologies used by their current customers—which provided the resources the firms needed to survive over the short term.

The second stream of ideas, originally taught by Bower (1970) and amplified by Burgelman (1983a, 1983b), describes the resource allocation process internal to the firm. These scholars suggest that most strategic proposals—to add capacity or develop new products or processes—take their fundamental shape at lower levels of hierarchical organizations. Bower observed that the allocation of funding amongst projects is substantially shaped by the extent to which managers at middle levels of the organization decide to support, or lend *impetus,* to some proposals and to withhold it from others. Bower also observed that risk management and career management were closely linked in the resource allocation process. Because the career costs to aspiring managers of having backed an ultimately unsuccessful project can be severe, their tendency was to back those projects where the demand for the product was assured.

Our study links these two streams by showing how the impetus that drives patterns of resource allocation (and hence innovation) within firms does not stem from autonomous decisions of risk-conscious managers. Rather, whether sufficient impetus coalesces behind a proposed innovation is largely determined by the presence or absence of current customers who can capably articulate a need for the innovation in question. There seems to be a powerful linkage from (1) the expectations and needs of a firm's most powerful customers for product improvements to (2) the types of innovative proposals which are given or denied impetus within the firm and which therefore are allocated the resources necessary to develop the requisite technological capabilities, to (3) the markets toward which firms will and will not target these innovations, which in turn lead to (4) the firms' ultimate commercial success or failure with the new technology.

A primary conclusion of this paper is that when significant customers demand it, sufficient impetus may develop so that large, bureaucratic firms can embark upon and successfully execute technologically difficult innovations—even those that require very different competencies than they initially possessed.[1] Conversely, we find that when a proposed innovation addresses the needs of small customers in remote or emerging markets that do not supply a significant share of the resources a firm currently needs for growth and survival, firms will find it difficult to succeed even at innovations that are technologically straightforward. This is because the requisite impetus does not develop, and the proposed innovations are starved of resources.

Our findings build upon the work of earlier scholars who have addressed the question of why leading firms may fail when faced with technological change. Cooper and Schendel (1976) found that new technologies often are initially deployed in new markets, and that these were generally brought into industries by entering firms. They observed that established firms confronted with new technology often intensified investment in traditional technical approaches, and that those that did make initial resource commitments to a new technology rarely maintained adequate resource commitments. Foster (1986) noted that at points when new technologies enter an industry, entrants seem to enjoy an "attacker's advantage" over incumbent firms. Henderson and Clark (1990) posited that entrant firms enjoyed a particular advantage over incumbents in architectural technology change.

We hope to add additional precision and insight to the work of these pioneering scholars, by stating more precisely the specific sorts of technological innovations that are likely initially to be deployed in new applications and the sorts that are likely to be used in mainstream markets from the beginning and to define the types of innovation in which we expect attackers to enjoy an advantage and the instances in which we expect incumbents to hold the upper hand. By presenting a model of the processes by which resource commitments are made, we hope partially to explain a puzzle posed but not resolved by each of these authors: *why* have incumbent firms generally intensified their commitments to conventional technology, while starving efforts to commercialize new technologies—even while the new technology was gaining ground in the market? Finally, by examining why established firms do these things, we hope to provide insights for how managers can more successfully address different types of technological change.

RESEARCH METHODS

Three very different classes of data were used in this study, to establish solid construct validity (Yin, 1989). The first was a database of the detailed product and performance specifications for every disk drive model announced by every firm participating in the world industry between 1975 and 1990—over 1,400 product models in all. These data came from *Disk/Trend Report,* the leading market research publication in the disk drive industry, and from product specification sheets obtained from the manufacturers themselves. The tables and other summary statistics reported in this paper were calculated from this database, unless otherwise noted. This data set is not a statistical sample but constitutes a complete census of companies and products for the world industry during the period studied.

The second type of information employed in the study relates to the strategies pursued, and the commercial success and failure, of each of the companies that announced the development of a rigid disk drive between 1976 and 1990. *Disk/Trend* reported each firm's rigid disk drive sales in each of these years, by product category and by market segment. Each monthly issue between 1976 and

---

[1] Evidence supporting this conclusion is provided below. In making this statement, we contest the conclusions of scholars such as Tushman and Anderson (1986), who have argued that incumbent firms are most threatened by attacking entrants when the innovation in question destroys, or does not build upon, the competence of the firm. We observe that established firms, though often at great cost, have led their industries in developing critical competence-destroying technologies, when the new technology was needed to meet existing customers' demands.

1990 of *Electronic Business* magazine, the most prominent trade publication covering the magnetic recording industry, was examined for information about disk drive manufacturers, their strategies and products. We used this information to verify the completeness of the *Disk/Trend* data[2] and to write a history of the disk drive industry describing the strategies and fortunes of firms in the industry (Christensen, 1993).

The third type of information employed in this study came from over 70 personal, unstructured interviews conducted with executives who are or have been associated with 21 disk drive manufacturing companies. Those interviewed included founders; chief executives; vice presidents of sales and marketing, engineering, and finance; and engineering, marketing, and managerial members of pivotal product development project teams. The firms whose executives were interviewed together account for over 80 percent of the disk drives produced in the world since the industry's inception. Data from these interviews were used to reconstruct, as accurately as possible, the decision-making processes associated with key innovations in each company's history. Wherever possible, accounts of the same decision were obtained from multiple sources, including former employees, to minimize problems with post hoc rationalization. Multiple employees were interviewed in 16 of the 21 companies.

The *Disk/Trend* data enabled us to measure the impact that each new component and architectural technology had on disk drive performance. Furthermore, it was possible to identify which firms were the first to develop and adopt each new technology and to trace the patterns of diffusion of each new technology through the world industry over time, amongst different types of firms. When analysis of the *Disk/Trend* data indicated a particular entrant or established firm had prominently led or lagged behind the industry in a particular innovation, we could determine the impact of that leadership or followership on the subsequent sales and market shares, by product-market segment, for each company.

Analysis of these data essentially enabled us to develop a theory of *what* will happen when different types of technological change occur—whether we would expect entrant and established firms to take leadership in their development. We then used our interview data to write case histories of key decisions in six companies to understand *why* those patterns of leadership and followership in technology development occur. These case studies covered entrant and established firms, over an extended period of time in which each of them made decisions to invest, or delay investing, in a variety of new technologies. These cases were selected in what Yin (1989) calls a multicase, nested experimental design, so that through pattern matching across cases, the external validity of the study's conclusions could be established.[3]

We studied the disk drive industry because its history is one of rapid change in technology and market structure. The world rigid disk drive market grew at a 27 percent annual rate to over $13 billion between 1975 and 1990. Of the 17 firms in the OEM industry in 1976, only one was still in operation in 1990. Over 130 firms entered the industry during this period, and more than 100 of them failed. The cost per megabyte (MB) of the average drive in constant 1990 dollars fell from $560 in 1976 to $5 in 1990. The physical size of a 100 MB drive shrank from 5,400 to 8 cubic inches over the same period. During this time, six architecturally distinct product generations emerged, and a new company rose to become market leader in four of these six generations. A description of disk drive technology that may be helpful for some readers is provided in Appendix 1.

TYPOLOGIES OF TECHNOLOGICAL CHANGE

Earlier scholars of technology change have argued that incumbent firms may stumble when technological change destroys the value of established technological competencies (Tushman and Anderson, 1986) or when new architectural technologies emerge (Henderson and Clark, 1990). For present purposes, however, we have found it useful to distinguish between those innovations that *sustained* the industry's rate of improvement in product performance (total capacity and recording density were the two most common measures) and those innovations that *disrupted* or redefined that performance trajectory (Dosi, 1982). The following two sections illustrate these concepts by describing prominent examples of trajectory-sustaining and trajectory-disrupting technologi-

---

[2] *Disk/Trend Report* identified 133 firms that participated in the disk drive industry in the period studied. The search of *Electronic Business* magazine yielded information on one additional firm, Peach Tree Technology, that never generated revenues and somehow had escaped detection by the *Disk/Trend* editors.

---

[3] Exhibit 5 (which refers to Yin, 1989, 35–37) describes this pattern matching.

EXHIBIT 1   Examples of Sustaining Technological Change in Componentry (Left) and Product Architecture (Right)

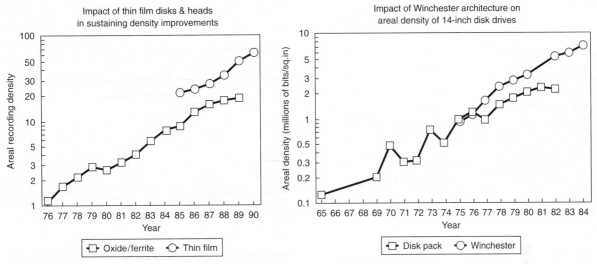

Source: Reprinted with permission from *Business History Review,* 1993, 67, p. 557.

cal changes in the industry's history. The subsequent sections then describe the role these innovations played in the industry's development, the processes through which incumbent and entrant firms responded to these different types of technological change, and the consequent successes and failures these firms experienced.

Sustaining Technological Changes

In the disk drive industry's history, most of the changes in competent technology and two of the six changes in architectural technology sustained or reinforced established trajectories of product performance improvement. Two examples of such technology change are shown in Exhibit 1. The left-most graph compares the average recording density of drives that employed conventional particulate oxide disk technology and ferrite head technology versus the average density of drives that employed new-technology thin-film heads and disks that were introduced in each of the years between 1976 and 1990. The improvements in the conventional approach are the result of consistent incremental advances such as grinding the ferrite heads to finer, more precise dimensions and using smaller and more finely dispersed oxide particles on the disk's surface. Note that the improvement in areal density obtainable with ferrite/oxide technology began to level off in the period's later years— suggesting a maturing technology S-curve (Foster,

1986). Note how thin-film head and disk technologies emerged to sustain the rate of performance improvement at its historical pace of 35 percent between 1984 and 1990.

The right-most graph in Exhibit 1 describes a sustaining technological change of a very different character: an innovation in product architecture. In this case, the 14-inch Winchester drive substituted for removable disk packs, which had been the dominant design between 1962 and 1978. Just as in the thin-film-for-ferrite/oxide substitution, the impact of Winchester technology was to sustain the historically established rate of performance improvement. Other important innovations (such as embedded servo systems, RLL, and PRML recording codes; higher RPM motors; and embedded SCSI, SMD, ESDI, and AT interfaces) also helped manufacturers sustain the rate of historical performance improvement that their customers had come to expect.[4] Hereafter in this paper,

---

[4] The examples of technology change presented in Exhibits 1 and 2 in this paper introduce some ambiguity to the unqualified term *discontinuity,* as it has been used by Dosi (1982), Tushman and Anderson (1986), and others. The innovations in head and disk technology described in the left graph of Exhibit 1 represent *positive discontinuities* in an established technological trajectory, while the development of trajectory-disrupting technologies charted in Exhibit 2 represent *negative* discontinuities. As will be shown below, established firms seemed quite capable of leading the industry over positive discontinuities. The

EXHIBIT 2   The Disruptive Impact on Performance Improvement of the 5.25-inch Versus the 8-inch Architecture

Attribute	8-inch drives	5.25-inch drives
Capacity (megabytes)	**60**	10
Volume (cubic inches)	566	150
Weight (pounds)	21	6
Access time (ms)	**30**	160
Cost per megabyte	**$50**	$200
Total unit cost	$3000	$2000

Key: Attributes valued highly in the minicomputer market in 1981 are presented in **boldface.**
Attributes valued in the emerging desktop computing market in 1981 are shown in *italics.*
Source. Analysis of *Disk/Trend Report* data; from Christensen (1992a: 90).

technological changes that have such a sustaining impact on an established trajectory of performance improvement are called *sustaining technologies.*

Disruptive technological changes

Most technological change in the industry's history consisted of sustaining innovations of the sort described above. In contrast, there were just a few trajectory-disrupting changes. The most important of these from a historical viewpoint were the architectural innovations that carried the industry from 14-inch diameter disks to diameters of 8, 5.25, and then 3.5 inches. The ways in which these innovations were disruptive are illustrated in Exhibit 2. Set in 1981, this table compares the attributes of a typical 5.25-inch drive—a new architecture that had been in the market for less than a year at that time—with those of a typical 8-inch drive, which by that time had become the standard drive used by minicomputer manufacturers. Note that along the dimensions of performance which were important to established minicomputer manufacturers—capacity, cost per megabyte, and access time—the 8-inch product was vastly superior. The 5.25-inch architecture did not address the needs of minicomputer manufacturers, as they perceived their needs at that time. On the other hand, the 5.25-inch architecture *did* possess attributes that appealed to the desktop personal computer market segment that was just emerging in

_____

negative ones were the points at which established firms generally lost their positions of industry leadership.

1980–82. It was small and lightweight—important features for this application. And it was priced at around $2,000, which means it could economically be incorporated in desktop machines. Hereafter in this paper, technologies such as this, which disrupt an established trajectory of performance improvement or redefine what performance means, are called *disruptive technologies.*

In general, sustaining technological changes appealed to established customers in existing, mainstream markets. They provided these customers with more of what they had come to expect. In contrast, disruptive technologies rarely could initially be employed in established markets. They tended instead to be valued in remote or emerging markets. This tendency consistently appears not just in disk drives, but across a range of industries (Rosenbloom and Christensen, 1995).

THE IMPACT OF SUSTAINING AND DISRUPTIVE TECHNOLOGIES ON INDUSTRY STRUCTURE

The history of sustaining and disruptive technological change in the disk drive industry is summarized in Exhibit 3. It begins in 1974, the year after IBM's first Winchester architecture model was introduced to challenge the dominant disk pack architectural design. Almost all drives then were sold to makers of mainframe computers. Note that in 1974 the median-priced mainframe computer was equipped with about 130 MB of hard disk capacity. The typical hard disk storage capacity supplied with the median-priced mainframe increased about 17 percent per year, so that by 1990 the typical mainframe was equipped with 1,300 MB of hard disk capacity. This growth in the use of hard disk memory per computer is mapped by the solid line emanating from point A in Exhibit 3. This trajectory was driven by user learning and software developments in the applications in which mainframes were used (Christensen and Rosenbloom, 1995).

The dashed line originating at point A measures the increase in the average capacity of 14-inch drives over the same period. Note that although the capacity of the average 14-inch drive was equal to the capacity shipped with the typical mainframe in 1974, the rate of increase in capacity provided within the 14-inch architecture exceeded the rate of increase in capacity demanded in the mainframe market—carrying this architecture toward high-end mainframes, scientific computers, and super-computers. Furthermore, note how the new 14-inch Winchester architecture sustained the capacity trajectory that

EXHIBIT 3 Patterns of Entry and Improvement in Disruptive Disk Drive Technologies

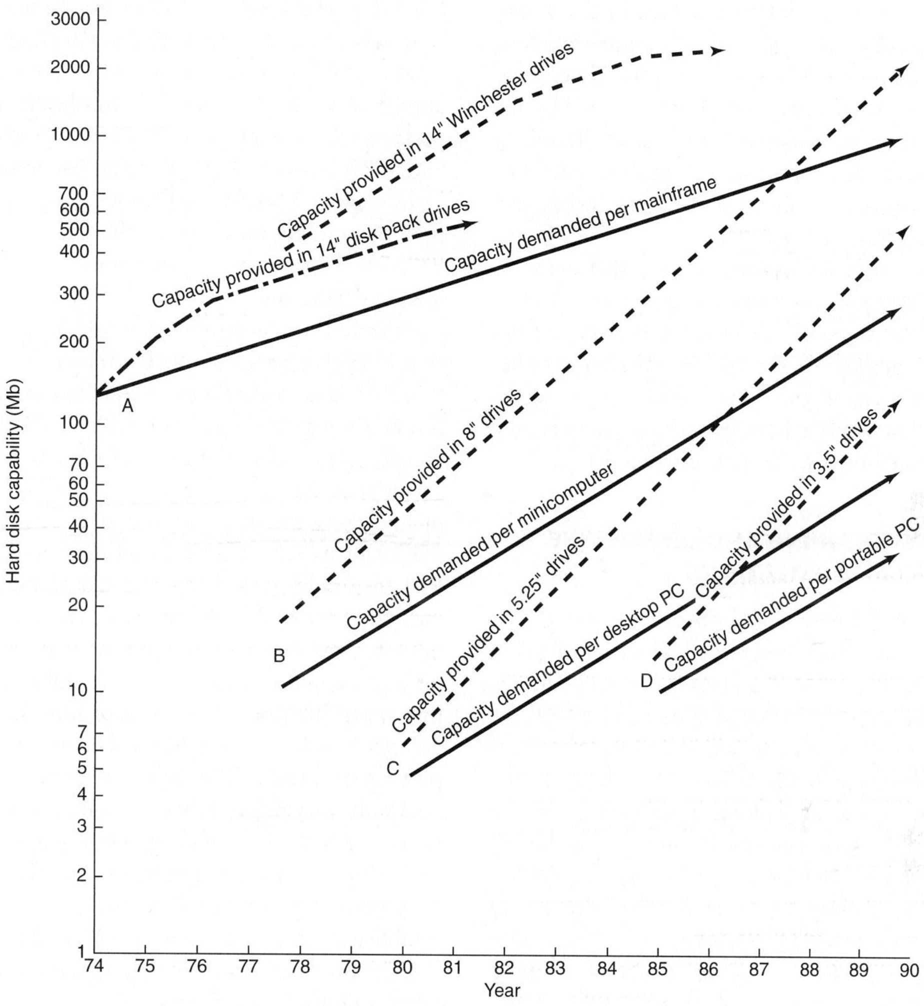

Source: Reprinted with permission from *Business History Review,* 1993, 67, p. 559.

had been established in the earlier removable disk pack architecture. Appendix 2 describes how these trajectories were calculated.

The solid trajectories emanating from points B, C, and D represent the average hard disk capacity *demanded* by computer buyers in each market segment, over time.[5] The dashed lines emanating from points B, C,

and D in Exhibit 3 measure trends in the average capacity that disk drive manufacturers were able to *provide* with each successive disk drive architecture. Note that with the exception of the 14-inch Winchester architecture, the maximum capacity initially available in each of these architectures was substantially *less* than the capacity required for the typical computer in the established market—these were *disruptive* innovations. As

---

[5] These trajectories represent the disk capacity *demanded* in each market because in each instance, greater disk capacity could have been supplied to users by the computer manufacturers, had the market de-

manded additional capacity at the cost for which it could be purchased at the time.

a consequence, the 8-, 5.25-, and 3.5-inch designs initially were rejected by the leading, established computer manufacturers and were deployed instead in emerging-market applications for disk drives: minicomputers, desktop PCs, and portable PCs, respectively. Note, however, that once these disruptive architectures became established in their new markets, the accumulation of hundreds of sustaining innovations pushed each architecture's performance ahead along very steep, and roughly parallel, trajectories.[6]

Note that the trajectory of improvement that the technology was able to *provide* within each architecture was nearly *double* the slope of the increase in capacity *demanded* in each market. As we will see, this disparity between what the technology could provide and what the market demanded seems to have been the primary source of leadership instability in the disk drive industry.

LEADERS IN SUSTAINING AND DISRUPTIVE TECHNOLOGICAL INNOVATIONS

To better understand why leading firms might successfully pioneer in the development and adoption of many new and difficult technologies and yet lose their positions of industry leadership by failing to implement others, we compared the innovative behavior of *established* firms with that of *entrant* firms, with respect to each of the sustaining and disruptive technological innovations in the history of the disk drive industry. Building upon the approach employed by Henderson and Clark (1990), we defined established firms as firms that had previously manufactured drives which employed an older, established technology, whereas entrant firms were those whose initial product upon entry into the industry employed the new component or architectural technology being analyzed. This approach was used because of this study's longitudinal character, looking at the performance of incumbents and entrants across a sequence of innovations.

In spite of the wide variety in the magnitudes and types of sustaining technological changes in the industry's history, the firms that led in their development and adoption were the industry's leading, established firms. Exhibit 4(a) depicts this leadership pattern for three representative sustaining technologies. In thin-film head

technology, it was Burroughs (1976), IBM (1979), and other established firms that first successfully incorporated thin-film heads in disk drives. In the 1981–86 period, when over 60 firms entered the rigid disk drive industry, only five of them (all commercial failures) attempted to do so using thin-film heads as a source of performance advantage in their initial products. All other entrant firms—even aggressively performance-oriented firms such as Maxtor and Conner Peripherals—found it preferable to cut their teeth on ferrite heads in the entry products, before tackling thin-film technology in subsequent generations.

Note the similar pattern in the development and adoption of RLL codes—a much simpler development than thin-film head technology—which consumed at most a few million dollars per firm. RLL enabled a 30 percent density improvement and therefore represented the type of inexpensive path to performance improvement that ought to be attractive to entrant firms. But in 1985, 11 of the 13 firms which introduced new models employing RLL technology were established firms, meaning that they had previously offered models based on MFM technology. Only two were entrants, meaning that their initial products employed RLL codes. Exhibit 4(a) also notes that six of the first seven firms to introduce Winchester architecture drives were established makers of drives employing the prior disk pack architecture.[7]

The history of literally every other sustaining innovation—such as embedded servo systems, zone-specific recording densities, higher RPM motors and the 2.5-inch Winchester architecture—reveals a similar pattern: the established firms led in the adoption of sustaining technology be it in componentry or architecture. Entrant firms followed. In other words, the failure of leading firms to stay atop the disk drive industry generally was not because they could not keep pace with the industry's movement along the dashed-line technological trajectories mapped in Exhibit 4. The leading incumbent firms effectively *led* the industry along those trajectories even though many of these were competency-destroying progressions in terms of technologies, skills, and manufacturing assets required (Tushman and Anderson, 1986).

In contrast, the firms that led the industry in introducing *disruptive* architectural technologies—in the moves to points B, C, and D in Exhibit 3—tended overwhelm-

---

[6] The parallel impact of sustaining innovations across these architectural generations results from the fact that the same sustaining technologies, in the form of componentry, were available simultaneously to manufacturers of each generation of disk drives (Christensen, 1992b).

[7] Note that the statistics shown in Exhibit 4 are not a sample—they represent the entire population of firms in each of the years shown offering models incorporating the technologies in question. For that reason, tests of statistical significance are not relevant in this case.

EXHIBIT 4   Trends in Technology Leadership and Followership in Sustaining Versus Disruptive Technologies

(a) Numbers of established and entrant firms introducing models employing selected trajectory-sustaining technologies

		1974	1975	1976	1977	1978	1979	1980	1981	1982	1983	1984	1985	1986	1987	1988
Thin-film heads	Entrants								1		1	2	1		1	4
	Established			1			1	1	3	5	6	8	12	15	17	22
RLL codes	Entrants											1	2	3	6	8
	Established											4	11	20	25	26
Winchester architecture	Entrants				1	4	9									
	Established	1		3	3	7	11									

(b) Numbers of established and entrant firms introducing models based upon disruptive architectural technologies

		1974	1975	1976	1977	1978	1979	1980	1981	1982	1983	1984	1985	1986	1987	1988
8-inch	Entrants					1	4	6	8							
	Established					0	2	5	5							
5.25-inch	Entrants							1	8	8	13					
	Established							1	2	8	11					
3.5-inch	Entrants											1	2	3	4	
	Established											0	1	1	4	

Note: Data are presented in these tables only for those years in which the new technologies were gaining widespread acceptance, to illustrate tendencies in technology leadership and followership. Once the technologies had become broadly accepted, the numbers of firms introducing models using them are no longer reported. Twelve years are covered in the thin-film head category because it took that long for thin-film heads to become broadly used in the marketplace. Only five years of history are reported for RLL codes because by 1988 the vast majority of established *and* entrant firms had adopted RLL codes. Four years of data are shown for new architectures, because any established firms that had not launched the new architecture within four years of its initial appearance in the market had been driven from the industry.

ingly to be *entrant,* rather than established firms. This is illustrated in Exhibit 4(b). It shows, for example, that in 1978 an entrant offered the industry's first 8-inch drive. By the end of the second year of that architecture's life (1979), six firms were offering 8-inch drives; two-thirds of them were entrants. Likewise, by the end of the second year of the 5.25-inch generation's life, 8 of the 10 firms offering 5.25-inch drives were entrants. Entrants similarly dominated the early population of firms offering 3.5-inch drives. In each of these generations, between half and two-thirds of the established manufacturers of the prior architectural generation *never* introduced a model in the new architecture. And those established drivemakers that did design and manufacture new architecture models did so with an average two-year lag behind the pioneering entrant firms. In this fast-paced industry, such slow response often proved fatal.

These patterns of leadership and followership in sustaining and disruptive technologies are reflected in the commercial success and failure of disk drive manufacturers. The ability of established firms to lead the industry in the sustaining innovations that powered the steep technological trajectories in Exhibit 4 often were technologically difficult, risky, and expensive. Yet in the history of this industry, there is no evidence that the firms that led in sustaining innovations gained market share by virtue of such technology leadership (Christensen, 1992b). This leadership enabled them to maintain their competitiveness only within specific technological trajectories. On the other hand, entrant firms' leadership advantages in disruptive innovations enabled them not only to capture new markets as they emerged, but (because the trajectories of technological progress were steeper than the trajectories of performance demanded) to invade and capture established markets as well.

Hence, all but one of the makers of 14-inch drives were driven from the mainframe computer market by entrant firms that got their start making 8-inch drives for minicomputers. The 8-inch drivemakers, in turn, were driven from the minicomputer market, and eventually the mainframe market, by firms which led in producing 5.25-inch drives for desktop computers. And the leading makers of 5.25-inch drives were driven from desktop and minicomputer applications by makers of 3.5-inch drives, as mapped in Exhibit 4.

We began this paper by posing a puzzle: why it was that firms which at one point could be esteemed as aggressive, innovative, customer-sensitive organizations could ignore or attend belatedly to technological innovations with enormous strategic importance. In the context of the preceding analysis of the disk drive industry, this question can be sharpened considerably. The established firms were, in fact, aggressive, innovative, and customer-sensitive in their approaches to sustaining innovations of every sort. But why was it that established firms could not lead their industry in disruptive architectural innovations? For it is only in these innovations that attackers demonstrated an advantage. And unfortunately for the leading established firms, this advantage enabled attacking entrant firms to topple the incumbent industry leaders each time a disruptive technology emerged.[8]

To understand why disruptive technological change was so consistently vexing to incumbent firms, we personally interviewed managers who played key roles in the industry's leading firms, as incumbents or entrants, when each of these disruptive technologies emerged. Our objective in these interviews was to reconstruct, as accurately and from as many points of view as possible, the forces that influenced these firms' decision-making processes relating to the development and commercialization of disruptive architectural technologies. We found the experiences of the firms, and the forces influencing their decisions, to be remarkably similar. In each instance, when confronted with disruptive technology change, developing the requisite *technology* was never a problem: prototypes of the new drives often had been developed before management was asked to make a decision. It was in the process of allocating scarce resources amongst competing product and technology development proposals, however, that disruptive projects got stalled. Programs addressing the needs of the firms' most powerful customers almost *always* preempted resources from the disruptive technologies, whose markets tended to be small and where customers' needs were poorly defined.

In the following section we have synthesized the data from case studies of the six firms we studied in particular depth, into a *six*-step model that describes the factors that influenced how resources were allocated across competing proposals to develop new sustaining versus disruptive technology in these firms. The struggle of Seagate Technology, the industry's dominant maker of 5.25-inch drives, to successfully commercialize the disruptive 3.5-inch drive, is recounted here to illustrate each of the

steps in the model. Short excerpts from a fuller report of other case histories (Christensen, 1992a) are also presented to illustrate what happened in specific companies at each point in the process. Exhibit 5 describes how the findings from each of the case studies support, or do not support, the principal propositions in the model. In Yin's (1989) terms, the high degree of literal and theoretical replication shown in Exhibit 5 and the extent of "pattern matching" across case studies where more than one firm encountered the same technological change lend high degrees of reliability and external validity to the model.[9]

A MODEL OF THE RESOURCE ALLOCATION PROCESS IN ESTABLISHED FIRMS FACED WITH DISRUPTIVE CHANGE

1. Although entrants were the leaders in *commercializing* disruptive technology, it did not start out that way: the first engineers to develop the disruptive architectures generally did so while employed by a leading established firm, using bootlegged resources. Their work was rarely initiated by senior management. While architecturally innovative, these designs almost always employed off-the-shelf components. For example, engineers at Seagate Technology, the leading 5.25-inch drive maker, were the second in the industry to develop working prototype 3.5-inch models, in 1985. They made over 80 prototype models before the issue of formal project approval was raised with senior management. The same thing happened earlier at Control Data, the dominant 14-inch drive-maker. Its engineers had designed working 8-inch drives internally, nearly two years before they appeared in the market.

2. The marketing organization then used its habitual procedure for testing the market appeal of new drives, by showing prototypes to lead customers of the exist-

---

[8] We believe this insight—that attacking firms have an advantage in disruptive innovations but not in sustaining ones—clarifies but is not in conflict with Foster's (1986) assertions about the attacker's advantage. The historical examples Foster uses to substantiate his theory generally seem to have been disruptive innovations.

[9] For readers who are unfamiliar with the work of scholars such as Yin (1989) and Campbell and Stanley (1966) on research methodology, a *literal* replication of a model occurs when an outcome happens as the model would predict. A *theoretical* replication of the model occurs when a different outcome happens than what would have been predicted by the model but when this outcome can be explained by elements in the model. In the instance here, the success of entrants and the failure of established firms at points of disruptive technology change are directly predicted by the model and would be classed as literal replications. Instances where an established firm succeeded in the face of disruptive technological change because it acted in a way that dealt with the factors in the model that typically precipitated failure would be classed as *theoretical* replications of the model. Several of these instances occurred in the industry's history, as explained later in this paper.

EXHIBIT 5 Support of Key Elements of Model Found in Each of Six in-Depth Case Studies

Companies studied:	Prototypes of disruptive architecture drive are developed internally, well before widespread industry adoption (model step 1).	Marketers show early prototypes to lead customers of prior architecture; they reject product; marketing issues pessimistic forecast (model step 2).	Project to commercialize disruptive product is shelved; company aggressively pursues sustaining innovations (model step 3).	New firms are established to commercialize disruptive architecture; they find new markets, where product's attributes are valued (model step 4).	Entrant firms which initially sold product only in new market improve performance faster than initial market requires, enabling them to attack established markets (model step 5).	In response to entrants' attack, established firms belatedly introduce disruptive product. Sales are largely to existing customers, cannibalizing sales of prior architecture products (model step 6).
Quantum Corp.	L	L	L,T	L,T	L	L,T
Conner Peripherals	L		L	L	L	L,T
Miniscribe	L		L	L	L	
Seagate Technology	L	L	L	L	L	L
Micropolis T	L	L,T	L,T	L	T	
Control Data	L	L	L,T	L,T	L	L,T

Note: An L in the matrix indicates that this step was a clear, explicit element in that firm's case history—in Yin's (1989) terms, a "literal replication." Where T is shown, the firm avoided the fate described in the model by explicitly recognizing the factors in the model and dealing with them in the manner described in the final section of this paper. These constitute what Yin calls theoretical replications of the model. Where no L or T is shown, that step was not a clear or prominent part of the firm's encounter with the disruptive technology being studied. Some firms studied confronted only one disruptive architecture. Miniscribe, for example, started making 5.25-inch drives generally in the pattern indicated by our model and was subsequently driven from the industry. Other firms, such as Quantum and Control Data, confronted a series of disruptive innovations and dealt with some of them differently than they did with others, as described in the last section of the paper. In such instances, an L and a T are entered in the matrix. As Yin points out, when multiple case studies are used to support a multielement model, as in this study, each cell in a matrix such as this constitutes an independent observation. Hence, the model is supported in 32 of the 36 observations.

ing product line, asking them to evaluate the new models.[10] In the Seagate case, again, marketers tested the new 3.5-inch drives with IBM and other makers of XT- and AT-class desktop personal computers—even though the drives, as shown in Exhibit 4, had significantly less capacity than in the mainstream desktop market demanded.

These customers showed little interest in the disruptive drives, because they did not address their need for higher performance within the established architectural framework. As Exhibit 3 shows, the established customers needed new drives that would take them *along* their existing performance trajectory. As a consequence, the marketing managers were unwilling to support the disruptive technology and offered pessimistic sales forecasts.

Generally, because the disruptive drives were targeted at emerging markets, initial forecasts of sales were small. In addition, because such products were simpler and offered lower performance, forecast profit margins were also lower than established firms had come to require. Financial analysts in established firms, therefore, joined their marketing colleagues in opposing the disruptive programs. As a result, in the ensuing allocation process resources were explicitly withdrawn, and the disruptive projects were slowly starved.

For example, when Seagate's main customer, IBM's PC division, rejected Seagate's 3.5-inch prototypes for insufficient capacity, sales forecasts were cut and senior managers shelved the program—just as 3.5-inch drives were becoming firmly established in laptops. "We needed a new model," recalled a former Seagate manager, "which could become the next ST412 [a very successful product generating $300 million sales annually in the desktop market that was near the end of its life cycle]. Our forecasts for the 3.5-inch drive were under $50 million because the laptop market was just emerging—and the 3.5-inch product just didn't fit the bill." And earlier, when engineers at Control Data, the leading 14-inch drive maker, developed its initial 8-inch drives, its customers were looking for an average of 300 MB per computer, whereas CDC's earliest 8-inch drives offered fewer than 60 MB. The 8-inch project was given low priority, and engineers assigned to its development kept getting pulled off to work on problems with 14-inch drives being designed for more important customers. Similar problems plagued the belated launches of Quantum's and Micropolis's 5.25-inch products.

3. In response to the needs of current customers, the marketing managers threw impetus behind alternative *sustaining* projects, such as incorporating better heads or developing new recording codes. These would give their customers what they wanted, could be targeted at large markets, and would generate the sales and profits required to maintain growth. Although they generally involved greater development expense, such sustaining investments appeared *far* less risky than investments in the disruptive technology, because the customers were there. The rationality of Seagate's decision to shelve the 3.5-inch drive in 1985–86, for example, is stark. Its view downmarket (in terms of Exhibit 3) was at a $50 million total market forecast for 3.5-inch drives in 1987. What gross margins it could achieve in that market were uncertain, but its manufacturing executives predicted that costs per megabyte in 3.5-inch drives would be much higher than in 5.25-inch products. Seagate's view upmarket was quite different. Volumes in 5.25-inch drives with capacities of 60–100 MB were forecast to be $500 million in size by 1987. And companies serving the 60–100 MB market were earning gross margins of 35–40 percent, whereas Seagate's margins in its high-volume 20 MB drives were between 25 and 30 percent. It simply did not make sense for Seagate to put resources behind the 3.5-inch drive, when competing proposals to move upmarket to develop its ST251 line of drives were also actively being evaluated.

After Seagate executives shelved the 3.5-inch project, it began introducing new 5.25-inch models at a dramatically accelerating rate. In the years 1985, 1986, and 1987, the numbers of new models it introduced each year as a percentage of the total number of its models on the market in the prior year were 57, 78, and 115 percent, respectively. And during the same

---

[10]This is consistent with Burgelman's observation that one of the greatest difficulties encountered by corporate entrepreneurs was finding the right "beta test sites," where products could be interactively developed and refined with customers. Generally, the entre to the customer was provided by the salesman who sold the firm's established product lines. This helped the firm develop new products for established markets but did not help it identify new applications for its new technology (Burgelman and Sayles, 1986, 76–80). Professor Rebecca Henderson pointed out to us that this tendency always to take new technologies to mainstream customers reflects a rather narrow *marketing* competence—that although these issues tend to be framed by many scholars as issues of technological competence, a firm's disabilities in finding new markets for new technologies may be its most serious innovative handicap.

period, Seagate incorporated complex and sophisticated new component technologies such as thin-film disks, voice coil actuators, RLL codes, and embedded SCSI interfaces. In each of our other case studies as well, the established firms introduced new models in their established architectures employing an array of new component technologies at an accelerating rate, after the new architectures began to be sold. The clear motivation of the established firms in doing this was to win the competitive wars against each other, rather than to prepare for an attack by entrants from below.

4. New companies, usually including members of the frustrated engineering teams from established firms, were formed to exploit the disruptive product architecture. For example, the founders of the leading 3.5-inch drivemaker, Conner Peripherals, were disaffected employees from Seagate and Miniscribe, the two largest 5.25-inch manufacturers. The founders of 8-inch drivemaker Micropolis came from Pertec, a 14-inch manufacturer; and the founders of Shugart and Quantum defected from Memorex.[11] The start-ups were as unsuccessful as their former employers in interesting established computer makers in the disruptive architecture. Consequently, they had to find *new* customers. The applications that emerged in this very uncertain, probing process were the minicomputer, the desktop personal computer, and the laptop (see Exhibit 3). These are obvious markets for hard drives in retrospect. But at the time, whether these would become significant markets for disk drives was highly uncertain. Micropolis was founded before the market for desk-side minicomputers and word processors, in which its products came to be used, emerged. Seagate was founded two years before IBM introduced its PC, when personal computers were simple toys for hobbyists. And Conner Peripherals got its start before Compaq knew the portable computer market had potential. The founders of these firms sold their products without a clear marketing strategy, essentially to whoever would buy them. Out of what was largely a trial-and-error approach to the market, the ultimately dominant applications for their products emerged.

5. Once the start-ups had found an operating base in new markets, they found that by adopting sustaining improvements in new component technologies,[12] they could increase the capacity of their drives at a faster rate than was required by their new market. As shown in Exhibit 3, they blazed trajectories of 50 percent annual improvement, fixing their sights on the large, established computer markets immediately above them on the performance scale. As noted above, the established firms' views downmarket, and the entrant firms' views upmarket, were asymmetrical. In contrast to the unattractive margins and market size the established firms saw when eyeing the new markets for simpler drives as they were emerging, the entrants tended to view the potential volumes and margins in the upscale, high-performance markets above them as highly attractive. Customers in these established markets eventually embraced the new architectures they had rejected earlier, because once their needs for capacity and speed were met, the new drives' smaller size and architectural simplicity made them cheaper, faster, and more reliable than the older architectures. For example, Seagate, which started in the desktop personal computer market, subsequently invaded and came to dominate the minicomputer, engineering workstation, and mainframe computer markets for disk drives. Seagate, in turn, was driven from the desktop personal computer market for disk drives by Conner and Quantum, the pioneering manufacturers of 3.5-inch drives.

6. When the smaller models began to invade established market segments, the drivemakers that had initially controlled those markets took their prototypes off the shelf, where they had been put in step (3), and defensively introduced them to defend their customer base in their own market.[13] By this time, of course, the new architecture had shed its disruptive character and had become fully performance-competitive with the larger drives in the established markets. Although some established manufacturers were able to defend their market positions through belated introduction of the new architecture, many found that the entrant firms had developed insurmountable advantages in manufacturing cost and design experience, and they

---

[11] Ultimately, nearly all North American manufacturers of disk drives can trace their founders' genealogy to IBM's San Jose division, which developed and manufactured its magnetic recording products (Christensen, 1993).

[12] In general, these component technologies were developed within the largest of the established firms that dominated the markets above these entrants, in terms of the technology and market trajectories mapped in Exhibit 3.

[13] Note that at this point, because the disruptive innovation invading below had become fully performance-competitive with the established technology, the innovation had essentially acquired the character of a sustaining innovation—it gave customers what they needed.

eventually withdrew from the market. For those established manufacturers that did succeed in introducing the new architectures, survival was the only reward. None of the firms we studied was ever able to win a significant share of the new market whose emergence had been enabled by the new architecture; the new drives simply cannibalized sales of older, larger-architecture products with existing customers. For example, as of 1991 almost none of Seagate's 3.5-inch drives had been sold to portable/laptop manufacturers: its 3.5-inch customers still were desktop computer manufacturers, and many of its 3.5-inch drives continued to be shipped with frames permitting them to be mounted in XT- and AT-class computers that had been designed to accommodate 5.25-inch drives. Control Data, the 14-inch leader, never captured even a 1 percent share of the minicomputer market. It introduced its 8-inch drives nearly three years after the pioneering start-ups did, and nearly all of its drives were sold to its existing mainframe customers. Miniscribe, Quantum, and Micropolis all had the same cannibalistic experience when they belatedly introduced disruptive-technology drives. They failed to capture a significant share of the new market and at best succeeded in defending a portion of their prior business.

There are curious asymmetries in the *ex post* risks and rewards associated with sustaining and disruptive innovations. Many of the sustaining innovations (such as thin-film heads, thin-film disks, and the 14-inch Winchester architecture) were *extremely* expensive and risky from a *technological* point of view. Yet because they addressed well-understood needs of known customers, perceived market risk was low; impetus coalesced; and resources were allocated with only prudent hesitation. Yet, although these innovations clearly helped the innovators retain their customers, there is no evidence from the industry's history that any firm was able to gain observable market share by virtue of such technology leadership.[14]

On the other hand, disruptive innovations were technologically straightforward: several established firms had already developed them by the time formal resource allocation decisions were made. But these were viewed as extremely risky, because the markets were not "there." The most successful of the entrants that accepted the risks of creating new markets for disruptive innovations generated billions in revenues upon foundations of architectural technology that cost at most a few million dollars to put into place.

We argue that although differences in luck, resource endowments, managerial competence, and bureaucratic agility matter, the patterns of technology leadership displayed by established and entrant firms in the disk drive industry accurately reflect differences in the fully informed, rational *ex ante* perceptions of risks and rewards held by managers in the two types of firms. In each of the companies studied, a key task of senior managers was to decide which of the many product and technology development programs continually being proposed to them should receive a formal allocation of resources. The criteria used in these decisions were essentially the total return perceived in each project, adjusted by the perceived riskiness of the project, as these data were presented to them by midlevel managers. Projects targeted at the known needs of big customers in established markets consistently won the rational debates over resource allocation. Sophisticated systems for planning and compensation ensured that this would be the case.[15]

The contrast between the innovative behavior of some *individuals* in the firm versus the manner in which the firm's *processes* allocated resources across competing projects is an important feature of this model.[16] In the cases studied, the pioneering engineers in established firms that developed disruptive-architecture drives were innovative not just in technology, but in their view of the market. They intuitively perceived opportunities for a

---

[14]Christensen (1992b) shows that there was no discernible first-mover advantage associated with trajectory-sustaining innovations to firms in the disk drive industry. In contrast, there were *very* powerful first-mover advantages to leaders in trajectory-disruptive innovations that fostered the creation of new markets.

[15]It is interesting that 20 years after Bower's (1970) study of resource allocation, we see in leading-edge systems for planning and compensation the same bias against risk taking. Morris and Ferguson's description of how IBM allowed Microsoft to gain control of PC operating system standards is centered on the role of mainframe producers in IBM's resource allocation process. In a 1990 interview with one of the authors, one of the most successful innovators in IBM history recounted how time and again he was forced to battle the controlling influence of middle-management's commitment to serve commercial mainframe customers.

[16]We are indebted to Professor Robert Burgelman for his comments on this issue. He has also noted, given the sequence of events we observed—where engineers inside the established firms began pursuing the disruptive product opportunity before the start-up entrants did—that timing matters a lot. It may be that when individuals in the established firms were pressing their ideas internally, they were too far ahead of the market. In the year or two that it took them to leave their employers, create new firms, and create new products, the nascent markets may have become more ready to accept the new drives.

very different disk drive. But organizational processes allocated resources based on rational assessments of data about returns and risks. Information provided by innovating engineers was at best hypothetical: without existing customers, they could only guess at the size of the market, the profitability of products, and required product performance. In contrast, current customers could articulate features, performance, and quantities they would purchase with *much* less ambiguity. Because of these differences in information clarity, firms were led toward particular sorts of innovations—many of which were extremely challenging and risky—and away from others. In the firms studied here, the issue does not seem so much to be innovativeness *per se,* as it is what *type* of innovation the firms' processes could facilitate.

In light of this research, the popular slogan "Stay close to your customers" (which is supported by the research of von Hippel, 1988, and others) appears not always to be robust advice. One instead might expect customers to lead their suppliers toward sustaining innovations and to provide no leadership—or even to explicitly *mis*lead—in instances of disruptive technology change. Henderson (1993) saw similar potential danger for being held captive by customers in her study of photolithographic aligner equipment manufacturers.

We close our discussion of the model with a final note. Neglect of disruptive technologies proved damaging to established drivemakers because the trajectory of performance improvement that the technology *provided* was steeper than the improvement trajectory *demanded* in individual markets (see Exhibit 4.) The mismatch in these trajectories provided pathways for the firms that entered new markets eventually to become performance-competitive in established markets as well. If the trajectories were parallel, we would expect disruptive technologies to be deployed in new markets and to stay there; each successive market would constitute a relatively stable niche market out of which technologies and firms would not migrate.

THE LINKAGE BETWEEN MODELS OF RESOURCE DEPENDENCE AND RESOURCE ALLOCATION

We mentioned at the outset that a contribution of this paper is that it establishes a linkage between the school of thought known as *resource dependence* (Pfeffer and Salancik, 1978) and the models of the resource allocation process proposed by Bower (1970) and Burgelman (1983a, 1983b). Our findings support many of the con-

clusions of the resource dependence theorists, who contend that a firm's scope for strategic change is strongly bounded by the interests of external entities (customers, in this study) who provide the resources the firm needs to survive. We show that the mechanism through which customers wield this power is the process in which impetus coalesces behind investments in sustaining technologies, directing resources to innovations that address current customers' needs.

But although our findings lend support to the theory of resource dependence, they decidedly do not support a contention that managers are powerless to change the strategies of their companies in directions that are inconsistent with the needs of their customers as resource providers (Pfeffer and Salancik, 1978, 263–265).[17] The evidence from this study is that managers can, in fact, change strategy—but that they can successfully do so only if their actions are consistent with, rather than in counteraction to, the principle of resource dependence. In the disk drive industry's history, three established firms achieved a measure of commercial success in disruptive technologies. Two did so by spinning out organizations that were completely independent, in terms of customer relationships, from the mainstream groups. The third launched the disruptive technology with extreme managerial effort, from within the mainstream organization. This paper closes by summarizing these case histories and their implications for theory.

Distinct Organizational Units for Small Drives at Control Data

Control Data (CDC) was the dominant manufacturer of 14-inch disk pack and Winchester drives sold into the OEM market between 1975 and 1982: its market share fluctuated between 55 and 62 percent. When the 8-inch architecture emerged in the late 1970s, CDC missed it by three years. It never captured more than 3–4 percent of the 8-inch market, and those 8-inch drives that it

---

[17] In Chapter 10 of Pfeffer and Salancik's (1978) book, for example, they assert that the manager's most valuable role is symbolic, and they cite a hypothetical example. When external forces induce hard times in a company, managers can usefully be fired—not because bringing in a new manager will make any difference to the performance of the organization, but because of the symbolic content of that action. It creates the *feeling* in the organization that something is being done to address this problem, even though it will have no effect. The evidence from these case studies does not support this assertion about the ability of managers to change the course of their organizations. *As long as managers act in a manner consistent with the forces of resource dependence,* it appears that they can, indeed, wield significant power.

did sell were sold almost exclusively to its established customer base of mainframe computer manufacturers. The reason given by those interviewed in this study was that engineers and marketers kept getting pulled off the 8-inch program to resolve problems in the launch of next-generation 14-inch products for CDC's mainstream customers.

CDC also launched its first 5.25-inch model two years after Seagate's pioneering product appeared in 1980. This time, however, CDC located its 5.25-inch effort in Oklahoma City—according to one manager, "not to escape CDC's Minneapolis engineering culture, but to isolate the [5.25-inch product] group from the company's mainstream customers. We needed an organization that could get excited about a $50,000 order. In Minneapolis [which derived nearly $1 billion from the sale of 14-inch drives in the mainframe market] you needed a million-dollar order just to turn anyone's head." Although it was late and CDC never reascended to its position of dominance, CDC's foray into 5.25-inch drives was profitable, and at times it commanded a 20 percent share of higher-capacity 5.25-inch drives.

Having learned from its experience in Oklahoma City, when CDC decided to attack the 3.5-inch market it set up yet another organization, in Simi Valley, California. This group shipped its first products in mid-1988, about 18 months behind Conner Peripherals, and enjoyed modest commercial success. The creation of these stand-alone organizations was CDC's way of handling the "strategic forcing" and "strategic context determination" challenges described by Burgelman (1983b, 1984).

Quantum Corporation and the 3.5-inch Hardcard

Quantum Corporation, a leading maker of 8-inch drives sold in the minicomputer market, introduced its first 5.25-inch product three years after those drives had first appeared in the market. As the 5.25-inch pioneers began to invade the minicomputer market from below, for all of the reasons described above, Quantum launched a 5.25-inch product and was temporarily successful in defending some of its existing customers by selling its 5.25-inch drive to them. But it never sold a single drive into the desktop PC market, and its overall sales began to sag. In 1984 a group of Quantum engineers saw a market for a thin 3.5-inch drive plugged into an expansion slot in IBM XT- and AT-class desktop computers—drives that would be sold to end users, rather than OEM computer manufacturers. Quantum financed and retained 80 percent ownership of this spin-off venture, called Plus Development Corporation, and set the company up in dif-

ferent facilities. Plus was extremely successful. As sales of Quantum's line of 8-inch drives began to evaporate in the mid-1980s, they were offset by Plus's growing "Hardcard" revenues. By 1987, sales of 8- and 5.25-inch products had largely evaporated. Quantum purchased the 20 percent of Plus it did not own, essentially closed down the old corporation, and installed Plus's executives in Quantum's most senior positions. They then reconfigured Plus's 3.5-inch products to appeal to desktop computer makers such as Apple, just as the capacity vector for 3.5-inch drives was invading the desktop, as shown in Exhibit 4. By 1994 the new Quantum had become the largest unit-volume producer of disk drives in the world. Quantum's spin-out of the Hardcard effort and its subsequent strategic reorientation appears to be an example of the processes of strategy change described in Burgelman (1991).

Micropolis: Transition Through Managerial Force

Managers at Micropolis Corporation, also an 8-inch drivemaker, employed a very different approach in which senior management initiated a disruptive program within the mainstream organization that made 8-inch drives. As early as 1982, Micropolis founder and CEO Stuart Mabon intuitively saw the trends mapped in Exhibit 4 and decided the firm needed to become primarily a maker of 5.25-inch drives. While initially hoping to keep adequate resources focused on the 8-inch line so that Micropolis could straddle both markets,[18] he assigned the company's premier engineers to the 5.25-inch program. Mabon recalls that it took "100 percent of his time and energy for 18 months" to keep adequate resources focused on the 5.25-inch program, because the organization's own mechanisms allocated resources to where the customers were: 8-inch drives. By 1984 Micropolis had failed to keep pace with competition in the minicomputer market for disk drives and withdrew its remaining 8-inch models. With Herculean effort, however, it did succeed in its 5.25-inch programs. Exhibit 6 shows why this was necessary: in the transition, Micropolis assumed a position on a very different technological trajectory (Dosi, 1982). In the process it had to walk away from every one

---

[18] The failure of Micropolis to maintain simultaneous competitive commitments to its established technology while adequately nurturing the 5.25-inch technology is consistent with the technological histories recounted in Utterback (1994). Utterback found historically that firms that attempted to develop radically new technology almost always tried simultaneously to maintain their commitments to the old, and that they almost always failed.

EXHIBIT 6   The Disruptive Impact of 5.25-inch Drives on the Market Position of Micropolis Corp

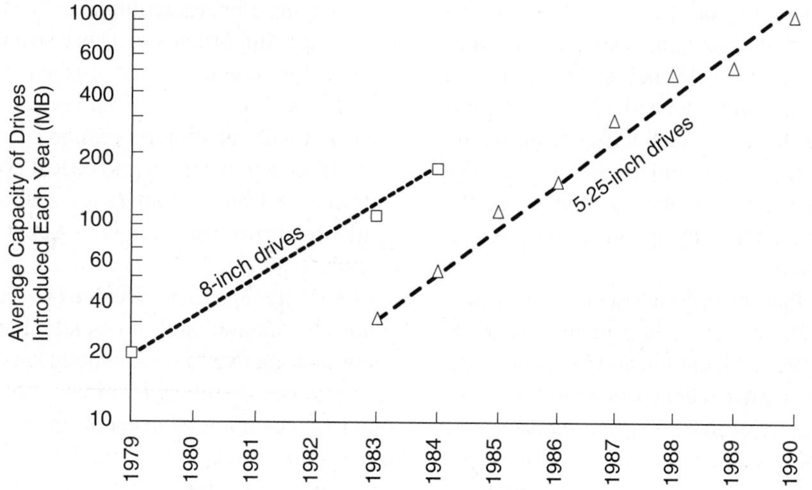

Average Capacity of Drives Introduced Each Year (MB)

8-inch drives

5.25-inch drives

of its major customers and replace the lost revenues with sales of the new product line to an entirely different group of desktop computer makers. Mabon remembers the experience as the most exhausting of his life. Micropolis aborted a 1989 attempt to launch its first 3.5-inch drive, and as of 1992 the company still had not introduced a 3.5-inch product.

Exhibit 7 arrays the experiences of the six companies we studied in depth, as they addressed disruptive technologies from within their mainstream organization and through independent organizations. Companies are classed as having been successful in this table if their market share in the new market enabled by the disruptive disk drive technology was at least 25 percent of its percentage share in the prior, established market in which it was dominant. Hence, Control Data, whose share of the 14-inch mainframe computer disk drive market often exceeded 60 percent, was classed as a failure in its attempt to sell 8-inch drives, because its share of minicomputer disk drives never exceeded 3 percent. Its share of 5.25-inch drives sold to the desktop workstation market, however, reached 20 percent, and it was therefore classed as a success in that effort. An organization was defined as being independent from the mainstream if it was geographically separated, was held accountable for full profit and loss, and included within it all of the functional units of a typical company (sales and marketing, manufacturing, finance, human resources, engineering, etc.).

In addition to the six firms studied in depth, Exhibit 7 lists other firms, shown in *italic type,* whose histories were researched through public sources and a more lim-

EXHIBIT 7   The Success and Failure of Companies Addressing Disruptive Technologies Through Mainstream Versus Independent Organizations

	Commercialized from within an independent organization	Commercialized from within the mainstream organization
Succeeded	Control Data 5.25-inch (L) Control Data 3.5-inch (L) Quantum 3.5-inch (L) *Maxtor 3.5-inch (L)*	Micropolis 5.25-inch (T)
Failed		Control Data 8-inch (L) Quantum 5.25-inch (L) Miniscribe 3.5-inch (L) Seagate 3.5-inch (L) Micropolis 3.5-inch (L) *Memorex 8-inch (L)* *Memorex 5.25-inch (L)* *Priam 5.25-inch (L)* *Century Data 8-inch (L)* *Ampex 8-inch (L)* *Ampex 5.25-inch (L)*

ited number of personal interviews. The L and T shown next to each company in the table, as in Exhibit 5, denote whether that firm's experience lends literal or theoretical support (Yin, 1989) to the proposition that managers can effect a strategy change despite resource dependence, by creating independent organizations that depend exclusively upon resources in the targeted market. Micropolis' transition from 8- to 5.25-inch drives is classed as a theoretical replication, because of the enormous managerial effort that was required to counteract the force of resource dependence in that transition.[19] Note that in every instance except Micropolis' 5.25-inch entry, firms that *fought* the forces of resource dependence by attempting to commercialize disruptive technology from within their mainstream organizations failed, as measured by *Disk/Trend* data. And the firms that *accounted for* the forces of resource dependence by spinning out independent organizations succeeded.

Note in Exhibit 7 that there do not seem to be strong firm or managerial effects, compared to the organizational effect. Control Data, Quantum, and Micropolis encountered multiple disruptive technologies; and *the same general managers sat atop these organizations across each of these transitions.* What seems to have distinguished these firms' successful from failed attempts to commercialize these disruptive technologies was not the talent of the managers *per se,* but whether the managers created organizationally distinct units to accomplish the task—where the forces of resource dependence could work in their favor, rather than against them. The successful cases cited here are the only ones in the industry's history in which a leading incumbent stayed atop its market when faced with disruptive technological change—and as a result, the number of data points in the top half of the matrix is limited. But these findings do suggest that, while the forces of resource dependence act as strong constraints on managerial discretion, managers can in fact manipulate those constraints effectively in order to achieve strategic change.

CONCLUSIONS

This study highlights an important issue for managers and scholars who strive to understand the reasons why strong, capably managed firms stumble when faced with particular types of technological change. While many scholars see the issue primarily as an issue of *technological competence,* we assert that at a deeper level it may be an issue of *investment.* We have observed that when competence was lacking, but impetus from customers to develop that competence was sufficiently strong, established firms successfully led their industries in developing the competencies required for sustaining technological change. Importantly, because sustaining technologies address the interests of established firms' existing customers, we saw that technological change could be achieved without strategy change.

Conversely, when technological competence existed, but impetus from customers was lacking, we saw consistently that firms were unable to commercialize what they already could do. This is because disruptive technologies initially tend to be saleable only in different markets whose economic and financial characteristics render them unattractive to established firms. Addressing these technologies therefore requires a change in strategy in order to attack a very different market. In the end, it appears that although the stumbles of these established firms are *associated* with technological change, the key issue appears to be firms' disabilities in changing strategy, not technology.

Our model is not presented as the path every firm follows when faced with disruptive technology. We believe, however, that it may contribute several insights for scholars interested in the factors that affect strategic change in firms. First, it notes that the allocation of resources to some product development and commercialization programs, and the denial of resources to others, is a key event or decision in the implementation of strategy. The model highlights the process by which impetus and consequent resources may be denied to technological opportunities that do not contribute to the needs of prominent customers. These findings suggest a causal relationship might exist between resource allocation processes, as modeled by Bower (1970) and Burgelman (1983a, 1983b), and the phenomenon of resource dependence (Pfeffer and Salancik, 1978). Our findings suggest that despite the powerful forces of resource dependence, however, managers can, in fact, wield considerable power, and wield it effectively, in changing the strategic course of their firms in directions other than those in which its resource providers are pulling it. By understanding the processes that link customer needs, impetus, and resource allocation, managers can align efforts to commercialize disruptive technology (which entails a change in strategy) with the forces of resource dependence. This involves managing disruptive technology in a manner that is out of the organizational and strategic context of mainstream organizations—where of necessity, incentives and resource allocation processes are designed to nourish sustaining innovations that address current customers' needs. In this way, the model and

---

[19] The success or failure of these other firms at each point of disruptive technology change was unambiguously determinable from *Disk/Trend Report* data. Similarly, whether these firms managed the launch of disruptive technology products from within their mainstream organization or through an organizationally separate unit was a matter of public record and general industry knowledge. Hence, there were no subjective judgments involved in constructing Exhibit 7.

these case studies illustrate the mechanisms through which autonomous and induced strategic behavior (Burgelman, 1983a) can affect, or fail to affect, a company's course.

Much additional research must be done. Efforts to explore the external validity and usefulness of the model through studies of sustaining and disruptive technological change in other industries has begun (Rosenbloom and Christensen, 1995), but much more is required. In addition, we hope that future researchers can develop clearer models for managerial action and strategic change in the face of disruptive technology change that are consistent with the principles of resource dependence and the processes of resource allocation.

ACKNOWLEDGMENTS

We gratefully acknowledge the financial support of the Harvard Business School Division of Research in conducting the research for this paper, and thank the editors of *Disk/Trend Report* for sharing their industry data with us. We are indebted to Professors Robert Burgelman of Stanford University, Rebecca Henderson of the Massachusetts Institute of Technology, and David Garvin and several of our other colleagues at the Harvard Business School, as well as the anonymous referees, for invaluable suggestions for improving earlier versions of this paper. Any remaining deficiencies are our sole responsibility.

REFERENCES

Bower, J. (1970). *Managing the Resource Allocation Process.* Irwin, Homewood, IL.

Burgelman, R. (1983a). "A model of the interaction of strategic behavior, corporate context, and the concept of strategy." *Academy of Management Review,* 3(1), pp. 61–69.

Burgelman, R. (1983b). "A process model of internal corporate venturing in the diversified major firm." *Administrative Science Quarterly,* **28,** pp. 223–244.

Burgelman, R. (1984). "Designs for corporate entrepreneurship in established firms." *California Management Review,* **26,** Spring, pp. 154–166.

Burgelman, R., (1991). "Intraorganizational ecology of strategy-making and organizational adaptation: Theory and field research." *Organization Science,* **2,** pp. 239–262.

Burgelman, R., and L. Sayles (1986). *Inside Corporate Innovation.* Free Press, New York.

Campbell, D. T., and J. C. Stanley (1966). *Experimental and Quasi-Experimental Designs for Research.* Houghton Mifflin, Boston, MA.

Christensen, C. M. (1992a). "The innovator's challenge: Understanding the influence of market demand on pro-

cesses of technology development in the rigid disk drive industry." D.B.A. dissertation, Graduate School of Business Administration, Harvard University.

Christensen, C. M. (1992b). "Exploring the limits of the technology S-curve." *Production and Operations Management,* **1,** pp. 334–366.

Christensen, C. M. (1993). "The rigid disk drive industry: A history of commercial and technological turbulence." *Business History Review,* **67,** pp. 531–588.

Christensen, C. M., and R. S. Rosenbloom (1995). "Explaining the attacker's advantage: Technological paradigms, organizational dynamics, and the value network." *Research Policy,* **24,** pp. 233–257.

Cooper, A., and D. Schendel (February 1976). "Strategic responses to technological threats." *Business Horizons,* **19,** pp. 61–69.

Data Sources: The Comprehensive Guide to the Information Processing Industry (annual). Ziff-Davis Publishing, New York.

Disk/Trend Report (annual). Disk/Trend, Inc., Mountain View, CA.

Dosi, G. (1982). "Technological paradigms and technological trajectories." *Research Policy,* **11,** pp. 147–162.

Foster, R. J. (1986). *Innovation: The Attacker's Advantage.* Summit Books, New York.

Henderson, R. M. (1993). "Keeping too close to your customers." Working paper, Sloan School of Management, Massachusetts Institute of Technology.

Henderson, R. M., and K. B. Clark (1990). "Architectural innovation: The reconfiguration of existing systems and the failure of established firms." *Administrative Science Quarterly,* **35,** pp. 9–30.

Pfeffer, J., and G. R. Salancik (1978). *The External Control of Organizations: A Resource Dependence Perspective.* Harper & Row, New York.

Rosenbloom, R. S., and C. M. Christensen (1995). "Technological discontinuities, organizational capabilities, and strategic commitments." *Industrial and Corporate Change,* **4,** pp. 655–685.

Tushman, M. L., and P. Anderson (1986). "Technological discontinuities and organizational environments." *Administrative Science Quarterly,* **31,** pp. 439–465.

Utterback, J. (1994). *Mastering the Dynamics of Innovation.* Harvard Business School Press, Boston, MA.

von Hippel, E. (1988). *The Sources of Innovation.* Oxford University Press, New York.

Yin, R. K. (1989). *Case Study Research: Design and Methods.* Sage, Newbury Park, CA.

APPENDIX 1: A BRIEF PRIMER ON HOW DISK DRIVES WORK

Rigid disk drives are comprised of one or more rotating disks—polished aluminum platters coated with magnetic material—mounted on a central spindle. Data are recorded and read on concentric tracks on the surfaces of these disks. Read-write heads—one each for the top and bottom surfaces of each disk on the spindle—are aerodynamically designed to fly a few millionths of an inch over the surface of the disk. They generally rest on the disk's surface when the drive is at rest, "take off" as the drive begins to spin, and "land" again when the disks stop. The heads are positioned over the proper track on the disk by an actuator motor, which moves the heads across the tracks in a fashion similar to the arm on a phonograph. The head is essentially a tiny electromagnet which, when current flows in one direction, orients the polarity of the magnetic domain on the disk's surface immediately beneath it. When the direction of current through the electromagnet reverses, its polarity changes. This induces an opposite switch of the polarity of the adjacent domain on the disk's surface as the disk spins beneath the head. In this manner, data are written in binary code on the disk. To read data, changes in magnetic field on the disk as it spins beneath the head are used to induce changes in the direction of current—essentially the reverse process of writing. Disk drives also include electronic circuitry enabling computers to control and communicate with the drive.

As in other magnetic recording products, *areal recording density* (measured in megabits per square inch of disk surface area, or mbpsi) was the pervasive measure of product performance in the disk drive industry. Historically, areal density in the industry has increased at a steady 35 percent annual rate. A drive's total capacity is the product of the available square inches on the top and bottom surfaces of the disks mounted on the spindle of the drive, multiplied by its areal recording density. Historically, the capacity of drives in a given product architecture has increased at about 50 percent annually. The difference between the 35 percent increase in areal density and the 50 percent increase in total capacity has come from mechanical engineering innovations, which enable manufacturers to squeeze additional disks and heads into a given size of drive.

APPENDIX 2: CALCULATION OF THE TRAJECTORIES MAPPED IN EXHIBIT 3

The trajectories mapped in Exhibit 3 were calculated as follows. Data on the capacity provided with computers in the mainframe, minicomputer, desktop personal computer, and portable computer classes were obtained from *Data Sources,* an annual publication that lists the technical specifications of all computer models available from each computer manufacturer. Where particular models were available with different features and configurations, the manufacturer provided *Data Sources* with a "typical" system configuration, with defined RAM capacity, performance specifications of peripheral equipment (including disk drives), list price, and year of introduction. In instances where a given computer model was offered for sale over a sequence of years, the hard disk capacity provided in the typical configuration generally increased. *Data Sources* divides computers into mainframe, mini/midrange, desktop personal, portable and laptop, and notebook computers. For each class of computers, all models available for sale in each year were ranked by price, and the hard disk capacity provided with the median-priced model was identified, for each year. The best-fit line through the resultant time series for each class of computer is plotted as the solid lines in Exhibit 3. These single solid lines are drawn in Exhibit 3 for expository simplification, to indicate the trend in typical machines. In reality, of course, there is a wide band around these lines. The leading and trailing edges of performance—the highest and lowest capacities offered with the most and least expensive computers—were substantially higher and lower, respectively, than the typical values mapped in Exhibit 3.

The dotted lines in Exhibit 3 represent the best-fit line through the unweighted average capacity of all disk drives introduced for sale in each given architecture, for each year. These data were taken from *Disk/Trend Report.* Again, for expository simplification, only this average line is shown. There was a wide band of capacities introduced for sale in each year, so that the highest-capacity drive introduced in each year was substantially above the average shown. Stated in another way, a distinction must be made between the full range of products available for purchase and those in typical systems of use. The upper and lower bands around the median and average trajectories in Exhibit 3 are generally parallel to the lines shown.

Because higher-capacity drives were available than the capacities offered with the median-priced systems, we state in the text that the solid-line trajectories in Exhibit 3 represent the capacities "demanded" in each market. In other words, the capacity per machine was not constrained by technological availability. Rather, it represents a *choice* for hard disk capacity, made by computer users, given the prevailing cost.

Making SMaL Big: SMaL Camera Technologies

> *If you differentiate a product too far from the market, you have to develop the market. If you don't differentiate it enough, you look the same as every other Joe. So in product definition, it is important to get the differentiation large enough to make the investment in the technology worthwhile yet small enough so it doesn't take six years to develop a market.*
> —Charles Sodini, Co-founder and Chairman,
> SMaL Camera Technologies

Clayton M. Christensen and Scott D. Anthony

"It is nice. I hate to say it, but it is nice," SMaL Camera Technologies (SMaL) CEO Maurizio Arienzo said begrudgingly. It was January 2003. Arienzo was sitting in a conference room in SMaL's Cambridge, Massachu-

Source: Senior Researcher Scott D. Anthony (M.B.A. '01) prepared this case under the supervision of Professor Clayton M. Christensen. HBS cases are developed solely as the basis for class discussion. Cases are not intended to serve as endorsements, sources of primary data, or illustrations of effective or ineffective management. Copyright © 2003 President and Fellows of Harvard College. To order copies or request permission to reproduce materials, call 1-800-545-7685, write Harvard Business School Publishing, Boston, MA 02163, or go to http://www.hbsp.harvard.edu. No part of this publication may be reproduced, stored in a retrieval system, used in a spreadsheet, or transmitted in any form or by any means—electronic, mechanical, photocopying, recording, or otherwise—without the permission of Harvard Business School.

setts, headquarters surrounded by digital cameras that a group of SMaL employees gathered in preparation for a trip to Las Vegas for the annual International Consumer Electronics Show. Arienzo was toying with a tiny Exilim digital camera made by Casio. The camera was just one of the many emerging competitors in the very-slim camera category that SMaL essentially created when it commercialized its revolutionary credit card-sized camera in 2002.

SMaL's first-generation technology had been a commercial success. In 2002, SMaL sold more than a half-million "kits" to its customers—manufacturers who used the kits to make low-priced digital still cameras. SMaL had more than $10 million in revenue in 2002. It was profitable in the second half of the year. But competitors had entered. Now, SMaL had to decide what to do for an encore. Should it continue to improve its basic technology and create more advanced cameras for the consumer market to compete with copycats? Should it step up existing efforts to penetrate the security and surveillance and automotive markets? Or should it try to bring its imaging technology into completely new markets, like cellular phones?

SMaL's senior management dreamed of ramping the company's annual revenues up past $100 million and issuing stock to the public in 2004 (see Exhibit 1 for financial projections). Deciding what came next could well determine if SMaL would ever hit it big. As Arienzo put it:

> For a startup, there really are three challenges. First, can you bring a first product to market? Second, can you make money by doing that or are you going to lose your shirt?

EXHIBIT 1 Financial Projections ($000s)

	2001	2002 1st Half	2002 2nd Half	2002 Total	2003	2004	2005
Revenues	433	1,554	9,210	10,764	27,250	64,217	101,262
Cost of Goods Sold	N/A	1,010	5,527	6,537	14,974	39,885	65,103
Gross Profits	433	544	3,683	4,227	12,276	24,332	36,159
Research and Development	2,671	1,206	2,631	3,837	9,795	12,610	13,878
Sales, General and Administrative	856	429	956	1,385	2,282	4,718	5,478
Total Expenses	3,527	1,635	3,587	5,222	12,077	17,328	19,356
Earnings Before Interest and Taxes	−3,094	−1,091	96	−995	199	7,004	16,803
Interest Income (Expense)	111	28	23	51	65	102	183
Pretax Income	−2,983	−1,063	119	−944	264	7,106	16,986
Taxes	0	0	0	0	0	2,487	5,945
Net Income	−2,983	−1,063	119	−944	264	4,619	11,041

Note: Figures have been disguised.
Source: Company documents.

Third, can you do an encore? Can you keep doing it over and over again? We've demonstrated we can bring a product to market. We shipped more than 3 million components in 2002. We made money doing so. We were profitable in the second half of the year. We had more than $10 million in revenue. We have demonstrated one and two. Now we have to go and do an encore.

SMAL'S BACKGROUND

SMaL originated in the labs of the Massachusetts Institute of Technology (MIT). In the early 1990s, MIT Professor Charles Sodini started toying with the idea of developing new imaging technology using complementary metal oxide semiconductor (CMOS) technology. "Around 1990 I thought about the fact that digital cameras might start to come into play in this world," Sodini recalled. "Why I thought about it, I don't know. That's my job. I'm not always right. I just thought that cameras were going to be an important thing."

Digital cameras are powered by a chip called an image sensor that turns light into digital images. Most cameras use what is known as charge-coupled device (CCD) technology. CCD chips have historically offered high picture quality but are proprietary and expensive to manufacture, largely because they come in a multiple-chip solution and require a dedicated manufacturing production line in a semiconductor factory. The use of CCD chips explains why first-generation digital cameras were so bulky and expensive. Camera companies that sought to have digital imaging replace traditional film-based imaging had to use CCD chips to produce a product that demanding customers would deem satisfactory.

CMOS chips are more generic. For example, personal computers use CMOS-based chips for the processor, graphics accelerators, networking, and a variety of other functions. It is possible to embed more "intelligence" on CMOS chips. CMOS-based chips historically had not been considered for imaging applications even though they are significantly cheaper to manufacture.

So Sodini and a core group of MIT colleagues set out to develop a CMOS image sensor. Many other researchers and companies had developed their own CMOS image sensors. But this particular MIT team sought to solve two endemic shortcomings of all digital cameras—regardless of whether they used CCD or CMOS chips. The first problem has plagued photographers since George Eastman developed the first camera more than 100 years ago: taking photographs in difficult lighting conditions. Any photographer knows that too

much light can wash out an image. Imagine trying to take a picture in daylight through a window. Even though your eye can see through the window, the camera cannot. Most cameras just can't handle contrast the way the human eye can. Sodini and one of his graduate students developed a way to adapt to various lighting conditions on a bulky computer-controlled test system. The student completed his Ph.D. and went on to work for a *Fortune* 500 semiconductor company.

The second fundamental challenge in image sensor design is minimizing the amount of power the sensor requires. Power consumption is of particular concern in portable devices such as digital cameras and cell phones, where battery power is at a premium. In order to develop the world's lowest power image sensor, Sodini teamed up with fellow MIT professor Hae-Seung [Harry] Lee, an expert in designing low-power mixed-signal chips that include both analog and digital functions on the same chip.

With this innovative imager technology in hand, Sodini worked with Keith Fife, one of the most gifted graduate students he had ever supervised, to develop a prototype video camera using the imager. While designing this camera, Keith used the imager's ability to adapt to varying brightness to develop a technology called "Autobrite®." In essence, Autobrite runs complicated algorithms and histograms to dynamically adjust each "pixel" in a picture to optimize its contrast. The resultant "wide dynamic range" improves picture quality in certain lighting situations. Exhibit 2 shows examples of how Autobrite can capture vital details of a scene with varying lighting conditions. For example, in the middle image, the picture without Autobrite fails to show the devious-looking intruder lurking outside the window. With Autobrite, the potential intruder is readily visible.

Once Fife completed the prototype camera in 1999, Sodini turned to two long-time MIT colleagues, Professors Ichiro Masaki and Lee, to build a company to commercialize the technology (see Exhibit 3 for the background of SMaL's CEO and founders). Masaki was an expert in "intelligent transportation" and machine vision and had deep connections in the automotive industry. SMaL Camera officially came into being in September 1999 (see Exhibit 4 for a timeline of key events).

Selecting a Target Market

After forming the company, the founders had to decide on a specific product to develop and a specific market to target. They thought the technology had obvious

EXHIBIT 2   Comparison Pictures: Standard Digital Cameras vs. SMaL's Cameras with Autobrite®

Source: Company documents.

EXHIBIT 3   Brief Biographies of SMaL's CEO and Founders

Maurizio Arienzo, Ph.D. (President and CEO): Over 20 years' experience in high-tech industries. Extensive involvement with CMOS technology. Prior to SMaL, served as VP and General Manager of ATI Technology where he led the business unit in charge of 3D graphic processors and boards for consumer and professional personal computers. Prior to ATI he led United Technologies' UTRC Division worldwide operations and a $100 million research and development program. Prior to UTC, he was with IBM for 14 years. At IBM his experience included Director of VLSI Design and Communications Technology. He instigated and led a radical shift from bipolar to CMOS technology for mainframe computers, as well as managed the Deep Blue Chess Project, which defeated world champion Garry Kasparov.

Keith Fife (Co-founder, VP of Engineering): Received Masters of Engineering degree from MIT studying algorithms and architecture for wide dynamic range image sensors. Expertise includes mechanical, electrical, and integrated circuit mixed-signal design. Experience in both system-level and device-level design from work at Compaq and Motorola. Winner of numerous awards in both technology and product design.

Hae-Seung Lee, Ph.D. (Co-founder and Treasurer): Joined MIT's faculty in 1984. Currently a Professor with the Department of Electrical Engineering and Computer Science. Research focused on analog to digital conversion, communications, and circuit design. Author or co-author of more than 80 journal and conference papers in the areas of analog and mixed-signal integrated circuits, particularly analog-to-digital converters, operational amplifiers, and microsensor interface circuits.

Ichiro Masaki, Ph.D. (Co-founder and Vice Chairman): Joined MIT's senior research staff in 1993. Currently the Director of the Intelligent Transportation Research Center at MIT's Microsystems Technology Labs, which tries to integrate multiple aspects of intelligent transportation systems. Principal fields of expertise are microsystems, machine vision, and intelligent transportation systems.

Charles G. Sodini, Ph.D. (Co-founder and Chairman): Joined MIT's faculty in 1983. Currently a Professor in the Department of Electrical Engineering and Computer Science. Research interests focus on integrated circuit and system design with emphasis on analog, RF, and memory circuits and systems. Ph.D. from the University of California-Berkeley. Previous working experience at Hewlett-Packard.

Source: Company documents.

application in three market segments. First, they could produce a consumer-focused digital still camera. Digital cameras had already entered the market and experienced significant growth (see Exhibit 5 for historic growth in U.S. digital camera sales). The second potential market was the security and surveillance market. The founders thought many corporations would be very interested in a digital video camera that did a better job of capturing images in difficult lighting situations. For example, most cameras in ATMs (Automated Teller Machine vestibules) are incapable of capturing clear images of anything outside the vestibule during the daytime. The third potential market was the automotive market. Automotive companies could use the technology for "smart" applications, such as a cruise control system that automatically adapted a vehicle's speed to adjust for the speed of surrounding vehicles. Masaki had several high-level contacts at both auto companies and tier-one suppliers.

The company decided to develop a slim camera to target the consumer segment. It would secondarily focus on the security and surveillance market with the long-term vision of selling to automotive companies.

The founders thought there was an opportunity to enter the consumer market because most digital cameras used CCD technology, which made them relatively bulky and expensive. Cameras that used CMOS still consumed significant power and therefore required large batteries. The key to making a slim camera was low power consumption (to use an extremely thin battery) and high integration (to ensure a low component count). Lee's expertise in these design techniques made this idea possible. Also, entering the consumer market provided a quick path to revenues, something all of the founders were interested in (see below). They ultimately dubbed the camera the "credit card" camera, because its dimensions closely mirrored a credit card.

Sodini explained the decision:

Besides the credit card camera, we decided to also get into the security and surveillance markets for a couple of reasons. First, the auto market was going to be a video market and we wanted to make sure we had some video capabilities. Second, the security and surveillance companies would really like this Autobrite or wide dynamic range technology so it would drive the technology. So the thinking was, if we got in the consumer space we would learn how to be low cost or at least maintain our cost and the security and surveillance space would allow us to have technology growth and keep pushing us from an engineering standpoint.

Arienzo agreed. Although the automotive opportunity seemed to be the largest of the three, entering the con-

EXHIBIT 4 Timeline of Key Events

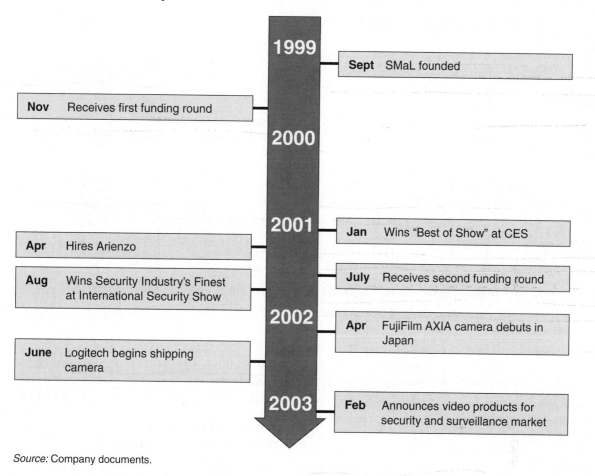

Source: Company documents.

sumer and security and surveillance markets first put SMaL on a path that increased its overall chances of success. He said:

> Not that many startups ever focus on automotive opportunities, because of the long lead times. You just can't justify investing five years' worth of R&D and losses before your first profit rolls in. Our chances of success go up if we say our consumer volumes show we have the capability to deliver in volume and our security cameras show we have the right technology. With these two things together we can successfully enter the automotive market.

Decent strategy [handwritten annotation in left margin]

Developing a Camera: Integration to Drive Down Power Consumption

SMaL started working on its credit card-sized camera by developing five essential components: a battery, an image sensor (with the Autobrite), an Application Specifics Integrated Circuit (ASIC) that handled most of the cam-

era's intelligence, a collapsible lens, and a viewfinder (through which users would look). SMaL custom designed each component. It had to. To make the camera thin, SMaL had to use an extremely thin (0.8 millimeter) lithium-polymer battery. To use a thin battery, SMaL had to have what is called "low power dissipation." Basically, the camera had to be extremely energy efficient, with each action draining a very small amount of the battery's power. Sodini explained that the only way to achieve this was to customize each piece of the camera:

> Achieving the lower power is not a silver bullet. It is doing all the circuits correctly and Harry is an expert in this. It is not a single patent or two patents. It is just knowing how to do it right. There are people who know how to do it but it is a very limited set of people worldwide. One wrong circuit and the power drains. Imagine you have the most complicated plumbing system in the world with all the valves and so on and one of the valves is left open. Water is going to

EXHIBIT 5   Growth in Digital Cameras

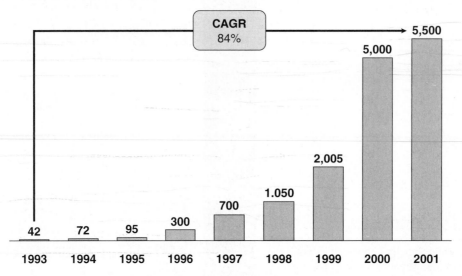

U.S digital camera shipments (000s)

Source: InfoTech Trends; Appliance/Statistical Review.

flow through that valve and the water level is going to drop. That's your battery running out. You need to get everything just right.

Ultimately, the SMaL team developed a 6-millimeter (¼″) thin camera—dubbed the "Ultra-Pocket®"—that was truly revolutionary (see Exhibit 6 for the camera's specifications). It was extremely small, claiming a place in *Guinness World Records* as the world's thinnest camera ever. It consumed almost no power. And it had Autobrite. But it looked, felt, and worked like any other digital camera. Users turned it on, clicked a button, and took pictures. They then downloaded the pictures through their computer's Universal Serial Bus (USB) port, during which time the battery automatically recharged itself.

SMaL's camera had limits, of course. The camera didn't have a flash. It didn't have an LCD display where users could see the picture they just took. Users couldn't zoom in and out. All of these features would require a larger battery and would increase the camera's size. Most importantly, picture resolution was relatively low. The number of picture elements, called "pixels," measures digital camera resolution. The higher the number of pixels, the sharper the image. Pictures taken with lower-resolution cameras could appear granular, especially when enlarged. By 2002, most cameras offered resolution ranging from 1 to 3 megapixels (million pixels). SMaL's camera had VGA resolution, which cor-

responded roughly to 0.3 megapixels. But SMaL still seemed to be on to something. Next, it had to go beyond the development stage and find a way to make money.

Financing Choices Drive Business Model Selection

The company faced an important decision very early in its history. It was 1999, and all of Sodini's advisers were pushing him to raise significant amounts of capital and quickly ramp up the company. But from the very beginning, SMaL intended to stay, well, small. Sodini said he never believed the hype of the late 1990s' bull market. "You don't get something for nothing. Two plus two does not equal eight," he said. "We did have two choices. We could go ahead and pump this thing up and flip it in a year. It wouldn't sustain but we could make a lot of money. Not that money doesn't mean anything, but our intention was to build a long-term sustainable company."

SMaL raised several million dollars from a Japanese company and consciously tried to live off that money. Sodini recalled receiving the first round of funding:

> We talked to Yokogawa Electric and they said they were interested. So they flew over on a Thursday. Later that day, we called our attorney. He said, "Do you have a term sheet?" I said, "No." He said, "When will it be done?" I said, "We need the final documents by 1 p.m. tomorrow." He thought we were nuts. But we got it signed. It was prob-

EXHIBIT 6   Specifications for SMaL's Ultra-Pocket®

Imager	640 x 480 (VGA) Color CMOS
Viewfinder	Optical
Focal Length, 35 mm Conversion Equivalent	47 mm
Aperture	F/3.8
Focus Range	2 ft. to infinity
Exposure Control	Automatic
Shutter Speed	1/30 to 1/15,000 sec.
Interface	USB
Power	Lithium polymer rechargeable battery (internal)
Dimensions	3.4" x 2.1" x 0.2" (world's thinnest)*
Weight	1.2 oz (35 g) including battery
Image Storage	8 MB internal flash memory; holds up to 26 VGA resolutions or 101 QVGA images

*Guinness World Records, 2002.
Source: Company documents.

ably the fastest funding I've ever heard of. The whole thing took about 24 hours.

Those funds were sufficient to allow SMaL to hire about 10 people and build its first prototype. In early 2001, SMaL took the prototype to the annual Consumer Electronics Show (CES) in Las Vegas. CES traditionally has been a launching pad for new technologies. The VCR, CDs, and DVDs all debuted at CES. Sodini recalled the decision to unveil the technology at CES:

> Keith's extremely hard work along with the rest of our "small" team got the camera sort of working at the end of 2000. We almost pulled out of CES twice because we were so far behind. The images it took were terrible. The software was terrible. The lens was blurry. We just weren't quite finished. The video prototype was working, so we could show that. We could show how Autobrite worked. And we could show what the credit card camera looked like.
>
> Well, we realized you can actually show stuff that doesn't work so well if you figure out how to show it. Nobody seemed to care that it didn't work because they had never seen a form factor like ours. They just couldn't believe it. We got inundated with people and press and then we ended up winning "Best of CES" with the credit card camera.

[handwritten note: Sounds familiar]

Buoyed with its success at CES, SMaL decided to ramp up. First, it hired Arienzo to be its CEO. Arienzo had a long history in technology-related industries. While at IBM he worked on a project team that designed the first CMOS-based mainframe. He had known the three SMaL founders for several years and had been serving as an informal advisor to the company. He described his decision to join SMaL:

> There are three important reasons I decided to join. First, I really wanted to get back to a startup environment because it is just exhilarating. It is a roller coaster ride. The second reason is that this area is definitely growing. I knew first hand how CMOS can come into a business, grow from the bottom, and slowly but surely chew it up. The perfect example is the CMOS mainframe. That chip replaced about 80 bipolar chips. This was another opportunity. The CCD is like the bipolar technology and CMOS can come in and really change the game. The third thing was I was going to do this with a group of people that I knew and trusted. That was very important. The environment is very, very important. We all wanted to do the same thing.

Armed with a CEO, SMaL went out and raised a second round of capital. The round included SMaL's original corporate investor and Stata Venture Partners, a venture capital fund founded by Boston high-tech legend Ray Stata. In the 1960s, Stata co-founded Analog Devices, one of the semiconductor industry's early pioneers. The second round of funding was significant but still less than $10 million.

Stata and Sodini had known each other for years. Also, Managing Partner Lee Barbieri said Stata Venture Partners was interested in SMaL because SMaL had a unique opportunity to create new markets. "The thing that stood out was that this technology had the opportunity to enter into market segments that were relatively unfulfilled," said Barbieri, who became a member of SMaL's Board of Directors. "It had broad appeal to several segments. That gives it a real sense of balance."

SMaL's limited capital impacted how it would commercialize its technology. Not only did it need to seek revenue opportunities quickly, it couldn't design a big organization. Sodini explained:

There was a lot of hand wringing. Everybody said, "Why don't we just sell it on QVC? We'll make more money." But you add up what it takes to touch a customer and it's a lot of people. . . . We're one step removed. Having a screen between you and the consumer at this size company is important. The whole idea was to not have to build a large organization in the early stages.

So SMaL started putting together a top-flight team, focusing initially on beefing up the engineering organization and the operations team with industry experts from IBM, Motorola, Compaq, etc. This team was instrumental in delivering the volumes and the quality of products in 2002. It deferred building internal marketing capabilities until mid-2002. It decided against building any distribution and manufacturing capabilities altogether. By 2003, it had about 35 employees.

Sodini said SMaL decided to focus on areas where it could build strong competitive advantage. "The manufacturing is a high fixed cost, low margin game. There are other people who can get that done," Sodini said. "What we have is 'product definition' and key technological components that allow us to capture value."

On the other hand, SMaL wanted to sell more than just individual components. Arienzo explained why selling just components can be tough. "It is very difficult. As soon as your customer knows what technology you are using and the size of your chip they know exactly what the chips are worth, what the costs are," he explained. "You are in a situation where your customer determines how much profit you are going to make. That is just a tough business to be in unless you have and keep major competitive advantages."

Instead of building entire cameras and becoming a consumer products company or producing just individual components, SMaL settled somewhere in the middle. It decided to produce kits (see Exhibit 7 for a picture of the kit components on a reference board). Each kit contained SMaL's proprietary subsystems. SMaL sold the kits to Original Equipment Manufacturers (OEMs) along with software and a "reference design" that guided manufacturing. The OEMs would insert the kit into a consumer camera for which they would do the industrial design (ID). In essence, the kit was an "interdependent" device that slotted into a "modular" consumer product architecture. The OEMs had freedom over the "look and feel" of the product but could not change any piece of the kit. OEMs would be responsible for all activities related to marketing and distribution. In essence, SMaL offloaded the investment required to build a market to the OEMs. It sold the kits in the $20 to $30 range.

Finding OEMs was not necessarily an easy task. Many large consumer electronics companies had established cameras that used proprietary CCD technology. Executive Director of Business Development Romney Williams explained the challenges SMaL faced. "When we show our solution to some companies, it can be very hard for us to change their thinking," Williams said. "If you look at their organizational structure and budgets, many have significant resources devoted to developing CCD technologies. They dismiss CMOS-based solutions as cheap and low quality. While certain CMOS cameras fit that description, others are good quality and therefore threatening."

SMaL's first OEM customer was FujiFilm AXIA, one of FujiFilm's sales and distribution divisions. Sodini explained the serendipitous way the FujiFilm relationship came about. "When I left CES I went to Japan to give a talk for MIT. The dean of engineering at MIT was there and I showed him this camera the night before my talk. He just fell in love with this thing. He was flashing it around, showing it to everyone," Sodini said. "So some guy comes up to me from FujiFilm and says he wants to talk to me."

FujiFilm AXIA agreed to distribute its "AXIA eye-plate ™," camera in Japan. It outsourced the actual camera manufacturing to a company in Hong Kong called IDT. SMaL's second customer was Logitech, a California-based computer peripheral company best known for its

EXHIBIT 7   SMaL's Ultra-Pocket Reference Board (Kit Components Circled)

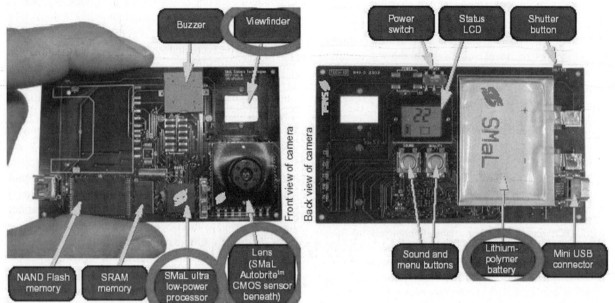

Source: Company documents.

affordable web cameras, mice, and keyboards. Logitech produced a SMaL-enabled camera called the Logitech Pocket Digital. SMaL's third customer ironically turned out to be IDT, who made cameras to sell outside of Japan under labels like Oregon Scientific. The cameras retailed for less than $150.

Other Imaging Startups

SMaL's go-to-market, financing, and business model approach proved an interesting contrast to Pixim and Foveon, two other imaging startup companies.

Pixim was trying to develop a new alternative to CCD and CMOS technology. Its Digital Pixel System, based on research at Stanford University, potentially combined the low cost of CMOS and the high performance of CCD chips. It put the entire functionality of a camera on a chip. CEO Bob Weinschenk said in 1999: "We have a disruptive technology."[1] Like SMaL, Pixim believed its technology could be used for a consumer camera, security and surveillance applications, and automotive appli-

cations. Unlike SMaL, Pixim focused on developing technology before finding market applications. It raised close to $40 million from leading venture capital companies like Mohr Davidow Ventures and Mayfield. It hired a seasoned management team. Legendary movie director Francis Ford Coppola served as an advisor. By 2003, it had changed its focus to hone in on opportunities in the security industry. In February 2003, it debuted its first product—a digital video camera purported to work under any lighting condition.

Foveon tried to leapfrog existing providers by developing high-quality image sensors for the professional-grade digital photography market. Its "X3" sensor chip claimed to capture three times the color resolution of existing digital cameras. Its investors included corporations such as National Semiconductor and Synaptics and venture capital firm New Enterprise Associates. In October 2002, Sigma (a Japanese company) became the first company to introduce a camera with Foveon's chip. Its camera cost about $1,800.[2]

[1] Pixim's Web site <www.pixim.com>; Dean Takashi, "Image is everything; Pixim looks to digital cameras to weather the chip malaise," *Red Herring,* June 2001.

[2] David Becker, "Release set for 'sharper' digicam chip," *CNET News,* September 23, 2002, <http://news.com.com/2100-1040-959038.html>.

SUCCESSES AND STRUGGLES TO DATE

The first batch of SMaL-powered cameras hit the Japanese market in April 2002 and the U.S. market in June 2002. It quickly became apparent that SMaL's combination of small size, novel technology, and low price filled a void.

Arienzo said he believed a SMaL-powered camera competed in a different way in the marketplace:

> We like to refer to the Ultra-Pocket as the Sony Walkman of digital cameras. Because its unprecedented portability and convenience fill needs that no other camera can, its unique benefits resonate very well with first-time digital camera buyers and existing owners of digital cameras alike. The camera's thinness and light weight [0.2 ounces] enable you to have it with you at all times. Its long battery life [500 to 1,000 images between charges—compared to 20 to 50 shots with most other digital cameras] means you never worry about the cost of replacing or the inconvenience of charging the battery. Autobrite enables spontaneous image-taking in bright lighting conditions, such as glare or backlit scenes. Lastly, the camera's combination of sleekness and value create strong "bang for your buck," mass-market appeal.

> You have your professional camera that you only take with you when you are going to a wedding or a graduation. You have to think about grabbing it before you leave home. The Ultra-Pocket is a different thing. It is a Walkman. This is the camera that you always have with you. My wife has one in her glove compartment and one in her pocketbook. My kids have one in their backpacks. I always have one in my shirt pocket, with my business cards. It is a different model. I believe this camera is not necessarily part of the same pie of digital photography that we have been observing up to now.

Arienzo gave an example of how SMaL's camera allowed people to do things that historically were difficult:

> For example, we have seen business people go into a meeting, pull out their Ultra-Pocket, and take pictures of everybody in the room. Then they download the pictures and match them with that person's business card. So now you have a person's business card and picture in your computer. Not that this was impossible before, but the unobtrusiveness of our camera allows this specific job to be done in a much more natural way. Our camera becomes a conversation piece, an ice breaker, or a fashion statement.

SMaL's approach also allowed it to get to market very quickly. "We have done most of the design and development work for OEMs," Arienzo said. "That turns into cost and time to market advantages. We signed the agreement with one of our OEMs in January, it made the announcement in May, it started shipping in June. This doesn't happen that often. It was extremely fast."

The approach created some challenges. SMaL was removed from its ultimate customer, the end user, and did not have a way to directly gather feedback about how customers used its product. Nonetheless, sales in 2002 ramped quickly, exceeding expectations. SMaL's inventive go-to-market strategy allowed it to have the market to itself for a period of time.

Barbieri said SMaL did an impressive job creating growth with very limited investment. "As far as the company goes, we're feeling very good about it," he said. "It has a good group of people. They delivered on a technology, getting it to market in a very difficult time. They have been very efficient using investment dollars and converting it to a viable product. Not all companies can do that."

But all was not rosy. SMaL faced real challenges. Viable competitors began to emerge in the low-end of the marketplace. SMaL had to decide what came next.

Emergence of Competitors

Once SMaL proved that a market existed for very small cameras, competitors entered in earnest. The first competitor was Casio's Exilim. Its edgy television commercial featured a woman wearing leather trousers sliding the camera into her back pocket. The camera had 2-megapixel resolution, a flash, and an LCD display. It sold for about $300 and was not as slim as SMaL's cameras.

Although Arienzo admitted the Exilim and other copycats offered attractive products, he still believed SMaL offered something unique:

> These guys saw our camera and liked the format. So they tried to cram everything they could into a credit card. Of course, they couldn't make it as thin as ours because it wouldn't work. So they put in a fatter battery. Once you put in a fatter battery you can put in a flash, you put in a display. You put everything in there. Of course, by the time you are done, you take this thing apart and there are three to four times as many components.

SMaL's bundle of a low price point, unique imaging technology, low power dissipation, and extremely small size may have remained unique. But SMaL's OEM customers began demanding that SMaL improve its product to better match the emerging features in the marketplace. Arienzo had to decide what to do.

WHAT NEXT?

In February 2003, SMaL could essentially take five different paths. It could try to produce better consumer camera kits to beat back competitors. It could redouble its efforts in the security and surveillance space. It could try to accelerate its efforts to crack the automotive market. It could try to enter the cellular phone camera market. Or it could try to take a "left turn" into completely new applications.

The options were not necessarily mutually exclusive. SMaL could split resources between opportunities. But SMaL still only had 35 employees. Unless it hired more engineers, taking on too many projects might overtax developers who were already working 18-hour days. If it spread itself too thin, SMaL risked never advancing past the development stage. If it focused all of its efforts on the wrong market, it could lose its chance for greatness. SMaL had to place a bet.

Option 1: Moving on Up

The most obvious path for SMaL to take would be to incrementally improve its product to better compete with entrants. Indeed, in February SMaL announced its next-generation kit that featured higher resolution (1.3 megapixels) and supported a flash. The camera was a little thicker than its predecessor but still quite thin. It still featured Autobrite. It still had low power dissipation.[3]

But should SMaL do even more? It could try to produce a kit offering 2.0-megapixel resolution, where the entry-level market seemed to be headed before the end of 2003. It could try to add on more advanced features. Its OEM customers were demanding it, but Arienzo was not sure if it was the right way to go:

> Our new product is higher quality and it is nearly as thin. We are putting in a flash. We're not increasing price that dramatically. We start talking to our OEMs and they say, "We like that. Can you do more? Can you do for $150 what your competitors are doing for $300?" To do that, we need to put in a display. Once you start putting in a display, you need to fatten the battery. You quickly are back to square zero. If we keep marching along this straight line we are go-

---

[3] SMaL Camera Technologies, "SMaL Camera Technologies Announces Availability of Next Generation Digital Imaging Kit to Enable World's Thinnest and Lightest 1.3-Megapixel Digital Cameras," February 3, 2003, <http://www.smalcamera.com/pressreleases/smal_up13_release.html>.

ing to be just as fat as they are. We may be cheaper. But we may not.

Even if SMaL did decide to race up its technological improvement trajectory, Arienzo knew it needed to select at least one other opportunity to focus on. He commented:

> We must maintain a trajectory to the common place where everybody else is going because if you don't, you can't sell. But you don't want to invest all of your marbles in that because you know you could die out there. You want to make sure your investments to get there are not too large because while you are working on the next generation you also want to be able to spend some of those resources on making a left turn.

Option 2: Step Up Security and Surveillance Efforts

At a security industry trade show in August 2001, SMaL introduced an early version of the Ultra-Wide W3000 product. It received the "Security Industry's Finest" award. Towards the end of 2001, Arienzo decided to create a separate team to further develop SMaL's security and surveillance offering. "One of our investors badly wanted to do security cameras with us," he said. "I discovered very quickly by the end of 2001 there was no way the small team that was doing the credit card camera could also do the security camera. So we had to start a separate team to do the video and keep them busy just on the video and not contaminate the two groups."

The team ultimately developed a series of video products to enter the security and surveillance market (see Exhibit 8 for product overviews). At one level, the products were quite similar to the consumer camera. They still had Autobrite, allowing superior performance in some situations. They still were digital. But they could capture moving images as well. And, the team developed a novel camera that captured an extremely wide, panoramic image. One feature allowed the panoramic camera to remain stationary and yet "pan" a room electronically. The camera constantly captured rectangular images of an entire room. By sampling different square sections of the scene (progressively moving from the left to the right), SMaL created the illusion that the stationary camera was in fact moving. "That camera really wows people," Sodini said. "When you see it on the TV you swear it is a moving camera but it is just standing still. It has a lot of interesting applications because with one camera you can cover a lot of range."

EXHIBIT 8 **Specifications for SMaL's Security and Surveillance Cameras**

W3000 Ultra-Wide with Autobrite®

SMaL's W3000 line of Ultra-Wide cameras with Autobrite is a revolution in the security and surveillance industry. It offers OEMs and large Systems Integrators the opportunity to add profitable new products to their security camera lineup. Ultra-Wide's unique features and benefits will result in clear differentiation in an increasingly competitive marketplace.

FEATURES

- Ultra-Wide 1920 × 480 resolution provides a unique three-times wide field of view
- The entire field of view is monitored at all times
- Autobrite ensures that details in both bright and dim areas of a scene are clearly visible
- No moving parts to wear out. All panning is completely automatic. Multiple panning and viewing options available.
- No fish-eye distortion and no image processing for distortion correction
- Built-in motion detection for intelligent monitoring, panning and event triggering
- Available in analog and IP-addressable formats

V1200C NetCam with Autobrite®

SMaL's V1200C NetCam with Autobrite is the first network camera to truly offer next generation surveillance. Unlike CCD network cameras, the V1200C is All-Digital "from the pixel to the picture" so it provides benefits no other network camera can.

The V1200C is the perfect Smart Camera platform. It has enough available processing power to run tomorrow's sophisticated image recognition applications like motion detection and object tracking.

FEATURES

- On-board processing power and Autobrite technology make the V1200C the perfect "smart camera" platform
- High-quality VGA streaming at a screaming 30 frames per second, the fastest in the industry today
- Three video operating modes for different network conditions and configurations: HTTP, UDP and TCP/IP
- Competitively priced compared with less featured network cameras

V1100C with Autobrite®

SMaL's V1100C with Autobrite is an integrated board-level solution that allows Security & Surveillance OEMs to introduce a new CCTV camera with unmatched dynamic range.

Now OEMs can offer a surveillance camera perfect for mixed lighting security settings that render traditional CCD cameras useless. And because the V1100C is a fully-integrated board-level solution built around SMaL's innovative image sensor and color processing ASIC, SMaL can get OEMs to market quickly. SMaL can also deliver finished cameras if desired.

FEATURES

- Features SMaL's 640 × 480 progressive scan image sensor with full 30fps frame rate
- Fully-integrated board-level solution ready for rapid integration into OEM's housings and product design
- Factory configurable image processing parameters and user features for OEM customization
- SMaL's modular platform offers future opportunities for network camera, smart camera and wide view camera products

Source: Company documents.

[handwritten margin notes: "like Ciena & HP", "need end to end solution to compete", "— Cams", "— recording", "— Monitors", "— Install etc."]

By January 2003, SMaL was ready to begin commercializing its technology but had begun to encounter some resistance from potential customers. SMaL's management believed the fragmented and risk-adverse nature of the industry posed a challenge. Corporations tend to be the primary purchasers of security and surveillance systems. They install cameras throughout the corporation and have a centralized facility where security personnel watch for any suspicious behavior. Numerous companies make security and surveillance systems. They sell these systems to installers, like Siemens Building Technology, ADT Security Services, and Diebold, Inc., which then sell systems to corporations.[4]

Although companies were increasingly concerned with security, SMaL asserted that the industry's fragmented nature made change difficult. "Security and surveillance is very conservative," Arienzo said. "You have

---

[4]"Tall expectations: Marked by exceptional performance in 2001, the security industry's largest systems integrators are poised for non-stop business through the remainder of this year," *Security Distribution and Marketing,* July 2002. Available from ABI/Inform.

these guys sitting in a 'glasshouse' watching 40 screens and you say, 'This is unbelievable. What are they doing? Why do you do it this way?' The industry within the next few years is going to undergo a transformation similar to when computers went to distributed computing, but it could take longer."

Sodini explained that existing companies had an established infrastructure that SMaL's solutions had to conform with. For instance, most video cameras send out their signals using "NTSC," an analog standard. SMaL had to convert its signal from digital to analog to conform to existing systems. This obviated one of SMaL's purported advantages—an all-digital solution.

Despite these challenges, the company's founders remained convinced that its product had a compelling value proposition. SMaL could redouble its efforts to reach this market. It could pull engineers off its consumer camera product and refocus them towards improving the security camera. Its product had won a prestigious award. Maybe all it needed to find success was more time and dedicated resources. After all, it had only recently begun attacking the market in earnest. Were more resources all it needed or would it have to change other things to find success?

Barbieri was quite convinced that SMaL would ultimately find success in this market. "Security is a huge opportunity," he said. "Our advantages in this space are substantial. I think the most difficult piece will be making sure we are partnered with the right companies."

Option 3: Speed up Automotive Efforts

SMaL's founders sensed in the company's early days that the best long-term bet for the company lay in the automotive market. Automotive companies had shown an increasing interest in "smart" applications like adaptive cruise control, intelligent mirrors, and so on. Williams noted that VGA resolution would be ample for these applications. Any image would be viewed through a small monitor in a dashboard, which probably would offer no better than VGA resolution.

SMaL had quietly been building the capability to go after the automotive opportunity. In 2002, it secured an agreement to work with a leading supplier to design and build components for smart applications. The problem with the automotive opportunity was that it required several more years of development. Even with its design win, SMaL would not see any significant revenue until 2005. But perhaps SMaL could try to accelerate that time

frame. Maybe if it pushed on the accelerator it could make the 2005 revenue stream much bigger.

Option 4: Cameras in Phones

SMaL could try to bring its imaging technology to other consumer domains. Perhaps the most obvious application would be to develop a camera to put in a cellular phone. Cameras in cellular phones had already proven to be a huge hit in Japan. J-Phone had attracted more than 5 million subscribers to its camera phone service by the middle of 2002.[5] Most industry experts predicted camera phones would be a huge hit in the Western world as well. The International Data Corporation estimated that consumers would buy close to 140 million camera-equipped phones in 2006.[6]

Leading cellular handset manufacturers like Nokia were very aware of the opportunity. They had two different ways to bring a camera phone to market. They could offer an integrated device with an embedded camera or they could let consumers attach an add-on module.

Either way, some of SMaL's technological advantages could prove compelling. Phones needed cameras that did not drain batteries. The cameras clearly had to be small. CMOS-based cameras would seem to have a real advantage because they were cheap and their image quality in this market was good enough.

Williams noted that SMaL had several options to go after the camera phone opportunity. It could try to develop a module to sell to phone manufacturers. This would require a full-scale development effort but could be a source of competitive advantage. It could partner with a company that sold chipsets to mobile phone manufacturers and work to bundle SMaL's image sensor. Or it could try to supply its imager to companies that were trying to develop camera modules. It was clear that SMaL would have to design something new—its existing five-part kit just wouldn't quite work for any of these opportunities.

Realizing any of these opportunities presented challenges. Because the market seemed so large, a plethora of companies were going after it. Many existing imaging companies were developing CCD-based camera modules to place in phones. The high levels of competition could quickly erode any profitability that module

---

[5] Paul De Bendern, "PluggedIn—Camera-phone combos face uncertain reception," *Reuters,* July 9, 2002.
[6] International Data Corporation, "Moving Pictures: The Future of Mobile Devices and Imaging." Presentation at CES, January 2003.

providers could squeeze from the solutions. As Barbieri said, "Within months there will be dozens of companies that take off-the-shelf components and put them together in a similar form factor."

Option 5: Making a Left Turn

The final option was to try to take imaging to a new place. SMaL's senior management believed it created a category when it developed the credit card–sized camera. Was there a way for it to make a "left turn" and bring imaging to other places where it was historically impossible?

For instance, Arienzo detailed a potential opportunity to bring imaging technology to law enforcement officials:

> One of my best friends has been working with a company in security and surveillance in Italy. Italian police cars have computers in their cars that are connected through the wireless network to the central system where they have everyone's pictures and fingerprints. One of the things we are talking about developing is a camera that can take a picture of a suspect and has a place to take their fingerprint. So when the police stop a suspect they can take their picture, take their fingerprint, download it onto the computer, and immediately get a full file on that person.

The problem with these sorts of opportunities was they tended to be difficult to find, could be of limited size, and could require substantial development work. As Williams said, "Our technology offers distinct technological advantages in numerous markets. But we just don't have the resources currently to take on a lot of custom development. So naturally, we want to identify high-volume, high-margin opportunities that require little engineering development."

Choices, Choices

Arienzo said he believed that SMaL ultimately would have a healthy mix of revenue between its three original target markets—consumer cameras, security and surveillance, and automotive. But how would SMaL get there? Arienzo put down the Exilim camera, framed his Ultra-Pocket with his other hand, and turned contemplative:

> What is it really that we have and how can we leverage this? Is there a different direction to go that would capitalize on the innovation that we have in a different dimension? This is a typical thing that happens. Competition is coming in. One of our OEMs says, "Can you do what the competi-

tion is doing but make it cheaper?" And we say, "Why do we want to do this cheaper? I am going to be second or third or fourth or fifth. I want to be the first one like I was before." I don't know the answer yet. We have a format that is attractive. We have the convenience. We have the Autobrite. We have the low power. The real challenge is where are the real opportunities and how do we go after them. We can take this everywhere. The key thing is to find where. And you definitely don't want to take it where everybody else is.

Disruption, Disintegration and the Dissipation of Differentiability

Clayton M. Christensen, Matt Verlinden, and George Westerman

This paper proposes a deductively derived model to help managers who preside over decisions to integrate or outsource to assess *ex ante* whether, when, and why it might be strategically and competitively important to develop internal capabilities to perform certain activities in-house and when it would be sensible and safe to outsource elements of value-added. Among the paper's conclusions are that the competitive advantage from vertical integration is strongest in tiers of the market where customers are under-served by the functionality or performance available from products in the market. Vertical integration tends to be a disadvantage when customers are over-served by the functionality available from products in the market. Vertically integrated firms will therefore often dominate in the most demanding tiers of markets that have grown to substantial size, while a horizontally stratified, or disintegrated, industry structure will often be the dominant business model in the tiers of the market that are less demanding of functionality.

1. INTRODUCTION

Whether to become or remain vertically integrated is a question of vast strategic importance in many industries. In recent years, firms such as Alcoa, Lucent, and General Motors, for whom vertical control over most steps in

Source: Industrial and Corporate Change, Volume 11, Number 5, 2002, pp. 955–993.

their value chains had historically constituted an important basis of competitive advantage, have sold upstream businesses that produced components or intermediate materials, in order to focus on the portions of their value chains that they consider to be core to their business. Others, like IBM, continue to own but are de-coupling upstream from downstream operations, tasking the former to sell components openly in the market and the latter to procure components from external suppliers when necessary to maintain competitiveness. In contrast, Microsoft is aggressively integrating downstream from its initial operating system products into a variety of applications software markets; Intel has integrated into chipsets and motherboards using its microprocessors; and telecommunications and entertainment companies have integrated together in bewildering ways.

Some business experts have praised these actions, while other reputable observers have reacted with skepticism. For example, IBM's management have been criticized for having outsourced the microprocessor and operating system of their personal computer from Intel and Microsoft, choosing to participate primarily in the design and assembly stages of value-added in their product. While history has proven the decision to have been unfortunate for IBM, at the time the decision was made it was judged by many as the right thing to do.[1] It has indeed been difficult to predict, a priori, which of these moves toward or away from vertical integration would be judged in retrospect as having been managerially astute and which would be viewed as strategically flawed. Too often for decisions as important as these, their wisdom can only be judged with the benefit of history.

This paper proposes a deductively derived model to help managers who preside over decisions to integrate or outsource to assess *ex ante* whether, when, and why it might be strategically and competitively important to develop internal capabilities to perform certain activities in-house and when it will be sensible and safe to outsource elements of value-added. Our conclusions are that:

1. The competitive advantage from vertical integration is strongest in tiers of the market where customers are under-served by the functionality or performance available from products in the market. Vertical integration tends to be a disadvantage when customers

are over-served by the functionality available from products in the market.

2. As a result of (1), vertically integrated firms will often dominate in the most demanding tiers of markets that have grown to substantial size, while a horizontally stratified, or disintegrated, industry structure will often be the dominant business model in the tiers of the market that are less demanding of functionality.

3. The tendencies listed in (1) and (2) occur in end-use markets for complete product systems, such as automobiles and computers. But they also can occur in the markets for subsystems and components, which themselves comprise multiple constituent parts and materials.

4. Most often, vertically integrated firms tend to dominate many markets at the outset. Because of the patterns observed in our earlier studies, however—in which the pace of technological progress proceeds at a faster rate than customers in any given tier of the market can utilize that progress—the dominant business model in any given tier of the market will tend to shift over time from vertically integrated firms to a horizontally stratified population of specialized firms.

5. The generalization in (4) can be reversed, however, when performance gaps emerge in markets due to discontinuous shifts in the functionality demanded by customers. When this occurs, the pendulum of competitive advantage is likely to swing back toward vertically integrated firms, as companies seek to compete with each other on the basis of superior product functionality again.

6. When the dominant business model in a tier of the market shifts from vertical integration to horizontal stratification, the ability to achieve above-average profitability tends to transfer from the firms that design and assemble end-use products that historically had not been good enough to those that build those subsystems which limit performance of the end-use system, and which therefore are not good enough.

These conclusions began to take their initial shape in studies of the patterns of vertical integration and disintegration in the disk drive industry, in which the pendulum of competitive advantage swung repeatedly between integrated and non-integrated firms, in various tiers of the market (Christensen, 1993, 1994; Chesbrough and Kusunoki, 2001). This paper's conclusions have not been built inductively from empirical analysis, however. They have been derived deductively by combining the results of the disk drive studies with other scholars' examinations

---

[1] See, for example, the discussion of IBM's outsourcing decision in *Fortune,* 14 April 1997.

of technological modularity (Ulrich, 1995; Sanchez and Mahoney, 1996; Baldwin and Clark, 1997), and with concepts of the drivers of change in the basis of competition (Christensen, 1996; Adner and Levinthal, 2001). In this paper we provide some preliminary but promising empirical evidence supporting the model and use the model to examine briefly the histories of the computer, automobile, software, photonics, financial services, and microprocessor industries, to suggest that the model might be more broadly useful. Our primary purpose in offering this paper is to invite other scholars to test empirically these hypotheses and thereby continue to build deeper understanding of the circumstances under which we might expect integration and non-integration to confer competitive advantage or disadvantage.

2. RELATIONSHIP TO PRIOR STUDIES OF VERTICAL INTEGRATION

The model presented in this paper does not address every rationale for vertical integration and disintegration. We believe, however, that it builds upon and extends the foundations laid by several important scholars who have studied the causal drivers behind integration. Stigler's (1951) causal model, echoing Adam Smith's (1776) original analysis of the specialization of labor, asserted that a driver of specialization was market size. He observed that many industries begin as vertically integrated ones due to their small size. They then increasingly become populated by specialist firms as they grow. Stigler posited that later in the life cycle, when demand begins to contract, industries consequently tend to reintegrate. Although we agree that scale is a factor, our model views scale often as an outcome of other factors that drive specialization, rather than as a fundamental causal driver of it.

Coase (1937) and Williamson (1985) introduced the role of transaction costs as the causal driver of the optimal boundaries of the organization. There are many types of transaction costs, including threat of intellectual property appropriation (Teece, 1986), lock-in (Williamson, 1979), asset specificity (Williamson, 1979; Klein *et al.*, 1978), and the challenges of coordinating interdependent investments (Chandler, 1977). Demsetz (1988) characterized transactions costs as the costs of search and maintenance, showing how these vary across the industrial life cycle. A stream of subsequent scholars within the transactions cost paradigm, including Teece (1986), Langlois (1994), Becker and Murphy (1992), Sanchez and Mahoney (1996), and Chesbrough and

Teece (1996), have identified a specific type of transactions cost—the challenge of coordination amongst diverse specialists—as a driver of managerial integration across such interfaces. Monteverde's (1995) construct of "unstructured technological dialogue" describes the management challenge when an interface between stages of value-added is inter-dependent and not well specified. Our model builds most directly upon Monteverde's concept.

Scholars working in a parallel stream have studied in engineering terms the concepts of architectural modularity, in order to define more precisely the conditions under which suppliers and customers of products and services might need to engage in structured versus unstructured technological dialogue (e.g., Henderson and Clark, 1990; Clark and Fujimoto, 1991; Christensen, 1994; Ulrich, 1995; Ulrich and Eppinger, 1995; Chesbrough and Kusunoki, 2001; and Baldwin and Clark, 2000).

The contribution we hope to make to the work of these scholars is to define the underlying factors that cause dialogue between customers and suppliers to be unstructured (which can entail high transactions costs if the dialogue transcends the boundaries of firms) or structured (which lowers transactions costs between firms). We also describe underlying mechanisms that may cause structured dialogue to become unstructured, and vice versa. In addition, our model helps explain why the power to earn attractive profits resides at specific locations in a value-added chain but not at others (Porter, 1985). It also specifies the factors that can cause the power to earn attractive profit to shift to other stages of value-added.

3. DEFINITIONS

The key unit of analysis in our model is the *interface* at which a supplier of value-added and a customer of that value-added interact—whether that interface is within or between organizations. It is at this interface that structured or unstructured dialogue occurs. The specific terms that scholars, such as those noted above, use to describe this dialogue vary (Billington and Fleming, 1998; Fixson, 2000). For our purposes, we assert that for structured dialog to occur across an interface between stages or elements of value-added, three conditions must be met.

1. The customer that procures or uses a piece of value-added must understand and be able to specify to its supplier which attributes or parameters of the product or service must be provided and to what tolerances.

2. Metrics for those attributes must exist, and the technology to measure those attributes must be available, reliable, and unambiguous.

3. The procuring company must understand the interactions or interdependencies between the attributes of what is provided and the performance of the system in which the procurer will use it. If there is any variation in what is provided, the procurer needs to understand how, when, and why it will affect the performance of the system (Taguchi and Clausing, 1990).

If these three conditions are met, then the interface between a provider of an element of value-added and its user can be termed a *modular* interface, across which structured technical dialogue can occur. At modular interfaces, the necessary information exists for a market to function efficiently. Modular interfaces can occur across the boundaries of companies and across boundaries of functional groups within a company (such as between product design and manufacturing). They can also occur between groups within a project team; and they can exist between individuals. Such interfaces occur in products, services, and systems of use. Henceforth in this paper, when we use the term *product,* we intend for it to apply to a service as well.

When these three conditions are not met at an interface, then we term it an *inter-dependent* interface,[2] across which *unstructured* technical dialogue must occur. At interdependent interfaces, the necessary information required for an efficiently functioning market does not exist. Management and integration, rather than markets, constitutes the most efficient coordinating mechanism across interdependent interfaces.[3]

Few products, services, or systems would be composed exclusively of modular or interdependent interfaces—suggesting that architectures that are entirely modular or entirely interdependent would be rare extremes at opposite ends of a spectrum. This also suggests that we could rarely characterize an entire industry as being dominated by integrated or specialized firms—because this is likely to vary at the interfaces of different

pieces of value-added. It will also vary, as shown below, by tier of the market.[4]

The use of these definitions in the model presented below yields results that are consistent with the findings of scholars such as Sanchez and Mahoney (1996) and Chesbrough and Teece (1996). We assert that if these three conditions of modularity—specifiability, measurability, and predictability—exist at any interface, it improves the potential for an efficiently functioning market to emerge at that interface. Markets are more effective coordinating mechanisms across modular interfaces than is managerial coordination. On the other hand, management will trump market coordination in cases where an interface is interdependent.

4. THE CAUSES OF SWINGS BETWEEN VERTICAL INTEGRATION AND STRATIFICATION

Many companies today are striving to outsource those elements of value-added that do not build upon their strengths and can therefore be procured more cost-effectively from suppliers. History has shown, however, that many industries pass through repeated cycles in which competitive advantage rests alternately with integrated and non-integrated business models (Christensen, 1994; Fine, 1998)—suggesting that decisions to integrate or disintegrate that make sense in one context can create disadvantages when things change.

Our studies of how disruptive innovations can cause well-managed companies to fail can shed some light on the drivers behind this cyclical pattern. Because this work has been reported elsewhere, it will only be briefly summarized here.[5] There are two elements to this model,

---

[2] Ulrich (1995) and others use the term "integral" to refer to interfaces where these conditions are not met, and Chesbrough and Teece (1996) use the term "systemic." We have chosen the term "interdependent" because it seems more descriptive of the situation. The other terms connote enough other meanings that we have chosen to employ this new term.
[3] This assertion mirrors Monteverde's conclusion that "Roughly speaking (since other things also matter), firm boundaries . . . should congeal around transactions rich in such technically necessary, unstructured dialog" (Monteverde, 1995: 1629).

[4] In earlier papers about these phenomena (Christensen and Rosenbloom, 1995; Christensen, 1997: ch. 2), we describe the existence of a "value network"—a nested ecosystem of suppliers and customers whose constituent companies share similar business models and process rhythms, which tend to move up-market and get disrupted as a group. The evidence in Section 5 of this paper suggests that all companies within a particular value network are not likely to uniformly employ modular or interdependent architectures. Elsewhere, Christensen suggests the existence of a "Law of Conservation of Modularity"—a generalization asserting that interfaces across sequential elements in a value-added chain are likely to be alternately interdependent and modular (Christensen, 2001).
[5] The initial findings that the pace of technological progress can outstrip the abilities of customers to utilize that progress were detailed in Christensen (1992a, b). Having assembled a complete census of data on every disk drive model introduced by each company in the world disk drive industry between 1970 and 1990, Christensen measured through regression analysis the trajectory of improvement in the storage capacity of each form factor of disk drives during this period. Then, using data on disk drive capacity actually used in various classes of computers,

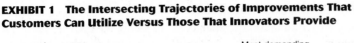

EXHIBIT 1   The Intersecting Trajectories of Improvements That Customers Can Utilize Versus Those That Innovators Provide

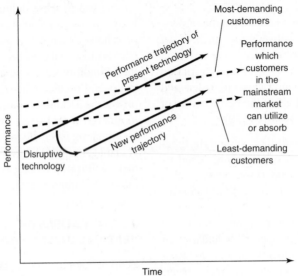

as depicted in Exhibit 1. The first asserts that in most markets there is a trajectory of performance improvement that customers can actually absorb or utilize over time, represented by the gently sloped lines. Secondly, as depicted by the steeply sloped lines, there is a distinctly different trajectory of performance improvement that the innovators in an industry provide to their market, as they introduce new and improved products. Our studies have shown that the trajectory of technological progress almost always outstrips the abilities of customers to utilize the improvement.

This means that companies whose product functionality is closely tuned to what customers in a tier of a market may need at one point in time typically improve products at such a rate that they overshoot what those same customers actually can utilize in later years. In other words, the functionality of a product can oversatisfy what less-demanding customers in lower tiers of the market need, even while customers in more demanding tiers of the market continue to need more functionality than even the best available products offer. It also means that "disruptive technologies"—simpler, more convenient products that initially do not perform well enough to be used in main-stream markets—can take root in undemanding tiers of the market and then improve at such a rapid rate that they can squarely address mainstream market needs in the future.

This model has been used to describe how minicomputers displaced mainframes, and how personal computers displaced minicomputers. It illustrates how hydraulic excavator manufacturers overthrew makers of cable shovel makers and how the Japanese automakers assaulted western car markets. It describes the mechanism through which steel minimills have been displac-

---

he measured through regression analysis the trajectory of improvement utilized by customers in various tiers of the market. These results were described in Christensen (1993), Christensen and Rosenbloom (1995), Bower and Christensen (1995), Rosenbloom and Christensen (1995), and Christensen and Bower (1996). Similar econometric analysis was used in Christensen (1997) to measure the trajectories of improvement in functionality that manufacturers of excavating equipment provided, in contrast to the trajectory of performance improvement that various types of contractors were able to utilize. The "disruptive technologies model" was inductively derived from these empirical analyses. Dan Monroe of Bell Laboratories (Monroe, 1999) and Mick Bass of Hewlett-Packard (Bass and Christensen, 2000) subsequently have empirically measured the same phenomena in semiconductor products. Christensen (1997) also uses the model in a deductive mode, comparing the predictions of the model to qualitative data about the histories of established and entrant companies in the computer, steel, retailing, motor controls, motorcycle, and accounting software industries. Subsequent studies have found the same phenomenon in medical education (Christensen and Armstrong, 1998), retailing (Christensen and Tedlow, 2000), healthcare (Christensen et al., 2000), macroeconomic growth (Christensen et al., 2001), and semiconductor products (Bass and Christensen, 2002). Professor Ron Adner and his colleagues (Adner, 1999; Adner and Levinthal, 2001; Adner and Zemsky, 2001) have recently examined the same phenomenon using deductive, modeling methods.

ing integrated mills; by which the packet-switched telecommunications infrastructure is disrupting the circuit-switched network; and many others. The model has been expanded and refined, using very different research methods, by Adner and his colleagues (Adner, 1999; Adner and Levinthal, 2001; Adner and Zemsky, 2001), among others.

During the early years of many industries, in the leftmost regions of Exhibit 1, product functionality is not good enough to satisfy the needs of customers in most tiers of the market. Competition during this era therefore focuses predominantly on product functionality: designing and producing higher-performing products is a fundamental mechanism by which companies strive to get ahead of each other (Christensen, 1996, 1997; Adner and Levinthal, 2001; Adner and Zemsky, 2001). These competitive pressures compel engineers to fit the pieces of their product together in new and untested ways in each successive product generation, as they work to wring as much performance as possible from the technology that is available. As a result, product designs tend to be interdependent, rather than modular, during this era: the design of each part tends to be contingent upon the design of other parts and upon the way they interact within the overall system architecture. There are often powerful inter-dependencies between design and manufacturing during this era that are similarly based in the competitive need to stretch functionality to the frontiers of what is possible.[6]

There are two reasons why interdependent architectures predominate during eras when product functionality is not yet good enough for what customers need. The first was articulated by Ulrich (1995), who showed that creating a modular architecture—especially one that is defined by industry standards—forces designers to compromise or back away from the frontier of what is technologically possible. At the left side of Exhibit 1, backing off is not competitively feasible. The second reason is that new technologies are often employed in the stages and tiers of an industry where competitors are stretching toward the frontier of functionality. It is when new tech-

nologies are used to do things that have never been done before that engineers most often encounter interdependent interfaces: they do not know what to specify, cannot accurately measure important attributes, and do not yet understand how variation in one subsystem will impact overall system performance. Unstructured technical dialogue is therefore the language required to compete successfully when a product's functionality is not good enough to address targeted customers' needs.

In early mainframe computers, for example, the logic circuitry could not be designed until the operating system was designed; the operating system could not be designed until the core memory was designed; and the core memory could not be designed until the logic circuitry had been designed. Manufacturing methods powerfully affected whether the system performed as it was designed to do. Everything depended upon everything else. A company could not have existed in that industry as an independent supplier of logic circuitry or operating systems or as a contract manufacturer because clear, modular interfaces had not yet been established to define how the parts would fit together. This implies that integrated companies can be expected to dominate at the interfaces between pieces of value-added where functionality is not good enough. The dominance of IBM in mainframe computers, Digital Equipment in minicomputers, General Motors and Ford in the automobile market, Alcoa in aluminum, Standard Oil in oil, and Xerox in photocopying are all examples of firms whose vertical integration conferred competitive advantage during an era when performance was not good enough.

Because these conditions often typify an industry during its early years, scholars such as Stigler (1951) and Chandler (1977) have observed that integrated firms generally comprise the predominant business model as most industries grow towards substantive mass. Certainly industries must achieve a certain critical mass in order to support specialized competitors. We assert, however, that the fundamental causality of integrated firms being dominant at the outset and then displaced by specialized ones is not the passage of time or a general evolution towards "maturity" or large scale *per se*. Rather, it is this causal sequence:

1. When functionality is not good enough to address what customers in a given tier of the market can utilize, firms compete by making better products.
2. In order to make the best possible products with the technology that is available, product architects tend to employ interdependent, proprietary architectures,

---

[6] Stuckey and White (1993) assert that industries will remain vertically integrated when there is *asset specificity* (a fixed asset is geographically so restricted that it is *de facto* tied to another asset), *technical specificity* (two pieces of equipment can work only with each other and will not easily work with others), and *human capital specificity* (people whose skills are of value only within a particular working relationship). In the parlance of this paper, each of these situations is architecturally *interdependent*.

because building a modular system around industry standards forces them to back away from the frontier of what is technologically possible. In tiers of the market where product functionality is not good enough, competitive conditions penalize companies that attempt to do this. New technologies are often employed in these conditions.

3. Because this entails unstructured technical dialogue, transactions costs are minimized through integration. Integration constitutes an important competitive advantage in managing the interdependencies in design, manufacturing, sales, service, and procurement during this period.[7]

When the functionality of available products surpasses what customers in a tier of a market can utilize, however, competition changes. Customers experience diminishing marginal utility from further improvements and consequently are less willing to reward further improvements with higher prices. Innovators therefore need to find other ways to compete profitably for the business of customers in tiers of the market who are over-served by functionality. Our research suggests that very often, speed to market becomes a critical dimension of competition in the lower-right regions of Exhibit 1. Similarly, the ability to conveniently customize the features and functions of products to the specific needs of customers in ever-smaller market niches becomes a critical trajectory of innovation that enables firms to get ahead of their competition and maintain profit margins (Pine, 1992; Christensen, 1996, 1997; Adner and Levinthal, 2001).

The efforts of disruptive competitors to be fast and flexible in this era of overshoot at the right side of Exhibit 1 forces them to create modular product designs in order to be competitive—because modularity creates

many more options for speed, cost reduction, and customization (Baldwin and Clark, 2000). When available functionality more than satisfies what customers can utilize, designers have the slack to back away from the frontier of what is technologically possible, in order to define modular architectures (Ulrich, 1995). Modularity often begins to take form in companies' proprietary interface specifications, which enable them to outsource components and subsystems at arm's length from other organizations (Sanchez and Mahoney, 1996). When one company's modular interface specifications become accepted by multiple competitors, they can become industry standards. Industry standard modularity enables firms that design and assemble products to introduce new and customized products even more rapidly than they could when interfaces were modular but proprietary, as designers and assemblers can mix and match the most effective components from the best suppliers.

Over time, the lower overheads and scale economies that focused component suppliers enjoy, coupled with the speed-to-market and flexibility advantages enjoyed by non-integrated assemblers, enable a population of horizontally stratified firms to displace vertically integrated firms (Grove, 1996; Fine, 1998; Baldwin and Clark, 2000). Modular specifications constitute sufficient information for an efficient market to work; and market-based coordination (structured technical dialogue) trumps managerial coordination across modular interfaces (Sanchez and Mahoney, 1996).

In summary, the chain of causality that shifts competitive advantage in a given tier of a market from integrated firms is this:

1. When the functionality of available products outstrips the ability of customers in a tier of the market to utilize further improvements, companies must compete differently to win the business of customers who are over-served by functionality. Innovations that facilitate speed to market and the ability to customize features and functions in response to the needs of customers in ever-smaller market niches become the trajectories of improvement that customers reward with premium prices.

2. Efforts to compete along these dimensions of speed, flexibility, and customization cause product architectures to evolve toward modularity. This facilitates speed and flexibility.

3. Modularity then enables independent, focused providers of individual pieces of value-added to thrive, because transactions cost−minimizing structured

---

[7]Stigler's (1951) observation that industries tend to reintegrate and consolidate as they became mature in their later stages also may not result from shrinking scale *per se*. We have written elsewhere that after the dimensions of innovation in functionality, reliability, and convenience are exhausted, price-based competition becomes predominant. It is possible that costs can be minimized most effectively from within an interdependent product architecture and integrated business model. For example, our conversations with some of Dell Computer's competitors have surfaced the possibility that Dell is over-serving the market in terms of convenience and customization—and that there are real overhead costs associated with its business model and product architecture. If an integrated supplier like IBM now offered to the market a single one-size-fits-all personal computer with more-than-enough microprocessor speed, display pixels, and memory capacity, it might possible be able to steal substantial share at the low end from Dell. It is possible, therefore, that the causality of what Stigler observed is the mechanism that we discuss here.

EXHIBIT 2   Overshooting the Functionality That Customers Can Utilize Triggers Change in the Way Companies Must Compete

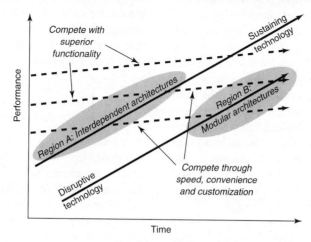

technical dialogue can occur. As a result, an industry which at one point was dominated by integrated firms becomes dominated by a population of specialized, non-integrated firms.

Exhibit 2 summarizes the conditions in which we would expect an industry to be characterized by functionality-based competition amongst integrated firms employing interdependent architectures (Region A) versus those in which the industry would be characterized by speed- and convenience-based competition within a population of specialized competitors who interact within modular architectures (Region B).[8]

A significant body of scholarship (e.g., Teece, 1986) has focused on the appropriability of knowledge as a critical factor affecting decisions to integrate or disintegrate. We hope that our model casts additional insight on this phenomenon as well. It implies that when the functionality of a product is not good enough to address customers' needs, the language of successful competition must be unstructured technical dialogue. The interactions through which this dialogue occurs are the "locations" where the organization's capabilities to design and manufacture better products reside. This tacit knowledge

or capability cannot be appropriated by competitors. When overshooting has occurred and competitive forces drive architectures toward modularity, however, then the capability for fitting the pieces of the product together which had resided in unstructured technical dialogue becomes embodied in the interface standards—structured technical dialogue—that define how the modules fit and work together. This enables competitors to appropriate what had been proprietary capability and know-how.

4.1 Case Evidence Supporting the Disintegration Model

The model presented above was deductively derived through a synthesis of various scholars' work. In this section we offer preliminary empirical evidence—some of it in the form of numerical analysis, some in the form of narrative history—that is consistent with the chain of causality in this model. In case studies of industries as diverse as disk drives, computers, financial services, and microprocessors, we observe a process similar to the one outlined above that transferred competitive advantage from integration towards non-integration. We summarize these observations in the following.

4.2 Evidence from the Disk Drive Industry

Our earlier research described how the performance of disk drives improved at a more rapid pace than the ability of customers in any given tier of the market could absorb those improvements. Over and over, this enabled

---

[8] The advent of a modular architecture in many cases seems associated with the emergence of a dominant design (Abernathy and Utterback, 1978; Christensen *et al.*, 1998). This association is not yet clear enough in our minds to say more than this. The possibility of this linkage, however, is something that we invite other scholars to study with us.

disruptive innovators piercing into the market's under-belly to displace the industry's leaders (Christensen and Rosenbloom, 1995; Christensen and Bower, 1996).

This continuous process of up-market migration implies (in the language of this paper) that architectural modularity is likely to occur in the least-demanding tiers of the market first and that at any point in time we should expect the most demanding tiers of the market, which are the most under-served by the functionality of available products, to be populated by more technologically inter-dependent products. Consequently, we would expect integrated firms' market positions to be strongest in the most demanding tiers of the market and the market shares of non-integrated firms to be strongest in the least-demanding, most over-served tiers of the market.

In our study of the disk drive industry, we devised a method to measure the degree to which the architecture of a drive was modular or interdependent. It is an indirect measure, but seems to support the notion that modularity appears first in the least-demanding tiers of the market, where the phenomenon of overshooting first occurs. The analysis suggests that modular architectures then migrate toward more demanding tiers of the market, as this on-going process of overshooting successively more demanding tiers of the market continues.

To do this analysis, we built a database of every model of disk drive introduced by any company in the world between 1975 and 1998 — 4334 models in all. This consti-tutes a complete product census for the industry in these years.[9] For each of these models, we had data on the types of components that were used in the drive — in-cluding hardware components and the types of firmware and software coding that were employed. We then esti-mated regression equations, in which the dependent vari-able was the recording density of the drive.[10] The inde-pendent variables were the year in which the drive was introduced, the size of the drive,[11] and the components that were used in the drive — represented by dummy vari-ables for each type or generation of component tech-nology. Where interviews with engineers suggested that interactions amongst components might affect the re-cording density achieved in a product, interaction terms were included in the analysis. The equation was esti-mated in the following form:

$$\ln(\text{Recording Density}) = B_1 + B_2(\text{Year}) +$$
$$B_3(\ln \text{Disk Diameter}) + B_4(\text{Component Dummy 1}) +$$
$$\ldots + B_n(\text{Component Dummy } n)$$

The coefficients that were estimated for each of the com-ponent dummy variables measured the extent to which the use of various component technologies added to or detracted from the recording density of the product. The coefficient of the year variable measured the annual im-provement in recording density that resulted from gen-eral, incremental advances that could not be linked to the use of particular new architectural, component, software, or firmware technology. Detailed results from this analy-sis are reported in Appendix 1. The adjusted R^2 was 0.95, indicating that the variables accounted for most of the variation in density across products in the sample.

This equation allowed us to estimate the expected recording density of each drive, given its size, the com-ponents that were used, and the year in which it was de-signed. We could then compare the expected density with the density that its engineers actually achieved. We called the ratio of the actual recording density to the ex-pected density the *architectural efficiency* of the drive and calculated this ratio for every disk drive model in the database.[12] An architectural efficiency ratio of 1.0 indi-cates that the engineers achieved exactly the expected density. Ratios above 1.0 indicate that, through clever product design, the engineers were able to wring more recording density out of the same set of components than the average engineer would have done. A ratio of less than 1.0 suggests that the drive's engineers got less-than-expected performance, given the components that they used.

---

[9] The data were obtained as a generous gift from Mr. James Porter, ed-itor of *Disk/Trend Report*. We have entered the data in a huge Excel spreadsheet and would be happy to share the data with colleagues who wish to analyze it further (available on request from C.M.C.). Although *Disk/Trend Report* recently ceased publication, the San Jose Public Li-brary holds past copies of the reports.

[10] Recording density is measured as the number of megabits of infor-mation that can be stored on a square inch of disk area.

[11] The diameter of the disk actually has a strong effect on the recording density that is feasible, because the inertial problems of precisely posi-tioning larger components over a particular track of data are much greater in large drives than small drives.

---

[12] Professor Marco Iansiti (Iansiti, 1997) used different methods to de-velop an analogous measure in his study of product design processes in the computer workstation industry. He labeled his measure "techno-logical yield." We prefer to use the term "architectural efficiency," to be consistent with earlier publications that employed this measure (Chris-tensen, 1992a,b) and because it is more descriptive of the phenomenon we are trying to measure. Whereas Iansiti compared what was theoret-ically achievable versus what was actually achieved, we have measured the average of all engineers' work versus the work of the individual product design teams that developed each of the products.

EXHIBIT 3   The Progress of Modular Architectures Through Progressively Demanding Tiers of the Disk Drive Market

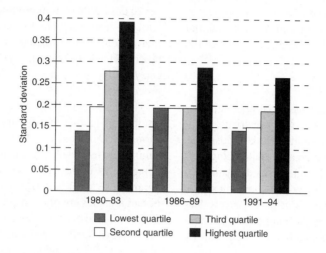

If the interface standards amongst the components were so completely defined that engineers had no degrees of freedom in designing how they would fit the components together in the drive's architecture—i.e., if the design were completely modular—then we would expect the architectural efficiency of the population of drives to be 1.0 and the standard deviation of architectural efficiency to be 0. The larger the standard deviation in the architectural efficiency of the product models in this population, the greater the scope for differentiated techniques for integrating components. In other words, the greater the standard deviation, the greater the degree of architectural interdependency in product designs. And the lower the standard deviation, the greater the degree of architectural modularity in the drive.

Exhibit 3 maps on its vertical axis the standard deviation of the architectural efficiency of drives sold into the desktop computer market between 1980 and 1995, by tier of the market—ranging from the drives in the lowest-capacity quartile at the front to those of the highest-capacity quartile in the back.[13] Fleming and Sorenson

(2001) used very different methods to arrive at a similar conclusion.

Note that the standard deviation increases from front to back—from the lowest quartile to the highest quartile in each of the periods—suggesting that the degree of interdependency was always greater in the most-demanding tiers of the market. While the degree of interdependence/modularity seems to have been stable over time in the lowest quartile of products, in the second, third, and fourth product quartiles the degree of interdependency decreased monotonically over time, as the ongoing process of overshooting and increased modularity progressed upward through tiers of the market. This suggests that the scope for product differentiation was always most limited in the lowest tiers of the market in which customers were most over-served and greatest in the most demanding tiers, where customers' thirst for improved performance still required more interdependent architectures. The stable standard deviation in the lowest tier of the market supports the notion that few products are entirely modular at every interface.[14]

---

[13] There is a common problem in analyses of this sort, as one of the reviewers of this paper pointed out. Quoting from the review letter, "[If] you plot the size of the residual at different levels of the dependent variable, [you often] find that the residual is larger on the larger end of the distribution of the dependent variable, and smaller at the smaller end of the distribution of the dependent variable. It would be very surprising to have found any other pattern, [because] it is common for errors to be heteroscedastic in proportion to the dependent variable." He or she is correct. It is for this reason that our measure of architectural efficiency we have used in these studies is the ratio of actual to expected record-

ing density, rather than the absolute magnitude of the residual. Using the ratio normalizes for the effect of the absolute magnitude. Indeed, had we not normalized in this way, the plot would have been extraordinarily misleading because recording densities have increased dramatically over the period.

[14] The only deviation from the trend towards increased modularity seems to have occurred in the late 1980s, when the drive makers in all tiers of the market began to use thin film heads. As Waid (1989) notes, thin film heads constituted a fundamentally interdependent technological challenge during the earliest years of their use, because many

As shown below, the industry's vertically integrated firms—particularly IBM—have dominated the most-demanding tiers of the market, while non-integrated manufacturers such as Quantum and Western Digital held the largest shares in the least-demanding end of the market.[15]

4.3 The Computer Industry

We do not have a similar set of detailed, component-level data for the computer industry as for disk drives, but it appears that a similar pattern holds in this industry as well. Products in the most performance-demanding tiers of the market are architecturally interdependent and proprietary and are supplied by integrated companies. The architectures of products targeted at progressively less performance-intensive tiers of the market are progressively more modular and are supplied by progressively less-integrated companies.

In the early years of digital computing, when the functionality of available products fell short of what the mainstream markets needed, the computer industry was dominated by integrated players such as IBM. Even today, the most demanding tiers of the mission-critical enterprise server business continue to be dominated by integrated companies such as Hewlett-Packard, IBM, and Silicon Graphics. Their products are technologically interdependent, built around proprietary reduced instruction set computer (RISC) microprocessors and proprietary UNIX operating systems whose key properties are interdependently designed and manufactured, largely in-house. The performance of their products has overshot what is utilized in all but the most demanding tiers of the market—where unit volumes are so small, in fact, that Silicon Graphics' once-spectacular growth trajectory has sputtered.

Products in the next-lower tiers of the server business are more modular in character. Sun Microsystems' Solaris operating system, for example, is rapidly becoming a standard. Predictably, this market tier is dominated by less-integrated manufacturers. Sun, for example, continues to design its own microprocessor and operating system but licenses them to competitors and outsources fabrication. Sun is aggressively pushing up-market to disrupt Hewlett-Packard, IBM, and Silicon Graphics, carrying its more modular architecture with it in the process.[16]

The less-demanding tiers comprising the business computing market are dominated by suppliers such as Compaq, Dell, and Gateway, whose products are consummately modular. These firms are not integrated; most components in their products are supplied by specialist companies. Manufacturing and the in-bound and out-bound logistics are often managed by contractors such as Solectron, and even the design of some products is being out-sourced. Dell, in particular, leverages its status as a non-integrated assembler of modular products to conveniently customize its computers to the specifications of individual customers and deliver the machines to their doorsteps within 48 hours. These firms began their histories squarely in the personal computer space and have aggressively carried modularity and disintegration up-market, disruptively stealing market share in the workstation and server space from Sun. As components get more capable, the non-integrated companies carry their modular architecture up-market—hence, disintegration is occurring in progressively more demanding tiers of the market.

4.4 Mortgage Banking

The mortgage banking industry has historically been dominated by integrated institutions such as savings banks and savings and loans institutions, which collected and serviced deposits, originated loans, evaluated borrowers' credit worthiness, assessed property values, closed loans, and serviced them. In terms of the definition of modularity noted above, there were no standard ways to measure the riskiness of a loan made to any borrower, and as a result, markets could not emerge at the interface of these stages of value-added.

Asset securitization and credit scoring systems that originated in the credit card industry essentially replaced bank officers' judgement with simple metrics —they brought modularity. With credit scoring came

---

elements of the drive's design were interdependent with elements of the thin film head design. This supports the point suggested above that when new technologies are used their interactions with other elements in the system design are not well understood.

[15] Some readers of earlier drafts of this paper have wondered whether, in the lower tiers of truly commoditized product markets, architectures might become interdependent again. If everybody in a significant portion of a market wanted exactly the same features and functions, and their desires were stable over time, the flexibility and options value of modularity might have little value (Baldwin and Clark, 2000). It then might be possible that a single interdependent product design would be a lowest-cost solution.

---

[16] The pattern in which these waves of disruptive technologies are sweeping through the tiers of the computing market is described in greater detail in Christensen and Verlinden (1999).

knowledge of which attributes of the borrower needed to be specified, and technology for measuring those attributes became known. Likewise, asset securitization transformed loans from non-standard assets with uncertain risks and returns to standardized units with easily measured risk and return. Credit scoring and securitization took root in the 1960s in the lowest tier of the lending market—credit cards of retailers such as Sears. These then migrated up-market, usurping open credit cards, auto loans, mortgage loans, and, most recently, small business loans. In each of these market tiers, integrated commercial and savings banks have been replaced by a horizontally stratified population of specialist firms such as MBNA, GMAC, GE Capital, Countrywide, and FNMA. Integrated banks' share of the mortgage market, for example, has eroded from over 90% in the 1960s to 39% by 1999. A population of specialized firms now originate most mortgages, perform credit checks, value collateral, close loans, and service them (Hodes and Hall, 1999).

4.5 Disintegration of the Microprocessor Industry

Our final case is the microprocessor industry. Although the microprocessor is a component within a modular personal computer, the microprocessor itself is a complex, technologically interdependent system. Projects to develop next-generation microprocessor platforms consume time and resources of a magnitude similar to those that were required to design new mainframe computers. Intel is an integrated company, designing for itself each element of the microprocessor in an interdependent, iterative process. Its "copy exactly" method of transferring designs into volume production is a testament to the complex and poorly understood interdependencies between design and manufacturing.

While the speed of complex instruction set (CISC) microprocessors has gotten fast enough that Intel and AMD are disrupting RISC microprocessor-based machines in the higher tiers of the market, their products have overshot the speed that typically is utilized in mainstream business applications. In fact, Monroe (1999) has shown that the Moore's Law pace at which transistors are being made available per area of silicon is outstripping the ability of circuit designers to utilize transistors by 40% each year. As a consequence, in the less performance-demanding tiers of the market, the architecture of microprocessors, such as the Intel Celeron processor, is becoming more modular (interview with Mr. Randy

Steck, Intel Architecture Labs, July 1999). And at the lowest end, for those chips in hand-held wireless digital appliances, companies like Tensilica have begun to offer web-based tools that enable applications developers to assemble from modular components custom-designed microprocessors and systems-on-a-chip whose features and functionality are tuned exactly to the requirements of the application. Design cycles for these modular microprocessors are measured in weeks, rather than years (Bass and Christensen, 2002).

The findings of Macher (2001) support these assertions. He has shown that integrated semiconductor manufacturers perform better than non-integrated ones in the most performance-demanding tiers of the market, whereas the opposite is the case in less-demanding tiers. Furthermore, with clearer design-for-manufacturing rules as an interface, chips positioned away from the leading edge are increasingly being fabricated in independent silicon foundries, which he shows are able to bring products to market much more rapidly than integrated firms.

4.6 Synthesis Across These Cases

Exhibit 4 summarizes the patterns revealed in this set of cases. It lists down the left-most column the causal chain in the model we are proposing. For each of the industries we have studied, an X in the cells of the table indicates where that phenomenon was observed.

4.7 Case Studies in Reintegration

The trajectory maps in Exhibits 1 and 2 suggest that the predominant business model in many industries generally will evolve from integrated firms toward non-integrated, specialized business models. But on occasion the trend has reversed itself, back towards integration. Other financial reasons for reintegration are considered in Section 5. The factor that seems to have driven the reascendance of integration as a source of competitive advantage, however, was the occurrence of a "performance gap"—an upward shift in the functionality that customers needed. In terms of Exhibits 1 and 2, this involves an upward shifting of the dotted, gently sloping lines to a new height. The emergence of these performance gaps can throw an industry back into a "Region A" situation, as depicted in Exhibit 2. When this happens, it demands again true managerial and technological reintegration, as innovators through unstructured technical dialogue are again forced to piece the components of their products together in unconventional and untested ways, in order to

EXHIBIT 4   Supporting Evidence in Case Studies for Key Elements of the Model

	Disk drives	Computers	Financial services	Micro- processors
1. At the outset, when available functionality is insufficient to meet customer needs in mainstream tiers of the market, product architectures are interdependent.	X	X	X	X
2. The industry is dominated at this time by vertically integrated firms.	X	X	X	X
3. The functionality provided by the leading integrated firms overshoots what customers in lower tiers of the market can utilize and are willing to pay for.	X	X		X
4. The basis of competition in those tiers of the market that are over-served in functionality changes. Speed to market and the ability to conveniently customize features and functions become competitively important.	X	X		X
5. Product architectures become modular to facilitate competition on new dimensions.	X	X	X	X
6. Modularity enables non-integrated firms to compete. In those tiers of the market in which overshooting and modularity have occurred, the industry tends to disintegrate; a horizontally stratified population of specialist firms displaces integrated ones.	X	X	X	X
7. Because the pace of technological progress proceeds faster than the ability of customers in given tiers of the market to absorb it, the sequence of events in steps 1–6 above recurs, in each progressively more demanding tier of the market.	X	X	X	X

push performance as close as possible to what customers have begun to demand. The following sections describe in some detail why and how this happened in disk drives and then recount a similar pattern in the software industry as well.

4.8 Reintegration in Disk Drives

Through most of the 1990s the 3.5-inch drive market was largely in Region B of Exhibit 2. These drives were used primarily in desktop personal computers, and their capacity—as big as 60 GB—had substantially overshot what customers actually were able to utilize in the mainstream tiers of that market. As shown above, the architecture of drives sold into this market was increasingly modular, especially in its less-demanding tiers. This meant that components from a variety of suppliers could be mixed and matched with predictable results in new product designs. This market, consequently, was dominated by less integrated companies—Seagate, Quantum, Western Digital, and Maxtor. IBM, the most extensively integrated competitor, has barely been able to sustain a foothold in that market.[17]

The 2.5-inch disk drive market, in contrast, was in Region A. Even though they emerged chronologically after the 3.5-inch drive, the functionality of 2.5-inch drives used in notebook computers was not yet good enough. The reason? Computer users attempted to use notebook computers for essentially the same applications as they used desktop computers. Because the 2.5-inch drives in notebooks have one-sixth the surface area for recording than their 3.5-inch desktop siblings,[18] for most of the

---

[17] We have deliberately used the term "less integrated" rather than "non-integrated" here because, by this point in the industry's history, all of these firms were integrated to some extent, positioned at various points along the spectrum. Seagate (especially after having acquired

Conner Peripherals) had a thriving disk-making operation and had a magneto-resistive (MR) head operation that was beginning to bear fruit. It had deep expertise in thin film head-making. Quantum designed its controller circuitry but outsourced everything else, including manufacturing. It had attempted to begin making MR heads by purchasing Digital Equipment's disk drive business but stumbled badly. By 1998 it had essentially passed the MR head hot potato to Matsushita Kotobuki Electric (MKE), its manufacturing partner, and MKE was laboring to learn how to make and integrate the heads. Western Digital and Maxtor were the least integrated. IBM was by far the most extensively integrated—especially in the linkages between its components, its research activities that supported advanced-technology components, and its read-write channel design activities. The main differences in integration between IBM and Seagate are in IBM's extensive research activities and in the manner in which IBM's engineers seem to be able to integrate their pieces of value-added—especially at the partial response, maximum likelihood (PRML)–MR head interface.

[18] Each 2.5-inch disk has half the recording area of a 3.5-inch disk, but because the 2.5-inch form factor is used in notebook computers, it must be much thinner, allowing fewer disks to be stacked on a spindle than in the 3.5-inch architecture.

1990s notebook computer users were largely dissatisfied with the capacity, weight, and power consumption of 2.5-inch drives. As a result, 2.5-inch drives were built around MR heads and PRML error detection codes—complex, non-standard technologies that required interdependent, iterative design processes in order to wring as much performance as possible out of these new technologies.[19]

The 2.5-inch drive market was dominated by the industry's most technologically integrated companies—IBM, Toshiba, Hitachi, and Fujitsu. Although this market had been served for a few years at its outset by non-integrated firms, as the character of customers' needs became clear, the non-integrated players with their modular product architectures were completely driven from that market. Their share fell from 96% in 1990 to 13% in 1996 and 3% in 1998, as the integrated firms learned to focus their diverse technological capabilities on the customers' needs for maximum recording density. Evidence of the re-ascendance of the integrated business model is summarized in Exhibit 5.

There is now some evidence that the capacity trajectory of 2.5-inch drives has begun to intersect with the capacity demanded in the notebook computer marketplace. This portends another pendulum swing towards modular architectures, shifting competitive advantage back toward non-integrated competitors in this particular market.

Chesbrough and Kusunoki (2001) describe the difficulties that non-integrated firms have escaping the "modularity trap" when an industry passes through a "technology phase shift," suggesting that if they consciously and capably manage the swings between interdependence and modularity, integrated firms ought to have long-term performance advantages over non-integrated firms. Our work supports their finding and perhaps adds a bit more specificity about the causes of "technology phase shifts," the "double helix" pattern that Fine (1998) observed, and the "architectural reconfigurations" that Henderson and Clark (1990) examined.

4.9 Personal Computer Software

Just like the 2.5-inch disk drive market, the personal computer software market when it coalesced was populated by non-integrated companies. Microsoft's DOS constituted a standard interface into which non-integrated software vendors such as WordPerfect, Borland, Lotus, and Harvard Graphics could "plug" their modules. But within a few years, as customers came to understand what they wanted, a "performance gap" emerged—PC users began demanding the ability to transport portions of graphics, spreadsheets, and word processing files into other types of file. This performance gap demanded integration, and Microsoft responded by creating non-standard, interdependent connections amongst its Windows operating system and its suite of office applications—and later its Internet Explorer. Almost overnight, Microsoft's non-integrated competitors vaporized.[20]

Today, however, the pendulum seems to be swinging in the other direction. The functionality and number of features in most of Microsoft's products have dramatically overshot what most of its customers actually are able to use. Non-integrated software firms writing to disruptive Internet protocols and the Java programming language, with their modular architectures, are capturing a

---

[19]Evidence that the architecture of 2.5-inch disk drives is interdependent rather than modular comes from many sources. This first was a set of twenty-four interviews conducted with engineering managers at IBM, the industry's most integrated company; Seagate, a partially integrated firm; Quantum, a non-integrated assembler of drives; and Read-Rite and Komag, which were non-integrated suppliers of heads and disks, respectively. In every case, they noted that in using PRML codes and MR heads (defined below) to maximize the density of 2.5-inch drives, they could not work with suppliers because they could not specify what suppliers had to deliver and could not measure what attributes of the heads were most critical for maximizing performance. They all attributed IBM's success in this market to its ability to conduct all of the required design and manufacturing in-house, in integrated teams. We also conducted statistical analyses of the phenomena, showing how the statistical significance of interaction terms between components in the regression equations described in the Appendix varied across 3.5-inch and 2.5-inch drives. We have not included those results in this paper because of length constraints, but they point to the same conclusion. Drives whose functionality is nearer to the frontier of feasibility have more interdependence in their architectures. The interdependency between these technologies occurs in what engineers in the industry call "the channel." MR heads offer a completely different, and much more sensitive, method for detecting changes in the flux field on a disk than prior inductive head technology—enabling much smaller magnetic domains to be created on disks. PRML software algorithms detect when errors in reading data might have occurred and, based upon patterns in other data, estimate what the missing or erroneous data are. The ability to maximize recording density by using the most advanced MR heads depends upon the ability of PRML coders to identify and correct error patterns, which arise because of the way the heads are designed. Both pieces of technology must be done interdependently. This is not the case with the technologies that are used away from the frontier of possibility, such as inductive thin film heads and run-length-limited (RLL) error-correction codes. Both can be procured and used off the shelf from third parties.

[20]It seems that the foresight of Microsoft's management team is a common interpretation of why Microsoft made this move toward interdependent architectures, whereas firms that were managed by less aggressive or competent teams, such as WordPerfect, Novell, and Lotus, missed this opportunity. To provoke discussion, we are specifically proposing that there is a more fundamental causality behind what happened: the performance gap forced integration, and Microsoft was in the best position to respond.

EXHIBIT 5 Contrast in 1998 Market Shares Held by Non-Integrated Versus Integrated Companies in the Over-Satisfied 3.5-Inch Market and the Under-Satisfied 2.5-Inch Market

Market shares in the 3.5-inch market (%)		Market shares in the 2.5-inch market (%)	
Integrated firms	8	Integrated firms	97
IBM	4	IBM	67
Toshiba	1	Toshiba	21
Hitachi	2	Hitachi	5
Fujitsu	1	Fujitsu	4
Less-integrated firms	87	Less-integrated firms	1
Seagate/Conner	33	Seagate/Conner	0
Quantum	23	Quantum	0
Western Digital	23	Western Digital	0
Maxtor	8	Maxtor	1
Others	5	Others	2
Total	100	Total	100

Source: Disk/Trend Report, 1999.

dominant share of Internet-oriented applications, in a classic disruptive technology fashion. Linux, an operating system whose modular architecture enables opensource devotees independently to maintain and improve elements of the system, is beginning to disintegrate certain tiers of the market as well.

These cases of reintegration constitute what Yin (1984) calls *theoretical* replications of the model proposed in this paper. The model suggests that overshooting the functionality required in a tier of the market precipitates a change in the basis of competition, which in turn causes product or service architectures to evolve from interdependency toward modularity. This in turn causes industry structures to evolve from vertical integration towards specialized stratification. In the cases described immediately above, the emergence of functionality gaps, or "under-shooting" caused this process to reverse itself towards integration.

5. SHIFTS IN THE LOCUS OF PROFITS

Our research also suggests that the stages of value-added in which attractive profits can be made tend to differ from the left to the right sides of the disruptive technologies map. During eras characterized by Region A in Exhibit 2, the largest vertically integrated firms, which engage in designing and assembling architecturally interdependent end-use products whose performance is not yet good enough, tend to capture a disproportionate share of their industry's profits. During the eras of horizontal stratification described as Region B, in contrast, the firms engaged in those same stages of value-added—

where more-than-good-enough modular products are designed and assembled—typically find it very difficult to earn more than subsistence profits. Whereas component suppliers tend to struggle to be profitable in Region A, in Region B the firms that supply technologically interdependent subsystems to the assemblers make the lion's share of profit.

The reason why the ability to earn attractive profits flips is that two factors that drive the ability to earn unusual profits—steep scale economics and the ability to create differentiated products—favor designers/assemblers in Region A and subsystem suppliers in Region B. In the next section we will recount in some detail how and why this happened in the disk drive industry and then suggest how the same phenomenon seems to be occurring in the computer, telecommunications, and automobile industries as well.

5.1 The Narrowing Scope for Differentiation

Modularity brings benefits of speed, lower cost, and technological flexibility, as Baldwin and Clark (2000) have described. Indeed, adopting modular product architectures is critical to survival in a world where, as suggested in Exhibit 2, the basis of competition centers upon speed to market and the ability to conveniently customize features and functions to the needs of specific sets of customers. Without modular architectures and disintegrated business models, firms in Region B simply could not compete effectively.

The downside of modularity is that it seems also to narrow the ability of competitors to differentiate their products through superior design. This was demonstrated in the analysis summarized in Exhibit 3, which described how the variability in the architectural efficiency of disk drives dropped as product architectures became more modular. In addition to losing the ability to differentiate products on the basis of performance, the designers and assemblers of modular products also lose their ability to differentiate on the basis of cost. The cost structure of non-integrated design/assembly firms tends to be dominated by variable, rather than fixed, costs. Because it is high fixed costs that give rise to steep scale economics, assemblers of modular products compete on relatively flat scale curves, meaning that small competitors can enjoy similar costs as larger ones.

In an attempt to illustratively measure the flattening of scale economics in a modular world, we collected data on the unit volumes, total costs, and product line complexity for each disk drive manufacturer and built a regression model that allowed us to estimate each manufacturer's cost, during each year, to produce a drive of a given capacity. The equation takes the form

$$\ln(\text{Product Cost}) = B_0 + B_1 \ln(\text{Drive Capacity}) + B_2 \ln(\text{Total Units Produced}) + B_3 \ln(\text{Product Line Complexity})$$

The variables are defined as follows: *Product Cost* is calculated by dividing the total operating costs in the company, exclusive of interest and taxes, by the number of disk drive units produced. Hence, we call this measure *fully allocated product cost*. *Drive Capacity* is the weighted average capacity of the disk drive units shipped each year by the company. This is an important variable, because higher-capacity drives are more costly to produce. We expected the coefficient of this variable to be positive. *Total Units Produced* is the total number of disk drives shipped during the year. We expected the coefficient of this variable to be negative, positing that as scale increased, unit costs would fall. *Product Line Com-*

plexity is the number of product families produced by the company in the year. We expected the coefficients of this variable to be positive—overhead costs per unit would increase as increasing complexity of the product line would demand higher management overheads.

All of the data required for this calculation were taken from *Disk/Trend Report*. The equation for the early 1980s, when modular architectures were just beginning to penetrate the industry, was

$$\ln(\text{cost/unit}) = 296.39 - 0.146(\text{year}) - 0.370 \ln(\text{unit volume}) + 0.126 \ln(\text{no. of families}) + 0.511 \ln(\text{weighted mean MB/unit})$$

t-statistics: $(-3.44)\ (-4.70)\ (1.68)\ (6.23)\ R^2 = 0.88$

The equation for the early 1990s, when modular architectures had become pervasive, was

$$\ln(\text{cost/unit}) = 322.22 - 0.160(\text{year}) - 0.15 \ln(\text{unit volume}) + 0.014 \ln(\text{no. of families}) + 0.544 \ln(\text{weighted mean MB/unit})$$

t-statistics: $(3.41)\ (-0.52)\ (0.12)\ (4.20)\ R^2 = 0.88$

Note how the scale coefficient fell and became statistically insignificant, as did the complexity coefficient (no. of families). We would expect both in a regime of modularity.

We estimated this equation for each year. The coefficient B_2 constituted a measure of the steepness of the scale economics in disk drive manufacturing at each point in the industry's history. Using this equation, we could then estimate what it would cost each manufacturer to make a drive of a given capacity, given the scale at which it produced in any year and the complexity of its product line, measured by the number of product families. The scale curve as it looked in the late 1980s is shown in Exhibit 6, which charts the fully allocated costs on the vertical axis and each firm's production volumes

EXHIBIT 6   Scale Economics in the Design and Assembly of Modular 3.5-Inch Drives in the Late 1980s

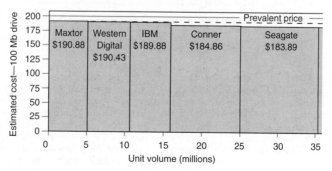

on the horizontal axis for a typical modular 100 MB 3.5-inch drive. It shows that the scale economics in design and assembly of modular disk drive designs were flat—small competitors could add this value almost as cost-effectively as the largest firms—because the cost structure was dominated by variable rather than fixed costs.

For the makers of modular disk drives, competition in the absence of performance and cost differentiability has been difficult and unrewarding. It is the users of disk drives, not the manufacturers, who have reaped the benefits of lower cost, more flexibility, and greater speed in product development that result from modularity. Typical gross margins for high-volume drives used in desktop personal computing fell from 35% in 1984 to become mired in the 10–15% range in the last years of that decade.

5.2 The Profitability of Component Manufacture

While the business of design and assembly of modular drives was a wearying race on an accelerating treadmill in Region B of Exhibit 2, the business of making heads and disks during this same period shifted progressively to Region A of Exhibit 2. In order to force the cost of disk drives ever-lower, designers could never be satisfied with the functionality (recording density achievable) of heads and disks—because the higher the recording density, the fewer the number of disk platters and heads required in the drive. As a consequence, over this period heads and disks themselves become more technologically interdependent assemblies of materials, creating substantial scope for product differentiation. The high fixed costs of designing and manufacturing thin film disks and MR heads steepened the scale economics in this slice of value-added as well. Exhibit 7 shows, for example, that Komag, the largest independent disk manufacturer (which also made the highest-performance disks in the industry),[21] had substantially lower costs than its competitors. Because products were differentiable and scale economics were steep, the leading independent component makers were highly profitable. In contrast to the 11% annual rate of return that the shareholders of non-

integrated disk drive assemblers received between 1988 and 1994, the leading component makers, Komag and Read-Rite, returned 38% annually to their shareholders.

In response to this shift in the stage of value-added in which attractive profits could be earned, some leading assemblers of drives began producing their own components. Exhibit 7 makes it easy to see why. Although their costs of production were higher than Komag's, the price at which assemblers were buying disks from Komag was determined where the supply and demand curves intersected—at the cost of the *marginal* supplier in the market—Akashic. As long as their scale enabled them to produce at greater volumes than the marginal supplier, and as long as the scale curve sloped steeply enough, these companies found disk-making to be a more attractive slice of value-added in which to participate than was design and assembly (see footnote 21). Hence, one of the leading non-integrated assemblers, Conner Peripherals, built an independent business to manufacture disks; and another, Seagate, developed businesses to make both disks and heads, which involved even steeper scale economics. These firms initially made components for internal consumption only, but ultimately found it compelling to sell to competing assemblers as well.[22] A number of analysts, in fact, reported that for many years in the 1990s over 100% of these firms' profits could be attributed to the value they captured in component manufacturing operations (meaning that they lost money in design and assembly). IBM subsequently has followed suit in selling components into the market as well.

It is important to note that while economists might call these firms' migration into making components "vertical integration," it would be more accurate to say that they established managerially and technologically independent business positions in the component-manufacturing stage of value-added. This stemmed from a very different motivation and entailed a very different management structure than did the requirement to create new, interdependent product architectures, built through

---

[21] The sources of these data were *Trend/Focus,* an annual market research report on the industry supplying components to the disk drive assemblers, and the engineering staff at Komag. Exhibit 7 was constructed with an economic model built in conjunction with the engineering staff at Komag, which estimated the cost of producing a disk of a given quality at various volumes. By inserting *Trend/Focus* data into the model, we developed estimates of the production costs of various competitors.

[22] By the late 1990s, Komag's profits had plummeted. But in an odd way, its collapse supports the thesis of this section. So many disk drive assemblers had been enticed into making their own disks because of the profitability of disk-making relative to final product assembly, that little merchant-market volume was available to Komag by the late 1990s. Its costs consequently rose and its profitability was decimated. But it was the profits that attracted the assemblers into disks, and not the requirement for technological and managerial coordination that drove this move to vertical integration. A similar fate befell Read-Rite, at least temporarily. Especially with the advent of magneto-resistive heads in the mid-1990s—an immature technology with steep scale economics—the design/assembly firms that could afford it brought as much head-making capacity in-house as possible.

EXHIBIT 7   Supply Curve for the Thin Film Disk Industry, 1994

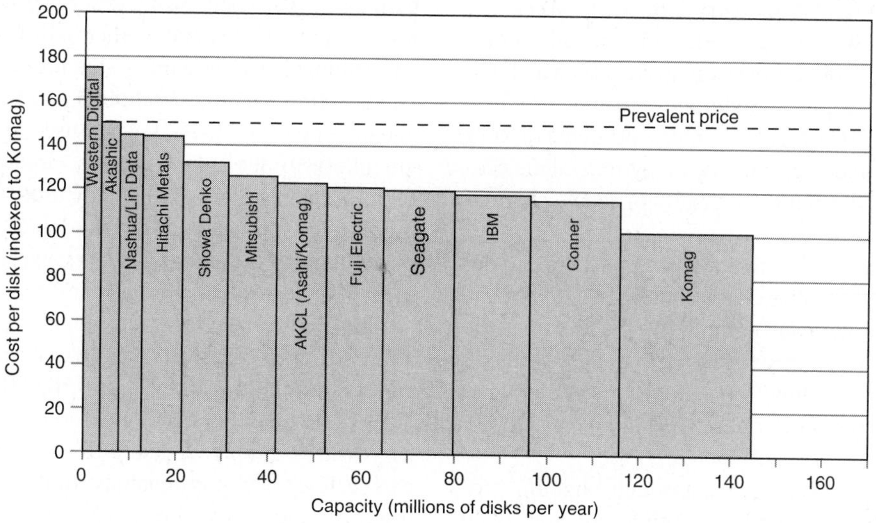

unstructured technical dialogue in response to the performance gaps described above.

Our conclusion, in essence, is that attractive profits tend to be earned where performance is not yet adequate relative to the needs of user in the next stage of value-added and where, therefore, product architectures are likely to be proprietary and interdependent in character. Because the pace of performance improvement typically outstrips the ability of customers to utilize that improvement, the places in the value chain that presently enjoy attractive profitability are likely to lose their ability to continue those levels of profitability, and vice versa. In the following, we will summarize how this same shift in the ability of designers/assemblers versus component suppliers to capture attractive profits occurred in computers and is beginning to happen in the automobile industry.

5.3 Shift in the Locus of Profitability in the Computer Industry

The largest firms that designed and assembled computers in the technologically interdependent era—particularly IBM and Digital Equipment—captured extraordinary profits because of the differentiability of their products and the high fixed costs (and consequently steep scale economics) in design and manufacturing. They wielded such power that most of their parts suppliers survived at subsistence levels of profitability. But, as personal computers with modular architectures came to dominate mainstream markets, the tables turned. How does a de-

signer of a modular personal computer in a firm such as Compaq create a better product than competitors such as Dell, Gateway, Hewlett-Packard, or IBM? Incorporate a faster microprocessor? A higher capacity hard drive? More megabytes of DRAM? In a consummately modular product there are so few degrees of design freedom that the only way to offer a better product is to offer higher-performance components, which competitors can also offer. When most costs are variable, the scale curve flattens substantially: it becomes difficult to assemble at lower costs too. As speed to market and the ability to mass-customize become the only dimensions along which assemblers of modular products can compete, firms in this stage of value-added can find competition to be an unrewarding race on an accelerating treadmill.[23]

The impact on the profitability of design and assembly in the computer value-added chain has been predictable. "In 1986, companies that built and sold computer systems captured about 80% of the total profits being generated in the computer industry. By 1991, however, systems makers were getting just 20%. The market

---

[23] The first firms to identify how the basis of competition amongst assemblers of modular products in over-served tiers of the market shifts to speed and customization can, in fact, do well for a time. This was certainly the case with Dell Computer and Chrysler, for example. The operations-based abilities to compete in these terms against other assemblers, however, can be replicated, as Porter (1996) notes. One of the foremost prophets of time-based competition, George Stalk, recognized the same unattractive end-game for modular assemblers (Stalk and Hout, 1990; Stalk, 1993).

re-allocated profits to the components makers" ("Deconstructing the Computer Industry," *Business Week,* 23 November 1992: 90–96). Indeed, in the modular era it has been interdependent subsystem makers such as Intel, Microsoft, and Applied Materials—whose products themselves are technologically interdependent, involve high fixed costs, and consequently enjoy steep scale economics—that have captured a disproportionate share of industry profits.

Strategists often use a "five forces" framework to describe where in the value chain competitive advantage and attractive profits can be built. We believe that the mechanism described here may define the dynamic, causal mechanisms behind the somewhat static characterizations of market power described in Porter's (1980, 1985) work.

This implies, of course, that through ongoing processes of overshooting and disruption, we are likely to see yet further shifts in the locus of power to earn profit in this industry. For example, as the functionality of operating systems, microprocessors, and MR heads becomes more than good enough and as disruptive hand-held wireless computing/communication devices emerge (which are not yet good enough) it is very possible that the power to earn attractive profits will migrate away from the "back-end" locations where it has resided to the stage of value-added where the end-use product is designed and assembled. We would welcome any efforts by other scholars to evaluate this hypothesis.[24]

5.4 The World Automotive Industry

Our final "case study" is not historical but is predictive: we will use the model to project how the structure of the world auto industry might evolve in response to the tendencies we have chronicled here. We hope that this case

study will help other scholars visualize better the implications of the mechanisms described above and assess how they might play out in other industries that presently are dominated by large integrated firms. Theory can only be built cumulatively if scholars' explanations of cause and effect can be falsified, when used to predict what we are likely to see under various circumstances (Kuhn, 1962; Kaplan, 1986). We hope that future scholars, looking through the lenses of our model, can see anomalous phenomena as the auto industry evolves, and bring better theory to the academy.

The performance of automobiles has overshot the ability of most customers to utilize it, on several dimensions. Autos today routinely go 150,000 miles and more. They often go out of fashion before they wear out. Many car owners simply cannot utilize even longer-lasting cars. While technology enables comfortably-sized cars to travel 30 and more miles per gallon of fuel (some new hybrid gas-electric vehicles get 80 m.p.g.), consumers' rush toward less efficient sport-utility vehicles suggests that the car makers have overshot on this dimension of performance as well. Although autos are capable of cruising at speeds exceeding 90 miles per hour, traffic laws will not allow it. The list could go on.

The major disruptive innovators in the world automotive industry in the last 30 years have been Japanese firms, such as Toyota, which entered North American and European markets with low-priced offerings and subsequently moved up-market in a classic disruptive fashion. Analysts have noted that a key tool used by these disruptive innovators to control costs and accelerate their product design cycle has been their use of a tiered supplier system (Dyer, 1996). Rather than designing and manufacturing their own components and performing all system design and assembly in-house, as General Motors and Ford traditionally had done, the disruptive Japanese innovators procured subsystems from a limited number of "Tier 1" suppliers, such as Nippon Denso. Their more modular product architectures, and the supplier infrastructure that mirrored them, helped the Japanese disruptors bring new designs to market much more rapidly than their American and European competitors.

Just as in computers, the basis of competition in the mainstream tiers of the automobile market is changing as the functionality of cars has overshot what is actually utilized by customers. Speed to market is increasingly important (Stalk and Hout, 1990; Clark and Fujimoto, 1991). Design cycles, which often took 6 years in the "Region A" era of the industry's history, have been shortened to 2 years today and are converging on 18 months.

---

[24] We have an additional hypothesis. Assemblers of modular products, such as Compaq Computer, increasingly outsource more and more value-added to contract manufacturers. Firms such as Solectron, Celestica, and Flextronics, for example, began as circuit board assemblers. They then integrated forward into assembling computer motherboards. They then advanced into assembling the entire computer; then into managing inbound and outbound supply chain logistics; and most recently, into the design of the products themselves. Why would the contract manufacturers find it attractive to integrate *into* the very stages of value-added that the computer companies found it attractive to get *out* of? The computer makers need to keep improving return on assets. When the assemblers of modular products cannot differentiate in performance or cost, they cannot improve the numerator of the return-on-assets ratio (ROA). They only have leverage over the denominator—they improve ROA—and they do this by outsourcing asset-intensive stages of value-added. This accentuates the "modularity trap" that Chesbrough and Kusunoki (2001) describe.

The ability to conveniently customize the features of each car for specific customers is emerging as a critical differentiator. For example, Toyota recently announced that its customers could custom-order cars for delivery within 5 days (Simison, 1999). The acceleration in time-to-market and improving ability to customize conveniently is being enabled by a steady modularization of the architecture.

To stay abreast of the frenetic pace of product development in the industry, General Motors has disintegrated by bundling its component-making companies into Delphi Corporation and spinning it off. Ford followed suit by spinning off Visteon.

To date, the industry seems to have evolved in a way that is quite consistent with the early steps in our model. If it continues to evolve along the path predicted by the model, we might expect the following developments in the coming years.

Ever-more-modular automobiles, comprised of increasingly standardized subsystems provided by Tier 1 suppliers, will likely take root initially at the lowest tiers of the market, amongst disruptive auto makers whose only hope for gaining a competitive edge is to introduce models faster than the competition and who want to flatten the scale curve.[25] These are firms that will want to be able to design and assemble autos with the lowest ratio of fixed to variable costs possible.[26] We would expect auto makers in the more sophisticated tiers of the market to remain more vertically integrated, longer into the future, than would auto makers at the low end.

As the Tier 1 module suppliers experience the freedom to make trade-offs within the subsystem in order to minimize cost and optimize performance, subject to the interface constraints specified by the car companies, the internal architecture of the subsystem will become progressively more interdependent. The Tier 1 suppliers will begin to see interactions amongst the components that they were unable to see when they were fragmented suppliers of individual parts. Hence, the performance of subsystems from different suppliers is likely to become more differentiated.

At the outset, the subsystems from which the modular autos will be built are unlikely to interface with each other according to industry standards—the interface specifications will continue to be detailed by the car designers. But there will likely come a point when cars come to be designed around the interface specifications that Tier 1 suppliers articulate.

The number of suppliers of subsystems in the world industry is then likely to drop, as a result of steepening scale economics in design and manufacturing of those interdependent products. In contrast, the scale economics in the design and manufacture of cars are likely to flatten, as the job of designing and assembling modular cars becomes ever simpler. In fact, it will become increasingly possible to design and accurately simulate the performance of cars on a computer. The number of auto brands, therefore, is likely to maintain steady or even increase, as barriers to entry erode.

Ironically, even though the functionality of cars has overshot what consumers can actually utilize, car makers will continue to strive to offer products that are better than the competition. Customers will be reluctant to pay for the superfluous functionality, but, given the choice between equally priced autos, consumers will always accept the one with better performance, even though they will pay little for it. This means that car makers that refuse to keep racing up-market will lose share and profits. Because the designs are modular, however, the only way for car companies to differentiate the performance of their products from those of competitors will be to offer the best subsystems. This means that, by definition, suppliers of subsystems will be in Region A, even as their customers, the car makers, are in Region B. Hence, the internal architecture of the subsystems will increasingly become interdependent. It will therefore be difficult for focused firms that make only one or a few of the components comprising the subsystem to survive.

As the automobile becomes progressively more modular and the subsystems more interdependent, the ability to capture a disproportionate share of the industry's profits will migrate from the car makers to the Tier 1 subsystem suppliers. This probably will not be the case with all subsystems in the automobile, however. Extraordinary profits will accrue to those suppliers whose subsystems are in Region A, which forces their designs toward the interdependent end of the architectural spectrum.

---

[25] Maynard (1998) points out that even General Motors is seriously considering implementing modular designs and assembly lines at the *low* end of its product line.

[26] Chrysler's recent entry into the Brazilian automobile market is an example of this. Because Chrysler was the thirteenth company to enter the Brazilian market, it could not justify the typical investment (usually hundreds of millions of dollars) required to build a traditional assembly facility, given the initial market share it could reasonably expect to capture. In order to achieve profitability at low volumes, Chrysler's strategy has been to modularize both the vehicle design and the assembly process. A few suppliers design and build major subsystems in their own plants. They deliver these major modules to the Chrysler line, where the modules fit together in far fewer steps, with far less capital investment, than typically required (White, 1998).

Subsystems which themselves perform beyond what the car makers need, and are therefore architecturally modular, are unlikely to generate abnormally attractive profits. Hence, the strategies that integrated manufacturers such as General Motors and Ford have followed in spinning off their components operations in order to be more cost- and speed-competitive in the stage of value-added where attractive profits formerly were made, mirror almost exactly IBM's decision to out-source the microprocessor and operating system to Intel and Microsoft, so that it could continue to design and assemble personal computers.

5.5 Implications for Integration and Outsourcing Strategies

We hope this model can add insights to two pieces of prevailing wisdom about industry structure and outsourcing. The first is about the general trend seen in most industries, where dominant, integrated firms over time give way to a horizontally stratified population of specialized firms (Chesbrough and Teece, 1996; Grove, 1996). Our contribution is that the causal mechanism that precipitates the vertical disintegration of industries may be the overshooting of the functionality that actually is utilized in certain tiers of the market. Overshooting precipitates a change in the basis of competition towards speed to market and the ability to conveniently customize features and functions. This, in turn, requires the modularization of product architectures which, finally, enables industry disintegration or deconstruction (Langlois and Robertson, 1992). This means that we would expect integrated firms to remain strong in tiers of the market that are under-served by the functionality of prevailing products and that industries will trend toward reintegration when shifts in what customers demand cause performance gaps to emerge.

The second insight relates to the simple rule that managers and consultants use in making outsourcing decisions—that firms should outsource components or services if it is not their core competence, or if somebody else can do it at lower cost. This logic almost always makes compelling sense on the surface. But this research suggests that this logic can lead a firm to outsource those pieces of value-added in which most of the industry's profit will be made in the future—and to retain activities in which it is difficult to create enduring, differentiable advantages versus competitors. Although these hypotheses require further study, it appears that the assemblers of modular items at any stage of the value chain—whether they be end-use products, subsystems, or components—

are likely to struggle to achieve competitive advantage and to earn attractive profits. Attractive profitability seems to flow from the point of customer contact back through the product system to the point at which unsatisfied demand for functionality, and therefore technological interdependency, exists. Hence, these dynamics can cause the point of attractive profitability to shift from the system provider to the subsystem or component providers—from the front end to the back end to the front end again—as these dynamics work through an industry.

ADDRESS FOR CORRESPONDENCE

Clayton M. Christensen, Harvard Business School.

REFERENCES

Abernathy, W., and J. Utterback (1978), "Patterns of industrial innovation," *Technology Review,* **50** (June–July), 40–47.

Adner, R. (1999), "A demand-based view of the emergence of competition: Demand structure and technology displacement," working paper, Insead.

Adner, R., and D. Levinthal (2001), "Demand heterogeneity and technology evolution: Implications for product and process innovation," *Management Science,* **47,** 611–628.

Adner, R., and P. Zemsky (2001), "Disruptive technologies and the emergence of competition," working paper, Insead.

Baldwin, C. Y., and K. B. Clark (1997), "Managing in an age of modularity," *Harvard Business Review,* **75**(September–October), 84–93.

Baldwin, C. Y., and K. B. Clark (2000), *Design Rules: The Power of Modularity.* MIT Press: Cambridge, MA.

Bass, M. J., and C. M. Christensen (2002), "The future of the microprocessor business," *IEEE Spectrum,* **39**(April), 34–39.

Becker, G. S., and K. M. Murphy (1992), "The division of labor, coordination cost, and knowledge," *Quarterly Journal of Economics,* **107,** 1137–1160.

Billington, C., and L. Fleming (1998), "Technological evolution, standard interfaces, and new market opportunities," *POMS Series in Technology and Operations Management,* 30–41.

Bower, J. L., and C. M. Christensen (1995), "Disruptive technologies: Catching the wave," *Harvard Business Review,* January–February.

Chandler, A. D. (1977), *The Visible Hand.* The Belknap Press of Harvard University Press: Cambridge, MA.

Chesbrough, H. W., and K. Kusunoki (2001), "The modularity trap: Innovation, technology phase shifts and the resulting limits of virtual organizations," in I. Nonaka and D. J. Teece (eds.), *Managing Industrial Knowledge.* Sage: London, ch. 10.

Chesbrough, H. W., and D. J. Teece (1996), "When is virtual virtuous?" *Harvard Business Review,* **74**(January–February), 65–74.

Christensen, C. (1992a), "Exploring the limits of the technology S-curve (parts 1 and 2)," *Production and Operations Management,* **1**, 334–366.

Christensen, C. M. (1992b), "The innovator's challenge," unpublished DBA thesis, Harvard Business School.

Christensen, C. M. (1993), "The rigid disk drive industry: A history of commercial and technological turbulence," *Business History Review,* **67**, 531–588.

Christensen, C. M. (1994), "The drivers of vertical disintegration," Harvard Business School working paper.

Christensen, C. M. (1996), "Patterns in the evolution of product competition," *European Management Journal,* **15**, 117–127.

Christensen, C. M. (1997), *The Innovator's Dilemma: When New Technologies Cause Great Firms to Fail.* Harvard Business School Press: Boston, MA.

Christensen, C. M. (2001), "The law of conservation of modularity," working paper, Harvard Business School.

Christensen, C. M., and E. Armstrong (1998), "Disruptive technologies: A credible threat to leading programs in continuing medical education?" *The Journal of Continuing Education in the Health Professions,* **18**, 69–80.

Christensen, C. M., and J. L. Bower (1996), "Customer power, strategic investment, and the failure of leading firms," *Strategic Management Journal,* **17**, 197–218.

Christensen, C. M., and R. S. Rosenbloom (1995), "Explaining the attacker's advantage: Technological paradigms, organizational dynamics, and the value network," *Research Policy,* **24**, 233–257.

Christensen, C. M., and R. S. Tedlow (2000), "Patterns of disruption in retailing," *Harvard Business Review,* **78** (January–February), 42–45.

Christensen, C. M., and M. Verlinden (1999), "Hewlett Packard's Merced decision," Harvard Business School case study #9-699-011.

Christensen, C. M., F. Suarez, and J. Utterback (1998), "Strategies for survival in fast-changing industries," *Management Science,* **44**, S207–S220.

Christensen, C. M., R. Bohmer, and J. Kenagy (2000), "Will disruptive innovations cure health care?" *Harvard Business Review,* **78**(September–October), 102–111.

Christensen, C. M., T. Craig, and S. Hart (2001), "The great disruption," *Foreign Affairs,* **80**, 80–95.

Clark, K. B., and T. Fujimoto (1991), *Product Development Performance.* Harvard Business School Press: Boston, MA.

Coase, R. H. (1937), "The nature of the firm," *Economica,* **4**, 386–405.

Demsetz, H. (1988), "The theory of the firm revisited," *Journal of Law, Economics and Organization,* **4**, 141–161.

Disk/Trend Report (1999), Disk/Trend Inc.: Mountain View, CA.

Dyer, J. (1996), "How Chrysler created an American keiretsu," *Harvard Business Review,* **74**(July–August), 42–56.

Fine, C. (1998), *Clockspeed.* Perseus Press: New York.

Fixson, S. (2000), "A taxonomy development: Mapping different product architectures," working paper, Technology, Management and Policy Program, Massachusetts Institute of Technology.

Fleming, L., and O. Sorenson (2001), "Technology as a complex adaptive system: Evidence from patent data," *Research Policy,* **130**, 1019–1039.

Grove, A. S. (1996), *Only the Paranoid Survive.* Doubleday: New York.

Henderson, R., and K. B. Clark (1990), "Architectural innovation: The reconfiguration of existing product technologies and the failure of established firms," *Administrative Science Quarterly,* **35**, 9–30.

Hodes, M. S., and G. W. Hall (1999), "Home run: Taking a closer look at internet mortgage finance," Goldman Sachs Investment Research.

Iansiti, M. (1997), *Technology Integration.* Harvard Business School Press: Boston, MA.

Kaplan, R. (1986), "The role for empirical research in management accounting," *Accounting, Organizations and Society,* **11**, 429–452.

Klein, B., R. Crawford, and A. Alchian (1978), "Vertical integration, appropriable rents, and the competitive contracting process," *Journal of Law and Economics,* **21**, 297–326.

Kuhn, T. (1962), *The Structure of Scientific Revolutions.* The University of Chicago Press: Chicago, IL.

Langlois, R. N. (1994), "Capabilities and vertical disintegration in process technology: The case of semiconductor fabrication equipment," working paper, CCC.

Langlois, R. N., and P. L. Robertson (1992), "Networks and innovation in a modular system: Lessons from the microcomputer and stereo component industries," *Research Policy,* **21**, 297–313.

Macher, J. T. (2001), "Vertical disintegration and process innovation in semiconductor manufacturing: Foundries vs. integrated producers," working paper, Robert E. McDonough School of Business, Georgetown University.

Maynard, M. (1998), "GM considers switch to modular assembly," *USA Today,* December 16, 2B.

Monroe, D. (1999), "The end of scaling: Disruption from below," in S. Luryi, J. Xu, and A. Zaslavsky (eds.), *Future Trends in Microelectronics: Beyond the Beaten Path.* Wiley: New York.

Monteverde, K. (1995), "Technical dialog as an incentive for vertical integration in the semiconductor industry," *Management Science,* **41**, 1624–1638.

Pine, B. J. (1992), *Mass Customization: The New Frontier in Business Competition.* Harvard Business School Press: Boston, MA.

Porter, M. (1980), *Competitive Strategy.* The Free Press: New York.

Porter, M. (1985), *Competitive Advantage.* The Free Press: New York.

Porter, M. (1996), "What is Strategy?" *Harvard Business Review,* **74**(November–December), 61.

Rosenbloom, R. S., and C. M. Christensen (1995), "Technological discontinuities, organizational capabilities, and strategic commitments," *Industrial and Corporate Change,* **3**, 655–685.

Sanchez, R., and J. T. Mahoney (1996), "Modularity, flexibility and knowledge management in product and organization design," *Strategic Management Journal,* **17** (Winter special issue), 63–76.

Simison, R. L. (1999), "Toyota develops a way to make a car within 5 days of a custom order," *Wall Street Journal,* 6 August, A4.

Smith, A. (1776), *The Wealth of Nations* [Modern Library: New York, 1994].

Stalk, G. (1993), "Japan's dark side of time," *Harvard Business Review,* **71**(July–August).

Stalk, G., and T. Hout (1990), *Competing Against Time.* The Free Press: New York.

Stigler, J. (1951), "The division of labor is limited by the extent of the market," *Journal of Political Economy,* **59**, 185–193.

Stuckey, J., and D. White (1993), "When and when not to vertically integrate," *McKinsey Quarterly,* no. 3, 3–27.

Taguchi, G., and D. Clausing (1990), "Robust quality," *Harvard Business Review,* **68**(January–February), 65–75.

Teece, D. (1986), "Profiting from technological innovation: Implications for integration, collaboration, licensing and public policy," *Research Policy,* **15**, 285–305.

Ulrich, K. (1995), "The role of product architecture in the manufacturing firm," *Research Policy,* **24**, 419–440.

Ulrich, K., and S. Eppinger (1995), *Product Design and Development.* McGraw-Hill: New York.

Waid, D. (1989), *Rigid Disk Drive Magnetic Head/Media Market and Technology Report.* Peripheral Research Corporation: Santa Barbara, CA.

White, G. L. (1998), "Chrysler makes inroads at plant in Brazil: modular assembly cuts costs at small factory," *Wall Street Journal Europe,* 14–15 August, 44.

Williamson, O. (1979), "Transactions cost economics: The governance of contractual relations," *Journal of Law and Economics,* **23**, 233–261.

Williamson, O. (1985), *The Economic Institutions of Capitalism.* Prentice-Hall: Englewood Cliffs, NJ.

Yin, R. (1984), *Case Study Research: Design and Methods.* Sage: Beverly Hills, CA.

APPENDIX 1: NOTES ON THE CALCULATION OF ARCHITECTURAL EFFICIENCY

To measure the abilities of different companies to extract performance from any given set of components, we conducted a multivariate regression analysis of the components used in 4334 disk drives introduced in the industry between 1979 and 1997. The equation estimated in this analysis measured the extent to which the year in which a product was introduced and the different components (represented by dummy variables) that were used contributed to the differences in areal recording density (megabits per square inch of disk surface) of different disk drive models. Essentially, the equation derived from this analysis allowed us to estimate, on average for the entire industry, what recording density could be achieved at a given point in time with any set of components. Likewise, the coefficients in this equation measured the improvement in recording density that we would expect the average engineer in the industry to have achieved by using each new component technology.

This equation was used to estimate the areal density that each disk drive manufacturer should have been able to achieve at the time each of its models was introduced, given the set of components used in that model. The ratio of the actual recording density of the product to the predicted density was termed the *architectural efficiency* of the drive. A ratio of 1.2 meant that the company's engineers got 20% greater density out of a given set of components than was average for the industry, whereas one of 0.8 meant that the company succeeded in only getting 80% of the recording density that would have been average for the industry, given the components that were used.

Iansiti (1997) introduced the concept of "technological yield." This is a measure of the differences in product performance that stem from clever product design, rather than from use of superior components.

Exhibit A1 presents the coefficients of variables in the equations that were estimated. The dependent variable in each case was the log of areal density. Following Christensen (1992a,b), the reference components were those in common use in 1979. In the database, the use of new-technology components was indicated with a system of dummy variables. The table below lists only those component, software, and architectural variables with *t*-statistics during at least one period >2.00. In addition, a few variables for unusual interfaces were not reproduced in this table, for the sake of brevity. Note that the adjusted R^2 of 0.951 suggests that these variables account for much of the variation in observed areal density among the models of disk drives designed over this period.

EXHIBIT A1 Coefficients of Variables

	Coefficient	t-statistic	Original technology to which the new technology's performance is compared
Constant	−0.913	−3.04	
Year of introduction	0.199	57.80	NA: this is a continuous, not dummy variable
Disk diameter	−0.00154	−9.69	none: continuous variable, in centimeters
New head and disk technologies			
MIG head	0.047	2.00	ferrite head
Thin film head	0.251	13.50	ferrite head
MR head	0.838	22.70	ferrite head
Thin film disk	0.188	9.45	particulate oxide disk
Interaction of thin film head and thin film disk	−0.295	−3.35	
Actuator technologies			
Stepper motor	−0.428	−18.30	voice coil motor
Torque motor	−0.157	−4.93	voice coil motor
Rotary actuator design	0.063	3.55	linear actuator design
Optical positioning system	−0.380	−3.75	stepper positioning
Dedicated surface servo	0.020	−1.27	stepper positioning
Embedded servo	0.169	8.67	stepper positioning
Recording/error correction codes			
2,7 RLL recording code	0.207	9.23	modified frequency modulation (MFM) code
1,7 or 8,9 RLL recording code	0.439	14.40	MFM code
0,4,4 PRML recording code	0.585	11.90	MFM code
0,6,6 PRML recording code	0.775	13.00	MFM code
Interfaces			
PC/AT	0.073	2.64	ST412 interface
SCSI	0.099	3.83	ST412 interface
SCSI2	0.197	6.43	ST412 interface
SCSI3	0.324	2.80	ST412 interface
SMD	0.356	11.80	ST412 interface
ESDI	0.214	6.96	ST412 interface
ANSI	0.226	2.53	ST412 interface
IBM	0.287	6.55	ST412 interface
Proprietary interfaces	0.113	3.54	ST412 interface
Other interfaces	0.314	10.30	ST412 interface
Other technologies			
Zone-specific bit recording rate	0.127	6.35	uniform rate regardless of distance from center
Ramp loaded heads	0.106	1.61	heads rise from surface of the disk
Number of observations	4334		
Adjusted R^2	0.951		

APPENDIX 2: NOTES ON THE CALCULATION OF THE INDUSTRY SUPPLY OR SCALE CURVE IN EXHIBIT 6

The purpose of this regression analysis was to calculate the steepness of scale economics in the stage of value-added involving the design and assembly of disk drives at various points in time over the industry's history. The companies whose data were used for these calculations were disk drive companies that were only engaged in de-

sign and assembly. Firms that not only designed and assembled, but also manufactured some or all of the components they used could not be included in the study, because reported costs could not be allocated accurately to the various stages of value-added. The data was drawn from *Disk/Trend Report,* as well as from the financial statements of the companies, for the years 1981–1989. The analysis could not be extended beyond 1989 because there were too few surviving firms engaged solely in the business of designing and assembling disk drives. Firms had either exited the industry, integrated into making disk drive components, or integrated into making other products.

The equation that was estimated was of the form

$$\ln(\text{cost/unit}) = B_0 + B_1(\text{year}) + B_2 \ln(\text{unit volume}) + B_3 \ln(\text{no. of product line complexity}) + B_4 \ln(\text{drive capacity})$$

The choice of these variables as the ones most likely to impact total cost was grounded in research conducted by the first author that has been synthesized in the Harvard Business School teaching case, "Michigan Manufacturing Corporation" (HBS case no. 9-694-051).

The variables were defined as follows: *cost/unit* was calculated by dividing the total operating costs in the company, exclusive of interest and taxes, by the number of disk drive units produced. Hence, this measure is the *fully allocated product cost* for each company, for each year. *Drive capacity* is the weighted average capacity of the disk drive units shipped each year by the company. This is an important control variable, because each company's product mix was differently distributed across tiers of the market, and higher-capacity drives are more costly to produce. We expected the coefficient of this variable to be positive. *Unit volume* is the total number of disk drives shipped during the year. We expected the coefficient of this variable to be positive. *Unit volume* is the total number of disk drives shipped during the year. We expected the coefficient of this variable to be negative, positing that firms with larger production scale would enjoy lower costs and that as any firm's production scale increased, its unit costs would fall. *Product line complexity* is the number of product families produced by the company in the year. We expected the coefficients of this variable to be positive—overhead costs per unit would increase as increasing complexity of the product line would demand higher management overheads. The definition of a product family was that used in Christensen (1992b).

We estimated coefficients for the equation for panels of years: 1981–1984 and 1986–1989. An alternative approach, to include a dummy variable for each year during this period, was not feasible because in some years there were fewer than thirty observations. The equation for the years 1981–1984, when modular architectures were just beginning to penetrate the industry, was

$$\ln(\text{cost/unit}) = 296.39 - 0.146(\text{year}) - 0.370 \ln(\text{unit volume}) + 0.126 \ln(\text{no. of families}) + 0.511 \ln(\text{weighted mean MB/unit})$$

t-statistics: $(-3.44)\,(-4.70)\,(1.68)\,(6.23)\; R^2 = 0.88$

The equation for the years 1986–1989, when modular architectures had become much more pervasive in 3.5-inch drives used in desktop computers, was

$$\ln(\text{cost/unit}) = 322.22 - 0.160(\text{year}) - 0.15 \ln(\text{unit volume}) + 0.014 \ln(\text{no. of families}) + 0.544 \ln(\text{weighted mean MB/unit})$$

t-statistics: $(3.41)\,(-0.52)\,(0.12)\,(4.20)\; R^2 = 0.88$

Several comparisons between these measurements merit mention. First, the year term is essentially a "catch-all," whose coefficient represents the year-to-year reduction in cost attributable to engineering and product technology improvements. The relative stability of the coefficients measured in the two time panels suggests that the variables in the equations vary independently and that probably no other important explanatory variables are missing from these estimations, which have interactions with the variables shown. The coefficient of the "weighted average megabytes per unit" variable was similarly stable, as we would expect: adding an extra megabyte of capacity to a drive ought to result in a predictable increment to cost.

Note how the coefficient of the unit volume variable was negative and statistically significantly different from zero, suggesting rather steep scale economics in the 1981–1984 period. The coefficient was statistically insignificant in the later period, suggesting that scale economics were not a significant driver of cost: the scale curve seems to have flattened. Similarly, the product line complexity variable, which was modestly significant during the era of architectural interdependency, was insignificant when modular architectures were more pervasive—reflecting the fact that modularity facilitates increased product variety without the significant cost penalties incurred when architectures are interdependent.

One reviewer of this paper noted that because of the large standard error of the coefficient of the scale variable in the second period, we actually cannot reject, based upon statistical analysis alone, the null hypothesis that scale economics might still have been steep during this period. Nonetheless, industry executives who have reviewed the work uniformly felt that there were almost no differences in cost across the five largest firms. We take this statistical analysis, therefore, to be consistent with the theory (a high proportion of variable to fixed costs flattens the scale curve), as well as consistent with the perceptions of industry executives.

INDUSTRY CONTEXT

CASE II-6

The U.S. Telecommunications Industry: 1996–1999

Eric Marti

This case describes key developments in the U.S. telecommunications industry since the passage of the Telecommunications Act of 1996. During this period, the industry saw considerable merger activity, increasing intensity of competition, the continued convergence between voice and data networks, and a number of technological innovations. In the wake of the act, long-distance service providers were attempting to enter local markets, while local carriers sought to provide long-distance and other services.

Moreover, telephone and cable companies were entering the market for high-speed data services, including Internet access, with telephone companies investing in DSL (digital subscriber line) technologies and cable companies investing in cable modems. As voice and data networks continued to converge, the importance of Internet Protocol (IP) technology and the viability of Internet telephony had become manifest. Wireless services continued their rapid growth, and new forms of wireless service were introduced, including broadband wireless.

IMPACT OF REGULATORY CHANGE

Passage of the Telecommunications Act (on February 8, 1996) set up three major battlefronts within the industry. First, it opened the $108.3 billion (1998 revenues) [1] market for local phone service to its first serious competition: AT&T, the nation's largest telecommunications company, was now permitted to get back into the local phone business, which it had been forced to leave 12 years earlier.

Second, the act allowed the incumbent local exchange carriers (ILECs) to enter the long-distance business, both within and outside of their service region: they could offer in-region long distance only after demonstrating that they had opened their local markets to competition, but they were free immediately to offer out-of-region long distance, without any precondition.

Third, the act shifted cable companies into a new strategic position: like ILECs, cable companies have wires into customers' homes—the coveted "last mile." Though the idea of cable telephony had been around for years, cable operators had been prohibited from offering phone service; the Telecommunications Act gave new life to the prospect of cable-based telecommunications.

and Dr. Andrew S. Grove, for use as a basis for class discussion. It draws upon earlier industry notes prepared by John W. Foster, Alva H. Taylor, and Raymond S. Bamford.
[1] *Preliminary Statistics of Common Carriers,* 1998 Edition, Federal Communications Commission, May 1999.

EXHIBIT 1   Selected Financial Data for RBOCs and GTE, 1990–1998

(in millions of dollars, except return on average equity is percentage)

	1998	1997	1996	1995	1994	1993	1992	1991	1990
Ameritech:									
Revenues	17,514	15,998	14,917	13,428	12,570	11,710	11,153	10,818	10,663
Net income (loss)	3,606	2,296	2,134	2,008	(1,064)	1,513	(400)	1,166	1,254
Cash flow from operating activities	4,810	4,510	3,743	3,557	3,430	3,189	3,288	2,804	2,886
Capital expenditures	2,982	2,641	2,440	2,120	1,877	2,092	2,237	2,152	2,116
Total assets	30,299	25,339	23,707	21,943	19,947	23,428	22,818	22,290	21,715
Stockholders' equity	10,897	8,308	7,687	7,015	6,055	7,845	6,992	8,097	7,732
Return on average equity (%)	36.20	28.71	29.03	30.72	16.84	20.39	17.84	14.73	16.26
Bell Atlantic:									
Revenues	31,566	30,368	13,081	13,430	13,791	12,990	12,647	12,280	12,298
Net income (loss)	2,965	2,455	1,882	1,858	(755)	1,403	1,341	(223)	1,313
Cash flow from operating activities	10,071	8,859	4,416	3,981	3,753	4,234	3,930	3,756	3,535
Capital expenditures	7,447	6,638	2,553	2,627	2,648	2,517	2,560	2,545	2,747
Total assets	55,144	53,964	24,856	24,157	24,272	29,544	28,100	27,882	27,999
Stockholders' equity	13,025	12,789	7,423	6,684	6,081	8,224	7,816	7,831	8,930
Return on average equity (%)	22.97	24.29	24.66	29.17	19.60	18.47	17.67	15.89	14.98
BellSouth:									
Revenues	23,123	20,633	19,040	17,886	16,845	15,880	15,149	14,446	14,345
Net income (loss)	3,259	3,261	2,863	(1,232)	2,160	880	1,618	1,472	1,632
Cash flow from operating activities	7,741	7,039	5,863	5,443	5,172	4,786	4,947	4,390	4,527
Capital expenditures	5,212	4,858	4,455	4,203	3,600	3,486	3,189	3,102	3,191
Total assets	39,410	36,301	32,568	31,880	34,397	32,873	31,463	30,942	30,207
Stockholders' equity	16,110	15,165	13,249	11,825	14,367	13,494	13,799	13,105	12,666
Return on average equity (%)	20.60	23.02	22.84	11.94	15.50	7.58	12.33	11.69	12.66
GTE:									
Revenues	25,473	23,260	21,339	19,957	19,944	19,748	19,984	19,621	18,374
Net income (loss)	2,172	2,794	2,798	(2,138)	2,451	900	(754)	1,580	1,541
Cash flow from operating activities	5,890	6,244	5,899	5,033	4,740	5,277	4,832	4,784	3,744
Capital expenditures	5,609	5,128	4,088	4,034	4,192	3,893	3,909	3,857	3,453
Total assets	43,615	42,142	38,422	37,019	42,500	41,575	42,144	42,437	33,769
Stockholders' equity	8,766	8,038	7,336	6,871	10,556	9,677	10,171	11,417	9,210
Return on average equity (%)	27.30	36.35	39.39	29.27	24.47	10.00	16.92	15.31	18.07

RBOCs

Regulators and legislators presumed that, as a result of the Telecommunications Act, the RBOCs would attempt to compete in each other's regions. But as a sector, the RBOCs' initial strategic reaction instead was to consolidate. In 1997, Pacific Telesis merged into SBC Communications (a $16 billion deal), while Bell Atlantic acquired Nynex for $25.6 billion. Moreover, further consolidation is in the works: Bell Atlantic is planning to acquire GTE (for $53 billion), and SBC wants to buy Ameritech (for $62 billion). Both deals await government approval. Meanwhile, cross-region competition among RBOCs has been virtually nonexistent. The major exception was SBC's acquisition of Southern New England Telecommunications for $5 billion in 1998, which gave the company a position in Bell Atlantic's territory.

Only two RBOCs—BellSouth and US West—had not merged with other companies, but in July 1999 US West agreed to be acquired for $35 billion by Denver-based Qwest Communications. Qwest, a long-distance company founded in 1988, has nearly completed an 18,815-mile fiber-optic network connecting 150 cities. If the deal goes through, BellSouth (which owns a 10 percent stake in Qwest) will be the only RBOC not to have entered the consolidation game. For Qwest, the US West acquisition would immediately provide a customer base to which it could market services on its state-of-the-art fiber system (see Exhibit 1).

EXHIBIT 1   (Continued)

	1998	1997	1996	1995	1994	1993	1992	1991	1990
Nynex*:									
Revenues			13,454	13,407	13,307	13,408	13,155	13,250	13,585
Net income (loss)			1,477	(1,850)	793	(394)	1,311	601	949
Cash flow from operating activities			3,689	3,648	3,700	3,655	3,506	3,246	2,875
Capital expenditures			2,905	3,188	3,012	2,717	2,450	2,499	2,493
Total assets			27,659	26,220	30,068	29,458	27,714	27,503	26,651
Stockholders' equity			7,059	6,079	8,581	8,416	9,724	9,120	9,149
Return on average equity (%)			20.49	14.59	9.33	(3.00)	13.92	6.58	10.25
Pacific Telesis**:									
Revenues			9,588	9,042	9,274	9,244	9,935	9,895	9,716
Net income (loss)			1,142	(2,312)	1,159	(1,504)	1,142	1,015	1,030
Cash flow from operating activities			2,592	2,769	2,947	2,727	3,053	2,659	2,760
Capital expenditures			2,454	2,002	1,631	1,800	2,056	1,867	1,937
Total assets			16,608	15,841	20,139	23,437	22,516	21,838	21,581
Stockholders' equity			2,773	2,190	5,233	7,786	8,251	7,729	7,401
Return on average equity (%)			42.60	28.24	17.45	2.38	14.29	13.42	13.47
SBC:									
Revenues	28,777	26,681	13,898	12,670	11,772	10,690	10,015	9,332	9,113
Net income (loss)	4,023	1,674	2,101	(930)	1,649	(845)	1,302	1,076	1,101
Cash flow from operating activities	8,381	7,596	4,824	4,021	3,967	3,441	3,615	2,893	2,671
Capital expenditures	5,927	6,230	3,027	2,336	2,350	2,221	2,144	1,826	1,778
Total assets	45,066	44,836	23,449	22,003	26,005	24,308	23,810	23,179	22,196
Stockholders' equity	12,780	10,520	6,835	6,256	8,356	7,609	9,304	8,859	8,581
Return on average equity (%)	34.53	14.75	31.22	24.18	20.66	16.97	14.33	13.26	13.00
US West:									
Revenues	12,378	11,479	11,168	9,484	9,176	10,294	10,281	10,577	9,957
Net income (loss)	1,508	1,527	1,501	1,184	1,150	(2,806)	(614)	553	1,199
Cash flow from operating activities	3,927	4,191	3,614	2,719	2,509	3,338	3,292	3,030	2,822
Capital expenditures	2,672	2,168	2,444	2,462	2,254	2,449	2,261	2,654	2,559
Total assets	18,407	17,667	16,915	16,585	15,944	20,680	27,964	27,854	27,050
Stockholders' equity	755	4,367	3,917	3,476	3,179	5,861	8,268	9,587	9,240
Return on average equity (%)		29.08	32.87	35.58	25.44	6.74	13.21	5.88	13.85

* Acquired by Bell Atlantic in 1996.
** Acquired by SBC in 1996.
Sources: Standard & Poor's, Market Guide, company reports.

The RBOCs all have their eyes on the $104 billion long-distance market, but as of August 1999—more than three years after passage of the Telecommunications Act—no RBOC had received FCC approval to offer long-distance service in its region. (That situation may soon change, however; some observers expect that Bell Atlantic may be granted permission to offer long-distance in New York sometime this year.) And though the RBOCs were immediately free to provide local and long-distance service outside of their regions, as a group they have pursued these opportunities only to a limited degree.

All of the RBOCs operate significant wireless businesses in their regions (as beneficiaries of the original cellular licenses that the FCC granted to the ILECs in 1984, plus additional licenses won in subsequent auctions). Moreover, since permitted by the Telecommunications Act of 1996, they now offer data services such as high-speed lines (e.g., T1, T3)[2] and Internet access.

A key area of RBOC vulnerability is their dependence on access fees, which accounted for 22.5 percent of their 1998 revenues.[3] The FCC is forcing the ILECs, over

---

[2] T1 and T3 refer to circuits capable of transmitting data at 1.5 megabits per second and 45 megabits per second, respectively.
[3] In 1998, the five RBOCs had combined revenues of $113 billion (from all sources); of that amount, $25.5 billion came from access fees. Data is from annual reports.

time, to reduce these rates toward the actual cost of providing access. Though there is some disagreement between the ILECs and IXCs (interexchange) over the true cost of access, the figure is significantly less than the 3–4 cents per minute that they now charge. (AT&T estimates the cost is .5 cent per minute.)[4] In any case, that revenue source is being eroded both by the FCC reduction mandate and by IXC strategies to bypass RBOC networks.

GTE

The Telecommunications Act of 1996 freed GTE immediately to enter any market—including long distance—without restriction, unlike the five Baby Bells. GTE built its own long-distance capabilities, and by the end of 1998 it had captured 2.7 million customers. With 1998 revenues of $25.5 billion, GTE has a strong position in each of the important telecom sectors, including local (23.5 million lines in 28 states), wireless (4.8 subscribers in 17 states), online services, and long distance.

In August 1997, GTE completed its acquisition of BBN, the Internet service provider credited with designing the Internet (and establishing the @ sign), for $616 million. AT&T had held a minority interest in BBN and had been rumored as a potential acquirer of BBN. GTE also is investing billions of dollars to build a private, 17,000-mile nationwide data network and has invested $485 million for a 20 percent share of Qwest's new network. GTE started to roll out high-speed DSL service in its region in June 1998, with plans to offer the service in 16 states.

As noted above, GTE has agreed to merge with Bell Atlantic. The combination would create the country's largest provider of local phone service (with 65.1 million lines), operating in 39 states and 76 of the top 100 markets nationwide. It would also become the largest wireless provider, with 11.4 million subscribers.

Long-Distance Carriers

In contrast to the RBOCs' reluctance to compete outside their regions, the long-distance players—AT&T, MCI WorldCom, Sprint, and others—have aggressively pursued strategies to expand the scale and scope of their operations (see Exhibit 2). Their moves are aimed both at enhancing their positions in long distance and at entering new markets, particularly the local service business and the fast-growing market for broadband data services.

Strategically, these companies are trying to develop the capability to offer customers a wide array of telecommunications services—one-stop shopping. AT&T is the most dramatic example of this strategy—the ultimate success of which remains to be seen. But it took a bold new CEO—C. Michael Armstrong, recruited in late 1997 from Hughes Electronics Corp.—to pull it off.

AT&T With Armstrong at the helm, AT&T embarked on a string of major acquisitions, beginning with the purchase of Teleport Communications Group for $11.3 billion[5] in January 1998, which gave it access to local service in 85 markets. As a result of the deal, AT&T expected to save about $1.25 billion in 1999 due to financial synergies and reduced local network access fees. Shortly after, the company struck a deal to acquire cable operator TCI—the nation's largest, with 13.5 million subscribers—for $58 billion (renaming the unit AT&T Broadband & Internet Services). Later that year, in October 1998, AT&T announced its $1.5 billion acquisition of Vanguard Cellular Systems, one of the largest cellular operators in the United States. Vanguard provided services to approximately 625,000 customers under the Cellular One brand name. This was followed in December 1998 by AT&T's $5 billion acquisition of IBM's Global Network Services, a data network service for corporations. Then, in May 1999, AT&T announced its bid to acquire Number 3 cable operator MediaOne—which had already negotiated a deal to be acquired by Number 2 cable operator Comcast. In the end, Comcast and AT&T worked out an agreement, with AT&T getting MediaOne—with 5 million customers—for $62 billion. The deal still awaits FCC approval (most analysts agree that it will be approved).

Having spent some $126 billion on these deals—plus $11.5 billion to acquire McCaw Cellular in 1994—AT&T is making one of the boldest gambits in U.S. corporate history. The reason is clear: its core business —long distance—is no longer a significant source of growth. The long-distance market, now rife with competition, has grown at an average annual rate of only 5.5 percent overall since 1990. Meanwhile, competition has cut AT&T's share of that sluggish market to 44.5 percent in 1997 (from 90 percent in 1984).[6] Nonetheless, AT&T relied on long distance for 86 percent of its 1998 revenues. So, even though the local phone market has

---

[4]"Plain Talk on the Future of Communications," speech by AT&T Chairman C. Michael Armstrong, September 29, 1998.

[5]Note: AT&T paid approximately 22 times revenue.
[6]*Long Distance Market Shares,* Federal Communications Commission, March 1999.

EXHIBIT 2   Selected Financial Data for Major Long-Distance Carriers, 1990–1998

(in millions of dollars, except for return on average equity is percentage)

	1998	1997	1996	1995	1994	1993	1992	1991	1990
AT&T:									
Revenues	53,223	51,319	52,184	79,609	75,094	67,156	64,904	63,089	55,977
Net income (loss)	6,398	4,638	5,908	139	4,710	(3,794)	3,807	522	2,735
Cash flow from operating activities	10,217	8,353	6,867	9,690	8,956	7,129	7,874	6,015	5,463
Capital expenditures	7,981	7,143	6,339	6,411	5,304	3,942	4,183	3,979	3,667
Total assets	59,550	58,635	55,552	88,884	79,262	60,766	57,188	53,355	43,775
Stockholders' equity	25,522	22,647	20,295	17,274	17,921	13,850	18,921	16,228	14,093
Return on average equity (%)	25.30	20.83	29.85	0.79	29.65	24.25	21.66	3.44	20.39
MCI*:									
Revenues		19,653	18,494	15,265	13,338	11,921	10,562	9,491	7,680
Net income (loss)		149	1,202	548	795	582	609	551	299
Cash flow from operating activities		3,488	3,144	2,979	2,355	1,978	1,726	1,271	1,549
Capital expenditures		3,828	3,347	2,866	2,897	1,733	1,272	1,377	1,274
Total assets		25,510	22,978	19,301	16,366	11,276	9,678	8,834	8,249
Stockholders' equity		11,311	10,661	9,602	9,004	4,713	3,150	2,959	2,340
Return on average equity (%)		1.36	11.86	5.89	11.58	15.93	19.29	19.71	12.46
Qwest:									
Revenues	2,243	697	231						
Net income (loss)	(844)	15	(7)						
Cash flow from operating activities	45	(36)	33						
Capital expenditures	1,413	346	57						
Total assets	8,068	1,398	264						
Stockholders' equity	4,238	382	9						
Return on average equity (%)		7.425	na						
Sprint:									
Revenues	17,134	14,874	14,045	12,765	12,662	11,368	9,230	8,780	8,345
Net income (loss)	415	953	1,184	395	891	55	457	368	309
Cash flow from operating activities	4,255	3,379	2,404	2,729	2,472	2,136	2,018	1,565	1,201
Capital expenditures	4,231	2,863	2,434	1,857	2,016	1,595	1,151	1,244	1,566
Total assets	33,231	18,185	16,953	15,196	14,936	14,149	10,188	10,464	10,553
Stockholders' equity	12,448	9,037	8,532	4,671	4,554	3,949	2,839	2,545	2,324
Return on average equity (%)	3.86	10.85	18.08	20.58	20.87	14.19	15.93	15.16	14.01
WorldCom:									
Revenues**	17,678	7,351	4,485	3,640	2,221	1,145	801	263	154
Net income (loss)	(2,669)	384	(2,213)	268	(122)	104	(6)	18	10
Cash flow from operating activities	4,085	1,318	798	616	261	151	84	42	27
Capital expenditures	5,418	2,645	657	356	192	36	58	19	13
Total assets	86,401	22,390	19,862	6,635	3,430	2,515	870	337	169
Stockholders' equity	45,003	13,510	12,960	2,187	1,827	1,622	343	100	39
Return on average equity (%)	(9.12)	2.70	(28.91)	12.49	(8.70)	9.77	(1.16)	25.39	28.66

*Acquired by WorldCom in 1998.

**WorldCom completed its acquisition of MCI on September 14, 1998, and accounted for the transaction as a purchase; accordingly, the operating results of MCI are included from the date of acquisition.

Sources: Standard & Poor's, Market Guide, company reports.

grown at an average annual rate of just 5.6 percent over the last five years, nearly 100 percent of those revenues have gone to the ILECs: taking share from the ILECs is at the heart of AT&T's game plan.

Driving AT&T's cable acquisition strategy are two key motives. First, cable systems have wires directly into customer homes, thereby enabling AT&T to bypass the ILECs' local loops ("last mile") and to avoid paying access charges. In 1998, AT&T spent $15.3 billion in access fees paid to local phone companies, which represented nearly 34 percent of its long-distance revenues of $45.6 billion. Second, coaxial cable is a broadband medium—it has the capacity to carry content at high speed, such as graphics, video, and audio. Based on this combination of bypass and bandwidth, AT&T hopes to build a nationwide system offering businesses and consumers a complete bundle of telecom services: local and long-distance phone service, cable, high-speed Internet access, and other advanced services (e.g., movies on demand).

Including the MediaOne acquisition, AT&T's cable network would pass 25.5 million homes (about a quarter of the nation's households), to which it could market cable phone services. Moreover, AT&T has agreements with Time Warner and Comcast (the Number 2 and 3 cable operators, respectively), to market AT&T phone services to their cable customers. This would extend the potential reach of AT&T's cable phone service to 60% of all households. AT&T is now testing cable phone service in several U.S. markets.

However, the job of creating a full-blown, advanced telecommunications network from a patchwork of cable systems is neither simple nor cheap. Most cable networks require significant upgrading in order to serve as two-way communications systems. According to *Fortune* magazine, upgrading systems to handle voice costs about $500 per subscriber and $700 to $1,200 for upgrades to carry high-speed data traffic.[7] And *Teletechnology* newsletter estimated that, as of the beginning of 1998, only 17 percent of cable infrastructure was ready for two-way communication.[8]

Cable networks, in their current state, are deficient as telecommunications systems in several ways. For example, the traditional "tree and branch" network architecture upon which most cable systems were originally based makes them very vulnerable to service outages: damage suffered at any point on the network interrupts traffic for all customers downstream. By contrast, the star or ring architectures employed by the ILECs provide redundant channels to minimize network outages. Moreover, while coax cable is capable of maintaining speed and data integrity over a relatively long distance from the trunk to the home, the trunk portion of the system, which carries traffic from the head-end to the distribution branches in neighborhoods, would have to be upgraded to fiber-optic.

The most important disadvantage to the cable infrastructure is that it was designed to provide one-way delivery of video, and systems must be retrofitted with switches and signal relays to allow for two-way transmission, as well as head-end equipment that can both send and receive transmissions. Other obstacles for the cable operators have been a lack of industry-wide standards for key technical components, such as servers, and having network transmission protocols which have hampered software development in such critical areas as billing and traffic monitoring systems, vital aspects of delivering high-quality customer service.

Cable operators also face significant organizational hurdles in attempting to convince users to entrust their mission-critical telephony needs to a cable provider. Cable operators must overcome the monopolist mind-set with which they have run their cable networks and for which they have earned a reputation for providing poor customer service while steadily increasing rates. In addition, cable operators lack network management experience, and have traditionally viewed themselves as participants in the entertainment business, focused on acquiring content and reselling it.

MCI WorldCom   As AT&T pursued its growth strategy, the other IXCs were not standing still. In late 1997, for example, Number 2 long-distance provider MCI announced that it would merge with the much smaller Number 4 provider, WorldCom, for $37 billion—a move that took the industry by surprise. The deal closed in September 1998, and the combined entity was renamed MCI WorldCom. GTE and British Telecom had also made runs at MCI, and in early 1997 MCI appeared to have been sold to BT for $20 billion. However, GTE upset that deal with a cash offer of $28 billion, and WorldCom bested GTE with an all-stock counteroffer initially worth $30 billion.

Prior to the MCI deal, WorldCom had approximately 5.5 percent of the U.S. market, including many highly profitable business customers. MCI added 22 million long-distance customers, which were also considered among the industry's most profitable.[9] The combined MCI WorldCom had 25 percent of the long-distance market and operations in 65 countries.

The MCI deal was the dramatic continuation of an aggressive acquisition strategy that WorldCom had been pursing since the early 1990s. It had already acquired MFS (in 1996) and Brooks Fiber (in 1997), two large fiber-based CLECs (competitive local-exchange carri-

---

[7] *Fortune,* July 5, 1999.
[8] *Teletechnology,* July 10, 1998.

[9] *Fortune,* November 10, 1997.

ers). Combining MCI's local service with its MFS and Brooks Fiber operations, the company spanned 100 of the top local markets. Previously, MCI had been struggling to build local networks in 30 cities, with losses of approximately $500 million on revenues of $500 million in 1997.[10] After the merger, MCI would leverage WorldCom's local networks rather than continue building its own.

MCI WorldCom planned to utilize its own local infrastructure, rather than RBOC service. According to Tim Price, CEO of MCI WorldCom's U.S. subsidiary, "We are going to be an absolute power. . . . Our local strategy has always been built upon infrastructure. . . . If most of my revenue came from residential customers, I would do resale. But most of my revenue comes from business-to-business sales."[11] MCI WorldCom is well-positioned to attract business customers: a high percentage of companies are concentrated in central cities, where MFS and Brooks Fiber had laid their networks, and the company's high-speed fiber infrastructure can handle corporations' growing data-traffic needs.

While domestic long distance accounted for two-thirds of MCI WorldCom's 1998 revenues of $30.4 billion, the company's major sources of growth lie elsewhere. In 1998, for example, revenues from domestic long distance grew by less than 9 percent from their 1997 level, versus far higher rates of increases in other segments: local services (80 percent), Internet services (69 percent), international services (59 percent), and data (28 percent).[12]

One noticeable gap in MCI WorldCom's offerings is wireless. The company has no significant cellular or PCS (personal communication service) operations, while its chief rivals lead these markets—AT&T in cellular and Sprint in PCS. This lack impinges on MCI WorldCom's ability to sell itself as a single source for corporate telecommunications needs. Most of MCI WorldCom's efforts in wireless are focused on data services. In the first half of 1999, MCI WorldCom announced deals to acquire SkyTel (the Number 2 paging service) as well as CAI Wireless and Wireless One (both providers of broadband wireless services).

Sprint Sprint, the Number 3 long-distance company with about a 10 percent share of the U.S. market, has not pursued an all-out acquisition strategy like AT&T and MCI WorldCom.[13] But it, too, has its eyes on local service and the growing data market. The company had 1998 revenues of $17.1 billion, two-thirds of which came from its long-distance operations. It also offers local service, with 7.6 million lines in 18 states. And Sprint PCS, a wholly owned unit, operates the nation's largest PCS system, with more than 3 million subscribers. PCS revenues in 1998 were $1.23 billion (though the unit actually incurred a net loss of $2.64 billion).[14]

In December 1998, Sprint launched an entirely new network infrastructure, called ION (integrated on-demand network), optimized to carry voice, video, and data. According to Sprint CEO and Chairman William Esrey, ION is Sprint's strategy to grow its data services business and to expand into local markets. The new network employs packet switched, ATM (asynchronous transfer mode) technology and supports the Internet protocol (IP). The company has invested $2 billion developing this network, and plans to spend an additional $400 million over the next two years. It expects improved efficiencies from the ION network to save the company $1 billion over the next five years.[15] Sprint ION services currently are available in a handful of cities to large businesses, which connect to the backbone via high-bandwidth lines (e.g., T1 or T3). Residential service in several markets is scheduled for the fall of 1999. The company will use a combination of digital subscriber line (DSL) service—via agreements with various CLECs that are now rolling out this service—and fixed wireless technologies[16] to provide high bandwidth for the "last mile" connecting residences to the ION network.

According to Sprint, ION offers "virtually unlimited bandwidth over a single existing telephone line for simultaneous voice, video calls, and data services."[17] Sprint predicted that the cost to deliver a typical voice call using the new network will drop by at least 70 percent and will allow full-motion video conferencing to be

---

[10] *Fortune,* October 27, 1997.
[11] *Fortune,* March 2, 1998.
[12] MCI WorldCom 1998 annual report.

[13] One notable exception is Sprint's acquisition of several wireless cable-TV companies in early 1999, including People's Choice TV (for $420 million), American Telecasting (for $167.8 million), Videotron USA (for $180 million), and Transworld Telecommunications (for $30 million). The acquisitions provide Sprint with broadband access to homes, enabling it to bypass ILEC access fees. (See *Wall Street Journal,* April 28, 1999, May 4, 1999, May 6, 1999, and *Network World,* May 10, 1999.
[14] Sprint 1998 annual report.
[15] Ibid.
[16] DSL and fixed wireless technologies are explained later in this note; see section on "Technological Developments" below.
[17] Sprint press release, June 2, 1998.

offered at lower cost than a typical long-distance call today.

In August 1998, Sprint launched a phone-to-phone Internet telephony service, called Callternatives, in Atlanta, Dallas, Los Angeles, San Francisco, and Seattle. The service allows calls throughout the United States— for 7.5 cents a minute—and to numerous international locations at rates of up to 75 percent less than circuit-switched service.[18] "I cannot say it clearly or loudly enough: Sprint is fully, completely committed to IP," said CEO Esrey.[19]

Qwest   In January 1998, Qwest Communications purchased long-distance carrier LCI in a $4.4 billion stock deal, which made Qwest the fourth-largest IXC in the United States, after AT&T, MCI WorldCom, and Sprint. For most of its history, Qwest had supplied network capacity and construction services to larger phone companies. But with the near completion of its fiber-optic coast-to-coast telecom network, the company is now competing to provide service to end users. Headed by Joe Nacchio, formerly the Number 3 executive at AT&T, the company has become an aggressive player in long-distance and data services.

Qwest, along with a new generation of telecommunication companies (including Level 3, IXC, and Williams), focuses on applying the latest communications technologies to the telecom industry. Qwest's state-of-the-art network is designed to deliver both voice and data packets at high speed. According to Nacchio, "People ask if we're telecom guys or Silicon Valley guys. I like to say that we are a Silicon Valley company on the other side of the Rockies. . . . The incumbents are not poised for data growth. They are plagued by proprietary technology and a collapsing pricing structure."[20]

The weak link in Qwest's position, however, is its lack of local access to end users. In 1998 Qwest tried to solve that problem by signing marketing deals with US West and Ameritech allowing Qwest to offer long-distance services to US West's and Ameritech's local customers. Qwest had signed up many customers for this service. However, AT&T and MCI sued, arguing that the arrangement violated the 1996 Telecommunications Act. The FCC agreed and in September 1998 rejected the deal.

The company launched three new initiatives to reach end users. First, the US West acquisition would give

Qwest immediate access to US West's 16 million customers, 50,000 of whom now subscribe to high-speed DSL service. Second, it recently invested $90 million for a 19 percent stake in Advanced Radio Telecom Corp., which is building a broadband wireless network in more than 40 U.S. markets. Finally, the company has local-access agreements with two CLEC start-ups—Covad Communications and Rhythms NetConnections—which are rolling out high-speed DSL services to an increasing number of markets.

CLECs

Since passage of the Telecommunications Act of 1996, activity among CLECs has moved into high gear. The overall number of CLECs jumped from 57 in 1995 to 146 in 1998,[21] many of them started directly in the wake of the Telecommunications Act. Their 1998 revenues were $3.3 billion (compared to $1.9 billion in 1997),[22] and they had 5.6 million lines in service, up from 1.6 million in 1997.[23] And by early 1999, CLECs' interconnections with ILECs numbered nearly 5,500—double the number from the year before.[24]

While some CLECs focus on opportunities to buy ILEC service at wholesale rates—which the Telecommunications Act requires ILECs to offer competitors— and resell it at a markup, most are installing some combination of their own lines (usually fiber-optic) and switches that interconnect with ILEC exchanges. Only the leanest of operators can make money on pure resale of ILEC facilities, because the gross margin is only about 15 percent. A facilities-based CLEC, however, can earn margins of 50 percent to 80 percent. (AT&T, MCI, and Sprint had all tried the resale game as an initial foray into local service, but they quit because none could make a profit. Indeed, AT&T lost an average of $3 per month on each subscriber.)[25]

Most CLECs focus on small to midsize business customers, who occupy urban office buildings and suburban industrial parks. Revenues from these dense clusters of high-volume customers are enough to justify the expense of installing lines to customer premises and laying the

---

[18]*Business Communications Review,* January 1, 1999.
[19]Cnet (news.com), July 16, 1998.
[20]*Fortune,* June 8, 1998.

[21]*Trends in Telephone Service,* Federal Communications Commission, February 1999.
[22]*Monitoring Report,* Federal Communications Commission, June 1999.
[23]*Business Communications Review,* June 1999.
[24]Interconnection statistic cited by US West CEO Solomon Trujillo in his speech "Assessing the Telecommunications Act of 1996: Is America Getting What Americans Want?" January 1, 1999.
[25]*Telephony,* March 16, 1998.

EXHIBIT 3   Selected Quarterly Financial Data for Several Emerging Data-CLECs

(all figures are in millions of dollars)

	30 June 99	31 March 99	31 December 98	30 September 98	30 June 98	31 March 98
Covad Communications:						
Revenues	10.8	5.6	2.8	1.6	0.8	0.6
Net income	(41.9)	(28.9)	(19.9)	(16.6)	(8.9)	(2.8)
Total assets	593.8	577.2	139.4	144.6	146.5	na
Total debt	353.8	358.5	142.9	138.0	133.1	na
Stockholders' equity	172.0	187.4	(24.7)	(6.4)	8.1	na
Northpoint Communications:						
Revenues	2.5	1.3	0.5	0.2	0.1	0.04
Net income	(37.9)	(23.4)	(15.9)	(7.8)	(3.3)	(1.9)
Total assets	503.1	131.0	60.5	na	na	na
Total debt	58.3	56.1	51.9	na	na	na
Stockholders' equity	425.0	47.6	(6.5)	na	na	na
Rhythms Netconnections:						
Revenues	1.6	0.7	0.3	0.2	0.1	0.01
Net income	(42.9)	(23.9)	(15.3)	(11.9)	(6.8)	(2.4)
Total assets	789.3	245.5	171.7	174.0	na	na
Total debt	494.3	163.7	158.2	152.9	na	na
Stockholders' equity	239.1	41.6	(6.7)	8.2	na	na

Sources: Market Guide, company reports.

fiber-optic rings that transport traffic to interconnections with ILEC or IXC exchanges. CLECs are especially aggressive in providing high-speed lines to businesses: according to *Telecommunications* magazine, "CLECs now get more than half of their profits from T1 service." Moreover, by some industry estimates, CLECs may control 40 percent of all T1 business by 2002.[26]

The CLECs remain highly fragmented, with a large number of small but growing players (see Exhibit 3). But just as AT&T acquired Teleport and WorldCom acquired MFS and Brooks Fiber, more consolidation in this sector can be expected.

TECHNOLOGICAL DEVELOPMENTS

While the effects of the Telecommunications Act on competition are being played out, technology is also bringing dramatic change to the industry. There are many recent innovations, but they can generally be divided into two categories: wireline technologies that enable high-speed transmission of content and new wireless technologies—including broadband—that provide further alternatives to wireline service.

Chief among the first category—the wire-based "broadband" technologies—are DSL, cable modems, and dense wavelength division multiplexing (DWDM).

DSL

Digital subscriber line (DSL) enables high-speed transmissions over the twisted-pair, copper telephone wire that is standard in most homes and residences. Many different variants of DSL have been developed, but the most common is ADSL (asymmetric DSL). It enables upstream communication (i.e., transmission from the customer premises) at a rate of 64–640 kilobits per second (Kbps) and downstream rates of up to 1.5 megabits per second (Mbps). Faster variants of DSL can achieve speeds of up to 52 Mbps. By comparison, today's fastest consumer dial-up modems operate at a maximum of 56 Kbps.

Though developed in the late 1980s and early 1990s, DSL technology was not commercially deployed until 1997. It requires customers to have a DSL modem connected to their equipment (typically connected to a computer), and the phone company also must have special DSL equipment at its switching facilities. One major limitation of DSL is that, for technical reasons, it is available only to customers located within a few thousand feet of the phone company's switching office (beyond that

---

[26] *Telecommunications*, April 1999.

distance, the signal degrades). With the current state of the technology, as much as 40 percent of the population does not have access to DSL.

Cable Modems

Cable modems are another innovation addressing the broadband issue. Though first introduced in the early 1990s—Zenith was one of the original developers of the technology—only in recent years have cable modems been installed in significant numbers. But with the arrival of the Internet in full force, residential demand for high-speed Internet connections has spurred usage of cable modems. Moreover, cable systems were originally designed for one-way transmission only; cable modems at the customer premises, therefore, cannot be deployed until the cable system is upgraded to accommodate two-way communications.

Cable modems can theoretically provide connections up to 10 Mbps. However, due to cable's tree-and-branch architecture—by which the system effectively is a large local area network—connection speed degrades as more people in the system are online at the same time. (DSL technology does not have this drawback because each subscriber's connection is a dedicated line to the phone company's exchange.) Even so, cable-modem connection speeds exceed by many times the 56 Kbps rates of today's standard modems.

The race is on between DSL and cable modems to deliver high-speed connections to residences and small businesses. So far, cable modems have the lead. In 1998, there were 500,000–700,000 cable-modem users versus 200,000–300,000 DSL subscribers nationwide (estimates for both technologies vary). Many analysts forecast this trend to continue. For example, research firm Jupiter Communications predicts that by 2002, cable modem users will outnumber DSL subscribers, 6.8 million to 3.4 million.[27]

DWDM

Another technology addressing wire-based broadband is DWDM (dense wavelength division multiplexing). Just as DSL technology enhances the capability of copper phone wire, DWDM does something similar for fiber-optic cable: it increases the transmission capacity of a fiber strand by dividing the light passing through it into many waves, each of which can carry a signal. Currently, DWDM can increase fiber-optic transmission by 80 times,[28] and further improvements are expected soon. (In its laboratories, Lucent Technologies has divided the light in a single fiber into 100 beams, each traveling at 10 billion bits per second, 10 times today's usual rate; the resulting capacity—1 trillion bits per second—is more than sufficient to handle all of North America's telecommunications needs.)[29] This is a great advantage to owners and developers of fiber-optic systems, because DWDM enables them to increase the effective capacity of existing fiber at far less expense than laying more fiber underground.

DWDM and other innovations have dramatically expanded the transmission capacity of fiber-optic networks. Indeed, Qwest—which has nearly completed construction of an 18,500-mile network—claims that its system has enough bandwidth to transmit the equivalent of the entire contents of the Library of Congress coast to coast in 20 seconds.[30] Moreover, Qwest is just one of five companies building extensive fiber-optic networks throughout the country: Frontier, IXC, Williams, and Level 3 have projects of similar scale in various stages of completion. All of this is in addition to the fiber-optic networks that AT&T, MCI WorldCom, and Sprint have in place, as well as the RBOCs' and CLECs' regional fiber backbones. This surge in fiber supply has spurred predictions of an imminent bandwidth glut. For example, Forrester Research, a market research firm, says the glut will start next year and will extend until 2005 or later.[31] Worldwide Renaissance, a consulting firm, comes to a similar conclusion: "within two years, the United States will have 400 times more telecommunications capacity than it had in 1998"—enough to handle 54 trillion simultaneous phone calls—yet "demand for space on networks to carry computer traffic, video, and voice calls will grow only 20 times."[32] In April 1999, *Forbes* reported that since June 1998, "the wholesale spot price of bandwidth is down 35 percent, thanks to ample supply."[33] And according to a recent MIT study, 83 percent of the bandwidth on AT&T's international fiber network goes unused.[34]

The new fiber firms, on the other hand, state their belief that demand will be virtually infinite, as new band-

---

[27] *Cable World*, May 24, 1999.

[28] *Technology Review*, March 1, 1999.

[29] *Business Week*, December 7, 1998.

[30] *Denver Rocky Mountain News*, February 14, 1999.

[31] *Fortune*, March 15, 1999.

[32] *The Boston Globe*, July 10, 1999; *Dallas Business Journal*, July 2, 1999.

[33] *Forbes*, April 19, 1999.

[34] *Data Communications*, May 7, 1999.

width-hungry applications reach businesses and consumers: video on demand, video teleconferencing and consumer videophones, TV-style programs on the Internet, and other multimedia-based communications. "I don't see a glut," said IXC CEO Benjamin Scott. "I see a big wave of demand."[35] Level 3 CEO James Crowe answers the glut predictions with this analogy from the computer industry: "Did Intel glut the microprocessor market by coming out with generation after generation of more powerful and cheaper micro-processors? Of course not. Demand just took off and sucked up the supply."[36] Of the five new fiber companies, Williams Communications is alone in its strategy of offering bandwidth only at wholesale; all the other firms offer—or will offer—services to end users.

Fixed Wireless

In the wireless area, a technology referred to as fixed wireless, or wireless local loop (WLL), offers another option to conventional wireline service. Rather than lay down cable and install wire into customer premises—a very expensive undertaking—providers of fixed wireless services mount receiving and transmitting equipment on the customer's rooftop at far less cost. This equipment sends and receives signals to and from a central tower, which serves as the switching facility that ties into the public phone system. There are several variants of this technology, distinguished primarily by the radiowave spectrum used and bandwidth capacity.

In recent years, the FCC has auctioned off licenses to different portions of spectrum for wireless services. An alphabet soup of technologies[37] has appeared:

- LMDS (local multipoint distribution system) operates in the 28 GHz to 31 GHz spectrum and provides transmission speeds ranging from 1.54 Mbps (T1 rate) to 45 Mbps (T3 rate).
- MMDS (multichannel multipoint distribution service) was originally designed to deliver cable TV programming over a wireless network (so-called wireless cable); it operates in the 2.5 GHz to 2.7 GHz spectrum and provides bandwidth of 128 Kbps to 3 Mbps.[38]

- DEMS (digital electronic message service) operates at 24 GHz and offers bandwidth up to 1.54 Mbps (Teligent is the leader in this area).
- Finally, broadband services are also available in the 39 GHz spectrum; WinStar and Advanced Radio Telecom lead the field. WinStar's Wireless Fiber service, for example, offers T1-level bandwidth of 1.54 Mbps.

INTERNET TELEPHONY

Another active development area is Internet telephony, particularly the use of the Internet for long-distance voice communications. The appeal is mainly economic: calls made over the Internet—whether voice or data—are not subject to the access fees that local phone companies charge for terminating standard long-distance calls. Given that long-distance companies now pay out a third of their revenues in access fees, avoiding those charges means huge cost savings.

But there are a few drawbacks to Internet telephony. The main one is the inferior audio quality of Internet calls versus conventional phone calls over circuit switched networks. In order to be transmitted over the Internet, the speaker's voice first must be digitized (turned into bits of data) and arranged in packets, then transmitted like any other data packets through the Internet's switches. But packet switching technology was not designed for voice communication: packets do not travel together in a steady stream along a single conduit—as does the signal in a standard analog call over the phone—and any single packet can be momentarily delayed at any switch on its path, or it can be dropped altogether. Such delays and losses cause the call to sound choppy or broken.

Though currently less than 1 percent of voice calls are carried over the Internet, analysts predict that figure to grow dramatically. One research group projects that by 2002, Internet-based voice calls will be a $9.4 billion market.[39] A number of companies have been started to exploit the cost advantage of Internet telephony. However, until the technology is developed to solve the audio quality problem—an area that's being actively researched—Internet telephony is likely to remain a minor niche. Nonetheless, all the major carriers—from AT&T and MCI WorldCom to the RBOCs—are investigating

---

[35] *Investor's Business Daily,* March 3, 1998.

[36] *Barron's,* June 14, 1999.

[37] Data on various fixed wireless technologies from "Annual Report and Analysis of Competitive Market Conditions with Respect to Commercial Mobile Services," Federal Communications Commission, June 24, 1999.

[38] This is the technology, for example, employed by the four wireless cable companies that Sprint acquired in early 1999. The FCC distrib-

uted MMDS licenses as early as 1984, but operators did not deploy MMDS for two-way communications, as Sprint and others now intend to use the technology. See *Network World,* May 10, 1999.

[39] *Network Computing,* March 8, 1999.

Internet telephony, and some now even offer this service in a limited way (e.g., Sprint's Callternatives service).

In a recent test of international call audio quality, IDT Corp.'s Net2Phone Direct—a service that allows phone-to-phone calling over IDT's proprietary packet switched network—scored 3.69, on a scale of 1 to 5, versus 4.10 for AT&T's conventional circuit switched service. This result suggests a narrower quality gap than many industry observers had expected. But the price gap was enormous: the IDT calls cost just 10 cents per minute, compared to $1.90 per minute for AT&T's peak business rate.[40]

The biggest bet on Internet telephony is being made by two young companies, Qwest and Level 3. Each is spending billions to build its own high-speed, packet-switched network based on Internet protocols. Level 3, for example, plans to spend $10 billion to build a 16,000-mile system connecting major U.S. cities and selected foreign markets (10 percent of which had been completed by mid-1999). Both firms believe that technological improvements will soon solve the quality issues of Internet telephony, leaving them with enormous cost advantages over circuit switched competitors. Those advantages are driven primarily by the swift pace at which router and fiber-optic technologies—two key elements of the new-generation networks—are increasing their price performance. Routers double their price performance every 20 months, while advances in optical technologies (e.g., DWDM) double fiber network performance every 10 months.[41] Level 3 chief executive James Crowe believes that the company will be able to offer prices 20 percent below those of established companies like AT&T and MCI WorldCom. But that's only the beginning. "We see no reason," Crowe recently told the press, "why we won't be able to drop our prices by 50 percent or more each year, once we get going."[42] Indeed, Level 3 claims it will be able to carry calls over its all-packet network for less than 4 percent of the cost of circuit switched service.[43]

EXPLOSIVE GROWTH OF DATA TRAFFIC

In addition to deregulation and technology, a third major trend is also driving change in the telecommunications industry: the explosive growth of data traffic and the consequent demand for broadband services. Data traffic includes transmission of fax, text, graphics, video, audio, and other nonvoice content. According to one research group, in 1999 data will have surpassed voice as a percentage of worldwide telecommunications content (when measured as bits transferred) and, by 2002, will account for 92 percent of worldwide content.[44] Faxes, for example, now account for some 40 percent of all long-distance telephone traffic.[45]

Alan Taffel, VP of business development for UUNet Technologies, Inc. (a subsidiary of MCI WorldCom that provides Internet access), told *Upside* magazine: "The load customers are placing on our network is doubling every three and a half months, and in some periods faster than that, which is equivalent to 1,000 percent per year."[46]

At the root of the data explosion is the information revolution: automated business processes such as electronic data interchange (EDI), for instance, generate large volumes of data that must be shuttled from party to party. Moreover, the tremendous rise in World Wide Web activity and Internet usage for email, newsgroups, and other communications translates into increased traffic over phone lines and Internet backbones.

BROADBAND

The dramatic growth in data traffic is driving another key trend in telecommunications: the growing demand for broadband services. Multimedia content—which is rich in graphics, audio, and video—requires far more bandwidth for its transmission than do ordinary voice calls (see Exhibit 4). While the backbones of today's phone networks (which are primarily fiber-optic cables) can handle the broadband needs of multimedia content, the bottleneck comes at the "last mile": the twisted-pair copper wire that runs into the home or business.

Much of what is happening today in the telecommunications industry centers on the problem of delivering broadband capability to the home or office. AT&T's push into cable, for instance, is as much an effort to provide broadband service to consumers as it is to win their local phone business: the company wants to bundle high-

---

[40] Ibid.
[41] *Barron's,* June 14, 1999.
[42] Ibid.
[43] *Information Week,* June 21, 1999.

[44] *America's Network,* May 15, 1998; data cited are from Insight Research Corp. (Parsippany, NJ).
[45] *Business Communications Review,* April 1999; statistic cited is from research firm IDC.
[46] *Upside,* July 1998.

EXHIBIT 4   Infrastructure Bandwidth Requirements

Media transmitted	Required bandwidth	Transmission infrastructure required[7]
Styled text	2–10 Kbps	Twisted-pair wire, coax cable, fiber-optic
Speech graded audio[1]	32–64 Kbps	Twisted-pair wire, coax cable, fiber-optic
Still images	10–128 Kbps	Twisted-pair wire, coax cable, fiber-optic
Low quality compressed video[2]	100 Kbps to 1.5 Mbps	Twisted-pair wire, coax cable, fiber-optic
High fidelity audio[3]	176 Kbps to 1.5 Mbps	Twisted-pair wire, coax cable, fiber-optic
Medium quality compressed video[4]	1.5–6 Mbps	Twisted-pair wire, coax cable, fiber-optic
High quality compressed video[5]	6–24 Mbps	Coax cable, fiber-optic
Visualization[6]	50–100 Mbps	Coax cable, fiber-optic

[1] Speech-graded audio (SGA) refers to audio that accompanies video, rather than ordinary voice telephony. SGA requires higher bandwidth due to the necessity of synchronizing audio with the video which it accompanies.
[2] Used in such applications as current digital videophone, low quality video typically saves bandwidth by transmitting 15 frames per second (vs. 30 fps for broadcast video), resulting in jerky images, and by using a very small display window often only 25% of the full screen size.
[3] High fidelity audio requires increased sampling rates to eliminate delays and gaps.
[4] Transmits 30 frames per second, providing better quality images and motion, but still limited to small display windows in uses such as delivery of CNN to a window on the user's PC, etc.
[5] Required for very high resolution workstations used in collaborative engineering and scientific design and research in networked configurations.
[6] Involves 3-D imaging of complex structures or designs, such as solid modeling and 3-D animation, which must be performed in real time.
[7] Achieving high-speed transmission rates on twisted-pair wire requires use of digital technologies such as DSL.
Source: Computer Technology Research Corp.

speed Internet access along with cable-TV and local phone service.

Several other developments on the broadband front deserve mention. One is the emerging new class of "data CLECs." These firms primarily focus on offering DSL service to small and midsize businesses, as well as the home-office customer. Taking advantage of surging demand for high-speed Internet connections—and the ILECs' slow pace in serving these customer segments—recent start-ups like NorthPoint Communications, Covad Communications, and Rhythms NetConnections have rolled out service throughout the country. Covad, for example, now offers service in 20 major markets. The company partners primarily with Internet service providers, who sell Covad's DSL service bundled with Internet access.

These data CLECs have experienced rapid growth. For the three months ended March 31, 1999, Covad's revenues totaled $5.6 million, up from $186,000 in the same period in 1998; NorthPoint's revenues totaled $1.3 million, up from $35,000; and Rhythms NetConnections' revenues totaled $660,000, up from $10,000.[47] Moreover, the stock market has favorably viewed the growth prospects of these firms, as evidenced by the recent market values of their stocks: $4.1 billion for Covad, $4.9 billion for NorthPoint, and $4.7 billion for Rhythms NetConnections (all as of July 14, 1999).

While the data CLECs typically focus on the broadband needs of business customers, high-speed cable networks have emerged to provide broadband to the home. The two leading services are At Home and Roadrunner, both of which were started within the last few years. At Home was founded in 1995 as a joint venture that included cable operators Comcast, Cox, and TCI. AT&T's acquisition of TCI gave it 26 percent ownership of At Home (and a controlling share of votes). At the end of 1998, At Home had 331,000 subscribers; Roadrunner, which is owned by Time Warner and began offering service in 1995, had 180,000 subscribers. Together, the two services accounted for nearly three-quarters of the estimated 700,000 subscribers to high-speed cable service.[48]

Also on the broadband scene are companies building wireless networks capable of high-speed transmission. In a fixed wireless system, a radio transmitter mounted on the customer's premises communicates with a central antenna site, which serves as the gateway to the phone system or Internet. The two most prominent entries in the broadband wireless arena are Teligent and WinStar. Like the data CLECs, they are targeting small and midsize businesses in major markets. Teligent, for example, which was founded in 1996, has entered 28 markets covering 83 million people and plans to enter 12 additional markets by the end of 1999. In addition to high-speed data services, Teligent also offers local and long-distance

[47] Revenue data from the companies' annual reports and SEC filings.

[48] *Quarterly Cable Statistics,* Bear Stearns, April 30, 1999.

service. Headed by former AT&T president Alex Mandl, Teligent has licenses to operate in 74 markets nationwide, all of which it plans to enter by the end of 2001.[49]

WinStar's strategy in broadband wireless has been to contract with owners of corporate real estate to secure access rights to buildings. By March 1999, the company had access rights to more than 4,800 commercial buildings, with plans to increase that number to 8,000 by year's end. It has licenses in more than 160 major markets, including all of the top 50 cities. The company now offers service in the top 30 U.S. markets and had 380,000 lines in service as of March 31, 1999. It will add 10 more U.S. markets by the end of 1999. The eventual network will cover more than 60 percent of the nation's small to medium-sized businesses.[50]

An interesting development on the broadband wireless front is the planned purchase, by AT&T unit Liberty Media Group, of Associated Group, Inc., which is Teligent's largest shareholder. If completed, the $3 billion deal would give AT&T a 41 percent stake in Teligent—and another weapon to bypass RBOCs in the battle for local phone business.

DEVELOPMENTS IN SATELLITE-BASED COMMUNICATIONS

Iridium

Iridium, the Motorola-led global phone venture, is to date the most ambitious effort in the satellite-based sector. Thus far, the results have been dismal. When the company launched its service on November 1, 1998, it promised to sign up 52,000 subscribers over the next five months and have revenues of $30 million; but by March 31, 1999, it had only 10,300 users and sales of just $1.45 million. Moreover, the company has quarterly payments of $100 million on $3.4 billion in debt, which it has been unable to meet.[51] In August 1999, Iridium filed for bankruptcy.

Iridium initially promoted its service as an alternative to cellular: the target market was globe-hopping businesspeople, some 5 million strong and growing. These folks, the thinking went, would use a single Iridium satellite phone to replace the several different cell phones required for each continent on which they traveled. But that plan did not work out, for several reasons. The Irid-

ium phone itself—which is 7 inches long, weighs 1 pound, and originally cost around $3,000—is much larger and heavier than today's palm-size cell phones. Moreover, it requires a line of sight to one of Iridium's 66 satellites, which means that it doesn't work indoors. And at $2 to $7 per minute, the usage charges were high. In June 1999, in response to market resistance, Iridium reduced the per minute fees to between $1.59 and $3.99 and lowered the handset cost to $1,495.[52]

Moreover, the company appears to have based its business plan on assumptions that did not hold up over time. For example, it had originally projected a cost of $2.5 billion to build the system, but that ballooned to $5 billion. Meanwhile, as Iridium was building the system, cellular service—against which Iridium was positioning itself—expanded rapidly, while its price declined. By the time Iridium became operational, the competitive landscape had shifted. As of this writing, Iridium's current management faces the challenges of working out a solution with its creditors and developing a revenue stream that has a hope of meeting operating expenses.

Teledesic

Iridium's problems notwithstanding, privately held Teledesic is marching ahead with its plans to build a satellite-based "Internet-in-the-Sky." Cost is perhaps the largest hurdle Teledesic must overcome in implementing its plans. Under its original plan to launch 840 satellites—when each satellite would have run $100 million to build and launch—the cost was prohibitive. Teledesic scaled back the number of satellites in its system to 288, and it has pushed back the targeted starting date for service to 2004. The company thus far has raised some $1.5 billion in equity investment, against a total projected development cost of $9 billion. In 1999, Teledesic signed agreements with Motorola as the prime contractor and with Lockheed Martin as the prime launch service. Motorola also is an investor in Teledesic.

Though Teledesic plans to offer voice capabilities over its system, its main focus is to provide wireless broadband service enabling computers to connect to the Internet and corporate intranets. Customers will have compact low-power terminals and antennas mounted on their rooftops, which will connect inside to a computer network or PC. Most users will have an uplink connec-

---

[49] Teligent data from company's website, www.teligent.com, July 1999.
[50] WinStar data from company's website, www.winstar.com, July 1999.
[51] Data on Iridium's problems from *Forbes,* June 14, 1999.
[52] Data on new pricing structure from the company's website, www .iridium.com, July 1999.

tion of up to 2 Mbps and a downlink connection of up to 64 Mbps; connection at 64 Mbps in both directions will be possible using special high-speed terminals.[53]

In contrast to Iridium's premium pricing strategy, Teledesic foresees end user rates comparable to those of wireline broadband services such as DSL or cable modem. However, Teledesic service will be marketed through a network of service partners, and these resellers will set rates for the areas they serve.

Teledesic will not be a lone player in the satellite-based broadband business—and it may not be the first. SkyBridge LP, a United States–based company led by French communications equipment giant Alcatel and other international partners, is building a system of 80 LEO satellites to offer broadband connectivity. It plans to have service available by 2001. Another potential entrant is Astrolink, a $3.5 billion venture led by Lockheed Martin that would employ four high-orbit satellites; start of service is scheduled for mid-2002. Hughes Electronics Corp. is also working on a broadband service called Spaceway, which would use eight high-orbit satellites to provide global Internet connectivity and which it plans to have in service by 2003.

INTERSECTION OF TELECOMMUNICATIONS AND IT INDUSTRIES

In 1999, telecommunications and information technologies are converging. A prime example, discussed above, is Internet telephony, which uses packet switching technology (originally intended to connect computers) to carry voice conversations. This convergence is bringing IT companies—hardware and software developers alike—into various aspects of the telecommunications business. One of the most visible IT companies moving into the telecom arena is Microsoft.

Microsoft's first major foray into telecommunications came in June1997, when it put up $1 billion for 11.5 percent of cable operator Comcast. Microsoft Chairman Bill Gates described the investment as part of his "vision of linking the PC and TV" to offer advanced "capabilities to deliver video, data and interactivity to the home."[54] Then, in December1998, Microsoft invested $200 million for a 1.3 percent stake in Qwest. Qwest will offer hosting services, built on Microsoft platforms, over its high-speed network.[55] In May1999, the software giant bought $5 bil-

lion of AT&T convertible securities and warrants (equivalent to equity of 3.4 percent). In return, AT&T agreed to license an additional 2.5 million copies of Microsoft's Windows CE software for its digital cable set-top units, with an option for 2.5 million more. This is in addition to an earlier 5-million unit commitment made by TCI in 1998 before being acquired by AT&T.[56] Also in May, Microsoft invested $600 million for a 4.25 percent stake in Nextel Communications, a provider of wireless services in 50 U.S. markets. Nextel customers will be able to use digital phones to access Microsoft's MSN Web portal as their gateway to a customized set of Internet services.[57] Microsoft has also made a number of moves overseas in telecom. In May it paid $120 million to acquire the Swedish firm Sendit, which provides a service that enables customers to view and send messages on their cell phones using Internet browser software. In addition, Microsoft invested more than $500 million in two U.K. cable operators, Telewest and NTL Inc., which are rolling out interactive, broadband service over their networks. And a $300 million investment for a 7.8 percent stake in United Pan-Europe Communications,[58] Europe's second-largest cable company, will put Windows CE software on digital set-top boxes in UPC's 3.4 million homes across Europe beginning next year.[59]

TRENDS FOR THE FUTURE

The future of the U.S. telecommunications industry will likely extend and amplify the trends in place today. The SBC-Ameritech, Bell Atlantic–GTE, and US West–Qwest mergers, if approved, will consolidate a significant segment of the industry, placing pressure on Bell-South—the only RBOC not in a merger deal—to find a growth strategy. More consolidation is also likely in both the wireless and cable sectors, in which hundreds of small and midsize companies operate. RBOCS will experience greater competition for local service, as the CLECs continue to cherry-pick business and home-office customers from the ILECs and as AT&T rolls out local phone service over its cable network.

Convergence of telecommunications and information technology will increasingly bring traditionally nontelecom companies—such as Microsoft, Cisco, 3Com, and others—into telecom-related businesses. For example,

---

[53] Teledesic data from company's website, www.teledesic.com, July 1999.
[54] *Chicago Sun-Times,* June 9, 1997.
[55] Dow Jones Business News, December 14, 1998.

[56] Deutsche Bank Research, May 10, 1999.
[57] Dow Jones Business News, May 28, 1999.
[58] Reuters English News Service, July 26, 1999.
[59] *New Media Markets* (London), June 3, 1999.

the operating-system battle between Microsoft's Windows CE and 3Com's Palm OS in handheld computers, in which 3Com enjoys a lead,[60] is extending into new generations of cell phones and wireless devices designed to take advantage of the emerging broadband services to connect to the Internet.

The growth of wireless services will continue to outpace growth in the wireline sector. The market penetration rate of cellular and PCS services in the United States at 26 percent is far less than in many other industrialized nations, such as Italy (36 percent), Japan (37 percent), and Finland (58 percent).[61] One research group forecasts a penetration rate of 54 percent by 2004.[62]

Another area certain to continue its rapid growth is the demand for high-speed Internet access, via technologies such as DSL, cable modems, and broadband wireless. Much of that growth will come from small-business and residential customers, for whom such services are only now becoming widely available. As expanded services and increased competition force prices down over the next few years, this market may experience explosive growth similar to that of cellular and PCS services in the 1980s and 1990s.

Finally, the market for Internet telephony will likely be another major growth area. As both audio quality and service improve, the dramatic cost savings will drive the market. As noted earlier, already the quality difference between circuit switched and packet switched calls (at least over IDT's IP network) is relatively small, while the price difference is enormous.

All of these trends add up to an increasingly competitive telecommunications industry. The predictable effects—as in all competitive marketplaces—will be a greater variety of offerings and declining prices. The two major wild cards are technological innovation and government regulation.

---

[60] *Business 2.0,* August 1999.
[61] *Business Week,* May 3, 1999.
[62] *Mobile Computing & Communications,* June 1999; the research report cited is "US Wireless Voice Market Forecast Update (1999–2004)," Strategy Analytics (Boston).

Slouching Toward Broadband

And what rough beast, its hour come round at last /
Slouches toward Bethlehem to be born?
—William Butler Yeats, "The Second Coming"

Robert A. Burgelman and Philip Meza

INTRODUCTION

With the twenty-first century underway, many people and businesses (and people with business plans) hoped that the time had come at last for broadband to enter the home. The prospect of consumer high-speed connections to the Internet, often defined as data transfer rates of around 200,000 bits per second (or 200 kilobits per second, kbs), promised a host of new uses for the Internet.[1] However, most consumers still only experienced the Internet at the limits of traditional dial-up modems: 56,000 bits per second (56 kbs) or slower.[2] For these unfortunates, the World Wide Web became the "World Wide Wait"; as it took several minutes for a graphic-rich and therefore bit-intensive Web page to download at those speeds. More advanced Internet applications, such as Web phone calls, video on demand, or Web broadcasts of music or television were haltingly slow or completely impractical at non-broadband speeds. It seemed to many

---

[1] Specifically, the FCC defines broadband as the ability to download (receive bits) and upload (transmit bits) at speeds of 200 kbs. The FCC chose 200 kbs because they believed that it was sufficient to provide the most popular forms of broadband, changing Web pages as quickly as one can turn the pages of a book and transmitting full-motion video.
[2] A modem is a device that modulates, or converts back and forth, between streams of digital signals from a digital device such as a computer, and analog signals that can be carried along conventional copper twisted pair telephone lines that were originally designed to carry voices. The modem demodulates incoming analog signals and converts them to digital signals for the digital device.

that the full benefits of the Internet as a delivery channel for much consumer-targeted advanced e-commerce or entertainment applications would have to wait until broadband became ubiquitous.

By the late 1990s, several technologies had been developed that promised to bring broadband Internet access to consumers. With the prospects of broadband service delivered via cable television coaxial lines, by telephone copper wire twisted pair using digital subscriber lines (DSL), and by satellites and other wireless systems, many analysts made sanguine predictions about the levels of broadband adoption among consumers in the United States and the European Union. By the end of 2001, about 10.7 million homes, or 16 percent of all homes online in the United States had high-speed Internet access, almost double from the year prior (Exhibit 1). In Britain, 290,000 consumers had high-speed access by 2001 and in the broader European Union, 17 percent of all homes with Internet access had broadband connections, more than double from the previous year.[3] While this growth was impressive, it was still below most analysts' expectations. Further, the United States lagged behind other countries in adopting consumer broadband: for example, South Korea had four times the per capita deployment of broadband to the home while Canada had twice the per capita number of the United States (Exhibit 2). Some studies predicted that the United States would fall to ninth place in consumer broadband penetration by 2005.[4] The reasons for the slower than expected adoption of broadband in the United States varied according to viewpoint. Some pointed to poor regulatory oversight and, as a function of this, the high cost of broadband services as the reason for slow adoption. Others blamed the slow adoption of broadband on a lack of popular broadband products, the so-called "killer applications," which would drive consumers to broadband. As Chairman of the United States Federal Communications Commission (FCC) Michael Powell pointed out, "Combined broadband availability is estimated to be almost 85 percent [in 2001]. The intriguing statistic is . . . only 12 percent of these households have chosen to subscribe."[5]

Big Bucks from Broadband, but for Whom

In 1987, economist Robert Solow coined the Solow Paradox saying, "you can see the computer age everywhere but in the productivity statistics." For much of the 1990s, businesses and economists were at a loss to find evidence that gains in information technology (IT) performance contributed much national economic growth. However, the second half of the 1990s saw marked productivity gains that many attributed in part to IT. In the first half of the decade, Gross Domestic Product (GDP) grew at an annual rate of 2.4 percent, compared to 4.1 percent annual growth in the second half of the decade. During the second half of the 1990s, the estimated rate of price decline for computers more than doubled from 15.1 to 32.1 percent.[6] Many economists pointed to networking as the crucial link between increased IT performance and productivity gains. Networks, essentially any connection between two or more computers, are made far more robust by broadband. Others pointed to broadband as an important potential catalyst for general economic growth in the United States. A Brookings Institution study conducted in July 2001 estimated that broadband could add $500 billion per year to the United States economy.[7] The study found consumers would benefit from enhanced online home shopping and entertainment services as well as from a variety of additional services. The researchers estimated that $400 billion per year could be derived from such services, while an additional $50 billion to $100 billion per year could be added to the economy from broadband-related gains experienced by manufacturers of computers, software, and entertainment products.

In the fourth quarter of 2001, e-commerce generated an estimated $25 billion in revenue worldwide.[8] The

---

[3] "Answers from Broadband Regulators," *The Financial Times,* December 20, 2001.
[4] According to TechNet, a technology industry research and political action group.
[5] Michael K. Powell, Chairman, FCC, at the National Summit on Broadband Deployment, Washington, D.C. October 25, 2001 (http://www .fcc.gov/Speeches/Powell/2001/spmkp110.html).

---

[6] Dale W. Jorgenson, "Information Technology and the U.S. Economy," *American Economic Review* 91, no. 1 (March 2001).
[7] Robert W. Crandall and Charles L. Jackson, "The $500 Billion Opportunity: The Potential Economic Benefit of Widespread Diffusion of Broadband Internet Access," The Brookings Institution, July 2001 (www.criterioneconomics.com/documents/ Crandall_Jackson_500_Billion_Opportunity_July_2001.pdf). The authors conclude that universal adoption of broadband in the United States (universal defined as equal to the 94 percent of U.S. households with at least one phone line) could provide consumers with economic benefits of up to $400 billion per year while producers of network equipment, household computers, ancillary equipment, software, and producers and distributors of entertainment products could benefit by as much as $100 billion per year (p. 2). It should be noted that this study was commissioned by the New York–based RBOC Verizon.
[8] Michael Pastore, "New Records Predicted for Holiday E Commerce," *E-Commerce News,* 21 October 2001.

EXHIBIT 1   Internet Access Data

U.S. Internet Access Subscriptions

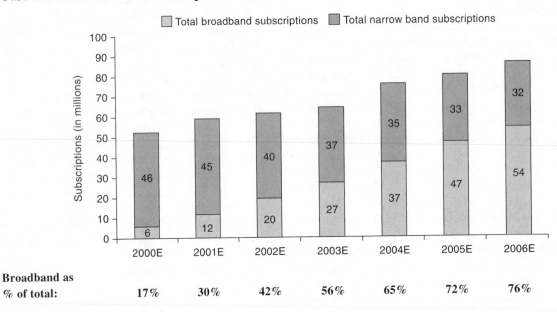

| Broadband as % of total: | 17% | 30% | 42% | 56% | 65% | 72% | 76% |

U.S. Internet Access Revenue

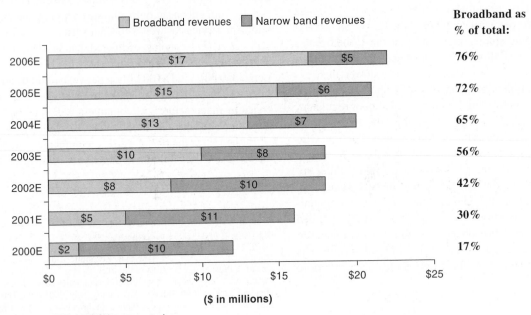

Source: ABN AMRO Incorporated.

EXHIBIT 2 Broadband Penetration per 100 Population

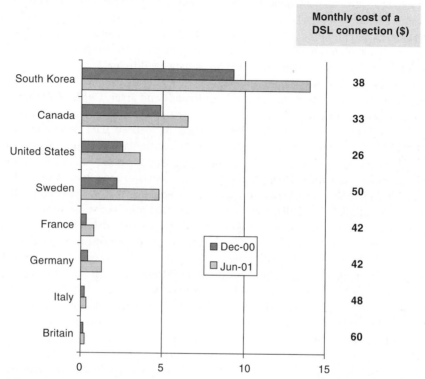

NB: Does not include service start-up costs. Monthly service costs varied in the United States.
Source: OECD; *The Economist.*

United States accounted for over 46 percent of that market. A mere ten years earlier that figure was close to zero. A May 1999 survey by Mercer Management Consulting in Washington, D.C., showed that people with high-speed access search for information and make purchases on-line at approximately double the rate of those with lower-speed analog modems.[9] In 1990, around 15 percent of U.S. households owned a computer. By 2000, more than 50 percent of U.S. households owned a computer, and by 2001, a similar percentage of households had access to the Internet. From 1996 to 2001, the average hours of Internet use per person soared in the United States. However, the growth in the average number of hours per person spent on the Internet is declining, even as Internet applications increase. Similarly, the rate of

consumer spending (in nominal dollars) on personal computers in the United States has declined for the past five years. Some suspect that this decline is the result of consumer frustration with narrowband access for increasingly broadband applications.[10]

FLAVORS OF BROADBAND

Broadband describes various technologies that transfer bits (whether they form an e-mail message, picture, spreadsheet, movie, phone call, etc.) at speeds far greater than possible by ordinary dial-up modems. Many broadband technologies currently available enable users to download at speeds exceeding a million bits per second.

[9] P. William Bane and Stephen P. Bradley, "The Light at the End of the Pipe," *Scientific American,* October 1999.

[10] Crandall and Jackson, "The $500 Billion Opportunity."

The power of broadband lies in the potential for new applications and services that are made possible by the transfer of information (bits) at such high speeds.

Broadband technologies also promised to change the economies and usage patterns of consumer Web access. Many Internet Service Providers (ISPs) offer unlimited use (flat rate) pricing packages. This was a boon in the United States, where most consumers were not directly charged for local calls and most consumers dialed into a local ISP phone number to access the Internet. When ISP AOL changed to flat rate access in the United States in December 1996, usage increased to 70 minutes per day from 14 minutes per day prior to all you can eat pricing. In Europe, AOL and other ISPs have also moved to flat rate pricing; however, local calls are often still metered in many European countries, inhibiting Internet usage. Regardless of call pricing policies, most consumers access the Internet via traditional phone lines, alternating between surfing the Web and using their (single) phone line for voice calls. If you are surfing the Web, you cannot be on the phone and vice versa. By contrast, broadband technologies do not interfere with a consumer's phone (voice) connection and thus can be left engaged—"always on" in the parlance.

Current Broadband Options

There are several methods currently available to deliver broadband to homes. In general, they provide bandwidth through standard telephone lines (copper wire twisted pair) already installed in homes, through cable TV coaxial cable, or via satellite. Each of these modes was originally designed for another purpose, for example voice telephone service or transmission of television signals. In the 1980s and 1990s, engineers began trying a variety of approaches to connect homes for high-speed data communications. This industry note describes three of them. The first two—broadband over cable TV lines and over phone lines—use clever technologies to wring the most out of existing wires to the home: hybrid fiber-coax makes use of the cable TV industry's infrastructure, which includes fiber-optic lines in addition to coaxial cable; the digital subscriber line (DSL), meanwhile, exploits frequencies much higher than those used to convey conversations to send high-speed data over pairs of copper telephone wires. Cable and DSL were by far the two leading technologies for delivering broadband to the home. Among the most economically developed nations in the world, the members of the Organization for Economic Cooperation and Development (OECD), cable led DSL in consumer broadband penetration. In 1999,

84 percent of consumer broadband subscribers used cable versus 16 percent with DSL. By the end of 2000, cable slipped to 55 percent versus 45 percent with DSL. By June 2001, cable edged out DSL by 51 percent to 49 percent.[11] The proportions in the United States were somewhat different.

Broadband over Cable TV Lines Cable television systems have emerged as the early leader in providing such high-speed data access in the home. Currently, cable accounts for 70 percent of consumer broadband in the United States. A cable television system is a company that lays and services coaxial cable and presents programming that is transmitted through the coaxial cable that runs into subscribers' homes and screws into their TVs or set-top boxes.[12] Cable television system operators are distinct from cable networks, which provide programming. However, some multiple systems operators (MSOs), or their parent companies, also own cable networks.

The same coaxial cable that runs into each cable subscriber's home is capable of delivering broadband Internet access (and telephone service too). To access the Internet, the subscriber must have a cable modem, a device that attaches to the cable just like a TV converter box but decodes and manipulates data rather than television signals. Beginning in the late 1980s, many cable companies began upgrading their networks with high capacity fiber optics to support delivery of enhanced, two-way services such as interactive television—which did not win broad consumer support—and video on demand (pay per view), which fared better. Broadband Internet access offered a new, rich market for this transmission capacity. By the mid-1990s, some cable companies introduced broadband Internet services for their subscribers. The hybrid fiber-coax (HFC) systems that cable companies laid with an eye to offering interactive TV and pay-per-view services offered consumers very large capacity for bit transmission. Just one of the many television channels offered to subscribers can carry almost 30 megabits per second (Mbs) to the home.[13]

---

[11] Sam Paltridge, "The Development of Broadband Access in OECD Countries," Organization for Economic Cooperation and Development (OECD), 29 October 2001 (http://www.oecd.org/pdf/M00020000/M00020255.pdf).

[12] An organization that owns two or more cable television systems is known as a multiple system operator (MSO). Prominent examples of MSOs include Comcast, Time Warner Cable, and Cox Communications.

[13] Milo Medin and Jay Rolls, "The Internet Via Cable," *Scientific American,* October 1999.

High capacity optical fibers connect the cable operator's central facility (the "head end") to each neighborhood area (the "node"), which typically encompasses about 1,000 homes, each a potential customer. In an HFC system, the data channel is shared among the homes linked by coax to the end of the local fiber-optic line. Thus, the actual data rate achieved in any individual home depends on the number of users sharing the channel at a given time.[14] Most cable broadband customers experience speeds of 1 megabit per second (mbs). There is also a lower-speed channel in the reverse direction to carry data from the home back to the Internet.

Cable operators stole a march on the telecommunications companies by offering broadband Internet access to consumers almost two years earlier than most regional Bell operating companies (RBOCs). Between the passage of the Telecommunications Act of 1996 and early 2001, the cable industry spend $42 billion to deploy broadband infrastructure in order to offer various advanced services such as high-speed Internet access, digital music, and telephony. By March 2001, U.S. cable companies gained their 4 millionth consumer broadband customer, double the number of broadband customers they had by the end of 1999. The success of the cable companies is credited with spurring telephone companies to offer their own consumer broadband services.

Broadband over Phone Lines   Currently, most broadband over telephone lines uses a variety of DSL technologies, which taken together are often abbreviated xDSL.[15] By the beginning of 2002, around 28 percent of all broadband subscribers in the United States used some version of DSL.

In the United States, DSL services was provided by RBOCs and Competitive Local Exchange Carriers (CLECs). In 2000, four of the leading five DSL providers were RBOCs (Exhibit 3).

The capacity of a communications channel depends on its bandwidth (the range of frequencies it can use) and its signal-to-noise ratio (which depends on the quality of the connection). In 1948, a Bell Lab scientist, Claude E. Shannon, calculated the theoretical transmission capacity of telephone lines at about 35 kbs. It took thirty years of modem development to attain that speed. Modems operating at 56 kbs achieve such rates by taking advantage

EXHIBIT 3   Top 5 DSL Companies by 2000

Company	Type	DSL Subscribers by 2000
SBC	RBOC	767,000
Verizon	RBOC	540,000
Covad	CLEC	274,000
Qwest	RBOC	255,000
Bell South	RBOC	215,000

NB: Covad filed Chapter 11 bankruptcy in August 2001.
Source: Sam Paltridge, "The Development of Broadband Access in OECD Countries," Organization for Economic Cooperation and Development (OECD), 29 October 2001 (http://www.oecd.org/pdf/M00020000/M00020255.pdf).

of digital connections that circumvent some sources of noise in transmissions toward the end user.[16] These modems are still limited to upload (signals sent toward the ISP) rates of 33.6 kbs.

There are several ways currently available to transmit data at high rates over the twisted pair of copper wire designed to convey phone calls and in place in almost every home in the United States. A technology known as integrated services digital network (ISDN), which transmits data at up to 128 kbs, had been gaining popularity since the mid-1990s. Much faster transmission speeds, operating at 1.544 mbs, have been available from T1 lines, initially developed to enable multiple voice connections using a single line. T1 has traditionally been priced for commercial voice access, which is much more costly and more than most people can afford for data access.

The twisted pair of copper telephone wire from a home typically runs to the local exchange carrier's central office containing a switch. A switch is a complex piece of equipment that routes telephone calls to other switches or phones as necessary. DSL service does not use the existing switching equipment. DSL switches are installed in the central office to exploit the full data-carrying capacity of the wires, which normal phone calls do not use. This allows DSL subscribers to simultaneously use the same twisted pair wire for telephone calls and data transmission. Most DSL technologies use a signal splitter installed at the subscriber's premises. Installation of the splitter required a phone company technician visit, which added to the start up costs of the service. A new technology, known as "splitterless DSL" or "G.Lite," made it possible to manage the splitting remotely from the central office. It was hoped that this

---

[14] Ibid.

[15] Asymetric DSL (ADSL) and Symetric DSL (SDSL) are the most popular forms of DSL in the world. In addition, other types of DSL include high–data-rate DSL (HDSL) and Very-high–rate DSL (VDSL).

[16] George T. Hawley, "Broadband by Phone," *Scientific American*, October 1999.

would help reduce the costs associated with initiating and providing DSL service. Companies such as Intel and Microsoft collaborated with phone companies to develop and disseminate the technology.

At present, DSL services can be provided to homes within a 4 to 5 kilometer radius from the telecommunication exchange or central office. The most widely deployed version is asymmetric DSL, or ADSL. It is capable of delivering 3 to 4 Mbs to the home and a slower rate back from the home, typically a small fraction of a megabit per second.

In the 1980s, engineer Joseph W. Lechleider proposed using a copper twisted pair phone line as a very high bandwidth channel, over the short distance from the end user to a telephone central office. He also proposed multilevel coding of the signal to further enhance performance. This transmission technique was called digital subscriber line. By the early 1990s, several firms had developed "high–data-rate" flavors of DSL (known as HDSL) that could transmit almost 800 kbs over a distance of four kilometers. Concurrent with the development of HDSL, John Cioffi of Stanford University demonstrated a signal coding technique called Discrete Multitone, using it to send more than 8 million bits per second through a telephone line more than 1.6 kilometers in length. The technique divided an overall bandwidth of about 1 MHz into 256 subchannels of about 4 kHz each. In essence, it created 256 virtual modems operating simultaneously over the same line. Originally, the Discrete Multitone approach was intended for sending entertainment video over telephone wires. Because such use relies principally on one-way transmission, most of the subchannels were devoted to the "downstream" signal (flowing toward the consumer), carrying about 6 Mbs, with about 0.6 Mbs available in the other direction. This asymmetric form of DSL has become known as ADSL, and the signal coding is now a worldwide standard.[17]

Satellite and Wireless Broadband Neither cable companies nor RBOCs enjoy reputations for sterling customer service. For RBOCs in particular, provisioning and servicing broadband customers has been a challenge. This is one reason some consumers hold out the hope for broadband service without going through cable companies or phone companies. Many of these consumers look to wireless broadband for the answer. Satellite and wireless broadband offer the newest modes for delivery of broadband Internet access to consumers. By 2002, these modes accounted for around 1 percent of all consumer broadband in the United States.

Satellite systems are currently the most widely used wireless broadband system. By early 2002, two companies, DirecPC and StarBand, provided two-way satellite-based Internet access of around 500 kbs, or approximately 10 times the speed of dial-up modems. This transmission rate was expected to improve within the next few years. These companies used geostationary satellites that orbit the earth 36,000 kilometers (22,000 miles) above the equator at the same speed as the earth's rotation (and thus appear from the ground to be stationary) to communicate with fixed-orientation dish antennas attached to customers' homes and use advanced signal processing to compensate for transmission delays caused by the great distances their radio signals must travel. As with satellite TV, trees and heavy rains can affect reception of the Internet signals. The services were generally aimed at consumers who could not receive DSL or cable broadband services.

Meanwhile, many cell phones currently in use in the United States provide Internet connections, albeit slowly in the 10 kbs range, or one-fifth of the speed of most dial-up modems. However, the next generation of cell phones, often referred to as third-generation or 3G technology, were expected to provide broadband access in the megabit per second range. This would enable cell phone handsets to receive and display full-motion video and multimedia applications. These applications were thought to have a "data stimulus effect" in which increased data use would not displace voice traffic but increase it. Handset makers and network providers stood to benefit from wireless broadband applications if they could overcome the relatively low wireless penetration rate in the United States. In 2002, only around 45 percent of the population owned a mobile phone, compared with 77 percent in the European Union.[18]

Broadband service to the home may also soon be provided by ground-based and wireless systems. Two systems, multi-channel multipoint distribution service (MMDS) and local multipoint distribution services (LMDS) can be used to provide wireless broadband Internet access. The basic premise behind wireless networks is that the major cost of installing any broadband system based on wire or fiber is not the cable itself but the labor to install it. Thus, they eschew wire lines. Instead,

---

[17] George T. Hawley, "Broadband by Phone," *Scientific American,* October 1999.

[18] Paul Taylor, "Next Generation Networks: Why 2.5G Reality Lies Behind 3G Claims," *The Financial Times,* March 20, 2002.

like cellular telephones, these networks use radio connections from a base station antenna to remote units at residences.[19] MMDS systems service customers within a range of approximately 15 miles of a base station and require a line of sight path between the base station and the consumer's premises. LMDS operate at frequencies 10 times higher than those used by MMDS and are attenuated by rainfall, foliage, and other obstacles.[20]

BROADBAND AND THE DIGITIZATION OF CONTENT

For the provider, broadband can be a conduit for the much-desired consumer "three-pack" of video, data, and phone service. While many business models awaited widespread consumer broadband and were indifferent as to how it was delivered, there were many powerful stakeholders interested in precisely how consumer broadband was delivered. These stakeholders included cable companies and telephone companies but also ISPs such as AOL and Microsoft's MSN and media content producers such as studios as well as broadcast and cable television networks.

Each of these content industries developed discretely because of the different economic factors involved in the creation and especially distribution of their respective products and because of regulatory forces preventing their combination. In addition, these products required discrete consumption: reading a paper book versus listening to a vinyl record on a phonograph or magnetic tape player (or later a CD player), viewing a movie in a theater versus watching it on television versus streaming it on the Web. Music was the first type of content to be digitized in the early 1980s. This represented a boon to music distributors (usually the copyright holders) who were involved early on in setting the technical standards underlying the standard.[21] During the 1990s, it became clear to content producers and distributors that most of the material they created and controlled could be digitized—converted into bits. Movies, music recordings, books, television broadcasts, and much more could be converted into digital files and hence distributed over the Internet.

While content providers were slow to adopt digital distribution of their wares over the Internet, other entrepreneurs did not wait. Music labels were the first to experience the technological shock to their distribution systems. A nineteen-year-old college student named Shawn Fanning developed a hybrid peer-to-peer program that facilitated the swapping of music files on the Internet.[22] Fanning found venture capital and started a company called Napster, a file swapping service. That company quickly gained devotees among college students who had access to high-speed lines on their campuses and in their dorms. But the audience did not stop there. Soon Napster was attracting twenty three million users who at its height swapped tens of millions of files and spawned a host of imitators. This was a clear demonstration to record labels, which owned most of the copyrights on the material being swapped, of the threat and opportunity represented by the Internet. While the courts struck down Napster's service as illegal, finding that it promoted copyright violations, other services were harder to stop. And file swapping did not end with music. Movie studios began to realize that their products were just as vulnerable—especially in a broadband world.

These files could be transmitted to and displayed by computers because they had been digitized: converted into a digital code that could be read by digital devices such as PCs, CD players, MP3 players, and like.[23] Similarly, movies could be digitized and distributed via the Internet and displayed on digital devices such as PCs. However, digitized movies created much larger files than digitized music. Narrowband data transmission rates are insufficient for a competitive, or even enjoyable, distribution channel for much other than music. The size of a typical three-minute song file exceeded 3 megabytes—over 25 million bits (there are 8 bits to the byte).[24] Swapping song files that approached audio CD quality was possible but feasible only between users with high-speed connections. With respect to movies, picture quality that compared to that given by a VHS tape and player would

[19] Robert P. Norcross, "Satellites: The Strategic Highground," *Scientific American,* October 1999.
[20] Crandall and Jackson, "The $500 Billion Opportunity."
[21] See Jeffrey H. Rohlfs, *Bandwagon Effects in High-Technology Industries* (Cambridge: MIT Press, 2001), for an interesting discussion of the network effects associated with compact-disc players and several other technologies and products.

[22] Peer-to-peer describes a network that enables a group of computer users with the same networking program (e.g., Napster) to connect with each other over the Internet and directly access files from each other's hard drives. For further information, see Professor Robert A. Burgelman and Philip Meza, "Peer-to-Peer Computing: Back to the Future," SM-76, Standard University Graduate School of Business.
[23] MP3 refers to Moving Picture Expert Group (MPEG) MPEG-1 Audio Layer-3, a standard and format for compressing sound data into a very small file while preserving the original level of sound quality when it is played. MP3 players are portable devices for storing and playing such files.
[24] Peter H. Lewis, "Napster Rocks the Web," *New York Times,* June 29, 2000.

EXHIBIT 4   Bandwidth Needed for Selected Applications

Application	Minimum bandwidth	Ideal bandwidth
Movies on Demand	1.5 Mbs	7 Mbs
Digital Television	1 Mbs	7 Mbs
Near Video on Demand	1 Mbs	1.5 Mbs–7 Mbs
Tele-Working	110 kbs	1.5 Mbs–7 Mbs
Distance Learning	110 kbs	7 Mbs
Videoconferencing	110 kbs	800 kbs
Audio on Demand	110 kbs	700 kbs
Video Telephony	70 kbs	200 kbs
Home Shopping	40 kbs	1.5 Mbs–7 Mbs
Tele-Gaming	40 kbs	600 kbs
Electronic Banking	40 kbs	400 kbs

Source: TechNet; Canada Broadband Task Force.

require data transmission rates of 500 kbs. A DVD-quality image would require 750 kbs (Exhibit 4). Even the low resolution (20 frames per second) and jerky image produced by streaming software in 2002 consumed a 300 kbs datastream for the duration of the transmission.[25] Compression standards such as those determined by the Moving Picture Experts Group (MPEG) reduced the size of digitized files by as much as a factor of 50 (a 200 gigabyte two-hour movie could be compressed to a 4 gigabyte DVD).[26]

Digitized files could be distributed via broadband connections and displayed on a variety of digital devices. This combination of broadband distribution and "media agnostic" devices (e.g., a PC that could play and even distribute the contents of a CD, MP3 file, or DVD) underscored the movement toward so-called convergence. Convergence meant different things to different people. For many, it represented the ability to combine the traditional functions of personal computers, CD players, televisions, telephones, and even movie theaters, because each could now display digitized data (e.g., songs, movies, phone calls) and distribute it via the Internet. Each of these forms of content were formerly distributed in separate ways. However, each was subject to digitization and hence delivery over the Internet; distribution made easier by broadband. Many media companies made explicit or implicit bets on convergence. Some studios

sought to buy distribution assets while companies with distribution assets bought content providers. Companies paid dearly to own both distribution and content assets. The increased bandwidth provided by broadband technologies enabled distribution assets to carry more data, while digitization of content allowed content owners to sell their products to a greater variety of people in an increasing number of ways.

SPEEDBUMPS ON THE INFORMATION SUPERHIGHWAY

Digitzation of content and broadband technologies combined increased the usefulness of a computer network that had been around since the 1960s: the Internet. Since its inception as a U.S. government–sponsored fault-tolerant communications network, able to function in times of emergency or disaster (such as when various sites, or nodes, along the network might be knocked out due to an earthquake or even nuclear attack), the Internet had been the purview mostly of academic and government researchers. By the early 1990s, as the Internet started to be used by the general population and businesses, some government and industry officials began referring to the Internet as the Information Superhighway (with speeds limited only by increasing data transmission rates) and pinned hopes for economic and social prosperity on the ability of the Internet to facilitate commerce, learning, and entertainment. For all of the popularity of the Internet, broadband technologies still have not appeared in the marketplace as rapidly as most observers had predicted. Nor has the broadband marketplace proven to be as competitive as was hoped.

It Is Costly to Widen Narrow Roads

In the wake of the deregulation of telecommunications prompted by the Telecommunications Act of 1996, RBOCs focused on defending themselves against competition from CLECs. RBOCs did whatever they could to undermine CLECs in consumer broadband, making it difficult for rival DSL start-ups to interconnect to the RBOC's equipment, and going so far as to bar rivals' technicians from bathroom facilities at switches.[27] Meanwhile, cable companies focused on consolidation rather than expansion into voice services. It was only with consumer broadband that cable companies and RBOCs began to compete with each other; cable compa-

---

[25]"Reality Check for Video on Demand," *The Economist*, June 21, 2001. NB: Movies in theaters are displayed at 24 frames per second; television in North America is broadcast at 30 frames per second. *Source:* Charles Petzold, *Code* (Redmond, Wash.: Microsoft Press, 1999).

[26]Petzold, p. 380.

[27]Stephanie N. Mehta, "How to Get Broadband Moving Again," *Fortune*, December 10, 2001.

nies offering high-speed Internet access and RBOCs offering DSL. Meanwhile, the rate of increase of Internet use in the United States started to decline. Some blame frustration with the slow download times produced by dial-up modems.

During 2001, the rate at which customers signed up for broadband declined. The number of DSL customers increased 20 percent the first quarter of 2001 but declined to a 14 percent increase in the second quarter of 2001. Meanwhile, the rate of broadband customer acquisition for cable companies declined 12 percent during the same period.[28]

At the same time, many RBOCs began to pull back on their DSL expansion plans. Sprint and the RBOC SBC Communications have both scaled back DSL expansion plans, and AT&T Wireless has eliminated its wireless broadband service. Other RBOCs became less aggressive about expanding DSL service into new regions, instead focusing on offering the service to areas they already served. Analysts estimated that it took RBOCs two years to recover the costs associated with installing and servicing a consumer DSL account. In addition, DSL service often eliminated the need for a second residential telephone line—a lucrative source of revenue for RBOCs. With the high profile closures of many DSL start-ups, the RBOCs had the field largely to themselves by 2002.[29]

For cable companies, there was still much uncertainty surrounding the disposition and impact of open access regulations. Time Warner's cable systems shared its system with EarthLink (a condition of the AOL–Time Warner merger.)

RBOCs and cable companies were involved in partnerships with the three leading ISPs in the United States to offer broadband service. For the ISPs, broadband offered a cheaper way to service members. ISP EarthLink estimated it spent around $3 on telecommunications and equipment costs for every $10 it earned from dial-up customers. The ISP estimated it spent $8 on those costs for every $10 it earned from broadband customers. EarthLink claimed it was more expensive for it to provide DSL service than cable broadband. The ISP retained about 30 percent of the revenue generated from its broadband service; the remaining 70 percent went to the DSL provider or cable company.[30]

Wi-Fi: A Potential Hot Spot for Broadband   For several years network enthusiasts toyed with applications emerging from a technical standard designated 802.11b, but more commonly called Wireless Fidelity or Wi-Fi. This networking standard governed wireless local area networks that could transfer data at speeds of up to 11 megabits per second, faster than the approximately 1 megabit per second that DSL provided and far faster than the 144 kilobit per second data transmission rates (but within a much shorter range) that third generation (3G) mobile service providers planned. Users communicated with Wi-Fi transmitters or base stations, known as "hot spots," via small antennas connected to devices such as desktop or laptop computers and personal digital assistants. For example, a DSL subscriber could connect his or her DSL modem to a Wi-Fi hot spot, in this case a base station, and enjoy wireless broadband access (for multiple devices) within a range of 150 feet or so, using small, easy to install equipment bought for between $100 and $300. While some hoped that Wi-Fi would make broadband more attractive to consumers, others noted that it was easy to share Wi-Fi connections, even between residences such as apartments, and observed that the networking standard raised the specter of broadband piracy, especially in densely populated areas.

Providers emerged that offered subscription-based Wi-Fi broadband Internet access via a growing network of hotels, coffee shops, airports, and other facilities. For example, by 2002, the ubiquitous Starbucks equipped 530 of its stores with hot spots and planned to offer Wi-Fi access in 70 percent of its 3,200 stores in North America.[31] Subscription rates varied, but some plans offered unlimited highspeed wireless Internet access to networks of Wi-Fi stations across the country for around $70 per month. Since Wi-Fi applications operated in unlicensed airwave spectrum, the frequencies used by devices such as baby monitors, these service providers did not face the same large costs of 3G cellular providers in acquiring their spectrum.

How to Get the Bandwagon Rolling

Consumer broadband deployment faced the bandwagon problem: costs would decrease and consumer benefit would increase as more people adopted consumer broadband (i.e., got aboard the "bandwagon").[32] However, the

[28]Dennis K. Berman and Shawn Young, "Bells Make a High-Speed Retreat from Broadband," *Wall Street Journal,* October 29, 2001.
[29]Ibid.
[30]Julia Angwin, "AOL, Microsoft, and EarthLink Now Pick Up Subscriber Race," *Wall Street Journal,* October 29, 2001.

[31]Amey Stone, "Special Report: The Wireless Net," *Business Week,* April 1, 2002.
[32]A bandwagon effect can be defined as the benefit a consumer enjoys as the result of others doing (or using) the same things as other

high cost of consumer broadband service dissuaded many potential users. This problem was complicated by the reluctance of suppliers to provide complementary products (e.g., high bandwidth services such as video on demand) until there was a sizeable group of consumers for the products.[33]

One thing was clear; it will cost a lot of money to get the bandwagon rolling. Estimates vary of the cost to deploy broadband to every home in the United States. Under current conditions, it costs between $1,000 and $2,000 per home to deploy broadband to a consumer. If one estimates there are 100,000,000 homes in the United States, the cost ranges from $100 billion to $200 billion. Some analysts estimate a larger total cost. FCC Commissioner Powell acknowledged the limited ability of government to drive the bandwagon. Powell said:

> I believe that the key measure is availability of service, not adoption rates. I emphasize availability, because there are many questions that remain as to what services consumers will value and to what degree they will be willing to subscribe. I am hesitant to let adoption rates drive government responses, for a developing market needs the cues produced by consumer free choice.[34]

Citing the gap between the estimated 85 percent of households in the United States that have access to broadband and the mere 12 percent that choose to subscribe,[35] Powell said: "Consumers may not yet value the services at the prices they are being offered. . . . This highlights the classic chicken and egg dilemma. Broadband applications that consumers value are not yet offered to justify broadband service, yet the lack of broadband subscribers inhibits subscription—similar problems exist in many network industries."

Powell cited four ways in which government could influence broadband deployment adoption: directly pay for a build-out by subsidizing consumers or providers; indirectly pay by offering tax incentives to consumers or providers; aggregate demand by using the government buying power; and remove legal barriers. The last tool would have a direct impact on the industries that hope to create and distribute content in a more converged world. Powell added:

> Clearly legal restraints can retard deployment of new services. The government can look at modifying or relaxing laws and regulations that impede deployment. . . . Much of what is holding back broadband content is caused by copyright holders trying to protect their goods in a digitized world. Stimulating content creation might involve a re-examination of the copyright laws. Arguably, VCRs would not be widely available today if Universal Studios had won its infringement case against Sony in 1984. They won in the Supreme Court by a vote of 5 to 4.

Powell touched on one significant force inhibiting consumer broadband deployment: copyright holders were pulling the brake.

Content providers were deeply concerned about the ability of consumers to pirate their products. Few large content providers, such as movie studios, record labels, and television broadcasters, had devised successful new business models that operated in the new era distinguished by digitization of content and broadband transmission and the convergence of vehicles of media consumption that they enabled. Entertainment companies looked to government for more stringent controls over the technologies that could enable content pirating. Technology companies such as PC builders and semiconductor makers balked, suggesting that new business models for entertainment companies were the answer to content piracy. Michael Eisner, Disney's Chairman and CEO, said that it was "easy to encourage us to overlook the pirates when you're making the sword," and doubted that any new business model could compete with digital copies that were free, flawless, and easily accessible.[36]

The Lights Go Out @Home

While broadband access was widely available in the United States, it was expensive, usually exceeding $50 per month, and often difficult to get. Furthermore, many service providers proved to be unstable. In 2001, two prominent DSL broadband suppliers, NorthPoint Com-

---

consumers. Jeffrey H. Rohlfs, *The Bandwagon Effect in High-Technology Industries* (Cambridge: MIT Press, 2001).

[33] See Rohlfs, *Bandwagon Effects,* for an interesting discussion of bandwagon or network effects associated with several technologies and products.

[34] Michael K. Powell, Chairman, FCC, at the National Summit on Broadband Deployment, Washington, D.C., October 25, 2001 (http://www.fcc.gov/Speeches/Powell/2001/spmkp110.html).

[35] In 2001, investment bank JP Morgan estimated that 73 percent of homes in the United States had access to cable broadband and 45 percent had access to DSL service. FCC Chairman Powell estimated that these constitute 85 percent of all households in the United States.

[36] Amy Harmon, "Piracy, or Innovation? It's Hollywood vs. High Tech," *The New York Times,* March 14, 2002.

munications and Rhythms NetConnections, went out of business, eventually selling to larger telecom companies, but leaving hundreds of thousands of mostly business customers without broadband service before the transition. In August 2001, Covad, another prominent CLEC, filed for Chapter 11 protection. A more prominent failure, this time in cable, was to follow.

In 1995, cable giants Comcast, Cox Communications, and TCI (later acquired by ATT Broadband) funded a company called @Home to offer broadband Internet access to consumers over cable lines. At the time, the company estimated it would cost between $500 and $1,000 per home (or $8 billion to $10 billion total) to upgrade the cable networks of its investors to carry broadband signal to consumers.[37] Even though this represented almost the entire market capitalization of the three cable companies, many had high hopes for @Home. In 1999, @Home paid $6.3 billion for the Internet portal Excite, in what was one of the largest Internet deals to that time. Unfortunately for @Home, the cost estimates to upgrade its constituent cable systems proved to be dramatically low.

In addition, infighting among its cable company investors added to @Home's problems. Also, regulatory issues surrounding "open access"—for example whether AT&T had to accept third party ISPs such as AOL on their systems—slowed the company. The technology downturn in 2000–2001 dealt the final blow. In September 2001, Excite@Home filed for Chapter 11 protection and prepared to discontinue service. This left 4.1 million subscribers, mostly consumers, scrambling to find new broadband service providers. At the same time that Excite@Home filed Chapter 11, AT&T offered to purchase essentially all of the company's broadband assets for $307 million in cash. However, three months later the deal fell apart and Excite@Home, having gone to court to win the right to disconnect customers, prepared to close its doors. Soon thereafter, AT&T sold its cable television business to Philadelphia-based cable operator Comcast for $47 billion in stock. This deal ended a yearlong auction for the business between Comcast, cable operator Cox Communications, and AOL Time Warner for the cable giant's assets. Software maker Microsoft financially supported both Comcast and Cox in their bids and even offered to infuse $4 billion to $5 billion into

ATT Broadband if the company decided to spurn the three offers.

A NATIONAL IMPERATIVE?

Some technology industry leaders had been increasingly vocal about the need for the United States to increase the penetration of consumer broadband in the country. Large technology companies such as Cisco, Intel, and Microsoft, as well as prominent technology investment bankers and venture capitalists, banded together to form TechNet, a technology industry advocacy group. TechNet and prominent technology industry leaders have framed the issue of consumer broadband penetration as a matter of national strategic importance.

John Chambers, the president and CEO of networking giant Cisco, said, "Broadband should be a national imperative for this country in the twenty-first century, just like putting a man on the moon was an imperative in the last century. . . . In order to stay competitive, educate the workforce, and increase productivity, the United States must have ubiquitous broadband." Intel's CEO Craig Barrett said, "It is critically important for the United States to adopt a national broadband policy that encourages investment in new broadband infrastructure, applications, and services—particularly new last mile broadband facilities. . . . Regulatory policies should encourage all companies to deploy these expensive and risky facilities."[38] These leaders are promoting a set of decidedly non–laissez-faire government policies to promote consumer broadband in the United States. These included asking the government to offer tax credits to help companies defray the costs of bringing broadband to poor and rural areas and exempting new RBOC broadband investments from federal regulation. Some observers noticed how strange it was for technology companies, who had a large financial stake in broadband deployment and who in the past had been critical of RBOC foot dragging, to come out in support of exempting RBOCs from federal regulation. FCC Chairman Powell seemed unsure whether such a national policy was warranted. He observed: "I caution, however, that we have to distinguish between a true market failure, and what is simply hard or challenging. . . . In struggling through the challenge it will be common for some to want to try and leap ahead

---

[37] Jason Krause, "Broadband's Tug of War," *The Standard,* December 11, 2000.

[38] "TechNet CEO's Call for National Broadband Policy," TechNet Press Release January 15, 2002 (http://www.technet.org/issues/updates// 2002-01-15.69.phtml).

by securing government assistance. Market failure might demand a government response, but market challenges should be left to market players."[39]

CONCLUSION

Clearly much was at stake with consumer broadband in the United States. Some looked at broadband as a catalyst for economic growth and a way to deliver the United States out of a recession, an economic downturn that hit the technology sector particularly hard. Others looked at consumer broadband as a national, strategic asset and suggested that the government take active steps to promote the deployment of consumer broadband. However, the forces influencing consumer broadband deployment in the United States were complex. What role, if any, the government could play would have to be balanced by market and technological forces that influenced consumer broadband in the United States.

---

[39] Michael K. Powell, Chairman, FCC, at the National Summit on Broadband Deployment, Washington, D.C., October 25, 2001 (http://www.fcc.gov/Speeches/Powell/2001/spmkp110.html).

The PC-Based Desktop Video-Conferencing Systems Industry in 1998

Osamu Suzuki

On February 26, 1998, PictureTel Corporation, the world market share leader in the videoconferencing systems industry, announced disappointing results for the fiscal year 1997 (PictureTel's historical financial performance is shown in Exhibit 1). Annual revenues were $466.4 million, declining 4.9 percent from the previous year. Net losses were $39.4 million compared to a net income of $32.2 million in 1996. One of the primary reasons for the sales decrease was overall market slowdown in the company's PC-based desktop videoconferencing systems business. Some securities analysts pointed to

Source: Copyright © 1998 by The Board of Trustees of the Leland Stanford Junior University. All rights reserved. Osamu Suzuki, M.B.A. 1998, prepared this case under the supervision of Professor Robert A. Burgelman as the basis for class discussion rather than to illustrate either effective or ineffective handling of an administrative situation.

EXHIBIT 1 PictureTel's Historical Financial Performance

($K)

	12/31/97	12/31/96	12/31/95	12/31/94	12/31/93	12/31/92	12/31/91
Revenue:	466,425	490,225	346,758	255,193	176,252	141,409	78,024
Product	417,115	451,119	319,017	232,226	158,627	127,551	69,988
Roll-about systems*	69.0%	65.0%	70.0%	76.0%	82.7%	79.4%	89.1%
Desktop systems*	9.0%	15.0%	15.0%	9.0%	0.3%	0.0%	0.0%
Multipoint control units*	11.0%	13.0%	7.0%	6.0%	7.0%	10.8%	0.6%
Service	49,310	39,106	27,741	22,967	17,625	13,858	8,036
Gross margin:	190,514	239,176	171,715	126,154	98,241	76,880	42,643
SG&A	167,841	133,028	101,229	86,218	60,374	46,484	26,739
R&D	79,523	65,134	46,184	38,327	29,192	21,280	10,154
EBIT	(55,490)	48,095	27,541	6,949	11,360	13,313	6,804
Net income	(39,398)	32,172	19,629	4,579	8,426	10,659	5,951
Total assets	355,051	386,254	288,141	216,699	187,425	165,713	144,857
Shareholders' equity	227,965	264,846	200,822	153,236	146,939	132,128	119,623
G.M./Revenue	40.8%	48.8%	49.5%	49.4%	55.7%	54.4%	54.7%
Net income/revenue	−8.4%	6.6%	5.7%	1.8%	4.8%	7.5%	7.6%
ROA	−20.0%	14.3%	10.9%	3.4%	6.4%	8.6%	7.9%
ROE	−21.3%	13.8%	11.1%	3.1%	6.0%	8.5%	9.0%

*% of total revenue
The acquisition of MultiLink was accounted for as a pooling of interests since the fiscal year 1996, before which figures are not available.
Source: PictureTel annual reports.

the delay in the anticipated introduction of a new LAN-based[1] desktop videoconferencing system as being the source of the soft demand. In addition, the business had experienced a drastic price decrease in its five-year history (Exhibit 2). Although the videoconferencing systems industry had seen significant progress, including standardization, in this decade, it had a long history of disappointment. This financial decline of the industry leader raised the question as to whether the demand was really there.

One factor that made the past few years different from earlier days was Intel Corporation's high-profile involvement in this industry (Intel's historical financial performance is shown in Exhibit 3). However, Intel also lowered its overall first-quarter revenue expectation as much as 10 percent on March 4. *Dataquest* said software applications had stagnated so that even the fastest PCs offered little benefit to the users. Shedding light on another aspect, an analyst at Hambrecht & Quist in San Francisco argued that the announcement signaled that lower PC prices were not necessarily causing PCs to reach more people. "It shows that demand isn't elastic," he said.[2] Some others pointed out that Intel's efforts to "make the PC it" in the home resulted in only limited success.[3] Participating in the PC-based desktop videoconferencing market had been one of the most strategic moves for

---

[1] LAN stands for local area network.
[2] *Wall Street Journal,* March 5, 1998.
[3] *Wall Street Journal,* February 12, 1998.

EXHIBIT 2   The Evolution of Industry-Wide Average Price for ISDN Based

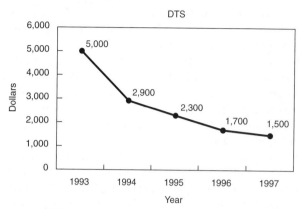

Source: TelSpan Publishing.

Intel during the last few years. Industry observers were wondering whether Intel would be able to create the new market on its own.

EARLY HISTORY OF THE VIDEOCONFERENCING SYSTEMS INDUSTRY

Since AT&T's introduction of the world's first Picturephone in 1964 at the New York World's Fair, videoconferencing systems (VCSs) had continuously disappointed people's expectations of two-way visual communication. Many devices were introduced by various companies,

EXHIBIT 3   Intel's Historical Financial Performance

($M)

	12/31/97	12/31/96	12/31/95	12/31/94	12/31/93	12/31/92	12/31/91
Revenue	25,070	20,847	16,202	11,521	8,782	5,844	4,779
COGS	9,945	9,164	7,811	5,576	3,252	2,557	2,316
Gross margin:	15,125	11,683	8,391	5,945	5,530	3,287	2,463
SG&A	2,891	2,322	1,843	1,447	1,168	1,017	765
R&D	2,347	1,808	1,296	1,111	970	780	618
EBIT	10,659	7,934	5,638	3,603	3,530	1,569	1,195
Net income	6,945	5,157	3,566	2,288	2,295	1,067	819
Total assets	28,880	23,735	17,504	13,816	11,344	8,089	6,292
Shareholders' equity	19,295	16,872	12,140	9,267	7,500	5,445	4,418
G.M./revenue	60.3%	56.0%	51.8%	51.6%	63.0%	56.2%	51.5%
Net income/revenue	27.7%	24.7%	22.0%	19.9%	26.1%	18.3%	17.1%
ROA	54.0%	38.5%	36.0%	28.6%	36.3%	21.8%	19.0%
ROE	51.2%	35.6%	33.3%	27.3%	35.5%	21.6%	18.5%

Source: Intel Corporation 10K form.

but no one had yet completely satisfied users' basic requirements (i.e., affordable and reliable communications), at least until the mid 1980s.

Problems abounded. First, devices had been prohibitively expensive. Not only did the VCS itself cost $250,000 on average, users were required to set up a special room in which to implement it. An additional expense was incurred to buy a high-bandwidth dedicated transmission line. For example, a T1 line was needed to accommodate data transmission rate up to 1,544 Kbps (kilobits per second). The worst problems came after implementation. Picture quality was low (rough, jerky, and dark) and different makers' VCSs did not talk to each other (i.e., there was no compatibility between competing products). As a result of all these problems, it seemed almost natural that most people chose to physically fly around the world rather than try to meet their colleagues over a VCS.

Higher Bandwidth Roll-About Systems: Compression Laboratories

A company called Compression Laboratories Inc. (CLI) brought about the first breakthroughs. In 1984, CLI launched a VCS that worked on much lower bandwidth (384 Kbps) than T1. Then, CLI continuously decreased the bandwidth requirement so that users could benefit from videoconferencing over public circuit switching transmission lines like ISDN (integrated services digital network). Starting from 1,544 Kbps in 1982, the minimum bandwidth requirements for commercially available systems had come all the way down to 56 Kbps by 1987. CLI had always stayed at the head of the race, developing ever-efficient video compression technology.

As required bandwidth was continuously declining, a new type of VCS called a roll-about system (RAS) was gaining popularity in the late 1980s. RASs, as the name indicates, could be moved around in the building, so users did not have to set up dedicated rooms for videoconferencing. To move VCSs around, VCSs needed to be more compact. This is where another important enabling technology came out: VLSI (very large scale integrated circuits). VLSI played a significant role in scaling down VCSs. Advanced VLSI technology enabled VCS manufacturers to place more and more transistors and other components on the limited size of a silicon chip. In this way, the size of those integrated components was significantly reduced. Thus, with the increasing use of VLSI technology, the cost of VCSs steadily decreased as components became smaller and systems more integrated, while offering greater functionality to the customers. CLI was supported by the ASIC (application specific integrated circuits) developer, Integrated Information Technology (currently 8×8) in developing proprietary chips for video compression.

Although CLI played an important role in improving video compression technology, its fundamental corporate strategy to capitalize on proprietary video compression technology led the company to diversify into other related markets, including high-definition TV and satellite broadcasting. This lack of focus and the company's strong belief that users would keep paying a premium for high-quality pictures was fatal to CLI. It made it difficult for the company to quickly respond to new competitors with a different approach.

Lower Bandwidth Roll-About Systems: PictureTel

PictureTel, founded in 1984 by a group of MIT graduates, started to focus on RASs that worked on still lower bandwidth (56–112 Kbps) than CLI's mainstream products, which typically worked on 384 Kbps bandwidth or higher. While CLI's products were superior in terms of picture quality, CLI underestimated the potential of PictureTel's substantial price advantage and users' reluctance to implement high-bandwidth lines. For example, in January 1991, PictureTel launched System 4000 at the list price of $40,000, whereas CLI's average list price was $56,000. With this price advantage, PictureTel tried to meet the needs of a new group of customers, who could be satisfied with less-than-TV-quality pictures. PictureTel also emphasized the use of third-party distribution, while CLI predominantly distributed through its own sales force.

As it turned out, CLI completely failed to respond to this challenge from the lower-end market. Ironically enough, CLI had been ahead of PictureTel in developing video compression algorithms for the lower-bandwidth systems. With PictureTel increasing market share at the expense of CLI's business, CLI responded by simply decreasing the list price (CLI's average unit price in 1992 decreased to $49,600). Unfortunately, CLI's proprietary ASIC approach did not allow it to profitably compete against PictureTel, which purchased programmable video compression chips from LSI Logic. By 1992, their market share was reversed: PictureTel rose from 40 percent in 1991 to 49 percent in 1992, while CLI went from 50 percent to 39 percent. Decreasing profit margins limited CLI's new product development investments. As a result, CLI failed to properly respond to the next industry wave (i.e., PC-based desktop videoconferencing systems or DTSs). CLI never reestablished its position in the newly emerging DTS segment and ended up being acquired by one of its competitors later. With CLI's decline, the position of industry leader was passed on to PictureTel.

PC-Based Desktop Systems: Intel's Entry

Since its divestiture of an "intrapreneurial operation" called Personal Computer Enhancement Operation (PCEO)[4] in 1984, Intel had been looking around for new PC applications which CEO Andrew Grove called "power hungry applications." PCEO's mission was "to provide enhancements to the basic PC systems being sold by Intel's PC OEM customers (Jim Johnson, vice president and general manager)."[5] PCEO's early results included ethernet adapter cards (installed into a standard PC expansion slot to connect with LANs) or fax modem.

In this context, a new task force, carved out as PCED Business Communications, was assigned the role of DTS development. Intel's decision to go into the DTS market seemed somewhat intuitive at this point. Asked whether market research convinced Intel that there was a huge potential for the DTS market, Andrew Grove replied, "Who the hell are you going to ask? This is a brand-new market. There's just something about live video on a computer screen. I can't walk away from it."[6] Patrick Gelsinger, who had been in charge of 486 development, was chosen to lead this group. This choice was controversial inside Intel since he was then responsible for the development of P6, the successor of the Pentium. Grove noted: "In many ways this is the test of it. We can't expect to succeed if we aren't willing to put our best people on the project."[7]

As for Intel's core microprocessor business, the period preceding the entry into the DTS market was a very busy one. With the March 1993 introduction of the Pentium, Intel was in a critical transition period. The Pentium was the first microprocessor specifically designed to compete against RISC[8] architecture microprocessors. Originally developed by MIPS, RISC chips were believed to have superior performance over a narrow range of processing intensive tasks, including 3D graphics or videos. Although the ACE consortium[9] had been disbanded by that time, new threats started to emerge from various new RISC projects, including the PowerPC of IBM, Apple, and Motorola (summer of 1993) and Digital Equipment's Alpha (late 1992). Also in May of the same year, Microsoft announced the release of Windows NT, which ran on the Intel architecture but also on MIPS' RISC architecture. In addition, Microsoft was working with both DEC and IBM to help them port NT to DEC's Alpha chip and IBM's PowerPC chip.

In the PC industry at large during this period, price competition between PC makers heated up. As a result, PC makers were not financially capable of promoting future usage for PCs. On the other hand, Intel had just succeeded in getting its local bus specification, called PCI (peripheral component interconnect), accepted as an industry standard. The effect was significant for the whole PC industry. By improving I/O (input-output) processing between PCs and such peripherals as disks, graphics adapter chips, or network adapters, PCI would boost PC system performance, eliminating the bottlenecks that had most negatively impacted overall functionality.

THE VCS INDUSTRY IN 1998: KEY ISSUES

Market Segments

In 1998, there were roughly three types of VCS segments in the market: roll-about systems, PC-based desktop systems, and multipoint control units.

The roll-about system (RAS) was the most popular VCS segment. In 1996, the worldwide market was estimated to be $635 million (up 15.5 percent from 1995, Exhibit 4). The United States (where 21 companies were

EXHIBIT 4 Worldwide RAS Market in 1996

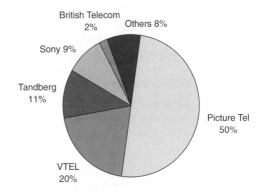

Total $635 million

Sources: Annual reports, 10K forms, *Telespan Publishing,* case writer's estimate.

---

[4] PCEO was later integrated back into Intel and renamed Personal Computer Enhancement Division.
[5] *Intel Corporation (E): New Directions for the 1990s,* Stanford Case.
[6] *Forbes,* December 6, 1993.
[7] *Intel Corporation (E): New Directions for the 1990s,* Stanford Case.
[8] Reduced instruction set computing.
[9] The industry consortium established in 1991 to develop and promote the RISC architecture microprocessor.

competing) was by far the biggest subsegment, totaling $478 million (up 24.1 percent from 1995). The RAS provided an integrated mobile cabinet with a TV-size display that is controlled through a tabletop board. The main usage of RAS was a point-to-point communication where two groups of people are involved in one meeting. The quality of motion picture was superior, 30 fps (frames per second),[10] transmitted either through T1 or ISDN. The average unit price varied between $15,000 and $90,000. Customers were primarily Fortune 1,000 type multinational companies, large health care providers, or distance education facilities. They were relatively less price sensitive. For them, ease of use or reliability of equipment were more important than price, since system failure could cause serious monetary as well as nonmonetary consequences. Starting in the fall of 1996, less expensive versions were coming to the market to stimulate acceptance as well as to respond to market erosion caused by the expansion of the PC-based desktop systems market. Some systems were priced as low as $10,000, seriously damaging traditionally RAS-focused companies' profitability.

The PC-based desktop system (DTS) was the second largest product segment (Exhibit 5). In 1996, the worldwide market was estimated to be $171 million (up 41.0 percent from 1995). The U.S. market, with 56 competitors, was again the biggest subsegment, totalling $111 million (up 40.3 percent from 1995). In terms of unit shipment, DTSs outpaced RASs for the first time in the U.S. market in 1996. Traditionally, DTSs were provided in a package consisting of a video compression board (commonly called codec[11] board, which is inserted into a PC), a camera, a microphone, and software that supports codec's video compression tasks. The mode of transmission was largely through ISDN and T1 and to a lesser extent hosted by LANs. Recently, firms introduced DTSs based on the Internet and on POTS (plain old telephone service).[12] Picture quality was acceptable but not as good as RASs especially for business users since most often the frame rate was limited to 15–25 fps. In addition to large corporations, major customers included SOHO (small offices, home offices), small business, and consumers. They tended to be much more price sensitive

EXHIBIT 5 Worldwide DTS Sales for Major Three Competitors

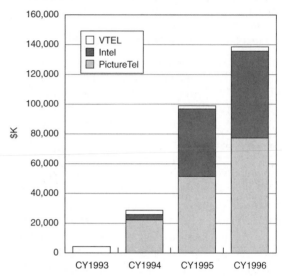

Sources: Annual reports, 10K and 10 Q forms, *Computer Reseller News, Computer World,* case writer's estimate.

than customers for the RAS market were. In a typical setting, participants were limited to two end-points, as in the case of RASs. Due to the small size of the display, usage was virtually limited to person-to-person videoconferencing. Another feature that critically differentiated DTSs from RASs was DTSs' collaboration applications, including the ability to exchange and work on spreadsheets and data files on videoconferencing displays. It was reported that the worldwide DTS market experienced a significant slowdown in 1997.

Both types of VCS described above were basically limited to point-to-point use. In other words, to have a videoconference between three or more end points, users needed to have special equipment called a multipoint control unit (MCU). MCUs involved highly complicated equipment that functioned as a gateway, interfacing with different proprietary VCSs and converting the transmission speed within them. MCUs' highly advanced features necessitated direct sales by the manufacturer due to the technical complications and need for extensive installation support. Unit price varied between $20,000 and $300,000, which only very price insensitive customers could afford. Major customers included manufacturers of RASs or DTSs, telecommunication carriers (e.g., AT&T, MCI, Sprint), and to a lesser degree, commercial customers, scientific institutes, and distance

---

[10]Frame rate is the most commonly used measure for picture quality. Since it only captures the "smoothness" of moving pictures, resolution or picture size should also be considered to evaluate real picture quality.
[11]Codec, formed from **co**der/**dec**oder.
[12]Conventional existing telephone lines.

learning facilities. Important purchase criteria were reliability, number of ports, and interconnectivity. More than 80 percent of sales for MCUs were generated in the United States (where the growth rate was 67 percent in 1996), out of the total worldwide market of $88 million (up 100 percent from 1995) in 1996. VideoServer dominated the U.S. market with 64 percent share, followed by Lucent Technologies.

Video Compression Technology

The decreased bandwidth requirement mentioned above was primarily due to improvements in video compression technology, one of the most important enabling technologies in the VCS industry. A conventional video image includes as much information as 90 million bps. It is too big for transmission over currently available transmission lines. Thus, the video image must be compressed or omitted when it goes through transmission lines and then decompressed or restored at the other end of the line. Video compression was a four-step process: preprocessing, encoding, decoding, and postprocessing. The first step removes high-frequency noise from the digitized picture. The second step employs a series of mathematical transformations defined by video compression algorithms to encode (i.e., compress) the picture. On the receiving end, in steps three and four, the process is reversed and the signal is decoded (i.e., decompressed) and cleaned of noise.[13]

The competition in the VCS industry had mainly focused on the improvement of the video compression algorithm; in other words, developing more efficient codec that executes the video compression algorithm. Under the constraint that the decompressed picture should be acceptable, companies competed to reduce the required bandwidth to send pictures of the same quality or to improve the picture quality given the same amount of transmission bandwidth. Exhibits 6 and 7 show the evolution of minimum required bandwidth for TV-quality VCSs (i.e., 30 fps pictures). Specifically, Exhibit 6 shows the actual and forecasted evolution, and Exhibit 7 shows the trend line.

In 1998, there were two options for designing a DTS codec: a traditional hardware-based solution and a recently developed software-based solution. The hardware-based solution utilized a dedicated video compression chip. Embedded on a codec board, the dedicated video compression chip was largely responsible for over-

all system performance. Multiple chip suppliers were available for DTS manufacturers. They included Toshiba (for PictureTel), Texas Instruments (for VTEL),[14] Integrated Information Technology (for Compression Laboratories), Motorola (for British Telecom), Lucent Technology (for C-Phone), and Graphics Communications Technologies (for a large group of Japanese codec makers). In the past few years, video compression chips had become a lot less expensive. For example, Lucent Technology's AVP lll was a quite powerful (16 billion operations per second) and versatile video compression chip that was compliant with several video compression standards. In 1998, it was provided at the unit price of $78 in quantities of 25,000. Its previous generation chip, AVP ll was priced $250 when it was first introduced in August 1994. The price fell to about $150 in only a year. In general, a hardware-based solution was adopted for ISDN-based DTSs.

On the other hand, the software-based solution relied on software to execute video compression algorithms with the help of a general-purpose microprocessor located in a host PC. This solution was born as a result of the recent advance in video compression algorithms that enabled videoconferencing over low-bandwidth transmission lines like POTS or Internet. One drawback with software-based solutions was that the picture quality suffered due to the limited bandwidth and the slower data processing by software codec. The introductory price for new generation general-purpose microprocessors had traditionally been more than $900.

The critical difference between ISDN-based DTSs and POTS- or Internet-based DTSs was the required amount of data processing. It was estimated to be at least 3,630 MIPS (millions of instructions per second) for ISDN-based DTSs. Since currently available general-purpose microprocessors are much slower, most companies adopted the hardware-based solution for ISDN-based DTSs. On the other hand, POTS- or Internet-based videoconferences followed a less complicated video compression algorithm for more limited data processing requirements. As a result, the software-based solution was a viable choice providing QCIF[15] (176 × 144 pixels) image quality at 3–15 fps frame rate. However, even in the case of POTS- or Internet-based videoconferencing, a solution based on a dedicated video compression

[13] *EDN,* May 22, 1997.

[14] VTEL insisted its system run on Intel's microprocessor. However, VTEL's products were not especially inexpensive, nor did they provide extraordinary profit margin to the company.
[15] Quarter common intermediate format.

EXHIBIT 6   The Evolution of Minimum Required Bandwidth for 30 FPS Pictures

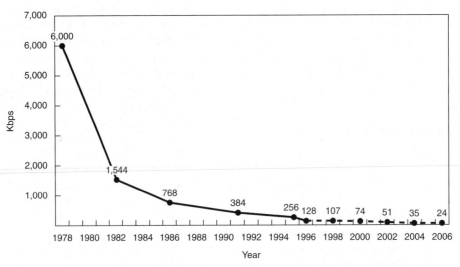

Sources: 10K form for Compression Labs and PictureTel, *Network World,* casewriter's forecast.

EXHIBIT 7   The Evolution of Minimum Required Bandwidth for 30 FPS Pictures (Trend Line)

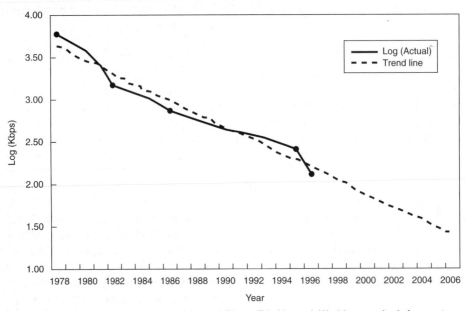

Sources: 10K forms for Compression Labs and PictureTel, *Network World,* casewriter's forecast.

chip was superior in both image quality (CIF,[16] 352 × 288 pixels) and frame rate (15 fps).

It was expected that powerful general-purpose microprocessors would take more and more of dedicated video compression chips' jobs in the future. However, at the same time, video compression algorithms also needed to be significantly improved to have acceptable picture quality on low-bandwidth lines like POTS.[17] Exhibit 8

---

[16]Common intermediate format.

[17]In 1998, transmission bandwidth over POTS was generally limited to 28.8 Kbps.

EXHIBIT 8 The Historical and Forecasted Microprocessor Power

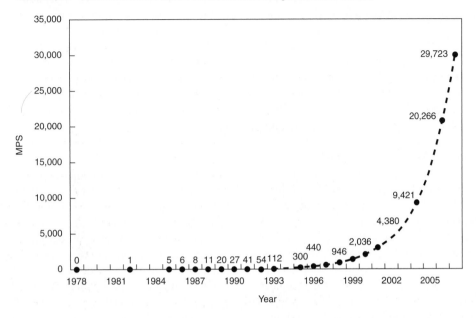

shows the historical and forecasted evolution of general-purpose microprocessor power.

Standardization of Video Compression Technology

Along with the significant decrease in required bandwidth, a critical issue the VCS industry needed to overcome was incompatibility between competing products. An international organization called International Telecommunication Union Telecommunication standardization sector (ITU-T) assumed this task and finally introduced the first VCS industry standard, H.320, in December 1990. It was an umbrella standard that contained some substandards, including H.261 for regulating image compression algorithms. H.320 as a whole mainly defined video signal (including sound) exchanges between different video-conferencing equipment over ISDN or T1. In other words, H.320 ensured the compatibility between different manufacturers' systems. In 1998, most manufacturers' product offerings complied with H.320. One important point with this standard was that VCS manufacturers agreed with the ITU-T to grant licenses, on a nonexclusive and nondiscriminatory basis and on fair and reasonable terms, to all manufacturers who wished to comply with the standards (this arrangement was made on all the other standards described below).

Although H.320 ensured the compatibility between competing products, it did not standardize the whole video compression process. As a result, incumbents were allowed to differentiate their products with proprietary video compression algorithms accumulated over the previous years, as long as they followed H.320 as a minimum common interface. Out of the four video compression steps discussed above, H.261 did not regulate preprocessing, encoding, or postprocessing. By regulating only decoding, the standard allowed codec designers leeway to develop proprietary video compression algorithms for controlling picture quality. Actually, most VCS makers provide their proprietary video compression algorithm in addition to the industry standard algorithm. In the case of PictureTel's RAS products, two systems attempted to communicate using the proprietary SG4 algorithm once they were connected. If that failed, they would drop down to the older version of SG4 and finally to H.261. In other words, H.261 was developed as the lowest common denominator to win all participants' acceptance.

While H.320 established itself as a real industry standard, ITU-T adopted another potentially important standard for the DTS market. T.120, which was approved in 1995, defined the exchange of data and graphical images among PCs, VCSs, and other graphical communication devices. It was extended in February 1996 for collaborative multimedia conferencing, wherein video, audio, and data information could be shared between end points in a multipoint setting. The effect of this standardization was significant since it contained possibilities for applications such as a file sharing or a whiteboard on videoconferencing display. For example, users at remote places were able to work on the same spreadsheet while simultaneously having PC-based videoconferencing. In 1998, the compliance to T.120 began to be a norm among major competitors.

In addition to T.120, ITU-T was preparing another class of standards in anticipation of rapidly emerging markets: Internet- or POTS-based VCSs. Ratified in October 1996, H.323 defined videoconferencing applications on LANs and WANs (wide area networks). It also standardized IP (Internet protocol)-based videoconferencing supported by TCP/IP,[18] bringing Internet-based VCSs into reality. H.324, initially approved in November 1995 and then ratified in October 1996, was a standard for videoconferencing and audioconferencing on POTS. Both H.323 and H.324 adopted H.263, an improved version of H.261, as the image compression standard. Because of the wide availability and low cost of POTS or Internet, Internet- and POTS-based videoconferencing were expected to ignite the need for VCSs among consumers.

There was the prospect that H.263 would merge with MPEG. MPEG (Moving Picture Experts Group) was an international standards-setting group involved in defining standards for data compression of moving pictures. Members were mainly home electronics companies trying to capture the huge business opportunities of multimedia. MPEG had secured the position of industry standards in such home electronics as CD-ROM and DVD. Therefore, it seemed critical for the VCS industry to at least maintain compatibility with these standards for the purpose of winning widespread consumer acceptance in the future. It was reported that "H.263 worked so well that the MPEG adopted H.263 as the basis for MPEG-4. MPEG and ITU-T are likely to converge on one recommendation for next generation products."[19]

Infrastructure (ISDN) and Installation

Unlike the situation in Japan or Europe, penetration of ISDN in the United States suffered a substantial delay. This was primarily due to the fact that there had not been any industry standard until February 1991. After the introduction of National ISDN 1, the number of ISDN installations had steadily increased to about one million lines in 1997 (Exhibit 9).

Another issue with ISDN was the wide discrepancy among initial installation costs. They varied depending on the region, between $65 (Denver) and $400 (St. Louis), with an average of $172.[20] In the case of corporate customers, volume discounting was applied, making the price structure more complicated. As for another start-up cost, ISDN modems (terminal adapters), which cost $300–$400, were rapidly becoming a commodity item due to the competition among PC peripheral vendors.[21] Several vendors, including 3Com, Diamond Multimedia Systems, Farallon Communications, and U.S. Robotics Access, went as far as setting up line provisioning services, which order the ISDN lines from the regional telephone company as well as prepare the line correctly in order to expedite sales.[22] Some telecommunication carriers offered substantial discounts on the VCSs if their ISDN service was ordered at the same time. For example, Pacific Bell bundled Intel's DTSs with ISDN installation for about half the cost of the two items purchased separately.

Exhibit 10 shows the evolution of minimum transmission costs required for available VCS. ISDN was continuously getting less expensive, reaching $0.6/hour in 1995. Monthly charges also varied depending on the region, ranging from $14 (Chicago) to $199 (Minneapolis), with an average of $55.[23] It was already as low as POTS in some regions (e.g., Chicago, Detroit).

Although ISDN had become affordable, the implementation of DTSs was still a painful process. The DTS providers were assisted by VARs (value added resellers), who provided consulting and installation support including setting up ISDNs (Exhibit 11). For VARs, these services were a more important source of profit than selling VCSs or related software (Exhibit 12).

From the customer's point of view, VARs were quite helpful mainly in two ways. First, connecting to ISDN was not an easy task. Placing an order with a local phone company required understanding various ISDN options and terminology. It also would be confusing to choose and correctly configure ISDN terminal adapters. And, for corporate customers, it was necessary to consider the coordination between existing network and ISDN lines.

---

[18] Transmission control protocol/Internet protocol.
[19] *EDN,* May 22, 1997.

[20] *Computer Technology Review,* August 1997.
[21] *Computer Reseller News,* May 19, 1997.
[22] Ibid.
[23] *Computer Technology Review,* August 1997.

EXHIBIT 9   The Evolution of ISDN-Installed Base in the United States

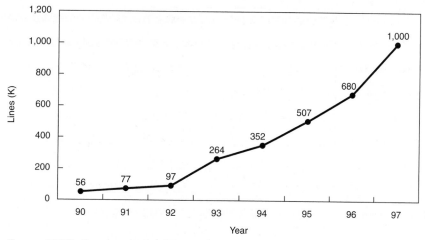

Source: OECD, Computer Industry Forecast.

EXHIBIT 10   The Evolution of Transmission Cost over ISDN

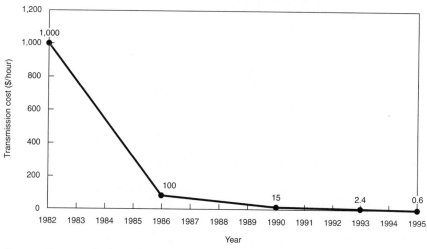

Sources: Compression Lab, *Wall Street Journal,* and others.

Second, choosing an appropriate DTS was reasonably difficult. Even if available bandwidth was the same, picture quality could be dramatically improved either through compliance to higher H.320 requirements or adoption of proprietary video compression algorithms. Specifically, each product (i.e., codec) allocated the available bandwidth differently to increase resolution and to increase frame rate. Some put more emphasis on resolution, while others emphasize frame rate (Exhibit 13). Also, picture quality differed significantly depending on existing network environments and lighting

and noise conditions in the room where the DTS was actually used. Such PC features as processing power, disk storage capacity, and monitor quality also influenced the performance of the DTS. As a result, selecting the most appropriate DTSs to each user's individual needs and situations was a very complicated task.

VARs assisted users with picking the best system by swapping the regular peripherals of a typical desktop system for higher-end cameras, monitors, mikes, and speakers, given various constraints at the customer's site. After the initial installation, training or maintenance

EXHIBIT 11   Value Added Services Resellers Offer Their VCS Customers

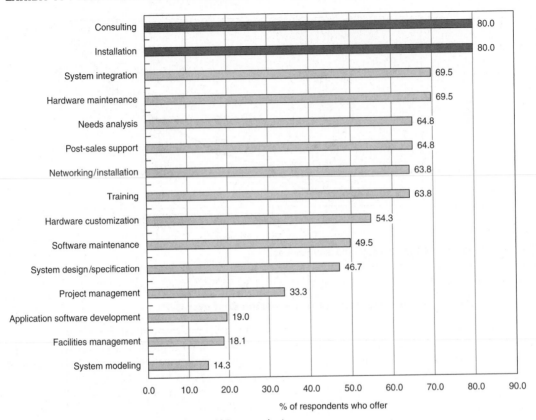

Source: *Computer Reseller News* survey on 105 respondents.

EXHIBIT 12   What Motivates Resellers to Offer Their Customers VCS Solutions?

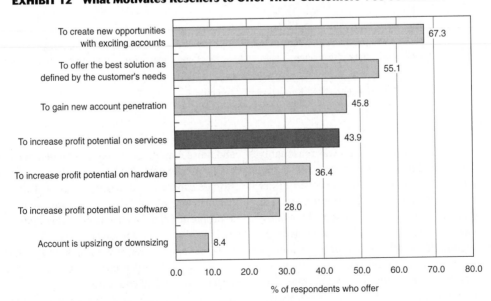

Source: *Computer Reseller News survey* on 107 respondents.

EXHIBIT 13 Trade-off in Bandwidth Allocation Between "Resolution" and "Frame Rate"

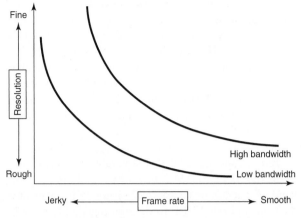

There can be infinite combinations of resolution and frame rate for each specific bandwidth. Picture size can be added creating three-dimensional trade-off.

EXHIBIT 14 PictureTel and Intel: Pricing History

Month	Company	Product	Price
Jul-93	PictureTel	LivePCS 100	$5,995
Jan-94	Intel	ProShare 200	$1,999
Jan-95	PictureTel	LivePCS 50	$2,495–$4,195
Nov-95	PictureTel	LivePCS 200	$1,995
Apr-96	Intel	ProShare 200	$1,499
May-96	PictureTel	Live200	$1,495–$2,445
Jun-97	Intel	Intel Business Video Conferencing with ProShare technology	$1,199

Sources: PictureTel, Intel.

was also provided from them to secure stable visual communication.

MAJOR COMPETITORS AND THEIR STRATEGIES IN 1998

PictureTel

In 1996, with a worldwide market share of 50 percent in the RAS segment (at $15,000–$50,000), PictureTel was clearly the industry leader. PictureTel had also established a superior market position in the DTS segment (at $1,995–$5,995) with 54.6 percent market share in the United States. Although no public data was available for 1997, PictureTel reported that it defended the position of market share leader in the worldwide ISDN-based DTS market. The company's broad and well-balanced product line was supplemented by MCUs (at $20,000–$300,000) sourced from VideoServer. The total installed base was more than 50,000 systems worldwide. The main source of revenue was RASs (69 percent of total sales), while since 1993, product offerings were rapidly expanding in DTSs (9 percent of total sales).

PictureTel's aggressive development of the ISDN-based DTS market was reflected in rapid price cuts matching those of Intel, who had much deeper pockets (Exhibit 14). On the other hand, PictureTel spent $40 million on the acquisition of MultiLink to acquire audioconferencing expertise used in MCUs (April 1997). As for the RAS market, PictureTel introduced a

highly sophisticated video compression algorithm called SG4 on April 1995 in its new flagship RAS (Concorde 4500, at $35,000–$50,000). It was an improved version of a previous generation algorithm (SG3) launched in 1991. In 1998, SG4 or SG3 was offered only for its RASs lines. Also in October 1996, PictureTel launched a relatively inexpensive portable RAS called SwiftSite as the industry's first compact conferencing system. The unit price was $8,995–$10,345, while the traditional average unit price for RASs had been $34,500. SwiftSite was designed to develop a new class of customers who could not afford RASs but had needs of group-to-group meetings between remote sites. It worked on ISDN providing 15 fps pictures.

Customer segment focus was relatively diverse compared to some other VCS manufacturers. PictureTel sold to Fortune 1,000 companies, as well as governments, telecommunication carriers, health care providers, and distance education facilities. PictureTel was organized based on product segment, not on customer segment.

PictureTel derived a substantial revenue stream from overseas (43 percent of total revenues in fiscal year 1997). This geographical diversification was realized mostly through responding to its multinational business customers' need to deal with a single vendor's equipment worldwide. Detailed revenue distribution in 1997 was as follows: United States, $286 million (down 10.9 percent from 1996); Europe, $107 million (down 3.7 percent from 1996); and Asia/Pacific, $73 million (up 26.6 percent from 1996).

One of PictureTel's biggest strengths was its extensive distribution network. Its domestic distribution agreements mainly included telecommunication solutions providers (Lucent Technologies, MCI, GTE, Southernwestern Bell, Ameritech, Pacific Bell) and to a lesser extent, distributors for PCs, peripherals, and software (CompuCom Systems, Ingram Micro). Also overseas,

PictureTel established distribution agreements mostly with such renowned telecommunication carriers as British Telecom, Nippon Telephone & Telegraph, Siemens, Telecom Italia, Deutsche Telekom, Alcatel, and France Telecom. As a result of these distribution agreements, 74 percent of total sales were made through third-party distributors securing better access to target customers. PictureTel also had entered into a nonexclusive agreement to develop and distribute low-end DTSs with Compaq (May 1994) and nonexclusive comarketing agreements and reselling agreements with AT&T and IBM.

To deal with the biggest potential drawback of the extensive use of third-party distributors (i.e., inferior customer support), PictureTel offered a comprehensive portfolio of consulting, design service, project management, installation and training, and maintenance, mostly by in-house staff. In addition to that, a one-year warranty for hardware and a 90-day warranty for software were provided to assure its product quality to customers. Gross margin for service business was estimated to be 30 percent.

PictureTel outsourced manufacturing of DTSs to several subcontractors. Those subcontractors also conducted quality testing at their sites according to PictureTel's specifications. In case of RASs, PictureTel purchased various components and assembled them into complete systems. Certain components were procured from single sources, even when multiple vendors were available, to maintain quality control and enhance the working relationship with suppliers.

On March 1998, PictureTel welcomed Bruce R. Bond, a former CEO of ANS Communications (a networking subsidiary of America Online), as a new CEO, replacing Norman E. Gaut, who had been in the position since January 1986.

Intel

Intel's first entry into the DTS market was through a codevelopment project with PictureTel, when PictureTel tried to develop its first DTS with IBM (for PC architecture) and Intel (for a video compression chip, called V3). However, after the introduction of the prototype in 1991, Intel dropped out of this apparently winning combination in August 1992. Intel's intentions were made clear when the company revealed its plan to push its proprietary video compression algorithm about a year and a half later. Intel chose to take the proprietary algorithm path because it viewed H.320 as being too demanding to implement on PC platforms at a reasonable cost. Also, as it turned out later, there seemed to be fundamental differences in product development philosophy between PictureTel and Intel. For example, Intel's DTSs were designed to compress pictures with a dedicated video compression chip and to decompress with a host microprocessor, while PictureTel's products relied on a dedicated video compression chip for compression/decompression functions. In addition, they significantly differed in how much ISDN bandwidth was allocated to data-sharing applications. Intel prioritized data sharing, while PictureTel emphasized video quality, therefore prolonging the data-sharing transaction.

In response, PictureTel picked up AT&T and then Toshiba (August 1993) as chip partners, eventually introducing its first DTS in July 1993. Intel, on the other hand, decided to make a $7 million equity investment in then third player VTEL to develop together new video compression software for DTS (October 1993).

Intel entered with its ISDN-based DTS, called ProShare, in January 1994, reportedly utilizing its own video compression chip 82750PD. Intel made a decision to compete as one of the participants, not as a component supplier. Andrew Grove talked about this decision: "Twice before [i.e., PCs and ethernet] we sat by and played the components supplier as a system business grew haphazardly. These things aren't an Erector set that jumps together on its own. Somebody has to package our technologies and sell them. This time we're going to go out and help create the market, build the systems as well as the components, and compete in the market place."[24]

With the launch of ProShare, Intel started to organize a consortium of PC makers named Personal Conference Work Group (PCWG). PCWG's primary purpose was to establish another industry standard around Intel's video compression algorithm "Indeo"[25] apart from H.320. PCWG insisted that H.320 was not appropriate to integrate existing PC architecture. In other words, H.320 did not yet cover standards for the kinds of interactive software vital to PC-based videoconferencing, such as screen sharing and document transfer. Although the H.320 provided better compression (or higher quality picture at a given bandwidth), Indeo was much more easily decoded on low-end microprocessors such as x86 series.

Intel leveraged its huge resources to gain control of the emerging industry. It was reported that the total spending in 1994 was as high as $100 million, including research, development, and promotion of ProShare;

---

[24] *Forbes,* December 6, 1993.
[25] Intel/**video.**

$8 million was allocated to the advertising budget. It was the second biggest only to the long-running "Intel Inside" effort. Major focus of advertisement was put on trade publications such as *InfoWorld, PC Week, Windows Magazine, PC World, PC Magazine, Information Week,* and *CommunicationsWeek.* Also, a series of 24 sales seminars in 13 cities around the country were planned during the first four months of the market launch.[26] During the course of trying to spread its clout in the DTS industry, Intel reached a distribution agreement for ProShare with CLI in exchange for a $2 million cash infusion (May 1994).

Although established players in the PC industry such as AT&T, Compaq, Lotus Development, Novell, and Hewlett-Packard joined PCWG, it eventually failed to win widespread support. Primarily due to the fact that H.320 had already established its installed base, establishing a different standard would only confuse the market. PCWG was virtually disbanded in February 1995, shortly after Microsoft expressed its support for H.320. Also, the emergence of the next industry standard (T.120) played a role in lessening the legitimacy of PCWG's claim that H.320 was not the appropriate standard for the DTS market. Despite the fact that Intel failed to establish a new ecosystem around its own video compression algorithm, it hardly seemed to care and kept pursuing an aggressive price-cutting strategy.

In 1998, Intel's product offering was focused on an ISDN/LAN-based DTS called Intel Business Video Conferencing 4.0 with ProShare technology ($1,199), a PC-based group conferencing system called Team Station system ($9,999), and POTS- or Internet-based DTS (Video Phone with ProShare technology). Video Phone was a software product preinstalled in Pentium-based PCs for free. For Video Phone, users had to buy an upgrade kit that included a video camera ($199) to actually have videoconferencing on their PCs.

Intel's ISDN/LAN-based DTSs were designed to rely on dedicated video compression chips only for compression tasks, enabling an aggressive pricing strategy to ignite the demand. In return, they satisfied only minimum requirements of industry standards like H.320 or H.323, while PictureTel complied with the highest requirements. In the U.S. DTS market segment, Intel was the second largest supplier with 29.5 percent market share in 1996. Recently, Intel intended to put more emphasis on LAN-based DTSs rather than ISDN-based DTSs.[27]

As for the distribution, for the first time in its history, Intel initially adopted "restricted distribution channels"[28] to better support and to educate business end users. One hundred fifty resellers were authorized from the 200–300 members of Intel's Advanced Network Reseller program. "We decided we needed to move from the commodity approach," said Gerry Greeve, director of sales and marketing for Personal Conference Division.[29] Later, the distribution channels were expanded to add telecommunication carriers and PC makers to high-end integrators and VARs. Starting with Compaq (October 1995) and then with IBM Intel gradually expanded the scope of marketing agreements in which the PC manufacturer provided specially configured PCs for corporate customers. It was estimated that the preconfiguration should add $700 or $800 to the price of a system. Intel also established distribution agreements with such telecommunication carriers as Ameritech, Bell Atlantic, Pacific Bell, AT&T, British Telecom, Deutsche Telekom, France Telecom, PTT Netherlands, Telecom Italia, Telefonica, and Nippon Telephone & Telegraph.

For the consumer market, some PC makers, including Hewlett-Packard, IBM, Sony, and Toshiba, distributed PCs with preinstalled video compression software. According to the company's press release, as of June 1997, over 2 million home PCs had been shipped with the Intel Video Phone software preinstalled.

As a part of continuous efforts to improve the functionality of its DTSs, Intel entered into a cross-licensing agreement with Microsoft, which had launched data and voice conferencing software called NetMeeting in June 1996.[30] Intel licensed the T.120 implementation for data conferencing from Microsoft, while Microsoft licensed H.323 protocol support for Internet telephony from Intel (August 1996). Microsoft added an H.323-compliant videoconferencing feature with the release of NetMeeting 2.0 in May 1997. The compatibility between ProShare and NetMeeting was assured by an agreement reached in June 1996.

VTEL

Founded in 1986, VTEL was the second largest RAS supplier in 1996, capturing 17.7 percent share of the U.S. market (VTEL's historical financial performance is

---

[26] *Business Marketing,* February 1994.
[27] *Computer Reseller News,* December 15, 1997.

[28] *Business Marketing,* February 1994.
[29] *Computer Reseller News,* February 14, 1994.
[30] Microsoft originally licensed data conferencing technologies from PictureTel.

EXHIBIT 15   VTEL's Historical Financial Performance

Alter the merger with CLI ($K)

	7/31/97	7/31/96*	12/31/95	12/31/94	12/31/93	12/31/92
Revenue:	191,023	96,962	191,074	169,189	126,547	121,098
Product	150,791	74,098	169,455	159,350	N.A.	N.A.
Service	40,232	22,864	21,619	9,839	N.A.	N.A.
Gross margin:	74,702	35,980	66,843	66,380	39,089	40,326
SG&A	65,399	38,842	62,511	52,502	N.A.	N.A.
R&D	24,460	16,274	21,283	19,004	N.A.	N.A.
EBIT	(44,283)	(18,507)	(17,214)	(476)	N.A.	N.A.
Net income	(52,054)	(18,507)	(53,843)	169	(12,817)	(1,796)
Total assets	131,135	175,092	223,061	178,086	170,469	137,010
Shareholders' equity	76,765	122,238	139,512	124,185	117,595	95,183
G.M./revenue	39.1%	37.1%	35.0%	39.2%	30.9%	33.3%
Net income/revenue	−27.3%	−19.1%	−28.2%	0.1%	−10.1%	−1.5%
ROA	−28.9%	−9.3%	−8.6%	−0.3%	N.A.	N.A.
ROE	−52.3%	−14.1%	−40.8%	0.1%	−12.0%	−1.9%

Before the merger with CLI ($K)

	7/31/96*	12/31/95	12/31/94	12/31/93	12/31/92	12/31/91
Revenue:	50,109	78,095	54,231	31,452	26,067	11,019
Product	34,564	68,156	52,157	30,534	N.A.	N.A.
Service	15,545	9,939	2,074	918	N.A.	N.A.
Gross margin:	19,173	39,425	27,837	14,619	13,048	4,796
SG&A	21,245	25,952	19,860	16,288	N.A.	N.A.
R&D	8,860	11,309	8,846	8,350	N.A.	N.A.
Operating income	(12,045)	2,084	(869)	(10,019)	718	(2,537)
Net income	(9,899)	3,739	62	(9,334)	1,487	(2,496)
Total assets	111,903	118,308	46,435	45,547	42,274	11,391
Shareholders' equity	94,416	103,838	37,223	36,258	38,306	6,376
G.M./revenue	38.3%	50.5%	51.3%	46.5%	50.1%	43.5%
Net income/revenue	−19.8%	4.8%	0.1%	−29.7%	5.7%	−22.7%
ROA	−10.5%	2.5%	−1.9%	−22.8%	2.7%	−22.3%
ROE	−10.0%	5.3%	0.2%	−25.0%	6.7%	−39.1%

*7 month result. ROA and ROE are adjusted for comparison purpose.
The acquisition of Integrated Communication Systems was accounted for as a purchase method.
Source: VTEL annual report.

shown in Exhibit 15). VTEL also provided proprietary MCUs, securing the third largest market share (11.4 percent) after VideoServer and Lucent Technologies. Although VTEL was also in the DTS segment ($2,495–$9,995), the product variety was limited to higher-end systems and its market share was less than 5 percent of the U.S. market.

VTEL's RASs were priced as relatively high-end RASs ($15,995–$72,000), clearly reflecting its corporate strategy to focus on the niche RAS segment. Worldwide installed base was about 22,000 units.

Among them, 1,500 systems were installed at health care providers, positioning VTEL as the largest health care VCS provider (50 percent market share). The acquisition of CLI in January of 1997 had strengthened its position in the high-end RAS segment, enhancing VTEL's CDV (compressed digital video) expertise. Another strength of VTEL's RAS line was its heavy emphasis on open hardware and software PC architectures, which provided familiar user interface to customers. In the MCU segment ($49,995–$146,990), VTEL aggressively pursued strengthening its proprietary position. Together with Accord Video Telecommunications, VTEL engaged in a strategic alliance to enhance the features of its proprietary MCUs.

VTEL's product development strategy was closely allied with Intel. Intel owned 7.2 percent of VTEL and had funded a part of VTEL's product development expenses. In return, VTEL licensed an H.261-compliant compression algorithm to Intel.

VTEL's market emphasis was narrowly focused on distance education, government, health care, and service and commercial customers. For each of them, VTEL established a corresponding Customer Business Unit in 1996. Detailed revenue distribution for the fourth quarter of the fiscal year 1997 was as follows: distance education, 26 percent; government, 25 percent; health care, 15 percent; and service and commercial customers, 34 percent.

As a natural consequence of this market focus, VTEL leveraged VARs specialized in selling to those target market segments in order to better access appropriate customer accounts. In addition to these specialized VARs, VTEL extensively utilized third-party distributors. They included major telecommunication carriers such as GTE, Ameritech, ATS, MCI, Southern Bell, Sprint, and US West, deriving 93 percent of total sales from indirect sales efforts. In the move to promote downstream integration, VTEL acquired Integrated Communication Systems (one of VTEL's existing VARs) to better support system integration, installation, and on-going maintenance efforts (November 1995).

In 1998, VTEL was shifting the focus of its marketing strategy from a channel push approach to a demand pull approach. While the previous approach focused on trade shows or aggressive sales practices targeted at distributors, the new approach tried to raise industry awareness among end users through advertising and public relations campaigns.[31]

VCS APPLICATIONS

In 1998, there were limited examples of actual and potential DTSs applications (some applications of RASs are also included since they may be good indicators of future DTSs applications).

Flagstar Bank (Bloomfield Hills, Michigan) has cut the time needed to obtain a mortgage from weeks to from one hour to five hours with the help of DTSs. They met the need to speed the way they received and processed loan applications from more than 4,400 loan originators (typically real estate agents) and mortgage brokers nationwide. Michael R Hillman, vice president of business development at Flagstar, said videoconferencing helped re-create the contact customers had 40 years ago, when they could visit a mortgage banker in their neighborhood. Since the system was instituted in March 1995 at Flagstar, more than 500 institutions nationwide had joined, installing Intel's DTSs at more than 600 sites. Virtual Mortgage Network (Newport Beach, California) also realized the same benefits through the use of DTSs.[32]

Hartness International (Greenville, South Carolina) is a manufacturer of packaging machinery that is geared to automating the packing process. Hartness designs and assembles sophisticated machines that are at the end of the production line. This machinery is designed to take finished bottled products and place them into their shipping cartons. Hartness used PictureTel's RAS as a cost-efficient and simple process to assist in the maintenance of its machinery. For example, if a machine breaks down, Hartness technicians are called from a customer site over video with a camera positioned on the factory floor. With this arrangement, technicians can see the machine, talk to the customer directly, and jointly develop an understanding of the problem. Technicians can interactively view situations and suggest changes without taking the machinery off line, where downtime costs on average $150 per minute. Also, by working "face to face," Hartness found it can solve problems more easily. Since about 80 percent of its customer service calls can be handled remotely, the VCS has become a cost-effective solution to sending technicians out to a customer site. Customers highly value this system since the cost of the video call is only $10 to $20 compared to hundreds or thousands of dollars wasted during downtime waiting for Hartness's engineers to arrive.[33]

Mobil Corporation (Houston, Texas) utilizes PictureTel's VCSs to keep the pipeline operation up and running as smoothly as possible, because the cost of a pipeline failure is about $500,000 per day. During a recent pipeline failure in Nigeria, repair materials and specifications

---

[31] *Advest, Inc.,* February 23, 1998.

[32] *Computer World,* October 14, 1996; *Communications Week,* September 18, 1996.

[33] PictureTel home page.

were in Singapore. The Singapore team shipped the material and then by communicating over videoconferencing helped the local team to fix the problem. Before using the VCS, the process would have taken far longer with repeated fax and phone calls slowing the process down. And, if the problem couldn't be resolved, the Singapore team would have had to fly to Nigeria, costing three days in travel and $1.5 million in revenue.[34]

Officials at Owens Corning Fiberglas (Toledo, Ohio) said it cut in half the time it took to bring to market an insulation product used in Whirlpool's appliances. Technical teams shared drawings at semiweekly desktop videoconferences on PictureTel's DTSs, improving the efficiency of collaborative work between remote sites.[35]

There is not much information on consumer applications. However, according to Intel's survey, the family segment most interested in visual communications is grandparents wishing to see children and grandchildren, followed by parents wishing to see children away at school.[36]

As for the customers' reservation price, some sources have provided quite consistent views. In a survey of 75 companies, David Boomstein, senior vice president at Applied Business Telecommunications (Livermore, California), found that 55 percent of business users would use a videoconference system if it cost about $1,000; 31 percent indicated they could afford to pay between $1,000 and $5,000 in 1994. The Yankee Group reached basically the same conclusion in a survey conducted in 1992. They found that 50 percent of respondents would purchase DTSs at a cost under $1,000, while only 18 percent would buy in the $3,000 to $5,000 range, and none above $5,000. Many Japanese interviewees mentioned that consumers would not pay more than $300 for consumer electronics, to which DTSs would be classified in retail market.

PROSPECTS OF THE PC-BASED DTS INDUSTRY BEYOND 1998

With the establishment of industry standards, such as H.323 or H.324, some new segments were emerging in the DTS market (Exhibit 16). They were low-bandwidth DTSs, which worked on either POTS or Internet. As was discussed above, since most low-bandwidth systems compressed video images through software running on a

microprocessor in a host PC, no dedicated video compression chip was included in the package. This was a primary reason why these low-bandwidth systems could be provided at a big price advantage compared to traditional high-bandwidth DTSs. List prices were less than $300 for most of them. The flip side of this price advantage was their picture quality. Since the amount of transmitted data was very limited, the picture quality was hardly acceptable (only 4–15 fps) for business use. As a result, the current market was virtually limited to consumer use. Many software development companies entered this segment, including White Pine Software, Creative Labs, and VDOnet. Some other companies including Boca Research and VCI HiTech chose a hardware-based solution utilizing Lucent Technology's AVP lll video compression chip.

Videophones were another recent market development. Wide product variety was available in this segment, ranging from a TV set-top box to conventional phone equipment with a small display. The price range also varied from $300 to as high as $6,000. Since their function was limited to videoconferencing, and picture quality was comparable only to low-bandwidth DTSs, the major target market was consumers and to a lesser extent small offices. Among these new products, the TV set-top box seemed to have a big potential since it was very easy to install and inexpensive ($300–$650). The installation could be as simple as conventional VCRs, while the low-bandwidth DTS required users to install an add-on kit like a video capture board or video compression software. As a result, TV set-top box providers mostly targeted those consumers who were relatively less familiar with handling PCs, while low-bandwidth DTSs found the most eager early adopters among PC enthusiasts. Major competitors in the TV set-top box market included C-Phone and 8 × 8. Both TV set-top boxes and low-bandwidth DTSs were distributed through consumer electronics retail channels like Fry's Electronics or CompUSA.

The other promising, but still difficult to materialize, class of DTS was the LAN-based DTS. LAN-based DTSs had been available with very limited success since InterVision System tried to crack this market as early as May 1993. Given the fact that almost 90 percent of PCs in large corporations are connected to LANs, LAN-based DTSs should be an ideal solution to bring videoconferencing to desktops. If DTSs are connected through LANs, users are not required to implement new wiring such as ISDN—you have POTS all the way down to the PCs.

---

[34] Ibid.
[35] *Computer World,* October 14, 1996.
[36] *Computer Retail Week,* June 17, 1996.

EXHIBIT 16   DTS Launch History

	ISDN based	Lan based	POTS based	Internet based
1992	Compression Labs (September)			
1993	AT&T (May) PictureTel (July) VTEL (3Q)	InterVision (March) Compression Labs (July)		
1994	Intel (January) VCON (June) Vivo Software (September)**	C-Phone (?) PictureTel (September) Intel (November)	Creative Labs (October)	
1995		Connectix (October)**		
1996	Zydacron (July)	Corel (February) VCON (September)	VCI HiTect (February) VD Onet (April)**,*** Intel (June)** Boca Research (August)	InSoft (January)** White Pine (March)** Specom (November)**
1997			C-Phone (February)* 8 × 8 (February)* Tekram Technology (June)**	Winnov (February)** Creative Labs (February)** Microsoft (May)** Intel (June)** VocalTec (August)** Smith Micro (October)** Connectix (December)**

*TV set-top box.
**Software-based DTS.
***VD Onet licenses Boca Research, Diamond Multimedia Systems, Gallant Computer, Tekram Technology, and 3 com.

However, because the basis of LANs' transmission mode was fundamentally different from that of other lines mentioned above (i.e., T1, ISDN, or POTS), reliable business quality videoconferencing was yet to be delivered on LAN-based DTSs. Since the LAN's inception in late 1970s, a transmission mode called packet switching had been adopted on it, while other traditional transmission lines for VCSs had been based on circuit switching. Under packet switching, data is packetized in either a variable or predefined chunk at the sending site and sent out only when the line is not occupied. Consequently, available bandwidth is very efficiently used since everyone is allowed to occupy only up to the necessary duration for sending each packet. This mode of transmission was ideal for most data transmissions between PCs since they are "bursty," in that periods of high data transfer rates are followed by relatively long periods during which no data is transmitted.

The flip side of this efficient use of bandwidth is that no one is guaranteed a specified QoS (quality of service), because the access to the network is not always available depending on the degree of congestion of the network. Specifically, a QoS guarantee implies a minimum bandwidth allocation and a maximum transmission delay,

which are critically important for real-time data transmissions. Under LAN environments, some data can be delayed or in some cases lost during the transmission for real-time applications such as videoconferencing. For this reason, VCS providers had focused their product development efforts mostly on DTSs based on circuit switching transmission, which guarantees QoS by securing necessary transmission capacity. LAN-based DTSs had been available for several years, but the consensus in the market was that the picture quality was unreliable, especially for business use. As a result, 95 percent of videoconference for business was currently done over ISDN using H.320.[37] In 1998, most of LAN-based DTSs were provided as hardware-based systems at the comparable price with ISDN-based DTSs.

Since packet switching was also adopted by WANs for most of data exchanges between PCs (major WANs protocols include IP, frame relay, and ATM),[38] the convergence between videoconferencing and PCs was the convergence between circuit switching and packet

---

[37] *Computer Reseller News*, December 15, 1997.
[38] Asynchronous transfer mode.

switching from a technology point of view. Reflecting the inherent technological difficulty underlying this challenge, the DTS providers were working with various network solution providers. PictureTel announced a co-development agreement with FORE Systems, which captured 24 percent share of the U.S. ATM WAN access switch market. PictureTel was also working with Concentric Network, a provider of IP-based network solutions. VTEL bet on frame relay, cooperating with Motorola and Memotec Communications. Motorola was one of major participants in the frame relay systems market, capturing 24 percent of the U.S. FRADs (frame relay access devices) market and 15 percent of the U.S. 56/64 Kbit CSU/DSUs (channel service units/data service units) market. Intel minimized the technological risk by being allied with Cisco Systems, which possessed a substantial presence both in frame relay and ATM markets: 58 percent of the U.S. router market and 21 percent of the U.S. ATM WAN access switch market.

EXHIBIT 1 Annual Revenues (in Millions)

	91	92	93	94	95	As of 9/30/96 (9 months)
SAP-Global (DM)	707	831	1102	1831	2696	2372
Americas* (DM)	81	98	232	636	1010	921
Americas ($)	49	63	146	394	711	614
Exchange rate as of December 31	1.664	1.562	1.654	1.616	1.421	1.5
Americas % of total market	12%	12%	21%	35%	37%	39%

Note: In both Germany and America, the composition of revenues was roughly the same, and had been quite stable:
   70% licensing of software and maintenance.
   20% implementation services by SAP's consultants.
   10% training of partners and project teams.
* Americas includes Canada, the United States, Mexico, Latin America, and Australia. U.S. operations account for 80–90% of Americas operations.
Source: SAP America.

CASE II·9

SAP America

Artemis March

In just three years, SAP America (the abbreviation stands for Systems, Applications, Programs in Data Processing and is pronounced S-A-P) had gone from relative obscurity to being the phenomenon of the corporate computing world. By the mid-1990s, it was well on its way to becoming a billion-dollar company, and the derivative business powered by its engine was estimated at over $9 billion (see Exhibit 1). Such growth had placed great strain on the organization's regionally decentralized structure.

In April 1996, Jeremy Coote, the newly appointed president, called a meeting of senior executives to decide how to reorganize for the future. One of the resulting changes was that consulting activities became a separate line of business. Coote had subsequently charged Eileen Basho, consulting's new vice president, with two major

Source: Copyright © 1996 by The President and Fellows of Harvard College. Research Associate Artemis March prepared this case under the supervision of Professor David A. Garvin as the basis for class discussion rather than to illustrate either effective or ineffective handling of an administrative situation.

tasks: developing a professional services strategy that would allow the company to move from global to midtier markets, and significantly reducing the time and costs of implementation.

COMPANY AND INDUSTRY BACKGROUND

SAP AG, the parent of SAP America, was the world's fifth-largest software firm and the leading producer of real-time, integrated applications software for client-server computing. Its R/3 product had quickly come to dominate the enterprise information systems (EIS) segment of the client-server market. R/3 software functioned as the central nervous system of a company, allowing an entire global enterprise to communicate and exchange data instantaneously and seamlessly throughout (see Exhibit 2 for a more complete description of the product).

SAP AG was founded in Walldorf, Germany, in 1972 by four young software engineers whose vision of an integrated software package had been turned down by their employer, IBM. Seven years later, they launched their first major EIS product, R/2, which was designed for mainframe computers. In 1989, they took their company public. Five years later, SAP's market capitalization was $15 billion, and over 75 percent of the common stock was still owned by the founding families.

Three of the founders had remained active in the daily running of the company and continued to sit on the ex-

EXHIBIT 2   R/3

R/3 was a standard software package that helped companies reorganize around processes rather than functions. It employed a three-tier architecture whose robustness, scaleability, and flexibility allowed it to meet the diverse demands of global and smaller customers as well as the needs of a broad range of industries. R/3's master file and client-server design made possible seamless and synchronous integration of data sharing across an enterprise, even through new releases of the product. This capability led SAP America's president Jeremy Coote to observe: "What you are buying from SAP is the breadth and scope of seamless integration, rather than a product."

By 1996, the cumulative investment in R/3 exceeded DM 3 billion and had been fully expensed. The scope of R/3's reach was massive; it cut across the entire enterprise, linking over 80% of all activities. The global nature of the product was reflected in its ability to automatically calculate exchange rates and to operate in multiple languages. Revenues from R/3 came from licensing users at a particular site and from annual maintenance fees which were a percentage of the original fee. Licensing fees depended on the number of users and their category of use; some users only read transactions, some carried out a limited set of transactions, while others used the full capacity of the system. Fees were higher for the more intensive categories of use.

R/3 was very open architecturally. This meant that a customer was not locked into an existing database, type of hardware, or any specific portion of their solution forever. R/3 could run on any of the major hardware platforms, operating systems, or relational databases. The product consisted of a large suite of applications modules in four broad areas—finance and control, materials management and production planning, sales and distribution, human resources—and the software took a process perspective on all of these activities. For example, on a quote-to-cash process, it delivered a quote on a product to a customer, priced it out, checked availability, procured materials, staged them, shipped the product, and collected the money.

The horizontal, process orientation of R/3 was designed into the software through configuration tables. A table was an arrangement of default settings through which data ran automatically. A major process could involve a few hundred tables, and changing one table had ripple effects on scores of others. Although R/3 was designed as a standard package, the software could be customized by changing the settings in the tables. Based on its preferences and operating requirements, a company decided on the settings for each table. In this way, it tailored the software to its needs but without changing any code.

Recently, the laborious process of changing every table by hand had been superseded by two major developments: SAP had encoded over 1,000 best practices into the software, and SAP had developed new modeling tools that automated the table-setting process. Best practices were scaleable business processes that had been drawn from 25 years of close collaboration between customers and developers. They were actually precise configurations of table settings that encoded the practices of industry leaders, serving as templates that other companies could use as a starting point for their own organizations.

New modeling tools such as Business Engineer also made it much easier to align standard templates with a customer's own processes. Business Engineer allowed customers to automatically reconfigure scores of tables to accommodate their changes to SAP processes. The tool allowed the application consultant to lift the template into the modeling tool, make it look like the customer's, and drive those parameters back into R/3. SAP had also developed a rapid implementation methodology called Accelerated SAP that drew from the best practices of field consultants, who collaborated to design the new methodology. It was specially tailored for mid-sized companies, who were unwilling to invest in extended implementation.

---

ecutive board. They were described as highly accessible, financially conservative, and as having kept the company "outrageously flat." They ran SAP AG on the basis of informal working relationships honed over long periods of time, consistently invested 20–25 percent of gross revenues in R&D, capitalized nothing, carried no debt, and did not book revenues until products were delivered. Almost 25 percent of the company's 7,000 employees were in R&D, and half were in professional services, which at SAP consisted of consulting and training.

The German (or AG) executive board was tightly linked to the product development organization and was involved in a variety of strategic decisions concerning the product, such as the functionality to be incorporated in new releases. Besides the founders, board members included the two top executives from the R&D organization and Paul Wahl, who joined the company in 1991 as

vice president for worldwide marketing but had spent most of his career in technology organizations.

Strategic Focus

In late 1991, prior to the R/3 launch, the AG board had spent at least two months discussing whether SAP should remain a product company, focused on selling software packages, or whether it should broaden to focus on solutions. Wahl, who had just joined the company, described the alternatives and some of the board's thinking:

A product has a defined functionality, and you hope to sell a lot of copies. So as a product company, you earn your revenues from license fees. A solutions company, on the other hand, gets a lot more of its revenues from services, and provides a more complete package that includes implementation as well as a wide range of other services.

But we knew that if R/3 were very successful and we were a solutions company, we would have to hire thousands of consultants. The board said, no, we are a product company. What we want is market penetration of our product. We want R/3 to become *the* business infrastructure, the de facto industry standard. So what we need to do is to sell as much software as we can, as fast as we can.

To do that, we needed strong alliances with partners. There was some concern that this choice could put us in a firefighting mode, where we had to fix our partners' mistakes. Saying that we were a product company also hurt the feelings of our own consulting people. But the choice focused us and put even more pressure on R&D to develop a superior product.

The board then had to decide how much of the services market generated by R/3 it would pursue itself and how much of the business it would leave to partners. SAP, it decided, would seek only 20–30 percent of the R/3 implementation business. In the United States, it would initially pursue even less. R/3 was introduced in Europe on July 1, 1992, and three months later in America, where sales took off quickly and then skyrocketed in 1994.

Coming to America

SAP AG began to expand internationally in the late 1980s and chose foreign subsidiaries as its vehicle. It established SAP America in 1988 as part of the Americas group, which also included Canada, Mexico, Latin America, and Australia. When the American subsidiary experienced management problems in mid-1992, top members of the German board parachuted in. After the dust settled, Klaus Besier became president, Wahl joined the American board, and Hasso Plattner, SAP's cofounder and de facto chief technologist, became chairman of the Americas organization, a position he continued to hold four years later. Besier soon added the title of chief operating officer; he became CEO early in 1994. Besier was described by a senior executive as a "dynamic leader, a marketeer par excellence, very directed and driven. He speaks well and has a strong physical presence. With Klaus, there is no pretense. What matters is getting the job done. His penchant is to build; the company has to be headed in a direction."

Charting a Course

To address the needs of the American market, Besier moved away from the German model in several respects, including the sales organization, target customer base, and organizational structure.

Commissioned Sales Force   SAP America had learned from R/2 that its product needed to be sold more heavily in America than in Europe and that a strong sales force was required to compete effectively. Alex Ott, vice president of global partnering, recalled: "We had no customer base, no market share, a handful of people, and a new product which ran on a new technology. We concluded that we must be quick on our feet, and have more feet on the street than anyone else." SAP America's managers decided that they needed a commission plan for R/3. Besier moved aggressively, putting the entire sales force (rather than just a pilot group, as had been agreed by the board) on commission. He also recruited more and more of the sales force from the ranks of professional salespeople, rather than engineers.

Target Customers   Besier's aggressive, entrepreneurial sales force believed that it could close deals with very large companies. Their first multimillion dollar sale, to Chevron, proved to be a watershed for SAP. The deal closed in December 1992; it punctured the belief that multinationals were married to their mainframes. R/3 more than met Chevron's tests for scaleability, volume, and speed; in fact, it outperformed SAP's major competitor by 300–800 percent. The product's architecture was validated, opening a floodgate to other large accounts. SAP America then set its sights on global companies with revenues of at least $2.5 billion. Eric Rubino, general counsel, recalled:

> The product was validated as being so superior to competitors' that we thought it really could become the de facto standard—if we could get it out there fast enough. We believed that we had a window of opportunity when no one could compete with us, but a window of only about two years.

Regional Organization   To move product as quickly as possible, SAP America established in January 1993 autonomous regional offices in San Francisco, Chicago, Atlanta, and Philadelphia. SAP headquarters remained in Philadelphia, but the corporate office, which continued to handle events, public relations, and advertising, was separated organizationally from the Northeast Region. Each region became a separate P&L (profit and loss) center, with its own presales, sales, consulting, and training services, all reporting to a regional vice president (RVP). Wahl explained:

> Initially, we thought about common resources for the regions. Then we decided that for each region to win strategic

deals, we needed to give them all of the autonomy and tools they needed to close the sale, as well as the services required to support the client.

The regions had significant flexibility in dealmaking. If they were negotiating licenses, for example, and the customer thought the fee was too high, they could offer free training or even free consulting to close the sale.

In 1995, each of the four regions was further divided into three districts, led by a district director. Like regional vice presidents, district directors were general managers who ran relatively complete businesses. Key aspects of the role were described by Robert (Bob) Salvucci, district manager for Philadelphia and, later, Coote's successor as RVP for the Northeast: "It's a fun job if you don't like a lot of structure and you like to handle a lot of things happening at once. You need high energy, a thick skin, and the ability to make rapid-fire decisions on the fly." Districts did not have separate P&L, however; for accounting and compensation purposes, they were considered part of the region. The compensation system was highly leveraged; that is, for regional, district, and other managers, it had a low base salary relative to market, but there was no cap on the upside potential. The variable portion of the compensation system was tied primarily to making individual, district, or regional software sales numbers. Because SAP stock was traded only in Europe, there were no stock options.

RESOURCING EXPLOSIVE GROWTH

The first Americas strategy meeting was held in Bermuda in the summer of 1993 and became something of a landmark event. Market acceptance of R/3 was now assured, and enthusiasm for the product was so great that explosive growth was anticipated. The group set a $1 billion revenue target for SAP America, to be reached by 1997. To achieve such massive growth, the executives concluded that they had to do three things: create an industry strategy to penetrate markets and build the installed base, rethink and vastly expand their partnership strategy, and dramatically ramp up their service and support capabilities.

An Industry Strategy: ICOEs

The executives developed a vertical industry strategy, to be delivered through industry centers of expertise, or ICOEs. ICOEs were to serve as a bridge between R/3 customers and the product development organization in Walldorf. Each would work closely with users in a par-

ticular industry, defining and prioritizing their requirements and then communicating them to developers to influence their design decisions and deployment of resources. This approach fit well with SAP's product philosophy. The base R/3 product was not expected to provide a 100 percent solution; it would meet only 80 percent of customers' needs, and ICOEs would provide the final 20 percent through customized software solutions and industry-specific consulting services.

At their meeting in Bermuda, the executives chose to establish ICOEs in six manufacturing sectors, including oil and gas, process industries, and high technology. By 1995, these markets accounted for 80 percent of SAP America's licensing revenues. Organizationally, the ICOEs were small, highly autonomous units, consisting of two to six presales and consulting experts, that nominally reported to a regional vice president. But they were in fact highly independent, and were led by directors who were extremely entrepreneurial and had been recruited because of their industry-specific knowledge.

Each of the six ICOE directors interpreted his role uniquely, giving different weight to one of three areas of activity: presales support, charting market direction, and liaison with product development. The high-tech ICOE, for example, concentrated on supporting customers and the SAP field sales force during the presales process, while the Process Industry ICOE built a formal, broad-based process to help customers define their requirements more clearly. These requirements were then prioritized for different user groups. User groups were highly organized within the SAP community; they had considerable power and served as a critical source of information and feedback.

Most ICOE directors spent considerable time in Germany building strong ties with influential developers and SAP AG board members. As one of them put it: "SAP works like the Senate. Lobbying and influence are essential for getting your industry's needs met in the next release of the product." Prior to the 1996 reorganization, the six ICOE directors had never met as a group; typically, they operated independently of one another and had little contact.

Partnering

To realize the company's ambitious growth goals, the range of partners and their level of investment in SAP would have to shift to unprecedented levels. Ott was given the task of leveraging external resources in the sales and implementation of SAP, while also managing

EXHIBIT 3   Types of Partners

Type	Characteristics	SAP certifies	Value to SAP	Value to partner	Examples
Alliance	Professional service firms that provide services and resources in sales and implementation of SAP products	Individuals in the firm have sufficient R/3 knowledge.	Leverage client relationships Leverage industry expertise Allow SAP to sell high volume of R/3 fast Allow R/3 to become de facto industry standard	Huge, lucrative SAP practice area	Price Waterhouse Andersen Consulting ICS/Deloitte CSC Index DDS, Inc.
Platform	Provide hardware on which R/3 runs	R/3 runs on the platform.	Ensure that SAP's technology is in sync with current and future platform technology Provide multiple platform choices to customer Leverage large marketing budgets of platform companies	Ensure that its current and future technology will support R/3 SAP is a market leader which drives their commodity product, part of channel strategy. Exploit SAP in their advertising	IBM* HP* Digital Apple AT&T Sun Microsystems Pyramid Telemarketing
Technology	Provide operating systems and databases through which R/3 runs	R/3 runs on operating system or under database.	Provide multiple choices to customer Ensure current and future compatibility	R/3 is core business application which must be able to support	Oracle Microsoft Intel
Complementary	Wide range of applications and software tools that run on top of or with R/3	Interoperability of R/3 and third-party software.	SAP does not provide 100% of software solution Leverage specialized software expertise of third parties	Use interoperability as marketing tool Use SAP as channel to sell product	

*Some partners, such as IBM or HP, have multiple partnering relationships with SAP—as providers of professional services, platforms, operating systems or middleware, and software product.
Source: SAP America.

the business side of partner relationships. He worked to develop partnering relationships in four categories: alliance, platform, technology, and complementary partners (see Exhibit 3). Allen Brault, director of the U.S. Partner Program, described the resulting network as an "ecosystem":

> Everyone is intertwined, with each firm tied into everyone else's success. If any component fails, it ripples throughout the entire system. Ultimately, the failure can be traced back

to SAP, because it means we have not worked closely enough with that partner.

Gaining Cooperation   SAP America chose to leverage alliance partner resources and expertise by leaving 80–90 percent of the consulting implementation business on the table. It would focus on selling the product and assisting with the initial installation; all other aspects of implementation or application were the province of

EXHIBIT 4   Alliance Partner Investment in SAP Practice: Number of SAP-Certified Consultants, Circa Early 1996

	Worldwide	United States
Price Waterhouse	1,800	1,100 (500 to be added in '96)
Andersen Consulting	2,700 (100/month to be added in '96)	N/A
ICS/Deloitte & Touche	1,400 (600 to be added in '96)	900
CSC	1,000	200
SAP America	750	180

N/A: not available.
Source: Aberdeen Group.

partners. To pursue this business, partners had to make substantial investments in their own SAP practices (Exhibit 4). After three years, the results were obvious; as Ott put it: "R/3 has been a gold mine for leading consulting firms." Brault explained why SAP had been so successful in getting these firms to invest in their SAP practices:

> Our approach is a complementary one, in that we have opened up a vast new business for our partners. We say, "We have a great product, and if you are willing to make the investment, we are not going to compete with you for the same consulting business." Traditionally, these firms have been reluctant to fund a practice around an outside vendor's product, because the vendors have often moved into consulting, making it difficult for them to compete effectively.

These relationships were further strengthened by changing business needs. In the early 1990s, the concepts and language of reengineering and business process redesign (BPR) became increasingly popular. Ott noted: "Consultants were talking about reengineering and BPR, but they did not yet have a tool to make their concepts fly." R/3 was just such a tool, for it could immediately embed redesigned processes in an integrated information system. R/3 could even lead the redesign process, as Coote observed:

> R/3 is packaged software, but it is so broad that it forces different parts of an organization to work together. Just to install the software and set the tables, every part of the company has to agree on some basic points: What is a customer? When do we do credit checks? What are the capacity limits of each of our factories?

In addition, R/3 included at least 800 best practices, which made it possible to shorten the BPR process and

lower the risks associated with installing custom software and integration. Instead of coming up with new process designs only to find that they could not be programmed into computer systems, designers could use R/3's process templates, which were preconfigured, and then modify them using automated modeling tools. Ott explained:

> The market will no longer pay for paper designs that can't be programmed. Our system is both very flexible and standardized: you can configure it according to customer needs, without modifying the underlying software or interfaces. For this reason, the big consulting firms have adopted R/3 into their BPR methodologies, and the process reengineers now design their "to be" scenarios with R/3 in mind.

Competency Centers   The openness of R/3 and its reliance on client-server architecture meant that customers had to make platform and technology decisions that they had not faced with R/2. SAP had to help them assess their options, while remaining neutral about their choices. This required an intimate familiarity with the ever-changing capabilities and constraints of platform and technology partners and an understanding of their ability to support R/3, which was itself constantly evolving. To address these needs, SAP America established Competency Centers with each of its platform and technology partners.

The centers provided a range of presales information to customers and were a focal point for the flow of knowledge between SAP and its partners. They were usually located at SAP headquarters in Philadelphia and occasionally on partners' premises. In each center, the partner provided a dedicated team of technical and applications consultants who were highly knowledgeable about their own product as well as R/3. The team worked with customers on such matters as the sizing and configuration of the computer system they would need and the required connectivity to other corporate systems. The Competency Centers had the systems in place to perform tests and benchmarking for R/3; these tests served as the basis for SAP's certification of hardware and technology partners. Certification was conducted by a group of 50 technologists based in Walldorf, under the direction of Wahl.

Managing the Relationship   Complementarity between R/3 and partners' business focus was but one part of SAP's approach to alliance relationships. Ott described its key characteristics: there could be no financial ties between SAP America and its partners, the relationship had to be mutually beneficial, and it could not be exclusive. The company had also established "rules of engagement" for partnering activities. Three of the most important were equal treatment at the same level, making the highest level partnering status (called *logo partner*) an earned one, and the establishment of clear criteria for promoting alliance partners to that status.

Every year, SAP America assembled its global alliance partners and shared with them its business plan and anticipated consulting needs. Forecasts were extremely accurate because SAP dominated the market, knew its pipeline, and was relatively certain of the deals that would close. It was then up to each of the partners to decide how much more they wanted to invest in training and how many additional resources, including the number of additional R/3 consultants, they would hire that year. Ott explained his approach:

> The cornerstone of the relationship is open, trustworthy conversations. I put our numbers on the table, and I never overstate our expectations. We have always hit our numbers; in fact, we've always exceeded them. In addition, I will not sign up new alliance partners to meet rising demand if the old ones can do it; I always give them rights of first refusal.
>
> Of course, our logo partners cannot plan together because that would be collusion. But by the size and nature of the large consulting firms, you have a pretty good idea of what they are likely to be willing to invest. I don't want to legally nail down these resources, however, because the relationship should be based on trust.

Ott's organization included a single global partner manager for each of the global alliance partners, as well as partner managers who were responsible for two or more smaller alliance relationships. The rules of engagement minimized conflict of interest by having each partner manager responsible for a single partner in a category. To ensure the best solution for customers, Ott insisted that his managers not be measured on the SAP-related revenue generated by partners. They were, however, responsible for managing all bilateral relationship issues of strategy, communication, education, and advocacy.

Under their direction, a master legal agreement was signed with each partner. It outlined SAP's obligation to train its partners, give them a copy of R/3 software, and assign partner managers. Partners were obligated to make "reasonable commercial efforts" to acquire and maintain a comprehensive knowledge of SAP and its products; live up to certain standards, such as keeping customer satisfaction above a threshold level; and dedicate a partner manager of their own to SAP. Alliance partners had to have a software implementation methodology that was appropriate for R/3. They were also required to attach a business plan to the legal agreement, outlining their expected commitments of resources for SAP consulting, broken down by markets and geography.

Partnership agreements could be terminated on a number of accounts; the most important was customer dissatisfaction. Based on an annual customer survey undertaken by an independent source, partners were rated on a 1–10 scale. Those whose weighted average scores exceeded a certain level achieved an award of excellence for the year; those that fell consistently below were warned of the need to improve. SAP ratcheted up the standard annually and was willing to use it to remove poor performers. In past years, two partners had been removed for this reason.

Professional Services

Professional services were those activities provided to customers for a fee; support activities, by contrast, had no fee attached. Consulting was the core of professional services, while training spanned both categories. It provided a source of revenue but had historically been run on a breakeven basis.

Consulting While a few SAP consultants worked directly for a particular ICOE, most reported to the region that hired them. Their solid reporting line was either to the district director or to the services director in the region. Because of the company's explosive growth, the hiring rate for consultants had been exceedingly steep (see Exhibit 5). Considerable learning took place on the job, since training lasted only 10 weeks. Although exact numbers were hard to come by, SAP believed that for every one of its own consultants, there were 8–10 in the outside SAP community. Basho, who had been district director in the New York metropolitan area before Besier named her vice president of consulting (with dotted line control), in January 1996, compared SAP's and partners' consultants:

> There is nothing that we do that our partners don't. But you could best describe our consultants as deep and theirs as broad. Our consultants bring in-depth product knowledge, and are always a little further ahead than partners on the product's capabilities and requirements.

SAP's consultants did two main kinds of work: basis consulting and applications consulting. Basis consultants put R/3 and its support system in place and ensured

EXHIBIT 5   SAP America Headcount

Year end	Sales	Consulting	Other	Total
1988	—	9	2	11
1989	5	22	12	39
1990	16	50	23	89
1991	30	114	43	187
1992	50	155	79	284
1993	118	220	73	411
1994	211	523	138	872
1995	230	679	361	1270
10/31/96	296	846	479	1621

Source: SAP America.

that the software was functioning correctly in a network. They knew what hardware configurations were needed to support the volume of transactions, how to convert the data from legacy systems to R/3's client-server approach, and how to load the software. Basis consultants were extremely valuable, and their skills had to be well leveraged. For every basis consultant, there were at least three applications consultants. Their primary responsibility was to work with the customer to identify their requirements and then customize the software configuration to match those requirements.

Because growth was so rapid, SAP America needed experienced managers immediately; it therefore hired its consulting managers from outside. As Bill Schwartz observed when he was hired as director of human resources in February 1996: "The expectation was that you were being brought in because you already knew the right thing to do, and you were expected just to do it." There was no career path for managers or consultants, and each region evolved its own definitions of managerial roles. Because of the long learning curve, it took nearly two years for SAP to begin getting a payback from its consultants. Unfortunately, with demand so high for anyone who knew anything about R/3, consultants began leaving in significant numbers by 1995. Some left to join a customer or a partner organization; more frequently, they left to set up their own R/3 consulting practices.

Training   During 1992–93, SAP developed scores of modules on product functionality. The Northeast region sequenced a number of these modules into a basic 10-week package that was used to train SAP's own consultants; the approach was quickly adopted by other regions. A five-week version of the course was then developed for partners, and customized versions were presented to customers' project implementation teams. SAP declined to pursue the end user training business for profit, even though by 1996 it was estimated to be a $600 million market.

To create a large-scale operation that could provide the quantity of external resources of the desired quality level, SAP America founded a Partner Academy in June 1994. Multiple locations were soon established in various parts of the country. Partner Academy's business side was under Ott's purview, and he ran it on a breakeven basis. Ott explained: "If our partners are going to invest so heavily in staffing up for R/3, I do not want to charge them on top of that." The cost of attending the Partner Academy was set at $1,000 per seat, but the fee was not always collected. By mid-1996, 5,000 outside consultants had gone through at least one cycle of training at one of the academy locations. Those who passed were certified as skilled for that release of the software.

Support and Infrastructure

One manager likened the 1993–95 period to "riding a rocket." During this period, very little attention was given to building infrastructure, except in the area of licensing and contracts.

Licensing and Contracts   When Eric Rubino was hired as general counsel in 1991, he found no systems or procedures in place to support the sales process. He recalled: "I would get a license in and wouldn't even know where it came from." To create order, Rubino generated standardized license agreements and a clear-cut proposal process; he also copyrighted the product. He observed: "Contract management is a tangible thing. For example, you must have a consistent message across regions. You must have consistent discounting policies, and be consistent in your concessions to customers." Rubino developed tools for training new contract administrators, noting: "If you are going to decentralize, you must put tools in place to empower contract administrators—who are not lawyers—to make business and legal decisions for the corporation, and train them to understand corporate positions."

Tools included standard pricing manuals that spelled out discounts and concessions and a contract manual that spelled out, paragraph by paragraph, what the license agreement meant in lay terms. The manual described very clearly what terms could be modified, the exact terms that could be used or added, and what language and wording could not be deleted. Before new administrators were sent out to the regions, they worked side by side with senior administrators for a month. Rubino also held a great many joint staff meetings on a regional basis, ensuring that regional contract administrators were aligned and consistent in their policies.

Administration   Between 1993 and 1995, there was little formal planning or budgeting. One result was great latitude in the interpretations of the few administrative systems that did exist. Meetings were rare, and offices were frequently empty because staff were in the field meeting with customers. In response, the regions got rid of the computers sitting on unused desks and gave every employee a laptop. Salvucci described the field environment:

> You were closing every deal you could, hiring people, opening offices, and building support. There were never enough resources to go around, so you were constantly finding and juggling resources, and being careful about the promises you made. Until Bill Schwartz came on board, all HR was outsourced, so there was no infrastructure you could turn to for new employees—or for new customers or resolving a problem. You were personally responsible for things like finding office space for new hires, getting them laptops, plugging into systems, and ensuring new people were trained.

Human Resources   Prior to Schwartz's arrival, SAP America's major HR concern was recruitment. The company knew what it had to offer people to bring them in but had little idea how its compensation system compared to others, let alone the percentile in which its base salaries should be. Salary grades and job titles existed on paper, but adherence to guidelines varied across regions. Schwartz found that even many senior managers did not take a traditional business perspective or give much thought to how their activities might impact people outside their regions. He observed:

> A director will want to promote some consultants, and will justify it in terms of employee retention. They don't think about a cost justification, or revenues versus costs. I will push back: "You are adding costs, but are you making money? Is there a strategy about whom you want to retain and whom you don't? Have you talked to other business directors about this? Have you considered the impact of your requests on my office? For instance, if I approve your requests, what precedent will it set for other regions?"

Building Infrastructure   By the spring of 1996, SAP America began paying far more attention to issues of organization, systems, and infrastructure. Schwartz had a one-word explanation for the change: "Kevin." Kevin McKay had joined the company in mid-1995 as CFO for the Americas, with a charter to build the internal side of the company and the goal of playing a major role in shaping strategic direction. Software, McKay emphasized, was a reference business, in which the need to build infrastructure was linked to the phase of the business. "Early on," he observed, "we needed some good toeholds, some key customer references. Our first big push was to establish our name and to position ourselves. That's the hull of the ship parting the waves." But he pointed out:

> Once you take ownership of a product, you must have a huge infrastructure to support it effectively. Behind the hull there has to be fuel and propulsion that is headed in the right direction. So we needed a hotline that follows the sun on a 7/24 [7 days a week, 24 hours a day] basis, consulting resources to size and implement the product, a whole group of partners to help position R/3 within the customer organization, and relationships with hardware partners to establish performance criteria on their platforms. We had to develop a curriculum to train people, and build our own consulting organization to make sure the implementation was done right.
>
> That was stage one. Now we are entering a different stage of maturity, where we have a huge responsibility to our installed base. Worldwide, we have 5,000 customers who are investing millions yearly in our product for their mission-critical activities. At this point we have to build the additional infrastructure to support our customer base.

To that end, McKay's first-year agenda in human resources included several initiatives: the creation of accurate, properly titled job descriptions, a market survey of salaries and benefits to serve as the basis for a total compensation strategy, and the development of a communications plan covering benefits and pay. Schwartz described the communications plan as "our effort to tell employees what they risk losing if they leave. We have very good benefits and profit sharing, but we just gave them to people. They weren't communicated, so they just became taken-for-granted entitlements. We need to tell people much more effectively what they've got here." Schwartz had also begun working on a long-term incentive plan, which included three-year vesting and a performance-unit plan pegged to SAP America's performance as a whole, and was actively recruiting someone to help direct career pathing, succession planning, and management development.

Sales and Implementation Process

Presales and Sales   The decision to purchase R/3 was often part of a strategic choice to run one's entire company differently. As a result, the sales cycle was a long one, especially for global clients. It often took a year or more to build relationships to the point where an opportunity arose that could be used to gain access for the 12–18 month presales and sales process. Account executives had to be able to identify and position these opportunities, while building consensus across divisions, countries, and multiple levels of the organization. In many cases, customers had never before made an enterprise-wide decision. Paul Melchiore, a global account executive, described the process:

> You hang out at the company for long stretches of time. You live there, building relationships, understanding the organization's complexity, its politics, its readiness for change, and putting a strategy together for your unique selling proposition. Sometimes you do a small project; if it goes well, you develop allies, gain some exposure, and can then begin selling the vision of what SAP can do across the board. You may meet 200–300 people during the selling process, all of whom are potential influencers. It may take a year or more to get the credibility to sell your vision at the top executive level. And when you get to that level, you may only get the opportunity to present for an hour, once.

Because the potential savings and strategic benefit from implementing R/3 were so large, a formal justification process was seldom required. Instead, global companies requested demonstrations, tests, and benchmarking to prove that SAP would work in their environment. This often required the involvement of SAP's partners. Salvucci described the role of the district director in the process:

> You need to be present at the beginning of the sales cycle to position the product and develop executive contacts that you will need later. You also have to find resources for a presales team, a sales team, and a consulting team to manage the sales cycle for the software. Because there is a sales cycle for the consulting partner, hardware, and database, you must spend a lot of time with them as well, putting together strategies.

Implementation Although no two installations were alike, outside partners like Andersen and Price Waterhouse usually took the lead role in R/3 project management and implementation. Because they integrated SAP product knowledge with their own implementation methodologies, each handled the process a little differently. The partner's consultants and customer's team members were dedicated full-time to the project, working together day in and day out.

SAP's basis and applications consultants, by contrast, usually served on multiple projects at the same time. They therefore attended meetings intermittently, assisting in the implementation process and providing expert advice and coaching about the product to both customers and partners. Each region's consultants used their own implementation methodology. Some customers did not want to rely on outside partners or required special skills; these installations SAP handled itself.

ORGANIZATIONAL CHALLENGES IN A SHIFTING MARKET

Despite its success, SAP America was facing a number of challenges and problems. By 1995, there were internal and external pressures, resulting from the company's explosive growth, stronger competition, and new strategic demands.

Internal Issues

The regions had different approaches to billing, overtime, and training and were not operating as a single company. Utilization of consultants, for example, could be 80–90 percent in one region and half of that in another. There were similar discrepancies in utilization rates in training centers. Nor was learning being transferred throughout the organization. Coote summarized the consequences: "We have not been leveraging our size, and have not been able to match our talent with the problem at hand. People are working separately on the same problem, so instead of fixing something once, we fix it four times."

Moreover, market perception was that SAP implementation was costly and lengthy. This perception was fueled by a number of damaging articles in the press that cited six-month projects taking four times longer than predicted, with an attendant rise in costs. The reality was more complex. As a backbone for all business processes, R/3 made possible projects of a scale that had not previously existed. When implementation was linked to the massive redesign of business processes, project scope escalated dramatically. As a result, it was difficult to disentangle the costs and time for implementing R/3 from the costs of effecting the major cultural and organizational changes associated with reengineering.

Strategic Shifts and Opportunities

By 1995, competitors' products had developed sufficient functionality to be considered viable alternatives to R/3.

SAP's largest competitor, Oracle, had an excellent database to which it had added an EIS application. As one manager observed: "What they want to sell is their database, so they use their application as a loss leader to gain control of the account. They are getting very aggressive and will do whatever it takes." Other firms had taken a modular approach, developing, for example, a strong HR module to gain entry, which could then be leveraged to sell other products over time. Baan had emulated SAP in some respects, but in order to land the Boeing account, was reputed to have revised its base product considerably—a path SAP had refused to take to win any order.

By 1996, SAP America had approximately 500 customers and 700 installations in North America; about half were *Fortune 500* companies. As McKay pointed out, one challenge was to harvest these accounts more completely: "We've sold modules and software to the top tier, but we haven't fully mined these accounts. We have the hunters out bagging the big global accounts, but now we have to bring in the farmer who works them over time." Coote identified another challenge: "We must dramatically increase the customer base so that we become the de facto standard." This meant continuing to close global deals, increasing sales in services markets, and moving into the midtier market where customers thought about R/3 in very different ways. Bryan Plug, president of SAP Canada, elaborated:

> Because of the complexity of their businesses, and their cultural belief that they are the best, big companies feel that they must invent their own business practices. So they want an implementation method that explores all the nuances and niches of R/3, and allows them to extract all the flexibility and functionality they can. They assemble the best software, the best process experts, and the best implementers, and are willing to make the necessary investments to stay on the leading edge.
>
> Midtier companies, on the other hand, are more pragmatic. They don't presume they can do it best. They are willing to find out what others have done, and see how closely it fits their situation. They are willing to adapt, and are looking for a guided tour through the software. All they want is a solution that will work for them.

The increased importance of the middle market had implications for the sales and implementation process as well. Salvucci explained: "You have to be able to pick up a phone, get to the top people, and get in the door. You are trying to close the order from the moment you arrive. You have to minimize the sales cycle, get a decision, and, if it isn't happening, move on."

REORGANIZATION

On February 1, 1996, Besier resigned from SAP America to head an Internet start-up. In the wake of his departure, a three-person office of the president was formed. Wahl was named CEO, but still spent about half of his time in Germany. Coote, who had joined SAP in 1988, become CFO of SAP America in 1990, and was at the time RVP of the largest region, the Northeast, was named president and took responsibility for the line organization. McKay continued as CFO and was named, in addition, chief operating officer for the Americas, adding training, internal systems, hotline, and other support to his responsibilities. Both McKay and Coote reported to Wahl.

A New Structure

On Saturday, April 13, 1996, Coote called a meeting of senior managers to discuss the best way to realign the company for the next wave of growth. His two primary objectives were for SAP America to act more as one company and to better leverage its size and skills. Coote's original proposal for the new organization was vertical industry segments, an idea that had been strongly favored by Besier. Some expectancy had built around this outcome, with the ICOE directors anticipating that they would become vice presidents. In presenting the proposal, Coote separated out the existing manufacturing ICOEs and also, for the first time, financial services, health care, and government. He explained: "I wanted to give everyone the same view of where we make money today and in the future. Today 75–80 percent of our revenues come from manufacturing companies. But our future growth is in services."

Lines of Business After a modest amount of discussion, the group concluded that although SAP America should continue to work toward a vertical organization, it was not yet ready to make the leap. It simply did not have the people to fill many of the vertical roles, and managers were not clear about the criteria to be used to form segments. For example, how many and which industry slices should they have? On what basis would such segments be formed? To which markets did they really want to dedicate resources? There was concern as well that SAP might again splinter into a dozen or so pieces, driving up overhead. The group therefore agreed rather quickly that for the next 18–20 months, they would organize around three major lines of business: sales, consulting, and training. In the weeks following the meeting, a more detailed organizational plan was developed, coupled with a new compensation plan. For directors and above, a portion of variable pay was now based on the performance of their line of business, and a portion was based on SAP America's performance overall.

Sales Sales was further subdivided into its own three lines of business by size of account; a fourth line, emerg-

ing markets, which involved the three new services markets, was added as well (see Exhibit 6). Peter Dunning, formerly RVP for the Southern region and newly named executive vice president, described the increased focus the reorganization gave him and his account executives in Global Sales:

> As RVP, I had 250 people; 80 percent of them were in consulting and support. The job was very maintenance intensive. Now I can focus on getting licensing revenues

EXHIBIT 6 SAP Organization Chart, May 1996

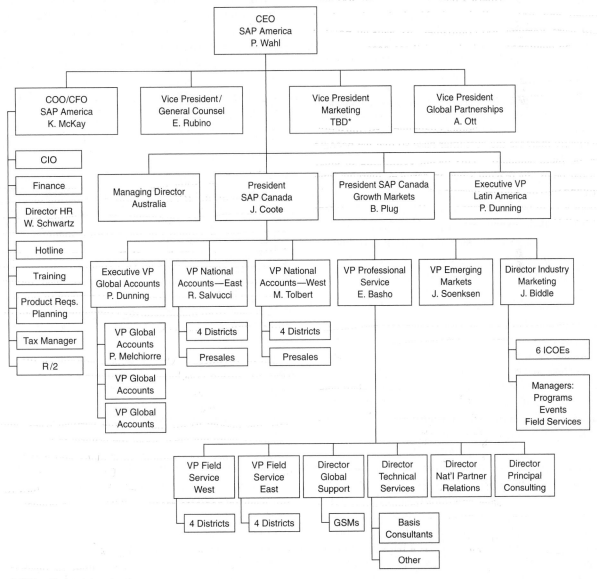

*TBD = To be determined
Source: SAP America.

from large accounts. We've gotten rid of the distractions—like geographic barriers and different sized accounts—for people who are good at global deals.

In anticipation of the next reorganization, Dunning set as one of his priorities the building of a virtual organization within global sales organized around industry expertise. More and more of his sales people would become specialists in particular industries.

ICOEs   The thorniest issue in the reorganization was what to do with the ICOEs. Coote outlined the situation:

> The ICOE directors were doing an excellent job, but they had each gone in separate directions. I wanted them to be more like program directors in a defense company or brand managers in a consumer products company who work across organizational boundaries. In reality, they were creating separate organizations within the company, and were beholden to no one. As a result, they were getting detached from the line. What we needed was to internalize their message into the mainstream of the organization.

After a great deal of discussion, the six manufacturing ICOEs became part of Jane Biddle's industry marketing group, reporting directly to Coote. Coote and Wahl had hired Biddle a few weeks earlier, anticipating that she would play a leadership role with the ICOEs. Biddle had 25 years of experience in software development, systems implementation, and marketing, knew all the ICOE directors, and had been to Walldorf many times because SAP had for years been the largest client of her strategic marketing firm.

Biddle had two broad objectives: bringing consistency and standardization to ICOE practices, including a single face to customers and the field, and developing an integrated approach to marketing within the company by spreading ICOE knowledge throughout SAP. One of her vehicles was a formalized business planning process, which required the ICOE directors to develop plans and present slides in a common format. Her next step in planning was to help them turn their strategic plans into operational plans and budgets. To bring the ICOE's industry knowledge into the line organization, Biddle's first step was to develop "solutions guides." Each was a primer on an industry and crafted the information to what a salesperson would want when talking with a potential customer. These guides were to be the basis for focused sales training, the first of its kind at SAP.

THE CHALLENGES IN PROFESSIONAL SERVICES

The reorganization gave Basho the 850-member consulting organization on a solid-line basis, rather than the dotted-line reporting she had had since January. She set as her top objective "to change both the myth and reality that SAP implementation is costly and complex." Coote had charged her as well with the goal of developing an implementation strategy for moving downmarket to midtier companies.

Professionalization

Even before the reorganization, Basho had taken steps to begin professionalizing the consulting organization. One of her first initiatives was to personally review each region. She first assembled a seven-page outline of the issues she intended to cover during her visit and sent it out several weeks in advance. She recalled: "The regions were shocked. First, because they got to see something in writing, and, second, because I sent them the request ahead of time." Another first was the attention Basho devoted to productivity and consistency across regions. She requested information on consultants' billable hours and then established targets for the end of 1996. In addition, she assigned a cross-regional group to develop a single implementation methodology for midtier companies and created another group to define an integrated set of consulting roles. Their work provided the input for Basho's recasting of the professional services organization and the development of multiple career paths.

Career Paths and Roles   Basho subdivided her consulting force into four groups: technical services, field consultants, principal consultants, and global support managers. Her technical services people were grouped by functional expertise; they included SAP's 200 basis consultants and experts who worked with emerging technologies. The field consulting group mirrored the national accounts sales force and had a four-step career path: applications consultant, lead consultant, consultant manager, and services director. Basho aligned each of her field directors with an ICOE director and made them accountable for bringing ICOE knowledge into the professional services organization. A new role, called principal consultant, was created for experienced consultants who aspired to excellence in consulting rather than positions in management. The role had considerable cachet; the first cadre of principal consultants immediately renamed themselves "platinum consultants" and created their own logo. Basho explained the importance of this option: "These were the people who were leaving SAP to establish independent practices. Within a couple of weeks of announcing the concept, a number of them had already contacted us and told us they want to come back."

Basho also split out the role of global support manager (GSM) and positioned GSMs at the front end of the sales process in a role equivalent to partner in a Big Six firm. There were 30 to 40 GSMs in total. Each was dedicated to a single account, mirroring the approach in sales. GSMs developed the overall implementation program for a new R/3 installation and coordinated SAP resources throughout the process.

Expectations and Behavior Basho and Schwartz worked together to clarify roles, procedures, and lines of authority in the new organization. In May, Basho convened a two-day meeting with her directors and managers, where she and Schwartz shared the stage. He recalled:

> We were all in the room together, and Eileen said: "When you want to promote someone, I want to see it first, and I want a justification. Bill is the last stop in the process, so don't go around me. He will support me and simply send it back." And I stood there nodding my head, "Yes."

Schwartz then explained how the consulting organization would work with his field HR people; this time, Basho nodded in affirmation. Following the meeting, several people observed that they had learned more about what was expected of them in the preceding two days than they had in the previous two years.

Customer Alternatives and Involvement

The key objectives of moving into the middle market (called national accounts at SAP America) and controlling implementation time and costs were both addressed by a new approach. Basho explained:

> In national accounts, we are going to go in and help customers size the project during the presales period. Using an estimating tool, we can draw a baseline for time, costs, and resources. Then we are going to explore alternative project approaches, and increase the choices a customer has on implementation. If they choose to work with one of our global alliance partners, we will position the partner. If they choose Accelerated SAP [SAP's new rapid implementation meth-

odology for national accounts], we can recommend a group of smaller partners who are certified implementers. Initially, I will have to subcontract these small partners in under me. Even though they have good people, they don't yet have a reputation for successful implementation.

Coote felt so strongly about getting a rapid implementation methodology in place that he had accelerated its timetable. Reorganizing by lines of business had made it easier, he thought, to adopt a strategy for the middle market that differed from past approaches. Salvucci, who now had national account sales responsibility, concurred:

> One of our strategies for selling in the middle market will be to engage our consulting organization early in the sales cycle, and put a stake in the ground for customers: if you want to use our methodology to install SAP, this is what you can expect in time and money. If our partners won't step up and meet these targets, we will do it ourselves. That does not mean we are going to go out and do all the consulting. We are not. What we are doing is putting a stake in the ground to increase our control over the process.

In the global market, Basho also intended to bring down implementation time and costs. She explained:

> I am also increasing our involvement with global accounts. From the beginning, global support managers are now strategically placed to deal directly with the customer's executive sponsor, and to educate the customer about how to use our partners more effectively. The GSM sets the implementation strategy, gets the right people onto the projects, and keeps the program from going off track.

Basho was keenly aware that this new approach would impact partner relationships, although she did not envision major changes in strategy. She observed: "Our partner strategy was and is sound. The problem is that we gave up too much control." Coote agreed, noting that SAP America's approach to global accounts was one of continuing evolution. He observed:

> We have to be more involved than in the past, and that means we have to refine the partnering model. In addition, our product has continued to evolve, and we have more tools available for automating some of the configuration work. Partners have to understand their changing role in the mix, and that the relationship will continue to change.

Crossing the Chasm—and Beyond

Geoffrey A. Moore

Virtually all contemporary thinking about high-tech marketing strategy has its roots in the Technology Adoption Life Cycle, a model which grew out of social research begun in the late 1950s about how communities respond to *discontinuous innovations.*

Truly discontinuous innovations are new products or services that require the end user and the marketplace to dramatically change their past behavior, with the promise of gaining equally dramatic new benefits. Applied to marketing, the model postulates that when a marketplace is confronted with the opportunity to switch to a new infrastructure paradigm—from typewriters, say, to word processors—customers self-segregate along an axis of risk aversion, with the risk-immune *innovators* moving to the forefront, asking—even demanding—to be first to try out the new opportunity, while the risk-allergic *laggards* retreat to the rear of the line (quills still firmly in hand). In between, the model identifies three additional communities—the *early adopters, early majority,* and *later majority.*

Graphically, the model is represented as a bell curve (Exhibit 1):

Each of the segments in the bell curve represents a standard deviation from the norm. Thus the early and late majority are one standard deviation from the norm, each comprising about a third of the total population, while the early adopters and laggards are two and the innovators three standard deviations away. The idea is that change will be adopted from left to right, with each constituency coming to the fore in sequence.

Prior to encountering this model, high-tech marketers were in desperate need of help. Most of us had grown up in a business environment where excellence in marketing was defined in reference to Procter & Gamble. In attempting to apply that company's approach to high tech, we were thrashing about miserably. In particular, the tools for marketing communications just weren't working right, and whenever we went to people for advice, they kept chastising us for making our messages too long, too complicated, and, well, too nerdy. When the Technology Adoption Life Cycle came upon the scene, we were delighted, because it helped explain why our communications got such enthusiastic responses from some customers and such chilly ones from others.

In order to make this model truly ours, we relabeled each of the five constituencies as follows:

1. **Innovators = *Technology enthusiasts.*** These are people who are fundamentally committed to new technology on the grounds that, sooner or later, it is bound to improve our lives. Moreover, they take pleasure in mastering its intricacies, just in fiddling with it, and they love to get their hands on the latest and greatest innovation. And thus they are typically the first customers for anything that is truly brand-new.

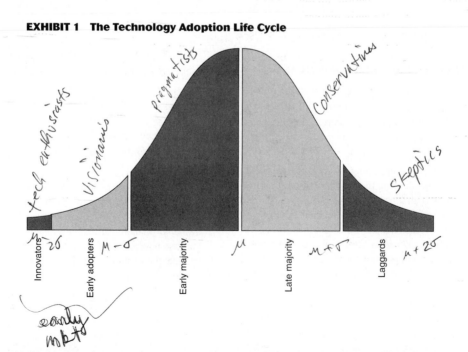

EXHIBIT 1   The Technology Adoption Life Cycle

Virtually all organizations support techies. In your own family there is likely to be one—and only one—person who can program the answering machine, set the clock on the VCR, and figure out the espresso machine. Same is true at the office. Who do you go to when you can't get the computer to work right? That is your techie.

From a marketing point of view, particularly in business-to-business sales, there is really only one drawback to techies: they don't have any money. What they have instead is influence. The reason we spend so much time with them is that they are the gatekeepers to the rest of the life cycle. If they pan a new product, no one else gives that product a second glance. Only with their endorsement can a discontinuous innovation get a hearing, and so we often "seed" (read "give") products to this community to gain their support.

2. **Early Adopters = *Visionaries*.** These are the true revolutionaries in business and government who want to use the discontinuity of any innovation to make a break with the past and start an entirely new future. Their expectation is that by being first to exploit the new capability they can achieve a dramatic and insurmountable competitive advantage over the old order.

Visionaries have an extraordinary influence on high tech because they are the first constituency who can and will bring real money to the table. In so doing, they provide at least as much seed funding for entrepreneurs as does the venture capital community. And because they tend to love the limelight, they also help publicize the new innovation, giving it a necessary boost to succeed in the early market.

But for all this there is a quid pro quo. Each visionary demands special modifications that no one else would dream of using, and quickly these demands begin to overtax the R&D resources of the fledgling enterprise. Sooner or later this forces companies to seek out a different kind of customer, one who really just wants what everybody else wants, a customer known as the pragmatist.

Taken together, technology enthusiasts and visionaries make up the *early market.* Although their personal motives are quite different, they are united by their drive to be the first, the techies desiring to *explore* and the visionaries desiring to *exploit* the new capability. No one else in the Technology Adoption Life Cycle has any interest in being first, as you can see from the remaining profiles:

3. **Early Majority = *Pragmatists*.** These people make the bulk of all technology infrastructure purchases. They do not love technology for its own sake, so are different from the techies, whom they are careful, nonetheless, to employ. Moreover, they believe in *evolution* not *revolution,* so they are not visionaries, either—indeed they shy away from them. Instead, they are interested in making their companies' systems work effectively. So they are neutral about technology and look to adopt innovations only after a proven track record of useful productivity improvement, including strong references from people they trust.

Pragmatists are the people most likely to be in charge of a company's mission-critical systems. They know this infrastructure is only marginally stable, and they are careful to protect it from novel intrusions. As such, they prove to be a tough nut to crack when the time comes for them to underwrite shifting to the new paradigm.

When they finally do make this shift, pragmatists prefer to buy from the market leader for two reasons. First, everyone else in the market makes their products work with the leader's, so while the leader's product may not be the best one, systems built upon it are going to be the most reliable. Second, the market leader attracts many third-party companies into its aftermarket, so that even when the leader is not responsive to customer requests, the marketplace as a whole is. As a result, pragmatists have determined that customers of market-leading vendors get a better overall value from the market.

4. **Late Majority = *Conservatives*.** These customers are pessimistic about their ability to gain any value from technology investments and undertake them only under duress—typically because the remaining alternative is to let the rest of the world pass them by. They are very price-sensitive, highly skeptical, and very demanding. Rarely do their demands get met, in part because they are unwilling to pay for any extra services, all of which only reconfirms their sour views of high tech.

Conservatives nonetheless represent a largely untapped opportunity for high-tech products, holding out the promise of a horde of new customers who can be brought into the market if handled with care, albeit presenting deep challenges to the vendors who elect to serve them. The key to winning their business and profiting is to simplify and commoditize systems to the point where they just work. Conservatives, in other words, are happy to buy several dozen of the world's most advanced microprocessors, as long as they are deeply embedded inside a BMW.

5. **Laggards = *Skeptics*.** These are the gadflies of high tech, the ones who delight in challenging the hype and puffery of high-tech marketing. They are not so much potential customers as ever-present critics. As such, the goal of high-tech marketing is not to sell to them but rather to sell around them.

Linked all together these five profiles make up the Technology Adoption Life Cycle. The idea of developing the market by working from one profile to the next provided the basis for high-tech marketing strategy in the 1980s. The desired progression went as follows:

- Begin by seeding new products with the *technology enthusiasts* so they can help you educate the *visionaries*.
- Once you have captured the *visionaries'* interest, do whatever it takes to make them satisfied customers so that they can serve as good references for the *pragmatists.*
- Gain the bulk of your revenue by serving *pragmatists,* ideally by becoming the market leader and setting the de facto standards.
- Leverage success with the *pragmatists* to generate sufficient volume and experience so that products become reliable enough and cheap enough to meet the needs of the *conservatives.*
- As for the *skeptics,* leave them to their own devices.

INTRODUCING THE CHASM

Unfortunately, as logical and attractive as this strategy appears in theory, in actual practice it did not work very often. Specifically, companies kept stumbling every time it came to making the transition from the visionaries to the pragmatists. The problem was that these two groups, although adjacent on the adoption life cycle, are so different in terms of underlying values as to make communication between them almost impossible, as the comparison in Exhibit 2 illustrates.

Perhaps the easiest way to epitomize the differences between these two groups is to contrast the way they use the phrase "I see." When visionaries say "I see," they do so *with their eyes closed.* That's how visionaries *see.* Pragmatists, on the other hand, like to see with their eyes open. They don't trust visionaries for the same reasons that they don't trust people who want to navigate using *the force.*

EXHIBIT 2

Visionaries	Pragmatists
Intuitive	Analytic
Support revolution	Support evolution
Contrarian	Conformist
Break away from the pack	Stay with the herd
Follow their own dictates	Consult with their colleagues
Take risks	Manage risks
Motivated by future opportunities	Motivated by present problems
Seek what is possible	Pursue what is probable

In short, visionaries think pragmatists are pedestrian, and pragmatists think visionaries are dangerous. As a result, visionaries, with their highly innovative—not to say hare-brained—projects do not make good references for pragmatists, and market development, instead of gliding across this transition point, stalls. Unfortunately, by the time that high-tech firms were getting this far into the market, they were so highly leveraged financially that any hiccup (and this stall tended to hit more like a whooping cough) would throw them into a tailspin—or, as we came to call it, *into the chasm* (Exhibit 3).

The idea of the chasm is a simple one. It says that whenever truly innovative high-tech products are first brought to market, they will initially enjoy a warm welcome in an *early market* made up of technology enthusiasts and visionaries but then will fall into a *chasm,* during which sales will falter and often plummet. If the products can successfully cross this chasm, they will gain acceptance within a *mainstream market* dominated by pragmatists and conservatives. Since for product-oriented enterprises virtually all high-tech wealth comes from this third phase of market development, crossing the chasm becomes an organizational imperative.

Unfortunately, too few innovative products were actually getting across. What was happening instead was that investors, flushed with the results of early-market acceptance, became impatient to see an immediate transition into a high-growth, high-profit mainstream marketplace. That, after all, was what the life cycle model predicted. When they got chasm results instead, they assumed that management was somehow at fault, and in trying to correct these faults, they ended up more often than not destabilizing operations to a point from which they could never recover.

Fortunately, as the chasm idea has caught on, this is all beginning to change.

EXHIBIT 3   The Chasm

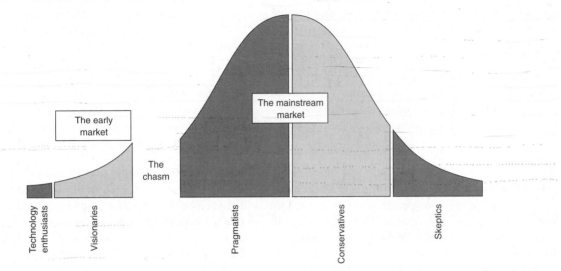

CROSSING THE CHASM

The fundamental strategy for making a successful "crossing" is based on a single observation: the main difference between the visionaries of the early market and the pragmatists in the mainstream is that the former are willing to bet "on the come" whereas the latter want to see solutions "in production" before they buy. That is, when a visionary sees that you have 80 percent of the solution to her problem, she says, "Great, let's get started right away on building the other 20 percent together." A pragmatist, on the other hand, says, "Wait a minute—aren't *you* supposed to be the one improving *my* productivity? I'll buy this thing when it's done but not before." Specifically, what pragmatists want, more than anything else, is a 100 percent solution to their problem—what we came to call the *whole product.*

The idea of the whole product has been around for some time, having initially been popularized by Theodore Levitt at Harvard and subsequently getting a lot of exposure in Silicon Valley from Bill Davidow's *Marketing High Technology.* In the context of the chasm, however, it took on a radically simplified meaning. Basically, the whole product became defined as *the minimum set of products and services necessary to ensure that the target customer will achieve his or her compelling reason to buy.* In this light, we saw that high-tech companies were prolonging their stays in the chasm because they were unable, or unwilling, to commit to taking any particular whole product all the way through to this level of completion.

Here's what would happen instead. The high-tech enterprise, sensing it was in the chasm, and realizing that the customer needed more than just the bare product itself, would set out to address this problem. Instead of focusing on a single target customer, however, management would invariably recoil from putting all its eggs in one basket. Instead, it would target four or five likely candidate segments with the idea of focusing intensively on whichever opportunity caught fire first.

This decision was followed by a round of customer visits with major customers from each of the target segments, during which "wish lists" of requirements were painstakingly extracted and recorded. These lists were then reviewed by a product marketing council made up of marketing and engineering managers who would extract from them the common themes, the most broadly requested enhancements. These were the "nuggets," or key requirements, which defined the next release. In this way, when the next release came out, true to its intent, it had something for everybody.

Unfortunately, however, it had *everything* for nobody. That is, no one group ever got 100 percent of its whole product requirements fulfilled. We never finished any one customer's list. *But that is precisely the requirement that pragmatists insist upon before they purchase.* Pragmatists therefore would praise our efforts, pat us on the back, but they would not buy our product. So after a round of development, which in turn required a round of funding, the company garnered a round of applause, but alas, not a round of sales.

It was only then that some of us came to the counter-intuitive—indeed horrifying—realization that *the only safe way to cross the chasm is in fact to put all your eggs in one basket.* That is, the key to a winning strategy is to identify a single beachhead of pragmatist customers in a mainstream market segment and to accelerate the formation of 100 percent of their whole product. The goal is to win a niche foothold in the mainstream as quickly as possible—that is what is meant by *crossing the chasm.*

AN EXAMPLE

When *Crossing the Chasm* was written, all its examples were drawn from companies who had crossed the chasm more or less inadvertently. That is, since we did not have a specified concept for this transition period (although many savvy investors and executives knew about it intuitively), it was hard to have an explicit strategy for negotiating the passage. Subsequently, however, companies have had a chance to incorporate these ideas into their plans with good success. One such company is Documentum.

Documentum is in the document management software business with high-end systems that were originally designed at Xerox. Virtually unknown until 1994, it had spent the early part of the 1990s in the chasm, limping along at a few million dollars per year in revenues, taking on a new visionary every year, with nothing much to show for it. In 1994, it came out of nowhere to become the overwhelmingly dominant supplier of systems to the pharmaceutical industry, beginning with the specific niche of Computer Aided New Drug Approval (CANDA). How was it able to do this?

At the end of 1993, in a series of management meetings, Documentum's executive team reviewed some 80 or so candidate beachhead segments. From these they narrowed it down to their target based on five criteria:

1. Is the target customer well funded and are they readily accessible to our sales force?
2. Do they have a compelling reason to buy?
3. Can we today, with the help of partners, deliver a whole product to fulfill that reason to buy?
4. Is there no entrenched competition that could prevent us from getting a fair shot at this business?
5. If we win this segment, can we leverage it to enter additional segments?

In the case of pharmaceutical companies, there was no question that they were well funded, and the target customer for this application is readily accessed, being a specific department whose sole job is to handle regulatory submissions. So it passed the first hurdle.

As to the compelling reason to buy, over the life of a typical patented drug, revenues average $400 million per year. Patents last for 17 years, but that period starts with patent award not regulatory approval. Every day of delay from that point on costs the drug company $1 million in lost revenue opportunity. That felt compelling enough for the team at Documentum.

It was the whole product that was the real challenge. The CANDA document set typically ranges from 200,000 to 500,000 pages, coming from scores of different sources, some computerized, many not. Documentum focused all its systems development and all its whole product marketing on pulling this specific set of highly diverse sources together. To do so it had to draw heavily on partnership resources from much larger vendors like Sun, Oracle, and CSC (Computer Sciences Corporation). But from their experience with a project funded by a visionary at Syntex, the company could see this was feasible, and so the segment passed this test.

As to competition, while other competitors were far bigger, more technically accepted, with more established user groups, none had really stepped up to the entire CANDA challenge. Through its special efforts Documentum felt it would be able to fundamentally change the economic equation and communicate that fact to the economic buyers.

And finally, if it won the CANDA application in pharmaceutical, it could readily expand forward both into other departments within pharmaceutical, such as manufacturing and R&D, as well as other FDA-regulated industries such as medical equipment and food processing.

What was the result of all this? In the space of a year, from the go-ahead in first quarter of 1994 to the end of that calendar year, Documentum garnered 30 of their top 40 target customers. In the same space of time their closest competitor won only one. Their revenue run-rate for that year tripled and is on target to triple again. They are the unquestioned market leader in this segment, which gives them far more influence than their size warrants. They can never be dislodged from this marketplace, indeed cannot, from the pharmaceutical industry's point of view, be allowed to go out of business. As such, they are now set up to attack the market from a position of strength and have strong prospects for market expansion. Such is the power of crossing the chasm.

The key point to close with here is the powerful impact on market development of gaining one's first niche in the mainstream. To cite another example, consider the difference between the current status of pagers and pen-based personal digital assistants in the market today. Most people don't carry either. But if you ask someone, if you carried a pager, do you think it would work? most people answer yes. When asked the same question about a PDA, most answer no. When asked why, they point to the fact that they have seen certain categories of people use pagers routinely—doctors, LAN administrators, and other people on call—whereas they do not know any group of people that uses PDAs routinely. As a result, they are much more willing to consider adopting the former than the latter. This is a key part of the reasoning behind gaining a beachhead. Not only does it gain you some immediate customers, it also makes it much easier for all future customers to buy in.

BEYOND THE CHASM

Inside the Tornado is focused on mapping the marketplace beyond the chasm. It focuses on three subsequent stages in the life cycle model, as illustrated by Exhibit 4.

The map divides up the landscape into six zones, which are characterized as follows:

1. *The Early Market,* a time of great excitement when customers are technology enthusiasts and visionaries looking to be first to get on board with the new paradigm.
2. *The Chasm,* a time of great despair, when the early-market's interest wanes but the mainstream market is still not comfortable with the immaturity of the solutions available.
3. *The Bowling Alley,* a period of niche-based adoption in advance of the general marketplace, driven by compelling customer needs and the willingness of vendors to craft niche-specific whole products.
4. *The Tornado,* a period of mass-market adoption, when the general marketplace switches over to the new infrastructure paradigm.
5. *Main Street,* a period of aftermarket development, when the base infrastructure has been deployed and the goal now is to flesh out its potential.
6. *End of Life,* which can come all too soon in high tech because of the semiconductor engine driving price/performance to unheard of levels, enabling wholly new paradigms to come to market and supplant the leaders who themselves had only just arrived.

The thesis is that business strategy must change dramatically as marketplaces move through these stages. The key points of its argument are as follows:

- The forces that operate in the bowling alley argue for a niche-based strategy that is highly customer-centric.
- Those in the tornado push in the opposite direction toward a mass-market strategy for deploying a common standard infrastructure.
- Then on Main Street market forces push back again toward a customer-centric approach, focusing on specific adaptations of this infrastructure for added value through mass customization.

EXHIBIT 4   The Landscape of the Technology Adoption Life Cycle

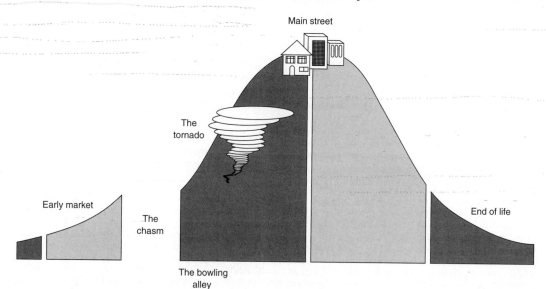

- Given these dramatic reversals in strategy, it is imperative that organizations be able to agree on where their markets are in the life cycle.
- In the meantime, the economic cataclysm of the tornado deconstructs and reconstructs the power structure in the market so rapidly that simply understanding who is friend and who is foe becomes a challenge.
- Within this newly emerging market structure, companies must compete for advantage based on their status within it.
- Positioning in this context consists of a company taking its rightful place in the hierarchy of power and defending it against challengers.
- And finally, moving fluidly from strategy to strategy is the ultimate challenge of any organization, demanding an extraordinarily flexible response from its management team.

With these directions in one hand and our map in the other we can now set out to follow our Yellow Brick Road.

READING II-7

Competing Technologies: An Overview*

> *Every steam carriage which passes along the street justifies the confidence placed in it; and unless the objectionable feature of the petrol carriage can be removed, it is bound to be driven from the road, to give place to its less objectionable rival, the steam-driven vehicle of the day.*
> —William Fletcher (1904)
> *Steam Carriages and Traction Engines,* p. xi

W. Brian Arthur

INTRODUCTION

When a new engineering or economic possibility comes along, usually there are several ways to carry it through. In the 1890s the motor carriage could be powered by

steam, or by gasoline, or by electric batteries. In more modern times nuclear power can be generated by light-water, or gas-cooled, or heavy-water, or sodium-cooled reactors. Solar energy can be generated by crystalline-silicon or amorphous-silicon technologies. An AIDS vaccine may eventually become possible by cell-type modification methods, or by chemical synthesis, or by anti-idio-type methods. Video recording can be carried out by Sony Betamax® or by VHS technologies.

In each case we can think of these methods or technologies as "competing" for a "market" of adopters.[1] They may compete unconsciously and *passively,* like species compete biologically, if adoptions of one technology displace or preclude adoptions of its rivals. Or they may compete consciously and *strategically* if they are products that can be priced and manipulated. (In this latter case, following nomenclature introduced in Arthur,[2] we will say they are *sponsored.*)

What makes competition between technologies interesting is that usually technologies become more attractive—more developed, more widespread, more useful—the more they are adopted. Thus competition between technologies usually becomes competition between bandwagons, and adoption markets display both a corresponding instability and a high degree of unpredictability.

Increased attractiveness caused by adoption, or what I will call increasing returns to adoption, can arise from several sources; but five are particularly important:

1. *Learning by using.*[3] Often the more a technology is adopted, the more it is used and the more is learned about it; therefore, the more it is developed and improved. A new airliner design, like the DC-8, for example, gains considerably in payload, passenger capacity, engine efficiency, and aerodynamics, as it achieves actual airline adoption and use.
2. *Network externalities.*[4] Often a technology offers advantages to "going along" with other adopters of it—to belonging to a network of users. The video tech-

Change and Economic Theory (New York: Columbia University Press, 1987), pp. 590–607.
[1] W. B. Arthur, "Competing Technologies and Lock-in by Historical Events: The Dynamics of Allocation Under Increasing Returns," Paper WP-83–90, International Institute for Applied Systems Analysis, Laxenburg, Austria, 1983.
[2] W. B. Arthur, "Information, Imitation and the Emergence of Technological Structures," mimeo, Stanford University, 1985.
[3] N. Rosenberg, *Inside the Black Box: Technology and Economics* (Cambridge, England: Cambridge University Press, 1982).
[4] M. Katz and C. Shapiro, "Network Externalities, Competition, and Compatibility," *American Economic Review* 75 (1985), pp. 424–40.

*I am grateful to Paul David, Giovanni Dosi, Frank Englmann, Christopher Freeman, Richard Nelson, Nathan Rosenberg, Gerald Silverberg, and Luc Soete for comments on this paper, and to participants at the May 1987 IFIAS meeting on Technical Change and Economic Theory, Maastricht, The Netherlands. In G. Dosi, ed., *Technical*

nology VHS is an example. The more other users there are, the more likely it is that the VHS adopter benefits from a greater availability and variety of VHS-recorded products.

3. *Scale economies in production.* Often, where a technology is embodied in a product, like the polaroid technology, the cost of the product falls as increased numbers of units of it are produced. Thus the technology can become more attractive in price as adoption increases.

4. *Informational increasing returns.* Often a technology that is more adopted enjoys the advantage of being better known and better understood. For the risk-averse, adopting it becomes more attractive if it is more widespread.

5. *Technological interrelatedness.*[5] Often, as a technology becomes more adopted, a number of other sub-technologies and products become part of its infrastructure. For example, the gasoline technology has a huge infrastructure of refineries, filling stations, and auto parts that rely on it. This puts it at an advantage in the sense that other technologies, if less adopted, may lack the requisite infrastructure or may require a partial dismantling of the more widespread technology's in-place infrastructure.

Of course, with any particular technology, several of these benefits to increased adoption may be mixed in and present together. Rarely do we have a pure source of increasing returns to adoption.

Whatever the source, if increasing returns to adoption are indeed present, they determine the character of competition between technologies. If one technology gets ahead by good fortune, it gains an advantage. It can then attract further adopters who might otherwise have gone along with one of its rivals, with the result that the adoption market may tip in its favor and may end up dominated by it.[6] Given other circumstances, of course, a different technology might have been favored early on, and *it* might have come to dominate the market. Thus in competitions between technologies with increasing returns, ordinarily there is more than one possible outcome. In economic terms there are multiple equilibria. To ascertain how the *actual* outcome is selected from these multiple candidate outcomes, we need to keep track of how adoptions of rival technologies build up (together with the small events that might influence these) and how they

eventually sway and tip the market. We need, in other words, to follow the dynamics of adoption.

Where competing technologies possess increasing returns, a number of very natural questions arise:

1. How can we model the adoption process when there is competition between increasing-return technologies and hence indeterminacy in the outcome?
2. What analytical techniques can be brought to bear on this increasing-return allocation problem? In particular, what techniques can help us determine the possible outcomes of the adoption process?
3. When technologies compete, under what circumstances *must* one technology—albeit an indeterminate one at the outset—achieve a monopoly and eventually take 100 percent of the adoption market? Under what circumstances will the market eventually be shared?
4. How does the "competing standards" case differ from the competing technologies one?
5. What difference does it make to have different sources of increasing returns: network externalities rather than learning effects, for example?
6. What policy issues arise in the competing technology case?
7. What major research questions remain to be answered?

In this paper I will provide an overview of my work on the competing technology problem, highlighting in particular the dynamic approach. Where possible I will connect my approach and results with those of others and I will mention open research problems. I begin with a review of the basic competing technologies model and then go on to discuss some of the questions raised above.

LOCK-IN BY SMALL EVENTS: A REVIEW OF THE BASIC MODEL

As one possible, simple model of competition between technologies with increasing returns,[7] imagine two unsponsored technologies, *A* and *B,* competing passively for a market of potential adopters who are replacing an old, inferior technology. As adoptions of *A* (or *B*) increase, learning-by-using takes place and improved versions of *A* (or *B*) become available, with correspondingly higher payoffs or returns to those adopting them. Each agent—each potential adopter—must choose either *A* or *B* when its time comes to replace the old technology.

[5] M. Frankel, "Obsolescence and Technological Change in a Maturing Economy," *American Economic Review* 45 (1955), pp. 296–319.
[6] Arthur, "Competing Technologies and Lock-in by Historical Events."
[7] Ibid.

EXHIBIT 1   Returns to Adopting _A_ or _B_, Given Previous Adoptions

Previous Adoptions	0	10	20	30	40	50	60	70	80	90	100
Technology _A_	10	11	12	13	14	15	16	17	18	19	20
Technology _B_	4	7	10	13	16	19	22	25	28	31	34

Once an agent chooses it sticks to its choice. The versions of _A_ or _B_ are fixed when adopted, so that agents are not affected by the choices of future adopters.

Suppose for a moment, in a preliminary version of this model, all agents are alike. And suppose that returns to adopting _A_ or _B_ rise with prior adoptions as in Exhibit 1. The dynamics of this preliminary model are trivial but instructive. The first agent chooses the higher-payoff technology—_A_ in this table. This bids the payoff of _A_ upward, so that the next agent a fortiori chooses _A_. _A_ continues to be chosen, with the result that the adoption process is locked in to _A_ from the start. Notice that _B_ cannot get a footing, even though if adopted it would eventually prove superior.

Already in this simple preliminary model, we see two properties that constantly recur with competing technologies: _potential inefficiency_ in the sense that the technology that takes the market need not be the one with the longer-term higher payoff to adopters; and _inflexibility_, or lock-in, in the sense that the left-behind technology would need to bridge a widening gap if it is to be chosen by adopters at all.

Although there are examples of technologies that lock out all rivals from the start, this preliminary model is still not very satisfactory. The outcome is either predetermined by whichever technology is initially superior or, if both are evenly matched, the outcome is razor-edged. In reality, adopters are not all alike and, at the outset of most competitions, some would naturally prefer technology _A_, and some technology _B_. If this were the case, the order in which early adopter types arrived would then become crucial, for it would decide how the market might tip.

Consider now a full model that shows this. We now allow two types of adopters, _R_ and _S_, with natural preferences for _A_ and _B_, respectively, and with payoffs as in Exhibit 2. Suppose each potential-adopter type is equally prevalent, but that the actual arrivals of _R_ and _S_ agents are subject to small unknown events outside the model, so to speak. Then all we can say is that it is equally likely that an _R_ or an _S_ will arrive next to make their choice. Initially at least, if an _R_-agent arrives at the adoption window to make its choice, it will adopt _A;_ if an _S_-agent arrives, it will adopt _B_. Thus the difference in adoptions between _A_

EXHIBIT 2   Returns to Adopting _A_ or _B_, Given n_A and n_B Previous Adopters of _A_ and _B_

	Technology A	Technology B
_R_-agent	$a_R + rn_A$	$b_R + rn_B$
_S_-agent	$a_S + sn_A$	$b_S + sn_B$

Note: The model assumes that $a_R > b_R$ and that $b_S > a_S$. Both _r_ and _s_ are positive.

and _B_ moves up or down by one unit depending on whether the next adopter is an _R_ or an _S;_ that is, it moves up or down with probability one-half. This process is a simple gambler's coin-toss random walk. There is only one complication. If by chance a large number of _R_-types cumulates in the line of choosers, _A_ will then be heavily adopted and hence improved in payoff. In fact, if _A_ gains a sufficient lead over _B_ in adoptions, it will pay _S_-types choosing to switch to _A_. Then both _R_- and _S_-types will be adopting _A_, and only _A_, from then on. The adoption process will then become locked in to technology _A_. Similarly, if a sufficient number of _S_-types had by chance arrived to adopt _B_ over _A, B_ would improve sufficiently to cause _R_-types to switch to _B_. The process would instead lock in to _B_ (see Exhibit 3). Our random walk is really a random walk with absorbing barriers on each side, the barriers corresponding to the lead in adoption it takes for each agent-type to switch its choice.

All this is fine. We can now use the well-worked-out theory of random walks to find out what happens to the adoption process in the long run. The important fact about a random walk with absorbing barriers is that absorption occurs eventually with certainty. Thus in the model I have described, the economy _must_ lock in to monopoly of one of the two technologies, _A_ or _B_, but _which_ technology is not predictable in advance. Also, the order of choice of agent is not averaged away. On the contrary, it decides the eventual market outcome. Thus, the process is _non-ergodic_—or more informally we can say that it is _path-dependent_ in the sense that the outcome depends on the way in which adoptions build up, that is, on the path the process takes. As before, the process becomes inflexible; once lock-in occurs the dominant technology continues to be chosen; hence it continues to im-

EXHIBIT 3 Difference in Adoptions: Random Walk With Absorbing Barriers

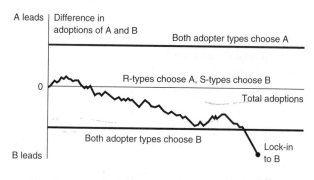

prove, so that an ever larger boost to the payoff of the excluded technology would be needed to resuscitate it. Further, it is easy to construct examples in which this greedy algorithm of each agent's taking the technology that pays off best at its time of choice may miss higher rewards to the future adoption and development of the excluded technology. As in the preliminary model, economic efficiency is not guaranteed.

This model, like all theoretical models, is obviously stylized. But it does capture an important general characteristic of competition between technologies with increasing returns. Where the competition is not dead at the outset, with a single technology dominating from the start, the adoption process is inherently unstable, and it can be swayed by the cumulation of small historical events, or small heterogeneities, or small differences in timing. Thus low-level events, stemming from the inevitable graininess present in the economy, can act to drive the process into the gravitational orbit of one of the two (or, with several technologies competing, many) possible outcomes. What we have in this simple model is order (the eventual adoption-share outcome) emerging from fluctuation (the inherent randomness in the arrival sequence). In modern terminology, our competing-technologies adoption process is therefore a *self-organizing process.*[8]

Of course, it could be objected that at some level—in some all-knowing Laplacian world—the arrival sequence in our model is foreordained, and that therefore the outcome that this sequence implies is foreordained, and that therefore our technology competition is deter-

minate and predictable. Ultimately this comes down to a question of modelling strategy. Where increasing returns are present, different patterns of small events—whether known or not—can lead to very different outcomes. If they are unknown at the outset, if for practical purposes they lie beneath the resolution of our model, we must treat them as random; so that unless we believe we know all events that can affect the buildup of adoptions and can therefore include them explicitly, models of technological competition must typically include a random component. In the model above, randomness was introduced by lack of knowledge of the arrival sequence of the adopters. But in other models it could have different sources. Randomness might, for example, enter in a homogeneous adopter-type model because technological improvements occur in part by unpredictable breakthroughs. The subject is new enough that even obvious extensions like this have not yet been studied. There may be a wide class of competing-technology models, but we would expect to see much the same properties as we found above upheld: inflexibility or lock-in of outcome, nonpredictability, possible inefficiency, and nonergodicity or path-dependence.

Do real-world competitions between technologies show these properties? Does the economy sometimes lock in to an inferior technology because of small, historical events? It appears that it does. Light-water reactors at present account for close to 100 percent of all U.S. nuclear power installations and about 80 percent of the world market. They were originally adapted from a highly compact unit designed to propel the first American nuclear submarine, the U.S.S. *Nautilus,* launched in 1954.[9] A series of circumstances—among them the U.S. Navy's role in early construction contracts, political expediency within the National Security Council, the behavior of key personages like Admiral Rickover, and the Euratom Program—acted to favor light water, so that learning and construction experience gained with light water early on locked the market in by the mid-1960s.[10] And yet the engineering literature consistently argues that, given equal development, the gas-cooled design would have been superior.[11]

[8] I. Prigogine, "Order Through Fluctuation: Self-Organization and Social System," in *Evolution and Consciousness,* ed. E. Jantsch and C. H. Waddington (New York, Addison-Wesley, 1976).

[9] A. M. Weinberg, "Power Reactors," *Scientific American* 191 (1954), pp. 33–39.
[10] R. Cowan, "Backing the Wrong Horse: Sequential Technology Choice Under Increasing Returns," doctoral dissertation, Stanford University, 1987.
[11] H. M. Agnew, "Gas-Cooled Nuclear Power Reactors," *Scientific American* 244 (1981), pp. 55–63.

Similarly, gasoline now dominates as the power source for automobiles. It may well be the superior alternative, but certainly in 1895 it was held to be the least promising option. It was hard to obtain in the right grade, it was dangerous, and it required more numerous and more sophisticated moving parts than steam. Throughout the period 1890–1920, developers, with predilections depending on their previous engineering experience, produced constantly improving versions of the steam, gasoline, and electric automobiles. But a series of circumstances—among them, in the North American case, unlikely ones like an 1895 horseless carriage competition which appears to have influenced Ransom Olds in his decision to switch from steam to gasoline, and an outbreak in 1914 of hoof-and-mouth disease that shut down horse troughs where steam cars drew water—gave gasoline enough of a lead that it subsequently proved unassailable.[12] Whether steam and electric cars, given equal development, could have been superior is not clear, but this question remains under constant debate in the engineering literature.[13]

Is lock-in to a possibly inferior technology permanent? Theoretically it is, where the source of increasing returns is learning by using, at least until yet newer technologies come along to render the dominant one obsolete. But lock-in need not be permanent if network externalities are the source. Here if a technology's advantage is mainly that most adopters are going along with it, a coordinated changeover to a superior collective choice can provide escape. In an important paper, Farrell and Saloner[14] showed that as long as agents know other agents' preferences, each will decide independently to switch if a superior alternative is available. But where they are uncertain of others' preferences and intentions, there can be excess inertia: each agent would benefit from holding the other technology but individually none dares change in case others do not follow.

Whatever the source of increasing returns in competitions between technologies, the presence of lock-in and

sudden release causes the economy to lose a certain smoothness of motion.

TECHNOLOGY STRUCTURE: THE PATH-DEPENDENT STRONG LAW OF LARGE NUMBERS

In the discussion so far, we have derived some basic ideas and properties of technology competition from a dynamic model with a very particular linear-returns-from-learning mechanism. We would like to be able to handle competing-technology problems with more general assumptions and returns-to-adoption mechanisms. In particular we are interested in qualitative questions such as whether, and under what circumstances, an adoption market must end up dominated by a single technology.

In thinking about the type of analytical framework we would need for more general versions of the problem, it seems important to preserve two properties: (1) that choices between alternative technologies are affected by the numbers of each alternative present in the adoption market at the time of choice; equivalently, that choices are affected by current market shares; (2) that small events outside the model may influence the process, so that a certain amount of randomness must be allowed for. Thus the state of the market may not determine the next choice, but rather the probability of each alternative being chosen.

Consider a dynamical system that abstracts and allows for these two properties. I will call it an *allocation process*. At each time that a choice occurs, a unit addition or allocation is made to one of K categories, with probabilities $p_1(x), p_2(x) \ldots, p_K(x)$, respectively, where this vector of probabilities p is a function of x, the vector giving the proportion of units currently in categories 1 to K (out of the total number n so far in all categories). In our competing technologies problem, this corresponds to a choice of one technology from K competing alternatives, each time of choice, with probabilities that depend upon the numbers of each alternative already adopted and therefore upon current adoption shares.[15] (For a given problem, if we know the source of randomness and the payoff-returns at each state of the market, we can, in principle at least, derive these probabilities as a function of adoption shares.)

[12]C. McLaughlin, "The Stanley Steamer: A Study in Unsuccessful Innovation," *Explorations in Entrepreneurial History* 7 (1954), pp. 37–47; W. B. Arthur, "Competing Technologies and Economic Prediction," *Options* (1984), International Institute for Applied Systems Analysis, Laxenburg, Austria.
[13]R. L. Burton, "Recent Advances in Vehicular Steam Engine Efficiency," Society of Automotive Engineers, Preprint 760340, 1976; W. C. Strack, "Condensers and Boilers for Steam-Powered Cars," NASA Technical Note TN D-5813, Washington, DC, 1970.
[14]J. Farrell and G. Saloner, "Standardization, Compatibility and Innovation," *Rand Journal of Economics* 16 (1985), pp. 70–83.

[15]If these probabilities depend on *numbers adopted* rather than directly on market shares we can write them as $p_1(nx), p_2(nx), p_k(nx)$. This becomes equivalent to a probability function p_n that depends on time n as well as adoption share x.

EXHIBIT 4   Probability of Adoption as a Function of Adoption Share

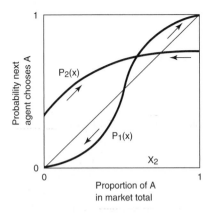

Our question is: what happens to the long-run proportions (or adoption shares) in such a dynamical system? What long-run technological structures can emerge? The standard probability-theory tool for this type of problem is the Strong Law of Large Numbers, which makes statements about long-run proportions in processes where increments are added at successive times. For example, if we successively add a unit to the category Heads with probability 1/2 in tossing a coin, the standard Strong Law tells us that the proportion of Heads must settle to 0.5. But we cannot use the standard Strong Law in our process. We do not have the required *independent* increments. Instead we have increments—unit adoptions or allocations to technologies 1 through K—which occur with probabilities influenced by past increments. We have a "coin" whose probability of Heads changes with the proportion of Heads tossed previously.

We can still generate a Strong Law for our dependent-increment process. Suppose we consider the mapping from present proportions, or adoption shares, to the probability of adoption, as with the two examples in Exhibit 4, where $K = 2$. We can see that where the probability of adoption A is higher than its market share, there would be a tendency in the allocation (or adoption) process for A to increase in proportion; and where it is lower, there would be a tendency for it to decrease. If the proportions or shares in each category settle down as total allocations increase, then they should settle down at a fixed point of this mapping. In 1983 Arthur, Ermoliev, and Kaniovski proved that (under certain technical conditions) indeed this conjecture is true.[16] Allocation pro-

cesses indeed settle down in the long run, with probability one, to an unchanging vector of proportions (adoption shares) represented by one of the fixed points of the mapping from proportions (or adoption shares) to the probability of adoption. They converge to a vector of adoption shares x where $x = p(x)$. Not all fixed points are eligible. Only "attracting," or stable, fixed points (ones that expected motions lead toward) can emerge as the long-run outcomes. (Thus in Exhibit 4 the possible long-run shares are 0 and 1 for the function p_1 and x_2 for the function p_2.) Of course, where there are multiple fixed points, *which* one is chosen depends on the path taken by the process: it depends upon the cumulation of the random events that occur along the way. This very general Strong Law for dependent-increment processes (which, following convention, I shall label AEK) generalizes the conventional Strong Law of Large Numbers.

The *allocation process* framework, with its corresponding Strong Law, applies to a wide variety of self-organizing, or autocatalytic, problems in economics and physics.[17] For our competing-technology purposes, however, we now have a powerful piece of machinery that enables us to investigate the possible long-run adoption outcomes under different adoption-market mechanisms. For a particular problem we would proceed in three steps:

1. Detail the particular mechanisms at work in the adoption process, paying special attention to returns functions, heterogeneities, and sources of randomness.
2. Use this knowledge to derive the probabilities of choice of each technology explicitly as a function of current adoption shares.
3. Use the AEK Strong Law to derive actual long-run possible adoption shares as the stable fixed points of the adoption-share-to-probability mapping.

---

[16] Hill, Lane, and Sudderth proved a version of this theorem in 1980 for the case $K = 2$ and p unchanging with time n. The informally stated

version in the text holds for $K \geq 2$ and for time-varying functions p_n provided they converge to a limiting function p. See W. B. Arthur, Y. M. Ermoliev, and Y. M. Kaniovski, "On Generalized Urn Schemes of the Polya Kind" (in Russian), *Kibernetika* 19 (1983), pp. 49–56; English trans. in *Cybernetics* 19, pp. 61–71; "Strong Laws for a Class of Path-Dependent Urn Processes," in *Proceedings of the International Conference on Stochastic Optimization,* Kiev, 1984, ed. Arkin et al. (Berlin: Springer, 1984); "Path-Dependent Processes and the Emergence of Macro-Structure," *European Journal of Operational Research* 30 (1987), pp. 294–303. Technically, the sequence of Borel functions p_n needs to converge to p at a rate faster than $1/n$ converges to zero; the set of fixed points of p needs to have a finite number of connected components; and for $K > 2$ convergence to a point rather than to a cycle or more complex attractor requires the deterministic dynamics formed by the expected motion of the process to be a gradient system. The 1986 paper is perhaps the best introduction to this theorem.
[17] Arthur, Ermoliev, and Kaniovski, "Strong Laws for a Class of Path-Dependent Urn Processes," and "Path-Dependent Processes and the

A number of studies now use this technique.[18] The "informational increasing returns" model of Arthur[19] is an example. In this model risk-averse potential adopters are uncertain about the actual payoff of two fixed pay-off technologies they can choose from. They gather information by polling some random sample of previous adopters. (Neither learning-by-using nor network effects are present.) Increasing returns come about because, if adopters of A are more numerous, the next chooser will likely sample more A's than B's, and will therefore be better informed on A. Being risk-averse, it will therefore choose A, with a probability that increases with A's proportion of x of the market. Application of the AEK Strong Law to a rigorous model of this mechanism yields precise circumstances under which informational-increasing returns allow stable fixed points only at the points $x = 0$ and $x = 1$. That is, it yields circumstances under which information-increasing returns alone cause eventual monopoly of A or of B with probability 1.

WHEN IS TECHNOLOGICAL MONOPOLY INEVITABLE?

Is it inevitable that one technology must eventually shut out the others when there are increasing returns to adoption? The answer is no. Consider a more general version of the heterogeneous-adopter–unknown-arrival-sequence model, in which there is now a continuum of agent types rather than just two. We can now think of agents—potential adopters—as distributed over adoption payoffs as in Exhibit 5. An adopter is chosen at random from this probability distribution each time a choice is to be made; and the distribution itself shifts either to the right or upward as returns to A or B increase with an adoption of either A or B, respectively. Monopoly—lock-in to a single technology—corresponds to the distribution of payoffs getting driven over the 45° line in this two-technology case. (We assume the distribution of adopter payoffs has "bounded support"—i.e., it does not tail off to infinity in any direction.) Where K technolo-

EXHIBIT 5 Payoffs to Adoption of *A* and *B* Under a Continuum of Adopter Types

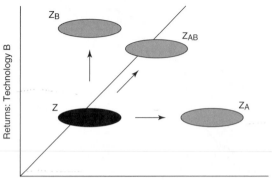

Note: At the outset, adopter payoffs lie in set Z. Adoptions of technology A only shift this set horizontally to the right as in Z_A. Adoptions of B only shift it vertically as in Z_B. Adoptions of A and B shift it diagonally as in Z_{AB}.

gies compete, we can use the AEK Strong Law to show that where there is no ceiling to the increasing returns (so that returns increase without bound as adoptions increase), then sooner or later one technology *must* by the cumulation of chance achieve sufficient adoption advantage to drive the distribution of adopters "over the line." With unbounded increasing returns eventual monopoly by a single technology is indeed inevitable.[20]

But where returns to adoption increase but are bounded, as when learning effects eventually become exhausted, monopoly is no longer inevitable. The reason is interesting. In this case, certain sequences of adopter types could bid the returns to both technologies upward more or less in concert. These technologies could then reach their "increasing returns ceilings" together, with adopter-type-payoffs still straddled across the 45° line (as with Z_{AB} in Exhibit 5), and thus with the adoption market shared from then on. But other adopter-arrival sequences may push the payoff distribution across the line early on. Thus with increasing returns to adoption that are bounded, the general finding is that some "event histories" dynamically will lead to a shared market; other event histories lead to monopoly.[21]

Exact conditions for monopoly in the strategic-competition case where technologies exist as sponsored

Emergence of Macro-Structure"; W. B. Arthur, "Industry Location and the Importance of History," Center for Economic Policy Research, Paper 84, Stanford, 1986; "Urban Systems and Historical Path-Dependence," in *Urban Systems and Infrastructure,* ed. R. Herman and J. Ausube, NAS/NAE Volume, 1987.

[18] See, for example, P. David, "Some New Standards for the Economics of Standardization in the Information Age," Paper 79, Center for Economic Policy Research, Stanford, 1986.

[19] Arthur, "Information, Imitation and the Emergence of Technological Structures."

[20] Arthur, "Industry Location and the Importance of History."

[21] Ibid.

products are not yet known. Hanson[22] explored a version of this IBM-versus-Apple problem, building on the basic linear-increasing-returns model above. He assumed that firms could price technologies and thereby manipulate adoption payoffs in a market where heterogeneous adopters arrived at random. Hanson was able to show in this stochastic-duopoly problem that firms would price low early on to gain adoptions, possibly even taking losses in an arm-wrestling match for market share. If both firms were evenly matched enough to stay in the market under these circumstances, then sooner or later the cumulation of chance events might allow one firm sufficient adoption advantage to tip the market in its favor. It would then have sufficient advantage to be able to raise its price and take monopoly profits, while keeping the other firm on the contestable margin of the market. Using AEK, Hanson was able to detail certain conditions under which monopoly by a single-technology-product would be inevitable. It is clear, however, that conditions can be constructed where the markets can also end up shared. For example, when increasing returns are bounded, and firms discount future income heavily so that they are mainly interested in present sales, neither firm may wish to price low early on. Neither might then eventually win the natural customers of the other and the result would be a shared market.

COMPETING STANDARDS AND THE ROLE OF EXPECTATIONS

The term *standard* has two meanings in the technology literature: that of a convention or code of practice, such as distributing alternating current at 110 volts or transmitting it at 60 hertz, and that of the technology or method or code that comes to dominate—that becomes "standard." Standards in the first sense—conventions—can compete much the same as method-technologies do, for a market of adherents, or users, or adopters. Competing standards raise somewhat different issues from competing technologies.[23] I will treat standards here only in

so far as they overlap with our dynamics-of-adoption problem.

With standards, learning, information, and production externalities are less important, and the main sources of increasing returns are network externalities and possibly technological interrelatedness. Both sources confer benefits if *future* adopters go along with one's choice. This introduces something not yet considered in our discussion—*expectations*.

Katz and Shapiro, in an important paper,[24] consider a static version of the problem of competing "networks" of different standards, in which "network externalities" accrue to increased network size. The networks are provided by firms which must determine network size in advance. It pays firms to provide large networks if potential adopters expect these networks to be large and thereby commit their choice to them. Therefore if, prior to adoption, sufficient numbers of agents believe that network A will have a large share of adopters, it will; but if sufficient numbers believe B will have a large share, *it* will. Katz and Shapiro showed that there could be multiple "fulfilled-expectation equilibria," that is, multiple sets of eventual network adoption shares that fulfill prior expectations.

In this simple but important model, expectations are given and fixed before the adoption process takes place. More realistically, if adoption were not instantaneous, potential adopters might change or modify their expectations as the fortunes of alternatives changed during the adoption process itself. One possible formulation[25] is to assume that agents form expectations in the shape of beliefs about the adoption process they are in. That is, they form probabilities on the future states of the adoption process—probabilities that are conditioned on the numbers of current adoptions of the competing alternatives. Thus these probabilities, or beliefs, change and respond as the adoption market changes. (We would have a *fulfilled-equilibrium-stochastic-process* if the *actual* adoption process that results from agents acting on these beliefs turns out to have conditional probabilities that are identical to the *believed* process.) In this model, if one standard, or technology, gets ahead by chance adoptions, its increased probability of doing well in the adoption market will further enhance expectations of its success.

[22] W. Hanson, "Bandwagons and Orphans: Dynamic Pricing of Competing Systems Subject to Decreasing Costs," doctoral dissertation, Stanford, 1985.

[23] See David, "Some New Standards for the Economics of Standardization in the Information Age." Also see J. Farrell and G. Saloner, "Installed Base and Compatibility," *American Economics Review* 76 (1986), pp. 940–55; "Standardization and Variety," *Economic Letters* (1986), pp. 71–74; and Standardization Compatibility, and Innovation."

[24] "Network Externalities, Competition, and Compatibility."

[25] W. B. Arthur, "Competing Technologies and Lock-in by Historical Events: The Dynamics of Allocation under Increasing Returns," revised from 1983 paper as Center for Economic Policy Research, Paper 43, Stanford, 1985.

Analysis here confirms the basic Katz and Shapiro finding. Adaptive or dynamic expectations act to destabilize further an already unstable situation: lock-in to monopoly positions now occurs more easily.

POLICY ISSUES

We have seen that in uncontrolled competitions between technologies with learning effects, or network externalities, or other sources of increasing returns to adoption, there is no guarantee that the fittest technology—the one with superior, long-run potential—will survive. There are therefore grounds for intervention.

Where a central authority with full information on future returns to alternative adoption paths knows which technology has superior long-run potential, it can of course attempt to tilt the market in favor of this technology. Timing is, of course, crucial here: [26] in Paul David's phrase there are only "narrow windows" in which policy would be effective. [27]

More often, though, it will not be clear in advance which technologies have most potential promise. The authorities then face the difficult problem of choosing which infant technologies to subsidize or bet on. This yields a version of the multiarm bandit problem (in which a gambler plays several arms of a multiarm bandit slot machine, trying to ascertain which has the highest probability of producing jackpots). Cowan [28] has shown that, where central authorities subsidize increasing-return technologies on the basis of their current estimates of future potential, locking into inferior technologies is less likely than in the uncontrolled adoption case. But it is still possible. An early run of bad luck with a potentially superior technology may cause the central authority, perfectly rationally, to abandon it. Even with central control, escape from inferior technological paths is not guaranteed. This finding is important for projects like the U.S. Strategic Defense Initiative, where ground-based excimer lasers, particle-beam weapons, X-ray lasers, homing vehicles, and other devices compete for government subsidy on the basis of expected long-run promise. Where each of these improves with development, it is likely that lock-in to one will occur; however,

it may not be lock-in to the one with superior long-run potential.

It may sometimes be desirable as a policy option to keep more than one technology alive, to avoid monopoly problems (if the technology is marketed), or to retain "requisite variety" as a hedge against shifts in the economic environment or against future "Chernobyl" revelations that the technology is unsafe. The question of using well-timed subsidies to prevent the adoption process tipping and shutting out technologies has not yet been looked at. But its structure—that of artificially stabilizing a naturally unstable dynamical process—is a standard one in stochastic feedback control theory.

SOME RESEARCH QUESTIONS

Several open or only partially resolved research questions have already been mentioned. Besides these, there are at least three major classes of problems that I believe would benefit from future study:

Recontracting Models

Where the source of increasing returns is learning-by-using, results would change little if adopters could re-enter the queue and change their choice at a future date. What counts with learning is the previous number of adoptions of a technology, not the fact that an agent is choosing a second time. [29] Where the source is network externalities, results *would* change substantially. In this case, with agents changing their preferences occasionally as well as striving to go along with the more prevalent alternative, recontracting or changing choice would take place as adoptions built up and might continue even when the market was at its full, saturated size. We would then have something akin to a stochastic version of the Farrell and Saloner model. [30] The important difference from our earlier models is that with "deaths" as well as "births" of adoptions allowed, increments to market-share position would tend to be of constant order of magnitude. Adoption processes with recontracting would therefore tend to show convergence in distribution rather than strong convergence, with punctuated equilibria possible in the shape of long sojourns near or at monopoly of one technology coupled with intermittent changeover

---

[26] Arthur, "Competing Technologies and Lock-in by Historical Events."
[27] "Some New Standards for the Economics of Standardization in the Information Age."
[28] "Backing the Wrong Horse."

[29] Agent arrivals, if second-time choosers, might, however, be dependent on the previous arrival sequence.
[30] "Standardization, Compatibility, and Innovation."

to monopoly by a different technology. This type of structure has counterparts in genetics, sociology and in far-from-equilibrium thermodynamics.[31] But it has not yet been studied in the technology context.

Empirical Studies

So far we have two excellent historical studies on the set of events and varied sources of increasing returns that led to dominance of the QWERTY typewriter keyboard[32] and the dominance of alternating current.[33] For most present-day uses, alternating current indeed appears to be superior to the alternative, direct current. The QWERTY keyboard, however, may be slightly inferior to the alternative Dvorak keyboard. Norman and Rumelhard[34] find Dvorak faster by 5 percent. Missing as yet, however, are detailed empirical studies of the actual choice-by-choice dynamics of technological competitions. For prominent competitions such as that between nuclear reactors it might be possible to put together a complete account of the adoption sequence and the events that accompanied it. This would allow identification and parameter estimation of the stochastic dynamics of an *actual* rather than a theoretical case.

Spatial Technological Competition

One of the striking features of the classical technology diffusion literature[35] is its concern with the spatial dimension—with the fact that a technology diffuses geographically as well as temporally. In the *competing* technologies problem, geographical diffusion would of course also be present. The spatial dimension would become particularly important if returns to adoption were affected by neighbors' choices. This was the case historically in competitions between railroad gauges[36] where it

was advantageous to adopt a gauge that neighboring railroads were using. The dynamics of spatial-technology competitions have not been explored yet. But they would resemble those of the well-known Ising model in physics and voter models in probability theory, where dipoles and voters respectively are influenced by the states of their nearest neighbors.[37] Here geographical clusters of localities locked in to different technologies might emerge, with long-run adoption structure depending crucially on the particular spatial increasing-returns mechanism at work.

CONCLUSION

In the classical literature on the economics of technology, a new and superior technology competes to replace an old and inferior one. In this new literature, two or more superior technologies compete with *each other*, possibly to replace an outmoded one. Competition assumes a stronger form. In the competing-technologies problem, the theory that emerges is a theory of nonconvex allocation. There are multiple equilibria—multiple possible long-run adoption-share outcomes. The cumulation of small random events drives the adoption process into the domain of one of these outcomes, not necessarily the most desirable one. And the increasing-returns advantage that accrues to the technology that achieves dominance keeps it locked in to its dominant position.

I have indicated that competing technologies are examples of self-organizing, order-through-fluctuation systems. They are also examples of evolutionary systems, although the mechanisms are quite different from the ones in Nelson and Winter.[38] Where competing technologies possess increasing returns to adoption, one technology can exercise competitive exclusion on the others; if it has a large proportion of natural adopters it will have a selectional advantage, and the importance of early events results in a founder effect mechanism akin to that in genetics.

The dynamical picture of the long-term economy that results is less like that of a sphere smoothly rolling on a flat surface, with its point of contact with the ground

[31] H. Haken, *Synergetics* (Berlin: Springer, 1978); W. Weidlich and G. Haag, *Concepts and Models of a Quantitative Sociology* (Berlin: Springer, 1983).

[32] P. David, "Clio and the Economics of QWERTY," *American Economic Review, Proceedings* 75 (1985), pp. 332–37.

[33] P. David and J. Bunn, "The Battle of the Systems and the Evolutionary Dynamics of Network Technology Rivalries," mimeo, Stanford, 1987.

[34] D. Norman and D. Rumelhart, "Studies of Typing from the LNR Research Group," in *Cognitive Aspects of Skilled Typewriting,* ed. W. Cooper (Berlin: Springer, 1983).

[35] Griliches, "Hybrid Corn: An Exploration in the Economics of Technological Change," *Econometrica* 25 (1957), pp. 501–22; P. David, "Clio and the Economics of QWERTY."

[36] D. Puffert, "Network Externalities and Technological Preference in the Selection of Railway Gauges," doctoral dissertation, Stanford, 1988.

[37] T. Liggett, "Interacting Markov Processes," in *Lecture Notes in Biomath 38* (Berlin: Springer, 1979).

[38] R. Nelson and S. Winter, *An Evolutionary Theory of Economic Change* (Harvard, MA: The Belknap Press of Harvard University Press, 1982).

unique and ever changing, and more like that of a poly-pod lurching down a slope. Where technologies compete, patterns—technology adoption structures—lock in. But as time passes and new technological competitions come about, the old patterns are changed, shaken up, and reformed, and in due course a new one is locked in.

To the extent that this happens, there may be theoretical limits as well as practical ones to the predictability of the economic future.

CASE II·10

Digital Distribution and the Music Industry in 2001

Napster was born a rock 'n roll technology, and like the greatest of rock stars, it was meant to die young. Even if by some miracle of science and law, Napster evolves into a legitimate new machine, the original dream of Napster—free, instant, infinite, easily accessible music for everyone—is done.
—Rolling Stone Magazine, February 17, 2001

Benjamin Cha and Kausik Rajgopal

I. INTRODUCTION

It was the twenty-first-century version of David vs. Goliath, and Goliath, it appeared, had finally won.

On March 7, 2001, federal judge Marilyn Hall Patel ordered Napster, Inc., the revolutionary music file-sharing service, to remove all copyright-protected songs from its directory. For two years, Napster had enabled millions of PC users to swap music files across the Inter-

net for free. This ruling effectively gave the music industry's record labels control over Napster. Judge Patel gave Napster three business days to comply with her ruling, once the record companies provided Napster with a list of songs in their copyright catalogue. This ruling seemed to bring to a close a long saga in the "new economy" era of the music industry: that of an upstart file-sharing service headquartered in Redwood City, California, challenging the long-held dominance of the record companies. From 1999 to 2001, Napster had been the Internet startup at the eye of the storm that had confounded the music industry's giants. The storm involved, amidst much acrimony against Napster, lawsuits worth over $1 billion from the record companies and recording artists alike.

The ruling came on the heels of months of legal jockeying by Napster and its allies, including U.S. Senate Judiciary Committee Chairman Orrin Hatch and the company's star legal counsel, David Boies.[1] Throughout the summer of 2000, Napster argued that its technology raised important questions about how copyright laws should be applied to the new digital medium. The record labels sued and the courts declared Napster's business fundamentally illegal and a violation of intellectual property laws. Napster appealed. Then, in October 2000, the media giant Bertelsmann AG, parent company to one of the plaintiffs in the lawsuit, BMG Entertainment, broke with its industry cohorts by announcing an alliance between Napster and its e-Commerce Group (BeCG).[2] Suddenly, it appeared that Napster had a chance for survival. That is, until February 13, 2001, when the Ninth Circuit Appeals Court declared that Napster was liable for its users' copyright infringements and had to stop its music trading. In a last ditch effort on the eve of the recording industry's prestigious annual Grammy Awards, Napster publicly announced a $1 billion royalty proposal to the record labels. The music labels scoffed at the offer, and shortly thereafter Judge Patel drove the final nail into Napster's coffin by reissuing her injunction against the young company.

The reaction was unanimous: this ended, for all practical purposes, Napster as its 63 million members had

---

[1] David Boies, attorney with Boies, Schiller, and Flexner LLP, represented the U.S. Government in its antitrust case against Microsoft and was Vice President Al Gore's chief counsel in arguments to the Supreme Court on the 2000 Florida ballot issue.

[2] Industry insiders say the deal was the final clash in a yearlong conflict between Bertelsmann and senior executives at BMG. The resignations of BMG's CEO, chairman, and president of new technology were announced in the weeks following the deal.

known it. But analysts were quick to point out that while Napster might be dead for the moment, alternative peer-to-peer services such as Gnutella were alive and well and might pose an even greater threat to the industry.[3] "The record industry has the advantage now of being able to get these songs off Napster any time they choose, but consumers will flee to all the other alternatives where the labels won't be able to control them," commented Forrester Research analyst Eric Scheirer.

More importantly, the Napster phenomenon had shown that there was enormous consumer demand for online access to music. Digitally distributed music was simply too convenient and compelling. In a short period, Napster had become one of the most popular destinations on the Internet and had given consumers everywhere access to millions of digitally encoded MP3 songs without requiring them to pay a cent to anyone.[4] In doing so, it had left an indelible stamp on American popular culture. And there were still dozens of digital music startups backed by hundreds of millions in venture capital dollars and by media giants such as Universal, MTV (Viacom), and AOL–Time Warner. A few had even gone public. Most, including Napster, had yet to make any money. Not only were these media conglomerates concerned with generating value from their music copyrights, they were also worried about the digitization of television and film content. If that happened, their copyright assets in those creative areas might be up for grabs as well. In order for these concerns to be addressed, the music copyright confusion had to be resolved first. And while incumbent record companies had successfully combated the Napster threat for now, it was clear that the Napster setback was only a battle in a larger war—over prospective digital music standards and their impact on power and profits in the music industry.

II. THE MUSIC INDUSTRY

A. The Players

By 2003, music was a $37 billion global market with unit sales of approximately 3.5 billion.[5] In 2000, industry earnings in the U.S. totaled approximately $14.3 billion with 1 billion units sold (Exhibit 1). About 65 percent of these units were sold as CDs, the dominant mode of music distribution. The U.S. market dominated the global market with approximately 38 percent share of global sales, followed by Japan (17 percent), the UK (8 percent), and Germany (7 percent).

Music was truly a global industry. Music produced in one region was easily consumed across the world. The supply chain for music was global, leading to a highly concentrated set of music companies that effectively controlled it. Consolidation during the 1980s and 1990s had led to an oligopoly with five major players dominating the business: Warner Music Group, BMG Entertainment, Sony Music Entertainment, Universal Music Group, and EMI. With the exception of EMI, a larger media and entertainment company owned each of these record companies: AOL–Time Warner, Bertelsmann AG, Sony Corporation, and Vivendi-Universal, respectively (Exhibit 2).

The record companies unquestionably controlled both the production and distribution of music, owning assets and influencing every aspect of the music value chain, from creation to eventual distribution. Each of the major labels had its own distinctive organization but did business in more or less the same way. Together they controlled over 80 percent of the global music market. Their market share in terms of net sales was estimated as follows: Universal—23 percent, Sony—20 percent, EMI—14 percent, Warner—13 percent, and BMG—12 percent.[6] As of March 2001, BMG and EMI were in discussions to merge with each other and this merger would reduce the number of large players to four.

B. The Value Chain (Exhibit 3)

Production The production of music involved the sourcing of artists and the actual creation of recorded music. Record companies had extensive Artist & Repertoire (A&R) departments which had the mandate of locating new artists and developing their music to production quality. This was one of the primary functions of record companies. Their talent pool was large and diverse—the next big hit was as likely to come out of a garage in Seattle as Julliard's jazz program. New acts were as likely to get called back after A&R managers had listened to their demo tapes as they were to be "discovered" when performing. A&R managers had significant bargaining power within record companies.

---

[3] Gnutella and peer-to-peer architecture is described in later sections.
[4] MP3 is a digital compression format for music (described in later sections).
[5] Year 2000, International Federation of the Phonographic Industry (IFPI).

[6] Music Business International World Music Report.

EXHIBIT 1 Music Shipments by Unit and Dollar Value, 1991–2000 (U.S. Market)

	1991	1992	1993	1994	1995	1996	1997	1998	1999	2000	% 99–00
CD	333	408	495	662	723	779	753	847	939	943	0.4
	$4,338	5,327	6,511	8,465	9,377	9,935	9,915	11,416	12,816	13,215	3.1
Cassette	360	366	340	345	273	225	173	159	124	76	(38.5)
	$3,020	3,116	2,916	2,976	2,304	1,905	1,523	1,420	1,062	626	(41.0)
LP/EP	5	2	1	2	2	3	3	3	3	2	(24.6)
	$29	14	11	18	25	37	33	34	32	28	(12.7)
Music video	6	8	11	11	13	17	19	27	20	18	(8.0)
	$118	157	213	231	220	236	324	508	377	282	(25.2)
DVD	—	—	—	—	—	—	—	1	3	3	35.2
	—	—	—	—	—	—	—	12	66	80	21.1
Total units	801	896	956	1,123	1,113	1,137	1,063	1,124	1,161	1,079	(7.0)
Total value	$7,834	9,024	10,047	12,068	12,320	12,534	12,237	13,724	14,585	14,323	(1.8)

Unit: millions, net after return; line items do not sum because of singles and other sales.
Source: Recording Industry Association of America (RIAA); http://www.riaa.com/pdf/year_end_2000.pdf.

EXHIBIT 2 Major Record Companies, Parent Companies, and Affiliates (as of 2001)

AOL–Time Warner	Bertelsmann	Sony Corporation	Vivendi-Universal
America Online	Random House	Sony Broadband Entertainment	Universal Pictures
Turner Broadcasting	Gruner+Jahr AG	Sony Pictures Entertainment	Universal Concerts
Home Box Office	RTL Group	Columbia TriStar Motion Picture Group	Universal Home Video
Time Inc.	Bertelsmann Arvato AG	Columbia Pictures	Universal TV & Network Group
Time Warner Trade Publishing	Direct Group	Sony Pictures Classics	European Television and Film Operations
Warner Bros.	Bertelsmann Springer	Columbia Home Entertainment	European IPS's and Telecom Operators
New Line Cinema	Barnes & Noble.com	Columbia TriStar Television	
Time Warner Cable	CDNow	Sony Computer Entertainment	

Warner Music Group	BMG Entertainment	Sony Music Entertainment	Universal Music Group	EMI
The Atlantic Group	Arista Records	American Recordings	A&M Records	Astralwerks
Elektra Entertainment Group	RCA Music Group	Columbia Records	Decca Record Company	Blue Note Records
London-Sire Records, Inc.	BMG Ariola	Epic Records	Deutsche Grammophone	Capitol Records
Rhino Entertainment	BMG Classics	550 Music	Geffen Records	Caroline Records
Warner Bros. Records	BMG Distribution	Harmony Records	Interscope Records	EMI Chrysalis
Warner Music International	BMG Music Publishing	Legacy Recordings	Island Def Jam Record Group	EMI Classics

EXHIBIT 2　**(continued)**

Warner Music Group	BMG Entertainment	Sony Music Entertainment	Universal Music Group	EMI
Warner/Chappell Music Inc.	Buddha Records	Loud Records	Mercury Records	Grand Royal Records
WEA Inc.	Jive	Razor Sharp	MCA Records	Matador Records
Alternative Distribution Alliance	Logic Records	Sony Music Soundtrax	Polydor	Parlophone
Warner Special Products Records	Loud			Records Virgin
Giant Merchandising	Milan Records Sonopress Wasabi Music Windham Hill	Untertainment Inc. The WORK Group Sony Wonder Sony Classical Sony Broadway	PolyGram Verve Music Group Universal Classics Motown Records	Virgin Records

Source: Company reports and company websites.

WARNER MUSIC GROUP

As of 2001, Warner Music Group (WMG) is headquartered in New York and is an operating division of AOL–Time Warner. Latest company figures show WMG's consolidated proforma revenues ended December 31, 2000, at $4.15 billion with EBITDA of $518 million. WMG is working closely with AOL on several digital music initiatives and is one of the leading supporters of the DVD-Audio format. WMG's WEA Manufacturing is one of the world's largest CD manufacturers as well as the number one DVD manufacturer.

AOL–Time Warner is the world's largest media and entertainment company and owns some of the industry's most renowned brands including Time Inc., Warner Bros., CNN, and America Online. AOL–Time Warner's businesses comprise Internet services and various online properties, several major television networks, magazine and book publishing, filmed entertainment, and cable systems in addition to music. Consolidated proforma revenues for the entire AOL–Time Warner group for the year ended December 31, 2000, were $36.21 billion with EBITDA of $8.27 billion.

BMG ENTERTAINMENT

BMG Entertainment (BMG) is headquartered in New York and is 100 percent owned by Bertelsmann AG of Gütersloh, Germany. Latest company figures show that consolidated revenues for BMG in fiscal year 1999/2000 totaled $4.7 billion. 55 percent of its business was derived from the North American market. EBITDA increased 27 percent from the previous year to $210 million.[1] BMG has almost 12,000 employees, and the company is the number two distributor of current albums in the U.S. market. BMG's Sonopress division is the third largest CD manufacturer worldwide.

Bertelsmann is the world's third-largest media company with operations in over 50 countries and over 76,000 employees. The Bertelsmann Foundation, the Mohn Family, and the Zeit Foundation together own 100 percent of the company (71 percent, 21 percent, and 8 percent, respectively). Latest company figures show that consolidated revenues for the group in fiscal year 1999/2000 increased by 24 percent year-on-year to $15.3 billion. EBITDA rose 41 percent to $1.7 billion.[2] Bertelsmann's operations include book, magazine and newspaper publishing and printing, television and radio (primarily in Europe), and interactive multimedia, in addition to BMG.

SONY MUSIC ENTERTAINMENT

Sony Music Entertainment is headquartered in New York and is a division of Sony Corporation of America (U.S. subsidiary of Sony Corporation Japan). Consolidated revenues for the fiscal year ended March 2000 were $6.7 billion. EBITDA figures for Sony Music are not published.

Sony Corporation is the largest audio-visual and information technology manufacturing company in the world and is one of the entertainment industry's leading companies. The Sony Corporation is a sprawling empire, which employs over 190,000 people worldwide across more than a thousand subsidiary companies. Sony's media and entertainment divisions operate motion picture production studios, television, digital media, home entertainment, and merchandise, among others. Sony Corporation's consolidated revenues for the year ended March 2000 were $63.1 billion and reported operating income totaled $2.3 billion. Sony is a supporter of the DVD-Audio format. Given Sony Music's association with Sony's consumer electronics divisions, the group has historically been an early adopter and developer of new formats such as the MiniDisc, Super Audio CD, DVD, and memory stick.

[1] Based on 1 U.S. $=1.08 Euros.
[2] Based on 1 U.S. $=1.08 Euros.

EXHIBIT 2 (continued)

UNIVERSAL MUSIC GROUP

Universal Music Group is headquartered in Universal City, California, and is owned by Vivendi-Universal. Latest company figures for Universal Music Group show proforma December 31, 2000, consolidated revenues at $6.12 billion and EBITDA of $1.07 billion.[3] The company has over 12,000 employees, and the company is the world's largest music company with 22.5 percent of world market share and 40 percent market share for classical music.

Vivendi-Universal is the new company created by the end-of-year 2000 merger of Vivendi, Seagram, and Canal+. Its businesses are separated into two divisions: Media & Communications and Environmental (which encompasses water, energy, and transportation). However, the 120,000 employee company is rapidly shedding its old-industry roots in the second division and the company has made public its intent to become a media and entertainment group. Vivendi-Universal operates Universal Studios, publishing and multimedia concerns, and Internet and telecommunications operations in addition to music. Latest Vivendi-Universal figures show proforma December 31, 2000, consolidated revenues at $48.63 billion and EBITDA of $6.68 billion.[4]

EMI

EMI is the only publicly listed and independent record company (headquartered and listed in London, U.K). Throughout 2000, EMI was courted by both Warner Music Group and BMG Entertainment for a potential acquisition, and as of March 2001 the company was in continuing negotiations with BMG for a merger. For the fiscal year ended March 31, 2000, EMI's consolidated revenues totaled $3.48 billion with EBITDA of $509 million.[5] EMI is one of the oldest record companies and has been in business for over 100 years. Like the other labels, EMI's operations encompass recording studios, CD manufacturing, distribution, record labels, and Internet initiatives. EMI is one of the industry's supporters of the DVD-Audio format and began releasing copyrights in this medium in 1998.

---

[3] Based on 1 U.S. $=1.08 Euros.
[4] Based on 1 U.S. $=1.08 Euros.
[5] Based on 1 U.K. pound=1.46 U.S. $.

Record companies provided artists with an up-front sum of cash that served as an advance on royalties. This amount ranged from $150,000 to $1 million depending on the artist and was intended to be applied to producing a full-length album which might cost in excess of $200,000 to cover production, staff, equipment, studio rental, and agency and legal fees. Artists did not actually begin receiving royalties until record companies recouped their advances. Typical record contracts provided artists with a mechanical royalty of between 8 and 10 percent of sales revenue from their work. Albums that sold 500,000 units were considered "gold" and sales of 1,000,000 units "platinum." Given the production costs involved, these were significant benchmarks for both artists and record companies.

In addition to A&R managers, record companies also kept successful producers, who had extensive experience in producing albums, on their payroll. New artists' music was often quite "raw" and the work of high quality producers could make or break an album. Producers might either be full-time employees of record companies or independent. Top quality producers had high bargaining power with record companies and received a cut of royalties going to artists.

Popular belief among rock musicians was that record companies represented the "unholy establishment," out to make money at the expense of the artists. "The record company is The Man," said one artist—"no two ways about it." However, other artists pointed out that record companies provided valuable functions such as studio production and promotion of new artists, all the while "dealing with the enormous egos that artists often bring with them." The treatment accorded to artists might also depend on the internal reputation of their A&R manager or producer—those with pre-established reputations commanded more resources for new artists they brought under their wings.

Manufacturing and Distribution Most major record companies had integrated CD manufacturing and music printing functions into their businesses. Producing the media involved pressing CDs, packaging, and creating the labeling and accompanying artwork. CD pressing operations involved an initial capital expenditure in excess of tens of millions of dollars in manufacturing facilities, and there were significant economies of scale for large production runs. CD pressing was a low-margin business and a cost center for the major record companies. For this reason, it was not attractive for new companies to enter the CD-manufacturing business alone. Many small labels outsourced the actual pressing of their media to the major record companies. This helped the record companies to manage their fixed manufacturing costs since it added scale to their production runs.

The major record companies also integrated distribution. Each of the five majors invested in extensive distribution infrastructure over time (warehouses, trucks, wholesale outlets) and this was another barrier to entry for new record companies or stand-alone distributors. During the last two decades of the twentieth century, distributors had locked in control key channels to the major retail outlets and had evolved into highly profitable and powerful divisions within each record company.

Promotion   With over 35,000 new albums coming to market every year, it was essential that record companies ensured that their artists were exposed to consumers who could make a purchase decision. A number of key marketing and promotional methods were used in the industry. The primary one was broadcast radio (AM/FM radio). Music videos, in-store merchandizing, advertising and cross-promotion, and concert touring also served as promotional tools. Advertising included billboards as well as magazine and newspaper advertising, which targeted the buyer demographic likely to listen to the album

EXHIBIT 3   Music Industry Value Chain

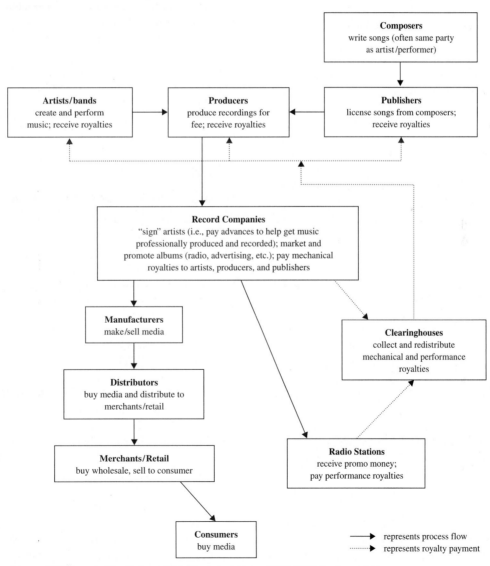

Source: IDC Report, *The Future of the Music Industry—MP3, DVD-Audio, and More.*

EXHIBIT 3 (continued)

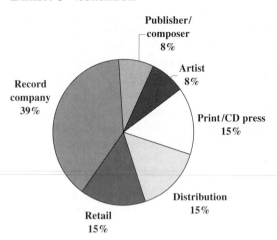

Source: IDC Report, *The Future of the Music Industry—MP3, DVD-Audio, and More,* mid-2000.

being promoted. Music videos were loss leaders, created and financed by record labels for artists to promote their popularity and album sales. The high costs behind producing quality music videos (over $1 million on average per video) prevented them from being sold on a per-unit basis like CDs. Record companies also promoted artists by financing their concert tours. Again, these were for the purpose of building identification and loyalty and were usually geared towards promoting an upcoming or newly released album. Most concerts, like music videos, were money losers.

Retail The last part of the value chain was the point of contact with the consumer. Large music retailers such as Tower Records, HMV, and others carried large catalogues and deep inventory to generate over 75 percent of total end-product CD sales. Such retailers focused on having the widest selection of music available to customers. Since such record stores usually occupied high-rent locations such as malls and high-traffic areas, they needed to generate high sales volumes and good product profit margins. In comparison, mass merchants whose main business was consumer electronics or other items used music as a way to draw traffic into stores but generated a much smaller percentage of overall CD sales.

Consumers and consumer tastes played an important role both in the development of music and the approach major record companies used to sign new artists. For example, on the creative side, a sudden "boy band" hit might generate much more creative talent from that genre—and in turn, a record company would increase its

talent search for artists producing a similar sound. Similarly, the emergence of new genres of music led to growth opportunities (e.g., alternative rock, acid jazz, house music). Consumers were also interested in new technologies that could enhance the listening experience—such technologies, however, should be significant enough to warrant the investment that came with purchasing that new technology.

Role of the Record Company Album production was a high-risk, high-payoff bet, and successful albums had to pay not just for their own costs but for the costs of all the failures as well. Record companies invested in expensive production studios, large manufacturing facilities, and extensive distribution infrastructure to get new music produced and then had to spend significant promotional money to get music out into the minds of consumers. Roughly 90 percent of albums ended up selling fewer than 10,000 copies, and a record company's initial financing costs for failures was not recoverable. From this standpoint, the music production business was not that different from the venture capital or pharmaceuticals businesses, where the company's economics depended on a "home-run" paying off the costs for a large number of failures.

C. Intellectual Property Protection

The music produced and distributed by record companies was considered protected intellectual property and was a key source of value to record companies because it erected regulatory barriers to copying previously distributed music. Once music had been released, intellectual property regulations prevented competitors from copying it. By restricting free competition on released music, the profits of the companies that produced and distributed the music in the first place were protected. Once competition was eliminated in this way for a particular music album, the pricing pressure on the album was also reduced—a record company could effectively charge the same price for a multi-platinum album over several years. In 2000, a copy of the U2 album *Joshua Tree* was retailing for the same inflation-adjusted price it sold for when it was released nearly two decades before. Music companies were very aware of the value of their intellectual property—industry executives referred to their assets as "copyrights" as opposed to "products" or "albums" or "artists."

Two types of intellectual property protections must be understood in order to appreciate the value provided by them to record companies. The first is "copyright," which is a term of intellectual property law that gives ownership to the creator of an artistic (or other) work and which prohibits unauthorized duplication, performance, or distribution of this creative work. The second is the music industry's current licensing structure, under which creative works are used for broadcast, manufacture, and performance and the copyright holder is paid royalties for its use (Exhibit 4).

The world of copyrights and licenses had historically been a far friendlier place for the record companies. These companies were now facing the unenviable challenge of sifting through various distribution technologies that posed a challenge to their distribution infrastructure and protected intellectual property. This task so pervaded the minds of music industry executives that a new term to describe the subject of digital protection of copyrights

---

EXHIBIT 4   Copyright Law and Music Licensing

COPYRIGHT LAW

The most basic copyright law is the Federal Copyright Law under which copyright owners are protected from the unauthorized reproduction, performance, or distribution of copyright protected works. Penalties for infringement can occur in both civil and criminal contexts. Traditionally, criminal penalties were only available for intentional acts undertaken for purposes of "commercial advantage" or "private financial gain." However, the No Electronic Theft Law of 1997 (the "NET Act") promulgated that sound recording infringements (including by digital means) can be criminally prosecuted even where no commercial gain is derived from the infringing activity. Additionally, the NET Act amended the definition of "commercial advantage or private financial gain" to include the receipt (or expectation of receipt) of anything of value, including receipt of other copyrighted works (as in MP3 trading). Punishment in such instances includes up to five years in prison and/or $250,000 fines. Individuals may also be civilly liable, regardless of whether the activity is for profit, for actual damages or lost profits, or for statutory damages up to $150,000 per work infringed. The Copyright Act stipulates a "personal use" doctrine that permits consumers who have legally purchased a recording to make copies of it, so long as the copies are played for personal use (e.g., taping a CD to play in one's car).

There are also a number of laws that relate to the digital distribution of music and online music listening. The Audio Home Recording Act of 1992 (AHRA) exempts consumers from lawsuits for copyright violations when they record music for their own private, noncommercial use. Importantly, the AHRA eases consumer access to advanced digital audio recording technologies (e.g., an advanced CD to DAT recording machine) but does not cover "multipurpose devices," such as a PC or CD-ROM drive.

The Digital Millennium Copyright Act of 1998 (DMCA) was a significant overhaul of international copyright law. The DMCA law delineates the responsibilities of Internet service providers (ISPs) in cases of infringement online. For example, the law formalizes a notice and takedown procedure between ISPs and copyright owners. It is now clear that when an ISP is aware it is posting or transmitting infringing content, the ISP must act to remove the infringing works or it may be liable for any resulting damages. However the DMCA protects ISPs from legal action if the ISP gives notice and requests takedown of infringing content. At the same time, the DMCA allows "webcasting" (i.e., the digital streaming of audio content, including music).

Companies ranging from CNN to MTV have sought to webcast. Under the DMCA, webcasters are given a statutory license to webcast, as long as they follow certain provisions (e.g., no more than two songs from the same artist can be played in a row, playlists cannot be pre-published, no user interactivity with the webcast is permitted).

MUSIC LICENSING

To use copyrighted material, one must obtain a license from the copyright holder. With music, there are two copyrighted works involved. The first is the "musical composition/work" (i.e., lyrics and notes on paper), which is usually owned by the songwriter and his or her music publisher. To perform a musical work (e.g., at a concert, on the radio) one must obtain a license from one of three performing rights organizations: the American Society of Composers, Authors and Publishers (ASCAP); Broadcast Music, Inc. (BMI); and SESAC Inc. (SESAC). These performance rights organizations collect money for the licenses and then pay it out as royalties to the composers and publishers. The Harry Fox Agency is responsible for granting licenses for the production and distribution of musical compositions.

The second copyrighted work is the "sound recording," which is the recording of an artist's performance of a given song. The record company that produced and released the recording usually owns this work, although sometimes the recording artist or producer is the owner. A license for this copyright is the most pertinent for digital music concerns. Similarly, the record companies have been the most reluctant to grant such licenses until digital rights management technology is well developed.

Each type of license has a number of subsets and special cases. Royalty structures are negotiated according to the relative bargaining power of individual artists and the other parties involved. For example, there are record company–artist contracts which stipulate that the mechanical license is built on a sliding scale, depending on the number of shipments, differing pay-outs for CDs, cassettes, DVDs, or downloads, or in some cases royalty-based deductions for studio costs or marketing expenses.

Sources: U.S. Copyright Office website, http://www.loc.gov/ copyright/title17, and *Copyright Basics* from http://www.riaa.com/ Copyright-What.cfm.

emerged within the industry—"digital rights management." Were it not for major disruption caused by the rise of digital technologies, this term would not exist.

III. DISRUPTION

A. The Emergence of MP3 and Online Access to Music

PC functionality in terms of speed, memory, graphics, and display technology grew rapidly through the 1990s. Technology advances combined with economical bandwidth (e.g., rising broadband adoption), innovations in consumer electronics devices, and improved Internet interactivity during this period enabled the desktop PC to become a powerful multimedia tool. Amidst this technology and Internet development, entertainment emerged as one of the most popular categories on the Internet—after search engines and portals, entertainment domains were more in demand than both "news and information" as well as finance- and investment-related websites (Exhibit 5).

With this phenomenon, a digital compression format for music called "MP3" emerged. MP3 is an abbreviation for "MPEG-1, Level 3," a section of the MPEG-1 standard for audio and video compression. MPEG standards were created by the Moving Picture Experts Group (MPEG), a working group of the International Standards Organization (ISO). What made MP3 immediately compelling was that with MP3 one could compress a music file to about a tenth of its original CD size. In comparison, most digital audio and video files were very large and memory-intensive and therefore unwieldy for storage or transport. MP3 was originally created by a partnership between consumer electronics company Thomson Multimedia (owner of the RCA brand) and the German Fraunhoffer Institute under the aegis of MPEG (Exhibit 6). These companies' roles in creating MP3 appeared to be no different than, say, Sony's or Microsoft's ongoing initiatives to create new formats or Philips' creation of the CD about 25 years earlier. However, the key difference between MP3 and digital formats created by Sony or Microsoft was that MP3 was licensed early and cheaply by the ISO. Therefore, the fact that the ISO was a nonprofit organization committed to promoting standardization worldwide had been pivotal in making MP3 the ubiquitous standard for digital music.

The process of creating an MP3 file by copying music from a CD was very easy. This was done through a process called "ripping," made easy by the availability of free Internet software. Consumers could convert CD

music into MP3 files in short order—it took less than 10 minutes for a consumer to "rip" a full-length CD into MP3 files. These files could then be played on the user's PC, e-mailed to friends, or distributed on the Internet. Because the files were digitally encoded there was no loss in audio quality, in theory, no matter how many times the file was copied.[7]

Hand-in-hand with the emergence of MP3 files came technology development by software companies and a frenzied birth of Internet startups, online initiatives from major media companies, and later, hardware device innovations by consumer electronics companies. While each used diverse Internet technologies and had differing business models, they all sought to leverage the Internet as a new distribution channel for music and a new way to introduce music to consumers. This caused concern in the recording industry establishment but remained a nebulous threat as very few startups were profitable and even fewer had access to record company copyrights. What's more, MP3 by itself was a technology without a significant user base; that was, until Napster became the launching pad for explosive growth in MP3 usage and the proliferation of unlicensed copyrights.

B. Napster

In January 1999, Northeastern University freshman Shawn Fanning wrote the Napster program to enable him to trade MP3 files with his peers.[8] Realizing that the software had far-reaching potential, Shawn incorporated Napster a few months later to commercialize it. The Napster vision from the very beginning was very simple and a direct challenge in the face of the music industry. While the record companies thought of music as a copyright asset for sale, Napster's founding vision was that music should be for "sharing" as opposed to for sale. Napster's strategy was built on this vision to create a worldwide community of listeners who shared their music with each other. During this time it was unclear whether Napster would focus on developing its technology or using the technology to make a viable business.

Visitors to the Napster website obtained a free downloadable software program which enabled them to swap MP3 files with other users who had registered with the system. Napster servers intermediated the music file sharing and offered a directory listing. The software offered key information such as the connection speeds to

---

[7] There is some debate about fidelity loss caused by truncation and download errors.

[8] A complete Napster chronology is outlined at the end of the Exhibits.

EXHIBIT 5 Home and Work Internet Audience, February 2001 (U.S. Market)

	Unique audience ('000)	Reach % (active)	Visits per person	Time per person	Pages per person*
Top categories (by domain)					
Search Engines/Portals & Communities	102,554	93.66	6.45	0:10:16	—
Entertainment (includes Music)	78,934	72.09	2.43	0:06:17	—
Telecom/Internet Services	78,861	72.02	3.53	0:06:39	—
Computers & Consumer Electronics	60,354	55.12	2.78	0:08:51	—
Multi-category Commerce	52,159	47.64	3.31	0:09:26	—
News & Information	51,781	47.29	3.32	0:10:16	—
Special Occasions	45,465	41.52	2.13	0:06:47	—
Finance/Insurance/Investment	41,669	38.06	3.24	0:19:38	—
Family & Lifestyles	38,128	34.82	1.99	0:09:02	—
Education & Careers	37,046	33.83	2.10	0:07:51	—
Government & Non-Profit	33,325	30.44	2.13	0:10:10	—
Travel	31,449	28.72	1.89	0:09:07	—
Home & Fashion	30,106	27.50	1.60	0:08:38	—
Top domains					
yahoo.com	60,568	55.32	12.05	1:14:13	172
aol.com	54,028	49.34	10.12	0:35:41	64
msn.com	53,155	48.55	11.58	0:49:05	159
microsoft.com	33,375	30.48	2.68	0:08:11	16
passport.com	27,628	25.23	9.02	0:09:58	30
geocities.com	25,972	23.72	2.70	0:07:27	15
go.com	23,550	21.51	4.18	0:21:48	44
netscape.com	19,443	17.76	9.36	0:28:27	43
amazon.com	19,436	17.75	2.19	0:12:10	23
bluemountain.com	19,186	17.52	2.14	0:10:31	17
ebay.com	17,546	16.02	9.78	1:39:54	301
lycos.com	16,362	14.94	3.32	0:13:17	44
excite.com	14,534	13.27	9.11	0:35:44	62
napster.com	14,528	13.27	5.12	0:10:31	19
nbci.com	14,355	13.11	3.43	0:10:15	18
flowgo.com	13,287	12.14	2.77	0:05:38	8
americangreetings.com	13,201	12.06	1.94	0:10:59	17
Top music domains					
napster.com	14,528	13.27	5.12	0:10:31	19
cdnow.com	4,849	4.43	2.04	0:07:46	19
bmgmusicservice.com	3,298	3.01	1.74	0:11:03	26
mp3.com	3,254	2.97	1.55	0:04:06	12
mp3s.com	1,985	1.81	1.64	0:03:16	6
getmusic.com	1,538	1.40	1.19	0:03:36	6
musicmatch.com	1,477	1.35	2.58	0:10:58	12
rollingstone.com	1,326	1.21	1.26	0:03:53	6
sonicnet.com	1,220	1.11	2.05	0:13:14	12
artistdirect.com	1,201	1.10	1.56	0:04:04	10
winamp.com	1,156	1.06	1.34	0:07:10	10
grammy.com	688	0.63	1.23	0:05:17	12
bmg.com	472	0.43	1.46	0:01:35	6
allmusic.com	427	0.39	2.48	0:08:43	22

*Not meaningful for categories.
Source: Nielsen/NetRatings Web usage Report, February 2001.

EXHIBIT 6 More on MP3 (MPEG-1, Level 3)

MP3, short for MPEG-1 Level 3, is the section within the Moving Picture Experts Group (MPEG) specification that deals with audio and video compression. The International Standards Organization (ISO) licenses MP3 algorithms for a nominal price (approximately $0.50 per player) to companies that develop MP3 codec products; i.e., software or hardware that plays MP3 music files. MP3 is a variable-bit codec, and users can determine the sampling rate at which the audio is encoded. At higher sampling rates, the audio maintains better fidelity to its original but results in less compression. For most consumers, MP3 files encoded at reasonable rates (96 kbps or 120 kbps) are virtually indistinguishable from CD sound.

Thomson Multimedia and the German Fraunhoffer Institute originally developed the MP3 codec. Thomson Multimedia is the world's fourth-largest consumer electronics group and develops, manufactures, and markets TVs, VCRs, camcorders, audio and communication appliances, satellite decoders, DVD players, and other audio-visual equipment. In the U.S., Thomson's most well-known brand is RCA, and the company has been licensed to manufacture and market a broad range of consumer electronics products for General Electric under the GE brand. The Fraunhoffer Institute is one of the leading organizations of applied research in Germany and operates 47 research centers in Germany with about 9,000 employees.

The ISO, a non-governmental organization, is a worldwide federation of national standards organizations from over 130 countries. Its mission is "to promote the development of standardization and related activities in the world with a view to facilitating the international exchange of goods and services, and to developing cooperation in the spheres of intellectual, scientific, technological, and economic activity."

Source: Moving Picture Experts Group, at http://www.mpeg.org/MPEG/index.html.

---

files being shared by other people, bit rates at which MP3 files were encoded (a proxy for sound quality), search capability by file name and artist name from the universe of file-sharers on the network at any given time, and a comprehensive directory of all music on its system. One could think of it as a real-time search engine for online music. Once a user identified a song they desired, they could download it from the other user's PC with relative ease. Songs could be downloaded in a matter of minutes. Once downloaded, a song could be played on a user's PC on demand, or with the right hardware, transferred onto a CD (a process called "burning") and then played on any traditional CD player. Software programs to play MP3 files on a PC were freely available over the Internet and were distributed by software vendors Microsoft, Music-Match, Nullsoft-Winamp (an AOL–Time Warner company), and RealNetworks who together had distributed hundreds of millions of them. Napster was a classic Internet-age "infomediary"—while it did not own MP3 files, the software to play them, or even the MP3 format, it enabled individuals around the world to connect their music with each other.

In November 1999, two weeks before Napster had even officially launched, the battle lines had been drawn. The 2.0 beta version of its software had already been distributed among online music aficionados. "I love it," wrote Marc Geiger of ArtistDirect, a competitor digital music site. "It's totally community-oriented and a pass-the-music play. It argues totally for the subscription model we have been yapping about." A *Wired* magazine article reported that "fans like Napster because it combines existing elements of the online music experience into a single application that allows people to talk about what music they like and trade files."[9] When Napster finally launched, the music industry was ready. The Recording Industry Association of America (RIAA), an industry group representing the major record companies, fired the first salvo. The RIAA sued Napster for promoting music piracy just two days after the website launched. Napster's official response to the suit announcement was instructive, capturing the company's vision in a nutshell. "We are about new artists, unknown music . . . about community and sharing," said then-Napster CEO Eileen Richardson. Those words seemed to make little difference to the record companies who claimed that Napster's file traffic "was virtually all unauthorized." Napster was clearly not making money from this service, since access was free. But from this moment on, Napster would grow accustomed to seeing itself in and out of courts making legal arguments about its business. Both Napster and its allies would continue to argue that copyright laws were simply not sufficient to govern music file sharing technologies. On the other side, the major record companies were unanimous in their arguments against the company.

As technology and Internet stocks led the March 2000 NASDAQ correction, and dot-com fallout began in earnest shortly thereafter, many questions about Internet music distribution were raised. Similar to many of its Internet startup kindred, Napster had yet to make any

---

[9]"Napster: Music Is for Sharing," by Jennifer Sullivan, *Wired News*, November 1, 1999.

money and had no foreseeable business model. But two months later in May, venture capitalists Hummer Winblad Venture Partners announced a $15 million Series C investment into the company. As part of the deal, Hummer Winblad partners Hank Barry and John Hummer joined the board of directors with Barry assuming the role of Napster's interim CEO. While Napster's valuation details were not made public, industry observers speculated that it was substantial, approaching at least several tens of millions of dollars. CEO Barry, who replaced Richardson, was a lawyer by training who had headed Cooley Godward's Technology Practice Group in Palo Alto and previously practiced in the entertainment law department of Paul, Weiss, Rifkind, Wharton & Garrison in New York before becoming a venture capitalist with Hummer. Barry made it his chief task to champion Napster's legal defense in the courts and the courts of public opinion. In a speech at Stanford's Graduate School of Business in late 2000 (Barry was a Stanford Law graduate), he underlined that Napster's original vision had still not changed: "We are a membership and community service for sharing music, not a music subscription service," he pointed out.[10] Barry also implied that what Napster was doing was legal and fell under the "fair use" doctrine of copyright law. He also sought to portray Napster as under attack primarily because it threatened the record companies' stranglehold on distribution.

Through March 2001, when Judge Patel effectively ordered it to shut down, Napster continued to be the focus of significant press coverage and popularity even though it had yet to make any money. With no advertising or marketing, Napster's user base had grown from a few thousand to tens of millions. The number of files available through its service had increased from tens of thousands to hundreds of millions. However, it appeared that Napster's notoriety was beginning to get the better of it. Despite the fact that music files were still widely available after the ruling, usage dropped substantially. Nevertheless, Napster continued to press its case and seek the public's support, forming a "Napster Action Network" and urging its members to write to Congress about reforming current laws governing the digital distribution of music. Both record industry executives and Napster were to appear as witnesses in a Senate Judiciary Committee hearing about online entertainment to be held the next month. It appeared unlikely that Congress would

rewrite any laws, but more than a few members of Congress had expressed concern about the rate at which record companies were licensing their copyrights to online music companies.

Peer-to-Peer Architecture[11] Much of the fervor over Napster was its "peer-to-peer" technology, a computing architecture that utilizes the unused computing power of distributed personal computers over the Internet. In early 2000, workers at AOL subsidiary Nullsoft released a mutant form of peer-to-peer architecture called Gnutella, and this program carried the Napster concept to the next level. Gnutella did not use a central server to match up users—instead, the software on a user's PC would connect itself to as many other Gnutella users as it could find on the Internet. Like Napster, it then permitted each user to download files from other users, but because there was no central server, there was no oversight and thus no entity to be held liable for the mass transfer of unlicensed copyrights. Gnutella could have displaced Napster's popularity and caused several orders of magnitude greater problems in the music and media industries. However, its clumsy user interface and slow technology development during Napster's rise prevented it from doing so. It remained to be seen whether this would change after the Napster ruling, and media executives everywhere were aware that Gnutella could pose an even greater threat.

The peer-to-peer architecture that both Napster and Gnutella popularized had significant implications for computing and digital content. It differed from the traditional client/server network architecture, in which some computers are dedicated to serving others, by its potential to disintermediate servers and give consumers enormous power. Even though peer-to-peer networks generally did not offer the same performance under heavy loads, by enabling users to share and trade digitized content on a mass scale it offered a twenty-first century extension of the book club and new ways of finding and experiencing content. At the time of the Napster ruling, numerous peer-to-peer systems were available over the Internet and development in the software community continued. With Napster, it appeared that this type of system was applicable and in demand for music files. However, it remained to be seen whether such a system could be used for other digitized content and most importantly, how it could be made secure and, thereafter, commercialized.

---

[10] Bishop Auditorium, Stanford Graduate School of Business, December 1, 2000.

[11] Peer-to-peer architecture is a broad topic and is discussed at length in Stanford Graduate School of Business Case SM-76.

C. Other Digital Music Alternatives (Exhibit 7)

Napster's ease of use and wide-ranging access to music files meant that it gained a large user base that others could not. But while Napster was able to gain wide popularity, there were still dozens of digital music initiatives in operation that offered technologies and models that might prove more successful. For example, online music sites MP3.com and MTV's Sonicnet had remained popular even while Napster captured most online music traffic. MP3.com, one of the earliest online music companies, was founded in 1997 with an original vision of becoming an MP3 download destination (a process described below). As the concept of MP3s became known, MP3.com attracted significant user and market attention and the company went public in mid-1999. Its early business life, however, was a warning sign for Napster. Six months after its IPO, the recording industry sued it for copyright infringement after it unveiled a new "digital storage service" (also described below). MP3.com would continue to find itself in and out of the courts for the rest of 2000.

Other online music companies such as ArtistDirect, Farmclub (Universal), Launch, Live365, RollingStone.com, and Yahoo! Music each unveiled their own digital music offerings. The range of technologies used by these companies and others was broad, and most sought to use the Internet as a distribution channel to offer consumers a new way to both discover and listen to music. Almost without exception, though, all online music companies suffered from a lack of digital rights management that would enable them to receive copyright licenses from the record companies. Without such licenses to this music, most companies were hard-pressed to turn a profit. Nevertheless consumer demand remained strong and digital music companies developed a few alternatives to Napster that might ultimately be used once digital rights management was built and licenses were, in fact, granted. Key examples included Internet radio, secure downloads, and online storage services.

Internet Radio/Streaming   Streaming technology, the bulk of which was developed by RealNetworks and Microsoft, provided consumers with instant audio or video entertainment but did not enable users to download content on to their PCs. Internet radio used streaming technology for a "webcast" that had the basic attributes of FM radio but offered a deeper level of interactivity (concurrent playlists, artist information, purchase opportunities, etc). A webcast was streamed over the UDP layer of the Internet and stored in a temporary buffer on a user's PC. This meant that there was limited "error recovery" of data packets and webcasted music could not be easily checked for quality. However, since music files were not downloaded and copied, a system under which content rights holders were compensated for each stream on a royalty basis continued to be a viable digital music alternative and one that the record companies continued to endorse. In 2000–2001, many stand-alone sites that offered consumers a directory of Internet radio sites were unveiled, and traditional FM radio stations also migrated a number of their broadcasts to the Internet to be webcasted. With streamed music, there is a technology constraint in that audio quality is usually no better than FM radio. Thus, streaming has so far only provided a lower quality PC-based solution to consumers who wish to own music to play on other devices. As the technology for streaming higher-quality audio continues to develop, webcasting may turn out to be an attractive option for music companies and consumers alike.

Downloads   In contrast to streaming, downloading involved moving an entire file before any part of it could be replayed. Once the file was downloaded, the PC user could replay it on demand, send it as an e-mail attachment, trade it as with Napster, or post it to a website. Once posted on the Web, it could then be downloaded through its hyperlink. The record labels were strongly averse to the downloading characteristics of MP3 and similar compression formats. The key issue for downloads as a distribution mechanism, as with peer-to-peer file sharing, was adequate copyright security and copy protection which did not yet exist; thus recipients were not required to pay for their downloads. The five majors therefore did not license their music catalogues to offer consumers the ability to download MP3 or other formatted files from their servers, even for a fee. Without a compelling catalogue of music content to offer, these companies found it difficult to attract visitors to their sites. Copy protection technology would be the solution to this problem It was also what all of the record companies required and was under development by many of the major software technology companies.

Online Storage   Companies such as MP3.com developed technology that enabled consumers to upload their CD collections to the companies' servers and gain access to their music wherever they had an Internet connection. They believed that consumers would ultimately come to think of recorded music as a service that they accessed, instead of a plastic disc that they played. The online stor-

EXHIBIT 7   Companies Active in Digital Music 2000–2001

Type	Companies	Business model
Record company	Warner, BMG, Sony, Universal, EMI, and numerous independent labels	Involved at all levels of value chain; business driven primarily by physical media sales (CDs). Most major record labels have initiated their own online distribution and/or content initiatives.
Music player software, compression/format technology, and streaming services & technology	Apple, Microsoft, MusicMatch, Nullsoft (AOL–Time Warner), RealNetworks, Yahoo!	Software and technology for PCs which allows the playback of multiple music formats including MP3 and enables consumers to stream music, convert CDs into digital format ("ripping"), record CDs ("burning"), mix music, and organize their music files. While much of this software is distributed for free, these companies charge businesses for streaming servers and sell software upgrades.
Music content/portal	AOL Music, ArtistDirect, Billboard, eMusic, Farmclub.com (Universal), GetMusic (BMG and Universal joint venture), Launch, Listen, MP3.com, MTV, Music.com, RollingStone, Sonicnet, Sony Music, Spin, Yahoo Music	Music news, directories, sampling, etc. Additionally, various creative artists operate their own sites. Primarily advertising supported. Some sites may offer or facilitate legal downloads, usually music promotions by record labels or unsigned artists. For-fee downloads have met with limited success. Businesses are primarily advertising supported.
Online CD merchants	Amazon, BMG Music Service, CDNow, TowerRecords.com	Physical CD sales.
Streaming music/Internet radio	Broadcast.com (Yahoo!), Echo Networks, Friskit, Launch, Live365, NetRadio, Shoutcast (AOL–Time Warner), Sonicnet (MTV), Spinner (AOL–Time Warner)	Internet delivered "radio" programming ("webcasting") that offers AM/FM equivalent listening but with broader reach and interactivity. Advertising supported.
Online digital music storage service	MP3.com, Musicbank, Nullsoft-Winamp (AOL–Time Warner)	Enables consumers to store their CD collections in digital format on third-party servers. Users can then access their music wherever there is an Internet connection. Supported by monthly subscription fees.
Peer-to-peer service/technology	Aimster, Flycode, Freenet, Gnutella, Napster, Scour Exchange (shut down)	Services and technologies that enable consumers to trade digitized content (e.g., music) via their peer-to-peer architectures.
Digital Rights Management (DRM) technology	IBM, Intel, InterTrust, Liquid Audio, Microsoft, Preview Systems, RealNetworks, Reciprocal	Copyright protection is the "holy grail" for digital music and digitized content. These companies are working to create secure formats that operate as stand-alone codecs or in combination with playback software. Businesses supported by licensing fees.
Compressed audio/MP3 device manufacturer	Aiwa, Compaq, Creative Labs, Intel, Iomega, Philips, RCA, Samsung, Sonicblue (Rio), Sony	Manufacture MP3 and other digital format consumer electronics devices for home, travel, and car. Some focus on flash memory and "memory sticks." Business driven by volume hardware device sales.

Source: Case author synthesis based on information from company websites.

age theory envisioned that content-based firms would no longer be producing actual artifacts for consumers to buy. While this model was highly dependent on widespread broadband adoption and eventual ubiquity of Internet-enabled devices, it appeared compelling because of the continuing decrease in storage costs and a growing consumer propensity to think about getting music online. If this vision came to pass, the online storage companies could effectively supplant retail stores as the intermediaries between record companies and consumers.

IV. INDUSTRY RESPONSE

The preceding discussion establishes a critical point for the music industry: electronic distribution through digitally compressed files was viable, was in demand, and posed several fundamental challenges to the dominance of the music industry oligopoly. It threatened copyright protection, showed the need for new strategies in the disrupted industry, and exposed a continuing war over standards and how to use the Internet as a distribution channel.

A. The Copyright Battle

The first challenge posed to the industry by what Napster represented was the threat to the most significant asset that underlay the record companies' power: the intellectual property protection afforded by copyright law. If music did not require a secure, physical, trackable receptacle for distribution (such as a CD), it became practically impossible for the record companies to control their copyrights. As Napster demonstrated, the music files were available for sharing among millions of users, even though no one actually purchased the files.

The record companies recognized this challenge and met it early. First, they continued to refuse to license their music catalogues to online music companies, in spite of pressure from Congress and their existing customers. Second, they sought legal recourse to what was essentially an attack on the source of their earnings. By 2000, they had filed over a billion dollars' worth of lawsuits against several digital music startups and had made Napster the focus of their attacks. While several file-sharing clones aspiring to offer the same functionality as Napster had also emerged, the record companies hoped to make Napster a precedent for any other file-sharing companies.

This legal challenge was highly successful in the courts. The courts ruled that the basis of copyright law remained intact even in an age of digital music distribution technology and that services like Napster were in clear violation of such a law. The record companies were able to effectively shut Napster down, unambiguously regaining the power they had always had over their music copyrights. But it appeared that the record companies had merely won one battle in their fight against Napster. They continued to deal with the strategic issues raised by Napster's emergence and to fight a larger war over secure digital standards.

B. Strategic Issues for Incumbents

Napster's emergence underlined several key strategic issues for the incumbents of the music industry. While every other incumbent drew daggers as soon as they saw Napster, one company separated itself from the pack and sought to partner with Napster. This was German media giant Bertelsmann AG, parent company of BMG Entertainment, Random House publishing, and others. The champion of the partnership internally was Bertelsmann eCommerce Group (BeCG), a corporate-level team responsible for the e-commerce strategy of Bertelsmann as a whole (Exhibit 8).

The partnership would transform Napster's vision and strategy from a company dedicated to free music to a company providing access to copyrighted music online for a monthly subscription fee. Bertelsmann could then use Napster as one of its distribution mechanisms to whet the appetite for consumers worldwide before they paid to buy its copyrighted music. Few details of the agreement were made available, but the substance of the deal included BeCG extending a $50 million loan to enable Napster to build a system that would charge users a subscription fee and give artists, songwriters, publishers, and music labels a cut. Once this system was developed, Bertelsmann promised to drop the lawsuit filed by its BMG unit and make its music catalogue available. The range of the monthly subscription fee was quoted to be between $4.95 and $6.95. The partnership agreement also gave Bertelsmann warrants to acquire a portion of Napster's equity in the future. As of March 2001, the partnership was still in effect, even though Napster's continued existence as a separate company was very much in doubt.

There were at least six strategic issues facing Bertelsmann and the other incumbent record companies. These included the creation of a viable and large user base with next to no advertising, the possibility of new and more annuity-like revenue streams from a digital subscription model, and the competitive advantage of being a gatekeeper to a new distribution infrastructure. In addition, they needed to better understand and use peer-to-peer architecture for other in-house content being digitized, the costs and benefits of investing in physical or digital distribution infrastructure, and the capabilities, drawbacks and implications of potential digital standards and distribution.

While the record companies spent millions each year on advertising and promotion to acquire and retain customers, Napster had rocketed to a large global user base with little advertising. Clearly, some of this had to do with the fact that Napster's service was free. But there were important lessons to be learned from how Napster had made a potential technology for online file sharing a viable one. Most importantly, Napster's model proved

EXHIBIT 8   Bertelsmann eCommerce Group (BeCG)

With the objective of leading Bertelsmann AG into the digital future, CEO Thomas Middlehoff put together Bertelsmann eCommerce Group (BeCG) in June 2000 by combining all of Bertelsmann's e-commerce companies and Internet holdings into one unit. As of March 2001 BeCG consisted of bol.com, CDNOW, BarnesandNoble.com, Napster, Bertelsmann Broadband Group, and the BMG Music Clubs. The group's stated objective is "to become the leading global e-community and e-commerce network with exclusive access to the largest selection of media content." BeCG is managed by a team of thirty executives, and the group's President and CEO is Andreas Schmidt. Before taking his position with BeCG, Schmidt was president and CEO of AOL Europe and prior to that served with Bertelsmann's Gruner + Jahr publishing division.

Source: Bertelsmann corporate website, http://www.Bertelsmann.com.

that there was large latent demand among everyday consumers (not just techno-geeks or hackers) for music distributed online. While the record companies had been aware that such demand existed, this tech-savvy and early-adopter population had largely emerged from outside their purview and, as such, the record companies were lagging behind in formulating a strategy to capture it.

There also emerged a creative new way to monetize this larger user base: through a subscription revenue model. On average, a consumer bought about five CDs a year at an average of $13 per CD. This generated annual revenue of $65 per consumer, but this revenue had a high variance. In other words, some consumers bought no CDs at all, others bought several more than five, etc. Incumbents saw that an online music distribution system could generate a small monthly subscription from consumers—and at a small nominal amount of even $4.95–6.95 per month, a record company could generate a revenue stream comparable with an average consumer buying five CDs. The advantage with this revenue stream was that the variance would be minimized, creating an annuity-based, reliable revenue source that had not previously existed in the music industry.

There were also wider competitive advantages that could be derived by making a bet on Napster. Whoever actually partnered with Napster could be in a gatekeeper position to extract rents from the other major record companies, should the technology prove to be a winner. Napster, in some sense, had already done all the

hard work of acquiring a large and loyal customer base. Whichever record company could help them monetize it could derive revenue, not just from the subscriptions for themselves, but potentially as a fraction of the subscriptions to the music of other record companies as well. Bertelsmann was now in this position, which could be a huge advantage for BMG's front-end. By controlling a popular new distribution infrastructure with a dedicated user base, artists could migrate to that label from the other record companies, fundamentally changing the power equation not just between artists and record companies, but among the record company oligopoly as well.

There was also something to be gained by having insight into a technology that could be applied to other digitized content. All but one of the record companies was part of a larger media conglomerate. While many had historically looked at technology as simply a tool for business, Bertelsmann may have believed that peer-to-peer architecture had shown technology could be more than just a tool but also the cornerstone for a company-wide strategy. Thomas Middlehoff, CEO of Bertelsmann said in an October 2000 speech at the Stanford Graduate School of Business prior to the announcement of the BeCG-Napster deal: "We should not be afraid of technology," pointing to an orientation Bertelsmann took to the emergence of new technologies.[12] BeCG may have seen that an alliance with Napster could stimulate company-wide learning for Bertelsmann on the viability and challenges of implementing peer-to-peer technologies across a wide array of businesses, not just music.

The fifth issue was a key question about the costs and benefits of continuing to invest in physical vs. distribution infrastructure. The more knowledge a record company had about online distribution, the better positioned it could be to determine an online/offline channel strategy. Before Napster, all the record companies had continued to make capital investment decisions on the order of several hundred million dollars in the existing physical production and distribution infrastructure. Inventory management was a non-trivial issue, with an estimated 30 percent of CDs returned each year. If digital distribution of music was viable, it threw into question how and why these regular capital investment decisions were made. On the question of digital distribution, the record companies were flying blind and did not have a granular appreciation for its benefits, implementation issues, and

---

[12] October 13, 2000; Bishop Auditorium, Stanford Graduate School of Business.

EXHIBIT 9   Online Music Spending Actual and Projected, 1999–2003 (U.S. Market)

	Physical product (CD's)	Digital downloads	Digital subscriptions	Total online music spending	% of total music market
1999	387	0	0	387	2.7%
2000	826	9	0	836	5.5%
2001	1,431	34	5	1,469	9.1%
2002	2,109	88	63	2,259	13.3%
2003	2,713	189	278	3,181	17.4%

Unit: $ millions.
Source: Media Metrix Online Music Report, 2001.

strategic challenges. However, digital distribution was the sum of Napster's business, and no other company had done it as well. The major record companies could learn from the intensive organizational experience and knowledge of any number of the digital music startups when it came to distributing music online. By partnering with Napster, a record company could learn more about digital distribution, better framing the costs and benefits of the distribution capital investment decision. This knowledge could be another competitive threat against the other record companies.

The final strategic question was the one that has been central to software and technology companies but not necessarily for the music and media industries: the competitive advantage conferred by owning the next distribution standard. This was the larger war that had been played out several times in the technology industry and could become the entire context under which the battle over Napster had been fought.

C. The Standards War

Throughout much of the 1980s and all of the 1990s, the music industry's undisputed distribution standard was the CD. Before the CD, the standard was tapes; before tapes, the standard was records. However, each of these standards shared one key attribute: they were secure, physical, trackable and very importantly, high fidelity–loss music receptacles. If one copied a CD on to a cassette tape, there was discernible loss in recording quality and fidelity that even non-audiophiles could hear. Digital formats such as MP3 changed the notion of formats in several important ways—MP3 was not secure, not physical, and not trackable in the sense that CDs or tapes were. And no matter how many times an MP3 file was copied there was no loss in recording quality or fidelity.[13]

Despite the attractiveness of digital formats, record companies had questioned, at a basic level, how much consumers wanted a digital versus physical media; i.e., did consumers desire a physical disc or tape that was packaged, had accompanying artwork, and was sold through a retail outlet that gave buyers a "retail experience"? There had been ample evidence to suggest that there was enormous demand for digitally distributed music—MP3 players were being introduced by the major consumer electronics companies; traffic to Napster and other online music destinations continued to grow; and PC manufacturers continued to advertise their PCs' multimedia functionality. On the other hand, some industry watchers proposed that digital music would make up a only small relative portion of overall music sales (Exhibit 9).

Physical Versus Digital Formats   Throughout the music industry's history, the distribution structure had been built to support a physical standard. In fact, before the MP3 format exploded on to the scene, several higher-fidelity physical formats were already being developed to take advantage of the existing physical distribution infrastructure. These physical formats included DVD-Audio (DVD-A), Super Audio CD (SACD), and MiniDisc (MD). DVD-A was a non-proprietary format using the same media as the fast-growing DVD-Video (DVD-V) market, and consumer electronics DVD players were introduced into the market in 1998. The official DVD specification was originally developed by a consortium of 10 companies including Hitachi, JVC, Matsushita, Mitsubishi, Philips, Pioneer, Sony, Thomson, Time Warner, and Toshiba. SACD was jointly developed by Sony and Philips and was essentially a CD-format which enabled extremely high-quality sound fidelity. The MD, a storage medium built on optical technology, was pioneered by Sony in 1991.

Throughout 2000 and by March 2001, it appeared that DVD-A was poised to gain the largest market over

---
[13]There is some debate about fidelity loss caused by truncation and download errors.

EXHIBIT 10 Audio Player Device Installed Base Actual and Projected, 1998–2003 (U.S. Market)

	1998	1999	2000	2001	2002	2003
DVD-A	—	196	968	3,127	7,000	12,663
Digital Format	62	791	2,688	6,786	13,090	22,154
CD	126,989	139,618	147,729	147,033	140,229	127,011

Unit: thousands.
N.B. The above projections for digital format devices do not include PCs, and projections for CD devices do not include CD-capable DVD players and PCs. Additionally, it must be noted that it is relatively easy for consumers to transfer digital format music files onto CDs (a process called "burning") with PC hardware or stand-alone devices. As such, it can be argued that digital formats may proliferate at a greater rate than shown because they can be backwards-compatible to the large installed base of CD players. IDC's projections were revised in March 2001 to reflect actual year 2000 sales, and new projections taking into account technology and market developments in late 2000. The only part of these projections that IDC made public was that compound annual growth rates of 51% were expected for digital format devices between 2000 and 2005.
Source: IDC Report, *The Future of the Music Industry—MP3, DVD-Audio, and More.*

SACD and MD, in spite of the hubbub over digital formats. Support for DVD was fueled by tremendous industry support and all the major media companies began releasing DVD movies in 1999. It was expected that their record company divisions would soon follow suit. Additionally, a key feature of DVD players was that they were expected to play CDs. While the SACD offered even better audio fidelity than DVD-A, its players and the medium itself were expensive to manufacture. MD was also not expected to command a large market because it was a proprietary format marketed by Sony. Because it was positioned as a home recording format with limited prerecorded content released on it, it had some potential to compete with digital formats, but this remained to be seen. Naturally, the CD was expected to continue dominating overall unit volumes due to its low cost, availability, industry support, consumer awareness, and installed base (Exhibit 10).

MP3 seemed to be able to challenge the viability of physical formats for a while, but the Napster legal resolution ensured that these physical formats—especially DVD-A—were still very viable potential standards. It is worthwhile to note that it took a decade for the commercial CD to replace the cassette tape in terms of unit shipments.[14] The record companies have invested heavily in the success of DVD-A and positioned themselves as its champions, using their marketing muscle to motivate customers to adopt it more quickly.

Security and Alternatives to MP3 With the proliferation of an unsecured MP3 format, several companies have worked to add security to both MP3 as well as other digital formats. Companies focused on developing a se-

cure MP3 format have tried two basic approaches, neither of which had yielded successful results by 2001. The first approach proposed packaging MP3 files in secure digital containers that could only be opened with an encrypt/decrypt key associated with a particular system or sent separately to the user. Developers concluded that this approach would not work because keys were too difficult to track and consumers would have very limited flexibility with transfer play (per the Copyright Law's "fair use" doctrine). The other proposed solution was an encryption technology that intertwined itself with the encoded MP3 file. Since it stayed with the file, the key could be anything from a hard-drive identification number to user information. Information held in the encryption code could be used to ensure copyright protection, establish new business models, or allow specific uses of the song (such as number of copies allowed or number of plays permitted). Several companies, including InterTrust, IBM, and Sony, were working on this type of technology.

Other companies, namely RealNetworks, Liquid Audio, and Microsoft, each developed their own end-to-end solutions which enabled music to be encoded into a secure non-MP3 format, compressed to a reasonable file size, purchased online, downloaded, and played. Each company also created back-end solutions to manage and track payments, enabling them to act as clearinghouses for downloaded music. Where these companies had not yet succeeded was in enlisting partners and record company affiliates, which they needed to form their ecosystem of music distribution, on the technology and infrastructure side as well as on the content side. With limited support from the five record companies, each end-to-end solution continued to develop at a different rate and this drove consumers back to the familiar MP3 format. As the latest entrant, IBM announced in January 2001 that it would begin offering the Electronic Media

---

[14]Another example is the continuing decline of the cassette format; see Exhibit 1.

EXHIBIT 11   Napster Chronology

1992
The Moving Picture Experts Group, a committee of engineers, finalizes a standard for squeezing audio into relatively small computer files. The standard, called MPEG-1 Layer 3, eventually becomes known as MP3.

April 1995
A startup called Progressive Networks unveils its RealAudio software, which "streams" music a bit at a time as PC users listen. Because slow Internet connection speeds make it impractical for most users to download music files all at once, even in compressed form, RealAudio quickly becomes the soundtrack for the Web.

April 1996
A site called TheDJ.com launches, using RealAudio's technology to broadcast 24 channels of music over the Internet. Eventually the site is renamed Spinner.com.

June 1997
As connection speeds increase, listeners who previously listened only to "streamed" music begin downloading complete files in the MP3 format. Many use a program called Winamp to listen to the files. Winamp is developed by software company Nullsoft, which later develops the peer-to-peer program Gnutella.

December 1997
Michael Robertson launches a site called MP3.com to serve as a repository for music in the MP3 format. The site focuses on little-known artists who agree to make their music available online.

September 1998
Diamond Multimedia introduces the Rio, a Walkman-like portable player for MP3 files, adding to the momentum of the format. Within weeks, the recording industry sues Diamond, fearing the Rio will spur copying.

October 1998
Congress passes the Digital Millennium Copyright Act in an effort to clamp down on the free-for-all world of Internet music.

January 1999
Shawn Fanning, a Northeastern University student, writes a program called Napster that lets Internet users easily share MP3 files. A few months later, Napster

Inc. is launched to commercialize the product.

June 1999
AOL agrees to pay $400 million in stock for Nullsoft and Spinner and later merges the two.

December 1999
The recording industry files a copyright infringement suit against Napster.

January 2000
MP3.com launches a new service called My.MP3.com that lets members scan in a CD once, then listen to a copy stored online anywhere, anytime. The move indicates that MP3.com needs popular music in addition to the small unknown bands it had focused on and quickly prompts a lawsuit by the recording industry.

March 2000
The group of programmers at Nullsoft who created the Winamp player release a file-sharing program called Gnutella that redoubles concern in the recording industry. Unlike Napster, Gnutella doesn't rely on a central computer and would be nearly impossible to shut down. Gnutella users quickly begin trading movie clips and music files over the Internet.

April 2000
Heavy-metal rock band Metallica sues Napster, escalating the profile of the fight between the Internet startup and the recording industry.

May 2000
Both MP3.com and Napster lose key decisions in the lawsuits against them, stepping up pressure on the startups to reach settlements with the recording industry. U.S. District Judge Marilyn Hall Patel rules that Napster is not entitled to "safe harbor" under the Digital Millennium Copyright Act.

June 2000
MP3.com settles lawsuits with Warner and BMG. The licensing deal calls for MP3.com to pay the labels whenever members store or listen to songs on MyMP3.com.

July 2000
Judge Patel grants the RIAA's request for a preliminary injunction against Napster and orders it to shut down. The Ninth Circuit Court of Appeals stays the lower court injunction.

October 2000
Despite the ongoing lawsuit, Bertelsmann crosses party lines and announces a partnership with Napster. Under the deal, Bertelsmann agrees to drop the lawsuit if Napster creates a new service that compensates copyright holders. Bertelsmann gains the right to buy a stake in Napster and agrees to make its music catalogue available to it once the new service is built.

November 2000
MP3.com settles its outstanding copyright infringement lawsuit with Universal Music Group for $53.4 million. It has now settled with all five major record labels. Total price tag: $170 million.

February 13, 2001
The Ninth Circuit Court of Appeals declares that it agrees with every legal argument put forth by the lower court when it issued the original injunction against Napster. The three-judge panel says that Napster must stop its users from sharing copyrighted material and tells the lower court judge to reissue the injunction. Equally ominous for Napster, the appeals court says that the Redwood City, California, company is liable for copyright infringement for the actions of its estimated tens of millions of users, a fact that could doom the company's plans to eventually make a profit from its service.

March 7, 2001
Judge Patel rewrites the injunction, ordering Napster to remove unauthorized copyright works within three days of receiving notice by the record companies. In the preceding weeks, traffic to Napster skyrockets as users scramble to download the last free music they can.

March 26, 2001
According to a press release by Napster, the total number of files available through its index at any one time has dropped by 57% from 370 million to 160 million, and the average number of files being shared by users has dropped by almost two-thirds from 198 to 74.

Source: Case author synthesis based primarily on company and public media information.

Management System (EMMS), which used technology developed by InterTrust and allowed consumers to pass along digital content containing controls on its use. IBM's system purported to be able to preset the number of times a song could be played before it would self-lock. However it was unclear if this system would prove to be viable, unlike previous ones offered by its competitors.

Still others have developed compression technologies for formats that could compete against MP3. Examples include Windows Media Audio (WMA) developed by Microsoft, ATRAC-3 developed by Sony and RealNetworks, Enhanced Perceptual Audio Coder (EPAC) by Lucent Technologies, a2b by AT&T, and Transform-Domain Weighted Interleave Vector Quantization (1 WinVQ) developed by Japan's NTT Human Interface Labs. While some of these formats offered compression and fidelity superior to MP3's, none have been able to receive consumer attention or industry support.

In what appeared to be an early move to prevent potential music industry disruption such as Napster, in late 1998 the Secure Digital Music Initiative (SDMI) was formed to define industry standards for secure digital music distribution. SDMI was able to garner the support of 180 companies and organizations representing key technology and consumer electronics companies, in addition to the major record companies. But by all accounts, by March 2001, SDMI had failed. The consortium repeatedly designed secure systems and challenged hackers to break them. Each time, hackers successfully did so, and in January 2001, SDMI Chairman Leonardo Chiariglione finally stepped down.[15] In his resignation speech, Chiariglione expressed frustration at repeated efforts by consortium members to exert their influence and veto power, which had gridlocked SDMI efforts, pointing both to industry and technology setbacks.[16]

A big hurdle faced by each company developing a secure format or system was that millions of songs had already been formatted into MP3, giving them a formidable installed base. As noted earlier, it was remarkably easy for consumers to "rip" music from CDs and convert them into the MP3 format using software widely distributed free over the Internet. Potentially the largest source of unprotected copyrighted files therefore existed in the CD collections of consumers everywhere. For this reason, the MP3-installed base had the potential to continue

growing rapidly, and digital rights management continued to be difficult to enforce.

If a digital format were to win the standards war, the physical distribution infrastructure built out by record companies, wholesalers, and retailers would be under direct attack. In that case, a variety of potential Internet-based distribution methods could contend to become the dominant method of distribution. The incumbents would then react in a hostile fashion by defending their existing investments in a purely physical distribution infrastructure. It was also possible that the record companies and others invested in the incumbent infrastructure could try to create a hybrid distribution system, where both brick-and-mortar infrastructure and online methods had a role.

V. CONCLUSION

Our music industry story began with a David vs. Goliath saga about Napster taking on the big record companies and threatening their dominance over the industry. However, even though Congress continued to hold hearings about online entertainment distribution, the Napster ruling was a clear victory for Goliath—it unequivocally held existing intellectual property laws intact and effectively ordered Napster to shut down. This has given the record companies oligopoly, and their larger parent company media groups a high level of comfort about their assets in the age of digital technology.

While most popular media accounts of the Napster debate have focused on its intellectual property ramifications, the rare convergence of digital technology and entrepreneurs willing to take on the music industry in the 1990s raised several key strategic issues for the incumbents. This case identified six such issues: the creation of a new and broad customer base; the possibility of an annuity versus per-unit revenue model; the gatekeeper advantage for a record company having proprietary access to a new distribution infrastructure; understanding of a new technology that could be applied across other digital content; the equally important need for organizational knowledge to balance physical and digital distribution strategy; and the strategy an incumbent should adopt with respect to the evolving war over standards.

The last issue merits special attention. If Napster was the vehicle for proliferating MP3's installed base and positioning it as a potential new standard, the fate of that standard continued to be very much in doubt. The standards war stood at a critical juncture as of the writing of this case. A digital rights management system embraced by all five major record companies did not yet exist.

---

[15] Ironically, Chiariglione was one of the original founders of the Moving Pictures Expert Group (MPEG), creators of MP3.
[16] Chiariglione comments from *Wired News,* January 24, 2001.

Interestingly, in the first week of April 2001, several high-profile online music deals were made public—Yahoo! announced a partnership with Universal and Sony Music to create the Duet subscription music service, AOL–Time Warner said it would join with Bertelsmann and EMI to license its music on a non-exclusive basis to RealNetworks and form the joint venture MusicNet; and Microsoft announced the first public test of MSN Music, a service designed to help consumers discover new songs and artists. These announcements pointed to a new willingness on the part of the record companies to venture deeper into digital technology. So while fundamental questions remained about whether the eventual standard would be physical, digital, or hybrid and about the implications for the music industry's value chain, it also appeared that some Davids and Goliaths were beginning to play to the same beat.

READING II-8

Finding the Balance: Intellectual Property in the Digital Age

Philip Meza and Robert A. Burgelman

INTRODUCTION

Intellectual property (IP) is protected by various forms of property rights. In the United States these rights are granted under legal vehicles, such as patents and copyrights described in the Constitution and expanded by Congress. Microprocessors and movies are considered IP, and their property rights are subject to legal protection; and so too are computer programs, photographs, paintings, sculptures, and even genetically altered mice.

IP laws are intended to balance the rights of the inventor or author with the needs of society. They were designed to promote creativity without unduly restricting dissemination of its fruits.

The concepts of IP rights trace back to the thirteenth century. The first recorded patent was awarded in 1421. By the sixteenth century, English law began to recognize copyright protections. While the precepts of IP rights are old and broadly accepted, recent events have put them in the news. For example, online retailer Amazon.com received a controversial process patent on its "1-click" ordering feature, in which an order is processed with a single keystroke.[1] Under a series of new laws and proposals, introduced or enacted in the late 1990s in the United States, Congress extended the terms of copyright protection for certain classes of IP and made illegal certain technologies that enabled the circumvention of copyright safeguards. Other changes were also making their way through Congress at that time.

Most industries, and particularly high technology and entertainment industries, rely upon IP rights to protect the huge investments needed to create products such as software programs, movies, and musical recordings. However, high technology companies such as PC makers and software developers and entertainment companies such as movie studios and recording companies increasingly found themselves at odds with each other over attempts to modify IP laws—particularly copyrights—to account for the risks of piracy and the opportunities for easy distribution of pirated IP resulting from the digitization of content and the Internet. With the specter of rampant piracy of perfect copies facilitated by digital technologies and broadband Internet access, content producers were slow to adopt digital distribution channels and sought to close down those, such as the popular file-swapping service Napster, which sprang up in the vacuum. Content producers lobbied Congress for a number of remedies to the threats they perceived from digitization and the Internet, such as extensions to copyrights, outlawing algorithms and programs to defeat anti-copying techniques on CDs and DVDs, and forcing device makers (PCs, PDAs, etc.) to build piracy detection systems into devices to inhibit copying.

[1] Amazon.com started offering its 1-click feature in September 1997 and received a patent for it in September 1999. The company sued rival Barnesandnoble.com in October 1999 for patent infringement over its own single click purchase process. In December 1999, Amazon obtained a preliminary injunction that forced its competitor to adopt a two-click system, but the injunction was overruled in February 2001. In March 2002, both sides reached an undisclosed out-of-court settlement.

Digital media (legitimate and otherwise) was one of the few bright spots for high technology companies in the middle of a deep and protracted recession. These demands left computer makers and builders of components such as microprocessors, software developers, and others between a rock and a hard place. Consumers disliked many of the anti-piracy technologies promoted by media companies because they often restricted legal (as well as illegal) uses of the technologies. High technology companies feared government intrusion, legislating what technologies they could and could not market. Many thought that digital media could provide compelling services (the "killer app") that would drive device sales and promote broadband uptake. The issues surrounding IP protection could either promote or inhibit digital media. As these complementors squared off, countless billions of dollars and much of the future of media and technology were at stake.

TYPES OF INTELLECTUAL PROPERTY RIGHTS

The three most prominent forms of IP property rights are patents, copyrights, and trademarks. Each protects different types of IP for various periods of time. Some types of IP qualify for property right protection from more than one of these vehicles; for example, some software programs are granted both copyrights and patents. However, most forms of IP are protected under one or another of these vehicles.

The type of IP determines the form of legal protection. Novel inventions or processes can qualify for patent protection; movies and recordings usually qualify for copyrights; trade names, logos, and commercial designs are protected by trademarks. These vehicles are very important to their owners. In 1998, patent licensing revenues exceeded $100 billion around the world.[2] According to a trade group, the copyright industry in the United States (book and music publishing, film production, radio and television broadcasting, and computer software development) accounted for $535.1 billion, or 5.24 percent of the United States Gross Domestic Product (GDP), and achieved estimated foreign sales and exports of $88.97 billion in 2001.[3]

Patents

A patent grants an inventor the right to exclude others from producing or using the inventor's discovery or invention for a set period of time. The first true patent was issued in 1421 by the Republic of Florence in Renaissance Italy. The recipient was the architect and inventor, Filippo Brunelleschi, for the design of his ship used to transport white marble used in his famous Duomo of Florence.[4] Twenty-eight years later in England in 1449, John of Utynam was awarded a 20-year monopoly for his glass-making process previously unknown in that country. In return for his monopoly, John of Utynam was required to teach his process to native Englishmen. That same function of passing on information is now fulfilled by the publication of a patent specification.[5]

In exchange for the right to exclude others from using, making, or selling the invention, an inventor discloses the details of the patented invention. Once issued, patents become public record. Failure to disclose the details concerning the invention can result in an invalid patent. In the United States, patent laws were enacted by Congress under the Constitution: "To promote the progress of science and useful arts, by securing for limited times to authors and inventors the exclusive right to their respective writings and discoveries."

In order to be patented, an invention must be novel, useful, and not of an obvious nature. The United States Patent and Trademark Office (USPTO), the federal agency charged with administering patent laws, will not grant a patent on an invention that was publicly used or available for sale by anyone, including the inventor, more than one year before the inventor filed a patent application. Identical or similar inventions that others publicly disclose anywhere in the world before an inventor files a patent application, known as "prior art," may prevent the inventor from obtaining patent protection because the invention would not be considered novel.

The invention must be useful for some purpose. However, an invention does not need to have commercial potential to be considered useful. A patent gives its owner the right to exclude others from making, using, or selling the specific invention in the United States. It does not confer the right to actually use the invention. Sometimes use is blocked by the need to employ other technologies or machines that are already patented by others. Such situations are often resolved by trading patent licenses.

[2] Kevin G. Rivette and David Kline, *Rembrandts in the Attic: Unlocking the Hidden Value of Patents,* Harvard Business School Press (Boston: 1999), p. 5.
[3] Press Release, "IIPA Economist Study Reveals Copyright Industries Remain a Driving Force in the U.S. Economy," 22 April 2002, http://www.iipa.com.
[4] Donald S. Chisum, *Principles of Patent Law: Cases and Materials,* Foundation Press (2001), 2nd ed., p. 10.
[5] http://www.derwent.com/patentfaq/history.html.

An invention that is considered obvious would be barred from patent protection. To determine whether an invention is non-obvious, patent examiners consider whether, "in light of known, similar products, processes, or designs, would a person of ordinary skill (but not extraordinary skill) working in the field related to the inventor's invention consider the differences between the invention and similar products, processes, or designs obvious?"[6]

There are three types of patents issued in the United States: Utility, Design, and Plant patents. Utility patents are the most common and cover four general types of inventions or discoveries:

- Processes: such as industrial or technical procedures, methods of doing business, and software (see below).
- Machines: combinations of mechanical and electrical elements, including special purpose computer systems, even if dynamically configured from a general purpose computer by software.
- Articles of manufacture: tangible, man-made, or manufactured items, generally including all products not considered "machines" or compositions of matter; they may include a CD-ROM or other physical embodiment of a software program.
- Compositions of matter: physical entities where the substance itself is the important element, such as chemical compositions, mixtures of ingredients, and new chemical compounds.

Design patents protect new, original, and ornamental design for an article of manufacture. Plant patents protect inventors who discover and asexually reproduce any distinct and new variety of plant.

In an important change for information technology companies, in 1981 the United States Supreme Court held that software-related inventions could be subject to patent protection. Prior to that decision, software had been excluded from patenting because the process of performing the program's function involved underlying mathematical algorithms, which were considered unpatentable. Software uses a non-physical process, operating electronically through the utilization of algorithms to control the output of the computer program. Mathematical algorithms have a functional application in computer programs, and thus can be protected under the Patent Act.

Not everything under the sun can be patented. Abstract ideas, mental processes, laws of nature, and physical phenomena are exempt from patent. For example, Charles Darwin could not have patented his theory of evolution and Albert Einstein did not need to bother the patent office with his formula for the theory of relativity; nor could a mineral or plant found in the wild be patented. Literary, dramatic, musical, or artistic works cannot be patented but are usually subject to copyright protection. (See below.)

Since the time of the Founding Fathers, patents were normally issued for a non-renewable period of 17 years, beginning from the date of issuance. Under a recent amendment prompted by the Agreement on Trade-Related Aspects of Intellectual Property (TRIPS) accompanying the Uruguay Round of the General Agreement on Tariffs and Trade (GATT), patent terms were extended to 20 years measured from the date of application.

Each patent application for an alleged new invention is reviewed by an examiner to determine whether it is entitled to a patent. In the past a model was required as part of a patent application; in most cases today, only a detailed specification is necessary.[7] If an application is rejected, the decision may be appealed to the Patents Office's Board of Appeals, with further or alternative review available from the United States Court of Appeals for the Federal Circuit, or in the United States District Court for the District of Columbia, and onward to the United States Supreme Court.

An issued patent can be overturned if prior art exists that demonstrates an invention was not novel or was obvious at the time the patent application was filed. For example, journals or trade publications that describe aspects of the patented invention may be sufficient to establish prior art and thus invalidate a patent.

Some software developers and other enterprises have sought and been awarded business method patents on software. Such patents prevent others from creating, using, or selling a program that performs the same process or function as the patented program, even if different underlying code is used. Many of these business method patents are controversial because they give patent protection to business processes, such as reverse auctions over the Internet (E-Bay) or easy "1-click" online purchase processes (Amazon.com), that critics contend are not novel.

For some companies, business processes—which can be patented—were far more valuable than the products

---

[6]http://www.chillingeffects.org/patent/faq.cgi.

[7]Some of these models turn up in antique fairs across the country and have been featured on the PBS television series "Antiques Roadshow."

they manufactured. For example, Dell Computers assembles PCs on a "build-to-order" basis that allows customers to configure the computers they are purchasing, either by themselves on the Internet or with the assistance of a Dell representative over toll-free phone lines. According to the company, much of Dell's success stemmed not just from it products, which were basically commodity items, but from its patents on the company's continuous-flow manufacturing, configuration, and customer service models. By 2003, Dell had over 80 patents (and counting) on its build-to-order direct sales model, covering its online customer-configurable ordering system, which was integrated into the company's manufacturing, inventory, distribution, and customer service operations. These patents not only impeded would-be build-to-order competitors, but also helped Dell secure better component pricing. In 1999, Dell and IBM announced a cross-license agreement valued at $16 billion. Dell received IBM components at lower costs while IBM licensed some of Dell's process patents.[8] Commenting on the value of patents to the company, Dell's director of intellectual property and assistant general counsel, Henry Garrana said, "This is our innovation—how we run the factory, how our ordering system allows customers to configure their PCs with whatever hardware and software they choose, how we advise customers of shipment—and we intend to protect that innovation."[9]

Copyrights

Compared to patents, copyright offers a less restrictive—but far longer-lasting—form of IP protection. Copyright protects the particular way in which a work, such as a poem, movie, or computer program is expressed. The earliest English copyright statutes were enacted in the sixteenth century. By 1710, England's Parliament passed the Statute of Anne, which granted works published after April 10, 1710, a copyright term of 14 years from the date of publication, and an additional term of 14 years if the author survived the original term. Works published prior to April 10, 1710, received a copyright term of 21 years from that date. In the newly independent United States, the Constitution provided Congress with a federal copyright power.

Copyright protects only physical representation of a given work and not the ideas, concepts, procedures, processes, or methods of operation that may underlie that representation. For example, while Disney's Mickey Mouse is protected by copyright (and other legal devices), the idea itself of a fun-loving rodent is not subject to copyright. In *NEC Corp. v. Intel Corp.*, in which NEC sought to have Intel's copyrights on its 8086 and 8088 microcodes invalidated, and in which Intel countersued for copyright infringement, a court found that microcodes (instructions that perform specific processing functions and are not program-addressable) can be copyrighted, but alternative microcodes that are not substantially similar, even though some of their subroutines may be similar because their underlying ideas were straightforward and capable of only a limited range of expression, do not infringe.[10] Thus, Intel's microcodes were proper subject matter for copyright, but NEC did not infringe such rights because its microcodes were not substantially similar. A copyright owner has the right to prevent others from making unauthorized, literal copies of the copyrighted work, but not from independently creating works that may tell similar stories in the case of novels or movies, or perform the same functions in the case of software. Thus, while the pioneering spreadsheet program Visicalc enjoyed copyright protection, others were free to develop software that performed similar functions.

In order to be copyrightable, a work must be "fixed" or recorded in some format and must be original, that is, independently created by its author. Copyright protection begins as soon as an original work is fixed in a tangible medium of expression. Creators may register their work with the United States Copyright Office, but that is not necessary to obtain full copyright protection. A work does not need to be novel (i.e., formerly unknown) or even lawful to be protected by copyright. For example, the fact that a federal judge found the file sharing service Napster unlawful did not in any way invalidate the copyright that Napster enjoyed on its software. Even obscene works can enjoy copyright protection.[11]

A copyright is ordinarily awarded to the creator or creators of a work for the life of the copyright. In the United States, beginning with the first Copyright Act in 1790, the initial terms of copyright were set at a term of

[8]David Kline, "The Best Offense Is a Pit Bull Patent Lawyer," *Business 2.0,* June 2000. "IBM, Dell Announce $16 Billion Technology Agreement, Believed to Be Largest Industry OEM Agreement Ever," Joint Dell-IBM Release, March 4, 1999.
[9]*Rembrandts in the Attic: Unlocking the Hidden Value of Patents,* p. 35.

[10]*NEC Corp. v. Intel Corp.,* 10 U.S.P.Q.2d (BNA) 1177 (N.D. Cal. 1989).
[11]*Mitchell Brothers Film Group v. Cinema Adult Theater,* 604 F.2d 852 (5th cer. 1979), cert. Denied, 445 U.S. 917 (1980).

14 years. The 1790 Act also provided that, if the author survived the initial term, he or his executors, administrators, or assigns could renew the copyright for another term of 14 years. Subsequent copyright acts expanded the terms of protection. In response to copyright extensions enacted in England, Congress passed the Copyright Act of 1831, which increased the copyright term to 28 years, with renewal available for an additional 14 years, matching the copyright extension granted by Parliament. In response to these actions, France extended its copyright terms to the life of the author plus 50 years, Russia extended its copyright term to life of the author plus 20 years, and perpetual rights were granted in Germany, Norway, and Sweden. In 1909, Congress expanded the initial copyright period to 28 years and increased the renewal term to 28 years.

After a series of brief extensions in the first half of the twentieth century, Congress passed the Copyright Act of 1976, enacting a term of life of the author plus 50 years for works created or published after January 1, 1978. This made United States copyright terms congruent with the Berne Convention for the Protection of Literary and Artistic Works, an international copyright treaty begun in 1886 and which the United States joined in 1989. Today both American and European copyrights, under the auspicies of the Berne Convention, run for 70 years beyond the life of the author. For "works made for hire," the copyright endures for a term of 95 years from the year of its first publication, or a term of 120 years from the year of its creation, whichever expires first.[12] Copyrights are transferable as property, at the discretion of the owner. In some cases, however, the actual creator is not considered the author of the work for copyright purposes. Work that is created by an employee in the course of employment is considered a "work for hire," and the employer is considered the author of the work for copyright purposes.[13]

Software was subject to copyright protection in the United States after Congress passed the 1976 Copyright Act. Prior to this Act, there had been uncertainty whether copyright law could protect software. This uncertainty stemmed from the fact that functional instructions and ideas—the heart of a computer program—are not copyrightable because they do not meet the minimal copyright requirement for creativity. Court decisions since the 1980s and congressional guidance led to the inclusion of computer programs and databases under copyright law.

When a copyright is awarded, the author is given a temporary monopoly in original creation. This monopoly takes the form of six rights in areas where the author retains exclusive control. These rights are:

(1) right of reproduction (i.e., copying),
(2) right to create derivative works,
(3) right to distribution,
(4) right to performance,
(5) right to display, and
(6) right to digital transmission.

Copyright protects the first two rights in both private and public contexts, whereas an author can only restrict the last four rights in the public sphere.[14] Any violations of these property rights are considered copyright infringement.

There are limitations to the property rights conveyed by copyright. The most prominent exception falls under "fair use." The doctrine of fair use allows the reproduction and use of copyrighted material for purposes such as criticism, parody, news reporting, as well as teaching and research.[15] The boundaries of fair use have been frequently challenged in court. Another limitation is the first sale doctrine. Under this provision, ownership of a physical copy of a copyrighted work, such as a book or record, permits a range of activities such as lending the item, reselling the item, disposing of the item, destroying the item, and so forth, but it does not permit copying the item in its entirety. That is because the transfer of the physical copy does not include transfer of the copyright to the work. This doctrine will be challenged by proposed legislation intended to fight piracy in an era when perfect digital copies of copyrighted work are easily made and distributed.

---

[12] See Copyright Act §303.

[13] An interesting court case decided in August 2002 involved many of the elements of copyright. A federal judge ruled that ownership of copyrights to 70 ballets created by famed choreographer Martha Graham between 1926 and 1991 belonged to the Martha Graham Center and not her designated heir. The Martha Graham Center claimed that because Graham was its employee, dances she created while she had that status from 1956 to 1991 were "work for hire" and belonged to the center. The judge agreed. In the ruling, the judge found ten of the contested dances (including the famous 1944 ballet, "Appalachian Spring") belonged in the public domain, and five belonged to individual commissioning organizations. For nine of the ballets, the judge ruled that neither the center nor Graham's heir had shown whether these dances were "published" (fixed) in the form of videos or films available to the public, with adequate copyright notice included, and thus were uncopyrighted.

[14] http://www.chillingeffects.org/copyright/faq.cgi#QID8.
[15] 17 U.S.C. §107.

Trademarks

Trademark protects names and images that are used to label goods or services. Articles subject to trademark include company or product names, images (e.g., Mickey Mouse), logos (e.g., Nike's "swoosh"), slogans (e.g., "Intel Inside"), and product design and product packaging (e.g., the distinctive Coca-Cola bottle, protected under a form of trademark known as trade dress).

Trademark property rights prohibit others from selling goods or services under the same or a confusingly similar name. However, trademark protection does allow for types of "fair uses" including product comparison and, similar to copyright, criticism, news reporting, and parody. The advent of the Internet has brought about Web-related trademark controversies, such as "cybersquatters" who register identical or similar well-known names with the idea of selling them at high prices to the trademark owner or other interested parties. Some Websites use well-known trademarked names in meta-tags for their sites so search engines will misdirect users to that site.

Trade Secrets

A trade secret is information of any sort that is valuable to its owner, is not generally known, and has been kept secret by the owner. Trade secrets are protected only under state laws. The Uniform Trade Secrets Act, in effect in a number of states, defines trade secrets as "information, including a formula, pattern, compilation, program, device, method, technique, or process that derives independent economic value from not being generally known and not being readily ascertainable and is subject to reasonable efforts to maintain secrecy." The concept of trade secrets dates back to ancient Roman law, which punished people who induced workers to divulge secrets pertaining to their master's commercial activities.

Trade secrets protection makes it illegal to deliberately copy an established commercial idea or information that a company keeps secret. Business information, such as customer lists, manufacturing processes, and formulas for producing products, can be protected by trade secret laws. Inventions and processes that are not patentable can be protected under trade secret law. Patent applicants generally rely on trade secret law to protect their inventions while the patent applications are pending.[16] In some cases, businesses prefer trade secret protection to patents. If Coca-Cola's inventor had applied

for a patent on the formula for the soft drink he created in the mid-1880s, that patent would have expired around 1903.[17] By leaving the formula unpatented, Coke has been able to defend its flavor under trade secret laws.

CATCHING UP WITH TECHNOLOGY

The pace of technology change often far exceeds the pace of legislation and jurisprudence, particularly concerning patents and copyrights. Sometimes the gap between technology and regulation can slow technological development; other times companies are able to negotiate solutions, in the absence of clear IP ownership, that enable them to exploit fast-paced technological changes. Technology companies in particular found that they needed to move faster than the legal and legislative mechanisms could turn. In order to exploit technological advances, even in the absence of clear IP ownership, some technology companies found it preferable to negotiate with competing IP proprietors—even before the dust had settled on competing claims—rather than wait to introduce new technologies to the marketplace.

Compromise and Cross License

An example of one such compromise was the legal dispute concerning the patent for the integrated circuit (IC)—the microchip that revolutionized computers. The IC was independently invented by Jack Kilby of Texas Instruments in July 1958 and Robert Noyce of Fairchild Electronics in January 1959. After undergoing separate patent reviews, each man was awarded a patent on his respective submission. After prolonged litigation, all the way to the U.S. Supreme Court, Noyce's patent was upheld, even though Kilby elucidated the invention six months sooner, on the strength of Noyce's more complete and more accurate description of his conception of the IC. However, the inventors and their respective companies felt the IC was far too important to bottle up while waiting for the courts to resolve the prolonged patent dispute. By 1966, before the first of what would be several court opinions was issued, Fairchild and TI agreed to grant licenses to the other (cross license) for integrated circuit production. Other companies that wanted to produce ICs had to negotiate a royalty with both Fairchild and TI (generally ranging from 2 to 4 percent of the licensee's profit from IC production). The IC brought

---

[16] http://profs.lp.findlaw.com/patents/patents_3.html.

[17] T. R. Reid, *The Chip,* Random House, (New York: 2001), p. 98.

Fairchild and TI hundreds of millions of dollars of royalties over the years.[18]

The company that Robert Noyce went on to co-found, Intel, is well-known for its fierce protection of its IP. However, in early 1995, Intel ended its seven-year patent and copyright dispute with competing microprocessor maker Advanced Micro Devices (AMD) concerning Intel's 386 and 486 microprocessor, not in a courtroom, but at the negotiating table. At the behest of a United States magistrate, the two companies worked out their differences in this long-running fight; under the settlement, all litigation involving each company was dropped. AMD was given a perpetual license to the microcode in the Intel 386 and 486 microprocessors but agreed that it has no right to copy any other Intel microcode, including that of the Pentium. Intel and AMD negotiated a new patent cross-license agreement that took effect January 1, 1996. AMD also dropped its antitrust case against Intel and agreed to make no more than 20 percent of its 486 processors using Intel microcode at foundries (independent microprocessor factories).[19]

Copyright Fights

Of the various forms of IP protection, none have proved as contentious over the past 100 years as copyright. Legal scholars, as well as businesses, realize that decisions concerning the scope and length of copyright protection are extraordinarily influential and impact the quantity, quality, and cost of future content.[20] The current battle over copyright places the interests of technology producers, such as PC makers, against those of copyright holders, content producers such as recording companies and movie studios. This tension stretches back into the early 20th century.

Blatant copyright infringement is as old as copyright protection itself. Sometimes, infringement was sanctioned, tacitly or overtly, by governments. When the United States was a developing country (and even after it had become economically well developed), U.S. law refused to recognize the copyrights of non-U.S. citizens. Foreign copyright holders, such as authors and composers, chaffed at the rampant piracy of their works in the United States. The author Charles Dickens, on his American lecture tours, was a vocal critic of the fact that his copyrights were not recognized in this country. The composer Sir Arthur Sullivan (of Gilbert and Sullivan) even went so far as to copyright some of his compositions under the names of United States citizens who in turn remitted to Sullivan royalties from this country.[21] Then as now, music was at the forefront of the tension between content owners and technology companies.

In England, at around the turn of the last century, legitimate music publishers tried a variety of schemes to protect copyrighted music. Publishers tried to institute expirations on sheet music, restricting the length of time people could perform sheet music before they were required to buy another copy. The British publishers asked England's postmaster general to block all music shipments from the United States.[22] They threatened to prosecute musicians who transposed songs into other keys. Finally, they persuaded Parliament to pass strong new anti-piracy legislation and then sought to enforce it.[23]

After much lobbying by copyright holding interests, Parliament acted. The Musical Copyright Act came into effect in England on October 1, 1902. On that day, the Music Publishers Association in England paid over one thousand anti-pirate vigilantes to roam the streets of London to search for and destroy pirate editions of songs in sheet-music bonfires, as well as beat up street hawkers who peddled pirated sheet music. As one music historian observed, "By showing the teeth in the new copyright law, the publishers scared off the great majority of music black-marketeers."[24]

Changes in technology have often had the effect of challenging the ability of copyright holders to protect their property. In 1908 music publishers sued makers of player piano rolls claiming that the paper piano rolls were based on the publishers' music, hence violating their copyrights. The Supreme Court ruled that piano rolls, holes punched in a specific pattern on a template made from a roll of paper that caused piano chords to be struck, were not close enough to published music to infringe on copyright as it then existed.[25] The next year Congress established the "mechanical license," which granted anyone the right to reproduce another's published music in return for a royalty set by law (Exhibit 1).

---

[18] For a further description of the concurrent development of the IC, see T. R. Reid, *The Chip*, Random House (New York: 2001), pp. 96–117.
[19] Brian Fuller, "AMD, Intel Finally Settle Dispute," *EE Times*, January 15, 1995.
[20] Paul Goldstein, *Copyright's Highway*, Hill and Wang (New York: 1994), p. 202.

[21] Charles C. Mann, "The Heavenly Juke Box," *The Atlantic Monthly*, September 2000.
[22] James Coover, *Music Publishing, Copyright, and Piracy in Victorian England*, Mansell (New York: 1985), pp. 18–19.
[23] Coover, *Music Publishing, Copyright, and Piracy in Victorian England*, pp. viii–ix.
[24] Music historian Professor James Coover, quoted in "The Heavenly Jukebox."
[25] *White-Smith Music Pub. Co. v. Apollo Co.*, 209 U.S. 1 (1908).

EXHIBIT 1   Copyright Royalty Rates Section 115, the Mechanical License

Date	Rate	Authority
1990–1977	2 cents	Copyright Act of 1909
January 1, 1978	2.75 cents or 0.5 cent per minute of playing time or fraction thereof, whichever is greater	Copyright Act of 1976
January 1, 1981	4 cents or 0.75 cent per minute of playing time or fraction thereof, whichever is greater	1980 Mechanical Rate Adjustment Proceeding
January 1, 1983	4.25 cents or 0.8 cent per minute of playing time or fraction thereof, whichever is greater	1980 Mechanical Rate Adjustment Proceeding
July 1, 1984	4.5 cents or 0.85 cent per minute of playing time or fraction thereof, whichever is greater	1980 Mechanical Rate Adjustment Proceeding
January 1, 1986	5 cents or 0.95 cent per minute of playing time or fraction thereof, whichever is greater	1980 Mechanical Rate Adjustment Proceeding
January 1, 1988 to December 31, 1989	5.25 cents or 1 cent per minute of playing time or fraction thereof, whichever is greater	17 U.S.C. 801 (b)(1) and 804; based upon the change in the Consumer Price Index from Dec. 1985 to Sept. 1987
January 1, 1990 to December 31, 1991	5.7 cents or 1.1 cents per minute of playing time or fraction thereof, whichever is greater	Consumer Price Index from Sept. 1987 to Sept. 1989
January 1, 1992 to December 31, 1993	6.25 cents or 1.2 cents per minute of playing time or fraction thereof, whichever is greater	Consumer Price Index from Sept. 1989 to Sept. 1991
January 1, 1994 to December 31, 1995	6.60 cents or 1.25 cents per minute of playing time or fraction thereof, whichever is greater	Consumer Price Index from Sept. 1991 to Sept. 1993
January 1, 1996 to December 31, 1997	6.95 cents or 1.3 cents per minute of playing time or fraction thereof, whichever is greater	Consumer Price Index from Sept. 1993 to Sept. 1995
January 1, 1998 to December 31, 1999	7.1 cents or 1.35 cents per minute of playing time or fraction thereof, whichever is greater	1997 Mechanical Rate Adjustment Proceeding
January 1, 2000 to December 31, 2001	7.55 cents or 1.45 cents per minute of playing time or fraction thereof, whichever is greater	1997 Mechanical Rate Adjustment Proceeding
January 1, 2002 to December 31, 2003	8.0 cents or 1.55 cents per minute of playing time or fraction thereof, whichever is greater	1997 Mechanical Rate Adjustment Proceeding
January 1, 2004 to December 31, 2005	8.5 cents or 1.65 cents per minute of playing time or fraction thereof, whichever is greater	1997 Mechanical Rate Adjustment Proceeding
January 1, 2006	9.1 cents or 1.75 cents per minute of playing time or fraction thereof, whichever is greater	1997 Mechanical Rate Adjustment Proceeding

Source: http://www.copyright.gov/carp/m200a.html.

Strangely, the 1909 copyright law contained a copyright exemption for the "reproduction or rendition of a musical composition by or upon coin-operated machines."[26] It took Congress over 50 years to close this loophole during which time the once lucrative coin-operated jukebox industry developed.[27]

Radio also caused worries for music copyright holders. In 1931, the American Society of Composers, Authors and Publishers (ASCAP), a group that licenses music and distributes royalties, claimed that the LaSalle Hotel in Kansas City, Missouri, violated their copyrights by playing songs broadcast on a radio show over speakers wired throughout the hotel. A court found that while the hotel could not legally perform the music without permission, it could project the music in the hotel if it were broadcast over the radio.[28] Under later revisions

---

[26] Copyright Act of March 4, 1909, ch. 320, § 1(e), 35 Stat. 1075 (1909).

[27] For a further discussion of this exemption, see Stanley Green, "Jukebox Piracy," *The Atlantic Monthly,* April 1962, Volume 209, No. 4, p. 136.

[28] *Buck v. Jewell-La Salle Realty Co.,* 283 U.S. 191 (1931).

to copyright laws, and subsequent court opinions, such performances would be subject to royalty payments. Throughout the 1930s ASCAP increased the license fees it charged for radio performances. Radio broadcasters decided to enter this market themselves and formed Broadcast Music, Inc. (BMI) to compete against ASCAP. BMI had little success in poaching ASCAP-affiliated artists, but did sign new artists and added Latin American songs to its catalog. In 1941, during a dispute over royalty rates, broadcasters pulled all ASCAP music off the air, instead playing public domain songs and BMI's catalog of new tunes and Latin American music. ASCAP songs stayed off the air for eight months before an agreement was reached with broadcasters. During the ASCAP "blackout," the group found that sales of their records and sheet music plummeted.[29]

The threat from photocopiers was addressed in 1968 when a medical publisher, Williams & Wilkins, sued the United States National Library of Medicine (NLM) for its practice of photocopying its journals for use by researchers without paying royalties. On appeal, the Supreme Court ruled that NLM's copying was fair use and thus not a copyright violation.[30]

Broadcast television companies twice sued community antenna television (CATV) stations (the precursor to cable television) over CATV retransmission of broadcast television signals. In two important cases in 1968 and 1974, courts found that CATV stations could retransmit broadcasts without violating any copyrights.[31] These findings greatly helped the development of cable television in the United States.

In 1984, movie studios took on the nascent home video recording (VCR) industry. Fearful of the impact that VCRs could have on the studios' ability to control its content, a group of movie studios, led by Universal Studios, sued Sony Corporation, maker of the Betamax video recorder. To the studios, the VCR represented a technology whose main purpose was to violate copyrights. An appeals court found in favor of the studios, and the case went to the Supreme Court. The Supreme Court, in a 5 to 4 decision, narrowly reversed the appeals court ruling and found that the ability of VCRs to record broadcast television for private viewing at a more con-

venient time ("time shifting" which was deemed fair use) represented a legitimate use for the technology.[32] At the time of the ruling, Jack Valenti, the Chairman of the Motion Picture Associate of America (MPAA), was quoted as saying, "The VCR is to the American film producer and the American public as the Boston strangler is to a woman home alone."

In the end, radio has proven to be an important complement to recorded music, and about one third of the annual revenue of major studios comes from home video sales.[33]

Going to Court and Going to Congress

Conflicting patent and copyright claims are open to judicial resolution. However, claims of infringement, or disputes about rightful ownership of IP are costly and time consuming to resolve. According to a 2001 survey conducted by the American Intellectual Property Lawyer's Association (AIPLA), a patent litigant can expect to spend at least $500,000 and up to $6 million to try a patent case. On average, a patent suit in which $1 million to $25 million is at risk costs $797,000 through discovery, and just under $1.5 million through trial, with some litigants reporting costs in excess of $2.5 million. For those cases in which more than $25 million is at risk, the average litigant can expect to spend $1.5 million through discovery and roughly $3 million if there is a trial. Many small companies cannot afford the money or time needed to fight a dispute.

While some patents have been controversial (e.g., business method or process patents) and left to the courts to decide, copyright issues over the years have been fraught with contention. The Supreme Court has weighed in on a number of copyright conflicts involving content producers. The Court has delivered numerous opinions that interpret a consistent view of the purpose of copyright. In 1932, the Court wrote, "The sole interest of the United States and the primary object in conferring the monopoly lie in the general benefits derived by the public from the labors of authors."[34] In 1948, the Court wrote, "The copyright law, like the patent statues, makes reward to the owner a secondary consideration."[35] In

[29] For more on the ASCAP blackout, see Goldstein *Copyright's Highway,* pp. 71–75.

[30] *Williams & Wilkins Co. v. The United States Records,* 420 U.S. 376 (1975).

[31] *Fortnightly Corp. v. United Artists Television, Inc.,* 392 U.S. 390 (1968) and *Teleprompter Corp. v. Columbia Broadcasting System, Inc.,* 415 U.S. 394 (1974).

[32] For an in-depth discussion of the Betamax case, see Robert A. Burgelman and Philip Meza, "A Look at Three Regulatory Forces Influencing Content and Distribution in the Motion Picture and Television Industries," SM-105, Stanford Graduate School of Business.

[33] James Lardner, "Hollywood vs. High-Tech," *Business 2.0,* May 2002.

[34] *Fox Film Corp. v. Doyal,* 286 U.S. 123, 127 (1932).

[35] *United States v. Paramount Pictures, Inc.,* 334 U.S. 131, 158 (1948).

1984, in the VCR case mentioned above, the Court wrote, "The primary objective of copyright is not to reward the labor of authors but to 'promote the Progress of Science and useful Arts.'"[36] However, it is within the purview of Congress to decide the term (length) of copyright protection.

Since 1962, Congress extended the term of copyright protection 11 times. Copyright scholar Paul Goldstein of Stanford Law School has written: ". . . the U.S. Congress has been far more consistent in extending rights against economically valuable uses than a strict showing of needed incentives would appear to indicate. . . . Congress has never once required authors or publishers to demonstrate that, in fact, they need the new right as an incentive to produce literary or artistic works."[37]

IP PROTECTION IN THE WAKE OF THE INTERNET

Compared to radios, photocopiers, and VCRs, digitization and the Internet represent a fundamentally different threat to the existing business models of copyright holders. Digital technology enables users to create perfect copies of movies and recordings and distribute them virtually without cost. Photocopiers did not threaten the fundamental business models of publishers. The VCR turned out to be a boon for studios, even though pirated analog VCR tapes did inflict financial harm on movie companies. Because the quality of pirated analog recordings was often lower and distribution was difficult to scale, these activities did not threaten the copyright owners in the same way as easily pirated DVDs or digital movie files distributed over the Internet. New digital technologies combined with the Internet created much more significant threats. Audio compression technologies, such as the MP3 algorithm, condense audio tracks into a twelfth of their original digital space. A CD copied ("ripped") into MP3 format could be sent over the Internet and downloaded on to someone's computer in minutes instead of hours.[38] Over the past few years, millions of often perfect or near perfect copies of copyrighted songs were available, for free, on various file sharing networks. By 2002, movies were starting to appear on these networks, sometimes as soon as they released to theaters. By 2003, recording companies suffered several years of declining sales—blaming online piracy for much of the slide.

In 1992, Congress passed the Audio Home Recording Act (AHRA), an amendment to the federal copyright law of 1976. Under the AHRA, all digital recording devices must incorporate a Serial Copy Management System (SCMS). This system allows digital recorders to make a first-generation copy of a digitally recorded work but does not allow a second-generation copy to be made from the first copy (users may still make as many first-generation copies as they want). The AHRA also provides for a royalty tax of up to $8 per new digital recording machine and 3 percent of the price of all digital audiotapes or discs. This tax is paid by the manufacturers of digital media devices and distributed to the copyright owners whose music is presumably being copied. In consideration of this tax, copyright owners agree to forever waive the right to claim copyright infringement against consumers using audio recording devices in their homes. This is commensurate with the fair use exception to copyright law, which allows consumers to make copies of copyrighted music for non-commercial purposes. The SCMS and royalty requirements apply only to digital audio recording devices. Because computers were not considered digital audio recording devices, they were not required to comply with the Serial Copy Management System requirement.[39]

The Sonny Bono Law: I Got You Babe for Another 20 Years

In 1998 entertainment companies vigorously lobbied Congress for two pieces of legislation that impacted their IP property rights. One extended the length of American copyrights, enacted under the Sonny Bono Copyright Term Extension Act (CTEA), introduced by Senator Orrin Hatch (R-Utah) and named for the late Congressman Sonny Bono (R-California), a former hit songwriter and performer who gained fame in the late 1960s performing with his former wife, Cher.

In 1976, Congress extended the term of copyright protection from 28 years, renewable once, to the life of the author plus 50 years. In 1998, under what became known as the Sonny Bono CTEA, Congress extended the term of copyright to life of the author plus 70 years and, with respect to "works made for hire," 95 years after publication or 120 years after creation, whichever expires first. Opponents sued the government, claiming that the extension was a violation of the First Amendment of

---

[36] *Sony Corp. v. Universal Studios, Inc.*, 464 U.S. 417, 429 (1984).
[37] Goldstein, *Copyright's Highway*, p. 172.
[38] "Music to Their Ears," *The Economist*, September 19, 2002.
[39] 2002 Duke L. & Tech. Rev. 0023.

the Constitution, which protects free speech.[40] The challenge was heard by the Supreme Court, which in January 2003, found that the Congress had the authority to set the terms for copyright protection, and the Supreme Court would defer to the Congress' determinations on copyright terms. The Court found that the First Amendment does not limit the Congress' power to extend copyright terms. Justice Ginsburg, writing for the majority, stated: "The First Amendment securely protects the freedom to make—or decline to make—one's own speech; it bears less heavily when speakers assert the right to make other people's speeches. To the extent such assertions raise First Amendment concerns, copyright's built-in free speech safeguards are generally adequate to address them. . . . Such safeguards include fair use, and the principle that copyright protects expressions, but not the ideas or facts contained in expressions."

Digital Millennium Copyright Act

The second, and far more controversial piece of legislation, the Digital Millennium Copyright Act (DMCA), was also enacted in 1998. This law declared that "no person shall circumvent a technological measure that effectively controls access to a work protected" by copyright. The DMCA made it a crime not only to copy a protected work, but to de-encrypt an encrypted work without authorization. The law also contained stipulations that made it illegal to manufacture, release, or sell any tools, hardware, or software designed to circumvent encryption of a copyrighted work. The DMCA contained provisions that gave ISPs and Web hosts "safe harbor" from copyright infringement claims if they implemented notices and removal procedures to eliminate infringing content. However, the law had the potential to make it illegal to manufacture and sell much of the software and hardware that technology companies hoped would make media over the Internet a common application and at the same time help pull them out of recession.

In January 2003, under the DMCA, a federal judge ordered Verizon Communications (a Regional Bell Operating Company formed from the mergers of Bell Atlantic, Nynex, and GTE) to give a record industry trade group the identity of an Internet subscriber suspected of making available unauthorized copies of several hundred songs. This marked a departure for recording companies that in the past had focused their legal efforts against on-line file sharing services such as Napster and others. Verizon appealed the decision.

Consumer Broadband and Digital Television Promotion Act

In March 2002, United States Senator Ernest F. Hollings (D-S.C.), chairman of the Senate Commerce Committee, and five co-sponsors, introduced legislation called the Consumer Broadband and Digital Television Promotion Act. The bill would require that new hardware and software, from CD players to television sets to computers, block unauthorized copying of copyrighted works. It would have movie studios, record labels, and others attach digital tags to a movie, song, or album that would encode rules about how it could be played, viewed, or copied on devices such as computers or digital TVs. Manufacturers and content owners would have a year to agree on technology to enforce these rules; after that, the Federal Communications Commission could impose a standard. It would then be illegal to manufacture devices that did not implement that standard.

Hollings said: "I believe the private sector is capable, through marketplace negotiations, of adopting standards that will ensure the secure transmission of copyrighted content on the Internet and over the airwaves. . . . But given the pace of private talks so far, the private sector needs a nudge."[41] The bill's supporters said the legislation was designed to stimulate the growth of high-speed Internet access and digital television. Supporters argued that consumers have been slow to adopt services such as broadband Internet access because there was not enough programming and content; and copyright owners will not provide that content online until they are sure people cannot make and distribute unauthorized copies. But opponents of the bill feared it would grant copyright owners too much control over how consumers use technology.

LOOKING FOR SOLUTIONS

Entertainment and computer companies also tried to resolve the issues for themselves. In January 2003, the Recording Industry Association of America (RIAA), a trade organization that represents the world's largest record companies, and the Business Software Alliance, a software-industry trade group, and the Computer Systems Policy Project, which represents leading hardware

---

[40] *Eldred et al. v. Ashcroft.*

[41] Mike Musgrove, "Hollings Proposes Copyright Defense," *The Washington Post,* March 22, 2002, p. E03.

EXHIBIT 2   Technology and Record Company Policy Principles

Issued jointly by Business Software Alliance (BSA), Computer Systems Policy Project (CSPP), and Recording Industry Association of America (RIAA).

Rapidly changing technology presents important new opportunities for distributing content and expanding consumer choice, but also pose new and difficult threats of piracy to the recording, software, and technology industries. Never has there been a greater need for dialogue and collaboration to determine how best to respond to these opportunities and challenges. Public policy battles in the Congress and the media in recent years require inter-industry constructive dialogue and concerted efforts to develop consensus approaches.

The undersigned organizations have therefore agreed upon a core set of principles that will govern our activities in the public and policy arenas during the 108th Congress. These principles are:

1. **Public Awareness.** Technology and record companies should jointly encourage and promote consumer awareness campaigns about the rights and wrongs of Internet use and digital copying. Such campaigns should be funded privately, but joint approaches to Congress for a federal role should also be considered.

2. **Consumer Expectations.** Technology and record companies agree that meeting the needs and expectations of our customers is critically important to the viability of our industries. Consumers are eager to enjoy new music and new technologies and record and technology companies are already addressing those needs. How companies satisfy consumer expectations is a business decision that should be driven by the dynamics of the marketplace, and should not be legislated or regulated.

3. **Enforcement.** Technology and record companies support private and governmental enforcement actions against infringers.

4. **Technical Protection Measures.** Technology and record companies have collaborated to develop, are using, and support the use of unilateral technical protection measures that limit unauthorized access, copying, or redistribution of products without government-imposed requirements for the incorporation of specific functionality in a computer or other device. Legislation should not limit the use or effectiveness of such measures. Technology and record compa-

nies agree that product labeling should endeavor to clearly inform consumers of the playability of content on devices they might own or use.

5. **Actions by Rightholders.** Technology and record companies support technical measures to limit illegal distribution of copyrighted works, subject to requirements that the measures be designed to be reasonable, are not destructive to networks, individual users' data or equipment, and do not violate individuals' legal rights to privacy or similar legally protected interests of individuals.

6. **Mandates.** Technology and record companies believe that technical protection measures dictated by the government (legislation or regulations mandating how these technologies should be designed, function and deployed, and what devices must do to respond to them) are not practical. The imposition of technical mandates is not the best way to serve the long-term interests of record companies, technology companies, and consumers. Technology can play an important role in providing safeguards against theft and piracy. The role of government, if needed at all, should be limited to enforcing compliance with voluntarily developed functional specifications reflecting consensus among affected interests. If government pursues the imposition of technical mandates, technology and record companies may act to ensure such rules neither prejudice nor ignore their interests.

7. **Improved Public Dialogue.** Technology and record companies agree to engage in constructive dialogue and look for common ground in policy debates.

The member companies of the **BSA** include: Adobe, Apple, Autodesk, Avid, Bentley Systems, Borland, Cisco Systems, CNC/Mastercam, Dell, Entrust, HP, IBM, Intel, Internet Security Systems, Intuit, Macromedia, Microsoft, Network Associates, Novell, PeopleSoft, SeeBeyond, Sybase, and Symantec.

The member companies of **CSPP** include: Dell Computer Corporation, Intel Corporation, Hewlett-Packard Company, Motorola Corporation, NCR Corporation, IBM Corporation, EMC Corporation, and Unisys Corporation.

The member companies of the **RIAA** include: BMG, EMI Recorded Music, Sony Music Entertainment, Universal Music Group, Warner Music Group.

Source: Business Software Alliance.

manufacturers, agreed on seven "policy principles" pertaining to their legislative activities; i.e., lobbying in Congress (Exhibit 2). While the principles were general, some[42] thought they represented a compromise between the two camps: The music industry would drop its support for compulsory anti-piracy technology ("How com-

panies satisfy consumer expectations is a business decision that should be driven by the dynamics of the marketplace, and should not be legislated or regulated")[43]; and the computer industry would drop its support for legislation such as the Digital Media Consumers' Rights

---

[42]"Unexpected Harmony," *The Economist,* January 23, 2003.

[43]"Technology and Record Company Policy Principles," issued jointly by the Business Software Alliance, Computer Systems Policy Project, and Recording Industry Association of America.

Act,[44] which would reaffirm fair use exemptions to copyright laws.

Significantly, the Motion Picture Association of America, a trade group of movie studios, did not participate in the call for compromise and continued to call for government action including the enforcement of technical anti-piracy measures such as digital rights management technologies.

Digital Rights Management

Digital Rights Management (DRM) is a phrase used to describe a combination of software encryption and new hardware, designed to make digital copying impossible without permission. Critics of DRM contend that the technology, and the framework of the laws that would support DRM, could erode consumer rights enjoyed under concepts such as fair use and the doctrine of first sale. Private copying that is now legal, for listening to music or reading text on more than one device, for example, would also become subject to the permission of the record company or publisher. PC makers, among others, worried that many aspects of DRM could hobble the ability of PCs to play digital media.

By 2002, some large music labels began to produce CDs embedded with forms of DRM technology. These were copy-protection programs designed to prevent disks from being played on PCs. Sony has developed its own anti-piracy technology, called key2audio, which prevented consumers from listening to CDs on any type of CD-ROM or DVD player. Sony announced in January 2002 that it had produced a total of 10 million discs for 500 different albums that could not be played on personal computers by using its key2audio program. A second version of the software, key2audio4PC, permitted listeners to play copy-protected CDs on their personal computers. But the discs were encrypted to limit usage to a single specific PC, preventing the user from playing the disc on alternative devices. BMG licensed anti-piracy technology that prevented consumers from reformatting songs into MP3 files and burning copies, or making them available on file-sharing systems. The software prevented listeners from playing the discs on CD-ROM drives and was also potentially damaging to amplifiers and speakers as well as having the ability to disable stand-alone CD burners.[45]

CONCLUSION

New information technologies have been important complements to content owners. Conflicts that developed as new business models adjusted to new technologies were usually hammered out through a combination of litigation, legislation, and compromise. This has not yet happened with digital technologies. Perfect digital copies made on PCs and their easy worldwide distribution via the Internet could fundamentally change the balance between the interests of content owners and the public. The fact that the two camps need each other has not yet brought about a compromise. Most of the activity, thus far, has been through litigation and legislation. Concepts such as fair use and the first sale doctrine could be sacrificed in favor of DRM technologies. Courts could tip the balance in favor of the public over the wants of content owners; and those industries could continue to lose hundreds of millions of dollars each year to piracy. Congress could legislate technological solutions that offered better protection to copyright owners but hobbled technology industries.

READING II-9

Note on New Drug Development in the United States

Stefan Thomke and Ashok Nimgade

In the early 1990s, the pharmaceutical industry was one of the largest and most profitable research and manufacturing businesses, with annual worldwide sales around $250 billion. The engine driving its growth was heavy investment in research and development. The top

---

Source: Copyright © 1998 by The President and Fellows of Harvard College. Professor Stefan Thomke and Research Associate Ashok Nimgade, M.D., prepared this note as the basis for class discussion. Some of the data presented are based on empirical studies conducted in the late 1980s and may have changed at the time of discussion. To order copies or request permission to reproduce materials, call 1-800-545-7685, write Harvard Business School Publishing, Boston, MA 02163, or go to http://hbsp.harvard.edu. No part of this publication may be reproduced, stored in a retrieval system, used in a spreadsheet, or transmitted in any form or by any means—electronic, mechanical, photocopying, recording, or otherwise—without the permission of Harvard Business School.

---

[44] Introduced in the Congress on 7 January 2003 by Rep. Rick Boucher (D-VA).
[45] 2002 Duke L. & Tech. Rev. 0023.

50 pharmaceutical companies worldwide spent around $25.4 billion in R&D, or almost 16 percent of their sales.[1]

For each therapeutic drug developed in the United States, the sponsoring pharmaceutical firms spent over $250 million, and the average time to market was 14.8 years (an increase of about 40 percent over the 1970s).[2] Estimated costs included both out-of-pocket costs, time costs (i.e., forgone investments as a result of investing in R&D before any returns are realized), and costs of failed projects. Although differing accounting techniques lead to varying estimates, new drug development has undoubtedly been costly, with high failure rates.

Clearly, such war-level–like marshalling of resources, involving thousands of highly trained individuals spanning continents, represented a vast difference from the millennia-old practice of healing through herbs. Yet, the basic principles guiding drug discovery through the centuries have remained unchanged: optimum therapy should combine medical efficacy with minimal side effects.

Even after the synthetic chemistry revolution of the mid-nineteenth century, modern drugmakers, like their forebears, continued turning to nature for clues. But where traditional herbalists might have used a mix of compounds found in a single herb, synthetic chemists attempted to isolate the solitary "active ingredient" from a plant (such as aspirin from willow). At the very least, this would allow for patentability.

To get this all-important patent and to develop new drugs more effectively, however, modern drug companies follow a very systematic R&D and approval process. What follows is a description of the steps that were required in the late 20th century to get a drug from the lab bench through the U.S. Food and Drug Administration (FDA) approval process—the world's most stringent drug approval process. Glaxo-Wellcome's anti-migraine drug sumatriptan (also known as Imitrex®) will be used to demonstrate new drug development challenges facing pharmaceutical firms. (See Exhibit 1.)

PHASES OF NEW DRUG DEVELOPMENT

Basic Research (About Two Years)

Classical drug discovery as practiced through much of the 19th and 20th centuries involved the initial screening of plants, microorganisms, and other naturally occurring

---

EXHIBIT 1   The Genesis of Glaxo's Sumatriptan

The history of modern drugs for migraine headaches finds an odd linkage with the persecution of witches several centuries ago in Europe and puritan New England. In these ages, young women who reported hallucinations (sometimes about flying) were labeled as witches. With the hindsight of centuries it appears likely that these women may have consumed rye infected by ergot, a type of fungus. Ergot and the drug LSD share a chemical relationship with the important nervous system signaling compound (neurotransmitter) called serotonin. Another related compound, ergotamine, became one of the first antimigraine drugs available. It was found to interact with a serotonin receptor to counteract the dilation of cranial blood vessels associated with the throbbing sensation experienced by migraine sufferers. However, Ergotamine's known side effects ranged from nausea, vomiting, muscle cramps, constriction of peripheral blood vessels, and even to physical dependence.

Ergotamine nonetheless pointed out the direction for future programs in antimigraine drug development. A leap in understanding occurred after the 1950s, when availability of synthetic serotonin allowed researchers to appreciate that several different receptors for serotonin existed in the body. By the 1970s, a particular branch (5-HT1) of the serotonin receptor family had been implicated with migraine. In the mid-1970s, Glaxo researcher P. P. A. Humphrey and colleagues started exploring a variety of serotonin-like compounds in the hopes of finding an effective antimigraine drug.

A breakthrough occurred when the Glaxo team discovered a compound that appeared to constrict cranial blood vessels. This led to a derivative compound (named AH25086) that acted in a much more selective fashion; that is, it exerted its antimigraine effects primarily at the sites where it was supposed to and not elsewhere.

This compound, unfortunately, could only be administered by injection, thereby limiting its usefulness to patients. Efforts to find a drug that could also be taken orally led to a derivative termed GR43175, which later became better known as sumatriptan (Imitrex®) (see Exhibit 7). Discovered in 1984, sumatriptan was to eventually become the first new medication in over a half-century specifically developed for treatment of migraines.

Source: From P. R. Saxena and M. D. Ferrari, "From Serotonin Receptor Classification to the Antimigraine Drug Sumatriptan," *Cephalgia* 12 (1992), pp. 187–196.

---

substances in order to find a "hit" or "lead" compound. Typically taking place in test tubes (in vitro) and lab animals (in vivo), this initial screening allowed for quicker,

---

[1] *Pharmaceutical Industry Summary,* Lehman Brothers (1996).
[2] U.S. Food and Drug Administration (FDA), "From Test Tube to Patient: New Drug Development in the United States," *FDA Consumer,* Special Issue (January 1995); J. DiMassi, H. Grabowsky, and L. Lasagna, "Cost of Innovation in the Pharmaceutical Industry," *Journal of Health Economics* 10 (1994); pp. 107–142.

cheaper, and safer testing than that using humans. In essence, the process was like trying to find, through trial and error, the right molecular key to open up a biochemical lock within the body. The keys were often found in odd places. For instance, cyclosporin, widely used to treat organ transplant patients, was isolated by a Finnish researcher from a mud extract. Perhaps a more common place to initiate massive screening programs, however, was in the vast collections, or libraries, of hundreds of thousands of compounds that most pharmaceutical companies retained over decades.

With this broad screening strategy, an average of only 1 out of every 10,000 compounds screened would eventually make it to the market. One strategy to beat these astronomical odds was to develop "me-too" versions of preexisting drugs—for example, there are more than 200 antibiotic versions, or analogues, of penicillin, which was discovered in the 1920s.

Yet another way to beat the 1:10,000 odds and create more revolutionary drugs involved understanding much more about the molecular locks (receptors) where therapeutic compounds were thought to act. But "disease processes are complex and involve a sequence of events," according to Rhonda Gruen, Ph.D., of Hoffmann-LaRoche.[3] "If you want to intervene in the disease process, you try to break it down into its component parts. . . . You would then select a particular step as a target for drug development." But even with this reductionist approach, which relied on newer technologies such as genetic engineering, the goal of creating drugs based on completely deterministic principles eluded scientists.

Regardless of which strategy was used to identify lead compounds, drug development involved painstaking iterative research, with organic chemists making analogues or modifications of existing leads. A single experienced chemist could generate around one new compound every 7 to 10 days, at a cost of $5,000–$10,000 per compound. This stage of the process could consume 124 chemist-years[4] and represented a critical path activity—a place of high leverage for speeding up the drug development cycle. Even newer methods of rapid drug compound generation, such as combinatorial chemistry, were carried out in conjunction with this careful, handcrafting of molecules at vital steps.

---

[3] US Food and Drug Administration FDA, "From Test Tube to Patient: New Drug Development in the United States," *FDA Consumer,* Special Issue (January 1995).

[4] R. G. Halliday, S. R. Walker, and C. E. Lumley, *Journal of Pharmaceutical Medicine* 2 (1992), pp. 139–154.

Preclinical (Biological) Screening (About Three Years)

Traditionally, out of 10,000 starting compounds, only 40 might make it to the next stage of preclinical testing. The preclinical trials involve animal testing to assess safety as well as to gather data on biological effects of drug candidates. Attention is particularly focused on the absorption, metabolism, and excretion of the drug in animals in order to find clues about what to expect in human trials. (See Exhibit 2.)

Clinical Trials (About Six Years)

Drugs making it through the animal studies (now termed Investigational New Drugs, or INDs) are finally put through the most expensive and time-consuming regulatory hurdles: human clinical trials monitored by the FDA. On average, roughly 1 in 10 of all drug candidates passes these trials and reaches the market. Increasing proportions of the total costs occurred with each of the three successive phases are described below.

Phase I: Safety Trials, One Year In this initial phase, the drug is tested for up to a year on one to two dozen healthy volunteers who are well-compensated for their participation. Often, very high doses are administered to determine potential toxicities and safe ranges. This phase, however, also yields invaluable information on the absorption, metabolism, and excretion of the drug in humans. (See Exhibit 3.)

EXHIBIT 2 Sumatriptan Enters Animal Trials

Where previously only a handful of researchers had been involved with the discovery of sumatriptan, a team of almost two dozen pharmacologists, toxicologists, and technicians were now involved with testing sumatriptan in animals several years.

Animal testing involved high doses of sumatriptan to discern toxic effects. These studies evaluated sumatriptan's safety even at levels several dozen times higher in concentration than human doses. The animal populations used included rats, mice, dogs, and even pregnant rabbits (to study the effect on unborns).[1]

Obviously, since animals do not suffer from anything easily recognizable as migraine in humans, the ultimate test of efficacy for sumatriptan would come from human clinical trials.

[1] *Imitrex*® *Injection Publication,* Glaxo Wellcome (1996).

EXHIBIT 3   Sumatriptan in Phase I Safety Trials

Phase I trials for sumatriptan were conducted initially in the United Kingdom and then also in the United States. In this phase, which lasted roughly a year in the United States but two years on a worldwide basis, some 300 healthy, paid volunteers worldwide were eventually tested with gradually increasing doses up to about 2.5 times the dose migraine patients would get.[1]

These studies indicated that sumatriptan was well tolerated in humans and also provided data on the pharmacokinetics of the new drug (how the human body processed this drug).[2]

---

[1] Interview with Donna Gutterman, Director of U.S. Medical Affairs, CNS/Anesthesia/Critical Care, Glaxo Wellcome (December 1997).
[2] *Imitrex®Injection Publication,* Glaxo Wellcome (1996).

EXHIBIT 4   Sumatriptan in Phase II Efficacy Trials

Some Phase II trials were started in the mid 1980s in the United Kingdom and were ramped up in the United States and elsewhere by 1988. Data collected from over 500 patients worldwide (more than 200 from the United States), showed significant acute efficacy in a variety of dosage forms (subcutaneous, oral, intranasal).[1]

---

[1] Interview with Donna Gutterman, Director of U.S. Medical Affairs, CNS/Anesthesia/Critical Care, Glaxo Wellcome (December 1997).

EXHIBIT 5   Sumatriptan in Phase III Trials

Starting in 1988, Glaxo tested sumatriptan worldwide on over 6,000 people in Phase III clinical trials. Entering sumatriptan into the extensive Phase III clinical trials represented a serious commitment for Glaxo. Until sumatriptan, no large-scale clinical studies had ever been conducted with anti-migraine drugs.[1]

A major phase of the trials took place in the United States in 1989, from May to November, at 61 sites and with over 1,100 patients suffering acutely from migraines. Extensive data was collected on each patient: medical history, physical exams, routine lab tests, vital signs, adverse effects, and subjective efficacy at various time intervals before and after administration of sumatriptan.[2]

The results showed efficacy, with some patients experiencing relief as early as 10 minutes after receiving sumatriptan. Four-fifths of sufferers experienced relief within two hours. Reported adverse effects included flushing, nausea, numbness, tingling, and dizziness.

Data from these and other trials in the United States and worldwide were collected for submission to the FDA into an enormous multivolume document titled the "New Drug Application" (NDA). The NDA for injectable Imitrex, which was filed in July 1990, covered over 4,332 patients.[3] A truck transported the millions of sheets of paper, bound in several hundred volumes from Glaxo's U.S. base at Research Triangle, North Carolina, to Washington, D.C. Market approval of the compound sumatriptan would ultimately rest on the FDA's assessment of data in the NDA.

---

[1] Interview with Donna Gutterman, Director of U.S. Medical Affairs, CNS/Anesthesia/Critical Care, Glaxo Wellcome (December 1997).
[2] R. K. Cady et al., "Treatment of acute migraine with subcutaneous sumatriptan," *Journal of American Medical Association* (June 5, 1991), pp. 2831–2835.
[3] FDA Committee Discussion, *Script* 1666 (November 6, 1991), p. 20.

---

12 yrs to here

Phase II: Efficacy Trials, Two Years   While Phase I marked the introduction of the new drug candidate into humans for the first time, Phase II represents the testing of the drug on human *patients.* This phase tests the drug candidate in up to several hundred volunteer patients based at participating hospitals. To ensure statistically relevant data, typically from this point onward in all human trials, a portion of the volunteers receives the drug while the others receive placebos, with the data-gathering clinicians themselves remaining ignorant ("blinded") about what each patient receives.

While this phase allows researchers to evaluate the drug's effectiveness, it also provides further information about adverse effects and optimum dosage levels. At the end of this phase, researchers confer with FDA regulatory authorities to determine whether to go on to Phase

1/3 pass through Phase II

III trials. Roughly one-third of all drug candidates typically survive Phase I and II. (See Exhibit 4.)

Phase III: Long-Term Efficacy Trials, Three Years   *14 yrs to here* *1/4 pass through phase 3*
Phase III trials is by far the most expensive phase of drug testing, involving thousands of volunteer patients at hospital sites scattered around the country and even overseas. In Phase III, researchers monitor long-term drug use for safety and optimum dosage levels. By studying far more patients over a longer period of time than in Phase II studies, they can uncover subtler and more insidious side effects. Over one-fourth of drug candidates pass this hurdle and move on to the FDA review stage. (See Exhibit 5.)

≈ 17 yrs

EXHIBIT 6 FDA Review for Sumatriptan

In October 1991, the FDA advisory committee voted unanimously to recommend approval of sumatriptan, moving it closer to full FDA approval. Although this committee's verdict was nonbinding, a positive recommendation was a sign that the FDA would most likely approve the drug.[1]

For some two years, the FDA and Glaxo researchers communicated with each other to fill in small gaps in the data or to clear up residual issues. In 1993, U.S. market approval for injectable sumatriptan was granted by the FDA (market approval for the oral form would come two years later). Market approval came almost a decade after the discovery of sumatriptan and about 15 years after the initial work of the sumatriptan team.[2]

Drugmakers at Glaxo and elsewhere continued searching for more selective and specific antimigraine compounds to provide patients even greater relief, the ultimate goal being complete cure and prevention of migraine. Driving some of the ongoing drug development research were newer findings that focused on nerve inflammation as opposed to just blood vessel dilation as the cause of migraine. (The contributions of vessel dilation and nerve inflammation to migraine genesis are not mutually exclusive, since one phenomenon most likely influences the other; for instance, even sumatriptan was found to have some effect on nerve inflammation.) Thus, several drug firms started searching other branches of the vast serotonin family for antimigraine activity.

Sumatriptan, however, would provide the yardstick by which future antimigraine compounds would be measured.

---

[1] FDA Committee Discussion, *Script* 1666 (November 6, 1991), p. 20.
[2] Interview with Donna Gutterman, Director of U.S. Medical Affairs, CNS/Anesthesia/Critical Care, Glaxo Wellcome (December 1997).

EXHIBIT 7 Sumatriptan Acting on Serotonin Receptor

(A) Receptors ("Locks") and Neurotransmitters ("keys")

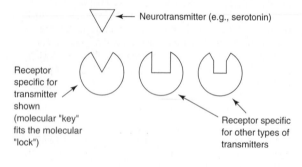

(B) Transmitting Messages via Neurotransmitters

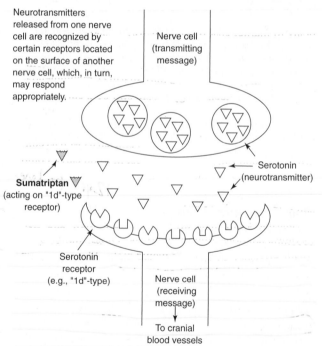

FDA Review (About Two to Three Years)

The NDA (new drug application) represents a tribute to the 20th century pharmaceutical industry's data-generating capacity, with its contents running into hundreds of thousands of pages. The NDA includes data not only on each patient, but also on the company's plans for producing and stocking the drug. Not surprisingly, the FDA committee has historically taken two to three years to review the NDA and make recommendations about marketing the drug. (Fortunately, the trend toward computer-assisted NDAs has already started to reduce this rather long review process.) Often, the FDA and sponsoring drug firms work closely to iron out potential problems with the data or other technical problems.

CASE II-11

Eli Lilly and Company: Drug Development Strategy

Stefan Thomke, Ashok Nimgade, and Paul Pospisil

On a sunny morning in February 1995, Project Manager Bianca Sharma looked out her office window at the Indianapolis skyline and contemplated the critical decisions facing Eli Lilly's R&D team, which was racing to develop a new generation anti-migraine drug. In a few hours, she would present her business recommendations on product development options to Lilly's Project Team Advisory Committee.

Lilly's new drug candidate promised to be unlike any other market entrant; as such, it could be positioned as the first of a new product subclass. One approach for Sharma's team, therefore, might be to field the best possible compound, even if that meant a further delay in market entry since exploring additional compounds would take time. However, not only would every month's delay to market cost revenue, it would also enable prior entrants to consolidate their market positions.

The role of a new technology, combinatorial chemistry, also might be factored into Sharma's recommendations. This new technology would still be a curiosity on the horizon had not two Lilly scientists seen its possibilities for speeding up the product development cycle. At the same time, the technology was untried as well as controversial, and Lilly, should it invest in it too early, could waste millions of dollars and months of research pursuing false leads. At a time of unprecedented market pressures, this was a huge risk.

Sharma knew that the stakes were high and her recommendations important to the choice the Project Team Advisory Committee would make. She once again turned to the data laid out on her desk.

THE PHARMACEUTICAL INDUSTRY IN THE MID-1990S

The worldwide pharmaceutical industry was one of the largest and most profitable of research and manufacturing businesses; by the mid-1990s, annual worldwide pharmaceutical sales were around $250 billion, with roughly 80 percent originating in the industrialized G7 nations. Top blockbuster drugs targeted diseases of particular concern to industrialized nations, such as depression, peptic ulcer disease, hypertension, and cholesterol-reduction. (See Exhibit 1.) These nations' aging population was also expected to provide a boost to the pharmaceutical market.

Being first to market with a new class of therapeutic agents was increasingly crucial for a product to be commercially successful, however. Quite often, the first three drugs introduced within a new product class would together control over 80 percent of the market. At the same time, the process of drug discovery, development, and clinical approval was extremely effort-intensive and expensive. Large pharmaceutical companies spent up to 15–20 percent of sales in R&D. In the United States, as part of an extensive, highly regulated safety approval process, each drug had to pass three phases of clinical trials under the scrutiny of the U.S. Food and Drug Administration (FDA): Phase I, which tested clinical safety, Phase II, which assessed drug efficacy, and Phase III, which tested adverse effects from long-term use (see Exhibit 2). For each successful product the sponsoring drug firm typically spent more than $230 million, with the average time to market being 14.8 years—over twice as long as it took the U.S. space program to get a man on the moon.[1]

In addition, the time required for a pharmaceutical drug to be approved substantially decreased the effective term of its patent protection. Under current law, a patent's term expired 20 years from the time the patent application was filed. (Prior to 1995, patent protection extended 17 years after the patent was issued.) But even with whatever patent protection remained by the time a drug reached the market, 7 out of 10 products failed to return a profit on a company's investment. Fortunately for these firms, sales of only a few products could provide exceptional returns. In the mid-1990s, 14 products had annual sales over $1 billion,[2] enabling profit margins of 15–20 percent. (See Exhibit 3.)

Source: Copyright © 1997 by the President and Fellows of Harvard College. Professor Stefan Thomke, Research Associate Ashok Nimgade, M.D., and Paul Pospisil, Ph.D., prepared this case as the basis for class discussion rather than to illustrate either effective or ineffective handling of an administrative situation.

[1] FDA (1995), "From Test Tube to Patient: New Drug Development in the United States," *FDA Consumer,* Special Issue January; J. DiMassi, R. Hansen, H. Grabowsky, and L. Lasagna (1994), "Cost of Innovation in the Pharmaceutical Industry," *Journal of Health Economics* 10, pp. 107–142.
[2] "World Pharma Firm League," *Marketletter,* July 3, 1995.

EXHIBIT 1   U.S. Pharmaceutical Market by Therapeutic Category, 1994

Drug category	1994 (U.S. $ billions)	2000 estimates (U.S. $ billions)	% Change of market share
Cardiology	15.4 (18%)	13.1 (13%)	(27)
Antibiotics	12.0 (14%)	8.1 (8%)	(42)
Gastrointestinal	11.1 (13%)	10.1 (10%)	(23)
Central nervous system	**6.8 (8%)**	**13.1 (13%)**	**62**
Respiratory	5.1 (6%)	8.1 (8%)	33
Lipid lowering	4.3 (5%)	5.0 (5%)	0
Cancer	4.3 (5%)	7.1 (7%)	40
Diabetes	3.4 (4%)	4.0 (4%)	0
Arthritis	3.4 (4%)	2.0 (2%)	(50)
Hematology	3.4 (4%)	7.1 (7%)	75
Imaging	2.6 (3%)	2.0 (2%)	(50)
Antiviral	2.6 (2%)	3.0 (3%)	100
Thrombotics	2.6 (2%)	2.0 (2%)	0
Immunology	.86 (1%)	2.0 (2%)	100
Osteoporosis	.86 (1%)	4.0 (4%)	300
Other	8.6 (10%)	10.1 (10%)	0
Total	**$85.6 billion (100%)**	**$100.9 billion (100%)**	

Source: Lehman Brothers Pharmaceutical Research, 1996.

Not surprisingly, because of long product development lead times and large marketing costs, combined with high risks, the pharmaceutical industry was dominated by large transnational companies, with the top 20 companies generating 47 percent of total sales.[3] Most major players were U.S. or European multinational pharmaceutical firms such as Merck & Co., Bristol-Myers-Squibb, Glaxo, and Eli Lilly; each had annual sales revenues running in the billions of dollars and employed several thousand employees worldwide. (See Exhibit 4.)

Meanwhile, drugmakers worldwide were facing increased public pressure to reduce prices of most pharmaceuticals. Whereas prior emphasis had been placed on drug safety and efficacy, cost became an additional important factor in the 1990s. In the United States, the rapid growth of managed care organizations and the implementation of cost-containment practices—including price controls, volume discounts, and substitution of cheaper generic products in hospital formularies—had greatly increased competitive pressures. Top pharmaceutical firms also faced substantial loss of dollar market share to generic products because of patent expirations. Within a few months of a drug going off patent, leading firms were often forced to slash prices by 80 percent.

Although pharmaceuticals accounted for only about a tenth of all health care costs in the United States and in many cases reduced need for more costly interventions like surgery, to consumers they represented a highly visible target. Pharmaceutical firms were often depicted as price-gougers, with retirees having to make substantial out-of-pocket payments for pills or AIDS patients spending thousands of dollars a year just for one drug. Given this environment, drugmakers, in order to have their new, higher-priced products included in hospital formularies, had to demonstrate that these products would yield substantial therapeutic and cost benefits over existing ones. According to Martin Haslanger, Ph.D., executive director of Research Technology and president of Sphinx Pharmaceuticals, "The marketplace will only reward innovation. It is no longer rewarding to make incremental improvements."[4]

Drugmakers confronted these market pressures in a variety of ways. At a strategic level, several firms responded by mergers that generated workforce reductions and other cost savings, while other firms invested heavily in, or acquired, innovative biotech companies in hopes of tapping new technologies. For all drugmakers, speeding the drug development cycle became a priority—for every week's delay to market, millions of revenue might be lost. Moreover, since the R&D phase of product development was largely under the internal con-

---

[3] Ibid.

[4] K. Heine, "Sphinx Paves the Way to Discover," *Focus*, Eli Lilly, March 1995.

EXHIBIT 2   Summary of Drug Development in the USA

New drug development in the early 1990s was a costly affair with high failure rates. For each therapeutic drug entering the market, pharmaceutical firms invested more than $230 million (estimates go up to $359 million) and 14.8 years (up from 4.3 years in the 1970s). Estimated costs include out-of-pocket expenses, costs of failed projects, and opportunity costs. A brief outline of the drug development process follows:

BASIC RESEARCH (ABOUT TWO YEARS)

This phase typically started through the initial screening of plants, microorganisms, and other naturally occurring substances to find a "hit" or "lead" compound. In a painstaking iterative process, organic chemists would then make analogues or modifications of existing leads. Although this stage typically cost a firm $30–50 million, it represented a point of great leverage for speeding up a firm's drug development process. Only 40 out of an initial 10,000 compounds might make it to the next stage of preclinical testing.

PRECLINICAL (BIOLOGICAL) SCREENING (ABOUT THREE YEARS)

Preclinical trials, which often overlapped the basic research phase, involved animal testing to assess drug safety and to gather data on biological effects (e.g., absorption, metabolism, and excretion). Only one in four drugs typically made it through this phase to enter human clinical testing as "investigational new drugs" (INDs).

HUMAN CLINICAL TRIALS (ABOUT SIX YEARS)

Investigational new drugs faced the FDA's regulatory hurdles, the most stringent and time-consuming approval process for therapeutic drugs in the world. Total costs for conducting clinical trials topped $200 million, but with increasing proportions of this cost occurring with each of the three successive phases described below.

Phase I Safety Trials (One Year)

In Phase I trials, researchers determined highest tolerated doses, toxicities, and safe ranges in one or two dozen healthy volunteers. This phase also yielded invaluable information on absorption, metabolism, and excretion of the drug in humans.

Phase II Efficacy Trials (Two Years)

Phase II tested efficacy of drug candidates in up to several hundred volunteer patients based at test sites composed of participating hospitals. To ensure statistically relevant data, from this point onward, a portion of the volunteers received the drug while the others received placebos. Roughly one-third of all drug candidates survived Phases I and II.

Phase III Long-Term Efficacy Trials (Three Years)

In the longest and most expensive phase of drug testing, researchers monitored drug use in thousands of volunteer patients for long-term safety, optimum dosage levels, and subtler adverse effects. Only about a fourth of all drug candidates survived Phases I, II, and III and moved on to the FDA review stage.

FDA REVIEW (ABOUT 2–3 YEARS)

Despite a trend toward computer-assisted applications, the hundreds of thousands of pages submitted in the new drug application (NDA) to the FDA represented a tribute to the pharmaceutical industry's data-generating capacity. The NDA included data on each patient, as well as on the company's plans for producing and stocking the drug. The FDA committee took up to three years to review the NDA. Even after approval, however, postmarketing surveillance by the FDA continued. Only one-tenth of all drug candidates entering clinical trials ultimately reached the market.

Sources: J. A. DiMasi (1995), "New Drug Development: Cost, Risk, and Complexity," *Drug Information Journal,* May; FDA (1995), "From Test Tube to Patient: New Drug Development in the United States," *FDA Consumer,* Special Issue, January; Kenneth I. Kaitin and Huub Houben (1995), "Worthwhile Persistence: The Process of New Drug Development," *Odyssey, The Glaxo-Wellcome Journal of Innovation in Healthcare,* June.

trol of the individual company, it represented a powerful leverage point for controlling time and cost. Hence, in an attempt to shorten the drug development cycle, many pharmaceutical firms raced to incorporate emerging breakthrough technologies such as genetic engineering, combinatorial chemistry, and high-throughput screening.

ELI LILLY AND COMPANY

Eli Lilly and Company was founded in Indianapolis, Indiana, in 1876 by Colonel Eli Lilly. A pharmaceutical chemist and Civil War veteran, Colonel Lilly was frustrated by the poor quality of medicines and "sideshow hucksterism" of his time. Over ensuing decades, his company went from a family-run firm to a global corporation: in the mid 1990s, Lilly, operating in 150 countries, was one of the world's largest pharmaceutical companies, with over 25,000 employees and 1994 sales of $5.7 billion.

Through much of the 20th century, Lilly was prominent in the traditional field of antibiotics. In the early 1980s, however, it made news by becoming the first marketer of a genetically engineered product when—through a collaboration with a biotechnology firm—it introduced human insulin. In the late 1980s, Lilly gained further public prominence by developing the innovative

EXHIBIT 3   Top 20 Prescription Drugs by Worldwide Sales, 1994

(Dollars in millions)

Rank 1994	Rank 1993	Product name	Product type	Marketer	World sales	% change from 1993	U.S. sales
1	1	Zantac	Ulcer therapy	Glaxo-Wellcome	$3,663	12	$2,280
2	2	Vasotec/Renitec	Hypertension treatment	Merck	2,185	6	975
3	4	Prilosec/Losec	Ulcer therapy	Astra & Merck	1,904	40	850
4	10	Zovirax	Herpes therapy	Glaxo-Wellcome	1,729	49	444
5	**6**	**Prozac**	**Antidepressant**	**Eli Lilly**	**1,665**	**38**	**1,180**
6	3	Capoten	Hypertension treatment	Bristol-Myers Squibb	1,500	2	581
7	5	Mevacor	Cholesterol reducer	Merck	1,345	3	1,115
8	8	Adalat line	Hypertension/Angina	Bayer	1,300	8	120
9	9	Cipro/Ciproxin	Anti-infective	Bayer	1,300	8	712
10	16	Zocor	Cholesterol reducer	Merck	1,255	39	400
11	11	Voltaren	Anti-arthritic	Ciba	1,192	5	269
12	7	Procardia line	Hypertension/Angina	Pfizer	1,177	(3)	1,177
13	12	Augmentin	Anti-infective	SmithKline Beecham	1,126	(3)	491
14	17	Sandimmune	Immunosuppressive	Sandoz	1,038	7	500
15	14	Cardizem line	Hypertension/Angina	Hoechst Marion	933	2	812
16	18	Rocephin	Anti-infective	Hoffman-La Roche	930	4	413
17	20	Premarin	Estrogen replacement	Wyeth-Ayerst	853	14	723
18	23	Neupogen	Bioresponse modifier	Amgen	829	15	617
19	22	Pepcid/Pepcidine	Ulcer therapy	Merck	820	12	625
20	**15**	**Ceclor**	**Anti-infective**	**Eli Lilly**	**$812**	**(11)**	**394**

Source: Derived from "Top 100 Drugs," *PharmaBusiness*, July 1995, p. 16; and "World Pharma Firm League," *Marketletter*, July 3, 1995.

EXHIBIT 4   Top 20 Firms Active in the Pharmaceutical Industry, 1994

(Dollars in millions, unless noted otherwise)

Company[a]	Total sales	R&D expense	EBIT	Net income	Return on equity (%)	Return on assets (%)	Employees (000s)
(1) Bayer, A. G.	$28,023	$2,050	$2,430	$1,271	11.9%	4.7%	146.7
(2) Ciba-Geigy	16,171	1,578	2,232	1,403	12.0	6.1	84.0
(3) Johnson & Johnson	15,734	1,278	2,867	2,006	28.2	12.8	81.5
(4) Merck & Co.	14,970	1,231	4,633	2,997	26.9	13.7	47.5
(5) Bristol-Myers Squibb	11,984	1,108	2,638	1,842	32.3	14.3	47.7
(6) Sandoz	11,639	1,199	NA	1,272	20.7	8.9	60.3
(7) Hoffman-La Roche	10,816	1,710	3,110	2,098	17.0	8.6	61.4
(8) SmithKline Beecham Plc	9,933	976	1,213	110	12.4	0.9	55.4
(9) Abbott Laboratories	9,156	964	2,228	1,517	37.5	17.8	49.5
(10) American Home Products Corp.	8,966	817	2,145	1,528	35.9	7.1	74.0
(11) Glaxo	8,484	1,287	2,826	1,955	25.2	16.1	47.4
(12) Pfizer Inc.	8,281	1,139	2,003	1,298	30.0	11.7	40.8
(13) Hoechst Celanese Corp.	7,794	313	(55)	186	5.9	2.3	29.2
(14) Tekeda Chemical Industries	7,778	677	1,124	518	7.7	4.5	11.0
(15) Eli Lilly and Company	**5,712**	**897**	**1,828**	**1,286**	**22.1**	**8.2**	**24.9**
(16) Sankyo Co. Ltd.	5,575	477	887	395	11.3	5.8	NA
(17) Schering-Plough	4,657	620	1,281	922	58.6	21.3	21.2
(18) Rhone-Poulenc Rorer	4,175	611	547	341	21.0	7.6	22.1
(19) Wellcome Plc—ADS	3,096	542	1,098	632	22.1	14.4	17.6
(20) Marion Merrell Dow Inc	$3,060	$462	$632	$438	20.5%	10.6%	9.4

[a]Some firms have substantial business activity outside pharmaceuticals which is included in these figures.
NA = not available.
Sources: Standard & Poor's; Compustat, Global Vantage.

antidepression drug fluoxetine (widely known by the brand name Prozac®).

By the 1990s, Lilly maintained major research divisions across a variety of treatment areas, including central nervous system disease, inflammatory disease, cardiovascular disease, cancer, and endocrinology (which dealt with hormonal diseases like diabetes and growth hormone deficiency). Its products ranged from the highly promising drug Zyprexa® for treating schizophrenia to Gemzar® for treating pancreatic cancer. For all its success, however, Lilly, like most other pharmaceutical firms, could not easily predict its next blockbuster. (See Exhibit 5.)

Nevertheless, Lilly had remained an industry leader through its 120-year history. By the early 1990s the company was expanding into allied businesses such as diagnostics and animal products. But it also faced high organizational costs and a dwindling product pipeline. An $11 billion drop in company stock value, from March 1991 to June 1993, signaled a loss of confidence in Lilly's competitiveness.

In 1993, under a newly appointed CEO, R. L. Tobias, Lilly sold its medical device and diagnostics unit in order to focus on vertically integrating drug discovery, development, production, and distribution. The new management slashed Lilly's workforce by 10 percent

EXHIBIT 5A   Eli Lilly and Company 1994 Financial Highlights

(Dollars in millions, except per share data)

	1994	1993	% change
Net sales	$5,712	$5,199	10%
R&D expenses	839	755	11
Income from continuing operations	1,185	465	155
Net income	1,286	480	168
Earnings per share:			
Income from continuing operations	4.10	1.58	159
Net income	4.45	1.63	173
As adjusted[a]			
Net income	1,398	1,336	5
Net income per share	4.84	4.54	7
Dividends paid per share	2.5	2.42	3
Capital expenditures	577	634	(9%)
Income from continuing operations as a percent of shares	20.7%	8.9%	
Return on assets	11.8%	5.2%	
Return on shareholders' equity	25.9%	10.2%	

[a]For 1994, reflects the result of operations without the impact of acquisitions (including Sphinx) and product recall.
For 1993, reflects results of operations without impact of restructuring.
Source: Eli Lilly and Company.

EXHIBIT 5B   Eli Lilly and Company Major Product Sales

(Dollars in millions)

Drug	Category 1994 sales	1994 sales	% of total Lilly sales	Launch year
Prozac	Antidepressant	$1,665	29%	1988
Ceclor	Antibiotic	812	14	1979
Humulin	Diabetes	665	12	1980
Axid	Gastrointestinal	487	9	1988
Vancocin	Antibiotic	249	4	1958
Humatrope	Growth Hormone	226	4	1987
Keflex	Antibiotic	140	2	1971
Lorabid	Antibiotic	$ 129	2%	1992

Source: Eli Lilly and Company.

EXHIBIT 6   Eli Lilly and Company—Organization

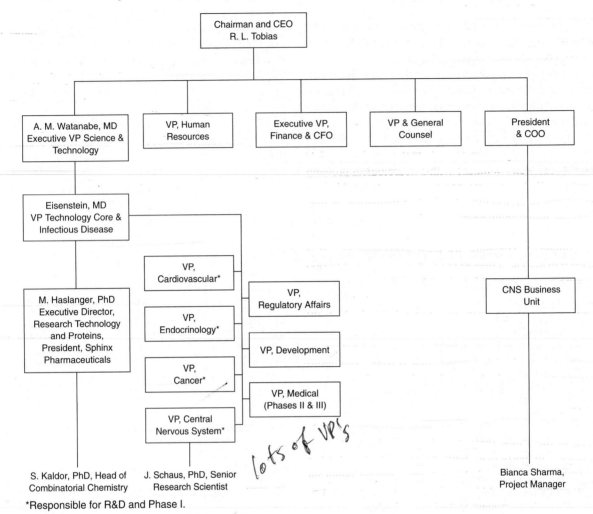

*Responsible for R&D and Phase I.

and acquired several key businesses and technologies that strengthened the core pharmaceutical business. The company also planned to restructure its research efforts to refill the product pipeline. As a result of these steps as well as several promising new products, Lilly's stock price substantially rose. (See Exhibit 6.)

INNOVATIONS IN THE NEW DRUG DEVELOPMENT PROCESS

Throughout history, drug discovery relied on the observations and experiments of naturalists and herbalists. Even in the 1990s, a fourth of all medical compounds, including aspirin and the widely used heart drug digitalis, derived originally from plant extracts.

Synthetic chemistry, whose roots lay in the 19th century, marked the first modern revolution in drug development. It made possible the development of compounds never before seen in nature, including more powerful and potent variations of naturally occurring compounds (such as the cephalosporin antibiotics that were variations of the naturally occurring penicillin). Synthetic chemistry also aided in the patenting of drugs and as such helped spawn the multinational drug industry.

Through much of the 20th century, however, drug discovery remained a labor-intensive process relying on inspiration, hard work, and luck. Metaphorically, drugs were molecular-sized keys that had to fit "locks," or targets (called receptors); chemists were the locksmiths. Indeed, they were effectively blind, or at least semiblind, locksmiths, for they had to make up thousands of different keys to find the one that matched. Doing so entailed synthesizing compounds, one at a time, which typically required 7 to 10 days and $5,000–$10,000 per compound. For each drug reaching the market firms spent an average of 124 chemist-years on synthesizing starting compounds,[5] a critical path activity. The time spent on synthesis represented a place of high leverage for speeding up the drug development cycle.

Newly synthesized molecular keys were tested by biologists, typically using animals that served as models for a disease (e.g., a mouse with a neurological problem similar to Parkinsonism). Most compounds would show no activity or be too toxic for further evaluation. A few, however, might show promise, and chemists would modify these "lead compounds" until a good clinical candidate emerged. Typically, for each successful drug that made it to market, a firm began with an average of 10,000 starting compounds. Of these, only 1,000 would make it to more extensive *in vitro* trials (i.e., outside living organisms in settings such as a test tube), of which 20 would be tested even more extensively *in vivo* (i.e., in the body of a living organism such as a mouse) before 10 compounds made it to human clinical trials. The entire process represented a long and costly commitment, with the human trials closely monitored by the government.

The next major revolutions in drug development, *genetic engineering* and *rational drug discovery,* crystallized in the 1980s through a deeper understanding of biology—in particular, how drugs worked and what receptors they targeted. Now drugs—Prozac being an early example—could be made by combining serendipity with working models of the human body.

With these revolutions, industry experts expected the R&D process to shift from a random screening approach toward a "rational" drug discovery process—a shift tantamount to replacing a shotgun with a viewfinder-equipped gun. Yet scientists still could not make accurate enough predictions about drug–receptor interactions, and drug discovery continued to remain a tedious, labor-intensive process, generating and then examining hundreds or thousands of related compounds. Although many drug firms had, over the decades, built libraries of hundreds of thousands of compounds, they had barely scratched the surface of the potential molecular diversity present on our planet.

Just as locksmiths could make thousands of differing keys based on just one template, so too could theoretical chemists envision creating hundreds of thousands or even millions of derivatives (or analogues) based around a relatively simple compound such as penicillin. Because of this staggering molecular diversity, drug makers tended to be uneasy, feeling that their particular drug on the market might by no means be the best, and that a rival firm would pluck out another, far better drug from the universe of related molecules—and it would eventually corner the market.

By the late 1980s, several biologists and chemists hoped that recent advances in synthetic chemistry, robotics, and information systems could tap this rich molecular diversity and allow for yet another major revolution in drug discovery: *combinatorial chemistry* (often shortened to "combichem") and its allied branch, *high-throughput screening.*

Combinatorial chemistry enabled a large collection, or library, of related chemical compounds to be quickly generated simultaneously. Instead of making one compound at a time, variations were created around the backbone of a basic molecular structure. With just a few building blocks chemists could create a large, diverse set of molecules just as locksmiths could make thousands of keys from one template using just a dozen different shaped cuts. (See Exhibit 7.) With the molecule serotonin, for example, up to several millions of related molecules could be generated—a staggering feat to accomplish manually.

The human body, in essence, was a master of combinatorial chemistry (and high-throughput screening), churning out over a trillion different antibodies (specialized proteins that help neutralize bacteria, toxins, or other invaders) by shuffling around different molecular components. In the laboratory, however, combinatorial chemistry presented a major difficulty: many processes involved in drug synthesis were not routine and required individual adjustments by skilled chemists. Likewise, the vital step of screening presented a major challenge. Potential drug molecules were traditionally tested, or screened, in live animals—a venture fraught with logistical difficulties, high expense, and considerable statistical variation. Using traditional screens, drug makers could hardly manage to sift through their own historical libraries of compounds, let alone the unprecedented volumes of compounds generated by combinatorial chemistry.

Given this slow pace of screening, scientists would often jump on early leads and become invested in them

---

[5] R. G. Halliday, S. R. Walker, and C. E. Lumley, *Journal of Pharmaceutical Medicine* 2 (1992), pp. 139–154.

EXHIBIT 7 **Principles of Combinatorial Chemistry**

Combinatorial chemistry is an emerging technology for generating a large collection, or library, of related chemical compounds rapidly, instead of having to make one compound at a time. This allows for creating variations around the backbone of a basic molecular structure. With just a few building blocks chemists can create a large, diverse set of molecules just as locksmiths can create thousands of keys from one template using just a dozen different shaped cuts.

Two major combinatorial chemistry systems—split-and-mix and parallel synthesis—came into wide usage. In split-and-mix synthesis, illustrated below, chemists synthesize compounds on surfaces of small beads. In each successive step, different beads are recombined and partitioned into different vessels. To each vessel, the next building block is added, and the process continues until the desired number of compounds has been created. Sensitive detection techniques can take advantage of small built-in differences between the starting beads to fish out the more promising combinations.

In parallel synthesis, different compounds are synthesized in separate vessels arrayed into columns and rows. No remixing of compounds occurs. Although this method yields fewer compounds, it yields higher purity of compounds.

The split-and-mix method works as follows (see table): in **Round 1**, different polymer beads are reacted with compound A in vessel 1, B in vessel 2, and C in vessel 3. These beads are then mixed together and then split into three vessels. In **Round 2**, building block D is added to Vessel 1, E to Vessel 2, and F to Vessel 3. Once more, these compounds are mixed and split again. In **Round 3**, building block G is added to Vessel 1, H to Vessel 2, and I to Vessel 3. Note that newly added building blocks are bolded. With each consecutive round, the number of compounds increases by a factor of 3.

Combinatorial Chemistry (the "Split-and-Mix" Method)*

Round	Vessel 1	Vessel 2	Vessel 3	Number of compounds
1	**A**	**B**	**C**	$3 (= 3^1)$
2	A**D**, B**D**, C**D**	A**E**, B**E**, C**E**	A**F**, B**F**, C**F**	$9 (= 3^2)$
3	AD**G**, BD**G**, CD**G**	AD**H**, BD**H**, CD**H**	AD**I**, BD**I**, CD**I**	$27 (= 3^3)$
	AE**G**, BE**G**, CE**G**	AE**H**, BE**H**, CE**H**	AE**I**, BE**I**, CE**I**	$27 (= 3^3)$
	AF**G**, BF**G**, CF**G**	AF**H**, BF**H**, CF**H**	AF**I**, BF**I**, CF**I**	
...	...	...	...	...
K	...	...	...	$(= 3^K)$

*S. Thomke, E. von Hippel, and R. Franke, "Modes of Experimentation: An Innovative Process—and Competitive—Variable," *Research Policy* 27 (1998).

---

at the expense of other promising new leads. The challenge, therefore, was to develop test tube–based screening methodologies amenable to automation. As Stephen Kaldor, a Lilly scientist, explained, "We needed a system that allowed us to evaluate and prioritize our leads simultaneously, rather than letting the clock decide which molecules we would work up."[6]

High-throughput screening was aimed at solving this problem. Using this technology, high-speed robots would perform a series of biological tests, or assays, on all members of a chemical library virtually simultaneously. A simple biochemical response based on the fit between a potential drug and its receptor could be visualized simply—for instance, through a color change—and thus could be used to pick out compounds that showed the desired activity.

Obviously, the greater the number of compounds generated through combinatorial chemistry, the greater the demand placed on screening. Thus, generating a library of millions of compounds could outstrip the capacity of a screen capable of processing only a thousand compounds a week. One popular strategy chemists experimented with to get around this dilemma was restricting combinatorial diversity to representatives from major families of a compound's analogues. In essence, this was like examining major branches and subbranches of a tree, rather than examining individual leaves.

For many traditional chemists in 1994, however, the larger issue centered around proving the merit of combinatorial chemistry. Although it looked promising in theory, it worked only for certain groups of compounds. Moreover, no new drug candidates had been uncovered by this new and untried technique.

---

[6] K. Heine, "Sphinx Paves the Way to Discover," *Focus,* Eli Lilly, March 1995.

COMBINATORIAL CHEMISTRY AT LILLY

The Technology Core Group of the research and development area of Lilly functioned as a separate division that supported the company's various research activities. In the early 1990s, this group recognized the potential promise of combinatorial chemistry and high-throughput screening and realized that other pharmaceutical firms were planning to acquire biotech firms with leading edge expertise in these areas.

Under direction of chemist Stephen Kaldor, Ph.D., Lilly started developing capabilities in combinatorial chemistry. Kaldor was charged with creating libraries, or collections, of compounds that could then be tested within the organization for therapeutic properties. In early March 1994, he gave a well-attended presentation on his team's work that helped disseminate knowledge of combinatorial chemistry through the organization.

In September 1994, as a vote of confidence in the new technology, Lilly acquired a financially strapped biotechnology firm named Sphinx Pharmaceuticals (of Durham–Research Triangle Park in North Carolina, and Cambridge, Massachusetts), which had leading expertise in combinatorial chemistry and high-throughput screening and boasted experts such as its vice president of research Michael Pavia, Ph.D. But it would be another year or more before Sphinx's capabilities could be integrated into Lilly's drug discovery division. At the same time, Kaldor's group made some remarkable progress. Normally, a Lilly chemist was able to synthesize one compound per week, and Lilly had a screening capacity of 50 compounds per week. By the end of 1994, Kaldor's group, using combinatorial chemistry and high-throughput screening, increased the capacity to screen compounds for biological activity around eight-fold, and the capacity to synthesize new compounds by a factor of 120.

DRUG DISCOVERY FOR CENTRAL NERVOUS SYSTEM (CNS) DISEASES

In the mid-1990s, roughly one billion people, or one-fifth of the world's people, suffered from a neurological or psychiatric disorder at one point in their lifetime. World Bank estimates revealed that central nervous system (CNS) diseases accounted for roughly 10 percent of all lifetime years lost to disease. Even "less severe" psychiatric conditions—for instance, clinical depression, severe insomnia (sleeplessness), and migraine, each of which affected over 10 percent of the population—could take a severe toll on society. For instance, depression

might predispose people to suicide, a point poignantly illustrated by the demise of the wife of Lilly CEO Randall Tobias. Because of similar tragedies, according to Tobias in a sobering journal interview, "we're spending over $1 billion a year in research and development. We don't know all the answers—and we need to keep going."[7]

Fortunately, modern medications had the potential to boost quality of life so dramatically that patients might end up taking medications regularly for years, with, for example, a depressive patient spending up to $25 a week for a daily Prozac regimen. This, of course, was a boon for drug makers in the small but growing CNS market, which had 1994 worldwide sales of $11.1 billion (80 percent originating in G7 nations).

Many CNS diseases were thought to result from imbalances of neurochemical agents (neurotransmitters) that transmitted signals between nerves. The number of active neurotransmitters normally present at any time was intricately controlled by biochemical mechanisms for production, storage, release, and rapid degradation of these agents. Scientists postulated that biochemical machinery dysfunctions leading to altered concentrations of certain neurotransmitters led to conditions ranging from panic disorder to obsessive compulsive disorder to depression.

Different neurotransmitters were known to activate different receptors just as different keys might open up different doorways. (See Exhibit 8.) Not surprisingly, various classes of neurotransmitters, such as dopamine, norepinephrine, and serotonin, were associated with differing diseases. Serotonin, for example, was associated with a variety of conditions ranging from depression to insomnia to aggression to migraine. Its wide-ranging effects in the body were a consequence of at least a dozen known types of receptors (molecular locks) in locations as varied as the digestive system and the nervous system where serotonin could act.

The serotonin family of molecules and receptors in the nervous system would play a large role in the fortunes of Lilly. Lilly's first billion dollar blockbuster antidepressant drug, Prozac, launched in 1988, very *selectively* boosted levels of serotonin to exert its therapeutic effects. Prior antidepressants, in contrast, had undesirable side-effects such as sedation, anxiety, and dry mouth because they nonselectively increased levels of several different neurotransmitters in addition to serotonin.

---

[7] "Lilly Rides a Mood Elevator," *Business Week,* November 11, 1996, p. 63.

try on existing drug?

EXHIBIT 8   Receptors and Neurotransmitters (Simplified Illustration)

(A) Receptors ("Locks") and Neurotransmitters

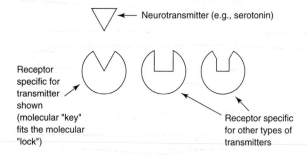

(B) Transmitting Messages via Neurotransmitters

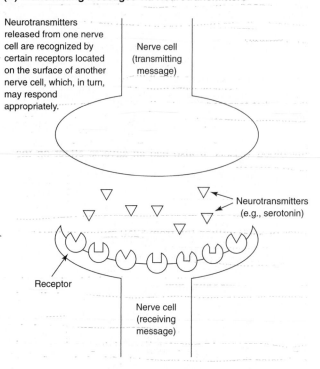

Prozac grew to become the world's fifth best-selling drug in 1994, its sales accounting for over a fourth of Lilly's revenues. (See Exhibits 3 and 5.) Leveraging on this success, Lilly's CNS research division grew to roughly a third of all company research efforts. The aggressive emergence of other direct competitors to Prozac, which itself would come off patent in 2003, lent urgency to Lilly's CNS projects. Even if Lilly could not produce another blockbuster such as Prozac, it needed other solid hits.

Lilly turned once more to serotonin.

LILLY'S MIGRAINE PROJECT

> *I cannot describe the pain because it was so severe, but you might imagine how it would feel if someone hammered a sharp nail into your eye and out your temple. The pain affected the entire side of my head, even causing me to vomit. To curb the pain, my doctor gave me an injection which only put me to sleep.*
> —Description of a migraine sufferer[8]

Migraine, a French word derived from the Greek *hemicrania,* referred to pain involving half the head at a time. Migraine afflicted 12 percent of the population, with a 3:1 preponderance in women; it was characterized by unilateral pulsating headaches often severe enough to restrict physical and mental activity. Historians of medicine speculated that visual disturbances experienced during migraines inspired Charles Dodgson (writing under the pseudonym Lewis Carroll) to describe various physical distortions his heroine Alice experienced in Wonderland.[9]

Traditional migraine therapies ranged from compresses to biofeedback to narcotic painkillers to tranquilizers. Some therapies dated back centuries: ancient Egyptians employed tight compresses around the scalp. Most therapeutic efforts focused on a theory, dating to the 1930s, that dilation of blood vessels in the lining of the brain caused migraine. It was only in the 1980s that scientists suspected that nerve inflammation involving the neurotransmitter serotonin played a role. By the

---

[8] http://www.painclinic.com/treatment.htm, 1996.

[9] L. A. Rolak, "Literary Neurologic Syndromes: The Alice in Wonderland Syndrome," *Archives of Neurology* 46 (1992), p. 353.

early 1990s, two classes of therapies existed: those directed at prophylaxis (with expected 1996 worldwide sales of $200 million) and therapeutics directed at treating acute attacks (with expected 1996 worldwide sales of $1.5 billion).

Lilly scientists hoped to capitalize on their expertise in serotonin research to find a drug for acute attacks of migraine. The stakes were high. The only recent drug on the market targeted specifically at migraine was Glaxo-Wellcome's sumatriptan (Imitrex®). Imitrex, launched in 1992, was a mildly effective drug that acted by constricting blood vessels; it also had an adverse effect on the heart's vessels, thereby limiting its use in many patients. In addition, the effects of Imitrex were very short lived for most patients. Yet Imitrex enjoyed almost 75 percent of the acute migraine market, with projected 1996 annual sales of $800 million (up from $250 million in 1993).

Many scientists, including those at Lilly, felt that the makers of Imitrex had followed the wrong path by trying to find a compound that constricted blood vessels (known as vasoconstriction). While Imitrex was believed to constrict blood vessels by mimicking serotonin, it affected a number of different serotonin subtypes, including the serotonin 1d receptor. Several drug makers raced to develop therapies that targeted the 1d subclass of serotonin receptors.

Lilly researchers, however, were not convinced that, of the variety of serotonin subtypes Imitrex was known to affect, the 1d receptor was involved in its antimigraine activity. By 1991, Synaptic Pharmaceutical Corporation (Paramus, New Jersey), Lilly's collaborator, had found (cloned) a new serotonin receptor subtype, the serotonin 1f receptor. Synaptic's scientists also demonstrated that Imitrex had affinity for the 1f receptor. Lilly and Synaptic scientists theorized that it was the serotonin 1f receptor which was specifically involved in migraine. In effect, they potentially held the biochemical anti-migraine lock (receptor) and now needed to find the right key.

This was no small task, for chemists could envision well over a million different variations of serotonin, any of which could prove the right key. The logical place to start looking, however, was in the 1,000 or so serotonin-like compounds in Lilly's extensive decades-old collection of 250,000 compounds.

From 1991 to early 1994, spearheaded by senior chemists John Schaus, Ph.D., and James Audia, Ph.D., along with scientists David Nelson, Ph.D., and Lee Phebus, Ph.D., in Lilly's Serotonin Working Group, researchers started out screening a few serotonin-like compounds weekly but later screened up to 20–30 com-

pounds per week from Lilly's serotonin collection.[10] By March 1994, out of over 1,000 previously synthesized serotonin-like compounds, one particularly good lead had been found. In addition, Lilly's experiments in which lab animals were administered these lead compounds showed further promise of the 1f serotonin receptors as treatment targets for migraine without the need for inducing vasoconstriction.

But the work was not over yet. Schaus explained this "lead identification" stage of drug discovery:

> In order to find a molecule that interacts with the target, you need to look in a systematic, iterative way. Some analogue of the initial, starting "key" will work, but is not likely to be potent or a good compound . . . [although] at least it is a good starting point.

Using traditional methods of creating derivatives, researchers found a better compound, named *LY329511*. In the iterative process of drug discovery, this now became the current lead against which further drug candidates would have to be tested. According to Schaus, LY329511 was:

> More than satisfactory with good affinity [for the receptor], activity, moderate selectivity [i.e., activity for that receptor alone], and oral activity, with moderate duration of effect. . . . There was a lot of excitement about taking it into clinicals. But we didn't know much about toxicology, and we hadn't explored other chemical modifications. We wanted to make another 100 derivatives—this might realistically take up to a year.

COMBINATORIAL CHEMISTRY AND LILLY'S MIGRAINE PROJECT

Fortunately, Schaus recalled fellow Lilly chemist Stephen Kaldor's March seminar on combinatorial chemistry. Both had obtained their chemistry Ph.D.s at Harvard, but at different times. Schaus, senior to Kaldor by several years, had originally attended the seminar because "Stephen is very bright. You want to follow what he's doing because it's sure to be interesting." Although Lilly's expertise in combinatorial chemistry still lagged behind that of specialized biotech firms, it was Kaldor whom he telephoned to say:

---

[10] This could be considered a "medium-throughput screen," and it contrasted favorably with technology available at the time of discovery of Prozac, when only one compound could be screened per week in a screening process involving crude rat brain extracts.

I greatly enjoyed your presentation and feel it may pertain to one of our serotonin projects. We are under time pressure to get an anti-migraine compound into clinical trials and, fortunately, already have a good "hit." We have started to generate analogues of this lead compound but I am intrigued about using combinatorial chemistry to explore other leads. The last thing I want to do, however, is go down a path not well thought out and which will need a lot of fixing later on.

In midsummer 1994, Schaus and Kaldor sat in the Contemplative Garden in the central courtyard of a large research building, an area where scientists often gathered for informal meetings, and discussed how they might collaborate. "I was delighted that John [Schaus] was willing to try our new technology for punching out analogues for his leads," Kaldor explained later. "But we were still working out bugs in our system; we were still interfacing extensive instrumentation and robotics with reproducible small-scale chemistry." The extent to which they should use combinatorial chemistry versus traditional chemistry to create new derivatives was difficult to decide. As an initial pilot effort, however, Kaldor agreed to make some 30–40 compounds, study the results, modify the search to make another 30–40 compounds, and continue in this iterative fashion. Traditional chemistry would be used at critical points.

The assay results on the first set of compounds showed that efforts should be focused on one subclass of derivatives. It was in the second batch of combichem compounds that they knew they had made a significant finding. A number of compounds showed significantly higher potency than LY329511. Detailed testing of these new compounds demonstrated that one of them, LY334370, was an improvement over LY329511. Importantly, it lacked the vasoconstricting adverse effects seen in the previous compound.

The company's philosophy of R&D management supported this ad hoc collaboration. As explained by Jim White, Ph.D., director of neural science research, "There's a lot of serendipity in science. We can't lead science. Historically, Lilly doesn't hire chemists to fill jobs. We left an open playing field in which Kaldor felt empowered to think." Lilly had created an R&D environment that attracted scientists from top universities; several Lilly scientists had studied under Nobel laureates.

But as word of this unusual collaboration spread through the company, even support from other superiors such as Ben Laguzza, Ph.D., director of neuroscience chemistry research, and Richard DiMarchi, Ph.D., vice president of endocrinology, could not shield the two scientists from criticism. According to Bill Heath, director of Target Validation and Screen Enablement:

Schaus came under heavy criticism. People felt he was engaging in "voodoo science," and that the collaboration would divert valuable screening capacity. Schaus and Kaldor were gutsy, taking a big gamble. Even the concept of high-throughput screening was met with skepticism. Few at Lilly believed we could collapse three years of screening into three months or even less. It's very easy to stop something you don't believe in.

"Traditional chemists saw combinatorial chemistry as a threat to their jobs," according to Laguzza. Although going from traditional to combinatorial chemistry might be crudely likened to going from handcrafting to a production line, Kaldor noted:

Combinatorial chemistry does not replace the wisdom or experience of conventional chemists. The tension centers around, instead, in how much we "subjugate" traditional medicinal chemistry to have it supply us intermediates. . . . much glory, after all, comes from the final product.

September 1994 witnessed indirect support for combinatorial chemistry in the form of Lilly's acquisition of Sphinx. Unfortunately, Sphinx's capabilities would not be able to be tapped for the migraine project since up to a year would be required to integrate its capabilities. (The two companies employed differing protocols for preparing materials for the screening process.)

The same month, however, also witnessed a broadside to the Kaldor-Schaus collaboration during a seminar Schaus presented on his research. The data on identifying potential antimigraine serotonin compounds were well received until Schaus showed work involving combinatorial chemistry. Since combinatorial chemistry–generated compounds were only 80–90 percent pure (as opposed to almost 100 percent purity for conventional syntheses), several audience members questioned the scientific value of the combinatorial chemistry data. Could promising signs of activity in some of the combinatorial chemistry–generated compounds, after all, be simply due to impurities?

Fortunately, Schaus could present favorable comparisons of studies with the same compounds synthesized via both traditional and combinatorial approaches. But this did not spare him from further criticism along purely logistical lines. Some argued he distracted the team's main efforts by testing an unproved technology. Others felt these experiments overloaded the company's biological screening assay, which was geared only for volumes generated by traditional approaches. But Schaus argued that "the benefits over the longer term of being able to synthesize many more compounds at once would far outweigh the extra time and effort over the short term."

Market-constricting?
non- to vessels

As Lilly scientists drew battle lines over combinatorial chemistry, Lilly managers prepared to debate decision choices in bringing an anti-migraine compound to clinical trials.

DIFFICULT CHOICES: THE PROJECT TEAM ADVISORY COMMITTEE (PTAC) MEETING

Migraine project manager Bianca Sharma, who held an M.B.A. as well as an advanced degree in biochemistry, looked forward with anticipation to the PTAC (pronounced "pee-tack") meeting, which would be dedicated primarily to the migraine project. The committee typically met for several hours each month and recommended whether (or how) compounds should go into clinical trials. The PTAC comprised some 20 high-level scientists and managers, including the president and VPs of Lilly Research Laboratories. Projects were voted on through an anonymous electronic scoring system, with the chairman, Dr. Douglas Morton, responsible for breaking deadlocks.

From the research scientist's viewpoint, the PTAC served primarily as a senior scientific peer review. For each project, it reviewed issues of safety as ascertained from animal studies, basic biology, and preclinical pharmacology (did the drug seem efficacious in animal models?) and chemistry (given constraints of time and money, had the company adequately surveyed all leads to field the best clinical candidate?). From the corporate strategist's viewpoint, however, PTAC also assessed market opportunities.

Representing the CNS business unit, Sharma's task was to present business recommendations on drug development options for the migraine project. Preparing for PTAC meetings, she had found, was an interdisciplinary effort that helped clarify issues of resource requirements and allocations. Sharma now mentally rehearsed what she felt were the three key business issues for her PTAC presentation.

Issue 1: Time to Market

In reviewing her spreadsheet model of market projections based on data from marketing (see Exhibit 9), Sharma realized that each month's delay to market would result not only in revenue losses, but also in opportunity cost from allowing prior serotonin-based entrants to consolidate their grasp on the market. Although time to market was of essence, it appeared that Lilly would most likely be the fourth or fifth serotonin-like compound to reach the market. But it would be the first serotonin **1f**-based compound. For this reason, some strategists ar-

gued, it was critical to take the time required to field the best possible compound. But how much of a delay was tolerable?

Sharma recalled a discussion with senior corporate strategist Amy Velasquez who commented on the new competitive challenges: "In the old days we could hold back our lead compound. Not now; today's market is more competitive and calls for 'hustle.'" Velasquez added, "If we had a backup, we could put it on hold until we see anything that creates a hitch. Then the backup could be turned on quickly." Unfortunately, no backup existed now.

On the other hand, Martin Haslanger had made a theoretical argument for holding back:

2 philosophies

> Sometimes it's almost better to be number two—a second fast-follower. The list of the top 100–200 best-selling drugs includes many good fast followers. The chances of getting to market in first place can be near zero because of the long series of low-probability steps involved in product development. For example, with Prozac, we went through some minefields to get to the market first. We almost did not make it at many points. Then, when we faced rough patches, our competitors were able to play up their products, to our detriment.

Issue 2: Diversity of Leads

Teece article

The second issue was intimately linked to the first. If Lilly were competing with unlimited time and resources on its side, it could take several similar leads simultaneously through the astronomically expensive clinical trials. But as Amy Velasquez had pointed out, "It is hard to justify two similar compounds racing down the track! The support infrastructure is enormous." Even if one lead were held back in favor of another, Haslanger noted certain intangible costs because "the following group will lose a sense of urgency." Like other drug makers, therefore, Lilly simply had to send the best available compound candidate through the maze of clinical trials. And candidate LY334370, as Sharma recalled, was a significant improvement over the already promising LY329511.

Thus, diversity of leads was extremely important but would have to be explored earlier in the drug discovery process. Combinatorial chemistry could make its biggest impact here. Exploring further molecular diversity would also help broaden patent claims.

Issue 3: Traditional or Combinatorial Chemistry?

Combinatorial chemistry promised to dramatically boost the ability to create, and thus explore, related compounds.

PART TWO: DESIGN AND IMPLEMENTATION OF TECHNOLOGY STRATEGY: AN EVOLUTIONARY PERSPECTIVE

EXHIBIT 9   Memo–Migraine Marketing Analysis

Memorandum

ATT'N: Bianca Sharma, Migraine Project Manager
FROM: Anh Thieu, Marketing
DATE: June 17, 1994

Here is some information excerpted from our marketing report on our migraine project:

Baseline projection: Based on current market data as well as prior experience, our projection is that our serotonin 1f-based compound will hit the market in 2001, and gradually build up market share by 2005 to its peak $300- to $500-million annual sales. (This is assuming that our product is indeed seen as more efficacious than 1d-based compounds.) Our models indicate that our drug could expect to remain at its peak levels for roughly another three years until competition would slowly erode market share to a negligible amount about two years before its patent expiration in 2012. (We discount revenue streams at 13% per annum.) Below are sundry items that went into our projection models:

- On average, each migraineur experiences 10–12 attacks per year, with mean duration of 9–24 hours. The frequency of attacks is greatest in the age group of 35–45 years. Only 55% of migraineurs sought medical treatment, and of these, only half were correctly identified as migraine. Thus, we feel that patient-education and physician-education could considerably expand the market for migraine. In fact, based on Gallup polls, perhaps about 40% of nonconsulters could be motivated to seek treatment. In this case, pharmaceutical firms can perhaps increase the total market size for new (serotonin-based) therapies by 3–4 times into a $3- to $4-billion market.
- Currently, two classes of migraine therapies exist: those directed at prophylaxis (which have expected 1996 worldwide sales of $200 million) and therapeutics directed at treating acute attacks (expected 1996 worldwide sales of $1.5 billion).
- Annual sales of our competitor Sumatriptan (Glaxo's Imitrex) since 1992 launch (note that only 10% of migraineurs are treated by sumatriptan):

Year	Sales ($ millions)	Sales growth (%)
1992	100	—
1993	250	175
1994	400	60
1995	525	40 (projected)
1996	800	50 (projected)

- In terms of migraineur preferences, 70% felt avoidance of cardiovascular adverse effects (such as those associated with sumatriptan) were important. Only 28% felt reduction in cost compared to sumatriptan was important.

With best regards, Anh

P.S. I am also including below some information on our marketing experience with Prozac, in case you find it interesting.

Market experience of Prozac—market share (percent):

Year	Prozac	Zoloft	Paxil	Desyrel	Pamelor
1990	22.6%	—	—	3.0%	8.3%
1991	18.9	—	—	2.5	9.6
1992	16.4	5.3	—	1.7	7.2
1993	14.7	10.0	4.3	1.1	2.3
1994	16.7%	11.6%	7.4%	0.8%	1.1%

Note: Prozac, Zoloft, and Paxil are from the new class of antidepressants ("Selective Serotonin Reuptake Inhibitors"); Desyrel and Pamelor are older antidepressants. Zoloft and Paxil were launched in 1992 and 1993, respectively.
Source: J. R. Brinemeyer et al., "Doctor's Orders," *New Rx Trends,* September Industry Report, November 7, 1995, Lehman Brothers.

A Lilly chemist could now create orders of magnitude more compounds in a given time period. Yet many Lilly scientists viewed the new technology with considerable mistrust, as it still had many unresolved problems and had never before been used to get a compound to clinical trials.

With the above issues in mind, Sharma next reviewed predictions various corporate experts had made about the impact of combinatorial chemistry on clinical trial outcomes (see Exhibit 10). In September 1994, she had polled six experts within the firm for their estimates about how combichem could affect chances of getting a drug candidate through clinical trials. At the same time, she asked them how these chances might impact time-to-market. Two of the experts she polled, Drs. John Lee and Edward Pan, were senior scientists working closely with the incipient Kaldor-Schaus collaboration; another two, Drs. Beverly Bourell and John Wecker, were traditional

EXHIBIT 10   Expert Estimates for Migraine Project

Participants (all participants had first-hand knowledge of the migraine project):
Dr. John Lee, Senior Scientist, Combichem Group
Dr. Edward Pan, Senior Scientist, Combichem Group
Dr. Beverly Bourell, Senior Scientist, Central Nervous System
Dr. John Wecker, Senior Scientist, Central Nervous System
Dr. Clare Pimentel, Senior Prozac Product Manager
Mr. Ashley Peck, Director of Corporate Marketing

Scenario 1: "If we bring our current lead migraine compound—'a bird in the hand'—to market with no further lead optimization, what do you feel is the chance of passing clinicals?"

Expert	Months delay	Chance of passing clinicals
Lee	0	8%
Pan	0	9
Bourell	0	12
Wecker	0	11
Pimentel	0	10
Peck	0	10%
Average		**10%**
Standard deviation		1.4

Scenario 2: "If we spend additional time seeking a better analogue of the current lead migraine compound using combinatorial chemistry, what do you feel is the chance of passing clinicals? At what cost in time required to reach the market?"

Expert	Months delay	Chance of passing clinicals
Lee	7	15%
Pan	6	14
Bourell	11	11
Wecker	12	11
Pimentel	8	10
Peck	10	11%
Average	**9.0**	**12%**
Standard deviation	2.4	2.0

Scenario 3: "If we go back to basic research and use combinatorial chemistry to try developing a new breakthrough migraine drug platform, what do you feel is the chance of passing clinicals? At what cost in time required to reach the market?"

Expert	Months delay	Chance of passing clinicals
Lee	12	20%
Pan	12	19
Bourell	26	13
Wecker	25	13
Pimentel	16	14
Peck	17	11%
Average	**18.0**	**15%**
Standard Deviation	6.2	3.6

chemists who had extensive experience with serotonin-based drugs and had raised their concerns in Schaus's presentation on his work with Kaldor. The final two were senior managers with scientific training—Dr. Clare Pimentel, a senior product manager from the Prozac program, and Ashley Peck, director of corporate marketing, who had worked closely with Lilly's R&D group for over 25 years. Sharma hoped that she could use the expert poll as an input to her projections but felt uneasy about the level of disagreement among the six experts on various development options. (See Exhibit 11.)

Then Sharma looked at her watch: the PTAC meeting was just two hours away.

EXHIBIT 11 Timeline

4000–2000 B.C.	• Ancient Egyptians develop compresses around skull to stop migraines (procedure still used in 1990s).
1876	• Eli Lilly founded in Indianapolis, Indiana, by Colonel Eli Lilly.
1970s	• Early research in Lilly on serotonin.
1980s	• Prozac launched on market in 1988.
1991	• Serotonin **1f** receptor cloned by Lilly's collaborator, Synaptic Pharmaceutical Corporation. Rapid screening procedures utilizing Synaptic's technology allow 20–30 compounds to be screened weekly.
	• CNS group starts screening serotonin-like compounds from Lilly's historical library (total 250,000 compounds). During next three years over 1,000 compounds will be screened.
1992	• Glaxo launches sumatriptan (Imitrex).
1994:	
March/April	• "Hot" lead compound found from the screen with good fit at the serotonin **1f** receptor.
	• Kaldor gives combinatorial chemistry seminar to an in-house audience at Lilly that includes Schaus. This serves as catalyst for Kaldor-Schaus collaboration.
March/June	• Improvements upon this lead made using traditional chemistry. Screening proceeds using an improved assay, which now tests 50 compounds per week.
September	• Sphinx acquired. Will take almost another year to integrate Sphinx's leading-edge technology in combichem and high-throughput screening
December	• Schaus presents seminar on his research to other CNS research group leaders. Able to demonstrate that combichem can lead to pure, quantifiable results.
1995:	
February	• PTAC (project approval committee) meets to discuss strategic choices in migraine project.
2001	• Projected launch, if approved, of Lilly's migraine product.
2003	• Patent protection of Prozac ends.

Source: Lilly migraine project dates: interviews conducted with Lilly personnel.

GLOSSARY

analogue A structural variation of a parent molecule. Useful analogue compounds may exhibit fewer adverse effects or might be therapeutic in smaller doses.

assay A test to determine properties of a chemical entity such as strength or purity or activity in a biological system.

central nervous system (CNS) disease Any disease primarily affecting behavior, movement, perception, or other components of the central nervous system. Examples include Alzheimer's disease, depression, and migraine.

combinatorial chemistry A branch of synthetic chemistry developed that allows for systematically generating large numbers of chemically diverse but related compounds. Combinatorial chemistry, thus, potentially allows drug makers to rapidly generate and explore thousands of compounds in just weeks in order to find promising compounds.

compound A distinct chemical entity formed by the union of two or more ingredients in a distinctive proportion. Drug compounds are formed from a distinctive proportion of differing chemical elements.

library A collection of differing compounds (analogous to a library of books), usually maintained for further study. Drug firms often maintain libraries of all compounds synthesized in the past by their scientists.

molecular diversity The importance of molecular diversity—analogous to diversity found within the human race—stems from the fact that even minor changes in molecular structure can tremendously alter function. As a result, drug makers seek to adequately explore molecular diversity of a promising drug's analogues in order to field the best possible drug.

neurotransmitter A molecular agent capable of transmitting signals from one nerve to another (e.g., serotonin) by acting upon specific receptors.

receptor A specialized protein located on or within cells in the body capable of detecting specific environmental changes. Receptors in the nervous system, once activated by neurotransmitters, will often trigger specific responses within the body.

screening The process of systematically examining a collection of compounds to find those with the most promise for a given purpose (such as drug development). *High-throughput screening* refers to the ability to screen a large number of compounds in a short time period—a capability needed to successfully apply combinatorial chemistry.

serotonin A compound (chemically termed 5-hydroxytryptamine) widely distributed in the body. Serotonin serves as a neurotransmitter by acting at different receptors in the nervous system, and has been implicated with conditions and behaviors as diverse as depression, migraine, sleep, and aggression.

serotonin receptors specialized proteins in the body capable of detecting and responding to serotonin. Within the body, over a dozen different subclasses (for instance, **1f** and **1d**) of serotonin receptors exist at sites ranging from the blood stream to the intestines to the nervous system. Analogues of serotonin may act in differing ways at differing subclasses of serotonin receptors.

synthetic chemistry The branch of chemistry dealing with the creation of compounds in the laboratory.

ORGANIZATIONAL CONTEXT

Gunfire at Sea:
A Case Study of Innovation

Elting E. Morison

In the early days of the last war when armaments of all kinds were in short supply, the British, I am told, made use of a venerable field piece that had come down to them from previous generations. The honorable past of this light artillery stretched back, in fact, to the Boer War. In the days of uncertainty after the fall of France, these guns, hitched to trucks, served as useful mobile units in the coast defense. But it was felt that the rapidity of fire could be increased. A time-motion expert was, therefore, called in to suggest ways to simplify the firing procedures. He watched one of the gun crews of five men at practice in the field for some time. Puzzled by certain aspects of the procedures, he took some slow-motion pictures of the soldiers performing the loading, aiming, and firing routines.

When he ran these pictures over once or twice, he noticed something that appeared odd to him. A moment before the firing, two members of the gun crew ceased all

activity and came to attention for a three-second interval extending throughout the discharge of the gun. He summoned an old colonel of artillery, showed him the pictures, and pointed out this strange behavior. What, he asked the colonel, did it mean. The colonel, too, was puzzled. He asked to see the pictures again. "Ah," he said when the performance was over, "I have it. They are holding the horses."

This story, true or not, and I am told it is true, suggests nicely the pain with which the human being accommodates himself to changing conditions. The tendency is apparently involuntary and immediate to protect oneself against the shock of change by continuing in the presence of altered situations the familiar habits, however incongruous, of the past.

Yet, if human beings are attached to the known, to the realm of things as they are, they also, regrettably for their peace of mind, are incessantly attracted to the unknown and things as they might be. As Ecclesiastes glumly pointed out, men persist in disordering their settled ways and beliefs by seeking out many inventions.

The point is obvious. Change has always been a constant in human affairs; today, indeed, it is one of the determining characteristics of our civilization. In our relatively shapeless social organization, the shifts from station to station are fast and easy. More important for our immediate purpose, America is fundamentally an industrial society in a time of tremendous technological development. We are thus constantly presented with new devices or new forms of power that in their refinement and extension continually bombard the fixed structure of our habits of mind and behavior. Under such conditions,

Source: Elting E. Morison, *Men, Machines, and Modern Times* (Cambridge: MIT Press, 1966). This essay was delivered as one of three lectures at the California Institute of Technology in 1950. It has been reprinted in various truncated forms a good many times since. This is the first time it has appeared as it was originally written.

our salvation, or at least our peace of mind; appears to depend upon how successfully we can in the future become what has been called in an excellent phrase a completely "adaptive society."

It is interesting, in view of all this, that so little investigation, relatively, has been made of the process of change and human responses to it. Recently, psychologists, sociologists, cultural anthropologists, and economists have addressed themselves to the subject with suggestive results. But we are still far from a full understanding of the process and still further from knowing how we can set about simplifying and assisting an individual's or a group's accommodation to new machines or new ideas.

With these things in mind, I thought it might be interesting and perhaps useful to examine historically a changing situation within a society; to see if from this examination we can discover how the new machines or ideas that introduced the changing situation developed; to see who introduces them, who resists them, what points of friction or tension in the social structure are produced by the innovation, and perhaps why they are produced and what, if anything, may be done about it. For this case study the introduction of continuous-aim firing in the United States Navy has been selected. The system, first devised by an English officer in 1898, was introduced in our Navy in the years 1900 to 1902.

I have chosen to study this episode for two reasons. First, a navy is not unlike a society that has been placed under laboratory conditions. Its dimensions are severely limited; it is beautifully ordered and articulated; it is relatively isolated from random influences. For these reasons the impact of change can be clearly discerned, the resulting dislocations in the structure easily discovered and marked out. In the second place, the development of continuous-aim firing rests upon mechanical devices. It therefore presents for study a concrete, durable situation. It is not like many other innovating reagents—a Manichean heresy, or Marxism, or the views of Sigmund Freud—that can be shoved and hauled out of shape by contending forces or conflicting prejudices. At all times we know exactly what continuous-aim firing really is. It will be well now to describe, as briefly as possible, what it really is. This will involve a short investigation of certain technical matters. I will not apologize, as I have been told I ought to do, for this preoccupation with how a naval gun is fired. For one thing, all that follows is understandable only if one understands how the gun goes off. For another thing, a knowledge of the underlying physical considerations may give a kind of elegance to the succeeding investigation of social implications. And now to the gun and the gunfire.

The governing fact in gunfire at sea is that the gun is mounted on an unstable platform, a rolling ship. This constant motion obviously complicates the problem of holding a steady aim. Before 1898 this problem was solved in the following elementary fashion. A gun pointer estimated the range of the target, ordinarily in the 1890s about 1,600 yards. He then raised the gun barrel to give the gun the elevation to carry the shell to the target at the estimated range. This elevating process was accomplished by turning a small wheel on the gun mount that operated the elevating gears. With the gun thus fixed for range, the gun pointer peered through open sights, not unlike those on a small rifle, and waited until the roll of the ship brought the sights on the target. He then pressed the firing button that discharged the gun. There were by 1898, on some naval guns, telescope sights which naturally greatly enlarged the image of the target for the gun pointer. But these sights were rarely used by gun pointers. They were lashed securely to the gun barrel, and, recoiling with the barrel, jammed back against the unwary pointer's eye. Therefore, when used at all, they were used only to take an initial sight for purposes of estimating the range before the gun was fired.

Notice now two things about the process. First of all, the rapidity of fire was controlled by the rolling period of the ship. Pointers had to wait for the one moment in the roll when the sights were brought on the target. Notice also this: There is in every pointer what is called a firing interval—that is, the time lag between his impulse to fire the gun and the translation of this impulse into the act of pressing the firing button. A pointer, because of this reaction time, could not wait to fire the gun until the exact moment when the roll of the ship brought the sights onto the target; he had to will to fire a little before, while the sights were off the target. Since the firing interval was an individual matter, varying obviously from man to man, each pointer had to estimate from long practice his own interval and compensate for it accordingly.

These things, together with others we need not here investigate, conspired to make gunfire at sea relatively uncertain and ineffective. The pointer, on a moving platform, estimating range and firing interval, shooting while his sight was off the target, became in a sense an individual artist.

In 1898, many of the uncertainties were removed from the process and the position of the gun pointer radically altered by the introduction of continuous-aim firing. The major change was that which enabled the gun pointer to keep his sight and gun barrel on the target throughout the roll of the ship. This was accomplished by altering the gear ratio in the elevating gear to permit a pointer to compensate for the roll of the vessel by rapidly elevating and depressing the gun. From this change another followed. With the possibility of maintaining the gun always on the target, the desirability of improved sights became immediately apparent. The advantages of the telescope sight as opposed to the open sight were for the first time fully realized. But the existing telescope sight, it will be recalled, moved with the recoil of the gun and jammed back against the eye of the gunner. To correct this, the sight was mounted on a sleeve that permitted the gun barrel to recoil through it without moving the telescope.

These two improvements in elevating gear and sighting eliminated the major uncertainties in gunfire at sea and greatly increased the possibilities of both accurate and rapid fire.

You must take my word for it, since the time allowed is small, that this changed naval gunnery from an art to a science, and that gunnery accuracy in the British and our Navy increased, as one student said, 3000 percent in six years. This does not mean much except to suggest a great increase in accuracy. The following comparative figures may mean a little more. In 1899 five ships of the North Atlantic Squadron fired five minutes each at a lightship hulk at the conventional range of 1,600 yards. After 25 minutes of banging away, two hits had been made on the sails of the elderly vessel. Six years later one naval gunner made 15 hits in one minute at a target 75 by 25 feet at the same range—1,600 yards; half of them hit in a bull's-eye 50 inches square.

Now with the instruments (the gun, elevating gear, and telescope), the method, and the results of continuous-aim firing in mind, let us turn to the subject of major interest: how was the idea, obviously so simple an idea, of continuous-aim firing developed, who introduced it into the United States Navy, and what was its reception?

The idea was the product of the fertile mind of the English officer Admiral Sir Percy Scott. He arrived at it in this way while, in 1898, he was the captain of H.M.S. *Scylla*. For the previous two or three years he had given much thought independently and almost alone in the British Navy to means of improving gunnery. One rough day, when the ship, at target practice, was pitching and rolling violently, he walked up and down the gun deck

watching his gun crews. Because of the heavy weather, they were making very bad scores. Scott noticed, however, that one pointer was appreciably more accurate than the rest. He watched this man with care, and saw, after a time, that he was unconsciously working his elevating gear back and forth in a partially successful effort to compensate for the roll of the vessel. It flashed through Scott's mind at that moment that here was the sovereign remedy for the problem of inaccurate fire. What one man could do partially and unconsciously perhaps all men could be trained to do consciously and completely.

Acting on this assumption, he did three things. First, in all the guns of the *Scylla,* he changed the gear ratio in the elevating gear, previously used only to set the gun in fixed position for range, so that a gunner could easily elevate and depress the gun to follow a target throughout the roll. Second, he rerigged his telescopes so that they would not be influenced by the recoil of the gun. Third, he rigged a small target at the mouth of the gun, which was moved up and down by a crank to simulate a moving target. By following this target as it moved and firing at it with a subcaliber rifle rigged in the breech of the gun, the pointer could practice every day. Thus equipped, the ship became a training ground for gunners. Where before the good pointer was an individual artist, pointers now became trained technicians, fairly uniform in their capacity to shoot. The effect was immediately felt. Within a year the *Scylla* established records that were remarkable.

At this point I should like to stop a minute to notice several things directly related to, and involved in, the process of innovation. To begin with, the personality of the innovator. I wish there were time to say a good deal about Admiral Sir Percy Scott. He was a wonderful man. Three small bits of evidence must here suffice, however. First, he had a certain mechanical ingenuity. Second, his personal life was shot through with frustration and bitterness. There was a divorce and a quarrel with that ambitious officer Lord Charles Beresford, the sounds of which, Scott liked to recall, penetrated to the last outposts of empire. Finally, he possessed, like Swift, a savage indignation directed ordinarily at the inelastic intelligence of all constituted authority, especially the British Admiralty.

There are other points worth mention here. Notice first that Scott was not responsible for the invention of the basic instruments that made the reform in gunnery possible. This reform rested upon the gun itself, which as a rifle had been in existence on ships for at least forty years; the elevating gear, which had been, in the form Scott found it, a part of the rifled gun from the beginning; and the telescope sight, which had been on shipboard at least eight years. Scott's contribution was to bring these three elements appropriately modified into a combination that made continuous-aim firing possible for the first time. Notice also that he was allowed to bring these elements into combination by accident, by watching the unconscious action of a gun pointer endeavoring through the operation of his elevating gear to correct partially for the roll of his vessel. Scott, as we have seen, had been interested in gunnery; he had thought about ways to increase accuracy by practice and improvement of existing machinery; but able as he was, he had not been able to produce on his own initiative and by his own thinking the essential idea and modify instruments to fit his purpose. Notice here, finally, the intricate interaction of chance, the intellectual climate, and Scott's mind. Fortune (in this case, the unaware gun pointer) indeed favors the prepared mind, but even fortune and the prepared mind need a favorable environment before they can conspire to produce sudden change. No intelligence can proceed very far above the threshold of existing data or the binding combinations of existing data.

All these elements that enter into what may be called original thinking interest me as a teacher. Deeply rooted in the pedagogical mind often enough is a sterile infatuation with "inert ideas"; there is thus always present in the profession the tendency to be diverted from the *process* by which these ideas, or indeed any ideas, are really produced. I well remember with what contempt a class of mine which was reading Leonardo da Vinci's *Notebooks* dismissed the author because he appeared to know no more mechanics than, as one wit in the class observed, a Vermont Republican farmer of the present day. This is perhaps the expected result produced by a method of instruction that too frequently implies that the great generalizations were the result, on the one hand, of chance—an apple falling in an orchard or a teapot boiling on the hearth—or, on the other hand, of some towering intelligence proceeding in isolation inexorably toward some prefigured idea, like evolution, for example.

This process by which new concepts appear, the interaction of fortune, intellectual climate, and the prepared imaginative mind, is an interesting subject for examination offered by any case study of innovation. It was a subject as Dr. Walter Cannon pointed out, that momentarily engaged the attention of Horace Walpole, whose lissome intelligence glided over the surface of so many ideas. In

reflecting upon the part played by chance in the development of new concepts, he recalled the story of the three princes of Serendip who set out to find some interesting object on a journey through their realm. They did not find the particular object of their search, but along the way they discovered many new things simply because they were looking for *something*. Walpole believed this intellectual method ought to be given a name, in honor of the founders, serendipity; and serendipity certainly exerts a considerable influence in what we call original thinking. There is an element of serendipity, for example, in Scott's chance discovery of continuous-aim firing in that he was, and had been, looking for some means to improve his target practice and stumbled upon a solution by observation that had never entered his head.

Serendipity, while recognizing the prepared mind, does tend to emphasize the role of chance in intellectual discovery. Its effect may be balanced by an anecdote that suggests the contribution of the adequately prepared mind. There has recently been much posthaste and romage in the land over the question of whether there really was a Renaissance. A scholar has recently argued in print that since the Middle Ages actually possessed many of the instruments and pieces of equipment associated with the Renaissance, the Renaissance could be said to exist as a defined period only in the mind of the historians such as Burckhardt. This view was entertainingly rebutted by the historian of art Panofsky, who pointed out that although Robert Grosseteste indeed did have a very rudimentary telescope, he used it to examine stalks of grain in a field down the street. Galileo, a Renaissance intelligence, pointed his telescope at the sky.

Here Panofsky is only saying in a provocative way that change and intellectual advance are the products of well-trained and well-stored inquisitive minds, minds that relieve us of "the terrible burden of inert ideas by throwing them into a new combination." Educators, nimble in the task of pouring the old wine of our heritage into the empty vessels that appear before them, might give thought to how to develop such independent, inquisitive minds.

But I have been off on a private venture of my own. Now to return to the story, the introduction of continuous-aim firing. In 1900 Percy Scott went out to the China Station as commanding officer of H.M.S. *Terrible*. In that ship he continued his training methods and his spectacular successes in naval gunnery. On the China Station he met up with an American junior officer, William S. Sims. Sims had little of the mechanical ingenuity of Percy Scott, but the two were drawn together by temperamental similarities that are worth noticing here. Sims had the same intolerance for what is called spit and polish and the same contempt for bureaucratic inertia as his British brother officer. He had for some years been concerned, as had Scott, with what he took to be the inefficiency of his own Navy. Just before he met Scott, for example, he had shipped out to China in the brand new pride of the fleet, the battleship *Kentucky.* After careful investigation and reflection he had informed his superiors in Washington that she was "not a battleship at all—but a crime against the white race." The spirit with which he pushed forward his efforts to reform the naval service can best be stated in his own words to a brother officer: "I am perfectly willing that those holding views differing from mine should continue to live, but with every fibre of my being I loathe indirection and shiftiness, and where it occurs in high place, and is used to save face at the expense of the vital interests of our great service (in which silly people place such a childlike trust), I want that man's blood and I will have it no matter what it costs me personally."

From Scott in 1900 Sims learned all there was to know about continuous-aim firing. He modified, with the Englishman's active assistance, the gear on his own ship and tried out the new system. After a few months' training, his experimental batteries began making remarkable records at target practice. Sure of the usefulness of his gunnery methods, Sims then turned to the task of educating the Navy at large. In 13 great official reports he documented the case for continuous-aim firing, supporting his arguments at every turn with a mass of factual data. Over a period of two years, he reiterated three principal points: first, he continually cited the records established by Scott's ships, the *Scylla* and the *Terrible,* and supported these with the accumulating data from his own tests on an American ship; second, he described the mechanisms used and the training procedures instituted by Scott and himself to obtain these records; third, he explained that our own mechanisms were not generally adequate without modification to meet the demands placed on them by continuous-aim firing. Our elevating gear, useful to raise or lower a gun slowly to fix it in position for the proper range, did not always work easily and rapidly enough to enable a gunner to follow a target with his gun throughout the roll of the ship. Sims also explained that such few telescope sights as there were on board our ships were useless. Their cross wires were so thick or coarse they obscured the target, and the sights had been attached to the gun in such a way that the recoil system

of the gun plunged the eyepiece against the eye of the gun pointer.

This was the substance not only of the first but of all the succeeding reports written on the subject of gunnery from the China Station. It will be interesting to see what response these met with in Washington. The response falls roughly into three easily identifiable stages.

First stage: At first, there was no response. Sims had directed his comments to the Bureau of Ordnance and the Bureau of Navigation; in both bureaus there was dead silence. The thing—claims and records of continuous-aim firing—was not credible. The reports were simply filed away and forgotten. Some indeed, it was later discovered to Sims's delight, were half-eaten-away by cockroaches.

Second stage: It is never pleasant for any man's best work to be left unnoticed by superiors, and it was an unpleasantness that Sims suffered extremely ill. In his later reports, beside the accumulating data he used to clinch his argument, he changed his tone. He used deliberately shocking language because, as he said, "They were furious at my first papers and stowed them away. I therefore made up my mind I would give these later papers such a form that they would be dangerous documents to leave neglected in the files." To another friend, he added, "I want scalps or nothing and if I can't have 'em I won't play."

Besides altering his tone, he took another step to be sure his views would receive attention. He sent copies of his reports to other officers in the fleet. Aware as a result that Sims's gunnery claims were being circulated and talked about, the men in Washington were then stirred to action. They responded, notably through the chief of the Bureau of Ordnance, who had general charge of the equipment used in gunnery practice, as follows: (1) our equipment was in general as good as the British; (2) since our equipment was as good, the trouble must be with the men, but the gun pointer and the training of gun pointers were the responsibility of the officers on the ships; and most significant (3) continuous-aim firing was impossible. Experiments had revealed that five men at work on the elevating gear of a six-inch gun could not produce the power necessary to compensate for a roll of five degrees in 10 seconds. These experiments and calculations demonstrated beyond peradventure or doubt that Scott's system of gunfire was not possible.

This was the second stage—the attempt to meet Sims's claims by logical, rational rebuttal. Only one difficulty is discoverable in these arguments; they were wrong at important points. To begin with, while there was little difference between the standard British equipment and the standard American equipment, the instruments on Scott's two ships, the *Scylla* and the *Terrible,* were far better than the standard equipment on our ships. Second, all the men could not be trained in continuous-aim firing until equipment was improved throughout the fleet. Third, the experiments with the elevating gear had been ingeniously contrived at the Washington Navy Yard—on solid ground. It had, therefore, been possible to dispense in the Bureau of Ordnance calculation with Newton's first law of motion, which naturally operated at sea to assist the gunner in elevating or depressing a gun mounted on a moving ship. Another difficulty was of course that continuous-aim firing was in use on Scott's and some of our own ships at the time the chief of the Bureau of Ordnance was writing that it was a mathematical impossibility. In every way I find this second stage, the apparent resort to reason, the most entertaining and instructive in our investigation of the responses to innovation.

Third stage: The rational period in the counterpoint between Sims and the Washington men was soon passed. It was followed by the third stage, that of name-calling—the *argumentum ad hominem.* Sims, of course, by the high temperature he was running and by his calculated overstatement, invited this. He was told in official endorsements on his reports that there were others quite as sincere and loyal as he and far less difficult; he was dismissed as a crackbrained egotist; he was called a deliberate falsifier of evidence.

The rising opposition and the character of the opposition were not calculated to discourage further efforts by Sims. It convinced him that he was being attacked by shifty, dishonest men who were the victims, as he said, of insufferable conceit and ignorance. He made up his mind, therefore, that he was prepared to go to any extent to obtain the "scalps" and the "blood" he was after. Accordingly, he, a lieutenant, took the extraordinary step of writing the President of the United States, Theodore Roosevelt, to inform him of the remarkable records of Scott's ships, of the inadequacy of our own gunnery routines and records, and of the refusal of the Navy Department to act. Roosevelt, who always liked to respond to such appeals when he conveniently could, brought Sims back from China late in 1902 and installed him as Inspector of Target Practice, a post the naval officer held throughout the remaining six years of the Administration. And when he left, after many spirited encounters we cannot here investigate, he was universally acclaimed as "the man who taught us how to shoot."

With this sequence of events (the chronological account of the innovation of continuous-aim firing) in mind, it is possible now to examine the evidence to see what light it may throw on our present interest: the origins of and responses to change in a society.

First, the origins. We have already analyzed briefly the origins of the idea. We have seen how Scott arrived at his notion. We must now ask ourselves, I think, why Sims so actively sought, almost alone among his brother officers, to introduce the idea into his service. It is particularly interesting here to notice again that neither Scott nor Sims invented the instruments on which the innovation rested. They did not urge their proposal, as might be expected, because of pride in the instruments of their own design. The telescope sight had first been placed on shipboard in 1892 by Bradley Fiske, an officer of great inventive capacity. In that year Fiske had even sketched out on paper the vague possibility of continuous-aim firing, but his sight was condemned by his commanding officer, Robley D. Evans, as of no use. In 1892 no one but Fiske in the Navy knew what to do with a telescope sight any more than Grosseteste had known in his time what to do with a telescope. And Fiske, instead of fighting for his telescope, turned his attention to a range finder. But six years later Sims, following the tracks of his brother officer, took over and became the engineer of the revolution. I would suggest, with some reservations, this explanation: Fiske, as an inventor, took his pleasure in great part from the design of the device. He lacked not so much the energy as the overriding sense of social necessity that would have enabled him to *force* revolutionary ideas on the service. Sims possessed this sense. In Fiske, who showed rare courage and integrity in other professional matters not intimately connected with the introduction of new weapons of his own design, we may here find the familiar plight of the engineer who often enough must watch the products of his ingenuity organized and promoted by other men. These other promotional men when they appear in the world of commerce are called entrepreneurs. In the world of ideas they are still entrepreneurs. Sims was one, a middle-aged man caught in the periphery (as a lieutenant) of the intricate webbing of a precisely organized society. Rank, the exact definition and limitation of a man's capacity at any given moment in his career, prevented Sims from discharging all his exploding energies into the purely routine channels of the peacetime Navy. At the height of his powers he was a junior officer standing watches on a ship cruising aimlessly in friendly foreign waters. The remarkable changes in systems of gunfire to which Scott introduced him gave him the opportunity to expend his energies quite legitimately against the encrusted hierarchy of his society. He was moved, it seems to me, in part by his genuine desire to improve his own profession but also in part by rebellion against tedium, against inefficiency from on high, and against the artificial limitations placed on his actions by the social structure, in his case, junior rank.

Now having briefly investigated the origins of the change, let us examine the reasons for what must be considered the weird response we have observed to this proposed change. Why this deeply rooted, aggressive, persistent hostility from Washington that was only broken up by the interference of Theodore Roosevelt? Here was a reform that greatly and demonstrably increased the fighting effectiveness of a service that maintains itself almost exclusively to fight. Why then this refusal to accept so carefully documented a case, a case proved incontestably by records and experience? Why should virtually all the rulers of a society so resolutely seek to reject a change that so markedly improved its chances for survival in any contest with competing societies? There are the obvious reasons that will occur to all of you—the source of the proposed reform was an obscure, junior officer 8,000 miles away; he was, and this is a significant factor, criticizing gear and machinery designed by the very men in the bureaus to whom he was sending his criticisms. And furthermore, Sims was seeking to introduce what he claimed were improvements in a field where improvements appeared unnecessary. Superiority in war, as in other things, is a relative matter, and the Spanish-American War had been won by the old system of gunnery. Therefore, it was superior even though of the 9,500 shots fired at various but close ranges, only 121 had found their mark.

These are the more obvious, and I think secondary or supporting, sources of opposition to Sims's proposed reforms. A less obvious cause appears by far the most important one. It has to do with the fact that the Navy is not only an armed force; it is a society. Men spend their whole lives in it and tend to find the definition of their whole being within it. In the 40 years following the Civil War, this society had been forced to accommodate itself to a series of technological changes—the steam turbine, the electric motor, the rifled shell of great explosive power, case-hardened steel armor, and all the rest of it. These changes wrought extraordinary changes in ship design, and, therefore, in the concepts of how ships were to be used; that is, in fleet tactics, and even in naval strategy. The Navy of this period is a paradise for the historian or sociologist in search of evidence bearing on a society's responses to change.

To these numerous innovations, producing as they did a spreading disorder throughout a service with heavy commitments to formal organization, the Navy responded with grudging pain. For example, sails were continued on our first-line ships long after they ceased to serve a useful purpose mechanically, but like the holding of the horses that no longer hauled the British field pieces, they assisted officers over the imposing hurdles of change. To a man raised in sail, a sail on an armored cruiser propelled through the water at 14 knots by a steam turbine was a cheering sight to see.

This reluctance to change with changing conditions was not limited to the blunter minds and less resilient imaginations in the service. As clear and untrammeled an intelligence as Alfred Thayer Mahan, a prophetic spirit in the realm of strategy, where he was unfettered by personal attachments of any kind, was occasionally at the mercy of the past. In 1906 he opposed the construction of battleships with single-caliber main batteries—that is, the modern battleship—because, he argued, such vessels would fight only at great ranges. These ranges would create in the sailor what Mahan felicitously called "the indisposition to close." They would thus undermine the physical and moral courage of a commander. They would, in other words, destroy the doctrine and the spirit, formulated by Nelson a century before, that no captain could go very far wrong who laid his ship alongside an enemy. The 14-inch rifle, which could place a shell upon a possible target six miles away, had long ago annihilated the Nelsonian doctrine. Mahan, of course, knew and recognized this fact; he was, as a man raised in sail, reluctant only to accept its full meaning, which was not that men were no longer brave, but that 100 years after the battle of the Nile they had to reveal their bravery in a different way.

Now the question still is, why this blind reaction to technological change, observed in the continuation of sail or in Mahan's contentions or in the opposition to continuous-aim firing? It is wrong to assume, as it is frequently assumed by civilians, that it springs exclusively from some causeless Bourbon distemper that invades the military mind. There is a sounder and more attractive base. The opposition, where it occurs, of the soldier and the sailor to such change springs from the normal human instinct to protect oneself, and more especially, one's way of life. Military organizations are societies built around and upon the prevailing weapons systems. Intuitively and quite correctly the military man feels that a change in weapon portends a change in the arrangements of his society. Think of it this way. Since the time that the memory of man runneth not to the contrary, the naval society has been built upon the surface vessel. Daily routines, habits of mind, social organization, physical accommodations, conventions, rituals, spiritual allegiances have been conditioned by the essential fact of the ship. What then happens to your society if the ship is displaced as the principal element by such a radically different weapon as the plane? The mores and structure of the society are immediately placed in jeopardy. They may, in fact, be wholly destroyed. It was the witty cliché of the 1920s that those naval officers who persisted in defending the battleship against the apparently superior claims of the carrier did so because the battleship was a more comfortable home. What, from one point of view, is a better argument? There is, as everyone knows, no place like home. Who has ever wanted to see the old place brought under the hammer by hostile forces whether they hold a mortgage or inhabit a flying machine?

This sentiment would appear to account in large part for the opposition to Sims; it was the product of an instinctive protective feeling, even if the reasons for this feeling were not overt or recognized. The years after 1902 proved how right, in their terms, the opposition was. From changes in gunnery flowed an extraordinary complex of changes: in shipboard routines, ship design, and fleet tactics. There was, too, a social change. In the days when gunnery was taken lightly, the gunnery officer was taken lightly. After 1903, he became one of the most significant and powerful members of a ship's company, and this shift of emphasis naturally was shortly reflected in promotion lists. Each one of these changes provoked a dislocation in the naval society, and with man's troubled foresight and natural indisposition to break up classic forms, the men in Washington withstood the Sims onslaught as long as they could. It is very significant that they withstood it until an agent from outside, outside and above, who was not clearly identified with the naval society, entered to force change.

This agent, the President of the United States, might reasonably and legitimately claim the credit for restoring our gunnery efficiency. But this restoration by *force majeure* was brought about at great cost to the service and men involved. Bitternesses, suspicions, wounds were made that it was impossible to conceal and were, in fact, never healed.

Now this entire episode may be summed up in five separate points:

1. The essential idea for change occurred in part by chance but in an environment that contained all the essential elements for change and to a mind prepared to recognize the possibility of change.

2. The basic elements, the gun, gear, and sight, were put in the environment by other men, men interested in designing machinery to serve different purposes or simply interested in the instruments themselves.

3. These elements were brought into successful combination by minds not interested in the instruments for themselves but in what they could do with them. These minds were, to be sure, interested in good gunnery, overtly and consciously. They may also, not so consciously, have been interested in the implied revolt that is present in the support of all change. Their temperaments and careers indeed support this view. From gunnery, Sims went on to attack ship designs, existing fleet tactics, and methods of promotion. He lived and died, as the service said, a stormy petrel, a man always on the attack against higher authority, a rebellious spirit; a rebel, fighting in excellent causes, but a rebel still who seems increasingly to have identified himself with the act of revolt against constituted authority.

4. He and his colleagues were opposed on this occasion by men who were apparently moved by three considerations: honest disbelief in the dramatic but substantiated claims of the new process, protection of the existing devices and instruments with which they identified themselves, and maintenance of the existing society with which they were identified.

5. The deadlock between those who sought change and those who sought to retain things as they were was broken only by an appeal to superior force, a force removed from and unidentified with the mores, conventions, devices of the society. This seems to me a very important point. The naval society in 1900 broke down in its effort to accommodate itself to a new situation. The appeal to Roosevelt is documentation for Mahan's great generalization that no military service should or can undertake to reform itself. It must seek assistance from outside.

Now with these five summary points in mind, it may be possible to seek, as suggested at the outset, a few larger implications from this story. What, if anything, may it suggest about the general process by which any society attempts to meet changing conditions?

There is, to begin with, a disturbing inference half-concealed in Mahan's statement that no military organization can reform itself. Certainly civilians would agree with this. We all know now that war and the preparation for war are too important, as Clemenceau said, to be left to the generals. But as I have said before, military organizations are really societies, more rigidly structured, more highly integrated, than most communities, but still societies. What then if we make this phrase to read, "No society can reform itself"? Is the process of adaptation to change, for example, too important to be left to human beings? This is a discouraging thought, and historically there is some cause to be discouraged. Societies have not been very successful in reforming themselves, accommodating to change, without pain and conflict.

This is a subject to which we may well address ourselves. Our society especially is built, as I have said, just as surely upon a changing technology as the Navy of the 1890s was built upon changing weapon systems. How then can we find the means to accept with less pain to ourselves and less damage to our social organization the dislocations in our society that are produced by innovation? I cannot, of course, give any satisfying answer to these difficult questions. But in thinking about the case study before us, an idea occurred to me that at least might warrant further investigation by men far more qualified than I.

A primary source of conflict and tension in our case study appears to lie in this great word I have used so often in the summary, the word *identification*. It cannot have escaped notice that some men identified themselves with their creations—sights, gun, gear, and so forth—and thus obtained a presumed satisfaction from the thing itself, a satisfaction that prevented them from thinking too closely on either the use or the defects of the thing; that others identified themselves with a settled way of life they had inherited or accepted with minor modification and thus found their satisfaction in attempting to maintain that way of life unchanged; and that still others identified themselves as rebellious spirits, men of the insurgent cast of mind, and thus obtained a satisfaction from the act of revolt itself.

This purely personal identification with a concept, a convention, or an attitude would appear to be a powerful barrier in the way of easily acceptable change. Here is an interesting primitive example. In the years from 1864 to 1871 ten steel companies in this country began making steel by the new Bessemer process. All but one of them at the outset imported from Great Britain English workmen familiar with the process. One, the Cambria Company, did not. In the first few years those companies with

British labor established an initial superiority. But by the end of the 1870s, Cambria had obtained a commanding lead over all competitors. The president of Cambria, R. W. Hunt, in seeking a cause for his company's success, assigned it almost exclusively to the labor policy.

We started the converter plant without a single man who had ever seen even the outside of a Bessemer plant. We thus had willing pupils with no prejudices and no reminiscences of what they had done in the old country.

The Bessemer process, like any new technique, had been constantly improved and refined in this period from 1864 to 1871. The British laborers of Cambria's competitors, secure in the performance of their own original techniques, resisted and resented all change. The Pennsylvania farm boys, untrammeled by the rituals and traditions of their craft, happily and rapidly adapted themselves to the constantly changing process. They ended by creating an unassailable competitive position for their company.

How then can we modify the dangerous effects of this word *identification*? And how much can we tamper with this identifying process? Our security—much of it, after all—comes from giving our allegiance to something greater than ourselves. These are difficult questions to which only the most tentative and provisional answers may here be proposed for consideration.

If one looks closely at this little case history, one discovers that the men involved were the victims of *severely limited* identifications. They were presumably all part of a society dedicated to the process of national defense, yet they persisted in aligning themselves with separate parts of that process—with the existing instruments of defense, with the existing customs of the society, or with the act of rebellion against the customs of the society. Of them all the insurgents had the best of it. They could, and did, say that the process of defense was improved by a gun that shot straighter and faster, and since they wanted such guns, they were unique among their fellows, patriots who sought only the larger object of improved defense. But this beguiling statement, even when coupled with the recognition that these men were right and extremely valuable and deserving of respect and admiration—this statement cannot conceal the fact that they were interested too in scalps and blood, so interested that they made their case a militant one and thus created an atmosphere in which self-respecting men could not capitulate without appearing either weak or wrong or both. So these limited identifications brought men into conflict with each other, and the conflict prevented them from arriving at a common acceptance of a change that presumably, as men interested in our total national defense, they would all find desirable.

It appears, therefore, if I am correct in my assessment, that we might spend some time and thought on the possibility of enlarging the sphere of our identifications from the part to the whole. For example, those Pennsylvania farm boys at the Cambria Steel Company were, apparently, much more interested in the manufacture of steel than in the preservation of any particular way of making steel. So I would suggest that in studying innovation, we look further into this possibility: the possibility that any group that exists for any purpose—the family, the factory, the educational institution—might begin by defining for itself its grand object and see to it that that grand object is communicated to every member of the group. Thus defined and communicated, it might serve as a unifying agent against the disruptive local allegiances of the inevitable smaller elements that compose any group. It may also serve as a means to increase the acceptability of any change that would assist in the more efficient achievement of the grand object.

There appears also a second possible way to combat the untoward influence of limited identifications. We are, I may repeat, a society based on technology in a time of prodigious technological advance, and a civilization committed irrevocably to the theory of evolution. These things mean that we believe in change; they suggest that if we are to survive in good health we must, in the phrase that I have used before, become an "adaptive society." By the word *adaptive* is meant the ability to extract the fullest possible returns from the opportunities at hand: the ability of Sir Percy Scott to select judiciously from the ideas and material presented both by the past and present and to throw them into a new combination. *Adaptive,* as here used, also means the kind of resilience that will enable us to accept fully and easily the best promises of changing circumstances without losing our sense of continuity or our essential integrity.

We are not yet emotionally an adaptive society, though we try systematically to develop forces that tend to make us one. We encourage the search for new inventions; we keep the mind stimulated, bright, and free to seek out fresh means of transport, communication, and energy; yet we remain, in part, appalled by the consequences of our ingenuity, and, too frequently, try to find security through the shoring up of ancient and irrelevant conventions, the extension of purely physical safeguards, or the delivery of decisions we ourselves should make into the keeping of superior authority like the state.

These solutions are not necessarily unnatural or wrong, but they historically have not been enough, and I suspect they never will be enough to give us the serenity and competence we seek.

If the preceding statements are correct, they suggest that we might give some attention to the construction of a new view of ourselves as a society which in time of great change identified with and obtained security and satisfaction from the wise and creative accommodation to change itself. Such a view rests, I think, upon a relatively greater reverence for the mere *process* of living in a society than we possess today, and a relatively smaller respect for and attachment to any special *product* of a society, a product either as finite as a bathroom fixture or as conceptual as a fixed and final definition of our Constitution or our democracy.

Historically such an identification with *process* as opposed to *product,* with adventurous selection and adaptation as opposed to simple retention and possessiveness, has been difficult to achieve collectively. The Roman of the early republic, the Italian of the late fifteenth and early sixteenth century, or the Englishman of Elizabeth's time appears to have been most successful in seizing the new opportunities while conserving as much of the heritage of the past as he found relevant and useful to his purpose.

We seem to have fallen on times similar to theirs, when many of the existing forms and schemes have lost meaning in the face of dramatically altering circumstances. Like them we may find at least part of our salvation in identifying ourselves with the adaptive process and thus share with them some of the joy, exuberance, satisfaction, and security with which they went out to meet their changing times.

I am painfully aware that in setting up my historical situation for examination I have, in a sense, artificially contrived it. I have been forced to cut away much, if not all, of the connecting tissue of historical evidence and to present you only with the bare bones and even with only a few of the bones. Thus, I am also aware, the episode has lost much of the subtlety, vitality, and attractive uncertainty of the real situation. There has, too, in the process, been inevitable distortion, but I hope the essential if exaggerated truth remains. I am also aware that I have erected elaborate hypotheses on the slender evidence provided by the single episode. My defense here is only that I have hoped to suggest possible approaches and methods of study and also possible fruitful areas of investigation in a subject that seems to me of critical importance in the life and welfare of our changing society.

Architectural Innovation: The Reconfiguration of Existing Product Technologies and the Failure of Established Firms

Rebecca M. Henderson and Kim B. Clark

The distinction between refining and improving an existing design and introducing a new concept that departs in a significant way from past practice is one of the central notions in the existing literature on technical innovation.[1] Incremental innovation introduces relatively minor changes to the existing product, exploits the potential of the established design, and often reinforces the dominance of established firms.[2] Although it draws from no dramatically new science, it often calls for considerable skill and ingenuity and, over time, has very significant economic consequences.[3] Radical innovation, in contrast, is based on a different set of engineering and scientific principles and often opens up whole new markets and potential applications.[4] Radical innovation often creates great difficulties for established firms[5] and can be the basis for the successful entry of new firms or even the redefinition of an industry.

Radical and incremental innovations have such different competitive consequences because they require different organizational capabilities. Organizational capabilities are difficult to create and costly to adjust.[6] Incremental innovation reinforces the capabilities of established organizations, while radical innovation forces them to ask a new set of questions, to draw on new technical and commercial skills, and to employ new problem-solving approaches.[7]

The distinction between radical and incremental innovation has produced important insights, but it is fundamentally incomplete. There is growing evidence that there are numerous technical innovations that involve apparently modest changes to the existing technology but that have quite dramatic competitive consequences.[8] The case of Xerox and small copiers and the case of RCA and the American radio receiver market are two examples.

Xerox, the pioneer of plain-paper copiers, was confronted in the mid-1970s with competitors offering copiers that were much smaller and more reliable than the traditional product. The new products required little new scientific or engineering knowledge, but despite the fact that Xerox had invented the core technologies and had enormous experience in the industry, it took the company almost eight years of missteps and false starts to introduce a competitive product into the market. In that time Xerox lost half of its market share and suffered serious financial problems.[9]

In the mid-1950s engineers at RCA's corporate research and development center developed a prototype of a portable, transistorized radio receiver. The new product used technology in which RCA was accomplished (transistors, radio circuits, speakers, tuning devices), but RCA

Source: Copyright © 1990 by Cornell University. *Administrative Science Quarterly* 35 (1990), pp. 9–30.

[1] E. Mansfield, *Industrial Research and Technical Innovation* (New York: Norton, 1968); M. Moch and E. V. Morse, "Size, Centralization and Organizational Adoption of Innovations," *American Sociological Review* 42 (1977), pp. 716–25; C. Freeman, *The Economics of Industrial Innovation,* 2d ed. (Cambridge, MA: MIT Press, 1982).

[2] R. Nelson and S. Winter, *An Evolutionary Theory of Economic Change* (Cambridge, MA: Harvard University Press, 1982); J. E. Ettlie, W. P. Bridges, and R. D. O'Keefe, "Organizational Strategy and Structural Differences for Radical vs. Incremental Innovation," *Management Science* 30 (1984), pp. 682–95; R. D. Dewar and J. E. Dutton, "The Adoption of Radical and Incremental Innovations; An Empirical Analysis," *Management Science* 32 (1986), pp. 1422–33; M. L. Tushman and P. Anderson, "Technological Discontinuities and Organizational Environments," *Administrative Science Quarterly* 31 (1986), pp. 439–65.

[3] S. Hollander, *The Sources of Increased Efficiency: A Study of Du Pont Rayon Plants* (Cambridge, MA: MIT Press, 1965).

[4] G. G. Dess and D. Beard, "Dimensions of Organizational Task Environments," *Administrative Science Quarterly* 29 (1984), pp. 52–73; Ettlie et al., "Organizational Strategy and Structural Differences for Radical vs. Incremental Innovation"; Dewar and Dutton, "The Adoption of Radical and Incremental Innovations."

[5] A. C. Cooper and D. Schendel, "Strategic Response to Technological Threats," *Business Horizons* 19 (1976), pp. 61–69; R. L. Daft, "Bureaucratic versus Nonbureaucratic Structure and the Process of Innovation and Change," in *Research in the Sociology of Organizations,* vol. 1, ed. S. B. Bacharach (Greenwich, CT: JAI Press, 1982), pp. 129–66; R. Rothwell, "The Role of Small Firms in the Emergence of New Technologies," in *Design, Innovation and Long Cycles in Economic Development,* ed. C. Freeman (London: Francis Pinter, 1986), pp. 251–48; Tushman and Anderson, "Technological Discontinuities and Organizational Environments."

[6] Nelson and Winter, *An Evolutionary Theory of Economic Change;* M. T. Hannan and J. Freeman, "Structural Inertia and Organizational Change," *American Sociological Review* 49 (1984), pp. 149–64.

[7] T. Burns and G. Stalker, *The Management of Innovation* (London: Tavistock, 1966); J. Hage, *Theories of Organization* (New York: Wiley Interscience, 1980); Ettlie et al., "Organizational Strategy and Structural Differences of Radical vs. Incremental Innovation"; Tushman and Anderson, "Technological Discontinuities and Organizational Environments."

[8] K. B. Clark, "Managing Technology in International Competition: The Case of Product Development in Response to Foreign Entry," in *International Competitiveness,* ed. M. Spence and H. Hazard (Cambridge, MA: Ballinger, 1987), pp. 27–74.

[9] Ibid.

saw little reason to pursue such an apparently inferior technology. In contrast, Sony, a small, relatively new company, used the small transistorized radio to gain entry into the U.S. market. Even after Sony's success was apparent, RCA remained a follower in the market as Sony introduced successive models with improved sound quality and FM capability. The irony of the situation was not lost on the R&D engineers: for many years Sony's radios were produced with technology licensed from RCA, yet RCA had great difficulty matching Sony's product in the marketplace.[10]

Existing models that rely on the simple distinction between radical and incremental innovation provide little insight into the reasons why such apparently minor or straightforward innovations should have such consequences. In this reading, we develop and apply a model that grew out of research in the automotive, machine tool, and ceramics industries that helps to explain how minor innovations can have great competitive consequences.

CONCEPTUAL FRAMEWORK

Component and Architectural Knowledge

In this paper, we focus on the problem of product development, taking as the unit of analysis a manufactured product sold to an end user and designed, engineered, and manufactured by a single product-development organization. We define innovations that change the way in which the components of a product are linked together, while leaving the core design concepts (and thus the basic knowledge underlying the components) untouched, as *architectural* innovation.[11] This is the kind of innovation that confronted Xerox and RCA. It destroys the usefulness of a firm's architectural knowledge but preserves the usefulness of its knowledge about the product's components.

This distinction between the product as a whole—the system—and the product in its parts—the components—has a long history in the design literature.[12] For example, a room fan's major components include the blade, the motor that drives it, the blade guard, the con-

trol system, and the mechanical housing. The overall architecture of the product lays out how the components will work together. Taken together, a fan's architecture and its components create a system for moving air in a room.

A component is defined here as a physically distinct portion of the product that embodies a core design concept[13] and performs a well-defined function. In the fan, a particular motor is a component of the design that delivers power to turn the fan. There are several design concepts one could use to deliver power. The choice of one of them—the decision to use an electric motor, for example—establishes a core concept of the design. The actual component—the electric motor—is then a physical implementation of this design concept.

The distinction between the product as a system and the product as a set of components underscores the idea that successful product development requires two types of knowledge. First, it requires component knowledge, or knowledge about each of the core design concepts and the way in which they are implemented in a particular component. Second, it requires architectural knowledge, or knowledge about the ways in which the components are integrated and linked together into a coherent whole. The distinction between architectural and component knowledge, or between the components themselves and the links between them, is a source of insight into the ways in which innovations differ from each other.

Types of Technological Change

The notion that there are different kinds of innovation, with different competitive effects, has been an important theme in the literature on technological innovation since Schumpeter.[14] Following Schumpeter's emphasis on creative destruction, the literature has characterized different kinds of innovations in terms of their impact on the established capabilities of the firm. This idea is used in Exhibit 1, which classifies innovations along two dimensions. The horizontal dimension captures an innovation's impact on components, while the vertical captures its impact on the linkages between components.[15] There are, of course, other ways to characterize different kinds of in-

[10] Ibid.

[11] In earlier drafts of this paper we referred to this type of innovation as *generational*. We are indebted to Professor Michael Tushman for his suggestion of the term *architectural*.

[12] D. L. Marples, "The Decisions of Engineering Design," *IEEE Transactions of Engineering Management* EM.8 (June 1961), pp. 55–71; C. Alexander, *Notes on the Synthesis of Form* (Cambridge, MA: Harvard University Press, 1964).

[13] K. B. Clark, "The Interaction of Design Hierarchies and Market Concepts in Technological Evolution." *Research Policy* 14 (1985), pp. 235–251.

[14] J. A. Schumpeter, *Capitalism, Socialism and Democracy* (Cambridge, MA: Harvard University Press, 1942).

[15] We are indebted to one of the anonymous *ASQ* reviewers for the suggestion that we use this matrix.

EXHIBIT 1   A Framework for Defining Innovation

Core concepts

	Reinforced	Overturned
Unchanged (Linkage between core concepts and components)	Incremental innovation	Modular innovation
Changed	Architectural innovation	Radical innovation

novation. But given the focus here on innovation and the development of new products, the framework outlined in Exhibit 1 is useful because it focuses on the impact of an innovation on the usefulness of the existing architectural and component knowledge of the firm.

Framed in this way, radical and incremental innovation are extreme points along both dimensions. Radical innovation establishes a new dominant design and, hence, a new set of core design concepts embodied in components that are linked together in a new architecture. Incremental innovation refines and extends an established design. Improvement occurs in individual components, but the underlying core design concepts, and the links between them, remain the same.

Exhibit 1 shows two further types of innovation: innovation that changes only the core design concepts of a technology and innovation that changes only the relationships between them. The former is a modular innovation, such as the replacement of analog with digital telephones. To the degree that one can simply replace an analog dialing device with a digital one, it is an innovation that changes a core design concept without changing the product's architecture. Our concern, however, is with the last type of innovation shown in the matrix: innovation that changes a product's architecture but leaves the components, and the core design concepts that they embody, unchanged.

The essence of an architectural innovation is the reconfiguration of an established system to link together existing components in a new way. This does not mean that the components themselves are untouched by architectural innovation. Architectural innovation is often triggered by a change in a component—perhaps size or some other subsidiary parameter of its design—that creates new interactions and new linkages with other components in the established product. The important point is that the core design concept behind each com-

ponent—as well as the associated scientific and engineering knowledge—remains the same.

We can illustrate the application of this framework with the example of the room air fan. If the established technology is that of large, electrically powered fans, mounted in the ceiling, with the motor hidden from view and insulated to dampen the noise, improvements in blade design or in the power of the motor would be incremental innovations. A move to central air conditioning would be a radical innovation. New components associated with compressors, refrigerants, and their associated controls would add whole new technical disciplines and new interrelationships. For the maker of large, ceiling-mounted room fans, however, the introduction of a portable fan would be an architectural innovation. While the primary components would be largely the same (e.g., blade, motor, control system), the architecture of the product would be quite different. There would be significant changes in the interactions between components. The smaller size and the colocation of the motor and the blade in the room would focus attention on new types of interaction between the motor size, the blade dimensions, and the amount of air that the fan could circulate, while shrinking the size of the apparatus would probably introduce new interactions between the performance of the blade and the weight of the housing.

The distinctions between radical, incremental, and architectural innovations are matters of degree. The intention here is not to defend the boundaries of a particular definition, particularly since there are several other dimensions on which it may be useful to define radical and incremental innovation. The use of the term *architectural innovation* is designed to draw attention to innovations that use many existing core design concepts in a new architecture and that therefore have a more significant impact on the relationships between components than on the technologies of the components themselves. The matrix in Exhibit 1 is designed to suggest that a given innovation may be less radical or more architectural, not to suggest that the world can be neatly divided into four quadrants.

These distinctions are important because they give us insight into why established firms often have a surprising degree of difficulty in adapting to architectural innovation. Incremental innovation tends to reinforce the competitive positions of established firms, since it builds on their core competencies[16] or is "competence

---

[16] W. J. Abernathy and K. B. Clark, "Innovation: Mapping the Winds of Creative Destruction," *Research Policy* 14 (1985), pp. 3–22.

enhancing."[17] In the terms of the framework developed here, it builds on the existing architectural and component knowledge of an organization. In contrast, radical innovation creates unmistakable challenges for established firms, since it destroys the usefulness of their existing capabilities. In our terms, it destroys the usefulness of both architectural and component knowledge.[18]

Architectural innovation presents established firms with a more subtle challenge. Much of what the firm knows is useful and needs to be applied in the new product, but some of what it knows is not only useful but may actually handicap the firm. Recognizing what is useful and what is not, and acquiring and applying new knowledge when necessary, may be quite difficult for an established firm because of the way knowledge—particularly architectural knowledge—is organized and managed.

The Evolution of Component and Architectural Knowledge

Two concepts are important to understanding the ways in which component and architectural knowledge are managed inside an organization. The first is that of a dominant design. Work by Abernathy and Utterback,[19] Rosenberg,[20] Clark,[21] and Sahal[22] and evidence from studies of several industries show that product technologies do not emerge fully developed at the outset of their commercial lives.[23] Technical evolution is usually characterized by periods of great experimentation followed by the acceptance of a dominant design. The second concept is that organizations build knowledge and capability around the recurrent tasks that they perform.[24] Thus one cannot understand the development of an organization's innovative capability or of its knowledge without understanding the way in which they are shaped by the organization's experience with an evolving technology.

The emergence of a new technology is usually a period of considerable confusion. There is little agreement about what the major subsystems of the product should be or how they should be put together. There is a great deal of experimentation.[25] For example, in the early days of the automobile industry, cars were built with gasoline, electric, or steam engines, with steering wheels or tillers, and with wooden or metal bodies.[26]

These periods of experimentation are brought to an end by the emergence of a dominant design.[27] A dominant design is characterized both by a set of core design concepts that correspond to the major functions performed by the product[28] and that are embodied in components and by a product architecture that defines the ways in which these components are integrated.[29] It is equivalent to the general acceptance of a particular product architecture and is characteristic of technical evolution in a very wide range of industries.[30] A dominant design often emerges in response to the opportunity to obtain economies of scale or to take advantage of externalities.[31] For example, the dominant design for the car encompassed not only the fact that it used a gasoline engine to provide motive force but also that it was connected to the wheels through a transmission and a drive train and was mounted on a frame rather than on the axles. A dominant design incorporates a range of basic choices about the design that are not revisited in every subsequent design. Once the dominant automobile design had been accepted, engineers did not reevaluate the decision to use a gasoline engine each time they de-

[17] Tushman and Anderson, "Technological Discontinuities and Organizational Environments."

[18] Cooper and Schendel, "Strategic Response to Technological Threats"; Daft, "Bureaucratic Versus Nonbureaucratic Structure and the Process of Innovation and Change"; Tushman and Anderson, "Technological Discontinuities and Organizational Environments."

[19] W. J. Abernathy and J. Utterback, "Patterns of Industrial Innovation," *Technology Review* (June–July 1978), pp. 40–47.

[20] N. Rosenberg, *Inside the Black Box: Technology and Economics* (Cambridge: Cambridge University Press, 1982).

[21] "The Interaction of Design Hierarchies and Market Concepts in Technological Evolution."

[22] D. Sahal, "Technological Guideposts and Innovation Avenues," *Research Policy* 14 (1986), pp. 61–82.

[23] E. Mansfield, *The Production and Application of New Industrial Technology* (New York: Norton, 1977).

[24] R. M. Cyert and J. G. March, *A Behavioral Theory of the Firm* (Englewood Cliffs, NJ: Prentice Hall, 1963); Nelson and Winter, *An Evolutionary Theory of Economic Change.*

[25] Burns and Stalker, *The Management of Innovation;* Clark, "The Interaction of Design Hierarchies and Market Concepts in Technological Evolution."

[26] W. J. Abernathy, *The Productivity Dilemma: Roadblock to Innovation in the Automobile Industry* (Baltimore: Johns Hopkins University Press, 1978).

[27] Abernathy and Utterback, "Patterns of Industrial Innovation"; Sahal, "Technological Guideposts and Innovation Avenues."

[28] Marples, "The Decisions of Engineering Design"; Alexander, *Notes on the Synthesis of Form;* Clark, "The Interaction of Design Hierarchies and Market Concepts in Technological Evolution."

[29] Clark, "The Interaction of Design Hierarchies and Market Concepts in Technological Evolution"; Sahal, "Technological Guideposts and Innovation Avenues."

[30] Clark, "The Interaction of Design Hierarchies and Market Concepts in Technological Evolution."

[31] R. L. Daft and K. E. Weick, "Towards a Model of Organizations as Interpretation Systems," *Academy of Management Review* 9 (1984), pp. 284–95; B. Arthur, "Competing Technologies: An Overview," in *Technical Change and Economic Theory,* ed. G. Dosi et al. (New York: Columbia University Press, 1988), pp. 590–607.

veloped a new design. Once any dominant design is established, the initial set of components is refined and elaborated, and progress takes the shape of improvements in the components within the framework of a stable architecture.

This evolutionary process had profound implications for the types of knowledge that an organization developing a new product requires, since an organization's knowledge and its information-processing capabilities are shaped by the nature of the tasks and the competitive environment that it faces.[32]

In the early stages of a technology's history, before the emergence of a dominant design, organizations competing to design successful products experiment with many different technologies. Since success in the market turns on the synthesis of unfamiliar technologies in creative new designs, organizations must actively develop both knowledge about alternative components and knowledge of how these components can be integrated. With the emergence of a dominant design, which signals the general acceptance of a single architecture, firms cease to invest in learning about alternative configurations of the established set of components. New component knowledge becomes more valuable to a firm than new architectural knowledge because competition between designs revolves around refinements in particular components. Successful organizations therefore switch their limited attention from learning a little about many different possible designs to learning a great deal about the dominant design. Once gasoline-powered cars had emerged as the technology of choice, competitive pressures in the industry strongly encouraged organizations to learn more about gasoline-fired engines. Pursuing refinements in steam- or electric-powered cars became much less attractive. The focus of active problem solving becomes the elaboration and refinement of knowledge about existing components within a framework of stable architectural knowledge.[33]

Since in an industry characterized by a dominant design, architectural knowledge is stable, it tends to become embedded in the practices and procedures of the organization. Several authors have noted the importance of various institutional devices like frameworks and routines in completing recurring tasks in an organization.[34] The focus in this paper, however, is on the role of communication channels, information filters, and problem-solving strategies in managing architectural knowledge.

Channels, Filters, and Strategies

An organization's communication channels, both those that are implicit in its formal organization (A reports to B) and those that are informal ("I always call Fred because he knows about X"), develop around those interactions within the organization that are critical to its task.[35] These are also the interactions that are critical to effective design. They are the relationships around which the organization builds architectural knowledge. Thus, an organization's communication channels will come to embody its architectural knowledge of the linkages between components that are critical to effective design. For example, as a dominant design for room fans emerges, an effective organization in the industry will organize itself around its conception of the product's primary components, since these are the key subtasks of the organization's design problem.[36] The organization may create a fan-blade group, a motor group, and so on. The communication channels that are created between these groups will reflect the organization's knowledge of the critical interactions between them. The fact that those working on the motor and the fan blade report to the same supervisor and meet weekly is an embodiment of the organization's architectural knowledge about the relationship between the motor and the fan blade.

The information filters of an organization also embody its architectural knowledge. An organization is constantly barraged with information. As the task that it faces stabilizes and becomes less ambiguous, the organization develops filters that allow it to identify immediately what is most crucial in its information stream.[37] The emergence of a dominant design and its gradual

[32] For simplicity, we will assume here that organizations can be assumed to act as boundedly rational entities, in the tradition of K. Arrow, *The Limits of Organization* (New York: Norton, 1974); Nelson and Winter, *An Evolutionary Theory of Economic Change.*

[33] G. Dosi, "Technological Paradigms and Technological Trajectories: A Suggested Interpretation of the Determinants and Directions of Technical Change," *Research Policy* 11 (1982), pp. 147–62; Clark, "The Interaction of Design Hierarchies and Market Concepts in Technological Evolution."

[34] J. Galbraith, *Designing Complex Organizations* (Reading, MA: Addison-Wesley, 1973); Nelson and Winter, *An Evolutionary Theory of Economic Change;* Daft and Weick, "Towards a Model of Organizations as Interpretation Systems."

[35] Galbraith, *Designing Complex Organizations;* Arrow, *The Limits of Organization.*

[36] H. Mintzberg, *The Structuring of Organizations* (Englewood Cliffs, NJ: Prentice Hall, 1979); E. von Hippel, "Task Partitioning: An Innovation Process Variable," *Research Policy* (1990).

[37] Arrow, *The Limits of Organization;* Daft and Weick, "Towards a Model of Organizations as Interpretation Systems."

elaboration molds the organization's filters so that they come to embody parts of its knowledge of the key relationships between the components of the technology. For instance, the relationships between the designers of motors and controllers for a room fan are likely to change over time as they are able to express the nature of the critical interaction between the motor and the controller in an increasingly precise way that allows them to ignore irrelevant information. The controller designers may discover that they need to know a great deal about the torque and power of the motor but almost nothing about the materials from which it is made. They will create information filters that reflect this knowledge.

As a product evolves, information filters and communication channels develop and help engineers to work efficiently, but the evolution of the product also means that engineers face recurring kinds of problems. Over time, engineers acquire a store of knowledge about solutions to the specific kinds of problems that have arisen in previous projects. When confronted with such a problem, the engineer does not reexamine all possible alternatives but, rather, focuses first on those that he or she has found to be helpful in solving previous problems. In effect, an organization's problem-solving strategies summarize what it has learned about fruitful ways to solve problems in its immediate environment.[38] Designers may use strategies of this sort in solving problems within components, but problem-solving strategies also reflect architectural knowledge, since they are likely to express part of an organization's knowledge about the component linkages that are crucial to the solution of routine problems. An organization designing fans might learn over time that the most effective way to design a quieter fan is to focus on the interactions between the motor and the housing.

The strategies designers use, their channels for communications, and their information filters emerge in an organization to help it cope with complexity. They are efficient precisely because they do not have to be actively created each time a need for them arises. Further, as they become familiar and effective, using them becomes natural. Like riding a bicycle, using a strategy, working in a channel, or employing a filter does not require detailed analysis and conscious, deliberate execution. Thus, the

operation of channels, filters, and strategies may become implicit in the organization.

Since architectural knowledge is stable once a dominant design has been accepted, it can be encoded in these forms and thus becomes implicit. Organizations that are actively engaged in incremental innovation, which occurs within the context of stable architectural knowledge, are thus likely to manage much of their architectural knowledge implicitly by embedding it in their communication channels, information filters, and problem-solving strategies. Component knowledge, in contrast, is more likely to be managed explicitly because it is a constant source of incremental innovation.

Problems Created by Architectural Innovation

Differences in the way in which architectural and component knowledge are managed within an experienced organization give us insight into why architectural innovation often creates problems for established firms. These problems have two sources. First, established organizations require significant time (and resources) to identify a particular innovation as architectural, since architectural innovation can often initially be accommodated within old frameworks. Radical innovation tends to be obviously radical—the need for new modes of learning and new skills becomes quickly apparent. But information that might warn the organization that a particular innovation is architectural may be screened out by the information filters and communication channels that embody old architectural knowledge. Since radical innovation changes the core design concepts of the product, it is immediately obvious that knowledge about how the old components interact with each other is obsolete. The introduction of new linkages, however, is much harder to spot. Since the core concepts of the design remain untouched, the organization may mistakenly believe that it understands the new technology. In the case of the fan company, the motor and the fan-blade designers will continue to talk to each other. The fact that they may be talking about the wrong things may only become apparent after there are significant failures or unexpected problems with the design.

The development of the jet aircraft industry provides an example of the impact of unexpected architectural innovation. The jet engine initially appeared to have important but straightforward implications for airframe technology. Established firms in the industry understood that they would need to develop jet engine expertise but failed to understand the ways in which its introduction would change the interactions between the engine and

[38]J. G. March and H. A. Simon, *Organizations* (New York: Wiley, 1958); M. A. Lyles and I. I. Mitroff, "Organizational Problem Formulation: An Empirical Study," *Administrative Science Quarterly* 25 (1980), pp. 102–19; Nelson and Winter, *An Evolutionary Theory of Economic Change.*

the rest of the plane in complex and subtle ways.[39] This failure was one of the factors that led to Boeing's rise to leadership in the industry.

This effect is analogous to the tendency of individuals to continue to rely on beliefs about the world that a rational evaluation of new information should lead them to discard.[40] Researchers have commented extensively on the ways in which organizations facing threats may continue to rely on their old frameworks—or in our terms on their old architectural knowledge—and hence misunderstand the nature of a threat. They shoehorn the bad news, or the unexpected new information, back into the patterns with which they are familiar.[41]

Once an organization has recognized the nature of an architectural innovation, it faces a second major source of problems: the need to build and to apply new architectural knowledge effectively. Simply recognizing that a new technology is architectural in character does not give an established organization the architectural knowledge that it needs. It must first switch to a new mode of learning and then invest time and resources in learning about the new architecture.[42] It is handicapped in its attempts to do this, both by the difficulty all organizations experience in switching from one mode of learning to another and by the fact that it must build new architectural knowledge in a context in which some of its old architectural knowledge may be irrelevant.

An established organization setting out to build new architectural knowledge must change its orientation from one of refinement within a stable architecture to one of active search for new solutions within a constantly changing context. As long as the dominant design remains stable, an organization can segment and specialize its knowledge and rely on standard operating procedures to design and develop products. Architectural innovation, in contrast, places a premium on exploration in design and the assimilation of new knowledge. Many organizations encounter difficulties in their attempts to make this type of transition.[43] New entrants, with smaller commitments to older ways of learning about the environment and organizing their knowledge, often find it easier to build the organizational flexibility that abandoning old architectural knowledge and building new requires.

Once an organization has succeeded in reorientating itself, the building of new architectural knowledge still takes time and resources. This learning may be quite subtle and difficult. New entrants to the industry must also build the architectural knowledge necessary to exploit an architectural innovation, but since they have no existing assets, they can optimize their organization and information-processing structures to exploit the potential of a new design. Established firms are faced with an awkward problem. Because their architectural knowledge is embedded in channels, filters, and strategies, the discovery process and the process of creating new information (and rooting out the old) usually takes time. The organization may be tempted to modify the channels, filters, and strategies that already exist rather than to incur the significant fixed costs and considerable organizational friction required to build new sets from scratch.[44] But it may be difficult to identify precisely which filters, channels, and problem-solving strategies need to be modified, and the attempt to build a new product with old (albeit modified) organizational tools can create significant problems.

The problems created by an architectural innovation are evident in the introduction of high-strength-low-alloy (HSLA) steel in automobile bodies in the 1970s. The new materials allowed body panels to be thinner and lighter but opened up a whole new set of interactions that were not contained in existing channels and strategies. One automaker's body-engineering group, using traditional methods, designed an HSLA hood for the engine compartment. The hoods, however, resonated and oscillated with engine vibrations during testing. On further investigation, it became apparent that the traditional methods for designing hoods worked just fine with traditional materials, although no one knew quite why. The

---

[39] R. Miller and D. Sawyers, *The Technical Development of Modern Aviation* (New York: Praeger, 1968); J. P. Gardiner, "Design Trajectories for Airplanes and Automobiles during the Past Fifty Years," in *Design, Innovation and Long Cycles in Economic Development*, ed. C. Freeman (London: Francis Pinter, 1986), pp. 121–41.

[40] D. Kahneman, P. Slovic, and A. Tversky, *Judgment Under Uncertainty: Heuristics and Biases* (Cambridge: Cambridge University Press, 1982).

[41] Lyles and Mitroff, "Organizational Problem Formulation"; J. E. Dutton and S. E. Jackson, "Categorizing Strategic Issues: Links to Organizational Action," *Academy of Management Review* 12 (1987), pp. 76–90; S. E. Jackson and J. E. Dutton, "Discerning Threats and Opportunities," *Administrative Science Quarterly* 33 (1988), pp. 370–87.

[42] M. R. Louis and R. I. Sutton, "Switching Cognitive Gears: From Habits of Mind to Active Thinking," working paper, School of Industrial Engineering, Stanford University, 1989.

[43] C. Argyris and D. Schön, *Organizational Learning* (Reading, MA: Addison-Wesley, 1978); K. E. Weick, "Cognitive Processes in Organizations," in *Research in Organizational Behavior*, vol. 1, ed. B. M. Staw and L. L. Cummings (Greenwich, CT: JAI Press, 1979), pp. 41–47; Louis and Sutton, "Switching Cognitive Gears."

[44] Arrow, *The Limits of Organization*.

knowledge embedded in established problem-solving strategies and communication channels was sufficient to achieve effective designs with established materials, but the new material created new interactions and required the engineers to build new knowledge about them.

Architectural innovation may thus have very significant competitive implications. Established organizations may invest heavily in the new innovation, interpreting it as an incremental extension of the existing technology or underestimating its impact on their embedded architectural knowledge. But new entrants to the industry may exploit its potential much more effectively, since they are not handicapped by a legacy of embedded and partially irrelevant architectural knowledge. We explore the validity of our framework through a brief summary of the competitive and technical history of the semiconductor photolithographic alignment equipment industry. Photolithographic aligners are sophisticated pieces of capital equipment used in the manufacture of integrated circuits. Their performance has improved dramatically over the last 25 years, and although the core technologies have changed only marginally since the technique was first invented, the industry has been characterized by great turbulence. Changes in market leadership have been frequent, the entry of new firms has occurred throughout the industry's history, and incumbents have often suffered sharp declines in market share following the introduction of equipment incorporating seemingly minor innovation. We believe that these events are explained by the intrusion of architectural innovation into the industry, and we use three episodes in the industry's history—particularly Canon's introduction of the proximity aligner and Kasper's response to it—to illustrate this idea in detail.

INNOVATION IN PHOTOLITHOGRAPHIC ALIGNMENT EQUIPMENT

Data

The data were collected during a two-year, field-based study of the photolithographic alignment equipment industry. The study was initially designed to serve as an exploration of the validity of the concept of architectural innovation, a concept originally developed by one of the authors during the course of his experience with the automobile and ceramics industry.[45]

The core of the data is a panel data set consisting of research and development costs and sales revenue by product for every product development project conducted between 1962, when work on the first commercial product began, and 1986. This data is supplemented by a detailed managerial and technical history of each project. The data were collected through research in both primary and secondary sources. The secondary sources, including trade journals, scientific journals, and consulting reports, were used to identify the companies that had been active in the industry and the products that they had introduced and to build up a preliminary picture of the industry's technical history.

Data were then collected about each product-development project by contacting directly at least one of the members of the product-development team and requesting an interview. Interviews were conducted over a 14-month period, from March 1987 to May 1988. During the course of the research, over a hundred people were interviewed. As far as possible, the interviewees included the senior design engineer for each project and a senior marketing executive from each firm. Other industry observers and participants, including chief executives, university scientists, skilled design engineers, and service managers were also interviewed. Interview data were supplemented whenever possible through the use of internal firm records. The majority of the interviews were semistructured and lasted about two hours. Respondents were asked to describe the technical, commercial, and managerial history of the product-development projects with which they were familiar and to discuss the technical and commercial success of the products that grew out of them.

In order to validate the data that were collected during this process, a brief history of product development for each equipment vendor was circulated to all the individuals who had been interviewed and to others who knew a firm's history well, and the accuracy of this account was discussed over the telephone in supplementary interviews. The same validation procedure was followed in the construction of the technical history of the industry. A technical history was constructed using interview data, published product literature, and the scientific press. This history was circulated to key individuals who had a detailed knowledge of the technical history of the industry, who corrected it as appropriate.

We chose to study the semiconductor photolithographic alignment equipment industry for two reasons. The first is that it is very different from the industries in which our framework was first formulated, since it is

---

[45]Clark, "Managing Technology in International Competition."

characterized by much smaller firms and a much faster rate of technological innovation. The second is that it provides several examples of the impact of architectural innovation on the competitive position of established firms. Photolithographic equipment has been shaken by four waves of architectural innovation, each of which resulted in a new entrant capturing the leadership of the industry. In order to ground the discussion of architectural innovation we provide a brief description of photolithographic technology.

The Technology

Photolithographic aligners are used to manufacture solid-state semiconductor devices. The production of semiconductors requires the transfer of small, intricate patterns to the surface of a wafer of semiconductor material such as silicon, and this process of transfer is known as lithography. The surface of the wafer is coated with a light-sensitive chemical, or "resist." The pattern that is to be transferred to the wafer surface is drawn onto a mask and the mask is used to block light as it falls onto the resist, so that only those portions of the resist defined by the mask are exposed to light. The light chemically transforms the resist so that it can be stripped away. The resulting pattern is then used as the basis for either the deposition of material onto the wafer surface or for the etching of the existing material on the surface of the wafer. The process may be repeated as many as 20 times during the manufacture of a semiconductor device, and each layer must be located precisely with respect to the previous layer.[46] Exhibit 2 gives a very simplified representation of this complex process.

A photolithographic aligner is used to position the mask relative to the wafer, to hold the two in place during exposure, and to expose the resist. Exhibit 3 shows a schematic diagram of a contact aligner, the first generation of alignment equipment developed. Improvement in alignment technology has meant improvement in minimum feature size, the size of the smallest pattern that can be produced on the wafer surface, yield, the percentage of wafers successfully processed, and throughput, the number of wafers the aligner can handle in a given time.

Contact aligners were the first photolithographic aligners to be used commercially. They use the mask's shadow to transfer the mask pattern to the wafer surface. The mask and the wafer are held in contact with each

---

[46]R. K. Watts and N. G. Einspruch, eds., *Lithography for VLSI, VLSI Electronics—Microstructure Science* (New York: Academic Press, 1987).

EXHIBIT 2 Schematic Representation of the Lithographic Process

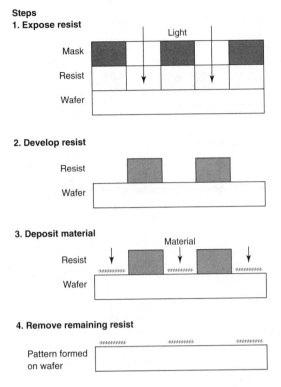

other, and light shining through the gaps in the mask falls on to the wafer surface. Contact aligners are simple and quick to use, but the need to bring the mask and the wafer into direct contact can damage the mask or contaminate the wafer. The first proximity aligner was introduced in 1973 to solve these problems.

In a proximity aligner the mask is held a small distance away from (in proximity to) the wafer surface, as shown in the simplified drawing in Exhibit 4. The separation of the mask and the wafer means that they are less likely to be damaged during exposure, but since the mask and wafer are separated from each other, light coming through the mask spreads out before it reaches the resist, and the mask's shadow is less well defined than it is in the case of a contact aligner. As a result, users switching to proximity aligners traded off some minimum feature size capability for increased yield.

The basic set of core design concepts that underlie optical photolithography—the use of a visible light source to transmit the image of the mask to the wafer, a lens or other device to focus the image of the mask on the wafer, an alignment system that uses visible light, and a mechanical system that holds the mask and the wafer in

EXHIBIT 3   Schematic Diagram of a Contact Aligner

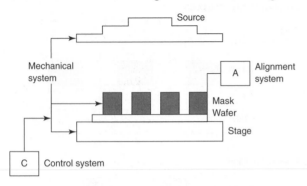

EXHIBIT 4   Schematic Diagram of a Proximity Aligner

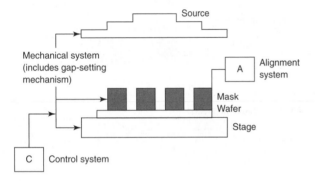

place—have remained unchanged since the technology was first developed, although aligner performance has improved dramatically. The minimum-feature-size capability of the first aligners was about 15 to 20 microns. Modern aligners are sometimes specified to have minimum feature sizes of less than half a micron.

Radical alternatives, making use of quite different core concepts, have been explored in the laboratory but have yet to be widely introduced into full-scale production. Aligners using x-rays and ion beams as sources have been developed, as have direct-write electron beam aligners, in which a focused beam of electrons is used to write directly on the wafer.[47] These technologies are clearly radical. Not only do they rely on quite different core concepts for the source, but they also use quite different mask, alignment, and lens technologies.

---

[47] T. H. P. Chang, M. Hatzakis, A. D. Wilson, and A. N. Broers, "Electron-Beam Lithography Draws a Finer Line," *Electronics* (May 1977), pp. 89–98; W. L. Brown, T. Venkatesan, and A. Wagner, "Ion Beam Lithography," *Solid State Technology* (August 1981), pp. 60–67; P. Burggraaf, "X-Ray Lithography: Optical's Heir," *Semiconductor International* (September 1983), pp. 60–67.

A constant stream of incremental innovation has been critical to optical photolithography's continuing success. The technology of each component has been significantly improved. Modern light sources are significantly more powerful and more uniform, and modern alignment systems are much more accurate. In addition, the technology has seen four waves of architectural innovation: the move from contact to proximity alignment, from proximity to scanning projection alignment, and from scanners to first- and then second-generation "steppers." Exhibit 5 summarizes the changes in the technology introduced by each generation. In each case the core technologies of optical lithography remained largely untouched, and much of the technical knowledge gained in building a previous generation could be transferred to the next. Yet, in each case, the industry leader was unable to make the transition.

Exhibit 6 shows share of deflated cumulative sales, 1962–1986, by generation of equipment for the leading firms. The first commercially successful aligner was introduced by Kulicke and Soffa in 1965. They were extremely successful and held nearly 100 percent of the (very small) market for the next nine years, but by 1974 Cobilt and Kasper had replaced them. In 1974 Perkin-Elmer entered the market with the scanning projection aligner and rapidly became the largest firm in the industry. GCA, in turn, replaced Perkin-Elmer through its introduction of the stepper, only to be supplanted by Nikon, which introduced the second-generation stepper.

In nearly every case, the established firm invested heavily in the next generation of equipment, only to meet with very little success. Our analysis of the industry's history suggests that a reliance on architectural knowledge derived from experience with the previous generation blinded the incumbent firms to critical aspects of the new technology. They thus underestimated its potential or built equipment that was markedly inferior to the equipment introduced by entrants.

The Kasper Saga

The case of Kasper Instruments and its response to Canon's introduction of the proximity printer illustrates some of the problems encountered by established firms. Kasper Instruments was founded in 1968 and by 1973 was a small but profitable firm supplying approximately half of the market for contact aligners. In 1973 Kasper introduced the first contact aligner to be equipped with proximity capability. Although nearly half of all the aligners that the firm sold from 1974 onward had this capability, Kasper aligners were only rarely used in prox-

EXHIBIT 5   A Summary of Architectural Innovation in Photolithographic Alignment Technology

Major changes

Equipment	Technology	Critical relationships between components
Proximity aligner	Mask and wafer separated during exposure.	Accuracy and stability of gap are a function of links between gap-setting mechanism and other components.
Scanning projection	Image of mask projected onto wafer by scanning reflective optics.	Interactions between lens and other components are critical to successful performance.
First-generation stepper	Image of mask projected through refractive lens. Image "stepped" across wafer.	Relationship between lens field size and source energy becomes significant determinant of throughput. Depth-of-focus characteristics—driven by relationship between source wavelength and lens numerical aperture—become critical. Interactions between stage and alignment system are critical.
Second-generation stepper	Introduction of "site-by-site" alignment and larger 5× lenses.	Throughput now driven by calibration and stepper stability. Relationship between lens and mechanical system becomes crucial means of controlling distortion.

Source: Field interviews, internal firm records; see R. M. Henderson. "The Failure of Established Firms in the Face of Technical Change: A Study of Photolithographic Alignment Equipment," Ph.D. dissertation, Harvard University, 1988.

EXHIBIT 6   Share of Deflated Cumulative Sales (%) 1962–1986, by Generation, for the Leading Optical Photolithographic Alignment Equipment Manufacturers*

Alignment equipment

Firm	Contact	Proximity	Scanners	Step and repeat (1)	Step and repeat (2)
Cobilt	44		<1		
Kasper	17	8		7	
Canon		67	21	9	
Perkin-Elmer			78	10	<1
GCA				55	12
Nikon					70
Total	61	75	99+	81	82+

*This measure is distorted by the fact that all of these products are still being sold. For second-generation step and repeat aligners this problem is particularly severe, since in 1966 this equipment was still in the early stages of its life cycle.
Source: Internal firm records, Dataquest, VLSI Research Inc.

imity mode, and sales declined steadily until the company left the industry in 1981. The widespread use of proximity aligners only occurred with the introduction and general adoption of Canon's proximity aligner in the late 1970s.

Clearly, the introduction of the proximity aligner is not a radical advance. The conceptual change involved was minor, and most proximity aligners can also be used as contact aligners. However, in a proximity aligner, a quite different set of relationships between components is critical to successful performance. The introduction of

the proximity aligner was thus an architectural innovation. In particular, in a proximity aligner, the relationships between the gap-setting mechanism and the other components of the aligner are significantly different.

In both contact and proximity aligners, the mask and the wafer surface must be parallel to each other during exposure if the quality of the final image on the wafer is to be adequate. This is relatively straightforward in a contact aligner, since the mask and the wafer are in direct contact with each other during exposure. The gap-setting mechanism is used only to separate the mask and the wafer during alignment. Its stability and accuracy have very little impact on the aligner's performance. In a proximity aligner, however, the accuracy and precision of the gap-setting mechanism are critical to the aligner's performance. The gap between the mask and the wafer must be precise and consistent across the mask and wafer surfaces if the aligner is to perform well. Thus, the gap-setting mechanism must locate the mask at exactly the right point above the wafer by dead reckoning and must then ensure that the mask is held exactly parallel to the wafer. Since the accuracy and stability of the mechanism is as much a function of the way in which it is integrated with the other components as it is of its own design; the relationships between the gap-setting mechanism and the other components of the aligner must change if the aligner is to perform well. Thus, the successful design of a proximity aligner requires both the acquisition of some new component knowledge—how to build a more accurate and more stable gap-setting mechanism—and the acquisition of new architectural knowledge.

Kasper's failure to understand the challenge posed by the proximity aligner is especially puzzling given its established position in the market and its depth of experience in photolithography. There were several highly skilled and imaginative designers at Kasper during the early 1970s. The group designed a steady stream of contact aligners, each incorporating significant incremental improvements. From 1968 to 1973, the minimum-feature-size capability of its contact aligners improved from fifteen to five microns.

But Kasper's very success in designing contact aligners was a major contributor to its inability to design a proximity aligner that could perform as successfully as Canon's. Canon's aligner was superficially very similar to Kasper's. It incorporated the same components and performed the same functions, but it performed them much more effectively because it incorporated a much more sophisticated understanding of the technical interrelationships that are fundamental to successful proximity alignment. Kasper failed to develop the particular component knowledge that would have enabled it to match Canon's design. More importantly, the architectural knowledge that Kasper had developed through its experience with the contact aligner had the effect of focusing its attention away from the new problems whose solution was critical to the design of a successful proximity aligner.

Kasper conceived of the proximity aligner as a modified contact aligner. Like the incremental improvements to the contact aligner before it, design of the proximity aligner was managed as a routine extension to the prod-

uct line. The gap-setting mechanism that was used in the contact aligner to align the mask and wafer with each other was slightly modified, and the new aligner was offered on the market. As a result, Kasper's proximity aligner did not perform well. The gap-setting mechanism was not sufficiently accurate or stable to ensure adequate performance, and the aligner was rarely used in its proximity mode. Kasper's failure to understand the obsolescence of its architectural knowledge is demonstrated graphically by two incidents.

The first is the firm's interpretation of early complaints about the accuracy of its gap-setting mechanism. In proximity alignment, misalignment of the mask and the wafer can be caused both by inaccuracies or instability in the gap-setting mechanism and by distortions introduced during processing. Kasper attributed many of the problems that users of its proximity equipment were experiencing to processing error, since it believed that processing error had been the primary source of problems with its contact aligner. The firm "knew" that its gap-setting mechanism was entirely adequate and, as a result, devoted very little time to improving its performance. In retrospect, this may seem like a wanton misuse of information, but it represented no more than a continued reliance on an information filter that had served the firm well historically.

The second illustration is provided by Kasper's response to Canon's initial introduction of a proximity aligner. The Canon aligner was evaluated by a team at Kasper and pronounced to be a copy of a Kasper machine. Kasper evaluated it against the criteria that it used for evaluating its own aligners—criteria that had been developed during its experience with contact aligners. The technical features that made Canon's aligner a significant advance, particularly the redesigned gap mechanism, were not observed because they were not considered important. The Canon aligner was pronounced to be "merely a copy" of the Kasper aligner.

Kasper's subsequent commercial failure was triggered by several factors. The company had problems designing an automatic alignment system of sufficient accuracy and in managing a high-volume manufacturing facility. It also suffered through several rapid changes of top management during the late 1970s. But the obsolescence of architectural knowledge brought about by the introduction of architectural innovation was a critical factor in its decline.

Kasper's failure stemmed primarily from failures of recognition: the knowledge that it had developed through its experience with the contact aligner made it difficult for the company to understand the ways in which Canon's proximity aligner was superior to its own. Similar problems with recognition show up in all four episodes of architectural innovation in the industry's history. The case of Perkin-Elmer and stepper technology is a case in point. By the late 1970s Perkin-Elmer had achieved market leadership with its scanning projection aligners, but the company failed to maintain that leadership when stepper technology came to dominate the industry in the early 1980s. When evaluating the two technologies, Perkin-Elmer engineers accurately forecast the progress of individual components in the two systems but failed to see how new interactions in component development— including better resist systems and improvements in lens design—would give stepper technology a decisive advantage.

GCA, the company that took leadership from Perkin-Elmer, was itself supplanted by Nikon, which introduced a second-generation stepper. Part of the problem for GCA was recognition, but much of its failure to master the new stepper technology lay in problems in implementation. Echoing Kasper, GCA first pronounced the Nikon stepper a "copy" of the GCA design. Even after GCA had fully recognized the threat posed by the second-generation stepper, its historical experience handicapped the company in its attempts to develop a competitive machine. GCA's engineers were organized by component, and cross-department communication channels were all structured around the architecture of the first-generation system. While GCA engineers were able to push the limits of the component technology, they had great difficulty understanding what Nikon had done to achieve its superior performance.

Nikon had changed aspects of the design—particularly the ways in which the optical system was integrated with the rest of the aligner—of which GCA's engineers had only limited understanding. Moreover, because these changes dealt with component interactions, there were few engineers responsible for developing this understanding. As a result, GCA's second-generation machines did not deliver the kind of performance that the market demanded. Like Kasper and Perkin-Elmer before them, GCA's sales languished and they lost market leadership. In all three cases, other factors also played a role in the firm's dramatic loss of market share, but a failure to respond effectively to architectural innovation was of critical importance.

DISCUSSION AND CONCLUSIONS

We have assumed that organizations are boundedly rational and, hence, that their knowledge and information processing structures come to mirror the internal structure of the product they are designing. This is clearly an approximation. It would be interesting to explore the ways in which the formulation of architectural and component knowledge is affected by factors such as the firm's history and culture. Similarly, we have assumed that architectural knowledge embedded in routines and channels becomes inert and hard to change. Future research designed to investigate information filters, problem-solving strategies, and communication channels in more detail could explore the extent to which this can be avoided.

The ideas developed here could also be linked to those of authors such as Abernathy and Clark,[48] who have drawn a distinction between innovation that challenges the technical capabilities of an organization and innovation that challenges the organization's knowledge of the market and of customer needs. Research could also examine the extent to which these insights are applicable to problems of process innovation and process development.

The empirical side of this paper could also be developed. While the idea of architectural innovation provides intriguing insights into the evolution of semiconductor photolithographic alignment equipment, further research could explore the extent to which it is a useful tool for understanding the impact of innovation in other industries.

The concept of architectural innovation and the related concepts of component and architectural knowledge have a number of important implications. These ideas not only give us a richer characterization of different types of innovation, but they open up new areas in understanding the connections between innovation and organizational capability. The paper suggests, for example, that we need to deepen our understanding of the traditional distinction between innovation that enhances and innovation that destroys competence within the firm, since the essence of architectural innovation is that it both enhances and destroys competence, often in subtle ways.

An architectural innovation's effect depends in a direct way on the nature of organizational learning. This paper not only underscores the role of organizational learning in innovation but suggests a new perspective on the problem. Given the evolutionary character of development and the prevalence of dominant designs, there appears to be a tendency for active learning among engineers to focus on improvements in performance within

---

[48]"Innovation."

a stable product architecture. In this context, learning means learning about components and the core concepts that underlie them. Given the way knowledge tends to be organized within the firm, learning about changes in the architecture of the product is unlikely to occur naturally. Learning about changes in architecture—about new interactions across components (and often across functional boundaries)—may therefore require explicit management and attention. But it may also be that learning about new architectures requires a different kind of organization and people with different skills. An organization that is structured to learn quickly and effectively about new component technology may be ineffective in learning about changes in product architecture. What drives effective learning about new architectures and how learning about components may be related to it are issues worth much further research.

These ideas also provide an intriguing perspective from which to understand the current fashion for cross-functional teams and more open organizational environments. These mechanisms may be responses to a perception of the danger of allowing architectural knowledge to become embedded within tacit or informal linkages.

To the degree that other tasks performed by organizations can also be described as a series of interlinked components within a relatively stable framework, the idea of architectural innovation yields insights into problems that reach beyond product development and design. To the degree that manufacturing, marketing, and finance rely on communication channels, information filters, and problem-solving strategies to integrate their work together, architectural innovation at the firm level may also be a significant issue.

Finally, an understanding of architectural innovation would be useful to discussions of the effect of technology on competitive strategy. Since architectural innovation has the potential to offer firms the opportunity to gain significant advantage over well-entrenched, dominant firms, we might expect less entrenched competitor firms to search actively for opportunities to introduce changes in product architecture in an industry. The evidence developed here and in other studies suggests that architectural innovation is quite prevalent. As an interpretive lens, architectural innovation may therefore prove quite useful in understanding technically based rivalry in a variety of industries.

Intel Corporation: The DRAM Decision

George W. Cogan and Robert A. Burgelman

INTRODUCTION

In November 1984, *Andy Grove,*[1] Intel's chief operating officer, stood in his office cubicle gazing out at Silicon Valley and thought about his company's future. The semiconductor industry which Intel had helped create 16 years earlier had entered what looked to be a prolonged cyclical downturn. Some operations had already been trimmed, but Grove believed the company would have to react again soon (see company financial data in Exhibit 2). The recession hit the company's Memory Components Division particularly hard. For much of the previous five years, memory components had been suffering under competitive pressure from the Japanese.

Since 1980, Intel had been losing its market position in *dynamic random-access memories (DRAMs)* as the industry average selling price per chip had declined much more rapidly than the 20 to 30 percent per year which was customary. The Japanese had taken the lead in unit sales of the latest generation of DRAMs, the 256 *kilobit* (256K) version, but Intel was fighting back with a program to leapfrog the Japanese in the product's next generation. Its $50 million 1 *megabit* (1 meg= 4 × 256K) research project was soon to produce working prototypes. Intel managers estimated they were ahead of the Japanese in the 1 meg device. Still, a debate was growing within the company about whether Intel could continue to compete in the commodity market of DRAMs. Grove was formulating his personal position on the matter.

It seemed clear that if Intel chose to continue with the DRAM product line, it would have to commit to at least one $150 million state-of-the-art *Class 10 production facility.* On the other hand, Intel's other businesses were much more profitable than memories; in an ROI framework, the microprocessor business deserved the majority of Intel's corporate resources. It was difficult for both Grove and *Gordon Moore,* Intel's chief executive

Source: Reprinted with permission of Graduate School of Business. Copyright © 1989 by The Board of Trustees of the Leland Stanford Junior University.
[1]Note: All italicized names appear with biographies in Exhibit 1; all italicized words appear with definitions in the technical appendix.

EXHIBIT 1 Biographies of Key Intel Personnel

Jack Carsten joined Intel from Texas Instruments and has held various high level management positions since then. In 1985 he was senior vice president and general manager of the Components Group.

Dennis Carter is a Harvard M.B.A. with an engineering background. He has worked in several areas of the company and is currently assistant to the president.

Sun Lin Chou received his B.S. and M.S. degrees in Electrical Engineering from MIT and his Ph.D. in electrical engineering from Stanford University. He joined Intel in 1971 and has managed the DRAM technology development group in Oregon since then.

Dov Frohman joined Intel from Fairchild in 1969. He was responsible for the invention of the EPROM. He currently manages Intel's design group in Israel.

Edward Gelbach joined Intel from Texas Instruments in 1969. He is currently senior vice president of sales.

Andrew Grove was born in Budapest. He received his B.S. from CCNY and his Ph.D. from Berkeley. After working at Fairchild Camera and Instrument for five years, he joined Intel in 1968. He has been president and chief operating officer since 1979.

Ted Hoff joined Intel as a designer in 1969. He headed the group that invented the microprocessor. Hoff left Intel in 1983.

Gordon Moore was born in San Francisco. He received his B.S. in chemistry from Berkeley and his Ph.D. in chemistry and physics from the California Institute of Technology. He worked as a member of the technical staff at Shockley Semiconductor from 1956 to 1987, and he founded Fairchild. He founded Intel in 1968 and is currently the chairman and CEO.

Robert Noyce was born in Burlington, Iowa. He received his B.S. from Grinnell College and his Ph.D. from MIT. He was a research engineer at Philco from 1953 to 1956, a research engineer at Shockley Transistor, and a founder and director of Fairchild Camera and Instrument. He is credited with coinventing (with Kilby at TI) the integrated circuit. He founded Intel and currently serves as vice chairman of the board of directors.

Bob Reed received his bachelor's degree from Middlebury College and his M.B.A. from the University of Chicago. He joined Intel in 1974. He was appointed chief financial officer in 1984.

Ron Smith received his bachelor's degree in physics from Gettysburg College and his M.S. and Ph.D. degrees in physics from the University of Minnesota. He joined Intel in 1978 as a device physicist in the Static Logic Technology Development Group. In 1985, he was manager of that group.

Dean Toombs joined Intel from Texas Instruments in 1983 with the express purpose of running the Memory Components Division.

Leslie Vadasz joined Intel in 1968 and has held a variety of senior management positions since then. He is currently senior vice president and director of the Corporate Strategic Staff.

Ron Whittier holds a Ph.D. in chemical engineering from Stanford University. He joined Intel in 1970. From 1975 until 1983, he managed the memory products division. In 1983, he became vice president and director of Business Development and Marketing Communications.

Albert Yu was born in Shanghai and holds a Ph.D. in electrical engineering from Stanford University. He joined Intel in 1975.

---

officer, to imagine an Intel without DRAMs. The memory business had made Intel, and was still by far the largest market segment in integrated circuits. Not the least of Grove's worries was how the investment community would react to Intel's decision to cede such a large market segment to the Japanese.

COMPANY BACKGROUND

Early History

On August 2, 1968, the *Palo Alto Times* announced that *Bob Noyce* and *Gordon Moore* had left Fairchild to form a new company. Andy Grove, who had been Moore's assistant director of research at Fairchild, also left to complete what the company's historians have called the triumvirate. The three were key technologists in the emerging solid-state electronics industry. Noyce had invented the integrated circuit (simultaneously with Jack Kilby at Texas Instruments), and Intel was the first company to specialize in making large-scale integrated circuits.

In mid-1969, Intel introduced its first product, a *bipolar static random-access memory (SRAM)* with a 64-bit storage capacity. The chip itself was less than a quarter of an inch on a side and contained nearly 400 *transistors*. While the SRAM had some small markets, Intel had set its sights on the growing computer memory business, then dominated by *magnetic core* technology. To attack the magnetic core business required at least a 10-fold reduction in cost per bit.

The Intel managers decided early on to pursue a new process technology in addition to the relatively proven bipolar process. The *metal-oxide-semiconductor* (MOS) process promised to lead to increased transistor density while simultaneously reducing the number of fabrication steps required to make a working chip. The process had been published in scientific journals, but serious manufacturability questions remained. MOS transistors consumed only a fraction of the power of a traditional bipolar transistor and thus could be more densely packed on the chip. But they were also very sensitive to trace amounts of impurities in processing, raising the question

EXHIBIT 2 Selected Intel Corporation Financial Data

	Year ended December 31								
	1976	1977	1978	1979	1980	1981	1982	1983	1984
Sales	226	283	400	663	854	788	900	1.122	1,629
COGS	117	144	196	313	399	458	542	624	883
Gross margin	109	139	204	350	455	330	358	498	746
R&D	21	28	41	67	96	116	131	142	180
SG&A	37	48	76	131	175	184	198	217	315
Operating profit	51	63	87	152	184	30	29	139	251
Interest and other			(1)	(3)	2	10	2	40	47
Profit before tax	51	63	86	149	186	40	31	179	298
Income tax	26	31	42	71	89	13		63	100
Net income	25	32	44	78	97	27	31	116	198
Depreciation	10	16	24	40	49	66	83	103	114
Capital invest	32	97	104	97	152	157	138	145	388

	December 31								
	1976	1977	1978	1979	1980	1981	1982	1983	1984
Cash and ST invest	26	39	28	34	127	115	85	389	230
Working capital	93	81	67	115	299	287	306	608	568
Fixed assets	30	80	160	217	321	412	462	504	778
Total assets	156	221	356	500	767	871	1,056	1,680	2,029
LT debt	0	0	0	0	150	150	197	127	146
Equity	109	149	205	303	432	488	552	1,122*	1,360
Employees	7,300	8,100	10,900	14,300	15,900	16,800	19,400	21,500	25,400
ROS	11.1%	11.3%	11.0%	11.8%	11.4%	3.4%	3.4%	10.3%	12.2%
ROA**	24.3%	20.5%	19.9%	21.9%	19.4%	3.5%	3.6%	11.0%	11.8%
ROE**	33.8%	29.4%	29.5%	38.0%	32.0%	6.3%	6.4%	21.0%	17.6%

Note: The first and second quarters of 1985 showed revenue of $375 million and $360 million and profit of $9 million and $11 million, respectively. The first and second quarters of 1984 showed revenue of $372 million and $410 million and profit of $54 million and $50 million, respectively.
*Includes $250 million proceeds from sale of 11% stake to IBM.
**Based on beginning-of-year asset (equity) values.
Source: Intel annual reports.

of whether their performance characteristics would remain stable over time.

Les Vadasz headed the MOS team of several engineers. In contrast to the bipolar effort, the MOS effort moved slowly. The primary problem was to develop a stable transistor *threshold voltage.* After a year of frustration and setbacks, Vadasz's team produced the first commercially available MOS SRAM, the 256-bit "1101." The successful processing sequence had several proprietary aspects which put Intel in the forefront of semiconductor technology development. Vadasz commented that at this early stage of development, the processing sequences had proprietary aspects, but were not always well understood.

Since the market for SRAMs was young, Intel had difficulty selling the new device. But the successful MOS process was immediately applied to the existing market for *shift registers* among mainframe computer makers. Shift register sales provided the company with a war chest of cash needed to weather its first semiconductor recession of 1970–1971.

Development of DRAM

Another technical innovation followed the 1101. Intel worked closely with Honeywell engineers to design and develop the first DRAM in 1970, the 1-kilobit "1103." While the SRAM required six MOS transistors per memory cell, the DRAM required only three transistors. With fewer elements in each memory cell, the 1103 contained more storage capacity in the same silicon area. While the new design allowed increased memory cell density, it also required a significant amount of external circuitry for *access* and *refresh.* An advertisement placed in computer trade journals in early 1971 announced: "THE END. CORES LOSE PRICE WAR TO NEW CHIP."

In spite of the price/performance advantage, customers had to be taught how to use the new device and convinced of its reliability. *Ed Gelbach,* VP of sales, remembered 1971:

> We could never find a customer that used them and yet we were shipping literally hundreds of thousands of them. They were all testing them and putting them in boards . . . but it seemed like none of the customers ever shipped machines with the part. My recurring nightmare was that all of those chips would be returned over a single weekend.

In order to speed the adoption of DRAMs, Intel started the Memory Systems Operations (MSO), which assembled 1103 chips along with the required peripheral controller circuitry for OEM sale into the computer maker market. Soon MSO was responsible for about 30 percent of Intel's business. By 1972, the 1103 was the largest selling integrated circuit in the world and accounted for over 90 percent of Intel's $23.4 million in revenue.

Gordon Moore called the 1103 "the most-difficult-to-use semiconductor product ever invented." Ironically, that may have helped its market success:

> There was a lot of resistance to semiconductor technology on the part of the core memory engineers. Core was a very difficult technology and required a great deal of engineering support. The engineers didn't embrace the 1103 until they realized that it too was a difficult technology and wouldn't make their skills irrelevant.

New DRAM Generations

From its early days, Intel was fighting a battle with processing yields. The early 1103's were produced on 2-inch–diameter silicon wafers, each containing about 250 devices. Of the 250, early 1103 runs produced an average of 25 fully functional devices, or an overall yield of 10 percent. *Ron Whittier,* general manager of the Memories Components Division from 1975 until 1983, said that throughout a product's life cycle, wafer yields increased continually as process improvements were developed. The productivity of the factory was also increased by changing the size of the wafer whenever silicon manufacturers developed techniques to grow larger silicon ingots and equipment manufacturers developed machines which could handle larger wafers. In 1972, *Albert Yu* headed a team which converted the bipolar process from 2-inch to 3-inch wafers, effectively doubling capacity.

In the early days, Vadasz recalled, MSO developed another strategy for increasing yield. Since it only took one defective memory cell (out of 1024 in the 1103) to make a chip dysfunctional, it seemed inefficient to throw away all defectives. MSO's scheme was to compensate for a defective memory cell using creative peripheral logic circuitry. The peripheral circuitry was designed to bypass the defective cells within each memory chip so that rejected 1103s could still be used. Since the scheme required extra 1103s in each system, Intel referred to the concept as redundancy.

Soon after Intel's early success, competitors entered the market for DRAMs and began to erode Intel's MOS process technology lead. By the mid-1970s, Intel was one of several companies vying to be the first at introducing the new generation of DRAM memories. Every three years, a new generation with four times as much capacity as its predecessor was developed (see Exhibit 3).

Vadasz recalled that even at the 4K and 16K level, Intel was struggling to keep up with its competitors. During the formative years of the DRAM market, the chip design was in rapid flux. A start-up company, MOSTEK, was able to take market share from Intel in the 4K generation by incorporating the peripheral circuitry required to manage the memory on the chip itself. Vadasz recalled: "The first DRAMs were not very user-friendly, and MOSTEK came out with a better product." MOSTEK introduced the concept of on-chip *multiplexing*, which allowed a smaller number of output pins to address the entire memory. Multiplexing started a trend in DRAMs towards user-friendliness.[2]

Vadasz commented:

> Even though you have invented the product, sometimes it is easier for new entrants to seize an opportunity and beat you to the punch. They are not encumbered by the same things you are. . . . The real problem in technological innovation is in anticipating the relevant issues. Once a technological "box" has been defined, it is easy for a team of great engineers to optimize everything in that box. Choosing the box is the hard part.

Intel's first 4K DRAM was redesigned to include the internal multiplexing logic. *Sun Lin Chou,* who was involved in the 4K DRAM development, said that in the revised version, Intel also implemented a one-transistor DRAM cell, which became the industry standard. While more challenging from a process technology standpoint, the reduction in the number of transistors allowed for a smaller chip size. The revised 4K version sold well, but time was short before the next generation.

---

[2] Eventually Intel sold MSO since the value added had been integrated onto the chip itself and the majority of MSO's customers had learned how to use DRAMs.

EXHIBIT 3   Product Introduction Timelines

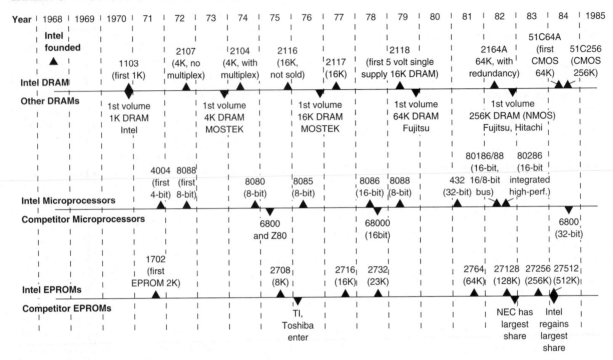

Note: 6800 and 68000 are Motorola Products. Z80 is a Zilog Product.
Source: Intel documents, Dataquest.

Dennis Carter described Intel's early strategy as "staying ahead of the experience curve using process technology."[3] According to Sun Lin Chou, a successful DRAM company participates in the early phase of each generation when low competitor yields and high demand support high prices.

> In fact, for the first two years, the demand for DRAMs to the first market entrant is semi-infinite. As soon as the leading vendor makes a new DRAM, he can crank his capacity to the maximum and he will be guaranteed of selling all his output. This is not true for more complex products such as a logic product with a new function where the customers have to first learn how to use it.

Each new generation required a quadrupling of the number of transistors contained on a chip. The driving force behind increased density was the ability to define patterns of ever narrower dimensions (functional equivalent of wires and components in a circuit) on the silicon wafer, to invent creative ways of reducing the required number and size of components per memory cell, and to make larger chips without defects. Each new generation reduced the minimum linewidth by a factor of about 0.7, from 5 µm at the 4K generation. The minimum linewidth was controlled primarily by the accuracy of the photolithography process, while the maximum chip size was determined by the ability to control the number of random defects on the wafer.[4]

While competition was tough even at the 4K level, a series of process innovations kept Intel amongst the memory leaders through the 16K DRAM generation (see Exhibit 3). Gordon Moore developed the strategy of using DRAMs as a technology driver. The latest process technology was developed using DRAMs and later transferred to other products. Early on in the company's de-

---

[3] The experience curve referred to the declining nature of industry-wide manufacturing costs over time due to experience. The semiconductor industry had a 70 percent experience curve (costs reduced by 30 percent for each doubling in cumulative volume). Companies who were not ahead of the curve for a particular product or generation suffered erosion of margins or market share.

[4] The size of the chip defines the area of the wafer which each process-induced defect can potentially damage. If the chip size is too large, yields are unacceptably low unless the defect level can be simultaneously reduced.

velopment, Intel managers decided to merge the research and manufacturing functions. Gordon Moore had been dissatisfied with the linkage between research and manufacturing at Fairchild. As a result, he had insisted that Intel perform all process research directly on the production line. Moore commented:

> Our strategy optimizes our ability to make fast incremental process technology improvements. We don't have a central corporate research lab. We tend to evaluate other research advances in light of how they will affect our businesses. For instance, while Texas Instruments has been funding a research effort in *gallium arsenide,* we have been watching gallium arsenide develop for the past 20 years. We're still silicon believers.

During the 1970s, Intel competed by developing new processes which were used to enhance product features or to enable new product families beyond memories. The *HMOS* (high-performance MOS) process enabled Intel to introduce the first 5-volt-single-power-supply 16K DRAM in 1979. Earlier offerings, including Intel's two previous 16K DRAMs (2116 and 2117), required that the user supply three separate voltages to the chip. The new product, the 2118, greatly simplified the user's design and production tasks. While Intel had lost market share with the 2116 and 2117, it was all alone with the 5-volt device and captured a price premium of double the industry average for three-power-supply 16K DRAMs in 1979 (see Exhibit 4). The DRAM technology development group focused a significant amount of its resources on developing Intel's third 16K DRAM offering while competitors concentrated on the 64K generation.

Intel management decided to focus on the single-power-supply 16K DRAM for two primary reasons: they projected a relatively long life cycle for the 16K generation due to the technical challenge in achieving the 64K generation, and they believed the one-power-supply process would eventually dominate the memory industry. They considered it too risky to tackle both the 64K DRAM generation and the single-power-supply technology in the same product.

The drive towards smaller and smaller geometries was achieved through improvements in both processing methodology and processing machinery. Dennis Carter explained that in the early years some processing steps were considered black magic and defined a company's competitive edge. As time went on, the movement of engineers between chip companies and the involvement of suppliers and equipment manufacturers in process development efforts led to a general leveling of process capability amongst Silicon Valley firms. Sun Lin Chou commented about the trends in processing:

> Process technology and equipment have become so complex and expensive to develop that no vendor can hope to do better than [its] competitors in every process step. The key to innovation is to be on par with your competitors on every process step, but to select one or two or three process features with the highest leverage and focus your efforts to gain leadership there. In DRAMs we focus on high-quality thin *dielectrics.*

The Invention of the EPROM

Albert Yu, vice president of development and general manager of the components division, said he usually associates the invention of any important product with one person. The EPROM (electrically programmable read-only memory) was invented by *Dov Frohman.* Yu said Frohman not only invented the product, but he also described the physical effect, saw that it could be applied to a memory device, designed the first part, and fabricated the first device.

Frohman's story has become legendary at Intel. As a recent hire from Fairchild in 1969, Frohman was assigned to help understand and remedy a strange phenomenon which was causing reliability problems with the MOS process. The problem involved the silicon gate structure. Frohman saw that the phenomenon could be explained by the existence of an unintentional *floating gate* within the MOS device. He realized that if a floating gate were intentionally constructed, a new type of programmable memory which would permanently store information could be built.

Frohman designed the first test devices and assembled a demonstration for Gordon Moore. According to Frohman:

> We put together a 16-bit array with primitive transistor packages sticking out of the 16 sockets, an oscilloscope and pulse generator, and we carted all this into Gordon's office. There were red bulbs to indicate the bits. This was all new to us, and we were thrashing around. We showed Gordon that by pushing the button you could program the device, and we demonstrated that it would hold a charge.

Later, it was discovered that ultraviolet light could be used to erase the memory. Moore committed the company to the production of the EPROM even though no one could tell where the device would have applications. Recalled Moore:

EXHIBIT 4 Market Information for DRAMs and Microprocessors

Product	1974	1975	1976	1977	1978	1979	1980	1981	1982	1983	1984
Worldwide unit shipments of DRAMs (in thousands)											
4K	615	5,290	28,010	57,415	77,190	70,010	31,165	13,040	4,635	2,400	2,250
16K 3PS*			50	2,008	20,785	69,868	182,955	215,760	263,050	239,210	120,690
16K 5V*					1	150	1,115	5,713	23,240	57,400	40,600
64K						36	441	12,631	103,965	371,340	851,600
256K									10	1,700	37,980
Worldwide yearly average selling prices of DRAMs ($/unit)											
4K	17.00	6.24	4.35	2.65	1.82	1.92	1.94	1.26	1.62	2.72	3.00
16K 3PS*			46.39	18.63	8.53	6.03	4.77	2.06	1.24	1.05	1.09
16K 5V*					150.00	17.67	7.38	3.84	2.23	1.98	2.07
64K						110.14	46.26	11.00	5.42	3.86	3.16
256K									150.00	47.66	17.90
Total market	10,455	33,010	124,163	189,559	317,932	562,339	961,785	621,775	905,506	1,885,745	3,593,242
Intel DRAM market share											
4K	82.9%	45.6%	18.7%	18.1%	14.3%	8.7%	3.2%	2.4%	2.3%	1.9%	1.4%
16K 3PS*			37.0%	27.9%	11.5%	4.4%	2.1%	66.5%	33.1%	11.7%	12.3%
16K 5V*						100.0%	94.0%	0.2%	1.5%	3.5%	1.7%
64K							0.7%				0.1%
Estimated revenue**	8,667	15,052	23,643	37,976	40,479	32,882	28,139	25,534	33,109	68,238	58,607

Achitecture (% units sold)	1976	1977	1978	1979	1980	1981	1982	1983	1984
Microprocessor sales history by architecture									
8-bit:									
Zilog (780)	2.2%	5.8%	12.4%	17.0%	21.1%	22.7%	23.4%	37.4%	35.1%
Intel (8080, 8088)	22.8%	36.6%	34.6%	38.9%	27.1%	19.7%	19.1%	22.3%	33.5%
Motorola (6800, 650X, 680X)	15.0%	13.0%	17.2%	20.8%	18.8%	21.1%	17.9%	14.8%	14.0%
Others	60.0%	44.6%	35.8%	23.3%	33.0%	36.5%	39.6%	25.5%	17.4%
Total 8-bit (million units)	n/a	n/a	n/a	12.5	22.4	33.8	47.9	67.8	75.1
Average selling price	n/a	n/a	n/a	$6.03	$4.60	$3.32	$3.18	$3.25	$4.06
16-bit:									
Zilog (Z8000)				1.4%	4.5%	3.4%	5.1%	5.8%	6.2%
Intel (80186/286,8086)			6.7%	14.0%	28.9%	31.7%	26.6%	32.1%	59.1%
Motorola (68000)						3.9%	5.8%	10.8%	20.2%
Others			93.3%	84.6%	66.6%	61.0%	62.5%	51.3%	14.5%
Total 16-bit (million units)	n/a	n/a	n/a	0.5	0.8	1.8	4.1	7.1	10.0
Average selling price			n/a	$30.29	$38.00	$16.96	$15.29	$14.25	$28.90

*16K 3PS refers to the industry-standard, three-power-supply DRAM. The 16K 5V model requires only one power supply.
**Sales of 1K DRAMs were negligible by 1977. Estimates are created by assuming Intel prices at average selling price. Casewriter estimates that by 1984 Intel DRAM sales were closer to $100 million. Losses to gross income due to DRAMs in 1984 were estimated by the casewriter to be between $20 million and $30 million.
†Architecture refers to company who originated design, not to manufacturer. For example, while Intel's designs captured 33.5% and 59.1% of the 8- and 16-bit segments, Intel's actual unit sales of microprocessors accounted for only 14.5% of total market sales in 1984. Licensing agreements with other vendors account for the remainder. Next to Intel, NEC was the second largest unit shipper of microprocessors at 13.5% of total units. Motorola captured fifth place behind Zilog (8.9%) and AMD (7.4%) with 7.3% of microprocessor unit sales in 1984.
Source: Dataquest

It was just another kind of memory at the time, and people saw it as a research and development device. Today, the likelihood of someone killing an effort like this one is very high, because we require a well-defined application to a market from the outset. This is especially so because we are not lacking in opportunities. There is still a lot of evolution left in the current technology. If you consider the possibilities for reducing line width, you can see another 12 years of evolution along the same curve.

The Invention of the Microprocessor

Ted Hoff invented the microprocessor. Intel had been hired by the Japanese firm Busicom to design and build a set of chips for a number of different calculators. Busicom had envisioned a set of around 15 chips designed to perform advanced calculator functions. Hoff suggested building a simpler set of just a few general-purpose chips which could be programmed to carry out each of the calculators' instructions.

He was the architect of the chip set which Federico Faggin and a team of designers implemented. The set included four chips: a central processing unit (CPU) called the 4004, a read-only memory (ROM) with custom instructions for calculator operation, a random-access memory (RAM), and a shift register for input/output buffering. It took nearly a year to convince Busicom that the novel approach would work, but by early 1970, Intel signed a $60,000 contract which gave Busicom proprietary rights to the design. The CPU chip, 4004, was eventually called a microprocessor.

While Intel produced chips for Busicom which were successfully made into 100,000 calculators,[5] a debate within the company developed about whether Intel should try to renegotiate the rights to the chip design. Hoff believed that Intel could use the devices as a general-purpose solution in many applications ranging from cash registers to street lights, and he lobbied heavily within the company.

Eventually, Intel decided to offer reduced pricing to Busicom in exchange for noncalculator rights to the design. Ed Gelbach remembered the management decision: "Originally, I think we saw it as a way to sell more memories and we were willing to make the investment on that basis." Busicom, in financial trouble, readily agreed to the proposal.

The 4004 was introduced in 1971. It contained 2,300 MOS transistors and could execute 60,000 instructions per second. Its performance was not as good as custom-designed logic, but Intel believed there was a significant market for it. Early on, it became apparent that Intel would have to educate its customers in order to sell the 4004. As a result, Gelbach's group developed the first of Intel's development aides, which were programming tools for the customer. By 1973 revenues from design aides exceeded microprocessor sales.

In tandem with the 4-bit 4004, Intel developed an 8-bit microprocessor, the 8008, which was introduced in April 1972. The 8008 was designed with a computer terminal company in mind, but was rejected by the company because it was too slow and required 20 support chips for operation.

In the meantime, Intel's advancements in static and dynamic RAMs had provided a new process technology which promised increased transistor switching speed. Intel had created an *NMOS* process, which was applied to the 8008. In addition, much of the functionality of the support chips was integrated into the new microprocessor, the 8080. As a result of process technology, the 8080 could execute 290,000 instructions per second. In addition, the 8080 required only six support chips for operation.

The introduction of the 8080 in April 1974 heralded the beginning of a new age in computing. The market for microprocessors exploded as new uses were developed. Intel was one year ahead of Motorola's introduction of the 6800 and eventually took nearly the entire 8-bit market. Even though the 6800 used an architecture more familiar to programmers, Intel offered more effective development aids and support systems. Several integrated circuit companies were licensed to produce the 8080 so that customers were assured of a second source of supply. Ed Gelbach remembered the mid-1970s as the good old days. At an initial selling price of $360 per chip, Intel paid for the 8080 research and development in the first five months of shipments.

Motorola and Zilog[6] continued to apply pressure in the 8-bit microprocessor marketplace (see Exhibit 4). But Intel's 16-bit microprocessor, the 8086, again was first to market by about one year when it was introduced in June 1978. Intel management decided that upward

---

[5] The casewriter noticed a Busicom calculator on Gordon Moore's desk. Moore also wore an Intel digital watch, which he called his $15 million watch, referring to Intel's ill-fated venture into the watch business. He said: "If anyone comes to me with an idea for a consumer product, all I have to do is look at my watch to get the answer. . . ."

[6] Zilog had been formed as a start-up by three Intel design engineers. Andy Grove commented that the loss of those engineers set back Intel's microprocessor program by as much as one year.

compatibility would be a critical feature of the 16-bit chip. While the 8086 could operate software developed originally for the 8080, it employed a new architecture which required new software for full exploitation. An 8-bit *bus* version of the new architecture, the 8088, was also introduced. For two years, Intel did not meet its sales forecasts for the 8086 family as customers purchased only sample quantities and worked on a new generation of software. In the meantime, Motorola introduced its own 16-bit microprocessor, the 68000, and appeared to be gaining momentum in the field.[7]

Recognizing that the 68000 represented a critical threat that could lock Intel out of the 16-bit market and potentially the next generation as well, Intel created a task force to attack the 68000. The project was called operation CRUSH. The project leader said: "We set out to generate 100,000 sales leads and get that down to 10,000 qualified leads resulting in 2,000 design wins in 1980." SWAT teams of engineering, applications, and marketing people were mobilized to travel anywhere in the world whenever a design win was threatened.

The CRUSH campaign emphasized Intel's systems approach, and produced 2,500 design wins in the first year. The most notable win was IBM's decision to use the 8088 in their first personal computer in 1981. IBM planned an open-architecture personal computer, and Intel's 8086 family defined the software standard. Intel sales representatives knew they won the IBM account several months before it was made public when the IBM Boca Raton office started placing orders for Intel's ICE-88 development systems. In 1981, 13 percent of Intel's sales were to IBM.

The project to develop the next microprocessor generation began in 1978. The 80186 and 80286 were designed to be upwardly compatible with the 8086, and to offer increased integration, internal memory management, and advanced software protection (security) capability. The 80286 was designed to operate with as few as four support chips. The 286 team developed product features through extensive field interviews, and created a list of over 50 potential applications ranging from business systems to industrial automation. Ironically, the applications list did not include personal computers, which later became the single largest application.

The 80286 was the most ambitious design effort ever undertaken at Intel. The chip contained 130,000 transistors (versus 29,000 for the 8086). Intel's computerized design tools were stretched to their limit. Four separate computer systems had to be used just to store the design. Design verification (a tool which checks that mask design correctly reflects schematic design) took four days of continuous computer operation. Several crises arose throughout the development period.

The 286 logic design supervisor recalled:

> At least once a year we went through a crisis that made us wonder whether we would get there or not. One was the chip size crisis. At one point, it looked like the chip would be as big as 340 mils on a side. That was so big that people outside the design team would roll on the floor laughing. They kind of enjoyed our misery. Chip designers love to hear that someone else's chip is too big, but when it happens to you, it's really serious stuff.

The design team of 24 people worked feverishly for three years to develop the first prototype. That device was fabricated in 1982 at Fab 3 in Livermore but did not operate with high enough speed. Gradually, all the bugs were worked out, and only one hurdle remained: developing the methodology to test the chips as they came off the line. Production was ready to start making the 80286 six months before the testing procedure could be developed. Intel had to develop computer tools in order to design the tests. The chip was introduced in 1983, 18 months later than originally planned.

In the meantime, Motorola was gaining momentum. Dennis Carter, who worked on marketing the 80286, said:

> The 68000 came out after the 8086 and it was having some success in the marketplace, but we weren't particularly concerned because we knew the 186 and 286 were on the horizon. We believed we would announce the 286, and everyone would flock to our door. But when we introduced it, the world perceived the 286 not as a powerful monster machine, but as a slight continuation of the 8086. It also seemed that a lot of startups were using Motorola, and that was real scary, because that's one indication of where the future is going to be.

Project CHECKMATE paralleled the earlier project CRUSH in concept. CHECKMATE task force members gave a series of seminars 200 different times to 20,000 engineers around the world. Rather than emphasizing performance specifications which Motorola could also use to advantage, the seminar stressed features which had been included at the request of the marketplace in 1978, such as *virtual memory addressing* and *multitasking*. Carter recalled:

---

[7] Motorola won the Apple computer account with the 68000. The 68000 architecture remains Apple's standard.

As a result, the design wins completely turned around. When we went into CHECKMATE, some market segments were three or four to one in favor of Motorola. By the time we finished, it had turned around the other way.

Synergies Between EPROMs and Microprocessors

No one foresaw that microprocessors would create a booming market for EPROMs. The original four-chip design for the 4004 was general purpose except for the ROM chip, which had to be customized (at the factory) for each application.

Although it was developed separately, the EPROM substituted for the ROM and provided two advantages: the designer of a custom product could develop and revise the ROM-resident microprocessor programs quickly, and smaller applications which could not afford the expense of a custom ROM could substitute off-the-shelf EPROMS. Ed Gelbach commented:

> It made sense to be able to reprogram the microprocessor instead of buying fixed ROMs for it. You could change your system overnight or every five minutes with EPROM.

Intel had a competitive advantage in the EPROM process, and retained a majority market share until the late 1970s. Competitors had trouble imitating Intel's "floating gate" process. *Ron Smith,* manager of Static/Logic Technology Development, said:

> If a device physicist were confronted with the EPROM out of the blue, he might be able to prove it won't work. The EPROM process has as much art as science in it, not only in the wafer fab, but in the packaging, testing, and reliability engineering.

In 1977, Intel introduced the 16K EPROM, 2716, which was compatible with any microprocessor system. All alone with the floating-gate process, Intel enjoyed a boom in EPROM sales for two years.

By 1981, the industry faced a cyclical downturn, and Intel's virtual monopoly on the EPROM market was challenged by several competitors, including the Japanese. The industry average selling prices for the 16K EPROM dropped by 75 percent in 1980. Intel management responded by accelerating the introduction of the 64K EPROM.

In the midst of a semiconductor recession, Intel decided to retrofit the brand new Fab 6 at Chandler, Arizona, with a new photolithography technology: *Stepper alignment.* Fab 6 had just come online and was idle (see Exhibit 5 for more detail on Intel facilities). The gamble was significant: "new process, new product, new plant,

and new people." The 64K EPROM (2764) team met very aggressive yield goals, and Intel was again leading the world in EPROM sales. By mid 1981, Fab 6 had produced hundreds of thousands of 2764s, and output was doubling every quarter.

Technology Development

The 2764 had been used by Intel's Santa Clara Technology Development Group to develop stepper alignment. Steppers allowed smaller feature definition and smaller die size,[8] but the capital equipment was an order of magnitude more expensive than conventional projection aligners. Because of the trend towards more expensive equipment and the growing need for a new generation of equipment for each generation of product, Intel modified its traditional philosophy of developing processes on fabrication lines.

From early on, Intel had divided its technology development into the three groups which represented the three major process areas: EPROM, DRAM, and logic. Competition between the groups for scarce resources in the Santa Clara facility had led to the decision to separate the groups geographically. By 1984, the three separate technology development groups were in three cities: EPROMs in Santa Clara, California; microprocessors and SRAMs in Livermore, California;[9] and DRAMs in Aloha, Oregon. While development of each technology was independent, management insisted on equipment standardization. Periodically, the groups got together, pooled information on equipment options, and agreed to purchase the same equipment.

Gordon Moore commented that resource allocation did not necessarily parallel the market fortunes of the process families:

> Allocation of resources to the different technology development groups is centralized by Andy and me. We want to maintain commonality. Also, we are old semiconductor guys. Ideally, one of the groups starts a new technology and the others follow. But for stepper technology this was not true; they all did it simultaneously.

The three groups each developed a distinctive style and distinctive competences which related to their product responsibilities (see Exhibit 6). The Santa Clara group was responsible for the EPROM and *EEPROM*

---

[8] Smaller die size leads to higher yield and lower manufacturing costs. If die size is reduced by 25 percent, manufacturing costs are typically reduced by at least 25 percent.
[9] The Livermore site was also a production facility in 1984.

EXHIBIT 5 Intel Facilities in 1984

Intel's wafer foundries

Fab area	Location	Year first opened	Original wafer size	Current wafer size	Technology development	Primary production focus
Ex Fab 1	Mountain View,	Purchased 1986	1″	Closed		
Fab 1	CA	1977	3″	4″	EPROM	Small number of EPROMs
Fab 2	Santa Clara, CA	1971	4″	4″	No	Logic
Fab 3	Santa Clara, CA	1973	3″	4″	Logic, SRAM	Logic and SRAM (was DRAM)
Fab 4	Livermore, CA	1979	4″	4″	No	Microcontrollers and EPROM
Fab 5	Aloha, OR	1979	4″	4″	DRAM	Pilot and DRAM
Fab 6	Aloha, OR	1980	4″	4″ and 6″	No	Logic, EPROM, Micro-controllers
Fab 7*	Chandler, AZ	1983	5″	6″	No	EPROM only
Fab 8	Albuquerque, NM	Scheduled 1985	6″	6″	No	EPROM
Fab 9	Jerusalem, Israel	Scheduled 1986	6″ plan		No	Under construction
Fab 10**	Rio Rancho, NM	Held at shell				
Fab 11**	Rio Rancho, NM	Held at shell				

*First 6″ fab area in world. Original 5″ facility used DRAMs for shakeout. 1981–82 recession delayed production and allowed installation of 6″ equipment. Process transfer to 6″ wafers was unexpectedly difficult and took over one year.
**These fab areas could be loaded with facilities and equipment and started in about two years

Intel's other worldwide facilities (excluding 50 sales offices)

Location	Date started	Product focus	Operation
Penang, Malaysia	1972	Broad	Component assembly and test
Manila, Philippines	1974	Broad	Component assembly and test
Haifa, Israel	1974	Logic	Design center
Barbados, West Indies	1977	Broad	Components assembly
Tsukuba, Japan	1881	Logic	Design center
Las Piedras, Puerto Rico	1981	Systems, DRAMs	Systems assembly, component test
Singapore	1984	Systems	Systems assembly

Source: Intel Documents.

(electrically erasable programmable read-only memory) products. They focused on the processing steps most critical to EPROMs, for example, the double polysilicon process used to create the floating gate. Similarly, the Livermore group concentrated on processes critical to logic devices.

The DRAM technology development group led the company in linewidth reduction. For example, the DRAM group was developing a 1-μm process while the logic group was developing a 1.5-μm process. Two key factors made DRAMs suitable as a technology driver: large demand for the latest DRAM generation (early high-volume manufacturing experience) and simplicity of integrating design and testing with process development.

Process specialization in all three technology areas limited the direct transferability of processing modules from one area to another, but DRAMs still provided a convenient vehicle for leading-edge process learning, and the DRAM group was highly regarded. Ron Whittier said:

In 1984, the memory technology development group represented Intel's best corporate resource for process development. People like Sun Lin Chou are a scarce resource in a technology-driven company. Sun Lin's group understands and executes process development better than any other group at Intel.

Dean Toombs described the DRAM group as different from the others because of the relationship between design and process engineers:

The DRAM designer is a specialist and more a device physicist than other designers. He focuses on the memory cell and has to understand where every electron in the structure is. There is more of a connection between the designer and the process engineer. The design and the process are de-

EXHIBIT 6 Technology Development Groups

	DRAM	EPROM	Logic/SRAM
Location	Aloha, OR	Santa Clara, CA	Livermore, CA
Product focus	Moderate, undertakes some basic research	Strong, little basic research; EPROM and EEPROM development.	Strong
Process/design interface	Design engineers highly specialized in DRAMs with device physics focus. Process and design development are highly interactive and in parallel.	Process and design less tightly coupled.	Process and design loosely coupled. Design engineers focus on circuit design. Process engineers focus on shrinking linewidth technologies.
Key distinctive technical competence	Thin dielectrics and pushing photolithography limits. Tend to lead Intel in geometry reduction. DRAMS are seen as technology driver. Currently the only group with a 1-micron technology	Problems specific to EPROM and EEPROM. Expertise in developing polysilicon and passivation processes. Also focused on pushing technology to 1 micron.	Processes to shrink existing products and increase yields. Currently developing new process for 386 microprocessor. Developing expertise in double layer metalization.
Number of personnel	120	120	120
1985 budget allocation*	$65 million	$65 million	$65 million
Other comments	DRAM technology development group considered by many to be the most competent group. Major effort in 1-meg DRAM development. Facility has low turnover.	Relatively high turnover to competing companies in Silicon Valley. Has successfully maintained Intel lead in EPROM technology.	Technology development takes place in facility used for production of logic products. Major project in developing 386 process.

*Case writer's estimate.

veloped together. In contrast, a logic designer is not as concerned with the details of a transistor's operation. The process is critical, but not as interactive with the design.

Intel Product Line and Situation in Late 1984

By the end of 1984, logic products (including microprocessors, *microcontrollers,* and peripherals) were the dominant source of Intel's revenue (see Exhibit 7). The company offered over 70 peripheral chips which worked in tandem with its microprocessor lines. The 80186 and 80286 were tremendously successful. In addition to the IBM PC business, Intel had locked up the IBM PC clone business with customers such as Compaq, who purchased microprocessors either from Intel or from one of its licensed second sources such as Advanced Micro Devices. The only serious 16-bit architectural competitor was Motorola,[10] although *Electronic News* had reported that 10 companies, including NEC, Hitachi, Mitsubishi, Fujitsu, and Zilog, were developing proprietary 32-bit

products, and National Semiconductor had already introduced its 32-bit offering. NEC's proprietary design effort was particularly interesting since NEC also supported Intel's microprocessor line as a second source.[11]

Intel had also developed a line of microcontrollers which integrated logic and memory (both SRAM and EPROM) to provide a self-sufficient, one-chip computer. One Intel manager suggested that integration of EPROM technology with logic was an effort to lift EPROMs from a commodity status. The microcontroller business had products in the 4-, 8-, and 16-bit market segments, which were used to control everything from house fans to complex satellites and had prices ranging from one thousand to several thousand dollars per chip.

Scheduled for introduction in late 1985 was the successor to the 286, the 32-bit 80386™ microprocessor.[12] According to one Intel manager, "Once again, Intel was

[10]Motorola's 68000 has a 16-bit bus but actually uses a 32-bit internal architecture.

[11]*Electronic News,* February 18, 1985. The article also reports that Fujitsu did not confirm rumors that it had a proprietary 32-bit design. Instead, Fujitsu indicated its development efforts were still centered on second source agreements with Intel.
[12]386 is a trademark of the Intel Corporation.

EXHIBIT 7   Composition of Revenues

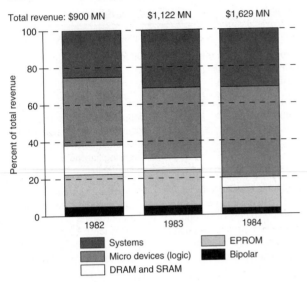

Total revenue: $900 MN $1,122 MN $1,629 MN

Legend:
- Systems
- Micro devices (logic)
- DRAM and SRAM
- EPROM
- Bipolar

Source: Dataquest.

betting the company on a new product." With 270,000 transistors, the 386 was even more complex than the 286. Intel had invested heavily in computerized design and simulation tools which made the design task run more smoothly. In 1984, Intel believed it had the best chip design capability in the world. However, Motorola had developed a strong 32-bit product, the 68020,[13] and was already in the marketplace winning designs, locking customers into its architecture.

The 80386 was scheduled to be one of the first products made with the new *complementary MOS (CMOS)* process (the 80C51 microcontroller and the 51C64 DRAM had both used versions of CMOS). It was also the first microprocessor to use stepper alignment; *double metalization,* and *plasma etching.* Development of the 386™ process was taking place in parallel with a new SRAM process at Livermore under the direction of Ron Smith. Ron Smith explained:

Our group was called the Static Logic Technology Development Group and our charter was to develop *scaling improvements*[14] for the logic and SRAM lines. SRAMs were to lead the company in scaling. We saw the SRAMs not only as a product line but as a vehicle for microprocessor development. The SRAM is an indispensable tool in developing

any new process. It is much easier to debug a process using memory components, because they are easier to test. That's why Intel traditionally uses memory products to develop a new technology.

In 1984, the Livermore group was developing two distinct processes, since the performance requirements for SRAMs and microprocessors differed. Although Intel had a good position in the low-volume, high-speed SRAM segment, it did not participate in the largest SRAM segment, which demanded higher density (more storage capacity).[15] The high-volume SRAM segment demanded a new four-transistor cell design and process. By contrast, the high-speed SRAM and the new 80386™ microprocessor both demanded a six-transistor CMOS design.

The high-volume SRAM process required a complex *polysilicon resistor* technology which was giving Smith's group difficulty. Smith described the environment as it had evolved in mid-1985:

Eventually, we decided to drop the poly resistor process and go with a six-transistor CMOS SRAM product so that we could focus our attention on the 386 development. Basically, we sacrificed the high-volume SRAM for the 386™.

To get an idea of the complexity of the 386™ development, compare it to the 286. The 286 team really comprised only six people. When it came time to develop the 386™, we had to come up with a double metalization process while at the same time reducing line widths to 1.5µm (from 2µm) and implementing the CMOS process. The 386™ process team had about 60 people: specialists in plasma etching, stepper alignment, chemical etching, and diffusion. If you compare the mask design for the 286 with the 386, you'll be able to tell how much area we saved by going to a double-layer metal. Lots of the 286 area was taken up with the routing of metal.

Gordon Moore described a linkage between market and technology development which may have contributed to the loss of a competitive SRAM product.

Product designers want to see their product in high volume. So, it is important to have volume in a product line to get high-quality designers on board. For instance, SRAMs received less attention for that reason than I wish they had. We had a strong position in high-speed SRAMs, but we gave it up without really making a conscious decision.

The systems business at Intel had continued to grow with the company and by the end of 1984 represented the same 30 percent of revenue that MSO had represented in

---

[13] Introduced in sample quantities in September 1984.
[14] Scaling improvements allowed Intel to reduce the chip size of existing products without expensive redesign. The reduced chip size led to reduced manufacturing costs.

[15] Intel's overall SRAM position had diminished significantly over the years as Japanese manufacturers gained market share.

1973. While a great deal of the systems business comprised development products aimed at microprocessor and microcontroller users, Intel also had vertically integrated into software development systems and single-board computers so that it could offer its customers options at several levels of integration.

Manufacturing and Process Fungibility

While tolerating some process proliferation within plants, Intel took great pains to standardize each facility as it expanded its manufacturing base. In 1973, Grove was pictured in a snapshot at his desk with a foot-long mock chip package. On its side was printed the McDonald's Golden Arches logo with "McIntel" substituted. Each Intel chip would "look and taste the same no matter which facility produced it."

As larger-diameter silicon wafers became available, Intel developed a process on one line and then transferred the technology to its other facilities. For example, a process for 4-inch-diameter wafers was first developed at Fab 3 in Livermore, California, by a team of three people. The team leader then supervised the start-up of Fab 5 in Aloha, Oregon, which was dedicated to 4-inch wafers. In 1983, after delaying start-up due to the 1981–82 recession, Intel was the first semiconductor company to use 6-inch wafers at Fab 7, Rio Rancho, New Mexico (see Exhibit 8).

By 1984, Intel had seven fab areas in the United States, all within a two-hour flight of headquarters in Santa Clara. Due to more stringent manufacturing standards, the cost of a fab area had risen dramatically since the 1970s. A new fab area fully equipped cost between $150 million and $200 million and took about two years to construct. The first overseas fab area had just opened in Jerusalem, Israel. *Jack Carsten,* senior vice president and general manager of the Components Group, commented in retrospect on the decision to locate in Israel:

Around the time we were deciding to put up a fab in Israel, I supported the idea of building a fab area in Japan. I had actually obtained leases on Japanese soil so that Intel could locate its first overseas fab area in Japan. That plant would have provided some insulation from currency fluctuations, but the Israel plant had tremendous government subsidies and a good labor market. A Japanese plant would have also put us into the pipeline of Japanese equipment vendors, and linked us into the Zaibatsu network. We could have tapped the expertise of Japanese DRAM technology development, silicon makers, mask makers, and the infrastructural support. This is what Texas Instruments did, because they had

a commitment to local manufacturing. Eventually, we chose Jerusalem, largely because of the subsidies. This is not to say that the Israel facility is bad. It is a fine facility, but it certainly can't offer currency hedging against the Japanese yen.

Nearly all (97 percent) manufacturing capacity was devoted to MOS devices. Within MOS, the majority of processing was NMOS, but there was a trend towards increased CMOS. Each production facility was more or less dedicated to a particular process family (DRAM, Logic, or EPROM), although some facilities manufactured more than one family. Within each family, some process sequences were sometimes customized to accommodate particular product performance needs. While the equipment within any fab area was similar, different fab areas had different generations of equipment, and some processes required more of a particular machine for line balancing. Gordon Moore commented on the proliferation of process technologies:

Over time, there has been a tendency to get more and more processes, and that complicates manufacturing allocations. In the past, we solved the problem by brutally getting out of businesses. But the customers didn't like that. For instance, we abdicated share in microcontrollers because we had to clean out somewhere to do other things.

While each facility could not produce every family of products, there was some fungibility between products and facilities. In times when demand was strong and capacity constrained sales, Intel division managers would get together monthly to decide how to load the factories. The chief financial officer, *Bob Reed,* described the process as being one that maximized margin per manufacturing activity:

Basically, there are three main process areas: fabrication, assembly, and test. Assembly is usually not a constraining factor—you can ramp it up as fast as you need to. Similarly, test can be ramped up in the short term. Fabrication (the front end of the process) is usually the bottleneck in times of tight capacity—it takes long lead times to increase capacity. Since fabrication is the constraining resource, fabrication is the key variable for assigning cost to products.

Each process sequence (EPROM, Logic, or DRAM) is assigned a total amount of manufacturing activity based on the number of steps it requires. Total company manufacturing costs are then allocated to products on the basis of manufacturing activity. For each product, the overall yield (number of good die at final test versus total number of die on starting wafer) is applied as a divisor to the process cost to arrive at a total cost per good part. The sales price per part

EXHIBIT 8   Sample of Cost Accounting Data for Selected Intel Products in 1984

Product	Process	Raw wafer cost	Number of mask layers	Number of activities	Cost per activity	Line yield	Cost per wafer	Die per 6" wafer	Wafer sort yield	Total cost per die	Package/ test cost per die	Yield at test	Total cost per chip	Average selling price	Contribution margin per chip
64K DRAM	NMOS DRAM	60	8	30	72.00	90%	2,467	1900	90%	1.44	0.45	90%	2.103	2.05	–2%
64K DRAM	CMOS DRAM	100	10	38	72.00	84%	3,376	1806	85%	2.20	0.45	90%	2.944	3.08	4%
256K DRAM	CMOS DRAM	100	10	38	72.00	83%	3,417	922	60%	6.18	0.65	90%	7.585	16.27	53%
64K EPROM	NMOS DRAM	60	12	48	72.00	79%	4,451	1582	75%	3.75	2.65	90%	7.112	8.15	13%
256K EPROM	NMOS EPROM	60	12	48	72.00	78%	4,508	756	60%	9.94	2.45	90%	13.764	21.00	34%
80286	LOGIC	60	10	40	72.00	90%	3,267	172	70%	27.13	2.00	85%	34.273	250.00	86%
80386 (samples)	1.5 μm LOGIC	100	13	50	72.00	90%	4,111	131	30%	104.61	15.00	85%	140.716	900.00	84%

Key:
Raw wafer cost: raw wafer cost differs depending on whether or not process is CMOS.
Number of mask layers: Refers to the number of times the wafer goes through the photolithography step.
Number of activities: Refers to the number of times the wafer is physically altered in the process.
Cost per activity: Basic unit of manufacturing for cost accounting purposes. Refers to the number of times the wafer is physically altered in the process.
Cost per activity: An average of worldwide manufacturing costs, including depreciation, materials, labor, and other facilities costs.
Line yield: Ratio of wafers started to wafers completed.
Die per 6" wafer: Number of devices on a 6" wafer (function of die size).
Wafer sort yield: Number of good die divided by total die after all processing is completed and before wafer is sawed and devices are packaged.
Total cost per die: Cost per wafer divided by number of good die per wafer at wafer sort test.
Packages/test cost: Cost of packaging and testing one device.
Yield at test: Number of devices entering packaging divided by number of devices which pass final test.
Total cost per chip: Total cost per die plus packaging and testing costs all divided by yield at test.
Source: Casewriter estimates.

is then used to calculate margin per part, and margin per activity (see Exhibit 8).

According to Reed, sometimes the numbers told a compelling story about the DRAM business. The difference between margin/activity for DRAMs and for the highest margin products could be an order of magnitude. Ron Whittier, general manager of the Memory Components Division from 1975 until 1983, felt that the system for plant allocation was a very good one:

Some companies really went too far by selling capacity to the highest bidder within the company. At Intel, a minimum production allocation would be assigned based on how much we needed to produce to maintain our long term market position. Basically, we used our independent distributors as buffers. In times when DRAM production was pressured by other products, we tapered sales to independent distributors while maintaining sales to large account customers.

Grove commented that since the distributors never accounted for more than 20 to 30 percent of Intel's DRAM business, they could not really account for the leveling in Intel's DRAM sales (see Exhibit 4).

Whittier also noted that DRAMs had at one time been the single largest product line and thus could not easily be entirely displaced by other products unless total capacity was decreased. The finance group thought of DRAMs as a "low ROI, high beta" product line. Bob Reed insisted that the DRAM manager sign a symbolic check equal to the margin foregone whenever high-margin products were bumped by DRAMs.

Ed Gelbach explained why Intel had stayed with the DRAM even though it looked less profitable than other products:

I was in favor of keeping DRAMs from a marketing strategy standpoint. A full-line supplier has a basic advantage in any sales situation. When you're competing with full-line suppliers, it helps to be able to offer a comparable line. Since customers often pay particular attention to their highest-dollar-volume vendor, it also pays to offer the commodity product since it is generally purchased in high volume. A more subtle reason boils down to reputation. Intel had been known to drop unprofitable products, sometimes leaving customers high and dry.

In board meetings, the question of DRAMs would often come up. I would support them from a market perspective, and Gordon [Moore] would support them because they were our technology driver. Andy [Grove] kept quiet on the subject. Even though it wasn't profitable, the board agreed to stay in it on the face of our arguments.

ENVIRONMENTAL FORCES

Bob Reed realized the entire U.S. semiconductor industry was in trouble even during the boom year of 1984.

Even though ROS for the industry was relatively high in 1984, asset turns were decreasing and ROA was low. The business had become too capital intensive. An astute observer could see that the U.S. industry as configured couldn't provide its investors with an adequate return when a new plant cost $150 million and took at least two years to build. Intel was virtually alone with a respectable ROE.

In 1985, the semiconductor industry was expected to enter into another in a series of cyclical down turns which seemed to occur every five years. The cause of the cyclical recessions was a classic case of oversupply and softening demand. Since 1980, a large amount of worldwide semiconductor fabrication capacity had been added, and the learning curve effect (increase in yields, decrease in chip size, etc.) added another 30 percent per year to worldwide capacity.

In the previous recession, Intel had been one of a few companies not to cut back its production workforce. While Intel did not have a no-layoff policy, during the 1981–82 recession Andy Grove had instituted the "125 percent solution." In that program all salaried employees were asked to work an additional 10 hours per week without additional compensation to accelerate product introductions. When the 1980 recession proved to be longer than expected, Intel instituted a 10 percent pay cut in addition to the 125 percent solution.

Intel had several groups of competitors (see Exhibit 9). The first were other U.S. full-line digital design and supply houses such as Motorola, National Semiconductor, and Texas Instruments (TI). Motorola had made the transition from a tube manufacturer in the 1950s to a diversified semiconductor and electronic systems manufacturer in the 1980s. It offered a full line of products competitive with Intel's, including DRAMs, microcontrollers, and microprocessors and was Intel's only serious challenger in microprocessor architecture. TI, while not renowned for its microprocessors, also had a complete product line, including a facility in Japan which was fabricating DRAMs.

The second category of competitor focused on process technology as opposed to design. That group was represented by AMD. While AMD produced a full line of component products, a significant portion was manufactured under license from Intel and others.

The third group included foreign competition, particularly Japanese. Japanese competitors included Hitachi,

EXHIBIT 9 Selected Competitor Data for 1984

FY 1984 (in millions of dollars)	Intel	National Semi-conductor	Texas Instruments	Advanced Micro Devices	Motorola	Hitachi	Toshiba	NEC	Fujitsu
Semiconductor sales	$1,201	$1,213	$2,484	$ 515	$2,319	$2,051	$1,516	$2,251	$1,190
Total sales	1,629	1,655	5,741	583	5,534	18,528	11,003	7,476	5,401
COGS	883	1,146	4,190	276	3,206	13,632	8,182	5,117	3,346
R&D	180	158	367	101	411	898	597	391	(incl.)
SG&A	315	247	491	108	1,064	3,367	2,758	1,443	1,453
Other	(48)	1	168		387		(1,106)	673	335
Profit	299	103	525	98	466	631	572	367	523
Profit after tax	198	64	316	71	387	709	250	189	297
Depreciation	113	115	422	43	353		627		374
Capital expenditure	388	278	705	129	783		1,192	883	747
Total assets	2,029	1,156	3,423	512	4,194	7,997			5,699
LT debt	146	24	380	27	531	1,379	1,830	1,524	915
Total equity	1,360	619	1,540	278	2,278	6,118	2,191	1,728	1,935

Semiconductor market share in 1984	Bipolar Digital	EPROM	DRAM and SRAM	MOS Micro-component	MOS logic	Linear	Discrete	Opto-electronic	Total (in millions)
AMD	5.4%	10.5%	0.5%	1.8%	0.1%	0.4%	1.3%	0.3%	$515
Fairchild	8.6%		0.1%	0.5%	0.7%	2.9%	0.8%	4.3%	665
Fujitsu	6.4%	11.1%	7.8%	3.7%	3.0%	0.8%	8.6%	4.3%	1,190
Hitachi	4.7%	17.4%	15.1%	3.7%	2.2%	3.7%			2,051
Intel	0.7%	16.0%	3.4%	23.0%	1.2%				1,201
Mitsubishi	2.6%	13.3%	4.0%	4.8%	0.4%	2.1%	3.7%	1.1%	964
Mostek			7.1%	1.7%	1.8%				467
Motorola	9.5%	1.1%	6.1%	9.0%	10.4%	5.5%	12.2%	1.6%	2,319
National	6.1%	4.2%	1.1%	3.6%	5.9%	8.9%	0.9%	1.2%	1,213
NEC	2.6%	5.8%	13.0%	12.7%	8.3%	5.9%	7.6%	2.8%	2,251
Philips	12.3%		0.7%	3.2%	3.7%	4.8%	4.4%	1.5%	1,325
TI	22.5%	10.5%	10.8%	3.6%	2.9%	8.4%	1.2%	4.1%	2,484
Toshiba	0.8%	3.6%	7.1%	2.2%	8.7%	4.7%	8.4%	8.8%	1,516
Others	14.4%	6.5%	21.3%	21.9%	50.3%	51.8%	50.9%	70.1%	10,900
Total market (in millions of dollars)	$4,783	$1,319	$4,906	$3,229	$3,493	$4,888	$4,986	$1,221	$29,061

Key:
MOS microcomponent: microprocessors, peripherals, and microcontrollers.
MOS logic: gate arrays, custom logic, and application-specific ICs.
Linear: operational amplifiers, comparators, and other analog devices.
Discrete: single transistors, diodes, and thyristors.
Optoelectronic: LEDs, semiconductor lasers, and solar cells.
Source: Dataquest and annual reports.

Fujitsu, NEC, Toshiba, and others. They had concentrated primarily on DRAM and SRAM products, although each also had a significant share of the EPROM market and served as second sources to U.S. microprocessor and microcontroller suppliers. Intel had second-source agreements for its microprocessor line with Fujitsu and NEC.

Several U.S. DRAM makers had accused Japanese manufacturers of dumping DRAMs at prices below cost throughout the early 1980s.

Industry observers saw that Japanese firms under the direction of MITI had targeted semiconductors as a strategic industry and were investing for the long term. In the years between 1980 and 1984, U.S. firms invested a total of 22 percent of sales in new plant and equipment while Japanese firms invested 40 percent. The result was that by 1983, Japanese total investment in semiconductors exceeded U.S. investment. Production yields of Japanese semiconductor companies exceeded those of U.S. producers by as much as 40%.[16]

DRAMs were not the only product under siege by the Japanese. *The Wall Street Journal* published a story in June 1984 which reported on a memo sent by Hitachi to its U.S. EPROM distributors. The memo said: "Quote 10% below their price; if they requote, go 10% again, don't quit until you win."[17]

Intel had been wary of Japanese semiconductor companies for some time and had sued NEC in 1982 when it alleged NEC copied its 8086 product without license. Peter Stoll, an 8086 designer at Intel, realized his chip had been copied when he discovered that NEC's 16-bit microprocessor had two transistors which were disconnected from the rest of the circuit at exactly the same place where he had disconnected them in a late revision of the Intel mask set.[18] This was considered evidence that NEC copied the chip without even understanding its design.

Bob Reed emphasized the importance of Intel's ability to protect its intellectual property:

If our primary value added is in our design capability, we've got to protect that with vigilance. We have a strict policy of pursuing anyone or any company that appropriates our intellectual property—design or process.

In this highly competitive environment, managers at Intel and other companies often had to consider the problem of spin-off companies. Key engineers had sometimes left Intel to form their own companies with venture capital help. Their departure would stall research at a minimum and, according to Gordon Moore, could be seen as diluting the U.S. industry's ability to compete. Spin-offs were sometimes accused of taking technology with them.[19]

DRAM SITUATION IN 1984

Loss of Leadership Position

By the end of 1984, Intel had lost significant market share in DRAMs (see Exhibits 4 and 9). The first real difficulties had come with the 64K generation. In 1980, Intel's 5-volt 16K DRAM was still a market success due to process innovations, and work was continuing on the 64K generation. DRAMs traditionally led the company in new technology development, and the 64K DRAM was no exception.

Ron Whittier said that to make the 64K version, the memory cell size was reduced, but the actual die size still had to be increased significantly. The DRAM group calculated that given current defect levels in manufacturing, the required die size would be too big. Based on the number of defects per square centimeter normally experienced in fabrication, the projected yield on the 64K DRAM would be too low to be acceptable. In order to boost yield, the group decided to build in redundancy at the chip level.

Whittier described the redundancy technology:

Essentially, you have a row-and-column addressing system on a memory chip. The periphery of the chip contains logic and refresh circuitry necessary to control and update the DRAM. In the 64K version, Intel added an extra column of memory elements so that in the event of a process-induced defect, the auxiliary column could be activated. There was a physical switch, or "fuse," built in to each column which could be addressed by the tester machinery. When a bad element was detected, current would be passed through the switch and would blow a "fuse," inactivating the defective column and kicking in the auxiliary column. In this fashion,

[16]Clyde Prestowitz, "While the best U.S. companies obtained yields of 50–60 percent, the best Japanese were getting 80–90 percent," *Trading Places,* 1988, p. 46.
[17]*The Wall Street Journal,* June 5, 1985.
[18]Clyde Prestowitz, *Trading Places,* 1988, p. 48.

[19]Intel had sued SEEQ for taking a technology for electrically erasable PROMS (EEPROMs). Excel, a spin-off from SEEQ was later sued by SEEQ. Note: Intel continued to pursue its own EEPROM process but eventually decided not to participate in that market because it was too small. A second engineering team left Intel on friendly terms to found Xicor. In 1985, Xicor and Intel were negotiating a joint research project.

a defective memory chip could be "reprogrammed" before shipment, and overall yield could be improved.

Dean Toombs, general manager of the memory components division after 1983, had worked on DRAMs at Texas Instruments (TI) before coming to Intel. Toombs said the discussion on redundancy was industrywide. At TI, engineers had concluded that at the 64K generation redundancy would not be economical and had deferred the discussion until the next generation. For the 64K generation, TI ultimately chose to focus on reducing the defect level in manufacturing.

Intel's redundancy program started out successfully. Two 64K DRAM projects were carried out in tandem, one nonredundant and the other redundant. Prior to production commitment, the redundant design was a clear winner, with yields over twice that of the nonredundant design.

Success quickly turned to failure as a subtle but fatal defect in the redundant technology showed up late in development. The fuse technology was less than perfect. The polysilicon fuse would blow during testing as designed, but a mysterious regrowth phenomenon was detected during accelerated aging tests. Sun Lin Chou commented:

> The failing-fuse problem was simply a case of not having done enough engineering early on. We just didn't fully characterize the process technology and the fusing mechanism.

The result was that the switch eliminating the defective column of memory cells was not permanent. In some cases, the device would revert to its original configuration after being in the field for some time—meaning the defective cell would again become a part of the memory. Errors would occur in which the device alternated randomly between the two states, meaning that at any given time the location of data stored in the memory became uncertain. In either case, the failures were not acceptable, and Intel could not develop a quick fix.

In the meantime, Japanese competitors were throwing capacity at 64K DRAMs and improving the underlying defect density problem which Intel's redundancy program had meant to address. Between July 1981 and August 1982, Japanese capacity for 64K DRAM production increased from 9 million to 66 million devices per year.[20] Whittier took a one-week trip to see Intel sales

engineers[21] and explain that Intel's 64K DRAM would be late:

> The sales force was very disappointed in the company's performance. Any sales force wants a commodity line. It's an easy sell and sometimes it's a big sell. That trip was perhaps the most difficult time in my whole career. When I announced we would be late with the product, the implication was that Intel would not be a factor in the 64K generation.

While the development team eventually fixed the fuse problem and was the first to introduce a redundant 64K DRAM, the 2164, its introduction was too late to achieve significant market penetration.

Attempts to Regain Leadership Position

Having assessed that they were behind in the 64K DRAM product generation, the DRAM group took another gamble. The development effort was shifted from NMOS to CMOS. The advantage of CMOS circuitry was lower power consumption and faster access time. Intel defined a set of targeted applications for the CMOS DRAM technology.[22] Whittier's strategy was to introduce the CMOS 64K and 256K DRAMs in 1984. The notion was that by creating a niche market with premium pricing, Intel could maintain a presence in the DRAM market while accelerating forward into a leadership position at the 1-meg generation.

Dean Toombs said that by the time he took over the Memory Components Division in 1983, things were "clicking along." Demand was in an upswing, and Intel seemed to have a technology strategy which could lead to dominance in the 1-meg DRAM market. Many of the 2164 sales in 1983 went to IBM, and in addition Intel sold IBM the 2164 production and design technology. Toombs recalled that in late 1983 and early 1984, the silicon cycle was on an upswing and memory product demand was at an all-time high. The memory components division's bookings exceeded its billings.

During the boom of late 1983 and early 1984, all of Intel's factories were running at capacity. Allocation of production capacity between products was necessary. The question facing the memory components division was how to effect the transition from NMOS to CMOS.

---

[21] Intel sales engineers sold Intel's entire product line but were supported by applications engineers in a ratio of one engineer to every two sales representatives.

[22] One such application was laptop computers, which place a premium on low-power consumption chips.

---

[20] Clyde Prestowitz, *Trading Places,* 1988, p. 44.

Toombs said the "hard decision" was made to completely phase out the NMOS line. All DRAM fabrication was consolidated in Oregon's Fab 5. Toombs suggested that the decision to "go CMOS" was consistent with Intel's general philosophy: to exploit new technology and create a lead against competitors based on proprietary knowledge.

The development of the CMOS 64K and 256K DRAMs took place in a facility adjacent to the Oregon production facility. While the development was not on the production line, there was a fairly smooth transition into manufacturing. The CMOS technology was more complex, requiring 11 to 12 masking steps versus 8 to 9 steps for NMOS. This resulted in a higher manufacturing cost for the CMOS process (see Exhibit 8).

The CMOS DRAM products were introduced in 1984 and priced at about one and a half to two times the prevailing NMOS price. Intel management developed a niche strategy: differentiate the product from other offerings and sell it on features. In addition to the CMOS feature, Intel offered an alternative memory organization which provided performance advantages in some applications. Intel sampled the products broadly to many customers and made many design wins, particularly in situations where other DRAMs had inadequate performance. The 256K chip was well-designed and executed. Sun Lin Chou commented:

> The 256K CMOS DRAM was the first DRAM product which did not have to go through some sort of design or process revision before or after going to market. With this product, we felt we were regaining our lead in DRAM technology after three generations.

The CMOS DRAMs started as a winning product family. Unfortunately, the market softened as 1984 went along. The price of NMOS DRAMs fell by 40 percent in one three-month period from May to August 1984. In the scramble and upheaval of the semiconductor market, Toombs said that Intel's differentiation message got lost. All suppliers were pushing products into the market, and Intel's superior product specifications seemed like just another ploy to get volume.

By late 1984, Intel's ability to make profits and, more importantly, to project future profits in DRAMs was limited. Said Toombs: "In a commodity marketplace, your staying power is a function of the size of your manufacturing base." According to Toombs, by late 1984, Intel was down to less than 4 percent of the 256K DRAM market and had lost its position entirely in 64K DRAMs.

On the other hand, the technical strategy seemed to work, since the first prototype of the 1-meg DRAM was expected in March 1985. However, as Sun Lin Chou indicated, Intel's technology strategy for the 1-meg DRAM had been different from that of previous generations:

> Our advanced capability in thin dielectric has allowed us to focus on reducing the minimum feature size to one micron instead of changing the entire cell design. Some memory leaders have chosen to scrap the traditional capacitor design, and are trying to move to a smaller "trench" capacitor which requires an entirely new generation of equipment and processing. While they are still at 1.2 to 1.5 microns, we've pushed the photolithography technology further. We may have to go to the trench capacitor in the next generation [4 megabit], but by then we will be able to take advantage of their learning.

Toombs believed that the DRAM technology development group had provided Intel with a unique product capability:

> The 1-meg DRAM will be a technically outstanding product, at least one and a half to two years ahead of any competition in application of CMOS. But the handwriting is on the wall. In order to make the DRAM business go, major capital investment is required and the payback just isn't there. The issue for 1985 is how to survive.

Jack Carsten believed it was critical for Intel to stay in the DRAM business. But in case the company was no longer willing to dedicate facilities to DRAMs, he felt a technology transfer deal should be made with a Korean chip manufacturer:

> The play I am proposing is to stop manufacture of the DRAMs, and to form an alliance with a large Korean company who has state-of-the-art capacity installed. We now have a functional 1-meg DRAM. Basically, Intel could support the business through an R&D alliance and be the technology leader.
>
> To be fair, you have to realize that the Koreans have state-of-the-art equipment, but are not yet expert at using it.[23] In order to make the technology transfer work, we would have to transfer 20 or so of our crack engineers to teach the Koreans how to make the 1-meg DRAM. Apart

---

[23] Note: In February 1985, Intel was to enter into an agreement with a Korean firm to transfer technology for two Intel parts. The technology had been developed at Intel to introduce the 8048 microcontroller (same generation as the 8085 microprocessor) and the 2764 EPROM (see Exhibit 3 for timeline). While those processes required 3- to 4-micron geometries, the 1-meg DRAM product required 1-micron geometries. The Korean company had annual semiconductor sales of about $10 million in 1984.

from the technology risk, there is the risk that we would create a new competitor. History is rife with examples of how technology transfers have backfired, and we've certainly been burned before. But, maybe there's some truth to the logic that the enemy of your enemy is your friend.

OPTIONS FOR DRAM

Grove could see several distinct options for the DRAM business: (1) drop it all together, (2) stay in the business as a niche player, (3) license the technology to another company, or (4) invest in DRAM capability at the 1-meg level and commit to a low-margin business.

As he reflected on the situation, he thought about how Intel had arrived at its current position:

At the 16K level, we were leading in both EPROM and DRAM products, but capacity was tight. We reduced our commitment to DRAMs in what was, in effect, a capital appropriations decision. Margins and customer dependence were both important in causing us to shift our focus to EPROMs.

Then came the lackluster 64K design. We stumbled and it was a burning embarrassment. Our market position was at 2 to 3 percent. You just can't win like that.

Gordon [Moore] is probably right when he says the only difference between DRAMs and EPROMs is that EPROMs never missed a turn. If you miss a turn, the game is over.

The bright side is that we might have lost a lot more if our 64K generation had been a success. Texas Instruments is probably losing more than five times what we are.

We have been trying to find a clever way to stay in this business without betting everything we have, but maybe there is none.

The key question is, Should we really commit to being a leader? Can we be? What is the cost if we try? What is the cost if we don't?

TECHNICAL APPENDIX

Access: In this context, refers to the circuitry which allows the DRAM user to read and write to specific locations of memory. Access time is a critical performance feature of DRAMs and refers to the amount of time it takes to read or write a bit of memory. Often DRAMs offer two different access modes, one that is bit by bit and one that writes or reads large amounts of data. The bit-by-bit rate is typically slower.

Bipolar: Refers to a generic type of transistor and to the family of processes used to make it. The bipolar transistor consumes more power than the MOS transistor but can be made to switch faster. Excessive power consump-

tion limits the density of bipolar products. The bipolar process is a relatively complex semiconductor process.

Bus: Refers to the communication backbone of the microprocessor. An 8-bit bus can transfer 8 bits of data at a time between the microprocessor and the outside world (memory or other peripherals). The 8-bit-bus version of the 8086 actually has a 16-bit internal bus. Each cycle within the chip can handle two cycles of data input.

Capacitor: A circuit element (transistors, resistors, capacitors) which consists of two metallike layers separated by a thin insulating film. In a typical integrated circuit the silicon substrate (wafer) acts as the first metallike layer. The silicon surface is oxidized to form the insulating layer (silicon dioxide) and then a polysilicon layer is deposited over the oxide to form the second metallike layer. In the context of DRAMs, the capacitor acts as an information storage device. When a positive charge is placed on one surface of a capacitor, a negative charge is induced on the opposite surface. The capacitor holds the charge for a limited period of time, and the presence of the charge indicates a bit (binary digit) of information. The ability of the capacitor to store charge is related to its area and the thickness of the insulating film. The thinner the insulator and the larger the surface area, the more charge a capacitor can store. (See *trench etched capacitor* for more information.)

Chip: Refers to the actual integrated circuit which is cut from the wafer after fabrication. Typical chips are 100–400 mils on a side and can contain several hundred thousand transistors. The chip is put into a package where microscopic wires are attached to the die and brought out of the package in larger pins which can be soldered into a printed circuit board.

Class 10 production facility: Semiconductor fabrication plants are perhaps the cleanest areas ever created. Airborne particulates such as dandruff, pollen, and other forms of dust are a major source of semiconductor manufacturing yield problems. One particle of dust settled on a silicon wafer is enough to ruin an entire chip. The class number of a facility refers to the amount of particulate in the air. Class X means that 1 cubic foot of air on average will contain X or fewer particles. A class 10 fabrication facility is designed with advanced air-filtering designed to eliminate turbulence. Operators wear specialized clothing and enter clean rooms only through air showers which remove contamination. To give a sense of the cleanliness, a typical hospital operating room is between class 1,000 and 10,000.

Complementary MOS (CMOS): Refers to a semiconductor process which can produce a specific configuration of transistors which include both NMOS and PMOS devices. A group of six transistors fabricated in CMOS forms the fundamental building block for Intel's latest generation of logic circuitry. The six-transistor cell is a bistable cell which is either in the on or off state. CMOS has the advantage of very low power consumption, since none of the transistors ever draws current except during the time when the six-transistor cell changes states from on to off. Laptop computers use exclusively CMOS integrated circuits.

Die: See *chip.*

Dielectrics: Refers to insulating materials. In semiconductor processing they include silicon dioxide, silicon nitride, silicon oxynitride, and others. Dielectrics are used in several areas of integrated circuits. In DRAMs, they are used for storage capacitors. In MOS transistors, they form the gate insulator.

Double metalization: Until the 80386, all of Intel's circuits employed only one layer of metalization. The design of logic circuitry (where interconnection between groups of transistors appears to be random) is greatly simplified by adding a second layer of metal. Although the processing sequence is complicated, double-layer metalization allows chip size to be reduced.

Dynamic random-access memory (DRAM): A variety of RAM which maximizes utilization of silicon "real estate" and minimizes power consumption per storage bit. Each bit of information is stored as a charge on a capacitor driven by one transistor. Since the charge dissipates rapidly even when power is constantly supplied to the device, the information within each memory location must be rewritten (refreshed) hundreds of times a second. While the refresh function was originally taken care of by external circuitry, the latest DRAM chips have onboard refresh circuitry. DRAMs are available in 8K, 16K, 64K, 256K, and most recently in 1-meg sizes. K stands for kilobit and refers to the chip's storage capacity. See *kilobit* definition.

Electrically erasable programmable read-only memory (EEPROM): A variety of ROM which can be erased and programmed at the user's factory. The device is similar to the EPROM except it can be erased electrically (without ultraviolet light).

Electrically programmable read-only memory (EPROM): A variety of ROM which can be erased and programmed at the user's factory. The classical EPROM comes with a quartz window in its package so that ultraviolet light can be used to erase its contents. Then each memory location can be programmed to permanently contain desired information. In applications where low volume or time constraints prevent the fabrication of a custom ROM, or where the user may intend to make future modifications to its nonvolatile memory, EPROM devices are used. Sometimes EPROMs are supplied without quartz windows (cheaper). Since ultraviolet light cannot get in to erase these devices, they are programmable only once.

Floating gate: This is the structure in an EPROM device which allows a memory cell to be programmed and later erased. The floating gate can be charged by applying a relatively high voltage to the region surrounding it. Electrical traps in the floating gate store electrons which reach the floating gate. The trapped electrons can be sensed by surrounding structures. When ultraviolet light is directed at the floating gate, the light has sufficient energy to excite the trapped electrons out of the floating gate, and the memory is erased. See *EPROM* definition.

Gallium arsenide: A semiconductor material with properties considered by many to be superior to silicon's. The fastest switching transistors are made with gallium arsenide. Difficulty and expense in device fabrication, as well as constant silicon device improvement, have led to a relatively small market for gallium arsenide products.

Gate oxide: This is a critical part of the MOS transistor which is typically formed by oxidizing the surface of a silicon wafer (to make silicon dioxide) in a high-temperature (1000° C) furnace. The gate itself is typically formed out of a deposited layer of polycrystalline silicon. See definitions for *threshold drift* and *MOS.*

HMOS: An Intel acronym standing for high-performance MOS. HMOS is an NMOS process, with small geometries. See *NMOS* definition.

Kilobit (1K): 2^{10} or 1024 bits. Each DRAM generation has four times as much capacity as its predecessor. Since computers operate in binary code, the actual memory contents are multiples of 2. Thus, the 1K generation has 2^{10} bits, the 4K generation has 2^{12} bits, the 16K generation has 2^{14} bits, the 64K generation has 2^{16} bits, and so on.

Magnetic core: A form of random-access computer memory utilizing ferrite cores to store information. This technology was made obsolete by silicon devices.

Megabit (1 meg): 2^{20} or 1,048,576 bits. See definitions for *kilobit* and *DRAM.*

Metal oxide semiconductor (MOS): Refers to a generic type of transistor (see definition of *transistor*) and to the family of processes used to make it. The switch in an MOS transistor is caused by the action of the metal (or polycrystalline silicon) gate on the "channel." MOS transistors come in two polarities: n-channel (NMOS) or p-channel (PMOS). To turn on a p-channel device, a negative voltage is put on the gate. The charge on the gate induces an opposite charge in the channel which completes the circuit between the source and the drain. When the voltage is removed, the channel no longer conducts. The n-channel device turns on with a positive voltage applied to the gate. The MOS process typically requires fewer processing steps than the bipolar process. The turn-on speed on MOS devices is controlled by fundamental physics (the mobility of electrons and positive charges in silicon) and the geometry of the device (as devices get smaller, they get faster).

Multiplexing: A generic term used in many areas of electronics. In the case of the 4K and later DRAM generations, multiplexing refers to a scheme adopted to economize on the number of output pins required to address each memory location. Instead of using one pin for each column and each row in the matrix of memory cells, multiplexing allows the 4K memory to be addressed with just 12 pins (it contains 2^{12} bits).

Multitasking: Refers to a microprocessor's ability to manage more than one task simultaneously. Multitasking is not simply a software feature. The ability to employ multitasking is embedded in the chip's architecture.

NMOS: See *MOS*. Several generations of logic were built on NMOS circuitry. A cell of six NMOS transistors replaced Intel's traditional PMOS logic family. NMOS transistors are faster than PMOS devices due to fundamental physical properties.

Plasma etching: A process which is used to define patterns on the silicon wafer during the fabrication process. Until the early 1980s, all etching was done with wet chemicals. Plasma etching improves control and linewidth accuracy. It takes place in a partial vacuum chamber. Gaseous chemicals are introduced into the wafer chamber and ionized using radio frequency power. The ionic species selectively etch different materials used to build the integrated circuit. Plasma chemistry is a new discipline which has been brought to bear on semiconductor processing in order to achieve smaller linewidths and better etching control.

Polycrystalline silicon (poly, polysilicon): A material which can be used as a conductor. In the wafer fabrication process, polycrystalline silicon is deposited on the wafer surface (usually in a low-pressure, high-temperature process) and etched in patterns to form connections between transistors. It is also used to form the gate structure of a transistor (the gate turns the transistor on or off), the floating gate of an EPROM cell (stores the state of the EPROM cell), and one side of the storage capacitor which makes up a DRAM cell. Its main advantage as a material in processing is that it serves as a conductor while also being able to withstand high-temperature processing. While other conductive materials (such as aluminum) cannot withstand the high temperatures required by wafer processing and must be applied only at the end of the process, poly can be applied in the middle of the process and subsequently be covered by other layers.

Polysilicon resistor: By varying the conditions under which polysilicon is deposited on a wafer, lines of polysilicon can be used to form resistor elements. The poly resistor process was difficult for Intel to execute.

Random-access memory (RAM): Formerly called direct-access memory. Family of information storage devices in which specific memory locations can be accessed (to retrieve or store information) in any sequence. This is distinct from sequential-access memory, in which data must be retrieved or stored in a specific order or sequence (example: magnetic tape memory, CCD memory, bubble memory). RAM is usually volatile memory. Thus, a constant power supply is required in order to retain stored information. Several processing technologies have been used to produce the two generic varieties of RAM, DRAM and SRAM.

Read-only memory (ROM): A variety of memory which contains a fixed set of information which cannot be altered, often referred to as nonvolatile memory. Within a typical computer system, ROM contains a sequence of data which has been embedded in the chip at the factory. Thus, ROM chips are custom-made for each application. Only one masking layer in a 10-layer fabrication process needs to be altered to change the information stored in a ROM.

Refresh: Since a dynamic RAM will hold data for only a fraction of a second before it is lost (the charge on the capacitor holds for only a fraction of a second before it leaks away), a useful DRAM must contain circuitry which can continually read and update the contents of each memory location. This circuitry is referred to as refresh circuitry.

Scaling improvements: Refers to the general process of decreasing linewidths in integrated circuits. In the early 80s, Intel's static/logic group focused on taking existing products and shrinking them to improve yield and increase manufacturing capacity. Devices would be shrunk proportionally (nearly), so that chip design would not have to be changed significantly.

Shift registers: A common type of sequential-access memory used in computer systems to manipulate strings of data.

Static random-access memory (SRAM): A RAM memory device which does not require refreshing as long as power is constantly applied. Each memory cell includes either four transistors and two resistors or six transistors. In comparison with DRAMs, fewer memory cells can be packed into the same area. SRAM memory can be made with faster access times than DRAM. The process for SRAM more closely resembles the process for logic devices. As a result, the on-chip memory contained in microprocessors is often SRAM.

Stepper alignment: The latest generation of photolithography processing is carried out on stepper aligners. The photolithography step has two key goals: to align the current mask layer to all previous layers and to transfer the narrowest possible line widths to the wafer. With traditional projection alignment, the pattern for the entire wafer is exposed at the same time. As wafer diameters increase and minimum geometries decrease, the alignment task becomes more difficult. The slightest thermal expansion or warpage will cause the devices on the edge of the wafer to be misaligned even when those in the center are aligned. Stepper aligners expose patterns across the wafer in several steps so that the runoff at the wafer edges can be minimized. At each step, the mask and the wafer are realigned. Stepper aligners are very sophisticated optical and mechanical devices, costing upwards of $1 million per unit.

Threshold drift: Refers to a phenomenon which causes the turn-on voltage of an MOS transistor to change over time. A certain critical voltage must be applied to the gate of an MOS transistor in order to turn it on. If the oxide insulator which separates the gate from the channel is not free of mobile ionic contamination, the threshold, or turn-on, voltage will drift or change over time making the device useless. One source of mobile ionic contamination is common table salt.

Transistor: First invented at Bell Labs in 1948, the transistor is a solid-state device which can be thought of as an electrical switch. It is a three-terminal device: voltage applied to one terminal opens and closes the circuit between the other two terminals. Transistors are the fundamental building block for electronic and logic circuitry. Configurations of transistors can execute logic functions. The first transistors replaced vacuum tubes and were fabricated one at a time by fusing three material layers together in a "sandwich" structure. Bob Noyce (Intel) and Jack Kilby (TI) invented the "planar transistor," which allows fabrication and interconnection of many transistors on one substrate. While many variations exist, two basic types of transistors dominate the current market: bipolar and MOS (or FET) transistors.

Trench etched capacitor: A traditional capacitor is formed on the surface of the silicon wafer (see *capacitor* definition) and occupies a significant portion of a DRAM cell's area. A trench etched capacitor conserves silicon surface area because its orientation is perpendicular to the wafer surface. Vertical trenches are formed using a relatively new technique called reactive ion etching in which the wafer is exposed to a plasma in a strong electric field. Some manufacturers have chosen to adopt the trench structure in order to produce the 1-meg generation of DRAMs. (Note that another method of maintaining storage capacity while reducing area is to reduce the insulator thickness. This has been the traditional method, but has become more difficult in recent generations. Thin-oxide capability is considered a key technological advantage. Current oxide [insulator] thicknesses are about 100 angstroms [one-hundred-millionth of a meter], considered to be near the limit of current manufacturing methods.)

Virtual memory addressing: This microprocessor feature allows the microprocessor to handle many users at the same time without confusing each user's tasks. More specifically, it refers to the microprocessor's ability to use its own protocol to keep track of memory locations regardless of the physical configuration of memory. For example, Intel's 80286 can assign up to one gigabyte of virtual memory addresses to different users. Those virtual memory addresses are then mapped into the physical memory addresses.

Wafer: A slice of silicon which serves as the substrate for integrated circuits. Each wafer contains up to several thousand chips. The first silicon wafers used in production were 2 inches in diameter. Most recently almost all of Intel's fabrication takes place on 6-inch-diameter wafers. In some processing steps such as diffusion, wafers are processed in batches of 25 to 50. Other processing steps such as photolithography take place on individual wafers, one at a time. As processing technology has become more and more complex and wafer size has increased, additional steps have been carried out on individual wafers as opposed to batches.

Strategic Dissonance

Robert A. Burgelman and Andrew S. Grove

Aligning corporate strategy and strategic action is a key top management responsibility. Such alignment is viewed by some as driven by the strategic intent of the CEO who sets ambitious targets within a 10 to 20 year time horizon, relentlessly develops the firm's capabilities, and transforms the basis of competition in the industry to the firm's advantage.[1] This is an inspiring view, to which many CEOs no doubt aspire. But it is a view premised on top managers having extraordinary foresight. Extraordinary foresight can, of course, always be assumed to explain successful strategies after the fact. But there is convincing evidence that it is very improbable in high-technology industries.[2]

If extraordinary foresight is unavailable, how can top management make strategic decisions in high-technology industries? Our answer to this central question is based on research concerning Intel Corporation's strategic evolution[3] as well as our analysis of more than a dozen case studies of major players in the information processing and telecommunications industries.[4]

STRATEGIC DISSONANCE

Our key premise is that in extremely dynamic industries[5] alignment between a firm's strategic intent and strategic action is not likely to last. Inevitably, strategic actions will begin to lead or lag strategic intent. Such divergences between intent and action cause "strategic dissonance" in the organization. While new strategic intent is necessary to lead the company out of strategic dissonance, our key proposition is that new strategic intent must be based on top management's capacity to take advantage of the conflicting information generated by strategic dissonance.

Not all dissonance, of course, is strategic. Companies continuously experience some level of dissonance as a result of routine disagreements and conflicts because no

Source: Reprinted from *California Management Review* 38/2 (Winter 1996): 8-28. Support from Stanford Business School's Strategic Management Program and from the Stanford Computer Industry Project are gratefully acknowledged. The administrative assistance of Jiranee Tongudai is much appreciated. We would also like to thank two anonymous reviewers and the editor for their helpful comments.

division of labor is ever perfect and no project ever unfolds exactly as planned. Companies need managers precisely to mediate and resolve these sorts of frictions. Dissonance, however, is strategic when it signals impending industry or corporate transformation. Here are three examples from Intel.

In 1970, newly founded Intel Corporation introduced dynamic random-access memory (DRAM) products in the market. DRAMs replaced magnetic core memory as the standard technology used by computers to store instructions and data as they executed programs, and Intel became the first successful semiconductor memory company in the world. Throughout the 1970s and early 1980s, DRAMs continued to be viewed as Intel's core business. While the DRAM industry grew tremendously during that period, the onslaught of Japanese entrants caused Intel's DRAM business to be hurt by the late 1970s. By the end of 1984, there was serious disagreement within the company regarding the importance of DRAMs in Intel's future. The disagreement had been latent for several years. It was resolved when, during 1984–85, Intel's top management completed the drawn out process of exiting from the DRAM business and realized that Intel had transformed itself from a memory company into a microprocessor company.

In 1990–91, Intel top management faced a strategic decision about what to do about the company's RISC architecture efforts. During the 1980s, a middle-level technical manager had developed the i860 RISC chip within Intel and had convinced several higher-level managers of its commercial potential. The technical development had been somewhat surreptitious because it was sold to top management as the development of a co-processor for the i486 chip but did in fact involve a stand-alone processor. The managers involved in the i860 project launched a successful marketing effort and top management had little real choice but to adopt the i860 as a new strategic product. Commercial success subsequently slowed down in the face of the competition of a plethora of other RISC chips. But large amounts of Intel's development resources had begun to flow to RISC architecture efforts and there had developed two camps within the company with different views about the future of RISC versus CISC. After a protracted debate, top management, in 1991, decided to reaffirm its commitment to the x86-CISC architecture and to scale down the RISC effort.

In November 1994, a flaw in the first release of the Pentium microprocessor—a routine event associated with most first releases of new microprocessors to OEMs—triggered a discussion among technical users on the Internet which was picked up quickly by CNN and other news media. Intel's initial reluctance to replace the flawed chips, except for those highly technical users that were likely to engage in mathematical operations that could be affected by the flaw,

EXHIBIT 1   Strategic Inflection Point

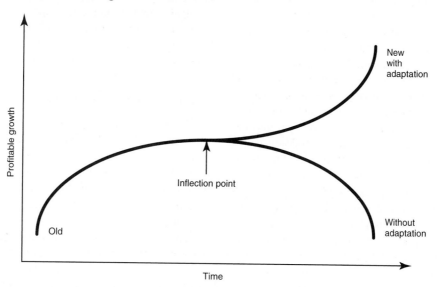

created an uproar and escalated the event into a full blown "Pentium processor crisis." While the national press hammered Intel for not being forthcoming enough in replacing the flawed products with no questions asked, Intel's OEM and distribution channel sales data indicated that demand for Pentium processors continued unabated. After several difficult weeks of internal debate, Intel top management decided to exchange all flawed Pentium processors for new ones simply upon request. By that time, Intel's top management had come to grips with the fact that Intel's prominence in end user space, in part as the result of the Intel Inside campaign started in April 1991, had dramatically changed the rules of the game for Intel, and probably for all high-technology companies marketing to end users.

Strategic Dissonance Signals a Strategic Inflection Point

A common thread running through these vignettes of strategic dissonance is that they signaled that Intel had reached (DRAM exit, Pentium processor crisis) or was about to reach (i860 RISC chip) what we call a "strategic inflection point" (SIP) in its development. *Inflection point* has a rigorous mathematical meaning[6] but here we use it more loosely—metaphorically—to describe the giving way of one type of industry dynamics to another; the change of one winning strategy into another; the replacement of an existing technological regime by a new one. These changes—witness the computer industry—create a "valley of death"[7] for the incumbents because they materially affect their profitable growth trajectories. If an incumbent's top management is able to come up

with new strategic intent that takes advantage of the new industry conditions, it can traverse the valley of death and enter a new era of profitable growth. Otherwise, it continues to survive with severely reduced performance prospects, or dies (see Exhibit 1).

Unfortunately, it is very difficult for anyone in an extremely dynamic industry, including top management, to clearly perceive the new industry equilibrium, winning strategy, or new technological regime that looms beyond an SIP. Think about a computer-generated image being morphed from one state to another—you cannot tell when one ends and the other starts; only the beginning (old image) and the end (new image) are clear. In between is a dizzying succession of intertwined, overlapping, blurred, fuzzy images.

So, how can top management know when dissonance is strategic—signaling an SIP—as opposed to a minor and/or transitory change in competitive dynamics, strategy, or technology? How to tell signal from noise? Sometimes the telling signs are quite obvious. For instance, in 1984, every clear-minded senior manager in the telecommunications industry had to realize that Judge Green's "Modified Final Judgement" inaugurated a period of momentous change that would transform the competitive dynamics in the industry in major ways.[8] In other instances, however, the telling signs may be subtle and intangible. For example, after the Japanese had become powerful players in DRAMs, Intel managers visiting Japan would come back with the feeling that they were viewed with newly found derision—"Something changed; it was different now," they would say upon return. It took Intel's top management several more years to realize that the competitive dynamics, the winning strategy, and the key technological competencies in the DRAM industry had fundamentally changed.

In the face of an SIP, voices sounding danger ahead will emerge. These voices usually rise from the middle-management ranks or from the sales organization: From people that know more because they spend time outdoors where the storm clouds of creative destruction gather force and—unaffected by company beliefs, dogmas, and rhetoric—start blowing into their face. Some will flag their concern to top management—and it's wise to pay heed as it would have been very wise to give serious weight to the troubled comments of the Intel travelers. Other middle managers will just quietly adjust their own work to respond to the strategic change. For instance, in the early 1980s Intel got down to one factory out of eight manufacturing DRAMs because the finance and production planning people (middle-level managers) month-by-month allocated scarce capacity from where it seemed unprofitable to where it seemed to be more fruitful. Often, these words and actions don't seem strategic at first glance: they seem peripheral. But it is wise to keep in mind that when spring comes, snow melts first at the periphery: That's where it is most exposed.

The Need for Strategic Recognition

Managing strategic dissonance requires "strategic recognition"—the capacity of top managers to appreciate the strategic importance of managerial initiatives *after* they have come about but *before* unequivocal environmental feedback is available. Top management's strategic recognition that the set of changing circumstances is an SIP happens in three key stages:

- Recognizing the growing divergence between what the company currently puts forth as its strategy and the actions taken by its managers—what we call here strategic dissonance.
- Asking the (anxiety provoking) question, "Is it one—an SIP?"
- Trying to discern the newly emerging strategic picture and providing a framework in which the divergence can be combated and new strategic intent formulated.

The method of resolution is broad debate, involving different technical, marketing, and strategic points of view and representatives of different levels in the organization. This takes time. Dealing with the strategic dissonance associated with an SIP is a fundamental test of the resilience of a company's culture and its leadership.

Strategic dissonance, strategic inflection point, and strategic recognition are the three interrelated key concepts that answer the question of how top management can decide on strategic intent in high-technology industries.

A FRAMEWORK FOR ANALYSIS

We propose a theoretical framework of five dynamic forces[9] that shape a company's evolution and the emergence of strategic dissonance (see Exhibit 2). This framework can help top managers determine whether manifestations of dissonance are strategic and/or ask questions that help surface latent signs of strategic dissonance.

The first of these forces—the *basis of competitive advantage* in the industry—is determined by the industry factors identified by Michael Porter[10] as key determinants of the attractiveness of an industry: bargaining power of customers and suppliers, the nature of the rivalry among incumbents, and the threat of new entrants and of substitution. Technological change, legislation, or government regulation can affect each of these elements and their relative importance. The second force concerns the company's *distinctive competence:* the competencies that have made it possible to develop a competitive advantage and to survive.[11] The third force is the company's *official corporate strategy* which reflects top management's beliefs about the basis of the firm's current success and anticipated changes in the familiar environment.[12] The fourth force—*strategic action*—is what the company actually does. Finally, the fifth force concerns the company's *internal selection environment* which mediates the link between corporate strategy and strategic action and the link between distinctive competence and the basis of competitive advantage. The internal selection environment comprises administrative elements (e.g., resource allocation rules) and cultural elements (e.g., norms governing internal communication).[13]

During some periods in a company's history, these five forces are in harmony: The company's distinctive competence is consistent with the basis of competition in the industry, its official strategy and the strategic actions of its managers are coaligned, and its internal selection environment is relatively peaceful with no signs of strategic dissonance.

This was the case at Intel in the early 1970s. Intel had established itself as a leader in semiconductor memories by pioneering a new semiconductor process called metal-oxide-silicon (MOS) technology. This process technology allowed Intel to increase the number of tran-

EXHIBIT 2   Dynamic Forces in Firm Evolution

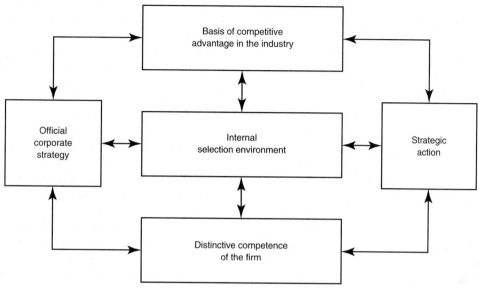

Source: R. A. Burgelman, "Fading Memories: A Process Theory of Strategic Business Exit in Dynamic Environments," *Administrative Science Quarterly,* 39, 1994.

sistors on a chip while simultaneously reducing its production cost. This, in turn, allowed Intel to successfully introduce the world's first DRAM into the market in 1970. While other companies, notably Advanced Memory Systems, had been able to design a working DRAM, they had failed to develop a process technology to manufacture the new device successfully in volume. Process technology became Intel's distinctive competence. During the next half a dozen years these competencies served Intel to remain the dominant competitor in the DRAM business. During that period, Intel's corporate strategy was to offer semiconductor memory chips as alternatives for mainframe computer memories, and this strategy guided Intel's strategic actions. The internal selection environment routinely allocated resources to semiconductor memories.

Over time, however, the dynamic forces shown in Exhibit 1 tend to diverge and their harmonious relationships are broken, thereby creating strategic dissonance in the organization.

SOURCES OF STRATEGIC DISSONANCE

Divergence of the Basis of Competition and Distinctive Competence

The most fundamental and often least readily visible source of strategic dissonance derives from a divergence between the changing basis of competition in the industry and the firm's distinctive competencies, the latter becoming less relevant for competitive advantage. This happened in Intel's DRAM business. In the late 1970s, Japanese entrants used their large-scale precision manufacturing skills to obtain high yields early on in new DRAM generations, thereby outcompeting Intel, which had much weaker manufacturing skills. High yields had great impact on unit cost, and this was a crucial advantage as DRAMs became a commodity product.

Companies often experience an inertial aftermath of success: They have become sharply aware of the competencies that made them successful against the initial competition and they continue to rely on these distinctive competencies even when the competition changes. Also, companies usually organize themselves in such a way that the employees representing these competencies are likely to have the greatest influence in the strategic decision making process. Changes in the basis of competition thus often evoke inertial responses by incumbents.[14] Intel's DRAM business, again, provides an example. Falling behind the Japanese, Intel tried to compete by creating advanced products based on the company's strong process technology skills. Process technology had been the technological competency that had given Intel its initial competitive advantage. Process technologists continued to play the dominant role in Intel's DRAM product development for the 16K (kilobit), 64K, 256K, and 1 Meg (megabit) generations, in spite of the industrywide shift in the basis of competition toward manufacturing competence.

On the other hand, strong technological competencies may also evolve in new, sometimes unanticipated, directions and provide the basis for generating new business opportunities. Important examples at Intel are the invention of erasable programmable read-only memories (EPROMs) and, even more so, the invention of the microprocessor. These developments have strategic repercussions for the company's existing core business and require difficult top management decisions. The successful EPROM and microprocessor businesses soon began to compete with Intel's relatively weak core DRAM business for scarce manufacturing resources. Later on, the increasingly strong microprocessor business also competed with the weakening EPROM business. This internal competition turned out to be advantageous for the company, transforming Intel gradually from a lagging "memory company" into a leading "microprocessor company." Evolving technological competence, however, may also create fundamental strategic dilemmas. The development of the i860 RISC processor at Intel, for instance, threatened to undermine the company's strong core microprocessor business based on the ×86 architecture.

In sum, firm-level competencies and the basis of competition in the industry often evolve along independent paths. Our framework suggests that dynamically matching firm-level distinctive competencies and the basis of competition in the industry is a tough top management challenge. It requires top management to closely watch the evolution of the industry structure as well as to be alert to the strategic implications of unanticipated new developments in the company's competencies.

Divergence Between Stated Strategy and Strategic Action

A second major source of strategic dissonance, one that is usually more readily visible, originates in the divergence between corporate strategy and strategic action. One driver of this divergence is inertia in corporate strategy.[15] Corporate strategy reflects top management's beliefs about the basis of success of the firm. Top managers usually rise through the ranks and are deeply influenced by their perception of what made the company successful. Intel's exit from the DRAM business, for instance, was delayed by the fact that top management was still holding on to Intel's identity as a memory company, even though the company had become a nonfactor in DRAMs

with 2–3 percent market share by 1985. IBM's slowness in taking advantage of the RISC microprocessor architecture (which it had invented in the mid-1970s)[16] was, no doubt, attributable, at least in part, to top management's perception of IBM as the leading "mainframe computer" company in the world. Similarly, Microsoft's relatively weak past strategy in networking operating systems probably was, in part, due to their corporate identity throughout the 1980s as the "desktop operating system" company. Intertwined with these inertial self-perceptions is emotional attachment on the part of top management to the business that made the company successful. As one middle-level manager put it in relation to Intel's exit from the DRAM business: "It was kind of like Ford getting out of cars."[17] Last, but not least, top management often hesitates to change the strategy because the consequences are not completely clear. For instance, Intel's slowness in moving away from defining itself as a memory company were, in part, due to the fact that DRAMs were viewed as the company's technology driver having been the largest volume product (in units) historically.

If inertia in corporate strategy leads to change that is too slow, top managers can also change the corporate strategy too fast—in ways that stretch beyond what the company is capable of doing and the market is ready to accept. In the early 1990s, Apple Computer's CEO John Sculley was clearly in front of his organization when he pushed the strategy of developing personal digital assistants (PDAs) and personally championed the Newton operating system. Sculley's strategic intent stretched beyond Apple's available innovative capabilities and the market's readiness. At the same time, Apple was facing a major battle in its core personal computer business after the barriers that separated the Macintosh's niche from the rest of the PC industry weakened in the face of the success of Windows 3.0. Sculley's ambitious strategy for PDAs required the development of new innovative capabilities while at the same time the demands of the PC business required major cultural change to achieve greater cost consciousness and discipline in product development. Apple could not do both, and Sculley's strategic goals thus created enormous, top-driven dissonance within the organization.[18]

The other drivers of this divergence are the independent strategic actions taken by middle-level managers. During the late 1970s and into the early 1980s, Intel's new EPROM and microprocessor businesses began to compete with the DRAM business for scarce manufacturing capacity. As noted earlier, middle-level managers in manufacturing planning allocated scarce manufacturing to the new, higher margin EPROM and microprocessor businesses, thereby gradually diminishing the role of DRAMs as Intel's core business. In 1984, another middle-level manager responsible for process technology development for static random-access memory (SRAM) and microprocessors made the crucial choice to support a new process technology that favored microprocessors and specialty memory products over commodity memories.[19] This decision effectively decoupled the commodity memory business from the rest of Intel's business. Ironically, this move turned out to be beneficial after the new strategic intent (Intel the "microprocessor company") was formulated.

While some actions may turn out to be helpful, there is also potential danger associated with strategic actions of middle-level managers that diverge from the official strategy. The technical and initial commercial success of the i860 RISC chip as an unplanned stand-alone processor created a strategic dilemma for Intel's top management and extremely strong, eventually divisive, tensions within the organization.

Role of the Internal Selection Environment

If the basis of competition in the industry, the company's distinctive competencies, the firm's official strategy, and the strategic actions of middle-level managers all start diverging from each other, how can a company possibly survive? Research suggests that in the face of an SIP, a company's internal selection environment may be more important for survival than its stated strategy.[20] The role of the internal selection environment is to regulate the allocation of the company's scarce resources—cash, competencies and capabilities, and senior management attention—to strategic action while the official strategy is in flux and new strategic intent has not yet been formulated and articulated.

A company can continue to be successful for some time if its internal selection environment selects actions that are consistent with competitive reality even while becoming decoupled from the official (stated or implicit) corporate strategy. The continued success provides then a time cushion for bringing corporate strategy back in line with strategic action. At Intel, for instance, the capacity allocation decisions favoring EPROMs and microprocessors over DRAMs were initially not driven by official corporate strategy. Rather, they were driven by the internal resource allocation rule—maximize margin-per-wafer-start—that favored products with greater profitability and hence greater competitive advantage in the external environment. The deteriorating competitive position of DRAMs required top management to make a

fundamental strategic choice in 1984: Stay in DRAMs and invest several hundred million dollars to get on a par with the market share leader in a commodity market, or exit from DRAMs and concentrate key resources to become a leading microprocessor company. This strategic choice was facilitated by the results of the internal selection processes which had already shifted the "mainstream" away from memories toward microprocessors.

The internal selection processes leading up to the formulation of new strategic goals critically depend on top management's strategic recognition capacity. One type of strategic recognition involves top management's ability to recognize the strategic importance of actions by middle-level managers who try to tie a new business initiative to the corporate strategy—providing legitimacy for the new business. For instance, the internal and external success of microprocessors eventually made top management realize that Intel's future lay with becoming a microprocessor company. A second type of strategic recognition involves top management's ability to recognize the strategic importance of actions of middle-level managers that diminish the legitimacy of an existing business and decouple it from the corporate strategy. As an example, the allocation of manufacturing capacity away from DRAMs and the decision by a middle-level manager to give up a process technology that was important for commodity memory products eventually helped top management recognize that DRAMs were no longer a core business for Intel.[21]

MANAGING STRATEGIC DISSONANCE

Strategic dissonance, strategic inflection points, and strategic recognition are tools for managing the major transformations that companies must bring about in the face of discontinuous change. As the company moves through the valley of death, the old and the new basis of competition, the old and the new distinctive competence, the old and the new strategy, and the old and new strategic action are all in play together. Exhibit 3 shows a picture of the transformation process.[22]

So, what are the characteristics of the internal selection environment and what are the top management behaviors that help a company take advantage of strategic dissonance and survive the turbulence of an SIP?

Help Internal Selection Reflect External Reality; Allow Dissent

Top management must help ensure that the firm's internal selection environment continues to reflect the real competitive pressures in the external environment. A

EXHIBIT 3   The Transformation Process

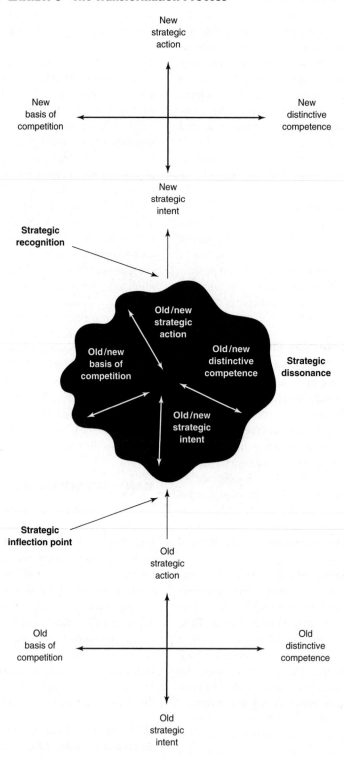

necessary condition is that the company has a management information system that reflects how its businesses are really doing in the competitive environment. This allows top management to ask sharp questions, on a regular basis, about why the company's businesses are performing the way they are. Intel's rule to allocate scarce manufacturing capacity based on margin-per-wafer-start, for instance, forced the DRAM middle-level managers to come up with their best strategic arguments for why the company should forgo profits by allocating scarce capacity to DRAMs. Constantly watching competitors—old and new—is mandatory behavior for top management. Why are they strong competitors? What do they do that we cannot do better? This is one set of questions senior managers should ask. In the DRAM case, for instance, Intel top management should have asked why the Japanese new entrants into the DRAM industry seemed to be getting much higher yields in manufacturing from the start.

It is also important that the firm's internal selection environment values dissent and controversy surrounding the interpretation of the data. This is difficult, because organizations are uncomfortable with internal dissent. Debating tough issues is only possible where people will speak their minds without fear of punishment. The debate between CISC and RISC at Intel during 1990–91 strained this ideal at Intel. The debate became acrimonious at times; different factions were beginning to engage in a civil war. People were voicing concerns: "How will I work for so and so when this is all over?" The DRAM crisis did likewise. A key role of top management is to provide an umbrella against such fears. Top management may not be competent to personally judge the issues but it is up to them to create a fear-free internal selection environment. So, our advice to top managers is, first, don't shut people up, and, second, if they disagreed and were right, congratulate them!

Don't Dismiss Strategic Dissonance

A company's capacity for getting through an SIP depends predominantly on a very human issue: How the top management reacts, emotionally, to strategic dissonance. This is no surprise. Business people, like all people, have emotions, and a lot of emotions are tied up in the status and well-being of their business. In spite of the best attempts at business and engineering schools to inculcate rational analysis, when the business gets into serious difficulties or key managerial assumptions are challenged, objective analysis takes second seat to personal/emotional reactions.

In fact, the top managers in charge are likely to go through some variation of the stages of dealing with a catastrophe:

$$\text{DENIAL} \rightarrow \text{ESCAPE or DIVERSION} \rightarrow$$
$$\text{ACCEPTANCE} \rightarrow \text{PERTINENT ACTION}$$

Denial is prevalent in the early stages of almost every instance. To appreciate this, read the annual report management letters of companies that, in retrospect, we know were facing an SIP. *Escape* refers to the personal actions of top managers. For instance, frequent public speeches on vague subjects given by CEOs of companies facing difficult times or the move of corporate headquarters away from the center of business action are signs of attempted escape. *Diversion,* by contrast, refers to the worst kind of escape, often involving major acquisitions unrelated to the core business that faces an SIP.

Effective top managers go through these first two stages as well, but they are able to move on to the *acceptance* and *pertinent action* stages before it is too late. Ineffective top managers are unable to do so and have to be removed. Those that replace them are not necessarily more capable but usually do not have the emotional investment in the current strategy. In our view, replacement of corporate leaders in the face of an SIP is far more motivated by the need to put distance between the present and the past than by getting someone "better." Intel's DRAM crisis became resolved when Grove went to see CEO Gordon Moore and asked him what a new top management would do if he and Moore were replaced. The answer was clear: Get out of DRAMs. Grove then suggested that Moore and he go through the revolving door, come back in, and do it themselves—a forced way to put distance between present and past.

Formulate New Strategic Intent Based on Strategic Recognition

Top management must try to surmise what the new equilibrium of forces in the industry will look like and what the new winning strategy will be, knowing that they cannot get it completely right. Getting out of the valley of death associated with an SIP requires top management to develop a mental image of what the industry will look like and the company should look like when it climbs out on the other side. Top management must use the information that is generated by strategic dissonance when trying to discern the true new shape of the company on the other side of the valley. It must be a realistic picture grounded in the company's distinctive competencies—

existing ones or new ones that are already being developed. For instance, when Intel finally got out of the DRAM business it had also become clear that the company had to be reconceptualized as a microprocessor rather than a memory company. By that time, Intel had moved from a silicon-based distinctive competence in memory products to a distinctive competence in implementing computer architectures in silicon chips.

Coming out of a difficult period, top management is more likely to have a sense of what they *don't* want the company to become before they know what they *do* want it to become. For instance, as middle-level managers in the DRAM business experienced difficulties in obtaining capacity allocations, they proposed, several times, that Intel restructure itself and give DRAMs their own manufacturing capability instead of sharing with other products. These requests helped top management decide that they did not want Intel principally to become a supplier of commodity type products. This decision was made before it was clear to top management that Intel would become a leading microprocessor company. Management writers use the word *vision* for this. But that is too lofty for our purpose. Leadership here implies changing with the environment and the organization. Reality must lead top management rather than the other way around. This is difficult because top management is expected to have vision.

Getting through the period of immense change requires reinventing—or perhaps rediscovering—the company's identity. Since companies and their leaders are shaped by their past, this is truly hard. If top management got its experience running a hardware company, how can they and their key staff imagine what it is to run a software company? Steve Jobs, for instance, must have struggled with that at NeXT. It is not surprising that it took many years before he was able to redefine NeXT as a software company and got rid of the desire to produce esthetically pleasing, well-designed "computers." Today, Intel is outgrowing its identity as a leading microprocessor company and faces the challenge of redefining itself as a company that wants to be a supplier of building blocks for the computing and communications industries.

Move from Strategic Intent to Strategic Action

Seeing, imagining, sensing the new shape of the company is only one step. Getting there requires more wrenching actions. These moves we have called strategic actions and they involve (re)assigning resources in order to pursue the new strategic intent. The fact is,

corporate strategy is realized by performing a series of such strategic actions, and not via strategic planning. Strategic plans are abstract, far away, and give managers a lot of chances to reconsider as they go along—so, they don't command the true attention their action-oriented counterparts do.

Clearly, the wisdom necessary to guide a company through transformational changes cannot, as a practical matter, reside only in the head of the CEO. If it did, he or she would have guided the company through those changes in the first place. If, on the other hand, the CEO comes from the outside, chances are he or she does not really understand the evolving subtleties in such situations. Middle managers have the hands-on exposure, but, by necessity their experience is specialized, not companywide.

What is needed is real-time mining of the middle managers' insights, exposing all that information to searing intellectual debate, and letting this ferment take place until the shape of the other side of the valley is sufficiently clear that a dedicated march in its direction is feasible. Once that starts, the ferment needs to stop, and all hands need to be committed to this new direction. We think, therefore, that there is an inverted-U type of relationship between the intensity and duration of constructive intellectual debate in a company and its long-term ability to manage through SIPs (see Exhibit 4).

At one extreme, too little intellectual debate means that middle managers do not challenge one another as long as the favor is reciprocated. The result: A lack of strategic dissonance and a hard fall off the curve. At the other extreme, too much intellectual debate paralyzes the company because most energy is used up seeking to win the debate for the sake of winning rather than for the sake of the company. Strategic action is delayed indefinitely and, again, there is a hard fall off the curve. So, during strategic dissonance, top management must let go some while they are not sure. (This is not easy: top management is paid for being sure!) But then they must pull strategic action and strategy back in line and direct the march. Strategic leadership means encouraging debate *and* bringing debate to a conclusion.[23]

Take Advantage of the "Bubble"

Top management must deliberately use the company's uncommitted resources that accumulate in good times— what we call the bubble—by responding to early signs of strategic dissonance and by supporting new initiatives before strategic dissonance emerges. This too is difficult, particularly so when the prospects of the mainstream

EXHIBIT 4   Relationship Between Adaptability and Internal Debate

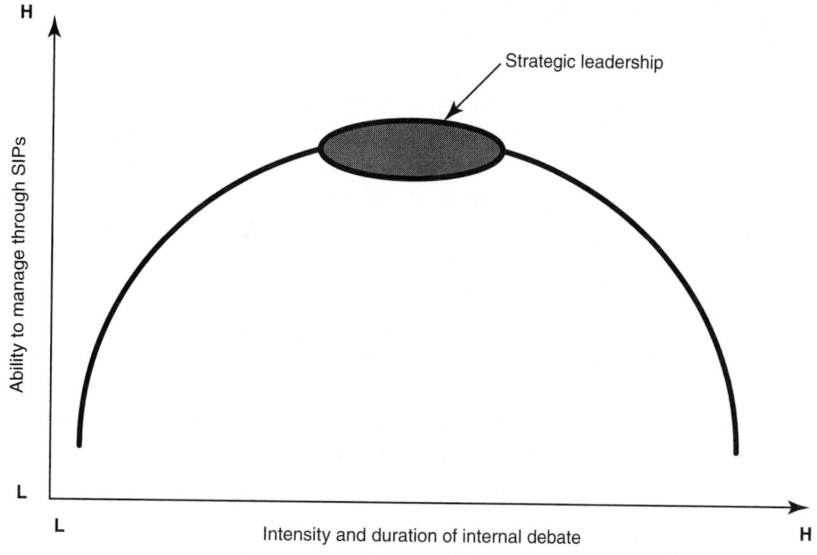

business in the foreseeable future continue to be favorable (abundant profits and growth expected) and everybody is very busy exploiting the existing opportunities. Senior and top management, under such circumstances, is likely to pay only lip service to supporting new initiatives; it is easy to delay action to "tomorrow." When the prospects are not so good, it is easier to take action. In the early 1990s, Apple Computer had about $1 billion in free cash, but the prospects of the mainstream PC business looked less good because Apple's niche was not growing and was threatened by Microsoft's Windows 3.0.[24] While the choice of strategic intent can be questioned, John Sculley deserves credit for anticipating the need for change in Apple's strategy and starting the change process.

Manage Unanticipated Invention

While senior management should constantly look for ways to harvest the benefits of unanticipated invention generated by the company's technological competencies, the first, and foremost, question should be, Is this invention useful to our core business? If not, where could we use it? Is the new area suggested by this invention of interest to us? Does it make use of other competencies we have? Implicit in these actions of senior management is the will to terminate investment in areas that, after careful examination, do not fit the firm. This may sound cold, but the willingness to terminate experiments has to be viewed as an integral part of the process of creating such experiments. If such will is lacking, eventually the

weight of accumulated and undisposed of experimentation will dissipate the bubble and inhibit the start of new ones.[25]

Culture Is the Key

The internal selection environment that we are describing is one in which there are both strong bottom-up and top-down forces. If the company is dominated by the top-down force, chances are that it will efficiently march in lockstep toward an important strategic intent, but the strategic intent better continue to be the right one. If the bottom-up force dominates, chances are that the company will drift aimlessly from one limited strategic intent to another and dissipate its resources. Obviously, if there is neither top-down nor bottom-up force, the company will experience something like "Brownian motion."

But how can these forces both be strong at the same time? They can, if the company has the rugged, confrontational/collegial culture that is desirable in high-technology industries. Such a culture has two attributes: First, it tolerates—even encourages—debate (at Intel, the name for it is *constructive confrontation*). These debates are vigorous, devoted to exploring issues, and indifferent of rank.[26] They are focused on finding what is best for the company (as opposed to the individual or group). Second, it is capable of making—and accepting—clear decisions; with the entire organization capable of supporting the decision.

An organization that has a culture that approximates these two requirements is a powerful adaptive (learning) organization. This is the culture that works best when top management has to navigate between letting chaos reign and reining in chaos. For instance, there was enormous contention in the CISC versus RISC debate. There was rebellion within the Microprocessor Group against its management. After a period of exhausting debate, everybody was ready for a clear new direction. While a few people decided to leave, the adoption and execution of the new direction unified everyone.

Other companies that have survived in extremely dynamic industries by transforming themselves probably have a similar set of characteristics, even though they shape them in their own way. Hewlett-Packard (HP), for instance, has such a culture (judging by the results), perhaps more so than any other large company. Their history has been and continues to be a series of transformations, all achieved by "peaceful means" in the hands of internal management. To see this, compare their ability to move from instruments to computers (and their growth spurt) with that of their major competitors in instruments. When computers moved from minicomputer-based technology to microprocessor-based technology, compare their performance with that of other minicomputer manufacturers. HP made the transformation while hardly working up a sweat. In recent years, HP has transformed itself again, becoming the world leader in desktop printing [27] and gradually working itself into a strong position in desktop computers. HP's culture is more "SIP-ready" than any we can think of.

CONCLUSION

We started this article by asking: How can top management in extremely dynamic environments decide on the right strategic intent? We have offered a conceptual framework and three interrelated key concepts—strategic dissonance, strategic inflection point, and strategic recognition—for answering that central question. Our conceptual framework helps examine the evolving linkages between a company's distinctive (core) competencies and the basis of competition in the industry, and its official corporate strategy and strategic action. The research underlying our framework has revealed that, over time, there will unavoidably emerge divergences between competence and basis of competition, and between strategy and action. We view these divergences as natural outcomes of the internal and external dynamic forces that move and shake companies and industries. We also view the strategic dissonance that these divergences create as an opportunity for top management to learn about the changing reality of the competitive world

that the company faces and the new opportunities generated by its own competencies. Strategic dissonance signals a strategic inflection point in the firm's development trajectory and alerts top management to the fact that the familiar picture of the industry is being morphed into a completely new one—involving a fundamental change in the basis of competition, requiring fundamentally different competencies, or both. Strategic recognition is top management's major tool for dealing with strategic dissonance and an SIP. Strategic recognition picks out of the mass of conflicting information the elements that can form the foundation for new, viable strategic goals. Top management's capacity for strategic recognition is enabled in major ways by the ability of the company's internal selection environment to distinguish signal from noise. This, in turn, depends on the comprehensiveness, depth, and rigor of intellectual debate among middle and top managers, which is the cultural feature most telling of a company's long-term ability to manage through SIPs.

NOTES

1. Gary Hamel and C. K. Prahalad, *Competing for the Future* (Boston, MA: Harvard Business School Press, 1994). These authors introduced the idea of "strategic intent." See Gary Hamel and C. K. Prahalad, "Strategic Intent," *Harvard Business Review* (May/June 1989).

2. A current example concerns the impact of the Internet on the computer and telecommunications industries. Few of the key players in these industries foresaw the speed and force with which the Internet has evolved during the last 18 months. For a general discussion of the difficulty of foreseeing the implications of new technologies, see Nathan Rosenberg, "Uncertainty and Technological Change," paper prepared for the Conference on Growth and Development: The Economics of the 21st Century, organized by the Center for Economic Policy Research of Stanford University, June 3–4, 1994.

3. This research is reported in Robert A. Burgelman, "Intraorganizational Ecology of Strategy Making and Organizational Adaptation: Theory and Field Research," *Organization Science* (August 1991); Robert A. Burgelman, "Fading Memories: A Process Theory of Strategic Business Exit in Dynamic Environments," *Administrative Science Quarterly* (March 1994); Robert A. Burgelman, "A Process Model of Strategic Business Exit: Implications for an Evolutionary Perspective on Strategy," *Strategic Management Journal* (Special Issue, Summer 1996).

4. These case studies are used in our M.B.A. elective course "Strategy and Action in the Information Processing Industry" at the Stanford Business School. Some of these cases were written at the Stanford Business School: George W.

Cogan and Robert A. Burgelman, "Intel Corporation (A): The DRAM Decision," 1990; Bruce K. Graham and Robert A. Burgelman, "Intel Corporation (B): Implementing the DRAM Decision," 1991; George W. Cogan and Robert A. Burgelman, "Intel Corporation (C): Strategy for the 1990s," 1991; Dan Steere and Robert A. Burgelman, "Intel Corporation (D): Microprocessors at the Crossroads, 1993; Dan Steere and Robert A. Burgelman, "Intel Corporation (E): New Directions for the 1990s," 1993; Alva H. Taylor, Robert A. Burgelman, and Andrew S. Grove, "A Note on the Telecommunications Industry in 1993," 1994; Alva H. Taylor, Robert A. Burgelman, and Andrew S. Grove, "The Wireless Communications Industry: After AT&T–McCaw," 1994; Thomas Kurian and Robert A. Burgelman, "The Operating Systems Industry in 1994," 1994; Jeffrey Skoll, David Zinman, and Robert A. Burgelman, "The Consumer Online Services Industry in 1995," 1995. Other cases, written at the Harvard Business School, include "The Global Semiconductor Industry in 1987"; "The Global Computer Industry; Note on the PC Network Software Industry, 1990"; "Microsoft's Networking Strategy; Mips Computer Systems (A)"; "Motorola and Japan (A); The Transformation of IBM"; "Apple Computer 1992, and Reshaping Apple Computer's Destiny," 1992. These are all published in David B. Yoffie, *Strategic Management in Information Technology* (Englewood Cliffs, NJ: Prentice Hall, 1994).

5. For a discussion of different types of dynamic environments, see Jeffrey Williams, "How Sustainable Is Your Competitive Advantage?" *California Management Review,* 34/3 (Spring 1992): 29–51. For a discussion of the managerial challenges of operating in "high-velocity" environments, see Kathleen Eisenhardt, "Speed and Strategic Choice: How Managers Accelerate Decision Making," *California Management Review,* 32/3 (Spring 1990): 39–54.

6. Mathematically, an inflection point is reached when the first derivative (the slope of the trajectory) becomes zero and the second derivative (the rate of change) changes sign (positive to negative or vice versa).

7. Andrew S. Grove, "PCs Trudge out of the Valley of Death," *The Wall Street Journal,* January 18, 1993; "Invest or Die," *Fortune,* February 22, 1993 (cover story).

8. Nevertheless, even in 1995 it is by no means obvious what the new competitive equilibrium in the telecommunications industry will look like; what the winning strategies and the dominant technologies will be. For instance, Bell Atlantic, one of the most aggressive regional Bell operating companies (RBOCs) planning to diversify into delivering video and television services, abruptly called a halt to its plans in April 1995. See "Bell Atlantic Halts Plan for Video Services," *The New York Times,* April 26, 1995. Recently, AT&T decided to split itself up into three parts— telecommunications services, telecommunications equipment, and computers—in order to be able to compete in a more focused way in each of these dynamic industries.

One reason for the split-up was that AT&T experienced enormous strategic dissonance as the RBOCs, in anticipation of the deregulation of the local exchange business, were increasingly reluctant to buy telecommunications equipment from a potential major rival.

9. Burgelman (March 1994), op. cit.

10. Michael E. Porter, *Competitive Strategy* (New York: Free Press, 1980).

11. The concept of distinctive competence was first proposed by Philip Selznick, *Leadership in Administration: A Sociological Interpretation* (New York: Harper & Row, 1957). Distinctive competence is similar to core competence, but emphasizes the relative uniqueness of the competencies that the company initially assembles and the evolutionary processes through which they evolve. As a result of these evolutionary processes, distinctive competencies have inertia and may become "competence traps." See Barbara Levitt and James March, "Organizational Learning," in W. Richard Scott, ed., *Annual Review of Sociology,* 14 (1988): 319–340. For a discussion of core competence see C. K. Prahalad and Gary Hamel, "The Core Competence of the Corporation," *Harvard Business Review* (May/June 1990).

12. See Robert A. Burgelman, "A Model of the Interaction of Strategic Behavior, Corporate Context, and the Concept of Strategy," *Academy of Management Review* (1983); Gordon Donaldson and Jay W. Lorsch, *Decision Making at the Top: The Shaping of Strategic Direction* (New York: Basic Books, 1983); Karl E. Weick, "Substitutes for Corporate Strategy," in David J. Teece, ed., *The Competitive Challenge* (Boston, MA: Ballinger, 1987).

13. Burgelman (March 1994), op. cit.

14. Arnold C. Cooper and Dan E. Schendel, "Strategic Responses to Technological Threats," *Business Horizons* (1976); William J. Abernathy, Kim B. Clark, and Alan M. Kantrow, *Industrial Renaissance: Producing a Competitive Future for America* (New York: Basic Books, 1983); Michael E. Tushman and Philip Anderson, "Technological Discontinuities and Organizational Environments," *Administrative Science Quarterly* (1986); Barbara Levitt and James March, "Organizational Learning," *Annual Review of Sociology,* 14 (1988); Rebecca M. Henderson and Kim B. Clark, "Architectural Innovation: The Reconfiguration of Existing Product Technologies and the Failure of Established Firms," *Administrative Science Quarterly* (1990); Dorothy Leonard-Barton, "Core Capabilities and Core Rigidities: A Paradox in Managing New Product Development," *Strategic Management Journal* (1992).

15. Michael T. Hannan and John H. Freeman, "Structural Inertia and Organizational Change," *American Sociological Review* (1984); Henry Mintzberg and James A. Waters, "Tracking Strategy in an Entrepreneurial Firm," *Academy of Management Journal* (1982); Danny Miller and Peter H. Friesen with the collaboration of Henry Mintzberg, *Organizations: A Quantum View* (Englewood Cliffs, NJ: Prentice Hall, 1984).

16. See for instance "Mips Computer Systems," in Yoffie (1994), op. cit.

17. Burgelman (March 1994), op. cit., p. 41.

18. See "Reshaping Apple Computer's Destiny 1992," in Yoffie (1994), op. cit.

19. See "Intel Corporation (A): The DRAM Decision," Stanford Business School Case PS-BP-256, p. 10.

20. See Burgelman (August 1991) and (March 1994), op. cit.

21. These two processes are called "strategic context determination" and "strategic context dissolution," respectively. See Burgelman (1996), op. cit.

22. A vivid example from the late 19th century concerns the transition from wind to steam as the dominant means for powering ships. For a while, some ship builders produced hybrids featuring both sails and steam engines. See R. N. Foster, *Innovation: The Attacker's Advantage* (New York: Summit, 1986). Today, in the face of uncertainty as to whether TDMA or CDMA will become the dominant technology in cellular telephony, some telecommunications companies are planning to bring out cellular phones that embody both technologies.

23. We think that strategic recognition and strategic leadership must meet the tests for "statesmanship," put forth by Henry A. Kissinger. Kissinger writes: "The ultimate test of statesmanship . . . is a combination of *insight and courage* [emphasis provided]. Insight leads to assessments that define a society's freedom of action, while courage enables the statesman to act on his convictions before they are generally understood. Great statesmen operate on the outer margin of their society's capabilities; weak statesmen tend to be overwhelmed by events." See Henry A. Kissinger, Review of "Churchill: The Unruly Giant" by Norman Rose, *The New York Times Book Review,* July 16, 1995, p. 7.

24. See "Reshaping Apple Computer's Destiny 1992," in Yoffie (1994), op. cit.

25. For an assessment framework, see Robert A. Burgelman, "Designs for Corporate Entrepreneurship in Established Firms," *California Management Review,* 26/3 (Spring 1984).

26. Andrew S. Grove, *High Output Management* (New York: Random House, 1983); Andrew S. Grove, "Breaking the Chain of Command," *Newsweek,* October 3, 1983. There is some useful social science literature on the quality of decision making in teams with dissent. One line of inquiry concerns the role of minority views in increasing group performance. There is evidence that distinct minority points of view help generate novel solutions that lead to improved group performance. See, for instance, Charlan Nemeth, "Style Without Status Expectations: The Special Contributions of Minorities," in Murray Webster and Martha Foschi, eds., *Status Generalization: New Theory and Research* (Stanford, CA: Stanford University Press, 1988). Another line of inquiry concerns the use of conflict as a means for improving decision effectiveness. Two techniques for introducing conflict in decision processes are "Devil's Advocate" and "Dialectical Inquiry." Devil's Advocate involves assigning an individual or group the task of criticizing a particular course of action. Dialectical Inquiry involves creating a debate between opposing views. See, for instance, Richard A. Cosier and Charles R. Schwenk, "Agreement and Thinking Alike: Ingredients for Poor Decisions," *Academy of Management Executive* (February 1990). Much of this research, however, is based on experiments involving students in contrived settings. A study of how Lyndon Johnson used George Ball as "devil's advocate" in top-level government decision making during the Vietnam war to isolate and defuse, rather than to integrate, a different point of view suggests the potential pitfalls of some of these techniques. See Irving L. Janis, *Victims of GroupThink* (Boston: Houghton Mifflin, 1972) and Irving L. Janis and Leon Mann, *Decision Making: A Psychological Analysis of Conflict, Choice, and Commitment* (New York: Free Press, 1977).

27. "How HP Used Tactics of the Japanese to Beat Them at Their Game," *The Wall Street Journal,* September 8, 1994.

CASE II-13

Intel Corporation: Strategy for the 1990s

George W. Cogan and Robert A. Burgelman

INTRODUCTION

The two years following Intel's decision to exit the DRAM business were difficult ones. Company revenues fell during 1985 and 1986 as Intel's top management discontinued several low-margin product lines and reduced the workforce of 25,400 by 7,200. Intel losses for 1986 exceeded $200 million. The entire industry suffered as it adjusted to the new Japanese capacity and slackening demand.

In 1987, Intel began to emerge from the recession. While the company adopted a sole sourcing strategy for its microprocessor products, demand grew dramatically for its 386™ microprocessor[1] product line. In the middle of 1989, the company's expected sales had nearly tripled to $3.1 billion. In 1989, it had the highest return on sales of any major semiconductor company in the world. (See Exhibits 1 and 2.)

Source: Reprinted with permission of Graduate School of Business. Copyright © 1989 by The Board of Trustees of the Leland Stanford Junior University.
[1] 386 is a trademark of Intel Corporation.

EXHIBIT 1   Selected Intel Corporation Financial Data (Dollars in Millions)

	Year ended December 31											
	1979	1980	1981	1982	1983	1984	1985	1986	1987	1988	1989	1990
Sales	663	854	788	900	1,122	1,629	1,364	1,265	1,907	2,875	3,127	3,921
COGS	313	399	458	542	624	883	943	861	1,043	1,506	1,721	1,930
Gross margin	350	455	330	358	498	746	421	404	864	1,369	1,406	1,991
R&D	67	96	116	131	142	180	195	228	260	318	365	517
SG&A	131	175	184	198	217	315	287	311	358	456	483	666
Operating profit	152	184	30	29	139	251	(61)	(135)	246	595	557	858
Interest and other	(3)	2	10	2	40	47	55	(76)	42	34	−96	336
Profit before tax	149	186	40	31	179	298	(6)	(211)	288	629	583	486
Income tax	71	89	13		63	100	(7)	8	40	176	192	336
Net income	78	97	27	31	116	198	1	(203)	248	453	391	650
Depreciation	40	49	66	83	103	114	166	173	171	210	190	292
Capital investment	97	152	157	138	145	388	236	154	301	477	351	680

	December 31											
	1979	1980	1981	1982	1983	1984	1985	1986	1987	1988	1989	1990
Cash and ST investment	34	127	115	85	389	230	188	74	630	970	1,064	1,785
Working capital	115	299	287	306	608	568	717	649	506	1,036	1,242	1,806
Fixed assets	217	321	412	462	504	778	848	779	891	1,122	1,284	1,658
Total assets	500	767	871	1,056	1,680	2,029	2,152	1,977	2,498	3,549	3,994	5,377
LT debt	0	150	150	197	127	146	270	287	298	479	412	345
Equity	303	432	488	552	1,122	1,360	1,421	1,245	1,276	2,080	2,549	3,592
Employees	14,300	15,900	16,800	19,400	21,500	25,400	21,300	18,200	19,200	20,800	22,000	24,600
ROS	11.8%	11.4%	3.4%	3.4%	10.3%	12.2%	0.1%	(16.0%)	13.0%	15.8%	12.5%	16.6%
ROA	21.9%	19.4%	3.5%	3.6%	11.0%	11.8%	0.5%	(9.4%)	9.9%	12.8%	9.8%	12.1%
ROE	38.0%	32.0%	6.3%	6.4%	21.0%	17.6%	0.1%	(14.3%)	19.5%	21.8%	15.3%	18.1%

Source: Intel annual reports.

EXHIBIT 2   Selected Competitor Data for 1988

FY 1988 (in millions)	Intel	National Semiconductor	Texas Instruments	Advanced Micro Devices	Motorola	Hitachi	Toshiba	NEC	Fujitsu
Total sales	2,874	1,648	6,294	1,125	8,250	39,800	28,579	21,893	16,374
COGS	1,505	1,280	5,778	661	5,040	29,535	20,583	15,120	10,713
R&D	318	264		208	incl.				
SG&A	456	236		224	1,957	8,259	7,115	5,863	4,704
Other	(36)	55		18	642	(643)	(122)	344	108
Profit	631	(187)	516	14	611	2,649	1,003	566	849
Profit after tax	453	(23)	366	19	445	1,094	485	204	337
Depreciation	211	184	389	153	543	2,351	1,412	1,310	1,094
Capital expenditure	477	277	628	131	873	2,333	1,469	2,016	1,527
Total assets	3,550	1,416	4,427	1,081	6,710	44,969	27,673	23,426	18,532
LT debt	479	52	623	130	343	3,462	4,423	3,576	2,413
Total equity 1987	1,276	1,013	1,885	623	3,008	14,607	4,061	3,523	4,660
Total equity 1988	2,080	848	2,243	645	3,375	16,148	5,743	4,784	6,616

Source: Annual reports.

As Andy Grove, Intel's CEO since 1987, described the emergence of the "new" Intel late in 1990, he wondered about the implications of the changing structure of the semiconductor industry on his company. He wondered what Intel's technology strategy should be and whether the Intel of the 1990s should plan to be a dominant player in the EPROM business. He also wondered about the emergence of RISC architecture and the implications that held for Intel's core microprocessor business. Finally, the growing importance of Intel's systems business raised some touchy issues about the company's relations with its customers.

DRAMS IN 1990

After the decision to stop developing the 1 meg DRAM in late 1984, Andy Grove had traveled to Portland to address the DRAM Technology Development Group. He had started his announcement to the group by saying: "Welcome to the mainstream of Intel."

While there had been significant resistance to the decision to exit DRAMs on the part of some high-level managers, the DRAM technology development group accepted the decision. Sun Lin Chou, then leader of the group, said:

> I guess one of the reasons that we didn't feel so bad about the DRAM decision is that we felt we had done our part by regaining a leading technical position with the 1 meg DRAM. We were allowed to continue development for several months, so that by the time we stopped, we had functioning 1 meg DRAM parts.
>
> The company was really caught in a no-win situation. We were trying harder and harder, but it seemed that our efforts would not lead to a big success.

Intel's experience in the DRAM marketplace mirrored that of several other U.S. competitors who also exited during the 1985–86 recession. In 1985, the entire DRAM market shrank by over 50 percent to $1.4 billion. However, by late 1987, demand once again began to outpace supply, and DRAM suppliers enjoyed market growth and renewed profitability. By 1987, Japanese companies controlled the overwhelming majority of the DRAM market since only two U.S. manufacturers, Texas Instruments and Micron Technology, remained.[2]

By 1990, Japanese companies commanded 87 percent of the $8 billion DRAM market, U.S. companies held about 8 percent, and Korean companies held the remain-

ing 5 percent.[3] Korean market share was likely to increase as Korean firms announced investment plans of over $4 billion by the early 1990s. In order to address marketing concerns that the company have a full product line, Intel, in 1987, had signed a long-term sourcing agreement with Samsung Semiconductor for DRAM chips under which Intel would market the Korean chips under its own name. *Electronic Buyer News* reported that Intel had sold more than 10 million 256K and 1-megabit DRAMs during 1988 through its commodity operation. Prevailing prices suggest that the DRAM reseller business generated well over $100 million in revenue by 1990.

The dramatic decline in U.S. position led some industry observers to predict the eventual downfall of the entire U.S. semiconductor industry. The concern over U.S. competitiveness and dependence on foreign suppliers led several companies to announce plans to form a joint DRAM venture. A group of semiconductor and computer companies[4] agreed in June 1989 to form U.S. Memories, Inc., investing an initial $50,000 each. The venture required $1 billion in capitalization over several years and intended to use IBM's design for a 4-megabit DRAM as its introductory product offering early in 1991. The unusual arrangement between competitors was likely to require federal antitrust clearance[5] and faced opposition from vocal critics.

NEW TECHNOLOGY DRIVERS

Until 1985, Intel managers thought of DRAMs as the company's technology driver. Historically, DRAMs had always been the first products to employ new technology. Even though it never went into production, the 1-megabit DRAM was Intel's first attempt at a 1-micron geometry. Sun Lin Chou said it was typical for DRAMs to precede logic products in linewidth reduction by at least one year.

In 1990, Sun Lin Chou expressed some skepticism in discussing the cumulative volume model for learning in the semiconductor industry:

---

[2] Although IBM does not sell DRAMs, it is one of the world's largest producers for its own internal uses.

[3] These figures do not include U.S. captive suppliers (IBM and AT&T). If captive suppliers are included, Japan's share of the U.S. market falls to 65 percent. Captive estimate from G. Gilder, *Microcosm* (New York: Simon and Schuster, 1989), p. 152.

[4] The group included Hewlett-Packard, Intel, IBM Corp., Digital Equipment Corp., LSI Logic Corp., National Semiconductor, and Advanced Micro Devices.

[5] *The Wall Street Journal*, June 21, 1989, p. B5, and *San Francisco Chronicle*, June 22, 1989, p. C1. Some companies (notably Apple and Sun Microsystems) were reluctant to invest in U.S. Memories, due to relationships with existing DRAM manufacturers. *San Francisco Chronicle*, September 26, 1989, p. C1.

The traditional model of a technology driver says that the more you do, the more high-volume products you run, the more productive you get. That means in order to stay on the leading edge, you need a product you can ramp into high-volume production rapidly. There is some truth to the model, but it can be carried to an extreme.

There are certainly ways of learning that can be carried out at much lower volumes. Our recent experience suggests that you can learn without massive volumes. If so, that takes away the requirement or urgency to have a traditional technology driver. We think it is possible to achieve mature yields by processing only about 10,000 wafers versus the old model's predicted requirement of 1,000,000 wafers. But you have to use intelligence.

You don't learn quickly when you increase volume by brute force. You have to learn by examining wafers. Learning is based on the number of wafers looked at, analyzed, and the number of effective corrective actions taken. Even if you have processed 1,000 wafers, the technical learning probably only came from the 10 wafers you analyzed. Technical learning is time- and engineering-constrained, not number-of-wafers–constrained.

There are also a great number of things you can do in an open loop system. For example, you can see or guess where particles are coming from and remove them without really knowing for sure whether they are a yield limiter. You don't take the time to get the data to justify the fix; you don't do a detailed study; you just fix what seems broken. You have an intuition about what to do. The Japanese have really led the way on this. You don't undertake an ROI analysis to figure out the cost/benefit for every little improvement. You just fix everything you can think of. Everyone can participate.

Craig Barrett, executive vice president and general manager of the Microcomputer Components Group, believed the importance of DRAMs to technology leadership had been overestimated by most industry observers:

At one time DRAMs really were a technology driver for Intel. DRAMs are still the single biggest product in the industry as a whole. They are about $8 billion to $10 billion of a $50 billion market. And they are certainly a learning vehicle for some.

When we got out of DRAMs we were concerned that we might suffer from the lack of volume. We tried to address that concern by selectively staying in the EPROM business. Even though the EPROM volume is not as big, it is a volume product. But, I would have to conclude that after two generations post DRAM we do not miss it as a technology driver.

I think that the industry used the notion of technology driver as a crutch. We were late waking up to the fact that we did not need to run volume in order to learn. There are other ways to be intelligent. You don't have to depend on volume if you depend on good engineering.

We have data to show that our learning as represented by lowering defect density has actually accelerated in the past two generations when plotted either as a function of time or as a function of cumulative wafers put through the fab. For each generation since 1985—1.5 micron, 1 micron, and most recently 0.8 microns—each defect density trend line is downward sloping with the most recent generations having the steepest slopes.

While we have some volume from our EPROM line and we make lots of efforts to transfer learning from one facility to another, we focus on basic techniques to accelerate learning: design of experiments, statistical process control, and just plain good engineering.

While we do have a lot of high-margin wafer starts, we still have a significant mixture of products. We have 256K EPROMs, 1 meg, 2 meg, and just recently 4 meg in addition to our microcontrollers, which are all very cost sensitive. We chose to stay in those commodity businesses partly because it does "keep us honest." Of course, it also represents a significant part of our revenue and it helps to amortize R&D expenditure.

Gerry Parker, vice president of Technology Development, had a slightly different perspective on the issue of technology drivers:

There is no single technology driver at Intel. We focus our technology development on logic and nonvolatile memory products. More than ever before, we watch what the rest of the industry is doing and try to follow trends. The DRAM is the industry's driver, because it is the highest volume product, and DRAM suppliers are the biggest equipment purchasers. There have been some really fascinating developments in the industry. I think that the entire industry paradigm has shifted in the past several years.

I spend a lot of time now following what the DRAM people are doing and talking with equipment manufacturers. A great deal of the know-how is now generated at the equipment suppliers. We try to stay in the mainstream by purchasing the most advanced equipment, but then we optimize it to maximum advantage for our products.

For example, I know that a certain stepper vendor is developing a new tool that will accommodate a certain maximum chip size. It will not be able to process larger chips. The size is driven by the needs of Toshiba's next-generation DRAM. They are building the equipment to satisfy the demands of their largest customer.

You can bet that all of Intel's next generation parts will be designed to capitalize on the DRAM tool. We will put that constraint on our designers. The equipment vendor will be tooled up to produce those steppers in volume and will be happy to supply us with a few machines. We could ask them to design a special tool for us, but it would be inferior because we wouldn't command the same level of attention that Toshiba gets.

Attitude is important and has led to the changes. The Japanese really have taught us something. They expect excellence from equipment vendors and make *them* develop the expertise to provide the best possible equipment. If a piece of equipment has a problem, the vendor is right there in the fab area fixing it and he can make appropriate changes on the next generation.

Our approach has traditionally been different. We would modify the equipment ourselves and not even tell the vendor. We sometimes didn't even let the vendors into our fabs. We have changed a lot in our openness, and we are beginning to use sole-source suppliers for each category of equipment, but we could still do more.

I was talking to a guy at Applied Materials, one of our equipment suppliers, about the differences between our approach and that of the Japanese. In Japan, all the technicians set the machines to the exact settings that are specified by Applied Materials. If the process doesn't work, Applied Materials gets blamed. In the United States, we tend to be more inventive: each technician sets the machine to an optimum that he has determined. When you operate like that, it becomes more difficult to blame the vendor when the yields are down.

As a result of this fundamental change in the equipment suppliers' role, learning now resides in the industry, not just in the company. That is a complete shift. Just to prove it, look at this example. A Japanese ball bearing company, NMB,[6] with no expertise in the semiconductor industry, had $500 million in excess cash and decided to get into the DRAM business. They got vendors to sell them equipment and set it up, and they contracted with consultants to sell them a process and get it running. In a short time they are the most automated semiconductor factory in the world. That would never have happened even five years ago.

I certainly don't want to minimize the importance of process development. NMB now has to go out and buy a new process for the next generation. There is plenty of process development that distinguishes companies from each other. But, the latest equipment is essential to getting the highest yields. Equipment vendors allow Intel and even new startups to keep up with the latest industry advances.

EPROM

By the end of 1986, Intel had exited the DRAM and SRAM businesses, stopped the development of E^2PROMs, sold its memory systems division, and sold its bubble memory subsidiary. Intel's only remaining position in memory businesses was in EPROMs. In 1986, Intel commanded a 21 percent share of the $910 million market versus 17 percent of an $860 million market two years earlier. In 1989, EPROMs were manufactured in five of Intel's fab sites.

Intel's continued dominance in the EPROM business arose partly from a successful legal battle against Hitachi and other Japanese companies accused of selling EPROMs below cost in the United States. Intel successfully fended off the attack through actions taken by the U.S. government.

In September 1986, Intel top management requested a middle-level manager to prepare a study of each memory business and make recommendations for Intel's long-term strategy. The manager recommended that Intel maintain its position in the EPROM business.

Intel top management decided to keep the EPROM operation as a relatively high volume product to drive learning, but primarily as an enabling technology for the microcontroller business. Intel's microcontrollers integrate EPROM functionality and use an EPROM process technology. In 1989, Intel remained the EPROM market leader with 21 percent market share of a $1 billion market.

Flash

The middle manager also recommended that the company devote resources to a new memory technology called *Flash*. He said:

People say necessity is the mother of invention, and it sounds trite, but it's true. Those two years [1985–86] at Intel were incredibly stressful for the entire company. But, out of that time emerged several paradigm changes.

One very important one was Flash memory. Flash is very similar to E^2PROM in functionality, but it is much cheaper to make. Basically, it costs less than EPROM, but you can erase it electrically instead of with light. This is a major cost/functionality discontinuity in EPROM semiconductor technology and has significant implications. One can envision low-end solid-state reprogrammable systems, for instance, as well as simpler field service for ROM/EPROM-based systems.

Contrasting Flash to DRAM reveals some interesting perspectives. Flash does not have the flexible write functionality of DRAM, but it is nonvolatile. Additionally, Flash is actually a simpler-to-manufacture read/write technology because it is not constrained by the need for a large capacitor in each memory cell. About 80 percent of the current DRAM cell is active whereas only 5 percent of the Flash cell

---

[6] For more on NMB, see Gilder, *Microcosm*, pp. 154–59. Takami Takahashi, NMB president, views DRAMs as the ultimate commodity: "A chip is merely a miniature ball bearing—flattened out, with a picture on it." In 1989, NMB was on a yearly sales run rate of $350 million, having reached sales of $200 million in 1988 on an estimated investment of $200 million in plant and equipment. The plant had a total of 160 employees working four shifts.

is. That means that Flash can shrink like mad. The best way to compete with the Japanese is to change the game.

Another paradigm change has resulted in our working on a truly parallel processor, or neural network, that uses a version of Flash technology. By making an analog instead of a digital device, we can develop a low-precision but very high performance "trainable analog/memory processor." It remains to be seen what applications will evolve from this capability but it has exciting possibilities.

If Flash leads to miniaturization of computers from portable to hand-held units, neural nets may solve handwriting recognition. This, combined with a notebook computer, would result in a very user-friendly tool for a large market.

As you think about it, Flash may ultimately have implications for the microprocessor business. If you look out far enough, you can see a whole new era for semiconductor technology.

By 1990, some industry observers began to recognize the potential for Flash as a replacement for conventional magnetic disc drives in laptop computers.[7] Some industry specialists noted that solid-state disks, when compared to traditional Winchester drives, can consume up to 300 times less power, are 15 times more durable, can withstand much more heat, and are up to 100 times faster. Other industry specialists, however, noted that there has been a 100-fold "shrink" in the size of 20- to 40-megabit drives since the late 1970s (from 2,300 cubic inches for the 14-inch drive to 23 cubic inches for the current 1-inch drive), and that during that time price has decreased by a factor of 10, and access time improved by a factor of 2.[8] Exhibit 3 shows projections of prices for various 2.5-inch disk drive capacities.

In the portable PC market, the London-based company Psion PLC already had plans to introduce two notebook computers in 1990 which would use Flash instead of magnetic storage. While the current installed base of portables is estimated at fewer than 5 million units, the future potential is estimated at more than 20 million.[9]

The market for ultraportables (falling between today's 6-pound notebook and the 1-pound pocket-type) was estimated to grow from fewer than 1 million in 1990 to 12 million in 1994.[10]

---

[7] Microsoft has decided to support the technology by releasing file-management software that lets MS-DOS treat Flash like disk drives.
[8] "You Can Take It with You," Forum on Portable Computers and Communications, Bear Stearns & Co., New York, October 2–3, 1990.
[9] Ibid.
[10] Ibid.

EXHIBIT 3 Cost/Drive over Time, 2.5″ 20–200 MB, Midyear OEM Quantities

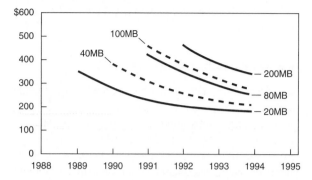

EXHIBIT 4 PC Card Cost Projection

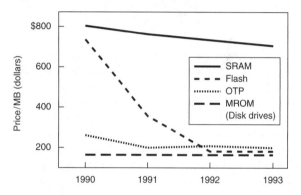

Although Flash was still more expensive than traditional magnetics, its learning curve was much steeper. Exhibit 4 shows price projections for different storage technologies.

In October 1990, Intel announced a credit-card size "Flash memory card" which will be available in 1- and 4-megabyte storage disks, and priced at $298 and $1,198, respectively. Intel said that the new storage drive will offer an important alternative to floppy and hard disk drives in portable computers, because it uses less power and offers improved performance. The reduced power demands, for instance, will extend battery life between 10 and 100 times for portable computers. The company expected to begin mass production of the Flash memory card in December.

By 1994, Intel predicted it would have a 16-megabit Flash chip. The chip would enable a cost-competitive alternative to the industry standard 40-megabyte hard drive on a credit-card size format.

Western Digital was reportedly developing Flash subsystems that can be managed like magnetic media, and can be interfaced into a system like a disk drive.[11] Texas Instruments was also developing its own Flash technology, which reportedly used less power than Intel's during data writing.

NEW MICROPROCESSOR STRATEGY

During the same week in October 1985 when Intel made the decision to close Fab 5 in Oregon for DRAM production, it announced shipment of the 32-bit 80386. The electronics industry received the 386™ microprocessor with great enthusiasm. Just one year later, in the third quarter of 1986, customers had completed development of new products, and the first products to contain the 386™ were shipped. By then, the new microprocessor had garnered over 200 design wins by virtue of its upward compatibility with existing personal computer software and its broad applications in other markets.

The power of the 386's ability to leverage previous software led to the most rapid ramp up of production for any microprocessor in Intel's history. By the end of 1987, just two years after introduction, Intel had shipped an estimated 800,000 units as compared to 50,000 for the earlier 8086 at two years after its introduction. By 1989, some analysts believed that Intel was too dependent on the i386™ and its support chips, estimating that they generated nearly $1 billion, or between 30 and 40 percent of revenue for the company during FY 1988.

A new corporate strategy added to Intel's early success with the 80386. During previous generations, Intel supported a cross-licensing agreement with AMD in which AMD acted as a second source and provided development of support chips. Intel's top management made the decision to make AMD perform under the existing agreement or be prepared to act as a sole source for the 386™.[12]

Craig Barrett described some of the factors which figured in the decision:

> Basically, Intel got to the point where it could generate enough customer confidence to pull it off. There were at least several forces at work.
>
> Our quality thrust of the early 1980s began to pay off in improved consistency on the manufacturing line and overall

better product quality. In addition, customer-vendor partnerships became more prevalent throughout our business. For example, we had recently started selling Ford a microcontroller product, the 8061. They proclaimed that total cost was more important than purchase price alone and decided to work with us closely and exclusively—sort of on the Japanese model. We learned a great deal from that which carried into our other customers and to our vendors.

> We had also decided to pursue a "vendor of choice" strategy in 1984 which led to improved customer satisfaction. Finally, the experience with earlier ×86 generations led us to believe that we could accurately forecast demand for the 386™ and put sufficient manufacturing capacity in place.
>
> With improved manufacturing consistency and better forecast accuracy, we realized that it wasn't always necessary to have a second source to keep the customer satisfied. And, as our second-source deal with AMD came unraveled, we put in the capability to never miss a shipment by adding strategic inventory and redundant capacity. And, since then we have never missed an 80386 customer commitment.
>
> The pitfalls of our strategy are obvious. You can fall on your own sword. And it only takes once to lose the confidence of your customers. Also, the business is sufficiently profitable that everyone is gunning for you. They try to make clones of your products or substitutes.

Bob Reed, chief financial officer, underlined the importance of intellectual property to Intel and to the semiconductor industry:

> Intel has looked around for an edge against competitors. When we look back 10 years from now we may see that intellectual property protection[13] saved the U.S. semiconductor market. The protection will essentially lead to a segmentation of the semiconductor industry into maybe 10 industries, all with leaders. Intel's sole source strategy for the i386™ is a good example of a winning strategy. Now Motorola is also a sole source.
>
> This does not imply a much more complicated contractual relationship with customers. For example, Intel has no penalty clauses for nondelivery of parts; however, we never miss a delivery. The stakes have been raised on both sides of the table.
>
> At Intel, the legal department has grown from 5 to 20 internal people in the past five years. In addition, we retain outside counsel. We vigorously pursue anyone who infringes on our intellectual property rights.

In order to support the sole-sourcing strategy, Intel converted their new Israel facility, originally designed

---

[11] Ibid.

[12] Intel believed that AMD did not earn rights to the 386™ design under the existing licensing agreements. Intel's decision led to a widely publicized dispute with AMD which was still in the final stages of binding arbitration at the time of this case development. IBM, however, continued to be allowed to manufacture Intel microprocessors for its own products.

---

[13] In a landmark decision in 1986, the U.S. Courts agreed with Intel that computer code embedded in silicon is covered by U.S. copyright laws, thus affording protection for Intel's chip designs.

EXHIBIT 5   Silicon Trends and PC Integration

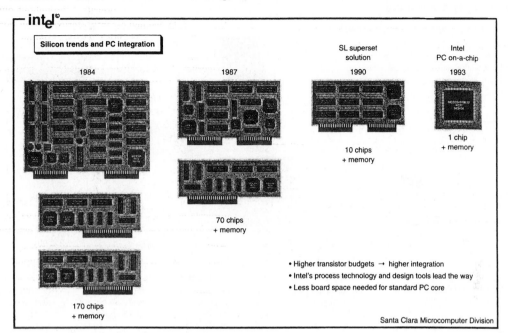

for EPROMs, to make microprocessor products. In addition, the Portland technology development group began developing a 1-micron version of the 386™, a significant reduction in chip size from the original 1.5-micron geometry.

While increased performance and the need for ever increasing price/performance advancements were the key force driving microprocessor development, high integration and increased functionality were also important. Increased functionality and integration depend on the ability to "shrink" the microprocessor, allowing more space to integrate new features. Jack Carsten, formerly an Intel senior vice president and currently a venture capitalist in Silicon Valley, said:

> Lots of people talk about the design team that developed Intel's 386™ chip. It's a great product. But, the great unsung heroes at Intel are the people who successfully developed the "shrink" technology for the 386™. That reduction in geometry led to higher performance parts as well as greatly increased yields.

Exhibit 5 shows the evolution of the result of the shrinking CPU technology.

Sun Lin Chou discussed the role of the Portland Technology Development group:

> In the past two years the situation has changed significantly. We don't just do process development in Portland. We have

designers in Portland who leverage our ability to make use of leading-edge technology sooner. Some of those designers are old DRAM designers who have retrained.

> In the old days, memory was always the first product to use a new process. First we would get the yields up on memory, then a couple of years later the logic product would use the process. Stabilize the process on memory, then do logic. Since logic takes longer to design, it is easier to do it that way. Now we are faced with no DRAM. The concept of technology driver has changed.

> Our challenge is to get logic products up on new processes sooner than we ever have before. To do that, we accelerate and integrate the design process. We use the Portland designers to design standard cells which can then be used by the chip designer groups. We also take existing logic parts that have proven designs and use the new standard cells to generate "shrink" designs.

> Instead of using memory to ramp production, we are now using logic products redesigned with smaller geometries. That is a fundamental change, because demand is not infinite for logic products. We may only have to use a small fraction of one fab's capacity to satisfy the world demand for a particular logic product.

> We also have a group of designers that actually work on new chip designs with the design group in Santa Clara. There was a lot of skepticism about having split design teams, but this arrangement allows us to have a set of designers who are much closer to the process. For example, the Portland design group designed the entire Cache RAM block that goes into the 80486™ chip.

EXHIBIT 6   Intel X86 Compatible Computers Will Dominate PCs, Workstations, Midrange, and Eventually All Computing

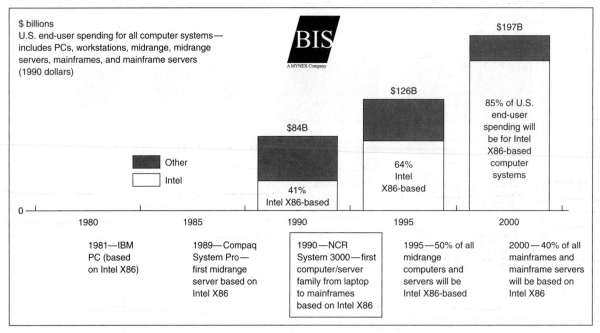

Source: BIS CAP International.

The 80486™[14] was introduced in April 1989. With over 1 million transistors, the *i*486™ microprocessor contains nearly four times the circuit elements in the 386™. The *i*486 had taken a total of 130 person-years in design effort, compared to 80 for the 386. It had benefited from a fourfold increase in proprietary specialized design tools created by Intel. The overall investment in the *i*486 development had been more than $200 million. In keeping with its strategy of upward compatibility, Intel has designed the new offering to run software developed for its predecessors. The *i*486™ was expected to be especially important in the growing market for a new class of "servers," which can store information for an entire corporation and send it out as needed to PCs in response to queries from different types of users (engineers, accountants, marketing specialists, senior executives). In 1990, the market for servers was projected to grow from $4 billion to $12 billion by 1994.[15]

RISC Versus CISC

By 1990, Intel had established a dominant position in the personal computer microprocessor business based on CISC (complex instruction set computing) design. Every manufacturer of advanced IBM-compatible personal computers had to purchase the 386 or 486 microprocessor from Intel. Similarly, those manufacturers or their customers had to purchase operating system software from Microsoft Corporation[16] in order to maintain backward compatibility with the thousands of programs already developed for the PC market. During 1990, NCR was the first Intel customer to decide to use Intel microprocessors throughout its entire product line. Some analysts believed that Intel's penetration in the CISC-microprocessor market would continue throughout the 1990s (see Exhibit 6).

In the meantime, a new market for microprocessors led to the proliferation of microprocessor designs. The

---

[14] 486 is a trademark of the Intel Corporation.
[15] *Business Week,* November 26, 1990, p. 122.

[16] Microsoft was the sole source for the IBM-PC operating system, MS-DOS. In conjunction with IBM, Microsoft also developed a new operating system, OS2, which took advantage of the 286 and 386's multitasking features, while maintaining backward compatibility.

engineering workstation market characterized by high-performance graphics and computation ability was pioneered by Sun Microsystems. In some of its earlier systems, Sun used the Intel 386 chip, but instead of MS-DOS chose the UNIX operating system.[17]

Scott McNealy, president of Sun Microsystems, believed that Intel was charging too much for its processors, so he initiated the development[18] of a new processor using a computing architecture called RISC (reduced instruction set computing).[19] Following a strategy of "open" standards, McNealy made the Sun RISC chip design (SPARC) available to his competitors.

In addition to the SPARC chip, several other RISC chips had reached the market place by 1990, including offerings from MIPS and Motorola. Each of the new RISC chips was capable of supporting some version of the UNIX operating system environment.

In 1990, various analysts were debating the future of RISC versus CISC. One analyst observed that while RISC microprocessors were simpler than CISC ones, the system logic that surrounds the RISC microprocessor is more complex, and that all the RISC does is to transfer system complexity from the microprocessor to the system logic. This analyst also noted that RISC is far behind CISC on the learning curve, and that, for instance, in 1990, Intel alone shipped over 8 million 32-bit CISC microprocessors, while the 10 RISC suppliers combined shipped no more than 200,000 units.[20]

Another analyst observed that the success of RISC versus CISC is likely to depend on whether a totally seamless software bridge can be created enabling all IBM-PC compatible application software to be run fast enough on UNIX-based machines. The question is

who could do that, and what their incentive would be to do so.[21]

THE *i*860™ STORY

In 1988, Intel's official response to RISC architecture was to call it "the technology of the have nots." As several companies announced new RISC chips, Intel developed an internal jargon referring to the competitor chips as YARPs, for "yet another RISC processor."

Yet, within the Intel design organization, a designer named Les Kohn had been trying for several years to initiate a RISC program:

> I joined the company in 1982 after working for National on their 32000 processor. At that time, I realized that RISC architecture had some definite technical advantages. That was very difficult to see from Intel's perspective of the ×86 architecture. So even at a technical level, there was no clear consensus that RISC is the right approach.
>
> Between 1982 and 1986, I made several proposals for RISC projects through the Intel product-planning system, but I wasn't successful. RISC was not an existing business and people were not convinced that the market was there. Also, the company had had a bad experience with a new architecture, the 432, which was not commercially successful. Experience makes skeptics. The design would have been way too big to do in a skunkworks.
>
> In 1986, I saw that our next generation processors would have 1 million transistor chips, and I started working on the idea of a RISC-based processor that would take full advantage of that technology. This proposal had more aggressive goals and was more convincing than previous ones. Several people, including Sai Wai Fu and Kanwar Chadha, got interested in the idea, and we drafted a product requirement document that outlined market size, pricing, and rough development cost. Then we had several breaks that made the project go.
>
> First of all, we positioned it as a co-processor to the 80486 and made sure that it could be justified on that basis. We designed it as a stand-alone processor, but made it very useful as an accessory to the 486™.
>
> We made sure it was very different from the ×86 family so that there would be no question in the customer's mind of which product to use. The real fortuitous part came when presentations to several large customers generated a lot of positive feedback to senior management. Feedback helps because at a technical level, senior managers are not experts.

---

[17] Unlike MS-DOS, the UNIX operating system is capable of taking advantage of the multiprocessing feature of the 386. In addition, UNIX is an "open" program and available from multiple sources (although many of the versions are not compatible).

[18] While Sun designed the RISC chip, it did not have chip-making expertise and farmed out the actual manufacturing of the chip to several silicon foundries.

[19] The RISC (reduced instruction set computing) actually preceded the CISC (complex instruction set computing) architecture. Instructions are in the lowest level commands a microprocessor responds to (such as "retrieve from memory" or "compare two numbers"). CISC microprocessors support between 100 and 150 instructions while RISC chips support 70 to 80. As a result of supporting fewer instructions, RISC chips have superior performance over a narrow range of tasks and can be optimized for a specific purpose. Through combinations of the reduced instruction set, the RISC architecture can be made to duplicate the more complex instructions of a CISC chip, but at a performance penalty.

[20] Sachs, Goldman, "The Future of Microprocessors," research report, April 23, 1990.

[21] Hambrecht & Quist, Inc., "Institutional Research: Intel Corporation," September 12, 1990.

There was also a whole group of customers who did not previously talk to Intel, because they were more interested in performance than compatibility. 3D graphics, workstation, and minicomputer accounts all got very interested. In the end, it looks like the *i*860[22] will generate a whole new business for Intel.

During the development of the RISC chip, it was code named the N10, and perceived by top management as a coprocessor for the *i*486™. The N10 had a 64-bit architecture with floating point and integer processing as well as enhanced graphics capability. According to Kohn, the chip utilized design concepts found in supercomputers. The design team of 50 wore tee shirts with a miniaturized CRAY supercomputer icon resting on a chip.

Kohn commented on Intel's unique position to produce a 1-million transistor RISC chip:

Intel has historically led the industry in having the most transistors—at least in terms of widely used, commercial microprocessors. To do it on the schedule we did it on requires a very close working relationship between technology development and the design teams.

In a lot of cases, RISC companies are working with external vendors for the fabrication of parts so they either have to design for the lowest common denominator of those technologies or they don't necessarily get access to the most advanced technology.

Another factor is the design tools. Intel made a strategic decision to invest in advanced CAD tools. Our new database manager allows us to manage the several thousand files that go into this chip. It made sure that people didn't make changes that got lost or that two different people weren't making changes to the same file at the same time. We also used a new generation of workstation-based circuit design that was very graphic, allowing the engineers to work directly with schematics and display results graphically.

In February 1989, Intel announced the *i*860 not as a co-processor, but rather as a stand-alone RISC processor. Top management decided to join the RISC processor race. Grove said:

We had our own marketing story for the chip, but our customers changed it. They said, "Listen, this isn't just a co-processor chip. This could be the central processor of a super technical workstation." Occasional sarcastic jibes aside, we're in no position now to dump on RISC as a technology. Our chip shows what the real potential of RISC is.[23]

Craig Barrett viewed the *i*860 as part of a rational strategy having emerged through the championing of a top-flight engineer:

There has been competition between the RISC and CISC architectures for some time. If we assume that the market will split, this gives us a position in both markets.

Intel's bread and butter clearly is still in the ×86 family. There is a 586 on the drawing board and a 686 planned to follow that. If there was ever any question of which comes first, it could be answered very quickly. But if there are enough people out there who want to buy YARPs, then we call the *i*860 a YARP killer. It is the highest-performance RISC processor on the market.

SYSTEMS BUSINESS

Les Vadasz became senior vice president and general manager of the Intel Systems Business in 1985. In 1988, the business had nearly kept pace with the dramatic microprocessor growth so that it accounted for about $750 million of Intel's $2.8 billion in sales. In 1990, it was expected to contribute over $1 billion.

Originally, the Systems Business provided technology to enable the growth of Intel's semiconductor business. For example, development systems, which allowed customers to design systems and write software for microprocessor applications, provided a significant portion of the revenue.

In 1985, top management had made the strategic decision to increase the systems business share of total revenue. Vadasz said:

In 1985, the systems business was still devoted to accelerating the deployment of our silicon technology. We were providing our customers multiple choices at different levels of integration. If they wanted microprocessors or board level products, we could provide either.

Now we are more like an independent business. We make a range of products: PC-compatibles for OEMs; mainframes through a joint venture[24]; and even parallel supercomputers based on the *i*386™ processors. We also make PC enhancement boards and sell them through retail channels. Microprocessor-based computer technology is the future, even in supercomputers.

We organize by having segmented strategies for each market. We must recognize that each of our segments requires a different business structure. For example, supercomputers and PCs require entirely different manufacturing

---

[22] 860 is a trademark of the Intel Corporation.
[23] *The Wall Street Journal*, February 28, 1989, pp. A1 and A8.

[24] BIIN Computer, a joint venture with Siemens, was founded in the summer of 1988 to develop a fault-tolerant computer. The joint venture was dissolved in October 1989.

disciplines. The PC enhancement business requires a retail understanding, its own sales force, a different kind of documentation, and, of course, its own product engineering.

As you grow, and stake out new territory, you test and develop new capabilities for the company. Each new capability can then be deployed into other areas. But, you must exercise discipline in how you use your capabilities.

Several of the businesses started as ventures in the Intel Development Organization (IDO), which Vadasz also heads. Vadasz continued:

IDO looks a bit like an internal venture capital fund. It is funded by the corporation and has its own mini board of Gordon Moore, Bob Reed, and me. It serves to isolate a new idea from the quarterly cycle of Intel's business. We create an isolated investment unit and see how it does. These units are managed with an iron hand, but on their own merits.

The guiding question at Intel is, Where can we add intellectual value? Some semiconductor people used to grow crystal ingots [raw material for semiconductors], but they found they could not add value there. Others, specializing in crystal growth, became more effective suppliers. DRAMs have become like that. Manufacturing DRAMs does not tell you how to make computers. The lowest-value-added component in the chain always tends to spread, so you get perfect competition in that area.

Some industry observers believed Intel's Systems Business represented a bold strategy which could alienate its customers. Not only did Intel have a sole-source position, but it could even be considered a potential competitor to some of its customers, companies such as Compaq, Tandy, and Olivetti.

QUESTIONS IN 1990

In reviewing the recent history of the company, Grove wondered how to top the "awesome $3 billion Intel." Among the U.S. semiconductor companies, Intel was clearly the leading performer in 1990, but what steps would be necessary to continue that performance?

During the strategic reorientation of 1985, Intel's top management had completely revised the company's strategic long-range planning (SLRP) system, and had resolved to emphasize a set of overriding corporate strategies which would guide lower levels in developing specific objectives. The three-point corporate strategy was:

1. Increase architectural and technological leadership.
2. Be our customers' preferred supplier.
3. Be a world-class manufacturer.

Five years later, this strategy still seemed right. The company continued to invest large amounts of resources in R&D (some $400 million in 1990) and its track record of innovation continued unabated.

However, some adjustments might be necessary. In particular, Grove wondered about the future role of the relatively low margin EPROMs in what was now "the microprocessor company." Should Intel get out of EPROMs to free resources for microprocessors, or should they continue, particularly in light of the potential future of Flash? He also questioned the role of RISC and the implications of Intel's endorsement of that technology. Was RISC a distortion of Intel's microprocessor strategy or part of it? What options could they pursue? Finally, he wanted to consider the larger environmental forces that could help or prevent Intel from sustaining its current growth and profitability throughout the 1990s.

CASE II-14

Managing Innovation at Nypro, Inc.

Rebecca Voorheis

Gordon Lankton, president and majority owner of Nypro, Inc., one of the world's leading makers of precision custom injection molded plastic parts, paused at the entrance to his Clinton, Massachusetts, plant, and put on his plastic hair cap and safety glasses. Passing a line of large Nestal molding machines, he entered a closet-sized room housing a single prototype molding machine—a machine that might represent Nypro's future. Lankton watched as a technician changed the mold in a minute flat, compared to the several hours necessary to change a

Source: Research Associate Rebecca Voorheis prepared this case under the supervision of Professor Clayton Christensen as the basis for class discussion rather than to illustrate either effective or ineffective handling of an administrative situation. Some of the data in this case have been disguised to protect the proprietary interests of the company. Copyright © 1995 by the President and Fellows of Harvard College. To order copies or request permission to reproduce materials, call 1-800-545-7685, write Harvard Business School Publishing, Boston, MA 02163, or go to http://www.hbsp.harvard.edu. No part of this publication may be reproduced, stored in a retrieval system, used in a spreadsheet, or transmitted in any form or by any means—electronic, mechanical, photocopying, recording, or otherwise—without the permission of Harvard Business School.

mold on the Nestal machine, Nypro's main production equipment. NovaPlast—the revolutionary molding machine which could mold a broad mix of low-volume precision parts without the cost penalty generally incurred in frequent machine setups—immediately started filling the magnetically clamped mold.

As Novaplast's servo screw pushed viscous plastic into the mold, Lankton reflected on the past and speculated about the future of Nypro. He wondered how he should begin integrating the NovaPlast machines into Nypro's 21 plants that spanned the globe. How fast should they be rolled out? Should Nypro build one plant dedicated to NovaPlast molding machines, or should the machines be scattered across Nypro's plant network?

BACKGROUND

Nypro's injection molding machines melted small beads of plastic material, then squeezed the material into a mold at high pressure, either with a hydraulically powered piston ram or screw operating inside a cylinder. Customers provided Nypro with detailed specifica-

tions for each product. Nypro's three divisions—consumer/industrial (32.2% of sales), health care (46.7%), and communications/electronics (21.1%)—logged 1994 sales of $165,983,000 and profits of $10,826,000, marking Nypro's ninth consecutive year of record performance (Exhibit 1).

The plastics injection molding industry historically had been populated by small, low-value-added molders—any person trained as a molder who could afford a molding machine could set up a business. Barriers to entry were low because there were few economies of scale. Differentiation was difficult. Nypro, founded as the Nylon Products Corporation in 1955, had been one of these small molders until Gordon Lankton, a Cornell-trained engineer, joined the company as general manager in 1962. Lankton followed a strategy of developing superior technology by focusing on large-scale molding jobs with demanding, technologically progressive customers. Through this focus, as the number of Nypro customers dropped from about 700 in 1980 to around 50 large, multi-national customers by 1995, its revenues per customer jumped from $60,000 to over $4 mil-

EXHIBIT 1   Nypro Financials

(Dollars in 1,000s)	Year ended			
	July 2, 1994	July 3, 1993	June 27, 1992	June 29, 1991
Net sales	165,983	135,829	119,856	100,201
Cost of sales	126,512	104,810	93,832	78,215
Gross profit	39,471	31,019	26,024	21,986
Expenses:				
Selling	7,244	6,826	5,978	5,546
General and admin.	16,807	11,481	9,972	8,035
Research and development	2,705	2,415	1,793	1,005
	26,756	20,722	17,743	14,586
Operating profit	12,715	10,297	8,281	7,400
Other income (expense):				
Other income, net	1,699	1,001	1,114	1,616
Interest expense	(1,502)	(846)	(978)	(1,216)
Interest income	450	260	417	515
Equity in net income of unconsolidated affiliates	605	464	202	(864)
Minority interests in (income) losses of consolidated subsidiaries	(77)	(97)	(13)	152
	1,175	782	742	203
Income before taxes	13,890	11,700	9,508	7,603
Income taxes	(3,064)	(3,194)	(3,002)	(2,450)
Net Income	10,826	8,506	6,506	5,153

lion.[1] Nypro was the fifth-largest plastics molder in the United States (the top four were devoted to the automobile industry). Before-tax profits averaged 17% of sales in an industry with a 4% average.

A key to Nypro's success was Lankton's view that maintaining a vigorous growth rate was not just the *result* of a successfully executed strategy, it was a key *input* in the formula for success. Lankton worried that if Nypro's growth stagnated, the best and most entrepreneurial people would leave the company. He explained:

> Innovative people like to go out and become entrepreneurs on their own. I want to create an atmosphere here that encourages them to stay. When growth slows, we get nervous because the entrepreneurial-types won't see opportunities here and will look elsewhere. A few years ago, we hit a revenue plateau at $50 million and we saw *lots* of people leave. I worry that as we get bigger, we can't keep growing at the same rate each year. How, then, can I maintain an entrepreneurial staff and facilitate innovation?

Lankton used a stock program to reward valuable employees.[2] To get into the program, an employee was selected based on a formula that measured years of service, pay level, and performance ratings (which were weighted most heavily). Four hundred employees were considered for stock ownership each June. Six to eight stockholders were chosen from this pool, from various levels within the company. Through retirement and attrition, the number of shareholders remained near 100. Stockholders chose the board of directors for Nypro.

STRUCTURING FOR INNOVATION

Nypro's organizational structure facilitated aggressive internal competition and constant attention to performance statistics that compared groups within the company. Many attributed Nypro's success in innovation to this internal rivalry—what one executive called "progress through conflict." This competitive spirit originated from Gordon Lankton himself and was fostered by Nypro's plant location strategy and its use of project teams.

Gordon Lankton

Gordon Lankton was a competitive person. He fostered rivalry in everything with which he became involved. For example, at a yearly management retreat at Duke University's Graduate School of Management, a team-building exercise entailed taking small teams to the center of Duke University's forest with the challenge to work cooperatively within the team to find a way out. "The goal quickly disintegrated into 'beat everyone else'" recalled Brian Jones, president of Nypro's Clinton, Massachusetts, operation. "We were in the middle of the woods discussing the best strategy with his team when Lankton's group went running by. *All* of the teams then started running, abandoning any deliberate strategy or teamwork." In another example, Lankton consistently insisted on running with the Puerto Rico plant manager, Jim Goodman, whenever he was in town. Goodman was both a Marine Corps veteran and a marathoner, while 61-year-old Lankton averaged one 10-minute mile per day. Lankton felt he had to beat Goodman, though, and each time struggled until he couldn't stay with him any longer.

Organizational Strategy

Nypro's manufacturing strategy was to build plants near its customers in vital markets. Its slogan, "Nypro is your local source for custom injection molding . . . worldwide," emphasized its commitment to customer service. Nypro's 21 plants were identical—with 20 to 24 Nestal molding machines in dust-free clean rooms, fed by materials through under-floor piping systems. Nypro set its plants at this size because scale economies were essentially exhausted at that level; two 20-machine plants could produce at equal or lower cost to a single 40-machine plant. Plants were tailored to the markets and companies they served. For example, Nypro's plant in Corvallis, Oregon, served the needs of Hewlett-Packard, and the plant in Gurnee, Illinois, specialized in the health care industry of northwest Chicago (Exhibit 2). Nypro's 1994 Annual Report explained:

> Our global customers want us to be truly global—that means doing the exact same thing in Shenzhen, China, that we do in Cayey, Puerto Rico. They want us to use the same machines, same process control, same mold technology, same procedures, same CAD systems—regardless of where we make their products around the world. . . . Nypro provides local capabilities to our customers who share our global outlook. In adding value, we operate where our customers operate, delivering exactly what they need, exactly when they need it.[3]

This decentralized location strategy had its strengths, as well as weaknesses. Randy Barko, Nypro's vice president of sales, explained:

---

[1] Thirty-five customers accounted for 80% of Nypro's business.
[2] Nypro was privately owned, so stock price was calculated at 12.5 times earnings.

[3] *Nypro Annual Report,* 1994, pp. 1, 7.

We are all these separate little units all over the world. Our challenge is to be responsive, entrepreneurial, and internally independent, but to be viewed by the outside world as one company. We want people to know that any Nypro plant they go to, anywhere in the world, is still Nypro. We want customers to know that wherever they are, they are going to find the same technology; the same materials; the same capability. The challenge with this strategy, of course, is innovation. Achieving uniformity across plants is easy—you identify a set of processes and procedures that do the job well, and implement them with instructions not to deviate. But that precludes innovation. And if you encourage people to innovate, you can quickly lose your consistency across plants.

Nypro management strongly felt that innovation was a result of competition. For example, the Burlington, North Carolina, plant, which was considered one of the most innovative molding plants in the world, began using dedicated, labeled hoses hooked to each machine for each of the different plastics used, in order to avoid cleanup costs and impurities in early shots. Word spread, and the Burlington plant became deluged with visitors from other Nypro locations. Brian Jones explained the visits:

> It's competition. There were a lot of innovations at Burlington that people studied, but they focused on the hoses. There's a sort of competitive marketplace in the company for good process ideas, as the plants compete against each other for the top ranking. Good ideas get snapped up fast and nobody buys into mediocre ideas.

To keep information on innovations flowing, each Nypro plant was organized as a company, with a board of directors composed of managers from other facilities. An internal company publication stated, "The Board of Directors concept is designed to bring a variety of disciplines from Nypro's experienced and qualified employees to the support of the General Managers of Nypro companies and joint ventures." The people in the table below, for example, are members of the Clinton plant's

Board of Directors. A significant exception to Nypro's policy of decentralization was in sales. Randy Barko, corporate vice president for sales in the Clinton corporate headquarters, personally approved every new customer and every major new customer program in the company. At least one salesperson was resident in each of the Nypro plants, but all salespeople were responsible directly to Barko, with only a dotted line relationship to the general manager of each company.

Teams

Nypro managed its customer relationships by establishing teams that focused on the product development and process improvement issues for each customer-specific project. Each team was headed by a program manager who was part of the engineering organization. While the program manager specialized in a specific industry, the rest of the team was composed of people from various disciplines. A team could include a mix of tooling engineers, quality engineers, sales contacts, plant representatives, process engineers, manufacturing engineers, and automation engineers. "These people may have worked on five different projects in the last six months, so they are bringing different expertise from different projects," Randy Barko, vice president of sales, explained, "The program manager has the overall responsibility of keeping the project going in one direction, but the team members will give him or her input along the way, having had the experience from other projects to bring to it."

The original members of a team consisted of Nypro engineers and engineers from the client company. This group of people, known as the Development Team, was expected to fully develop the new product idea and process innovations. Once engineering and development were done and the product was in production, the Development Team was phased out and a new team was put together—the Continuous Improvement Team. Continuous Improvement teams comprised manufacturing, quality control, materials procurement, and marketing people. Representatives of similar functions at the client

Clinton board member	Position	Other boards serving on
Alfonso Berrios	Info.Tech, Puerto Rico	
Rick Bourgeois	corporate controller	NP Medical
Frank Brand	outside director	Nypro Inc.
Rick Hoeske	vice president, engineering	Puerto Rico, Singapore
Dave Parker	salesman, northeast	
Paddy Woods	general manager, Ireland plant	North Carolina

EXHIBIT 2 Nypro's Worldwide Plant Locations, Fiscal Year 1994

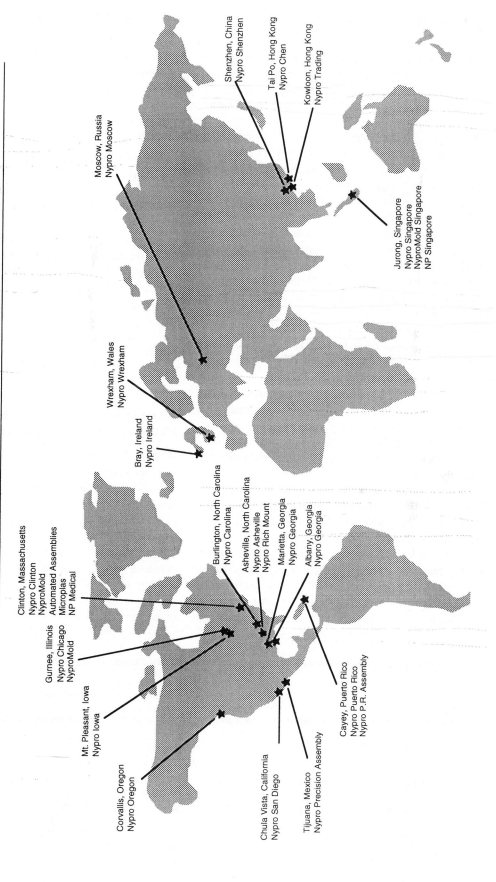

WORLDWIDE LOCATIONS

Nypro

Clinton, Massachusetts
Nypro Clinton
NyproMold
Automated Assemblies
Microplas
NP Medical

Gurnee, Illinois
Nypro Chicago
NyproMold

Mt. Pleasant, Iowa
Nypro Iowa

Corvallis, Oregon
Nypro Oregon

Chula Vista, California
Nypro San Diego

Tijuana, Mexico
Nypro Precision Assembly

Cayey, Puerto Rico
Nypro Puerto Rico
Nypro P.R. Assembly

Burlington, North Carolina
Nypro Carolina

Asheville, North Carolina
Nypro Asheville
Nypro Rich Mount

Marietta, Georgia
Nypro Georgia

Albany, Georgia
Nypro Georgia

Bray, Ireland
Nypro Ireland

Wrexham, Wales
Nypro Wrexham

Moscow, Russia
Nypro Moscow

Shenzhen, China
Nypro Shenzhen

Tai Po, Hong Kong
Nypro Chen

Kowloon, Hong Kong
Nypro Trading

Jurong, Singapore
Nypro Singapore
NyproMold Singapore
NP Singapore

company, and frequently a representative of Nypro's suppliers, also joined the team. Because of this dual-team system, there was always a team of people responsible for every product Nypro produced, for as long as it was in production.

In one project, for example, the Continuous Improvement Team was still in existence even after 10 years of production at Nypro. That year, the team member representing Nypro's materials supplier suggested using a more expensive plastic that he felt might increase yields far downstream, in Nypro's *customer's* process. In just one year the customer's production cost fell by $25 million—a savings that dwarfed the total value of the plastic components the customer was buying from Nypro.

If a team became stagnant in its innovative strategy, Nypro management would change some of the people on the team to get a different perspective on the project. Brian Jones explained, "We get people on teams where they have to get out of their comfort zone. Teams are composed of a vertical and horizontal slice of the company. Each project group kept a constant watch over the others to monitor what other teams were coming up with. If one team innovated its process in a beneficial way, Nypro management would spread information about the success. Subsequently, in the "internal market" for innovations, other teams could use the same innovation in their own projects.

Gordon Lankton distributed performance results of all the divisions throughout the company. Internal corporate reports highlighted both the successes of the best plants and the failures of the worst (Exhibit 3). It was important to Lankton that comparisons were always made *between* plants or teams (which numbered almost 90)—never between individuals, or between a unit's present and past performance. Performance statistics were gathered on a quarterly basis, and results and plans for

improvement were discussed at annual management meetings. Because the projects teams worked on vastly different projects, Nypro developed unique standards of performance. The following questions were asked by a business review committee in evaluating a Development or Continuous Improvement Team:

- How well did you help the customer get its product to market?
- Was the *customer's* product commercially successful?
- Did you help the customer attack the market in a new and different way?
- Did the customer achieve its strategic goal?
- Did you get a contract as an exclusive supplier?
- Did you ink a long-term contract?
- Have you made steady and significant improvements beyond your original targets for margins, revenues, quality, and cycle time?
- How are your financial, accounting, and profit/loss results?
- Can you make the product faster than you did at first?

MANAGING THE DEVELOPMENT AND ADOPTION OF NEW TECHNOLOGIES

Because Nypro's teams specialized in *custom* molding—making by contract parts which its customers designed—the company's scope for innovation was in process, not product. Most ideas for process improvement emerged as Nypro's Continuous Improvement teams worked to solve production and profitability problems for its customers. Nypro's far-flung network of close-to-customer plants made managing these activities challenging, and involved answering four questions: (1) what process innovations had actually occurred? (2) which of these innovations were important enough to be adapted

EXHIBIT 3   Examples of Statistics Used to Compare Plants' Performance

Nypro plant	Machine utilization	On-time shipments	Customer return incidents (per machine, per year)	Materials as % of sales	% Sales change, 1994–1995
Clinton	75%	92%	2	23.4%	13.8%
Puerto Rico	80%	97%	2.3	43.7%	−4.4%
Oregon	51%	100%	0	51.7%	NA
Georgia	70%	98%	1.4	49.7%	100%
China	65%	100%	NA	46.5%	NA
Singapore	69%	100%	.7	43.5%	10%
Chicago	49%	88%	.3	35.8%	NA
Ireland	72%	98%	.8	45.1%	21.8%

in other plants? (3) how could the innovation be transferred from the team that developed it to other teams and plants? and (4) how could Nypro standardize the new way of doing things?

The following examples illustrate some of these challenges.

The Vistakon Project

Nypro's concept of Continuous Improvement teams was born when its engineers were challenged in a contract with Johnson & Johnson's Vistakon division to make molds for disposable contact lenses with substantially less variation in the degree of vision correction for lenses of a given power than Bausch and Lomb, Vistakon's leading competitor, was able to achieve. Nypro ultimately learned to make molds with a $\pm5\mu$m variation—a $50\times$ reduction in dimensional variability over the tightest that had been achieved in the industry until that time, and an achievement that reinforced Nypro's reputation as a capable specialty molder.[4]

Even though the product development effort had been successful, Nypro's parts were so critical in Vistakon's quality- and price-sensitive production process that Nypro had to keep its Development Team in place long after volume production had started. The ensuing efforts at improvement were so cooperation-intensive that the Nypro team found it necessary to integrate with Vistakon's team in order to exchange information efficiently. By sharing with each other on-line manufacturing data, the Vistakon/Nypro team dramatically increased production quality. Nypro and Vistakon personnel each could call up information on production rates, inventory levels, and production schedules, machine-by-machine, in each other's plants. Once the news of the success of Nypro's Vistakon team began to spread, other teams in the company started inquiring about the "Continuous Improvement Team" (CIT) system developed during the project, and began implementing integrated teams with their customers, also with successful results in efficiency and process improvements. Management then stepped in to standardize the CIT system. Thereafter, as a standard procedure, Nypro crafted an agreement with each new customer stating that the parties would establish a joint Continuous Improvement Team to work together to reduce cost and improve profitability for both sides. Barko described the benefit:

Customers in the past never talked to the injection molders about what the product was really used for, what the critical elements of it were. It was just, "Here's a print, here's a dimension—make it." The Vistakon project opened up a whole new thought process of how the product is used and what the critical elements of the products are.

Another of the Vistakon team's innovations that proved popular in Nypro's internal market for process improvements related to moldmaking. Making a mold for plastics injection molding is a significant cost which increases exponentially with the precision of the mold. Injection molders therefore traditionally only made molds as precise as the customer requested. However, Nypro's teams realized upon seeing the results of the Vistakon project that extreme precision in moldmaking was probably worth the cost. As other post-Vistakon teams began to explore ways they could improve, more and more of them began adopting the extreme standard of precision the Vistakon team had used in making its molds. Ultimately the cost and quality benefits of this practice became clear to management, and they established a new ground rule: if the tolerance requested by the customer was $\pm$X, Nypro would design its molds as if the tolerance demanded were $\pm\frac{1}{2}$X.

The Reach Toothbrush Project: Bi-Component Molding

In the early 1990s, Johnson & Johnson's dental care division contracted with Nypro's Puerto Rico company to mold Reach® brand toothbrushes. J&J wanted the brush handle made from two different plastic materials— a rigid plastic for the main structure, with a coating of soft, rubbery material on the top and bottom of the handle for a better grip. Nypro's Puerto Rico engineers figured out how to make the two-component handle in a single stroke or cycle of the molding machine. The technique, dubbed bi-component molding, proved critical to making the popular product to the customer's targeted cost, and the news of the Puerto Rican team's success spread throughout the company. Because Nypro's teams were evaluated on whether their customers' products were commercially successful, other CIT teams began proposing to *their* customers that bi-component molding could be used to give their next-generation products a better hand feel. Soft-handled products such as Crayola's Munchkin-brand baby spoons were the result. Transferring bi-component molding know-how kept the Puerto Rican team busy, but the recognition they received as winners in the internal team competition made it worthwhile.

[4]*Molding the Impossible: The NYPRO/Vistakon Disposable Contact Lens Project.* Harvard Business School case No. 694-062 (November 23, 1994).

Innovations in Plant Design

The clean-room manufacturing philosophy for which Nypro was famous also was a bottom-up innovation. Warren Brooks, a manager of a production facility in Clinton, decided to make his plant as clean as a hospital operating room in the late 1970s. Brooks was convinced that an immaculate production facility was crucial to efficient operation—not only visual cleanliness, but particle size, air circulation, air quality, and other exacting details. He presented the idea to Nypro management, which felt the idea was excessive. But because the divisions were run separately at the time, Brooks could glean resources from his division when the corporate staff wouldn't fund it. In 1979, he established Nypro's first clean-room facility. Brooks filtered the air in the production facility to diminish dust, had workers wear gowns and plastic hair-coverings, cleared the floor of all extraneous obstacles, and installed piping under the floors to supply the viscous plastic material. It rapidly paid off in terms of product quality and employee productivity. The clean room structure was then adopted by the Puerto Rico plant manager. Over the next five years corporate management realized the advantage of clean parts molding and dictated that each plant built thereafter would be a clean-room facility.

The visual factory—where each office, conference room, cafeteria, and other gathering place or working space at Nypro had a view onto the production floor—became a standard design through a similar process. Visual factory designs ensured that no one was removed from the "minute-by-minute urgency and immediate reaction times" that were essential to Nypro's success as a manufacturer, according to Brian Jones.

The visual factory grew out of the sales and marketing function at Nypro-Clinton, which found that customers who were untrained in molding could greatly benefit from seeing the production process so they could conceptualize Nypro's value as a supplier and molder. To obviate customers' having to don hair caps, safety goggles, shoe guards, and other safety equipment in order to view the production facility, they installed viewing windows around the Clinton's production floor. Soon it became clear that having everyone—employees and customers alike—in visual contact with the production floor was a great benefit to the entire operation. In 1985 the visual factory was adopted as a standard plant design.

MRP2 Systems

Some Nypro innovations were initiated by senior management, as was the case with Nypro's MRP2 production planning software. In 1995, Nypro management was in the fifth year of asking each of the plant locations to adopt a common MRP2 (manufacturing resource planning) software system. Nypro's MRP2 system integrated resource planning and capacity requirements with information technology, CAD/CAM, total quality management, and process control—bringing each of the Nypro plants together under one software system which would allow them to communicate about production planning, both inside Nypro and with the customer. The Puerto Rico plant was the first to accept the technology, in 1990. Other plant managers had been reluctant to implement the software, though. Each manager wanted a highly customized system which would allow his or her plant to best compete, as opposed to a standardized system.

To spur adoption, management established a special team, headed by Dan Gorman, to implement the MRP2 system. The team had a sales-type role—it was responsible for persuading each plant to accept the technology. Brian Jones stated, "The plants would tell you that the Clinton team has no authority, but it does. And it actually has a lot of capability in specializing design and making implementation easier."

After a few years of struggling to convince the plants to implement the system, Gorman's team decided to establish the system at Clinton and let the other plant locations observe its performance. Simultaneously, the MRP2 team began talking to customers about what the software meant and how it could be used, hoping the customers would demand the technology at their respective Nypro locations. Finally, by early 1995 the MRP2 system was beginning to gain momentum at Nypro: all domestic plants were in some stage of adapting the MRP2 system to their specific needs, though none of them had fully implemented it.

DEALING WITH A SHIFTING BASIS OF COMPETITION

Nypro was once far ahead of its competitors in terms of the precision it could achieve in its molded parts. By 1995, however, several other molders had improved their processes to levels competitive with Nypro's ability—and those levels seemed more than adequate for the vast majority of customers at present.

Increasingly, Nypro's marketers found they needed to quote shorter delivery times in order to capture business, and to do this, Nypro had been forced to help its tooling suppliers reduce their lead times from an average of 20 weeks to 6 weeks. Randy Barko explained:

Time is our focus today. It's the driving force of all current projects. One thing we always say is, "Lights work 24 hours a day." That doesn't mean you want everybody to work 24 hours a day, but it forces you to focus on not losing any productive hours. When you are saying it's going to take you four weeks to build a tool, you are saying it's four weeks times seven days times 24 hours. How much of that is nonvalue-added time?

"We have one customer now who wants parts from a sample mold within four weeks," Barko continued. "Eventually they are going to want it in two weeks, then one week. A mold in four weeks, even six months ago, would have been difficult to even fathom." To squeeze lead time, Nypro had begun sending the customer's CAD files to its toolmaker to initiate work on the mold, even while they were still finalizing what the mold would cost. "There just wasn't time to go through a whole big long quoting process and negotiating back and forth," Barko explained. "If they want it in four weeks, price isn't the most important thing. We trust each other. We know we're going to agree on the cost. So why hold things up for it?"

THE NOVAPLAST ROLL-OUT

In 1990 on his annual trip around the world to observe new developments in the plastics injection molding industry Gordon Lankton saw a molding machine at a Japanese VCR and automotive parts manufacturing plant which he felt might address the market for low-volume, high-mix, quick-turnaround business—a market that Nypro historically had been unable to supply. Lankton was interested because as more and more companies began competing on bases of speed and variety, this segment of the molding business was growing rapidly. After his trip, Lankton gave an internal Nypro team, headed by Curt Watkins, the task of studying the machine, which Nypro dubbed NovaPlast.

Traditionally, high-volume precision molders such as Nypro had used very big, expensive equipment which required several hours in set-up time to change the molds used. These high fixed set-up costs made the low-volume, high-mix market unprofitable to them, and Lankton felt that the market was not well served by world-class molders as a result. Curt Watkins stated, "We never looked at low-volume, high-mix markets because we weren't competitive." When a customer had a small job with specialized molding needs, Nypro often would contract with an independent molder to provide the low-

EXHIBIT 4   NovaPlast Characteristics (from an Internal Nypro Publication)

- **What is it?**
  small machine molding
  cost effective, short run, low-volume production
  ultimate quality, high-precision injection molding
  short lead time, low cavitation
  production quantity specific
  one minute mold changes
  "lights out" operation
  just in time deliveries

- **Scope**
  prototyping, product development
  market introductions
  low-volume production
  ramp-up to high-volume production
  lower capital investment
  concurrent engineering

- **Project/product criteria**
  mold base sizes $4 \times 5''$ and $6 \times 6''$
  maximum cavitation = 4
  1.75" maximum part height
  minimum/maximum mold stack height = 5" to 10"
  3-level design complexity
  yearly production requirements = 1 million/year or less
  material usage = 30 lbs./hour maximum
  maximum part surface area = 2 to 8 square inches

EXHIBIT 5   Relative Costs of Nestal and NovaPlast, Indexed at 100

	Conventional machine	NovaPlast
Capital cost	100	50
Tooling	100	25–30
Set up time	100	<1
Run time	100	50
Staffing	100	20

volume parts. When the volume reached a certain level, Nypro would shift production to its own facilities.

NovaPlast was a small machine in size and capacity. The size of the molds it could accommodate, and therefore the number of cavities NovaPlast could fill in one molding cycle, was limited. However, the molds could be changed in a matter of minutes with minimal labor effort, as Exhibits 4 and 5 show. Barko described how it worked.

NovaPlast minimizes nonvalue-added activities with functions like magnetic clamping and automatic preheating. You can slide the mold into the machine, then just push the button and magnetically it's clamped into place. You have eliminated all nonvalue-added activity—messing with molds and mold clamps for hours.

It's like a game show. NovaPlast opens three possible doors for Nypro, with a "prize" behind each. Door number one is typical of what NovaPlast was intended for—a short-run business, quickly timed and repeated small requirements for the next ten years. Behind door number two, NovaPlast is used for development-type projects where you need to get something to market in a short period of time. Maybe you build single cavity tooling to get it to market. Behind door number three, there are a lot of other jobs running at Nypro in bigger machines and in bigger molds that we can downsize. We can also use NovaPlast for long-runs and ultra-fine precision molding, as long as a new mold is made to fit the machine.

Nypro ordered a prototype high-precision NovaPlast machine from a custom builder, and by late 1994 it was in operation at the Clinton plant. Nypro had begun some projects on NovaPlast and was introducing the technology to customers. The NovaPlast development, marketing, and sales teams were centralized at Nypro's Clinton headquarters. Seeking early orders for parts compatible with the NovaPlast machine was critical to the development strategy, because Nypro needed to learn how the machine could be used.[5] These orders had begun arriving in early 1995.

In Nypro's experience there was a relatively steep and protracted learning curve associated with every new class of equipment. Understanding how settings for temperature, pressure, and dwell time interacted with mold design to affect the dimensional variability in molded parts—and understanding how to control the factors that contributed to variability—were difficult problems that needed to be worked out on each new class of machine. Because NovaPlast machines were new to the industry, these issues promised to be particularly vexing.

The issue Nypro's management team needed to resolve was how and where, within Nypro's structure, to build this understanding of how to mold with NovaPlast machines, and how to leverage that capability in the marketplace. It then needed to determine how to disseminate the machines and that knowledge across the company. Three options had begun to emerge from discussions on the issue.

The first option—and probably the most popular one with senior management—was to build a new plant that would employ *only* NovaPlast machines. The arguments for this were, first, engineering efficiency: all of the knowledge created about the NovaPlast equipment would best be concentrated in one place; and second, focus: the other systems for serving the high-mix, fast-response, low-volume-per-part—systems such as bidding, order entry, toolmaking, production scheduling, and inventory control—were different enough from those required to sustain Nypro's mainstream business that a distinct organization needed to be established to focus on these unique tasks. Furthermore, Lankton felt that centralizing development would facilitate his and Watkins' personal oversight of the project.

The second option was to install two or three machines in each of Nypro's plants. The arguments supporting this option were, first, that the market was distributed across the territories served by each plant, and that close-to-customer manufacturing was particularly important in this segment of the market. Indeed, many of Nypro's high-volume customers also bought low-volume parts from other vendors. Second, this option would put many more engineers and marketers, in different competitive environments, to work on the problem of how to control and exploit the NovaPlast. With a larger variety of solutions investigated, it was possible that better technology would emerge than would be developed under the first option described above.

The third option would be not to roll NovaPlast out across the company at all, but to focus on making it successful at a single plant. If it emerged as a profitable addition to that plant's arsenal of competitive weapons, then Nypro's "internal market" for innovation would take over, and the effort would roll itself out, if it were judged to be commercially valuable. The logic supporting this option was that Nypro's internal market had a great track record at spotting winning innovations.

As Lankton watched his technician work with the NovaPlast, he sensed that the time for making his decision was near. The technology was advancing and the orders were arriving. This technology appeared to be the best bet Nypro had for maintaining the vigorous growth rate Lankton felt his $200 million company needed to maintain its vitality.

---

[5] Nypro would accept a NovaPlast project only if the customer's mold cavitation fit the machine.

Intraorganizational Ecology of Strategy Making and Organizational Adaptation: Theory and Field Research

Robert A. Burgelman

This paper presents an intraorganizational ecological perspective on strategy making, and examines how internal selection may combine with external selection to explain organizational change and survival. The perspective serves to illuminate data from a field study of the evolution of Intel Corporation's corporate strategy. The data, in turn, are used to refine and deepen the conceptual framework. Relationships between induced and autonomous strategic processes and four modes of organizational adaptation are discussed. Apparent paradoxes associated with structural inertia and strategic reorientation arguments are elucidated and several new propositions derived. The paper proposes that consistently successful organizations are characterized by top managements who spend efforts on building the induced and autonomous strategic processes, as well as concerning themselves with the content of strategy; that such organizations simultaneously exercise induced and autonomous processes; and that successful reorientations in organizations are likely to have been preceded by internal experimentation and selection processes offered through the autonomous process.

The emergence of an ecological perspective, producing new insights in organizational change and adaptation (e.g., Carroll 1988, Hannan and Freeman 1989), has triggered several debates in organizational science that are important for the field of strategic management. One debate centers around the issue of environmental determinism versus strategic choice (Child 1972, Aldrich 1979, Astley and Van de Ven 1983, Bourgeois 1984, Hrebiniak and Joyce 1985). Another debate concerns the relative importance of selection and adaptation in explaining organizational change and survival (Miles and Cameron 1982, Hannan and Freeman 1984, Singh et al. 1986). These sorts of debates have sometimes been interpreted

as reflecting a fundamental opposition between the ideas of ecology and strategy.

The present paper is based on the premise that there need not be a fundamental opposition of ecological and strategic perspectives, and that a fruitful integration of these ideas is possible in some ways. To do so, the paper uses the variation-selection-retention framework of cultural evolutionary theory (Campbell 1969, Aldrich 1979, Weick 1979) which has previously been applied to strategy making by western (Burgelman 1983a) as well as Japanese (Kagono et al. 1985) scholars. The paper extends earlier work by addressing research questions motivated by the evolutionary perspective. Some of these concern strategy content and process: How does the content of an organization's strategy come about and how does it evolve? How do strategy-making processes take shape over time? Of particular interest for this paper are questions concerning some of the connections between strategy-making processes and different forms of organizational change and adaptation: what, if any, is the link between strategy making and inertia? Which sorts of strategy-making processes lead to major strategic change that is survival-enhancing? The paper uses field research at Intel Corporation, a leading semiconductor company, to explore these questions.

The purposes of the paper are twofold. First, the paper proposes the usefulness of an *intraorganizational* ecological perspective on strategy making. An organization is viewed as an ecology of strategic initiatives which emerge in patterned ways and compete for limited organizational resources so as to increase their relative importance within the organization. Strategy results, in part, from selection and retention operating on internal variation associated with strategic initiatives. Variation in strategic initiatives comes about, in part, as the result of individual strategies seeking expression of their special skills and career advancement through the pursuit of different types of strategic initiatives. Selection works through administrative and cultural mechanisms regulating the allocation of attention and resources to different areas of strategic initiative. Retention takes the form of organizational-level learning and distinctive competence, embodied in various ways—organizational goal definition, domain delineation, and shared views of organizational character. In this perspective, strategic initiatives rather than individuals are the unit of analysis (Cohen and Machalek 1988).

Second, the paper proposes patterned links between the intraorganizational ecological processes and different forms of adaptation that have previously been

Source: Reprinted from *Organization Science* 2/3(August 1991). Copyright © 1991 by The Institute of Management Services. Used with permission.

identified in the literature. More specifically, the paper suggests how opposing ideas concerning expected consequences of major strategic change (Hannan and Freeman 1984, Tushman and Romanelli 1985) can possibly be reconciled. This, in turn, suggests directions for further research.

The next section of the paper discusses a field study carried out at Intel Corporation. The following two sections examine, first, strategic content and process from an evolutionary perspective and, second, relationships between strategy-making processes and modes of organizational adaptation. Throughout these sections, references to and vignettes from the Intel study are provided. The discussion section presents conclusions from the research and several propositions derived from it. The final section presents implications for theory and further research.

A FIELD STUDY OF INTEL CORPORATION

To explore the research questions motivated by the evolutionary perspective, a field study of the evolution of Intel Corporation's corporate strategy was carried out. Intel is a leading semiconductor company which has survived for more than 20 years as an independent company in an extremely dynamic industry. The firm grew from $1 million of sales in 1968 to almost $3 billion in 1989. Profits rose from a loss of $2 million in 1969 to $453 million in 1988.

After initial interviews with CEO Andrew S. Grove and his assistant, Dennis Carter, it was decided to focus the first stage of the research on Intel's decision, in 1985, to exit from the dynamic random-access memory (DRAM) business. The second stage of the research focused on the period since 1985 and Intel's current strategy. The study, encompassing archival data collection as well as interviews, was carried out during the period August 1988–October 1989. Company documents describing Intel's history, industry publications, and other written materials were analyzed. Some 20 key Intel managers were interviewed, many of them repeatedly. Some top managers who had previously left the company were included as well. The research is embodied in two case studies (Cogan and Burgelman 1989a,b).

The research began with a broad examination of how Intel's strategy as a "memory company" had taken shape in the early years and then focused on the decision to exit DRAMs. In 1985, Intel was faced with a large cyclical downturn in the semiconductor industry, and fierce Japanese price competition in DRAMs. The firm expected a loss of more than $100 million in 1986, yet needed to invest several hundred million dollars in new plant and equipment if it wanted to be competitive for the next generation of DRAMs. Top management decided that exit from DRAMs was the best alternative for Intel. Managers from different levels and different functional and business groups who had been involved in and/or affected by the decision were asked to discuss the causes of Intel's exit and the aftermath of the decision. Looking at numerical archival data, it was a surprise to find that DRAMs had been a relatively small part of Intel's business for several years before the decision to exit was actually made.

Intel's market share in DRAMs was only 3.4 percent, ranking ninth in the industry, in 1985. Yet there was a pervasive feeling among the interviewees that getting out of DRAMs had been perhaps the most momentous decision in Intel's history. The research then sought to understand Intel's evolution from a "memory" company in 1968 to a "microcomputer" company in 1985. This evolution is illustrated in Exhibit 1.

The second stage of the research focused on events since 1985, covering several key strategic areas, including the development of Intel's major complex instruction set computing (CISC) microprocessor business (the ×86 product family); the evolution of the strategic importance of the erasable programmable read-only memory (EPROM) business; Intel's experience with the application specific integrated circuits (ASICS) business; the emergence and spinoff of the electrically erasable programmable read-only memory (EEPROM) venture; the growing importance of the systems business; the emergence of reduced instruction set computing (RISC) processors as part of Intel's strategy; and questions regarding the potential strategic importance of a new form of memory called FLASH. While most of the research was retrospective, the research period was long enough to observe some strategic decisions in real time, especially the decision to adopt RISC as part of Intel's corporate strategy, and the current uncertainty about FLASH memories.

The field study was guided by an evolutionary framework, derived from earlier research (Burgelman 1983a), which posits the existence of induced and autonomous processes in strategy making. The induced process concerns initiatives that are within the scope of the organization's current strategy and build on existing organizational learning; the autonomous process concerns initiatives that emerge outside of it and provide the potential for new organizational learning. These processes

EXHIBIT 1   Intel's Evolution from Memory Company to Microcomputer Company

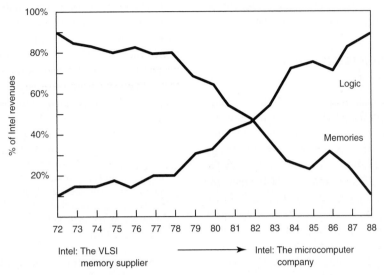

Source: Intel Corporation.

are considered important determinants of the evolution of the organization's strategy. The field data serve to test, to some extent, the validity of this framework. Campbell (1975) discusses several conditions for making a single case study useful as a probe for theory, two of which can be addressed in relation to the Intel study: (1) keeping track of confirming and disconfirming observations; (2) choosing the theory without knowledge of the confirmatory value of the case study. First, while initially not intended to serve as a test of an evolutionary theory of strategy making, the study does offer confirmatory support for the existence of the strategic processes proposed in the framework. Disconfirming observations were not systematically sought out, but some unexpected findings are presented that suggest the need for some amendment of the theory. Second, the availability of Intel as a research site was a fortuitous event and the researchers did not know whether the Intel case study would show support for the evolutionary framework or not. They were not familiar with the strategic management approaches of Intel. Also, many of the open-ended interviews were done by the research assistant who was not involved in developing the conceptual framework. This limited somewhat the potential for confirmatory bias in the data collection. The research assistant wrote up detailed interview transcriptions which were analyzed together with data collected by the author.

While offering support for the existence of the proposed strategy-making processes, the research also offers the opportunity to refine and deepen some of the ideas underlying the initial conceptual framework. The paper reflects iterations between theory and data, using the data to identify some new aspects of an evolutionary perspective on strategy-making processes. In the context of grounded theorizing (Glaser and Strauss 1967), the paper intends to move from theory building based on research in substantive areas, such as internal corporate venturing (Burgelman 1983b), to a more general theory of strategy-making processes in organizations. The theory concerns corporate strategy rather than business strategy, and substantive strategy making rather than corporate restructuring (Snow and Hambrick 1980).

The research has several limitations. It concerns a single high-tech organization still run by some of its founders. The firm has grown up in a cyclical but very expansive industry. And it is a successful organization. Clearly it would be useful to study a larger sample also including failing organizations. On the other hand, by concentrating on one organization with 20 years of continuity in leadership, the research could access sources with intimate knowledge of the details of the firm's evolution and could examine in depth how the organization had dealt with partial failure — and the threat of complete failure — at a critical point in its history. Also, the semiconductor industry has previously been studied by organizational ecologists (e.g., Brittain and Freeman 1980, Boeker 1989), but no in-depth study of the strategy making of semiconductor firms is currently available.

INTRAORGANIZATIONAL ECOLOGY OF STRATEGY MAKING

Research on strategy-making processes can be classified in terms of two primary foci (Snow and Hambrick 1980). Some scholars, focusing on strategic change, have documented major epochs (Mintzberg 1978, Mintzberg and Waters 1982), periods of quantum change (Miller and Friesen 1984), and reorientations (Tushman and Romanelli 1985) in strategy making. Others have documented the *ongoing* process of strategy making in organizations (e.g., Quinn 1982). The evolutionary framework encompassing induced and autonomous strategic processes builds on both streams of work. This section discusses the induced and autonomous processes in terms of variation-selection-retention mechanisms, and uses them to elucidate strategy making at Intel.

Induced Strategic Process

Retention   Consider a newly founded and successful organization like Intel in the late 1960s. Whether initial success is the result of co513mpetence or luck, top management's role is to articulate an organizational strategy that will help secure continued survival. Such a strategy is likely to be based, at least in part, on retrospective sense making and attempts to capture top management's learning about the basis for the organization's success. The strategy is embodied in the managers who rose to (or stayed at) the top while pursuing a particular set of strategic initiatives. It is also embodied in oral and written statements regarding the technical/economic as well as cultural factors—such as key values and company traditions—perceived to be associated with past success (Pettigrew 1979, Beyer 1981, Haggerty 1981, Donaldson and Lorsch 1983, March 1981b, Pfeffer 1981, Weick 1987). Organizational strategy, conceived in this fashion, identifies the distinctive competences of the organization, defines its goals, delineates its action domain, and defines its character (Selznick 1957, Andrews 1971, McKelvey and Aldrich 1983). The organizational strategy may be expressed in substantive rules and prescriptions, referring to the technical/economic and cultural factors (March 1981a, Nelson and Winter 1982) which guide organizational-level strategic action and induce strategic initiatives in line with it at lower levels. Through the ap-

plication of these rules and prescriptions, strategic decisions are joined over time (Freeman and Boeker 1984), distinct patterns of organizational-level strategy are realized (Miles and Snow 1978, Mintzberg 1978, Miller and Friesen 1984), and the organization's character is maintained (Selznick 1957).

The Intel study illustrates this evolutionary perspective on organizational strategy. Les Vadasz, a top level manager, described how Intel's strategy making had evolved:

> Intel was a successful start-up in the late 60s, and one of the first things I did (when asked to think about strategic planning) was to try to understand what led to Intel's success. The reasons for success were embedded in the combined talents of the group that was in charge. We had a "sense" about the technology and the business which led to a series of correct decisions.

Having a "sense" about the technology meant that Intel's top management understood that silicon rather than metal was the key material for memories and that process technology was the driver of the memory business. In fact, it was manufacturing prowess that made it possible for Intel to succeed with DRAMs where other memory start-ups (such as Advanced Memory Systems) had previously failed. Andy Grove, in charge of engineering and manufacturing in the early days, and other team members solved the technical problems with silicon-based memories, and were able to get Intel's production yields to surpass the threshold for viability in the market against core memories. Once the fundamental manufacturing problems had been solved, Intel's technological efforts focused on how to get more transistors on the same amount of silicon real estate. The ability to make smaller and denser devices was the result of Intel's research and was kept proprietary. Top management also believed that initial success was associated with using small business teams, which affected the way Intel tried to implement its strategy as it grew larger. While Intel's success with silicon-based memories set the stage for a fundamental transformation of the computer industry, such transformation was not the founders' purpose; they simply saw the entrepreneurial opportunity of offering replacement parts for mainframe computer memories (Gilder 1989).

Of course, an organizational strategy largely based on retrospective rationality does not preclude prospectively rational efforts on the part of top management. One upper-level manager at Intel expressed this as follows: "Grove has been preaching: 'Make the tough decisions! Don't do something tomorrow because you did it today.'"

However, as will be seen later on, Grove himself experienced how difficult it was to actually do this.

Selection Research suggests that the awareness of a firm's strategy is likely to be concentrated at the top level of the organization (Hambrick 1981), and that there may be less than full agreement on what the firm's distinctive competences are (Stevenson 1976, Snow and Hrebiniak 1980). Also, as an organization grows, strategy making becomes increasingly differentiated over multiple levels of management (Williamson 1970) and the strategy can no longer be directly communicated in substantive detail to all levels of management. Participants differentially situated in the organization are likely to perceive different strategies as having the best potential for their own and the organization's advancement. This provides an important source of internal variation, as individuals who possess data, ideas, motivation, and resources all strive to undertake specialized initiatives. But unless an organization is able to establish internal selection mechanisms to maintain a level of coherence, it seems likely that the strategy eventually will become unrealized (Mintzberg 1978). Top management is expected, therefore, to establish a structural context encompassing administrative (Bower 1970) and cultural (Ouchi 1980) mechanisms. Administrative mechanisms include, among others, strategic planning and control systems, approaches to measuring and rewarding managers, and rules governing resource allocation. Cultural mechanisms include, among others, socialization rituals and behavioral norms (do's and don'ts). Different forms of structural context provide more or less tight coupling between the organizational strategy and strategic initiatives of managers at various levels (e.g., Chandler 1962, Mintzberg 1979, Rumelt 1974, Williamson 1970, Haspeslagh 1983).

The Intel data support the importance of having the induced process driven by top management strategic intent, and also offer insight in the consequences of losing the coupling between strategic initiatives of middle managers and strategic intent. Commenting on the evolution of Intel's strategic long-range planning (SLRP) process, Les Vadasz described the efforts to establish an induced process:

> As the company grew, we tried to replicate the environment that had led to making "correct" decisions by forming relatively small business units and creating a bottom-up strategic planning system. However, that became very unwieldy. The notion of pushing decisions down may have been a good one, but the task-relevant maturity was not great enough. Managers started gaming with the system. One key

symptom was that new ideas were often co-opted by groups and molded to fit immediate needs rather than developed as originally intended. The system is now more top-down. A high-level group sets the corporate strategy, and business units operate within that locus. Business units must focus on a few things and do them right. Neither the old nor the new system is perfect. . . . Some managers complain that their "sandbox" is too well defined.

CEO Grove elaborated on the problems of letting middle-level managers drive the induced process in the face of unclear top management strategic intent:

> The SLRP process turned into an embarrassment. Top management didn't really have the guts to call the shots, so we were trying to get middle management to come up with strategies and then taking pot shots at them. It wasn't clear whether middle management had either positional or informational power.
>
> In addition to being unpleasant, the system resulted in unrealistically high projections. One year, someone had the idea to put all the previous SLRP forecasts for unit sales on one chart along with the actual growth for the same period. The result was a series of "hockey sticks" which demonstrated the ineffectiveness of the process.

The data also confirm that rules concerning resource allocation are a potent part of structural context (Bower 1970). Intel was the first company able to manufacture and market DRAMs successfully and viewed itself as the "memory company." As one manager put it, "In a way, DRAMs created Intel." However, as new business opportunities in EPROMs and microprocessors were pursued, and competed for resources, DRAMs began to lose out. As a result of adopting a resource allocation rule that shifted resources systematically to products that maximized margin per manufacturing activity, DRAMs found it very difficult to continue to obtain capital investment in competition with other products. In fact, the VP of finance at Intel insisted, at one point, that the DRAM manager sign a symbolic check equal to the margin forgone when high-margin products were bumped by DRAMs. So even though most managers at Intel continued to believe the mythology (the "self-evident truth" as CEO Andrew Grove put it) of Intel as a memory company, the effect of these capital investment decisions was that Intel became a microprocessor company during the early 80s. The mythology was kept alive, in part, because important amounts of resources continued to flow to DRAM R&D (estimated at one-third of the total of about $195 million in 1985).

The data suggest that Intel's internal selection processes were consistent with the selection pressures in the external environment. Resources were allocated to the more profitable businesses rather than to DRAMs, even though a major change in organization-level strategy had not yet been explicitly made. Given the relative size of the capital investments involved (hundreds of millions of dollars), this was extremely important. Eventually, of course, the discrepancy between internal selection and organizational strategy needed to be resolved.

The finding of a significant discrepancy between the internal selection mechanisms and the organizational strategy suggests that the induced strategic process may be driven more by the structural context than by the strategy (Bower 1970): managers may respond more to incentives than to directions. In addition, this finding suggests that the induced process can continue to be effective if the internal selection mechanisms reflect the selective pressures of the environment, even while becoming decoupled from the espoused organizational strategy. In this situation, positive performance provides a time cushion for bringing organizational strategy in line with structural context. One expects that the opposite would not hold. That is, internal selection mechanisms coupled strongly to the organizational strategy but not reflecting the selective pressures of the environment are not likely to be associated with effectiveness of the induced process. Recognizing the importance of internal selection being linked directly to environmental pressures as well as to organizational strategy provides a refinement of earlier theory concerning strategy and structure.

Variation   The induced strategic process is intended to preserve the coupling of strategic initiatives at operational levels with the organization's strategy through shaping managers' perceptions about which types of initiatives are likely to be supported by the organization. As a consequence, the induced process may have a variation-reduction effect on the set of strategic initiatives that it spawns. In the Intel case, Chairman Gordon Moore addressed this issue in relation to Intel's strategy in 1989:

> We can do variations on present businesses very well, but doing something new is more difficult. Today, the likelihood of someone killing an effort like the one of Dov Frohman [inventor of the EPROM] is very high, because you need a well-defined application to a market from the outset. This is especially so because we are not looking for additional opportunities. There is still a lot of evolution left in the current technology. If you consider the possibilities with reducing linewidth, you can see another 12 years of evolution along the same curve.

Gordon Moore's observations also seem to imply that the induced process depends on the growth opportunities remaining in the current domain. To the extent that these growth opportunities are perceived to be high, it is expected that top management will favor initiatives that fit with the current strategy.

Of course, this does not imply that there is no planned variation in the induced process. Clearly, there is room for core technology advances, new product development for existing product families, new approaches to marketing and manufacturing, and so on. Hundreds of examples of such planned variations could be documented at Intel. And these variations are not always small, since new equipment, for instance, may require very large investments. Later in this paper, the adaptive implications of the variation-reduction tendency of the induced process will be further examined.

Autonomous Strategic Process

Variation   Studies of public organizations (e.g., Daft and Becker 1978, Lewis 1980) and of private organizations (e.g., Shepard 1967, Kidder 1981, Kanter 1982, Burgelman 1983b, Mintzberg and McHugh 1985) suggest that, at any given time, some individuals or small groups are likely to try to get their organization to engage in activities that are outside of the scope of its current strategy. As the Intel examples provided below may illustrate, such autonomous initiatives are often significantly different from induced ones in terms of technology employed, customer functions served, and/or customer groups targeted. They often derive from new combinations of individual and organizational skills and capabilities (Penrose 1968, Teece 1982) that are not currently recognized as distinctive or centrally important to the firm. While autonomous initiatives are probably quite often triggered by ideas or events external to the organization, they involve more than imitation in order to be of evolutionary importance for the organization's strategy. Imitation usually does not lead to sustainable competitive advantage. Autonomous initiatives are important for the firm's evolution to the extent that they involve the creation of new competences that may combine in unique ways with the resources and competences already available to the organization. While autonomous initiatives often emerge fortuitously and are difficult to predict, they are usually not random because they are rooted in and constrained by the evolving competence set of the organization (McKelvey and Aldrich 1983).

Autonomous initiatives can originate at all levels of management. But they are most likely to emerge at a level where managers are directly in contact with new technological developments and changes in market conditions, and have some budgetary discretion. As the organization grows, they are increasingly likely to emerge at levels below top management, even in the case of a company like Intel where senior executives have strong technical backgrounds.

The Intel study shows that, in spite of Gordon Moore's concerns, the autonomous strategic process is not easily suppressed. This is illustrated by a recent example of how Intel got into the RISC processor business with its i860 processor.[1]

The i860 Story. The story of Intel's entrance into the RISC (reduced instruction set computing) processor business details the emergence of a new product family which may ultimately challenge Intel's core microprocessor strategy. It illustrates the ability of an astute technologist, Les Kohn, to test the boundaries of the currently articulated corporate strategy and to modify them. Intel's deliberate corporate strategy was *not* to enter the RISC business, but rather to focus on the extremely successful ×86 architecture. Kohn had been attempting to get Intel into the RISC processor business since he joined the company in 1982. As he puts it: "RISC was not an existing business and people were not convinced a market was there." In fact, the strength of the organization's aversion to RISC architectures was demonstrated by the corporate argot, YARP, for "Yet Another RISC Processor." While talking in understated terms about his approach, it seemed clear that Kohn had a deliberate strategy which could be viewed as surreptitious from the perspective of corporate strategy. He mentioned that there was some realization at levels below top management that "Intel needed to broaden beyond the 386[2] market, but there was no agreement on what to do and how to do it." He also intimated that "There were various contenders at different points." From a technical point of view, Kohn believed that RISC architecture had intrinsic advantages over CISC architecture. However, he had learned from several more straightforward attempts at the product approval process that an approach which supported rather than challenged the status quo would be more likely successful. Also, the investment needed was too large to do the development "under the table." His solution was to disguise his product. Andrew Grove, Intel's CEO, mentioned that Kohn sold the design to top management as a co-processor, rather than a stand-alone processor. Kohn confirmed that "We designed it as a stand-alone processor, but made it very useful as an accessory to the i486."[3] By the time top management realized

what their "co-processor" was, Kohn, with the help of two other champions, had already lined up a customer base for the stand-alone processor, a base he suggested was different than the companies who purchase the 486 chips; in Kohn's own words, "a lot of customers who before did not even talk to Intel." Thus Kohn could argue that he was broadening Intel's business rather than cannibalizing it. During 1989 Intel's top management decided to amend the corporate strategy to incorporate the RISC chip business.

Another example, still in a much earlier stage, concerns a new type of memory, called FLASH. A middle-level manager who is currently championing FLASH memories at Intel emphasized that FLASH might ultimately provide a replacement for the microprocessor business. Asked to describe life as a champion at Intel, this manager said:

> You have to be naive, but mature enough to realize that the process takes a long time. You have to be sensitive to political toes. You have to be a religious zealot, but not too religious because then you lose your credibility. Finally, you have to succeed. . . . It is most difficult to champion a product that threatens the company's [current] business.

Selection At the time it emerges, the importance of an autonomous strategic initiative in relation to the firm's current strategy remains more or less indeterminate. To resolve the indeterminacy, the strategic context for the new initiative must become clear to, and accepted by, top management. Strategic context determination processes (Burgelman 1983b, Haspeslagh 1983) allow autonomous initiatives to be internally evaluated and selected outside the regular structural context, usually through the interactions of various types of champions and top management, and may lead to a change in the organization's strategy. Such amendments, in turn, integrate the new business activities with the induced strategic process.

Strategic context determination processes may be among the more elusive, volatile, and precarious decision processes in organizations. They deal with highly equivocal inputs and are therefore expected to involve relatively few rules but many interlocked cycles for their assembly (Daft and Weick 1984, Weick 1979). That is, they require much iterative, substantive interaction between managers from different levels in the organization. In contrast to the structural context, which selects initiatives that are consistent with an ex ante vision, strategic context determination processes select initiatives for which the vision becomes articulated ex post (Burgelman 1983c). They require that viability be established, in both the internal and external environments, at each

---

[1] i860 is a trademark of the Intel Corporation.
[2] 386 is a trademark of the Intel Corporation.
[3] i486 is a trademark of the Intel Corporation.

intermediate stage of their development. As the process unfolds, and more information becomes available, top management is able to evaluate the adaptive potential of the new activities for the organization. From an evolutionary point of view, only after it has become reasonably certain that an autonomous initiative is viable can it legitimately become part of the organizational strategy. In a study of the autonomous strategic process in the area of marketing strategy, Hutt, Reingen, and Ronchetto (1988) operationalize the process in terms of network analysis, communication patterns, and coalition building. They conclude: "If the efforts of the product and organizational champions are successful, the autonomous strategic initiative blends into the firm's formal planning routine and concept of strategy" (1988, p. 16).

Commenting on how the strategic context for a potential new business gets defined at Intel, Les Vadasz, who had been responsible for Intel's internal corporate venturing efforts, mentioned that these efforts require alternative avenues for obtaining resources so that the new business has a chance to demonstrate its viability. This is illustrated with Intel's add-on-boards venture.

> *The Add-On Boards Story.* Some middle-level managers had the idea to develop add-on boards for personal computers. The strategic planning process initially rejected the idea since channels of distribution were too different. The idea, however, was able to get support through Intel's internal corporate venturing program and became a separate business. After success of the business became evident, the venture was folded back into Intel's Systems business.

In a similar vein, the general manager of the components development group said he keeps the process fluid by "carving out a certain amount of resources for unplanned things. Usually you need no more than a million dollars to get something going." These examples suggest that the availability of "unabsorbed slack" (e.g., Singh 1986) may be an important factor affecting the rate at which autonomous strategic behavior can be supported within the organization.

Retention Both EPROMs and microprocessors were the result of unplanned initiatives that were outside of the scope of the strategy of the early 70s. These initiatives had been able to obtain resources because top management recognized *some* of their potential *after* they had come into existence. Obtaining resources allowed the new initiatives to demonstrate their viability in the environment. The evolutionary success of microprocessors and the accompanying shift in relative importance in Intel's action domain from memory (low design con-

tent) to microprocessor (high design content) had important consequences for the evolution of Intel's distinctive competences. As differences in process technology leveled among competitors in the industry, distinctive competences in circuit design increasingly became the new basis for Intel's competitive advantage. And, as customers had to be taught what the powerful microprocessors could do for them, it also lead Intel to develop new distinctive marketing capabilities (Davidow 1986).

The RISC story, presented earlier, is important because it shows how the autonomous strategic process allows the organization to become more clearly aware of, and prepare itself to cope with, environmental variations that have already come into play and might potentially threaten its competitive position. RISC had been invented at IBM but had remained dormant until it found a major application in work stations. Craig Barrett, a top level manager, pointed out that RISC is still viewed as relatively less important than CISC in Intel's strategy, but that its availability makes it possible for Intel to be a strong competitor in what may become an important new market:

> Intel's bread and butter is in the ×86 product family. There is a 586[4] on the drawing board and a 686 planned to follow that. If there was ever any question of which comes first, it could be answered quickly. But if there are enough people out there who want to buy YARPs, then we call the i860 a YARP killer. It is the highest performance RISC processor on the market.

Kohn's autonomous efforts now make it possible for Intel to be prepared in case RISC would ever pose a threat to CISC.

Autonomous initiatives provide the organization with an internal window on future, potentially major environmental variations in markets and technologies, and with strategic options. This may perhaps be the case with FLASH memories. While the implications of FLASH may eventually be less revolutionary than its champion predicts, and the strategic context for FLASH so far remains unclear at Intel, this champion's efforts offer Intel top management the opportunity to anticipate and evaluate a potential environmental variation.

Sometimes, the strategic context for a new business cannot be successfully defined, and the business dies out or spins off. The Intel data reveal that, in some instances, a failed attempt to define the strategic context for an initiative outside the scope of the current strategy may nev-

---

[4] 586 and 686 are trademarks of the Intel Corporation.

ertheless lead to a sharper articulation of the firm's strategy. An example (in this case resulting from imitation) is provided with the application specific integrated circuit (ASIC) venture. Intel had been late moving into ASICs. Tens of millions of dollars were invested for a fast ramp up, and a separate division was established. However, top management soon realized that ASIC was simply a delivery vehicle for circuit designs. As one middle level manager observed, "In ASIC the customer added all the value. So we realized that we should add the value ourselves." The separate division was eventually folded back into Intel's mainstream as the corporate focus on design as a competitive advantage was adopted by the entire organization. Later on, Intel disengaged from ASICs in fact because its core design skills were different.

Managing the autonomous strategic process seems difficult. The history of areas such as Silicon Valley indicates that autonomous strategic initiatives in established firms often result in the creation of new firms, rather than in new businesses for the firms where they originated. Many internal entrepreneurs seem to have left reluctantly because of lack of organizational support. In the Intel case, one example, among others, concerns a group involved in EEPROMs, who left after a majority of top management determined that EEPROMs were too small and specialized. The group formed a venture called Xicor. On the other hand, autonomous initiatives can have a dissipating effect on the spawning organization's resources and/or distinctive competence. Resources can be spread thin if too many autonomous initiatives are supported, perhaps at the expense of the mainstream businesses. Distinctive competences can be diluted or lost if an autonomous initiative is not internally supported and important talent decides to leave the firm, with or without the help of venture capital. (It is interesting to note that Intel significantly increased its legal staff during the 80s in order to better be able to protect its intellectual property.) Yet sometimes it seems quite clear, in retrospect, that an established company lost out severely because it failed to capitalize on autonomous initiatives (this is well illustrated, for instance, in the case of Bendix Corporation and electronic fuel injection; see Porter 1981). Later in this paper, the adaptive implications of the variation-increasing tendency of the autonomous strategic process will be further discussed.

Rationality of Strategy Making as Internal Selection

From the perspective of the organization, the rationality of the induced strategic process seems clear. In this process, intentional strategy may serve the organization to leverage—do as much as possible with—its currently available learning, to fully exploit the opportunities associated with the current action domain. From the perspective of individual managers, operating in the induced process would seem attractive. This is so because the organizational learning, guiding participants operating in the induced process, is likely to have been achieved at significant organizational and individual costs (Langton 1984). For instance, top managers may remember former colleagues who tried to do different things and suffered high costs in terms of their career progress, or they may recall instances where the organization tried something different—say, an unrelated diversification move—and it ended up being very costly. Participants at lower levels can be expected to be aware of this and therefore motivated to pursue initiatives in line with the current strategy. Induced initiatives allow managers to propose projects that take advantage of the available organizational learning, rather than to incur the potentially high costs of new individually driven learning associated with pursuing projects through the autonomous process. The induced process is part of the organization's regular opportunity structures for career advancement.

But why then are some managers willing to engage in autonomous strategic behavior? March (1988) observes that their motivation may be rooted in (*a*) an "obligatory logic" or (*b*) a "consequential logic." Managers operating within an obligatory logic engage in autonomous initiatives because it is congruent with their self-image. Managers operating within a consequential logic may feel that they have capabilities and skills that make autonomous initiatives no riskier than induced ones, or because they want to emulate colleagues who have received unusually high internal rewards for successfully pursuing a highly risky autonomous initiative, or they pursue it because they expect to receive venture capital support if no internal support is forthcoming. From the viewpoint of consequential logic, managers may see the autonomous process as an alternative opportunity structure for career progress if they consider that their access to the opportunity structure as defined by the induced process is limited, for instance, because of previous "bad luck" with performance outcomes, poor prospects of available opportunities in the induced process, or because other strategists have already preempted access to the induced process.

The organization may, within resource constraints, rationally tolerate autonomous strategic initiatives because it offers, as the Intel data suggest, opportunities to explore and extend the boundaries of its capabilities set, to engage new environmental niches in which environmental forces such as competition or institutional pressures (e.g., DiMaggio and Powell 1983) are as yet not as strong (Astley 1985, Burgelman 1983c, Itami 1983), to help the organization enter new niches that have already been opened up by others and which might eventually pose a threat to the current strategy, or to learn about future potential variations in markets and technologies. In the autonomous strategic process, myopically purposeful (McKelvey 1982) initiatives by individuals may help the organization find out what its intentions could be. The possibilities for participants to engage in opportunistic behavior (Bower 1970, Williamson 1970, Rumelt 1987, Cohen and Machalek 1988), however, underscore the importance of the structural and strategic contexts.

Structural and strategic contexts, together, constitute internal selection processes operating on strategic initiatives. The effectiveness of internal selection processes may depend on how closely they correspond to the selection pressures exerted by the current external environment, while simultaneously allowing new environments to be sought out. As seen earlier, at Intel there seemed to exist a close correspondence between key parts of the structural context and the current external environment: resource allocation in the induced process favored business activities that were able to get high returns in the current external environment. At the same time, Intel kept open the possibility to activate processes of strategic context determination through which new, unplanned business activities got a chance to obtain resources to demonstrate their viability.

STRATEGY MAKING AND ORGANIZATIONAL ADAPTATION

The view of strategy making as an intraorganizational ecological process yields a new theoretical question: how important are internal selection processes for explaining continued organizational survival? This question can be addressed by linking the induced and autonomous processes to different forms of adaptation identified previously in the literature: (1) relative inertia (Hannan and Freeman 1984), (2) adjustment (Snow and Hambrick 1980), (3) reorientation (Tushman and Romanelli 1985), and a new form proposed here; (4) strategic renewal.

The Adaptation Paradox Revisited

Relative Inertia Overcoming the liabilities of newness (Stinchcombe 1965) requires organizations to de-velop a capacity for reliability and accountability in their transactions with the environment (Hannan and Freeman 1984) and to structure themselves so as to be considered legitimate (e.g., DiMaggio and Powell 1983). But doing so may create structural inertia (Hannan and Freeman 1984). Paradoxically, adaptation to existing environmental demands may reduce the organization's capacity to adapt to future changes in the environment or to seek out new environments.

The existence of an induced strategic process seems to be consistent with *relative inertia* arguments. Relative inertia means that the rate of strategic change that the organization can implement will, in the long run, be lower than the rate of change in the environment (Hannan and Freeman 1984). Some ecological research has shown that the inertial consequences of environmental selection are likely to affect the core features of an organization (Scott 1981, Hannan and Freeman 1984, Singh et al. 1986). While the difference between core and peripheral features of organizations has not been definitively established, it seems reasonable to view a firm's strategy as a core feature. Because the strategy is rooted in organizational experience and learning, top managers are likely to be reluctant to make frequent changes in it. As noted earlier, research (e.g., Mintzberg and Waters 1982, Miller and Friesen 1984, Tushman and Romanelli 1985) suggests that an organization's strategy tends to remain in place for extended periods of time. So it seems plausible in many instances to expect the evolution of the strategy to be inert relative to the accumulation of changes in the environment (Snow and Hambrick 1980).

The Intel case provides further insight in this. The articulation of corporate strategy in terms of microprocessor leadership versus memory leadership came almost five years after the company had stopped being a major player in DRAMs. Reflecting on how difficult it had been to get top management to come to grips with this change, Andrew Grove observed:

> Don't ask managers, "What is your strategy?" Look at what they do! Because people will pretend. . . . The fact is that we had become a nonfactor in DRAMs, with 2–3 percent market share. The DRAM business just passed us by! Yet, in 1985, many people were still holding to the "self-evident truth" that Intel was a memory company. One of the toughest challenges is to make people see that these self-evident truths are no longer true.

Intel's top management took a long time to finalize a decision that had been in the making since the early 80s. Several managers pointed out in the interviews that the decision could and should have been made sooner. The delay was, in part, caused by the fact that some managers sensed that the existing organizational strategy was no longer adequate and that there were competing views about what the new organizational strategy should be. There was still an important group of managers who believed that DRAMs were critically important to Intel. Some of the top technologists saw DRAMs as the technology driver of the corporation. This group was convinced that DRAMs, being the largest volume product, were key to Intel's learning curve. Some of the top salespeople also saw the need for offering a complete product line to the customer. Top management as a group, it seems, was watching how the organization sorted out the conflicting views. CEO Grove observed:

> By mid-1984, some middle-level managers had made the decision to adopt a new process technology which inherently favored logic [microprocessor] rather than the memory advances, thereby limiting the decision space within which top management could operate. The faction representing the ×86 microprocessor business won the debate even though the 386 had not yet become the big revenue generator that it eventually would become.

While clearly demonstrating a degree of relative inertia, Intel's exit decision was not too late. Intel lost a lot of money in DRAMs but the hemorrhaging was stopped before its viability became threatened. In fact, Intel lost less money than its competitors, including the Japanese. So, why was Intel's relative inertia as low as it was? The data suggest that this was not due, in first instance, to a prescient or exceptionally agile top management, but to the way in which the internal selection processes were allowed to work themselves out.

An atmosphere in which strategic ideas can be freely championed and fully contested by anyone with relevant information or insight may be a key factor in developing internal selection processes that maximize the probability of generating viable organizational strategies. Such processes generate strategic change that is neither too slow nor too fast (Hambrick and D'Aveni 1988, Levitt and March 1988). They take time to develop and have a large tacit component. That is, it is difficult to provide a full explanation of how they actually work. The role of founders, such as Bob Noyce, Gordon Moore, and Andy Grove at Intel, seems important in setting the initial tone and maintaining continuity. The data suggest that the influence of top management in strategy making at Intel was undeniably very strong, but that there was also a perception on the part of most managers that, most of the

time, knowledge and facts tend to win over positional power at Intel. The possibility for a young engineer like Les Kohn to directly interact with the CEO on substantive technical issues and to be able to prevail on the merits of the argument is a vivid illustration of that. It is also illustrated in CEO Grove's view on his role in decisions to continue to support or not a business activity:

> You need to be able to be ambiguous in some circumstances. You dance around it a bit, until a wider and wider group in the company becomes clear about it. That's why continued argument is important. Intel is a very open system. No one is ever told to shut up, but you are asked to come up with better arguments. People are allowed to be persistent.

Once the decision to exit DRAMs was made, top management showed strong intent to implement it. In the face of some lingering opposition, Grove himself took charge and made several organizational and personnel changes. Perhaps most important, from a symbolic point of view, he visited several groups affected by the decision and addressed them with the phrase, "Welcome to the Mainstream Intel," that is, Intel the microprocessor company, thereby ratifying the results of the internal selection processes that had been going on for several years. Top management also reassigned the highly regarded memory R&D group to microprocessors, thereby protecting the firm's distinctive technical competences.

Adjustment Inherent tendencies toward relative inertia in organizational strategy do not preclude adjustments (Snow and Hambrick 1980) in the strategy. Such adjustments leave the overall strategy in place and operate on more peripheral features. Recent ecological research suggests that some types of peripheral changes may enhance an organization's life chances (Singh et al. 1986). Adjustments are to a large extent deliberate, reflecting strategic choice and managerial discretion (Hambrick and Finkelstein 1987), and are instances of nonrandom adaptation.

The Intel study offers several examples of deliberate adjustments that were made to try to stay viable in the DRAM business. Some of these involved efforts to differentiate Intel's DRAM offering from the commodity business; others involved efforts to reduce cost and design time. One move involved the introduction of the first 5-volt 16K DRAM in 1980 (differentiation). Another move involved introducing "redundancy" in the 64K DRAM design in order to increase yields (cost reduction). Still another move was to "go CMOS" for the

64K and 256K (differentiation). A final move involved focusing on "thin dielectrics" for the 1 Meg DRAM in order to reduce the minimum feature size to 1 micron instead of changing the entire cell design (cost reduction). None of these moves, however, was sufficient to make DRAMs viable again as a business for Intel. Eventually, as was noted earlier, the decision to exit became unavoidable.

Relative inertia and adjustment both seem possible outcomes of the induced strategic process. Relative inertia does not preclude adjustment, and adjustments may temporarily result in improved performance. In the long run, however, cumulative environmental selection pressures are expected to overwhelm adjustments effected through the induced strategic process, and it seems likely that the strategy itself will eventually have to change in major ways.

Theory (Hannan and Freeman 1984) and empirical evidence (Singh et al. 1986) suggest that major strategic changes are governed by environmental selection processes. That is, such changes subject the organization to powerful environmental pressures and are likely thereby to reduce the chances of survival. On the other hand, Tushman and Romanelli (1985) suggest that strategic reorientations, which imply major changes in the concept of strategy, are an integral part of a punctuated equilibrium model of firm evolution. Firms that do not reorient when major changes are necessary, or reorient when the need for such changes is not compelling, they argue, will see their life chances reduced. The seeming contradiction between these two positions can be resolved in terms of the role of the autonomous strategic process, as explained below.

Reorientation Major changes in the strategy seem likely to upset the induced strategic process in fundamental ways. The necessity for a major strategic change suggests that selective pressures from environmental variations have made the organization's capacity for relatively modest adjustments largely irrelevant. At first, threat-rigidity (Staw, Sandelands, and Dutton 1981) may lead top management to reaffirm familiar approaches. For instance, Cooper and Schendel (1976) found that established firms, confronted with the threat of radically new technologies, were likely to increase their efforts to improve the existing technology rather than switch to the new technology, even after the latter had passed the threshold of viability. Eventually, however, confronted with chronic low performance, top management is more likely to take major risks (March 1981b, Singh 1986)

by making extreme and vacillating changes in the strategy, potentially involving a complete change of domain (Hambrick and D'Aveni 1988). When an organization finds itself in a precarious situation, reorientation may be perceived by top management as necessary to maintain or regain viability (Miles and Cameron 1982), and may be better than doing nothing. However, as March (1981b) has observed, organizations facing bad times, and therefore following riskier and riskier strategies, may simultaneously increase their chances of survival through the present crisis but also reduce their life expectancy: "For those organizations that do not survive, efforts to survive will have speeded the process of failure" (1981b, p. 567).

Strategic Renewal Major changes in the strategy effected through the autonomous strategic process, however, need not be completely governed by external selection processes. Autonomous strategic initiatives, as seen in the Intel case, offer opportunities to open new niches or provide early warning of impending radical, external changes. To the extent that strategic context determination processes are effectively activated, the organization may learn new capabilities and skills in anticipation of making major changes in its strategy, but without knowing in advance how it should be changed. Changes of this sort form the basis for "strategic renewal"—major strategic change preceded by internal experimentation and selection. In the Intel case, EPROMs and microprocessors, like the recent i860 (RISC) chip, were unplanned developments, but Intel management was capable of recognizing the importance of these developments after they had occurred, and keeping them inside the firm through shifts in resource allocation.

Reorientations are *not* expected outcomes of the autonomous strategic process. Consistent with the view of organizational ecology (Hannan and Freeman 1984), environmental selection is expected to govern reorientations, because reorientations seem fundamentally incompatible with strategy making as an organizational learning process based on internal experimentation and selection. Reorientations inherently seem to involve "betting the organization" because they eliminate a good deal of its cumulative learning. On the other hand, strategic renewal—major strategic change preceded by internal experimentation and selection—is the critical outcome of the autonomous process through which an organization can indefinitely maintain adaptive.

Exhibit 2 summarizes the analysis of the induced and autonomous strategic processes and their proposed ties to modes of organizational adaptation.

EXHIBIT 2 Intraorganizational Ecology of Strategy Making and Organizational Adaptation: Intraorganizational Ecological Processes

	Variation	Selection	Retention	Ties to adaptation
Induced	Strategic initiatives seeking resources for projects that correspond to internal selection pressures of structural content, fit with the current organizational strategy, and offer access to regular opportunity structure for career advancement. Originate at operational level but intended to be driven by top management's ex ante vision. Enhanced by availability of growth opportunities remaining in current action domain. Radically new induced initiatives initiated by top management.	Initiatives selected through administrative mechanisms (e.g., strategic planning) and/or cultural influencing (e.g., reference to key values). Differential allocation of resources to different areas of strategic initiative. Key is that internal selection reflects current external selection pressures. Major changes in structural content.	1. Organizational learning about basics for past/current survival (variously embodied). 2. Distinctive competencies (variously embodied). 3. Organizational goals. 4. Organizational action domain. 5. Organizational character. All of these elements integrated in ex ante vision. Major changes in the dimensions of organizational strategy.	1. *Relative inertia.* Organizational survival is due to a good fit of internal selection processes with the environment. Survival motivates conservatism on the part of top management and desire to leverage existing organizational learning through induced process. Reluctance to change organizational strategy. 2. *Adjustment.* Relatively minor changes in strategy to accommodate environmental change. 3. *Reorientation.* Major changes in strategy in response to major environment change.
Autonomous	Strategic initiatives outside scope of current strategy. Driven by operational-level managers seeking to use their skills in new combinations with organization's distinctive circumstances and, in some cases, seeking career advancement through alternative opportunity structure. Enhanced by availability of unabsorbed slack.	Defining strategic context for new initiatives through: • finding resources outside regular resource allocation process; • demonstrating visibility in external environment through entrepreneurial activity; • mobilizing internal support on the part of upper-level managers; • developing new competencies/skills; • setting stage for an amendment in the organizational strategy.	Changes in organizational learning, distinctive competence, and selective importance of new activities in total domain activity, which, cumulatively, lead top management to recognize that a major change in strategy is necessary and feasible. Lead to new, ex post vision. Once formally ratified, new vision becomes part of the basis for the induced process.	4. *Strategic renewal.* Major change in organizational strategy preceded by internal experimentation and selection offers organization possibilities for anticipatory adaptation to new environmental demands and/or to enter new niches.

DISCUSSION

Organizations are both creators and prisoners of their environments (Miles and Cameron 1982). Organizational survival depends to a significant extent on the adjustment and renewal capacities of strategy-making processes. Such processes are an emergent property of organizations and may be differentially distributed within a population of organizations. Firms overcome the liabilities of newness by accumulating and leveraging organizational learning, and by deliberately combining distinctive competences in the induced process. Adjustments effected through the induced strategic process serve the organization in its attempts to remain adaptive over some range of environmental variation and over a certain time horizon (Chakravarthy 1982, Burgelman 1983c). The autonomous strategic process, on the other hand, helps organizations develop, appropriate, and retain new learning. Strategic renewal through internal experimentation and selection offers an organization the possibility to remain adaptive over a wider range of environmental variation and a longer time horizon (Chakravarthy 1982, Burgelman 1983c).

Selection and adaptation have sometimes been viewed as alternative explanations in organizational research (e.g., Singh et al. 1986). The analysis presented in this paper suggests that they may be viewed, to some extent, as complementary: selection processes at the intraorganizational level, working themselves out through the strategy-making processes, may generate strategies that are adaptive at the organizational level.

Structural and strategic contexts thus emerge as critical process design parameters from this analysis. In the induced strategic process, top management's role is to ensure the pursuit of an intended strategy through administrative and cultural mechanisms that couple operational-level strategic initiatives with the intended strategy. Doing so makes it possible for the organization to build on past success and to exploit the opportunities associated with the current domain. However, the Intel study also suggests that it is important that the structural context reflect the selective pressures of the environment. This provides a reality test for the organizational strategy. In the autonomous strategic process, top management's role is strategic recognition rather than strategic planning (Burgelman 1983c, Van de Ven 1986). Top management needs to facilitate the activation of strategic context determination processes to find out which of the autonomous initiatives have adaptive value for the organization and deserve to become part of the organization's strategy. The proposed importance of a continued concern with managing strategic processes, as well as with strategy content (or "strategic choice") at any given time, is consistent with a wide range of research findings (e.g., Hedberg, Nystrom, and Starbuck 1976; Bower and Doz 1979; Padgett 1980). More formally,

PROPOSITION 1. *Firms that are relatively successful over long periods of time, say, 10 years or more, will be characterized by top managements that are concerned with building the quality of the organization's induced and autonomous strategic processes as well as with the content of the strategy itself.*

Combining induced and autonomous processes in their strategy making would seem to give organizations a chance to outsmart or outrun the selective pressures associated with environmental variations. The analysis suggests that organizations may have to keep both processes in play at all times, even though this means that the organization never completely maximizes its efforts in the current domain. This implies that strategic intent and internal entrepreneurship, separately, are not sufficient for organizational survival (e.g., Hamel and Prahalad 1989). Both are needed *simultaneously*. The ability to maintain these different concerns simultaneously seemed to be missing in the failing corporations studied by Hambrick and D'Aveni (1988), who found that failing firms tended to operate either in an inactive (no strategic change) or hyperactive (excessive and vacillating change) mode. This also implies that a sequential approach involving, for instance, sequences of reorientation and convergence (Tushman and Romanelli 1985) may not be optimal in the long run. More formally,

PROPOSITION 2. *Firms that are relatively successful over long periods of time, say, 10 years or more, will be characterized by maintaining top-driven strategic intent while simultaneously maintaining bottom-up driven internal experimentation and selection processes.*

The analysis also suggests that successful reorientations, as defined by Tushman and Romanelli (1985), are likely to be *preceded* by internal experimentation and selection processes effected through the autonomous strategic process. More formally,

PROPOSITION 3. *The population of firms with successful strategic reorientations will contain a significantly higher proportion of firms whose strategic reorientations were preceded by internal experimentation and selection processes than the population of firms with failing strategic reorientations.*

Of course, these propositions do not imply that there is only one way to organize the strategic processes or that managers should get overly absorbed in the details of these processes. Also, there does not seem to be a fixed optimal ratio in terms of emphasis on induced versus autonomous processes. At different times in an organization's development, different emphases on the induced and autonomous strategic processes may be warranted, and there may not be a fixed series of stages in firm evolution as some researchers seem to suggest (e.g., Kimberly and Miles 1980, Miller and Friesen 1984). Old firms may continue to be able to act like young ones, even though young ones may not be equally able to act like old ones. The renewal capacity associated with the autonomous strategic process may enable organizations to negate the inevitability of aging and decline. By the same token, it may expose them again, to some extent, to the liabilities of newness (Hannan and Freeman 1984).

The intraorganizational ecological perspective has offered useful insights into Intel's strategic evolution. Intel may have survived as an independent company, in part, because it was able to recognize important internal variations that were externally viable, and to allocate resources to these through the internal selection mechanisms, almost in spite of the pervasive desire to continue to be a "memory company." The procrastination in finalizing the DRAM-exit decision, and Gordon Moore's current concerns about the inexorable tendency toward narrowing down the technology base of the firm suggest some inertial tendencies in Intel's strategic process. But events like the emergence of the i860 (RISC) chip also suggest that the autonomous strategic process is still alive and well. Although Intel went through a major strategic change—from "memory company" to "microcomputer company"—it did not do so through a dramatic and sudden reorientation. Instead, unplanned, autonomous processes were allowed to run their courses, with many losers and some winners. And as these processes unfolded, the company developed new learning that made the ratification of the strategic change a reasonably safe bet for top management.

IMPLICATIONS AND CONCLUSIONS

This paper has offered an intraorganizational ecological perspective on strategy making and organizational adaptation. The framework proposes balancing of variation-reduction and variation-increasing mechanisms. It suggests that one process leads to relative inertia and incremental adjustments, while the other expands the

firm's domain and renews the organization's distinctive competence base, countering inertia and serving some of the functions of a reorientation. The research reported here provides some confirmation of the existence of these two processes, suggests some amendments to the initial conceptual framework, and offers additional insights into the working of the processes.

The research is a part of emergent efforts to integrate evolutionary views of strategy making and organization. These efforts recognize the importance of some forms of rationality and learning and the need to go beyond biological evolutionary arguments (e.g., Langton 1984, Boyd and Richerson 1985, Gould 1987). They reflect a belief that evolutionary theory may be useful for integrating insights from organizational ecology, rational adaptation, and random transformation perspectives (Hannan and Freeman 1984). Other seeds for such a synthesis already exist. Economic evolutionists (Nelson and Winter 1982, Winter 1990) provide a detailed theoretical picture of some of the mechanisms of inheritance, selection, and survival. Organizational evolutionists have shown that some forms of organizational change are adaptive while others reduce an organization's life chances (e.g., Singh et al. 1986), and that the "imprinting" effects of founding characteristics of organizations affect subsequent rates of organizational change (Tucker et al. 1990, Boeker 1989). This paper sketches the outlines of an intraorganizational perspective on strategy making and proposes this as a fourth level in the hierarchy of ecological systems which currently comprises only organization, population, and community levels (Carroll 1984, Astley 1985, Aldrich and Auster 1986). Incorporating this additional level may facilitate the rapprochement between ideas of ecology and strategy, and enhance the prospects of an evolutionary theory of organizations (Burgelman and Singh 1987).

The intraorganizational perspective on strategy making also extends frameworks presented by Mintzberg (1978) and Quinn (1982) in the strategic management literature. It does so by documenting more explicitly some of the sources of emergent strategy, by further elucidating the organizational decision processes through which emergent strategies become part of realized strategies (strategic context determination), by identifying feedback mechanisms between realized and intended strategy, and by providing some evidence that logical incrementalism is likely to be variation reducing and may need to be augmented with an autonomous strategic process to enhance long-term organizational survival. The perspective presented in the paper adds some additional dynamism to these earlier frameworks and draws more explicit attention to the simultaneity of multiple strategy-making processes in organizations.

Implications for Theory and Future Research

Several specific avenues for further research derive from the propositions discussed earlier. For instance, future research could examine whether consistently successful firms are characterized by top managements' spending efforts on building each organization's strategy-making processes; whether such firms simultaneously exercise induced and autonomous strategic processes; and whether successful reorientations are more likely to be preceded by internal experimentation and selection processes effected through the autonomous strategic process than are the unsuccessful ones.

Effective internal selection seems to depend on top management's capacities to adjust the structural and strategic contexts in the organization. Discovering the determinants of such capacities and how the latter relate to rates of adjustment and strategic renewal remains an important agenda for further research (March 1981b, Hannan and Freeman 1984). Future research could also examine the possibilities that there may be an optimal level of ambiguity in the concept of strategy (March 1978) and an optimal degree of coupling in the structural context (Weick 1976). This would require studying the working of strategy-making processes in different types of organizations, such as generalists versus specialists (Freeman and Hannan 1983) or defenders, prospectors, analyzers, and reactors (Miles and Snow 1978), and under different types of environmental conditions (e.g., Freeman and Hannan 1983, Eisenhardt 1989). This, in turn, may raise further questions about the relationships between strategy making and organization form, provide deeper insight into the distinction between core and peripheral features, and elucidate the mechanisms that determine structural features and their transformation—that is, organizational morphology.

For internal selection mechanisms to be useful, organizations must generate internal variation. That is, they must motivate strategic initiatives on the part of their participants. As a result of internal selection, some participants may win big and others may lose big. But the genius of surviving organizations lies in their ability to benefit from both winning and losing individual strategic initiatives through their capacity for learning. This suggests an organizational-level analogy to societal-level processes described by Rosenberg and Birdzell (1986). Rosenberg and Birdzell provide some evidence for how

Western capitalism has used decentralized entrepreneurialism: it has allowed innovators to bear the losses of failed experiments and to gain the profits of successful ones, and it has benefited from both in terms of growth. This analogy also suggests a link between strategy making and "foolishness" (March 1981b). Organizations may use individual-level "foolishness" to enhance organizational-level survival in somewhat the same way that organizational-level foolishness may enhance the survival chances of a system of organizations. March views organizational foolishness as a form of altruism, but it might be possible to link such individual-level behavior to the idea that strategy making may be viewed as part of the organization's opportunity structures for career advancement.

This, in turn, motivates interest in further examining how the Barnard-March-Simon theory of inducements and contributions may be realized. It raises, for instance, the issue of how the balance between inducements and contributions may be different in the induced and autonomous strategic processes and how shifting balances may affect organizational adaptation. It also directs attention to the effects that external resource constraints (e.g., remaining growth opportunities in an organization's current action domain) and internal resource constraints (e.g., "sustainable growth" [Donaldson and Lorsch 1983]) and "unabsorbed slack" (e.g., Singh 1986) may have on the degree to which induced and autonomous strategic initiatives are supported during any given period in the firm's history. These links open new directions for research.

In conclusion, the theory and field research presented in this paper suggest that the opposite views of blind natural selection or prescient and comprehensive strategic planning as the basis for understanding organizational adaptation both are too narrow. The pure environmental-selection view misses the additional insights that can be obtained from considering internal selection. The pure strategic-planning view misses the ecological components altogether. Rich behavioral phenomena are currently being documented in a variety of studies and will have to be accounted for by equally rich theories of organizations. An intraorganizational ecological perspective on strategy making seems likely to provide a useful input to organization theory. It also suggests the need to reconsider important precepts of received strategic management theory.[5]

---

[5] Acknowledgements: Support from the Strategic Management Program and from the BF America Faculty Fellowship of Stanford Uni-

REFERENCES

Aldrich, Howard E. (1979). *Organizations and Environments.* Englewood Cliffs, NJ: Prentice Hall.

——— and Ellen R. Auster (1986). "Even Dwarfs Started Small: Liabilities of Age and Size and Their Strategic Implications," in Larry L. Cummings and Barry Staw (Eds.), *Research in Organizational Behavior.* Greenwich, CT: JAI Press, 8, 165–198.

Andrews, Kenneth (1971). *A Concept of Corporate Strategy.* Homewood, IL: Irwin.

Astley, W. Graham (1985). "The Two Ecologies: Population and Community Perspectives on Organizational Evolution." *Administrative Science Quarterly,* 30, 224–241.

——— and Andrew H. Van de Ven (1983). "Central Perspectives and Debates in Organization Theory." *Administrative Science Quarterly,* 29, 245–273.

Beyer, Janice M. (1981). "Ideologies, Values and Decision Making in Organizations." In Paul E. Nystrom and William H. Starbuck (Eds.), *Handbook of Organization Design.* New York: Oxford University Press, 2, 166–202.

Boeker, Warren (1989). "Strategic Change: The Effects of Founding and History." *Academy of Management Journal,* 32, 489–515.

Bourgeois, L. J., III (1984). "Strategic Management and Determinism." *Academy of Management Review,* 9, 586–596.

Bower, Joseph L. (1970). *Managing the Resource Allocation Process.* Boston, MA: Graduate School of Business Administration, Harvard University.

——— and Yves Doz (1979). "Strategy Formulation: A Social and Political Process." In Dan E. Schendel and Charles W. Hofer (Eds.), *Strategic Management.* Boston: Little, Brown and Company, 152–166.

Boyd, Robert, and Peter J. Richerson (1985). *Culture and the Evolutionary Process.* Chicago: The University of Chicago Press.

Brittain, Jack W., and John Freeman (1980). "Organizational Proliferation and Density Dependent Selection: Organizational Evolution in the Semiconductor Industry." In John R. Kimberly and Robert H. Miles (Eds.), *The Organizational Life Cycle.* San Francisco: Josey-Bass.

Burgelman, Robert A. (1983a). "A Model of the Interaction of Strategic Behavior, Corporate Context, and the Concept of Strategy." *Academy of Management Review,* 8, I, 61–70.

——— (1983b). "A Process Model of Internal Corporate Venturing in the Diversified Major Firm." *Administrative Science Quarterly,* 28, 223–244.2

Burgelman, Robert A. (1983c). "Corporate Entrepreneurship and Strategic Management: Insights from a Process Study." *Management Science,* 29, 1349–1364.

——— and Jitendra V. Singh (1987). "Strategy and Organization: An Evolutionary Approach." Paper presented at the Annual Meetings of the Academy of Management, New Orleans, August.

Campbell, Donald T. (1969). "Variation and Selective Retention in Sociocultural Evolution." *General Systems,* 14, 69–85.

——— (1975). "Degrees of Freedom and the Case Study." *Comparative Political Studies,* 8, 178–193.

Carroll, Glenn R. (1984). "Organizational Ecology." *Annual Review of Sociology,* 10, 71–93.

——— (1988), *Ecological Models of Organizations.* Cambridge, MA: Ballinger.

Chakravarty, Balaji S. (1982). "Adaptation: A Promising Metaphor for Strategic Management." *Academy of Management Review,* 7, 1, 35–44.

Chandler, Alfred D. (1962). *Strategy and Structure.* Cambridge, MA: MIT Press.

Child, John (1972). "Organization Structure, Environment, and Performance: The Role of Strategic Choice." *Sociology,* 6, 1–22.

Cogan, George W., and Robert A. Burgelman (1989a). "Intel Corporation (A): The DRAM Decision." Stanford Business School Case PS-BP-256.

——— and ——— (1989b). "Intel Corporation (B): Strategy for the 1990s." Stanford Business School Case.

Cohen, Lawrence E., and Richard Machalek (1988). "A General Theory of Expropriative Crime: An Evolutionary Ecological Model." *American Journal of Sociology,* 94, 465–501.

Cooper, Arnold C., and Dan E. Schendel. (1976). "Strategic Responses to Technological Threats." *Business Horizons* (February), 61–63.

Daft, Richard L., and Sellwyn W. Becker (1978). *The Innovative Organization.* New York: Eisevier.

——— and Karl E. Weick (1984). "Toward a Model of Organizations as Interpretation Systems." *Academy of Management Review,* 9, 284–295.

Davidow, William H. (1986). *Marketing High Technology: An Insider's View.* New York: The Free Press.

DiMaggio, Paul J., and Walter W. Powell (1983). "The Iron Cage Revisited: Institutional Isomorphism and Collective Rationality in Organizational Fields." *American Sociological Review,* 48, 147–160.

Donaldson, Gordon, and Jay W. Lorsch (1983). *Decision Making at the Top.* New York: Basic Books.

Eisenhardt, K. M. (1989). "Making Fast Strategic Decisions in High Velocity Environments." *Academy of Management Journal,* 32, 543–576.

versity's Graduate School of Business is gratefully acknowledged. Glenn Carroll, Don Hambrick, Arie Lewin, Jim March, Ann Miner, Brian Mittman, Jeffrey Pfeffer, Dick Scott, Jitendra Singh and anonymous *Organization Science* reviewers have provided helpful and encouraging comments along the way, shaping the arguments presented in this paper. The outstanding research assistance of George W. Cogan and the generous collaboration of Intel Corporation are much appreciated. The conclusions reached in this paper are my own. Thanks also to Jiranee Kovartana for excellent administrative assistance.

Freeman, John, and Michael T. Hannan (1983). "Niche Width and the Dynamics of Organizational Populations." *American Journal of Sociology,* 88, 1116–1145.

—— and Warren Boeker (1984). "The Ecological Analysis of Business Strategy." *California Management Review,* 26, Spring, 73–86.

Gilder, George (1989). *Microcosm.* New York: Simon and Schuster.

Glaser, Barney G., and Anselm L. Strauss (1967). *The Discovery of Grounded Theory.* Chicago, IL: Aldine.

Gould, Stephen Jay (1987). "The Panda's Thumb of Technology." *Natural History* (January), 14–23.

Haggerty, Patrick E. (1981). "The Corporation and Innovation." *Strategic Management Journal,* 2, 97–118.

Hambrick, Donald C. (1981). "Strategic Awareness Within Top Management Teams." *Strategic Management Journal,* 2, 263–279.

—— and Sidney Finkelstein (1987). "Managerial Discretion: A Bridge Between Polar Views of Organizational Outcomes." In Larry L. Cummings and Barry Staw (Eds.), *Research in Organizational Behavior.* Greenwich, CT: JAI Press, 4, 369–406.

—— and Richard A. D'Aveni (1988). "Large Corporate Failures as Downward Spirals." *Administrative Science Quarterly,* 33, 1–23.

Hamel, Gary, and C. K. Prahalad (1989). "Strategic Intent." *Harvard Business Review,* 67 (May–June), 63–76.

Hannan, Michael T., and John H. Freeman (1984). "Structural Inertia and Organizational Change." *American Sociological Review,* 49, 149–164.

—— and —— (1989). *Organizational Ecology.* Cambridge, MA: Harvard University Press.

Haspeslagh, Philippe (1983), "Portfolio Planning Approaches and the Strategic Management Process in Diversified Industrial Companies." Doctoral dissertation, Harvard Business School.

Hedberg, Bo L. T., Paul C. Nystrom, and William H. Starbuck (1976). "Camping on Seesaws: Prescriptions for a Self-Designing Organization." *Administrative Science Quarterly,* 21, 41–65.

Hrebiniak, Lawrence G., and William J. Joyce (1985). "Organizational Adaptation: Strategic Choice and Environmental Determinism." *Administrative Science Quarterly,* 30, 336–349.

Hutt, Michael D., Peter H. Reingen, and John J. Ronchetto, Jr. (1988). "Tracing Emergent Processes in Marketing Strategy Formation." *Journal of Marketing,* 52, 4–19.

Itami, Hiroyuki (1983). "The Case for Unbalanced Growth of the Firm." Research Paper Series #681, Graduate School of Business, Stanford University.

Kagono, Tadao, Ikujiro Nonaka, Kryonori Sakakibara, and Akihiro Okumura (1985). *Strategic Versus Evolutionary Management.* New York: North-Holland.

Kanter, Rogabeth M. (1982). "Middle Managers as Innovators." *Harvard Business Review,* 60 (July–August), 95–105.

Kidder, Tracy (1981). *The Soul of a New Machine.* Boston: Little Brown.

Kimberly, John R., and Robert H. Miles (1980). *The Organizational Life Cycle.* San Francisco: Jossey-Bass.

Langton, John (1984). "The Ecological Theory of Bureaucracy: The Case of Josiah Wedgewood and the British Pottery Industry." *Administrative Science Quarterly,* 29, 330–354.

Levitt, Barbara, and James G. March (1988). "Organizational Learning." *Annual Review of Sociology,* 14, 319–340.

Lewis, Eugene (1980). *Public Entrepreneurship.* Bloomington, IN: Indiana University Press.

March, James G. (1978). "Bounded Rationality, Ambiguity, and the Engineering of Choice." *Bell Journal of Economics and Management Science,* 9, 435–457.

—— (1981a). "Decisions in Organizations and Theories of Choice." In Andrew H. Van de Ven and William F. Joyce (Eds.), *Perspectives on Organization Design and Behavior.* New York: Wiley.

—— (1981b). "Footnotes to Organizational Change." *Administrative Science Quarterly,* 26, 563–577.

—— (1988). "Wild Ideas: The Catechism of Heresy." *Stanford Magazine* (Spring).

McKelvey, Bill (1982). *Organizational Systematics: Taxonomy, Evolution, Classification.* Berkeley and Los Angeles, CA: University of California Press.

—— and Howard E. Aldrich (1983). "Populations, Organizations and Applied Organizational Sciences." *Administrative Science Quarterly,* 28, 101–128.

Miles, Raymond E., and Charles C. Snow (1978). *Organizational Strategy, Structure, and Process.* New York: McGraw-Hill.

Miles, Robert H., and Kim Cameron (1982). *Coffin Nails and Corporate Strategies.* Englewood Cliffs, NJ: Prentice Hall.

Miller, Danny, and Peter H. Friesen with the collaboration of Henry Mintzberg (1984). *Organizations: A Quantum View.* Englewood Cliffs, NJ: Prentice Hall.

Mintzberg, Henry (1978). "Patterns in Strategy Formation." *Management Science,* 24, 934–948.

—— (1979). *The Structuring of Organizations.* Englewood Cliffs, NJ: Prentice Hall.

—— and James A. Waters (1982). "Tracking Strategy in an Entrepreneurial Firm." *Academy of Management Journal,* 25, 465–499.

—— and Alexandra McHugh (1985). "Strategy Formation in an Adhocracy." *Administrative Science Quarterly,* 30, 160–197.

Nelson, Richard R., and Sidney G. Winter (1982). *An Evolutionary Theory of Economic Change.* Cambridge, MA: Harvard University Press.

Ouchi, William (1980). "Markets, Bureaucracies, and Clans." *Administrative Science Quarterly,* 25, 129–141.

Padgett, John F. (1980). "Managing Garbage Can Hierarchies." *Administrative Science Quarterly,* 25, 583–604.

Penrose, Edith T. (1968). *The Theory of the Growth of the Firm.* Oxford: Basil Blackwell.

Pettigrew, Andrew (1979). "On Studying Organization Cultures." *Administrative Science Quarterly,* 24, 570–581.

Pfeffer, Jeffrey (1981). "Management as Symbolic Action: The Creation and Maintenance of Organizational Paradigms." In Barry Staw (Ed.), *Research in Organizational Behavior,* Greenwich, CT: JAI Press, 3, 1–52.

Porter, Michael E. (1981). "Bendix Corporation," (A)-(9-378-257-rev. '81), HBS Case Services, Harvard Business School.

Quinn, James Brian (1982). *Strategies for Change.* Homewood, IL: Irwin.

Rosenberg, Nathan, and L. E. Birdzell, Jr. (1986). *How the West Grew Rich.* New York: Basic Books.

Rumelt, Richard P. (1974). *Strategy, Structure, and Economic Performance.* Boston: Graduate School of Business Administration, Harvard University.

——— (1987). "Theory, Strategy and Entrepreneurship." In David J. Teece (Ed.), *The Competitive Challenge.* Cambridge, MA: Ballinger, 137–158.

Scott, W. Richard (1981). *Organizations: Rational, Natural, and Open Systems.* Englewood Cliffs, NJ: Prentice Hall.

Selznick, Philip (1957). *Leadership in Administration.* New York: Harper and Row.

Shephard, Herbert A. (1967). "Innovation-Resisting and Innovation-Producing Organizations." *Journal of Business,* 40, 470–477.

Singh, Jitendra V. (1986). "Performance, Slack, and Risk-Taking in Organizational Decision Making." *Academy of Management Journal,* 29, 562–585.

———, Robert J. House, and David J. Tucker (1986). "Organizational Change and Organizational Mortality." *Administrative Science Quarterly,* 31, 587–611.

Snow, Charles C., and Lawrence G. Hrebinlak (1980). "Strategy, Distinctive Competence, and Organizational Performance." *Administrative Science Quarterly,* 25, 317–336.

——— and Donald C. Hambrick (1980). "Measuring Organizational Strategies: Some Theoretical and Methodological Problems." *Academy of Management Review,* 5, 527–538.

Staw, Barry, Lance E. Sandelands, and Jane E. Dutton (1981). "Thrust-Rigidity Effects in Organizational Behavior: A Multilevel Analysis." *Administrative Science Quarterly,* 26, 147–160.

Stevenson, Howard E. (1976). "Defining Corporate Strengths and Weaknesses." *Sloan Management Review* 17, 51–58.

Stinchcombe, Arthur L. (1965). "Social Structure and Organizations." In March, J. G. (Ed.), *Handbook of Organizations.* Chicago: Rand McNally.

Teece, David J. (1982). "Towards an Economic Theory of the Multi-Product Firm." *Journal of Economic Behavior Organization,* 3, 39–63.

Tucker, David J., Jitendra V. Singh, and Agnes G. Meinhard (1990). "Founding Characteristics, Imprinting and Organizational Change." In Singh, J. V. (Ed.), *Organizational Evolution: New Directions.* Newbury, CA: Sage Publications.

Tushman, Michael L., and Elaine Romanelli (1985). "Organizational Evolution: A Metamorphosis Model of Convergence and Reorientation." In L. L. Cummings and Barry Staw (Eds.), *Research in Organizational Behavior.* Greenwich, CT: JAI Press, 7, 71–222.

Van de Ven, Andrew H. (1986). "Central Problems in the Management of Innovation." *Management Science,* 32, 4, 590–607.

Weick, Karl E. (1976). "Educational Organizations of Loosely Coupled Systems." *Administrative Science Quarterly,* 21, 1–19.

——— (1979). *The Social Psychology of Organizing.* Reading, MA: Addison-Wesley.

——— (1987). "Substitutes for Corporate Strategy." In David J. Teece (Ed.), *The Competitive Challenge.* Boston: Ballinger.

Williamson, Oliver E. (1970). *Corporate Control and Business Behavior.* Englewood Cliffs, NJ: Prentice Hall.

Winter, Sidney G. (1990). "Survival, Selection and Inheritance in Evolutionary Theories of Organization." In Singh, J. V. (Ed.), *Organizational Evolution: New Directions.* Newbury Park, CA: Sage Publications.

CASE II-15

Hewlett-Packard: The Flight of the Kittyhawk

Gregory C. Rogers

In 1903, on a windy beach in Kitty Hawk, North Carolina, Orville and Wilbur Wright demonstrated that sustained flight was possible. Though their plane only flew 120 feet on the first attempt, they flew farther and higher on each successive trial. The two brothers stood at the threshold of a new era in transportation.

In June of 1992, Hewlett-Packard (HP) introduced the smallest hard disk drive in the world, named the Kittyhawk. The drive's disks were 1.3 inches in diameter; the unit was not much larger than two postage stamps (see Exhibit 1 for a picture of the Kittyhawk). The first version of the Kittyhawk supplied 20 megabytes of storage

Source: Copyright © 1997 by The President and Fellows of Harvard College. Research Associate Gregory C. Rogers prepared this case under the supervision of Professor Clayton Christensen as the basis for class discussion rather than to illustrate either effective or ineffective handling of an administrative situation. Some of the names and data in this case have been disguised to protect the interests of the company.

EXHIBIT 1   The Hewlett-Packard 1.3-Inch Kittyhawk Disk Drive

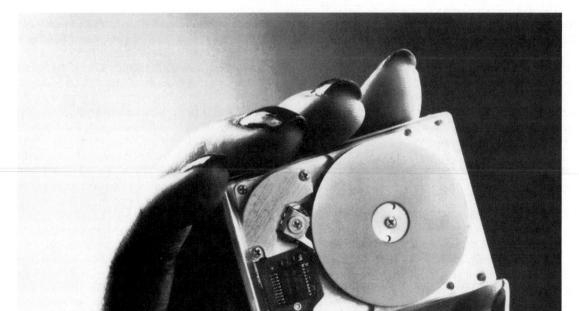

and had unique componentry enabling the drive to withstand a 3-foot drop without any data loss. The possible applications of the drive in the mobile computing market seemed endless, and the team at HP responsible for launching the Kittyhawk eagerly anticipated the takeoff of their newest innovation.

RIGID DISK DRIVES

Rigid disk drives (commonly called hard drives) were magnetic information storage and retrieval devices used with computers. The first rigid disk drive, invented in 1956 by engineers in IBM's San Jose, California, laboratories, was the size of two large refrigerators placed side by side. It could store 5 megabytes (MB) of information. The technological progress since that time was remarkable. Drives wrote and read information in the same sort of binary code that computers used. Most disk drives consisted of a read-write head that was mounted at the end of an arm which swung over the surface of a rotating disk in much the same way that a phonograph needle and arm reached over a record; disks, which were aluminum or glass platters coated with magnetic material; at least

two electrical motors—a spin motor that drove the rotation of the disks and an actuator motor that moved the head to the desired position over the disk; and a variety of electronic circuits that controlled the drive's operation and its interface with the computer.

The read-write head was a tiny electromagnet, whose polarity changed whenever the direction of the electrical current running through it changed. Data were written onto disks by sending electrical pulses through the head's electromagnet to create minute magnetic flux fields that oriented the magnetic polarity of particles (the domain) on the disk surface immediately beneath the head. With domains being given either positive or negative polarity in this way, information could be stored in binary code. Data could be retrieved from the disk's surface by reversing this process. A disk drive's architecture was categorized by the size of the disk's diameter (i.e., a 3.5-inch disk drive).

THE DISK MEMORY STORAGE DIVISION

From Hewlett-Packard's earliest beginnings as an electronic instruments company to its domination of the

EXHIBIT 2 HP's Mass Storage Group Organization Chart (1992)

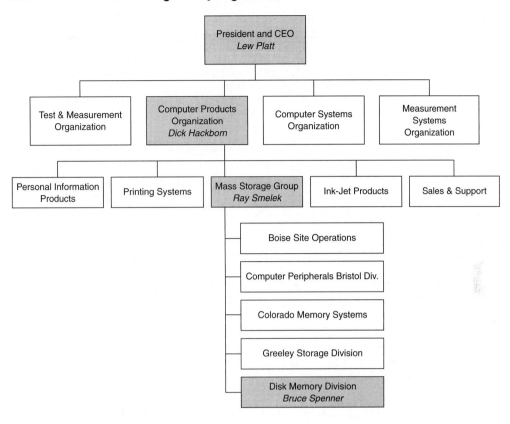

printer industry, the HP culture deeply valued technical innovation as a key to success. HP employed a management by objective (MBO) process to focus its businesses on financial goals and its people on the potential paths of innovation and strategy to achieve such goals. HP favored a decentralized organizational structure so as to allow its businesses a freedom of decision making and movement.

HP had four major business organizations—Test & Measurement, Computer Systems, Measurement Systems, and Computer Products. Of these four, the Computer Products Organization consisted of the company's laser printer, ink-jet printer, personal computer, and mass storage product groups. The Mass Storage Product Group developed and managed HP's storage technologies (see Exhibit 2 for the Mass Storage Group's organization chart). The Disk Memory Division (DMD), which was responsible for developing and launching the Kittyhawk and other disk drive models, resided within the Mass Storage Group.

Based in Boise, Idaho, DMD's disk drive sales in 1992 reached $519 million, approximately 80 percent of which was derived from OEM orders and the rest from HP's internal computer businesses.[1] HP's corporate net revenue was at $16 billion. (See Exhibit 3 for a 10-year comparison of HP corporate revenues versus its disk drive revenues.) At the same time, the industry leaders, IBM and Seagate Technology, had disk drive sales of $4 billion and $3 billion, respectively.[2]

Although small in comparison to some of the other disk drive manufacturers, DMD had a profitable position within the market. It concentrated on high-performance products within the 5.25- and 3.5-inch architectures that supplied healthy profit margins to the division. Consequently, HP's product line offered a substantially higher capacity in megabytes than the industry norm (see Exhibit 4). For many of DMD's R&D engineers, the most

---

[1] 1993 Disk/Trend Report.
[2] Ibid.

EXHIBIT 3   HP Corporate Net Revenue Versus Disk Drive Revenue (1983–1992)

(Fiscal Year Ends October 31–Dollars in Millions)

	1983	1984	1985	1986	1987	1988	1989	1990	1991	1992
Corporate net revenues	4710.0	6044.0	6505.0	7102.0	8090.0	9831.0	11899.0	13200.0	14494.0	16410.0
Disk drive revenues	269.1	315.5	259.1	251.3	328.1	420.6	533.4	402.2	280.7	519.4
Disk drive revenues as a percentage of corporate's	5.7%	5.2%	4.0%	3.5%	4.1%	4.3%	4.5%	3.0%	2.0%	3.2%

Source: Disk/Trend Report.

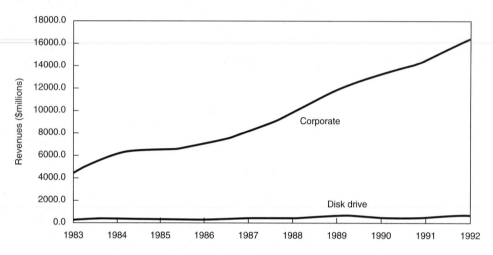

sought after projects were the ones that developed the next generation drives that furnished ever higher capacities and faster access times. Concentrating on the high-end engineering workstation and network server markets, DMD had been among the first in the industry to introduce 1 and 2 gigabyte drives.[3] These disk drives were extremely successful in the marketplace.

THE KITTYHAWK

Genesis of the Idea

Bruce Spenner, the general manager of the Disk Memory Division, came to HP in 1978 from teaching electrical engineering at Washington University in St. Louis. A few years after joining HP Labs, he was a part of the company's top priority project to implement reduced instruction set computing (RISC) architecture into HP's minicomputers and workstations. While other computer companies didn't fully believe the benefits of RISC and balked in implementation, HP's full commitment to the architecture made it the leader in UNIX computing.

Described by employees as not the typical "meet the numbers" manager, Spenner was widely viewed as a visionary and risk taker. At HP Labs, his responsibilities soon expanded into overseeing a software laboratory that produced major new breakthroughs under his watch. Dick Hackborn, who had built HP's highly successful printer business and was now executive vice president in charge of the company's Computer Products Organization, liked Spenner's concept-driven thinking. In 1990, Ray Smelek, G. M. of the Mass Storage Product Group, promoted Spenner to general manager of the Disk Memory Division.

DMD was an anomaly within HP. It had been selling drives externally to OEMs since 1984, and, though profitable, DMD was still a niche player from a disk drive industry perspective. In contrast, HP as a whole took pride in its ability to be a market leader. Bothered by DMD's position, Spenner often asked, "How can we make HP a major player in the disk drive industry? Why don't we have 20 percent market share? How can DMD become the next printer business for HP?" Questions like these sparked Spenner's entrepreneurial spirit. By 1991, he was convinced that a new disk drive architecture with an innovative design could take the computing market by storm, and that HP was the company to create it.

---

[3] 1 gigabyte is equivalent to 1,000 megabytes.

EXHIBIT 4   A Comparison of HP's Product Position, Relative to Other Leading Disk Drive Makers

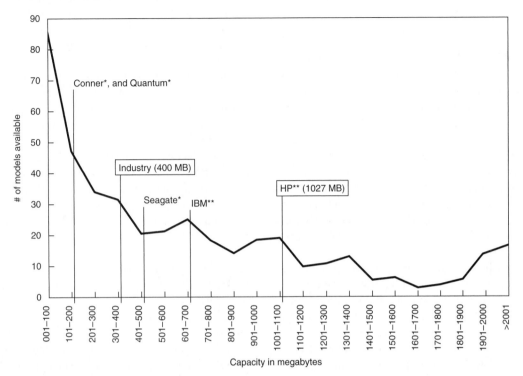

Source: 1992 Disk/Trend Report.
Vertical lines indicate the capacity of the median model sold by DMD and Principal Competitions, compared to the industry.
*Focus on desktop and notebook personal computers.
**Focus on engineering workstation, file servers, and other large computers.

DMD had established itself in the 5.25- and 3.5-inch markets, but by 1992 had not introduced a 2.5-inch drive of the sort used in notebook computers. Spenner felt the competitors within that market—particularly Conner, Quantum, and Western Digital—were too strong to attack directly, and that to succeed, HP needed to go beyond any existing architecture. He believed in Dick Hackborn's favorite maxim: "Never take a fortified hill."

Thus, Spenner wanted to attack an entirely new hill. He envisioned the future of storage in the form of large data library servers fed and utilized by client computers (desktop and notebook PCs) and, in the future, hand-held computers. Hand-held computers and other very small forms of computing represented an emerging market for which DMD could make a suitably small disk drive. Spenner had found his hill. He wanted a disk drive that not only served the computing marketplace but transcended the traditional market boundaries and could be used in any product that used a microprocessor.

To receive approval to initiate the project, Spenner decided to present the idea directly to Dick Hackborn. He assigned one of his engineers, George Drennan, to scope out different design concepts. Drennan reported back with several different sized rectangular boxes, each one representing a possible choice in size for HP's new drive. The largest represented a 2.5-inch drive, the smallest a 1.3-inch. Over lunch in early 1991, Spenner placed in front of Dick Hackborn the different sized boxes, explained his vision of a new disk drive, and asked, "Well, which one shall it be?" Hackborn looked them over, and to Spenner's surprise, he picked up the 1.3-inch box and said, "Do this one." This approval was all that Spenner needed. "Hackborn had such respect within the HP organization," stated one engineer, "That once he said 'Do something,' everyone seemed to fall into line." Soon after Hackborn had given approval for the project, so too did Ray Smelek. At the time, the Computer Products Organization had just reported record earnings for fiscal

1990. Hackborn and Smelek agreed that DMD could afford the financial risks of the Kittyhawk. Much of the necessary investment could be covered by profits from the division's 1 and 2 gigabyte products.

The Project Team

Despite Kittyhawk's heavyweight endorsements, DMD's functional management and most of the R&D section managers hesitated to support the 1.3-inch drive. They felt that the investment in a new, small architecture would conflict with the needs of the division to stay atop of its established markets. In the race for multi-gigabyte drives, Seagate and Maxtor were neck and neck with DMD, and the industry's volume leaders, Quantum and Conner were nipping at their heels. They felt that the division's priorities should be to its next-generation higher-gigabyte product lines, not to a tiny drive whose market was yet unclear.

Spenner had expected this reaction, and moved to separate the 1.3-inch project from the rest of the division. Accordingly, the project team moved operations out of DMD's main building into trailers located at a remote corner of the division site. Spenner considered Kittyhawk the division's highest priority project and afforded the team the power to make timely decisions. One team member viewed Kittyhawk as an engineer's dream project: "We were basically a start-up business with the speed and flexibility of entrepreneurs but with also the financial and technical backing of a successful high-tech company." The project also received executive support from the top ranks of HP. Dick Hackborn and Lew Platt, HP's CEO, often visited the project trailers to see how the development was progressing.

Spenner wanted to make sure that the Kittyhawk was not governed by the division's traditional development processes. In order to speed Kittyhawk to the market, he gave the Kittyhawk team autonomy to develop the drive, find new markets, and cultivate a customer base.

The core project team, formed in May of 1991, contained three functional representatives (manufacturing, marketing, and R&D) with a program manager from R&D, Rick Seymour, as the leader. It was not hard to fill these positions. Spenner looked for risk-takers that would be more excited by the market potential of a 1.3-inch drive than by its technological capabilities. These core members were not necessarily experienced in developing new architectures or cultivating emerging markets but were considered to be can-do people. Rick Seymour had been an R&D section manager for DMD with a manufacturing background in disk drive heads and me-

dia. Although having never led the development of a new architecture, he had the reputation for quick thinking and action that Spenner believed necessary to make the project succeed. Jeff White, the marketing manager, had joined HP a few years earlier with an M.B.A. and had a similar reputation.

Like Spenner with the core of the team, the Kittyhawk's managers carefully chose their staff. Although recruiting from other HP divisions as well, they mostly selected exceptional employees from within DMD. "Because of the priority of our project, if we wanted someone from the division's next generation 2-gigabyte project," said Seymour, "we got him. No questions asked."

The core team was wary of team members who would bring with them HP's cultural biases. To reinforce how differently the team needed to work, David Woito, the project's R&D manager, required all engineers to sign a creed before they could join the Kittyhawk team: *"I am going to build a small, dumb, cheap disk drive!"* Two engineers would not sign the statement and returned to HP mainstream.

To ensure that the team functioned well, the core team extensively researched team dynamics and group development literature. When setting up their work areas, team members who had to coordinate together had their desks next to each other. "Our organization was a state of the art team," boasted a member.

The Project Parameters

Spenner drafted a project charter for Kittyhawk, which consisted of five goals:

1. Introduce the Kittyhawk in 12 months, from start to finish.
2. Accomplish a break-even time (BET) of less than 36 months (see Exhibit 5). BET was the time it took to repay the negative cash flow incurred in developing and launching the product.
3. Achieve a $100 million revenue rate in two years after launch.
4. To be the first 1.3-inch drive on the market—"the first on a new hill."
5. Grow faster than the disk drive market to help HP become a significant industry leader. Thus, revenue growth rate had to be around 35 percent.

Although aggressive, Spenner's charter did not appear to be out of reach. HP's average cycle time for new disk drive platform development was 18 months. Because they could leverage off of technology that DMD had been developing for its larger drives, the project team be-

**EXHIBIT 5   Hewlett-Packard's Method for Evaluating Project Success:
The Break-Even Time Calculation**

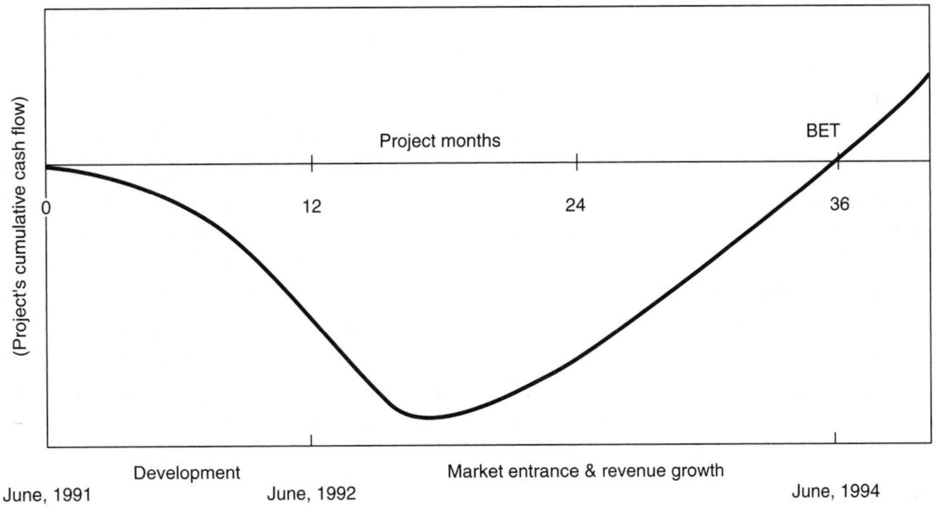

This schedule was a standard HP format for measuring project success.

lieved that they could attain the 12-month introduction date. In addition, although three times higher than had been originally forecast, the $100 million dollar revenue rate was thought to be possible by focusing on and cornering high-growth market areas.

Finding the Kittyhawk Market

One week after the start of the project in June of 1991, Seymour and White arrived at the Consumer Electronics Show in Chicago to look at some market possibilities for the Kittyhawk. They ignored the desktop and notebook computer sections of the show, fortified hills that they were, and searched for the newest mobile computing products—hand-held and pen-based computers, otherwise known as personal digital assistants (PDAs). Although still in the fledgling stages of development, PDAs offered some interesting possibilities for a 1.3″ drive.

After interviewing several leading PDA developers in the mobile computing section, Seymour and White came upon a booth that was the size of about eight or nine other booths combined—the Nintendo exhibition. There they found a labyrinth of interactive games and turned to each other with the same awestruck reaction: "Look at all the storage possibilities here! We could fit 50 of these games onto one Kittyhawk." They pulled the Nintendo marketing manager aside and asked him if Nintendo might be interested in a new, small storage device for its game cartridges. The Nintendo manager replied, "Absolutely, the software writers' dream is to have more cheap storage.

We're always looking to create more complex games." He then emphasized that the imperative word here was *cheap,* more accurately about $50. As they left, Seymour asked, "How many of these game cartridges do you ship per year?" "Well, to give you an idea," the manager responded, "in the Christmas season we ship about 1.5 million per day."

After returning to Boise, White continued market research for the project. He read research reports on new markets in electronics and contacted companies to explore their future product plans. White also talked to many people within HP itself in his search for insight about where the electronics industry was going to explode. White compiled a list of five possibilities: mobile information technologies, communications technologies, consumer electronics, automotive electronics, and some new developments in standard computer technology.

After considerable deliberation over these target markets, the Kittyhawk team narrowed the strategy for the Kittyhawk down to two possibilities, either a disk drive specifically focused at the mobile computing market or a drive so inexpensive that it could be used in applications where disk drives previously had not been economically feasible. The team struggled between these two choices. Seymour and White had not forgotten their experience in the Nintendo exhibition, certainly not the "1.5 million" statistic. But at the same time, they also believed that a $50 disk drive, by itself, might not spawn a large market fast enough to achieve Bruce Spenner's desired break-even time. The lowest unit cost that had been achieved thus far in the industry for a fully featured disk drive of any capacity was about $130. For the industry as a whole, this $130 seemed to have acted as a cost floor of sorts—it cost that much to purchase and assemble the basic components. Designers were able to reduce the cost per megabyte by persistently increasing the megabytes per drive. But the cost *per drive* seemed to stubbornly remain above $130. Hence, designing a $50 drive would require a significant design breakthrough.

Mobile computing markets would require breakthrough technologies of a very different sort—in particular, the ability to pack more megabytes of information per square inch of disk surface than had even been done in a small drive. But if they could do it, the market seemed attractive. Every company that was developing a PDA showed intense interest whenever White or someone from his marketing staff asked if they could use a smaller disk drive. White noted, "Mobile computing was still in its infancy when the Kittyhawk was being developed. Everyone who knew something about technology thought that PDAs would be the next biggest thing to hit the market." Companies like Apple, IBM, Motorola, AT&T, and even HP were investing hundreds of millions of dollars in the development of their own PDAs.

Because the mobile computing market volume seemed nearer at hand, the team decided that the best strategy would be to start by designing a drive suited for the mobile computing market and then eventually, through high-volume production, reach the $50 price point through volume manufacturing and next-generation product redesign. From their beach head in mobile computing, the team imagined a disk drive that would be utilized in all sorts of consumer electronics like Nintendo game cartridges and cellular phones. They saw it used as a "super" floppy disk, where computer users could carry the Kittyhawk around in their pockets with programs already loaded onto it, and be able to sit down at public-access computers, plug in the 1.3-inch drive, and begin using the applications that they brought with them. The team reveled in the possibilities.

Seymour subsequently presented a three page strategy document to Spenner. On each page, in bold lettering, was printed one objective:

- Lead industry in 1.3-inch form factor.
- Ride the mobile computing explosion to get to low cost.
- "I'll sell you a drive for $49.95"

Rick Seymour explained the simplicity behind these objectives: "This was not a 20-page strategy that you would ordinarily see with a project of this magnitude. Instead, we just wanted people to start to imagine the immense possibilities of the Kittyhawk."

To give Spenner reassurance that mobile computing represented the right high-growth market for the Kittyhawk, the team contracted with a highly reputable market research firm that specialized in high-tech markets, to independently gauge the magnitude of Kittyhawk's opportunity. The firm typically would talk to existing customers and industry experts to analyze where the market was headed. However, in this market, when it was not yet clear who the larger customers would ultimately be, the firm found that its normal methodologies led it nowhere. White recalled, "It was like trying to learn Swahili without the help of anyone else who knows the language. The research firm ended up talking to us more than anyone else. Naturally, they came to believe what we believed."

As White worked with budding PDA makers, some of the clearest early input came from Dayton Electronics Corporation, a leading computer maker that was developing a pen-based computer to be used as an electronic clipboard by delivery personnel in over-night package delivery companies. Dayton's lead customer had a specification that the computer had to be able to withstand a 3-foot drop onto concrete. At the time, the average hard disk drive could withstand a drop, while operating, of about 3 inches without data loss.

Other of the Kittyhawk's design specifications were taken from HP's Corvallis Division. Whereas most notebook and sub-notebook computers employed 2.5-inch drives, the Austin Division was designing a "super" sub-notebook that would not have space for a 2.5-inch drive. As a result, the Kittyhawk team worked closely with the Austin group to meet their operating requirements—particularly, low weight and low power consumption.

Through their work with PDA developers, the Kittyhawk team developed a view about which of the PDA developers would succeed. They felt that those handheld computers that addressed an application-specific niche in the market—such as Dayton's PDA for package delivery—would be more likely to succeed because of the focused functionality they required. Portable check-in devices for car rental companies had similar characteristics.

The Competitors

Seymour and White felt that two technologies might compete with Kittyhawk. The first was Flash memory, a

EXHIBIT 6   The Pattern in Reduction of Disk Surface in New, Small Architectures

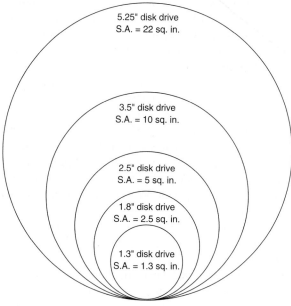

5.25" disk drive
S.A. = 22 sq. in.

3.5" disk drive
S.A. = 10 sq. in.

2.5" disk drive
S.A. = 5 sq. in.

1.8" disk drive
S.A. = 2.5 sq. in.

1.3" disk drive
S.A. = 1.3 sq. in.

Surface Area $= \pi R^2$

nonvolatile integrated memory circuit that retained information stored on it even if the power was turned off. Because it had no moving parts, Flash was exceptionally rugged. Although the Flash chip commanded about $50 per megabyte, 10 times more expensive than the average disk drive, it became competitive with disk memory at the small end. Six megabytes of Flash memory cost about $300. Because of the apparent unit cost floor for disk drives discussed above, this meant that for very low capacity drives, Flash memory would be more closely cost-competitive than for higher capacity drives. The Kittyhawk engineers considered the dynamics of this competition when deciding that their 1.3-inch drive should have at least 20 megabytes of storage.

The second potential competitor was the 1.8-inch disk drive. Although not yet available when the Kittyhawk project started, industry sources believed that several other companies planned to introduce 1.8-inch models in 1992. Historically, in the progression from 8-inch to 5.25-inch, 3.5-inch to 2.5-inch disks, the surface area per disk in each new architecture was half of the preceding generation's surface area (Exhibit 6 shows this pattern). Hence, a 1.8-inch drive would be the industry's most predictable next step after the 2.5-inch drive; the Kittyhawk essentially leapfrogged ahead one generation beyond the 1.8-inch form factor. Seymour tended to dis-

count the 1.8-inch threat, however. Though it would have greater capacity, it would be larger and consume more power.

The Product

Seymour deliberately worked to instill fear amongst his colleagues. "I wanted the team to imagine that everyone in the industry was going to beat us to the punch." Integral Peripherals' introduction of the first 1.8-inch disk drive for sub-notebook computers in September 1991 spurred the Kittyhawk group to move even faster. "We traded most everything to meet the schedule: performance, features, cost—everything but reliability," said Seymour. Though Seymour and White felt they probably had a 12-month lead on the competition, they told everyone 6 months to elevate the sense of urgency.

Designing the Kittyhawk to meet the key performance mandates White's market research had identified—the 3-foot drop and 20 MB of capacity, in particular—required that three unique technologies be developed. The first was a new substrate material for the disks. Disks in larger drives generally consisted of polished platters of aluminum that were coated with thin films of magnetic metal. To meet the height requirement of the Kittyhawk, these disks needed to be reduced to the thickness of foil—making aluminum an unsuitably weak substrate. The project team developed, with a supplier, a glass substrate which was thin but strong enough. It could be polished so flat and smooth that heads could fly closer to the disk, allowing data to be packed more densely. Team members believed that this disk technology, combined with other custom components, would allow the Kittyhawk to reach up to 200 megabytes of capacity by 1995.

The second technology was a new level of integration for the Kittyhawk's electronics. Fortunately, since 1989 a group of DMD engineers had been working on the problem of managing the drive's operations and computer interface within a much smaller number of custom-designed integrated circuits. While a typical 1.8-inch disk drive had 20 to 30 chips, the Kittyhawk team integrated even better functionality on only 5 chips. This meant that the 1.3-inch module would use less power, would be lighter, and would be manufacturable at lower cost.

The key to meeting the 3-foot drop requirement centered on a proprietary six-axis piezoelectric accelerometer. This was a shock-sensing mechanism that could detect impending impact on both linear and rotational axes and cause the drive to revert to a mode that protected against data loss—acting much like an air-bag collision sensor on an automobile. Rick Seymour described his initial reaction to the innovation: "The technology was amazing. An elegant design all around. The only problem was that this component alone cost over $10 to make. But, man, was it cool."

The project team decided not to manufacture their drive in-house. They looked instead for an external supplier with a proven expertise in miniaturized manufacturing, and found a perfect match in Japan's Citizen Watch Corporation. Citizen designed and built an automated production line for the Kittyhawk. Prepared for future growth, the line had a capacity of 150,000 units per month.

The Kittyhawk was introduced right on schedule in June of 1992, exactly 12 months from the beginning of development. Although retired and not having been present at a product launch in ten years, William Hewlett, HP's cofounder, presided at the press conference announcing the Kittyhawk's launch. It measured 0.4 inch by 2 inches by 1.44 inches and weighed about 1 ounce. The Kittyhawk was almost half the total size and one-third the weight of the 1.8-inch disk drives that had been introduced to market just months before. The Kittyhawk announcement garnered more press coverage than any new product announcement in the history of Hewlett Packard. The design won several prestigious technology and new product awards for 1992. CEO Lew Platt developed the habit of carrying a Kittyhawk in his pocket as a conversation piece for customers and analysts.

Seymour wasn't sure how he felt about all the attention. "The great news was that we were in a project with a lot of visibility. That was also the bad news. We had unbelievable support. If we made the Kittyhawk fly, it would fly high, but if it crashed, there was going to be one hell of an explosion."

HP shipped its first Kittyhawk on June 23, with high volume OEM pricing at about $250. Based on their read of the market, the Kittyhawk's marketing staff was projecting the next two-year demand from the PDA market to be over 500,000 units. At this pricing, Kittyhawk looked as it if would achieve Spenner's objectives both for revenue rate and break-even time.

The Customers

By July of 1992, the Kittyhawk team had design wins in new PDAs being developed at six computer companies. It appeared to be besting both Flash memory and the 1.8-inch drive for the most attractive applications. The team also got design wins in other applications. One example

was with a company which utilized the drive as backup storage in the portable check-in devices it made for car rental companies. The demand for the Kittyhawk looked to be on target with the project's goals. What's more, many of these customers at the time were considered to be the bluest of blue chip companies—Apple, IBM, and even HP itself.

In its third month of production, however, the project hit a road bump. HP's Corvallis Division decided that a 1.3-inch drive would not be able to meet the future storage requirements of its super sub-notebook computers. Even though the Kittyhawk team had plans to introduce a second-generation drive with 40 megabytes, that would still not be enough. Corvallis instead decided to use Integral Peripherals' 1.8-inch drive. Kittyhawk had lost its first major potential customer.

An even bigger road bump was that the PDA market never emerged as expected. For most of the PDAs, Kittyhawk's performance was more than sufficient. But other new technologies upon which the PDAs depended, such as handwriting recognition software and new integrated circuitry, proved to be inadequate. Literally every PDA manufacturer found its PDA sales to be disappointing, and most withdrew from the market. The hand-held computers that were commercially successful tended to be technologically modest, lower-priced devices whose needs for storage could be economically satisfied by Flash memory chips.

But there was never an unambiguous, definitive signal to the team that the PDA market wouldn't materialize. It seemed that for every customer that stumbled, such as Apple with its Newton, another reputable, technologically competent customer stepped up with a different type of PDA which it was confident would hit the right price and performance points in the market. Hence, though Kittyhawk's volume ramp was delayed, prosperity always seemed right around the corner. For example, just as HP announced the Kittyhawk II with 43 MB of storage that withstood 10 percent greater shock and consumed 25 percent less power than the Kittyhawk I, a major computer company, Chicago Controls, designed Kittyhawk into an industrial pen-based device for recording and analyzing data for statistical process control in manufacturing plants. Kittyhawk's ruggedness was attractive because stored data would remain intact despite any rough handling that might occur on the factory floor. Microsoft was creating a version of its PC operating system with graphical interface for this particular PDA. The requirements were that the operating system had to be able to fit on the soon-to-be-introduced 40-megabyte

Kittyhawk and still leave enough capacity for other programs. White's own research with end users supported Chicago Controls' enthusiasm for this product: if it took off, it alone would catapult Kittyhawk back on plan.

To bolster HP's commitment to Kittyhawk, Seymour brokered a meeting between Spenner, Smelek, and Chicago Controls' CEO, and it worked. They left reassured with the Kittyhawk's potential. Shortly after the meeting, however, Microsoft announced that its operating system for this application would need more than the 43 MB of storage the Kittyhawk offered. This derailed the whole concept of this PDA for factory control.

Even while prosperity kept looming around the next corner in mobile computing, several unexpected customers started to show interest in HP's 1.3-inch drive. The first was a Japanese company whose portable word processor printed Japanese Kanji (Chinese characters) when words were spelled on its keyboard. The device was used in both the home and office. It required a storage device that not only had enough capacity to store the necessary translation programs but also could withstand the shocks to which portable devices were exposed. The Kittyhawk's shock resistance also attracted manufacturers of cash registers. Most of the newest cash registers

were run through an operating system that recorded daily transactions within a central computer system. The manufacturers were looking for a storage drive that could act as a backup if the central computer failed while also being able to withstand the shock from the slamming shut of the cash register drawer. The 20-megabyte Kittyhawk served the needs of both these applications perfectly.

Another customer saw the Kittyhawk as a "film cartridge" which could be removed from the digital camera it was developing, and inserted into viewing and printing devices. The Kittyhawk's shock resistance was particularly attractive for this application. The camera's success depended on two enabling technologies. The first was rugged storage. Although Flash memory could solve this piece of the puzzle, the Kittyhawk served the need better due to its lower cost per megabyte. The second technology was a charge-coupled device (CCD) that transformed images into digital format. The CCD technology ultimately proved technically feasible, but unfortunately its cost pushed the camera's retail price to $1,500, where unit volumes were disappointing.

As a result, the list of Kittyhawk customers (shown in Exhibit 7) was very different from what the team had originally planned.

EXHIBIT 7   Planned Versus Actual Production Levels and Product Applications

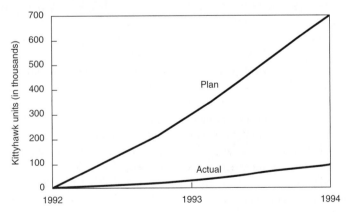

Planned versus actual major product

Plan:	Actual:	# of units sold over the life of the project (000s)
• Personal digital assistants	• Japanese word processors	100
• Sub-notebooks	• Personal digital assistants	35
• Hard copy devices	• Digital cameras	20
• Printers	• Cash registers	8
• Copiers	• Telecom switching systems	2
• Fax machines		

A New Beginning?

Despite this string of disappointments peppered by a few successes from unexpected quarters, interest in the Kittyhawk kept rolling in to Jeff White's marketing team—interest from highly credible companies with solid new product ideas. These seemed to fall into two groups. The first were those described above—where the Kittyhawk's ruggedness based upon its accelerometer technology was its most prized attribute. The second group of potential customers were sounding a very different theme: they needed a cheap, simple drive priced at around $50.

"It took a couple of years of the Kittyhawk being in the marketplace before people figured out what they needed," White recalled. "Before the Kittyhawk, most of our customers never even thought about disk storage as a way to improve their products. The Kittyhawk got them thinking, and then they started coming to us with what they really wanted." Nintendo, for example, showed the Kittyhawk team an entertainment system they had already designed, unbeknownst to HP, with a slot for a Kittyhawk drive to be plugged in—a module that could contain many more games, with much more sophisticated graphics, than Nintendo's conventional cartridge approach. "The system is all set," the Nintendo representative persuaded. "All you have to do is sell us your drive for $50." When White protested that the Kittyhawk's accelerometer alone (required for shock resistance) rendered the $50 price impossible, Nintendo responded that they didn't need the accelerometer—they just needed 20 megabytes at $50, cheap and simple.

A fax machine manufacturer explored with the team the possibility of offering an embedded Kittyhawk as an option in its high-end model to handle graphics-intensive transmission. "I learned pretty early on that you don't want to be designed in as an option," White recalled. "You want to be part of their standard product, or you have no way of forecasting what kind of volume you're looking at." White pointed at one of the customer's lower-priced fax machines and asked how many of those they sold. To the answer of 5 million units per year, Seymour responded, "That's interesting. Could you use the Kittyhawk for those?" The customer reviewed his materials list and answered, "Sure, as long as you can deliver the drive to us for $48." "How about if we hit $100?" Seymour queried. The customer shook his head and said, "If you hit $52 we still couldn't use it." White recalled 10 other companies with similar propositions at the $50 price point.

In mid-1994, Seymour convened a meeting of the Kittyhawk core team to determine their response to these developments. Three alternatives emerged from the discussion. The first was to continue to pursue the ruggedness-based applications that were beginning to coalesce. The problem with this strategy was that the ramp to high volumes was sure to be slow and unpredictable—because the customers generally were pursuing new applications themselves, and their success depended on many developments besides the Kittyhawk. The team was losing its confidence that such a business could get big enough fast enough to merit continued interest from HP management.

The second option was to leverage the ruggedness and electronics integration technologies the team had developed to create a superior 2.5-inch drive for notebook computers. This would pit HP against formidable, high-volume competitors such as Quantum, Conner, Seagate, and Western Digital in the mainstream market. But some team members felt HP could become a viable player at the high end of that market, earning enough of a price premium for its ruggedness that it could be a profitable competitor.

The team felt most enthusiastic, however, about the third option—a $50 drive. "Designing something so cheap and simple would be a huge challenge," Seymour predicted. "But with what we learned the first time around, we felt we could do it. Designing a 40 MB 1.3-inch drive that could drop 3-feet onto a concrete floor was no simple feat, either. The $50 drive would be a very different challenge, but it probably wouldn't be more difficult."

Making money at Hewlett-Packard with a $50 drive would require a very different overhead structure than the one Seymour had built in his push to get the Kittyhawk into the market in a year, so he approached Spenner and Smelek with his proposal. "I told them I didn't think the Kittyhawk, as currently conceived, was ever going to pay off like we needed—but that in the process of learning this lesson, we had found where the real market was. But it would take another considerable investment, and about 10–12 more months for a redesign and relaunch."

It was clear, however, that DMD management had neither the enthusiasm nor the profit cushion for another run. Because many of the division's best engineers had been transferred from high-end drive development into the 1.3-inch effort, DMD had not had the resources to develop a competitive 4-gigabyte hard drive. Without a new top-model drive in its core product line, DMD's revenues started to flatten. On September 7, 1994, HP announced that it would discontinue its 20- and 40-megabyte Kittyhawk disk drives. Its production levels were far below those initially forecast (see Exhibit 5). "We're disappointed to have to cancel our market-leading HP Kittyhawk," said Bruce Spenner in a press release. "HP keeps its individual business units tightly focused on key market segments with good to excellent prospects. When those markets don't yield as expected, HP minimizes its exposure to additional risk and makes difficult decisions such as this one."

When Ray Smelek gathered the Kittyhawk team together to inform them of the decision to shut down the project, he told them, "I took the risk. You guys executed beautifully." The crash of the Kittyhawk was not nearly as devastating as the team had imagined. No one was fired. In fact several project members were promoted, including Rick Seymour and Jeff White. Seymour was placed in charge of developing a 9-gigabyte drive with many of the ex-Kittyhawk members comprising the new team. White became its OEM marketing manager. The primary problem the team experienced after the end of the project was reintegrating themselves back into the division. Some employees who had not been a part of Kittyhawk felt resentful that the project had disassociated itself from the rest of DMD.

Seymour recounted: "I've never seen a failed project from which so many of the team members would have been willing to do it all over again in a heartbeat. Most of the members came to me at some point after the project had ended and said, 'Rick, that was the most fun I've ever had.'"

READING II-14

Meeting the Challenge of Disruptive Change

Clayton M. Christensen and Michael Overdorf

These are scary times for managers in big companies. Even before the Internet and globalization, their track record for dealing with major, disruptive change was not good. Out of hundreds of department stores, for example, only one—Dayton Hudson—became a leader in discount retailing. Not one of the minicomputer companies succeeded in the personal computer business. Med-

Source: Clayton M. Christensen is a professor of business administration at Harvard Business School in Boston and the author of *The Innovator's Dilemma: When New Technologies Cause Great Firms to Fail*

ical and business schools are struggling—and failing—to change their curricula fast enough to train the types of doctors and managers their markets need. The list could go on.

It's not that managers in big companies can't see disruptive changes coming. Usually they can. Nor do they lack resources to confront them. Most big companies have talented managers and specialists, strong product portfolios, first-rate technological know-how, and deep pockets. What managers lack is a habit of thinking about their organization's capabilities as carefully as they think about individual people's capabilities.

One of the hallmarks of a great manager is the ability to identify the right person for the right job and to train employees to succeed at the jobs they're given. But unfortunately, most managers assume that if each person working on a project is well matched to the job, then the organization in which they work will be, too. Often that is not the case. One could put two sets of identically capable people to work in different organizations, and what they accomplished would be significantly different. That's because organizations themselves—independent of the people and other resources in them—have capabilities. To succeed consistently, good managers need to be skilled not just in assessing people but also in assessing the abilities and disabilities of their organization as a whole.

This article offers managers a framework to help them understand what their organizations are capable of accomplishing. It will show them how their company's disabilities become more sharply defined even as its core capabilities grow. It will give them a way to recognize different kinds of change and make appropriate organizational responses to the opportunities that arise from each. And it will offer some bottom-line advice that runs counter to much that's assumed in our can-do business culture: if an organization faces major change—a disruptive innovation, perhaps—the worst possible approach may be to make drastic adjustments to the existing organization. In trying to transform an enterprise, managers can destroy the very capabilities that sustain it.

Before rushing into the breach, managers must understand precisely what types of change the existing organization is capable and incapable of handling. To help them do that, we'll first take a systematic look at how to recognize a company's core capabilities on an organizational

(Harvard Business School Press, 1997). Michael Overdorf is a Dean's Research Fellow at Harvard Business School. Reprinted by permission of *Harvard Business Review,* March–April 2000. Copyright © by The President and Fellows of Harvard College; all rights reserved.

level and then examine how those capabilities migrate as companies grow and mature.

WHERE CAPABILITIES RESIDE

Our research suggests that three factors affect what an organization can and cannot do: its resources, its processes, and its values. When thinking about what sorts of innovations their organization will be able to embrace, managers need to assess how each of these factors might affect their organization's capacity to change.

Resources

When they ask the question "What can this company do?" the place most managers look for the answer is in its resources—both the tangible ones like people, equipment, technologies, and cash, and the less tangible ones like product designs, information, brands, and relationships with suppliers, distributors, and customers. Without doubt, access to abundant, high-quality resources increases an organization's chances of coping with change. But resource analysis doesn't come close to telling the whole story.

Processes

The second factor that affects what a company can and cannot do is its processes. By processes, we mean the patterns of interaction, coordination, communication, and decision making employees use to transform resources into products and services of greater worth. Such examples as the processes that govern product development, manufacturing, and budgeting come immediately to mind. Some processes are formal, in the sense that they are explicitly defined and documented. Others are informal: they are routines or ways of working that evolve over time. The former tend to be more visible, the latter less visible.

One of the dilemmas of management is that processes, by their very nature, are set up so that employees perform tasks in a consistent way, time after time. They are *meant* not to change or, if they must change, to change through tightly controlled procedures. When people use a process to do the task it was designed for, it is likely to perform efficiently. But when the same process is used to tackle a very different task, it is likely to perform sluggishly. Companies focused on developing and winning FDA approval for new drug compounds, for example, often prove inept at developing and winning approval for medical devices because the second task entails very different ways of working. In fact, a process that creates the

capability to execute one task concurrently defines disabilities in executing other tasks.[1]

The most important capabilities and concurrent disabilities aren't necessarily embodied in the most visible processes, like logistics, development, manufacturing, or customer service. In fact, they are more likely to be in the less visible, background processes that support decisions about where to invest resources—those that define how market research is habitually done, how such analysis is translated into financial projections, how plans and budgets are negotiated internally, and so on. It is in those processes that many organizations' most serious disabilities in coping with change reside.

Values

The third factor that affects what an organization can and cannot do is its values. Sometimes the phrase "corporate values" carries an ethical connotation: one thinks of the principles that ensure patient well-being for Johnson & Johnson or that guide decisions about employee safety at Alcoa. But within our framework, "values" has a broader meaning. We define an organization's values as the standards by which employees set priorities that enable them to judge whether an order is attractive or unattractive, whether a customer is more important or less important, whether an idea for a new product is attractive or marginal, and so on. Prioritization decisions are made by employees at every level. Among salespeople, they consist of on-the-spot, day-to-day decisions about which products to push with customers and which to deemphasize. At the executive tiers, they often take the form of decisions to invest, or not, in new products, services, and processes.

The larger and more complex a company becomes, the more important it is for senior managers to train employees throughout the organization to make independent decisions about priorities that are consistent with the strategic direction and the business model of the company. A key metric of good management, in fact, is whether such clear, consistent values have permeated the organization.

But consistent, broadly understood values also define what an organization cannot do. A company's values reflect its cost structure or its business model because those define the rules its employees must follow for the company to prosper. If, for example, a company's overhead costs require it to achieve gross profit margins of

---

[1] See Dorothy Leonard-Barton, "Core Capabilities and Core Rigidities: A Paradox in Managing New Product Development," *Strategic Management Journal* (summer, 1992).

40%, then a value or decision rule will have evolved that encourages middle managers to kill ideas that promise gross margins below 40%. Such an organization would be incapable of commercializing projects targeting low-margin markets—such as those in e-commerce—even though another organization's values, driven by a very different cost structure, might facilitate the success of the same project.

Different companies, of course, embody different values. But we want to focus on two sets of values in particular that tend to evolve in most companies in very predictable ways. The inexorable evolution of these two values is what makes companies progressively less capable of addressing disruptive change successfully.

As in the previous example, the first value dictates the way the company judges acceptable gross margins. As companies add features and functions to their products and services, trying to capture more attractive customers in premium tiers of their markets, they often add overhead cost. As a result, gross margins that were once attractive become unattractive. For instance, Toyota entered the North American market with the Corona model, which targeted the lower end of the market. As that segment became crowded with look-alike models from Honda, Mazda, and Nissan, competition drove down profit margins. To improve its margins, Toyota then developed more sophisticated cars targeted at higher tiers. The process of developing cars like the Camry and the Lexus added costs to Toyota's operation. It subsequently decided to exit the lower end of the market; the margins had become unacceptable because the company's cost structure, and consequently its values, had changed.

In a departure from that pattern, Toyota recently introduced the Echo model, hoping to rejoin the entry-level tier with a $10,000 car. It is one thing for Toyota's senior management to decide to launch this new model. It's another for the many people in the Toyota system—including its dealers—to agree that selling more cars at lower margins is a better way to boost profits and equity values than selling more Camrys, Avalons, and Lexuses. Only time will tell whether Toyota can manage this down-market move. To be successful with the Echo, Toyota's management will have to swim against a very strong current—the current of its own corporate values.

The second value relates to how big a business opportunity has to be before it can be interesting. Because a company's stock price represents the discounted present value of its projected earnings stream, most managers feel compelled not just to maintain growth but to maintain a constant rate of growth. For a $40 million company

to grow 25%, for instance, it needs to find $10 million in new business the next year. But a $40 billion company needs to find $10 billion in new business the next year to grow at that same rate. It follows that an opportunity that excites a small company isn't big enough to be interesting to a large company. One of the bittersweet results of success, in fact, is that as companies become large, they lose the ability to enter small, emerging markets. This disability is not caused by a change in the resources within the companies—their resources typically are vast. Rather, it's caused by an evolution in values.

The problem is magnified when companies suddenly become much bigger through mergers or acquisitions. Executives and Wall Street financiers who engineer megamergers between already-huge pharmaceutical companies, for example, need to take this effect into account. Although their merged research organizations might have more resources to throw at new product development, their commercial organizations will probably have lost their appetites for all but the biggest blockbuster drugs. This constitutes a very real disability in managing innovation. The same problem crops up in high-tech industries as well. In many ways, Hewlett-Packard's recent decision to split itself into two companies is rooted in its recognition of this problem.

THE MIGRATION OF CAPABILITIES

In the start-up stages of an organization, much of what gets done is attributable to resources—people, in particular. The addition or departure of a few key people can profoundly influence its success. Over time, however, the locus of the organization's capabilities shifts toward its processes and values. As people address recurrent tasks, processes become defined. And as the business model takes shape and it becomes clear which types of business need to be accorded highest priority, values coalesce. In fact, one reason that many soaring young companies flame out after an IPO based on a single hot product is that their initial success is grounded in resources—often the founding engineers—and they fail to develop processes that can create a sequence of hot products.

Avid Technology, a producer of digital-editing systems for television, is an apt case in point. Avid's well-received technology removed tedium from the video-editing process. On the back of its star product, Avid's stock rose from $16 a share at its 1993 IPO to $49 in mid-1995. However, the strains of being a one-trick pony soon emerged as Avid faced a saturated market, rising inventories and receivables, increased competition, and shareholder lawsuits. Customers loved the product, but Avid's lack of effective processes for consistently developing new products and for controlling quality, delivery, and service ultimately tripped the company and sent its stock back down.

By contrast, at highly successful firms such as McKinsey & Company, the processes and values have become so powerful that it almost doesn't matter which people get assigned to which project teams. Hundreds of MBAs join the firm every year, and almost as many leave. But the company is able to crank out high-quality work year after year because its core capabilities are rooted in its processes and values rather than in its resources.

When a company's processes and values are being formed in its early and middle years, the founder typically has a profound impact. The founder usually has strong opinions about how employees should do their work and what the organization's priorities need to be. If the founder's judgments are flawed, of course, the company will likely fail. But if they're sound, employees will experience for themselves the validity of the founder's problem-solving and decision-making methods. Thus processes become defined. Likewise, if the company becomes financially successful by allocating resources according to criteria that reflect the founder's priorities, the company's values coalesce around those criteria.

As successful companies mature, employees gradually come to assume that the processes and priorities they've used so successfully so often are the right way to do their work. Once that happens and employees begin to follow processes and decide priorities by assumption rather than by conscious choice, those processes and values come to constitute the organization's culture.[2] As companies grow from a few employees to hundreds and thousands of them, the challenge of getting all employees to agree on what needs to be done and how can be daunting for even the best managers. Culture is a powerful management tool in those situations. It enables employees to act autonomously but causes them to act consistently.

Hence, the factors that define an organization's capabilities and disabilities evolve over time—they start in resources; then move to visible, articulated processes and values; and migrate finally to culture. As long as the or-

ganization continues to face the same sorts of problems that its processes and values were designed to address, managing the organization can be straightforward. But because those factors also define what an organization cannot do, they constitute disabilities when the problems facing the company change fundamentally. When the organization's capabilities reside primarily in its people, changing capabilities to address the new problems is relatively simple. But when the capabilities have come to reside in processes and values, and especially when they have become embedded in culture, change can be extraordinarily difficult. (See the sidebar "Digital's Dilemma.")

SUSTAINING VERSUS DISRUPTIVE INNOVATION

Successful companies, no matter what the source of their capabilities, are pretty good at responding to evolutionary changes in their markets—what in *The Innovator's Dilemma* (Harvard Business School, 1997), Clayton Christensen referred to as *sustaining innovation*. Where they run into trouble is in handling or initiating revolutionary changes in their markets, or dealing with *disruptive innovation*.

Sustaining technologies are innovations that make a product or service perform better in ways that customers in the mainstream market already value. Compaq's early adoption of Intel's 32-bit 386 microprocessor instead of the 16-bit 286 chip was a sustaining innovation. So was Merrill Lynch's introduction of its Cash Management Account, which allowed customers to write checks against their equity accounts. Those were breakthrough innovations that sustained the best customers of these companies by providing something better than had previously been available.

Disruptive innovations create an entirely new market through the introduction of a new kind of product or service, one that's actually worse, initially, as judged by the performance metrics that mainstream customers value. Charles Schwab's initial entry as a bare-bones discount broker was a disruptive innovation relative to the offerings of full-service brokers like Merrill Lynch. Merrill Lynch's best customers wanted more than Schwab-like services. Early personal computers were a disruptive innovation relative to mainframes and minicomputers. PCs were not powerful enough to run the computing applications that existed at the time they were introduced. These innovations were disruptive in that they didn't address the next-generation needs of leading customers in existing markets. They had other attributes, of course, that en-

---

[2]Our description of the development of an organization's culture draws heavily from Edgar Schein's research, as first laid out in his book *Organizational Culture and Leadership* (Jossey-Bass Publishers, 1985).

Digital's Dilemma

A lot of business thinkers have analyzed Digital Equipment Corporation's abrupt fall from grace. Most have concluded that Digital simply read the market very badly. But if we look at the company's fate through the lens of our framework, a different picture emerges.

Digital was a spectacularly successful maker of minicomputers from the 1960s through the 1980s. One might have been tempted to assert, when personal computers first appeared in the market around 1980, that Digital's core capability was in building computers. But if that were the case, why did the company stumble?

Clearly, Digital had the resources to succeed in personal computers. Its engineers routinely designed computers that were far more sophisticated than PCs. The company had plenty of cash, a great brand, good technology, and so on. But it did not have the processes to succeed in the personal computer business. Minicomputer companies designed most of the key components of their computers internally and then integrated those components into proprietary configurations. Designing a new product platform took two to three years. Digital manufactured most of its own components and assembled them in a batch mode. It sold directly to corporate engineering organizations. Those processes worked extremely well in the minicomputer business.

PC makers, by contrast, outsourced most components from the best suppliers around the globe. New computer designs, made up of modular componets, had to be completed in six to 12 months. The computers were manufactured in high-volume assembly lines and sold through retailers to consumers and businesses. None of these processes existed within Digital. In other words, although the people working at the company had the ability to design, build, and sell personal computers profitably, they were working in an organization that was incapable of doing so because its processes had been designed and had evolved to do other tasks well.

Similarly, because of its overhead costs, Digital had to adopt a set of values that dictated, "If it generates 50% gross margins or more, it's good business. If it generates less than 40% margins, it's not worth doing." Management had to ensure that all employees gave priority to projects according to these criteria or the company couldn't make money. Because PCs generated lower margins, they did not fit with Digital's values. The company's criteria for setting priorities always placed higher-performance minicomputers ahead of personal computers in the resource-allocation process.

Digital could have created a different organization that would have honed the different processes and values required to succeed in PCs—as IBM did. But Digital's mainstream organization simply was incapable of succeeding at the job.

---

abled new market applications to emerge—and the disruptive innovations improved so rapidly that they ultimately could address the needs of customers in the mainstream of the market as well.

Sustaining innovations are nearly always developed and introduced by established industry leaders. But those same companies never introduce—or cope well with—disruptive innovations. Why? Our resources-processes-values framework holds the answer. Industry leaders are organized to develop and introduce sustaining technologies. Month after month, year after year, they launch new and improved products to gain an edge over the competition. They do so by developing processes for evaluating the technological potential of sustaining innovations and for assessing their customers' needs for alternatives. Investment in sustaining technology also fits in with the values of leading companies in that they promise higher margins from better products sold to leading-edge customers.

Disruptive innovations occur so intermittently that no company has a routine process for handling them. Furthermore, because disruptive products nearly always promise lower profit margins per unit sold and are not attractive to the company's best customers, they're inconsistent with the established company's values. Merrill Lynch had the resources—the people, money, and technology—required to succeed at the sustaining innovations (Cash Management Account) and the disruptive innovations (bare-bones discount brokering) that it has confronted in recent history. But its processes and values supported only the sustaining innovation: they became disabilities when the company needed to understand and confront the discount and on-line brokerage businesses.

The reason, therefore, that large companies often surrender emerging growth markets is that smaller, disruptive companies are actually more capable of pursuing them. Start-ups lack resources, but that doesn't matter. Their values can embrace small markets, and their cost structures can accommodate low margins. Their market research and resource allocation processes allow managers to proceed intuitively; every decision need not be backed by careful research and analysis. All these advantages add up to the ability to embrace and even initiate disruptive change. But how can a large company develop those capabilities?

CREATING CAPABILITIES TO COPE WITH CHANGE

Despite beliefs spawned by popular change-management and reengineering programs, processes are not nearly as flexible or adaptable as resources are—and values are even less so. So whether addressing sustaining or disruptive innovations, when an organization needs new processes and values—because it needs new capabilities—managers must create a new organizational space where those capabilities can be developed. There are three possible ways to do that. Managers can

- create new organizational structures within corporate boundaries in which new processes can be developed,
- spin out an independent organization from the existing organization and develop within it the new processes and values required to solve the new problem,
- acquire a different organization whose processes and values closely match the requirements of the new task.

Creating New Capabilities Internally

When a company's capabilities reside in its processes, and when new challenges require new processes—that is, when they require different people or groups in a company to interact differently and at a different pace than they habitually have done—managers need to pull the relevant people out of the existing organization and draw a new boundary around a new group. Often, organizational boundaries were first drawn to facilitate the operation of existing processes, and they impede the creation of new processes. New team boundaries facilitate new patterns of working together that ultimately can coalesce as new processes. In *Revolutionizing Product Development* (The Free Press, 1992), Steven Wheelwright and Kim Clark referred to these structures as "heavyweight teams."

These teams are entirely dedicated to the new challenge, team members are physically located together, and each member is charged with assuming personal responsibility for the success of the entire project. At Chrysler, for example, the boundaries of the groups within its product development organization historically had been defined by components—power train, electrical systems, and so on. But to accelerate auto development, Chrysler needed to focus not on components but on automobile platforms—the minivan, small car, Jeep, and

truck, for example—so it created heavyweight teams. Although these organizational units aren't as good at focusing on component design, they facilitated the definition of new processes that were much faster and more efficient in integrating various subsystems into new car designs. Companies as diverse as Medtronic for its cardiac pacemakers, IBM for its disk drives, and Eli Lilly for its new blockbuster drug Zyprexa have used heavyweight teams as vehicles for creating new processes so they could develop better products faster.

Creating Capabilities Through a Spinout Organization

When the mainstream organization's values would render it incapable of allocating resources to an innovation project, the company should spin it out as a new venture. Large organizations cannot be expected to allocate the critical financial and human resources needed to build a strong position in small, emerging markets. And it is very difficult for a company whose cost structure is tailored to compete in high-end markets to be profitable in low-end markets as well. Spinouts are very much in vogue among managers in old-line companies struggling with the question of how to address the Internet. But that's not always appropriate. When a disruptive innovation requires a different cost structure in order to be profitable and competitive, or when the current size of the opportunity is insignificant relative to the growth needs of the mainstream organization, then—and only then—is a spinout organization required.

Hewlett-Packard's laser-printer division in Boise, Idaho, was hugely successful, enjoying high margins and a reputation for superior product quality. Unfortunately, its ink-jet project, which represented a disruptive innovation, languished inside the mainstream HP printer business. Although the processes for developing the two types of printers were basically the same, there was a difference in values. To thrive in the ink-jet market, HP needed to be comfortable with lower gross margins and a smaller market than its laser printers commanded, and it needed to be willing to embrace relatively lower performance standards. It was not until HP's managers decided to transfer the unit to a separate division in Vancouver, British Columbia, with the goal of competing head-to-head with its own laser business, that the ink-jet business finally became successful.

How separate does such an effort need to be? A new physical location isn't always necessary. The primary requirement is that the project not be forced to compete for resources with projects in the mainstream organization.

As we have seen, projects that are inconsistent with a company's mainstream values will naturally be accorded lowest priority. Whether the independent organization is physically separate is less important than its independence from the normal decision-making criteria in the resource allocation process. The sidebar "Fitting the Tool to the Task" goes into more detail about what kind of innovation challenge is best met by which organizational structure.

Manager think that developing a new operation necessarily means abandoning the old one, and they're loathe to do that since it works perfectly well for what it was designed to do. But when disruptive change appears on the horizon, managers need to assemble the capabilities to confront that change before it affects the mainstream business. They actually need to run two businesses in tandem—one whose processes are tuned to the existing business model and another that is geared toward the new model. Merrill Lynch, for example, has accomplished an impressive global expansion of its institutional financial services through careful execution of its existing planning, acquisition, and partnership processes. Now, however, faced with the on-line world, the company is required to plan, acquire, and form partnerships more rapidly. Does that mean Merrill Lynch should change the processes that have worked so well in its traditional investment-banking business? Doing so would be disastrous, if we consider the question through the lens of our framework. Instead, Merrill should retain the old processes when working with the existing business (there are probably a few billion dollars still to be made under the old business model!) and create additional processes to deal with the new class of problems.

One word of warning: in our studies of this challenge, we have never seen a company succeed in addressing a change that disrupts its mainstream values without the personal, attentive oversight of the CEO—precisely because of the power of values in shaping the normal resource allocation process. Only the CEO can ensure that the new organization gets the required resources and is free to create processes and values that are appropriate to the new challenge. CEOs who view spinouts as a tool to get disruptive threats off their personal agendas are almost certain to meet with failure. We have seen no exceptions to this rule.

Creating Capabilities Through Acquisitions

Just as innovating managers need to make separate assessments of the capabilities and disabilities that reside in their company's resources, processes, and values, so must they do the same with acquisitions when seeking to buy capabilities. Companies that successfully gain new capabilities through acquisitions are those that know where those capabilities reside in the acquisition and assimilate them accordingly. Acquiring managers begin by asking, "What created the value that I just paid so dearly for? Did I justify the price because of the acquisition's resources? Or was a substantial portion of its worth created by processes and values?"

If the capabilities being purchased are embedded in an acquired company's processes and values, then the last thing the acquiring manager should do is integrate the acquisition into the parent organization. Integration will vaporize the processes and values of the acquired firm. Once the acquisition's managers are forced to adopt the buyer's way of doing business, its capabilities will disappear. A better strategy is to let the business stand alone and to infuse the parent's resources into the acquired company's processes and values. This approach truly constitutes the acquisition of new capabilities.

If, however, the acquired company's resources were the reason for its success and the primary rationale for the acquisition, then integrating it into the parent can make a lot of sense. Essentially, that means plugging the acquired people, products, technology, and customers into the parent's processes as a way of leveraging the parent's existing capabilities.

The perils of the ongoing DaimlerChrysler merger can be better understood in this light. Chrysler had few resources that could be considered unique. Its recent success in the market was rooted in its processes—particularly in its processes for designing products and integrating the efforts of its subsystem suppliers. What is the best way for Daimler to leverage Chrysler's capabilities? Wall Street is pressuring management to consolidate the two organizations to cut costs. But if the two companies are integrated, the very processes that made Chrysler such an attractive acquisition will likely be compromised.

The situation is reminiscent of IBM's 1984 acquisition of the telecommunications company Rolm. There wasn't anything in Rolm's pool of resources that IBM didn't already have. Rather, it was Rolm's processes for developing and finding new markets for PBX products that mattered. Initially, IBM recognized the value in preserving the informal and unconventional culture of the Rolm organization, which stood in stark contrast to IBM's methodical style. However, in 1987 IBM terminated Rolm's subsidiary status and decided to fully integrate the company into its own corporate structure. IBM's managers soon learned the folly of that decision.

Fitting the Tool to the Task

Suppose that an organization needs to react to or initiate an innovation. The matrix illustrated below can help managers understand what kind of team should work on the project and what organizational structure that team needs to work within. The vertical axis asks the manager to measure the extent to which the organization's existing processes are suited to getting the new job done effectively. The horizontal axis asks managers to assess whether the organization's values will permit the company to allocate the resources the new initiative needs.

In region A, the project is a good fit with the company's processes and values, so no new capabilities are called for. A functional or a lightweight team can tackle the project within the existing organizational structure. A functional team works on function-specific issues, then passes the project on to the next function. A lightweight team is cross-functional, but team members stay under the control of their respective functional managers.

In region B, the project is a good fit with the company's values but not with its processes. It presents the organization with new types of problems and therefore requires new types of interactions and coordination among groups and individuals. The team, like the team in region A, is working on a sustaining rather than a disruptive innovation. In this case, a heavy-weight team is a good bet, but the project can be executed within the mainstream company. A heavyweight team—whose members work solely on the project and are expected to behave like general managers, shouldering responsibility for the project's success—is designed so that new processes and new ways of working together can emerge.

In region C, the manager faces a disruptive change that doesn't fit the organization's existing processes or values. To ensure success, the manager should create a spinout organization and commission a heavyweight development team to tackle the challenge. The spinout will allow the project to be governed by different values—a different cost structure, for example, with lower profit margins. The heavyweight team (as in region B) will ensure that new processes can emerge.

Similarly, in region D, when a manager faces a disruptive change that fits the organization's current processes but doesn't fit its values, the key to success almost always lies in commissioning a heavyweight development team to work in a spinout. Development may occasionally happen successfully in-house, but successful commercialization will require a spinout.

Unfortunately, most companies employ a one-size-fits-all organizing strategy, using lightweight or functional teams for programs of every size and character. But such teams are tools for exploiting established capabilities. And among those few companies that have accepted the heavyweight gospel, many have attempted to organize *all* of their development teams in a heavyweight fashion. Ideally, each company should tailor the team structure and organizational location to the process and values required by each project.

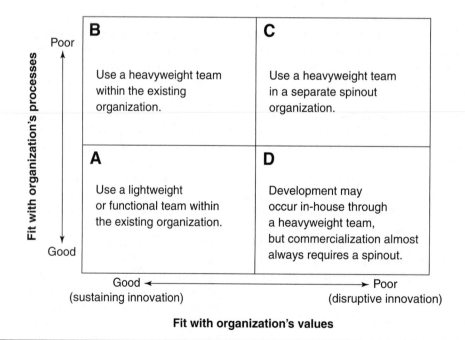

When they tried to push Rolm's resources—its products and its customers—through the processes that had been honed in the large-computer business, the Rolm business stumbled badly. And it was impossible for a computer company whose values had been whetted on profit margins of 18% to get excited about products with much lower profit margins. IBM's integration of Rolm destroyed the very source of the deal's original worth. DaimlerChrysler, bowing to the investment community's drumbeat for efficiency savings, now stands on the edge of the same precipice. Often, it seems, financial analysts have a better intuition about the value of resources than they do about the value of processes.

By contrast, Cisco Systems' acquisitions process has worked well because, we would argue, it has kept resources, processes, and values in the right perspective. Between 1993 and 1997, it primarily acquired small companies that were less than two years old, early-stage organizations whose market value was built primarily upon their resources, particularly their engineers and products. Cisco plugged those resources into its own effective development, logistics, manufacturing, and marketing processes and threw away whatever nascent processes and values came with the acquisitions because those weren't what it had paid for. On a couple of occasions when the company acquired a larger, more mature organization—notably its 1996 acquisition of Strata-Com—Cisco did not integrate. Rather, it let StrataCom stand alone and infused Cisco's substantial resources into StrataCom's organization to help it grow more rapidly.[3]

Managers whose organizations are confronting change must first determine whether they have the resources required to succeed. They then need to ask a separate question: Does the organization have the processes and values it needs to succeed in this new situation? Asking this second question is not as instinctive for most managers because the processes by which work is done and the values by which employees make their decisions have served them well in the past. What we hope this framework introduces into managers' thinking is the idea that the very capabilities that make their organizations effective also define their disabilities. In that regard, a little time spent soul-searching for honest answers to the following questions will pay off handsomely: Are the processes by which work habitually gets done in the organization appropriate for this new problem? And will the values of the organization cause this initiative to get high priority or to languish?

If the answers to those questions are no, it's okay. Understanding a problem is the most crucial step in solving it. Wishful thinking about these issues can set teams that need to innovate on a course fraught with roadblocks, second-guessing, and frustration. The reason that innovation often seems to be so difficult for established companies is that they employ highly capable people and then set them to work within organizational structures whose processes and values weren't designed for the task at hand. Ensuring that capable people are ensconced in capable organizations is a major responsibility of management in a transformational age such as ours.

---

[3] See Charles A. Holloway, Stephen C. Wheelwright, and Nicole Tempest, "Cisco Systems, Inc.: Post-Acquisition Manufacturing Integration," a case published jointly by the Stanford and Harvard business schools, 1998.

STRATEGIC ACTION

READING II-15

Strategic Intent

Gary Hamel and C. K. Prahalad

Today managers in many industries are working hard to match the competitive advantages of their new global rivals. They are moving manufacturing offshore in search of lower labor costs, rationalizing product lines to capture global scale economies, instituting quality circles and just-in-time production, and adopting Japanese human resource practices. When competitiveness still seems out of reach, they form strategic alliances—often with the very companies that upset the competitive balance in the first place.

Important as these initiatives are, few of them go beyond mere imitation. Too many companies are expending enormous energy simply to reproduce the cost and quality advantages their global competitors already enjoy. Imitation may be the sincerest form of flattery, but it will not lead to competitive revitalization. Strategies based on imitation are transparent to competitors who have already mastered them. Moreover, successful competitors rarely stand still. So it is not surprising that many executives feel trapped in a seemingly endless game of catch-up—regularly surprised by the new accomplishments of their rivals.

Source: Reprinted from *Harvard Business Review,* May–June 1989, pp. 63–76.

For these executives and their companies, regaining competitiveness will mean rethinking many of the basic concepts of strategy.[1] As "strategy" has blossomed, the competitiveness of Western companies has withered. This may be coincidence, but we think not. We believe that the application of concepts such as "strategic fit" (between resources and opportunities), "generic strategies" (low cost versus differentiation versus focus), and the "strategy hierarchy" (goals, strategies, and tactics) has often abetted the process of competitiveness decline. The new global competitors approach strategy from a perspective that is fundamentally different from that which underpins Western management thought. Against such competitors, marginal adjustments to current orthodoxies are no more likely to produce competitive revitalization than are marginal improvements in operating efficiency. (The box insert "Remaking Strategy" describes our research and summarizes the two contrasting approaches to strategy we see in large, multinational companies.)

Few Western companies have an enviable track record anticipating the moves of new global competitors. Why? The explanation begins with the way most companies have approached competitor analysis. Typically, competitor analysis focuses on the existing resources

[1] Among the first to apply the concept of strategy to management were H. Igor Ansoff in *Corporate Strategy: An Analytic Approach to Business Policy for Growth and Expansion* (New York: McGraw-Hill, 1965), and Kenneth R. Andrews in *The Concept of Corporate Strategy* (Homewood, IL: Dow Jones-Irwin, 1971).

(human, technical, and financial) of present competitors. The only companies seen as a threat are those with the resources to erode margins and market share in the next planning period. Resourcefulness, the pace at which new competitive advantages are being built, rarely enters in.

In this respect, traditional competitor analysis is like a snapshot of a moving car. By itself, the photograph yields little information about the car's speed or direction—whether the driver is out for a quiet Sunday drive or warming up for the Grand Prix. Yet many managers have learned through painful experience that a business's initial resource endowment (whether bountiful or meager) is an unreliable predictor of future global success.

Think back. In 1970, few Japanese companies possessed the resource base, manufacturing volume, or tech-

nical prowess of U.S. and European industry leaders. Komatsu was less than 35 percent as large as Caterpillar (measured by sales), was scarcely represented outside Japan, and relied on just one product line—small bulldozers—for most of its revenue. Honda was smaller than American Motors and had not yet begun to export cars to the United States. Canon's first halting steps in the reprographics business looked pitifully small compared with the $4 billion Xerox powerhouse.

If Western managers had extended their competitor analysis to include these companies, it would merely have underlined how dramatic the resource discrepancies between them were. Yet by 1985, Komatsu was a $2.8 billion company with a product scope encompassing a broad range of earth-moving equipment, industrial robots, and semiconductors. Honda manufactured almost

Remaking Strategy

Over the last 10 years, our research on global competition, international alliances, and multinational management has brought us into close contact with senior managers in America, Europe, and Japan. As we tried to unravel the reasons for success and surrender in global markets, we became more and more suspicious that executives in Western and Far Eastern companies often operated with very different conceptions of competitive strategy. Understanding these differences, we thought, might help explain the conduct and outcome of competitive battles as well as supplement traditional explanations for Japan's ascendance and the West's decline.

We began by mapping the implicit strategy models of managers who had participated in our research. Then we built detailed histories of selected competitive battles. We searched for evidence of divergent views of strategy, competitive advantage, and the role of top management.

Two contrasting models of strategy emerged. One, which most Western managers will recognize, centers on the problem of maintaining strategic fit. The other centers on the problems of leveraging resources. The two are not mutually exclusive, but they represent a significant difference in emphasis—an emphasis that deeply affects how competitive battles get played out over time.

Both models recognize the problem of competing in a hostile environment with limited resources. But while the emphasis in the first is on trimming ambitions to match available resources, the emphasis in the second is on leveraging resources to reach seemingly unattainable goals.

Both models recognize that relative competitive advantage determines relative profitability. The first emphasizes the search for advantages that are inherently sustainable; the second emphasizes the need to accelerate organizational learning to outpace competitors in building new advantages.

Both models recognize the difficulty of competing against larger competitors. But while the first leads to a search for

niches (or simply dissuades the company from challenging an entrenched competitor), the second produces a quest for new rules that can devalue the incumbent's advantages.

Both models recognize that balance in the scope of an organization's activities reduces risk. The first seeks to reduce financial risk by building a balanced portfolio of cash-generating and cash-consuming businesses. The second seeks to reduce competitive risk by ensuring a well-balanced and sufficiently broad portfolio of advantages.

Both models recognize the need to disaggregate the organization in a way that allows top management to differentiate among the investment needs of various planning units. In the first model, resources are allocated to product-market units in which relatedness is defined by common products, channels, and customers. Each business is assumed to own all the critical skills it needs to execute its strategy successfully. In the second, investments are made in core competences (microprocessor controls or electronic imaging, for example) as well as in product-market units. By tracking these investments across businesses, top management works to assure that the plans of individual strategic units don't undermine future developments by default.

Both models recognize the need for consistency in action across organizational levels. In the first, consistency between corporate and business levels is largely a matter of conforming to financial objectives. Consistency between business and functional levels comes by tightly restricting the means the business uses to achieve its strategy—establishing standard operating procedures, defining the served market, adhering to accepted industry practices. In the second model, business-corporate consistency comes from allegiance to a particular strategic intent. Business-functional consistency comes from allegiance to intermediate-term goals, or challenges, with lower level employees encouraged to invent how those goals will be achieved.

as many cars worldwide in 1987 as Chrysler. Canon had matched Xerox's global unit market share.

The lesson is clear: assessing the current tactical advantages of known competitors will not help you understand the resolution, stamina, and inventiveness of potential competitors. Sun-tzu, a Chinese military strategist, made the point 3,000 years ago: "All men can see the tactics whereby I conquer," he wrote, "but what none can see is the strategy out of which great victory is evolved."

Companies that have risen to global leadership over the past 20 years invariably began with ambitions that were out of all proportion to their resources and capabilities. But they created an obsession with winning at all levels of the organization and then sustained that obsession over the 10- to 20-year quest for global leadership. We term this obsession *strategic intent.*

On the one hand, strategic intent envisions a desired leadership position and establishes the criterion the organization will use to chart its progress. Komatsu set out to "Encircle Caterpillar." Canon sought to "Beat Xerox." Honda strove to become a second Ford—an automotive pioneer. All are expressions of strategic intent.

At the same time, strategic intent is more than simply unfettered ambition. (Many companies possess an ambitious strategic intent yet fall short of their goals.) The concept also encompasses an active management process that includes focusing the organization's attention on the essence of winning, motivating people by communicating the value of the target, leaving room for individual and team contributions, sustaining enthusiasm by providing new operational definitions as circumstances change, and using intent consistently to guide resource allocations.

Strategic intent captures the essence of winning. The Apollo program—landing a man on the moon ahead of the Soviets—was as competitively focused as Komatsu's drive against Caterpillar. The space program became the scorecard for America's technology race with the USSR. In the turbulent information technology industry, it was hard to pick a single competitor as a target, so NEC's strategic intent, set in the early 1970s, was to acquire the technologies that would put it in the best position to exploit the convergence of computing and telecommunications. Other industry observers foresaw this convergence, but only NEC made convergence the guiding theme for subsequent strategic decisions by adopting "computing and communications" as its intent. For Coca-Cola, strategic intent has been to put a Coke within "arm's reach" of every consumer in the world.

Strategic intent is stable over time. In battles for global leadership, one of the most critical tasks is to lengthen the organization's attention span. Strategic intent provides consistency to short-term action, while leaving room for reinterpretation as new opportunities emerge. At Komatsu, encircling Caterpillar encompassed a succession of medium-term programs aimed at exploiting specific weaknesses in Caterpillar or building particular competitive advantages. When Caterpillar threatened Komatsu in Japan, for example, Komatsu responded by first improving quality, then driving down costs, then cultivating export markets, and then underwriting new product development.

Strategic intent sets a target that deserves personal effort and commitment. Ask the chairmen of many American corporations how they measure their contributions to their companies' success and you're likely to get an answer expressed in terms of shareholder wealth. In a company that possesses a strategic intent, top management is more likely to talk in terms of global market leadership. Market share leadership typically yields shareholder wealth, to be sure. But the two goals do not have the same motivational impact. It is hard to imagine middle managers, let alone blue-collar employees, waking up each day with the sole thought of creating more shareholder wealth. But mightn't they feel different given the challenge to "Beat Benz"—the rallying cry at one Japanese auto producer? Strategic intent gives employees the only goal that is worthy of commitment: to unseat the best or remain the best, worldwide.

Many companies are more familiar with strategic planning than they are with strategic intent. The planning process typically acts as a "feasibility sieve." Strategies are accepted or rejected on the basis of whether managers can be precise about the how as well as the what of their plans. Are the milestones clear? Do we have the necessary skills and resources? How will competitors react? Has the market been thoroughly researched? In one form or another, the admonition "Be realistic!" is given to line managers at almost every turn.

But can you *plan* for global leadership? Did Komatsu, Canon, and Honda have detailed, 20-year "strategies" for attacking Western markets? Are Japanese and Korean managers better planners than their Western counterparts? No. As valuable as strategic planning is, global leadership is an objective that lies outside the range of planning. We know of few companies with highly developed planning systems that have managed to set a strategic intent. As tests of strategic fit become more stringent, goals that cannot be planned for fall by the wayside. Yet companies that are afraid to commit to goals that lie outside the range of planning are unlikely to become global leaders.

Although strategic planning is billed as a way of becoming more future oriented, most managers, when pressed, will admit that their strategic plans reveal more about today's problems than tomorrow's opportunities. With a fresh set of problems confronting managers at the beginning of every planning cycle, focus often shifts dramatically from year to year. And with the pace of change accelerating in most industries, the predictive horizon is becoming shorter and shorter. So plans do little more than project the present forward incrementally. The goal of strategic intent is to fold the future back into the present. The important question is not, "How will next year be different from this year?" but, "What must we do differently next year to get closer to our strategic intent?" Only with a carefully articulated and adhered to strategic intent will a succession of year-on-year plans sum up to global leadership.

Just as you cannot plan a 10- to 20-year quest for global leadership, the chance of falling into a leadership position by accident is also remote. We don't believe that global leadership comes from an undirected process of intrapreneurship. Nor is it the product of a skunk works or other techniques for internal venturing. Behind such programs lies a nihilistic assumption: the organization is so hidebound, so orthodox ridden that the only way to innovate is to put a few bright people in a dark room, pour in some money, and hope that something wonderful will happen. In this "Silicon Valley" approach to innovation, the only role for top managers is to retrofit their corporate strategy to the entrepreneurial successes that emerge from below. Here the value added of top management is low indeed.

Sadly, this view of innovation may be consistent with the reality in many large companies.[2] On the one hand, top management lacks any particular point of view about desirable ends beyond satisfying shareholders and keeping raiders at bay. On the other, the planning format, reward criteria, definition of served market, and belief in accepted industry practice all work together to tightly constrain the range of available means. As a result, innovation is necessarily an isolated activity. Growth depends more on the inventive capacity of individuals and small

teams than on the ability of top management to aggregate the efforts of multiple teams towards an ambitious strategic intent.

In companies that overcame resource constraints to build leadership positions, we see a different relationship between means and ends. While strategic intent is clear about ends, it is flexible as to means—it leaves room for improvisation. Achieving strategic intent requires enormous creativity with respect to means: witness Fujitsu's use of strategic alliances in Europe to attack IBM. But this creativity comes in the service of a clearly prescribed end. Creativity is unbridled, but not uncorralled, because top management establishes the criterion against which employees can pretest the logic of their initiatives. Middle managers must do more than deliver on promised financial targets; they must also deliver on the broad direction implicit in their organization's strategic intent.

Strategic intent implies a sizable stretch for an organization. Current capabilities and resources will not suffice. This forces the organization to be more inventive, to make the most of limited resources. Whereas the traditional view of strategy focuses on the degree of fit between existing resources and current opportunities, strategic intent creates an extreme misfit between resources and ambitions. Top management then challenges the organization to close the gap by systematically building new advantages. For Canon this meant first understanding Xerox's patents, then licensing technology to create a product that would yield early market experience, then gearing up internal R&D efforts, then licensing its own technology to other manufacturers to fund further R&D, then entering market segments in Japan and Europe where Xerox was weak, and so on.

In this respect, strategic intent is like a marathon run in 400-meter sprints. No one knows what the terrain will look like at mile 26, so the role of top management is to focus the organization's attention on the ground to be covered in the next 400 meters. In several companies, management did this by presenting the organization with a series of corporate challenges, each specifying the next hill in the race to achieve strategic intent. One year the challenge might be quality; the next, total customer care; the next, entry into new markets; the next, a rejuvenated product line. As this example indicates, corporate challenges are a way to stage the acquisition of new competitive advantages, a way to identify the focal point for employees' efforts in the near to medium term. As with strategic intent, top management is specific about the ends—reducing product development times by

[2]Robert A. Burgelman, "A Process Model of Internal Corporate Venturing in the Diversified Major Firm," *Administrative Science Quarterly,* June 1983.

75 percent, for example—but less prescriptive about the means.

Like strategic intent, challenges stretch the organization. To preempt Xerox in the personal copier business, Canon set its engineers a target price of $1,000 for a home copier. At the time, Canon's least expensive copier sold for several thousand dollars. Trying to reduce the cost of existing models would not have given Canon the radical price performance improvement it needed to delay or deter Xerox's entry into personal copiers. Instead, Canon engineers were challenged to reinvent the copier—a challenge they met by substituting a disposable cartridge for the complex image-transfer mechanism used in other copiers.

Corporate challenges come from analyzing competitors as well as from the foreseeable pattern of industry evolution. Together these reveal potential competitive openings and identify the new skills the organization will need to take the initiative away from better positioned players. Exhibit 1, "Building Competitive Advan-

tage at Komatsu," illustrates the way challenges helped that company achieve its intent.

For a challenge to be effective, individuals and teams throughout the organization must understand it and see its implications for their own jobs. Companies that set corporate challenges to create new competitive advantages (as Ford and IBM did with quality improvement) quickly discover that engaging the entire organization requires top management to:

- *Create a sense of urgency,* or quasi crisis, by amplifying weak signals in the environment that point up the need to improve, instead of allowing inaction to precipitate a real crisis. Komatsu, for example, budgeted on the basis of worst case exchange rates that overvalued the yen.
- *Develop a competitor focus at every level through widespread use of competitive intelligence.* Every employee should be able to benchmark his or her efforts against best-in-class competitors so that the challenge

EXHIBIT 1 Building Competitive Advantage at Komatsu

Protect Komatsu's home market against Caterpillar	Reduce costs while maintaining quality	Make Komatsu an international enterprise and build export markets	Respond to external shocks that threaten markets	Create new products and markets
Early 1960s: Licensing deals with Cummins Engine, International Harvester, and Bucyrus-Erie to acquire technology and establish benchmarks	**1965:** C D (Cost Down) Program **1966:** Total C D program	**Early 1960s:** Develop Eastern bloc countries **1967:** Komatsu Europe marketing subsidiary established **1970:** Komatsu America established	**1976:** V-10 program to reduce costs by 10% while maintaining quality; reduce parts by 20%; rationalize manufacturing system **1977:** ¥ 180 program to budget company-wide for 180 yen to the dollar when exchange rate was 240	**Late 1970s:** Accelerate product development to expand line **1979:** Future and Frontiers program to identify new businesses based on society's needs and company's know-how
1961: Project A (for Ace) to advance the product quality of Komatsu's small-and medium-sized bulldozers above Caterpillar's		**1972:** Project B to improve the durability and reliability and to reduce costs of large bulldozers **1972:** Project C to improve payloaders	**1979:** Project E to establish teams to redouble cost and quality efforts in response to oil crisis	**1981:** EPOCHS program to reconcile greater product variety with improved production efficiencies
1962: Quality Circles companywide to provide training for all employees		**1972:** Project D to improve hydraulic excavators **1974:** Established pre-sales and service department to assist newly industrializing countries in construction projects		

becomes personal. For example, Ford showed production-line workers videotapes of operations at Mazda's most efficient plant.

- *Provide employees with the skills they need to work effectively*—training in statistical tools, problem solving, value engineering, and team building, for example.
- *Give the organization time to digest one challenge before launching another.* When competing initiatives overload the organization, middle managers often try to protect their people from the whipsaw of shifting priorities. But this "wait and see if they're serious this time" attitude ultimately destroys the credibility of corporate challenges.
- *Establish clear milestones and review mechanisms* to track progress and ensure that internal recognition and rewards reinforce desired behavior. The goal is to make the challenge inescapable for everyone in the company.

It is important to distinguish between the process of managing corporate challenges and the advantages that the process creates. Whatever the actual challenge may be—quality, cost, value engineering, or something else—there is the same need to engage employees intellectually and emotionally in the development of new skills. In each case, the challenge will take root only if senior executives and lower level employees feel a reciprocal responsibility for competitiveness.

We believe workers in many companies have been asked to take a disproportionate share of the blame for competitive failure. In one U.S. company, for example, management had sought a 40 percent wage-package concession from hourly employees to bring labor costs into line with Far Eastern competitors. The result was a long strike and, ultimately, a 10 percent wage concession from employees on the line. However, direct labor costs in manufacturing accounted for less than 15 percent of total value added. The company thus succeeded in demoralizing its entire blue-collar work force for the sake of a 1.5 percent reduction in total costs. Ironically, further analysis showed that their competitors' most significant cost savings came not from lower hourly wages but from better work methods invented by employees. You can imagine how eager the U.S. workers were to make similar contributions after the strike and concessions. Contrast this situation with what happened at Nissan when the yen strengthened: top management took a big pay cut and then asked middle managers and line employees to sacrifice relatively less.

Reciprocal responsibility means shared gain and shared pain. In too many companies, the pain of revitalization falls almost exclusively on the employees least responsible for the enterprise's decline. Too often, workers are asked to commit to corporate goals without any matching commitment from top management—be it employment security, gain sharing, or an ability to influence the direction of the business. This one-sided approach to regaining competitiveness keeps many companies from harnessing the intellectual horsepower of their employees.

Creating a sense of reciprocal responsibility is crucial because competitiveness ultimately depends on the pace at which a company embeds new advantages deep within its organization, not on its stock of advantages at any given time. Thus, we need to expand the concept of competitive advantage beyond the scorecard many managers now use: Are my costs lower? Will my product command a price premium?

Few competitive advantages are long lasting. Uncovering a new competitive advantage is a bit like getting a hot tip on a stock: the first person to act on the insight makes more money than the last. When the experience curve was young, a company that built capacity ahead of competitors, dropped prices to fill plants, and reduced costs as volume rose went to the bank. The first mover traded on the fact that competitors undervalued market share—they didn't price to capture additional share because they didn't understand how market share leadership could be translated into lower costs and better margins. But there is no more undervalued market share when each of 20 semiconductor companies builds enough capacity to serve 10 percent of the world market.

Keeping score of existing advantages is not the same as building new advantages. The essence of strategy lies in creating tomorrow's competitive advantages faster than competitors mimic the ones you possess today. In the 1960s, Japanese producers relied on labor and capital cost advantages. As Western manufacturers began to move production offshore, Japanese companies accelerated their investment in process technology and created scale and quality advantages. Then as their U.S. and European competitors rationalized manufacturing, they added another string to their bow by accelerating the rate of product development. Then they built global brands. Then they deskilled competitors through alliances and outsourcing deals. The moral? An organization's capacity to improve existing skills and learn new ones is the most defensible competitive advantage of all.

To achieve a strategic intent, a company must usually take on larger, better financed competitors. That means carefully managing competitive engagements so that scarce resources are conserved. Managers cannot do that simply by playing the same game better—making marginal improvements to competitors' technology and business practices. Instead, they must fundamentally change the game in ways that disadvantage incumbents—devising novel approaches to market entry, advantage building, and competitive warfare. For smart competitors, the goal is not competitive imitation but competitive innovation, the art of containing competitive risks within manageable proportions.

Four approaches to competitive innovation are evident in the global expansion of Japanese companies: building layers of advantage, searching for loose bricks, changing the terms of engagement, and competing through collaboration.

The wider a company's portfolio of advantages, the less risk it faces in competitive battles. New global competitors have built such portfolios by steadily expanding their arsenals of competitive weapons. They have moved inexorably from less defensible advantages such as low wage costs to more defensible advantages like global brands. The Japanese color television industry illustrates this layering process.

By 1967, Japan had become the largest producer of black-and-white television sets. By 1970, it was closing the gap in color televisions. Japanese manufacturers used their competitive advantage—at that time, primarily, low labor costs—to build a base in the private-label business, then moved quickly to establish world-scale plants. This investment gave them additional layers of advantage— quality and reliability—as well as further cost reductions from process improvements. At the same time, they recognized that these cost-based advantages were vulnerable to changes in labor costs, process and product technology, exchange rates, and trade policy. So throughout the 1970s, they also invested heavily in building channels and brands, thus creating another layer of advantage, a global franchise. In the late 1970s, they enlarged the scope of their products and businesses to amortize these grand investments, and by 1980 all the major players— Matsushita, Sharp, Toshiba, Hitachi, Sanyo—had established related sets of businesses that could support global marketing investments. More recently, they have been investing in regional manufacturing and design centers to tailor their products more closely to national markets.

These manufacturers thought of the various sources of competitive advantage as mutually desirable layers, not mutually exclusive choices. What some call competitive suicide—pursuing both cost and differentiation— is exactly what many competitors strive for.[3] Using flexible manufacturing technologies and better marketing intelligence, they are moving away from standardized "world products" to products like Mazda's mini-van, developed in California expressly for the U.S. market.

Another approach to competitive innovation— searching for loose bricks—exploits the benefits of surprise, which is just as useful in business battles as it is in war. Particularly in the early stages of a war for global markets, successful new competitors work to stay below the response threshold of their larger, more powerful rivals. Staking out underdefended territory is one way to do this.

To find loose bricks, managers must have few orthodoxies about how to break into a market or challenge a competitor. For example, in one large U.S. multinational, we asked several country managers to describe what a Japanese competitor was doing in the local market. The first executive said: "They're coming at us in the low end. Japanese companies always come in at the bottom." The second speaker found the comment interesting but disagreed: "They don't offer any low-end products in my market, but they have some exciting stuff at the top end. We really should reverse engineer that thing." Another colleague told still another story. "They haven't taken any business away from me," he said, "but they've just made me a great offer to supply components." In each country, their Japanese competitor had found a different loose brick.

The search for loose bricks begins with a careful analysis of the competitor's conventional wisdom: How does the company define its "served market"? What activities are most profitable? Which geographic markets are too troublesome to enter? The objective is not to find a corner of the industry (or niche) where larger competitors seldom tread but to build a base of attack just outside the market territory that industry leaders currently occupy. The goal is an uncontested profit sanctuary, which could be a particular product segment (the "low end" in motorcycles), a slice of the value chain (components in the computer industry), or a particular geographic market (Eastern Europe).

When Honda took on leaders in the motorcycle industry, for example, it began with products that were just

---

[3] For example, see M. E. Porter, *Competitive Strategy* (New York: Free Press, 1980).

outside the conventional definition of the leaders' product-market domains. As a result, it could build a base of operations in underdefended territory and then use that base to launch an expanded attack. What many competitors failed to see was Honda's strategic intent and its growing competence in engines and power trains. Yet even as Honda was selling 50cc motorcycles in the United States, it was already racing larger bikes in Europe—assembling the design skills and technology it would need for a systematic expansion across the entire spectrum of motor-related businesses.

Honda's progress in creating a core competence in engines should have warned competitors that it might enter a series of seemingly unrelated industries—automobiles, lawn mowers, marine engines, generators. But with each company fixated on its own market, the threat of Honda's horizontal diversification went unnoticed. Today companies like Matsushita and Toshiba are similarly poised to move in unexpected ways across industry boundaries. In protecting loose bricks, companies must extend their peripheral vision by tracking and anticipating the migration of global competitors across product segments, businesses, national markets, value-added stages, and distribution channels.

Changing the terms of engagement—refusing to accept the front runner's definition of industry and segment boundaries—represents still another form of competitive innovation. Canon's entry into the copier business illustrates this approach.

During the 1970s, both Kodak and IBM tried to match Xerox's business system in terms of segmentation, products, distribution, service, and pricing. As a result, Xerox had no trouble decoding the new entrants' intentions and developing countermoves. IBM eventually withdrew from the copier business, while Kodak remains a distant second in the large copier market that Xerox still dominates.

Canon, on the other hand, changed the terms of competitive engagement. While Xerox built a wide range of copiers, Canon standardized machines and components to reduce costs. Canon chose to distribute through office-product dealers rather than try to match Xerox's huge direct sales force. It also avoided the need to create a national service network by designing reliability and serviceability into its product and then delegating service responsibility to the dealers. Canon copiers were sold rather than leased, freeing Canon from the burden of financing the lease base. Finally, instead of selling to the heads of corporate duplicating departments, Canon appealed to secretaries and department managers who wanted distributed copying. At each stage, Canon neatly sidestepped a potential barrier to entry.

Canon's experience suggests that there is an important distinction between barriers to entry and barriers to imitation. Competitors that tried to match Xerox's business system had to pay the same entry costs—the barriers to imitation were high. But Canon dramatically reduced the barriers to entry by changing the rules of the game.

Changing the rules also short-circuited Xerox's ability to retaliate quickly against its new rival. Confronted with the need to rethink its business strategy and organization, Xerox was paralyzed for a time. Xerox managers realized that the faster they downsized the product line, developed new channels, and improved reliability, the faster they would erode the company's traditional profit base. What might have been seen as critical success factors—Xerox's national sales force and service network, its large installed base of leased machines, and its reliance on service revenues—instead became barriers to retaliation. In this sense, competitive innovation is like judo: the goal is to use a larger competitor's weight against it. And that happens not by matching the leader's capabilities but by developing contrasting capabilities of one's own.

Competitive innovation works on the premise that a successful competitor is likely to be wedded to a "recipe" for success. That's why the most effective weapon new competitors possess is probably a clean sheet of paper. And why an incumbent's greatest vulnerability is its belief in accepted practice.

Through licensing, outsourcing agreements, and joint ventures, it is sometimes possible to win without fighting. For example, Fujitsu's alliances in Europe with Siemens and STC (Britain's largest computer maker) and in the United States with Amdahl yield manufacturing volume and access to Western markets. In the early 1980s, Matsushita established a joint venture with Thorn (in the United Kingdom), Telefunken (in Germany), and Thomson (in France), which allowed it to quickly multiply the forces arrayed against Philips in the battle for leadership in the European VCR business. In fighting larger global rivals by proxy, Japanese companies have adopted a maxim as old as human conflict itself: my enemy's enemy is my friend.

Hijacking the development efforts of potential rivals is another goal of competitive collaboration. In the consumer electronics war, Japanese competitors attacked traditional businesses like TVs and hi-fis while volunteering to manufacture "next generation" products like VCRs, camcorders, and compact disc players for Western rivals. They hoped their rivals would ratchet down development spending, and in most cases that is precisely what happened. But companies that abandoned their own development efforts seldom reemerged as serious competitors in subsequent new product battles.

Collaboration can also be used to calibrate competitors' strengths and weaknesses. Toyota's joint venture with GM, and Mazda's with Ford, give these automakers an invaluable vantage point for assessing the progress their U.S. rivals have made in cost reduction, quality, and technology. They can also learn how GM and Ford compete—when they will fight and when they won't. Of course, the reverse is also true: Ford and GM have an equal opportunity to learn from their partner-competitors.

The route to competitive revitalization we have been mapping implies a new view of strategy. Strategic intent assures consistency in resource allocation over the long term. Clearly articulated corporate challenges focus the efforts of individuals in the medium term. Finally, competitive innovation helps reduce competitive risk in the short term. This consistency in the long term, focus in the medium term, and inventiveness and involvement in the short term provide the key to leveraging limited resources in pursuit of ambitious goals. But just as there is a process of winning, so there is a process of surrender. Revitalization requires understanding that process too.

Given their technological leadership and access to large regional markets, how did U.S. and European companies lose their apparent birthright to dominate global industries? There is no simple answer. Few companies recognize the value of documenting failure. Fewer still search their own managerial orthodoxies for the seeds of competitive surrender. But we believe there is a pathology of surrender (summarized in "The Process of Surrender") that gives some important clues.

It is not very comforting to think that the essence of Western strategic thought can be reduced to eight rules for excellence, seven S's, five competitive forces, four product life cycle stages, three generic strategies, and innumerable two-by-two matrices. Yet for the past 20 years, "advances" in strategy have taken the form of ever more typologies, heuristics, and laundry lists, often with dubious empirical bases. Moreover, even reasonable concepts like the product life cycle, experience curve, product portfolios, and generic strategies often have toxic side effects: They reduce the number of strategic options management is willing to consider. They create a preference for selling businesses rather than defending them. They yield predictable strategies that rivals easily decode.

Strategy "recipes" limit opportunities for competitive innovation. A company may have 40 businesses and only four strategies—invest, hold, harvest, or divest. Too often strategy is seen as a positioning exercise in which options are tested by how they fit the existing industry structure. But current industry structure reflects the strengths of the industry leader; and playing by the leader's rules is usually competitive suicide.

Armed with concepts like segmentation, the value chain, competitor benchmarking, strategic groups, and mobility barriers, many managers have become better and better at drawing industry maps. But while they have been busy map making, their competitors have been moving entire continents. The strategist's goal is not to find a niche within the existing industry space but to create new space that is uniquely suited to the company's own strengths, space that is off the map.[4]

This is particularly true now that industry boundaries are becoming more and more unstable. In industries such as financial services and communications, rapidly changing technology, deregulation, and globalization have undermined the value of traditional industry analysis. Map-making skills are worth little in the epicenter of an earthquake. But an industry in upheaval presents opportunities for ambitious companies to redraw the map in their favor, so long as they can think outside traditional industry boundaries.

Concepts like "mature" and "declining" are largely definitional. What most executives mean when they label a business mature is that sales growth has stagnated in their current geographic markets for existing products sold through existing channels. In such cases, it's not the industry that is mature, but the executives' conception of the industry. Asked if the piano business was mature, a senior executive in Yamaha replied, "Only if we can't take any market share from anybody anywhere in the world and still make money. And anyway, we're not in the 'piano' business, we're in the 'keyboard' business." Year after year, Sony has revitalized its radio and tape recorder businesses, despite the fact that other manufacturers long ago abandoned these businesses as mature.

A narrow concept of maturity can foreclose a company from a broad stream of future opportunities. In the 1970s, several U.S. companies thought that consumer electronics had become a mature industry. What could

---

[4] Strategic frameworks for resource allocation in diversified companies are summarized in Charles W. Hofer and Dan E. Schendel, *Strategy Formulation: Analytical Concepts* (St. Paul, MN: West Publishing, 1978).

The Process of Surrender

In the battles for global leadership that have taken place during the last two decades, we have seen a pattern of competitive attack and retrenchment that was remarkably similar across industries. We call this the process of surrender.

The process started with unseen intent. Not possessing long-term, competitor-focused goals themselves, Western companies did not ascribe such intentions to their rivals. They also calculated the threat posed by potential competitors in terms of their existing resources rather than their resourcefulness. This led to systematic underestimation of smaller rivals who were fast gaining technology through licensing arrangements, acquiring market understanding from downstream OEM partners, and improving product quality and manufacturing productivity through companywide employee involvement programs. Oblivious of the strategic intent and intangible advantages of their rivals, American and European businesses were caught off guard.

Adding to the competitive surprise was the fact that the new entrants typically attacked the periphery of a market (Honda in small motorcycles, Yamaha in grand pianos, Toshiba in small black-and-white televisions) before going head-to-head with incumbents. Incumbents often misread these attacks, seeing them as part of a niche strategy and not as a search for "loose bricks." Unconventional market entry strategies (minority holdings in less-developed countries, use of nontraditional channels, extensive corporate advertising) were ignored or dismissed as quirky. For example, managers we spoke with said Japanese companies' position in the European computer industry was nonexistent. In terms of brand share that's nearly true, but the Japanese control as much as one-third of the manufacturing value added in the hardware sales of European-based computer businesses. Similarly, German auto producers claimed to feel unconcerned over the proclivity of Japanese producers to move upmarket. But with its low-end models under tremendous pressure from Japanese producers, Porsche has now announced that it will no longer make "entry level" cars.

Western managers often misinterpreted their rivals' tactics. They believed that Japanese and Korean companies were competing solely on the basis of cost and quality. This typically produced a partial response to those competitors' initiatives: moving manufacturing offshore, outsourcing, or instituting a quality program. Seldom was the full extent of the competitive threat appreciated—the multiple layers of advantage, the expansion across related product segments, the development of global brand positions. Imitating the currently visible tactics of rivals put Western businesses into a perpetual catch-up trap. One by one, companies lost battles and came to see surrender as inevitable. Surrender was not inevitable, of course, but the attack was staged in a way that disguised ultimate intentions and sidestepped direct confrontation.

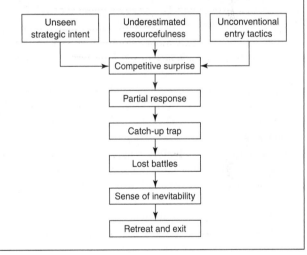

When Does Surrender Become Inevitable?

possibly top the color TV? they asked themselves. RCA and GE, distracted by opportunities in more "attractive" industries like mainframe computers, left Japanese producers with a virtual monopoly in VCRs, camcorders, and compact disc players. Ironically, the TV business, once thought mature, is on the verge of a dramatic renaissance. A $20 billion-a-year business will be created when high-definition television is launched in the United States. But the pioneers of television may capture only a small part of this bonanza.

Most of the tools of strategic analysis are focused domestically. Few force managers to consider global opportunities and threats. For example, portfolio planning portrays top management's investment options as an array of businesses rather than as an array of geographic markets. The result is predictable: as businesses come under attack from foreign competitors, the company attempts to abandon them and enter others in which the forces of global competition are not yet so strong. In the short term, this may be an appropriate response to waning competitiveness, but there are fewer and fewer businesses in which a domestic-oriented company can find refuge. We seldom hear such companies asking: Can we move into emerging markets overseas ahead of our global rivals and prolong the profitability of this business? Can we counterattack in our global competitors' home markets and slow the pace of their expansion? A senior executive in one successful global company made a telling comment: "We're glad to find a competitor managing by the portfolio concept—we can almost predict how much share we'll have to take away to put the business on the CEO's 'sell list.'"

Companies can also be overcommitted to organizational recipes, such as SBUs (strategic business units) and the decentralization an SBU structure implies. Decentralization is seductive because it places the responsibility for success or failure squarely on the shoulders of line managers. Each business is assumed to have all the resources it needs to execute its strategies successfully, and in this no-excuses environment, it is hard for top management to fail. But desirable as clear lines of responsibility and accountability are, competitive revitalization requires positive value added from top management.

Few companies with a strong SBU orientation have built successful global distribution and brand positions. Investments in a global brand franchise typically transcend the resources and risk propensity of a single business. While some Western companies have had global brand positions for 30 or 40 years or more—Heinz, Siemens, IBM, Ford, and Kodak, for example—it is hard to identify any American or European company that has created new global brand franchise in the last 10 to 15 years. Yet Japanese companies have created a score or more—NEC, Fujitsu, Panasonic (Matsushita), Toshiba, Sony, Seiko, Epson, Canon, Minolta, and Honda, among them.

General Electric's situation is typical. In many of its businesses, this American giant has been almost unknown in Europe and Asia. GE made no coordinated effort to build a global corporate franchise. Any GE business with international ambitions had to bear the burden of establishing its credibility and credentials in the new market alone. Not surprisingly, some once-strong GE businesses opted out of the difficult task of building a global brand position. In contrast, smaller Korean companies like Samsung, Daewoo, and Lucky Gold Star are busy building global-brand umbrellas that will ease market entry for a whole range of businesses. The underlying principle is simple: economies of scope may be as important as economies of scale in entering global markets. But capturing economies of scope demands inter-business coordination that only top management can provide.

We believe that inflexible SBU-type organizations have also contributed to the deskilling of some companies. For a single SBU, incapable of sustaining investment in a core competence such as semiconductors, optical media, or combustion engines, the only way to remain competitive is to purchase key components from potential (often Japanese or Korean) competitors. For an SBU defined in product-market terms, competitiveness means offering an end product that is competitive in price and performance. But that gives an SBU manager little incentive to distinguish between external sourcing that achieves "product embodied" competitiveness and internal development that yields deeply embedded organizational competences that can be exploited across multiple businesses. Where upstream component manufacturing activities are seen as cost centers with cost-plus transfer pricing, additional investment in the core activity may seem a less profitable use of capital than investment in downstream activities. To make matters worse, internal accounting data may not reflect the competitive value of retaining control over core competence.

Together a shared global corporate brand franchise and shared core competence act as mortar in many Japanese companies. Lacking this mortar, a company's businesses are truly loose bricks—easily knocked out by global competitors that steadily invest in core competences. Such competitors can co-opt domestically oriented companies into long-term sourcing dependence and capture the economies of scope of global brand investment through interbusiness coordination.

Last in decentralization's list of dangers is the standard of managerial performance typically used in SBU organizations. In many companies, business unit managers are rewarded solely on the basis of their performance against return on investment targets. Unfortunately, that often leads to denominator management because executives soon discover that reductions in investment and head count—the denominator—"improve" the financial ratios by which they are measured more easily than growth in the numerator—revenues. It also fosters a hair-trigger sensitivity to industry downturns that can be very costly. Managers who are quick to reduce investment and dismiss workers find it takes much longer to regain lost skills and catch up on investment when the industry turns upward again. As a result, they lose market share in every business cycle. Particularly in industries where there is fierce competition for the best people and where competitors invest relentlessly, denominator management creates a retrenchment ratchet.

The concept of the general manager as a movable peg reinforces the problem of denominator management. Business schools are guilty here because they have perpetuated the notion that a manager with net present value calculations in one hand and portfolio planning in the other can manage any business anywhere.

In many diversified companies, top management evaluates line managers on numbers alone because no other basis for dialogue exists. Managers move so many times as part of their "career development" that they often do not understand the nuances of the businesses they are managing. At GE, for example, one fast-track manager heading an important new venture had moved across five businesses in five years. His series of quick successes finally came to an end when he confronted a Japanese competitor whose managers had been plodding along in the same business for more than a decade.

Regardless of ability and effort, fast-track managers are unlikely to develop the deep business knowledge they need to discuss technology options, competitors' strategies, and global opportunities substantively. Invariably, therefore, discussions gravitate to "the numbers," while the value added of managers is limited to the financial and planning savvy they carry from job to job. Knowledge of the company's internal planning and accounting systems substitutes for substantive knowledge of the business, making competitive innovation unlikely.

When managers know that their assignments have a two- to three-year time frame, they feel great pressure to create a good track record fast. This pressure often takes one of two forms. Either the manager does not commit to goals whose time line extends beyond his or her expected tenure. Or ambitious goals are adopted and squeezed into an unrealistically short time frame. Aiming to be number one in a business is the essence of strategic intent, but imposing a three- to four-year horizon on the effort simply invites disaster. Acquisitions are made with little attention to the problems of integration. The organization becomes overloaded with initiatives. Collaborative ventures are formed without adequate attention to competitive consequences.

Almost every strategic management theory and nearly every corporate planning system is premised on a strategy hierarchy in which corporate goals guide business unit strategies and business unit strategies guide functional tactics.[5] In this hierarchy, senior management makes strategy and lower levels execute it. The dichotomy between formulation and implementation is familiar and widely accepted. But the strategy hierarchy undermines competitiveness by fostering an elitist view of management that tends to disenfranchise most of the organization. Employees fail to identify with corporate goals or involve themselves deeply in the work of becoming more competitive.

The strategy hierarchy isn't the only explanation for an elitist view of management, of course. The myths that grow up around successful top managers—"Lee Iacocca saved Chrysler," "De Benedetti rescued Olivetti," "John Sculley turned Apple around"—perpetuate it. So does the turbulent business environment. Middle managers buffeted by circumstances that seem to be beyond their control desperately want to believe that top management has all the answers. And top management, in turn, hesitates to admit it does not for fear of demoralizing lower level employees.

The result of all this is often a code of silence in which the full extent of a company's competitiveness problem is not widely shared. We interviewed business unit managers in one company, for example, who were extremely anxious because top management wasn't talking openly about the competitive challenges the company faced. They assumed the lack of communication indicated a lack of awareness on their senior managers' part. But when asked whether they were open with their own employees, these same managers replied that while they could face up to the problems, the people below them could not. Indeed, the only time the workforce heard about the company's competitiveness problems was during wage negotiations when problems were used to extract concessions.

Unfortunately, a threat that everyone perceives but no one talks about creates more anxiety than a threat that has been clearly identified and made the focal point for the problem-solving efforts of the entire company. That is one reason honesty and humility on the part of top management may be the first prerequisite of revitalization. Another reason is the need to make participation more than a buzzword.

Programs such as quality circles and total customer service often fall short of expectations because management does not recognize that successful implementation requires more than administrative structures. Difficulties in embedding new capabilities are typically put down to "communication" problems, with the unstated assumption that if only downward communication were more effective—"if only middle management would get the message straight"—the new program would quickly take root. The need for upward communication is often ignored, or assumed to mean nothing more than feedback. In contrast, Japanese companies win, not because they have smarter managers, but because they have developed ways to harness the "wisdom of the anthill." They realize that top managers are a bit like the astronauts who circle the earth in the space shuttle. It may be the astronauts who get all the glory, but everyone knows that the real intelligence behind the mission is located firmly on the ground.

---

[5] For example, see P. Lorange and R. F. Vancil, *Strategic Planning Systems* (Englewood Cliffs, NJ: Prentice Hall, 1977).

Where strategy formulation is an elitist activity it is also difficult to produce truly creative strategies. For one thing, there are not enough heads and points of view in divisional or corporate planning departments to challenge conventional wisdom. For another, creative strategies seldom emerge from the annual planning ritual. The starting point for next year's strategy is almost always this year's strategy. Improvements are incremental. The company sticks to the segments and territories it knows, even though the real opportunities may be elsewhere. The impetus for Canon's pioneering entry into the personal copier business came from an overseas sales subsidiary—not from planners in Japan.

The goal of the strategy hierarchy remains valid—to ensure consistency up and down the organization. But this consistency is better derived from a clearly articulated strategic intent than from inflexibly applied top-down plans. In the 1990s, the challenge will be to enfranchise employees to invent the means to accomplish ambitious ends.

We seldom found cautious administrators among the top managements of companies that came from behind to challenge incumbents for global leadership. But in studying organizations that had surrendered, we invariably found senior managers who, for whatever reason, lacked the courage to commit their companies to heroic goals—goals that lay beyond the reach of planning and existing resources. The conservative goals they set failed to generate pressure and enthusiasm for competitive innovation or give the organization much useful guidance. Financial targets and vague mission statements just cannot provide the consistent direction that is a prerequisite for winning a global competitive war.

This kind of conservatism is usually blamed on the financial markets. But we believe that in most cases investors' so-called short-term orientation simply reflects their lack of confidence in the ability of senior managers to conceive and deliver stretch goals. The chairman of one company complained bitterly that even after it improved return on capital employed to over 40 percent (by ruthlessly divesting lackluster businesses and downsizing others), the stock market held the company to an 8:1 price/earnings ratio. Of course the market's message was clear: "We don't trust you. You've shown no ability to achieve profitable growth. Just cut out the slack, manage the denominators, and perhaps you'll be taken over by a company that can use your resources more creatively." Very little in the track record of most large Western companies warrants the confidence of the stock market. Investors aren't hopelessly short-term; they're justifiably skeptical.

We believe that top management's caution reflects a lack of confidence in its own ability to involve the entire organization in revitalization—as opposed to simply raising financial targets. Developing faith in the organization's ability to deliver on tough goals, motivating it to do so, focusing its attention long enough to internalize new capabilities—this is the real challenge for top management. Only by rising to this challenge will senior managers gain the courage they need to commit themselves and their companies to global leadership.

READING II-16

Strategy as Vector and the Inertia of Coevolutionary Lock-In

Robert A. Burgelman

To examine the consequences of a period of extraordinary success for the long-term adaptive capability of a firm's strategy-making process, this comparative longitudinal study of Andy Grove's tenure as Intel Corporation's chief executive officer (CEO) documents how he moved Intel's strategy-making process from an internal-ecology model to the classical rational-actor model during 1987–1998. His creation of a highly successful strategy vector pursued through an extremely focused induced-strategy process led to coevolutionary lock-in with the personal computer market segment, in which Intel's strategy making became increasingly tied to its existing product market. Intracompany analysis of four new business development cases highlights the inertial consequences of coevolutionary lock-in. The paper examines implications of coevolutionary lock-in in terms of its effect on balanc-

Source: Reprinted from *Administrative Science Quarterly,* 47 (2002): 325–357. The research for this paper was critically dependent on my case writing and teaching collaboration with Andrew S. Grove, Intel's former CEO and current chairman, since 1988. The generous collaboration of Intel Corporation and its managers in this research is much appreciated. James G. March and Ezra W. Zuckerman offered many useful comments on an earlier draft. I am especially indebted to Jim March for drawing attention to coevolutionary lock-in as a phenomenon of organizational adaptation. The ideas of this paper were significantly sharpened as the result of challenging comments and queries of the *ASQ* reviewers and Christine Oliver, its editor. Thanks also to managing editor Linda Johanson for helpful editorial suggestions.

ing induced and autonomous strategy processes and exploitation and exploration in organizational learning.

There is a vast literature ascribing the success of a company to the vision, strategy, and leadership approach of its CEO. Some of these accounts put the CEO at center stage (e.g., Welch, 2001); others put him or her more modestly in the background (e.g., Collins, 2001). Organizational and strategic management researchers, however, have long highlighted the difficulties leaders encounter in aligning organizational action in the pursuit of strategic intent (e.g., Mintzberg, Ahlstrand, and Lampel, 1998). Recent work in organizational ecology (e.g., Barnett and Hansen, 1996), the behavioral theory of the firm (e.g., Levinthal and March, 1993), and neo-institutional theory (e.g., Zuckerman, 2000) continues to illuminate the external and internal limitations facing top management. Yet we still understand little about why some firms have periods of extraordinary success, what the role of the CEO is in heralding and leading the organization through such periods, and what the consequences are of such periods for strategy making thereafter. While organizational researchers are mostly concerned with ordinary states and expect regression toward the mean to wash out fluctuations over time, periods of extraordinary success have potentially important consequences for the strategy-making process as a long-term adaptive organizational capability; that is, spanning multiple generations of CEOs.

Longitudinal field-based research of strategy making at Intel Corporation during Andy Grove's tenure as chief executive officer (CEO) offered the opportunity to study a period of extraordinary corporate success and its consequences for the company's strategy-making process. Intel seemed a particularly interesting research site because it is one of the most important firms of the digital age (Gilder, 1989; Isaacson, 1997) and its evolution highlights the fundamental technological and economic forces that characterize digital industries (e.g., Arthur, 1987). The research could be used to compare Grove's strategy-making approach to that of his predecessor (Gordon Moore) and successor (Craig Barrett) and thus could examine his efficacy as CEO within the context of Intel as an evolving system over time.

Andy Grove succeeded Gordon Moore as CEO in 1987 at the time that Intel was recovering from defeat in its original semiconductor memory business and refocusing on its microprocessor business (Burgelman, 1994). He held the position until early 1998. Between 1987 and 1998, Intel became the clear winner with its microprocessors in the personal computer (PC) market segment. Intel's revenues grew from $1.9 billion to $25.1 billion—an increase of 29.4 percent per annum—and net income grew from $248 million to $6.9 billion—an increase of 39.5 percent per annum. In 1998, however, Intel's growth in the core business slowed down significantly. Also it had become clear that new business development was relatively unsuccessful during Grove's tenure as CEO. In 1997, Craig Barrett, then Intel's chief operating officer (COO), observed that Intel's core microprocessor business had begun to resemble a creosote bush, a desert plant that poisons the ground around it, preventing other plants from growing nearby. The creosote bush metaphor raised potentially interesting questions about the strategic consequences of Intel's ability to dominate in the PC market segment. It drew attention to the phenomenon of coevolutionary lock-in: a positive feedback process that increasingly ties the previous success of a company's strategy to that of its existing product-market environment, thereby making it difficult to change strategic direction. Despite the attention given to winner-take-all competition in digital industries (e.g., Arthur, 1987) and the role of inertia in organizational and industry evolution (e.g., Hannan and Freeman, 1977, 1984), researchers have paid little attention to how coevolutionary lock-in comes about and may become a significant source of strategic inertia. This study addresses this gap. It seeks to shed light on the role of the CEO in creating a strategy-making process that leads to coevolutionary lock-in and what its implications are for organizational adaptation.

Grove described his approach as "vectoring" Intel's strategy-making process. Vector—a quantity having direction and magnitude, denoted by a line drawn from its original to its final position (*Oxford English Dictionary*)—seems an apt metaphor to describe his efforts to align strategy and action. By creating a strategy vector, Grove was able to drive Intel in the intended direction with a total force equal to all the forces at its disposition. The paper examines the long-term adaptive implications of Grove's strategic leadership approach, which seemed to approximate the classical rational-actor model (Allison and Zelikow, 1999; Bendor and Hammond, 1992), and contrasts it with that of his predecessor.

COEVOLUTIONARY LOCK-IN IN FIRM EVOLUTION

Informed by evolutionary organization theory (e.g., Aldrich, 1999; Baum and McKelvey, 1999), earlier research on Intel before Grove became CEO suggested that effective strategy making may be as much about creating an environment in which middle management makes strategic decisions as it is about strategy making in the classical sense and that the role of top management might be to recognize transitions rather than to initiate them (Burgelman, 1994). These findings were consistent with an internal ecology model of strategy making, which was conceptualized in terms of induced and autonomous strategy processes (Burgelman, 1991). Induced strategy exploits initiatives that are within the scope of a company's current strategy and that extend it further in its current product-market environment. Autonomous strategy exploits initiatives that emerge through exploration outside of the scope of the current strategy and that provide the basis for entering into new product-market environments. Intel's strategy making before Grove became CEO resembled an internal-ecology model in which induced (memory-related) and autonomous (microprocessor-related) initiatives competed for the company's scarce resources based on their success in the external competitive environment. This paper documents how Grove's successful strategy vector created a highly focused induced strategy process, which moved Intel's strategy making away from the internal-ecology model and closer to the rational-actor model. It shows how positive environmental feedback associated with the successful strategy vector caused coevolutionary lock-in and how this can illuminate time-paced evolution (Gersick, 1994; Brown and Eisenhardt, 1997) and the dynamics of competitive intensity (Barnett, 1997).

Strategic Inertia of Coevolutionary Lock-In

This paper's detailed ethnographic data also document new sources of strategic inertia that may be the unintended consequence of coevolutionary lock-in. Systemic sources of inertia associated with coevolutionary lock-in provide additional insight into structural inertia (Hannan and Freeman, 1984). They help elucidate the dynamics of the evolving relative efficiency of internal selection (Miller, 1999; Lovas and Ghoshal, 2000) and external selection (Sorenson, 2000), as a company's product-market environment matures, and of the rate and direction of innovation relative to environmental evolution as firms grow large (Sørensen and Stuart, 2000). Study of the psychological sources of inertia associated with coevolutionary lock-in can be used to assess Prahalad and Bettis's (1986) contention that executives become ingrained with beliefs about causes and effects that may not hold after the environment changes. And they help sort out Audia, Locke, and Smith's (2000) argument that success tends to increase decision makers' feelings of self-

efficacy from that of Miller and Chen (1994), who suggest that it causes complacency, understood as drifting without further attempts at improvement. These psychological sources of strategic inertia draw attention to the potential limitations of evolution guided by the strategic intent of the CEO (Lovas and Ghoshal, 2000). Most important for the purposes of this paper, the various sources of strategic inertia associated with coevolutionary lock-in have implications for maintaining a balance between induced and autonomous strategy processes and between exploitation and exploration in organizational learning. They help connect these ideas, which are rooted in evolutionary organization theory (Burgelman, 1991; March, 1991), with related ideas of the modern economic theory of the firm (Rotemberg and Saloner, 1994, 2000).

RESEARCH METHOD

The research reported in this paper is part of a longitudinal multistage, nested case study design (e.g., Yin, 1984; Leonard-Barton, 1990) focused on major periods of Intel's history (Burgelman, 2002). These include Epoch I: Intel the memory company (1968–1985); Epoch II: Intel the microprocessor company (1985–1998); and Epoch III: Intel the Internet building-block company (beyond 1998). These three epochs correspond roughly to the tenure of Gordon Moore, Andy Grove, and Craig Barrett as Intel's CEOs.

Data Collection

Interview Data. For this paper, which focuses on Intel's Epoch II, I used data from 63 informants, collected mostly through interviews I and/or a research associate conducted and through informal interactions. Informal interactions sometimes involved a research associate. Others took place in the strategic long-range planning sessions I observed, in executive education sessions I taught for senior Intel executives, and through working with Intel staff in preparing for executive education sessions. I also had access to transcripts of interviews conducted and tape-recorded by Intel consultants. The list of these informants and their positions in the organization is provided in Exhibit 1. Managers from different levels, different functional groups, and different businesses were involved. Throughout the research period, I used informal discussions with many current and former Intel employees to corroborate data obtained from the formal interviews.

Most interviews lasted between one and two hours and focused on key events, people, and issues. Key events involved, for instance, the introduction of successive

EXHIBIT 1   Informants Providing Data Concerning Epoch II (1988–1998)

Name and most relevant job during Epoch II	Interview	Informal interaction
1. Gordon Moore, chairman	X	X
2. Andy Grove, CEO	X	X
3. Craig Barrett, COO	X	X
4. Gerry Parker, executive VP, Technology and Mfg. Group	X	X
5. Paul Otellini, executive VP, Intel Architecture Business Group	X	X
6. Frank Gill, executive VP, Intel Products Group; gen. mgr., Networking	X	X
7. Les Vadasz, senior VP, Corporate Business Development Group	X	X
8. Albert Yu, senior VP, Microprocessor Products Group	X	X
9. Ron Whittier, senior VP, Intel Architecture Labs, Content Group	X	X
10. Andy Bryant, senior VP and CFO	X	X
11. Sean Maloney, senior VP, Sales and Marketing Group		X
12. Dennis Carter, VP, Corporate Marketing Group	X	X
13. Ron Smith, VP, gen. mgr., Chipsets	X	X
14. Patrick Gelsinger, VP, gen. mgr., Proshare	X	X
15. Mike Aymar, VP, Desktop Products Group, Hood River	X	X
16. Mark Christensen, VP, gen. mgr., Networking (late 1990s)	X	X
17. John Miner, VP, Enterprise Server Group		X
18. Hans Geyer, VP, gen. mgr., Flash Products Division		X
19. Patty Murray, VP, Human Resources		X
20. Harold Hughes, VP and CFO, mid-1990s	X	X
21. John Davies, VP, Consumer Marketing Desktop Prod. Grp., Hood River	X	
22. Avram Miller, VP, Corporate Development Group, Hood River	X	
23. Jim Johnson, gen. mgr., PC Enhancement Organization (late 1980s)	X	X
24. Claude Leglise, marketing director, i860 (late 1980s)	X	X
25. Steve McGeady, gen. mgr., Home Media Lab (mid-1990s)	X	X
26. Scott Darling, gen. mgr., Busin. Com. Prod. Grp., Proshare (late 1990s)	X	X
27. Sandra Morris, manager, Intel Prod. Grp. (mid-1990s)	X	X
28. Tom Yan, mgr. development, OEM Prod. and Syst. Div., Hood River	X	
29. Dick Pashley, gen. mgr., Flash Memory Division (early 1990s)	X	X
30. Warren Evans, Business Process Network, Planning	X	X
31. Renee James, technical assistant to Andy Grove (mid-1990s)	X	X
32. Katherine Yetts, technical assistant to Craig Barrett (mid-1990s)	X	X
33. Michael Bruck, program manager, Content Group	X	X
34. Vin Dham, program manager, Pentium processor (early 1990s)	X	X
35. Richard Wirt, director, Software, IAL	X	X
36. Les Kohn, technical manager, i860 processor (late 1980s)	X	
37. Bruce McCormick, manager, Flash (mid-1980s)	X	
38. Sally Fundakowski, manager, CMG (early 1990s)	X	
39. Tom Macdonald, marketing director, 386 and 486 processors	X	
40. Jim Yasso, mgr., Desktop Prd. Grp. and Microp. Prd. Grp. (mid-1990s)	X	
41. Don Whiteside, gen. mgr., Digital Imaging and Video Division	X	
43. Lori Wigle, strat. mkting. dir., Digital Imaging and Video Division	X	
43. Tom Willis, manager, Corporate Business Development Group	X	
44. Dave Williams, director, Home Media Lab	X	
45. Dave Cobbley, director, Home Media Lab	X	
46. Rob Siegel, program manager, Hood River	X	X
47. Ganesh Moorthy, mgr., Appliance and Comp. Div. (Deskt. Prod. Grp.)	X	
48. Krish Bandura, engineer, Hood River	X	
49. Roy Coppinger, product mgr., OEM Prod. and Syst. Div., Hood River	X	
50. Eric Mentzer, marketing manager, Chipsets	X*	X
51. Andy Wilhelm, technical manager, Chipsets	X*	
52. Andy Beran, finance manager, Chipsets	X*	
53. Tom Bruegel, finance manager, Networking (mid-1990s)	X*	
54. Dan Sweeney, marketing program mgr., Networking (mid-1990s)	X*	
55. Steve Cassell, engineering mgr., Networking (early 1990s)	X*	

(continues)

EXHIBIT 1 **(continued)**

Name and most relevant job during Epoch II	Interview	Informal interaction
56. Kirby Dyess, mkting. mgr., PC Enhancem. Org. (late 1980s)	X*	X
57. Susan Studd, human res. mgr., PC Enhancem. Org. (late 1980s)	X*	X
58. Gerry Greve, marketing director, Proshare (mid-1990s)	X*	
60. Laura Finney, finance manager, Proshare (mid-1990s)	X*	
61. Taymoor Arshi, engineering manager, Proshare (mid-1990s)	X*	
62. Mark Olson, product marketing manager, Microproc. Prod. Grp.		X
63. John Sutherland, manager, Systems Management Division		X

*These interviews were tape-recorded by Intel consultants, and transcripts of the raw recorded interview data were made available to this author.

generations of microprocessors. Key people were individuals or groups from different functional areas or different hierarchical levels who made critical decisions or made proposals that, while not necessarily implemented, triggered high-level reconsideration of strategic issues. Key issues included, for instance, how to allocate resources to different businesses, how to resolve internal competition between different microprocessor architectures, and how to enter into new businesses. Most interviews were not tape-recorded (exceptions are listed in Exhibit 1), but the interviewers made extensive notes. Many of the interviews were done together with research associates. Transcripts of the research associates' notes showed agreement on the substantive content of the interviews. This provided some confidence that the data were valid and reliable.

Archival Data. Archival data, such as documents describing the company's history, annual reports, and reports to financial analysts, were obtained from Intel. Additional archival data were obtained from outside sources, such as industry publications and financial analysts' reports and business press articles about Intel and the semiconductor and computer industries. The archival data could be juxtaposed with the interview data to check for potential systematic biases in retrospective accounts of past strategy.

Case Teaching as a Data Source. The interview and archival data were used to write several case studies about the role of strategy making in Intel's evolution during the period that Grove was CEO (Cogan and Burgelman, 1991; Steere and Burgelman, 1993a, 1993b; Fine and Burgelman, 1997; Bamford and Burgelman, 1997a, 1997b; Bamford and Burgelman, 1998; Suzuki and Burgelman, 1998; Burgelman, Carter, and Bamford, 1999). Lengthy discussions with the research associates involved in writing these cases provided me with an op-

portunity at each writing to check whether they thought my interpretation of the data was consistent with theirs, providing an additional check on internal validity (e.g., Dyck and Starke, 1999). Grove taught these cases in Stanford Business School's M.B.A. program throughout the research period. This yielded rich additional data as he reflected on Intel's strategic situation in class. It provided a window into the mind of the CEO as strategic thinker that has rarely been matched in previous studies.

Multilevel Comparative Analyses

I adopted the methodology of grounded theorizing (Glaser and Strauss, 1967) to analyze the field data. While grounded theorizing requires care not to use data simply as illustrations of preconceived theoretical ideas, analysis is only possible within a theoretical perspective. With this in mind, I used three interrelated conceptual frameworks generated through grounded theorizing in earlier work. Together, these frameworks form an evolutionary research lens to perform a multilevel comparative analysis of Intel's strategy making during Andy Grove's tenure as CEO. At the company level, the analysis is comparative with respect to time. I examined Intel's strategy making during Epoch II with a framework including induced and autonomous strategy processes (Burgelman, 1991) and compared it with Epoch I. At the company-environment interface level, the analysis is also comparative with respect to time. I examined the coevolution of Intel's strategy with the PC industry during Epoch II, leading to lock-in, with a framework of internal and external forces driving company evolution (Burgelman, 1994) and compared it with Epoch I. The forces taken into account in this framework include the basis of competitive advantage in the industry, the firm's distinctive competencies, its official corporate strategy, its strategic actions, and its internal selection environment. At the intracompany level, the analysis compares new business development efforts during Epoch II. The process model of internal corporate venturing (Burgelman, 1983), which identifies the interlocking key activities of multiple levels of management involved in internal new business development, helped in examining the behavioral details of the development of four cases in the context of Intel's strategy-making process.

Strengths and Limitations of the Research

By concentrating on one firm and tracking one CEO throughout his tenure, I had access to sources with intimate knowledge of the details of the company's strategy making. It also allowed me to become familiar with "the manager's temporal and contextual frame of reference" (Van de Ven, 1992: 181). Because I had virtually unlimited research access to the company throughout the twelve-year research period, I was able to obtain input from different levels of management, which provided a basis for triangulation and made it possible to maintain an appropriate level of distance and neutrality, while capitalizing on the teaching collaboration with Andy Grove. Nevertheless, the research has several limitations. First, it focused on a single high-tech company run by one of the founding team members. Also, during Grove's tenure as CEO, the PC industry expanded enormously, and fortuitous circumstances contributed to giving Intel the opportunity to become a driving force. Finally, during the study, I kept track of the evolving fortunes of Intel's competitors, but it would have been fruitful to study these other organizations systematically if time and access had permitted it.

COEVOLUTIONARY LOCK-IN OF STRATEGY AND ENVIRONMENT

Grove's Strategy Vector

During Epoch II, Gordon Moore remained as Chairman and Craig Barrett served as chief operating officer (COO). Looking back in 1999, Andy Grove pointed out that "At no point in Intel's history has it been a solo show. It's never been only one person leading the organization. Our tradition is somewhat of a shared power structure." Nevertheless, many insiders confirmed that Andy Grove drove strategy making during Epoch II. Exhibit 2 provides a chronology of selected key instances throughout Epoch II when it was clear that Grove made the difference in how Intel took strategic action in the core microprocessor business.

The data presented in Exhibit 2 show that Grove's role in driving Intel's strategy making relied more on strategic recognition than on foresight. Intel had been lucky to

invent the microprocessor and even more lucky to obtain the design win for the IBM PC. But it was ex post facto strategic recognition of the importance of these fortuitous events that set Intel on its highly successful course. An article in *The New York Times* in 1988 pointed out that it was "irksome to competitors . . . that there is a fair amount of luck involved in all of this [Intel's success]." Responding to this, Andy Grove was quoted as saying, "There is such a thing as luck and then you grab it and exploit it" (Pollack, 1988). Grove sometimes also called it "earned luck" (Schlender, 1989). Exhibit 2 indicates that the ability to get the organization to follow up on the mandates that Grove imposed based on his strategic recognition was another defining characteristic of Grove's leadership. Contrasting Grove's strengths to those of cofounder Robert Noyce and his own, Gordon Moore said, "Andy is a true manager. He is very detail oriented. He has strong follow-up—he never trusted that anyone would do what they were asked unless there was follow-up—and he is strongly data driven."

Focusing Intel on the Microprocessor Business. Exhibit 2 indicates that toward the end of Epoch I, then-COO Grove recognized that Intel's future lay in microprocessors rather than memory products. To make sure that the organization would be committed to the new microprocessor-focused strategy when he became CEO, Grove made major changes in Intel's senior management. He recalled,

> The Grove leadership approach consisted of trying to persuade and sell the new strategic approach to the management team. . . . After some period of time, the new strategy had traction with some managers and it did not have traction with some others. The people who did not get traction—they may have provided lip service to the new strategy, but their actions were not so supportive—the approach was to remove these people from positions where they could choke progress. We moved them around to other positions where they couldn't impede progress. This worked for a period of time. But when it became obvious that they were in a position that was not so important or influential, several of them left. We didn't actually have to fire anyone, nor were we happy that they left. But they were not happy being in a non-core activity.

Intel's new corporate strategy reflected key lessons that top management had learned from the DRAM (dynamic random access memory) exit. In the context of a case discussion in an MBA class in the early 1990s, Grove said,

> We learned that we had to get around the companies that had subjugated us in DRAM. We learned that high market share

EXHIBIT 2 Company Level of Analysis: Andy Grove's Impact on Intel's Strategy Making During Epoch II*

Selected key instances	Strategic recognition	Strategic action
Transition to Epoch II: Focusing Intel on microprocessors as chief operating officer (mid-1980s)		
Ed Gelbach (Sales VP and director): "In board meetings the question of DRAM would often come up. I would support them from a market perspective, and Gordon [Moore] would support them because they were our technology driver. Andy [Grove] kept quiet on the subject." *Jack Carsten (GM Components Division):* "Grove said: 'Don't worry about the memory business; it is not important to our future.'" *Another senior executive:* "Grove has been preaching: 'Make the tough decisions! Don't do tomorrow something because you did it today.'"	*COO Andy Grove:* "I stayed quiet because I didn't know what to do, initially." *COO Andy Grove:* "It's not always clear why you do certain things. You do a lot of things instinctively, without knowing why you're doing it. I knew we had to get out of DRAMs and put all our brightest on microprocessors." *COO Andy Grove:* "I recall going to see Gordon (Moore) and asking him what a new management would do if we were replaced. The answer was clear: Get out of DRAMs. So, I suggested to Gordon that we go through the revolving door, come back in, and just do it ourselves."	Grove removes Carsten as GM Components Division in summer 1985. Grove moves Sunlin Chou and the DRAM Technology Development Group to microprocessors. Grove goes to Oregon in October 1985 and tells the organization, "Welcome to the mainstream of Intel."
Resolving the battle between i860 (RISC) and ×86 (CISC) microprocessors within Intel (1991)		
Dennis Carter (VP Corporate Marketing): "In the end, Andy [Grove] resolved the debate. He essentially did a compromise that favored CISC."	*Andy Grove in February 1991:* "The strategy process reflects the company's culture. You can look at it positively or negatively. Positively, it looks like a Darwinian process: We let the best ideas win; we adapt by ruthlessly exiting businesses; we provide autonomy, and top management is the referee who waits to see who wins and then re-articulates the strategy; we match evolving skills with evolving opportunities. Negatively, it looks like we have no strategy; we have no staying power; we are reactive, try and move somewhere else if we fail; we lack focus."	Grove did not allow the planned introduction of both 486c and 486r processors that would have signaled a planned transition path from CISC to RISC. The i860 business was to continue by that name and was soon halted in early 1991. *Andy Grove in November 1992:* "It was a confusing period for Intel. . . . The i860 was a very successful renegade product that could have destroyed the virtuous circle enjoyed by the Intel Architecture. . . . Intel was helping RISC by legitimizing it. . . ."
Identifying the magnitude of capital investment as Intel's new differentiator (1993)		
Direct observation during SLRP 1993: In his kick-off presentation, Grove identified Intel's successive key strategic differentiators throughout its evolution: silicon technology competence (1970s), design competence (mid-1980s), intellectual property (late 1980s), and brand preference (early 1990s). He then suggested that the increasingly large capital investments necessary for next generation processors had become the new differentiator for the next several years.	*Andy Grove:* Pointing to the great uncertainty associated with these capital investments, Grove posited that they would provide Intel with a new competitive advantage. He asked, rhetorically, "Who is going to invest $5 billion on speculation?"	Grove was willing to make these large bets. During the remaining four years of his tenure as CEO, Intel invested $13.5 billion in plant, property, and equipment. In 1997, Craig Barrett said, "It's a risk to go out and spend billions of dollars on these manufacturing plants. But if we didn't, we couldn't possibly reap the benefits. We're going down the road at 150 miles per hour, and we know there's a brick wall someplace, but the worst thing we can do is stop too soon and let someone else pass us" (Reinhardt, Sager, and Burrows, 1997: 71).

Selected key instances	Strategic recognition	Strategic action
Resolving conflict around "Intel Inside" between Corporate Marketing and Intel Products Group		
Direct observation during SLRP 1993: At the end of SLRP the objectives as stated in 1992 were revisited in light of the discussions during the 1993 SLRP. The third objective in 1992 was "Manage the Intel and Intel Inside brands for significant return and long-term advantage." Grove felt that this objective had to be restated in light of the intense conflicts that had broken into the open between CMG (Dennis Carter) and IPG (Frank Gill) during the SLRP 1993 discussions.	*Andy Grove:* "This is a lame statement. And yet it is the inflection point—[similar] to what happened with the transition from memories to microprocessors. This involves a dialectic. It is a move from a single space to a dual one. This duality is all over the place. It is a continuation of the change from OEM to a distribution channel."	Grove decides: "Dennis [Carter] and Frank [Gill] must rephrase this. It must be words that will affect hundreds of people that work for them and are fighting over it. The new words [must make sure] we get credit for what we do for our [end-user] customers: ease-of-use, richness, upgradability; and who our customers *could* be."
Supporting Intel's motherboard business in the face of organizational resistance (mid-1990s)		
Harold Hughes (former CFO): "Andy was always brilliant at identifying threats to our business. For example, on the motherboard business, Andy and I clashed. I said that we were never going to make any money on motherboards. But they did push adoption of our microprocessors. Our motherboard business allowed the little [OEMs] to stay competitive."	*Andy Grove:* "I have been rabid about four things in my career at Intel: motherboards, Intel Inside, chipsets, and videoconferencing."	Grove supported the development of the motherboard business in spite of strong opposition of the microprocessor division, whose OEM customers complained vigorously about Intel's vertical integration strategy, and in the face of reservations on the part of the CFO.
Supporting the chipset business to drive industry adoption of Intel technology (mid-1990s)		
Several executives pointed out that Andy Grove initially did not support the development of the chipset business based on the new Peripheral Component Interconnect (PCI) bus technology but, rather, wanted to introduce the new technology as an enabling technology into the PC industry with a consortium-based effort.	After the chipset business became very successful, Andy Grove changed his mind about chipsets as a strategic business for Intel.	Grove then began to view the chipset business as an important tool for supporting the corporate strategy. Andy Bryant (CFO) said, "At a time when motherboard pricing was extremely competitive, the motherboard division decided not to use Intel's chipsets because they were more costly than third-party alternatives—even though they provided superior performance. . . . Grove ruled that the long-term interests of the company required moving advanced technology into the market place, and that we should forgo short-term returns for the long-term benefits."
Driving Intel to meet the threat of the growth of the low end of the PC market segment (1997)		
Direct observation during SLRP in September 1997: Grove was very concerned about recent developments in the PC market segment. He felt that Intel's top management was failing to see the strategic implications of the rapid growth in demand for below-$1,000 PCs.	*Andy Grove during his SLRP kickoff:* "We say we have a top-to-bottom strategy. But we don't act top-to-bottom, because Intel has low-end phobia. . . . But the low end is not going away. . . . The data about desktop sales at the retail, reseller, and direct level all show a downward trend in price: $500 in about a year! I have not seen that before. And the volumes at the low end are up. So, the good news about segment zero is that we have it on our road map. The bad news is that we don't have an engineered product."	Grove articulated a new mandate, requiring the assignment of a large number of engineers to the task of developing a microprocessor specifically for the low-end market segment.

In about six months the team developed a new product called the Celeron processor, which made it possible for Intel to regain market segment share against AMD in the low end by early 1999. |

(continues)

EXHIBIT 2   (continued)

Selected key instances	Strategic recognition	Strategic action
Driving Intel to meet the threat of the growth of the low end of the PC market segment (1997)		
		In early 1999, Paul Otellini observed, "We've made a lot of progress on the low end. One year ago in the sub-$1,000 market segment our share was about 38 percent. We then lost some ground, but we have regained share, so we're at about 38 percent again."
Looking back: Grove's influence on the PC industry during Epoch II		
Gordon Moore (chairman emeritus) in 1999: "When he became CEO, he really jumped on the opportunity to organize the industry. I wasn't so inclined to do this. He likes public exposure more than I did, and he has a stronger feeling about where he fits in. . . . Andy has had a tremendous impact on what's going on outside."		

*Abbreviations and terms used in this table are as follows: DRAM = dynamic random access memory; RISC = reduced instruction set computing; CISC = complex instruction set computing; and SLRP = strategic long-range planning. The motherboard is the main integrated circuit board in a PC; it contains the microprocessor, the memory, and other support chips. A chipset is the set of support chips for the microprocessor; for example, a chip that controls computer graphics. Bus refers to the set of electrical connections between a microprocessor and the other chips on an integrated circuit board. The speed of communication allowed by the bus affects PC performance. The PCI bus architecture increased speed significantly over the previous bus standard.
+ Executive interviewed for Epoch I study, not listed in Exhibit 1.

was critical for success and that to get market share we had to be willing to invest in manufacturing capacity. Such investments involve big bets because they have to be made in advance of actual demand. We learned that commodity businesses are unattractive, so we didn't want to license out our intellectual property anymore.

General-purpose microprocessors were a disruptive technology (Christensen and Bower, 1996). Microprocessor development was subject to Moore's Law, which posits that computing power doubles every 18 months and is available at the same price. Andy Grove was among the first to recognize that, in contrast to the vertically integrated mainframe and minicomputer industries, the PC industry followed a "horizontal" model in which a component manufacturer's products needed to be able to work with other component manufacturers' products (Grove, 1993, 1996). Grove's "vertical" and "horizontal" were a precursor to what economists call "closed" and "open" models of industry organization (Farrell, Monroe, and Saloner, 1998: 144). Success in the horizontal PC industry was governed by increasing returns to adoption, a new economic force (e.g., Arthur, 1987) that was initially not well understood by most industry partici-

pants. Increasing returns to adoption meant that a technological platform, like Intel's $\times 86$ microprocessors, became increasingly valuable the more people were using it. Achieving a high installed base was key to creating a virtuous circle. While economies of scale and economies of learning were important determinants of the relative success of different industry participants competing within the same microprocessor architecture, increasing returns to adoption strongly affected competition between different architectures.

Resolving the Internal Battle Between CISC and RISC.   The $\times 86$ architecture was based on complex instruction set computing (CISC). During the mid-1980s, however, Intel's autonomous strategy process generated the development of a microprocessor (the i860) based on a new architecture called reduced instruction set computing (RISC). Internal champions of the i860 had been able to generate support from workstation original equipment manufacturers (OEMs), which were new customers for Intel. During 1989–90, the autonomous and somewhat surreptitious development of the i860 and its initial market success looked like a potentially adaptive variation (Burgelman, 1991). But the new microprocessor soon created significant confusion inside the company that reflected external confusion about the importance of the RISC architecture for the future development of the PC. The internal confusion manifested itself in the emergence of two warring camps within Intel's microprocessor development group (MPG). Each camp had its external supporters. Andy Grove said that Microsoft supported the i860. Compaq, however, strongly supported the ×86 architecture. According to Grove, within a short period of time, the RISC camp had been able to claim about 50 percent of the microprocessor development resources because there was no clear corporate strategy regarding RISC (personal communication). Some within Intel proposed to create a transition path from the ×86 architecture to the RISC architecture by bringing out two versions of the i486, one called i486c and the other i486r, but this proposal ran into strong resistance from Dennis Carter, Intel's senior marketing executive during most of Epoch II, who feared that it would undermine Intel's brand identity. In part motivated by the negative consequences that a similar battle between CISC and RISC was having within rival Motorola (Tredennick, 1991), Grove eventually resolved the situation. Exhibit 2 quotes Dennis Carter on how Grove decided the issue. It also reports Grove's growing concerns about Intel's strategy-making process. The episode strengthened his determination to fully exploit Intel's favorable strategic position with the ×86 architecture. He said, "The commitment to the ×86 architecture vectorized everybody at Intel in the same direction."

Effectively Driving Strategy Making in the Core Business. The significance of the rise and fall of the i860 microprocessor lies primarily in the effect it had on Grove's efforts to further strengthen Intel's induced strategy process. Exhibit 2 shows that Grove had come to the conclusion that Intel's Darwinian strategy process was perhaps a guise for lack of a clear strategy. His efforts to vectorize everybody at Intel in the same direction in 1991 created an induced strategy process superbly suited for exploiting the rich opportunities in the PC market segment of the microprocessor industry. Several entries in Exhibit 2 describe how Grove drove Intel's strategy making in the core business during the remainder of Epoch II. He showed keen insight into the successive strategic differentiators that had formed the basis of Intel's competitive advantage in the past and emphasized the importance of large capital investments for competitive advantage for the remainder of the 1990s. He forced senior executives to resolve the frictions that were emerging between corporate marketing's concerns about protecting the Intel brand and the needs of businesses outside the core microprocessor business. He forced the motherboard business to adopt Intel's more advanced but also more expensive PCI chipset technology in the face of resistance of both the motherboard managers and the finance organization. Toward the end of Epoch II, Grove forced the microprocessor business to face up to the dangerous threat posed by the rapidly growing low end of the PC market. He recognized that Intel's "low-end phobia" was preventing it from meeting the challenge posed by this major environmental shift and directed Intel to engage in a crash effort to develop the Celeron processor to meet it. Finally, as Gordon Moore observed, Grove's strategy vector gave Intel the opportunity to drive its external environment; that is, the development of the PC market segment.

Intel's Narrow Business Strategy

Already in 1989 then-Chairman Gordon Moore had observed that CEO Andy Grove had significantly narrowed Intel's strategic focus, but he also predicted that the growth potential of the microprocessor business would not make that a problem in the next twelve years (Burgelman, 1991). Looking back in 1998 and comparing Intel's strategy during Epoch II and Epoch I, Grove said, "The most significant thing was the transformation of the company from a broadly positioned, across-the-board semiconductor supplier that did OK to a highly focused, highly tuned producer of microprocessors, which did better than OK" (Kawamoto and Galante, 1998). Many senior executives confirmed that Grove forced a distinct shift in the strategy-making process toward a narrow business strategy focused on microprocessors for the PC market segment. Exhibit 3 provides evidence of this shift. The views expressed in Exhibit 3 touch on various aspects of the strategic leadership approach Grove used to focus Intel's induced strategy process narrowly on the microprocessor business. They include setting clear objectives and establishing a structural context (Bower, 1970; Burgelman, 1983), including strategic planning, organization structure, and resource allocation, to align strategy and action.

Unambiguous Strategic Objectives. Intel's strategic focus became ingrained in the strategy-making process through the setting of clear and consistent objectives. Intel's number one objective was to strengthen the position of Intel microprocessors in the evolving computer industry. A related objective was to "make the PC it," which became somewhat of a rallying cry. Grove viewed the PC

EXHIBIT 3 Company Level of Analysis: Views on Intel's Narrow Business Strategy During Epoch II

Gordon Moore (1989):
"Over time . . . Intel has narrowed and narrowed its technological interests. Andy [Grove] has been instrumental in this. . . . We can do variations on present businesses very well. But doing something new is more difficult."

Gerry Parker (1989):
"We could now manufacture everything in one and one-half plants. That's obscene. You need a broad product base—EPROM [electrically programmable read-only memory] is a natural. . . ."

Les Vadasz (1988):
"The system [strategic long-range planning] is now [in the late 1980s] more top-down. A high-level group sets the corporate strategy, and business units operate within that focus. Business units must focus on a few things and do them right. . . . Some managers complain that their 'sandbox' is too well defined."

A senior executive (1995):
"Intel may be too focused too soon. We have narrowed our range of experimentation too fast from 360 degrees to 180 and then to 90. The code words are: You don't have a business plan; your strategy is vague."

"We must narrow down from a 360 degree scan to 20, but even so we still have 20 things to do. Andy [Grove], however, wants a 'laser short.'"

Frank Gill (1997):
"In 1994–95, Andy [Grove] would tell me, 'Frank, I make a billion dollars in profit per quarter and you make a billion dollars in revenue per year. This is all distraction, so focus on Job 1.'"

Another senior executive (1998):
". . . a lot . . . is driven from Job 1, because every six months we have an SLRP [strategic long-range planning meeting]. Andy [Grove] stands up and says . . . here is a problem. And everyone says . . . we can go do wonderful things to solve that problem."

Craig Barrett (1999):
"[During the second epoch] we became much more verticalized behind IA and related businesses. Now we are more broad. . . . This requires less top down management and more P&L and line management."

A third senior executive (1999):
"Barrett is very different from Grove. First, he's encouraging new ideas. . . . Andy wouldn't have let that happen. Craig made it happen. . . . Second is behavior. If you have a good idea, overwhelm it with resources: What do you need? Do what it takes. Come back with a prize. . . . That's a different style."

A fourth senior executive (1999):
"But I am more concerned about Andy [Grove] because of his singular focus. Andy says that PCs are becoming a commodity. So, we must focus on servers and not let Sun [Microsystems] capture this. It is like going back to the old days."

"Barrett at some point will be expected to set the corporate strategy; and if he doesn't, Andy [Grove] will."

---

as the ideal tool for computing as well as for communications and even for entertainment. Intel also made a distinction between "Job 1" and "Job 2." Job 1 encompassed everything that had to do with making the Intel architecture more successful. Job 2 involved the development of new businesses around the core business.

CEO-Driven Strategic Planning. Grove said that he had used changes in the company's strategic long-range planning process (SLRP) to redefine the content of the new corporate strategy and get the organization to execute it:

> In 1987, we blew up the SLRP process. Formerly it had been a very bottom-up process, but there was no strategic framework. Each of the different groups was supposed to come up with the strategy for their group, and then we would try to piece them together like a jigsaw puzzle. By '87, I was so frustrated with the whole thing that I started the process of turning the SLRP process on its head. I said, "I'm going to tell you what the strategy is." I started with a detailed discussion of the environmental issues, which led to a series of strategic mandates. I did not consult the organization. I did this myself, along with the help of my technical assistant at the time, Dennis Carter. . . . I became very directive in prescribing the strategic direction from the top down. This defined the strategy for all of the groups, and it provided a strategic framework for different groups at different levels of management. It's very hard to reach through several layers of management to communicate the strategy and the vision. SLRP became a tool for doing that.

Typically, Grove's SLRP kickoff speech was followed by a two-hour presentation in which he addressed Intel's strategic challenges, presented his vision of what was happening in the industry, and identified high-level trends. The remainder of the three-day meeting involved presentations by Intel's senior executives concerning specific issues and topics. They worked across product and functional groups to put their presentation together, with the help of a staff member. These executives had been given their assignment without knowing in advance what Grove was going to present. Dennis Carter pointed out that this was viewed as a tough assignment, dreaded by some, and that instances of strategic dissonance surfaced immediately.

Centralized Organization Structure.   During Grove's tenure as CEO, Intel's organization structure became highly centralized. In the words of one senior executive, "Intel was organized around funneling things up to Gordon, Andy, and Craig." Intel was structured as a matrix, with various corporate functions on one side and various product groups on the other. Each product group carried profit and loss responsibility for its respective market, but no product group controlled all of the functional resources needed to execute its strategy. The functional groups were responsible for supporting the product groups and for cultivating necessary expertise across the organization. The functional groups were highly stable so as to develop capabilities, while he product groups were constantly redefined in order to match the evolving product-market environment. Given the importance of microprocessors in Intel's new corporate strategy, and the relentless pace with which new product generations needed to be developed, manufactured, and marketed, coordination among all the groups was critical.

Tightly Managed Resource Allocation.   The resource allocation process strongly favored Intel's core microprocessor business. As one executive observed in 1999:

> Virtually every single quarter, the requests outweigh the willingness to spend. We would end up ZBB-ing [zero-based budgeting] the lower ROI projects. The larger ROI projects were almost always related to the mainstream CPU [microprocessor] business. Therefore, if you were not part of the mainstream business, you needed to be very spirited and very perseverant to drive your projects through that process every quarter. I knew they were great businesses by any other metric, just not compared to the microprocessor business. . . . If you were in a non-core business, it was tough.

Complementary Strategic Thrusts

Comparing Epoch II with Epoch I, Craig Barrett said in 1999, "We became the industry driving force." Exhibit 4

identifies key dynamics of the PC market segment between the early 1980s and 1998. It also identifies several complementary strategic thrusts, briefly discussed next, that made it possible for Intel to drive the PC market segment. These complementary thrusts did not reflect a comprehensive ex ante formulated strategic plan to take control of the PC market segment. Rather, Grove's successful narrow business strategy set in motion a positive feedback process that extended the number and magnitude of strategic responsibilities that Intel needed to take on to sustain its position as driver of the PC market segment. These, in turn, reinforced the induced strategy process.

Sole-Source Supplier.   The installed base of $\times 86$ microprocessors created by IBM's success in the PC market segment (with Intel's 8088 and 80286 microprocessors) had significantly and fortuitously shifted bargaining power in Intel's favor. Understanding the implications of increasing returns to adoption offered Intel the opportunity to become sole-source supplier of microprocessors for the PC market segment as of the 80386 microprocessor generation. Nevertheless, this was a bold move given IBM's still very powerful position in the industry. Looking back, Grove said, "What good is the 386 if IBM doesn't adopt it? . . . We were chewing our nails until 1986, when Compaq adopted the 386. IBM adopted it the next year." Intel was able to keep rival AMD tied up in the courts over intellectual property rights disputes, which allowed it to remain the sole source for the 386 processor for four years. The 386 microprocessor was succeeded by the i486, which was introduced in April 1989. It again took four years (until the summer of 1993) before AMD was able to launch its first 486-compatible processors.

Investing in Manufacturing.   One of the imperatives associated with the sole-source strategy was that Intel needed to become a world-class manufacturer. Exhibit 4 shows the large and rapidly increasing capital investments Intel made during Epoch II. Intel's new manufacturing prowess depended on a new distinctive competence: close integration of the Microprocessor Group's chip designs and process technology and manufacturing competencies within the Technology and Manufacturing Group. Intel became renowned for its ability to optimize the manufacturing process of a new chip design and then to roll out that process to Intel's other plants using the "copy exact" principle.

EXHIBIT 4 Company-Environment-Interface-Level of Analysis: Highlights of Coevolution of Intel's Narrow Business Strategy and PC Market Segment, Epoch II

PC market segment

1981–84	1985	1986 1987	1988 1989 1990 1991	1992 1993 1994	1995 1996	1997	1998
IBM introduces PC/XT/AT with an Intel chip and Microsoft operating system.	Large installed base for IBM PC/XT/AT; Compaq has emerged as a viable competitor; Intel and Microsoft are the fortuitous beneficiaries of a "virtuous circle."	Compaq first with 386 PC; IBM follows.	Clone PC manufacturers are gaining share.	Commoditization of PCs: intense margin pressure for PC OEMs; threat from IBM-Apple-Motorola RISC alliance does not materialize.	Internet emerges: threat of the network computer (NC).	Growth in demand for below-$1,000 PC is a real threat to Intel; NC threat does not materialize.	AMD [Advanced Micro Devices] gains market segment share on the low end.

Intel strategy

1981–84	1985	1986 1987 1988	1989 1990 1991	1992 1993 1994	1995 1996	1997	1998
8088 and 80286 chips for IBM PCs; cross-license other chip manufacturers; Intel initially not fully aware of importance of PC for its future.	Decision to be sole source for new 80386 processor and to maintain product leadership; "Red X" end-user marketing campaign.	Court battle with AMD about intellectual property rights for ×86 microprocessors prevents AMD from entering the 386 market for four years; same for 486.	Intel is sole source for i486 processor; "Intel Inside" end-user marketing campaign; Intel develops an ecosystem; i860 battle resolved; Intel creates IAL to enable the PC industry.	Intel is sole source for new Pentium processor; Intel vertically integrates into motherboards and chipsets, which are decisively helpful in Pentium launch; Pentium flaw crisis and resolution.	Intel introduces Pentium Pro for workstations with Windows NT; AMD litigation for 386 and 486 settled; Microsoft pressures Intel to stop its native signal processing (NSP) project.	Intel introduces Pentium with MMX and later in the year Pentium II.	Intel introduces Celeron processor to combat AMD on the low end; Pentium II Xeon for workstations/servers.

	1985	1986	1987	1988	1989	1990	1991	1992	1993	1994	1995	1996	1997	1998
Reven. ($ billion)	1.4	1.3	1.9	2.9	3.1	3.9	4.8	5.8	8.8	11.5	16.2	20.8	25.1	26.3
Profits ($ b)	0.0	−0.2	0.2	0.5	0.4	0.7	0.8	1.1	2.3	2.3	3.6	5.2	6.9	6.1
Cap. invest. ($ b)	0.24	0.15	0.3	0.5	0.4	0.7	0.9	1.2	1.9	2.4	3.6	3.0	4.5	4.0
R&D exp. ($ b)	0.19	0.23	0.3	0.3	0.4	0.5	0.6	0.8	1.0	1.1	1.3	1.8	2.3	2.7

Pacing the Race Through Product Leadership. Exhibit 4 shows the rapid pace of product introductions between 1993 and early 1998: Pentium (1993), Pentium Pro (1995), Pentium MMX (1997), Pentium II (1997), and the Celeron (1998) processors. This time-driven product introduction strategy, however, reflected deep intuition for the feasible pace of development of the PC industry. In an M.B.A. class in fall 1994, Andy Grove revealed that he had learned from studying the data that the peak-to-peak production across microprocessor generations for 386 and 486 microprocessors had been about three years and would be the same for the Pentium processor. Based on this, Grove assumed that the next generation microprocessor, the P6, would follow the same adoption cycle, which informed the timing of Intel's next major capital investment decisions.

Building Brand with End Users. In April 1990, Intel launched its first "Intel Inside" campaign. Aimed directly at end users, rather than Intel's traditional PC OEM customers, the campaign sought to influence customers to ask for Intel microprocessors specifically when they purchased a PC. Major OEMs such as Compaq and IBM initially refused to participate in some elements because they felt that Intel Inside decreased their ability to differentiate their products from the competition, but eventually all of them carried the Intel Inside logo on their products, in part because Intel engaged in massive co-marketing campaigns with the OEMs. From 1990 to 1993, Intel invested more than $500 million in end-user marketing campaigns. Paradoxically, the Pentium flaw crisis of November–December 1994, which, according to Grove, "shook Intel to its core," in some ways indicated the powerful impact of Intel's branding strategy on end users.

Introducing Industry-Enabling Technologies. Increased competition among a growing number of PC OEMs created intense pressure on their profit margins. Combined with its successful sole-source strategy, this gave Intel the ability to appropriate a large part of the available profits in the PC market segment. This created a positive feedback loop, which increasingly shifted the center of industry influence from the PC OEMs to Intel (and to Microsoft) during the 1990s. Only the largest PC OEM customers could afford to do much research and development (R&D). Other OEMs became increasingly dependent on Intel for technological innovation. Intel created the Intel Architecture Labs (IAL) for the purpose of developing new technologies that would remove technological bottlenecks preventing PCs from taking full advantage of the increased processing power of new-generation microprocessors. These technologies were offered to the OEM customers for free or for nominal royalty payments.

Cultivating an Ecosystem of Complementors. The most important complementary product for Intel's microprocessors was Microsoft's Windows operating system software. Andy Grove described the relationship between Microsoft and Intel as "two companies joined at the hip." While constantly vying for perceived leadership of the PC industry and jealously guarding their own spheres of influence (software for Microsoft and hardware for Intel), most of the time the two companies were able to maintain their symbiotic relationship throughout Grove's tenure as CEO. Intel also invested in creating internal support groups to help other independent software vendors develop applications requiring high processor power to stimulate demand for its next generation processors. Intel provided its partners with advance information about its next microprocessor designs and support products.

Forward Integration into Chipsets and Motherboards. Intel's chipsets and motherboards made it possible to leverage its strong strategic position in microprocessors by enabling OEM customers, who did not have the resources to develop these system-level products, to introduce PCs with Intel's latest microprocessors. This is turn was helpful in reducing its dependency on the stronger OEMs, in case the latter were reluctant to stay with Intel's road map for developing next-generation microprocessors. This actually happened when some major OEMs initially decided to wait to introduce Pentium processor–based PCs, and Intel enabled Packard Bell and Dell to take the lead.

Successful Coevolution Turns into Inertia

During Epoch II, in contrast to Epoch I, Intel's distinctive competencies continued to evolve with the basis of competition in the PC market segment of the microprocessor industry, and the official strategy clearly drove strategic action, leveraging both position and distinctive competence. This gave the company great momentum between 1987 and 1997, which is reflected in revenue growth and profit growth (Exhibit 4). In late 1998, Intel's stock market valuation surpassed $200 billion for the first time.

Lock-In. Intel's narrow business strategy tied its success increasingly to that of the PC market segment. By 1993, 486 microprocessors accounted for 75 percent of the company's revenues of $8.8 billion and 85 percent of its $2.3 billion in net profit. By 1998, 80 percent of Intel's $26.3 billion in revenues and just about all of its $6.1 billion in net profits came from microprocessors. Signaling the company's extreme dependence on the prospects of its product-market environment, revenues grew only 5 percent, and net income declined 13 percent during 1998, in part as a result of the unexpectedly rapid relative growth of the low end of the PC market segment. Exhibit 4 shows the increasingly large capital and R&D investments that needed to be made to keep driving the coevolutionary process. Also, Intel's dependence on the OEM customers as a distribution channel for its microprocessor products made forward integration into systems products difficult. Intel's strong interdependence with Microsoft impeded strategic initiatives in the software area. In one widely noted case—Intel's Native Signal Processing (NSP) initiative to augment the microprocessor's video capability (Exhibit 4)—Grove admitted that Intel "caved" in the face of Microsoft's displeasure (Schlender, 1996).

Inertia. By 1997, Intel's road map for the development of next generations of microprocessors determined its long-term development trajectory, which was not easily changed. While Intel had put mechanisms in place that allowed very fast response to short-term contingencies affecting the road map, Dennis Carter explained that the ability to make quick adjustments, paradoxically, reinforced the company's strategic focus and the lock-in with the PC market segment. The successful crash effort to develop the Celeron processor, however, signaled that while Intel's lock-in with the PC market segment remained strong, the lock-in of the PC market segment with Intel was perhaps loosening. Also, toward the end of 1996, Andy Grove was beginning to worry about the effect Intel's strong influence with its OEM customers was having on its strategy-making process. In an M.B.A. class discussion in fall 1996, Grove said, "There is a hidden danger of Intel becoming very good at this. It is that we become good at one thing only."

COEVOLUTIONARY LOCK-IN AND STRATEGIC INERTIA

Reduced Capacity for New Business Development

By 1997, then-COO Craig Barrett did not believe that Intel could sustain its historical growth rate and profitability solely with microprocessors. Barrett realized that

Intel's intense focus on microprocessors had made it difficult for new ventures to thrive inside Intel (hence, his use of the creosote bush metaphor mentioned earlier). Different groups in the company continued to explore a multitude of new business ideas (Burgelman, Carter, and Bamford, 1999), but Intel's autonomous strategy process had become less able to exploit new business opportunities. Dennis Carter noted that outbound marketing (delivering a technology to the market) dominated inbound marketing (finding new market needs that could be met by technology). Frank Gill, an executive vice president in charge of Intel's new business development during most of Epoch II, pointed out that Intel's matrix organization did not provide managers with much opportunity to learn to make trade-offs among various functional considerations. This impeded the development of new generations of general managers able to develop new businesses. Also, business-level general managers must resolve the initial ambiguity about the correct strategy of a new business, but in the corporate context this is not sufficient. To continue to obtain corporate support the process of strategic context determination must be activated, which helps link the new business strategy to the corporate strategy. This explorative, iterative process involves multiple levels of management in building a new strategic thrust for the corporation (Burgelman, 1983).

During fall 1999, Andy Grove reflected on the slowing down of growth in the core microprocessor business and his efforts to develop new businesses during Epoch II: "The old CEO knew that this was coming. He tried like hell to develop new business opportunities, but they almost all turned into [dirt]." Public data support Grove's contention that he knew relatively early on that Intel would have to transform itself again. Already in 1993, he had said, "Our people have navigated successfully through one transformation, so perhaps it won't be as hard to sign them up for another one. But success can trap you. The more successful we are as a microprocessor company, the more difficult it will be to become something else. To take advantage of some opportunities I see ahead, we're going to have to transform ourselves again. The time to do it is while our business is still strong" (Grove, 1993: 60).

While Grove recognized the need for strategic renewal, difficulties in developing new businesses during Epoch II suggest that he and Intel were subject to sources of strategic inertia associated with coevolutionary lock-in. Exhibit 5 identifies these two sources of strategic inertia. The ProShare case shows that the CEO's active involvement in driving new business development is likely

EXHIBIT 5 Company Level of Analysis: Coevolutionary Lock-in and Sources of Strategic Inertia During Epoch II

Views from below	Intel's strategic intent	Strategic action
1. If strategic, apply logic of core business strategy.		
Intel's strategy for videoconferencing (ProShare)		
Patrick Gelsinger (GM, ProShare): "ProShare was viewed as a horizontal capability—that was Andy's [Grove] wish." "We could have acted on the vertical markets six months sooner if Andy had not had such a strong opinion." *Another ProShare executive:* "There wasn't a debate about it, there wasn't even a discussion. . . . Andy had already trained the organization, meaning Intel, that periodically he gets all these flashes of an idea." *Frank Gill (senior executive):* "It was not being out of the loop so much as not being sure. . . . [I thought] maybe the throwing of massive resources at it would work. I didn't know for sure and Andy and Pat were quite confident.	Grove's intent was to make videoconferencing an integral capability of the PC. To this end, he favored a frontal assault on the entire PC market segment, rather than targeting vertical segments first.	Grove assigned Patrick Gelsinger, in charge at the time of the next-generation microprocessor development, to ProShare. *Grove:* "Moving Pat off of P6, a product on which the future of our company truly depends, to run this new initiative was a very controversial step. But in many ways this is the test of it." Grove continued to be deeply involved in the strategic decision making until 1996, when he asked Frank Gill to scale down the effort, which involved some 700 people at the time. *Grove in 1999:* "We assumed that just because it could be done technically there would be high demand. I was an enthusiastic user and supporter, but I've stopped using it. . . . If we were to do it over again, our approach would be not so much like the Normandy invasion, but more of a vertical focus. . . . We brought a style and conceptual approach to an area where it did not work."
Intel's strategy for bringing the PC into the living room (Hood River)		
Rob Siegel (project manager) and his team identified the target applications and uses for the Hood River product. The design called for the use of Intel's 233 MHz Pentium II processor, the highest performance CPU at the time. *By August 1996, Siegel:* ". . . we had accomplished a lot. We had Microsoft doing what we wanted them to do, and we had established an impressive customer list. In addition, the Product Line Business Plan presentation went well. We received the highest rating, and Andy Grove came up with the phrase, 'Hijack the TV,' which became our rallying cry."	*Andy Grove:* "'The PC is it,' Grove declares. 'That sums up Intel's business plan and rallying cry.' 'Some think the information superhighway will come through their TV,' Grove proclaimed. . . . '[But] the information tool of the future is on your desk, not in your living room'" (Burstein and Kline, 1995: 24).	Siegel and his team continued their efforts through the fall of 1996. But they ran into funding problems when the idea of a "network computer" (NC) gained some tracking under the impulse of Oracle's Larry Ellison, and the Desktop Product Group (DPG) reallocated resources to meet the perceived threat to the core business. Siegel was able to get funding reinstated, but the market for Hood River did not develop as planned. In early 1997, Mike Aymar (GM of DPG) halted the venture. *Aymar:* "Originally we expected the venture to . . . generate demand for another 1 million PCs per year. But market projections were for various vendors worldwide to ship only in the tens of thousands of units in '97 and '98. . . . This was insufficient.
2. If "non-strategic," pay as you go.		
PCI Chipsets as a new business		
Andy Beran (Finance Mgr.): "We never would have gotten into the business if we had to fight for internal capacity. . . .	*Ron Smith (GM, chipset busin.):* Regarding his intent to develop the chipset business based on Intel's new PCI technol-	Senior Microprocessor Group executives supported Smith's efforts to develop the chipset business. Smith was able to use

(continues)

EXHIBIT 5 (continued)

Views from below	Intel's strategic intent	Strategic action
2. If "non-strategic," pay as you go.		
PCI Chipsets as a new business		
It always would have looked like a lower [return] to the processors."	ogy: "Andy Grove told me that we had no damn business doing PCI . . . That was early on. He and I had a heated discussion about it. . . . He basically said something to the effect of who do we think we are, a chip company thinking we are going to drive an I/O bus standard."	the new PCI technology to wrest control of chipsets away from the PC OEMs and make the chipsets an important tool for supporting the launch of Intel's new Pentium processor. With Smith having succeeded in the face of corporate ambivalence, Grove wrote Smith a note saying, "And I said it couldn't be done." From then on, Grove viewed the chipset business as strategically important for the core business.
Beran noted that top management let them keep the cash they generated with old products to fund the development of chipset business: "At the point where that wasn't enough, we were already successful enough to keep going."		
Randy Wilhelm (Technical Mgr.): "There was some doubt, I think, in certain parts of Intel that we were able to push a bus standard, whereas in the past we had always had key OEMs pushing the bus standard."		
Eric Mentzer (Marketing Mgr.): "They said, we don't believe you guys are going to be successful, so we don't want you going into those accounts. . . . The processor division was out telling the field sales force and the customers, don't use this; use the low-risk thing."		
Networking as a new business		
Frank Gill (GM, Networking): "First, in the early 1990s, there was Andy Grove's ability to get everybody to focus on job 1. . . . Any other activity was viewed as a distraction. . . . A second factor was that . . . since all the planning activity involving Andy was focused on job 1, he did not have sufficient insight or knowledge to meaningfully contribute to our networking and connectivity businesses."	*Grove:* "There was a time when I could have flipped a switch between videoconferencing and networking."	Grove funded both opportunities, but he said, "Much more funding was going to videoconferencing."
"In 1994–95, Andy would tell me, 'Frank, I make a billion dollars in profit per quarter and you make a billion dollars in revenue per year. This is all distraction, so focus on Job 1.'"	"I have been rabid about four things in my career at Intel: motherboards, Intel Inside, chipsets, and videoconferencing. What if I had been equally rabid about networking? Intel could be a very different company."	Grove did not allow much time for discussions of the networking business during the strategic long-range planning sessions of the early-to-mid-1990s.
"Networking was forced to live quarter by quarter. Any time we did not make the planned quarterly numbers, we were put on notice and I got lots of questions about why we were wasting energy in this area."	Reflecting on strategic discussions concerning the networking business with Frank Gill, Grove said, "I am not happy with statements that are somewhat right, but mostly wrong. Maybe I am too good for my own good. I weed out all the weeds, but also some of the potential seeds. . . . Barrett is more comfortable with leaving strategy a bit more murky, undefined."	*As of 1997, Frank Gill:* "Mark [Christensen] clearly got networking better connected within Intel. He came up with the fast Ethernet 'big pipes need big processors' notion and building remote management hooks into the network cards. He also put more focus on OEM customers where Intel had channel power."
Mark Christensen (Gill's successor): "For the first six years, from 1991 to 1997, it was basically 'pay your own way' for growth. If you didn't grow, you had the threat of getting downsized. Much of the funding was being funneled into programs that would help microprocessor growth—Job 1."		After 1997, networking was viewed as part of the corporate strategy, leading to a major acquisition and full corporate support for growing the business.

to impose the logic of the successful core business in an area in which it may not apply, thereby impeding development of an appropriate business strategy and simultaneously inducing escalation of commitment. The Hood River case shows that even if the CEO is not actively involved, he or she may cast a shadow of influence that also impedes the development of an appropriate strategy for the new business, even though not inducing escalation of commitment. The chipset case shows some of the major difficulties a new business must overcome to get corporate support if the CEO initially views it as an enabler only of the core business. The networking case shows that these difficulties are exacerbated if the link with the core business cannot be easily established, thereby limiting its growth funding to the resources that it can generate on its own. Exhibit 6 summarizes the compara-

tive analysis of these four cases using the process model of internal corporate venturing (Burgelman, 1983). The process model identifies key interlocking activities of different levels of management (corporate, middle, and venture) in the core (definition and impetus) and overlaying (structural context and strategic context) subprocesses of venture development.

Strategic Inertia I: If Strategic, Apply Logic of Core Strategy

The Proshare Case.   The ProShare venture's purpose was to make videoconferencing a standard PC capability, which would help create additional demand for microprocessor power. Grove's strategic intent determined the strategic context for the venture from the start (Exhibit 5). His support shielded the venture from the strong

EXHIBIT 6   Intra-Company Level of Analysis: Comparative Process Model Analysis of Four New Business Development Cases During Epoch II

Leadership activities by management level and subprocess*	ProShare	Hood River	Chipsets	Networking Until 1997	Networking Changes after 1997
Corporate management level:					
Definition: Monitoring	From the start	From the start	Fly under radar	Little interest	Strong
Impetus: Authorizing	From the start	Erratic	Pay as you go	Pay as you go	Strong
Strategic context: Rationalizing	Premature	Didn't get to	Lagging (link to Pentium)	Lagging	Link to core
Structural context: Structuring;	Suspended	Strong influence	Strong influence	Strong influence	Adjusted
Selecting (links structural and strategic contexts)	Suspended	Strong influence	Strong influence	Strong influence	Adjusted
Middle management level:					
Definition: Coaching	Limited	Limited	Strong	Strong	
Impetus: Strategic building;	Didn't get to	Didn't get to	Not necessary	Limited	Strong
Organizational championing (links impetus and strategic context)	Not necessary	Didn't get to	Strong	Give up	Strong
Strategic context: Delineating	Premature	Didn't get to	Strong	Limited	Strong
Structural context: Negotiating	Not necessary	Ineffective	Strong	Defensive	Strong
Venture management level:					
Definition: Technical and need linking;	Limited effectiveness	Ineffective	Effective	Effective	
Product championing (links definition and impetus)	Not necessary	Ineffective	Effective	Effective	
Impetus: Strategic forcing	Limited effectiveness	Ineffective	Effective	Effective	
Strategic context: e.g., bootlegging	Little room	Not possible	Anticipate Pentium	Limited	
Structural context: Questioning	Little room	Ineffective	Work around	Work around	

*Source: Burgelman, 1983.

selection pressures of the structural context, in particular Intel's rigorous financial reviews. Grove got deeply involved in monitoring the definition of the venture strategy and in authorizing funding of its development (Exhibit 6). In a fall 1999 discussion with an M.B.A. class, Grove mentioned that Intel had spent about $750 million on the unsuccessful venture. His insistence on applying the horizontal, frontal assault strategy of the microprocessor business to ProShare reduced the degrees of freedom of the executives in charge of the new business development effort (Exhibit 5). Pat Gelsinger's task was to deliver a technology to the market in the same way that Intel delivered next-generation microprocessors to the market. Technical and need-linking efforts were limited in their effectiveness; discipline-instilling, product-championing efforts were not required to secure resources internally; and the effectiveness of strategic-forcing efforts to secure a fast-growing beachhead in the market was limited (Exhibit 6). Frank Gill, the senior executive positioned between Grove and Gelsinger, was left—or rather, as he put it, "able to stay"—out of the loop. With Grove performing the role of Gill in the strategic context determination process, the discipline-instilling organizational championing efforts—requiring Gill to convince peers, as well as top management, that the continuation of the videoconferencing venture was in the long-term interest of the corporation—were not required (Exhibit 6). Finally, as a consequence of the early and sustained support from the CEO, the opportunity costs associated with ProShare were not considered until 1996, when Gill was asked to scale the venture down (Exhibit 5).

The Hood River Case. The Hood River venture's purpose was to bring the PC into the living room as an electronic entertainment device. Hood River was started as a seed project with initial funding from Intel's Corporate Business Development group in February 1996. The venture's strategy was influenced from the start by Grove's publicly stated strategic intent that the "PC is it," which was taken to heart by Rob Siegel the project leader (Exhibit 5). This drove the technical and need-linking efforts in the Hood River product definition. Since there was no direct and forceful support from the CEO for this project, the selective effects of the structural context were very strong (Exhibit 6). This was evident when funding was temporarily cut off without warning in December 1996 to harness resources in the face of the perceived threat of the "network computer" (NC) to Intel's core business. In-

effective technical and need-linking activities made it difficult to collaborate with the consumer electronics OEMs, who had a very different view of the market and the technology required. Siegel tried to pursue product-championing activities, but, as a relative newcomer, he could not exert influence in the network of resource-controlling relationships of Intel's matrix. Strategic forcing never got started, as no consumer electronics OEMs or PC OEMs were willing to adopt the Hood River product concept (Exhibit 6). As a result, Michael Aymar, the middle-level executive, had no foundation to build on and could not continue to ask top management for support. He stopped funding Hood River in 1997 (Exhibit 5).

Strategic Inertia II:
If Non-Strategic, Pay as You Go

The PCI Chipset Case. Intel Architecture Labs developed the PCI bus technology in the early 1990s. Top management's initial intention was to organize a consortium to bring PCI to the PC industry as an enabling technology for the core microprocessor business, as the previous bus standard was too slow to take advantage of increased processing power. Determination of the strategic context of the PCI chipset venture was lagging because Grove was opposed to the idea of turning PCI chipsets into a business (Exhibit 5). Ron Smith nevertheless decided to pursue PCI chipsets as a new business. He tried to "fly under the radar" to protect the venture from close top management scrutiny to build a viable business foundation (Exhibit 6). He assembled a team of experienced functional managers who were well connected with the rest of the corporation and could access resources that would otherwise not be available. These managers engaged in careful technical and need linking to define Intel's chipset opportunity. Realizing they would not be able to secure scarce manufacturing capacity internally against the more profitable microprocessors, their product-championing efforts took the form of contracting with outside manufacturers. Smith convinced his team that winning inside required winning outside through successful strategic forcing (Exhibit 6). Each year, the venture delivered more than it had promised, which gave senior executives such as Albert Yu, Paul Otellini, and Craig Barrett a reason for supporting it in the face of Andy Grove's doubts. The chipset venture's potential was sufficiently large that no additional business opportunities needed to be found to reach critical mass. Ron Smith did not have to engage in strategic building, which requires the agglomeration of additional business opportunities through internal transfer of projects and/or through carefully targeted acquisitions, and could focus on coaching the venture team. Also, Smith had anticipated that the PCI chipset would be important for facilitating the launch of the Pentium processor in 1993 and had instructed the team to design the chipset accordingly. Smith's prediction turned out to be correct, which facilitated the determination of the strategic context later on (Exhibit 6). Eventually, Grove concluded that the chipset venture was an important business for Intel. His retroactive rationalization concluded the process of strategic context determination. From then on it had his full support.

The Networking Business Case.   In the early 1990s, Frank Gill's charter was to develop new businesses for Intel, but because of the enormous growth of the core business, Andy Grove began to view these efforts as a distraction. Grove felt that Gill was too much focused on the success of the networking business and not enough on that of the core business. Grove also felt uncomfortable with the lack of clarity of the networking strategy (Exhibit 5). Gill pointed out that Grove had been totally focused on the core microprocessor business and that the strategic long-range planning process (SLRP) spent little time on businesses that were not considered strategic. Top management looked at networking as an industry enabler, rather than as a new business. Gill gave up on the organizational championing efforts in the face of peer resistance and top management's recalcitrance and focused on short-term financial performance to protect the business (Exhibit 6). This created a vicious circle. Unsuccessful organizational championing limited the amount of corporate resources made available for the networking business, which limited the scope of the strategic building activities that Gill could engage in: large acquisitions were simply not permitted. And this, in turn, limited the growth of the business in the fast growing industry to what could be achieved with the strategic forcing activities based on the internally developed products. Fortunately, these were the result of effective technical and need linking and experienced strong market acceptance. The effectiveness of these activities was at least in part the result of Gill's strong coaching of his team and successful shielding of the networking business from top management. Only in 1997, when a new general manager was able to show the importance of networking for the microprocessor business and for Intel's future growth

was its strategic context determined, and it received full top management support.

DISCUSSION AND CONCLUSIONS
Coevolutionary Lock-In

This study shows how Andy Grove was able to take advantage of the fortuitous circumstances Intel faced in its microprocessor business with the rapid ascendance of the IBM PC and to turn good luck into a strategy vector. He made Intel focus on a narrow business strategy and established an induced strategy process that tightly aligned strategy and action and produced extraordinary success. His deep understanding of the forces that gave rise to the strategy vector also gave him great confidence in dealing with several crises that challenged it. This study, however, also reveals the complex reciprocal causation between Grove's strategic intent and the structures and processes that he put in place and how the very success of the strategy vector resulted in the emergence of coevolutionary lock-in and impeded new business development. Although Grove was a master of strategy, who knew that Intel would have to transform itself again eventually, he and Intel were subject to inescapable evolutionary dilemmas associated with the dynamics of coevolutionary lock-in.

Intel's success as the sole source of the highest value component of PCs made it increasingly able to appropriate the available rents in the PC market segment. But this asymmetry created a positive feedback loop, requiring Intel to make more and more of the investments necessary to enable adoption of next-generation microprocessors. These complementary strategic thrusts helped Intel to control its external environment (Pfeffer and Salancik, 1978), but they also increasingly tied its strategic direction and economic fortunes to the evolution of the PC market segment. Coevolutionary lock-in engendered by strategic dominance entangled Intel in a system of relationships that reduced its freedom of action, a paradox well articulated by J. G. March: "You can have autonomy or you can have power but you cannot have both. Power depends on linkages and linkages destroy autonomy" (personal communication).

As a driving force of the PC market segment, Intel was able to influence the pace of industry change. Such time-paced strategy is a powerful alternative to event-paced strategy (Gersick, 1994; Brown and Eisenhardt, 1997). It allows a company to dictate the pace of strategic change that other players—customers, competitors, suppliers, and complement—must adhere to. Intel's time-paced strategy, however, did not simply try to impose its strategic intent on the product-market environment unilaterally. Grove had learned that there was a natural adoption cycle in the PC market segment, with a period of about three years between the maximum ramp-up for different microprocessor generations. He also knew that Intel could not expect to change that much. At the same time, having put in place the competencies and support infrastructure to deliver new generations of microprocessors to the PC market segment, Intel had a strong internal drive to do so. Intel's time-paced strategy thus reinforced the lock-in with the PC market segment. Also, Intel was able to win the two defining battles in the microprocessor market segment—against other Intel architecture suppliers and against the RISC architecture—that Grove had identified in late 1993. But Intel's competitive intensity increasingly specialized the company's competitive repertoire for the PC market segment (Barnett, 1997), further reinforcing coevolutionary lock-in.

Intel's introduction of the Celeron processor in 1998 to counter AMD at the low end of the PC market segment testifies to the company's relentless competitive intensity. The need for a crash effort to introduce the Celeron processor, however, also suggests that Intel, while continuing to innovate at a high rate with its Pentium processor product family, had begun to produce innovations that were less in tune with evolving environmental demands (Sørensen and Stuart, 2000). Intel seemed to have difficulties recognizing that the importance of the external selection environment relative to the internal selection environment was increasing toward the end of Epoch II (Sorenson, 2000). Intel's difficulties in this respect seem consistent with the observation that in successful organizations there will be a natural tendency for internal selective-retentive processes to dominate external ones (Miller, 1999: 94). Coevolutionary lock-in may thus be an extension and further elucidation of the sources of structural inertia (Hannan and Freeman, 1984).

Extraordinary success associated with coevolutionary lock-in heightened Andy Grove's confidence in the logic of the core business strategy (e.g., Prahalad and Bettis, 1986). But Grove's direct involvement in ProShare made it difficult for the middle-level executive in charge to develop a strategy that was appropriate for the new business and to act in accordance with an objective analysis of the situation. Grove's approach in the ProShare case supports Audia, Locke, and Smith's (2000) suggestion that success may increase a decision maker's feelings of self-efficacy. It confirms that the inertia of success is often best understood in terms of the strength of the decision maker's beliefs in the validity of the current strategy, rather than in terms of complacency or drifting without further attempts at improvement (Miller and Chen, 1994). It also supports Miller's (1994) finding that decision-making styles tend to be more extreme during periods following success than during periods following poor or mediocre performance. Grove eventually came to realize this, but his strong involvement early on, before major market and technical uncertainties had been reduced, led to escalation of commitment and prevented scaling down or timely exit from the failing business. This raises important questions about the limitations of using top management's strategic intent as a means for guided evolution (Lovas and Ghoshal, 2000). Within Intel's induced-strategy process, guided evolution worked fine: Many new projects related to the strategic intent expressed in the microprocessor road map were useful variations that were effectively selected and retained. When Grove tried to use strategic intent to shape new variations that were not commensurate with the logic of the core business, however, the result was misguided evolution.

Much of Intel's R&D investments went into technologies that complemented the microprocessor and thereby offered opportunities to launch new businesses, but the company rarely attempted to do so. One reason for this was that any technology advance that enriched the PC market segment was likely to create more demand for microprocessors, which had very high margins. Thus, it was generally more valuable in the short run to give away technology and quickly disseminate it in the market, rather than try to build a business around it. This suggests the powerful effect that financial strategy and capital market considerations may have on product-market strategy. It also indicates, however, another strong structural inertial consequence of coevolutionary lock-in. As Intel's extraordinary lucrative core business continued to grow very fast in the mid-1990s, Grove began to consider non-core business development as a distraction. Consequently, it was increasingly difficult for non-core new businesses to command top management attention and corporate resources. This was exacerbated by Intel's structural context, which facilitated execution of the core business strategy but was less able to deal with non-core new business development: Strategic planning was almost exclusively focused on the core business. New general management talent was not easily developed in Intel's matrix organization. Resource allocation favored the core business, and new businesses were constantly in danger of experiencing random shocks when critical resources were taken away to cope with a perceived threat to the core business. The measurement and reward system was unforgiving for deviations from objectives, even though new business strategies require such flexibility. While many new ideas continued to emerge, the structural context made it difficult to activate the process of strategic context determination, necessary to link the new business to the corporate strategy.

Implications for Theory

The causes and consequences of coevolutionary lock-in suggest that this little-noticed process might help illuminate some of the inescapable dilemmas in the natural dynamics of organizational adaptation. It also helps connect ideas about the internal ecology of strategy making, the modern economic theory of the firm, and an evolutionary perspective on organizational learning.

Organizational Adaptation. Previous findings based on a study of Intel's transformation during Epoch I (Burgelman, 1991, 1994) supported the proposition that companies that are successful over long periods of time maintain top-driven strategic intent, through the induced strategy process, while simultaneously maintaining bottoms-up driven strategic renewal, through the autonomous strategy process. Recent efforts by scholars to formalize parts of the induced and autonomous strategy processes framework seem to support this proposition. In Rotemberg's and Saloner's (2000) mathematical model, the firm employs a visionary CEO who is consistently biased in favor of certain projects but who leaves the door open for pursuing sufficiently good opportunities outside the existing vision. They have shown that this may offer greater profit-maximizing possibilities than committing to a narrow business strategy (Rotemberg and Saloner, 1994). They showed the important role played by objective middle managers supporting promising projects outside the CEO's vision. Importantly, they also showed that the CEO must not interfere with the autonomy of middle managers in allocating resources to autonomous projects.

The study of Grove's tenure as CEO initially cast doubt on the importance of the autonomous strategy process. Like other great leaders, Grove was able to recognize the unique opportunities facing Intel and to mobilize his organization to exploit them by creating an extremely focused induced strategy process. If the growth of the PC

market segment had continued unabated, Intel's induced strategy process would probably have sufficed to secure continued adaptation, reducing thereby further the relevance of the autonomous strategy process. This would have undermined the validity of the internal ecology perspective on strategy making. Toward the end of Epoch II, however, it became clear that Intel's future growth would also depend on new business development and that the strategies for new businesses might have to be defined by general managers who were closer to the front line. Inertial consequences of coevolutionary lock-in, however, had significantly reduced the effectiveness of Intel's autonomous strategy process. Exhibit 7 provides a schematic representation of the paper's core theoretical idea: A company's relentless and successful pursuit of a narrow business strategy through the induced strategy process may produce coevolutionary lock-in and reduce the effectiveness of the autonomous strategy process, which weakens a company's long-term adaptation.

The heavy lines in Exhibit 7 indicate the reinforcement of Intel's induced strategy process, the creation of the strategy vector, and the coevolutionary lock-in with the PC market segment that it engendered. Exhibit 7 also shows the impact of the sources of inertia associated with coevolutionary lock-in on the autonomous strategy process. Some initiatives that needed to be pursued through the autonomous strategy process were erroneously subjected to the logic of the induced strategy process (Strategic Inertia I); others faced Intel's reduced ability to activate strategic context determination processes (Strategic Inertia II).

Exhibit 7 illuminates inescapable evolutionary dilemmas arising in the natural dynamics of organizational adaptation. Grove's strategic leadership approximated the classical rational-actor model in pursuing Intel's enormous opportunity in the PC market segment, but at the cost of reducing Intel's capability to develop new businesses. Was this a mistake? This study suggests that objective necessities arising from the coevolutionary lock-in of the induced strategy process and the product-market environment were a major cause of the relative neglect of the autonomous strategy process. The resource requirements of pursuing the microprocessor business, especially top management time and attention, did not leave much room for alternative pursuits. And the short-term opportunity costs of pursuing the microprocessor business were perceived as low. Also, it seems quite possible that Andy Grove passed on the CEO baton to Craig Barrett in early 1998 when he realized that a

EXHIBIT 7 Effects of a Strategy Vector on the Internal Ecology of Strategy Making

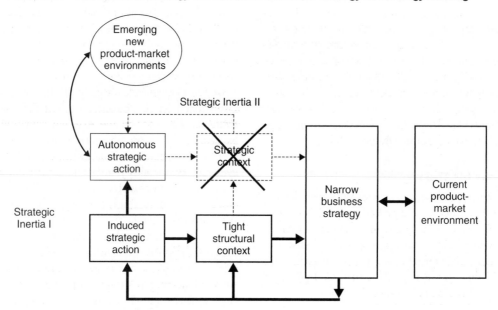

new, less singularly focused strategic leadership approach was necessary and there was still time to rebuild Intel's new business development capability. Alternatively, might an effort to maintain the internal ecology of strategy making have severely hampered the firm? Does optimal long-term adaptation follow a punctuated equilibrium pattern (e.g., Tushman and Romanelli, 1985), perhaps involving a series of discrete periods, each focused on maximally exploiting the available opportunities, rather than a more continuous evolutionary process of balancing exploitation of available opportunities at a given time with preparing the ground for future growth opportunities? This study cannot definitively answer these alternative questions. Its findings suggest, however, that without major acquisitions, the likelihood of moving instantaneously and discontinuously from one period's opportunity frontier to that of another is low. For instance, it took more than ten years for microprocessors to become Intel's new core business. In 2002, Intel management realized that large new businesses do not emerge fully formed out of the blue. Recognizing the possibility of alternative developmental paths, this paper's identification of coevolutionary lock-in nevertheless casts new light on the role of strategy making as a long-term adaptive organizational capability. This advance of administrative science provides company leaders responsible for designing the strategy-making pro-

cess with a conceptual framework for considering more explicitly and sooner the trade-offs involved in balancing induced and autonomous strategic processes and exploitation and exploration in organizational learning.

Strategy and Learning   This study's findings raise the question of whether induced and autonomous strategy processes are fundamentally at odds with one another or can be effectively pursued simultaneously. Maintaining the simultaneity of induced (variation reducing) and autonomous (variation increasing) strategy processes may involve difficulties similar to maintaining a balance between exploitation and exploration processes in organizational learning (March, 1991). Both processes compete for limited resources, and company leaders necessarily make tradeoffs between them. Given the extraordinary opportunities Intel faced in the core business, focusing on learning that increased its mean performance rather than on learning that could increase the variance of performance seemed rational (March, 1991: 82). Also, Grove's ability to vectorize everybody at Intel in the same direction led to quick convergence of individual beliefs (strategic initiatives) and the organizational code (the corporate strategy) (March, 1991: 75). Intel experienced turnover because the lowest 10 percent of individual performers were systematically replaced, but this also ensured the rapid socialization of new employees to Intel's organizational code because they were keen to understand Intel's performance expectations, which were clearly tied to implementing the core strategy. Overall, Intel's induced strategy process during Grove's tenure as CEO favored organizational learning that was maximally concerned with exploitation.

Exploration involves experimentation (March, 1991) and is viewed here through the lens of the autonomous strategy process, which dissects exploration into autonomous strategic initiatives and the process of strategic context determination. The strategic context determination process, which depends critically on the general management abilities of middle-level executives, helps companies turn exploration efforts into new exploitation opportunities. The distinction between exploratory initiatives and the strategic context determination process helps explain the mixed record of new business development during Intel's Epoch II. In spite of Grove's efforts to vectorize everybody in the same direction, numerous autonomous strategic initiatives continued to emerge, indicating continued attempts at exploration. The decrease in Intel's capacity to activate strategic context determination processes, however, prevented the company from exploiting the more viable autonomous initiatives. Strategic context determination processes thus appear to be the crucial nexus between exploration and exploitation and key to balancing induced and autonomous strategy processes effectively. Strategic context determination processes complement a company's structural context in important ways. They make it possible to suspend the selective effects of the structural context, which almost unavoidably tends to become fine-tuned for supporting top management's current strategic intent. And they serve to create links between autonomous strategic action and the company's strategy, thereby amending it. The capacity to activate and successfully complete such processes can be viewed as a measure of the intelligence of the company's internal selection environment and may be at the very heart of strategy making as an adaptive organizational capability.

This study's main contributions concern the natural dynamics of organizational adaptation. An evolutionary perspective on strategy making helps bridge and extend related ideas about the benefits and potential opportunity costs of narrow business strategies in the modern economic theory of the firm and ideas about exploitation and exploration in theory about organizational learning. Fine-grained detail of a strategy-making process approximating the classical rational-actor model suggests that the pursuit of focus and efficiency may also become the

potential enemy of effective exploration and strategic renewal. Strong positive environmental feedback strengthens the relative importance of the internal selection environment but also causes coevolutionary lock-in, which is a double-edged sword: Strategic dominance begets dependence. The relative dominance of the internal selection environment may last a long time, more than ten years in the case of Intel's Epoch II, but eventually cumulative changes in the external selection environment are likely to reduce its efficiency. Coevolutionary lock-in exacerbates tendencies toward structural inertia in novel and potentially insidious ways because it affects the balance between induced and autonomous strategy processes and a company's ability to develop new businesses, and hence the long-term adaptive capability of its strategy-making process.

Conclusions from a single case study warrant healthy caution, but by examining a case of extraordinarily successful CEO-driven strategy making that approximated the classical rational-actor model, this paper provides further support for the internal-ecology model of strategy making as an adaptive organizational capability. There is little doubt that companies that find themselves in the fortuitous circumstances that Intel faced in the PC market segment after its defeat in the DRAM business can greatly benefit from a leader with an exceptional ability to capitalize on them. Yet the benefits of the rational-actor model must be tempered by the realization that in dynamic environments, even in digital industries characterized by winner-take-all competition, the relative strength of the company's strategy vector will eventually decline, because the forces that make periods of extraordinary success possible are unlikely to last forever. The inertial consequences of coevolutionary lock-in, however, are likely to linger on if company leaders do not address them. An organization's long-term adaptation, spanning multiple generations of CEOs, may therefore critically depend on maintaining the strategic renewal capability of its internal ecology of strategy making.

REFERENCES

Aldrich, H. 1999. *Organizations Evolving.* London: Sage.

Allison, G., and P. Zelikow. 1999. *Essence of Decision: Explaining the Cuban Missile Crisis,* 2d ed. New York: Addison Wesley Longman.

Arthur, B. 1987. "Competing technologies: An overview." In G. Dosi (ed.), *Technical Change and Economic Theory,* 590–607. New York: Columbia University Press.

Audia, P. G., E. A. Locke, and K. G. Smith. 2000. "The paradox of success: An archival and a laboratory study of strategic persistence following radical environmental change." *Academy of Management Journal,* 43: 837–853.

Bamford, Raymond S., and Robert A. Burgelman. 1997a. "Intel Corporation: The Hood River Project (A)." Stanford Business School Case SM-49A.

————. 1997b. "Intel Corporation: The Hood River Project (B)." Stanford Business School Case SM-49B.

————. 1998. "Intel's strategic position in the family room, 1998." Stanford Business School Case SM-50.

Barnett, W. P. 1997. "The dynamics of competitive intensity." *Administrative Science Quarterly,* 42:128–160.

Barnett, W. P., and M. T. Hansen. 1996. "The red queen in organizational evolution." *Strategic Management Journal,* Summer Special Issue, 17: 139–157.

Baum, J. A. C., and B. McKelvey (eds.). 1999. *Variations in Organization Science: In Honor of Donald T. Campbell.* Thousand Oaks, CA: Sage.

Bendor, J., and T. H. Hammond. 1992. "Rethinking Allison's models." *American Political Science Review,* 86: 301–322.

Bower, J. L. 1970. *Managing the Resource Allocation Process.* Boston: Harvard Business School Press.

Brown, S. L., and K. M. Eisenhardt. 1997. "The art of continuous change: Linking complexity theory and time-paced evolution in relentlessly shifting organizations." *Administrative Science Quarterly,* 42: 1–34.

Burgelman, R. A. 1983. "A process model of internal corporate venturing in the diversified major firm." *Administrative Science Quarterly,* 28: 223–244.

————. 1991. "Intraorganizational ecology of strategy making and organizational adaptation: Theory and field research." *Organization Science,* 2: 239–262.

————. 1994. "Fading memories: A process theory of strategic business exit in dynamic environments." *Administrative Science Quarterly,* 39: 24–56.

————. 2002. *Strategy Is Destiny: How Strategy-Making Shapes a Company's Future.* New York: Free Press.

Burgelman, R. A., D. L. Carter, and R. S. Bamford. 1999. "Intel Corporation: The evolution of an adaptive organization." Stanford Business School Case SM-65.

Burstein, D., and D. Kline. 1995. "In the square-off between TV and computer, the smart money might be on the boob tube." *Los Angeles Times,* October 29.

Christensen, C. M., and J. L. Bower. 1996. "Customer power, strategic investment, and the failure of leading firms." *Strategic Management Journal,* 17: 197–218.

Cogan, G. W., and R. A. Burgelman. 1991. "Intel Corporation (C): Strategies for the 1990s." Stanford Business School Case PS-BP-256C.

Collins, J. C. 2001. *Good to Great.* New York: HarperBusiness.

Dyck, B., and F. A. Starke. 1999. "The formation of breakaway organizations: Observations and a process model." *Administrative Science Quarterly,* 44: 792–822.

Farrell, J., H. K. Monroe, and G. Saloner. 1998. "The vertical organization of industry: Systems competition versus component competition." *Journal of Economics and Management Strategy,* 7: 143–182.

Fine, K. M., and R. A. Burgelman. 1997. "Intel Corporation (F): Going Beyond Success in 1997." Stanford Business School Case S-BP-256F.

Gersick, C. J. G. 1994. "Pacing strategic change: The case of a new venture." *Academy of Management Journal,* 37: 9–45.

Gilder, G. 1989. *Microcosm: The Quantum Revolution in Economics and Technology.* New York: Simon and Schuster.

Glaser, B. G., and A. L. Strauss. 1967. The Discovery of Grounded Theory. Chicago: Aldine.

Grove, A. S. 1993. "How Intel makes spending pay off." *Fortune,* February 22: 57–61.

————. 1996. *Only the Paranoid Survive.* New York: Double Day.

Hannan, M. T., and J. Freeman. 1977. "The population ecology of organizations." *American Journal of Sociology,* 83: 929–984.

————. 1984. "Structural inertia and organizational change." *American Sociological Review,* 49: 149–164.

Isaacson, W. 1997. "The microchip is the dynamo of a new economy driven by the passion of Intel's Andrew Grove." *Time,* December 29: 46–51.

Kawamoto, D., and S. Galante. 1998. "The legacy of Andy Grove." *CNET,* March 26.

Leonard-Barton, D. 1990. "A dual methodology for case studies: Synergistic use of a longitudinal single site with replicated multiple sites." *Organization Science,* 1: 248–266.

Levinthal, D., and J. G. March. 1993. "The myopia of learning." *Strategic Management Journal,* Winter Special Issue, 14: 95–112.

Lovas, B., and S. Ghoshal. 2000. "Strategy as guided evolution." *Strategic Management Journal,* 21: 875–896.

March, J. G. 1991. "Exploration and exploitation in organizational learning." *Organization Science,* 1: 71–87.

Miller, D. 1994. "What happens after success: The perils of excellence." *Journal of Management Studies,* 31: 85–102.

————. 1999. "Selection processes inside organizations: The self-reinforcing consequences of success." In J. A. C. Baum and B. McKelvey (eds.), *Variations in Organization Science: In Honor of Donald T. Campbell,* 93–109. Thousand Oaks, CA: Sage.

Miller, D., and M.-J. Chen. 1994. "Sources and consequences of competitive inertia: A study of the U.S. airline industry." *Administrative Science Quarterly,* 39: 1–23.

Mintzberg, H., B. Ahlstrand, and J. Lampel. 1998. *Strategy Safari.* New York: Free Press.

Pfeffer, J. and G. R. Salancik. 1978. *The External Control of Organizations.* New York: Harper & Row.

Pollack, A. 1988. "An 'awesome' Intel corners its market." *The New York Times,* April 3.

Prahalad, C. K., and R. A. Bettis. 1986. "The dominant logic: A new linkage between diversity and performance." *Strategic Management Journal,* 7: 485–501.

Reinhardt, A., I. Sager, and P. Burrows. 1997. "Can Andy Grove keep profits up in an era of cheap PCs? *Business Week,* December 22.

Rotemberg, J. J., and G. Saloner. 1994. "The benefits of narrow business strategies." *American Economic Review,* 84: 1330–1349.

———. 2000. "Visionaries, managers, and strategic direction." *RAND Journal of Economics,* 31: 693–716.

Schlender, B. R. 1989. "Intel produces a chip packing huge power and wide ambitions." *Wall Street Journal,* February 28.

———. 1996. "A conversation with the lords of Wintel." *Fortune,* July 8.

Sorenson, O. 2000. "Letting the market work for you: An evolutionary perspective on product strategy." *Strategic Management Journal,* 21: 577–592.

Sørensen, J. B., and T. Stuart. 2000. "Aging, obsolescence and organizational innovation." *Administrative Science Quarterly,* 45: 81–112.

Steere D., and R. A. Burgelman. 1993a. "Intel Corporation (D): Microprocessors at the Crossroads." Stanford Business School Case S-BP-256D.

———. 1993b. "Intel Corporation (E): New Directions for the 1990s." Stanford Business School Case S-BP-256E.

Suzuki, O., and Robert A. Burgelman. 1998. "The PC-Based Desktop Videoconferencing Systems Industry in 1998." Stanford Business School Case SM-51.

Tredennick, N. 1991. "1991: The Year of the RISC." *Microprocessor Report,* February 6, 1991: 16.

Tushman, M. E., and E. Romanelli. 1985. "Organization evolution: A metamorphosis model of convergence and reorientation." In Barry M. Staw and L. L. Cummings (eds.), *Research in Organizational Behavior,* 7: 171–222. Greenwich, CT: JAI Press.

Van de Ven, A. H. 1992. "Suggestions for studying strategy process: A research note." *Strategic Management Journal,* Summer Special Issue, 13: 169–188.

Welch, Jack, with J. A. Byrne. 2001. *Jack.* New York: Warner Business.

Yin, R. K. 1984. *Case Study Research.* Applied Social Research Methods Series, 5. Beverly Hills, CA: Sage.

Zuckerman, E. W. 2000. "Focusing the corporate product: Securities analysts and de-diversification." *Administrative Science Quarterly,* 45: 591–619.

CASE II-16

Inside Microsoft: The Untold Story of How the Internet Forced Bill Gates to Reverse Course

Paul Carroll

Until six months ago, it looked as if Microsoft might, in fact, be lost in cyberspace. It was so far behind Internet upstarts that industry analysts wondered if the company whose software dominated the PC era might be sidelined in a new age of Internet computing.
—*Business Week,* July 15, 1996

DRIVING EVERYTHING

Even if Gates and his executives had had an inkling of the Web's trajectory, they had more pressing concerns. Government regulators were in the midst of a huge probe into Microsoft's alleged anticompetitive practices. A hush-hush group was creating a service to rival America Online Inc. Another was building "superhighway" goodies—video servers for interactive TV, programs for set-top boxes, and so on. Most importantly, legions of programmers were jamming to finish what would become Windows 95.

Microsoft's public reaction to the Web remained muted until last fall, when the Web's momentum was too great to ignore—as was the threat to Microsoft. Some 20 million people were surfing the Net without using Microsoft software. Worse, the Web—with a boost from Sun Microsystems' Java programming language—was emerging as a new "platform" to challenge Windows' hegemony on the PC.

Gates had had enough. On December 7, he staged an all-day program for analysts, journalists, and customers to show that Microsoft had every intention of playing—and winning—in the new software game. It would make Web browsers, Web servers, and "Web-ize" existing Microsoft programs. It would even license Sun's Java—whatever it took. . . .

The impact of those products has yet to be felt, but the speed and intensity of Microsoft's offensive has already changed the calculus of competitors and analysts. "People aren't asking anymore if Microsoft will be killed by the Internet but whether Microsoft will dominate the Internet," says Scott Winkler, vice president at market researcher Gartner Group Inc.

Indeed, in just six months, Gates had done what few executives have dared. He has taken a thriving, $8 billion, 20,000-employee company and done a massive about-face. "I can't think of one corporation that has had this kind of success and after 20 years just stopped and decided to reinvent itself from the ground up," says Jeffrey Katzenberg, a principal of DreamWorks SKG, which has a joint venture with Microsoft. "What they're doing is decisive, quick, and breathtaking."

Gates, a keen student of business history, has been intensely aware of how other market-leading companies—from General Motors Corp. to IBM—have stumbled when their top executives failed to read the signs of fundamental change in their industries. Tackling that problem was a prominent theme in his best-seller, *The Road Ahead,* published last fall. "I don't know of any examples where a leader was totally energized and focused on the new opportunities where they totally missed it," he says.

Here, for the first time, is the inside story of Microsoft's dramatic turnabout. It's a tale full of twists, turns, miscues, and even a fatefully timed illness. And it's a story of how three young programmers became Net preachers, spreading the gospel and peppering management with email that eventually helped get Gates and his team to act.

The Web-izing of Microsoft begins in February 1994, when Steven Sinofsky, Gates's technical assistant, returned to his alma mater, Cornell University, on a recruiting trip. Snowed in at the Ithaca, New York, airport, he headed back to the Cornell campus. That's when he saw it: students dashing between classes, tapping into terminals, and getting their email and course lists off the Net.

The Internet had spread like wildfire. It was no longer the network for the technically savvy—as it had been seven years earlier when Sinofsky was studying there—but a tool used by students and faculty to communicate with colleagues on campus and around the world. He dashed off a breathless email message called "Cornell is WIRED!" to Gates and his technical staff.

The response from one of Gates's staff: Someone in networking has been "bugging us about this same stuff. Maybe you should get together." The other guy was J. Allard. While being recruited in 1991, the cherub-faced programmer had worried whether Microsoft "had

a clue about the Internet." He signed on anyway, figuring he could help make the company hip to the Net. In 1992, Allard was the only Microsoft programmer who had it on his business card: Program Manager, Internet Technologies. "I was a lonely voice," he recalls.

FIXING BUGS

Allard's job was building TCP/IP, the Net communications format, into Microsoft LAN Manager and Windows for Workgroups. TCP/IP had long been standard on Unix computers made by companies such as Sun Microsystems. But for Microsoft, says Allard, it was just a "checkbox item"—ordered by Executive Vice President Steven A. Ballmer. "I don't know what it is. I don't want to know what it is. My customers are screaming about it. Make the pain go away," Allard recalls Ballmer saying.

In an unsanctioned project in early 1993, Allard oversaw the development of Microsoft's first Internet server—a computer that could link Microsoft to other Net sites. It was programmed to distribute test copies of the TCP/IP code to customers. Soon, they were posting other bug fixes, and it became one of the 10 most-used servers on the Net.

Little of this was registering with top management, though. Gates, then 37, and his lieutenants had never seen the Net in use the way the incoming legions of 20-somethings had. And with so much riding on the Windows rewrite, they had little time for new projects.

Allard was increasingly frustrated. The Net was abuzz over Mosaic, a "browser" program created by a precocious computer science undergraduate at the University of Illinois and posted on the Net for anyone to download. Suddenly, the Web had an easy, point-and-click format—for the masses. On January 25, 1994, he penned a call-to-arms memo titled "Windows: The Next Killer Application for the Internet."

Allard recommended building a Mosaic-like browser and including TCP/IP in Chicago, the code name for what became Win95. This memo also introduced the language that would become Microsoft's battle cry nearly two years later: "Embrace" Internet standards, and "extend" Windows to the Net. Says Allard: "I finally just couldn't take it anymore. I felt the company just didn't get it."

Once Sinofsky weighed in, things started happening. The two began talking, and Sinofsky soon got a Net connection. "I dragged people into my office kicking and screaming," says Sinofsky. "I got people excited about this stuff." Among the infected was Gates. "When Sinofsky started talking about the phenomenon he'd seen at Cornell and [showing] me Gopher and the early Web stuff . . . it caught my attention," says Gates. "I thought, 'That's a good thing.'"

The boss gave the go-ahead for an executive retreat to discuss the Net. That was a key breakthrough: At Microsoft, such gatherings convene when Gates feels execs need to focus on a critical issue. On April 5, 1994, two months after Sinofsky's Cornell visit, top brass holed up at the Shumway Mansion in nearby Kirkland, Washington, a 1909 estate used for conferences. Gates and his chiefs pored over a 300-page Internet briefing compiled by Sinofsky. At issue: How important was the Internet? And how much should Microsoft invest in it?

BABY STEPS

In one breakout group, Allard tangled with Russell Siegelman, who was heading Marvel, the code name for what's now the Microsoft Network online service. Allard argued that instead of being proprietary, Marvel should be based on Web standards. Seigelman held his ground—and won. It was a decision that would later cost millions to reverse.

Still, Net progress was made: TCP/IP would be integrated into Win95 and Windows NT, the version of Windows that runs network-server computers. The sales team was told to use the Web to dispense marketing information. The applications group agreed to give Word, the word processing program, the ability to create Web pages.

Next, Gates jumped deeper into the process by devoting much of his April Think Week—a semiannual retreat—to the Internet. His April 16 memo, "Internet Strategy and Technical Goals," contained the first signs of a growing corporate commitment. "We want to and will invest resources to be a leader in Internet support," wrote Gates.

It was a first step, albeit a measured one. "I don't think he knew how much to bet yet," says Allard. But board member David F. Marquardt did: he recalls that he was "amazed" that Microsoft was putting so little into the Net. "They weren't in Silicon Valley. When you're here, you feel it all around you," says Marquardt, a general partner at Technology Venture Investors in Menlo Park, California. He broached the subject at the April board meeting that year. Gates's response? "His view was that

the Internet was free," says Marquardt. "There's no money to be made there. Why is that an interesting business?"

To an increasingly important group of competitors, it was clear there was a huge opportunity—and if Microsoft didn't pursue it, they might be able to undo the behemoth's software dominance. Sun, Netscape, Oracle, IBM, and others saw their chance to reset the rules on the Net.

So did the Net start-ups that were multiplying like cells. Yahoo!, Lycos, InfoSeek, PointCast—dozens were rushing into the vacuum where Microsoft wasn't. The most high-profile of these was headed by James H. Clark, who resigned as chairman of the company he founded, Silicon Graphics Inc., and latched on to the Internet opportunity. He had the goose that laid the golden egg: Marc Andreessen, that 23-year-old University of Illinois programmer. Netscape Communications (originally Mosaic Communications) was founded on April 4, 1994, the eve of the Shumway retreat. By October, it was downloading its Navigator browser across the Internet.

In the spring of 1994, the Net was exploding. Millions of PC users were logging on. There were some 21,700 commercial Websites, up from 9,000 in 1991. Even IBM had a home page, complete with a greeting from Chairman Louis V. Gerstner Jr. So did General Electric, Tupperware, Volvo, and Hyatt Hotels. Time Warner had Pathfinder, which featured electronic versions of its magazines. Increasingly, the Net, not interactive TV, looked like the route to the Info Highway. Grasping that, Sun Microsystems began adapting a software language for interactive TV into what would become Java.

That April, at the Spring Comdex trade show, Sinofsky saw Booklink, a browser owned by CMG Information Services. He showed it to Brad A. Silverberg, then head of Microsoft's Win95 business. Execs began negotiating to license the technology. But as the talks dragged on, AOL swooped in and bought BookLink for $30 million in November. Says Silverberg: "That woke us up. We had to be a lot more aggressive, a lot more lively. Time was ticking faster in this new world."

During this period, Gates was crafting a strategy for Microsoft in the emerging wired world. But as outlined in his October 1994 memo, "Sea Change," the approach was to use existing Microsoft products. Other Microsoftians were becoming convinced that the Internet was the way.

One was Benjamin W. Slivka, now 35 and project leader for Internet Explorer, Microsoft's browser. In mid-1994, he and three other programmers were looking into what features to plan for the successor to Win95. He got his Internet hookup and soon knew the answer: On August 15, he sent email to his small band, saying they needed a browser and might even get one ready for Win95. When Netscape's Navigator hit the Net that fall, Slivka checked it out, then grabbed six people and mapped out the browser features for Win95.

To get the work done faster, one of his programmers took a shopping trip—to Spyglass Inc. in Naperville, Illinois, a Netscape rival. It was an ironic moment for Spyglass CEO Douglas P. Colbeth. Six months earlier, he had come calling on Microsoft—only to be rebuffed. "Typically, they said, 'We'll build it ourselves,'" says Colbeth. But by late 1994, Netscape was beginning its ascent and Microsoft was eager to deal. It signed a Spyglass license on December 16.

NETWORK NEWS

Still, going into 1995, Microsoft management was focused on Chicago. Originally scheduled for December 1994, it had been pushed back to mid-1995 and would emerge, finally, as Win95 that August. The company was scrambling to complete Windows NT for the corporate market, too. "Those were the focus," says Gates, "and the Internet was like an underlying rumble."

Gates had also ordered that Microsoft Network should make its debut in Chicago. The MSN story is loaded with might-have-beens. In December 1992, when Siegelman started the planning, the Net was hardly a showstopper. The real star was AOL, a Windows-based online service that was gaining members at a rapid clip. So in May 1993, Gates approved Siegelman's plan for a rival service that would have a big advantage—the software needed to use it would be included in Win95.

In fall of 1993, the MSN team ramped up to get done in time to come out with Chicago. But, heeding the Net rumblings, Gates agreed to let Rob Glaser, a longtime Microsoft exec who had pioneered the push into multimedia, do an analysis of how the Net affected MSN. His conclusion: Microsoft should "radically change" the strategy and make the online service part of the Net.

Then, fate stepped in. In November 1993, Siegelman, age 34, suffered a brain hemorrhage. He would recover but his absence prompted the normally relentless Glaser to ease up. He presented his plan to Siegelman's staff, but with the boss away and the team already stressed out, he didn't push hard. "We just couldn't afford to spend a lot of energy changing our plan," says Jeffrey Lill, a former MSN team member. Adds Glaser: "I felt the stars were

not aligning for Microsoft to really understand the Net early."

Besides, MSN was a high-profile project. Gates unveiled the planned service in a keynote speech at Comdex in November 1994, and within weeks persuaded Tele-Communications Inc. to pony up $125 million for a 20 percent stake in MSN. TCI chief John C. Malone had been on the verge of investing that amount in rival AOL. But, says AOL CEO Steven M. Case, "In the final hour, Gates persuaded him—implored him—not to invest in AOL." Three weeks later, Microsoft paid $16.4 million for 15 percent of UUNet Technologies, Inc., which now carries MSN traffic.

Despite MSN, by May 1995, Gates was sounding the Internet alarm. He issued "The Internet Tidal Wave," a memo that hit on the themes that had been reverberating throughout Silicon Valley. He declared that the net was the "most important single development" since the IBM PC. "I have gone through several stages of increasing my views of its importance. Now, I assign the Internet the highest level," he wrote.

On May 27, Slivka issued his own alarm, titled "The Web Is the Next Platform." He warned that the Web had the potential to supersede Windows. Says Slivka: "I don't know if I actually believed it would happen. But I wanted to make a point."

There was a growing sense among Microsoft execs that the Internet opportunity had to be seized—before it slipped to others. On June 1, 40 of them gathered at the Red Lion Inn in Bellevue, Washington, to brainstorm Net strategy. Gates gave a 20-minute talk on the "Internet Tidal Wave." Slivka's scheduled 15-minute talk ended up lasting more than an hour. "I got some people riled up," he says. At one point, Slivka proposed that Microsoft give away some software on the Net, as Netscape was doing. Gates, he recalls, "called me a communist."

Executives also went through every Net project that Microsoft had in the works and got their first peek at Java. The reaction? "Like the early reaction to my memo, it was lukewarm," says Allard.

Only after Win95 was shipping in August did Microsoft put full force into the Net. "In the three or four months before, there were symptoms that this thing was really accelerating," Gates says. "I said, 'O.K., once we get Windows 95 shipped, I'm really going to put a lot of thinking into how this affects our strategy. Can we have a strategy where we bet on the Internet and assume it's really going to drive demand for PCs and software? And how would that reshape our strategy?'"

Gates had no time to lose. On August 8, 1995, Netscape seized the spotlight with a spectacular initial public offering—which soared from 28 to 58 the first day and launched a bull market in Internet stocks. Chairman Clark became a paper billionaire 18 months after launching his company. Gates didn't hit that milestone until Microsoft was 12 years old.

Netscape was gaining more than a following on Wall Street. It had Microsoft-like dominance in the Web-browser business and was signing up blue-chip customers who were building Websites with the Netscape server program. Meanwhile, all of computerdom was getting jazzed about Java, the Sun software that would make it possible to zap programs as well as Web pages over the Net. That scheme threatened to make the Web a place where Windows mattered not at all. On November 16, Goldman, Sachs & Co. removed Microsoft's stock from its "recommended for purchase" list because of Internet concerns.

The message was clear: If Microsoft didn't want to be eclipsed in the network-computing era, it was going to have to play on the Internet—and it would have to play by Net rules. It would have to accept the Internet standards—embrace them—and try to hold on to its kingpin position by extending them with Microsoft embellishments.

Microsoft shifted to Internet time, with the bombastic Ballmer beating the tempo. Recalls Gates: "Ballmer is saying, 'Well, where are we?' We're saying, 'Well, we have a lot of pieces, but it's not as comprehensive as it should be.' Ballmer is saying, 'Make it comprehensive, and have an event. In fact, pick a date, and you'll have it comprehensive by then.'"

The date was set: Paul A. Maritz, group vice president for platforms, would pull together an elaborate Internet summit for December 7. Microsoft would announce plans for browsers, Web servers, and a new Web-based MSN—and other initiatives. Holed up in the boardroom, Maritz listened for two days as execs streamed through with their plans. Richard Tong, a Microsoft general manager, hit the road, picking the brains of Net consultants. Slivka's group wrote a 14-page memo on how Microsoft could get 30 percent of the browser market. It suggested getting AOL and Compuserve Inc. to license Microsoft's browser.

TRASH TALK

At 8 P.M. on December 6, Microsoft's top execs gathered at the Seattle Center auditorium for a dress rehearsal. They carefully went through each presentation. Gates even noodled with the language on the slides. (At the same time, executives from Microsoft and Sun were working through the night on a Java licensing agreement.) By midnight, the show was ready—until a PR exec told Gates the presentations were overwhelming. They needed a three-point summary for reporters. An exhausted Gates slumped to the floor, Ballmer next to him. Everyone waited, unsure if Gates was thinking or furious. Finally he blurted out: "I just want them to get that we're hard-core about the Internet!"

Since then, there has been no looking back. Microsoft employees tuned in to closed-circuit TV to hear the Internet briefing, got the speeches by email, and later received videotape copies. Gates wanted it perfectly clear what the new marching orders were. He need not have worried, notes Chris Peters, vice president of the Vermeer Product Unit. "If the chairman says success is defined as *that,* you will get a lot of *that!*"

Today, the Microsoft organization is pumped. "The thing that really motivates us is paranoia and competition," says Maritz. The day after Microsoft's December 7 splash, Netscape CEO James L. Barksdale was asked about the threat Microsoft posed. His joking response: "God is on our side." That was like putting a match to dry kindling. "It's the kind of stuff that gets people up in a locker room," says Silverberg, who now heads Microsoft's Internet division. "I want to thank Netscape. All this trash talk helped get us motivated."

Microsoft is using more than school spirit. Within days of the summit, insiders say, it tried to buy Excite. The start-up's "search-engine" technology, like that of its better-known rival Yahoo!, would help make MSN a useful gateway to the rest of the Web. Insiders say Microsoft offered $75 million, but Excite turned it down after investment bankers said they could get more by going public. On April 4, Excite went public and is now valued at $84 million. Microsoft's next bid, an estimated $130 million offer for Vermeer Technologies Inc., a start-up with scant sales, succeeded. Vermeer's highly regarded Front-Page is used for creating Web pages.

On February 12, Microsoft unveiled a key weapon in its contest with Netscape: the Internet Information Server. Some 90,000 free copies have been downloaded to date. March brought another major coup: From under the nose of Netscape, Microsoft snared a deal to have its

Internet Explorer used as the primary Web browser on AOL. In exchange, Microsoft offered a big concession: putting AOL in Win95, ending an exclusive edge for MSN. Microsoft was on its way from Web wannabe to Web contender. Says Intel Corp. CEO Andrew S. Grove: "That was a masterpiece of pragmatic business attitude."

In June, Microsoft turned its attention to intranets—corporate networks built on Internet technology. On June 13, it outlined an initiative centered on Windows NT 4.0, due late this summer. It will be crammed with Web features, including FrontPage and a new search program. That's attractive to outfits such as Merrill Lynch & Co. that would prefer one supplier for conventional software and the newer Net applications. It's rolling out a trading system around 25,000 Windows PCs and 1,200 NT servers—with intranet and Internet connections.

Bill Gates is counting on customers such as Merrill Lynch to stand by as his company fills in the remaining holes in its Internet strategy. Microsoft still lags in programs for collaboration and electronic commerce, for instance.

The Net upstarts that goaded Microsoft say it's missing a lot more than a few pieces. They claim what's coming out of Redmond is mainly talk. "It doesn't take long to write an ad," sniffs Sun Microsystems CEO Scott McNealy. Gates concedes his work is not done. "We're not saying we're out of the woods on this one," he says. "We have more than a year of incredible execution that we have to do." That's Internet time, mind you.

CASE II-17

Charles Schwab & Co., Inc., in 1999

Margot Sutherland and Kelly DuBois

> *It may sound simple, but the real key is anticipating what kinds of products and services investors are going to want. Like Wayne Gretsky, we want to skate where the puck is going to be.*[1]
> —Charles Schwab, 1998

With the June 1, 1999, edition of the *Wall Street Journal* spread before him, Dave Pottruck, president and co-CEO

of Charles Schwab Corporation (CSC), contemplated a piece of news that was about to send shock waves through the brokerage community. The newspaper had just announced Merrill Lynch's decision to launch online trading on December 1, 1999. Customers at Merrill Lynch would be able to trade online for $29.95/trade or, for a minimum annual fee of $1,500, make as many trades as they wanted. Now that Merrill Lynch had joined the online trading revolution, Pottruck wondered, how would this affect Charles Schwab & Co., Inc. (Schwab), and what should the company do in response?

COMPANY STRUCTURE

As of 1999, Charles Schwab & Co., Inc., was CSC's principal subsidiary.[2] Schwab provided securities brokerage and related financial services to 6.1 million active customer accounts. The company had 304 branch offices in 47 states as well as offices in Puerto Rico, the United Kingdom, and the Virgin Islands. Schwab employed 13,300 employees and was 40 percent employee owned.

Customer assets were $561 billion in June 1999. In 1998, Schwab had attracted $80.8 billion in net new customer assets and opened 1,380,000 new accounts. Revenue for 1998 was $2.7 billion (Exhibits 1, 2, 3, 4 and 5). The company operated in four main areas:

• The retail services segment allowed individual investors to make trades through four channels: at branch offices, through representatives at call centers, via automated telephone service, and on the Internet. Schwab also offered referrals to independent fee-based investment advisors.

Kelly DuBois prepared this case under the supervision of Professor Robert Burgelman as the basis for class discussion rather than to illustrate either effective or ineffective handling of an administrative situation. The case was updated from an earlier version prepared by Jeff Maggioncalda in 1996. To order copies or request permission to reproduce materials contact our distributor, Harvard Business School Publishing at 1-800-545-7685, or write Harvard Business School Publishing, Boston, MA 02163. No part of this publication may be reproduced, stored in a retrieval system, used in a spreadsheet, or transmitted in any form or by any means—electronic, mechanical, photocopying, recording, or otherwise—without permission. Version: (C) 11/16/99.
[1] Rebecca McReynolds, "Doing It the Schwab Way," *USBanker*, July 1998, p. 47.
[2] Other subsidiaries included Charles Schwab Europe (CSE), a retail securities brokerage firm in the United Kingdom, Charles Schwab Investment Management (CSIM), the investment advisor for Schwab's proprietary mutual funds, and Mayer & Schweitzer (M&S), a market maker in Nasdaq and other securities providing trade execution services to broker-dealers and institutional customers.

EXHIBIT 1   Charles Schwab & Co., Inc., Growth in Assets, Revenues, and Net Income, 1993–1998.

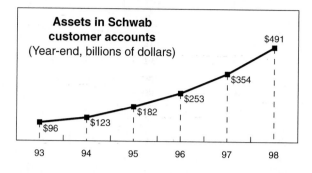

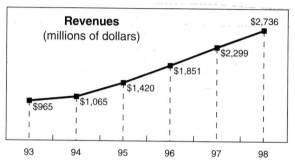

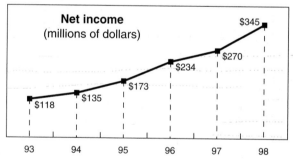

Source: Charles Schwab & Co., Inc., 1998 Annual Report.

- Schwab provided custodial, trading, and support services to 5,400 independent investment managers. In 1998, these managers had $146.4 billion in client assets at Schwab.
- The Mutual Fund Marketplace allowed customers to invest in over 1,600 mutual funds from 261 fund families, including 1,024 Mutual Fund OneSource funds.
- The capital market segment provided trade execution services in Nasdaq, exchange-listed and other securities primarily to broker-dealers and institutional customers. The unit accounted for approximately 650 personnel and over 10 percent of revenues.

SCHWAB THE INNOVATOR: 1971–1995

Schwab was incorporated as a brokerage firm in 1971 in California by Charles Schwab, a Stanford M.B.A. It didn't take long for the company to establish itself as an innovator in the industry. A defining moment for the firm came in 1975, when the scope of opportunities in the retail investment sector underwent a dramatic change.

Up until "May Day" in 1975, brokerage commissions were regulated by the government. Regulation prevented wide variations in the prices customers could be charged to buy and sell securities. Following deregulation in 1975, a group of brokerage firms reduced commissions to almost half that of the standard full service firms. Discounters offered cheap execution of stock trades for people who knew what they wanted to buy or sell. The discounters benefited from a growing population of informed individual investors who had access to financial information from newspapers, finance-related cable television programming, and magazines.

Charles Schwab decided to take advantage of the new opportunities offered by deregulation. His company would not sell advice on which securities to buy and when to sell as the full-service brokerage firms did. Instead, Schwab would focus on providing informed investors with low-cost access to security transactions.

From the beginning, the company invested heavily in technology as a way to lower costs. For instance, Schwab spent $2 million on a used IBM mainframe in 1977 even though it lacked a sufficient customer base to fully utilize it. In 1985, Schwab was one of the first firms to recognize that the personal computer could be used as a distribution channel for financial services. That year, Schwab introduced a DOS-based software product called Equalizer that allowed retail investors to conduct online transactions and research via their personal computers. Then in the late 1980s and on into the early 1990s, Schwab developed several technology-based services that would become central components of its business:

TeleBroker

Schwab recognized that telephones could be used as ubiquitous access and transaction devices and in 1989 introduced TeleBroker, a fully automated telephone system that allowed customers to retrieve real-time stock quotes and place orders. Although many customers continued to place orders through standard Schwab customer service representatives, Schwab offered a 10 percent discount for full electronic transactions. In 1995, 80 million calls (75 percent of total) and more than 15 million trades were

EXHIBIT 2   Charles Schwab & Co., Inc. Financial and Operating Highlights, 1993–1998

(In millions, except per share amounts and as noted)

| | Growth rates | | | | | | | |
| | Com-pounded Annual | | | | | | | |
	5-year, 1993–1998	1-year, 1997–1998	1998	1997[1]	1996	1995	1994	1993
Revenues [2]	23%	19%	$2,736	$2,299	$1,851	$1,420	$1,065	$ 965
Net income	24%	29%	$ 348	$ 270	$ 234	$ 173	$ 135	$ 118
Basic earnings per share [3]	24%	28%	$ .88	$ .69	$ .60	$ .45	$ .35	$ .30
Diluted earnings per share [3]	24%	29%	$ .85	$ .66	$ .58	$ .43	$ .34	$ .29
Dividends declared per common share [3]	31%	16%	$.1080	$.0933	$.0800	$.0622	$.0416	$.0281
Weighted-average common shares outstanding—diluted [3]			412	409	404	402	394	401
Closing market price per share (at year-end) [3]	64%	101%	$56.19	$27.96	$14.22	$ 8.94	$ 5.17	$ 4.80
Book value per common share (at year-end) [3]	30%	24%	$ 3.55	$ 2.87	$ 2.17	$ 1.62	$ 1.21	$ .97
Number of common stockholders of record (at year-end, in thousands)	33%		7.1	7.1	2.7	2.1	1.9	1.7
Pre-tax profit margin			21.1%	19.5%	21.3%	19.5%	21.1%	21.4%
After-tax profit margin			12.7%	11.8%	12.6%	12.2%	12.7%	12.2%
Borrowings (at year-end)	14%	(3%)	$351	$361	$ 284	$ 246	$ 171	$ 185
Stockholders' equity (at year-end)	30%	25%	$1,429	$1,145	$ 855	$ 633	$ 467	$ 379
Return on stockholders' equity			27%	27%	31%	31%	32%	37%
Full-time equivalent employees (at year-end, in thousands)	15%	5%	13.3	12.7	10.4	9.2	6.5	6.5
Selected cash flow highlights								
Net income plus depreciation and amortization	25%	23%	$ 487	$ 395	$ 332	$ 241	$ 190	$ 162
Capital expenditures—cash purchases of equipment, office facilities and property, net	19%	33%	$ 185	$ 139	$ 160	$ 166	$ 32	$ 77
Cash dividends paid	31%	16%	$43	$ 37	$ 31	$ 24	$ 16	$ 11

Source: Charles Schwab & Co., Inc., 1998 annual report.
[1] 1997 includes charges for a litigation settlement of $24 million after-tax.
[2] $.06 per share for both basic and diluted earnings per share.
[3] Revenues are presented net of interest expense. Reflects the December 1998 three-for-two common stock split.

handled electronically, and service was offered in English, Spanish, Mandarin, and Cantonese.[3] If TeleBroker transactions had been considered an independent brokerage service, it would have been the third largest discount brokerage in the world in 1995.

To service this telephone system, Schwab invested $15- to $20 million in four regional customer service telephone centers. Schwab did not make direct branch telephone numbers publicly available; instead, virtually all calls were routed to the call centers, which handled customers' requests 24 hours a day. Pooling efficiencies resulted in nearly all customer calls being answered within three rings and hold times of less than one minute.

SchwabLink

To expand its reach to more customers and to leverage its valuable brand better, in 1991 Schwab introduced a service for fee-based financial advisors called SchwabLink. SchwabLink provided fee-based advisors with back-office custodial services. Advisors could plug into Schwab's computers to trade both Schwab and

---

[3] Cost estimate based on data provided in *Fortune*, June 1, 1992.

EXHIBIT 3   Charles Schwab & Co., Inc. Consolidated Statements of Income, 1996–1998

(In thousands, except per share amounts)

Year ended December 31	1998	1997	1996
Revenues:			
Commissions	$1,309,383	$1,174,023	$954,129
Mutual fund service fees	559,241	427,673	311,067
Interest revenue, net of interest expense of $651,881 in 1998, $546,483 in 1997, and 425,872 in 1996	475,617	353,552	254,988
Principal transactions	286,754	257,985	256,902
Other	105,226	85,517	73,836
Total	2,736,221	2,298,750	1,815,922
Expenses excluding interest:			
Compensation and benefits	1,162,823	961,824	766,377
Communications	206,139	182,739	164,756
Occupancy and equipment	200,951	154,181	130,494
Advertising and market development	154,981	129,550	38,987
Depreciation and amortization	138,477	124,682	98,342
Professional services	87,504	69,583	52,055
Commissions, clearance, and floor brokerage	82,981	91,933	80,674
Other	125,821	137,011	80,174
Total	2,159,677	1,851,503	1,456,859
Income before taxes on income	576,544	447,247	394,063
Taxes on income	228,082	176,970	160,260
Net income	$348,462	$270,277	233,803
Weighted-average common shares outstanding—diluted*	411,505	408,863	403,652
Earnings per share*			
Basic	$.88	$.69	$.60
Diluted	$. 85	$.66	$.58
Dividends declared per common share*	$.1080	$.0933	$.0800

*Reflects the December 1998 three-for-two common stock split.
Source: Charles Schwab & Co., Inc., 1998 annual report.

non-Schwab products. They could outsource all transaction, record-keeping, and statement preparation duties to Schwab's computerized system for a fee based on the number of transactions and the size of customer assets. As a result, Schwab retained the customer account and assets and better utilized the capacity of its back-office computer systems.

Schwab's relationship with independent, fee-based advisors allowed it to reach more customers, to sell more product, and to provide its customers, although indirectly, with investment advice. Although advisors were not forced to purchase Schwab products using SchwabLink, many did. By 1995, Schwab had attracted more than 5,600 advisors who had brought in $52 billion in assets (28 percent of total customer assets) and generated commissions representing 13 percent of total commissions.

The company had amassed 82 percent of all assets available from fee-based advisors.[4] Schwab paid close attention to the needs of these financial advisors, improving their relationship by offering more powerful software products.

To provide greater assistance to customers seeking investment advice, Schwab began AdvisorSource, a referral service, in June of 1995. Unlike commissioned advisors who were compensated based on the types and amounts of securities they sold, fee-based advisors charged an annual fee based on customer assets to help an individual set up and manage his or her investment

---

[4] Alyssa A. Lappen, "Charles Schwab's Search for the Next Paradigm." *Institutional Investor,* April 1996, p. 64.

EXHIBIT 4   Charles Schwab & Co., Inc. Consolidated Balance Sheets, 1997–1998

(In thousands, except per share amounts)

December 31	1998	1997
Assets		
Cash and cash equivalents	$ 1,155,928	$ 797,477
Cash and investments required to be segregated under federal or other regulations		
(including resale agreements of $7,608,067 in 1998 and $4,707,187 in 1997)	10,242,943	6,774,024
Receivable from brokers, dealers, and clearing organizations	334,334	267,070
Receivable from customers—net	9,646,140	7,751,513
Securities owned—at market value	242,115	282,569
Equipment, office facilities, and property—net	396,163	342,273
Intangible assets—net	46,274	55,854
Other assets	200,493	210,957
Total	$22,264,390	$16,481,707
Liabilities and stockholders equity		
Drafts payable	$ 324,597	$ 268,644
Payable to brokers, dealers, and clearing organizations	1,422,300	1,122,663
Payable to customers	18,119,622	13,106,202
Accrued expenses and other liabilities	618,249	478,032
Borrowings	351,000	361,049
Total liabilities	20,835,768	15,336,590
Stockholders' equity:		
Preferred stock—9,940 shares authorized; $.01 par value per share; none issued		
Common stock—500,000 shares authorized; $.01 par value per share; 401,883		
shares issued and outstanding in 1998 and 401,533 shares issued in 1997*	4,019	2,677
Additional paid-in capital	213,312	241,422
Retained earnings	1,254,953	955,496
Treasury stock—2,630 shares in 1997, at cost*		(35,401)
Unearned ESOP shares	(1,088)	(2,769)
Unamortized restricted stock compensation	(43,882)	(17,228)
Foreign currency translation adjustment	1,308	920
Total stockholders' equity	1,428,622	1,145,117
Total	$22,264,390	$16,481,707

*Reflects the December 1998 three-for-two common stock split.
Source: Charles Schwab & Co., Inc., 1998 annual report.

portfolio. For this reason, fee-based advisors were recognized to be more objective and less committed to pushing certain financial products at the expense of a client's real needs.

In order to be referred to Schwab customers, financial advisors had to meet Schwab's stringent criteria. Advisors were assessed on the basis of experience, customer satisfaction, turnover, and assets under management. They also had to pass a due diligence process that involved financial, legal, regulatory, and credit background checks. The majority of advisors in the market place were very small in size. Referrals were carried out on a one-to-one basis, built on trust. The referral of a customer to an advisor was done by the branch. Branch in-

vestment specialists were required to know the advisor and the market segment that the advisor targeted so that a proper match could be made. By 1996, the service had signed up 320 prescreened fee-based advisors in 30 states to whom Schwab referred interested customers. In exchange, Schwab received 30 percent of the advisor's fees in the first year, 25 percent in the second year, 20 percent in the third year, and nothing in following years.

OneSource

In 1992 Schwab introduced the Schwab Mutual Fund OneSource program, a revolutionary fund supermarket that helped customers purchase Schwab and non-Schwab no-load mutual funds with greater ease and without paying transaction fees. With OneSource, customers could purchase no-load funds from a variety of fund families. Purchases were made instantly from customers' own brokerage accounts using any of Schwab's trading interfaces, including customer sales representatives and Tele-Broker. Additionally, Schwab sent customers a consolidated periodic statement reflecting portfolio changes and balances from all funds purchased through OneSource. Customers also received a year-end tax statement.

Schwab generated revenue from OneSource by charging fund providers a 25 to 35 basis point fee (0.25 percent to 0.35 percent of customer assets) for listing the fund in the fund supermarket and providing shareholder servicing. OneSource provided an exceptional distribution channel for the fund providers, especially the smaller ones who lacked substantial advertising budgets, and off-loaded all record-keeping and transactional duties to Schwab's back-office computers. Schwab's investments in its telephone customer support systems, its branch network, its trading software, its tremendous back-office processing capabilities, and its brand made it especially qualified to offer a mutual fund supermarket.

Participating in OneSource was a risky decision for fund providers, however, since Schwab controlled each customer relationship and provided only an aggregated statement of all shareholders to each fund provider. Because Schwab made it so easy for customers to purchase and redeem shares, customer loyalty to any fund family was low and customers frequently switched among fund families. To reduce this churn, in 1995 Schwab started to levy a fee on customers engaged in frequent short-term redemptions. When investors did redeem their mutual fund shares, nearly 99 percent of the money remained in a Schwab brokerage account, primarily because Schwab offered the only money market funds in the OneSource program and therefore captured idle investor funds following redemption. Schwab earned 60 basis points on money market accounts and 100 basis points on equities.

Building the technological infrastructure for OneSource was costly. Schwab equipped each fund provider with a computer and a direct communication line to Schwab's computers at a cost of approximately $300,000 per provider, including 43 fund families offering no-load mutual funds, 40 fund families offering funds only to fee-based advisers, and 174 fund families offering transaction-fee funds that had custody agreements with Schwab. According to Sanford Bernstein, fully half of Schwab's technology budget between 1990 and 1993 was dedicated to building the OneSource infrastructure. As of mid-1996, Schwab had invested more than $150

million in the OneSource program. "We invested heavily in the systems and process, Thank God," explained Schwab's executive vice president of its mutual fund business. "We are in effect a transfer agency that is open to the public." [5]

From 1993 to 1995, customer assets held by Schwab that had been purchased through OneSource, excluding Schwab's proprietary funds, grew from $8.3 billion to $23.9 billion, an annual rate of 70 percent. These assets generated almost 25 percent of Schwab's total money management revenues. Nearly half of all the money flowing into Schwab's OneSource program came from the network of 5,600 fee-based advisors, who benefited not only from Schwab's record-keeping and back-office services but also from its wide selection and absence of fees. Unlike commissioned brokers such as the 13,500 employed by Merrill Lynch, Schwab's advisor partners had a broader selection of funds from which to choose. As the head of one front-end-load fund manager said, "The fee-only advisers will be the death of people like us. Dealers used to sell us, but now they can draw from whatever [inventory] is appropriate." [6]

Indeed, Charles Schwab himself proclaimed the advantage he provided by offering such a broad selection and criticized the strategy of the full service brokerages that offered only their own products:

> It's the same game, the same flaw as in Apple [Computer]. They were a closed architecture. They contained things. They got a higher price on their PCs, a higher price on their software. That is a flawed long-term business strategy. . . . An intelligent, self-reliant person doesn't want to be in a closed architecture. They're too smart for that.

With OneSource, Schwab became the primary gateway through which customers could easily and cost-effectively buy and sell mutual funds. Increasingly, fund providers had no choice but to pay Schwab the 25 to 35 basis points and lose customer contact if they wanted such a powerful distribution channel. One of Schwab's primary fund competitors, T. Rowe Price, had yet to offer any funds through OneSource. "Schwab is just a utility," remarked its marketing director. "It is eminently copyable." [7]

Competitors such as Fidelity attempted to mimic Schwab's success by introducing their own mutual fund supermarkets, but had little success. After almost three

[5] Ibid., p. 66.
[6] Ibid., p. 68.
[7] Ibid., p. 64.

years, Fidelity's FundsNetwork had gathered only $2 billion of assets in no-load funds outside of Fidelity's family of funds.

Schwab in 1995

Schwab's early strategy proved exceptionally successful. The firm had not been afraid to be innovative in its thinking. For instance, Schwab had solidified its reputation as a low-cost broker in 1991 when it purchased Nasdaq market maker Mayer and Schweitzer, a move that gave Schwab some control over bid-ask spreads.[8] At most brokerages, effective prices to customers could be far different from advertised prices because the brokerages obtained different bid-ask spreads. Schwab's purchase was a forward-integrating move that allowed the firm to procure better spreads than many of its competitors.

But clearly Schwab owed much of its success to the heavy investments it had made in technology and automation systems, which allowed the company to build extremely cost-effective operations. Schwab's compensation and benefits costs as a percentage of revenues were substantially lower than the rest of the industry. Much of this cost saving was passed on to customers in the form of lower commissions. Schwab also used its low-cost structure to fund aggressive marketing campaigns, typically featuring the likeness of Charles Schwab. In 1995, Schwab spent almost double the average level of advertising and communications expenditures for brokerage firms as a group. Schwab's advertising investments paid off. From 1990 to 1995, Schwab more than doubled its customer base to 3.2 million customers. Schwab's brand achieved 71 percent awareness and its quality of management and reputation both ranked first in a 1994 *Wall Street Journal* survey of customer perceptions of brokerage firms.

With customers came assets and transactions. From 1990 to 1995, Schwab grew its customer assets from $31 billion to $182 billion, a rate of 42 percent per year. These assets generated revenues of $1.4 billion in 1995, with over half that number from commissions (Exhibit 5). From 1993 to 1995, Schwab increased its commissions primarily by growing the number of active customer accounts 26 percent. Favorable market performance in 1995 led customers to trade more frequently, resulting in an 11 percent increase in transactions per active account. Schwab's average commission per trade was generally $70–$75. By year-end 1995, Schwab's commissions represented over half the total commissions earned by all discounters (Exhibit 6).

Although Schwab did not invest heavily in bricks and mortar, it did lease branch offices throughout the United States. Schwab believed that customers liked to know that there was a physical place where their money resided and that they could speak face to face with brokerage representatives. From 1990 to 1995, Schwab increased its branch network from 120 to 239 branches in 46 states, Puerto Rico, and London. In 1996, branches were staffed with 7 to 10 employees, all of whom focused on customer-related activities such as orientation, education, and investment counseling and following up on leads generated by regional call centers.

By the mid-90s, Schwab appealed to a specific type of investor—one who was educated, felt comfortable trading securities without advice, sought lower prices, and typically felt comfortable using technology. In fact, about two-thirds of Schwab's customers had personal computers in their homes, about twice as many as the overall population.[9] The average age of Schwab's customer was 47, 10 years less than the industry average. Although Schwab contended that it made a significant commitment to better understanding its customer base, its reputation for customer knowledge was poor. "Fidelity used to know more about Schwab's customers than Schwab did," remarked one insider in 1996. "What they had built were transaction systems. What they need[ed] [was] customer information."[10] Distance between Schwab and its customer base was, to some degree, intentional. As Schwab reported in its financial statements, "Schwab's customer service delivery systems reduce the dependency on the need for personal relationships between Schwab's customers and employees to generate orders. Schwab does not generally assign customers to individual employees."

THE EVOLVING BROKERAGE INDUSTRY

Mid-1990s: The Rise of the Internet

In 1995 the Internet caught everyone by surprise with its potential to quickly and profoundly change the econom-

---

[8] The bid-ask spread is the difference between the sales price (ask) and purchase price (bid) and is collected by the market maker, the firm that actually brokers the transaction between buyer and seller.

[9] Spokesman Tom Taggart in James F. Peltz, "The Cutting Edge; Markets and Modems," *LA Times,* Section D, p. 1, August 5, 1996.
[10] "Chuck Schwab's Search for the New Paradigm," *Institutional Investor,* April 1996, p. 70.

EXHIBIT 5   Charles Schwab & Co., Inc. Composition of Revenues, 1995–1998

Composition of revenues	1998	1997	1996	1995
Commissions	**48%**	51%	52%	53%
Principal transactions	**10**	11	14	13
Total trading revenues	**58**	62	66	66
Mutual fund service fees	**20**	19	17	15
Net interest revenue	**17**	15	14	15
Other	**5**	4	3	3
Total non-trading revenues	**42**	38	34	33
Total	**100%**	100%	100%	*99%

*Total does not add up to 100% due to rounding.
Source: Charles Schwab & Co., Inc. 1998 annual report.

EXHIBIT 6   Market Shares of Estimated Retail Commissions

	Schwab commissions ($ millions)	Discounters' commissions ($ millions)	Estimated industry commissions ($ millions)	Discounters' share of retail commission	Schwab share of discounters' commission	Schwab share of retail commission
1985	$ 126	$ 299	$ 5,492	5.4%	42.2%	2.3%
1986	203	539	6,982	7.7	37.6	2.9
1987	297	718	8,449	8.5	41.4	3.5
1988	186	482	5,860	8.2	38.6	3.2
1989	229	580	6,767	8.6	39.5	3.4
1990	244	613	5,919	10.4	39.8	4.1
1991	349	773	7,059	11.0	45.1	4.9
1992	441	999	7,723	12.9	44.1	5.7
1993	552	1,283	9,138	14.0	43.0	6.0
1994	546	1,305	9,003	14.5	41.8	6.1
1995	751	1,446	10,665	13.6	51.9	7.0
1996	954	1,777	12,266	14.5	53.7	7.8
1997	1,174	2,048	14,221	14.4	57.3	8.3
1998	1,309	n/a	n/a	n/a	n/a	n/a

Note: NYSE member discounters vs. all NYSE firms.
Source: Securities Industry Fact Book, 1997, and Schwab annual reports, 1995–1998.

ics of the brokerage industry. In October of that year, Schwab introduced e.Schwab, a product that provided investors with account and research information over the Internet and that was designed for the computer-savvy investor who required little or no telephone-based customer service and communicated primarily by electronic mail. By the end of 1995, more than 15 percent of Schwab's 15 million transactions were initiated from personal computers.[11]

In contrast to full-service brokers, Schwab had been quick to respond to the emerging Internet. Few full-service brokers even acknowledged the Internet in 1995;

those who did cautioned investors about security flaws. Charles Schwab had decided that the Internet was a high priority for the company. Four months after Schwab told his executive vice president for Electronic Brokerage that he wanted website trading, Schwab's Web Trading service was up and running, providing trading and account information services on the World Wide Web. In early 1996, Schwab announced an upgraded e.Schwab and became the first major brokerage to offer trading via the Internet.

Within the brokerage industry, debate on how use of the Internet would change customer behavior ranged widely. Some thought the Internet would enable customers to make more of their own decisions. For instance, Internet tools for sorting and ranking information were a

[11] "On Technology's Leading, Not Bleeding Edge," *Institutional Investor,* April 1996, p. 69.

valuable aid to investors for such tasks as picking the best mutual funds. But, on the other hand, many in the brokerage community thought that the abundance of information on the Internet would convince customers they needed more assistance than ever before to sift through the data and the choices available to them.

Another question that brokers puzzled over was how the transfer of knowledge, information, and functionality to end users through the Internet would affect their businesses as more and more people began to use online services. By 2003, Forrester projected that 9.7 million U.S. households would manage more than $3 trillion online. Forrester's estimate represented 19 percent of retail investment assets and predicted 20.4 million online accounts.

New Entrants in the Industry

While many of the established brokerages were debating their next moves, new firms entered the scene and forged ahead. Internet technology, based on open standards and scalable microprocessor computing power, offered low costs at substantially lower volumes than the larger mainframes that dominated the brokerage industry. As a result, costs that were once typically fixed became far more variable, and entry into the industry could be achieved with far less trading volume.

Electronic brokers such as E*Trade and eBroker sprang up and offered prices as low as $12 per trade, a tenth the price of a trade at a full-service brokerage. In three months in 1996, E*Trade watched Web-based trading grow from zero to 20 percent of their total volume. E*Trade's trading system consisted of one million lines of code and fast Internet server computers which reportedly cost about $12 million.[12] By May of 1996 there were estimated to be 800,000 online brokerage accounts (1 percent of total) and Internet usage continued to grow rapidly.

The profile of the typical Internet investor was similar to the typical Schwab customer: the median age of E*Trade's customers was 40, three-quarters of them had two or more university degrees, and they were active traders who used the Web to buy or sell three times a week. To a large degree, the Web-based brokerage firms were attractive to Schwab's most profitable customers—those who traded often and usually through electronic channels.

By mid-1996, competition among online traders had increased considerably: 13 online trading channels existed in addition to Schwab. Furthermore, prices had dropped rapidly between 1993 and 1996. E*Trade had reduced prices seven times since launching trading on its proprietary system in 1993. When introduced, e.Schwab trades were priced at $39 for up to 1,000 shares, substantially higher than many on-line competitors. In July of 1996, Schwab reduced its e.Schwab price to $29.95 for up to 1,000 shares of stock, stating that it was passing on cost savings to its investors. In December 1996 Schwab's Web Trading service provided a 20 percent discount off Schwab's regular trading commissions. Although Schwab's offerings were not at the low end of the price range, they did receive favorable ratings for overall value and service.

Late 1990s: Online Trading Gains Momentum

By 1998, online trading was a compelling force in the brokerage industry. The growth in popularity of online stock trades surprised many in the industry. In 1998, 14 percent of all stock trades were executed online, up 50 percent from 1997. In 1999 estimates of the total number of online trading accounts in the United States ranged widely. Bancorp's Piper Jaffray estimated that between 1997 and 1998, the number of accounts had nearly doubled from 3.7 million to 7.3 million. Forrester Research, however, estimated that fewer than 2.2 million U.S. households traded online at the beginning of 1999.

The most immediate and obvious advantage of online brokerages for knowledgeable investors was cost savings. Online commissions dropped 50 percent in 1997 as competition for investors increased. In May 1999, the cost of a trade varied from $8 at Ameritrade to $29.95 at Schwab. Trades executed at full-service brokers were much higher, estimated at $116.[13] Frequent traders (those who traded from their accounts between 28 and 62 times a year) traded at the lower price firms, Datek and Discover. In contrast, Schwab's customers traded less frequently, averaging under 12 trades per year (Exhibits 7, 8).

As online websites evolved, they began to provide readily available, mostly free financial information to investors. Gideon Sasson, president for electronic brokerage at Charles Schwab, described how the Internet had shifted the power structure in favor of the customer. "The

---

[12] Tim Jackson, "Brokers Tremble as E*Trade Takes Off," *Financial Times,* March 11, 1996, p. 15.

[13] William Glasgall, "The Investor Revolution," *Business Week,* February 22, 1999, p. 113.

EXHIBIT 7 Online Assets and Trades per Account, 9/98–12/98 (Assets in Thousands)

Rank	Firm	Asset	Rank	Firm	Trades/ qtr.
1	Schwab	79	1	Datek	15.5
2	Fidelity	67	2	Discover	6.9
3	Waterhouse	58	3	SURETRADE	6.4
4	NDB	43	4	Waterhouse	5.9
5	Discover	42	5	Ameritrade	4.9
6	Ameritrade	42	6	E*Trade	4.2
7	Datek	24	7	NDB	3.8
8	E*Trade	22	8	Schwab	2.8
9	DLJ	17	9	DLJ	1.7
10	SURETRADE	10	10	Fidelity	1.2
	Weighted average	58		Weighted average	3.1

Source: Piper Jaffray Inc.

world before the Internet was one where few had access to information, and the rest of us had to listen to them." Sasson believed that the Internet had the power to change the structure of the brokerage industry by democratizing the distribution of investment information. "In the old world, people were account numbers. Online, it's more about *how* than *what:* 'Don't tell me what to do. Tell me how to do it!'"[14]

In 1998, assets held at online brokerages equaled one-eighth of the total amount of assets held at the top five brokers in the country.[15] By 1999 it was estimated that there were about 100 online brokerages. Full-service firms could no longer ignore the inroads that online brokerages were making in gathering customer assets and began to add online investing to their services in 1998 and 1999. They found that some of their best clients had opened online accounts to execute trades. In 1998, PaineWebber surveyed its customers and found that 8 percent had already opened online accounts and that 30 percent said they planned to in the next year.[16] Once it began offering online service, Morgan Stanley Dean Witter discovered that some of its best clients were using it. The 60,000 clients that used its Clientserv service had four times the assets and five times the revenue of the av-

erage account. "We were floored. It's been consistently our best clients," the firm reported.[17]

As the full-service brokers came on board in 1999, however, Schwab was already a force to contend with. In June, Schwab reported 2.5 million active online accounts, an increase of 1.3 million accounts from year-end 1997. Customer assets in online accounts totaled $219 billion, 39 percent of the total $561 billion of funds invested through Schwab. Schwab was the top Internet brokerage firm and handled almost one-third of all Internet trades. Even though Schwab's share was estimated to be more than double that of the next largest competitor, the company carefully watched the Internet strategies of companies like E*Trade.

E*Trade and Beyond: New Models of the Brokerage Firm

E*Trade Group Inc. was incorporated in California in 1982 and began to provide online investing services to self-directed investors through its website in February 1996. The company was headquartered in Palo Alto and in 1998 was reported to employ 1,200 people and to operate one retail office. The company was the first Internet company to make money, but it lost $712,000 in 1998 after generating revenues of $245 million. In the first quarter of fiscal 1999, the company lost a further $13.2 million (Exhibits 9, 10, and 11).

In 1998, E*Trade had over 676,000 customer accounts with assets under management of over $11.2 billion. In 1998, the company's reported goal was to replicate full-service firms' spectrum of services electronically, but without using human brokers or building branches. The firm was trying to move away from selling only discount trading and aimed to offer a variety of financial services.

As companies like E*Trade sought to reshape the brokerage industry, Schwab was actively developing an alternative model to the full-service brokerage exemplified by firms like Merrill Lynch and Dean Witter. Pottruck described Schwab's challenge:

> The real opportunity for us is to go after their customers. Of the $13 trillion in investable household assets, $12 trillion is invested in banks and full-commission firms. We've been cheaper for 25 years, yet those customers are still there. So it's not price that's keeping them from coming to us but the level of service they believe they can get from Schwab. Our job is to have prospects understand that Schwab can provide a new model of a full-service investing firm—not a cheaper

---

[14] Jaime Punishill, Bill Doyle, Michael E. Gazala, and Tell Metzger, "Net Investing Goes Mainstream," *Forrester Report,* March 1999, p. 19.
[15] William Glasgall, "The Investor Revolution," *Business Week,* February 22, 1999, p. 114.
[16] Ibid., p. 115.

[17] Ibid., p. 116.

EXHIBIT 8 Wiring Wall Street

	Type of brokerage	Commission on each trade and/or annual fee	Minimum balance	Additional services or notes
Merrill Lynch*	Discount Full service	$29.95 a trade. 1% of assets a year.	$20,000 None	Details not yet available. Minimum annual fee is $1,500.
Prudential	Full service	$24.95 a trade plus a fee of 0.25 to 1.5% of assets a year.	$100,000	Minimum annual fee is $1,500.
Citigroup	Discount	$19.95 a trade.	None	Research reports available for as little as $1.25.
	Full service**	Fee of 0.5 to 2% of assets.	$100,000	Minimum annual fee is $1,500.
Paine Webber**	Full service	Fee of 0.5 to 2.5% of assets.	$50,000	Minimum annual fee of $357, varies according to number of trades.
DLJ Direct	Discount	$20 a trade plus 2 cents a share for trades over 1,000 shares.	None	With credit approval can trade up to $15,000. Accounts with $100,00 get free research reports. Some access to initial public offerings.
Discover Brokerage Direct***	Discount	$14.95 a trade up to 5,000 shares of listed stocks, no limit on Nasdaq stocks.	$2,000	Can buy Morgan Stanley research reports, free for accounts with $100,000. Some access to initial public offerings.
Schwab	Combination	$29.95 a trade up to 1,000 shares.	$2,500	Assets management service for $100,000 portfolios, fee is 1% of assets. Accounts with $500,000 get free research reports.
E*Trade	Discount	$14.95 a trade up to 1,000 shares.	$1,000	Free research reports after 30 trades a quarter.
Fidelity Investments	Combination	$14.95 a trade plus 2 cents a share for trades over 1,000 shares.	$2,000	Requires more than 36 trades over 12 months.

*Services planned for later this year.
**Discount trading through Citibank; full-service through Salomon Smith Barney.
***Subsidiary of Morgan Stanley Dean Witter.
Source: Excerpted from Gretchen Morgenson, "Call Off the Death Watch for Brokers" *New York Times,* June 6, 1999. Reproduced with permission.

model of what Merrill Lynch is but a very different model. For example, our brokers aren't paid a percentage of the commission a customer generates, so there's no question of conflict of interest.[18] (See Exhibit 12.)

Schwab's model was based on providing investors with the degree of advice and service they wanted, through the channel they preferred. Executive VP Daniel Leemon,

Schwab's chief strategist, believed that Schwab would succeed in growing a new sort of firm in retail investment. But exactly what kind of customer could the company hope to win?

Leemon divided the 30 million U.S. households that had brokerage accounts into three types of investors: about 12 million were "delegators," people who wanted to offload the investment chores to others. At the other end of the spectrum were 3 million largely self-directed investors. In the middle were 15 million households that

[18] "Where Will Schwab Go Next?" *Money Magazine,* May 1999, p. 56.

EXHIBIT 9   E*Trade Group, Inc. Consolidated Statements of Operations, 1996–1998

(In thousands, except per share amounts)

	Years ended September 30		
	1998	**1997**	**1996**
Revenues:			
Transaction revenues[a]	$162,097	$109,659	$44,178
Interest, net of interest expense	56,019	25,265	4,813
International	7,031	4,000	—
Other	20,135	17,471	13,529
Net revenues	$245,282	$156,395	$62,520
Cost of services	$111,832	$ 73,381	$38,027
Operating expenses:			
Selling and marketing	$ 71,293	$ 28,160	$10,944
Technology development	32,916	13,547	4,699
General and administrative	30,906	16,847	8,238
Total operating expenses	$135,115	$ 58,554	$23,881
Total cost of services and operating expenses	$246,947	$131,935	$61,908
Pre-tax income (loss)	($1,665)	$ 24,460	$612
Income tax expense (benefit)	(953)	9,425	(555)
Net income (loss)	($712)	$ 15,035	$ 1,167
Net income (loss per share):			
Basic	($0.02)	$0.46	$0.06
Diluted	($0.02)	$0.42	$0.04
Shares used in computation of net income (loss) per share:			
Basic	42,285	32,352	19,641
Diluted	42,285	35,874	29,932

[a] Interest is presented net of interest expense of $39,714, $14,909, and $2,224 for fiscal years ended September 30, 1998, 1997, 1996, respectively.
Source: E*Trade Group, Inc., Form 10-K, annual report.

Leemon called the "validators"—people who knew what they wanted, but at times needed some information and advice to confirm it. Leemon pointed out that the "validators" usually turned to full-service firms for support. He believed that Schwab could win over the validators with the right mix of information, advice, and technology.[19]

Although Charles Schwab believed that price was important to consumers, he believed trust was key—customers wanted to deal with companies they trusted that provided good service. Schwab described his vision of how people would handle their personal finances in the future:

It's as simple as turning on your computer, and right there are all the pockets of your financial life on the screen from your 401(k) and IRA to your brokerage and bank accounts. We'll be the consolidator, the integrator. We'll be the utopia.[20]

In 1999, Schwab's website was evolving toward that vision. The site, www.Schwab.com, included trading reports, research from Standard & Poor's and investment banks, insider trading reports from Vickers, live interviews with CEOs, and an equity screening service that found stocks that met customers' criteria. Instead of selling advice, Schwab offered two sets of opinions: Hambrecht & Quist and Credit Suisse First Boston. In

---

[19] Jeffrey Laderman, "Remaking Schwab: As Commissions Fall and Investors Crave Advice, the Discount Broker Bets Big on the Web," *Business Week*, May 25, 1998.

[20] Eric Schonfeld, "Schwab Puts It All Online," *Fortune Magazine*, December 7, 1998.

EXHIBIT 10   E*Trade Group, Inc. Consolidated Balance Sheets 1997, 1998

(In thousands, except share amounts)

	September 30 1998	1997
Assets		
Current assets:		
Cash and equivalents	$21,834	$23,234
Cash and investments required to be segregated under federal or other regulations	5,000	15,001
Investment securities	502,534	191,958
Brokerage receivables—net	1,310,235	724,365
Other assets	$11,635	6,970
Total current assets	$1,851,238	961,578
Property and equipment—net	48,128	19,995
Investments	58,342	5,519
Related party receivables	3,719	3,259
Others assets	7,491	5,121
Total assets	$1,968,918	$995,442
Liabilities and stockholders' equity		
Liabilities:		
Brokerage payables	$1,184,917	$681,106
Bank loan payables	—	9,400
Accounts payable, accrued liabilities and other	73,765	21,542
Total liabilities	$1,258,682	$712,048
Commitments and contingencies:		
Stockholders' equity: Common stock. $.01 par: shares authorized, 150,000,000;		
shares issued and outstanding 1998, 56,603,291; 1997, 39,949,768	$566	$399
Additional paid-in capital	681,624	266,953
Retained earnings	15,310	16,022
Cumulative translation adjustment	210	—
Unrealized gain on available-for-sale securities, net of tax	12,526	—
Total stockholders' equity	710,236	$283,374
Total liabilities and stockholders' equity	$1,968,918	995,442

Source: E*Trade Group, Inc., Form 10-K, annual report.

EXHIBIT 11   E*Trade Group, Inc. Composition of Revenues, 1996–1998

	Years ended September 30		
	1998	1997	1996
Revenues:			
Transaction revenues	66.1%	70.1%	70.7%
Interest, net of interest			
expense	22.8	16.2	7.7
International	2.9	2.5	—
Other	8.2	11.2	21.6
Net revenues	100.0%	100.0%	100.0%

Source: E*Trade Group, Inc., Form 10-K, annual report.

addition, Schwab reported analysts' upgrades and downgrades from all brokerage firms. A retirement planner allowed customers to calculate the holdings of their non-Schwab retirement accounts along with their Schwab investments to determine if their retirement goals were on track.

Dave Pottruck hoped to create a "clicks and mortar" firm that united best-of-breed technology and people. Schwab's multichannel method of service delivery provided access and choice, offering customers service wherever they happened to be. The Web had become a popular option, but Schwab representatives were still available in branch offices and at call centers to assist investors in developing asset allocation strategies and in evaluating their investment choices. Customers appreci-

EXHIBIT 12   Full-Commission Brokers Have Over One-Third of the Market

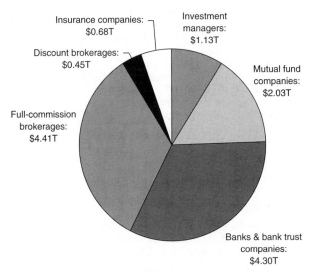

Insurance companies: $0.68T

Investment managers: $1.13T

Discount brokerages: $0.45T

Mutual fund companies: $2.03T

Full-commission brokerages: $4.41T

Banks & bank trust companies: $4.30T

Source: E*Trade Group, Inc., Form 10-K, annual report.

ated Schwab's branches: 70 percent of new accounts were opened in a branch, even though 80 percent of trades at Schwab took place online. Furthermore, the AdvisorSource referral service had proven extremely popular. Since 1995, more than 6,000 investors had hired an advisor from Schwab's AdvisorSource service. In June 1999, 400 fee-based advisors managed a total of $4 billion in Schwab customer assets. During the first quarter of 1999, Schwab reported a 47 percent increase in referrals to advisors from the same period in 1998.

Managing Growth at Schwab

Between 1993 and 1999, Schwab's growth had been extremely rapid. Customer assets had grown from $96 billion in 1993 to $561 billion in June 1999. Revenue had nearly tripled between 1993 and 1998, and earnings had grown at an average annual rate of 26 percent (Exhibit 1).

By 1999, the company had 13,300 employees, 300 percent more than in 1993. Fifty-five percent of Schwab's employees had been with the company two years or less. And Schwab had to continue to recruit aggressively to keep up with the company's growth. In April 1999, Schwab placed an ad in the *Wall Street Journal* announcing that the company was "looking for 1,000 people who want(ed) to change the way the world invest[ed]."

In an organization of Schwab's size, energizing and motivating employees was crucial to growing the business. Management at Schwab firmly believed that doing things the Schwab way started with communicating the

company's vision and then giving the work force the power to act. On March 13, 1999, Schwab held a day-long companywide event called VisionQuest. Through interactive sessions, employees learned about Schwab's role in the investment market, changes in the financial services industry, and timely issues such as baby boomers and the Internet.

Evelyn Dilsaver, a senior vice president at Schwab and a Stanford Executive Program graduate from 1996, commented that Schwab's key characteristic was to "be able to turn on a dime, adapting quickly to change." She emphasized that being a "change junkie" was critical at Schwab, and that employee input was essential in formulating that change. Schwab gave employees the power to create change and the technology to implement it. As Dawn Lepore, Schwab's chief information officer put it, "We have a culture that embraces technology. We have 14,000 employees, but we think of ourselves as having 14,000 technologists."

The integration of e.Schwab into the mainstream at Schwab exemplified the company's operating style. Looking back on e.Schwab's origins in 1996, Dave Pottruck recalled how the group had started out as a small team that reported directly to him. In the race to online trading, Schwab was competing with the new small online brokerages like E*Trade. "So we needed a group that felt like they did: nimble, unshackled from the larger bureaucracy," said Pottruck.[21] But a couple of years later, as Schwab's online service became more popular, the company realized that e.Schwab could not remain a separate business. It would have to be integrated into the larger organization, and that meant repricing core products, renovating systems, and retraining employees.[22] In short, from 1998 on, every Schwab employee had to understand how Schwab and the Internet fit together.

Management felt that bringing the Internet into the mainstream of the company wasn't violating company culture at all. Clearly, one of the forces behind the company's meteoric growth was Schwab's ongoing commitment to growing its technological systems. In 1998, for instance, the company spent $201 million on occupancy and equipment—up from $154 million in 1997 and $130 million in 1996.[23] The increase was due, in large part, to the company's investment in technology. Dave Pottruck thought of Schwab as "a financial services company on the outside and a technology company on

[21] Ibid., p. 96.
[22] Stewart Alsop, "E or Be Eaten," *Fortune,* November 8, 1999, p. 87.
[23] Charles Schwab, annual report, 1998.

EXHIBIT 13   Service Outages at Online Brokerages, January 1, 1999–April 1, 1999

Brokerage	Date of outage	Duration	Cause
Charles Schwab	March 1	25 minutes	Unforeseen limitation in storage-management software.
	February 24	90 minutes	Memory space available in the main console region of the primary mainframe was exhausted.
	February 17	15 minutes	Configuration error in DB/2.
	January 8	35 minutes	Configuration error resulting from moving Web traffic over to a second, new mainframe.
E*Trade Group	February 5	60 minutes	Problems with new server installation.
	February 4	60 minutes	Problems with new server installation.
	February 3	120 minutes	Problems with new server installation.

Source: Reproduced with permission from "Weathering a Market Storm," *Network World*, April 12, 1999, p. 41.

the inside." Charles Schwab agreed. "In many ways," he said, "technology is the driver and enabler of all we do, and it's been Schwab's hallmark to enable customers to interact directly with technology themselves."

As Schwab grew, the performance of its technological systems had a critical impact, not only on the delivery of financial services, but also on the perception in the marketplace of Schwab's brand. This was illustrated in 1998 and 1999 when enormous surges of interest and activity in online trading caused capacity-related problems for several online brokers, including Schwab (Exhibit 13).

Matching capacity with growth had proven to be a tremendous challenge: daily online trades at Schwab had risen from 11,800 in 1996 to over 200,000 in 1999.[24] (See Exhibit 14.) When Schwab's systems did go down, the company reacted by increasing customer service on other channels, so that if clients couldn't enter a trade through the Internet, they could go to a phone, or go directly to a Schwab office. Fred Matteson, executive vice president of information technology at Schwab, pointed out that overall, Schwab's record showed that the outages had totaled only 6.1 hours of downtime, one-tenth of 1 percent of all the trading hours, or, across 252 trading days, 99.89 percent availability.

NEW INITIATIVES IN 1999

Though growth had brought challenges, management at Schwab continued working to position the company for even greater future growth. In early 1999, Schwab embarked on several new initiatives to grow the company by reaching out to its most profitable clients. At the time, 25 percent of Schwab's customers accounted for 80 per-

cent of the firm's revenue, and Schwab planned new services targeted at these affluent investors.

For example, Schwab was working on an email service that would monitor portfolios and contact clients when stocks made significant moves up or down. The service would also alert clients to mutual funds or stocks that more closely met their needs than existing holdings. Schwab also was joining with lead underwriters to give Schwab customers access to key initial public offerings. The company was considering the use of database marketing techniques to pitch issues to likely investors for initial public offerings.

To attract more big customers, Schwab had a new cash management account in the works called Schwab One Access. The product would feature bill-paying capability, full Internet access, a cash machine card, a high rate of interest on cash balances, and stock trading. In 1999, 1,500 clients were testing the product, which was scheduled for roll out in 2000.

In early 1999, the company proposed a new suite of services called Signature Services, offering three levels of premium service with increasing levels of personal attention. Benefits, which depended on assets invested and number of trades per year, included priority status in the phone queue and a special website with additional investment research features (Signature Service level), access to highly-trained brokers (Signature Gold level), and priority access to initial public offerings (Signature Platinum level).[25]

The company planned to open at least 200 new offices and to offer on-site training sessions and seminars. On the international front, the company expanded operations in

---

[24] Saroja Girishankar, "E-Biz Sites Push for 100% Uptime," *Internetweek*, Issue 760, April 12, 1999, p. 1.

[25] The Signature Service plan required $100,000 and 12 annual trades, Signature Gold required $500,000 and 24 annual trades, and Signature Platinum required $1,000,000 and 48 annual trades.

EXHIBIT 14   Charles Schwab & Co., Inc. Trading Activity, 1996–1998

(In thousands)

Daily average trades	1998	1997	1996
Revenue trades:			
Online	56.3	26.8	11.8
TeleBroker and VoiceBroker	8.2	12.2	11.9
Regional customer telephone service centers, branch offices, and other	32.7	32.8	30.3
Total	97.2	71.8	54.0
Mutual fund OneSource trades:			
Online	18.0	12.8	8.4
TeleBroker and VoiceBroker	1.0	1.3	1.2
Regional customer telephone service centers, branch offices, and other	21.3	20.1	17.6
Total	40.3	34.2	27.2
Total daily average trades:			
Online	74.3	39.6	20.2
TeleBroker and VoiceBroker	9.2	13.5	13.1
Regional customer telephone service centers, branch offices, and other	54.0	52.9	47.9
Total	137.5	106.0	81.2

Source: Charles Schwab & Co., Inc., 1998 annual report.

the United Kingdom and Canada and had plans for the Japanese market. Pottruck commented, "I wouldn't be surprised to see us operating in 15 leading countries two or three years down the road."

JUNE 1999: THE COMPETITIVE ENVIRONMENT WIDENS

By mid-1999, Schwab's business model had proven successful compared against online brokers like E*Trade. But Merrill Lynch's announcement of upcoming online trading meant there would be pressure from the other direction. Pottruck was now faced with addressing the competitive challenge of full-service brokerage firms like Merrill Lynch; he was also about to be faced with the emergence of new financial dot.coms from firms like Bank One.

Merrill Lynch & Co., Inc.

Merrill Lynch was the big player in the full-service brokerage business. The company provided investment, financing, advisory, insurance, and related products and services on a global basis, including securities brokerage, investment banking, asset management, securities clearance services, equity, debt and economic research, banking, and insurance. The firm's customer base included individual investors, small businesses, corporations, governments and governmental agencies, and financial institutions.

Merrill Lynch entered the online trading business with a transaction fee of $29.95/trade or a minimum annual fee of $1,500 per year for unlimited trading. The company had launched an extensive ad campaign that touted the annual fee plan, highlighting the benefit of having access to financial advice from a Merrill Lynch broker. It was reported that the company entered the business of online brokerage in an attempt to act from a position of strength rather than a position of weakness.[26] In 1998, commissions from listed securities and over-the-counter sales at Merrill Lynch were over $3 billion dollars, but represented only 18 percent of revenues. Merrill Lynch managed nearly $1.5 trillion in customer assets, almost triple what clients invested at Schwab. Of Merrill's clients, 400,000 used Merrill Online to manage their accounts, which totaled $300 billion in assets.[27] The firm was considered a powerhouse in investment banking and asset management. But Schwab had created tremors at Merrill Lynch, and on Wall Street in general, when its market capitalization topped $36 billion in June 1999, surging past Merrill Lynch's $26 billion market capitalization (Exhibits 15, 16 and 17).

[26]Charles Gasparino, "Horning In: Facing Internet Threat, Merrill to Offer Trading Online for Low Fees," *Wall Street Journal,* June 1, 1999, p. 1.
[27]Joseph Kahn, "Schwab Lands Feet First on Net," *New York Times,* Business Day section, February 10, 1999.

EXHIBIT 15 Merrill Lynch & Co. Inc. Composition of Revenues, 1996–1998

	(%) 1998	(%) 1997	(%) 1996
Revenues:			
Commissions:			
Listed and over-the-counter	18	17	16
Mutual funds	11	10	10
Other	4	4	4
Interest and dividends	6	6	8
Principal transactions	15	24	26
Investment banking	19	18	15
Asset management and			
portfolio service fees	24	18	18
Other	4	3	4
Net revenues	100	100	100

Source: Charles Schwab & Co., Inc., 1998 annual report.

WingspanBank.com

Less than a month had passed since Merrill Lynch had announced its strategy to provide online trading and investment services when Dave Pottruck learned that yet another competitor had entered the ring. On June 24, Bank One announced that it had established a new business unit, WingspanBank.com, to sell a range of financial services over the Internet.

Bank One Corporation, headquartered in Chicago, Illinois, held over $250 billion in assets, operated 2,000 offices in 14 states, and maintained a nationwide network of ATMs. WingspanBank was a virtual bank through which financial services could be distributed over the Internet. The new bank offered checking accounts, certificates of deposit, credit cards, mortgages, insurance,

EXHIBIT 16 Merrill Lynch & Co. Inc. Consolidated Balance Sheets 1997, 1998

	Year ended last Friday in December		
	1998	**1997**	**1996**
Revenues:			
Commissions	$5,799	$4,995	$4,085
Interest and dividends	19,314	17,299	13,125
Principal transactions	2,651	3,827	3,531
Investment banking	3,264	2,876	2,022
Asset management and portfolio service fees	4,202	3,002	2,431
Other	623	500	519
Total revenues	$35,853	$32,499	$25,713
Interest Expense	18,306	16,243	12,092
Net revenues	$17,547	$16,256	$13,621
Non-interest expenses:			
Compensation and benefits	$9,199	$8,333	$7,012
Communications and technology	1,749	1,255	1,010
Occupancy and related depreciation	867	736	742
Advertising and market development	688	613	527
Brokerage, clearing, and exchange fees	683	525	433
Professional fees	552	520	385
Goodwill amortization	226	65	50
Provision for costs related to staff reductions	430	—	—
Other	1,057	1,098	834
Total non-interest expenses	$15,451	$13,145	$10,993
Earning before income taxes and dividends on preferred securities issued by subsidiaries	$2,096	$3,111	$2,628
Income tax expense	713	1,129	980
Dividends on preferred securities issued by subsidiaries	124	47	—
Net earnings	$1,259	$1,935	$1,648
Net earnings applicable to common stockholders	$1,220	$1,896	$1,602
Earnings per common share:			
Basic	$3.43	$5.57	$4.63
Diluted	$3.00	$4.79	$4.08

Source: Merrill Lynch 1998 annual report.

EXHIBIT 17 Merrill Lynch & Co. Inc. Consolidated Balance Sheets, 1997, 1998

	December 25, 1998	December 26, 1997
Cash and cash equivalents	$ 12,530	$ 12,073
Cash and securities segregated for regulatory purposes		
or deposited with clearing organizations	6,590	5,357
Receivables under resale agreements and securities borrowed transactions	87,713	107,443
Marketable investment securities	4,605	3,309
Trading assets, at fair value		
Equities and convertible debentures	25,318	24,031
Contractual agreements	21,979	21,205
Corporate debt and preferred stock	21,166	32,537
U.S. government and agencies	15,421	9,848
Non-U.S. governments and agencies	7,474	10,221
Mortgages, mortgage-backed, and asset-backed	7,023	7,312
Other	3,358	2,937
	101,739	108,091
Securities received as collateral, net of securities pledged as collateral	6,106	—
Total	$107,845	$108,091
Securities pledged as collateral	8,184	—
Other receivables		
Customers *(net of allowance for doubtful accounts of $48 in 1998 and $50 in 1997)*	29,559	27,319
Brokers and dealers	8.872	5,182
Interest and other	9,278	8,185
Total	$ 47,709	$ 40,686
Investments of insurance subsidiaries	4,485	4,833
Loans, notes, and mortgages *(net of allowance for loan*		
losses of $124 in 1998 and $130 in 1997)	7,687	4,310
Other investments	2,590	1,829
Equipment and facilities *(net of accumulated depreciation and amortization*		
of $3,482 in 1998 and $2,955 in 1997)	2.761	2,099
Goodwill *(net of accumulated amortization of $338 in 1998 and $131 in 1997)*	$5,364	5,467
Other assets	1,741	1,483
Total assets	$299,804	$296,980

Source: Merrill Lynch 1998 annual report.

mutual funds, electronic bill payment, brokerage services, and online trading. On its new website, the bank boasted that "never before in the history of financial services, has there been a more versatile, more powerful, one-stop resource available."

Dave Pottruck scrolled through the bank's website and discovered that the company offered free research, stock quotes, news, and trading for $19.95 per trade of up to 1,000 shares. The site also offered 250 no-transaction-fee, no-load mutual funds from the Wingspan Fund Marketplace in addition to another 7,000 mutual funds. The site provided consumers with a list of investment options and products based on the information they provided. Broker-assisted trading was also available for an additional fee (a percentage of the value of the stocks traded.)

Bank One planned to launch an extensive marketing plan to promote WingspanBank. George McCain, a Wingspan spokesman, estimated that marketing the initiative would cost $100 million to $150 million over the course of the year. The plan would target people whose lifestyles were built entirely around the Internet. Bank One wasn't the only financial services company that was marketing heavily. E*Trade was reputed to have spent $150 million on marketing over the past year, over 50 percent of revenue.[28]

CONCLUSION

With this news in the back of his mind, Pottruck considered what the competitive dynamics of the brokerage industry were likely to be over the course of the next six months. Merrill Lynch, E*Trade, WingspanBank, and Schwab, although competing for similar customers, appeared to be doing so from very different starting points. Pottruck described the challenges facing Schwab:

> Schwab now competes with both the high and low end of the brokerage business—but the competitive space is even more complex. Schwab also competes with combinations of firms. The firm is home to all of the financial investments of only half of our customers. For the rest, Schwab's assets under management represent between 25 percent and 75 percent of our customer's money. The richer Schwab's customers are, the smaller our share of their wallet!

Pottruck began to consider Schwab's next steps in light of these competitors. How could Schwab maintain its growth trajectory in the face of so many, varied competitors? What other firms might enter the space? How could Schwab protect and grow its existing customer base? Was Schwab getting "squeezed in the middle" or could it create a "category of one"?

CASE II-18

Amazon.com: Evolution of the E-Tailer

We are not a retailer and we are not a technology company. We are a customer company.
—Jeff Bezos, Founder, CEO, Amazon.com, February 2001[1]

Robert A. Burgelman and Philip Meza

INTRODUCTION

Since going online in July 1995, Amazon.com grew from a tiny warehouse containing the "Earth's Biggest Bookstore,"[2] to the leading Internet retailer in the world. The company's growth was phenomenal: it expanded from books to offering 28 million items across numerous categories and acquired 29 million global customers along the way. In 1999, Amazon's founder and chief executive officer Jeff Bezos was named *Time Magazine*'s Man of the Year. By 2000, according to Interbrand, Amazon.com became the forty-eighth most valuable brand in the world, embodying the principle of electronic commerce for people worldwide.[3]

However, that global growth came at a price. By late 2000, Amazon's U.S. books/music/movies segment had lost $2.3 billion and Amazon had borrowed $2.1 billion for the sake of its international investments. Its share price, which had ascended to vertiginous heights in 1999, had plummeted. (See Exhibit 1.) By late 2000 and early 2001, a few analysts were beginning to question Amazon's ability to survive until it reached profitability, although such dire forecasts were hotly contested by the

---

[1] All quotes from Jeff Bezos are from the authors' interview on February 5, 2001, unless otherwise cited. Subsequent quotes from this interview will not be cited.
[2] Amazon.com prospectus (S-1) March 24, 1997, p. 2.
[3] Daniel Bögler and Andrew Edgecliffe-Johnson, "Jeff Bezos: The Man of Last Year, Revisited," *Financial Times,* December 27, 2000.

EXHIBIT 1   Share Prices of Selected Companies and the NASDAQ Composite Index

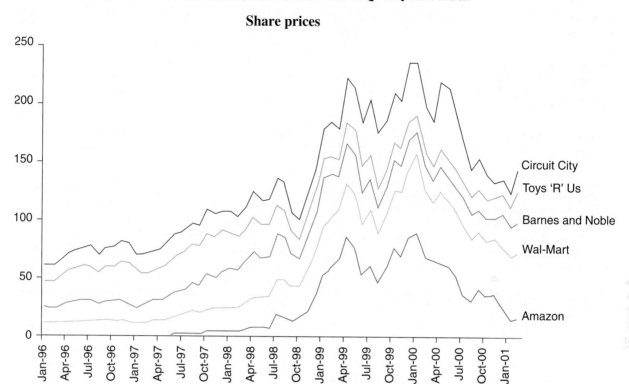

Share prices

Circuit City
Toys 'R' Us
Barnes and Noble
Wal-Mart
Amazon

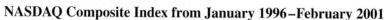

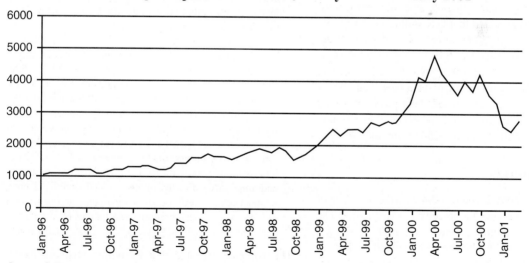

NASDAQ Composite Index from January 1996–February 2001

Source: © Thompson Financial Datastream. All Rights Reserved.

company and other analysts. Still, on the heels of a technology and Internet stock shakeout that stripped billions of dollars from the valuations of Internet-related stocks and saw many once high-flying Web companies close their doors, 2001 was a watershed year for the company.

Asked in early 2001 what were the key bridges that Amazon must cross over the next three years, Bezos did not hesitate:

> First is profitability by fourth quarter 2001. We want to make the company as a whole profitable so that the U.S. businesses subsidize international business. This past quarter, the U.S. books, music, and video business had a profitability of 2 percent of sales with an operating loss, and business as a whole had a 6 percent operating loss. The majority of investment is in International.
>
> Second is to take advantage of the opportunity to be the first truly global retailer.
>
> Third is to expand product selection.
>
> Fourth is to institutionalize at Amazon the ability to continually innovate. This is still the "Kitty Hawk" era of e-commerce. We want to innovate on a large scale. The very DNA we have [must code for] inventiveness. This has to be owned by all employees.

Amazon's DNA may code for inventiveness: the company had evolved over the past five years from selling other distributors' book inventories to owning a national and then global fulfillment system for a wide range of categories. The potential market size was enormous. Jupiter research estimated that U.S. online sales reached almost $12 billion in 2000, up 66 percent from 1999. However, that was still a small drop in the bucket compared to the $2.7 trillion spent on U.S. retail sales in 2000. If estimates were correct, and between 4 and 8 percent of all U.S. retail sales would take place online by mid-decade, then Amazon would be in a good position to capture a piece of that $125 to $250 billion market.[4]

IN THE BEGINNING

Jeff Bezos founded Amazon in 1994 with the intention of riding the Internet wave he perceived as inevitable. The then thirty-two-year-old vice president at D. E. Shaw, a New York City based brokerage firm, noticed the incredible current and projected growth of Web sites and Internet access. Bezos was particularly optimistic about online retail opportunities and set out to develop a business model to leverage growth in Internet access in the United

States. After researching a variety of retail categories, Bezos selected bookselling, believing that an online business model offered superior economics to established competitors in the physical world.

In the prospectus to Amazon.com's initial public offering ("IPO"), the company drew a comparison between an online book retailer and traditional competitors:

> Amazon.com was founded to capitalize on the opportunity for online book retailing. The Company believes that the retail book industry is particularly suited to online retailing for many compelling reasons. An online bookseller has virtually unlimited online shelf space and can offer customers a vast selection through an efficient search and retrieval interface. This is particularly valuable in the book market because the extraordinary number of different items precludes even the largest physical bookstore from economically stocking more than a small minority of available titles. In addition, by serving a large and global market through centralized distribution and operations, online booksellers can realize significant structural cost advantages relative to traditional booksellers.[5]

In particular, Amazon.com's management cited important key advantages of its online business model to the traditional book retailing industry:

> Several characteristics of the traditional book industry have created inefficiencies for all participants. Physical store-based book retailers must make significant investments in inventory, real estate, and personnel for each retail location. This capital and real estate intensive business model, among other things, limits the amount of inventory that can be economically carried in any location. The average superstore stocks less than 10 percent of the estimated 1.5 million English-language books believed to be in print, which limits customer selection and available retail shelf space for the majority of published titles. In addition, publishers typically offer generous rights of return to their customers and, as a result, effectively bear the risk of their customers' demand forecasting which encourages over ordering. As a result, returns in the book industry are high, creating substantial additional costs. Finally, publishers and traditional book retailers cannot easily obtain demographic and behavioral data about customers, limiting opportunities for direct marketing and personalized services.[6]

The company boasted that its online business model was superior to those of brick and mortar competitors. Amazon.com's IPO was hugely successful, selling over 3 million shares at $18 per share.

---

[4] Jeff Fisher, "Clicks for Bricks," *Newsweek,* February 12, 2001.

[5] Amazon.com Prospectus (S-1), March 24, 1997, p. 4.
[6] Ibid., p. 23.

GET BIG FAST

Since its IPO, Amazon grew as if it had a hyperactive corporate pituitary gland—even by Internet standards. (See Exhibit 2.) Bezos told *Fortune Magazine,* "Our initial strategy was very focused and very uni-dimensional. . . . It was GBF: Get Big Fast."[7] Indeed, Bezos still regards the company's audacious start—offering 1 million titles—as one of his best corporate decisions.

> What once looked foolish can seem smart now. When we started the company on July 16, 1995, we offered one million titles. We were advised by very knowledgeable people to offer only three hundred thousand titles. That was twice the size of the inventory carried by the largest physical bookstores. The catalog was hard for us, but doable. Obtaining the books was really hard. But the success generated word of mouth.

[7] Katrina Brooker, "Beautiful Dreamer," *Fortune,* December 18, 2000.

In 1998, Amazon started selling music, videos, and DVDs and expanded overseas facilities in England and Germany to sell books. (See Exhibit 3.) Bezos described Amazon's expansion into new categories as a customer-led evolution. He recalled:

> Our evolution [beyond books] came as the result of customer requests. We got a constant stream of e-mails from customers asking for other products. As a result, we launched music, selling only popular music titles. Surprisingly, most of the e-mails that followed were requests for classical music.

In 1999, Amazon continued to expand its category offerings, adding products such as electronics, toys, and software to its U.S. operations and music to its European operations. That year the company also added entirely new businesses; it introduced both co-branded auctions and zShops Marketplaces. The revenue models for these types of businesses were fundamentally different from Amazon's initial model. Amazon's storefront model, while more efficient than brick and mortar competitors,

EXHIBIT 2 Amazon Financial Data

Quarterly income statement

	30-Jun-01	31-Mar-01	31-Dec-00	30-Sep-00	30-Jun-00
Sales—Core Business	667.6	700.4	972.4	637.9	577.9
Total Sales	**667.6**	**700.4**	**972.4**	**637.9**	**−577.9**
Cost of Goods Sold	487.9	517.8	748.1	470.6	441.8
SG&A Expense	143.0	160.9	214.5	164.6	158.3
Depreciation	53.2	53.7	78.1	83.3	88.6
Research & Development	64.7	70.3	69.8	71.2	67.1
Unusual Inc/Exp	58.7	114.3	184.1	11.8	2.4
Total Expenses	**807.5**	**917.0**	**1,294.5**	**801.4**	**758.3**
Interest Expense, Non-Oper	−35.1	−33.7	−36.1	−33.8	−33.4
Other—Net	16.9	39.9	−149.4	25.1	7.0
Pre-Tax Income	**−158.0**	**−210.4**	**−507.6**	**−172.2**	**−206.7**
Income Taxes	0.0	0.0	0.0	0.0	0.0
Income After Taxes	**−158.0**	**−210.4**	**−507.6**	**−172.2**	**−206.7**
Equity in Affiliates	−10.3	−13.2	−37.6	−68.3	−110.5
Net Income (Excluding E&D)	***−168.4***	***−223.6***	***−545.1***	***−240.5***	***−317.2***
Accounting change	0.0	−10.5	0.0	0.0	0.0
Net Income (Including E&D)	***−168.4***	***−234.1***	***−545.1***	***−240.5***	***−317.2***
Primary EPS Excluding E&D	−0.47	−0.63	−1.53	−0.68	−0.91
Primary EPS Including E&D	−0.47	−0.66	−1.53	−0.68	−0.91
Dividends per Common Share	0.00	0.00	0.00	0.00	0.00
Shares to Calculate Primary EPS (millions of shares)	359.8	357.4	355.7	354.0	349.9

NB: E&D stands for Extraordinary Items and Depreciation
Source: Company Reports; OneSource.

EXHIBIT 2 (continued)

Historical income statement 1997–2000

	Year ended December 31				Quarters ended fiscal year 2001			Quarters ended for fiscal year 2000		
	2000	1999	1998	1997	30-Jun-01	31-Mar-01	31-Dec	30-Sep	30-Jun	31-Mar
Net sales	$2,761,983	$1,639,839	$609,819	$147,787	$667,625	$700,356	$972,360	$637,858	$577,876	$573,889
Cost of sales	2,106,206	1,349,194	476,155	118,969	487,905	517,759	748,060	470,579	441,812	445,755
Gross profit	655,777	290,645	133,664	28,818	179,720	182,597	224,300	167,279	136,064	128,134
	23.7%	17.7%	21.9%	19.5%	26.9%	26.1%	23.1%	26.2%	23.5%	22.3%
Operating expenses:										
Fulfillment	414,509	237,312	65,227	15,944	85,583	98,248	131,027	96,421	87,597	99,463
Marketing	179,980	175,838	67,427	24,133	34,658	36,638	55,196	41,921	42,216	40,648
Technology and content	269,326	159,722	46,424	13,384	64,710	70,284	69,791	71,159	67,132	61,244
General and administrative	108,962	70,144	15,618	6,741	22,778	26,028	28,232	26,217	28,468	26,045
Stock-based compensation[1]	24,797	30,618	1,889	1,211	2,351	2,916	(1,112)	4,091	8,166	13,652
Amortization of good will and other intangibles[1]	321,772	214,694	42,599	—	50,830	50,831	79,210	79,194	80,413	82,955
Impairment-related and other[1]	200,311	8,072	3,535	—	58,650	114,260	184,052	11,791	2,449	2,019
Total operating expenses	1,519,657	896,400	242,719	61,413	319,560	399,205	546,396	330,794	316,441	326,026
Loss from operations	(863,880)	(605,755)	(109,055)	(32,595)	(139,840)	(216,608)	(322,096)	(163,515)	(180,377)	(197,892)
Interest income	40,821	45,451	14,053	1,901	6,807	9,950	10,979	9,402	10,314	10,126
Interest expense	(130,921)	(84,566)	(26,639)	(326)	(35,148)	(33,748)	(36,094)	(33,809)	(33,397)	(27,621)
Other income (expense)	(10,058)	1,671	—	—	(1,178)	(3,884)	(5,365)	3,353	(3,272)	(4,774)
Non-cash investment gains and losses[1]	(142,639)	—	—	—	11,315	33,857	(155,005)	12,366	—	—
Net interest income (expense) and other	(242,797)	(37,444)	(12,586)	1,575	(18,204)	6,175	(185,485)	(8,688)	(26,355)	(22,269)
Loss before equity in losses of equity-method investees	(1,106,677)	(643,199)	(121,641)	(31,020)	(158,044)	(210,433)	(507,581)	(172,203)	(206,732)	(220,161)
Equity in losses of equity-method investees, net[1]	(304,596)	(76,769)	(2,905)	—	(10,315)	(13,175)	(37,559)	(68,321)	(110,452)	(88,264)
Cumulative effect of change in accounting	—	—	—	—	—	(10,523)	—	—	—	—
Net loss	$(1,411,273)	$(719,968)	$(124,546)	$(31,020)	$(168,359)	$(234,131)	$(545,140)	$(240,524)	$(317,184)	$(308,425)
Basic and diluted loss per share	$(4.02)	$(2.20)	$(0.42)	$(0.12)	$(0.47)	$(0.66)	$(1.53)	$(0.68)	$(0.91)	$(0.90)
Basic and diluted loss per share—pro forma	$(1.19)	$(1.19)	$(0.25)	$(0.11)	$(0.16)	$(0.21)	$(0.25)	$(0.25)	$(0.33)	$(0.35)
Shares used in computation of basic and diluted loss per share	350,873	326,753	296,344	260,682	359,752	357,424	355,681	353,954	349,886	343,884

[1] Amounts excluded from pro forma calculations.
Source: Company reports.

EXHIBIT 2 (continued)

	Quarters ended for fiscal year 1999				Quarters ended for fiscal year 1998				Quarters ended for fiscal year 1997			
	31-Dec	30-Sep	30-Jun	31-Mar	31-Dec	30-Sep	30-Jun	31-Mar	31-Dec	30-Sep	30-Jun	31-Mar
Net sales	$676,042	$355,777	$314,377	$293,643	$252,828	$153,648	$115,982	$87,361	$66,040	$37,887	$27,855	$16,005
Cost of sales	588,196	285,300	246,846	228,852	199,475	118,823	89,794	68,063	53,127	30,717	22,641	12,484
Gross profit	87,846	70,477	67,531	64,791	53,353	34,825	26,188	19,298	12,913	7,170	5,214	3,521
	13.0%	19.8%	21.5%	22.1%	21.1%	22.7%	22.6%	22.1%	19.6%	18.9%	18.7%	22%
Operating expenses:												
Fulfillment	107,070	53,707	42,374	34,161	26,797	16,906	12,612	8,912	6,837	3,996	3,335	1,777
Marketing	72,354	33,135	43,793	26,556	21,581	20,497	14,356	10,993	9,943	7,409	4,636	2,146
Technology and content	57,720	44,451	34,149	23,402	17,194	13,288	8,745	7,197	5,118	3,845	2,856	1,565
General and administrative	26,051	18,382	14,468	11,243	5,413	4,936	3,273	1,996	2,007	1,898	1,718	1,118
Stock-based compensation[1]	14,049	11,789	4,669	111	298	1,214	192	185	333	339	340	199
Amortization of good will and other intangibles[1]	82,301	74,343	37,150	20,900	20,452	16,737	5,410	—	—	—	—	—
Impairment-related and other[1]	2,085	1,779	3,809	399	1,281	2,254	—	—	—	—	—	—
Total operating expenses	361,630	237,586	180,412	116,772	93,016	75,832	44,588	29,283	24,237	17,486	12,885	6,805
Loss from operations	(273,784)	(167,109)	(112,881)	(51,981)	(39,663)	(41,007)	(18,400)	(9,985)	(11,324)	(10,316)	(7,671)	(3,284)
Interest income	8,972	12,699	12,860	10,920	4,263	4,755	3,390	1,645	783	688	366	64
Interest expense	(18,142)	(21,470)	(28,320)	(16,634)	(8,622)	(8,419)	(7,569)	(2,029)	(267)	(19)	(40)	—
Other income (expense)	(366)	2,159	(73)	(49)	—	—	—	—	—	—	—	—
Non-cash investment gains and losses[1]	—	—	—	—	—	—	—	—	—	—	—	—
Net interest income (expense) and other	(9,536)	(6,612)	(15,533)	(5,763)	(4,359)	(3,664)	(4,179)	(384)	516	669	326	64
Loss before equity in losses of equity-method investees	(283,320)	(173,721)	(128,414)	(57,744)	(44,022)	(44,671)	(22,579)	(10,369)	(10,808)	(9,647)	(7,345)	(3,220)
Equity in losses of equity-method investees, net[1]	(39,893)	(23,359)	(9,594)	(3,923)	(2,405)	(500)	—	—	—	—	—	—
Cumulative effect of change in accounting	—	—	—	—	—	—	—	—	—	—	—	—
Net loss	$(323,213)	$(197,080)	$(138,008)	$(61,667)	$(46,427)	$(45,171)	$(22,579)	$(10,369)	$(10,808)	$(9,647)	$(7,345)	$(3,220)
Basic and diluted loss per share	$(0.69)	$(0.59)	$(0.43)	$(0.20)	$(0.15)	$(0.15)	$(0.08)	$(0.04)	$(0.04)	$(0.04)	$(0.03)	$(0.01)
Basic and diluted loss per share—pro forma	$(9.55)	$(0.26)	$(0.26)	$(0.12)	$(0.07)	$(0.08)	$(0.06)	$(0.04)	$(0.04)	$(0.03)	$(0.03)	$(0.01)
Shares used in computation of basic and diluted loss per share	338,389	332,488	322,340	313,794	308,778	301,405	292,554	282,636	278,826	275,190	255,840	232,860

[1] Amounts excluded from pro forma calculations.
Source: Company reports.

EXHIBIT 2 (continued)

Historical balance sheets

	30-Jun 2001	31-Mar 2001	31-Dec 2000	30-Sep 2000	30-Jun 2000	31-Mar 2000	31-Dec 2000	30-Sep 1999 (unaudited)	30-Jun 1999 (unaudited)	31-Mar 1999 (unaudited)
ASSETS										
Current assets:										
Cash and cash equivalents	$462,949	$446,944	$822,435	$647,048	$720,377	$755,132	$133,309	$ 73,542	$ 105,757	$ 72,881
Marketable securities	146,020	196,029	278,087	252,976	187,244	253,749	572,879	832,143	1,038,480	1,370,084
Inventories	129,035	155,562	174,563	163,880	172,360	172,257	220,646	118,793	59,387	45,236
Prepaid expenses and other current assets	71,353	57,175	86,044	88,061	76,864	82,004	79,643	55,590	53,334	37,077
Total current assets	809,357	855,710	1,361,129	1,151,965	1,156,845	1,263,142	1,006,477	1,080,068	1,256,958	1,525,278
Fixed assets, net	292,422	304,179	366,416	352,290	344,042	334,396	317,613	221,243	156,333	60,600
Goodwill, net	89,002	123,996	158,990	383,996	441,240	471,748	534,699	514,098	563,884	153,763
Other intangibles, net	63,893	80,424	96,335	136,474	155,538	175,444	195,445	189,370	172,245	3,978
Investments in equity-method investees	12,223	22,539	52,073	91,131	211,715	271,542	226,727	156,157	102,361	23,817
Other equity investments	24,729	28,503	40,177	73,345	88,261	150,782	144,735	40,113	3,659	3,849
Other assets	53,410	54,804	60,049	54,306	53,294	54,882	40,154	38,750	42,774	41,699
Total assets	$1,345,036	$1,470,155	$2,135,169	$2,243,507	$2,450,935	$2,721,936	$2,465,850	$2,239,799	$2,298,214	$1,812,984
LIABILITIES AND STOCKHOLDERS' EQUITY (DEFICIT)										
Current liabilities:										
Accounts payable	$257,976	$257,411	$485,383	$304,709	$286,239	$255,797	$463,026	$236,711	$165,983	$133,018
Accrued expenses and other current liabilities	241,149	217,613	272,683	148,953	137,079	137,008	176,208	95,728	72,603	47,728
Unearned revenue	86,945	93,661	131,117	142,046	115,566	134,758	54,790	2,411	5,525	4,546
Interest payable	43,833	16,720	69,196	35,056	41,213	15,812	24,888	10,045	23,960	9,107
Current portion of long-term debt and other	18,337	19,305	16,577	17,213	17,731	15,983	14,322	12,776	9,873	7,186
Total current liabilities	648,240	604,710	974,956	647,977	597,828	559,358	733,234	357,671	277,944	201,585
Long-term debt and other	2,126,727	2,118,856	2,127,464	2,082,697	2,131,531	2,136,961	1,466,338	1,462,203	1,449,224	1,533,862
Commitments and contingencies										
Stockholders' equity (deficit):										
Preferred stock, $0.01 per value:										
Authorized shares—500,000										
Issued and outstanding shares—none										

EXHIBIT 2 (continued)

	30-Jun 2001	31-Mar 2001	31-Dec 2000	30-Sep 2000	30-Jun 2000	31-Mar 2000	31-Dec 2000	30-Sep 1999 (unaudited)	30-Jun 1999 (unaudited)	31-Mar 1999 (unaudited)
Common stock, $0.01 par value: Authorized shares—5,000,000 Issued and outstanding shares	3,622	3,588	3,571	3,561	3,554	3,500	3,452	3,393	3,364	3,228
Additional paid-in capital	1,356,216	1,344,083	1,388,303	1,342,574	1,335,733	1,293,761	1,194,369	1,026,484	976,571	303,701
Stock-based compensation	(10,132)	(10,532)	(13,448)	(19,504)	(25,410)	(34,889)	(47,806)	(32,180)	(37,743)	(1,275)
Accumulated other comprehensive income (loss)	(83,846)	(63,118)	(2,376)	(65,637)	(84,664)	(46,302)	(1,709)	(18,957)	(9,411)	(4,390)
Accumulated deficit	(2,695,791)	(2,527,432)	(2,293,301)	(1,748,161)	(1,507,637)	(1,190,453)	(882,028)	(558,815)	(361,735)	(223,727)
Total stockholders' equity (deficit)	(1,429,931)	(1,253,411)	(967,251)	(487,167)	(278,424)	25,617	266,278	419,925	571,046	77,537
Total liabilities and stockholders' equity	$1,345,036	$1,470,155	$2,135,169	$2,243,507	FI2,450,935	$2,721,936	$2,465,850	$2,239,799	$2,298,214	$1,812,984

	30-Jun 2001	31-Mar 2001	31-Dec 2000	30-Sep 2000	30-Jun 2000	31-Mar 2000	31-Dec 2000	30-Sep 1999	30-Jun 1999	31-Mar 1999
Key Metrics—quarterly										
Inventory turns—annualized	13.71	12.55	17.68	11.20	10.26	9.08	13.86	12.81	18.88	24.50
A/P days	48.12	44.74	59.69	59.57	58.96	51.65	72.42	76.33	61.19	52.89
Inventory days	24.07	27.04	21.47	32.04	35.50	34.78	34.51	38.31	21.89	17.99
A/R days	2.63	1.54	0.73	3.86	4.77	4.62	1.54	2.83	3.91	3.08
Operating cycle	(21.42)	(16.17)	(41.28)	(44.52)	(43.93)	(37.95)	(57.02)	(60.69)	(38.40)	(25.32)
Days in period	91	90	92	92	91	90	92	92	91	91

EXHIBIT 2 (continued)

	31-Dec 1998	30-Sep 1998 (Unaudited)	30-Jun 1998 (Unaudited)	31-Mar 1998 (Unaudited)	31-Dec 1997	30-Sep 1997 (unaudited)	30-Jun 1997 (unaudited)	31-Mar 1997 (unaudited)
ASSETS								
Current assets:								
Cash and cash equivalents	$71,583	$76,320	$328,351	$98,662	$110,119	$45,177	$6,847	$2,799
Marketable securities	301,862	260,940	8,261	18,659	15,258	3,494	50,220	4,346
Inventories	29,501	19,772	17,035	11,674	8,971	2,732	1,652	939
Prepaid expenses and other current assets	21,308	17,625	12,679	4,486	3,363	1,824	1,189	942
Total current assets	424,254	374,657	366,326	133,481	137,709	53,227	59,908	9,026
Fixed assets, net	29,791	23,821	15,587	10,276	9,726	4,801	3,832	2,605
Goodwill, net	174,052	207,070	52,398	—	—	—	—	—
Other intangibles, net	4,586	5,994	2	—	—	—	—	—
Investments in equity-method investees	7,740	—	—	—	—	—	—	—
Other equity investments	—	—	8,246	—	—	—	—	—
Other assets	8,037	8,172	7,907	2,343	2,409	350	331	196
Total assets	$648,460	$619,714	$450,466	$46,100	$149,844	$58,378	$64,071	$11,827
LIABILITIES AND STOCKHOLDERS' EQUITY (DEFICIT)								
Current liabilities:								
Accounts payable	$113,273	$60,046	$47,780	$34,610	$33,027	$15,659	$10,395	$5,685
Accrued expenses and other current liabilities	47,484	37,545	23,110	11,782	8,871	4,415	6,857	3,353
Unearned revenue	—	1,064	909	627	816	—	—	—
Interest payable	10	116	85	1,260	177	—	—	—
Current portion of long-term debt and other	808	684	751	1,297	1,660	228	156	653
Total current liabilities	161,575	99,455	72,635	49,576	44,551	20,302	17,408	9,691
Long-term debt and other	348,140	340,495	332,406	76,702	76,702	181	181	—
Commitments and contingencies								
Stockholders' equity (deficit):								
Preferred stock, $0.01 per value: Authorized shares—500,000 Issued and outstanding shares—none	—	—	—	—	—	—	—	—

EXHIBIT 2 (continued)

	30-Jun 2001	31-Mar 2001	31-Dec 2000	30-Sep 2000	30-Jun 2000	31-Mar 2000	31-Dec 2000	30-Sep 1999 (unaudited)
Common stock, $0.01 par value:								
Authorized shares—5,000,000								
Issued and outstanding shares	3,186	3,114	2,982	2,904	2,898	2,868	2,868	2,088
Additional paid-in capital	297,438	294,636	114,247	66,294	65,137	64,009	63,332	12,833
Stock-based compensation	(1,625)	(2,943)	(1,301)	(1,493)	(1,930)	(2,291)	(2,659)	(3,090)
Accumulated other comprehensive income (loss)	1,806	590	(41)	—	—	—	—	—
Accumulated deficit	(162,060)	(115,633)	(70,462)	(47,883)	(37,514)	(26,691)	(17,059)	(9,701)
Total stockholders' equity (deficit)	138,745	179,764	45,425	19,822	28,591	37,895	46,482	2,136
Total liabilities and stockholders' equity	$648,460	$619,714	$450,466	$146,100	$149,844	$58,378	$64,071	$11,827

Key Metrics—quarterly	31-Dec 1998	30-Sep 1998	30-Jun 1998	31-Mar 1998	31-Dec 1997	30-Sep 1997	30-Jun 1997	31-Mar 1997
Inventory turns—annualized	32	26	25	26	36	56	70	
A/P days	52	46	48	46	57	47	42	
Inventory days	14	15	17	16	16	8	7	
A/R days	3	3	3	1	1	1	1	
Operating cycle	(36)	(28)	(28)	(30)	(40)	(38)	(34)	
Days in period	92	92	91	91	92	92	91	

EXHIBIT 2 (continued)

Formulas used in computations

Inventory turns
3 months COGS $\times$ 4 $\div$ Average of Inventory for current quarter and Inventory for prior quarter

AP days
Accounts payable $\times$ Number of days in quarter $\div$ Current quarter COGS

Inventory days
Inventory $\times$ Days in quarter $\div$ Current quarter COGS

AR days
Average of AR—ending and AR—beginning $\times$ 365 $\div$ (Quarter revenue $\times$ 4)

Operating cycle
Inventory days + Accounts receivable days − Accounts payable days

still had a significant capital component, since the company had to make investments in inventory and fulfillment. In Amazon's new businesses, the company acted as an agent by facilitating transactions and taking a fee. For example, Amazon's zShops were a virtual shopping mall, where sellers could quickly set up an electronic storefront. Amazon charged sellers $39.99 a month to list up to five thousand items, $0.10 for every additional item listed, and a completion fee of 1.25 to 5 percent of the final price. Amazon Payments, the company's credit card processing system, allowed it to monitor zShop transactions and allowed sellers to avoid the bother of transaction payment processing. By the first quarter of 2001, the partnerships started to pay off. Amazon's alliances, including high profile agreements with Toys 'R' Us and drugstore.com, generated gross profit margins of 67 percent, compared to 23 percent gross margins across the rest of the company.[8]

By the end of 1999, Amazon began to leverage its impressive traffic numbers by creating the Amazon Commerce Network ("ACN"), acting as a portal for other retailers, taking fees and equity in addition to direct investments. From 1998 to the end of 2000, Amazon opened thirty-one stores selling 28 million items—everything from books to barbeques.

On December 28, 2000, Amazon opened an online bargain outlet store. The company reduced prices up to 70 percent on a variety of items. While the company offered discounted items in all of its categories, it thought the outlet would be particularly successful with consumer electronics and toys. Analysts thought the outlet would serve as a vehicle to liquidate excess inventory from Amazon's stores and zShops. Amazon.com expected to soon see its inventory balance drop to less than $175 million, down 20 percent from the fourth quarter 2000. Analysts estimated the inventory-carrying cost of excess merchandise was approximately 20 to 30 percent of the cost of inventory. (See Exhibit 4.) Thus, margins started taking a hit when clearance markdowns reached over 50 percent.[9]

The Joy of a Negative Operating Cycle

A key advantage of Amazon's business model, particularly with respect to brick and mortar competitors, was the company's negative operating cycle. Amazon received credit card payment from customers within a few days of purchase, but it did not pay its vendors for thirty to sixty days of sale. In addition, Amazon did not actually carry in inventory many of the products it sold, relying instead on suppliers to provide fast fulfillment and shifting inventory risk to its vendors in the process. According to Amazon, its typical operating cycle was around (−) forty-one days. Amazon estimated that the typical book retailing operating cycle was around (+) seventy-eight days. Thus Amazon generated interest on the full sale price (cost of goods and gross margin) for over a month.

Getting Physical

While negative operating cycles offered one important source of advantage over brick and mortar competitors, Amazon sought to reap even larger efficiencies from its

---

[8] Andrew Edgecliffe-Johnson, "Amazon Links Start to Pay Off," *Financial Times,* April 25, 2001.

[9] "Amazon.com's New Outlet Store Confirms 'Deal' Mentality on Web," *DSN Retailing Today,* January 22, 2001, p. 6.

EXHIBIT 3   Selected Data for Books and Music in the U.S.

Estimated revenue, printing expenses and inventories for book publishers: 1998 and 1999

	($ 000)		
	1999	**1998**	**% Change**
Revenue total	$24,129	$22,480	7.3
Sources of revenue			
Revenue from the sale of printed material	19,840	18,622	6.5
Total revenue from the sale of electronic or non-printed material (except audio)	2,434	2,168	12.2
Multimedia	811	748	8.4
Online	1,623	1,420	14.3
Revenue from the sale of audio books	198	191	3.8
Revenue from the sale of publication rights	247	235	5.2
Contract printing	361	428	−15.7
Other revenues	1,048	836	25.5
Expenses			
Purchased printing	1,104	3,908	5.0
Total inventories at end of year	2,984	2,737	9.0
Finished goods and work-in-process	2,723	2,510	8.5
Materials, supplies, fuel, etc.	261	227	14.6

Source: U.S. Census Bureau.

Estimated revenue, book publishers: 1998 and 1999

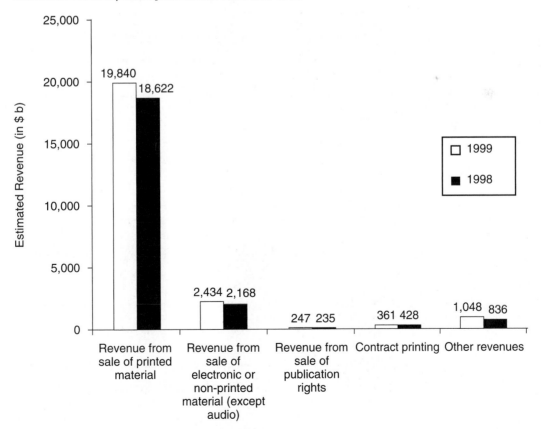

Source: Publishers Weekly, 248(9): February 26, 2001.

EXHIBIT 3 (continued)
Online music buyers and sales, 1999–2001

Number of music buyers online (000)

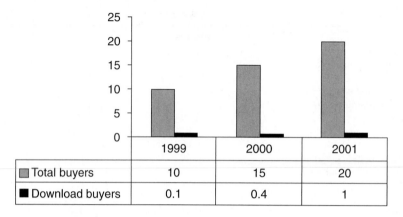

	1999	2000	2001
▨ Total buyers	10	15	20
■ Download buyers	0.1	0.4	1

Online music sales ($ mil)

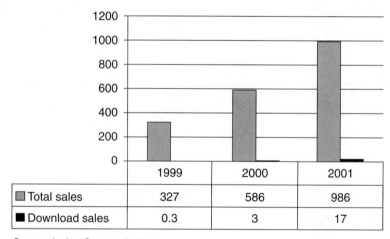

	1999	2000	2001
▨ Total sales	327	586	986
■ Download sales	0.3	3	17

Source: Jupiter Communications.

Total music sales in billions

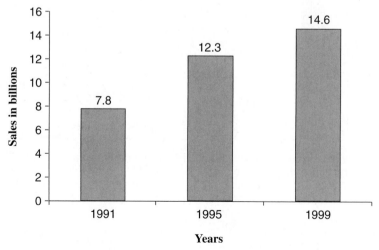

Source: Industry Standard, August 28, 2000.

EXHIBIT 4   Amazon Annualized Inventory Turns

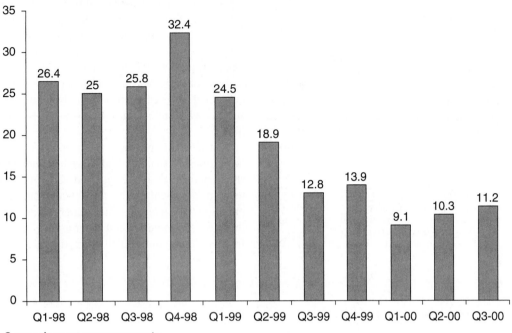

Source: Amazon company reports.

comparative lack of physical infrastructure. The business model, as described in Amazon's prospectus, called for a minimum of bricks.

> The Company sources product from a network of book distributors and publishers. The Company carries minimal inventory and relies to a large extent on rapid fulfillment from major distributors and wholesalers which carry a broad selection of titles. The Company purchases a substantial majority of its products from Ingram and B&T. Ingram is the single largest supplier and accounted for 59 percent of the Company's inventory purchases in 1996. Of the more than 2.5 million titles offered by the Company, up to 400,000 are currently supplied by book distributors and wholesalers, including Ingram and B&T. . . . The Company utilizes automated interfaces for sorting and organizing its orders to enable it to achieve the most rapid and economic purchase and delivery terms possible. The Company's proprietary software selects the orders that can be filled quickly via electronic interfaces with vendors, and forwards remaining orders to its special order group. Under the Company's arrangements with its distributors, electronically ordered books often are shipped by the distributor within hours of receipt of an order from Amazon.com. The Company has developed customized information systems and dedicated ordering personnel that specialize in sourcing hard-to-find

books. The Company currently processes all sales through its warehouse in Seattle.[10]

This worked when Amazon offered only books. However, as the company expanded its offerings, it necessarily expanded its infrastructure. In 1999, Amazon built twelve distribution centers in the United States, adding over 3 million square feet, at a cost of $200 million.

WHAT DO YOU OWN?

By 1999, Bezos had pinned his hopes on synergy developing from Amazon's e-commerce technology platform, brand power, and fulfillment infrastructure that he had quickly built in the United States and overseas. In the company's 1999 Annual Report, Letter to Shareholders, Bezos wrote:

> At a recent event at the Stanford University campus, a young woman came to the microphone and asked me a great question: "I have one hundred shares of Amazon.com. What do I own?"

---

[10] Amazon SEC Form 424B1, June 15, 1997.

I was surprised that I had not heard the question before, at least not so simply put. What do you own? You own a piece of the leading e-commerce platform.

The Amazon.com platform is comprised of brand, customers, technology, distribution capability, deep e-commerce expertise, and a great team with a passion for innovation and a passion for serving customers well. . . . We believed we have reached a "tipping point,"[11] where this platform allows us to launch a new e-commerce business faster, with higher quality of customers experience, a lower incremental cost, a higher chance of success, and a clear path to scale and profitability than perhaps any company.[12]

---

[11] "Tipping Point" is the concept that small changes will have little or no effect on a system until a critical mass is reached. Then further small changes "tip" the system and a large effect is observed.
[12] Amazon.com, *1999 Annual Report,* Letter to Shareholders, p. 2.

Competitors

Amazon did not fit comfortably into existing industry categories. When asked whether Amazon was really a software company—its key asset being its information systems—Bezos replied, "I always think of that as a semantic issue. We are not a retailer and we are not a technology company. We are a customer company." Still, discussion of likely competitors usually included companies such as Wal-Mart, Barnes & Noble, and Kmart. (See Exhibit 5.)

Not surprisingly, competition from Wal-Mart loomed large in Bezo's mind. Wal-Mart had more than 3,600 stores across the globe, boasted state-of-the-art inventory management skills, and owned one of the best brands in mass retailing. The retailer had also moved onto the Web. Customers could order a wide range of goods from walmart.com, which were delivered a few days

---

EXHIBIT 5   Selected Financial Information

	12/31/2000	9/30/2000	6/30/2000	3/31/2000
Net sales				
U.S. books, music, and DVD/video	$511,671	$399,905	$385,275	$401,415
U.S. electronics, tools, and kitchen	220,203	97,597	91,755	74,596
Total U.S. retail	731,874	497,502	477,030	476,011
U.S. services	95,601	52,691	27,453	22,746
Total U.S.	827,475	550,193	504,483	498,757
International	144,885	87,665	73,393	75,132
Consolidated totals	972,360	637,858	577,876	573,889
Gross profit				
U.S. books, music, and DVD/video	138,989	108,746	86,862	82,855
U.S. Electronics, tools, and kitchen	22,407	8,940	6,249	7,059
Total U.S. retail	161,396	117,686	93,111	89,914
U.S. services	36,672	30,711	26,667	22,184
Total U.S.	198,068	148,397	119,778	112,098
International	26,232	18,882	16,286	16,036
Consolidated totals	224,300	167,279	136,064	128,134
Pro forma income (loss) from operations				
U.S. books, music, and DVD/video	39,122	24,688	10,056	(2,425)
U.S. electronics, tools, and kitchen	(72,725)	(60,839)	(69,077)	(67,249)
Total U.S. retail	(33,603)	(36,151)	(59,021)	(69,674)
U.S. services	17,207	7,281	4,175	(2,144)
Total U.S.	(16,396)	(28,870)	(54,846)	(71,818)
International	(43,550)	(39,569)	(34,503)	(27,448)
Consolidated totals	$(59,946)	$(68,439)	$(89,349)	$(99,266)

Source: Amazon.com.

later. Or customers could order products through the Web site and pick them up from their local Wal-Mart store.

Similarly, Kmart's Bluelight.com, a partnership with Softbank and Martha Stewart Living Omnimedia, leveraged Kmart's vast physical presence. As with Wal-Mart, Bluelight placed Web kiosks in each of Kmart's 1,100 stores in the United States. In May 2000, Bluelight launched a free ISP service, gaining four million subscribers in four months.

The number two–ranked online bookseller behind Amazon, B&N.com, was also integrating into the physi-

cal network of 550 superstores owned by Barnes & Noble, which controlled 40 percent of the online bookstore. New service counters were installed to enable customers to log on to B&N.com to order any book or other product through the Web site. Customers could pick up their orders at the store or have them delivered. (At the time of this writing, delivery was limited to the New York area.) In addition, customers who bought books or music CDs through B&N.com were able to return items to Barnes & Noble stores for credit or exchange.

EXHIBIT 5 (continued)
Income statements for Barnesandnoble.com, Barnes and Noble, Inc., Wal-Mart Stores, Inc., Kmart, and Circuit City for financial year 2000

	Barnesand noble.com 31-Dec-2000	Barnes and Nobles Inc. 29-Jan-2000	Wal-Mart 31-Jan-2000	K-Mart 31-Jan-2001	Circuit City 29-Feb-2000i
($ 000, except EPS)					
Sales—Core Business	320.1	3,486.0	165,013.0	37,028.0	12,614.4
Sales—Other			1,796.0		
Total Sales	**320.1**	**3,486.0**	**166,809.0**	**37,028.0**	**12,614.4**
Cost of Goods Sold	261.8	2,483.7	129,664.0	29,658.0	9,751.8
SG&A Expense	194.5	651.1	27,040.0	7,415.0	2,309.6
Interest Expense			1,022.0		24.2
Depreciation	47.8	112.3			
Research & Development	40.4	6.8			
Unusual Inc/Exp	75.1				
Total Expenses	**619.6**	**3,253.9**	**157,726.0**	**37,073.0**	**12,085.6**
Interest Net	23.7	−23.8		−287.0	
		10.3			
Pre-Tax Income	**−275.7**	**218.6**	**9,083.0**	**−332.0**	**528.8**
Income Taxes	0.0	89.6	3,338.0	−134.0	200.9
Income After Taxes	**−275.7**	**129.0**	**5,745.0**	**−198.0**	**327.8**
Preferred Dividends				−36.0	
Interest Adj for Primary EPS					
Minority Interests			−170.0		
Net Income Before E&D	**−275.7**	**129.0**	**5,575.0**	**−198.0**	**327.8**
Accounting Change		−4.5	−198.0		
Discontinued Operations					−130.2
Extraordinary Items					
Net Income After E&D	**−275.7**	**124.5**	**5,377.0**	**−198.0**	**197.6**
Preferred Dividends				−36.0	
Income Av. to Common Shareholders				−234.0	
Dividends per Common Share			0.20		0.07
Shares to Calculate Primary EPS (millions of shares)	147.4	69.0	4,451.0	482.0	201.3
Primary EPS Excluding E&D	−1.87	1.87	1.21	−0.49	1.63
Primary EPS Including E&D	−1.87	1.80	1.25	−0.49	0.98

NB: E = extraordinary items, D = discontinued operations.
Source: Company reports.

EXHIBIT 5 (continued)
Sales per employee of Barnesandnoble.com, Barnes and Noble, Inc., Wal-Mart Stores, Inc., and Kmart in fiscal year 2000 ($ M)

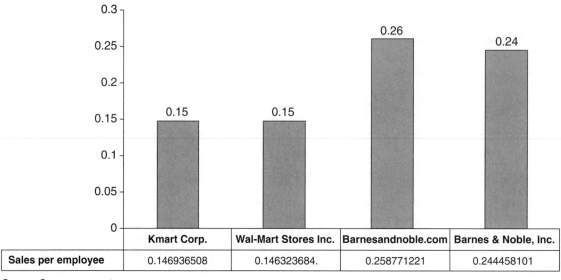

	Kmart Corp.	Wal-Mart Stores Inc.	Barnesandnoble.com	Barnes & Noble, Inc.
Sales per employee	0.146936508	0.146323684.	0.258771221	0.244458101

Source: Company reports.

AFTER THE FALL

The year 2000 marked the end of a steady increase in the NASDAQ. From its all time high of 5,049 on March 10, 2000, the exchange lost 59 percent of its value in the following twelve months. A long list of famous Internet companies lost the majority of their value; many closed their doors. By many measures, 2000 was a good year for Amazon. Revenues totaled $2.8 billion dollars, an increase of 68 percent over 1999. Not surprisingly, the best growth was in new domestic categories, e.g., tools and hardware and consumer electronics, with sequential revenue increases of 317 percent in fiscal 2000 to $683 million. Amazon's international segment also experienced significant growth, up 127 percent year over year to $381 million in 2000. The international growth reduced the impact of Amazon's traditional U.S. books/music/movie segment, which accounted for just over 60 percent of consolidated sales in 2000, down from 80 percent in 1999. Amazon increased its cumulative customer base 16 percent to 29 million through the addition of 4.1 million customers during the forth quarter of 2000. Of the 4.1 million new customers added, about 1.1 million were international customers, which increased Amazon's total international client base to 5 million customers, a boost of 72 percent.

Also by the fourth quarter 2000, twelve-month sales per active customer reached $134, up from $130 in the previous quarter, and customer acquisition costs declined from $15 in the third quarter to $13 by the end of the year. Repeat customers comprised 75 percent of total orders for the fourth quarter, up from 73 percent from the previous year.[13]

Despite the relatively robust performance in 2000, Amazon expected sales growth in 2001 to slow to 20–30 percent, or around $3.4 billion, far below the 43 percent growth previously expected. In an effort to drive toward profitability, the company laid off 1,300 employees comprising 15 percent of its workforce. Amazon also closed one of its twelve distribution centers and one of its nine customer service centers.[14]

AMAZON TODAY

Speaking about Amazon.com today, Bezos said:

Our mission is to be the earth's most customer-centric company. We intend to do this through actions in three categories:

- Listen: the traditional definition applies;
- Invent: because you can listen to customers, but they don't always know what they want or what is possible;

---

[13] S. Rashtchy, "Amazon.com," U.S. Bancorp Piper Jaffray Inc., January 31, 2001.
[14] *Business Week,* February 12, 2000, p. 39.

- Personalize: we are investing heavily in personalization technology.

We want to set a new worldwide standard for customer centricity. Our vision is to build a place where people can come to find and buy whatever they want online. The first and foremost step is to build the discovery mechanisms [that customers can use to find] products. We want to build a place where people can find anything with a capital "A."

Summing up his vision for the company, Bezos said: "We don't see it as our job to sell people things as much as it is to help people make purchase decisions. It's a subtle but important difference."

Amazon created one way of making that "help" pay. The company announced that it planned to start charging publishers for recommending selected titles in e-mail promotions to Amazon customers. Publishers would be charged as much as $10,000 per title to be spotlighted in the e-mail. Amazon would also require publishers to purchase advertising spots on its Web pages, pushing the total cost up to $17,000. In the past, the online retailer had recommended books for free in those e-mails. The titles were selected by Amazon editors solely according to content. Amazon still planned to recommend books it considered worthwhile for free via e-mails. Amazon said it would disclose which e-mails were paid advertisements.[15]

Touching Atoms vs. Streaming Bits

For many investors, part of Amazon's financial charm stemmed from its fundamental business model, the negative operating cycle it allowed, and the other efficiencies associated with and expected of Web-based businesses. But there always had been a fulfillment component to Amazon's primary business model, whereby employees actually had to "touch" items (often referred to as picking and packing, whereby items are picked from inventory shelves and packed into a box for shipping). Amazon expanded its categories of offerings and its geographic presence, and it also expanded its infrastructure. Bezos said:

The first day, 5½ years ago, we touched every book the customer bought. There are few ways to reliably get products to customers without touching the products. It's part of the path to maturation. I have heard a story, maybe it's apocryphal, that Henry Ford had to go into iron ore mining because there wasn't enough iron ore available in the country at the time.

Asked if Amazon's fundamental business model would continue to span Web vision and fulfillment skills, Bezos said:

There will always be products that require [our touching]. We will have a competence [in distribution] that will be hard to compete with . . . real competence from our distribution network.

Most businesses have two things in the physical world in which they are excellent. Look at Wal-Mart. Its physical attributes are excellent: greeters, clean stores, right locations, and it has the lowest cost structures. It is a rare business that has only a single competency.

There are many cases where we do not touch the products, for example, Drugstore.com. The physical distribution of pharmaceuticals is very different from the physical distribution of the products we got good at distributing.

Bezos described the type of product that Amazon wanted to offer.

The items we touch should have two attributes:

- Conveyable, i.e., on a conveyer belt and smaller than a bread box
- Nonperishable

We have millions of SKUs (stock keeping units) in our distribution center network. It's difficult to ship singles, from a selection of millions, to individuals.

Bezos viewed Amazon's distribution facility a key competitive advantage. Yet, Amazon enjoyed a much higher valuation than even best of breed retailers with state-of-the-art distribution skills. For example, while companies in the Standard & Poor's 500 had an average PE multiple of eighteen, most retailers generate only single digit PE ratios.

GETTING PERSONAL

What then separates Amazon from other retailers? For many observers it is the potential power of the data generated by millions of transactions. Bezos said:

We use collaborative filtering, a statistical method that looks at your purchase history, compares it to other customers, builds a statistical aggregate electronic "soul mate" that tells you what your soul mate has purchased that you have not.

But it's still early. The algorithms themselves are hard and they are constrained by processing power.

For Bezos, personalization would be a hallmark of the Amazon brand and experience. He observed, "The business reason to do personalization is so that we build a deep relationship with customers that they would miss

---

[15] *Wall Street Journal*, February 7, 2001, p. B1.

if they went away." Bezos saw Amazon as a mix of Web skills (including e-commerce platform and payment mechanisms) and fulfillment expertise. Bezos summed up: "These come together at software."

But for *You* the Price Is . . .

That software was increasingly sophisticated. For example, by drawing on known demographics and purchase history, algorithms could estimate a buyer's price elasticity for a given item and raise or lower a price to meet the maximum that an individual was likely to pay. This practice was known as dynamic pricing. Broadly speaking, prices were free to move in response to demand, supply, aggregate buying, reverse auctions, or haggling. Jupiter research projected that revenue from these online dynamic pricing formats would reach $1 billion in 2000 and grow to $7 billion by 2004.[16] While dynamic pricing was not a new concept, shops in high-income areas often charged more for items than shops in lower income areas. When wedded to Web technology and customer-specific databases, the practice could become a powerful tool for maximizing pricing and margins. For brick and mortar sellers, tests of price elasticities could be expensive and time consuming. Therefore, most sellers confined tests to a narrow range of prices on a limited number of items. By contrast, Web-based sellers could easily perform continuous, real-time price testing that produced immediate customer responses. For example, if a seller wanted to know the sales impact of a 5 percent price increase, he or she could conduct a test by charging every fiftieth visitor this increased price. By studying responses, researchers could gain important insights into the role price plays in customers' buying decisions.[17]

One high-profile example of Web-based dynamic pricing in practice occurred with Amazon in September 2000. Users in a chat room on the DVDtalk.com Web site noticed that some Amazon customers paid more for given DVDs than others. The visitors noticed that Amazon's prices seemed higher for regular customers. One chat room visitor said, "They [Amazon] must figure that with repeat customers they have 'won' them over and they can charge them slightly higher prices since they are loyal and don't mind and/or won't notice that they are being charged three to five percent more for some items." When the chat room visitors complained about the pricing variation to Amazon, the company's spokesman Bill

Curry replied, "It was done to determine consumer responses to different discount levels . . . this was a pure and simple price test. This was not dynamic pricing. We don't do that and have no plans to ever do that." However, in an e-mail response to an individual DVDTalk.com member, another Amazon representative wrote, "I would first like to send along my most sincere apology for any confusion or frustration caused by our dynamic price test. Dynamic testing of a customer base is a common practice among both brick and mortar and Internet companies." Indeed, Curry later observed, "Dynamic pricing is stupid, because people will find out. Fortunately, it only took us two instances to see this."[18]

Still, Jupiter Research believed dynamic pricing practices would increase in the online retail industry. Jupiter expected customers to receive offers to which they were more likely to respond based on a variety of factors including "purchase history, including lifetime customer value and demonstrated price sensitivity; clickstream history (site versioning based on affiliate and advertising linkage); preferences and interests reported by customers; and products purchased by other individuals with similar purchase patterns, demographic, or psychographic profiles."[19]

THE AMAZON EFFECT

In the e-tailing world, Amazon had quickly become the proverbial eight hundred pound gorilla. Bezos and others credited the company's innovativeness for its success. Indeed, Amazon originated or quickly adopted a host of innovations that set it apart from the prevailing competition.

Amazon's "one-click" check out process offered one contentious example. In September 1997, Amazon launched a system that allowed shoppers to buy items without completing long registration and shipping forms—a chore shoppers found tedious and that inhibited buying. Instead, Amazon designed software and redesigned its processes to allow repeat buyers to purchase items by clicking one button. Two years later Amazon was awarded a patent on its one-click process.

In 1998, B&N.com introduced a similar one-click service. Amazon sued and in December 1999 was awarded an injunction in U.S. District Court in Seattle. In February 2001, the U.S. Court of Appeals in Washington D.C. issued a unanimous decision to overturn the injunction

---

[16] Jupiter Research, Forecasts and Projections, Commerce Infrastructure, August 2000.
[17] Michael V. Marin, "Virtual Pricing," *The McKinsey Quarterly,* no. 4, 2000.

[18] David Streitfeld, "On the Web, Price Tags Blur; What You Pay Could Depend on Who You Are," *The Washington Post,* September 27, 2000.
[19] Michele Rosenshein, "Dynamic Merchandising," Jupiter Research, Vol. 5, October 24, 2000.

awarded in 1999. Both sides were scheduled to go to trial over the issue in September 2001.

Meanwhile, independent booksellers looked to join forces to compete with Amazon. According to the Book Industry Study Group, a market research firm, independent booksellers owned a 15.2 percent share of the nearly 1.1 billion adult consumer books sold in the United States in 1999, down from their 19.5 percent share in 1995. Similarly, national chains also saw their market share slip, falling to 24.6 percent in 1999 from 25.5 percent in 1995. Book e-tailers, led by Amazon, garnered 5.4 percent of the overall market in 1999, up from 0.4 percent in 1997, the first year for which data is available.[20]

To combat the market share loss, independent booksellers set up their own Web site and some joined forces with companies such as BookSite.com, an online clearinghouse and database-management firm that let independent booksellers set up their own Web pages, backed up by BookSite's online title list and delivery system. BookSite had two hundred independent bookstores as members, each with annual revenue of $250,000 or more. Members maintain their own individual storefronts on the Web, but pay a fee of about $2,500 a year for access to BookSite's book-title database, search-engine software, and access to warehouses of book distributors, such as Ingram Book Group, the distributor featured prominently in Amazon's prospectus.

BookSite's founder said, "I think there's an image that independent booksellers are kind of shy little fellows sitting in the corner crying . . . That's not the case. There's a whole cadre of booksellers out there carrying on the battle."[21]

BookSite, however, would soon have some competition. The American Booksellers Association, a trade group representing small bookstores, was in March 2001 testing Booksense.com. Part of a larger marketing plan to raise the profile of independent booksellers nationwide, Booksense would offer the same kind of back-office e-commerce services as BookSite, including fulfillment and distribution and a database of titles. Booksense would charge its members $100 a month and 4.25 percent of the store's online sales.[22]

BookSite had 1.2 million titles, and Booksense planned to offer 2.4 million titles using a database it licensed from Baker & Taylor Corp., the distributor formerly used exclusively by Amazon before it deployed its own internal-fulfillment system.

BookSite and Booksense would each depend to some degree on their wholesaler partners to fulfill orders.

One analyst estimated the size of the online book sales market at $1.44 billion in 2000, or 7.5 percent of the estimated $19 billion in total consumer book sales for that year. But he estimated that by 2003, the online market could increase 90 percent to $2.7 billion. Total book sales were projected to grow only 18 percent, to $22.5 billion.[23]

CONCLUSION

It was clear that Amazon had matured far beyond the initial online business concept described in its 1995 prospectus. What was less clear was what the company would become in the future, what kind of business model it should adopt, and how such a model should be valued. Like that woman from Stanford, shareholders would want to know what they had bought and where Amazon was going. Amazon innovated and created a new form of retail organization. The question was whether the new form was viable or whether existing firms could imitate and incorporate some the features of the new form to enhance their own survival chances in the quickly changing retail ecology.

Display Technologies, Inc. (Abridged)

Jonathan West and H. Kent Bowen

In late May 1993, Toru Shima, president of Display Technologies Incorporated (DTI), confronted a choice many managers would envy. His success at manufacturing light-weight, color display screens for notebook computers had resulted in an increasing number of requests from his customers asking for substantial

---

[20] Scott Eden, "Independent Booksellers Hope to Find Strength in Numbers," *Wall Street Journal*, July 17, 2000.
[21] Ibid.
[22] Ibid.
[23] Ibid.

Source: Copyright © 1998 by The President and Fellows of Harvard College. Professor Jonathan West and H. Kent Bowen prepared this case as the basis for class discussion rather than to illustrate either effective or ineffective handling of an administrative situation. This case is an abridgement of Harvard Business School Case 9-697-117.

increases in output. These flat-panel color screens, known as LCDs (liquid crystal displays), had become hot sellers, as customers demanded ever-increasing performance and lighter weight from their portable computers.

Since Shima's main customers were also his company's owners (DTI was a joint venture of Toshiba and IBM Japan), he could hardly refuse their request. Toshiba and IBM could use every screen Shima's plant produced. Both companies were amassing a growing backlog of notebook computer orders. Shima's work force had already raised output from the original 10,000 units per month to the current 50,000 per month. His people, machines, and systems were stretched. Now he was being pressed to raise production to 100,000 per month.

Shima was not sure how best to meet these expectations. He knew the task would be tough. The type of LCDs DTI made were extraordinarily difficult to manufacture. They required hundreds of delicate steps, each performed on some of the most expensive, state-of-the-art manufacturing technology in the electronics business. Few firms had substantial experience with color LCDs, but every company building them was racing to supply rapidly growing demand. There were multiple obstacles to increased output by these firms: none of them had figured out all the manufacturing process complexities, and both the technology itself and product requirements (such as screen size) were changing rapidly.

Shima's choices seemed to be among three possibilities: (1) focus on increasing yields on his existing production line, (2) add capacity by building a second line similar to the existing one, or (3) shift to a new production technology with larger glass sheets that would allow twice as many screens to be built in the same time. Shima wanted to weigh his options carefully before deciding. If successful, each option would meet the short-term projected needs of his customers. However, Shima's past experience and instincts told him that the probability of success varied by option, and the choice he made would have strategic ramifications well into the future.

BACKGROUND

Both IBM and Toshiba had long been leaders in the world computer and electronics industries (Exhibit 1). In the 1980s, they were in the forefront of an industry-wide shift to smaller and more portable personal computers. Toshiba had pioneered a highly successful "notebook" computer (designed to be as portable as a notebook) in 1985. (Exhibit 2 shows a photo of a Toshiba portable personal computer.) IBM introduced its first notebook computer 1988, following its launch of a personal computer in 1981. These innovative notebook products relied upon advances in component technologies: more durable batteries, miniature disk drives, tiny printed circuit boards, and smaller, lighter display screens.

Light-weight, compact screens had been a critical bottleneck in the move to portability. Conventional screen technologies used for desk-top monitors (cathode ray tubes, or CRTs) were far too heavy, bulky, and power consuming for truly portable computers. The development of *flat-panel displays—thin, light*-weight screens with acceptable resolution in color—was critical to the success of notebook computer products. *Liquid crystal displays (LCDs)* (whose manufacturing process is described briefly below) were by far the most popular type of flat-panel displays.

Toshiba and IBM had chosen to develop a thin-film transistor (TFT) active-matrix version of the LCD. An *active matrix* screen provided faster response and sharper contrasts than the passive-matrix technology that was used on earlier flat-panel screens and LCDs for watches and calculators. Active-matrix LCDs were made by sandwiching a layer of special liquid crystal material between sheets of glass to create a full-color display. When voltage was applied to the liquid crystal, millions of tiny, separate light sources (called pixels) were turned on or off. To create a coherent image, each pixel had to be controlled by a separate transistor that instructed each pixel when and how to turn on. In the *thin-film transistor (TFT)* version of this technology used by Toshiba and IBM, the transistors were processed into a very thin layer (film) on the surface of sheets of glass. The addition of this thin layer of transistors, critical to the performance of the product, presented complex manufacturing challenges.

The Joint Venture Decision

In the early 1980s, both IBM and Toshiba pursued independent research projects to develop flat-panel displays. By the mid-1980s, IBM had developed an advanced TFT-LCD but did not yet have an economically viable high-volume manufacturing process. When Toshiba's central research and development center announced a 9.5-inch active matrix TFT-LCD in December 1985, Kiyoji Ishida, director of IBM's Yamato Laboratory in Japan, approached Toshiba for discussions about a joint venture.[1] He was impressed by Toshiba's experience

---

[1] Note: Display screens are measured diagonally, as are television screens.

EXHIBIT 1   The World's 20 Largest Computer and Electronics Companies (1993, by Sales)

Company	Country	Sales ($ billion)	Assets ($ billion)	Stockholders' equity ($ billion)	Employees
International Business Machines	United States	65.1	86.7	27.6	308,010
General Electric	United States	62.2	192.9	23.5	268,000
Hitachi	Japan	61.5	76.7	25.8	331,505
Matsushita Electric Industrial	Japan	57.5	75.6	30.1	252,075
Siemens	Germany	51.4	50.8	13.5	413,000
Samsung Group	South Korea	49.6	48.0	6.4	188,558
Toshiba Corporation	Japan	37.5	49.3	10.1	173,000
Philips Electronics	Netherlands	33.3	26.9	5.0	252,200
Sony	Japan	31.5	39.7	12.5	126,000
ABB Asea Brown Boveri	Switzerland	30.5	25.9	4.1	213,407
Alcatel Alsthom	France	30.5	44.2	9.0	203,000
NEC	Japan	28.4	34.9	7.1	140,969
Daewoo	South Korea	28.3	39.3	5.1	78,727
Fujitsu	Japan	27.9	33.1	9.7	161,974
Mitsubishi Electric	Japan	26.5	30.7	7.1	107,859
Hewlett-Packard	United States	16.4	13.7	7.5	92,600
Canon	Japan	15.3	17.2	5.7	67,227
Electrolux	Sweden	14.0	10.4	2.0	119,200
Digital Equipment	United States	14.0	11.3	4.9	113,800
Thomson	France	13.4	18.0	1.4	100,800

Source: Fortune, 26 July 1993.

EXHIBIT 2   Toshiba's Portable Personal Computer, with 10.4-inch TFT-LCD Display

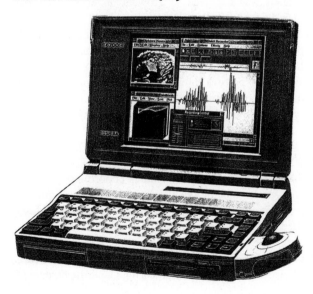

with semiconductor manufacturing and believed Toshiba could be the partner IBM needed to develop an effective manufacturing process quickly. Ishida recalled his motivation in seeking to collaborate with Toshiba:

IBM's research laboratory [in Yorktown Heights, New York] is dedicated to fundamental research and is not designed for work on commercial products. IBM wanted to gain access to Toshiba's knowledge and experience with high-volume manufacturing. Each company's capabilities complemented the other.

For Toshiba, IBM offered fundamental technologies and the possibility of sharing the enormous anticipated cost of the facilities required to manufacture LCDs in volume. Tsuyoshi Kawanishi, Toshiba's senior executive vice president for partnerships and alliances, explained Toshiba's motivation for seeking an alliance with IBM:

> The key was to establish a win-win situation for two competent partners. IBM could offer its brand equity in the PC world, its PC interface applications, and the depth of its research. Toshiba could offer semiconductor process technologies that were applicable to LCD production and close relationships with equipment vendors.

In the late 1980s, electronics industry engineers disagreed about which of several competing technologies offered the most promising road to a successful—and manufacturable—color LCD. After examining the available options, IBM and Toshiba decided that, although TFT-LCD appeared to be the most expensive option, its picture quality was best and it promised the overall highest-quality product. Kawanishi recalled:

> It was my firm conviction that customers would not compromise once they saw the superior quality of our new TFT-LCD product. From my experience in the semiconductor industry, I believed the production cost problems could be overcome by increasing productivity. We had achieved a 20 percent annual [cost] improvement in DRAMs.[2]
>
> In the highly capital-intensive LCD industry, where technology evolves day by day, it is very important to be one of the pioneers. The empirical rule says that the top three vendors can make money, numbers four and five will break even, and the other entrants and followers will lose money. The sooner you invest, the more likely you are to benefit from [the early stages of the product life cycle] when the product's market price is still relatively high.

The two companies signed an initial two-year joint development agreement in August 1986, establishing a 50-person joint-research team of IBM and Toshiba engineers based at IBM's Yamato Laboratory. The engineers shared results from previous research and their experience with process technologies. By May 1988 they were able to announce a prototype 14-inch TFT-LCD.

At the conclusion of their first two-year agreement, the two companies signed a contract to begin manufacturing. They established Display Technologies Incorporated (DTI) in August 1988 as an equally owned joint venture to manufacture large, color LCDs. A new production facility was completed in May 1991 next to Toshiba's conventional LCD manufacturing facilities at Himeji City, 600 kilometers west of Tokyo. By the time production got under way four months later, the company employed 130 people and was committed to produce more than 10 varieties of TFT-LCD panels. Each parent company contracted to buy 50 percent of the output. Each sought somewhat different versions. Toshiba wanted several 9.5-inch as well as 10.4-inch versions, whereas IBM sought mainly 10.4-inch models. By May of 1993, each parent company had invested more than $125 million in the firm. DTI had about 600 total employees, of which 120 were engineers, 30 managers, and 80 manufacturing/maintenance engineers. To continue to meet the demands for new models, space at the current

EXHIBIT 3 Projected Worldwide Demand for Large-Format (Greater Than 8-inch) TFT-LCD Screens (1995 Projections Shown Depending on Price)

	Price per screen	Volume (millions of units)
1991 (actual)	$2,100	0.5
1992 (actual)	1,600	1.2
1993 (estimated)	1,200	3.5
1995 (estimated)		
Scenario 1	720	5.0
Scenario 2	640	6.2
Scenario 3	560	8.0
Scenario 4	480	10.5
Scenario 5	400	17.0

manufacturing site was being developed for the product development group; this space was expected to be fully functional in less than a year.

Sales Growth and Competition

Sales of LCD screens accelerated in the late 1980s. Industry analysts estimated that by the year 2000, demand for LCD screens would grow to at least $20 billion—perhaps as high as $40 billion. Demand for TFT-LCD screens was expected to grow at an even faster rate than demand for all LCDs. Demand for TFT-LCDs was 27 percent of total LCD demand in 1992, and was expected to reach 54% of total LCD demand in 1995. Large-format TFT-LCDs (greater than 8 inches) were a significant portion (projected to grow from 81 percent to 83 percent between 1992 and 1995) of all TFT-LCD screens produced.

In 1993 Japanese producers supplied 95 percent of the world market for passive-matrix LCDs and nearly 100 percent of the newer active-matrix LCDs. Some saw the LCD market as a tremendous opportunity—"a second semiconductor business"—for Japanese industry.

Many in the industry believed, however, that the speed with which the market could expand would depend on how fast the prices of LCDs declined (see, for example, Exhibit 3). Sakae Arai, senior manager of Toshiba's LCD Device Marketing and Engineering Department, agreed:

> Cost is key. A color LCD costs more than five times as much as a CRT. In 1993, the factory production cost for a 14-inch CRT was $200–$300. If LCD prices could be cut so that they were only two or three times as much as those of CRTs, the LCD market could really take off—especially in areas such as workstations and PCs, which look particularly

---

[2] DRAM (dynamic random access memory) was a low-cost, commonly used type of semiconductor memory chip. Since DRAMs, like TFT-LCDs, were transistor-based products, Shima hoped that his experience with DRAMs would provide valuable insights into TFT-LCD manufacturing.

promising. Offices in Japan are often very small. There is little room for desktop equipment. The use of notebook-type word processors and notebook PCs should continue to increase. And along with the growing use of office automation equipment, demands for [reducing equipment size] are getting stronger.

The potential size of the market was attractive to many microelectronic companies. Several Japanese firms had already begun production and others planned to enter. Sharp Corporation had emerged as the early leader and largest TFT-LCD manufacturer. With the industry's largest LCD volumes, Sharp enjoyed economies of scale in production. As an early entrant, it had accumulated considerable manufacturing skill. It produced small color LCDs, used in audio/visual products such as VCRs and hand-held video cameras. As well as supplying its own divisions, Sharp also sold LCDs to PC vendors, including Compaq, Apple, Toshiba, and IBM.

NEC was the second largest TFT-LCD manufacturer. NEC was the largest PC maker in Japan, with 50 percent domestic market share. Most of NEC's LCD production had so far been dedicated to meeting its own needs.

By 1993 worldwide production of color LCDs suitable for computers was poised to expand rapidly. Hitachi, Matsushita, and ADI were producing small quantities of color TFT-LCDs. At least three other major Japanese electronics companies (Hoshiden, Matsushita, and Sanyo) planned to begin producing computer-sized color LCDs (most had produced smaller LCDs for several years). Three Korean manufacturers with extensive experience in semiconductors (Samsung, Goldstar, and Hyundai) were also ready to begin production. In addition, a half-billion dollar consortium sponsored by the U.S. Advanced Research Projects Agency was investigating ways to stimulate U.S. firms to enter the business with radical, new technologies.

THE MANUFACTURING PROCESS

TFT-LCDs posed many of the same manufacturing challenges as other semiconductor chips (such as memories and microprocessors), but TFT-LCDs were characterized by several unique features that resulted in especially tricky problems for manufacturing managers and engineers. Gaining an acceptable yield (a high proportion of good output from a process or subprocess) was particularly difficult. Moreover, the failure rate from each step cumulated, so that the final yield from the entire process was only the proportion remaining after many steps, any

one of which could introduce a defect. For example, in 1993, the yields of the three major process steps were 75 percent, 70 percent, and 85 percent, resulting in an overall yield of $(.75)(.70)(.85) = 44.6$ percent. Almost all of the defects introduced during the three major process steps were identified at the end of the entire process during functional testing. The yields at each process step were inferred from the type of defects identified in the final functional test.

Semiconductor chips were produced in batches of hundreds on each 5- to 8-inch diameter wafer (a *wafer* is a sheet of material, also called a substrate, on which the chips are made). Thus, many defect-free chips could usually be selected from those on the wafer, even if some were damaged or contaminated. In contrast, in TFT-LCD production, the total glass panel—itself larger than an entire chip wafer—had to be kept defect free to obtain a good display screen.

Manufacture of TFT-LCDs called for three types of production processes: the transistor-array process, to produce the intricate grid of transistors that controlled the light pixels; the cell-formation process, to construct the layer of liquid crystal that created the image; and the module-assembly process, to assemble the finished product (see Exhibit 4). Some testing was carried out at the end of each of the three processes, although most defects could not be identified until functional testing at the end of the entire process.

The *transistor-array* was constructed by depositing millions of transistors on a glass sheet that was later cut into two 10.4-inch LCD panels per sheet. The production process used for this step was similar to that employed by large-scale integrated circuit manufacture: deposition of layers of conducting and insulating materials on a base layer of material, using photolithography and etching. These steps were repeated six to nine times, each time creating an additional layer. At the end of the process, the glass sheet was cut to form two separate panels. The throughput time of the transistor-array process was two weeks. DTI's yield from the transistor-array process was about 75 percent in 1993.

The *cell-formation process* injected liquid crystal material into a narrow space between the coated surfaces of two glass sheets, one of which held the transistor array, the other of which had an array of similarly small color filter dots (red, blue, and green). (The color filter was a purchased component.) The glass plates were separated by a 0.5-micron gap and liquid crystal was injected into the gap using a vacuum process. The resulting unit was known as a "cell." Light polarizers were attached to the

EXHIBIT 4   Process Flow–Large-Format TFT-LCD Panels

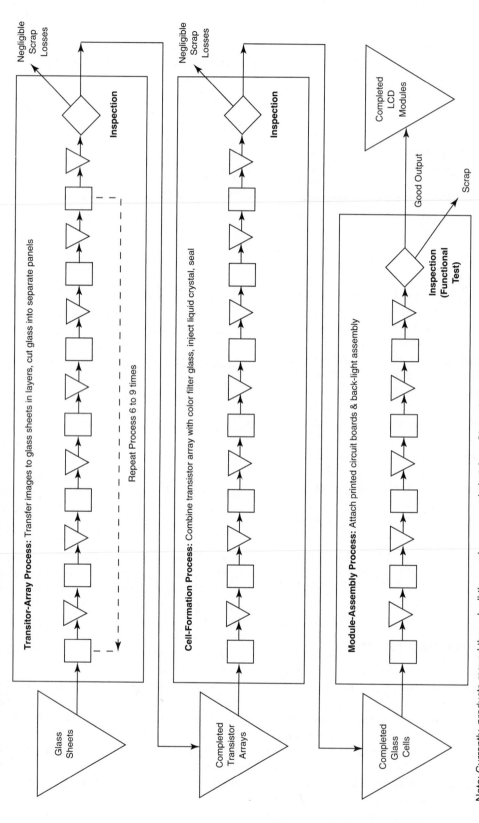

Note: Currently, products moved through all three subprocesses in batches. Glass sheets moved through the transistor-array process in batches of 25. Each sheet was cut into two panels at the end of the transistor-array process. Two panels were lost due to dust protection, so batches of 48 panels moved through the cell-formation and module-assembly processes.

cell after completion. The throughput time of the cell-formation process was one week. DTI's yield from the cell-formation process was about 70 percent in 1993.

The *module-assembly* process assembled a complete TFT-LCD unit. The glass-and-liquid-crystal layer was linked to a printed circuit board (each of the individual transistors had to be connected to the board to allow control of the pixels), drive circuit, and backlight assembly. The throughput time of the module-assembly process was one day (two shifts). DTI's yield from the module-assembly process was about 85 percent in 1993.

The single largest cause of defects was tiny particles of dust. Akihiro Fukatsu, of Toshiba's Material and Liquid Crystal Display Group, explained:

> If a single dust particle remains in the LCD panel, the corrupted spot will ruin an entire LCD panel. The human eye is extremely sensitive to color. It can detect even a slight variance in color density.
>
> Every production step contains the hidden possibility of contamination from airborne dust, people's sweat, skin flakes, or hair. Ideally, automation should be used to minimize the number of people in the clean room. Equipment control is also key, since [tiny particles arising from the equipment at any step in the process] can remain in the panel.

Much of the challenge in manufacturing LCDs arose from the need to overcome these problems. Toshiba's semiconductor-process experience was valuable in this task, since successful semiconductor manufacture also called for meticulous attention to detail on the part of all equipment operators and precise discipline in clean-room practices. (See Exhibit 5 for a photograph of DTI's clean room in the Himeji City plant.)

As a market leader in DRAMs, Toshiba had developed considerable expertise in this field, and Shima himself was widely regarded as an industry leader in this area. Much of this know-how could be transferred to TFT-LCD manufacture. Although dust-control management in TFT-LCD production was not as "numerically severe" as that in semiconductor manufacture—it called for removal only of particles larger than 0.5 microns, whereas semiconductor manufacture demanded removal of particles as small as 0.18 microns—the much larger size of LCD screens made dust control demands particularly stringent. In TFT-LCD production, even a single dust particle on the large panel could destroy an entire screen.

The glass required for the panels was also a very sensitive and difficult material to handle. It easily became electrostatically charged (in which case it actually attracted particles) and was inherently brittle. To ensure the necessary near-perfect transparency, it had to be kept impeccably clean throughout the entire process.

Early Production Success

Production at the new site began slowly but soon improved. DTI engineering director Hidenori Akiyoshi revealed:

> We actually started from nothing. Nobody, us included, had any experience with large-format TFT-LCD mass production. Although a test production run had been carried out by Toshiba's laboratory, a lot of unexpected problems were waiting for us as we ramped up. When we started production, the overall line yield was far below 10 percent, primarily due to equipment problems.
>
> First, we decided that we should work with equipment vendors. This helped us raise the yield to 25 percent. Then, we faced electrostatic and particle-defect problems. It turned out these had been introduced by previous steps, but became apparent only later. We had to alter steps in the process repeatedly.

Eventually, yields stabilized around 45 percent. Management focused next on raising output. Overcoming problems with output was achieved by meticulously examining each step, first to identify, and then to remove, all unnecessary action—no matter how small. One such improvement, for example, reduced robot arm movements by two seconds. According to Akiyoshi:

> This accumulation of time-reducing activities eventually made improvements of [many minutes]—even an hour, in the long run. DTI management also shortened the idle time between each step by [about 15 percent]. This kind of activity would have been meaningless until the yield reached a certain level, since workers and equipment would be idle in the subsequent steps under the low-yield production line.

The TFT-array process was run as a batch process, with 25 sheets of glass substrate per batch. In each batch, one sheet was used to protect the others from dust; another was used for sampling inspection. Thus two sheets were lost from the output of each batch. After the yield stabilized, Akiyoshi decided to eliminate sampling inspection to increase output to 24 sheets per batch. Since each sheet of glass was cut into two panels (screens), this resulted in an output (before yield losses) of 48 screens per batch.

EXHIBIT 5   DTI Himeji Plant Clean Room

SHIMA'S CHALLENGE

As Akiyoshi and his engineering group labored to raise output at DTI, Toshiba and IBM sought a new leader for the fledgling company. On 25 May 1992, they appointed Toru Shima as DTI's president.

Shima began his career with Toshiba in 1961 as a semiconductor engineer. In 1976, he was promoted to senior manager, and in 1987 he was appointed president of Tohoku Semiconductor Incorporated, a strategic joint venture between Toshiba and Motorola. In 1989, he became general manager of Toshiba's Memory Division, which produced the world's largest-selling 1-megabit DRAM. Toshiba's development of this product was regarded by many industry observers as the single most-successful semiconductor development program ever. Since 1985, Shima had taught part-time at Osaka University, helping master's degree students grasp the intricacies of semiconductor manufacture.

Now he would be confronted by large, color LCDs, perhaps the most difficult electronics-manufacturing challenge of his career. Shima stressed what he called the "four Ms" of manufacturing: machines, materials, methods, and man. He sought improvements in all four to raise DTI's output.

Machines   Shima believed that one key to raising output was the total elimination of "doka-tei" (significant equipment breakdowns). He developed a 24-hour, on-site support system, in which equipment vendors stayed at the plant round-the-clock for the first three to six months after installation to support the new equipment. The plan succeeded. Equipment failures were prevented and utilization rates improved dramatically.

Another key was to prevent "choko-tei" (minor breakdowns). Attacking this problem, Shima implemented "visual control" of processes and improved operator training. Under the new system, all operators could monitor the process themselves and undertake routine maintenance of their own equipment.

To further improve machine utilization, Shima moved the plant to three-shift, 24-hour operation, with one shift dedicated to equipment maintenance and repair. During the other two shifts, each eight hours in length, the equipment was operational and producing product 85 percent of the time. Taken together, these three measures increased the mean time between equipment failure by 300 percent.

Materials   Shima found that material costs in LCD manufacturing were considerably higher than in semiconductor manufacturing, where they were about 20 percent of cost (Exhibits 6a and 6b). He therefore placed special stress on working with materials suppliers to reduce the cost of all major materials: color filters, backlight units, and printed circuit boards (PCBs). Toshiba's research division established joint efforts with several suppliers to tackle this task.

Methods   Shima scrutinized the entire production process to optimize line balance and locate bottlenecks between various process steps. His goal, again, was output maximization. He sought the assistance of two groups: Toshiba's semiconductor engineers, to transplant

EXHIBIT 6A   Large-Format (Greater Than 8 Inches) TFT-LCD Bill of Materials

Bill of materials: each large-format TFT-LCD panel required the following items:

TFT array		$ 23
Cell assembly		$133
Including:		
Light polarizer	$ 5	
Glass	15	
Liquid crystal	2	
Color filter	110	
Spacer and miscellaneous materials	1	
Module assembly		188

Including: TAB connector, backlight unit, printed circuit board, anisotropic conductive film, flexible printed circuit, cable, shield cable, frame, silicon, rubber

Total materials	$344

EXHIBIT 6B   Large-Format TFT-LCD Cost Breakdown for Each Good Unit (Panel) of Output Produced

(1993, at 45% Yield)

Materials[a]	$ 764
Depreciation and overhead	300
Labor	110
Total cost (at 45% yield)	**$1,174**
Selling price	$1,200

[a]Materials cost exceeds material cost stated in Exhibit 6a due to yield losses resulting in scrap.

methodologies established in DRAM manufacturing—particularly helpful in improving the transistor-array steps—and Toshiba's passive-matrix LCD engineers, now located next door, who were valuable in streamlining the cell-formation processes. Through hard and tedious work and based on deep understanding, each process had to be brought under control and made capable.

Man   To heighten each employee's sense of responsibility for the process, especially of dust reduction, Shima established what he termed the "Doctor Particle" system. Dozens of operators were appointed as a Doctor Particle, charged with investigating all root causes of particle/dust formation and developing recommendations to eliminate the underlying problems. The resulting reduction of contamination was credited with raising yield in key steps by an additional 30 percent. Shima's aim was to ensure that, after yields reached an acceptable level, responsibility for further improvement would move entirely to the operators.

Production management was not, however, Shima's only challenge. He also needed to blend two disparate corporate cultures. To help meld his employees into a single culture, he established a rule that prevented employees from mentioning the names of their parent companies. If employees mentioned their originating firm during a meeting, they were required to place a 10-yen coin into a big jar in the meeting room. Eventually, Shima said, it became difficult to determine from which firm any particular employee came.

THE CHOICES IN MAY 1993

By 1993, DTI had attained a monthly production of 50,000 panels. DTI's market share of computer-sized (large-format) TFT-LCD screens had grown to approximately 17 percent of the total. IBM's newly introduced Think Pad notebook PC, using DTI's 10.4-inch panel, was a huge success. DTI led the notebook PC display industry, and the 10.4-inch size became standard.

But success caused further challenges. Toshiba and IBM now wanted DTI to raise production to 100,000 panels per month. Toshiba sold almost 600,000 notebook computers in 1992, giving it the largest share of the world market. IBM ranked fifth. Looking forward, Toshiba and IBM believed that at least 50 percent of notebook PCs would use a TFT-LCD by 1997, meaning that even more substantial increases in output would soon be needed.

Shima had to plan to meet these demands, but he also had to watch—and further reduce—current production costs. Toshiba's Sakae Arai projected sharply increased cost and price competition within a few years:

> By 1996, if each manufacturer implements their proposed investment plans (see Exhibit 7), the demand-supply conditions will reverse. Price erosion will surely follow. We need to prepare for this by achieving cost competitiveness for the longer term.

Shima's experience with DRAM production also told him that he could soon be subject—simultaneously—to the need for both rapid volume increases and steep cost reductions, as competitors gained experience. (Typical DRAM volume and cost curves are shown in Exhibits 8a, 8b, and 8c.) His plan would therefore have to meet current production demands, but also take into account future volume-increase and cost-reduction needs.

As he considered his options, Shima believed that, in the short term at least, he had to choose among three possible solutions for doubling output (see Exhibit 9):

1. **Continue to focus on improving output in the existing line.** Shima was not content with the present yield and output of the existing process. He believed that even though considerable improvement had been achieved so far and much of the technology was novel, with additional help from 30 additional engineers and technicians, the existing operators could probably double the monthly output by significantly increasing

EXHIBIT 7   Large-Format (Greater Than 8 Inches) TFT-LCD Production Plans (Announced Production Plans as of May 1993)

Company name	Plant location[a]	Start-up of new lines	Current monthly production	Planned total monthly capacity (1995)	Planned investment ($ U.S. millions)
Sharp	Tenri	June 1994	150,000	250,000	$950
	Mie	2nd half 1995		150,000	(1993–1995)
NEC	Kagoshima	December 1993	80,000	100,000	$760
	Akita	December 1994		50,000	(1993–1996)
Hitachi	Mobara	Winter 1994	5,000	30,000	$285
Hoshiden	Kobe	Spring 1994	none	60,000	$95
Fujitsu	Yonago	Spring 1994	none	15,000	$257
					(through 1997)
Matsushita	Ishikawa	April 1994	10,000	30,000	(undisclosed)
Advanced Display (ADI)	Kumamoto	February 1994	2,000	40,000	$127.5
		Summer 1996		100,000 (1996)	
DTI	Himeji City		50,000	100,000	?
Total monthly			**297,000**	**925,000**	

[a] All plants located in Japan.

EXHIBIT 8A   DRAM Worldwide Shipments (Millions of Units), by Production Generation

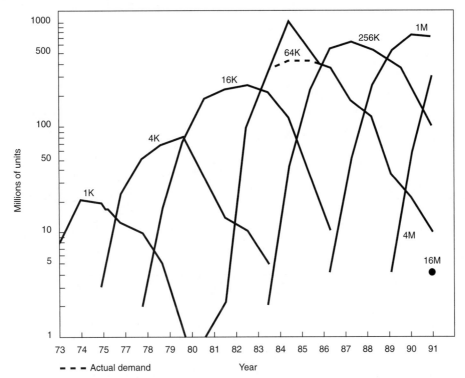

- - - Actual demand   Year

The above graph shows shipment volumes for each successive generation of DRAMs. (Note semi-log scale.) The curve labels refer to the memory size (in bits) per DRAM chip. For example, 1 K denotes the generation of DRAMS with 1,000 bytes per chip, and 4 M denotes the generation of DRAMS with 4 million bytes per chip.

yield. (Thus, the number of operators was not expected to change as yields increased.) The most optimistic timing would require 6 months, but it could take as long as 24 months. During this period, the necessary experimentation would also result in lost production (estimated at 18 percent of the monthly production) during the improvement process. Shima also saw other opportunities for cost reduction. Any increases in output would reduce the per unit cost of depreciation and labor; yield increases would also lower material scrap costs.

2. **Duplicate the existing production line.** Under this option, DTI could simply replicate its existing technology. It could utilize all that had been learned from experience with the current production line and could anticipate accurately what would be the output of the new line. Importantly, the new line could be housed in

the existing plant and ramped up quickly. Shima estimated that in nine months, he could acquire the equipment for the new line and install it in additional cleanroom space that had been designed originally into the plant. A couple of months thereafter, the new line could be functioning at the same level of output as the existing line. The cost implications of such a choice would need to be weighed carefully; estimates were for about $200 million for capital investment for the second production line and adaptation of the current facilities and shared infrastructure. Choosing this approach, however, might limit improvements of the current process. Shima knew that it would be difficult for his workforce to concentrate on improving the old line while they were installing the new one.

3. **Invest in a radically new line employing new technologies.** Several new production technologies had

EXHIBIT 8B DRAM Price Trends (1983–1993)

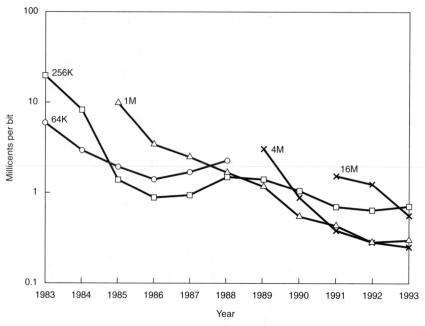

Source: ICE. In the above graph, 64 K denotes DRAMs with 64,000 bits per chip, 4 M denotes DRAMs with 4 million bytes per chip, etc. DRAM price trends (1983–1993).

EXHIBIT 8C DRAM Water Fabrication Facility Costs

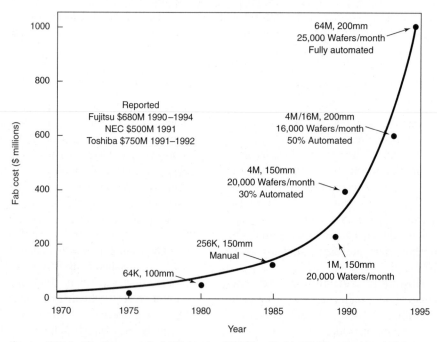

Source: ICE. In the above graph, 64 K denotes DRAMs with 64,000 bits per chip, 4 M denotes DRAMs with 4 million bytes per chip, etc. DRAM price trends (1983–1993).

EXHIBIT 9 Three Options to Raise Output to 100,0000 Units/Month

Option 1: Improve existing production process

Significantly improve yields and cycle time:

Estimated time to completion:	6–24 months
Capital expenditure:	$5 million
Engineering resources required:	30 engineers*
Production disruption estimate:	18%

Option 2: Duplicate existing line

Estimated time to completion:	9 months
Capital expenditure:	$200 million
Engineering resources required:	50 engineers*
Production disruption estimate:	0%

Option 3: Introduce new production technology

Larger substrates, single-piece flow process:

Estimated time to completion:	15–30 months
Capital expenditure:	$300 million
Engineering resources required:	120 engineers*
Production disruption estimate:	0%

*The fully loaded cost per engineer was estimated to be $100,000 per year.

been developed on the pilot-production line in Toshiba's Fukaya plant that could potentially be applied to large-format TFT-LCD production. The two most important innovations employed larger glass substrates (the sheets from which the panels were made) and a more advanced handling system. By using larger 360 mm × 465 mm (about 14-inch × 18-inch) substrates, the new system could potentially produce four 10.4-inch panels from each substrate, as opposed to the two panels produced from the existing substrate size of 300 mm × 400 mm (about 11.8-inch × 15.7-inch). This required different versions of the expensive equipment used for the original line and the design of new jigs, fixtures, and handling equipment.

The new handling system would allow a shift from the current batch system to more of a single-piece flow process. Roughly two dozen substrates were processed as a batch under the current system. The large substrate size required for LCDs, however, made it difficult to maintain conformity. Quality varied between individual substrates in each batch. In addition, under the existing batch system, processing equipment had to be sufficiently large to handle dozens of glass substrates at once. Robots were needed to load and unload the trays between processing steps, at which time the fragile glass edges of the panels occasionally became damaged.

Shima thought these problems would have become impossible to resolve under the old system coupled with the even-larger substrates that would be needed by a new line. The proposed handling system, devised to overcome these problems, moved to a single-piece flow process. For example, with the new system, in the coating step in the transistor-array process, a substrate would flow from coating to baking without loading and unloading. This would remove the risk of damage and loss of time during the changeover from one machine to another. The new system cycle time currently was 120 seconds. If Shima could achieve the same overall 45 percent yield as the existing TFT-LCD line, this cycle time would need to be cut to 12 seconds to enable the desired 100 percent productivity increase.

While together the elements of this shift in process technology promised a 100 percent increase in output, the new system had not yet been tested in actual production. Shima knew the new system would require considerable unproven equipment and substantial experimentation before it met the yield and output goals of his current line. It was likely to take 15 to 30 months to get the new technology running relatively smoothly.

The technology did promise, however, to make DTI a pioneer in the next generation production technology. With the new technology, DTI could potentially preempt its competitors in the race to establish standards. By establishing his equipment as the industry standard, Shima hoped to encourage equipment suppliers to lock into DTI's technology, reducing the cost of future expansion and allowing more-rapid depreciation of current equipment. One rumor predicted, however, that Sharp would soon move to 450 mm × 370 mm (17.7-inch × 14.6-inch) substrates, each yielding six 8.4-inch panels; another suggested that NEC planned to produce 370 mm × 470 mm (14.6-inch × 18.5-inch) substrates, each yielding four 10.4-inch panels. If the biggest equipment vendors adopted these as industry standards, DTI's specifications would require costly customized equipment. The option of moving to the new process technology was predicted to require an investment of at least $300 million for a line running at about 45 percent yield that could produce 100,000 panels per month.

Shima was not sure how to weigh all the implications of his choice. One thing, however, was certain. Both his company's competitors and owners would maintain their pressure. As significant and costly as this decision was, there was the added dimension of urgency to capture the future—rather than just react to the present problem.

Rambus Inc.

We are like a chip company which does everything
other than build and sell the chips.[1]
—Rambus CEO Geoff Tate

Vik Murthy and Paul Staelin

INTRODUCTION

As March 2001 began, officials at Rambus Inc. anxiously awaited court rulings. In the United States Rambus was sued by the large memory chip manufacturers Micron Technology and Hyundai Electronics. Meanwhile, Rambus sued memory chipmaker Infineon in the United States and Germany while also suing Micron in Italy. The courts would rule on Rambus's control over two of three prevailing standards of dynamic random access memory (DRAM) for computers. Meanwhile, turbulence in the public financial markets was affecting the entire technology sector. Rambus stock was now trading below $17, over 85 percent below its fifty-two–week high (but still over three times higher than its May 1997 IPO price). Amid this backdrop, Rambus's senior management team remained focused on broadening the adoption of the company's proprietary Rambus DRAM (RDRAM) technology, particularly in the markets for personal computers, servers, consumer electronics, and networking devices.

Headquartered in Los Altos, California, Rambus designed and licensed technology that accelerated the speed at which multiple chips in a memory system interfaced with one another. This technology served to enhance the performance and cost-effectiveness of computers, consumer electronics, and other electronic systems.

[1] February 14, 2001, interview with ON24 i-Network (www.on24.com).

The company's business model had two important aspects: (1) Rambus marketed its technology to original equipment manufacturers (OEM) to encourage them to design Rambus technology into their products, and (2) Rambus licensed its proprietary technology to semiconductor companies to manufacture and sell memory solutions (memory and logic integrated circuits) that incorporated Rambus interface technology.

This business model placed Rambus in a delicate position. Since Rambus focused on its core competence in technology design, it did not manufacture any of the chips that were supplied to its primary OEM customers. As a result, it had to maintain favorable business relationships with chip suppliers, who, as the middlemen between Rambus and OEMs, exerted considerable influence over the price and supply of DRAM chips. In addition, Rambus had to ensure that its technology would work optimally with the technology of powerful and influential hardware manufacturers, particularly Intel, the dominant supplier of microprocessors and a significant supplier of motherboards to computer OEMs. Intel's CEO recently hinted at some strain in the relationship between Rambus and Intel. Rambus also needed to balance its interests with the interests of its business partners in maximizing shareholder value, particularly with regard to maintaining a technological lead over its competitors, defending its intellectual property from legal attacks, and earning an appropriate rate of return for the use of its intellectual property.

Despite the delicacy of its strategic position, by 2001 Rambus had claimed a significant portion of the memory value chain with its high performance systems and broad intellectual property. This feat was achieved largely by prominent distribution through Dell. In response, Rambus's competitors challenged its patents and developed competing standards and protocols. Rambus was going to be severely threatened by these competitors given its relative small size, and it was already feeling the impact of their aggressive strategic responses. High litigation expenses increased the company's marketing, general, and administrative costs by 43 percent or $2.8 million from the third to the fourth quarter of 2000. In a fourth quarter conference call, Rambus CFO Gary Harmon warned that legal costs would continue to exceed expectations in coming months. However, during the call, Harmon also noted that he expected Rambus's operating margins to reach 52 percent by December 2001. Such remarkable projected operating margins reaffirmed that Rambus was still a force in the DRAM industry.

DRAM INDUSTRY

In 1970, Intel Corporation developed the 1-kilobit "1103"—the first DRAM—in collaboration with Honeywell. The primary advantage of DRAM over static random access memory (SRAM)—the prevailing standard at the time—was that DRAM required one-sixth the transistors per bit of information that SRAM did and, as a result, took up significantly less area per bit. This afforded DRAM a sizable cost advantage over SRAM. However, DRAM required logic to both access and refresh the data contained in the memory. This requirement led Intel to develop function-specific groups of chips ("chipsets" or "controllers") that performed these two tasks. DRAM chips, in combination with the chipsets, provided full memory functionality. In the resulting architecture of the computer memory system, the computer's microprocessor accessed the DRAM indirectly through the chipsets, making the chipsets the means by which the microprocessor accessed data housed in the memory chip (Exhibit 1).

Soon after Intel's invention, other competitors entered the DRAM market and the industry quickly exhibited a pattern of introducing a new generation of technology with four times the memory capacity every three years (Exhibit 2). In the early 1980s, large Japanese manufacturers aggressively targeted the DRAM industry. Japanese DRAM manufacturers invested 40 percent of sales in new plant and equipment between 1980 and 1984, compared to only 22 percent for U.S. DRAM manufacturers. As a result of this aggressive policy, by 1983 total Japanese investment in semiconductors exceeded U.S. investment. Industry observers pointed out that Japanese firms had targeted DRAM as a strategic industry and

EXHIBIT 1   Computer System Architecture

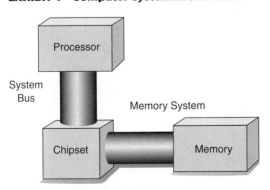

Source: Rambus Web site (http://www.rambus.com).

EXHIBIT 2   Evolution of DRAM Densities

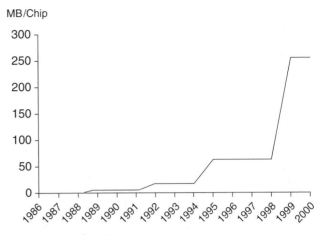

Source: Paul Staelin.

were investing for the long term. By 1984, production yields of the Japanese semiconductor manufacturers were reported to exceed those of the U.S. manufacturers by as much as 40 percent. Several U.S. manufacturers subsequently accused the Japanese firms of "dumping" DRAMs at prices below cost. In the mid- and late 1980s, Intel and several other U.S. manufacturers exited the DRAM industry.

By 1990, Japanese firms accounted for 87 percent of the $8 billion DRAM market. In comparison, U.S. firms accounted for 8 percent, and Korean firms accounted for the remaining 5 percent. In the early 1990s, Korean manufacturers announced plans to invest $4 billion in the DRAM industry. By the end of the decade, Korean DRAM manufacturers had captured the dominant market position. In 1999, the two top DRAM manufacturers—Samsung and Hyundai—were Korean; each controlled over 20 percent of the market. Five of the remaining top ten manufacturers were Japanese firms, representing roughly 24 percent of the market. Only two non–Pacific Rim firms, Micron (U.S.) and Infineon (Germany), were among the top ten DRAM manufacturers, with a combined 24 percent market share.

The DRAM industry was highly concentrated in 1999, with the top three firms representing nearly 60 percent of all industry sales and the top ten manufacturers representing nearly 95 percent (Exhibit 3). Despite the industry evolutions described above, little had changed with regard to the industry's structure. The primary customers were still OEMs, and PCs still represented the

EXHIBIT 3   DRAM and Semiconductor Industry Structure

Top 10 DRAM manufacturers 1999 worldwide shipments ($ millions)			Top 10 semiconducor manufacturers Actual 1999, estimated 2000 revenues ($ millions)					
Company	Worldwide shipments	Market share	Company	1999 Rank	2000 Rank	1999 Revenues	2000 Revenues	Market share
Samsung	4,750	22.9%	Intel	1	1	26,806	29,750	13.4%
Hyundai	4,212	20.3%	Toshiba	3	2	7,618	11,214	5.0%
Micron	3,319	16.0%	NEC	2	3	9,210	11,081	5.0%
NEC	1,716	8.3%	Samsung	4	4	7,125	10,800	4.9%
Infineon	1,665	8.0%	Texas Instruments	5	5	7,120	9,100	4.1%
Hitachi	1,080	5.2%	Motorola	6	6	6,394	8,000	3.6%
Toshiba	933	4.5%	ST Microelectronics	9	7	5,077	7,948	3.6%
Mitsubishi	681	3.3%	Hitachi	7	8	5,554	7,282	3.3%
Fujitsu	551	2.7%	Hyundai	11	9	4,830	6,887	3.1%
Mosel-Vitelic	495	2.4%	Infineon Technologies	8	10	5,223	6,715	3.0%
Total	**20,742**	**100.0%**	**Total**			**169,136**	**222,082**	**100.0%**

Source: Cahners In-Stat Group; Dataquest.

majority of all DRAM sales. Capital expenditures still remained the most significant expense for DRAM manufacturers, and was a sizeable barrier to entry for new firms. Furthermore, different strategies were adopted among the major DRAM manufacturers. Vendors such as Samsung, Toshiba, and NEC focused on process technology innovation, whereas other vendors such as Micron focused instead on cost leadership.

The basic memory architecture, pioneered in 1970, of combining chipsets and DRAM chips still prevailed in 2001. Yet, the memory density of DRAM chips had continued to increase dramatically. Despite these rapid memory density advancements, the speed advancements of DRAM chips were small compared to those of the microprocessor. This comparative lag was illustrated by the fact that the typical operating frequency of mainstream processors had increased from 5 MHz in 1980 to over 1 GHz in 2001, while the typical operating frequency of standard DRAM chips had evolved to only 133 MHz (Exhibit 4). As a result, by 2001, the bottlenecks in most PCs, workstations, and game consoles came from the memory subsystem.

By 2001, three types of DRAM were commonly used. Most computer systems still employed synchronous dynamic RAM, or SDRAM. The main difference between SDRAM and its predecessors was that it was synchronized with the system clock that governed the speed of the microprocessor. In so doing, SDRAM reduced the

EXHIBIT 4   Evolution of Microprocessor and DRAM Speeds

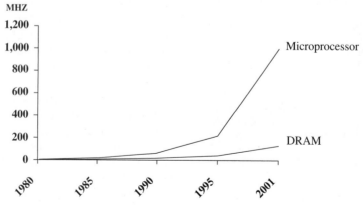

Source: Paul Staelin.

time necessary for the microprocessor to retrieve data from memory chips. DDR SDRAM (double-data-rate SDRAM) essentially doubled the speed of SDRAM by employing advanced synchronization and signaling techniques. This format was championed by an industry coalition of memory manufacturers called JEDEC (Joint Electronic Device Engineering Council), and introduced for sale in the fall of 2000. RDRAM, a competing proprietary format developed by Rambus, was introduced for use in PCs in late 1999. By March 2001, Rambus had established licensing agreements with six of the top ten DRAM manufacturers for all three formats.

In 2001, DRAM was available in 16 MB, 32 MB, 64 MB, 128 MB, and 256 MB modules. Retail prices for these models varied by capacity, vendor, and format. In February 2001, SDRAM sold at below $0.50 per MB; DDR SDRAM sold at under $1.00 per MB; and RDRAM, in contrast, sold at roughly $2.00 per MB (Exhibit 5).

RAMBUS'S EMERGENCE

Company Background

Rambus was founded in March 1990 by two former Stanford University graduate students, Mike Farmwald (CS PhD '81) and Mark Horowitz (EE PhD '84 and EE Professor, Computer Systems Laboratory), who foresaw that memory would become a bottleneck in computer systems. Although both founders had an interest in applying their technology to the computer industry, their hopes of seeing their technology adopted in computer main memory systems were dashed when talks with Intel in 1990 to have Rambus serve as the high-speed memory solution for the 486 computer fizzled. Not to be deterred, the company shifted direction to focus on computer graphics. Early Rambus customers in this arena included Nintendo and Cirrus Logic. A 1992 article described Rambus as follows:

> The problem Rambus addresses is well known to systems designers: The data transfer rate of memory ICs lags behind a processor's ability to handle data. . . . And as display resolutions increase and customers clamor for true color, costs are driven up due to the memory needed to supply pixels at a high rate for flicker-free display. Animation graphics and video also require high data transfer rates to display images in real time.[2]

Rambus Technology

Rambus technology served to increase the rate at which data was transferred between memory devices (DRAM chips) and microprocessors and controllers. This increased rate allowed semiconductor memory devices to keep pace with faster generations of microprocessors and controllers, and thus support the accelerating data transfer requirements of multimedia and other high-bandwidth applications. The performance of a computer or other device was typically constrained by the speed of its slowest component. In the past, that component had been the microprocessor. In recent years, however, as Moore's Law[3] continued to hold, memory subsystems, rather than the central microprocessor, had become the bottleneck. These memory subsystems stored the instructions and data needed by increasingly more powerful microprocessors.

Rambus technology represented a paradigm shift in DRAM system design. Instead of merely combining disparate components as traditional DRAM designers had done, Rambus took a systems-level approach, and designed each component to optimize the performance of the overall memory system. As a result, its RDRAM was capable of transferring data through a simplified bus (the channel that relayed requests for data between the microprocessor and the memory) at significantly higher frequencies than conventional memory systems. Rambus was able to significantly improve both the peak performance and the sustained performance of the memory system relative to other DRAM solutions. However, Rambus technology was not compatible with the DRAM technologies that preceded it.

Rambus's new memory system had two equally important parts: the physical layer and the signal layer (see Appendix for additional detail). The physical layer created an efficient memory bus between the logic chipset and the memory, and the signal layer efficiently transferred data along that bus. The hardware system, when combined with the signaling technologies, allowed not only high peak data transfer speeds, but also sustained system performance in excess of 90 percent of the peak rate. By comparison, other technologies sustained system performance at approximately 60 percent of the peak rate. By 2001, the company's basic RDRAM systems provided 800 MHz peak performance, and its higher-end

---

[2] D. L. Andrews, *Byte Magazine*, 1992.

[3] Moore's Law states that the density of transistors on a silicon chip doubles every eighteen months while the price for increasing the density remains constant.

EXHIBIT 5   Recent Memory Chip Pricing Trends

Price/MB

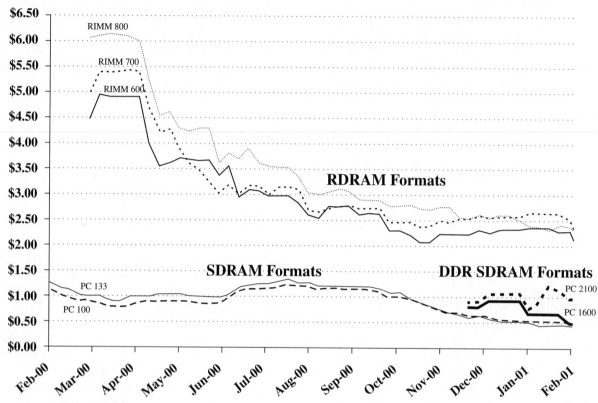

Source: http://members.home.net/smsperling.

technologies allowed 1.6 GHz and 3.1 GHz capability, respectively (Exhibit 6).

Research and Development

The future competitiveness of Rambus depended on the success of its continuing research and development efforts. Rambus had assembled a team of engineers that represented each of the diverse capabilities required to design system-level memory architectures: computer architecture, digital and analog circuit design and layout, DRAM and logic semiconductor processes, packaging, printed circuit board (PCB) routing, and high speed testing. As of September 30, 2000, Rambus employed 110 people in its engineering departments, over 70 of whom held advanced technical degrees. Although Rambus incurred research and development expenses of $11.5 million in 2000, a substantial portion of the company's total engineering costs were allocated to "cost of contract revenues." The company's customers required a high level

of technical support. Rambus's total engineering expenditures in 2000 were $23.6 million.

Rambus Technology in the Marketplace

The primary markets for RDRAM were PCs, workstations, and consumer products. In the PC/workstation market, Rambus memory technology was used to provide high-bandwidth memory connections to Intel Pentium III and Pentium 4 microprocessors. An Intel-developed chipset for the Pentium III (employing Rambus technology) had been successful in the workstation market and, as a result, Rambus was fully established in that segment. Workstations were estimated to represent 5 percent of the overall $27 billion DRAM industry. Graphics applications, an earlier Rambus target market, constituted approximately 4 percent of the industry while servers constituted another 5–6 percent.

In 1999 and 2000, Rambus's chipset targeted for the mainstream PC market had been less successful due to a

EXHIBIT 6   Memory Format Performance Comparisons

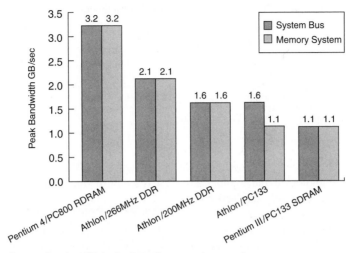

Source: Rambus Web site (http://www.rambus.com).

EXHIBIT 7   DRAM Market Segmentation

Revenue share by category

Category	1999	2000	2001E
PC	54%	56%	58%
Upgrade modules	20%	19%	19%
Servers	6%	6%	5%
Graphics	6%	4%	4%
Workstations	5%	5%	5%
Games	3%	3%	3%
Other	6%	6%	7%
Total 2000 market = $27.0 billion			

Source: IDC; Dataquest.

variety of factors including bandwidth limitations inherent in the chipset and the high cost of RDRAMs compared to standard memory. Despite these setbacks, it was expected that Rambus's share of the PC DRAM segment would grow. As the largest segment of the DRAM market, the PC segment (including upgrade modules) was estimated to represent upwards of 75 percent of the annual $27 billion DRAM manufacturing industry. Furthermore, it was estimated that Intel-specified architectures influenced 70–80 percent of sales in this category (Exhibit 7).[4]

Rambus memory had also begun to make inroads into various consumer products segments, which constituted

---
[4]Peter Clarke, "Siemens Jumps on Rambus Bandwagon in License Deal," *EETimes*, August 25, 1997.

approximately 5 percent of the DRAM market. Nintendo 64 game consoles had used an earlier version of Rambus technology while the Sony Playstation 2 used current Rambus technology. Other consumer applications for Rambus memory systems were digital TVs, VCRs, printers, communications equipment (such as networking hardware), and set-top boxes (which had been recently introduced in Japan). Some speculated that, in the post PC era, demand for memory bandwidth would only grow, as handheld devices, game machines, MP3 players, high-definition televisions, and VCRs proliferated. Currently, the size of these ancillary markets was negligible.

Rambus developed its RDRAM-compatible technology to be manufactured using standard industry processes. However, because of the inclusion of the extra Rambus interface circuitry and other core features, RDRAMs were somewhat larger than standard SDRAMs. In addition, RDRAMs used newer chip scale packaging and required high-speed testers. While the marginal cost of testing with the new equipment was comparable to that of standard equipment, there were additional lead-time and capital requirements for manufacturers producing RDRAM.

Rambus's Strategy

The dominant tenet of Rambus's strategy was to popularize use of its proprietary technology among semiconductor and systems manufacturers. The company received an approximate 2 percent royalty rate from the sale of every RDRAM chip. Furthermore, Rambus earned a royalty rate of about 3 to 5 percent on the sale

EXHIBIT 8 Estimated RDRAM Share of DRAM Market

Source	Revenue share of overall DRAM market			
	2000	2001	2002	2003
In-Stat	8%	25%	45%	55%
Dataquest	12%	33%	50%	62%
IC Insights	8%	10%	20%	n/a
Estimated market size	**$27 Billion**	**$35 billion**	**$47 billion**	**$60 billion**

Source: http://www.sharkeyestreme.com/hardware/guides/pentium4/8.shtml.

of every controller chip that interfaced with its RDRAM. After initially applying its technology to the graphics applications market, Rambus concurrently targeted computer workstations and consumer appliances. By early 1998, Rambus appeared to be gaining traction in these segments. In March of that year, the company reported that chips designed using its RDRAM technology exceeded $1 billion in sales, and that the company had twenty royalty-based licensees, including the industry's fourteen largest DRAM manufacturers. By 2001, sales of RDRAM chips were projected to constitute anywhere from one-tenth to one-third of the $30 billion plus DRAM industry (Exhibit 8).

Rambus's narrow focus on intellectual property meant that it did not have to commit significant resources to capital expenditures, and could capitalize on its strengths in design and development. This afforded the company economies of scope, which it could pass on to the memory chip manufacturers that licensed its technology. In a 1998 speech, Rambus board member Bill Davidow commented on the advantages that Rambus brought to its partners:

> [Memory manufacturers] so frequently focus on what they pay for the technology rather than the benefits they get. I believe Rambus has saved and will save the semiconductor industry billions of dollars. Partners individually have each paid a fraction of what it would cost to develop that technology themselves.[5]

One of the ways in which Rambus attempted to speed adoption of the RDRAM format was to couple its technology with leading systems manufacturers. By 2001, Rambus had relationships with a number of leading systems technology companies, including Intel, IBM, Hewlett-Packard, Texas Instruments, LSI Logic, NEC, and Toshiba. Of these relationships, the Intel relationship was the most significant to Rambus.

The Intel Relationship

The linchpin of Rambus's strategy for popularizing the use of RDRAM was getting Intel to support its standard. In November 1996, Rambus entered into a development and license agreement with Intel in which RDRAM would serve as the main memory format for the Intel Pentium III microprocessor. Under Intel's 1996 agreement with Rambus, the CPU manufacturer committed to support the RDRAM with its controller chips. Also under the agreement, if Intel met certain RDRAM controller chip production and sales targets, they earned stock warrants for up to 4 percent ownership of Rambus and a seat on the board. A 1997 *PC Magazine* article commented on Intel's motivations for pursuing a relationship with Rambus.

> Memory chipmakers [claim] that Intel . . . is locking vendors out of the specification development in such a way that it can bring high-performance Rambus-based systems on the market before its competitors get hold of the specifications. It is believed that Intel can synchronize certain microprocessor chip designs with new memory technologies in such a way that by changing certain specifications on the fly, this technology can ruin the performance of Cyrix, AMD, and even Motorola-based systems while improving its own. In other words, change parameters and protocols at a critical moment after other processor houses have committed to an earlier design. Currently Intel controls the microprocessor market, the support chip set market, and the motherboard market. It now sees the memory market as another one in which it should profit.[6]

An alternative viewpoint was that Intel was simply trying to grow the market for PCs by continuously trying

---

[5]Craig Matsumoto, "Wall Street Wary of IP Companies," *EE Times,* March 27, 1998.

[6]John C. Dvorak, "Inside Track," *PC Magazine,* August 1997.

to improve the performance of the PC in a way that was discernible to the end-user. In order to accomplish this in the late 1990s, Intel had to address the shortcomings of conventional memory. This was where Rambus came in.

However, the Intel-Rambus agreement had proven to be rather turbulent for both parties. Between 1996 and 1998, Intel had developed and begun producing two Rambus controllers as part of new chipsets. One, designed for use in workstations, was released on time. The other, the Intel 820 chipset, meant for use in the PC market, had suffered high-profile delays because of technical problems. The 820 had experienced production delays because of technical glitches rumored to be the result of the difficulties of working with Rambus technology compounded by Intel's shift to a 0.13 micron production process. Despite Intel's reassurances that its product roadmap would continue to center around Rambus technology, rumors persisted that the Intel-Rambus relationship was strained. These rumors came to a head in October 2000 when Intel CEO Craig Barrett invited speculation that his company's relationship with Rambus was turning acrimonious in an interview with *The Financial Times.*

> We made a big bet on Rambus and it did not work out. In retrospect, it was a mistake to be dependent on a third party for a technology that gates your performance. We hoped we were partners with a company that would concentrate on technology innovation rather than seeking to collect a toll from other companies.

Industry observers speculated that Barrett's comments were motivated in part by Rambus's recent campaign to collect royalties from memory chip manufacturers for SDRAM and DDR SDRAM memory technology after Intel recanted its commitment to use only RDRAM in its next-generation Pentium 4 platform. Intel officials later clarified Barrett's statement as referring only to Intel's Timna processor, a Rambus-optimized low-end processor that was cancelled before its launch because of problems with a translation hub that would have allowed the Timna processor to operate with SDRAM. "We still are believers in RDRAM for high-performance desktop applications," Barrett said. "In fact, the Pentium 4 product introduction is an RDRAM microprocessor."

In February 2001, at its developers' forum, Intel announced that it would be offering rebates to RDRAM chip manufacturers in an effort to mitigate the price premium of RDRAM systems compared to SDRAM systems. In addition, the three leading RDRAM chip manufacturers—Samsung, Toshiba, and Elpida[7]—announced that they were ramping up their production volumes. Furthermore, Barrett once again appeared to be expressing public support for the Rambus standard: "If RDRAM comes down and it's only 10 or 15 percent more expensive than SDRAM or competing technologies by year-end, we think the performance enhancement we get with RDRAM will carry the day."[8] Moreover, Intel officials announced their intention to expand their use of RDRAM memory into the market for PCs selling below $1,000. The rationale for Intel's renewed support of Rambus appeared to be the importance of its Pentium 4 launch:

> Intel's corporate health depends on quickly ramping the Pentium 4 processor and on seeing the memory vendors sharply increase RDRAM shipments. For now, Intel's 850 is the only chip set to support the Pentium 4, and the 850 only supports RDRAMs.[9]

CHALLENGES

Competitive Environment

The semiconductor market was highly competitive and subject to price erosion, cyclical buying patterns, short product life cycles, and rapid technology changes. In this competitive environment, most DRAM manufacturers produced higher frequency versions of standard DRAM such as SDRAMs, which competed with RDRAMs. In order to achieve performance comparable to that of RDRAM systems with these more conventional types of DRAM, large parallel memory architectures needed to be put in place. These complicated architectures were significantly more expensive to design and build than conventional DRAM systems.

Rambus's technical success had been due largely to the systems-level approach with which it addressed the memory bottleneck. In the late nineties, competitors had begun to take a similar approach and Rambus believed that its principal competition would eventually come from its RDRAM-compatible licensees and prospective licensees. Some DRAM manufacturers had begun to produce DDR SDRAM, which was designed to double

---

[7] Elpida is a DRAM manufacturing joint venture between NEC and Hyundai.

[8] Edward F. Moltzen, "Challenges on Intel's Horizon," *Computer Reseller News,* March 2, 2001.

[9] David Lammers, "Intel Looks to Move Past False Starts with Rambus," *EE Times,* March 1, 2001.

the memory bandwidth of SDRAMs without increasing clock frequency. While Rambus had successfully negotiated SDRAM-compatible licenses with some of the leading DRAM manufacturers that included royalty payments on DDR SDRAM, three major memory chip manufacturers had not agreed to a license. Infineon, Micron, and Hyundai were opposed to paying for third-party technology.

In 1997, a consortium of major memory chip manufacturers led by Hyundai Electronics and Micron Technology attempted to introduce a competing standard of memory called synchronous link DRAM (SLDRAM). Designed as a stopgap memory solution, SLDRAM would have supported microprocessors at speeds of 400 MHz, and potentially up to 800 MHz. In addition, the memory makers claimed that their SLDRAM standard would consume less power than prevailing memory technologies, and would cost less than the Rambus proprietary RDRAM.[10] The prospects for SLDRAM faded, however, when the technology struggled to achieve the support of major systems companies.

In early 2000, another consortium of major memory chip manufacturers (Micron, Infineon, Hyundai) contested Rambus's intellectual property rights to the DDR SDRAM standard. If they proved successful in U.S. and German courts, a parallel situation would exist to 1997 whereby an industry consortium would be advancing a rival standard to Rambus's RDRAM. Yet, the control of a technology standard by a consortium raised coordination problems, particularly with regard to manufacturing specifications. In 1998, an industry design engineer pointed out that:

> DDR presents much more difficult issues in signaling and data transfer. I believe there has to be some sort of governing body creating a comprehensive spec similar to the one we have for PC-100 [SDRAM]. Otherwise it is not clear that the industry can make DDR producible.[11]

Some industry observers questioned the ability of standards bodies to present a viable alternative to the proprietary technology of a third party. Within standards bodies, coordination problems could be compounded by the disputes of rivals within the consortium seeking to advance their own individual interests. A third-party

technology company could potentially mitigate this problem by serving as a neutral intermediary. In addition, observers noted that third-party technology companies gained advantages of focus and specialization that could not be matched by those within a consortium.

The late nineties had also seen the emergence of "embedded DRAM" in which logic and DRAM circuitry were included in the same chip, eliminating the need for chip interface circuitry and, as a result, the Rambus performance advantage. Despite its comparatively higher cost, however, such an implementation was well suited for applications in which space and energy savings were important, such as laptops and graphics subsystems. These markets tended not to be Rambus's focus.

Actual vs. Perceived Technical Advantage

Despite the large disparity between bus performances, the performance disparity between RDRAM and DDR/SDRAM systems at the user level was less pronounced. Despite the 156 percent bus performance advantage of Pentium 4/RDRAM over Athlon/266 MHz DDR, professional video editors using a Pentium 4/RDRAM platform could achieve only 32 percent better performance than those using an Athlon/266 MHz or Pentium III/PC133 platform. In addition, Mad Onion's WebMark2001 benchmark measures found that the Pentium 4/RDRAM platform performed 13 percent faster than the Athlon/266 MHz DDR platform and 28 percent faster than the Pentium III/SDRAM platform on emerging internet and e-commerce applications representative of current and future usage patterns for e-Business users (Exhibit 9).

Rambus appeared well positioned to exploit the emergence of data-rich content and applications on the Internet. Many argued that since streaming video and audio required significant memory bandwidth, the speed advantages of RDRAM compared to SDRAM and other DRAM solutions would become more evident to the end-user as use of more complex data became more common. Improved performance would be particularly noticeable if microprocessor speeds continued to increase faster than standard memory speeds.

Pending Litigation

In 2001, the litigation in which Rambus found itself embroiled centered around the company's claims that it owned patents that covered two memory standards, SDRAM and DDR SDRAM, which competed with Rambus's proprietary RDRAM. In 2000, Rambus began vigorously enforcing these patents through legal action.

---

[10]Owen Linderholm, "No More Memory Bottlenecks," *Windows Magazine,* January 1998.
[11]Ron Wilson, "Warning Alarm Sounds on Implications of PC-100 Memory Bus," *EE Times,* April 10, 1998.

EXHIBIT 9   Performance Benchmarks of Leading DRAM Formats

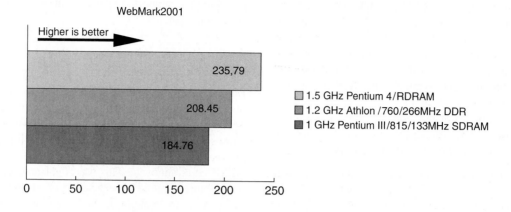

WebMark2001

Higher is better

235,79
208.45
184.76

☐ 1.5 GHz Pentium 4/RDRAM
◼ 1.2 GHz Athlon /760/266MHz DDR
◼ 1 GHz Pentium III/815/133MHz SDRAM

0   50   100   150   200   250

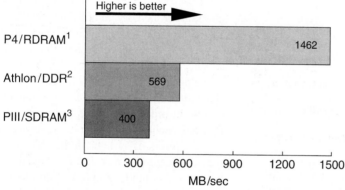

Si Soft Sandra 2000 memory benchmark
CPU Windows 98 SE

Higher is better

P4/RDRAM[1]   1462

Athlon/DDR[2]   569

PIII/SDRAM[3]   400

0   300   600   900   1200   1500

MB/sec

[1] 1.5 GHz Pentium 4 processor with 800 MHz RDRAM memory
[2] 1.2 GHz Athlon processor with 266 MHz DDR memory
[3] 1 GHz Pentium III processor with 133 MHz SDRAM memory
Sisoft Sandra 2000 Memory Benchmark MB/sec CPU Windows 98 SE
Source: http://www.sharkeyextreme.com/hardware/guides/pentium4/8.shtml.

In June 2000, two of the top ten DRAM manufacturers—Toshiba and Hitachi—agreed to pay royalties to Rambus for not only its RDRAM technology, but also for SDRAM and DDR SDRAM chips. While specific details of the royalty agreements were not disclosed, it was speculated that Rambus charged a 0.5–1 percent royalty on SDRAM chips, and a 2–3 percent royalty on DDR SDRAM chips.

Rambus . . . claims it has patents on basically every kind of PC memory being manufactured today and has bent many manufacturers to its will. Its flagship design, known as Di-

rect Rambus DRAM, isn't part of any of the lawsuits. But it hasn't yet generated as much as the company had hoped from memory manufacturers. Rambus DRAM chips are more complex and more expensive to manufacture than conventional memory. . . . Seeing a chance for additional revenue, Rambus threw down the gauntlet by asserting patents on an alternative to Rambus's technology known as Double Data Rate DRAM, and on the older standard memory known as synchronous DRAM.[12]

---

[12] Arik Hesseldahl, "Rambus Investors Lose Their Minds," *Forbes,* March 16, 2001.

By the end of 2000, Rambus had agreements in place with six of the top ten DRAM manufacturers (comprising 51 percent of the overall DRAM industry) to earn royalties on all three of the leading DRAM standards (see chart below). Nonetheless, significant uncertainty surrounded the outcome of the company's lawsuits with Infineon, Micron, and Hyundai—the fate of the company's existing SDRAM and DDR royalty arrangements with various DRAM manufacturers was therefore uncertain. It was also unclear that litigation would proceed to completion. As noted by an industry observer:

> A quick look at history shows that none of these cases even have to go to trial. Rambus filed a patent suit against Hitachi in January 2000 both in the U.S. and in Germany. About six months later, the two companies agreed on royalties that Hitachi would pay Rambus.[13]

DRAM manufacturer	Global DRAM market share	Details of relationship with Rambus
1. Samsung	24%	Agreed to pay Rambus royalties on all 3 standards
2. Hyundai	**20%**	**Suing Rambus for anti-competitive behavior in U.S.**
3. Micron	**17%**	**Suing Rambus for anti-competitive behavior in U.S.**
4. NEC	10%	Agreed to pay Rambus royalties on all 3 standards
5. Infineon	**8%**	**Sued by Rambus for patent infringement in U.S. and Germany. Suing Rambus for anti-competitive behavior**
6. Toshiba	8%	Agreed to pay Rambus royalties on all 3 standards
7. Mitsubishi	4%	Agreed to pay Rambus royalties on all 3 standards
8. Fujitsu	3%	No deal in place, awaiting outcome of U.S. and German verdicts
9. Hitachi	3%	Agreed to pay Rambus royalties on all 3 standards
10. Oki	2%	Agreed to pay Rambus royalties on all 3 standards

In mid-March 2001, Rambus's stock price tumbled 50 percent after a Virginia judge ruled against the company in a pretrial hearing in the lawsuit with Infineon Technologies. U.S. District Court Judge Robert Payne said Rambus's key terms defining the scope of their patents were not supported by claims made by inventors in seeking the patents.[14]

Development of New Constraints and Dependencies

Rambus technology eased an emerging memory bottleneck before it became acute by accelerating the rate at which bits of information could travel through a computer system. Yet, the system-level approach of the Rambus architecture potentially slowed the rate at which OEMs could innovate. This was true because Rambus's architecture required a greater level of interplay between memory component players and equipment manufacturers than was required by simpler memory technologies. This increased interplay complicated product development for OEMs and increased the costs of developing RDRAM-based products by more than just the price differential for memory components. Some argued that this cost differential was only temporary as Rambus technology represented a discontinuous innovation that required advancement along a new learning curve.

Rambus's system-level approach required different skills than the ones most DRAM manufacturers possessed. In order to organize the entire memory system, Rambus needed to orchestrate the design efforts of the manufacturers of systems, logic chipsets, microprocessors, and memory chips. The skills required to effectively influence and guide the product development processes of such diverse and loosely coupled players were quite distinct from the pure engineering skills required to produce a DRAM with four times the memory capacity every three years. As a result, Rambus faced a potential constraint on qualified engineering talent.

The adoption of Rambus technology was accelerated because it leveraged the existing memory architecture of the CPU, logic chipset, and memory modules. Thus, Rambus was not dependent on the emergence of another technology elsewhere on the motherboard to drive this adoption. However, the continued adoption of the Rambus system depended strongly on two factors: (1) the continued rapid improvement of microprocessor speeds (which would exacerbate the role of the memory as the bottleneck); and (2) the development of memory-intensive, real time software applications. This was true

---

[13]Caroline Humer, "Patently Uncertain: Ruling Against Rambus Further Muddles Its Future," TheStreet.com, March 19, 2001 (http://www.thestreet.com/tech/semis/1349202.html).

[14]Timna Tanners, "Rambus Dips Further as Judge Questions Patents," *Reuters,* March 16, 2001.

because hardware product cycles tended to precede software product cycles. In the past, Microsoft had typically pioneered these software applications (e.g., Windows, Office). In the face of the government's anti-trust inquiry into Microsoft's business practices, however, it was unclear whether the pace of new applications development would slow.

CONCLUSION

With Intel's backing, Rambus grew its revenue stream dramatically. For the year ended September 30, 2000, Rambus earned revenues of $72 million, up nearly tenfold from five years earlier (Exhibit 10). In addition, the company was beginning to see the scale advantages that its business model afforded, as profitability, asset turnover, and working capital intensity also showed dramatic improvement (Exhibit 11). Nonetheless, Rambus was still among the smallest players in the semiconductor industry and its competitors had responded to its efforts by challenging its patents and developing competing standards and protocols. The major memory chip manufacturers collectively had over $20 billion in revenues in 1999.

EXHIBIT 10 Rambus Consolidated Income Statements (1995–2000)

All figures in $000's, except per share data

	Year ending September 30					
	1995	**1996**	**1997**	**1998**	**1999**	**2000**
Revenues						
Contract revenues	7,364	11,205	20,186	28,727	35,353	39,683
Royalties	–	65	5,829	9,137	8,017	32,628
Total Revenues	**7,364**	**11,270**	**26,015**	**37,864**	**43,370**	**72,311**
Year Over Year Growth		*53%*	*131%*	*46%*	*15%*	*67%*
Costs of Goods Sold						
Cost of Contract Revenues	(5,236)	(4,821)	(5,491)	(8,988)	(12,232)	(12,093)
Gross Profit	**2,128**	**6,449**	**20,524**	**28,876**	**31,138**	**60,218**
Gross Margin	*29%*	*57%*	*79%*	*76%*	*72%*	*83%*
Operating Expenses						
Research and Development	(3,117)	(5,218)	(9,815)	(9,649)	(8,123)	(11,501)
Marketing General and Administrative	(5,064)	(5,799)	(8,755)	(11,260)	(13,516)	(21,140)
Employee Stock-Related Compensation Expense	–	–	–	–	–	(171,085)
Total Operating Expenses	**(8,181)**	**(11,017)**	**(18,570)**	**(20,909)**	**(21,639)**	**(203,726)**
Operating Income (Loss)	**(6,053)**	**(4,568)**	**1,954**	**7,967**	**9,499**	**(143,508)**
Operating Margin[1]	*−82%*	*−41%*	*8%*	*21%*	*22%*	*38%*
Interest and Other Income, Net	619	737	1,536	3,413	4,346	4,714
Interest expense	(297)	(298)	(194)	(52)	(7)	–
Income (Loss) Before Income Taxes	**(5,731)**	**(4,129)**	**3,296**	**11,328**	**13,838**	**(138,794)**
Provision For/Benefit From Income taxes	(1,289)	(286)	(1,315)	(4,540)	(5,120)	32,667
Net Income (Loss)	**(7,020)**	**(4,415)**	**1,981**	**6,788**	**8,718**	**(106,127)**
Return on Sales[1]	*−95%*	*−39%*	*8%*	*18%*	*20%*	*90%*
Net Income (Loss) Per Share—Basic	**$(1.24)**	**$(0.73)**	**$0.09**	**$0.07**	**$0.09**	**$(1.10)**
Net Income (Loss) Per Share—Diluted	**n/a**	**n/a**	**n/a**	**$0.07**	**$0.09**	**$(1.10)**
Number of shares used in per share calculations:						
Basic	5,665	6,088	21,711	90,816	93,328	96,487
Diluted	n/a	n/a	n/a	97,504	100,208	96,487

Notes:
[1] Excludes non-cash employee stock-related compensation expense
Source: Rambus.

EXHIBIT 11   Rambus Consolidated Balance Sheets (1995–2000)

	Year ending September 30					
	1995	1996	1997	1998	1999	2000
Current Assets						
Cash and Cash Equivalents	977	742	20,641	25,798	14,982	63,093
Marketable Securities	13,173	7,812	51,184	53,913	72,158	59,127
Accounts Receivable	1,206	718	925	1,913	1,499	68
Prepaid and Deferred Tax Assets	—	—	5,974	7,829	7,579	17,661
Prepaid Expenses and Other Current Assets	840	873	2,033	2,340	2,260	2,988
Total Current Assets	**16,196**	**10,145**	**80,757**	**91,793**	**98,478**	**142,937**
Property and Equipment, Net	1,598	2,340	4,338	3,989	4,232	6,724
Marketable Securities, Long-Term	—	—	986	8,357	5,658	7,548
Restricted Cash	—	—	—	—	2,500	2,500
Other Assets	513	383	1,797	6,848	4,905	59,922
Total Assets	**18,307**	**12,868**	**87,878**	**110,987**	**115,773**	**219,631**
Current Liabilities						
Accounts Payable[1]	205	228	378	459	265	1,850
Income Tax Payable[1]	76	84	3,292	12	—	74
Accrued Salaries and Benefits[1]	304	338	1,454	1,940	3,090	3,504
Other Accrued Liabilities[1]	528	587	1,042	1,017	1,070	3,604
Current Portion of						
Capital Lease Obligations	929	753	382	130	—	—
Deferred Revenue	9,721	13,082	24,473	28,617	32,279	24,155
Total Current Liabilities	**11,763**	**15,072**	**31,021**	**32,175**	**36,704**	**33,187**
Capital Lease Obligations, Less Current Portion	687	544	130	—	—	—
Deferred Revenue, Less Current Portion	13,793	9,396	30,066	37,020	17,505	24,122
Total Liabilities	**26,243**	**25,012**	**61,217**	**69,195**	**54,209**	**57,309**
Stockholders' Equity (Deficit)						
Convertible Preferred Stock, $0.001 Par Value	11	11	—	—	—	—
Common Stock, $0.001 Par Value[2]	24	24	88	92	95	97
Additional Paid-in Capital	22,088	22,323	59,799	67,548	78,503	285,885
Stockholder's Notes Receivable	—	—	(680)	—	—	—
Deferred Stock-Based Compensation	—	—	—	—	—	(571)
Accumulated Deficit	(30,077)	(34,492)	(32,511)	(25,723)	(17,005)	(123,132)
Accumulated Other Comprehensive Loss	29	1	(35)	(125)	(29)	43
Total Shareholders' Equity	**(7,936)**	**(12,144)**	**26,661**	**41,792**	**61,564**	**162,322**
Total Liabilities and Shareholders' Equity	**18,307**	**12,868**	**87,878**	**110,987**	**115,773**	**219,631**
Return On Assets[3]	−38%	−34%	2%	6%	8%	30%
Return On Equity[3]	88%	36%	7%	16%	14%	40%

Notes:
[1] Casewriter's estimate for 1995
[2] Adjusted for 4 for 1 stock split in May 2000
[3] Excludes non-cash employee stock-related compensation expense
Source: Rambus.

The ongoing court battle with three large memory chip manufacturers, as well as the dynamics of its relationships with OEMs and systems companies raised several questions about Rambus's future prospects. How could Rambus guarantee the efficacy of its royalty and license income stream when it, in fact, did not manufacture a tangible product? How could Rambus prevent larger, better-capitalized memory chip manufacturers from locking the much smaller company out of the DRAM industry? What strategies could the company pursue to distance itself from potential competitors? How could Rambus improve its negotiating position with its business partners?

Primary Elements of a Rambus-Based System

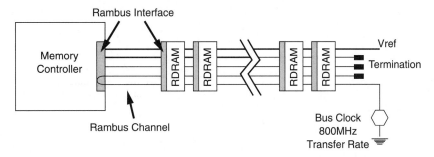

APPENDIX: RAMBUS TECHNOLOGY

The Physical Layer

The physical layer of the Rambus solution was comprised of three parts: the Rambus Channel, the Rambus Interface, and the Rambus DRAM (RDRAM).

Unlike conventional DRAM systems, the Rambus Channel incorporated a system-level specification and, as a result, systems using Rambus Channels could operate at full rated speeds. In contrast, systems using conventional DRAMs could not typically operate at full rated speeds because specifications for separate components within the system (like set-up time, hold time, and so on) varied. The Rambus Channel was capable of transferring data at rates up to 800 MHz per second. Each Rambus channel supported up to 32 RDRAMs.

The Rambus Interface was comprised of circuitry that controlled the signal layer of the system and ensured that each component interacted appropriately with the system. As a result, this Interface circuitry was resident in each component of the Rambus Channel, including the logic circuitry and the RDRAM.

The Rambus DRAM, or RDRAM, is a specialized DRAM that incorporates the Rambus interface circuitry.

The Signal Layer

The signaling protocol developed by Rambus was designed to leverage the benefits of the system-level design specifications of the physical layer. Rambus had developed three signaling technologies: Rambus Signaling Layer (RSL), Quad Rambus Signaling Layer (QRSL), and Quad Serializer/De-serializer (Serdes).

In 1992, Rambus introduced its first signaling technology, Rambus Signaling Layer (RSL), which addressed the chip interconnect bottleneck by providing semiconductor manufacturers with ten times the bandwidth, or 500 MHz, than was used in PCs. By 2000, RSL had evolved to support data rates of up to 800 MHz for PC applications and as high as 1.066 GHz in certain "short channel" applications.

During 2000, Rambus introduced its next-generation signaling technology, Quad Rambus Signaling Layer (QRSL), which allowed data to be transferred at 1.6 gigabits/second per pin, twice as fast as the Rambus RSL technology currently shipping in PCs and in the Sony PlayStation®2. Implementing multi-level signaling, QRSL transferred two bits per edge using four voltage levels. QRSL was thought to be most ideal for consumer, graphics, and networking applications.

In addition, Rambus introduced a new signaling technology called Quad Serializer/De-serializer (SerDes), which were 4×3.125 Gb/s serial links for point-to-point serial interconnect applications.

3

ENACTMENT OF TECHNOLOGY STRATEGY—DEVELOPING A FIRM'S INNOVATIVE CAPABILITIES

In Part II, we discussed the design and evolution of a firm's technology strategy. Technological competencies and capabilities were viewed as the foundation of technology strategy. The evolution of technology strategy was examined in the context of a matrix of generative selective forces that shape innovation processes within the firm, within an industry, and in the broader system encompassing multiple industries or major segments within an industry. In Part III we take a somewhat different perspective, examining how a firm's innovative activities reflect its technology strategy and how the enactment of technology strategy serves to further develop its innovative capabilities.

657

Technology strategy is enacted through the performance of a sequence of key tasks (see Part Four), which serves to augment the firm's existing technological competences and to build new ones. At the start of this sequence is technology sourcing. In order to stay ahead of competitors, high-technology firms must source technology on a continuous basis. While many firms source some of their technology through licensing arrangements, R&D with other firms, consortia, strategic alliances, joint ventures, and acquisitions, high-technology firms must source the bulk of their new technology internally through investments in R&D. At the end of the sequence of key tasks is technical support and field service—companies selling technical equipment, for instance, need a capability to service the equipment and to train and keep their users up-to-date. Between technology sourcing and technical support are key tasks associated with the major corporate innovation challenges: the development of new products and new businesses.

INNOVATION CHALLENGES IN ESTABLISHED FIRMS

New Product and New Business Development

The major innovation challenges facing established firms derive from the evolutionary process model of strategy making. This model, reproduced in Exhibit 1, distinguishes between *induced* and *autonomous* strategic processes.

Induced strategic action takes place in light of the firm's corporate strategy and in relation to its familiar external environments. Corporate strategy reflects top management's beliefs about the basis of the firm's past and current success.[1] These beliefs determine what the firm views as its distinctive (or core) competences and what the product-market domain is in which it can successfully compete. While in small firms corporate strategy and strategic action are usually closely linked, larger firms typically require the creation of a structural context to secure the link between strategy and action. The structural context serves to select strategic initiatives that fit with the corporate strategy and leverage the organizational learning on which the corporate strategy is based. The structural context encompasses administrative (e.g., resource allocation rules) and cultural (e.g., rules of expected behavior) mechanisms.

Autonomous strategic action is outside the scope of the current corporate strategy and opens up new environmental niches. Successful, autonomous initiatives lead to an amendment of the firm's concept of strategy through the process of strategic context determination. This involves middle-level managers in formulating a broader strategy for the initiatives of internal entrepreneurs and acting as organizational champions to convince top management to support these initiatives. The autonomous strategic process is guided by the strategic recognition capacity of senior and top managers, rather than by strategic planning.[2]

Exploiting Innovation Opportunities in the Induced Process Typically, technological innovations associated with the induced process are incremental or architectural.[3] They emerge, in part, from the firm's R&D investments. Incremental or architectural innovations are not necessarily small innovations; for instance, developing a new air frame for the next-generation aircraft is an incremental (and perhaps, in part, architectural) innova-

EXHIBIT 1   An Evolutionary Framework of the Strategy-Making Process in Established Firms

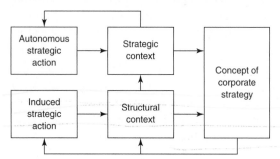

[1] R. A. Burgelman, "A Model of the Interaction of Strategic Behavior, Corporate Context, and the Concept of Strategy," *Academy of Management Review* 8 (1983), pp. 61–70; "Intraorganizational Ecology of Strategy Making and Organizational Adaptation: Theory and Field Research," *Organization Science* 2 (1991); "Fading Memories: A Process Theory of Strategic Business Exit in Dynamic Environments," *Administrative Science Quarterly* 39 (1994), pp. 24–56; G. Donaldson and J. Lorsch, *Decision Making at the Top* (New York: Basic Books, 1983); K. Weick, "Substitutes for Corporate Strategy," in D. J. Teece, ed., *The Competitive Challenge* (Cambridge, Mass.: Ballinger, 1987), pp. 221–34.
[2] R. A. Burgelman, "Corporate Entrepreneurship and Strategic Management: Insights from a Process Study," *Management Science* 29 (1983), pp. 1649–64; "Intraorganizational Ecology"; and "Fading Memories."
[3] R. M. Henderson and K. B. Clark, "Architectural Innovation: The Reconfiguration of Existing Product Technologies and the Failure of Established Firms," *Administrative Science Quarterly* 35 (1990), pp. 9–30.

tion project for Boeing because it is well understood in the context of that firm's corporate strategy. But such a project involves a commitment of billions of dollars. Innovation in the induced process is also likely to shift from the "fluid" to the "specific" state (increased importance of process innovation relative to product innovation)[4] as products reach the mature stage in the life cycle of their underlying technologies. Adjusting to the changing basis of competition entailed by this shift often poses difficult managerial problems.[5] In the short to medium term, managing incremental and architectural innovations is the most significant innovation challenge facing established firms. In the longer term, managing disruptive innovations of the sort that create new growth businesses typically prove to be most vexing. To meet this challenge, firms must develop strong but flexible product and process development capabilities, so that appropriate processes are employed in each situation.

Exploiting Innovation Opportunities in the Autonomous Process Typically, technological innovations associated with the autonomous process are radical.[6] Such opportunities emerge somewhat unexpectedly or serendipitously from the firm's R&D investments, especially corporate research. Radical innovations are not necessarily large, at least not initially. For instance, electronic fuel injection (EFI) was invented at Bendix Corporation by an individual engineer; now, however, EFI is a $100 million-plus segment in the automotive supply industry. Similarly, Steve Jobs and Steve Wozniak developed the personal computer in a garage, and total sales in the personal computer industry exceeded $100 billion in 1995.

The innovation challenge posed by the autonomous strategic process is important for a firm's long-term survival and development, particularly because as firms grow large their capacity to maintain a growth rate based on pursuing opportunities in their mainstream areas of business eventually diminishes. Sooner or later, firms—Apple and IBM alike—must find and exploit growth opportunities in marginally related (or even unrelated) areas of business. Systematic research shows that such diversification is difficult and risky. Not surprisingly, various authors have argued that firms should maintain

the "common thread"[7] and "stick to the knitting."[8] This may be good advice for firms that have not sufficiently exploited additional opportunities in their mainstream businesses through the induced strategic process; however, it overlooks the fundamental growth problem. To meet the innovation challenge associated with the autonomous process, firms must develop a capability to manage internal entrepreneurship.

A Balancing Act Firms must also balance the relative emphasis on these two key challenges throughout their development. This is difficult, in part because the two innovation challenges require different management approaches, and there is a strong tendency for firms to address the challenges sequentially rather than simultaneously.[9]

The remainder of this discussion focuses on the management of corporate research and corporate entrepreneurship. It highlights the innovation challenge associated with the autonomous process; the challenge associated with the induced process—new product development—is discussed in Part Four.

STRATEGIC MANAGEMENT OF CORPORATE RESEARCH

Because of its long-range time horizon, high risk, and exploratory orientation, corporate research poses especially subtle and complex strategic management issues. Established high-technology firms typically spend a significant fraction of their resources—at least 5 to 10 percent of sales—on R&D activities. Most of these resources are allocated to R&D projects for mainstream businesses, but a sizable fraction—10 to 15 percent of the total R&D budget—is often spent on corporate research.[10] Corporate research is truly long-range, high-risk, and exploratory. The effort of Monsanto in the biotechnology area is an example as is the establishment of the Palo Alto Research Center (PARC) by Xerox in 1970.[11] There are important issues associated with the strategic management of R&D activities in general, such as (1) whether the firm is putting its R&D dollars into those areas of technology that will

[4] W. Abernathy, *The Productivity Dilemma* (Baltimore: The Johns Hopkins University Press, 1978).
[5] Burgelman, "Fading Memories."
[6] A. Cooper and D. Schendel, "Strategic Responses to Technological Threats," *Business Horizons,* 1976, pp. 61–69; R. A. Burgelman, "A Process Model of Internal Corporate Venturing in the Diversified Major Firm," *Administrative Science Quarterly* 28 (1983), pp. 223–44; Henderson and Clark, "Architectural Innovation."

[7] H. I. Ansoff, *Corporate Strategy* (New York: McGraw-Hill, 1965).
[8] T. J. Peters and R. H. Waterman, *In Search of Excellence* (New York: Harper & Row, 1983).
[9] R. A. Burgelman, "Managing the Internal Corporate Venturing Process," *Sloan Management Review,* Winter 1984, pp. 33–48.
[10] R. S. Rosenbloom and A. Kantrow, "The Nurturing of Corporate Research," *Harvard Business Review,* January–February 1982.
[11] B. Uttal, "The Lab That Ran Away from Xerox," *Fortune,* September 5, 1983.

EXHIBIT 2   The Functions of Corporate Research

The research charter must be specified.
The research charter represents the shared understanding of the mission that research is expected to fulfill.

		New strategic directions	Support of existing businesses
Innovations by:	Improving and strengthening understanding of technologies in use	Diversifying to new applications and markets	Identifying product and process improvements
	Discoveries and developing new technologies	Diversifying to entirely new businesses	Developing new processes for established products
Corporate service by:	Intelligence	Opening windows on new science and technology	Assessing threats and opportunities
	Human resources	Recruiting new kinds of skills	Recruiting talented people with high potential
	Technology transfer	Identifying acquisition candidates with needed technological expertise	Recruiting for all divisions, from corporate research to operations

Source: R. S. Rosenbloom and A. M. Kantrow, "The Nurturing of Corporate Research," *Harvard Business Review,* January–February 1982, pp. 115–23.

provide the highest economic returns and (2) how tightly R&D projects are linked to business objectives in those promising areas of technology.[12]

The Functions of Corporate Research

Rosenbloom and Kantrow[13] have provided a useful overview of the functions of corporate research; it indicates that corporate research helps meet the innovation challenges associated with the induced and autonomous strategic processes (see Exhibit 2).

Support of Existing Businesses (Induced Process)
As Exhibit 2 suggests, activities in support of the firm's existing business comprise improvements in existing products and processes. Often, the corporate research group will have high-level experts in certain areas of science that divisional R&D groups or product developers cannot afford for themselves exclusively. Corporate research also can provide several services to the rest of the corporation: (1) help divisional R&D groups assess technological threats and opportunities through high quality intelligence work, (2) assist divisional R&D with their human resource management by helping recruit talented technical personnel, and (3) facilitate transfers of technology from corporate research to divisional R&D or product development groups.

New Strategic Directions (Autonomous Process)
The key contribution of a corporate research capability, however, is to discover new areas of technology that may form the basis of entirely new businesses. For example, Du Pont's invention of nylon, Corning's invention of optical fiber, and EMI's invention of the CT scanner created entirely new businesses for these firms. IBM's contributions to high-temperature superconductivity may one day pay off in new but as yet unimagined business opportunities. Rosenbloom and Kantrow[14] point out that corporate research may help a firm keep a window open on new science and technology, and Cohen and Levinthal[15] found that corporate research increases the firm's "absorptive capacity" of new technology. Furthermore, having top-level scientists at corporate R&D may help in the recruitment of other top technical personnel. Finally, corporate research may help in identifying acquisition candidates with the necessary technical expertise.

Effectively Using the Output of Corporate Research
Corporate research's role is to generate new technologies, some of which can be used effectively in the various parts of the organization responsible for new product development for existing businesses (induced strategic process). The transfer of technology from research to devel-

[12]R. N. Foster, "Linking R&D to Strategy," *The McKinsey Quarterly,* Winter 1981.
[13]"The Nurturing of Corporate Research."
[14]Ibid.
[15]W. M. Cohen and D. A. Levinthal, "Absorptive Capacity: A New Perspective on Learning and Innovation," *Administrative Science Quarterly* 35 (1990), pp. 128–52.

opment, however, is a nontrivial problem for most firms. (See Reading III-2.)

Corporate research also generates technologies that cannot easily find a home in the firm's existing product development infrastructure. These require special arrangements to facilitate the technologies (autonomous strategic process). Later in this chapter a framework for designing such arrangements is presented.

Managing Key Interfaces

Corporate Research—Divisional R&D Interface (Induced Process)

Managing the interface between corporate research and divisional R&D is difficult because of the differing orientations and expectations of the groups involved.[16] Scientists in divisional labs or people in product development usually want to commission experimental studies or obtain expert help from corporate research. They tend to see corporate research as providing a service and expect corporate research to be responsive to their initiations and requests. Corporate research, on the other hand, tends to see itself as carrying out work at the frontier of areas of science that promise to be of great importance to the firm's long-term success and resists being asked to perform low-level technical problem solving. Members of corporate research want to be considered "advisers" who initiate improvements in the research programs of divisional R&D. Given these different expectations, careful use of administrative, geographical, and personal linkages is important to manage the interfaces effectively. These linkages are illustrated in Exhibit 3.

Geographical linkages are the physical proximity among R&D groups. Research conducted by Allen,[17] for instance, has shown the importance of proximity for communication among R&D personnel. Administrative linkages comprise the authority relationships of different groups; that is, whether they report to the same superior. To the extent they do, it is of course easier to impose formal collaboration. Personal linkages refer to the informal network of contacts researchers develop in the firm. While the most elusive, these ties probably have the greatest impact on the quality of collaboration among research personnel.

Corporate Research—Business Research Interface (Autonomous Process)

Developing new areas of business based on corporate research is an entrepreneurial

EXHIBIT 3 Linkages Among R&D Units

		Geographical			
		Closed		Open	
		Personal		Personal	
		Closed	Open	Closed	Open
Administrative	Closed	Tight coupling			
	Open				No coupling

task. It necessitates linking new technological solutions to market needs and obtaining additional resources to create a commercially viable new business and thus requires inputs from corporate research and business research specialists. Managing the interface between corporate research and business research specialists, such as the interface between corporate research and divisional R&D, is difficult. Burgelman and Sayles[18] have identified several factors that affect the interface between corporate research and business research professionals (see Exhibit 4).

The work environments of corporate research and business research professionals are quite different. Corporate researchers operate in the well-established tradition of scientific research and have clearly described positions in the research management hierarchy (bench scientist, group leader, R&D manager, etc.). The scientific method guiding their work is well codified, and the databases they use are to a great extent systematic and objective. Moreover, the time pressures encountered are mostly self-generated because it is difficult for management to significantly compress the time needed to carry out critical experiments and virtually impossible to order scientific breakthroughs. The time to complete a scientific study is to a large extent determined by the logic of the scientific method. Business research professionals, on the other hand, operate in a less well defined research tradition and their work hierarchy is often less clearly defined. Their methods tend to be more ad hoc and less codified, and their databases tend to be less systematic and more subjective. Business research professionals are more likely to encounter externally generated time pressures (e.g., from customers with technical problems) that determine the time period within which a solution must be found.

---

[16]R. A. Burgelman and L. R. Sayles, *Inside Corporate Innovation* (New York: Free Press, 1986).

[17]T. J. Allen, *Managing the Flow of Technology* (Cambridge, Mass.: MIT Press, 1977).

---

[18]*Inside Corporate Innovation.*

EXHIBIT 4   Systematic Differences Between Business and R&D People

	R&D people	Business research people
Work environment		
1. Structure	Well defined: existence of research tradition; clearly described positions	Ill defined: no real research tradition; positions less clearly defined
2. Methods	Scientific and codified	Ad hoc and uncodified
3. Database	Systematic and objective	Unsystematic and largely subjective
4. Work and time pressures	Mostly internal; how long does it take?	Mostly external; how long do we have?
Professional orientations		
5. Operating assumptions	Serendipity	Planning
6. Goals	"New" ideas; can it be improved?	"Big" ideas; does it work?
7. Performance criteria	Quality of investigation	Quantity of results
Quality of personnel		
8. Educational background	Ph.D.	Master's
9. Experience	Deep and focused	Broad and diverse
Personal interests		
10. Career objectives	Become venture manager?	Become venture manager?

Source: Burgelman and Sayles, *Inside Corporate Innovation* (New York: Free Press, 1986).

The professional orientations of the two groups are also somewhat different. Corporate scientists consider serendipity (and the concomitant unpredictability) a way of life and are mostly interested in pursuing new ideas and finding ways to improve technical performance in major ways. Corporate scientists expect their work to be evaluated primarily on the quality of the investigation rather than the commercial usefulness of its results. Business research professionals, on the other hand, usually operate in a planning framework requiring predictable commercial results. They are interested in the commercial impact of a technical idea rather than its novelty, and in whether it will solve a technical customer need within acceptable cost parameters.

Finally, differences in background and personal interests may impede effective interaction among the groups. Corporate scientists typically have Ph.D.s and have built experience through deep and focused research. Conversely, business research professionals often do not have Ph.D.s and have had broader and more diverse experiences.

Linking Corporate Research to Corporate Development Strategy

Providing a clear charter for corporate research (see Exhibit 2) is important to facilitate its strategic management. In addition, top management must ensure that corporate research supports the firm's corporate development strategy. This requires that top management establish an ef-

fective process for deciding which new businesses and competences the firm wants to develop. Having a clear corporate development strategy makes it easier for top management to assess the strategic importance of different research areas with the help of the firm's chief scientist, corporate vice president of technology, or other senior representative of R&D.

Assessing Technological Opportunity   Rosenberg[19] outlines how the high uncertainty involved in technological changes makes it extremely difficult to assess associated business opportunities even after their technological feasibility has been established. For instance, one of the most important applications of the laser has been telecommunications. However, "patent lawyers at Bell Labs were initially unwilling even to apply for a patent on the laser, on the grounds that such invention had no possible relevance to the telephone industry."[20] Rosenberg goes on to discuss five dimensions of the fundamental uncertainty that constrain the ability to predict the value of radically new technologies:

1. Technological innovations come into the world in primitive conditions and with properties and charac-

---

[19] N. Rosenberg, "Uncertainty and Technological Change," paper prepared for the Conference on Growth and Development: The Economics of the 21st Century, organized by the Center for Economic Policy Research of Stanford University, June 3–4, 1994.
[20] Ibid., p. 5.

teristics whose usefulness cannot be immediately appreciated (e.g., the laser was not an obvious substitute for something that already existed).

2. The impact of technological innovations often depends on improvements in complementary inventions (e.g., the usefulness of the laser in telecommunications depended on the availability of fiber optics).

3. Major technological innovations often constitute entirely new technological systems, but it is difficult to conceptualize such systems (e.g., the telephone was originally conceptualized as primarily a business instrument).

4. Major technological innovations often had their origins in attempts to solve very specific problems and lead to unanticipated uses (e.g., the steam engine was invented specifically as a device for pumping water out of flooded mines).

5. The ultimate impact of technological innovations depends on the ability to effectively link them to specific categories of human needs (e.g., it was David Sarnoff, not Marconi, who linked the possibility of wireless communication to extended human needs).

Assessing technological opportunities is an integral task of top corporate research management. Rosenbloom and Kantrow[21] report criteria used by George Pake, former vice president of corporate research at Xerox, to assess technological opportunities. Pake asked the following questions:

- Are first-class researchers available to pursue them?
- Is major investment likely to yield major advances?
- How many years will it take before we see useful results?
- How many failures and successes have others had in this area?

If a proposal survived this initial screening and before committing resources, Pake and others at Xerox then asked,

- Can the expert technology be obtained from vendors or through acquisition?
- What costs would be incurred by displacing an existing research program to implement the new proposal?
- Is there enough hope that a successful result can be transferred downstream?
- Will the necessary capital be available?

Clearly, answering these kinds of questions involves qualitative judgment as well as quantitative analysis. The capacity of top management to evaluate the quality of the

thinking of R&D managers, group leaders, and bench scientists in corporate research is crucial here. As the case on Du Pont's miracle fiber Kevlar in this section will illustrate, often the technical dimensions of these opportunities are much easier to predict than the nature of the market for the innovations.

The Role of Different Levels of Corporate Research Management   The key operational levels in corporate research are as follows:

- Technicians (usually having a bachelor's or master's degree in science or engineering and responsible for helping scientists with the implementation of experiments, data analysis, etc.);
- Bench scientists (usually having a fairly recent Ph.D. in science or engineering and responsible for specific research projects);
- Group leaders (usually having a Ph.D. in science or engineering and a strong track record as a "respected peer" in their specialty and responsible for a number of bench scientists and their projects);
- R&D managers (senior managers to whom a number of group leaders report); and
- Director of corporate R&D (responsible for the overall corporate research effort).[22]

The director of corporate research will usually report to a vice president in charge of all the firm's R&D and technology efforts. Sometimes, the firm will have a chief scientist and/or a scientist advisory board to help the CEO and top management with decisions concerning R&D and technology. Also, sometimes the firm will have a parallel ladder of scientific positions to recognize the levels of achievement of scientists who do not wish to become "managers."

While the ultimate responsibility for corporate research rests with top management, Burgelman and Sayles[23] found that many critical decisions are actually made by senior (but not top) managers. R&D managers established general directions and broad research programs for their group leaders and the bench scientists that report to them, but for the most part tried to keep their staff honest by asking questions and demanding reviews. A critical factor seemed to be the intellectual respect the R&D manager commanded from not being easily snowed by the researchers. Also, the group leader played a very important role in making substantive judgments.

---

[21] "The Nurturing of Corporate Research," p. 121.

[22] Burgelman and Sayles, *Inside Corporate Innovation.*
[23] Ibid.

Group leaders experienced most intensely the tension between relevance of a scientific area to the corporation and the need to do good science. At the same time, group leaders were often involved in starting a new venture based on corporate research. They usually were sufficiently close to the actual research work to fully understand how a particular technical solution might satisfy a market need and were sufficiently familiar with, and networked in, the corporate environment to be able to act as product champion.

Allocating Resources to Corporate Research   Once areas of corporate research receive top management support based on their relevance to corporate strategy and the abundance of their technological opportunities, resources can be allocated to them. Corporate research, however, is inherently inertial: To overcome the conceptual and empirical hurdles associated with discovery and invention, scientists need to be tenacious and persistent. Not surprisingly, the trajectories of corporate strategy and corporate research are likely to diverge. Also, technological opportunities may not materialize at the rate or the magnitude originally anticipated. While it would be dysfunctional to disrupt the long-term horizon of corporate research projects, it is necessary to monitor the pattern of resource allocation. The strategic management of corporate research requires both rigorous scientific scrutiny by research management and close financial scrutiny by business management. Some companies, notably Merck, have found it useful to apply an options valuation framework to investments in corporate research.[24]

MANAGING CORPORATE ENTREPRENEURSHIP

The Managerial Challenge Posed by Autonomous Strategic Action

Technology-based internal entrepreneurial activity often emerges spontaneously.[25] This is not surprising because firms almost continuously bring in new talent that interacts with the firm's existing resources, competencies, and capabilities in ways that cannot be fully anticipated.[26] Here are some examples:

- In 1966, calculators were largely mechanized. A young man working for one of the calculator companies brought a model for an electronic calculator to Hewlett-Packard. His own firm was not interested in it because they didn't have the electronic capability. In spite of unfavorable market research forecasts, William Hewlett personally championed the project.[27]
- In 1980, Sam H. Eletr, a manager in Hewlett-Packard's labs, tried to persuade the company's new product people to get into biotechnology. "I was laughed out of the room," he said. But venture capitalists didn't laugh. They persuaded Mr. Eletr to quit Hewlett-Packard and staked him $5.2 million to start a new company. Its product was gene machines, which make DNA, the basic material of the genetic code—and the essential raw material in the burgeoning business of genetic engineering. Several years later, Hewlett-Packard formed a joint venture with Genentech Inc. to develop tools for biotechnology. One product it has considered is gene machines.[28]

How should corporate management deal with autonomous strategic initiatives? Clearly, not every new initiative can or should be supported. Yet it seems reasonable to ask whether the top management of the firms in these examples made a strategic decision not to pursue the initiatives of their internal entrepreneurs. From a strategic management perspective, it is insufficient to reject the electronic calculator because "we don't have an electronics capability" or the gene-making machine because "we are not in biotechnology." There must have been important competencies in the firm that allowed the internal entrepreneurs to come up with their idea and perhaps even develop a prototype. Even if there was no apparent relationship with current capabilities and skills, it was important for top management to consider the potential implications of the initiative for the firm's strategic position. In the case of calculators, for instance, top management of the mechanical calculator firm might be expected to have considered the strategic implications of someone else bringing an electronic calculator to market successfully. Often they do not, however. Because autonomous action explores the boundaries of the firm's set of core and distinctive competencies and the corresponding product-market opportunities, it is a vital part of the strategic process in established firms.

autonomous actions forces looking beyond current competencies

[24] N. A. Nichols, "Scientific Management at Merck: An Interview with CFO Judy Lewent," *Harvard Business Review,* January–February 1994.
[25] Burgelman, "A Process Model."
[26] E. T. Penrose, *The Theory of the Growth of the Firm* (Oxford: Blackwell, 1968).

[27] R. M. Atherton and D. M. Crites, "Hewlett-Packard: A 1975–1978 Review," Harvard Case Services, Boston, Mass. 1980.
[28] "After Slow Start, Gene Machines Approach a Period of Fast Growth and Steady Profits," *The Wall Street Journal,* December 13, 1983.

EXHIBIT 5 Interface Problems Involving the NVD

	NVD–operating divisions interfaces	NVD–corporate management interfaces
Strategic interferences	• Domain protection issues • Synergy considerations	• Lack of diversification strategy • Limits to rate of strategic change that can be absorbed • Effects on corporate image
Administrative/cultural frictions	• Rigidities resulting from management system • Personnel transfer issues	• Circumvention of corporate rules and regulations • Inadequate measurement and reward systems • Resistance to institutionalization

Source: Adapted from R. A. Burgelman, "Managing the New Venture Division: Research Findings and Implications for Strategic Management," *Strategic Management Journal,* January–March 1985.

The Use of New Venture Divisions

One way top management has tried to take advantage of the autonomous strategic initiatives that often emerged based on technologies developed in corporate research was to create a separate new venture division, or NVD. The premise was that internal entrepreneurs should be allowed to pursue ventures unencumbered by the constraints of the firm's mainstream business management. Having reached critical mass, a new venture could then be transferred to an operating division as a new business unit or department or, if sufficiently large, the venture could become a freestanding division in its own right. The prospect of becoming the general manager of a major new business in the corporate context was a strong incentive for would-be corporate entrepreneurs. Fast[29] and Burgelman and Sayles,[30] however, have documented serious problems associated with the NVD design. The problems as documented by Burgelman[31] are summarized in Exhibit 5.

NVD–Operating Division Interface Problems In the NVD's interface with the operating divisions, potential strategic interferences revolve around product-market domain and synergy issues. The product-market domain of new ventures is meant to involve business areas outside the strategies of the operating divisions, but down the road there are often conflicts of strategic interests. For instance, an operating division may want to absorb a new venture while its manager is still trying to demonstrate

that it will be sufficiently large to warrant creating a separate division. Also, an operating division may be concerned if the sales force of a new venture begins to contact its existing customers.

Besides potential strategic interferences, administrative frictions may emerge. A uniform corporate management system may make it difficult for a new venture to get resources from an operating division because divisional managers feel they have to stick to their action plans (which do not include helping fledgling ventures). Personnel transfers between divisions and new ventures are difficult when capable divisional personnel are concerned about being reintegrated in the corporate mainstream if a new venture folds.

NVD–Corporate Management Interface Problems A key problem facing the NVD is that the firm lacks a clear corporate diversification strategy. In addition, corporate management often has no clear idea about the rate of strategic change the firm can sustain. Finally, top management may belatedly become concerned about the effects of a venture's activities on the corporate image. For instance, if a venture sold a deficient piece of equipment, the ramifications for the corporation would extend far beyond the effects on the venture itself. Not being sure what to expect, top management often adopts a vacillating stance toward new ventures. Venture managers are aware of this and realize they have only limited time to make a mark. This puts enormous pressure on venture managers to show fast growth within a narrow time window.

Administrative frictions in the NVD–corporate management interface sometimes result from the venture's occasional circumvention of corporate rules and regulations: Sometimes the venture manager will feel compelled to cut corners in corporate standard operating procedures in order to survive. Also, the lack of measurement

[29] N. D. Fast, *The Rise and Fall of Corporate New Venture Divisions* (Ann Arbor, Mich.: U.M.I. Research Press, 1979).
[30] Burgelman and Sayles, *Inside Corporate Innovation.*
[31] R. A. Burgelman, "Managing the New Venture Division: Research Findings and Implications for Strategic Management," *Strategic Management Journal,* 1985.

and reward systems tailored to the tasks of developing a new venture may motivate dysfunctional actions. For example, if the size of a business (sales volume or number of personnel) is the major criterion for managerial compensation, it should come as no surprise that venture managers will try to grow their venture quickly, sometimes at the expense of other considerations. Furthermore, venture managers are likely to resist attempts on the part of corporate management to institutionalize their venture—to act more like the rest of the corporation—as long as they feel that the corporate ways and means are impeding their struggle for success in the market as well as in the internal corporate context.

A Framework for Assessing Internal Entrepreneurial Initiatives

How can corporate management improve its capacity to deal with autonomous strategic action if simply putting such an initiative in a separate new venture division often does not work? A first step in addressing this question is recognizing that different ventures have different needs and not all ventures can be effectively treated in the same way. The next step is to develop an analytical framework that can be used to assess entrepreneurial initiatives and that leads to tentative conclusions about the use of a variety of organization design alternatives to effectively structure the relationship between entrepreneurial initiatives and the corporation. The proposed conceptual framework focuses on two key dimensions of strategic decision making concerning internal entrepreneurial proposals: the expected strategic importance for corporate development and the degree to which proposals are related to the core capabilities of the corporation (i.e., their operational relatedness). (See Exhibit 6.)

Assessing Strategic Importance Assessing strategic importance involves considering the implications of an entrepreneurial initiative for the firm's product-market position. In the example of gene machines at Hewlett-Packard, the assessment of strategic importance would address the question of whether failing to pursue the initiative would prevent the corporation from moving into bioelectronics, a potentially important new area of electronic instrumentation.

How can management assess the strategic importance of an entrepreneurial initiative? While this is an important responsibility, it often is one for which top management is not well equipped. Corporate-level managers in established firms tend to rise through the ranks, having earned their reputation as head of one or more of the firm's operating divisions. By the time they reach the top manage-

EXHIBIT 6 Toward an Assessment Framework

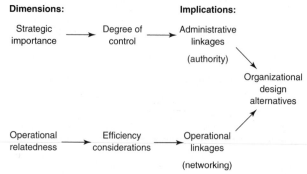

Key dimensions and their implications

Source: R. A. Burgelman, "Managing Corporate Entrepreneurship: New Structures for Implementing Technological Innovation," *Technology in Society* (December 1985), pp. 91–103.

ment level, they have developed a highly reliable frame of reference to evaluate business strategies and resource allocation proposals pertaining to the corporation's main lines of business. By the same token, their substantive knowledge of new technologies and markets is limited. Top management tends to rely on corporate staff, consultants, and informal interactions with colleagues from other companies to assess new business fields. Such information sources have merit, but they are no substitute for efforts to understand the substantive issues associated with an autonomous initiative. Top managers depend on middle-level managers, who are closer to new technologies and markets and who champion autonomous initiatives based on their own substantive assessments. Such interactions improve top management's capacity to make strategically sound assessments. Examples of critical issues to be addressed in these substantive interactions are as follows:

- How does this initiative maintain the firm's capacity to move in areas where major current or potential competitors might move?
- How does this help the firm determine where *not* to go?
- How does it help the firm create new defensible niches?
- How does it help mobilize the organization?
- To what extent could it put the firm at risk?
- When should the firm get out of it if it does not seem to work?
- What is missing in the analysis?

Strategic assessment may result in characterizing a proposal as *very* or *not at all* important. In other cases, the situation will be more ambiguous and lead to assessments such as "important for the time being" or "may be important in the future." Key to the usefulness of the analysis is that such assessments are based on specific, substantive factors.

Assessing Operational Relatedness Operational relatedness concerns the degree to which an entrepreneurial initiative requires competencies and capabilities that differ from the corporation's core competencies. Entrepreneurial initiatives typically are based on new competencies and may have the potential for positive or negative synergies with existing competencies/capabilities. Also, internal entrepreneurs often weave together pieces of technology and knowledge from separate parts of the organization that would otherwise remain unused.

In order to be able to make the required assessment of operational relatedness, corporate management again needs to rely on substantive interactions with middle-level managers who champion entrepreneurial projects. Critical issues and questions to be addressed include:

- What key capabilities are required to make this project successful?
- Where, how, and when will the firm get them if it doesn't have them yet, and at what cost?
- Who else might be able to do this, perhaps better?
- How will these new capabilities affect the capacities currently employed in the firm's mainstream business?
- What other areas may possibly require successful innovative efforts if the firm moves forward with this project?
- What is missing in the analysis?

To help top management with this assessment it is useful to develop a competencies/capabilities inventory that indicates how they are deployed in the firm's current businesses. In light of this, new initiatives will sometimes be classified as *very* or *not at all* related. In other cases, the situation will lead to a *partly related* assessment. These assessments should again be made in specific, substantive terms for each initiative.

Design Alternatives for Corporate Entrepreneurship

Having assessed an entrepreneurial initiative in terms of its strategic importance and operational relatedness, corporate management must choose an organization design for structuring the relationship between the new business opportunity and the corporation that is commensurate with its position in the assessment framework. This involves various combinations of administrative and operational linkages.

Determining Administrative Linkages The assessment of strategic importance has implications for the degree of control corporate management must maintain over the new business development. The premise is that firms, like individuals, want to exert control over the factors likely to affect their strategic position and thus their freedom to act and pursue their objectives. This, in turn, has implications for the administrative linkages to be established. If strategic importance is high, strong administrative linkages are in order. This means, basically, that the new business must be folded into the existing structural context of the firm. Corporate management will want a say in the strategic management of the new business through direct reporting relationships as well as involvement in planning and budgeting processes and in trade-offs between the strategic concerns of the new and existing businesses. Measurement and reward systems must reflect clearly articulated strategic objectives for the new business development.

Low strategic importance, on the other hand, should lead corporate management to examine how the new business can best be spun off. In more ambiguous situations where strategic importance is judged to be somewhat unclear, corporate management should relax the structural context and allow the new business some leeway in its strategic management. In such situations, the strategic context of the new business remains to be determined. This requires mechanisms facilitating substantive interaction between middle and corporate levels of management and measurement and reward systems capable of dealing with as yet unclear performance dimensions and strategic objectives.

Determining Operational Linkages The degree of operational relatedness has implications for the efficiency with which both the new and the existing businesses can be managed. The premise here is that firms seek to organize their operations in such a way that synergies are maximized while the cost of transactions across internal organizational boundaries is minimized. This, in turn, has implications for the required operational linkages. If operational relatedness is judged to be high, tight coupling of the operations of the new and existing businesses is in order. Corporate management should ensure that both new and existing capabilities and skills are employed well through integration of work flows, adequate mutual adjustment between resource users through lateral relations at the operational level, and free flows of information and know-how through regular contacts between professionals in the new and existing businesses.

In contrast, low operational relatedness may require complete decoupling of the operations of new and existing businesses to avoid interferences. In situations where operational relatedness is partial and not completely clear, loose coupling seems most adequate. In such situations, the work flows of new and existing businesses should remain basically separate, and mutual adjustment is achieved through individual integrator roles or task force types of mechanisms, rather than directly through the operational-level managers. Information and know-how flows, however, remain uninhibited. Exhibit 6 summarizes the key dimensions and their implications of the assessment framework.

Choosing Design Alternatives

Various combinations of administrative and operational linkages produce different design alternatives. Exhibit 7 shows nine such design alternatives.

The design alternatives discussed here are not exhaustive, and the scales for the different dimensions used in the assessment framework remain rudimentary. Much room is left for refinement through further research. By the same token, the framework represented in Exhibit 7 provides a conceptual underpinning for a number of practices adopted by established firms.

Direct Integration High strategic importance and operational relatedness require strong administrative and operational linkages. This means there is a need to integrate the new business directly into the mainstream of

EXHIBIT 7 Organization Designs for Corporate Entrepreneurship

Design alternatives

Operational relatedness		Very important	Uncertain	Not important
Unrelated		3 Special business units	6 Independent business units	9 Complete spin-off
Partly related		2 New product department	5 New venture division	8 Contracting
Strongly related		1 Direct integration	4 Micro new venture department	7 Nurturing and contracting

Strategic importance

Source: R. A. Burgelman, "Designs for Corporate Entrepreneurship in Established Firms," *California Management Review* (Spring 1984), pp. 154–66.

the corporation. Such integration must anticipate internal resistance for reasons well documented in the organizational change literature. The role of "champions"—those who know the workings of the current system very well—is likely to be important in such situations. The need for direct integration is perhaps strongest in highly integrated firms, where radical changes in product concept and/or in process technologies could threaten the overall strategic position of the firm. For instance, the development of "float glass" by Pilkington Glass, Ltd., had immediate and far-ranging implications for all glass makers, including Pilkington.[32]

New Product Department High strategic importance and partial operational relatedness require a combination of strong administrative and medium-strong operational linkages. This may be achieved by creating a separate department around an entrepreneurial project in that part (division or group) of the operating system where the potential for sharing capabilities and skills is significant. Corporate management should monitor the project's strategic development in substantive terms and not allow it to be folded ("buried") into the overall strategic planning of that division or group. For instance, there was strong resistance to developing electronic fuel injection (EFI) in the Automotive Group at Bendix Corporation. Only when a new group-level manager took charge and brought in new technical competences was EFI seriously pursued by Bendix. By that time, however, Bosch, which had licensed the technology from Bendix, was far ahead in EFI.

Special Business Units High strategic importance and low operational relatedness may require the creation of specially dedicated new business units. Strong administrative linkages are necessary to ensure the attainment of explicit strategic objectives within specified time horizons throughout the development process. It will often be necessary to integrate some of these business units into a new operating division in the corporate structure. IBM's use of the special business unit (SBU) design to enter the personal computer (PC) business is an example. In the mid-1980s, the SBU was disbanded and the PC activities were folded into IBM's mainstream organization. Corning Inc. has been able to use wholly owned subsidiaries to capitalize on new opportunities that emerge, at least in part, from its considerable corporate R&D efforts.

[32]B. Twiss, *Managing Technological Innovation* (London: Longman, 1980).

Micro New Ventures Department   Uncertain strategic importance and high operational relatedness seem typical for the "peripheral" projects that are likely to emerge in the operating divisions on a rather continuous basis. For such projects, administrative linkages should be loose. The venture manager should be allowed to develop a strategy within budget and time constraints but should otherwise not be limited by current or divisional or even corporate level strategies. Operational linkages should be strong, to take advantage of the existing capabilities and skills and to facilitate transferring back newly developed ones. Norman Fast[33] has discussed a "micro" new ventures division design that would seem to fit the conditions specified here. Fast describes how the Du Pont company, during the 1970s, moved away from a corporate new venture division to scale down the type of new ventures pursued and to tie these more strongly to the firm's operating divisions.

New Venture Division (NVD)   This design is proposed for situations of maximum ambiguity in the assessment framework. The NVD may serve best as a "nucleation" function. It provides a fluid internal environment for projects with the potential to create major new business thrusts for the corporation but of which the strategic importance remains to be determined as the development process unfolds. Administrative linkages should be fairly loose. Middle-level managers supervising a few ventures are expected to develop "middle range" strategies for new fields of business: bringing together projects that may exist in various parts of the corporation and/or can be acquired externally and integrating these with some of the venture projects they supervise to build sizable new businesses. Operational linkages should also be fairly loose yet sufficiently developed to facilitate the transfer of relevant know-how and information concerning capabilities and skills. Long time horizons—8 to 12 years—are necessary, but ventures should not be allowed to languish. High-quality middle-level managers are crucial to make this design work.

Independent Business Units   Uncertain strategic importance and negligible operational relatedness may make this arrangement appropriate. The firm may want to maintain controlling ownership with correspondingly strong board representation but also offer part of the ownership to partners and to the venture's management. This

provides corporate management with the option either to bring the venture into the corporation as a wholly owned subsidiary at a later date or to spin it off completely. IBM, during the early 1980s, had several independent business units,[34] most of which were later spun off. An example of joint ownership is provided by the way Bank of America organized its venture capital business.[35]

Nurturing plus Contracting   In some cases, an entrepreneurial proposal may be considered unimportant for the firm's corporate development strategy yet be strongly related to its operational capabilities and skills. Such ventures typically will address market niches that are too small for the company to serve profitably but that offer opportunities for a small business. Top management may want to help such entrepreneurs spin off from the corporation and may, in fact, help the entrepreneur set up his or her business. This provides a known and, in all likelihood, friendly competitor in those niches, keeping out other ones. Instead of administrative or ownership linkages, there may be a basis for long-term contracting relationships in which the corporation can profitably supply the entrepreneur with some of its excess capabilities and skills. Strong operational linkages related to these contracts may facilitate transfer of new or improved skills developed by the entrepreneur.

Contracting   The possibilities for nurturing would seem to diminish as the required capabilities and skills of the new business are less related. Yet there may still be opportunities for profitable technology licensing arrangements and for learning about new or improved capabilities and skills through some form of operational linkages.

Complete Spin-Off   If strategic importance and operational relatedness are both low, complete spin-off may be most appropriate. A decision based on a careful assessment of both dimensions is likely to lead to a well-founded decision from the perception of both the corporation and the internal entrepreneur.

Implementing Design Alternatives

In order to implement designs for corporate entrepreneurship effectively, three major issues and potential

---

[33] *The Rise and Fall of Corporate New Venture Divisions.*

[34] "Meet the New Lean, Mean IBM," *Fortune,* June 13, 1983, p. 78.
[35] "Despite Greater Risks, More Banks Turn to Venture-Capital Business," *The Wall Street Journal,* November 28, 1983.

problems must be considered. First, corporate management and the internal entrepreneur should view the assessment framework as a tool to clarify—at a particular moment—their community of interests and interdependencies and to structure a non–zero sum game. Second, corporate management must establish measurement and reward systems capable of accommodating the incentive requirements of different designs.[36] Third, as the development process unfolds, new information may modify the perceived strategic importance and operational relatedness, which may require a renegotiation of the organization design. The organization design framework must thus be used dynamically, with ventures potentially moving from one type of arrangement to another.

To deal effectively with implementation issues and potential problems, corporate management must recognize internal entrepreneurs as "strategists" and perhaps even encourage them to think as such. This is necessary because the stability of the relationship will depend on both parties' feeling that they have achieved their individual interests to the greatest extent, given the structure of the situation. On the part of corporate management, this implies attempts to appropriate benefits from the entrepreneurial endeavor, but only to the extent that they can provide the entrepreneur with the opportunity to be more successful than if he or she were to go it alone. This, in turn, requires simultaneously generous policies to help internal entrepreneurs based on a sound assessment of their proposals and unequivocal determination to protect proprietary corporate capabilities and skills vigorously. During the early 1980s, companies in Silicon Valley, for instance, increased their legal staffs in part to defend themselves from the siphoning off of intellectual property by unwanted spin-offs.[37]

CONCLUSION

In his early work, Schumpeter[38] distinguished between entrepreneurial and managerial types of economic activity. The role of the Schumpeterian entrepreneur was to change the pattern of resource allocation in the economy. In the process of innovation, entrepreneurs created a gale of "creative destruction." In his later work, Schumpeter[39] viewed large organizations as the main engine of the innovation process. While there have been doubts about the innovative capability of large established corporations, there is little doubt that they continue to play a key role in innovation. Through their ability to fund corporate research, large established corporations provide a substratum of discovery and invention that feeds the innovation process. Many start-ups have been built on ideas that originated within large established corporations. The spin-offs from Hewlett-Packard, Intel, and Apple, for instance, testify to this. Large established corporations thus fulfill an important function that could not easily be performed by small firms or by the government. Also, it is sometimes argued that the innovation process in large established corporations is more costly than in start-ups. But this ignores the fact that many start-ups are usually competing to bring a new product to market and that most of these fail. If the costs incurred by all the failing start-ups were considered together with the cost of the winning start-up to calculate the total cost of the innovation, it is not clear that the innovation process involving start-ups would always be more efficient than that involving large established firms.

Here we argue that the early Schumpeterian process is, to some extent, reenacted in established corporations. Established corporations maintain their growth and their long-term viability by taking advantage of internal entrepreneurs' exploration of the potential of the dynamic resource combinations that they have assembled. Internal entrepreneurs, like external ones, enact new opportunities and change the resource allocation pattern within the firm. To facilitate and manage this process better, new organization designs are necessary. This, in turn, requires a richer theory of the firm and a more nuanced view of the role of hierarchies, contracts, and markets. The conceptual foundations of these developments are currently being laid in such fields as the economics of internal organization, agency theory, the theory of legal contracts, and evolutionary theories of strategy and organization. As usual, practitioners are already experimenting with new organizational forms and arrangements. In the process, they generate new data and lay the basis for new research questions. A better understanding of the process of corporate entrepreneurship will facilitate the collaboration between firms and their internal entrepreneurs.

---

[36] B. Holmstrom, "Agency Cost and Innovation," *Journal of Economic Behavior and Organization* 12 (1989), pp. 305–27.

[37] "Spin Offs Mount in Silicon Valley," *The New York Times,* January 3, 1984.

[38] J. A. Schumpeter, *The Theory of Economic Development* (Cambridge, Mass.: Harvard University Press, 1934).

[39] J. A. Schumpeter, *Capitalism, Socialism, and Democracy* (N.Y.; Harper and Brothers, 1942).

INTERNAL AND EXTERNAL SOURCES OF TECHNOLOGY

The Lab That Ran Away from Xerox

Bro Uttal

On a golden hillside in sight of Stanford University nestles Xerox's Palo Alto Research Center, a mecca for talented researchers—and an embarrassment. For the $150 million it has lavished on PARC in 14 years, Xerox has reaped far less than it expected. Yet upstart companies have turned the ideas born there into a crop of promising products. Confides George Pake, Xerox's scholarly research vice president: "My friends tease me by calling PARC a national resource."

Not that the center has been utterly barren of benefits for Xerox. The company's prowess in designing custom chips, to be used in future copiers, comes largely from PARC. So do its promising capabilities in computer-aided design and artificial intelligence. PARC did most of the research for Xerox's laser printers, now a $250-million-a-year business growing at 45 percent annually and expected to turn a profit in 1984.

But Xerox hasn't cashed in on PARC's exciting research on computerized office systems, which was the center's original reason for being. According to Stanford J. Garrett, a security analyst who follows Xerox for Paine Webber, the company's office systems business

Source: Reprinted with permission from the September 5, 1983, issue of *Fortune* magazine. © 1983 by Time, Inc. All rights reserved.

lost a horrific $120 million last year and will probably drop $80 million in 1983. "Xerox has got a lot out of PARC," says Garrett, "but not nearly as much as it could have or should have."

Why has Xerox had trouble translating first-rate research into money-making products? Partly because the process takes time at any large company—often close to a decade. Sheer size slows decision making, and the need to concentrate on existing businesses impairs management's ability to move deftly into small, fast-changing markets. This is a special problem for Xerox, still overwhelmingly a one-product company whose copiers accounted for three-quarters of last year's $8.5 billion in revenues and almost all the $1.2 billion in operating profits.

Serious organizational flaws, acknowledged by high Xerox executives, have also proved a handicap. PARC had weak ties to the rest of Xerox, and the rest of Xerox had no channel for marketing products based on the researchers' efforts. The company has revamped office equipment marketing five times in the last six years. "Xerox has creaked, twisted, and groaned trying to find out how to use PARC's work," says an insider. While Xerox has groaned, disgruntled researchers have left in frustration. These Xeroids, as they call themselves, have showered PARC's concepts—for designing personal computers, office equipment, and other products—on competing companies.

PARC's influence outside the walls of Xerox is an ironic tribute to the ambitious vision of the man who founded the center in 1969. C. Peter McColough, then

671

Xerox's president, charged PARC with providing the technology Xerox needed to become "an architect of information" in the office. The new center, in a mutedly elegant three-story building whose rock-garden atria foster meditation, quickly lured many of the nation's leading computer scientists, offering what an alumnus calls "a blank check and 10 years without corporate interference."

Roughly half of PARC's money went for research in computer science and half for research in the physical sciences. Most of the glamour radiated from the computer crew. Members were notorious for long hair and beards and for working at all hours—sometimes shoeless and shirtless. They held raucous weekly meetings in the "bean-bag room," where people tossed around blue-sky concepts while reclining on huge pellet-filled hassocks. PARC's hotshots were not just playing at being geniuses. Before long, computer scientists recognized PARC as the leading source of research on how people interact with computers.

The hands-off policy at Xerox's headquarters in Stamford, Connecticut, proved a double-edged sword. PARC researchers used their freedom to explore concepts for personal computing that have since swept the industry. All sorts of computers, including some from Apple and IBM, now offer "bit-mapped" displays, which PARC championed 10 years ago. Such displays link each of the thousands of dots on a video screen to a bit of information stored in computer memory, thus allowing the computer to change each dot and create very fine-grained images. Apple's new, easy-to-use Lisa flaunts a display that can be divided into "windows" for viewing several pieces of work at once, as well as a pointing device, or "mouse," for giving commands. PARC did the lion's share of work on both ideas.

But Xerox's loose management also encouraged PARC to overstep its charter, which was to do research, not nuts-and-bolts product development. By the mid-1970s, the center was hard at work on the Alto, an expensive machine with some of the attributes of a personal computer, which was supposed to serve as a research prototype. Alto and its software became so popular inside Xerox, where PARC installed a couple of thousand of the systems, that some renegade researchers began to see them as commercial products. Out of top management's sight, they slaved like distillers of moonshine whiskey to develop the Alto for the market.

Product development, however, was the turf of another Xerox group, which was championing a rival machine called the Star, later to reach the market as Xerox's 8010 workstation. Unlike a personal computer, which generally relies on its own processing power and memory, the Star worked well only when linked with other Xerox equipment. (See "Xerox Xooms toward the Office of the Future," *Fortune,* May 18, 1981.)

PARC rebels not only took on the development group, but also dominated a Xerox unit set up to test-market research prototypes. This group got over 100 Altos installed in the White House, both houses of Congress, and a few companies and universities. Unwilling to support rival machines, Xerox guillotined the Alto and in 1980 liquidated the whole test-marketing group.

Veterans of that group have been the chief evangelists of PARC technology. John Ellenby, one of the unit's managers, later founded Grid Systems. His Compass computer approximates some prescient PARC concepts first used in the Alto. It's portable, uses a bit-mapped display, and easily hooks up with remote computers. At $8,000 to $12,000, the Compass sounds too costly to be popular, but Grid expects revenues of more than $28 million in 1983, its first full year of operations; in August, Grid said it was on the verge of profitability.

Another manager of the test-marketing unit, Ben Wegbreit, had previously been one of PARC's brightest technical talents. Convergent Technologies of Santa Clara, California, founded in 1979 to make workstations, picked off Wegbreit and two colleagues to design software. Convergent's word processing program shows some of its origins in the form of a "piece table," a type of software developed at PARC. It allows computers with fairly small memories to process long documents. It does this by storing only the changes made when editing, along with the original version, instead of the original plus a full-length edited version, as other programs do. Conveniences like that have helped Convergent land contracts that could produce some $450 million in sales to big computer companies that haven't developed their own desktop systems.

Charles Simonyi, who defected from Hungary at 17, styles himself "the messenger RNA of the PARC virus." He worked at the center for seven years, mostly on Bravo, a text-editing software program for the Alto that never reached the market. "We weren't supposed to do programs like that," he confesses, "so Bravo started out as a subterfuge. But when people at Xerox saw it, they wanted to use it inside the company. Bravo was why people used Altos, just as VisiCalc was the reason people bought the Apple II." Simonyi expected some brilliant executive to see his product's market potential. "That wasn't dumb," he says, "but it was naive to assume such a person would come from Xerox." Simonyi found a warmer welcome at

Microsoft Corporation, based in Bellevue, Washington, which rang up $50 million in sales of personal-computer software in the year ended last June. A big chunk of this year's sales, which should approach $100 million, will come from Microsoft Word, a streamlined version of Bravo.

Lisa is the unkindest cut of all. In December 1979, Steve Jobs, then Apple's vice chairman, visited PARC with some colleagues to poke around. They saw Smalltalk, a set of programming tools. "Their eyes bugged out," recalls Lawrence Tesler, who helped develop Smalltalk. "They understood its significance better than anyone else who had visited." Seven months later, Jobs hired Tesler, having decided to use many Smalltalk features in the Lisa.

The Lisa had to be priced at $10,000, two to four times Jobs' earlier estimates. But it seems to be taking off. Apple claims to have shipped as many Lisas in July, the first month they were available, as Xerox has shipped Stars, or 8010s, in 19 months of availability. The Star, which embodies many concepts used in the Lisa, has been ill-starred. The influential *Seybold Report on Professional Computing* calls it "a jack-of-all-trades which does none really well." Sales suffered initially because some of the Star's software was late in coming to market.

Office equipment analysts have started referring to PARC-style systems as "Lisalike," not "Starlike." Apple's next computer, Macintosh, scheduled to ripen into a commercial product by the end of this year, could further identify Apple with PARC's ideas. The engineering manager for Macintosh came from PARC, where his last big project was a personal computer.

From this, Xerox might appear to have muffed the chance to make it big in personal computers with PARC's creations. Some Xeroids are sure the company could have been an early winner if only it had launched a less expensive Alto in the late 1970s. Unlike the Star, the Alto was an "open" computer, easy for outsiders to program. Independently written software has helped touch off the personal computer explosion, so the dissidents have a point. Because the Star is "closed," outsiders can't write programs for it.

To mourn the Alto, though, is to blame unfairly those who killed it. Xerox was out to produce office equipment, and no office equipment supplier, including IBM, foresaw that personal computers would compete with their wares. It was inconceivable that the cost of computer memory would decline 31 percent a year, as it has for the last five years, or that today's microcomputers would be as powerful as yesterday's mainframe computers. Xerox and its ilk concentrated not on freestanding personal computers but on clusters of workstations that share the use of computer hardware. That way, customers could spread high hardware costs across many workers. And suppliers could defray the costs of their prized sales forces with big-ticket orders.

Besides, Xerox had, and still has, ulterior motives in the office. Competition in the copier market keeps growing, and the company's chief aim has been to protect copier installations by strengthening its control of large, lucrative accounts. Companies that can sell complete office systems—workstations with reliable software, printers, and data-storage devices, all linked into a network—have a stronger lock on their customers than do suppliers of stand-alone equipment. Thus, the Star, which works well only when hooked up with other Xerox gear, seemed to fit the company's strategy better than freestanding little computers would.

The complete-system approach, moreover, was more compatible with Xerox's expansive ways of thinking than the alternative of making piecemeal improvements on an individual machine like the Alto. Big companies often can't make the modest efforts needed to probe emerging markets. "It's a problem when you're getting your feet wet in a new business," says Jack Goldman, formerly Xerox's research chief. "In a large company, every product must be a home run to justify the costs of marketing and development."

That has been especially true at Xerox, which owes its existence to xerography, one of the longest homers on record. Top management "followed the big-bank strategy," says one veteran. "They wanted to build absolutely the best office system instead of taking things bit by bit." At PARC, the company's urge to build the best at the expense of the merely better, like an Alto, had its own name: biggerism.

Biggerism could pay off in some ways, to be sure. Xerox has big hopes for Ethernet, a PARC-invented network that uses a cable and translating devices to connect different types of office equipment. By souping up the performance of PARC's original version of Ethernet, Xerox drastically raised the cost of hooking up, to as much as $5,000 per connection. That move discouraged sales and deterred other equipment makers from adapting their machines to talk through Ethernet. But now, improved chip technology has sliced the cost of connecting by about two-thirds. Over 70 office equipment makers are using Ethernet or plan to, including Apple. The temporary setback helped keep Ethernet from becoming *the* industry standard, but it is *a* standard. (The only other company likely to set a standard is IBM.)

Xerox still thinks PARC's work can produce some big hits. No one is more convinced than John Shoch, a remarkably hard-boiled former PARC researcher who became the company's office systems chief last October. His first priority is to expand the number of Xerox products that will communicate over Ethernet (20 do now, including laser printers and facsimile machines). Making a winner out of the Star will take more effort. Because the technology is old and the system tries to do so many things, the workstation seems expensive and inept in many functions, especially compared to Lisa.

Shoch wants to bring out a less costly version of the $15,000 Star, which he sees as one claw of a pincer's movement to narrow the Lisa's potential market share. The other claw, in his view, will be IBM's personal computer armed with a Lisa-like set of programs written by VisiCorp. Priced at some $7,000, that system won't compete directly with the Star but will be far cheaper than the Lisa. It will also tap into Ethernet—thanks to a helping hand from Xerox. Says Shoch: "There's going to be a squeeze between the lower priced Star and commodity-type computers that run better software. It'll be a tough place to compete."

The company's support of PARC has never wavered. This year's budget of $35 million or so will set a record. But changes have taken place. Last March, Xerox appointed a new director of PARC, William Spencer. A veteran of two decades at Bell Labs, Spencer admires AT&T's ability to transfer technology out of the lab by attaching satellite labs to major manufacturing plants. "PARC's main shortcoming," he feels, "has been a lack of management attention. We started things that didn't match what was going on in other parts of Xerox."

Spencer is trying to produce a better fit by meeting a couple of times a year at PARC with Xerox's division managers, some of whom haven't visited for years. Every three weeks or so he breakfasts with Shoch, and they've started a joint hiring program: some new researchers will spend their first year or so at PARC, then join the office systems group.

Time is on Spencer's side. Having taken its lumps in the office systems business, Xerox has a better fix on what kinds of products make sense. While Shoch's division still struggles to discover a successful way of selling office systems, PARC, having created much of the technology McColough sought, is stepping up its work on a new frontier: very-large–scale integrated circuits used for everything from diagnosing copier breakdowns to connecting personal computers with mainframes. "The foundation for our future will be the next generation of

chips," says Spencer, who originally came to PARC to set up a line for making them. "Office systems is a smaller part of our work now."

When a company wants to make it big in a new business, a solid base of technology is necessary. But it's hardly sufficient. Without a clear understanding of corporate strategy and pressure from a hungry marketing group, even the best technologists can get out of hand. The tricky part is to strike a balance between encouraging creativity and getting your money's worth.

CASE III-1

Du Pont Kevlar® Aramid Industrial Fiber

Clayton Christensen

As Howard W. Swank, general manager of Du Pont's Textile Fibers Department, headed toward his Wilmington office on the morning of February 27, 1974, he knew that in a few hours he would soon face some stiff questions from the company's Executive Committee. Entering the lobby of the Nemours Building he glanced at the huge John McCoy mural from the 1939 New York World's Fair, which proclaimed in image and word Du Pont's motto, "Better Things for Better Living . . . Through Chemistry." Less than a week earlier, he had submitted to the X-Committee, as it was known in Du Pont parlance, the first of a three-part appropriation request for capital to build a 50-million pounds/year plant for the manufacture of Kevlar® Aramid fiber, his department's newest development—a miracle fiber of extraordinarily complex chemistry that was pound-for-pound five times stronger than steel. Kevlar truly was, Swank believed, a better

Source: Professor Clayton Christensen prepared this case as the basis for class discussion rather than to illustrate either effective or ineffective handling of an administrative situation. It is an abridgment of a longer case, "Du Pont Kevlar® Aramid Industrial Fiber," No. 391-146, written by Professor David A. Hounshell, Marvin Bower Fellow, under the supervision of Professor Richard S. Rosenbloom. Copyright © 1998 by the President and Fellows of Harvard College. To order copies or request permission to reproduce materials, call 1-800-545-7685, write Harvard Business School Publishing, Boston, MA 02163, or go to http://www.hbsp.harvard.edu. No part of this publication may be reproduced, stored in a retrieval system, used in a spreadsheet, or transmitted in any form or by any means—electronic, mechanical, photocopying, recording, or otherwise—without the permission of Harvard Business School.

thing for better living. Swank had been the general manager of Textile Fibers throughout Kevlar's development, so he was intimately familiar with the situation and how the X-Committee viewed the project. He had asked for the first $82 million of the total projected cost of $332 million. This initial sum would be used to pay for partial design of the plant, preparation of more accurate construction cost estimates, and payment of cancellation costs of long-time delivery equipment for the first commercial Kevlar plant.

Swank hoped that he had made a convincing case for the appropriation in his formal request. Kevlar was not unknown to the X-Committee, because it had been funding the fiber's development since 1971 and its members had been as amazed as anyone about Kevlar's properties. Barely three years earlier, Swank had made his first presentation to the X-Committee about Kevlar, then known as Fiber B-1. At that time he had briefed the committee on Fiber B-1's history, its properties, and its anticipated markets, and he had requested the committee's appropriation of $8.9 million for a Market Development Facility (MDF) in which enough of the new fiber could be made to determine more precisely the potential market and manufacturing costs for the fiber. Swank also asked the committee to designate the Fiber B-1 program as a New Venture Development, effective January 1, 1971, which meant that the program's cost would be reported below the annual profit/loss statement of the Textile Fibers Department and thus not reflect negatively on the department's performance. The Executive Committee had granted Swank's requests, and the Fiber B-1 project had gotten off to a good start.

PRECURSOR TECHNOLOGIES TO KEVLAR

Du Pont had been the pioneer of polyamides—nylon—in the 1930s and, subsequently, had advanced polymer chemistry from a black art to a science through a fundamental research program in its Central Research Department. Nylon had been commercialized in 1940, and earnings from it had fueled the company's growth and earnings in the post–World War II era. Since 1940 Du Pont's chemists in the Textile Fibers Department had developed a greater understanding of the relationship between the molecular structure of given polymers (i.e., how molecules are arranged, how the chains are shaped, the architecture of bonds) and the physical properties of those polymers (such as strength, melting point, and stiffness). The Textile Fibers Department's Pioneering Research Laboratory had accumulated enough theoretical understanding and empirical evidence to develop

tools that enabled chemists to predict with remarkable accuracy how a given polymer would perform in certain applications when spun into a fiber.

Equipped with these tools, Du Pont's chemists had theorized that a new polyamide might be synthesized that could be stable at higher temperatures than ordinary nylon. If spun into a fiber, this might be used in high-temperature applications such as fire-fighting garments, upholstery on airplanes, and other industrial uses. Du Pont scientists took a major step toward this goal in 1950, when they found a way to form polymers at room temperature at the interface of two liquids in different phases (comparable to the interface of salad oil and vinegar when left undisturbed). "Interfacial" polymerization gave chemists a technique to prepare literally tens of thousands of polymers that had previously been impossible to synthesize. By 1953, they had evolved away from this two-phase system, learning how the polymers could simply precipitate out of a single-phase low-temperature solution.

Although researchers employing other polymerization methods had failed repeatedly, in 1959 a small team of chemists—Paul Morgan, Stephanie Kwolek, and Wilfred Sweeney—volunteered to use this technique, labeled "solution polymerization," to synthesize this new high-temperature polyamide. Even as several of their colleagues were congratulating each other for not getting "stuck" on the project, the team succeeded in preparing a high-molecular weight, soluble aromatic polyamide. As predicted, the new polymer remained stable at very high temperatures. After further work to improve and simplify the process, the team recognized that they had developed a patentable polymer that was both thermally and chemically stable. This was trademarked in 1963 as Nomex aromatic polyamide (later reclassified as Nomex Aramid when Du Pont won a new classification for aromatic polyamides). Du Pont's experience with the commercialization of Nomex would figure heavily in its decision-making about the commercialization of Kevlar.

Development of Nomex progressed satisfactorily at the Du Pont laboratory in Waynesboro, Virginia, and in 1961, the Textile Fibers Department received authorization from the X-Committee to build a one million–pound pilot plant in Richmond, Virginia, where Du Pont was permanently shutting down its rayon manufacturing capacity. The pilot plant would produce both Nomex fibers and paper. Starting up in 1963, the pilot plant produced Nomex papers, used for electrical insulating purposes, substituting for the natural mineral mica. This product quickly won the interest of Boeing and Lockheed and

EXHIBIT 1 Textile Fiber Department's Major New Products, 1960–1972

Investment name of product (type)	Date discovered	Date commercialized	R&D costs ($ millions)	Cumulative precommercial losses by 1973 ($ millions)
Lycra spandex fiber	1953	1962	$25	$115
Reemay spunbonded polyester	1958	1965	a	
Typar spunbonded polypropylene	1958	1966	a	
Tyvek® spunbonded polyethylene	c. 1958	1967	a	$265
Nomex Aramid fiber	1954	1967	a	
Qiana® nylon	c. 1960	1968	a	

a Pre-commercial R&D costs for each of these fibers averaged about $45 million, with a range of $25 to $60 million.

approval of the Underwriter's Laboratory as an electrical insulating material. The market development of Nomex fibers, however, was slower owing to several factors—including the lack of light-stable dyes for the fibers. These problems notwithstanding, the X-Committee authorized in 1965 the construction of a 9 million pounds per year commercial plant for Nomex at the Richmond site, which started up in 1967.

Despite the appearance of smooth sailing, however, Nomex's development had come at a high cost. Pre-commercial R&D expenses exceeded $50 million, at that time the greatest sum of money Du Pont had ever spent on a project. Sales of Nomex fell short of expectations, and the plant operated well below capacity for at least six years. Moreover, the plant was plagued with operating problems, and its fiber and paper products required improvements before they could earn broader market acceptance. This confirmed what Du Pont's managers already knew implicitly: that market growth for an industrial product like Nomex will generally be a slow, uncertain, and tedious process, because customers are rarely willing to substitute unknown materials for the tried-and-true in their *established* products; the risks of jeopardizing satisfactory streams of profit were simply too great. With few exceptions, the initial uses for Nomex were in *new* products that Du Pont's customers were themselves just developing.

Thus Nomex lost money during its first four years and was generating only marginal operating earnings when Swank submitted his authorization request for the Kevlar plant.[1] The company had made a cash commitment to Nomex that approached $100 million before it had any

hope of turning the corner on the product. Moreover, the Textile Fibers Department had a number of other "problem children," as one member of the Executive Committee called them, including Reemay, Typar, Tyvek, and Qiana. During the 1960s, the department had developed and commercialized these new products, each with high pre-commercial R&D costs, comparatively high plant investments, and uncommonly high initial operating losses. Up through 1973, these "problem children," whose histories are recounted in Exhibit 1, sustained operating losses totaling $440 million on an investment of about $320 million. Indeed, only one big new product commercialized during the 1960s, Lycra spandex fiber, became financially successful in a relatively short period of time after commercial plant start up. Swank also knew that the Executive Committee had been closely following the performance of his department (see Exhibit 2) and especially its major products, nylon, Dacron polyester, and Orlon acrylic fibers—which were experiencing record or near-record sales but whose earnings were softening under increased competition (see Exhibits 3 and 4). The operating earnings on these major fibers accounted for 50% of the corporation's earnings during the 1960s.

EXHIBIT 2 Du Pont Company and Textile Fibers Department Performance, 1960–1973 ($ Millions)

	Du Pont		Fibers Department	
	Sales	Earnings	Sales	Earnings
1960	$2,143	$251	$ 172	$124
1962	2,407	309	815	159
1964	2,761	343	972	180
1966	3,159	372	1,087	163
1968	3,455	362	1,299	175
1972	4,961	418	1,885	184
1973	6,008	579	2,283	243

[1] "Operating earnings" was Du Pont's terminology for a product's profits before tax considerations and departmental burden were taken into account.

EXHIBIT 3   Major Fiber Products: Operating Earnings, 1961–1970 ($ Millions)

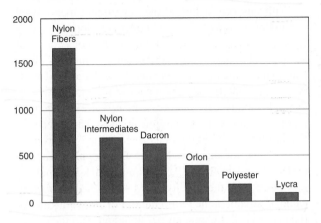

KEVLAR'S DEVELOPMENT

Kevlar's development was closely related to that of Nomex. In 1965, Stephanie Kwolek and Paul Morgan succeeded in synthesizing the polymer and spinning it into a fiber. As soon as she achieved this objective, however, Kwolek realized that she had made not just another laboratory curiosity but a polymer of great scientific and (potentially) commercial importance. Her synthesis product was a hazy, low-viscosity fluid. But when she stirred it, the fluid became opalescent. She had synthesized the first liquid crystalline (or anisotropic) polymer. Liquid crystalline polymers form chains that are highly organized in parallel arrays. Kwolek showed that this molecular orientation persisted when the opalescent fluid was spun into a fiber and that fibers so made were, like Nomex,

EXHIBIT 4   Du Pont World Fiber Shipments, 1940–1973: Rayon, Acetate, Nylon, Orlon, Dacron

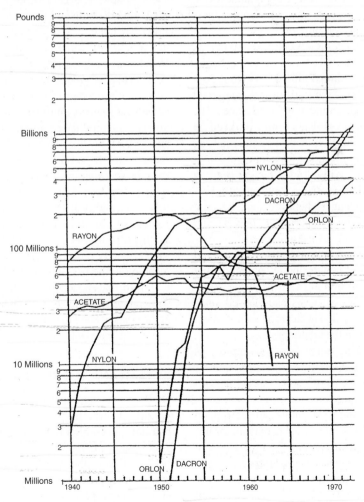

stable at high temperatures. But unlike Nomex, these fibers were very strong and stiff—more than seven times stiffer than nylon or Dacron fibers.

By 1969, using fiber made at the small experimental spinning works in Du Pont's Pioneering Research Laboratory, the Textile Fibers Department began to put out small samples of Kwolek's discovery, code-named Fiber B, to selected tire companies for evaluation as a tire cord material and to key aircraft manufacturers for assessment as a reinforcement in plastic composites. Altogether, the tire companies made about 200 test tires from Fiber B and demonstrated that these tires had "outstanding product performance, superior to all known incumbents."

Two problems plagued Fiber B's commercial potential, however. First, despite projections of producing it in multi-million–pound quantities, the estimated costs of producing Fiber B—involving intermediates manufacture, polymerization, and spinning—were simply too high, especially for the tire cord market. Moreover, to achieve adequate adhesion to rubber, tire makers had to apply adhesive to Fiber B under extraordinarily high tensions. Manufacturers would resist Fiber B for this reason alone.

When in 1970 these problems were judged intractable, Pioneering Research went back to the drawing board. Two years later, they had refined Fiber B to give it 50% greater tenacity and slightly higher stiffness. It continued to exhibit excellent high-temperature resistance. The Textile Fibers Department's managers were so keen on this new fiber, labeled Fiber B-1, that they had requested in early 1971 a $23 million Market Development Facility (MDF), in Richmond, without ever having put any Fiber B-1 out to tire and to aerospace companies for preliminary assessment. Managers believed that, because Fiber B-1's properties were so superior to Fiber B's and because the department understood quite well how customers in the tire and aerospace industries valued and evaluated the properties of new materials, precious time would be wasted if construction of an MDF were delayed. Already, more than five years had elapsed since Kwolek had first spun Fiber B. The department had spent $5.7 million on the fiber in the laboratory.

The Textile Fibers Department moved as rapidly as possible with the Fiber B-1 MDF because its managers wanted to get on top of events that were rapidly unfolding in both the tire cord market and the aircraft and aerospace industries. Swank and his deputies had determined to speed the start up of the MDF by using existing prototype (i.e., not designed with commercial production in mind) technology and plant space. Their intention was to get as much Fiber B-1 as possible into the market from the plant. By December 1971 the MDF had been put together and started up with an initial capacity of 125 pounds per hour.

With this goal achieved the department then moved toward the design of a larger Market Development Facility which would contain prototype technology for all of the critical elements of a projected commercial plant. This plant would not only generate critically needed product but also additional design data and, importantly, cost data. The annual capacity of this plant was expected ultimately to approach six million pounds. The Executive Committee approved the department's major appropriation request for this new Market Development Facility (MDF-II) in late April 1972 and made an additional appropriation for the facility in May 1973. This facility came on stream in the fourth quarter of 1973 with an initial capacity of 900 pounds per hour and with the potential of being reamed out to two or three times that level. By the end of 1973, the department had produced over a million pounds of fiber in MDF-I and MDF-II, at average costs somewhat over $20 per pound. The department's R&D organization had made major improvements to the Fiber B-1 manufacturing process, and the resulting product was greatly improved. By this time, Du Pont had trademarked Fiber B-1 as Kevlar Aramid fiber.

The Textile Fibers Department's 1971 projections for costs and its scenario for commercialization had slipped somewhat, but no more so than similar projections for almost any product commercialized by the department since 1950. Swank had hoped in 1972 that commercial facilities might be started up as early as late 1974. Basing their projections on the admittedly skimpy laboratory-scale production data, engineers and other development personnel had projected that a 20-million–pound plant costing $112 million could generate a net return on investment of between 10% and 20% if operating at 90% sales/capacity ratio (a figure the department anticipated reaching in the fifth commercial year). They concluded, therefore, that capacity would have to be raised to achieve sufficient economies of scale in order to produce Kevlar at the costs needed to penetrate the tire cord industry and composite materials markets.

KEVLAR AND THE TIRE MARKET

Du Pont had been a major player in the tire business from its earliest years. In cooperation with Goodyear, Du Pont had introduced high-tenacity rayon tire cord in the mid-1930s, and by early 1940, it had largely displaced cotton tire cord. After the war, Du Pont introduced nylon tire cord, which possessed superior strength, modulus, and elongation properties to those of rayon. Nylon captured

Process : invent material ⇒ build factory ⇒ Test in mkt. for Mkt Dev much of rayon's market share, but it suffered one major flaw: it flatspotted. When nylon-reinforced tires were cold they developed a squareness that caused a thumpy ride until the tire warmed up and rounded out. Automakers were unwilling to buy nylon-reinforced tires as original equipment because they feared losing new car sales because of their initially thumpy ride. Du Pont had spent millions trying to eliminate nylon's flatspotting but without success. In the early 1960s the company and several of Du Pont's competitors had introduced a polyester tire cord and adhesive system that eliminated the flatspotting problem. Hence, tire manufacturers were able to choose from rayon, nylon, or polyester tire cord depending on what segment within the market they wanted to target. (See Exhibit 5 for trends in tire cord consumption.)

While Du Pont and its competitors were investing heavily in new polyester tire cord capacity, another development was already evident: the radial tire. In 1970, few Americans knew anything about radial tires: only 1% of the tires sold in the United States were radials compared to 40% in Europe.

If the tire industry took the step to radials—and Du Pont had a clear indication from General Motors that it wanted to have radials on its cars by 1975—Du Pont stood to lose in a big way. With radial tires, the bulk of the tire cord was the belting, which ran around the circumference of the tire in the direction of travel. Only about one third of the tire cord went into the carcass, as radial bands that ran perpendicular to the line of travel, from one bead of the tire to the other (the bead was the thick ridge of rubber that contacted the wheel rim). Neither nylon nor polyester possessed the properties necessary to make a tire cord for radial belts. Fiberglass might capture some of the belting market, but it possessed some very severe limitations in flex life, adhesion, and durability. Steel, a new product that was already going into bias-belted tires, appeared to be the logical belt of choice. Du Pont had no hope of securing a position in either fiberglass or steel; they were beyond the bounds of the company's traditional practice in the chemical industry. Hence, Du Pont needed to win the belting market for Kevlar, pre-empting steel.

trouble in tire mkt.

Kevlar appeared to the managers of the Textile Fibers Department as the product to maintain the company's tire cord business if not command the industry. Pound-for-pound, Kevlar was four to five times stronger than steel. In tires, Kevlar's tenacity and modulus were superior to steel tire cord; only in the measure of elongation was it inferior, but it was still within acceptable bounds. Steel tire cord was in short supply in the United States, and prices had risen recently to 60¢ per pound. Du Pont hoped to move rapidly with Kevlar, thereby preempting steel-belted radial tire manufacture. Many U.S. manufacturers appeared to be reticent to enter the steel cord business or to expand their limited capacity. Steel tire cord manufacture was comparatively labor intensive.

Economics of production—for both steel and Kevlar—would ultimately determine the victor. Du Pont had no control over how steel tire cord would develop. But because Kevlar had performed extremely well in trade evaluations of hundreds of thousands of bias-belted and radial tires, the department's managers were confident that if Kevlar could be priced at not more than 4 to 4.8 times the price of steel (what they called the "replacement ratio") Kevlar could compete successfully and gain market share. Moreover, it held three advantages over steel. First, it was lighter, making for a more energy-efficient and smoother ride. Second, unlike steel, it could be used on tire manufacturing equipment that handled rayon, nylon, polyester, and glass cords. Third, some manufacturers had experienced problems in handling steel in the construction of large radial truck tires; with Kevlar, they had not had this problem. Du Pont predicted that the total market for belt fibers would approach 500 million pounds by 1980. With these advantages, Kevlar might become a major earner in Du Pont's fiber family.

Tire manufacturers gave every indication of being willing to adopt Kevlar. In 1973, a major American tire company quietly substituted Kevlar for rayon belts in some of its radial tires at the rate of about 1500 tires per month. Goodyear initiated a big promotional campaign for its Double Eagle super-premium radial tire, belted with Flexten, the tire company's trademarked cord made from Kevlar. In fact eight tire companies worldwide were selling Kevlar-belted radial tires in the highest-performance tiers of their product lines, and 13 firms had manufactured more than 50,000 Kevlar carcass truck tires.

The Kevlar MDF-II was hard-pressed to meet the tire industry's demand for Kevlar. With the facility operating at capacity it was difficult to take the plant off-line to engineer process and product improvements—but nonetheless, several important enhancements had been achieved.

EXHIBIT 5 Tire Cord Consumption, 1970–1973 (Millions of Pounds)

Year	Steel	Poly-ester	Nylon	Fiber-glass	Kevlar	Rayon	Total
1970	3	150	265	35		86	539
1971	5	179	276	36		113	609
1972	24	222	291	37		94	668
1973	60	242	274	34		73	683

The Textile Fibers Department, with its enormous experience in the economics of scaling up fiber manufacturing processes, projected that a 50-million–pound Kevlar plant would provide the necessary economies of scale for Kevlar to compete with steel tire cord. Moreover, Kevlar promised to be able to compete as a reinforcement material in non-tire rubber applications such as belts and hoses.

other opps

KEVLAR IN COMPOSITE MATERIALS

The same promise and the same uncertainties for Kevlar existed in composite materials applications in the aircraft and aerospace industries. Composite materials—fiber-reinforced materials possessing the strength of aluminum alloys and steel but at significantly less weight—were in their infancy when Kevlar was first discovered. Nomex had been adopted by both Boeing and Lockheed in non-structural aircraft panel composites, securing for Du Pont a significant entry into the composite materials market. Kevlar's strength and modulus might allow it to enter structural composites as well. *Cannibalize Nomex?*

Airframe manufacturers placed a value on saving weight at $50 per pound, and if weight savings began to compound in aircraft design, thereby leading to major reductions in the weight of structural components, value added could go to as high as $150 per pound.

Fiberglass composites (made up of 50% to 60% glass fibers in a solid plastic matrix of epoxy or phenolic resins) had opened up and now dominated this market. Although stronger than metals along the reinforcement fiber axis, fiberglass composites were considerably weaker in other directions. Moreover, they fatigued more easily than metal and had low impact-resistance.

Kevlar's density was lower than glass fibers while possessing roughly the same tensile strength and a higher modulus. Substituting Kevlar for fiberglass meant weight reductions of at least 25%, suggesting added value of about $25 per pound in aircraft. Pricing the fiber at $10 to $15 per pound could bring high demand for Kevlar. The Textile Fibers Department had worked with a major aircraft manufacturer in its composite materials screening tests, and Kevlar seemed likely to help them resolve some serious weight problems with a new aircraft design when used in non-structural applications. And Kevlar drew attention from aircraft and aerospace companies for another reason: it absorbed radar. Kevlar might well become a big product for a new generation of top-secret military aircraft and missiles.

Military Apps

In the aircraft and aerospace markets, Kevlar would have to compete not only against fiberglass, but also carbon and boron fibers and possibly even aluminum fibers.

Already at least ten United States, British, and Japanese companies were supplying carbon fibers at $80 to $400 per pound. Kevlar possessed weight and strength advantages over carbon fibers, but composites made from carbon fibers were three times as stiff as similarly made Kevlar composites and therefore possessed greater attractiveness in structural applications. But carbon fibers had some severe production and handling problems, and Du Pont's technical staff thought that mixed-fiber composites of carbon and Kevlar might offer superior performance.

Boron fibers also were growing as a composite-reinforcing material. Boron was twice as stiff as Kevlar, but it sold at $200 to $300 per pound. Du Pont projected that boron fiber costs would fall to $50 to $100 when produced in million-pound quantities.

Managers believed that Kevlar had excellent opportunities in the aircraft and aerospace markets. But they warned that beyond the immediate substitution of Kevlar for fiberglass in non-structural applications, penetration in these markets would be slow because of the industry's need to prove out plastic composites in general and Kevlar in particular. They thought that demand for Kevlar in these markets might reach 11 million pounds by 1980.

THE CORPORATE CONTEXT, 1974

In addition to these uncertainties about the use of Kevlar fiber in the tire and aerospace industries, Du Pont's senior managers had one other concern. The Executive Committee understood that its decision on the Kevlar plant would mean not only a commitment of investment capital, but several years of operating losses. For several years Du Pont had been performing at levels below its historical norm. Even though sales had steadily increased since 1968, earnings had dipped. The Executive Committee knew that its 1960s commitment to a New Ventures Program intended to provide long-term growth and greater earnings had hurt the company in the short run. But the "New Ventures Era," as it had become known, was drawing to a close. (Indeed, in the early 1970s, the Executive Committee privately viewed the program as a failure.) To improve performance, the X-Committee had to watch its capital expenditures very carefully. The committee had invested a record amount of capital in 1973—$781 million, up from the 1972 record of $561 million. Prospects for capital expenditures for 1974 looked even more frightening. If the X-Committee granted all of the requests coming up from the departments (which it had historically done), the capital commitments would swell to well over $1 billion at a time when the company's cash reserves were running low for the first time in decades. (See Exhibit 6.)

EXHIBIT 6 E. I. du Pont de Nemours & Company Financial and Operating Data, 1947–1974

	Sales ($ million)	Operating income ($ million)	Operating investment ($ million)	Net return on operating investment (%)	Income from GM stock ($ million)	Construction expenditures ($ million)	% income paid as dividends (%)	Long-term debt ($ million)	Investment per employee ($ thousands)
1947	$ 783	$ 78	$ 1,016	7.7%	$ 42	$ 116	83%	$ 0	$14
1950	1,298	187	1,408	13.3	121	114	82	0	18
1953	1,750	153	1,866	8.2	83	135	78	0	20
1956	1,888	255	2,252	11.3	128	157	80	0	25
1959	2,114	288	2,745	10.5	131	174	79	0	33
1962	2,407	305	3,341	9.1	147	245	79	0	37
1965	3,400	419	5,238	8.6	—	369	68	43	42
1968	3,931	380	6,784	6.4	—	355	69	114	49
1971	4,371	357	7,700	4.9	—	474	68	236	64
1974	6,910	404	10,521	4.2	—	1,038	67	793	77

Source: Du Pont Company Annual Reports.

THE EXECUTIVE COMMITTEE'S DECISION

Accompanied by his assistant general managers, Howard Swank made his journey to the ninth floor of the Du Pont Building to answer questions about Kevlar raised by the Executive Committee and to advocate building the big commercial Kevlar plant. Swank felt strongly that Du Pont needed to build this plant to achieve the necessary economies of scale for Kevlar, thus allowing Du Pont to prosper during the market's transition to radial tires and to provide a clear statement to customers from the tire and aerospace industries that Kevlar was here to stay. The Kevlar venture was full of risks, but the Textile Fibers Department had been taking big risks throughout Swank's 35-year career in the department. Would the Executive Committee be willing to risk another $332 million for the uncertain rewards offered by the miracle fiber Kevlar? Swank would soon find out.

READING III-2

Transforming Invention into Innovation: The Conceptualization Stage

Robert A. Burgelman and Leonard R. Sayles

Understandably we think of strategy formulation as top management work. Most employees, even quite high-level managerial employees, take the goals of the business as a given. But in the high-technology world, strategy often revolves around the innovation activities of relatively low-level technical and business people. To be sure, their decisions will require ratification by top management. Nevertheless the reality is that those closer to the emerging technology will seek to define the business opportunity.

Creating a new business opportunity, however, goes beyond "invention." "Innovation" involves welding marketplace opportunities with inventive technology and new technical knowledge. This requires substantial skill and it is by no means a simple decision making process. For instance, a new plastic could or might be translated

---

Note: This is Chapter 3 of a book-length, detailed examination of the processes of technological innovation at a major corporation whose identity has been disguised as United Corporation. See Burgelman, R. & Sayles, L., *Inside Corporate Innovation,* New York: The Free Press, 1986. The quotations in this reading are all from employees and managers of United Corporation.

into any number of new products. Since there are still very many implementation unknowns as to how a laboratory breakthrough can be more completely understood, modified, and controlled—and eventually mass-produced economically—selecting the commercial applications of any new discovery is highly problematic. Marketing new products resulting from technological break-throughs is equally problematic. Depending on future technological developments, which are still unknown, one or more markets *may* be visible. But these markets can also be elusive, particularly when one is dealing with products that users have not previously experienced.

To lead to the development of a potentially successful new business, the marketing strategy must also take into account corporate interests. Further investment in business development will be forthcoming only if the definitions of the product and market are in a field that the company considers consistent with its legitimate domain, present and future. The process whereby the link between a new business and the corporate context becomes established involves complex strategic activities on the part of various levels of management; project initiators must (and do) attempt to anticipate whether a new development *could possibly* be acceptable given the "fabric" of the corporation. The notion of the "fabric" of the corporation is inherently vague, never quite completely delineated; it is always in the process of being stretched as a result of the strategic initiations that people at the operational level are attempting to engage in.

Thus three elements must be brought together by R&D managers and/or new-venture managers in their efforts at strategy formulation: (1) technical competency, (2) market need, and (3) corporate interest. How is this done? Whose job should it be? How can management evaluate whether it is being done effectively? Does a new venture fail because some failure is inevitable with all the unknowns present when the strategy must be formulated, or because the managerial patterns and practices in making the decision were faulty? To answer these questions one needs to know something about the process by which these decisions are made. And by process we mean how individual managers and scientists link up those three elements.

The history of corporate innovation is replete with the development of exciting new technical breakthroughs that did not lead to viable products. And, in fact, there is no reason to believe that most new knowledge has any immediate application. Basic researchers have warned that this is true, but there is the natural temptation to believe that new laboratory phenomena *must* have commercial implications and more naively, that the more interesting the breakthrough the greater is its commercial value.

In contrast, there are always efforts to define a market need and seek to "invent-to-order" a product for that need. The government occasionally even publishes lists of the most-wanted inventions, but such presumed market inducements, in themselves, don't seem to produce relevant new technologies.

CONCEPTUALIZATION OF NEW BUSINESS OPPORTUNITIES

The evolution of the method of managing this process at United appears to be similar to that which has taken place in many corporate R&D functions. Initially, when it was recognized that some welding of specializations was necessary, it was hoped that R&D could add market specialists on an ad hoc basis—as advisors or consultants when necessary. Gradually, as recognition of the importance of the marketing side grew, a permanent, formalized "business research function" was added to the R&D function to help shape new ventures and increase the odds that new products would be successfully commercialized.

Some senior managers expected that the market specialists would gradually take the lead in strategy formulation by seeking to define research objectives. Others assumed the scientists and business researchers would work together.

The managerial initiatives associated with R&D at this exploratory stage can be defined in three alternative patterns:

1. Marketing-oriented managers can direct scientists into what appear to be exciting markets with assured high demand. (This is often called, in fact, "demand pull.") Here innovation, the need, is father to (or mother to) the new "invention."
2. Scientists, attuned to the realities of the corporation's interests, look for new technologies and scientific breakthroughs with good commercialization potential. (This is called "technology push.")
3. Marketing and scientific specialists work together, bringing their own skills to a joint endeavor to develop new technology with sound market possibilities.

Any of these three patterns is a good theoretical possibility, but only one predominated at United.

THE PREDOMINANCE OF "TECHNOLOGY PUSH"

At United, it was clear that most new-product efforts got their initial definition on the basis of "technology push."[1] In part, this reflected the need for highly sophisticated knowledge about science and technology, about what is feasible and what isn't, about what the odds are that something can be accomplished, and about what the resulting new product is likely to have in the way of basic characteristics. While it sounds feasible that dialogues should occur between business and science spokespeople, they may be less constructive at this very early stage than they obviously are at a somewhat later stage of the development process. An example may show why the "partnership" arrangement is not as productive as would be presumed:

> The laboratory has pioneered in developing a new high-strength material. Given its characteristics market research said the new material's ideal application was vehicle parts, because of its strength-to-weight ratio. Furthermore, given their knowledge of motor vehicle manufacturers, market research proposed one or two vehicle parts that would represent an ideal market to penetrate. Unfortunately these specific uses would require further technological breakthroughs that would be incredibly difficult to guarantee. In fact, the laboratory scientists estimated that there might be only a handful of researchers in the world who could make the needed technological advances. The market researchers never could appreciate why it was so difficult to go from the basic discovery to the ultimate commercial application they had envisioned.

There will be dozens if not hundreds of such trade-offs among cost, feasibility, and application that require a great deal of technical knowledge and experience. In addition, United placed great emphasis on what it called attaining a "sustainable position." It sought to have a "technological lock" on any new product. While it is questionable that patents represent an absolute barrier to competition, United sought to develop unique, patentable technologies.

It is not surprising then that the major trade-offs and early decisions at United were made inside the head of a single technically trained person. Usually this individual would be a technologist who wanted to accomplish an impressive business goal such as developing a product that would have enormous economic implications. These scientist-entrepreneurs took it upon themselves to link up their conception of what ideas are marketable with new technological discoveries coming both from within and outside of their own laboratory.

They often traveled around the world gleaning information on potentially marketable scientific breakthroughs. Their goal was to tie together emerging knowledge with a challenging technical issue or problem.

Here is a typical example of how an R&D scientist develops interests and seeks to develop projects that will lead to new products.

Opportunities, in my view, come up as technical problems. As a result of certain interest trends in my division, I had gotten interested in molecules that had been heated up to high temperatures. Because the technical problems usually turn out to be quite different than they are initially defined, I come to see much more fundamental questions . . . which is what led me to engage in research at the frontiers of organic chemistry.

In the field at the time there was one particular technical problem that interested me . . . a very difficult to control transformation process. There was a researcher in France who had learned how to exercise fine control. I thought that if I could really learn how the process works, how to control it, it would surely have some real business applications.

Essentially these scientists—through reading and contacts in the field—identify exciting frontier areas in their respective fields that appear to have some conceivable relationship to what have been defined as corporate interests. They also of course seek to link up new developments that have been created in other parts of their corporate R&D world, that is, the R&D sectors of the operating divisions.

Ten years ago I and others became aware of the fact that our corporation was developing substantial new technology in one aspect of the electronic controls field. This led to a separate division being created, and I began working on controls as applied to the health field, but with the recession it became difficult to get a heavy R&D commitment to that area. Therefore I was pleased when I got shifted to the corporate R&D labs which had a health-related technology program. There we looked for health applications of the kind of technology we were developing that would be a major market.

About this time I visited another lab of the corporation and I met a scientist there who had developed a unique but related technology that could be developed, I felt, into a product that would be far superior to anything in the field.

Broadly speaking, the experienced technologist looks for ideas and scientific breakthroughs that might provide new-product leverage. Often this means linking up work being done in the corporate R&D laboratory with data being generated in some other organization. Through personal contacts, reading, and attending meetings the scientist does what management personnel call "environmental scanning," that is, seeking to see some synthesis or synergy between ideas and fields of knowledge that competitors may have missed

We were pursuing a field of inquiry relating to some development going on in one of the operating divisions and I thought I should try to put the two together. When I began working with them, I gained access to some complementary research in a government laboratory on the West Coast

EXHIBIT 1 The Flow of Activities in the "Technology Push" Model

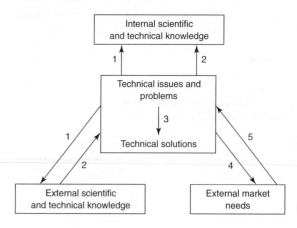

that they had been collaborating with. I was now getting close to something that might have some real commercial possibilities.

This is what management should expect of its R&D personnel: the ability not only to conduct relevant research but to monitor and link up with other relevant work wherever it may be going on, and to see some overall pattern or implication in these diverse streams.

Exhibit 1 represents a model embodying the typical sequence of "linkages" followed in the evolution of a technology-driven exploratory strategy.

Such linkages can fail, of course, even when technical personnel find interesting problems and possible solutions but when their ideas do not match corporate interests and cannot be woven into the corporate "fabric":

In another case, I was interested in high-temperature materials and that got me into boron chemistry. This was also the result of my interacting with colleagues in academia. I began to get interested in making these boron-based materials less expensively, but these materials were outside of the corporation's experience. There was some interest in the Defense Department and we came very close to proving its business importance, but the linking-up failed; we couldn't get corporate management interested; it was out of their realm.

Thus, the technologist still faces the problem of gaining financial support for his conception. This is the classic chicken-and-egg problem. It is difficult to "prove" the usefulness of this new approach without adequate funding. But adequate funding usually depends upon being able to show very good data and results, which in turn require that funding. "Bootleg research" is one first step around this vicious circle.

At times changing circumstances convert a skimpily supported effort to an all-out campaign. The energy crisis of a couple of years ago was one of the most profound stimulants.

> We had been working on new types of insulation for years but when the energy crisis occurred everyone realized that we might have a number of immediate applications. I knew of our experience and work in this area and I formulated a proposal for a 2- to 5-year effort for our top management review committee. As an additional impetus I was able to show that moving on this front would help us move in a direction that had *often* been talked about in the *corporation*—*getting out of* becoming a basic supplier of commodity-type materials into higher-margined finished products.

Problems with "Technology Push"

But such enthusiasm and confidence cannot compensate for some defects inherent in an overemphasis on "technology push." Perhaps the most obvious is that a scientist-entrepreneur's orientation toward understanding some basic phenomenon and solving a *tough* technological problem will tend to encourage market applications that are the most easily researched and evaluated.

> In one of our cases, a new material being developed was applied to a rather easily fabricated consumer product. In fact, as a marketing person added later to the project later discovered, the real potential application was in a very different class of product.

A more serious pitfall of technology-driven projects is that they are more likely to get locked into a particular technical solution.

> The company developed an interest in a high-technology area in the biological field. The efforts were directed by a Ph.D. who some years before had developed an innovative method of separating materials at the molecular level. Such separation was an important step in producing certain new products in which we became interested. But, as we later realized, Dr. X's technique, as interesting as it was, wasn't the best way of making the transition to large-scale manufacture. But as long as Dr. X was in charge, alternative methods would not be explored.

Of course, one could argue—with some justification—that if Dr. X hadn't helped make the initial technological breakthrough the company might not have become interested in this particular biological field. However, at the early conceptual stage it is important to keep options open. A specific technological innovation may have hidden defects or may turn out to be less useful than predicted for the class of end products that are most marketable. As long as the key decisions are being made

primarily by the "father of the invention" it is possible that ends will be confused with means. Here is another example:

> Another researcher developed a new type of seed tape which was designed for large-scale agricultural use. Further exploration disclosed that such a process would be useful primarily in greenhouses growing seedlings, not in open fields. The real market opportunity was seen now as producing transplants rather than simply a new seed carrier (i.e., the tape).

A related pitfall of the "technology push" mode is that there is a tendency to address the needs of atypical users and to invoke their acceptance of the new product, process, or system as evidence for the existence of a new business "opportunity." The scientist-entrepreneur has a knack for coming up with convincing evidence to demonstrate the "interest" of prospective users. As one scientist-turned-business manager put it, "If you address yourself to the 'right' people in any market, you will hear them say: 'Wow! This is what we have been waiting for.' [2] This process of selectively addressing atypical potential customers is especially dangerous if the technical linking-up process has not been adequately performed to begin with. Early success with an inadequate technical system used by an atypical customer can lead to the erroneous projection of market potential.

While we have said that successful technologists-entrepreneurs do concern themselves with the user marketplace (and the corporate marketplace for ideas), they are limited in the sophistication with which they can do this. Those with business training and experience, particularly in analyzing and estimating markets, can make an important contribution. In fact, it is often felt that such people should take the initiative in defining a new-product strategy.

"NEED PULL" DOMINANCE

Experienced management consultants like McKinsey believe that R&D can be targeted—in advance—by specific market goals:

> An experienced photochemist, Dr. Hans Schleussner, owner-manager of a medium-sized West German pharmaceutical company, put together a three-person team to work on a project to develop blood substitutes. It took them just 2 1/2 years to find a plasma substitute, which led to the establishment of a new business for Schleussner, revived the entire market for gelatine preparations, and left the large pharmaceutical companies to catch up, at great expense, over the next 3 to 4 years.[3]

EXHIBIT 2 The Flow of Activities in the "Need Pull" Model

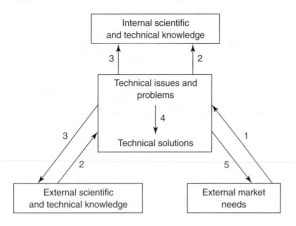

From a personnel point of view, a major distinction of "need pull" from "technology push" is a division of labor. In the "need pull" model, the definition and exploration of markets are usually handled by a business/marketing-trained specialist. This individual's identification of a high-potential market initiates a search process for inside- or outside-the-firm technical knowledge that might be used to develop an innovative product to enter that market.

The actual sequence we observed is depicted in Exhibit 2.

Experienced new-venture managers recognize that market needs have to be defined in terms that avoid the following two extremes: superficial broad generalizations (e.g., "materials for home building") or very narrow applications with limited potential (e.g., "cabinet hinge material"). To bridge these extremes, a narrowing or focusing process takes place. But this too has its own problems. In particular, the process breeds confusion for the R&D people, who must keep redesigning their technology to fit a perpetually moving target. Or, immediate market demands may override a consideration of more fundamental long-range trends. For instance, in the early 1970s a company called "Accuracy" acquiesced to its salespeople's demand for a process control system that would use both digital and analog computers, ignoring the trend that would make analog computers obsolete.[4]

Also, too many market-oriented compromises can destroy a basically sound innovative idea. John Newhouse[5] tells the story of an aeronautical engineer with American Airlines who foresaw the need for smaller jets. He wanted to develop a two-engine, relatively lightweight plane seating *150* passengers, which would fill the airline's need for a practical, economical plane to fly out of LaGuardia to the Midwest. As McDonnell Douglas and Lockheed explored other customer requirements, they saw that there was a need for more range and climbing ability—with the resulting addition of more weight. A plane with more weight required a third engine; this led to the development of the DC-10 and the L-1011, two planes with essentially the same design. The market for a smaller plane was completely missed and was eventually filled first by a European manufacturer with the A-300B aircraft (Airbus Industrie).

Following the same line of thought, users or customers often do not have a clear idea of their own needs with respect to a truly new product, and "conventional wisdom" about customers or users can kill a potentially successful innovation. *The New York Times* recently told about a GE engineer who invented the cassette in 1952, "But he left his important invention to gather dust after a GE executive told him, 'There is no future in tape.'"[6]

When the sought-for innovation is going to be an element in a larger system manufactured by an outside user, the market research problems can be most complex and there will be great leeway for error.

> We were designing a key component for aircraft using our new Z material. The more we looked the more we realized how much we needed to understand the interaction of almost all of the components and particularly the effect of stressful usage and what future maintenance people will want and how they will operate. Simply designing a first-rate component was a long way from the solution.
>
> So you learn that you cannot seek to develop a new part in isolation; you need to analyze all the stresses in the system as they impact the part and then translate these into requirements of your new high-strength material and see how you can design it to minimize the more costly elements.

If one of the risks of "technology push" is developing a solution for which there turns out to be no problem, the "need pull" approach faces the possibly greater risk of not being able to generate the required technology to solve an existing problem either in-house or through acquisition. Said one participant from the business side:

> Many applications have started with a given technology. The problem is then to see how you build a business with that technology, how to acquire a proprietary position and capitalize on it. Our "plating" business actually started with a focus on the larger market and the identification of opportunities, and we then tried to develop the technology. It's a more risky approach. You might do a lot of fine work but never reach your goals. One alternative way is to use an acquisition strategy. But that is very risky too. Even if you buy ten com-

panies, there can still be an eleventh one that has the real key to the technology.

Perhaps the most serious shortcoming of "need pull" is the absence of a "true believer." For the new-business market analyst, this potential product is but one of a number that may be in the process of being researched. There is no assurance that even "if it flies" it will be backed up by the new-business marketing specialist. Not only is future promise lacking as an additional motivation, but there is no past commitment. After all, the idea is usually not the brainchild of the analyst who has been assigned to investigate its commercial potential.

In contrast, the technical person who becomes a "product champion" has a sense of being identified with an idea or a discovery or at least with a systematic line of research reflecting his or her own competencies and interest. Even more importantly, in United as in many corporate R&D laboratories, a successful definition of a new-product venture can bring with it the possibility of major advancement. It can become a vehicle for increased visibility, for becoming a new-venture manager and even the head of a major new business. And as we have noted before, some scientists in corporate laboratories find these highly appealing prospects; they really do want to jump from pure research to pure management.

Projects at this exploratory stage meet lots of resistance in the laboratory, the marketplace, and the corporate budget process. To some extent their viability depends upon gaining momentum—giving key managers the sense that this project has favorable odds and is moving forward. Hence, a degree of initial success is necessary to attract interest and support.

THE DOUBLE LINKING REQUIRED

We have been describing the technical-linking and need-linking processes. Both are necessary for successful innovation.

Technical linking requires someone who can combine a promising technical problem (e.g., increasing the durability of a fiber)—one that is recognized as falling within the broad boundaries of the corporation's domains of interest—with external and/or internal scientific knowledge. The researcher-conceptualizer views the *solution* of this technical problem as both feasible and relevant. It is by means of the technical sophistication possessed by the researcher-conceptualizer that this individual can recognize that this is a sensible, realistic problem to be working on at this time. The process of technical linking leads to the realization that working on a particular problem

represents taking a "logical" step forward, one that may lead to a possible technological breakthrough with profitable consequences for the corporation.

The other linking-up that must be undertaken at the same time relates to needs. It represents the ability to perceive interrelationships between these existing or potential technical breakthroughs in the laboratory and actual or potential market demand. Essentially this linking asserts that if X can be accomplished, and routinized—commercialized within a suitable price range—then there will be a market of this size.

"TECHNOLOGY PUSH" AND "NEED PULL" MODELS COMPARED

Below we have summarized the deficiencies and shortcomings of the two approaches to strategy formulation at the exploratory stage:

"TECHNOLOGY PUSH"	"NEED PULL"
• Start with what easily can be researched and evaluated	• Look at needs that are easily identified but with minor potential
• Address the needs of the atypical user	• Continue to change the definition of the "opportunity"; "miss the opportunity"
• Get locked into one technical solution	• Lack a "champion" or "true believer"

CORPORATE INTERESTS

New-venture projects of the nature described here typically fall outside of the current strategy of the firm. To be sure, as we described earlier, top management seeks to define the industries and business that it would find appealing. To the extent that these go beyond the interests of the operating divisions, however, they are so broadly defined (for example, "health," "food," or "energy") as to be virtually useless as a guide for concrete action. In fact, what we found was the emergence of new fields out of small areas of commercial activity related to specific projects originating at the operational level. This was most clear from the analysis of the written documents at United. In 1975, the corporate long-range plan for the new-venture division read:

> Instead of dealing with an ever-growing number of separate arenas, attention should be focused on a critical few major fields, within each of which arenas may be expanded, grouped together, or added.

EXHIBIT 3   Three Elements Requiring Linkage

1 Relevant "problems"	2 Technology sources	3 Market demand
As defined by top management's professed "interests"	Researcher's personal interests	Marketer's personal search
Problems of operating divisions	Existing corporate expertise	Areas of customer dissatisfaction
New opportunities created by external events	New technological developments	Potential for new need satisfaction

Yet no matter who seeks to be the proponent of a new venture and argue its viability, ultimately it must be accepted by higher management. Proponents of new ventures, therefore, needed to understand what kind of project would be acceptable to top management. Even more important, it seemed, was their capability to stay away from projects that would be perceived by top management as *not* consistent with the external image of the firm, or that might lead to dangerous potential legal liabilities. In the health field, for instance, people knew that top management was concerned about entering therapeutic rather than diagnostic segments.

Thus, the three elements must be considered together in order to define a viable new business opportunity (Exhibit 3).

It was, then, perhaps not surprisingly, a group leader who usually turned out to be the driving force in the definition of a new business opportunity. Such people have enough contact with the substantive research process to understand and direct the technical-linking process, sufficient contact with the business side to think in terms of market needs, and the organizational experience required to understand how new technological breakthroughs could be "woven into the fabric" of the firm.

EFFECTIVE CONCEPTUALIZATION

Such successful managers are synthesizers, able to put together and link ongoing technical streams with existing corporate commitments and directions and then to relate these to market needs. Success is dependent on the simultaneous, almost serendipitous occurrence of a number of mutually compatible requirements and resources. The link to the market is frequently neglected: the explicit requirements of customers, competitive pressures, size and durability of the demand, and opportunities for synergies and economies of scale.

A remarkable example of the importance of having people who can perform the *double* linking process is provided by the story of Steve Jobs of Apple Computer visiting Xerox's Palo Alto Research Center:

In December 1979, Steve Jobs, then Apple's vice-chairman, visited PARC with some colleagues to poke around. They saw "smalltalk," a set of programming tools. "Their eyes bugged out," recalls Lawrence Tesler who helped develop "smalltalk." "They understood its significance better than anyone else who had visited." Seven months later, Jobs hired Tesler, having decided to use many "smalltalk" features in the Lisa.[7]

Here is a carefully conceptualized strategy that meets our criteria:

United's focus should be on certain special organic acids that have a very complex molecular structure, are difficult to synthesize and where various governmental and market forces assure a premium price for the output of the type of processing we will be doing and where a number of related products can be developed that will allow us to build an economical multipurpose facility.

A small number of development managers have the skill and insight to combine the technological and market emphases at this very early stage of the cycle. The example below represents one of the most successful innovations we followed:

I had worked in the computer field and knew the importance of matching a technology with the market configuration. When I took on the Z project I soon learned that the technology we were utilizing had also been adopted by another company seeking to enter this same market.

My company had gotten very interested in a novel idea being developed by one of the scientists in one of our satellite laboratories. After some discussion it was clear that this could be directly applied to the development of a new line of diagnostic instruments that would have major advantages over what is now being produced. The scientist, however, was very rigid: the equipment had to follow his original conceptions and breakthroughs.

As Z project manager I insisted on doing market research, and from that learned of customer needs that would not be satisfied by the original conception. We also learned that there was a substantial market to be tapped having to do with the reagents needed to operate the equipment. So we ended up with a radical departure, using only the nucleus of the scientist's physical concepts. We added a very different data "reader," a minicomputer, and so forth.

Even when the two processes—technology and market linkages—are combined there is no guarantee of success. The following case is typical of how a company develops interests in funding a new area of development and some of the ensuing problems:

> The corporation recognized there might be some commercial potential in its filtration expertise. I wrote a position paper on the state of the art in this field and where we stood. It was decided we should do further work in the area. In the course of our R&D work we developed a unique product that seemed to have applications to the pollution problems of one particular major industry. We even were able to develop a test installation.
>
> I now had proof of a well-operating installation, so I asked myself how many of these installations could be needed in the market: ten thousand or so? Now I had to make a judgment as to how many of these potential customers were likely to go our way. To do so, you must know the alternatives for these customers; you must talk to the pollution control people. Then you must put together these facts, and on this basis—what people have told you—you make your projections.
>
> Eventually, a market study was done that said that there was not going to be a big enough market for a gas separation method but there was a hint in the report—and it was really just a hint—that there just might be an opportunity for liquid filtering. So we got into it and soon found out that the product we had was not adequate!

A CLASSIFICATION SCHEME

As we review the examples above, it seems relatively easy to allot them to one of the cells in the matrix shown in Exhibit 4. While we would be hard-pressed to provide statistical proof, the most successful ventures appeared to be those in quadrant II (double linking).

Most new ventures in R&D-oriented corporations appear to be in the domain of technology. The technology managers concentrate on linking up inside and outside knowledge in the development of prototype solutions (product, process, or system) that will also be consistent with some market or need analysis. As that is defined and there is some proof of technical feasibility, the first business plans are conceptualized.

INNOVATION TRAPS

While at times there is extraordinarily good fortune and the original conceptualization turns out to be the best, more realistically better definitions are made when there

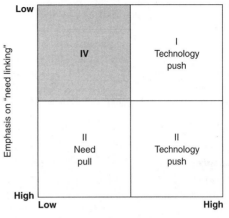

EXHIBIT 4   Emphasis on "Technical Linking" and "Need Linking"

is flexibility and modification. Innovative technology stimulates the search for commercial applications. Efforts to explore potential business applications reveal defects in the original technological conception leading to the search for modified or different technological approaches. For such flexibility to be present during conceptualization it is important that scientists maintain their perspective. Being overly committed or identified with a given "solution" can injure the scientist's ability to realistically appraise technological breakthroughs in the light of market considerations. Such scientists observably err by defining the problems with which they are coping in such narrow terms that only one solution, namely "their" solution, will do.

Management can evaluate the quality of their developmental personnel by observing which individuals have the flexibility to modify or even drop technical solutions in the light of new data, new constraints, or need-derived problems. Such researchers may begin a project with great enthusiasm for a specific breakthrough they have made or have become familiar with, but as their research progresses they are able to spot the flaws in this particular technology and seek alternatives. Often the alternatives can turn out to be even more worthwhile than the original breakthrough.

> During the early days of the National Aeronautics and Space Administration (NASA) science program it was decided to orbit a telescope, and the chief scientist evolved a design that included a very costly lens that could be produced only in one foreign laboratory. Both the cost and the delay inherent in procuring that particular lens motivated the person to link the chief scientist with the engineers who

would actually be responsible for the satellite, and the need for that particular lens was challenged. The proponent of the lens insisted that it was the only one that would provide the resolution power that designated use demanded. When he was told that it could not be procured because the whole program would suffer costly delays, he was able to modify another lens that had been developed in the United States. The cost was a fraction of the original estimate of the foreign lens and the new lens proved even more powerful than the original specifications demanded.[8]

There can also be too much flexibility. On the market side this can reflect itself in unrealistic demands for invention or technical solutions because "this is what the market demands." Sometimes this leads to expectations and even promises to management that can't be delivered. Those in charge of marketing may be unresponsive to what scientists say is feasible or deliverable. In this case the wish is not father to the child, so to speak.

There may also be too much flexibility on the technical side when, for instance, scientists jump in too quickly to fill a niche that has been defined by top management or the environment as timely and obviously supportable. When it is too easy to get funding and encouragement, scientists may fail to "do their homework" and may rush to implement a new technology that has not been worked through and questioned adequately, or seek to find an "all-purpose" solution to a broad and complex problem like the energy crisis.

Finally, a trap can exist at this conceptualization stage when the market success of the innovation is too dependent on a potentially variable environmental component of the market. United got trapped into developing costly or cumbersome pollution control systems that could only be viable with a strict level of governmental enforcement of certain regulations. Similar mistakes can be made when it is assumed in a cavalier fashion that a given resource that is now in short supply will always be in short supply or, alternatively, that a surplus of a given resource will exist forever.

NOTES

1. The concepts of "technology push" and "need pull" were introduced by Donald Schon. See D. Schon, *Technology and Social Change,* Delacorte, New York, 1967.
2. Another recent example is from Gould, Inc. In 1981, Gould followed its successful K-100 logic analyzer with an oversophisticated and over-priced K-101 model. As one former Gould manager put it, the K-101 was a product that "only the lunatic fringe of the customer base would appreciate." See "Gould Reshapes Itself into High-Tech Outfit Amid Much Turmoil," *Wall Street Journal,* October 3, 1984.
3. H. Henzler, "Functional Dogmas That Frustrate Strategy," *McKinsey Quarterly,* Winter 1982, p. 26. See also F. W. Gluck and R. N. Foster, "Managing Technological Change: A Box of Cigars for Brad," *Harvard Business Review,* 55, September–October 1978.
4. *Wall Street Journal,* September 3, 1981.
5. J. Newhouse, *The Sporty Game,* Knopf, New York, 1982.
6. *New York Times,* August 4, 1982.
7. "The Lab That Ran Away from Xerox," *Fortune,* September 5, 1983, p. 100.
8. L. R. Sayles and M. Chandler, *Managing Large Systems,* Harper & Row, New York, 1971.

READING III-3

Technology Markets, Technology Organization, and Appropriating the Returns from Research

Clayton M. Christensen and Henry W. Chesbrough

ABSTRACT

This paper recounts three phases of the evolution of two key hard disk drive technologies from the early 1970s until the late 1990s. Contrary to recent research that predicts a trend towards greater modularity, this history shows that key disk drive technologies evolved from technological interdependence to technological modularity, and then cycled back to interdependence. Organizational structures generally remained inert during these shifts, until the most recent period.

From this history, we inductively derive a contingency framework of the technological and organizational factors that affect a company's ability to capture the returns from its research. In our framework, the state of the technology and the organizational configuration of the firm must be aligned with each other, in order to appropriate

Source: Harvard Business School Working Paper Series, 2001. We wish to thank Professors Ken Kusunoki, Keith Pavitt, Richard Rosenbloom, James Utterback, Jonathan West, Steven Wheelwright; Drs. Michael Raynor and Philip Roussel; and Matt Verlinden for their invaluable assistance in improving earlier drafts of this paper.

these returns. The proper alignment varies with these two factors. We analyze the component choices in each of 3,894 disk drive models, and find that disk drive heads appear to be more interdependent than thin film disks. We also find that firms that make their own heads are able to achieve higher technical performance from their designs than do firms that make their own disks.

We conclude that firms must develop and retain systems level knowledge on the one hand, and make more aggressive use of intermediate markets when feasible on the other hand, if they are to profit from their research investments as the character of their key technologies shifts over time.

I. INTRODUCTION

Scholars have long noted that the technology of the firm shapes the organization of that firm (Burns and Stalker, 1961; Woodward, 1960). More recent scholarship has shown that the organization of the firm also conditions its ability to profit from its innovation activities (Teece, 1986). A number of scholars have examined the role of the type of technology in the ability of incumbent firms to adapt to innovation opportunities (Abernathy and Utterback, 1978; Tushman and Anderson, 1986; Anderson and Tushman, 1990; Henderson and Clark, 1990; Christensen, 1997). Some have argued that the organizational strategy of the firm must be aligned with the type of technology they choose to develop (Chesbrough and Teece, 1996; Tushman and O'Reilly, 1997).

This paper builds on this prior research by developing a contingency framework for firms to align their organizational strategy with the technology that they are pursuing. It advances the idea that the character of technology is not static; rather, it evolves from one type which we will term interdependent (to be defined below) to an opposite type we will term modular (also to be defined below). As a given architecture reaches its technical performance limits, an impetus is created to discover new technologies, which causes the evolution to cycle from modularity within the architecture back to an interdependent new architecture. As the technology shifts from one phase to the other, the optimal organizational configuration of the firm must also shift, if the firm is to continue to capture value from its innovation activities.

Our conception highlights the role of intermediate markets, which arise in the interfaces between research, development, design, and manufacturing. The presence or absence of these markets is determined by the character of the technology, where modular technologies are asso-

ciated with significant intermediate markets, while interdependent technologies imply sparse intermediate markets. Every company's organization of its technology development efforts must take the presence or absence of these markets into account.

The remainder of the paper is organized as follows. In the second section, we provide a history of technological changes in the heads and media of a hard disk drive used for storing data in a computer. This section shows the evolution of technology towards greater modularity and the corresponding response of firms. In the third section, we introduce a more recent history of a new technological advance in the drive industry, which moved the industry away from modularity, and towards more interdependent technological solutions. We sketch the organizational responses of firms to this change as well. In the fourth section, we analyze data from 3,894 disk drive models and examine the contrasting behavior of head and disk componentry in disk drives. We then develop our framework as a hypothesis that explains organizational alignment with the character of technology. The fifth section offers conclusions and directions for further research.

II: THE EVOLUTION OF KEY DISK DRIVE TECHNOLOGIES

Definitions

Before reviewing the history of key disk drive component technologies, it will be helpful to define several important terms. *Components* are devices fabricated from materials that are the building blocks of intermediate or end-use products. Components embody the fundamental technological concepts upon which products are based (Henderson and Clark, 1990). For example, the magnetic data recording technology upon which tape and disk drives are based resides in the recording heads, tapes, and disks employed in the products. Optical recording products employ different technology, embodied in different components. The *architecture* of products and components defines the working relationship amongst the components and/or materials of which they are comprised. The following history is part of a larger, detailed research program investigating the patterns of technology development in that industry in the United States and also in Japan (see Christensen, 1993, 1997; and Chesbrough, 1999a, 1999b).

For most of the first three decades in the computer industry's history, IBM was the undisputed leader in developing and manufacturing a range of data storage products based upon magnetic recording technology. In a manner modeled by Abernathy & Utterback (1978), the early years of IBM's magnetic recording technology development were characterized by extensive experimentation with product design. IBM first began using magnetic tape storage with its early computers in 1953. In 1956, engineers at its newly established magnetic information storage laboratories in San Jose, California, completed development of the world's first machine to store data on rigid rotating disks. Named the RAMAC (for Random Access Method for Accounting and Control), the world's first disk drive took the space of two large side-by-side refrigerators; stored data on fifty 24-inch disks mounted on a single spindle; and for all this, packed 5 megabytes (MB) of capacity.

The IBM RAMAC was an *architectural* innovation—its inventors used known technology and available materials in new ways to craft a machine that worked (Henderson and Clark, 1990). This is frequently the case in the development of new categories of products—initial models often employ known technology and commercially available materials and components.

These earliest disk drives worked, but rarely worked well. In fact, the earliest customers did not have clear definitions of which attributes of the product would be the most important. This understanding could only coalesce as these early products began to be used.[1]

Between 1956 and 1964, the dimensions of performance along which customers needed improvement became clear, and innovating firms began to be pressured by customers and competitors to advance along this technological trajectory (Dosi, 1982). IBM initially was able to find these improvements within the network of component suppliers it had cultivated around its San Jose development and manufacturing operations. By the mid-1960s, however, IBM determined that its independent component suppliers could not provide the rate of improvement in component performance that it required, and the company integrated backward into designing and producing many of its components. This required IBM, in turn, to begin *research* activities that would yield the advanced technology to be embodied in those components. This was the genesis, in about 1964, of the company's research activities in magnetic recording. As it did this, IBM's innovative energies shifted away from the architectural creativity that was so important to the establishment of the product category, and focused instead on improving the materials and components employed in the product.[2]

Technological Interdependence

IBM was not simply integrated upstream into components and materials in order to assure supply. It had to employ highly integrated product development processes as well, because the design of most components depended upon the way other components were designed and upon the design of the product's architecture. The interaction between the components and the architecture was not well understood, and was continually shifting as each element advanced. When component interactions within a system are not well characterized and understood, we term the architecture *interdependent* (Ulrich, 1995). As Christensen and Verlinden (2000) have shown, the need to eke maximum technological performance out of a design forces companies to employ interdependent architectures.

As the dominant manufacturer of magnetic recording products in the 1960s and 1970s, IBM was best able to afford the research costs inherent in being in the component business and had the scale and scope required to manage interdependent design problems. But *every* firm that wanted to play in the disk drive industry during these years had to incur these costs or exit the industry. The advanced components required to keep pace with the industry's technological trajectory were not commercially available, because the technologies were rapidly evolving and poorly understood. Hence, each of the early participants in the industry—including Burroughs, Control Data, Univac, Honeywell, Storage Technology, Digital Equipment, Xerox, Ampex, Fujitsu, Hitachi, and NEC—integrated backward into the manufacture of components and the research required to support their development. Suppliers of earlier ferrite core heads were unable to continue to offer new components in this market, and the component supply in disk drives became almost entirely captive.

The interdependence of disk drive technologies at this time was both a blessing and a curse. It was a blessing in that it created a pervasive barrier to entry in the industry. Independent manufacturers of most components could not exist because their would-be customers were unable to specify what they needed, and the interaction of variability in key component parameters on the performance of other components was not well understood. In industry parlance, firms could not "fully characterize their technology" and how it would perform under a wide range of conditions.

But technological interdependence was also a curse in that it made the product design process costly and managerially difficult. It would be far simpler if a project manager could in essence say to one group, "You go off and design the head"; to another group, "You design the disk"; and so on, and then assemble the pieces together at the end. They could not do this, however, unless they could specify to each of these groups which attributes of their components they needed to meet and to what tolerances. They needed to be able to measure these attributes unambiguously; and they needed to understand how changes in the design of one component would affect the required design of other components. In other words, technological modularity could vastly simplify the problems of management by obviating the need for so much interaction during development (Sanchez and Mahoney, 1996).

IBM took a major step toward a modular architectural design in 1964, at the same time that it designed its first modular mainframe computer, the IBM Series 360 (Pugh et al., 1991; Baldwin and Clark, 2000). However, while the technical design of the 360 was far more modular than earlier IBM designs, there were no decoupling markets for components to supplant managerial coordination across the interface between components and product design, as Christensen and Verlinden (2000) and Baldwin and Clark (2000) suggest may ultimately happen. The supply of components in system 360- and 370-class mainframes remained almost entirely captive.

This is because at the outset the interface standards amongst the modules were internal and proprietary. Under such conditions of "internal modularity," companies such as IBM could subcontract the design and manufacture of components to third-party suppliers, while its competitors could not use those same unmodified components. Later, through reverse engineering, departing employees, and technical conferences, IBM's internal interfaces became better understood and emerged as industry standards. Then "market modularity" occurred and new entrants could offer components using widely accepted interface standards. It took several years after IBM and its competitors achieved internal modularity before market modularity emerged. And as the following case histories and analysis show, it happened much faster in disks than in heads.

We define architectures as modular when their constituent components meet the following conditions:

1. The required attributes of components in the system can be specified.
2. Tools and equipment exist to verify that the required attributes of components have been met.
3. The interactions between the components in the architecture are well understood, and the effects of changes to components upon the system can be predicted.[3]

Modularity brought to IBM and its competitors all of the benefits in speed, flexibility, and design cost savings that Baldwin and Clark (2000) describe. But it brought problems as well. The same specifications, measurement

technology, and understanding of interactions that enabled internal component development groups to work at arms length with product designers made it possible for external suppliers to produce components that would meet those same specifications. This shifted the sources of value-added in disk drives, a shift that would prove difficult for vertically integrated producers with captive component supply operations to manage.

This shift occurred in three phases: the emergence of (1) thin film heads, (2) thin film disks, and (3) magneto-resistive head technologies. Each of these phases entailed the integration of everything from basic science through end product design, and all exemplify the management challenge of coordinating the disparate character of materials, components, and the design of products that can use those components. However, they had very different paths of diffusion into the market and hence comprise something of a natural experiment.

Thin Film Heads

IBM's original recording head design, called ferrite heads, consisted of an electromagnet formed by coiling fine copper wire around ferrite (iron oxide) cores. By the mid-1970s, recording head technology had become modular enough that a market for standard-design heads had emerged. These were supplied by independent manufacturers such as Applied Magnetics.

A primary factor limiting recording density was the size and precision of these electromagnets. Ferrite heads had to be ground mechanically to achieve desired tolerances, and by the mid-1970s, many felt the performance limits of ground ferrite heads were being approached. As early as 1965, researchers posited that by sputtering thin films of metal on the recording head and then using photolithography to etch electromagnets on the head's surface, smaller but more powerful electromagnets could result, enabling more precise orientation of smaller magnetic domains on the disk surface. Starting in about 1965 in its Yorktown Heights, New York, research center, IBM alone wrestled with understanding basic scientific issues in the physics of magnetic recording and the properties of new materials—issues that needed to be better understood before the feasibility of thin film head development could be realistically assessed. This phase of foundation-building scientific inquiry lasted about six years. By 1971, no thin film heads existed, but the *concept*—the technological feasibility—had been worked out through theory and general experimentation. IBM proudly announced its conceptual breakthrough in 1971.

IBM's announcement spurred its rivals to begin their own thin film research and development activities.

Although thin film photolithography was well established in the semiconductor industry, its application to recording heads proved extraordinarily difficult. Read-write heads required much thicker films than did integrated circuits; the surfaces to be coated were often at different levels; and they had to be sloped in order to "fly" over the spinning disk surface. Nonetheless, IBM's announcement indicated that these challenges could be surmounted.

Once working thin film head prototypes had been made and tested (by about 1976), a manufacturing process engineering effort was initiated, and the tortuous process of designing the component into a new disk drive model was begun. This was tortuous because the thin film head was an interdependent technology—the design of the head depended upon the design of other components in the system and upon the architecture of the system itself. And the designs of these other elements of the product in turn were predicated on the design of the head. Product development teams intending to employ thin film technology therefore had to do their work in a tightly integrated manner, because of these complex, poorly understood technological interactions. And because of the modularity of earlier designs, none of them had a practiced process for doing this: the earlier, well-understood design rules were now obsolete, and the new rules had to be discovered via trial and error.

Burroughs' experience exemplified how challenging this was. Burroughs was the first disk drive maker to announce a model employing thin film heads, in 1976, but it was never able to ship the product. Its failure was not because it couldn't make the thin-film heads. It was because Burroughs was unable to account for the new, complex technological interactions inherent in thin film technology. They couldn't make the *product* work.

IBM shipped its first product that used thin film heads in 1979—14 years after its underlying scientific research had been initiated, and 8 years after it began purposeful component development. The cost of IBM's total thin film head effort has been estimated at over $300 million (in 1970s dollars). Despite this magnitude of investment, the vertical integration and investments in research that supported advanced component development paid off handsomely for IBM. It was able to capture the proprietary value of the technologies it developed because of the technologically interdependent character of the disk drive. Even if proprietary technology had leaked out of IBM embodied in an engineer or a document, competitors could not directly use it, unless they also possessed the integrative design capability to design simultaneously the other components as they designed the head and the product architecture and then possessed the skill to ramp the resulting design into volume manufacturing. A leading market researcher commented as late as 1986 that:

> Very high entry costs combined with a veritable mine field of technical traps has kept the number of independent thin-film head suppliers down to a handful; even IBM, developer of the technology, had formidable problems in bringing this technology to market.[4]

Thin Film Disks

In contrast to the way in which the developers of thin film heads were able to capture the fruits of their investment in technology, the case of thin film disk development illustrates how modularity enables other firms to appropriate technology that was developed internally. Thin film disks provide a natural contrasting case. They embodied many of the same materials concepts. The technology emerged shortly after thin film heads. Both technologies were pursued by independent component manufacturers, with the backing of prominent venture capital firms. Yet thin film disks diffused into the market far more rapidly than did thin film heads.

Recording disks originally were made by coating flat aluminum platters with microscopic particles of iron oxide. By the mid-1970s, engineers sensed that this technology was approaching two insurmountable barriers to improvement. By nature, there were unusable interstitial spaces amongst even the most tightly packed of the needle-shaped oxide particles. These spaces could not store magnetic information. The second problem was that variation in the height of the particles on the disk limited engineers' ability to fly heads closer to the disks. The technological solution to these constraints, thin film disks, consisted of plated aluminum platters that were sputter-coated with thin films of a magnetic metal a few angstroms thick. Thin film disk development was initiated in about 1976 in IBM's research center and at Xerox's Palo Alto Research Center (PARC). Thin film disk development is estimated to have cost each of these firms between $50 million and $100 million.

Diffusion of Thin Film Disk and Head Technology into the Market

The thin film head and the thin film disk were both substantially new component technologies, as defined by Henderson & Clark (1990). Yet the interdependent character of the head, and the modular character of the disk, made the first technology very difficult for other firms to incorporate into new designs and the second relatively easy.

IBM's introduction of its new thin film heads and disks in a limited number of high-end models stimulated demand for the new componentry amongst certain independent, non-integrated disk drive manufacturers. These independent firms, such as Maxtor and Micropolis, were those that pushed, through innovative (some would say "daring") system design, a much more aggressive posture than the vertically integrated manufacturers were typically inclined to adopt. These "bleeding edge" manufacturers that most needed the advanced componentry were, more or less directly, competitors of IBM. But IBM viewed its proprietary access to advanced componentry as its primary competitive advantage and was unwilling to sell its components in the external marketplace.

Sensing this demand for advanced components, venture capitalists recruited key IBM and Xerox engineers into new start-up firms to produce and sell the new-technology components to bleeding-edge disk drive makers in the OEM market. The industry's leading thin film disk manufacturer, Komag, and the leading thin film head manufacturer, Read-Rite, both started in this manner, in 1983. These firms perceived an opportunity to supply advanced component technologies to independent drive manufacturers. Their formation constitutes a sort of natural experiment, in that entry into thin film heads involved commercializing an interdependent technology, while entry into media involved a modular technology. Yet both were backed enthusiastically by Silicon Valley venture capitalists.

Initially, Komag was much more successful in selling its thin film disks than Read-Rite was in selling its thin film heads. The technological modularity of disks constituted sufficient information for a decoupling market to emerge between Komag as supplier and non-integrated designers and assemblers of drives, such as Maxtor. All three elements of modularity existed: Komag's customers could specify what they needed; clear metrics allowed supplier and customer to communicate expectations and verify results on the same test equipment; and the ability to predict how variation in disk attributes would interact with the performance of other elements of the system facilitated the buying and selling of disks in the open market. As the top chart in Exhibit 1 shows, this decoupling market was so much more effective than managerial coordination at the component/product design interface that the non-integrated firms were much more aggressive in adopting the new disks than were the integrated firms, even though it was the integrated firms that had paid to develop the technology. For example, in 1986 85% of the products introduced by non-integrated disk drive makers

used thin film disks, whereas only 20% of the models introduced by integrated drive makers that year used thin film disks.

The top chart in Exhibit 1 illustrates the dual-edged organizational impact of a technology shift from interdependent to modular. Those organizations that utilized intermediate markets for their components (i.e., buying and selling disks and heads in the open market) were able to exploit the modular technology quite effectively. Those organizations that continued to pursue vertically coordinated and constrained strategies ended up moving much more slowly and were slower to incorporate this improved technology. In IBM's case, they led in the creation of thin film disk technology but lagged in the deployment of that technology, so that IBM's research leaked out into the industry before IBM made effective use of it. IBM's vertically controlled strategy, which had served it well during the interdependent phase of disk drive technology, did not fit well with the now-modular character of the technology.

The bottom chart in Exhibit 1 shows a different story for thin film heads, however. It was the *integrated* firms that led in their development and use. A few non-integrated firms attempted to employ thin film heads in fits and starts between 1983 and 1986, but their attempts were ineffective. Complaints from both sides of the transaction typified the challenge. One disk drive design engineer said, "The (independent) thin film head suppliers just aren't reliable. We tell them what we need, and they ship heads to us that just won't work." And the head supplier lamented, "The customers just don't know what they want. They give us a spec, and we deliver exactly what they ask for. Then they call us and complain that the heads won't work."

In our assessment, this problem was not an issue of the reliability of the head supplier. It was an issue of technological interdependence. Drive makers did not know which attributes they needed to specify; clear measurement methods did not exist; and variation in certain attributes of the heads interacted with the performance of the disk drive system in unpredictable ways. This is why the disk drive makers concluded that the heads they had received "wouldn't work." Between 1979 and 1986, therefore, the interdependent nature of the technology essentially kept thin film heads proprietary to IBM and its integrated competitors. Hence, in 1986, while 85% of the drives introduced by non-integrated companies were using thin film disks, only 8% of those models used thin film heads.

The design and manufacture of thin film disks was radically difficult technology on a number of dimensions, as

EXHIBIT 1 Impact of Modularity on the Ability of Integrated and Non-Integrated Firms to Exploit New Thin Film Technologies

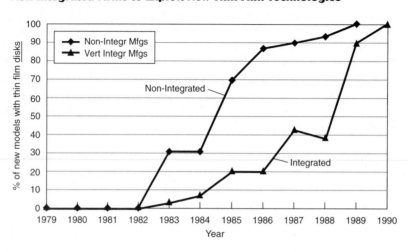

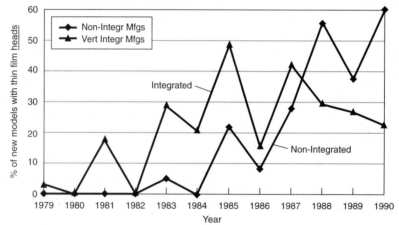

thin film heads had been before. However, incorporating thin film disks into new disk drive product designs was much simpler than for thin film heads—because the new disks were *modular* in character. Specifically:

1. Disk drive product designers knew what attributes of thin film disks needed to be specified, and to what tolerances. For example, the definition of what constituted a surface defect, the maximum allowable interstitial spacing, the variation in particle flatness and diameter of the disks, could be specified quite precisely to an independent group that would design and manufacture the disks.

2. Standard metrics for each of these attributes existed, and the technology to perform reliable measurements was available, such as test equipment and instrumentation. For example, the spin stands that helped to

characterize the earlier oxide media worked for this new media as well.

3. The science underlying this technology was well enough understood that the interactions between the thickness of the sputtered metal layer, the coercivity of the media, and other elements of the disk drive design could be modeled. This meant that variation in these key parameters could be accounted for, and designs of the other portions of the drive ultimately could be made robust to such variability (Clausing and Taguchi, 1990).

4. As a result of conditions 1–3 above, a number of viable suppliers were able to enter, creating an intermediate market for components. Users of intermediate products can manage suppliers at arms length and can switch between suppliers at little or no cost. Suppliers can similarly add and drop customers with little cost

incurred. Technical modularity enables organizational modularity (Sanchez and Mahoney, 1996).

These conditions gave rise to the entry of new supplier firms that offered thin film disks as stand-alone component items for disk drive firms to design into their drives.

Starting in 1987 the situation in thin film heads also changed. With eight years of experience with the technology under the belts of industry engineers, the uncertainties about attributes, tolerances, and interactions that had kept thin film heads an interdependent technology became resolved—and as thin film heads acquired a modular character, their use by non-integrated companies mushroomed. It then became more straightforward for non-integrated designers and assemblers of disk drives to procure the heads from non-integrated suppliers like Read-Rite. While Komag, the disk maker, had been financially viable from its inception, Read-Rite struggled to stave off bankruptcy until 1988, when it finally turned its first profit on $28 million in sales. Enabled by modularity, its revenues then rocketed 86% per year, to $345 million in 1992.

IBM's position in drives suffered as a result of this new competition. The technological advantages its drives had enjoyed through advanced componentry were eroded as competing firms incorporated leading edge components into their designs. Worse, IBM's position in its systems business had deteriorated as well. This placed IBM's drive business in a quandary: how to profit from its enormous research commitments in magnetic storage, when new entrants were able to produce technologically equivalent designs, and its own systems business was under attack?

This conundrum overlooks a possible solution IBM could have used, but chose not to pursue: the option of unbundling its drives from its systems, and selling the drives on the intermediate market to other computer manufacturers. IBM chose not to do this, in large part because they did not wish to enable their computer competitors by allowing them to buy the same technology that IBM used. Because IBM did not so empower its storage business, it limited its storage market penetration to its own systems market.

Upstream in the value chain, IBM's component businesses also were *not* free to sell their products to outside disk drive firms. This limited their volume and scale economies to that which IBM's disk drive business could support. This impaired their ability to gain greater volume and spread their high fixed development costs over a greater number of units (Klepper, 1996). Competing firms sold their technology to as many customers as they could, achieving production volumes well above IBM's own vol-umes. Competing firms could even justify the addition of new manufacturing capacity ahead of IBM. IBM thus became a high cost supplier of component technologies they had originally invented. IBM's more expensive drives, in turn, burdened IBM's systems products with higher disk drive costs than they otherwise would have had. The advent of modularity in product and component designs thus induced a vicious circle for IBM.

Once the technology had become modular, it would have been far more profitable for IBM to find *external* customers for its component technologies than to have relied entirely upon what componentry would be needed within IBM itself. Similarly, IBM would have done better to allow its disk drives to be sold to competing firms, in order to build greater volumes, reduce costs, and spread the R&D costs over more units. In other words, the organizational strategy that might have maximized IBM's return on its investments in advanced component technologies would have been (1) to use its components internally as long as the technologies were interdependent and then (2) to aggressively sell them in the external marketplace after they had become modular.

Japanese Disk Drive Firms' Organizational Response to Disk Drive Technology Shifts

While the strategy noted in the previous paragraph smacks strongly of retrospective analysis, the contemporaneous behavior of Japanese disk drive firms actually followed an organizational approach very much like the one advised. The Japanese disk drive firms watched IBM's technology activities very closely. Japanese disk drive research and development in this period consisted chiefly of reverse engineering IBM's breakthroughs in magnetic storage materials and components and then applying these results within their own proprietary computer systems architectures. While they followed IBM's technical actions closely, though, Japanese firms did not imitate IBM's organizational policies. If IBM's systems business did not evidence a need for a hard disk drive, IBM's storage division did not develop that drive. By contrast, Fujitsu, Hitachi, NEC, and Toshiba often developed hard disk drives well in advance of their internal systems needs. Fujitsu's first 5.25″ and 3.5″ drives, for example, were sold primarily on an OEM basis to other computer companies; Fujitsu's internal consumption amounted to less than 10% of the first year's sales of these drives.

The adaptation of the leading Japanese firms can be seen from Exhibit 2. In 1982, each firm had some limited sales of OEM drives, while IBM's drive sales were entirely to IBM itself. By 1986, as volumes in disk drives

EXHIBIT 2   OEM and Captive Sales of IBM and Japanese HDD Firms, 1982 and 1986

	1982 % captive revenues	1982 % OEM revenues	1986 % captive revenues	1986 % OEM revenues
IBM	100	0	100	0
Fujitsu	75	25	65	35
Hitachi	90	10	80	20
NEC	95	5	67	33
Toshiba	95	5	45	55

Sources: Estimated Market Shares, Disk/Trend Reports, 1983, 1987.

expanded, the OEM business for each Japanese company grew even more, so that OEM became a significant business for each of the companies. Toshiba went even further: more than half its revenues came from outside customers by 1986.

The decentralized organizational policy of Japanese drive firms allowed their storage units to compete for design wins in systems markets, even in those markets where the downstream Japanese systems division had not (yet) entered. As a result, Japanese drives were sold in greater volume than they would have, had they followed IBM's organizational policy. This policy also provided a second beneficial effect. If the systems division of a Japanese firm stumbled in making the transition from one systems market to another (i.e., from mainframes and minicomputers to workstations and PCs in the mid-1980s), its storage division was not prevented from entering that market through sales to outside manufacturers. This allowed Japanese disk drive manufacturers to navigate systems market shifts that frustrated firms like IBM. Finally, if and when the systems divisions did enter the systems market, they were supported by an already established internal drive supplier, whose costs were lower as a result of volumes generated through outside sales.

MR Technology: Research Advances Induce New Technological Interdependence

The story of disk drive component technology evolution does not end with the emergence of modular technologies. In 1992, IBM announced that its researchers had developed a new and very different type of recording head technology, called *magneto-resistive* (MR) heads. MR technology offered the potential to increase the recording density of disk drives by a factor of 10 over thin film heads. MR technology is based on the change in the resistance of certain materials in the presence of a magnetic field. A sensor measures the induced changes, which can be made much smaller than was previously achievable

with thin film technology. The MR head that induces these changes was an intensely interdependent technology—even more so than was the case with thin film heads—in that the design of the disks, actuator mechanisms, and read-write channels depended upon the design of the head—and vice versa. The complexity of the MR heads was well illustrated by an IBM engineer's statements at its announcement; "We don't fully understand the physics involved, but we can replicate the event."

While the creation and development of the MR head was a technical marvel in itself, its incorporation into disk drive designs proved to be challenging as well. As in the earlier case of the initial thin firm heads, the established design rules and models that links head componentry with associated disks, electronics, and encoding technologies had to be thrown out. Once again, IBM had a strong lead in the technology and enjoyed a significant performance advantage from its integrated components and drives.

IBM's announcement of MR technology again caused its rivals to imitate its breakthrough. However, such imitation proved difficult. Statements by non-integrated designers and assemblers of disk drives and by executives of read-write head manufacturing companies, trying to incorporate MR heads into their drives, echoed almost verbatim the statements made twelve years earlier about thin film heads. Disk drive designers complained that MR heads sold by the independent head suppliers just weren't reliable—that most of the heads they deliver wouldn't work. And the head suppliers complained that they gave their customers exactly what they specified—the problem was that they didn't know what they needed. It was not an issue of being reliable. It was an issue of interdependent technology. And try as they might, for at least the first five years after IBM announced its MR head, nobody in the United States but IBM had the integrated perspective required to utilize the MR head effectively.

Quantum and Seagate, the largest OEM drive makers, were each subsequently forced to integrate into making their own MR heads and to engage in the research and technology development efforts required to support advanced componentry development, integration, and manufacturing.[5] Seagate reportedly had to "tune" its hard disk designs to get its MR heads to work. Even Komag, the leading thin film disk maker, decided to acquire Dastek, a struggling head manufacturer with a fledgling MR capability, so that it could design disks that would work with MR heads. Between 1992 and 1998, the market share of vertically integrated disk drive manufacturers had rebounded from 55% to 80%, and IBM's research capability once again became the envy of the industry.

This time, however, under Gerstner's leadership, IBM changed its organizational strategy. Leveraging its MR technology advantage, IBM aggressively entered the OEM disk drive market, selling its drives to numerous computer makers.[6] IBM's OEM market sales of disk drives, all of which employed IBM's MR heads, grew from zero in 1992 to almost $3 billion by 1997 (*Disk/Trend,* 1998). For the first time, IBM sold its drives into markets ahead of its own systems. For the first time, IBM even initiated new disk drive designs that were intended for external customers rather than for IBM itself. Non-integrated disk drive companies such as Western Digital and Maxtor in the U.S. and NEC and Toshiba in Japan struggled mightily, working with their independent head suppliers to keep up with the pace of density improvement that IBM forged. All fell behind. These non-integrated firms found themselves in an organizational trap, where they lacked the internal systems knowledge of MR's technical interdependencies to extricate themselves (Chesbrough & Kusunoki, 2001).

Later in the 1990s, MR technology became better understood and hence more modular. Independent head makers could now offer MR heads. At the same time though, IBM began to offer its MR heads themselves to independent drive makers. IBM's component volumes soon expanded beyond its own disk drive requirements, which in turn had expanded beyond IBM's own systems requirements. While this gave rival drive makers access to leading edge technology, IBM likely believed that the gains from the expanded volumes it garnered from selling its components outweighed whatever costs were incurred from having competing firms using its component technology. And of course, IBM's drive division would benefit from this greater component volume in the form of lower costs for the heads it used, making its drives still more competitive for both its OEM customers and internal systems customers. IBM's policy thus created a virtuous circle, replacing the vicious one created by its earlier insistence on captive-only supply policies towards its component technologies.

V. AN EMPIRICAL EVALUATION OF ARCHITECTURAL EFFICIENCY

The evidence presented so far has been limited to a few salient firms. To examine our arguments in detail across the entire industry, we have constructed an analysis of 3,894 individual disk drive models to evaluate some aspects of our theory in the larger industry. Our dependent variable is a measure of what we term the "architectural efficiency" of each disk drive. Intuitively, this measure captures the ability of drive makers to achieve high density designs out of their individual disk drive components. Higher densities reflect greater technical efficiencies, because fewer heads and disks are needed to achieve the same storage capacity. We defined architectural efficiency to be the actual areal density achieved by each disk drive, relative to a predicted average areal density achieved by all firms utilizing the same underlying components in the drive designed in the same year. Areal density is measured in millions of bits per square inch.

The predicted average areal density measure for all drives using those components is derived from compiling data on all the *Disk/Trend* measures of product parameters. The relationship of each of these components and the resulting areal density of the drive model is estimated, which generates coefficient estimates for the individual components in the population of disk drive models. These coefficient estimates are then applied to the actual component specifications of each drive model, to determine a predicted average areal density (see Exhibit 3).

With these two measures in hand, we then divide "predicted areal density" into the *actual* areal density of each product model, to create the "architectural efficiency" measure.[7]

$$\text{Architectural efficiency} = \frac{\text{Actual areal density in that specific drive model}}{\text{Calculated average areal density from those components}}$$

Our analysis suggests that companies will vary in their ability to employ interdependent technologies in early stages of their deployment. Disk drive firms all must design their products using major components such as disks and heads in their designs. Companies vary in whether they make the heads and media themselves or not, and our analysis above suggests that this difference ought to matter. If this is so, then we should be able to observe differences in their architectural efficiency; i.e., in the areal density they actually achieve in the products they ship. More particularly, we ought to expect disk drive models with thin film and MR heads to behave differently from thin film disks. The interdependence of the former creates complexities that ought to impair architectural efficiency, at least initially, while thin film disks ought not to exhibit such inefficiency.

Exhibit 4 shows the results of regressing architectural efficiency for 3,894 disk drive models that shipped from 1980 through 1995. The coefficients for thin film disks is significant and positive in the first model for the

EXHIBIT 3 Summary Statistics and Correlations of HDD Components

Variable	#Obs	Mean	Std. Dev.	Min	Max
arch_eff	3894	1.051612	.3288623	.096	3.132
TF_head	3894	.3145865	.4644106	0	1
MR_head	3894	.0354391	.1849107	0	1
TF_disk	3894	.6640986	.4723653	0	1
own_head	3894	.3816127	.4858447	0	1
own_disk	3894	.4958911	.5000473	0	1
owntfdsk	3894	.3325629	.4711919	0	1
owntfhd	3894	.13585	.3426732	0	1
ownMRhd	3894	.0354391	.1849107	0	1

	arch_eff	TF_head	MR_head	TF_disk	own_head	own_disk	owntfdsk	
arch_eff	1.0000							
TF_head	−0.0411	1.0000						
MR_head	0.0731	−0.1299	1.0000					
TF_disk	−0.0476	0.3214	0.1363	1.0000				
own_head	0.0878	0.0700	0.2440	−0.0480	1.0000			
own_disk	0.0736	0.0570	0.1683	0.0137	0.7127	1.0000		
owntfdsk	0.0302	0.1850	0.2450	0.5020	0.4610	0.7117	1.0000	
owntfhd	−0.0043	0.5853	−0.0760	0.1376	0.5047	0.3398	0.3692	1.000
ownMRhd	0.0731	−0.1299	1.0000	0.1363	0.2440	0.1683	0.2450	−0.0760

EXHIBIT 4 Regression Analyses of Heads and Disks upon Architectural Efficiency

	All Models (1)	1980–1986 (2)	1987–1993 (3)	1994–1995 (4)
Constant	1.003	1.020**	0.793**	1.249**
	0.033	0.043	0.031	0.040
TF_head	−0.001	0.139	−0.013	−0.074
	0.016	0.063	0.016	0.042
TF_disk	0.116**	0.109*	0.153**	<dropped[1]>
	0.021	0.053	0.025	
MR_head	−0.028	NA	NA	0.158*
	0.034			0.072
own_head	0.089**	0.088*	0.102**	−0.233**
	0.018	0.041	0.020	0.085
own_disk	0.012	−0.033	0.076*	0.150**
	0.022	0.039	0.032	0.042
Own thin film head	−0.022	−0.057	−0.015	0.099
	0.024	0.091	0.024	0.090
Own thin film disk	0.002	0.157	−0.081	<dropped>
	0.023	0.087	0.031	
Year dummies	<included>			
Observations	3894	979	2502	413
Chi-square	19.94	4.86	13.27	5.77
Adjusted R-squared	0.10	0.04	0.06	0.06

* $p < .05$
** $p - .01$
[1] By 1994, all disk media was thin film.

overall sample and in three partitioned samples for 1980–1986, 1987–1993, and 1994–1995 that follow. Drive models with thin film disks achieved higher architectural efficiencies in these data, both overall and in each period.

The behavior for thin film heads, by contrast, is insignificant in the overall sample. However, the behavior of this variable changes markedly over the three periods. Drive models with thin film heads initially achieve a significantly higher architectural efficiency in the period from 1980 to 1986. As discussed above, this is the period when thin film heads were almost exclusively captive. From 1986 to 1993 and in 1994 to 1995, however, the influence is insignificant. As discussed above, this is when thin film heads transitioned to become less interdependent and more modular, and drive makers began to incorporate merchant thin film heads into their designs.

The architectural efficiency of drive models with MR heads is not significant in the overall sample. However, MR heads only entered into the *Disk/Trend* specification tables in 1994. In the sub-sample of those drives, its usage is significantly and positively related to architectural efficiency.

When we track whether firms make these components or not, we find a statistically significant effect for firms that make their own heads and not for firms that make their own disks. Firms who make their own heads appear to actually enhance the architectural efficiency of their product designs. Making one's own disks does not similarly enhance the architectural efficiency of the models using those disks, with the exception of the period from 1985 to 1993. Interaction terms for making one's own thin film heads and thin film disks are not significant. However, the degree of correlation of these interaction terms with whether or not firms make their heads and disks is high, 0.505 for heads, and 0.712 for disks. Thus, the interpretation of the variables for making one's own heads and disks is hard to disentangle from the interaction terms. The interaction term for making one's own MR heads (not shown in the regression model) is 1.000, reflecting the lack of an effective merchant market for MR heads in 1994 and 1995.

These results are generally supportive of our theory. We expect the degree of interdependence in a component like thin film heads and MR heads to vary over time. The behavior of the thin film head variable performs very much as we would predict. We would also predict that firms making an interdependent technology component ought to achieve more technical efficiency. We would predict that firms making a modular component (here, thin film disks) ought not to realize such a benefit. Thin film disks are associated with higher architecture efficiency, regardless of whether one makes them or buys them.

There are other interpretations possible for these results. Companies choose whether or not to make their own components for other reasons beyond improving the areal density of their designs, such as reducing the cost of the components or assuring the supply of critical components. We lack reliable measures of production volumes by model that could isolate these issues from the question of technical design efficiency.

However, any alternative theory must account for the varying influence of thin film heads over time, relative to thin film disks. An alternative theory must also explain why making heads is associated with architectural efficiency, while making disks is not. Both were important component technology advances that arose from similar materials science at approximately the same time in the industry. Both components were supported by startup companies seeking to create merchant markets for these components. Yet the two components have quite different effects on architectural efficiency. Our evidence is at least consistent with the argument that thin film heads (and later, MR heads) were interdependent technologies during the early 1980s, while thin film disks were not. And companies that made these interdependent technologies may have been able to eke more performance out of the interdependent technologies, relative to companies coordinating with external suppliers. There does not appear to be a similar performance benefit for firms making a less interdependent component, such as thin film media.

VI. IMPLICATIONS FOR ALIGNING ORGANIZATIONAL STRUCTURE WITH TECHNOLOGICAL CHARACTER

With interdependent technologies, product designers do not know which of the many attributes of a component need to be specified to particular tolerances in order to have the product perform as expected when the components are assembled together. Unambiguous methods to measure these attributes may not exist, and engineers may be unable to predict or model how variation in the attributes of some components will affect the required design of other elements of the product. In Kaufman's (1993) lexicon, these interdependent conditions create a "rugged landscape" that complicates the development of solutions to improve the product.[8] Under conditions of technological interdependence, optimal component designs and the product architecture can only be defined iteratively and interactively by an integrated development organization. Much of the knowledge of effective integration may be tacit in form, making it hard to transmit within the firm and even harder to share across firms (Monteverde, 1995). These conditions make it difficult, if not impossible, for firms to enter the intermediate markets as suppliers. Pure modularity and pure technological interdependence are, of course, extreme boundary conditions. Most products and technologies exist somewhere along a continuum between these extremes (Brusoni and Prencipe, 2001).

At the other end of the value-added spectrum, we might say that a modular interface between product design and manufacturing exists when clear, explicit design rules exist[9] and when new engineers can readily be taught how changes in product design affect manufacturing process parameters. Modularity at this interface enables an arm's-length relationship between design and manufacturing. It can enable a decoupling market to emerge at this interface, which can deconstruct a previously internal supply chain into a network of suppliers (Langlois, 1992; Christensen and Rosenbloom, 1995). Entry can occur on both sides of the interface, with design-based entrants buying from entrants specializing in manufacturing. Technological interdependence, by contrast, exists at this interface when clear design-for-manufacturing rules do not exist and when the impact of changes in product design on the cost and quality of the manufacturing process can only be discovered through trial and error prototyping. This is often the case with scale-up situations in many process-based industries (Pisano, 1996).[10]

Firms can employ differing possible organizational strategies to coordinate their decisions across technical interfaces. One ideal type is a decentralized or autonomous organizational approach. Here we mean that the business unit in question has the autonomy to source technology from, and sell its products to, whomever it chooses. For example, a decentralized firm could obtain materials, components, or entire products from any source it wished and sell them through a variety of internal and external channels. By contrast, a centralized firm constrains its selection at each of these interface points to a single source, usually an internal captive source, and limits the sale of products to its own distribution channels.

Our usage of these terms does not correspond exactly with the economist's idea of vertical integration. There, the fundamental determinant is the ownership of the assets. Our usage takes into account the possibility that ownership may not fully specify the coordination of those assets. Our terms are intended to focus attention on the *management* of these technical assets, as opposed to their ownership. We have in mind the distinction between the use of markets and prices to coordinate actions and the use of managerial processes to coordinate actions.[11]

Whenever technological modularity conditions exist as defined above, they create sufficient information to enable markets to coordinate at arm's length the interactions between technological components and the systems that use these components. Modularity also enables intermediate markets to emerge at the interfaces between components within a system. These markets, which this paper labels "decoupling markets," make it difficult for firms that develop new technology in upstream research

to capture the technology's value in the downstream markets for end-use products.

Firms that follow decentralized organizational strategies (as defined above) effectively match their internal organization to these modular technological characteristics. Decentralization enables units within the firm to buy and sell independently in these decoupling markets, and frees them from corporate dictates to use captive sources when market conditions make this choice unwise. However, when the condition opposite to modularity exists—which this paper calls technological *interdependence*[12]—then managerial coordination, rather than markets, provides the most effective mechanisms to coordinate the interfaces between these stages. Here, the requisite information of how the different elements function together is not well defined, and interactions between elements are poorly understood. Under such conditions of technological interdependence, decoupling markets do not function effectively, and close coordination outside of the market is required to make the technology perform effectively. As Ulrich (1995) has shown, integral technologies also achieve better product performance (at the expense of flexibility), relative to more modular architectures.

The comparative benefits of internal coordination arise from Williamson's (1975, 1985) concepts of markets vs. hierarchies. Due to the complexities inherent in interdependent technologies, their numerous technical interactions cannot be fully characterized and are only poorly understood. Under these conditions, markets do not function effectively and can even be hazardous. A customer cannot fully specify his requirements to a buyer and cannot predict how the component or subsystem will affect his system. When these problems arise, bargaining costs ensue. The usual recourse in the market would be to switch suppliers. Because the interdependencies are poorly understood, though, bringing in another supplier may only introduce new technical problems, which again may be viewed differently by the different parties to the transaction. Technological interdependence undermines the ability to discipline one supplier by switching to another. To achieve the close coordination and to facilitate rapid mutual adjustment between interdependent technologies, administrative coordination outside of the market is required to develop the technology effectively.

These comparative advantages in technically interdependent regimes, though, lose their efficacy when technology has shifted to become modular in character. With modular technology, even complex components can be substituted for one another in a system. Enough codified information now exists to enable markets to coordinate the integration of technology across the interfaces between stages of value added. Rival suppliers with interchangeable products discipline one another to promote strong competition within these interfaces, resulting in more rapid advances in technology and lower prices to systems customers of those component products.

In these circumstances, decentralized firms, and even virtual firms are "virtuous" (Chesbrough and Teece, 1996), compared to firms that continue to manage these coordination activities inside the firm. The earlier information advantages within the firm have been rendered insignificant by the advent of technical interface standards. The incentive characteristics within firms remain low-powered, but this now becomes an impediment, instead of a virtue. The presence of established standards permits multiple firms to compete at each level of technology. Since markets can now function effectively to coordinate technical development within these standards, high powered incentives lead to more advanced technology sooner. The presence of alternate credible sources similarly resolves potential appropriability problems, because suppliers have alternate customers, and customers have alternate suppliers.

Firms that follow decentralized organizational strategies effectively match their internal organization to these modular technological characteristics. For these firms, focusing within a single layer of technology harnesses the strong incentives and high volumes available through the market. The ability of modular interfaces to coordinate their actions within a larger systems architecture mitigates coordination hazards and enables these firms to move fast.

The Cyclical Character of Modularity and Interdependence

Despite the advantages of technological modularity in product design, modularity is not necessarily a stable end-state. Every architecture has its performance limits, and eventually a new architecture must be established to transcend these limits. This new architecture, in turn, emerges only fitfully and is not fully characterized at its inception. Technologies can thus cycle over time between modularity and interdependence. Such shifts have implications for how firms need to realign themselves in order to capture value from their innovation investments. Our history of recent technical developments in the disk drive industry provides two illustrations of such a shift from modular to interdependent technology. First was the shift from iron ferrite heads to thin film heads. Second was the subsequent shift from now-mature thin film heads to magneto-resistive (MR) heads.

EXHIBIT 5 Technology-Organization Alignment Matrix

	Modular	Interdependent
Decentralized organization	Proper alignment Value realized only within technology layer No inefficient interactions	Misalignment Can't manage interactions Insufficient infrastructure
Centralized organization	Misalignment Unnecessary internal coordination Reduced scale economies	Proper alignment Value realized through the system Effective management of hard to define interactions

We do not regard either modularity or interdependence as an end-state. Instead, technological and scientific discovery can cause the nature of technology to cycle from modularity to interdependence and (later) back to modularity. Our model implies that firms must be prepared to adjust their organizational approach to the nature of the technology they pursue, in order to profit from that technology. The overall conclusion from our framework is a contingent approach towards organizing for innovation. This contingency framework is shown in Exhibit 5.

Our framework implies that the ability to create and capture value from technology must vary with the type of technology and the organizational approach of the firm. As technologies evolve, there is a critical shift in where value can be added and captured within an architecture. Interdependent technologies enable firms to create and capture value in two discrete ways: one through the use of superior components, and the other through superior architectural combinations of those components. With the advent of modularity, though, the latter source of value-added is obliterated. Firms can only expect to profit from their value-added within their level of the technology and cannot expect to recover any value from their systems integration capabilities.

The optimal alignment in Exhibit 5 runs from the upper left quadrant, in periods of technical modularity, to the lower right quadrant, in periods of technical interdependence. The "off diagonal" quadrants reflect a misalignment of organizational structure with the character of technology. Firms in the lower left quadrant err by imposing inappropriate overheads on the technology and

EXHIBIT 6 IBM's Movement Along the Technology-Organization Alignment Matrix

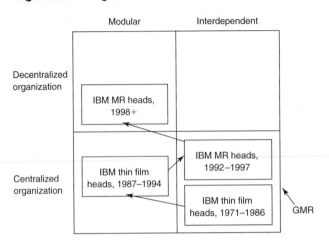

overly restricting the market for internal technology deployment. Firms in the upper right quadrant err by attempting to coordinate interdependent technology through arm's-length relationships.

Exhibit 6 depicts a summary of IBM's alignment with regard to disk drive heads that illustrates our model of technology and organizational alignment. In the beginning, from 1971 to 1986, IBM was properly aligned in the lower right hand quadrant. The interdependent technology could not be adequately characterized to enable its sale to other firms, so IBM was correct to restrict deployment to its own disk drives. As the technology became more modular, intermediate sales became feasible. However, IBM eschewed any change to its centralized organizational approach. This caused IBM to become misaligned and moved its position into the lower left quadrant of the matrix in Exhibit 5. With the advent of MR heads in 1992, technological interdependence re-emerged, causing IBM to become properly aligned again. Now that MR heads are becoming more modular, IBM itself has become more decentralized and is actively selling its components in the intermediate market. This choice has moved IBM into the upper left quadrant. At the same time, a new technology, called giant magneto-resistive heads (GMR), is coming into the market. We expect that this will initially be an interdependent technology as well, which will then become more modular over time. We expect GMR to be deployed initially only on captive disk drives and then to shift to intermediate markets as its interactions with other elements of the disk drive architecture become better understood.

VII. CONCLUSION AND DIRECTIONS FOR FUTURE RESEARCH

We have presented a framework that links the position of a technology along the spectrum from interdependent to modular states and on companies' organizational strategies from centralized to decentralized. When firms properly align their organizational strategy with the state of technology, they are more able to capture the returns on their R&D investments. As noted above, because these ideas are grounded in a single industry study, their implications can only constitute hypotheses, which need to be evaluated through further research. The utility of our framework must be judged by the insights it contributes to our understanding of managing technology. We believe that the framework offers a few important insights.

Recent scholars have called attention to the problem of technology "leaking" out of a corporation's research laboratory into the market, potentially threatening the continued viability of central research labs at IBM, Xerox, and Lucent (Rosenbloom and Spencer, 1996). Our analysis frames this question of leakage with the following question: is the technology interdependent, or is it modular? We would predict that interdependent technology will not leak out of the lab into the market. However, it will also have trouble transferring inside the firm, unless the firm makes the other interdependent technologies that are required to make the technology work. On the other hand, modular technologies out of the research lab will transfer readily within the firm. But its modular character makes it likely that it will leak out as well. Thus, our framework complements and extends the received literature on the appropriability of technology. Our framework shows how the ability to appropriate returns from research may vary between firms in an industry and even within a single firm in that industry, over time.

A second insight is that modularity is not an end-state of technological evolution. We think that the recent enthusiasm for modularity (e.g., Baldwin and Clark, 2000) pays insufficient attention to the dynamics of technical advance. Every architecture contains a technical performance limit. At some point, that architecture must be transcended, if technical advance is to continue. Our history suggests that technological architectures may cycle between modular and interdependent states as they advance. This suggests that the organizational responses to the powerful insights offered by modularity must include responses that acknowledge the possible return to an interdependent state. This implies that organizations must develop greater organizational flexibility and must retain a high level of systems knowledge, even when they procure (or supply) components in intermediate markets (Brusoni and Prencipe, 2001).

Failure to retain this systems knowledge could result in a "modularity trap," where the buying firm no longer possesses the systems knowledge to incorporate new (interdependent) component technologies effectively into its systems (Chesbrough and Kusunoki, 2001). We note how previously decentralized firms that prospered during the modular phase of technology in their industry, such as Microsoft and Intel, are now making substantial investments in basic research on systems architectures themselves. Such investments would make little sense if their core architectures were expected to remain modular indefinitely. We think these new research investments might create the systems knowledge needed to pursue, and profit from, more interdependent technological architectures for these firms if and when such technology shifts occur in the personal and enterprise computing industries.

A third insight is a deeper understanding of the benefits and problems of a centralized approach to managing technology. The framework shows what internal managers understand deeply: that being internally integrated helps to manage the complexities involved with interdependent technologies (Ulrich, 1995). Once these complexities become more fully characterized, though, intermediate markets can arise, and markets become superior methods of coordinating technological developments (Langlois and Robertson, 1995; Monteverde, 1995; Baldwin and Clark, 2000). Internal managers may not be sufficiently aware of these intermediate markets or of the resulting implications for their organizational approach.

A fourth insight is the role of these intermediate markets themselves. While the state of characterized knowledge may be difficult to perceive (except in hindsight), there are discernible metrics that can be perceived. The presence of new entrant suppliers, the capabilities of test equipment and design tools, and the ability to adequately specify and verify requirements are all observable constituent parts of these intermediate markets. These items comprise early indicators of an impending shift towards modularity. As these elements become increasingly effective, the technology base is likely to become increasingly modular.

Further research could extend each of the above insights. Examining a firm's ability to appropriate the returns from its research investments makes appropriability partially endogenous to the firm and potentially amenable to its strategy and organization. Novak and Eppinger (2001) have found that automotive manufacturers vary in their choice of architecture, and that their choice influences their decisions of whether or not to vertically integrate. Their data may enable them to conduct tests of the dynamics of this decision, to determine whether it varied over time for individual firms.

Our assertion of a cycle of technological evolution, from modular to interdependent (and back), would benefit greatly from careful historical analysis of other technologies and the organizational response of firms to the different states of characterized knowledge of the technology over time. Brusoni and Prencipe (2001) offer two brief histories of aircraft engines and chemical engineering. Each history shows the enduring value of retaining systems integration knowledge, even if some portions of the value chain are outsourced (though the authors do not observe the saliency of intermediate markets in those settings that we find here in our history).

Finally, more study along the lines of Monteverde (1995) is needed of the key component elements in intermediate markets, such as studying the effects of improving test equipment or advances in design tools on the technical information being modeled. If our framework is correct, there may be powerful predictive information available from closely studying these enabling advances. These artifacts may be associated with the necessary knowledge required to coordinate components within an architecture and presage a shift towards greater technological modularity.

REFERENCES

Abernathy, W., and J. Utterback. 1978. "Patterns of industrial innovation." *Technology Review* (June–July), 40–47.

Anderson, Philip, and Michael Tushman. 1990. "Technological discontinuities and dominant designs: A cyclical model of technological change." *Administraive Science Quarterly,* vol. 35: 604–633.

Baldwin, C., and K. B. Clark. 2000. *Design Rules: The Power of Modularity* (MIT Press, Cambridge, MA).

Bridenbaugh, P. 1993. "The future of industrial research, or postcards from the edge of the abyss," in R. Rosenbloom, and W. J. Spencer (eds.), *Engines of Innovation* (Harvard Business School Press, Boston, MA), 1996.

Brusoni, Stefano, and Andrea Prencipe. 2001. "Unpacking the black box of modularity: Technologies, products, and organizations." *Industrial and Corporate Change,* vol. 10 (1): 179–205.

Burgelman, R., and L. R. Sayles. 1986. *Inside Corporate Innovation* (The Free Press, New York).

Chandler, A. D. 1977. *The Visible Hand* (The Ballinger Press of Harvard University Press, Cambridge, MA).

Chesbrough, H. W. 1999a. "Arrested development: The experience of European hard disk drive firms in comparison with U.S. and Japanese firms." *Journal of Evolutionary Economics,* special issue editor, Steven Klepper, vol. 9(3): 287–330.

Chesbrough, H. W. 1999b. "The differing organizational impact of technological change: A comparative theory of national institutional factors." *Industrial and Corporate Change* 8(3): 447–485.

Chesbrough, H., and K. Kusunoki. 2001. "The modularity trap: Innovation, technology phases shifts and the resulting limits of virtual organizations," in Nonaka and Teece (eds.), *Knowledge and the Firm* (Oxford University Press), forthcoming.

Chesbrough, H. W., and D. J. Teece. 1996. "When is virtual virtuous? Organizing for innovation." *Harvard Business Review* (January–February), 65–74.

Christensen, C. M. 1993. The rigid disk drive industry: A history of commercial and technological turbulence. *Business History Review,* vol. 67(4), Winter, 531–588.

Christensen, C. M. 1997. *The Innovator's Dilemma: When New Technology Causes Great Firms to Fail* (Harvard Business School Press, Boston, MA).

Christensen, C. M., and Joseph L. Bower. 1996. "Customer power, technology investment, and the failure of leading firms." *Strategic Management Journal,* vol. 17, 197–218.

Christensen, C. M., and R. S. Rosenbloom. 1995. "Explaining the attacker's advantage: Technological paradigms, organizational dynamics, and the value network." *Research Policy,* vol. 24, 233–257.

Christensen, C. M., F. Suarez, and J. Utterback. 1998. "Strategies for survival in fast changing industries." *Management Science,* vol. 44(12).

Christensen, C. M., and M. Verlinden. 2000. *Disruption, Disintegration, and the Dissipation of Differentiability.* Working Paper #00-074, Harvard Business School.

Constant, E. W. 1980. *The Origins of the Turbojet Revolution* (The Johns Hopkins University Press, Baltimore).

Dosi, G. 1982. "Technological paradigms and technological trajectories." *Research Policy,* vol. 11, 147–162.

Eccles, R. G., and H. C. White. 1988. "Price and authority in inter-profit center transactions." *American Journal of Sociology,* vol. 94 (Supplement): S17–S51.

Ferguson, C., and C. Morris. 1993. *Computer Wars: The Fall of IBM and the Future of Global Technology* (Times Books, New York).

Fine, Charles, and Daniel Whitney. 1996. "Is the Make Versus Buy Decision a Core Competence?" Working paper, MIT International Motor Vehicle Program.

Gomory, R. 1989. "From the ladder of science to the product development cycle." *Harvard Business Review* 67 (November–December), 99–105.

Griliches, Z. 1986. "Productivity, R&D and basic research at the firm level in the 1970s." *American Economic Review* (March).

Henderson, R. 1994. "The evolution of integrative capability: Innovation in cardiovascular drug design." *Industrial and Corporate Change,* vol. 3(3), 607–630.

Henderson, R. M., and K. B. Clark. 1990. "Architectural innovation: The reconfiguration of existing systems and the failure of established firms." *Administrative Science Quarterly* (March), 9–30.

Hounshell, D. A. 1991. "Du Pont Kevlar Aramid Industrial Fiber." Harvard Business School Case No. 9-391-146.

Hounshell, D. A. 1996. "The evolution of industrial research in the United States," in R. Rosenbloom and W. J. Spencer (eds.), *Engines of Innovation* (Harvard Business School Press, Boston).

Hounshell, D. A., and J. K. Smith. 1988. *Science and Corporate Strategy* (Cambridge University Press, New York).

Iansiti, M., and T. Khanna. 1995. "Technological evolution, system architecture and the obsolescence of firm capabilities." *Industrial and Corporate Change,* vol. 4(2), 333–361.

IBM Corporation. 1984. *How One Company's Zest for Technological Innovation Helped Build the Computer Industry* (pamphlet).

Kauffman, Stuart. 1993. *Origins of Order: Self-Organization and Selection in Evolution* (Oxford University Press, New York).

Klein, B., R. Crawford, and A. Alchian. 1978. "Vertical integration, appropriable rents, and the competitive contracting process." *Journal of Law and Economics* 21:297–326.

Klepper, S. 1996. "Entry, exit, growth, and innovation over the product life cycle." *The American Economic Review* (June).

Langlois, Richard. N. 1992. "External economies and economic progress: The case of the microcomputer industry." *Business History Review* 66, vol. 1:1–52.

Langlois, Richard. N., and Paul Robertson. 1995. *Firms, Markets, and Economic Change: A Dynamic Theory of Business Institutions* (Routledge, London, England).

Levin, R. C., A.K. Levorick, R. R. Nelson, and S. G. Winter. 1987. "Appropriating the returns from industrial research and development." *Brookings Papers on Economic Activity* (3):783–820.

Masten, S. 1988. "A legal basis for the firm." *Journal of Law, Economics, and Organization.* vol. 4 (1):181–198.

Monteverde, K. 1995. "Technical dialog as an incentive for vertical integration in the semiconductor industry." *Management Science,* vol. 41 (October): 1624–1638.

Moore, G. E. 1996. "Some personal perspectives on research in the semiconductor industry," in R. S. Rosenbloom and W. J. Spencer (eds.), *Engines of Innovation* (Harvard Business School Press, Boston).

Mowery, D., and N. Rosenberg. 1989. *Technology and the Pursuit of Economic Growth* (Cambridge University Press, New York).

Mueller, W. F. 1962. "The origins of the basic inventions underlying Du Pont's major product and process inventions, 1920 to 1950," in R. Nelson (ed.), *The Rate and Direction of Inventive Activity* (Princeton University Press, Princeton, NJ).

Mueller, W. F., and Tilton. 1969. "R&D costs as a barrier to entry." *Canadian Journal of Economics,* vol. 2 (November), 576.

Novak, Sharon, and Steven Eppinger. 2001. "Sourcing by design: Product complexity and the supply chain." Forthcoming, *Rand Journal of Economics.*

Pavitt, K. L. R., 1991, "What makes basic research economically useful?" *Research Policy,* vol. 20, 109–119.

Penrose, E. 1959. *The Theory of the Growth of the Firm* (M. E. Sharpe, Inc., Armonk, New York).

Pisano, G. 1996. *The Development Factory: Unlocking the Potential of Process Innovation* (Harvard Business School Press, Boston, MA).

Pugh, E., L. Johnson, and J. Palmer. 1991. *IBM's 360 and Early 370 Systems* (MIT Press: Cambridge, MA).

Reich, L. S. 1985. *The Making of Industrial Research* (Cambridge University Press, New York).

Rosenberg, N. 1982. *Inside the Black Box: Technology and Economics* (Cambridge University Press, Cambridge).

Rosenberg, N. 1990. "Why do firms do basic research (with their own money)?" *Research Policy,* vol. 19, 165–174.

Sahal, D. 1981. *Patterns of Technological Innovation* (Addison-Wesley, London).

Sanchez, R. and J. T. Mahoney. 1996. "Modularity, flexibility, and knowledge management in product and organization design." *Strategic Management Journal,* vol. 17 (Winter Special Issue), 63–76.

Solow, R. 1957. "Technological change and the aggregate production function." *Review of Economics and Statistics,* vol. 39, 312–320.

Taguchi, G. and D. Clausing. 1990. "Robust quality." *Harvard Business Review* (January–February), 65–75.

Teece, David J. 1976. *The Multinational Corporation and the Resource Cost of International Technology Transfer* (Ballinger, Cambridge, MA).

Teece, D. 1986. "Profiting from technological innovation: Implications for integration, collaboration, licensing and public policy." *Research Policy,* vol. 15, 285–305.

Teece, David J., Gary P. Pisano, and Amy Shuen. 1997. "Dynamic capabilities and strategic management." *Strategic Management Journal* 18 (7):509–533.

Tushman, M., and C. O'Reilly. 1997. *Winning Through Innovation* (Harvard Business School Press, Boston, MA).

Tushman, M., and P. Anderson. 1986. "Technological discontinuities and organizational environments." *Administrative Science Quarterly,* vol. 31: 439–465.

Ulrich, Karl. 1995. "The role of product architecture in the manufacturing firm." *Research Policy,* vol. 24.

Ulrich, K. T., and S. D. Eppinger. 1995. *Product Design and Development* (McGraw-Hill, Inc., New York).

Utterback, J. M 1982. "The innovation process," in M. Tushman and W. Moore (eds.), *Readings in the Management of Innovation* (Pitman Books, Ltd., Marshfield, MA).

Utterback, J. M. 1994. *Mastering the Dynamics of Innovation* (Harvard Business School Press, Boston, MA).

Williamson, O. E. 1975. *Markets and Hierarchies: Analysis and Antitrust Implications* (The Free Press, New York).

Williamson, O. E. 1985. *The Economic Institutions of Capitalism* (The Free Press: New York).

END NOTES

1. Rosenberg (1982) has shown that this is common: what constitutes good performance, although obvious in retrospect, is rarely apparent as new product-markets emerge. Because the products simply were not available, customers rarely thought insightfully about how they would be used. This convergence amongst a group of customers toward a common rank-ordering of important performance attributes defines what Dosi (1982) calls a technological paradigm.

2. Utterback's (1994) work on the dynamics of innovation suggests that in the initial stages of most industries' evolution, the rate of product innovation is high. This rate ultimately subsides when a dominant design emerges. This enables an increase in the rate of process innovation. Other work suggests that, within the product innovation phase of Utterback's model, there are really *two* stages—a period of architectural innovation, followed by a period in which the focus is on component-level product innovation. This phase may last for an extended period, well after the emergence of dominant designs. This is a principal finding of Henderson & Clark (1990), who also found that firms' initial focus on architectural innovation shifts toward a subsequent component focus.

They point out that, as a result, firms' abilities at architectural innovation atrophy through disuse, while their abilities to innovate in certain types of componentry are enhanced. Iansiti and Khanna (1995) have also shown that underneath what appears to have been a steady, incremental pace of improvement in an assembled product (mainframe computers) are an array of component-level innovations over time, some of which are quite radical in character. Christensen, Suarez, and Utterback (1998) show that the dominant design of disk drives was defined long before several important component-level innovations such as thin film and magneto-resistive heads, as discussed later in this paper.

3. In Christensen and Raynor's (2001) terms, modular architectures are specifiable, verifiable, and predictable.

4. Dennis Waid, R*igid Disk Drive Heads and Media: A Technology and Marketing Report* (Saratoga, CA: The Technology Assessment Group, 1986).

5. In the MR head area, a longstanding alliance between Quantum and MKE required the partners to form a 50-50 joint venture, MKQC, to be responsible for the design, development, and production of Quantum's MR heads, this despite the ability of the two firms to coordinate a longstanding alliance during the modular phase of the technology without any joint equity ownership structures in the past. In early 1999, Quantum and MKE announced the termination of their joint development programs in MR head technology. Quantum now sources external MR heads.

6. While MR technology disk drives were interdependent at the component level, these drives plugged and played with the standard drive interfaces with computers, so that these drives had a ready OEM market available to them. As noted in the following paragraph, it would take another five years before IBM could sell the MR heads themselves as OEM components.

7. An example might help to illustrate the concept. The IBM 2.5" Travelstar LP 2360 (code named "Bolero") shipped in 1995. It incorporated IBM's MR head in its design, along with a thin film disk, run length limited (RLL) code, and other component features. Its actual areal density was 644 million bits per inch. The average areal density for product models with the same components as the IBM Travelstar was calculated to be 390 million bits per square inch. We construct the measure of architectural efficiency by taking 644 million bits per inch and dividing that by the calculated average of 390 million bits per square inch for drives that used the same components. In this case, the model's architectural efficiency was 1.651.

8. More formally, greater interdependence among n different components implies a higher value for k, the measure of the interactions among the n components.

9. An example where such rules have emerged is in the use of design languages in ASICs, such as Verilog, that map circuit designs directly to chip layout and eventual fabrication. The advent of these languages has helped to facilitate the emergence of the so-called "fabless" semiconductor firms and the emergence of foundries that are dedicated to the production of other firms' chip designs.

10. Pisano's notion of "learning before doing" corresponds closely with the idea of modularity, since learning before doing presumes the existence of well-characterized models of how interactions will likely behave when put into higher volume manufacturing. "Learning by doing" on the other hand fits well with interdependence in that significant trial and error is required before processes can be scaled up.

11. A highly decentralized firm might own upstream materials and component assets (and hence meet the economist's definition of vertical integration) but rely upon market forces and market prices to define the interactions between upstream and downstream stages of a value-added chain. See Eccles and White, 1992, and our discussion of Fujitsu's approach to MR head technology below.

12. This term is developed in Eppinger and Ulrich, 1995. One of us has earlier termed this technology *systemic* (Chesbrough & Teece, 1996). We adopt the term *interdependent* here to highlight the organizational implications of this type of technology and to dispel any confusion around "systems technology" vs. "systemic technology" that might arise from readers with engineering and scientific backgrounds. In addition, the term *modularity* seems to have found widespread use in the technology and organization literature (Henderson and Clark, 1990; Sanchez & Mahoney, 1996; Baldwin and Clark, 2000), and we adopt it here.

READING III-4

The Transfer of Technology from Research to Development

H. Cohen, S. Keller, and D. Streeter

In this paper, we will discuss some observations we have made in our own laboratories on the transfer of technology from research to development. We have tried to assemble "data" on transfers or attempted transfers that have occurred over the past 15 years. We have inspected these findings to see whether some common features could be recognized.

Source: Reprinted with permission from *Research Management* 22, no. 3 (May 1979), pp. 11–17. *Note: The authors of this paper all worked in the Research Division of IBM.*

IBM's Research Division is a separate division of the company, independent of product groups and reporting directly to the chief operating executives in the corporate office. The division is not, however, a staff advisory group but is charged with two major functions: to contribute to the technologies required for the product line by supporting current technologies and by finding new alternatives, and to contribute to those fields of science which underlie present product technologies and which may provide future ones. Product development is carried out in the laboratories of the groups' development divisions. There are 27 of these throughout the world. Thus, our Research Division, with its three laboratories in Yorktown Heights, San Jose, and Zurich, faces a development community about 10 times our size, well spread geographically, and covering a very large range of technical areas. In only one case, at San Jose, are research and development laboratories located at the same site.

Since completing the data taking and analysis reported here, we have used some of the notions to help guide research managers and project leaders with new transfers as they have come about. In doing this, we have begun to perceive other aspects that we hope will bear further generalizations, perhaps in later reports. In addition, we have added to our divisional staff a full-time marketing representative as program manager for technology transfer, and a full-time cost estimator. The former serves to make the corporate and divisional marketing representatives knowledgeable about our work and to bring their requirements to us. The latter helps us prepare our case with our development colleagues.

METHODOLOGY

First, let us set out some terminology. Transfers will be called successful if the technology has moved from research to a development laboratory and then has become a product or a part of a product or an important enhancement of a production process. A nonsuccessful transfer will be one in which the technology has left research but has not appeared as a product. A nontransfer refers to research projects that were intended for transfer but were never accepted in development.

We began our study with two parallel steps: first, we wrote down the "well-known" lore in the company having to do with the transfer problem; and second, we examined a long list of all the projects in the laboratories over a 15-year period that we felt were intended to be transferred (remember that part of our mission has always been to work in science as well as in applied projects).

The prejudices about what was required for a good transfer were collected from research and development managers and staff members who had been involved in transfers. Here are some of them:

1. There must be an advanced technology group in the receiving organization to enable transfer to take place. (*Advanced technology* is the term used in the company for an advanced effort in the development laboratory not directly supporting a currently planned product but aimed at follow-on or replacement products.)
2. Advanced technology competes with research, often blocking transfer.
3. Transfer occurs when "outsiders" recognize the value of the technology. These outsiders may be external to the company, or they may be internal users of the technology but not prospective developers.
4. The external marketplace can play an effective role in pressuring a transfer to take place.
5. Once a project has transferred, it is useful to maintain some level of work in research, overlapping and complementing the newly initiated work in the division.
6. There should be joint participation, by research and development, when the project is still in research. The transfer can be most easily facilitated with the transfer of people from the joint program to the receiving organization.
7. Physical proximity of research to the receiving organization is important.

We examined the long list of projects and divided it into new lists of successful, nonsuccessful, and nontransfers. From these, we chose projects that represented the functional areas of our research programs: logic and memory, storage, input/output and communications, systems and programming, and computer applications. We actually reviewed only 18 projects so that we can certainly make no claims to completeness even within our own laboratories. A description of each of the case histories is given in the Appendix. Furthermore, we conducted our examination in an "anthropological" mode of observation and discussion through interviews without trying to quantify results. We have, therefore, arrived at some views and suggestions and not at hard-and-fast conclusions or rules of conduct.

From the original prejudices or "lore" noted above, we produced an interviewing guide and then interviewed more than 50 people who were involved in the transfers. Most, but not all, of these are or were in the research division so that we have more a research view than a general one. Case histories were prepared for each of the projects. The case histories and key factor suggestions were reviewed, testing the original prejudices, sometimes replacing or confirming them, sometimes adding new factors of interest. We finally replaced the original list with a new set of factors or ingredients of a transfer to which we gave an ordering of importance. In the following two sections, we will discuss these technology transfer factors in order of relative importance. In the discussion, we will point out examples from specific projects to help explain the factors.

Primary Factors

Technical Understanding It is essential that research understand the main technical issues of the technology before passing it on. This may seem obvious. However, in some cases we studied this did not seem to be true, and this is why we believe the technical base for each project must be considered carefully. In the germanium project, while the materials and processing problems were understood, the limitations in the advantages of germanium over silicon became apparent only after several years of research activity. These had less to do with devices that were created and more to do with device implementation in packaging and circuitry.

In addition, the target of achieving a very high speed device, a rather restricted goal, could also be achieved with silicon, whose development was continuing to make progress. Another example can be drawn from the beam addressable file project. There were problems in obtaining the laser arrays for addressing and problems in obtaining a material with the desired properties. At the same time, research tried very early in the game to obtain development assistance in the program. It turned out that this was premature. In addition, we had not successfully evaluated the benefits of this technology over what was available in the conventional magnetic recording. Since we didn't have the technology in hand (lack of addressing arrays or appropriate materials) and since we had not fully assessed the advantages over existing technology and the latter's limitations or lack of them, the project was destined to be unsuccessful insofar as the transfer process was concerned.

When a research project is aimed at transferring to development toward product status, it is important to understand where it will fit in the product line and what requirements must be met to reach that fit. While research cannot do its own marketing, it cannot waste time solving problems that don't exist or producing technology that cannot be sold by IBM. A basic ingredient of a technology is its cost. This can be considered at least in a pre-liminary estimate fashion for hardware but is, obviously, very difficult for programming. Both of the large systems projects we referred to failed in this respect.

Fortunately, for devices, circuits, and other hardware, the research work itself requires that at least one possible means of manufacturing be exhibited. Alternatives and improvements can be left for development and manufacturing engineering. For software, especially systems programming, "manufacture" or implementation in development is not well understood. Research results in software have not seemed to have directly affected eventual implementation methods.

Feasibility Several projects never demonstrated the feasibility of research concepts because the time pressures forced transfer before demonstration could be accomplished. One thing that we learned was that we have to sometimes bridle our enthusiasm to keep from pushing an idea before we understand it well enough and can demonstrate its feasibility. Research and the receiving division must reach an agreement on what constitutes feasibility. Clearly, this will depend on the topic. For an algorithm such as the Fast Fourier Transform, the requirement is a running program that does better than existing methods. For hardware it will be a working device or even a system of components, performing a function, together with a demonstrated fabrication methodology. The program in magnetic films for memories is one in which feasibility was shown. However, magnetic films never became a product due to advances made in core memories and the quick growth in semiconductor memory technology.

In some cases, there are entire application systems or languages where the feasibility implies acceptability to the end user. This might be an end user in, say, medical diagnosis or the airline business, and must involve some kind of joint study with real users before feasibility can be demonstrated.

Advanced Development Overlap For those projects that are transferred out, research must determine whether to maintain activity, either to support development or to defend its concepts, or to explore advanced or related technologies. The successful research development of FETs was followed by an abrupt discontinuation of almost all research in semiconductors for a short period. This was a mistake. The difficulty experienced in getting the development division to pick up the one-device memory cell in 1967 may have been partly due to a relative disinterest by research management in semiconductors just at that time as it turned its attention to other areas.

In planning applied projects, and especially as they near transfer, careful preparations have to be made for the proper kind of overlap program. For certain research projects, in particular, systems work, the creation of a special, advanced development effort is often the answer to problems of scaling-up or to answer questions of marketability or economic feasibility before making a full product commitment. This may require bringing to the research laboratories new kinds of people. For example, with APL, a complete working system with customers was running before transfer.

Growth Potential   There have been several research programs that suffered from being too narrowly aimed at a specific need and not having clear paths to technical growth and to growth in product applicability. Examples of this are the germanium and the beam addressable file programs.

Unless there is a prospect of technical advancement, the transfer may not be successful due to the fact that existing technologies "stretch" themselves. The challenge of a new technology forces an existing one to extend itself, to advance its goals, to expand its potential in the face of competition. Frequently, this stretching removes the advantages of this challenge, resulting in its demise. This was exactly the case with the beam addressable file. The germanium project and the magnetic thin-film program afford other examples. The cryogenic computer work of the early 1960s is another example. The thin superconducting film memories developed at that time lost out to the advances being made by magnetic films and the cryotron logic lost out to the constant advances made by silicon circuitry. In all of these cases, not enough attention was paid to the growth potential in the new technology.

While research could perhaps take credit for stimulating or forcing advances in the existing technologies by offering competing alternatives, it certainly can't be the organization's major ambition or goal. To avoid being caught itself, Research has to constantly and carefully look over its shoulder at what is coming along.

Existence of an Advocate   No matter how elegant the research results are or how much benefit they appear to have for the company, someone in research must take the responsibility to see that the results reach the right place. Our study indicates that a strong proponent actively selling the research results is necessary for transfer. It is obviously not sufficient; the several projects that failed to transfer or failed to become products also had research champions. Properly timed seminars for publicizing and explaining transferable research concepts have been helpful when used. The effectiveness of the research champion has been enhanced in several cases via a push-pull provided by an external champion.

Advanced Technology Activities in a Development Laboratory   The major conclusion is that advanced technology programs in the development laboratories are helpful and often necessary for transfer from research. In a very clear-cut fashion, the presence of "ad tech" groups aided in our moving electron beam technology and magnetic bubbles work from research to development. Both of these transfers have and are taking place continuously. Materials and knowledge of materials processing, device and circuit invention, and application techniques have all moved out. Interest in electron beam fabrication methods was high enough amongst individuals in ad tech, and their connection to research was useful in smoothing the way. With respect to bubbles, the ad tech lab in development had the talents and experience to pick up its technology. Thus, without formal contracting or negotiating, the presence of skilled and research-minded people in the development labs, and their relative freedom from close-in product demands, made it easier to effect the transfer.

In other hardware projects, divisional ad tech has served a critical function and has often looked to be competitive or even obstructional to research. Our case studies show that most of the time, the higher hurdles created by ad tech skepticism or resistance were, in the end, beneficial. For LSI-FET (large-scale integration–field effect transmitter), research had to do the work and carry materials processing, device and circuit design, and design automation very far along, further than the research image of itself was comfortable with. However, the results were convincing, the corporation took on FETs in a confirmed fashion, and research benefited by having seasoned people in silicon technology, ready for subsequent efforts.

There is a similar record for magnetic films. The initial hurdles put up by the relevant development organization required very solid results and a thorough involvement of research people, not only in technology but also in systems usage and its economy. In the cases of the already mentioned beam addressable file and germanium programs, ad tech groups were correctly negative. By and large, having an ad tech activity in a divisional development laboratory is a positive asset to technology transfers.

All of the above is relevant to hardware technology. In the case of software activities, the picture is not as clear. In one case, that of APL, it was protected and developed slowly inside research. While it created its technology, it also created a user audience and usage patterns. Keeping it in research longer than might have been thought desirable had the benefit of producing a new language and tools for its operation, not seriously reduced in effectiveness by having to comply with then-current marketing philosophy. Thus, research, willing or not, provided the advanced technology phase for APL.

There is a class of programming results that really does not require very much further development. The FFT, VM Monitor, and ASTAP contributions were passed on fairly directly, but in each case the successful transfer came about by negotiating what level of programming would be acceptable.

In general, in the software area it is a little more difficult to define the role of ad tech groups in the development sector.

External Pressures For many of the hardware projects that were transferred and for some of the software ones, the presence of some form of the same technology in a competitor's laboratory or a product announcement has helped transfer. For our work in LSI-FETs, most of the industry was beginning preparation for FET componentry while our components development groups were still concentrating on bipolars. Research was able to draw attention to the competition when it was needed. For magnetic thin films, a competitor had announced a memory product before our product was close to announcement, but it was clear from the published work of research activities in several laboratories that a number of companies were working on magnetic films. At the time we were urging a development lab to become interested in electron beam technology, some manufacturers were publicly talking about methods and preliminary results. Reports of work on bubbles at other laboratories have kept product development people interested enough to make the continuous transfer that is occurring easier.

In other projects, however, there was no competitive pressure. In the applications area, cryptography and Fast Fourier Transforms were unique to research and IBM. The beam addressable file was not specifically pushed by competitors, although their people had similar projects under way. In the S.S.A., there was an immediate development following the research work in order to fulfill a government contract.

In general, for hardware, parallel activity elsewhere has helped research to transfer to development. It has also created an external standard against which to judge the research progress and achievement. When there is no outside activity we can expect greater difficulty in making judgments ourselves and in transferring.

For the applications results, external pressure has not played an important role. For the systems and programming transfers, competition has played a part in the past and may again in the future.

Joint Programs Joint programs can have several forms. They can involve support by money or by people. They may involve research people in development laboratories or development people in our laboratories. The most interesting observation from our case studies is that there was no joint activity in any of the systems and programming projects. There may have been a number of reasons, but for the most part this seemed to have been because of an inability by research to convince development managers that our ideas were any better or might be more productive than their own.

There were (or are) activities involving jointly planned programs or lending of people in LSI-FET, magnetic bubbles, and magnetic thin films. In the germanium and electron beam projects, research took on development people in training or as a mode of entry hiring into the company. In general, we conclude that joint programs are good to have but do not ensure success.

Secondary Factors

Timeliness Timeliness may enter in several ways. For one, research may try to provide a new or unique technology early because there are other candidates for a new product. More often research will have to be concerned about product cycles and when entry of improvements or even a new technology in a conventional product area is feasible. Good timing is important but it is not sufficient for successful transfer. If what we have is good enough, timeliness may not even be necessary.

Internal Users In addition to the useful pressure that external competition may create in helping to move a technology to the development laboratories, in some cases internal IBM users can play a similar role. A demand from hardware systems people, in one of the development labs, for low-cost, high-density FET circuitry helped in getting our divisional components people to pick up the research results. Internal use of APL helped create pressure on the sales side of the business. Hopefully, internal users of magnetic bubbles will grow and augment the market for device and circuit manufacture. If such internal-user demands do not naturally arise, perhaps research labs should stimulate them.

Government Contracts In one of the cases studied, magnetic bubbles, the presence of a government contract was useful in furthering the research work itself and in providing a good stimulus for transfer. In the early days of magnetic thin-film research, contracts were helpful in getting started in the technology. Another contract supported some early work in sparse matrices. The difficulty of the government's requirements for the Social Security Page Reader forced a collaboration between research and development that probably would not have taken place otherwise. The collaboration produced technical advances that were useful in subsequent products. In effect, the stiff external requirements forced the development groups to look to research for advanced work.

High-Level Involvement Occasionally, research has turned to corporate management for help in transfer. This was true in the case of LSI-FETs. At other times, staff committees were involved. In general, however, this has not been an important or even an effective mechanism for research to use.

Individual Corporate Responsibility In one case, cryptography, an individual with a corporate watchdog role was useful. In general, this is rare and this may be important only when there is a totally new area of technical endeavor, such as cryptography, for us to deal with.

Proximity In practically no case was the proximity of a development laboratory to a research laboratory an important factor. At times, being close was convenient and saved money, but no transfer failed because of distance.

APPENDIX: THE 18 CASE STUDY PROJECTS

Large-Scale Integration–N-Channel Field Effect Transistors (Successful)

In 1963, the Yorktown Heights laboratory began work on integrated silicon circuitry. This included silicon processing techniques, involving considerable physics and chemistry, device and circuit design, light table development for mask making and other optical lithographic requirements, and a design automation program. The devices were primarily FETs—field effect transistors—but the methodology evolved proved to be useful for bipolar devices and circuits as well. The general idea of large-scale integration was transferred to the component development laboratories in 1966, but it was not until 1968 that the specific technology for FET was finally adopted. This transfer provided the basis for IBM's main memories of the early 1970s and for the logic in most of the company's terminals and small machines in the same period.

Electron Beam Fabrication Methods (Successful)

In the early 1960s, the Yorktown Heights laboratory used electron beams to produce an optically read storage disk. Its original use was as the dictionary in a Russian translation system. Some of this early "photostore" technology was transferred as early as 1963 into special-purpose storage products. From that time on, there were a number of parallel research activities: the beam column itself including an improved filament, the software to automatically run circuit patterns, and, importantly, efficient sensitive resists for the lithographic processing. These were transferred continuously into the component development laboratories beginning about 1966. Electron beam fabrication methods are now in use in the lithographic processes of circuit chips.

The Germanium Program (Nontransfer)

Germanium has a higher mobility than silicon and, in the early days of transistors, was widely used for point contact and junction transistors. With the coming of integration in the early 1960s, there was a brief period of competition between germanium and silicon for use in integrated circuits. The Yorktown laboratory started a program in 1964 which was supported by funds from the Components Development Division. With this support, the program grew to a rather large size. As the silicon technology advanced, the germanium studies experimented with low-temperature environments (liquid nitrogen) to gain further speed and other advantages. Both were aimed at a high-speed circuit requirement for a large computing system which was in design at the time. By 1968, however, it had become apparent that although germanium might meet the requirements of speed for this particular computer project, the power required to attain these speeds was very high. Although this was also true of silicon, silicon had much more attractive characteristics at medium and low speeds and appeared to have greater growth and extendability prospects. The project was terminated in 1968, and the use of germanium in computer circuitry has disappeared.

One Device Memory Cell (Unsuccessful)

Until 1966, integrated circuits for memory in the research laboratory and in development in IBM had used a number of transistors for each memory cell. A cell is the physical location of memory bit storage. At this time, a research staff member invented a memory circuit, which required only one device, and a patent was issued in 1968. Attempts were made to interest the development laboratories in this circuit which gave a very large decrease in cell area and therefore represented a primary means of increasing memory density on a chip and increasing speed. Unfortunately, other designs had already been adopted for current development in 1967 and little headway was made. Eventually, cell designs of this kind did appear in IBM memory technology but an early lead was lost.

Magnetic Thin Film Memory (Unsuccessful)

Early work on using thin magnetic films to form memories was carried on in IBM, Lincoln Laboratories, Univac, and other laboratories. In 1960, joint preliminary studies by IBM research and a development group resulted in a research project in the Zurich laboratory. This was successful to the extent that the technology was brought from Zurich to Yorktown Heights and with further work was transferred to a components development laboratory. By 1964, a product design for a very fast memory was completed. Plans were made to use the memories in a large computer. In research, further activity produced new technical ideas for other versions of thin film memories. While all of this was happening in magnetic thin films, the major memory product was ferrite cores which were being continuously improved as to size and speed. Also, the first transistor memories were being considered. In the end, only one computer system with a fast magnetic thin film memory was shipped. It had made its goals but the technology, by 1968, had been overtaken by transistor memories. In 1969, efforts were terminated by both research and development.

Beam Addressable Storage (Nontransfer)

In the mid-1960s, before the serious advent of magnetic bubbles as a storage candidate, much thought was given to replacing magnetic induction recording with a beam addressable storage system. To gain high bit density, magnetic domain sizes on disks and tapes have been continuously reduced, hence requiring the magnetic head to move closer to the disk surface. As the head-to-surface gap becomes smaller, design and operational control become more difficult and more costly. Beam addressed disk storage did not have this limitation and therefore looked interesting. A research project was under way in the San Jose laboratory by 1968. It used a magneto-optic effect: originally a europium oxide–coated disk was written on by a light beam produced by low-temperature injection lasers. At first, the disk surface materials also had

to be operated at liquid nitrogen temperatures. New disk coatings were found and plans were made to do the work necessary to bring continuously operating room temperature semiconductor lasers into the system. A deeper understanding of the physical mechanisms involved in the transduction of light energy through a thermal phase to a change in magnetic phase was studied. As all of this was being done, the magnetic induction recording technology in the neighboring development laboratory was spurred to significant improvements. Higher densities of magnetic bits and dramatically smaller head-to-disk gaps were found feasible. The projected densities and costs of magnetic induction recording became equal to or better than those set out as goals for the beam addressable project, and it was terminated.

Magnetic Bubbles (Successful)

Although IBM researchers had worked with the interesting garnet crystal materials and were aware of magnetic effects themselves and those observed at the Bell Laboratories and Philips Eindhoven laboratory, it was not until the announcement by the Bell Labs of its bubble technology and its patent in the area that interest was really spurred. Research groups were formed in 1969, and a small NASA contract was accepted in 1971 calling for a simple operating chip with bubbles of rather large diameter. The contract was completed in 1972. New materials, including an amorphous substitute for the garnet crystals, began to come out of the research activities. Inventions of new bubble devices and of a new system concept, the bubble lattice file, appeared. However, efforts to interest the component development laboratories and computer system development groups in the company were not successful. Research then undertook a campaign to interest not only the technology developers in the company but also future systems users. Finally, the storage development laboratory became interested and early research work was transferred. Research continues to work on advanced concepts in bubble storage.

Copier Technology (Successful)

In the early 1960s, relatively basic work was started in the San Jose Research laboratory on organic photoconductors. Although there was not a specific product goal in mind, it was thought that microfilms or perhaps copiers might require such photosensitive materials. The early studies led to the discovery of a very high–sensitivity photoconductor just at the time when technology for an office copier was required. A robot model was built to show that the new material would work. Since this was a new product area, there was no development group to accept the work. Eventually some of the research people carried the technology into development while others created an advanced technology group for the development division.

Social Security Page Readers (Successful)

Character and pattern recognition had been a research field in the computer sciences all throughout the 1950s. In the early 1960s, the Yorktown Heights group developed a system for character recognition with multiple scanners and software and hardware for processing recognition logic flexible enough to operate on a wide variety of fonts. In product development, however, character recognition concentrated on special single fonts such as might be employed in a bank check reader. When the Social Security Administration requested a multifont page reader in 1963, the research facility and its processing experience was used to show feasibility. A joint effort was carried on by research and the development laboratory for two years involving transfers of people both ways. When the page reader product was delivered to the Social Security Administration, a large number of the research concepts were included.

System Y (Unsuccessful) and
System A (Unsuccessful)

These were two large projects—one in the mid-1960s, the other in the early 1970s. One dealt with an advanced hardware design for a computer and the other a software architecture. We cannot discuss these projects in any detail because some of the results are still sensitive. However, they were similar in the following respect: in each there were some extremely interesting and potentially powerful concepts developed while they were in research (Yorktown Heights). In both cases, this was only a short period of time, one year, and before these concepts could be worked to any degree of feasibility, the projects were moved almost intact into a development program. In hindsight, it appears now that not enough understanding was provided during the research period.

APL (Successful)

The concepts of the APL language were brought to IBM by the research staff member who conceived of them at Harvard. The language was unique in that it developed a new notation and syntax and, among other attractive features, allowed for the powerful operators on vectors and matrices that are desired by people in many kinds of math-

ematical applications in science. After a trial as a batch system, a time-sharing implementation was created, nominally for use in the Yorktown Heights laboratory. Classes were taught and very quickly a large number of researchers began to use the system. Other users came on to the system from other parts of IBM. All of this was carried on relatively informally, and as the user set grew and the language became well known it served as a proof to the development and marketing groups in the company that APL deserved to become a product. This finally happened in 1970.

M-44 (Successful)

This was the local name at the Yorktown Heights laboratory for a project in the early 1960s that tested concepts for virtual memory and virtual machines. An older computer was physically modified and a new operating system created to try out the ideas. For example, the notion of paging, bringing blocks of data from disk or drum to main memory in an ordered fashion so as to give the user the impression of an enhanced or virtual memory, was tested by literally coding algorithms and trying them out. The virtual machine concept was first used in this experimental system. The research results were positive and were quickly transferred to development groups for use in time-sharing systems in the late 1960s and virtual memory and machine systems in the 1970s.

VM Monitor/Statistics-Generating
Package (Successful)

These are two related software programs that enable users of VM, one of IBM's main operating systems, to measure the performance of their workload on the systems. The programs were developed in Yorktown Heights for use on the local computing systems to help understand computing efficiency and improvements. They were transferred relatively smoothly to a development division and have become part of the VM system provided for customers.

Cryptography (Successful)

Data security became an issue in IBM in the late 1960s. Corporate responsibility was assigned to an individual who stimulated interest and activities amongst the mathematicians at Yorktown Heights. Simultaneously, others in the laboratory were coding and designing hardware for some new encryption methods. Attempts were made in 1970 to interest advanced technology groups in the terminal development laboratories, but there were no takers. However, in 1971, a special product was produced by the same development laboratory for a banking customer. The cryptographic code developed by that laboratory was sent to Yorktown Heights for testing and it was easily broken. The new technology, ideas, hardware, and software that had been under way at research were quickly put into use instead, and the transfer was effected. An enhanced version of these codes has now become the federal cryptographic standard.

Fast Fourier Transform (Successful)

This now well-known algorithm came into being in its present easily computed form through the joint efforts of two IBMers in research and a staff member of the Bell Labs in 1963. The algorithm was suggested to solve a particular problem in low-temperature physics and programmed at Yorktown Heights. Its amazing usefulness was publicized and propagated to IBM customers and scientists by reports, papers, newsletters, and a large number of personal contacts. Within four years' time, programs were available, special hardware was under development, and the algorithm was on its way to becoming one of the most widely used in all of scientific computing. Important extensions are still being made.

ASTAP (Successful)

This is an acronym for an internal IBM circuit analysis program. Between 1963 and 1975, mathematicians in the Yorktown Heights laboratory made a number of contributions. Two of these, methods for handling "stiff" differential equations and for dealing efficiently with sparse matrices, have made huge improvements in circuit analysis running times. They have also led to a large number of independent mathematical investigations by workers in the field in a number of other institutions.

Graphic Document System (Unsuccessful)

This project began as a possible solution to the problem of mapping electric utility holdings. It was stimulated by a known customer need and it allowed field maps, roughly sketched on the job, to be easily and swiftly transformed into properly dimensioned, annotated, and rectified maps. The system used special hardware and required new software. It was used in a test with one of the major regional utility companies and proved effective in this trial. Using the mapping system as a base, a drafting system was also evolved and tested in one of IBM's development laboratories. Both projects have since wandered through a number of development projects in both domestic and European development laboratories, but no products have resulted.

READING III-5

Absorptive Capacity: A New Perspective on Learning and Innovation

Wesley M. Cohen and Daniel A. Levinthal

INTRODUCTION

Outside sources of knowledge are often critical to the innovation process, whatever the organizational level at which the innovating unit is defined. While the example of Japan illustrates the point saliently at the national level,[1] it is also true of entire industries, as pointed out by Brock[2] in the case of computers and by Peck[3] in the case of aluminum. At the organizational level, March and Simon[4] suggested most innovations result from borrowing rather than invention. This observation is supported by extensive research on the sources of innovation.[5] Finally, the importance to innovative performance of information originating from other internal units in the firm, outside the formal innovating unit (i.e., the R&D lab), such as marketing and manufacturing, is well understood.[6]

Source: Reprinted with permission from *Administrative Science Quarterly* 35 (1990), pp. 128–52.

[1] D. E. Westney and K. Sakakibara, "The Role of Japan-Based R&D in Global Technology Strategy," in *Technology in the Modern Corporation,* ed. M. Hurowitch (London: Pergamon, 1986), pp. 217–32; E. Mansfield, "The Speed and Cost of Industrial Innovation in Japan and the United States: External vs. Internal Technology," *Management Science* 34, no. 10 (1988), pp. 1157–68; N. Rosenberg and W. E. Steinmueller, "Why Are Americans Such Poor Imitators?" *American Economic Review* 78, no. 2 (1988), pp. 229–34.

[2] G. W. Brock, *The U.S. Computer Industry* (Cambridge, MA: Ballinger, 1975).

[3] M. J. Peck, "Inventions in the Postwar American Aluminum Industry," in *The Rate and Direction of Inventive Activity,* ed. R. R. Nelson (Princeton: Princeton University Press, 1962), pp. 279–98.

[4] J. G. March and H. A. Simon, *Organizations* (New York: Wiley, 1958).

[5] For example: W. F. Mueller, "The Origins of the Basic Inventions Underlying DuPont's Major Product and Process Innovations, 1920 to 1950," in *The Rate and Direction of Inventive Activity,* ed. R. R. Nelson (Princeton: Princeton University Press, 1962), pp. 323–58; D. Hamberg, "Invention in the Industrial Research Laboratory," *Journal of Political Economy* 71 (1963), pp. 95–115; S. Myers and D. C. Marquis, "Successful Industrial Innovations," Washington, DC: National Science Foundation, NSF 69–17, 1969; R. Johnston and M. Gibbons, "Characteristics of Information Usage in Technological Innovation," *IEEE Transactions on Engineering Management* 22 (1975), pp. 27–34; E. von Hippel, *The Sources of Innovation* (New York: Oxford University Press, 1988).

[6] E. Mansfield, *Economics of Technological Change* (New York: Norton, 1968).

The ability to exploit external knowledge is thus a critical component of innovative capabilities. We argue that the ability to evaluate and utilize outside knowledge is largely a function of the level of prior related knowledge. At the most elemental level, this prior knowledge includes basic skills or even a shared language but may also include knowledge of the most recent scientific or technological developments in a given field. Thus, prior related knowledge confers an ability to recognize the value of new information, assimilate it, and apply it to commercial ends. These abilities collectively constitute what we call a firm's absorptive capacity.

At the level of the firm—the innovating unit that is the focus here—absorptive capacity is generated in a variety of ways. Research shows that firms that conduct their own R&D are better able to use externally available information.[7] This implies that absorptive capacity may be created as a byproduct of a firm's R&D investment. Other work suggests that absorptive capacity may also be developed as a byproduct of a firm's manufacturing operations. Abernathy[8] and Rosenberg[9] have noted that through direct involvement in manufacturing, a firm is better able to recognize and exploit new information relevant to a particular product-market. Production experience provides the firm with the background necessary both to recognize the value of, and implement methods to reorganize or automate, particular manufacturing processes. Firms also invest in absorptive capacity directly, as when they send personnel for advanced technical training. The concept of absorptive capacity can best be developed through an examination of the cognitive structures that underlie learning.

Cognitive Structures

The premise of the notion of absorptive capacity is that the organization needs prior related knowledge to assimilate and use new knowledge. Studies in the area of cognitive and behavioral sciences at the individual level both justify and enrich this observation. Research on memory development suggests that accumulated prior knowledge increases both the ability to put new knowledge into memory, what we would refer to as the acquisition of knowledge, and the ability to recall and use it. With respect to the acquisition of knowledge, Bower and Hilgard[10] suggested that memory development is self-reinforcing in that the more objects, patterns, and concepts are stored in memory, the more readily is new information about these constructs acquired and the more facile is the individual in using them in new settings.

Some psychologists suggest that prior knowledge enhances learning because memory—or the storage of knowledge—is developed by associative learning in which events are recorded into memory by establishing linkages with preexisting concepts. Thus, Bower and Hilgard[11] suggested that the breadth of categories into which prior knowledge is organized, the differentiation of those categories, and the linkages across them permit individuals to make sense of and, in turn, acquire new knowledge. In the context of learning a language, Lindsay and Norman[12] suggested the problem in learning words is not a result of lack of exposure to them but that "to understand complex phrases, much more is needed than exposure to the words: a large body of knowledge must first be accumulated. After all, a word is simply a label for a set of structures within the memory system, so the structures must exist before the word can be considered learned." Lindsay and Norman further suggested that knowledge may be nominally acquired but not well utilized subsequently because the individual did not already possess the appropriate contextual knowledge necessary to make the new knowledge fully intelligible.

The notion that prior knowledge facilitates the learning of new related knowledge can be extended to include the case in which the knowledge in question may itself be a set of learning skills. There may be a transfer of learning skills across bodies of knowledge that are organized and expressed in similar ways. As a consequence, experience or performance on one learning task may influence and improve performance on some subsequent learning task.[13] This progressive improvement in the performance of learning tasks is a form of knowledge transfer that had been referred to as "learning to learn."[14] Estes,[15] however, suggested that the term "learning to learn" is a misnomer

[7] J. E. Tilton, *International Diffusion of Technology: The Case of Semiconductors* (Washington, DC: Brookings Institution, 1971); T. J. Allen, *Managing the Flow of Technology* (Cambridge, MA: MIT Press, 1977); D. C. Mowery, "The Relationship Between Intrafirm and Contractual Forms of Industrial Research in American Manufacturing, 1900–1940," *Explorations in Economic History* 20 (1983), pp. 351–74.

[8] W. J. Abernathy, *The Productivity Dilemma* (Baltimore: Johns Hopkins University Press, 1978).

[9] N. Rosenberg, *Inside the Black Box: Technology and Economics* (New York: Cambridge University Press, 1982).

[10] G. H. Bower and E. R. Hilgard, *Theories of Learning* (Englewood Cliffs, NJ: Prentice Hall, 1981).

[11] Ibid.

[12] P. H. Lindsay and D. A. Norman, *Human Information Processing* (Orlando, FL: Academic Press, 1977).

[13] H. C. Ellis, *The Transfer of Learning* (New York: Macmillan, 1965).

[14] Ibid; W. K. Estes, *Learning Theory and Mental Development* (New York: Academic Press, 1970).

[15] Estes, *Learning Theory and Mental Development*.

in that prior experience with a learning task does not necessarily improve performance because an individual knows how to learn (i.e., form new associations) better, but that an individual may simply have accumulated more prior knowledge so that he or she needs to learn less to attain a given level of performance. Notwithstanding what it is about prior learning experience that may affect subsequent performance, both explanations of the relationship between early learning and subsequent performance emphasize the importance of prior knowledge for learning.

The effect of prior learning experience on subsequent learning tasks can be observed in a variety of tasks. For instance, Ellis suggested that "students who have thoroughly mastered the principles of algebra find it easier to grasp advanced work in mathematics such as calculus."[16] Further illustration is provided by Anderson, Farrell, and Sauers,[17] who compared students learning LISP as a first programming language with students learning LISP after having learned Pascal. The Pascal students learned LISP much more effectively, in part because they better appreciated the semantics of various programming concepts.

The literature also suggests that problem-solving skills develop similarly. In this case, problem-solving methods and heuristics typically constitute the prior knowledge that permits individuals to acquire related problem-solving capabilities. In their work on the development of computer programming skills, Pirolli and Anderson[18] found that almost all students developed new programs by analogy-to-example programs and that their success was determined by how well they understood why these examples worked.

We argue that problem solving and learning capabilities are so similar that there is little reason to differentiate their modes of development, although exactly what is learned may differ: learning capabilities involve the development of the capacity to assimilate existing knowledge, while problem-solving skills represent a capacity to create new knowledge. Supporting the point that there is little difference between the two, Bradshaw, Langley, and Simon[19] and Simon[20] suggested that the sort of necessary preconditions for successful learning that we have identified do not differ from the preconditions required for problem solving and, in turn, for the creative process. Moreover, they argued that the processes themselves do not differ much. The prior possession of relevant knowledge and skill is what gives rise to creativity, permitting the sorts of associations and linkages that may have never been considered before. Likewise, Ellis[21] suggested that Harlow's[22] findings on the development of learning sets provide a possible explanation for the behavioral phenomenon of "insight" that typically refers to the rapid solution of a problem. Thus, the psychology literature suggests that creative capacity and what we call absorptive capacity are quite similar.

To develop an effective absorptive capacity, whether it be for general knowledge or problem solving or learning skills, it is insufficient merely to expose an individual briefly to the relevant prior knowledge. Intensity of effort is critical. With regard to storing knowledge in memory, Lindsay and Norman[23] noted that the more deeply the material is processed—the more effort used, the more processing makes use of associations between the items to be learned and knowledge already in the memory—the better will be the later retrieval of the item. Similarly, learning-set theory[24] implies that important aspects of learning how to solve problems are built up over many practice trials on related problems. Indeed, Harlow[25] suggested that if practice with a particular type of problem is discontinued before it is reliably learned, then little transfer will occur to the next series of problems. Therefore, he concluded that considerable time and effort should be spent on early problems before moving on to more complex problems.

Two related ideas are implicit in the notion that the ability to assimilate information is a function of the richness of the preexisting knowledge structure: learning is cumulative, and learning performance is greatest when the object of learning is related to what is already known. As a result, learning is more difficult in novel domains, and, more generally, an individual's expertise—what he or she knows well—will change only incrementally. The above discussion also suggests that diversity of knowl-

[16] Ellis, *The Transfer of Learning.*

[17] J. R. Anderson, R. Farrell, and R. Sauers, "Learning to Program in LISP," *Cognitive Science* 8 (1984), pp. 87–129.

[18] P. L. Pirolli and J. R. Anderson, "The Role of Learning from Example in the Acquisition of Recursive Programming Skill," *Canadian Journal of Psychology* 39 (1985), pp. 240–72.

[19] G. F. Bradshaw, P. W. Langley, and H. A. Simon, "Studying Scientific Discovery by Computer Simulation," *Science* 222 (1983), pp. 971–75.

[20] H. A. Simon, "What We Know About the Creative Process," in *Frontiers in Creative and Innovative Management,* ed. R. L. Kuhn (Cambridge, MA: Ballinger, 1985), pp. 3–20.

[21] Ellis, *The Transfer of Learning.*

[22] H. F. Harlow, "The Formation of Learning Sets," *Psychological Review* 56 (1949), pp. 51–65; "Learning Set and Error Factor Theory," in *Psychology: A Study of Science,* vol. 2, ed. S. Koch (New York: McGraw-Hill, 1959), pp. 492–537.

[23] *Human Information Processing.*

[24] Harlow, "The Formation of Learning Sets" and "Learning Set and Error Factor Theory."

[25] "Learning Set and Error Factor Theory."

edge plays an important role. In a setting in which there is uncertainty about the knowledge domains from which potentially useful information may emerge, a diverse background provides a more robust basis for learning because it increases the prospect that incoming information will relate to what is already known. In addition to strengthening assimilative powers, knowledge diversity also facilitates the innovative process by enabling the individual to make novel associations and linkages.

From Individual to Organizational Absorptive Capacity

An organization's absorptive capacity will depend on the absorptive capacities of its individual members. To this extent, the development of an organization's absorptive capacity will build on prior investment in the development of its constituent, individual absorptive capacities, and, like individuals' absorptive capacities, organizational absorptive capacity will tend to develop cumulatively. A firm's absorptive capacity is not, however, simply the sum of the absorptive capacities of its employees, and it is therefore useful to consider what aspects of absorptive capacity are distinctly organizational. Absorptive capacity refers not only to the acquisition or assimilation of information by an organization but also to the organization's ability to exploit it. Therefore, an organization's absorptive capacity does not simply depend on the organization's direct interface with the external environment. It also depends on transfers of knowledge across and within subunits that may be quite removed from the original point of entry. Thus, to understand the sources of a firm's absorptive capacity, we focus on the structure of communication between the external environment and the organization, as well as among the subunits of the organization, and also on the character and distribution of expertise within the organization.

Communication systems may rely on specialized actors to transfer information from the environment or may involve less structured patterns. The problem of designing communication structures cannot be disentangled from the distribution of expertise in the organization. The firm's absorptive capacity depends on the individuals who stand at the interface of either the firm and the external environment or at the interface between subunits within the firm. That interface function may be diffused across individuals or be quite centralized. When the expertise of most individuals within the organization differs considerably from that of external actors who can provide useful information, some members of the group are likely to assume relatively centralized "gatekeeping"

or "boundary-spanning" roles.[26] For technical information that is difficult for internal staff to assimilate, a gatekeeper both monitors the environment and translates the technical information into a form understandable to the research group. In contrast, if external information is closely related to ongoing activity, then external information is readily assimilated and gatekeepers or boundary-spanners are not so necessary for translating information. Even in this setting, however, gatekeepers may emerge to the extent that such role specialization relieves others from having to monitor the environment.

A difficulty may emerge under conditions of rapid and uncertain technical change, however, when this interface function is centralized. When information flows are somewhat random and it is not clear where in the firm or subunit a piece of outside knowledge is best applied, a centralized gatekeeper may not provide an effective link to the environment. Under such circumstances, it is best for the organization to expose a fairly broad range of prospective "receptors" to the environment. Such an organization would exhibit the organic structure of Burns and Stalker,[27] which is more adaptable "when problems and requirements for action arise which cannot be broken down and distributed among specialist roles within a clearly defined hierarchy."

Even when a gatekeeper is important, his or her individual absorptive capacity does not constitute the absorptive capacity of his or her unit within the firm. The ease or difficulty of the internal communication process and, in turn, the level of organizational absorptive capacity are not only a function of the gatekeeper's capabilities but also of the expertise of those individuals to whom the gatekeeper is transmitting the information. Therefore, relying on a small set of technological gatekeepers may not be sufficient; the group as a whole must have some level of relevant background knowledge, and when knowledge structures are highly differentiated, the requisite level of background may be rather high.

The background knowledge required by the group as a whole for effective communication with the gatekeeper highlights the more general point that shared knowledge and expertise are essential for communication. At the most basic level, the relevant knowledge that permits effective communication both within and across subunits

---

[26] Allen, *Managing the Flow of Technology;* M. L. Tushman, "Special Boundary Roles in the Innovation Process," *Administrative Science Quarterly* 22 (1977), pp. 587–605.
[27] T. Burns and G. M. Stalker, *The Management of Innovation* (London: Tavistock, 1961), p. 6.

consists of shared language and symbols.[28] With regard to the absorptive capacity of the firm as a whole, there may, however, be a trade-off in the efficiency of internal communication against the ability of the subunit to assimilate and exploit information originating from other subunits or the environment. This can be seen as a trade-off between inward-looking versus outward-looking absorptive capacities. While both of these components are necessary for effective organizational learning, excessive dominance by one or the other will be dysfunctional. If all actors in the organization share the same specialized language, they will be effective in communicating with one another, but they may not be able to tap into diverse external knowledge sources. In the limit, an internal language, coding scheme, or, more generally, any particular body of expertise could become sufficiently overlapping and specialized that it impedes the incorporation of outside knowledge and results in the pathology of the not-invented-here (NIH) syndrome. This may explain Katz and Allen's[29] findings that the level of external communication and communication with other project groups declines with project-group tenure.

This trade-off between outward- and inward-looking components of absorptive capacity focuses our attention on how the relationship between knowledge sharing and knowledge diversity across individuals affects the development of organizational absorptive capacity. While some overlap of knowledge across individuals is necessary for internal communication, there are benefits to diversity of knowledge structures across individuals that parallel the benefits to diversity of knowledge within individuals. As Simon[30] pointed out, diverse knowledge structures coexisting in the same mind elicit the sort of learning and problem solving that yields innovation. If there exists a sufficient level of knowledge overlap to ensure effective communication, interactions across individuals who each possess diverse and different knowledge structures will augment the organization's capacity for making novel linkages and associations—innovating—beyond what any one individual can achieve. Utterback,[31] summarizing research on task performance and innovation, noted that diversity in the work setting "stimulates the generation of new ideas." Thus, as with Nelson and Winter's[32] view of organizational capabilities, an organization's absorptive capacity is not resident in any single individual but depends on the links across a mosaic of individual capabilities.

Beyond diverse knowledge structures, the sort of knowledge that individuals should possess to enhance organizational absorptive capacity is also important. Critical knowledge does not simply include substantive, technical knowledge; it also includes awareness of where useful complementary expertise resides within and outside the organization. This sort of knowledge can be knowledge of who knows what, who can help with what problem, or who can exploit new information. With regard to external relationships, von Hippel[33] (1988) has shown the importance for innovation of close relationships with both buyers and suppliers. To the extent that an organization develops a broad and active network of internal and external relationships, individuals' awareness of others' capabilities and knowledge will be strengthened. As a result, individual absorptive capacities are leveraged all the more, and the organization's absorptive capacity is strengthened.

The observation that the ideal knowledge structure for an organizational subunit should reflect only partially overlapping knowledge complemented by nonoverlapping diverse knowledge suggests an organizational trade-off between diversity and commonality of knowledge across individuals. While common knowledge improves communication, commonality should not be carried so far that diversity across individuals is substantially diminished. Likewise, division of labor promoting gains from specialization should not be pushed so far that communication is undermined. The difficulties posed by excessive specialization suggest some liabilities of pursuing production efficiencies via learning by doing under conditions of rapid technical change in which absorptive capacity is important. In learning by doing, the firm be-

[28] R. Dearborn and H. A. Simon, "Selective Perception in Executives," *Sociometry* 21 (1958), pp. 140–44; D. Katz and R. L. Kahn, *The Social Psychology of Organizations* (New York: Wiley, 1966); T. J. Allen and S. D. Cohen, "Information Flows in R&D Labs," *Administrative Science Quarterly* 20 (1969), pp. 12–19; M. L. Tushman, "Technical Communication in R&D Laboratories: The Impact of Project Work Characteristics," *Administrative Science Quarterly* 21 (1978), pp. 624–44; T. R. Zenger and B. S. Lawrence, "Organizational Demography: The Differential Effects of Age and Tenure Distributions on Technical Communication," *Academy of Management Journal* 32 (1989), pp. 353–76.
[29] R. Katz and T. J. Allen, "Investigating the Not Invented Here (NIH) Syndrome: A Look at the Performance, Tenure, and Communication Patterns of 50 R&D Project Groups," *R&D Management* 12 (1982), pp. 7–12.
[30] "What We Know About the Creative Process."

[31] J. M. Utterback, "The Process of Technological Innovation Within the Firm," *Academy of Management Journal* 12 (1971), pp. 75–88.
[32] R. R. Nelson and S. Winter, *An Evolutionary Theory of Economic Change* (Cambridge, MA: Harvard University Press, 1982).
[33] *The Sources of Innovation.*

comes more practiced and hence more capable at activities in which it is already engaged. Learning by doing does not contribute to the diversity that is critical to learning about or creating something that is relatively new. Moreover, the notion of "remembering by doing"[34] suggests that the focus on one class of activity entailed by learning by doing may effectively diminish the diversity of background that an individual or organization may have at one time possessed and, consequently, undercut organizational absorptive capacity and innovative performance.

It has become generally accepted that complementary functions within the organization ought to be tightly intermeshed, recognizing that some amount of redundancy in expertise may be desirable to create what can be called cross-function absorptive capacities. Cross-function interfaces that affect organizational absorptive capacity and innovative performance include, for example, the relationships between corporate and divisional R&D labs or, more generally, the relationships among the R&D, design, manufacturing, and marketing functions.[35] Close linkages between design and manufacturing are often credited for the relative success of Japanese firms in moving products rapidly from the design stage through development and manufacturing.[36] Clark and Fujimoto[37] argued that overlapping product development cycles facilitate communication and coordination across organizational subunits. They found that the speed of product development is strongly influenced by the links between problem-solving cycles and that successful linking requires "direct personal contacts across functions, liaison roles at each unit, cross-functional task forces, cross-functional project teams, and a system of 'product manager as integrator.'"[38] In contrast, a process in which one unit simply hands off the design to another unit is likely to suffer greater difficulties.

Some management practices also appear to reflect the belief that an excessive degree of overlap in functions may reduce the firm's absorptive capacity and that diversity of backgrounds is useful. The Japanese practice of rotating their R&D personnel through marketing and manufacturing operations, for example, while creating knowledge overlap, also enhances the diversity of background of their personnel. Often involving the assignment of technical personnel to other functions for several years, this practice also suggests that some intensity of experience in each of the complementary knowledge domains is necessary to put an effective absorptive capacity in place; breadth of knowledge cannot be superficial to be effective.

The discussion thus far has focused on internal mechanisms that influence the organization's absorptive capacity. A question remains as to whether absorptive capacity needs to be internally developed or to what extent a firm may simply buy it via, for example, hiring new personnel, contracting for consulting services, or even through corporate acquisitions. We suggest that the effectiveness of such options is somewhat limited when the absorptive capacity in question is to be integrated with the firm's other activities. A critical component of the requisite absorptive capacity for certain types of information, such as those associated with product and process innovation, is often firm-specific and therefore cannot be bought and quickly integrated into the firm. This is reflected in Lee and Allen's[39] findings that considerable time lags are associated with the integration of new technical staff, particularly those concerned with process and product development. To integrate certain classes of complex and sophisticated technological knowledge successfully into the firm's activities, the firm requires an existing internal staff of technologists and scientists who are both competent in their fields and are familiar with the firm's idiosyncratic needs, organizational procedures, routines, complementary capabilities, and extramural relationships. As implied by the discussion above, such diversity of knowledge structures must coexist to some degree in the same minds. Moreover, as Nelson and Winter's[40] (1982) analysis suggests, much of the detailed knowledge of organizational routines and objectives that permit a firm and its R&D labs to function is tacit. As a consequence, such critical complementary knowledge is acquired only through experience within the firm. Illustrating our general argument, Vyssotsky,[41] justifying the placement of Bell Labs within AT&T, argued:

> For research and development to yield effective results for Bell System, it has to be done by . . . creative people who

[34] Nelson and Winter, *An Evolutionary Theory of Economic Change.*
[35] Mansfield, *Economics of Technological Change,* pp. 86–88.
[36] Westney and Sakakibara, "The Role of Japan-Based R&D in Global Technology Strategy."
[37] K. B. Clark and T. Fujimoto, "Overlapping Problem-Solving in Product Development," technical report, Harvard Business School, 1987.
[38] Ibid., p. 24.

[39] D. M. S. Lee and T. J. Allen, "Integrating New Technical Staff: Implications for Acquiring New Technology," *Management Science* 28 (1982), pp. 1405–20.
[40] *An Evolutionary Theory of Economic Change.*
[41] V. A. Vyssotsky, "The Innovation Process at Bell Labs," technical report, Bell Laboratories, 1977.

understand as much as they possibly can about the technical state of the art, and about Bell System and what System's problems are. The R&D people must be free to think up new approaches, and they must also be closely coupled to the problems and challenges where innovation is needed. This combination, if one is lucky, will result in insights which help the Bell System. That's why we have Bell Labs in Bell System, instead of having all our R&D done by outside organizations.

Path Dependence and Absorptive Capacity

Our discussion of the character of absorptive capacity and its role in assimilating and exploiting knowledge suggests a simple generalization that applies at both the individual and organizational levels: prior knowledge permits the assimilation and exploitation of new knowledge. Some portion of that prior knowledge should be very closely related to the new knowledge to facilitate assimilation, and some fraction of that knowledge must be fairly diverse, although still related, to permit effective, creative utilization of the new knowledge. This simple notion that prior knowledge underlies absorptive capacity has important implications for the development of absorptive capacity over time and, in turn, for the innovative performance of organizations. The basic role of prior knowledge suggests two features of absorptive capacity that will affect innovative performance in an evolving, uncertain environment.[42] Accumulating absorptive capacity in one period will permit its more efficient accumulation in the next. By having already developed some absorptive capacity in a particular area, a firm may more readily accumulate what additional knowledge it needs in the subsequent periods in order to exploit any critical external knowledge that may become available. Second, the possession of related expertise will permit the firm to better understand and therefore evaluate the import of intermediate technological advances that provide signals as to the eventual merit of a new technological development. Thus, in an uncertain environment, absorptive capacity affects expectation formation, permitting the firm to predict more accurately the nature and commercial potential of technological advances. These revised expectations, in turn, condition the incentive to invest in absorptive capacity subsequently. These two features of absorptive capacity—cumulativeness and its effect on expectation formation—imply that its development is domain specific and is path or history dependent.

The cumulativeness of absorptive capacity and its effect on expectation formation suggest an extreme case of path dependence in which once a firm ceases investing in its absorptive capacity in a quickly moving field, it may never assimilate and exploit new information in that field, regardless of the value of that information. There are two reasons for the emergence of this condition, which we term *lockout*.[43] First, if the firm does not develop its absorptive capacity in some initial period, then its beliefs about the technological opportunities present in a given field will tend not to change over time because the firm may not be aware of the significance of signals that would otherwise revise its expectations. As a result, the firm does not invest in absorptive capacity and, when new opportunities subsequently emerge, the firm may not appreciate them. Compounding this effect, to the extent that prior knowledge facilitates the subsequent development of absorptive capacity, the lack of early investment in absorptive capacity makes it more costly to develop a given level of it in a subsequent period. Consequently, a low initial investment in absorptive capacity diminishes the attractiveness of investing in subsequent periods even if the firm becomes aware of technological opportunities.[44] This possibility of firms being locked out of subsequent technological developments has recently become a matter of concern with respect to industrial policy. For instance, Reich[45] declaims against Monsanto's exit from "float-zone" silicon manufacturing because he believes that the decision may be an irreversible exit from a technology, in that "each new generation of technology builds on that which came before," and that "once off the technological escalator it's difficult to get back on" (p. 64).

Thus, the cumulative quality of absorptive capacity and its role in conditioning the updating of expectations are forces that tend to confine firms to operating in a particular technological domain. If firms do not invest in developing absorptive capacity in a particular area of expertise early on, it may not be in their interest to develop that capacity subsequently, even after major advances in the field. Thus, the pattern of inertia that Nelson and

---

[42] W. M. Cohen and D. A. Levinthal, "Fortune Favors the Prepared Firm," technical report, Dept. of Social and Decision Sciences, Carnegie Mellon University, 1989.

[43] Ibid.

[44] A similar result emerges from models of adaptive learning. B. Levitt and J. G. March, "Organizational Learning," *Annual Review of Sociology* 14 (1988), pp. 319–40, noted that "a competency trap can occur when favorable performance with an inferior procedure leads an organization to accumulate more experience with it, thus keeping experience with a superior procedure inadequate to make it rewarding to use" (p. 322).

[45] R. B. Reich, "The Rise of Techno-Nationalism," *Atlantic*, May 1987, pp. 63–69.

Winter[46] highlighted as a central feature of firm behavior may emerge as an implication of rational behavior in a model in which absorptive capacity is cumulative and contributes to expectation formation. The not-invented-here syndrome, in which firms resist accepting innovative ideas from the environment, may also at times reflect what we call lockout. Such ideas may be too distant from the firm's existing knowledge base—its absorptive capacity—to be either appreciated or accessed. In this particular setting, NIH may be pathological behavior only in retrospect. The firm need not have acted irrationally in the development of the capabilities that yields the NIH syndrome as its apparent outcome.

A form of self-reinforcing behavior similar to lockout may also result from the influence of absorptive capacity on organizations' goals or aspiration levels. This argument builds on the behavioral view of organizational innovation that has been molded in large part by the work of March and Simon.[47] In March and Simon's framework, innovative activity is instigated due to a failure to reach some aspiration level. Departing from their model, we suggest that a firm's aspiration level in a technologically progressive environment is not simply determined by past performance or the performance of reference organizations. It also depends on the firm's absorptive capacity. The greater the organization's expertise and associated absorptive capacity, the more sensitive it is likely to be to emerging technological opportunities and the more likely its aspiration level will be defined in terms of the opportunities present in the technical environment rather than strictly in terms of performance measures. Thus, organizations with higher levels of absorptive capacity will tend to be more proactive, exploiting opportunities present in the environment, independent of current performance. Alternatively, organizations that have a modest absorptive capacity will tend to be reactive, searching for new alternatives in response to failure on some performance criterion that is not defined in terms of technical change per se (profitability, market share, etc.).

A systematic and enduring neglect of technical opportunities may result from the effect of absorptive capacity on the organization's aspiration level when innovative activity (e.g., R&D) contributes to absorptive capacity, which is often the case in technologically progressive environments. The reason is that the firm's aspiration level then depends on the very innovative activity that is triggered by a failure to meet the aspiration level itself. If the firm engages in little innovative activity, and is therefore relatively insensitive to the opportunities in the external environment, it will have a low aspiration level with regard to the exploitation of new technology, which in turn implies that it will continue to devote little effort to innovation. This creates a self-reinforcing cycle. Likewise, if an organization has a high aspiration level, influenced by externally generated technical opportunities, it will conduct more innovative activity and thereby increase its awareness of outside opportunities. Consequently, its aspiration level will remain high. This argument implies that reactive and proactive modes of firm behavior should remain rather stable over time. Thus, some organizations (like Hewlett-Packard and Sony) have the requisite technical knowledge to respond proactively to the opportunities present in the environment. These firms do not wait for failure on some performance dimension but aggressively seek out new opportunities to exploit and develop their technological capabilities.[48]

The concept of dynamically self-reinforcing behavior that may lead to the neglect of new technological developments provides some insight into the difficulties firms face when the technological basis of an industry changes—what Schumpeter[49] called "the process of creative destruction." For instance, the change from electromechanical devices to electronic ones in the calculator industry resulted in the exit of a number of firms and a radical change in the market structure.[50] This is an example of what Tushman and Anderson[51] termed competence-destroying technical change. A firm without a prior technological base in a particular field may not be able to acquire one readily if absorptive capacity is cumulative. In addition, a firm may be blind to new developments in fields in which it is not investing if its updating capability is low. Accordingly, our argument implies that firms may not realize that they should be developing their absorptive capacity due to an irony associated with

---

[46] *An Evolutionary Theory of Economic Change.*
[47] *Organizations.*

[48] This argument that such reactive and proactive behavior may coexist in an industry over the long run assumes that there is slack in the selection environment and that technologically progressive behavior is not essential to survival. One can, alternatively, identify a number of industries, such as semiconductors, in which it appears that only firms that aggressively exploit technical opportunities survive.
[49] J. A. Schumpeter, *Capitalism, Socialism and Democracy* (New York: Harper and Row, 1942).
[50] B. A. Majumdar, *Innovations, Product Developments and Technology Transfers: An Empirical Study of Dynamic Competitive Advantage. The Case of Electronic Calculators* (Lanham, MD: University Press of America, 1982).
[51] M. L. Tushman and P. Anderson, "Technological Discontinuities and Organizational Environments," *Administrative Science Quarterly* 31 (1986), pp. 439–65.

its valuation: the firm needs to have some absorptive capacity already to value it appropriately.

Absorptive Capacity and R&D Investment

The prior discussion does not address the question of whether we can empirically evaluate the importance of absorptive capacity for innovation. There is a key insight that permits empirical tests of the implications of absorptive capacity for innovative activity. Since technical change within an industry—typically incremental in character[52]—is often closely related to a firm's ongoing R&D activity, a firm's ability to exploit external knowledge is often generated as a byproduct of its R&D. We may therefore consider a firm's R&D as satisfying two functions: we assume that R&D not only generates new knowledge but also contributes to the firm's absorptive capacity.[53] If absorptive capacity is important, and R&D contributes to it, then whatever conditions, the firm's incentives to learn (i.e., to build absorptive capacity) should also influence R&D spending. We may therefore consider the responsiveness of R&D activity to learning incentives as an indication of the empirical importance of absorptive capacity. The empirical challenge then is to understand the impact of the characteristics of the learning environment on R&D spending.

We construct a simple static model of firm R&D intensity, which is defined as R&D divided by sales. Normalization of R&D by firm sales controls for the effect of firm size, which affects the return per unit of R&D effort. This model is developed in the broader context of what applied economists have come to believe to be the three classes of industry-level determinants of R&D intensity: demand, appropriability, and technological opportunity conditions.[54] Demand is often characterized by the level of sales and the price elasticity of demand. The latter indicates the degree to which a firm's revenue will increase due to a reduction in price. For example, in the case of a process innovation that reduces the cost of production and, in turn, the product price, the price elasticity of demand reflects the associated change in total revenue that influences the economic return to innovative effort. Appropriability conditions refer to the degree to which firms capture the profits associated with their innovative activity and are often considered to reflect the degree to which valuable knowledge spills out into the public domain. The emphasis here is on valuable knowledge, because if a competitor's knowledge spills out but the competitor has already exploited a first-mover advantage in the marketplace, this knowledge is no longer valuable to the firm and does not constitute a spillover by our definition. The level of spillovers, in turn, depends on the strength of patents within an industry, the efficacy of secrecy, and/or first-mover advantages. Technological opportunity represents how costly it is for the firm to achieve some normalized unit of technical advance in a given industry. As typically conceived, there are two dimensions of technological opportunity.[55] The first, incorporated in our model, refers simply to the quantity of extraindustry technological knowledge, such as that originating from government or university labs, that effectively complements and therefore leverages the firm's own knowledge output. The second dimension of technological opportunity is the degree to which a unit of new knowledge improves the technological performance of the firm's manufacturing processes or products and, in turn, the firm's profits. For example, given the vitality of the underlying science and technology, an advance in knowledge promises to yield much larger product-performance payoffs in the semiconductor industry than in steel.[56]

The basic model of how absorptive capacity affects the determination of R&D expenditures is represented diagrammatically in Exhibit 1. We postulate that learning incentives will have a direct effect on R&D spending. We also suggest that where the effect of other determinants, such as technological opportunity and appropriability, depend on the firm's or rivals' assimilation of knowledge, absorptive capacity—and therefore learning incentives—will mediate those effects. Finally, we suggest that the effect of appropriability conditions (i.e., spillovers) will be conditioned by competitor interdependence. In this context, we define interdependence as the

---

[52] Rosenberg and Steinmueller, "Why Are Americans Such Poor Imitators?"

[53] We refer readers interested in the details of the theoretical and subsequent empirical analysis and results to W. M. Cohen and D. A. Levinthal, "Innovation and Learning: The Two Faces of R&D," *Economic Journal* 99 (1989), pp. 569–96, from which the following discussion is drawn.

[54] W. M. Cohen and R. C. Levin, "Empirical Studies of Innovation and Market Structure," in *Handbook of Industrial Organization,* ed. R. C. Schmalensee and R. Willig (Amsterdam: Elsevier, 1989), pp. 1059–1107.

[55] Ibid.

[56] This second dimension is incorporated in the model developed in Cohen and Levinthal, "Innovation and Learning." We do not incorporate this second dimension in the present model because all the qualitative theoretical and empirical results associated with this second dimension of technology opportunity are the same as those associated with the first considered here.

EXHIBIT 1   Model of Absorptive Capacity and R&D Incentives

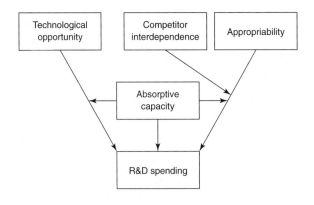

extent to which a rival's technical advances diminish the firm's profits.

Two factors will affect a firm's incentives to learn and, therefore, its incentives to invest in absorptive capacity via its R&D expenditures. First is the quantity of knowledge to be assimilated and exploited: the more there is, the greater the incentive. Second is the difficulty (or, conversely, the ease) of learning. Some types of information are more difficult to assimilate and use than others. We interpret this to mean that per unit of knowledge, the cost of its absorption may vary depending on the characteristics of that knowledge. As learning is more difficult, more prior knowledge has to have been accumulated via R&D for effective learning to occur. As a result, this is a more costly learning environment. In such a setting, R&D is more important to building absorptive capacity and the more R&D effort the firm will need to have expended to achieve some level of absorptive capacity. Thus, for a given level of a firm's own R&D, the level of absorptive capacity is diminished in environments in which it is more difficult to learn. In addition, we are suggesting that a more difficult learning environment increases the marginal effect of R&D on absorptive capacity. In contrast, in environments in which learning is less demanding, a firm's own R&D has little impact on its absorptive capacity. In the extreme case in which external knowledge can be assimilated without any specialized expertise, a firm's own R&D would have no effect on its absorptive capacity.

We have argued that the ease of learning is in turn determined by the characteristics of the underlying scientific and technological knowledge. Although it is difficult to specify a priori all the relevant characteristics of knowl-

edge affecting the ease of learning, they would include the complexity of the knowledge to be assimilated and the degree to which the outside knowledge is targeted to the needs and concerns of the firm. When outside knowledge is less targeted to the firm's particular needs and concerns, a firm's own R&D becomes more important in permitting it to recognize the value of the knowledge, assimilate, and exploit it. Sources that produce less targeted knowledge would include university labs involved in basic research, while more targeted knowledge may be generated by contract research labs, or input suppliers. In addition, the degree to which a field is cumulative, or the field's pace of advance, should also affect how critical R&D is to the development of absorptive capacity. The more that findings in a field build on prior findings, the more necessary is an understanding of prior research to the assimilation of subsequent findings. The pace of advance of a field affects the importance of R&D to developing absorptive capacity because the faster the pace of knowledge generation, the larger the staff required to keep abreast of new developments. Finally, following Nelson and Winter,[57] the less explicit and codified the relevant knowledge the more difficult it is to assimilate.

To structure the analysis, we assumed that firms purposefully invest in R&D to generate profit and take into account R&D's dual role in both directly generating new knowledge and contributing to absorptive capacity. Knowledge is assumed to be useful to the firm in that increments to a firm's own knowledge increase the firm's profits while increments to rivals' knowledge diminish them. We posit a simple model of the generation of a firm's technological knowledge that takes into account the major sources of technological knowledge utilized by a firm: the firm's own R&D knowledge that originates with its competitors' R&D, spillovers, and that which originates outside the industry. Exhibit 2 provides a stylized representation of this model in which, first, the firm generates new knowledge directly through its own R&D, and second, extramural knowledge, drawn from competitors as well as extraindustry sources such as government and university labs, also contributes to the firm's knowledge. A central feature of the model is that the firm's absorptive capacity determines the extent to which this extramural knowledge is utilized, and this absorptive capacity itself depends on the firm's own R&D. Because of this mediating function, absorptive capacity influences the effects of appropriability and technological

---

[57] *An Evolutionary Theory of Economic Change.*

EXHIBIT 2   Model of Sources of a Firm's Technical Knowledge

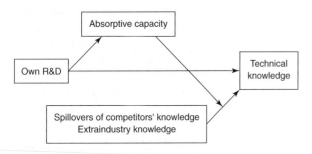

opportunity conditions on R&D spending. Thus, the effects of appropriability and technological opportunity are not independent of R&D itself.

A key assumption in the model is that exploitation of competitors' research findings is realized through the interaction of the firm's absorptive capacity with competitors' spillovers. This interaction signifies that a firm is unable to assimilate externally available knowledge passively. Rather, to utilize the accessible R&D output of its competitors, the firm invests in its absorptive capacity by conducting R&D. Exhibit 2 also illustrates that, like its assimilation of competitors' R&D output, a firm's assimilation of extraindustry knowledge—the dimension of technological opportunity considered here—is constrained by its absorptive capacity. According to our model, therefore, the factors that affect learning incentives (i.e., the ease of learning and the quantity of available knowledge) influence the effects of appropriability and technological opportunity conditions on R&D.

Direct Effect of Ease of Learning   As shown formally in Cohen and Levinthal,[58] this model implies that as the ease of learning diminishes, learning becomes more dependent on a firm's own R&D, and R&D spending increases because of two effects. First, the marginal impact of R&D on absorptive capacity is greater in more difficult learning environments. As the learning environment becomes more difficult, however, there is a second, more subtle effect. Since, ceteris paribus, a more difficult learning environment lowers firms' absorptive capacities, R&D activity becomes more of a private good in the sense that competitors are now less able to tap into the firm's R&D findings that spill out.

Technological Opportunity   We predict that an increase in technological opportunity—the amount of

available relevant external technical knowledge—will elicit more R&D in more difficult learning environments. Greater technological opportunity signifies greater amounts of external information, which increase the firm's incentive to build absorptive capacity, and a more challenging learning environment increases the level of R&D necessary to build absorptive capacity.

Appropriability   We predict that spillovers will provide, in part, a positive incentive to conduct R&D due to the interaction of spillovers with an endogenous absorptive capacity. Traditionally, spillovers have been considered only a deterrent to R&D activity.[59] In the standard view, a firm's incentive to invest in R&D is diminished to the extent that any findings from such activities are exploited by competitors and thereby diminish the innovator's own profits. In our framework, however, this negative appropriability incentive associated with spillovers is counter-balanced by a positive absorptive-capacity-building incentive. The more of its competitors' spillovers there are out there, the more incentive the firm has to invest in its own R&D, which permits it to exploit those spillovers.

We have shown elsewhere[60] that when this absorption incentive is large, as when learning is difficult, spillovers may actually encourage R&D. The relative magnitude of the absorption incentive is greater when firms within an industry are less interdependent in the sense that rivals' technical advances have less of an effect on the firm's own profits. With less interdependence, the degree to which rivals gain from the firm's R&D spillovers at the firm's expense diminishes relative to the benefit of being able to exploit the rivals' spillovers. Either a more competitive market structure or a higher price elasticity of demand for the firm's product can diminish interdependence in an industry.

METHODS

Data and Measures

To test the predictions of our framework for R&D activity, we used cross-sectional survey data on technological opportunity and appropriability conditions in the Amer-

---

[58] "Innovation and Learning."

[59] For example: R. R. Nelson, "The Simple Economics of Basic Research," *Journal of Political Economy* 67 (1959), pp. 297–306; K. J. Arrow, "Economic Welfare and the Allocation of Resources for Invention," in *The Rate and Direction of Inventive Activity,* ed. R. R. Nelson (Princeton, NJ: Princeton University Press, 1962), pp. 609–25; M. A. Spence, "Cost Reduction, Competition, and Industry Performance," *Econometrica* 52 (1984), pp. 101–22.

[60] Cohen and Levinthal, "Innovation and Learning."

ican manufacturing sector collected from R&D lab managers by Levin et al.,[61] and the Federal Trade Commission's Line of Business Program data on business unit sales, transfers, and R&D expenditures. The dependent variable, R&D intensity, was defined as company-financed business-unit research and development expenditures, expressed as a percentage of business unit sales and transfers over the period 1975 through 1977. The data on inter-industry differences in technological opportunity and appropriability are industry (line of business) mean scores computed as an average over all respondents within a given industry. The sample consists of 1,719 business units representing 318 firms in 151 lines of business.

The data pose two estimation issues. First, some 24 percent of the firms performed no R&D in at least one year. If the independent variables reflect both the probability of conducting R&D, as well as the amount of R&D spending, then a Tobit analysis would be appropriate. Alternatively, a firm may require some initial level of absorptive capacity before it is influenced by the characteristics of the learning environment. In this case, the variables reflecting the ease of learning only affect the amount of R&D conducted by firms engaging in R&D activity and not the probability of engaging in R&D activity. In light of the uncertainty over the appropriate estimation technique, we explored the robustness of the results by analyzing a Tobit and an OLS (or GLS) specification. The second estimation issue is the presence of heteroscedasticity. We found the assumption of homoscedasticity to be violated, with the logarithm of the error variance being a linear function of the exogenous variables and the number of respondents to Levin et al.'s survey.[62] Unless otherwise noted, the results we report in this section reflect robust effects that hold across three different estimation methods, including ordinary least squares (OLS), generalized least squares (GLS) in which we adjust for heteroscedasticity, and Tobit, which was used when we included the observations for which R&D expenditures were zero.

We tested our predictions in the context of an empirical model of business unit R&D intensity in which technological opportunity, appropriability, and demand conditions are considered as the principal industry-level determinants of firms' R&D spending. While data constraints do not permit observation of the direct effect of the ease of learning or its determinants on firms' R&D spending, we were able to examine how these variables condition the influence on R&D of technological opportunity and appropriability conditions.

Technological opportunity was assessed with variables measuring the "relevance" or "importance" for technological progress in each line of business of what are considered to be two critical sources of technological opportunity—the science base of the industry and extraindustry sources of knowledge.[63] These measures are drawn from Levin et al.'s survey, in which R&D managers indicated on a 7-point Likert scale the relevance of 11 basic and applied fields of science and the importance of external sources of knowledge to technological progress in a line of business. The basic fields of science include biology, chemistry, mathematics, and physics, and the applied fields of science include agricultural science, applied math/operations research, computer science, geology, materials science, medical science, and metallurgy.[64] The five extraindustry sources of knowledge considered here included equipment suppliers (EQUIPTECH), materials suppliers (MATERIAL-TECH), downstream users of the industry's products (USERTECH), government laboratories and agencies (GOVTECH), and universities (UNIVTECH). We interpreted the measures of the relevance or importance of each field or knowledge source to index the relative quantity of knowledge generated by that field or source that is potentially useful. We then distinguished across the 11 scientific fields and the five extraindustry knowledge source variables on the basis of the ease of learning associated with each. We suggested above that one important determinant of the ease of learning is the degree to which outside knowledge is targeted to a firm's needs and concerns. One can readily distinguish among both the 11 fields and the five extraindustry knowledge sources on that basis. The knowledge associated with the basic sciences is typically less targeted than that associated with the applied sciences. We also distinguished among the extraindustry knowledge sources on the same basis. A priori, we ranked university labs, government labs, materials suppliers, and equipment suppliers as providing increasingly more targeted knowledge to firms. We did not rank the relative effect of knowledge originating

[61] R. C. Levin, A. K. Klevorick, R. R. Nelson, and S. G. Winter, "Questionnaire on Industrial Research and Development," Dept. of Economics, Yale University, 1983; "Appropriating the Returns from Industrial R&D," *Brookings Papers on Economic Activity,* 1987, pp. 783–820.
[62] Ibid.

[63] Cohen and Levin, "Empirical Studies of Innovation and Market Structure."
[64] Although geology was classed as a basic science by Levin et al. (see note 61), we classed it as an applied science because of its inductive methodology and intensive use by firms in the extractive sector.

from users because, as suggested by von Hippel,[65] users will often provide a product idea to potential suppliers, but the informativeness of the "solution concept" is quite variable. Therefore, the targeted quality of the information is variable as well.

To represent intraindustry spillovers of R&D, we employed measures from Levin et al.'s survey of the effectiveness of six mechanisms used by firms to capture and protect the competitive advantages of new processes and new products: patents to prevent duplication, patents to secure royalty income, secrecy, lead time, moving quickly down the learning curve, and complementary sales and service efforts. We employed the maximum value of the effectiveness scores attained by these mechanisms as our measure of appropriability or spillovers and label this variable APPROPRIABILITY; a high level of APPROPRIABILITY reflects a low level of spillovers.

In our theory, we predicted an interaction effect by which, as the ease of learning diminishes, or firms become less interdependent, the effect of spillovers on R&D spending should become more positive (or less negative). In the absence of any direct measure of the ease of learning, we distinguished categorically between those industries in which basic science was more relevant to technical progress than the relatively more targeted applied sciences and assumed that learning was generally less difficult in industries that fell into the latter category. Thus, we created a dummy variable, DUMBAS, that equals 1 when the average value of the relevance scores associated with the basic fields exceeds that associated with the applied fields and that equals 0 otherwise. We specified the dummy variable, DUMAPP, analogously. To capture the interdependence of firms, we employed measures of industries' competitiveness as represented by each industry's four-firm concentration ratio (C4) and industry-level estimates of the price elasticity of demand (PELAS).

To further control for industry demand conditions, we used industry estimates developed by Levin[66] of price elasticity (PELAS) and income elasticity (INCELAS) and a demand time-shift parameter (DGROWTH). Finally, we included another control variable that may also reflect technological opportunity, industry maturity. We used a somewhat crude measure of industry maturity, NEWPLANT, that measures the percentage of an indus-

try's property, plant, and equipment installed within the preceding five years.

RESULTS

Technological Opportunity

Our theory suggests that when the targeted quality of knowledge is less (i.e., learning is more difficult), an increase in the relevance (i.e., quantity) of knowledge should have a more positive effect on R&D intensity. Therefore, the coefficient estimates of the variables measuring the relevance of the four basic scientific fields should exceed those of the variables measuring the relevance of the seven applied scientific fields. Confirming the prediction, Exhibit 3 indicates that the estimated coefficients for the applied sciences are, with the exception of computer science, lower than that for the basic sciences. The similarity of the estimate of the effect of the relevance of computer science, an applied science, to those of some of the basic sciences suggests that the assumption may not be correct that only one determinant of the ease of learning, the targeted quality of the field, varies systematically across the fields of applied and basic science. Another determinant of the ease of learning postulated above is a field's pace of advance, where faster pace should require more R&D to permit assimilation, and the pace of advance in computer science has been relatively rapid over the past two decades.

To further test the prediction that the coefficient values of the less targeted, basic-science field variables would exceed those of the applied fields, we estimated a specification, otherwise identical to the first, in which we constrained the coefficients of the basic sciences to be the same and the coefficients of the applied sciences to be the same. This shows the effect on R&D spending when the overall technological opportunity associated with basic science and applied science, respectively, changes. The constrained coefficient estimates of the effect of the technological opportunity associated with the basic and applied sciences are significantly different (at the $p < .01$ level) across all estimation methods, with the former equal to .189 and the latter equal to $-.080$ in the GLS estimation. Therefore, relative to the effect of an increase in the technological opportunity associated with applied science, an increase in that associated with basic science elicits more R&D.

Our predicted ranking of the coefficient magnitudes associated with the extraindustry sources of knowledge, reflecting increasingly targeted knowledge from these sources, is largely confirmed. The coefficient estimate for

[65] E. von Hippel, "Successful Industrial Products from Customer Ideas," *Journal of Marketing* 42 (1978), pp. 39–49.
[66] R. C. Levin, "Toward an Empirical Model of Schumpeterian Competition," Technical Report, Dept. of Economics, Yale University, 1981.

EXHIBIT 3   Analysis of R&D Intensity

	Regression coefficient		
Variable	OLS ($N = 1{,}302$)	GLS ($N = 1{,}302$)	Tobit ($N = 1{,}719$)
Intercept	−5.184**	−2.355*	−4.086**
	(1.522)	(1.037)	(1.461)
APPROPRIABILITY × C4	.213	.342**	.368**
	(.128)	(.103)	(.130)
APPROPRIABILITY × PELAS	−.192	−.200*	−.176
	(.106)	(.091)	(.103)
APPROPRIABILITY × DUMAPP	.448*	.248	.211
	(.202)	(.143)	(.194)
APPROPRIABILITY × DUMBAS	.302	.174	.094
	(.208)	(.144)	(.206)
USERTECH	.470**	.397**	.612**
	(.104)	(.069)	(.107)
UNIVTECH	.374**	.318**	.395**
	(.131)	(.091)	(.147)
GOVTECH	.221*	.069	.137
	(.106)	(.079)	(.107)
MATERIALTECH	−.258**	−.074	−.303**
	(.098)	(.070)	(.100)
EQUIPTECH	−.401**	−.484**	−.574**
	(.111)	(.077)	(.117)
Biology	.314**	.185**	.276*
	(.102)	(.071)	(.114)
Chemistry	.289**	.081	.191*
	(.084)	(.062)	(.088)
Math	.184	.151	.123
	(.131)	(.097)	(.143)
Physics	.373**	.323**	.310*
	(.117)	(.091)	(.128)
Agricultural science	−.441**	−.273**	−.308**
	(.088)	(.064)	(.099)
Applied math/operations research	−.237	−.117	−.366*
	(.148)	(.102)	(.152)
Computer science	.294*	.116	.433**
	(.124)	(.090)	(.122)
Geology	−.363**	−.240**	−.365**
	(.084)	(.061)	(.097)
Materials science	−.110	−.150	.116
	(.125)	(.095)	(.118)
Medical science	−.179	−.133	−.133
	(.093)	(.070)	(.103)
Metallurgy	−.315**	−.195**	−.393**
	(.077)	(.053)	(.089)
NEWPLANT	.057**	.049**	.045**
	(.008)	(.006)	(.007)
PELAS	.936	1.082*	.892
	(.611)	(.527)	(.573)
INCELAS	1.077**	.587**	1.112**
	(.170)	(.131)	(.188)
DGROWTH	.068	−.074	.004
	(.090)	(.053)	(.105)
	.287		

*$p < .05$; ** $< .01$.
Standard errors are in parentheses.
Source: W. M. Cohen and D. A. Levinthal, "Innovation and Learning: The Two Faces of R&D," *Economic Journal* 99 (1989), pp. 590–591, 569–96.

the importance of knowledge originating from universities exceeds that for government labs, which, in turn, is greater than that for materials suppliers, which exceeds that for equipment suppliers. The difference between coefficient values is statistically significant in the case of government sources versus materials suppliers for both the OLS and Tobit results ($p < .01$) and in the case of materials suppliers versus equipment suppliers in the GLS results ($p < .01$). While we had no prediction regarding the coefficient value for USERTECH, the consistently high value of the coefficient estimate may reflect some element of demand conditions. Consistent with this, we have observed the variable USERTECH to be significantly correlated with measures of the importance of product differentiation.[67]

Appropriability

The results largely support the prediction that the ease of learning conditions the effect of knowledge spillovers. The effect on R&D intensity of increasing appropriability (i.e., diminishing spillovers) was significantly greater ($p < .05$) in those industries in which the applied sciences are more relevant to innovation than the basic sciences. This result suggests that the positive absorption incentive associated with spillovers is greater in industries in which the difficulty of learning is greater. Second, there is a significant positive effect ($p < .01$) of the interaction between market concentration and the appropriability level. As market concentration increases (indexing a diminution in competitiveness), the positive effect of a given appropriability level on R&D intensity increases, as predicted. Likewise, the effect of the interaction of the price elasticity of demand and the level of appropriability is negative (but only significant at $p < .05$ in the GLS estimate), providing additional support for the proposition that the positive effect of spillovers will increase in industries in which firms are less interdependent. The results suggest that the learning environment affects the impact of spillovers on R&D spending and that the importance of the positive absorptive-capacity-building incentive relative to that of the negative appropriability incentive is conditioned by the degree of competitor interdependence.

While we have shown that the learning environment modifies the effect of appropriability conditions, the question remains whether spillovers may, on balance, actually encourage R&D in some industries. To explore this pos-

sibility, we examined the effect of spillovers in the four two-digit SIC code level industries for which our sample contains enough lines of business to permit separate industry regressions. These include SICs 20 (food processing), 28 (chemicals), 35 (machinery), and 36 (electrical equipment). Due to the reduction in the degrees of freedom for industry-level variables, we simplified the estimating equation to consider only the direct effect of APPROPRIABILITY, and the science field variables were summarized as the maximum relevance scores attained by the basic and applied fields, respectively. In SICs 28 and 36, the effect of the APPROPRIABILITY variable was negative and significant at conventional levels, implying that R&D intensity rises with spillovers. In the Tobit results, the sign was also positive for SICs 28 and 36, but the coefficient estimates were not quite significant at the .05 confidence level. Thus, in SICs 28 (chemicals) and 36 (electrical equipment), R&D intensity rose with spillovers when we controlled for other industry-level variables conventionally thought to drive R&D spending, including technological opportunity and demand conditions. Although the analyses showing a positive effect of spillovers in these two industry groups do not represent a direct test of our model, the results suggest, particularly when considered with the interaction results, that the positive absorption incentive associated with spillovers may be sufficiently strong in some cases to more than offset the negative appropriability incentive.

IMPLICATIONS FOR INNOVATIVE ACTIVITY

Drawing on our prior work,[68] we offer some implications of absorptive capacity for the analysis of other innovative activities, including basic research, the adoption and diffusion of innovations, and decisions to participate in cooperative R&D ventures, that follow from the preceding analyses.

The observation that R&D creates a capacity to assimilate and exploit new knowledge provides a ready explanation of why some firms may invest in basic research even when the preponderance of findings spills out into the public domain. Specifically, firms may conduct basic research less for particular results than to be able to provide themselves with the general background knowledge that would permit them to exploit rapidly useful scientific

---

[67] Compare Cohen and Levinthal, "Innovation and Learning."

[68] Ibid.; W. M. Cohen and D. A. Levinthal, "Participation in Cooperative Research Ventures and the Cost of Learning," technical report, Dept. of Social and Decision Sciences, Carnegie Mellon University, 1987.

and technological knowledge through their own innovations or to be able to respond quickly—become a fast second—when competitors come up with a major advance.[69] In terms of our discussion of the cognitive and organizational aspects of absorptive capacity, we may think of basic research as broadening the firm's knowledge base to create critical overlap with new knowledge and providing it with the deeper understanding that is useful for exploiting new technical developments that build on rapidly advancing science and technology.

This perspective on the role of basic research offers a rather different view of the determinants of basic research than that which has dominated thinking in this area for the 30 years since Nelson's[70] seminal article. Nelson hypothesized that more diversified firms will invest more heavily in basic research because, assuming imperfect markets for information, they will be better able to exploit its wide-ranging and unpredictable results. Nelson thus saw product-market diversification as one of the key determinants of basic research.[71] Emphasizing the role of basic research in firm learning, our perspective redirects attention from what happens to the knowledge outputs from the innovation process to the nature of the knowledge inputs themselves. Considering that absorptive capacity tends to be specific to a field or knowledge domain means that the type of knowledge that the firm believes it may have to exploit will affect the sort of research the firm conducts. From this vantage point, we would conjecture that as a firm's technological progress becomes more closely tied to advances in basic science (as has been the case in pharmaceuticals), a firm will increase its basic research, whatever its degree of product-market diversification. We also suggest, with reference to all firm research, not just basic research, that as the fields underlying technical advance within an industry become more diverse, we may expect firms to increase their R&D as they develop absorptive capacities in each of the relevant fields. For example, as automobile manufacturing comes to draw more heavily on newer fields such as microelectronics and ceramics, we expect that manufacturers will expand their basic and applied research efforts to better evaluate and exploit new findings in these areas.

The findings on the role of absorptive capacity and the ways in which it may be developed also have implications for the analysis of the adoption and diffusion of innovations. Our perspective implies that the ease of learning, and thus technology adoption, is affected by the degree to which an innovation is related to the preexisting knowledge base of prospective users. For example, personal computers diffused more rapidly at the outset among consumers and firms who had prior experience on mainframes or minicomputers. Likewise, software engineering practices seem to be adopted more readily by programmers with previous Pascal rather than Fortran experience because the structure of Pascal more closely reflects some of the underlying principles of software engineering.[72] Our argument also suggests that an innovation that is fully incorporated in capital equipment will diffuse more rapidly than more disembodied innovations that require some complementary expertise on the part of potential users. This is one of the anticipated benefits of making computers more user-friendly.

The importance of absorptive capacity also helps explain some recent findings regarding firms' cooperative research ventures. First, Link[73] has observed that cooperative research ventures are actually found more typically in industries that employ more mature technologies rather than in industries in which technology is moving ahead quickly—as seems to be suggested by the popular press. Second, it has been observed that cooperative ventures that have been initiated to pursue basic research, as well as more applied research objectives, have been subject over the years to increasing pressure to focus on more short-term research objectives.[74] The simple notion that it is important to consider the costs of assimilating and exploiting knowledge from such ventures provides at least a partial explanation for these phenomena. Many cooperative ventures are initiated in areas in which the cost to access the output of the venture is low, or they often gravitate toward such areas over time. Conversely,

---

[69] N. Rosenberg, "Why Do Firms Do Basic Research (with Their Own Money)?" *Research Policy* 1990.

[70] "The Simple Economics of Basic Research."

[71] Markets for information often fail because they inherently represent a situation of information asymmetry in which the less informed party cannot properly value the information he or she wishes to purchase, and the more informed party, acting self-interestedly, attempts to exploit that inability. See O. E. Williamson, *Markets and Hierarchies: Analysis and Antitrust Implications* (New York: Free Press, 1975).

[72] G. Smith, W. M. Cohen, W. Hefley, and D. A. Levinthal, "Understanding the Adoption of Ada: A Field Study Report," technical report, Software Engineering Institute, Carnegie Mellon University, 1989.

[73] A. N. Link, "Cooperative Research Activity in U.S. Manufacturing," technical report, University of North Carolina, Greensboro, 1987.

[74] D. C. Mowery and N. Rosenberg, *Technology and the Pursuit of Economic Growth* (New York: Cambridge University Press, 1989).

those who are attempting to encourage cooperative research ventures in quickly advancing fields should recognize that the direct participation in the venture should represent only a portion of the resources that it will take to benefit from the venture. Participating firms also must be prepared to invest internally in the absorptive capacity that will permit effective exploitation of the venture's knowledge output.

CONCLUSION

Our empirical analysis of R&D investment suggested that firms are in fact sensitive to the characteristics of the learning environment in which they operate. Thus, absorptive capacity appears to be part of a firm's decision calculus in allocating resources for innovative activity. Despite these findings, because absorptive capacity is intangible and its benefits are indirect, one can have little confidence that the appropriate level, to say nothing of the optimal level, of investment in absorptive capacity is reached. Thus, while we have proposed a model to explain R&D investment, in which R&D both generates innovation and facilitates learning, the development of this model may ultimately be as valuable for the prescriptive analysis of organizational policies as its application may be as a positive model of firm behavior.

An important question from a prescriptive perspective is, When is a firm most likely to under-invest in absorptive capacity to its own long-run detriment? Absorptive capacity is more likely to be developed and maintained as a byproduct of routine activity when the knowledge domain that the firm wishes to exploit is closely related to its current knowledge base. When, however, a firm wishes to acquire and use knowledge that is unrelated to its ongoing activity, then the firm must dedicate effort exclusively to creating absorptive capacity (i.e., absorptive capacity is not a byproduct). In this case, absorptive capacity may not even occur to the firm as an investment alternative. Even if it does, due to the intangible nature of absorptive capacity, a firm may be reluctant to sacrifice current output as well as gains from specialization to permit its technical personnel to acquire the requisite breadth of knowledge that would permit absorption of knowledge from new domains. Thus, while the current discussion addresses key features of organizational structure that determine a firm's absorptive capacity and provides evidence that investment is responsive to the need to develop this capability, more research is necessary to understand the decision processes that determine organizations' investments in absorptive capacity.

NEC: A New R&D Site in Princeton

Walter Kuemmerle and Kiichiro Kobayashi

"Yes, you have heard correctly. I just learned that Dawon Kahng died yesterday." Daizaburo Shinoda's voice was hoarse. He felt sad and overwhelmed as he conveyed this news to Michiyuki Uenohara, the managing director of NEC, in Japan. Over the last few years, Kahng had become both a valuable colleague and a good friend to Daizaburo Shinoda. They had worked very closely since the start-up of NEC Research Institute, Inc. (NECI), in Princeton, New Jersey. Shinoda, a senior manager of NEC Corporation, had been appointed vice president of NECI in 1989, and Kahng was its first president. The two men had many discussions concerning not only NECI's strategy but its day-to-day operations; they had also seen each other socially. The sudden death of Kahng was a shock to Shinoda, and he was uncertain about what to do next.

NEC CORPORATION: COMPANY BACKGROUND

NEC in 1992

NEC's total revenue for fiscal year 1992 was $28.37 billion, with net income of $115 million; total assets were $30.69 billion, and the number of employees was about 40,000, making the NEC Corporation one of the biggest companies in Japan (second in total revenues in electronics companies). (See Exhibits 1a and 1b for NEC's financial statements.) Its business was concentrated in three fields: computers, communication appliances, and electronics devices. NEC's global market share of personal computers was about 11.4 percent (third in the global market). Its share of communication appliances was about 6.0 percent (fourth in the global market), and the semiconductor share was 18.9 percent (second in the global market). NEC was one of the few electronics companies that had developed three well-balanced fields in the past few decades; by contrast, IBM focused on computers and AT&T on communications.

Source: Copyright © 1998 by The President and Fellows of Harvard College. Professor Walter Kuemmerle and Visiting Scholar Kiichiro Kobayashi, Ph.D., prepared this case as the basis for class discussion rather than to illustrate either effective or ineffective handling of an administrative situation.

EXHIBIT 1A   NEC Corporation Annual Income Statement

($ millions, except per share)	March 92	March 91	March 90	March 89
Sales	$28,374.80	$26,232.60	$21,798.50	$23,178.90
Cost of goods sold	17,181.40	15,501.30	13,191.70	14,485.70
Gross profit	$11,193.40	10,731.30	8,606.80	8,693.20
Selling, general, and admin. expenses	8,508.41	7,569.97	5,869.88	6,011.90
Operating income before depreciation	2,684.99	3,161.33	2,736.92	2,682.01
Depreciation, depletion & amortization	1,771.77	1,639.66	1,259.89	1,292.47
Operating profit	913.214	1,521.67	1,477.03	1,389.54
Interest expense	813.714	763.092	573.031	543.767
Nonoperating income/expense	344.685	233.085	275.285	238.895
Special items	0	0	0	0
Pre-tax income	445.113	991.603	1,179.31	1,084.68
Total income taxes	342.850	681.199	668.146	656.12
Minority interest	−9.308	13.127	13.766	16.226
Income before extraordinary items & discontinued operations	111.571	360.277	497.399	412.338
Preferred dividends	0	0	0	0
Available for common	111.571	360.277	497.399	412.338
Savings due to common stock equivalents	0	0	0	0
Adjusted available for common	111.571	360.277	497.399	412.338
Extraordinary items	3.286	25.418	41.962	72.451
Discontinued operations	0	0	0	0
Adjusted net income	$114.857	$385.695	$539.361	$484.789

NEC Corp.—ADR	March 92	March 91	March 90	March 89
Earnings per share (primary)—excluding extra items & discontinued operations	$0.37	$1.14	$1.55	$1.32
Earnings per share (primary)—including extra items & discontinued operations	0.38	1.21	1.67	1.54
Earnings per share (fully diluted)—excluding extra items and discontinued operations	0.37	1.14	1.55	1.32
Earnings per share (fully diluted)—including extra items and discontinued operations	0.38	1.21	1.67	1.54
EPS from operations	NA	NA	NA	NA
Dividends per share	0.39	0.35	0.34	0.34

Source: S&P Compustat.

Corporate History

Started as a joint U.S.-Japanese enterprise, NEC was established in 1899 as a telephone manufacturer, financed by the Western Electric Company (a manufacturing division of AT&T). Not until after the Second World War did NEC become a consumer-oriented firm, when Koji Kobayashi, then managing director, initiated a plan to establish radio wireless communications as the company's new core business. This was made possible once the Japanese government had deregulated electric wave frequencies. The company went on to develop satellite communication systems with the Hughes Corporation in the 1960s—systems that subsequently transmitted such news as the assassination of President Kennedy and events like the Tokyo Olympic Games.

Meanwhile, in the 1950s, Kobayashi had recognized that entering the computer business would be critical if the company was to advance in its communications businesses. "Communication devices have no information processing function," he noted. "On the other hand, computers can't transfer information. Combining these tools will make it possible to create new technology and business chances." In 1958 NEC introduced its first mainframe computers, which then were not compatible with IBM machines. NEC reigned as the top computer manufacturer in Japan until it gave way to the Fujitsu

EXHIBIT 1B   NEC Corporation Annual Balance Sheets

($ millions)	March 92	March 91	March 90	March 89
Assets				
Cash & equivalents	$ 3,614.89	$ 3,239.20	$ 2,745.31	$ 3,896.17
Net receivables	7,341.93	7,142.15	6,242.52	6,492.98
Inventories	6,495.25	5,660.86	4,657.58	5,140.09
Prepaid expenses	@CF	@CF	@CF	@CF
Other current assets	539.052	586.829	513.437	442.097
Total current assets	17,991.10	16,629.00	14,158.80	15,971.30
Gross plant, property & equipment	19,132.21	16,451.30	13,135.07	12,912.48
Accumulated depreciation	10,732.50	8,963.17	7,073.46	7,124.80
Net plant, property & equipment	8,399.71	7,488.13	6,061.61	5,787.68
Investments at equity	979.436	875.305	748.918	827.654
Other investments	1,634.72	1,514.82	1,221.48	1,419.72
Other assets	1,680.85	1,361.73	1,125.58	1,154.60
Total assets	$30,685.80	$27,869.00	$23,316.40	$25,160.90
Liabilities				
Long-term debt due in one year	$1,218.13	$532.326	$431.772	$563.857
Notes payable	5,275.46	4,515.05	3,977.58	4,328.03
Accounts payable	5,551.34	6,075.34	5,167.05	5,449.19
Taxes payable	71.729	361.553	419.165	401.211
Accrued expenses	0	0	0	0
Other current liabilities	3,001.08	2,648.77	2,413.35	2,492.51
Total current liabilities	15,117.70	14,133.00	12,408.90	13,234.80
Long-term debt	6,201.80	4,954.55	3,715.68	4,462.64
Deferred taxes	0	0	0	0
Investment tax credit	0	0	0	0
Minority interest	394.79	380.794	332.62	311.895
Other liabilities	2,367.35	2,152.87	1,763.12	1,968.49
Total liabilities	$24,081.64	$21,621.21	$18,220.31	$19,977.82
Equity				
Common stock	1,415.43	1,331.33	1,109.81	1,202.81
Capital surplus	2,235.73	2,104.13	1,700.94	1,842.86
Retained earnings	2,953.02	2,812.38	2,285.44	2,144.04
Less: Treasury stock	0.022	0.064	0.082	6.534
Common equity	6,604.16	6,247.77	5,096.11	5,183.16
Total equity	6,604.16	6,247.77	5,096.11	5,183.16
Total liabilities & equity	30,685.80	27,869.00	23,316.40	25,160.90
Common shares outstanding	307.829	307.662	303.926	298.648

Source: S&P Compustat.

Corporation in 1968. NEC launched its personal computer business in the early 1980s; soon thereafter, its 98PC series conquered the market.

NEC had a long history in manufacturing electronic parts, starting with vacuum tubes in 1928, transistors in 1954, and integrated circuits in 1961—these products were for internal use, however. In 1967, NEC established an electronics parts division as a new key business because it realized that electronics devices would enable communication devices and computers to be linked. Because semiconductors were a volume business, a huge amount of capital had to be invested so accumulated production volume could be added and unit costs reduced. To take advantage of economies of scale, NEC sought a worldwide market, expanding its semiconductor business through the 1970s and 1980s. In 1983, it established a large semiconductor factory at Livingston (United Kingdom), and another at LSI (Roseville, California) in 1984. In 1992, NEC's 18.9 percent share of the global semiconductor market was second only to Intel.

Developing the C&C Corporate Vision

Concentrating on computers and communications (C&C) became NEC's corporate goal. This vision also included electronics devices. In 1977, at the International Tele-communication Conference in Atlanta, Kobayashi had stated, "Computers and communications will be integrated through semiconductors in the near future. This will be possible technologically." Computers and communication technology had not been integrated at that time in technology and business, but Kobayashi realized the necessity of doing so—he had propounded the idea when pushing NEC to enter the computer business in the first place. Moreover, ever since Kobayashi introduced the concept of C&C in Atlanta, this approach was acknowledged as being important in many technological fields worldwide.

At the same time, C&C defined NEC's strategic domain. Kobayashi strongly recognized the necessity of simple and meaningful catch phrases that could represent the code of conduct for all NEC employees. He also realized that NEC had to "renovate" its business structure. When it had been a subcontractor, NEC only needed to listen to what customers suggested; but entering into the computer business meant it had to make decisions itself—from product development to marketing. NEC had to be proactive in running its organization, and this meant changing its corporate culture. The C&C vision became the motivation for NEC to change from being a subcontractor to becoming a market-oriented electronics company.

Two Excellent Leaders

When Koji Kobayashi was named president of NEC in 1964, about 63 percent of total sales came from government-related companies; the subcontractor business was low risk–low return (i.e., it was stable but profit was thin). Kobayashi thus promoted the computer and semiconductor businesses forcefully while at the same time deciding to withdraw from the atomic power plant business because it required considerable investment. He also introduced the division profit center system in 1965 in order to improve the company's overall efficiency. Then, as his ideas evolved, in 1977 he created the C&C long-term corporate vision while also leading various initiatives to improve NEC's short-term profitability.

When Tadahiro Sekimoto became president in 1980, he viewed himself as responsible for carrying the C&C corporate vision forward. A scientist by training, he also had broad experience in the company's various business sectors. He established channels for consumer products

throughout Japan and raised NEC's corporate image by executing a large-scale campaign for the C&C strategy.

These two leaders, Kobayashi and Sekimoto, were essential to the "renovation" of NEC. Not only were they responsible for creating and promoting the corporate vision, they consistently—and tenaciously—held to the C&C strategy: It took nearly 20 years for the computer business to become a key division in the firm. (See Exhibit 2 for NEC's Organization Chart.) "It takes a few decades for potential technology to be put to practical use," Kobayashi had often remarked. In addition, Kobayashi and Sekimoto increased public awareness of the company and enhanced its prestige; doing so was essential if NEC was to change its focus from subcontracting towards consumer electronics. They both promoted volume sales and established advertising campaigns, which advanced a positive corporate image. Finally, they collaborated with other electronics companies, such as Hughes in the satellite communication business, RCA and GE in the semiconductor business, and, later, Microsoft in the personal computer business. Strategic alliances made it possible for NEC to gain access to external resources and accelerate its entry into the market.

Past R&D Policy at NEC

From 1985 on, NEC had spent roughly 8.3 percent of total sales a year in R&D expenses (compared with about 5–6 percent in other electronics firms). About 95 percent of the R&D budget was distributed to the business division laboratories, where new product development was carried out, with the remainder allocated to the central lab. Electronics firms needed to have a wide variety of technologies, to combine several key technologies, and to develop new products as quickly as possible, and NEC was no exception. Its laboratories explored a wide variety of research fields, including psychology, sociology, anthropology, biology, and civil engineering, in addition to electronics-related technologies.

Michiyuki Uenohara was key in establishing NEC's R&D policy. He had been with Bell Laboratories in the United States and was renowned for developing a communication satellite receiver. Joining NEC in 1967 as the head of the device development division in NEC's central laboratory, he went on to develop the semiconductor laser, the optical converter, and fifth-generation computer languages. Uenohara promoted technology fusion within NEC's R&D resources: "Combining several technological resources makes it possible to develop new technologies," he noted. Uenohara also stressed both R&D efficiency and business-related R&D strategy. "We should

EXHIBIT 2 Organization Chart of NEC

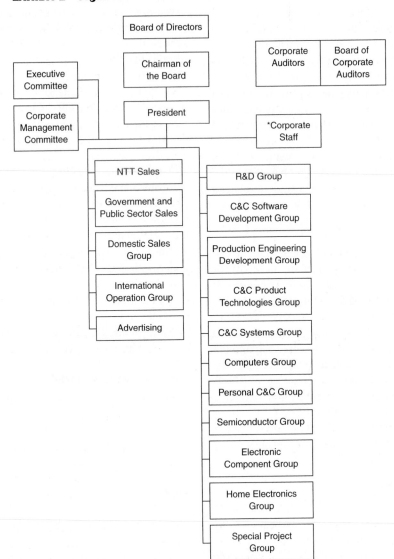

Source: Annual report.

select some technologies which are common to our business divisions as the key technologies of our company," he said, and thus initiated joint research projects, directly sponsored by business divisions.

ENVIRONMENTAL CHANGES

In the late 1980s, Japanese electronics manufacturers faced a turning point as the country's fundamental economic structure was altered due to a slowdown in growth.

During the prior two decades, Japanese companies in general were able to avoid taking risks in developing new technologies by importing fundamental technologies from abroad. They continued to focus on products' quality, cost, and functionality, investing huge amounts of capital in manufacturing processes and aiming at high-volume production. This operations-oriented strategy worked very well in times of rapid growth and brought good economic performance. But the end of such economic growth compelled Japanese firms to jettison their catch-up approach and instead to create innovative technologies themselves. It was no longer feasible to rely mainly on importing scientific knowledge from Western countries.

Further, the rapid progress of information technology and global-level competition in the late 1980s had made the economic world smaller. As more and more advanced knowledge emerged around the world, companies from many countries established strategic sites in foreign countries in order to access new information as well as markets. They also had to move new products from development to market very quickly. At the same time, as technology and specialization advanced rapidly, it became more difficult for companies to harness all necessary technologies through their own R&D activities. Consequently, they were forming strategic alliances with other firms, laboratories, and universities that held a competitive edge technologically. As a result of these realities, Japanese companies had to build global R&D networks that tapped into new centers of knowledge and to commercialize products globally.

At the industry level, the establishment of de facto standards represented a critical success factor in the electronics arena, and, moreover, the de facto standard-setting competition had proceeded rapidly. Cooperation and competition therefore-coexisted. This phenomenon forced electronics companies to predict future technology directions as precisely as they could; to gain a comprehensive understanding of technology trends; to target and create a core competence; and to forge strategic alliances in which they would be a key player.

Rethinking and redefining the industry, however, remained a problem. Deregulation and technological changes had altered the traditional concept of industry as being focused on the end-product, and made it possible for new companies to enter or segment markets as important intermediary players. Electronics companies were forced to realize that the industry's boundaries represented a variable that was not given but that had to be managed. This, in turn, forced companies to establish core competences within the wide field of electronics and to introduce new products through R&D activities. As such, building new knowledge as well as global technological presence became a central issue of corporate strategy in the electronics industry.

NEC'S NEW R&D SITE IN PRINCETON

Preparation for New R&D Site

In 1984, Michiyuki Uenohara, the senior managing director of NEC (who was also in charge of the company's entire R&D effort), and Dawon Kahng began to discuss plans for a new R&D lab. Recognizing that it was no longer possible to introduce new technologies from abroad, the two set about implementing their visionary plans for a basic research facility of NEC.

Both Uenohara and Kahng held degrees from Ohio State University and had been scientists together at Bell Laboratories, where Kahng developed the MOS transistor. At the time, Bell Labs indicated to him that putting this invention to practical use would be extremely difficult. But Japanese manufacturers did succeed in both "practical" and mass production. Impressed, Kahng decided to join NEC.

Two years later, in 1986, Daizaburo Shinoda, who had previously managed laboratories at NEC, joined Uenohara and Kahng to help shape the company's basic research laboratories in foreign countries. Shinoda also realized the importance of basic research: Japanese manufacturers had previously only nurtured and taken advantage of Western technologies but now had to develop new research on their own.

In 1987, the plan of establishing a new R&D site (the Uenohara Proposal) was submitted to NEC's top management and approved. Tadahiro Sekimoto, NEC's CEO, also had been thinking about the necessity of creating and absorbing new technological knowledge, so he was in favor of the plan. Shinoda recalled:

> Basic research will require risk taking and long-term investment, so it is very important for top management to recognize the necessity of basic research. Basic research does not always produce instant results for corporate economic performance in the short run. This is why basic research needs commitment from the top management. The top management of NEC recognized that basic research is essential for the company's survival, and it is also the social responsibility of the company that strives to be a world leader.

In January 1988, NEC assembled a small but powerful team of senior managers, including Tsuneya Kato, the managing director of NEC who was also in charge of the R&D group, Shinoda, and Kahng, to carry the plan forward. Combining outstanding scientific experience, technical expertise, and managerial know-how, the team members reported directly to the top of the company and were deeply involved in the management and supervision of NEC's R&D strategy.

Objectives of New R&D Site

In June 1988, NEC registered a new company in the United States, the NEC Research Institute, Inc. (NECI). Shinoda and Kahng established NECI's six main objectives:

1. To contribute to the progress of knowledge and information in the 21st century.
2. To contribute to the NEC's C&C businesses.
3. To contribute to society as a whole in the arts and sciences.
4. To establish NEC's scientific presence, and raise its corporate image globally.
5. To develop new technological knowledge and transfer it to other NEC laboratories.
6. To attract talented scientists who were essential to NEC.

Which Location?

Several sites for NECI were proposed, including Boston (Massachusetts), Palo Alto (California), and Princeton (New Jersey). (See Exhibit 3 for a comparison of locations.) Shinoda and Kahng believed it was important to establish a new basic research laboratory in a relatively quiet place that was also an academic center so the best possible work could be done over a sustained period of time. They were worried that Boston might be too fast-paced for basic research activities and ruled out California because proximity to Europe was important. Shinoda and Kahng therefore selected Princeton, noting in a joint paper:

> The reason why we chose Princeton was that it was located among regional clusters of scientific excellence, and it would be easy to absorb new sources of knowledge. There are many scientific institutes around Princeton, the Bell Laboratories, the IBM Research Institute, the SRI Institute, and so on. Princeton is also a convenient place to do collaborative research because of its proximity to such universities as Princeton University, Columbia University, and Yale Uni-

versity. Moreover, NEC has its U.S. headquarters in New York, which is also easily reached from Princeton.

Starting and Managing Princeton

In October 1988, after the decision to locate in Princeton had been made, Shinoda and Kahng began recruiting senior-level researchers. Because they believed that the level and prestige of the laboratory depended on the technical abilities of researchers, they aimed to hire prominent local scientists, thereby demonstrating their seriousness to local scientific communities. "There are three tasks of top management in establishing a basic research laboratory," Shinoda said. "First, it is necessary to attract as many very excellent researchers as possible. Second, we must develop a research agenda for the new site. And third, we must entrust them with research."

The NEC Princeton laboratory was opened in 1989, with 37 employees; a year later there were 66. Kahng became the president and Shinoda the executive vice president; three of the four management members were Americans. The laboratory's basic operational policies were as follows:

1. To focus on the basic research of innovative computer technology.
2. To promote the interfacing between physical science and computer science.
3. To acquire intellectual property rights by applying for patents quickly.
4. To promote synergy between the Princeton lab and other NEC labs.
5. To absorb knowledge from the Princeton scientific community.

EXHIBIT 3 Area Comparison

	Palo Alto Area	Boston Area	Princeton Area
Population	1,601,600	3,827,300	329,900
Per-capita income	19,245	18,136	19,980
Households	540,500	1,426,300	117,900
Median income	49,298	45,549	45,505
Retail sales ($1000)	15,301,562	27,351,804	3,012,711
Car registration	1,002,371	2,000,185	180,197
# of colleges & universities	156 (CA)	75 (MA)	32 (NJ)
Bachelor's degree or higher (%)	32.6%	34.4%	29.5%
University enrollment	165,585	361,605	30,867
# of airports	33 (CA)	8 (MA)	3 (NJ)
Fortune 500 headquarter cities	52 (SF + LA)	14 (Boston)	18 (NJ) 47 (NY)
# of employees (manufacturers)	275,700	377,700	39,800
Other NEC facilities	None	Development Lab	NEC U.S. (NY)

Source: United States Statistical Yearbook (various issues).

EXHIBIT 4   Computer Science Research Field

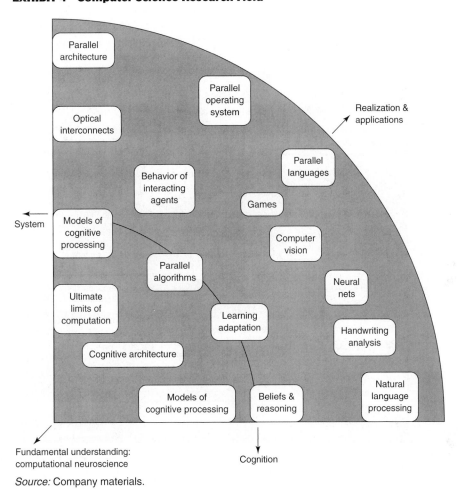

Source: Company materials.

Shinoda and Kahng paid close attention to the site's research agenda. Writing about the new laboratory, they commented:

> Setting a research agenda is the essential task for initial managers because it defines the characteristics of the new R&D site. We focused on computer sciences and physical sciences because we have the corporate vision [C&C]. In order to link the new site into the company, we had to pay close attention to the Princeton laboratory's research agenda, and create mechanisms to integrate it into NEC's overall strategic goal, C&C.

Therefore, Shinoda and Kahng decided that NECI should concentrate on basic research in computer-related technology (i.e., physical science and computer science) because NEC's direction was informed by the Computer and Communication business domain (see Exhibits 4 and 5).

Regarding the laboratory's structure, Shinoda noted at a press conference:

> Basic research needs an appropriate organizational structure and management in order to flourish. We should not take any steps to hinder a researcher's work. We think that basic research should not be managed from above. One important thing in managing a basic research laboratory is not to administer to researchers, but to create an atmosphere that fosters the intellectual interaction between researchers. We insist on the freedom of research, so we adopted the flat management structure with no reporting hierarchy, which provided the best academic environment of self-directed research. Each researcher is given a research budget based on position.

EXHIBIT 5   Physical Science Research Field

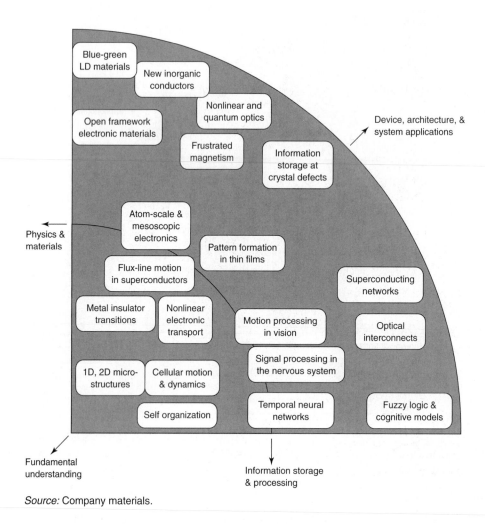

Source: Company materials.

C. W. Gear, the laboratory's scientific vice president, elaborated:

> The NEC Research Institute has a basic research mission and is one of a few industrial research laboratories in the world. If I am asked, "Are you free to do whatever you want at the Institute?" I answer, "No, we are free to do what we think will contribute to the company." Good basic research is not managed from above, but it has to be managed by the researcher by himself. This Institute has a mission: to contribute to the future of computing and communication—areas in which the parent company is a big player.

In both the physical science and the computer science division, the research organization included a range of positions, from vice president to intern (see Exhibit 6 for an organization chart of NEC Princeton). The two vice presidents and eight fellow scientists constituted the Board of Fellows, which discussed the laboratory's research direction and decided its R&D strategy in cooperation with NEC.

In the research organization's flat management structure, researchers were directly linked to the vice president in charge of their divisions; there was no reporting hierarchy between the researchers, but they sometimes did joint research. Senior research scientists and research scientists were accompanied by a senior research associate or research associate, who served as assistants.

Vice presidents were responsible for managing their individual divisions. Fellow scientists were required to have more than 23 years of research experience, as well

EXHIBIT 6   Organization Chart of NEC Princeton

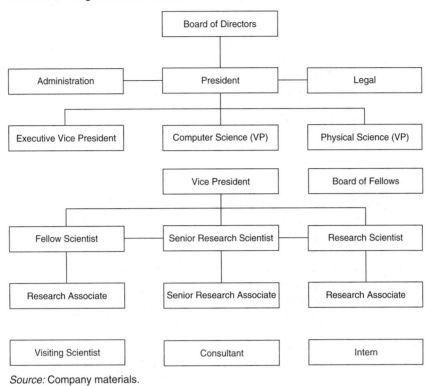

Source: Company materials.

as an international reputation in their research area. Senior research scientists had to be leaders in the academic community, with 10 to 20 years of research experience. Research scientists, who had fewer than 10 years of research experience, were hired on the strength of their research papers. All vice presidents, fellow scientists, senior research scientists, and research scientists were required to have Ph.D. degrees. Research budgets were based on position; there were no research proposals to write and no proposals to review.

Senior research associates and research associates, who were engaged in developing and programming software, designing hardware, analyzing quantitative data, and writing research reports, had to hold either a bachelor's or a master's degree. The Princeton laboratory also encouraged visiting employees (scientists/scholars, consultants, and interns) in order to stimulate the exchange of technological information. Visiting scholars usually stayed at the Princeton laboratory for one year and were engaged in joint research. Consultants were non-regular employees with special expertise, while interns were Ph.D. candidates working under the supervision of scientists.

Evaluation system

Shinoda and Kahng realized they had to determine appropriate incentive structures and employment contracts before they began to hire employees, for once the evaluation system was established, it would be very difficult to change. The system would also define the research evaluation criteria as well as the activities of most scientists. The two men decided that the assessment of scientists should be carried out once a year. Each scientist had to submit a report about his or her own research for the past three years, including research results, activities within NECI, activities outside NECI, publications, and the number of patents applied for.

At the first stage of review, the assessment committee, comprising a few upper level scientists, formulated an evaluation draft sheet that included suggestions about what the individual scientist needed to improve. When the committee decided to promote a scientist, they asked for opinions outside of NECI for reference.

The evaluation draft was submitted to the appropriate vice president and fellow scientist upon completion, who discussed whether the suggestions of the evaluation group should have been made and revised the assessment sheet if necessary. The result was submitted to the Board of Fellows and a final assessment made. This final evaluation determined the researcher's income for the next year. Meanwhile, scientists received their final evaluation sheets and could submit a written report to their superior if they objected to the results.

NECI's evaluation system was based on what each scientist contributed to the laboratory, but also focused on academic contributions in the past three years and what the individual scientist expected to accomplish in the future.

Global Scientific Collaboration

Shinoda and Kahng recognized that R&D sites abroad were often good at combining knowledge from different scientific fields into new ideas and technologies because they were open to the local scientific community. NEC's laboratories in Japan were very focused on existing product lines and very close to the business sectors, so they could not contribute sufficiently to pioneering projects. Hence, NEC established its basic research laboratory in the United States. In another joint paper, Shinoda and Khang expressed their opinion about openness of basic research:

> We also assure scientists that they have the freedom to publish the results of their research in refereed academic journals. We know that it is essential for researchers to have a prominent reputation in academia. At the same time, openness of fundamental research results brings a lot of benefits to the company, such as applying for patents, establishing intellectual property rights, receiving patent royalties, and attracting other excellent scientists.

Shinoda and Kahng envisioned two functions for the Princeton laboratory: "One is to access new knowledge and absorb new research results by promoting collaborative research with foreign scientific communities. The other is to become a good consultant for all NEC's laboratories, by exchanging NECI researchers with other NEC laboratories" (see Exhibit 7 for Shinoda's and Kahng's vision for NEC).

Realizing that they had to hire renowned local scientists as the laboratory group leaders, Shinoda and Kahng noted, "We had to staff them with the right people because the ability of the scientists defines the quality and prestige of the laboratory. It is essential to hire prominent and promising scientists in order to access and absorb new knowledge from the local scientific community." If they succeeded in hiring talented scientists who were part of the local scientific community, they felt confident they could attract junior scientists with very high poten-

EXHIBIT 7 Shinoda's and Kahng's Vision for R&D at NEC

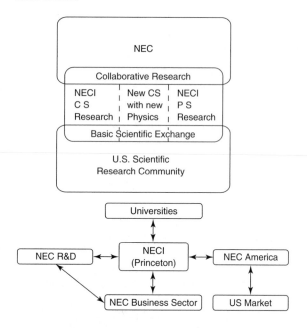

CS = Computer Science
PS = Physical Science
Source: Company materials.

tial, and target the right university institutes and scholars for joint research projects. Gear elaborated:

> For NEC, the Institute is an important component of its industrial-academic interaction program. Opening in a similar culture to that of Princeton University, it is easier for the Institute scientists to interact with outside scientists. We have a flow of visitors—at any given time our scientific staff is enlarged about 30 percent by visitors ranging from students to faculty on sabbatical. We learn from these visitors and they can learn from us. This Institute is supposed to contribute new knowledge, and it does this by publishing all of its work in literature that is accessible to the public. This is a recognition that openness of fundamental research has many benefits.

To make the Princeton laboratory a good technology consultant for all of NEC, and to make this new site part of the NEC community, Shinoda and Kahng needed to create mechanisms to integrate it into the firm's overall strategic goals. They planned several ways by which the U.S. and the Japanese scientists could be in contact with each other in cooperation with senior NEC R&D management in Japan. Shinoda explained:

> Nothing can replace face-to-face contact between active researchers. Therefore, a lot of scientists from both NEC and

EXHIBIT 8   Results of Research at NECI

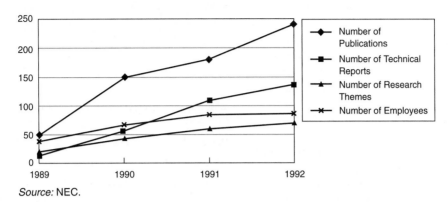

Source: NEC.

NECI spend time visiting other NEC R&D sites. We pay special attention in order to make sure that newly hired scientists were aware of the resources that existed within the company. Through collaborations with scientists in the company's several research laboratories, the scientists at the Princeton laboratory get an appreciation of the critical problems the company faced in the near future.

The first R&D strategy exchange meeting between NEC Japan and NECI was held in November 1989; nine months later the first result of joint research about computer science between NEC and NECI came out. New ideas started moving from the Princeton laboratory to the rest of the company, as Shinoda and Kahng created direct links among researchers across different sites, stimulating the exchange of knowledge. For NECI as a whole, research results increased year by year (see Exhibits 8–10 for Results of Research at NECI, R&D at NEC, and NECI's cost structure).

Leaders of the New R&D Site

The initial leader of an R&D site had a powerful impact not only on the culture of the site, but also on its long-term research agenda and performance. As Shinoda said, "Laboratory leaders should be prominent scientists and managers who will be able to fulfill their responsibilities, to absorb new scientific knowledge, and to nurture ties between the new sites and the local scientific community." At the Princeton laboratory, Kahng, a prominent local scientist, was also a former fellow of Bell Laboratories and had been in contact with many other prominent scientists in the United States. He also attracted many young potential researchers because of his strong reputation. From the beginning, he commanded respect in the scientific community surrounding the laboratory.

For his part, Shinoda was a highly skilled manager at NEC. He understood company politics and felt strongly

EXHIBIT 9   R&D at NEC

	1970	1980	1990	1992
Number of researchers at corporate lab in Japan	700	919	1,148	1,293
Percentage of sales of R&D	7.4	6.0	8.4	9.5

Source: NEC.

EXHIBIT 10   NECI Cost Structure ($ million)

	1989	1990	1991	1992
Initial cost	20.0			
Running cost	10.0	16.3	19.9	20.6

Source: NEC.

that a basic research laboratory was needed. Not everyone agreed with him, and he had to overcome these peoples' doubts. He recalled:

> My initial task was to persuade the objectors about the value of an R&D site in the United States. I insisted that basic research would pay off, and outlined four reasons why I felt sure I was correct. First, a basic laboratory would be able to acquire scientific property rights that would eventually bring profits to the company. Second, the laboratory would establish core technology which would lead to competitive advantages: the company has to develop prominent core competence in order to collaborate with other companies advantageously. Third, scientists in basic research would become the most reliable consultants for the company. And finally, building a basic research laboratory would raise the corporate image of NEC and attract many talented people from outside the company who would become the company's strategic assets.

Beyond being respected scientists and skilled managers, Kahng and Shinoda shared a strong strategic vision, which enabled the Princeton laboratory to start off smoothly. They had a comprehensive understanding of technological trends and the new dynamics of global R&D; they also had in-depth knowledge of both Japanese and non-Japanese cultures. As such, they were well-positioned to integrate the Princeton laboratory into NEC's existing R&D network (see Exhibits 11 and 12 for resumes of Kahng and Shinoda).

What Next?

Kahng's sudden death in 1992 came as a great shock to Shinoda, who faced a difficult decision and complex challenges (see Exhibit 13 for a review of the flow of events regarding NECI). First, he had to decide who should succeed Kahng. Second, he had to continue to promote collaboration between NECI and other NEC laboratories. Finally, NEC was planning on establishing several

new R&D sites abroad. As the number of the company's R&D sites grew, Shinoda and his fellow R&D leaders would face the increasingly challenging task of coordinating NEC's global R&D network.

EXHIBIT 12   Curriculum Vitae of Dr. Daizaburo Shinoda

Name:	Daizaburo Shinoda, Ph.D.
Date of Birth:	July 9, 1931
Place of Birth:	Tokyo, Japan
Education:	1958—Graduated from Kyoto University (Chemistry)
	1960—M. A. in chemistry from Kyoto University
	1973—Doctor of Science from Kyoto University
Work Experience:	1960—Joined NEC (basic laboratory)
	1976–1986—Held the positions of Manager, Ultra-LSI Research Laboratory, and General Manager, Fundamental Research Laboratories
	1987—Served as Vice President, Research and Development, at NEC Corporation. Currently assigned to the NEC Research Institute as Executive Vice President

Source: NEC.

EXHIBIT 11   Curriculum Vitae of Dr. Dawon Kahng

Name:	Dawon Kahng, Ph.D.
Date of Birth:	May 4, 1931
Place of Birth:	Seoul, Republic of Korea
Education:	1955—Graduated from Seoul University (Physics)
	1959—Ph.D. from Ohio State University (Electrical Engineering)
Work Experience:	1957—Joined Bell Telephone Laboratories, Inc.
	1984—Supervisor at Bell Telephone Laboratories, Inc.
	—Naturalized in the United States
	—Fellow at AT&A Bell Laboratories
	1987—Retired AT&T Bell Laboratories
Achievements:	Invented Si MOS transistors, now used at basic elements of LSI
	Developed luminescence in the visible and charge coupled devices
	Invented nonvolatile semiconductor memories (currently used as EPROM, EEPROM)
Membership:	Member of Sigma Xi and Pi Mu Epsilon
	Fellow of IEEE (1972)
Awards:	Recipient, Stuart Ballantine Gold Medal of the Franklin Institute, Pennsylvania

Source: NEC.

EXHIBIT 13   Flow of Events

1984:	Uenohara/Kahng planning sessions
1986:	Shinoda joins
1987:	Uenohara proposal to NEC top management
1988:	Project team for new R&D site put together
	NEC Research Institute registered in U.S.
	Started hiring senior researchers
1989:	NEC Princeton Laboratory opens
	Application for the first patent in U.S.
1990:	U.S.–Japan R&D strategy conference
	U.S.–Japan joint research starts
1991:	Researcher evaluation system starts
1992:	Dawon Kahng dies

Source: NEC.

CASE III-3

Cisco Systems, Inc.: Acquisition Integration for Manufacturing

Nicole Tempest and Christian G. Kasper

David Keller, vice president of manufacturing, new product introduction, and technology at Cisco Systems, Inc. (Cisco), hung up the phone and sat back to think about the challenges that lay ahead. He had just spent the last hour talking with Gary Wilder, director of manufacturing operations, and Dick Swee, vice president of engineering, at Summa Four Inc. (Summa Four)—a systems company which developed and manufactured programmable switches used in the development of telephony applications. Cisco had announced in July 1998 that it had reached an agreement to acquire publicly held Summa Four for $116 million in stock. The conversation had been about the major effort that lay ahead to integrate the two companies' manufacturing organizations. While the deal was not expected to officially close until November 1998, Keller had called Wilder and Swee to give them an overview of how Cisco managed these types of integration projects so that they could begin to prepare the Summa Four organization.

Keller had reviewed the due diligence report on Summa Four written by a team from his department and knew that the integration process would be complex. While Cisco had made 25 acquisitions prior to the Summa Four acquisition, most had been of Silicon Valley–based software or preproduction hardware companies which had small (if any) manufacturing organizations. The Summa Four acquisition had the potential to be different. Summa Four was a 22-year-old hardware company with $42 million in revenues, over 200 employees, one manufacturing plant located in Manchester, New Hampshire, and a full line of products being shipped. Summa Four represented one of Cisco's largest acquisitions to date in terms of current revenues and employees.

Keller was concerned about just how difficult the acquisition integration process would be from a manufacturing standpoint. How would they treat Summa Four's legacy and next generation products? Where would they be manufactured? How would Cisco deal with Summa Four's suppliers? Did it make sense to keep the Manchester plant operating? If so, for how long? What risks did Cisco face during the integration process and what could be done to help mitigate those risks?

CISCO OVERVIEW

Cisco Systems, founded in 1984 by Leonard Bosack and Sandy Lerner—a husband-and-wife team of computer specialists at Stanford University—grew out of a project to tie together disparate computer networks on campus. Bosack and Lerner developed the first "multiprotocol" router—a specialized microcomputer that sat between two or more networks (even those with different operating systems) and allowed those networks to "talk" to each other by deciphering, translating, and funneling data between them. As Bosack explained back then: "We network networks."[1] Cisco's technology opened up the potential for linking all of the world's disparate computer networks together in much the same way as different telephone networks were linked around the world. Technology pioneered by Cisco provided the functionality for the World Wide Web.

As the global Internet and corporate Intranets grew in importance, so too did Cisco. With an early foothold in this rapidly growing industry, Cisco quickly became the leader in the data networking equipment market—the "plumbing" of the Internet. By 1998, most of the large-scale routers that powered the Internet were made by Cisco. While routers and switches continued to be Cisco's core products, the company's product line had expanded to include a broad range of other networking solutions, including website management tools, dial-up and other access solutions, Internet appliances, and network management software. (See Exhibit 1 for a list of Cisco's product categories.) Cisco's broad product line enabled it to offer customers an "end-to-end" network solution—an option which over 50 percent of Fortune 500 companies were actively considering, according to Cisco. By 1998 the company held the number one or number two position in 14 of the 15 markets in which it competed. As a result,

Source: Copyright © 1999 by The President and Fellows of Harvard College. Nicole Tempest, Associate Director of the HBS California Research Center, and Dean's Research Fellow Christian G. Kasper prepared this case under the supervision of Professor Steven C. Wheelwright and Charles A. Halloway, Kleiner Perkins Caufield and Byers Professor of Management at Stanford University's Graduate School of Business, as the basis for class discussion rather than to illustrate either effective or ineffective handling of an administrative situation.

---

[1] *The San Francisco Chronicle,* February 17, 1990.

EXHIBIT 1   Cisco Product Categories

Product category	Description
High-end routers	Cisco's high-end platforms for the most mission-critical networks
WAN switches	Wide area networking switching for frame relay and ATM, plus network access devices
LAN switches	Local area networking switching for workgroup networks
Hubs	Devices to link small workgroups in local networks
Access products	Scalable products for remote access
Web scaling products and technologies	Products that provide Internet access, security, scalability, and management
Security products	Comprehensive solutions for network protection and enabling Internet business applications
InterWorks for SNA	Availability, scalability, performance, flexibility, and management for IBM/SNA networks
IOS software	Cisco's Internetworking Operating System software
Network management	Network management solutions that offer end-to-end network management for any Cisco-based network

Source: www.cisco.com.

Cisco had become a safe decision for large companies. As one industry analyst commented, "I have heard from a number of really large clients: 'It's like IBM in the old days—you won't get fired for choosing them.'"[2]

In 1996 Cisco entered the $250 billion telecom equipment market, which was undergoing significant change due to rapid advances in technology. Whereas historically there had been three separate types of networks—phone networks for transmitting voice, computer networks for transmitting data, and broadcast networks for transmitting video—advances in digitization had allowed voice, data, and video all to be translated into the ones and zeros of computer language. This, in turn, made it possible to transmit all three over *one* network in a more efficient and economical manner. As a result, phone companies were beginning to replace their century-old voice-only networks with new networks capable of carrying voice, data, and video. By positioning its products for this mar-

ket, Cisco was competing with a far larger group of rivals than it had in the past—including Lucent Technologies and Nortel. In June 1998 Cisco scored a major victory against these rivals when Sprint selected Cisco to be the primary supplier of its new data and telephone network.

Having received its initial funding from the venture capital firm Sequoia Capital, Cisco went public in February 1990, closing its first day of trading with a market value of $222 million. Just 8 years later, Cisco's market value topped the significant $100 billion mark, reaching that mark faster than any company in history and stripping Microsoft of the previous record of 11 years. Between 1989 and 1998 Cisco's revenues grew at a compound annual rate of 89 percent, from $28 million to $8.5 billion, and with traffic on the Internet doubling every four months, Cisco continued to have significant growth potential. (See Exhibit 2 for Cisco's financials).

Cisco's Business Strategy

Cisco's business strategy reflected the experience of CEO John Chambers and Chairman John Morgridge. Morgridge, who had been CEO of Cisco from 1988 to 1995, established many of Cisco's core business principles, including the importance of customer satisfaction, time to market, and frugality. Chambers, who took over as CEO in January 1995, spent most of his career at IBM and Wang, and watched both companies suffer crippling declines as a result of not adapting to changing market conditions quickly enough. Morgridge, Chambers, and Ed Kozel—then Cisco's chief technology officer—crafted a strategic plan for Cisco in 1993, which was still being executed in 1998. The plan consisted of four main components:

1. Assemble a broad product line in order to provide customers one-stop shopping for networking solutions.
2. Systematize the acquisition process.
3. Define industry-wide software standards for networking equipment.
4. Pick the right strategic partners.

An inherent part of Cisco's strategy was using acquisitions and partnerships to gain access to new technologies. This strategy was relatively unique in the high-tech world, where many companies viewed looking to the outside for technological help as a sign of weakness. However, Chambers believed that this was just the sort of insular thinking that had led to IBM's and Wang's downfall. He viewed partnerships and acquisitions as the most efficient means of offering customers an end-to-end networking solution and developing next generation prod-

---

[2] *Wired News*, March 1997.

EXHIBIT 2   Cisco Systems, Inc, Selected Financial Data, Five Years Ended July 25, 1998

(in thousands, except per share amounts)

	1998	1997	1996	1995	1994
Net sales	$8,458,777	$6,440,171	$4,096,007	$2,232,652	$1,334,436
Net income	$1,350,072[a]	$1,048,679[b]	$ 913,324	$ 456,489[c]	$ 322,981
Net income per common share—basic[d]	$ 0.88	$ 0.71	$ 0.64	$ 0.33	$ 0.25
Net income per share—diluted[d]	$ 0.84[a]	$ 0.68[b]	$ 0.61	$ 0.32[c]	$ 0.24
Shares used in per share calculation—basic[d]	1,533,869	1,485,986	1,437,030	1,367,453	1,296,023
Shares used in per share calculation—diluted[d]	1,608,173	1,551,039	1,490,078	1,425,247	1,342,213
Total assets	$8,916,705	$5,451,984	$3,630,232	$1,911,949	$1,129,034

[a] Net income and net income per share include purchased research and development expenses of $594 million and realized gains on the sale of a minority stock investment of $5 million. Pro forma net income and diluted net income per share, excluding these nonrecurring items net of tax, would have been $1,878,988 and $1.17, respectively.
[b] Net income and net income per share include purchased research and development expenses of $508 million and realized gains on the sale of a minority stock investment of $153 million. Pro forma net income and diluted net income per share, excluding these nonrecurring items net of tax, would have been $1,413,893 and $0.91, respectively.
[c] Net income and net income per share include purchased research and development expenses of $96 million. Pro forma net income and diluted net income per share, excluding these nonrecurring items net of tax, would have been $515,723 and $0.36, respectively.
[d] Reflects the three-for-two stock split effective September 1998.
Source: Annual Report 1998.

ucts. For example, Cisco's partnership with Microsoft enabled the company to develop a new technology for making networks more intelligent in just 18 months. Cisco insiders estimated that it would have taken Cisco four years to develop the product itself without the Microsoft partnership.

Cisco's Manufacturing Philosophy and Organization

From its beginnings, Cisco was structured as a highly centralized organization. Morgridge believed that too many start-up companies decentralized too quickly, and therefore were unable to benefit from the advantages of scale and control associated with a centralized organization. However, in 1995 Cisco established three separate "lines of business"—Enterprise, Small/Medium Business, and Service Provider—each of which had two to nine separate "business units" reporting to them. Although Cisco had begun to move to a more decentralized structure, most of the company's functional areas still remained centralized as of mid-1998, including manufacturing, customer support, finance, information technology, human resources, and sales. Only engineering and marketing were decentralized at the business unit level.

Cisco operated three manufacturing facilities: two in San Jose, "Tasman" and "Walsh," and a third in South San Jose, "Silver Creek." Tasman and Walsh were Cisco's first manufacturing plants and they produced most of Cisco's enterprise routers and LAN switches. The Silver Creek facility was inherited through the 1996 acquisition of StrataCom, Inc., and it produced most of Cisco's high-

end Internet backbone products for service providers (e.g., Sprint, MCI). In addition to these three owned and operated manufacturing facilities, Cisco utilized "external factories" to outsource production of some of its high-volume products. (See Exhibit 3 for Cisco's manufacturing department organization chart.)

Cisco's manufacturing strategy was heavily dependent on outsourcing. The company outsourced many manufacturing activities, such as board stuffing and board testing, to contract manufacturers since these activities required a significant investment in "bricks and mortar," were less scaleable, and generated lower returns relative to Cisco's core business. For example, in the case of Cisco's higher-end, more highly configured products, Cisco would outsource subassembly, bring in completed subsystems, and conduct final testing and assembly in-house, in one of its three manufacturing facilities. At the other end of the spectrum, Cisco utilized external factories to build, test, and ship its less configured, high volume products, such as its low-end routers. Carl Redfield, senior vice president of manufacturing and logistics at Cisco, explained the strategy: "I want my people focusing on the intellectual portion, establishing the supply base, qualifying new suppliers, and developing better processes, not managing direct labor." We supply the intellect; they supply the labor.[3]

---

[3] Timothy Laseter, *Balanced Sourcing* (San Francisco: Jossey-Bass, 1998).

EXHIBIT 3 Cisco's Manufacturing Organization (as of 7/98)

```
                        ┌─────────────────────────────┐
                        │      Carl Redfield          │
                        │  Senior Vice President      │
                        │  Manufacturing and Logistics│
                        └─────────────────────────────┘
                                      │
                              ┌─────────────────────────────┐
                              │      Connie Keay            │
                              │  Executive Assistant        │
                              │  Manufacturing Administration│
                              └─────────────────────────────┘
```

Mike Campi	Tom Fallon	Linc Holland	David Keller	Randy Pond
Vice President	Vice President and	Vice President and	Vice President	Vice President and
Global Supply Management	Plant Manager Silver Creek	Plant Manager External Manufacturing	Manufacturing Technology and NPI	Plant Manager Tasman/Walsh

Rebecca Jacoby	Bob Spiegel	Curtis Montgomery	Karen Schmidt	Frank Atter
Director	Director	Director	Director	Controller
Manufacturing Planning	Manufacturing Information Services	Manufacturing Quality	Human Resources	Manufacturing Finance

Tom Fallon, vice president and plant manager at Cisco, added: "If we can make it cheaper, we do. But even then, we look for suppliers who can match our costs. Strategically we want to outsource."[4]

Approximately 25 percent of Cisco's revenue and 50 percent of its unit volume was manufactured and shipped out of external factories. While external factories were not owned by Cisco, and their employees were not Cisco employees, Cisco did supply them with Cisco information systems and test systems to ensure that they met Cisco's standards for quality and customer satisfaction.

CISCO'S ACQUISITION STRATEGY

Cisco regarded acquisitions primarily as a means to secure technology and scarce intellectual assets. As Chambers commented: "Most people forget that in a high-tech acquisition, you really are acquiring only people. That's why so many of them fail. At what we pay, $500,000 to $2 million an employee, we are not acquiring current market share. We are acquiring futures."[5]

Cisco had three primary goals for ensuring the success of its acquisitions. These were, in order of importance: (1) employee retention, (2) follow-up on new product development, and (3) return on investment.

Employee Retention

Since the employees of acquired companies were critical to the success of the acquisition, Cisco went to great efforts to retain them. Cisco itself was basically just the combination of 25 different organizations that had merged over time. Integration success was due in large part to the very organized, methodical approach that Cisco took toward managing the experience of acquired employees. In the words of a senior human resources manager, "Our objective during the acquisition and transition is to make the employees whole." That is, their efforts were focused on ensuring that employees maintained comparable—if not better—financial consideration and benefits as they transitioned to Cisco's policies and plans.

The responsibilities of the human resources (HR) department began even before the acquisition was consummated. A team of HR professionals typically would spend several weeks with the acquisition candidate developing a transition plan. The plan would map the changes and time frame required to smoothly transfer the personnel,

---

[4] Ibid.
[5] *Business Week*, August 31, 1998.

benefits, and compensation policies of the acquired company to Cisco. Based on a belief that people don't like change—especially change they can't predict—Cisco's HR professionals went to great lengths to tailor the specifics of the transition plan to the needs of the acquired company's employees. For example, Cisco added a new health care provider to its employee benefit options so that the acquired employees were able to keep their existing doctors.

After the acquisition closed, Cisco's HR team would spend another six to seven weeks on-site executing the transition plan. This would give them the opportunity to review the details of the plan with the acquired firm's management before rolling it out to all the employees. The rollout process typically centered on small group discussions with Cisco's HR team and employees from the acquired company. Furthermore, Cisco usually insisted that the acquired company's management team play an active role in educating their own employees.

For the employees of the acquired firm, working for Cisco required a number of significant changes to their compensation. One of the most significant issues was that Cisco required all employees to waive their rights to accelerated vesting on their existing stock options—an event usually triggered by an acquisition—before the deal closed. In return, employees would receive an equivalent value of Cisco options for all of their company's unvested options. In addition, they offered a retention bonus at the end of the first and second years. Given the historically strong performance of Cisco's stock, there was usually little resistance to the new compensation package.

The employees of the acquired companies also benefited from Cisco's history of explosive growth and need for skilled workers. Of its first 25 acquisitions, only two required layoffs, and every redundant person had the opportunity to apply for any Cisco job opening worldwide. Since Cisco typically had 300–600 job openings available at any one time, this represented an attractive option for redundant employees. Part of this policy stemmed from Chamber's experience as vice president of U.S. operations at Wang where he was given the unpopular and heart-wrenching task of laying off 4,000 of Wang's 10,000-person workforce. He vowed to never face this situation again.

These policies had met with great success in the past. The employee turnover rate for acquisitions was only 8 percent, the same level as for Cisco's long-term employees. Approximately one in five Cisco employees and one-third of Cisco's top management positions were filled by people who had come from acquired companies, and

these individuals continued to promote an environment that welcomed acquired employees into its ranks.

New Product Development

Successful new product development required both technical expertise and management talent in order to understand the market, translate market needs into a product, and deliver that product to market quickly. Cisco's new product introduction (NPI) process required that input from marketing, engineering, and manufacturing was incorporated into the product design to ensure that products were designed for functionality, manufacturability, testability, and cost-effectiveness. Since Cisco viewed acquisitions as a means of introducing new products, it was important for Cisco to accelerate the acquired company's new product development efforts. Cisco had found that the most effective way to do this was for the acquired company to adopt Cisco's cross-functional, systematic NPI process. (See Exhibit 4 for a detailed description of Cisco's NPI process.)

More than simply adding to its list of offerings, Cisco saw product development as a high-leverage item. Cisco's goal was to quickly convert newly acquired products to its own NPI process and hopefully reap significant sales volume improvements. This required Cisco to quickly assess where each of the company's products was in the development process. With this information, Cisco could make an informed decision about which products to convert to the NPI process, and which products were too far along in their development to benefit from the change. Although Cisco tried to convert as many new products as possible, typically only the early-stage-development products would use the new process.

Return on Investment

Cisco also looked for acquisitions to generate a high return on investment. The key to accomplishing this was to quickly and effectively leverage Cisco's powerful sales organization and third party distributors (value added resellers, or VARs) to sell the acquired company's products. Charles Giancarlo, vice president for global alliances at Cisco, reiterated Cisco's focus on generating results quickly following an acquisition: "If there are no results in three to six months, people begin to question the acquisition. If you have good short-term results, it's virtuous cycle."[6]

In order to generate results quickly, Cisco made every attempt to have the acquired company's products appear

---

[6] *Business Week,* August 31, 1998.

EXHIBIT 4   Cisco's New Product Introduction Process

Cisco's NPI process involved three phases: strategy and planning, execution, and deployment. The process also included a series of checkpoints between the "strategy and planning" and "deployment" stage to help instill rigor and discipline into the new product introduction process. The multiple checkpoints ensured that there was both a shared vision for the new product and a commitment to allocate sufficient resources to it.

The "concept commit checkpoint" came at the beginning of the strategy and planning phase. This checkpoint ensured that a cross-functional team had approved both the product requirement document (PRD) and the business plan attached to it, and was willing to commit resources sufficient to get to the product design point. By the end of the strategy and planning phase, designers would have developed a definitive design specification for the product.

Next the product had to clear the "execution checkpoint" which ensured that the cross-functional team agreed on both the design specifications and the revised PRD, and was committed to dedicating the resources required to ship the product on a particular date. In the execution phase, the engineering group worked with manufacturing to develop and test prototypes. Manufacturing would conduct a thorough design for manufacturability (DFM) review early in the prototype development process and would help the engineering group develop a product that was easily testable on the Autotest system.

Close to the end of the execution phase—about a month before the first product was shipped—the product had to pass the "orderability checkpoint." This was a manufacturing-driven checkpoint that ensured that the product had passed a rigorous set of criterion before being posted on Cisco's website. The manufacturing group used the test to ensure they could hit the ship date and meet the expected ramp up in demand. The check list included questions such as:

- Has the product completed and passed its development test?
- Has the product been beta tested, and is the feedback good?
- Are the results from the software tests positive?
- Do we have suppliers lined up? Can they make the parts?
- Do we have reasonable yields at the prototype stage?

Once the product passed the orderability check point, it was added to Cisco's price list, and it entered into the deployment phase where it was either slated for "unlimited release" or "controlled release." Products slated for unlimited release were typically those that were in high demand, had completed all the development milestones, and for which Cisco had significant capacity to build, test, ship, and service. Products slated for controlled release were typically those that still faced some degree of design risk. For example, the product could have received compliance approval in some, but not all geographic areas (i.e., approved for the United States, but not yet for Europe). In these cases, Cisco would restrict output as a way of controlling the risk involved in the product launch.

Two to three months after the first product had been shipped, the product faced yet another manufacturing checkpoint, known as the "time to quality and volume" (TTQV) checkpoint. This checkpoint—which included analyses on yields and costs—was designed to ensure that the manufacturing group could make the product cost-effectively at high volumes. The TTQV checkpoint was conducted two to three months after production had begun so that sufficient run-rate data could be collected and used for analysis. Once the product had passed this checkpoint, it was produced according to its own rollout plan and lifecycle.

---

on Cisco's price list on the day the deal closed so that Cisco's sales force could immediately begin to sell the new products. The power of leveraging Cisco's sales and distribution channels alone could result in a two- to five-times ramp up in the acquired company's volume. Effectively leveraging its distribution channels in this manner was one of the key drivers behind the significant growth in Cisco's revenues.

Types of Acquisitions

Cisco made its first acquisition in 1993, when it purchased Crescendo Communications—a LAN-switching company—for $97 million. By mid-1998, Cisco had announced 29 acquisitions worth about $7 billion and had made noncontrolling investments in 40 companies—three of which Cisco later acquired.[7] (See Exhibit 5 for a list of Cisco's acquisitions.) Cisco's target was to have 30 percent of its revenue come from acquisition and development (A&D) efforts and 70 percent from internal research and development (R&D) efforts. Proposals for specific acquisition candidates often came directly from Cisco's business units, based on feedback from customers. Cisco would then screen these potential candidates against a well-defined set of criteria (see Exhibit 6).

Cisco's acquisitions spanned a range of companies producing different types of products, at different points in their lifecycles. There were essentially four types of acquisitions: software companies, "pre-production" hardware companies, small hardware companies shipping product, and mature hardware companies. The complexity of the integration process, and the level of resources dedicated to the effort, varied depending on the type of acquisition. From a manufacturing standpoint, software companies and preproduction companies were the least complex to integrate into Cisco, since these types of

---

[7] *San Jose Mercury News,* October 12, 1998.

EXHIBIT 5 Cisco's Acquisitions

Data[a]	Company	Business description	Alignment with Cisco line of business	Approximate acquisition price ($MM)	Approximate number of employees
10/98	Selsius Systems	Supplier of network PBX systems for high-quality telephony over IP networks	Enterprise	$145 (stock+cash)	51
9/98	Clarity Wireless Corporation	Wireless communication technology for computer networking and the internet service markets	Service provider	$157 (stock)	39
8/98	American Internet Corporation	Software for IP address management and Internet access	Service provider	$56 (stock)	50
7/98	Summa Four, Inc.	Open programmable digital switching systems	Service provider	$116 (stock)	210
5/98	CLASS Data Systems	Network management software	Enterprise	$50 (stock+cash)	34
3/98	Precept Software, Inc.	Multimedia networking software	IOS technologies[b]	$84 (stock)	50
3/98	NetSpeed, Inc.	Standards-based DSL technology	Service provider	$236 (stock)	140
2/98	WheelGroup Corporation	Intrusion detection and security scanning software	IOS technologies	$124 (stock)	75
12/97	LightSpeed International, Inc.	Voice signaling technologies	Service provider	$160 (stock)	70
7/97	Dagaz (Integrated Network Corporation)	Broadband networking products	Service provider	$126 (stock)	30
6/97	Ardent Communications Corp.	Combined communications support for compressed voice, LAN, data, and video traffic across public and private frame relay and asynchronous transfer mode (ATM) networks	Service provider	$156 (stock)	40
6/97	Global Internet Software Group	Windows NT security	Small/medium business	$40 (cash)	20
6/97	Skystone Systems Corp.	High-speed synchronous optical Networking/synchronous digital hierarchy (SONET/SDH) technology	Service provider	$102 (stock+cash)	40
3/97	Telescend	Wide area network access products	Service provider	Terms not disclosed	NA
12/96	Metaplex, Inc.	Network products for the IBM enterprise marketplace	Enterprise	Terms not disclosed	20
10/96	Netsys Technologies	Network infrastructure management and performance analysis software	Service provider	$79 (stock)	50

(continued)

EXHIBIT 5 (continued)

Data[a]	Company	Business description	Alignment with Cisco line of business	Approximate acquisition price ($MM)	Approximate number of employees
9/86	Granite Systems, Inc.	Standard-based multilayer Gigabit Ethernet switching technologies	Enterprise	$220 (stock)	50
8/96	Nashoba Networks, Inc.	Token ring switching technologies	Enterprise	$100 (stock)	40
7/96	Telebit Corp's MICA Technologies	Modem ISDN channel aggregation (MICA) technologies	Service provider	$200 (cash)	288
4/96	StrataCom, Inc.	ATM and frame relay high-speed wide area network switching equipment	Service provider	$4,666 (stock)	625
1/96	TGV Software, Inc.	Internet software products for connecting disparate and computer systems over local area, enterprise-wide global computing networks	Small/medium business	$138 (stock)	130+
10/95	Network Translation, Inc.	Network address translation and Internet firewall hardware and software	Small/medium business	Terms not disclosed	10
9/95	Grand Junction, Inc.	Fast Ethernet (100Base-T) and Ethernet switching products	Small/medium business	$400 (stock)	85
9/95	Internet Junction, Inc.	Internet gateway software connecting desktop users with the Internet	Small/medium business	$5.5 (stock)	10
8/95	Combinet, Inc.	ISDN remote-access networking products	Small/medium business	$132 (stock)	100
12/94	LightStream, Corp.	Enterprise ATM switching, workgroup ATM switching, LAN switching and routing	Service provider	$120 (cash)	60+
10/94	Kalpana, Inc.	LAN switching products	Enterprise	$240 (stock)	150
8/94	Newport Systems Solutions, Inc.	Software-based routers for remote network sites	Small/medium business	$91 (stock)	55
9/93	Crescendo Communications	High-performance workgroup networking products	Enterprise	$97 (stock)	60

[a] Date of announcement.
[b] Internetworking operating system.
Source: www.cisco.com, literature search.

EXHIBIT 6   Screening Criteria for Potential Acquisition Candidates

Screening criteria	Means of achieving criteria
Offer both short-term and long-term win/wins for Cisco and the acquired company.	• Have a complementary technology that fills in a need in Cisco's core product space • Have a technology that can be delivered through Cisco's existing distribution channels • Have a technology and products which can be supported by Cisco's support organization • Are able to leverage Cisco's existing infrastructure and resource base to increase its overall value
Share a common vision and chemistry with Cisco	• Have a similar understanding and vision of the market • Have a similar culture • Have a similar risk-taking style
Are located (preferably) in Silicon Valley or near one of Cisco's remote sites	• Have company headquarters and most manufacturing facilities close to one of Cisco's main sites

companies typically did not have a manufacturing organization in place or an existing customer backlog to satisfy. At the other end of the spectrum, small hardware companies shipping product and mature hardware companies were the most complex to integrate. In fact, the complexity of the integration process had far more to do with the company's stage of development than with its acquisition price. For example, the manufacturing integration process for a $300 million acquisition of a preproduction company could be far easier than for a $100 million acquisition of a hardware company that was already shipping product. Keller compared the effort involved in integrating preproduction companies to companies already shipping product:

> The integration of preproduction companies tends to be less difficult than integrating companies that are already shipping product, since we can have more influence and add more value on the manufacturing side, and there isn't a lot we have to "undo." We can integrate the company into our operations and set them up on our systems right from the start.

While Cisco had made several acquisitions of software, preproduction hardware, and small hardware companies already shipping product, as of 1998 Cisco had made only one acquisition of a mature hardware company—the acquisition of StrataCom in 1996. (See Exhibit 7 for examples of acquisitions by type.)

CISCO'S ACQUISITION INTEGRATION PROCESS

Before agreeing to the terms of an acquisition, Cisco conducted thorough due diligence on the company. A project manager from Cisco's business development group would coordinate the overall due diligence process, in which a cross-functional team—comprising representatives from marketing and engineering within Cisco's business units and representatives from Cisco's centralized manufacturing organization—conducted a detailed assessment of the acquisition candidate's business processes. For example, the manufacturing due diligence team reviewed the company's manufacturing processes, identified risks, provided input to valuation discussions, and scoped the work that would be required to integrate the two companies if the deal were to close. The manufacturing due diligence process centered around a one- to two-day visit to the company to see and discuss a number of details regarding their technology, manufacturing and engineering processes, and organization. Prior to the due diligence session, Cisco would send an outline of issues for discussion to the heads of the manufacturing and engineering groups at the company to help prepare for the visit. (See Exhibit 8 for a sample list of manufacturing due diligence issues.)

After the acquisition had closed, Cisco would move forward with its postacquisition integration process. Although each of Cisco's acquisitions was unique and required a customized integration approach based on a comprehensive understanding of the company, there were 10 common steps that were mandatory. The mandatory steps centered on converting the acquired company to Cisco's manufacturing systems, processes, and methodologies. While the time allotted for completing these steps could vary, ultimately the "Cisco way" would be put into place. Cisco described these steps as "stakes in the

EXHIBIT 7   Examples of Acquisitions by Type

Acquisition type	Description	Examples of acquisitions by type
Software companies	These companies designed and sold software—primarily engineering companies. Since they were not involved in the hardware side of the business, they did not have a manufacturing organization. As a result, this type of acquisition required the least amount of involvement from the Cisco manufacturing organization during the integration process.	American Internet Corporation CLASS Data Systems Precept Software, Inc. WheelGroup Corporation LightSpeed International, Inc. Global Internet Software Group Netsys Technologies TGV Software, Inc. Internet Junction, Inc.
Preproduction hardware companies	These companies had a technology Cisco wanted, but they were not yet shipping any product. Frequently these companies had developed a prototype, but the product was not yet designed for manufacturability. This type of acquisition was relatively straight-forward from a manufacturing integration standpoint, since there was no existing infrastructure with which to contend and no existing customer order backlog to satisfy.	Clarity Wireless Corporation Dagaz Ardent Communications Group Skystone Systems Corp. Telescend Granite Systems, Inc. Nashoba Networks, Inc. Telebit Corp's MICA Technologies
Small hardware companies shipping product	These small companies—sometimes private, sometimes public—were shipping product to a limited installed base of customers. Cisco would typically acquire these companies for their engineering team and the potential they offered for developing next generation products. These companies typically had some sort of enterprise resource planning (ERP) system in place, but often would not have the manufacturing standards of a mature company. This type of acquisition proved to be more complex then pre-production companies since the integration process had to proceed without impacting the continuity of supply to existing customers.	Summa Four, Inc. NetSpeed Inc. Network Translation, Inc. Grand Junction, Inc. Combinet, Inc. Kalpana, Inc. LightStream Corp. Newport Systems Solutions, Inc. Crescendo Communications
Mature hardware companies	These large, mature companies typically had a substantial customer base. They had established manufacturing processes in place and were ISO-certified (International Organization for Standardization). This type of acquisition took far longer to integrate due to the complexity of decisions that had to be made. However, in this type of acquisition both companies would have significant resources to dedicate to the integration process, thereby facilitating the effort.	StrataCom, Inc.

ground." On the other hand, certain decisions—such as how to handle the integration of an acquired company's employees and manufacturing plants—varied from acquisition to acquisition and required significant management judgment. (See Exhibit 9 for a diagram of the integration process.)

In both cases, Cisco utilized a "scenario planning" approach to make decisions about what to do and how fast to do it. The scenario planning approach took into account Cisco's business objectives for the acquisition, information on the company gathered from the due diligence effort, and projected outcomes under various integration scenarios (e.g., higher volumes, merging plants). The approach was used to help outline alternatives and generate consensus regarding recommendations.

Manufacturing Integration Team

Cisco organized a manufacturing integration team to manage the postacquisition process. Cisco's approach was to appoint one of the senior managers within the *acquired* company as the integration team leader. Tony Crabb, previously the vice president of manufacturing for StrataCom (before becoming director of manufacturing at Cisco), was chosen to lead the StrataCom integration team. Crabb reflected on the impact of Cisco's approach to leading the integration process:

EXHIBIT 8   Sample List of Manufacturing Due Diligence Issues

Issues	Sample questions
Target market dynamics	• What was the demand forecast? • What were the gross margin targets?
Product portfolio	• What was the product set? • What was the development status on new products?
Manufacturing technology	• What was their process for designing products for manufacturability, testability, cost, cycle time, and volume?
Verification process	• How did they conduct internal and external design verification?
Supply base and order fulfillment	• Who was on their approved vendor and subcontractor list? • How did they manage their material pipeline and inventory?
Development, release, and manufacturing process	• What was their philosophy on design? • How much were they influenced by sales versus engineering? • Did they utilize cross-functional teams in the development process?
Manufacturing process competencies	• Did they have any specific manufacturing core competencies that should be taken into consideration?
Organizational structure	• How were they organized? • How many people were in each area?
Leadership/management competencies	• What was the skill level of the workforce as a whole? • What were the leadership capabilities of the management team?

EXHIBIT 9   Postacquisition Integration Steps

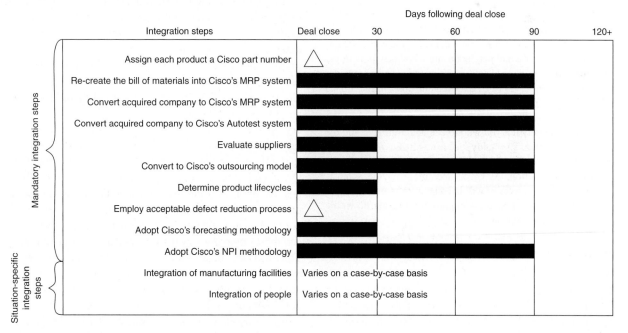

Source: Casewriter interviews.

From the perspective of employees within the acquired company, it's pretty important to see someone they know and trust leading the integration effort. If it were a Cisco person leading the process, they would feel as if it were being imposed upon them, and therefore resent the process. On the other hand, if it's someone they know, it's easier for them to ask questions and feel a part of the process.

The balance of the integration team was comprised of experienced members of both organizations. The overall team was then divided into sub-teams that were responsible for leading key business process conversion tasks.

Based on experience from several acquisitions, Cisco also had developed the "buddy system" approach. The buddy system involved appointing an experienced Cisco employee to be the "manager of the intangibles" within both engineering and manufacturing organizations of the acquired company, and swapping a handful of Cisco employees with employees from the acquired company. Both the manager of intangibles and the on-site Cisco staff would assist employees from the acquired company with questions regarding how to access information and get things done within the Cisco organization. While the manager-of-intangibles position had no official reporting structure beneath it, the role was considered a critical part of the integration process and was reserved for strong performers within the Cisco organization. Crabb described how the buddy system worked in the Strata-Com acquisition:

> One of the keys to success in the StrataCom integration process was to have Cisco people within the StrataCom organization, so that we had people on site who knew how to get information from the big Cisco organization. As an outsider you don't know how to get even the most basic things done—like how to get a new ID badge. But, by having a Cisco person sitting in the cube right next to you, he or she can immediately tell you who to call and even give you the person's number. The buddy system de-stresses a lot of angst about how to do things and how to be productive within the Cisco organization. As Cisco does more remote acquisitions, the buddy system will become even more important because you won't have the opportunity to walk down the hall and talk to someone.

Mandatory Integration Steps

As soon as the manufacturing integration team was created, work began on the mandatory components of the integration process. The mandatory steps provided a clearly articulated plan for achieving fast and seamless integration. From the customer's perspective, Cisco wanted to make it appear that the acquired company was a part of Cisco from the day the deal closed. Yet, Cisco was very aware that massive and unilateral changes could potentially have enormous disruptive effects. Cisco's mandatory steps drew on the experience gained from numerous previous acquisitions and provided a framework and timeline for the integration team to tackle their job (see Exhibit 10 for more details on the mandatory integration steps).

The mandatory steps effectively broke down into three primary categories: merging information systems, aligning current processes, and implementing ongoing methodologies. The merging of information systems involved both the materials resource planning system (MRP) and the product testing system (Autotest). Due to the large number of acquisitions undertaken, it would have been incredibly complex and redundant for Cisco to maintain multiple systems. Thus, the integration team was tasked with transitioning the acquired company to Cisco's MRP and Autotest systems in a staged process that typically achieved full integration within 90 days. Although an aggressive timeline, the rapid implementation of the Autotest system ensured that the product quality would meet Cisco's standards. The move to Cisco's MRP system not only aided the sales staff in placing orders for the new product, but also helped identify opportunities for part consolidation and supplier rationalization.

In aligning the acquired company's current processes with Cisco's, the integration team focused on three areas: evaluating suppliers, assessing outsourcing options, and determining product lifecycles. In the first area, the integration team reviewed the suppliers of the acquired company, with the ultimate goal of transitioning them to Cisco's vendors. Supplier choice was a difficult decision, and factors such as continuity of supply, on-time delivery, quality, customer support, and cost were all taken into consideration. The second area, assessing outsourcing options, examined the role that outsourced manufacturing could play in the acquired company. Cisco relied heavily upon outsourcing, and mandated that all piece part assembly and board level testing be outsourced. A comprehensive outsourcing plan was crafted to move the acquired company toward optimal use of outsourcing. The third area, determining product lifecycle, was one of the most important tasks of the integration team. The acquired company's products needed to be segmented by development phase so that appropriate decisions could be made about their integration into Cisco's organization. In all, these steps were usually completed within 90 days of the time of the merger.

EXHIBIT 10 Mandatory Manufacturing Integration Steps

ASSIGN EACH OF THE ACQUIRED COMPANY'S PRODUCTS A NEW CISCO PRODUCT NUMBER

Cisco assigned a new product number to each of the acquired company's products that would be entered into Cisco's MRP (manufacturing resource planning) database. At the initial phase, there would be no other details on the product (e.g., parts, cost data) in the database, so a transaction could not be fully conducted electronically through Cisco's MRP database. Instead, if a customer placed an order for one of the acquired company's products, Cisco would transfer the order internally (by phone, email, or fax) to the acquired company's order desk for fulfillment. The acquired company would then make, test, and ship the product from its facilities. However, all of this was done behind the scenes, from the customer's perspective, they were dealing directly with Cisco. (See the following illustration.)

Order and Product Flow

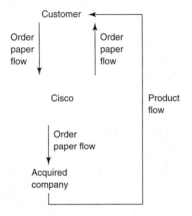

RE-CREATE THE BILL OF MATERIALS IN CISCO'S MRP DATABASE

The next step was to recreate the bill of materials for each of the acquired company's products into Cisco's MRP database. This involved a detailed part-mapping process whereby a team from Cisco's component engineering group would analyze each specific part that went into each product to determine if an identical part was already used by Cisco—and therefore already in the MRP database. The process involved an extensive review of each part's data sheet, since parts that seemed identical on the surface could be ever-so-slightly different in reality. If an exact match were found, then the part would be given the existing Cisco part's number. If no match were found, then the part would be given a new part number. Since it was a detailed and time-consuming process, often taking up to 90 days to complete, the detailed part-by-part mapping would not be done for those products that were slated for short-term production or end of life.

While the primary goal of the part-mapping process was to "get it done," a secondary goal was to identify opportunities to consolidate parts and vendors. Cisco's goal was to utilize ex-

isting, preapproved vendors where possible and minimize the growth of its parts database. In other words, if the acquired company was buying a part that was almost identical to one that Cisco was already buying from another vendor, the team would flag it as an opportunity for near-term substitution. However, since the overarching goal was to integrate the parts data into Cisco's MRP database, only the obvious substitution opportunities were identified during this process. As Crabb described it: "We'll take all the low-hanging fruit, but we don't try to do everything at this point."

CONVERT THE ACQUIRED COMPANY TO CISCO'S MRP SYSTEM

Once all the parts had been given Cisco part numbers, Cisco would convert the company over to Cisco's MRP system. Unlike some of its competitors, Cisco did not believe in running multiple MRP systems in parallel, instead, Cisco made it mandatory for acquired companies to convert to Cisco's MRP system. However, in some cases, Cisco would recommend that the acquired company keep its own MRP system in place for its short term production products or end of life products. Once the company had converted to Cisco's MRP system, Cisco had all the necessary infrastructure required to plan, build, and ship the acquired company's products. Typically conversion to Cisco's MRP system would take place within 90 days of close.

CONVERT THE ACQUIRED COMPANY TO CISCO'S AUTOTEST SYSTEM

Cisco considered its Autotest system—a software-based automated testing system that measured the functionality and configuration of products—to be an essential component of its overall quality control process. The system worked by running data from the manufacturing process through a set of test "scripts." The Autotest system analyzed the data and determined whether the product passed or failed the tests, and under what conditions. The Autotest system was networked to Cisco's MRP system, enabling it also to test final product configuration to ensure that it matched the customer's order. Since Cisco sold many built-to-order, highly configurable products, there were numerous opportunities to make mistakes. The Autotest system gave the operator an almost foolproof way to ensure that the right product was being shipped to the customer. Cisco's external factories and subassembly contractors were also networked into the Autotest system.

If Cisco decided to continue operating an acquired company's plant for an extended period of time, then Cisco would require that the Autotest system be implemented in the acquired company's manufacturing facility. To set up the Autotest system, the integration team had to first determine whether the company had a set of written diagnostics for each product, since diagnostics were needed to write the test scripts. If the company did not have written diagnostics—which was typically the case—then development engineers from the relevant Cisco business unit would work with engineers from the acquired company to write diagnostics for the Autotest system.

continued

On average it took three months to get the Autotest system up and running in an acquired company; however, it could take longer in cases where the engineering department was making significant changes to product design. During the period in which the Autotest system was being set up, Cisco depended on the acquired company's existing test processes for quality control—usually a set of PC-driven tests that required an operator to enter the script coding, run the test, and watch the results on the computer screen. While these types of tests were adequate for a small company, they were prone to human error, which was why Cisco mandated conversion to the Autotest system. In the best case scenario, the implementation of the Autotest system would coincide with the ramp up in the acquired company's production volume.

EVALUATE SUPPLIERS

Cisco's supply operations (supply ops) group evaluated, approved, and managed suppliers for both Cisco and its acquired companies. To qualify as an approved Cisco vendor, the vendor had to meet predetermined financial and business criteria, such as:

- Cisco could represent no more than 20% of the supplier's business, so that fluctuations in Cisco's demand did not threaten continuity of supply,
- The vendor had to be in solid financial standing, and
- The vendor had to rate highly on a quarterly scorecard administered by Cisco which measured performance against a series of criteria, including on-time delivery, lead time, quality level, customer support, and cost.

Cisco's supply ops group began to evaluate an acquired company's suppliers during the due diligence process to identify any risks to continuity of supply following the acquisition. Within 30 days of close the supply ops group was expected to have developed a plan for how to handle the supplier base. The goal was to convert the acquired companies to Cisco suppliers over time. However, the desire to use Cisco vendors had to be weighed against the impact the conversion would have on the continuity of supply and the development time for new products—in addition to the cost of the effort. As a result, Cisco rarely made supplier changes for products slated for short-term production or end of life. For products slated for long-term production and new products, Cisco's supply ops group evaluated new suppliers using the same criteria used to add suppliers to Cisco's approved vendor list. Marc Beckman, senior manager of global supply management for electronic components at Cisco, explained:

> We want to be able to influence supplier selection decisions just like we do here at Cisco. On the other hand, we don't want to impact the acquired company's business in a negative way. If we can switch to an existing Cisco supplier without having an adverse impact on their business, then we do. If we think it will have a real adverse impact, then we won't make the switch; we'll approve the vendor, but only for that *particular* product. If it's a critical supplier for a new product and we're too far down the road on development to switch, then we'll evaluate the proposed supplier and analyze the risks on a case by case basis.
>
> One thing we are sensitive about is the effect our decisions have on suppliers who have been supporting the ac-

quired company over a period of time. We will often evaluate the impact of switching suppliers on the existing suppliers, and if the impact appears severe, we will try to work out an arrangement whereby they can support the product for a period of time until they can readdress their customer base.

CONVERT TO CISCO'S OUTSOURCING MODEL

Cisco required that the companies that it acquired convert to its outsourced manufacturing model as well. There were essentially three levels of outsourcing: piece part assembly, board level testing, and final assembly and testing. As a rule, Cisco always outsourced the first two to contract manufacturers. They also outsourced the third—final assembly and testing—in the case of products fulfilled by external factories. If the acquired company were operating under a highly vertically integrated production model, Cisco developed a transition plan for outsourcing the piece part assembly and intermediate testing activities, at a minimum. However, for products slated for short-term production or end of life, Cisco would often leave their in-house manufacturing processes in place. Cisco had also explored the possibility of leveraging its contract manufacturers to produce, fulfill, and provide aftersale support for products slated for end of life—but had not yet tested this option. Cisco's goal was to have a comprehensive outsourcing plan in place within 90 days of the close.

DETERMINE PRODUCT LIFECYCLES

In order to determine how to treat each of the acquired company's products, the manufacturing group first needed to determine how long Cisco planned to manufacture and support each product. Due to their importance, a first pass at these decisions was typically made within 30 days of the close. In order to make these decisions, the manufacturing team carefully reviewed the business case underlying the acquisition. In some cases Cisco acquired a company for its current line of products—meaning that most of its products would be slated for long-term production. In other cases, Cisco acquired the company for its potential to develop next generation products, rather than for its existing products—meaning that many of the existing products would be slated for short term production or positioned for end of life. However, even if a product were slated for end of life, it would be phased out over time, rather than eliminated outright, since Cisco's goal was to assure continuity of supply to the acquired company's customers immediately following the acquisition.

EMPLOY AN ACCEPTABLE DEFECT REDUCTION PROCESS

Cisco required that a basic statistical process control mechanisms be put in place to track yield and failure data on a daily and weekly basis. While the Autotest sytem would ultimately produce these data, Cisco mandated that the acquired company have an acceptable process in place at the time of the close for charting the data—even if it were a manual process.

ADOPT CISCO'S FORECASTING METHODOLOGY

Following an acquisition, Cisco continued to depend on the acquired company to provide product booking forecasts, since Cisco believed that the acquired company was most familiar with the demands of its own customers and marketplace. However, the acquired company would submit its forecasts to

Cisco's business unit–level marketing group to discuss and revise, if needed. Input from Cisco's business-level marketing group was essential since they had the experience to project the implications of leveraging Cisco's sales and distribution channels on an acquired company's production volume. Since the forecast would ultimately be entered into Cisco's MRP system and drive production decisions, it was important to reach consensus on it. As a result, Cisco required that acquired companies adopt Cisco's approach to forecasting within 30 days of the close.

Cisco required both a monthly review as well as a transaction-level forecast, and was just as interested in the assumptions that were used to develop the forecasts as in the forecasts themselves. Cisco required that acquired companies adopt Cisco's "envelope of demand" methodology of monthly forecasting, which entailed providing a set of quantified upside and downside ranges to the forecast. As part of the forecast, the marketing group included detailed assumptions about what would need to happen to achieve the upside and downside forecasts (e.g., three accounts would need to sign contracts to meet the upside forecast) and they provided probability assessments for these scenarios. By providing analytical rigor behind a set of ranges to the forecast, the marketing group helped the manufacturing group determine the types and levels of buffers to set up in manufacturing.

ADOPT CISCO'S NEW PRODUCT INTRODUCTION (NPI) METHODOLOGY

Cisco required that the companies it acquired adopt Cisco's NPI process for its new product development where feasible (sometimes new products were too far along the development process to convert to Cisco's NPI process). On the day the deal closed, Cisco would make a determination as to which new products were early enough in their development cycle to convert to Cisco's NPI process, and within 90 days of the close, the NPI process would be implemented.

The last category of mandatory integration steps was the implementation of ongoing methodologies, including defect reduction, forecasting, and new product introductions. To reduce defects, Cisco required the acquired company to immediately implement statistical process controls. While this functionality would later be provided by the Autotest system, quickly reducing and maintaining low defect rates was a crucial driver of financial performance. Cisco also required that the acquired company adopt its forecasting methodology within 30 days of the close of the deal. Forecasting at Cisco stressed the joint development of production and sales volume predictions between Cisco's business unit–level marketing group and the management of the acquired company. Cisco believed there was great value in the analytical rigor of a detailed plan with clearly articulated assumptions. Finally, the integration team implemented Cisco's new product introduction methodology. Within 90 days of purchase, the new company would use Cisco's NPI model—including cross-functional teams—on all products that were early enough in their development cycle to benefit.

Situation-Specific Integration Steps

While Cisco had a number of mandatory integration steps, it handled manufacturing facility and employee integration issues on a situation-specific basis. On the manufacturing facility side, the preliminary question was whether to leave the acquired facilities essentially intact, fully integrate them into Cisco's facilities, or any one of many options in between. The time required to reach decisions on these issues and implement a transition plan also varied widely from acquisition to acquisition. A team, made up of staff from Cisco's new product introduction group, considered a number of factors in making their recommendations on how to treat an acquired company's production facilities. These factors included the business plan for the acquired company (e.g., projected volumes, ramp-up timing, product lifecycles), the competencies of the acquired company's production facilities (e.g., quality controls, production processes), an affordability assessment (e.g., how can we maximize the value of the company's products?), and an assessment of other intangibles (e.g., how would a plant closure affect the R&D and engineering effort?).

During the period the team was developing the recommendation on whether and when to merge plants, Cisco would continue to operate out of the acquired company's production facility. However, since Cisco was ultimately accountable for the quality of the products coming out of the acquired company's plants, the team would frequently audit the company's quality control processes to ensure that they met Cisco's standards. In addition, Cisco mandated that its acquired companies implement certain of its engineering and manufacturing procedures in their production facilities and go through an ISO (International Organization for Standardization) audit of those procedures within six to twelve months.

In terms of employee integration, Cisco would customize a plan to meet the needs of the acquired company's labor force. Cisco would offer employees flexibility around the transition process (e.g., timing of geographic moves), in addition to the traditional economic incentives. For example, they might be given the option to continue working at the acquired company's

EXHIBIT 11   Summa Four's Product Line

Product name	VCO/Series 80	VCO/Series 20	VCO/4K
Introduction date	February 1995	September 1996	March 1998
Description	High-density open-programmable switch used for application development, highly distributed intelligent peripheral implementations, and scaleable transport deployments in both wireline and wireless networks	Same functionality as VCO/Series 80, but offers a smaller footprint and rack-mountable design which makes it suitable for turnkey integration with other application systems	World's highest density open-programmable switch
Density	2,048 time slots	2,048 time slots	4,096 time slots
Fully NEBS compliant	Yes	No	Yes

Source: www.summafour.com, casewriter interview.

plant for as long as the facility was maintained; move to one of Cisco's production facilities in California; or move into another part of the Cisco organization (e.g., quality control, field service). Cisco believed in being open, honest, sensitive, and flexible with the employees of the acquired company during the postacquisition integration process.

THE SUMMA FOUR ACQUISITION

Founded in 1976, Summa Four had become a leading provider of open programmable digital switching systems, sold primarily to telecommunications service providers worldwide (i.e., AT&T, MCI, Sprint, British Telecom). By 1998, Summa Four had installed over 2,000 switches in over 30 countries. Approximately 50 percent of its systems were installed outside the United States. Customers used Summa Four's open programmable switching platforms for basic call switching as well as for delivering value added services, such as voice mail, calling card applications, voice-activated dialing, intelligent 800-call routing, and voice and fax messaging. Summa Four was also developing a next-generation product, code-named Project Alpha,[8] that represented the industry's first standards-based open programmable switch.

Due to the deregulation of the telecommunications industry, service providers were in a fierce, competitive race to develop and deliver these types of enhanced services to their customers. Prior to the advent of open programmable switching technology, service providers typically used large-scale proprietary central office switches.

The proprietary nature of these switches made service providers dependent on their switching equipment vendors to help develop new services. However, open programmable switches allowed service providers to develop or purchase their own applications, which reduced development costs and accelerated time to market. Summa Four's company vision was to "provide open, intelligent, standards-based switches to telecom service providers worldwide, fundamentally changing the cost and time-to-market for deploying new networks and services."

Cisco announced it would acquire the Manchester, New Hampshire–based company in July 1998. The acquisition was intended to enable Cisco to offer value added telephony applications to telecommunication service providers, and extend these services to IP (Internet protocol) networks, which were able to transmit voice, data, and video.

Summa Four Product Line

Summa Four's product line included the VCO Series/20, the VCO Series/80, and the VCO/4K—all of which were highly configurable and built to order. While Project Alpha was still in the development phase at the time of the acquisition, and over a year away from product launch, it was a key reason behind Cisco's interest in Summa Four.

All products in the VCO family shared a similar architecture and many of the same features. (See Exhibit 11 for an overview of Summa Four's products.) The key distinguishing feature among them was their time slot density (the greater the time slots, the more lines could run in and out of the switch). The VCO Series/80—introduced in February 1995—offered a nonblocking switching matrix of 2,048 time slots. In addition, the Series/80 was fully NEBS (Network Equipment Building Systems) compliant—meaning that it conformed to a

---

[8] Name has been disguised.

specific set of environmental compatibility criteria (e.g., physical protection, electromagnetic compatibility, and electrical safety) that most of the large telecommunication service providers required. Smaller telecommunication service providers were often willing to work with products that were not fully NEBS compliant in order to gain a particular design advantage or reduce costs.

The VCO Series/20—introduced in September 1996—offered the same number of time slots as the Series/80, but was a far smaller unit than the Series/80. Its small footprint and rack-mountable design made it well-suited for turnkey integration with other application subsystems. However, the Series/20 was not fully NEBS compliant, due to trade-offs in design that would have been required to comply with NEBS standards. Both the VCO Series/20 and VCO Series/80 were considered mature products and the plan was to migrate customers to the VCO/4K over time.

The VCO/4K was Summa Four's newest and most advanced product. Introduced in March 1998, the VCO/4K was the world's highest density programmable switch. It offered a nonblocking switching matrix of 4,096 time slots, was fully NEBS compliant, and included all of the other features common to the Series/20 and Series/80. While the VCO/4K was still in field trial deployment, it was ramping-up faster than expected. While the initial signs were positive, Cisco would have to wait to see the market's reaction to the 4K before it could make a determination about its potential lifespan. If the 4K turned out to be a highly successful product and the decision was made to keep its production in Manchester, Cisco would need to invest in both equipment and labor in order to increase the capacity of the Manchester manufacturing facility. Given that Cisco's California manufacturing facilities had additional capacity and had all the key testing infrastructure in place, Cisco was unsure of whether this type of investment into Summa Four's Manchester facility was prudent.

Summa Four Organization

In September of 1998, the idea of being acquired by Cisco was still very new to Summa Four's employees. At the time of the acquisition announcement, Summa Four had 210 employees, including 65 development engineers and 23 employees in the manufacturing organization. While there was a good deal of excitement about the prospect of working for Cisco, a number of employees voiced reservations. One manager said, "This is an exciting time, but I worry that a number of changes are going to be forced down our throats."

One of the areas that attracted the most concern was the cultural implications of being acquired by a much larger firm. Summa Four's management knew that they were just one of many in a long line of Cisco acquisitions. They had built their business in a simple functional organization, where personal connections and informal processes allowed for quick action. In a larger organization, effective problem solving would likely require a host of specialists and multiple organizational units, resulting in a far more complex process. Some employees worried that the feel of working in the high-energy world of a small business would be lost. Dick Swee captured much of this sentiment when he said, "There is a big difference between a $10 billion organization and a $50 million organization. We've been used to the feel of a small company, and that is certainly going to change."

There was also concern about the level of influence that Summa Four employees would be able to exert within Cisco. It was unclear what role their current products would play among the Cisco offerings, and their ability to guide the integration process might be severely limited. With well over 10,000 people working for Cisco, Summa Four employees worried that Cisco would not be very receptive to their input. However, with the New England job market so hot, at least there would be attractive alternatives for most of the experienced engineers if things didn't work out.

Summa Four Manufacturing

Summa Four's headquarters and manufacturing plant shared the same facility in Manchester, which was less than an hour away from one of Cisco's remote R&D facilities, located in Chelmsford, Massachusetts. Cisco's due diligence team found Summa Four's plant to be clean, orderly, and efficient. Summa Four's plant compared favorably to many of the other plants that Cisco had acquired. However, the plant used a homegrown, PC-based test system that was far less automated than Cisco's Autotest system. Summa Four's MRP system was from Symix, a supplier of systems for midrange manufacturers of discrete, configurable products. It did not appear that the Symix software was compatible with Cisco's MRP system.

As for its manufacturing processes, Summa Four had moved toward more and more outsourcing with each generation of products. For example, almost all of the assembly and testing for Summa Four's early VCO Series/20 and Series/80 products was conducted in-house, including power supply assembly and board testing. On the other hand, in the case of its newer VCO/4K product, Summa Four had outsourced most of the piece part assembly.

Suppliers

Summa four purchased approximately 5,000 individual parts from 250 suppliers, 85 of whom were new to Cisco. While the Summa Four acquisition was far smaller than the $4.6 billion acquisition of StrataCom in 1996, Summa Four had a comparable number of parts and suppliers to StrataCom, reflecting the complexity of the Summa Four integration process. Of some concern was the fact that approximately 200 of Summa Four's parts were sole-sourced, meaning that only one vendor supplied each of those parts, which created a pricing and continuity-of-supply risk.

Fortuitously, Summa Four had recently contracted with Sanmina—a Cisco approved backplane and chassis integration company—to do subassembly for its VCO/4K product. Sanmina had quickly become one of Summa Four's major suppliers. Cisco considered Sanmina to be a potential candidate for testing the idea of leveraging a contract manufacturer to handle the production, fulfillment, and aftersale support of manufacture products in the future.

DECISIONS AHEAD

Keller anticipated that the postacquisition integration of Summa Four would be relatively complex given the company's remote location, its line of legacy products, and its number of employees. In a week's time he would have to present his recommendations on how to integrate Summa Four's products, plant, and people. His initial thoughts were that it would make the most sense to transfer the Alpha generation to the main Cisco facility and leave the other products where they were, to eventually be phased out. While this appeared to be the easiest route to take, would it deliver the type of returns that Cisco had come to expect? What would he do with the Manchester plant if expected demand were to increase dramatically? What were the risks inherent in these choices? What would be the impact on retaining Summa Four's key employees?

As Keller sat back to consider these issues, he received a phone call informing him of yet another Cisco acquisition on the horizon, this time of Selsius Systems of Texas—a maker of products which allowed companies to combine voice and data communications on their corporate networks. Keller knew that Summa Four would likely serve as a role model for the Selsius acquisition integration process and potentially many more to come. He

knew that he would have to think very carefully about the myriad of integration issues facing Cisco with the Summa Four acquisition.

CASE III-4

PlaceWare: Issues in Structuring a Xerox Technology Spinout

Henry Chesbrough and Christina Darwall

> *Not everything we start ends up fitting with our businesses later on. Many of the ideas we work on here involve a paradigm shift in order to deliver value. So sometimes we must work particularly hard to find the "architecture of the revenues." Since the creation of the CIC [Corporate Innovation Committee] here at Xerox, there has been a growing appreciation for the struggle to create a value proposition for our research output and for the fact that this struggle is as valuable as inventing the technology itself.*
> —John Seely Brown, chief scientist of the Xerox Corporation and director of the Xerox Palo Alto Research Center

Richard Bruce gazed at the golden California hills stretching out beyond Xerox Corporation's Palo Alto Research Center (PARC) offices in June 1996, as he mulled over his team's next steps. The team had just received word that the Xerox CIC had agreed to spin out the PlaceWare technology, subject to certain requirements. Although happy about the outcome, Bruce knew several potentially conflicting issues had to be resolved if the spinout was to be successful. Xerox required continued access to the technology after it spun out, it wanted to make a reasonable return on the money it had invested in the technology so far, and it was unwilling to invest further money in the technology. The PlaceWare software developers had their own needs and desires that had to be addressed if they were to be motivated to continue working with the technology. Finally, whoever ended up funding the spinout would have issues that had to be addressed.

Bruce knew they had to obtain additional funding as soon as possible because Xerox's investment would stop by year end. He had to come up with a proposed structure for the spinout of PlaceWare that resolved the needs of the various parties, and he had to do it soon.

THE CORPORATE INNOVATION COMMITTEE

Although Xerox had traditionally—and famously—experienced difficulty in profiting from its research achievements at PARC,[1] a recent review of projects under way in Xerox's research labs[2] convinced managers that the company had a wealth of ideas ripe for commercialization. According to Rafik Loutfy, vice president of strategy, Planning, and Innovation, the review illustrated that

> Xerox really needed a process for examining how best to commercialize the corporation's software and solutions technologies. We have over $1 billion invested in R&D, but much of this technology has no clear path to the market. Moreover, our corporate planning process [Xerox 2005] established a corporate goal to grow at strong double-digit rates—well above the growth rate of our existing businesses. Since our software and solutions technologies are in fast-growing markets, we felt we should be able to help Xerox reach its corporate goals by developing better processes to commercialize technology.

Xerox had experimented with various mechanisms to commercialize its technology. It had established and funded a separate company, LiveWorks, to develop and market interactive whiteboards.[3] Richard Bruce had been the interim president of this subsidiary. When he returned to PARC, an outside CEO was brought in, who requested and received $25 million in additional capital. The company proved unable to turn a profit, however, and was subsequently shut down.

Xerox also experimented with an internal venture capital (VC) operation, Xerox Technology Ventures (XTV),[4] which had enjoyed significant financial success from its initial round of investments from 1989 to 1996.[5] How-

ever, since the fund could invest only in technologies ready to be pursued independently from the lab,[6] Xerox management felt strongly that this VC structure did not allow XTV to harness the potential synergies available to the corporation from its technologies. But technologies that with further development might benefit the overall corporation did not lend themselves to an independent VC structure, since XTV did not assign any value to increased Xerox corporate profits resulting from the technology.

Xerox terminated XTV in the latter half of 1996, to be replaced with a different process intended to identify and select technologies that might benefit the corporation overall, once additional funding, support, and direction were provided for them. This new process—essentially an internal incubator—was called Xerox New Enterprises (XNE). In parallel with XNE, Xerox established a process to spin out other technologies that, while commercially promising, did not suggest synergies with Xerox business units. A "funnel" of research projects identified at each research lab was then screened, selected, evaluated, and commercialized. Only a certain portion of the screened technologies moved onto the evaluation process, and only some of those were actually commercialized outside the company, as shown in Exhibit 1.

To manage this process the Corporate Innovation Committee (CIC) was formed; the group was charged with screening potential candidate projects and managing this outplacement process.

Mark Myers, senior vice president of Corporate Research and Technology and cochair of the CIC, explained the options for commercializing technologies.

> When we evaluate technologies for spinout, we filter candidate technologies into four categories: (1) The ones that our business units are willing to fund get top priority and are effectively sponsored by the business units. (2) Technologies that the business units are not willing to acquire, but the Xerox New Enterprise Board (XNE) is willing to support, get second priority[7] (3) Spinning the technology out to the venture community. If we're not interested in the technology for ourselves, it may be best for the employees and for

---

[1] PARC was responsible for many salient technologies in the personal computer industry, including Ethernet networking software, bitmapped graphics operating systems, and scalable software printer fonts. These were successfully commercialized by others—3Com, Apple Computer, and Adobe, respectively. See Douglas Smith and Robert Alexander, *Fumbling the Future* (New York: William Morrow, 1988).

[2] In 1996, Xerox had significant research facilities in Palo Alto, California; Rochester, New York; Cambridge, England; Grenoble, France; and Toronto, Canada.

[3] With these boards, a user's writing on one board could be displayed on another, and vice versa. The boards came in varying sizes, from a single unit in individual offices to entire walls of conference rooms.

[4] See HBS Case No. 295-127, "Xerox Technology Ventures."

[5] One conservative calculation determined that the initial $30 million invested by Xerox had yielded at least $219 million in capital gains as

of 1996, for an internal rate of return of 56 percent. By comparison, the internal rate of return for other VC funds established in 1989 was 13.7 percent. See HBS Case 298-109, "Xerox Technology Ventures: January 1997."

[6] These technologies could even compete against Xerox's own business units, and the venture capital structure would prevent Xerox from s topping this competition—even though Xerox funded the venture through XTV.

[7] See "Inxight: Incubating a Xerox Technology Spinout," HBS Case No. 699-019 by Prof. Henry Chesbrough for the experience of one XNE managed project.

EXHIBIT 1   The CIC/XNE Project Funnel

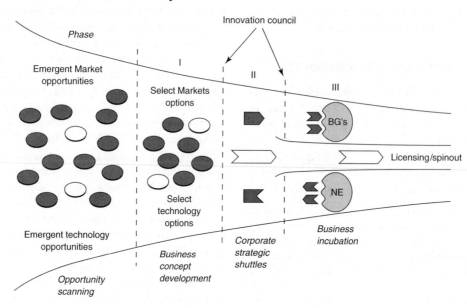

Xerox to spin the thing out. There may even be an opportunity for the spinout to be a supplier to Xerox later on. And of course, (4) we don't commercialize it, and instead keep it in the labs.

The CIC process was headed by Rafik Loutfy, who reported to Myers and his staff. Among the issues they had to address was how to compare different technologies serving different markets. Loutfy's team thus created common criteria for projects presenting their business case to the CIC. Loutfy pointed out, at the same time "while we put a lot of work into developing the content of these presentations, the other half of the CIC's concern was the credibility of the presenters. If they are not credible themselves, then whatever promises or projections they make are immediately discounted."

PLACEWARE BACKGROUND

The original impetus for PlaceWare technology came from multiuser domains (MUDs). Chat rooms, news groups, and usenets were all examples of MUDs, which had been around since the beginning of the Internet itself. The first MUD, developed in England in 1979, was a text-based online environment in which a "community" of participants played. Unlike computer games of the time in which players interacted only with the game, MUDs allowed users who didn't otherwise know each other to interact together while they all progressed

through the MUD environment. Eventually a few MUD programs emerged that were almost entirely programmable by participants. Using programming tools, the participants themselves could build new activities and enhance existing ones, effectively creating their own online environments. One of these MUDs, designed by a Canadian graduate student, used a fairly straightforward but powerful object-oriented programming language. As such, it was called MUD object-oriented (MOO).

Pavel Curtis, a project leader in the Computer Sciences Laboratory at Xerox PARC, had long been interested in programming languages; he had joined PARC in 1983, and subsequently worked on a variety of language-related projects. In the summer of 1990, when the pace of his major research project slowed, he became intrigued with MUDs. After extensive research, he came across MOO. Curtis remembered his reaction to the Canadian student's work:

> It wasn't perfect, of course [what language is?], but he seemed to have made many fewer of the mistakes made by most language-design amateurs. There were even features that were original.... I decided that it would be fun to work with [the student] on the future evolution of his language. I approached him about this (on the MOO of course) and he was receptive.[8]

---

[8]Pavel Curtis, "High Wired," online memorandum, pp. 3–4.

When Curtis was encouraged to choose a character name for himself upon entering the MOO world, he chose "Lambda," a major keyword in the programming language he had been working on for some time at Xerox PARC. He became deeply involved in the MOO, eventually revising the server used for managing the environment; indeed, he named it LambdaMOO. Moreover, several of his colleagues joined in, building the server's core libraries and providing new functionality. Curtis recalled:

> The collaborative feel of it was fascinating as we worked closely together from our separate offices thousands of miles apart, as we had good-natured arguments about the relative merits of American and Australian spellings of English words, and as we eventually became joined by other hackers, legendary programmers, and fellow researchers. But what was most fascinating was the community that was forming, a community with hundreds of people, all learning about LambdaMOO and coming to see what it was all about.[9]

Early in 1991, as Curtis was preparing for his annual performance appraisal, he realized that he had spent most of the past year working on MUD and MOO. He wrote a document about the technical aspects of his work to discuss with his lab manager, who later advised him not to let this fascinating line of inquiry get in the way of his major area of research. Nonetheless, in February 1991, LambdaMOO was announced and released to the public. Ultimately, it became the most successful public MUD of the time, whose community numbered some 10,000 people.

LAMBDAMOO EVOLVES INTO JUPITER

By 1992, PARC management itself concluded that extending the technology that had gone into creating LambdaMOO should become a major area of research. The project was renamed Jupiter and additional researchers, including Dave Nichols and Bob Kravacic, were assigned to the effort. Nichols had joined PARC in 1990 and worked on a project to provide collaborative filtering of electronic mail and news. Associated with PARC since 1984, Kravacic had previously focused on artificial intelligence and the LISP programming language.

Jupiter was envisioned as a multiuser, multimedia infrastructure supporting long-term remote collaboration with shared applications (tools) and multicast audio and visual communication. By integrating content with communications facilities, the project hoped to provide what Xerox PARC researchers viewed as the optimal infrastructure for community interaction. They also believed that a metaphor of physical space—"rooms" with different activities/content within a "house" for participants— would make the notion of "community" intuitively apparent.

In early 1994 Mike Dixon joined the team. He had been with PARC since 1991 and was instrumental in developing a number of important products, co-designing, for example, the real-time control architecture used in Xerox copier and printer products. Then, in October, Richard Bruce, a PARC researcher who had left to become CEO of LiveWorks, returned. When he first joined PARC in 1982, Bruce focused on hardware systems technology; now, however, he wanted to shift his attention to software. His lab manager suggested that he learn MOO and write some applications, and thus Bruce joined the Jupiter team.

Meanwhile, PARC management decided to include the Jupiter project on its "PARC tour" as one of the featured projects demonstrated to visitors—outsiders as well as people from numerous business units. One demonstration showed 80 PARC researchers collaborating on different projects through the PARC server. Visitors were uniformly impressed, though many could not determine exactly how to employ such a powerful capability in their own business units.

A variety of events subsequently affected Jupiter. First, research team members considered the project finished in mid-1995; the tools were available to allow users to build applications, as they did in LambdaMOO—only now these applications could employ voice and visual images in addition to text. Second, they wanted the technology released to the public, as the LambdaMOO technology had been. They felt that as they had been able to learn a lot from observing how large communities of people used LambdaMOO, they could likewise learn a great deal from observing how people used Jupiter. The researchers also began discussing plans for a very broadly based next generation of the technology.

PARC management, however, had misgivings about releasing Jupiter to the public. John Seely Brown, director of PARC and chief scientist of the Xerox Corporation, and Mark Myers began discussing how Xerox needed to be more systematic about cutting-edge technologies; the company had to determine a technology's "value propositions" and then build business models based on them. It was obvious that the company was serious about reaping dividends from its investments in technology development and did not see how giving Jupiter away would

---

[9]Ibid., p. 5.

provide any obvious return for Xerox and its shareholders. If a technology did not fit with any of Xerox's current businesses, another way had to be found to capture the value it created. Richard Bruce, for his part, determined to find opportunities for the Jupiter technology.

Jupiter Market Opportunities

Bruce spent several months visiting various Xerox businesses to see whether the technology could be applied internally. He recalled one potential opportunity:

> A fairly senior sales executive spent three months at PARC at the same time I was working on this project. She helped me think about how we might use the technology inside and I spoke with many national account managers and business unit managers to discuss their communications problems. But people inside the Xerox sales organization did not even use email at that time and so it was hard for them to envision how to use Jupiter. It became clear to me that it would be 10 years before our business processes would be sophisticated enough to use this technology.

Bruce and Jupiter researcher Nichols then ran a series of internal meetings where the Jupiter technology was compared with other existing technologies against specific market opportunities. They first brain-stormed 31 different scenarios in which the Jupiter technology could be used and then developed in more detail the 6 that they thought had the most potential:

1. An online bookstore—which would represent any online retail opportunity.
2. Medical consultation among several physicians, meant to represent occasional expert interactions.
3. Business collaboration (in contrast to the medical consultation, this represented longer-term, more frequent interactions among a larger number of people).
4. A "project wall," an online version of a large physical wall used to post project information, meant to represent internal collaboration within a firm.
5. Virtual professional conferences or conventions.
6. A toner manufacturing plant, meant to represent any manufacturing facility where communal access to information would be needed.

The technologies against which Bruce and Nichols compared Jupiter included the Web (with software that allowed users on the same Web page to be aware of one another and communicate using text and audio),[10] online services such as America Online (AOL) and CompuServe, and desktop video conferencing services such as those offered by ProShare and PictureTel. Bruce and Nichols evaluated the four technologies against 3 to 10 variables in each of the six scenarios, ranking the technologies on a scale from 1 to 10 in terms of how well they addressed each key variable.

The resulting opportunity matrix, finished in the fall of 1995, suggested that the Jupiter technology had its biggest competitive advantage in the online retailing opportunity (see Exhibit 2). When the team subsequently talked with retailers about using the Jupiter technology for their online sites, however, they found little interest. The retailers were united in their belief that one of the primary reasons to have an online site was to *get rid* of salespeople, and the Jupiter notion of a retail website included interactions—not only sales person-to-customer, but customer-to-customer. Although the online retail opportunity wasn't pursued, the group believed that they had nonetheless gained an insight about the technology: Jupiter was superior in situations where there were casual meetings and high amounts of interaction among many people. In particular, Jupiter allowed for significant richness in the applications being shared by the people using it.

JUPITER EVOLVES INTO PLACEWARE

While Bruce was pursuing market opportunities, researchers were pursuing the technology's next generation, which came to be called PlaceWare.[11] It would be Java-based and run on the World Wide Web. PlaceWare's architecture consisted of a layer that ran on the client systems that provided access to the content to be shared, plus a set of RPCs (remote procedure calls) that resided on the client system linking the client to the server. The server, in turn, hosted the platform and the applications creating the content and maintained the master version of all content being shared. Kravacic, one of the software developers, described some of PlaceWare's capabilities:

> We had developed algorithms for managing shared data, which was displayed in the windows at the client [system], and we had a list of objects that could be shared: integers, lists, strings. Our guarantees were that the users would all see the same objects. However, whenever two people were editing the same object in the same app[lication] at the same time, we had to resolve contention issues. Of course, if they were editing different objects in the same app, we'd display what each was writing in real time.

---

[10] One example of such software was Ubique. A lower-end version of this software was NetMeeting by Microsoft, while Lotus Notes was another text-based platform.

[11] First it was renamed Network Places, then Net Places, and eventually PlaceWare.

EXHIBIT 2 Jupiter Opportunity Matrix

September 1995	Jupiter	Web	Online service	Digital video system
Bookstore:				
Mobile user state	9	3	3	2
Tools	9	7	5	8
Custom stacks	9	7	5	9
Browse merchandise	9	9	9	7
Reading groups	10	7	7	3
Task-based casual conversation	10	7	5	2
Custom connections	9	4	4	2
Marketing flyers	10	8	5	5
Switch between synchronous and asynchronous	10	2	1	6
Total bookstore points	85	54	44	44
Business collaboration:				
Audio	5	5	1	9
Video	4	1	1	9
Shared editing	9	1	1	7
Shared general application	1	1	1	9
Persistent connection	9	9	1	5
Organization	9	8	5	5
Mobile/remote connection	10	5	5	3
Total business collaboration points	47	30	15	47
Professional society meetings:				
Nametag/identification	10	5	5	2
Proceedings of meeting	7	9	5	6
Participation at meeting	10	4	6	6
Total professional society points	27	18	16	14
Remote medical consultation:				
Artifacts	6	3	1	9
Telepointing	1	3	1	10
Experts to consult	6	3	2	9
Total medical consultation points	13	9	4	28
Toner factory:[a]				
Video monitor processes	10	1	1	9
Conference on a problem	10	3	3	10
General connection to users	10	10	5	10
Monitor plan status nonvideo	5	5	2	5
Create multimedia record of problem	8	4	4	8
Total toner factory points	43	23	15	42
Project wall:[b]				
Permanent recordable area	8	8	5	3
Large	4	4	4	4
Public	8	9	3	1
Up-to-date	10	9	10	10
Simultaneous use	7	6	2	5
Total project wall points	37	36	24	23

Note: Rating from 1–10 for each attribute in each application; 10= highest, 1 = lowest.
[a] A vertical application for large Xerox copier systems.
[b] A vertical application for Xerox's LiveWorks' boards.

The server had much to track: the state of connections with each user, what the user could access, what areas the user was authorized to visit, and where the user had complete "authoring rights" versus "view only" capabilities. And, this "state of information" had to be maintained in real time for all active users. The team had already demonstrated such ability with 80 users on the Jupiter system and believed they could scale the number of users up to 500. Within two to three years, as servers, connections, and client personal computers increased in speed, the team felt

EXHIBIT 3   PlaceWare Technology Diagram

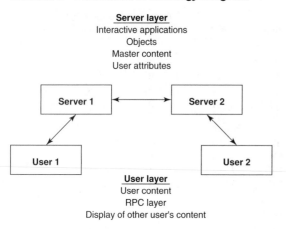

that they could handle over 1,000 users. Exhibit 3 provides a schematic view of the PlaceWare architecture.

Nonetheless, the development process faced numerous difficulties, given the state of both Java and the Internet at the time. Kravacic elaborated:

> One of the things we were fighting was that the browsers were taking over the audio channel. It was hard to write a standard way to transmit audio, because each browser handled that aspect of it differently, even though they all implemented Java.
>
> Netscape was a browser that gave us real problems. You couldn't load multiple [Java] applets because under certain conditions . . . the screen might freeze, or you might get the Windows dialog box "death message." We were seeing crashes with frequent regularity. "Pure virtual function call" was one error message. "Memory access violation" was another one. In Netscape, the colors on the screen painter were always wrong, and you might write in a window, only to find the browser writing the information outside the window. Though some of this was what any Java developer was then fighting, we were pushing areas of the code that weren't being pushed elsewhere, so I think we were uncovering even more headaches than usual.

Despite the problems encountered transferring their technology to an open system, the move to Java was considered critical, as Dixon recalled:

> With Jupiter, we were in a hurry to get something out. Our goal had been to get the programming tools out quickly and then study how people used them to interact and build their own online communities, but management said that it was too valuable to give away. Now, we . . . were considering spinning the technology out, where the technology had to be "productized." But Jupiter really wasn't capable of being

productized. We were stuck unless we could find a way to re-do the system—almost starting from scratch—with Java.

Because the researchers believed that Java was the answer to developing the next-generation product, they were determined to resolve some of the problems they were encountering. Curtis and Dixon paid a visit to Sun Microsystems' JavaSoft team in the fall of 1995, at the same time as Bruce and his colleagues were developing the opportunities matrix. After a lengthy and contentious meeting, the Java team said that it was unable to help because it already had too much to do getting the current code out to the market. Leaving depressed, Curtis and Dixon drew up a list of what they could accomplish without changing Java, but it wasn't inspiring. They worked late into the night—when Dixon had a breakthrough insight. He recalled:

> We wanted the system to be "viral"—contagious—so that it didn't have to be reinstalled each time. We didn't want a client-server system. We wanted a server-server system. I decided that what we needed was a very thin client. We only needed to provide the most basic "hooks" at the client, and these we could write in Java and give away over a phone line.[12] The revenue opportunity, and the vast majority of the code, could be server-based. This greatly reduced our dependence on the browser software code.

Jupiter researchers were so excited about Dixon's idea that they immediately held meetings about spinning out the technology. At the time, however, they believed that a spinout would, depending on how it was structured, mean handing over the technology to someone else—on the outside—who would then productize it and perhaps write applications for it. "We were really a platform in search of an application," Kravacic said. "Our position was kind of like a company marketing an operating system. To get people to use our platform and write apps for it, we needed to convince people to do so based on being a solid company, with lots of 'seats'[13] for the developer of the app."

They considered companies like Netscape, AOL, and Sun/JavaSoft as potential partners who could quickly make their technology ubiquitous at the client end. They also thought of Hewlett-Packard, and other similar companies, as candidates for marketing the server-based

---

[12] This was similar to Netscape's early distribution of its browser code in 1994—when the company offered free 90-day trial copies of Navigator that could be downloaded to users. While users were supposed to pay after the expiration period, many did not.

[13] Licenses of many higher-end software products were sold on a "per seat" basis, referring to the products at the time. If Company X had a license for 500 seats, it then could have up to 500 active users at a time.

product. The team estimated that any commercial version of their code would require 100,000 to 200,000 lines of code, plus extensive documentation, particularly if it were to be used by another firm to do development.

All this suggested the possibility of a licensing arrangement between Xerox and one or more partners, thereby allowing technology to be commercialized through firms with ties to millions of customers. But should such a license be exclusive or nonexclusive? An exclusive license provided much greater incentive for the licensee to make the additional effort and investments needed to push the technology into the market. If the wrong licensee were selected, however, the technology might hit a dead end. Such dead ends could be avoided with a nonexclusive arrangement, but each partner also would have less incentive to push the technology as well as the ability to free-ride on the investments and effort made by the other licensees.

After exploratory conversations with some potential partners, who indicated some limited interest, the group realized that further development work would be needed before anything could be delivered. It was also clear that these potential partners were more interested in what PlaceWare could do to advance their own businesses than they were in the overall potential for PlaceWare itself. Finally, the developers realized that control over the future direction of PlaceWare could shift to these partner firms if they did a licensing deal, whether exclusive or nonexclusive—and they were uneasy about losing control.

In sum, the developers believed that their vision of the next Jupiter generation would mesh well with the burgeoning movement toward the Web. What they had developed to share resources, manage "resource contention," track user attributes, and so on, was directly relevant. Their belief in the Internet phenomenon, meanwhile, had been validated by the Netscape IPO. Initially priced at $15, that company's stock rose to $71 at the end of the first day of trading, establishing a market value of over $4 billion for a 16-month-old company. To the researchers, the 1995 Netscape IPO was significant to the PlaceWare team—not because of the valuation it fetched, but because of Netscape's licensing of Java. This promised the availability of tens or even hundreds of millions of machines that had the building blocks for the interactive communications capabilities that PlaceWare could provide. The group felt some urgency to move quickly; they were concerned that the Web was exploding (see Exhibit 4) and that they might become a footnote if they failed to get to market soon.

THE BUSINESS CASE FOR PLACEWARE

In November 1995, Bruce and Curtis paid a visit to a well-known Kleiner, Perkins venture capitalist—who was not encouraging. This echoed the message from all the VCs with whom they had met: there was "too much" technology and "no real product."

Bruce then began holding meetings with the researchers to discuss their commitment to a spinout. Researchers, he learned, were concerned about lifestyle issues, worried, for instance that a spinout couldn't possibly maintain the PARC work environment. He recalled:

EXHIBIT 4   Web Server Growth Comparison

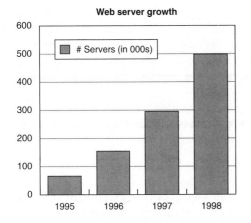

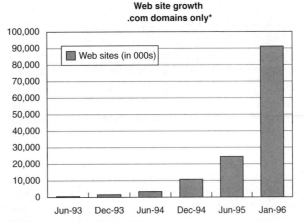

*Excludes .gov and .edu domains.

Source: Xerox market research.

When I was in those meetings, I felt—but couldn't say at the time—that in fact their lifestyles *would* change fairly dramatically; eventually they figured this out. Xerox PARC researchers come to PARC for the academic freedom, not for the money, and so their motivations are often different from many others here in Silicon Valley.

Realizing he needed additional resources to assemble a complete business plan for PlaceWare, Bruce held informal conversations with Bill Shott about how a spinout might work. Shott was leaving Network Computing Devices (NCD) where, as vice president of marketing, he had been involved with building one of the first Web browsers; now he was interested in pursuing real-time Web-based products. In January 1996, John Seely Brown authorized Bruce to hire Shott to help develop the spinout plan.

During the first half of 1996, Shott brought in a variety of potential users for demonstrations and discussions about potential PlaceWare applications. The "matrix of opportunities" helped point the team in a general direction, but Shott believed that developers needed specific input from real potential customers in order to create a good business model for the spinout. Companies such as 3Com, Adobe, Clarify, Cisco, Hewlett-Packard, and NewsCorp visited. Hewlett-Packard was interested in building an application for its second-line support engineers to train their first-line support engineers. NewsCorp had just bought an online news service and was interested in an "auditorium" application where thousands of people could enter an auditorium and have a "conversation" and interactions with celebrities such as Madonna.

Overall, visitors—whether companies or VCs—were consistently intrigued by the technology and impressed with the quality and depth of the research team. Bruce repeatedly said that "any one of them could be the chief technology officer of a Silicon Valley company." In addition, VCs made it clear that they were investing a lot of money in the Internet space—that there was a paradigm shift occurring and that they were investing significant funds because they knew that at least a few of their investments would hit it really big.

Shott viewed the opportunity identification process as an iterative one. He explained:

> We tried measuring each option against the technology and then cycling back to the next option. We knew that we had the advantages of scale and interaction when compared to other technologies. We could also see a continuum on which we fit, from Presentations (hierarchical) to Classrooms (participative) to true Collaboration. We didn't want to compete with Microsoft's NetMeeting, so the collaborative positioning wasn't too attractive. HP was actually interested in using our technology for online classrooms, but we did not view the training market as attractive since training budgets were so easily cut. NewsCorp's auditorium application seemed to intrigue them, but we thought it was too simple an approach and recommended they build it themselves.

Meanwhile, Bruce and Shott worked on a business plan that presented PlaceWare as a technology platform for a variety of alternative applications. For example, the business plan emphasized that the Web was moving from a broadcast model to an interactive model, and PlaceWare had an opportunity to become the leading comprehensive interaction infrastructure for enterprises. They calculated that PlaceWare would need approximately $7 million in equity capital over the next two years, and that if things went well, the business could exceed $100 million in five years' time (see Exhibit 5 for the executive summary of the PlaceWare business plan presented to the CIC).

PLACEWARE MEETS THE CIC

As Bruce and Shott finalized the business plan and a slide presentation for the CIC meeting, they calculated that Xerox had spent about $6 million in R&D expenses over the past five years on the Jupiter technology and wanted to present a credible case for how Xerox could realize a return on this investment. The business plan focused on how PlaceWare could capitalize on what the team perceived as a movement toward true interactivity on the Web. Although several companies offered some interactive capabilities, the PlaceWare team saw an opportunity to offer *all* interactive capabilities—including text, audio, and video—as integrated services whose functions and presentation were consistent. The team proposed to target the "customer interaction" market, which they defined as anyone engaged in an interactive process for professional purposes. By analyzing market research, the team estimated that 10 percent of Internet server owners could benefit from interacting directly with customers on their Web sites.

Prior to the meeting, Bruce and Shott had met individually with key members of the CIC to discuss potential issues, as Bruce recalled:

> We knew that each person on the CIC had different objectives and concerns. Some were worried about our having done a thorough job checking out the potential to use the technology inside or losing the research talent of the PlaceWare team. Others were worried about the odds of the spinout succeeding, as they were concerned about the effect on Xerox's reputation if the spinout should fail. Some were

EXHIBIT 5 Highlights of the PlaceWare Business Plan

EXECUTIVE OVERVIEW

The World Wide Web is moving through distinct stages of development. In the first stage, "Publishing," most Web sites were essentially electronic versions of print documents, consisting mainly of static text and images with hyperlinks to related static sites. Currently in the second stage, "Infobase," Web sites serve as gateways to computational resources such as databases accessed through search engines. In the emerging third stage, "Interaction," Web sites are becoming venues—places—for developing truly interactive communities for business, government, and affinity groups of all kinds.

Interactive capabilities, including electronic mail, threaded forums, and real-time audio and video, are available today and, in fact, account for an enormous amount of traffic on the Internet. But they are typically offered as independent services with no consistency in function or presentation, limiting their practicality and appeal. Full realization of the Internet's potential requires a seamless integration of interaction with content, providing the user with a unified interface to all Internet functionality.

True interactivity will allow Web businesses to move from a broadcast model to an interactive model, encouraging what have been more-or-less passive audiences to become participants, with all the qualities this word implies: identity, involvement, and loyalty. True interactivity will allow companies offering goods and services to gain significant efficiencies by increasing customer interaction while cutting costs and will increase employee productivity in enterprises large and small by allowing cross-functional teams and employee communities to interact as if they were sitting in adjacent cubicles.

To achieve enhanced interactivity on the World Wide Web, we have created PlaceWare, a platform that seamlessly integrates Web-based content with communication and interaction capabilities. Through links to a PlaceWare server, Web sites will offer visitors awareness of other visitors currently on the site, common windows for live interaction with chat, audio, video, shared applications, and mobile objects. PlaceWare will also provide customers with means to easily develop new applications.

MARKET

By analyzing Web site category data from Point Communications, a market research firm, we estimate that 10% of Internet server owners can benefit from interacting directly with customers on their Web sites. Since communication is the primary purpose of Intranets, we believe that 25% of Intranet servers will implement PlaceWare interactivity. Based on these estimates and market saturation within four years, we project a market size of 11,000 servers in 1997, growing to 700,000 servers in 2000.

COMPETITION

The major competition will come from platform vendors, specifically Netscape, Microsoft, and Quarterdeck. These companies, however, have not yet developed architectures that provide the level of integrated functionality of PlaceWare. They are at least 12 months behind, and their solutions will suffer from major deficiencies: security, integration of content with interactivity, scalability, access to tools, and the development environment.

BUSINESS MODEL

To capture value to the customer, the company will tier its product line based on major increases in functionality. PlaceWare will price the different versions of the server as well as the applications as a function of the number of simultaneous users. To maximize development of third-party applications, PlaceWare will provide a low-priced server for the developer and give away the software developer kit. The company will stimulate mass adoption with low-priced servers for new simultaneous users and will build a revenue stream from its installed base with annual product upgrades and maintenance contracts. Finally, the company will price fees for support and upgrades relatively high to capture value from future server enhancements. Additional income will be derived from the sale of shared tools.

FINANCIALS

	1996	1997	1998	1999	2000
Profit and loss statement (six months):					
Revenue	$ 0	$4,037,407	$23,228,549	$66,444,211	$141,681,899
Cost of goods sold	0	184,215	1,314,098	4,651,095	11,334,552
Gross margin	0	3,853,192	21,914,451	61,793,116	130,347,348
Department expenses	1,648,431	5,934,681	19,380,587	50,497,600	97,760,511
Other expenses	226,272	516,120	878,207	1,546,996	3,299,269
Pre-tax profits	(1,874,703)	(2,597,609)	1,655,657	9,748,520	29,287,568
Cash flow statement:					
Sources	0	2,966,612	20,160,824	66,326,177	139,796,523
Uses	1,670,324	6,631,094	20,538,883	59,850,205	119,511,830
Increase (decrease) in cash	(1,670,324)	(3,664,482)	(378,059)	6,475,971	20,284,694
Cash at beginning of period	4,000,000	5,329,676	1,665,194	1,287,136	7,763,107
Cash at end of period	2,329,676	1,665,194	1,287,136	7,763,107	28,047,800
Capital raised	4,000,000	3,000,000			
Head count	27	51	126	220	472

interested in Xerox's equity stake and still others in Xerox's rights to the technology.

The June CIC Meeting

The PlaceWare technology and business plan were presented to the CIC at its first meeting in June 1996, along with three other technologies. Shott made the PlaceWare presentation. Bruce felt it was critical that Shott make the PlaceWare presentation. Whereas PARC researchers did not have much credibility with the business managers in Xerox; Shott, as an outside consultant with a strong business background, would. The biggest issue at the CIC meeting, said Bruce, was the employees' percentage of equity ownership.

> Andy Garman put up some numbers showing Xerox getting a 40 percent to 50 percent ownership on a premoney valuation of $8 million to $10 million, which some of us viewed as totally unrealistic. We also discussed the fact that Xerox had a policy of not negotiating with employees, only with venture capitalists. Of course, VCs care about their own interests first, the employees' interests second, and Xerox's interests third.

Garman managed the review process for PlaceWare. His role was to screen the PlaceWare technology and evaluate its potential, both within Xerox and as an independent entity. He described his reactions:

> It was obvious that there were no business divisions inside Xerox ready to use PlaceWare. The high-end production systems unit saw some value for them, but only as a narrow vertical application to link Xerox to its largest customers. This would have ignored the value of the technology as a horizontal systems technology, and would have distorted its development and lost its potential value. And, if the technology did spin out, the large systems unit could be an early customer, and get much of its value that way anyhow. In fact, my biggest challenge during the period when I was evaluating this technology was keeping the developers from walking out the door and doing it on their own. There were some patents we had filed, but these were fairly narrow in scope, and there wasn't any code that was commercial grade over which we could claim ownership.

Mark Myers also recalled the discussion:

> Jupiter was an interesting, PARC-like project, about people interacting with one another in an electronic community. This technology appealed to out researchers in the PARC, Grenoble, and Cambridge research labs. But it wasn't seen as a source of competitive advantage for Xerox. Also, the user base for PlaceWare outside of our research labs was hard to see. I saw the spinout as a good outcome, both for Xerox and for the founders.

In the end, CIC members voted to spin out PlaceWare, concluding that it was unlikely to be of strategic value in terms of synergy with any of Xerox's current businesses, and that a spinout would bring the corporation the highest expected value for the technology. Andy Garman recalled the marching orders with which he left the CIC meeting:

> Because Xerox was interested in the financial opportunity, continued access to the technology, and the treatment of the researchers, I left the CIC meeting with a series of constraints:
> 1. Xerox didn't want to invest any additional money.
> 2. Xerox required broad access to the technology, now and in the future.
> 3. Xerox wanted the ownership percentage for the principals to be below a certain level. This might seem odd, but their position was actually pretty reasonable. They didn't want some researcher in Rochester working on mainstream technology to perceive that some PARC researchers working on exotic stuff were getting rich. It's an adverse incentives problem, because how Xerox treats one researcher influences how other researchers feel.

THE SPINOUT STRUCTURING DECISION

After numerous discussions with Garman and some preliminary meetings with outside parties such as venture capitalists, Bruce felt there were four alternate ways in which to structure a spinout of PlaceWare from PARC. One method would be executing a licensing agreement with one or more other companies that would transfer the responsibility for executing the business plan to the licensing company (who would then presumably invest the additional $7 million or so to finance the further development of the technology). This would provide some up-front money to Xerox and, depending on the deal, might also include an ongoing royalty stream of payments over time. Licenses could be either exclusive or nonexclusive, and Bruce knew that the motivations of the other partner(s) depended on the way in which the license was crafted. The PlaceWare development team had indicated, though, that they were worried that licensing might result in losing control over the future of their ideas. Moreover, it wasn't clear what financial benefit, if any, the team would receive beyond long-term consulting to document and transfer the code.

A second approach would be to enter into a strategic alliance with one or more firms to pursue the further development of the PlaceWare code. Xerox would contribute the technology developed to date, while the alliance partner would finance the further development of the technology and focus it on areas that leveraged the partner's existing businesses. Possible allies included firms like Netscape, AOL, Sun/Java-Soft, HP, or even NewsCorp. This approach would enable the development team to continue influencing both the development and direction of the project, though each potential ally would be interested in different directions; it also seemed to take advantage of the Internet explosion under way in the market. Bruce believed that an alliance would require Xerox to invest additional funds, however, as allies would expect Xerox not only to contribute the ideas generated to date, but also actual working code—and potentially to develop some specific applications that utilized that code as well. Bruce wondered how Xerox management would respond to an option that required them to invest further in PlaceWare, before any value could be returned to the corporation.

A third approach was taking the PlaceWare ideas and development team out to the venture community to attract financing. This would shift the project out of a research mode and strongly into a "get it out the door" mode. Bruce believed that the venture community excelled in commercializing technology in this way. This approach also promised an attractive upside opportunity for Xerox if the venture succeeded. Bruce knew that the development team would likely share in that upside as well, but it came with substantial risk. If the spinout did not develop a commercially successful product, it would be shut down, and the team members fired. At the moment, there seemed to be no immediate "home run" use for the technology. Finally, Bruce wondered what valuation Xerox could expect from the VC community for the money it would have invested in developing the technology so far.

A fourth approach would be to "bootstrap" the start-up. This would mean pursuing the technology commercialization in a much lower-cost way—for example, by paying lower salaries, working out of the cheapest space available, and using "angels" (private investors) for initial capital instead of venture capitalists. Bruce had heard that venture capital firms needed to invest at least $2 million to $3 million per company to justify their time and effort, while angel investors were willing to supply as little as $25,000.[14] Bruce saw this as the highest-risk approach—one that would severely impact the family-friendly lifestyles they had all enjoyed at PARC. If they could hit upon a winning use for the technology though, this path arguably promised the highest reward for the team, and might provide a better return for Xerox as well.

THE VIEW FROM THE DECK

As Bruce soaked up the warm California sun, he pondered his next steps. In the employee area, the group had to decide who would be leaving Xerox PARC and in what way. Did all the team members have to leave PARC? Did those who left have to leave PARC permanently or could they take a leave of absence? Regarding fundraising, Bruce knew he would be working with Garman, who was in charge of negotiating the terms for the spinout—although Brown would have final approval. Bruce knew that they needed to start targeting sources of capital immediately as they could not actually leave and set up shop until they were funded. He also knew that if they couldn't get funding by the end of the current calendar year, they would not be funded by Xerox the following year, and therefore would either have to give up the spinout or quit PARC.

Bruce felt that employee issues and fundraising were connected. He knew that if they went the venture capital or angel investor route and spun out an independent company, he himself would need to go with the spinout in some capacity to facilitate, since they didn't have a CEO already on board. He wasn't sure that he was ready to leave PARC permanently himself, and he knew the risks involved after his experience with LiveWorks. Shott had decided that if the venture were funded, he would join the company as vice president of marketing; while if a licensing deal or strategic alliance were executed, he did not see an ongoing role for himself. Staring at the hills before him, Bruce realized that it was time to decide how Xerox should structure the spinout of the PlaceWare technology.

READING III-6

Making Sense of Corporate Venture Capital

Henry W. Chesbrough

Large companies have long sensed the potential value of investing in external start-ups. More often than not, though, they just can't seem to get it right.

Recall the mad dash to invest in new ventures in the late 1990s—and then the hasty retreat as the economy

---

[14]For more information on angel investors in Silicon Valley, see "Band of Angels," HBS Case No. 898-188.

turned. Nearly one-third of the companies actively investing corporate funds in start-ups in September 2000 had stopped making such investments 12 months later, according to the research firm Venture Economics, and during the same period, the amount of corporate money invested in start-ups fell by 80%. This decline in investments was part of a historic pattern of advance and retreat, but the swings in recent years were even wider than before: Quarterly corporate venture-capital investments in start-ups rose from $468 million at the end of 1998 to $6.2 billion at the beginning of 2000 and then tumbled to $848 million in the third quarter of 2001. While private VC investments also ebb and flow as the economy changes, the shifts in corporate VC investments have been particularly dramatic.

Such inconsistent behavior certainly contributes to the low regard with which many private venture capitalists view in-house corporate VC operations. In their eyes, the wild swings are further evidence that big companies have neither the stomach nor the agility to manage investments in high-risk, fast-paced environments. They also point to some high-profile missteps by individual companies to support this conclusion. Those missteps have, in turn, tended to make some companies hesitant to launch programs to invest in external start-ups, even in good times.

A number of companies, however, have defied this stereotype of the bumbling corporate behemoth and have continued to make investments in new ventures. Even as substantial numbers of corporate venture capitalists have headed for the exits in the past year and a half, some big companies—including Intel, Microsoft, and Qualcomm—have publicly committed themselves to continued high levels of investment. Others—such as Merck, Lilly, and Millennium Pharmaceuticals—have actually come in the door as others have left. What gives these optimists their confidence? More generally, why have some companies' forays into venture capital been successful, generating significant growth for their own businesses?

To answer these questions, we need an organized way to think about corporate venture capital, a framework that can help a company decide whether it should invest in a particular start-up by first understanding what kind of benefit might be realized from the investment. This article offers such a framework, one that also suggests when—that is, in what kind of economic climates—different types of investment are likely to make sense.

But first, let's briefly define corporate venture capital. We use the term to describe the investment of corporate funds directly in external start-up companies. Our defini-tion excludes investments made through an external fund managed by a third party, even if the investment vehicle is funded by and specifically designed to meet the objectives of a single investing company. It also excludes investments that fall under the more general rubric of "corporate venturing"—for example, the funding of new internal ventures that, while distinct from a company's core business and granted some organizational autonomy, remain legally part of the company. Our definition does include, however, investments made in start-ups that a company has already spun off as independent businesses.

Our framework helps explain why certain types of corporate VC investments proliferate only when financial returns are high, why other types persist in good times and in bad, and why still others make little sense in any phase of the business cycle. It can also help companies evaluate their existing and potential VC investments and determine when and how to use corporate VC as an instrument of strategic growth.

THE DUAL DIMENSIONS OF CORPORATE VC

A corporate VC investment is defined by two characteristics: its objective and the degree to which the operations of the investing company and the start-up are linked. Although companies typically have a range of objectives for their VC investments, this type of funding usually advances one of two fundamental goals. Some investments are strategic: They are made primarily to increase the sales and profits of the corporation's own businesses. A company making a strategic investment seeks to identify and exploit synergies between itself and a new venture. For example, Lucent Venture Partners, which invests the telecommunications equipment maker's funds in external companies, makes investments in start-ups that are focused on infrastructure or services for voice or data networks. Many of these companies have formal alliances with Lucent to help sell Lucent's equipment alongside their own offerings. While Lucent would clearly like to make money on its investments in these start-ups, it is willing to accept low returns if its own businesses perform better as a result of the investments.

The other investment objective is financial, wherein a company is mainly looking for attractive returns. Here, a corporation seeks to do as well as or better than private VC investors, due to what it sees as its superior knowledge of markets and technologies, its strong balance sheet, and its ability to be a patient investor. In addition, a company's brand may signal the quality of the start-up to other investors and potential customers, ultimately returning rewards to the original investor. For example, Dell Ventures, Dell Computer's in-house VC operation, has made numerous Internet investments that it has expected to earn attractive returns. While the company hopes that the investments will help its own business grow, the main rationale for the investments has been the possibility of high financial returns.

The second defining characteristic of corporate VC investments is the degree to which companies in the investment portfolio are linked to the investing company's current operational capabilities—that is, its resources and processes. For example, a start-up with strong links to the investing company might make use of that company's manufacturing plants, distribution channels, technology, or brand. It might adopt the investing company's business practices to build, sell, or service its products.

Sometimes, of course, a company's own resources and processes can become liabilities rather than capabilities, particularly when it faces new markets or disruptive technologies.[1] An external venture may offer the investing company an opportunity to build new and different capabilities—ones that could threaten the viability of current corporate capabilities. Housing these capabilities in a separate legal entity can insulate them from internal efforts to undermine them. If the venture and its processes fare well, the corporation can then evaluate whether and how to adapt its own processes to be more like those of the start-up. In rare cases, the company may even decide to acquire the venture.

FOUR WAYS TO INVEST

Clearly, neither of these two dimensions of corporate investing—strategic versus financial and tightly linked versus loosely linked—is an either-or proposition. Most investments will fall somewhere along a spectrum between the two poles of each pair of attributes. Still, overlaying the two dimensions creates a useful framework to help a company assess its current and potential VC investments. (See the exhibit "Mapping Your Corporate VC Investments" for a depiction of these distinct types of corporate venture capital.)

---

[1] See Dorothy Leonard-Barton, "Core Capabilities and Core Rigidities: A Paradox in Managing New Product Development," *Strategic Management Journal,* summer 1992, for a discussion of how companies' capabilities can become liabilities. For an introduction to disruptive technologies, see Clayton M. Christensen, *The Innovator's Dilemma: When New Technologies Cause Great Firms to Fail* (Harvard Business School Press, 1997).

Driving Investments

This type of investment is characterized by a strategic rationale and tight links between a start-up and the operations of the investing company. For instance, Agilent Technologies created a VC operation to invest in three strategic areas—life sciences, wireless communications, and optical communications—that it has identified as key to its growth. The VC arm works closely with the company's existing businesses to share information, qualify investment opportunities, and connect portfolio companies to Agilent's own initiatives. For example, Agilent has recently invested in a start-up company making wireless radio-frequency devices, a product area Agilent plans to explore in its own business. If this investment is successful, Agilent's future business will benefit; if it fails, Agilent will get a valuable early warning about pitfalls to avoid in that business.

Similarly, Microsoft has earmarked more than $1 billion to invest in start-up companies that could help advance its new Internet services architecture, ".Net." This Microsoft technology—which will enable its Windows platform to provide a variety of Internet services—is a contender to set the standards for the next generation of products and services over the Web. Microsoft is funding start-up firms that will exploit its architecture and, in so doing, promote the adoption of the Microsoft standard over rival approaches from Sun Microsystems and IBM. The start-ups are tightly linked to Microsoft's operations through the Windows software and tools that the company provides to them for the development of their own products.

The strategic value of Microsoft's .Net investments is highlighted by the company's decision to make them in the shadow of earlier VC investment losses. The company has written off staggering sums—$980 million in the third quarter of 2000 alone—in its corporate VC portfolio. But rather than backing off, Microsoft is charging ahead with new .Net investments. Because they could help the company win the battle over the next Internet services standard—a major strategic victory—it is willing to risk substantial financial losses.

Although it's clear that many driving investments can advance a corporate strategy, there are limits to what they can achieve. The tight coupling of these investments with a company's current processes means that these investments will sustain the current strategy. They will be unlikely to help a corporation cope with disruptive strategies or to identify new opportunities when the company must go beyond its current capabilities to respond to a change in the environment. If a corporation wants to transcend current strategy and processes, it should not rely on driving investments, which are ill suited for these tasks.

Enabling Investments

In this mode of VC investing, a company still makes investments primarily for strategic reasons but does not couple the venture tightly with its own operations. The theory is that a successful investment will enable a company's own businesses to benefit but that a strong operational link between the start-up and the company isn't necessary to realize that benefit. This may seem too good to be true. How can a company's strategy benefit if its operations are not tightly linked to the venture? One answer lies in the notion of complementarity: Having one product makes a person want another. A company can take advantage of this notion by using its VC investments to stimulate the development of the ecosystem in which it operates—that is, the suppliers, customers, and third-party developers that make goods and services that stimulate demand for the company's own offerings.

Intel Capital, the investment arm of the semiconductor giant, is a paradigmatic example of a company making enabling investments. Back in the early 1990s, long before corporate venture capital was fashionable, Intel realized it could benefit from nurturing start-ups making complementary products: Demand for them could spur increased demand for Intel's own microprocessor products. So Intel invested in hundreds of companies whose products—such as video, audio, and graphics hardware and software—required increasingly powerful microprocessors inside the computers they ran on, thereby stimulating sales of Intel Pentium chips. Whereas Microsoft's VC investments in start-ups seek to establish a new standard, in Intel's case, the investments have mainly been aimed at increasing its revenue by boosting sales within the current Wintel operating system standard.

Intel Capital's enormous VC investment portfolio has been the subject of some derision. Critics charge that Intel engages in "drive-by investing." They argue that the company cannot possibly coordinate with its own operations—or even effectively monitor—the more than 800 investments it has made in the past decade. But this criticism misses the point of Intel's investment strategy. The strategic value to Intel lies not in its ability to coordinate its operations with the companies in its investment portfolio but rather in the increased demand for Intel's own products generated by its portfolio companies. Intel need not closely manage every investment because it typically coinvests alongside VC firms that direct the ventures' growth and monitor their performance.

Intel itself may have added to the confusion about its investment rationale by widely touting the financial returns it earned in recent years. The high returns were in fact secondary to Intel's strategic objectives, merely making Intel's investments more affordable. The strategic benefits of these enabling investments have spurred Intel to continue with this type of funding, despite its recent investment losses, just as the strategic benefits of the driving investments help to offset Microsoft's recent losses. (Note that not all of Intel's VC investments would be characterized as enabling. Some clearly are driving investments, including those the company has made in companies in its supply chain. And, as we will see below,

---

Mapping Your Corporate VC Investments

Combining an assessment of your company's corporate objective—strategic or financial—with an analysis of the degree of linkage—tight or loose—between your operation and a start-up receiving your funding reveals the four types and purposes of corporate VC investments.

	Corporate investment objective	
Link to operational capability	strategic	financial
tight	**Driving** advances strategy of current business	**Emergent** allows exploration of potential new businesses
loose	**Enabling** complements strategy of current business	**Passive** provides financial returns only

other Intel investments fall into another category in our framework.)

The investments made by Merck's new VC unit illustrate another kind of enabling investment. Rather than increasing demand for Merck's products, the company's investments are designed to support technologies that could enhance its profitability by streamlining the way it does business. For example, Merck has invested in start-up companies developing ways to cut the time required to recruit appropriate patients for clinical trials of new drugs Merck's relationship with the start-ups is that of an investor and a customer. But if these ventures succeed, Merck will be able to use their methods to move its drugs more rapidly through the clinical trials necessary to obtain FDA approval, leaving it more time to market a drug before its patent expires. The company estimates that speeding up the patient recruitment process could ultimately add millions of dollars *per month* to Merck's bottom line. Again, Merck need not enjoy a high financial return on these investments to realize their strategic benefits.

But enabling investments have their limits, too. These vehicles will be justified only if they can capture a substantial portion of the market growth they stimulate. When Intel grows its ecosystem, it is also growing the market for competitors like Advanced Micro Devices. Because Intel's market position is strong, it can expect to realize most of the increased demand in the market. Intel's smaller rival AMD, by contrast, could not afford to create demand in a similar fashion because it would not capture enough of the increase to justify its investments.

Emergent Investments

A company makes these kinds of investments in start-ups that have tight links to its operating capabilities but that offer little to enhance its current strategy. Nevertheless, if the business environment shifts or if a company's strategy changes, such a new venture might suddenly become strategically valuable. This gives it an optionlike strategic upside beyond whatever financial returns it generates. For example, a company may sense an opportunity in a strategic "whitespace"—a new market with a new set of customers. Exploring the potential of such a market is often difficult for a company focused on serving its current market. Investing in a start-up willing and able to enter this uncharted territory—selling real products to real customers—provides information that could never be gleaned from the hypothetical questions of a market research survey. If the market seems to hold potential, the investing company may choose to shift its course.

Thus, while the immediate benefits, if any, of such investments are financial, the ultimate return may result from exercising the strategic option. In that sense, emergent investments complement the benefits of driving investments, which are designed only to further the company's current strategy.

A strong operational link between a company and its start-up can take various forms. It may mean sharing technology, as with the start-ups spun off from Lucent Technologies. (See the sidebar "Lucent Hedges Its Bets.") Lucent also sometimes shares production facilities and sales channels with the newly independent ventures, improving the efficiency of its own production and distribution operations by allowing them to run at a higher capacity.

Or the links might take the form of product use. In 1997, Intel invested in a start-up called Berkeley Networks. Berkeley used existing Intel processors to make low-cost switches and routers for communications networks—a new market for Intel products. At the time, Intel was happy to see its products used in this rather novel way. But with little likelihood that Berkeley's business would create much incremental demand for its products and no other apparent strategic upside for itself, Intel saw the investment as primarily a financial one.

As Intel performed its due diligence on its investment, though, it began to see the outlines of a possible strategy shift, one that might result in the widespread use of its products in network switches. Initially, this view was controversial within the company: At the time, Intel's communications business was focused on making products (for example, network interface cards for PC networks) that were compatible with the prevailing Ethernet network standard. Since the Berkeley approach competed with the Ethernet standard, Intel had to balance the benefits of promoting a new network architecture that used Intel's core Pentium products against the threat that the Berkeley-inspired architecture posed to Ethernet networks. After some sharp, internal disagreements—and after the value of Berkeley Networks began to grow—Intel decided to adapt its strategy to pursue this opportunity, culminating in the Intel Internet Exchange Architecture, launched in 1999. The investment in Berkeley Networks helped Intel identify a promising opportunity more quickly than it might have otherwise.

Of course, many options never become valuable, and many emergent investments will never be important to an organization's strategy. It is important to let these options lapse and settle for whatever financial returns have been earned. Thus, managing these investments requires

Lucent Hedges Its Bets

A good example of an emergent investments strategy—in which a company invests in external startups that are closely linked to its operating capabilities but not to its current strategy—involves a company's putting money into a technology it actually developed. Lucent's New Ventures Group (which is separate from Lucent's external VC arm, Lucent Venture Partners) is charged with identifying underutilized technologies within the company's Bell Labs and spinning off the most promising of them as independent start-up companies. Lucent then invests in those companies, typically on its own in the first round of financing but with other investors later on. The company is mainly looking for a profitable return on these investments. But the investments may also hold the potential for significant future strategic returns.

Indeed, three of the more than 30 technology spin-offs created so far by the New Ventures Group have been reacquired by Lucent. Ultimately, those technologies were deemed strategically valuable to the company, either because the market had changed or because the technology had progressed further than had been expected. One such spin-off is Lucent Digital Video, which created analog-to-digital converters that enable audio and video content to move on analog networks. After the New Ventures Group spun out this business, Lucent began winning new business by selling its own equipment in combination with the new company's products. It soon became clear that digital technology would unlock significant growth for Lucent, so it chose to reacquire the company. If the New Ventures Group had not created and financed this spin-off, this key strategic benefit might not have become apparent.

That's because the New Ventures Group forces technology out of the lab. Whenever the group identifies a candidate technology for spin-off, a countdown starts within Lucent's business units. Within the limited time frame, if one of the units doesn't commit to using the technology, the New Ventures Group gets the opportunity to spin it off. Thus, the technology, instead of stagnating or dying on the shelf, actually gets used—in a new venture if not in one of Lucent's business units.

The Corporation as Money Manager

One corporate best practice in the 1960s and 1970s involved identifying diversification opportunities in order to smooth out volatility in revenue and profits. Companies thought that this practice would appeal to shareholders and would command higher stock prices. But modern financial portfolio theory pointed out a critical flaw in this thinking: Shareholders could diversify their own portfolios and did not need corporations to do it for them. Indeed, such diversification is no longer viewed as a positive benefit for shareholders, and many conglomerates actually trade at a diversification discount rather than at a premium.

A similar situation arises in what we call passive corporate VC investing. These investments are uncoupled from the corporation's strategy and its operating capabilities and are justified largely by the prospect of financial gains. But shareholders have plenty of other ways to invest in early-stage companies and can seek such prospective gains on their own, without assistance from a corporate VC program. Companies can justify VC investments if they add value for their shareholders in ways that the shareholders cannot do themselves. But although companies might argue that their core businesses give them superior knowledge of technologies and markets and thus advantages over other investors in identifying start-ups likely to deliver healthy financial returns, evidence of this is scarce.

balancing financial discipline with strategic potential. Many companies err by throwing good money after bad. Partnering with private VC funds, and following their lead, is one way to impose financial discipline on the process.

Passive Investments

In this mode of VC investment, the ventures are not connected to the corporation's own strategy and are only loosely linked to the corporation's operational capabilities. Consequently, the corporation lacks the means to actively advance its own business through these investments. And despite the perception of some companies that they enjoy technology or market knowledge that gives them advantages over other investors, the recent flight of corporate VC suggests otherwise. Thus, in passive venturing, a corporation is just another investor subject to the vagaries of financial returns in the private equity market. Indeed, this type of investing is arguably a misuse of shareholders' funds. (For a fuller discussion, see the sidebar "The Corporation as Money Manager.")

For example, Dell Ventures poured money into ventures that had only tangential connections with Dell's own strategy. Yes, these ventures would have increased demand for personal computers and servers if they had succeeded, but Dell's market share was not high enough to allow it to capture much of the gain from that increased demand. When the value of its investments collapsed last year, no potential strategic benefit remained—as would have been the case with an emergent investment—to compensate for the financial losses.

INVESTMENTS FOR ALL SEASONS

Seen in this light, it is not surprising that corporate VC investors—many of which fit the description of passive investors—tend to head for the exits when the markets turn down. Similarly, emergent investments are more appropriate when the economy is booming and the likelihood of solid financial returns offsets the uncertainty of any strategic benefit.

By contrast, enabling and driving investments have more staying power. Granted, enabling investments may retreat somewhat in difficult times. When financial returns are down, enabling investments become more expensive and thus less attractive when compared with other, more conventional, business development mechanisms—such as advertising or promotional expenses—that a company can use to further its strategy. But as the decisions by companies such as Intel and Merck indicate, enabling investments can hold long-term benefits.

And low financial returns ought to have little impact on driving investments. After all, these investments are not justified by their financial returns but rather by their strong potential to positively affect the company's own business. As the decisions by companies such as Microsoft suggest, a decrease in the rate of return on VC investments shouldn't undermine that rationale.

Thus, while corporate VC investments have generated decidedly uneven financial returns, they should not be judged primarily on that basis. They should be thought of as important ways for a company to fuel the growth of its business. Driving, enabling, and emergent investments can, in different ways, each foster the growth of a company's current businesses; emergent investments can identify and spark the growth of future businesses. (The exhibit "Paths to Growth" shows six ways the different kinds of corporate VC investments can generate growth.)

Paths to Growth

A corporation's investments in external start-up companies can advance its own growth on a number of strategic fronts.

Growing Your Current Businesses

	Investment	Type	Example
Promoting a standard	In start-ups making products and services that promote the adoption of a technology standard you own or are backing	Driving	Microsoft's investment in companies supporting .Net, its Internet services architecture
Stimulating demand	In start-ups developing complementary products and services that increase demand for your own	Enabling	Intel's investment in companies whose products require its Pentium processor
Leveraging underutilized technology	In companies you have spun off in order to commercialize an unused and nonstrategic technology	Emergent	Lucent's investment in companies built around a technology that Lucent deems a misfit with its current strategy

Growing Your Future Businesses

	Investment	Type	Example
Experimenting with new capabilities	In ventures developing interesting new business processes unrelated to or possibly in conflict with your current ones	Emergent	Cisco's investment in communications technologies that it later acquires and deploys internally
Developing a backup technology	In companies developing alternative technologies, as hedges against your current technology direction	Emergent	Intel's investment in a company developing a networking technology that could supplant one that Intel participates in
Exploring strategic whitespace	In companies serving customers in new markets, thereby providing an indicator of those markets' potential	Emergent	Panasonic's investment in start-ups pursuing the convergence of home computing and entertainment

Regardless of whether growth is desired in present or future businesses, a company needs a clear-eyed view of its strategy and its operational capabilities. It needs the discipline to build its investment portfolio with these parameters in mind. And it needs to manage its investments to capture the latent strategic benefits in its portfolio rather than chasing the evanescent promise of high financial returns in the venture capital market. If it follows these precepts, a company's VC investments will survive during general downturns in venture capital investment and will ultimately generate valuable growth for its shareholders.

LINKING NEW TECHNOLOGY AND NOVEL CUSTOMER NEEDS

CASE III-5

Innovation at 3M Corporation

Stefan Thomke and Ashok Nimgade

On the evening of October 23, 1997, Rita Shor, senior product specialist at 3M, looked across the conference room at her team from the Medical-Surgical Markets Division. She wondered when to draw to a close the intense ongoing debate on the nature of the team's recommendations to the Health Care Unit's senior management. A hand-picked group of talented individuals, the team had embarked on a new method for understanding customer needs, called Lead User Research. But this initiative to introduce leading-edge market research methods into 3M's legendary innovation process had now grown into a revolutionary series of recommendations that threatened to rip apart the division.

While senior management wanted the Lead User team to execute a manageable project involving surgical draping material to protect surgery patients from infections, the team now wanted to rewrite the entire business unit's strategy statement to also include more proactive products or services that would permit the *upstream containment*

of infectious agents such as germs. This went against the incrementalist approach that for so long had pervaded 3M. After all, as Mary Sonnack, division scientist and an internal 3M consultant on the new Lead User methodology, noted, "3M gets so much revenue from incremental products . . . like a blue Post-it note instead of just a yellow one."

Outside the window, the late autumn breeze rippled through the tall Minnesota grass—a seasonal reminder that it had been a year since the group first embarked on the Lead User process (see Exhibit 1). The method, including training, had called for fewer than six months to be dedicated to the entire process. But the lengthy commitment from participants as well as 3M senior management might just pay off if it took the Medical-Surgical Markets Division from a stagnating business to a reinvigorated enterprise. Clearly, however, unless the team came up with successful product ideas and effective positioning, the new methodology for product innovation would die with the winter frost. And so might the entire business unit.

HISTORY OF 3M CORPORATION[1]

In 1902, on the banks of Lake Superior, five investors got together to excavate what they thought was high-quality corundum, a mineral almost as hard as diamond that

[1] Much of the information on 3M history comes from G. C. Nicholson, "Keeping Innovation Alive," *Research-Technology Management* 41, no. 3 (May/June 1998), pp. 34–40, and *3M Annual Report, 1998.*

EXHIBIT 1   Important Milestones

1902	Minnesota Mining and Manufacturing founded.
1948	3M Steri-Drape® Surgical Drape introduced.
1961	Medical Products Division, the first 3M division dedicated solely to health care, founded.
1993	
May	MIT Professor Eric von Hippel contacts Mary Sonnack to see if 3M would help test Lead User methodology. Sonnack would spend the entire next year at MIT to learn and help formalize the Lead User methodology and initiate the involvement of psychologist Joan Churchill in the later part of the year.
1996	
June	Rita Shor given task of finding breakthrough products for Medical-Surgical Markets Division. Shor approaches Mary Sonnack after hearing Sonnack lecture internally at 3M about Lead User methodology.
September–October	Stage 1 of Medical-Surgical Markets Division Lead User project starts. Shor's product development team meets with Mary Sonnack.
End of October	Stage 2 starts.
December	Stage 3 starts. The product development team decides to search internationally for breakthrough ideas on surgical draping.
1997	
January–March	Medical-Surgical Markets Division team visits South America and Asia for breakthrough ideas on surgical draping.
April	Lead user meetings/workshops result in several concepts. Team starts search for appropriate lead users.
June–July	New management in Medical-Surgical Markets Division seeks justification for Lead User process and wants accelerated outcome. The team convinces new management to maintain support. Stage 4 starts.
August	Large 2.5-day Lead User workshop with 11 outside experts and 11 3M insiders.
October 27	Scheduled date for Medical-Surgical Markets Division team's presentation to management concerning recommendations generated from Lead User process.
November	Medical-Surgical Markets Division management's deadline for resource allocation for product concepts generated from Lead User process.

manufacturers used for producing abrasives. What they dug up under the banner of the Minnesota Mining and Manufacturing Company, however, turned out low-grade and worthless. After filling one $20 order, the venture folded up its mining operations and turned instead to the sandpaper business. Here, disaster struck again: the abrasives they had imported from Spain refused to stick to the sandpaper.

Research and development (R&D) then at 3M, as the company became known, took place in a primitive laboratory so small the sole technician had to back out to let the boss in. The young technician figured out the problem after plunging some sandpaper into water and noting an oil slick. Follow-up investigations revealed that during shipment from Spain, an ocean storm had caused olive oil to leak into the abrasive material. This insight allowed for fixing the sandpaper problem while also establishing the emphasis on technology and innovativeness at 3M.

By 1916, survival assured, the company started paying stock dividends. The firm, now headquartered in St. Paul,

Minnesota, initially stayed close to abrasives, developing the world's first waterproof sandpaper in the early 1920s. 3M technicians began bypassing purchasing agents in order to better understand product needs. Often, they walked into factories and workplaces and talked directly to workers, an unheard of practice that yielded unexpected dividends.

While visiting an autobody shop in the 1920s, for instance, Richard Drew, a young lab assistant, heard a torrent of screams and curses. Workers had apparently just ruined a two-tone paint job when paint peeled away as they removed glued newspaper strips used as masking materials. Back in the lab, while working with a new and crinkly backing material for sandpaper, Drew came up with the idea that would provide the world with masking tape. To spend the long hours needed to perfect the new tape, however, he had ignored a direct order from the company head to put all his efforts into improving a preexisting product. Drew's success helped spawn the legend of the subversive 3M inventor and the 3M aphorism: "It's better to seek forgiveness than to ask for permission." It also helped inspire a "get out of the way" attitude on the part of management toward product developers. At the same time, Drew had opened up another "core technology" for 3M. A few years later, in fact, Drew went on to also invent Scotch® brand cellophane tape, which would help the company prosper through the Great Depression.

Over the decades, 3M enjoyed national and global growth as well as a reputation for remaining a "hothouse" of innovation. "We'll make any damn thing we can make money on," stated a past 3M president, Richard Carlton.[2] According to the *International Directory of Company Histories:*

> Observers and outsiders frequently describe 3M in terms approaching awe. 3M earns such respect because of its improbable, almost defiantly non-corporate nature. The company is gigantic, yet it is as innovative and as full of growth potential as though it were a small venture.[3]

3M inventors did not share directly in product royalties; rather, the firm hoped that individual love for discovery would drive innovation. 3M sought to encourage innovation through a variety of means, including awards for innovation as well as in-house grants for innovative projects. The company also allowed all staff to spend 15 percent of their time to explore new ideas outside of assigned responsibilities. Post-it® Notes were developed on the 15 percent time scheme by 3M inventor Art Fry, who first used a weak adhesive to produce convenient hymnal markers for his music recitals.

3M also employed a "dual ladder" approach that allowed senior, technically inclined individuals with attractive career opportunities to advance, without having to switch to management. In addition, the company held internal showcases for products and ideas to help encourage interdepartmental cross-pollination, or "bootlegging" of discoveries. As a result of these steps, 3M employees tended not to move to other companies.

The 3M model of expansion involved splintering off decentralized units based on new key product areas that were sufficiently different from prior key technologies. The first core technology from the 1920s had been adhesives and sandpaper. By the late 1990s, however, over 30 key technologies existed at 3M. Much market growth for 3M also came from finding new twists to existing product platforms: for instance, digital "Post-it Software

Notes," or the use of 3M's Thinsulate®, first introduced in 1978 for apparel, in reducing sound in automobiles.

In the 1990s, 3M operated with four objectives: producing 30 percent of sales from products that did not exist four years earlier—an attempt to accelerate away from the incrementalism that had served as an engine for growth in the past few decades; greater than 10 percent annual growth in earnings per share; greater than 27 percent return on capital employed; and 20–25 percent return on equity. It also sought to change the mix of new products to emphasize products truly new to the world, instead of line extensions, which typically had provided two out of three new product sales dollars. By 1997, completely new products produced two out of three sales dollars.

To achieve high rates of innovation 3M placed a heavy emphasis on R&D. In 1997, it employed 4,500 scientists, engineers, and technicians in the United States, and another 2,000 overseas. On average, 3M spent 6.5–7.0 cents of every sales dollar on laboratory-based R&D, which amounted to just over $1 billion in 1997—not including process engineering and quality control expenses. In 1997, 3M companies operated in more than 60 countries, and overseas businesses generated half of the firm's $15.07 billion in revenue and half of its $2.7 billion in operating income. 3M employed 75,000 workers, of whom 36,000 were outside the United States. (See Exhibits 2 and 3.)

The Medical Products Division, the first 3M division dedicated solely to health care, was founded in 1961. A decade later, the Health Care Group at 3M provided an umbrella for all health-related product divisions, including the Medical-Surgical Markets Division. By 1997, 3M could claim over 10,000 health-related products, ranging from surgical drapes to dental fillings to respirators to software. By 1994, Health Care sales topped $2 billion.[4]

Innovation at 3M in the 1990s

Product teams at 3M typically involved skunk works teams primarily comprising technical individuals; teams also involved process engineers to help ensure that the particular product under development could be efficiently made. These engineers also provided teams with feedback about 3M's manufacturing capabilities. The entire team faced no risk if an idea flopped—indeed, there might even be a celebration. In case of failures, members of disbanded teams could go on to other projects. Although failures were often celebrated, each technical person's

---

[2] *International Directory of Company Histories,* vol. 1 (Chicago/London: St. James Press, 1988), p. 499.
[3] Ibid.

[4] 3M brochure entitled "3M Health Care," 1996.

EXHIBIT 2 Selected 3M Financial Data (Dollars in Millions, except per Share Data)

	1995	1996	1997
Sales	$13,460	$14,236	$15,070
Cost of goods sold	6,861	7,216	7,710
Gross profit	6,599	7,020	7,360
Selling, general, and administrative expense	3,440	3,646	3,815
Depreciation, depletion, and amortization	859	883	870
Operating profit	2,300	2,491	2,675
Net income (after taxes)	$976	$1,526	$2,121
Other Data:			
EPS (primary)—excluding extra items and discontinued operations	3.11	3.63	5.14
Dividends per share	1.88	1.92	2.12
ROA (%)	9%	11%	16%
ROE (%)	19%	24%	36%
Market value	27,791	34,597	33,121
R&D expenses	883	947	

Source: 3M financial reports.

EXHIBIT 3 3M Revenue by Classes of Products/Services (Dollars in Millions)

	1995	1996	1997E	1998E
Tape products	$ 2,042	$ 2,096	$ 2,215	$ 2,370
Abrasive products	1,220	1,270	1,375	1,510
Automotive and chemical products	1,328	1,460	1,620	1,800
Connecting and insulating products	1,470	1,564	1,688	1,850
Consumer and office products	2,272	2,460	2,672	2,925
Health care products	2,221	2,356	2,545	2,775
Safety and personal care products	1,220	1,301	1,385	1,505
All other products	1,687	1,729	1,835	1,980
Total	$13,460	$14,236	$15,335	$16,715

Source: R. P. Curran, "Minnesota Mining & Manufacturing Co.—Company Report," *Merrill Lynch Capital Markets*, New York, July 11, 1997.

output over one or two years would be evaluated as a whole. The 3M mythology allowed for technical employees to take matters in their own hands—as exemplified by the Post-it notes story.

Marketing input traditionally came from current customers and sales representatives. Product developers focused on finding new angles or twists on early trends. At the same time, few market researchers worked at 3M; only one market researcher served 900 engineers. Instead, the firm hired out for market research reports from smaller market research firms. To identify market needs and trends, 3M product developers in the health care unit, for instance, utilized several tools:

• Data from sales representatives with daily contact with physicians or registered nurses.

• Focus groups: for example, one business unit within the Medical-Surgical Division would gather some 30 nurses biannually from across the nation in a room for obtaining reactions to proposed products.
• Customer evaluations of currently marketed products.
• Site visits by 3M scientists and technologists to observe physicians and nurses at work, with the intent to identify unforeseen needs.
• Data on risk factors for diseases.

Several disadvantages to these methods had become apparent over the years. A major disadvantage was that the information obtained was not necessarily proprietary. Anyone, for example, could open up a medical textbook to find key risk factors for diseases. Attempts to seek more proprietary information through, say, focus groups provided virtually no clue about market needs some 5 to 10 years down the road. While visiting customers provided an opportunity for Thomas Edison–type "innovations by serendipity," customers were somewhat blind about their own needs, and thus could not provide clues about developing revolutionary products.

Even these customer visits, although traditionally a part of 3M, had often become deemphasized during the past few decades of successful growth through incremental innovation. This often led to situations where, as Mary Sonnack, division scientist and 3M internal consultant, pointed out: "Typically, one or two product developers or even marketers think of a product, then they throw it over the wall to the commercializers." As a result, thousands of 3M product concepts and inventions awaited markets and languished on drawing boards and R&D labs.

The Medical-Surgical Markets Division

Over the past century, a few medical pioneers, including Benjamin Lister and Florence Nightingale, had demonstrated that the cleanliness of health care providers and the hospital environment could reduce the rate of new infections in patients. Previously, patients died on account of the hospital nearly as much as because of what put them there in the first place. It took several decades, however, for the pendulum to swing within the medical establishment from ridiculing such a stress on sanitation to mandating high standards of hygiene among health professionals. As a result, surgeons and attending staff now scrubbed with an almost ritualistic devotion using antiseptic detergents and donned sterile clothing and foot covers before entering operating rooms.

What was being operated upon was also antiseptically prepared, or "prepped," for surgery. Thus, operating teams carefully established "sterile fields" on the skin around the pertinent area, freeing it from microbial contamination. A key part of this process involved use of surgical drapes, which served to isolate the "field of surgery" from all other potential sources of infection, including the rest of the patient's body, the operating table, the anesthesiologist's equipment, and all members of the surgical team. But the diversity of the microbial world constantly challenged this artificial fortress. As a result, medical personnel had to remain vigilant about catheters and tubes along which agents of infections could migrate into the patient.

From midcentury on, surgical operating rooms became a product developer's dream come true. Product categories dedicated to preserving sterility included razors and clippers for shaving hair, presurgical soaps for scrubbing hands, sterile surgical gloves and masks, drapes,

handwashes, antibiotics, lavages for washing away excess blood in a sterile fashion, sponges with or without handles, antiseptic solutions, and dressings.

The surgical drapes business unit within the Medical-Surgical Division focused largely on reducing infections from the skin through surgical drapes and surgical prepping. For 3M, the drape business represented one extension of 3M masking tape inventor Richard Drew's attempts to meet the needs of autobody workshops. By the mid-1990s, 3M was highly penetrated in one niche of surgical drapes which brought the company over $100 million in yearly sales. But sales in the United States had limited growth remaining in these market niches. Overseas markets were limited by the high cost of 3M products, when converted into local currencies.

Most surgical drape products were developed using the equivalent of one full-time product developer and generated about $1 million in sales each. Occasionally, a $1- to $20 million product would come along, but these big products were becoming fewer and fewer. Typically, it would take about two years to get a surgical drape product out from initial product conception to market. In the best case, this could be shortened to a year; in worse cases, it could take up to four years.

The surgical drapes section of the Medical-Surgical Markets Division had discovered the hard way that technological excellence by itself meant little. In the early 1990s, for instance, the division had spent three years developing a virus-proof gown that would let water vapor but not viruses pass through the fabric through microscopic pinholes. This manufacturing feat, however, came in just as managed care was taking hold. Although customers loved the fabric, the 10–15 percent price premium banished the product into a tiny niche in the European market.

By 1996, the business unit had gone almost a decade with only one successful product. Senior management charged Rita Shor with the mandate of developing a breakthrough product within the existing business strategy. She was assigned to the task not only because of her seniority, having been at the division 11 years, but also because she was considered creative and a consensus builder.

LEAD USER RESEARCH AT 3M'S MEDICAL-SURGICAL MARKETS DIVISION

Shor realized, at the outset, that 3M's traditional methods for understanding customer and market needs would not suffice. Market research reports provided an abundance of data but contained little useful information for conceptualizing a breakthrough product. She recalled, however, an in-house lecture given a few weeks before by Mary Sonnack, a 3M division scientist and consultant who had become increasingly involved with new product development using a new methodology termed *Lead User research,* which she had studied at the Massachusetts Institute of Technology (MIT). Shor wondered if this might provide the key to a breakthrough product.

The premise of this novel methodology was that certain consumers experienced needs ahead of other consumers and that some of the former would seek to innovate on their own. By tapping the expertise of these "lead users," manufacturers could find invaluable sources of innovation. Lead users had often already created innovations to solve their own leading-edge needs—familiar examples were "white-out" (Liquid Paper), invented by a secretary for correcting typographical mistakes, and the sports drink Gatorade, developed in Florida with invaluable input from athletes.

3M's experience with traditional market research had been disappointing; it had not led to the kinds of innovations senior management wanted for the marketplace. As Chuck Harstad, former vice president of the Commercial and Office Supply Division and now vice president of Corporate Marketing, recalled:

> At the end of the day, we didn't learn anything from our market research department. 3M had to find new ways to identify leading-edge customer needs and develop concepts for breakthrough products and services. Traditional market research methods couldn't deliver the goods. And product developers would not assume ownership for understanding customer needs because they considered that to be the responsibility of market researchers. So we ended up eliminating the market research department to learn about customer needs!

Sonnack, under mandate from Harstad to seek out newer and better customer-focused product development processes, thought that Lead User research fit well with 3M's customer-focused philosophy (see Exhibit 4). In 1994, she began an unusual year-long stay at MIT to study with Professor Eric von Hippel, who had pioneered Lead User research. For von Hippel, the collaboration represented a way to develop a step-by-step methodology for practitioners and seek further validation of Lead User concepts. Since he had not charted out a how-to manual, he started this process with the help of Sonnack and Minnesota organizational psychologist Joan Churchill.

One of Sonnack's and Churchill's goals was to disseminate the Lead User process throughout 3M. Support for the new methodology existed at high levels within the company. William Coyne, 3M's head of research and de-

velopment, for instance, was fairly critical of the strategic planning process because he felt that "traditional strategic planning does not leave enough room for innovation. And innovation cannot be planned ahead of time." This view did not go unchallenged within 3M's senior management and represented a radical departure from the incrementalist approach to innovation. "Strategic planning looks in the rearview mirror and cannot keep up with the rate of change in today's markets," added Coyne. "We need to understand leading-edge customer needs to change the basis of competition." Widespread adoption of the Lead User process could help get 3M back to its roots of working more closely with customers and understanding such market needs.

Through one of Sonnack's in-house lectures, Shor first heard about the new methodology. In June of 1996, she telephoned Sonnack to say:

> Our business unit has been going nowhere. While we are number one in the surgical drapes market niche, and pull in over a hundred million in yearly sales, we are stagnating. We need to find new customer needs we haven't thought of before. If we don't bring in radically new ways of looking for products, upper management may have little choice but to sell off the business.

At the time, Sonnack's and Churchill's in-house consulting schedule was crowded. But Shor's degree of commitment appeared to match Sonnack's enthusiasm for the new methodology, and the two women agreed to meet. Were the Medical-Surgical Markets Division to focus product development based on the Lead User method it would become one of the first divisions at 3M to do so. During their preliminary meeting, Sonnack warned Shor about the need for high-level commitment from both team members and their management.

Selling the new approach to senior management would use much of Shor's time and efforts. At first, senior management had balked at such a large commitment. But Shor pointed out that an adequate human resources commitment to the new methodology might prove more cost-effective than having 10–15 people working disjointedly. She tactfully reminded management that far more human resources were often redeployed for attacking technical problems that developed later in the product development process: "3M can pour a hundred thousand dollars at the drop of a hat for a production problem late in the product development process, but it is not used to doing so for such an early stage." Finally, however, Shor obtained support from her senior management to assemble a product innovation team on the basis of creativity and enthusiasm from the Medical-Surgical Markets Division.

EXHIBIT 4 Lead User Research Methodology

If the outer appearance of things matched their inner nature, there would be no point to science.

—Galileo

The Lead User method, pioneered by Professor Eric von Hippel of the Massachusetts Institute of Technology (MIT), provides a means to unearth product development opportunities that are not immediately obvious by traditional methods. It allows for accurately forecasting market opportunities by tapping the expertise and experience base of "lead users," the individuals or firms that experience needs *ahead* of the market segment in which they operate. Lead users may lead in either the *target* or *analogous* markets. Some lead users may be involved with just one or more of the important *attributes* of the problems faced by users in the target market.

Ideally, Lead User methods allow new product development to flow out of a sensitive understanding of product features that will matter most to customers several years later. Specific benefits of Lead User methods include: richer and more reliable information on the needs of emerging customer needs, better products and service concepts since these come out of better data on quality needs, and acceleration of the product and service development process.

These benefits, however, come only after substantial commitment of resources on the part of the sponsoring firm. Research indicates that three elements remain necessary for success in the Lead User process: *supportive management*, use of *a cross-disciplinary team of highly skilled people*, and a clear *understanding of the principles of Lead User research*.

Success of the study relies heavily on selecting a talented core team. Typically, the team consists of four to six people from marketing and technical departments, with one member serving as project leader. These team members typically spend 12 to 15 hours per week for the entire project on a Lead User project. This high level of immersion fosters creative thought and sustains project momentum.

Lead User projects typically take five or six months, in which time the four to six people involved spend up to a third of their time on the project. Conducting a Lead User study involves four stages, as described below, with typical time commitments provided in parentheses:

- *Stage I: Project Planning (4–6 weeks)* In this "homework," or scouting, phase of the study, the team identifies the types of markets and new products of interest, and the desired level of innovation. For instance, does the company seek a "breakthrough" product or does it wish to merely extend current product or service lines? At the same time, the team identifies key business constraints. The team typically starts Stage I by informally interviewing industry experts, including customers, suppliers, and internal company managers, to get a feel for current trends and market needs. This lays the groundwork for developing strategies for future data collection and for helping focus on key market trends.

- *Stage II: Trends/Needs Identification (5–6 weeks)* The ultimate goal of this stage is to select a specific need-related trend(s) to focus upon for the remainder of the study. Typically a four-day team workshop kicks off this stage. In this workshop, members digest the information collected during Stage I to get a sense of the "conventional wisdom" relating to trends and

market needs. Thereafter, the focus shifts to finding top experts, through querying experts, telephone "networking," scanning literature, and consulting with in-house colleagues. Thereafter, telephone interviews can start. Three or four weeks into Stage II, the team generally develops a good understanding of major trends and is now positioned for the vital task of "framing" the customer need that can be addressed by a new product or service. These initial ideas are reworked and refined throughout this stage.

- *Stage III: Preliminary Concept Generation (5–6 weeks)* In this stage, the group acquires a more precise understanding of the needs it has selected as the area of focus. The team begins to generate preliminary concepts involving ideal attributes and features that will best meet customer needs. The team also seeks to informally assess business potential for the product or service being conceptualized. The team continues interviewing lead user experts for technical knowledge that pertains to concept generation. Toward the end of Stage III, the team meets with key managers involved with implementing concepts after completion of the entire project to confirm that identified needs and initial concepts fit well with important business interests.

- *Stage IV: Final Concept Generation (5–6 weeks)* In this stage, the team takes the preliminary concept developed in Stage III toward completion. Participants in this stage seek to ensure that all possible solutions have been explored. Activity in Stage IV centers around a 1- to 2-day Lead User workshop with invited lead users to improve and add to the preliminary concepts. Typically, 15–18 people attend this workshop, of which a third may come from the project team and from in-house technical or marketing divisions. In these workshops, subgroups consisting of in-house personnel as well as invited experts discuss independent parts of the problem to generate alternative product concepts. Thereafter, the entire group evaluates the concepts in terms of technical feasibility, market appeal, and management priorities. Finally, the entire group arrives at consensus on the most commercially promising concepts and develops recommendations for further steps to refine them.

After the workshop, the team refines the preliminary concept on the basis of knowledge gained from the workshop. At a meeting with managers, the team presents the proposed products or services, covering design principles. The team comes prepared with solid evidence about why customers would be willing to pay for them. For any concept chosen for commercialization, at least one member of the Lead User team should remain involved in further steps needed to take the concept to market. This helps fully leverage the vast body of knowledge captured through the Lead User method.

While Lead User methodology stresses qualitative probing of the right questions over the traditional focus on quantifiable questions, ongoing studies seek to compare performance of the new method with traditional methods.

Source: This section draws from E. von Hippel, J. Churchill, M. Sonnack, *Breakthrough Products and Services with Lead User Research* (Cambridge, Mass. and Minneapolis, Minn.: Lead User Concepts, Inc., 1998, Oxford University Press). For a detailed discussion and description of Lead User research, see also S. Thomke and A. Nimgade, *"Note on Lead User Research,"* Harvard Business School Case No. 669-014.

In a few weeks she was able to assemble an impressive interdisciplinary team.[5]

All team members were to commit half their time to the project. But as it turned out, several team members found that their managers still expected them to perform most of their traditional duties. As a result, much of the team work took place on Saturdays or outside the office at restaurants. The team sought in a disciplined manner to follow a project schedule with four stages prescribed by the Lead User research methodology (see Exhibit 4).

Stage I: Project Planning (~1.5 months at 3M)

Stage I goals: In this "homework," or scouting, stage of the study, which typically lasted 4–6 weeks, teams identified the types of markets and new products of interest, and the desired level of innovation.

In September of 1996, as the first stage started, Sonnack and Churchill sat in on Shor's early Lead User team meetings to focus the process. The two coleaders probed the team with questions like, "What do you know about this market . . . what don't you know?" "How about reimbursement policies?" "How important is the skin itself as a source of infection?" The team met for four hours each week in a conference room lined with some 20 flip charts so that ideas could be jotted down quickly. Between meetings, team members would search the Internet, literature, and their people network for information on relevant topics. Through this process, the team built up an invaluable database of information. For instance, it learned that 30 percent of infections occurred from the patient's own skin—a figure that highlighted the need for good surgical drapes.

Stage II: Trends/Needs Identification (~1.5 months at 3M)

Stage II goals: The ultimate goal of this stage, which typically lasted 5–6 weeks, was to select a specific need-related trend(s) to focus upon for the remainder of the study. Typically a four-day team workshop kicked off this stage.

The 3M team started Stage II with a five-day workshop intended to make sense of all the information gathered in Stage I. Through the workshop, which marked the culmination of all weekly meetings thus far, the team developed the following parameters for a breakthrough product: It should conform to the body, prove more effective than current products, and be easy to apply and remove.

The team, by now, had reached a stage where secondary literature could no longer add much of value. The second half of the workshop provided a turning point for the next phase of research: identifying appropriate expertise residing in experts at the leading-edge of practice. The team undertook intensive group brainstorming about identifying appropriate experts to contact for more ideas and information from analogous areas of product development. Towards this end, workshop leaders encouraged participants to "step outside the box" because the most logical person might not prove the most appropriate expert. Through the rest of this stage, team members collected information from these identified experts.

Team members started talking over the telephone to a wide range of experts ranging from veterinary sciences to medics from the U.S. Mobile Army Surgical Hospital (MASH) unit in Bosnia. The MASH unit, discovered by team coleader John Pournoor, had been considered a potential lead user because of its needs for portable, inexpensive, and flexible products. Product flexibility would ideally allow for low inventory, a prime consideration for a mobile medical unit. Hospitals, in contrast, could stock dozens of different product sizes and types. Interestingly, the MASH physicians did not fully realize their own need for manageable inventories since they focused on problems of communications, computerization, and telemedicine in the field; thus, they were not the lead users the team was looking for.

Although the MASH physicians would not be able to collaborate more intimately with the 3M Medical-Surgical Markets Division, this stage turned up other experts—from the theater makeup business to veterinary sciences to oceanographers—who would contribute to later stages.

Stage III at 3M: Preliminary Concept Generation (~6 months)

Stage III Goals: In this stage, which typically lasted 4–8 months, lead user groups acquired a more precise understanding of market needs in the selected areas of focus. The teams began to generate preliminary concepts involving ideal attributes and features that would best meet customer needs.

By casting a wide net for product concepts, the division's business unit rapidly realized it knew precious little about the needs of customers outside the developed world. While sanitary conditions in the developed world had long since moved infectious disease down the roster of major killers (below causes such as cardiovascular dis-

---

[5] The Medical-Surgical Markets Division (MSMD) team included: Rita Shor, senior product specialist; Susan Hiestand, business manager with a marketing background; John Pournoor, polymer chemist; Matt Scholz, senior research specialist; Maurice Kuypers, market development supervisor; and Mark Johnson, process development specialist, Medical Products Resource Division.

ease and cancer), in the developing world infectious diseases were still major killers. If 3M hoped to find a breakthrough infection control product here, however, the team quickly realized it should visit several emerging market sites. The majority of new growth opportunities might lie here, even though disposable products were not popular or affordable.

Through December and January 1997, the team broke up into groups of two and traveled to hospitals in South America and Asia. Shor and Pournoor visited Malaysia, Korea, Indonesia, and India. This was the first time the Medical-Surgical Markets Division had sent product developers, rather than marketers, to visit potential customers. It allowed the 3M team members to see how operating room personnel coped with infection challenges of extreme environments. According to Shor:

> While we saw some excellent, world-class hospitals in India, we also observed hospitals in which surgeons operated barefoot and even we visitors had to take off our shoes. For surgical field preparation, these teams used cloth (often with holes) that provided no resistance to fluids migrating to the wound itself! Sometimes, surgeons would use pieces of raincoat to cover over the patient's groin and other dirtier areas to keep microbes from migrating. Some surgeons used antibiotics wholesale, since these seemed cheaper to them than disposable drapes. . . . Often, only in side-conversations would surgeons reveal that surgical infection was a problem. We also quickly realized that many other nations did not care about labor-savings from our products. Labor was inexpensive and unlikely to be replaced or reduced. As a result, we realized we should not overengineer our products for these markets.

The international fact-finding trips lengthened the expected duration of Stage III almost fourfold. While they yielded invaluable information about extreme environments and international market needs, they turned up no experts on lead use in terms of product efficacy.

With an eye toward bringing the project to a useful culmination, individual team members, under Sonnack's and Churchill's guidance, continued searching for appropriate lead users that might actually help develop product concepts. Team members continued talking with customers, academics, and industry experts, as well as searching through refereed journals and the Internet. The team found no single lead user with the exact set of specifications that the proposed 3M breakthrough product or products would need. Instead, a variety of lead users were found with expertise about different relevant attributes.

Commenting on the often painstaking search for an appropriate expert, Pournoor felt, "It is like finding a partner for marriage." Some experts came from traditional backgrounds—for instance, an expert on infection control that consulted with the U.S. government Centers for Disease Control. Sometimes experts were found in the least likely places. During the premiere of the *Lion King* show in Minneapolis, for instance, a team member ended up chatting backstage with one of the makeup artists. As it turned out, the artist's husband, himself a makeup artist, had consulted with an orthopedic products firm. This makeup artist possessed specialized knowledge about the application of materials to the skin, which the team eventually felt would prove useful for developing breakthrough products.

How to pool together the combined knowledge and talent of this diverse array of knowledge to develop product concepts would prove the challenge of the final project stage.

Stage IV at 3M: Final Concept Generation (~3 months)

Stage IV goals: In this stage, which typically lasts 2–4 months, Lead User teams take preliminary concepts developed in Stage III toward completion and also seek to ensure that all possible solutions have been explored. This stage centers around a workshop with invited lead users.

In the summer of 1997, bad luck struck the team in the form of a change in senior management. Thus far, the team had kept upper management apprised of the team's progress because "that way, when you make recommendations and submit proposals, there are no surprises."[6] The new business unit manager, Sam Dunlop, was one of the rare managers to come with a traditional market research background. His vision was aligned with the old 3M strategy of incremental growth in high-margin products. Dunlop had accepted the new post against his will, with the mandate to "stop the hemorrhage of profits and reconsolidate the division." He was close to retirement, and over the past few years none of the units he headed had thrived.

In an initial meeting with team leaders, Dunlop stated more than once, "We must not tax the current operating income!" Although he recognized the need for departing from traditional product development, the focus on finding "wild-eyed" lead users made him uncomfortable. His marketing training had stressed logic and quantifiable data, which could be collected and analyzed in a predictable, linear fashion. The Lead User methodology, in

---

[6] "Teamwork with a Twist Helps 3M'ers Think Differently," *3M Stemwinder*, April 15, 1998.

contrast, collected qualitative data from people, with new questions leading to new concepts, which in turn started up a new cycle of questions that begged further answers. Where the process would ultimately lead was never known with full certainty at the project's start. As a temporary compromise, Dunlop reduced the Lead User team by one member and made his opposition to the project quite clear.

Shor and her team had to sell the program starting from scratch, reminding the new managers about how inefficient the old ways of developing products had been. One tactic was to invite some of the business managers to join several team brainstorming sessions. This, according to Pournoor, "got them out of the box," and made them more receptive. Nonetheless, team members remained uncomfortably aware of the watchdogs of corporate profitability nipping at their ankles.

* * * * *

Even with the project green light blinking anemically, the team finally decided to center the Stage IV workshop around the bold question, "Is there a revolutionary approach to infection control?" In deference to management's concern with the near-term bottomline, however, the team decided to focus specifically on product efficacy and cost. Rita Shor expressed the workshop goals to 11 3M personnel (see Exhibit 5) and 11 outside experts (see Exhibit 6) that had gathered on August 8 at a St. Paul hotel:

> By the end of the workshop, we want at least three product concepts that could dramatically improve microbial control in the surgical setting of today and tomorrow, with significant cost savings for surgeons in the United States and in the rest of the world. We seek breakthrough innovations that range from being so big as to render obsolete the current system, or, alternatively, so simple that they would use our existing technologies in a new ways.

All assembled experts signed intellectual property rights to 3M, but received modest financial remuneration in the form of an honorarium. The workshop lasted two and a half days, a period, described by Lead User team coleader John Pournoor, a veteran of many product development focus groups, as "not too long and not too short." This length of time allowed for two to three iterations of concepts.

In the introductory session, group members introduced themselves and discussed how their backgrounds might pertain to the task on hand. The group of experts, varying in age from 35 to 79, came from disciplines ranging from dermatology to makeup artistry to veteri-

EXHIBIT 5   3M Staff Participating in the Stage IV Workshop

Lead User team members:
- Rita Shor, Senior Product Specialist, Medical-Surgical Markets Division (MSMD), and Lead User team coleader
- Susan Hiestand, Business Manager, MSMD
- John Pournoor, Ph.D., Research Specialist, MSMD, and Lead User team coleader
- Matt Scholz, Senior Research Specialist, MSMD
- Maurice Kuypers, Market Development Supervisor, MSMD
- Mark Johnson, Process Development Specialist, MSMD

Lead User team consultants:
- Joan Churchill, Ph.D., Clinical Psychologist
- Mary Sonnack, Division Scientist and Internal 3M Consultant

Other 3M staff members involved:
- *Microbiologist:* Joanne Bartkus, Ph.D., Clinical Studies
- *Business Development Manager:* German Chamorro, 3M Latin America
- *Synthetic Chemist:* John Dell, Ph.D., Senior Research Specialist
- *Organic Chemist:* Roger Olsen, R&D Manager
- *Marketing Manager:* Nicola Stevens
- *Product Designer:* Joy Packard

nary sciences (see Exhibit 6). The workshop was divided into exercise sessions lasting several hours each. For each session, participants divided up into smaller groups of three to five individuals. Although groups constantly changed, "An element of competition among groups developed," according to Pournoor. "This reminded me of my old work at Boeing, where we'd have two different teams working in parallel on the same project."

Group members and facilitators faced at least four major challenges. The first arose from the lack of structure found in many corporate meetings. As a result, some groups tended to flounder during much of the exercise sessions. In a surprisingly large number of sessions, however, teams adhered to a strict schedule, which served to shepherd them toward solutions in the last few minutes.

A second challenge came from introverted and extroverted participants. Initially, for instance, the makeup artist, according to Pournoor, "felt intimidated by all the big words being thrown around, and I think he began to wonder what he was doing there. As time went on, however, his expertise and our needs converged. He contributed more and more." By contrast, the surgeon tended to squash all new ideas that arose early in the session. During a break, however, the veterinarian took him aside, saying, "Do you remember how during your training you were under someone's thumb? Well, that's what you're doing to us." After reflecting upon these words, the surgeon actually stayed up much of that night searching the

EXHIBIT 6   Outside Experts Participating in the Stage IV Workshop

EXPERTISE ON ADVANCED METHODS
FOR UNDERSTANDING BACTERIA

- **General surgeon and chemist** *(M.D., Ph.D.)*, possessed considerable experience in minimally invasive surgery with very ill patients as well as epidemiological expertise. *Area of innovation:* understanding surgical contamination.
- **Dermatologist/surgeon** *(M.D.)*, had worked on laser excision of skin cancer and possessed expertise on skin infection. *Area of innovation:* surgical wound healing.

EXPERTISE ON METHODS
FOR "FAST TRACK" TO MARKET

- **Antimicrobial pharmacologist** *(Ph.D.)*, had chaired the Food and Drug Administration Antimicrobial Committee for pharmaceutical drugs and had worked with skin care and pharmaceutical products for 30 years. He had worked on a similar product focus group that had led "tortuously" to the anti-cold medication Nyquil. *Area of innovation:* antimicrobial agents.

EXPERTISE ON ADVANCED AGENTS TO KILL BACTERIA

- **Disease control expert** *(M.S.)*, a water purifying expert who had worked for the Centers for Disease Control (appearing here as a private consultant) and had a background in epidemiology and hospital staff-mediated infections. *Area of innovation:* expertise in controlling infections in wet environments as evinced by getting a flood-stricken hospital back in operation with antiseptic systems working within six days.
- **Antimicrobial chemist** *(Ph.D.)*, with training in synthetic organic chemistry, held over 50 patents in better delivery of antiseptic solutions and had also researched synthetic materials used to make artificial skin. *Area of innovation:* delivery of antiseptic solutions.
- **Biologist** *(Ph.D.)*, had started out researching meat industry infection but ended up appreciating the need for preventive medicine through "looking upstream" for the earlier sources of infection involving livestock. *Area of innovation:* study of the relationship between different microorganisms; development of light and reduced fat cheese.
- **Biochemical engineer** *(Ph.D.)*, university professor who worked in the areas of tissue engineering and sterilization. *Area of innovation:* tissue engineering and sterilization.

EXPERTISE ON EASE OF APPLICATION TO SKIN

- **Hollywood makeup artist,** had served as a consultant to an orthopedic products firm. *Area of innovation:* application of materials and cosmetics to the skin.
- **Veterinarian surgeon** *(D.V.M.)*, explained his presence on the panel in terms of the extreme challenges infection control in animals poses since, in his words, animals "have hair, do not bathe, and carry no insurance!" Veterinarian input, thus, could help address an extreme end of the spectrum of human infection that was traditionally neglected. *Area of innovation:* surgical techniques and implant design, for which he had won the 1996 veterinarian "Practitioner of the Year" award.
- **"Creative health practitioner"** *(M.D.)*, a psychiatrist with a B.S. in microbiology, also had a background in assessment of performance of paint products. *Area of innovation:* assessment of chemical applications on hard surfaces.
- **Polymer chemist,** who had also studied acupuncture, in addition to polymers. *Area of innovation:* study of acupuncture, polymers, and rheology (the study of the flow of matter).

Internet for new information, and thereafter went on to encourage other team members' contributions.

A third challenge came from finding ways to marry very creative ideas with technical feasibility. A rare nexus of lead user need and technological reality occurred following a period when the veterinarian stopped to reflect on his view of the ideal operating room:

> I—and probably most surgeons—want to focus on only one area on the operating table. I don't want to see anything except what I'm focused on, especially when I'm tired or under stress. With this in mind, could we create a material that we could quickly pull out of the wall or a box and place directly over the patient to create an infection barrier? Such a material should ideally draw the surgeon's attention to only the area being operated upon. This would prove valuable because time is of the essence, and surgery is a waltz that must be performed correctly every single time.

Subsequent brainstorming identified a preexisting material found in 3M's current line of products as possi-

bly capable of bringing the veterinarian's needs to product reality. This exchange of ideas ended up forming the basis of one of the workshop's key product concept recommendations.

The fourth challenge lay in navigating a sea of facts. Here, an intricate interplay of questions and answers between experts from a diverse range of interrelated disciplines helped keep the entire product development process afloat. For example, one participant asked, "How do we make all these antimicrobial materials stick to the patient's body?" The makeup artist, heretofore in the background, pulled open his large binder of dozens of prefabricated/premade concoctions of skin-adhesive materials that 3M would have otherwise missed. By the end of the ensuing discussion, he ended up sketching a product concept for layering materials onto surfaces with smooth contours that could be shown to the other participants.

In the course of several sessions, the invitees successfully rose to the challenges facing them and generated

---

EXHIBIT 7   Excerpt from Memo on Product Recommendations

The abbreviated descriptions below are the Lead User team's recommendations for three product lines for the Medical-Surgical Markets Division (MSMD). (Note that these are the leading contenders from the six concepts that came out of the final product development workshop.)

1. **The "Economy" line.** The MSMD should consider a line of surgical drapes using a combination of low-cost materials. Preexisting 3M adhesives and fastening devices may provide a variety of ways for sticking the materials to the body. A one-size-fits-all strategy and time-saving dispensing systems will boost product acceptance in the current cost-containment environment as well as in developing countries. (Impetus for this product line, in fact, came out of the divisional fact-finding trips to the developing world.) Following the veterinarian lead user's advice, these materials should allow focus on only the part of the body being operated upon. Being based on preexisting 3M technologies, this represents an incremental proposal. *[handwritten: what's different? cheaper?]*

2. **The "Skin Doctor" line** [see Exhibit 8]. The MSMD should consider a line of hand-held devices resembling handheld vacuums for antimicrobial protection. These devices would layer antimicrobial substances onto surfaces being operated upon. An advanced generation of the Skin Doctor could potentially operate in two modes: a vacuum mode, which could mop up surface liquids, in addition to the original layering mode. Impetus for this came from the Lead User workshop. Being based on preexisting 3M technologies, this also represents an incremental proposal.

3. **Antimicrobial "armor" line.** Currently, 3M focuses on only surface infections and thus ignores other infection control markets that include blood borne, urinary tract, and respiratory infections. An armor product line would use 3M technologies to "armor" catheters and tubes from unwelcome microscopic visitors. This line would represent a breakthrough product because it is consistent with the current business strategy of reactive infection control but would provide the company entry into a new $2 billion market.

---

numerous product concepts. In the final session, the group met as a whole to rate and prioritize all concepts on the basis of commercial appeal and technical feasibility. Finally, team members agreed upon the next steps for refining the leading candidates (see Exhibit 7). The external experts ended up rating the workshops highly, from an A− to A+ largely because, in Shor's words, "They'd been in brain-storming sessions where everybody tossed out ideas, but this time, they got to turn the ideas into concrete concepts . . ."[7] (see Exhibit 8). *[handwritten: felt like they contributed]*

After the lead users and other invitees had left town, the product development team from the Medical-Surgical Markets Division met to decide upon its final recommendations to senior management. The team felt the following "metrics" should be used for ranking the product development concepts that had arisen from the recent workshop: *[handwritten: Prioritization]*

• Customer preference for the new products.
• Creation of new growth for the division, with the goal of double-digit annual growth. Creation of new businesses and industries that could change the basis of competition for the business unit.
• Boosted global presence of the division.
• Higher growth for the rest of 3M through, as much as possible, incorporation of proprietary 3M technology with patent protection.

The team ended up with three product recommendations that involved an "economy" line with a strong focus on cost, a "skin doctor" line, and an antimicrobial "armor" line (see Exhibit 7). The first two recommendations represented straightforward linear extensions of existing 3M product lines. The last, the team thought, represented a departure from past activities, and might thus open the door to new business opportunities. The team felt solidly confident in presenting these three recommendations to senior management, especially given the scope for synergy with 3M's existing activities and business unit strategy. For instance, all these proposed product lines could potentially boost sales from preexisting 3M products that helped reduce microbial contamination. As another example, the first proposal could also draw from a preexisting line of 3M drapes. *[handwritten: new + likes + company]*

It was the fourth recommendation, however, that divided the team and formed the basis for a long, heated discussion among the team members.

THE FIFTH RECOMMENDATION: EVOLUTION OR REVOLUTION?

Over the past few months, the product development team had become increasingly aware of a gaping hole in medical knowledge involving infection containment. Discussions with lead users and associated experts indicated that the medical community still groped for ways to prevent infections and was easily swayed by any report that

---

[7]"Lead User Research Picks Up the Pace of 3M Innovation," *3M Stemwinder,* September 24, 1997.

EXHIBIT 8 Drawing of the "Skin Doctor" Product Concept Generated During the Lead User Workshop

appeared credible. No health care company had yet stepped in to take leadership in the area of early intervention in the disease process. Thus a vacuum existed in which 3M could find a new growth area.

For the fourth recommendation, therefore, the product development team had begun thinking about rewriting the business unit's strategy statement to include *upstream containment* of infections or, in other words, to keep infections from happening by precautionary upstream measures. Entering the area of upstream containment, however, meant becoming adept at a new set of skills and knowledge. It meant, for example, being able to track early contamination and its possible consequences in a health care facility—not only detecting specific contaminants but also identifying and, depending on their risk level, targeting individuals for interventions.

The new approach thus called for much more sophistication than the traditional industrial viewpoint, which held one patient just as deserving as the next of the latest surgical drape or the newest handwash. With the new approach, for instance, a malnourished patient might be targeted for nutritional interventions in addition to standard interventions, and diabetic patients might be identified for extra antibiotic coverage.

At 3M, such sophistication called for combining technologies from more than one core area or from areas in which 3M lacked depth. In particular, the product development team recognized the need to combine technologies from its Medical-Surgical Division with diagnostics. But because the term *diagnostics* held a negative connotation at 3M—following the brief and unhappy acquisi-

tion of a small diagnostics company in the 1980s—the team diplomatically substituted the word *detection* in wording its recommendations.

The very need for diplomacy with phrasing of recommendations brought home the ramifications of a shift in direction. "While traditional product development team members at 3M face no immediate consequences for failures," according to Pournoor, the polymer chemist, "we were actually thinking about challenging the entire business strategy. We were crossing boundaries. . . . I think this resulted from using the Lead User methodology, which, in addition to allowing us to gather and use information differently than before, also provided emotional support for change. Team members no longer felt like 'lone-rangers,' as they might have under the traditional regime."

In the evening before the final recommendations were to be presented, the team met to resolve a deadlock over the fourth recommendation. Maurice Kuypers, the market development supervisor, sparked the debate by stating, "We don't want the Lead User methodology to be viewed as a means for fomenting revolution. We already have three great product recommendations. If the team proceeds too quickly with the fourth recommendation, senior management may pull the plug on everything: the product recommendations as well as the Lead User method itself."

Mark Johnson, the process development specialist, countered, "When I started with this method, I thought we were just going to develop new products. But now, talking with these lead user experts has shown me that what we were planning was not too effective anyway. We should seriously question our unit's business strategy."

Susan Hiestand, the business unit manager, chipped in: "Wasn't our mandate to find breakthroughs? We were warned that with the Lead User method we will never be able to predict the final outcome or the path we will end up taking. Well, here we are with our breakthrough: It's not a product you can drop on your foot; it turns out to be a process or a service!"

"I think in the back of his mind," John Pournoor warned, "Dunlop would not mind seeing this process fail. Let's not give him any excuses for scrapping everything we've worked and sacrificed for, with our extra hours of hard work on this process. Let's focus on the first three recommendations, plant a few seeds about infection prevention, and draw the managers into making the intellectual leap themselves. Let them become the revolutionaries . . . or 'corporate visionaries.'"

Rita Shor looked at her watch. In less than an hour she would have to draw the discussion to a close and seek consensus. She recalled how in the final workshop, the sessions often floundered until very close to the end, when miraculously the group would arrive at consensus. But that—as invaluable to fostering creativity as it had proven—now seemed like playing a board game on a rainy day. Today's decisions would ripple through the very real world of business, with the future of a sizable business unit at stake.

Note on Lead User Research[1]

Stefan Thomke and Ashok Nimgade

Jim Sanchez, a Bose Speakers Professional Products manager with responsibility for developing new products, was pleasantly surprised by the high quality of the background music he heard when he walked into a Boston-area Strawberries, a local chain of CD stores. On investigation he found that the manager had bought several Bose speakers designed for home use and asked

---

Source: Copyright © 1998 by The President and Fellows of Harvard College. Professor Stefan Thomke and Research Associate Ashok Nimgade, M.D., prepared this case as the basis for class discussion rather than to illustrate either effective or ineffective handling of an administrative situation.
[1]Much of the information comes from E. von Hippel, J. Churchill, M. Sonnack, *Breakthrough Products and Services with Lead User Research* (Cambridge, Mass., and Minneapolis, Minn.: Lead User Concepts, Inc., 1998, from Oxford University Press).

electricians to install them "somehow." At that time, in the late 1980s, none of the available speakers were designed for mounting from above, but an electrician had wrapped metal straps around the speaker boxes to suspend them over people's heads—not necessarily safely. Sanchez went back to his office with Polaroid pictures of some of the improvised installations. Bose engineers quickly built prototypes, which they took back to Strawberries for further testing. This serendipitous discovery of a "lead user" need led Bose to successfully pioneer high fidelity speakers for the background music market.[2]

WHO ARE LEAD USERS?

Most people are familiar with the concept of lead users at an intuitive level. Many customer products have, after all, been developed by lead users. The prototype for protein-based hair conditioners, for instance, came from daring women in the 1950s who experimented with homemade concoctions containing beer or eggs to impart more body and shine. Familiar consumer products ranging from Gatorade to graham cracker crust to sport bras to mountain bikes to surf boards all stem from consumer ideas and innovations.

For any market or product, there will almost always be individuals who experience needs ahead of everyone else. An intuitive notion of lead users based on the above examples, however, can prove misleading. Lead users are not necessarily recognized "opinion leaders" in a field. Rather, they lead with respect to cutting-edge applications of important market and technical trends. They generally experience needs *ahead* of the market segment in which they operate (see Exhibit 1). Three types of lead users exist:

1. Lead users in the *target* application. This may include lead users who have actually experimented with developing prototypes. The Strawberries CD chain store example provides a good illustration of this group of lead users.
2. Lead users in *analogous* markets—that is, in fields with similar applications. For instance, a health care firm interested in antibacterial control products for humans might actually find a lead user from the veterinarian sciences.
3. Lead users involved with the more important *attributes* of problems faced by users in the target market. For instance, a refrigeration manufacturing firm may find lead users from the supercomputer industry,

---

[2]For a fuller account of this example, see Ibid., pp. 1:20–1:21.

EXHIBIT 1   Position of Lead User Relative to Market

CHARACTERISTICS OF LEAD USERS

1. Lead users have new product or service needs that will be general in a marketplace, but they face them months or years before the bulk of the market encounters them.
2. Lead users expect to benefit significantly by finding a solution to their needs. As a result, they often develop new products or services themselves because they can't or don't want to wait for them to become available commercially.
3. Lead users are not the same as "early adopters"— users who are among the first people to purchase an existing product or service (see figure below). Lead users are facing needs for products and services that *do not exist* on the market.

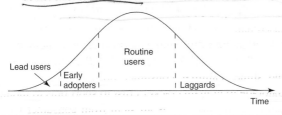

where cooling technology plays an important role in running the computers.

Obviously, a wealth of information pertaining to product development resides in lead users. Finding these people, however, is generally not easy. Casual surveys cannot always unearth them. Appropriate lead users may dwell upon untrodden ways, proving as elusive as Wordsworth's violet by a mossy stone "half-hidden from the eye." Even if one does find someone with the right technical background, that person may not prove the best communicator. One might end up sitting on a mother lode with no idea of how to extract anything of value.

LEAD USER RESEARCH METHODOLOGY

Lead User research, pioneered by Professor Eric von Hippel of the Massachusetts Institute of Technology (MIT), provides a means of accurately forecasting market opportunities by systematically tapping the expertise and experience base of lead users. The Lead User method, developed by von Hippel in conjunction with 3M scientist and internal consultant Mary Sonnack and organizational psychologist Joan Churchill, allows new product development to arise from a sensitive understanding of product features that, ideally, will matter most to customers several years later.

Several successful Lead User studies have helped corroborate the usefulness of Lead User methods in settings ranging from health care to telecommunications to food. With increasing experience in Lead User methodology, its benefits and challenges have become more apparent over time. The specific benefits of Lead User methods include:

- Access to richer and more reliable information on emerging customer needs than can be provided through traditional marketing research. Lead User methods, however, complement, not replace, the need for traditional marketing research.
- Development of better products and service concepts since these come out of better data on consumers' likely needs.
- Acceleration of the product and service development process.

Specific challenges to successfully using the Lead User methodology also exist. These include:

- Difficulty in predicting the pathway from start to finish. Because of the unexpected twists and turns projects take, the ultimate path followed may not be obvious without the benefit of hindsight. At certain stages, therefore, financiers and divisional superiors can be left with sweaty palms.
- The high level of commitment needed in terms of quality and quantity of human resources. One study indicates that management in major U.S. firms commits only a small portion of the innovation budget for early market research and concept development.[3] The bias in most firms is to view the truly important work as commencing with formal product and process development.
- Difficulties in assessing any given individual's participation in a team-based effort. This can prove problematic for assessing royalties or promotions.

CONDUCTING A LEAD USER STUDY

In the 1980s, a major food corporation identified two intersecting trends that seemed the most promising for developing a new snack food: a growing public interest in healthy foods and an interest in amateur or "weekend" athleticism. With this knowledge, they turned to Professor von Hippel for help. Thus was launched the "Olympic Snack" project, one of the earliest Lead User studies conducted.

Von Hippel and management consultant Lee Meadows launched a Lead User study with the intent of developing new healthy snack foods that would contribute to athletic

---

[3] R. G. Cooper, *Winning at New Products* (Reading, Mass.: Addison-Wesley Publishing Company, 1994).

performance. The two began the study by scanning sport magazines aimed at serious amateur athletes as well as research articles in sport nutrition. In their reading they found solid evidence linking some kinds of snacks to performance enhancement during and after athletic events. Satisfied that the project was feasible, they next conducted telephone interviews with elite athletes including Olympians, prominent coaches, and nutrition scientists. Through these interviews they identified a small group of innovative lead users that they felt could contribute to developing the "Olympic Snack." These lead users included an national medal-winning weight lifter, a nutrition scientist who had worked with an elite navy combat group, and a competitive bicycle racer.

It became apparent that knowledge about performance-enhancing foods was segmented between nutritionists and athletes. Nutritionists were more knowledgeable about what snacks should contain and how their consumption should be timed. They cared little about taste. The athletes, on the other hand, knew how snacks should be formulated for easy consumption in the midst of competition. Towards the end of the study, to focus on these two areas of knowledge, von Hippel and Meadows ran two different concept development workshops: one aimed at capturing the knowledge of the nutritionists and the other aimed at capturing the taste preferences of athletes. The combined knowledge from these workshops led to the development of concepts for a very novel line of healthy snacks.[4]

The Olympic Snack story illustrates how most Lead User projects work. The team typically begins with a little to a moderate amount of knowledge about the arena within which it expects to work. (Note that the Olympic Snack example is atypical in utilizing two external consultants rather than an inside team to conduct the entire study.) Initially the team must do its homework to develop a familiarity with the field. Thereafter, the study focuses on tapping unpublished knowledge that resides in leading-edge users and experts. Holding workshops with lead users toward the end of the study allows the firm to capture what is hopefully the world's finest assemblage of living knowledge crucial to the particular product development. The entire process, while vigorous, stresses qualitative validity over statistical reliability—a feature that in an age of increasing quantification makes many market researchers queasy.

Lead User projects based within companies can take five or six months but get faster with experience. During this time corporate team members involved spend 12 to 15 hours per week—or roughly up to a third of their time—

on the project for its entire duration. This high level of immersion fosters creative thought and sustains project momentum. Lower levels of commitment, experience has shown, tend to make projects drag on and also bog down attempts to figure out where the team has left off.

As one might imagine, given the need for such commitment, the study's success relies heavily on selecting a talented core team and receiving strong support from senior management. Typically, a corporate team consists of four to six people, including representatives from marketing and technical departments. One or two members serve as project leaders. This team size appears to be large enough to generate diverse perspectives, yet small enough to facilitate team logistics and rapid team decision making. Ideal team members have a deep and broad knowledge base relevant to the topic, remain open to new approaches, and enjoy thinking creatively.

In conducting a Lead User study, four stages can be defined (see also Exhibits 2 and 3). In reading descriptions of these stages below, it is useful to reflect on the Olympic Snack example.

Stage I: Project Planning (4–6 Weeks)

This is essentially the "homework," or scouting, phase of the study in which the team identifies types of markets and new products of interest it seeks to target. These markets and products, of course, should fit within the firm's key business goals and constraints. The team also seeks to define the desired level of innovation. For instance, does the company seek a breakthrough product or does it wish to merely extend current product or service lines?

At a tactical level, the team begins Stage I by getting grounded in the project, by reading trade journals, browsing through market surveys and market data, searching the Internet, or informally interviewing industry experts, who may include customers, suppliers, and internal company managers, to get a feel for current trends and market needs. Next, the group develops a specific data collection plan, focused on key questions (such as market trends) as well as key resources (appropriate experts and trade literature).

The challenge for most Lead User studies is to avoid downplaying the importance of this stage. The base of knowledge developed here will reap dividends down the road. According to Lead User process consultant Joan Churchill, "The lead user process is a very disciplined process. Teams that look for 'quick fixes' can end up disillusioned once they realize how much study is needed before getting to the 'fun stuff.' Teams that leapfrog the

---

[4]For a fuller account of this example, see E. von Hippel et al., *Breakthrough Products and Services with Lead User Research,* pp. 1: 16–1:17.

EXHIBIT 2   Summary of Lead User Research Process

STAGE 1: PREPARING TO LAUNCH THE LEAD USER PROJECT

Key management activities

- Select the new product/service areas of interest.
- Designate a cross-disciplinary research team of 4–6 people to implement the project.

Key team activities

- Refine the focus through discussions with key stakeholders.
- Develop a data collection plan.

STAGE 2: IDENTIFYING TRENDS AND KEY CUSTOMER NEEDS

Key team activities

- Broadly explore trends through interviews with lead use experts and reading in the trade literature.
- Select the markets and core needs that will be the focus of concept development.

STAGE 3: EXPLORE LEAD USER NEEDS AND SOLUTIONS

Key team activities

- Generate preliminary solution concepts by interviewing lead users and lead use experts.
- Collect market data for a business case.
- Present needs data and preliminary solutions to management.

STAGE 4: IMPROVE SOLUTION CONCEPTS WITH LEAD USERS AND EXPERTS

Key team activities

- Hold a 2–3 day workshop to further develop concepts.
- Finalize concepts and develop a written new product or service proposal.
- Review the project output with management.

After the workshop

- Test appeal of the concept(s) on target market(s).
- Hand-off the concept(s) for commercialization.

Source: E. von Hippel et al., *Breakthrough Products and Services with Land User Research*, p. 2:21.

EXHIBIT 3   Major Lead User Research Activities and Suggested Time Allocations

Stage/major activities	Who	Suggested time by activity
Stage 1: Project Planning		**4-6 weeks total**
• Develop master plan.	Project planners	10+ hrs. (over 1 month)
• Learn about the current marketplace.	Project team	3–4 weeks
• Further refine the project focus.		
Stage 2: Trends/Needs Identification		**5–6 weeks total**
• Conduct literature searches.	Individual team members	10+ hrs. per week
• Interview top experts.	Whole project team	1+ hr. (weekly meeting)
• Interpret/analyze data, select specific needs to focus on.		
Stage 3: Preliminary Concept Generation		**5–6 weeks total**
• Interview lead users and experts.	Individual team members	10+ hrs. per week
• Gather data for business case.	Whole project team	1+ hr. (weekly meeting)
• Define new product or service requirements, generate concepts.		
Stage 4: Final Concept Development		**5–6 weeks total**
• Plan Lead User workshop.	Individual members	10+ hrs. (over 2 weeks)
• Invite participants.		2–3 days (typical length of workshop)
• Hold workshop—improve concepts with lead user/experts.		2+ weeks
• Finalize concepts.	Whole project team	10+ hrs. (2–3 meetings)
Project Wrap-Up		**2–3 meetings**
• Evaluate project outcomes.	Management/project team	10+ hrs. (2–3 meetings)
• Plan next commercialization steps.		

Approximate length of Project: 4–6 Months

(With increasing experience and team members who dedicate over 50% of their time, the duration of a study can be reduced.)

Source: E. von Hippel et al. *Breakthrough Products and Services with Lead User Research*, p. 3:9.

first stage by immediately starting to look for lead users may set themselves up for failure."[5]

Stage II: Trends/Needs Identification (5–6 Weeks)

At this stage the team officially launches its Lead User study. The ultimate goal is to select a specific need-related trend(s) to focus upon for the remainder of the study. In the Olympic Snacks example, for instance, the team decided to address two intersecting trends involving a growing interest in healthy foods and an interest in amateur athleticism.

The team initiates the trend and market investigation with a focused, comprehensive trade literature review pertaining to the project. This helps provide a sense of the conventional wisdom relating to trends and market needs. Experience shows that a four-day team workshop provides the best way to kick off this stage. In the first two days of this session, members browse through reading material selected by the team during Stage I. Every two or three hours, group discussions cover what members are learning from the reading.

The next two days of this workshop lay the groundwork for interviewing lead users as well as lead use experts—individuals who, while not necessarily lead users, possess expertise relevant to lead use. In a half-day session, the team prepares an interview guide that covers key questions to explore with experts. The team spends another half-day conducting warm-up interviews with local experts. The reason for this heavy emphasis, as Churchill points out, is that "some technical people at corporations have never seen a customer face-to-face; and not many have good interviewing skills."[6]

The process of finding top experts involves querying industrial gurus, scanning literature, searching the Internet, and consulting with in-house colleagues. Telephone "networking" also helps identify appropriate experts. Interviewing typically takes place over the telephone, but it can also occur in person for certain experts with vital information.

Three or four weeks into Stage II, the team generally develops a good understanding of major trends and is now positioned for the vital task of framing the customer need that can be addressed by a new product or service. This needs framing typically occurs through a series of meetings spread over two weeks, during which the team evaluates, interprets, and combines the data collected from readings and interviews.

Thereafter, teams typically take another two weeks to rework and refine initial ideas on needs framing in light of further interviews and readings. This allows the team to zero in on the data directly pertaining to the project focus and set aside extraneous information.

Example

Top executives at a company that manufactured hearing aids concluded that for their product development goals an ideal new product line would have several key features: it would yield profitability of $1- to $5 million in its first year, and over $20 million in later years. Furthermore, this product line would utilize existing company technologies and existing marketing channels. Instead of scouring the world—in the manner of lamas seeking the next dalai lama—for products already born, the firm executives turned to a Lead User study.

To kick off the lead user project, 20 people from each of the firm's departments participated in a half-day brainstorming session. Of several product concepts discussed, the most promising was a low-cost, quality hearing instrument to address the needs of people in their 50s suffering from early hearing loss. Current products on the market ignored the needs of this segment of the population.

At the end of the brainstorming session, the team envisioned the new product line as being inexpensive (under $200), easy to use (with no need for adjustment by users or audiologists), and with significantly improved sound quality without acoustic feedback or background noise. Each early assumption about a product attribute led to new questions about which the team felt it had to learn more. Consider, the following:

- Demographics: A rapidly growing number of people over 50 years old would suffer from mild to moderate hearing loss. New question: How many of these people are actually buying hearing aids? What features are they seeking?
- Product usage: The new product line would appeal to people in their 50s concerned with the cosmetics of hearing aids. New question: What cosmetic features would prove important to this population of aging baby boomers?
- Technology: Leading-edge products appear increasingly simple to use. New question: What new technologies in our own and other fields can help create an easy-to-use, "one size fits all" type of hearing aids?

After this needs-framing exercise, the team found itself ready to enter the next phase.[7]

---

[5] Interview with Joan Churchill, August 1998.
[6] Ibid.

[7] For a fuller account of this example, see E. von Hippel et al., *Breakthrough Products and Services with Lead User Research*, pp. 3:5–3:6.

Stage III: Preliminary Concept Generation (5–6 Weeks)

With Stage III, all potential analogies to armchair philosophizing end: The team now begins to generate preliminary concepts. First, however, the group must acquire a more precise understanding of the focal area. This understanding arises from the iterative process of seeking solutions to questions, which in turn generates further questions. The team continues interviewing lead user experts for technical knowledge that pertains to concept generation.

Many of the interviews occur at the lead user's own place of business. This provides invaluable information that the lead user might find commonplace and not worthwhile expressing, or information hard to explain over the telephone (e.g., through annotated demonstrations like "At this point, I turn my home-crafted wood stake thus . . . before the vampire eludes my grasp").

For concepts generated in this stage, the team must start outlining the attributes and features the ideal product should have, along with benefits and values offered to targeted customers and key design features. (Recall in the hearing aid example how the team addressed these key issues.) The team seeks to informally assess business potential for the product or service being conceptualized.

Toward the end of Stage III, the team meets with key managers responsible for implementing product development concepts that will ultimately rise from the Lead User project. By now, the team should be armed with some verifying evidence that the identified needs and preliminary solution ideas do indeed represent good business opportunities. This involves providing data on size and profitability of the targeted market as well as analysis of competitive offerings to make sure that preliminary concepts offer unique benefits and value to target customers.

Stage IV: Final Concept Generation (5–6 Weeks)

In Stage IV, the team takes the preliminary concept developed in Stage III toward completion. Activity in this stage generally centers around a Lead User workshop of up to two or three days. The workshop serves to fill in missing pieces in the preliminary concepts developed in Stage III as well as to ensure that all possible solutions have been explored. During the workshop, the team works intensively with lead users and lead use experts to improve and add to the preliminary concepts.

Example

A manufacturer of hardware products planning to develop abrasives for smooth surfaces that are difficult to sand down (e.g., banisters, chair legs, decorative moldings) ended up inviting to the workshop held during Stage IV lead users that included a designer of early American furniture, an internationally renowned wood sculptor, and a specialist in guitar design and refurbishment. All these lead users were experts in the sanding of compound curves in wood (either by hand or under factory production conditions). Several design prototypes for viable products emerged from this confluence of diverse talents.[8]

A well-orchestrated workshop proves crucial for success. Typically, 15 to 18 people attend a Stage IV workshop, of which a third may come from the project team and from in-house technical or marketing divisions. The remaining attendees are lead users or lead use experts. While many of these may already have been identified in Stage II, further probing may be required to find people with appropriate expertise. Well over a month of planning may go into designing and scheduling the workshop.

At the very beginning of the workshop, which ideally is held off-site in pleasant surroundings, people take turns explaining their expertise and interests. The group then discusses the problem area and reviews background information. Because 15 to 18 people cannot discuss any matter efficiently, let alone civilly, much of the workshop occurs in subgroups, each of which discusses independent parts of the problem. Through the remainder of the workshop, these small groups are formed and re-formed for efficient cross-pollination of ideas and viewpoints.

Towards the end of the workshop, different subgroups are charged with generating alternative product concepts. Friendly rivalry among subgroups often spurs inventiveness and even the quest for increasingly novel solutions. Thereafter, the entire group meets to systematically evaluate the generated product concepts in terms of technical feasibility, market appeal, and management priorities. The entire group arrives at consensus on the most commercially promising concepts and develops recommendations for further steps to refine them. Here, the vast array of expertise allows for virtually instantaneous feedback. According to Rita Shor, a 3M product developer who led a Lead User study for developing surgical product concepts:

As concepts in our Lead User workshop were being developed, it was especially useful to get *immediate* feedback from the surgeons and microbiologists and skin bacteria specialists. Because of the high level of expertise and actual field experience that the external attendees brought to the workshop, the group generated ideas faster and explored

---

[8]For a fuller account of this example, see E. von Hippel et al., *Breakthrough Products and Services with Lead User Research*, pp. 4:18–4:19.

them more deeply than would have been possible in one-to-one interviews.[9]

Obviously, the synergy from this meeting of minds provides one reason why most lead users and lead use experts are literally signing away intellectual property rights to innovations and product concepts that may stem from such workshops. Most invitees generally realize that on their own they may be unlikely to develop the particular innovations. Furthermore, many lead users and lead use experts enjoy contributing to innovations, even if only for the sake of innovation, and find such workshops intellectually stimulating. For some invitees, it provides a welcome change from an intellectual isolation. Too many lead users, to return to Wordsworth, have remained like a solitary star in a sky.

Example
For the hearing aid Lead User workshop, the sponsoring firm had identified several key attributes that the ideal product should have. This made it easier to think about lead users the firm should invite for interviews and workshop attendance. As you read the list of desirable attributes below, you may think of yet more potential lead users and lead use experts than the firm identified.

- Attribute 1—cosmetic appeal. Lead users/experts identified: cosmetic dentistry specialists; manufacturers of upscale costume jewelry.
- Attribute 2—customizable low-cost tubing. Lead users/experts identified: medical tubing suppliers; manufacturers/suppliers of amplifiers for professional football teams.
- Attribute 3—low acoustical feedback/minimal amplification of unwanted sound. Lead users/experts identified: specialists in tiny circuitry and digital technology applications in the video and music industries.
- Attribute 4—ease of purchase (without need for ear exams or special fittings). Lead users/experts identified: opticians who had pioneered sales of contact lenses through mass retailers; major retailers that sold eyeglasses and offered on-site eye exams.

Afterward, the team refines the preliminary concept on the basis of knowledge gained from the workshop with lead users and lead use experts who attended that meeting. The team presents senior managers with information about the proposed products or services, providing solid evidence about why customers would be willing to pay for them. Among the visual tools found useful

for this meeting are sketches of the concepts and video-taped clips from the Lead User workshop.

After the Project: Testing the Concepts
Since lead users are not the same as routine users in a target market, concepts should be tested on ordinary consumers in the target market. The nature of validation required varies from firm to firm, depending on how much commercial promise concept evaluators anticipate the concept to hold.

Quite often, quantitative methods for evaluating routine products do a poor job of evaluating the novel functions and benefits offered by breakthrough products and services. For this reason, many Lead User project managers evaluate concepts based on small groups of users in the target markets as well as on their own judgment. In some cases, however, because of considerations of secrecy, some firms have opted to skip this testing on routine users.

At least one member of the lead user team should help shepherd the product or service concept through the next development phases to ensure that the expertise built through the entire process of the study is fully deployed. This also helps ensure that innovative products do not get tangled in a web of "business as usual" practices. For instance, after the Olympic Snack study, the sponsoring firm planned to test the new product line the way it tested all its other products: on housewives shopping in supermarkets. Only timely intervention from the lead user product champion steered testing toward the target market of weekend athletes.

Increasing experience with Lead User methodology over the years suggests that three elements are necessary for a successful study:

1. *Supportive management* that will provide the project the creditability and long-term commitment required.
2. The use of a *cross-discipline Lead Use study team of highly skilled people* comprising the very best people with years of experience, creativity, and good team skills.
3. A clear *understanding of the principles of Lead User research,* which may gain further from use of a consultant who can coach the process through the nuances of the method.

By its very nature, innovation remains an unpredictable process that does not lend itself to lockstep algorithms. The methods described above may provide a key to the successful courtship of the muse of innovation.

---

[9] Ibid., p. 7:6.

CASE III·6

What's the BIG Idea?

*Eventually, 15 years from now, we'd like to be the
worldwide inventors' brand. So when two guys in a pub
in Dublin come up with something, they'll know where
to take it. Think about it—if you come up with an idea,
what are you going to do with it? Ninety-nine percent
of the world doesn't have any of the experience, access,
or resources that you need to take the thing on the back
of the envelope and turn it into a product. How many
great ideas are never realized because of that?*
—Michael Collins, Founder and CEO, Big Idea Group

Clayton M. Christensen and Scott D. Anthony

It was September 2001, and Michael Collins (Harvard
Business School '92) was in a decidedly good mood as
he finished an early morning conference call with one of
his most productive inventors. Collins, the founder and
CEO of Big Idea Group (BIG), was trying to hammer out
the details of a line of card games he hoped to pitch to a
toy company later that month. Collins had met this inventor several months ago at one of his company's Big
Idea Hunts, where scores of inventors would converge at
a local hotel to present their ideas to BIG. Discussions
like these reminded Collins why he founded BIG—an
intermediary between inventors and idea-buying companies in the kids' industry. Not only did he get the chance
to have day-to-day interactions with inventors, he had the
chance to make a substantial amount of money doing it!

Collins turned his attention to an e-mail from BIG's
chairman, George d'Arbeloff, with the latest revisions to
a sponsorship agreement the two of them had been working on for the past several weeks. The agreement was
with a leading tool manufacturer that wanted BIG to apply its process to assist the manufacturer's own innovation efforts. As Collins read through d'Arbeloff's com-

Source: Research Associate Scott D. Anthony prepared this case
(9-602-105, November 14, 2001) under the supervision of Professor
Clayton M. Christensen. Harvard Business School cases are developed
solely as the basis for class discussion. Cases are not intended to serve
as endorsements, sources of primary data, or illustrations of effective or
ineffective management. Copyright © 2001 President and Fellows of
Harvard College. To order copies or request permission to reproduce
materials, call 1-800-545-7685, write Harvard Business School Publishing, Boston, MA 02163, or go to http://www.hbsp.harvard.edu. No
part of this publication may be reproduced, stored in a retrieval system,
used in a spreadsheet, or transmitted in any form or by any means—
electronic, mechanical, photocopying, recording, or otherwise—without the permission of Harvard Business School.

ments, he absentmindedly played with one of his own inventions, a miniature bendable astronaut, that sat beside
his computer. Collins *knew* that the process he had developed to take ideas as a resource and transform them
into valuable products worked in the kids' industry; he
thought that it could work in numerous other industries.
But he wondered—was it really the process that proved
so successful or was it his own unique ability to manage
all the moving parts that made up the process? He also
wondered if he would be able to find the right people to
extend BIG into other industries. If he could, BIG had
the opportunity to be a tremendously successful and profitable company. "The big question is: Can you take innovation and turn it into a business?" Collins said. "People
will say this is Mike Collins, Inc.—more of a 'practice'
than a company. I plan on proving them wrong."

BECOMING BIG: MICHAEL COLLINS'S BACKGROUND

Upon graduating from Dartmouth College with a degree
in engineering in 1986, Collins went to work for TA Associates, a leading Boston-based venture capital firm.
After spending four years at TA, he entered the Harvard
Business School. While exploring his options after grad-
uation, he attended a speech by noted investor Warren
Buffett. Collins recalled Buffett's career advice to a student questioner: "He said: First, find the smartest person
you can work for and convince them to hire you and
second, be in an industry you really love. That was very
good advice."

While Collins was at HBS, his father would send him
the sports page from their Wisconsin hometown newspaper. On the back of the sports page was a human interest
section, and one day Collins noticed a story about a group
of 300 girls waiting in a rainstorm for a chance to buy a
product from Pleasant Company, a Wisconsin-based doll
company run by charismatic founder Pleasant Rowland.
Collins remarked, "I figured that any company that created that kind of demand must be doing something right
and had to have someone very sharp running it. I eventually decided I wanted to be part of that. So I just walked
in the front door and said, 'I want to work here.'" By the
end of the day, Collins had been hired.

After working with Pleasant for a year, Collins struck
out alone, founding a toy catalog company called Kid
Galaxy. Two and a half years later, Collins stumbled onto
the concept of Bendos (see Exhibit 1 for examples of Bendos), which rapidly proved successful. Collins recalled:

EXHIBIT 1   Bendos Examples

**Allie the
Best Friend**

**Chopper the
Motorcycle Cop**

**Chief
the Executive**

**Flip the
Acrobat**

**Ms. Brighton
the Teacher**

**Prof. Neutron
the Scientist**

Source: Bendos Web site (http://www.bendos.com).

We were doing a catalog photo shoot for a line of wooden vehicle toys. We'd created some bendable characters—Bendos—as props to accompany the vehicles. We found out that the kids could have cared less about the vehicles, but they loved the Bendos. In fact, when we went to pack up, the kids had taken all our samples. On the way back from the photo shoot, I got on the phone with product development and we had 32 characters done in about a month.

I had spent years working my butt off, managing a business from soup to nuts, and we were just getting by. All of a sudden, we had a hot product and it was so much easier. It became very clear to me that value creation—at least in this industry—was all about innovative products.

With the success of Bendos, Collins was inspired to see if he could combine his knowledge of the kids' space with the venture capital process to create a new way of managing innovation. He hired his own replacement at Kid Galaxy and resigned.

KIDS' INDUSTRY OVERVIEW

As the label "kids' industry" is extremely broad and contains subsegments such as clothing, accessories, and toys, it is difficult to provide precise statistics about BIG's key target market. The closest proxy is likely to be the toy industry. With almost $30 billion in retail sales in 2000, the U.S. toy industry was extremely large and contained a multiplicity of segments (see Exhibit 2 for key industry statistics). Retailers ranged from large, well-known companies like Toys "R" Us to smaller gift stores that sold impulse toys near their displays. More than 50 percent of toys were sold in one of the top four retailers—Wal-Mart, Toys "R" Us, Kmart, and Target. Retailers purchased toys from a disparate array of distributors and wholesalers running the gamut from large corporations like Hasbro and Mattel to smaller niche players like Kid Galaxy, Basic Fun, and Learning Curve.

The largest category by far was video games, with reported U.S. retail sales of more than $6 billion. However, there were numerous other robust categories. For example, there was more than $500 million in shipments in categories ranging from fashion dolls to plush toys to skating accessories.

While these statistics indicate there still was an appetite for toys, Collins pointed to some trends that demonstrated that the future was not as bright. Kids were "aging" more quickly, growing out of toys and into other activities such as sports and music at a younger and younger age. In addition, high-tech gadgets—from CD players to cell phones—were competing for their dollars.

And in an era where personalization and niche markets were becoming increasingly important, retailers used to mass-market promotions were finding it hard to adapt. Finally, the old strategy of riding a great license (hit movies, TV shows, books, etc.) seemed to be a greater gamble than ever with so many recent properties failing to generate enthusiasm for merchandise.

Key toy manufacturers such as Hasbro and Mattel had struggled for years to develop innovative new products that did not rely on tie-ins with movies such as Star Wars. One industry executive commented: "We're in a period of lack of innovation, a lack of imagination. People are licensed out. People are going with what they know."[1] Andy Gatto, a senior vice president at Toys "R" Us with responsibility for product development, echoed the sentiment that the industry had been lacking innovation recently, which he said presented an opportunity for BIG:

> At a macro level, I would suggest that you are looking at an industry that hasn't really been growth-centered for the past decade or so. Those of us who depend on fresh content and building brands around innovative platforms are reaching out to whatever resources we can to find that innovation. [BIG's] timing was perfect. There is a need. If they can deliver on that need, they will have a very bright future.

HOW TO MAKE IT BIG: PHILOSOPHY AND PROCESSES

Collins founded BIG in July 2000 (see Exhibit 3 for a timeline of key events and Exhibit 4 for brief management biographies). The basic concept was to create a company that would tap into the incredible entrepreneurial power of legions of individual inventors. Collins and d'Arbeloff positioned the company as an intermediary between inventors and idea-buying companies—both manufacturers and retailers—and created a detailed process that resembled one found in the venture capital industry. As Collins noted, "Our model is a lot like venture capital because it's deal flow. It's picking which one percent of the projects you're going to work on, and then cutting the deal. In addition, BIG's organization chart will look more like a VC firm's than a typical company, with partners responsible for each vertical market."

While Collins brought his entrepreneurial flair and innovation background to the table, d'Arbeloff offered more nuts-and-bolts business experience. D'Arbeloff had

---

[1] Anne D'Innocenzio, "Toy makers resurrect dormant toys to make them must-haves," Associated Press Newswires, 4 February 2001.

EXHIBIT 2   Toy Industry Statistics

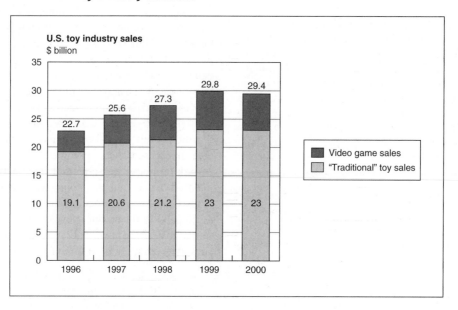

U.S. toy industry sales
$ billion

Year	"Traditional" toy sales	Total
1996	19.1	22.7
1997	20.6	25.6
1998	21.2	27.3
1999	23	29.8
2000	23	29.4

Legend:
- Video game sales
- "Traditional" toy sales

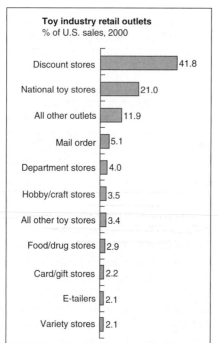

Toy industry retail outlets
% of U.S. sales, 2000

Outlet	%
Discount stores	41.8
National toy stores	21.0
All other outlets	11.9
Mail order	5.1
Department stores	4.0
Hobby/craft stores	3.5
All other toy stores	3.4
Food/drug stores	2.9
Card/gift stores	2.2
E-tailers	2.1
Variety stores	2.1

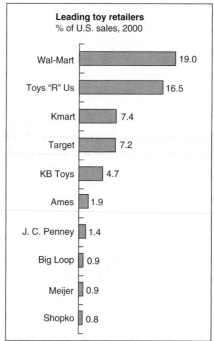

Leading toy retailers
% of U.S. sales, 2000

Retailer	%
Wal-Mart	19.0
Toys "R" Us	16.5
Kmart	7.4
Target	7.2
KB Toys	4.7
Ames	1.9
J. C. Penney	1.4
Big Loop	0.9
Meijer	0.9
Shopko	0.8

Source: Compiled by the casewriter based on statistics from the Toy Industry Association (available at http://www.toy-tia.org/industry/statistics).

a long and successful career at Teradyne, a Boston-based test equipment manufacturing and service company. There he held a series of management positions, including leadership of one of the company's largest product groups. (d'Arbeloff's brother, Alex, was the founder and long-time CEO of Teradyne). D'Arbeloff, who became BIG's chairman in October 2000, met Collins through his wife. He remarked, "Mike and I kind of hit it off. And, as it turns out, we complement each other. I've run a large company. I'm interested in business problems. I'm

EXHIBIT 3   Timeline of Key Events

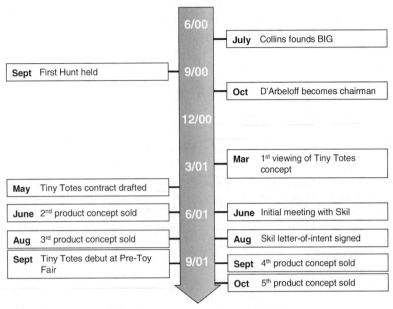

Sept First Hunt held	**July** Collins founds BIG
	Oct D'Arbeloff becomes chairman
	Mar 1st viewing of Tiny Totes concept
May Tiny Totes contract drafted	
June 2nd product concept sold	**June** Initial meeting with Skil
Aug 3rd product concept sold	**Aug** Skil letter-of-intent signed
Sept Tiny Totes debut at Pre-Toy Fair	**Sept** 4th product concept sold
	Oct 5th product concept sold

Timeline dates: 6/00, 9/00, 12/00, 3/01, 6/01, 9/01

Source: Company documents.

EXHIBIT 4   Brief Management Biographies

Michael Collins (CEO): Worked for four years at TA Associates, a Boston-based VC firm. Founded Kid Galaxy, a specialty toy company and producer of award-winning Bendos line. Recruited management team and non-venture capital board members. Graduated from Dartmouth College with degree in engineering. Received M.B.A. from Harvard Business School.

George d'Arbeloff (Chairman of Advisory Board): Diverse experiences during 30-year career with Teradyne, most recently running $800 million semiconductor test business. Served as CEO of $2.6 million point-of-sale system provider. Graduated from Harvard College with degree in engineering.

Ted Gutelius (Advisory Board Member): President Warner Capital Resources, a proprietary database of accredited angel investors.

Jeffrey Kennis (Advisory Board Member): President, Enchanted Moments, New England sales group for kid's products.

Beth Obermiller (Vice President, Kids): Extensive background in children's products. Served as managing editor at Perfection Learning and executive editor at Pleasant Company. Served as vice president of product development at Kid Galaxy. Received B.A. in English from Grinnell College and M.A. from University of Michigan.

Heather Hill (BIG Scoop Editor): Experienced researcher, writer, and editor. Helped research and manage trend research division at Big Blue Dot. Served as project manager and editor at *Parents' Choice Magazine* and Houghton Mifflin. Has B.A. in history from Wheaton College.

Source: Company documents.

---

good at executive-to-executive relationships and have negotiated lots of contracts. Mike pushes me and I contain Mike."

Basic Philosophy

The basic philosophy underlying BIG's process was that invention comes from many different places and in very

unpredictable ways, not just via well-funded product development departments within large companies. Though product development departments could come up with great ideas and were strong at evolving existing product lines, they would often exclude from the process thousands of individual "tinker-ers." While in some industries product development demanded high levels of centralized expenditures, Collins believed that others had virtually flat product development scale curves, implying no real advantage to spending $20 million versus $2,000 to develop a prototype. In industries that fell in the latter category, thousands of independent innovators were busy in garages and basements around the world, creating a fertile ground that the new product development groups of even the largest companies often could not match. As Collins noted:

> Corporations have their own product development departments and, yes, they're coming up with good things. But what we do is help capture the power of parallel processing for innovation. An inventor in Des Moines might see a problem or an opportunity and produce a great idea. But most companies don't try to access that resource. They keep being dragged back to the day-to-day: worrying about their sales in South Carolina or having too many "X11s" and not enough "X12s."

Since its inception, BIG had enjoyed close relations with Toys "R" Us, a leading U.S.-based toy retailer with more than $11 billion in worldwide sales. Gatto said that the BIG concept added value by providing a fresh perspective on the product development process:

> The creative process is sometimes subjective as opposed to objective. It is nice to have an objective third-party point of view because they look at it from a much purer perspective than we can. If someone brings in a product in a category that's under-performing and people are just emotionally down and drained by that category, insiders might not give something innovative a fair shake.
>
> However, someone from the outside that isn't tainted by the most recent up-to-the-minute sales information looking at the same product might bring a whole different perspective.

With his personal background as an inventor, Collins also had a strong belief that individual inventors were a resource to be treasured and handled carefully rather than belittled or exploited. "As an inventor, I think I have a sensitivity to what they go through," Collins asserted. "They want to have their day in court. And if our evaluation is negative, they want to know that too. All they ask is to be treated fairly, truthfully, and respectfully."

Process

BIG followed a four-step process that it termed its "innovation engine" (displayed in Exhibit 5), which involved: 1) generating idea flow; 2) "winnowing" ideas down to those with the best potential; 3) researching, prototyping, and refining concepts for evaluation; and 4) selling a concept to a manufacturer, retailer, or entrepreneur. As d'Arbeloff put it, "We find em, fix em, and sell em."

Step 1: Generating Ideas BIG had six primary sources of generating "superior idea flow." The six were all somewhat interconnected and created a reinforcing network of inventors and idea flows.

Hunts: Perhaps the most inventive and intriguing source of potential inventions were the company's "Big Idea Hunts," which Collins termed a "kind of Antiques Roadshow for kids' products." While individual companies had run product contests before, BIG was unique in acting as a middleman, not representing a single company.

Typically BIG held six events a year, three in the spring and three in the fall, staged at various locales across the country. To generate interest, BIG would run a series of advertisements in local newspapers and trade journals (see Exhibit 6 for a sample advertisement) prior to the Hunt. For the Hunt itself, BIG would rent out a hotel conference room for a weekend and invite local inventors to come show their concepts to a panel of industry experts. BIG attempted to make the Hunts as fun as possible, and offered cash prizes to "winning" submissions. In return, they asked inventors to pay a modest $35 fee for presenting up to three ideas.

The Hunts often attracted an eclectic group of people. "You see an incredible cross-section of humanity," Collins said. "From a Harley-Davidson motorcyclist who has a balsa wood airplane concept to a retired toy executive who comes in with a PowerPoint presentation and a $15,000 prototype. You see it all, and they all have a story."

Bob Bushnell, a music-shop owner from a suburb of Minneapolis, first encountered BIG at a local Hunt. Bushnell began creating games in the late 1960s. While he had come up with dozens of concepts, he'd never found a venue to commercialize any of his ideas. He happened to see one of BIG's ads and decided to attend the Hunt. Bushnell said, "The important thing with the Big Idea Group is that you are actually seeing somebody—and I think that garners trust, confidence, and encouragement. Those are three things that I never got any other way."

Collins agreed that one of the primary goals of the Hunts was to get out and mingle with the inventor community—and to treat inventors as professionals. Every inventor met not just with Collins but also with a panel of experts recruited by BIG to review concepts. As Collins said: "Everybody gets a chance to show their idea to a

EXHIBIT 5 BIG's "Innovation Engine"

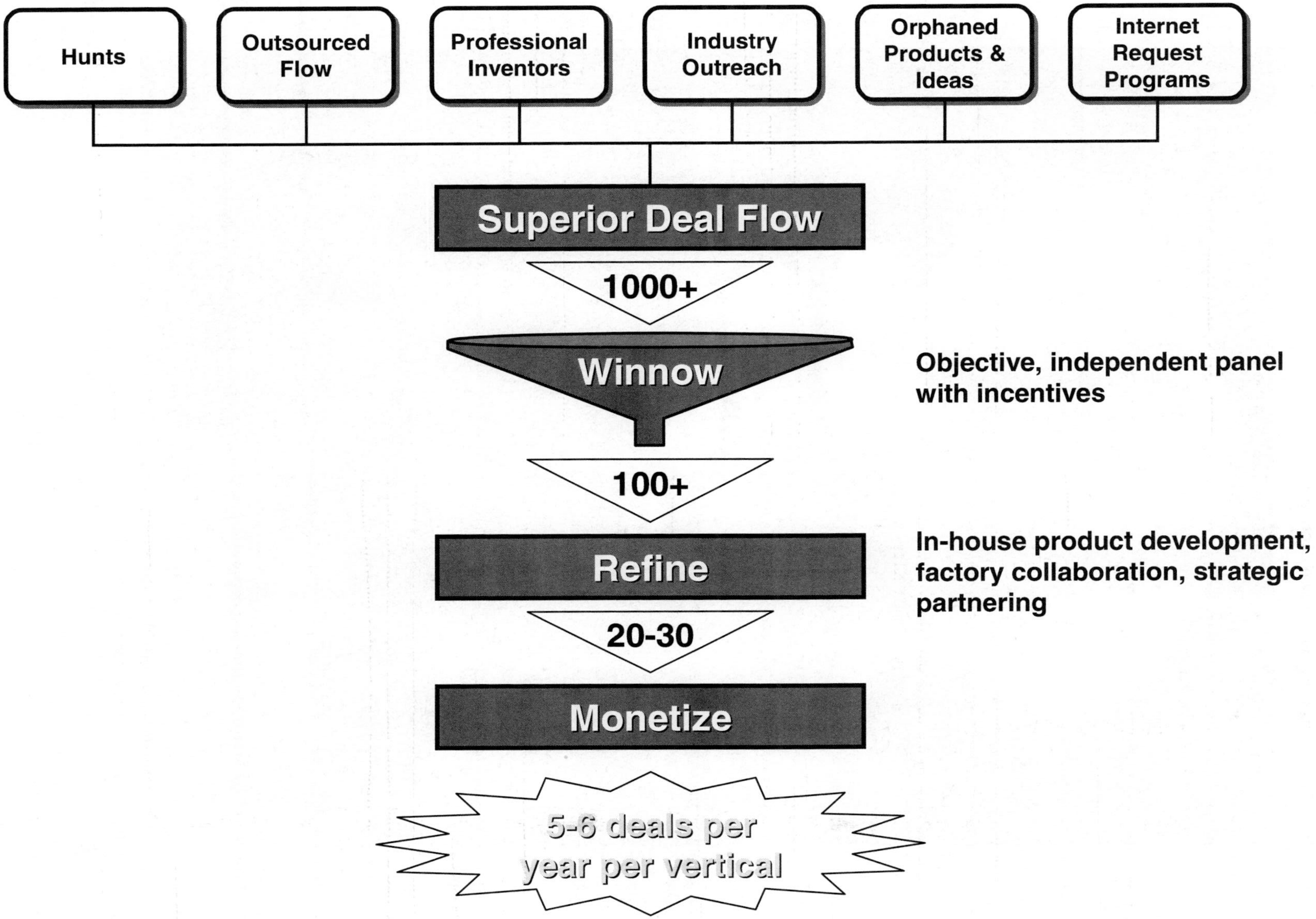

Source: Company documents.

EXHIBIT 6   Big Idea Hunt Advertisement

Source: Company documents.

group of industry professionals. Even if a concept strikes us as weak, we give the inventor as much constructive feedback as possible. We think this is very important. There's also a certain discipline in doing a Hunt on a regular basis that we find valuable. It keeps us from fixating on concepts that might be OK, but not great."

Outsourced Flow: As BIG began working more intimately with toy companies, the companies realized that they too might be able to tap into the BIG process. Major toy companies often got dozens of unsolicited idea submissions a month, and many had no formalized way to separate good ideas from bad. "A number of companies get a dozen to two dozen unsolicited submissions a week. They might not even open them—they just put them straight into the Dumpster," Collins said. "Some even have a policy where callers get a voice recording that essentially says: 'We don't look at outside inventions. Call the industry association.'"

Toys "R" Us encountered this problem and thought BIG might be able to help. It outsourced its unsolicited inventor and vendor submissions to BIG for evaluation, winnowing, and refining. "I give companies like TRU credit," Collins said. "Instead of discarding the inventions, they send them to us. We work up the promising ones and meet quarterly. It's good for TRU, good for us, and good for the inventor."

Gatto said Toys "R" Us decided to outsource its submissions because good ideas may have been slipping through the cracks:

> We are inundated with requests from consumers and amateur inventors who think they have great ideas. But I have a relatively lean group of people who are pretty heavily engaged in the day-to-day of making our business go. If I were to entertain every one of these propositions that came in by mail or fax, I would need a staff of people just to handle this segment.
>
> It's a matter of utilizing our resources in the most effective way. From an infrastructure perspective, I would find it difficult to give this high enough priority to do it internally.

Professional Inventors: Through its Hunts and by word of mouth, BIG began to build a network of "professional" inventors who could work closely with BIG on new kids' concepts. Sometimes these inventors brought in concepts themselves. Other times they helped evaluate an idea or added their own thoughts and design work to another inventor's concept. These professionals also helped BIG make key connections to more inventors and to manufacturers or retailers.

In addition to having contacts with individuals, BIG cultivated relationships with inventor communities. BIG became a member of the United Inventors Association,

one of the largest inventor organizations in the United States, and publicized Hunts through that organization as well as via direct mailings to local inventor groups.

Industry Outreach: Another method of improving idea flow arose from BIG's dedication to produce and publish research on industry trends. Beginning in February 2001, BIG began to publish some of its trend research in a free monthly Web newsletter, The BIG Scoop (www.bigscoop.net). As of October 2001, the publication had a base of more than 2,000 subscribers, including both industry personnel and inventors. The Scoop generated inquiries about BIG's services and helped demonstrate the company's industry knowledge. In addition, Collins said it disciplined BIG to keep a careful watch on trends that could inspire innovative products.

Collins said that BIG received some of the same benefits—awareness and validation—from its association with Toys "R" Us, which allowed BIG to interact with executives from major companies such as Procter and Gamble and Waterpik.

Orphaned Products: Several toy companies that BIG worked with had "orphaned" products that they had either never brought to market or had stopped developing and promoting. BIG could put those products into their process and see if a revitalized line could emerge. Collins pointed to Lincoln Logs as an example of an orphaned product, although BIG was not involved in its rebirth. Lincoln Logs—small plastic and wooden pieces that could be assembled into structures—were a classic American toy, developed in 1916 by the son of noted architect Frank Lloyd Wright. The line enjoyed decades of successful sales. But by the late 1990s, Hasbro had stopped spending serious money on development and marketing of the product, and revenues had shrunk to insignificant levels. Then in February 1999, K'Nex—a toy company noted for its creative product design—signed a licensing agreement with Hasbro. K'Nex re-launched Lincoln Logs the following year. Once again the line proved a hit, with a K'Nex executive commenting that it was selling "three times more product than expected." [2]

Internet & Newsletter Request Program: Through its Web site and a newsletter, BIG solicited suggestions from inventors in specific areas. This solicitation program helped BIG add to lines under consideration or already in development. While the idea flow that resulted from this solicitation was less than that seen from the Hunts, the concepts were more targeted.

---

[2] Stacy Botwinick, "Knock on wood," *Playthings,* 1 September 2000.

Collins estimated that from all these sources, BIG had seen more than 1,500 ideas from its inception up through September 2001, at a rate that has grown to almost 200 ideas a month.

Step 2: Winnowing   The next critical step for BIG was to "winnow" the number of ideas that it had into a manageable number to refine and then take to kids' companies. Much like venture capitalists who receive hundreds of business plans but elect to invest in only a handful of companies, BIG chose to pursue only the highest potential ideas.

In the course of the Hunts, a panel of industry experts led by Collins handled the winnowing process. The panel did not have a formal process for deciding what ideas to pursue, and ultimate decision-making power rested with Collins. Collins commented on the evaluation process:

> There's a consensus approach with a leader, who in the kids' space is me. Like a venture partner, I solicit everybody's input. We meet the inventor, ask questions, and fill out a one-page evaluation form [displayed in Exhibit 7] to help structure the debate. Later we discuss the concept in private. At the end of the weekend, we create a list of the best five to seven ideas. Although we can't know or call everything right in the kids' market, the great ideas usually jump out. Concepts that you show to almost anyone and they get it—those are the BIG ideas.

Collins said that he came up with the idea for the panels because he thinks that fairly appraising innovations requires a breadth of knowledge, experience, and taste. "The panel reflects the reality that we're going to see a wide range of concepts," he noted. "You don't want a personal bias—or lack of knowledge—to kill something that has potential. You want a lot of people's reactions."

BIG paid panelists $1,000 a weekend for their participation. While individual panelists could be the same from weekend to weekend, BIG tried to mix up the members to get a variety of backgrounds and perspectives. Though panelists did not receive any direct incentive payments in the form of "equity" in concepts, Collins said a potential panelist had never turned down an offer to participate. BIG had developed a pool of approximately 15 panelists culled from Collins's increasingly large network of contacts within the industry. Collins said BIG pursued panelists both proactively and "opportunistically," and was always looking for "good athletes" with broad industry experience.

Liz Knight, a Hasbro veteran who had spent the last 14 years as an inventor and designer in the children's product area, participated in two different panels. Knight, who had known Collins for several years, said she agreed to participate in the panels because she enjoyed "seeing how other people are approaching things. There are so many ideas out there. Inventors will think they have a great idea, but often all they have is a germ of an idea—which can expand into 100 different directions."

While that lack of refinement can be frustrating, Knight noted that it also stimulated her: "It inspires me. It gives me exposure to new ideas."

As for evaluating what she sees, Knight said she did not follow a formal process for deciding what was a good idea. "You see it and you know it—and you know it because of your experience and exposure to ideas," she said.

To evaluate concepts received outside the context of the Hunts, Collins drew on a number of sources. Professional inventors, designers, consultants, and in-house staff helped critique and refine ideas, applying the same criteria as those used for Hunt submissions.

Step 3: Refinement   Once BIG winnowed the pool of ideas down to a manageable number, it would work closely with the inventor—much like venture capitalists become intimately involved with operating companies in their portfolios—to refine concepts to make them more appealing to kids' companies. Here, BIG would draw on its existing knowledge of what companies were looking for in new products. Either the original inventor or a stable of outside contractors would refine the concept and produce the appropriate material for presentations.

The typical innovation would take three to six months to refine. Refinements could involve competitive research, repositioning, design, engineering, field-testing, trademark and/or patent research, sourcing and costing, as well as presentation preparation. In cases where the inventor was involved in the refinement, the collaboration had the extra benefit of leading to a closer relationship between BIG and the inventor.

While d'Arbeloff said BIG would not develop a detailed "business plan" for the concept, it did "a fair amount of research on the idea" to make sure the opportunity was sufficiently lucrative and could be manufactured profitably. "We clearly don't want to present an idea to a company unless we understand the potential, not only for us, but also for the company to whom we are selling the idea," d'Arbeloff said.

Gatto noted that the refining stage was particularly important because Toys "R" Us would be more excited to pursue something that it "recognized" as opposed to a rough concept. BIG is "good at taking a concept to the next level," Gatto said. "If someone comes in with a rather crude idea, BIG can sometimes embellish that idea and make it into something that is more on target.

EXHIBIT 7 Big Idea Hunt Concept Evaluation Form

Kids' Product Hunt
BIG Evaluation Form

Product Name: _____

Inventor Name: _____

Panelist Name: _____

Appeal of product   1   2   3   4   5   6   7   8   9   10

Size of market   1   2   3   4   5   6   7   8   9   10

Strength of competition   1   2   3   4   5   6   7   8   9   10

Longevity/extendability/defensibility   1   2   3   4   5   6   7   8   9   10

Ease of sale   1   2   3   4   5   6   7   8   9   10

OVERALL SCORE   1   2   3   4   5   6   7   8   9   10

Possible Prospects: _____
_____
_____

To Do's in Order to Show: _____
_____
_____
_____

Panelist Signature: _____

Date: _____

Source: Company documents.

Sometimes ideas have a better chance of making the cut if somebody has taken them through that 'plussing up' exercise before they get here."

Step 4: Capturing Value   With a refined product concept, BIG would approach manufacturers, retailers, or entrepreneurs that it thought would best be able to commercialize the idea. Depending on the concept, BIG would target companies ranging from industry behemoths like Toys "R" Us or Mattel to smaller companies like Basic Fun, a niche player that specialized in key chains and related accessories. BIG had three primary ways to monetize a product idea: license the product to a company like Basic Fun, develop the concept internally as a private-label product that either BIG or a company like Toys "R" Us would sub-contract to a private-label manufacturer, or bundle several concepts to sell to an entrepreneur.

As of September 2001, BIG had monetized 35 different products through five contracts—four licensing deals and one private label. All of the licensing deals featured these terms:

- An **advance** of up to $100,000 that BIG would split equally with the inventor.
- A **royalty** of 2% to 10% of wholesale revenue. Inventors would get half of the royalty fee, up to a maximum of 3%. For example, a 5% royalty fee would be split in half. On an 8% royalty, BIG would receive 5% and the inventor 3%.
- A **guarantee** of minimum royalties of up to $100,000 that BIG would split evenly with the inventor.

Individual deals could end up being quite lucrative for individual inventors. Bushnell, the game inventor, created a series of card games that BIG sold to Toys "R" Us. "I had planned to not do anything with the games that I had for another 10 years," Bushnell said. "It was going to be a retirement project. Now it could be my retirement."

Both Collins and d'Arbeloff said they were pleased by their progress to date. The fact that they had successfully monetized separate concepts in three successive months indicated growing momentum. While both pointed to the process they had created as key to BIG's success, it was clear that Collins himself was an integral factor as well. Various participants called Collins "the rainmaker" and said his industry knowledge, personality, and inventive flair were critical to BIG's success.

The Tiny Totes Case Study

Susan Kern, a mother living in Indianapolis, firmly believed that she had the right stuff to come up with com-

EXHIBIT 8   Tiny Totes Example

Source: Company documents.

pelling toys. Since the 1980s she had spent countless hours trying to break into the industry as an inventor, working with an agent who would represent her concepts to toy companies. Frustrated by her lack of success, she happened to see an ad in *Playthings* magazine for one of BIG's Hunts. She contacted the group with a number of concepts that she and two of her friends—one an artist and one a costume designer—had developed. Since they couldn't make it in person to the Hunt, the three put together a videotape and had a conference call with BIG (BIG normally met in person with inventors, but would allow "virtual" or phone presentations at the request of the inventor).

The concept was a small purse-like item, eventually named "Tiny Totes" (see Exhibit 8 for product info). The miniature bags could be worn on girls' hands or ankles and contained tiny collectibles. According to Collins, the panel instantly knew that this idea had real potential:

> The panel knew that the area of teen fashion accessories is hot. At an earlier and earlier age, girls are giving up Barbie and going to the mall. They like little things and they like to collect. We understood intuitively the market, the opportunity, the macro trends. We also knew that, though the idea needed some work before it was ready to show, there were definitely companies where this would fit. I've heard people call it a "prepared mind." It's your experience, knowledge, and gut that tell you when you see something great.

Knight participated in the panel that saw the original Tiny Totes concept. Like Collins, she knew right away that the concept could be powerful. "The product targeted the market of young girls and what they like, which is little collective things," she said. "It hit what was hot—

key chains—but gave it a twist so that it wasn't just another key chain."

Over the next several months, BIG worked with the three inventors to refine the concept, do some preliminary costing, and create a list of companies that seemed to have the appropriate distribution to market the product. While BIG approached Toys "R" Us and Hasbro, it eventually sold the idea to Basic Fun, which, according to Collins, had "the perfect distribution for this product and expertise in miniatures. They are big enough to really run with the opportunity, but small enough to care about the line." BIG showed the product to Basic Fun in April 2001, had a contract drafted by May, and signed the contract in June. In September 2001, the product debuted at Pre-Toy Fair.

Collins said that without BIG, the invention would probably have never made it to the market:

> The reality is, that product would have probably died on the vine for a number of reasons. First, the inventors weren't sure who to take the concept to. And even if they had found the right company, that company might not have taken the time to look at the product—or see the potential if they actually did review it. Because by the time we presented Tiny Totes, we'd redesigned, re-engineered, and packaged it.

Kern agreed that BIG played a vital role in bringing Tiny Totes from concept to reality. "The chance after all of these years to have this very knowledgeable go-between—you can't put a price tag on that," she said. The success with Tiny Totes energized Kern, who with her two friends continued to work on new ideas. "This stuff just pops in my head," she explained. "I find out

what's fun for me. Then we solve it as a team. We just do what we want."

Financing/Business Model

As of September 2001, BIG had raised approximately $850,000 in relatively small chunks from angel investors. Since BIG was positioned as a middleman that did not hold inventory, it did not require major investments or expensive overhead. As d'Arbeloff noted, "Our business model is interesting because we generate high profits for relatively little revenue since overhead is so low. It's like venture capital."

Collins did point out some important differences between venture capital and the BIG concept. "Venture capital is a great business model. You make investments with other people's money and you get 25 percent of the gain. But you have to have a fund, and working with a company can be a decade-long commitment," he noted. "With BIG, I get equity for value-added, not capital. And our equity is in a portfolio of ideas and product lines, not companies."

BIG's business plan projected that it would be profitable in 2002 and would generate $12 million in profit by 2006 (see Exhibit 9 for key financial projections). However, to meet that plan, BIG knew it had to expand beyond its initial focus in the kids' industry into other vertical markets.

HITTING THE BIG TIME: WHAT NEXT?

In April 2001, with a growing sense that their entry into the kids' industry was proving to be quite successful, Collins and d'Arbeloff turned their thoughts to the next

EXHIBIT 9 Financial Projections ($ 000s)

	2001	2002	2003	2004	2005	2006
Revenues						
Advances	80	140	210	320	420	570
Corporate Services	100	150	230	300	380	450
Sponsorships	0	750	1,500	2,250	3,000	4,000
Total Operating Revenue	180	1,040	1,940	2,870	3,800	5,020
Operating Expenses	600	1,200	1,800	2,400	3,000	3,600
Operating Profit (Loss)	(420)	(160)	140	470	800	1,420
Royalties/Direct Import	0	250	1,180	3,050	6,150	10,980
Total Profit	(420)	90	1,320	3,520	6,950	12,400
KEY ASSUMPTIONS						
Number of vertical markets	1	2	3	4	5	6
Number of deals	5	9	14	21	28	38
Number of "home run" deals	0	1	1	1	2	2
Average royalty per deal	5%	5%	5%	5%	5%	5%

Source: Company documents.

"vertical" they could attack. Almost since the inception of the business, Collins and d'Arbeloff had thought that the "home and garden" industry would be a natural place to extend their business model. In fact, they received confirmation that home and garden had potential from an unexpected source. Collins recalled:

> There's a program at Tuck Business School where top undergraduates can go through a month-long "boot camp." Last summer, right when I started the business, they wanted to do a case on us. The assignment was what markets should we go into next and why. They provided a lot of research confirming the potential of the home and garden market. It's a big opportunity and the kind of market where independent inventors can easily come up with something.

The Home and Garden Industry

The U.S. home and garden or do-it-yourself industry dwarfed the toy industry, with the National Retail Hardware Association reporting more than $160 billion in retail sales in 2000 (see Exhibit 10 for industry facts and figures). Like the kids' industry, home and garden is made up of numerous discrete subsegments with many different kinds of retailers. While in 2000 the top 25 chains—dominated by the two big national chains, Home Depot and Lowe's—controlled almost 50 percent of all retail sales, there were almost 40,000 outlets run by smaller companies outside that top 25. As in the kids' market, there were a wide number of suppliers to the industry, ranging from well-recognized consumer brands like Craftsman, Hunter, and Kohler to specialty brands known largely to home improvement aficionados.

Finding a Sponsor

While BIG received angel financing to go after the kids' industry, Collins and d'Arbeloff decided to seek sponsorship from home and garden companies that were looking for ways to augment their product development efforts. Collins explained the rationale for seeking sponsors: "In the first place, revenue is better than equity. In addition, there's going to be huge advantage to having a close relationship with sponsors. We've learned that with Toys "R" Us. Working with companies and knowing what their culture is, who the decision-makers are, and where they want to head strategically will help us in all facets of our initiative."

A BIG angel investor put Collins and d'Arbeloff in touch with Skil-Bosch, a 77-year-old tool company based in Chicago. BIG set up a meeting with Skil-Bosch in Chicago in June 2001. As d'Arbeloff recalled, "Mike and I sat down to meet with the president of the company and

one of his staff. We'd put together a slide presentation and were about halfway through it when the president said, 'I've got it, let's go. How much?'" Collins quickly proposed $750,000, the sum BIG spent a year on the kids' space and the estimated amount that would be needed for home and garden. Skil-Bosch agreed to foot a significant portion of that sum and become lead sponsor of the program. In return, it received the right of first refusal on any ideas within its scope of business that were generated by the BIG process. The two companies signed a letter of intent in August 2001 and formally launched the program in September 2001.

Ann Dow, director of innovation and advanced development at the Skil-Bosch Power Tool Company, said that it decided to partner with BIG to look for ideas outside of its traditional market segments. "We recognize that there are a lot of inventors in our categories and many of their ideas go untapped because people don't know or can't locate the appropriate people within a company to share their ideas," Dow said. "Internally, we're not organized to proactively contact external inventors to see what else is out there—that's how BIG adds value."

Dow added that Skil-Bosch hoped its partnership with BIG would produce at least one big idea along with several smaller ideas each year. Additionally, it anticipated the collaboration would create a "pipeline" of new ideas. "The tool category is extremely competitive right now and companies can't compete on cost alone," Dow explained. "You must demonstrate added value to end users, and we believe this will be driven by providing innovative solutions to their problems. Innovation can come from anywhere, and BIG's process provides just one avenue out of many to help drive creative solutions."

The BIG Issue: Is the Process Transferable?

With the next vertical industry selected and a lead sponsor locked up, BIG now needed to turn its attention to actually making the home and garden opportunity happen. Collins and d'Arbeloff had a host of complicated issues they needed to sort out. Were there overlooked inventors in the industry that were sitting on worthwhile products? Would the process that worked so successfully in the kids' space transfer to an industry that was much different? Could they find the right person to manage the home and garden business unit? And, perhaps most importantly, was BIG really creating a sustainable business with substantial barriers to entry, or would its success invite a slew of copycats that BIG could not defend against?

Presence of Products   Collins and d'Arbeloff were convinced that there were inventors who had developed

EXHIBIT 10 Home Improvement Industry Facts and Figures

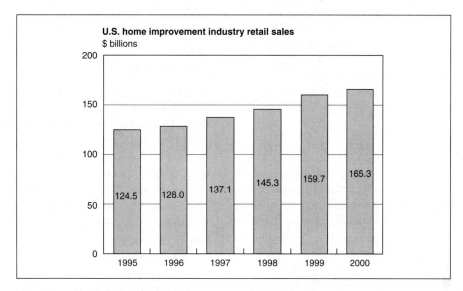

U.S. home improvement industry retail sales
$ billions

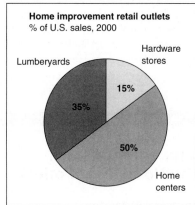

Home improvement retail outlets
% of U.S. sales, 2000

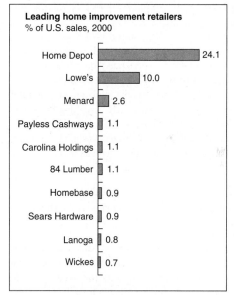

Leading home improvement retailers
% of U.S. sales, 2000

Source: Compiled by the casewriter based on statistics from the National Retail Hardware Association (available at http://www.nrha.org/markmeas.html).

potentially valuable products in the home and garden space. At annual shows like Yankee Inventor Expo, a number of inventors routinely displayed ideas that fit the home and garden market. In addition, some of BIG's inventors in the kids' space had home and garden concepts in development.

Process BIG intended to employ the same process that had proven so successful in the kids' industry. It planned to develop a network of inventors to generate deal flow

through Hunts and related activities. While Collins recognized the Hunts might be smaller—"we might see 30–40 people during the course of a weekend instead of 100"—he still thought the events would be a valuable way to tap in to the inventor community. BIG would again assemble panels of industry experts to evaluate the inventions gathered through its generation process. As of September 2001, BIG had begun to think about who were the right people to have on its panel, with Skil-Bosch providing an initial list of potential contacts.

The rest of the process would be similar to the one BIG followed in the kids' space. Ideas would be evaluated and winnowed down from the initial list. Then BIG would follow the same steps of adding value to concepts and monetizing them through deals with the appropriate companies. Although both Collins and d'Arbeloff admitted the process would need to evolve as BIG learned more about the industry, they were confident that their basic system would work.

Finding the Right Stuff   Perhaps the most critical issue facing BIG was finding the manager to head up the home and garden initiative. While existing staff would handle the launch, Collins recognized that it would be necessary to quickly add additional, separate resources to manage the new vertical industry. D'Arbeloff said that hiring the right person would be key to BIG's successful expansion beyond the kids' industry. "I think one of the challenges is finding the Mike Collins of home and garden," he remarked. Collins added what he viewed as the necessary skills for the job:

> I think it's as much a function of personality, creativity, and intelligence as it is domain experience. You can acquire domain expertise in a pretty short period of time with smart panelists and good sponsors. But the job is broad: coaching inventors, working with creative staff, assessing concepts, selling products, negotiating deals, etc. You have to be able to meet with CEOs for strategic discussions in the morning and then discuss a portable toilet seat with an inventor in the afternoon.

Dow said Skil-Bosch was confident that the BIG process was repeatable in other industries with the right leader:

> The key to the process is the leader. Mike calls himself the rainmaker, and he is key. I've sat in on a couple of the Hunts that he's done. He understands the toy category inside and out, so he can successfully lead and drive the conversations with inventors. He recruits additional panelists to provide diversity, balance, and objectivity, but he's the main driver. BIG's challenge is to identify a "Mike" in the home and garden segment.

Building BIG Barriers   Collins said he believed that BIG's system created a virtuous cycle that built potent barriers to entry. Through its idea generation process, BIG formed a network of hundreds of potential inventors. As it worked closely with companies, it learned what ideas were most likely to be successful and could send that feedback to its inventor community to generate more profitable ideas. "I do think there's great value in the network you create and the business partnerships you establish," Collins said. "You could replicate our process, but you can't replicate the human side of the business."

CONCLUSION

It had been quite a year for Collins and d'Arbeloff, and they both were excited about the opportunity before them. D'Arbeloff remarked that in contrast to his first (failed) startup venture, which came nowhere close to meeting business plan targets, "In this venture, we've done everything we said we would. In fact, we've done more than we'd promised." The pair believed that they had found a new, highly profitable way to handle the innovation process. But questions certainly remained. As Collins remarked:

> Big Idea Group is like any invention. We saw a need, developed a prototype, and have experimented to get it right. A few things haven't worked out, but we keep learning and getting smarter. Home and garden is a big step. We don't know if it will work as we envisioned. If it doesn't, we'll try a new approach—just like any good inventor.

CASE III-7

Intel Corporation: The Hood River Project

Raymond S. Bamford

> *Intel's traditional OEMs and consumer electronics companies are driving towards increased integration of computers and consumer electronics products. . . . Entertainment media, both audio and video, are transitioning to digital formats. . . . The computer is uniquely positioned to add value in this world of digital media. . . . To take advantage of this opportunity, the computer must be positioned at the logical center of the entertainment control point in the home—tightly integrating microprocessor power with consumer electronics equipment.*
> —Hood River Market Requirements Document, 8/30/96

As the clock struck midnight in his office on December 15, 1996, Rob Siegel leaned back in his chair and thought more about the future of Hood River, the project he had led since its inception almost a year earlier.[1] The central goal of Hood River was to define the standards and establish a market presence for the PC in the living room, and Siegel and his team felt that they had made good progress toward achieving these goals. However, the Hood River team had recently encountered a series of challenges and setbacks. In October, while Siegel was attending a speaking engagement at a prominent East Coast business school, the funding for Hood River had been suddenly cut without his input having been solicited. Although Siegel had succeeded in getting the funding reinstated, his team remained somewhat anxious and unsure about their future. Later that same month, senior management had begun questioning some of the fundamental aspects of the product design, which caused additional anxiety. Then in early December, the organization into which Siegel reported was reorganized. Rather than reporting directly to the general manager of the Desktop Products Division, Siegel would report through a marketing vice president.

Siegel believed that Hood River would continue to face difficult challenges within Intel, and he thought seriously about whether it would be best to spin off the program as a separate company. Les Vadasz, who headed Corporate Business Development (CBD), would control that decision. Siegel's first job at Intel had been in CBD, and CBD had provided the seed financing for Hood River. Siegel had regular contact with Vadasz, and was planning to meet with him later that week. Siegel wondered whether he should make a formal request to spin off Hood River, and if so, how he should go about making and justifying his request. As Siegel walked out of his office to head home, he wondered about his future at Intel and realized that he would have to make some decisions quickly (see Exhibit 1 for Siegel's biography).

INTEL BACKGROUND

Intel was founded in 1968 by Robert Noyce and Gordon Moore, two legends in the emerging field of solid-state electronics. Noyce and Moore were soon joined by their new director of operations, Andy Grove. Grove took responsibility for building the organization, and shaped the culture of the company with his focus and aggressive-

ness. Recalled Moore, "Andy always made it hard on me. I would be all excited that we were under budget or ahead of schedule on a product—and he'd ask why we couldn't do it faster and cheaper. He got very interested in the art of management, and that served us very well."[2] Grove became Intel's president in 1979, its CEO in 1987, and its chairman in 1997. (Exhibit 2 shows Intel's mission, objectives and values.)

Throughout its history, Intel's strategy had focused on technology leadership, first-mover advantage, and the dominance of horizontal markets. Intel engineers invented most of the important building blocks of the digital age, including the SRAM (static random-access memory), the DRAM (dynamic random-access memory), the EPROM (electrically programmable read-only memory), the EEPROM (electrically erasable programmable read-only memory), and the microprocessor.

By 1996, Intel had established itself as the dominant player in the semiconductor industry, and one of the most powerful companies in the computer industry. Intel's microprocessors could be found in more than 90 percent of personal computers, and, along with Microsoft's Windows NT operating system, in a rapidly growing percentage of computer workstations and servers. Intel-based systems were increasingly penetrating corporate data centers, where they were displacing systems based on RISC (reduced instruction set computing)[3] technology. Intel was a leading player in the markets for chipsets[4] and motherboards.[5] Intel was also a major player in the markets for flash memory,[6] embedded control chips,[7] and a variety of networking and communications products, including video conferencing.

During the 10-year period between 1987 and 1996, Intel achieved exceptional financial performance (see Exhibit 3). Sales of Pentium microprocessors and related board-level products comprised about 80 percent of the company's revenues and a substantial majority of its

---

[1] The names of some of the players in this case have been disguised.

[2] "Why Andy Grove Can't Stop," *Fortune*, July 10, 1995.
[3] RISC chips were manufactured by companies such as Hewlett-Packard, Sun Microsystems, Digital, and IBM, which tied their chips to their own versions of Unix.
[4] Chipsets perform the essential logic functions surrounding the microprocessor.
[5] Motherboards combine microprocessors and chipsets on a circuit board to form the basic subsystem of a computer.
[6] Flash memory is commonly used in products such as computers and mobile phones, and has the advantages of being easily programmable and capable of saving data even after power is turned off.
[7] Embedded control chips are designed into cellular phones, laser printers, automobile engines, automobile braking systems, hard disk drives, home appliances, and the like.

EXHIBIT 1 Rob Siegel Resume

OVERVIEW

Over ten years' experience in high technology spanning the semiconductor, software and hard drive industries. An entrepreneurial and experienced leader with a proven track record in new market creation, venture investing, strategic alliance development, international sales and marketing.

WORK EXPERIENCE

Intel Corporation   Santa Clara, CA; 1994–Present
Manager, Corporate Business Development
- Closed five investments in 12 months totaling $10 million; investments ranged in size from $5 million to $150K
- Formulated and initiated Intel's strategies in multi-player gaming, virtual worlds, PC/consumer electronics convergence and 3-D graphics; worked with product groups to implement strategic directions
- Led strategic alliance with Autodesk for Pentium Pro launch

Other
- Led a cross-functional team of 25 people and delivered to Intel's executive staff key products and issues for all of Intel's consumer markets for the three year period 1997–1999
- Introduced Intel to the Starbright Foundation and led Intel's initiative to donate $500K worth of computers to a test program bringing virtual worlds to children dying of cancer

Sun Microsystems   Palo Alto, CA; 1993–1994
Consultant (concurrent to graduate work studies)
- Researched and recommended both market opportunities and product ideas for Sun's technology that became Java; outlined potential alliances and launch strategies

Quantum Corporation   Milpitas, CA; Summer, 1993
Product Marketing Intern
- Designed and implemented new pricing and forecasting system for $500 million hard drive distribution channel; prepared customer materials for sales force on new, high volume hard drive product lines; determined financial impact of withholding distribution of one product and closing domestic factory

GeoWorks   Berkeley, CA; 1990–1992
Manager, International Sales and Marketing
- Responsible for sales to hardware companies in the U.S., Far East and Europe, including Philips, Sony, NEC, Samsung, Canon and others, for bundling software with personal computers and PDAs; in charge of all associated pricing and contract negotiations; managed the delivery of software, documentation and marketing requirements

Bain and Company   San Francisco, CA; 1989–1990
Associate Consultant
- Designed and programmed pricing system and account profitability tool for $600 million company
- Converted tool to client's DEC mini-computer system and managed national roll-out of 82 branch sites

Berkeley Softworks (now GeoWorks)   Berkeley, CA; 1986–1989
Marketing Assistant (Full-time work concurrent with completion of undergraduate degree)
- SYSOP for company's online technical support to users and developers
- Designed and created end user newsletters and documents for advertising and packaging
- Co-authored three software manuals

EDUCATION

Stanford University, M.B.A.; June 1994
—Co-Editor in chief, *The Reporter,* High Tech Club

University of California, Berkeley, B.A. Political Science; May 1989
—3.8 GPA, High Honors, Phi Beta Kappa, Delta Chi Fraternity

MISCELLANEOUS

Lead researcher for *Only the Paranoid Survive,* by Andy Grove
Campaign Chairman for GeoWorks' United Way campaigns, 1990–1992
Hit .222 at Los Angeles Dodger's Adult Fantasy Baseball Camp

EXHIBIT 2   Intel's Mission, Objectives, and Values, 1996

OUR MISSION:

Do a great job for our customers, employees and stockholders by being the preeminent building block supplier to the computing industry worldwide.

OUR OBJECTIVES:

1. **Strengthen the #1 position of Intel microprocessors in the new computing industry.**
   - Make high performance Intel Architecture processors the preferred choice for desktop, server, and mobile market segments.
   - Make the Intel Architecture PC the platform of choice for authoring and visualization of digital content.
   - Provide strategic leadership/guidance to the industry to assure an adequate supply of PC components.
   - Rapidly grow Pentium® processor PC shipments and increase Intel's influence in Asia, Latin America, and Eastern Europe.
   - Help our segment-leading, market-making, and regional brand customers to be successful through fastest time to market.
   - Make the Pentium® Pro processor the CPU of choice for the 32-bit corporate desktop, workstation, and server market segments.

2. **Make the high-performance PC "IT" and establish Intel as the leading PC communications company.**
   - Have the high-performance PC recognized as the indispensable tool for work, learning, and play on the net and off the net.
   - Develop technologies and common industry specifications to enable the PC to support real-time multimedia communication (RMC) applications:
     —Accelerate the deployment of RMC applications into the home, business, and mobile market segments.
     —Extend the availability of RMC to online services and the Internet.
   - Engage the new media industry and assure the timely availability of RMC digital content for the Intel Architecture PC.
   - Build successful businesses in selected networking and communication market segments.

3. **Harness the Internet "energy" as a source of applications for high performance PCs.**
   - Help develop an Intel Architecture–based Internet Dream Machine and provide a well-integrated, cost-effective access/presence server to small and medium businesses.
   - Make the Intel Architecture PC the port of choice for all Internet systems and application software; encourage and aid the Internet ISV industry to enrich their applications with RMC capabilities.
   - Be a leading user of Internet technologies inside of Intel including providing an awesome Intel corporate website.
   - Market and evangelize the high-performance Intel Architecture PC as a superior device for on-the-net and off-the-net applications.

4. **Excel at Intel basics.**
   - Be the "no excuses" supplier of choice to our customers.
   - Continuously improve our performance to Intel values.
   - Build and fill the industry's best factories with leading edge products and processes.
   - Make our Information Technology systems a competitive advantage.
   - Align our semiconductor business and capacity to support growth in the PC and cellular phone markets.

OUR VALUES:

Discipline

The complexity of our work and tough business environment demand a high degree of self discipline.

We strive to:
- Conduct business with uncompromising integrity and professionalism.
- Clearly communicate intentions and expectations.
- Make and meet commitments.
- Properly plan, fund, and staff projects.
- Pay attention to detail.

Results Orientation

We are results oriented.

We strive to:
- Set challenging goals.
- Execute flawlessly.
- Focus on output.
- Assume responsibility.
- Confront and solve problems.

Risk Taking

To succeed we must maintain our innovative environment.

We strive to:
- Embrace change.
- Challenge the status quo.
- Listen to all ideas and viewpoints.
- Encourage and reward informed risk taking.
- Learn from our successes and mistakes.

Great Place to Work

A productive and challenging work environment is key to our success.

We strive to:
- Be open and direct.
- Work as a team with respect and trust for each other.
- Manage performance fairly and firmly.
- Recognize and reward accomplishments.
- Maintain a safe and neat workplace.
- Be an asset to the community.
- Have fun!

Customer Orientation

Partnerships with our customers and other business partners are essential for our mutual success.

We strive to:
- Listen to our partners well.
- Communicate mutual intentions and expectations.
- Deliver innovative and competitive products and services.
- Make it easy to work with us.

Quality

Our business requires continuous improvement of our performance to our Mission and Values.

We strive to:
- Set challenging and competitive goals.
- Do the right things right.
- Excel at Intel basics.
- Continuously learn, develop, and improve.
- Take pride in our work.

EXHIBIT 3   Intel Financial Highlights

Intel income statement, 1994–1996 ($ millions)

	1996	1995	1994
Net revenues	$20,847	$16,202	$11,521
Cost of sale	9,164	7,811	5,576
Research and development	1,808	1,296	1,111
Marketing, general and administrative	2,322	1,843	1,447
Operating costs and expenses	$13,294	$10,950	$ 8,134
Operating income	**$ 7,553**	**$ 5,252**	**$ 3,387**
Interest expense	(25)	(29)	(57)
Interest income and other, net	406	415	273
Income before taxes	**$ 7,934**	**$ 5,638**	**$ 3,603**
Provision for taxes	2,777	2,072	1,315
Net income	**$ 5,157**	**$ 3,566**	**$ 2,288**
Earnings per share	**$5.81**	**$4.03**	**$2.62**

Source: Intel Annual Report, 1996.

Intel stock price 12/31/93–12/31/96, $ per share

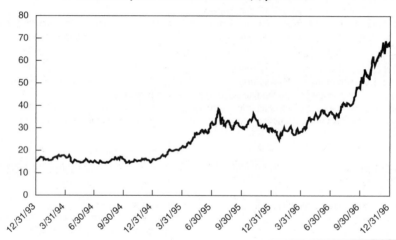

Net revenue, 1987–1996

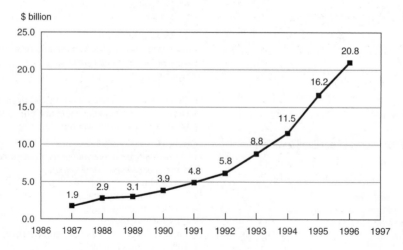

EXHIBIT 3 *(continued)*

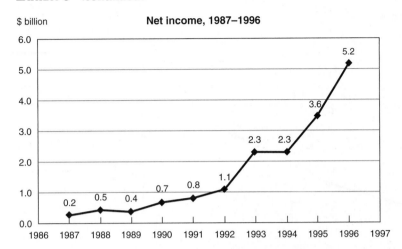

$ billion — Net income, 1987–1996

1996 revenue by product	
Microprocessors	$14.9 B
Chipsets	$1.4 B
Motherboards	$1.2–2.0 B
Networking	$1.0–2.0 B
Flash memory	$950 M
Embedded controllers	$530 M
Video conferencing	$33.5 M

Source: Intel, *Dataquest*

EXHIBIT 4 **The Evolution of Intel's Microprocessors**

Processor	Clock speed (MHz)	Die size (mm²)	Number of transistors (millions)	Date of release
486DX	25	165	1.2	April 1989
486SX	16	316	1.2	September 1991
486DX2	50	230	1.2	March 1992
Pentium	60	294	3.1	March 1993
486DX4	75,100	87	1.6	March 1994
Pentium Pro	150, 200	196	5.5	November 1995
Pentium MMX	166	128	4.5	January 1997
Pentium II	233, 300	203	7.5	May 1997
Pentium MMX Mobile	200, 233	95	4.5	September 1997

Source: PC Magazine, 9/23/97; Intel.

gross margin in 1996.[8] Revenue increased from $1.9 billion to $20.8 billion, an increase of 30.5 percent per annum. Net income grew from $248 million to $5.2 billion, an increase of 40.3 percent per annum. And Intel's stock price, adjusted for stock splits, grew from $3 5/16 per share at the end of 1987 to $65 15/32 at the end of 1996, an increase of 39.3 percent per annum. Intel operating activities generated $8.7 billion in cash in 1996, up from $4.0 billion and $2.9 billion in 1995 and 1994, respectively. At the end of 1996, Intel employed approximately 48,500 people worldwide.

Intel's strategy was to continually introduce higher performance microprocessors. The company had recently introduced higher performance members of the Pentium microprocessor family, the Pentium with MMX™ and the Pentium II. (Exhibit 4 shows the evolution of Intel's microprocessors and the relentless pace of new product introductions.) To drive demand toward the newer products, Intel cultivated new businesses and worked with the software industry to develop compelling applications that would take advantage of this higher performance. To implement its strategy, Intel aggressively invested in both R&D and production capacity for its high-performance chips (see Exhibit 5). Production investment decisions were usually made long before demand for these chips could be ascertained. Intel's capital investments in property, plant, and equipment had grown from $302 million in 1987 to $3.6 billion in 1995 and $3.0 billion in 1996. At the end of 1996, Intel's capital forecast for 1997 was $4.5 billion.[9]

---

[8] Intel and *Dataquest*.

[9] http://www.fool.com/Calls/1997/calls970116b.htm.

EXHIBIT 5 Intel Investments, 1987–1996

Research and development

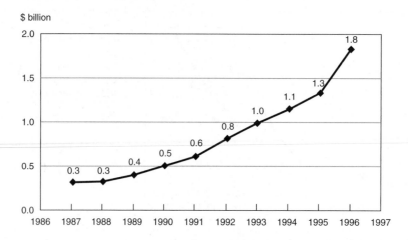

Capital additions to plant, property, and equipment

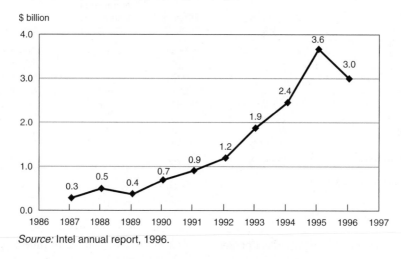

Source: Intel annual report, 1996.

In 1996, Intel was organized in a matrix structure consisting of both product and functional groups (see Exhibit 6). The product groups included Desktop Products Group (DPG), Mobile & Handheld Products Group (MHPG), Enterprise Products Group (EPG), Internet & Communications Group (ICG), and Content Group (CG). The functional groups included Sales & Marketing Group (SMG), Corporate Business Development (CBD), Technology & Manufacturing Group (TMG), and Microprocessor Products Group (MPG). A typical feature of Intel's organization was for groups to be headed by two people, known as "two-in-a-box," which usually included one person with a technical orientation and another one

with a business orientation. At the top of the organization chart, Andy Grove, Craig Barrett, and Gordon Moore were shown as three-in-a-box. (Exhibit 7 shows biographies of some of Intel's senior managers.)

CORPORATE BUSINESS DEVELOPMENT (CBD)

Corporate Business Development (CBD) performed an important function within Intel by making outside equity investments in strategic companies, by making acquisitions, and by financing technology or business ideas that were generated internally within Intel. CBD was led by Les Vadasz, who had been among Intel's first employees.

EXHIBIT 6   Intel Organization Chart

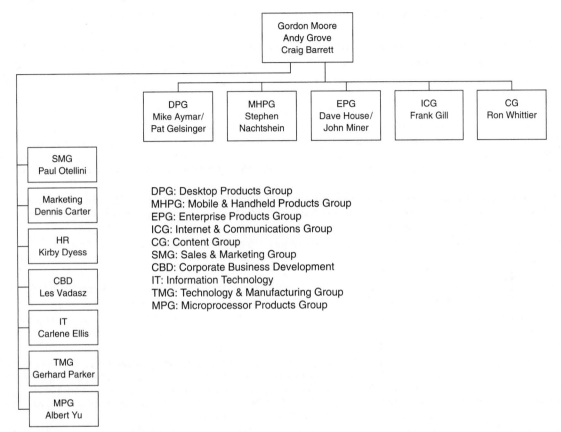

DPG: Desktop Products Group
MHPG: Mobile & Handheld Products Group
EPG: Enterprise Products Group
ICG: Internet & Communications Group
CG: Content Group
SMG: Sales & Marketing Group
CBD: Corporate Business Development
IT: Information Technology
TMG: Technology & Manufacturing Group
MPG: Microprocessor Products Group

Avram Miller, vice president of Corporate Business Development and a direct report to Vadasz, had been at Intel for 13 years and described his role as that of "a troublemaker that makes Intel do things that they don't want to do, driving major objectives that do not fit the Intel core." By Intel's standards, CBD was a very small group, composed of approximately a dozen people, with a very flat organizational structure (see Exhibit 8). According to Rob Siegel:

There are two types of people in CBD. There are those that are associated with a particular business group (with a solid reporting line to the business unit and a dotted line to CBD). These people are looking for technologies for the business unit's core business, and can get funding from Vadasz for things like a license in a new technology. There are also those people that belong to CBD proper. These are the "crazies" who don't really fit in and tend to have a longer time frame on the areas that they explore.

CBD performed three types of activities. First, CBD played a role like that of a venture capitalist, making equity investments in independent start-up companies and completing technology transfers or licensing agreements. Second, CBD managed strategic relationships with other companies. Third, CBD funded seed programs within Intel, such as Hood River, where CBD gave budget relief to business groups in exchange for engineers that staff the program. Explaining the first role of CBD, which constituted the vast majority of CBD's activities, Vadasz said:

CBD seeks to accelerate the creation of new market ecosystems, in part by using our financial resources. This amounts to about 80 percent of what we're doing. The best example of this is what we're doing in visual computing for the PC. The PC has been a distant laggard relative to the Mac, SGI, and Sun. But over the last few years we made a large investment in our own R&D to improve the platform. At the same time, we made a number of investments in hardware and software companies to accelerate their plans to adapt their products to the new Intel platforms. On the other hand, sometimes our investments are focused on improving our own capabilities to deliver our products. We may need a piece of technology per se for our own needs, such as the next generation wafer stepper for our new generation of silicon manufacturing. We need to be sure that the technology

EXHIBIT 7   Intel Executive Officers, December 1996

Craig R. Barrett (age 57) has been chief operating officer since 1993; a director of Intel since 1992; and executive vice president since 1990.

Andrew S. Grove (age 60) has been a director of Intel since 1974; president since 1979; and chief executive officer since 1987.

Gordon E. Moore (age 67) has been a director of Intel since 1968 and chairman of the board since 1979.

Leslie L. Vadasz (age 60) has been a director of Intel since 1988 and senior vice president and director of corporate business development since 1991.

Frank C. Gill (age 53) has been executive vice president and general manager, Internet and Communications Group, since 1996. Prior to that, Mr. Gill was senior vice president and general manager, Intel Products Group, from 1991 to 1996.

Paul S. Otellini (age 46) has been executive vice president, director, Sales and Marketing Group, since 1996. Prior to that Mr. Otellini was senior vice president, director, Sales and Marketing Group, from 1994 to 1996; senior vice president and general manager, Microprocessor Products Group, from 1992 to 1994; and vice president and general manager, Microprocessor Products Group, from 1991 to 1992.

Gerard H. Parker (age 53) has been executive vice president and general manager, Technology and Manufacturing Group, since 1996. Prior to that, Dr. Parker was senior vice president and general manager, Technology and Manufacturing Group, from 1992 to 1996, and vice president and general manager, Technology and Manufacturing Group, from 1990 to 1992.

Ronald J. Whittier (age 60) has been senior vice president and general manager, Content Group, since 1995. Prior to that, Mr. Whittier was senior vice president and general manager, Intel Architecture Laboratories, from 1993 to 1995, and vice president and general manager, Software Technology Group, from 1991 to 1992.

Albert Y. C. Yu (age 55) has been senior vice president and general manager, Microprocessor Products Group, since 1993. Prior to that, Dr. Yu was vice president and general manager, Microprocessor Products Group, from 1991 to 1993.

Michael A. Aymar (age 49) has been vice president and general manager, Desktop Products Group, since 1995. Prior to that, Mr. Aymar was vice president and general manager, Intel486 Microprocessor Division, from 1994 to 1995, and vice president and general manager, Mobile Computing Group, from 1991 to 1994.

Patrick P. Gelsinger (age 35) has been vice president and general manager, Desktop Products Group, since 1996. Prior to that, Mr. Gelsinger was vice president, Internet and Communications Group, and general manager, ICG Product Development, from 1995 to 1996; vice president, Intel Products Group, and general manager, Personal Conferencing Division, from 1993 to 1995; vice president, Intel Products Group, and general manager, PC Enhancement Division-Business Communications, from 1992 to 1993; and general manager, D 6, Microprocessor Development, from 1991 to 1992.

John H. F. Miner (age 41) has been vice president and general manager, Enterprise Server Group, since 1996. Prior to that, Mr. Miner was vice president, Desktop Products Group, and general manager, OEM Products and Services Division, from 1995 to 1996; general manager, OEM Products and Services Division, from 1993 to 1995, and general manager, OEM Modules Operation, from 1992 to 1993.

Stephen P. Nachtsheim (age 51) has been vice president and general manager, Mobile/Handheld Products Group, since 1995. Prior to that, Mr. Nachtsheim was vice president and general manager, Mobile and Home Products Group, from 1994 to 1995, and general manager of European Intel Products Group, from 1990 to 1994.

EXHIBIT 8   Corporate Business Development (CBD) Organization

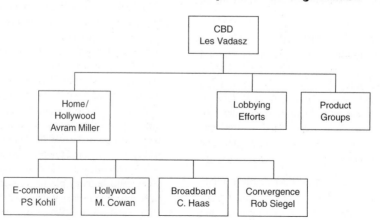

that we depend on is delivered in a timely manner. This amounts to about 20 percent of what we're doing.

Managing strategic relationships and funding seed programs were relatively minor activities for CBD. CBD funded approximately 2–3 seed programs each year on average, and 4 or 5 seed programs were typically active at any one time. In the case of seed programs, CBD provided the initial financing, but eventually project management and funding were transferred to one of the business units. According to Avram Miller, "This does not always work very well. Because if the business units don't care initially about the project, they probably won't care later either. It's the corporate immune system that takes over."

Vadasz commented:

One of the biggest dangers for big companies is not being able to manage small amounts of money. For some top managers, these new ventures are trivial stuff. But these ventures are necessary to stay on the bleeding edge. On the other hand, you can easily overspend too early. I have done this various times in my life! . . . CBD is finding out that we let go of products too early, when they are still too weak. . . . Thus, there is a continuous dilemma: how to create a nurturing environment and minimize the transition issues into the main line of business. Because every main line business will consume your resources and more! Perhaps these projects need some continuous oversight from CBD or others after the transfer.

One important implication of Intel's organization structure was that power and control over resources were distributed across the organization. Even senior managers relied on resources outside of their direct control to achieve their goals. In order to effectively get things done within Intel, managers needed to build relationships across the organization and have the ability to garner support from one's colleagues.

THE PC IN THE LIVING ROOM: THE GENESIS OF HOOD RIVER

Rob Siegel: Corporate Entrepreneur

Rob Siegel joined Intel in August 1994, soon after graduating from Stanford's Graduate School of Business. Siegel had originally received an offer from Intel's Corporate Marketing Group. However, for several years Siegel had known Avram Miller, from CBD, who was exploring new ways that people could use computers. After several discussions with Miller, Siegel decided to join CBD. Within CBD, Siegel was initially involved

with a broad range of activities, including 3D graphics, multiplayer computer games, "virtual worlds," and telephony issues. Siegel had been very pleased with his career at Intel. After 15 months on the job, Siegel had already been promoted once when he was approached by Les Vadasz and Avram Miller to explore "how to move bits around the home." According to Avram Miller:

Rob had done a number of good deals in the new media area, within my strategic framework. He was young, talented, and eager to do more, so I was wrestling with what his next challenge would be. I was interested in Rob's career and wanted to see him grow. I felt that Rob needed something more challenging, so I looked to stick him somewhere that would make him uncomfortable.

Internal Events

Hood River was spawned by a number of events both internal and external to Intel. In early 1995, few people within Intel were focused on "digital convergence," the increasing overlap between the computing, communications, and consumer electronics industries. Siegel recalled that during the SLRP[10] of mid-1995, the question was raised of how to put the PC in the living room, and 60 people started yelling at each other, each with a different opinion on the issue."

Les Vadasz and Avram Miller had already been considering the opportunity for the PC in the living room. In his house Vadasz had installed a big media room that used expensive hardware devices to connect the different components. According to Vadasz:

Hood River sprang, in part, from my personal experience with building a high-end media room in my home. I had a rack full of equipment and a controller, but the current approach is brain dead, and the so-called ease of use of consumer electronics devices is a myth. Given that the PC is an intelligent interactive device, why not give the PC a role in the consumer electronics space?

Initially, the project did not appear attractive to Siegel who saw only "dead ends and dead bodies" in this area. He elaborated:

A number of high-profile people were working in this area, but everybody was losing money. There were a number of dead bodies in the convergence space, and even more in set-top boxes. One high-profile venture had already lost $43 million in venture money. . . . I originally hesitated

---

[10] SLRP, or strategic long-range planning, pronounced "slurp," was a meeting attended by Intel's most senior executives to discuss important issues related to corporate strategy.

because this looked like something where a lot of smart people had failed inside and outside Intel.

According to Avram Miller:

> Les and I had been kicking around the idea of the PC in the living room, and we encouraged Rob to look into it. Initially, Rob was not very interested. Rob now had to develop the entire strategy, which was a new task for him. At first Rob accomplished little. But then he came up with the Hood River concept.

Siegel recalled that he had taken several months, from August to November of 1995, to study the problem. Siegel had purchased about $5,000 worth of common electronics equipment, and together with several engineers, took the equipment apart and asked what could be put into a PC. By December 1995, things started to click and Siegel saw the opportunity to do a seed program around the convergence of the PC with consumer electronic devices. In addition to the encouragement from Vadasz and Miller, Siegel had been introduced to Eric Albertson, an engineer from OPSD in Oregon, who had been hired in October 1995 to work on new form factor products. Albertson's ideas had much in common with Siegel's own vision, and the two began to collaborate.

External Events

By 1996, more than 34 percent of U.S. households owned a PC, up from 18 percent in 1990. This figure was projected to rise by 55 percent by the year 2000. Of the households not expected to own a PC, the two most common reasons were that they did not need one, or could not afford one.[11] In contrast, television sets were in approximately 98 percent of U.S. homes.[12]

The average U.S. home contained a number of consumer electronics devices that provide entertainment and communications, including TVs, stereo sound systems, VCRs, game consoles, telephones and answering machines, and fax machines. In 1995 and 1996, many analysts believed that the integration of these devices was the next logical step. Across a broad spectrum of industries, including entertainment, telecommunication, cable, consumer electronics, and computing, there was tremendous enthusiasm around interactive multimedia and the "convergence" of these various industries.

In late 1995, a debate was being conducted as to whether the PC or the TV would become the dominant device of the future. Andy Grove had described this battle as the "war for eyeballs." He clearly believed in the PC. "The PC is it," said Grove. "That sums up Intel's business plan and rallying cry. Some think the information superhighway will come through their TV. The information tool of the future is on your desk, not in your living room."[13] According to Nicholas Negroponte, the best-selling author and new-media futurist, by the year 2000, "many Americans will be watching TV in the upper-right-hand corner of their PCs."[14] *Business Week* ran a cover story describing the huge industry activity to develop new products for the family room, saying "dozens of computer and consumer electronics companies are flocking to the digital convergence market. . . . For the consumer electronics camp, the PC/TV information appliance is, potentially, the next big thing—the first new product category to hit the industry since camcorders."[15]

Other observers had different views. According to another market research firm, the PC and the television set were "diverging rather than converging. . . . The TV set has remained essentially unchanged for decades and sold at a low price, whereas the PC is a dynamic, complex, and expensive product. TV viewers are passive consumers constrained by prices. PC users, on the other hand, are busy, wealthy, make their own decisions, seek efficiency, and expect to interact."[16]

In 1995, Gateway 2000 (a major PC manufacturer) planned to introduce their Destination product, which combined a multimedia PC with a big-screen television. Destination was designed for the family room, and cost approximately $4,000. Based on their market research, Gateway found that the product had high appeal among both early adopters and families with children younger than 12 years old, where users had significant PC experience and household income greater than $50,000. Gateway also found strong interest among first-time PC buyers who owned multiple gadgets in the home. Upon seeing a prelaunch version of the product, both Rob Siegel and Avram Miller said, "That's it!"

---

[11] *Dataquest,* 1996.

[12] Jupiter Communications, 1996.

[13] "The Square Off Between the TV and Computer," *Los Angeles Times,* October 29, 1995.

[14] "Personal Computers: Television on Your PC," *The New York Times,* March 14, 1995.

[15] "Defending the Living Room; How TV Makers Tend to Fend off Cyberlopers," *Business Week,* June 26, 1996.

[16] "Report Undermines Wedding Plans for TV and PC," *The New York Times,* November 1, 1995.

HOOD RIVER SEED PROGRAM

Through his analysis, Siegel identified three phases of home computing, which consisted of "the PC today, the PC as it moves into the family room, and the PC anywhere in the home, where everything talks to everything else." Siegel argued against pursuing the last option because "it was a black hole, both from a technical and a user model perspective." Within the home, the PC had already penetrated the den and home office. Siegel believed that the living room was "where Hood River [would] continue the PC's march." Siegel put together a proposal for a seed program. This proposal defined the Hood River product, proposed goals for the seed program, and suggested metrics for measuring the success of the seed program.

The purpose of the seed program was to determine whether the product would sell and if there was a legitimate business opportunity for the PC in the living room. If successful, Hood River would increase the total available market for Intel products by creating new users and new uses for PCs. Siegel believed that Hood River would allow Intel to influence consumer electronics companies to introduce PC-centric entertainment systems; to facilitate the development of relevant standards, such as home networks and wireless keyboards and peripherals; and to persuade content and software developers to target the family room PC with new applications. According to Vadasz:

> The primary objective of Hood River was to engage the PC and consumer electronics industries and see where there is an opportunity. The home is one of the few frontiers left. We need a network that ties telephony, audiovisual capabilities, and data all together in the home. The merging of these components is what we need. Once that is accomplished, many new things can happen.

The specific objectives of the seed program were (1) to build a reference design and a prototype to demonstrate consumer electronic capabilities, including high-end audio and video, on a PC; (2) to develop a marketing and partner strategy for the new product; and (3) to integrate the new venture into core Intel products and systems within the Desktop Products Group (DPG). According to Vadasz, "I wanted Hood River to have a dotted line into DPG because I wanted a home for it by the time it would need real money."

Desktop Products Group (DPG)

The Desktop Products Group (DPG) was responsible for all desktop computer products at Intel. DPG sold products to over 1,000 customers, mostly original equipment manufacturers (OEMs), none of which represented more than 10 percent of total revenues. DPG was run as a profit center, and generated a significant percentage of Intel's overall revenue and profits. DPG was run by Mike Aymar, who was two-in-a-box originally with Carl Everett and then with Patrick Gelsinger, who replaced Everett toward the end of 1996. Several organizations were matrixed with DPG, including the groups that built chipsets and microprocessors,[17] while the motherboard group, called the OEM Products & Services Division (OPSD), reported directly into DPG.

In early 1996, OPSD, which had only recently been integrated into DPG, had responsibility for designing and building Intel's motherboard products. OPSD's primary mission was to accelerate the adoption of Intel's latest processors and systems. OPSD had a marketing group that had responsibility for detailed product marketing. The market for motherboards was characterized by rapid technological change and extremely rapid new product introductions. As a result, the OPSD business planning model was very short-term, with a horizon of approximately 16 weeks. In early 1996, OPSD was headed by John Miner. After Miner was promoted to run Enterprise Products Group, Tom Yan and Steve Werner were chosen to run OPSD (two-in-a-box) and reported directly to Aymar.

The Hood River Venture Team

On February 2, 1996, the seed program was approved and Siegel was selected to run the program. Explained Siegel, "Aymar wanted someone with fire in his belly, and Miller was willing to let me do it." Siegel had asked for $2.5 million in funding for 15 months, but received $1.2 million for 5 months. The program was named Hood River after a popular surfing spot in Oregon. In February 1996, Siegel had a solid-line reporting relationship to Avram Miller in CBD and a dotted-line reporting relationship to Michael Aymar in DPG.

Within DPG, the Hood River project split into two parts, with the market creation and product concept work being done in Santa Clara, California, and the systems and product implementation work being done in Oregon within OPSD. Siegel, working out of Santa Clara, was responsible for the high-level product concept and product definition, as well as evangelizing the product, interfacing with customers, and understanding the market.

---

[17] The microprocessor group effectively worked with all of the product groups, including DPG.

EXHIBIT 9 Hood River Organization Structure

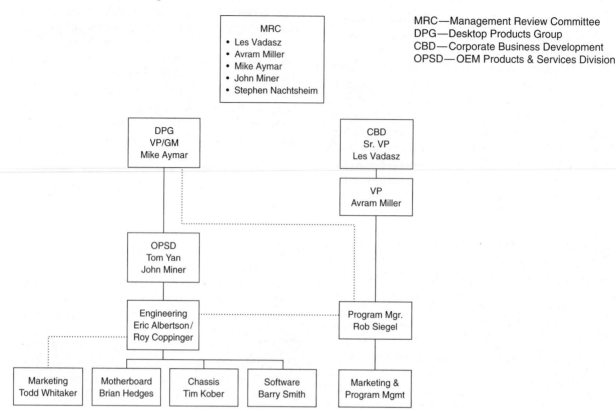

Krish Bandaru, who reported to Siegel, worked with ISVs and hardware vendors to inculcate in them the Hood River vision. Before Bandaru came on board, Siegel had been allocated 25 percent of one technical marketing engineer who reported to another manager within DPG. However, this engineer ended up doing 0 percent work for Hood River in actuality.

The OPSD marketing group in Oregon had responsibility for product marketing, which included the detailed product specifications. Todd Whitaker handled product marketing for Hood River within OPSD. Eric Albertson was the engineering manager in OPSD for Hood River, and he had a lateral relationship with Siegel. Albertson reported to Tom Yan and Steve Werner in DPG (see Exhibit 9). Yan managed the development group, which included software, hardware, and systems engineers.

Following Intel's normal procedures, Siegel also established a management review committee (MRC) for Hood River. The purpose of the MRC meetings was to update management on the status of the program, and to fa-

cilitate executive input and oversight. The MRC included Les Vadasz, Avram Miller, Michael Aymar, John Miner (vice president and general manager, Enterprise Server Group), and Stephen Nachtsheim (vice president and general manager, Mobile/Handheld Products Group).

The remainder of the case describes the evolution of the Hood River program between February and December 1996.

FEBRUARY–MAY 1996

For the first few months of the program, Siegel focused on defining the product and writing marketing requirements. He and his team conducted preliminary market research, which suggested that consumers associated the living room with entertainment, whereas they associated the PC in the den with productivity applications. This meant that Hood River would need to do entertainment well. Siegel also researched the market value of selected segments of the consumer electronics industry (see Ex-

EXHIBIT 10   Retail Market Value of Selected Segments, 1995

$ billions

	U.S.	Japan	W. Europe	Total
Television	$10.9	$ 8.1	$ 8.7	$ 27.7
VCR	3.9	3.5	3.7	11.1
Home audio	4.4	2.1	6.8	13.3
Camcorder	2.7	2.0	1.6	6.3
DBS	1.5	0.1	0.8	2.4
Computers	20.0	6.3	13.5	39.8
Total	**$43.3**	**$22.2**	**$35.2**	**$100.7**

Source: BIT, Intel.

hibit 10). Siegel and his team explored the available technology, where they discovered that the biggest cost of a living room PC was for the monitor. By May, OPSD had approximately 10 engineers allocated to Hood River.

The Hood River Product Concept

Based on his early research and analysis, Siegel began to define the Hood River product concept. Siegel expected that the Hood River product would be positioned at the high end of the family room PC market, selling for $3,500 or higher (see Exhibit 11). Siegel projected that the market for this product would be "tens of thousands in 1996 (for the first year after product launch), [and] hundreds of thousands in 1997 (for the subsequent 12-month period)."

There were four major components to the product, which included communications, audio and video, computer hardware, and software. (See Exhibit 12 for additional detail.) Siegel and his team identified the target applications and uses for the Hood River product, which included: communications applications, such as telephony integration, Internet connectivity, video conferencing, and virtual worlds; consumer electronics capabilities, such as CD juke boxes, VCR programming, and digital video discs (DVD); entertainment application such as video games, social games, and "edutainment"; productivity applications such as email, information retrieval, and word processing; and new applications such as enhanced broadcasting and home control capabilities. The design called for the use of Intel's 233 MHz Pentium II processor, their highest performance CPU at the time.

OEM CUSTOMERS

One question that Siegel faced was which OEM customers to target, and whether PC or consumer electron-

EXHIBIT 11   The Family Room PC Market Segments

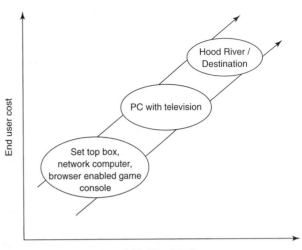

The family room PC market segment will be defined by several physical configurations, likely clustered around three price points: $250–750, $1,000–2,000, and $2,000+.... Efforts by Sega and Nintendo to add browser capabilities to their game machines . . . and the much discussed network computer, as espoused by Oracle and Sun, . . . fit into the low-end of the category. . . .

The high-end products in this category are best exemplified by Gateway's Destination product, Net TV's first commercial offering, and the forthcoming PCTV that is being developed by Compaq and Thomson. All of these products use high-end Intel microprocessors and are sold with large display screens. . . .

One of the key defining aspects of this latter segment of the market is that the PC is the centerpiece of the consumer's entertainment center, whereas the lower two segments relegate computing power and the PC to periphery or add-on status.

—Hood River Market Requirements Document

Source: Intel.

ics companies would make the best partners. Consumer electronics had the clear advantage in terms of ease of use, low maintenance, low cost, quality audio and video, and reliability. However, PCs had the advantage in terms of several applications, such as those for personal productivity, education, communication, and reading. Siegel also considered the unique strengths that each particular company offered in terms of manufacturing skills, brand, and technology, while also considering the similarity of their vision with that of Hood River. Based on this analysis, Siegel identified five initial target customers, which included Sony, Toshiba, Matsushita, Compaq, and Thomson Electronics.

EXHIBIT 12 Hood River Major Components, May 1996

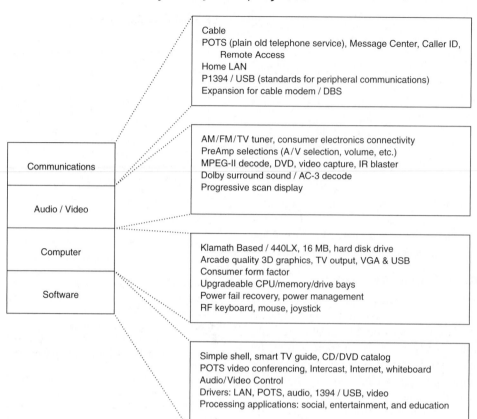

During this time, Siegel could not talk directly to OEM customers, but did speak with some partners, such as those for audio and video components. Avram Miller explained:

> It gets more difficult when you start to work with our primary customers. . . . You're put under much greater scrutiny. . . . If you're working in a new area, such as networking, nobody is likely to bother you. But everything that's a PC is another story.

Complementors/Partners

In order to offer a completely integrated product for the living room, Siegel and his team worked with a number of third parties, including audio companies such as Harman, Bose, and Yamaha; software companies for a wide variety of applications and standards; and peripheral manufacturers for keyboards, joysticks, toys, and the like. Hood River was dependent upon the establishment of a number of technology standards, including those for video decoding (MPEG),[18] digital access to source material (DVD),[19] wireless peripherals (IR or RF),[20] home local area networks, and simple and reliable connectivity of consumer electronic equipment (IEEE 1394).[21]

Hood River was also dependent upon Microsoft for many important features. For example, Hood River required the operating system to provide power management features, known as Instant-On, which would allow the product to instantly turn on and be ready to use. Microsoft planned to add this functionality to Memphis,

---

[18] MPEG: Moving Picture Expert Group, an International Organization for Standardization (ISO) standard for audio and video compression.
[19] DVD: digital video disks, a CD sized disc that can hold audio, video, and computer data and provide theater quality sound.
[20] IR: Infrared; RF: radio frequency.
[21] IEEE 1394: a high speed serial bus standard for transferring audio, video, and control signals between the computer and external consumer electronics equipment.

their next major operating system release after Windows 95, scheduled for mid-1997. However it was not certain that this release would be ready soon enough to accommodate Hood River's current schedule.

In May 1996, Microsoft's planned "Entertainment PC" had much in common with Intel's vision for the living room PC. The primary differences were that Microsoft was looking to use a lower-end CPU, such as the 150 MHz Pentium; they envisioned a sealed case, which would make it difficult for users to upgrade the CPU or memory; and they were focused primarily on offering multimedia applications, rather than providing a living room PC per se.

Key Issues

During this period, some challenges arose. OPSD had begun to staff up for Hood River, but according to Krish Bandaru:

> We weren't able to hand pick anyone up in Oregon. Most of the engineers in Oregon were excellent motherboard designers, but they had no real drive or vision for the HR program in particular. We were asking them to do something outside of their normal structure and being in a separate state didn't help matters.

OPSD had only recently been integrated with DPG, so there was some apparent redundancy between DPG marketing and OPSD marketing. The dispersed nature of the organization created additional challenges. According to Siegel:

> There were a number of groups throughout Intel that were able to get working in this area, but nobody was really in charge. I could only influence the others because I had passion for the product and Aymar's ear. Yet, coordinating all these groups and guiding them along the path of my vision was my task. OPSD had just been integrated into DPG, but it was still a loose federation. Some of the people in OPSD didn't want to be involved [with Hood River] and their marketing group was wondering why they needed me. OPSD marketing thought that I was part of corporate marketing and that I was doing their job.

Management Review Committee I, May 1996

In May 1996, Hood River had its first MRC review. Siegel walked through market data, including buying patterns, the size of the market, projections for worldwide sales, and how the likely customers compared to Intel's target customers. Siegel also discussed some of the technological details, including specifications, usage models, and some of the more important differences between the TV and the PC. Siegel presented a timeline that showed product availability in advance of "back to school '97" and the 1997 Christmas season.

Based on projected costs at that time, Siegel estimated that the Hood River product would be priced at approximately $4,700 with a monitor, which was significantly higher than their original target. Therefore, the Hood River team planned to explore areas where they might reduce costs. By the May MRC, Siegel and his team had spent approximately $100,000, or about 8 percent of their $1.2 million budget. As a result of the meeting, the MRC gave Siegel approval to continue with Hood River. In particular, Siegel received approval to begin contacting and working with customers and lining up partners.

JUNE–AUGUST 1996

After the May MRC, Siegel began to talk to more companies, especially OEM customers and Microsoft, and he continued the market research. In addition, Siegel refined the Hood River product concept, which called for a quiet, fanless design; wireless peripherals; and front panel connectors for camcorders, joysticks, controls, and an LCD panel. Siegel and his team also worked to define distribution channels, a corporate marketing strategy, standards efforts, and business development requirements. By August, OPSD had increased staffing to approximately 35 engineers.

Hood River Product Concept

Siegel and his team expanded their research to include primary market research of end users. The research suggested that the most popular applications were easy VCR programming, a video phone, information retrieval, DVD, traditional PC applications, and the remote retrieval of phone messages (see Exhibit 13). Most potential customers seemed to view the Hood River product as a TV with a PC component, rather than as a replacement for a PC. Siegel predicted that Hood River would be able to achieve sales volume of 250,000 units in 1997, and 2 million units in 1998.

OEM CUSTOMERS

During the summer of 1996, Siegel and his team engaged a number of potential customers for Hood River, including AST, Fujitsu, Goldstar, IBM, Matsushita, NEC, Packard Bell, Sharp, Sony, and Toshiba. Sony, IBM, and Matsushita appeared most promising.

EXHIBIT 13   Market Survey Results–Application Rankings: Relative Preference Index

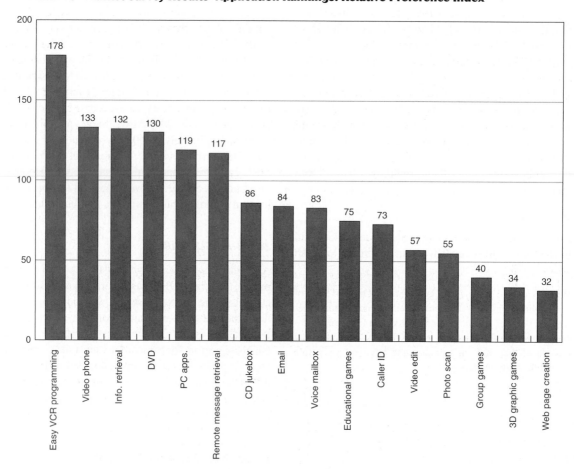

Intel had recently helped Sony enter the PC market by building their motherboards, so OPSD had good relations with the Sony engineers. Given Sony's expertise in consumer electronics, Hood River was the next logical step in the relationship. Sony was planning a product called the Home Entertainment Station that was scheduled for release in 1998. Sony planned the product to be modular in nature with a very small form factor.

In June, Siegel had his first meeting with Sony. Sony's product concept for the living room PC had much in common with Intel's; however, there were several significant issues that needed to be addressed. For example, Intel planned to use the Pentium II processor for Hood River, whereas Sony was planning to use the 486 processor. In addition, Sony was proposing a smaller form factor, they were targeting a lower price point, and they were willing to accept fewer integrated features in favor of a more modular design, where additional components could be sold separately to augment the system. According to

Siegel, "It turned out to be a very bad meeting. And afterwards Aymar was just laughing, telling me that I had learned a lot that day on the differences between our industries." Despite these challenges, in August 1996, Siegel believed with an 85 percent confidence factor that Sony would be won as a customer.

Siegel followed the initial Sony meeting with a two week trip to Japan that included visits with Sharp, Matsushita, JVC, NEC, and Fujitsu. According to Siegel:

During these meetings we discerned the six laws of the consumer electronics industry, which we compared to the five laws of the PC industry. The six laws of the electronics industry were that it's a hardware-driven market, de facto standards dominate, technology changes slowly, price points are in the range of $500 versus $2,000 for PCs, boxes are not expandable, and ease of use drives sales.

By comparison, the five laws of the PC industry were that the hardware/software spiral and the virtuous circle are fixed; standards lead to volume; technology changes very rapidly; the high end drives the market; and price, place, and promotion—the 3 Ps—are essential. I realized that for the PC to succeed in the family room, our product would have to fit within the consumer electronics ecology, and that we would have to make the product sexy.

The primary issues to resolve with Matsushita, for instance, were to more clearly define the relationship between the two companies on the product, and to agree on motherboard and system specifications. Matsushita was actively working on a family room PC project called AccessVision, and their product vision was closely aligned with Intel's. Matsushita had carefully explored a variety of family room computer scenarios, and seemed eager to partner with Intel to bring a product to market both in Japan and the United States. In August 1996, Siegel estimated that the Matsushita partnership would succeed with an 85 percent confidence factor.

Siegel also had detailed discussions with IBM. In 1996, IBM's strategy was focused on enabling network-centric computing, and the IBM Aptiva extended this strategy to home computing. IBM agreed to work with Intel to define a motherboard, which they would purchase from Intel. IBM also expressed interest in procuring the entire chassis from Intel if Intel could add sufficient value. The two companies shared market research data and were planning the details of their expected working relationship. However, there were some differences. IBM was focusing their differentiation on home networking and the control of the home, and had some different ideas about form factor as well. It was also unclear what the exact nature of the relationship between the two companies would be. For example, would IBM buy motherboards from Intel or actually do the work themselves? In August 1996, Siegel estimated that the IBM partnership would be successful with a 90 percent confidence factor.

Complementors/Partners

During this period, Siegel and his team continued to make progress with independent software vendors (ISVs), independent hardware vendors (IHVs), and Microsoft.

On the ISV front, Siegel was targeting 5 family room applications for "back to school '97" and 10 applications by Christmas '97. Siegel expected to specify the target companies and finalize the presentation by September 6th, to complete first meetings by October 4th, and to close accounts by October 31st. This activity was owned collectively by both the Content Group and OPSD.

Working with IHVs, Siegel hoped to have eight IHV products shipping with Hood River by the second half of

'97. These products would include enhanced audio receivers, speakers, and CD juke boxes; peripherals such as joysticks, keyboards, and headsets; and video cameras. Siegel planned to specify target companies by September 15th, to complete first meetings by September 30th, and to close accounts by October 31st. This task was owned by DPG (a different group from Siegel's).

Siegel and his team also continued to work with Microsoft with the goals of enlisting their "full strategic support for the family room computer category." Siegel and his team succeeded in influencing Microsoft to include the key software components required by Hood River in the upcoming release of Memphis. These key software components were advanced power management features ("Instant-On"), digital audio, drivers for the 1394 standard, and support for wireless peripherals. These issues were discussed in weekly meetings with Microsoft.

Key Issues

Siegel had identified a number of software challenges related to the product concept. The user interface had several challenges, including allowing viewing from a distance of 10 feet, supporting wireless input and output, and seamlessly controlling the consumer electronic devices. It was difficult for the software to support broadcast TV enhancements and high-quality DVD playing. There were difficulties supporting the concurrent operation of certain applications, such as DVDs and answering machines. In addition, Hood River depended upon Microsoft for the Instant-On functionality typical of consumer electronics devices. According to Ron Whittier, senior vice president and general manager of the Content Group,

> The integration of the application set onto the platform is a problem. We can do each application individually, but it is hard to do them all because the integration is not at all straightforward. We also have a problem supporting some of the individual applications. What was and still is the most difficult issue is the user interface. Hood River assumes PC familiarity in its UI design. The navigation between applications is much more complex than moving from channel to channel on the TV. Hood River was designed for the computer-literate person. But most consumers are coming from a TV orientation.

There were additional challenges as well. Hood River faced thermal challenges due to the fanless design, which was necessary for quiet operation. The standard for communications among wireless peripherals had not been fully defined. And the plan to enhance TV images was still being investigated by the Intel Architecture Lab (IAL).[22]

In July 1996, Hood River encountered two organizational challenges. First, Mike Aymar put Siegel in charge of the product line business plan (PLBP) for consumer products within DPG. This was an important and strategic plan; however, it was also very challenging to complete. As a result, Siegel worked exclusively on the business plan during July and therefore lost time on Hood River. On the other hand, this planning work gave Siegel a vehicle for gaining visibility for Hood River, and according to Siegel, "the family room became a topic for the first time in front of the ESM [executive staff meeting]."[23]

Second, Eric Albertson left the company and was replaced as engineering manager by Roy Coppinger, who took responsibility for implementation. Coppinger was very disciplined and detail oriented, but not especially passionate about Hood River. According to Coppinger:

> I established communication with other Intel groups for technology, in particular Intel Architecture Lab [IAL] and Internet Communications Group [ICG]. But I let the existing players, like Mike Aymar and Rob Siegel, manage the project. I did not become a champion for funding. But I was responsible for execution. I was the lead person for discussions with Microsoft, which was very important, because Memphis was viewed as the basis of the product by Intel, so that we wouldn't have to write code ourselves for features [like Instant-On].

Management Review Committee II, August 1996

The second MRC had originally been scheduled for the end of June, but was delayed until August due to Siegel's involvement with the product line business plan. At the August MRC, Siegel presented a functional demo of the product that included TV channel surfing, a big-screen gaming application, VCR programming, a DVD movie, and a CD changer. Siegel outlined the description of the Hood River product, including its primary features and distinguishing characteristics (see Exhibit 14). In particular, the functional demo showed the quiet, fanless design and the front panel connectors for camcorders, joysticks, controls, and an LCD panel.

---

[22]Note: IAL was expected to deliver the software components that tuned MPEG-II and AC3 codecs with the Pentium II processor and integrated them with the DVD player.

[23]The executive staff meetings include all of Intel's most senior managers.

EXHIBIT 14   Hood River Product Description, August 1996

"A dazzling, full function entertainment computer for the family room."

Primary Features
- Big screen, 3D games
- DVD surround sound movies
- Video phone
- Intercast
- Home message center
- Web browsing/Net games
- New social, team games

Distinguishing Characteristics
- Fits in the family room ecology
  —Quiet consumer electronics chassis
  —Complements existing consumer electronics appliances, such as TV, VCR, stereo, etc.
  —Wireless input devices
- Controls other consumer electronics products
- Higher quality audio and video
- Enhanced TV/VCR viewing (stretch goal for HR1)

Siegel felt that the product and customer updates "were great," and that the market research had been valuable, despite his observation that "Vadasz hates market research." The next issue was to get customers such as Sony and Toshiba to actually develop products that would connect to the PC. According to Siegel:

> By August we had accomplished a lot. We had Microsoft doing what we wanted them to do, and we had established an impressive customer list. In addition, the product line business plan presentation went extremely well. We received the highest rating, and [Andy] Grove came up with the phrase "Hijack the TV," which became our rallying cry.

The budget issue did not come up until the end of the meeting. According to Siegel:

> We only had three minutes left in the meeting when I came to the slide on the budget request. With such limited time I probably should not have put this up. But I did, and we asked for $2.5 million. Vadasz asked, "Is this still a seed program? Why should I spend more money on this?" I had told others that I would get Vadasz to continue the funding, which had helped me get their support. It became a smoke-filled room, with Vadasz, Aymar, and John Miner all involved with the decision. At the end of the meeting Miller said, "Hood River is no longer a seed, but rather a full tree." . . . I said, "Yes, but it doesn't have any roots yet." The meeting ended inconclusively on the budget issue. Later, we ended up with a deal behind the scenes where Vadasz funded another $1.3 million, which would pay for Hood

River through the end of 1996, but it would be in DPG's budget for 1997.

SEPTEMBER–NOVEMBER 1996

After the MRC, Siegel put the finishing touches on the formal markets requirement document (MRD) and prepared the budget for 1997. Siegel proposed a $10 to $15 million budget that would fund Hood River through 1997 within DPG. This budget included all of Hood River spending, including engineering, marketing, and relationship management with ISVs and IHVs. Although it was a large budget, much to Siegel's satisfaction, the budget was approved in late September. Siegel continued to engage OEM customers and partners, while OPSD continued product development. By October, OPSD had increased staffing for Hood River to approximately 50 engineers.

Hood River Product Concept

The completed MRD was consistent with Siegel's earlier concepts. The key features of Hood River as specified by the MRD included: the Pentium II microprocessor; the 440 LX chipset for arcade quality graphics; a DVD drive for playing digital movies, audio CDs, and CD-ROMs; a wireless keyboard, mouse, and joystick for untethered control of the device; and a highly reliable and tightly integrated environment.

In addition, the MRD called for a wide array of software applications and technologies to be integrated into the Hood River product. In part, these applications and technologies would provide the following characteristics: high-quality television viewing; consumer quality audio support; the ability to control new and existing audio and video equipment; arcade quality graphics; Instant-On capabilities; consumer electronics look, feel, and reliability; minimal ambient noise; and readable text of Windows applications at a distance of 10 feet (see Exhibit 15 for additional details).

During this period the Hood River design team made good progress on the design. In December 1996, the project was basically on schedule. The motherboard was about 70 percent complete, the chassis was about 60 percent complete, and the software[24] was about 40 percent complete.

---

[24] Intel was developing software tools to allow OEMs to customize the user interface, and software drivers to control consumer electronics devices.

OEMS

During this period, consumer electronic companies and Intel had two debates over key design issues. The first debate concerned which microprocessor would be used. Consumer electronic companies preferred a less expensive microprocessor. Intel wanted a high-end microprocessor. According to Krish Bandaru, "Hood River is supposed to be a robust entertainment computer—and at Intel that means a PC with a high-end Pentium processor." The second debate concerned the basic look and feel of the system. Consumer electronics companies wanted a small, quiet, easy-to-use product that cost less than $2,000. Their vision was to take a modular approach that consisted of low-cost components that could be connected via the 1394 protocol. They believed that a modular product would allow customers to buy the system in pieces, reducing up-front costs. According to Tom Yan:

> With this approach, you could have a PC piece that was in the den and operated from the living room. This is of course a different model than what Intel likes, because Intel would like to have a PC in the living room and in the den. Also, consumer electronic companies want more features, but for a lower cost than the PC. Since the PC has already become a low-margin product due to commoditization, this is impossible.

Sony had emerged as one of the key customers for Hood River. According to Todd Whitaker, "In October, Sony began to back off" in their support and enthusiasm for Hood River. Siegel saw the situation slightly differently. He said, "Sony continued to challenge us, just as they had from the beginning, but they did not waver any more so than normal."

Compaq was working on a product similar to Hood River for the living room, called PC Theater, that they were close to launching in the fall of 1996. Their product did not use motherboards or components from Hood River, and was based on a Pentium processor, not the Pentium II. Siegel had visited with Compaq over the summer, and began collaborating with them by sharing market research data and comparing plans. Even if they chose not to use Hood River, Siegel believed that their efforts in this segment would facilitate his own market creation efforts. Coppinger also began discussions with Compaq's PC Theater team, but said, "This group was not in the mainstream of Compaq, and it looked like they were underresourced, just like Hood River."

EXHIBIT 15 Key Hood River Applications and Technologies

Software integration	Software shell that sits atop Windows 9X to provide friendly user interface; drivers and low-level APIs for controlling and integrating consumer electronic equipment and other devices.
Consumer quality audio system	Audio system to provide support for both digital and analog equipment; system to support a DVD player, an AC-3 enabled receiver, and digital speakers, as well as existing receivers, CD players, and so on.
Quality display for broadcast TV	System should provide a large display suitable for use as a TV or computer monitor; if possible, line-doublers, which can improve TV image quality, should be incorporated.
Wireless input devices	Keyboard, joystick, mouse, and other input devices must operate without wires; a standard must be established for these devices; the system should be able to accommodate either IR (infrared) or RF (radio frequency) technology, at the discretion of the OEM.
DVD video playback	System must offer DVD playback quality that meets or exceeds that offered by dedicated consumer players.
MPEG-1 encode ready	System must support real-time capture and MPEG-1 frame compression.
IEEE 1394 enabled	Key OEMs, including IBM, Sony, Compaq, and HP, all require support for IEEE 1394 by 2H97; IEEE 1394 will be the main interconnectivity standard for transferring audio, video, and control signals between the computer and consumer electronics devices.
Arcade quality 3D	Hood River must be the premier home gaming platform; system must support 3D performance that meets or exceeds the quality and performance of 1996 arcade systems and state-of-the-art 1997 game consoles.
Telephony integration	System must offer full-featured computer telephony integration.
Video telephony	With video phone being named as the second most desired application, system should support consumer video telephony via POTS,* ISDN, and the like.
Omni-directional microphone	To support telephony applications, system must provide an effective microphone for both individual and group use.
Digital camera and camcorder	To support video telephony and consumer authoring, system must interface with analog camcorders and digital cameras (still and video).
Intercast technology	System should incorporate intercast technology, which allows additional data and content to be transmitted through a conventional TV signal.
Power management	System must be able to move from idle state to full functionality in a reasonable time to process random inputs, such as phone calls or user input (e.g., turning unit on).
Internet excellence	Browsers for the platform should support state-of-the-art technologies in 2H97 (such as HTML, VRML, Java, etc.)
Information retrieval	The system should have the perception of being "Always On"; value added software such as the PointCast Network should be included, at the discretion of the OEM.
Connecting a standard PC monitor	The system should allow the use of an additional VGA monitor for traditional productivity application such as word processing, spreadsheets, and household finance programs.
Consumer appliance features	The system should support traditional consumer electronics features for form factor, setup, reliability, and noise levels.
System upgradability	System must allow microprocessor, memory, and hard disk drive to be updated in an easy "plug and play" manner.

*POTS (plain old telephone service).
Source: Hood River market requirements document.

Complementors/Partners

During this period Siegel and his team made steady progress evangelizing to partners and working on standards efforts. Siegel established a program to encourage ISVs to develop applications specifically for the family room. He published design guidelines for these applications that would improve their usability in the family room. Intel offered to help fund the development of selected applications by prepaying royalties, and by December 1996, Siegel had reviewed a number of proposals from interested ISVs. On the standards front, Siegel and his team had helped to develop standards for wireless keyboards and joysticks, and for connecting living room PCs to large screen monitors.

Although Intel had persuaded Microsoft to add to Memphis the necessary features for Hood River, Intel could not control Microsoft's development schedule. By December 1996, the schedule for Memphis had begun to slip, and there were ominous signs that it could be further delayed. According to Tom Yan, "We are dependent upon Microsoft to create the right functionality and usability. We were looking to Memphis to deliver the type of support that we are looking for."

Key Issues

Additional market data was coming in from multiple OEM customers who had already released products in this segment. According to Tom Yan:

> The results of their efforts were coming in and their machines were selling less than 1,000 per month. Thus, market evidence suggests that the opportunity is relatively small. Also, some of them have used low-end microprocessors, which do not show good PC performance but deliver good consumer electronics capabilities. As an example, one of the PC suppliers offers a product for $1,999 that combines a segment zero (low-end) microprocessor with DVD. However, consumers could buy DVD for $500 and a low-end PC for less than $1,000. Others have high-end processors but mediocre consumer electronics features. Nobody has done both well. Hood River wants to do both, but at a price point that is too high.

Another challenge that occurred was that new technologies emerged as the market development work was being conducted, which made it difficult to match the technologies and the markets. Tom Yan explained:

> Some aspects of the technology are not ready yet, and we are trying to force-fit today's technology into a new category that needs new technology. An example of this is the line-doubling technology which allows video images for TV content to appear smoother and clearer. At the start of Hood River, this technology was available but was very expensive. It could be found in home theater systems that cost as much as $10,000. Now this technology had been integrated into chips for PCs for a price of about $50. And these prices will decline further in the future.

Another important piece of technology that was missing was the 1394 standard, which would provide a high-speed digital connection between devices.

An External Threat: The NetPC

Around this time, the network computer (NC) emerged as a potential threat to Intel's core business. Companies like Sun Microsystems, Oracle, Netscape, and IBM were evangelizing a new computing paradigm, based on "thin clients" and "fat servers," that they claimed would dra-

matically reduce the total cost of ownership (TCO) of desktop computers—especially maintenance and management costs.[25] The NC was expected to include low-end processors running Sun's Java software—they would not include Intel's microprocessors or Microsoft's Windows operating systems.

Intel's response to this external threat was focused and swift. OPSD was given the charter to design a low-end PC, called the NetPC, which would include a Pentium processor and PC management software from Intel that would reduce the TCO of Intel PCs. OPSD quickly ramped up efforts for the NetPC, growing staff to approximately 70 engineers by October 1996. As a result, the NetPC competed for some of the same resources as Hood River. Todd Whitaker noted, "We respond extremely well to threats, but perhaps not so well to opportunities."

Crisis Strikes

In late October, Siegel was speaking at a class at Harvard Business School when his pager went off. The call was from Krish Bandaru, who told him that funding for Hood River had been cut. Tom Yan and Carl Everett (who was "two-in-a-box" with Aymar) had made the decision jointly, and Yan had sent an email to the engineering team to communicate the decision. Siegel received a number of voice messages from members of the engineering team looking for additional information and asking questions such as whether they still had jobs. Siegel responded quickly and aggressively. He recalled:

> I called Aymar right away, and also sent a strongly worded email to ask about the decision. In essence I asked, "How can we take risks in this company if they always end up in the same place—defending the status quo?" . . .

Aymar subsequently reinstated the funding. However, the apparent vulnerability of the program created anxiety within the engineering team.

By late November, Michael Aymar was unhappy with the lack of enthusiasm from customers and he began to question all of the assumptions about the program. Especially as a result of concerns voiced by Sony, Aymar questioned the decision to use the Pentium II, and called for a detailed cost analysis of the Pentium II versus the Pentium with MMX. According to Krish Bandaru:

> The engineers did a complete cost analysis that compared the two platforms. We found that there is no significant cost

---

[25] Some analysts, such as the Gartner Group, had reported that the cost of maintaining and managing PCs in corporate environments was many times more expensive than the original cost of the PC itself.

benefit from using the Pentium with MMX. And there are important advantages to using the Pentium II, along with the 440LX chipset. The 440LX enables AGP[26] graphics and combined with the Pentium II satisfies the market requirement for arcade quality graphics. However, the 440LX doesn't work with any other processor. You couldn't get AGP with the Pentium with MMX from Intel. . . . Also, it's part of Intel's business model to always be looking for compelling reasons for customers to upgrade [to the latest processor], and at that time, any "new" platform had to focus on this "sell-up" message.

According to Siegel:

In the end, we discovered that we could only save about $200 with this change, which moved our expected price from $2,400 to $2,200—still above our target price of $1,900 [excluding the monitor].

The decision was made to continue with the Pentium II. However, the processor questioning caused additional turmoil within the engineering team.

In December, DPG was reorganized. Rather than reporting directly to Mike Aymar, Siegel was made to report to John Davies, who was responsible for consumer marketing and had recently been promoted to VP. According to Davies:

Hood River has the second biggest staffing in terms of engineering in OPSD. So it is a big investment, but without a payback visible within 18–24 months. We know that we have to try to sign up more OEMs quickly.

He continued:

It is interesting to see what we are trying to do with Hood River, which is to put the PC in the living room where it doesn't fit. You can think about interesting demos using the PC in the living room, like Star Trek games and so on. But there are some key challenges. First, nobody is using the PC in the family room. It's the last thing on my mind when I come home. In fact, I want to get away from it. Second, there is the chicken or egg problem. You need applications, but you can only get them if you have an installed base. With zero installed base, there is definitely a software problem.

DECISION TIME

The Hood River project had now entered a critical stage. Siegel recognized that the project had "had its ups and downs" and that it had been "especially hurt by Everett's [and Yan's] funding decision." The project had lost time,

customers were not committed, and at a time when the importance of coordinating and influencing the various constituencies within Intel had peaked, Siegel found himself with even less formal authority.

Siegel still believed in the program and felt passionate about the product concept. However, he was beginning to have doubts about the viability of the project within Intel. He believed that with direct ownership and control of the program's technical and marketing resources, he would make the program successful. Siegel even had discussions with one venture capital firm, which made him confident that he could secure external funding for the project.

In December 1996, Siegel considered several options. He could request that Hood River be spun off as a separate company, with funding from Intel or a venture capital firm. Les Vadasz from CBD would have to approve that decision. Siegel could also request that Hood River be established as a separate division within Intel, with himself as general manager. This decision would have to be supported by Vadasz, Mike Aymar, and probably Intel top management as well. Siegel also considered whether the current arrangement could be salvaged, and if so, how he should proceed. Finally, Siegel wondered if there were other options that he had not yet considered. Siegel realized that in the coming days he would have to decide which course of action to pursue, and how to justify his request.

READING III-8

Discovery-Driven Planning

Rita Gunther McGrath and Ian C. MacMillan

Business lore is full of stories about smart companies that incur huge losses when they enter unknown territory—new alliances, new markets, new products, new technologies. The Walt Disney Company's 1992 foray into Europe with its theme park had accumulated losses of more than $1 billion by 1994. Zapmail, a fax product, cost Federal Express Corporation $600 million before it was dropped. Polaroid lost $200 million when it ventured into

Source: Copyright © 1995 by the President and Fellows of Harvard College. All rights reserved.
*The authors wish to thank Shiuchi Matsuda of Waseda University's Entrepreneurial Research Unit for providing case material on Kao's floppy disk venture.

---

[26]AGP: accelerated graphics port, which offered arcade quality graphics capabilities.

instant movies. Why do such efforts often defeat even experienced, smart companies? One obvious answer is that strategic ventures are inherently risky: The probability of failure simply comes with the territory. But many failures could be prevented or their cost contained if senior managers approached innovative ventures with the right planning and control tools.

Discovery-driven planning is a practical tool that acknowledges the difference between planning for a new venture and planning for a more conventional line of business. Conventional planning operates on the premise that managers can extrapolate future results from a well-understood and predictable platform of past experience. One expects predictions to be accurate because they are based on solid knowledge rather than on assumptions. In platform-based planning, a venture's deviations from plan are a bad thing.

The platform-based approach may make sense for ongoing businesses, but it is sheer folly when applied to new ventures. By definition, new ventures call for a company to envision what is unknown, uncertain, and not yet obvious to the competition. The safe, reliable, predictable knowledge of the well-understood business has not yet emerged. Instead, managers must make do with assumptions about the possible futures on which new businesses are based. New ventures are undertaken with a high ratio of assumption to knowledge. With ongoing businesses, one expects the ratio to be the exact opposite. Because assumptions about the unknown generally turn out to be wrong, new ventures inevitably experience deviations—often huge ones—from their original planned targets. Indeed, new ventures frequently require fundamental redirection.

Rather than trying to force startups into the planning methodologies for existing predictable and well-understood businesses, discovery-driven planning acknowledges that at the start of a new venture, little is known and much is assumed. When platform-based planning is used, assumptions underlying a plan are treated as facts—givens to be baked into the plan—rather than as best-guess estimates to be tested and questioned. Companies then forge ahead on the basis of those buried assumptions. In contrast, discovery-driven planning systematically converts assumptions into knowledge as a strategic venture unfolds. When new data are uncovered, they are incorporated into the evolving plan. The real potential of the venture is discovered as it develops—hence the term discovery-driven planning. The approach imposes disciplines different from, but no less precise than, the disciplines used in conventional planning.

EURO DISNEY AND THE PLATFORM-BASED APPROACH

Even the best companies can run into serious trouble if they don't recognize the assumptions buried in their plans. The Walt Disney Company, a 49% owner of Euro Disney (now called Disneyland Paris), is known as an astute manager of theme parks. Its success has not been confined to the United States: Tokyo Disneyland has been a financial and public relations success almost from its opening in 1983. Euro Disney is another story, however. By 1993, attendance approached 1 million visitors each month, making the park Europe's most popular paid tourist destination. Then why did it lose so much money?

In planning Euro Disney in 1986, Disney made projections that drew on its experience from its other parks. The company expected half of the revenue to come from admissions, the other half from hotels, food, and merchandise. Although by 1993, Euro Disney had succeeded in reaching its target of 11 million admissions, to do so it had been forced to drop adult ticket prices drastically. The average spending per visit was far below plan and added to the red ink.

The point is not to play Monday-morning quarterback with Disney's experience but to demonstrate an approach that could have revealed flawed assumptions and mitigated the resulting losses. The discipline of systematically identifying key assumptions would have highlighted the business plan's vulnerabilities. Let us look at each source of revenue in turn.

Admissions Price

In Japan and the United States, Disney found its price by raising it over time, letting early visitors go back home and talk up the park to their neighbors. But the planners of Euro Disney assumed that they could hit their target number of visitors even if they started out with an admission price of more than $40 per adult. A major recession in Europe and the determination of the French government to keep the franc strong exacerbated the problem and led to low attendance. Although companies cannot control macroeconomic events, they can highlight and test their pricing assumptions. Euro Disney's prices were very high compared with those of other theme attractions in Europe, such as the aqua palaces, which charged low entry fees and allowed visitors to build their own menus by paying for each attraction individually. By 1993, Euro Disney not only had been forced to make a sharp price reduction to secure its target visitors, it had also lost the benefits of early-stage word of mouth. The talking-up phenomenon is especially important in Europe, as Disney could have gauged from the way word of mouth had benefited Club Med.

Hotel Accommodations

Based on its experience in other markets, Disney assumed that people would stay an average of four days in the park's five hotels. The average stay in 1993 was only two days. Had the assumption been highlighted, it might have been challenged: Since Euro Disney opened with only 15 rides, compared with 45 at Disney World, people could do them all in a single day.

Food

Park visitors in the United States and Japan "graze" all day. At Euro Disney, the buried assumption was that Europeans would do the same. Euro Disney's restaurants, therefore, were designed for all-day streams of grazers. When floods of visitors tried to follow the European custom of dining at noon, Disney was unable to seat them. Angry visitors left the park to eat, and they conveyed their anger to their friends and neighbors back home.

Merchandise

Although Disney did forecast lower sales per visitor in Europe than in the United States and Japan, the company assumed that Europeans would buy a similar mix of cloth goods and print items. Instead, Euro Disney fell short of plan when visitors bought a far smaller proportion of high-margin items such as T-shirts and hats than expected. Disney could have tested the buried assumption before forecasting sales: Disney's retail stores in European cities sell many fewer of the high-margin cloth items and far more of the low-margin print items.

Disney is not alone. Other companies have paid a significant price for pursuing platform-based ventures built on implicit assumptions that turn out to be faulty. Such ventures are usually undertaken without careful up-front identification and validation of those assumptions, which often are unconscious. We repeatedly observed that the following four planning errors are characteristic of this approach:

- *Companies don't have hard data but, once a few key decisions are made, proceed as though their assumptions were facts.* Euro Disney's implicit assumptions regarding the way visitors would use hotels and restaurants are good examples.
- *Companies have all the hard data they need to check assumptions but fail to see the implications.* After making assumptions based on a subset of the available

> # Some Dangerous Implicit Assumptions
>
> 1. Customers will buy our product because we think it's a good product.
> 2. Customers will buy our product because it's technically superior.
> 3. Customers will agree with our perception that the product is "great."
> 4. Customers run no risk in buying from us instead of continuing to buy from their past suppliers.
> 5. The product will sell itself.
> 6. Distributors are desperate to stock and service the product.
> 7. We can develop the product on time and on budget.
> 8. We will have no trouble attracting the right staff.
> 9. Competitors will respond rationally.
> 10. We can insulate our product from competition.
> 11. We will be able to hold down prices while gaining share rapidly.
> 12. The rest of our company will gladly support our strategy and provide help as needed.

data, they proceed without ever testing those assumptions. Federal Express based Zapmail on the assumption that there would be a substantial demand for four-hour delivery of documents faxed from FedEx center to FedEx center. What went unchallenged was the implicit assumption that customers would not be able to afford their own fax machines before long. If that assumption had been unearthed, FedEx would have been more likely to take into account the plunging prices and increasing sales of fax machines for the office and, later, for the home.

- *Companies possess all the data necessary to determine that a real opportunity exists but make implicit and inappropriate assumptions about their ability to implement their plan.* Exxon lost $200 million on its office automation business by implicitly assuming that it could build a direct sales and service support capability to compete head-to-head with IBM and Xerox.
- *Companies start off with the right data, but they implicitly assume a static environment and thus fail to notice until too late that a key variable has changed.* Polaroid lost $200 million from Polavision instant movies by assuming that a three minute cassette costing $7 would compete effectively against a half-hour videotape costing $20. Polaroid implicitly assumed that the high cost of equipment for videotaping and playback would remain prohibitive for most consumers. Meanwhile, companies pursuing those technologies steadily drove

down costs. (See the exhibit "Some Dangerous Implicit Assumptions.")

DISCOVERY-DRIVEN PLANNING: AN ILLUSTRATIVE CASE

Discovery-driven planning offers a systematic way to uncover the dangerous implicit assumptions that would otherwise slip unnoticed and thus unchallenged into the plan. The process imposes a strict discipline that is captured in four related documents: a *reverse income statement,* which models the basic economics of the business; *pro forma operations specs,* which lay out the operations needed to run the business; a *key assumptions checklist,* which is used to ensure that assumptions are checked; and a *milestone planning chart,* which specifies the assumptions to be tested at each project milestone. As the venture unfolds and new data are uncovered, each of the documents is updated.

To demonstrate how this tool works, we will apply it retrospectively to Kao Corporation's highly successful entry into the floppy disk business in 1988. We deliberately draw on no inside information about Kao or its planning process but instead use the kind of limited public knowledge that often is all that any company would have at the start of a new venture.

The Company

Japan's Kao Corporation was a successful supplier of surfactants to the magnetic-media (floppy disk) industry. In 1981, the company began to study the potential for becoming a player in floppy disks by leveraging the surfactant technology it had developed in its core businesses, soap and cosmetics. Kao's managers realized that they had learned enough process knowledge from their floppy disk customers to supplement their own skills in surface chemistry. They believed they could produce floppy disks at a much lower cost and higher quality than other companies offered at that time. Kao's surfactant competencies were particularly valuable because the quality of the floppy disk's surface is crucial for its reliability. For a company in a mature industry, the opportunity to move current product into a growth industry was highly attractive.

The Market

By the end of 1986, the demand for floppy disks was 500 million in the United States, 100 million in Europe, and 50 million in Japan, with growth estimated at 40% per year, compounded. This meant that by 1993, the

global market would be approaching 3 billion disks, of which about a third would be in the original equipment manufacturer (OEM) market, namely such big-volume purchasers of disks as IBM, Apple, and Microsoft, which use disks to distribute their software. OEM industry prices were expected to be about 180 yen per disk by 1993. Quality and reliability have always been important product characteristics for OEMs such as software houses because defective disks have a devastating impact on customers' perceptions of the company's overall quality.

The Reverse Income Statement

Discovery-driven planning starts with the bottom line. For Kao, back when it began to consider its options, the question was whether the floppy disk venture had the potential to enhance the company's competitive position and financial performance significantly. If not, why should Kao incur the risk and uncertainty of a major strategic venture?

Here, we impose the first discipline, which is to plan the venture using a reverse income statement, which runs from the bottom line up. (See the exhibit "First, Start with a Reverse Income Statement.") Instead of starting with estimates of revenues and working down the income statement to derive profits, we start with *required profits.* We then work our way up the profit and loss to determine how much revenue it will take to deliver the level of profits we require and how much cost can be allowed. The underlying philosophy is to impose revenue and cost disciplines by baking profitability into the plan at the outset: Required profits equal necessary revenues minus allowable costs.

At Kao in 1988, management might have started with these figures: net sales, about 500 billion yen; income before taxes, about 40 billion yen; and return on sales (ROS), 7.5%. Given such figures, how big must the floppy disk

First, Start with a Reverse Income Statement

The goal here is to determine the value of success quickly. If the venture can't deliver significant returns, it may not be worth the risk.

Total Figures
Required profits to add 10% to total profits = 4 billion yen
Necessary revenues to deliver 10% sales margin =
   40 billion yen
Allowable costs to deliver 10% sales margin = 36 billion yen

Per Unit Figures
Required unit sales at 160 yen per unit = 250 million units
Necessary percentage of world market share of OEM unit
   sales = 25%
Allowable costs per unit for 10% sales margin = 144 yen

opportunity be to justify Kao's attention? Every company will set its own hurdles. We believe that a strategic venture should have the potential to enhance total profits by at least 10%. Moreover, to compensate for the increased risk, it should deliver greater profitability than reinvesting in the existing businesses would. Again, for purposes of illustration, assume that Kao demands a risk premium of 33% greater profitability. Since Kao's return on sales is 7.5%, it will require 10%.

If we use the Kao data, we find that the required profit for the floppy disk venture would be 4 billion yen (10% × 40 billion). To deliver 4 billion yen in profit with a 10% return on sales implies a business with 40 billion yen in sales.

Assuming that, despite its superior quality, Kao will have to price competitively to gain share as a new entrant, it should set a target price of 160 yen per disk. That translates into unit sales of 250 million disks (40 billion yen in sales divided by 160 yen per disk). By imposing these simple performance measures at the start (1988), we quickly establish both the scale and scope of the venture: Kao would need to capture 25% of the total world OEM market (25% of 1 billion disks) by 1993. Given what is known about the size of the market, Kao clearly must be prepared to compete globally from the outset, making major commitments not only to manufacturing but also to selling.

Continuing up the profit and loss, we next calculate allowable costs: If Kao is to capture 10% margin on a price of 160 yen per disk, the total cost to manufacture, sell, and distribute the disks worldwide cannot exceed 144 yen per disk. The reverse income statement makes clear immediately that the challenge for the floppy disk venture will be to keep a lid on expenses.

The Pro Forma Operations Specs and the Assumptions Checklist

The second discipline in the process is to construct pro forma operations specs laying out the activities required to produce, sell, service, and deliver the product or service to the customer. Together, those activities comprise the venture's allowable costs. At first, the operations specs can be modeled on a simple spreadsheet without investing in more than a few telephone calls or on-line searches to get basic data. If an idea holds together, it is possible to identify and test underlying assumptions, constantly fleshing out and correcting the model in light of new information. When a company uses this cumulative approach, major flaws in the business concept soon become obvious, and poor concepts can be abandoned long before significant investments are made.

We believe it is essential to use industry standards for building a realistic picture of what the business has to look like to be competitive. Every industry has its own pressures—which determine normal rates of return in that industry—as well as standard performance measures such as asset-to-sales ratios, industry profit margins, plant utilization, and so on. In a globally competitive environment, no sane manager should expect to escape the competitive discipline that is captured and measured in industry standards. These standards are readily available from investment analysts and business information services. In countries with information sources that are less well developed than those in the United States, key industry parameters are still used by investment bankers and, more specifically, by those commercial bankers who specialize in loans to the particular industry. For those getting into a new industry, the best approach is to adapt standards from similar industries.

Note that we do not begin with an elaborate analysis of product or service attributes or an in-depth market study. That comes later. Initially, we are simply trying to capture the venture's embedded assumptions. The basic discipline is to spell out clearly and realistically where the venture will have to match existing industry standards and in what one or two places managers expect to excel and how they expect to do so.

Kao's managers in 1988 might have considered performance standards for the floppy disk industry. Because there would be no reason to believe that Kao could use standard production equipment any better than established competitors could, it would want to plan to match industry performance on measures relating to equipment use. Kao would ascertain, for example, that the effective production capacity per line was 25 disks per minute in the industry; and the effective life of production equipment was three years. Kao's advantage was in surface chemistry and surface physics, which could improve quality and reduce the cost of materials, thus improving margins. When Kao planned its materials cost, it would want to turn that advantage into a specific challenge for manufacturing: Beat the industry standard for materials cost by 25%. The formal framing of operational challenges is an important step in discovery-driven planning. In our experience, people who are good in design and operations can be galvanized by clearly articulated challenges. That was the case at Canon, for example, when Keizo Yamaji challenged the engineers to develop a personal copier that required minimal service and cost less than $1,000, and the Canon engineers rose to the occasion.

A company can test the initial assumptions against experience with similar situations, the advice of experts in the industry, or published information sources. The point is not to demand the highest degree of accuracy but to build a reasonable model of the economics and logistics of the venture and to assess the order of magnitude of the challenges. Later, the company can analyze where the plan is most sensitive to wrong assumptions and do more formal checks. Consultants to the industry—bankers, suppliers, potential customers, and distributors—often can provide low-cost and surprisingly accurate information.

The company must build a picture of the activities that are needed to carry out the business and the costs. Hence in the pro forma operations specs, we ask how many orders are needed to deliver 250 million units in sales; then how many sales calls it will take to secure those orders; then how many salespeople it will take to make the sales calls, given the fact that they are selling to a global OEM market; then how much it will cost in sales-force compensation. (See the exhibit "Second, Lay Out All the Activities Needed to Run the Venture.") Each assumption can be checked, at first somewhat roughly and then with increasing precision. Readers might disagree with our first-cut estimates. That is fine—so might Kao Corporation. Reasonable disagreement triggers discussion and, perhaps, adjustments to the spreadsheet. The evolving document is doing its job if it becomes the catalyst for such discussion.

The third discipline of discovery-driven planning is to compile an assumption checklist to ensure that each assumption is flagged, discussed, and checked as the venture unfolds. (See the exhibit "Third, Track All Assumptions.")

The entire process is looped back into a revised reverse income statement, in which one can see if the entire business proposition hangs together. (See the exhibit "Fourth, Revise the Reverse Income Statement") If it doesn't, the process must be repeated until the performance requirements and industry standards can be met; otherwise, the venture should be scrapped.

Milestone Planning

Conventional planning approaches tend to focus managers on meeting plan, usually an impossible goal for a venture rife with assumptions. It is also counterproductive—insistence on meeting plan actually prevents learning. Managers can formally plan to learn by using milestone events to test assumptions.

Milestone planning is by now a familiar technique for monitoring the progress of new ventures. The basic idea, as described by Zenas Block and Ian C. MacMillan in the book *Corporate Venturing* (Harvard Business School Press, 1993), is to postpone major commitments of resources until the evidence from the previous milestone

Second, Lay Out All the Activities Needed to Run the Venture

PRO FORMA OPERATIONS SPECS

1. Sales
Required disk sales = 250 million disks
Average order size (Assumption 8) = 10,000 disks
Orders required (250 million/10,000) = 25,000

Number of calls to make a sale (Assumption 9) = 4
Sales calls required (4 × 25,000) = 100,000 per year

Calls per day per salesperson (Assumption 10) = 2
Annual salesperson days (100,000/2) = 50,000
Sales force for 250 days per year (Assumption 11)
  50,000 salesperson days/250 = 200 people

Salary per salesperson = 10 million yen (Assumption 12)
Total sales-force salary cost (10 million yen × 200)
  = 2 billion yen

2. Manufacturing
Quality specification of disk surface: 50% fewer flaws than best competitor (Assumption 15)

Annual production capacity per line = 25 per minute
  × 1440 minutes per day × 348 days (Assumption 16)
  = 12.5 million disks
Production lines needed (250 million disks/12.5 million disks per line) = 20 lines

Production staffing (30 per line [Assumption 17]
  × 20 lines) = 600 workers

Salary per worker = 5 million yen (Assumption 18)
Total production salaries (600 × 5 million yen) = 3 billion yen

Materials costs per disk = 20 yen (Assumption 19)
Total materials cost (20 × 250 million disks) = 5 billion yen
Packaging per 10 disks = 40 yen (Assumption 20)
Total packaging costs (40 × 25 million packages)
  = 1 billion yen

3. Shipping
Containers needed per order of 10,000 disks = 1
  (Assumption 13)
Shipping cost per container = 100,000 yen (Assumption 14)
Total shipping costs (25,000 orders × 100,000 yen)
  = 2.5 billion yen

4. Equipment and Depreciation
Fixed asset investment to sales = 1:1 (Assumption 5)
  = 40 billion yen
Equipment life = 3 years (Assumption 7)
Annual depreciation (40 billion yen/3 years)
  = 13.3 billion yen

Third, Track All Assumptions

Keeping a checklist is an important discipline to ensure that each assumption is flagged and tested as a venture unfolds.

Assumption	Measurement
1. Profit margin	10% of sales
2. Revenues	40 billion yen
3. Unit selling price	160 yen
4. 1993 world OEM market	1 billion disks
5. Fixed asset investment to sales	1:1
6. Effective production capacity per line	25 disks per minute
7. Effective life of equipment	3 years
8. Average OEM order size	10,000 disks
9. Sales calls per OEM order	4 calls per order
10. Sales calls per salesperson per day	2 calls per day
11. Selling days per year	250 days
12. Annual salesperson's salary	10 million yen
13. Containers required per order	1 container
14. Shipping cost per container	100,000 yen
15. Quality level needed to get customers to switch % fewer flaws per disk than top competitor	50%
16. Production days per year	348 days
17. Workers per production line per day (10 per line for 3 shifts)	30 per line
18. Annual manufacturing worker's salary	5 million yen
19. Materials costs per disk	20 yen
20. Packaging costs per 10 disks	40 yen
21. Allowable administration costs (see revised reverse income statement)	9.2 billion yen

Fourth, Revise the Reverse Income Statement

Now, with better data, one can see if the entire business proposition hangs together.

Required margin	10% return on sales
Required profit	4 billion yen
Necessary revenues	40 billion yen
Allowable costs	36 billion yen
Sales-force salaries	2.0 billion yen
Manufacturing salaries	3.0 billion yen
Disk materials	5.0 billion yen
Packaging	1.0 billion yen
Shipping	2.5 billion yen
Depreciation	13.3 billion yen
Allowable administration and overhead costs	9.2 billion yen (Assumption 21)
Per-unit figures	
Selling price	160 yen
Total costs	144 yen
Disk materials costs	20 yen

event signals that the risk of taking the next step is justified. What we are proposing here is an expanded use of the tool to support the discipline of transforming assumptions into knowledge.

Going back to what Kao might have been thinking in 1988, recall that the floppy disk venture would require a 40-billion-yen investment in fixed assets alone. Before investing such a large sum, Kao would certainly have wanted to find ways to test the most critical assumptions underlying the three major challenges of the venture:

- capturing 25% global market share with a 20-yen-per-disk discount and superior quality;
- maintaining at least the same asset productivity as the average competitor and producing a floppy disk at 90% of the estimated total costs of existing competitors; and
- using superior raw materials and applied surface technology to produce superior-quality disks for 20 yen per unit instead of the industry standard of 27 yen per unit.

For serious challenges like those, it may be worth spending resources to create specific milestone events to test the assumptions before launching a 40-billion-yen venture. For instance, Kao might subcontract prototype production so that sophisticated OEM customers could conduct technical tests on the proposed disk. If the prototypes survive the tests, then, rather than rest on the assumption that it can capture significant business at the target price, Kao might subcontract production of a large batch of floppy disks for resale to customers. It could thus test the appetite of the OEM market for price discounting from a newcomer.

Similarly, for testing its ability to cope with the second and third challenges once the Kao prototype has been de-veloped, it might be worthwhile to buy out a small existing floppy disk manufacturer and apply the technology in an established plant rather than try to start up a greenfield operation. Once Kao can demonstrate its ability to produce disks at the required quality and cost in the small plant, it can move ahead with its own full-scale plants.

Deliberate assumption-testing milestones are depicted in the exhibit "Finally, Plan to Test Assumptions at Milestones," which also shows some of the other typical milestones that occur in most major ventures. The assumptions that should be tested at each milestone are

Finally, Plan to Test Assumptions at Milestones

Milestone event—namely, the completion of:	Assumptions to be tested
1. Initial data search and preliminary feasibility analysis	4: 1993 would OEM Market 8: Average OEM order size 9: Sales calls per OEM order 10: Sales calls per salesperson per day 11: Salespeople needed for 250 selling days per year 12: Annual sales person's salary 13: Containers required per order. 14: Shipping cost per container 16: Production days per year 18: Annual manufacturing worker's salary
2. Prototype batches produced	15: Quality to get customers to switch 19: Materials costs per disk
3. Technical testing by customers	3: Unit selling price 15: Quality to get customers to switch
4. Subcontracted production	19: Materials costs per disk
5. Sales of subcontracted production	1: Profit margin 2: Revenues 3: Unit selling price 8: Average OEM order size 9: Sales calls per OEM order 10: Sales calls per salesperson per day 12: Annual salesperson's salary 15: Quality to get customers to switch
6. Purchase of an existing plant	5: Fixed asset investment to sales 7: Effective life of equipment
7. Pilot production at purchased plant	6: Effective production capacity per line 16: Production days per year 17: Workers per production line per day 18: Annual manufacturing worker's salary 19: Materials costs per disk 20: Packaging costs per 10 disks
8. Competitor reaction	1: Profit margin 2: Revenues 3: Unit selling price
9. Product redesign	19: Materials costs per disk 20: Packaging costs per 10 disks
10. Major repricing analysis	1: Profit margin 2: Revenues 3: Unit selling price 4: 1993 world OEM market
11. Plant redesign	5: Fixed asset investment to sales 6: Effective production capacity per line 19: Materials costs per disk

listed with appropriate numbers from the assumption checklist.

In practice, it is wise to designate a *keeper of the assumptions*—someone whose formal task is to ensure that assumptions are checked and updated as each milestone is reached and that the revised assumptions are incorporated into successive iterations of the four discovery-driven planning documents. Without a specific person dedicated to following up, it is highly unlikely that individuals, up to their armpits in project pressures, will be able to coordinate the updating independently.

Discovery-driven planning is a powerful tool for any significant strategic undertaking that is fraught with uncertainty—new-product or market ventures, technology development, joint ventures, strategic alliances, even major systems redevelopment. Unlike platform-based planning, in which much is known, discovery-driven planning forces managers to articulate what they don't know, and it forces a discipline for learning. As a planning tool, it thus raises the visibility of the make-or-break uncertainties common to new ventures and helps managers address them at the lowest possible cost.

READING III-9

Living on the Fault Line

Geoffrey Moore

The fault line upon which technology-enabled businesses are built is the technology adoption life cycle. It causes dramatic shifts in alignment among the various strata that make up the competitive-advantage hierarchy. As a result, competitive-advantage positions that once seemed secure are abruptly overthrown, and management teams on the verge of congratulating themselves now must scramble to recover. Here's how it plays out.

Before a disruptive technology can be assimilated into a mainstream marketplace, it must pass through multiple phases of adoption during which the market behaves in different ways specific to each phase. The end goal of all these mutations is to create and populate a sustainable value chain that can transform the new technology into reliable, deployable offerings. We call this goal Main

Source: Chapter 4 from Geoffrey Moore, *Living on the Fault Line,* New York, Harper Business, 2000.

Street, a state of business maturity in which technology-enabled businesses resemble most other sectors of the economy.

To reach Main Street, however, technology-enabled markets must pass through three prior phases. There are thus four phases of adoption in all, and each one rewards a very different market development strategy. Indeed, the competitive-advantage strategy that brings success in any one phase causes failure at the next stage. This creates extraordinary management challenges for organizations that develop momentum and inertia around any one stage.

Depending on when and how your company rose to prominence, you could have gone through your last technology adoption life cycle several years or several decades ago. That will determine to some degree your familiarity with the material covered in this paper. Its goal is simply to lay out the market dynamics involved so that they can be readily understood by all involved in setting strategy.

I would like to start by reminding everyone once again that the fault line, this thing that is driving us all crazy even as it brings enormous wealth creation into the economy, is all Moore's fault! Not me, not Geoffrey Moore—*Gordon Moore!* To be specific, Moore's law, which observes that the semiconductor industry doubles the price/performance of its products roughly every eighteen months, is at the heart of the continuous eruption of disruptive technologies that has characterized the last twenty years. You can just do so much more new weird stuff nowadays than you ever could before because there is so much more horsepower to do it with. Moreover, as these disruptions build upon previous disruptions, both their frequency and their cumulative impact are increasing, so that we all feel like we are riding up a monstrous wave that shows no sign yet of cresting.

The Internet is in some sense a culmination of all this disruption and at the same time the starting point for another even bigger wave. Because it will radically shift power and wealth creation in virtually every sector of business, it is in effect a fault line running under the entire world economy. The offer it makes is at once exhilarating and terrifying—totally change what you are doing (terror) in order to achieve an order of magnitude greater effectiveness (exhilaration). This is the classic fault-line offer—discontinuous innovation enabled by disruptive technology. It has been studied at length under the heading *diffusion of innovation,* and the model that best describes its impact is the technology adoption life cycle.

THE TECHNOLOGY ADOPTION LIFE CYCLE

The technology adoption life cycle models the response of any given population to the offer of a discontinuous innovation, one that forces the abandonment of traditional infrastructure and systems for the promise of a heretofore unavailable set of benefits. It represents this response as a bell curve, separating out five subpopulations, as illustrated in Exhibit 1.

The bell curve represents the total population of people exposed to a new technology offer. The various segments of the curve represent the percentage of people predicted to adopt one or another of the five different strategies for determining when and why to switch allegiance from the old to the new. The five strategies unfold sequentially as follows:

1. The *technology enthusiast* strategy is to adopt the new technology upon its first appearance, in large part just to explore its properties to determine if it is "cool." The actual benefits provided may not even be of interest to this constituency, but the mechanism by which they are provided is of great interest. If they are entertained by the mechanism, they often adopt the product just to be able to show it off.
2. The *visionary* strategy is to adopt the new technology as a means for capturing a dramatic advantage over competitors who do not adopt it. The goal here is to be first to deploy an advantaged system and use that head start to leapfrog over the competition, establishing a position so far out in front that the sector realigns around its new leader. Visionaries are mavericks who want to break away from the herd and differentiate themselves dramatically.
3. The *pragmatist* strategy is directly opposed to the visionary. It wants to stay with the herd, adopting the new technology if and only if everyone else does as well. The goal here is to use the wisdom of the marketplace to sort out what's valuable and then to be a fast follower once the new direction has clearly emerged. Pragmatists consult each other frequently about who's adopting what in an effort to stay current but do not commit to any major change without seeing successful implementations elsewhere first.
4. The *conservative* strategy is to stick with the old technology for as long as possible (a) because it works (b) because it is familiar, and (c) because it is paid for. By putting off the transition to the new platform, conservatives conserve cash and avoid hitting the learning curve, making themselves more productive in the short run. Long term, when they do switch, the system is more completely debugged, and that works to their advantage as well. The downside of the strategy is that they grow increasingly out of touch for the period they don't adopt and can, if they wait too long, get isolated in old technology that simply will not map to the new world.
5. Finally, the *skeptic* strategy is to debunk the entire technology as a false start and refuse to adopt it at all. This is a winning tactic for those technologies that never do gain mainstream market acceptance. For those that do, however, it creates extreme versions of the isolation problems conservatives face.

Each of these strategies has validity in its own right, and a single individual is perfectly capable of choosing different strategies for different offers. But for any given technology, the market will develop in a characteristic pattern due to the aggregate effects of a population distributing its choices in the proportions outlined by the bell curve. The resulting market development model looks like the one shown in the Exhibit 2.

The model segments the evolution of a technology-based market as follows:

- The first phase, or *early market,* is a time when early adopters (technology enthusiasts and visionaries) take up the innovation while the pragmatic majority holds

EXHIBIT 1   The Technology Adoption Life Cycle

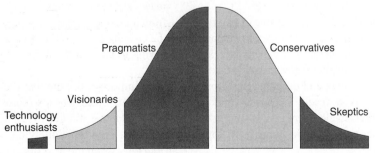

EXHIBIT 2   Technology-Enabled Market Development

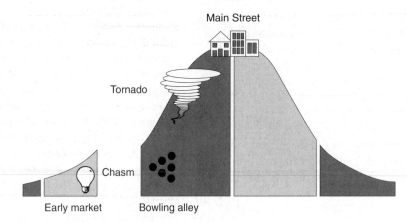

back. The market development goal at this stage is to gain a few prestigious flagship customers who help publicize the technology and celebrate its potential benefits.

- The early market is followed by a *chasm*, a period of no adoption, when the early adopters have already made their choices, but the pragmatist majority is still holding back. The barrier to further progress is that pragmatists are looking to other pragmatists to be references, but no one wants to go first. The market development goal at this stage is to target an initial beach-head segment of pragmatists who can lead the second wave of adoption.

- In the development of most technology-enabled markets, specific niches of pragmatic customers adopt the new technology before the general pragmatist population. We call this period the *bowling alley* because the market development goal is to use the first group of adopters as references to help win over the next group, and the next, and so on. Typically the "head bowling pin" is a niche of pragmatists who have a major business problem that cannot be solved with current technology but that does respond to a solution built around the new innovation. These are the *department managers in charge of a broken, mission-critical process. . . .* Once this first group starts to move it takes much less of a motive to overcome the inertia of the next group.

- As pragmatist adoption builds in niches, one of two futures emerges. In one, adoption continues to remain localized to niche markets, creating a pattern we call "bowling alley forever." In this pattern, each niche's solution is relatively complex and differentiated from every other niche's. As a result, no mass market emerges, and the market development goal is simply to expand existing niches and create new ones as the opportunity arises.

In the other pattern, a "killer app" emerges—a single application of the innovative technology that provides a compelling benefit that can be standardized across multiple niches. The killer app transforms niche adoption into mass adoption, creating an enormous uptick in demand for the new technology across a wide range of sectors. We call this period the *tornado* because the onrush of mass demand is so swift it creates a vortex that sucks the supply out of the market and puts the category into hypergrowth for a number of years. The market development goal here is to win as much market share as possible during a period when the entire market is choosing its supplier for the new class of technology-enabled offering.

- Once the supply side of the market finally catches up with the backlog of demand, the tornado phase subsides, and the market reaches a state we call *Main Street*. The new technology has been broadly deployed and, with the support of conservatives, now settles down to a (hopefully) long engagement as the incumbent technology. The market development goal here is to continuously improve the value of the offering, decreasing its base costs, and recouping margins by increasing the number of value-adding extensions that can supplement it. The ultimate extension in many cases is to convert the offering from a product sale to a services subscription, allowing the customer to gain the benefit of the product without having to take on the responsibility for maintaining it.

It is important to note that the end of the technology adoption life cycle does not represent the end of technology's productive market life. The category of offering can be sustained indefinitely on Main Street, coming to an end only when the next discontinuous innovation renders the prior technology obsolete. Indeed, despite all the emphasis on shortening life cycles, Main Street markets normally last for decades after complete absorption of the enabling technology—witness the car, the telephone, the television, the personal computer, and the cell phone. Importantly, however, the marketplace pecking order set by market share that emerges during the bowling alley and tornado phases tends to persist for the life of Main Street. That is, while Main Street represents the final and lasting distribution of competitive advantage, its boundaries get set prior to arrival. Thus success in every prior stage in the life cycle is key to building sustainable Main Street market success.

WHERE WE ARE HEADED

In this paper we are going to work through the dynamics of each of these stages, focusing on three elements, as follows:

1. *What the market is trying to accomplish independent of the desires of any individual participant within it.* The framework for this discussion will be the value-chain model and how, at each stage of the market, different relationships are privileged and come to the fore. The goal here is to describe the forces at work in the market and to set the context for what any individual company can hope to accomplish at each phase.
2. *What kinds of competitive advantage are useful at each stage.* The framework here will be the competitive-advantage hierarchy model and how, at each stage of the market, different forms of competitive advantage are privileged. The goal here is to align company ambition with market intention and to focus company management on the right critical success factors for each phase. What makes this so challenging on the execution front, where making a strong commitment to a single value discipline is the preferred tactic, is that at each stage the market rewards two of the four value disciplines and penalizes the remaining two.
3. *What impact success at each stage has on stock price.* The framework here will be the GAP/CAP valuation model and how, at each stage of the market, GAP and CAP can be expected to mutate. The goal here is to align management with shareholders, displacing the P&L statement with stock valuation as the key metric for company performance for all the market phases leading up to Main Street, where the two will finally rejoin each other to interoperate to the same end.

At the end of this review, we will have a comprehensive framework for understanding how to manage for shareholder value at each stage in the development of a technology-enabled market. We will, in other words, know the drill. The goal is to have no ambiguity on this front. That will then leave us with the extraordinary challenge of transforming our organizations to execute to this agenda. . . .

One last word of warning. The surgeon general is concerned that the remainder of this paper may cause *market model vertigo.* There are a total of sixteen diagrams in the paper as a whole, which vastly exceeds the recommended limit for vehicles of this size. All I can do is beg your indulgence. If I could have found a way to do this with fewer, I would have. So please, fasten your seat belts for the duration of this flight, and if need be, arm yourself with one of those little bags.

STAGE-ONE ADOPTION: THE EARLY MARKET

Value-Chain Strategy

The early market begins with the ambitions of two constituencies who live at opposite ends of the value chain (see Exhibit 3).

EXHIBIT 3 Early-Market Value Chain

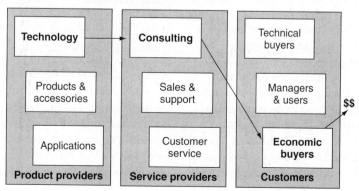

On the left is the *technology provider,* the supplier of the discontinuous innovation, with ambitions of constructing an entirely new marketplace based on a new platform. On the right are one or more visionary executives, in the role of *economic buyer,* who also have ambitions of their own. They want to rearchitect the marketplaces they participate in to install their company as the new market leader—and they want to do it fast. They see in the new technology an opportunity to disrupt the established order and insert themselves into the lead.

Between these two poles, however, there is at present no existing value chain that can link their ambitions. Indeed, the existing value chain is appalled by them. There is, however, one institution in the market that can bridge the gulf between the two, can transform the technology provider's magic into the economic buyer's dream, and that is the *consulting firm.* Rather than try to incubate a value chain in the marketplace, this consultancy will instead create a temporary value chain to serve a single project's specific needs. That is, they will pull together the products, the applications, the sales and support, the customer service, and in extreme cases even substitute their own people for the customer's technical buyer (and even for the customer's end users), all to make the value chain work *in a single instance for a single customer.*

Needless to say, this is an expensive proposition. But if it pays off, if the sponsoring company really does leapfrog over its competition in a new market order, then the visionary becomes a hero, and whatever money was spent was pocket change by comparison to the appreciation in the customer company's stock price.

So much for the primary players in the early-market value chain. Every other constituency exists in some marginalized role. Thus products are not yet really productized, and applications exist primarily in presentations as opposed to in the real world. In the services sector, sales, support, and customer service are all organizations that are just ramping up. Technical buyers in corporations are leery of taking responsibility for anything this immature, and managers and end users in general think it is way too early to be reengineering their functions. Note that these constituencies are not deleted from the diagram—they are very much present during an early-market project—but they are treated more as obstacles than as allies.

What makes the early-market value chain distinctive is that the consulting services function is playing many, many roles. To do so, it must operate inefficiently in that it must take responsibility for tasks for which it has no previous experience and no currently trained resource. People who can rise to this challenge are scarce, and thus

the organization must bill out its services at rates that substantially exceed those of standard contract labor. Moreover, since there is as yet no market for the new technology, once the project is done, there is not likely to be another like it in the pipeline, and thus the resources and their learning will be dispersed. Again, this drives up the costs of the project as they cannot be amortized across other efforts. Thus scarcity creates inefficiency, which in turn further exacerbates scarcity.

The end result is that neither the value chain nor the market persist past the end of the project (hence the absence of an arrow showing how money recycles to create additional business). In the early market, that is, customer sales are so few and far between that each effectively must be treated as a one-time event. Service providers can make money under this model, although it is a challenge to do so; product providers simply cannot. Although the customer is not price senstive, and thus does not require a discount to close the sale, there simply is not enough repeatable business to make the economics of a product-focused business model work out.

Competitive-Advantage Strategy

In a market with no persistent value chain, what kind of competitive advantage can a sponsor of discontinuous innovation hope to leverage or achieve?

As Exhibit 4 indicates, the primary competitive-advantage strategy for the early market consists in being first to catch the new technology wave. This is often called *first-mover advantage.* Amazon.com, by catching the Web retail wave first, has created a powerful brand that its competitors cannot hope to replicate, regardless of how much they spend. By being first to introduce auctions onto the Web, eBay gained first-mover advantage also, so that even when assaulted by an alliance of extremely powerful companies—Microsoft, Dell, Lycos, Excite— it has been able to sustain market share. Four years into Web advertising, the top ten sites, with Yahoo! leading the list, garner as much as 85 percent of the total spending— largely because of first-mover advantage. The SABRE system for airline and other travel-related reservations has had a similar track record, even as Apollo and Galileo and others have entered the market. Same with United Airlines' and American Airlines' frequent-flyer systems.

In every case, first-mover advantage equates to getting the market started around your unique approach and making the others play catch-up. It is a great strategy—when it works. The risk, of course, is that the market never goes forward to adopt the paradigm. At the time when the visionaries make their moves, this is a high probability.

EXHIBIT 4 Competitive Advantage in the Early Market

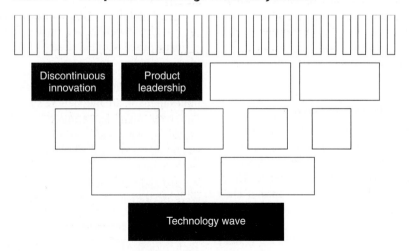

Visionaries are always bucking the odds in that most markets, like most mutations, die out before they can reproduce themselves sufficiently to gain persistence. Indeed, market creation is very much like the origin of species in nature, with the early market equating to the emergence of at least a few vital representatives of the new order.

The key metric of competitive advantage at this stage is simply the existence of proof of having one or more such representatives. For the technology provider, the test is one or more major corporate commitments from prestigious customers who champion the new paradigm as a platform for change in their industries. For the customer, the test is whether on top of this new platform an industry-changing offer can be promulgated. Neither measure is financial. Neither measure uses market share. The goal in both cases is just to validate the category. That puts the new wave on the map, enters it in the race.

The benefit to the company sponsoring this new initiative is that it gets a lot of attention. This attracts prospective customers to it at no additional cost of marketing. It also positions it as something of a thought leader in its industry. At the same time, however, it starts a timer ticking, with the expectation that within some definable period dramatic results will appear. If they do not, then the customers lose face, and the technology providers lose their company.

To sum up, for technology providers competitive advantage comes solely from positioning for a future market and not from gaining value-chain or market-segment advantage in an immediately exploitable market. There is a key implication here for corporate strategy—at this point in the life cycle one should not invest to build either value-chain or market-segment advantage. Thus, the technology-providing organization should not at this point be ramping up sales, marketing, customer service, manufacturing, procurement, logistics, human resources, information systems, or even financial projections. The only supply-side institution that should be making such plans is the professional services organization, which, because it is not tied to any particular new technology, can amortize its investment across a portfolio of "all the new stuff." For everyone else on the supply side, however, early-market build-up of infrastructure is bad strategy.

On the customer side, the primary competitive advantage to exploit is time. First-mover advantage decays, so this is a competition that goes to the swift. Prudence is not the order of the day—the whole enterprise is by definition imprudent—and should be supplanted instead by aggressive risk taking. The goal is not to be stupid or ostentatious but rather to act boldly on the assumption that the envisioned market, which today does not exist, will emerge before the investment capital runs out. One can manage the capital to some degree, but one cannot wait and see; one must bet on the come. This is the fundamental premise of venture capital, and this approach is standard procedure in Silicon Valley. But elsewhere, with other types of capital, or operating within established corporations, this mode appears reckless in the extreme, and forces accumulate quickly to tone down its aggressiveness.

This is the pattern of events chronicled in *The Innovator's Dilemma*. Ironically, although recurrent management reviews represent an attempt to reduce risk, their effect is actually to increase it. Once one has entered into a time-based competition, the one resource that must not be wasted is time, and that is precisely what does get wasted as sponsoring institutions deflect more and more management energy into investment justification instead of market creation.

Value Disciplines for the Early Market

In order to execute on a winning agenda, management teams must understand that the early market rewards discontinuous innovation and product leadership and penalizes customer intimacy and operational excellence. Thus optimal results are gained by elevating the former and suppressing the latter, as follows:

Elevate: *Discontinuous Innovation, Product Leadership*

The early market is driven by the demands of visionaries for offerings that create dramatic competitive advantages of the sort that would allow them to leapfrog over the other players in their industry. Only discontinuous innovation offers such advantage. In order to field that innovation, however, it must be transformed into a product offering that can be put to work in the real world. Hence the need for product leadership.

Suppress: *Customer Intimacy, Operational Excellence*

When technologies are this new, there are no target markets as yet and thus customer intimacy is not practical. Moreover, discontinuous innovations demand enormous customer tolerance and sacrifice as they get debugged, again not a time for celebrating putting the customer first. At the same time, because everything is so new and so much is yet to be discovered, it is equally impractical to target operational excellence. There is just too much new product, process, and procedure to invent and then shake out before pursuing this value discipline would be reasonable. Instead, . . . one has to make peace with the strategy "Go ugly early."

Looking at the above, it is not surprising that engineering-led organizations, who resonate with the value disciplines in favor, are much more successful at early-market initiatives than marketing-led or operations-led organizations, who lean toward the value disciplines that should be suppressed. Going forward, as we look at each subsequent phase of the life cycle, we will see that the rewarded and penalized disciplines change and so will the types of organizations that can be most successful.

Stock Price Implications

Technology-oriented investors take great interest in early-market developments, hoping to get in on the "next big thing" before the bulk of investors catch on to it. At the same time, however, they are wary of falling prey to a lot of hope that never turns into sustainable competitive advantage. Their dilemma is reflected in Exhibit 5.

The chart calls attention to both the positive and negative implications of what has been accomplished— namely, that a few customers have made a major commitment to the new technology. On the positive side, this can be taken as proof of the concept that there is a true GAP. This is a big step up from theoretical GAP, and it calls into being the *shadow* of a GAP/CAP chart.

On the negative side, however, there is no proof of any CAP. There is no evidence of a sustainable marketplace as yet. That is why we have a shadow of a chart. Because there is no persistent value chain in view, it is not clear yet exactly how much ground has been captured. Hence the question marks: Is this, or is this not, the next big thing?

EXHIBIT 5   Impact of Early-Market Success on Stock Price

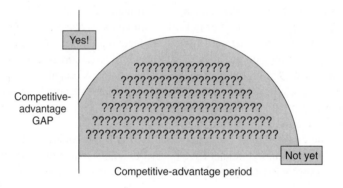

Nonetheless, if the company sponsoring the innovation is a venture-capital-backed start-up, the impact of early-market success is huge. Consider that its first round of funding was based on the current market value of a wing, a prayer, and the founding team's personal reputations. To get a second round at a higher valuation, it needed to garner at least one flagship customer. Now it has. Depending on how high the flag got raised and how broadly it unfurled, second-round valuations can enjoy increases of several hundred percent or more. Where has this new value come from? It has nothing to do with the actual revenues or earnings, although the bigger the deal, the better. Instead, it has everything to do with the usefulness of the new customer in communicating the value proposition of the company and demonstrating first-mover advantage. That is what captures the imagination and enthusiasm of the second-round investor. So winning a flagship deal in the early market is a very big deal for start-ups.

For large public companies, however, the issue is more problematic. Here total corporate revenues and earnings play such a dominant role in valuation that the communication of early-market wins, which typically do not show up in the numbers, must be managed carefully in order to extract shareholder value. The key audience to influence is the investment analyst community, so this communication must typically be channeled through the investor relations department. Unfortunately, that department tends over time to become "financially focused," falling prey to P&L myopia, because that is the orientation to which investment analysts default in their interrogations. To break free from this, the CEO has to be the communicator of the win, positioning it not as a financial event but rather as a market-making one, and holding up that single customer win as an icon for potential future streams of earnings.

If this approach is successful, a public company's stock will move gently upward on a halo effect. In general, however, history has shown that public companies tend to underplay early-market wins in their investor relations. This creates a relatively blank canvas upon which start-ups can paint. This used to be of no consequence because investment analysts would follow only public companies. But in the age of the Internet the transition from private to public comes so early in the life of a company that analysts must cover the start-ups if they are to have any chance of winning their IPO business. And once these analysts have gotten engaged with the idea of the next market, that begins to affect their valuation ideas about the established market. In short, it is becoming increas-ingly unwise for the investor relations team at established companies to neglect early-market events, both within their company and in the marketplace around them.

To wrap up this account of market development strategy for the early market, the core focus is on winning a few flagship customers in order to demonstrate to the marketplace and to investors that the company has first-mover advantage in catching a new wave of technology. These communications are targeted to the visionaries and other forward-thinking members of the market. Pragmatists in the same marketplace overhear these communications, not without interest. This may be the next thing they adopt—but not yet. Moving the first set of those pragmatists into the adoption window is the next market development challenge.

STAGE-TWO ADOPTION: CROSSING THE CHASM INTO THE BOWLING ALLEY

For technologies to gain persistent marketplace acceptance, they must cross the chasm and take up a position on the other side. Now we are in the realm of the pragmatists. To get pragmatists to move at all, companies must rethink their marketing objective from the early market. There the goal was to win a customer, and then another, and another. To cross the chasm, however, you have to *win a herd*. Here's why:

- Pragmatists only feel comfortable moving in herds. That's why they ask for references and use word of mouth as their primary source of advice on technology purchase decisions. Selling individual pragmatists on acting ahead of the herd is possible but very painful, and the cost of sales more than eats up the margin in the sale itself.
- Pragmatists evaluate the entire value chain, not just the specific product offer, when buying into a new technology. Value chains form around herds, not individual customers. There has to be enough repeatable business in the pipeline to reward an investment in specializing in the new technology. Sporadic deals, regardless of how big they are, do not create persistent value chains.

The visible metric for crossing the chasm, therefore, is to *make a market* and *create a value chain* where there were no market and no value chain before. This is a difficult undertaking. To increase its chances for success, and to decrease the time it takes to achieve, it is best to focus the effort on creating a niche market first before trying to create a mass market. It is simply prudent to minimize the number of variables at risk.

EXHIBIT 6   Bowling Alley Value Chain

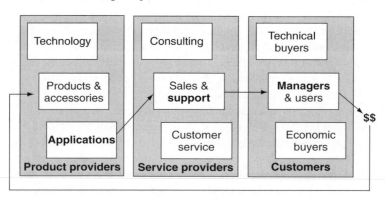

Think of a niche market as a self-contained system of commerce with its own local set of specialized needs and wants. Isolated from the mainstream market, which does not serve these special needs, it offers a *value-chain incubator* for emerging technology-enabled markets. That is, its isolation protects the fragile new chain from direct competitive attacks from the incumbent value chain. The customer community, in effect, nurtures the fledgling enterprise because it hopes to gain great benefit from it.

Value-Chain Strategy

To visualize the changes in moving from the early market to the bowling alley, let us return to our value-chain diagram, this time focusing on a new set of market makers as shown in Exhibit 6.

At the right-hand end of the chain, the *managers* in the customer domain represent the preassembled herd, an aggregation of relatively homogeneous demand. These are the department managers in charge of a broken, mission-critical process, all huddled in a mass. At the other end, the *application provider* in the product domain offers a relatively homogeneous solution to this herd's problem. It will bring its solution to market through a sales and support organization where it is the *support function* that really counts. That is because at the outset of a market the remaining value-chain partners are just getting recruited and cannot be relied upon to assemble the whole product correctly on their own. Later on these same partners will compete to take over the support function—and the enlightened application provider will let them, as it will greatly expand its market and its reach—but for now it is all just too new. So the application provider's support team must take the lead in working through all the glitches until a working whole product is in place, even when the problem is with someone else's part of the offering and not their own.

Note that the money-recycling arrow has now been restored to the diagram. This is the whole point of the niche-market strategy. We are now creating for the first time a self-funding persistent market where the economic gains of the customer lead to increasing and ongoing investment in the products and services that bring them about. Even if no other market ever adopts this technology, it will still be economically viable to maintain this niche. To be sure, the returns will not be all that the investors hoped for, but it will not be a total bust either. That is because niche markets have persistent competitive advantages that allow them to sustain themselves even when the marketplace in general is unsupportive of their efforts. Moreover, if the value chain extends its reach into additional niches, then it can add market growth to its already attractive price margins to produce highly attractive returns indeed.

The major beneficiary of this strategy is the application providers. It is they who harness the new wave of technology to the specific needs of the target segment, and they who rally the rest of the value chain to support this effort. Because the application provider is the company that really does "make the market," it gains a dominant market-specific competitive advantage during this market formation period. This advantage will persist indefinitely, even after the technology adoption life cycle goes forward, since once any market falls into a particular pecking order, it is loath to change.

Everyone else in the value chain—the core technology providers, the hardware and software product companies, the business consultants and the systems integrators, the customer service staff, and even the client's own technical staff—all happily take a backseat. That's because they will all be operating primarily as cost-effective generalists, making relatively minor modifications to their way of doing business, whereas the application vendor,

EXHIBIT 7 Competitive Advantage in the Bowling Alley

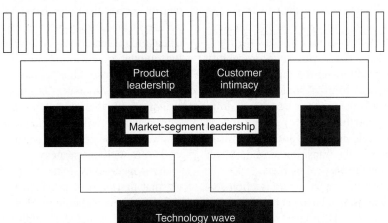

interacting intimately with the problem-owning department managers, must operate as a value-creating specialist and invest significantly to be able to do so effectively.

Competitive-Advantage Strategy

The competitive-advantage strategy for this stage of technology adoption looks like Exhibit 7.

The ability to harness the technology wave to solve the critical problem of one or more specific niche markets is what creates power at this stage, and that power goes primarily to the application provider. As more and more of the pragmatist department managers in the niche see their colleagues getting out of the soup, they, too, will come forward and insist on buying this vendor's application. Thus every other company in the value chain becomes dependent on that one vendor's good graces to get into the good deals. In effect, this creates a form of value-chain domination, but it is restricted solely to the niches served, and so it has very different properties—and a very different valuation—from the kind of broad horizontal-market domination we will see develop inside the tornado.

Because they reap the bulk of the rewards, it is relatively easy for application providers to understand and adopt niche marketing, especially if the alternative is to spend another year in the chasm. It is much more problematic, however, for a platform product or a transaction services company to embrace it. Their business plans are normally predicated on either broad horizontal adoption across a multitude of business segments or a broad cross-section of consumers. They are not well positioned to go after niche markets. Vertical industry domain expertise holds little value for them, and voluntarily subordinating themselves to an application vendor just to gain entry into

one little niche seems like a huge price to pay. Moreover, even if the tactic proves successful, the resulting order stream will be relatively modest and, worse, may inappropriately cause the rest of the market to misperceive the company as a niche player. For all these very good reasons, platform-products and transaction-services vendors tend to shy away from taking the niche approach to crossing the chasm. And yet it is still a mistake. Here's why.

As we shall see shortly, platform products are optimized for tornado markets, and transaction-services offers are optimized for Main Street markets. Those are the phases of the life cycle in which they will shine. So their strategy should be to accelerate technology adoption to get to "their" phase as quickly as possible. Time spent in the chasm for either strategy represents a huge opportunity cost, giving their competitors a chance to catch up to first-mover advantage while making no progress for themselves at all. This makes exiting the chasm as quickly as possible their top strategic imperative—hence their need to perform the admittedly unnatural act of niche marketing. To be sure, it is a little bit like asking a caterpillar who has a stated goal to be a butterfly to first spin itself into a cocoon and melt—the intermediate step is so disconnected from the end result that it is hard to warrant taking it. But there is now sufficient history to show that not taking the step is fatal—as demonstrated by the market development failures of ISDN networking, object-oriented databases, IBM's OS/2 operating system, pen-based PCs, infrared connectivity protocols, and artificial intelligence.

To be sure, once an initial niche market is established, the winning strategy for platform products and transaction services does indeed split off from the application providers. For the latter, the most powerful path forward is to stay in the bowling alley—this is their sweet spot—expanding niche to niche, following a bowling pin strategy. In this manner, such companies can chew their way through multiple markets with a very high probability of securing dominant positions in the majority of their niches. It is a "bowling alley forever" strategy focused on *preserving complexity* in order to create a source of profit margins for themselves and their service partners. It ends up trading off massive scale in favor of locally dominant roles and eventually makes the transition to Main Street as a leader in a set of mature vertical markets.

By contrast, for platform-product and transaction-services companies, the goal should be to get beyond niches altogether as soon as possible. Their quest instead should be for a single, general-purpose "killer app"—a word-processing program, a spreadsheet, e-mail, voice-mail, a Website, an e-commerce server—something that can be adopted by whole sectors of the economy all at once, thereby leveraging their horizontal business models' strength in being able to scale rapidly. But students of the life cycle should note that in the era prior to pervasive word processing, there were segment-specific solutions for lawyers, doctors, consultants, and governmental functions. These were a critical stepping stone toward getting to a mass market.

Value Disciplines for the Bowling Alley

To execute on a niche strategy in an emerging technology-enabled market, companies must realign their value discipline orientation to meet a new set of market priorities, as follows:

Elevate: *Product Leadership, Customer Intimacy*

The bowling alley is driven by the demands of pragmatists for a whole product that will fix a broken mission-critical business process. The fact that the process will not respond to conventional treatment calls out the need for product leadership. The fact that the required whole product will have to integrate elements specific to a particular vertical segment calls out the need for customer intimacy.

Suppress: *Discontinuous Innovation, Operational Excellence*

Pragmatist department managers under pressure to fix a broken process have neither the time nor the resources to support debugging a discontinuous innovation. At the same time, their need for special attention is incompatible with the kind of standardization needed for operational excellence.

Marketing-led organizations are best at crossing the chasm, specifically those that combine strong domain expertise in the targeted market segment with a solutions orientation. Operations-led organizations struggle with the amount of customization required that cannot be amortized across other segments, all of which offends their sense of efficiency. Engineering-led organizations struggle with the lack of product symmetry resulting from heavily privileging one niche's set of issues over a whole raft of other needed enhancements.

To win with this strategy, the critical success factor is focus—specifically, focus on doing whatever it takes to get that first herd of pragmatist customers to adopt en masse the new technology. Hedging one's bet by sponsoring forays targeted at additional herds at the same time is bad strategy. Both engineering- and operations-oriented organizations, however, are drawn to this approach because they fear that the company is putting all its eggs into one basket. Of course, that is precisely what it *is* doing. The reason it is good strategy to do so is that only by creating critical mass can one move a market and bring into existence a new value chain. Unless they can leverage tornado winds blowing in other markets, alternative initiatives subtract from the needed mass and, ironically, increase rather than decrease market risk.

Stock Price Implications

To help management teams of public corporations support what will at first seem to be an overly focused market development effort, it helps to show them the impact bowling alley success can have on stock price. Exhibit 8 illustrates the GAP/CAP implications of winning a niche market.

The size of the darkly shaded curve represents the valuation gained from winning market leadership in the first niche or head pin. It is a function of the amount of market share gained coming from sales of the new category in that niche. At The Chasm Group we use a three-tiered ranking system, as follows:

30 percent share of new sales and you can call yourself: **A leader**

50 percent share of new sales and you can call yourself: **The leader**

70 percent share of new sales and you can call yourself: **The dominator**

For the bowling alley strategy to work properly, companies must become "the dominator" in the first niche they attack and then achieve "the leader" status in the next one or two. After that, any of the three rankings contributes to

EXHIBIT 8 Impact of Chasm-Crossing Success on Stock Prices

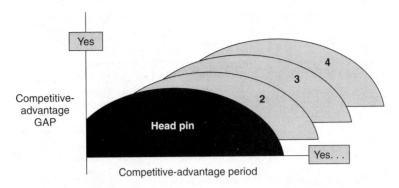

the overall market-share momentum in the sector. The rationale for these rules is that at the outset the pragmatist herd must hear a clear consensus forming around a single solution set, else they will dither in their purchase decisions and the market-capture effort will lose momentum.

So let us suppose in the head-pin niche you gain dominator status, and you have some additional niches under development: What is all that worth to investors? First, as the dominator of the first niche, it means you have a very high GAP, else others would have taken a larger percentage of the new sales. Second, it means you have secured a long CAP *for that niche* because now that the value chain has formed around your standards, there are huge barriers to entry for competitors and barriers to exit for customers and partners. So, unlike the early market, where you created *potential* shareholder value, now you have created *actual* shareholder value—hence the darker shading of the first curve.

For the first time, therefore, Wall Street can estimate with confidence the present value of future earnings at least within this one niche. For a start-up company in the application software sector, that estimate can be enough to merit a public offering. That is, a dominator position can be expected to generate high-quality earnings for a long period of time, and if these are your company's first earnings, they open up a promising future.

But if you are already a public company with a substantial earnings flow in place, then the impact on your P&L from adding the new niche may be negligible. Without a vision for how local niche dominance can be leveraged into additional niches, only modest shareholder value can be gained. You simply must go farther with the story to gain the uptick in stock price. That is why we labeled the CAP axis "Yes. . . ." To overcome lingering investment concern about future market size, it is critical to communicate the larger vision, educating the investor via

the bowling alley metaphor, showing how the company will grow forward into a second, third, and fourth niche, each time securing a strong leadership position with high GAP and long CAP.

Finally, if you are a platform-product or transaction-services company, you may worry that your investors will become confused by too much emphasis on what is in essence a niche-market success. In such cases management is often tempted to downplay their market-making achievement. This is a big mistake. Crossing the chasm is a major accomplishment, and you must take credit for it. The goal is to announce mainstream market acceptance for your new offering, citing all the buzz that has formed around you in the targeted niche market, and "creatively" interpret that as a harbinger of the mass adoption just around the corner. If you do not do this yourself, you leave the door open for some other competitor coming out of some other niche to claim this achievement for itself.

To wrap up our discussion of managing for shareholder value in the bowling alley, the core focus at this stage is on value-chain creation and market-segment domination, both leading to persistent competitive advantage, particularly for application providers. For all others at this stage, crossing the chasm is a critical transition vehicle to future competitive-advantage positions. The most powerful of these are created inside the tornado.

STAGE-THREE ADOPTION: INSIDE THE TORNADO

A tornado occurs whenever pragmatists across a variety of market sectors all decide simultaneously that it is time to adopt a new paradigm—in other words, when the pragmatist herd stampedes. This creates a dramatic spike in demand, vastly exceeding the currently available supply,

EXHIBIT 9   Tornado Value Chains

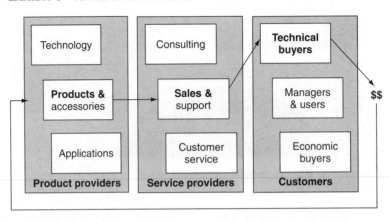

calling entire categories of vendors to reconfigure their offerings to meet the needs of a new value chain.

Value-Chain Strategy

The overriding market force that is shaping the tornado value chain is the desire for everyone in the market, beginning with the customer but quickly passing through to all the vendors, to drive the transition to a new paradigm as quickly as possible. That calls to the fore the three constituencies that are highlighted in Exhibit 9.

Each of these constituencies is well positioned to benefit from standardization for rapid deployment.

• In the product sphere, its is *products,* not technology and not applications, that get the privileged position. The problem with technology is that it is too malleable to be mass-produced and thus does not lend itself to rapid proliferation of common, standard infrastructure. The problem with applications is that they must be customized to sector-specific processes, and so again they do not deploy as rapidly as desired. By contrast, products, and specifically those that serve as platforms for a broad range of applications, are the ideal engine for paradigm proliferation.

Now, to be sure, there must be at least one application that warrants the purchase of the platform in the first place, but in a tornado that application must be essentially the same for every sector. Such an application is called "the killer app," and it becomes the focus for horizontal expansion across multiple sectors of the economy. *Accounting* was the killer app for mainframes, *manufacturing automation* for minicomputers, *word processing* for PCs, *computer-aided design* for

workstations, and *electronic mail* for local area networks. But in every case, it was the platform product providers, not the killer app vendors, who were ultimately the big tornado winners because as other applications came on-line, they created still more demand for their platforms.

• In the services sphere, it is the sales and support function, with the emphasis on *sales,* that carries the day. The drawback with consulting is that its projects are too complex, take too long, and require resources that are too scarce to ever permit a tornado to go forward. The drawback with customer service is that it is too focused on serving existing customers at a time when the over-whelming emphasis has to be on acquiring new customers.

Generating sales in the tornado is not a problem of winning over the customer so much as it is of beating the competition. It is critical, therefore, to field the most competitive sales force you can at this time. Because so much wealth is changing hands, and because the long-term consequences of market share are so great, tornado sales tactics are brutal, and sales aggressiveness is the core discipline. This is the time when nice guys do finish last.

On the support side, the key issue is to get new customers up and running on a minimal system as quickly as possible and then move on to the next new customer. The more cookie-cutter the process, the faster it replicates, and the more new customers you can absorb. The push is for operational excellence, not customer intimacy. This is not a normal support profile, so once again focusing the team on the right value discipline is a critical executive responsibility.

- On the customer side of the value chain, it is the *technical buyer,* not the end-user departments and not the economic buyer, who becomes the key focus. The problem with end users is that they inevitably seek customization to meet their department-specific needs. Not only is such complexity contrary to the vendor's wishes, it also works against the host institution's imperative to roll out the new infrastructure to everyone in the company as quickly as possible. Such rapid deployment requires a one-size-fits-all approach for the initial roll-out, something that the technical buyer understands far better than the end user. It is also not the time to court senior executives in their role as economic buyers. Once the tornado is under way, they sense the need to get over to the new infrastructure and delegate the task, including the selection process, to their technical staff.

When technical buyers become the target customer, their compelling reason to buy drives sales outcomes. High on their list is conformance to common standards, followed by market leadership status, which initially is signaled by partnerships with other market leaders, and later on confirmed by market share. The technical buyers' biggest challenge is systems integration, and this is where the support function can contribute to faster roll-outs by building standard interfaces to the most prevalent legacy systems.

The tornado, in essence, is one big land grab—a fierce struggle to capture as many new customers as possible during the pragmatist stampede to the new paradigm. Increasing shareholder value revolves entirely around max- imizing market share, and to that end there are three sources of competitive-advantage leverage to exploit.

Competitive-Advantage Strategy

The power of the tornado comes from the simultaneous unleashing of the bottom two layers of the competitive-advantage hierarchy, as highlighted in Exhibit 10.

The primary source of competitive advantage is simply to be riding the new technology wave as it enters into its tornado phase. Mass-market adoption is an awesome market creation force that wreaks havoc on installed bases rooted in old technology. As the incumbents retreat under the impact of this force to protect their increasingly conservative installed bases, your company advances with the new wave of adoption to occupy their lost ground. This is *category advantage* at work, and it alone will enhance your stock price—hence the scramble of every vendor in the sector to position themselves on the bandwagon of whatever this hot new category is.

The second element of competitive advantage derives from the potential institutionalization of key market-making companies as value-chain leaders or dominators. . . . That is, for each element in the value chain, tornado markets seek out a single market-leading provider to set the de facto standards for that component. That role normally goes to the company that garners the most new customers early in the race. In addition, when a single company can gain power over the rest of the value chain, typically by leveraging the power to withhold its proprietary technology and thereby stymie the entire offer, the market accords even more privilege to it.

EXHIBIT 10 Competitive Advantage in the Tornado

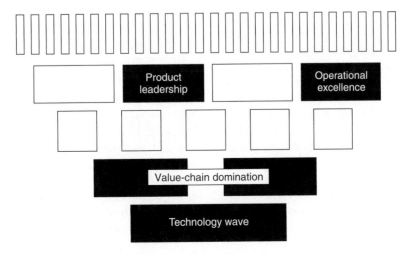

The power of market-share leadership is rooted in the pragmatist preference to make the safe buy by going with the market leader. That is, rather than rely on their own judgment, pragmatists prefer to rely on the group's. Once that judgment has been made clear, once one vendor has emerged as the favorite, then pragmatists naturally gravitate to that choice, which of course further increases that company's market share, intensifying its gravitational attraction.

This cycle of positive feedback not only spontaneously generates market leaders, but once they are generated, works to keep them in place. That is, the value-chain advantage a market leader gains over its direct competitors is that it has become the default choice for any other company in the chain to round out its offers. Thus the company gains sales that it never initiated and gets invited into deals its competitors never see. Such sales not only add to revenues but to margins, since the absence of competition removes much of the pressure to discount price. In short, winning the market-share prize is a very sweet deal, which, if it is not working for you, is working against you. Hence the need to focus all guns on market share.

Thus the essence of tornado strategy is simply to capture the maximum number of customers in the minimum amount of time and to minimize all other efforts. At each moment the winning strategy is to strike and move on, strike and move on. Anything you can do to slow down a competitor along the way is gravy. What you must not do is voluntarily slow yourself down, not even for a customer. That is, during the tornado *customer acquisition* takes temporary priority over *customer satisfaction*. The entire pragmatist herd is switching from the old to the new—not a frequent event. As customers, in other words, they are temporarily "up for grabs." Once they choose their new vendor, they will be highly reluctant to consider changing yet again. So either you win these customers now, or you risk losing them *for the life of the paradigm.*

And then there is the super grand prize bonanza of tornado market development to which we have already alluded, namely, gaining *value-chain power over the other vendors in the value chain.* As noted, this occurs when a single vendor has monopoly control of a crucial element in the value chain, the way Microsoft and Intel each do for the personal computer, the way Cisco does for the Internet, the way Qualcomm appears to do for the future of wireless telephony. In such cases, as the market tornado unfolds, the standard whole product that forms around the killer app incorporates a piece of your proprietary technology. Going forward, for the value-chain offering

as a whole to evolve, it must take your technology along with it—and there is no substitute for it. This makes everyone in the chain dependent upon you, which in turn allows you to orchestrate the behavior of the rest of the chain. This can include pressuring value-chain partners to adopt or support some of your less successful products so that you gain power across a much broader portion of your product line than its actual features and benefits would normally merit.

Value Disciplines for the Tornado

Whatever position one achieves during the tornado market depends largely on your company's ability to execute a market-share land-grab strategy. To this end, the market rewards a third alignment of value disciplines, as follows:

Elevate: *Product Leadership, Operational Excellence*

The tornado is driven by the demands of infrastructure buyers for standard, reliable offerings suitable for rapid mass deployment. Here product leadership gets translated into shipping the next release with the new set of features ahead of the competition and thereby grabbing additional market share from them. Operational excellence is critical to this effort because if there is any hiccup in the process, the market can still shift to an alternative vendor, with major market-share consequences that will last for the duration of the paradigm.

Suppress: *Discontinuous Innovation, Customer Intimacy*

Any form of discontinuous innovation during a tornado creates opportunity for error, putting rapid mass deployment at risk, and is thus anathema. Customer intimacy is also suppressed for the duration of the roll-out for the same reason, sacrificed to the end of achieving reliable, consistent deployment. Once the infrastructure is set in place, then there will be time to come back and meet customer-specific requests.

Operations-led organizations tend to have the edge in a tornado, where meeting deadlines, shipping in quantity, and minimizing returns all take priority over innovation and customer delight. Marketing-led organizations, by contrast, typically flounder because they cannot bear to relinquish their commitment to customer intimacy and customer satisfaction. They need to realize that, in a tornado, just getting the new systems installed and working properly is grounds for customer satisfaction.

Stock Price Implications

When it comes to investor returns, the tornado is the greatest wealth-creation force on the planet. It plays out to two end games depending on whether the market develops around proprietary technology or open-systems standards. In markets that develop under the influence of a proprietary technology, the roles of leader, challenger, and follower take on the following pattern:

- **Gorilla.** The market-share leader in a tornado with proprietary architectural control, this company creates massive shareholder value by gaining value-chain-domination power and forcing the rest of the market to serve its ends. Microsoft, Intel, and Cisco are all gorillas.
- **Chimp.** A direct challenger to the gorilla, this company also has proprietary technology, but it has lost the competition to establish the market's de facto standard. Once the market becomes aware of this outcome, it throws more and more of its business to the gorilla, effectively expelling the chimp from the standard value chain. Chimps have no recourse except to retreat into niche markets where they can make themselves over into "local gorillas," focusing on specialized applications where their non-standard technology is acceptable because of the exceptional added value they supply. Apple's Macintosh, Digital's Alpha chip, and Bay Network's Wellfleet routers are all chimps.
- **Monkey.** A follower of the gorilla, this company licenses the gorilla's architecture to offer a low-cost substitute for its products that is compatible with the de facto standard. Price-sensitive customers in the market are happy to support monkeys *as a class.* They do not, however, support any particular monkey as a company, and as a result monkeys can never gain lasting market share. As soon as a cheaper, better offer comes along, the market immediately shifts its allegiance to it. Attempting to buy market share, therefore, is always a losing strategy. The correct strategy instead is to opportunistically take advantage of holes in the gorilla's product line and to move on as soon as they are filled. Hitachi with its mainframes (cloning IBM's standards) and AMD with its K-series microprocessors (cloning Intel's) are both monkeys.

In contrast to the above, when tornado markets evolve in the absence of proprietary architectural control, the competitive dynamics within the hierarchy play out very differently. Such markets are frequently termed "open-systems markets," and to understand their dynamics executives need a second set of terms, as follows:

- **King.** The market leader in an open-systems tornado, this company has outexecuted its competition early on and is now enjoying the increasing-returns effects of market-share leadership. But unlike gorillas, kings have no proprietary technology to keep customers from exiting or competitors from entering their market. As a result, they can always be replaced, and thus the valuations of kings are significantly lower than those of gorillas. In the PC market, IBM was the original king, then Compaq, and now Dell.
- **Prince.** The market challenger in an open-systems tornado, this company's long-term prospects are dramatically different from the chimp's. That's because a prince can substitute for a king, whereas a chimp cannot substitute for a gorilla. Open-systems markets embrace princes as a mechanism to keep kings responsive to the rest of the chain's needs. In the PC market, Compaq began as a prince, as did Dell. HP has always been and still is a prince.
- **Serf.** A market follower in an open-systems tornado, this company has even less power than a monkey, since princes already serve as price competition for kings. As a result, it must discount even further to get its products purchased. As a class, serfs are significant because they can drag prices down to a point where even the king's business becomes unprofitable. In the PC market, the no-name "white box" PCs that are assembled by hundreds of resellers represent the serfs—and about one-third of the total market.

Now let's see how investors value these different roles in the context of relative competitive advantage. First, for markets where proprietary architectural control is a factor, see Exhibit 11.

Note first the huge market cap of the gorilla. As we have already discussed, it gains a very high GAP because it has a monopoly on a critical piece of new technology without which the tornado market cannot function. Moreover, since there is no substitute for its component, the company also has a very long CAP, essentially equivalent to the CAP of the whole market category. It is no accident that at the time of this writing, Microsoft and Cisco have the two highest market caps in the world.

Turning to the chimp, note, too, that it has a high GAP. That is because it, too, has proprietary technology for which there is no substitute. Unfortunately, however, this technology is not the de facto standard, and thus its CAP

EXHIBIT 11 Impact of Tornado Success on Stock Price (Proprietary Technologies)

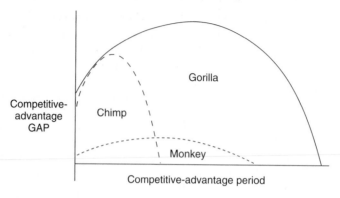

EXHIBIT 12 Impact of Tornado Success on Stock Price (Open Systems)

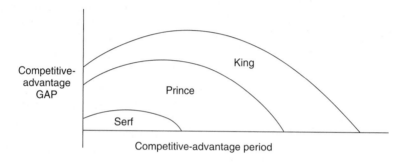

is severely limited. It can expand into niche markets where the gorilla chooses not to compete, but it has no chance in a head-to-head battle.

A monkey's prospects are just the opposite. It has a long CAP but can generate no significant GAP. That is, because its offers are compatible with the de facto standard, it can benefit from the category's persistence. However, since its presence is not required, its CAP is not as long as the gorilla's. Moreover, since it has no unique offer, it cannot generate any GAP to speak of except through price discounts. In short, monkeys do not make for good long-term investments.

In contrast to the foregoing, Exhibit 12 reflects valuations in an open-systems competition.

Here the king and the prince are on more equal footing, with the serf trailing. In this type of market, brand and distribution are the critical success factors. Serfs typically have neither, hence their minuscule market caps. Princes, by contrast, can challenge market-leading kings on either front. In the PC market, in particular, exploiting new channels of distribution has led to several changes in the hierarchy, first when Compaq used its retail skills to

unseat IBM, and then when Dell used its direct-selling skills to unseat Compaq. On the GAP axis, because all players must conform to a common standard, they end up competing on price to some degree, which reduces the maximum attainable GAP for any company, even the king. This has long-term consequences for every company in the market.

It is important to remember, however, that while a tornado market is in full swing, everybody gains simply by virtue of tornado demand far exceeding tornado supply. That is, the tornado creates an extended period of shortages that allow all companies to charge premium prices during this phase. Thus all stocks in the category tend to gain in valuation initially, and only after the competition sorts itself out, and the market implications of the various roles is understood, do stock prices adjust to meet these charts.

To wrap up our discussion of the tornado, the core focus is on grabbing as much market share as one can during this period of exceptional opportunity. Relatively early on in the process, these land grabs resolve themselves into one or the other of the two patterns we have just discussed, and companies end up in one of the six roles just reviewed. Once this has happened, the best strategy is to accept the role the market assigns you and execute as efficiently as possible from within that position for the duration of the tornado. Any fighting to change roles will only confuse the market and slow its adoption of your offerings. Your goal instead should be to build the biggest possible installed base as a prelude for a prolonged stint on Main Street.

STAGE-FOUR ADOPTION: ON MAIN STREET

Main Street begins as the market-share frenzy that drives tornado winds subsides. The overwhelming bulk of the pragmatists in the market have chosen their vendor, made their initial purchases, and rolled out the first phase of a multiphase deployment. Only a fraction of the total forecastable sales in the segment have actually been made at this point, but from here on out the market-share boundaries are relatively fixed. This has significant implications for the value chain.

Value-Chain Strategy

Here is the fourth and final mutation in the value chain. This one will endure for the life of the paradigm. In effect, it is the value chain we have been setting up all along (see Exhibit 13).

There is a key change underlying this entire value chain, which is that the technology adoption life cycle as a whole has evolved from the pragmatist to the conservative agenda, and every constituency in the value chain is affected by this change. Let's start with the customer.

When companies adopt new paradigms, conservative customers at first hang back, preferring to eke out some

last bit of value from the old system. But once it is clear that the new system must supplant the old one, then they seek to put their stamp on the new vendor relationship. They remind all these new arrivals that most of the promises that were made on behalf of their products and services are as yet far from true, and they work to keep everyone focused on making incremental improvements going forward. In effect, they transform what heretofore was a discontinuous innovation into what will from now on be a system of continuous innovation.

In mature—or maturing—markets, both the economic buyer and the technical buyer recede in importance. The economic buyer is no longer looking for competitive advantage or to support a manager in fixing a broken business process; now the issue is simply staying within budget, and that can be delegated. And the technical buyer is no longer concerned about how to either manage or postpone the introduction of a disruptive technology; now the concern is simply to stay compliant with established standards, and that, too, can be delegated. Even within the user community, the managers are now taking the new system for granted, assuming that it must be doing pretty much what it was bought to do (a naive, but all too frequent point of view). Thus it is only *end users,* the people who actually interact with the system on a frequent basis, that (a) know anything about how it really works, and (b) have a stake in sponsoring improvements to it.

If these end users do not voice their desires, then the offering becomes a complete commodity, with the purchasing department driving a *supplier relationship* going forward. If they do voice their desires, however, and gain their managers' approval, then end users can drive a *vendor relationship,* a condition that allows a company to

EXHIBIT 13   Main Street Value Chain

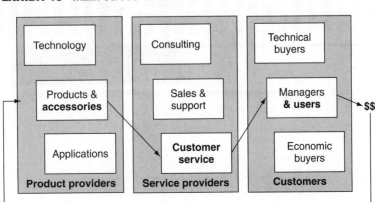

earn margins above commodity levels. We are long past the time for customers to embrace you in a *strategic partner relationship,* something that is confined to earlier phases in the life cycle.

To earn preferred margins from end-user sponsorship, focus shifts to those aspects of the value chain that end users can directly experience. On the product side, this suppresses the importance of technology, platform products, and even the core of the application. All these are still important, but they are more directly experienced by the technical buyer than the end user. By contrast, any product element that is consumable, as well as any change to the surface of the application, is highly user visible. It is here that minor enhancements for a modest increase in price can generate dramatic changes in gross profit margin, the way, for example, the cup holder has done in the automotive industry.

Lucrative as the accessories and consumables business is on Main Street, however, an even bigger opportunity lies in what we call the product-service shift. What customers used to value and buy as products becomes reconceived as service offerings—shifting the burden of system maintenance from the customer back to the vendor. Thus the move from answering machine to voicemail, from videotapes to pay-per-view, from bar bells to health clubs. This same shift is also the basis for an economy that enables the outsourcing of context. . . .

The primary organization tasked with masterminding this shift is *customer service.* Historically this has been a challenge because that organization was not constructed nor were its personnel recruited with the thought that it would eventually become a lead contributor to the P&L and market valuation of the company. In the age of the Internet, however, investors are now actively pursuing companies that have been founded from day one with just such an agenda in mind.

Competitive-Advantage Strategy

Competitive advantage on Main Street lives entirely at the top of the hierarchy, as shown in Exhibit 14.

The technology wave has crested and broken and no longer provides market development leverage. The value chain is already formed, and whatever place you have in it is not going to change without massive and usually unwarranted investment. There is always the possibility of you finding an underserved market segment here or there, but the speed of market penetration now will be much slower, the impact on any local value chain much less, and thus the rewards more modest than they would have been during the bowling alley phase. And so it is that we get to the domain of company execution, to which we shall turn in a moment, and differentiated offerings.

There are classically two types of differentiation strategies that succeed on Main Street. The first is being the low-cost provider, a strategy that works best in commodity markets where it is not the end user but the purchasing manager acting as economic buyer who is the real decision maker. The other type is a customer-delight strategy, which works best in consumer markets or in business markets where the end user is permitted to behave as a consumer. The more a market matures, the more likely your company has to deliver on both of these propositions to be competitive. To do so it must gravitate toward a product or service deployment strategy called *mass customization.*

EXHIBIT 14   Competitive Advantage on Main Street

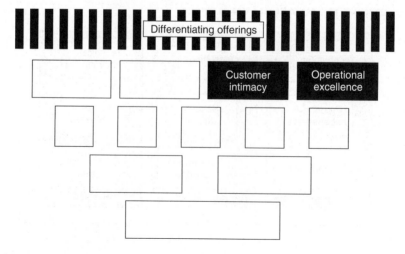

Mass customization separates any offering into a *surface* and a *substructure*. The surface is what the end user experiences. It is here that changes are made to enhance that experience. This is the *customization* portion of the offer. By contrast, the substructure is the necessary delivery vehicle for the entire performance, but it is not directly experienced by the end user. The goal here is to provide maximum reliability at the lowest possible cost, and the preferred tactic is to reduce variability and increase standardization to achieve high volume. This is the *mass* portion of the offer.

To combine the two without sacrificing the benefits of either, the customizing portion must often be done downstream in the value chain in a separate step from the mass portion. This typically leads to a need to redesign the value chain, creating new opportunities for service providers to create customization value at the point of customer contact. Think of how cell phones are provided, and you get the idea. Everything upstream from the retail outlet is totally standardized; everything downstream is customizable—the phone itself, its accessories, service options, program pricing, and the like. Prior to retail, everything is sold as a commodity; after retail, it is a value-added offering.

The implications of this restructuring of the market are far-reaching, and not just for service providers. Consumables have the same potential to deliver customized value. Consider, for example, the razor-to-razor-blade transition in Gillette's history, or Kodak's move from cameras to film, or HP's transition from inkjet printers to inkjet cartridges. In every case once Main Street is reached, it is the consumable at the surface, and not the underlying engine at the core, that becomes the basis of differentiation and the locus of high profit margins.

Alternatively, service transactions can also replace the serviced commodity as the locus of value creation. This has been the case in the automobile industry, where the bulk of the profits are made not from selling new cars but from financing the purchase, insuring the vehicle, supplying the consumables, and providing the maintenance services. In every case margins are affected by the end user's experience during these transactions. That is why companies like Lexus have been so successful with their customer-care offers. It is also why traditional car dealerships are failing with their customer-unfriendly approach to purchase and financing, driving their customers to brokers and to the Web instead.

In large part the promise of the Internet is based on it being a universal platform for value-adding customization in Main Street value chains. The systems are not yet completely in place to fulfill this proposition today, but forward-thinking executives and enlightened investors can see how with incremental improvements they will be able to generate scaleable, low-cost, high-touch offerings of the sort that create attractive profit margins on Main Street.

Value Disciplines

To execute on this strategy of mass customization, companies as elsewhere in the life cycle must learn to elevate one pair of value disciplines and suppress the other:

Elevate: *Operational Excellence, Customer Intimacy* Main Street markets are supported by conservative customers seeking incremental gains in value. These can be achieved either through decreasing the costs of the current set of offers—the domain of operational excellence—or by introducing a new set of offers improved through readily absorbed continuous innovations—the domain of customer intimacy.

Suppress: *Discontinuous Innovation, Product Leadership*

Discontinuous innovation runs directly contrary to the interests of Main Street customers and is simply not welcome. Even offers based on product leadership are problematic. If they require retooling the existing infrastructure, they usually just aren't worth it. What development teams must realize is that now product improvements should be focused either on keeping the core product viable, with operational excellence as a guide, or on making cosmetic changes at the surface, with customer intimacy providing the direction.

Of all the pairings, this particular set should be the most familiar to established companies in mature markets. They should see themselves as the champions of the first pair, and those wretched dotcoms assaulting their marketplace as the purveyors of the second. Note that in this pairing the established company's existing customers are very much on its side, not on the dotcoms'. That's because they, like the company itself, are ruled by conservative interests. It is instead the flock of new customers who are entering the tornado for the next big thing that are undermining this company's stock price going forward.

Stock Price Implications

The returns from Main Street business models are based on the assumption that the market is not under a technology-enabled attack and can be forecast to last indefinitely in its present state. Within that context, investor returns are created by selling modestly profitable offerings on a repeatable basis with very low cost of sales.

EXHIBIT 15   Impact of Main Street Success on Stock Price

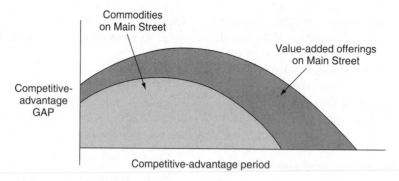

EXHIBIT 16   Impact of Paradigm Threat on Main Street Stock Price

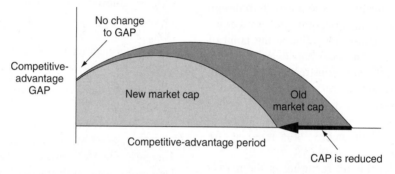

This is possible only when you are selling to an *existing loyal customer*. The mortal enemy of the Main Street model is churn—a continual enrollment of new customers at high cost of sales accompanied by a continual loss of existing customers, the most profitable to retain.

Companies that are able to minimize churn and maximize gains from existing customers generate one of two types of valuation depending on whether they follow a commodity or a value-added strategy (see Exhibit 15).

GAPs for companies in commodity businesses on Main Street are rarely high. Customer power, which is at its nadir during the tornado, reasserts itself on Main Street to create negotiating leverage. Moreover, since commodities are by definition substitutable, they have relatively low company CAPs as well. (The *category's* CAP, by contrast, is very long—we will have the salt business with us for some time to come.) Progress in such businesses is made by cost-reducing internal processes, particularly in the substructure, but even here, as competitors make the same adjustments, the savings must be passed on to the customer rather than reserved for the shareholder.

Creating value-added offerings through mass customization for end users is the preferred way to resist this erosion in margins. These offers increase GAP modestly—representing the premium end users will pay to

get what they really want. They also create modest switching costs—once you get what you really want it is hard to go back—thereby increasing CAP as well. Both these effects work only up to a point of tolerance, after which competitive pricing can and will override their influence. Nonetheless, because the volume of sales on Main Street is so high, and the bulk of the business-enabling investment has already been amortized, it is here that most of the profits in any economy are made. And these do go to the shareholders.

Thus it is that blue-chip stocks are created. Decade after decade they demonstrate themselves to be earnings machines, creating modest but predictable growth in both revenues and earnings accompanied by a remarkable lack of volatility in stock price. These stocks, and the New York Stock Exchange, have been the bastion of the American economy for the greater part of the twentieth century.

All this value is put at risk, however, whenever a disruptive technology paradigm appears. The question its arrival poses for investors is, will the old category delivered by the incumbent value chain persist, or will the new category delivered by a new value chain eliminate it? If the new paradigm is seen to be winning that battle, then the devaluation scenario shown in Exhibit 16 comes into play.

Note that GAP is unchanged. Indeed, for the immediate future there is little question that the Main Street vendors will have the more advantaged, better differentiated offers. No, instead it is *CAP* that comes under attack. The stock market's assessment of the competitive-advantage equation is that eventually the new paradigm will indeed win out. The incumbent companies are given a window to embrace the new paradigm themselves, but if they do not, then the market discounts their valuation dramatically, even if they are producing impressive P&L performances in their current quarter. That is, all the Main Street earnings beyond a given window that were forecast to go to the incumbent, based on its current market share, will now be forecast to go to one or another of the new challengers. This effectively removes those earnings from the incumbent's anticipated future earnings—hence the reduction in valuation.

(. . .)

IMPLICATIONS OF LIVING ON THE FAULT LINE

Consider how many different value-chain permutations we have examined in the course of a technology-enabled market developing through its various stages. To summarize them the four market states are shown in a side-by-side comparison table in Exhibit 17.

Exhibit 17 maps the working out of the competitive-advantage hierarchy over the course of a technology-enabled market's development. The columns lay out the life-cycle phases these markets evolve through. The rows lay out the changes in focus that organizations must make to adapt to this evolution. The first row sets forth the layer in the competitive-advantage hierarchy that has the most impact during each phase. The next three rows highlight the value-chain elements that create the most impact during the phase because they are best suited to leveraging the type of competitive advantage available. Finally, the last row recaps the stock price result of achiev-

ing the competitive-advantage position during each phase of the life cycle.

I hope and trust by now that the logic behind these various combinations is clear. Forces in the marketplace cause them to come about regardless of whether or not the companies involved want them to. As a result, they lay out the world of "what is."

Even a cursory glance, however, shows that the changes companies have to make in order to adapt to these forces are dramatic indeed. Moreover, the time allotted to make them is painfully short. As a result, it should surprise no one that few real-world organizations are very good at actually making them. Indeed, the larger and more successful a company becomes, the less likely it is to attempt making them at all.

It is essentially a problem of inertia. Once you get a certain amount of mass moving in any given direction, the price for changing that direction begins to exceed the return on making the change. Increasingly the logic of trade-offs says let things go forward as they are. Yes, it creates problems, but not as many as trying to change course would. Over time, however, as these problems continue to be left untended, their consequences build, until eventually the cost for *not changing* does indeed exceed the price of change. But by that time things are typically so far out of control, and the time horizon for change has become so immediate, that the inertia-driven organization simply cannot make the turn and crashes into a wall instead.

(. . .)

SUMMARY OF KEY POINTS

The main idea of this paper is that technology-enabled markets evolve through four distinct stages, each of which calls for a dramatically different strategic approach. Specifically, here are the key observations:

EXHIBIT 17   Four Market States

	Early market	Bowling alley	Tornado	Main Street
Primary competitive advantage	Catching technology wave	Market-segment domination	Market-share leadership	Differentiated offerings
Product focus	Technology	Applications	Platform products	Consumables
Service focus	Consulting	Support	Sales	Customer service
Customer focus	Economic buyer	Department manager	Technical buyer	End user
Stock price implications	High GAP, No CAP	High GAP, Long CAP (niche)	High GAP, Long CAP (mass)	Low GAP, Long CAP

1. Different roles in the *value chain* rise to prominence and recede from it at different points in the life cycle. The implication is that every dog has its day but that some days it's just not your turn to be the dog. The implication of that is *live with it*.
2. Different forms of *competitive advantage* are rewarded at different stages in the life cycle, as illustrated by the competitive-advantage hierarchy model.
3. Different *value disciplines* are rewarded or penalized at different stages in the life cycle, as illustrated by the value disciplines model.
4. Finally, different *stock price implications* are attached to operations that have successfully mastered the challenges of each phase in the life cycle, as illustrated by the GAP/CAP charts for each phase.
5. To ask any given organization to excel at all phases of the life cycle at all times is a good recipe for creating chaos—yet that is exactly what the high-tech marketplace demands of its leading companies.

(. . .)

INTERNAL CORPORATE VENTURING

Cultivating Capabilities to Innovate: Booz Allen & Hamilton

Clayton M. Christensen and Bret Baird

In May 1997, Brian Dickie, president of Booz Allen & Hamilton, was flying back to New York from a successful client meeting along with Frank Varasano, managing partner of the New York office and also head of the firm's Special Interest Group on Innovation. "You know, Frank," Dickie reflected, "we're much better at helping our clients learn how to innovate than we are at managing our own innovation processes. We're constantly developing breakthrough ideas in the course of our client work but we have a spotty track record in distilling these ideas and taking them to the market. We need to apply our own doctrine on market learning, cycle time, and organizing for innovation to ourselves. There are differences, of course, between the product development needs of a consulting firm and operating companies, but I think that in this case the shoemaker could do with a new set of shoes."

Source: Copyright © 1997 by The President and Fellows of Harvard College. Professor Clayton M. Christensen and Research Associate Bret Baird prepared this case as the basis for class discussion rather than to illustrate either effective or ineffective handling of an administrative situation.

HISTORICAL PERSPECTIVE

In 1997, Booz Allen & Hamilton (BA&H)—a firm which prided itself on helping its clients achieve real change in their businesses—was itself well into a sustained, multiyear self-renewal program. Founded in 1914, Booz Allen had blossomed into one of the world's largest consultancies, providing managerial and technological advice to senior managers of businesses and governments. The firm now comprised two essentially independent business sectors: the Worldwide Technology Business (WTB), a group based in Washington, D.C., that provided managerial and technology consulting primarily to the U.S. government, and the Worldwide Commercial Business (WCB), headquartered in New York, which provided management consulting services to major companies globally. In 1996, WCB accounted for over $600 million in client billings and employed almost 2,000 consultants working out of 30 offices worldwide.

Booz Allen's WCB defined its mission as helping the top management of the world's major companies to shape their agendas and to design and drive strategic change. The business model the firm historically had followed differed from that of many of its competitors. Its teams of experts offered clients "integrated solutions"—most projects involved assisting clients with strategy questions, operations improvements, and information technologies. Its strategy was to employ whatever services or concepts were needed to help clients improve their performance. Booz Allen's most direct competitor, McKinsey and Company, had long followed a similar strategy. In contrast, many of the high-growth, high-profile firms that had entered the consulting industry in recent decades had built their practices around particular "products"—concepts or services that could be sold and used in a relatively standard way with a variety of clients. The Boston Consulting Group (BCG), for example, had achieved prominence by conducting experience curve and business portfolio analyses for clients. Similarly, Monitor & Co. was known for its five-forces industry analysis, Gemini for its process reengineering, Integral for its aggregate project planning, and so on. Although they had built their initial reputations around these focused products, most of these firms, in order to continue to grow, had evolved their business models to resemble more closely the one that Booz Allen had followed.

Until the late 1980s, Booz Allen had essentially been an affiliation of individual partners' fiefdoms. "We were basically an artists' colony," observed Dickie. Partners serviced their own clients under what was little more than a shared administrative structure and brand name. They were rewarded for the revenue they personally brought to the firm and had little incentive to help other partners build their own profitable client relationships. Under this structure, there were few incentives to share knowledge and innovations across the partnership. Learning tended to occur at the individual and client team level, stimulated by particular engagements. While some informal networks existed, there was no explicit mechanism for sharing new insights beyond individual offices. Knowledge could not accumulate in a way that was readily accessible in the firm. Indeed, there were arguably incentives not to build on the insights that prior consulting teams might have developed: the Booz Allen culture prized the ability to develop new and innovative solutions to client problems, and borrowing someone else's ideas was considered uncreative. It added little to a consultant's or partner's stature. As a result, "wheels were being reinvented" time and again.

IMPLEMENTING STRATEGIC CHANGE

In 1987, Booz Allen took the first step in what Dickie called "learning to compete as an institution rather than as a confederation of individuals." The firm established a new partner compensation system that would better align partners' incentives with the strategic interests of the firm. In place of highly variable individual bonuses, partners in future would each receive a uniform percentage bonus on their base compensation, depending on the overall results of the firm. Base compensation in turn would be determined according to a combination of seniority and contribution to the institution on five dimensions of which revenue generation was only one element. The decisions on base compensation slotting levels would be taken, according to published rules, by the partner's principal team on a peer appraisal basis. This process both increased trust and transparency and gave the teams of partners a powerful means of influencing the behavior of their members, because, as one partner noted, "Money means something in this firm, but so does pride." Not wholly unexpectedly, not all partners welcomed these changes and in fact several prominent players eventually departed because they could not adapt from the earlier ethic of independence to a cooperative model. This new system proved to be a critical precursor to subsequent watershed achievements, because it helped Booz Allen become more capable of concerted action and strategic change.

Several years later, in 1994, Booz Allen embarked on a radically new strategy, called "Vision 2000" (soon abbreviated to V2K), which launched three major thrusts. First, the company established a "target client paradigm" under which it would concentrate on serving fewer clients with far more expansive and enduring relationships than before. Second, it would serve these clients by deploying "Triple Crown" client service teams comprising partners and consultants selected for their expertise in (1) strategy, organization, and industry knowledge, (2) operations and change management, and (3) information technology. These multifunctional teams would be able to deliver the full range of the firm's expertise as well as devise creative, high-impact cross-functional solutions for the client. Third, V2K committed to building a "knowledge engine" to better distill and deploy the firm's learning and ideas. "It is not enough," said Joanne Bessler, the firm's partner in charge of people development, "for us to promise our clients teams of very smart people who are committed to working exceptionally hard on their behalf. We must also deliver the full, accumulated learning of Booz Allen & Hamilton."

"Managing knowledge, becoming a learning organization," reflected Chuck Lucier, the firm's first chief knowledge officer, "is a huge challenge."

> All of our learning takes place at the individual or the project team level. We are a very decentralized organization, and teams keep getting disbanded and reformed. Moreover, for obvious reasons, we follow a very strict code of confidentiality in talking about our work even among ourselves. It's very conceivable that different teams could be addressing the same issues in complete isolation from one

another. In fact, it is more than conceivable, it is certain: there is a remarkable synchronicity in the issues on clients' agendas and in new ideas emerging in the field of business.

In designing the knowledge engine, Lucier championed three thrusts. The first of these was a matrix-type reorganization in which the columns were functional practices (strategic leadership, operations, and information technology) and the rows were industry practices, such as financial services or communications, media and technology, and so on. Most partners and staff would live within both an industry practice (called a professional community) and a functional practice. Knowledge in each area would be built through research, training programs and, "most importantly," noted Lucier, "since this is an apprenticeship business, staffing rotations on engagements."

In addition to the formal practice structure, Booz Allen launched "virtual" organizations, "special interest groups" (SIGs), to identify and consolidate what was known within the firm on particular subjects, to shape new "service offerings" for clients that were built upon these insights, and to assemble experts who could help partners sell and deliver these new offerings to their clients as the needs of clients created such opportunities. The topics addressed by the 12 SIGs ranged from new business models, innovation, and sourcing to conglomerates in emerging markets and strategic wargaming.

The third building block of the Knowledge Program was the creation of Knowledge-On-Line (KOL), an electronic warehousing and delivery system that enabled all consultants to access information on industries, technologies, markets, and companies that had been generated by prior BA&H client teams. Client reports from which confidential information had been removed were also often accessible through KOL. "We knew a lot of stuff; but nobody knew what it was, or where it was," recalled Lucier. "This was a critical problem, especially for junior people, who did not know which projects had been done in the past and by whom." The first version of KOL came online in 1995 and was soon followed by KOL version 2 in November 1996, which used Web-based technology to enable navigation by using key word searches. By 1997, KOL stored over 4,000 documents and was used routinely by 70 percent of staff worldwide.

In addition to capturing knowledge internally, Lucier sought to sponsor greater innovation by establishing a series of research linkages to business schools and by encouraging the publication of intellectual capital. By 1997, Booz Allen was engaged in 11 significant joint programs with leading academics and, through both its practices and SIGs, was publishing a series of *Viewpoints* publications, with titles such as "Leveraging Suppliers: The Extended Enterprise," "Consolidation in Capital Markets," and "Convergence in the Media and Telecommunications Industries." The firm also launched the *Journal of Strategy & Business* as a challenger to the *Harvard Business Review.* By 1997, *JSB* had achieved a circulation of 60,000 and was awarded the Folio Editorial Excellence Award by the business publishing industry.

To look back, the impact that implementing V2K had on Booz Allen seemed remarkable. The firm was growing at 25 percent annual rates, and profitability per partner, Dickie estimated, was at the high end of the industry. As planned, the number of clients served had been pared from over 1,000 to 200, meaning that average revenues per client relationship had increased more than 10-fold from the prior decade. Extensive client relationships, generating $10 million to $20 million in billings per year, were not uncommon. "This focus and scale has made a huge difference on the impact that we are having on our clients' performance," said Varasano. "Think about it. Even for a firm of our size, what impact could we be having on the agenda of Client number 999?"

LEVERAGING THE FIRM'S KNOWLEDGE

With three years of the knowledge program under their belt, Booz Allen's senior partners were now evaluating how successful it had been in meeting its twin objectives: (1) to make engagement teams more efficient in creating and delivering value to clients, and (2) to fuel the growth engine that was crucial to maintaining the vitality of the firm, by renewing and expanding existing client relationships and penetrating new ones. "We have certainly created a powerful set of resources," noted Steve Wheeler, the leader of the firm's marketing practice. "And we've made our ideas and knowledge much more visible and accessible. But we have not fully followed through on adapting our *processes,* or in building new processes, to capture all the benefits that we could."

Making Booz Allen Client Teams More Efficient

The benefits of leveraging what earlier BA&H client teams had learned, to get up to speed efficiently and start adding value to clients faster, were clear to everyone in the firm: fewer wheels would be reinvented. Leveraging past client team experiences into ongoing projects typically involved three dimensions. In order of increasing difficulty, these were (1) acquiring information about the structure and economics of the industry or market,

(2) applying the frameworks or models developed in previous engagements to the present client's situation, and (3) benefiting from lessons learned about the process of managing previous projects of a similar character, to avoid repeating the mistakes of the past, and utilize all that could be known about best practices across all of Booz Allen.

The extent to which prior experience could be used to help new project teams do their work more efficiently was illustrated in a sequence of projects that Frank Varasano had led, which involved identifying and deploying best practices within clients' engineering projects, with the goal of radically shortening product-development time. This technique was first developed well before KOL in a 1990–1992 project with Evandale Corporation, one of the world's largest aerospace concerns, in which Booz Allen consultants analyzed the performance of a large set of Evandale's engineering project teams to identify the most time- and cost-effective methods for performing certain classes of tasks that recurred in every project. By helping Evandale managers understand the best practices that had been demonstrated by an Evandale team in the past, and then helping ongoing teams to employ each of these practices, Booz Allen and Evandale reduced the cost of developing products by 30 percent, and reduced its development cycle significantly. This saved Evandale tens of millions of dollars in product development cost and enabled it to pull ahead of competitors by introducing next generation products at a faster pace. Varasano subsequently developed a similar program in 1993 at Defense General Corporation, one of the world's largest shipbuilders, and then at Toledo Motor, a major auto manufacturer, in 1995.

Matt Magleby, one of the principals[1] on the team responsible for the Toledo Motor project, recalled how he had to get up to speed in the days before KOL:

> Frank Varasano had enough experience and knowledge from the previous projects to convince Toledo Motor that we could do it, and to describe the basic methodology. But given the nature of partners' work, the real knowledge of how to analyze and implement best practices was in the heads of the people who had done the projects. By the time we got to Toledo, most of these people had been promoted, were entrenched in other clients, or had graduated from the firm.
>
> Fortunately, one member of the original team at Evandale was available and was able to surface a file box containing many of the original working papers from our ar-

chives in San Francisco. These included documentation of a four-step methodology which we incorporated as the foundation of our work.

> This process framework, really only took us 10 percent to 20 percent of the distance we ultimately had to travel to really deliver the value to Toledo Motor. Where our learning really got its start was in piloting the four-step process in two specific pieces of Toledo Motor's development process. This is where Booz Allen excels: targeting a problem and figuring out how to solve it. These pilots took our team's knowledge of how to identify and deliver the best practices results from 20 percent to 70 percent. We then generalized the approach and replicated the process in different parts of Toledo's development process. We delivered the rest of the benefit as we customized these methods to each engineering team's unique situation.
>
> I think that if KOL had been available when we began Toledo, our starting platform might have been 40 percent instead of 20 percent. A lot of that would be benchmark information on product-development processes, referrals to experts, and so on. But given all the nuances about Toledo's situation that were so different from Evandale or Defense General, it would be hard to transfer more learning than this about how to do the analysis and implementation through a medium like KOL.
>
> On the other hand, if we used the same team over and over, we would start at 70 percent plus. We could define a relatively routinized process and set of analyses and knock them dead in a fraction of the time it took at Toledo Motor.
>
> The key question is whether I or anyone else would want to do this. Well, I could handle it a couple of more times, but then I'd want out. It would get pretty routine, and I didn't come to work here for routine. I want variety. I want to learn new things. And besides, I want to make partner. If we took this show on the road and stamped out Best Practices Engineering projects for client after client, we'd make a ton of money for the firm and I would establish my credibility as an expert in an important field. But when you come up for partner you have to have played a key role in building major client relationships. Becoming a product expert is a far less common path. This means I need to stay at Toledo Motor, bringing solutions to other problems we can help them with.

Other consulting firms had built substantial practices upon the alternative business model described by Magleby: focusing on developing only a few concepts or service offerings, and then selling these service offerings multiple times to a sequence of clients. While focusing made the work less diverse, it also made capturing and transferring the learnings of previous teams easier. Further, with discrete teams repeatedly applying their model for a series of clients, they were able to build "capabilities" that were rooted in a common, repeatable way of structuring their work.

But within Booz Allen's culture, the alternative business model was unappealing. "The idea that we would *product-ize* a few frameworks or ideas, and then go around selling it to whoever would buy, with a one-size-fits-all mentality—we'd just never do it. It is crass commercialization, pure and simple," noted a prominent partner. Keith Oliver, managing partner in the firm's London office, was slightly more charitable:

> To use a manufacturing comparison, those kinds of firms are a bit like an assembly process, chunking out relatively standard products over and over again. Booz Allen is a custom job shop. Everything we do has a large tailored component to it.

By 1997, consensus was building that SIGs were not as effective in transferring capabilities as had originally been hoped, although they had produced a steady current of new ideas and marketing material that had been taken to a broad range of clients. SIGs, as noted above, were groups of principals and partners with specific shared interests, brought together under an informal structure. They were not physically located in the same office, and were not exempted from client work, but instead communicated through meetings, phone and computer, organizing and proposing ideas pertinent to their specific topics. "Part of the problem in pulling together what we know and then passing it on to others is that this work is never as high a priority as client work," confessed a partner. "I've got three large BA&H client teams working under me, I chair an important administrative committee, and I have responsibility for a special interest group. Quite frankly, the SIG is fifth, in order of priority."

Leveraging Prior Insights to Fuel Future Growth

The other primary benefit that Dickie and his partners hoped Booz Allen could reap from its investments in the knowledge program was to find better ways to leverage the insights that were being created, identified, and codified in the firm into even more extensive relationships with existing clients and new client relationships as well.

To the partners at Booz Allen, like the officers of most professional firms, maintaining the company's growth rate was a paramount concern. Keith Oliver reflected:

> Growth creates a virtuous cycle. It gives your most talented people faster opportunities to expand their responsibilities and progress in the firm. This makes it easier to attract more talented people, who in turn help you grow even more. We've seen what has happened to some of our competitors, when their growth stopped. Opportunities for personal ad-

vancement become much more limited, and your best junior people begin to leave. It gets more difficult to recruit good people, and therefore more difficult to return to robust growth. Strategically, almost nothing is as high a priority as maintaining growth.

Experience as well as recurrent market research showed that clients expected their top management consultants to bring them a steady stream of new ideas, and that bringing good ideas to the table was one of the best ways to penetrate new clients. Two alternative processes (not mutually exclusive) were being extensively discussed at the senior levels of the partnership, for utilizing Booz Allen's best ideas to create new avenues for growth.

A Free Market System

Some characterized the primary mechanism that Booz Allen employed to bring new service offerings to its clients as an internal free-market system. Much like products on display in an open market, ideas for how to add value or solve problems for clients existed everywhere at Booz Allen. "Ideas are in the air here—like steel in Sheffield," said Dickie. Many of these ideas had been born in successful client projects of the past, such as Booz Allen's methods for identifying and implementing "Best Demonstrated Practices" in engineering project management, described above. Others originated in specific research by a practice or by a special interest group.

Lauren Matt, a senior associate, added:

> Not all of these ideas, of course, are original to Booz Allen. News about new service offerings that other consulting firms have developed for their clients, or frameworks for understanding problems that come out of business schools, spreads very fast in the consulting industry. They are easy to replicate.

For example, Booz Allen had been among the first consultancies to offer capabilities-based strategy to its clients. Within a very short time, key competitors such as BCG, Bain, and McKinsey had each built substantial practices in this field. BCG's ideas for time-based competition, as another example, had been quickly emulated by its major competitors, including Booz Allen.

Like customers in a marketplace, Booz Allen partners could pick and choose among these frameworks, methods, and potential service offerings that had been developed in other client settings, and introduce these to both new and established clients as they saw the opportunity. As long as the models or methods helped partners address the needs of their clients, it did not matter if the offerings were homegrown, imported from academics, or drawn from other consultancies. This system, in theory, allowed Booz Allen to be responsive in offering its clients state-of-the-art thinking on their most challenging problems, as those problems emerged.

"But we have problems in this internal market of service offerings, just like you have problems in any market," noted Joanne Bessler. "The notion of perfect markets is predicated on there being perfect information," she observed. "And although KOL, *Viewpoints,* and our presentations at practice meetings and home office meetings have raised the visibility of what ideas and offerings have been developed and used elsewhere in the company, most of us only really understand those offerings that we have had personal experience with, or that have been done immediately around us—in our office, or by our friends." Hence, Dickie and Varasano were convinced that a number of high-potential service offerings were underutilized or even languishing in the internal market, because information about them had not been effectively disseminated.

Tied to this issue of dissemination was who in the firm used the KOL information system. A group of Booz Allen employees polled during the writing of this case about how the KOL resource was being utilized in the firm indicated that once a project had been agreed with a client, Booz Allen client teams tapped into the KOL database extensively for data on the industry, on competitors, on relevant technologies, and so on. Information on scheduling and project management techniques that earlier client teams in similar situations had employed—whether downloaded directly from KOL or learned by interviewing experienced individuals to which the KOL network referred them—was also heavily utilized by client teams. By far, the heaviest users of KOL were associates, usually the most junior members of the client teams, who sought this sort of information as background learning at the beginning of client engagements. There were far fewer searchers of the database for ideas about new services that might be offered to clients. "The fact is that we just do not read information until we feel a need for it," noted partner Gerry Adolph. "It seems clear that those responsible for selling new business do not see as great a need for the information in KOL."

Another cultural factor that constrained the rate at which some Booz Allen partners utilized new ideas for service offerings from the internal market was an innate reluctance to apply those service offerings which were perceived to fundamentally change the way business was conducted with clients or which might require further development or refinement. Frank Varasano explained:

Many partners are supportive in trying new cutting-edge service offerings with clients. But there are also many partners who are surprisingly set in their ways, unwilling to endorse enthusiastically an approach that is different from their traditional, accepted way of thinking—even if it might be superior in important respects. We need to convert these partners to begin embracing new techniques and incorporating them in their own practices—even if they are not yet fully fleshed out, with all the *i*'s dotted and the *t*'s crossed. This requires a little less perfectionism, and a good deal more willingness to experiment and learn while doing. We must be willing too, to invite our clients to partner with us on work at the frontier.

From Varasano's perspective, this was a classic "time to market" problem. Booz Allen was often a pioneer in developing new concepts, but the cultural tendency toward conservatism and perfectionism often held the firm back from exploiting ideas during "the early phases" of their life cycles. "We often talk ourselves into being a fast-follower rather than the leader," Varasano noted.

> I worry about this. Our major clients have become very, very sophisticated purchasers of consulting services. The ones that automatically come back to Booz Allen solely because the CEO has a long-standing relationship with one of our partners are rare today. Clients monitor which firms do the best work on what types of problems. If we don't stay right at the state of the art in each of our practice areas by learning about and applying the best we have to offer, these relationships that we have worked so hard to build will erode.

Varasano noted, for example, that many of the most innovative ideas about sourcing strategy and supply chain management in the industry had existed within Booz Allen for several years before the topic became hot in the consulting market. But because Booz Allen had not aggressively transferred and exploited the concepts, other firms—particularly AT Kearney—had developed a stronger reputation as the leader in this field. The same had happened with the process reengineering wave that swept through the consulting industry in the early 1990s. Booz Allen client teams had been helping their clients streamline business and production processes for years, but it was not until other firms coined the term *reengineering*—and popularized and marketed the concept through articles and seminars—that the growth in this market took off.[2] Booz Allen captured its fair share of this market but missed the opportunity to define it.

---

[2] An example of this approach of proactively marketing a new consulting service is exemplified by Michael Hammer in his article "Reengineering Work: Don't Automate, Obliterate," *Harvard Business Review,* July–August, 1990, pp. 104–112, and through the subsequent series of seminars which Hammer offered through his firm, CSC-Index.

Varasano summarized the dilemma:

We've performed a lot of work in sourcing and reengineering—there's no question that they've contributed to our growth and improved our overall service offering to our clients. The question I wonder about, however, is whether we could have grown at a substantially *faster* rate, if we had seized the perception of leadership in the marketplace, which we *could* have done, given the quality of our experience. We have a very strong culture and a definite position in the marketplace relative to our competitors. The issue is whether an efficiently functioning internal "free market" is the capability we'll need to keep driving the growth of the firm, given the increasing importance of time to market with innovations in our industry. Even if we make our internal market much nearer to a "perfect" one, through information technology and effective organizational structures, I wonder whether 10 years from now, will we look back and view this as a capability or a *dis*ability?

Campaign Selling

An alternative mode of managing innovation in new service offerings that was being piloted at Booz Allen was for the senior partners to become much more proactive in deciding which, of all the potential new service offerings that were surfacing in the company, had the highest potential for generating new growth. Whereas the firm's efforts to make the internal marketplace work better had focused on making partners *aware* of the new service offerings that they could draw upon, this alternative demanded that certain senior partners take on the role of *champions* for these new service offerings. These champions would travel throughout Booz Allen's worldwide network, energetically teaching the staffs at each office what these new service offerings were, describing the benefits that earlier Booz Allen clients had realized from implementing the work of BA&H client teams, and suggesting how to sell these new services to current and potential clients. This process of drumming up internal enthusiasm for new service offerings had been dubbed campaign selling.

Although it had never been attempted in a persistent manner, past attempts at campaign selling had met with only limited success. In the realm of supply chain–related service offerings, for example, Carolyn Willcox, a principal in the firm's Cleveland office, developed a set of ideas about sourcing strategy that she and her colleagues had developed through client work between 1990 and 1992. Willcox authored a *Viewpoints* publication that described her framework in 1993. As this was circulated internally, Paul Peterson, one of the firm's most senior and respected partners, was intrigued with the ideas

and impressed with Willcox's initiative. He suggested that she aim her publications more directly to CEOs in the auto industry, sensing that Willcox's new spin on the sourcing problem might generate substantial business there. Willcox then authored a new *Viewpoint* piece showing how the sourcing strategy framework could be applied to autos. Only one client project resulted, in 1993, however—and that came from a mass mailing sent directly to company executives, rather than from Booz Allen partners offering the ideas to their existing clients.

Meanwhile, Willcox continued to champion her ideas with missionary fervor, capturing another client from the oil industry, based on another *Viewpoints* article about the oil industry that she wrote a year later. As members of Booz Allen's worldwide community became aware of Willcox's work, she became a key resource person for sourcing problems via email, as well as a focal point for new ideas on the subject. Eventually she became the hub of a sourcing practitioner network, which enabled Booz Allen consultants who had encountered sourcing issues in their client work to share methods by exchanging experiences. This network later became one of Booz Allen's special interest groups, with Willcox as the head.

While Willcox's efforts served to organize the knowledge and kept the sourcing strategy concepts alive, sourcing never turned into a major revenue-generating service offering. It was during this same period that A. T. Kearny developed its own sourcing program and built its industry-leading reputation around it.

Another test of the firm's ability to "push" ideas for new service offerings through the partners and into clients through campaign selling followed from the sequence of projects involving best practices in engineering, described above, which had begun in 1990. In each engagement, the BA&H client teams working under Varasano's oversight successfully streamlined the clients' engineering processes, generating ongoing savings that were a significant multiple of the cost of the project. All three projects had won Booz Allen's Professional Excellence Award, given annually to a few project teams across the worldwide practice that demonstrated outstanding achievement in creating value for clients and in adding to the firm's base of intellectual capital.

Despite the success of these projects and Varasano's reputation in the firm, however, by 1997 no one else within the Booz Allen partnership, utilizing his or her own initiative, had sold a service modeled after the firm's string of successes at Evandale, Defense General, and Toledo Motor. This was a frustration to Varasano. Having seen the power of the methodology "to drive results

EXHIBIT 1   Booz Allen & Hamilton's Value and Mission Statement

VALUES

Booz Allen & Hamilton's aim is to build and sustain a preeminent, worldwide consulting firm—serving significant clients on important issues of management and technology and providing our people with a matchless opportunity for personal and professional growth and for contribution both within the firm and in the larger arena of family, clients, and community.

CLIENTS' INTERESTS COME FIRST

We measure our success in terms of the benefits that accrue to our clients from our work. In seeking these benefits for our clients, we are committed to the highest levels of professionalism:

- Objectivity—scrupulous intellectual honesty and the courage to "tell it like it is."
- Creativity—an openness to diversity of ideas and opinions.
- Quality results—that reflect the contributions of the best people working together in teams drawn from multiple disciplines.
- Value—in excess of our fees.

We seek full partnership with our clients from concept through implementation and we recognize that enduring client relationships, based on trust and mutual respect, are among the Firm's most valuable assets.

The foundation of our dedication to clients' interests is our commitment to the Firm and its people.

The firm	Our people
We are the beneficiaries of Booz Allen's priceless heritage, which includes: • A respected name. • Challenging work. • Stimulating clients and associates. • A rich environment for personal growth and development. • Financial strengths. • Opportunity to share in the wealth we generate, initially as employees and ultimately as owners. We take pride in this heritage. We are committed to the spirit of partnership as we build an enduring global franchise. We recognize the worth of individuals and we respect each other's contributions. We behave in accordance with high ethical standards and subordinate our interest to the good of the whole Firm.	The Firm provides membership in one of the most distinguished professional services institutions in the world. We pledge a working environment—enriched by a diversity of professional disciplines, personal styles, and business systems—that provides employees with: • Challenge and motivation. • Maximum opportunity for, and assistance towards, personal development as professionals. • Personal and professional freedom consistent with the interests of our clients and the Firm. • Superior financial rewards for superior performance. We pledge a performance appraisal system that is fair and dedicated to fostering career that is mutually rewarding for individuals and the Firm. We recognize all who share in the Booz Allen & Hamilton experience as special people.

We hold the firm in trust for generations to come and accept responsibility to pass on a strengthened heritage to our successors.

right to the bottom line with three major, sophisticated clients," he had developed a passionate zeal about the potential of Best Practices Engineering as a new service offering for the company. "This is *powerful*," he emphasized. "And *nobody* besides Booz Allen can do this! We should be doing it in 50 different countries—all over the world." Varasano initially marketed the service on his own. Then, in the beginning of 1997, he subsequently took to the road, "pounding the pavement," to stimulate interest amongst his partners to sell similar programs to other major clients. One new large client resulted from these efforts, although Varasano had hoped for more.

Dickie reflected on the dilemma. Those firms that rode on the growth wave of a major "product"—such as A. T. Kearney with sourcing or Gemini with reengineering—had done so by dedicating a very large fraction of their practices to this one thing, selling it and doing it over and over again.

This is a very different model from providing highly customized solutions to general managers' problems on a relationship basis. It requires a different business system, and I doubt if you can optimize on both. The more standardized your service offering, the less likely you are to be creative and innovative and the more vulnerable you are to disintermediation by lower-tier competitors. You could grow your way into a less attractive competitive and professional space.

Despite the tension among the various models, Dickie and Varasano were in full agreement that the free market system needed to be both improved and supplemented by other approaches. Varasano summed up:

The challenge is not producing the content—we are constantly coming up with bright ideas and new concepts, and we are learning to develop even more through extended enterprise relationships with other institutions. What we need to do is to install processes which select the most important new ideas and then roll them out through our partners to a large set of clients. We need processes to test ideas through internal and external market research; we need processes to package the ideas and communicate them; and we need incentives for partners to use them. This can't be a static system. We need a learning machine which continually captures innovations on the front line and transforms them into powerful new offerings to our clients. Everyone wins.

As their plane touched down at La Guardia, Dickie and Varasano agreed that they had isolated the right question; they scheduled to meet the following week to decide on the next steps.

CASE III-9

Cisco Systems, Inc.: Implementing ERP

Mark Cotteleer

Pete Solvik, Cisco Systems CIO, considered the last remaining line item of his ERP implementation budget. Cisco had a history of rewarding performance with cash bonuses, but the amount allocated for rewarding the ERP team, over $200,000, was unprecedented. To be sure, they had delivered a lot in a time frame that no one had believed possible. It had not been easy either. The team members, Solvik included, had taken a risk in joining the project. Rewards should, and would, be generous. The size of the bonus pool, though, made Solvik think: they had done well, but how well? What had gone right? What had gone wrong? Given another project of this magnitude and risk, would they be able to do it again?

HISTORY OF CISCO

Cisco Systems, Inc., was founded by two Stanford computer scientists in 1984 and became publicly traded in 1990. The company's primary product is the "router," the combination of hardware and software that acts as a traffic cop on the complex TCP/IP networks that make up the Internet (as well as corporate "Intranets"). With the

rise of Internet technologies, demand for Cisco's products boomed and the company soon began to dominate its markets. By 1997, its first year on the *Fortune* 500, Cisco ranked among the top five companies in return on revenues and return on assets. (See Exhibit 1 for Cisco's financial performance.) Only two other companies, Intel and Microsoft, have ever matched this feat. Perhaps even more impressive, on July 17, 1998, just 14 years after being founded, Cisco's market capitalization passed the $100 billion mark (15 times 1997 sales). Some industry pundits have predicted that Cisco will be the third dominant company—joining Microsoft and Intel—to shape the digital revolution.

Don Valentine, partner of Sequoia Capital and vice chairman of the board of Cisco,[1] was the first to invest in Cisco; he took a chance on the young company when other venture capitalists were more cautious. One way Valentine protected his $2.5 million initial investment was by reserving the right to bring in professional management when he deemed it appropriate.

In 1988, Valentine hired John Morgridge as CEO. Morgridge, an experienced executive in the computer industry, immediately began to build a professional management team. This team soon clashed with the founders and, after Cisco's initial public offering in 1990, both founders sold all of their stock and left the company. This departure left Morgridge free to continue his plans to install an extremely disciplined management structure.

Morgridge believed that many Silicon Valley firms decentralized too quickly and did not appreciate the proven ability of the functional organization to grow without sacrificing control. Accordingly, Morgridge maintained a centralized functional organization that is still in place today. While product marketing and R&D are now decentralized into three "lines of business" (Enterprise, Small/Medium Business, and Service Provider), the manufacturing, customer support, finance, human resources, IT, and sales organizations remain centralized.

HISTORY OF IT AT CISCO

Pete Solvik joined Cisco in January 1993 as the company's new CIO. At the time, Cisco was a $500 million company running a UNIX-based software package to support its core transaction processing. The functional areas

Source: Copyright © 1998 by The President and Fellows of Harvard College. Doctoral candidate Mark Cotteleer prepared this case at the HBS California Research Center under the supervision of Professors Robert D. Austin and Richard L. Nolan as the basis for class discussion rather than to illustrate either effective or ineffective handling of an administrative situation.

[1] Don Valentine was previously the outside executive chairman of the board of Cisco. Cisco has maintained its chairman of the board as an outside director. Currently, John Morgridge serves as an outside director and chairman of the board.

EXHIBIT 1   Financials and Other Cisco Statistics

Years ended	July 25, 1998	July 26, 1997	July 28, 1996	July 30, 1995
Net sales	$8,458,777,000	$6,440,171,000	$4,096,007,000	$2,232,652,000
Income before provisions for income taxes	$2,302,466,000	$1,888,872,000	$1,464,825,000	$737,977,000
Net income[1] [2] [3]	$1,350,072,000	$1,048,679,000	$913,324,000	$456,489,000
Net income per common share (diluted)[4]	$0.84	$0.68	$0.61	$0.32
Shares used in per share calculation (diluted)	1,608,173,000	1,551,039,000	1,490,078,000	1,425,247,000
Total assets	$8,916,705,000	$5,451,984,000	$3,630,232,000	$1,991,949,000
Stock price the Friday before fiscal year end[5]	$65.167	$35.417	$22.833	$12.458
Number of employees[6]	15,000	11,000	8,782	4,086
Net sales per employee	$563,918	$585,470	$466,409	$546,415
Net income per employee	$90,005	$95,334	$103,999	$111,720

[1] Net income and net income per share in 1998 include purchased research and development expenses of $94 million and realized gains on the sale of a minority stock investment of $5 million. Pro forma net income and diluted net income per share, excluding these nonrecurring items net of tax, would have been $1,878,988,000 and $1.17, respectively.

[2] In 1997, net income and net income per share include purchased research and development expenses of $508 million and realized gains on the sale of a minority stock investment of $153 million. Pro forma net income and diluted net income per share, excluding these nonrecurring items net of tax, would have been $1,413,893,000 and $0.91, respectively.

[3] In 1995, net income and net income per share include purchased research and development expenses of $96 million. Pro forma net income and diluted net income per share, excluding these nonrecurring items net of tax, would have been $515,723,000 and $0.36, respectively.

[4] Reflects the three-for-two stock split effective September 1998.

[5] Stock prices reflect a two-for-one split effective February 1996, a three-for-two split effective November 1997, and a three-for-two split effective September 1998.

[6] Number of employees was taken from respective 10K forms.

Source: 1998 annual report and 1998 10K form.

supported by the package included financial, manufacturing, and order entry systems. Cisco was "far and away" the biggest customer of the software vendor that supported the application.[2] Solvik's experience and the company's significant growth prospects convinced him that Cisco needed a change.

> We wanted to grow to $5 billion-plus. The application didn't provide the degree of redundancy, reliability, and maintainability we needed. We weren't able to make changes to the application to meet our business needs anymore. It had become too much spaghetti, too customized. The software vendor did offer [an upgraded version], but when we looked at it we thought, "By the time we're done our systems will be more reliable and have higher redundancy but it will still be a package for $300 million companies and we're a $1 billion dollar company."

Solvik's initial inclination was to avoid an ERP solution. Instead, he planned to let each functional area make its own decisions regarding the application and timing of its move. Keeping with Cisco's strong tradition of standardization, however, all functional areas would be required to use common architecture and databases. This approach was consistent with the organizational and budgetary structures that Solvik had installed upon his

arrival. Solvik felt strongly that budgetary decisions on IT expenditures be made by functional areas while the IT organization reported along solid lines to him. Solvik's objection to ERP solutions was also born out of concerns about the types of "megaprojects" that ERP implementations often became.

A DEFINING MOMENT

In the following year, little progress was made. Randy Pond, a director in manufacturing[3] and eventual coleader of the project, described the dilemma facing the functional areas in late 1993:

> We knew we were in trouble if we did not do something. Anything we did would just run over the legacy systems we had in place. It turned into an effort to constantly band-aid our existing systems. None of us were individually going to go out and buy a package. . . . The disruption to the business for me to go to the board and say, "Okay, manufacturing wants to spend $5- or $6 million dollars to buy a package and by the way it will take a year or more to get in . . ." was too much to justify. None of us was going to throw out the legacies and do something big.

---

[2] Most customers of the software vendors ranged from $50 million to $250 million in revenue.

[3] Subsequent to the implementation Randy Pond was promoted to the vice president level in manufacturing at Cisco.

The systems replacement difficulties of functional areas perpetuated the deterioration of Cisco's legacy environment. Incremental modification continued while the company sustained an 80 percent annual growth rate. Systems outages became routine. Product shortcomings exacerbated the difficulties of recovering from outages.

Finally, in January of 1994, Cisco's legacy environment failed so dramatically that the shortcomings of the existing systems could be ignored no longer. An unauthorized method for accessing the core application database—a workaround that was itself motivated by the inability of the system to perform—malfunctioned, corrupting Cisco's central database. As a result, the company was largely shut down for two days.

Cisco's struggle to recover from this major shutdown brought home the fact that the company's systems were on the brink of total failure. Solvik, Pond, and a number of other Cisco managers came to the conclusion that the autonomous approach to systems replacement they had adopted was not going to be sufficient. An alternative approach was needed. Solvik described what they did:

> We said, "we can't wait casually by while Order Entry, Finance, and Manufacturing go out and make three separate decisions." It would take too long to get those applications in place. We needed to take faster action. At that point we got sponsorship from the SVP of Manufacturing, Carl Redfield. He was with Digital before Cisco, in PC manufacturing. He took the lead and said, "OK let's get on with this. . . . let's start from the manufacturing perspective, and see if we can get the Order Entry and Financial groups in the company interested in doing a single integrated replacement of all the applications instead of taking a longer time doing separate projects." And so in February, about a month after the [company shutdown], we went about putting together a team to do an investigation to replace the application.

Redfield understood from previous large-scale implementation experiences at Digital how "monolithic" IT projects could take on lives of their own. He echoed Solvik's concerns about project size and had strong views about how Cisco should approach a large implementation project.

> I knew we wanted to do this quickly. We were not going to do a phased implementation, we would do it all at once. We were not going to allow a lot of customization either. There is a tendency in MRP systems[4] for people to want the sys-

tem to mirror their method of operation instead of retraining people to do things the way the system intended them. This takes a lot longer. Also, we wanted to create a schedule that was doable and make it a priority in the company as opposed to a second tier kind of effort.

SELECTING AN ERP PRODUCT

Cisco's management team realized that implementing to meet *business* needs would require heavy involvement from the business community. This could not be an IT-only initiative. It was critically important to get the very best people they could find. Solvik elaborated: "It was our orientation that in pulling people out of their jobs [to work on the project] if it was easy then we were picking the wrong people. We pulled people out that the business absolutely did not want to give up."

Consistent with the need for a strong Cisco team, the company would also need strong partners. Solvik and Redfield felt it was particularly important to work with an integration partner that could assist in both the selection and implementation of whichever solution the company chose. Great technical skills and business knowledge were a prerequisite. Solvik explained the choice of KPMG as the integration partner:

> KPMG came in and saw an opportunity to really build a business around putting in these applications. They also saw this as kind of a defining opportunity, to work with us on this project. As opposed to some other firms that wanted to bring in a lot of "greenies," KPMG was building a practice of people that were very experienced in the industry. For instance, the program manager that they put on the job, Mark Lee, had been director of IT for a company in Texas that had put in various parts of an ERP system.

With KPMG on board, the team of about 20 people turned to the software market with a multipronged approach for identifying the best software packages. The team's strategy was to build as much knowledge as possible by leveraging the experiences of others. They asked large corporations and the "Big Six" accounting firms what they knew. They also tapped research sources such as Gartner.[5] By orienting the selection process to what people were actually using and continuing to emphasize decision speed, Cisco narrowed the field to five packages within two days. After a week of evaluating the packages at a high level, the team decided on two prime candidates, Oracle and another major player in the ERP market. Pond

---

[4] MRP (material requirements planning) represents a class of systems, often thought of as predecessors of ERP, that focus on planning the material requirements for production. Forecast or actual demand is fed to MRP either manually or from other types of systems. MRP functionality is embedded in the offerings of all leading ERP vendors.

---

[5] The Gartner Group is a leading industry resource for information on ERP and other information systems and manufacturing related research.

recalled that size was an issue in the selection. "We decided that we should not put Cisco's future in the hands of a company that was significantly smaller than we were."

The team spent 10 days writing a request for proposals (RFPs) to send to the vendors. Vendors were given two weeks to respond. While vendors prepared their responses, the Cisco team continued its "due diligence" by visiting a series of reference clients offered by each vendor. Following Cisco's analysis of the RFP responses, each vendor was invited in for a three-day software demonstration and asked to show how their package could meet Cisco's information processing requirements. Cisco provided sample data and vendors illustrated how key requirements were met (or not met) by the software.

Selection of Oracle was based on a variety of factors. Redfield described three of the major decision points:

> First, this project was being driven pretty strongly by manufacturing and Oracle had a better manufacturing capability than the other vendor. Second, they made a number of promises regarding the long-term development of functionality in the package.[6] The other part of it was the flexibility offered by Oracle's being close by.[7]

Cisco also had reason to believe that Oracle was particularly motivated to make the project a success. Pond provided his impression of Oracle's situation: "Oracle wanted this win badly. We ended up getting a super deal. There are, however, a lot of strings attached. We do references, allow site visits, and in general talk to many companies that are involved in making this decision." The Cisco project would be the first major implementation of a new release of the Oracle ERP product. Oracle was touting the new version as having major improvements in support of manufacturing. A successful implementation at Cisco would launch the new release on a very favorable trajectory.

From inception to final selection the Cisco team had spent 75 days. The final choice was team based. Solvik described how the decision was made and presented to the vendors:

> The team internally made the choice and informed the vendors. There was no major process we had to go through with management to "approve" the selection. We just said, "Oracle you won; [other vendor] you lost." Then we went on to contract negotiations with Oracle and putting a proposal

together for our board of directors. The focus immediately turned to issues of how long the project would take, and how much it would cost. The team decided, "Yes, we will do this and we ought to go forward with the project." So now at the very end of April we were putting the whole plan together.

GOING TO THE BOARD

Before going to the board for approval, the team needed to answer two very important questions: How much would it cost and how long would it take? They knew their executives were worried that a big project might spin out of control and deliver substandard results. Despite the risks, the team took a pragmatic approach to estimating project requirements. Solvik described the process:

> Our quarters go August to October, November to January, February to April, and May to July.[8] So right here on May 1, beginning of the fourth quarter, we are asking, "How long should it take to do a project to replace all of our core systems?" This is truly how it went. We said, "You know we can't implement in the fourth quarter. The auditors will have a complete cow." If it takes a year we will be implementing fourth quarter, and that won't work. We thought it really should take 15 months, July or August a year later. Tom Herbert, the program manager, said there's no way we are going to take 15 months to get this done. That's ridiculous. So we started going in the opposite direction and said well can we do it in five months? That just didn't seem right. Understand we did not have a scope yet. In the end we basically settled that we wanted to go live at the beginning of Q3, so we would be completely stable for Q4. [See Exhibit 2 for a summary of milestone ERP implementation dates.]

That took care of setting a target date. Next came the task of estimating a project budget. Once again, Cisco was aggressive: "After we set a date, we estimated budgets. We put this whole thing together without really being that far into this program. We just looked at how much it touched" (Pete Solvik). Instead of developing a formal business case (i.e., a financial analysis) to demonstrate the impact that the project would have on the company, the team chose to focus on the issues that had sparked the analysis in the first place. In Solvik's view, Cisco had little choice but to move. He explained his approach to the situation:

> We said that we had this big outage in January. That we were the biggest customer of our current software vendor and that

---

[6] Redfield later notes that not all of these promises were met in the time frame agreed to during contract negotiations.
[7] Oracle and Cisco world headquarters are both located in the Silicon Valley approximately 20 miles from each other.

[8] Cisco's financial year-end is July 31.

EXHIBIT 2   Summary of Milestone ERP Implementation Dates

Project Kickoff	June 2, 1994
Prototype Setup Complete	July 22, 1994
Implementation Team Training	July 31, 1994
Process, Key Data, Modification Designs Complete	August 31, 1994
Functional Process Approval	September 30, 1994
Hardware Benchmark and Capacity Plan Validated	October 15, 1994
Critical Interfaces, Modifications, and Reports Complete	December 1, 1994
Procedures and End User Documentation Complete	December 16, 1994
Conference Room Pilot Complete—Go/No Go Decision	December 22, 1994
End User Training Begins	January 3, 1995
Data Conversion Complete	January 27, 1995
Go Live!	January 30, 1995

Source: Cisco ERP Steering Committee Report, October 20, 1994.

EXHIBIT 3   Breakdown of Implementation Costs for Cisco ERP Implementation

The Project Budget Estimate Did Not Include Estimates of the Cost of Cisco Personnel Time Beyond Some Members of the Core Team.

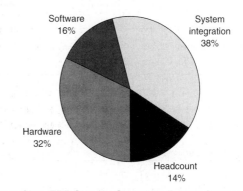

Source: Cisco ERP Steering Committee Report, October 20, 1994.

the vendor was being bought by another company. It was unclear who was going to support our existing systems and we needed to do something. The reliability, the scalability, and the modifiability of our current applications would not support our anticipated future growth. We needed either upgrades to the new version of the current application or we needed to replace it. If we replaced it, we could either do it in parts or do it as a whole. We evaluated those three alternatives, talked about the pros and cons of each alternative, and recommended that we replace our systems, big-bang, with one ERP solution. We committed to do it in nine months for $15 million for the whole thing. (See Exhibit 3 for a breakdown of project costs.)

Although Cisco was, to some extent, compelled to implement ERP, proceeding without a formal economic justification was also a matter of management philosophy. As Redfield put it:

You don't approach this kind of thing from a justification perspective. Cost avoidance is not an appropriate way to look at it. You really need to look at it like, "Hey, we are going to do business this way." You are institutionalizing a business model for your organization.

At $15 million, the project would constitute the single largest capital project ever approved by the company. Members of the team prepared to take this number to senior management with some trepidation. The first meeting with CEO Morgridge did nothing to alleviate their concerns. Pond described the meeting with Morgridge this way:

Pete Solvik, Tom Herbert, and I took the proposal to Morgridge and the reaction was pretty interesting. He made the comment, "You know, careers are lost over much less money than this." Pete and I were as white as a sheet of paper. We knew that if we failed that we were going to get shot. Failure is not something the business took to well, especially with this kind of money.

But Morgridge okayed taking the project proposal to the board. Unfortunately for Pond and Solvik, the reception was not much warmer there. Pond described what happened:

Before we even get the first slide up I hear the chairman speaking from the back of the room. He says, "How much?" I said I was getting to it and he responded: "I hate surprises. Just put the slide up right now." After I put it up he said, "Oh my God, there better be a lot of good slides. . . ."

There were, and the board ended up approving the project.[9] In the weeks and months following the meeting, Morgridge did his part by making it clear to the rest of Cisco that the ERP project was a priority. The project emerged as one of the company's top seven goals for the year. "Everybody in the company knew this was

---

[9] Pond adds that the cause for approval was aided by the fact that the legacy systems crashed on the day of the board meeting. "The day of the meeting, [the legacy system] went down. We were able to walk into the board meeting and say 'It's down again.' It was really a compelling story."

Exhibit 4   Cisco ERP Implementation Team Structure

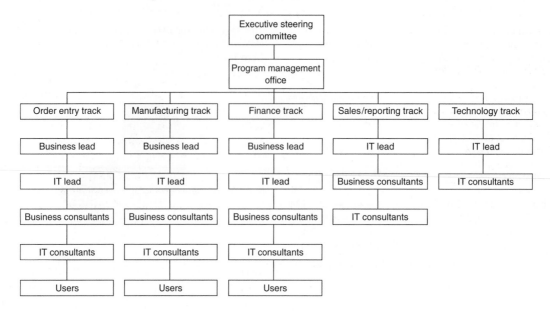

happening and it was a priority for the business," Pond explained.

BUILDING THE IMPLEMENTATION TEAM

With board approval in hand, the core ERP team lost no time in setting up a structure for the implementation. One of their first acts was to extend Cisco's relationship with KPMG through the end of the implementation. This decision was made based on KPMG's performance through the software selection process and the firm's continued commitment to staff the project with its most seasoned personnel.

Proceeding with implementation also meant that the team had to expand from its core 20 members to about 100, representing a cross section of Cisco's business community.[10] Again, the team sought only the very best for inclusion on the project. One of the rules of engagement for those working on the implementation was that it was short-term in duration and did not represent a career change for those involved. The effort was framed to those who would work on it as a challenge, a "throw down the gauntlet sort of thing." By this time, getting people to work on the team was not a problem. Elizabeth Fee, an

implementation team recruit, describes how the assignment was viewed: "They handpicked the best and the brightest for this team. To each person it was a career advancement possibility. People did it because it was something different, it was *the* opportunity, you were hand picked."

Team members from across Cisco were placed onto one of five "tracks" (process area teams). Each track had a Cisco information systems leader, a Cisco business leader, business and IT consultants from either KPMG or Oracle, and additional personnel from the business as team members (see Exhibit 4 for a diagram of Cisco's ERP team structure). Tracks were managed from a "Project Management Office" which included Cisco's business project manager, Tom Herbert, and Mark Lee, the KPMG project manager.

Sitting atop the entire project management structure was an executive steering committee consisting of the VP of Manufacturing, the VP of Customer Advocacy, the Corporate Controller, Solvik, Oracle's senior VP of Applications, and the partner-in-charge of West Coast Consulting for KPMG. The presence on the steering committee of such high-level executives from Oracle and KPMG was indicative of the importance these organizations placed on the project's success.

The ERP team's strategy for using the steering committee was to relieve them of the need to intervene directly in the management of the project. The committee's

---

[10]Total employment at Cisco was estimated at the time to be 2,500 people.

role was to provide high-level sponsorship for the project, to ensure visibility, and to motivate the team. The team aimed to make steering committee meetings celebratory events. To ensure this, they focused on addressing steering committee member's questions before meetings.

IMPLEMENTING ORACLE

The team's implementation strategy employed a development technique referred to as "rapid iterative prototyping." Using this approach, team members broke the implementation into a series of phases called conference room pilots (CRPs). The purpose of each CRP was to build on previous work to develop a deeper understanding of the software and how it functioned within the business environment.

CRP0

The first CRP (CRP0) began with training the implementation team and setting up the technical environment. Here the team worked in two parallel efforts. The first effort focused on getting the team trained on the Oracle applications. Cisco directed Oracle to compress its normal five-day training classes into two 16-hour days. In a two-week period the majority of team members participated in this "immersion" training for the entire application suite. While this was happening, a small "tiger team" was engaged in the second effort, getting the applications up and running.

Following training and setup of the system, the core team met in a session designed to quickly configure the Oracle package. Team members from all areas of the company were "locked" together in an off-site meeting to discuss and decide on the appropriate setting for the hundreds of parameters embedded within the software. Team members were joined by specialists from Oracle and KPMG. Solvik described the experience, its intensity, and results:

> There are all these configurable options on how are you going to run the systems. You set literally hundreds of parameters in these applications. So we went off-site two days, 40 people, and everybody's homework assignment was for that off-site meeting, maybe three or four weeks into the project at this stage, was to come in with an 80-20 recommendation on how to configure the system. We met all day and into the night for two days, going down to the "nth-degree" on how we were going to make this thing run for us. Oracle experts, with KPMG experts, with Cisco business people, Cisco IT people, let's talk about GL, let's talk about Chart of Ac-

counts, talk about this and talk about that. I call it the 1 percent effort that gave us 80 percent accuracy on how we would run this application, as opposed to a typical ERP approach, where you go off for six months, and overanalyze it to death. We had this three to four weeks into the project and we ended up being about 80 percent accurate in terms of how we could do this.

One week after this meeting the team completed CRP0 with a demonstration of the software's capacity to take a Cisco order all the way through the company's business process (quote-to-cash).

An important realization coming out of CRP0 was that Cisco would not be able to adhere to one of its early goals for the implementation—to avoid modification of the ERP software. Avoiding modification was important because changes tend to be firm-specific and make migration to future application releases difficult and time consuming. The team's experiences during the first phase of the project indicated that without a significant number of changes the software would not be able to effectively support the company. By the time one month had passed, it was clear that some changes would be required. Within two months after that it became clear that some of the changes would be substantial.

CRP1

Building on the lessons learned in CRP0, the implementation team immediately embarked on CRP1. With the team now fully staffed up, the goal of this phase of the project was for each track to make the system work within their specific area. As in earlier work, the emphasis was on getting the system to accommodate Cisco processes without modification. During CRP1, team members generated detailed scripts that documented the purpose for and procedures used to complete a process (see Exhibit 5 for a sample business process script). In order to ensure that all contingencies were accounted for, business process prototype tracking sheets were developed. (See Exhibit 6 for a sample prototype tracking sheet.) In contrast to CRP0, team members carefully documented the issues they ran across during their modeling. Issues were addressed in weekly three-hour meetings held by the Program Management Office. During these meetings the track leaders from each area worked together to resolve the issues and push the project forward. Modeling during this phase confirmed the concerns about the software. There were huge numbers of business processes that the software could not support.

EXHIBIT 5   Sample Business Process Script

ATP PROCESS:

Scope: This process will define how the Available To Promise process will work. This process will include how to enter information into the ATP, how to maintain ATP, how to access ATP information and how the information should be used.

Policy:
All Sales Orders will be assigned a scheduled ship date based upon the ATP dates.
Master Scheduling will maintain ATP information.
Request Date will be left blank if customer did not specify a request date.
Schedule date will be entered one week out from today's date.

Process for order scheduling:

CS Rep
1) Enter Order per Order Entry process.
2) Input Customer Request Date per Order Entry Process.
3) If Order is Government Rated or Express complete order line items per Order Entry process.
   a) After Booking of order, hit Page Down.
   b) Choose Order . . . (Order Action Quick Pick).
   c) Choose ATP Inquiry Order.
   d) When complete, hit Page Down again.
   e) Choose View Schedule Results.
   f) If ATP date matched Scheduled date and no failure reasons are listed below, go to step g. If errors exist, order must be scheduled into Group Available Date or have parameters changed in order.
   g) Choose Page Down again and select Choose Order.
   h) Choose Demand Order: System will state scheduling complete.
4) If order does not follow above, book the order per the Order Entry Process.
   a) Order will be submitted to Demand Interface automatically.
   b) If date is available, order will interface.
   c) If date is not available, order will remain in eligible status after demand interface has run.

Order Sched.
5) Run Process Exception Report (\Navigate Other Report Run).
   a) Choose Report under Type.
   b) Choose Process Exception Report.
   c) Choose Demand Interface for Program Name.
   d) Choose date range for order rejects.
   e) Submit report (F5).
6) Run Online ATP process to determine first available date for order to ship.
   a) Go into the Order (\Navigate Orders Enter).
   b) Query to bring up order that failed scheduling.
   c) Hit Page Down key.
   d) Choose Order. . . (Order Action Quick Pick).
   e) Choose ATP Inquiry Order.
   f) Choose View Schedule Results.
   g) If ATP Date matched Scheduled Date and no failure reasons are listed below, go to step h. If errors exist, order must be scheduled into Group Available Date or have parameters changed in order.
   h) Choose Page Down again and select Choose Order.
   i) Choose Demand Order: System will state scheduling complete.

ATP SYSTEM ISSUES
1) Report for Process Exceptions currently requires the Demand Interface Concurrent Manager ID be used (due to bug).
2) Table read by Demand Interface is never purged or cleaned up. As a result, records of failure will not be purged after success has occurred. Need to clear the Demand Interface table prior to each run somehow.
3) Process Exception Report will need to sort by Order Request Date.
4) Modification to default Promise Date from the Schedule Date after Demand Interface has occurred once. Future changes to Schedule Date should not affect Request Date.

ATP PROCESS ISSUES
1) Who will own the decision to use product from another demand class? Under what guidelines?
2) Who will determine which orders will slip out in order to add an order to an ATP date? Under what guidelines?
3) How can we guarantee that when Master Scheduling increases an ATP, that the order that required that date receives it? (Hand-off issue)

EXHIBIT 5 *(continued)*

4) How will DOA orders work so that they are shipped ASAP?
5) Should Customer Service be allowed to use the Buffer (DO NOT USE) demand class for any reservations?
6) What are exact definitions of Promise Date, Schedule Date, and Request Date? How will they be populated?
7) How should we control the use of Master Scheduling's Do Not Use/Buffer demand class?

COMMENTARY: PROCESS ISSUE NUMBER 1

Responsibility for this lie entirely within Customer Service Organization for demand classes that service customer segments. CS should not be allowed to move available quantity from Non-Revenue Demand Class without an approval from Master Scheduling (to avoid impacting the revenue plan) or from the Buffer Demand Class.

COMMENTARY: PROCESS ISSUE NUMBER 2

Open Issue: CS to own resolution on this.

COMMENTARY: PROCESS ISSUE NUMBER 3

Master Scheduling will change the demand class on the order and online interface the order if the product is available, to avoid confusing communication issues (to be tested in Conference Room Pilot).

COMMENTARY: PROCESS ISSUE NUMBER 5

Elizabeth and Kevin will work on this with Master Scheduling to determine best way to handle.

COMMENTARY: PROCESS ISSUE NUMBER 6

No.

COMMENTARY: PROCESS ISSUE NUMBER 7

Request Date is customer's requested ship from Cisco date. Promise Date is the date that Cisco has committed to ship the order to the customer. Schedule Date is the date used by Manufacturing to assign ATP and to notify CS of changes to the Production Date once an order has been missed.

The implementation team's response to the gaps found in the system was to develop a means for categorizing and evaluating each one individually. "All modification requests were classified as red, yellow, or green. Each one went to the track leads and anything that was a red had to go to the steering committee for approval." There were not many reds, but there were some (see Exhibit 7 for list of "red" modifications). In the end, 30 developers were needed for three months just to modify Oracle to support the business.[11] Elizabeth Fee described the process.

> When we realized we were not going to be able to go live "vanilla," we began to work on our modification strategy.

The months of July and August were focused on which modifications were we going to do? What's real and what's not? In some cases the user would be saying, "You know, the date used to be the first thing you type and in Oracle it's the fourth." In other cases it was the realization that we would have to hire 100 people on the shop floor to open and close work orders if we did not figure out a way to automate it.

Discovery of the need to modify Oracle led to some unplanned changes in the project plan and budget. In addition to the identification of required modifications, the implementation team also determined that the Oracle package would not adequately support the aftersales support needs of the company. As a result, the team embarked on a concurrent effort to evaluate and select a service support package. The package was selected and implemented on a schedule that matched the overall implementation schedule. Cisco planned to go live on both packages on the same day.

CRP2 and CRP3

As CRP1 turned into CRP2, and summer turned into fall, the implementation team found itself in the thickest, most difficult part of the implementation. Project scope had expanded to include major modifications, and a new

---

[11] When designing the modifications required for the system, Cisco made a concerted effort to stay "out of the core application code." "Core" code is the central programming logic on which application processing is based. Core code modifications are often not supported by the software vendor and can complicate a firm's ability to upgrade existing software with new releases. In Cisco's case, most modifications avoided touching the core code, relying instead on the addition of database fields and technically simple screen changes. In those cases where the core code was altered (usually to bypass certain processing), Cisco personnel worked with Oracle consultants and software engineers to identify appropriate changes. In several cases, Cisco modifications were later incorporated into Oracle's core product.

EXHIBIT 6   Sample Prototype Tracking Sheet

#	A — Application	B — Type	C — Related modules	D — Required	E — Comments	F — Status
1						
2	**Application**	**Type**	**Related modules**	**Required**	**Comments**	**Status**
3	**Financials & general ledger**					
4	System setup					
5	Accounting flexfield structure	Flexfield	All	Yes	5 segments	Done
6	Value set and values—Company	Flexfield	All	Yes	3 digit	Done
7	Value set and values—Department	Flexfield	All	Yes	6 digit	Done
8	Value set and values—Account	Flexfield	All	Yes	5 digit	Done
9	Value set and values—Project	Flexfield	All	Yes	4 digit	Done
10	Value set and values—Product	Flexfield	All	Yes	3 digit	Done
11	Calendar period types	Accounting	All	Yes	4-4-5 calendar	Done
12	Calendar periods	Accounting	All	Yes		Done
13	Currencies	Accounting	All	Yes	USD	Done
14	Sets of books	Accounting	All	Yes	14 sets of books	Done
15	Functional setup					
16	Account hierarchies and rollup groups	Accounting	All			Ongoing
17	Cross validation rules	Accounting	All			
18	Security rules	Accounting	All			
19	Shorthand aliases	Accounting	All			
20	Suspense accounts and intercompany accounts	Accounting	All			Done
21	Statistical units of measure	Accounting	All			Done
22	Accounting flexfield combinations	Accounting	All			
23	Daily conversion rate types	Translation	All			Done
24	Rates	Translation	All			
25	Summary accounts and templates	Summary	GL			
26	JE sources and categories	JE	GL	Yes		Done
27	Functional test cases					
28	Manual journal entries	JE	GL			
29	Recurring journal entries	JE	GL			
30	Mass allocation formulae—Rent allocation	JE	GL			
31	Reversing journal entries	JE	GL			
32	Journal import	JE	GL			
33	Online inquiry	Inquiry	GL			
34	Translation	Translation	GL			
35	Define budget and budget organization	Budget	GL			

EXHIBIT 7   Cisco ERP Implementation List of "Red" Modifications

Packout:
- Creates a "traveler" (i.e., a list of items to be configured) for build purposes; queues travelers by production cell so that each cell can print its own documentation (and not some other cell's) on demand.
- At the time the carton is being filled, allows barcode scanning to record contents of each box. Assigns a box tracking number and prompts for product serial number entry. Serial numbers are stored for future use and to prevent issuance of duplicates.
- Backflushes inventory from the system when the carton is closed.
- Determines if the box is ready for shipment or waiting for consolidation with other boxes and routes it to correct shipping location. If box is ready for shipment, it is released. If box is ready for consolidation the carton is tracked through its receipt at a consolidation center.
- Identifies last box in a ship set (delivery set) as it is received at a consolidation center and flags personnel to prepare the shipment.

Canada:
- Creates a separate installation of the general ledger and accounts payables with a separate set of books and separate currency.
- Allows transfer of data for Cisco general ledger consolidation.

Product configurator:
- Enables Cisco to input "rules" regarding orderability (physical and technical constraints on ordering) in a logical fashion rather than through code.
- Is tied to order entry—as an order is booked, the order is validated against the configurator.

OE form:
- Alters process for translating discounts from major order lines to subsidiary lines. Also changes manner in which pricing information is loaded into Oracle.
- Creates the ability to allow for landed cost data to be entered on an order.
- Creates the ability to allow for multinational orders—where the billing location is in the U.S. but the shipment is out of the United States.
- Adds new fields to capture additional sales order data.
- Adds a trigger at bookings to call the configurator.

Net change bookings:
- Creates information "synopsis" of the bookings on a daily basis.
- Creates a log of all order activity (plus or minus) which then is used by multiple other systems for reporting.

Sales agent splits:
- Creates a new form to enter sales agent information.
- Allows for assignment of sales credit to multiple agents with percentage allocation.

---

aftersales support package. One other major scope change also loomed. Because the downstream impacts of the project were much greater than expected, the team decided to tackle some larger technical issues. Whereas before systems had tended to communicate directly with one another (i.e., "point to point"), a new approach would now be employed in which all data communication would take place via a "data warehouse." Utilization of a data warehouse would allow all of Cisco's applications to access a single source for their information needs.

The scope changes meant further shifts in the utilization of Cisco's resources, especially for the company's 100-person IT department. The technical nature of most of the scope changes meant that this group bore most of the responsibility for the project additions. Solvik described the result:

> Basically all the rest of the IT group started decommitting from their other projects. They said "we have to spend our time just absorbing the fact that the core systems in the company are changing. We are needing to divert more and more energy and more and more resources towards the project." IT did nothing else that year. We also decided not to convert

any history as part of this project. Instead the data warehouse group created the capability to report historical and future in an integrated data conversion. We renumbered our customers; we renumbered our products; and we changed our bill-of-materials structure. We changed fundamentally all of our underlying data in the company and the data warehouse became the bridging system that would span history and future together.

By the end of CRP2, the first round of modifications was in place and running. During this time the implementation team continued to deepen its understanding of the Oracle and Service packages and to determine how to best make them work for Cisco. The final goal of CRP2 was to begin testing the system, both hardware and software, to see how well it would stand up to the processing load and transaction volumes required to run Cisco's growing business.

CRP3's focus was on testing the full system and assessing the company's readiness to "go live." A final test was conducted with a full complement of users to see how the system would perform, front to back, with a full transaction load. The implementation team executed these tests by capturing a full day's worth of actual business data and "rerunning" it on a Saturday in January. Team members watched as each track, in turn, executed a simulated day's worth of work. With this test completed to the entire team's satisfaction, everyone felt ready for cut-over in February. Pond described the ceremony that concluded CRP3:

> At the end of CRP3 each one of the functional leads presented their piece of the process and said "yes or no" on whether they were ready to go. We did each of them separately and then put everyone in the same room and made them nod their heads and say "we should go.". . . And then we turned the damn thing on. . . .

CUTTING OVER TO THE ORACLE

> *[After cutover] I wouldn't say the company hit the wall, but I would say we had major day-to-day challenges that needed to be solved quickly to avoid significant impact to the company. For example, our on-time ship, shipping on the date we commit to the customer, fell from 95 percent to about 75 percent; it was still not miserable but it was not good.*
> —Pete Solvik

The initial success of Cisco's cutover to Oracle was, to say the least, something less than what was expected. Overall business performance plummeted as users attempted to deal with a new system that proved to be disturbingly unstable. On average, the system went down nearly once a day. The primary problem, as it turned out, was with the hardware architecture and sizing. Ordinarily correcting the deficiency would have required the purchase of additional hardware, thus increasing the total project expenditure. But Cisco had asked for, and gotten, an unusual contract from the hardware vendor. In their contract Cisco purchased equipment based on a promised capability rather than a specific configuration. As a result, the onus for fixing the hardware performance problems fell completely on the hardware vendor.

A second problem had to do with the ability of the software itself to handle the transaction volume required in the Cisco environment. The design of the application exacerbated hardware problems by inefficiently processing common tasks. In retrospect, it was clear where the company had gone wrong in its final testing of the system. As Pond put it: "Some things were seriously broken at big data volumes, . . . and we have a huge database. Our mistake was that we did not test the system with a big enough database attached to it." In testing the system, Cisco had run individual processes sequentially rather than at the same time. In addition, only a partially loaded database

was used. After cutover, when all processes were running together over a fully converted database, the system lacked the capacity to process the required load.

The next two months were some of the most trying of the entire implementation. This was particularly true for the IT staff as it tried to grapple with the technical difficulties brought on by bringing the new system up. Fee described what it was like at this time:

> It was tough, really stressful. This was a big thing, one of the top company initiatives. There was a lot of focus on getting it done. We were working really long hours; making decisions that would affect the company going forward. . . . We always knew we would make it. It was always a "when," not an "if." There were [many] things you did not like about [the software].

ERP project status became the number one agenda item for weekly executive staff meetings. Strong vendor commitment from Oracle, the hardware vendor, and KPMG lead to an eventual stabilization of the software and improved performance. Solvik described the environment:

> So for about 60 days we were in complete SWAT-team mode to get this thing turned around. For example the president of the hardware vendor was our executive sponsor. This vendor probably had 30 people on site at one point. They were all over it. They lost money on this big time. It was great for them to get such a great reference, but it was a tough experience for them. Remember we had bought a capability. Everything they did to add capacity was out of their own pocket.

AFTER STABILIZATION

The technical problems associated with the Oracle implementation proved to be short lived. Over the course of the next three months Cisco and its vendors, working together, stabilized and added capacity to the system. The implementation ordeal concluded with a celebration party for the team and company management. Several members of Cisco's board of directors also attended. Feelings were running high that the new information systems would fulfill the promise of supporting the rapid growth that the company was expecting.

As he signed off on his recommendation for the bonus distribution, Solvik thought about the approach they had taken toward the implementation. "Total systems replacement for $15 million in nine months, who would have thought we could do it?" He tried to think about the decisions he and the team had made during the course of the implementation. What factors had made the difference between success and failure? Where had they been smart? Where had they been just plain lucky? Could they do it again if they had to?

CASE III-10

R. R. Donnelley & Sons: The Digital Division

Artemis March

"My biggest worry," said Barbara (Barb) Schetter, vice president and general manager of R. R. Donnelley's Digital Division, "is that we don't become an orphan. We could build up the division and even meet our revenue numbers, yet still not be embraced by the rest of the organization." Indeed, by early June 1995, many group and division managers at the $4.9 billion printing giant had yet to sign on to the strategic potential of digital technology or accept the Digital Division as the most appropriate locale for the business. Some still saw digital printing as a technology in search of a market. Others had indicated that if they did decide to embrace digital printing, they might do so on their own.

These concerns were very much on the minds of Schetter and Mary Lee Schneider, the division's director of marketing, as they sat down for a meeting on June 7, 1995. In two weeks Schneider was scheduled to make a presentation to one of Donnelley's business groups, Book Publishing Services, which was deciding whether to move into digital technology on its own or to bring its digital work to the division. Schetter and Schneider were hoping to craft a plan that would convince the Books Group to come to them. But they were still struggling to find convincing arguments and the right set of incentives.

COMPANY AND INDUSTRY BACKGROUND

R. R. Donnelley & Sons was founded in 1864. By 1995, it had become the world's largest commercial printer, with 41,000 employees in 22 countries. A privately held, family-run, Chicago-based company for almost a century, Donnelley went public in 1956; the first outsider was named chairman 20 years later. Donnelley had begun

printing telephone directories and the Montgomery Ward catalog in the late 1800s, and still generated 60 percent of its revenues from directories, catalogs, and magazines (see Exhibits 1 and 2). Its major customers were telephone operating companies, retail and direct-mail merchandisers, and publishers of books, magazines, and software. In 1995, the company was organized into 38 divisions; the divisions, in turn, were collected into eight business groups, which were part of three sectors.

Organization and Incentives

At Donnelley, manufacturing and sales were the core functions. Schneider observed:

> In this company, you either make it or you sell it. Our divisions are therefore organized around manufacturing assets [i.e., plants].[1] The trim size of the magazine, the binding requirements of the book—that's how we look at structure.

Highly autonomous, division managers were vice presidents who could choose the printing jobs they wanted to run and the equipment they wanted to buy. They sought the most profitable jobs because they were held accountable for operating profit, based on targets set during the budgeting process. Division P&Ls reflected plant revenues and costs, as well as allocations of corporate and selling expenses. Because most sales forces were aligned with business groups rather than divisions, each had a sales expense ratio that was applied to the work it sold into any plant.

Until 1991, division managers' incentive compensation was tied to their particular division's profit performance. This formula was subsequently changed in the oldest parts of the company, such as commercial printing, where the assets of individual divisions were similar and could be used for the same type of work. In these parts of the company, division-level incentives became groupwide in 1991, and sectorwide in 1993. As Jeff Majestic, financial director of the Information Services Group, explained:

> We couldn't move work around when each division wanted to maximize its own profitability. Now the division directors ask, "What is the most profitable way to run this job for Donnelley?" because they can make the best decision for the company without its affecting their incentive pay.

With few exceptions, division managers reported to business group presidents. Each business group contained several plants (divisions), as well as its own sales

---

[1] Although the fit was not perfect, Donnelley employees used the terms *division, plant,* and *assets* interchangeably.

EXHIBIT 1   Financial Highlights

Thousands of Dollars (except per Share Data)	Year ending December 31	
	1994	1993
Operating performance:		
Net sales	$4,888,786	$4,387,761*
Earnings from operations	459,431	415,607*
Net income	268,603	245,920*
Operating cash flow**	582,066	520.724*
Per common share:		
Net income	$ 1.75	$1.59*
Dividends	0.60	0.54
Other selected financial data:		
Capital investments	$ 545,651	$ 484,255
Working capital	551,480	424,473
Total assets	4,452,143	3,654,026
Total debt to total capitalization ratio	38.6%	27.8%
Return on average equity	14.1%	13.3%*

*Excluding the effects of one-time items in 1993 for a restructuring charge, required accounting changes for postretirement benefits and income taxes, and the deferred income tax charge related to the increase in the federal statutory income tax rate.
**Operating cash flow represents net income from operations, excluding one-time items, plus depreciation and amortization.
Source: Annual report.

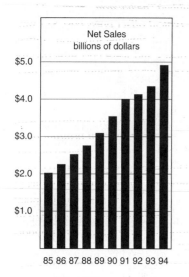

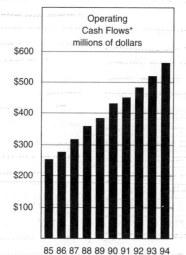

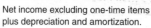
Net income excluding one-time items plus depreciation and amortization.

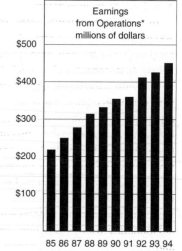
*Excluding one-time items.

force and such staff functions as marketing and finance. Group P&Ls were therefore the aggregate of their plants' P&Ls, and business presidents' incentive compensation was tied to the profits and losses of those plants. According to one senior manager:

This incentive system creates a tremendous bias for the business group presidents to deploy their sales forces to fill their assets. The sales force is an expense to its home group; you only benefit from it if they sell against your assets.

Salespeople worked solely on commission and were paid no matter what they sold or to whose assets the work was assigned. Technically, salespeople were free to sell work that was printed at any plant in the Donnelley system. But because sales managers' incentives, like those

EXHIBIT 2   Sales and Customers by Business Category (% of Consolidated Sales).

Catalogs	Magazines—18%	Books—13%	Metromail—5%
Lands' End	TV Guide	Random House	Procter & Gamble
L. L. Bean	Family Circle	Simon & Schuster	First Card
Eddie Bauer	Time	Harcourt Brace	Mutual of Omaha
J. Crew	Glamour	HarperCollins	Whirlpool
	People	Bantam Doubleday	
	Reader's Digest		
Retailers	**Telephone Directories—12%**	**Financial—5%**	**Software/Hardware—16%**
Wal-Mart	Sprint	Merrill Lynch	Microsoft
JC Penney	Ameritech	Smith Barney	IBM
Kmart	Nynex	Paine Webber	WordPerfect
Service Merchandise	Bell Atlantic	Goldman Sachs	Quicken
Toys "R" Us	Southwestern Bell	Schwab & Co.	
	US West		

31%

Source: R. R. Donnelley.

of business group presidents, were tied to the profitability of their particular group, there was considerable pressure to fill the home group's plants with profitable jobs. In a typical group, the salesforce sold 80–95 percent of its volume to its own plants.

In total, Donnelley's sales force numbered nearly 500 people. They were often described as the company's greatest strength, and sold primarily to print buyers, whose first consideration tended to be cost per page. Salespeople developed considerable knowledge about their customers, particularly on the operational side; they might become quite involved, for example, in helping a catalog customer reduce inventory and shorten cycle times. Most of Donnelley's upper management had come from sales, and many sales representatives did extremely well financially. CEO John Walter reportedly said that after being a sales representative, it took him six jobs to make equivalent money. Marketing, a recent innovation at Donnelley, for the most part supported the sales forces and focused on current customer needs, rather than creating long-term strategies.

Sectors were also a relatively recent addition to the organization. They were formed in 1993, when the president of Donnelley resigned. Instead of naming a successor, Walter clustered the business groups into three sectors: Commercial Print, Networked Services, and Information Resources. Each business group president reported to one of the three sector presidents, who were also executive vice presidents of the corporation. Together, Walter, the sector presidents, and key corporate staff formed Donnelley's management committee.

The Traditional Print Business

Donnelley's traditional businesses were geared to long printing runs on gravure and offset/web presses. These enormous machines, dubbed "heavy iron," required large capital investments. A typical offset press cost $12 million, and a gravure press cost considerably more. Offset presses used film and plates and were cost-effective for runs of 25,000 to 500,000, while gravure presses used etched copper cylinders and were employed for run lengths of 500,000 or more.

The company considered long-term relationships with customers to be the key to its commercial printing business. About 70 percent of this business was based on contracts of 3 to 10 years. Donnelley's strategy was to secure multiyear "enabling contracts," worth tens of millions of dollars, from select customers and to then build a plant specifically for each one, with equipment dedicated to its needs. Resource allocation likewise followed this opportunistic approach. While most people at the company viewed enabling contracts as the secret of the firm's success, others raised concerns. Allen Cubell, director of strategic planning for the Commercial Print Sector, noted: "You get an emergent strategy based on opportunities, as opposed to selecting the right opportunity based on a strategic assessment of alternatives."

The traditional print business was one of high fixed and low variable costs: the longer the run length on heavy iron, the lower the cost per page. Technology projects initiated by the corporate Technology Center and the divisions kept Donnelley's $3.7 billion asset base at the forefront of these traditional, electro-mechanical print technologies, while allowing some tailoring and customization. Majestic explained what customized binding equipment could do, using a Donnelley customer, the *Farm Journal,* as an example:

> Subscribers to this magazine include farmers of all kinds, and our customer wants to target the variable portions of the magazine to each of their interests. At the same time, we want to save the customer money. We do that by mailing according to zip code—in fact, by carrier route. Our binding lines allow us to assemble different versions of the magazine according to subscribers' interests, and then have them come off the equipment in zip code sequence, all correctly addressed. In total, we do 66,000 versions of the *Farm Journal!*

Industry Shifts and New Technologies

Industry trends were moving increasingly toward such local, targeted communications, often called "mass customization." Long-time customers such as *TV Guide* wanted shorter runs, more versions, tailored inserts, and greater use of color. Newer customers like Microsoft put a premium on speed, simultaneous global distribution, and the ability to revise materials quickly. All customers faced sharply rising postal rates and paper prices, which, along with increased inventory, warehousing, and shipping costs, were creating incentives to develop alternative, electronic media and new channels of distribution.

Imaging technologies had been fairly stable since the development of offset/web printing in the 1960s, but major changes were underway, largely because of the rapid spread of office computing. Schetter noted: "Last year, for the first time more paper was produced on desktops than on web presses." Desktop publishing, which emerged on a large scale in the late 1980s, integrated many craft-based, front-end, editorial, and prepress operations, and triggered their migration away from traditional production sites in the publishing and printing industries. The economic impact was significant, as Schneider observed: "The craft side of the business that we made big money on—stripping, color correction, etching—has migrated to the hands of the document creator."

Filmless printing technologies, such as digital four-color and computer-to-plate, were expected to have an even more profound impact. By eliminating the demanding intermediate steps of converting to film, these technologies would significantly reduce cycle times and chemical pollution. Digital four-color printing went the furthest, eliminating plates altogether and printing directly from computer files. It allowed short run, four-color printing whose image was infinitely customizable, and could be delivered in variable quantities as often as

desired. This capability, together with the low cost (approximately $200,000 in 1995) and small size of digital presses meant that they did not need to operate in a manufacturing environment but could be sited at distribution points anywhere in the world, even on customers' own premises. Rory Cowan, president of the Information Resources Sector and a staunch advocate of digital technology, summarized the likely impact: "Digital technology will atomize the printing industry the way the microprocessor did the computer industry." In 1995, digital growth was forecast at around 16 percent annually, while traditional printing was expected to grow by 3 percent.

Emerging Competition

In 1995, at least 55,000 printing companies operated worldwide. Most had fewer than 25 employees. Donnelley, with 6 percent of the $80 billion print market, was larger than its next nine rivals combined. Threats, however, were emerging from several directions, largely because of new technologies and new entrants to the business.

Online service providers and software packagers were making four-color images available electronically, at the same time that color printers were improving rapidly in quality and migrating to homes and small businesses. Smaller printing companies were building alliances, among themselves and with firms that had high-capacity networks for transmitting files. For example, AT&T had recently forged a multiparty agreement in which Adobe Systems and Quark provided the software to compose documents directly on computers; Xerox provided the software to compress and decompress document files before and after transmission; and digital print manufacturers provided the hardware. Moore Graphics and EDS had announced similar plans. Pulled together, these offerings provided the infrastructure to support networks of local printing companies and link them with retail chains such as Sir Speedy. Schetter explained the implications: "Digital print is rapidly migrating to retail. With these alliances, a small printer can now look like a very large printer."

THE DIGITAL VISION

One Donnelley executive alert to these changes was Cowan, who over the years had championed a series of efforts, including the formation of the Digital Division, to focus the company's attention on the opportunities of digital technology. Cowan joined Donnelley in 1986, when the company he then owned, CSA press, was acquired by the printing giant. Ten years earlier, while still in business school, he had bought CSA from his father and grown it into a $20 million printer of documentation books and bundles for the software industry. In 1987, Cowan was named senior vice president of sales for Documentation Services (soon renamed Global Software), Donnelley's first major nontraditional business group. Global Software served companies such as Microsoft, Apple, and IBM that needed to reproduce and distribute technical documentation in a variety of formats worldwide. By 1990, the business had quintupled in sales to several hundred million dollars, and Cowan was promoted to group vice president.

Throughout this period, Cowan attempted to build his new business in parallel with the old. Rather than directly challenging the traditional organization and values, he preferred, in his words, "to create a new business and have it drip on the culture." He viewed Donnelley as being "like IBM in 1983—PCs are coming in, but management has grown up in a mainframe world." Global Software therefore sought and developed a younger breed of managers, more of them women and all of them comfortable with computers. Epitomizing the breed was Janet Clarke, manager of the group's hardware sales force, who in 1985 had sought out IBM's PC division and made a crucial $50 million sale.

In 1991, Cowan was promoted again, and became Donnelley's sole executive vice president. He was effectively the number two person in the company, with responsibility for Global Software, Books, Financial, Information Services, and Metromail, as well as the corporate Technology Center. Meanwhile, he was becoming convinced that "value was leaving the book" and began exploring how Donnelley's traditional scale advantages could be preserved in a digital future.

A New Business Model

As Cowan saw it, digital presses were an essential enabling technology, but were unlikely, by themselves, to provide Donnelley with enduring competitive advantage. Instead, he believed that economies of scale would come from an information architecture that linked Donnelley with upstream "content owners" and downstream customers. Donnelley would become an electronic warehouse and distributor, with the critical ability to print on demand. In the early 1990s, Cowan began developing the broad outlines of a new business model based on these concepts, with distributed digital printing at its core.

In the new world, publishers would send data files of their manuscripts to Donnelley, where they would be retained in a database. When a bookstore needed copies of a particular book, it would contact Donnelley, and the files would be printed in the appropriate numbers, bound, and shipped; Donnelley would simultaneously send a check to the publisher for the necessary royalties. This process eliminated a range of costly steps, including warehousing and inventory, that represented roughly 60 percent of book publishers' costs. The approach also avoided the usual mismatching of demand and inventory. Because data files could be printed anywhere in the world—preferably in a print-on-demand (POD) site that Donnelley located near the final point of sale—end user stock could be replenished within 24 hours. To make the model work, Donnelley would need to develop and control four database systems: a transaction management system for triggering and managing the purchasing process, a system for royalty accounting and payment, an object-oriented database for managing the intellectual property, and a manufacturing database for directing the digital printing presses.

The underlying economics and selling process would be fundamentally different from traditional printing. Once the digitalized document was in the database, virtually no time or setup costs would be required to convert it to a final product in nearly any quantity. Cost per copy would thus be independent of run length, constant rather than declining. Costs would be higher than offset/web or gravure for long runs, but lower for short runs. Moreover, on-demand printing would have an enormous effect on customers' total system costs when warehousing, transportation, obsolescence, and throwaways were factored in. Total cycle time would be reduced by orders of magnitude—from 20 days to 2 or 3, and, if necessary, to a single day. Customization also offered the opportunity for more tailored marketing and better sales, so new selling approaches were likely to be needed.

For these reasons, Cowan suspected that a new division, dedicated to this approach, would be required, rather than simply spreading digital technology throughout the company. He recalled:

> I did not want to put two digital presses in every plant. They wouldn't see the light of day. They would be wonderful toys, but would be swallowed up if they were scattered.

Economic and Technical Validation

Between 1991 and 1993, Cowan began selling his vision within the firm, particularly to senior management. He established a venture capital fund to invest in new print-related technologies, and put a Donnelley executive on the board of each venture. And he asked the corporate Technology Center to research the capabilities and costs of new imaging technologies, to determine Donnelley's potential competitive advantage in a "digital future." A small group of technologists were assigned the task. They soon dubbed themselves the Field of Dreams Team, after the movie that spawned the phrase "build it, and they will come."

The team began by establishing close contact with technology suppliers such as Xeikon, a Belgian manufacturer of digital presses that was partially funded by Cowan's venture capital fund. Team members provided direction for Xeikon's development work, as well as oversight and monitoring. When prototypes became available, they conducted over 200 beta tests, using data files solicited from Donnelley customers. These tests produced estimates of throughputs, machine stability, and the readiness of the technology for full-scale manufacturing. Costs were higher than expected: the presses were expensive, required skilled and dedicated operators, and used more toner than anticipated. Nonetheless, for run lengths of 2,000 or less, digital's per unit costs were lower than the costs of offset printing.

Traditionally, Donnelley's competitive advantage had come from the scale economies associated with heavy iron. Cowan asked the team to determine whether scale advantages existed in digital technology, based on investments in information architecture and databases rather than the manufacturing process itself. Surprisingly, team members found that, in addition to these economies, Donnelley's ability to negotiate volume discounts and its efficiencies in using sophisticated production control systems and multiple presses provided advantages even in manufacturing. As team member Grant Miller noted, "We found that scale is good, and that we could make money at digital printing."

As part of their ongoing work, the team made numerous presentations about the technology to Donnelley marketing staff and customers. Miller alone made presentations to more than 60 major customers. He recalled:

> Internally, people thought digital was a good idea, but no one wanted it because it was outside their core business. They all had some potential digital work, but didn't know enough about the markets and were scared of an unproven technology. Customers, on the other hand, almost jumped up and down, even though they too didn't know what to do with the new technology, or were themselves just starting to convert to digital format.

To improve the odds of successful adoption, Cowan sought to link the Technology Center's work more closely with Donnelley's businesses. In 1993, he asked Schetter, who was then running a Financial Services printing facility, to join the Tech Center and informally manage the emerging digital effort. The goal, Cowan indicated, was to find a home for digital within Donnelley, or at least to spark a major digital program. One early candidate for this role, the Magazines Group, shelved its digital initiative just prior to launch because the new sector president wanted the group to focus on long run, high volume markets instead. Shortly thereafter, Donnelley launched an ambitious reengineering effort, with important consequences for digital's development.

REENGINEERING THE TECHNOLOGY DEVELOPMENT PROCESS

Between January and April 1994, seven teams worked to reengineer the processes of the corporate center. One, headed by James (Jim) Turner, who had come to Donnelley from IBM and was senior vice president for technology and head of the Technology Center, was assigned the task of improving the technology development process. Schneider, who had been actively involved in the Magazine Group's canceled digital program, was also a member of the team.

The Existing Process

The group quickly discovered, Turner recalled, "that all the technology development processes were ad hoc." Projects were not chosen on the basis of customer needs, nor were their economics carefully screened. Instead, senior managers with clout got their projects funded, particularly when they were identified and championed early in the budgeting cycle. One result was that resource decisions were often governed by a "first pig to the trough" mentality. Bootleg projects gained momentum once they secured highly placed sponsors; at that point they were rarely canceled. Technology projects seldom had financial gatekeepers, and there were no formal reviews of how development money was being spent. Division and marketing managers played a minor role in guiding technology development. Turner summarized the traditional approach:

> There were no limits on spending, no deliverables, and you could spend as much as a million dollars investigating a technology. No one was looking. There were no gates at the beginning. No one was saying "go/no go."

After analyzing 10 years of projects, the team also discovered that Donnelley, while often first with new technologies, rarely realized their full market potential. Miller explained:

EXHIBIT 3 Technology Development Process

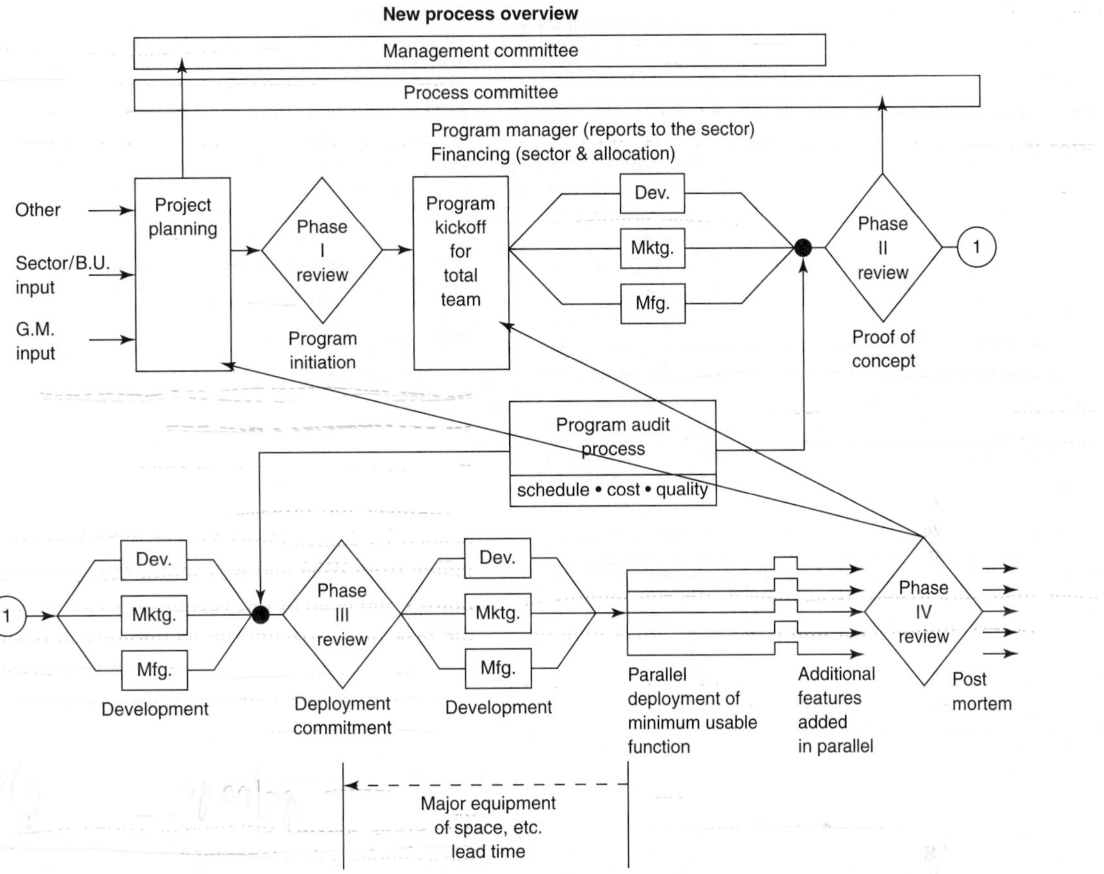

New process overview

Source: R. R. Donnelley.

We at the Tech Center would roll the technology out to one plant; they would try it, we would refine it, and then we'd take it to the next plant. With 38 plants, that takes a long time. They also wind up with different versions, and we had to support all them all.

Manufacturing managers could, and often did, say: "We'll take it later after you've gotten the bugs out," or, "We'll do our own version on our own equipment." The reengineering team discovered that divisions were spending, on their own, an amount equal to the Technology Center's budget, primarily on information systems technology and incremental technology improvements that were not transferred or transferable to other divisions. As a result, no one technology or information system worked across the company or across groups in a sector; some did not even work across closely related divisions.

The Redesigned Process

To overcome these problems, Turner's team devised a new process, guided by the objectives of greater speed, improved financial data and checkpoints, and better connections with the divisions. The underlying philosophy, Turner noted, was that "discipline does not have to mean bureaucracy."

The new process consisted of four structured phases. Each phase concluded with a formal review that specified deliverables to be met before the next phase could begin (see Exhibits 3 and 4). The divisions were offered incentives to take a broader, shared approach: corporate would pay half the bill if projects were at least sectorwide, and all projects were assigned to cross-functional teams, with representatives from marketing, manufacturing, and development. Teams operated through a matrix. Developers

EXHIBIT 4 Deliverables for Phase Reviews

Phase review requirement

Phase I (Program Initiation)*	Phase II (Proof of Concept)	Phase III (Deployment Commitment)	Phase IV (Post Mortem)

• SWAG** analysis
  • Financial benefits
  • Cost of development/deployment
  • Capital requirements
  • Revenue stream
  • Cost savings
• Schedule of development/deployment
• Make vs. buy
• Skilled set of people
• Initial market assessment
• Set maximum $ that can be spent prior to next justification
• Approval by sector president/sr. VP Technology
	• Rigorous financial review
	• Detailed
	  • Development schedule
	  • Deployment schedule
	  • Cost of development/deployment
	  • Capital requirements
	  • Cost savings
	  • Ongoing cost estimates
	  • Revenue stream
	  • Marketing plan
	  • Implementation plan
	• Completed program audit
	• Determine capital commitment, lead time to meet deployment schedule.
	• Set maximum $ that can be spent prior to next justification
	• Approval by sector president/sr. VP Technology
		• Final financial
		  • Financial justification
		  • Deployment schedule
		  • Capital requirements
		  • Market assessment
		• Completed second program audit
		• Approval by sector president/sr. VP Technology
		• OK to deploy
			• Metrics
			• Actual vs. planned
			  • Costs
			  • Schedules
			  • Function vs release
			  • Field performances
			  • Installation problems
			  • Lessons learned
			• Roles and responsibility problems
			• Process problems

*Up to $100,000 can be spent without completing Phase I requirements.
**SWAG = "scientific wild-assed guess."
Source: R. R. Donnelley.

continued to report to the Technology Center, while marketing and manufacturing representatives continued to report to their business groups. But they all also reported to a program manager, who was appointed by the appropriate sector or group president. Together, the program managers met monthly to decide on future projects, with Turner acting as their self-described coach and mentor. He observed:

> The program managers run this process; they are the ones empowered to make decisions. If there are complaints from the business presidents, I say to them, "The program managers report to you. You go after them if you're not getting value."

The process was triggered when a new technology or concept was deemed worthy of investigation. An ad hoc Technology Center team was formed and could spend up to $100,000 of strategic development funds to investigate the idea. Preliminary project and financial planning had to be completed within two months; the idea was not to be studied to death. At the end of two months, the project faced a Phase I review in which Turner, the relevant business groups, vendors, and other key players decided whether a formal program should be initiated. If the decision was yes, a program manager and cross-functional team were assigned. There were no limits on how much money this team could request to prove the concept in the next phase; the point was to move as quickly as necessary. Phase II and III reviews were rigorous financial checkpoints, and no project could receive major funding without first completing a successful Phase III review. Once a project passed a review, it had a green light until the next one; the only person empowered to stop a project between reviews was the program manager. Turner observed:

> With this system we are inviting senior management to stop meddling in technology programs. In the past, that was understandable, given our poor financial discipline. But not with the new process.

Turner believed strongly in the broad applicability of these techniques; he was convinced that the redesigned process could even be extended to new business creation:

> I see project management as being identical with process management, whatever the process. It's the Deming cycle: plan-do-check-get feedback. That's process management in a nutshell, and it's also what good project management is all

about. You could even run a new business through this process; you'd just present business plans at phase reviews instead of simple IRRs.

FROM VISION TO REALITY

The digital project was the first to tie into the newly revised technology development process. In April 1994, Barb Schetter was named program manager, with the objective of creating a new digital color printing business. She continued to report informally to Cowan. Because the project was already under way, it was grandfathered in at Phase III of the development process, and its Phase III review was scheduled for June. Schetter observed:

> Until we developed this new approach to technology development, digital was wandering. Then all of a sudden, we were catapulted into a process that gave us structure, hurdles, and credibility, allowing us to set dates, have meetings with general management, and get through the CFO's office.

The project's cross-functional team included Schneider for marketing, Lew Waltman for manufacturing, and Miller for development. They quickly dubbed themselves the Trapeze Team because they felt that they were "working without a net." The scheduling of the Phase III review meant that the team had to establish the existence of a market, identify possible applications, construct a deployment schedule and funding plan, and define the scope of the business in only two months. Every week, the team held day-long meetings, assembling cost estimates, integrating plans, crafting a preliminary design, rolling up projected costs and revenues, and generating an IRR that, in Schetter's words, "showed ourselves and others that we could roll out a division that could make money." During this period the team also began securing several digital presses, determining where the facility would be located, defining the database and transaction systems, obtaining the necessary capital appropriations, and creating a marketing plan.

Meanwhile, Schetter was making the case for a dedicated digital division to Cowan and other members of senior management. She recalled her reasoning—and the reaction to it:

> We had to get moved out of the Tech Center and into a P&L area, where we would also get HR and financial resources. I thought digital should be its own standalone business unit, with its own complete P&L, because our finances and marketing would be so dramatically different and because, with growth, we would become huge. They said absolutely not; they saw digital only as a [manufacturing] division.

Following the Phase III review, Schetter redoubled her efforts. This time, in addition to Cowan, she targeted Bart Faber, president of the Information Services Group (ISG), and asked to be moved there. On July 1, 1994, she was successful: Schetter was named vice president and general manager of the Digital Division, reporting directly to Faber. The division would have its own P&L, with marketing and a freestanding sales force reporting to Schetter.

The Information Services Group

ISG, digital's new home, was characterized by Faber as a

> greenhouse group that incubates small, internally generated divisions and manages a portfolio of venture capital investments. Those investments are our over-the-horizon radar to look at new technologies that may impact our core businesses and new ways that our customers will distribute information.

The businesses were unified, in part, by the goal of creating a "scaleable digital architecture," in which a single database drove outputs to diverse media. Faber observed: "Selling information in only one medium doesn't give you enough revenue to build a robust business model; you have to reslice it and remarket it." Daniel Hamburger, ISG's vice president for marketing and business development, added:

> We are laying a digital architecture for the company. Eventually, even commercial printing will be done by this new technology. From the same image database, we will be able to print at any scale, using any print technology, or deliver the image in any other form the customer wants—CD-ROM, fax, or online. The entire process, including the formatting for a particular medium, will be automated.

Faber had established several additional criteria for these new businesses: they should have the potential to grow twice as fast as the corporation, reach at least $100 million in sales, and achieve an above-average ROA. Because each ISG division was unique and their plants did not produce interchangeable work, division managers' incentives focused on divisional, rather than group, performance.

ISG's 60-member sales force, which sold about 85 percent of its $280 million volume outside the group's divisions, was often challenged to get their work into non-ISG plants. Faber observed:

> We are not tied to heavy iron, and other group's plants often throw my reps' stuff out. To succeed, they have to offer better priced, more profitable work. So my reps tend to be tougher, to leap on new businesses that are struggling for work and still answer the phone when they call.

like our dig wireless, phono, etc.

The ISG sales force targeted industries such as financial services, pharmaceuticals, and health care, where the primary focus was not publishing; salespeople worked not only with purchasing agents, but with marketing and senior managers, trying to meet their business and print requirements. As such, they tended to bundle together Donnelley products, and to include database services in the package.

In addition to the group salesforce, each of ISG's divisions had its own small, dedicated sales force. Faber noted:

> I have found that if a new business doesn't have control over its sales destiny, it has little chance of succeeding. It will wind up a second- or third-tier priority in most of Donnelley's other sales organizations. We have learned to build a dedicated sales force for all our new businesses.

BUILDING THE DIVISION

On becoming vice president and division general manager, Schetter's first decision was to "pick a date and drive to it." She chose November 11, 1994, noting that "with even a few digital presses we could be up and running; not perfect or full scale, but by then we could be a real business." Funding was delayed by several months, however, as the $40 million budget was finalized, and the start date for the new operation was moved to January 1995.

Operations and Technology

Memphis, Tennessee, was chosen as the site of the first digital facility, primarily because it was the central processing and distribution point of Federal Express. By locating close to the FedEx runway, the division gained several hours of work time each day, and could offer rapid, reliable delivery even without dispersed print-on-demand (POD) facilities or a complete database management system. In essence, Memphis offered "virtually distributed manufacturing" from a single location.

Manufacturing director Lew Waltman's immediate task was to test and operationalize the digital technology. Eleven digital presses were selected from three vendors. Each had strengths for different kinds of jobs, and the aim was to integrate the presses into an operation that would be the industry's low-cost digital producer. As Waltman noted, the challenge was enormous:

> There are very few pieces of this model anchored in any way. You cannot go somewhere else, observe for a day, and say, "Yes, we're running it properly." The equipment is new, and most of it is unproven.

Working with a third-party vendor, Waltman and his team also began building the transaction system and database to hold customers' content. A customer's order would trigger the transaction system, which would then access the right content, send it to the appropriate digital press, and pull together the printed pieces for the customer. New functional capabilities were added rapidly. By mid-1995, the system could accommodate Macintoshes as well as the original PC-based machines, and would soon be reconfigured so customers could do their own invoicing. In addition, the division developed three software tools that allowed customers to manipulate and vary the content in Memphis's database without ever leaving their offices. Target-IT allowed customers to pick, pull, and compose their own pages, depending on what they wanted to promote in a particular week. Send-IT allowed customers to send orders by dragging and dropping an icon on their desktop computers, while Order-IT allowed them to assemble the order itself.

These developments aligned closely with Faber's view of the division's purpose:

> The Digital Division is an attempt to take three distinct value creation devices—a content management system, a transactions management system, and digital imaging technology—and combine them to create a new product. They have a very different value that way, and allow us to get significantly higher margins. If we simply put Xeikon presses in each of our existing divisions, we would end up selling short-run printing jobs the same way that we sell longer runs—as images on pieces of paper. With the atomization of the printing industry, that wouldn't be very profitable.

Organization, Reporting Relationships, and Roles

In August 1994, Walter and Cowan asked Janet Clarke, now a Donnelley senior vice president, to head the Digital Division and become Schetter's boss (see Exhibit 5 for a partial organization chart). Clarke would report directly to Faber and would also manage half of the ISG sales force. Faber explained:

> By adding a sales animal like Janet to the mix, we covered the major weakness of a strong and seasoned team, added some capabilities we didn't have, and ensured our getting better sales performance. We could hold Janet responsible for some value.

Clarke added: "This was a people decision, not a strategy or structure decision." Schetter agreed, noting that

> Janet provides the balance. She is building the business from a customer base. She doesn't say to me, "I need a trans-

EXHIBIT 5   Partial Organization Chart, 1995

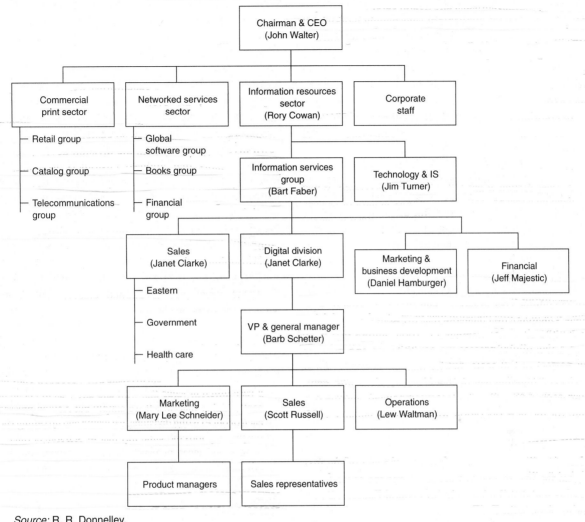

Source: R. R. Donnelley.

action system at less than $X per order." That's what Bart does. Rather, Janet asks, "Are we ready to sell?" Right now the issue is revenues, but once we get them, it will be our ability to deliver. The delivery of the Digital Division—that's my responsibility and not anyone else's.

Clarke, who was based in New York, described her role:

I spend my time as little as possible on [affecting] whether capital appropriations will be approved, or whether the plug will be pulled on the equipment, or the project management of the administrative system. I have a weekly conference call with Barb and her direct reports, and I go to Chicago fairly often. But my focus is on external sales, on things outside our radar scope, and for that, the best place is New York.

My job is to create robust revenue streams that use the advantages of the division and make it grow the way Global Software did in the 1980s. My job is to leverage digital for the whole company. I see the division as an incubator, from which we can figure out the opportunities for proliferating the technology, and can then integrate them into the business.

Clarke felt accountable for meeting revenue and marketing plan objectives, for monitoring technical and financial performance against division plan, for aligning the division strategy with company objectives, and for keeping the division's efforts broad enough to be transformational. She had chosen not to focus on internal lobbying at the sector or executive level, and had asked Faber

need for large inventories

to manage these relationships. She would, however, meet with senior-level customers to influence their thinking—what she called an "education and demand-creation function." She would also meet with customer influencers (such as consultants and advertising agency presidents) as a route to "backing into" their customers. Like Cowan and Faber, she would monitor technology developments, verifying her perceptions with investment bankers and analysts. Her role in dealing with "stray cats at a high level," was "catalytic . . . keeping Rory's vision . . . and being an ambassador for the company."

To supplement these efforts, Clarke organized her portion of the ISG sales force into three vertical teams: health care, federal government, and the eastern U.S. region, with the latter encompassing retail banking, credit cards, and high-end consumer marketing. She not only spent time with her sales managers and representatives, but also made sales calls, especially when a potential new customer or new area was involved.

In addition to Clarke's ISG sales force, the Digital Division was seeking revenue through Donnelley's other sales forces, for which Schneider, now the division's director of marketing, and her product managers provided technical and product support. The Digital Division was also building its own small sales force under Scott Russell, who had been at Xerox for 11 years and was hired by Schetter as sales manager in April 1995. By June, he was actively searching for six sales reps who, in his words, were both "hunters and farmers—people who can aggressively go after business, who have the confidence and know-how to close hard and professionally, and can farm and build relationships."

offer extra incentives?

Marketing and Sales Strategy

Target Markets To identify target markets, Schetter and Schneider developed a matrix from interviews with customers and Donnelley's marketing directors. Potential applications for short-run digital printing were first characterized by operating characteristics (e.g., turnaround time, paper requirements, repetitive database needs). The technology's capabilities were then mapped against these cells, and targets were established; they were continually updated based on experience in the marketplace. The primary near-term candidates were customers already using a digital format such as desktop publishing but who were encountering problems such as high physical distribution costs or high information obsolescence. Other potential candidates were those with unmet printing needs such as a desire for overnight delivery to multiple sites, increased customization of print materials, or

growing need for color. Based on this analysis, magazine reprints, corporate literature, marketing and product literature for pharmaceuticals and health care, and advance, liquidation, and prospecting catalogs were identified as target markets for 1995.

tgt. mkt

Positioning Because the Digital Division would offer services that differed quite a lot from Donnelley's traditional businesses, new marketing strategies were required. The division was not selling specific printing jobs in well-defined markets; instead, it offered a business capability that allowed customers to carry out printing in new ways, resulting in cost reductions and revenue enhancement. As Schneider put it: "We sometimes say we're not selling printing anymore; we're selling a marketing tool. We are teaching people to do things differently."

In most companies, the process of disseminating corporate literature and documents, whether for direct selling purposes or general information, was undermanaged, if managed at all. Typically, people scattered throughout the organization made piecemeal decisions about the production and distribution of reports, pamphlets, advertising, and other printed material. The result was literature that was costly to produce, expensive to inventory, and frequently out of date. Digital printing offered a much more effective approach, one that was likely to reduce the total costs associated with documents and printing. Moreover, by introducing new capabilities—the creation of short-run, on-demand, customized materials—digital printing could also increase customers' revenues by allowing greater market segmentation and more focused selling. To profit from these opportunities, however, most customers had to rethink the way that they conceived, produced, stored, and distributed their print materials.

To illustrate, Schneider cited a telephone operating company that produced generic corporate publications and marketing materials. These documents had never been customized and quickly became outdated. There were lengthy time gaps between updates, and salespeople had to root among "dead documents," stashed in dozens of cubbyholes, before sales calls. The digital alternative, Schneider noted, was an infinitely customizable "living document database"; electronic inventory would replace physical inventory, and each sales office would have a terminal with a "window into the materials of theirs that we have in Memphis." She elaborated:

> We're teaching them to think of their information as something that is alive and needs to be updated. There are two pieces, the content and the customers, and they need to be well matched. We're telling them to reengineer the way they

Key is to show machetes at co's that they can have a competitive advantage over other comp.

SECTION THREE: INTERNAL CORPORATE VENTURING **901**

gather and produce their information, publish it, and store it, so that the content is current and targeted to individual customers.

Unfortunately, the activities that Schneider hoped to re-engineer—which she termed the "literature management process"—had not yet been identified as a process by most customers. Thus, a major aspect of selling the division's services was helping customers recognize that they already had an implicit process for creating, managing, storing, and distributing literature, and that with digital technology the process could be reengineered to reduce total costs and enhance revenues. This required sophisticated positioning, as Clarke explained:

> We are selling to customers who sell to customers, rather than to people whose business is publishing. In essence, we are providing tools for marketing. So instead of calling on customers in the print procurement area, who only want to know the price per page, we are talking to senior people about their systems costs and total competitive advantage.

Consultative Selling   The multiple selling challenges, in turn, affected the sales approach. According to Russell:

> I don't want print reps on my sales force; it's not about printing. I want people who can find the right members of the organization, articulate digital's advantages, make them aware of their need for services, and help them see things in a new way. Our job is to lead customers, not be led by them. We don't want to meet current requirements, but to ferret out deeper, unmet needs and then satisfy them.

In fact, Schneider had discovered that if she or her product managers could provide proof of revenue enhancement, companies became more open to rethinking their literature management process. She observed:

> Our goal with a customer is to get to a prototype job, and compare the response it generates with their usual response rate. In every case so far, we have gotten a significantly higher rate—maybe two or three times what the customer was getting before. With that evidence, inertia is overcome, and it's like a runaway train. We suddenly have a champion within the organization.

To develop additional sales opportunities and better cross-industry data, the division was funding research with five partner-customers to measure the response rates of generic versus customized marketing messages.

Like Clarke, Schneider and Russell also viewed client influencers, such as consulting firms and advertising agencies, as an important leverage point, and planned to focus sales attention there. Russell noted:

These channels magnify and expand our reach. We are in start-up mode, so people are at a premium, and we need to engage outsiders to spread our message. I also discovered very quickly that focusing on channels was a way to avoid conflict with the traditional Donnelley sales force. With corporate clients, I was running into, "That's our account," or, "We have a big deal pending there and we don't want anything else going on there right now" all the time.

Mobilizing Sales   In fact, the Digital Division had to motivate three overlapping and potentially conflicting sales forces: the division's own sales reps, the ISG sales force, and the sales forces of other business groups. One problem was that if Russell or Clarke wanted an existing account reassigned to someone in their own group—who would then get credit for the sale—they first had to petition an account adjudication board. Schneider noted, "If you go through too many of those, you get a bad reputation as a group." Faber, however, was comfortable with the situation, and saw the need for diverse sales forces. He observed:

> In my view, it's better to have sales conflict and overcoverage than to be missing sales. The tension keeps everybody on their toes. It can be a little messy, but creation usually is.

One fallout of Donnelley's complex incentive structure was that business group leaders, sales managers, and sales representatives did not always see eye to eye. Clarke explained:

> Getting the middle of the organization to buy in is tough. Business group presidents and sales managers will not encourage their people to spend time selling the services of the Digital Division because the profits will accrue to another group. We therefore focused our incentives at the rep level because we needed the support of the complete Donnelley sales force.

To that end, Clarke had proposed an aggressive commission plan to motivate other groups' reps to sell work into Memphis. It included a "kicker," to be paid by the Digital Division, based on the page price of the work sold relative to a preestablished page price. Although more aggressive than most plans, such incentives were not uncommon, as Faber explained:

> When you are trying to get new businesses going, you really have to provide sales reps with special incentives. You are offering products and services that they don't know anything about. So you have to spend money to make it lucrative for them to learn about your business and become interested in it.

CHALLENGES OF INTERNAL ACCEPTANCE

By June 1995, the Memphis facility was up and running. But expected sales had not yet materialized, and the Digital Division was under intense financial pressure. Faber wanted to see profits by the fourth quarter, and a break-even year in 1996. He noted:

> We at Donnelley demand early profits from our new businesses. It's hard to be unprofitable around here for even a few years, unless you are making clear progress and it's part of a long-term plan. I have to run Digital as a strong stand-alone business because a marginal or unsuccessful organization won't convert anybody. The best way to convince people at Donnelley is to be successful.

As a result, Faber was not in favor of expanding the division or building other print-on-demand (POD) sites until Memphis was working well.

Schetter, by contrast, believed that the Digital Division represented an entirely new model, where the traditional incremental approach to investment was unlikely to succeed. She observed:

> You have to have large databases that integrate the software of multiple operating systems at multiple geographic locations. Our success depends on developing these new skill sets which are hard to find. We need an organized approach to expansion beginning right now.

Schetter's biggest concern, however, was being embraced by the business groups. She explained:

> We have not, as a company, stood up and said, "Short-run, on-demand, color printing and the associated delivery systems are a strategic initiative." There is no companywide rollout plan. We had envisioned a real pull for this capability, throughout Donnelley and from multiple customers. Instead, it has been more "wait and see" from the management committee. They say, "Let's see" if the business model proves out. "Let's see" if the transactions processing system pans out. Instead of taking a companywide position that digital is a strategic necessity, they're waiting for enablers who will pay the bill, and have said to the business group presidents, "You can use the Digital Division if you want, or you can do it on your own."

An immediate issue had arisen with the Books Group, which had a single digital press that had received few resources. Within 60 days, the group would decide whether it would invest in digital printing on a larger scale, or move its growing digital business to the Digital Division. Schetter and Schneider were trying to develop a presentation that would convince Books managers that the Digital Division offered the better opportunity. The question was, what arguments and incentives would be most effective?

CASE III-11

3M Optical Systems: Managing Corporate Entrepreneurship

Christopher A. Bartlett and Afroze Mohammed

In January 1992, Andy Wong faced an important decision. As manager of the Optical Systems (OS) business unit, how should he proceed with the Authorization for Expenditure presented to him by his management team working on a new computer privacy screen? Despite two previous market failures, the group assured him that the totally redesigned product would now succeed. Although Wong had great confidence in his team, he was also aware that the credibility of the unit, and even his own personal reputation, had been damaged in recent years. He believed in the privacy screen project, but he was also very conscious that he would soon need to get funding for the unit's other two development projects. He reflected on his options:

> The problem with the formal approval process is that, because it involves so many layers, there are lots of opportunities to kill ideas. So, one of my main jobs is to manage that process. One alternative is to use informal channels and seek support from some of my mentors higher in the organization, but that's an option you have to use carefully, and not too frequently. And of course, a final possibility would be to try to restructure the project so that we can do it within the unit without seeking approval through either the formal or informal systems.

At the same time, Wong's boss Paul Guehler, division vice president of the Safety and Security Systems Division (SSSD), was also worried about the OS unit. Although it was the smallest of SSSD's five business units, it occupied more of his time than any of the others. Optical Systems had been losing money since its formation

---

Source: Copyright © 1994 by The President and Fellows of Harvard College. Professor Christopher A. Bartlett and Research Associate Afroze Mohammed prepared this case as the basis for class discussion rather than to illustrate either effective or ineffective handling of an administrative situation.

as a business unit in 1979, and there were many in the division who felt it should start paying its way by milking its existing business rather than continuing to invest in new ones such as the privacy screen. Guehler reflected on his concerns:

> When I was asked to head this division, I was given a short list of priorities. Number one was, Clean up Optical Systems. . . . The priority is to demonstrate the unit's economic viability, but it also has to protect its credibility. They have a second, unrelated project that may need an additional $5 million investment, but they tell me it could develop into a $200 million business.

3M: PROFILE OF AN INNOVATIVE COMPANY

Founded in 1902 to mine abrasive minerals in Minnesota, by 1992, 3M[1] had evolved into a highly diversified global company whose $14 billion sales were generated by a portfolio of thousands of products managed through the company's 3,900 profit centers located within 47 divisions and sold through its organizations in 57 countries worldwide. Its well-deserved reputation for innovativeness was reflected in a long-standing company objective that 25 percent of its sales be generated by products introduced within the last five years. The company's new CEO, "Desi" DeSimone, had recently emphasized the need for even greater efforts in this area of 3M's distinctive capability by raising the objective to 30 percent of sales from products introduced within the past *four* years.

The Founding Philosophy

After a difficult first quarter century during which it evolved from a mining company to a sandpaper manufacturer, 3M's fortunes took a dramatic turnaround in the 1920s when a couple of young inventors applied the company's coating and adhesive know-how to develop two products—waterproof sandpaper and adhesive tape—that differentiated its commodity product line. From that time on, management developed a commitment both to building the company's core technologies and to creating an environment in which people could draw on them to innovate—"to stimulate ordinary people to produce extraordinary performances," as 3Mers put it.

By the early 1990s, 3M had developed a pool of over 100 technologies, extending from its roots in abrasives, adhesives, and coating processes to specialized high-tech expertise in areas as diverse as micro-interconnection, digital imaging, and transdermal drug delivery. To main-

tain its technological leadership, 3M maintained over 100 laboratories worldwide. The company funded these R&D efforts at a rate of between 6 percent and 7 percent of sales—twice the average rate for U.S. industrial companies, and amounting to $914 million in 1991.

To ensure that this technology was developed and applied effectively, 3M tried to ensure an innovative and creative environment. The value put on individual initiative was reflected in "the 15 percent rule" which allowed employees to devote up to 15 percent of their time on nonprogram activities that were related to innovative ideas they believed could be of value to the company. Project teams were formed around the most creative developments, and these were funded incrementally to allow the idea to be market-tested under the oft-repeated principle of "make a little, sell a little." Projects that survived the rigorous stage-by-stage review became departments, and departments that grew into substantial businesses were spun off as new divisions which seeded their own new set of projects to meet the 30 percent new product sales objective. The process had become self-perpetuating and was institutionalized as the company's "grow and divide" philosophy.

But the decentralized organization was held to demanding performance standards. In addition to the sales from new product targets, each division was expected to contribute to the corporate objectives of inflation-adjusted sales growth of 10 percent, pre-tax profit margins of 20 percent, and return on capital employed of 27 percent. As one ex-CEO explained, "We recognize some of our businesses as established but none as mature, and exempt none of them from striving to meet our standards for growth and profitability."

A vital component of the 3M machine was a structure and a culture that facilitated the linking and leveraging of the widely dispersed pockets of knowledge and expertise. Early in their careers, all employees learned that "products belong to divisions, but technology belongs to the company." A variety of organizational means were employed to encourage managers and scientists alike to develop extensive informal networks. Routinely, people called on experts wherever they were in the company to solicit advice or to ask them to work with them on a project. Cross-divisional "loans" of technical personnel were common.

The New Priorities

While these well-established policies and practices remained central within 3M, the 1980s brought a slowing of economic growth, an increase in the pace of technology development, and an intensification of global competition that led management to impose more discipline, coordination, and control on their increasingly diverse and widespread businesses. This was particularly true after 1986 when Alan "Jake" Jacobson became CEO. Under the pressure of his tough productivity program, the company reduced the labor content in its products by 35 percent and average manufacturing cycle time by 21 percent. Coupled with this new emphasis to "do more, faster with less" came a new focus on competitive strategy that encouraged managers not only to work on developing differentiated products, but also on creating defensible product-market positions.

As part of this new competitive focus, the company also began to change some aspects of 3M's vaunted innovative product-development process. In response to the pressure for faster development and implementation of innovations, the old model of the technological genius making a breakthrough in the laboratory was increasingly supplemented by teams of scientists, production engineers, and marketers working together from the outset. The need for speed also put pressure on the old "make a little, sell a little" philosophy. Particularly in some high-tech areas, the company was having to supplement the traditional approach with a model that allowed major front-end technological decisions and financial commitments. To facilitate this shift, Jacobson introduced the "Pacing Program," which aimed at identifying, among the thousands of projects in progress at any time within 3M, the hundred or so which could "change the basis of competition," and ensuring they received the funding and management attention they deserved.

On assuming the CEO's position in 1991, "Desi" DeSimone was determined to build on the disciplined legacy Jacobson had left. At the same time, however, he recognized the importance of protecting 3M's legacy of innovation-based entrepreneurship and the need to tolerate "well-intentioned failure." While the company had to be highly selective in supporting the ideas bubbling up, and equally firm about cutting off projects that were not achieving their objectives, it had to do so without damaging front-line initiative or threatening the careers of those who became project champions.

Like his predecessors, DeSimone celebrated the tenacity of front-line entrepreneurs fighting for their projects, and loved to tell the story about how as a division general manager he had repeatedly tried to stop a development team that was working on insulated materials. Despite his efforts, the team persisted, eventually developing the highly successful Thinsulate brand insulation widely used in outer garments. DeSimone explained the delicate management balance between discipline and flexibility:

> At the center of 3M's values are a respect for the individual and a commitment to creating an entrepreneurial environment where innovation flourishes. That requires managers to have respect for ideas coming up from below. They have to ask, "What do you see that I am missing?" And they may have to close their eyes for a while, or leave the door open a crack when someone is absolutely insistent that their idea has value. But in the end, there has to be performance. We can't allow every project to continue indefinitely. So we start to starve it. We force it to show it can survive.

BIRTH OF A BUSINESS

In 1979, the Optical Systems business unit was created to exploit light control film, a product based on 3M's innovation of microlouver technology (see Exhibit 1 for a brief description). This technology, which was considered to have substantial potential by many, already had a 15-year history in 3M, having begun its life in the New Business Ventures Division (NBVD) as "a technology in search of a market." The plastic film with its closely spaced microlouvers simulating a mini venetian blind, seemed to have many potential applications from window treatment to ski goggles, but despite the best efforts of NBVD, only one major user was found—3M's own Visual Products Division. The overhead projectors of the time created a glare problem for the presenter, and division product engineers became interested in the idea of placing a sheet of light control film beneath the glass projection stage. Although the film was expensive, it was effective, and was used on the top-end projector models.

When the NBVD was disbanded in 1979 on the belief that new businesses were more effectively developed within a "mother" division, management recognized that the optical microlouver technology was not going to develop beyond overhead projector screens if it was left in Visual Products. Bundled together with several other optical technologies with undefined applications, it became one of the assets of a new free-standing Optical Systems (OS) unit that reported directly to the group vice president of the Traffic and Personal Safety Products Group.

Despite these changes, the OS group continued to struggle, developing marginal products from its grab-bag of optical technologies, from magnifying lenses for rear projection television, to condensing lenses for microfilm

EXHIBIT 1   Light Control Film: Description and Potential Applications

PRODUCT DESCRIPTION

3M light control film (LCF) is a thin plastic film containing closely spaced black microlouvers. The film simulates a tiny venetian blind to shield out unwanted ambient light and direct display light of electronic instrumentation (Figure A).

Figure A

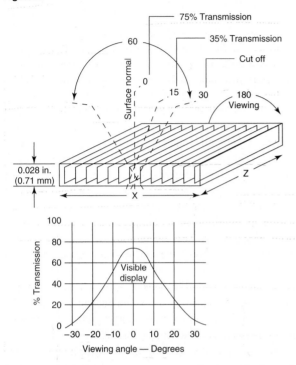

POTENTIAL APPLICATIONS

- **Privacy viewing:** Light control film allows for controlling viewing, so that unauthorized observers will have their line of sight blocked (e.g., on CRTs or Automatic Teller Machines, or ATMs) (Figure B).

Figure B

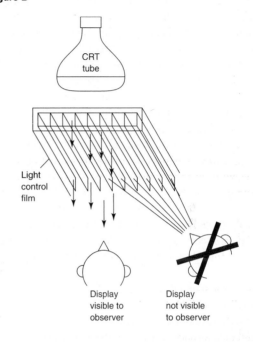

- **Sunlight readability:** Light control film microlouvers help block out annoying off-axis light while maximizing the transmission from the display to the viewer. The result is improved display contrast with little loss of brightness (Figure C).

Figure C

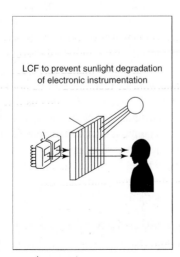

- **Light directing:** Light Control Film directs light to where it is needed or away from where it is not. It eliminates night time window reflections in automotive and aeronautical applications. It can also be used to hide the light source in incandescent lighting application (Figure D).

Figure D

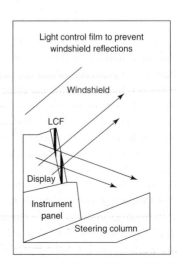

Source: Company documents.

readers. Light control film using the microlouver technology found its best application on automobile dashboards, where it controlled windshield reflection. But in the price-sensitive auto market, the product was regarded as an expensive luxury that did not add greatly to the perceived value of the car. Some products were sold at prices calculated on the basis of optimistic expectation of manufacturing cost reductions that were never realized. As a consequence, the unit was losing money at the rate of $3 to $5 million a year into the mid-1980s.

By this time, morale in the unit was low, with many losing confidence that they could build a viable business. But not Ron Mitsch, R&D vice president for the Life Sciences Sector, of which the Traffic and Personal Safety Products Group was part. When he became involved in the interviewing process for the open position for a new lab manager for OS, he convinced Andy Wong that the job represented a great opportunity. As an 11-year 3M veteran, Wong had spent most of his career in one of 3M's more mature divisions, but was beginning to get bored. Because Mitsch had previously acted as a kind of mentor, he trusted his judgment about the opportunities of working in a unit he saw as "exciting, stimulating, and kind of risky." Yet he was unprepared for the problems he soon encountered.

Under increasing pressure to boost performance, the OS unit's manager undertook a major rationalization of its diverse portfolio soon after Andy joined in late 1984. In the short term, this move exacerbated rather than improved the financial situation, since several of the projects were making contributions to the unit's overhead costs. A subsequent downsizing did little to boost OS's sagging morale. Through this turmoil, Wong tried to identify the unit's core technologies and unique competencies so he could recruit the right talent to focus on them. He decided he would build its capabilities around the emerging field of microreplication, a technology that involved creating microscopic structures in plastic to produce certain optical performers such as the louvered light control film. He then began using his personal network as well as formal channels to identify key technical specialists who could contribute to his objectives.

Through the mid-1980s, pressure to close the unit continued, but it had a staunch defender in Ron Mitsch, who in 1986 had been appointed vice president of the Traffic and Personal Safety Products Group. In 1987, Mitsch asked Wong to expand his responsibilities by taking on manufacturing as well. Despite his lack of prior experience, Wong tackled this new responsibility energetically. With the help of his key manufacturing experts, he analyzed the situation and came to the conclusion that the unit had been devoting too much attention to the latest exciting invention, an approach that tended to focus people on conceptual visions rather than on operating realities.

To redirect attention to the practical problems, Wong developed a three-year manufacturing strategy. For two years they concentrated on streamlining processes at their small plant in Petaluma, California, hoping to win the credibility and support for new investments. Next, OS's lab and manufacturing teams collaborated to develop a new extrusion process for light control film. On the basis of their record of improvements, the unit won approval to purchase an extruder, thus permitting them to consolidate manufacturing operations in Petaluma rather than simply assembling components from their other 3M plants. With much greater control over their own costs, quality, and scheduling, Wong estimated that between 1987 and 1990, manufacturing costs were reduced by 50 percent while quality was improved.

In 1988, Mitsch decided that the OS unit was beyond the incubation stage where it needed to be kept as a group-level development project. Believing it now had to prove itself as part of an operating division, he merged the unit into his group's Safety and Security Systems Division (SSSD) as one of five emerging businesses being developed under that divisional umbrella. (Exhibit 2 shows the OS unit's location in 3M's organization.)

UNDER NEW MANAGEMENT

In late 1989, a year after OS had been folded into SSSD, Andy Wong was asked to take over as the business manager of the unit. The business that Wong was appointed to lead was still in difficulty. While costs had been trimmed through technology focus and manufacturing economies, many of those gains had been offset by a declining sales volume. After several years of selling light control film for auto instrumentation applications, OS decided to deemphasize this application because it was unprofitable. Another major application, the "light bar" for the Mercury Sable's headlights was also canceled in 1990, partly due to a styling change, partly due to Ford's need to lower costs. The problem was, no major new applications were being developed to replace these and other sales declines. With OS losses increasing, this situation became the new business manager's first priority.

From Ammunition to Aiming Device

In Wong's mind, the need was clear. He had spent five years creating "the ammunition"—the technological competence and the manufacturing capability. Now what

EXHIBIT 2   OS Unit in the 3M Organization

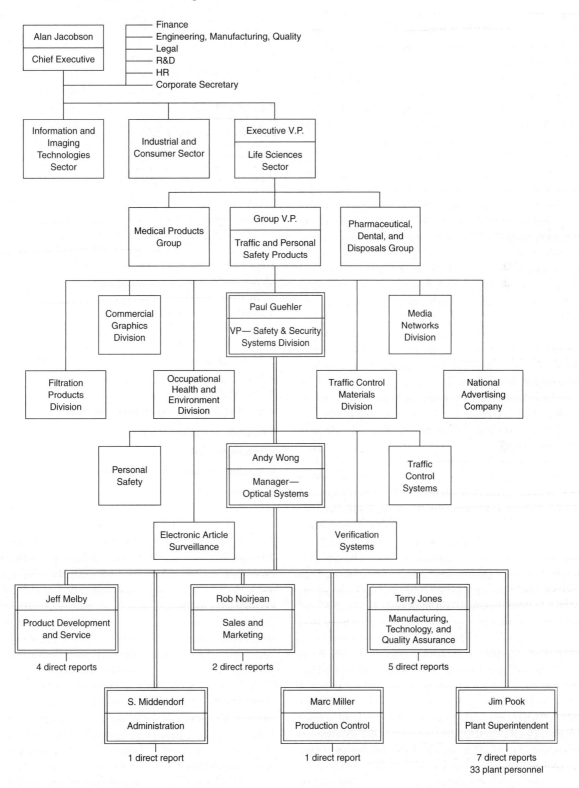

he felt was needed was "an aiming device"—a means to direct those internal assets towards external opportunities. The unit's existing four-person sales force scattered around the country working with specific customers on specific projects did not provide either the targeting or the power Wong was looking for. He wanted a professional marketing manager.

Wong took his argument to the division vice president for SSSD, but in a corporate environment of cost control, and with the OS unit's track record, he received a cool reception. But Wong was determined, and asked if he could take his request to the group vice president, Ron Mitsch. Fortunately for Wong, Mitsch had remained not only a believer in the potential of optical technologies, but also a personal mentor. He approved the new position, but only if OS would cut one of his unit's technical positions.

Wong then began searching for the best candidate for the job, using personal contacts and references as well as formal personnel channels. One of those who heard about the opening was Rob Noirjean, whose nine-year 3M career had seen him develop from a salesman to a marketing manager in the Office Documents System Division. In a hallway conversation, a friend told him that a marketing manager's position had recently been approved for a high-risk emerging business called Optical Systems. Like Wong, Noirjean saw such an opportunity as exciting. And if it didn't work out, at least it would provide good experience for his next assignment. He submitted his application, and was selected over more than a dozen other internal candidates.

Soon after Noirjean joined OS in February 1990, Wong asked him to focus his attention on identifying applications for the microlouvered light control film. Reviewing past applications but eliminating markets that would continue to demand high up-front engineering costs for one-time sales, Noirjean defined 11 broad areas of potential (see Exhibit 3 for Noirjean's list). Wong then suggested he try to develop a sense of priority by investigating each of these markets for three months at a time. The first two market opportunities Noirjean decided to focus on were specialty lighting and privacy viewing.

After six months of customer interviews and focus groups, he became excited about a handful of specific applications—museum lighting, where the value added would justify the high cost; automatic teller machines (ATMs), where controlled viewing through light control film provided a desirable privacy feature; and government computing, where some sales had also been made to the Customs and Immigration Services on the same basis of privacy viewing for the workstation operator. Yet even as

EXHIBIT 3   Noirjean's List of Potential Markets

- **Specialty lighting applications**
  - Museum lighting
  - Architectural lighting
  - Task lighting
  - Hospital lighting (bed lamps)
  - Film processing lighting
- **Privacy viewing**
  - ATM
  - Government computing
  - Corporate computing
  - Hospital radiology departments
- **Electronic display applications**
  - LED
  - PDP
  - Vacuum fluorescent
  - Electroluminescent
  - CRT (i.e., airport control tower display)
- **Automotive lighting**
  - Courtesy lighting
  - Map lights
- **Outdoor electronic display**
  - Gas pump displays
  - Industrial use displays
- **Avionic display lighting**
- **Copiers**
  - Internal directional lighting
- **Analog gauge lighting applications**
- **Machine vision applications**
- **Automotive CRTs**
- **Automotive switches and displays**

Source: Company document.

he explored these options, he became discouraged. Initial advertising generated leads among museums, but they were not translating into sales. Market research on teller machines indicated that banks were removing the privacy screens because some customers complained that they could not read the screen easily. And customs officers who dubbed the pilot products "the privacy screens from hell," had often taken the filters off their terminals complaining of eye strain due to glare reflection.

To better understand the problems of the "privacy screens from hell," Noirjean persuaded a secretary in his office to install one of the filters on her computer screen. With some experimentation, the excessive glare problem was solved. Meanwhile, however, the secretary had become increasingly attached to her test screen's privacy benefits. As an ex-salesman with an eye well practiced at scanning purchasing agents' offices for clues of competitive bids, Noirjean was sensitive to the value of office privacy, and recognized that workstation screens often contained sensitive information that the operator did not want passers-by or office visitors to read. Intuitively, he began focusing on a previously unidentified application he defined as "corporate computing."

Tightening the Standards

In October 1990, as Noirjean was continuing his market research, Paul Guehler arrived as SSSD's new divisional vice president. Reflecting the more disciplined approach that 3M top management had begun to emphasize, Guehler made it clear that despite the fact that OS represented less than 1/10 of the division's sales, it would be getting a lot of his attention:

> My impression was that the unit had been churning for the previous five years, at least. Because their results had never matched the high potential of their very visible technology, the management had become defensive, isolated, and sometimes almost secretive about their activities. And although they had the support of one or two top executives in 3M, they lacked broad credibility elsewhere in the organization. My job was to help develop the people to develop the business.

From the OS business unit, the new management style seemed threatening. At an informational meeting that the new vice president held with division staff, he openly acknowledged to the assembled group that if OS didn't perform, it would not be around next year. "It certainly added a sense of urgency to what we were doing," recalled Rob Noirjean. Andy Wong also found the situation had changed for him. Not only was there a new division vice president, but his long time mentor and project supporter Ron Mitsch had been promoted to senior vice president of Corporate R&D, and was no longer directly responsible for the SSSD in which the OS unit was located. Wong reflected how the change of bosses affected his role:

> I viewed my role as business unit manager encompassing four major responsibilities. First, I had to attract and retain good people—not always an easy task in a unit under threat. Then I had to build the team's motivation and commitment to the project. I think we achieved that. Everyone really believed in what we were doing, and we were all prepared to fight for it. Third, I had to ensure we kept making progress towards our objective. But because we first concentrated on building our internal capabilities—our ammunition—it was difficult to recognize progress until we began to fire it at market opportunities. Finally, I had a responsibility to keep senior management in the boat, not only by demonstrating steady progress, but also by painting a picture of the

cathedral we were building. It was this fourth role that began to dominate when Ron moved on to his new job and Paul took over the division.

Guehler's approach to managing the OS unit was what he described as a "give and take" strategy: he was willing to offer support and invest in the business, but he also took resources away and forced them to meet their financial objectives:

> First, they had to define clearly their core businesses. I helped them focus on three opportunities—computer filters, electronic display lighting enhancement, and automotive optics. The last one was a well-established segment and would help them survive while they tried to prove the first two. Next, I had to get them to open up, to communicate, to get more support particularly within the division. I forced them to commit their ideas to paper, to add multiple scenarios to their planning, and most of all, to articulate and defend their ideas. What they needed was discipline.

Testing the Business

With no budget remaining for additional market research and under pressure to bring a product to market fast, Noirjean decided to pursue the recently identified corporate computing opportunity. He conducted an informal survey among secretaries in another 3M division to determine their need for computer screen privacy, and the product attributes most important to them. On the basis of this information, he developed his marketing proposal for a new product—a computer privacy filter for general office applications.

Although several anti-glare screens existed on the market, the proposed product would open an entirely new privacy screen segment, and because of the new pressures, Noirjean needed to bring it to market quickly with little investment. He proposed taking light control film, cutting and shaping it to fit various monitor sizes, then packaging and selling it through computer supply distributors. The proposed product would be priced to distributors at $70, and by adding the distributors' normal 100 percent markup, the suggested retail price was set at $140, although many were expected to be sold below that level—perhaps as low as $99. Apart from minimum investment in packaging and inventories, both of which were commitments that the OS unit could fund internally, no major additional investment was required. It took little persuasion to get Andy Wong to agree to the proposal.

Implementing the plan was also relatively simple, and in February 1991, the first custom privacy filters were shipped. Sales gradually rose, reaching a level of about $10,000 a month—good basic demand, but far from the "home run" the unit needed. Growth stalled out due to two basic problems. First, distributors kept calling for different sizes of the screens, each of which was cut and formed to conform to the size and curvature of variously shaped models of computer screens. Within nine months, OS inventories listed more than 100 sizes. Another problem related to the perceived value of the screen. Although most appreciated its performance, the initial consumer reaction to paying over $100 for a formed sheet of plastic was one of surprise. By summer, Noirjean and the other OS managers had decided to redesign and relaunch the screen.

Their decision was to put the filter in standard size frames which would hang over the front of the monitor rather than fit exactly on the screen. To minimize investment, they negotiated a supply agreement for two standard size frames with a company selling an antiglare computer screen. With a redesigned package and brochure, they relaunched the product in October 1991.

However, even as this product was launched, Noirjean was aware that it would not meet the market need. Consumer reply cards he was receiving from users of the first-generation privacy screen were beginning to show a pattern in their responses. Typically scoring the product a "three" on a five-point scale, the comments indicated that while people loved the privacy feature, many of them complained that the screen created an uncomfortable glare. Feedback on the new universal screen design confirmed the perception. While there was a decline in distributor complaints about size availability and consumer comments about perceived value, the reply cards continued to highlight the glare problem.

While sales increased to around $20,000 a month, many in the SSSD saw the new privacy screen as yet another minor product from a group unable to fulfill its promises. But within the OS unit, everyone remained convinced they could make this product a winner.

THE NEW MULTIPROTECTION FILTER

Through selling the privacy screen, Noirjean became aware of the substantial sales volume being generated by the simpler and more commonplace antiglare filters that had been on the market for several years. As he conducted further market research, he became increasingly convinced that they had to reposition their product to overlap into this booming product market segment. He was also aware that such a decision would involve substantial new investment.

To respond to the new disciplined approach, the team prepared for their product relaunch by working through a four-phase development process that Guehler had insti-

tuted. Noirjean took primary responsibility for Phase I—the definition of a clear product and market concept.

Phase I: Developing the Product Concept

Noirjean's market research identified that there was a total potential untapped market of over 30 million PCs in the United States. Selling to this market, the antiglare filter market had developed into a $70 million business by 1991, and was growing at 20 percent annually. (Exhibit 4 presents key data from this study.) The market had become increasingly competitive, with the four largest players being Acco, a leading manufacturer of office supplies and therefore having good channel access; Polaroid, a company with a good brand image and a strong reputation in light filtering lenses; Fellowes, an office products manufacturer and supplier to the banking and financial service industry; and Optical Coating Laboratory Inc., the pioneer of the antiglare computer filters in the market. (Exhibit 5 provides a brief profile of each competitor.)

The products these companies supplied were quite similar; indeed all except Optical Coating Laboratory bought the coated glass from the same supplier. They differentiated their products by the design of the frame, through branding, and increasingly on price. As Noirjean prepared his Phase I analysis, he concluded that 3M

EXHIBIT 4 Multiprotection Filter Market Research Summary Data

New PC installations (1990):

Personal computers sold in 1990:	11.6 million
• for business use only (i.e., excluding home use and laptop)	5.9 million
• which 3M filters would fit (estimated at 90% of units)	5.3 million

Existing PC installations (pre-1990):

Number of pre-1990 PCs	60.0 million
Business use only	30.5 million
3M filter size coverage	27.4 million

Total potential market in 1990 | **32.7 million**

Stanford Resources estimates:

Total number of antiglare filters sold in U.S. in 1990		1.3 million
Total estimated market value (at distributor prices):	1990	$53.0 million
	1991	$70.0 million
	1995	$136.0 million
Estimated CAGR	1990–1995	20.3%

Note: Privacy filter is a "new to the world" product with unknown market potential.

Source: Company document (some data disguised).

EXHIBIT 5   Summary Competitive Profile

OPTICAL COATING LABORATORIES INC. (OCLI)

OCLI is the market leader with an estimated 37% market share. They reached the market through data supply and OEM channels. OCLI also private labels filters for large customers and sells directly to monitor manufacturers. OCLI does not have a privacy filter. They do not have a strong distribution position through the office supply channel.

Frame design(s): Side hanging universal, center mount, and contoured "profile" mount.

		Features		
Models	**U.S. distribution price**	**Anti-glare**	**Anti-radiation/static**	**Glass**
Vantage	$25.00	Yes	No	Yes
Professional Plus	49.00	Yes	Yes—98%	Yes
E-Shield	75.00	Yes	Yes—99.9%	Yes

ACCO

ACCO is a strong supplier to the office supply market. They offer two filters similar to our AF100 and AF200 in two sizes, 12″ by 13″ and 14″ by 15″, and hold approximately 14% of the filter market. Presently they do not have an extra large size like 3M's XL size. We have heard that ACCO may introduce a privacy filter using a Sumitomo technology that makes the screen go out of focus from the side rather than darken like our privacy filter.

Frame design(s): Side hanging universal.

		Features		
Models	**U.S. distribution price**	**Anti-glare**	**Anti-radiation/static**	**Glass**
ACCO GS	$26.53	Yes	No	Yes
ACCO VS	44.98	Yes	Yes—98%	Yes

FELLOWES

Fellowes is a strong supplier to the office supply channel and also to both computer and office supply superstores. They offer two products similar to our AF100 and AF200 which together hold 13% market share. They do not have privacy but they are searching for a supplier to provide this feature. Although Fellowes offers a side-hanging frame design, customers tend to feel it is flimsy. The hanging arm requires velcro to hold it in place since it is too short. Fellowes frame design is usually the lowest priced.

Frame design(s): Side hanging universal, center mount, and contoured "profile" mount.

		Features		
Models	**U.S. distribution price**	**Anti-glare**	**Anti-radiation/static**	**Glass**
Fellowes Anti-glare	$24.98	Yes	No	Yes
Fellowes Anti-glare/radiation	40.78	Yes	Yes—98%	Yes

POLAROID

Polaroid is a supplier to both the computer and office supply distributors. They sell low-cost plastic filters in two sizes (10″ by 13″ and 14″ by 15″), and one high-cost glass filter. Polaroid offers a universal mounting but it requires adhesive to hold it on the monitor. The performance of their plastic filters is not at the level of glass anti-glare filters. They have an estimated 11% share of the filter market.

Frame Design(s): Side hanging universal, center mount, and contoured "profile" mount.

		Features		
Models	**U.S. distribution price**	**Anti-glare**	**Anti-radiation/static**	**Glass**
CP60	$20.00	Yes	No	No
CP60 SC	32.00	Yes	Yes—98%	No
CP90	60.00	Yes	Yes—98%	Yes

OTHERS

A variety of other smaller suppliers (Sunflex, Norad, COS, Eyesaver, Optech, etc.) together account for around 25% of the market.

would have two important sources of advantage over competitive products—the unique privacy filter feature, and distribution offered by the company's access to office supply channels through its Commercial Office Supply Division (COSD) and to computer distribution outlets through the Data Storage Markets Division (DSMD).

In order to ensure the appropriate expertise and support for the development process, Wong asked his lab manager, Jeff Melby, to lead a cross-functional new product introduction team. From Noirjean's analysis, the team specified a product they felt would be truly top of the line in this segment. In addition to the antiglare and contrast enhancement offered by existing products, it would incorporate an electrically conductive coating which, when grounded, would prevent static electricity and dust buildup on the screen. This coating also proved effective in blocking 99.9 percent of low frequency E-field electromagnetic radiation which some reports (still inconclusive and somewhat controversial) had associated with health risks including miscarriages and leukemia. Finally, the filter would offer 3M's unique privacy feature, which was expected to be of increasing importance as the trend to open plan office design continued.

At the Phase I review meeting, the main concern was whether such a screen could be produced economically. Initial estimates suggested that adding all these features might result in a retail price approaching $300—clearly infeasible for an option on a $500 monitor. Noirjean's research suggested that the list price for such a product would have to be well under $200—a specification whose feasibility would have to be confirmed in Phase II.

Phase II: Undertaking the Feasibility Assessment

Having gained agreement on the broad concept, the unit's next challenge was to determine whether the product defined by Noirjean's research and Melby's team was technologically feasible within the prescribed cost parameters. To investigate this issue, Melby assigned two development subteams to explore the technical feasibility of both the glass specifications and the screen frame. Right away both teams began to involve people, resources, and expertise from many other parts of 3M and from the outside. (See Exhibit 6 for team membership.) Melby explained the philosophy:

> Management had been pounding on us to do more with less—and we certainly had very little! So we began drawing outsiders onto our team. In 3M's technical community we all have our personal networks of contacts, and the culture is one where you just have to ask for help and it's available. For ex-

EXHIBIT 6 3M Multiprotection Filters—Management Team Structure and Phase Status

New product introduction team members

S. Cobb	Laboratory
K. Fox	Quality Assurance
K. Castro	Quality Assurance
T. Jones	Manufacturing Technology
M. Miller	Manufacturing
D. Kingston	Lamination Development
K. Bramble	Packaging
V. Linse	Filter Assembly
J. Melby	Laboratory (leader)
S. Middendorf	Program Administrator
R. Noirjean	Marketing
S. Theirl	Product Development
J. Packard[a]	Corporate Hardgoods Engineering
J. Drake[a]	Surgical Products Division
Representative[b]	Injection Moulder
Representative[b]	Coating Subcontractor

[a] Member from other 3M unit.
[b] Non-3M team member.
Source: Company document.

ample, we drew on experts in our Specialty Film Division who had expertise in film lamination, our Optics Technology Center for their knowledge about film surface roughness, and our Corporate Process Technology Lab for advice on surface adhesion. We put all that expertise together in our work with a glass coater who had access to optical lamination capability, and together, we developed a proprietary process for laminating their coated glass with our microlouver film.

The frame design subteam also found ways to tap into a wide range of internal and external expertise that allowed it to develop a universal frame with a simple customizing adjustment that could be mounted without adhesives. They located an outside injection moulder and invited him to participate as a team member. They also tapped into internal expertise of the corporate Hardgoods Engineering Services and an engineer in Surgical Products Division who Wong had heard was an excellent hardware design person. With the help from Paul Guehler to win clearance with their bosses, both individuals were drafted as team members.

The team jelled quickly and soon came up with a unique design, as Rob Noirjean described:

> It was amazing how well everyone worked together, even the outsiders we pulled onto the team. We all knew what we needed to do, we all had complete faith in each other, and we all shared an absolute belief that we were developing a winning product. I guess it was because everyone sensed this was our last shot. . . . We did some benchmarking of our competitors' products, and eventually designed an inexpen-

EXHIBIT 7 Excerpt from Multiprotection Filter Business Plan

Summary filter sales and profit forecast

	1991 (Act)	1992 (6 months)	1993	1994
Forecast filter sales ($ 000)	180	1,000	10,000	20,000
Forecast operating income (%)	N.A.	1%	15%	20%

Summary risk analysis and response—3M multiprotection filters

Risk	Level	Plan
Light control film	Low	• Continue Petaluma supply
Supply		• Continue cost reduction • New equipment
Adhesive supply	Low	• Qualify second source
Lamination source	Low/medium	• Develop close partnership with key component vendor • Document process • Qualify second source • Develop new process
Laminate durability	Low	• Qualify per IBM Class C • Audit program with traceability
Frame source	Low	• Support molder insure capacity • 3M owns tooling • Document process
Back-order status	Low	• Ensure component supply and filter assembly capacity
Low sales demand	Low	• Introduce all necessary features plus privacy • Quality product line • In-place distribution • Sales support package • Replace competitors • 3M name
Existing competition	Low/medium	• Leverage 3M distribution • Sell product family • Offer same or better features and benefits
Emerging competition	Low/medium	• Leverage 3M distribution • Patent new and higher performance filter • Patent frame/hanger • Leverage 3M global presence/technical support • Business agreements with vendors • Offer package of benefits to overcome price issue

Source: Company document (some data disguised).

sive frame with all their features and a unique innovation. While the competition had to offer seven sizes of each of their models, we developed a squeeze adjustment feature that allowed us to offer only two.

Preparing Phase III: Developing the Business Plan

With agreement that the technical questions had been answered, the OS team was now ready to move into the Phase III Development process that led to the Phase IV Introduction stage. Before they could do so, however,

they were required to attach hard cost estimates and sales forecasts to the broad product concepts and design parameters they had developed. The new frame had been designed not only with market differentiation in mind; it also aimed at reducing supporting inventory levels and minimizing the tooling investment. Nonetheless, the final calculations arrived at an investment authorization request for $750,000 primarily for new moulds and assembly equipment.

The business plan also required the team to develop sales forecasts and risk assessments (see Exhibit 7). Rob

Noirjean, who prepared much of the data used in the plan, acknowledged that his forecast of $1 million of sales in the first six months faced a good deal of skepticism. And his estimate of worldwide sales of $10 million in 1993 was dismissed by some as being nothing more than a way of showing a one-year payback on the investment. Said Noirjean:

> The forecasts seemed high to many of them, especially compared to our sales of the first two generations of the product. But we tried to point out that they were a drop in the bucket compared to the total PC market size. . . . There are always a lot of soft facts in these presentations, and because 90 percent of new products fail, we knew management's role was to challenge the logic and expose the risks. Paul had certainly done that in the Phase I and II reviews, and we expected even tougher questioning in this style. . . . There certainly was a lot of doubt in the division. People were openly saying that we were just planning to throw money down a black hole again with this project. But we really believed our numbers.

Some concern also centered on the likely competitive response from the companies already established in the computer filter market. The OS team was aware that Sumitomo Chemical had developed a film that was clear when viewed head on, but caused objects to appear blurry from the side. Sumitomo had even approached 3M to determine their interest in the technology. Observed Noirjean:

> When we tested their product, end users told us they didn't like the feeling it gave them when they moved their heads and the screen went out of focus. . . . It is probably as expensive to produce as our louvered film, so that's not an advantage. Still, it could be a threat if an existing filter product incorporates it.

Finally, some worried that achieving the forecast sales volume at a distributor price of $79 (recommended retail $175) would require substantial support in sales and distribution. The OS team was assuming that they could access the office market channels through 3M's Commercial Office Supply Division (COSD) and the computer distribution outlets through Data Storage Markets Division (DSMD). But while corporate management strongly encouraged cross-divisional marketing efforts, units like COSD and DSMD still had to choose carefully among the products offered to them so that their specialized sales forces would not become overwhelmed and inefficient. Indeed, COSD had rejected OS's previous requests to distribute its earlier-model privacy screens, predicting (correctly, as it turned out) that those products would not have broad enough market appeal. And despite Paul Guehler's urging, the OS team had not yet persuaded either division to commit to distributing the new product.

Apparently the doubts and concerns about OS and its twice-failed screen were being taken seriously. While he was working on the business plan, Rob Noirjean received a request for information about the unit's sales from 1986 to the present. When he asked why management wanted ancient history, he was told it was for a review to decide the OS unit's future:

> You feel a bit like those guys on a submarine in the old war movies when someone calls out, "Torpedo off the port bow." But there's nothing to do but keep going and hope you can go fast enough so you get by it. As a team, we were all totally confident in the new product and completely committed to making it work. We just hoped we would be given the opportunity.

Meanwhile, Andy Wong continued to feel pressure. The situation in OS contrasted sharply with the other four units in SSSD, two of which were sponsoring new products that had been nominated to the company's highly visible and prestigious Pacing Program. Because profits were reported by business unit, everyone was aware that the OS unit was pulling down the division's overall performance numbers. Yet here was Wong trying to support not only the privacy screen proposal, but also another risky project that the unit was developing—a brightness enhancement product for electronic display applications that internal champions claimed was a potential $200 million a year business. One senior manager within the division asked Wong if OS wouldn't be better off switching from his aggressive but unsuccessful growth mode to a harvest strategy. By reassigning people to other units and cutting off R&D, the business unit could generate a profit with its ongoing auto components sales. While it would eventually put OS out of business, it was a strategy that would probably help Wong's personal evaluations, which had been low for the last three years.

Bottom of the Ninth, Two Out

In early 1992, some key decisions had to be made. For Andy Wong the question was, should he back the authorization for expenditure for the proposed computer filter? And if so, how should he seek support? Essentially he had four options: to postpone or reject the proposal; to try to fund it within his unit by outsourcing a standard frame, cutting inventory, and taking a more incremental approach; to try to get divisional funding; or to take the proposal to one of his senior-level mentors for support.

At the same time, Paul Guehler knew that he, too, may soon have to respond to this latest attempt to revive the privacy screen project after two previously unsuccessful launches of this product. He had five business units to develop, and because funding decisions put the whole division's credibility on the line, he wanted to ensure that other managers in the division were supportive of new initiatives. He also knew that within a year or so OS planned to ask for another $5 million for its promising electronic display brightness enhancement project. He reflected on the situation:

> Their credibility within SSSD and the corporation was pretty low. Two of our other business units had Pacing Program projects and were getting high level corporate attention and support. Meanwhile, Optical Systems was still losing $3 million on sales of $10 million. Some people felt it was time to pull the plug.

READING III-10

Managing the Internal Corporate Venturing Process: Some Recommendations for Practice

R. A. Burgelman

Internal corporate venturing (ICV) is an important avenue for corporate growth and diversification.[1] Systematic research, however, suggests that developing entirely new businesses in the context of established firms is very difficult even when a separate new venture division is created for this purpose.[2]

Source: Reprinted from *Sloan Management Review,* Winter 1984, vol. 25, no. 2, pp. 33–48, by permission of the publisher. © 1984 by Sloan Management Review Association. All rights reserved.

[1] For a detailed company background, see "*3M: Profile of an Innovating Company,*" No. 395-016.

[2] An overview of early studies on new ventures is provided in E. von Hippel, "Successful and Failing Internal Corporate Ventures: An Empirical Analysis," *Industrial Marketing Management* 6, pp. 163–74. Von Hippel has noted the great diversity of new venture practices. Some of this diversity, however, may be due to a somewhat unclear distinction between new product development and new business development. Von Hippel also identifies some key factors associated with success and failure of new ventures but does not document how the *process* takes shape.

Concerning the use of the new venture division (NVD) design, see N. D. Fast, "The Future of Industrial New Venture Departments," *In-*

STAGE MODELS OF ICV

Typical conceptualizations of ICV use a "stage model" approach.[3] Stage models provide a framework for discussing many important problems concerning the sequential development of new ventures. They focus on within-stage problems as well as on issues pertaining to the transition between stages. They emphasize the different requirements of different stages in terms of key tasks, people, structural arrangements, leadership styles, and the like. The problems most naturally addressed in a stage model are the ones that are important in growing any new business. But, many of the more difficult problems generated and encountered by ICV result from growing a new business in the context of an established organization. They result from the fact that strategic activities related to ICV take place at different levels of management simultaneously. Such problems are not easily incorporated in a stage model and tend to be discussed only in somewhat cursory fashion.

A PROCESS MODEL OF ICV

Recently, I have proposed a new model based on the findings of an exploratory study of the complete process through which new ventures take shape in the context of the new venture division (NVD) in large, diversified firms.[4] Exhibit 1 shows the "process model" of ICV. The methodology of the study is briefly described in the Appendix.

Exhibit 1 shows the *core* processes of ICV as well as the *overlaying* processes (the corporate context) in which the core processes take shape. The core processes of ICV comprise the activities through which a new business becomes defined and its development gains impetus in the corporation. The core processes subsume the managerial problems and issues that are typically addressed in stage models of ICV. The overlaying processes comprise the activities through which the strategic and structural contexts are determined. Structural context refers to the various organizational and administrative mechanisms put in place by corporate management to implement the

---

dustrial Marketing Management 8, pp. 264–79. Fast has observed the precarious, unstable function of NVD in many firms. He explains the evolution in terms of shifts in corporate strategy and/or in the political position of the NVD.

[3] For a recent example of a stage model, see J. R. Galbraith, "The Stages of Growth," *Journal of Business Strategy,* 1983.

[4] R. A. Burgelman, "A Process Model of Internal Corporate Venturing in the Diversified Major Firm," *Administrative Science Quarterly* 28 (1983), pp. 223–44.

EXHIBIT 1   Key and Peripheral Activities in a Process Model of ICV

		Core processes		Overlaying processes	
		Definition	Impetus	Strategic context	Structural context
Levels	Corporate management	Monitoring	Authorizing	Rationalizing	Structuring
	New venture division management	Coaching stewardship	Strategic building	Organizational championing Selecting Delineating	Negotiating
	Group leader/venture manager	Technical and need linking Product championing	Strategic forcing	Gatekeeping idea generating bootlegging	Questioning

☐ = Key activities

current corporate strategy. Strategic context refers to the process through which the current corporate strategy is extended to accommodate the new business resulting from ICV efforts. Both the core and overlaying processes involve key activities (the shaded area) and more peripheral activities (the nonshaded area) situated at different levels of the organization.

MAJOR PROBLEMS IN THE ICV PROCESS

The process model indicates that ICV involves the interlocking strategic activities of managers at different levels in the organization. These strategic activities are enacted without an existing master plan in which they all neatly fit together. Exhibit 2 provides an overview of some of the problematic aspects of the strategic situation at each level in each of the processes that constitute ICV.

Vicious Circles in the Definition Process

At the corporate level, managers tend to have a highly reliable frame of reference to evaluate business strategies and resource allocation proposals pertaining to the main lines of business of the corporation. By the same token, their capacity to deal with substantive issues of new business opportunities is limited, and their expectations concerning what can be accomplished in a short time framework are often somewhat unrealistic. Also, ICV proposals compete for scarce top management time. Their relatively small size combined with the relative difficulty in assessing their merit make it at the outset seem uneconomical for top management to allocate much of their time to them. Not surprisingly, top managers tend to *monitor* ICV activities from a distance.

Middle-level managers in corporate R&D (where new ventures usually originate) experience a tension between their resource *stewardship* and *coaching* responsibilities. Such managers tend to be most concerned about maintaining the integrity of the R&D work environment, which is quite different from a business-oriented work environment.[5] They are comfortable with managing relatively slow moving exploratory research projects and well-defined development projects. But they are reluctant to commit significant amounts of resources (especially people) to suddenly fast-moving areas of new development activity which fall outside of the scope of their current plans and which have not yet demonstrated technical and commercial feasibility.

Operational-level managers typically struggle to conceptualize their still somewhat nebulous (at least to outsiders) business ideas, which makes communication with management difficult. The results of their *technical* and *need-linking* efforts often go against conventional corporate wisdom. They cannot clearly specify the development path of their projects, and cannot demonstrate in advance that the resources they need will be used effectively in uncharted domains.

Demonstrating Technical Feasibility   The lack of articulation between different levels of management results in a vicious circle in resource procurement. Resources can be obtained if technical feasibility is demonstrated,

---

[5] These differences are discussed in greater depth in R. A. Burgelman, "Managing Innovating Systems: A Study of the Process of Internal Corporate Venturing," doctoral dissertation, Columbia University, 1980.

EXHIBIT 2   Major Problems in the ICV Process

Levels	Core processes		Overlaying processes	
	Definition	Impetus	Strategic context	Structural context
Corporate management	Top management lacks the capacity to assess the merits of specific new venture proposals for corporate development.	Top management relies on purely quantitative growth results to continue support for a new venture.	Top management considers ICV as insurance against mainstream business going bad. ICV objectives are ambiguous and shifting erratically.	Top management relies on reactive structural changes to deal with problems related to ICV.
NVD management	Middle-level managers in corporate R&D are not capable of coaching ICV project initiators.	Middle-level managers in new business development find it difficult to balance strategic building efforts with efforts to coach the venture managers.	Middle-level managers struggle to delineate the boundaries of a new business field. They spend significant amounts of time on political activities to maintain corporate support.	Middle-level managers struggle with unanticipated structural impediments to new venture activities. No incentive for star performers to engage in ICV activities.
Group leader, Venture leader	Project initiators cannot convincingly demonstrate in advance that resources will be used effectively. They need to engage in scavenging to get resources.	Venture managers find it difficult to balance strategic forcing efforts with efforts to develop the administrative framework of the emerging ventures.	Project initiators do not have a clear idea which kind of ICV projects will be viable in the corporate context. Bootlegging is necessary to get a new idea tested.	Venture managers do not have a clear idea what type of performance will be rewarded except fast growth.

but demonstration itself requires resources. *Product championing* activities serve to break through this vicious circle. Using bootlegging and scavenging tactics, the successful project champion is able to provide positive information reassuring middle-level management and providing them with a basis for claiming support for ICV projects in their formal plans. This dynamic explains the somewhat surprising finding that middle-level managers often encourage and do not just tolerate such subrosa activities.

Demonstrating Commercial Feasibility   Even when a technically demonstrated product, process, or system exists, corporate management is often reluctant to start commercialization efforts because they are unsure about the firm's capabilities to effectively do so. To overcome such hesitancies, product champions engage in corner cutting: activities which deviate from the official corporate ways and means (e.g., contacting customers from other divisions for tryouts, hiring sales people in disguise). Or they may choose an approach that is more acceptable in the light of corporate management's concerns but which may not be optimal from the long-term strategic point of view (e.g., propose a joint venture with another firm).

Managerial Dilemmas in the Impetus Process

Product championing resulting in preliminary demonstration of technical and commercial viability of a new product, process, or system and sets the stage for the impetus process. In the course of the impetus process, an ICV project receives "venture status;" that is, it becomes a quasi-independent new business with its own budget and general manager. Often the product champion becomes the venture manager. Even though there are misgivings expressed about it, this happens naturally. First, for the product champion this constitutes the big, but also the only, reward. Second, there is usually just nobody else around who could take over and continue the momentum of the development process.

Continued impetus depends on the *strategic forcing* efforts of the venture manager level: attaining a significant sales volume and market share position within a limited time horizon.[6] Strategic forcing efforts center

---

[6] The need for strategic forcing is also consistent with the findings that suggest that attaining large market share fast at the cost of early profitability is critical for venture survival. R. Biggadike, "The Risky Business of Diversification," *Harvard Business Review* 57 (May–June 1979), pp. 103–11.

around the original product, process, or system. To implement a strategy of fast growth, the venture manager attracts generalist helpers who can cover a number of different functional areas reasonably well. With the growth of the venture organization and under competitive pressures due to product maturation, efficiency considerations become increasingly important. New functional managers are brought in to replace the generalists. They tend to emphasize the development of routines, standard operating procedures, and the establishment of an administrative framework for the venture. This, however, is time-consuming and detracts from the all-out efforts to grow fast. Thus, the venture manager is increasingly faced with a dilemmatic situation: continuing to force growth versus building the organization of the venture. Growth concerns tend to win out, and organization building is more or less purposefully neglected.

Whilst the venture manager creates a "beachhead" for the new business, the middle level engages in *strategic building* efforts to sustain the impetus process. Such efforts involve the conceptualization of a master strategy for the broader new field within which the venture can fit. They also involve the integration of projects existing elsewhere in the corporation and/or of small firms that can be acquired with the burgeoning venture. These efforts become increasingly important as the strategic forcing activities of the venture manager reach their limit. At the same time, the administrative problems created by the strategic forcing efforts require increasingly the attention of the venture manager's manager. Hence, like the venture manager, the middle-level manager is also confronted with a serious dilemma: focusing on expanding the scope of the new business versus spending time coaching the (often recalcitrant) venture manager and building the organization. Given the overwhelming importance of growth, the coaching activities and organization building tend to be more or less purposefully neglected.

Corporate-level management's decision to *authorize* further resource allocations to a new venture are to a large extent dependent on the credibility of the managers involved. Credibility, in turn, depends primarily on the quantitative results produced. Corporate management tends to develop somewhat unrealistic expectations about new ventures. They send strong signals concerning the importance of making an impact on the overall corporate position soon. This, not surprisingly, reinforces the emphasis of the middle and operational levels of management on achieving growth.

New Product Development Lags Behind The lack of attention to building the administrative framework of the new venture prevents it from developing a continuous flow of new products. Lacking carefully designed relationships between R&D, engineering, marketing, and manufacturing, new product schedules are delayed and completed new products often show serious flaws.

The Demise of the Venture Manager Major discontinuities in new product development put more stress on the middle-level manager to find supplementary products elsewhere to help maintain the growth rate. This, in turn, leads to even less emphasis on coaching the venture manager. The new product development problems also tend to exacerbate the tensions between the venture manager and the functional managers. Eventually, the need to stabilize the venture organization is likely to lead to the demise of the venture manager.

The Indeterminate Strategic Context of ICV

The problems encountered in the core processes of ICV are more readily understood when examining the overlaying processes within which ICV development takes shape. Corporate management's objectives concerning ICV tend to be ambiguous. Top management does not really know which specific new businesses they want until the latter have taken some concrete form and size, and decisions must be made whether to integrate them or not in the corporate portfolio through a process of *retroactive rationalizing.*

Middle-level managers struggle with *delineating* the boundaries of a new business. They are aware that corporate management is interested in broadly defined areas like the "health field" or "energy." But it is only through the middle-level manager's strategic building and the concomitant articulation of a master strategy for the ongoing venture initiatives that the new business fields become concretely delineated and the possible new strategic directions determined.

At the operational level, managers engage in *gatekeeping, idea generating,* and preliminary *bootlegging* activities which may lead to the definition of ICV projects in new areas and/or in new business fields which are already emerging as a result of the ongoing ICV activities. These activities are autonomous because they are basically independent of the current strategy of the firm. Managers at this level have no clear idea at the outset which kinds of ICV projects will be viable in the corporation, but they seem to have a sense for avoiding those that have no chance of receiving support (e.g., because there have been some earlier failures in the area, or there are some potential legal liabilities associated with it).

Determining the Strategic Context   The indeterminateness of the strategic context of ICV requires middle-level managers to engage in *organizational championing* activities.[7] Such activities are of a political nature, and time-consuming. They require an upward orientation (as one venture manager put it) which is very different from the venture manager level's substantive and downward (hands-on) orientation. The middle-level manager must also spend time to work out the frictions with the operating system that may exist when the strategies of the venture and of mainstream businesses interfere with each other. The need for these activities tends to reduce further the amount of time and effort spent by the middle level on coaching the venture manager.

Oscillations of Corporate Strategy   New ventures take between 8 and 12 years on the average to become mature, profitable new businesses.[8] Top management's time horizon, however, is usually limited to three to five years. Corporate management's objectives tend to be shifting: new ventures are viewed by top management as insurance against mainstream business going bad rather than as a corporate objective per se.[9] Middle managers are aware that there are short-term windows for corporate acceptance which must be taken advantage of. This also puts pressure on them to grow new ventures as fast as possible.

**The Selective Pressures
of the Structural Context**

Top management establishes a structural context to support the corporate strategy. The structural context provides strategic actors at operational and middle levels

of management with signals concerning the types of projects that are likely to be supported and rewarded. It operates as a selection mechanism on the strategic behavior in the organization. ICV projects, by definition, fall outside the scope of the current corporate strategy and must overcome the selective pressures of the structural context.

The Incompleteness of the Structural Context   Establishing a separate new venture division facilitates the definition and early impetus processes of ICV projects. But, by itself, the new venture division constitutes an incomplete structural context. In the absence of measurement and reward systems tailored specifically to the requirements of new venture activities, venture managers do not have a clear idea what performance is expected from them except in terms of reaching a large size for their new business fast. Middle-level managers of the new venture division experience resistance from managers in the operating divisions when activities overlap. Ad hoc negotiations and reliance on political savvy substitute for long-term based, joint optimization arrangements. This leads, eventually, to severe friction between ICV and mainstream business activities.[10]

Reactive Changes in the Structural Context   When ICV activities expand beyond a level that corporate management finds opportune to support in light of their assessment of the prospects of mainstream business activities, or when some highly visible failures occur, changes are effected in the structural context to consolidate ICV activities. These changes seem reactive and indicative of the lack of a clear strategy for diversification in the firm.[11]

MANAGING THE CORPORATE CONTEXT OF ICV

The process model suggests that, at the corporate level of analysis, ICV is based on *experimentation and selection,* not a strategic planning process.[12] It is characterized by ambiguity, discontinuity, even an element of anarchy. Having identified some of the major problems in the ICV

---

[7]The importance of the middle-level manager in ICV was already recognized by Von Hippel, "Successful and Failing Internal Corporate Ventures." I. Kusiatin, "The Process and Capacity for Diversification Through Internal Development," doctoral dissertation, Harvard University, 1976; and M. A. Maidique, "Entrepreneurs, Champions, and Technological Innovations," *Sloan Management Review* 21, pp. 59–76, also have discussed the role of a "manager champion" or "executive champion."

[8]Biggadike, "The Risky Business."

[9]R. A. Peterson and D. G. Berger, "Entrepreneurship in Organizations: Evidence from the Popular Music Industry," *Administrative Science Quarterly* 16 (1971), pp. 97–106.

[10]These frictions are discussed in more detail in R. A. Burgelman, "Managing the New Venture Division: Research Findings and Implications for Strategic Management," *Strategic Management Journal* 6 (1985), pp. 39–54.

[11]Ibid.

[12]This argument is further developed in R. A. Burgelman, "Corporate Entrepreneurship and Strategic Management: Insights from a Process Study," *Management Science* 29 (1983), pp. 1349–64.

EXHIBIT 3   Recommendations for Making ICV Strategy Work Better

Levels	Core processes		Overlaying processes	
	Definition	Impetus	Strategic context	Structural context
Corporate management	ICV proposals are evaluated in light of corporate development strategy. Conscious efforts are made to avoid subjection to conventional corporate wisdom.	New venture progress is evaluated in substantive terms by top managers who have experience in organizational championing.	A process is in place for developing a long-term corporate development strategy. This strategy takes shape as a result of an ongoing interactive learning process involving top and middle levels of management.	Managers with successful ICV experience are appointed to top management. Top management is rewarded financially and symbolically for long-term corporate development success.
NVD management	Middle-level managers in corporate R&D are selected who have both technical depth and business knowledge necessary to determine minimum amount of resources for project, and who can coach star players.	Middle-level managers are responsible for the use and development of venture managers as scarce resources of the corporation, and facilitate intrafirm project transfers if the new business strategy warrants it.	Substantive interaction between corporate- and middle-level management leads to clarifying the merits of a new business field in light of the corporate development strategy.	Star performers at middle level are attracted to ICV activities. Collaboration of mainstream middle level with ICV activities is rewarded. Integrating mechanisms can easily be mobilized.
Group leader, Venture leader	Project initiators are encouraged to integrate technical and business perspectives. They are provided access to resources. Project initiators can be rewarded other than by becoming venture managers.	Venture managers are responsible for developing the functional capabilities of emerging venture organizations, and for codification of what has been learned in terms of required functional capabilities while pursuing the new business opportunity.	Slack resources determine the level of the emergence of mutant ideas. Existence of substantive corporate development strategy provides preliminary self-selection of mutant ideas.	A wide array of venture structures and supporting measurement and reward systems clarifies expected performance for ICV personnel.

process, managers can propose recommendations for improving the strategic management of ICV. These can serve to alleviate, if not eliminate, these problems by making the corporate context more hospitable to ICV. Improvement of the overlaying process will, presumably, allow management to focus more on the problems that are inherent in the core processes and less on those that result from having to "fight the system." Exhibit 3 summarizes the recommendations.

Elaborating the Strategic Context of ICV

Top management should recognize that ICV is an important source of strategic renewal for the firm, and not just insurance against poor mainstream business prospects. ICV should therefore be considered an integral and continuous part of the strategy-making process.

The Need for a Corporate Development Strategy   To dampen the oscillations in corporate support for ICV, top

management should create a process for developing an explicit and substantive long-term (10 to 12 years) strategy for corporate development, supported by a resource generation and allocation strategy. Both should be based on ongoing efforts to determine the remaining growth opportunities in the current mainstream businesses and the resource levels necessary to exploit them. Given the corporate objectives for growth and profitability, a resource pool should be reserved for activities outside the mainstream business. This pool should not be affected by short-term fluctuations in current mainstream activities. ICV as well as other types of activities (e.g., acquisitions) should be funded out of this pool. The existence of this pool of slack resources would allow top management to affect the rate at which new venture initiatives will emerge, if not their particular content.[13] This ap-

---

[13] Ibid.

proach reflects a broader concept of strategy making than maintaining corporate R&D at a certain percentage of sales.

Substantive Assessment of Venture Strategies To more effectively determine the strategic context of ICV, and to reduce the political emphasis in organizational championing activities, top management should increase its capacity to make substantive assessments of the merits of new ventures for corporate development. Top management should learn to assess better the strategic importance to corporate development and the degree of relatedness to core corporate capabilities of ICV projects.[14]

One way to achieve this capability is for top management to include members with significant experience in new business development in the top management team. In addition, top management should require middle-level organizational champions to explain how a new field of business would further the corporate development objectives in *substantive* rather than purely numerical terms. Middle-level managers should have to explain how they create value from the *corporate point of view* with the new ventures they sponsor. Operational-level managers would then have a better chance to find out early which of the possible directions their envisaged projects could take and will be more likely to receive corporate support.

Such increased emphasis on the part of top management would not necessarily mean having greater input in the specific directions of exploratory corporate R&D. Rather, it would increase their influence on the *business directions* that grow out of the exploratory R&D substratum.

Refining the Structural Context

Top management also needs to fine-tune the structural context and make it more compatible with the requirements of ICV.

More Deliberate Use of the New Venture Division (NVD) Often, the NVD becomes the recipient of "misfit" and "orphan" projects existing in the operating sys-

tem, and serves as the trial ground for possibly ill-conceived business ideas of the corporate R&D department. In some instances, greater efforts would seem to be in order to assess the possibilities of accommodating new venture initiatives in the mainstream businesses rather than transferring them to the NVD. In other instances, projects should be developed using external venture arrangements or be spun off. Such decisions should be based on an examination of where a project fits in the strategic context. They should be easily implementable by having a wide range of structures for venture-corporation relationships available.

Also, the NVD is a mechanism for *decoupling* the activities of new ventures and those of mainstream businesses. But this decoupling usually cannot be perfect. Hence, integrative mechanisms (e.g., "steering committees") should be established to deal constructively with conflicts that will unavoidably and unpredictably arise.

Finally, top management should facilitate greater acceptance of differences between the management processes of the NVD and the mainstream businesses. This may lead, for instance, to more careful personnel assignment policies and to greater flexibility in hiring and firing policies in the NVD to reflect the special needs of emerging businesses.

Such measures to use the NVD more deliberately (and selectively) will reduce the likelihood of reactive changes in the structural context.

Measurement and Reward Systems in Support of ICV Perhaps the most difficult aspect of the structural context concerns how to provide incentives for top management to seriously and continuously support ICV as part of corporate strategy making. Corporate history writing might be an effective mechanism to achieve this. This would involve the careful tracing and periodical publication (e.g., a special section in annual reports) of decisions whose positive or negative results may become clear only 10 or more years after the fact. Corporate leaders (like political ones) would, presumably, make efforts to preserve their position in corporate history.[15]

To reduce the destructive emphasis on fast growth at middle and operational levels of management, the

---

[14]These two dimensions would seem to be important in deciding what type of arrangements to use. For instance, high strategic importance and high degree of relatedness might suggest the need to integrate the new project directly into the mainstream businesses (even if there is resistance). Very low strategic importance and very low degree of relatedness might suggest complete spin-off as the best approach. The NVD would seem to be most adequate for more ambiguous situations on both dimensions.

[15]Some firms seem to have developed the position of corporate historian. Without underestimating the difficulties such a position is likely to encounter, one can imagine the possibility of structuring it in such a way that the relevant data would be recorded. Another instance, possibly a board-appointed committee, could periodically interpret this data along the lines suggested.

measurement and reward system must be tailored to the special nature of the managerial work involved in ICV. This would mean, for instance, greater emphasis on accomplishments in the areas of problem finding, problem solving, and know-how development than on volume of dollars managed. Efforts to develop the venture organization and the venture manager should also be included. These measures will alleviate the problems resulting from the pressures to grow fast, and more emphasis will be given by middle managers to coaching their venture managers, and to the administrative development problems of new ventures which otherwise tend to be neglected. More flexible systems for measuring and rewarding performance should accompany the greater flexibility in structuring the venture–corporate relations mentioned earlier. In general, the higher the degree of relatedness (the more dependent the new venture is on the firm's resources) and the lower the expected strategic importance for corporate development, the lower the rewards the internal entrepreneurs will be able to negotiate. Milestone points could be agreed upon to revise the negotiations as the venture evolves. To make such processes symmetrical (and more acceptable to the non-entrepreneurial participants in the organization), the internal entrepreneurs should be required to substitute negotiated for regular membership awards and benefits.

Furthermore, to attract "top performers" in the mainstream businesses of the corporation to ICV activities, at least a few spots on the top management team should always be filled with managers who have had significant experience in new business development. This will facilitate the determination of the strategic context and will eliminate the perception that NVD participants are not part of the real world and thus have not much chance to advance in the corporation as a result of ICV experience.[16]

At the operational level, where some managerial failures are virtually unavoidable given the experimentation and selection nature of the ICV process, top management should create a reasonably foolproof safety net. Product champions at this level should not have to feel that running the business is the only possible reward for getting it started. Systematic search for and screening of potential venture managers should make it easier to provide a successor for the product champion *in time*. Avenues for recycling product champions/venture managers should

be developed and/or their reentry into the mainstream businesses facilitated.

MANAGING THE CORE PROCESSES OF ICV

Increasing top management's capacity to manage the corporate context of ICV will, in turn, facilitate the management of the core processes of ICV development. To alleviate some of the specific problems mentioned earlier, some further recommendations can be proposed.

Managing the Definition Process

The ICV projects in my study typically started with an initiative at the group leader level (first-level supervisor) in the corporate R&D department. Such initiatives were rooted in the periphery of the corporate technological capabilities, reflected the creative insight and entrepreneurial drive of the initiator, and were influenced by the latter's perception of the chances of getting the venture eventually accepted by top management as a major new area for the firm.

Of the many ICV projects that start the definition process, only a few reach "venture" status. Some of the ones that do not make it to that transition may find a home for further development as a new product line in one of the operating divisions; others may just be stopped, and result only in an extension of the corporation's knowledge base. Some of the ones that do not make it, however, could possibly have succeeded, and some of the ones that do obtain venture status should not have. Timely assessment of the true potential of an ICV project remains a difficult problem. This follows from the very nature of such projects: the many uncertainties around the technical and marketing aspects of the new business, and the fact that each case is significantly different from all others. These factors make it quite difficult to develop standardized evaluation procedures and development programs without screening to death truly innovative projects.

Managing the definition process effectively thus poses serious challenges for middle-level managers in the corporate R&D department. They must facilitate the integration of technical and business perspectives, and must maintain a lifeline to the technology developed in corporate R&D as the project takes off. As stated earlier, the need for product championing efforts, if excessive, may cut that lifeline early on and lead to severe discontinuities in new product development after the project has reached the venture stage. The middle-level manager's efforts must facilitate both the product championing efforts and the continued development of the technology

---

[16] As some people in my study pointed out, there is no need to take the risks of new business development if you are identified as a star performer. Such performers are put in charge of the large, established businesses where their capabilities will presumably have maximum leverage.

base, by putting the former in perspective and by making sure that the interface between R&D and business people works smoothly.

Facilitating the Integration of R&D—Business Perspectives   To facilitate the integration of technical and business perspectives, the middle manager must understand the operating logic of both groups and must avoid getting bogged down in technical details, yet have sufficient technical depth to be respected by the R&D people. Such managers must be able to motivate the R&D people to collaborate with the business people toward the formulation of business objectives against which progress can be measured. The articulation of business objectives is especially important for the venture's relations with corporate management if the latter become more actively involved in ICV and develop a greater capacity to evaluate the fit of new projects with the corporate development strategy.

Middle-level managers in R&D must be capable to make the two groups give and take in a process of mutual adjustment toward the common goal of advancing the progress of the new business project. One of the key things here is creating mutual respect between technical and business people. Example setting by the R&D manager of showing respect for the business people's contribution is likely to have a carryover effect on the attitudes of the other R&D people. Regular meetings between the two groups to evaluate, as peers, the contribution of the different members of the team is likely to lead to much better integrated efforts.

The Middle Manager as Coach   Such meetings also provide a vehicle for better coaching the product champion. The latter is really the motor of the ICV project in this stage of development. There are some similarities between this role and that of the star player in a sports team. Often, the situation with respect to product champions as star players is viewed in either-or terms: either they can do their thing, and then chances are that we will succeed, but there will be discontinuities, not fully exploited ancillary opportunities, and so on; or, we harness them, and they won't play.

A more balanced approach is possible if the R&D manager uses a process in which the product champion is recognized as the star player, but is, at times, challenged to maintain breadth by having to respond to queries like:

- How is the team benefiting more from this particular action than from others that the team may think to be important?

- How will the continuity of the efforts of the team be preserved?
- What will be the next step?

To back up this approach, the middle manager should have a say in how to reward the members on the team differently. This, of course, refers back to the determination of the structural context, and reemphasizes the importance at the corporate level to recognize that different reward systems are necessary for different types of business activities.

Managing the Impetus Process

Pursuing fast growth and administrative development of the venture simultaneously is a major challenge during the impetus process. This challenge, which exists for any start-up business, is especially difficult for one in the context of an established firm. This is so because managers in ICV, typically, have less control over the selection of key venture personnel yet, at the same time, have more ready access to a wide array of corporate resources.[17] Thus, there is much less pressure on the venture manager and the middle-level manager to show progress in building the organization than there is to show growth.

The Venture Manager as Organization Builder   A more adequate measurement and reward system should force the venture manager to balance the two concerns better. The venture manager should have leeway in hiring and firing decisions but should also be held responsible for the development of new functional capabilities and the administrative framework of the venture. This would reduce the probability of major discontinuities in new product development mentioned earlier. In addition, it will provide the corporation with codified know-how and information which can be transferred to other parts of the firm, or to other new ventures even if the one from which it is derived ultimately fails as a business. Know-how and information thus become important outputs of the ICV process, in addition to sales and profit dollars.

Often, the product champion will not have the required capabilities to achieve these additional objectives. In such cases, the product champion should be warned that the business will probably have to be taken away from him or her at some later date unless the capability to handle the growing complexity of the new business

---

[17] Often, new ventures seem to be used for assigning personnel who do not fit well in the mainstream businesses (or are out of a job there).

organization is demonstrated. The availability of compensatory rewards and of avenues for recycling the venture manager would make it possible for management to tackle deteriorating managerial conditions in the new business organization with greater fortitude. Furthermore, the availability of a competent replacement (as a result of systematic corporate search) may induce the product champion to relinquish the venture rather than see it go under.

The Middle-Level Manager as Corporate Strategist

Increasing the capacity of top management to assess new venture projects will reduce the need for organizational championing and free up time for the middle-level manager for more intensive coaching of the venture manager in his or her efforts to build the venture organization. This aspect of the middle-level manager's job should also be more explicitly considered in the measurement and reward system at this level.

The encouragement of star performers at the middle level to get involved in new business development will also enhance their key role in the development of corporate strategy. By getting deeply involved in new business development, such middle-level managers will not only learn to manage the ICV process, they will also get to know the new businesses which may be part of the mainstream by the time they reach top-level positions. Because new ventures often intersect with multiple parts of mainstream businesses, they will learn what the corporate capabilities and skills—and the shortcomings in them—are, and learn to articulate new strategies and build new businesses based on new combinations of corporate capabilities and skills. This, in turn, may also enhance the realization of the possibilities for new operational synergies existing in the firm. Middle-level managers thus become crucial linking and technology transfer mechanisms in the corporation.

CONCLUSION: NO PANACEAS

The recommendations presented in this paper may make the ICV development a better managed process; that is, one less completely governed by the process of "natural selection." Yet the implication is not that this process can or should become a planned one, or that the fundamentally discontinuous nature of entrepreneurial activity can be avoided. Ultimately, ICV remains an uncomfortable process for the large, complex organization as it upsets its carefully evolved routines and planning mechanisms,

threatens its internal equilibrium of interests, and requires a revision of the very image it has of itself.

The motor of corporate innovation consists of the strategic behaviors of individuals at different levels, willing to put their reputation and their career on the line in the pursuit of the big opportunity. As individuals, they act against and/or in spite of the system; not because they value corner cutting and risk taking per se, but because they must respond to the logic of the situation. And for radical innovation to take place, that logic entails—as Schumpeter posited some 70 years ago—the escape from routine; that is, from the very stuff of which large, complex organizations traditionally are made. Yet, the success of such innovations is ultimately dependent on whether they can become institutionalized. This may pose the most important challenge for managers of large, established firms in the 1980s.

This paper has proposed that managers can make a strategy involving radical innovations work better if they increase their capacity to conceptualize the organization's innovation efforts in process model terms. The recommendations, based on this point of view, should result in a somewhat better use of the individual entrepreneurial resources of the corporation, and thereby in an improvement of the corporate entrepreneurial capability.

APPENDIX: A FIELD STUDY OF ICV

A qualitative method was chosen as the best way to arrive at an encompassing view of the ICV process.

Research Setting

The research was carried out in one large, U.S.-based, high-technology firm of the diversified major type which I shall refer to as GAMMA. GAMMA had traditionally produced and sold various commodities in large volume, but it had also tried to diversify through the internal development of new products, processes, and systems so as to get closer to the final user or consumer and to catch a greater portion of the total value added in the chain from raw materials to end products. During the 1960s, diversification efforts were carried out within existing operating divisions, but in the early 1970s, the company established a separate new venture division (NVD).

Data were obtained on the functioning of the NVD. The charters of its various departments, the job descriptions of the major positions in the division, the reporting relationships and mechanisms of coordination, and the reward system were studied. Data were also obtained on the relationships of the NVD with the rest of the corporation. In particular, the collaboration between the corporate R&D department and divisional R&D groups was studied. Finally, data were also obtained on the role of the NVD in the implementation of the corporate strategy of unrelated diversification. These data describe the historical evolution of the structural context of ICV development at GAMMA before and during the research period.

The bulk of the data was collected in studying the six major ICV projects in progress at GAMMA at the time of the research. These ranged from a case where the business objectives were still being defined to one where the venture had reached a sales volume of $35 million.

Data Collection

In addition to the participants in the six ICV projects, I interviewed NVD administrators, people from several operating divisions, and one person from corporate management. In all, 61 people were interviewed. The interviews were unstructured and took from one and a half to four and a half hours. Tape recordings were not made, but the interviewer took notes in shorthand. The interviewer usually began with an open-ended invitation to tell about work-related activities, then directed the discussion toward three major aspects of the ICV development process: (1) the evolution over time of a project, (2) the involvement of different functional groups in the development process, and (3) the involvement of different hierarchical levels in the development process. Respondents were asked to link particular statements they made to statements of other respondents on the same issues or problems and to give examples, where appropriate. After completing an interview, the interviewer made a typewritten copy of the conversation. All in all, about 435 legal-size pages of typewritten field notes resulted from these interviews.

The research also involved the study of documents. As could be expected, the ICV project participants relied little on written procedures in their day-to-day working relationships with other participants. One key set of documents, however, was the set of written corporate long-range plans concerning the NVD and each of the ICV projects. These official descriptions of the evolution of each project between 1973 and 1977 were compared with the interview data.

Finally, occasional behavioral observations were made, for example, when other people would call or stop by during an interview or in informal discussions during lunch at the research site. These observations, though not systematic, led to the formulation of new questions for further interviews.

READING III-11

Ambidextrous Organizations: Managing Evolutionary and Revolutionary Change

Michael L. Tushman and Charles A. O'Reilly III

All managers face problems in overcoming inertia and implementing innovation and change. But why is this problem such an enduring one? Organizations are filled with sensible people and usually led by smart managers. Why is anything but incremental change often so difficult for the most successful organizations? And why are the patterns of success and failure so prevalent across industries and over time? To remain successful over long periods, managers and organizations must be ambidextrous—able to implement both incremental and revolutionary change.

PATTERNS IN ORGANIZATION EVOLUTION

Across industries there is a pattern in which success often precedes failure. But industry-level studies aren't very helpful for illustrating what actually went wrong. Why are managers sometimes ineffective in making the transition from strength to strength? To understand this we need to look inside firms and understand the forces impinging on management as they wrestle with managing innovation and change. To do this, let's examine the history of two firms, RCA semiconductors and Seiko watches, as they dealt with the syndrome of success followed by failure.

The stark reality of the challenge of discontinuous change can be seen in Exhibit 1. This is a listing of the leading semiconductor firms over a 40-year period. In the mid-1950s, vacuum tubes represented roughly a $700 million market. At this time, the leading firms in the then state-of-the-art technology of vacuum tubes included great technology companies such as RCA, Sylvania, Raytheon, and Westinghouse. Yet between 1955 and 1995, there was almost a complete turnover in industry leadership. With the advent of the transistor, a

Source: Reprinted with permission from *California Management Review*, 38/4 (Summer 1996): 8–30. Some of the ideas contained in this article are elaborated upon in Michael L. Tushman and Charles A. O'Reilly III, *Winning Through Innovation: A Practical Guide to Leading Organizational Change and Renewal* (Boston, MA: Harvard Business School Press, 1997).

EXHIBIT 1 Semiconductor Industry, 1955–1995

1955 (vacuum tubes)	1955 (transistors)	1965 (semiconductors)	1975 (integrated circuits)	1982 (VLSI)	1995 (submicron)
1. R.C.A.	Hughes	TI	TI	Motorola	Intel
2. Sylvania	Transitron	Fairchild	Fairchild	TI	NEC
3. General Electric	Philco	Motorola	National	NEC	Toshiba
4. Raytheon	Sylvania	GI	Intel	Hitachi	Hitachi
5. Westinghouse	TI	GE	Motorola	National	Motorola
6. Amperex	GE	RCA	Rockwell	Toshiba	Samsung
7. National Video	RCA	Sprague	GI	Intel	TI
8. Rawland	Westinghouse	Philco	RCA	Philips	Fujitsu
9. Eimac	Motorola	Transitron	Philips	Fujitsu	Mitsubishi
10. Lansdale	Clevite	Raytheon	AMD	Fairchild	Philips

Source: Adapted from R. Foster, *Innovation. The Attacker's Advantage* (New York, NY: Summit Books, 1986).

major technological discontinuity, we see the beginnings of a remarkable shakeout. By 1965, new firms such as Motorola and Texas Instruments had become important players while Sylvania and RCA had begun to fade. Over the next 20 years still other upstart companies like Intel, Toshiba, and Hitachi became the new leaders while Sylvania and RCA exited the product class.

Why should this pattern emerge? Is it that managers and technologists in 1955 in firms like Westinghouse, RCA, and Sylvania didn't understand the technology? This seems implausible. In fact, many vacuum tube producers did enter the transistor market, suggesting that they not only understood the technology, but saw it as important. RCA was initially successful at making the transition. While from the outside it appeared that they had committed themselves to transistors, the inside picture was very different.

Within RCA, there were bitter disputes about whether the company should enter the transistor business and cannibalize their profitable tube business. On one side, there were reasonable arguments that the transistor business was new and the profits uncertain. Others, without knowing whether transistors would be successful, felt that it was too risky not to pursue the new technology. But even if RCA were to enter the solid-state business, there were thorny issues about how to organize it within the company. How could they manage both technologies? Should the solid-state division report to the head of the electronics group, a person steeped in vacuum tube expertise?

With its great wealth of marketing, financial, and technological resources, RCA decided to enter the business. Historically, it is common for successful firms to experiment with new technologies.[1] Xerox, for example, developed user-interface and software technologies, yet left it to Apple and Microsoft to implement them. West-

ern Union developed the technology for telephony and allowed American Bell (AT&T) to capture the benefits. Almost all relatively wealthy firms can afford to explore new technologies. Like many firms before them, RCA management recognized the problems of trying to play two different technological games but were ultimately unable to resolve them. In the absence of a clear strategy and the cultural differences required to compete in both markets, RCA failed.

In his study of this industry, Richard Foster (then a director at McKinsey & Company) notes,

Of the 10 leaders in vacuum tubes in 1955 only two were left in 1975. There were three variants of error in these case histories. First is the decision not to invest in the new technology. The second is to invest but picking the wrong technology. The third variant is cultural. Companies failed because of their inability to play two games at once: To be both effective defenders of what quickly became old technologies and effective attackers with new technologies.[2]

Senior managers in these firms fell victim to their previous success and their inability to play two games simultaneously. New firms, like Intel and Motorola, were not saddled with this internal conflict and inertia. As they grew, they were able to re-create themselves, while other firms remained trapped.

In contrast to RCA, consider Hattori-Seiko's watch business. While Seiko was the dominant Japanese watch producer in the 1960s, they were a small player in global markets (see Exhibit 2). Bolstered by an aspiration to be a global leader in the watch business, and informed by internal experimentation between alternative oscillation technologies (quartz, mechanical, and tuning fork), Seiko's senior management team made a bold bet. In the mid-1960s, Seiko transformed itself from being merely a

EXHIBIT 2   Employment in the Swiss Watch Industry, 1955–1985

Year	No. of firms	No. of employees
1955	2300	70,000
1965	1900	84,000
1970	1600	89,000
1975	1200	63,000
1980	900	47,000
1985	600	32,000

mechanical watch firm into being both a quartz and mechanical watch company. This move into low-cost, high-quality watches triggered wholesale change within Seiko and, in turn, within the worldwide watch industry. As transistors replaced vacuum tubes (to RCA's chagrin), quartz movement watches replaced mechanical watches. Even though the Swiss had invented both the quartz and tuning fork movements, at this juncture in history they moved to reinvest in mechanical movements. As Seiko and other Japanese firms prospered, the Swiss watch industry drastically suffered. By 1980, SSIH, the largest Swiss watch firm, was less than half the size of Seiko. Eventually, SSIH and Asuag, the two largest Swiss firms, went bankrupt. It would not be until after these firms were taken over by the Swiss banks and transformed by Nicholas Hayek that the Swiss would move to recapture the watch market.

The real test of leadership, then, is to be able to compete successfully by both increasing the alignment or fit among strategy, structure, culture, and processes, while simultaneously preparing for the inevitable revolutions required by discontinuous environmental change. This requires organizational and management skills to compete in a mature market (where cost, efficiency, and incremental innovation are key) *and* to develop new products and services (where radical innovation, speed, and flexibility are critical). A focus on either one of these skill sets is conceptually easy. Unfortunately, focusing on only one guarantees short-term success but long-term failure. Managers need to be able to do both at the same time; that is, they need to be ambidextrous. Juggling provides a metaphor. A juggler who is very good at manipulating a single ball is not interesting. It is only when the juggler can handle multiple balls at one time that his or her skill is respected.

These short examples are only two illustrations of the pattern by which organizations evolve: periods of incremental change punctuated by discontinuous or revolutionary change. Long-term success is marked by increasing alignment among strategy, structure, people,

and culture through incremental or evolutionary change punctuated by discontinuous or revolutionary change that requires the simultaneous shift in strategy, structure, people, and culture. These discontinuous changes are almost always driven either by organizational performance problems or by major shifts in the organization's environment, such as technological or competitive shifts. Where those less successful firms (e.g., SSIH, RCA) react to environmental jolts, those more successful firms proactively initiate innovations that reshape their market (e.g., Seiko).[3]

WHAT'S HAPPENING? UNDERSTANDING PATTERNS OF ORGANIZATIONAL EVOLUTION

These patterns in organization evolution are not unique. Almost all successful organizations evolve through relatively long periods of incremental change punctuated by environmental shifts and revolutionary change. These discontinuities may be driven by technology, competitors, regulatory events, or significant changes in economic and political conditions. For example, deregulation in the financial services and airline industries led to waves of mergers and failures as firms scrambled to reorient themselves to the new competitive environment. Major political changes in Eastern Europe and South Africa have had a similar impact. The combination of the European Union and the emergence of global competition in the automobile and electronics industries has shifted the basis of competition in these markets. Technological change in microprocessors has altered the face of the computer industry.

The sobering fact is that the cliché about the increasing pace of change seems to be true. Sooner or later, discontinuities upset the congruence that has been a part of the organization's success. Unless their competitive environment remains stable—an increasingly unlikely condition in today's world—firms must confront revolutionary change. The underlying cause of this pattern can be found in an unlikely place: evolutionary biology.

Innovation Patterns over Time

For many years, biological evolutionary theory proposed that the process of adaptation occurred gradually over long time periods. The process was assumed to be one of variation, selection, and retention. Variations occurred naturally within species across generations. Those variations that were most adapted to the environment would, over time, enable a species to survive and reproduce. This form would be selected in that it endured while less adaptable forms reproduced less productively and would diminish over time. For instance, if the world became colder and snowier, animals who were whiter and had heavier coats would be advantaged and more likely to survive. As climatic changes affected vegetation, those species with longer necks or stronger beaks might do better. In this way, variation led to adaptation and fitness, which was subsequently retained across generations. In this early view, the environment changed gradually and species adapted slowly to these changes. There is ample evidence that this view has validity.

But this perspective missed a crucial question: What happened if the environment was characterized, not by gradual change, but periodic discontinuities? What about rapid changes in temperature, or dramatic shifts in the availability of food? Under these conditions, a reliance on gradual change was a one-way ticket to extinction. Instead of slow change, discontinuities required a different version of Darwinian theory—that of punctuated equilibria in which long periods of gradual change were interrupted periodically by massive discontinuities. What then? Under these conditions, survival or selection goes to those species with the characteristics needed to exploit the new environment. Evolution progresses through long periods of incremental change punctuated by brief periods of revolutionary or discontinuous change.

So it seems to be with organizations. An entire subfield of research on organizations has demonstrated many similarities between populations of insects and animals and populations of organizations. This field, known as "organizational ecology," has successfully applied models of population ecology to the study of sets of organizations in areas as diverse as wineries, newspapers, automobiles, biotech companies, and restaurants.[4] The results confirm that populations of organizations are subject to ecological pressures in which they evolve through periods of incremental adaptation punctuated by discontinuities. Variations in organizational strategy and form are more or less suitable for different environmental conditions. Those organizations and managers who are most able to adapt to a given market or competitive environment will prosper. Over time, the fittest survive—until there is a major discontinuity. At that point, managers of firms are faced with the challenge of reconstituting their organizations to adjust to the new environment. Managers who try to adapt to discontinuities through incremental adjustment are unlikely to succeed. The processes of variation, selection, and retention that winnow the fittest of animal populations seem to apply to organizations as well.

To understand how this dynamic affects organizations, we need to consider two fundamental ideas; how organizations grow and evolve, and how discontinuities affect this process. Armed with this understanding, we

can then show how managers can cope with evolutionary and revolutionary change.

Organizational Growth and Evolution There is a pattern that describes organizational growth. All organizations evolve following the familiar S-curve shown in Exhibit 3. For instance, consider the history of Apple Computer and how it grew. In its inception, Apple was not so much an organization as a small group of people trying to design, produce, and sell a new product, the personal computer. With success, came the beginnings of a formal organization, assigned roles and responsibilities, some rudimentary systems for accounting and payroll, and a culture based on the shared expectations among employees about innovation, commitment, and speed. Success at this stage was seen in terms of congruence among the strategy, structure, people, and culture. Those who fit the Apple values and subscribed to the cultural norms stayed. Those who found the Jobs and Wozniak vision too cultish left. This early structure was aligned with the strategy and the critical tasks needed to implement it. Success flowed not only from having a new product with desirable features, but also from the ability of the organization to design, manufacture, market, and distribute the new PC. The systems in place tracked those outcomes and processes that were important for the implementation of a single product strategy. Congruence among the elements of the organization is a key to high performance across industries.

As the firm continued its successful growth, several inexorable changes occurred. First, it got larger. As this occurred, more structure and systems were added. Although this trend toward professionalization was resisted by Jobs (who referred to professional managers as "bozos"), the new structures and procedures were required for efficiency and control. Without them, chaos would have reigned. As Apple got older, new norms were developed about what was important and acceptable and what would not be tolerated. The culture changed to reflect the new challenges. Success at Apple and at other firms is based on learning what works and what doesn't.

Inevitably, even Apple's strategy had to change. What used to be a single-product firm (selling the Apple PC and then its successor, the Apple II) now sold a broader range of products in increasingly competitive markets. Instead of a focused strategy, the emphasis shifted to a marketwide emphasis. Not only was Apple selling to personal computer users, but also to the educational and industrial markets. This strategic shift required further adjustment to the structure, people, culture, and critical tasks. What worked in a smaller, more focused firm was

EXHIBIT 3 Punctuated Equilibrium and Organizational Evolution

Over time, the fit among business unit strategy, skills, and culture evolves to reflect changing markets and technology. When these changes occur, managers need to realign their units to reflect their new strategic challenges.

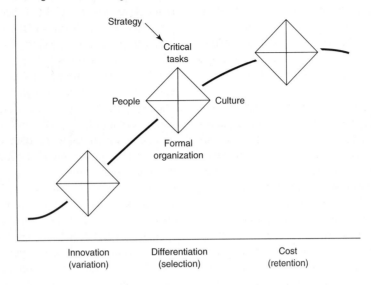

no longer adequate for the larger, more differentiated Apple. Success at this phase of evolution required management's ability to realign the organization to insure congruence with the strategy. The well-publicized ouster of Steve Jobs by Apple's board of directors reflected the board's judgment that John Sculley had the skills necessary to lead a larger, more diversified company. Jobs's approach was fine for a smaller, more focused firm but inappropriate for the challenges Apple faced in the mid-1980s.

Over an even longer period of success, there are inevitably more changes—sometimes driven by technology, sometimes by competition, customers, or regulation, sometimes by new strategies and ways of competing. As the product class matures, the basis of competition shifts. While in the early stages of a product class, competition is based on product variation, in the later stages competition shifts to features, efficiency, and cost. In the evolution of Apple, this can be seen as the IBM PC and the clones emerged. The Windows operating system loosened the grip Apple had maintained on the easy-to-use graphical interface and triggered a battle between three incompatible operating systems—the Mac, IBM's OS/2, and Microsoft Windows. Once Windows became the industry standard in operating systems, the basis of competition shifted to cost, quality and efficiency. Faced with these realities, Apple managers once again had to re-balance the congruence among strategy, struc-

ture, people, and culture. Success comes from being able to outdo the competition in this new environment. So the board of directors replaced Sculley as CEO in 1994 with Michael Spindler, who was seen as having the operational skills needed to run the company in a mature market. Spindler's task was to emphasize the efficiencies and lower margins required in today's markets and reshape Apple to compete in this new market. With Apple's performance stagnant, its board chose a turnaround expert, Gil Amelio, to finish what Spindler could not do.

Notice how Apple evolved over a 20-year period. Incremental or evolutionary change was punctuated by discontinuous or revolutionary change as the firm moved through the three stages of growth in the product class; innovation, differentiation, and maturity. Each of these stages required different competencies, strategies, structures, cultures, and leadership skills. These changes are what drives performance. But while absolutely necessary for short-term success, incremental change is not sufficient for long-term success. It is not by chance that Steve Jobs was successful at Apple until the market became more differentiated and demanded the skills of John Sculley. Nor is it surprising that, as the industry consolidated and competition emphasized costs, operations-oriented managers such as Michael Spindler and, in turn, Gil Amelio were selected to reorient Apple.

To succeed over the long haul, firms have to periodically reorient themselves by adopting new strategies and structures that are necessary to accommodate changing environmental conditions. These shifts often occur through discontinuous changes—simultaneous shifts in strategy, structures, skills, and culture. If an environment is stable and changes only gradually, as is the case in industries such as cement, it is possible for an organization to evolve slowly through continuous incremental change. But many managers have learned (to their stockholders' chagrin) that slow evolutionary change in a fast-changing world is, as it was for the dinosaurs, a path to the boneyard.

Technology Cycles   Although organizational growth by itself can lead to a periodic need for discontinuous change, there is another more fundamental process occurring that results in punctuated change. This is a pervasive phenomenon that occurs across industries and is not widely appreciated by managers. Yet it is critical to understanding when and why revolutionary change is necessary: This is the dynamic of product, service, and process innovation, dominant designs, and substitution events which together make up technology cycles. Exhibit 4 shows the general outline of this process.[5]

In any product or service class (e.g., microprocessors, automobiles, baby diapers, cash management accounts) there is a common pattern of competition that describes the development of the class over time. As shown in Exhibit 4, technology cycles begin with a proliferation of

innovation in products or services as the new product or service gains acceptance. Think, for example, of the introduction of VCRs. Initially, only a few customers bought them. Over time, as demand increased, there was increasing competition between Beta and VHS. At some point, a design emerged that became the standard preferred by customers (i.e., VHS). Once this occurred, the basis of competition shifted to price and features, not basic product or service design. The emergence of this *dominant design* transforms competition in the product class.[6] Once it is clear that a dominant design has emerged, the basis of competition shifts to process innovation, driving down costs, and adding features. Instead of competing through product or service innovation, successful strategies now emphasize compatibility with the standard and productivity improvement. This competition continues until there is a major new product, service, or process substitution event and the technology cycle kicks off again as the basis of competition shifts back again to product or service variation (e.g., CDs replacing audio tapes). As technology cycles evolve, bases of competition shift within the market. As organizations change their strategies, they must also realign their organizations to accomplish the new strategic objectives. This usually requires a revolutionary change.

A short illustration from the development of the automobile will help show how dramatic these changes can

EXHIBIT 4   Two Invisible Forces: Technology Cycles and Evolution

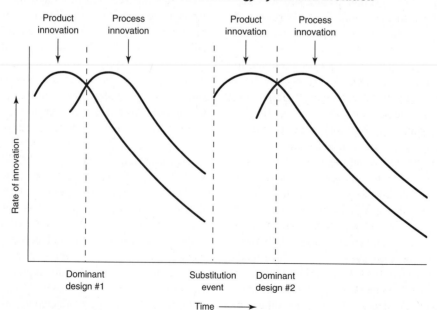

Source: Adapted from J. Utterback, *Mastering the Dynamics of Innovation* (Boston, MA: Harvard Business School Press, 1994).

be for organizations. At the turn of the century, bicycles and horse-driven carriages were threatened by the "horseless carriage," soon to be called the automobile. Early in this new product class there was substantial competition among alternative technologies. For instance, there were several competing alternative energy sources—steam, battery, and internal combustion engines. There were also different steering mechanisms and arrangements for passenger compartments. In a fairly short period of time, however, there emerged a consensus that certain features were to be standard—that is, a dominant design emerged. This consisted of an internal combustion engine, steering wheel on the left (in the U.S.), brake pedal on the right, and clutch on the left (this dominant design was epitomized in the Ford Model T). Once this standard emerged, the basis of competition shifted from variations in what an automobile looked like and how it was powered to features and cost. The new competitive arena emphasized lower prices and differentiated market segments, not product variation. The imperative for managers was to change their strategies and organizations to compete in this market. Those that were unable to manage this transition failed. Similar patterns can be seen in almost all product classes (e.g., computers, telephones, fast foods, retail stores).

With a little imagination, it is easy to feel what the managerial challenges are in this environment. Holding aside the pressures of growth and success, managers must continually readjust their strategies and realign their organizations to reflect the underlying dynamics of technological change in their markets. These changes are not driven by fad or fashion but reflect the imperatives of fundamental change in the technology. This dynamic is a powerful cause of punctuated equilibria and can demand revolutionary rather than incremental change. This pattern occurs across industries as diverse as computers and cement; the only issue is the frequency with which these cycles repeat themselves. Faced with a discontinuity, the option of incremental change is not likely to be viable. The danger is that, facing discontinuous change, firms that have been successful may suffer from life-threatening inertia—inertia that results from the very congruence that made the firm successful in the first place.

THE SUCCESS SYNDROME: CONGRUENCE AS A MANAGERIAL TRAP

Managers, as architects of their organizations, are responsible for designing their units in ways that best fit their strategic challenges. Internal congruence among strategy, structure, culture, and people drives short-term performance.[7] Between 1915 and 1960, General Radio had a strategy of high-quality, high-priced electronic equipment with a loose functional structure, strong internal promotion practices, and engineering dominance in decision making. All these things worked together to provide a highly congruent system and, in turn, a highly successful organization. However, the strategy and organizational congruence that made General Radio a success for 50 years became, in the face of major competitive and technological change, a recipe for failure in the 1960s. It was only after a revolutionary change that included a new strategy and simultaneous shifts in structure, people, and culture that the new company, renamed GenRad, was able to compete again against the likes of Hewlett-Packard and Tektronix.[8]

Successful companies learn what works well and incorporate this into their operations. This is what organizational learning is about; using feedback from the market to continually refine the organization to get better and better at accomplishing its mission. A lack of congruence (or internal inconsistency in strategy, structure, culture, and people) is usually associated with a firm's current performance problems. Further, since the fit between strategy, structure, people, and processes is never perfect, achieving congruence is an ongoing process requiring continuous improvement and incremental change. With evolutionary change, managers are able to incrementally alter their organizations. Given that these changes are comparatively small, the incongruence injected by the change is controllable. The process of making incremental changes is well known and the uncertainty created for people affected by such changes is within tolerable limits. The overall system adapts, but it is not transformed.

When done effectively, evolutionary change of this sort is a crucial part of short-term success. But there is a dark side to this success. As we described with Apple, success resulted in the company becoming larger and older. Older, larger firms develop structural and cultural inertia—the organizational equivalent of high cholesterol. Exhibit 5 shows the paradox of success. As companies grow, they develop structures and systems to handle the increased complexity of the work. These structures and systems are interlinked so that proposed changes become more difficult, more costly, and require more time to implement, especially if they are more than small, incremental modifications. This results in *structural inertia*—a resistance to change rooted in the size, complexity, and interdependence in the organization's structures, systems, procedures, and processes.

EXHIBIT 5   The Success Syndrome

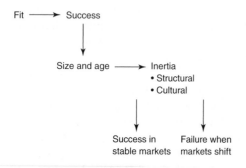

Quite different and significantly more pervasive than structural inertia is the *cultural inertia* that comes from age and success. As organizations get older, part of their learning is embedded in the shared expectations about how things are to be done. These are sometimes seen in the informal norms, values, social networks and in myths, stories, and heroes that have evolved over time. The more successful an organization has been, the more institutionalized or ingrained these norms, values, and lessons become. The more institutionalized these norms, values, and stories are, the greater the cultural inertia—the greater the organizational complacency and arrogance. In relatively stable environments, the firm's culture is a critical component of its success. Culture is an effective way of controlling and coordinating people without elaborate and rigid formal control systems. Yet, when confronted with discontinuous change, the very culture that fostered success can quickly become a significant barrier to change. When Lou Gerstner took over as CEO at IBM, he recognized that simply crafting a new strategy was not the solution to IBM's predicament. In his view, "Fixing the culture is the most critical—and the most difficult—part of a corporate transformation."[9] Cultural inertia, because it is so ephemeral and difficult to attack directly, is a key reason managers often fail to successfully introduce revolutionary change—even when they know that it is needed.

THE PARADOX OF CULTURE

The paradox of culture in helping or hindering companies as they compete can be seen in many ways. Consider, for example, the list of companies shown in Exhibit 6. These are firms about which there have recently been stories in the business press and in which the culture of the firm was seen as a part of the organization's success or failure. What is notable about this list is its diversity. The importance of organizational culture transcends country, industry, and firm size. Whether they are electronics giant Samsung, a Hong Kong bank, U.S. conglomerate Allied Signal, a high-tech firm such as Applied Materials or a low-tech company such as Nordstrom, or car manufacturers Nissan, Rover, or General Motors, culture appears to be a critical factor in the performance of the company. The language used in describing the importance of culture is often similar. Yukata Kume, president of Nissan, observed:

> The most challenging task I faced when I became president five years ago was to reform the corporate culture. . . . I decided that the major reason for our suffering or business predicament lay within Nissan itself.[10]

Jack Welch at GE commented on the future demands on organizations: "In the nineties the heroes, the winners, will be entire companies that have developed cultures that instead of fearing the pace of change, relish it."[11]

While news articles about successes and failures are not proof of anything, they offer an interesting window on the concerns of practicing managers and savvy journalists. Whether the issue is can Nike successfully export its "Just do it" culture to help drive global growth, or can Nokia, a Finnish maker of mobile phones, shed its stodgy culture in time to compete in the fast-moving telecommunications market, the managerial challenges are similar: How can managers diagnose and actively shape organizational cultures to both execute today's strategies and create the capabilities to innovate for tomorrow's competitive demands? To help focus and frame the crucial issue of managing culture, let's reflect on a few examples in which organizational culture helped firms succeed or was a significant part of their problem in adapting to new circumstances.

Here's the Good News

First, consider the remarkable transformation of British Airways. In 1981, British Airways lost almost $1 billion. Their customers often referred to the airline's initials "BA" as standing for "Bloody Awful." Ask any frequent flyer for his or her experiences on BA during this period and horror stories will emerge. Even the employees were embarrassed. One employee acknowledged that "I remember going to parties in the late 1970s, and if you wanted to have a civilized conversation, you didn't actually say that you worked for British Airways, because it got you talking about people's last travel experience, which was usually an unpleasant one."[12] When the announcement was made by the British government that the firm was to be privatized, the *Financial Times* newspaper sniffed that it might be that some investors would

EXHIBIT 6   Firms Recently Mentioned in the Business Press

Culture as a factor in success or difficulty

Hewlett-Packard	British Airways	Federal Express
Oki Electric	Kodak	Sears
Johnson & Johnson	Allied Signal	Deutsche Bank
General Electric	Home Depot	Pepsico
Silicon Graphics	McKinsey	Philips
Motorola	Royal Dutch/Shell	Bausch & Lomb
Levi Strauss	Southwest Airlines	Applied Materials
Microsoft	PPG	General Motors
Samsung	Nike	Wal-Mart
Siemens	Saturn	Boeing
Nordstrom	IBM	Nissan
Procter & Gamble	Tenneco	Rover
Coca Cola	Broken Hill Proprietary	Ford
Lucky-Goldstar	Goldman, Sachs	NUMMI
SBC Warburg	Westinghouse	United Airlines
Apple	Bear Stearns	British Petroleum
Swiss Bank Corp	Rubbermaid	Unilever
Nokia	Matsushita	Salomon
Intel	Chrysler	Kao
Aetna	Medtronics	

buy the stock, but only because "every market has a few masochists."

A scant five years later, however, BA's profits were the highest in the industry, 94 percent of its employees bought stock in 1987 when the firm went public, and passengers were making statements like the following: "I can't tell you how my memory of British Airways as a company and the experience I had 10 years ago contrasts with today. The improvement in service is truly remarkable." What accounts for this turnaround? The answer is largely to be found in the cultural revolution engineered by top management, Lord King, and Sir Colin Marshall.

After deciding that they were in the service business rather than the transportation business, British Airways put virtually its entire 37,000 person workforce through a two-day culture change program entitled "Putting People First." Almost all of the 1,400 managers went through a five-day version entitled "Managing People First" (MPF). On the surface this program is not conceptually unique. What separates MPF from most management training sessions is its magnitude, the consistency with which it was applied, and the support of top management. Colin Marshall, the chief executive officer, has called it the "single most important program now in operation" at BA and has addressed almost all of the 64 MPF classes.[13]

The emphasis on the culture change effort at BA was on instilling the new culture, establishing an evaluation scheme that measured not only what managers did but how they did it, and a compensation program with bonuses up to 20 percent based on how managers behave. Managers at BA appreciate that any airline can load passengers on a plane and fly them across the Atlantic. BA understands that they are in the service business and any competitive advantage has to be in the service they offer customers. As Bob Nelson, head of the program, noted, "The issue with customer service is that you can train monkeys to smile and make eye-contact, but what the hell do you do when you get a nonstandard requirement?"[14]

With essentially the same workforce, flying largely the same routes, and using the same technology, British Airways has become one of the world's leading airlines. Its competitive advantage is not in strategy or technology but in a culture shared throughout the organization that provides a level of service that competitors have found difficult to imitate. The lesson that we need to explore is how senior managers were successful in managing the culture to provide competitive advantage. What was it that they did that their competitors have been unable to do?

Similar success stories abound. Consider a phenomenon in the retail clothing industry, Nordstrom. While firms like Federated, Macy's, and Carter-Hawley-Hale have wrestled with bankruptcy, Nordstrom has grown from 36 stores and 9,000 employees in 1983 to 76 stores and over 35,000 employees by 1995, with average sales per square foot double the industry average. What accounts for Nordstrom's competitive advantage? A close reading of the strategy literature will quickly suggest that it is not the usual factors such as barriers to entry, power over suppliers and customers, or lack of industry rivalry. The retail industry is quite competitive and buyers and suppliers move easily from one firm to another. It isn't location, merchandise, appearance of the stores, or even the piano in the lobby. Each of these is easily imitable. Rather, as anyone who has shopped Nordstrom knows, it is the remarkable service that Nordstrom provides that differentiates it from its competitors. To deliver this service, Nordstrom relies not on the extensive formal controls manifest in policies, procedures, and close supervision, but rather on its culture, which is characterized by a set of norms and values that provide for a *social* control system. This social control system is used to coordinate activities in the face of the need for change and allows Nordstrom to meet the nonstandard requirements that are the true test of service.

Here's the Bad News

Until now we have told happy stories, ones in which managers have successfully used organizational culture to provide competitive advantage. But there are equally unhappy stories to tell as well; ones in which the culture of the firm is sometimes linked to failure. And, as suggested earlier, the paradox is often that it is the culture associated with the earlier success of the firm that becomes a part of its downfall. Think briefly about two icons of American business success and the difficulties they currently face: IBM and Sears. (While we use IBM and Sears, the phenomenon is worldwide.)

Between 1990 and 1993, IBM lost a total of $14 billion, with an $8.1 billion loss in 1993 alone. How could this happen? Certainly the computer business is a complex one. IBM was and is a very large firm, which complicates the decision-making process. Nevertheless, numerous presumably smart people were employed specifically to anticipate changes and insure that the firm was prepared to meet them. How, then, can we account for this failure, a failure that has cost almost 200,000 people their jobs and shareholders a loss of billions of dollars? It would be wrong to underestimate the complex difficulties in managing a firm of IBM's size. Certainly the answer must include aspects of strategy, organizational design, technology, and people.

However, perhaps the most important part of the answer to this question, and certainly a part of any solution, is in the culture of IBM; a culture characterized by an inward focus, extensive procedures for resolving issues through consensus and "push back," an arrogance bred by previous success, and a sense of entitlement that guar-

anteed jobs without a reciprocal *quid pro quo* by some employees. This culture—masquerading under the old IBM basic beliefs in excellence, customer satisfaction, and respect for the individual—was manifest in norms that led to a preoccupation with internal procedures rather than understanding the reality of the changing market. In his letter to the shareholders in the 1993 annual report, CEO Lou Gerstner states, "We have been too bureaucratic and too preoccupied with our own view of the world." He sees as one of his toughest and most critical tasks to change this entrenched and patriarchical culture into one characterized by a sense of urgency. Without this shift, he believes IBM will continue to squander its talent and technology.

While occurring in a very different industrial context, a similar drama is playing out at Sears, the great American retailer. Again, the picture is a complicated one and it would be wrong to oversimplify it. The broad outlines of the problem are, however, easily visible. Until 1991, Sears was the largest retailer in the United States with over 800 stores and 500,000 employees, including over 6,000 at headquarters in the Sears Tower in Chicago. For decades it was the family department store for America, a place where one could buy everything from clothes to tools to kitchen appliances. However, by the mid-1980s, trouble had begun to surface. Market share had fallen 15 percent from its high in the 70s, the stock price had dropped by 40 percent since Edward Brennan had become CEO in 1985, and chronic high costs hindered Sears from matching the prices of competitors such as Wal-Mart, Kmart, Circuit City, the Home Depot, and other low-cost specialty stores.[15]

Under Brennan's leadership, Sears made a number of strategic changes in attempts to halt the slide. Yet the execution of the strategy was dismal. Observers and analysts attributed the failure to Brennan's inability to revamp the old Sears culture that, as one respected analyst noted, was a

> culture rooted in a long tradition of dominating the retailing industry. . . . But this success bred in Sears executives an arrogance and an internal focus that was almost xenophobic." Another observed that "the main problem with Sears is that its managers and executives are 'Sears-ized'—so indoctrinated in the lore of past glories and so entrenched in an overwhelming bureaucracy that they cannot change easily.[16]

The old Sears culture, like the old IBM culture, was a product of their success: proud, inward-looking, and resistant to change.

The lesson is a simple one: organizational culture is a key to both short-term success *and,* unless managed correctly, long-term failure. Culture can provide competitive advantage, but as we have seen, it can also create obstacles to the innovation and change necessary to be successful. In the face of significant changes in technology, regulation, or competition, great managers understand this dynamic and effectively manage *both* the short-term demands for increasing congruence and bolstering today's culture *and* the periodic need to transform their organization and re-create their unit's culture. These organizational transformations involve fundamental shifts in the firm's structure and systems as well as in its culture and competencies. Where change in structure and systems is relatively simple, change in culture is not. The issue of actively managing organization cultures that can handle both incremental and discontinuous change is perhaps the most demanding aspect in the management of strategic innovation and change.

AMBIDEXTROUS ORGANIZATIONS: MASTERING EVOLUTIONARY AND REVOLUTIONARY CHANGE

The dilemma confronting managers and organizations is clear. In the short run they must constantly increase the fit or alignment of strategy, structure, and culture. This is the world of evolutionary change. But this is not enough for sustained success. In the long run, managers may be required to destroy the very alignment that has made their organizations successful. For managers, this means operating part of the time in a world characterized by periods of relatively stability and incremental innovation, and part of the time in a world characterized by revolutionary change. These contrasting managerial demands require that managers periodically destroy what has been created in order to reconstruct a new organization better suited for the next wave of competition or technology.[17]

Ambidextrous organizations are needed if the success paradox is to be overcome. The ability to simultaneously pursue both incremental and discontinuous innovation and change results from hosting multiple contradictory structures, processes, and cultures within the same firm. There are good examples of companies and managers who have succeeded in balancing these tensions. To illustrate more concretely how firms can do this, consider three successful ambidextrous organizations. Hewlett-Packard (HP), Johnson & Johnson (J&J), and ABB (Asea Brown Boveri). Each of these has been able to compete in mature market segments through incremental innovation and in emerging markets and technologies through discontinuous innovation. Each has been successful at

winning by engaging in both evolutionary and revolutionary change.

At one level they are very different companies. HP competes in markets like instruments, computers, and networks. J&J is in consumer products, pharmaceuticals, and professional medical products ranging from sutures to endoscopic surgical equipment. ABB sells power plants, electrical transmission equipment, transportation systems, and environmental controls. Yet each of them has been able to be periodically renew itself and to produce streams of innovation. HP has gone from an instrument company to a minicomputer firm to a personal computer and network company. J&J has moved from consumer products to pharmaceuticals. ABB transformed itself from a slow heavy engineering company based primarily in Sweden and Switzerland to an aggressive global competitor with major investments in Eastern Europe and the Far East. In spite of their differences, each has been ambidextrous in similar ways.

Organizational Architectures

Although the combined size of these three companies represents over 350,000 employees, each has found a common way to remain small by emphasizing autonomous groups. For instance, J&J has over 165 separate operating companies that scramble relentlessly for new products and markets. ABB relies on over 5,000 profit centers with an average of 50 people in each. These centers operate like small businesses. HP has over 50 separate divisions and a policy of splitting divisions whenever a unit gets larger than a thousand or so people. The logic in these organizations is to keep units small and autonomous so that employees feel a sense of ownership and are responsible for their own results. This encourages a culture of autonomy and risk taking that could not exist in a large, centralized organization. In the words of Ralph Larsen, CEO of J&J, this approach "provides a sense of ownership and responsibility for a business you simply cannot get any other way."[18]

But the reliance on small, autonomous units is not gained at the expense of firm size or speed in execution. These companies also retain the benefits of size, especially in marketing and manufacturing. ABB continually reevaluates where it locates its worldwide manufacturing sites. J&J uses its brand name and marketing might to leverage new products and technologies. HP uses its relationships with retailers developed from its printer business to market and distribute its new personal computer line. But these firms accomplish this without the top-heavy staffs found at other firms. Barnevik reduced

ABB's hierarchy to four levels and a headquarters staff of 150 and purposely keeps the structure fluid. At J&J headquarters, there are roughly a thousand people, but no strategic planning is done by corporate. The role of the center is to set the vision and review the performance of the 165 operating companies. At HP, the former CEO, John Young, recognized in the early 1990s that the more centralized structure that HP had adopted in the 1980s to coordinate their mini-computer business had resulted in a suffocating bureaucracy that was no longer appropriate. He wiped it out, flattening the hierarchy and dramatically reducing the role of the center.

In these companies, size is used to leverage economies of scale and scope, not to become a checker and controller that slows the organization down. The focus is on keeping decisions as close to the customer or the technology as possible. The role of headquarters is to facilitate operations and make them go faster and better. Staff have only the expertise that the field wants and needs. Reward systems are designed to be appropriate to the nature of the business unit and emphasize results and risk taking. Barnevik characterizes this as his 7-3 formula; better to make decisions quickly and be right 7 out of 10 times than waste time trying to find a perfect solution. At J&J this is expressed as a tolerance for certain types of failure; a tolerance that extends to congratulating managers who take informed risks, even if they fail. There is a delicate balance among size, autonomy, teamwork, and speed which these ambidextrous organizations are able to engineer. An important part of the solution is massive decentralization of decision making, but with consistency attained through individual accountability, information sharing, and strong financial control. But why doesn't this result in fragmentation and a loss of synergy? The answer is found in the use of social control.

Multiple Cultures

A second commonality across these firms is their reliance on strong social controls.[19] They are simultaneously tight and loose. They are tight in that the corporate culture in each is broadly shared and emphasizes norms critical for innovation such as openness, autonomy, initiative, and risk taking. The culture is loose in that the manner in which these common values are expressed varies according to the type of innovation required. At HP, managers value the openness and consensus needed to develop new technologies. Yet when implementation is critical, managers recognize that this consensus can be fatal. One senior manager in charge of bringing out a new workstation prominently posted a sign saying, "This is not a democracy." At J&J, the emphasis on autonomy

allows managers to routinely go against the wishes of senior management, sometimes with big successes and sometimes with failures. Yet in the changing hospital supply sector of their business, managers recognized that the cherished J&J autonomy was stopping these companies from coordinating the service demanded by their hospital customers. So, in this part of J&J, a decision was made to take away some of the autonomy and centralize services. CEO Larsen refers to this as J&J companies having common standards but unique personalities.

A common overall culture is the glue that holds these companies together. The key in these firms is a reliance on a strong, widely shared corporate culture to promote integration across the company and to encourage identification and sharing of information and resources—something that would never occur without shared values. The culture also provides consistency and promotes trust and predictability. Whether it is the Credo at J&J, the HP Way, or ABB's Policy Bible, these norms and values provide the glue that keeps these organizations together. Yet, at the same time, individual units entertain widely varying subcultures appropriate to their particular businesses. For example, although the HP Way is visible in all HP units worldwide, there are distinct differences between the new video server unit and an old-line instrument division. What constitutes risk taking at a mature division differs from the risk taking emphasized at a unit struggling with a brand new technology. At J&J, the Credo's emphasis on customers and employees can be seen as easily in the Philippines as in corporate headquarters in New Brunswick, New Jersey. But the operating culture in the Tylenol division is distinctly more conservative than the culture in a new medical products company.

This tight-loose aspect of the culture is crucial for ambidextrous organizations. It is supported by a common vision and by supportive leaders who both encourage the culture and know enough to allow appropriate variations to occur across business units. These companies promote both local autonomy and risk taking and ensure local responsibility and accountability through strong, consistent financial control systems. Managers aren't second-guessed by headquarters. Strategy flows from the bottom up. Thus, at HP the $7 billion printer business emerged not because of strategic foresight and planning at HP's headquarters, but rather due to the entrepreneurial flair of a small group of managers who had the freedom to pursue what was believed to be a small market. The same approach allows J&J and ABB to enter small niche markets or develop unproven technologies without the burdens of a centralized bureaucratic control system. On the other hand, in return for the autonomy they are granted, there are strong expectations of performance. Managers who don't deliver are replaced.

Ambidextrous Managers

Managing units that pursue widely different strategies and that have varied structures and cultures is a juggling act not all managers are comfortable with. At ABB, this role is described as "preaching and persuading." At HP, managers are low-key, modest team players who have learned how to manage this tension over their long tenures with the company. At HP, they also lead by persuasion. "As CEO my job is to encourage people to work together, to experiment, to try things, but I can't order them to do it," says Lew Platt.[20] Larsen at J&J echoes this theme, emphasizing the need for lower level managers to come up with solutions and encouraging reasonable failures. Larsen claims that the role is one of a symphony conductor rather than a general.

One of the explanations for this special ability is the relatively long tenure managers have in these organizations and the continual reinforcement of the social control system. Often, these leaders are low-keyed but embody the culture and act as visible symbols of it. As a group the senior team continually reinforces the core values of autonomy, teamwork, initiative, accountability, and innovation. They ensure that the organization avoids becoming arrogant and remains willing to learn from its competitors. Observers of all three of these companies have commented on their modesty or humility in constantly striving to renew themselves. Rather than becoming complacent, these organizations are guided by leaders who venerate the past but are willing to change continuously to meet the future.

The bottom line is that ambidextrous organizations learn by the same mechanism that sometimes kills successful firms: variation, selection, and retention. They promote variation through strong efforts to decentralize, to eliminate bureaucracy, to encourage individual autonomy and accountability, and to experiment and take risks. This promotes wide variations in products, technologies, and markets. It is what allows the managers of an old HP instrument division to push their technology and establish a new division dedicated to video servers. These firms also select "winners" in markets and technologies by staying close to their customers, by being quick to respond to market signals, and by having clear mechanisms to "kill" products and projects. This selection process allowed the development of computer printers at HP to move from a venture that was begun without formal approval to the point where it now accounts for almost 40 percent of HP's profits. Finally, technologies, products, markets, and even senior managers are retained by the market, not by a remote, inwardly focused central staff many hierarchical levels removed from real customers. The corporate vision provides the compass by which senior managers can make decisions about which of the many alternative businesses and technologies to invest in, but the market is the ultimate arbiter of the winners and losers. Just as success or failure in the marketplace is Darwinian, so too is the method by which ambidextrous organizations learn. They have figured out how to harness this power within their companies and organize and manage accordingly.

SUMMARY

Managers must be prepared to cannibalize their own business at times of industry transitions. While this is easy in concept, these organizational transitions are quite difficult in practice. Success brings with it inertia and dynamic conservatism. Four hundred years ago, Niccolò Machiavelli noted:

> There is no more delicate matter to take in hand, nor more dangerous to conduct, nor more doubtful in its success, than to be a leader in the introduction of changes. For he who innovates will have for enemies all those who are well off under the old order of things, and only lukewarm supporters in those who might be better off under the new.[21]

While there are clear benefits to proactive change, only a small minority of farsighted firms initiate discontinuous change before a performance decline. Part of this stems from the risks of proactive change. One reason for RCA's failure to compete in the solid-state market or for SSIH's inability to compete in quartz movements came from the divisive internal disputes over the risks of sacrificing a certain revenue stream from vacuum tubes and mechanical watches for the uncertain profits from transistors and quartz watches. However, great managers are willing to take this step. Andy Grove of Intel puts it succinctly, "There is at least one point in the history of any company when you have to change dramatically to rise to the next performance level. Miss the moment and you start to decline."[22]

NOTES

1. A. Cooper and C. Smith, "How Established Firms Respond to Threatening Technologies," *Academy of Management Executive*, 16/2 (1992): 92–120.

2. R. Foster, *Innovation: The Attacker's Advantage* (New York, NY: Summit Books, 1986), p. 134.

3. B. Virany, M. Tushman, and E. Romanelli, "Executive Succession and Organization Outcomes in Turbulent Environments," *Organization Science,* 3 (1992): 72–92; E. Romanelli and M. Tushman, "Organization Transformation as Punctuated Equilibrium," *Academy of Management Journal,* 37 (1994): 1141–1166; M. Tushman and L. Rosenkopf, "On the Organizational Determinants of Technological Change: Towards a Sociology of Technological Evolution," in B. Staw and L. Cummings, eds., *Research in Organization Behavior,* Vol. 14 (Greenwich, CT: JAI Press, 1992); D. Miller, "The Architecture of Simplicity," *Academy of Management Review,* 18 (1993): 116–138; A. Meyer, G. Brooks, and J. Goes, "Environmental Jolts and Industry Revolutions," *Strategic Management Journal,* 6 (1990): 48–76.

4. There is an extensive literature studying organizations using models from population ecology. A number of excellent reviews of this approach are available in M. Hannan and G. Carroll, *Dynamics of Organizational Populations* (New York, NY: Oxford University Press, 1992); G. Carroll and M. Hannan, eds., *Organizations in Industry: Strategy, Structure & Selection* (New York, NY: Oxford University Press, 1995); and J. Baum and J. Singh, eds., *Evolutionary Dynamics of Organizations* (New York, NY: Oxford University Press, 1994).

5. M. Tushman and L. Rosenkopf, "On the Organizational Determinants of Technological Change: Towards a Sociology of Technological Evolution," in B. Staw and L. Cummings, eds., *Research in Organization Behavior,* Vol. 14 (Greenwich, CT: JAI Press, 1992); M. Tushman and P. Anderson, "Technological Discontinuities and Organization Environments," *Administrative Science Quarterly,* 31 (1986): 439–465; W. Abernathy and K. Clark, "Innovation: Mapping the Winds of Creative Destruction," *Research Policy,* 1985, pp. 3–22; J. Wade, "Dynamics of Organizational Communities and Technological Bandwagons," *Strategic Management Journal,* 16 (1995): 111–133; J. Baum and H. Korn, "Dominant Designs and Population Dynamics in Telecommunications Services," *Social Science Research,* 24 (1995): 97–135.

6. For a more complete treatment of this subject, see J. Utterback, *Mastering the Dynamics of Innovation* (Boston, MA: Harvard Business School Press, 1994). See also R. Burgelman & A. Grove, "Strategic Dissonance," *California Management Review,* 38/2 (Winter 1996): 8–28.

7. D. Nadler and M. Tushman, *Competing by Design* (New York, NY: Oxford University Press, in press); D. Nadler and M. Tushman, "Beyond Charismatic Leaders: Leadership and Organization Change," *California Management Review* (Winter 1990): 77–90.

8. See M. Tushman, W. Newman, and E. Romanelli, "Convergence and Upheaval: Managing the Unsteady Pace of Organizational Evolution," *California Management Review,* 29/1 (Fall 1986): 29–44.

9. L. Hays, "Gerstner Is Struggling as He Tries to Change Ingrained IBM Culture," *Wall Street Journal,* May 13, 1994.

10. J. Kotter and N. Rothbard, "Cultural Change at Nissan Motors," *Harvard Business School Case,* #9-491-079, July 28, 1993.

11. "Today's Leaders Look to Tomorrow," *Fortune,* March 26, 1990, p. 31.

12. J. Leahey, "Changing the Culture at British Airways," *Harvard Business School Case,* #9-491-009, 1990.

13. L. Bruce, "British Airways Jolts Staff with a Cultural Revolution," *International Management,* March 7, 1987, pp. 36–38.

14. Ibid.

15. See, for example, D. Katz, *The Big Store: Inside the Crisis and Revolution at Sears* (New York, NY: Viking, 1987); S. Caminiti, "Sears' Need: More Speed," *Fortune,* July 15, 1991, pp. 88–90.

16. S. Strom, "Further Prescriptions for the Convalescent Sears," *New York Times,* October 10, 1992.

17. D. Hurst, *Crisis and Renewal* (Boston, MA: Harvard Business School Press, 1995); R. Burgelman, "Intraorganizational Ecology of Strategy Making and Organizational Adaptation," *Organizational Science,* 2/3 (1991): 239–262; K. Eisenhardt and B. Tabrizi, "Acceleration Adaptive Processes," *Administrative Science Quarterly,* 40/1 (1995): 84–110; J. Morone, *Winning in High Tech Markets* (Boston, MA: Harvard Business School Press, 1993); M. Iansiti and K. Clark, "Integration and Dynamic Capability," *Industry and Corporation Change,* 3/3 (1994): 557–606; D. Leonard-Barton, *Wellsprings of Knowledge* (Boston, MA: Harvard Business School Press, 1995).

18. J. Weber, "A Big Company That Works," *Business Week,* May 4, 1992, p. 125.

19. See C. O'Reilly, "Corporations, Culture, and Commitment: Motivation and Social Control in Organizations," *California Management Review,* 31/4 (Summer 1989): 9–25; or C. O'Reilly and J. Chatman, "Culture as Social Control: Corporations, Cults, and Commitment," in B. Staw and L. Cummings, eds., *Research in Organizational Behavior,* Vol. 18 (Greenwich, CT: JAI Press, 1996).

20. A Deutschman, "How HP Continues to Grow and Grow," *Fortune,* May 2, 1994, p. 100.

21. N. Machiavelli, *The Prince,* translated by L.P.S. de Alvarez (Dallas, TX: University of Dallas Press, 1974).

22. S. Sherman, "Andy Grove: How Intel Makes Spending Pay Off," *Fortune,* February 22, 1993, p. 58.

ENACTMENT OF TECHNOLOGY STRATEGY— CREATING AND IMPLEMENTING A DEVELOPMENT STRATEGY

In technology-intensive environments, development projects are where the action is. They're where the "rubber meets the road." Through a combination of product and process enhancement activities development projects can provide a host of benefits for an organization. First, they can lead to market success in a rapidly changing, intensely competitive setting. New products and their associated manufacturing processes and delivery systems can leapfrog the competition, create strong barriers that

939

others must hurdle just to stay in the game, and establish a leadership position as a dominant design. Furthermore, they can be the vehicle for entering new distribution channels and garnering new customers, and they can complement existing offerings by rounding out the line and targeting untapped niches.

Nearly as important as the promise of market success is the impact that effectively executed development projects can have on resource utilization: They not only capitalize on prior research efforts, but also leverage and enhance existing assets. What sales force or factory won't perform better with a new product that is hot in the marketplace than with an old, no longer distinctive product? Additionally, new products and new processes provide the means for an organization to overcome past weaknesses and establish an even stronger resource base for the future.

Still a third area of promise associated with the commercialization of new products and processes is that of organizational renewal and change. Organizations consist of people, and people become excited when they see growth opportunities being captured by new products and processes. Furthermore, the adoption and implementation of new technologies that transform aging assets can enable a business to recruit, train, and develop better people than its competitors. Being part of the team that succeeds in achieving its development goals is rewarding and fulfilling.

Unfortunately, far too often the reality surrounding many development projects is that although they begin with great expectations on the part of all involved, they fall far short in the end. See Exhibit 1 as an example. Even projects with milestone dates, resource plans, and aggressive market goals often slip as they encounter unexpected problems and organizational miscues, arriving late and no longer on target for the marketplace.

Why is it that so many development projects fail to deliver fully on their planned goals and anticipated benefits? Why do firms—even those that explicitly recognize the importance of product development—find it so challenging to focus resources

EXHIBIT 1   The Reality of Many Development Projects: Schedule Slippage in the A14 Stereo Project

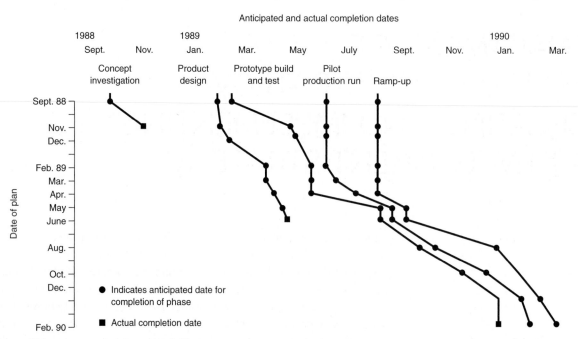

Source: Adapted from S. C. Wheelwright and K. B. Clark, *Revolutionizing Product Development* (New York: Free Press, 1992), p. 11.

EXHIBIT 2   Timing and Impact of Management Attention and Influence

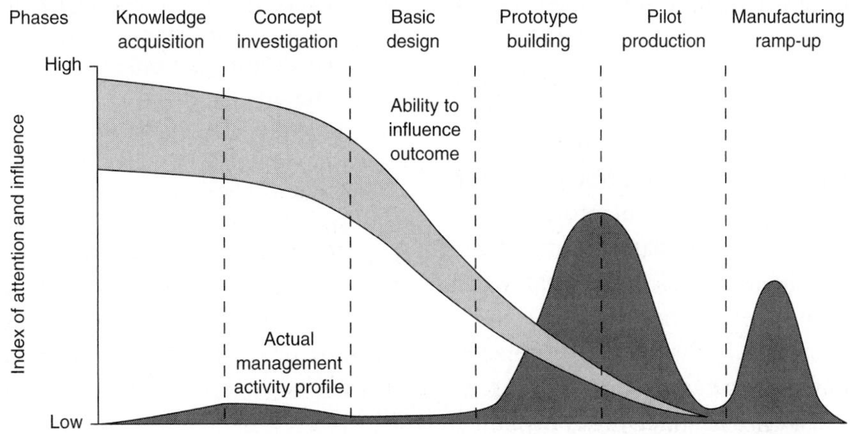

Source: R. H. Hayes, S. C. Wheelwright, and K. B. Clark, *Dynamic Manufacturing* (New York: Free Press, 1988), p. 279. See also F. Gluck and R. Foster, "Managing Technological Change: A Box of Cigars for Brad," *Harvard Business Review,* September–October 1975, p. 141.

and execute projects as intended? Additionally, why don't the increased dosages of management attention that inevitably result when major projects slip seem to have any impact on project effectiveness?

The perspective of this discussion is that an organization can achieve robust and predictable development capabilities that will achieve their intended goals in the marketplace, within the organization, and for the individuals involved. However, doing so requires a host of skills, tools, and concepts that in many instances differ significantly from the natural inclinations common in organizations. At the core of this need for change is management itself. In too many instances, management at all levels fails to provide the leadership required for success. The heart of the problem is management, but management is also the solution.

The magnitude of the change required on management's part is captured clearly by Exhibit 2. As illustrated, most senior managers play little, if any, role in the early stages (knowledge acquisition, concept investigation, and basic design) of a development effort. Once a project progresses to the point of building prototypes and trying to demonstrate the performance characteristics (or lack thereof) of those prototypes, management comes to life and remains attentive until prototyping problems have

been resolved. When the product is introduced, all too often customers discover a number of remaining issues and problems, and management again focuses its attention on the effort.

The problem with such a pattern is that management is only reactive. As suggested by the shaded curves in Exhibit 2, the greatest amount of management's energy on the project is expended when the ability to influence its outcome is at a minimum. It would be far more effective to focus management attention and effort on development activity at the front end or even the preproject phase of development. To do so, however, management must have the appropriate skills, tools, and methods to provide the foundation for a different type of involvement in development. Once accomplished, management can then spend a far greater portion of its energies assessing the lessons learned from individual projects, using them to improve development capability on an ongoing basis, and laying the groundwork for subsequent projects.

The remainder of this discussion is organized around three areas of management activity: preproject or front-end planning, project execution, and postproject learning. This combined set of management activities is what constitutes the development strategy for a business. The concepts, frameworks, and tools that have been found particularly effective in each of these areas will be described, and the subsequent readings and case studies will elaborate on those and illustrate their use in practice. This discussion begins by providing an overview of development strategy and a detailed examination of the preproject stages, including a descriptive framework for categorizing individual development projects into different types. Next, four alternative team structures for organizing the resources used to carry out a development effort are outlined. These can be used effectively to match individual project needs and requirements with the organization's resources and business objectives. The final portion of this discussion focuses on specific ways an organization can learn across a series of development efforts and apply that learning to achieve continual improvement in development speed, productivity, and quality. In addition, an expanded role for management in achieving longer-term development goals is outlined.

DEVELOPMENT STRATEGY AND PREPROJECT MANAGEMENT

While individual development projects are where much of the action is, senior management can have its greatest leverage in the preproject stages. There are two quite different views, however, as to the nature of senior management's role in these preproject activities. Both appear to be based on a similar overall concept of how development activity can be planned and managed, but the specific senior management activities under each approach are radically different, as are the results. We'll refer to the more frequently encountered approach as the *traditional senior management approach* and the alternative as the *development strategy leadership approach.*

The overall conceptual view of development activity for both approaches is that of the development funnel, shown in Exhibit 3. As suggested in this figure, organizations encounter a range of product ideas and concepts that can be investigated as potential new products and processes. From that range of possibilities, the organization must pick a handful of specific projects to which resources will be applied, with the goal of creating on-target, on-time, on-budget products and processes that can be introduced to the marketplace in an effective and efficient manner.

The *traditional role* of senior management in the development funnel is to select, consider (screen), and evaluate a handful of project ideas from all of those available, and then make "go/no-go" decisions with regard to those projects. Senior management thus reacts to the possibilities raised from throughout the organization (and perhaps adds a few ideas of its own) and commits resources to get selected projects developed and into the marketplace. Unfortunately, this traditional view has several shortcomings and weaknesses.

First, it assumes that the set of concepts proposed by the organization adequately covers the firm's opportunities and needs for new products and processes. Second, it assumes that senior management will have the required information to decide properly which product ideas to develop, in the context of ongoing business and product line strategies. Third, this view presumes that advanced development and technology work will have occurred before each development project receives its initial funding and approval. Finally, it assumes that senior management will adequately consider the capacity and resources requirements for prospective individual projects and for the mix of projects already approved. Unfortunately, few of these assumptions hold in practice, and the traditional approach ends up, again, being reactive, piecemeal, and tactical rather than proactive, comprehensive, and strategic.

A much more effective way to achieve the full potential of senior management involvement in development activity is the *development strategy leadership approach.* While based fundamentally on the idea of the development funnel, it creates a far more proactive role for senior management and incorporates a number of tools and techniques that facilitate senior management effec-

EXHIBIT 3   The Development Funnel

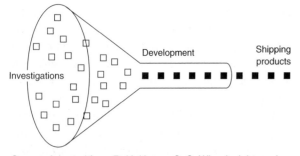

Investigations
Development
Shipping products

Source: Adapted from R. H. Hayes, S. C. Wheelwright, and K. B. Clark, *Dynamic Manufacturing* (New York: Free Press, 1988), p. 295.

tiveness. First, it seeks to put senior management in the position of motivating, guiding, and leading the organization to create the best set of projects. This includes articulating a set of criteria for what would constitute the "correct set" of development projects and connecting the process by which those criteria are applied with product, market, and technology strategies. Senior management thus helps to ensure that selected projects make the best use of existing resources, fit with ongoing business strategies, and are likely to achieve the firm's development objectives. Development projects are the means by which a firm enhances its capabilities; the aggregate set of approved projects is the basis for creating the development capabilities the firm needs and desires in the future.

A second way in which this approach creates substantial leverage is by placing senior management in the position of setting guidelines, general boundaries, and charters for individual projects so that those assigned to carry out such projects can focus their energies in the ways most likely to fulfill senior management's expectations. Thus, this approach avoids having senior management involved in too much of the detailed specification-setting refinements and instead emphasizes broad boundaries that differentiate projects and set clear objectives for what each project is to accomplish.

Third, after creating an appropriate set of projects and defining the boundaries and charters for each project within that set, senior management is in a much better position to make resource allocation and timing decisions that recognize available development capacity and the need to avoid overcommitting scarce resources. It is easier to track a handful of on-target projects than to jump from one project to another as the organization gradually recognizes that its development resources are overcommitted by a factor of two or three. Having contracted with individual development teams as to the charter and bounds of each project, senior management can focus its attention on providing tools and support so that all approved projects move ahead on schedule, rather than constantly reallocating resources in response to current crises and delays.

The results of such a development strategy leadership approach have been described by Clark and Fujimoto in their study of the worldwide automotive industry.[1] These authors looked at major new car development programs

in European, American, and Japanese auto companies and measured results in terms of project cycle time, resource requirements, and product quality. Their findings confirm that automotive companies that use the traditional approach take 20–25 percent longer, require almost twice as many engineering hours, and tend to have significantly lower product quality than do firms at which senior management follows the development strategy leadership approach. Clark and Fujimoto also discovered that the benefits of the latter approach were becoming sufficiently clear that the major auto companies following the traditional approach were focusing significant energy and resources on developing the ability to pursue the development strategy leadership approach.

To understand what is required of senior management to carry out this new approach effectively, it is helpful to examine its three distinctive activities. The following subsections discuss how senior management can create the right set of projects, charter and bound individual projects within that aggregate set, and then balance the supply and demand of resources to best achieve the firm's development objectives.

Creating the Aggregate Set of Projects

For an organization to get the most out of its development resources, it is essential that the right mix of projects—those that use available resources to support existing market segments and to open up new market segments while appropriately utilizing new technologies—get created and proposed to the organization. In terms of the funnel in Exhibit 3, this process can be compared to widening the mouth of the funnel so that a complete range of alternatives is investigated before specific choices are made. This task, however, goes beyond simply encouraging the generation of more ideas; it involves combining and bundling ideas that will allow the organization to cover most effectively the needed areas of new product and process development. Thus, it is essentially a matter of creating and defining the alternatives that the firm can pursue, not simply investigating and screening those that naturally arise.

One way to characterize and organize this task is by using a two-dimensional diagram (see Exhibit 4) that defines individual projects according to the degree of change in the product and manufacturing process they entail. The greater the degree of change along either dimension, the more resources that are likely to be needed in completing that project.

[1]K. B. Clark and T. Fujimoto, *Product eDevelopment Performance* (Boston: Harvard Business School Press, 1991).

EXHIBIT 4   Creating the Mix of Product/Process Development Projects

```
┌──────────────┐
│ Research and │
│  advanced    │
│ development  │
└──────────────┘
                          Process changes

                  New        Next      Single    Tuning
                  core     generation   dept.      and
                process     process    upgrade  incremental

         New      ┌ ─ ─ ─ ┐ ─ ─ ─ ─ ─ ─ ─ ─ ─ ─ ─ ─ ─
         core     │ Unique                              │
        product   │ radical                             │
                  │                                     │
       Next generation │                                │
        of core product │   Platform or next generation │
  Product          │                                    │
  changes          │          ┌ ─ ─ ─ ─ ─ ─ ─ ─ ─ ─ ─ ┐
       Addition to │          │                         │
     product family│          │     Enhancements,       │
                   │          │     hybrids, and        │
                   │          │     derivatives         │
      Add-ons and  │          │                         │
     enhancements  │          │              Sustaining │
                   └ ─ ─ ─ ─ ─ ┴ ─ ─ ─ ─ ─ ─ ─ ─ ─ ─ ─ ┘
```

Source: Adapted from S. C. Wheelwright and K. B. Clark, *Revolutionizing Product Development* (New York: Free Press, 1992), p. 93.

The two-dimensional construct of Exhibit 4 (called the *aggregate project matrix*) classifies individual projects into five types. The three central types—derivative/enhancement/hybrid, platform/next generation, and unique/radical—are known as *commercial development projects.* They lead to new products and processes, providing the benefits typically sought through the application of development resources. The fourth category—sustaining—often uses similar development resources as commercial development projects, but it does not create new products or processes. Rather, sustaining projects maintain or support existing products and processes or tailor them for a single customer. When new commercial development efforts are introduced to the marketplace before they are fully ready, the sustaining effort needed to make engineering change orders and other modifications so that products will perform up to customer expectations can be substantial. One reason for explicitly identifying such sustaining projects is to recognize the resource needs of those projects and the fact that they can often divert attention from the more traditional, more visible, and higher leverage development efforts.

The fifth category—research and advanced development—is generally the technical precursor to a commercial development effort. These projects prove the feasibility of a given product or process concept and validate the existence of the technical knowledge and invention required to make the concept a commercial success. Because invention and technical exploration so often yield unpredictable outcomes, research and advanced development usually precede a commercial development project to ensure that development activities will have a very high probability of technical and market success.

Some companies that have used this aggregate project matrix tool have opted to plot "technology risk" on the vertical axis—ranging from little technological uncertainty at the bottom to substantial uncertainty at the top end. They assess the technical risk entailed in both product *and* process projects on this single dimension. This allows them to measure the intended market impact of the project on the horizontal axis. Projects positioned at the right side of the matrix are replacement products, targeting existing customers in existing markets. Projects in the middle aim to strengthen the company's market share in existing markets that it does not currently serve well. Projects that are positioned at the left end of this continuum are charged with creating new markets. Whether executives use technology-market axes or product-process axes, the characterization of project types noted in Exhibit 4 still applies.

For any ongoing business, a mix of all five types of projects is essential to long-term success. While the majority tend to be created, defined, and resourced within the organization, it is possible for some portion to be subcontracted or partnered with other organizations. For instance, it is not unusual for a business to develop relationships with an industry association group or a university, with the intent of having that group be the source of much of the research and advanced development effort needed by the business. Similarly, firms will often acquire another business to gain ownership of a unique/radical new product or process, or will subcontract to a service organization or field support group part of the sustaining effort needed for the existing product line. It is less common that firms will subcontract or partner platform/next–generation efforts unless these happen to be the first such efforts or represent a diversification move. The key point is that one of senior management's roles is to recognize explicitly the needs of its business for an appropriate mix of these projects and then to determine the most effective way to get those projects completed—whether in-house, through acquisitions, with a partner, or with a subcontractor.

The proportion of effort needed in each of these five areas depends in part on the firm's strategy, but also on the technical opportunities available and the maturity of the firm's product lines. For instance, a large firm that dominates many of its markets, tends to have a broad product line, and may contemplate only incremental changes in its basic technology (such as Kodak in its film business) is likely to support a few selected research and advanced development projects and an occasional platform/next-generation effort (such as developing a whole new line of film), but it will focus most of its development resources on enhancement/derivative/hybrid projects or on sustaining and supporting its existing product lines. In the biotech industry, on the other hand, a firm might spend the vast majority of its development resources on research and advanced development, unique/radical projects, and an occasional wholly new platform. Such a firm would view itself as part of a young, emerging industry in which the leverage is in establishing strong positions in whole new areas with radical new products.

As a general rule, a company that is seeking to accelerate its growth rate would focus a larger proportion of its development resources on platform and breakthrough projects. A company whose strategic mandate was to wring maximum profit from its investments in R&D would likely focus most of its resources at derivative and sustaining projects.

There is no single best mix of projects for every company or even for all the companies in a single industry. What is important is for senior management to understand where the opportunities exist, where the payback will be greatest, and what mix and proportion of different types of projects will best enable the firm to accomplish its business strategy.

Chartering and Bounding Individual Projects

After deciding on the mix and proportion of project types, senior management needs to help create expectations as to what individual projects are intended to accomplish, where they fit in the overall set of projects, and what resources will be made available to the team executing each project. Here again, using the five types of projects is one way for management to establish and bound individual project expectations and temper and balance project objectives and resources. For instance, *derivative projects* can range from cost-reduced versions of existing products to add-ons or enhancements for an existing production process. Development work on a derivative project typically will take less time and fewer resources and be constrained in its performance achievements by the existing platform product or process from which it is derived. They typically target markets and customers that exist and are well understood. Thus, these projects typically require less creativity and are more predictable in their outcomes.

Breakthrough projects, on the other hand, involve significant changes to existing products and processes and require much more creativity, greater degrees of freedom, and more time and resources. Like the initial efforts to develop the compact disc or fiber optics, they create whole new product and process categories that can define a new market. Their results and requirements are much less certain than those of derivative projects and typically require a more experienced and aggressive effort. They tend to be high risk and high return, both to the organization and to those who work on them.

Because breakthrough products often incorporate revolutionary new technologies or materials, they may require dramatic changes in manufacturing processes. This requires that the development team be given considerable latitude in designing both the product and the process. Often this includes providing access to a variety of advanced development projects and their results so that multiple new technologies can be called upon to achieve the dramatic results expected.

Platform projects, which fall in the middle of the commercial development spectrum, are considerably harder to define and bound because they need to be compatible with existing products and processes and yet be sufficiently new and bold that they can serve as a basis for subsequent derivatives, enhancements, and other variations of a basic product/process. For instance, Honda's 1990 Accord line is a new platform that replaced its 1986 platform. Honda introduced a number of significant changes in both product and process but no fundamentally new technologies. Similarly, in the early 1990s, Kodak's single-use camera—available in several different versions—was built off a single platform, while the over 200 versions of Sony's Walkman were derived from one of three platforms, each of which was overhauled and redesigned (i.e., a new generation was created) every two or three years. The extendability of a platform—the range of derivative products that can be built with small incremental investment using the core platform design—is in fact a key metric of how good a platform design is.

EXHIBIT 5   Creating Product Families Via Development Projects

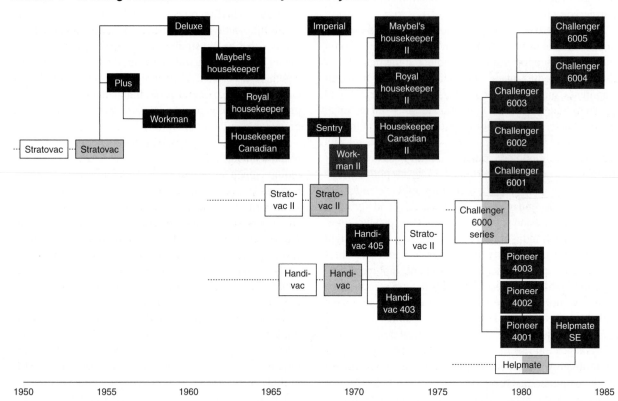

Source: S. C. Wheelwright and W. E. Sasser Jr., "The New Product Development Map," *Harvard Business Review*, May–June 1989, pp. 112–25.

How individual projects are chartered and bounded is important in giving focus and purpose to the development team charged with completing each project. The resulting product line, its basic architecture, its product families, and its range of variations will be the consequence of the set of breakthrough, platform, and derivative projects pursued in development. Organizations have discovered tremendous advantage in differentiating types of development projects such that they can leverage scarce development resources, address markets appropriately, and provide distinctive products offering competitive advantage. Chartering and bounding individual projects is a critical step contributing to the organization's success in achieving these goals. An example of how this might play out over time is shown in Exhibit 5 for a fictitious vacuum cleaner company. The exhibit outlines three generations of product, each involving one or more new platforms and a number of carefully selected and positioned derivative projects aimed at different segments and distribution channels. Senior management can play a

pivotal role in creating and guiding product and process generations and architectures.

Developing and Applying Resources to Selected Development Projects

It is perhaps easiest to understand senior management's role in providing and allocating resources by identifying the two most common problems firms have in this area: undertaking many more projects than can possibly be completed with the available resources and assigning critical resources to work on several projects concurrently. Both problems reflect a lack of discipline and management's unwillingness to make hard choices. Generally, the impact of these problems is far more detrimental and pervasive than most organizations recognize. A simple example can help to illustrate the consequences.

Suppose a firm has a total of 80 full-time development and design people available to work on commercial development projects (derivative, platform, and breakthrough). This means that a total of 960 people-months

EXHIBIT 6 Typical Development Capacity Predicament

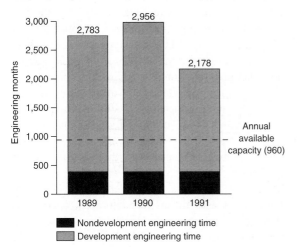

Source: S. C. Wheelwright and K. B. Clark, "Creating Project Plans to Focus Product Development," *Harvard Business Review,* March–April 1992.

can be allocated each year to these three types of development projects. Experience in industries as diverse as computers, scientific instruments, medical devices, and pharmaceuticals suggests that resources are typically overcommitted to the extent shown in Exhibit 6. As suggested, the representative firm with 80 full-time employees engaged in development activity might find that over one-third of the time actually available is spent on nondevelopment engineering tasks (such as sustaining engineering or other special requests the organization might place on these resources). Even more importantly, however, if one were to take all the projects currently considered active and estimate the amount of resources (in development people-months) required for completion and consider their desired completion dates, one would find that the firm had overcommitted its available development capacity by a factor of two or three. That is, the vast majority of firms have many more projects under way than they have resources to staff and complete the projects by the desired introduction dates. This puts development activity in a catch-22 mode: Priorities continually shift and people are moved from one project to another as the organization robs Peter to pay Paul in hopes of completing projects as scheduled. Of course, everybody knows that project commitments far exceed resources, making a game out of who will get priority and what projects will slip.

In addition, because there are not sufficient resources for all projects, the tendency is to commit particularly

critical resources to as many as six or eight concurrent projects. Unfortunately, recent studies suggest that over-committing individual resources actually reduces their effective capacity. That is, overcommitted individuals end up spending additional time going to meetings, getting back up to speed, correcting trivial errors, and so forth, thereby reducing their effective development capacity when it is most needed. This further exacerbates the overcommitment problem, leading inevitably to frustration, disappointment, and burnout.

In fact, the concept that an engineer, scientist, or marketing person is assigned to work simultaneously on multiple projects is quite misleading. In reality, at any point in time each person can work on only one project. The others sit, waiting to be worked on. If the people in a development organization are, on average, assigned to four projects each, an average of only one project is getting worked on. The other three projects are sitting in the intellectual equivalent of work-in-process inventory (WIP). This has the same impact on the speed and quality of development that WIP has on a manufacturing organization.

When we observe a small, seemingly faster company beat a larger, more ponderous competitor to market, it often is the simple result of the small company's engineers having only one project to focus upon—they have no WIP to slow them down. When larger firms allow their product line breadth to reflect itself in multiple project assignments per engineer, it slows the company down. The root cause of the difference is not company size per se. It is the number of projects in WIP.

Senior management must have the discipline to decide which projects are most important, to charter and bound those projects appropriately, and to commit to projects only up to the point at which capacity will allow completion of all the resourced projects. For most organizations, this means cutting the current number of projects by one-half to two-thirds—a difficult pill to swallow. It always seems easier to pretend that all projects underway could be completed if everyone worked harder and longer. Experience suggests that this is a fiction and that the best way to complete more projects on time, on budget, and on target is to do fewer projects and to assign scarce resources to, at most, one major and one minor project. However, when an organization has historically done the opposite, it requires senior management commitment and leadership to make this new set of principles a reality and to impose the discipline needed to avoid the all-too-common overcommitment. As chaos is reduced and focus on development resources increases, it is much easier for senior management to identify the additional resources and capabilities that are required and justified and to make appropriate changes. This puts senior management in a proactive role, helping to build the organization's development capabilities, rather than leaving it in a reactive role that inevitably dissipates much of the development activities' potential effectiveness.

In summary, senior management can have its greatest impact, either positive or negative, during the preproject phase. By shifting to a proactive mode and adhering to a handful of principles and guidelines, senior management can help the entire organization leverage its existing capabilities and enhance its future capabilities. Much of this can be done around the aggregate project plan framework of Exhibit 4 and the repeated application of the following eight-step procedure:

1. Define the primary types of commercial development, advanced development, and sustaining activity projects.
2. Determine the FTEs (full-time equivalents) and cycle time requirements for representative projects of each of those types.
3. Identify existing resources and compare those with the capacity required to complete existing projects on time.
4. Compute the implied capacity utilization from Step 3 and make the adjustments to bring supply and demand into balance.
5. Determine the mix of project types required in the future to achieve the firm's business objectives.
6. Estimate the number of projects of each type that can be undertaken to provide the desired mix and yet not overcommit existing development resources.
7. Create and define the set of specific projects that will be underway at various points of time in the future.
8. Work to increase the productivity of the development resources, thereby enhancing development capacity and capability in future time periods.

The case studies about Kirkham Instruments and Medtronic in this section describe two companies' attempts to use the aggregate project planning tool to manage new product development more effectively. Kirkham stumbled badly, while Medtronic boosted its fortunes dramatically by using this method.

PROJECT ORGANIZATION AND MANAGEMENT

Effective product and process development requires the integration of specialized capabilities. Such integration is difficult in most circumstances but particularly challenging as organizations grow and mature and as functional groups become more specialized. Even the way these functions are organized creates complications for development activity: Marketing typically is organized by product families and market segments; engineering is organized around functional disciplines and technical focus; manufacturing is often a mix of functions, process technologies, and product/market structures. The result is that, in firms of any substantial size, organizing and leading an effective development effort that integrates the tasks required on the part of all the functions is a major challenge.

If any one word has been used excessively in the past few years as a means to capture the opportunity available from more effective project management, it is *teams*. Unfortunately, much of the literature on product-development teams does little to distinguish among different types of teams, the characteristics that make one team more appropriate in a given setting than another, and the ways in which different types of teams can be managed most effectively. A particularly useful perspective on the range of development teams that an organization might apply to a given development project is that provided by Clark and Fujimoto,[2] whose classification arrays teams along a spectrum: from those that are largely functionally oriented, with only loose connections across the functions, to those that are autonomous and integrated, with only loose connections to the individual functions. This spectrum is summarized in Exhibit 7. While such a classification scheme is not unique, it is a useful way to organize quite different structures associated with very different leadership roles, each of which has its own strengths and weaknesses.

Functional Team Structure

In the traditional functional organization typical of many large, mature firms, people are grouped primarily by discipline, each working under the direction of a specialized subfunction manager and a senior functional manager. The different subfunctions and functions coordinate ideas through detailed specifications that all parties agree to at the outset and through occasional meetings at which issues that cut across groups are discussed. Over time, primary responsibility for a development effort passes

---

[2] Ibid.

EXHIBIT 7 Types of Development Teams

1. Functional structure

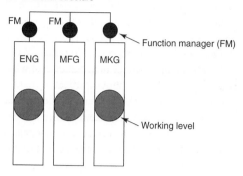

2. Lightweight project manager

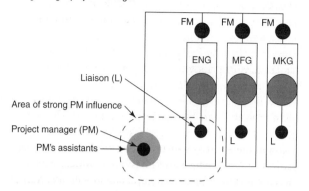

3. Heavyweight product manager

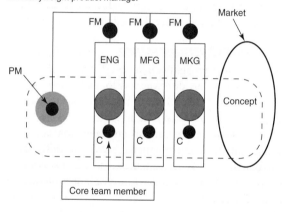

4. Autonomous project team

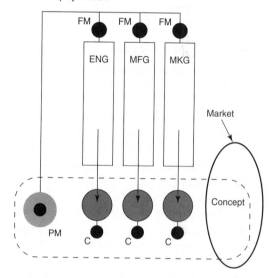

Source: K. B. Clark and S. C. Wheelwright, "Organizing and Leading 'Heavyweight' Development Teams," *California Management Review* 34, no. (1992), pp. 9–28.

sequentially—although often not smoothly—from one function to the next, a transfer often referred to as "throwing it over the wall."

The functional development team structure has several advantages and disadvantages. One strength is that managers who control a project's resources also control the performance of individual tasks in their functional area. Thus, responsibility and authority are usually aligned. However, tasks must be subdivided at the project's outset—the entire development process must be unpacked into separable, somewhat independent subactivities. But on most development efforts, not all required tasks are known at the outset, nor can they all be subdivided easily or realistically. When a product's architecture is modular, a functional team structure typically works well. When there are unpredictable interdependencies in the work to be done by two functional organizations, functional teams impede success. Coordination and integration often suffer.

Another major strength of this approach is that because most career paths are functional, at least until a general management level is reached. The work done on a project is judged, evaluated, and rewarded by the same subfunction and functional managers who make decisions about career paths. The associated disadvantage is that individual contributions to a development project tend to be judged largely independently of overall project success. The frequently cited tenet is that individuals cannot be evaluated fairly on outcomes over which they lack control. But as a practical matter, that often means that those directly involved in the details of the project are not responsible for the overall results finally achieved.

Finally, the functional project organization brings specialized expertise to bear on the key technical issues. The same person or small group of people may be responsible for the design of a particular component or subsystem over a long series of development efforts. Thus, the functions and subfunctions capture and apply the benefits of prior experience and become the keepers of the organization's depth of knowledge over time and across projects. The disadvantage is that every development project differs in its objectives and performance requirements, and it is unlikely that specialists developing a single component will do so very differently on one project compared to another. The best component or subsystem is defined by technical parameters in the areas of their expertise, rather than by overall system characteristics or specific customer requirements dictated by the unique market at which the development effort is aimed.

Lightweight Team Structure

As in the functional development structure, those assigned to the lightweight team reside physically in their functional areas, but each functional organization designates a liaison person to represent it on the project coordinating committee. These liaisons work with a lightweight project manager, usually a design engineer or product marketing manager, who coordinates different functions' activities. This approach usually occurs as an add-on to a traditional functional organization, with a functional liaison having that role added to his or her duties. The overall coordination assignment of the lightweight project manager, however, tends not to be present in the traditional functional structure.

It is important to recognize that project managers are lightweight in two significant respects. First, they are generally middle- or junior-level people who, despite considerable expertise, have little status or influence in the organization. Such people have spent a handful of years in a function, and the present assignment is seen as a broadening experience—a chance for them to move out of the function. Second, although they are responsible for informing and coordinating the activities of the functional organizations, the key resources (including engineers on the project) remain under the control of their respective functional managers. The lightweight project manager does not have power to reassign people or reallocate resources and instead concentrates on confirming schedules, updating timelines, and expediting across groups. Such project leaders typically spend no more than 25 percent of their time on a single project.

The primary strengths and weaknesses of the lightweight project team are those of the functional project structure, but now at least one person over the course of the project looks across functions and seeks to ensure that individual tasks—especially those on the critical path—get done in a timely function and that everyone is kept aware of potential cross-functional issues and what is going on elsewhere in this particular project.

Thus, improved communication and coordination are what an organization expects when moving from a functional to a lightweight team structure. Because power still resides with the subfunction and functional managers, however, hopes for improved efficiency, speed, and project quality are seldom realized fully. Moreover, lightweight project leaders find themselves tolerated at best and often ignored or even preempted. This can easily become a no-win situation for the individual thus assigned.

Heavyweight Team Structure

In contrast to the lightweight setup, the heavyweight project manager has direct access to, and responsibility for, the vast majority of those involved in the project. Such leaders are heavyweights in two respects. First, they are senior managers within the organization and may even outrank the functional managers. In addition to having expertise and experience, they also wield significant organizational clout. Second, heavyweight leaders have primary influence over the people working on the development effort and supervise their work directly through key functional people on the core teams. Often the core group of people is dedicated and physically colocated with the heavyweight project leader. However, the longer-term career development of individual contributors continues to rest not with the project leader—although that heavyweight leader makes significant input to individual performance evaluations—but with the functional manager, because members are not assigned to a project team permanently.

The heavyweight team structure has a number of advantages and strengths, along with associated weaknesses. In many instances, the advantages of the team approach bring with them potential disadvantages that may hurt development performance if not recognized and averted. Take, for example, the advantages of ownership and commitment, one of the most striking advantages of the heavyweight team. Identifying with the product and creating a sense of esprit de corps motivate core team members to extend themselves and do what is needed to help the team succeed. But such teams sometimes expand the definition of their role and the scope of the project and get carried away with themselves and their abilities. Even when the team does stay focused, the rest of the organization may see itself as second-class. Although the core team may not make the distinction explicit, it happens because the team has responsibilities and authority beyond those commonly given to functional team members. Thus, such projects inadvertently can become the "haves" and other, smaller projects the "have-nots" with regard to key resources and management attention.

Another potential concern is that the heavyweight team will want the same control over secondary activities (such as prototyping, analytical testing, and quality assurance) that it has over the primary tasks performed by dedicated team members. Thus, when waiting for these secondary tasks to be performed, the team's natural response is to demand top priority from the support organization or to be allowed to go outside and subcontract to independent groups. While these may sometimes be the appropriate choices, senior management must establish make-buy guidelines and clear priorities applicable to all projects—perhaps changing service levels provided by support groups—or have support groups provide capacity and advisory technical services but let team members do more of the actual task work in these support areas. Whatever actions the organization takes, the challenge is to achieve a balance between the needs of the individual heavyweight project and of the broader organization.

Another advantage of the heavyweight team is the integration and integrity it provides through a system solution to a set of customer needs. Getting all of the components and subsystems to complement one another and to address effectively the fundamental requirements of the core customer segment can result in a winning platform product/process. The team achieves an effective system design by using generalist skills applied by broadly trained team members, with fewer specialists and, on occasion, less depth in individual component solutions and technical problem solving. The extent of these implications is aptly illustrated by the nature of the teams Clark and Fujimoto encountered in their study of the auto industry.[3] Clark and Fujimoto found that for U.S. auto firms in the mid-1980s, typical platform projects organized under a traditional functional or lightweight team structure entailed full-time work for several months by approximately 1,500 engineers. In contrast, a handful of

Japanese platform projects carried out by heavyweight teams utilized only 250 engineers working full-time for several months. The implications of 250 versus 1,500 full-time equivalents (FTEs) with regard to breadth of tasks, degree of specialization, and need for coordination are significant and help explain major differences in project results as measured by product integrity, development cycle time, and engineering resource utilization.

But the lack of depth may also be a disadvantage of the heavyweight team. Some individual components or subassemblies may not attain the same level of technical excellence they would under a more traditional functional team structure. For instance, generalists may develop a windshield wiper system that is complementary with and integrated into the total car system and its core concept. But they also may embed in their design potential weaknesses or flaws that could have been caught by a functional team of specialists who had developed a long series of windshield wipers. To counter this potential disadvantage, many organizations order more testing of completed units to discover possible flaws, and have components and subassemblies reviewed by expert specialists. In some cases the quality assurance function has expanded its role to ensure that sufficient technical specialists review designs at appropriate points so that such weaknesses can be discovered early and their detrimental effects minimized.

Autonomous Team Structure

With the autonomous team structure, or "tiger team," individuals from the different functional areas are formally assigned, dedicated, and colocated to the project team. The project leader, a heavyweight in the organization, is given full control over the resources contributed by the different functional groups. Furthermore, the project leader becomes the sole evaluator of the contribution made by individual team members. In essence, the autonomous team is given a clean sheet of paper; it is not required to follow existing organizational practices and procedures but is instead allowed to create its own. This includes establishing incentives and rewards as well as norms for behavior. However, the team will be held fully accountable for the final results of the project: Success or failure is its responsibility and no one else's.

The fundamental strength of the autonomous team structure is focus. Everything the individual team members and team leader do is concentrated on making the project successful. Thus, tiger teams can excel at rapid, efficient new product and process development. They

---

[3] Ibid.

handle cross-functional integration in a particularly effective manner, possibly because they attract and select team participants much more freely than do the other project structures. Tiger teams, however, take little or nothing as given. They are more likely to expand the bounds of their project definition and tackle redesigns of the entire product, its components, and subassemblies rather than look for opportunities to utilize existing materials, designs, and organizational relationships. Their solution may be unique, making it more difficult to fold the resulting product and process—and in many cases, the team members themselves—back into the traditional organization upon project completion. As a consequence, tiger teams often become the birthplace of new business units or they experience unusually high turnover following project completion.

Senior managers, because they are asked to delegate much more responsibility and control to the team and its project leader than under any other organization structure, often become nervous at the prospects of a tiger team. Unless clear guidelines have been established in advance, it is extremely difficult during the project for senior managers to make midcourse corrections or exercise substantial influence without destroying the team. More than one team has gotten away from senior management and created major problems.

One aspect of selecting an appropriate team structure that should readily be apparent is the need to match that team structure not only with the capabilities and resources of the organization, but also with the type of project that is to be assigned to the development team. While many different considerations are important in such a matching of the team structure to the type of project, it is generally the case that projects requiring deep technical excellence are best done under a functional structure. Projects requiring an outstanding system solution, such as are typical of new platforms or next generation product concepts, are often best done by a heavyweight project team. In most instances, younger, less experienced workers on a lightweight project team can handle derivative and enhancement projects, thus gaining valuable training. Because many of the choices are constrained by the platform from which the derivative or enhancement comes, such lightweight teams are able to deliver quite effectively. Finally, radical or breakthrough projects, as often associated with the very first generation of a whole new product or process, are often best carried out by a more autonomous tiger team.

As a general rule, if the overall product architecture is not likely to change (so that the habitual patterns of interaction, communication, and coordination that have evolved in the past do not need to change) then functional or lightweight teams perform well. They are tools to exploit existing processes. In circumstances of significant architectural change, which mandate that different people interact with different people over different topics and with different timing than has historically been required, then heavyweight and autonomous teams work best. These teams are tools to create *new* processes.

Looking across different industries, it is also quite clear that the maturity of an industry and its technologies can have a direct bearing on the type of development team structure most likely to be found in the companies within that particular industry. For most start-up companies, the entire organization is often an autonomous tiger team simply because everyone is focused on a new product or process, and that is where the company's future lies. As second and third generations of the dominant product and process are developed, they too may continue to be carried out by a heavyweight project team consisting of virtually all the senior managers in the business. This is likely to be the case particularly where the company can grow substantially with a fairly narrow product line and simply by introducing succeeding generations of new products in that line. However, as companies mature and expand, adding multiple product lines, because some of those product lines require many more resources of a sustaining and operating nature, it is likely that they will shift their basic business organization to a functional structure. Thus, it is natural at that point to have product and process development also take on a more functional appearance, with the vast majority of resources being owned by the functions and the tasks being conducted under the direction of those individual functions.

That functional structure for the basic organization as well as its development efforts may then continue for years and even decades if a firm dominates its industry and if the rate of technical change is not too great. However, such a firm may become slow and less responsive over time. Like many of the industrial giants of the 1980s and early 1990s, it may find itself challenged as new technologies, competitors, and markets create a rapid onslaught of new product and process development opportunities. The functional structure is simply unable to keep up with all of those possibilities in a timely fashion. At that point such a large organization may start adding lightweight project coordinators in hopes of avoiding drastic organizational restructuring moves, while seeking diligently to improve its product development activities. Finally, it may become painfully obvious that on a few critical projects a totally new approach is needed. Some firms will choose to do that with a tiger team removed from the main organization; others might seek to develop a new capability for implementing heavyweight project teams. Industries such as automobiles, steel, and pharmaceuticals have followed patterns not unlike that just described.

The challenge for any single firm is to make sure that its dominant approach to organizing development teams matches its environment and its strategic imperatives and that the firm develops capabilities and resources that allow it to apply alternative modes when they are deemed most appropriate for particular projects. Especially critical is making sure that the organization's human resource selection, training, and development policies as well as its organizational systems provide the mix of skills in the quantities needed by the overall development strategy. In theory, an organization might well choose to develop a portfolio of approaches that would cover all four types of development team structures in order to match them to a full range of development projects it seeks to undertake. However, experience suggests that most organizations have a tendency to adopt a dominant orientation or a standard approach to leading and organizing development projects. That dominant orientation in firms determines what is easy and likely to work and what is hard and likely to be less effective. It thus determines the range of approaches and projects a firm can hope to apply and carry out.

Of the four development team structures outlined in Exhibit 7, two typically represent dominant orientations—the functional structure and the heavyweight team. Firms whose basic systems, skills, practices, and mechanisms are functional, for example, will find it relatively easy to implement lightweight teams. The lightweight setup is largely functional with an overlay of light coordination. Moving to a heavyweight team, however, is much more difficult and is unlikely to be fully successful if the functional structure remains the dominant orientation. Without basic changes in systems, practices, attitudes, and behaviors, attempts to add a heavyweight team capability in what is essentially a functional organization may create a "middleweight" approach but is unlikely to build a heavyweight team.

In contrast, firms that have teams as their dominant orientation and have built their systems, training efforts, communication structures, and patterns of leadership around heavyweight teams will find it relatively easy to implement autonomous tiger teams. However, even though the heavyweight team has a functional organiza-

tion carrying out some of its detailed work and support activities, conducting lightweight or even functional projects often involves adjustments in the standard approach, and their lightweight teams are likely to be somewhat "heavier" than if their dominant orientation were functional.

The experience of Chaparral Steel illustrates the challenges and advantages of building capability for several approaches in development. Located in Midlothian, Texas, 30 miles south of Dallas, by the early 1990s Chaparral was producing well over 1 million tons per year of steel products used in forging (high alloy) and construction (structural) products. Using an electric furnace, a continuous caster, and a rolling mill to convert steel scrap into various milled products, Chaparral had continued to improve its performance through a variety of product and process development efforts. Chaparral defined three types of projects: major advanced development, platform, and incremental. Projects of the first type might require an expenditure of $3 million to $5 million over a period of three to five years but would provide a breakthrough product or process. Platform projects might require $500,000 to $1 million in development expenses and take 12 to 24 months to execute. Incremental projects typically would incur development expenditures of $100,000 to $200,000, last a few months, and provide very quick payback. At any point in time the organization might have 40 or 50 development projects underway, of which no more than a couple would be major advanced development efforts, perhaps three to five would be platform efforts, and the remainder would be incremental efforts.

Because of the cost competitiveness of its industry and the operating demands required for profitable products and processes, Chaparral has chosen to conduct all of its development efforts on its factory floor and staff them primarily with line people. However, the team structure and project leadership used for each of the three types varies considerably. Incremental projects are almost all done by functional subgroups with a lightweight project manager. With so many projects going on and with projects so common, everyone understands the role of the lightweight project manager and wants to be supportive: They know, at some point, they will be one of those lightweight project managers and will desire the same kind of treatment. Thus, the support and cooperation provided to lightweight project managers tend to be substantially greater than in many traditional functional organizations. The platform projects are headed up by heavyweight project managers who have probably been department managers; following completion of the platform effort, they will go back to being a department manager. The advanced development projects are put under the direction of one of seven general foremen who report directly to the vice president of manufacturing (or one of the other vice presidents). These major projects start as advanced development efforts; once technical feasibility is proven, they quickly become breakthrough projects but with little or no change in team composition.

This mix of approaches has served Chaparral well in addressing the range of development opportunities and challenges faced in its business. Depending on the mix of technical depth, the coordination and integration of known tasks, the level of system integration, and the degree of breakthrough and new thinking required, Chaparral can pick a team structure, project manager, and overall management approach that make sense for the situation. Expectations have been established over more than a decade, and thus procedures and approaches—as well as their governing principles—are well known throughout the organization.

Tools That Aid Development Project Completion

An area of substantial promise for improving the consistency and performance of development teams is that of new tools and techniques. Many of these are computer-based and range from computer-aided design/computer-aided manufacturing (CAD/CAM) systems used by mechanical engineers and others, to computer-aided engineering and drafting systems used by designers and architects, and on to finite-element analyses used by material scientists and others. In addition, new computer simulation and analytical tools are being developed to aid chemists and physicists in such diverse areas as consumer products and pharmaceuticals.

While numerous advances in the nature and application of such computer-based tools are likely to occur in the coming decade, other "low-tech" tools are also being developed and finding wide acceptance. A tool such as quality function deployment (QFD) developed first at Toyota and now applied throughout a number of industries is a systematic procedure for linking customer requirements to design parameters. Thus, it serves to apply rigor and completeness to cross-functional problem-solving activities that are common in most complex, system-based development efforts.[4] Even such organizational

processes as just-in-time (JIT), value added analysis, and fast cycle time techniques are proving useful when applied to the tasks of new product and new process development. This coming decade is likely to see a number of these tools applied much more broadly and systematically in building an organization's development capabilities.

Finally, a number of more traditional tools that long have been considered an important part of new product and process development methodologies are likely to be enhanced, extended, and even completely rethought to make them more effective in the competitive environment of the 1990s. One example of such a traditional tool is prototyping. Physical models and prototypes are used by various engineering disciplines to test product and process concepts and multiple iterations in the design and development process. Clearly, computers have extended and enhanced the way in which such prototypes can be created and subsequently analyzed. As technologies continue to advance, the sophistication and range of prototyping activities will advance as well.

LEARNING ACROSS DEVELOPMENT PROJECTS

In a world of intense international competition where customers are sophisticated and demanding and technologies are diverse and dramatic in their effects, organizations that stand still in product and process development will neither prosper nor survive. The ability to sustain significant improvements in development over long periods of time rests on the capability to learn from experience. What is crucial in improving development is insight and understanding about how the organization works in practice. Studies that benchmark the best practice among competitors or that generate new concepts and frameworks may prove valuable in establishing perspective, but solving the problems that limit performance requires a detailed understanding of the root causes of those problems as they play out in the specific circumstances of the organization's development process. Thus, learning from experience is crucial. In the context of product and process development, learning from experience means learning from development projects.

But organizational learning is not a natural outcome of development projects, even in successful development efforts. There seem to be two fundamental problems. The first is that the performance that matters is often a result

---

[4]See Chapter 9 in S. C. Wheelwright and K. B. Clark, *Revolutionizing Product Development* (New York: Free Press, 1992). See also J. R. Hauser and D. Clausing, "The House of Quality," *Harvard Business Review,* May–June 1988, pp. 63–73.

of complex interactions within the overall development system. Moreover, the connection between cause and effect may be separated significantly in time and place. In some instances, for example, the outcomes of interest are only evident at the conclusion of the project. While symptoms and potential causes may be observed by individuals at various points along the development path, systematic investigation requires observation of the outcomes followed by an analysis that looks back to find the underlying causes. The second problem is that incentives in the organization favor pressing forward to the next project. Without concerted effort and focused attention on learning from the project that has just been completed, it is unlikely that engineers, marketers, or manufacturers will naturally devote time and energy to yesterday's problems. Most companies learn very little from their development experience. Those that do learn and understand the power in improvement do have developed tools and methods to help people—individually and collectively—gain insight and understanding and focus energy and attention on the problem of learning. While relatively little has been written and systematically studied with regard to how organizations learn about development activity and create capabilities to carry out such activities more effectively, a handful of observations can be made.

First, for an organization to learn across development projects, management must focus attention on the *need* for such learning. The way most organizations learn is within the functions along which they are organized, where those functions carry out repetitive tasks and gradually develop tools, systems, and procedures that incorporate their past experience and enable them to conduct those tasks more effectively. Since most development efforts are cross-functional or at least the leverage often occurs at the interfaces of the functions, learning about development requires a cross-functional perspective. Recent experience would suggest that project leaders are often in the best position to recognize the need for such learning and to capture the experiences of the development efforts they have been involved in and turn those into systems, tools, and procedures that others in the organization can apply. However, that requires that project leadership become a significant step in multiple career paths and an assignment that one might retain for an extended period of time. For example, an organization might well have younger project leaders start as lightweight coordinators and then gradually move to bigger projects, eventually becoming heavyweight project managers. A cadre of project leaders within the organization might then be developed who have a strong vested interest in capturing and applying the learning from individual development efforts.

A second observation is that learning from past development experience requires that lessons be identified, analyzed, captured, and then incorporated into the way the organization carries out its development activity. A particularly useful tool, but one not yet widely applied, is that of the *project audit*. This might well be undertaken by a cross-functional team (prior to its being assigned responsibility for a development project) that examines a recently completed project, compares it to other recently completed development efforts, and identifies high-leverage areas of opportunity where new tools, systems, or procedures might be of great benefit.

A third observation is that if improving development capability is important, senior management will need to provide leadership and guidance—with regard to goals and objectives but also in terms of resources, organizational attention, and new skills. Thus, an essential aspect of a development strategy for a given business is not just identifying the set of projects to be undertaken, the development team structures for doing so, or the tools and techniques to be used by the team. These are all important, but in addition forethought must be given to how the organization will learn, how that learning will be captured, the way in which it subsequently will be applied, and the results to be expected. Like so many issues, effective commercialization of products and processes depends on good management.

NEW PRODUCT DEVELOPMENT

For 2/19

CASE IV-1

Product Development at Dell Computer Corporation

Stefan Thomke, Vish V. Krishnan, and Ashok Nimgade

On an October afternoon in 1993, Mark Holliday, new head of Dell's Portable Division, laid down his papers and greeted key members of Dell's portable computer product development team now entering the conference room. The room occupied a corner of the firm's office park building on the outskirts of Austin, Texas.

Holliday had called the meeting in hopes the group could reach a consensus on recommendations for developing a new line of laptop computers. Dell did not currently market any portable computers. Its first line of portables, discontinued just a year earlier, had had technical problems—just the day before, in fact, the company announced a callback of some 17,000 units. Meanwhile, the lack of portables represented a gaping hole in the company's product line. Given the firm's sagging stock performance, the investment community was closely watching each and every move Dell made.

Source: Copyright © 1998 by The President and Fellows of Harvard College. Professor Stefan Thomke, University of Texas Professor Vish V. Krishnan, and Research Associate Ashok Nimgade, M.D., prepared this case as the basis for class discussion rather than to illustrate either effective or ineffective handling of an administrative situation. Names and company-confidential data have been disguised.

differentiate through battery life

One way that Holliday and the product development team hoped to differentiate the new Dell line of laptops was through battery life. Batteries lasted less than three hours before needing recharging—a considerable inconvenience for executives trying to work on airline flights or on the road. But the new lithium ion (LiOn; pronounced "lee-on") technology being developed at Sony, one of Dell's manufacturing partners, promised to drastically extend laptop usage time without recharging. Unfortunately, since Sony was working to resolve some battery charging issues, LiOn technology was not yet qualified to be used in laptops.

A successful new line of portables, especially with cutting-edge LiOn technology, could catapult Dell back into the portable computer market. As a former engineer with prior computer industry experience on both coasts, Holliday realized, however, that premature commitment to an unproven technology could yield another fiasco for Dell in the laptop market. The discussion around this issue was sure to prove lively.

THE PERSONAL COMPUTER INDUSTRY

Although the first digital computer was designed by Charles Babbage in the 1830s, the limitations of contemporary materials and manufacturing capabilities confined his vision primarily to the drawing board.[1] Not until

---

[1] Some of the information in this section derives from D. Narayandas and V. K. Rangan, "Dell Computer Corporation," Harvard Business School Case No. 596-058.

957

World War II did armies of engineers create factory-sized computers, such as the 50-foot Mark I at Harvard or the aptly named Colossus in London, capable of undertaking simple mathematical operations or breaking enemy codes.[2] Like dinosaurs, these early computers yielded way to more agile successors.

Technological breakthroughs over the decades allowed for dramatic size reductions with concomitant increases in computing power. Through the 1960s and 1970s, only government (especially defense) and big business could tap the power of computers. But as microchips replaced transistors and wiring, and manufacturing technologies improved, it appeared inevitable that the intersecting trends of miniaturization and lowered prices would ultimately place microcomputers at the disposal of individuals.

The microcomputer revolution started in the 1970s, with machines catering to hobbyists and "hackers." In July 1974, an electronic magazine promoted a printed circuit board that came with an instruction book for simulations. Known as the Mark 8 computer, over a thousand units were sold at $1,000 each, prompting the appearance of rival products. The market for similar machines grew to nearly 100,000 by 1977, thanks to several key developments: improved microprocessors, a standard operating system, increased availability of software, disk drives (which replaced cumbersome tape storage devices), and cheaper memory. Technology could now put more computing power on someone's desk than existed in the huge 50-foot machines of World War II.

Apple Computer and IBM

Through the late 1970s and 1980s, Apple Computer, a California-based firm, successfully commercialized an intuitively easy-to-use interface. Apple's engineers set the technological pace by cramming in as much new technology into products as possible, often working around the clock for days on end before a market launch. The firm drew on an entirely new cadre of users, primarily in the educational and hobbyist market. Business uses for the small computers, however, remained limited.

Initially, only a handful of larger firms like Texas Instruments and Zenith entered the business segment of the microcomputer market. To put matters in perspective, the Goliath-sized IBM's annual $1.5 billion R&D budget in the early 1980s alone loomed 50 percent larger than the entire microcomputer market. But IBM, and other giants

such as Hewlett-Packard and DEC, which made business-oriented, closet-sized mainframe and miniframe computers, could no longer ignore the meteoric 30 percent annual growth of the microcomputer market.

To play catch-up, IBM rapidly leveraged off its traditional corporate base and strong direct sales and service organization. It outsourced hardware and software components to launch its IBM Personal Computer in 1981. Working with Microsoft, IBM created a new operating system that it made available to all personal computer manufacturers; this "open architecture" policy encouraged third parties to develop IBM-compatible software. Apple, in the meantime, kept its technologically superior system proprietary. In a world of two incompatible operating systems, however, the IBM juggernaut eroded Apple market share. By 1983, IBM enjoyed 42 percent of the microcomputer market, with gross profits as high as 25 percent.

Enter the Clones

Even IBM could not meet the corporate demand for microcomputers that it had unleashed. During the 1980s, personal computer sales were to grow from ground level to $40 billion. Much of this growth came from manufacturers of IBM-compatible machines, termed IBM clones. Most notable of these cloners was Texas-based Compaq, which in just five years joined IBM and Apple in the pantheon of the top three-selling retail brand names. Lacking a sales force, Compaq sold through recruited independent full-service retail dealers. (Some 5,000 computer stores had sprung up in the United States by the late 1980s, spurred by an explosion of hardware and software.)

By 1990, microcomputers accounted for 40 percent of all computers sold, and technological breakthroughs and competition helped drive down the costs of manufacturing the machines. For instance, the cost of processing a million instructions per minute fell from $75,000 in 1980 to $2,000 by 1991. The cost of storing a megabyte of information dropped from $250 in 1980 to $75 in 1991. Lower costs, increasing numbers of software applications, friendlier interfaces (including Microsoft's popular Windows operating system for IBM-compatible computers), and the entry of new manufacturers and distributors all boosted public demand. In 1993, personal computers sold faster than video cassette recorders and almost as fast as TVs.[3] The British journal *The Economist* proclaimed:

---

[2] *Encyclopedia Britannica,* 1991, Chicago: University of Chicago.

[3] S. Lohr, "How Did Dell Computer Stumble?" *The New York Times,* May 28, 1993, Sec. D, p. 1.

"Once an icon of technological wizardry, personal computers have become a commodity. . . . And customers are less willing to pay for service and hand-holding."[4]

THE HISTORY OF DELL

In 1983, Michael Dell, a freshman at the University of Texas, Austin, started upgrading IBM-compatible personal computers and literally hawked them door-to-door to local businesses.[5] With inventory piling up in his dorm room and crowding his roommate, Dell moved off-campus—and informed his parents of plans to drop out of school at the end of the year. To avoid parental fury, he agreed to return to his premed curriculum if business proved disappointing. But with $180,000 in personal computer sales during his very first month, Dell never returned. (See Exhibit 1.)

He soon started buying and assembling components himself in order to sell computers under his own name directly to customers.[6] High growth rates and attractive margins allowed him to fund growth internally, and he began fielding orders for up to a hundred computers at a time from large oil companies and government agencies. Buyers wanted to meet directly with Dell, however, which created a dilemma: "We had to clean up our workshop," Dell later confessed, "buy some suits and ties, and get ready for meeting America's largest corporations face-to-face."

Dell's seat-of-the-pants operations matched the needs of his computer-literate customers, who demanded quality at a reasonable price. In the years to come, Dell would start a 24-hour complaint hotline and offer a supply of backup replacement equipment. By upgrading IBM-compatibles with the latest microprocessors and peripheral technologies at low costs, Dell's company grew to $6 million by 1985. That year, the firm introduced its own brand of personal computers and ended with $70 million in sales.

By 1990, Dell Computers fielded a broad line of personal computers, winning several trade magazine awards for products and services. Michael Dell himself gained

[4] *The Economist*, November 2, 1991.
[5] Some of the information in this section derives from D. Narayandas and V. K. Rangan, "Dell Computer Corporation," Harvard Business School Case No. 596-058.
[6] A. Server, "Michael Dell Turns the PC World Inside Out," *Fortune*, September 8, 1997, pp. 76–80ff.

EXHIBIT 1 Timeline

1984		Michael Dell Founds Dell Computer Corporation.
1985		Dell offers first personal computer of its own design.
1987		International expansion begins, with opening of subsidiary in the United Kingdom. Manufacturing will start there in 1990.
1988		Dell goes public.
1991		Dell introduces its first notebook computer.
1992		The company joins ranks of *Fortune* 500.
1993		
	January	Michael Dell first hears about Sony's lithium ion battery technology in Tokyo.
	March	Amid great uncertainty at Dell about fate of its laptop line, Dell reorganizes its portable division.
	May	After 14 consecutive quarters with rising stock profits, the firm reports that its profits had been slashed to $10 million, half of projected profits. Dell's stock plunged $7 a share to $25 on the day of this announcement.
	August	Market decisions are made about new laptop computer line.
	October	Dell recalls 17,000 discontinued notebooks after three machines were returned by owners reporting such technical problems as smoke or melted spots.

the distinction of becoming the wealthiest person in Texas.

The Dell Business Model

Dell Computer used the same principle to sell computers as Michael Dell had devised during his college venture: eliminate the middle man. The company focused on selling customized products directly via mail to savvy customers. Large clients, which included *Fortune 500* firms, government agencies, and universities, generally demanded reliability and compatibility with existing computers. Competitors in this arena included resellers of leading brands such as IBM, Compaq, and Hewlett-Packard. For clients from small to medium businesses, Dell's primary competitors were mail order firms such as Gateway 2000.

Dell serviced its customers with combinations of home-based telephone representatives and field-based representatives. By tracking historical sales records online, Dell could assess purchase patterns to better respond to customer needs. With direct marketing, in Michael Dell's words, "you actually get to have a relationship with the customer. And that creates valuable information, which, in turn, allows us to leverage our relationships with both suppliers and customers."[7]

Dell assured product quality by extensively pretesting all the configuration options it offered. Once customers called in orders, customized configuration details were sent on "spec sheets" to the appropriate assembly line (an assembly line in Austin for U.S. customers, and a plant in Ireland for European customers). Assembly proceeded in a manner similar to that for automobiles. It started with a chassis upon which an appropriate motherboard, memory, microprocessor, video card, and other peripherals were installed and then wired. Next, the appropriate software was loaded, and the entire machine was sent to the "burn in" area for four to eight hours of testing. Quality checking occurred at several points along the line. Finally, the machine would be packaged along with manuals and shipped, typically in three to five days after order receipt (a week longer for orders over 100 machines).

A 24-hour telephone support system comprising well-trained technical representatives provided the first post-shipment level of support. This team was able to help Dell's computer-savvy customers diagnose and solve problems themselves 91 percent of the time.[8] A room in Austin the size of a football field, with 760 cubicles with telephones, housed this team within the heart of Dell's sales representatives.[9]

Dell maintained a month's worth of component inventory, but its suppliers generally carried supplemental buffer stock that could be immediately shipped. Outsourcing provided several advantages, according to Michael Dell: "There are fewer things to manage, fewer things to go wrong. You don't have the drag effect of taking 50,000 people with you."[10] Smaller inventory also allowed new technologies to be adopted quicker, and product development cycles to move faster.

By creating close, coordinated relationships with its suppliers, vendors, and third-party maintenance providers, Dell created the illusion that its customers were dealing with just one large, well-run company. "The supplier effectively becomes our partner," according to Michael Dell.[11] "The rule we follow is to have as few partners as possible. And they will last as long as they maintain their leadership in technology and quality." This relationship also provided Dell with a front-row seat to new technologies its suppliers developed.

Dell Computer Stumbles

By 1990, Dell's success had spawned imitators such as Gateway 2000 and CompuAdd, which also enjoyed low overhead through mail-order sales. IBM and Compaq also announced plans for entering the direct mail order business. Compaq, at the same time, sparked off a price war by announcing a 30 percent cut in its prices.

Meanwhile, feeling the pinch of competition, Dell had expanded into the retail market to attract smaller customers who preferred shopping in showrooms. The new markets spurred Dell's annual sales from $890 million in 1991 to more than $2 billion a year later, overshooting the company's 1992 sales target by half a billion dollars. (See Exhibit 2.)

The rapid pace caught Dell in a cash crunch. In 1993, after 14 consecutive quarters with rising profits, the firm reported that its profits had been slashed to $10 million, half of what it had projected. Dell stock plunged $7 a share, to $25, on the day of this announcement.[12] Industry observers began speculating about the end of the Dell miracle. Michael Dell, they feared, had lost his legendary attention to detail and his ability to take cues from direct contact with customers and engineers. At any rate, several weaknesses had started to show in the company.

The first problem was that retail selling proved contrary to the spartanism of Dell's traditional direct model. Dell lost the advantage of being able to turn over inventory 12 times a year—twice as fast as its competitors—making it increasingly hard to find a premium in this market. Gateway, in the meantime, stuck to the direct model, growing from $275 million sales in 1990 to $914 million in 1992, with a promise of yet more growth to come.

The second problem involved the lack of senior management capable of guiding the firm toward maturity. Michael Dell became aware of this and hired several sen-

[7] J. Magretta, "The Power of Virtual Integration: An Interview with Dell Computer's Michael Dell," *Harvard Business Review,* March–April 1998, pp. 73–84.
[8] *Business Week,* July 1, 1991.
[9] S. Lohr, "How Did Dell Computer Stumble?" *The New York Times,* May 28, 1993, p. D1.
[10] J. Magretta, "The Power of Virtual Integration: An Interview with Dell Computer's Michael Dell," *Harvard Business Review,* March–April 1998, pp. 73–84.

[11] Ibid.
[12] S. Lohr, "How Did Dell Computer Stumble?" *The New York Times,* May 28, 1993, p. D1.

EXHIBIT 2   Dell Computer Corporation–Selected Sales and Financial Data

(a) Sales by products and segments (1991–1993)

	1991	1992	1993
Net sales ($ m)	$890	$2,014	$2,873
Products:			
Desktops	90%	88%	94%
Laptops	10%	12%	2%
Servers			4%
Market segment sales:			
Relationship	59%	61%	64%
Transaction	41%	39%	36%
Markets:			
U.S.	72.8%	72.5%	70.9%
Europe	27.2%	27.5%	27.2%
Asia			1.9%

Source: D. Narayandas and V. K. Rangan, "Dell Computer Corporation," Harvard Business School Case No. 596-058.

(b) Selected financial data (dollars in millions, except per share data)

	1991	1992
Net sales	890	2,014
Cost of goods sold	594	1,545
Gross profit	296	469
Selling, general and administrative expense	214	310
Depreciation, depletion, & amortization	14	20
Operating profit	69	139
Net income (after taxes)	51	102
Other data:		
EPS (primary)—excluding extra items and discounted operations	0.18	0.32
Dividends per share	0	0
ROA (%)	9%	11%
ROE (%)	19%	28%
Market value	761	1,705
R&D expenses	42	49

Source: Dell financial reports.

ior executives from larger firms such as Motorola to handle Dell's expanding operations.[13]

A third problem involved the lack of structure in Dell's product development process, symbolized, as some thought, by Dell's disastrous foray into the portable computer market.

---

[13] A. Server, "Michael Dell Turns the PC World Inside Out," *Fortune,* September 8, 1997, pp. 76–80ff.

Product Development at Dell

In accordance with its strategy of commoditization, Dell's R&D budget was smaller than most other large computer firms. This also went hand in hand with Michael Dell's philosophy of spartanism that permeated the entire organization. A modest one-story converted industrial warehouse with fluorescent lights and cubicles housed Dell's management and product development professionals.

In this setting, product development at Dell in the early 90s had remained an informal process, run by autonomous teams that often centered around experienced developers. While such an approach delivered several successful products, the results were neither consistent nor predictable. The informality of the process meant that risks were not assessed rigorously in making project investment decisions, nor were the project bounds tightly established. Project execution experienced enormous variability depending on the project leader in charge. In many projects, team members did not all share the same vision of the project's objectives. Designed products were frequently "thrown over the wall" to manufacturing, and in some cases quality issues were addressed too late in the development process.

Some experienced managers began advocating a more structured approach. But engineers, used to a freewheeling approach, decried formality, which they felt had the potential to lock out creativity. But after one computer project had to be canceled following an investment of several million dollars, Dell's senior management realized the need for a more structured approach adapted to the increasingly rapid product development cycles in the computer industry.

With input from industrial and academic consultants, Dell management started in early 1993 to organize product development around core teams of development professionals from several different functions. These teams, led by nominated core team leaders, were to take charge of the product's success from start to finish. Thus, through daily contact between different core team members, and through phase reviews, core teams hoped to avoid the pitfalls of the previous era. At phase reviews, typically slated for every three months, development work was to be reviewed, technical and market risks assessed, and funding for the next phase approved. The new process had the following phases (see Exhibit 3):

1. *Profile Phase:* The product development team arrived at a product and market definition, resulting in a two- to three-page "product features guide."
2. *Planning Phase:* Product team members developed a detailed business case for the product, which senior

EXHIBIT 3   Dell's New 18-Month Development Process

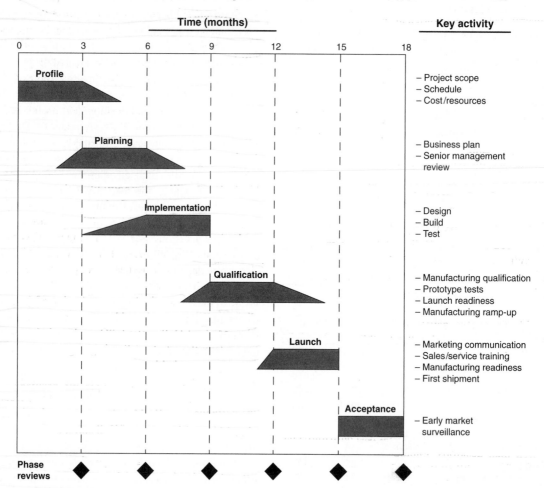

executives subsequently scrutinized for underlying assumptions and financial impact. This ensured that product developers paid enough attention to business issues before investing in the subsequent expensive phases.

3. *Implementation Phase:* The product development team designed, built, and tested functional prototypes of the proposed product. This phase also marked the commencement of the development of instruction manuals and service plans. At the end of this phase, orders for long lead time tooling were placed with suppliers, resulting in a major financial commitment to Dell.

4. *Qualification Phase:* The product development team built production prototypes of the proposed product. Prototypes were distributed to key customers to obtain their feedback on potential product improvements. Sales force training also began during this phase.

5. *Launch Phase:* The entire customer buying experience, from opening the packed finished product to running various software applications, was exhaustively tested. Production was ramped up and early customer shipments were made toward the end of the launch phase.

6. *Acceptance Phase:* The team collected customer feedback about the product for up to three months after launch. The phase was completed with an acceptance report that compared the results achieved with planned objectives and included a summary of lessons learned in the spirit of continuous improvement.

Through much of 1993, however, informality prevailed while the new process was being put in place, and core teams often approached the new process in spirit only.

THE PORTABLE COMPUTER INDUSTRY

For several years, technological and pricing breakthroughs promised to free personal computers from the desktop.[14] Although Osborne marketed the first portable computers in 1981, the machines remained only a small market presence throughout the 1980s. Most weighed over 20 pounds and were derogatorily termed "luggables." Many suffered from severe quality problems because manufacturers viewed the computers as "shrunken desktops." (See Exhibit 4.)

Nevertheless, by the end of the decade, the quality of portability itself gave these machines gross margins that were typically 3 to 5 percent above desktops. When several leading computer firms entered the portable field, it was predicted that the market would soon soar. Such predictions forced firms like Dell to determine the appropriate product balance among desktops, portables, and servers (microprocessor systems that created local networks between different computers and communication devices).

Portable computer development relied on several technological breakthroughs: flat liquid crystal display screens developed in Japan, which took substantially less space than traditional cathode ray tubes; compact hard drive disks that consumed less energy; and improved battery technology, which allowed over an hour of operations before needing to be recharged.

Manufacturing portables involved less hardware customization than desktops. Laptops, however, often enjoyed more feature differentiation than desktops. Overall, higher workmanship and quality went into these machines given the harsher range of conditions they would face in use. Portables underwent a commensurately challenging array of tests including exposure to shock, vibration, drops, and accelerations.

In 1993, portables were classified as laptops if they weighed between 4.5 and 8 pounds, and sub-notebooks if they weighed under 4 pounds.

DELL'S LATITUDE DEVELOPMENT PROJECT

Early Setback in Portable Computers

In 1991, Dell came out with its first line of portable computers. At Dell's assembly line, the chassis with dis-

play and motherboard came prepackaged from outside vendors; only the microprocessor, hard disk drive, and memory were added in the assembly line, followed by software. Through software and communications capabilities, it was possible to create significant personalization. And personalization remained Dell's forte.

In 1992, with portables accounting for 17 percent of Dell's sales, rumors circulated about quality problems, ranging from faulty battery packs to unreliable screens to frequent power failures to broken hinges. Dell's notebooks, based on older 386 microprocessors, were consequently slower than the 486-based machines fielded by rivals. Even Dell's commodity-like prices could not draw sufficient buyers, many of whom wanted machines that would keep them competitive in the business arena.

Early in 1993, in what was shaping into the company's *annus horribilis*, Dell canceled a new line of laptops under development, since these were deemed too slow and expensive. A subsequent write-off of $20 million in associated expenses sparked a reorganization of the portables division. When questioned by a reporter about the portables, Michael Dell replied, "One plane is late and these guys claim the whole airline is going down the tube. . . . These guys are babies."[15]

Michael Dell had a point, for the desktops division had racked up unit volume increases of 155 percent over the previous year. By May, however, notebook sales had slipped to just 6 percent of Dell sales, at a time when the company had envisioned portables to account for 20–25 percent of sales. Dell's portable division, one Dell official admitted, suffered from "significant underinvestment" and a "shrunken desktop mentality."[16] Rivals, in the meantime, reported strong portable sales: a Compaq notebook with the more advanced 486 microprocessor, for instance, broke a market launch record for all Compaq products.[17]

In a vote of confidence, however, Bill Gates, chairman of Microsoft and himself a Dell desktop user, stated, "Dell is a super-solid company. They'll get on top of the situation."[18] But Dell went on to post a $75.7 million second-quarter loss. Company officials blamed years of

---

[14] Some of the information in this section derives from D. Narayandas and V. K. Rangan, "Dell Computer Corporation," Harvard Business School Case No. 596-058.

[15] S. Lohr, "How Did Dell Computer Stumble?" *The New York Times*, May 28, 1993, p. D1.

[16] S. Lohr, "Dell's Second Stab at Portables," *The New York Times*, February 22, 1994, p. D1.

[17] T. Hayes, "Dell's Profit and Stock Plummet," *The New York Times*, May 26, 1993, p. D1.

[18] S. Lohr, "How Did Dell Computer Stumble?" *The New York Times*, May 28, 1993, p. D1.

EXHIBIT 4   Portable Computer Market Data

(a) Portable computer market size (millions of units)

	World	United States
1992	4.3	2.2
1993	6.2	2.9
1994*	7.4	3.2
1995*	8.9	3.7

*IDC projections for laptop market.

(b) Personal computer market size (millions of units) by vendor

	1987	1989	1991	1992	1993
IBM	28.0	16.9	14.1	11.7	14.0
Compaq	7.5	4.4	4.1	5.7	9.6
Apple	14.0	10.7	13.8	13.2	13.9
Dell	—	0.9	1.6	3.7	5.4
AST/Tandy	2.0	1.7	2.7	2.7	3.6
Gateway	—	0.2	2.5	3.6	4.4
Packard Bell	—	3.3	4.7	5.3	6.7
HP	—	NA	NA	NA	NA
DEC	—	NA	NA	NA	NA
Others	40.0	61.9	56.5	54.1	42.4

Source: John Steffens, *Computer Industry Forecasts and New Games—Strategic Competition in the PC Revolution* (Pergamon Press, 1994), cited in D. Narayandas and V. K. Rangan, "Dell Computer Corporation," Harvard Business School Case No. 596-058, Rev. March 11, 1996.

(c) U.S. personal computer market growth

	1988	1990	1992	Projected 1994	Projected 1996
Desktops:					
Sales (billion $)	20.05	20.78	22.52	25.06	33.0
Units (000s)	8,100	8,750	9,835	11,802	13,100
Portables:					
Sales (billion $)	3.28	3.87	4.75	8.48	11.6
Units (000s)	1,130	1,540	2,150	3,800	5,400
Servers:					
Sales (billion $)	1.64	2.97	5.47	8.11	12.5
Units (000s)	195	338	457	739	1,250

Source: BIS Strategic Decisions, Inc., cited in D. Narayandas and V. K. Rangan, "Dell Computer Corporation," Harvard Business School Case No. 596-058.

explosive growth, which they claimed strained company performance ranging from inventory management to product forecasting.

Unintentionally rubbing salt in the wound, three owners of Dell portables returned their machines during the fall because they had noted smoke or melted spots on the plastic housing. Investigating engineers found a weakness in an electronic circuitry component: under physical stresses such as jiggling the power cord and AC adapter, the component could sometimes crack.[19] In October 1993, Dell recalled 17,000 notebooks. The company's direct relationship with customers, it turned out, had facilitated tracking down the owners.

Commenting on Dell's woes, industry analyst Steve Ablondi noted, "This industry moves so fast that you can

[19] K. Jones, "Dell Recalls Thousands of Notebook Computers," *The New York Times,* October 9, 1993, Sec. 1, p. 47.

EXHIBIT 5   Dell's Organizational Structure and the Notebook Development Team (1993)

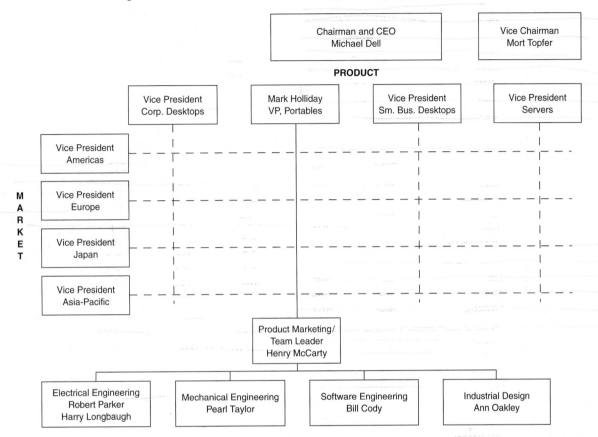

get thrown off the merry-go-round on one side and still get back on the other side . . . so Dell can come back from the dead in the portable business."[20] When Dell announced plans for launching a new line of notebooks in 1993, named the Latitude series, Michael Dell himself acknowledged that "it's very, very important for us to get this right."

The Next Generation: Choosing Which Features to Emphasize

To prepare for the challenges ahead, Dell reorganized its portable division. In spring 1993, Mark Holliday, the division's new head, immediately formed a core team that was charged with developing a new portable product to be launched in late fall 1994. The nucleus of the team included Robert Parker and Harry Longbaugh, electrical

engineers, Pearl Taylor, a mechanical engineer, Ann Oakley, an industrial designer, and Bill Cody, a software engineer. Henry McCarty, the product marketer, headed the team, which reported to Holliday. Holliday, in turn, reported directly to Michael Dell (see Exhibit 5).

Part of the reason for the reorganization was to speed decision making in an industry with ever-shortening product development cycles. By 1993, it took Dell 18 months to take an idea to production, of which some 14 months were involved with development. Once specification data were available, the process of tooling took four–five months. Product life cycles, by way of comparison, lasted roughly three years. The team expected to spend $10 million on the product development effort that would hopefully resuscitate Dell's portable computer line.

The first task the team faced involved taking stock of the situation. Within Dell there was great controversy about the future of the portables market—about its growth, pricing and marketing strategy, and resources needed to implement a successful strategy. Within the

---

[20] S. Lohr, "Dell's Second Stab at Portables," *The New York Times*, February 22, 1994, p. D1.

Strategys should come down from above.

team there was some debate about whether to enter the subnotebook market rather than just focus on notebooks. Which features to emphasize formed a large question. Some features engineers had to think about were not immediately obvious to customers—for instance, safety, microchip specifications, and component supply. While product developers thought along 10 or more dimensions, individual customers only thought along 2 or 3. With this in mind, McCarty, the product marketer, and some of the engineers on the team talked with customers, strategized about incorporating new technologies, and even started lining up suppliers.[21]

Safety should be given to know did it get through UL?

In the summer of 1993, early in the "profile phase," a discussion panel comprising all team members debated which features to highlight in a new line of laptops. Market research indicated that several features rated high in the minds of laptop consumers: price, microprocessor choice, battery life, screen resolution, reliability, weight, and size (see Exhibit 6). Dell considered emphasizing battery life—a feature that ranked only behind price and microprocessor choice.

Battery Life as a Value-Adding Feature

The consideration to highlight battery life grew out of a serendipitous encounter in January 1993 in Tokyo. Michael Dell recounted how after a meeting with one of Dell's primary manufacturing partners, Sony, someone ran up to him saying:

> "Oh, Mr. Dell, please wait one minute. I'm from Sony's power technology company. We have a new power-system technology we want to explain to you." And I remember thinking, Is this guy going to try to sell me a power plant? He starts showing me chart after chart about the performance of lithium ion batteries. "This is wonderful," I tell him. "And if it's true, we're going to put this in every notebook computer we make."[22]

According to a senior manager at Dell, "Michael has a great memory for these types of details, and he filed it away." When the company sought to reenter the laptop market, Michael Dell pulled out this piece of information for his engineers to contemplate.

At the time, most portable computers used nickel metal hydride (NiHi) rechargeable batteries (see Exhibit 7).

---

[21] Ibid.
[22] J. Magretta, "The Power of Virtual Integration: An Interview with Dell Computer's Michael Dell," *Harvard Business Review,* March–April 1998, pp. 73–84.

EXHIBIT 6   Marketing Memo

MEMO:	**PERSONAL COMPUTER MARKET**
ATTENTION:	Henry McCarty
FROM:	Gordon Lillie, Marketing
DATE:	August 15, 1993

Here is the summary market information you requested: we think Dell may capture 2.5% of the market with a good product, but even up to 3 percent with a superb product. If our gross margins average a fourth of our average price of $2400 over the life of the product, then expected margins over the three-year product cycle would be close to a half-billion dollars. Our models lead us to believe that each month's delay in product development would lead to a loss of about 4% of sales.

Market research shows that most laptop users already have considerable experience with desktops, and that new consumers are more likely to buy a desktop rather than a laptop. But portables are increasingly bought as the primary computer. In 1992, a fourth of portables were bought for this purpose by business customers of all sizes. At the same time, portables were also being purchased to replace desktops. (IDC Customer Directions and Buying Behavior, Year-End Surveys.)

P.S. I am also including marketing information about market size and product features that went into our deliberations.

Top 10 Notebook Evaluation Criteria for Actual Business Customer Purchases

Criterion	Incidence %
Price	54
Microprocessor	35
Battery life	27
Screen resolution	15
Reliability	11
Weight	9
Hard drive storage	6
Durability	3
Compatibility	3
Speed	1

Source: IDC Customer Directions and Buying Behavior, Year-End Surveys.

Top Six Leading Brands for Portables Among 1993 Business Customers

Brand	Purchases
IBM	34%
Compaq	51%
Toshiba	32%
Dell	7%
NEC	8%
Gateway	2%

Source: IDC Customer Directions and Buying Behavior, Year-End Surveys.

EXHIBIT 7   Battery Technology

Life is a search after power.
—Ralph Waldo Emerson

Batteries are energy storage devices that convert chemical energy into electrical energy in order to power attached devices. The first operable battery dates back to 1800, when Italian physicist Alessandro Volta devised the "voltaic pile," a simple arrangement of zinc and silver plates and salt water. Like most batteries to follow, this exploited the different electron-attracting properties of two different metals to deliver sustainable currents. But almost a century of further developments would be needed for the first commercial applications of batteries.

Battery technology remained a slow-moving field through much of the 20th century. Development of rechargeable batteries, however, helped power the automobile revolution, and decades later opened up use of small portable devices such as portable computers. In the early 1990s, computer batteries in widespread use were of the rechargeable nickel metal hydride (NiHi) and nickel-cadmium (NiCad) types. These batteries suffered from two major deficiencies, however: First, they would only recharge up to the point where they had been discharged. Users could take care of this annoying "memory effect" by occasionally allowing fully charged batteries to discharge all the way. Second, the NiCad batteries contained heavy metals that posed environmental health hazards if improperly disposed. (A serious consideration, given that if all the nickel-cadmium batteries produced each year in the Western World were lined up side by side, they would circle the Earth four times.)*

These two deficiencies, combined with the short times between recharges, conspired to make battery technology a bottleneck for growth of the portable computer industry. By the early 1990s, manufacturers in Japan (which produced half the world's NiCad batteries), Europe, and the United States raced to develop better products for the $800 million portable computer battery industry.** One promising innovation came from lithium ion technology. Plain lithium had already found prior use in the nonrechargeable button-sized batteries that powered watches and cameras for up to years. Chemical innovations now allowed for building lithium ion batteries without size limitations that could be recharged safely. These toxin-free batteries could pack perhaps three times more energy as a NiHi battery of the same size and possessed no memory effect. Furthermore, these could be recharged even more rapidly.

But lithium in larger batteries had a worrisome tendency to separate and pose an explosion hazard. Some battery developers had even given up on the quest, following minor calamities in their laboratories. An unknown number of companies, however, remained in the race for lithium ion technology.

A final hurdle for all new battery technologies involved testing. Actually, this was often not much of a hurdle at all given that little standardization existed for testing conditions. Manufacturers, thus, could claim long battery lives based on tests run under low power demand, thus creating a spate of "lies, damn lies, and battery lies." But scrupulous battery manufacturers often hired independent battery testing outfits to conduct two types of tests: "sprint tests," which ran systems at maximal power demand, and "steeplechase" tests, which mimicked the more typical patterns of intermittent use.

Source: Dell Marketing Division.
*F. E. Katrak and I. S. Servi, "Battle of the Nickel Links," *Electronic Engineering Times,* February 4, 1991, p. 52.
**P. J. Barry, "Valence Technology, Inc.—Company Report," C. J. Lawrence, Inc., 1993.

Under optimal conditions, NiHi batteries typically provided fewer than three hours of power at normal usage. But these batteries suffered from an annoying tendency to recharge only a fraction of their full capacity unless properly managed—a problem referred to as "battery memory." Furthermore, if not properly disposed of, they could release heavy metal toxins into the environment.

In contrast, lithium ion (LiOn), the technology the Sony engineer had mentioned to Michael Dell, suffered from neither of these deficiencies and promised longer recharge lives. LiOn was just starting to be used in camcorders. Thus far, however, no one had figured out how to power larger devices like computers using LiOn technology, especially given the tendency of lithium in larger batteries to separate and even explode. Some battery developers had shelved their LiOn development efforts, out of concern that safety and reliability problems might precipitate expensive product recalls and litigation. Some companies, however, kept at it. Toshiba was known to have a good start, but conceivably Sony engineers might be ahead.

It remained unclear if customers were as excited about new developments in batteries. Focus groups showed that new customers would not necessarily view portables with LiOn as better than portables with traditional batteries. But Michael Dell did not worry about this. As he pointed out, "The customer doesn't come to you and say, 'Boy, I really like lithium ion batteries. I can't wait to get my hands on some lithium ion.' The customer says, 'I want a notebook computer that lasts the whole day. I don't want it to run out when I'm on the plane.'"[23] Furthermore, among experienced customers—Dell's traditional customer base—battery life proved more important.

Thus, the product development team began viewing the LiOn battery as a tangible feature mirroring the new Latitude computers' overall quality. The new technology could potentially boost the entire product line's market size by anchoring product image in a business with sales cycles of only six to nine months. In the worldwide portable computer market, with annual sales of 11 million units, Dell's management believed that a good Dell product might recapture its old market share of 2.5 percent, and a superb product might even gain 3 percent.

The Next Generation: Which Battery?

A new battery technology was not the only computer powering option available to the product development team. Another possibility for doubling battery time could come from allowing users to eject the disk drive and replace it with a second battery—a strategy that, in Shakespeare's words, "gives to every power a double power." Essentially, Dell could choose between better fuel or a bigger gas tank—two tanks, in fact. The product development team agreed with Henry McCarty, however, that the dual battery option alone would not make customers perceive the Latitude line as leading technologically.[24]

Thus, at the end of the profile phase where a decision had to be made, Holliday and his team entertained only a few realistic development options:

1. *Continue with a proven battery technology (NiHi):* Dell could continue placing traditional batteries into its Latitude notebooks. McCarty and Taylor, the mechanical engineer, favored this option. This would take less space than the LiOn battery and thus allow for packing in some other features such as communications control or memory management accessories. All members of Dell's portables division agreed about the viability of this proven option, which would involve no delays and deliver a good Dell product. On the other hand, this option would provide limited product differentiation in an increasingly competitive market.

2. *Go with the new battery technology (LiOn):* Dell could incorporate new lithium ion batteries into the notebooks. Parker and Longbaugh, both electrical engineers, championed this option. This option would

mean incorporating an unproven and more expensive technology, which would also take up more space than conventional batteries. The new batteries were thicker than traditional batteries, requiring 40 cubic millimeters' more space—valuable space that could be used for other features. Because of uncertainty over the new technology, other leading manufacturers, such as Compaq, had decided to delay using LiOn technology. Sony (which currently turned out 100,000 rechargeable plain lithium batteries a month for cellular telephones)[25] had yet to complete testing and ramping up production capabilities for LiOn. In fact, if Dell committed to the batteries, it would most likely end up using all of Sony's production for the next few years.

3. *Defer commitment to either battery technology:* Dell could continue to pursue the laptop development without committing to either battery technology at the current phase review. Buying just two or three months would not pose a major problem, but deferring the decision until the qualification phase review, or another nine months—the time McCarty estimated it would take for Sony to provide conclusive test data—was another matter. The Dell team could potentially defer commitment until this point using either one of the following two approaches:

- The team could "overdesign" the battery space and the rest of the product to accommodate either battery. This implied that the mechanical engineering and industrial design groups would design the product to ensure that the thicker LiOn battery would fit as well. In addition—and Parker felt this was the harder requirement—the battery charging circuitry and software would have to remain compatible with either system. McCarty felt that the resulting bulkier product would be less attractive to the customer, and the variable cost of overdesigning could be as large as 2 percent of margins on each unit.
- Alternatively the team could follow a "dual path" approach in which two different products are developed independently—one using LiOn and the other using NiHi battery technology. The fixed cost of duplicating engineering activities and tooling meant an additional expense of $2.5 million. These costs stemmed from performing parallel electrical configuration and battery management software, and from tooling, among other engineering tasks. These estimates, of course, did not include the potential

---

[23] Ibid.
[24] In addition to addressing the issue of power supply, Dell engineers also were working on power management tools that let users determine power demand. For instance, maneuvers such as dimming the screen or shutting down non-essential programs could lower energy usage.

---

[25] "Recharged: The Battery Market," *The Economist,* May 2, 1992.

What other differences will the line have? (except for not smoking?)

SECTION ONE: NEW PRODUCT DEVELOPMENT **969**

I don't agree —

demoralization of engineers that would result from discarding half the craftsmanship in the final product and the opportunity cost of pulling developers away from other projects.

The October Meeting

As he called the meeting to order, Holliday indicated that he would encourage divergent viewpoints on the various options.

Taylor, the mechanical engineer, sparked the discussion: "We really can't afford the risk of delivering one failed product on top of another," she pointed out. "For this round, let's stick to NiHi and get a reliable product out the door. Let's not defer our decision: It runs counter to our new product development process which requires us to commit now. I mean, too much informality and delayed commitment in the past led us to scrap a $20 million product development project midstream. Isn't that why we reorganized the portables division and installed the new development process?"

Parker, the electrical engineer, interjected: "I think we need to get LiOn in our product somehow. That's what will hit our users between the eyes and add value to the entire line. And just think that a successful product could use all of Sony's new batteries and could lock out our competitors from LiOn technology. We could get a strong technical edge on the market." *(single source dangerous)*

"That's playing with fire!" McCarty, the marketer and team leader, responded. "I see so many question marks about Sony's supply capabilities that a small LiOn supply could choke our own ability to deliver portables. Remember that we want to use the new technology to build market share? So even if we boost product price to make up for smaller quantity, we may not meet our sales objectives. And let's not ignore the technical risks that make me feel uncomfortable."

"That's why we bother examining all branches of the decision tree," Holliday quietly reminded everyone and thought of the recent analysis that McCarty had prepared for him (see Exhibit 8).

do financial analysis

EXHIBIT 8 McCarty's Data on the Different Development Options

Estimates

Forecasted market size (1995–97)	= 11 million units per year
Potential Dell market share (good product, e.g., NiHi)	= 2.5% (or 825,000 units over 3 years)
Potential Dell market share (superb product, e.g., LiOn)	= 3.0% (or 990,000 units over 3 years)
Average price per unit over life of product	= $2,400
Average gross margin per unit over life of product	= $600
Expected product life	= 3 years
Cost of each month delay in development schedule	= 4% of unit sales
Expected length of development schedule	= 18 months (incl. acceptance phase)
Expected cost of development effort	= $10 million

small Δ + delay time + Sony risk

Option 1: Continue a proven battery technology (NiHi)
- Confidence = 100% (likelihood that it works as expected)
- Net margin = 825,000 units × $600/unit − $10 M   = $485 M

Option 2: Go with the new battery technology (LiOn)
- Confidence = 60% (likelihood that it works as expected); risky!!!
- Net margin (if LiOn works) = 990,000 units × $600/unit − $10 M   = $584 M *× .6*
- Net margin (if LiOn fails) = (825,000 units × 0.5) × $600/unit − ($10 + 0.3 × $10) = $234.5 M *× .4*
- If LiOn fails at launch, a switch to NiHi would require substantial rework (70% of original schedule and 30% of cost). Because competitors would have an established product on the market before them, Dell would lose about 50% of projected units sold.
- If LiOn causes a failure, there could be spillover effects into the desktop business. Dell's reputation for quality could be tarnished.

expected value 350.4 + 93.8 = 444.2 M

des in parallel – insurance – come out w/NiH – forthahead, use as test bed

Option 3: Defer commitment until qualification phase review (dual development *or* overdesign)
- If dual development paths[a] Estimated additional fixed cost = $2.5 million
- If product is overdesigned[b] Estimated additional variable cost = 0.5% of revenue (2% of margin)
- Gross margin (if LiOn works) = 990,000 units × $600/unit = $594 M (before additional cost)
- Gross margin (if LiOn fails) = 825,000 units × $600/unit = $495 M (before additional cost)
- The analysis assumes that Sony will give us enough information at the end of the qualification phase to determine with full certainty if LiOn will work or fail. If it fails, Dell can drop it and revert to option 1.

leverage what you can — platform reuse

[a] These are the actual project costs incurred. They include additional designers and engineers, material and tooling costs, etc. if we follow a dual path until the qualification phase review. The costs do not include the product opportunities we would forgo if we had to pull people away from other projects.
[b] Because of the LiOn battery's different dimensions and properties, we would have to "overdesign" the computer case, the charging circuitry, and battery management software to accommodate either battery technology, which would add about $12 cost per unit.

"I think deferring our decision is the way to go," said Oakley, the industrial designer. "Worst case, if the LiOn option looks bad, we'd revert to NiHi and lose some valuable internal space that could have supported other features. I know there are other costs, too, but staying flexible isn't a straight gamble; it's just half a gamble."

Longbaugh, the other electrical engineer, threw up his hands. "Listen, you don't rob a stagecoach by perching on the fence. Let's make up our minds one way or the other now. Dell has always had a strong culture of commitment and this doesn't seem right. I, for one, think LiOn is a really neat technology. I suggest we go straight to LiOn, keeping in mind that if it does flop, we could still develop a product with our proven battery technology."

Cody, the software engineer, slipped in the last words before a break in the meeting:

> True, but if it fails, think of the substantial rework needed— we've estimated the rework to require 70 percent of the original schedule and 30 percent of the $10 million development cost. And Henry [McCarty] thinks that the resulting late market entry would likely halve projected unit sales. And any technical fiasco could severely tarnish our reputation, and lead to spillover effects in our desktop business. Let's not fan a brush fire!

Looking out the conference room windows at the sun setting over the Texan landscape, Holliday reflected on how Dell had helped catalyze Austin's booming high-tech economy. Dell had flourished in the Texas Hill Country, relying on its unique model of making and selling computers. Now Wall Street and the business world scrutinized its every move. *The New York Times* had noted:

> In the fast-paced personal computer industry, the real test of a company's mettle is not if it slips, but whether it can recover quickly. . . . Unless Dell comes back with a strong portable business, the company risks being relegated to second-rate status in the personal computer industry.[26]

Yet after suffering from the prior setback, Holliday personally felt that his product development team had nothing more to lose—not in terms of revenue nor even worker morale. Once again, Holliday watched his colleagues enter the conference room and seat themselves around the table. He then called the meeting back to order. It was time to make a decision.

---

[26] S. Lohr, "Dell's Second Stab at Portables," *The New York Times,* February 22, 1994, p. D1.

READING IV-I

Communication Between Engineering and Production: A Critical Factor

H. E. Riggs

Extensive communication between engineering and production is critical to implementing the firm's technical policy. Communication must be both formal and informal. Informal communication should be encouraged in all the ways that have become common in high-technology companies, from "beer busts" to technical symposia to off-site, multiday discussion sessions.

Regardless of the amount of informal communication, formal communication is also essential. The formal communication system between engineering and production must deal with three important related, but distinct, challenges:

1. Introducing new products from the development laboratory to the production floor.
2. Providing the optimum—neither maximum nor minimum—level of documentation on existing products.
3. Facilitating orderly and cost-effective changes to products now in production.

INTRODUCING NEW PRODUCTS TO MANUFACTURING

Handing over the new product from engineering to manufacturing tests the cooperation and communication between engineering and production personnel as does no other activity. The high-technology company that manages this transition well stands to gain timing, cost, and quality advantages that can have substantial payoffs in the marketplace.

Where departmental barriers are high and engineers are encouraged or permitted to be myopic, design engineers will attempt to maximize product performance and manufacturing engineers will try to redesign the product to reduce its cost. Such a two-step process is highly inefficient and very time-consuming. Optimizing across the conflicting priorities of cost and performance—often called value engineering—must be the responsibility of

---

Source: From: *Managing High-Technology Companies.* Copyright © 1983 Van Nostrand Reinhold Company.

everybody engaged in new product creation, including marketing managers who have a hand in setting the new product's target specifications.

Extensive communication must both precede and follow the formal transition from engineering to production. Periodic product design meetings that involve design engineers, manufacturing engineers, and material planners (and sometimes product managers from marketing and others as well) should be held monthly during the early design stage and perhaps weekly just prior to and following the "hand over" of the new product from engineering to production. In these meetings, the design staff consults with manufacturing personnel regarding design alternatives under consideration and gains insight into the issues of producibility as the product or system is being designed. Realistic tolerances are specified, and engineers are encouraged not to tighten tolerances to expedite design or to gain an additional margin of safety. (Excessively tight tolerances almost always increase manufacturing costs.) Manufacturing should share with the design team its experience with present vendors and subcontractors as engineering is selecting sources for parts or processing for the new product or system.

Both manufacturing and engineering personnel must be aware that the design process is generally not complete when manufacturing commences. Design errors that need attention may be uncovered, change requests initiated by manufacturing to facilitate fabrication or assembly must be evaluated, and operating performance that met specifications in the laboratory but cannot be replicated on the manufacturing floor must be reassessed. Proper reliance on prototype units and pilot production runs before full-scale production is attempted can reduce costly errors.

Prototype, Pilot, and Production Runs

Engineering typically produces prototypes (the first one or two units of a new product or system). The engineers and design technicians construct them at considerable cost, frequently building and rebuilding them. They use techniques appropriate to the lab but inappropriate to full-scale production—"breadboards" instead of printed circuit boards and fabricated instead of cast metal or injection-molded parts—in order to facilitate design changes and minimize tooling costs and lead times. These prototypes, which are often necessarily quite different physically from the units ultimately supplied to customers, should be both thoroughly tested in the laboratory and subjected to some field testing. The purpose of pro-

totypes is to prove design concepts and confirm product specifications.

Once the basic design concepts have been proven in prototype and satisfactory operating specifications have been met, a pilot production run (the production of a limited quantity) should be initiated. The design used for the pilot production run should be the one that is expected to be used in full-scale production—for example, breadboards are now replaced with printed circuit boards, and substantially more investment is made in tooling. The purpose of the pilot production run is to test product producibility and to work out any bugs in the final design before the company scales up to full production. (When total anticipated volume of the product or system is small, this pilot production step can be eliminated.)

In some companies, pilot production runs are undertaken by the engineering department and, in others, by the manufacturing department. The exact reporting relationship is not particularly significant. What is important is to recognize that pilot production runs are inevitably the joint responsibility of engineering and production.

Freezing Designs

Before full-scale production is undertaken, the design must be frozen, after which time formal engineering change notices are the only mechanism for effecting changes. In the absence of a pilot production run (and sometimes even with it), the point at which design becomes final, or frozen, is often unclear. At the prototype stage, the design must be allowed to remain fluid, permitting design changes at minimum cost and documentation. But it is human nature to seek almost endlessly for small improvements and refinements. This propensity is as true for the design engineer who is a parent of the new product as it is for the artist in her sculpture or the writer in his manuscript. Just as editorial changes are expensive to effect once the manuscript has been set in type, so product design changes are expensive to effect once manufacturing has commenced.

Thus, at some point, the design of the new product must be frozen, and both manufacturing and engineering must agree upon that point. Subsequent design changes can no longer be made unilaterally by the design engineer, as they could during the prototype phase.

You can often gain important timing and cost advantages by freezing certain portions of the design before other portions. For example, in a complex computer-based system, the selection of the system's minicomputer can and should be frozen long before other portions of the system are designed, in order to provide sufficient time for the programmers to develop the necessary software and for purchasing to negotiate OEM contracts with the minicomputer supplier. Sequential freezing is appropriate: Freeze parts or components known to have long procurement lead times early; leave standard components and those parts requiring little or no tooling unfrozen until late in the design cycle. A complex design project can usefully be subjected to PERT (program evaluation and review technique) analysis to reveal the critical design concepts or components that need early freezing. This process of sequential freezing of portions of the design implies close working relationships and much communication throughout the engineering organization and between engineering and production.

Top managers of high-technology companies should see to it that procedures for freezing designs are both established and adhered to.

Using a Skunk Works

Some technology-based companies have successfully used an unusual organizational technique to expedite new product design and introduction. When a new product requires (1) a number of engineering disciplines, (2) careful attention to manufacturability and cost, and (3) a telescoping of the design and introduction stages, a separate task force may be created, drawing personnel from a number of functional departments in the company. When this task force is assigned separate facilities, sometimes with extra security against industrial espionage, these facilities are often referred to as the skunk works.

The objective is to recapture the advantage of the small company: high motivation, focused purpose on a single product, system, or process, and intensive and informal communication with a minimum of organizational barriers. The task force is accorded (or assumes) high prestige in the organization, and assignment to it is eagerly sought. Extra resources are typically made available to the task force.

Arguing against the establishment of a skunk works is the fact that creating one or a series of these task forces can be disruptive to the organization. Other development projects may be interrupted and key technical personnel assigned to the task force may be unavailable for informal counsel and advice on projects to which they are not formally assigned. Acceleration of the design can also cause some loss of efficiency.

This organizational device should be used only when competitive conditions demand fast action, either to pro-

tect an existing market position or to gain a jump on anticipated competition. Although the device has proved highly effective in a number of instances, resulting in a dramatic product unveiling that left both customers and competitors in awe, its overuse reduces the opportunities for specialization, economies of scale (experience curve economies), and routinizing of procedures.

A variation on this organizational device is to assign a group of engineers to "follow" a new design through the laboratory and onto the production floor. That is, rather than turning over its design (and prototypes) to manufacturing engineering, a portion or all of the engineering design team is assigned the responsibility for moving with the product from the design engineering organization to the manufacturing engineering organization. The trade-off is that the "following" engineers will know the new product in detail, thus eliminating the need for manufacturing engineers to learn the new product, but will be less experienced and probably less capable in attacking the problems of producibility and tooling. However, a design engineer who has spent some time wrestling with new products from a manufacturing engineering viewpoint will be a more effective design engineer when he or she returns to the laboratory and another new product. Again, a type of job rotation has occurred.

Moving from Single to Multiple Products

Many emerging technical companies—that is, small but rapidly growing companies—encounter real turmoil as they move from relying on a single product to offering multiple products to the market. A small technology-based business focusing on designing and manufacturing a single product is often wonderfully efficient. It minimizes conflicting priorities because all hands are devoted to the single product. As the business grows and more product lines are added to the company's portfolio, choices must be made. The general management task suddenly becomes much more complex.

In engineering, the task of product maintenance engineering on the older products competes for attention with new product development. The need for standardization of components and subassemblies across product lines becomes evident. Compromises between standardization and optimum price/performance suddenly become necessary.

In manufacturing, quality problems that remained under control because of the undivided attention of manufacturing and engineering on the single product line now drift out of control as technical attention is diffused across many products. The existence of multiple products on the manufacturing floor complicates production scheduling. These products require both unique and common skills and often incorporate common parts or subassemblies that ought to be produced in larger lots.

The interaction between engineering and manufacturing was extensive on the company's first product line. This intimate, one-on-one communication needs to be continued on the newer products, but coordination on older products needs to be more routinized.

A key test for an emerging high-technology company is its ability to move successfully from engineering and producing a single product to engineering and producing a portfolio of product lines. The transition requires that a manufacturing engineering function be established, as well as a data base and reference system to aid in standardizing components. Task assignments in engineering must clearly recognize the dual responsibility of product maintenance and product development. A formal documentation and engineering change request system must replace the informal communication that sufficed when the company was small and produced only one product.

ENGINEERING DOCUMENTATION

Formal communication between engineering and production demands product and process documentation: drawings, bills of material (parts lists), schematics, assembly prints, software listings, and many other elements of paperwork (and now, increasingly, microfiche, computer data bases, videotapes, and other media). Most of these communication media are created by engineering and represent the detailed specification of the product to be produced or the process to be operated.

Level of Detail

A persistent dilemma facing management in high-technology companies is the decision of just how much detail to incorporate into the documentation of particular products and processes. Detailed documentation, taking the form of prints, parts lists, assembly drawing, process and assembly instructions, and sometimes audio, video, and other nonprinted media, is expensive to create, control, and update. However, skimpy documentation may be risky, allowing design changes to be effected without thorough review. Such incomplete documentation may also inhibit accurate and complete communication among the functional departments of the business.

The dilemma is resolved primarily on the basis of the relative importance the high-technology company places on manufacturing flexibility and product costs. Very detailed documentation is required when (1) production volumes are high, (2) automation and tooling are relied upon to reduce costs, and (3) less skilled manufacturing labor is to be utilized. More elaborate documentation is a prerequisite to the aggressive pursuit of learning curve economies. Such elaborate documentation is not justified, however, when volumes are small, a skilled workforce can be relied upon to operate with limited instructions, and design changes are implemented at a rapid rate. As a general rule, more documentation is appropriate, justified, and necessary as one moves along the continuum from custom to standard products.

High-technology companies most frequently err on the side of too little documentation. This tendency is not surprising. In the early stages of the life of products and technologies, a minimum of documentation is appropriate. As the company, products, and technologies mature, there is a reluctance to invest engineering time and attention in paperwork on existing products rather than in designing new products. Companies that neglect documentation, however, find they are forever running to catch up with the required documentation.

General managers must strike the proper balance between too much documentation and too little. Despite protests to the contrary from most manufacturing managers, more complete and thorough documentation is not always appropriate. The right balance is a function of the overall business strategy and of the position of the particular product or product family within the product-process matrix. When the strategy is geared to a succession of new, high-technology products, skimpy documentation is both appropriate and cost effective. When the strategy depends upon achieving learning curve economies—the company is operating down and to the right on the product-process matrix—complete, up-to-date, and reliable documentation is essential.

Effects on Inventory Control

Effective inventory planning and control requires very accurate bills of material (that is, listings of individual parts, components, and subassemblies that go into a finished product). Inaccurate or incomplete bills of material preclude using sophisticated planning techniques, such as MRP. The result is that excessive raw material inventories are held in order to guard against shortages. Moreover, the omission of one or more parts from a bill of materials can cause a halt in the assembly process while the missing part is located. The result is that in-process inventories also balloon. Thus, improved inventory control in high-technology companies, an objective stressed repeatedly throughout this book, requires the active participation of engineering, as well as of the production and finance departments.

PROCESSING ENGINEERING CHANGES ON EXISTING PRODUCTS

Life in a technology-based business would be substantially simplified if all documentation, once created, could be relied upon to be both accurate and stable. Neither condition is easily achieved when both technology and product change is an ever-present fact of life. All engineering changes, whether to improve performance or to reduce costs, must be reflected in changed documentation. In addition, design errors uncovered by engineering or manufacturing personnel (and sometimes by field service personnel) must be corrected and the corrections incorporated into the documentation system.

Thus, requests for changes to existing products can—and should—emanate from all corners of the organization:

1. From engineering to take advantage of new technology or to incorporate a new product feature.
2. From the field service organization to improve reliability or to facilitate field repair.
3. From purchasing to take advantage of a new supplier or a lower price of a substitute component.
4. From marketing to improve the competitive posture of the product.
5. From manufacturing engineering to permit the use of more sophisticated tooling.
6. From production and inventory planning to permit standardization of components across product lines.
7. From production supervisors to reduce tolerances, and thereby costs, or to facilitate processing or assembly in some other way.

Just as requests for changes can emanate from all corners of the organization, so implemented changes affect all corners of the organization, including particularly purchasing, inventory control, marketing, field service, production supervision, and cost accounting. Because these organizational units will be affected by the change, they must have a hand in deciding whether the requested change should be adopted (and when), and they must be notified in a timely fashion of approved changes.

The number of change requests may be very high—in the tens for a simple product, the hundreds for a complex instrument, and the thousands for a comprehensive system. Each change is likely to have a ripple or domino effect on documentation. For example, the change of a single component may require a change in the drawing on which it first appears, on one or more bills of materials, on drawings of parts or assemblies farther up the product tree, on assembly instruction sheets, and so forth. Each change may have both obvious and not-so-obvious consequences; these need to be anticipated, evaluated, and, if appropriate, tested.

Technical companies should develop and institute formal procedures and paper flow systems to be certain that all necessary documents are changed as required, that changes do not become incorporated into the documentation before they are appropriately authorized, and that all affected individuals and groups within the organization are aware of the nature and effective date of the change in sufficient time to adapt accordingly. The process must be both rapid and thorough, but it also must be routine, if production and engineering activities are not to grind to a halt either as a result of a preoccupation with processing changes or a lack of coordination among the changes themselves.

Discipline must be built into the engineering change request system so that procedures are not short-circuited. If control of documentation is lost, the following conditions can occur:

1. Quality problems multiply as exact specifications of components become impossible to trace and unanticipated consequences arise from unauthorized design changes.
2. Inventory investments and write-offs increase as parts are made obsolete without notice and the production cycle lengthens because newly specified parts are not planned and acquired in a timely manner.
3. Manufacturing labor costs escalate as expediting, troubleshooting, and additional setups consume both direct and indirect labor-hours.

Proper handling of engineering changes is the bugaboo of documentation methods in many high-technology companies.

COST AND BENEFIT TRADE-OFFS

All changes have both benefits and costs, even those that simply correct drawing errors. The challenge is to make the proper trade-off. Engineering changes that alter the physical specifications of particular components may render obsolete present components now in inventory and necessitate rescheduling of manufacturing work orders or purchase orders with vendors. Such obsolescence and rescheduling costs must be weighed against the advantages to be achieved from the change to decide both if and when the change should be effected. The optimum decision is often to delay the change until present inventories are depleted, until new vendors can be brought on stream, or until other conditions occur that will minimize disruption.

Some changes—for example, in computer software—must be expedited to fix a bug in a particular program, with notification rushed to various parts of the organization and to customers. Other changes in the software—changes designed to enhance capabilities or improve execution efficiencies—should be saved up and incorporated with other alterations in periodic rereleases of entirely new generations of software. Changing software documentation is expensive, and such changes typically require changes in operating, training, and service manuals as well. Batching changes may be efficient, but this advantage must be weighed against the disadvantage of delaying the introduction of an improved product to the marketplace.

The initiator of a change request may be unaware of the full ramifications of the proposed change. A change in part M may require an adaptation of part P or assembly T, expensive reworking of tooling, or a change in maintenance procedure that must be communicated to customers and the field service force. The possibility that the benefit sought from the engineering change request could be more expeditiously accomplished by an alternative change must be evaluated. For example, a problem that could be corrected by a hardware change might also be correctable by a less expensive software change.

Evaluate all changes on the basis of costs and benefits. Making the trade-offs between the costs and the benefits of change is complicated within most high-technology companies by the fact that the relevant data on both costs and benefits are not readily available to the decision maker. Manufacturing cost penalties or savings may be ascertainable (although even here most cost accounting systems do not reveal the incremental costs), but the tangible and intangible benefits or costs associated with changes in competitive position, in ease of field maintenance, or in vendor relationships are often uncertain. The costs of effecting the change—engineering time, clerical effort on documentation, renegotiation by purchas-

ing, and possible scrapping of inventory—must be factored into the decision.

Engineering change requests must be routed for approval through each affected department: design engineering, manufacturing engineering, material planning, quality assurance, and field service. (In some companies still other departments should formally approve changes.) Each of the evaluators must be alert to the possible need to solicit input from other functions, such as marketing or finance. Checklists and rules of thumb may help streamline the process. An engineering change committee, which is responsible for making the final cost-benefit trade-off when disputes arise, should be constituted.

NEW MODELS VERSUS INCREMENTAL CHANGES

I spoke earlier of the importance of freezing new product design, and now I have suggested that engineering changes may occur in large numbers. What factors should management consider in deciding how much product evolution to permit through the engineering change request mechanism?

First, saving up (or batching) engineering change requests in order to effect many changes at one time can have distinct advantages in reducing implementation costs. Disruptions in both production and engineering are minimized.

More important advantages often attend the introduction of a brand new model or line of a product. First, the company's image in the marketplace may be enhanced when it introduces a new product or model that delivers significantly improved performance. The opportunity may exist to leapfrog the competition. A series of incremental changes may not have the same marketing impact on customers as the introduction of a new product, and competitors may be better able to react to, and sell against, a series of small improvements. When these conditions are present—as they usually are—management should restrict product evolution through small, incremental changes, even when such changes would result in some improvement in performance.

The engineering staff may benefit from an opportunity to start over on a product line, to incorporate new technology or new design concepts that cannot be utilized given the constraints of the present product. Such starting over is, of course, expensive, but new competitors entering the market are not constrained by present products. Thus, if the removal of such constraints represents an important design advantage, management should be certain that its own design engineers are not denied that advantage. For example, the full benefits of a new software language probably cannot be realized without starting over, and the maximum benefit of VLSI circuits is not realized by designing incrementally from present products.

Relatedly, new models or product lines, rather than incrementally improved present products, often permit adoption of manufacturing techniques that provide the company with significant cost and quality advantages. The use of robots in fabrication and assembly typically requires some product redesign to make optimum use of the robots' capabilities. The opportunities for automation may not be evident or, if evident, may not be economically justified if product design is accepted as a given. The concept of the product-process matrix presumes that both product design and process design are subject to changes and that the changes can and should be related.

The case should not be overstated, however. A market leader, such as IBM in mainframe computers, may need to pay particular attention to thwarting competitors' attempts to copy (often referred to as "reverse engineer") its products. A continuing series of well-planned design changes can severely complicate the process of reverse engineering and permit the leader to sustain a technological and performance edge over its competitors.

ALLOCATION OF ENGINEERING RESOURCES

Related to this problem of new products versus incremental changes is the inherent risk in high-technology companies that excessive engineering resources will be diverted from the truly new product to service the existing products. New products are the lifeblood of such companies; the more the company relies on technology to differentiate itself from competitors, the more this statement holds. Two sources of diversion are prevalent: product line maintenance and customer "specials."

In this paper, I have been emphasizing that continuing engineering of existing products is not unimportant, particularly as production seeks to improve product manufacturability and reduce its costs and as the need for improved documentation is realized. But such maintenance must not be permitted to consume all engineering resources.

Customers' requests for product modifications to meet their particular requirements consume precious engineering resources. The more the company accommodates such requests for specials, the more the company takes on the aspects of an engineering consulting firm

rather than a manufacturing company. When important customers make such requests, they may have to be accommodated. But too often technology-based companies drift into producing increasing numbers of specials when such activity is clearly not consistent with their overall strategy.

The balanced allocation of engineering resources, assuring adequate attention to the development of truly new products, is an important challenge to general managers. When the dominant view in the councils of management is production, excessive investment in product maintenance engineering will result. When the dominant view is marketing, excessive pressure for accommodating customers' requests for specials may result—to be followed soon by dissatisfaction at the slow pace of new product development. When the dominant view in management councils is development, essential product maintenance engineering may be shortchanged and very attractive opportunities for specials may be overlooked. No such myopic views can be permitted to dominate.

Communication between production and engineering is particularly intense, and often necessarily nonroutine, in connection with introducing new products onto the production floor from the engineering laboratory. Prototype and pilot production runs can assist in the transfer, as can mutual agreement on timely freezing of the design. The more dependent the company is on process technology, rather than state-of-the-art product technology, the more thorough must be the product and process documentation. Because documentation is both expensive and difficult to control, high-technology companies typically underemphasize it. To maintain careful control of products, processes, quality, costs, and inventory investments, you must subject suggested changes in existing products to strict and well-defined procedures to be certain that the myriad potential ramifications of the change are fully evaluated. In formulating its engineering change policy, the high-technology company should consider the trade-off between introducing a new model and permitting product evolution by means of a series of incremental changes. The policy must also assure that engineering resources are not so committed to product maintenance and customer specials that new product development is shortchanged.

READING IV·2

The New Product Learning Cycle

M. A. Maidique and B. J. Zirger

This paper summarizes our extensive study ($n = 158$) of new product success and failure in the electronics industry. Conventional "external factor" explanations of commercial product failure based on the state of the economy, foreign competition, and lack of funding, were found not to be major contributors to product failure in this industry. On the other hand, factors that can be strongly influenced by management such as coordination of the create, make, and market functions, the quality and frequency of customers' communications, value of the product to the customer, and the quality and efficiency of technical management explained the majority of the variance between successful and unsuccessful products. From these findings a framework for understanding and managing the new product development process that places learning and communication in the center stage was developed.

Successes and failures in our sample were strongly interrelated. The knowledge gained from failures was often instrumental in achieving subsequent successes, while success in turn often resulted in unlearning the very process that led to the original success. This observation has led us to postulate a new product "learning cycle model" in which commercial successes and failures alternate in an irregular pattern of learning and unlearning.

1. INTRODUCTION

Many factors influence product success. That much is generally agreed upon by researchers in the field. The product, the firm's organizational linkages, the competitive environment, and the market can all play important roles. On the other hand, the results of research on new product success and failure[1] are reminiscent of George Orwell's *Animal Farm* in that some factors seem to be "more equal than others." But, exactly which set of factors predominates seems to be, at least in part, a function

of both the methodology and the specific population studied by the researcher.[2]

The Stanford Innovation Project (SINPRO)

In a survey of 158 products in the electronics industry, half successes and half failures, we developed our own list of major determinants of new product success.[3] The eight principal factors we identified are listed below roughly in the order of their statistical significance. Products are likely to be successful if:

1. The developing organization, through in-depth understanding of the customers and the marketplace, introduces a product with a high performance-to-cost ratio.
2. The create, make, and market functions are well coordinated and interfaced.
3. The product provides a high contribution margin to the firm.
4. The new product benefits significantly from the existing technological and marketing strengths of the developing business units.
5. The developing organization is proficient in marketing and commits a significant amount of its resources to selling and promoting the product.
6. The R & D process is well planned and coordinated.
7. There is a high level of management support for the product from the product conception stage to its launch into the market.
8. The product is an early market entrant.

The study that led to these conclusions consisted of two exploratory surveys described in detail elsewhere.[4] The first survey was open-ended and was divided into two sections. In the first part we asked the respondent to select a pair of innovations, one success and one failure. Successes and failures were differentiated by financial criteria. The second section of the original survey asked respondents to list in their own words the factors they believed contributed to the product's outcome. Seventy-nine senior managers of high-technology companies completed this questionnaire.

The follow-up survey was structured into 60 variables derived from three sources: (1) analysis of the results of the first survey, (2) review of the open literature,

Source: Research Policy, December 1985. © 1985, Elsevier Science Publishers B.V. (North-Holland). Reprinted with permission.
[1] R. C. Cooper, "A Process Model for Industrial New Product Development," *IEEE Transactions on Engineering Management,* EM-30, no. 1 (1983), pp. 2–11.

[2] M. A. Maidique and B. J. Zirger, "A Study of Success and Failure in Product Innovation: The Case of the U.S. Electronics Industry," *IEEE Transactions on Engineering Management,* EM-31, no. 4 (1984) pp. 192–203.
[3] Ibid.
[4] Ibid.

and (3) the authors' own extensive experience in high-technology product development. Each respondent, on the basis of the original two innovations identified in survey 1, was asked to determine for each variable whether it impacted the outcome of the success, failure, neither, or both. Survey 2 was completed by 59 of the original 79 managers.

The results from these two initial surveys were reported earlier.[5] To summarize, we conducted several statistical analyses for each variable and innovation type, including determination of means and standard deviations, binomial significance, and clustering. Exhibit 1 shows the binomial significance for the 37 variables which differentiated between success and failure. Combining our statistical results with the content analysis of the initial survey, we derived the eight propositions listed earlier.

Using these eight factors as a starting point, we then developed a block diagram of the new product development process that focuses on the product characteristics and the functional interrelationships and competences that are most influential in determining new product success or failure (Exhibit 2). In our view, the innovation process is a constant struggle between the forces of change and the status quo. Differences in perceptions between the innovator and the customer and also between the groups that make the building blocks of the innovation process—engineering, marketing, and manufacturing—all conspire to shunt new product development or to deflect it from the path of success. Effective management attempts to integrate these constituencies and to allocate resources in a way that makes the new possible. These ideas are the basis of a model of the new product development process that we describe more fully and validate empirically in a forthcoming paper.[6]

The eight propositions resulting from our analysis were the objective "truths" that resulted from statistical analysis of our large sample of new product successes and failures. Though coincident in their salient aspects with the work of others,[7] these results, however, did not fully satisfy us. Had we missed important variables in our structured surveys? Had our respondents understood our questions? Had we failed to detect significant relations between some of the variables we identified—or

between these and some yet undiscovered factors? How valid were our final generalizations? And most important, what were the underlying conceptual messages in this list of factors? In short, we were concerned that perhaps our statistical analysis might have blurred important ideas.

Reflecting on his research on the individual psyche, Carl Jung once put it this way:[8]

> The statistical method shows the facts in the light of the average, but does not give a picture of their empirical reality. While reflecting an indisputable aspect of reality, it can falsify the actual truth in a most misleading way. . . . The distinctive thing about real facts, however, is their individuality. Not to put too fine a point on it, one could say that the real picture consists of nothing but exceptions to the rule, and that, in consequence, reality has predominately the characteristic of irregularity.

Such irregularities have caused one of the most experienced researchers in the field to wonder out loud if any fundamental commonalities exist at all in new product successes. "Perhaps," Cooper observed, "the problem is so complex, and each case so unique, that attempts to develop generalized solutions are in vain."[9]

2. METHODOLOGY

To address the concerns noted above, we prepared individual in-depth case studies for 40 of the original 158 products to search for methodological flaws or significant irregularities that might challenge the results of our statistical analysis (Exhibit 1). The case studies were prepared under the supervision of the authors by 45 graduate assistants.[10] Seventeen West Coast electronics firms which had participated in the 1982 Stanford-AEA Exec-

[5] Ibid.
[6] B. J. Zirger and M. A. Maidique (forthcoming), "Empirical Testing of a Conceptual Model of Successful New Product Development," to be submitted to *Management Science.*
[7] Cooper, "Process Model."

[8] C. G. Jung, *The Undiscovered Self* (New American Library, 1957), p. 17.
[9] R. C. Cooper, "The Dimensions of Industrial New Product Success and Failure," *Journal of Marketing* 43 (1979), p. 102.
[10] The authors wish to express their appreciation to the following graduate students and doctoral candidates, who assisted in preparation of the individual case studies: P. Achi, G. Ananthasubramanianium, R. Angangco, C. Badger, B. Billerbeck, R. Cannon, D. Chinn, L. Christian, B. Connor, A. Dahlen, S. Demetrescu, B. Drobenko, R. Farros, H. Finger, H. Jagadish, L. Girault-Cuevas, R. Guior, T. Hardison, Y. Honda, J. Jover, C. Koo, T. Kuneida, S. Kuraski, M. Lacayo, D. Lampaya, D. Ledakis, L. Lei, R. Ling, S. Makmuri, P. Matlock, C. Mungale, R. Oritz, B. Raschle, R. Reis, B. Russ, E. Saenger, J. Sanghani, V. Sanvido, F. Sasselli, R. Simon, P. Stamats, R. Stauffer, L. Taurel, B. Walsh, F. Zustak.

EXHIBIT 1   Significant Variables from Survey 2 Grouped by Index Variable

Successful innovations were:	Number of observations	Cumulative binomial	Significance rating
1. Better matched with user needs.			
Better matched to customer needs.	44	8.53 E-09	+++
Developed by teams which more fully understood user needs.	44	1.27 E-05	+++
Accepted more quickly by users.	49	7.01 E-04	---
2. Planned more effectively and efficiently.			
Forecast more accurately (market).	43	1.25 E-07	+++
Developed with a clearer market strategy.	45	1.24 E-04	+++
Formalized on paper sooner.	45	3.30 E-03	+++
Developed with less variance between actual and budgeted expenses.	46	2.70 E-02	--
Expected initially to be more commercially successful.			
3. Higher in benefit-to-cost ratio.	42	8.21 E-02	+
Priced with higher profit margins.	51	6.06 E-08	+++
Allowed greater pricing flexibility.	52	1.02 E-06	+++
More significant with respect to benefit-to-cost ratio.			
4. Developed by better-coupled organizations.	43	6.86 E-03	+++
Developed by better-coupled functional divisions.	39	1.68 E-07	+++
5. More efficiently developed.			
Less plagued by after-sales problems.	35	5.84 E-05	---
Developed with fewer personnel changes on the project team.	28	6.27 E-03	---
Impacted by fewer changes during production.	41	1.38 E-02	--
Developed with a more experienced project team.	39	2.66 E-02	++
Changed less after production commenced.	47	7.19 E-02	-
Developed on a more compressed time schedule.	39	9.98 E-02	+
6. More actively marketed and sold.			
More actively publicized and advertised.	39	4.74 E-03	+++
Promoted by a larger sales force.	28	6.27 E-03	+++
Coupled with a marketing effort to educate users.	37	1.00 E-02	++
7. Closer to the firm's areas of expertise.			
Aided more by in-house basic research.	25	7.32 E-03	+++
Required fewer new marketing channels.	25	7.32 E-03	---
Closer to the main business area of firm.	30	8.06 E-03	+++
More influenced by corporate reputation.	29	3.07 E-02	++
Less dependent on existing products in the market.	36	6.62 E-02	-
Required less diversification from traditional markets.	24	7.58 E-02	-
8. Introduced to the market earlier than competition.			
In the market longer before competing products introduced.	44	1.13 E-02	++
First-to-the-market type products.	39	1.19 E-02	++
More offensive innovations.	46	5.19 E-02	+
Generally not second-to-the-market products.	36	6.62 E-02	-
9. Supported more by management.			
Supported more by senior management.	31	1.66 E-03	+++
Potentially more impactful on the careers of the project team members.	32	5.51 E-02	+
Developed with a more senior project leader.	39	9.98 E-02	+
10. Technically superior.			
Closer to the state-of-the-art technology.	36	3.26 E-02	++
More difficult for competition to copy.	45	3.62 E-02	++
More radical with respect to world technology.	42	8.21 E-02	+

EXHIBIT 2   Diagram of the Critical Elements of the New Product Development Process

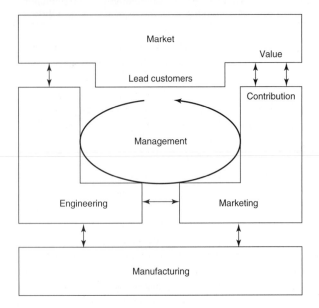

This paper reports how these case studies and the associated interview transcripts enriched our earlier conclusions. In section 3, we begin to clarify the terms that we had employed in our survey, specifically *user needs* and *product value*. In section 4, we explore the meaning of success. The case studies led us to expand our concept of success and failure beyond the one-dimensional confines of financial return. Indeed, success and failure often appear to be close partners, not adversaries, in organizational and business development. Finally, in section 5, we postulate an evolutionary model of new product development, which we believe leads to a better understanding of the relationship between success and failure. For many of the propositions we present here, we lack the analytical support that underlies the eight factors identified in our original research. Nonetheless, we feel that these findings, which we hope will help to illuminate further research—including our own—are as important as our statistical results.

3. DEFINING "USER NEEDS" AND "PRODUCT VALUE"

The detailed case studies largely reinforced the principal findings of the overall study.[11] But the case studies also enriched some of the findings from structured questionnaires by providing fresh insights on several of the key variables. In this paper, we focus on the most important and perhaps the least specific variable, "understanding of the market" and "user needs" which is believed to result in products with "high value."

One of the principal findings of our large sample survey was that "user needs" and "customer and market understanding" are of central importance in predicting new product success or failure, a result that parallels the findings of the pioneering SAPPHO pairwise comparison study.[12] This result, however, does little to illuminate how a firm goes about achieving such understanding. What's more, citing user needs ex post factor as a key explicatory variable in product success can be simply disregarded as tautological. Of course, it can be argued the company "understood" user needs if the product was

utive Institute and in our original two surveys served as sites for the 20 case studies. This subset of the original product pairs served as the subject of analysis for the case studies. Two or more project assistants interviewed managers and technologists and prepared written reports that included interview transcripts or summaries, background information on the firm, the competitive environment, the product development process, the characteristics of each of the two products, validation of the original Survey 2, and a critical review of the factors that contributed to success or failure in each case. Overall, 101 managers and technologists were interviewed in 148 hours of interviews.

Most of the companies supplied the research teams with detailed financial, marketing, and design information regarding each one of the products, including in some cases internal memoranda that traced the products' development histories. Because of the confidentiality of this data, we must not identify any of the firms, much as we would like to thank them for their contributions to the project. In some cases, to illustrate a point, we have chosen to use examples from the public domain, or from published cases we or others have written about, and we may mention a company by name; however, the companies that collaborated with the project are either left anonymous or given fictitious names which, when first introduced, are placed in quotation marks.

---

[11] Maidique and Zirger, "A Study of Success."

[12] R. Rothwell, C. Freeman, A. Horley, V. I. P. Jervis, Z. B. Robertson, and J. Townsend, "SAPPHO Updated—Project SAPPHO, Phase II," *Research Policy* 3 (1974), pp. 258–91. See also C. Freeman, *The Economics of Industrial Innovation* (Harmondsworth: Penguin Books, 1974), pp. 161–97.

successful. Expanding on such criticisms, Mowery and Rosenberg have pointed out that the term *user need* is in any event vague and lacks the precision with which economists define related market variables such as demand.[13] What seems to be important, however, is to determine whether there are identifiable ex post/ante actions that organizations take that develop and refine the firm's understanding of the customer's needs.

In most of the instances in which interviewees indicated a product has succeeded because of "better understanding of customer needs," they were able to support this view by citing specific actions or events. Both the experiential background of the management and developing team as well as actions taken during the development and launch process were viewed as important.

One line of argument went thus: We understood customer needs because the managers, engineers, and marketing people associated with the product were people with long-term experience in the technology and/or market. In such a situation, some executives argue, very little market research is required because the company's management has been close to the customer and to the dynamics of his changing requirements all along. As the group vice president of a major instrument manufacturer explained, "We were able to set the right design objectives, particularly cost goals, because we knew the business, *we could manage by the gut* (author's emphasis)."

This approach was evident in other firms also. When "Perfecto," a leading U.S. process equipment manufacturer, induced by a request from one of its European customers, commissioned a domestic market survey to assess potential demand for a new product that combined the functions of two of its existing products, the result was almost unanimously negative. Because of a quirk in the process flow in U.S. plants (which differed from European plants), domestic customers did not immediately see significant value in the integrated product. Notwithstanding the market survey data, Perfecto executives continued to believe that the product would prove to be highly cost-effective for their worldwide customers. Buoyed by enthusiasm in Europe and a feeling of deep understanding of his customers that was the result of 13 years of experience in the numerically controlled process equipment market, Perfecto's president gave the project the go-ahead. His experience and self-confidence

paid off. There was ultimately a significant demand for the new machine on both sides of the Atlantic.

These experience-based explanations, however, are only partially useful blueprints for action. The argument simply says that experienced people do better at new product development than the inexperienced, a hypothesis confirmed by our earlier research and that of others.[14]

Most of our informants, however, characterized the capture of "user needs" in action-oriented terms. For the successful product in the dyad, they described the company as having more openly, frequently, carefully, and continuously solicited and obtained customer reaction before, after, and during the initiation of the development and launch process. In some cases, the attempt to get customer reaction went to an extreme. "Electrotest," a test equipment manufacturer, conducted design reviews for a successful new product at its lead customers' plants. In general, the successful products were the result of ideas which originated with the customers, filtered by experienced managers. In one case, customers were reported to have "demanded" that an instrument manufacturer develop a new logic tester. As a rule, the development process for the successful products was characterized by frequent and in-depth customer interaction at all levels and throughout the development and launch process. While we did not find (and did not look for) what Von Hippel discovered in his careful research on electronic instruments, that users had in many cases already developed the company's next product, it was clear that, more so than any other constituency, they could point out the ideas that would result in future product successes.[15]

But when listening to customers, it's not enough to simply put in time. It is of paramount importance to listen to potential users without preconceptions or hidden agendas. Some companies become enamored with a new product concept and fail to test the idea against the reality of the marketplace. Not surprisingly, they find later that either the benefit to the customer was more obvious to the firm than to the customer himself or the product benefits were so specific that the market was limited to the original customer. For these reasons, the president of an automated test equipment manufacturer provided the following admonition: "When listening to customers, clear your mind of what you'd like to hear—Zen listening."

---

[13] D. Mowery and N. Rosenberg, "The Influence of Market Demand upon Innovation: A Critical Review of Some Recent Empirical Studies," *Research Policy* 8 (1979), pp. 101–53.

[14] A. C. Cooper and A. V. Bruno, "Success Among High-Technology Firms," *Business Horizons* 20, no. 2 (1977), pp. 16–22.
[15] E. A. von Hippel, "Users as Innovators," *Technology Review,* no. 5 (1976), pp. 212–39.

Unless this careful listening cascades throughout the company's organization and is continually "market"-checked, new products will not have the value to the customer that results in a significant commercial success. A predominant characteristic of the 20 successful industrial products that we examined in our case studies is that they resulted in almost immediate economic benefits to their users, not simply in terms of reduced direct manufacturing or operating costs. The successful products seemed to respond to the utility function of potential customers, which included such considerations as quality, service, reliability, ease of use, and compatibility.

Low cost or extraordinary technical performance per se did not result in commercial success. Unsuccessful products were often technological marvels that received technical excellence awards and were written up in prestigious journals. But typically such extraordinary technical performance comes at a high price and is often not necessary. "Very high performance, at a very high price. This is the story behind virtually every one of our new product failures," is how a general manager at "International Instruments," an instrument manufacturer with a reputation for technical excellence, described the majority of his new product disappointments.

In contrast to this phenotype, new product successes tend to have a dramatic impact on the customer's profit-and-loss account directly or indirectly. "Miltec," an electronic systems manufacturer, reported that its successful electronic counter saved its users 70 percent in labor costs and downtime. "Informatics," a computer peripheral manufacturer, developed a very successful magnetic head that was not only IBM compatible but also 20 percent cheaper and it offered a three times greater performance advantage. An integrated satellite navigation receiver developed by "Marine Technology," a communications firm, so drastically reduced on-board downtime in merchant marine ships in comparison to the older modular models that the company was overwhelmed by orders. The first 300 units paid for the $2.5 million R & D investment; overall, 7,000 units were sold. By comparison, the unsuccessful products provided little economic benefit. Not only were they usually high priced but also often they were plagued by quality and reliability problems, both of which translate into additional costs for the user.

4. HOW SHOULD PRODUCT SUCCESS BE MEASURED?

Our original surveys used a unidimensional success taxonomy. Success was defined along a simple financial

EXHIBIT 3   Distribution of Successes and Failures by Degree of Success/Failure for Case Studies

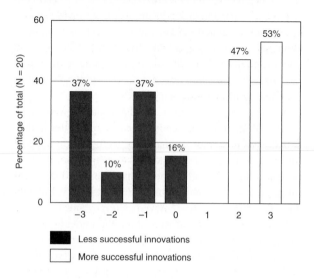

axis. Successful products produced a high return while unsuccessful products resulted in less than break-even returns. Using this measure, our population of successes and failures combined to form a clearly bimodal distribution (Exhibit 3) that reinforced our assumption that we were dealing with two distinct classes of phenomena. While obtaining and plotting this type of data went beyond what most prior success-failure researchers had deemed necessary to provide, our detailed case studies lead us to conclude that this may not have been enough.

Success is defined as the achievement of something desired, planned, or attempted. While financial return is one of the most easily quantifiable industrial performance yardsticks, it is far from the only important one. New product "failures" can result in other important by-products: organizational, technological, and market development. Some of the new product failures that we studied led to dead ends and resulted in very limited organizational growth. On the other hand, many others—the majority—were important milestones in the development of the innovating firm. Some were the clear basis for major successes that followed shortly thereafter.

International Instruments, a large electronics firm, developed a new instrument based on a new semiconductor technology (diode arrays) that the firm had not yet used in one of its commercial products. The instrument, though technically excellent, was developed for a new market where the company did not have its traditionally keen sense of what value meant to the customer. Few units were sold and the product was classified as a failure. On the other hand, the experience gained with the diode array technology became the basis for enhancement of other product families based on this newly gained technical knowledge. Secondly, the organization learned about the characteristics of the new market through the diode array product, and, armed with new insights, a redesigned product was developed that was a commercial success. Was the diode array product really a failure, its developers asked?

In this and other cases we observed, the failure contributed naturally to the subsequent successes by augmenting the organization's knowledge of new markets or technologies or by building the strength of the organization itself. An example from the public domain illustrates this point. After Apple Computer had been buffeted by the manufacturing and reliability problems that plagued the Apple III launch, which caused Apple to lose its lead in the personal computer market and to yield a large slice of the market to IBM, Apple's chairman summed up the experience thus: "There is no question that the Apple III was our most maturing experience. Luckily, it happened when we were years ahead of the competition. It was a perfect time to learn."[16] As demonstrated by the manufacturing quality of the Apple IIe and IIc machines, Apple, that is the Apple II division, learned a great deal from the Apple III mishaps. Indeed, Sahal has pointed out that success in the development of new technologies is a matter of learning.[17] "There are few innovations," he points out, "without a history of lost labor. What eventually makes most techniques possible is the object lesson learned from past failures." In his classic study of technological failures, Whyte argues that most advances in engineering have been accomplished by turning failure into success.[18] To Whyte, engineering development is a process of learning from past failures.

Few would think of the Boeing Company and its suppliers as a good illustration of Sahal's and Whyte's arguments. Rosenberg, however, has pointed out that early 707s, for many years considered the safest of airplanes, went into unexplainable dives from high-altitude flights. The fan-jet turbine blades used in the jumbo jet par excellence, Boeing's famed 747, failed frequently under stress in the 1969–70 period.[19] Despite these object lessons, or perhaps because of them, Boeing makes more than half of the jet-powered commercial airliners sold outside of the Soviet bloc. According to the executive vice president of the Boeing Commercial Airplane Company, himself a preeminent jet aircraft designer, "We are good partly because we build so many airplanes. We learn from our mistakes, and each of our airplanes absorbs everything we have learned from earlier models and from other airplanes."[20]

Learning by Doing, Using, and Failing

It has long been recognized that there is a strong learning curve associated with manufacturing activity. Arrow characterized the learning that comes from developing increasing skill in manufacturing as "learning by doing."[21] Learning by doing results in lower labor costs. The concept of improvement by learning from experience has been subsequently elaborated by the Boston Consulting Group and others to include improvements in production process, management systems, distribution, sales, advertising, worker training, and motivation. This enhanced learning process, which has been shown for many products to reduce full costs by a predictable percentage every time volume doubles, is called the experience curve.[22]

Rosenberg, based on his study of the aircraft industry, has proposed a different kind of learning process, "learning by using."[23] Rosenberg distinguishes between learning that is "internal" and "external" to the production process. Internal learning results from experience with manufacturing the product, "learning by doing"; external learning is the result of what happens when users have the opportunity to use the product for extended periods of time. Under such circumstances, two types of useful knowledge may be derived by the developing organization. One kind of learning (embodied) results in design modifications that improve performance, usability, or reliability; a second kind of learning (disembodied) results in improved operation of the original or the subsequently modified product.

[16]M. A. Maidique, J. S. Gable, and S. Tylka, *"Apple Computer (A) and (B),"* Case #S-BP-229(B) (Stanford Business School Central Services, Graduate School of Business, Rm. 1, Stanford, CA, 1983). See also M. A. Maidique and C. C. Swanger, *"Apple Computer: The First Ten Years,"* Case #PS-BP-245 (Stanford Business School Central Services, Graduate School of Business, Rm. 1, Stanford, CA, 1985).

[17]D. Sahal, *Patterns of Technological Innovation* (Reading, Mass.: Addison-Wesley Publishing, 1981), p. 306.

[18]R. R. Whyte, *Engineering Progress Through Trouble* (London: Institution of Mechanical Engineers, 1975).

[19]N. Rosenberg, *Inside the Black Box, Technology and Economics* (Cambridge: Cambridge University Press, 1982), pp. 124–26.

[20]J. Newhouse, *The Sporty Game* (New York: Alfred A. Knopf, 1982), p. 7.

[21]K. Arrow, "The Economic Implications of Learning by Doing," *Review of Economic Studies,* June 1962.

[22]B. Henderson, *Perspectives on Experience* (Boston Consulting Group, 1968) (third printing, 1972).

[23]Arrow, "Economic Implications," pp. 120–40.

EXHIBIT 4   A Model of Internal and External Learning

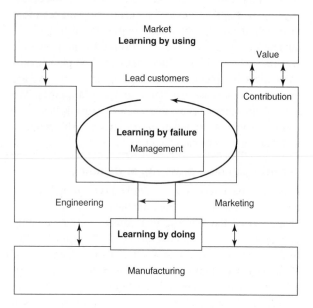

In our study, we found another type of external learning, a "learning by failing," which resulted in the development of new market approaches, new product concepts, and new technological alternatives based on the failure of one or more earlier attempts (Exhibit 4). When a product succeeds, user experience acts as a feedback signal to the alert manufacturer that can be converted into design or operating improvements (learning by using). For products that generate negligible sales volume, little learning by using takes place. On the other hand, products that fail act as important probes into user space that can capture important information about what it would take to make a brand new effort successful, which sometimes makes them the catalyst for major reorientations. In this sense, a new product is the ultimate market study. For truly new products it may be the only effective means of sensing market attitudes. According to one of our respondents, a vice president of engineering of "California Computer," a computer peripherals manufacturer, "No one really knows if a truly new product is worth anything until it has been in the market and its potential has been assessed."

Another dimension of "learning by failing" relates to organizational development. A failure helps to identify weak links in the organization and to inoculate strong parts of the organization against the same failure pattern. The aftermath of the Apple III resulted in numerous terminations at Apple Computer, from the president to the project manager of the Apple III project. Those remaining, aided by new personnel, accounted for the well-implemented Apple III redesign and reintroduction program and the highly successful Apple IIe follow-on product.[24]

When the carryover of learning from one product to another is recognized, it becomes clear that the full measure of a product's impact can only be determined by viewing it in the context of both the products that preceded it and those that followed. While useful information can be obtained by focusing on individual products or pairs of products, *the product family is a far superior unit of analysis from which to derive prescriptions for practicing managers.* The product family incorporates the interrelationship between products, the learning from failures as well as from successes. Thus, it is to product families, including false starts, not to individual products, that financial measures of success should be more appropriately applied.

Consider a triplet of communications products developed over a 10-year period by an electronics system manufacturer. For several years, Marine Technology had developed and marketed commercial and military navigation systems. These systems were composed of separate components manufactured by others, such as a receiver, teletype, and a minicomputer, none of which was specifically designed for the harsh marine environment. Additionally, this multicomponent approach, though technically satisfactory, took up a great deal of space, which is at a premium on the bridge of a ship. Each of Marine Technology's new product generations attempted to further reduce the number of components in the system. By 1975, a bulky HP minicomputer was the only outboard component.

The need for a compact, rugged, integrated navigation system had thus been abundantly clear to Marine Technology engineers and salespeople. Therefore, when microprocessors became available in the early 1970s, it was not surprising that Marine Technology's general manager initiated a program to develop a new lightweight integrated navigation system specially designed for the marine environment. The product was developed by a closely knit design team that spent six to eight months working with potential customers, and later market testing prototypes. Two years later, the company introduced the MT-1, the world's first microprocessor-

---

[24]Maidique, Gable, and Tylka, *"Apple Computer (A) and (B)."* Also, Maidique and Swanger, *"Apple Computer: The First Ten Years."*

based integrated navigation system. The product was an instant success. Over 7,000 units were sold at a price of $25,000 per unit. At this price, margins exceeded 50 percent.

Shortly after the success of the MT-1 was established, engineering proposed a new product (the MT-2) to Marine Technology's newly appointed president. The MT-2 was to be about one-sixth the volume of the MT-1 and substantially cheaper in price. The president was so impressed with a model of the proposed product that he directed a team, staffed in part by the original MT-1 design team members, to proceed in a top secret effort to develop the MT-2. The team worked in isolation; only a handful of upper management and marketing people were aware of the project. Three and a half years and $3.5 million later, the team had been able—by sacrificing some features—to shrink the product as promised to one-sixth the size of the MT-1 and to reduce the price to about $10,000. But almost simultaneously with the completion of the MT-2's development, a competitor had introduced an equivalent product for $6,000. Furthermore, the product's small size was not considered a major advantage. Key customers indicated the previous product was "compact enough." The company attempted to eliminate some additional features to tailor the product to the consumer navigation market, but it found that it was far too expensive for this market, yet performance and quality were too low for its traditional commercial and military markets. The product was an abject economic failure. Most of the inventory had to be sold below the cost.

A third product in the line, the MT-3, however, capitalized on the lessons of the MT-2 failure. The new MT-3 was directed specifically at the consumer market. Price, not size, was the key goal. Within two years, the MT-3 was introduced at a price of $3,000. Like the MT-1, it was a major commercial success for the company. Over 1,500 have been sold and the company had a backlog of 600 orders in 1982 when the case histories were completed.

At the outset of this abbreviated product family vignette, we said the family consisted of three products. In a strict sense, this is correct, but in reality there were four products, starting with what we will call the MT-0, the archaic modular system. The MT-0 was instrumental to the success of the MT-1. Through the experience with customers that it provided, it served to communicate to the company that size and reliability improvements would be highly valued by customers in the commercial and military markets in which the company operated. With the appearance of microprocessor technology, what

remained was a technical challenge, usually a smaller barrier to success than deciphering how to tailor a new technology to the wants of the relevant set of customers, as the company found out through the MT-2.

The success of the MT-1 was misread by the company to mean, "the smaller, the more successful," rather than, "the better we understand what is important to the customer, the more successful." The company had implicitly made an inappropriate trade-off between performance, size, and cost. They acted as if they had the secret to success—compact size—and by shutting off its design team from its new as well as its old customers ensured that they would not learn from them the real secrets to success in the continually evolving market environment. It remained for the failure of the MT-2 to bring home to management that, by virtue of its new design, the company was now appealing to a new customer group that had different values from its traditional commercial and military customer. Equipped with this new learning, the company was now able to develop the successful MT-3.

5. THE NEW PRODUCT LEARNING CYCLE

There are several lessons to be learned from the history of Marine Technology's interrelated succession of products. First, their experience clearly illustrates the importance of precursors and follow-on products in assessing product success. To what extent, for instance, was the M-2 truly a failure, or, alternatively, how necessary was such a product to pave the way for the successful MT-3? With hindsight one can always argue that the company should have been able to go directly to the MT-3, but wasn't to some extent the learning experience of the MT-2 necessary? Secondly, the story illustrates once again the importance of in-depth customer understanding as well as continuous interaction with potential customers throughout the development process even at the risk of revealing some proprietary information. Whatever learning might have been possible before entering the consumer market was shunted aside by the company's secretive practices.

The product evolution pattern of "Computronics," a start-up computer systems manufacturer, reinforces these findings. One of Computronics' founders had developed a new product idea for turnkey computer inventory control systems for jobbers (small distributors) in one of the basic industries. From his experience as a jobber in this industry, he knew that it was virgin territory for a well-conceived and supported computerized system. During the development process, the company enlisted the support of the relevant industry association. Association members offered product suggestions, criticized product development, and ultimately the association endorsed the product for use by its members. The first Compu-100 system was shipped in 1973. Ten years later, largely on the strength of this product and its accessories, corporate sales had doubled several times and reached nearly $100 million, and the company dominated the jobber market.

As the company's market share increased, however, management recognized that new markets would have to be addressed if rapid growth was to continue. In early 1977, the company decided to take what seemed a very logical step to develop a system that would address the needs of the large wholesale distributors in the industry. Based on its earlier successes, the company planned to take this closely related market by storm. After a few visits to warehousing distributors, the product specifications were established and development began under the leadership of a new division established to serve the high end of the business. Since no one at Computronics had firsthand experience with this higher level segment of the distribution system, a software package was purchased from a small software company, but it took a crash program and several programmers a year to rewrite the package so that it was compatible with Computronics hardware. After testing the Compu-200 at two sites, the company hired a team of additional sales representatives and prepared for a national rollout. Ten million dollars of sales were projected for the first year.

First-year revenues, however, were minimal. Even three years after the launch, the product had yet to achieve the first year's target revenue. What had happened? The new market would appear at first glance to be a perfect fit with Computronics' skills and experience, yet a closer examination revealed considerable differences in the new customer environment which, nonetheless, were brushed away in a cavalier manner by Computronics' management, who were basking in the glow of the Compu-100's success.

As organizations in such a euphoric state often do, Computronics grossly underestimated the task at hand. The large market for warehousing distributor inventory systems was attractive to major competitors such as IBM and DEC. But only a cursory study of the new customers and their buying habits was carried out. The tacit assumption was that large warehousing distributors were simply grown-up jobbers. Yet these new customers were now much more sophisticated, had used data processing equipment for other functions, and generally required

and developed their own specialized software. Increased competition and radically greater customer sophistication combined to require that Computronics be represented by a highly experienced and competent sales force. But because of the hurry to launch the product, Computronics skipped the customary training for sales representatives and launched the field sales force into a new area for the firm: the complex long-term business of selling large items ($480,000 each) to a technically knowledgeable customer. By believing that repeating past practices would reproduce past successes, Computronics had turned success into failure.

"Every victory," Carl Jung once wrote, "contains the germ of a future defeat."[25] Starbuck and his colleagues have observed that successful organizations accumulate surplus resources that allow them to loosen their connections to their environments and to achieve greater autonomy, but they explain, "This autonomy reduces the sensitivity of organizations to changing environmental conditions. . . . [O]rganizations become less able to perceive what is happening so they fantasize about their environments and it may happen that reality intrudes only occasionally and marginally on these fantasies."[26] Fantasies create a myth of invincibility, yet an old Chinese proverb says, "There is no greater disaster than taking on an enemy lightly."[27]

Marine Technology's management fantasized that it had the secret of success: smaller is better. Computronics had a fantasy that similarly extrapolated its past victories: new markets will be like old markets. This is a pattern that repeats itself over and over in business. We have already alluded to one of the best publicized contemporary examples of this phenomenon: Apple Computer's Apple III on the heels of its colossally successful Apple II precursor. Even IBM is not exempt from this cycle. After taking one-third of the market with its PC (personal computer) despite its late entry, a senior executive at the IBM PC Division stated, "We can do anything."[28] "Anything" did not, as it happens, include the follow-on product to the PC, the PCjr, which—in contrast to the original PC—was not adequately test marketed to determine how consumers would react to its design features and

[25] C. G. Jung, *Psychological Reflections* (New York: Princeton University Press, 1970), p. 188.
[26] W. Starbuck, A. Greve, and B. L. Hedberg, "Responding to Crisis," *Journal of Business Administration,* no. 9 (1978), pp. 111–37.
[27] Lao Tzu, *Tao Te Ching* (New York: Penguin Books, 1983), p. 131.
[28] D. Le Grande, as quoted in "How IBM Made Junior an Underachiever," *Business Week,* June 25, 1984, p. 106.

ultimately had to be dropped from the IBM product line. IBM and Computronics, however, have both, at least temporarily, become more humble. Both are soliciting customer inputs so that they can redesign their disappointments.

The flow from success to failure, and back to success again, at Marine Technology illustrated a rhythm that we were to encounter repeatedly in our investigations. In the simplest terms, failure is the ultimate teacher. From its lessons the persistent build their successes. Success, on the other hand, often breeds complacency. Moreover, success seems to create a tendency to ignore the basics, to believe that heroics are a substitute for sound business practice. As the general manager of "Automatrix," a test equipment manufacturer, pointed out, "It's hard, very hard, to learn from your successes." Ironically, success can breed failure for firms that continue to view the future through the prism of present victories, especially in a dynamic industry environment.

These observations have led us to propose a model of new product success and failure in which successes and failures alternate with an irregular rhythm. This is not to say that for every success there must be a complementing failure. Most industrial products—about three out of five—succeed despite popular myths to the contrary.[29] For some highly successful companies, as many as three out of four new products may be commercially successful. Most companies continuously learn by using, through their successful new products, and—as in the case of Marine Technology—they continuously develop improved designs. This is what most new product efforts are about—minor variations on existing themes.

But continued variations on a theme do not always lead to major successes. In time, further variations are no longer profitable, and the company usually decides to depart from the original theme by adopting a new technology—microprocessors, lasers, optics—or to attack a new market—consumer, industrial, government— or, alternatively, organizational changes, defections, or promotions destroy part of the memory of the organization so that the old now seems like the new. Changes in any of these three dimensions can result in an economic failure, or, in our terms, new learning about a technology, a market, or about the strengths and weaknesses of a newly formed group as shown in Exhibit 5, an extension of the familiar product–customer matrix originally pro-

EXHIBIT 5 Learning by Moving Away from Home Base

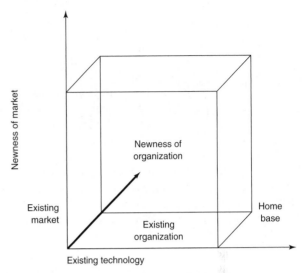

posed by Ansoff.[30] This recurrent cycle of success and failure is shown graphically in Exhibit 6.

In the model, a sequence of successes is followed by either a major organizational change, changes in product design, technology, or market directions that prompt an economic failure, which in turn spurs a new learning pattern. The model assumes a competitive marketplace, however, and is less likely to be applicable to a monopolistic situation in which a single firm dictates the relationship between customer and supplier. A second caveat is that while the pattern is roughly depicted as regular, in general it will be irregular, but the cycle of oscillation between economic success and failure, we believe, will still hold.

5.1 Success as a Stochastic Process

Success in new products is never assured. Too many uncontrolled external variables influence the outcome. Occasional or even frequent failure is a way of life for product innovations. As Addison reminds us in his *Cato,* "'Tis not in mortals to command success."[31] But while it is not possible to assure the outcome of any one product

---

[29] R. G. Cooper, "Most Products *Do* Succeed," *Research Management,* November–December 1983, pp. 20–25.

[30] H. I. Ansoff, *Corporate Strategy* (New York: McGraw-Hill, 1965), pp. 131–33.
[31] J. Bartlett, *Bartlett's Familiar Quotations,* 14th ed. (New York: Little, Brown, 1968), p. 393.

EXHIBIT 6 A Typical New Product Evolution Pattern

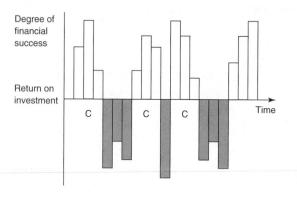

☐ Successful innovation
▨ Unsuccessful innovation
C = Market, technology, or organizational changes

trial, it is possible to increase the likelihood that a product or group of products will be successful. Addison goes on to add, "We'll do more, Sempronius, *we'll deserve it*" (authors' emphasis). The eight factors that we identified at the outset of this article, and the cyclic model we propose, are an attempt to help managers conceptualize the new product development process so as to improve the proportion of economic successes. But on the other hand, it would be a mistake to attempt to increase the number of successes by reducing new product risk to zero by cautious, deliberate management. In the process, rewards may be also reduced to the same level.

Failure, as we have tried to argue, is part and parcel of the learning process that ultimately results in success. Sahal sums up the process thus: "What eventually makes the development of new techniques possible is the object lesson learned from past failures . . . profit by example."[32] The important thing is to have a balance between successes and failures that results in attractive returns. Here a lesson from experienced venture capitalists, masters at the success forecasting game, is useful. As part of another research project, the authors have interviewed some of the nation's most successful and experienced venture capital investors whose portfolios have generally shown gains of 25 to 35 percent over the past 10 years. Given a large pot of opportunities, experienced venture capitalists believe they can select a group that will on the average yield an excellent return, yet few pro-

fessionals are so sanguine that they believe that they can with certainty foretell any one success; they've seen too many of their dreams fail to meet expectations.

A new product developed by "Electrosystems," a military electronics company, seemed to fit a venture capitalist's dream. The company's new product, a phase-locked loop, had its origin with one of its key customers, the requisite technology was within its area of expertise, and a powerful executive championed the product throughout its development. A large market was anticipated. Thus far, a good bet, one might conclude. What's more, the resulting product was a high-quality instrument. Yet the product brought little in the way of revenues to the firm, for an alternative technology that solved the same problem in a cheaper way was simultaneously developed and introduced by a competitor.

Five years later, again spurred by a customer requirement, Electrosystems developed an electronic counter as part of a well-funded and visibly championed development program. This time, however, the product saved the customer 70 percent of his labor costs, considerably reduced his downtime, and there was no alternative technology on the horizon. This product was very successful. The point here is not that the product that ultimately produced a cost advantage to the customer was more successful. That much is self-evident. The point is that at the outset both products looked like they would provide important advantages to the customer. After all, they both originated with customers. Both projects were well managed and funded and technologically successful. Yet one met with unpredictable external competition that blunted its potential contribution. The company did not simply fail and then succeed. It succeeded because it pursued both seemingly attractive opportunities. In other words, success generally requires not one but several, sometimes numerous, well-managed trials. This realization prompted one of our wisest interviewees, the chief engineer of "Metalex," an instrument manufacturer, to sit back and say, "I've found the more diligent you are, the more luck you have."

This is the way both venture capitalists and many experienced high-technology product developers view the new product process. Venture capitalists who have compiled statistics on the process have found that only 60 percent of new ventures result in commercial success; the rest are a partial or complete loss. (Not surprisingly, this is about the same batting average that Cooper found in his study of industrial products.) About 40 to 50 percent of new venture-capital backed ventures produce reasonable returns, and only 10 to 15 percent result in out-

---

[32] Sahal, *Patterns.*

standing investments. But it can be easily computed that such a combination of investments can produce a 25 to 30 percent return or more as a portfolio.

5.2 New Research Directions

Our research on new product success and failure has led us to reconsider our unit of analysis. Choosing the new product as the basic unit of analysis has many advantages. New products are clearly identifiable entities. This facilitates gathering research data. New products have individualized sales forecasts and return on investment criteria, and managements generally know whether these criteria are satisfied. "Successes" can be culled from "failures."

Our results, however, indicate that if financial measures of success are to be applied as criteria, a more appropriate unit of analysis is the product family. Before an individual product is classified as a failure, its contribution to organizational growth, market development, or technological advance must be gauged. New products strongly influence the performance of their successors and in turn are a function of the victories and defeats of their predecessors. Before the laurels are handed over to a winning team, an examination should be made of the market, technological, and organizational base from which the team launched its victory (Exhibit 5).

One of IBM's most notable product disasters was the Stretch computer. IBM set out to develop the world's most advanced computer, and, after spending $20 million in the 1960s for development, only a few units were sold.

On the heels of the Stretch fiasco came one of the most successful products of all time, the IBM 360 series. But when IBM set out to distribute kudos, it recognized that much of the technology in the IBM 360 was derived from work done on the Stretch computer by Stephen Dunwell, once the scapegoat for the Stretch "setback." Subsequently, Mr. Dunwell was made an IBM fellow, a very prestigious position at IBM that carries many unique perks.[33] As Newton once said, "If I have seen far it is because I stood on the shoulders of giants."[34]

We were able to gain insight into this familial product interrelationship because our success-failure dyads were often members of the same product family. But even though they were interrelated, they represented only a truncated segment of a product family. Nonetheless, in some sites, for example Marine Technology, we were able to collect data on three or four members of a product family. On the other hand, our efforts, to date, fall far short of a systematic study of product families. This is the central task of the next stage of our research.

Our limited results, however, bring into question research that focuses on the product as the unit of analysis, including our own. Consider one of our principal research findings, which is also buttressed by the findings of several prior investigators: successful products benefit from existing strengths of the developing business unit. The implication of this finding is that organizations should be wary of exploring new territories. In contrast to this result, our observations would lead us to argue just the opposite, that firms should continuously explore new territories even if the risk of failure is magnified.[35] The payoff is the learning that will come from the "failures" which will pave the way for future successes.

Careful validation of the cyclic model of product development proposed here could have other important consequences for our understanding of technology-based firms. If indeed the pattern proposed in Exhibit 6 is generalizable to firms that are continuously attempting to adapt to new markets and technologies, then there are important implications for management practice.

First, the model implies that new product development success pivots on the effectiveness of intra- and intercompany learning. This conclusion puts a premium on devising a managerial style and structure that serves to catalyze internal and external communication. Second, by implicitly taking a long-term view of the product development process, the model emphasizes the importance of long-term relationships with employees, customers, and suppliers. Out of such a view comes a high level of understanding, and therefore of tolerance for failure to achieve commercial success at any one given point in the product line trajectory. Firms need to learn that product development is a journey, not a destination. These preliminary findings are compatible with an exploratory study of new product development in five large

---

[33] T. Wise, "IBM's $5B Gamble," *Fortune,* September 1966; "A Rocky Road to the Marketplace," *Fortune,* October 1966. Also, Bob Evans, personal communication (Mr. Evans was program manager for the IBM 360 system).
[34] J. Bartlett, *Barlett's Familiar Quotations,* 13th ed. (New York: Little, Brown, 1968), p. 379.

[35] In an exploratory study of the relationship between the degree of "newness" of a firm's portfolio of products and its economic performance, the authors concluded that some "newness" results in better economic performance than "no newness." M. H. Meyer and E. B. Roberts, *New Product Strategy in Small High-Technology Firms,* WP #1428-1-84 (Sloan School of Management, Massachusetts Institute of Technology, May 1984).

successful Japanese companies completed by Imai and his colleagues.[36] One of the principal findings of their research was that the firms studied were characterized by an almost "fanatical devotion towards learning—both within organizational membership [sic] and with outside members of the interorganizational network." This learning, according to the authors, played a key role in facilitating successful new product development. It appears that when successful at new product development, small and large U.S. companies operate in a very similar manner to the best-managed Japanese firms.

Many key questions, however, remain to be settled. Is there an optimal balance between successes and failures? Are Japanese firms susceptible to the same oscillating pattern between success and failure as American firms? How does this balance change across industries? How can tolerance for failure be communicated without distorting the ultimate need for economic success? How can a firm learn from the failures of others? Are there characteristic success-failure patterns for a group of firms competing in the same industry? These and other related questions will occupy us in the next phase of our research.

CASE IV·2

Eli Lilly: The Evista Project

Matthew C. Verlinden

In early 1998, Dr. August "Gus" Watanabe, executive vice president of science and technology for Eli Lilly and president of Lilly Research Laboratories (see Exhibits 1 and 2), looked out his office window towards downtown Indianapolis. He was contemplating the future commercialization path for Lilly's new, potential blockbuster drug, Evista, which had received FDA approval on December 9, 1997, for the prevention of postmenopausal

---

Source: Copyright © 1999 by The President and Fellows of Harvard College. Research Associate Matthew C. Verlinden prepared this case under the supervision of Professor Steven C. Wheelwright as the basis for class discussion rather than to illustrate either effective or ineffective handling of an administrative situation.

[36] K. Imai, I. Nonaka, and H. Takeuchi, *Managing the New Product Development Process: How Japanese Companies Learn and Unlearn,* Institute of Business Research, Hitotsubashi University, Kunitachi (Tokyo, Japan, 1982), pp. 1–60. See also P. R. Lawrence and D. Dyer, *Renewing American Industry* (New York: The Free Press, 1983), p. 8.

osteoporosis. Evista, generically known as raloxifene hydrochloride, would be entering the estrogen replacement market, a market that had worldwide sales in excess of $1 billion in 1997.[1]

Of even wider significance was the fact that in initial trials, Evista appeared to lower the incidence of breast cancer and reduced total LDL in postmenopausal women without the negative side effect profiles of currently available estrogen replacement therapies. The potential of this new therapeutic drug and its impact on Lilly could be enormous. Some analysts predicted that Evista might become a $1 billion drug for the company.[2] With this in mind, Watanabe knew that the decision on how best to commercialize Evista would have a profound effect on Lilly's well-being. Should Lilly follow their traditional approach to commercialization? Or should Lilly follow a course more in line with the development approach adopted for Evista in early 1995, which would require the organization to transform its heavyweight product development team into a focused product (commercialization) team? In a senior management meeting later in the day, Watanabe would have to make a recommendation.

COMPANY BACKGROUND

Eli Lilly and Company was incorporated in 1901 to pursue the drug manufacturing business founded in Indianapolis, Indiana, in 1876 by Colonel Eli Lilly. A pharmaceutical chemist and a U.S. Civil War veteran, Colonel Lilly founded the company to improve the quality of medicinal products by introducing scientific methods into the product development process.

In the 1920s, Lilly launched its first major blockbuster drug—insulin. Developed with the research team of Frederick Banting and Charles Best, of the University of Toronto, the new therapy revolutionized the treatment of diabetes. The insulin product family and the treatment of endocrine diseases remained a focal point of Lilly's research throughout the 20th century. In the 1980s, Lilly introduced Humulin, the world's first human health care product created by using recombinant DNA technology. In 1997, insulin products accounted for nearly 13 percent of Lilly's worldwide revenues, with sales of more than $1 billion.[3]

---

[1] Jennifer Fron Mauer, "Eli Lilly Inches Up 0.4% as Evista Gets Expected FDA Okay," *Dow Jones Newswires,* December 10, 1997.
[2] Ibid.
[3] Eli Lilly 1997 annual report.

Both Big mkts.

EXHIBIT 1 Senior Management Organizational Chart (Effective July 1, 1998)

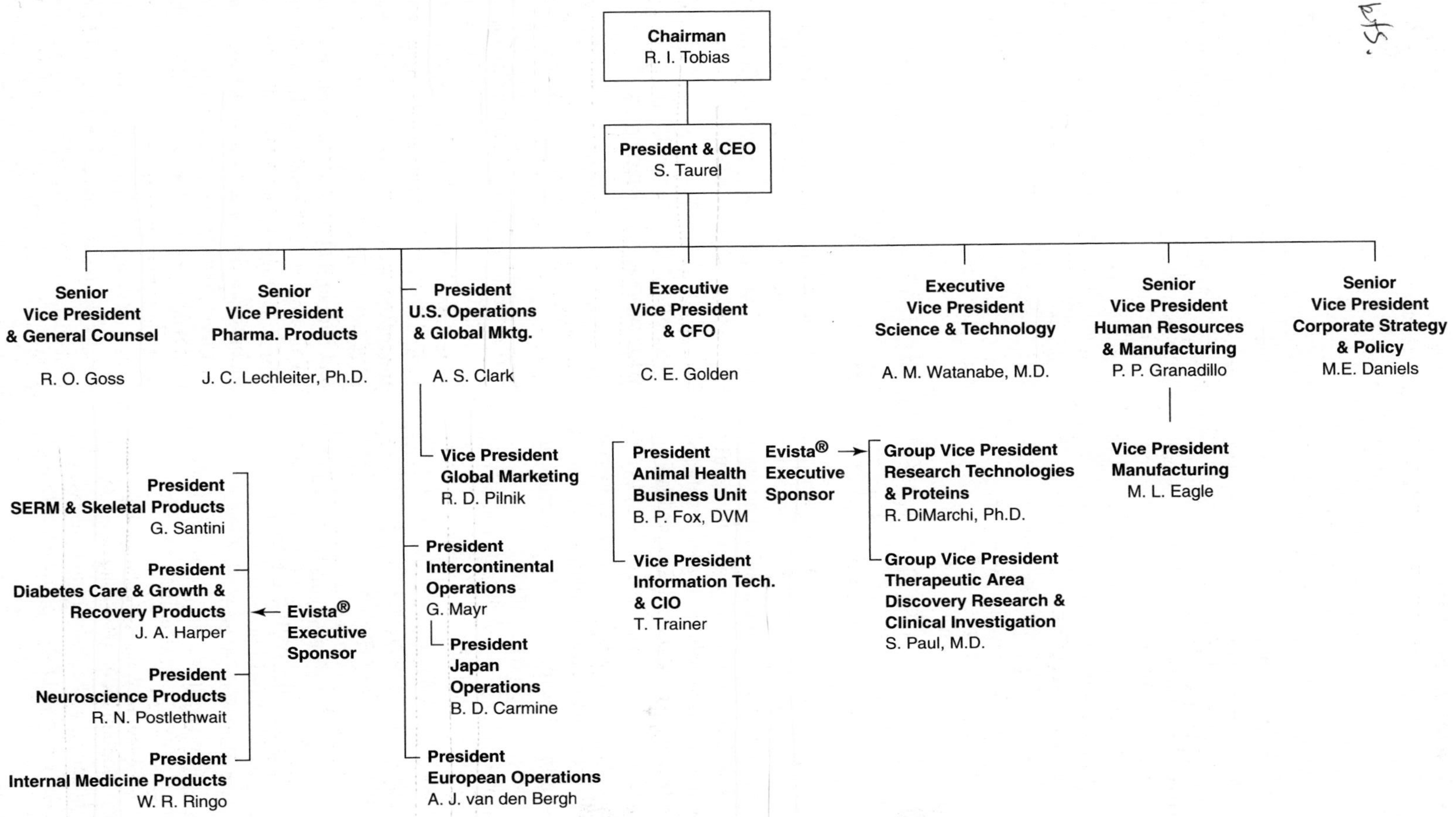

Chairman
R. I. Tobias

President & CEO
S. Taurel

Senior Vice President & General Counsel
R. O. Goss

Senior Vice President Pharma. Products
J. C. Lechleiter, Ph.D.

President
SERM & Skeletal Products
G. Santini

President
Diabetes Care & Growth & Recovery Products
J. A. Harper

President
Neuroscience Products
R. N. Postlethwait

President
Internal Medicine Products
W. R. Ringo

Evista® Executive Sponsor

President U.S. Operations & Global Mktg.
A. S. Clark

Vice President Global Marketing
R. D. Pilnik

President Intercontinental Operations
G. Mayr

President Japan Operations
B. D. Carmine

President European Operations
A. J. van den Bergh

Executive Vice President & CFO
C. E. Golden

President Animal Health Business Unit
B. P. Fox, DVM

Vice President Information Tech. & CIO
T. Trainer

Evista® Executive Sponsor

Executive Vice President Science & Technology
A. M. Watanabe, M.D.

Group Vice President Research Technologies & Proteins
R. DiMarchi, Ph.D.

Group Vice President Therapeutic Area Discovery Research & Clinical Investigation
S. Paul, M.D.

Senior Vice President Human Resources & Manufacturing
P. P. Granadillo

Vice President Manufacturing
M. L. Eagle

Senior Vice President Corporate Strategy & Policy
M.E. Daniels

Source: Company documents.

EXHIBIT 2 R&D Organizational Chart

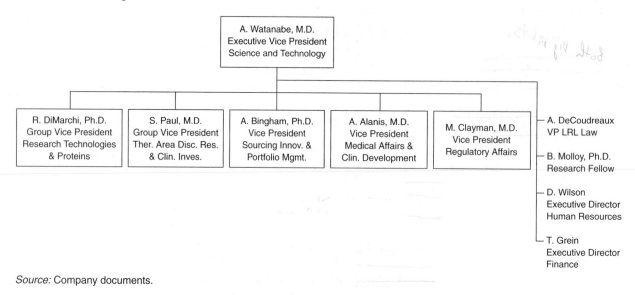

Source: Company documents.

In addition, Lilly had developed a number of important new anti-infectives in the 1950s, including long-acting, orally administered penicillin products and erythromycin, which was the first of its kind in a major new class of antibiotics called macrolides. It also developed, during that decade, the first agents of the cephalosporin antibiotic class and, subsequently, Ceclor, the world's top-selling antibiotic. As with therapeutics, for endocrine disease, anti-infectives remained an important focal point in 1997, representing 15 percent of Lilly's worldwide revenues, with sales of almost $1.3 billion.[4]

With the launch of Prozac in 1986, Lilly established itself as a leader in the development of drugs for central nervous system and related diseases. In 1996, Lilly launched the blockbuster drug Zyprexa, generically known as olanzapine. Zyprexa was approved by the Food and Drug Administration (FDA) on October 2, 1996, as a new antipsychotic agent for the treatment of schizophrenia. In its first 12 months on the market, Zyprexa accumulated sales of $550 million, making it the most successful first-year drug product, ever.

In addition to development of anti-infectives and therapeutics for central nervous system and endocrine diseases, Lilly, since its restructuring in 1994 (discussed below), had focused the remainder of its drug development efforts on fighting cancer and cardiovascular diseases. In the early 1990s, Lilly received FDA approval for ReoPro,

a cardiovascular, antiplatelet agent, and Gemzar, an oncology product. In 1997 sales of ReoPro and Gemzar were $254 million and $175 million, respectively.

THE DRUG DEVELOPMENT AND APPROVAL PROCESS

The commercialization of a new therapeutic drug in the United States comprised four stages—discovery, development, registration, and launch, a process best be described as long, complex, and risky (see Exhibit 3).

In the *discovery stage,* large numbers of molecules were screened for therapeutic efficacy. For just one approved drug, pharmaceutical companies often had to screen upwards of 10,000 molecules. After a molecule passed this initial screening, it faced extensive toxicological and animal tests. If the molecule passed these tests, the pharmaceutical manufacturer applied to test the compound in humans, and development was started.

In the *development stage,* the pharmaceutical manufacturer's first step was to file an investigational new drug (IND) application with the FDA. The IND was necessary to begin testing in humans. A typical IND might be more than 2,000 pages long and include information about preclinical testing and a description of proposed clinical trials. Unless the FDA ordered a hold, clinical trials were permitted to start 30 days after the application was filed upon final approval by a review board created at the institution or institutions where the trials were being

---

[4] Ibid.

**EXHIBIT 3   Standard Clinical Stages of Drug Development and Corresponding Success Rates
Using Conventional Product Development Approach**

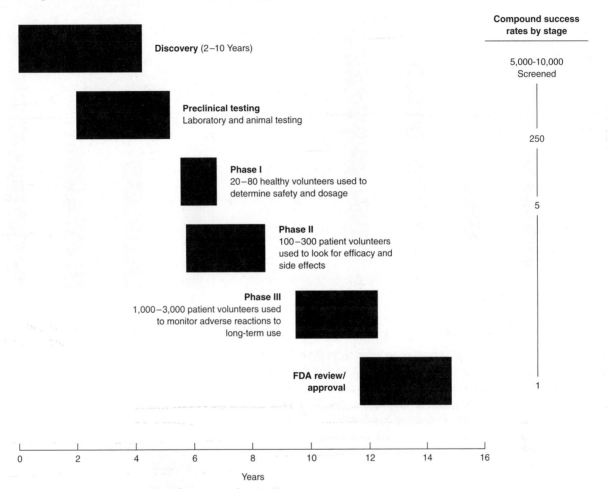

Compound success
rates by stage

Discovery (2–10 Years)

5,000-10,000
Screened

Preclinical testing
Laboratory and animal testing

250

Phase I
20–80 healthy volunteers used to
determine safety and dosage

5

Phase II
100–300 patient volunteers
used to look for efficacy and
side effects

Phase III
1,000–3,000 patient volunteers used
to monitor adverse reactions to
long-term use

FDA review/
approval

1

0   2   4   6   8   10   12   14   16

Years

Source: Pharmaceutical Research & Manufacturers Association.

low success rate of developed drugs.

conducted. Of the drugs entering clinical trials between 1980 and 1984, only 23.5 percent were expected to become marketed drugs.[5]

Clinical trials (part of the development stage) were conducted in three phases. In Phase I, safety studies were conducted on 20 to 100 healthy volunteers. Potential side effects were identified, and a dosage range was determined. Phase II trials determined the drug's effectiveness. Approximately 100 to 300 volunteers who had the targeted disease participated. Phase III trials, used to

monitor the development of adverse reactions to long-term use, typically involved 1,000 to 3,000 patients (and sometimes thousands more) in clinics and hospitals. Patients were closely monitored during this stage to assess the drug's efficacy and safety. Following the completion of Phase III trials was registration.

In the *registration stage,* a company compiled all information from these trials and, if the data successfully demonstrated safety and efficacy, they were submitted as a new drug application (NDA) to the FDA. Containing all the scientific information the company had gathered, NDAs typically were 100,000 pages long and required large-scale and increasingly lengthy and complex efforts to prepare for submission (see Exhibits 4 and 5).

[5] J. A. DiMasi, "Success Rates for New Drugs Entering Clinical Testing in the United States," *Clinical Pharmacology,* July 1995.

EXHIBIT 4   New Drug Applications Required Increasingly More Patients and More Data

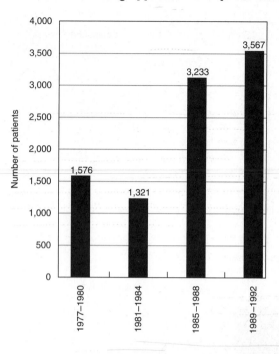

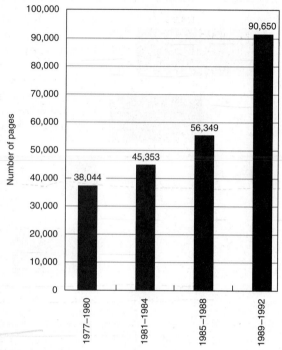

Source: "The Contribution of the Pharmaceutical Industry: What's at Stake for America," Boston Consulting Group, September 1993.

EXHIBIT 5   Average Number of Clinical Trials per New Drug Application

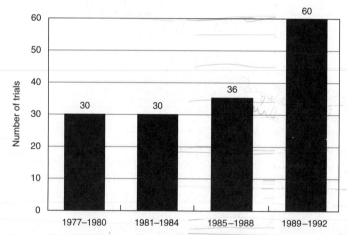

Source: "The Contribution of the Pharmaceutical Industry: What's at Stake for America," Boston Consulting Group, September 1993.

Ded hase FCC pt 15 emissions to pass

prep before Approval

The *commercialization stage* officially began with the FDA's approval to market the drug, although pharmaceutical companies started preparing for commercialization several months before the expected approval date. The most important aspect of the FDA's approval was what "indication" would be permitted on the label, that is, which disease(s) the drug could be used to treat and whether the drug had proven efficacy in the prevention of the disease(s) or in its treatment. Simply put, the indication on the label, to a large extent, determined market potential.

indication ⟹ market potential

R&D IN THE PHARMACEUTICAL INDUSTRY

Research-based pharmaceutical companies spent 19.4 percent of sales on R&D in 1995 (see Exhibit 6), a figure suggesting the importance the pharmaceutical industry placed on discovering and commercializing new therapeutics. And while R&D had always been critical, the advent of formularies in both the public and private sectors magnified the importance of productivity in R&D.

Formularies were instituted in both the private and public sector as a way of managing health care costs. A formulary was a list of prescription drugs that health care insurers would reimburse a patient for. Formularies added to the downward price pressure put on pharmaceutical manufacturers in four ways.

First, wherever possible, only prescriptions for generic substitutions of branded drugs were reimbursed. Second, health care insurers negotiated a bulk discount rate from the pharmaceutical manufacturer for any drug listed on their formulary. Third, even if more than one drug might have the same therapeutic effect, only one would be listed on the formulary for reimbursement.

price pressures ↓ ↓ ↓

EXHIBIT 6   R&D as a Percentage of Sales for Research-Based Pharmaceutical Companies and U.S. Industrial Sectors, 1995

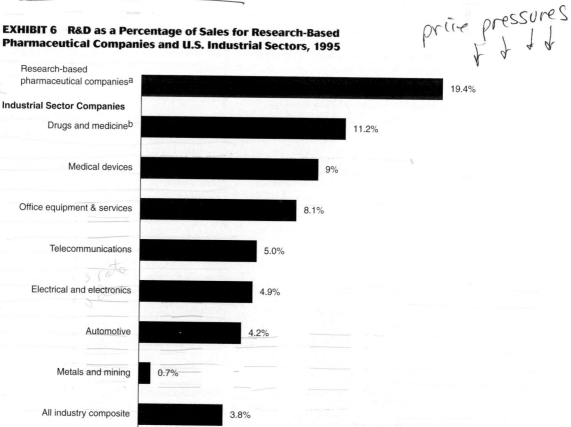

Research-based pharmaceutical companies[a] — 19.4%

Industrial Sector Companies

Drugs and medicine[b] — 11.2%

Medical devices — 9%

Office equipment & services — 8.1%

Telecommunications — 5.0%

Electrical and electronics — 4.9%

Automotive — 4.2%

Metals and mining — 0.7%

All industry composite — 3.8%

Source: PhRMA 1997, based on data from *PhRMA Annual Survey* and *Standard & Poor's Compustat,* a division of McGraw-Hill.

[a]"Research-based pharmaceutical companies" based on ethical pharmaceutical sales and ethical pharmaceutical R&D only.

[b]"Drugs and Medicine" category based on total R&D and sales for companies classified within the "drug and medicine" sector tabulated by *Standard & Poor's Compustat,* a division of McGraw-Hill.

EXHIBIT 7   **R&D Expenditures as a Percentage of Sales, Research-Based Pharmaceutical Companies, 1980–1997**

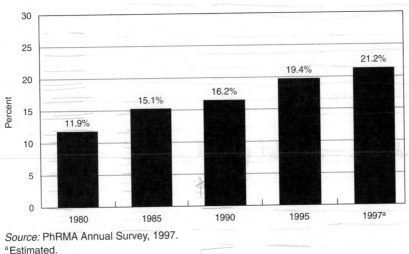

Source: PhRMA Annual Survey, 1997.
[a] Estimated.

For example, there were at least three drugs a physician could prescribe for the treatment of allergies, any one of which had essentially the same therapeutic effect. Therefore, the health care insurer had significant leverage to lower price by pitting one pharmaceutical manufacturer against another in a price war and only approving one of the three drugs for reimbursement. Fourth, health care insurers as well as independent pharmacies sought to maintain the fewest number of drugs as possible on their formularies in order to lower their own inventory overhead costs. "Me-too" drugs (branded nongeneric equivalents) were removed from formulary lists and inventories because they were seen as unnecessary.

The result was even more pressure on R&D organizations to develop radically new, differentiated, and more efficacious therapeutics. Otherwise, a newly developed drug would not be placed on a formulary after being approved by the FDA. At the same time, R&D expenditures were increasing (see Exhibit 7). The cost of bringing a new therapeutic drug to market had risen rapidly over the past two decades (see Exhibit 8); major drivers of development costs, including the number of required clinical trials and patients in each trial, had doubled.[6] During the 1990s, the average time required to develop a drug increased to 15 years (see Exhibit 9), thereby increasing the cost of capital needed for R&D. By 1997, the cost of

developing a new therapeutic had risen to more than $500M.[7]

Patent Protection

The combination of high development costs and long development times made intellectual property protection essential. Patent protection for the pharmaceutical industry covered the therapeutic molecule itself as well as, in many cases, the process by which the molecule was manufactured. Patents offered research-based pharmaceutical companies the protection they needed to recoup their R&D investments and generate returns.

Patents were particularly effective in the pharmaceutical industry vis-à-vis other industries because they were granted for the molecule itself, with the benefit of the molecule being specific to its structure and atomic composition. Thus, changing one bond in the chemical structure of an anticancer therapeutic might change it from being a powerful tool used to fight disease into a useless placebo or, worse, a lethal toxin.

While patents offered pharmaceutical companies the ability to protect their intellectual property, a finite patent life also implied a tremendous pressure to develop and commercialize new therapeutic drugs as quickly as possible. Longer development times directly consumed the company's profits by reducing its drug's exclusivity in the marketplace.

[6] "The Contribution of Pharmaceutical Companies: What's at Stake for America," the Boston Consulting Group, September 1993.

[7] Pharmaceutical Research and Manufacturers 1997 annual report.

EXHIBIT 8   Cost of Developing a New Drug

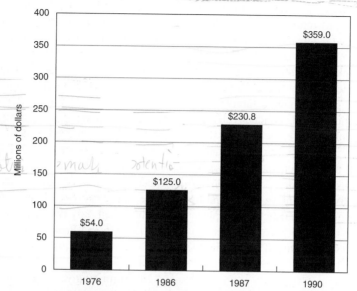

Source: U.S. Congress, Office of Technology Assessment, *Pharmaceutical R&D: Costs, Risks, and Rewards,* February 1993.
Note: Pre-tax estimated R&D costs are per new chemical entity as of the time of market approval. Cost includes capital and out-of-pocket costs; pre-tax capitalized costs are for drugs that entered clinical trials during the late 1970s.

EXHIBIT 9   Total Drug Development Time from Synthesis to Approval

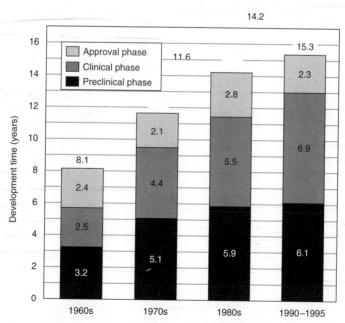

Source: Tufts Center for the Study of Drug Development, 1997.

[handwritten margin notes: "Dell — clones come out immediately — Dell was a clone" / "Drugs — clones often 17 yrs or so." / "Much less costly Wow!" / "Dell + Lilly poor perf" / "not con not pref" / "Gov interven" / "both re-stru" / "Both improve prod dev process."]

During the 1980s, the profitable lifetime for drugs in the United States—the time companies had to recoup development costs and generate returns for stockholders and funding for R&D—significantly shortened. This was due to the passage of the Hatch-Waxman Act of 1984, which allowed for the quick approval of generic copies of branded therapeutics, once a patent had expired.

Hatch-Waxman allowed generic manufacturers to circumvent the safety and efficacy trials conducted by the original patent holder simply by referencing the safety and efficacy data in the originator's patent. If the manufacturer could demonstrate that the generic had the same active ingredients as in the original drug, it could avoid retesting, thereby saving five to eight years in time to market and considerable cost. For research-based pharmaceutical companies, the increased pressure to recoup R&D investments, due to a shorter time of exclusivity—12 years as opposed to 14 to 17 years pre Hatch-Waxman—was substantial.

First-Mover Advantage

The creation of a new therapeutic *class* meant monopoly rents for the manufacturer. In 1986, Lilly received FDA approval to launch Prozac, its first blockbuster drug for central nervous system and related diseases. Prozac was the first of its kind in a new and important therapeutic class of drugs called selective serotonin reuptake inhibitors (SSRI), used for the treatment of depression. Prozac revolutionized the treatment of depression by its improved efficacy and a greatly reduced side effect profile. The drug was an instant success, reaching sales of $96 million in 1988, $313 million in 1989, and $645 million in 1990.

Not until 1992 did the FDA approve other SSRIs. That year, Pfizer launched Zoloft and SmithKline introduced Paxil. By this time, however, Lilly had established its hold on the marketplace, with Prozac sales topping $1 billion. Lilly maintained the lion's share of this market. In 1997, Prozac sales, of almost $2.5 billion, accounted for over 30 percent of Lilly's worldwide revenues, and Prozac represented 44 percent of worldwide sales in this therapeutic area; Zoloft and Paxil sales stood at $1.4 billion each.

DRUG DEVELOPMENT AT LILLY

When Gus Watanabe assumed leadership of Lilly Research Laboratories (LRL) in 1994, one of his primary goals was to improve the product-development process.

After serving as chairman of the department of medicine at Indiana University, Watanabe had joined Lilly in 1990 as vice president in charge of cardiovascular research. During the next several years he assumed increasing responsibility and in 1994 was promoted to executive vice president of science and technology, responsible for all of Lilly's research and development efforts.

Watanabe and other LRL senior managers were acutely aware that product development deadlines were not being met. Indeed, timelines for product development milestones were moved back monthly, if not quarterly. "Timelines didn't mean very much," affirmed one researcher. "It was almost expected that you wouldn't make your deadlines." Indeed, from 1985 to 1995, Lilly had launched only two major new therapeutics: Humulin® in 1986 and Prozac® in 1987. In an industry where R&D productivity was critical, this poor performance was a major issue.

Not surprisingly, this performance had taken its toll, particularly in income growth from 1991 to 1995 (see Exhibit 10). In addition, from early 1992 to mid-1993, Lilly lost $18 billion in market capitalization.[8] Combined with this dry spell in R&D productivity was the onslaught of *discontinuous* change in the competitive landscape. Many governments—including those of Germany, Spain, Italy, and the United Kingdom—imposed policies affecting the pricing and usage of medicines. Concurrently, the United States began grappling with health care reform.

In 1992 and 1993, Lilly restructured to better align itself with the changing marketplace. In mid-1993, Randall Tobias was appointed chairman and chief executive officer; in January 1994, Lilly announced that it was separating its medical devices and diagnostics businesses from its core pharmaceutical business to "better focus its resources on global pharmaceutical operations and further maximize shareholder value." As a result, in June, Guidant Corporation was formed, consisting of five of Lilly's nine medical device and diagnostics businesses; in December, 20 percent of Guidant's stock was offered to the public, with Lilly retaining an 80% equity share. Also in 1994, Lilly purchased PCS Health Systems, a managed pharmaceutical care company.

Lilly was determined to focus its efforts on its core pharmaceutical businesses, expand its reach in this sector, and enter an elite group of top-tier pharmaceutical

---

[8] Eli Lilly 1997 annual report.

EXHIBIT 10 Net Sales and Net Income for 1989 to 1997

	1989	1990	1991	1992[a]	1993[b]	1994	1995	1996	1997
Net sales	4,175.6	5,192.6	5,725.7	6,167.3	5,198.5	5,711.6	6,763.8	7,346.6	8,517.6
Net income (loss)	939.5	1,127.3	1,314.7	708.7	480.2	838.7	2,290.9	1,523.5	(385.1)[c]
Prozac									2,559.2
Anti-infective									1,272.5
Insulins									1,073.3
Zyprexa									730.2
Animal Health									589.8
ReoPro									254.4
Gemzar									174.8
Other									1,863.4

Note: Figures readjusted to exclude net sales and net income from businesses which formed Guidant.
[a] Reflects restructuring changes.
[b] Net sales from "discontinued operations" have been excluded.
[c] Reflects write-down of investment in PCS Health Systems Inc.
Source: Company annual report.

companies. To that end, on June 5, 1995, Lilly announced that it planned to sell its remaining equity in Guidant.

Function-Based Product Development

As LRL's senior management searched for causes of Lilly's product development problems, they encountered a number of disturbing facts—not the least of which was that it was almost impossible to diagnose specific reasons for delay in detail because product development resources were shared across all of LRL, with little accountability on a project-by-project basis. Furthermore, there were no systems to track resources and measure progress except at the macro level.

Staffing, as well, was a serious issue. Project managers were generally assigned four to five projects to manage, with functional team members also assigned to four or five projects. This might seem an efficient use of resources theoretically, but in practice a team member could rarely, if ever, focus on a particular project long enough to be effective. Thus, someone would be called to fight a fire on one project while simultaneously being responsible for important work on another. Once again, assigning accountability, tracking individual performance, and relating that to project progress were all extremely difficult.

Also contributing to significant delays was the fact that teams often met only monthly to decide important project issues. Compounding this problem was the absence of detailed project plans, which would have forced team members to plan for future uncertainties, determine internal and external interdependencies, and forecast future potential road blocks.

THE DEVELOPMENT OF EVISTA®

On January 13, 1995, Watanabe announced the formation of two heavyweight product development teams "to expedite the successful, timely introductions of selected drug candidates"—a turning point in Lilly's drug development history. Each team (one each for Evista and Zyprexa) was to "focus exclusively on a single compound during Phase III clinical trials." These dedicated, colocated, and cross-functional groups represented a significant departure from Lilly's traditional approach to drug development, whose management was characterized by the loose coordination of contributing functions. Effective product development required the integration of specialized capabilities. Integration was difficult in most circumstances, but was particularly challenging at Lilly, with its strong functional groups, extensive specialization, large numbers of people, and multiple, ongoing operating pressures.[9]

The teams were created specifically in response to Lilly's quest to reduce the time to market for major new compounds and to maximize the effectiveness of its global commercialization process. But the effort also

[9] Adapted from Clark and Wheelwright, "Organizing and Leading 'Heavyweight' Development Teams," *California Management Review,* Spring 1992.

marked Watanabe's determination to revitalize Lilly's drug development process. Formal announcements were posted to formally introduce the teams to the Lilly organization, indicating the importance they were being given. Behind the scenes, the teams quickly adopted the behavior of acting as if they had carte blanche power when requesting resources from the functions.

This would later come back to haunt the teams, however, most particularly Evista. The Zyprexa team would later be nicknamed "the big dogs" but the Evista team was called "the big pigs." The rest of the Lilly organization palpably resented the teams because of their free access to resources and senior management attention.

Heavyweight Teams

A number of key characteristics defined a heavyweight team at Lilly.[10] First, as indicated in Watanabe's announcement of their formation, the teams were each given a very clear business charter "to focus exclusively on the development of a single compound." Second, each team was colocated and cross-functional, although there was a five-month delay in colocating the Zyprexa team because of constraints on available space at Lilly headquarters. Third, the teams were each led by a heavyweight project manager. Fourth, each team took responsibility for the substance of the work, how the work was accomplished, and the ensuing results. Ownership and commitment were two striking characteristics of these teams, with each creating a "contract book" that explicitly detailed deliverables and timelines. Last, each team had two executive sponsors, one from LRL and one from the business group, who guided the team and worked to resolve conflicts between the team and the rest of the Lilly organization.

For both the Zyprexa and Evista teams, the heavyweight project managers played a pivotal role. The team leader had direct access to and responsibility for the work of everyone involved in the project. In fact, the term *heavyweight* was used to describe the project manager for two principal reasons. First, the team leader was a senior manager of the organization, having, as such, significant expertise and experience as well as organizational clout. Second, heavyweight leaders had primary influence over the people working on development of the drug and supervised their work directly through key functional people on the core team. While the long-term career development continued to rest with the functional man-

ager, the heavyweight project leader also made significant contributions to individual performance evaluations.

Also characterizing heavyweight teams at Lilly was the emphasis on developing a "system solution" for a set of customer needs as opposed to having functional groups focus on their own "end states." Thus, getting all the necessary components and subsystems to complement one another *and* win approval from the FDA *and* effectively address the needs of the prescribing physicians, health care insurers, and patients' physicians differentiated the heavyweight team approach from Lilly's previous development process.

While Watanabe clearly embraced the heavyweight team approach to developing Zyprexa and Evista, he had a number of concerns about how these teams would affect and work with the rest of the Lilly organization. Watanabe had known that by their very nature—being product-focused, and needing strong, independent leadership, broad skills and cross-functional perspective, and clear missions—heavyweight teams might conflict with Lilly's functional organization and raise questions about senior management's influence and control. And even the advantages of the team approach brought with them potential disadvantages, such as alienating the rest of the Lilly organization, that could hurt other development activities and efforts if not recognized and averted. Watanabe recognized that the challenges of managing heavyweight teams, particularly as they were Lilly's first, would be no easy task for the senior management team.

Zyprexa

Zyprexa had the potential to be both a huge medical milestone in the treatment of schizophrenia and a blockbuster drug for Lilly. Schizophrenia, a clinical syndrome affecting 1 percent of the world's population, was characterized by the presence of positive psychotic symptoms, such as delusions and hallucinations, and negative symptoms, such as diminished emotions and low motivation. People with schizophrenia often had difficulty distinguishing fantasy from reality, thinking clearly, and managing emotions. They had lost their social skills, their schooling and jobs, or their ability to communicate. Schizophrenia, long considered one of the most chronic and debilitating of mental illnesses, was estimated to cost $65 billion in health care costs and lost resources in 1997.

Standard schizophrenia drugs had long carried the risk of side effects such as rigidity, Parkinson's-disease–like tremors, and involuntary movements that left some patients flailing their arms and biting their tongues. The

---

[10] Ibid.

drug Clozapine changed schizophrenia treatment by fighting the symptoms and largely avoiding the troubling movements, but it posed another risk: a potentially fatal blood illness. Patients taking Clozapine had to have their blood drawn every week to test for the potential disorder.

The challenge was to develop better drugs that avoided the side effects of both standard therapy and Clozapine. The first, Risperal, went on the market in 1994.

When the announcement to form two heavyweight teams was made, Zyprexa, generically known as olanzapine, was eight months into Phase III trials, with the group responsible for its development recruiting patients into the large-scale, long-term study. Although the recruitment process had not been going well, many of the group's functional members resisted the conversion to a heavyweight team structure, deeming it an unwanted midstream change of course. This resistance was a hurdle senior management was determined to overcome.

Because space constraints at Lilly made colocating the team in one central area initially impossible, the functional members—coming from toxicology, project management, manufacturing, marketing, regulatory, information technology, statistics, and medical—remained physically located within their departments. Not until May 1995 were most team members able to colocate. During the interim, they carried on with business-as-usual practices, even though their reporting structures and work assignments had been formally changed.

Team members continued to be guided by the priorities of their functional goals rather than acting as a cohesive team, however, even after colocation. Work was sometimes passed from one function to the next ("throwing it over the wall") instead of being accomplished through a truly integrated, team-based approach. Coordination and integration remained difficult, as was communication between team members from different functions, because they often did not fully understand each others' work. This lack of coordination became starkly apparent during the collection and analysis of clinical data from the Phase III trials, as the NDA submission date neared.

Two functions were particularly critical to this data preparation effort: systems analysts, who created the computer database used to collect and analyze data efficiently, and statisticians, who analyzed the data from the database. Unfortunately, the system analysts were frustrated by the statisticians' constant requests to modify the database. The statisticians were frustrated by the system analysts' inability (through lack of knowledge) to construct a database yielding data the statisticians needed

to prepare an NDA. This mutual frustration lasted until early June, one month after the team had colocated. At that point, the two functional groups lost their identity as systems analysts and statisticians and gained a new one—members of the Zyprexa team. One system analyst remarked to a senior manager, "I finally understand what the statisticians do."

Then, in mid-July, only two months before the NDA's planned submission, a system analyst discovered a database error that would cause at least a four-week delay. The team's initial reaction was shock, but after a meeting held the day of the discovery and attended by all members (functions), a recovery plan was drawn up. By the end of the week, the Zyprexa team had a new database and was back on course. By working around the clock, it was able to submit documents to the FDA for approval right on schedule—just seven months after the team was formed.

Not only was the Zyprexa team able to dramatically streamline its efforts and accelerate the timeline, it became extremely efficient at forecasting the future. For example, a member of the European drug regulatory agency had faxed a number of detailed questions to the team regarding therapeutic activity, dosing, and clinical results. Having anticipated questions of this nature, the Zyprexa team faxed a response to Europe overnight. The European regulatory official subsequently noted that he had never before received such accurate and definitive information so quickly.

On September 27, 1996, the FDA approved Zyprexa for treating schizophrenia. The Zyprexa® team had shaved months from the process and had proven to themselves and to others at Lilly that the heavyweight team structure could indeed result in dramatic leaps in speed and quality. The Evista® team had a role model.

Evista

Lilly had begun testing raloxifene as an agent for treating breast cancer in the 1980s. Although raloxifene was an estrogen replacement therapeutic (for women), as was common for that time, Phase I trials were conducted on men to avoid any possible significant negative hormonal side effects on women; once safety concerns were allayed, the drug was then tested to determine its efficacy in treating breast cancer in women. Unfortunately, raloxifene failed to show efficacy in this trial.

When Watanabe announced the formation of a heavyweight team to develop raloxifene under the name Evista, in January 1995, Phase II trials had already indicated that raloxifene might be effective in treating osteoporosis.

With a market potential for Lilly of over $1 billion, the race to rapidly develop and commercialize Evista had begun.

As LRL's senior management staff had decided that executive sponsorship should be shared between an executive in the business unit and one in its organization, Jim Harper, then president of Women's Health Business, represented the business unit, with Dr. Richard M. DiMarchi, then vice president of endocrine research and clinical investigation, representing LRL. The next question was who should lead the team. LRL senior management understood that for the team to be successful, the project leader needed a strong sense of vision, had to command respect within Lilly, be perceived as an expert on the targeted disease or a closely related area, and be able to interface well with external organizations and regulatory bodies. Dr. John Termine was selected as vice president in charge of the Evista program. Termine, who joined Lilly in 1991, had extensive experience in clinical research on bone as the chief of the Bone Research Branch, National Institute of Dental Research, the chief of the Skeletal Biology Section of Bone Research Branch, and the acting chief on a rotational basis of the Laboratory of Biological Structure, National Institute of Dental Research.

Reporting to Termine were marketing, medical, and program administration (see Exhibit 11). As administration director, Dr. Gary Kaiser reported to Termine and was responsible for managing operations, project management, and manufacturing. Dr. Will Dere, who also reported to Termine, was responsible for all medical aspects including physician team members, clinical research staff, information technology, biostatistics, medical writing, and clinical operations. Rounding out Termine's staff was the global marketing director who managed publications, market research, product management, and regional market management.

In November 1993, 14 months before the Evista team was formed, senior management and key middle managers, involved at the time in the development of raloxifene, decided their commercialization strategy for Evista would be to seek approval for the label indication of "prevention" (see Exhibit 12). Osteoporosis was most commonly defined as occurring when bone density fell below two standard deviations from the bone density norm of a healthy young adult. Prevention of osteoporosis was

EXHIBIT 11   Evista® Organization Chart–January 1998

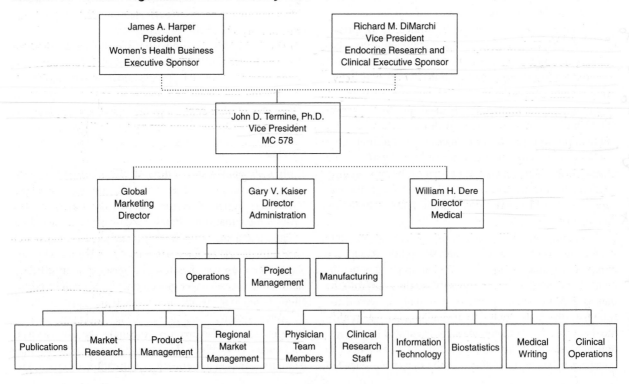

EXHIBIT 12   Delineation of Osteoporosis

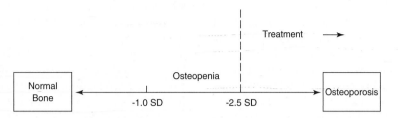

defined as increasing or preserving bone density. Treatment of osteoporosis meant preventing the occurrence of new osteoporotic fractures. Given these definitions, there were a number of reasons why Lilly's commercialization strategy was to target the prevention—rather than a treatment—indication first.

First, had Lilly wanted the FDA to approve a label indication for the treatment of osteoporosis, it would need to add two to three years to the approval process because longer-term studies were required for this indication, the patient group had to be much larger, and the necessary bone density and fracture data simply took more time to generate. Lilly also wanted to get the brand "Evista" to the market as quickly as possible, and "Evista" could be used only when the FDA approved the drug. Moreover, Lilly felt that there was a great deal of education to be conducted within the medical community and wanted to start this process as soon as possible.

When the Evista heavyweight team was formed in January 1995, it revisited the existing strategy to move forward first with the prevention indication. The heavyweight team supported the earlier decision, realizing its important market implications. Although a first approved label indication for Evista as a preventive for osteoporosis (as opposed to a treatment) would not have the same cachet with doctors and particularly with patients, the team felt that time to market and, particularly, establishing the Evista brand were critical even though the prevention indication would be a more difficult sell than would a treatment indication.

In March 1997, Lilly reviewed the 24-month Phase III data necessary for the prevention indication; on June 8, the Evista team submitted all documentation to the FDA for the approval of Evista® as a preventative for osteoporosis.

The first step in the final approval process was to have the data package reviewed by an FDA scientific advisory board, which for Evista comprised "thought leaders" and medical experts on endocrine and metabolic diseases.

On November 20, 1997, the advisory board voted on whether the FDA should approve Evista for the prevention of osteoporosis in postmenopausal women.

On December 9, 1997, at 11:56 P.M., four minutes before the expiration of the six-month rapid approval deadline, the FDA faxed its letter of approval to Lilly. The Evista® team members, who had gathered around the fax machine, rejoiced.

The strategy had worked. The Evista team had proven itself to the FDA and to the Lilly organization. Months had been cut from the timeline. In fact, the Evista team itself had accelerated the schedule. Senior management estimates were that at least 18 months had been saved compared to Lilly's conventional development process. The Evista team, a landmark in Lilly's history, was able to successfully coordinate clinical trials of 12,000 patients on a worldwide basis. The effort demanded unique leverage of Lilly's IT systems and a great deal of innovation—both of which the heavyweight team was well suited for.

The Evista team's IT group had been leveraged to provide worldwide remote patient data entry, significantly increasing the speed and accuracy of data acquisition. This was in stark contrast to the traditional approach of having paper forms filled out by local clinics and sent to Indianapolis for processing by data entry personnel who were unfamiliar with the data. The Evista team also constructed a worldwide database so that regulatory experts around the world could access information and access regulatory questions quickly and easily. The NDA submission itself was in both paper and electronic form. Regulatory officials could thereby easily access and search for information on a specific subject.

Even the FDA review of the package insert was done electronically and in real time. A conference room in Indianapolis was linked to a similar room at FDA headquarters in Rockville, Maryland. The text for the label indication appeared simultaneously at Lilly and the FDA, allowing the two groups to work on the label in real time instead of sending letters back and forth. According to the FDA, the simultaneous review of the label indication was "the wave of the future."

The cross-functional, heavyweight-team approach had allowed Lilly to shave at least 15 months from the development process. Furthermore, the "prevention strategy" was credited with saving over one year from the process by eliminating the need for bone fracture data. The team had also focused a large share of its resources on convincing the FDA that Evista was an estrogen-equivalent medicine with an improved benefit/risk profile that deserved a priority review. And by qualifying for rapid approval of Evista, another six months had been shaved from the development time. Since 1995, the team had worked around the clock, exhibiting a remarkable esprit de corps.

THE COMMERCIALIZATION OF EVISTA

In the months leading up to FDA approval, Lilly senior management struggled with the question of how best to commercialize Evista. Traditionally, the technical staff, including medical and manufacturing staff, would hand off the drug to sales and marketing so that technical staff

EXHIBIT 13 List of Launch Activities

Determine global pricing policy and communicate to affiliates.

Develop manufacturing logistics plan, including final packages, labels, and cartons, and final preparation of primary bulk and formulation manufacturing sites.

Develop market plans to support the new product and conduct ongoing market research.

Obtain preliminary approval for any necessary exportation/importation of bulk or finished product stock.

Final design and printing of promotional materials.

Fill the supply line—Manufacture and fill the product prior to regulatory approval. Immediately upon approval, ship to marketing affiliate of approval country.

Initiate pricing and reimbursement negotiations, prior to regulatory approval if possible.

Conduct sales launch meetings upon approval.

Develop and submit pharmacopoeia monograph.

Prepare to transfer learning from early launching countries to later launching countries.

Create clinical trial database for global access of clinical results.

Create and implement clinical response network for rapid response and data accumulation of patient complaints and any adverse results.

Source: Company documents.

members could quickly become involved in new efforts, where their expertise was critical.

Senior management, however, was considering a different approach for Evista, one following upon that of heavyweight development teams. Technical team members, particularly key members of the medical staff, would continue to follow Evista through commercialization. Some senior managers believed this might have the beneficial effect of reducing hand-off problems, ensuring that expertise in the product would not be lost when it mattered most (see Exhibit 13). Some managers believed this continuity would also enable technical staff members to gain marketplace experience, which was foreign to most. It also meant that they could focus their efforts and thereby increase their effectiveness.

The issue of limited resources—especially human resources—had historically been a bottleneck for Lilly's drug development efforts. Prior to the use of heavyweight teams, Lilly senior management had conducted a diagnostic to determine areas of improvement in their product development process. One major discovery was that a handful of key personnel were spread over a large number of projects. This staffing pattern was the result of a limited number of personnel having the breadth and depth of experience needed to effectively drive development projects. That lack of experienced personnel had not been solved by the use of heavyweight teams.

In fact, the use of heavyweight teams had served to emphasize and highlight this point because of the discipline it had brought to Lilly's product development process—specifically the staffing resource allocation process. Senior management was therefore caught in a quandary between staffing a heavyweight team to commercialize Evista, thereby reducing further the availability of key technical personnel available for other projects, or sticking with the traditional approach of assigning those key technical personnel to several projects simultaneously, violating one of the staffing principles for heavyweight teams. The creation of a heavyweight team for the commercialization of Evista would necessarily mean that other projects would have to be delayed or suspended, at least until additional technical resources could be hired or developed.

Senior management realized that the creation of a heavyweight team to commercialize Evista would also perpetuate the feelings of some in the Lilly organization that the Evista team truly was "the big pigs," particularly among those whose projects were to suffer as a result of the staffing allocations proposed for Evista. And while the development of Evista was clearly a success on a number of dimensions, there were those in the organization who still believed that any project would have succeeded given the resources that the Evista® team had access to. Senior management wondered how it could get buy-in from those in the organization who still did not believe in this product development process, while continuing the evolution and application of the use of heavyweight teams at Lilly.

There were other senior managers, however, who felt if technical members were allowed to stay with Evista through its commercialization process, which would take several years, Lilly's technical expertise could be diminished and marginalized, having a particularly negative impact on the functions. And several functions were already reeling from a lack of resources, since many of the people who had been on the Evista development team were key sources of medical and technical expertise. This was an especially acute issue because Lilly intended to make Evista a cornerstone of its women's health care business, given its potential efficacy in preventing breast cancer and heart disease. There were simply not enough experts to go around, and for many in Lilly, the needs for such experts outside the Evista launch were every bit as compelling as the needs within Evista.

One possible solution was to increase the percentage of revenues spent on R&D at Lilly. Although Lilly had increased the amount of funds going to R&D it was still below the industry's norm. In 1997, Lilly spent 16.2 percent of revenues on R&D. The industry's average was 19.4 percent. Surely, additional funds could help diminish capacity constraints and ease resource allocation tensions within the organization. However, it wasn't clear that an increase could come out of profits, without hurting Lilly's market value. Yet no other function felt they could cut back their spending without impacting their ability to support new product development efforts.

As senior management gathered to discuss these issues, Watanabe knew that the decision on how to commercialize Evista would have as much impact as his earlier decision to use heavyweight teams to develop raloxifene and olanzapine and could affect the entire Lilly organization. Watanabe wondered what criteria senior management should use to decide this issue? Should the decision be based on a strategic commitment to improve Lilly's development process in one fell swoop? What would be the organizational cost of suspending or delaying other projects? How could Lilly maximize the success of Evista, given the investment already made and the desire to make it a platform product? If Lilly adopted heavyweight teams for both development and commercialization, where would the resources come from to adequately staff and support these teams, while maintaining the viability of other projects that did not have the benefit of being heavyweight projects?

CASE IV-3

Team New Zealand

Alan MacCormack

Doug Peterson leaned back in his chair and twisted the cap off another Steinlager. The Wharf Cafe had grown crowded and smoky since the meeting had started. "We really have to get ourselves a proper conference room next time," he thought, as he stared out over a misty, gray Auckland harbor.

It was late May 1994. Peterson had been working on the design of New Zealand's 1995 America's Cup yacht for over a year. As lead designer, he had conceived the original concept and recruited the design team, which, for the first time, was making extensive use of sophisticated computer-aided design and simulation tools. Now, as the team assembled for its weekly review after the day's sailing, the time had come to commit to the construction of the new yacht.

Peterson pondered the decision they faced. The budget allowed for two yachts to be built; however, there were several strategies they could take with regard to their design. Should they build two yachts with *similar* hull and keel designs, so they could vary the details of the keel design and race them against each other to assess potential improvements? Should they build two yachts with hulls optimized for *different* sailing conditions? Or should they build one yacht now, but delay building the second, waiting till after another round of prototype tests, while they experimented with the first one on the water?

The decision they made in the next hour would profoundly affect their chances of winning in San Diego and becoming only the second team in 145 years to win the Cup from the Americans.

THE AMERICA'S CUP

In 1851, the Royal Yacht Squadron of England offered a silver trophy, called the Hundred Guinea Mug, to the winner of a sailing race run around the Isle of Wight, a small island off the south coast. Open to all nations, the race attracted 15 English entries and only one foreign challenger—the eventual winner, America. The Hundred Guinea Mug thereafter became known as the America's Cup, in honor of its first winner, and when the last surviving owner of the victorious team donated it to the New York Yacht Club, it was decided that challengers from other countries should be allowed to compete for the trophy in a "friendly competition between foreign nations." The rules for these races were defined in a document called "The Deed of the Gift."

The first America's Cup challenge was held in 1870. Over the next 30 years, the American defenders successfully defended against teams from England, Scotland, Canada, and Ireland. At this time, participants were not limited in design, hence boats varied greatly in both size and power. However, since the European challengers were required by the rules to cross the stormy North Atlantic under their own sail power, their boats were often heavily built and slower than the Americans'. Races were often one-sided affairs, of little interest to spectators.

In 1920, the rules were changed to specify the use of J-class designs, enormous single-masted boats over 100 feet long, with masts 120 feet high and a crew of 40. While races became closer, ultimately, the results were the same. Between 1920 and 1937, the Americans made another four successful defenses. After a long break due to World War II, J-class boats were ruled too expensive, and a new 12-meter class was created, with 65-foot long hulls, 90-foot masts, and a crew of 11. The rules were changed so that challengers' boats could be transported to the race site by ship rather than having to sail. As designs converged, racing became even tighter. Even so, between 1958 and 1980, the Americans defended successfully another eight times.

In 1983, the longest winning streak in sports history—132 years—ended when the revolutionary Australia II, with a radical and controversial "winged keel," defeated Liberty, under the helmsmanship of Dennis Conner. In 1987, however, Conner regained the cup in Perth with Stars & Stripes, racing for the San Diego Yacht Club. The next year, a team from New Zealand, exploiting a clause in "The Deed of Gift," challenged Conner with a huge boat nicknamed "The Big One." Without time to redesign, Conner defended successfully with a 60-foot ultralight catamaran, the first use of a double-hull in the America's Cup.

In 1992, a new yacht class was defined for the lighter winds of San Diego. The International America's Cup Class (IACC) required boats of 75 feet in length, with 110-foot masts and a crew of 16. By using advanced materials, boats became lighter for their size, and hence faster in the light winds. While America 3 eventually defeated the Italian challenger in the final, the 1992 races were enormously expensive. The American defender built five boats, the Italian challenger four. Both spent over $60 million. It was decided in the future to reduce expenses; each team would be limited to only two boats, with further limits on the use of sails and other equipment.

The 1995 cup races would follow a round-robin format. First, the boats would be divided into two groups: the defenders, from the country of the current cup holders, and the challengers, from all other nations. The racing would then be divided into three parts. In the first, which will start in January, the challengers will race against each other for the right to enter the final (this will be called the Louis Vuitton Cup). In the second, which will run simultaneously with the first, yachts from the host country will race for the right to defend. Finally, in May, the winning challenger team will race against the winning defender team for the America's Cup. Boat designs will be allowed to evolve between each race, until the start of the final.

Typical time differences between first- and second-placed boats would usually be less than one minute.

THE DESIGN OF A RACING YACHT

The design of a present-day racing yacht comprises four essential elements—the hull, the keel, the mast, and the sails (see Exhibit 1). The objective of the design team is to produce a light boat with as low a drag factor as possible. The structure, however, must also have the strength and stability to cope with highly variable wind and sea conditions. To achieve this balance, teams rely heavily on the skills and experience of the lead designer to make many critical trade-offs during the design process.

The bulk of the initial design work focuses on the hull and keel, as these are on the critical path for the construction of the yacht. To develop these, designers have

EXHIBIT 1   Schematic of a Recent Racing Yacht

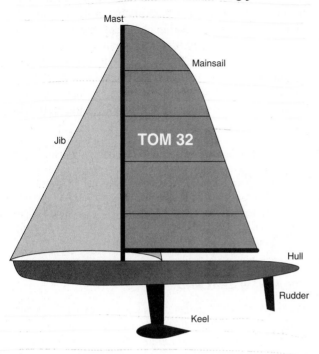

traditionally relied on what is known as the "tank-and-tunnel" process for getting feedback on performance. This process entails construction of a series of scaled-down physical prototypes which are tested in a wind tunnel and a towing tank (a large swimming pool equipped with a winch at one end, which tows the prototype down the middle) providing data on the amount of drag generated by a particular design.

During the initial stages of a typical yacht development, five to six physical prototypes are built at one-quarter scale (20 feet) and subject to testing in the wind tunnel and towing tank. Fabrication and testing of these prototypes takes several months and costs about $50,000 per prototype. Data on the performance of each of these designs are analyzed to assess relative performance characteristics and used to project potential design enhancements. A further set of prototypes is then built, and the whole process repeated. This series of prototype iterations typically occurs three or four times prior to freezing the design for construction. As Peterson explained:

> The tank-and-tunnel method is a design process where experimentation occurs in bursts. Every couple of months, you get back the results of your experiments. As a result, there is a limit to the number of design iterations you can

perform. A typical project can rarely afford more than 20 prototypes, due to time and money constraints. In each design cycle, you have to rely on big gains in performance.

THE USE OF SIMULATION IN DESIGN

The design of the critical surfaces on a present-day racing yacht is a complex activity. The presence of many interactions means it is not easy to predict the effect of even small changes in the structure. The system is "chaotic," and predicting its behavior is much like trying to predict the weather. While traditional tank-and-tunnel design methods rely on experienced designers and informed trial and error to overcome such complexity, the advent of cheap computer hardware and automated design tools have led to rapid advances in the possibility of simulating designs.

Modern yacht design makes use of several tools to help automate the process. Among the most important are finite element analysis (FEA), a tool which analyzes the structural characteristics of a design; computational fluid dynamics (CFD) programs, which help simulate the flow of water over the yacht's critical surfaces; and velocity prediction programs (VPPs), which predict how fast a particular design will be in a given set of wind and sea conditions.

CFD programs were originally developed for the aerospace industry, traditionally being used to model the flow of air over an aircraft's control surfaces. The software is "panel-based," the structure first being "broken up" into many small panels, each of which is represented by a set of mathematical equations. The program links these panels together to form a model of the complete design, then solves a set of equations governed by fluid mechanics theory to calculate the pressures and flows at the surface. While CFD had been around since the 1960s, its application to yacht design was a recent phenomenon as the teams began design work for the 1995 America's Cup. In its initial applications, it had met with only limited success, and opinions were mixed as to its usefulness.

Advantages of Simulation

The major advantages of simulation over traditional design methods fall into three main areas. It is cheaper and faster than constructing physical prototypes, it generates more insight into why particular designs are better or worse than others, and it avoids problems associated with "scaling up" the design from a physical prototype to the real world.

The primary advantage of simulation is in its speed and cost. While programs often require a significant amount of computing memory and processing power, once a basic design has been configured, design iterations can be run in a matter of hours, at little cost. The only limitation on how many iterations can be conducted relates to the amount of computer power available and, more important, the capacity of the design team to interpret results. In general, the bottleneck becomes a team's ability to generate and evaluate new configurations, not its ability to test them.

Another important advantage of simulation is that it establishes an understanding of the trade-offs involved with alternative design choices. Although tank-and-tunnel methods give a good indication of the overall performance of a design, they do not help the designer interpret why one design is performing better than another. CFD, by comparison, can show the pressure distributions and flows around a hull or keel which generate the drag produced by a given design.

A final advantage of simulation is that it avoids the problems of "scale-up." This occurs when the use of scaled-down models introduces distortions which affect the accuracy of test results. For example, certain types of drag, generated by the chaotic nature of a fluid flowing over a surface, are very sensitive to scale; hence, results from reduced-scale physical models are likely to be inaccurate. The use of simulation avoids such a bias.

Drawbacks of Simulation

Although simulation has many advantages over tank-and-tunnel tests, these tools are complementary nevertheless. As Peterson emphasized, "Even with all the simulation in the world, no one is going to commit $3 million to a yacht without towing it down a tank first!" Physical prototypes are used extensively early in the design process to set the basic parameters of the hull and keel. Once these have been defined, simulation is used to help optimize their shape.

The importance of simulation is greatly increased once the hull and keel have been built. CFD can be used to substantially improve the performance of the yacht through the design of aerodynamic wings which attach to the bulb at the bottom of the keel (the lead weight which gives a yacht its stability). In the run-up to a major race program, extensive testing and refinement of these appendages occurs, driven by the results of simulating different designs. These changes can lead to substantial improvements in performance.

Ultimately, however, all of these tools are only as good as the designer in whose hands they are placed. The lead designer is responsible for putting together the initial concept, without which no amount of simulation will yield a good design. Also in charge of directing the experimentation strategy, the designer is the person who says "what to try next." The concept design and experimentation strategy together provide critical "stakes in the ground" and a sense of direction—activities for which automated design tools provide little help. As Peterson noted:

> The CFD program can't design a yacht from scratch without conceptual input. It doesn't know what parameters it should be optimizing. Consider designing a golf ball to fly as far as possible off the tee. The computer won't tell you the ball should have dimples, but if you specify this as a design parameter, it will find the optimal dimple pattern and density for you.

TEAM NEW ZEALAND

During May 1993, general manager Peter Blake began putting together the team of people who would work together for over two years in an effort to win the America's Cup. The Team New Zealand syndicate comprised about 50 people, with activities split between team management, design and construction, and the crew, skippered by Olympic Gold medalist Russell Coutts (see Exhibit 2).

The budget for the syndicate, raised from corporate sponsors in New Zealand, was $20 million. While comparable to the budgets of other teams, Team New Zealand had decided to build two boats, rather than one, due to the experimental benefits this would give them during the testing period. Given the full cost of a boat, mast, keel, and sail program was around $3 million to $4 million, it was clear from the start that the money for other resources would be severely limited. The team would need to be small, focused, and highly motivated, with everyone adopting multiple roles.

Blake's philosophy in running the team was to have all the critical people on board from the beginning. On 24th May 1993, the team assembled for the first time. Rather than dive straight into the detail of design and crew training, they spent the first three weeks working together with an external consultant to outline the mission for the team and a vision of how they would work together. Peterson described the process:

> We spent a lot of time going over why certain teams had won or lost in the past. What we found was that unsuccessful efforts were often driven by one or two personalities, be they designer-driven, skipper-driven, or owner-driven. Suc-

EXHIBIT 2   Team New Zealand Syndicate: Key Staff Members

Syndicate head:	Peter Blake
Yacht Club:	Royal New Zealand Yacht Squadron
Syndicate budget:	Estimated $20 million
Team sponsors:	ENZA (New Zealand Apple and Pear Board)
	Lion Nathan (Steinlager)
	Lotteries Commission
	Television New Zealand
	Toyota New Zealand
Management	
Campaign public relations:	Alan Sefton
Campaign business manager:	Ross Blackman
Lead Crew	
Skipper:	Russell Coutts
Navigator:	Tom Schnackenberg
Afterguard:	Brad Butterworth
	Rick Dodson
	Murray Jones
Design Team	
Chief Designers	Doug Peterson
	Laurie Davidson
Computational dynamicist	David Egan
Aero/hydro dynamicist	Richard Karn
Performance analyst	Peter Jackson
Structures/weather	David Alan-Williams
Construction	
Construction chief	Tim Gurr
Structural experts	Wayne Smith
	Mike Drummond
	Chris Mitchell
	Neil Wilkinson

cessful teams were truly "managed," not dominated by one voice. Hence we wanted to run the syndicate in a democratic fashion. When we had differences of opinion on which direction to go, we'd put it to a vote. One of the most important outputs of the three weeks was the mission statement, which described the way that things would run. Above all, we stressed open communication and dissemination of knowledge, even to the extreme of running classes on yacht design and weather forecasting for anyone who was interested.

With the three-week "vision thing" behind them, the staff at last assumed their more traditional roles. The crew began training, using the yachts which had been built for the last America's Cup, and the design team began work on the concepts for the new design.

The Design Process

Doug Peterson was appointed to lead the design team. An American by birth, Peterson had extensive experience with designing boats and racing yachts. Peterson had no formal design or engineering training, but had been designing boats for as long as he could remember: "This is what I have always done. I can remember when I was in high school, I would spend all my time designing boats on pieces of scrap paper instead of paying attention in class." About 30 years and thousands of designs later, he was considered to be one of the world's leading yacht designers. His latest achievement was the design of the America 3 boat, the America's Cup winner in 1992. Peterson was given responsibility for developing the overall design concept for the Team New Zealand boat, specifying test models, analyzing results, and developing construction plans.

As the design team planned to make extensive use of automated design and simulation tools, Peterson assembled a mix of experienced yacht designers and simulation experts. Among them, Dave Egan was recruited to run the design simulations. Egan's appointment brought to the team prior experience in simulating yacht designs and a working knowledge of the required computer hardware, having previously been a sales agent for Silicon Graphics.

The design was initially driven by Peterson, who defined the initial boat concept and specified an implementation plan. Peterson drew upon the knowledge he had accumulated with the America 3 team to put his first thoughts to paper. Given America 3 had built five boats, each of which was significantly different in design, he had a lot of experience to help him. During the design process, the America 3 team had conducted over 65 prototype tests in the wind tunnel alone.

Egan's first job was to code this concept design into a geometry model for the simulation program, providing a baseline for performance. With this accomplished, design iterations and performance simulations began in November 1993. The initial simulations focused primarily on the design of the hull, with relatively simple keel variations. The team would have to commit to the hull design in May 1994, in order for construction to begin.

The Simulation Effort

Running CFD required substantial amounts of computer power. For example, to simulate the keel required coding 13,000 individual panels as part of the modeling program, creating data files of 6 to 8 gigabytes in size. While several syndicates were using similar analytical programs, the resources available to them and strategies they followed differed considerably.

Most syndicates had lined up large corporations to help with the task, allowing processing to be performed on the largest and latest supercomputers. Young America, for example, had over a million dollars of computer time available to them, through a partnership that included both Cray and Boeing. Boeing ran the design simulations on Cray supercomputers based in their headquarters in Seattle, using advanced CFD software developed for their aerospace needs. These machines were among the world's fastest computers, each costing several million dollars. Every few weeks, the Boeing engineers would run large batches of simulations and feed back their results to the Young America designers in San Diego. This allowed them to test a massive number of experimental designs.

The strategy adopted by Team New Zealand reflected the resource constraints presented by the budget. The team decided to use a small network of workstations which could be operated locally. Given the poor history CFD simulation had in yacht design, Egan was given less than $100,000 to cover personnel, hardware, and software. As he recalls:

> The early days of the project were a constant challenge to find resources. We were running around companies looking for computer time. At one, we managed to grab a 16 processor Challenge computer for a month prior to its being commissioned. The MIS guy never knew what happened! Then we gained access to a SunSparc2 workstation. Soon, however, the rising number of design iterations we needed to explore began to exceed its capacity.

As luck would have it, during Christmas 1993, Jim Clark, the CEO of Silicon Graphics, was in New Zealand having his yacht refitted. A keen sailor, Clark had invited several members of the team aboard his yacht. Over dinner, as he learned of their predicament, he immediately offered the INDY workstation installed in his yacht for the team to use. As Egan explains:

> Making contact with Jim was extremely timely. Although we declined the offer of his waterproof INDY, he did put us in touch with the local SGI office. They gave us access to the spare cycles on their demonstration machines, a four-processor Challenge server, and a couple of workstations.

The involvement of Silicon Graphics in the project grew with time. The company eventually became a sponsor of the team and lent a lot of computing equipment to the effort. This effectively increased the syndicate's simulation budget significantly. With a combination of workstations, the team could now simulate a new design every two or three hours. It gave the team immediate access to experimentation as the equipment was located a few feet from the dock. Egan emphasized the benefits of this approach compared with the tank-and-tunnel tests:

> Instead of relying on a few big leaps, we had the ability to continually design, test, and refine our ideas. The team would often hold informal discussions on design issues, sketch some schematics on the back of a beer mat, and ask me to run the numbers. Using traditional design methods would have meant waiting months for results, and by that time, our thinking would have evolved so much that the reason for the experiment would long since have been forgotten.
>
> We considered the crew our customers, in charge of what went into the design. They needed to drive the process. By having a computing strategy based upon local workstations, we had the ability to display results of simulations to them using flow-fill graphics. How we demonstrated the difference between two designs turned out to be a powerful marketing tool to help convince the crew of the benefits.

Team New Zealand's approach to simulation was extremely practical, heavily influenced by Peterson's experience. As he explained:

> Dave [Egan] was very realistic on the uses and limitations of CFD. In practice, if you start with a bad design, simulation won't get you anywhere near a good one. Some of the other syndicates let CFD drive their process. The Australians, for example, had some really deep simulation experts, and see where that got them.[1] At the end of the day, the real performance advantage is in the initial design. Everything else from there on in is just incremental improvement.
>
> Take the velocity prediction program. Trying to work out how the sails will perform is an extremely unreliable science. There's so much variability in the air flow. I told them to tweak it until they got the answer I expected; then we looked at the coefficients to see if they looked reasonable. In the end, it doesn't matter. All you're looking at is the differences between alternative designs. No one really believes we can accurately predict the time we'll put up over the course in San Diego.

During the six months between November 1993 and May 1994, the team cycled through building physical prototypes for tank-and-tunnel testing three times, building 14 scaled-down models. The first set of prototypes provided a performance baseline for the initial concept, allowing the team to parameterize the velocity prediction program and establish an estimate of the time around the

---

[1] The Australian boat sank in one of the early trials while racing against Team New Zealand.

course in San Diego. For the second and third set of prototypes, Peterson attempted to improve upon the initial design using a combination of experience and the flow-fill pictures generated by the CFD program. The improvements were significant, with the best prototype from the third set of tests bettering the time of the initial concept design by over two minutes. Egan described the situation as of early May:

> We were emerging with a robust design for the hull and keel. We had reduced the drag considerably over the concept design, but now, each new prototype was giving us less and less improvement. The third set of prototype tests, which we'd just got back, produced less than half the improvement of the second. There was a strong argument that the most improvement potential was now in the keel appendages, where a lot of enhancements can be made through the design and placement of the wings. To run those experiments, however, you have to put a real yacht in the water.

Testing of the actual boat in the water would be combined with CFD simulation of the keel. The two would have to be used together, since historically only about a third of the changes suggested by CFD resulted in "real" improvements to the design.

"TWO BOATS, OR NOT TWO BOATS, THAT IS THE QUESTION"

In late May 1994, the syndicate was faced with a major decision. Construction of the first yacht was planned to begin next month for an August delivery (boat construction took about two months). This would leave about four months for travel to San Diego, testing, and improvements before racing was to begin in January. However, the initial budget had provided money for two boats, and there were several theories on how to get the best value from the second one.

One option was to commit to building two yachts now for delivery in August. This way, the yachts could be used in combination to conduct test iterations on the keel wings. Another option was to build only one yacht now, use this to begin testing different keel wings, and meanwhile conduct another round of prototype testing on the basic hull and keel design. The second boat could then be built just prior to the start of the qualifying competition in January.

Building two boats now would allow Team New Zealand to put two boats in the water at the same time. Egan articulated the perceived logic behind a two-boat testing program:

The two-boat testing philosophy is driven by the fact that the sea is a noisy environment in which to run experiments. If we build two yachts of similar design, we gain the ability to run better experiments. We can put two keels with different wing designs on each boat, race them, and see how much difference there is. Then we can swap the keels and make sure the results hold for the other boat and crew. This way, there is no argument over whether the wind or sea conditions affected the results. The problem is especially relevant, given the improvements that come from changes to the keel wings are relatively small, in the order of two or three seconds over the whole course. Detecting these differences in noisy conditions is extremely difficult. Just a minor change in wind speed between two trials can easily swamp the effect of a design change.

In the past, teams using a two-boat testing program had shown that it was possible to run and verify the performance of a different keel wing design practically every 24 hours, particularly if the two boats were identical. During the day, while the crew were on the water, the simulation team would analyze hundreds of potential improvements to the keel appendages and select one or two which appeared most promising. Overnight, the construction team would work on the new designs and have them ready to sail the next morning. When the crew arrived, they would take the boats racing to verify whether the design changes produced real improvements.

With only one boat, alternative keel designs had to be removed and fitted during the sailing day. If conditions changed, the crew would often have to sail each design a number of times to identify which was better. As a result, verifying the results of design changes was slower than with two boats. Therefore, some argued that the differences in improvement speed between one- and two-boat testing would soon add up.

Building only one boat now traded the benefits of rapid feedback inherent in a two-boat testing process in favor of another cycle of testing prior to committing to the second yacht. Proponents of this approach argued that although the improvement potential in the basic design of the hull and keel had diminished, another cycle of tank-and-tunnel tests was still attractive. At the same time, running experiments with different keel appendages, even with only one boat, would still produce significant design enhancements. In combination, these two activities would yield greater overall improvement to the design and in addition would give the team the flexibility of building the second boat later in the development cycle. Building two boats now, they argued, was a waste of money and opportunity, particularly if these were identical.

Team New Zealand were not alone in having a budget big enough for two boats. As they tapped the sailing grapevine, however, other syndicates were taking diverse approaches.

The Japanese syndicate had decided to stagger the construction of their boats, opting to conduct another round of prototype tests before committing to the second one.

The leading Australian syndicate was building two boats simultaneously, but each was of very different design.

None of the three American defenders had decided to build two boats, despite having budgets of similar size to that of the New Zealand team. They had spent the money on other items, including more prototypes and iterations for tank-and-tunnel testing.

Team New Zealand's decision boiled down to three basic options: building two identical boats now; building two different boats now, perhaps one following one of Peterson's more aggressive concepts that hadn't made it to the wind tunnel yet; and building one boat now and one boat after some additional testing.

READING IV-3

Organizing and Leading "Heavyweight" Development Teams

Kim B. Clark and Steven C. Wheelwright

Effective product and process development requires the integration of specialized capabilities. Integrating is difficult in most circumstances, but is particularly challenging in large, mature firms with strong functional groups, extensive specialization, large numbers of people, and multiple, ongoing operating pressures. In such firms, development projects are the exception rather than the primary focus of attention. Even for people working on development projects, years of experience and the estab-

Source: © 1992 by The Regents of the University of California. Reprinted from the *California Management Review,* Volume 34, Number 3, Spring 1992. By permission of The Regents. Adapted from Chapter 8 of Steven C. Wheelwright and Kim B. Clark, *Revolutionizing Product Development: Quantum Leaps in Speed, Efficiency, and Quality* (New York, NY: Free Press, 1992).

lished systems—covering everything from career paths to performance evaluation, and from reporting relationships to breadth of job definitions—create both physical and organizational distance from other people in the organization. The functions themselves are organized in a way that creates further complications: the marketing organization is based on product families and market segments, engineering around functional disciplines and technical focus, and manufacturing on a mix between functional and product market structures. The result is that in large, mature firms, organizing and leading an effective development effort is a major undertaking. This is especially true for organizations whose traditionally stable markets and competitive environments are threatened by new entrants, new technologies, and rapidly changing customer demands.

This article zeros in on one type of team structure— "heavyweight" project teams—that seems particularly promising in today's fast-paced world yet is strikingly absent in many mature companies. Our research shows that when managed effectively, heavyweight teams offer improved communication, stronger identification with and commitment to a project, and a focus on cross-functional problem solving. Our research also reveals, however, that these teams are not so easily managed and contain unique issues and challenges.

Heavyweight project teams are one of four types of team structures. We begin by describing each of them briefly. We then explore heavyweight teams in detail, compare them with the alternative forms, and point out specific challenges and their solutions in managing the heavyweight team organization. We conclude with an example of the changes necessary in individual behavior for heavyweight teams to be effective. Although heavyweight teams are a different way of organizing, they are more than a new structure; they represent a fundamentally different way of working. To the extent that both the team members and the surrounding organization recognize that phenomenon, the heavyweight team begins to realize its full potential.

TYPES OF DEVELOPMENT PROJECT TEAMS

Exhibit 1 illustrates the four dominant team structures we have observed in our studies of development projects: functional, lightweight, heavyweight, and autonomous (or tiger). These forms are described below, along with their associated project leadership roles, strengths, and weaknesses. Heavyweight teams are examined in detail in the subsequent section.

EXHIBIT 1   Types of Development Teams

A. Functional team structure

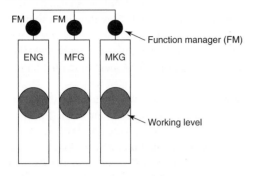

B. Lightweight team structure

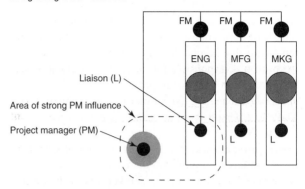

C. Heavyweight team structure

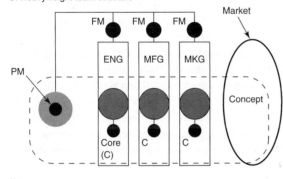

D. Autonomous team structure

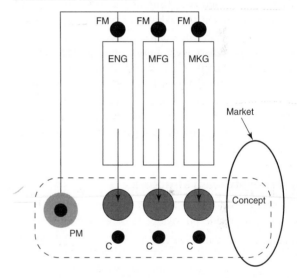

Functional Team Structure

In the traditional functional organization found in larger, more mature firms, people are grouped principally by discipline, each working under the direction of a specialized subfunction manager and a senior functional manager. The different subfunctions and functions coordinate ideas through detailed specifications all parties agree to at the outset, and through occasional meetings where issues that cut across groups are discussed. Over time, primary responsibility for the project passes sequentially— although often not smoothly—from one function to the next, a transfer frequently termed *throwing it over the wall.*

The functional team structure has several advantages and associated disadvantages. One strength is that those

managers who control the project's resources also control task performance in their functional area; thus, responsibility and authority are usually aligned. However, tasks must be subdivided at the project's outset (i.e., the entire development process is decomposed into separable, somewhat independent activities). But on most development efforts, not all required tasks are known at the outset, nor can they all be easily and realistically subdivided. Coordination and integration can suffer as a result.

Another major strength of this approach is that, because most career paths are functional in nature until a general management level is reached, the work done on a project is judged, evaluated, and rewarded by the same subfunction and functional managers who make the decisions about career paths. The associated disadvantage is that individual contributions to a development project tend to be judged largely independently of overall project success. The traditional tenet cited is that individuals cannot be evaluated fairly on outcomes over which they have little or no control. But as a practical matter, that often means that no one directly involved in the details of the project is responsible for the results finally achieved.

Finally, the functional project organization brings specialized expertise to bear on the key technical issues. The same person or small group of people may be responsible for the design of a particular component or subsystem over a wide range of development efforts. Thus the functions and subfunctions capture the benefits of prior experience and become the keepers of the organization's depth of knowledge while ensuring that it is systematically applied over time and across projects. The disadvantage is that every development project differs in its objectives and performance requirements, and it is unlikely that specialists developing a single component will do so very differently on one project than on another. The "best" component or subsystem is defined by technical parameters in the areas of their expertise rather than by overall system characteristics or specific customer requirements dictated by the unique market the development effort aims for.

Lightweight Team Structure

Like the functional structure, those assigned to the lightweight team reside physically in their functional areas, but each functional organization designates a liaison person to "represent" it on a project coordinating committee. These liaison representatives work with a "lightweight project manager," usually a design engineer or product marketing manager, who coordinates different functions' activities. This approach usually figures as an add-on to a traditional functional organization, with the functional liaison person having that role added to his or her other duties. The overall coordination assignment of lightweight project manager, however, tends not to be present in the traditional functional team structure.

The project manager is a "lightweight" in two important aspects. First, he or she is generally a middle- or junior-level person who, despite considerable expertise, usually has little status or influence in the organization. Such people have spent a handful of years in a function, and this assignment is seen as a "broadening experience," a chance for them to move out of that function. Second, although they are responsible for informing and coordinating the activities of the functional organiza-

tions, the key resources (including engineers on the project) remain under the control of their respective functional managers. The lightweight project manager does not have power to reassign people or reallocate resources and instead confirms schedules, updates time lines, and expedites across groups. Typically, such project leaders spend no more than 25 percent of their time on a single project.

The primary strengths and weaknesses of the lightweight project team are those of the functional project structure. But now at least one person over the course of the project looks across functions and seeks to ensure that individual tasks—especially those on the critical path—get done in a timely fashion, and that everyone is kept aware of potential cross-functional issues and what is going on elsewhere on this particular project.

Thus, improved communication and coordination are what an organization expects when moving from a functional to a lightweight team structure. Yet, because power still resides with the subfunction and functional managers, hopes for improved efficiency, speed, and project quality are seldom realized. Moreover, lightweight project leaders find themselves tolerated at best, and often ignored and even preempted. This can easily become a "no-win" situation for the individual thus assigned.

Heavyweight Team Structure

In contrast to the lightweight setup, the heavyweight project manager has direct access to and responsibility for the work of all those involved in the project. Such leaders are "heavyweights" in two respects. First, they are senior managers within the organization; they may even outrank the functional managers. Hence, in addition to having expertise and experience, they also wield significant organizational clout. Second, heavyweight leaders have primary influence over the people working on the development effort and supervise their work directly through key functional people on the core teams. Often, the core group of people are dedicated and physically colocated with the heavyweight project leader. However, the longer-term career development of individual contributors continues to rest not with the project leader—although that heavyweight leader makes significant input to individual performance evaluations—but with the functional manager, because members are not assigned to a project team on a permanent basis.

The heavyweight team structure has a number of advantages and strengths, along with associated weaknesses. Because this team structure is observed much less frequently in practice and yet seems to have tremendous potential for a wide range of organizations, it will be discussed in detail in the next section.

Autonomous Team Structure

With the autonomous team structure, often called the "tiger team," individuals from the different functional areas are formally assigned, dedicated, and colocated to the project team. The project leader, a "heavyweight" in the organization, is given full control over the resources contributed by the different functional groups. Furthermore, that project leader becomes the sole evaluator of the contribution made by individual team members.

In essence, the autonomous team is given a "clean sheet of paper"; it is not required to follow existing organizational practices and procedures, but is allowed to create its own. This includes establishing incentives and rewards as well as norms for behavior. However, the team will be held fully accountable for the final results of the project: Success or failure is its responsibility and no one else's.

The fundamental strength of the autonomous team structure is focus. Everything the individual team members and the team leader do is concentrated on making the project successful. Thus, tiger teams can excel at rapid, efficient new product and new process development. They handle cross-functional integration in a particularly effective manner, possibly because they attract and select team participants much more freely than the other project structures.

Tiger teams, however, take little or nothing as "given"; they are likely to expand the bounds of their project definition and tackle redesign of the entire product, its components, and subassemblies, rather than looking for opportunities to utilize existing materials, designs, and organizational relationships. Their solution may be unique, making it more difficult to fold the resulting product and process—and, in many cases, the team members themselves—back into the traditional organization upon project completion. As a consequence, tiger teams often become the birthplace of new business units or they experience unusually high turnover following project completion.

Senior managers often become nervous at the prospects of a tiger team because they are asked to delegate much more responsibility and control to the team and its project leader than under any of the other organization structures. Unless clear guidelines have been established in advance, it is extremely difficult during the project for senior managers to make midcourse corrections or exercise substantial influence without destroying the team. More than one team has "gotten away" from senior management and created major problems.

THE HEAVYWEIGHT TEAM STRUCTURE

The best way to begin understanding the potential of heavyweight teams is to consider an example of their success, in this case, Motorola's experience in developing its Bandit line of pagers.

The Bandit Pager Heavyweight Team

This development team within the Motorola Communications Sector was given a project charter to develop an automated, on-shore, profitable production operation for its high-volume Bravo pager line. (This is the belt-worn pager that Motorola sold from the mid-1980s into the early 1990s.) The core team consisted of a heavyweight project leader and a handful of dedicated and colocated individuals, who represented industrial engineering, robotics, process engineering, procurement, and product design/CIM. The need for these functions was dictated by the Bandit platform automation project and its focus on manufacturing technology with a minimal change in product technology. In addition, human resource and accounting/finance representatives were part of the core team. The human resource person was particularly active early on as subteam positions were defined and jobs posted throughout Motorola's Communications Sector and played an important subsequent role in training and development of operating support people. The accounting/finance person was invaluable in "costing out" different options and performing detailed analyses of options and choices identified during the course of the project.

An eighth member of the core team was a Hewlett-Packard employee. Hewlett-Packard was chosen as the vendor for the "software backplane," providing an HP 3000 computer and the integrated software communication network that linked individual automated workstations, downloaded controls and instructions during production operations, and captured quality and other operating performance data. Because HP support was vital to the project's success, it was felt essential they be represented on the core team.

The core team was housed in a corner of the Motorola Telecommunications engineering/manufacturing facility. The team chose to enclose in glass the area where the automated production line was to be set up so that others in the factory could track the progress, offer suggestions, and adopt the lessons learned from it in their own production and engineering environments. The team called their project Bandit to indicate a willingness to "take" ideas from literally anywhere.

The heavyweight project leader, Scott Shamlin, who was described by team members as "a crusader," "a renegade," and "a workaholic," became the champion for the Bandit effort. A hands-on manager who played a major role in stimulating and facilitating communication across functions, he helped to articulate a vision of the Bandit line and to infuse it into the detailed work of the project team. His goal was to make sure the new manufacturing process worked for the pager line, but would provide real insight for many other production lines in Motorola's Communications Sector.

The Bandit core team started by creating a contract book that established the blueprint and work plan for the team's efforts and its performance expectations; all core team members and senior management signed on to the document. Initially, the team's executive sponsor—although not formally identified as such—was George Fisher, the sector executive. He made the original investment proposal to the board of directors and was an early champion and supporter, as well as direct supervisor in selecting the project leader and helping get the team underway. Subsequently, the vice president and general manager of the Paging Products division filled the role of executive sponsor.

Throughout the project, the heavyweight team took responsibility for the substance of its work, the means by which it was accomplished, and its results. The project was completed in 18 months as per the contract book, which represented about half the time of a normal project of such magnitude. Further, the automated production operation was up and running with process tolerances of five sigma (i.e., the degree of precision achieved by the manufacturing processes) at the end of 18 months. Ongoing production verified that the cost objectives (substantially reduced direct costs and improved profit margins) had indeed been met, and product reliability was even higher than the standards already achieved on the off-shore versions of the Bravo product. Finally, a variety of lessons were successfully transferred to other parts of the sector's operations, and additional heavyweight teams have proven the viability and robustness of the approach in Motorola's business and further refined its effectiveness throughout the corporation.

The Challenge of Heavyweight Teams

Motorola's experience underscores heavyweight teams' potential power, but it also makes clear that creating an effective heavyweight team capability is more than merely selecting a leader and forming a team. By their very nature—being product (or process) focused, and needing strong, independent leadership, broad skills and cross-functional perspective, and clear missions—heavyweight teams may conflict with the functional organization and raise questions about senior management's influence and control. And even the advantages of the team approach bring with them potential disadvantages that may hurt development performance if not recognized and averted.

Take, for example, the advantages of ownership and commitment, one of the most striking advantages of the heavyweight team. Identifying with the product and creating a sense of esprit de corps motivate core team members to extend themselves and do what needs to be done to help the team succeed. But such teams sometimes expand the definition of their role and the scope of the project, and they get carried away with themselves and their abilities. We have seen heavyweight teams turn into autonomous tiger teams and go off on a tangent because senior executives gave insufficient direction and the bounds of the team were only vaguely specified at the outset. And even if the team stays focused, the rest of the organization may see themselves as "second class." Although the core team may not make that distinction explicit, it happens because the team has responsibilities and authority beyond those commonly given to functional team members. Thus, such projects inadvertently can become the "haves" and other, smaller projects the "have-nots" with regard to key resources and management attention.

Support activities are particularly vulnerable to an excess of ownership and commitment. Often the heavyweight team will want the same control over secondary support activities as it has over the primary tasks performed by dedicated team members. When waiting for prototypes to be constructed, analytical tests to be performed, or quality assurance procedures to be conducted, the team's natural response is to "demand" top priority from the support organization or to be allowed to go outside and subcontract to independent groups. While these may sometimes be the appropriate choices, senior management should establish make-buy guidelines and clear priorities applicable to all projects—perhaps changing service levels provided by support groups (rather than maintaining the traditional emphasis on resource utilization)—or have support groups provide capacity and advisory technical services but let team members do more of the actual task work in those support areas. Whatever actions the organization takes, the challenge is to achieve a balance between the needs of the individual project and the needs of the broader organization.

Another advantage the heavyweight team brings is the integration and integrity it provides through a system solution to a set of customer needs. Getting all the components and subsystems to complement one another and to address effectively the fundamental requirements of the core customer segment can result in a winning platform product and/or process. The team achieves an effective system design by using generalist skills applied by broadly trained team members, with fewer specialists and, on occasion, less depth in individual component solutions and technical problem solving.

The extent of these implications is aptly illustrated by the nature of the teams Clark and Fujimoto studied in the auto industry.[1] They found that for U.S. auto firms in the mid-1980s, typical platform projects—organized under a traditional functional or lightweight team structure—entailed full-time work for several months by approximately 1,500 engineers. In contrast, a handful of Japanese platform projects—carried out by heavyweight teams—utilized only 250 engineers working full-time for several months. The implications of 250 versus 1,500 full-time equivalents (FTEs) with regard to breadth of tasks, degree of specialization, and need for coordination are significant and help explain the differences in project results as measured by product integrity, development cycle time, and engineering resource utilization.

But that lack of depth may disclose a disadvantage. Some individual components or subassemblies may not attain the same level of technical excellence they would under a more traditional functional team structure. For instance, generalists may develop a windshield wiper system that is complementary with and integrated into the total car system and its core concept. But they also may embed in their design some potential weaknesses or flaws that might have been caught by a functional team of specialists who had designed a long series of windshield wipers. To counter this potential disadvantage, many organizations order more testing of completed units to discover such possible flaws and have components and subassemblies reviewed by expert specialists. In some cases, the quality assurance function has expanded its role to make sure sufficient technical specialists review designs at appropriate points so that such weaknesses can be minimized.

[1] See Kim B. Clark and Takahiro Fujimoto, *Product Development Performance* (Boston, MA: Harvard Business School Press, 1991).

Managing the Challenges of Heavyweight Teams

Problems with depth in technical solutions and allocations of support resources suggest the tension that exists between heavyweight teams and the functional groups where much of the work gets done. The problem with the teams exceeding their bounds reflects in part how teams manage themselves, in part how boundaries are set, and in part the ongoing relationship between the team and senior management. Dealing with these issues requires mechanisms and practices that reinforce the team's basic thrust—ownership, focus, system architecture, integrity—and yet improve its ability to take advantage of the strengths of the supporting functional organization—technical depth, consistency across projects, senior management direction. We have grouped the mechanisms and problems into six categories of management action: the project charter, the contract, staffing, leadership, team responsibility, and the executive sponsor.

The Project Charter A heavyweight project team needs a clear mission. A way to capture that mission concisely is in an explicit, measurable project charter that sets broad performance objectives and usually is articulated even before the core team is selected. Thus, joining the core team includes accepting the charter established by senior management. A typical charter for a heavyweight project would be the following:

> The resulting product will be selected and ramped by Company X during Quarter 4 of calendar year 1991, at a minimum of a 20 percent gross margin.

This charter is representative of an industrial products firm whose product goes into a system sold by its customers. Company X is the leading customer for a certain family of products, and this project is dedicated to developing the next generation platform offering in that family. If the heavyweight program results in that platform product being chosen by the leading customer in the segment by a certain date and at a certain gross margin, it will have demonstrated that the next generation platform is not only viable, but likely to be very successful over the next three to five years. Industries and settings where such a charter might be found would include a microprocessor being developed for a new computer system, a diesel engine for the heavy equipment industry, or a certain type of slitting and folding piece of equipment for the newspaper printing press industry. Even in a medical diagnostics business with hundreds of customers, a goal

EXHIBIT 2   Heavyweight Team, Contract Book—Major Sections

- Executive summary
- Business plan and purposes
- Development plan
  —Schedule
  —Materials
  —Resources
- Product design plan
- Quality plan
- Manufacturing plan
- Project deliverables
- Performance measurement and incentives

of "capturing 30 percent of market purchases in the second 12 months during which the product is offered" sets a clear charter for the team.

The Contract Book   Whereas a charter lays out the mission in broad terms, the contract book defines, in detail, the basic plan to achieve the stated goal. A contract book is created as soon as the core team and heavyweight project leader have been designated and given the charter by senior management. Basically, the team develops its own detailed work plan for conducting the project, estimates the resources required, and outlines the results to be achieved and against which it is willing to be evaluated. (The table of contents of a typical heavyweight team contract book is shown in Exhibit 2.) Such documents range from 25 to 100 pages, depending on the complexity of the project and level of detail desired by the team and senior management before proceeding. A common practice following negotiation and acceptance of this contract is for the individuals from the team and senior management to sign the contract book as an indication of their commitment to honor the plan and achieve those results.

The core team may take anywhere from a long week to a few months to create and complete the contract book; Motorola, for example, after several years of experience, has decided that a maximum of seven days should be allowed for this activity. Having watched other heavyweight teams—particularly in organizations with no prior experience in using such a structure—take up to several months, we can appreciate why Motorola has nicknamed this the "blitz phase" and decided that the time allowed should be kept to a minimum.

Staffing   As suggested in Exhibit 1, a heavyweight team includes a group of core cross-functional team members who are dedicated (and usually physically colocated) for

the duration of the development effort. Typically there is one core team member from each primary function of the organization; for instance, in several electronics firms we have observed core teams consisting of six functional participants—design engineering, marketing, quality assurance, manufacturing, finance, and human resources. (Occasionally, design will be represented by two core team members, one each for hardware and software engineering.) Individually, core team members represent their functions and provide leadership for their functions' inputs to the project. Collectively, they constitute a management team that works under the direction of the heavyweight project manager and takes responsibility for managing the overall development effort.

While other participants—especially from design engineering early on and manufacturing later on—may frequently be dedicated to a heavyweight team for several months, they usually are not made part of the core team though they may well be colocated and, over time, develop the same level of ownership and commitment to the project as core team members. The primary difference is that the core team manages the total project and the coordination and integration of individual functional efforts, whereas other dedicated team members work primarily within a single function or subfunction.

Whether these temporarily dedicated team members are actually part of the core team is an issue firms handle in different ways, but those with considerable experience tend to distinguish between core and other dedicated (and often colocated) team members. The difference is one of management responsibility for the core group that is not shared equally by the others. Also, it is primarily the half a dozen members of the core group who will be dedicated throughout the project, with other contributors having a portion of their time reassigned before this heavyweight project is completed.

Whether physical colocation is essential is likewise questioned in such teams. We have seen it work both ways. Given the complexity of development projects, and especially the uncertainty and ambiguity often associated with those assigned to heavyweight teams, physical colocation is preferable to even the best of online communication approaches. Problems that arise in real time are much more likely to be addressed effectively with all of the functions represented and present than when they are separate and must either wait for a periodic meeting or use remote communication links to open up cross-functional discussions.

A final issue is whether an individual can be a core team member on more than one heavyweight team si-

EXHIBIT 3   Project Manager Profile

	Lightweight (limited)	Heavyweight (extensive)
Span of coordination responsibilities	├──────────────────────────────┤	
Duration of responsibilities	├──────────────────────────────┤	
Responsible for specs, cost, layout, components	├──────────────────────────────┤	
Working level contact with engineers	├──────────────────────────────┤	
Direct contact with customers	├──────────────────────────────┤	
Multilingual/multidisciplined skills	├──────────────────────────────┤	
Role in conflict resolution	├──────────────────────────────┤	
Marketing imagination/concept champion	├──────────────────────────────┤	
Influence in: engineering	├──────────────────────────────┤	
marketing	├──────────────────────────────┤	
manufacturing	├──────────────────────────────┤	

multaneously. If the rule for a core team member is that 70 percent or more of his or her time must be spent on the heavyweight project, then the answer to this question is no. Frequently, however, a choice must be made between someone being on two core teams—for example, from the finance or human resource function—or putting a different individual on one of those teams who has neither the experience nor stature to be a full peer with the other core team members. Most experienced organizations we have seen opt to put the same person on two teams to ensure the peer relationship and level of contribution required, even though it means having one person on two teams and with two desks. They then work diligently to develop other people in the function so that multiple team assignments will not be necessary in the future.

Sometimes multiple assignments will also be justified on the basis that a function such as finance does not need a full-time person on a project. In most instances, however, a variety of potential value-adding tasks exist that are broader than finance's traditional contribution. A person largely dedicated to the core team will search for those opportunities and the project will be better because of it. The risk of allowing core team members to be assigned to multiple projects is that they are neither available when their inputs are most needed nor as committed to project success as their peers. They become secondary core team members, and the full potential of the heavyweight team structure fails to be realized.

Project Leadership   Heavyweight teams require a distinctive style of leadership. A number of differences between lightweight and heavyweight project managers are highlighted in Exhibit 3. Three of those are particularly distinctive. First, a heavyweight leader manages, leads, and evaluates other members of the core team and is also the person to whom the core team reports throughout the project's duration. Another characteristic is that rather than being either neutral or a facilitator with regard to problem solving and conflict resolution, these leaders see themselves as championing the basic concept around which the platform product and/or process is being shaped. They make sure that those who work on subtasks of the project understand that concept. Thus they play a central role in ensuring the system integrity of the final product and/or process.

Finally, the heavyweight project manager carries out his or her role in a very different fashion than the lightweight project manager. Most lightweights spend the bulk of their time working at a desk, with paper. They revise schedules, get frequent updates, and encourage people to meet previously agreed upon deadlines. The heavyweight project manager spends little time at a desk, is out talking to project contributors, and makes sure that decisions are made and implemented whenever and wherever needed. Some of the ways in which the heavyweight project manager achieves project results are highlighted by the five roles illustrated in Exhibit 4 for a heavyweight project manager on a platform development project in the auto industry.

The *first role* of the heavyweight project manager is to provide for the team a direct interpretation of the market and customer needs. This involves gathering market data directly from customers, dealers, and industry shows, as

EXHIBIT 4 The Heavyweight Project Manager

Role	Description
Direct market interpreter	First-hand information, dealer visits, auto shows; has own marketing budget, market study team, direct contact, and discussions with customers
Multilingual translator	Fluency in language of customers, engineers, marketers, stylists; translator between customer experience/requirements and engineering specifications
Direct engineering manager	Direct contact, orchestra conductor, evangelist of conceptual integrity, and coordinator of component development; direct eye-to-eye discussions with working level engineers; shows up in drafting room, looks over engineers' shoulders
Program manager "in motion"	Out of the office, not too many meetings, not too much paperwork, face-to-face communication; conflict resolution manager
Concept infuser	Concept guardian; confronts conflicts; not only reacts but implements own philosophy; ultimate decision maker; coordination of details and creation of harmony

well as through systematic study and contact with the firm's marketing organization. A *second role* is to become a multilingual translator, not just taking marketing information to the various functions involved in the project, but being fluent in the language of each of those functions and making sure the translation and communication going on among the functions—particularly between customer needs and product specifications—are done effectively.

A *third role* is the direct engineering manager, orchestrating, directing, and coordinating the various engineering subfunctions. Given the size of many development programs and the number of types of engineering disciplines involved, the project manager must be able to work directly with each engineering subfunction on a day-to-day basis and ensure that their work will indeed integrate and support that of others, so the chosen product concept can be effectively executed.

A *fourth role* is best described as staying in motion: out of the office conducting face-to-face sessions, and highlighting and resolving potential conflicts as soon as possible. Part of this role entails energizing and pacing the overall effort and its key subparts.

A *final role* is that of concept champion. Here the heavyweight project manager becomes the guardian of the concept and not only reacts and responds to the interests of others, but also sees that the choices made are consistent and in harmony with the basic concept. This requires a careful blend of communication and teaching skills so that individual contributors and their groups understand the core concept and have sufficient conflict resolution skills to ensure that any tough issues are addressed in a timely fashion.

It should be apparent from this description that heavyweight project managers earn the respect and right to carry out these roles based on prior experience, carefully developed skills, and status earned over time, rather than simply being designated "leader" by senior management. A qualified heavyweight project manager is a prerequisite to an effective heavyweight team structure.

Team Member Responsibilities Heavyweight team members have responsibilities beyond their usual functional assignment. As illustrated in Exhibit 5, these are of two primary types. Functional hat responsibilities are

EXHIBIT 5 Responsibilities of Heavyweight Core Team Members

Functional hat accountabilities:
• Ensuring functional expertise on the project
• Representing the functional perspective on the project
• Ensuring that subobjectives are met that depend on their function
• Ensuring that functional issues impacting the team are raised proactively within the team

Team hat accountabilities:
• Sharing responsibility for team results
• Reconstituting tasks and content
• Establishing reporting and other organizational relationships
• Participating in monitoring and improving team performance
• Sharing responsibility for ensuring effective team processes
• Examining issues from an executive point of view (Answering the question, "Is this the appropriate business response for the company?")
• Understanding, recognizing, and responsibly challenging the boundaries of the project and team process

those accepted by the individual core team member as representative of his or her function. For example, the core team member from marketing is responsible for ensuring that appropriate marketing expertise is brought to the project, that a marketing perspective is provided on all key issues, that project subobjectives dependent on the marketing function are met in a timely fashion, and that marketing issues that impact other functions are raised proactively within the team.

But each core team member also wears a team hat. In addition to representing a function, each member shares responsibility with the heavyweight project manager for the procedures followed by the team, and for the overall results that those procedures deliver. The core team is accountable for the success of the project, and it can blame no one but itself if it fails to manage the project, execute the tasks, and deliver the performance agreed upon at the outset.

Finally, beyond being accountable for tasks in their own function, core team members are responsible for how those tasks are subdivided, organized, and accomplished. Unlike the traditional functional development structure, which takes as given the subdivision of tasks and the means by which those tasks will be conducted and completed, the core heavyweight team is given the power and responsibility to change the substance of those tasks to improve the performance of the project. Since this is a role that core team members do not play under a lightweight or functional team structure, it is often the most difficult for them to accept fully and learn to apply. It is essential, however, if the heavyweight team is to realize its full potential.

The Executive Sponsor With so much more accountability delegated to the project team, establishing effective relationships with senior management requires special mechanisms. Senior management needs to retain the ability to guide the project and its leader while empowering the team to lead and act, a responsibility usually taken by an executive sponsor—typically the vice president of engineering, marketing, or manufacturing for the business unit. This sponsor becomes the coach and mentor for the heavyweight project leader and core team and seeks to maintain close, ongoing contact with the team's efforts. In addition, the executive sponsor serves as a liaison. If other members of senior management—including the functional heads—have concerns or inputs to voice, or need current information on project status, these are communicated through the executive sponsor.

This reduces the number of mixed signals received by the team and clarifies for the organization the reporting and evaluation relationship between the team and senior management. It also encourages the executive sponsor to set appropriate limits and bounds on the team so that organizational surprises are avoided.

Often the executive sponsor and core team identify those areas where the team clearly has decision-making power and control, and they distinguish them from areas requiring review. An electronics firm that has used heavyweight teams for some time dedicates one meeting early on between the executive sponsor and the core team to generating a list of areas where the executive sponsor expects to provide oversight and be consulted; these areas are of great concern to the entire executive staff and team actions may well raise policy issues for the larger organization. In this firm, the executive staff wants to maintain some control over:

- Resource commitment—head count, fixed costs, and major expenses outside the approved contract book plan;
- Pricing for major customers and major accounts;
- Potential slips in major milestone dates (the executive sponsor wants early warning and recovery plans);
- Plans for transitioning from development project to operating status;
- Thorough reviews at major milestones or every three months, whichever occurs sooner;
- Review of incentive rewards that have companywide implications for consistency and equity; and
- Cross-project issues such as resource optimization, prioritization, and balance.

Identifying such areas at the outset can help the executive sponsor and the core team better carry out their assigned responsibilities. It also helps other executives feel more comfortable working through the executive sponsor, since they know these "boundary issues" have been articulated and are jointly understood.

THE NECESSITY OF FUNDAMENTAL CHANGE

Compared to a traditional functional organization, creating a team that is "heavy"—one with effective leadership, strong problem-solving skills, and the ability to integrate across functions—requires basic changes in the way development works. But it also requires change in the fundamental behavior of engineers, designers, manufacturers, and marketers in their day-to-day work. An episode in a computer company with no previous experience with heavyweight teams illustrates the depth of change required to realize fully these teams' power.[2]

Two teams, A and B, were charged with development of a small computer system and had market introduction targets within the next 12 months. While each core team was colocated and held regular meetings, there was one overlapping core team member (from finance/accounting). Each team was charged with developing a new computer system for their individual target markets but by chance, both products were to use an identical, custom-designed microprocessor chip in addition to other unique and standard chips.

The challenge of changing behavior in creating an effective heavyweight team structure was highlighted when each team sent this identical, custom-designed chip—the "supercontroller"—to the vendor for pilot production. The vendor quoted a 20-week turnaround to both teams. At that time, the supercontroller chip was already on the critical path for Team B, with a planned turnaround of 11 weeks. Thus, every week saved on that chip would save one week in the overall project schedule, and Team B already suspected that it would be late in meeting its initial market introduction target date. When the 20-week vendor lead time issue first came up in a Team B meeting, Jim, the core team member from engineering, responded very much as he had on prior, functionally structured development efforts: Because initial prototypes were engineering's responsibility, he reported that they were working on accelerating the delivery date, but that the vendor was a large company, with which the computer manufacturer did substantial business, and known for its slowness. Suggestions from other core team members on how to accelerate the delivery were politely rebuffed, including one to have a senior executive contact his or her counterpart at the vendor. Jim knew the traditional approach to such issues and did not perceive a need, responsibility, or authority to alter it significantly.

For Team A, the original quote of 20-week turnaround still left a little slack, and thus initially the supercontroller chip was not on the critical path. Within a couple of weeks, however, it was, given other changes in the activities and schedule, and the issue was immediately raised at the team's weekly meeting. Fred, the core team member from manufacturing (who historically would not have been involved in an early engineering proto-

type), stated that he thought the turnaround time quoted was too long and that he would try to reduce it. At the next meeting, Fred brought some good news: through discussions with the vendor, he had been able to get a commitment that pulled in the delivery of the supercontroller chip by 11 weeks! Furthermore, Fred thought that the quote might be reduced even further by a phone call from one of the computer manufacturer's senior executives to a contact of his at the vendor.

Two days later, at a regular Team B meeting, the supercontroller chip again came up during the status review, and no change from the original schedule was identified. Since the finance person, Ann, served on both teams and had been present at Team A's meeting, she described Team A's success in reducing the cycle time. Jim responded that he was aware that Team A had made such efforts, but that the information was not correct, and the original 20-week delivery date still held. Furthermore, Jim indicated that Fred's efforts (from Team A) had caused some uncertainty and disruption internally, and in the future it was important that Team A not take such initiatives before coordinating with Team B. Jim stated that this was particularly true when an outside vendor was involved, and he closed the topic by saying that a meeting to clear up the situation would be held that afternoon with Fred from Team A and Team B's engineering and purchasing people.

The next afternoon, at his Team A meeting, Fred confirmed the accelerated delivery schedule for the supercontroller chip. Eleven weeks had indeed been clipped out of the schedule to the benefit of both Teams A and B. Subsequently, Jim confirmed the revised schedule would apply to his team as well, although he was displeased that Fred had abrogated "standard operating procedure" to achieve it. Curious about the differences in perspective, Ann decided to learn more about why Team A had identified an obstacle and removed it from its path, yet Team B had identified an identical obstacle and failed to move it at all.

As Fred pointed out, Jim was the engineering manager responsible for development of the supercontroller chip; he knew the chip's technical requirements, but had little experience dealing with chip vendors and their production processes. (He had long been a specialist.) Without that experience, he had a hard time pushing back against the vendor's "standard line." But Fred's manufacturing experience with several chip vendors enabled him to calibrate the vendor's dates against his best-case experience and understand what the vendor needed to do to meet a substantially earlier commitment.

---

[2] Adapted from a description provided by Dr. Christopher Meyer, Strategic Alignment Group, Los Altos, CA.

Moreover, because Fred had bought into a clear team charter, whose path the delayed chip would block, and because he had relevant experience, it did not make sense to live with the vendor's initial commitment, and thus he sought to change it. In contrast, Jim—who had worked in the traditional functional organization for many years—saw vendor relations on a pilot build as part of his functional job, but did not believe that contravening standard practices to get the vendor to shorten the cycle time was his responsibility, within the range of his authority, or even in the best long-term interest of his function. He was more concerned with avoiding conflict and not roiling the water than with achieving the overarching goal of the team.

It is interesting to note that in Team B, engineering raised the issue and, while unwilling to take aggressive steps to resolve it, also blocked others' attempts. In Team A, however, while the issue came up initially through engineering, Fred in manufacturing proactively went after it. In the case of Team B, getting a prototype chip returned from a vendor was still being treated as an "engineering responsibility," whereas in the case of Team A, it was treated as a "team responsibility." Since Fred was the person best qualified to attack that issue, he did so.

Both Team A and Team B had a charter, a contract, a colocated core team staffed with generalists, a project leader, articulated responsibilities, and an executive sponsor. Yet Jim's and Fred's understandings of what these things meant for them personally and for the team at the detailed, working level were quite different. While the teams had been through similar training and team start-up processes, Jim apparently saw the new approach as a different organizational framework within which work would get done as before. In contrast, Fred seemed to see it as an opportunity to work in a different way—to take responsibility for reconfiguring tasks, drawing on new skills, and reallocating resources, where required, for getting the job done in the best way possible.

Although both teams were "heavyweight" in theory, Fred's team was much "heavier" in its operation and impact. Our research suggests that heaviness is not just a matter of structure and mechanism, but of attitudes and behavior. Firms that try to create heavyweight teams without making the deep changes needed to realize the power in the team's structure will find this team approach problematic. Those intent on using teams for platform projects and willing to make the basic changes we have discussed here can enjoy substantial advantages of focus, integration, and effectiveness.

READING IV-4

The Power of Product Integrity

Kim B. Clark and Takahiro Fujimoto

Some companies consistently develop products that succeed with customers. Other companies often fall short. What differentiates them is integrity. Every product reflects the organization and the development process that created it. Companies that consistently develop successful products—products with integrity—are themselves coherent and integrated. Moreover, this coherence is distinguishable not just at the level of structure and strategy but also, and more important, at the level of day-to-day work and individual understanding. Companies with organizational integrity possess a source of competitive advantage that rivals cannot easily match.

The primacy of integrity, in products and organizations alike, begins with the role new products play in industrial competition and with the difficulty of competing on performance or price alone. New products have always fascinated and excited customers, of course. Henry Ford's Model A made front-page news after near-riots erupted outside dealers' showrooms. But today, in industries ranging from cars and computers to jet engines and industrial controls, new products are the focal point of competition. Developing high-quality products faster, more efficiently, and more effectively tops the competitive agenda for senior managers around the world.

Three familiar forces explain why product development has become so important. In the last two decades, intense international competition, rapid technological advances, and sophisticated, demanding customers have made "good enough" unsatisfactory in more and more consumer and industrial markets. Yet the very same forces are also making product integrity harder and harder to achieve.

Consider what happened when Mazda and Honda each introduced four-wheel steering to the Japanese auto market in 1987. Although the two steering systems used different technologies—Mazda's was based on electronic control, while Honda's was mechanical—they were equally sophisticated, economical, and reliable. Ten years earlier, both versions probably would have met with success. No longer. A majority of Honda's customers chose to install four-wheel steering in their new cars; Mazda's system sold poorly and was widely regarded as a failure.

Why did consumers respond so differently? Product integrity. Honda put its four-wheel steering system into the Prelude, a two-door coupe with a sporty, progressive image that matched consumers' ideas about the technology. The product's concept and the new component fit together seamlessly; the car sent a coherent message to its potential purchasers. In contrast, Mazda introduced its four-wheel steering system in the 626, a five-door hatchback that consumers associated with safety and dependability. The result was a mismatch between the car's conservative, family image and its racy steering system. Too sophisticated to be swayed by technology alone (as might have been the case a decade before), Mazda's potential customers saw no reason to buy a car that did not satisfy their expectations in every respect, including "feel." (Mazda's new advertising slogan, "It just feels right," suggests the company's managers took this lesson to heart.)

Product integrity is much broader than basic functionality or technical performance. Customers who have accumulated experience with a product expect new models to balance basic functions and economy with more subtle characteristics. Consumers expect new products to harmonize with their values and lifestyles. Industrial customers expect them to mesh with existing components in a work system or a production process. The extent to which a new product achieves this balance is a measure of its integrity. (One of integrity's primary metrics is market share, which reflects how well a product attracts and satisfies customers over time.)

Product integrity has both an internal and an external dimension. Internal integrity refers to the consistency between a product's function and its structure: the parts fit smoothly, the components match and work well together, the layout maximizes the available space. Organizationally, internal integrity is achieved mainly through cross-functional coordination within the company and with suppliers. Efforts to enhance internal integrity through this kind of coordination have become standard practice among product developers in recent years.

External integrity refers to the consistency between a product's performance and customers' expectations. In turbulent markets like those in which Honda and Mazda were competing, external integrity is critical to a new product's competitiveness. Yet for the most part, external integrity is an underexploited opportunity. Companies assign responsibility for anticipating what customers will want to one or more functional groups (the product

EXHIBIT 1   Focus on Development

What are the sources of superior performance in product development? What accounts for the wide differences in performance among companies in the same industry? To answer those questions, we studied 29 major development projects in 20 automobile companies around the world. (Three companies are headquartered in the United States, eight in Japan, and nine in Europe.) The projects ranged from micro-mini cars and small vans to large luxury sedans, with suggested retail prices from $4,300 to more than $40,000. Our research methods included structured and unstructured interviews, questionnaires, and statistical analysis. Throughout the study, we strove to develop a consistent set of data (including both measures of performance and patterns of organization and management) so that we could identify the constants among projects that differed greatly in scope and complexity.

We chose to concentrate on the automobile industry because it is a microcosm of the new industrial competition. In 1970, a handful of auto companies competed on a global scale with products for every market segment; today more than 20 do. Customers have grown more discerning, sophisticated, and demanding. The number of models has multiplied, even as growth has slowed, and technology is ever-more complex and diverse. In 1970, for example, the traditional V-8 engine with 3-speed automatic transmission and rear-wheel drive was the technology of choice for 80% of the cars produced in the United States. By the early 1980s, consumers could choose among 34 alternative configurations. In this environment, fast, efficient, effective product development has become the focal point of competition and managerial action.

planners in marketing, for example, or the testers in product engineering). But they give little or no attention to integrating a clear sense of customer expectations into the work of the product development organization as a whole.

Of course, there are exceptions. In a six-year study of new product development (see Exhibit 1), we found a handful of companies that consistently created products with integrity. What set these companies apart was their seamless pattern of organization and management. The way people did their jobs, the way decisions were made, the way suppliers were integrated into the company's own efforts—everything cohered and supported company strategy. If keeping the product line fresh and varied was a goal, speed and flexibility were apparent at every step in the development process, as were the habits and assumptions that accustom people and organizations to being flexible and to solving problems quickly. For example, product plans relied on large numbers of parts from suppliers who focused on meeting tight schedules and high quality standards even when designs changed late in the day. Product and process engineers jointly developed body panels and the dies to make them through informal, intense interactions that cut out unnecessary mistakes and solved problems on the spot. Production people built high-quality prototypes that tested the design against the realities of commercial production early in the game and so eliminated expensive delays and rework later on.

The examples we draw on in this article all come from the auto industry. We chose to look at a single industry worldwide so that we could identify the factors that separate outstanding performers from competitors making similar products for similar markets around the globe. But our basic findings apply to businesses as diverse as semiconductors, soup, and commercial construction. Wherever managers face a turbulent, intensely competitive market, product integrity—and the capacity to create it—can provide a sustainable competitive advantage.

THE POWER OF A PRODUCT CONCEPT

Products are tangible objects—things you can see, touch, and use. Yet the process of developing new products depends as much on the flow of information as it does on the flow of materials. Consider how a new product starts and ends.

Before a customer unpacks a new laptop computer or sets up a high-speed packaging machine, and long before a new car rolls off the showroom floor, the product (or some early version of it) begins as an idea. Next, that idea is embodied in progressively more detailed and concrete forms: Ideas turn into designs, designs into drawings, drawings into blueprints, blueprints into prototypes, and so on, until a finished product emerges from the factory. When it is finally in customers' hands, the product is converted into information once again.

If this last statement sounds odd, think about what actually happens when a potential buyer test-drives a new car. Seated behind the wheel, the customer receives a barrage of messages about the vehicle's performance. Some of these messages are delivered directly by the car: the feel of the acceleration, the responsiveness of the steering system, the noise of the engine, the heft of a door. Others come indirectly: the look on people's faces as the car goes by, comments from passengers, the driver's recollection of the car's advertising campaign. All these messages influence the customer's evaluation, which will largely depend on how he or she interprets them. In essence, the customer is consuming the product *experience,* not the physical product itself.

Developing this experience—and the car that will embody it—begins with the creation of a product concept. A powerful product concept specifies how the new car's basic functions, structures, and messages will attract and satisfy its target customers. In sum, it defines the character of the product from a customer's perspective.

The phrase *pocket rocket,* for example, captures the basic concept for a sporty version of a subcompact car. Small, light, and fast, a pocket rocket should also have quick, responsive handling and an aggressive design. While the car should sell at a premium compared with the base model, it should still be affordable. And the driving experience should be fun: quick at the getaway, nimble in the turns, and very fast on the straightaways. Many other design and engineering details would need definition, of course, for the car to achieve its objectives. But the basic concept of an affordable and fun-to-drive pocket rocket would be critical in guiding and focusing creative ideas and decisions.

By definition, product concepts are elusive and equivocal. So it is not surprising that when key project participants are asked to relate the concept for a new vehicle, four divergent notions of value emerge. Those for whom the product concept means *what the product does* will couch their description in terms of performance and technical functions. Others, for whom the concept means *what the product is,* will describe the car's packaging, configuration, and main component technologies. Others, for whom product concept is synonymous with *whom the product serves,* will describe target customers. Still others, reflecting their interpretation of the concept as *what the product means to customers,* will respond thematically, describing the car's character, personality, image, and feel.

The most powerful product concepts include all these dimensions. They are often presented as images or metaphors (like pocket rocket) that can evoke many different aspects of the new product's message without compromising its essential meaning. Honda Motors is one of the few auto companies that make the generation of a strong product concept the first step in their development process.

When Honda's engineers began to design the third-generation (or 1986) Accord in the early 1980s, they did not start with a sketch of a car. The engineers started with a concept—"man maximum, machine minimum"—that captured in a short, evocative phrase the way they wanted customers to feel about the car. The concept and the car have been remarkably successful: since 1982, the Accord has been one of the best-selling cars in the United States; in 1989, it was the top-selling car. Yet when it was time to design the 1990 Accord, Honda listened to the market, not to its own success. Market trends were indicating a shift away from sporty sedans toward family models. To satisfy future customers' expectations—and to reposition the Accord, moving it up-market just a bit—the 1990 model would have to send a new set of product messages.

As the first step in developing an integrated product concept, the Accord's project manager (the term Honda uses is *large product leader*) led a series of small group discussions involving close to 100 people in all. These early brainstorming sessions involved people from many parts of the organization, including body engineering, chassis engineering, interior design, and exterior design. In line with Honda tradition, the groups developed two competing concepts in parallel. The subject of the discussions was abstract: What would be expected of a family sedan in the 1990s. Participants talked frequently about "adult taste" and "fashionability" and eventually came to a consensus on the message the new model would deliver to customers—"an adult sense of reliability." The ideal family car would allow the driver to transport family and friends with confidence, whatever the weather or road conditions; passengers would always feel safe and secure.

This message was still too abstract to guide the product and process engineers who would later be making concrete choices about the new Accord's specifications, parts, and manufacturing processes. So the next step was finding an image that would personify the car's message to consumers. The image the product leader and his team emerged with was "a rugby player in a business suit." It evoked rugged, physical contact, sportsmanship, and gentlemanly behavior—disparate qualities the new car would have to convey. The image was also concrete enough to translate clearly into design details. The decision to replace the old Accord's retractable headlamps with headlights made with a pioneering technology developed by Honda's supplier, Stanley, is a good example. To the designers and engineers, the new lights' totally transparent cover glass symbolized the will of a rugby player looking into the future calmly, with clear eyes.

The next and last step in creating the Accord's product concept was to break down the rugby player image into specific attributes the new car would have to possess. Five sets of key words captured what the product leader envisioned: "open-minded," "friendly communication," "tough spirit," "stress-free," and "love forever." Individually and as a whole, these key words reinforced the car's message to consumers. "Tough spirit" in a car,

for example, meant maneuverability, power, and sure handling in extreme driving conditions, while "love forever" translated into long-term reliability and customer satisfaction. Throughout the course of the project, these phrases provided a kind of shorthand to help people make coherent design and hardware choices in the face of competing demands. Moreover, they were a powerful spur to innovation.

Consider this small slice of the process. To approximate the rugby player's reliability and composure ("stress-free"), the engineers had to eliminate all unnecessary stress from the car. In technical terms, this meant improving the car's NVH, or noise, vibration, and harshness characteristics. That, in turn, depended on reducing the "three gangs of noise," engine noise, wind noise, and road noise.

To reduce engine noise, the product engineers chose a newly developed balance shaft that rotated twice as fast as the engine and offset its vibration. The shaft made the Accord's compact 4-cylinder engine as quiet as a V-6 and conserved space in the process. But since the shaft was effective only when the engine was turning over reasonably quickly, the product engineers also had to design a new electrically controlled engine mount to minimize vibration when the engine was idling.

Moreover, once the engine was quieter, other sources of noise became apparent. The engineers learned that the floor was amplifying noise from the engine, as was the roof, which resonated with the engine's vibration and created unpleasant, low-frequency booming sounds. To solve these problems, the engineers inserted paper honeycomb structures 12 to 13 millimeters thick in the roof lining—a solution that also improved the roof's structural rigidity and contributed to the car's tough spirit. They also redesigned the body floor, creating a new sandwich structure of asphalt and sheet steel, which similarly strengthened the body shell.

Multiply this example hundreds of times over and it is clear why a strong product concept is so important. At its core, the development process is a complex system for solving problems and making decisions. Product concepts like those developed at Honda give people a clear framework for finding solutions and making decisions that complement one another and ultimately contribute to product integrity.

ORGANIZING FOR INTEGRITY

When cars were designed and developed by a handful of engineers working under the direction of a Henry Ford, a

Gottlieb Daimler, or a Kiichiro Toyota, organization was not an issue. What mattered were the engineers' skills, the group's chemistry, and the master's guidance. These are still vital to product integrity, but the organizational challenge has become immeasurably more complex. Developing a new car involves hundreds (if not thousands) of people working on specialized pieces of the project in many different locations for months or even years at a time. Whether their efforts have integrity—whether the car performs superbly and delights customers—will depend on how the company organizes development and the nature of the leadership it creates.

Efforts to organize development effectively are rooted in the search for solutions to two basic problems. One is designing, building, and testing the product's parts and subsystems so that every element achieves a high level of performance. In a car, this means that the brakes hold on wet or icy roads, the suspension gives a smooth ride on rough roads, the car corners well on sharp turns, and so on. Because performance at this level is driven by expertise and deep understanding, some specialization, both for individuals and for the organization, is essential. Yet specialization is a double-edged sword. By complicating communication and coordination across the organization, it complicates the second problem that development organizations face: achieving product integrity.

When markets were relatively stable, product life cycles long, and customers concerned most with technical performance, companies could achieve product integrity through strong functional organizations. Managers could commit whatever resources and time it took to make products that worked well, and external integrity (matching the product to customer expectations) was simply a by-product of those efforts. But as competition intensified and customers' needs and wants grew harder to predict, integration became an explicit goal for most product developers. By the late 1980s, even the most resolutely functional development organizations had established formal mechanisms such as coordination committees, engineering liaisons, project managers, matrix structures, and cross-functional teams to improve product development.

Structural mechanisms like these are only a small part of achieving product integrity, however. At best—when they are reinforced and supported by the behaviors, attitudes, and skills of people in every part of the development organization—they speed problem solving and improve the quality of the solutions. But by design, they are focused inward; they do not address integrity's external dimension. So unless the company makes a deliberate effort to integrate customers into the development process, it is likely to create products that are fresh and technologically advanced and that provide good value but that often fall short with sophisticated consumers.

For this reason, external integration is the single most important task for new product development. It represents a conscious organizational effort to enhance the external integrity of the development process by matching the philosophy and details of product design to the expectations of target customers. Generating a distinctive product concept that anticipates future customers' needs and wants is the first step in external integration. Infusing this concept into drawings, plans, detailed designs, and, ultimately, the product itself is the substance of its ongoing work.

To get some sense of how thorough (and hard) this infusion process actually is, consider a few of the conflicts Honda faced during the planning stage for the third-generation Accord.

The vehicle's product concept (man maximum, machine minimum) included maximum space and visibility for the occupants, minimum space for the car's mechanisms, a wide, low body for aesthetics, superb handling and stability, and superior economy in operation. To convey a feeling of spaciousness, the design called for a low engine hood and a larger-than-usual front window. Both features increased the driver's visibility and sense of interaction with the outside world. But the window size also meant that the cabin would get uncomfortably hot on sunny days unless the car had a big air conditioner—as well as a powerful engine to run it.

A large engine—the obvious solution—was precluded by the decision to keep the hood low, since the only suspension system that would work was an expensive, double-wishbone construction that narrowed the engine chamber. (See Exhibit 2.) And in any case, the engineers wanted the engine to be light so that the car would handle sharply.

The height of the hood became a battlefield, with body, engine, and chassis engineers warring over millimeters. What made the conflict constructive—it ultimately led to the development of a new engine that was both compact and powerful—was the fact that all the combatants understood what the Accord had to achieve. Guided by the large product leader, who saw every argument as an opportunity to reinforce the car's basic concept, the engineers could see their work through future customers' eyes.

As Honda's experience indicates, external integration extends deeply into the development organization, and

EXHIBIT 2   Double Wishbone Front Suspension

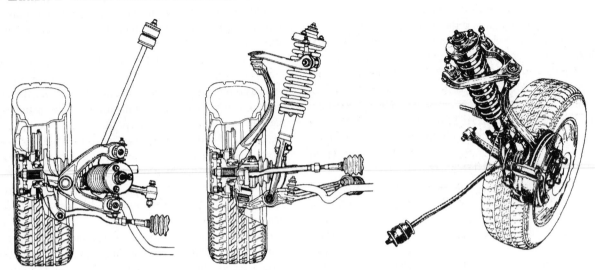

it involves much more than being "market oriented" or "customer driven." It begins with customers, to be sure, since the best concept developers invariably supplement the cooked information they get from marketing specialists with raw data they gather themselves. But strong product concepts also include a healthy measure of what we call "market imagination": they encompass what customers say they want and what the concept's creators *imagine* customers will want three or more years into the future. Remembering that customers know only existing products and existing technologies, they avoid the trap of being too close to customers—and designing products that will be out-of-date before they are even manufactured.

Interestingly, companies that are heavily driven by market data tend to slip on external integrity. As a rule, these companies have well-equipped marketing organizations with great expertise in formal research, and they are adept at using data from focus groups, product clinics, and the like to develop customer profiles. But these methods rarely lead to distinctive product concepts. In fact, to the extent that they limit or suppress the imaginations of product designers, they can actually harm a new product's future competitiveness.

How auto companies organize for external integration—and how much power they invest in their integrators—varies greatly. Some companies create an explicit role for an "external integrator" and assign it to people in a few functional units (testers in engineering, for example, and product planners in marketing). Others assign all their external integrators to a single specialized unit, which may be independent or organized by product. Sim-

ilarly, the work of concept creation and concept realization may be broken up among different groups in the development organization or consolidated under one leader, as it is at Honda.

We have already seen how advantageous consolidating responsibility can be for enhancing external integration. This approach is equally successful in achieving internal integrity.

One of the thorniest issues in creating a strong product concept is when (and how) to involve functional specialists other than those who make up the product development team. As we saw with the Accord, the product concept has clear repercussions for every aspect of the development process, from design and layout to cost and manufacturability. So on the one hand, front-loading input and information from specialists downstream is highly desirable. On the other hand, broad downstream involvement can easily jeopardize the distinctiveness and clarity of a product concept if (as often happens) negotiations and battles among powerful functions lead to political compromises and patchwork solutions.

The fact that working-level engineers were involved in the concept stage of the Accord's development was essential to its product integrity. Faced with tough choices about the car's front end, the engineers had not only a clear concept to guide them but also one they felt they owned. Moreover, their solution—the new engine—enhanced the Accord's internal integrity by raising its level of technical performance. (See Exhibits 3 and 4.) At the same time, internal demands and functional constraints never compromised the Accord's basic concept.

EXHIBIT 3   1990 Honda Accord Valve Train

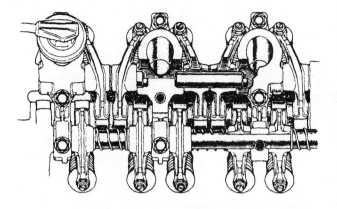

EXHIBIT 4   Second-Order Balance System

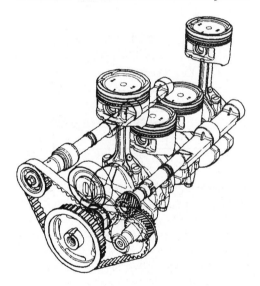

Like many of the other product managers we spoke with, the Accord's product leader knew that democracy without clear concept leadership is the archenemy of distinctive products.

There are other ways to balance downstream expertise with strong concept leadership, of course. (One of Honda's rivals also makes early cross-functional negotiations an important part of its new product development work, for example, but gives a small group of concept creators and assistants six months or so to establish the concept first, before the negotiations begin.) The important point is that integrity depends on striking a balance between the two. Companies that trade off one for the other sacrifice both product and organizational integrity. Those that place sole responsibility for the product con-

cept with a specialized unit (often one within marketing) end up with lots of last-minute design and engineering changes. Conversely, companies that initiate senior-level, cross-functional negotiations at the very start of every project usually find themselves with undistinguished products.

The integration that leads to product integrity does not surface in organization charts alone, nor is it synonymous with the creation of cross-functional teams, the implementation of "design for manufacturing," or any other useful organizational formula for overhauling development work. Ironically, efforts to increase integration can even undermine it if the integrating mechanisms are misconstructed or if the organization is unprepared for the change. At one U.S. auto company, we found a very coherent cross-functional project team with great spirit and purpose. But the team was made up solely of liaisons and included none of the working engineers actually responsible for drawings and prototypes. So for the most part, engineers ignored the team, whose existence only masked the lack of true integration.

What distinguishes outstanding product developers is the consistency between their formal structures and the informal organization that accomplishes the real work of development. In the case of the Honda Accord, we have seen some important characteristics of such consistency: the company's preference for firsthand information and direct (sometimes conflict-full) discussion; the way specialists are respected but never deified; the constant stream of early, informal communication (even at the risk of creating confusion or inefficiencies in the short run); and, most important, the primacy of strong concept leadership.

INTEGRITY'S CHAMPION: THE HEAVYWEIGHT PRODUCT MANAGER

The key to product integrity is leadership. Product managers in companies whose products consistently succeed accomplish two things without fail. They focus the whole development organization on customer satisfaction. And they devise processes (both formal and informal) for creating powerful product concepts and infusing them into the details of production and design. In our lexicon, they are "heavyweight" product managers, and they differ significantly from their lighter weight counterparts in other companies.

During the 1980s, product managers began to appear at more and more of the world's auto companies. In most cases, the title means relatively little. The position adds

EXHIBIT 5 Four-Door Sedan Exterior Dimensions

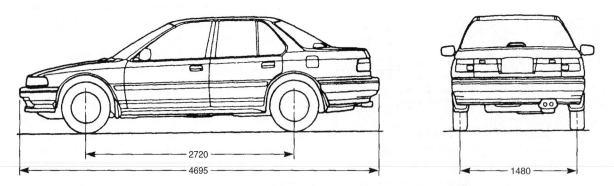

EXHIBIT 6 Four-Door Sedan Interior Dimensions and Four-Door Sedan Visibility

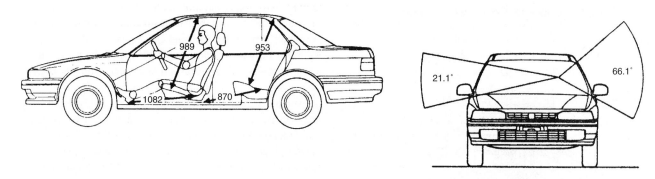

another box to the organization chart, but the organization's basic structure is still heavily functional. Product managers in these companies coordinate development activities through liaison representatives from each of the engineering departments. They have no direct access to working-level engineers, no contact with marketing, and no concept responsibility. Their positions have less status and power than the functional managers' do, and they have little influence outside of product engineering (and only limited influence within it). Their job is to collect information on the status of work, to help functional groups resolve conflicts, and to facilitate completion of the project's overall goals. They do not actually impair a product's integrity, but neither can they contribute much to it.

The contrast with the heavyweight's job could not be more striking. In a few auto companies, product managers play a role that simply does not exist in other automakers' development organizations. Like the Accord's large product leader, they are deeply involved in creating a strong product concept. Then, as the concept's guardians, they keep the concept alive and infuse it into every aspect of the new product's design. As one heavy-

weight product manager told us, "We listen to process engineers. We listen to plant managers. But we make the final decisions. Above all, we cannot make any compromise on the concept. The concept is the soul of the vehicle; we cannot sell it."

Guardianship like this is crucial because the product concept can get lost so easily in the complexity of actually designing, planning, and building a new car. The problems that preoccupied the Accord's product engineers were often almost imperceptibly small: a three-millimeter gap between the window glass and the body; the tiny chips on the car's sills that come from stones kicked up on the road; a minuscule gap between the hood and the body. But problems like these are the stuff of product integrity: All the magic is in the details. (See Exhibits 5 and 6.)

Keeping track of those details, however, is no easy matter. Nor is it easy to keep the product concept fresh and clear in many people's minds during the months (and years) that development consumes. For that reason, heavyweight product managers must be a little like evangelists, with the product concept as their Bible and the work of exhorting, preaching, and reminding as their mission. To paraphrase an assistant product manager in one of the heavyweight organizations, subtle nuances such as the car's taste and character have to be built into the design by fine-tuning. They cannot be expressed completely in planning documents, no matter how detailed those may be. So the product manager has to interact continuously with the engineers to communicate his intentions and to refresh and reinforce their understanding of the product concept.

As concept guardians, heavyweight product managers draw on both personal credibility and expertise and the organizational clout that comes with the job. Themselves engineers by training, heavyweight product managers have a broad knowledge of the product and process engineering required to develop an entire vehicle. Years of experience with their companies give their words weight and increase their influence with people over whom they have no formal authority.

Product planners and engineers working on the detailed design of specific parts typically fall into this category. Yet as we have seen, the substance of their work is vital to a new car's integrity. To track design decisions and ensure that the concept is being translated accurately, heavyweight managers communicate daily with the functional engineering departments. They also intervene directly when decisions about parts or components that are particularly problematic or central to the product concept are being made. From a functional point of view, this is clearly a breach of organizational etiquette. But in practice, this intervention is usually readily accepted, in part because it is backed by tradition but mostly because of the product manager's credibility. When heavyweights visit bench-level engineers, they come to discuss substantive issues and their input is usually welcome. They are not making courtesy calls or engaging in morale-building exercises.

Organizationally, the heavyweight manager effectively functions as the product's general manager. In addition to concept-related duties, the responsibilities that come with the job include: coordinating production and sales as well as engineering; coordinating the entire project from concept to market; signing off on specification, cost-target, layout, and major component choices; and maintaining direct contact with existing and potential customers. Some of this work occurs through liaison representatives (although the liaisons themselves are "heavier" than they are in the lightweight organizations since they also serve as local project leaders within their functional groups). But there is no mistaking the heavyweights' clout: engineering departments typically report to them (which ones depends on the internal linkages the company wishes to emphasize). Heavyweights are also well supplied with formal procedures like design review and control of prototype scheduling that give them leverage throughout the organization.

Still, probably the best measure of a product manager's weight is the amount of time that formal meetings and paperwork consume. Lightweight product managers are much like high-level clerks. They spend most of the day reading memos, writing reports, and going to meetings. Heavyweights, in contrast, are invariably "out"— with engineers, plant people, dealers, and customers. "This job can't be done without wearing out my shoes," one experienced manager commented. "Since I'm asking other engineers for favors, I shouldn't ask them to come to me. I have to go and talk to them."

What lies behind "product managers in motion" is the central role that information plays in bringing new products to life. Take the heavyweight's interaction with customers. Talented product managers spend hours watching people on the street, observing styles, and listening to conversations. Department stores, sports arenas, museums, and discotheques are all part of their "market research" beat.

Heavyweight product managers are equally active in their relations with the test engineers. Like the product manager, test engineers stand in for the customer. When they evaluate a suspension system or test-drive a new car, they are rehearsing the experience the future customer with consume. To do this successfully, in ways that will ensure product integrity, the test engineers must know what to look for. In other words, they must be crystal clear on the product concept.

Heavyweight product managers make sure this clarity exists. They often test-drive vehicles and talk about their experiences with the test engineers. Many can and do evaluate the car's performance on the test track and show up almost daily during critical tests. They also seize every opportunity to build good communication channels and deepen their ties with younger engineers. One product manager said he welcomed disagreements among the test engineers because they gave him a good reason to go out to the proving ground and talk about product concepts with younger people with whom he would not otherwise interact.

If we reverse direction to look at how heavyweight product managers promote internal integrity, the same kind of behavior and activities come to the fore. Direct contact with product engineers and testers, for example, not only reinforces the product concept but also strengthens the links between functions, speeds up decision making and problem solving, and makes it easier to coordinate work flows. In fact, almost everything a product manager does to infuse the concept into the details makes the organization itself work better and faster. The reason is the strong customer orientation that the product concept—and product manager—convey.

The product manager's job touches every part of the new product process. Indeed, heavyweight product managers have to be "multilingual," fluent in the languages of customers, marketers, engineers, and designers. On one side, this means being able to translate an evocative concept like the pocket rocket into specific targets like "maximum speed 250 kilometers per hour" and "drag coefficient less than 0.3" that detail-oriented engineers can easily grasp. On the other side, it means being able to assess and communicate what a "0.3 drag coefficient" will mean to customers. (The fact that the translation process from customer to engineer is generally harder than that from engineer to customer explains why engineering tends to be the heavyweight product managers' native tongue.)

Because development organizations are continually involved in changing one form of information into another, face-to-face conversations and informal relationships are their life's blood. Heavyweight managers understand this and act on it. Aware that product concepts cannot be communicated in written documents alone (any more than the feel and sensibility of a new car can be captured in words alone), they travel constantly—telling stories, coining phrases, and generally making sure that nothing important gets lost in translation.

THE IMPROVEMENT ETHIC

How a company develops new products says a great deal about what that company is and does. For most companies, the journey toward competing on integrity began during the 1980s. Quite possibly, it was inaugurated with a commitment to total quality or to reducing the lead time for developing new products. Heavyweight product management constitutes the next step on that journey. Taking it leads down one of two paths.

Some companies introduce a heavyweight product management system modestly and incrementally. A typical progression might go like this: shift from a strictly functional setup to a lightweight system, with the integrator responsible only for product engineering; expand the product manager's sphere to include new tasks such as product planning or product-process coordination;

then raise the product manager's rank, appoint people with strong reputations to the job, and assign them one project rather than a few to focus their attention and expand their influence. Senior managers that face deep resistance from their functional units often choose this path.

Other companies (particularly smaller players) take a faster, more direct route. One Japanese company leapt to a strong product manager system to introduce a new model. Backed by the widespread belief that the project might well determine the company's future, senior management created an unusually heavy product manager to run it. An executive vice president with many years of experience became the product manager, with department heads from engineering, production, and planning acting as his liaisons and as project leaders within their functional groups. With these changes, management sent a clear signal that the company could no longer survive in its traditional form.

The project succeeded, and today the product is seen as the company's turnaround effort, its reentry as a competitor after years of ineffectual products. The project itself became a model for subsequent changes (including the creation of a product manager office) in the regular development organization.

How a company changes its organization and the speed with which it moves will depend on its position and the competitive threat it faces. But all successful efforts have three common themes: a unifying driver, new blood, and institutional tenacity. (See Exhibit 7, which describes Ford Motor Company's progress toward becoming a heavyweight organization.)

Just as engineers need a vision of the overall product to guide their efforts in developing a new car, the people involved in changing an organization need an objective that captures their imaginations. Where changes have taken hold, senior managers have linked them to competition and the drive for tangible advantage in the marketplace.

During the 1980s, the quest for faster development lead time was particularly powerful in driving such efforts. But lead time is not an end in itself. Rather, its pursuit leads people to do things that improve the system overall. In this respect, lead time is like inventory in a just-in-time manufacturing system: Reducing work-in-process inventory is somewhat effective, but attacking the root causes of excess inventory truly changes the system.

Companies that successfully focus on lead time generally emphasize changes in internal integration. Product integrity can drive companies to higher performance.

EXHIBIT 7   The Case for Heavyweight Product Management

In the early 1980s, successful products filled the Ford Motor Company's scrapbooks but not its dealers' showrooms. Its cars were widely criticized. Quality was far below competitive standards. Market share was falling. In addition, the company's financial position was woeful, and layoffs were ongoing, among white-collar staff and factory workers alike. By the end of the decade, history was repeating itself: The Ford Explorer, introduced in the spring of 1990, may prove to be Ford's most successful product introduction ever. Despite the fact that it debuted in a down market, the four-door, four-wheel-drive sport-utility vehicle has sold phenomenally well. Rugged yet refined, the Explorer gets all the important details right, from exterior styling to the components and interior design.

Behind the Explorer lay a decade of changes in Ford's management, culture, and product development organization. The changes began in the dark days of the early 1980s with the emergence of new leaders in Ford's executive offices and in design studios. Their herald was the Taurus, introduced in 1985. Designed to be a family vehicle with the styling, handling, and ride of a sophisticated European sedan, the car offered a distinctive yet integrated package in which advanced aerodynamic styling was matched with a newly developed chassis with independent rear suspension and a front-wheel-drive layout. The car's interior, which minimized the chrome and wood paneling that were traditional in American roadsters, had a definite European flavor. So did the ride and the way the car handled: The steering was much more responsive, and the ride was tighter and firmer.

The development efforts that produced the Taurus set in motion profound changes within the Ford engineering, manufacturing, and marketing organizations. Traditionally, Ford's development efforts had been driven by very strong functional managers. In developing the Taurus, however, Ford turned to the "Team Taurus," whose core included principals from all the major functions and activities involved in the creation of the new car. The team was headed by Lew Veraldi, at the time in charge of large-car programs at Ford, and it served to coordinate and integrate the development program at the senior management level.

Team Taurus was the first step on a long path of organizational, attitudinal, and procedural change. As development of the Taurus went ahead, it became clear that integrated development required more than the creation of a team and that there was more to achieving integrity than linking the functions under the direction of a single manager. So the next step in Ford's evolution was the development of the "concept to customer" process, or C to C.

The C to C process took shape during the mid-1980s, as Ford sought aggressively to cut lead time, improve quality, and continue to bring attractive products to market. Led by a hand-picked group of engineers and product planners, the C to C project focused on devising a new architecture for product development: Its members identified critical milestones, decision points, criteria for decision making, and patterns of responsibility and functional involvement. This architecture was then implemented step by step, in ongoing programs as well as in new efforts.

At about the same time, in 1987, Ford formalized the program manager structure that had evolved out of the Taurus experience. (*Program manager* is the term Ford uses for the position we call product manager.) As part of this structure, senior management affirmed the centrality of cross-functional teams working under the direction of a strong program manager. Moreover, cross-functional integration was reinforced at the operating level as well as at the strategy level. The change in marketing's role is a good example: instead of adding their input through reports and memoranda, marketing people (led by the program manager) meet directly with designers and engineers to discuss concept development and key decisions about features, layout, and components. Similarly, program managers have been given responsibility for critical functions like product planning and layout, where many of the integrative decisions are made.

In successive programs, Ford has refined its approach and pushed integration further and further. The strength of the program managers has also increased. The results are visible in the products Ford developed during the latter part of the 1980s—and in their sales. Beginning with the Taurus, Ford has scored impressive market successes with a number of its new cars: the Lincoln Continental, which expanded Lincoln's share of the luxury market; the Thunderbird Super Coupe, which compares favorably with European high-performance sedans; the Probe, the result of a joint development project with Mazda and which enthusiasts generally rate higher than Mazda's own effort, the MX6; and the sport-utility Explorer.

Managed well, the drive to create products that fire the imagination gives the implementation of a heavyweight system energy and direction.

Of the many change efforts we have seen, the most successful were led by new people. Some were new to the company, but most came from within the organization. Sometimes viewed as mavericks, they saw the potential for change where others saw more of the same. A company cannot change everyone. It can, however, create new leaders and empower people who are attuned to the new direction the company has to take. It can also find nontraditional ways to identify and develop heavyweight product managers for the future, such as apprenticeship systems.

Moving to a heavier product manager structure is a process of discovery—one the U.S. auto company with the ineffectual cross-functional team we described earlier knows very well. Like many others, that company has discovered that changes in organizational structure are important but insufficient. To create a true team, greater change—particularly in the behavior of traditionally powerful functional managers—is needed.

The journey to heavyweight product management is hard, surprisingly so for many managers. Those who succeed do so because they have tenacity. Outstanding companies understand that projects end but the journey doesn't. The challenge to learn from experience and continuously improve is always there.

Yet in company after company, the same problems crop up over and over. Why do most companies learn so little from their product development projects? The explanation is simple: At the end of every project, there is pressure to move on to the next. The cost of this tunnel vision is very high. Those few companies that work at continuous improvement achieve a significant competitive edge. Moving to a more effective development organization can be the basis for instilling an ethic of continuous improvement. Companies that compete on integrity exercise that ethic every day.

Author note: We gratefully acknowledge the help of Nobuhiko Kawamoto, CEO of Honda Motor Company, and Tateomi Miyoshi, large product leader for the Honda Accord.

BUILDING COMPETENCES/ CAPABILITIES THROUGH NEW PRODUCT DEVELOPMENT

for 2/26/05

CASE IV-4

Braun AG: The KF 40 Coffee Machine (Abridged)

Karen Freeze

"If we're going to do it, we've got to quit stalling," exclaimed Albrecht Jestädt,[1] head of development for a new coffeemaker at Braun AG. "I've said all I can about polypropylene, and I'm convinced we can go with it," he added, taking another sip of his beer.

At the end of a day in January 1983, Jestädt and his colleagues were discussing Braun's newest design: an elegant, cylindrical coffeemaker, called the KF 40, destined for the middle and upper end of the mass market. To meet management's cost targets, however, they would have to use polypropylene, a much less expensive plastic than Braun's traditional material, and whether so doing would jeopardize Braun's reputation for quality was a matter of intense debate throughout the company. Unlike the very expensive polycarbonate, Braun's traditional material, polypropylene could not be molded into large, complicated parts (like the KF 40's "tank") without suffering "sink" marks on surfaces that were supposed to be

why not paint?

flawlessly even. So the designers had devised a solution that involved a major departure from the smooth, winter-white surfaces characteristic of all Braun household products. (See Exhibit 1 for a prototype.)

"The decision is obvious," claimed Gilbert Greaves, business director for household products. "We need this product *now,* and we have to stop being quite so picky."

"I think we should be picky," said Hartwig Kahlcke, the industrial designer on the project. "But we feel that the rippled design for the tank actually enhances the surface appearance, without compromise."

"Maybe," said Hartmut Stroth, recently appointed director of corporate communications. "But it's no trivial matter. It's true that if we lose a year, we might not get in the market at all. Yet *nothing* is worth losing our reputation for superior quality. Not even the mass market." Stroth, who had served for over a decade in various communications positions at Braun, was very sensitive to the importance of Braun's "visual equity" and the need for maintaining it: "Not only do we have to think hard about how this corrugated surface design would fit into the Braun 'look,' but also about what that look represents. The idea of using design to mask sink marks bothers me in principle, and it may not work in practice, especially if the stuff doesn't hold up. I'm anything but risk-averse in this business, but I need to be convinced." *diff on quality* *many do it*

"Then let's go ahead with the trial tooling," Kahlcke responded. "The chairman has already OK'd it; maybe that will convince you." Not waiting for Stroth's response, Kahlcke inquired about the chairman's views to date. "I know he liked the design, and I know he wants

[1] See Appendix for identification and pronunciation glossary.

1035

EXHIBIT 1 Two Views of the KF 40

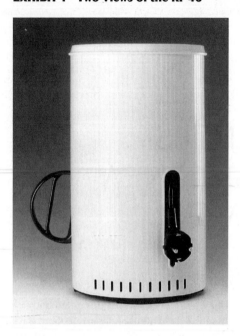

the product. What does he think about the material at this point?"

"You tell me," answered Lorne Waxlax, chairman of the board and Braun's CEO. He would have to make the ultimate decision and had just dropped in, as was his custom, to get the latest thinking on the KF 40.

CEO down in the details a bit, no?

COMPANY BACKGROUND: BRAUN BY DESIGN

Braun AG began as a family-owned radio and small appliance business founded in 1921 by Max Braun.[2] In the 1940s, Braun developed a novelty, the electric razor, which he introduced in 1950. After Braun's death in 1951, his sons, Artur and Erwin, took over, and three years later they asked their friend, Fritz Eichler, an artist then working in the theater, to help them find a new approach to their struggling business. In 1955, looking for an architect to help build a new office building, the company hired Dieter Rams, just two years out of architecture school.

Rams became Eichler's protégé, and together they built a small, intense design department at the company's headquarters in Kronberg, Germany. Convinced they could change the taste of their fellow citizens, Eichler, Rams, and colleagues set out to design and build a

new kind of product. (See Exhibit 2 for Rams' 10 commandments of good design.)

Eichler and Rams believed that their design philosophy should permeate the company, providing a recognizable identity not only in its products, but in every aspect of its relations with customers. (See Exhibit 3, "The Principles of Braun's Corporate Identity.") In Rams's

EXHIBIT 2 Ten Principles of Good Design

1. Good design is innovative.
2. Good design enhances the usefulness of a product.
3. Good design is aesthetic.
4. Good design displays the logical structure of a product; its form follows its function.
5. Good design is unobtrusive.
6. Good design is honest.
7. Good design is enduring.
8. Good design is consistent right down to details.
9. Good design is ecologically conscious.
10. Good design is minimal design.

"Braun has an uncompromising commitment towards the pursuit of excellence in performance-oriented design. Every product designed and manufactured by Braun must adhere to these commandments of good design. So, too, should every consumer demand such quality in the selection of a product—be it furniture, clothing, an automobile or a home appliance."

—Dieter Rams
Braun's Chief Designer

---

[2] AG = Aktiengesellschaft (joint stock company).

EXHIBIT 3   The Principles of Braun's Corporate Identity

Braun regards the consumer as a *partner* in its business, not as an *object* of its strategy that is open to manipulation.

Braun believes that consumer desires relate to genuine needs, and employs its expertise, inventiveness, know-how, etc., to satisfy these needs.

Braun seeks to satisfy these needs in an optimal way, perhaps even better than the consumer expects.

However, Braun refuses to persuade people to buy its products on the basis of presentation which meets—or pretends to meet—entirely different needs (which are not amenable to rational consideration) for prestige, ego-support, ostentatious consumption, cosmetic effectiveness, etc.

Braun refuses to exploit human weaknesses to improve its results, and rejects any means of "hidden persuasion."

Braun also rejects all methods involving purely superficial attraction: in place of this, it has demonstrated that firm concentration on product design which is as good and functional as possible—including external aspects—is also experienced as aesthetically satisfying.

view, achieving that identity required top management support of good design, and teamwork—constant interaction among disciplines. But designers also needed certain responsibilities and authority; otherwise, they would arrive, at most, at "superficial product cosmetics."

According to Rams, designers needed four things. First, they had to be responsible for configuring all elements of the product that would influence its final appearance. Second, designers needed the authority to determine the dimensions of a product (e.g., the positioning and ergonomic design of its operating functions); third, they must be the ones to decide on surface structures, colors, product labeling, and imprinting; fourth, they needed to cooperate with the engineers on construction problems (e.g., manufacturability) whenever the form of a product directly depended on the construction.

Although Rams was not without critics, his work was an effective counterweight to the popular assumption that designers merely dreamed up the external form of a product. Moreover, he adamantly stood by his own definition of "functional": that the purpose of good design is to fulfill the *primary function* of a product, including its need to be appealing to the user so it would be a welcome object in his or her environment.

By the mid-1970s Braun had built a thriving business, primarily in small home appliances (e.g., shavers, coffeemakers, and mixers), with additional sales in consumer electronics (e.g., cameras and hi-fi equipment). Further,

the Braun design group was succeeding in its mission. One of its first products, a heavy-duty kitchen mixer (1957), was still in production and selling well. Most famous was their shaver, familiar to men all over the world. Many Braun products had won design awards; 36 of them, including Braun's first coffeemaker, had found a permanent place in New York's Museum of Modern Art.[3]

The company's mission was carried out not only in its products, but also in its people. The company's principles had permeated its corporate consciousness and were second nature even at lower levels in the organization. Almost any employee could tell a visitor that Braun's values were embodied in its products, which had to have three characteristics: (a) first-class design, (b) superior quality, and (c) functions or features ahead of the competition. "We'll never bring out just a me-too product," echoed in every department.

The Gillette Connection

In 1967, the Braun brothers sold the company to an American consumer products giant, Gillette, well known for its mass-produced, mass-marketed products like razors, blades, and toiletries that had been marketed in Europe since the turn of the 20th century. For the first several years, Gillette left Braun's product strategy intact while infusing some of its management expertise into the organization. In fact, very few people knew that this German company *par excellence* had an American owner. But Braun soon began to expand its operations in other countries and extend its target markets beyond the opinion leaders it had originally cultivated. For example, in 1971, Lorne Waxlax, a Gillette manager since 1958, took charge of Braun's Spanish plant. He largely refocused the operation, emphasizing product development, sophisticated manufacturing, market research, and television advertising. The plant manufactured Braun's first successful mass-produced kitchen appliance, the hand blender, and served as the training ground for Braun's mass-produced appliance motors. By the early 1980s, Braun sales exceeded $400 million (see Exhibit 4).

BRAUN'S ORGANIZATION AND OPERATIONS

Braun AG in 1983 was organized into three main functions: business management, technical operations, and

---

[3] A testimony to the appeal of Braun products was the emergence of a Braun Collectors Club (Braun-Design Sammler, later the FreundesKreis Braun-Design). Its members, entirely independently from the company, collected Braun products and published a newsletter.

EXHIBIT 4   Braun Group Financial Information
(*Millions of Dollars*)

	1980	1981	1982
Net sales	$496.1	$451.4	$403.4
Profit from operations	23.6	22.8	33.3
Identifiable assets	384.3	325.2	301.5
Capital expenditures	21.5	23.6	20.4
Depreciation	17.3	18.9	16.6

group sales. (See organization chart in Exhibit 5.) Business management, a coordinating group established in 1976, was essentially strategic marketing. Until Gillette came along, Braun had assumed that if one made a good product, it would sell. And it generally did. But in 1975, marketing became more important, as the domestic and international marketing people came together under a single group. A director for each product group reported to the head of business management, as did the director of communications, which included packaging.

Old ways/ Strategy

Technical Operations

Braun invested heavily in technology, and all key technically related disciplines were based at company headquarters under Dr. Thomas H. Thomsen, recently appointed director of technical operations. Previously, he had been head of engineering for Gillette in both London and Boston. Technical operations comprised four functional groups: R&D, Manufacturing, Quality Assurance, and Industrial Design.

R&D   The research and development department employed 220 people and included scientists and engineers working on advanced technology, as well as those involved in product development. R&D was headed by Dr. Peter Hexner, an American ex-army colonel who had directed Gillette's advanced technology department for

EXHIBIT 5   Corporate Structure

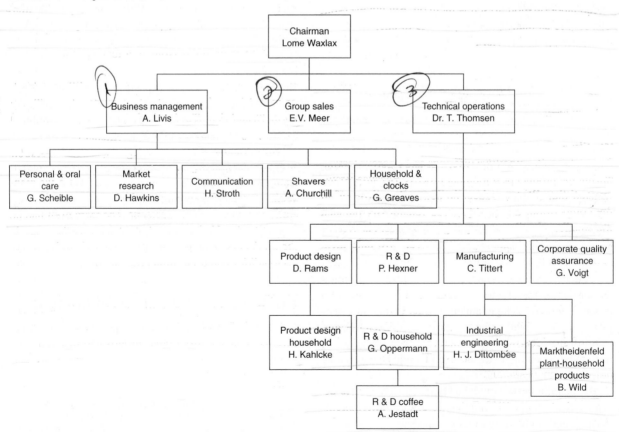

10 years. He commented on the challenge of balancing technology with the demands of design: "We have the classic conflicts. Design wants an elegant shaver a centimeter thick, and I have to knock reality into their heads: 'You can't fit a motor into a case a centimeter thick.'"

Engineering Process development and manufacturing engineering were part of the manufacturing organization, which managed Braun's component and assembly plants. Over three-quarters of Braun's manufacturing activity took place in its two large state-of-the-art plants in Walldürn and Marktheidenfeld (smaller operations were located in Spain, Ireland, Mexico, Argentina, and Brazil). Because of German labor's high cost, the manufacturing organization was continually pressured to produce efficiently, particularly in a plant like Marktheidenfeld that produced a wide variety of low-volume products including kitchen appliances. (For example, the plant produced around 700 units of the KF-35 coffeemaker per day.) While efforts to improve operations included automation, especially assembly, more challenging was designing a product so it required minimal assembly. "Anyone can make a cheap product with many parts and hire cheap labor offshore to screw them on. But not everyone can reduce as many parts as possible to one," said Bernard Wild, plant director at Marktheidenfeld.

> We can prove that advanced industrial nations don't have to forfeit manufacturing just because their labor costs are high. Our resources are in our brains and imaginations—our know-how.

Quality Assurance Quality assurance was responsible for analysis of competitive offerings and rigorous testing during the product development process. Because Braun insisted that all its products be better than those of all the competition, the quality group relentlessly pursued the smallest detail with very high standards. As Werner Utsch, a quality engineer, commented, "We take them apart down to the last screw."

Industrial Design The fourth group in technical operations, industrial design, had an impact on the company far beyond its 16-member size. Indeed, Dieter Rams, head of the department, felt that small size was an important ingredient in its success. The department employed seven designers, most of whom had won the Braun Prize, a design award the firm had offered to design students since 1968. By 1983 Rams's international stature often resulted in his being equated with Braun de-

sign almost exclusively. Yet he found this star status awkward: "I constantly have to stress that I don't do everything; I'm simply the motor that drives the department. I try to give other people the credit they deserve."

Until recently, Rams had reported only to the chairman. But because of time limitations, Waxlax assigned industrial design to technical operations, where most problems could be solved. The direct line to the chairman remained, but was used only for the most important issues and impasses. Rams noted, "I've had a good understanding with every chairman I've worked with. But often designers aren't so lucky. We often educate business management people to the point where they begin to understand design and are supportive to us, but then they leave."

PRODUCT DEVELOPMENT: THE TRIANGLE OF POWER–DESIGN, TECHNOLOGY, MARKETING

Product development had been relatively informal until 1980, when three people, representing R&D, business management, and manufacturing engineering, came together to develop procedures to make the process more operational and efficient. The result was a product development manual, introduced in 1981, that covered the responsibilities of key persons in a team (called an MTS team, for marketing-technology-strategy), definitions of elements in project development (e.g., different kinds of models), product specification guide, stages ("categories"), and signoff points in the process. (See Exhibit 6 for the project manual's table of contents.)

The "product program manager" (PPM) was responsible for maintaining these procedures; he or she chaired team meetings and represented the team vis-à-vis management, reporting directly to the head of technical operations or business management. The team itself had no formal leader. Various people took over as the stage in the product development process dictated, and stronger personalities could be influential; Jestädt, for example, first as product program manager, then as R&D manager for coffee, had quickly emerged as the de facto leader of the coffee machine project. (See Exhibit 7 for the PPM's and team's formal responsibilities.) In addition to the core team, people from other groups and disciplines—sometimes as many as 40—became involved as the project proceeded.

The team's monthly reports to the chairman had a standard format, divided into four sections: Description, Status, Further Steps, and Problems (or Risks). Although

EXHIBIT 6   Contents of Product Development Handbook

	Chapter
Project Procedures for New Products	**1**
Introduction	1.1
Goals	1.2
Assumptions	1.3
Tasks, Competence, Responsibilities	**2**
Project team	2.1
Project manager	2.2
Project team representatives	2.3
Project Development Procedure	**3**
Assumptions/principles	3.1
Implementation	3.2
Definition of terms	3.3
Exceptions	3.4
Project Profile	**4**
Explanations	4.1
Forms for project profile	4.2
Project Reporting	**5**
Project book	5.1
Reporting to the chairman	5.2
Summary	**6**
Product development flow chart	6.1

these monthly reviews were considered effective in motivating people to move toward the project goal, Waxlax did not like to use them as a threat:

> The trick is to know whether the deadline is truly viable or not. It's easy for marketing to insist on a deadline—they don't have to do the work. I believe the engineers know better than I how fast the team can go, and for that reason I don't want to force it unduly.

Waxlax saw the meetings as an efficient way to keep up to date on all that was going on and to keep on top of problems and conflicts as they arose. He didn't believe in minimizing conflict, but saw it as positive for the company: "It's often the guy who is against something who forces it to become better." He also viewed the monthly meetings as "a chance for me to encourage people," he added.

The point at which a project became formal and began to adhere to the *Projektablauf* [Project Procedures] varied. If, for example, a project had proceeded informally rather far in its development before entering the formal product development process, it might simply be formalized and have product specifications delineated. In its early stages, a project like the KF 40 might have pro-

vided monthly reports to the chairman for some time before becoming a formal project. (See Exhibit 8 for the Braun product development process line.)

Industrial Design's Role

The industrial design department played a central role in development, particularly at the front end of the process. Because most key disciplines at Braun were located in the same building, much communication about development took place informally, and no one really kept track of where ideas came from and when they first got together with a colleague from another department. That design, because of its reputation, often received disproportionate credit for a product occasionally irked some engineers and scientists, whose contributions were less visible. Well aware of this problem, the company's chairman accepted the responsibility of keeping the rivalry healthy.

Industrial design's relationship to other departments varied. Within the "triangle of power" (design-technology-marketing), design felt most akin to technology. The designers kept up with new developments in such fields as materials science, for example. "We understand technology, so when we have an idea, it is not unrealistic technically. We don't come up with totally impossible ideas," explained Rams. Likewise, with manufacturing, the group knew what it meant to design a product for manufacturability; if they were having difficulties, all they had to do was to go down the hall and across the parking lot to the engineering building. Such interaction among all disciplines was daily fare at Braun.

Marketing was something else, however. Business management often had conflicts with design because, said the marketers, the latter insisted on certain principles that were not always viable in the marketplace. "The problem with designers," Greaves, director of household products, sighed, "is that they think they design for eternity. Rams will hand me a 1965 design and expect me to go for it today." Sometimes the conflicts were trivial. For example, "one time we argued with Kahlcke (an industrial designer) over the baseplate of the mixer. Because of his obsession with details, he wanted it changed. I told him that was ridiculous, since no one would ever see it," recounted Greaves. "The cord storage was not in the base, so there was no reason whatsoever to turn the mixer over. But Kahlcke got his way!"

People in industrial design had a different perspective. Noted Rams: "I don't mind if technology has greater influence than design; we understand each other and can work things out. But when marketing gets power, it can

EXHIBIT 7   Formal Responsibilities of the Project Manager and Project Team Members

The Project Team

Tasks
- Collective development of the project goals and procedures (the Project Profile) on the basis of the product concept determined by the MTS team as well as the product profile.
- The assignment of functional-specific tasks to the relevant team member.
- The independent solving of problems in order to reach the goals articulated by the project profile.
- The development of alternatives when deviations from the project profile are necessary and the formulation of written proposals for changes for approval of the MTS team.

Authority
- Shortening of the planned course of product development when possible through changes in the project profile.

Responsibility
- The responsibility of the project team consists of the responsibility of the individual team members and the project manager.

The Project Manager

Tasks
- Overall coordination of the project from planning to production startup and control over fulfillment of project goals.
- Requisition of representatives from functional departments and the establishment of a project team.
- Calling and running of project meetings; preparation of meeting reports.
- Maintenance of the Project Book.
- Written records of project assignments.
- Planning and implementation of phase reviews at the end of each development category and whenever needed.
- Reports to product line manager.

Authority
- The right to direct information from team members and their superiors in the respective departments.
- The right to make necessary changes in the project profile and to submit written proposals for changes for approval by the MTS team.

Responsibility
- For coordination of
  - individual assignments in all functions.
  - project procedures.
  - information flow (including among team members).
  - supervision of costs, deadlines, and performance in accordance with the project profile.
- For the content of the project profile and project reports.
- For assuring that any changes in the product objectives set by the MTS team are made only in exceptional circumstances and only with the approval of the MTS team.

The Team Members

Tasks
- Handling of tasks in their functional area.
- Assure readiness, in cooperation with the product line supervisor, for their department's contribution to the project.
- Timely reports to the project manager about the completion of their department's tasks or deviation therefrom, in accordance with the project profile.
- Communicate information from their product line superior and other colleagues in their department.
- Nominate further representatives from their department (in agreement with the product line supervisor).

Authority
- Each team member can request that the project manager call a team meeting.
- Each team member has operating room, within the project profile, for solving problems.

Responsibility
- The team members of individual departments bear responsibility for the technical performance of their part of the work.
- The team members are responsible for ensuring the flow of information from their departments that pertains to the project.

Source: From *Handbuch Projektablauf von neuen Produkten,* section 2.

EXHIBIT 8 Product Development Procedures Outline and Definitions

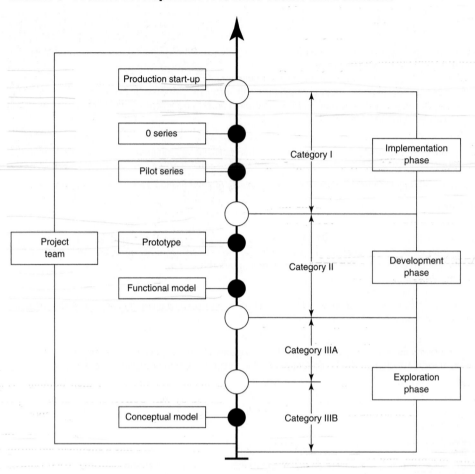

be bad." For example, sometimes marketing got its way with regard to color. "Why should we pay attention to color fads? Just because red cars are popular one year, why should we have a red hairdryer? It is not integral to the design."

A NEW STRATEGY

Lorne Waxlax became chairman of Braun in 1980. After his five-year stint in Spain, he had managed Braun's non–Central European export business for three years, and then headed business management for two. Waxlax had long wanted to encourage Braun to get rid of cameras and hi-fi and to focus more effectively on its core technologies in the personal care and appliance businesses. As chairman, Waxlax could proceed with this strategy.

While narrowing the product line, Waxlax also saw opportunity in six segments of the consumer appliance business: coffeemakers, irons, toasters, hairdryers, shavers, and food preparation products. They were big, and they were constant; the market for coffeemakers in Europe alone was over 9 million units per year. Even a small percentage share would make a good business, but Waxlax was "always going for a big share." Both business management and Braun's designers eagerly embraced this new strategy. Rams made very clear his philosophy: good design should be for everyone.

By 1983 Braun was well established in several product families. Electric shavers were its biggest and most widely marketed product line, accounting for half the company's revenues. In many countries Braun held first place in market share; wherever it was present, it was among the top three. The household division, whose image was represented by its classic kitchen machine, produced coffeemakers, mixers, juice presses, food processors, food choppers, and irons as well. In the personal care area, hairdryers and curling irons were the most successful, having achieved market leadership in Europe. Braun's exports were continuing to grow: In 1982 exports accounted for 75 percent of its turnover.

Waxlax and his top managers wished to focus on Braun's core products and expertise, its reputation for excellence in design, and the opportunities within grasp at the upper end of the mass market. Balancing these three dimensions of the company—technology, design, and business management—while maintaining the integrity of its corporate mission was management's key challenge.

COFFEEMAKERS: THE KF 40 PROJECT

One August day in 1981, when half of Germany was on holiday and the other half getting ready to leave, Waxlax wrote a memo to Gilbert Greaves, asking him to check into the possibilities for Braun in coffeemakers, a key element in the new strategy. Braun had entered the coffeemaker business in 1972 with the KF 20, a novel cylindrical design that won many design awards and was enthroned in the Museum of Modern Art in New York. (See Exhibit 9.) Available in strong red and yellow, it had entered the consciousness of upper-income coffee drinkers in both Europe and the United States. It was, however, a very expensive machine, and expensive to produce, retailing at about DM 120.

EXHIBIT 9   KF 20

EXHIBIT 10   KF 35

A few years later, the company introduced the KF 35, a sleeker version of the then popular "L-shape" epitomized by Mr. Coffee. It cost about 40 percent less than the KF 20 to produce, retailing at about DM 90. The design department was not fully satisfied with it: " I always thought it looked like a chemical lab sitting on the table," declared Rams, disdainfully. (See Exhibit 10.) The unit enjoyed only average sales, about 150,000 units annually.

The Competition

Braun's major competitors in the middle-to-high-end coffee machine segment were two German companies, Krups and Rowenta. Braun's market research defined this segment in terms of price points: DM 70 retail or above. In Germany and France, two of the biggest markets for coffeemakers, half the units were sold in that range. The market researchers were confident that a new Braun coffeemaker family offered across the entire spectrum, from DM 72 to DM 136, would be competitive in Europe, where the greater part of the market (about 70 percent of 9 million units annually) was for replacements. An open question was how soon Krups and Rowenta would copy Braun's design, as was their custom.

The U.S. market was considerably less certain, yet crucial if Braun was to attain a volume permitting a tolerable return on investment. "You don't go for the small appliance business because of the margins. You have to have high volumes," remarked Waxlax. Americans had been introduced to filter coffee systems through Mr. Coffee, a low-end product. Would they be willing to pay for Braun quality? With the currency exchange rate at DM 2.40 to $1.00, it was reasonable to expect imports to the United States to grow. The market for filter coffee machines was already running at about 11 million units, and penetration was still low. Braun's distribution system in the United States was practically nonexistent, however, and Waxlax wondered if it could be sufficiently developed in time.

What the "KF 35 Successor" Has to Be

Upon receiving Waxlax's coffee machine memo in August 1981, Greaves set to work with his people and in two months came up with a rough description of a product Braun could sell:

> It should have a shortened filter, slimmer jug [than the competition]; it should come in different colors, the water tank should be opaque, the tubes should be completely covered up, the filter should be tight and compact, the thermal jug should be more elegant, lighter, handier, taller, slimmer, and presentable on the coffee table.

That idea, which marketing articulated in October 1981, evolved into a "product profile" that Greaves circulated to key people on December 2, 1981. In this memo Greaves discussed, as Waxlax had asked, the issue of the cost/volume relationship and presented the direct costs and price points in connection with assumed volumes. He also analyzed the market segments and defined those segments where Braun could realistically compete. He determined that (*a*) a range of models—at least two—would be necessary; (*b*) this range was defined so that it could be constructed on a "building block system" to "minimize tooling investments"; and (*c*) the range would enable Braun to compete in medium to high price segments, at retail prices about DM 70. This would mean that Braun had to compete with key players—Krups, Rowenta, Siemens, and AEG—on features, not price. To be profitable, it would have to cost fully one-third less in direct costs than the KF 35, or 60 percent less than the KF 20. (See Exhibit 11 for summary of Greaves' memo.)

When the document was sent to R&D for feasibility analyses, R&D's first reaction to the target costs was "Nonsense! You can't make a coffeemaker for DM 23 in this company!"[4] Nor did engineering take the idea well:

"To be honest," confessed Hans-Jürgen Dittombée, manager of industrial engineering, "we thought the cost targets were impossible. We are responsible for technical planning and didn't see how we could get there."

Working with Greaves on the project was a young, energetic product program manager, Albrecht Jestädt, a mechanical engineer with experience in production and engineering. Upon hearing R&D's and Engineering's reactions, Jestädt refused to take no for an answer and set about looking for alternatives. If Braun can't manufacture it, at least we can sell an OEM product that we design, he reasoned. Over the next year, he explored options in and outside of Germany and managed to find a manufacturer in Switzerland who could meet the cost requirements.

The KF 40: Problem Solving in Development

In the meanwhile Jestädt and the designer for household products, Hartwig Kahlcke, teamed up and began to develop the product. Kahlcke, a quiet contrast to the ebullient Jestädt, had come to the design department 10 years earlier and worked on the KF 35. Kahlcke had also dealt extensively with the Spanish group because they did so many household products. "We share a vision," Jestädt declared, "and we're both willing to do what we must to realize it." That vision had as its starting point the KF 20 and its still novel cylindrical design. How could they use the cylinder within the cost parameters? They had to use less material and only one heating element to start with. "Our first design was really terrific—the water tank completely surrounded the filter. But then we realized that we had to think modularly, so manufacturing costs would be minimized, and so we had to drop it," Jestädt recalled.

Jestädt and Kahlcke knew that the cylindrical form not only was appealing, but it used less material than the "chemical lab," the KF 35. Going back and forth they came up with five or six blue foam models before settling on what they believed was the optimal configuration: a cylinder within a cylinder, operating on the same principle as the KF 35 but much more compact. The main novelty: It would be operated from the front, and thus it would take less space and look even slimmer on the kitchen counter. (See Exhibit 12 for the initial concept.)

---

[4] Direct costs [DC] at Braun included only labor and materials, not the myriad of other costs involved in producing a product, such as nonlabor manufacturing costs, development costs, capital investment, etc.

EXHIBIT 11   Excerpts from Memorandum "Product Profile—Coffee Machine Range"
(from Gilbert Greaves to G. Voight)

December 2, 1981

Background

A key element in determining the viability of a filter-coffee machine entry is the investment/volume required. The problem is that volume depends on the range offered. [But a wide range] necessitates different tools for housings, water tanks, etc., thus increasing the investment cost for entry.

A further element determining the range is price segmentation. In Germany 52% of the unit volume is sold under DM 59; [this would require] a direct cost we cannot realistically expect from Braun.

Conclusions

1. A range of models will be needed.
2. A range has been defined which can be constructed on a "building block" system to minimize tooling investments. *platform re-use*
3. This range will enable Braun to compete in medium to high price segment only . . . retail sales prices above 70 DM. We will have to compete on feature, not on price.

This document [based on a market survey] will serve as an input to R&D to evaluate costs, feasibility, and timing based on the [following] volume estimates.

Range

The Braun range will be differentiated from competition by the following characteristics:

1. The premium model in the range will have a thermal flask. Into this thermal flask the coffee can be filtered direct. Coffee can be held off the hot plate in the flask at 80 degrees Celsius for 45 minutes. This prevents evaporation and aroma loss.
2. All models in the Braun range will be compatible with a special "Coffee ground dispenser." This stores 500g of ground coffee in an airtight hopper and has a metering system allowing the coffee ground to be dispensed by cups into the coffee machine filter.
3. All models in the Braun range will have a laterally pivoting filter allowing the filter to be swung out of the machine and underneath the hopper so that the consumer does not need to handle the coffee ground at any time. The filter can be lifted out to dispense with the paper filter and coffee ground.

The range will consist of the following models:

why so many? Is there really this much segmentation?

	1	2	3	4	5	6	7
	kill it			*kill it*			
Standard Features							
Cup à 125 cc	8	8	8	12	12	12	12
Anti Drip	x	x	x	x	x	x	x
Pivoting Filter	x	x	x	x	x	x	x
Translucent Tank	x	x	x	x	x	x	x
Pilot Switch	x	x	x	x	x	x	x
Warming Plate	x	x	x	x	x	x	x
Cord Compartment	x	x	x	x	x	x	x
Optional Features							
Glass Jug	x	x	x	x	x	x	
Thermal Jug							x
Coffee Dispenser			x			x	x
Calcification Indicator			x			x	x
Detachable Tank		x	x		x	x	x
Fixed Tank	x			x			
Target Direct Cost	22	23	29	24	25	31	36
Target Price Point DM	74	78	99	82	85	105	122
Target Price Point £	18.5	19.5	24.75	20.5	21.25	26.25	30.5

Annual Volume Assumptions(000)   *close   close*

	1	2	3	4	5	6	7	Total
Year 1	150	50	60	50	50	40	100	500
Year 2	225	75	90	75	75	60	150	750
Year 3	300	100	120	100	100	80	200	1,000

EXHIBIT 12   KF 40—Initial Concept

A Single Heating Element

At the same time, other disciplines continued working on the project. R&D, after exclaiming "impossible" at the very idea, took up the challenge and looked at how to get the cost out of the heating element and many other dimensions of the machine. The cost target presupposed a single heating element for both heating the water and keeping the coffee hot, rather than the two needed for the KF 20. Within those parameters, they finally decided that they could go for aluminum rather than copper in the heating element, which would be cheaper, but it would mean different dimensions for the various parts because of differences in conductivity. Keeping the coffee temperature at 82°C was considered an absolute must by the designers and marketing alike, even though they knew it was essentially an insoluble problem because of the level of time that coffee might be held.

How to Attach a Handle Invisibly

R&D also responded to new design concepts. Kahlcke and Rams, for example, wanted to glue the handle on the pot and asked Engineering to explore adhesives. The design reasons were both aesthetic and functional: The conventional means of attaching the handle to the coffee jug was the metal band, which both interrupted the line of the jug and collected dirt. In the course of working on the adhesives, it had become clear that manufacturing engineering would have to design an automated gluing process, in order to keep the costs down. The good news by

spring 1983 was that the design and manufacturing process was expected to cost less than the conventional metal-band method. R&D still had not found the ideal adhesive, however, one that would hold for years under heat, impact, and moisture.

Stop That Drip!

R&D had other challenges. The marketing people had found that an anti-drip device would be very attractive for customers, but Braun wanted to go at least one step beyond the competition. The idea was to prevent drips either from the filter (when one pulls out the coffeepot) or from the water tube (when one swings the filter out). It was supposed to be a relatively easy assignment but, as Gunter Oppermann, head of R&D for household products, pointed out, "Simple is most difficult," and that was what the project was about. The drip-stop was a case in point. "It has to be dual-action (stopping the flow when either the pot *or* the filter was pulled out), and we have to go around some outside patents. We thought about toilet flushers as a model and started from there. We didn't want the device to stick, and yet it must be sturdy."

When a Coffeemaker Makes Coffee

Quality assurance was working on several aspects of the new machine, including its end product. "We found that we didn't really know anything about coffee," quality engineer Werner Utsch confessed, "so we had to analyze and test some more, and that has led us to work with the coffee producers." The tests revealed valuable information: "We have found that our competition doesn't know much about coffee either." The next step would be blind taste tests, for which they needed a functional model.

What Does the Market Tell Us?

The market researchers continued gathering data as well. In October 1982 they tested the thermal jug concept and determined that it would be an essential selling feature. The next month they tested filter systems; the swivel filter won hands down. At this time, contrary to results a year earlier, the market wanted a detachable, transparent water tank. It was "significantly preferred over a nontransparent one" and "should be included . . . if the price is not prohibitive to the customer." (See Exhibit 13 for market test results.) Jestädt and Kahlcke had, however, already developed a modular design that could not accommodate a transparent tank.

To Design Means to Think

Operating from the principle that "no parts = no assembly costs," Jestädt and Kahlcke were striving to col-

EXHIBIT 13

January 10, 1983

Report on Coffee Maker Tests

Title	Date of Report		Comments
	Month	*Year*	
Coffee machine group discussions	10	1981	Desired improvements of the Braun coffee machine with thermal jug: Shortened filter, slimmer jug, should come in different colors, the water tank should be opaque, the tubes should be completely covered up, the filter should be tight and compact, the thermal jug should be more elegant, lighter, handier, taller, slimmer, and presentable on the coffee table.
Thermos jug concept	10	1982	The concept of a thermos jug with aroma test protective lid is preferred by the majority of respondents over a conventional glass jug with removable hot plate. There's a theoretical potential for a detachable heating or heat protection device.
Coffee filter system	11	1982	The best filter system for our new coffee acceptance test machine would be a swivel filter and the best water tank would be a transparent one.
Coffee machine features	12	1982	BMR would recommend the following concept test features to be considered for the new coffee machine range: built-in decalcifier, jug with heat and aroma preservation, swivel filter system, transparent detachable water tank, capacity 10–12 cups.

Source: Company documents.

lapse the number of parts into as few as possible. This was where Rams' motto, "To design means to think [Designarbeit ist Denkarbeit]," converged with Bernard Wild's view of Braun's know-how. Working with machine tool experts headed by Friedhelm Bau, Jestädt and Kahlcke had designed a configuration that incorporated many large and small parts that in the past would have been screwed together. The water tank was now part of the appliance housing, and the whole large piece, known simply as the "tank," was now central to their product concept, for it accounted for a good chunk of the savings in assembly costs. (See Exhibit 14.) It was, however, the largest, most complicated part ever attempted in polypropylene injection molding at Braun, and as such would be risky. (Exhibit 15 explains injection molding.)

The Manufacturing Challenge

Manufacturing and toolmaking engineers were involved from the beginning of the project. Bernard Wild had prepared an analysis of plant requirements in order to achieve the projected volumes for the new coffeemaker. As soon as polypropylene was proposed, Bau's toolmaking department started working with plastic suppliers and toolmakers in Berlin, who had experience with designing large tools for polypropylene. Bau was convinced that the large tank could be molded on the three 330-ton

EXHIBIT 14 The KF 40 Tank

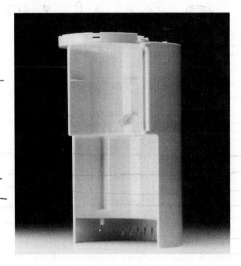

molding machines (presses) available at Marktheidenfelt. One machine could make 1,500 moldings (tank units) per day. With estimated volumes at 500,000 the first year, ramping up to 2,000,000 units the fourth year, the plant needed to be prepared to manufacture 10,000 units per day, given the 220 days per year that the plant operated. They were assuming a one-minute cycle time for the

---

EXHIBIT 15   Note on Injection Molding

Injection-molding technology permits the high-speed molding of thin, often complex parts out of metal or plastic. It involves (a) melting the material to a liquid state; (b) injecting the liquid under pressure into a metal mold; (c) waiting a number of seconds until the liquid cools and solidifies; (d) opening the mold; (e) withdrawing the part; (f) closing the mold again. To be precise and consistent, the process needs computer controls and robotized handling.

The easiest form to mold in this way is the cone, because it comes out from the mold easily. As soon as there are straight sides and protruding features, the design problem is vastly more complicated. Industrial designers, engineers, and tool designers work together to develop a design that can be produced effectively. For example, the mold needs to open at some point, and a flash line, preferably a very thin one, will show. The designers need to determine where the line's effects are minimal and design the mold accordingly.

In the case of plastic injection molding, the material is not held in liquid form. Rather, it is fed to the machine in small beads, like small white beans, which are melted instantly under pressure at the nozzle. This way the temperature can be controlled and there is less waste.

An important point in the design of a mold is the cooling rate of the plastic. This rate is determined by the properties of the plastic itself and by the shape of the part—its thickness at any given point and the distance of that point from the nozzle through which the liquid is injected. Because the part cannot be

removed until all of it has solidified, these problems must be taken into consideration when designing the part. Moreover, the injection temperature of the plastic and the temperature of the cooling water have to be kept constant via computer controls.

A mold may be very complicated, with more than one axis. Then the order in which the parts of the mold are opened and removed has to be carefully thought through. The "tank" part of the Braun coffee machine incorporated parts that would conventionally have been cast in at least five separate components and then screwed or snapped together. To save labor costs, the company invested in knowledge and tooling up front. This enabled them to keep production in high-wage Germany.

Some plastics are easier to cast than others. Those with low density, like polypropylene, are less stable, and this needs to be compensated for in the design of large parts. A large wall, for example, needs to be thicker or have a supporting shape built into the design. Because of the design implications of the variations in plastics, the same mold cannot be used for multiple kinds of plastic.

The quality of the molded part is determined not only by the design of the mold, but also by the interior surface finish of the mold. The quality of the metal, usually a special alloy steel, and the finishing technology used (e.g., erosion, grinding, polishing) determine how well a mold can meet its tolerances and how long it will last.

"tank" part, but could not be certain of it. They could start with three molds (or "tools"), one each for the 10- and 12-cup units and one for the thermal carafe, but they preferred to have the flexibility offered by five molds—two each for the 10- and 12-cup units.

If the product took off as expected, they would need four more molding machines and at least as many molds. Each machine cost about DM 500,000. The estimated cost for each tank mold was DM 250,000 and the lead time for tooling was around nine months for the large molds. Because the molds were not interchangeable for various types of plastics, the choice of plastic was crucial to engineering's planning.

Polypropylene: A Question of Braun-ness

Braun had pioneered in the use of plastics as early as the 1950s, when it rejected fake wood and overstuffed designs for its products. Its designers, engineers, and toolmakers were experienced in making both clear and opaque parts from several different kinds of plastic. For the outer housing of its appliances, the company had traditionally used polycarbonate, a dense, stable material that could be fashioned into precision parts with smooth

surfaces. Polycarbonate was, however, too expensive for the new coffee machine's requirements.

For that reason, Jestädt had begun working with ABS, which sold for about half of polycarbonate's going rate (see Exhibit 16). Even that, as it turned out, would probably be too expensive. The alternative, polypropylene, was the material of choice for low-end producers, but had never before been considered by Braun, except for interior parts that could benefit from its lower density and other features. The amount of polypropylene needed for each KF 40 unit was estimated at 700–950 grams. The problem with polypropylene for use in injection molding was its instability during the cooling process. Having a lower specific weight than the denser plastics, it tended to shrink unevenly and fall off, or "sink," at edges and meeting points. The resultant "sink marks" marred the surface and looked "cheap." Nor did polypropylene become as rigid as the more expensive materials, thus posing additional design challenges. Large parts were therefore especially vulnerable to a flimsy feel and had to be designed with the need to control that problem. It might mean thicker walls or a shape in the mold that would buttress the form from within.

EXHIBIT 16 Properties of Plastics

	Polycarbonate	ABS	Polypropylene
Cost DM/kg (1983)	85. DM	3.95 DM	2.8 DM
Specific weight	1.2	1.05	0.9
Melting temp.	220°C	200°C	165°–170°C
Softening temp.	160°C	140°C	120°C
Color-fastness	yes	no	yes
Shrinkage	0.5–0.7%	0.3–0.9%	0.3–2.5%
			(1–2.5% unfilled)

[handwritten: Shrinkage Jerry]

When polypropylene was first suggested, many colleagues familiar with its problems immediately objected: It will not be a *Braun* product if we use this cheap stuff, they warned. Despite such adamant objections, Jestädt and Kahlcke began working with chemical suppliers and toolmakers to explore ways of improving the quality of polypropylene parts. In fall 1982 they achieved a breakthrough: Why not let necessity be the mother of design in this case? If we can't get a perfectly smooth surface, let's minimize the effect of the sink marks by treating the surface in some way. This inspiration led to the idea for a corrugated surface that would both mask flaws and actually enhance the design as well.

NO! said the purists, for whom Braun design was synonymous with absolutely smooth, winter-white surfaces. "It's a compromise," said Utsch, "and I don't like compromises." Utsch, head of quality assurance for the project, kept pointing to polypropylene's tendency to scratch: "It's just too soft. Even a fingernail can scratch it. And if you wipe it off with the same sponge you wiped the counter off with, you can scratch it with food particles or coffee grounds." Even Rams was skeptical at first, but eventually came to support the solution. "It is the obvious way to go, given the project requirements."

Polypropylene did have some advantages other than its price, Oppermann pointed out: "It doesn't absorb water, so it won't stain easily. And, as far as we can tell, it won't get brittle as fast as polycarbonate, so it won't chip easily."

Jestädt, ever confident, explored further. Willing to take risks, R&D director Hexner supported R&D's involvement in trying to make polypropylene work. Like everyone else, he knew that if it didn't work, it would be extremely costly. "They are talking about a *huge* and very complicated tool for the tank. If it doesn't work, we'll have to throw it away and be another year behind." But Hexner didn't see any choice: "We've been given the job of making this thing at a ridiculous cost. My people say that it's possible only with polypropylene, and I

agree." To Hexner the "purists" were entirely unrealistic. "If a Braun product *has* to have a smooth surface, then you have two choices: Go with flaws, or forget it. And that is ridiculous!"

Hexner's boss, Dr. Thomsen, did not think it ridiculous to consider further choices. Nor did Waxlax. "We could make a business with, say, ABS. But it would be a different business," Thomsen contended. Waxlax was worried about the U.S. market implications: "We'd either have to drop the U.S. market, and that means low volumes, or restrict it to the higher-priced department store segment."

Jestädt and Kahlcke, meanwhile, were not insensitive to the design concerns. The ridges of the corrugated surface would have to be absolutely smooth, with no peaks or valleys, so that they would not catch any dirt. That job was turned over to the toolmakers. By the end of 1982 Bau's department was confident that the job could be done using the 330-ton molding machines at Marktheidenfeld. An outside consultant had suggested that the molding machines should be larger (500-ton) for a part the size of the tank, but that would mean an additional investment of DM 2 million for two new machines and upgrades of the old machines. Because the larger machines were much slower than the smaller ones, it would take five of them to produce the same number of units per day as the three 330-ton machines could produce.

The OEM Threat

In December 1982, Jestädt had presented his plan for a Swiss company to manufacture the new design. At the same meeting, someone brought in a cheap DM 29 coffeemaker from a supermarket and challenged those present, "If these guys can sell a coffeemaker for DM 29, you can surely make one for DM 23." As the discussion proceeded, the group realized that the new design was so special that it would be dangerous to let it out to a subcontractor; they would have to keep it inside in order to assure a competitive lead.

[handwritten: kills the cost model.]

[handwritten: where else could costs be cut electronics? switches?]

EXHIBIT 17   Project Report, Coffee Maker KF 40

January 26, 1983

Product description:

KF 40:   10-cup version with swinging filter, anti-drip, and cord storage
         DC target: FY 1982/83: 23.50 DM
KF 45:   same as the KF 40, but with switch for brewing 3–4 cups
         DC target: FY 1982/83: 24.30 DM

Status:

Blueprints for the construction of a functional model have been prepared, and it is currently being built.

Further steps:

- Prepare drawings for parts and tools   by 28 January 1983
- Requisition parts and tools; produce the   by 18 March 1983
  authorization request
- Have the authorization request approved   by 29 April 1983
- Finish the functional model   by 25 March 1983
- Test the functional model by QC   by 16 May 1983
- Build the design model   by 30 March 1983
- Complete drawings for tool orders   by 16 May 1983
- Go or no-go decision   by 17 May 1983
  If go, then Category I release
- Planned start-up of production   April 1984

Risks:

The above schedule does not include the production of prototypes. Only if the tests of the functional model reveal no major problems will it be possible to meet the planned deadlines.

Project: Coffee Makers KF 40 and KF 45   Signed: A Jestädt, Project Mgr.
Project Number: 542   Date: 26 January 1983   Version: 1

[handwritten margin note: Challenge moving to lower mkt segments]

[handwritten margin note: is only cost + time × cost of ...]

At that point it was proposed to take three months and build a trial tool to test the material; Waxlax approved DM 140,000 for the test and the tool, if the team chose to take that step. The proposal was, according to a project report for December 12, simply to "clarify if polypropylene is suitable for the appliance housing material." That was the point, according to Dittombée of industrial engineering. "I am confident that we can master polypropylene *technically*," he said, "but the discussion is about whether *Braun* can—or should—use it." For the purists, such a trial was far better than ordering the production dies and finding out polypropylene wouldn't work in this design and product.

A Material Decision

Over the next four months the coffeemaker project became more intense. At the report to management at the end of January 1983, drawings for the functional model were presented, and a schedule established (see Exhibit 17). The new 10-cup coffeemaker now had a

name: the KF 40. A second model, the KF 45, would have a 3–4 cup switch, costing one DM more. According to this schedule, the functional model would be ready by the end of March, with final tool drawings complete on May 16. The formal go/no-go decision would be made on May 17, followed by a "category I" signoff, which released the drawings so that tools could be ordered. Production ramp-up was estimated to begin in April of 1984, to reach 3,000 units per day within three months.

All this assumed that the KF 40 could be made with polypropylene and that all the other problems, such as the drip-stop, could be solved in time. By producing this schedule, business management had already cast its vote of confidence. Waxlax knew that Greaves tended to be conservative in his forecasts, and therefore one didn't have to worry about unrealistic figures in his analyses. Neither engineering nor design wanted to be pushed, however, and that Waxlax respected. The decision was a strategic one: a big risk—but one with a big payoff if they succeeded. The risk was not so much financial, though a million DM in molds and two years in development costs would not be insignificant. Should they go ahead without trial tooling, take three months for the trial test, rethink their positioning with a more expensive plas- tic, or walk away from the project? What risks were they willing to take and how far should they go before modifying the business strategy? Waxlax intended to take his time in listening to all points of view.

APPENDIX: IDENTIFICATION AND PRONUNCIATION GLOSSARY

Friedhelm **Bau** [Freedhelm Bow, as in "now"]	Manager, Machine Tools
Max **Braun** [Brown]	Founder, Braun AG
Artur and Erwin **Braun**	Sons and heirs of Max
Hans-Jürgen **Dittombée**	Manager, Industrial Engineering
Fritz **Eichler** [Ei as in Einstein]	Former director of design; member, board of directors
Gilbert **Greaves**	Business director, Household Products
Peter **Hexner**	Director of R&D
Albrecht **Jestädt** [Ahlbrecht *Ye*-shtet]	Mechanical engineer
Hartwig **Kahlcke** [Hartvig *Kahl*-keh]	Industrial designer, Household Products
Krups [Kroops]	Major German home appliance firm
Marktheidenfeld [Markt-*haydn*-felt]	Plant where KF 40 will be manufactured
Gunter **Oppermann** [Goonter Operman as in "open"]	Manager, R&D Household Products
Dieter **Rams** [Deeter Rahms]	Director of Design
Rowenta [Roventa]	Major German home appliance firm
Hartmut **Stroth** [Hartmoot Strote]	Director of Communications
Thomas H. **Thomsen**	Director of Technical Operations
Werner **Utsch** [Verner Ootsh]	Quality engineer, Household Products
Lorne **Waxlax**	Chairman, Braun AG
Bernard **Wild** [Bearnard Vealt]	Plant manager, Marktheidenfeld

Creating Project Plans to Focus Product Development

Steven C. Wheelwright and Kim B. Clark

The long-term competitiveness of any manufacturing company depends ultimately on the success of its product development capabilities. New product development holds hope for improving market position and financial performance, creating new industry standards and new niche markets, and even renewing the organization. Yet few development projects fully deliver on their early promises. The fact is, much can and does go wrong during development. In some instances, poor leadership or the absence of essential skills is to blame. But often problems arise from the way companies approach the development process. They lack what we call an "aggregate project plan."

Consider the case of a large scientific instruments company we will call PreQuip. In mid-1989, senior management became alarmed about a rash of late product development projects. For some months, the development budget had been rising even as the number of completed projects declined. And many of the projects in the development pipeline no longer seemed to reflect the needs of

Source: Reprinted by permission of *Harvard Business Review,* March–April 1992. Copyright © 1992 by The President and Fellows of Harvard College; all rights reserved.

PART FOUR: ENACTMENT OF TECHNOLOGY STRATEGY—CREATING AND IMPLEMENTING A DEVELOPMENT STRATEGY

EXHIBIT 1   PreQuip's Development Predicament: Overcommitted Resources

PreQuip had 960 engineering months each year to allocate to development work. But combining the time it would take to keep its current 30 projects on schedule with the time engineers spent doing nonproject development work, the company found it had overcommitted its development resources for the next three years by a factor of three.

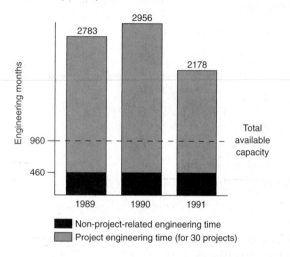

Non-project-related engineering time

Project engineering time (for 30 projects)

the market. Management was especially troubled because it had believed its annual business plan provided the guidance that the marketing and engineering departments needed to generate and schedule projects.

To get to the root of the problem, the chief executive first asked senior managers to compile a list of all the current development projects. They discovered that 30 projects were under way—far more than anticipated, and, they suspected, far more than the organization could support. Further analysis revealed that the company had two to three times more development work than it was capable of completing over its three-year development planning horizon. (See Exhibit 1.)

With such a strain on resources, delays were inevitable. When a project ran into trouble, engineers from other projects were reassigned or, more commonly, asked to add the crisis project to their already long list of active projects. The more projects they added, the more their productivity dropped. The reshuffling caused delays in other projects, and the effects cascaded. Furthermore, as deadlines slipped and development costs rose, project managers faced pressure to cut corners and compromise quality just to keep their projects moving forward.

The senior management team also discovered that the majority of PreQuip's development resources—primarily engineers and support staff—was not focused on the projects most critical to the business. When ques-

tioned, project leaders admitted that the strategic objectives outlined in the annual business plan had little bearing on project selection. Instead, they chose projects because engineers found the technical problems challenging or because customers or the marketing department requested them. PreQuip had no formal process for choosing among development projects. As long as there was money in the budget or the person making the request had sufficient clout, the head of the development department had no option but to accept additional project requests.

Many engineers were not only working on noncritical projects but also spending as much as 50 percent of their time on non-project-related work. They responded to requests from manufacturing for help with problems on previous products, from field sales for help with customer problems, from quality assurance for help with reliability problems, and from purchasing for help with qualifying vendors. In addition to spending considerable time fixing problems on previously introduced products, engineers spent many hours in "information" and "update" meetings. In short, they spent too little time developing the right new products, experimenting with new technologies, or addressing new markets.

PreQuip's story is hardly unique. Most organizations we are familiar with spend their time putting out fires and pursuing projects aimed at catching up to their competitors. They have far too many projects going at once and all too often seriously over-commit their development resources. They spend too much time dealing with short-term pressures and not enough time on the strategic mission of product development.

Indeed, in most organizations, management directs all its attention to individual projects—it micromanages project development. But no single project defines a company's future or its market growth over time; the "set" of projects does. Companies need to devote more attention to managing the set and mix of projects. In particular, they should focus on how resources are allocated between projects. Management must plan how the project set evolves over time, which new projects get added when, and what role each project should play in the overall development effort.

The aggregate project plan addresses all of these issues. To create a plan, management categorizes projects based on the amount of resources they consume and on how they will contribute to the company's product line. Then, by mapping the project types, management can see where gaps exist in the development strategy and make more informed decisions about what types of projects to add and when to add them. Sequencing projects carefully, in turn, gives management greater control of resource allocation and utilization. The project map also reveals where development capabilities need to be strong. Over time, companies can focus on adding critical resources and on developing the skills of individual contributors, project leaders, and teams.

Finally, an aggregate plan will enable management to improve the way it manages the development function. Simply adding projects to the active list—a common practice at many companies—endangers the long-term health of the development process. Management needs to create a set of projects that is consistent with the company's development strategies rather than selecting individual projects from a long list of ad hoc proposals. And management must become involved in the development process *before* projects get started, even before they are fully defined. It is not appropriate to give one department—say, engineering or marketing—sole responsibility for initiating all projects because it is usually not in a position to determine every project's strategic worth.

Indeed, most companies—including PreQuip—should start the reformation process by eliminating or postponing the lion's share of their existing projects, eventually supplanting them with a new set of projects that fits the business strategy and the capacity constraints. The aggregate project plan provides a framework for addressing this difficult task.

HOW TO MAP PROJECTS

The first step in creating an aggregate project plan is to define and map the different types of development projects; defining projects by type provides useful information about how resources should be allocated. The two dimensions we have found most useful for classifying are the degree of change in the product and the degree of change in the manufacturing process. The greater the change along either dimension, the more resources are needed.

Using this construct, we have divided projects into five types. The first three—derivative, breakthrough, and platform—are commercial development projects. The remaining two categories are research and development, which is the precursor to commercial development, and alliances and partnerships, which can be either commercial or basic research. (See Exhibit 2.)

Each of the five project types requires a unique combination of development resources and management styles. Understanding how the categories differ helps managers predict the distribution of resources accurately and allows for better planning and sequencing of projects over time. Here is a brief description of each category:

Derivative projects range from cost-reduced versions of existing products to add-ons or enhancements for an existing production process. For example, Kodak's wide-angle, single-use 35 mm camera, the Stretch, was derived from the no-frills Fun Saver introduced in 1990. Designing the Stretch was primarily a matter of changing the lens.

Development work on derivative projects typically falls into three categories: incremental product changes, say, new packaging or a new feature, with little or no manufacturing process change; incremental process changes, like a lower cost manufacturing process, improved reliability, or a minor change in materials used, with little or no product change; and incremental changes on both dimensions. Because design changes are usually minor, incremental projects typically are more clearly bounded and require substantially fewer development resources than the other categories. And because derivative projects are completed in a few months, ongoing management involvement is minimal.

Breakthrough projects are at the other end of the development spectrum because they involve significant changes to existing products and processes. Successful breakthrough projects establish core products and processes that differ fundamentally from previous generations. Like compact discs and fiber-optics cable, they create a whole new product category that can define a new market.

Because breakthrough products often incorporate revolutionary new technologies or materials, they usually require revolutionary manufacturing processes. Management should give development teams considerable latitude in designing new processes, rather than force them to work with existing plant and equipment, operating techniques, or supplier networks.

Platform projects are in the middle of the development spectrum and are thus harder to define. They entail more product and/or process changes than derivatives do, but they don't introduce the untried new technologies or materials that breakthrough products do. Honda's 1990 Accord line is an example of a new platform in the auto industry: Honda introduced a number of manufacturing process and product changes but no fundamentally new technologies. In the computer market, IBM's PS/2 is a personal computer platform; in consumer products, Procter & Gamble's Liquid Tide is the platform for a whole line of Tide brand products.

EXHIBIT 2   Mapping the Five Types of Development Projects

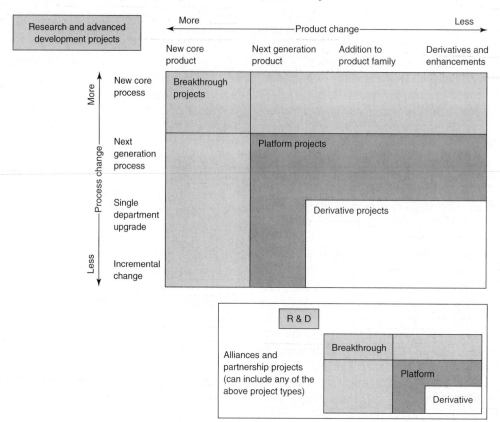

Well-planned and well-executed platform products typically offer fundamental improvements in cost, quality, and performance over preceding generations. They introduce improvements across a range of performance dimensions—speed, functionality, size, weight. (Derivatives, on the other hand, usually introduce changes along only one or two dimensions.) Platforms also represent a significantly better system solution for the customer. Because of the extent of changes involved, successful platforms require considerable up-front planning and the involvement of not only engineering but also marketing, manufacturing, and senior management.

Companies target new platforms to meet the needs of a core group of customers but design them for easy modification into derivatives through the addition, substitution, or removal of features. Well-designed platforms also provide a smooth migration path between generations so neither the customer nor the distribution channel is disrupted.

Consider Intel's 80486 microprocessor, the fourth in a series. The 486 introduced a number of performance im-

provements; it targeted a core customer group—the high-end PC/workstation user—but variations addressed the needs of other users; and with software compatibility between the 386 and the 486, the 486 provided an easy migration path for existing customers. Over the life of the 486 platform, Intel will introduce a host of derivative products, each offering some variation in speed, cost, and performance and each able to leverage the process and product innovations of the original platform.

Platforms offer considerable competitive leverage and the potential to increase market penetration, yet many companies systematically underinvest in them. The reasons vary, but the most common is that management lacks an awareness of the strategic value of platforms and fails to create well-thought-out platform projects. To address the problem, companies should recognize explicitly the need for platforms and develop guidelines for making them a central part of the aggregate project plan.

Research and development is the creation of the know-how and know-why of new materials and technologies that eventually translate into commercial development. Even though R&D lies outside the boundaries of commercial development, we include it here for two reasons: It is the precursor to product and process development; and, in terms of future resource allocation, employees move between basic research and commercial development. Thus R&D projects compete with commercial development projects for resources. Because R&D is a creative, high-risk process, companies have different expectations about results and different strategies for funding and managing it than they do for commercial development. These differences can indeed be great, but a close relationship between R&D and commercial development is essential to ensure an appropriate balance and a smooth conversion of ideas into products.

Alliances and partnerships, which also lie outside the boundaries of the development map, can be formed to pursue any type of project—R&D, breakthrough, platform, or derivative. As such, the amount and type of development resources and management attention needed for projects in this category can vary widely.

Even though partnerships are an integral part of the project development process, many companies fail to include them in their project planning. They often separate the management of partnerships from the rest of the development organization and fail to provide them with enough development resources. Even when the partner company takes full responsibility for a project, the acquiring company must devote in-house resources to monitor the project, capture the new knowledge being created, and prepare for the manufacturing and sales of the new product.

All five development categories are vital for creating a development organization that is responsive to the market. Each type of project plays a different role, each requires different levels and mixes of resources, and each generates very different results. Relying on only one or two categories for the bulk of the development work invariably leads to suboptimal use of resources, an unbalanced product offering, and eventually, a less than competitive market position.

PREQUIP'S PROJECT MAP

Using these five project types, PreQuip set about changing its project mix as the first step toward reforming the product development process. It started by matching its existing project list to the five categories. PreQuip's product line consisted of four kinds of analytic instruments—mass spectrometers, gas and liquid chromatographs, and data handling and processing equipment—

that identified and isolated chemical compounds, gases, and liquids. Its customers included scientific laboratories, chemical companies, and oil refineries—users that needed to measure and test accurately the purity of raw materials, intermediate by-products, and finished products.

PreQuip's management asked some very basic questions in its attempt to delineate the categories. What exactly was a breakthrough product? Would a three-dimensional graphics display constitute a breakthrough? How was a platform defined? Was a full-featured mass spectrometer considered a platform? How about a derivative? Was a mass spectrometer with additional software a derivative?

None of these questions was easy to answer. But after much analysis and debate, the management team agreed on the major characteristics for each project type and assigned most of PreQuip's 30 projects to one of the five categories. The map revealed just how uneven the distribution of projects had become—for instance, less than 20 percent of the company's projects were classified as platforms. (See Exhibit 3.)

Management then turned its attention to those development projects that did not fit into any category. Some projects required substantial resources but did not represent breakthroughs. Others were more complicated than derivative projects but did not fall into PreQuip's definition of platforms. While frustrating, these dilemmas opened managers' eyes to the fact that some projects made little strategic sense. Why spend huge amounts of money developing products that at best would produce only incremental sales? The realization triggered a reexamination of PreQuip's customer needs in *all* product categories.

Consider mass spectrometers, instruments that identify the chemical composition of a compound. PreQuip was a top-of-the-line producer of mass spectrometers, offering a whole series of high-performance equipment with all the latest features but at a significant price premium. While this strategy had worked in the past, it no longer made sense in a maturing market; the evolution of mass spectrometer technology was predictable and well defined, and many competitors were able to offer the same capabilities, often at lower prices.

Increasingly, customers were putting greater emphasis on price in the purchasing decision. Some customers also wanted mass spectrometers that were easier to use and modular so they could be integrated into their own systems. Others demanded units with casings that could withstand harsh industrial environments. Still

EXHIBIT 3   Before: PreQuip's Development Process Was Chaotic . . .

Each circle represents a PreQuip development project; the size correlates to the amount of development resources the project requires

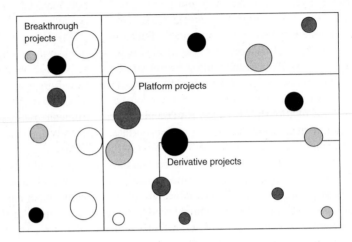

- ● Mass spectrometers
- ● Liquid chromatographs
- ○ Gas chromatographs
- ● Data processing and handling products

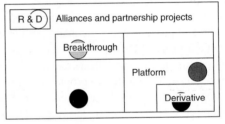

others required faster operating speeds, additional data storage, or self-diagnostic capabilities.

Taking all these customer requirements into account, PreQuip used the project map to rethink its mass spectrometer line. It envisaged a single platform complemented with a series of derivative products, each with a different set of options and each serving a different customer niche. By combining some new product design ideas—modularity and simplicity—with some features that were currently under development, PreQuip created the concept of the C-101 platform, a low-priced, general-purpose mass spectrometer. In part because of its modularity, the product was designed to be simpler and cheaper to manufacture, which also helped to improve its overall quality and reliability. By adding software and a few new features, PreQuip could easily create derivatives, all of which could be assembled and tested on a single production line. In one case, a variant of the C-101 was planned for the high-end laboratory market. By

strengthening the casing and eliminating some features, PreQuip also created a product for the industrial market.

Mapping out the new mass spectrometer line and the three other product lines was not painless. It took a number of months and involved a reconceptualization of the product lines, close management, and considerable customer involvement. To provide additional focus, PreQuip separated the engineering resources into three categories: basic R&D projects; existing products and customers, now a part of the manufacturing organization; and commercial product development.

To determine the number of breakthrough, platform, derivative, and partnership projects that could be sustained at any time, the company first estimated the average number of engineering months for each type of project based on past experience. It then allocated available engineering resources according to its desired mix of projects; about 50 percent to platform projects, 20 percent to derivative projects, and 10 percent each to break-

EXHIBIT 4   After PreQuip's Development Process Was Manageable

By mid-1990, PreQuip had reduced the number of development projects, including R & D, from 30 to 11, all defined and strategically positioned within the 5 project types.

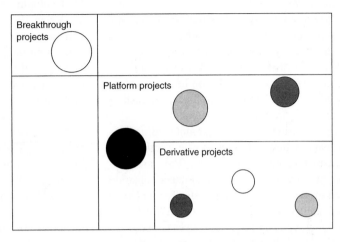

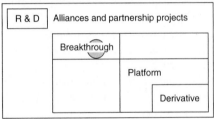

● Mass spectrometers

● Liquid chromatographs

○ Gas chromatographs

○ Data processing and handling products

through projects and partnerships. PreQuip then selected specific projects, confident that it would not overallocate its resources.

In the end, PreQuip canceled more than two-thirds of its development projects, including some high-profile pet projects of senior managers. When the dust had settled in mid-1990, PreQuip had just 11 projects: three platforms, one breakthrough, three derivatives, one partnership, and three projects in basic R&D. (See Exhibit 4.)

The changes led to some impressive gains: between 1989 and 1991, PreQuip's commercial development productivity improved by a factor of three. Fewer projects meant more actual work got done, and more work meant more products. To avoid overcommitting resources and to improve productivity further, the company built a "capacity cushion" into its plan. It assigned only 75 full-time-equivalent engineers out of a possible 80 to the eight commercial development projects. By leaving a small percent of development capacity uncommitted, PreQuip was better prepared to take advantage of unex-

pected opportunities and to deal with crises when they arose.

FOCUS ON THE PLATFORM

PreQuip's development map served as a basis for reallocating resources and for rethinking the mix of projects. Just as important, however, PreQuip no longer thought about projects in isolation; breakthrough projects shaped the new platforms, which defined the derivatives. In all four product lines, platforms played a particularly important role in the development strategy. This was not surprising considering the maturity of PreQuip's industry. For many companies, the more mature the industry, the more important it is to focus on platform projects.

Consider the typical industry life cycle. In the early stages of growth, innovative, dynamic companies gain market position with products that have dramatically superior performance along one or two dimensions. Whether they know it or not, these companies employ a breakthrough-platform strategy. But as the industry develops and the opportunity for breakthrough products decreases—often because the technology is shared more broadly—competitors try to satisfy increasingly sophisticated customers by rapidly making incremental improvements to existing products. Consciously or not, they adopt a strategy based on derivative projects. As happened with PreQuip, this approach ultimately leads to a proliferation of product lines and overcommitment of development resources. The solution lies in developing a few well-designed platform products, on each of which a generation of products can be built.

In the hospital bed industry, for example, companies that design, manufacture, sell, and service electric beds have faced a mature market for years. They are constantly under pressure to help their customers constrain capital expenditures and operating costs. Technologies are stable and many design changes are minor. Each generation of product typically lasts 8 to 12 years, and companies spend most of their time and energy developing derivative products. As a result, companies find themselves with large and unwieldy product lines.

In the 1980s, Hill-Rom, a leading electric-bed manufacturer, sought a new product strategy to help contain costs and maintain market share. Like other bed makers, its product development process was reactive and mired in too many low-payoff derivative projects. The company would design whatever the customer—a single hospital or nursing home—wanted, even if it meant significant commitments of development resources.

The new strategy involved a dramatic shift toward leveraging development and manufacturing resources. Hill-Rom decided to focus on hospitals and largely withdraw from the nursing home segment, as well as limit the product line by developing two new platform products—the Centra and the Century. The Centra was a high-priced product with built-in electronic controls, including communications capabilities. The Century was a simpler, less complex design with fewer features. The products built off each platform shared common parts and manufacturing processes and provided the customer with a number of add-on options. By focusing development efforts on two platforms, Hill-Rom was able to introduce new technologies and new product features into the market faster and more systematically, directly affecting patient recovery and hospital staff productivity. This strategy led to a less chaotic development cycle as well as lower unit cost, higher product quality, and more satisfied customers.

For companies that must react to constant changes in fashion and consumer tastes, a different relationship between platform and derivative projects makes sense. For example, Sony has pioneered its "hyper-variety" strategy in developing the Walkman: it directs the bulk of its Walkman development efforts at creating derivatives, enhancements, hybrids, and line extensions that offer something tailored to every niche, distribution channel, and competitor's product. As a result, in 1990, Sony dominated the personal audio system market with over 200 models based on just three platforms.

Platforms are critical to any product development effort, but there is no one ideal mix of projects that fits all companies. Every company must pursue the projects that match its opportunities, business strategy, and available resources. Of course, the mix evolves over time as projects move out of development into production, as business strategies change, as new markets emerge, and as resources are enhanced. Management needs to revisit the project mix on a regular basis—in some cases every six months; in others, every year or so.

STEADY STREAM SEQUENCING: PREQUIP PLANS FUTURE DEVELOPMENT

Periodically evaluating the product mix keeps development activities on the right track. Companies must decide how to sequence projects over time, how the set of projects should evolve with the business strategy, and how to build development capabilities through such projects. The decisions about changing the mix are neither easy nor straightforward. Without an aggregate project plan, most companies cannot even begin to formulate a strategy for making those decisions.

PreQuip was no different. Before adopting an aggregate project plan, the company had no concept of project mix and no understanding of sequencing. Whenever someone with authority had an idea worth pursuing, the development department added the project to its active list. With the evolution of a project plan, PreQuip developed an initial mix and elevated the sequencing decision to a strategic responsibility of senior management. Management scheduled projects at evenly spaced intervals to ensure a "steady stream" of development projects. (See Exhibit 5.)

A representative example of PreQuip's new strategy for sequencing projects is its new mass spectrometer, or C series. Introduced into the development cycle in late 1989, the C-101 was the first platform conceived as a sys-

EXHIBIT 5 Prequip's Project Sequence

Project type	Development resources committed at mid-1990 (% of total engineering time)	Project description	Project number	Sequencing 1990 / 1991
R & D	(Separate)	Advanced pump	RD-1	(1990 ──────── 1991 →)
		Electronic sensors	RD-2	───────────
		Software	RD-3	────────
Breakthrough	12.5%	Fully automated self-diagnostic system for gas chromatograph	BX-3	────────
Platform	52.5	Liquid chromatograph	A series	A-502 ──────── →
		Gas chromatograph	B series	B-502
		Mass spectrometer	C series	C-101 ───── C-201
		Data processing and handling equipment	D series	DX-52 ───── DX-82 →
Derivative	18.75	Liquid chromatograph	A series	A-311 A-321 A-502X
		Gas chromatograph	B series	B-22 B-32
		Mass spectrometer	C series	C-1/X C-1/Z C-101Z
		Data processing and handling equipment	D series	D-333 D-433
Partnership	10.0	Medical/chemical diagnostic system	VMH	────────

tem built around the new modular design. Aimed at the middle to upper end of the market, it was a versatile, modular unit for the laboratory that incorporated many of the existing electromechanical features into the new software. The C-101 was scheduled to enter manufacturing prototyping in the third quarter of 1990.

PreQuip positioned the C-1/X, the first derivative of the C-101, for the industrial market. It had a rugged casing designed for extreme environments and fewer software features than the C-101. It entered the development process about the time the C-101 moved into manufacturing prototyping and was staffed initially with two designers whose activities on the C-101 were drawing to a close.

Very similar to the C-1/X was the C-1/Z, a unit designed for the European market. The C-1/X team was expanded to work on both the C-1/X and the C-1/Z. The C-1/Z had some unique software and a different display and packaging but the same modular design. PreQuip's marketing department scheduled the C-101 to be introduced about six months before the C-1/X and the C-1/Z, thus permitting the company to reach a number of markets quickly with new products.

To leverage accumulated knowledge and experience, senior management assigned the team that worked on the C-1/X and the C-1/Z to the C-201 project, the next generation spectrometer scheduled to replace the C-101. It too was of a modular design but with more computer power and greater software functionality. The C-201 also incorporated a number of manufacturing process improvements gleaned from manufacturing the C-101.

To provide a smooth market transition from the C-101 to the C-201, management assigned the remainder of the C-101 team to develop the C-101X, a follow-on derivative project. The C-101X was positioned as an improvement over the C-101 to attract customers who were in the market for a low-end mass spectrometer but were unwilling to settle for the aging technology of the C-101. Just as important, the project was an ideal way to gather market data that could be used to develop the C-201.

PreQuip applied this same strategy across the other three product categories. Every other year it planned a new platform, followed by two or three derivatives spaced at appropriate intervals. Typically, when a team finished work on a platform, management assigned part of the team to derivative projects and part to other projects. A year or so later, a new team would form to work on the next platform, with some members having worked on the preceding generation and others not. This steady stream sequencing strategy worked to improve the company's overall market position while encouraging knowledge transfer and more rapid, systematic resource development.

AN ALTERNATIVE: SECONDARY WAVE PLANNING

While the steady stream approach served PreQuip well, companies in different industries might consider alternative strategies. For instance, a "secondary wave" strategy may be more appropriate for companies that, like Hill-Rom, have multiple product lines, each with its own base platforms but with more time between succeeding generations of a particular platform.

The strategy works like this. A development team begins work on a next generation platform. Once the company completes that project, the key people from the team start work on another platform for a different product family. Management leaves the recently introduced platform on the market for a couple of years with few derivatives introduced. As that platform begins to age and competitors' newer platforms challenge it, the company refocuses development resources on a set of derivatives in order to strengthen and extend the viability of the product line's existing platform. The wave of derivative projects extends the platform life and upgrades product offerings, but it also provides experience and feedback to the people working on the product line and prepares them for the next generation platform development. They receive feedback from the market on the previous platform, information on competitors' platform offerings, and information on emerging market needs. Key people then bring that information together to define the next platform and the cycle begins again, built around a team, many of whose members have just completed the wave of derivative products.

A variation on the secondary wave strategy, one used with considerable success by Kodak, involves compressing the time between market introduction of major platforms. Rather than going off to work on another product family's platform following one platform's introduction, the majority of the development team goes to work immediately on a set of derivative products. This requires a more compressed and careful assessment of the market's response to the just-introduced platform and much shorter feedback loops regarding competitors' products. If done right, however, companies can build momentum and capture significant incremental market share. Once the flurry of derivative products has passed, the team goes to work on the next generation platform project for the same product family.

Before 1987, Kodak conducted a series of advanced development projects to explore alternative single-use 35 mm cameras—a roll of film packaged in an inexpensive camera. Once used, the film is processed and the camera discarded or recycled. During 1987, a group of Kodak development engineers worked on the first platform project, which resulted in the market introduction and volume production of the Fling 35 mm camera in January 1988. (The product was later renamed the Fun Saver.) As the platform neared completion, management reassigned the front-end development staff to two derivative projects: the Stretch, a panoramic, double-wide image version of the Fling, and the Weekend, a waterproof version.

By the end of 1988, Kodak had introduced both derivative cameras and was shipping them in volume. True to the definition of a derivative, both the Stretch and the Weekend took far fewer development resources and far less time than the Fling. They also required less new tooling and process engineering since they leveraged the existing automation and manufacturing process. The development team then went to work on the next generation platform product—a Fun Saver with a built-in flash.

No matter which strategy a company uses to plan its platform-derivative mix—steady stream or secondary wave—it must have well-defined platforms. The most advanced companies further improve their competitive position by speeding up the rate at which they introduce new platforms. Indeed, in a number of industries we've studied, the companies that introduced new platforms at the fastest rate were usually able to capture the greatest market share over time.

In the auto industry, for example, different companies follow quite different sequencing schedules, with markedly different results. According to data collected in the late 1980s, European car companies changed the platform for a given product, on average, every 12 years, U.S. companies every 8 years, and Japanese companies every 4 years. A number of factors explain the differences in platform development cycles—historical and cultural differences, longer development lead times, and differences in development productivity.[1]

---

[1] Based on research by Kim B. Clark and Takahiro Fujimoto. See their article, "The Power of Product Integrity," *Harvard Business Review*, November–December 1990, p. 107.

In both Europe and the United States, the engineering hours and tooling costs of new products were much higher than in Japan. This translated into lower development costs for Japanese car makers, which allowed faster payback and shorter economic lives for all models. As a consequence, the Japanese could profitably conduct more projects and make more frequent and more extensive changes than both their European and U.S. competitors and thus were better positioned to satisfy customers' needs and capture market share.

THE LONG-TERM GOAL: BUILDING CRITICAL CAPABILITIES

Possibly the greatest value of an aggregate project plan over the long-term is its ability to shape and build development capabilities, both individual and organizational. It provides a vehicle for training development engineers, marketers, and manufacturing people in the different skill sets needed by the company. For instance, some less experienced engineers initially may be better suited to work on derivative projects, while others might have technical skills more suited for breakthrough projects. The aggregate project plan lets companies play to employees' strengths and broaden their careers and abilities over time. (See Exhibit 6.)

Thinking about skill development in terms of the aggregate project plan is most important for developing competent team leaders. Take, for instance, an engineer with five years of experience moving to become a project leader. Management might assign her to lead a derivative project first. It is an ideal training ground because derivative projects are the best defined, the least complex, and usually the shortest in duration of all project types. After the project is completed successfully, she might get promoted to lead a larger derivative project and then a platform project. And if she distinguishes herself there and has the other required skills, she might be given the opportunity to work on a breakthrough project.

In addition to creating a formal career path within the sphere of development activities, companies should also focus on moving key engineers and other development participants between advanced research and commercial development. This is necessary to keep the transfer of technology fresh and creative and to reward engineers who keep their R&D efforts focused on commercial developments.

Honda is one company that delineates clearly between advanced research and product development—the two kinds of projects are managed and organized differ-

EXHIBIT 6 Eight Steps of an Aggregate Project Plan

1. Define project types as either breakthrough, platform, derivative, R&D, or partnered projects.
2. Identify existing projects and classify by project type.
3. Estimate the average time and resources needed for each project type based on past experience.
4. Identify existing resource capacity.
5. Determine the desired mix of projects.
6. Estimate the number of projects that existing resources can support.
7. Decide which specific projects to pursue.
8. Work to improve development capabilities.

ently and are approached with very different expectations. Development engineers tend to have broader skills, while researchers' are usually more specialized. However, Honda encourages its engineers to move from one type of project to another if they demonstrate an idea that management believes may result in a commercially viable innovation. For example, Honda's new lean-burning engine, introduced in the 1992 Civic, began as an advanced research project headed by Hideyo Miyano. As the project moved from research to commercial development, Miyano moved too, playing the role of project champion throughout the entire development process.

Besides improving people's skills, the aggregate project plan can be used to identify weaknesses in capabilities, improve development processes, and incorporate new tools and techniques into the development environment. The project plan helps identify where companies need to make changes and how those changes are connected to product and process development.

As PreQuip developed an aggregate project plan, for example, it identified a number of gaps in its capabilities. In the case of the mass spectrometer, the demand for more software functionality meant PreQuip had to develop an expertise in software development. And with an emphasis on cost, modularity, and reliability, PreQuip also had to focus on improving its industrial design skills.

As part of its strategy to improve design skills, the company introduced a new computer-aided design system into its engineering department, using the aggregate project plan as its guide. Management knew that one of the platform project teams was particularly adept with computer applications, so it chose that project as the pilot for the new CAD system. Over the life of the project, the team's proficiency with the new system grew. When the project ended, management dispersed team members to other projects so they could train other engineers in using the new CAD system.

As PreQuip discovered, developing an aggregate project plan involves a relatively simple and straightforward procedure. But carrying it out—moving from a poorly managed collection of ad hoc projects to a robust set that matches and reinforces the business strategy—requires hard choices and discipline.

At all the companies we have studied, the difficulty of those choices makes imperative strong leadership and early involvement from senior management. Without management's active participation and direction, organizations find it next to impossible to kill or postpone projects and to resist the short-term pressures that drive them to spend most of their time and resources fighting fires.

Getting to an aggregate project plan is not easy, but working through the process is a crucial part of creating a sustainable development strategy. Indeed, while the specific plan is extremely important, the planning process itself is even more so. The plan will change as events unfold and managers make adjustments. But choosing the mix, determining the number of projects the resources can support, defining the sequence, and picking the right projects raise crucial questions about how product and process development ought to be linked to the company's competitive opportunities. Creating an aggregate project plan gives direction and clarity to the overall development effort and helps lay the foundation for outstanding performance.

CASE IV-5

Improving the Product Development Process at Kirkham Instruments Corporation

Clayton M. Christensen

"This was quite a week," Kathleen Quinn said to herself as she pulled onto the M-25 Motorway near her offices in the western London suburb of Slough late in the fall of 1995. Quinn, vice president for research and develop-

Source: Professor Clayton M. Christensen prepared this case as the basis for class discussion rather than to illustrate either effective or inef-

ment at Kirkham Instruments Corporation, had just completed with about 40 of her colleagues a week-long seminar at a nearby executive conference center on managing new product development, conducted by several faculty members from the Harvard Business School. "I've been a part of a lot of change management and re-engineering efforts which clearly had been doomed from the start," she reflected. "But this one is going to work. I've never seen management so united about anything like this. That aggregate project planning idea just makes so much sense. I hope we get busy implementing it all."

Kirkham Instruments was a closely held manufacturer of laboratory analytical equipment with 1995 turnover of £450 million.[1] The company was organized into four divisions: the Mass Spectrometer Division; the Chromatography Division, which made gas and liquid chromatographs; the Optical Equipment Division, which made optical comparators, microscopes, and related equipment; and Waterloo Instruments Ltd., a Belgian manufacturer of electron microscopes and x-ray diffraction equipment, which Kirkham had acquired in 1992. As Exhibit 1 shows, most of Kirkham's recent growth had come from its Mass Spectrometer and Chromatography divisions. Its optical product lines were in mature or declining markets, and the Waterloo Division, through acquired amidst high hopes of growth and profitability, had been struggling to remain viable in the face of formidable competition from American, German, and Japanese manufacturers. Kirkham's three British divisions were each housed in the company's complex of laboratory, manufacturing, warehouse, and office buildings in Slough.

About 40% of Kirkham's turnover came from customers in the United Kingdom, where it was the dominant maker of laboratory instruments. Another 25% came from countries in continental Europe, and 30% came from the Middle Eastern and Asia—particularly India, Saudi Arabia, and China, where rapidly growing

fective handling of an administrative situation. Copyright © 1997 by the President and Fellows of Harvard College. To order copies or request permission to reproduce materials, call 1-800-545-7685 or write Harvard Business School Publishing, Boston, MA 02163. No part of this publication may be reproduced, stored in a retrieval system, used in a spreadsheet, or transmitted in any form or by any means—electronic, mechanical, photocopying, recording, or otherwise—without the permission of Harvard Business School.

[1] "Turnover" was the term most English-speaking Europeans used instead of the North American term "revenue." In 1995, one British pound was worth approximately 1.60 U.S. dollars.

EXHIBIT 1   Turnover of Kirkham Instruments and Its Divisions, 1989–1996

Divisional turnover	1989	1991	1993	1994	1995	1996 (est.)
Mass spectrometer	112	130	151	166	175	176
Chromatography	62	81	105	120	130	138
Optical equipment	42	44	36	39	40	41
Waterloo Instruments			122	116	105	110
Total corporation	216	255	414	441	450	465

Note: Waterloo Instruments, Ltd., was acquired in 1992.

and increasingly sophisticated chemical companies comprised a very attractive market.

KIRKHAM INSTRUMENTS' STRUCTURE FOR NEW PRODUCT DEVELOPMENT

Quinn had begun her career with a four-year stint as a bench development engineer in the Optical Equipment Division, after receiving her doctorate in analytical chemistry from the University of Sussex. She had then taken a position as a manager of product development in the Chromatography Division; became vice president for engineering and development in that division; and in 1992 had been promoted to Kirkham's corporate staff. As vice president for research and development, Quinn had responsibility for a group of 45 scientists and engineers who developed new "technology platforms"—competencies in emerging technologies which might in the future constitute the basis for new product lines in the company. Quinn also managed a central software support group, which serviced the increasing need in each of the product divisions for greater software content in new products. As a member of Kirkham's board of managing directors, Quinn played a major role in corporate decisions to allocate funds for new product development in each of the company divisions. Quinn chaired the corporation's Development Council, comprised of herself and the four divisional vice presidents of engineering and development.

Historically, decisions on new product development funding had been left exclusively to the product divisions. Michael Donaldson, Kirkham Instruments' chief executive, had moved to centralize new product decision making in the early 1990s, in response to the growing desire of many customers to link the functions of multiple pieces of laboratory equipment into integrated systems. These systems permitted scientists to collect and analyze

data on materials samples that were generated on different specialized instruments. This meant that Kirkham Instruments needed to more closely coordinate developments in new equipment with desired features in the analytical software; and to coordinate the design of new features and the market introduction timing of new instruments from different divisions.

Quinn, as Kirkham's first corporate vice president for research and development, had found the process of centrally coordinating the development of new products a formidable task. The managing directors of the instrument divisions each had agreed that a more coordinated approach to managing product development had become essential. Nonetheless, they had retained responsibility for the turnover and profitability of their respective divisions, and for defining and implementing a strategy that would achieve their divisions' objectives. Indeed, despite the trend toward the purchase of integrated systems by laboratories, the majority of each division's turnover came from the sale of stand-alone products. In mass spectrometers, in particular, there was a rapidly growing market for small, self-contained portable units that could be transported to field locations to test the compliance to environmental regulations of effluents from manufacturing facilities. Hence, even though Quinn played a coordinative and oversight role and managed her own groups for software and advanced development, most projects to develop next-generation instruments continued to be managed by the managing directors for engineering and product development in the divisions. Exhibit 2 maps this organizational structure.

THE NEW PRODUCT DEVELOPMENT SEMINAR

The course on new product development which Quinn had just completed had been conducted by three Harvard Business School (HBS) professors who had been

EXHIBIT 2   The Organizational Structure of Kirkham Instruments

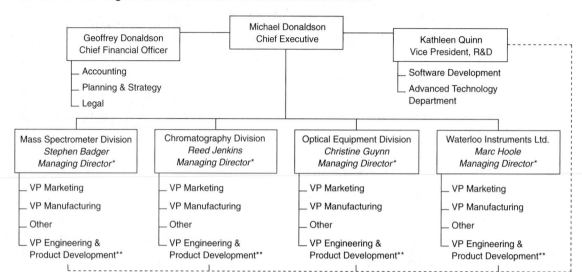

*Member, Executive Committee
**Member, Corporate Development Council

studying the problems of managing new product development in a variety of industries for nearly a decade. Their findings had come to the attention of Michael Donaldson, who was struck by the similarity of the problems the professors had identified, to those Kirkham Instruments was encountering. Donaldson was intrigued that the methods of managing these problems the professors were advocating might work at Kirkham, and asked Quinn to invite them to conduct a week-long seminar to convey what they had learned. For an unassuming fee, the professors had agreed to undertake the project.

In addition to Kathleen Quinn, Michael Donaldson, and corporate CFO Geoffrey Donaldson,[2] those who attended the seminar included the managing directors and board members from each division. The boards were comprised of the divisional vice presidents for sales & marketing, engineering and product development, manufacturing, finance, and human resources. Quinn had reserved three hours in the schedule at the end of each day for the boards to discuss the applicability of the day's concepts to their situation, and to devise an action plan for how they would implement the ideas when they returned to their regular work the next week. On the final day of the seminar, the managing director of each division had presented his or her action plan to Donaldson. As the seminar ended, Donaldson rose to thank the participants for their enthusiastic participation in the event, and then pointed to Quinn with an assignment: "Kathleen, someone in the company has got to own this problem of implementing these changes—to understand what needs to be done, to help the boards implement their action plans, and to keep me fully informed of what is working, and what is not. This is now your job. I look forward to what you, and everyone here, can do with what we have learned this week."

KEY CONCEPTS FROM THE COURSE

The action plans that had been presented by the four divisions' managing directors that morning had three elements in common. These were first, that Kirkham Instruments' technology and product development system was attempting to function far beyond its capacity: most marketers and engineers were assigned to work concurrently on between three to six projects. It was the sense of those at the seminar that to balance the company's capacity to execute projects with its project load, they needed to cancel or postpone at least half of the projects that were currently underway. Quinn smiled as she recalled all the heads nodding in agreement when their instructor had showed a chart which described how the productivity of

[2]The Donaldson brothers, grandsons of Kirkham Instruments' founder, were the major shareholders of the company.

EXHIBIT 3   The Impact of Multiple Concurrent Project Assignments on the Productivity of Development Personnel

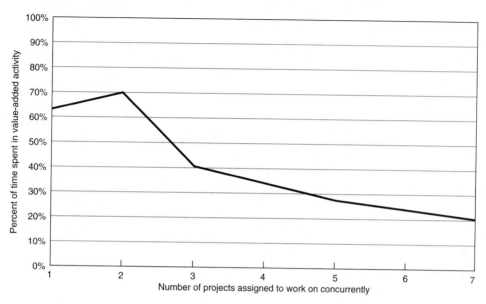

EXHIBIT 4   An Aggregate Project Planning Framework

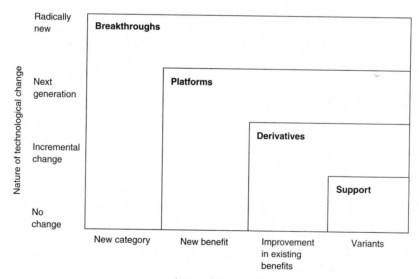

development personnel declined as the number of projects on which they were concurrently assigned to work, increased (the chart is reproduced as Exhibit 3).

The second concept everyone seemed determined to adopt was what the HBS trio called an aggregate project plan. They had presented a typology of projects—breakthrough, platform, derivative, and support—whose characteristics were defined by the axes on a *technology-market map,* shown in Exhibit 4. During the course the division boards had each tried to plot their current set of development projects on such a map. Each had concluded that to some degree they needed to focus more resources on projects of breakthrough or platform character, since these would constitute the basis for future growth.

EXHIBIT 5   The Product Development Funnel, with Its Phases, Documents, and Gates

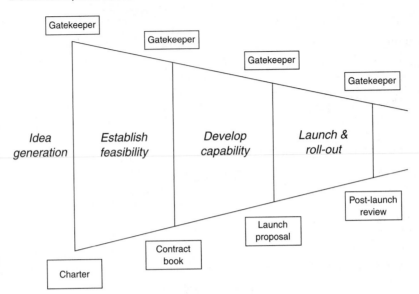

The third concept related to management of the development funnel—the way the divisions initiated and funded projects, assessed their progress, and made decisions about whether projects should be launched, killed, or continued. (The funnel framework discussed at the seminar is reproduced as Exhibit 5). The boards seemed unanimous in their belief that they needed to get better about killing projects. Aside from that conclusion, however, Quinn had not sensed from the seminar discussions the same degree of unanimity amongst board members about what more they should do to improve the management of their funnels. Each division already had its own system for project planning and documentation, and for reviewing progress at key milestones. Hence, during a comment period in the seminar one divisional marketing VP commented, "If it's not broken, why fix it?" But the manufacturing VP in the same division disagreed: "Our whole process is a sham. We have a written process, but nobody ever follows it. You've heard of the Golden Rule (He who has the gold makes the rules)? Well, there are a lot of people around here who have little pots of gold, and so we have lots of different rules."

THE FIRST STEPS OF IMPLEMENTATION

On Tuesday morning, November 23—just 4 days after the seminar had concluded—Michael Donaldson convened a special executive committee meeting, attended by Quinn, Geoff Donaldson, and the four division man-

aging directors: Stephen Badger (mass spectrometers), Reed Jenkins (chromatography), Christine Guynn (optical), and Marc Hoole (Waterloo). The only item on Donaldson's agenda was implementation of the new development system. Quinn opened the discussion: "I've thought a lot about each of your action plans, and it seems pretty clear that our highest priority needs to be to cut back the number of projects we're trying to push through the system—probably by half. What do you think?"

After polling the managing directors and finding that each agreed with the need, Donaldson concluded, "I think you've read everyone's opinion well, Kathleen. How should we proceed?"

Quinn passed out a sheet of paper. "Well, I've made a listing of all the projects we have underway, with the project managers' best estimates for how many person-months will be required to complete them. It's hard to believe, but it looks like we've got about 150 projects underway. I know there's going to be a lot of discussion on some of these, but I thought we might be able to make some fast progress by finding some projects that we all agree are low priorities. I think it's important to act on at least some of this, before we lose momentum."

After glancing over Quinn's list, Badger commented, "This list isn't accurate. You've got the T-300 project as taking 30 person-months, scheduled for launch next April. We stopped working on that one last July. And we've just started a new one that isn't even listed here, that will take a lot of resources."

"I agree that the list isn't accurate," added Guynn, who had just been promoted to her position from her previous post as marketing VP for chromatography products. "Just thinking back on my time in chromatography, I can think of four or five things that are soaking up a lot of time there, that aren't on this list. That's because they never write up a formal authorization request there until the project is almost finished. And some of the things you've listed for my division aren't anywhere near the size you've listed here. The XL20 comparator upgrade, for example, is really just half of an engineer for 6 weeks. You've got it down as way, way too big. I wouldn't even call it a project. Without even studying the list, I can see two or three others that are so minor that they shouldn't even be on the list. I think we'd just be wasting our time going over this today, Kathleen. We need something more accurate to work from."

Quinn defended her list. "Look. We've got to start somewhere. This isn't my data. It came from *your* people. I think it's the most accurate list we can come up with. For example, Steve, the T-300 project is alive and kicking—I guess there's a customer that wants to put it in four or five different labs, from what they tell me, so they've started working on it again." Quinn defended the accuracy of her list against several more complaints, but made little headway.

Finally, Donaldson broke in. "We're not going to get anywhere with this. Why don't we table the list idea, and ask you each to come back in two weeks with a definitive, accurate listing of all the projects in your divisions. Then we at least will have a common starting point. Kathleen, is there anything else we can do while we wait for this?"

"I've been thinking about it too," Marc Hoole interrupted. "I've got a real problem with just coming in and hacking out half of the projects. The facts are that for every one of those projects, there are people in the company who believe the project is absolutely essential for our future. It's definitional: If someone important didn't think the project was important, we'd never have started it. If we just go in and cancel things without laying a careful foundation of understanding for what we're doing, I'm afraid all hell will break loose. This can't just be a top-down effort."

"I have an alternative proposal for getting things going," Hoole continued. "I think we should put everyone in the company whose job relates in any way to new product development, through a condensed, one-day version of the HBS course. If they have the same understanding of the issues that we all have in this room, then I think the difficult decisions will be easier to make. People will know *why* we're doing what we're doing."

After a discussion, everyone agreed that a broader training effort was a better way to start. Donaldson asked, "Kathleen, do you think you could take our employees through such a session? We're talking about roughly 200 people. What do you think?"

"Well, I understand the basic concepts," Quinn responded. "But what really made last week so powerful was all of the stories, and all of the deep examples, that those professors used to help us internalize the material. If we're going take a day of the time of 200 people, we ought to do it right. We should get one of the Harvard faculty to come back. In particular, I think Tim Derrick would do a great job for us." The others in the group readily agreed that this would be a good investment, and Quinn promised to line Professor Derrick up as soon as possible. The conversation in the meeting then turned to other pressing operating issues. Because of Harvard's end-of-term schedule and the intervening holiday period, Quinn and Derrick were not able to convene the one-day crash course until Monday, February 16.

PORTFOLIO CHARTS, FUNNELS, AND KIRKHAM'S QUARTERLY EXECUTIVE CONFERENCES

To coordinate the product development, manufacturing, and marketing activities of Kirkham Instruments' four divisions, and to help corporate management stay abreast of the details in each business, for years Donaldson had convened a Quarterly Executive Conference on the first two business days of each quarter. The Donaldson brothers, Quinn, and the divisional managing directors attended the full two days, with a half day allocated to review the performance and plans for each of the four divisions. Other managers would also be invited to attend portions of the conference, to make presentations or participate in decisions that specifically impacted their responsibilities.

In mid-January 1996, Donaldson walked into Quinn's office with a proposal. "Kathleen, I think we were right to schedule that crash training course with Derrick next month. But I really sense that we're losing momentum. It's been nearly two months since we finished the course, and when I look around for what's changed, I see business as usual. I have an idea for how we can get things moving, though. I'd like us to use those portfolio charts and funnels Derrick showed us, as a standard format for reviewing product development in the Quarterly Executive Conferences, starting in April. I've always had a hard time keeping track of what division is doing what project, and what stage of development each is in. It would be nifty if the managing directors could always show a bubble chart showing their portfolio of projects. We could see at a glance whether we were comfortable with the mix of projects, like Derrick was saying—you know, whether we are doing enough breakthroughs and platforms, and so on."

"Sure," Quinn responded. "I think that would be a great idea. I think even just standardizing our vocabulary: using terms like breakthroughs, platforms, funnels, and contract books would be valuable. And do you know what else we could do? We could ask the managing directors to give us, on a single sheet of paper, a funnel showing which projects are in which stage. Remember how Derrick laid those out? First they're in the idea phase; then they pass through the charter gate into the feasibility stage of the funnel; then they go through the contract book gate to the capability development phase; then through the launch proposal gate; and so on. We could put the name of each project on a little bubble, and put each in its position in the funnel. We could color the platforms, derivatives, and breakthroughs differently, so you could see at a glance where everything is."

"That's great," affirmed Donaldson. "This will have to wait until the crash course is finished so the troops know what these tools are. But as soon as Derrick has finished could you call the Development Council together and tell them we need the first charts on April 1?"

Tim Derrick conducted the one-day condensed version of the week-long seminar in a full auditorium to about 250 employees on February 16. It went well, as everyone had expected. Quinn noticed that the crowd seemed to resonate even more strongly to Derrick's overload-inefficiency chart (Exhibit 3), and resolved to reinvigorate the management committee's enthusiasm for achieving a better balance between load and capacity. At the close of the day's meetings, Donaldson gave a rousing endorsement of Derrick's recommendations, and urged everyone to support Kathleen Quinn's efforts to lead the implementation. Quinn then explained that the first steps in implementation would be to put together the funnel and aggregate project plan charts, and asked everyone to cooperate when their vice president for engineering and development asked them for help.

CUTTING THE NUMBER OF PROJECTS

Derrick stayed overnight to attend Donaldson's Executive Committee Meeting the next morning. The main agenda item was to finalize the listing of projects under-

way, and to begin, if possible, cutting the lowest priority projects. Quinn met Derrick for breakfast, to update him on what had transpired since the November seminar: I've got to warn you, Tim, that we're not as far along in this as we had hoped we'd be. We all know we've got to cut back on the number of projects, but it has taken this long just to get a listing of projects that we agree is accurate, so that we can begin prioritizing."

"You're kidding," Derrick protested. "When we talked on the phone in December, you said you'd get the projects defined, prioritized, and trimmed last December. What happened?"

"You wouldn't believe how hard it is to come up with numbers everyone agrees on!" Quinn answered. "We decided we really needed to know exactly how far beyond our capacity we were operating, so that we didn't cut more projects than we had to. The managing directors each gave me their project lists before our meeting in December. As I assembled a master list, I couldn't believe how different it was from the one I had generated. A lot of the smaller projects had just disappeared from the list. I think they were figuring that if some of their pet projects didn't get on the list, they could be completed and launched before the gears of our new process even get going. And do you remember that my data in November had forecast us operating at 225% of capacity in the first quarter of 1996 with declining rates into the future? Well, when I added up the managing directors' numbers, they showed us operating at only 135% of capacity in the first quarter—hardly enough to get worried about. You can see what the forecast looks like from this chart (included as Exhibit 6). You can imagine all the picking at the accuracy of the project list and the numbers for each project when I tried to start the prioritization process at that meeting last December.

"Then with all the year-end pressures, we just had to set this work aside for a month or so, until things were operating normally again. Even *I* have been too busy to work on this. But we've finally got a listing of projects which I think everyone will agree is accurate. I think we'll finally be able to make some real headway on prioritizing and cutting projects today—especially with you here to put some discipline in us!"

When Donaldson's meeting began later that morning of February 17, Donaldson turned the agenda to Quinn, who quickly handed it to Derrick with the question, "I think we've finally agreed that this is the set of projects we need to consider. There are 124 of them. How do you think we should go about prioritizing these, so that we can cut back on the lower priority ones?"

EXHIBIT 6 **Quinn's Initial Estimate of Project Overload, Compared to the Sum of Estimates Compiled from Managing Directors' Project Lists in February 1996**

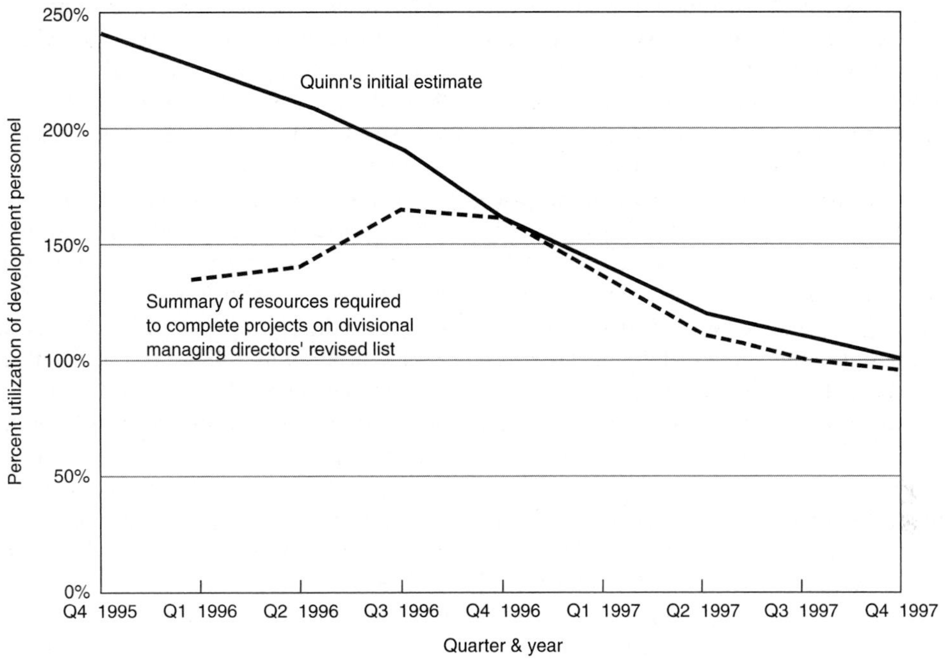

"Well," Derrick began, "if you remember from our seminar, the whole reason for the aggregate project planning tool is that it can help you link tightly your strategy with the set of projects that you execute. The way to go about this exercise is to set your strategy out as the criteria, and then assess which projects really fit, and which don't."

"We should be able to do that," Quinn added. "We just went through a strategy process last year, where we came up with a corporate goal and vision statement, and a strategy. I actually have an old transparency of the strategy here. Why don't I put it up on the screen, and then we can refer to it as we go down the list." Quinn then showed the statement of strategy, which was,

> The strategy of Kirkham Instruments is to grow profitably by designing, manufacturing, and marketing analytical instruments of exceptional quality worldwide. We will do this by understanding and anticipating the evolving needs of leading-edge customers, and to lead our industry in introducing products that address those needs.

Derrick then began taking the group down the list of 124 projects, trying to reach a consensus on the fit of each project to the strategy, by asking the group to classify projects as A, B, or C projects (with A being the

clearest fit fit with strategy). One hour later, before moving to project #11 on the list, Derrick interrupted the group. "I think I see a pattern here. We have 6 A projects, and 4 on which we can't agree between A & B. I don't think this will work."

"Do you know what the problem is?" volunteered Stephen Badger of the Spectrometer Division. "The strategy is so vague and general, almost any project fits. The only measure of strategic fit, actually, is growth and profitability. The A projects are the ones that look like they'll generate the most turnover and profit. It's that simple. Either we need to go back and re-do our strategy, to make it a lot more specific about what kinds of products and projects are our highest priorities, or we just need to call a spade a spade—calculate the return on investment for each project, and then prioritize them that way."

"I'm not going to let us open up that strategy thing again," Geoffrey Donaldson asserted. "We put a lot of time and thought into that strategy. I think it's sound. We *all* think it's sound. The problem is to *implement* it, not re-open it." In a whispered aside to Derrick, Donaldson then recounted how the Executive Committee had gone on a three-day retreat the previous summer into England's Lakes District, to hammer out a new strategy.

Donaldson recalled that the meeting at times had been very acrimonious, as different managing directors had very different opinions about what the future course of the company ought to be. "Just getting to the statement that we have here was a big achievement," he concluded.

"I agree with Geoff," added Christine Guynn. "It's a perfectly good strategy. We just need to get more sophisticated and accurate about the way we evaluate projects. Because the projections used in ROI calculations are just guesses anyway, everyone just games the system, so that we can't trust the numbers and have to rank projects based on politics and power. I know about a consulting firm, though, that has a methodology for scoring development projects using a number of different criteria. Maybe we should get them to help us. They would give us good, quantitative measures that would help us make decisions—not just which projects to cut, but which to put on the fast track, and so on."

In the ensuing discussion, Guynn's proposal gained substantial support. Donaldson then proposed, and the group agreed, that Kathleen Quinn would contact the firm and get the project going, if the price was reasonable. Donaldson then took the group through the host of other issues on the agenda, frequently asking for Derrick's input.

Quinn subsequently engaged the consulting firm, Fetzer-Woolley & Associates. The project started on April 15, and was slated to take about five months to complete. By early May, it had become clear to Quinn that Fetzer-Woolley required a far more intense level of support, in terms of the data they were requesting, than she had the time to give. Quinn consequently negotiated with Geoff Donaldson for the services of a member of Donaldson's planning staff, Cydney Peterson, who was assigned to work full-time managing the interface with Fetzer-Woolley. Peterson had joined Kirkham Instruments two years earlier after completing a 3-year stint in the London office of the American consultancy, Bain & Company. Bringing Peterson into the effort allowed Quinn to focus her energies more fully on her responsibilities to oversee the development of the critical software components of several key product development efforts, which had fallen behind schedule.

THE QUARTERLY EXECUTIVE CONFERENCE

On April 1, 1996, Marc Hoole, managing director of Waterloo Instruments Ltd., opened his portion of Donaldson's Quarterly Executive Conference by showing his aggregate project plan and funnel, which are reproduced

as Exhibit 7. Hoole had spent ten minutes describing several of his projects, when Donaldson broke in. "These tools are great, aren't they? I don't think we need to talk more about the project specifics. It's all right there. The position on the horizontal axis tells me what it's going to do in the market, and the vertical axis helps me understand the risk we're looking at. Are you comfortable with your portfolio, Marc?"

"We are," Hoole responded. "We're spending about 10% on breakthroughs, 30% on platforms, 60% on derivatives. Isn't that what Professor Derrick said good companies ought to be doing?" Donaldson then quizzed Hoole on the six projects in his funnel diagram which were nearing or had passed the launched gate.

Over the two-day conference, the other managing directors showed their portfolios and funnels, to similar effect. Donaldson suggested, and the others agreed, that these tools should become a regular part of the Quarterly Executive Conference. They liked the concise way they depicted what the divisions were working on.

The next week, Quinn called David Stock, VP of engineering and development at Waterloo, to compliment him on his work, and to be sure he understood that Donaldson would be expecting updated aggregate project plans at each of his quarterly conferences.

"You're kidding," Stock responded. "Those things are hell to put together. *You* have no idea, and I'm *sure* Donaldson has no idea, how much work is involved in putting together one of those aggregate project plan matrices. First, we've got to go through all of this data collection so we know what's on the matrix, and what's off. Then we need to know how big to draw each bubble. And then, we argued and argued about whether something was a breakthrough or a platform, or about whether a project's objective was to generate entirely new benefits to customers, or simply give us better performance to sell to existing customers. And you're telling me we've got to go through that drill once each quarter, just to put some pretty Powerpoint chart at Michael Donaldson's fingertips? What a nightmare. Is it worth all of this, really?"

"That's what he wants," Quinn responded. "I think it's worth a lot to have an informed senior management team. And I bet it gets easier."

PROGRESS IN PROJECT DOCUMENTATION AND GATEKEEPING

The funnel tools introduced in the seminar related to the use of documents and the establishment of "gates," or decision points, at clear junctures in the development fun-

EXHIBIT 7   Waterloo Instruments' Planning and Development

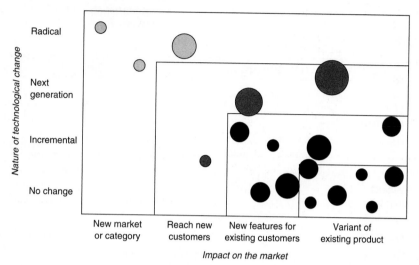

Aggregate project plan as of April 1, 1996

Development funnel as of April 1, 1996

Feasibility   Capability launch & roll-out

nel. The HBS faculty had recommended (see Exhibit 5) that product ideas be admitted formally into the funnel as funded projects with a project *charter*—a one-page document that described the concept, the role of the product in the company's product line architecture, and its aggregate project plan. The charter was designed to force project managers from the very beginning to integrate cross-functional viewpoints on every new product. Inputs on design for manufacturing; field service issues; pricing; how the company's sales representatives might react to the product; how it would be advertised; and so on: these issues needed to be addressed in the charter. Typically few answers could be given at such an early stage,

but if the charter forced the team to ask such questions early, the probability that all of the pieces of the puzzle would fit well together in the end, would be increased. The points at which these documents were submitted to management were called "gates." And senior management, acting as "gatekeepers," would then determine whether projects should be allowed to pass further along the funnel.

Quinn hoped that adopting this set of documents would be the easiest of the recommendations of the HBS faculty to implement, so in January of 1996 she had asked each member of her Development Council to ask each of his or her project managers to submit a project

EXHIBIT 8   A Sampling of Activities to Be Completed in Each of the Seven Phases of the Kirkham Instruments Product Development Process, Adopted in 1994

DOCUMENT TYPE:	DATA SHEET		DOCUMENT ID: WANG ID:	18-0295 7327x
TITLE:	Product Delivery Process Checklist			
DRAFT DATE:	00/00/00	**REVISION CODE:**	OA	**PAGE:**	1 of 7

17-0006 Product Delivery Process

Phase	Responsibility	Signature/Date Complete
(0) *Product Concept*		
Conduct Market Research/ Create Product Concept Document Create Draft MEC	Commercial Dev.	_____
Perform Preliminary Feasibility Studies	Product Dev.	_____
Approve Funding for Phase 1	BU Management	_____
Appoint Program Manager	Bu Management	_____
(1) *Product Definition*		
Appoint Cross-Functional Team	BU Management	_____
Complete Quality Function Deployment of Customer Requirements	Program Manager	_____
Finalize MEC	Commercial Dev.	_____
Define Program Strategy (including organization, legal, regulatory, marketing, development, and manufacturing strategies)	Program Manager	_____
Present Program Proposal to Business Unit Management	Program Manager	_____
Develop Phase 2 Plan	Program Mgr./Team	_____
Phase Closure Review	Project Team	_____
(2) *Product Requirements*		
Identify Critical Supplier(s) and Initiate Preliminary Qualification	Prod. Dev./QA	_____

charter or contract book, depending on the stage of completion of the project, for each project currently underway in his or her organization. Kirkham Instruments had been using a seven-phase "Product Delivery Process" for project management which the Development Council had adopted in 1994. The council members, working through staff associates, had painstakingly defined the development process in a manual which detailed what steps projects should go through in each phase, what in-

formation should be provided to senior executives at each decision point, and what criteria needed to be met in order to pass projects on to the next phase. (See Exhibit 8, for a sampling of pages from this manual.) Quinn wanted to switch to the much simpler three-phased system advocated by the HBS faculty group. Because the 1994 process already required project managers to create a project plan and to submit written reports in order to get management approval to pass to the next phase of the

EXHIBIT 8 (continued)

17-0006 Product Delivery Process

Phase	Responsibility	Signature/Date Complete
Identify Approval Team Members	Tech. Leader/ Program Mgr.	_____
Identify Technical Review Team Members	Tech. Leader	_____
Create Marketing Notice	Commercial Dev.	_____
Develop Program Timeline	Program Mgr./Team	_____
Complete Phase 2 Documentation	Project Team	_____
Instrument/Software Good Start Review	Project Team/ Mgmt. Board	_____
Phase Closure Review	Project Team	_____
(3) *Formulation/Design*		
Optimize Reagents/Assays (Bench-Level)	Tech. Leader	_____
Initiate New Raw Material(s)/Component Validation	Tech. Leader QA/ Pkg. Eng.	_____
Draft Preclinical Testing Protocol	Tech. Leader	_____
Draft Manufacturing Plan	Manufacturing	_____
Reagent/Assay Good Start Review	Project Team/ Mgmt. Board	_____
Create Initial Hazard Analysis	Tech. Leader	_____
Develop System Design Specification	Tech. Leader	_____
Communicate Product Architecture Using Renderings/Mock-Ups	Tech. Leader	_____
Perform Initial System Testing (including reagents, if applicable)	Tech. Leader	_____
Develop Preliminary Software Prototype and Breadboards	Tech. Leader	_____
Complete Phase 3 Documentation	Project Team	_____
Phase Closure Review	Project Team	_____

FINAL REVIEW: _____ **DATE:** _____

process, Quinn anticipated that project managers would simply have to re-package their most recent document, as either a charter or contract book, in order to comply with the new system. To make the gate documents easily accessible to the gatekeepers, who were the divisional managing directors, Quinn asked that all documents be posted in Kirkham Instruments' Lotus Notes system.

The faculty group had not recommended a specific form for these documents—suggesting that because their purpose was to force a discipline in thinking and cross-functional integration, the exact form of each document might vary, depending on project type. The charter for a breakthrough project, for example, would be expected to differ from what a derivative product's charter would look like. Hence, Quinn, after expressing support for this approach, did not specify to the Development Council members a particular format for the project documents.

By May 1996, charters or contract books for 37 projects had appeared in the Lotus Notes system. Quinn was disappointed as she reviewed these documents. Whereas the approach had been intended to force early, frequent, and even counter-intuitive cross-functional interaction from the inception of projects, it was clear that Kirkham Instruments' project managers and members simply did not have an intuition for how to do this, or even for why it was important. For example, Quinn remembered Derrick saying that in writing the project charter, teams might want to hypothesize what impression they wanted potential customers to have when they saw the first advertisements for the new product in the trade magazines in which Kirkham's divisions promoted their products. By thinking together about this from the outset, the team could then be sure that the product's features and styling were consistent with the impression they wanted to create with customers. Yet of the 21 project charters Quinn reviewed, not a single one reflected any advertising agency input. And there appeared to have been no input whatsoever from field service in most of the charters.

In a telephone conversation with Derrick in late May, Quinn observed that "Many of these documents were written by a single individual. And those which were team efforts, were put together by people who already habitually worked together. For example, the product planning people in our marketing departments have always had good relationships with product engineering. The charters and contract books all seem to reflect that."

To try to force project managers into earlier and richer patterns of interaction with people in other functional areas, Quinn designed a template for charters and contract books, which listed the topics that needed to be addressed in each document. She sent a memo with this template attached, to the divisional vice presidents of engineering and development in June, urging that its purpose was to encourage broader, out-of-the-box thinking, and was not simply another form to be filled out.

THE IMPLEMENTATION AUDIT

At the Quarterly Executive Conference in July 1996, Michael Donaldson asked the divisional managing directors how they felt the new system for managing new product development was working. The consensus was that they all felt much better informed about the status of projects, and were anxious for the Fetzer-Woolley evaluation of the potential of each project, which was due for completion in October. Each believed that with a more rigorous project evaluation methodology, they would be able to take a much more proactive role in prioritizing, accelerating, or killing projects.

"I hear what you're saying," Donaldson reacted. "I must say, however, that after the seminar last November, I somehow thought that things would change much more dramatically than they have. I suggest we invite Tim Derrick back for a few days; let him muck around and ask a lot of questions, and then give us a report of what he finds at our October Executive Conference."

Quinn extended the invitation to Derrick, who spent several days in late September interviewing members of the Executive Committee, several project managers, and a range of team members representing marketing, engineering, and manufacturing disciplines. He then synthesized and presented his findings at the Quarterly Executive Conference on October 1. As his summary transparency (reproduced in Exhibit 9) shows, it was a disappointing audit. Communication from the project teams to senior executives had improved, but at a cost which project managers deemed onerous. One project had been canceled.

"One of the most frightening things I've seen," Derrick observed, "is that project managers and members have lost their enthusiasm for this effort. And in some ways, the credibility of management has been damaged. Our crash course last February created expectations that some fundamental problems with the way Kirkham Instruments developed products would change, and things haven't changed. A number of people said they were just going to wait this one out, like they've waited out other programs in the past."

Derrick remarked that in addition to the added work which producing the planning charts and gate documents imposed on project managers, the most significant change they had perceived was that the divisional managing directors had become much more demanding of proof of a project's return on investment, at the charter gate to the funnel. As a result, a completely new *de facto* phase of the funnel had been created in front of the charter gate, in what was to have been a simple, low-budget "idea phase." Proponents of new project ideas were having to spend substantial resources to generate the information on technical feasibility and market potential, in order to get into the formal funnel with formal funding. "I think what has happened," Derrick noted, "is that everyone intuitively understands that you are working on too many things. But because you've not explicitly canceled any ongoing projects (about 16 had been com-

EXHIBIT 9   Professor Derrick's Conclusions from the September 1996 Audit

1. The primary use of the aggregate project planning tool has been to aid in upward communication—from project managers to managing directors, and to corporate management—about what the projects are. The tool has not yet been used effectively to link strategy with new product development.

2. The documents—charters and contract books—are also being used largely as communication tools. They have not been used to change the way or the timing in which the multi-functional aspects of each project are pulled together.

3. The decision-making behavior of gatekeepers has not been altered in the ways we had intended. Instead of using strategy as the primary criterion at the initial charter gate, they have actually become much more demanding of evidence of market potential and technological feasibility, before they will formally approve the charter.

4. The impact of this is that much work is being done, out of the sight of management, to obtain the evidence or results required in order to be approved at the charter gate. Essentially, we are forcing the start of projects outside of the funnel, thus circumventing our desire to control the number of projects in-house.

5. Projects are not reviewed on a regular rhythm. When a project falls behind on a critical milestone, its advocates find it easy to "hide" from review, until they have achieved the milestone.

6. The template for project documents introduced in June is most often used as a perfunctory checklist. There is little evidence that the process of writing gate documents is prodding people to think deeply in a cross-functional sense. Gatekeepers are just as guilty. They check to be sure each topic on the template has been addressed. The extent to which they demand that rigorous thinking be reflected in the documents is highly variable.

7. Employees are still working on 3–6 projects per person.

8. Project leaders really are not well trained in project management.

9. Personnel transfer inhibits embedding the new way of working in the culture. "As soon as I get someone up to speed, she gets transferred."

10. Rank-and-file employees are very skeptical that anything will change. They still see management as somewhat arbitrary or inconsistent in the way they do or do not make important decisions.

pleted in the past 10 months), the gatekeepers seem to have significantly raised the bar that projects must clear in order to get into the funnel. So you are moving slowly toward one of the important objectives of the system, but by very counterproductive means. Unfortunately, it looks as if the raising of the evidence bar at the beginning of the funnel is screening out ideas for breakthrough and platform projects."

Following the meeting, Quinn offered to drive Derrick back to Heathrow's Terminal 4, to get some additional time to talk. "Kathleen," Derrick began, "I wonder what impact the Fetzer-Woolley report will have on the Executive Committee. Do you think they'll accept the consultants' valuations of the projects, or will all the old disagreements that prevented action a year ago just resurface in this new context?"

"I actually think it will help," Quinn responded. "It's interesting. The Executive Committee needs numbers. That's how they make decisions. When the group needs to resolve an issue that hasn't been reduced to numbers, we seem to get bogged down. It's like we all speak different languages. But when alternatives can be expressed quantitatively, we can clip through decisions at quite a brisk rate. The numbers seem to make things so clear."

"What I don't understand about that," Derrick countered, "is that the only way Fetzer-Woolley is going to come up with numbers is to take the judgment of the people involved in each project and somehow quantify it. Why is it that the Executive Committee can't just make decisions on the basis of their own judgment? Why do they need to translate judgment into numbers, just so they can exercise judgment?"

"I think you've hit upon the answer, Tim. The issue is translation. The people on the Executive Committee don't speak the same language. They all bring to the table a different view on what our most important competencies are, what our most promising opportunities are, what our biggest problems are, and so on. This means that they apply different criteria to the same issue. Translating projects' potential into numbers puts it all into a common language that everyone understands," Quinn observed.

Derrick concluded, "I see what you mean. But I worry that they aren't going to trust the translators. They'll look at the translation—the numbers—and they'll say, 'Fetzer-Woolley didn't translate this one accurately. They didn't take this and that into account, and if they had, this project would rank a lot higher than they show it here. We just can't believe these numbers because some consultancy cranked them through their black box.' Then you're right back where you started. I hope I'm wrong, Kathleen. Because quite frankly, this has been a disappointing few days."

We've Got Rhythm!
Medtronic Corporation's
Cardiac Pacemaker Business

Clayton M. Christensen

The legacy of Medtronic Corporation, the company that created the cardiac pacemaker industry, is a proud one. Starting from its earliest pacemakers, which had to be carried outside the body, Medtronic had achieved dramatic improvements in the functionality, size, and reliability of these devices. In so doing it had extended the lives, and improved the quality of life, of hundreds of thousands of people in whom pacemakers had been implanted. The pacemaker has been designated as one of the ten most outstanding engineering achievements in the world over the past 50 years, along with the digital computer and the Apollo 11 moon landing.[1]

Medtronic, which in 1995 booked operating profit of $300 million on revenues of $1.7 billion, had been founded in 1957 in Minneapolis, Minnesota, by Earl Bakken, a researcher and inventor who had to his credit patents on several of the crucial technologies that led to the modern heart pacemaker. Pacemakers were small, battery-powered devices which, when implanted within a patient, helped a malfunctioning heart to beat in a steady, fixed rhythm. Because Medtronic was the first entrant into the pacemaker field and built a strong technological lead, it enjoyed a substantial portion (over 70%) of the market share for cardiac pacing through the 1960s.

Building upon Medtronic's legacy of leadership was not easy, however. In the face of increasing competition, rapid technological change, and tightening market and

Source: Professor Clayton M. Christensen prepared this case as the basis for class discussion rather than to illustrate either effective or ineffective handling of an administrative situation. Some of the data and names in this case have been disguised to protect the proprietary interests of the company. Copyright © 1997 by the President and Fellows of Harvard College. To order copies or request permission to reproduce materials, call 1-800-545-7685, write Harvard Business School Publishing, Boston, MA 02163, or go to http://www.hbsp.harvard.edu. No part of this publication may be reproduced, stored in a retrieval system, used in a spreadsheet, or transmitted in any form or by any means— electronic, mechanical, photocopying, recording, or otherwise—without the permission of Harvard Business School.
[1] This citation was made by the National Society of Professional Engineers in 1984.

regulatory demands for product quality, Medtronic saw its market share cut by more than half between 1970 and 1986. Though it had invested heavily in technology and product development over this period, much of that investment had been unproductive. Many projects failed to produce product designs that could be launched competitively, and the features and functionality of most of the products the company was able to launch lagged behind the competition. Several key employees left the company, seeing greater opportunity to develop their new pacemaker product ideas in new start-ups rather than within Medtronic. These competitors proved much faster than Medtronic at developing new products that advanced the state-of-the-art in pacemaking. Medtronic was also pummeled by two major product recalls related to product quality problems. Observers felt the company would have lost even more of the market during this period, were it not for its strong worldwide salesforce and the lingering legacy of its brand reputation amongst surgeons, the primary customer group.

Management changes which were initiated in the late 1980s, however, had sparked a dramatic reversal in the company's fortunes, and by 1996 the company had regained its position of product and market leadership. By all accounts, it was in front and pulling away from its competitors. On a pleasant Minneapolis spring afternoon in 1996, several members of the team that managed this turnaround—Steve Mahle, president of the Brady Pacing Business; Mike Stevens, general manager of the Pulse Generator & Programming Systems (PGPS) Division; Bill Murray, general manager of the MicroRel component manufacturing subsidiary; Director of Marketing Paula Skjefte (pronounced Sheftee); and Director of Product Development Technology Don Deyo—gathered to assess the progress they had made since they had taken the helm of the troubled division in the late 1980s. They were also anxious to understand whether the management structure and the processes, values, and resources they had created to achieve this turn-around were capable of maintaining the company's successful momentum in the future. This case recounts their achievements and concerns.

MEDTRONIC'S BRADY PACING BUSINESS

Medtronic's Brady Business Unit designed and built pacemakers that delivered a rhythm of electrical impulses to remedy a disorder called bradycardia, in which the heart's electrical system does not generate pulses to cause the heart to beat rapidly enough to sustain the body's normal activity, as described in Appendix 1.[2] Amongst its other businesses, Medtronic also had a Tachycardia Business Unit, whose products addressed the opposite malfunction—when the heart's electrical system generated too many beats. Because of the prevalence of bradycardia relative to other disorders in cardiac patients, the Brady Business Unit historically had delivered most of Medtronic's revenues, and an even larger share of its profits. Consequently, the health and vitality of the Brady Business strongly affected the corporation's overall financial performance.

The Brady Business Unit worked hand-in-glove with the component divisions of Medtronic in product development efforts, as shown in Exhibit 1. The Promeon Division, for example, developed new technologies to power pacemakers. In the early years of the industry's history in particular, battery technology had been a pivotal selling point because the battery could not be replaced: once it was depleted, a new pacemaker had to be implanted. Another division, MicroRel, designed and fabricated the critical hybrid microelectronic circuits in Medtronic's pacemakers. Located in Tempe, Arizona, it supplied proprietary circuitry to all of Medtronic's businesses. Work with MicroRel was viewed as a crucial connection in the development of new pacemakers, because of the increasing importance that integrated circuit (IC) technology played within these devices. Perhaps the most critical division for the Brady Business was Pulse Generators & Programming Systems (PGPS), headed by Mike Stevens. Unlike the other two component divisions that shared their services and output with other parts of Medtronic, PGPS focused on developing new products for bradycardia pacing, by translating customer and market-based inputs into product designs, and then worked closely with manufacturing to produce the final products. This involved design and assembly of the pacemaker as well as the programming unit, which typically sat on a table in the cath lab or operating room where the implantation was performed. Programming units allowed physicians to tailor the firmware in the pacemaker so that the frequency of the pulses it generated and a number of other attributes of the device matched the needs of each individual patient. The leads which carried electrical impulses from the pulse generator to the wall of the heart were designed by a separate leads group within the Brady Pacing Business Unit headed by Warren Watson.

HOW THE PACEMAKING LEADER LOST ITS RHYTHM

Product development at Medtronic historically had been supervised by its functional managers, who were intimately involved with each development effort during the company's early years. However, as the company grew, the functional managers became increasingly absorbed by operating responsibilities in their own functional organizations, making coordination across functions, in practice if not intent, a lower priority. The company responded by creating a group of project managers to coordinate the work of various functional groups. While this helped, most major decisions still had to be passed by the functional managers—"A legacy of how decisions had been made that still lingered in the organization," according to a long-time employee. The project managers' job was to try to get decisions to be made by the functional leadership—they only had minor authority to make decisions themselves.

"Planning new products is actually a lot more difficult in a business like this than it looks," reflected another experienced executive. "In some businesses the problem is a lack of great ideas. But in our situation—with rapidly changing technological possibilities, some darned good competitors and thousands of cardiologists out there with ideas for all kinds of new features, the opposite is true: We've always had *too* many ideas for new products. In our functional organization, without a single, coordinated process or person to articulate a product plan or strategy, development projects just started everywhere. When you had a good idea, you'd mock up something— either a real prototype or something on paper—and carry it around with you. Then when you'd run into Earl Bakken or another powerful manager in the hall, you'd corner him, pull your idea out of your pocket, and try to get him to support it. If his reaction seemed positive, then you would use that leverage to get a few friends to help you push it along. At some point you'd go to the engineering manager to get formal resources."

"The problem with this system was *not* that we were working on bad ideas. Most of them were technically sound and made market sense," commented Don Deyo, an experienced engineer and currently Director of Product Development and Technology. "We were trying to do

---

[2]The term "brady" derives from a Latin root meaning "slow." The opposite cardiac pacing disorder, tachycardia, took its name from a Latin root meaning "fast."

EXHIBIT 1 A Partial Organization Chart of Medtronic

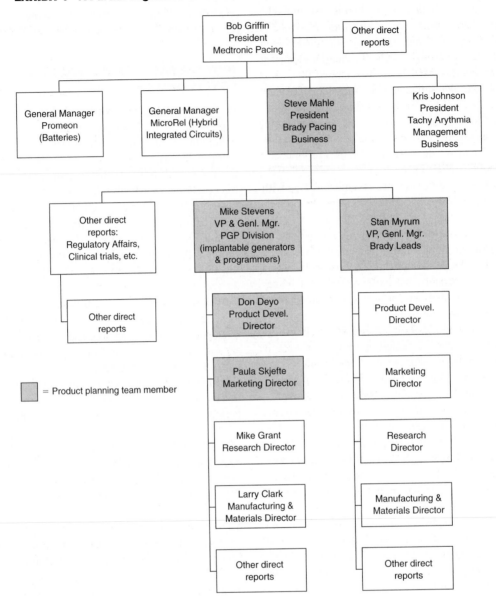

too many things, and no project got the focus and attention needed to get it done right. It was taking too long to get anything to market. We never got good at releasing new products, because you only get good at things you do a lot. Those that we did introduce often followed the lead of competitors. That's what happens when you continually try to respond to every new idea to come along."

"The problem then fed on itself," reflected Mike Stevens, general manager. "The development people would tell me that they could never get anything to market because marketing kept changing the product description in the middle of the projects. And the marketing people would say that it took so long for engineering to get anything done, that by the time they got around to completing something, the market demands would have changed. When customer requirements evolve faster than you can develop products, it becomes a vicious spiral."

In environments like that, it is *very* difficult to plan product families," Stevens continued. "If the company launched a product that subsequently could be modified or extended to create derivative models, it was a stroke of luck." Because of the *ad hoc* way in which new product development projects were conceived, Medtronic's project pipeline was made up of incongruous development cycles. Projects were separated according to whether they were single- or dual-chamber platforms. Each new model had largely its own unique circuitry, components, testing programs, casing, and battery. Due to the high costs of developing all these parts of the pacemaker, project managers battled each other for resources.

Although the company's reputation and strong sales-force relationships with surgeons kept disaster at bay, the company's performance suffered as a result of its disabilities in development. Between 1970 and 1986, it was almost always a competitor, not Medtronic, that introduced major new improvements to the market. For example, Cordis introduced the world's first programmable pacemaker in 1972; Medtronic followed in 1980. Cardiac Pacemakers Inc., a Medtronic spin-off, pioneered the first pacemaker with a long-life lithium battery in 1974. Even though the technology was available from a third-party supplier, Medtronic did not get its lithium battery-powered product out the door until 1978.

Although Medtronic introduced its first dual-chamber pacemaker during this period, it did not follow it with an improved dual chamber device for another eight years. Deyo explained, "We were working on next-generation dual-chamber products during all of those eight years. The problem was that just as we'd get ready to announce a new product, a competitor would come out with something better. So we'd force the funnel open again to allow for this new input, re-scope the project, and try to leap ahead of the competitor. Then just as we'd get ready with the improved version, a competitor would come in ahead of us with an even better product; and so on."

"I got so that I just didn't want to answer the phone because I was afraid there would be a salesman on the line wanting to know when we were going to come out with a product that was comparable to something a competitor had introduced," recalled Paula Skjefte, director of marketing. "I just couldn't give him an answer."

Field product failures compounded the problems caused by Medtronic's long development cycle. Its Xytron pacemaker line was recalled in 1976 after several units failed following implantation. And a few years later, physicians found that the leads on some pacemak-

ers they had implanted had disintegrated, so that the pacemakers' output was not getting transmitted to their patients' hearts. In total, Medtronic was forced to issue four different product advisories to warn that certain models were susceptible to malfunction. The result of these factors was a massive loss of share, from 70% in 1970 to 29% in 1986, as shown in Exhibit 2. Still, however, due to significant growth in the market, the company continued to report record sales and profits over this period, and for many in the company there was no cause for alarm.

"Medtronic was a really nice Minneapolis company," Don Deyo noted. This reflected in many ways the values of Medtronic's founder, who had a genuine reverence for every employee's contributions to the company's success. "But somehow in the mid-1970s, Deyo noted, "This attitude got out of hand. We dominated the market, and were very profitable. Because there was so little pressure on the business, we lost our intensity and willingness to focus our efforts."

A HOME RUN SAVES THE DAY

The company's decline was arrested in 1986—more by good fortune than any change in management practice, however. In the early 1980s a project leader, Ken Anderson, championed an idea for a "rate-responsive" pacemaker—a device which could sense when changes in body activity required the heart to beat faster or slower, and stimulated the heart to beat accordingly. Although most cardiologists Anderson spoke to thought the idea was impractical, and despite the indifference of most of Medtronic's staff, Anderson won the support of the general manager, and the two of them set up a dedicated team to pursue the idea. Its product, dubbed *Activitrax,* worked—technologically and in the marketplace. Cardiologists found its single-chamber design easy to implant, and its effect was nearly as good for patients as a dual-chamber pacemaker. Patients reported feeling stronger, because it would cause their hearts to beat more rapidly when they were working hard or exercising. And they reported feeling more rested in the morning, because *Activitrax* paced their hearts to beat more slowly when they were asleep.

The dramatic *Activitrax* therapeutic breakthrough literally saved Medtronic, because no other new platform products were ready for introduction until 1992. It did not, however, alter the way the company developed products.

EXHIBIT 2 **Changes in the Market Shares of Leading Pacemaker Manufacturers**

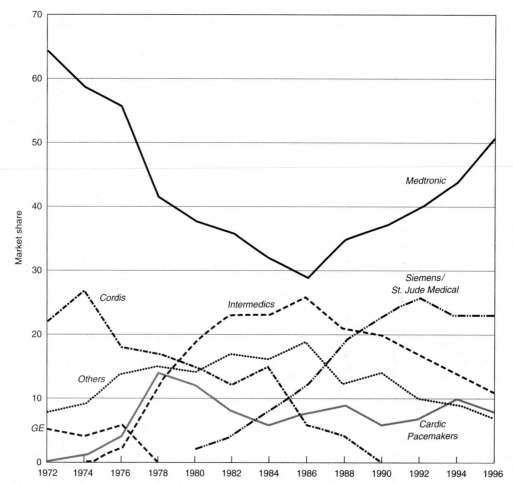

Notes: Over this period, ownership of several of these companies changed hands. Intermedics was acquired by Sulzer in the early 1990s. St. Jude Medical acquired the pacemaker business of Siemens; and Cardiac Pacemakers, a division of Eli Lilly, was spun off along with other of Lilly's medical device companies into an independent corporation called Guidant.
Source: Casewriter's estimates, synthesized from data provided by the company, by investment analysts, and by David Gobeli and William Rudelius in "Managing Innovation: Lessons from the Cardiac-Pacing Industry," *Sloan Management Review* (26), Summer, 1985, pp. 24–43.

THE TURNAROUND IN PRODUCT DEVELOPMENT

Though Medtronic's market position was helped by the success of Activitrax and by a serious product recall suffered by a principal competitor, the most dramatic changes in the company's market position were instigated when Mike Stevens was assigned to be vice president for product development of the PGPS Division in 1987. Stevens' career with Medtronic had begun in 1973, when Motorola decided to shut down its hybrid circuit manufacturing operation near Phoenix. Stevens and several other employees of the Motorola facility decided to continue the operation and obtained financing from Medtronic, which had been a major customer.

Stevens had watched Medtronic's struggles in product development from a supplier's viewpoint. "Though I didn't have a background in product development, I saw much of Medtronic's problem as Management 101. We had very strong functional roles. People were being measured by cost centers, and there was no accountability for the delay or failure of a new product. I felt the basic values and ethics of the company were still really strong.

But what needed work were its *processes*. I felt if we could get those straightened out, then we could bring the Brady business back to its past glory."

Stevens summarized key elements of his management philosophy as follows:

1. Commitments are sacred. The more responsibility you give to people to control their destiny, the more you can and must hold them accountable.
2. Create a sense of urgency by contrasting the excitement of bringing new therapy to patients, versus the consequences if your competitors are there first with better solutions. Don't waste time with excess travel or off-site meetings.
3. Are happy employees productive, or are productive employees happy? Stevens believed the latter, whereas Medtronic management had been acting as if the former were true.
4. Do nothing that separates management and employees. Management means responsibility, not status.

5. You only get what you measure.
6. Focus on gaining market share. Over time, this is the most accurate measure of your success.

Managers in the PGPS Division got a taste of Stevens' belief that commitments are sacred when, shortly after arriving at Medtronic, he held management to the project milestones they had agreed upon at the beginning of fiscal year 1988. Their incentive compensation was tied to these objectives, and 1988 was the first year in memory that management did not receive year-end bonuses that were tied to objectives.

Measuring Product Development Performance

Stevens implemented his measurement philosophy by focusing on four measures of product development performance, which corresponded to the achievements he wanted the organization to focus upon. These are described here:

Focus	Measure	Stevens' comments
Speed	Cycle time	"This is the time required to get a new product into the market. If I measure this, there isn't much else I need to measure. It forces you to do the other things right in product development, because you can't make mistakes, and you can't waste time."
Cost	Fully allocated unit product costs	"The reason we focus on fully allocated cost, rather than just viewing functional costs or direct product costs, is that it gets you thinking about market share, and the impact that unit volumes can have on your financial success. This is healthy thinking."
Innovativeness	Product performance relative to competitors	"This translates into market share, pure and simple."
Product quality	Field performance—defects per million	"In our business, you can't afford a field failure—because our patients count on us, and doctors can choose to go elsewhere."

Most people in PGPS welcomed Stevens' attitude. One commented, "I was just getting started as a project manager, and Mike was a breath of fresh air. His priorities were clear; I knew where he stood. He had a very different management style: very firm, assertive, thoughtful and focused. He was execution-oriented, and really held people accountable."

Processes and Practices

"This isn't a story about great management," Stevens emphasized. "It's a story about putting into place a set of

processes that helped a great team of people be as productive as they could be." The processes Stevens instituted had the following features:

1. *Speed* "Being fast to market eliminates *so* many other problems," commented Steve Mahle, who took over as president of the Brady Pacing Business in 1990. "The slowest part of our process was actually in deciding what needed to be done. We used to spend *lots* of time debating what we should do. One of Mike's greatest achievements was in cleaning up the front end. He did this by articulating very clearly what our

EXHIBIT 3   Process by Which New Product Concepts Were Defined at Medtronic

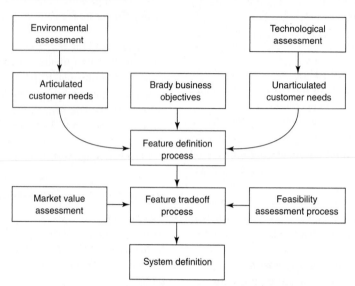

Note: throughout this process, as customers' needs were balanced against business objectives and technological feasibility, the marketing members of the Medtronic development teams repeatedly sought customers' feedback to the tradeoffs that were being contemplated.

strategy was, so that there were well-defined criteria that could guide these decisions. Then he created a process to get those decisions made."

Exhibit 3 describes the process by which new products were defined. An assessment of the competitive and customer environment was combined with a technology assessment to define the business objectives of each new product, and to clarify what the financial and competitive contributions of the new product needed to be. Stevens, who by 1991 had become division general manager, reviewed new product ideas according to their potential for meeting those business objectives. His staff, comprised of the managers of the division's marketing, research, development, technology, finance, human resources, and manufacturing functions, participated in this review with Stevens.

2. *Platform Strategy* Since product ideas in the earlier regime had originated in disparate parts of the organization and were approved and funded in independent decisions, it was quite common that products that required significant investments of time and money were not leveraged with derivative products that could extend their life and market reach. The highly successful Activitrax model, for example, did not spawn a single derivative product that offered different features, performance, or price points to the market. To devise an effective product line architecture built around product platforms, Mahle established a product planning team comprised of himself, Mike Stevens, Paula Skjefte, Don Deyo, and Stan Myrum, vice president and general manager of the business unit's leads division. This team defined a platform strategy around three key elements.

The first element was that the initial platform product had to be designed to accommodate the full range of derivative models from it, without significant redesign. "In other words," Stevens explained, "We designed the highest-performance, most fully featured version of the product at the outset." Medtronic then created derivatives by de-featuring and de-rating certain elements of that design, so that it could address other tiers of the market as well.

The second element of the platform strategy was enabled by the first. Historically, Medtronic had introduced new pacemaker features on its single-chamber models first, because they were technologically simpler to design and build. Once the features were accepted and the technology perfected in the single-chamber platform, the features were then moved up-market onto the dual-chamber platform. "The effect of this," Paula Skjefte noted, "was to force a lot of our lead physicians to continue focusing on single-chamber devices just so they could utilize our newest features. Once we began designing the platform to accommodate the full range of derivative models we planned to spin off from it, we didn't face the same constraint—it was just as easy to put the most advanced features on the dual-chamber model. This gave us a much clearer progression from basic, simple devices for the low end of the market to high-performance, fully featured models at the high end.

Skjefte continued, "The way we used to play in the low end of the market was to discount the price of our old model, after we had introduced a new one. This was ironic. Because we were reducing the cost of our products with each generation, we sold our high-cost models at the lowest prices, and our low-cost, newest models at the highest prices." The result was that there was little incentive to maintain a strong presence in lower tiers of the market. Under the new strategy, Medtronic addressed lower price points in its market with the simplest versions of its new lower-cost platforms. Hence, even as Medtronic was assuming a leadership role in features and functionality in higher tiers of the market, it strengthened its position in the low end as well.

The third aspect of Medtronic's platform strategy was to change the way platforms were defined. Formerly, Medtronic had thought of platforms in terms of physical architecture. Hence, it was inconceivable that a dual-chamber device could have been levered off of a single-chamber device platform. The projects were executed by completely different teams, and their designs therefore diverged from the very beginning. Under the new strategy, advances in microelectronics technology enabled so many of the most important capabilities to be designed into the hybrid circuit, that the circuit design constituted the platform. This circuit could then be modified quite readily, often through firmware modifications, to enable or disable particular features in the design of derivative products.

"I couldn't say whether Medtronic's decision to integrate backward into hybrid circuit production by starting MicroRel was good luck or good management," Stevens reflected. "But at this point the expert-

ise we have developed in circuit design and production is an enormous advantage. Our competitors outsource their hybrid circuits. But we have found that the hybrid is so integral to our functionality and our standards in quality and specifications, that suppliers just can't meet what we need. We can outsource things that are a little bit more modular—things that aren't so integral to the essence of our product. And being vertically integrated helps with speed. We can go down to MicroRel and shift priorities if something needs to be done quickly. We are also vertically integrated with our battery development and manufacturing."

Medtronic faced two particular challenges in implementing its platform strategy, Stevens reflected. "First, we learned that we needed to have the technology building blocks in place, before we could begin a platform project. Product development is not technology development—you can't have the uncertainties of advanced technology development on the critical path of a rhythmically executed product development project. Technology takes time to put into place, and it requires consistency in strategy and management methods, to tie advanced technology development with product development in a consistent, useful way. The second challenge we encountered was that platform projects required *much* more interaction and coordination amongst various individuals and groups in the company—within engineering, and across engineering, manufacturing, marketing, and finance—than other projects. You can't have a 'one-size-fits-all' habit of organizing and managing development teams, if you're really serious about a platform strategy."

Indeed, Stevens' decision to vest platform development teams with much greater decision-making authority—essentially making project managers the peers of functional managers—had a pervasive and sometimes disruptive impact on many in the organization. Heavyweight project managers with dedicated teams—from research, development, and marketing—oversaw the development of every platform. Other project managers, working under the supervision of the platform manager, took responsibility for derivative projects extending off of each platform. This represented a significant shift in the job of the company's functional managers. Their charge became providing trained, capable people to staff projects, and developing new technology platforms. "It became very clear, very quickly," observed Bill Murray, an electrical engineer turned project manager, "That project management was the path for career advancement. Even some of the functional managers left their positions to become project managers."

3. ***Project Documentation*** Previous agreements to initiate a project were often made verbally. "It was amazing how many misunderstandings and disagreements seemed to survive those verbal contracts," Don Deyo recalled. "You could leave a meeting thinking you had agreed on something, and learn a few months later that you hadn't. Then when we had to change something, the marketing and engineering people were always accusing each other of violating an earlier agreement. It's amazing in a setup like that, how easy it is legitimately and honestly to find someone else at fault." One way Stevens implemented his credo that commitments are sacred was to require two documents to be written at the start of the development phase of each project: a *Product Description* document, written by marketing, which detailed the customer requirements, product definition, and clinical performance expectations of the product; and the *Product Specification* document, written by engineering. This detailed the technical and cost specifications that the product would have to meet in order to meet the Product Description. Stevens required marketing to sign off on the Product Specification, certifying that there was a technical specification corresponding to each requirement in the Product Description. Similarly, engineering had to sign off on the Product Description, as a double-check that marketing and engineering were synchronized.

4. ***Phase Definition*** Stevens and Mahle defined a system of phases and project reviews, to which all projects would be subject. Projects started in a *business analysis phase,* in which the Product Description was written and the financial benefits of the project to Medtronic were estimated. Following review of the business case, the project would enter the *demonstration phase.* Here, the technological feasibility of the project was probed, to avoid putting the necessity of inventing something on the critical path of a development program. Rapid prototyping was emphasized in this phase, to identify problems and possible solutions as quickly as possible. If a product idea required a technology that was not well developed, Medtronic would shelve the idea, preferring to wait until the approach had been developed and proven in other markets. The Product Specification was prepared during this phase, and consistency with the Product Description was verified.

The major executive review came after the demonstration phase, where the proposed product's technological potential, competitive activity and market needs, and its volume, profit, and return on investment projections were rigorously reviewed. "I call this our *Commitment Review,*" noted Mahle. "I believe that language conveys intent. We had been plagued by waffling and compromise, and weren't doing what we said we would do." At one commitment review on a critical product, in fact, Mahle asked the team to stand up and make a verbal pledge to deliver to the customers and patients what they had said they would. "I believe in the power of personal commitment. Management tools are important, but tools alone won't do it."

Following the commitment review, projects went into the *development* or *commitment phase* of the process. "In the first two phases we have a lot of product ideas falling out or getting canceled, because we decide the market or technology just isn't there," Stevens commented. "But once projects enter the commitment phase, we expect 100% of them to be technically and commercially successful. There is no narrowing of the funnel after that."

The product planning team, which as noted above was responsible for establishing the product line architecture, also had responsibility for conducting the major phase reviews for each project.

5. ***Rhythm*** "There's a lot of uncertainty in new product development," noted Stevens. "You don't want to create additional uncertainty by the way you manage. The more predictability you can build into the development environment, the more productive your efforts will be." Stevens implemented this philosophy in two steps. First, he and Mahle fixed a date each month, a year in advance, when phase reviews would be held. Project teams approaching a review milestone thus could always count on Mahle and Stevens being available, to review their progress. Second, the management team established a schedule, far into the future, according to which new products would be developed and launched. "Of course we don't know what these specific products will be," said Stevens. "But we know the technology will always change, and we know the competition will always be trying to get ahead. It's like publishing a train schedule. It helps people to know when the next projects are scheduled to leave the station."

In retrospect, one benefit of setting a "train schedule" in advance was that there was less clamoring amongst Medtronic's marketers to revise objectives to include additional functionality or features after projects had begun. "In our troubled days," recalled Mahle, "No one knew when the next project was going to be started, let alone finished. Because of this, whenever a competitor came out with something, or an important physician came up with an important new idea, our marketing people were desperate to revise the charter of the product currently under development, to include that features. If they didn't get it on this train, when would they ever get it? Once we had a train schedule, they could relax. If we froze the spec and their feature or idea didn't make it on this one, they knew that in another 18–24 months, another train would be leaving the station, and they could get their idea on that one."

6. *Market Inputs* Medtronic also systematized the ways in which the company got input from customers, by revitalizing two eight-person physician review boards, which had previously been functioning but which had lost their impact on company policy, for each of Medtronic's pacemaker lines. These boards met twice each year to give inputs on the performance of existing models and suggest what functionality and features the company might incorporate in new models. "A big challenge with these boards," noted Paula Skjefte, was that "there is a strong tendency just to have experts on our boards. Life would be easier if we did that, but we wouldn't be getting the whole picture. Joe Average Cardiologist only spends about 2% of his practice on pacemakers. He's just not interested in spending a whole day on our board advising us about pacemakers. We want to be able to satisfy all the cus-

tomers, from the experts who want do their own programming, to the cardiologists who just want to get the pacemaker going with no hassle. Taking the pulse of the less demanding end of the market is actually a huge challenge." Once these boards were properly constituted and functioning, they became critical to Medtronic's ability to define the right pacing systems to meet clinical and customer needs.

RESULTS TO DATE

The results of the Medtronic team's efforts to put discipline into the Brady Pacing Division's product development operations have been remarkable, as summarized in Exhibits 2 and 4. The time required to develop new platform products was reduced by 75% between 1986 and 1996. Fully allocated product cost per unit fell 30%. Manufacturing defects per million units dropped by a factor of 4; and the number of field failures over the life of an implant dropped by 90%. And the company's share of the Brady Pacemaker market increased from 29% in 1986, to 51% in 1996. Medtronic was the leader in every segment of the market.

From July 1995 to July 1996, Medtronic replaced 100% of its products with new models. It was able to access every segment of the market, and became the highest-volume competitor in each—with ten derivative products built around a single platform technology.

"What's interesting," Paula Skjefte observed, "is now to see some of our competitors doing the same thing as we did in the past. There is a vicious cycle that almost got us, and is starting to hurt them. It looks like this: 1. When their share starts to decline, they start arguing over what

EXHIBIT 4   Improvements in New Product Development Performance at Medtronic, 1986–1996

Year	Platform name	Time* req'd. to develop platform	# of derivative models designed from this platform	Fully allocated manufacturing cost* per unit	Manufacturing defects* per million units	Manufacturing throughput time (days)
1986	Activitrax	160	1	140		30
1987						
1988						
1989						14
1990				120		
1991						
1992	Elite	140	1			
1993					270	
1994				110	150	8
1995	Thera	100	41	100	100	7

Note: To protect the company's proprietary interests, numbers in the third, fifth, and sixth columns whose headings are denoted by an asterisk (*) are indexed, where 1995 = 100

needs to be done and how to do it. They start more and more projects into the system, to placate these diverse opinions. 2. Because they aren't focused, it causes delays, and Medtronic gets its product out first. 3. They have to redirect their project to respond to our product, which slows them down. 4. They panic because we are getting way ahead, and try to make sure that the flagship product they are trying to launch has all the features and functions that will boost it ahead of the competition. 5. This takes even longer—forcing them either to introduce products that are not functionally competitive, or to rush something into the market that is potentially faulty, just to get something out there. 6. The effect of this is that they spend all the money required to develop and launch products, but it is wasted because it does not generate profitable revenue."

Stevens added, "People ask us what the secret is, to make a development organization work effectively. I tell them there aren't any magic bullets that kill the problems. It's just discipline. You need to do what you say needs to be done. You need to be in it for the long haul. There are no quick fixes. It's interesting how many people leave these conversations and then go off in search of an easier answer from some guru somewhere. It's amazing that the obvious isn't so obvious."

CHALLENGES FOR THE FUTURE

Success brought a new set of challenges to the Medtronic team, however. Internally, it was becoming clear that the job of changing company practices and culture would never be finished. Stevens noted, for example, that Medtronic's career path system constituted one of the most vexing challenges to implementing improvements. "When your best people are moving on every two or three years, you can never just sit back and say, 'It's working.' Because we're always losing the people we've trained, the understanding of what we're doing and why we're doing it has a very short half-life. We have to keep training and teaching and coaching. I suppose that someday these values and processes will become so ingrained that working this way will just be a part of our culture. But we sure aren't there yet. And probably by the time it gets deeply ingrained here, we'll need to unlearn this because something even better has come along."

"The new marketing challenges are formidable as well," Skjefte remarked. "We've always measured the performance of our products in terms of their therapeutic benefit—the extent to which the pacemaker can mimic the normal functioning of the heart's electrical system.

Now we have dual-chamber pacemakers whose rate varies with the patient's activity, whose batteries have a life far longer than the life expectancy of most implant recipients. Fifteen years ago pacemakers were not programmable. Today, our most advanced models have 200 parameters, which can be reprogrammed non-invasively using RF (radio frequency) technology. Today our models can sense and store all kinds of data about irregularities and other abnormal events in a patient's heart. Doctors can download this data with RF technology, simply by placing a device near the patient's chest. How much more do we need? I worry that we're getting to the point that "better" will no longer be valued as "better" by the mainstream cardiologists. How do you develop a stream of improved products if customers are genuinely happy with the performance and features in the products that they have today? In the future we'll need to change the rules of the game. We've got to figure out how to add value in different ways."

"Catching up to competitors was a very different challenge than it is now, to stay a generation *ahead* of them—because now we're the ones needing to define what the product generations must be," Don Deyo added.

Fortunately for Medtronic, experts continued to forecast strong growth for the pacemaker market into the foreseeable future, thanks to the bulge in the population most likely to need pacemakers created by the aging of the relatively prosperous "baby boom" generation in Western Europe, Japan, and North America. In addition to this growth, the large potential-markets for pacemakers in other parts of Asia, Latin America, and Eastern Europe, where economic growth was making advanced medical technology more affordable, defined even greater growth possibilities. This was especially true if the price of pacemakers (currently priced between $2,000 and $7,500, depending upon features and functionality) could be reduced significantly.

It also appeared in 1996 that the industry's competitive landscape had stabilized. Whereas 15 firms had entered the world pacemaker industry between 1965 and 1980, by 1996 only five of them remained. Medtronic claimed half of the market; St. Jude Medical (formerly Siemens) held 23%; Sulzer Intermedics 11%; and Guidant (recently divested by Eli Lilly) and Biotronik, a German firm focusing primarily in developing regions of the world, each accounted for 8%. Though several of these competitors were reeling from the rapid pace of product development that Medtronic had set, they were capable companies with substantial financial depth. In North America in particular, efforts of managed care providers to purchase larger volumes from fewer, highly capable suppliers with broad product lines had substantially raised the barriers to future would-be entrants into the industry.

"We've set some very different goals," added Steve Mahle. "We want to bring pacing to less developed countries. This will be a challenge to Medtronic, because our culture won't allow us to bring them substandard therapy just to make it affordable. We've got to find a way to bring them *appropriate* therapy at an affordable price. This will likely involve *very* advanced technology, and a massive effort at physician education. And we've got to figure out how to do all of this profitably.

"In developed countries, where we do 95% of our volume, our goal is to see that every patient has access not just to pacemaking therapy, but to *optimum* therapy—where the technology in their pacemakers is matched to their disease. For example, ten years ago only 30% of patients were receiving dual-chamber pacemakers. Today we're at 50%, but 70% really need them. This requires that we no longer just sell devices," Mahle continued. "We have to educate physicians, and help insurance providers understand that they should reimburse patients for devices that provide optimum therapy."

Skjefte described another dimension of the marketing challenge: "Now that we've taken the technological lead, we've got to work much more closely with our customers to understand how to make *them* more successful and profitable by using our products. This means not just the *physician* customers—cardiologists, electrophysiologists, and surgeons—but hospital management, payors, and buying groups.

Helping these customers become more profitable by using Medtronic devices loomed as a huge challenge, because the priority each placed on various aspects of a pacing system was different, and because the customers themselves often weren't structured to understand what was profitable for them. As an example, Medtronic had recently lost a major account, the Intermountain Cardiology Clinic in Salt Lake City, to a competitor which had undercut Medtronic's pacemaker price by nearly $1,000 per device. Although the Medtronic device was easier to program as the pacemaker was being installed, those responsible for maximizing the profitability of the clinic's "cath lab" (the operating room where pacemakers were implanted) determined that they would nonetheless maximize the cath lab's profitability by using the less expensive pacemaker.

The follow-up of patients with newly implanted pacemakers at this clinic was managed by a different out-patient profit center, however, and for *them,* use of the competing pacemaker proved much *more* expensive. All new pacemakers required some adjustments a few weeks after implantation, to address unique aspects of each patient's disease and lifestyle. Because Medtronic's product recorded data about the patient's heart functions within the pacemaker itself and allowed physicians to download and analyze this data and adjust the pacemaker easily through an RF device held close to the patient's chest, all necessary adjustments could be done in a single, 30-minute visit. The competitor's system, in contrast, required the patient to visit the out-patient clinic twice for adjustments, taking approximately 1.5 hours per visit. In addition, during the time between these visits (about two weeks) the patient had to carry a $500 "holter monitor" on his or her belt 24 hours per day, which recorded the heart functions as detected by a set of electrodes taped to the patient's chest. These additional monitoring and adjustment costs overwhelmed the money saved by purchasing the cheaper pacemaker. But because the savings and added expenses were incurred within two different profit centers of the clinic, it took enormous effort for Medtronic's salesforce to win back the business.

"These customers not only speak a different language than our traditional physician customers, but their knowledge and preferences are very heavily influenced by what pieces of the therapeutic puzzle they have responsibility for," Skjefe worried. "Somehow we've got to restructure our sales and marketing teams to better understand and address their concerns."

APPENDIX: THE CARDIAC PACEMAKER

Rhythmic contractions of the heart which pump blood through the body are stimulated by electrical impulses from the nervous system. Cardiac pacemakers either supplement or entirely replace the heart's own malfunctioning electric system. The heart contains four chambers—the right and left atria (singular: atrium) and the right and left ventricles. Blood flows from the veins of the body into the right atrium where it collects, and then is pumped into the right ventricle. The blood is pumped from the right ventricle to the lungs to obtain oxygen, and is then pumped into the left ventricle. The blood, now refreshed with oxygen, is then pumped from the left ventricle through arteries to all parts of the body.

To initiate the proper sequence of contractions, a normal electrical impulse originates in the sinoatrial (SA) node in the right atrium. This impulse then spreads

EXHIBIT 5   The Cardiac Pacemaker

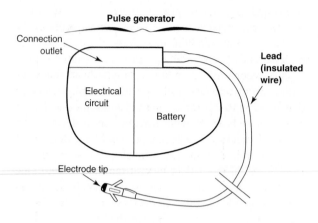

throughout both atria and stimulates atrial contraction. The electrical signal continues on to the ventricles through the atrioventricular (AV) node which delays the signal approximately 1/10 of a second to allow for the ventricles to fill with blood. When the ventricles complete their contraction, the signal is initiated once again in the SA node, creating a steady rhythm of heart beats.

Heart conditions necessitating a cardiac pacemaker can result from malfunction in any stage of this electrical system. Problems usually arise within the SA node and/or the AV conduction pathways, resulting in a slow, fast, or irregular heart rhythm. When the SA node malfunctions, the proper electrical impulses will not be generated to contract the atria and the ventricles at correct intervals. Patients with this condition suffer from sinus bradycardia: Their hearts beat at a persistently slow rate. When the AV node and its neurological pathways malfunction, the electrical signal that has just stimulated atrial contraction is blocked from initiating ventricle contraction. Consequently, a patient suffering from atrioventricular blockage would have a normal atrial beat but the ventricular rate would be too slow.

As diagrammed in Exhibit 5, the main body of the pacemaker is called the *pulse generator,* comprised primarily of electrical circuitry and the battery. An insulated wire called the *lead* connects this circuitry to the inside wall of one of the heart's chambers. The electrical impulse is created by the pulse generator and then delivered to the heart's muscle through the lead.

The first pacemakers employed a single-chamber system: They had one lead which was attached to the

right ventricle. These devices paced the heart at a fixed rate (usually 70 to 80 beats per minute), independently of the heart's intrinsic rhythm and changes in body activity. Because the heart and the implantable pacemaker were operating independently, the pacing was called "asynchronous."

The next generation of single-chamber pacemakers, which Medtronic invented in the mid-1960s, paced the heart on "demand," meaning that if the heart beat on its own, the pacemaker did not send a pacing impulse to the heart.

In 1981, Intermedics Corporation, an industry entrant whose founders included several former Medtronic employees, introduced the first dual-chamber pacemaker. This design utilized two leads—one in the right atrium and one in the right ventricle, which could sense and record the activity of both chambers and make sure that their contractions were synchronized. The dual-chamber pacemaker was capable of varying the heart rate by sensing or "tracking" atrial activity and then pacing the ventricle accordingly. Synchronizing atrial-ventricular contractions afforded the patient more flexibility in activity.

Pacemakers were implanted beneath the patient's skin near the heart, in a relatively simple procedure. Immediately prior to implantation, most pacemakers were placed in a programming device which typically sat on a table in the cath lab or operating room where the implantation was performed. This allowed the physician to program the firmware in the pacemaker so that the frequency of the pulses it generated and a number of other attributes of the device could be tailored to the needs of each individual patient.

The lead on the single-chamber design was implanted into the right ventricle relatively easily. Attaching the lead of the dual-chamber pacemaker, however, required much greater surgical skill, because the locations in the atrium were tricky to access, and attaching the lead to the smooth atrial chamber wall was difficult. This difficulty, coupled with its higher cost, had kept the dual-chamber pacemaker's share of the total market at about 20% throughout the 1980s, despite its superior functionality. Device and procedural innovations in the 1990s had reduced these barriers, however, so that use of dual-chamber devices became much more common.

The New Product Development Map

Steven C. Wheelwright and W. Earl Sasser, Jr.

No business activity is more heralded for its promise and approached with more justified optimism than the development and manufacture of new products. Whether in mature businesses like automobiles and electrical appliances, or more dynamic ones like computers, managers correctly view new products as a chance to get a jump on the competition.

Ideally, a successful new product can set industry standards—standards that become another company's barrier to entry—or open up crucial new markets. Think of the Sony Walkman. New products are good for the organization. They tend to exploit as yet untapped R&D discoveries and revitalize the engineering corps. New product campaigns offer top managers opportunities to reorganize and to get more out of a sales force, factory, or field service network, for example. New products capitalize on old investments.

Perhaps the most exciting benefit, though, is the most intangible: corporate renewal and redirection. The excitement, imagination, and growth associated with the introduction of a new product invigorate the company's best people and enhance the company's ability to recruit new forces. New products build confidence and momentum.

Unfortunately, these great promises of new product development are seldom fully realized. Products half make it; people burn out. To understand why, let's look at some of the more obvious pitfalls.

1. *The moving target.* Too often the basic product concept misses a shifting market. Or companies may make assumptions about channels of distribution that just don't hold up. Sometimes the project gets into trouble because of inconsistencies in focus; you start building a stripped-down version and wind up with a load of options. The project time lengthens, and longer projects invariably drift more and more from their initial target. Classic market misses include the Ford Edsel in the mid-1950s and Texas Instruments' home computer in the late 1970s. Even very success-

ful products like Apple's Macintosh line of personal computers can have a rocky beginning.

2. *Lack of product distinctiveness.* This risk is high when designers fail to consider a full range of alternatives to meet customer needs. If the organization gets locked into a concept too quickly, it may not bring differing perspectives to the analysis. The market may dry up, or the critical technologies may be sufficiently widespread that imitators appear out of nowhere. Plus Development introduced Hardcard, a hard disk that fits into a PC expansion slot, after a year and a half of development work. The company thought it had a unique product with at least a nine-month lead on competitors. But by the fifth day of the industry show where Hardcard was introduced, a competitor was showing a prototype of a competing version. And within three months, the competitor was shipping its new product.

3. *Unexpected technical problems.* Delays and cost overruns can often be traced to overestimates of the company's technical capabilities or simply to its lack of depth and resources. Projects can suffer delays and stall midcourse if essential inventions are not completed and drawn into the designers' repertoire before the product development project starts. An industrial controls company we know encountered both problems: It changed a part from metal to plastic only to discover that its manufacturing processes could not hold the required tolerances and also that its supplier could not provide raw material of consistent quality.

4. *Mismatches between functions.* Often one part of the organization will have unrealistic or even impossible expectations of another. Engineering may design a product that the company's factories cannot produce, for example, or at least not consistently at low cost and with high quality. Similarly, engineering may design features into products that marketing's established distribution channels or selling approach cannot exploit. In planning its requirements, manufacturing may assume an unchanging mix of new products, while marketing mistakenly assumes that manufacturing can alter its mix dramatically on short notice. One of the most startling mismatches we've encountered was created by an aerospace company whose manufacturing group built an assembly plant too small to accommodate the wing-span of the plane it ultimately had to produce.

Thus new products often fail because companies misunderstand the most promising markets and channels of distribution and because they misapprehend their own technological strengths or the product's technological challenges. Nothing can eliminate all the risks, but clearly the most important thing to do early on when developing a new product is to get all contributors to the process communicating: marketing with manufacturing, R&D with both. Products fail from a lack of planning; planning fails from a lack of information.

Developing a new generation of products is a lot like taking a journey into the wilderness. Who would dream of setting off without a map? Of course, you would try to clarify the purpose of the journey and make sure that needed equipment is available and in order. But once committed to the trip, you need a map of the terrain, something everybody can study—the focus for discussion, the basis for planning alternative courses. Knowing where you've come from and where you are is essential to knowing how to get where you want to go.

MAPPING EXISTING PRODUCTS

We have often used this analogy of a map with corporate managers involved in product development, and gradu-

EXHIBIT 1   Generic Product Development Map

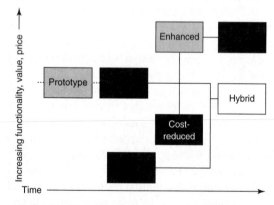

─────── **Development work** Concept; functional prototype
▨ **Engineering prototype** Leads to pilot production and ramp-up offering
■ **Core** Refined from initial prototype; becomes the standard offering

Leveraged products
▨ **Enhanced** Adds distinctive features to the core for identified market segments
■ **Customized** Distinctive features in small lots built for specific distribution channels of customers
■ **Cost-reduced** Stripped-down and/or low manufacturing cost version of core product for low end
☐ **Hybrid** A new design, developed by merging characteristics of two core products

ally it became clear to us that an actual map is needed, not just an analogy. Managers need a way to see the evolution of a company's product lines—the "where we are"—in order to expose the markets and technologies that have been driving the evolution—the "where we've come from." Such a map presents the evolution of current product lines in a summary yet strikingly clear way so that all functional areas in the organization can respond to a common vision. The map provides a basis for sharing information. And by enabling managers to compare the assumptions underlying current product lines with the ideal assumptions of new research, it points to new market opportunities and technological challenges. Why, for example, should an organization build for department stores when speciality discount outlets are the emerging channels of distribution? Why bend metals when you can mold ceramics?

Exhibit 1 illustrates a generic map that indicates how the product offerings in one generation may be related to each other. These relations are the building blocks that allow us to track the evolution of product families from one generation to another.

The map categorizes product offerings (and the development efforts they entail) as "core" and "leveraged" products, and divides leveraged products into "enhanced," "customized," "cost reduced," and "hybrid" products. (These designations seem to cover most cases, but managers should feel free to add whatever other categories they need.) A core product is the engineering platform, providing the basis for further enhancements. The core product is the initial, standard product introduced. It changes little from year to year and is often the benchmark against which consumers compare the rest of the product line.

Enhanced products are developed from the core design; distinctive features are added for various, more discriminating markets. Enhanced products are the first products leveraged from the capabilities put in place to produce the core and the first aimed at new or extended market opportunities. Often companies even identify them as enhanced versions, for example, IBM's Display-Write 3.1 is an enhanced version of DisplayWrite 3. But a leveraged product isn't necessarily more costly: The idea is simply to get more out of a fixed process—more "bang for the buck." As companies leverage high-end products, they may customize them in smaller lots for specific channels or to give consumers more choice. The cost-reduced model starts with essentially the same technology and design as the core product but is a stripped-down version, often with less expensive materials and lower factory costs, aimed at a price-sensitive market. (Think of the old Chevrolet Biscayne, which was many times the vehicle of choice for taxicabs and business fleets.)

Finally, there is the hybrid product, developed out of two cores. The initial two-stage thermostat products—accommodating a daytime and nighttime temperature setting—were hybrids of a traditional thermostat product and high-end, programmable thermostat lines.

On the generic map, from left to right is calendar time, and from bottom to top designates lower to higher added value or functionality, which usually also means a shift from cheaper to more expensive products.

These distinctions—core, hybrid, and the others—are immediately useful because they give managers a way of thinking about their products more rigorously and less anecdotally. But the various turns on the product map—the various "leverage points"—also serve as crucial indicators of previous management assumptions about the corporate strengths and market forces shaping product evolutions.

A map that shows a proliferation of enhanced products toward the high end, for example, says something important about the market opportunities managers identified after they had introduced the core. A map's configuration raises necessary questions about dominant channels of distribution—then and now. That products could have been leveraged in particular ways, moreover, says

something important about in-house technological and manufacturing capabilities—capabilities that may still exist or may need changing. The map generates the right discussions. When managers know how and why they have leveraged products in the past, they know better how to leverage the company in the present.

THE FIRST GENERATION

How can managers plan, develop, and position a set of products—that is, how do they build a dynamic map? With the generic map in mind, let us track offerings from generation to generation, as shown in Exhibit 2. Imagine a very simple line of vacuum cleaners, Coolidge Corporation's "Stratovac," introduced, say, in 1952. The core product, the Stratovac, was a canister-type appliance with a 2.5 horsepower motor. Constructed mainly from cut and stamped metals, it was distributed through department stores and hardware chains.

The following year, reaching for the somewhat more affluent suburban household, Coolidge brought out the "Stratovac Plus," an enhanced Stratovac delivered in a choice of three colors, with a 4 horsepower motor and a recoiling cord. In 1959, the company introduced the "Stratovac Deluxe"—a Stratovac Plus with a vacuum resistance sensor (which cut off the power when the bag was full) and a power head with a rotating brush for deep pile or shag carpeting. By 1959, the basic Stratovac

EXHIBIT 2 The First Generation of Coolidge Vacuum Cleaners (1952–1968)

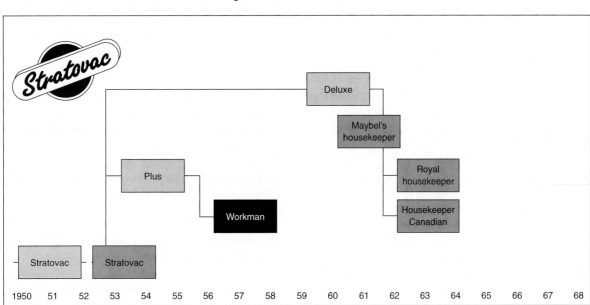

cost $89, the Stratovac Plus, $109, and the Stratovac Deluxe, $159.

To reach the industrial market at $79, Coolidge had decided to offer the "Stratovac Workman," a stripped-down Plus model—one color, no recoiling cord. That was introduced in 1956. And when Deluxe sales rocketed, Coolidge offered Maybel's department store chain a customized version of it, the Stratovac "Maybel's Housekeeper." This came out in 1960, in Maybel's blue gray, with the power head. The price was "only" $129. (Coolidge eventually customized the "House-keeper Canadian" for the Simpton's chain in Canada and the "Royal Housekeeper" for the Mid-Lakes chain in England.)

Again, this is a simple product line, but even so, the map raises interesting questions, especially for younger managers who came after this era. Why the Stratovac Plus? Why a proliferation of products toward the high end?

In fact, during the 1950s, most companies marketed home appliances through department stores with product families visibly shaped by the distribution channels. Products stood side by side in the stores, to be demonstrated by a salesperson. The markup was similar for each product on the floor.

What differentiated products in product families at the time was an appliance manufacturer's reach to satisfy more or less obvious customer segments—customers differentiated by factors like income and marital status. (In the 1950s, most vacuum cleaner purchasers were women, with more or less money, time, and patience.)

How Coolidge leveraged its products also points to certain fixed—and not especially unique—manufacturing capabilities. During the 1950s, company engineers designed appliances for manual assembly and traditional notions of economies of scale. By the end of the 1950s, Coolidge acquired new vacuum sensor innovations from the auto industry. It also learned certain flexible manufacturing techniques, making different colors and options possible.

By 1958, Coolidge had solved most of the technical problems of the Stratovac line and had recruited a number of ambitious design engineers to integrate vacuum sensor and power heads into the line. The life cycle of the product—including development time, which stretched back to 1949—was typical for core products of that time: 10 to 15 years. Demand for the Stratovac remained strong throughout the 1950s, and Coolidge sold to department stores in roughly the same proportion as its competition, except for companies organized around the door-to-door trade.

The company's increased (and not fully utilized) technical competence and the steadiness of its key distribution channels are crucial pieces of information to add to the map (see Exhibit 3). The map summarizes technical competence in the oval beneath the product lines and Coolidge's gross sales by distribution channel in the box graph. The fastest growing distribution channel in the industry—in this case, department stores—is shaded for emphasis.

THE SECOND GENERATION

With so much technical talent in-house, and a society growing increasingly affluent, Coolidge could not be expected to rest on the Stratovac's success indefinitely. Sales were steady, but by the mid-1960s customers assumed there would be some innovations. The age of plastics was dawning; the vanguard of the baby boom was taking apartments; it was the "new and improved" era.

Moreover, marketing people at Coolidge began to detect a new potential market at the low end. People who had relied on their Stratovacs for a decade were looking around for a second, lighter weight appliance for quick cleanups or for the workroom or garage. Lighter weight and cheaper naturally meant more reliance on plastic components.

In the early 1960s, Coolidge managers decided on two product families, each with its own core product (see Exhibit 4). The design team that had brought out the old core Stratovac would handle the "Stratovac II," and company new hires would design a second line, the all-plastic, mass-produced "Handivac" ("any color, so long as it's beige").

The Stratovac II, introduced in 1968, was heavier and had a 4.3 horsepower motor, resulting in a slightly noisier operation, "jet noise," which the marketing people reasoned would actually increase respect for its power. Half of the case was now plastic for a "streamlined" appearance. The core Stratovac II boasted a new dust-bag system, which virtually eliminated the need for handling dust. A retractable cord was also standard.

The Stratovac II "Sentry," an enhanced version of the core, included electronic controls for variable speed and came in many colors. The Stratovac II "Imperial," like the old Deluxe model, came with the power head. The Stratovac II Workman continued to sell steadily to the

EXHIBIT 3   The First Generation of Coolidge Vacuum Cleaners (1952–1968)

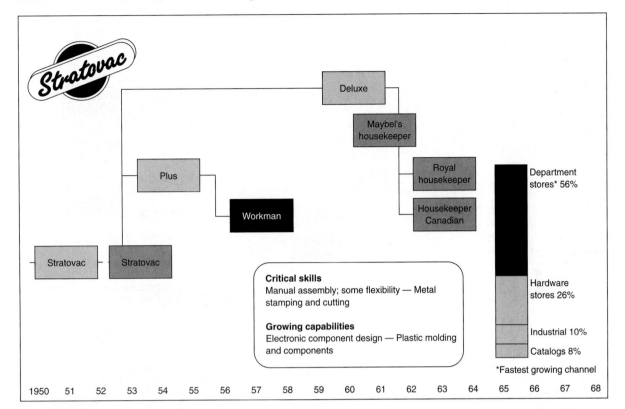

light industrial market, as did the Stratovac II House-keeper line to the department store chains that still sold the vast majority of units.

Most notable about the Stratovac II was how little changed it was, certainly on the manufacturing end. Assembly was still chiefly manual, along the lines of the 1950s—no priority given to modularity, design for manufacturability, or any of the considerations that would drive designers later on. There was some outsourcing of components to Mexico and Taiwan but no real attention to automation. The only significant change in the Stratovac II came in 1973, when inflationary pressures pushed management to develop a fully plastic casing and critical plastic components—in effect, a hybrid developed by merging technologies of the high-end vacuum cleaner with the low-end Handivac.

Handivac, the second core product, introduced in 1969, was something of a disappointment—mostly because of the inexperience of the team managing its development. Reliability was a problem, given Handivac's

almost complete dependence on plastic components, components subjected to higher than expected temperatures from an old, slightly updated 2.5 horsepower motor. Weight was also a problem: It was not as light as promised. Mass-production lines, which were partially automated, were considered a success when they were finally debugged.

Perhaps the greatest problem with the Handivac, however, was the fact that, like the Stratovac II, it was sold mainly through department stores and hardware chains, where markups were too large to permit it a significant advantage over the more expensive core product. Handivac sold for $79, while the Stratovac II sold for $99. Handivac managers tried to cut costs by going to an overseas supplier for a lighter weight, somewhat less powerful motor—over the vehement objections of Stratovac II designers, who had depended on Handivac's participation in their motor plant to keep their own costs in line.

Eventually, Handivac introduced a cost-reduced "Handivac 403," which sold for $69, importing a 3.0

EXHIBIT 4   The First and Second Generations of Coolidge Vacuum Cleaners (1952–1978)

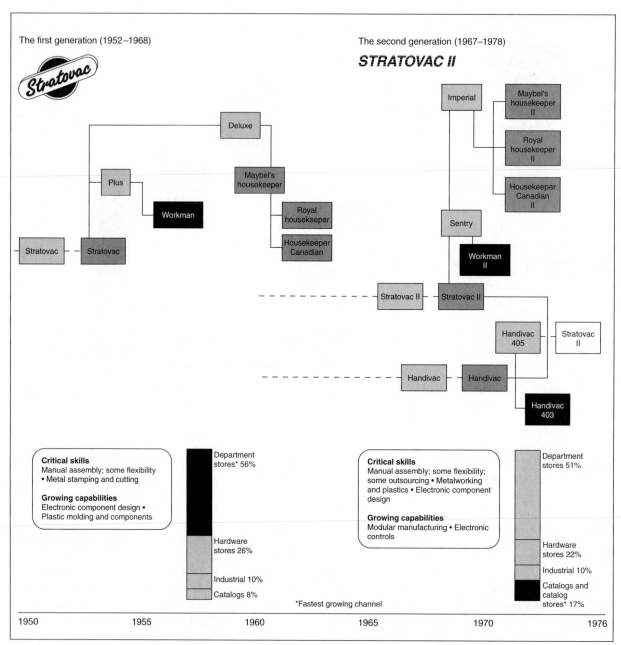

horsepower motor and cord subassembly from Japan. The enhanced "405" sold for $83. Handivac engineers began at this time to interact with Japanese manufacturing managers. But there were still no distribution channels where Handivac could enjoy the "price busting" opportunity it needed. The most promising channel, though hardly dominant, was the growing chains of catalog stores, which sold the Handivac 403 for $63, a 10 percent reduction in the department store price.

THE THIRD GENERATION

During 1976 and 1977, a number of external and internal pressures led to a redesign of the entire product line. Department stores were still the major source of revenue, but competitors were proliferating and the Stratovac II group felt the need to offer an increasing number of more enhanced and more customized products to maintain demand at the profitable high end. Consumers would pay a premium, marketing people believed, only if the company could produce so many versions that all customers felt they were getting the right color with the right options. Moreover, Coolidge had canvassed Stratovac II customers, who hadn't appreciated the "jet sound," as designers had assumed. Bulk was also a problem, as was the vacuum's unattractive look.

Inside the company, Coolidge's two design teams had become more cooperative, particularly as the advantages of molded plastic became obvious to everyone. The hybrid Stratovac II, which had been redesigned in plastic wherever possible, was something of a victory for the young Handivac designers over the more traditional group. Flexibility and cost were the keys to satisfying many markets, and plastics answered both needs. Eventually the more traditional designers also came to see the advantage of going to Japan for a smaller, lighter, more reliable motor—and for a number of subassemblies critical to the company's goal of offering arrays of options.

Concurrently in the mid-1970s, the Handivac designers were pressing for a complete merging of the design engineering teams and for studying Japanese manufacturing techniques. They argued that if flexibility, cost, and quality were going to be crucial, the manufacturing people would have to become more involved in product design. The young guard also believed that Coolidge could produce motors domestically—at required levels of quality—if it adopted certain innovations in machine tool and winding automation and instituted statistical process control at its existing motor plant.

Where the younger design group still lacked credibility, however, was on the bottom line. Top management was reluctant to give up on a two-track approach when the Handivac group had failed to deliver an appliance that made even as much as the Housekeeper line. The number of catalog stores was growing, and newer discount appliance chains were springing up in big cities, but the Handivac faced intense competition. Could the younger designers hope to come in with enough products, offering enough features, and at low enough costs to meet this competition?

In the end, Coolidge management decided to develop two core product families in its third generation (see Exhibit 4). The Stratovac II team redesigned the high-end vacuum cleaner in six models, the "Challenger 6000"

series. All appliances in this series came with a power head and a new bag system. By steps—6001, 6002, and upward—consumers could buy increasingly sophisticated electronic controls. And they could order the 6004 and 6005 in an array of colors.

The 6000 series was constructed almost entirely of molded plastic. Manufacturing came up with an automated way of applying hot sealant to critical seams, and the Challenger's motor was quieter. Top management agreed with the younger engineers that a more advanced motor factory could be constructed in the United States. The design teams didn't merge, but they found themselves working more closely together and increasingly with manufacturing.

The traditional design group simultaneously came out with the "Pioneer 4000" series. This was a middle-range product, somewhat smaller than the Challenger 6000, and not offering a power head. The marketing people felt that department stores would want a cost-reduced model to compete with the proliferating "economy" products that discount chains were now offering. (The 4001, 4002, and 4003 were distinguished, again, by electronic controls.) The Pioneer 4000 series was leveraged largely from the Challenger 6000 as a cost-reduced version.

Since both series offered stripped-down models, Coolidge did not introduce a specific industrial product and eliminated the Workman. Coolidge executives also believed that it was no longer worthwhile to customize models for particular department stores where margins were shrinking, so they eliminated the Housekeeper line.

A year after they introduced the Challenger 6000, the Handivac team brought out its new series of products, the "Helpmate." With minor modifications, Helpmate was customized as "Helpmate SE," targeted at different low-end market segments—college students, apartment dwellers, do-it-yourselfers, and the industrial market. The cleaner was lightweight. Attachments varied, as did graphic design: The company expected a Spartan gray color and a longer hose to appeal to commercial customers and bright pastels and different size brushes to appeal to women college students.

The key to the Helpmate line, however, was its manufacturing. The motor was no longer outsourced, and designers worked with manufacturing engineers on modular components and subassemblies. Top management agreed to set aside manufacturing space in the assembly plants for cellular construction of the Helpmate so that the company could respond quickly to demand for particular models. And Helpmate came in at two-thirds the price of the Pioneer 4000.

There was still some debate among Helpmate's product development team members about most likely channels. Some saw it designed only for discount chains and catalog stores, which by 1978 had pretty much eclipsed hardware stores. Others saw the Helpmate as a low-end product for department stores too. In the end, Helpmate was a smash in the discount stores and all but disappeared from department stores.

THE NEXT GENERATION?

Imagine that Coolidge managers are gathered in 1985 to consider the company's future. Their three-generation map has simplified a great deal of information—information the managers might intuitively understand but could not have looked at so clearly before. Where can they go from here?

Looking at their map, it's clear that Coolidge's product offerings are not appropriately matched to the new environment. They have aimed most of their products at department stores, and now discount chains are growing at a tremendous rate. They had devoted too much attention to figuring out how to leverage products at the high end, when the big battle was shaping up at the low end. Now Coolidge's managers wonder how long it will be before power options and accessories show up on cheaper, sturdier import lines distributed to high-volume outlets.

More growth in the company's manufacturing capabilities is obviously very important now. The map indicates the growing reciprocity between design and manufacturing engineers, owing largely to the initiatives of the younger design group. It would not be hard to imagine a merging of all engineering groups and the use of temporary dedicated development teams at this point. Product life cycles have obviously been shrinking; designers have to think fast now and cooperate across functional lines. To bring out a new line of inexpensive products that are both reliable and varied in options, Coolidge will need automated, flexible manufacturing systems. This development means bringing all parts of the company together—designers with marketing, manufacturing with both. It means, interestingly enough, a need for even clearer, more complete new product development maps.

The finished product development map presented in Exhibit 5 may appear elementary, but managers who have mapped their products' evolution have experienced substantial payoff in several areas. First, the map can be extremely useful to product development efforts. It helps focus development projects and limit their scope, making them more manageable. The map helps set specifications and targets for individual projects, provides a context for relating concurrent projects to one another, and indicates how the sequence of projects capitalizes on the company's previous investments. These benefits do much to minimize the likelihood of encountering two of the pitfalls we identified at the outset of this article, the moving target and the lack of product distinctiveness.

A second important benefit is the motivation the map provides the various functional groups—all with a stake in effective product development—to develop their own complementary strategies. As illustrated in the Coolidge Corporation example, the product development map raises a number of issues regarding distribution channels, product technology, and manufacturing approaches that must be answered in all parts of the company if the map is to represent the organization's agreed-on direction.

This point brings up the need for "submaps" in each functional area. In the Coolidge case, the first couple of product generations may not have shown the need for a more careful distribution channel map, but by the third the need is painfully clear. Capturing other strategic marketing variables in, say, a price map, a competitive product positioning map, and a customer map would enable the marketing function to identify and present important trends in the marketplace, define targets for future product offerings, and provide guidance for developing and committing sales and marketing resources.

Equally apparent by the third generation is the need for supporting maps in design engineering. A set of design engineering submaps can produce a clearer sense of the mix of engineering talent the company requires, how it should be organized and focused, and the rate at which the company should bring new technologies into future product generations. These maps would not only help managers integrate design resources with product development efforts but would also ensure that they hire and train new employees in a timely and effective manner and that they focus new project tools (such as computer-aided engineering) on pressing product development needs. The key is achieving technical agreement in advance of product development.

Toward the end of the third generation at Coolidge, the map reveals the need for more detailed manufacturing functional maps to bring out issues raised in the "critical skills" oval. Such maps would focus on strategic issues relating to manufacturing facilities, vendor relationships, and automation technology.

Again, the development of such functional submaps not only benefits manufacturing but also helps the company maximize the return on new product development

EXHIBIT 5   The Coolidge Vacuum Cleaner

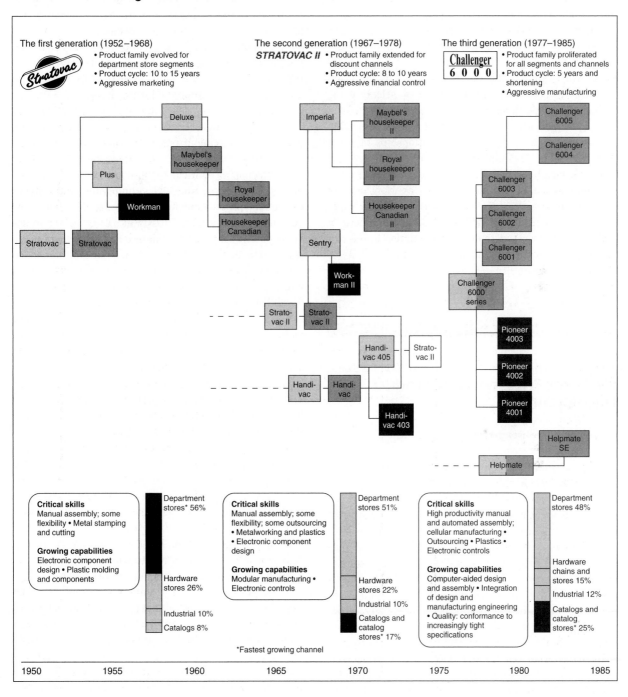

resources. The most interesting and useful benefits will come out of debates about what to put in the submaps.

Submaps capture the essence of the functional strategies, and when integrated with the new product development map, serve to tie those functional strategies together and provide both a foundation and a process for achieving a company's business strategy. The whole process facilitates the cross-functional discussion and resolution of strategic issues. How often have well-intentioned functional managers met to discuss their various substrategies only to have those from other functions tune out within the first two minutes, as the discussion becomes too technical, too detailed, or simply too parochial to comprehend?

Mapping provides a process for planning that avoids too much detail (like budgeting) and too much parochialism (like traditional functional strategy sessions). Managers will inevitably develop linkages across the organization by going through the steps of selecting the resources or factors to develop into a map, identifying the key dimensions to capture in the map, reviewing historical data to understand the relationships of those dimensions, and examining what is likely to drive future versions of the map. Functions can share their maps to communicate, refine, and agree on important product strategy choices. It is the sharing of functional capabilities—capabilities applied in a systematic, repetitive fashion to product development opportunities—that will become the company's competitive advantage.

Accelerating the Design-Build-Test Cycle for Effective New Product Development

Steven C. Wheelwright and Kim B. Clark

Perhaps no topic has gained such widespread attention among managers in recent years as effective new product development. Rapid, high-quality, on-target new product development is central to competition in industries ranging from consumer packaged goods to electronics, from appliances to pharmaceuticals, and from automobiles to steel. Firms that consistently define, resource, and execute new product development projects significantly more effectively and efficiently than their competitors are rewarded by significant strategic advantage.

Speed is at the heart of that advantage. But it must be speed born of enduring capability. Indeed, the themes that characterize outstanding development projects—clarity of objectives, focus on time to market, integration inside and out, high-quality prototypes, and strong lead-

Source: Adapted from Steven C. Wheelwright and Kim B. Clark, *Revolutionizing Product Development* (New York: Free Press, 1992). Reprinted by permission of *International Marketing Review* 11(1994), pp. 32–46.

ership, to name a few—reflect capabilities that allow the firm to move quickly and efficiently to develop attractive products and manufacturing processes. The power of such capabilities lies in the competitive leverage they provide. A firm that develops high-quality products rapidly may pursue several competitive options. It may start a new product development project at the same time as competitors, but introduce the product to the market much sooner. Alternatively, it may delay the beginning of a new development project in order to acquire better information about market developments, customer requirements, or critical technologies, introducing its product at the same time as its competitors but bringing to market a product much better suited to the needs of its customers. Furthermore, it may use its resources to develop additional products that more closely meet the demands of specific customer niches. Whatever the mix of customer targeting, speed to market, and product breadth a firm chooses to pursue, its advantages in fundamental capabilities provide a competitive edge.

The advantage of such capability has been widely recognized in the worldwide auto industry. By the late 1980s, leading Japanese auto firms (most notably Toyota and Honda) were developing major new cars (or "platforms") in 36 months and replacing existing product generations every four years. European and U.S. auto firms were taking approximately 60 months to develop similar projects, expending considerably more resources, and replacing existing product generations every eight-plus years.[1] This rapid development gave the leading Japanese firms significant advantages in forecasting customer preferences and offering newer designs (on average), faster paybacks, and more innovative products incorporating newer technologies. The evident power of development led Chrysler, Ford, and General Motors, as well as many European firms, to launch major efforts to revamp their approach to product development.

Competitive advantage results in large part from the way work gets done during the process of development. Especially important is the way in which engineering (both design and manufacturing process) and marketing combine technical detail—specific dimensions, parts parameters, materials, and components—into a coherent whole that more than meets customer expectations, even when such expectations are difficult to identify.

The magic in a winning new product or a superior process is in the details. Understanding how individuals,

---

[1] See Kim B. Clark and Takahiro Fujimoto, *Product Development Performance* (Boston: HBS Press, 1991).

work groups, and organizations carry out problem solving in product and process engineering, field service, and manufacturing is central to accelerated new product development. In this context a "problem" occurs when developers encounter a gap between the current design (or plan, process, or prototype) and customer requirements. For example, in the development of a medical diagnostic instrument, prototype testing and interaction with customers might reveal that nurses and technicians experience a glare on the display that makes it difficult to read. The customers' experience signals the existence of a problem, but does not define it precisely. Excessive glare could be the result of an inappropriate display angle, inappropriate materials, the absence of control in the manufacturing process, or any number of underlying causes. Although there may be a team member responsible for the display, solving excessive glare is likely to involve issues that extend beyond that narrow functional domain. Thus, the problem cuts across disciplines and perhaps even functions.

How the development team takes action to close such a gap—the way it frames and defines the problem, generates alternatives, organizes and conducts tasks, and implements solutions—determines the speed, efficiency, and effectiveness of problem solving. Where such problems are critical to overall system performance, drive program lead time, involve significant resources, or have decisive influence on a customer's perception of the product or process as a whole, the effectiveness of problem solving at the detailed local level can have a powerful influence on the overall performance of the development process. Effective problem solving at the working level is not a sufficient condition for overall success, but in our experience, it is a critical and necessary part of an outstanding development process.

An understanding of effective problem solving in development is essential for everyone involved in development teams, and particularly crucial for general managers. Our research and experience have led us to conclude that the role of the general manager is to build capability and create effective processes in the organization. Carrying out that role requires an in-depth understanding of the problem-solving process at the working level. General managers need to understand the process not only because changes often provide significant leverage for improving development, but also because such an understanding can be an important guide in making investment decisions about processes and capabilities. Furthermore, deep understanding may be useful as general managers make decisions about specific projects. With a

framework for thinking about detailed problem solving and an understanding of modern methods and systems, general managers will be in a much better position to evaluate the potential and progress of specific products or processes under development. Finally, such understanding can enable a general manager to assess and strengthen existing development capabilities so that accelerated product development can become a source of competitive advantage.

In the next section, we examine in detail the design-build-test cycle that, for most development projects for manufactured products, is the fundamental building block of effective and efficient problem solving. We include a description of alternative modes of problem solving and their implications for organizational skills and capabilities. Next we examine how superior capabilities at conducting the design-build-test cycle can be used to make dramatic improvements in individual product development efforts. Utilizing faster rates of organizational learning is at the heart of such improvements.

Having examined how the effectiveness of an individual development project benefits from such basic problem-solving capability, in the final section we consider how a firm can leverage that ability into a competitive advantage across a series of projects. Throughout the paper we use a number of examples from our research to illustrate key concepts and ideas. While each situation is unique, our hope is to show how managers in a wide range of development settings may develop and apply effective patterns of problem solving.

A. PROBLEM SOLVING IN NEW PRODUCT DEVELOPMENT

Solving problems during development is a learning process. No matter how much an engineer, a marketer, or a manufacturer may know about a given problem, there are always aspects of a new system that must be understood before an effective design can be developed. Except for the easiest of problems, developers are unlikely to come up with a complete design in a single iteration. Instead, developers go through several iterations, learning a little more about the problem and alternative solutions each time before converging to a final design and detailed specifications.

The Design-Build-Test Cycle

Each iteration or problem-solving cycle consists of the three phases illustrated in Exhibit 1. In the *design phase*, a developer frames the problem and establishes goals

EXHIBIT 1   The Design-Build-Test Cycle in Product-Development Problem Solving

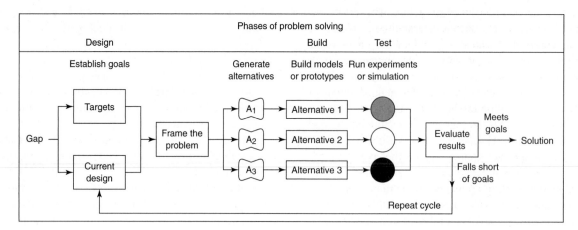

for the problem-solving process. Problem framing is crucial, since the apparent gaps in performance that we observe are often caused by underlying conditions that are difficult to observe and characterize. A problem with noise in the winding mechanism of a 35mm camera, for example, may be caused by the type of material, gear width, or a variety of other design parameters, including the precision of the manufacturing process. The frame put on a problem also depends on how objectives are defined. In the case of noise, for example, it may be apparent because of customer feedback that the old design had undesirable noise characteristics. A clear objective of the new system could be, therefore, to reduce noise below a given threshold level. A deeper understanding of the problem, however, may suggest that customers like to hear the rewind system working. Thus, the objective may not be simply to reduce noise below some threshold, but rather to create the right kind of sound—a sound that is distinct but soft and nonabrasive.

Once the developer has framed the problem, the next step in the design phase is to generate alternatives. Based on the developer's understanding of the relationship between design parameters and customer attributes, several designs for physical models may be appropriate. The purpose of the alternative designs may be to explore the relationship between design parameters and specific customer attributes. If the particular design cycle under discussion comes at a later stage of development, the purpose of the alternative designs may be to refine an established concept.

In the second or *build phase* of the problem-solving cycle, working models of the design alternatives are built

that allow for testing. Depending upon what a developer is trying to learn, the working models may take several forms. At an early stage of gear development on a 35mm camera, for example, a developer may implement alternatives electronically in a computer-aided design (CAD) workstation, using the computer to display graphically and visually the gears' characteristics. For some purposes it may be useful to take the build phase one step further, creating alternatives using easy-to-work-with materials such as plastic or soft metals. While computer simulation may provide sufficient information to arrive at effective solutions, later-stage testing and development may require building physical prototypes using materials and production processes reasonably close to those used in a commercial process.

In the third or *test phase* of the problem-solving cycle, working models, prototypes, or computer-generated images are tested. Depending upon the purposes of the problem-solving cycle, the tests may focus on a particular dimension or may involve full-scale system evaluation. In the case of gear noise, for example, an early testing scheme may examine the decibel level generated by alternative designs. Such a test could be run in a testing laboratory and the results used to generate an understanding of the connection between different design parameters and the overall noise level. Subsequently, given designs may be implemented with prototype parts and tested with potential customers.

Although conducting tests appears relatively straightforward, in practice getting good information out of the testing phase requires careful forethought and skillful execution of a test plan. In a laboratory setting, test engineers worry about things such as accuracy, precision, and the ability to calibrate measurements. In addition, tests are subject to random variation caused by fluctuations in the environment that have not been accounted for or controlled. In order to cope with such randomness from vibration, temperature, humidity, and even stray magnetic fields, engineers often repeat tests to identify the amount of noise in the testing process. But even when engineers have well-designed procedures to deal with random variation and have established instruments and processes to ensure accurate and precise measurement, there is still the problem of fidelity. Fidelity refers to the extent to which the test being conducted reflects the actual case of interest. With respect to gears in the film rewind system, for example, will a laboratory test of decibel levels reflect the way customers will perceive noise when using the camera? Are customers involved in the field tests representative of the customers they are trying to reach? Are test conditions effectively representative of the mode in which the camera will be used?

A single design-build-test cycle generates insight and information about the connection between specific design parameters and customer attributes. That information becomes the basis for a new design-build-test cycle and the process continues until developers arrive at a solution—a design—that meets requirements. Thus, the effectiveness of problem solving in development depends not only on the speed, productivity, and quality of each individual step in the cycle, but also on the number of cycles required to achieve a solution. The number of cycles depends directly on the extent to which activities at each of the problem-solving steps are linked and integrated.

The challenge in effective problem solving, therefore, is both to execute individual elements of the cycle (and individual cycles) rapidly and well and to link individual cycles so that solutions are coherent. As pressure for improved performance in lead time, cost, and quality has increased, firms have adopted a variety of methods to improve the execution and linkage of problem-solving cycles. At first glance, many of these methods appear to be little more than applied common sense—plan your work, think before you act, consider the consequences, and do it right the first time. While common sense is an all-too-rare commodity, there is more to structured methods—such as quality function deployment (QFD), design for manufacturability (DFM), and computer-aided engineering (CAE)—than a straightforward application of what everyone already knows. The difficulty is in finding a method and logic that works where people, infor-

mation, objectives, and capabilities interact in a complex system.

Methods of Communication in Problem Solving

At the heart of such methods, and indeed underlying any design-build-test cycle, is the extent to which problem solving is truly integrated. This shows up most forcibly in relationships between individuals or engineering groups where the output of one's problem-solving cycle is the input for the other's. Consider, for example, the relationship between a design group responsible for designing a plastic part and a process engineering group responsible for designing the mold that will be used to produce it. The upstream group—in this case, the part designers—solves its design problem by establishing the part's physical dimensions, how it will interface with other parts in the system, its surface characteristics, and the particular material to be used in its construction. All these solutions—dimensions, tolerances, interfaces, surface characteristics, and materials—become inputs into the downstream organization's design problem—in this case, the design of molds to be used in the production of the part. The mold designer's problem is to create a mold (or set of molds, particularly if the part is to be produced in volume) that will give the part its shape and surface characteristics, but will also be sufficiently durable, cost-effective, and operational that the part can be manufactured in volume (can withstand repeated use without breaking or sticking) reliably at low cost. How these two engineering groups work together determines the extent of integration in the design and development of the part and its associated mold and directly impacts the effectiveness of their joint design-build-test cycle in achieving development objectives.

The choices firms make about communication between upstream and downstream groups and how to link the actual work in time shape the nature of cross-functional integration. The key issue is the extent to which work is done in parallel. Exhibit 2 puts the communication patterns together with different approaches to parallel activity to create four modes of upstream-downstream interaction.

The first panel depicts the *serial/batch* mode of interaction. This is a classic relationship in which the downstream group waits to begin its work until the upstream group has completely finished its design. The completed design is transmitted to the downstream group in a one-shot transmission of information. This one-way, "batch"

EXHIBIT 2   Four Modes of Upstream-Downstream Interaction

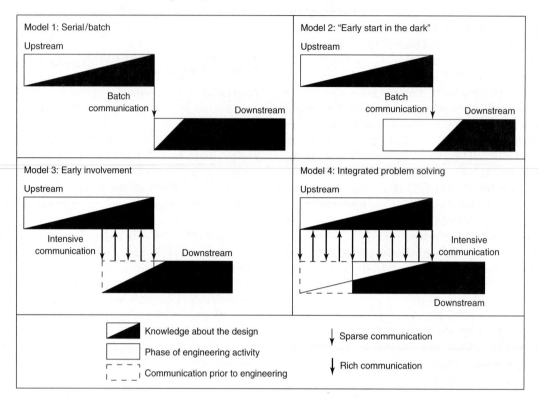

style of communication may not convey all of the important nuances and background to the final design, nor does it necessarily comprehend the strengths and opportunities afforded by the downstream group. In that sense, the problem solving that lies behind the design of the product and that will produce the design of the mold is not integrated.

The second mode—the *early start in the dark*—links the upstream and downstream groups in time, but continues to employ a batch style of communication. This mode of interaction often occurs where the downstream group faces a deadline that it feels cannot be met without an early start on the project. But the upstream group communicates only at the end of its work, so the downstream group in effect has to begin in the dark. When the completed upstream design arrives, the downstream group may be surprised by the design and experience a period of confusion as it tries to adjust its work. While the net result may be some reduction in overall lead time, the extent of the surprise and confusion can often be sufficient to make the process longer than the process

in mode one. Although the downstream and upstream groups work in parallel, and in this sense are "concurrent," in actuality they operate without information and the problem-solving cycles in the two organizations are not linked.

The third mode—the *early involvement* mode—begins to move toward real integration. In this mode the upstream and downstream players engage in two-way communication of preliminary, fragmentary information, although the upstream group is still involved in the design of the part well before the downstream group begins its work. Thus, while the downstream group develops insight about the emerging design and participates through feedback and interaction in the design process, it waits until the design is complete before undertaking problem solving in its own domain. The downstream group benefits from early involvement in two ways. First, the part design reflects a much better understanding of the issues confronting the process engineers than was true in either modes one or two. Second, the mold designers themselves have a much better sense of the issues and objectives embodied in the design. The net effect is that they are able to complete their work with fewer delays and downstream changes. In this sense, problem solving in the downstream and upstream groups is much more integrated.

The last mode in Exhibit 2—*integrated problem solving*—links the upstream and downstream groups in time and in the pattern of communication. In this mode, downstream engineers not only participate in ongoing dialogue with their upstream counterparts, but use that information and insight to get a flying start on their own work. This changes the content of the downstream work in the early phases of upstream design and is also likely to change fundamentally the content of communication between the two groups. Whereas in mode three the content of feedback from downstream engineers had to rely on past practice, theoretical knowledge, and engineering judgment, under integrated problem solving that feedback will also reflect actual practice in attempting to implement the upstream design.

Communication that is rich, bilateral, and intense is an important, even essential, element of integrated problem solving. Where problem solving between upstream and downstream groups is intimately connected, the practice of "throwing the design (blueprints) over the wall"—inherent in mode one—will not support timely mutual adaptation of product and process design. What is needed to capture the nuance and detail important for joint problem solving is face-to-face discussion, direct observation, interaction with physical prototypes, and computer-based representations. Moreover, that intimate, rich pattern of communication must occur in a timely way so that action may be taken to avoid costly mistakes downstream.

Integrated problem solving during the design-build-test cycle relies on early action by the downstream group, dense, rich dialogue between upstream and downstream participants, and a style of problem solving that is broader and more comprehensive than one experiences in the more narrow functional focus inherent in mode one. Indeed, effective integration places heavy demands on the organization. The engineering process must link problem-solving cycles in time; communication must be rich, precise, and intense; and the relationship between upstream and downstream groups must support and reinforce early and frequent exchange of constraints, ideas, and objectives. Moreover, because problem solving across traditional functional boundaries occurs in real time, the capacity for quick and effective action is

critical. Thus, effective integration relies on a specific set of capabilities, attitudes, and relationships that management must enhance and build over time.

B. UTILIZING SUPERIOR DESIGN-BUILD-TEST CAPABILITIES TO ACHIEVE RAPID NEW PRODUCT DEVELOPMENT

During the course of a product development project, the major design-build-test cycles involve the creation of prototypes or the testing of the production process in a pilot plant. Carrying out prototype or pilot production cycles well can have a decisive impact on the overall development effort. Consider, for example, prototyping data gathered from three firms in the major appliance industry during the mid-1980s. These data, and the design-build-test cycles they reflect, are summarized in Exhibit 3.

Differences in lead time among these firms are striking. A major new product development effort ranges from 12 to 22 months and 14 to 20 months at Companies A and B, respectively, whereas at Company C, it takes 36 months. Looking at where that total time is spent reveals a very different pattern for the two faster firms than for Company C. The source of that difference is reflected in the number and duration of the design-build-test cycles needed by each firm.

At Companies A and B, a major development effort requires three primary prototyping cycles. Each cycle involves design, building prototypes, and then testing and evaluating those units. The initial cycle for Companies A and B consists of taking the product concept, preparing sample drawings, building and testing a prototype unit based on the initial drawings, and then revising the design to complete the final drawings. While there are undoubtedly some small subcycles, the allocation of calendar time suggests they must be relatively minor if this first cycle takes from 7 to 14 months. Subsequently, these two companies do a second cycle which takes three to six months and involves preparing tooling for the factory, producing samples from that tooling, assembling units from such sample parts (as part of a prepilot production run), and complete testing of the resulting units. Finally, these firms engage in a third cycle of one to three months—the pilot production run—where revisions from the second cycle are incorporated into the final product and process designs, and the entire system is tested by building pilot production units. Customers evaluate those units, final revisions are made, and plans

EXHIBIT 3 Prototype Cycles and Design Timetables (in Months): Major Appliances

Event /activity	Companies A & B design-build-test (prototyping) cycles	Company A	Company B	Company C	Company C design-build-test (prototyping) cycles
Prefeasibility scoping		1–3	2–6	3	
Drawing for feasibility, sample		1–2	1–2	1	Cycle
Build sample		1–2	1	1	(1)
Test sample		2–5	2	3	
	Cycle (1)				
Drawings for design geometry		design		2	
Build design geometry		frozen		2	Cycle
Test design geometry				3	(2)
Complete drawings for issue		2	2	1	
Build evaluation models				2	Cycle
Test evaluation models (drawing release)				3	(3)
Tool release			2		
Tooling time	Cycle (2)	2–4	2–3	6	Cycle
Inspect samples				2	(4)
Prepare and conduct prepilot run				1	
Testing of product		1	1	2	
Prepare and conduct pilot run	Cycle (3)			1	Cycle
Prepare for production		2–3	1	3	(5)
Total development Project cycle time		12–22 months	14–20 months	36 months	

for volume production of the new product are approved. Market rollout and production ramp-up then follow.

In stark contrast, Company C engages in five separate design-build-test cycles. The first cycle, planned to take 10 months, is analogous to the first cycle at Companies A and B, but ends without completion of a fully functional prototype unit. A second cycle of six months is required to refine the design geometry, tolerances, and physical relationship of the subassemblies. The results of those two cycles then are combined into a third cycle, which takes five months and builds a handful of final engineering models that can be tested and evaluated. The output of that third cycle is a set of final revisions to the engineering drawings.

Company C's fourth cycle is analogous to the second cycle at Companies A and B, but requires 11 months versus the 3 to 6 required by the other two firms. Its aim at all three companies is to procure and test the tooling and to plan and carry out a prepilot production run. The prototypes built during the prepilot run are then tested thoroughly, and final revisions are made to the design of the product and its manufacturing process. Finally, Company C engages in a fifth prototyping and test cycle— pilot production—that is analogous to the third cycle

pursued at Companies A and B. However, Company C requires four months rather than the one to three months required by Companies A and B.

It is instructive to contrast the substantive differences between Companies A and B and Company C. One difference is that activity and cycle durations in the first two firms generally are anticipated to vary from project to project, whereas Company C anticipates that the planned duration of each cycle will be the same on every project. An even more striking difference is Company C's sequence of five design-build-test cycles. Companies A and B have compressed the time from concept to preproduction, while Company C has subdivided project steps to reduce complexity and "level of concurrency." Their intent has been to reduce what they perceive as the risks of costly mistakes. However, Company C, like Companies A and B, would claim that it is pushing hard to reduce its product development cycle time. So why does it use five cycles instead of three?

The explanation for the number and duration of the cycles at Company C lies in how rapidly their organization solves problems, learns, and converges to a final design. Because of poor communication, a narrow technical focus, and an excessively segmented process, Company C needs five cycles to reach a final design that can be produced in volume. Furthermore, because of the way Company C handles the sequence of individual activities and the way it structures and manages the project, it also needs more time to complete each cycle. If management arbitrarily were to cut that time or eliminate one or two cycles, many issues would go unresolved, leading to serious problems in production and the field.

Conceptually, any development project can be thought of (and usually is, at least implicitly) as a sequence of design-build-test cycles. Within each cycle, the prototype serves as a focal point for problem solving, testing, communication, and conflict resolution. Furthermore, it forces specificity in design, provides feedback about the choices made thus far, and highlights remaining unresolved issues. By creating a physical embodiment of the design's current state, engineers are able to study critical issues of functionality, marketing can test and explore customer needs and reactions, and manufacturing can determine the feasibility and options it has for producing the product in volume.

But in spite of prototyping's substantial potential and leverage, Company C treats it as a technical and tactical concern. Even after reviewing the data in Exhibit 3, management at Company C did not conceive of prototyping as a management tool. They did not grasp the nature of the process and its potential role in making development work more effectively. The same seems to hold true even for industries where new product development is the basis of competition, and the speed of development and resulting product performance is the focus of the firm's stated strategy. For example, in the engineering workstation segment of the computer industry, where firms such as Sun Microsystems, DEC, Hewlett-Packard, and IBM compete for a large, growing market, recent studies reveal differences in the number and duration of such cycles even greater than in major appliances—from as few as 3 cycles with durations as short as 100 days each, to as many as 11 cycles with durations as long as 200 days each.[2] Furthermore, the variety of ways in which prototyping cycles are managed and linked to the product development effort itself are as numerous as the number of firms in the industry.

---

[2] For additional information on prototyping in the workstation industry, see David Ellison ande Steven C. Wheelwright, "The Prototyping of PCBs in Engineering Workstation Development Projects," Harvard Business School working paper, 1991.

C. TURNING RAPID PRODUCT DEVELOPMENT CAPABILITY INTO COMPETITIVE ADVANTAGE

Rapidly executing design-build-test cycles may allow a firm to shorten its lead time on a particular project, but competitive advantage derives from the ability to consistently execute rapid development in a series of projects over time. With that capability, the firm may not only get to market more effectively, but in fact change the rules of the game. The interaction between two consumer electronics firms—firms we will call Northern and Southern—illustrates how such a competitive advantage might take shape and influence the nature of competition over repeated generations of product development activity.

Northern and Southern Electronics competed head-to-head in the compact stereo market. Until 1985, both Northern and Southern followed standard industry cycles in new product development, pricing, and manufacturing costs. With a product development cycle of 18 to 20 months, both firms introduced new generations of product every two years. Between major generation changes in products there were frequent model upgrades and price declines as the cost of key components and manufacturing fell with increasing volume. Thus, until the mid-1980s, both Southern and Northern had prices and costs that tracked each other closely, and both mirrored industry averages (see Exhibit 4A).

EXHIBIT 4A Standard Competitive Patterns for the Compact Stereo Market

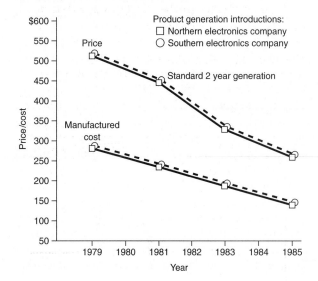

EXHIBIT 4B   Competition on Rapid Development Capabilities in the Compact Stereo Market

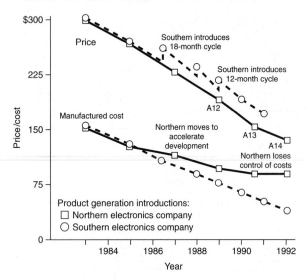

In the early 1980s, stimulated by the efforts of its new vice president of engineering, Southern embarked on a concerted effort to reduce its product development lead time. Without compromising quality, the entire organization began to develop the skills and characteristics associated with rapid, on-target design-build-test cycles. Stronger leadership, more effective cross-functional integration, greater attention to issues of manufacturability and design, more effective prototyping, and a revamped development process gradually led to a reduction in development lead time from 18 to 12 months.

As Exhibit 4B suggests, Southern began to make competitive use of its new development capability in early 1986. At that point it broke with industry tradition and introduced its next generation of stereo product about six months sooner than expected. With a more advanced system and superior performance, Southern was able to command a premium price in the marketplace. Although Northern followed six months later on a standard cycle, its next generation stereo was unable to command its traditional market share. As a result, Northern's volume increased more slowly than expected and its cost position began to erode slightly relative to Southern.

Southern Electronics introduced its next generation product 18 months later in the fall of 1987. Once again the product achieved a premium price in the market. However, Southern did not fully exploit its premium pricing opportunity. Instead, it lowered prices somewhat

to increase further its market share. At that point, not only was Northern behind in product features and technology, but Southern's aggressive pricing posture put even more pressure on Northern's sales volume and margins. Although Northern fought back with price discounts, increased advertising, and promotions to dealers, it was unable to stem the erosion of its historical market position. The result was an even greater disparity in the cost positions of Northern and Southern Electronics.

In late 1988, Northern introduced its next generation stereo system, the A12. Developed under the motto "Beat Southern," Northern's executives felt that the A12 would be the product to regain its former competitive position in the market. Much to their surprise, however, the roll-out of the A12 in early 1989 was met by Southern's introduction of its next generation stereo system: Southern had moved to a 12-month product introduction cycle in late 1988. At that point Northern was a full generation of technology behind Southern in its market offerings. Northern's management determined that the only course of action open was to accelerate development of the next generation system, the A13. They thus embarked on a crash development effort to bring the A13 to market in early 1990. At the same time, Northern began development of the A14, which was targeted for the Christmas 1990 selling season. The A14 was to get back into the competitive ball game on solid footing—a "close the gap" strategy.

While Northern's strategic intent was to catch up to Southern with accelerated product development, the reality was much different. Northern brought the A13 to market in early 1990, but the development process was so hectic and the ramp-up in manufacturing so strained that the company effectively lost control of its costs. The product came to market but was much more expensive and less effective than the company had planned. Because of its many problems, scarce development resources that were to have been moved to the A14 in early 1990 were focused instead on correcting problems and cleaning up the A13's design. To make matters worse, Southern continued to follow its 12-month introduction cycle and actually beat Northern to the market with its next generation product. The result for Northern was a further erosion in margins and market position.

Without making fundamental changes in its development process, which Northern management considered neither necessary nor within the charter of those working on the A14, Northern's attempt to push ahead with the A14 for the 1990 Christmas season was a dismal failure.

The A14 product had so many problems in the field and was so expensive to manufacture that the product line became a serious financial drain on the company.

The key to Southern's success in the compact stereo market was its consistent ability to bring excellent products to market before its competitors. This ability was rooted in fundamental changes management had made in its development process. These included obtaining broad-based organizational and individual buy-in to key project goals at the onset and empowering and encouraging development teams to modify the development process. Teaching the organization the skills and attitudes needed for integrated problem solving, and then reconfiguring the design-build-test cycles to utilize fully that newfound problem-solving skill, were central to Southern's improved development capability. In addition it harnessed that capability to a marketing and pricing strategy that was well targeted at Northern's weaknesses. In effect, Southern changed the nature of competition in the industry; Northern was forced to play a game for which it was ill-suited—a game Northern never fully comprehended until it was years behind in capability.

Southern Electronics' ability to bring a competitive product to market more rapidly than its chief rivals created three potential sources of advantage:

- *Quality of design*—more timely, on-target product offerings.
- *Performance*—more rapid use of emerging technologies.
- *Market share and margins*—more flexibility in pricing and share goals.

We have observed such advantages in a number of fast-cycle competitors in a wide range of industries. Firms such as Honda in automobiles, Applied Materials in semiconductor production equipment, ACS in angioplasty, Sony in audio products, Matsushita in VCRs, Philips in computer monitors, Hill-Rom in hospital beds, and Quantum in disk drives have made the ability to bring outstanding products to market rapidly a central feature of their competitive strategy. Once achieved, and subsequently maintained as the organization grows, an advantage built around fast-cycle capability founded on superior design-build-test skills seems to be strong and enduring.

Perhaps the most powerful effect of such capability is its leverage in changing the nature of competition. By improving development productivity and shortening the time between product generations, a firm such as Southern strengthened its own position and made painfully clear the weaknesses of its rival's approach to new product development. Although Northern may have faced competitive difficulties no matter how it responded to the Southern challenge; by attempting accelerated development in the context of its traditional systems, Northern created internal confusion, strained its resources, and reduced the effectiveness of its development organization. In addition, previously enthusiastic, capable, and hardworking product managers became frustrated and disappointed.

This is what has happened in the auto industry and is currently under way in many other industries. It is what makes the acceleration of design-build-test cycles through fundamental change in the problem-solving process such a strategic advantage and a matter of utmost concern for senior management.

PART FIVE

CONCLUSION: INNOVATION CHALLENGES IN ESTABLISHED FIRMS

We began this book by addressing the question of how general managers should integrate technology and innovation in their firm's strategy. Within the framework of an evolutionary theoretical perspective, Part II provided insights into the substance and enactment of a comprehensive and integrated technology strategy. In Parts III and IV, we examined the ways in which technology strategy is enacted in practice. We end the book by recapitulating some of its major themes in terms of key innovation challenges faced by the top management of established firms.

Throughout this book, we have posited that the innovation challenges facing established firms exist at a number of levels. One challenge entails exploiting a firm's existing opportunities to the fullest; relatively few are available, and they vanish if not seized. The materials on using product development to augment and renew a firm's capabilities provide useful tools to help the general manager meet this challenge. But this is not enough; existing opportunities will eventually be exhausted, and today's success is no guarantee for tomorrow's. Thus a second challenge involves generating entirely new opportunities, as discussed in the materials on corporate research, entrepreneurship, and innovation.

A third challenge involves balancing the portfolio of existing and new opportunities over time. This task is particularly difficult for two reasons: Resources at any given time are limited, and new and existing innovation opportunities require that conflicting management approaches be exercised simultaneously. As noted in Part III, most companies are more comfortable pursuing these challenges in sequence. Notable exceptions, however, exist: The 3M company has, for decades, continued to reinvent itself from within; Intel Corporation has transformed itself from a memory company to a microcomputer company and is now transforming itself into an Internet building block company; and Hewlett-Packard Company has evolved twice—from an instrument company into a computer company and, more recently, into the world's leading laser and inkjet printer company.

It seems appropriate to conclude this book with a set of case studies that offers a window on how the key innovation challenges are managed in some of the world's leading high-technology companies. The final cases provide an opportunity to revisit, in some depth, many of the themes that make studying the materials in this book so worthwhile.

CASE V-1

Apple Computer, 1999

Mary Kwak and David B. Yoffie

Observing Apple Computer in the 1990s was like watching a melodrama unfold. In five years, Apple had four

CEOs (John Sculley, Mike Spindler, Gil Amelio, and Steve Jobs). As each new chief executive took control, the company went through one reorganization after another. By July 1997, Apple had surrendered two-thirds of its market share, losses topped $1.6 billion, and shares were trading near all-time lows. (See Exhibit 1.) Soon competitor Michael Dell was recommending that Apple throw in the towel: "I'd shut it down and give the money back to the shareholders."[1] But as Apple entered 1999, many loyalists hoped that the melodrama was over. Co-founder Steve Jobs had come to Apple's rescue when the company was at its lowest point. Jobs loved to shock, and after taking the reins at Apple, he unleashed a series of dramatic moves. Perhaps most stunning was his decision to make peace with Microsoft, Apple's archenemy. After signing a long-term cross-licensing agreement, Jobs gave Bill Gates an equity stake in the company for $150 million.[2] Jobs then ended Spindler's cloning strategy and went on to kill the Newton, John Sculley's pride and joy. But Jobs's boldest gambit was the iMac, a cleverly designed, low-priced Macintosh that took the market by storm in 1998. By early 1999, Jobs had reversed course on nearly every aspect of his predecessors' strategies and delivered five consecutive quarters of profits. With unit sales and gross margin also on the rise, the same question was on everyone's mind: was this another blip, or could Steve Jobs make Apple "insanely great" again?

APPLE'S HISTORY

The Early Years

Steve Jobs and Steve Wozniak, a pair of 20-something college dropouts, founded Apple Computer on April Fool's Day 1976.[3] Working out of the Jobs family garage in Los Altos, California, they built a computer circuit board they named the Apple I. Within several months, they had made 200 sales and taken on a new partner: A. C. "Mike" Markkula, Jr., a freshly minted millionaire who had retired from Intel at the age of 33. Markkula, who was instrumental in attracting venture capital, was the experienced businessman on the team, Wozniak was the technical genius, and Jobs was the visionary who sought "to change the world through technology." Jobs made it Apple's mission to bring an easy-to-use computer to every man, woman, and child. In April 1978, the company launched the Apple II, a relatively simple machine that ordinary people could use straight out of

Source: Copyright © 1999 by The President and Fellows of Harvard College. Research Associate Mary Kwak and Professor David B. Yoffie prepared this case as the basis for class discussion rather than to illustrate either effective or ineffective handling of an administrative situation.

EXHIBIT 1 Apple Computer: Selected Financial Information, 1981–1998

($ millions, except employee and per share data)

	1Q1999	1998	1997	1996	1995	1994	1993	1992	1991	1986	1981
Net sales	1,710	5,941	7,081	9,833	11,062	9,189	7,977	7,087	6,309	1,902	334
Cost of sales	1,228	4,462	5,713	8,865	8,204	6,846	5,249	3,991	3,314	891	170
Research and development	76	310	485	604	614	564	665	602	583	128	21
Selling, general and administrative	279	908	1,286	1,568	1,583	1,384	1,632	1,687	1,740	610	77
Operating income (loss)	127	261	(1,070)	(1,383)	684	522	110	806	447	274	66
Net income (loss)	152	309	(1,045)	(816)	424	310	87	530	310	154	39
Cash, cash equivalents, and short-term investments	2,578	2,300	1,459	1,745	952	1,258	892	1,436	893	576	73
Accounts receivable, net	913	955	1,035	1,496	1,931	1,581	1,382	1,087	907	263	42
Inventories	25	78	437	662	1,775	1,088	1,507	580	672	109	104
Net property, plant, and equipment	344	348	486	598	711	667	660	462	448	222	31
Total assets	4,592	4,289	4,233	5,364	6,231	5,303	5,171	4,224	3,494	1,160	255
Total current liabilities	1,484	1,520	1,818	2,003	2,325	1,944	2,508	1,426	1,217	138	70
Total shareholders' equity	1,923	1,642	1,200	2,058	2,901	2,383	2,026	2,187	1,767	694	177
Cash dividends paid	—	—	—	14	58	57	56	57	57	—	—
Permanent full-time employees	NA	6,658	8,437	10,896	13,191	11,287	11,963	12,166	12,386	4,950	2,456
International sales/sales	47%	45%	50%	52%	48%	46%	45%	45%	45%	26%	27%
Gross margin	26%*	25%	19%	10%	26%	25%	34%	44%	47%	53%	49%
R&D/sales	5%*	5%	7%	6%	6%	6%	8%	8%	9%	7%	6%
SG&A/sales	16%*	15%	18%	16%	14%	15%	20%	24%	28%	32%	23%
Return on sales	7%*	5%	NM	NM	4%	3%	1%	7%	5%	8%	12%
Return on assets	9%*	7%	NM	NM	7%	6%	2%	14%	10%	15%	24%
Return on equity	26%*	22%	NM	NM	16%	14%	4%	27%	19%	25%	38%
Stock price low	$28.50**	$13.50	$12.75	$16.00	$31.63	$24.63	$22.00	$41.50	$40.25	$10.88	$7.13
Stock price high	$47.31**	$43.75	$29.75	$35.50	$50.13	$43.75	$65.25	$70.00	$73.25	$21.94	$17.38
P/E ratio at year-end	10.9***	17.5	NM	NM	9.2	14.9	40.1	13.8	21.9	16.8	27.7
Market value at year-end	4,604***	5,540	1,671	2,598	3,911	4,676	3,397	7,067	6,650	2,578	1,224

*12-month trailing average. ** Between October 1, 1998, and March 1, 1999. ***As of March 1, 1999. NA = not available; NM = not meaningful.

All information is on a fiscal-year basis, other than share price data, which are on a calendar-year basis. Apple's fiscal year ends in September.

Source: Apple financial reports, Datastream International, and Standard & Poor's Compustat.

EXHIBIT 2   Apple's Share of the Worldwide Personal Computer Market, 1980–98

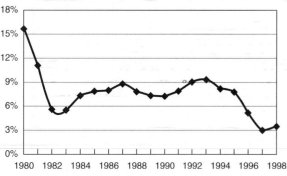

Source: InfoCorp, International Data Corp., Dataquest.

the box. The Apple II set off a computing revolution that drove the personal computer (PC) industry to $1 billion in annual sales in less than three years. Apple quickly became the industry leader, selling more than 100,000 Apple IIs to homes, schools, and small businesses by the end of 1980. (See Exhibit 2.) In December 1980, Apple went public, making its founders multimillionaires. (See Exhibit 3.)

Apple's competitive position changed fundamentally when IBM entered the PC market in 1981. The IBM PC, which relied on Microsoft's DOS operating system and a microprocessor from Intel, was stolid and gray when compared to the graphics- and sound-enhanced Apple II. But the IBM PC was a relatively "open" system that other manufacturers could clone. By contrast, Apple's computers relied on proprietary designs that only Apple could produce. As IBM-compatibles proliferated, Apple's revenues continued to grow, but its market share dropped sharply, falling to 6.2 percent in 1982.[4]

Apple's first response to the IBM-compatible onslaught was the Lisa, a stunning next generation machine. The Lisa, which Jobs named after his daughter, was the first personal computer to use a graphical user interface (GUI) and a point-and-click mouse. This combination eliminated the need to type in complicated commands. The Lisa also featured a windowing system that allowed several applications to run at the same time. However, it was incompatible with the IBM standard and even with the Apple II. Priced at $10,000, the Lisa found few buyers, and Apple dropped it soon after its launch in 1983. Instead, the company focused on developing a cheaper machine with many of the same advanced features. Steve Jobs personally oversaw the project, pam-

pering his troops with fresh-squeezed orange juice while exhorting them to create something "insanely great." The result was the Macintosh, which was introduced in a memorable blitz of publicity in early 1984.

The Mac marked a breakthrough in ease of use, industrial design, and technical elegance, but its slow performance and the lack of Mac-compatible software limited sales. Between 1983 and 1984, Apple's net income fell 17 percent, leaving the company in crisis by the end of the year. In April 1985, Apple's board removed Jobs from an operational role. Several months later, Jobs left Apple to found a new company named NeXT. These moves left John Sculley, the CEO who had been recruited from Pepsi-Cola in 1983, alone at the helm. Armed with a Wharton M.B.A., Sculley had led Pepsi's charge against Coke in the United States. Now he hoped to use his marketing savvy and operational expertise to drive Apple to similar heights.

The Sculley Years, 1985–93

Sculley sought to exploit Apple's capabilities in graphics and design to make the company a leader in desktop publishing, as well as education. He also moved aggressively to bring Apple into the corporate world. Sculley began Apple's turnaround with the January 1986 launch of the Macintosh Plus, which had almost 10 times the memory of the original Mac. By then, Apple's "evangelism" among software developers had also begun to bear fruit, yielding programs like Aldus (later Adobe) PageMaker and Microsoft Excel. The combination of superior software and peripherals, such as laser printers, gave the Macintosh unmatched capabilities in desktop publishing. All of these factors contributed to an explosion in sales and turned Apple into a global brand. By 1990, revenues reached $5.6 billion, while Apple's worldwide market share stabilized around 8 percent. In the education market, which contributed roughly half of Apple's U.S. revenue, the company's share was more than 50 percent. Apple had $1 billion in cash and was the most profitable personal computer company in the world.

Apple's Position in 1990 Apple controlled the only significant hardware and software alternative to the IBM standard. The company practiced horizontal and vertical integration to a greater extent than any other PC company, with the exception of IBM. Apple typically designed its products from scratch, specifying unique chips, disk drives, monitors, and even unusual shapes for its computers' chassis. While it never backward integrated

EXHIBIT 3   Adjusted Daily Closing Share Price, Apple Computer, 1980–99

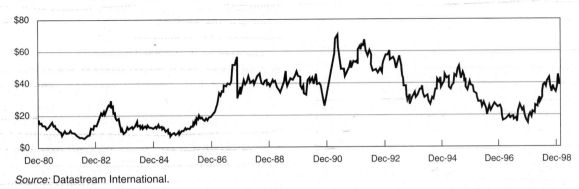

Source: Datastream International.

into microprocessors—which were supplied exclusively by Motorola—the company manufactured and assembled most of its own products in state-of-the-art factories in California. Apple also developed (*a*) its own proprietary operating system (OS), which was bundled with the Mac, (*b*) Mac applications software (through its subsidiary, Claris), and (*c*) many peripherals, such as printers.

Analysts generally considered Apple's products to be more versatile than comparable IBM-compatible machines. In 1990, IBM-compatibles narrowed the gap in ease of use when Microsoft released Windows 3.0. But in many core software technologies, such as multimedia, Apple retained a two-year lead. In addition, since Apple controlled all aspects of the computer, it could offer customers a complete desktop solution, including hardware, software, and peripherals, that allowed customers to "plug and play." Adding extra hardware and software to a Mac was almost as easy as plugging speakers into a stereo system. By contrast, users often struggled to add hardware or software to IBM-compatible PCs. This led one analyst to comment, "The majority of IBM and compatible users 'put up' with their machines, but Apple's customers 'love' their Macs."[5]

This love affair with the Mac allowed Apple to sell its premium products at a premium price. Top-of-the-line Macs went for as much as $10,000, and gross profit hovered around an enviable 50 percent. However, senior executives at Apple realized that trouble was brewing. As IBM-compatible prices dropped, Macs looked increasingly overpriced. As John Sculley explained, "We were increasingly viewed as the 'BMW' of the computer industry. Our portfolio of Macintoshes was almost exclusively high-end, premium-priced computers. . . . Without lower prices, we would be stuck selling to our installed base."[6] Moreover, Apple's cost structure was high: Apple devoted 9 percent of sales to research and development

(R&D), compared to 5 percent at Compaq, and only 1 percent for many IBM-clone manufacturers. These concerns led Dan Eilers, then vice president of strategic planning at Apple, to conclude: "The company was on a glide path to history."

Sculley believed "drastic action" was necessary in order to get Apple back on track. In his words, there would be no "sacred cows": "We still want to change the world, but we have to transform the company and industry for it to work."

Macs   Beginning in 1990, Sculley moved to reposition Apple in the mainstream "with products and prices designed to regain market share." This meant cheaper computers with mass-market appeal. He also sought to maintain Apple's technological lead by bringing out "hit products" every 6 to 12 months. In October 1990, Apple shipped the Mac Classic, a $999 computer intended to compete head-to-head with low-priced IBM clones. One year later, Apple launched the Powerbook notebook computer to rave reviews. By the end of 1991, 80 percent of Apple's sales volume was coming from new products, as opposed to 35 percent the previous year.

Despite these signs of strength, Sculley believed that Apple had to form a "federation" of corporate alliances in order to become more open, penetrate a broader market, and strengthen its technology base. In 1991, he led Apple into a close relationship with its foremost rival, IBM. This alliance had three major strands. First, Apple and IBM formed a joint venture, named Taligent, that was intended to create a revolutionary operating system incorporating the latest advances in software technology. At the time, it cost around $500 million to develop a next generation OS; subsequently, marginal costs were close to zero. Second, Apple committed to switch from Motorola's microprocessors to IBM's new PowerPC chip, while IBM agreed to license its technology to Motorola, in order to guarantee Apple a second source. Sculley believed that the PowerPC could help Apple to leapfrog Intel. Third, Apple and IBM formed another joint venture, named Kaleida, to create a common language for multimedia applications. One of Kaleida's projects was to write software for set-top boxes for interactive TV.

Apple's alliance with IBM was announced in a blaze of publicity in October 1991. By contrast, a second cooperative effort, involving Intel and Novell, was kept strictly under wraps. In early 1992, Sculley authorized a secret effort, codenamed "Star Trek," to rework the Mac OS to run on Intel chips. By November, Apple had a working prototype of the Mac OS on an Intel-based PC.

Other Products Although Sculley was a marketer by training, he took the post of chief technology officer (CTO) in March 1990. Sculley believed strongly that Apple had to change the rules of the game to thrive in the coming decade. He told his sales force in late 1991, "The industry must once again become innovation-driven, move away from commodity status, and provide value added products and services. I believe that Apple has a chance to make a difference." In his new role as CTO, Sculley championed a new product category he called personal digital assistants (PDAs)—handheld electronic organizers with wireless communications capability. Sculley believed that Apple's expertise in user-friendly software would give it an edge as computers and consumer electronics converged. In addition, he hoped that moving into a new market would lessen the pressure to compete on price.

Internal Changes Sculley argued that it was essential for Apple to become a low-cost producer in order to be competitive in the marketplace. One of his first moves in 1985 was to cut the workforce by 20 percent. In 1991, as pricing pressure hit Apple, the company again moved to reduce its headcount by 10 percent. Apple also sought to move much of its manufacturing to subcontractors and adopted a tougher line toward distribution and development partners. However, these actions were not enough to sustain Apple's profitability. With gross margin headed toward 34 percent, 14 points below Apple's 10-year average, and Sculley's decision to commute from Connecticut to the West Coast, the board "promoted" Sculley to chairman in June 1993 and appointed Michael Spindler, the company president, as the new CEO. Five months later, Sculley resigned to become the CEO of Spectrum Technologies, a small telecommunications firm in Con-

necticut. After three months, claiming he had been misled, Sculley left Spectrum amid an SEC investigation and allegations of stock manipulation by members of Spectrum's board.

The Spindler Years, 1993–95

Spindler was a German-born engineer who came to know Mike Markkula while working at Intel. As the head of Apple Europe, he tripled his division's revenues between 1988 and 1990, eventually accounting for 25% of Apple's sales worldwide.[7] Internally, people viewed Spindler as a strong operating manager, whose no-nonsense style contrasted sharply with Sculley's high-level focus on marketing and technology strategies. Yet despite their differences, Spindler continued to follow Sculley's strategy of rolling out hit products, expanding distribution, and committing Apple to compete aggressively on price. In one of his first public moves as CEO, Spindler declared that he would never allow Apple's products to be competitively overpriced again. In addition, Spindler tried to refocus the company on its core markets: the kindergarten-through-high-school and desktop publishing segments, where Apple held 60 percent and 80 percent share respectively.[8]

Macs By 1994, it was estimated that Apple had sold 25 million computers worldwide. (See Exhibit 4.) Over the years, groups within Apple had considered a number of plans to broaden the Mac platform's reach. These included putting the Mac interface on top of Microsoft's DOS operating system; "porting," or rewriting, the Mac OS to run on Intel chips (Star Trek); and allowing other companies to manufacture Mac clones. In January 1994, after years of intense internal debates, Spindler announced that Apple had chosen the third option, which had first been proposed in 1985 by, of all people, Bill Gates. Apple designated only a handful of companies to make Mac clones, including Power Computing, a start-up with ties to Olivetti; Radius, a manufacturer of Apple peripherals; and Motorola. The average price for a Mac OS license was approximately $50 per copy.

At the same time, Apple continued its efforts to stay one step ahead of the IBM-compatible world. In March 1994, Apple tried to reestablish itself as a technology leader with the launch of the PowerMac. Apple's newest computer was based on the PowerPC microprocessor, which improved performance two- to eightfold over the previous generation of Macs. In the first few months, PowerPC chips also had a significant price/performance advantage over Intel microprocessors. However, the

EXHIBIT 4   Shipments and Installed Base of Various Microprocessors, 1991–98

(Millions of dollars)

	1991	1992	1993	1994	1995	1996	1997	1998
Total shipments of Intel technologies								
Units shipped	20.2	30.6	41.4	47.8	60.1	76.0	90.0	105.0
Installed base	91.6	122.2	163.6	211.4	271.5	347.5	437.5	542.5
Motorola (680X0)								
Units shipped	3.3	3.9	4.5	3.9	1.1	0.8	0.5	0.2
Installed base	12.6	16.5	21.0	24.9	26.0	26.8	27.3	27.5
PowerPC								
Units shipped	0	0	0	0.8	3.0	4.0	2.8	3.5
Installed base	0	0	0	0.8	3.8	7.8	10.6	14.1
Total shipments of Motorola and PowerPC technologies								
Units shipped	3.3	3.9	4.5	4.7	4.1	4.8	3.3	3.7
Installed base	12.6	16.5	21.0	25.7	29.8	34.6	37.9	41.6

Note: 5% to 10% of total microprocessor shipments go into non-PC end products. Roughly 30% of the total installed base represented older technologies (early X86-generation and early 68000-series) that were probably no longer in use.
Source: Dataquest, InfoCorp, and casewriter estimates.

PowerPC's advantages turned out to be fleeting, and by late 1994, Macs were selling for a premium of almost $1,000 over comparable Intel-based machines. In the summer of 1995, Apple cut prices by 25 percent, and unit sales surged. By the fall, Apple had briefly regained its position as the leading seller of personal computers in the United States. But Apple was clearly losing momentum: a 1995 *Computerworld* survey of 140 corporate computer system managers found that none of the Windows users would consider buying a Macintosh, but more than half the Apple users expected to buy an Intel-based PC.[9]

Spindler, like Sculley, had hoped that a revolutionary new operating system would turn the picture around, but the prospects for a breakthrough were fading fast. At the end of 1995, Apple and IBM parted ways on Taligent and Kaleida. After spending $550 million to $600 million, neither side wanted to switch to the new technology.[10] IBM remained committed to UNIX, OS/2, and Windows as its core operating systems, while Apple continued to focus on improving the Mac OS.

International Expansion   Spindler set continued international growth as a key objective for Apple. In 1992, 45 percent of the company's sales came from outside the United States. One of the markets where Apple had enjoyed particular success was Japan, where the coexistence of multiple proprietary standards kept personal computer prices significantly higher than in the rest of the world. In 1993, Apple held 14 percent of the Japanese market, second only to NEC.[11] However, Fujitsu launched a ferocious price war in 1995. Although Apple responded by cutting prices, its market share began to erode, and gross margins collapsed. Within one year, Japan went from Apple's most profitable to one of its least profitable divisions.

Spindler also targeted China, one of the fastest-growing computer markets. Spindler set an ambitious goal: 15 to 16 percent market share in China by the year 2000.[12] In 1992, Chinese consumers bought only 190,000 PCs: 93 percent were Intel-based machines, and 2 percent came from Apple. However, analysts predicted that China would purchase 50 million personal computers annually by 2010, making it one of the largest markets in the world. In addition, Apple's software was widely believed to offer the best solution for handling Chinese characters.

Other Products   Spindler launched the Newton MessagePad, Apple's first personal digital assistant, in August 1993. However, the handheld device was months behind schedule, lacked the revolutionary anytime/anywhere communications capability Sculley had promised, and was notoriously poor at handwriting recognition. By the end of the year, Apple had sold only 80,000 MessagePads. Apple's second new venture, eWorld, debuted in January 1994. An online service exclusively for

Mac users, eWorld was intended to compete with Prodigy and AOL. However, eWorld never developed any momentum and was canceled in March 1996.

Internal Changes Spindler moved quickly to cut costs, announcing within weeks of his appointment that Apple would lay off 2,500 employees, or 16 percent of its workforce worldwide. At the same time, Apple reduced spending on R&D to 6 percent of sales. Spindler improved efficiency and cut development cycles from 24 months to 9, but serious operational problems remained. Poor forecasting and a dearth of key parts left Apple unable to meet demand for its best-selling products, while older lines languished on the shelf. In mid-January 1996, Apple reported a $69 million loss for the latest quarter and announced that 1,300 workers would be laid off.[13] Two weeks later, Gilbert Amelio, an Apple director, replaced Spindler as CEO.

The Amelio Years, 1996–97

Amelio, like Spindler, came from an engineering background. After turning around Rockwell International's semiconductor business, he was hired to do the same at National Semiconductor. Apple's board of directors enticed Amelio with a very lucrative golden parachute, hoping that he could repeat his magic one more time. When Amelio arrived, the company was in a desperate state. The stock price was at its lowest point in more than a decade, and Sun Microsystems, as well as Larry Ellison at Oracle, had expressed interest in taking over Apple. Amelio's first move as CEO was to kill the idea of a merger with Sun or a buyout by Ellison. Instead, he set out to improve operations by streamlining Apple's product line, slashing the payroll, and rebuilding cash reserves. He also planned to push Apple into higher-margin segments, such as servers, Internet access devices, and PDAs. Four months after Amelio arrived, he proclaimed that Apple would return to its historical premium-priced differentiation strategy. He declared that just as MagLite could sell its flashlights for huge premiums over ordinary flashlights, Apple should be able to sell Macintoshes at a huge premium over Intel-based PCs.[14] But Amelio had little time to make his strategy work. After 17 months, his inability to restore profitability precipitated his ouster by the board.

Macs Amelio's efforts to reposition Apple as a premium brand were hampered by growing concerns about quality, support, and software availability. In particular,

Apple had difficulty recovering from a 1995 setback, when two PowerBooks caught on fire, pushing the Macintosh image to an all-time low. Apple's worldwide market share dropped from 6 percent to 3 percent on Amelio's watch.[15] In the core education market, the company's market share fell from 41 percent to 27 percent.[16]

Apple executives continued to hope that a brand-new operating system would restore the platform's technological lead. But these efforts were in disarray. Amelio decided to cut Apple's losses by canceling the repeatedly delayed next generation Mac OS, which had already cost more than $500 million in R&D. Instead, in December 1996, he announced that Apple would acquire NeXT Software and that NeXT's founder, Steve Jobs, would return to Apple as a part-time adviser. NeXT's OS, NeXTStep, had a lead in a few technical areas over Microsoft. However, its market share was tiny, and it could not run Mac software. Amelio believed that Apple would need 12 to 18 months to build Rhapsody, a version of NeXTStep designed for top-of-the-line Macintoshes and network servers. Rhapsody was intended to allow developers to write applications that would run both on Apple's systems and on Windows. In the meantime, Apple released two updates to the Mac OS: Mac OS 7.6 in January 1997 and Mac OS 8 in July.

Other Products Apple's efforts in other markets were also faltering. By mid-1997, Newton had only 6 percent of the handheld market, which was dominated by 3Com's PalmPilot (66 percent) and products based on Microsoft's Windows CE (20 percent).[17] In addition, Apple was developing set-top box technology for the next generation of TVs, which fared even worse. In December 1996, Apple and its Japanese partner introduced the Pippin, a $500 device that allowed users to play games, send email, and surf the Web on a TV. The Pippin faced stiff competition and reportedly sold only 12,000 units in the United States before the project was abandoned in early 1998.[18]

Internal Changes Amelio had hired an entirely new senior staff and led the company through three reorganizations. He cut 2,800 workers from the payroll, beginning in April 1996, and in March 1997, Apple announced that another 4,100 would go.[19] Yet despite these austerity moves, Apple lost $1.6 billion from January 1996 through June 1997, and on July 2, 1997, the company's share price sank to a 12-year low. One week later, Amelio was forced out, and Steve Jobs—the mastermind of the Apple I, the Apple II, and the Macintosh—moved back into the executive suite after 12 years in exile. Jobs im-

EXHIBIT 5 **Personal Computer Average Selling Prices, 1997–2001**

	1997	1998	1999	2000	2001	CAGR, 1997–2001 (%)
Desktops	$1,812	$1,625	$1,494	$1,440	$1,388	−6%
Portables	2,616	2,323	2,191	2,098	2,060	−6
PC servers	7,447	6,957	7,037	6,875	6,667	−3
Total	$2,082	$1,882	$1,776	$1,709	$1,655	−6%

CAGR = compound annual growth rate.
Source: Adapted from Robert Cihra, "PC Industry Report," ING Baring Furman Selz LLC, October 9, 1998.

mediately recruited a new board of directors, including his personal friend Larry Ellison, the CEO of Oracle, and Jerry York, the former CFO of IBM.[20] In September, Jobs, who also remained head of Pixar Animation Studios, the maker of *Toy Story* and *A Bug's Life,* became Apple's interim CEO.

For Apple to survive into the next millennium, Jobs knew that he would have to take a new approach. Jobs's first task was to figure out a strategy that would reposition Apple in the evolving personal computer industry. The PC industry had changed dramatically since Jobs left Apple in 1985. All of the old formulas followed by his predecessors had underestimated the intensity and rapidity of change in the industry. Jobs was not going to make the same mistakes!

THE EVOLVING PERSONAL COMPUTER INDUSTRY

By 1999, personal computers had become a $170-billion global industry. From its earliest days in the mid-1970s, the industry had experienced explosive growth, dramatically altering the landscape of competition. Apple pioneered the first usable "personal" computing devices, but IBM was the company that brought PCs into the mainstream. IBM's brand name and product quality helped it to capture the lion's share of the market in the early 1980s, including almost 70 percent of the Fortune 1,000. At the time, many customers shunned IBM-compatible clones due to fears about quality, compatibility, reliability, and service. In addition, corporate buyers relied heavily on well-known retail outlets, such as Computer-Land, which only had space for four or five major brands on their shelves. In the mid-1980s, the typical retailer carried three core premium brands: Apple, which was the leader in user-friendliness and applications like desktop publishing; IBM, which was the premium-priced, industry standard; and Compaq, which built IBM-compatible machines with a strong reputation for quality and high

performance. The multitude of smaller clone companies had to compete for the remaining one or two spaces on the retailer's shelves.

IBM's dominance of the PC industry started to erode in the late 1980s, as buyers increasingly viewed PCs as commodities. IBM tried to boost its margins by building a more proprietary PC, but instead, it lost more than half of its market share, as well as its claim to be the standard bearer for the industry. By the early 1990s, "Wintel" (Microsoft **Win**dows and **Intel** microprocessors) had replaced "IBM-compatible" as the dominant standard. Throughout the 1990s, thousands of manufacturers, ranging from Compaq and Dell to no-name cloners, built personal computers around standard building blocks from Microsoft and Intel. By 1999, there were almost 400 million PCs installed around the world. The United States remained the largest market, accounting for approximately 40 percent of total shipments, followed by Western Europe (25 percent), Asia/Pacific (including Japan) (20 percent), and the "rest of the world" (Latin America, Eastern Europe, the Middle East, Africa, and Canada) (15 percent).[21] Annual PC unit growth averaged roughly 18 percent in the 1990s, and analysts predicted growth rates in the 13 percent to 15 percent range through 2005, with the largest increases occurring in the Asia/Pacific (excluding Japan) and the "rest of the world." Revenue growth, however, was unlikely to keep pace with unit shipments. (See Exhibit 5.) In more mature markets, such as the United States, where 50 percent of households owned PCs, slowing growth, combined with dropping component prices, was generating intensified competition on price. By early 1999, sub-$600 PCs (which usually sold without a monitor) accounted for almost 20 percent of U.S. retail sales.[22]

PC Manufacturing

The PC was a relatively simple device. Using a screwdriver, a person with relatively little technological sophistication could assemble a PC from four, widely available types of components: a microprocessor (the brains of the PC), a motherboard (the main circuit board), memory storage, and peripherals (the monitor, keyboard, mouse, etc.). Most manufacturers also bundled their PCs with an operating system. While the first PC was a desktop machine, by the late 1990s, there was a wide range of form factors, including laptops, notebooks, sub-notebooks, workstations (more powerful desktops), and servers (computers that acted as the backbone for networks of PCs).

In early 1999, it cost roughly $800 to produce a basic desktop PC, using off-the-shelf components, that would retail for $999. The single largest element of cost was the microprocessor, which ranged in price from $50 to over $600 for the latest Pentium chip. The other main components of the box—the motherboard, hard drive, memory, chassis, power, and packaging—cost around $250 to $350. The keyboard, mouse, modem, CD-ROM and floppy drives, and speakers totaled $90 to $140; a basic monitor cost around $100; and Windows 98 and labor added $50 each. A manufacturer could push its retail price down toward $499 by using a less powerful microprocessor, cutting back on hard drive capacity and memory, and offering lower-quality peripherals. Or it could build a machine that would sell for $2,499, incorporating a state-of-the-art microprocessor, a larger hard drive, more memory, a digital video disk (DVD-ROM) drive instead of a CD-ROM, a high-quality monitor, and additional software, such as Microsoft's Office productivity suite.

As components became increasingly standardized, PC makers cut spending on R&D. In the early 1980s, the leading PC manufacturers spent 5 percent of sales, on average, on R&D. By the late 1990s, the average was down to 1.5 to 2 percent. Apple, at 5 percent, was at the high end of the scale. At the low end, Gateway, a leading direct marketer of PCs, kept R&D below 1 percent of sales by relying on close relationships with its suppliers to keep its products up to date. More and more, rather than invest heavily in R&D, PC companies looked to innovations in manufacturing, distribution, and marketing to give them a competitive edge. Many firms, for example, turned to contract manufacturers to produce both components and entire PCs. (In the 1980s, by contrast, leading PC companies had generally kept key design, engineering, and manufacturing activities in-house.) Contractors initially shaved costs by handling simple manufacturing operations at flexible, high-volume plants in low-cost locations. Over time, they moved into more complex areas, such as design, prototyping, and testing. In some cases, companies that were sinking in the brand-name mar-

ket shifted into contract manufacturing. Taiwan-based Acer, for example, built home-oriented Aptiva computers for IBM.

In addition, many PC manufacturers sought to streamline their operations by moving from a build-to-stock model to a build-to-order or configure-to-order approach. If a company built to stock, it would forecast sales, purchase components, build computers to preestablished specifications, and accumulate inventory in advance of sales. In the build-to-order model, the manufacturer began building a PC only after an order had been received, relying on just-in-time delivery of parts by suppliers located near the PC assembly plant. In the configure-to-order case, which was also known as channel assembly, the manufacturer shipped a PC chassis, complete with motherboard and power supply, to a distributor. The distributor then relied on a small inventory of components to configure PCs to customer specifications as orders arrived.

By moving from build-to-stock to build-to-order, a company could potentially reduce its costs by 10 percent.[23] Roughly half of these savings came from cuts in inventory carrying costs and product returns. The remaining savings were due to a decline in price protection costs. Manufacturers incurred price protection costs by guaranteeing distributors against revenue losses resulting from future price cuts. By the late 1990s, these costs were climbing as the prices of key components—including microprocessors, memory, and hard disk drives—plunged. It was estimated that average component cost reductions reached 1 percent per week in the spring of 1998, twice the industry's historical average.[24]

Buyers and Distribution

PC buyers fell into four broad categories: business, government, education, and home. (See Exhibit 6.) In 1998, the business market accounted for roughly 60 percent of all PCs sold in the United States, government and education each accounted for 8 percent of total shipments, and the home market made up the rest.[25] Worldwide, large corporations, educational institutions, and government agencies were believed to account for more than one-third of spending on PCs, while small- and medium-size businesses (usually called SOHO, for small office, home office) accounted for one-half, and consumers for the rest.[26] The major criteria guiding PC purchases tended to vary by market segment. While price was critical to all segments, home users were generally the most sensitive to cost, while business customers put somewhat greater emphasis on service. Education buyers focused on a

Shift from 80's to 90's
inhouse → outsource

EXHIBIT 6 Personal Computer Vendors' Rankings Within Customer Segments Worldwide

	Home	Small office	Small business	Large business	Government	Education
Compaq	2	1	1	1	1	2
Dell	8	2	3	2	2	4
IBM	3	3	2	3	3	3
Hewlett-Packard	4	5	5	4	4	9
Gateway	5	4	8	7	6	5
Packard Bell NEC	1	10	10	9	9	8
Apple	7	7	9	10	10	1
Acer	9	8	4	8	8	10
Toshiba	10	6	6	5	5	7
Fujitsu	6	9	7	6	7	6

Small office = sites with fewer than 10 employees; small business = sites with 10 to 99 employees.
Note: Rankings are based on unit shipment data for the third quarter of 1998.
Source: International Data Corp.

EXHIBIT 7 Worldwide Personal Computer Market, 1995–98

(% of unit shipments)

	1995	1996	1997	1998	Unit growth, 1997–98 (%)
Compaq	10.0	10.4	13.4	14.4	21%
IBM	8.2	8.9	9.0	8.8	10
Dell	3.2	4.3	5.9	8.6	64
Hewlett-Packard	3.5	4.3	5.3	6.4	35
Packard Bell NEC	7.3	6.1	5.2	4.5	−3
Gateway	NA	2.8	3.3	4.0	36
Fujitsu	NA	3.7	3.7	3.7	13
Toshiba	NA	3.9	4.1	3.5	−5
Apple	8.0	5.3	3.2	3.4	17
Total shipments (thousands of units)	58,888	69,231	80,063	89,824	12%

NA = not available.
Source: International Data Corp.

combination of price and the availability of appropriate software.

In the 1980s, most PC buyers were relatively unsophisticated first-time customers. Many were intimidated by the technology and placed great emphasis on service, support, and compatibility in their buying decisions. In general, they bought no more than a few PCs at a time and preferred to buy established brands through full-service computer dealers. In the early 1990s, however, as customers became more knowledgeable about PCs, a variety of alternative channels emerged.

Corporate information technology managers and purchasing departments, often operating under tight budgets, began to buy large numbers of PCs directly from manufacturers or their distributors. Superstores, such as Staples, Wal-Mart, and Costco, catered to the consumer

and SOHO markets. Mail order outlets, which offered computers and peripherals at 30 to 50 percent discounts, also saw a sharp increase in demand. In addition, value added resellers (VARs) emerged to fulfill the growing business demand for networked PCs. VARs purchased PCs from a manufacturer or distributor and configured them with hardware and software to meet specific customers' needs. VARs were particularly important in the small business market, which accounted for nearly one-quarter of PC shipments in the United States.[27]

In the late 1990s, fueled by the explosion of the Internet, a growing number of manufacturers began to market PCs directly to customers over the World Wide Web. In the United States, roughly 22 percent of PCs were distributed through direct channels. National resellers, which operated networks of sales and service centers, accounted

EXHIBIT 8   Apple Competitors: Selected Financial Information, 1993–98

($ millions)

	1998	1997	1996	1995	1994	1993
Compaq						
Total revenues	31,169	24,584	20,009	16,675	12,605	8,873
Cost of sales	23,980	17,833	14,855	12,291	8,885	6,188
R&D	1,353	817	695	552	458	436
SG&A	4,978*	2,947	2,507	2,186	1,859	1,549
Net income	(2,743)*	1,855	1,318	893	988	19
Total assets	23,051	14,631	12,331	9,637	7,862	5,752
Total current liabilities	10,733	5,202	4,741	3,356	2,739	2,098
Total stockholders' equity	11,351	9,429	7,290	5,757	4,644	3,468
Gross margin	23%	27%	26%	26%	30%	30%
R&D/sales	4%	3%	3%	3%	4%	5%
SG&A/sales	16%	12%	13%	13%	15%	17%
Return on sales	NM	8%	7%	5%	8%	0%
Market value at year-end	71,400	42,771	20,141	12,758	10,207	6,103
Dell Computer						
Total revenues	12,327	7,759	5,296	3,475	2,873	2,014
Cost of sales	9,605	6,093	4,229	2,737	2,440	1,564
R&D	204	126	95	65	49	42
SG&A	1,202	826	595	424	423	268
Net income	944	518	272	149	(36)	102
Total assets	4,268	2,993	2,148	1,594	1,140	927
Total current liabilities	2,697	1,658	939	752	538	494
Total stockholders' equity	1,293	806	973	652	471	369
Gross margin	22%	21%	20%	21%	15%	22%
R&D/sales	2%	2%	2%	2%	2%	2%
SG&A/sales	10%	11%	11%	12%	15%	13%
Return on sales	8%	7%	5%	4%	NM	5%
Market value at year-end	93,113	27,421	9,569	3,223	1,613	850
IBM						
Total revenues	81,667	78,508	75,947	71,940	64,052	62,716
Cost of sales	50,795	47,889	45,408	41,573	38,768	38,568
R&D	5,046	4,877	4,654	4,170	4,363	5,558
SG&A	16,662	16,634	16,854	16,766	15,916	18,282
Net income	6,328	6,093	5,429	4,178	3,021	(8,101)
Total assets	86,100	81,499	81,132	80,292	81,091	81,113
Total current liabilities	36,827	33,507	34,000	31,648	29,226	33,150
Total stockholders' equity	19,433	19,816	21,628	22,423	23,413	19,738
Gross margin	38%	39%	40%	42%	39%	39%
R&D/sales	6%	6%	6%	6%	7%	9%
SG&A/sales	20%	21%	22%	23%	25%	29%
Return on sales	8%	8%	7%	6%	5%	NM
Market value at year-end	170,151	101,713	78,408	51,016	43,157	32,681

for 33 percent of sales. Independent VARs were responsible for 15 percent of sales, and retail channels, such as Circuit City and CompUSA, accounted for the rest.[28] Each channel appealed to a different mix of buyers. Retail customers, for example, were more likely to be first-time buyers, while customers in direct channels tended to be "power users" looking for sophisticated PCs.

PC Manufacturers

The three top vendors—Compaq, IBM, and Dell— accounted for 30 percent of PC shipments in 1998.[29] (See Exhibit 7.) Compaq was the market leader with a full range of PCs, from sub-$1,000 desktops to servers selling for tens of thousands of dollars. Dell was a direct-sales pioneer and the fastest-growing computer company

EXHIBIT 8 **(continued)**

($ millions)

	1998	1997	1996	1995	1994	1993
			Intel			
Net revenues	26,273	25,070	20,847	16,202	11,521	8,782
Cost of sales	12,144	9,945	9,164	7,811	5,576	3,252
R&D	2,509	2,347	1,808	1,296	1,111	970
SG&A	3,076	2,891	2,322	1,843	1,447	1,168
Net income	6,068	6,945	5,157	3,566	2,288	2,295
Total assets	31,471	28,880	23,735	17,504	13,816	11,344
Total current liabilities	5,804	6,020	4,863	3,619	3,024	2,433
Total stockholders' equity	23,377	19,295	16,872	12,140	9,267	7,500
Gross margin	54%	60%	56%	52%	52%	63%
R&D/sales	10%	9%	9%	8%	10%	11%
SG&A/sales	12%	12%	11%	11%	13%	13%
Return on sales	23%	28%	25%	22%	20%	26%
Market value at year-end	197,644	114,718	107,447	46,603	26,470	25,928
			Microsoft			
Total revenues	14,484	11,358	8,671	5,937	4,649	3,753
Cost of sales	1,197	1,085	1,188	877	763	633
R&D	2,798	1,925	1,432	860	610	470
SG&A	3,845	3,218	2,973	2,162	1,550	1,324
Net income	4,490	3,454	2,195	1,453	1,146	953
Total assets	22,357	14,387	10,093	7,210	5,363	3,805
Total current liabilities	5,730	3,610	2,425	1,347	913	563
Total stockholders' equity	16,627	10,777	7,543	5,738	4,450	3,242
Gross margin	92%	90%	86%	85%	84%	83%
R&D/sales	19%	17%	17%	14%	13%	13%
SG&A/sales	27%	28%	34%	36%	33%	35%
Return on sales	31%	30%	25%	24%	25%	25%
Market value at year-end	345,826	155,965	98,752	51,975	35,598	22,882

*Reflects a $3.2 billion charge for purchased in-process technology arising from the acquisition of Digital Equipment Corp. Figures given here for R&D generally excluded such changes.
NM = not meaningful.
Note: All information is on a fall-year basis, other than market value data, which are on a calendar-year. The fiscal year ends in January for Dell, in June for Microsoft, and in December for Compaq, Intel, and IBM.
Sources: Company financial reports, Disclosure, Datastream International.

in the world. Meanwhile, IBM, which once held 30 per-cent of the market, was just managing to hang on ahead of Dell. Below this top tier were a number of well-known brands, including Hewlett-Packard, Acer, Fujitsu, Gate-way, Packard Bell NEC, and Toshiba. In addition, "white boxes"—PCs without national brands, assembled prima-rily by small resellers and specialty retailers—accounted for 23 percent of the market in North America, 50 per-cent in Europe and Asia, and 90 percent in China.[30] From Steve Jobs's perspective, however, the main challengers remained Compaq, IBM, and Dell.

Compaq Founded in 1982, Compaq was the first com-pany to sell a successful IBM-compatible clone. In 1983,

Compaq generated more than $100 million in revenue, setting a U.S. record for first-year sales. Fifteen years later, revenues soared to $31 billion, making Compaq, which had recently acquired Tandem Computers and Digital Equipment Corporation, the second-largest com-puter company in the world. (See Exhibit 8.) Compaq's original strategy was to sell PCs that offered more power or features at prices close to IBM's. The company sought to stay ahead of the technological curve by engineer-ing its products from scratch and manufacturing many key components in-house. In 1986, it even scooped IBM by introducing the first PC to use Intel's powerful new 80386 chip. At the beginning of the 1990s, Compaq stumbled, as younger, more aggressive rivals moved in with cheaper PCs and direct service and support—all of which Compaq lacked. However, the company recovered by slashing costs, especially in engineering, and bringing out a new line of lower-priced machines. In the late 1990s, in response to renewed pressure from direct sellers, Compaq again reexamined its approach to building and selling PCs. The result was a hybrid model, incorporating aspects of the direct sellers' approach. Compaq began to implement build-to-order and configure-to-order programs in order to streamline production. At the same time, the company, which had historically relied on a vast distribution network, moved into direct sales. The Internet accounted for 8 to 10 percent of Compaq's sales in early 1999.[31] In addition, the company planned to use Digital's 22,000-person services unit to sell everything from notebooks to UNIX servers to corporations.

IBM   With 1998 sales of $82 billion, IBM was the largest computer company in the world. Hardware sales generated 42 percent of revenue, services accounted for 29 percent, software contributed 17 percent, and maintenance and rentals and financing made up the rest. Historically, IBM's trademark had been its sweeping horizontal and vertical integration. This strategy had driven IBM to a dominant position in mainframe computers. However, the company failed to secure ownership of the PC platform, instead allowing Microsoft and Intel to seize control of two critical components—the OS and the microprocessor. In the mid-1980s, IBM earned 25 to 30 percent of the revenues generated by the PC business worldwide.[32] But as competitors turned out cheaper and, in some cases, superior products, IBM's market share began to decline. In 1994, IBM's PC business lost $1 billion and forfeited the number one spot in worldwide PC shipments for the first time.[33] The company responded by streamlining its operations, launching the industry's first channel assembly program in 1996. By 1997, IBM had farmed out the assembly of more than 30 percent of its desktop PCs.[34] In addition, it began to match its rivals on price and expanded the range of products available directly through direct marketing. By 1998, IBM did $7 million in online sales each day.[35] Despite these moves, IBM's PC business remained a drag on company earnings, and its market share stalled around 9 percent.[36] Nonetheless, the company remained a major force in notebook computers, as well as in large corporate accounts.

Dell   Michael Dell started selling computers out of his dorm room at the University of Texas—Austin in 1984.

Dell Computer's first product was an IBM PC clone, which sold through computer magazines for 50 percent off IBM's price. By 1998, Dell offered a full line of desktops, notebooks, workstations, and servers, in addition to software, service, and support. The company had $12.3 billion in sales, and its website generated $14 million in revenue each day. Dell executives attributed their success to the company's distinctive business model, which centered on direct sales and build-to-order manufacturing. Dell needed only 36 hours after taking an order to ship a computer out the door. Consequently, in 1998, Dell maintained nine days of inventory, compared to Compaq's 27. Cost savings such as these allowed the company to maintain high margins while undercutting rivals' prices by 10 to 15 percent.[37] Moreover, the Dell model made it possible to offer products that precisely matched customer needs. Customers could use Dell's website to design the exact configuration of hardware and software that they required and find out immediately how much it would cost. In addition, Dell offered Premier Pages for larger "relationship" accounts. These were customized pages on customer intranets that automated the purchasing process. Relationship customers accounted for roughly 40 percent of Dell's customer base; "transactional" customers, who regarded each purchase as a one-time event, made up 30 percent; and the remaining 30 percent were a mix.[38]

Suppliers and Complements

There were two categories of suppliers to the PC industry: those supplying products that had many sources, such as memory chips, disk drives, and keyboards, and those supplying products that came from a small number of sources, notably microprocessors and operating systems. The components in the first category were widely available at highly competitive prices. Components in the second category were dominated by two firms: Intel and Microsoft.

Microprocessors (CPUs)   Microprocessors were the hardware "brains" of a computer. In 1998, the market for Intel-compatible chips was more than $20 billion, compared to less than $1 billion for PowerPC chips for the Mac.[39] While Intel held a monopoly on the 80386 market from 1986 through 1991, the market became more competitive in the 1990s. AMD, National Semiconductor (which owned Cyrix), IBM, TI, and a variety of international semiconductor companies challenged Intel in 386-, 486-, and Pentium-class microprocessors. Nonetheless, Intel remained the market leader by creating a powerful brand with its "Intel Inside" campaign, rapidly releasing new products, and slashing prices. Throughout the 1990s, Intel usually cut CPU prices by up to 50 percent per year. AMD made significant inroads into Intel's retail market share toward the end of the decade by promising to undercut Intel's prices by 25 percent. But AMD and Intel's other CPU competitors rarely earned any money on their microprocessor businesses, while Intel generated over $6 billion in profits in 1997 and 1998 on $25- to $26 billion in revenue. The U.S. Federal Trade Commission brought an antitrust action against Intel in 1998, but the two sides reached preliminary agreement on a settlement in March 1999.

Operating Systems   Operating systems were large pieces of software that managed a PC's resources and supported applications. Microsoft dominated the PC operating system market following the launch of the IBM PC. In the 1980s, Microsoft sold MS DOS, a relatively crude OS, to hardware manufacturers for $15 per PC. DOS was much harder to use than the Mac OS, but it gained a wide audience because it was available on cheap IBM-compatible clones. In 1990, Microsoft started to challenge Apple's technical supremacy by introducing Windows 3.0, followed one year later by Windows 3.1. Windows was a graphical user interface that cost $15, on top of the $15 cost of DOS. While Windows 3.1 was widely adopted, it remained markedly inferior to the Mac OS. It was only in 1995 that Microsoft significantly narrowed the gap, with the release of Windows 95. Windows 95, which retailed at $89, was an instant success, selling roughly 50 million copies in its first year. Microsoft received an average of $40 for every copy of Windows 95 sold. In 1998, Microsoft upgraded its operating system again to Windows 98, raising prices to $45 to $50 per copy. It was estimated that 90 percent of new PCs worldwide shipped with Windows 95 or 98.

Microsoft was under attack on a number of fronts by 1999. Sun Microsystems, a leading manufacturer of workstations, was promoting Java, a new software language, as a multiplatform alternative to Windows.[40] In addition, Microsoft was on the defensive in a major antitrust case in the United States. Federal and state attorneys argued that Microsoft had illegally leveraged its monopoly position in operating systems in order to penetrate the Web browser market. Yet despite these challenges, the company's financial performance remained strong, and the stock market crowned Microsoft as the most valuable company in the world.

Application Software   The value of an operating system was tied directly to the quantity and quality of application software that was available on that platform. The Apple II, for example, was a hit in businesses because it supported VisiCalc, the first electronic spreadsheet. Other important PC application segments included word processing, presentation graphics, databases, desktop publishing, personal finance, education, entertainment, and the Internet. Throughout the 1990s, the number of applications available on PCs exploded while average selling prices for PC software collapsed. Microsoft was the number one seller of applications for both the Macintosh and Wintel PCs. However, tens of thousands of small independent software vendors (ISVs) wrote the majority of PC applications. According to the Software Publishers Association, North American sales of PC application software reached $10.6 billion in 1996.[41] Software for Windows made up 81 percent of the total, while Mac programs accounted for 11 percent. Sales of Windows-based applications increased 16.3 percent between 1995 and 1996, while Mac application sales fell 23 percent.

Alternative Technologies

By the late 1990s, personal computers, inspired largely by Apple, were far easier to use than they had been 20 years before. They were also entering the price range of consumer electronics for the first time. By the end of 1998, PCs were available for $399. Nonetheless, a number of analysts believed that PCs had reached the end of the line. Lou Gerstner made the point most dramatically in IBM's 1998 annual report. In his letter to shareholders, IBM's chairman and CEO wrote, "The PC era is over." Others, such as Microsoft senior executive Craig Mundie, took a more moderate line: "This isn't the post-PC era; it's the PC-plus era."[42]

Few observers predicted that personal computers would disappear. Instead, they expected a variety of simpler personal computing devices to supplement and, to some extent, replace PCs. Some of these devices, such as the network computer, resembled the PC. (The network computer was a stripped-down machine that relied on a server to store data and applications.) Other devices looked more like consumer electronics, including handheld PDAs, smart phones, game consoles, and TV set-top boxes. In the spring of 1999, US West unveiled plans to sell Web phones that would support email and Internet access, while Sony announced that it would introduce a Web-capable successor to the PlayStation video console within a year. The consumer electronics giant, which had sold 50 million PlayStations, planned to

EXHIBIT 9   The Macintosh (1984) and the iMac (1998)

Source: Courtesy of Apple of Computer, Inc. iMac photo by Terry Hefferman.

invest $1 billion to $2 billion in the chips that would drive PlayStation 2.

APPLE TURNAROUND?

After returning as Apple's leader, Steve Jobs moved quickly to shake things up. On August 6, 1997, he announced that Microsoft had agreed to invest $150 million in its longtime rival and confirmed its commitment to developing core products, such as Office, for the Mac. While the Apple faithful booed and hissed, the news sent Apple stock to a 52-week high, and Apple's board soon signaled its faith in Jobs by deferring the search for a permanent CEO.

Macs   Jobs, who had long opposed cloning, abruptly brought the Macintosh licensing program to an end. Since the announcement of the first licensing agreement, clones had reached 20 percent of Macintosh unit sales, while the value of the Mac market had fallen 11 percent.[43] Convinced that clones were cannibalizing Apple's installed base, Jobs refused to license Apple's latest OS to the major clone manufacturers. In addition, Apple spent $110 million to acquire the assets of leading cloner Power Computing, including its license for the Mac OS.[44] Apple did grant a license to Taiwan-based Umax Data Systems, which sold largely into markets where Apple was weak, such as Asia and the sub-$1,000 segment. But Umax, which reported that it had lost money on its clone operations, ceased to manufacture Mac-compatible systems in 1998.[45]

Jobs also strengthened and consolidated Apple's product range, reducing the number of lines from 15 to 3. In November 1997, Apple introduced the G3 Power Macs, a series of high-end computers that were based on a powerful new PowerPC chip. G3 systems, which were targeted at business users, could also be used as network servers. Macintosh shipments increased in the quarter following their launch for the first time in two years. In May 1998, Apple followed up with a line of G3 Power-Books, which was also well-received. However, Jobs's greatest coup was the launch of the iMac—"the Internet-age computer for the rest of us"—in August 1998. (See Exhibit 9.) Priced at $1,299, the iMac was Apple's first entry in the low-priced consumer market. The iMac lacked a floppy disk drive but incorporated a CD-ROM drive and modem, all housed in a distinctive translucent teal-and-white case. It also supported "plug-and-play" peripherals, such as printers, that were designed for Wintel machines. (Previous-generation machines required peripherals that were built for the Apple platform.) One month after the iMac's launch, Emachines, a company that made its name in sub-$600 PCs, announced plans to offer an iMac-lookalike with an Intel chip. Emachines's knockoff was expected to sell for $799 in mid-1999.

The iMac was Jobs at his best. Jobs initiated the project shortly after taking over at Apple and pushed it to completion in only 10 months. In his words, the iMac was "designed . . . to deliver the things consumers care about most—the excitement of the Internet and the simplicity of the Mac."[46] Jobs saw the iMac as a breakthrough product, just like the original Mac, and he hoped that it would restore the luster to Apple's brand. Apple spent $100 million to promote the iMac, in its largest advertising campaign to date.[47] Billboards went up across the United States, announcing, "I think, therefore iMac," and after Apple expanded the line to include five "fruit" flavors (blueberry was the most popular), candy-colored iMacs danced across TV screens nationwide, to the musical accompaniment of the Rolling Stones. Plenty of free publicity, generated by the first exciting new Apple product in years, also helped Apple sell 278,000 iMacs in the first six weeks, making the iMac the best-selling computer in company history. Discounting by retailers pushed sales to 800,000 by the end of the year. According to one study, 32 percent of iMac purchasers were new computer buyers, while 13 percent were replacing Wintel machines.[48]

The iMac launch was only the most lavish example of Jobs's efforts to reenergize Apple's image. Soon after coming on board, he rehired TBWA Chiat/Day, the agency that designed the ads for the original Mac, and began to promote Apple with the quirky "Think different" campaign, which featured iconoclastic visionaries such as Albert Einstein and John Lennon. Jobs and TBWA Chiat/Day also sought to repeat their success in launching the Mac with a memorable Super Bowl spot in

1984.[49] While the first ad had cleverly played off George Orwell's vision of a totalitarian future, casting Apple as a spirited insurgent against massive IBM, the 1999 version enlisted Hal, the human-like computer from the movie *2001,* to pitch Apple's cause.

Jobs hoped that creating new excitement around Apple would bring developers back to the Apple platform, in addition to raising sales. However, when he took charge, the strategy for a successor to the Mac OS was still unclear. While Microsoft had a clear roadmap to replace Windows 95 and Windows 98 ultimately with Windows NT, many ISVs were uncertain about the future of Apple's OS, in particular because Rhapsody (the Mac version of Jobs's NeXT OS) would be largely incompatible with previous versions of the Mac OS. Jobs's strategy was to split the Rhapsody project into two tracks. Rhapsody became Mac OS X server, an operating system for high-end products, such as network servers. In addition, Apple developers adapted some of its advanced features for use in Mac OS X, a new version of the Mac OS that would support older applications. Mac OS X server debuted in January 1999, and Mac OS X was slated for release in early 2000. In the meantime, Apple continued to update its existing operating system, issuing interim releases in January and October 1998 and in May 1999.[50]

Apple also redoubled its efforts to woo and support important developers, assigning an "evangelist" to look after each of its partners. Developers soon noticed the change. According to a senior executive at Adobe Systems, which sold around $300 million in Macintosh software each year, "In the last few years it was impossible for any developer to work with them. We couldn't rely on anything they said. We were absolutely convinced they were going to die." However, he continued, there had been "a 180-degree turnaround" since Jobs had taken charge.[51]

Other Products In February 1998, Jobs shut down Apple's Newton division, which produced the MessagePad and the eMate, a portable computer aimed at the education market. Apple had spent roughly $500 million to develop these products over six years.[52] This move was part of Jobs's campaign to streamline Apple's business, which also slashed new project plans by 70 percent.[53]

Internal Changes Jobs made it a top priority to improve Apple's operating efficiency. One of his first moves was to cut company perks, forcing most employees to travel coach and ending Apple's popular paid sabbatical

EXHIBIT 10 Personal Computer Manufacturers

Operating performance

	1995	1996	1997	1998
Gross margin (%)				
Apple	26	10	19	25
Compaq	26	26	27	23
Dell	21	20	21	22
Gateway	16	19	17	21
Inventory turnover				
Apple	6	7	10	17
Compaq	6	9	13	13
Dell	11	12	18	40
Gateway	18	16	20	28
Velocity ("earns times turns")				
Apple	156	70	190	425
Compaq	156	234	351	299
Dell	231	240	378	880
Gateway	288	304	340	588
Cash conversion cycle* (days)				
Apple	76	74	53	25
Compaq	88	62	28	31
Dell	38	37	14	(6)
Gateway	28	25	15	2

*Cash conversion cycle = Average number of days of sales in inventory + Average number of days of sales in accounts receivable − Average number of days of sales in accounts payable.
Note: Data are on a fiscal-year basis. The fiscal year ends in January for Dell, in September for Apple, and in December for Compaq and Gateway.
Source: Company financial reports.

plan. Jobs also pruned Apple's organization, eliminating units that duplicated efforts and centralizing responsibility for functions, such as marketing, in companywide groups. Following restructuring efforts that had begun in 1996, Apple continued to reduce headcount, close facilities, and outsource manufacturing tasks. In addition, Jobs revamped Apple's distribution system, eliminating thousands of smaller outlets and expanding Apple's presence in national chains. In November 1997, Apple launched a website to sell Macs directly to consumers for the first time. While the website did not offer lower prices, it allowed customers to order custom-designed systems. In announcing this move, Jobs showed off a bull's-eye plastered across a picture of Michael Dell and declared, "We're coming after you, buddy."[54]

By early 1999, Jobs's efforts were paying off. After five profitable quarters, Apple had $2.6 billion in cash

EXHIBIT 11   Apple's Market Position, Fall 1998

Market	Apple's installed base	Share of installed base	Share of unit shipments
Consumers	10 million	17%	3%
Education	6 million	44%	25%
Design and publishing	6 million*	36%	27%

*The 6 million figure represents Apple's installed base in the business market as a whole; most of these customers are in the design and publishing segment.
Source: Data from Apple, cited in Jim Davis, "Apple's 5-Step Recovery Plan," *CNET News. com,* October 23, 1998.

and short-term investments. Inventory was down to two days worth of sales, and Apple had cut its cash conversion cycle from 44 to 13 days. (See Exhibit 10.) Gross margin was headed up, and as Fred Anderson, Apple's CFO, proudly announced, revenues, unit shipments, and earnings had all increased in the same quarter for the first time in more than three years.[55]

APPLE'S STRATEGY GOING FORWARD

Some observers doubted the sustainability of Apple's turnaround, but Jobs was supremely confident about the future of his company. As he explained in late 1998:

> The whole strategy for Apple now is, if you will, to be the Sony of the computer business. . . . Computers have a bright future. The question is, where can Apple fit in? Dell and Compaq and Hewlett-Packard sell mainly to the corporate market. Yet there's this whole consumer market, which hardly anybody with the right skills is focusing on.
>
> In audio and video electronics, Sony has a consumer products division, which is their core, and a professional business, which serves broadcasters. Well, our professional business is our design/publishing business, and our consumer business is education and pure consumers. [See Exhibit 11.] The consumer business is pretty cool because it's very high-volume and you really get to interact with individual customers.
>
> Beyond that, Apple's the only PC company left that makes the whole widget—hardware and software.[56]
>
> We own one of only two high-volume operating systems in the world. Everyone completely overlooks this. Microsoft has come to believe that offering an operating system is like printing money. Well, Dell can't print money. Compaq can't print money. But Apple can print money.[57]

ENDNOTES

1. Jai Singh, "Dell: Apple Should Close Shop," *CNET News.com,* October 6, 1997.
2. Louise Kehoe, "Ailing Apple Unveils Link with Microsoft," *Financial Times,* August 7, 1997.
3. This discussion of Apple's history is largely based on Jim Carlton, *Apple: The Inside Story of Intrigue, Egomania, and Business Blunders* (New York: Times Business/Random House, 1997), and "Apple Computer 1992," HBS No. 792–081.
4. Data from Dataquest, cited in Carlton, *Apple,* p. 11.
5. "Apple Computer 1992."
6. Unless otherwise attributed, all quotes from Apple executives are drawn from "Apple Computer 1992."
7. Carlton, *Apple,* p. 123.
8. By contrast, Apple's market share in corporations was only 6 percent. *Ibid.,* p. 273.
9. "Apple Computer 1996," HBS No. 796–126.
10. Charles McCoy, "Apple, IBM Kill Kaleida Labs Venture," *The Wall Street Journal,* November 20, 1995.
11. Jonathan Friedland, "Mac Attack," *Far Eastern Economic Review,* May 12, 1994.
12. "Apple Computer in China, 1993," HBS No. 794–100.
13. Louise Kehoe, "Apple Shares Drop Sharply," *Financial Times,* January 19, 1996.
14. John Simons, "A Bushel of Hope for Apple," *U.S. News & World Report,* July 29, 1996.
15. Jim Carlton and Lee Gomes, "Apple Computer Chief Amelio Is Ousted," *The Wall Street Journal,* July 10, 1997.
16. Jim Davis, "Apple Losing Education Share," *CNET News.com,* February 19, 1998.
17. Randolph Court, "Apple Dumps Newton," *Wired News,* February 27, 1998.
18. Michael Lyster, "Game Consoles Could Be New Web Device King," *Investor's Business Daily,* March 23, 1998.
19. Dawn Kawamoto and Anthony Lazarus, "Apple Lays Off Thousands," *CNET News.com,* March 14, 1997.
20. Peter Burrows, "Is This Apple's Grand Plan?" *Business Week,* August 25, 1997.
21. Robert Cihra, "PC Industry Report," ING Baring Furman Selz LLC, October 9, 1998, p. 11.
22. Data from PC Data, cited in David P. Hamilton, "PCs for Under $600 Seize a Chunk of the Market," *The Wall Street Journal,* March 26, 1999.
23. Robert P. Anastasi et al., "The Computer Sales Channel," The Robinson-Humphrey Co. Inc., August 25, 1997, p. 11.
24. Cihra, "PC Industry Report," p. 6.

25. *U.S. Industry and Trade Outlook 1998: Computer Equipment* (New York: DRI/McGraw-Hill, Standard & Poor's) Washington, D.C.: U.S. Dept. of Commerce/International Trade Administration; pp. 27–12, 27–13.

26. Cihra, "PC Industry Report," pp. 9–10.

27. IDC press release, November 9, 1998.

28. "Dell Online," HBS No. 598–116, pp. 7–8.

29. Dataquest press release, January 29, 1999.

30. Stephen Shankland, "Who Really Makes PCs?" *CNET News.com,* February 9, 1999.

31. Sandeep Junnarkar, "Compaq Mimics Dell, Gateway's Approach," *CNET News.com,* January 29, 1999.

32. Data from InfoCorp, cited in "Apple Computer 1992," p. 17.

33. Bart Ziegler, "IBM Tries, and Fails, to Fix PC Business," *The Wall Street Journal,* February 22, 1995.

34. Raju Narisetti, "How IBM Turned Around Its Ailing PC Division," *The Wall Street Journal,* March 12, 1998.

35. Ira Sager, "At IBM, Nothing but Blue Sky—for Now," *Business Week,* November 30, 1998.

36. IBM's Personal Systems unit lost $992 million (pre-tax) on sales of $12.8 billion in 1998; $161 million on sales of $14.3 billion in 1997; and $39 million on sales of $13.9 billion in 1996.

37. Gary McWilliams, "Whirlwind on the Web," *Business Week,* April 7, 1997.

38. "Dell Online," p. 4.

39. David Kirkpatrick, "The Second Coming of Apple," *Fortune,* November 9, 1998.

40. Sun claimed that developers could use Java to write applications that would run on any operating system, using a piece of software known as a Java virtual machine. By breaking the link between applications and the OS, this would make it easier for PCs with a small installed base to compete with Wintel machines.

41. Software Publishers Association press release, March 31, 1997.

42. John Markoff, "Fight of the (Next) Century: Converging Technologies Put Sony and Microsoft on a Collision Course," *The New York Times,* March 7, 1999.

43. Laurie J. Flynn, "Apple Sending Clone Makers Mixed Signals," *The New York Times,* August 11, 1997.

44. Dawn Kawamoto, "Apple Paid More Than Planned for Power," *CNET News.com,* May 11, 1998.

45. "Umax Lost Money on Mac Clones," *CNET News.com,* May 21, 1998.

46. Apple Computer press release, May 6, 1998.

47. Jim Carlton, "Apple Computer Is Prepared to Launch a Massive Marketing Blitz for iMac," *The Wall Street Journal,* August 14, 1998.

48. Jim Davis, "Apple's iMac Blossoms," *CNET News.com.*

49. The "1984" commercial that launched the Mac can be viewed at the website of TBWA Chiat/Day: http://www.chiatday.com/product/historical_work/tv/1984/1984.html.

50. Jim Davis, "OS X Is the Future for Apple," *CNET News.com,* May 11, 1998; Jim Davis, "Apple's Software Strategy Stays the Course," *CNET News.com,* May 10, 1999.

51. Kirkpatrick, "The Second Coming of Apple."

52. Carlton, *Apple,* pp. 235, 238.

53. Pete Burrows, "A Peek at Steve Jobs' Plan," *Business Week,* November 17, 1997.

54. Jim Davis, "Power Macs, Sales Plan Unveiled," *CNET News.com,* November 10, 1997.

55. Jim Davis, "Apple Posts $152 Million in Profits," *CNET News.com,* January 13, 1999.

56. Brent Schlender, "The Three Faces of Steve," *Fortune,* November 9, 1998.

57. Kirkpatrick, "The Second Coming of Apple."

C A S E   V - 2

Intel Beyond 2003: Looking for Its Third Act

> *There are no second acts in American lives.*
> —F. Scott Fitzgerald, *The Last Tycoon*

Robert A. Burgelman and Philip Meza

INTRODUCTION

There had been a second act for Intel. The company first came to prominence under the leadership of Robert Noyce, co-inventor of the integrated circuit,[1] and Gordon E. Moore, who first described the phenomenon, later

Source: Professor Robert A. Burgelman and Philip Meza prepared this case as the basis for class discussion rather than to illustrate either effective or ineffective handling of an administrative situation. This case may be used in conjunction with "Intel Corporation (A): The DRAM Decision," S-BP-256, and "Intel Corporation: The Evolution of an Adaptive Organization," SM-65, Stanford Graduate School of Business. Copyright © 2002 by the Board of Trustees of the Leland Stanford Junior University. All rights reserved. To order copies or request permission to reproduce materials, e-mail the Case Writing Office at cwo@gsb.stanford.edu or write Case Writing Office, Stanford Graduate School of Business, 518 Memorial Way, Stanford University, Stanford, CA 94305-5015. No part of this publication may be reproduced, stored in a retrieval system, used in a spreadsheet, or transmitted in any form or by any means—electronic, mechanical, photocopying, recording, or otherwise—without the permission of the Stanford Graduate School of Business.

[1] Robert Noyce, then of Fairchild Semiconductor, and Jack S. Kilby, of Texas Instruments (TI), both independently created designs and prototypes for an integrated circuit (IC) within a few months of each other in

called "Moore's Law,"[2] that has governed integrated circuit development since 1965. Intel had been the pioneering maker of computer memory chips in the 1970s.[3] When this market became commoditized in the mid-1980s, and pressures from Japanese memory chip manufacturers marginalized the company, Intel had been forced to look for its next big idea. The company found it in what had started as a small side project for Intel early in its history: microprocessors. In 1985, Intel bet the company on developing and selling leading-edge microprocessors that powered the rapid rise of personal computers (PCs).

Under the direction of Andrew S. Grove, who succeeded Gordon Moore as CEO in 1987, Intel became a major driver of the development of the PC market segment. Intel dominated the market segment for microprocessors, winning up to a 90 percent share of the PC segment of that market. Operating systems produced by Microsoft attained similar market share in the PC segment. Together, Intel and Microsoft created the so-called "Wintel" standard that made both companies extraordinarily valuable.[4] For most of the 1990s, microprocessors for PCs represented more than 80 percent of Intel's annual revenue and all of its profits. Intel and its investors became accustomed to extraordinary success as the company rode a 15-year wave of exploding growth in demand for its microprocessors. Through most of the 1990s, Intel's annual revenue grew at a compound annual growth rate (CAGR) of 25 percent, reaching a peak CAGR of 36 percent in 1996. By 1998, however, sales of PCs and the microprocessors that powered them began to slow. In 2000, revenue grew by only 15 percent, and dropped by 21 percent in 2001. Intel's operations, apart from its core PC microprocessor activities, were losing money (Exhibit 1).

As of 1997, Craig Barrett, Intel's COO at the time, became concerned about the company's growth depending entirely on microprocessors for the PC market segment. He also worried that the microprocessor business had become, for Intel, like a "creosote bush": a desert plant that poisons the ground around it so that no other plants can grow nearby. Barrett succeeded Andy Grove as Intel's CEO in 1998. Under his direction Intel began to search for growth in areas beyond its core PC microprocessor market segment, redefining itself as an Internet building block company. He also initiated executive development programs to augment Intel's leadership capability for new business development.

Over the next several years, Intel spent more than $10 billion in acquisitions, buying companies in the communications and networking industries, and also invested heavily in Internet-related services. Several billions of dollars of those investments came to nothing, as Intel bought its way into markets it soon exited. Nevertheless, by 2002 Intel's corporate strategy had broadened to encompass three strategic business areas: Intel Architecture Group (IAG), which created building blocks for desktop, mobile, and server businesses; Intel Communications Group (ICG), which sold building blocks to the telecommunications industry; and Wireless Computing and Communications Group (WCCG), which sold building blocks to the wireless communications industry. General managers who were long-term Intel employees ran each of these businesses. Parallel to these business groups remained powerful functional organizations: Intel Capital, Technology and Manufacturing Group (TMG), Sales and Marketing Group (SMG), Finance, and Human Resources, among others.

By late 2002, amid the most prolonged technology recession in the memories of Intel's long-serving senior executives, the company had refocused, and was directing its financial and engineering muscle toward its new concept of the convergence of communications and computing at the chip level. Intel's new mission was now captured in six key words: Silicon Leadership; Architectural Innovation; and Worldwide Opportunity. Intel also decided to maintain its traditionally high levels of capital expenditure and R&D investments in order to be in a strong strategic position when the recession ended

---

1958/1959. After an extended and complicated legal wrangling over the patent, an appeals court found for Noyce. However, both inventors agreed that the other was a genuine co-inventor and Fairchild and TI agreed to cross license the IC. Robert Noyce died in 1990. Jack Kilby was awarded one half of the 2000 Nobel Prize in Physics in recognition for his "part in inventing the integrated circuit." Nobel Prizes are not awarded posthumously.

[2] Gordon E. Moore, "Cramming More Components onto Integrated Circuits," *Electronics,* April 19, 1965. Moore's Law describes the exponential growth in the number of transistors that could occur on an integrated circuit every year or two, and predicts its continuation—which has held true for over 35 years. The impact of Moore's Law was predicted (presciently) in a cartoon in that 1965 article which depicted "Handy Home Computers" being sold next to notions and cosmetics in a department store.

[3] Intel's first products, static random access memory (SRAM) chips and later dynamic random access memory (DRAM) chips, were designed to replace the magnetic core memory then standard on mainframe computers.

[4] For an in-depth review and analysis of key strategic events at Intel including its exit from the memory business and entrance into the PC microprocessor business, see R. A. Burgelman, *Strategy Is Destiny* (New York: Free Press, 2002).

EXHIBIT 1   Intel Selected Summary Financial Information

Operating segment information

($ millions)	Q3 2002	Q2 2002	Q1 2002	Q4 2001	Q3 2001	Q2 2001	Q1 2001	Q4 2000	Q3 2000	Full Year 2001	Full Year 2000
Intel Architecture Group[1]											
Revenues	5,407	5,213	5,768	5,793	5,393	5,127	5,133	6,851	7,039	21,446	27,301
Operating profit	1,405	1,362	1,802	1,813	1,329	1,444	1,666	3,211	3,347	6,252	12,511
Intel Communications Group[2]											
Revenues	482	536	518	590	580	635	775	924	948	2,580	3,483
Operating loss	(177)	(127)	(150)	(129)	(218)	(235)	(153)	67	102	(735)	(319)
Wireless Communications and Computing Group[3]											
Revenues	586	532	459	518	509	510	695	819	667	2,232	2,669
Operating loss	(30)	(98)	(68)	(20)	(59)	(158)	(19)	161	149	(256)	(608)
All other[4]											
Revenues	29	38	36	82	63	62	74	108	77	281	273
Operating loss	(234)	(498)	(269)	(656)	(663)	(834)	(852)	(863)	(741)	(3,005)	(3,043)
Total											
Revenues	6,504	6,319	6,781	6,983	6,545	6,334	6,677	8,702	8,731	26,539	33,726
Operating profit	964	639	1,315	1,008	389	217	642	2,576	2,857	2,256	10,395

[1] Intel Architecture Group products include microprocessors, motherboards, and other related board-level products, including chipsets.
[2] Intel Communications Group products include Ethernet connectivity products, network processing components, embedded control chips, and optical components.
[3] Wireless Communications and Computing Group products include flash memory, application processors, and cellular chipsets for cellular handsets and handheld devices.
[4] The "all other" category includes acquisition-related costs, including amortization of identified intangibles, in-process research and development, and write-offs of acquisition-related intangibles. The "all other" category also includes the results of the Web hosting business. In addition, the "all other" category includes certain corporate-level operating expenses, including a portion of profit-dependent bonus and other expenses that are not allocated to the operating segments. In Q2 2002, "all other" included the charge for impairment of identified intangibles, primarily related to the previous acquisition of Xircom, as well as the charge related to winding down the Web hosting business. For quarters in 2001, "all other" includes goodwill amortization, whereas goodwill is no longer amortized beginning in 2002.
Source: Company reports.

Intel percent of revenue by group, 2001

Group	% total revenue 2001
Intel Architecture Group (IAG)	81
Intel Communications Group (ICG)	10
Wireless Communications and Computing Group (WCCG)	8.5
New Business Group (NBG)	0.5

EXHIBIT 1   (continued)

Selected financial data 1995–2001

(In millions)

Year	Net revenues	Cost of sales	Research and development	Operating income	Net income	Employees at year end
2001	$26,539	$13,487	$3,796	$2,256	$1,291	83.4
2000	$33,726	$12,650	$3,897	$10,395	$10,535	86.1
1999	$29,389	$11,836	$3,111	$9,767	$7,314	70.2
1998	$26,273	$12,088	$2,509	$8,379	$6,068	64.5
1997	$25,070	$9,945	$2,347	$9,887	$6,945	63.7
1996	$20,847	$9,164	$1,808	$7,553	$5,157	48.5
1995	$16,202	$7,811	$1,296	$5,252	$3,566	41.6

Source: Company reports.

Intel income statement data, most recent 7 quarters

(In millions, except per share amounts)

	Q3 2002	Q2 2002	Q1 2002	Q4 2001	Q3 2001	Q2 2001	Q1 2001
Net revenues	**$6,504**	**$6,319**	**$6,781**	**$6,983**	**$6,545**	**$6,334**	**$6,677**
Cost of sales	$3,331	$3,350	$3,301	$3,402	$3,553	$3,307	$3,225
Research and development	$1,006	$1,024	$982	$952	$930	$919	$995
Marketing, general and administrative	$1,095	$1,063	$1,072	$1,071	$1,064	$1,174	$1,155
Amortization of goodwill	$0	$0	$0	$405	$447	$417	$441
Amortization of acquisition-related intangibles and costs	$102	$229	$111	$145	$162	$177	$144
Purchased in-process research and development	$6	$14	$0	$0	$0	$123	$75
Operating costs and expenses	$5,540	$5,680	$5,466	$5,975	$6,156	$6,117	$6,035
Operating income	**$964**	**$639**	**$1,315**	**$1,008**	**$389**	**$217**	**$642**
Gains (losses) on equity securities, net	($96)	($59)	($46)	($287)	($182)	$3	$0
Interest and other	$49	$43	$48	$73	($70)	$126	$264
Income before taxes	**$917**	**$623**	**$1,317**	**$794**	**$137**	**$346**	**$906**
Income taxes	$231	$177	$381	$290	$31	$150	$421
Net income	**$686**	**$446**	**$936**	**$504**	**$106**	**$196**	**$485**
Basic earnings per share	**$0.10**	**$0.07**	**$0.14**	**$0.08**	**$0.02**	**$0.03**	**$0.07**
Diluted earnings per share	**$0.10**	**$0.07**	**$0.14**	**$0.07**	**$0.02**	**$0.03**	**$0.07**
Common shares outstanding	**6,646**	**6,677**	**6,684**	**6,698**	**6,718**	**6,725**	**6,721**
Common shares assuming dilution	6,712	6,803	6,861	6,851	6,876	6,889	6,899
Gross margin % of revenues	49%	47%	51%	51%	46%	48%	52%
Research & dev. % of revenues	15%	16%	14%	14%	14%	15%	15%
Mktg. gen. & admin. % of revenues	17%	17%	16%	15%	16%	19%	17%
Income before taxes % of revenues	14%	10%	19%	11%	2%	5%	14%
Net income % of revenues	11%	7%	14%	7%	2%	3%	7%
Pro forma information excluding acquisition-related costs:							
Pro forma operating costs and expenses	$5,432	$5,437	$5,355	$5,425	$5,547	$5,400	$5,375
Pro forma operating income	$1,072	$882	$1,426	$1,558	$998	$934	$1,302
pro forma net income	**$768**	**$620**	**$1,022**	**$998**	**$655**	**$854**	**$1,099**
Pro forma net income							
Basic EPS excl. acquisition-related costs	**$0.12**	**$0.09**	**$0.15**	**$0.15**	**$0.10**	**$0.13**	**$0.16**
Diluted EPS excl. acquisition-related costs	**$0.11**	**$0.09**	**$0.15**	**$0.15**	**$0.10**	**$0.12**	**$0.16**

Source: Company reports.

EXHIBIT 1 **(continued)**

Intel balance sheet data, most recent 7 quarters

	Q3 2002	Q2 2002	Q1 2002	Q4 2001	Q3 2001	Q2 2001	Q1 2001
Current assets:							
Cash and short-term investments	$9,615	$8,957	$9,231	$10,326	$9,158	$9,340	$10,058
Trading assets—fixed income	$1,313	$1,185	$1,047	$836	$726	$813	$1,123
Trading assets—equities	$89	$187	$256	$74	$67	$77	$107
Trading assets—SERP	$225	$278	$314	$314	$266	$335	$315
Total trading assets	$1,627	$1,650	$1,617	$1,224	$1,059	$1,225	$1,545
Accounts receivable	$3,089	$2,907	$2,883	$2,607	$3,043	$2,904	$3,432
Inventories:							
Raw materials	$286	$242	$265	$237	$297	$379	$406
Work in process	$1,520	$1,393	$1,301	$1,316	$1,308	$1,431	$1,367
Finished goods	$675	$870	$914	$700	$746	$1,016	$879
Subtotal inventories	$2,481	$2,505	$2,480	$2,253	$2,351	$2,826	$2,652
Deferred tax assets and other	$1,233	$1,182	$1,278	$1,223	$1,256	$1,010	$1,052
Total current assets	**$18,045**	**$17,201**	**$17,489**	**$17,633**	**$16,867**	**$17,305**	**$18,739**
Property, plant and equipment, net	**$17,970**	**$18,176**	**$18,314**	**$18,121**	**$18,138**	**$17,828**	**$16,774**
Marketable strategic equity securities	**$56**	**$96**	**$129**	**$155**	**$165**	**$649**	**$1,159**
Other long-term investments	**$1,182**	**$1,438**	**$1,605**	**$1,319**	**$1,249**	**$1,094**	**$1,141**
Goodwill, net	**$4,334**	**$4,338**	**$4,338**	**$4,330**	**$4,714**	**$5,300**	**$5,037**
Other assets	**$2,049**	**$2,249**	**$2,514**	**$2,837**	**$3,098**	**$3,448**	**$3,399**
Total assets	**$43,636**	**$43,498**	**$44,389**	**$44,395**	**$44,231**	**$45,624**	**$46,249**
Current liabilities:							
Short-term debt	$317	$383	$412	$409	$302	$411	$479
Accounts payable and accrued liabilities	$4,492	$4,195	$4,604	$4,755	$4,616	$4,984	$5,398
Deferred income on shipments to distributors	$512	$498	$572	$418	$507	$549	$648
Income taxes payable	$960	$672	$1,017	$988	$768	$869	$862
Total current liabilties	**$6,281**	**$5,748**	**$6,605**	**$6,570**	**$6,193**	**$6,813**	**$7,387**
Long-term debt	**$1,000**	**$1,081**	**$1,064**	**$1,050**	**$972**	**$928**	**$704**
Deferred tax liabilities	**$1,048**	**$1,089**	**$860**	**$945**	**$1,164**	**$1,145**	**$1,240**
Total stockholders' equity	**$35,307**	**$35,580**	**$35,860**	**$35,830**	**$35,902**	**$36,738**	**$36,918**
Total liabilities and stockholders' equity	**$43,636**	**$43,498**	**$44,389**	**$44,395**	**$44,231**	**$45,624**	**$46,249**

Source: Company reports.

Intel supplemental financial and other information, most recent 7 quarters

	Q3 2002	Q2 2002	Q1 2002	Q4 2001	Q3 2001	Q2 2001	Q1 2001
GEOGRAPHIC REVENUES:							
Americas	32%	35%	33%	33%	37%	37%	35%
Asia-Pacific	38%	38%	36%	35%	31%	31%	28%
Europe	23%	20%	23%	25%	25%	22%	25%
Japan	7%	7%	8%	7%	7%	10%	12%
CASH INVESTMENTS:							
Cash and short-term investments	$9,615	$8,957	$9,231	$10,326	$9,158	$9,340	$10,058
Trading assets—fixed income	$1,313	$1,185	$1,047	$836	$726	$813	$1,123
Total cash investments	$10,928	$10,142	$10,278	$11,162	$9,884	$10,153	$11,181
INTEL CAPITAL PORTFOLIO:							
Trading assets—equity securities	$89	$187	$256	$74	$67	$77	$107
Marketable strategic equity securities	$56	$96	$129	$155	$165	$649	$1,159
Other strategic investments	$1,169	$1,177	$1,241	$1,499	$1,772	$1,985	$2,032
Total Intel capital portfolio	$1,314	$1,460	$1,626	$1,728	$2,004	$2,711	$3,298

EXHIBIT 1 **(continued)**

Intel supplemental financial and other information, most recent 7 quarters

	Q3 2002	Q2 2002	Q1 2002	Q4 2001	Q3 2001	Q2 2001	Q1 2001
SELECTED CASH FLOW INFORMATION:							
Depreciation	$1,136	$1,135	$1,161	$1,093	$1,054	$1,050	$934
Amortization of goodwill	$0	$0	$0	$405	$447	$417	$441
Amortization of acquisition-related intangibles and costs	$102	$229	$111	$145	$162	$177	$144
Purchased in-process research and development	$6	$14	$0	$0	$0	$123	$75
Capital spending	($955)	($1,115)	($1,430)	($1,136)	($1,365)	($2,144)	($2,664)
Stock repurchase program	($1,001)	($1,002)	($1,005)	($1,003)	($1,002)	($1,002)	($1,001)
Proceeds from sales of shares to employees, tax benefit & other	$279	$239	$360	$298	$314	$224	$356
Dividends paid	($133)	($134)	($134)	($134)	($135)	($135)	($134)
Net cash used for acquisitions	($7)	($50)	$0	($4)	$0	($381)	($498)
SHARE INFORMATION (adjusted for stock splits):							
Average common shares outstanding	6,646	6,677	6,684	6,698	6,718	6,725	6,721
Dilutive effect of:							
Stock options	66	126	177	153	158	164	178
Convertible notes	0	0	0	0	0	0	0
Common shares assuming dilution	6,712	6,803	6,861	6,851	6,876	6,889	6,899
STOCK BUYBACK:							
BUYBACK ACTIVITY:							
Shares repurchased	56.6	37.2	30.9	35.0	34.9	34.1	29.4
Cumulative shares repurchased	1,651.4	1,594.8	1,557.6	1,526.7	1,491.7	1,456.8	1,422.7
OTHER INFORMATION:							
Employees (in thousands)	81.7	83.2	82.9	83.4	86.2	88.2	90.2
Day sales outstanding	36	37	37	37	38	39	40

Source: Company reports.

Intel consolidated statements of income, 1995–2001

Three years ended December 29
(In millions—except per share amounts)

	2001	2000	1999	1998	1997	1996	1995
Net revenues	**$26,539**	**$33,726**	**$29,389**	**$26,273**	**$25,070**	**$20,847**	**$16,202**
Cost of sales	13,487	12,650	11,836	12,088	9,945	9,164	1,296
Research and development	3,796	3,897	3,111	2,509	2,347	1,808	1,843
Marketing, general and administrative	4,464	5,089	3,872	3,076	2,891	2,322	1,843
Amortization of goodwill and other acquisition-related intangibles and costs	2,338	1,586	411	56	—		
Purchased in-process research and development	198	109	392	165	—	—	—
Operating costs and expenses	24,283	23,331	19,622	17,894	15,183	13,294	10,950
Operating income	**2,256**	**10,395**	**9,767**	**8,379**	**9,887**	**7,553**	**5,252**
Interest expenses				(34)	(27)	(25)	(29)

EXHIBIT 1 (continued)

Intel consolidated statements of income, 1995–2001

Three years ended December 29
(In millions—except per share amounts)

	2001	2000	1999	1998	1997	1996	1995
Gains (losses) on equity securities, net	(466)	3,759	883	—	—	—	
Interest and other, net	393	987	578	792	799	406	415
Income before taxes	**2,183**	**15,141**	**11,228**	**9,137**	**10,659**	**7,934**	**5,638**
Provision for taxes	892	4,606	3,914	3,069	3,714	2,777	2,072
Net income	**$1,291**	**$10,535**	**$7,314**	**$6,068**	**$6,945**	**$5,157**	**$3,566**
Basic earnings per common share	**$0.19**	**$1.57**	**$1.10**	**$1.82**	**$2.12**	**$1.57**	**$4.03**
Diluted earnings per common share	**$0.19**	**$1.51**	**$1.05**	**$1.73**	**$1.93**	**$1.45**	
Weighted average common shares outstanding	**6,716**	**6,709**	**6,648**	**3,336**	**3,271**	**3,290**	
Dilutive effect of:							
Employee stock options				159	204	187	
1998 Step-up warrants				22	115	74	
Weighted average common shares outstanding, assuming dilution	**6,879**	**6,986**	**6,940**	**3,517**	**3,590**	**3,551**	**884**

Source: Company reports.

Intel consolidated balance sheets, 1995–2001

(In millions—except par value)

	2001	2000	1999	1998	1997	1996	1995
Assets							
Current assets:							
Cash and cash equivalents	$7,970	$2,976	$3,695	$2,038	$4,102	$4,165	$1,463
Short-term investments	2,356	10,497	7,705	5,272	5,630	3,742	995
Trading assets	1,224	350	388	316	195	87	—
Accounts receivable, net of allowance for doubtful accounts of $68 ($84 in 2000)	2,607	4,129	3,700	3,527	3,438	3,723	3,116
Inventories	2,253	2,241	1,478	1,582	1,697	1,293	2,004
Deferred tax assets	958	721	673	618	676	570	408
Other current assets	265	236	180	122	129	104	111
Total current assets	**17,633**	**21,150**	**17,819**	**13,475**	**15,867**	**13,684**	**8,097**
Property, plant and equipment:							
Land and buildings	10,709	7,416	7,246	6,297	5,113	4,372	3,145
Machinery and equipment	21,605	15,994	14,851	13,149	10,577	8,729	7,099
Construction in progress	2,042	4,843	1,460	1,622	2,437	1,161	1,548
	34,356	28,253	23,557	21,068	18,127	14,262	11,792
Less accumulated depreciation	16,235	13,240	11,842	9,459	7,461	5,775	4,321
Property, plant and equipment, net	**18,121**	**15,013**	**11,715**	**11,609**	**10,666**	**8,487**	**7,471**
Marketable strategic equity securities	155	1,915	7,121				
Other long-term investments	1,319	1,797	790	5,365	1,839	1,353	1,653

EXHIBIT 1 (continued)

Intel consolidated balance sheets, 1995–2001

(In millions—except par value)

	2001	2000	1999	1998	1997	1996	1995
Goodwill, net	4,330	4,977					
Acquisition-related intangibles, net	797	964	4,934				
Other assets	2,040	2,129	1,470	1,022	508	211	283
Total assets	$44,395	$47,945	$43,849	$31,471	$28,880	$23,735	$17,504
Liabilities and stockholder's equity							
Current liabilities:							
Short-term debt	$409	$378	$230	$159	$212	$389	$346
Long-term debt redeemable within one year				—	110		
Accounts payable	1,769	2,387	1,370	1,244	1,407	969	864
Accrued compensation and benefits	1,179	1,696	1,454	1,285	1,268	1,128	758
Deferred income on shipments to distributors	418	674	609	606	516	474	304
Accrued advertising	560	782	582	458	500	410	218
Other accrued liabilities	1,247	1,440	1,159	1,094	842	507	328
Income taxes payable	988	1,293	1,695	958	1,165	986	801
Total current liabilities	6,570	8,650	7,099	5,804	6,020	4,863	3,619
Long-term debt	1,050	707	955	702	448	728	400
Deferred tax liabilities	945	1,266	3,130	1,387	1,076	997	620
Put warrants			130	201	2,041	275	725
Commitments and contingencies							
Stockholders' equity:							
Preferred stock, $0.001 par value, 50 shares authorized; none issued	—	—			—		
Common stock, $0.001 par value,	8,833	8,486	7,316	4,822	3,311	2,897	2,583
Acquisition-related unearned stock compensation	(178)	(97)					
Accumulated other comprehensive income	25	195					
Retained earnings	27,150	28,738	21,428	17,952	15,926	13,975	9,557
Accumulated other comprehensive income			3,791	603	58		
Total stockholders' equity	35,830	37,322	32,535	23,377	19,295	16,872	12,140
Total liabilities and stockholders' equity	$44,395	$47,945	$43,849	$31,471	$28,880	$23,735	$17,504

Source: Company reports.

Intel consolidated statements of cash flows, 1995–2001

(In millions)

	2001	2000	1999	1998	1997	1996	1995
Cash and cash equivalents, beginning of year	$2,976	$3,695	$2,038	$4,102	$4,165	$1,463	$1,180
Cash flows provided by (used for) operating activities:							
Net income	1,291	10,535	7,314	6,068	6,945	5,157	3,566

EXHIBIT 1 **(continued)**

Intel consolidated statements of cash flows, 1995–2001

(In millions)

	2001	2000	1999	1998	1997	1996	1995
Adjustments to reconcile net income to net cash provided by (used for) operating activities:							
Depreciation	4,131	3,249	3,186	2,807	2,192	1,888	1,371
Net loss on retirement of property, plant and equipment	119	139	193	282	130	120	75
Amortization of goodwill and other acquisition-related intangibles and costs	2,338	1,586	411				8
Purchased in-process research and development	198	109	392	165	—	—	
Gains (losses) on equity investments, net	466	(3,759)	(883)				
Gain (loss) on investment in Convera	196	(117)	—				
Deferred taxes	(519)	(130)	(219)	77	6	179	346
Tax benefits from employee stock plans	435	887	506	415	224	196	116
Changes in assets and liabilities:							
Trading assets	898	38	(72)				
Accounts receivable	1,561	(384)	153	(38)	285	(607)	(1,138)
Inventories	24	(731)	169	167	(404)	711	(835)
Accounts payable	(673)	978	79	(180)	438	105	289
Accrued compensation and benefits	(524)	231	127	17	140	370	170
Income taxes payable	(270)	(362)	726	(211)	179	185	**372**
Other assets and liabilities	(1,017)	558	(819)	249	(21)	439	(324)
Total adjustments	7,363	2,292	4,021	3,123	3,063	3,586	450
Net cash provided by operating activities	**8,654**	**12,827**	**11,435**	**9,191**	**10,008**	**8,743**	**4,016**
Cash flows provided by (used for) investing activities:							
Additions to property, plant and equipment	(7,309)	(6,674)	(3,403)	(3,557)	(4,501)	(3,024)	(3,550)
Purchase of Chips & Technologies, Inc., net of cash acquired				(321)	—	—	—
Purchase of Digital Equipment Corporation semiconductor operations				(585)	—	—	—

EXHIBIT 1 (continued)

Intel consolidated statements of cash flows, 1995–2001

(In millions)

	2001	2000	1999	1998	1997	1996	1995
Acquisitions, net of cash acquired	(883)	(2,317)	(2,979)	(906)			
Purchases of available-for-sale investments	(7,141)	(17,188)	(7,055)	(10,925)	(9,224)	(4,683)	(685)
Sales of available-for-sale investments				201	153	225	114
Maturities and sales of available-for-sale investments	15,398	17,124	7,987	8,681	6,713	2,214	1,444
Other investing activities	(260)	(980)	(799)				
Net cash used for investing activities	**(195)**	**(10,035)**	**(6,249)**	**(6,506)**	**(6,859)**	**(5,268)**	**(2,677)**
Cash flows provided by (used for) financing activities:							
Increase (decrease) in short-term debt, net	23	138	69	(83)	(177)	43	(179)
Additions to long-term debt	306	77	118	169	172	317	—
Repayment and retirement of long-term debt	(10)	(46)	—	—	(300)	—	(4)
Proceeds from sales of shares through employee stock plans and other	762	797	543	507	317	257	192
Proceeds from sales of put warrants	—	—	20		288	56	85
Repurchase and retirement of common stock	(4,008)	(4,007)	(4,612)		(3,372)	(1,302)	(1,034)
Payment of dividends to stockholders	(538)	(470)	(366)		(180)	(148)	(116)
Proceeds from exercises of 1998 step-up warrants				1,620	40	4	
Net cash used for financing activities	**(3,465)**	**(3,511)**	**(4,228)**	**(4,749)**	**(3,212)**	**(773)**	**(1,056)**
Net increase (decrease) in cash and cash equivalents	**4,994**	**(719)**	**(1,657)**	**(2,064)**	**(63)**	**(2,702)**	**283**
Cash and cash equivalents, end of year	**$ 7,970**	**$ 2,976**	**$ 3,695**	**$ 2,038**	**$ 4,102**	**$ 4,165**	**$ 1,463**
Supplemental disclosures of cash flow information:							
Cash paid during the year for:							
Interest	$ 53	$ 43	$ 40	$ 40	$ 37	$ 51	$ 182
Income taxes	$ 1,208	$ 4,209	$ 2,899	$ 2,784	$ 3,305	$ 2,217	$ 1,209
			*$ 3,305	*$ 2,217	*$ 1,209		

*Certain 1997 and 1996 amounts have been reclassified to conform to the 1998 presentation.
Source: Company reports.

EXHIBIT 2   Intel Capital Expenditure (CapEx) 2001 and 2002

2001: $7.3 billion	2002: $5.5 billion
300 mm	300 mm
22% of total capital	56% of total capital
27% of fab capital	72% of fab capital
0.13 micron and smaller	0.13 micron and smaller
60% of total capital	73% of total capital
78% of fab capital	95% of fab capital

Source: Andy Bryant, "To Recovery and Beyond," Intel Spring Analysts' Meeting, April 25, 2002.

(Exhibit 2). Some financial analysts, however, had begun to question Intel's heavy capital investments. In November 2002, Intel's stock was trading at $18.80, down from $72.84 at its peak in July 2000, and the price/earnings (P/E) ratio was at a low of 47.96 in the trailing 12 months, compared to a 5-year high of 162.62 (Exhibit 3).[5]

Looking beyond 2002, Intel's top management faced some big strategic questions: Would the envisaged convergence materialize and give Intel the opportunity to extend the company's position and competencies into lucrative new markets? How likely was it for Intel to get a return on the enormous investments in manufacturing and technology it was making in the face of major market uncertainties? Was Intel's executive leadership bench strong and deep enough to address the various challenges associated with the widened corporate strategic scope? Was Intel's organization optimally structured to implement the new corporate strategy? Would Intel find a successful third act?

LET CHAOS REIGN, THEN REIN IN CHAOS[6]

Internet Euphoria

During 1998–2001, Intel invested heavily in industries outside its traditional areas of expertise, buying its way into communications, information appliances, and Internet services. Barrett decentralized the company and restructured business groups three times in three years.[7] Within two years, Intel shuttered many of its operations in

these new areas. Barrett described events at Intel over the past few years: "There was a little roadkill along the way. We diverged into other elements of the Internet. Our actions since 1999 were partially driven by environmental factors, in particular the dotcom meltdown, the telecom meltdown, and the internationalization of business."[8]

The roadkill that Barrett mentioned included Intel's forays into services, organized under a new group called Intel Online Services (IOS), and system products, organized under another new group called Communications Products Group (CPG). In a little over two years the company spent $4 billion acquiring server farms and manufacturing servers, acquiring Web casting services, and even producing MP3 players and toy digital microscopes. In 2001, Intel dissolved CPG and stopped making network servers and routers after some of its biggest customers, including Dell Computer, Compaq, and Cisco Systems, complained about Intel's competition in their markets. In 2002, Intel also dropped most of its Internet services operations and dissolved IOS. Barrett said, "I do regret our forays into services businesses like streaming media and Intel Online. These were our contributions to the dotcom euphoria."

Remembering the Importance of Execution

For much of the 1990s, under Barrett's tenure as COO, Intel earned a reputation for flawless execution. The company's technological prowess, manufacturing excellence, and financial power kept at bay most competitors in its core PC microprocessor market segment. Over the past few years, however, Intel suffered hiccups in its core markets.

Reflecting on these events since he assumed the CEO job, Barrett said:

Two things happened: We stumbled and took our eye off the ball.

We did not execute well because we didn't follow our own methodology. For example, we had to recall some motherboards. With the management changes and because we were growing too fast, we did not follow our own best-known methods.

We used to use leapfrog teams to speed up innovation. These teams worked on technologies that were a generation ahead of the technologies just being introduced. We purposely abandoned the leapfrog strategy, which was put in place to facilitate product development during the four years between major microprocessor architecture innovations.

---

[5] Intel stock price at market close on 15 November 2002. PE ratio comparisons as of 8 November 2002.

[6] See Andrew S. Grove, *Only the Paranoid Survive* (New York: Doubleday, 1996), p. 123. Grove writes, "Getting through a strategic inflection point involves confusion, uncertainty, and disorder, both on a personal level and if you are in management on a strategic level for the enterprise as a whole."

[7] Cliff Edwards and Ira Sager, "Can Craig Barrett Reverse Intel's Slide?" *Business Week,* October 4, 2001.

[8] All quotes from Craig Barrett are from the authors' interview on 30 October 2002. Subsequent quotes from this interview will not be cited.

**EXHIBIT 3 Intel Selected Share Price, Volume and Price/Earnings (P/E) Data
December 31, 1996–September 9, 2002**

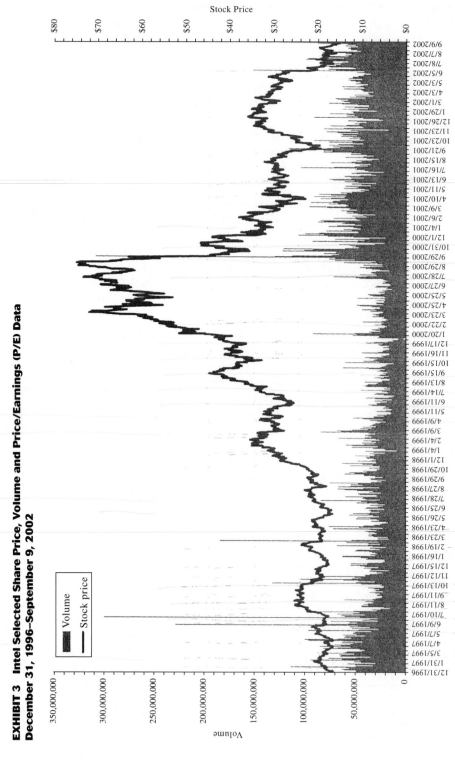

Source: Thompson Financial.

Intel PE ratio data

Year	Intel average P/E ratio
1992	12.3
1993	11.3
1994	10.7
1995	13.9
1996	14.2
1997	20.6
1998	24.3
1999	29.5
2000	36.1
2001	55.0

(As of 8 Nov 2002)	Intel	Semiconductor industry	Technology sector	S & P 500
P/E ratio (TTM)	47.96	47.73	34.76	24.74
P/E high (past 5 years)	162.62	91.96	67.14	49.33
P/E low (past 5 years)	17.46	16.64	19.90	16.90

TTM = trailing 12 months.
Source: ValueLine Investment Survey; OneSource.

With Itanium [see below], we cut back on parallel design teams for the desktop. This left a gap in technology. The gap made it easier for our competitors to compete with us. This was a conscious decision to make a structural change in the development cycle. But without perfect execution, the hole got bigger.

Some observers noted that Barrett, when he became CEO, needed as good a COO as he had been under Grove. For a time, Barrett tried to play both roles, but found it difficult to juggle the demands. Barrett said, "The problems were further exacerbated by the internationalization of business. Do you spend time in factories or in new, emerging markets?" In January 2002, Barrett named Paul Otellini to the position of president and COO. Barrett described Otellini as "Mr. Inside," with his hands on all of the levers at the company, much as Barrett had worked the switches when he had been COO. Meanwhile, Barrett continued his role as "Mr. Outside," orbiting the company that now spanned the globe to a degree that it never had before, setting strategies and direction.

Barrett's "Mr. Inside," President and COO Paul Otellini, offered his assessment on Intel over the past few years: "Craig took over at a time that coincided with industry, technology, and with hindsight, company change. The specter of the Internet and dotcom became catalysts to take action. Before Craig's changes, we did not have expertise in communications, beyond copper Ethernets. We obtained important communications architectures from our acquisitions.[9]

The company learned lessons from its failures over the past few years. Otellini said, "IOS was an orthogonal departure for us. Just as Microma[10] was about fashion and not technology, Web hosting turned out to be about consulting and not technology."

According to Otellini, "Where we are today, we are better off than if we had not taken those excursions. We have hitched ourselves to communications as a means to capitalize on Internet growth. It focuses on what we are good at: architectures and silicon. Silicon is the engine that will make convergence between communications and computing happen. Silicon is the template upon which to embed architectures." Otellini explained further:

We are incredibly strong in computing. We will lever that strength to become a first mover in communications. In five years, if communications and computing are separate activities at Intel, we've failed. Intel understands software tools and architectures that can be reproduced by the hundreds of millions. We understand:

- Computer Architectures
- Microprocessors
- Core Logic
- Memory
- Communications architectures and silicon

All of these things are central in a range of devices from servers to phones.

Intel's New Focus

By 2002, Intel had gained new focus. Barrett described Intel as a stool with four legs. The company would be supported by R&D; capital expenditure; its branding program; and increasingly, its venture capital investments through Intel Capital. These would serve as the company's foundation as Intel sought opportunities in silicon and digital computing and communications architectures around the world.

Barrett said Intel's organizational structure was now straightforward: "We have five business units. Three are microprocessor-oriented: these are Mobile, Desktop, and Server-Enterprise. In addition Intel is organized around handheld devices and network and communication infrastructure" (Exhibit 4).

For Barrett, the distractions of the past few years were now behind the company: "We are refocused on silicon, architectures, and worldwide business opportunities for the core business. This has led to the crystallization of our strategy. Our mission statement hasn't changed, but the definition of 'building blocks' of the Internet has become clearer."

The convergence of communications and computing architectures seemed a natural extension for the company to Barrett: "Silicon devices incorporating both logic and communications capability are important now. Our R&D budget goes into communications and the convergence of communication and computing. The branding program continues, plus Intel Capital has spent $150 million to fund communications investments, particularly in 802.11." [802.11 refers to a group of specifications governing wireless fidelity (WiFi), a high-frequency wireless local area network protocol.] In 2001, Intel spent $3.8 billion on research and development, 31 percent of

---

[9] All quotes from Paul Otellini are from the authors' interview on 9 October 2002, unless otherwise indicated. Subsequent quotes from this interview will not be cited.

[10] In 1972, Intel acquired Microma, a solid-state watch company, with the hope that it would provide an outlet for EPROM chips. The foray into watches failed and Intel left the watch business in 1977. Gordon Moore referred to the Microma watch he wore as his "$15 million watch." He said in 1988, "If anybody comes to me with an idea for a consumer product, all I have to do is look at my watch to get the answer." *Source:* R. A. Burgelman, *Strategy Is Destiny* (New York: Free Press, 2002) p. 115, and Intel Company Museum, Santa Clara, CA.

EXHIBIT 4   Intel Organization Chart 2002

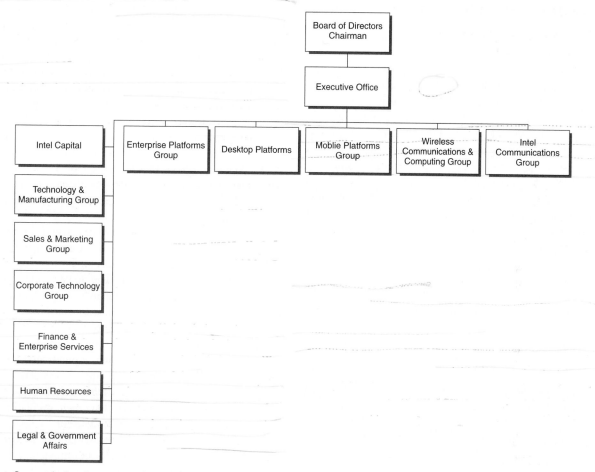

Source: Authors' reconstruction; company reports.

which went to communications investments. In 2002, Intel would spend $4.1 billion on R&D, with 30 percent going to communication. In both years, the largest portion of R&D spending was directed toward silicon products and processes.[11]

To Intel's mission of "Silicon Leadership, Architectural Innovation, and Worldwide Opportunity," Barrett added one further challenge: "Our goal is to be *one generation ahead* in each of these three areas."

Now that the company had refocused and redefined itself, President and COO Paul Otellini looked to the future:

I have been chartered with growing the earnings of the company. Figuring out where the opportunities are over the next five years and refining our bets. We are also figuring out learning and culture. Half of our employees have been here five years or less and have never seen a recession in their working lives. We must spend time creating the institutional learning [needed to carry the company forward].

Otellini depended upon that classic Intel asset to propel the company to the future: "We will take advantage of the world's greatest manufacturing network. Our manufacturing capabilities are either our best asset or worst liability because of the sunk costs."[12]

---

[11] Andy Bryant, "To Recovery and Beyond," Intel Spring Analysts' Meeting, April 25, 2002. According to Bryant, manufacturing accounted for more spending in 2002 due to costs associated with tooling fabs to produce on silicon wafers with wafer areas of 90 nm.

[12] It cost around $2.5 billion to build a fab, and Intel estimated that a fab depreciated by $500 million per year, whether or not it was active.

BEYOND 2002: INTEL'S FUNCTIONAL ORGANIZATIONS

Technology and Manufacturing: Feeding the Giant

Intel relied on its manufacturing arm, the Technology and Manufacturing Group (TMG) to help the company obtain scale economies and manufacturing leadership. About 25 percent of Intel's R&D budget was dedicated to supporting TMG. Intel's manufacturing infrastructure was like a giant: great to have on your side to wield against enemies, but hungry and expensive to feed.

For Intel's Chairman Andy Grove, "Capacity is strategy." "Henry Ford used [capacity] to revolutionize the automobile industry; the Japanese used it to push us out of the memory-chip business 25 years ago; we used it a decade ago to ignite the explosion of the PC industry. Now we're using it again so we can broaden our business beyond the PC,"[13] said Grove. Intel planned to spend $10 billion over the next two years on fabs. Bryant indicated that three 300 mm fabs equaled the capacity of seven 200 mm fabs.[14] In spite of the prolonged recession in technology, Intel continued to push the state-of-the-art in manufacturing technology.

Foundries: When You Look Fabless Intel believed that the superior returns from its process technology advances would push the company further ahead of its competition, threatening their ability to maintain their current business models. Pat Gelsinger, Intel's chief technology officer (CTO), explained:

> Unless you are a certain size, you can't afford to manufacture. Simple return on investment (ROI) states you can't economically produce microprocessors using 300 mm wafers unless you sell $5–$6 billion in revenue. Less volume and you can't get the ROI. Further, with each factory costing at least $2.5 billion to build and with a two-year technology cycle, you can't stay current with less than $1.25 billion per year in capital investments.[15]

Gelsinger thought that the increasing costs of manufacturing would force some companies to abandon some or all of their fabs in favor of foundries. Foundries are fabs for hire, owned by companies that specialize in chip manufacturing, as opposed to integrated design manufacturers (IDMs), which design, manufacture, and market their own semiconductors. The economic rationale behind the foundry model is that their focus on manufacturing allows them to make more efficient use of the large amounts of capital required to build fabs. The advent of foundries over the last decade has created a class of "fabless" chip design houses. But the real hope for future growth for foundries came from production outsourced by IDMs, electronics companies that had once relied on in-house chip manufacturing.

The leading foundry companies, Taiwan Semiconductor Manufacturing (TSMC) and its local rival United Microelectronics (UMC), together accounted for nearly two-thirds of the global market in made-to-order integrated circuits. Some analysts believed that the continued downturn in the semiconductor industry would boost this outsourcing model. Outsourcing to large foundries by IDMs actually declined from 13 percent of their output at the end of 2000 to around 7–8 percent in late 2002, as the big electronics companies struggled to keep their own production lines employed. However, many observers expected more IDMs to give up production in favor of going fabless. The economics were compelling: some analysts estimated TSMC's breakeven capacity utilization rate at around 44 percent, while UMC's was estimated at around 50–55 percent. Most IDMs only managed to break even at higher rates of 60–70 percent utilization.[16]

Intel and many of its most important competitors owned their own fabs. Sunlin Chou, Intel senior vice president and general manager of TMG, described the virtues Intel perceived it derived from its position as an IDM:

> Intel has both the integration advantage of an IDM, and the high production volumes that give the multi-factory scale advantage enjoyed by foundries. Integration enables us to develop technologies that are optimized for our products, and to ramp them smoothly and rapidly into volume production, while avoiding the yield and reliability problems that others (particularly foundries) have reportedly had with 130 nm technologies. Scale gives us economic benefits, keeps us cost competitive, and generates revenue to pay for R&D and future capacity. This combination of integration and scale is becoming scarcer in the industry and increases our competitive advantage.[17]

Being a successful IDM involved more than just throwing funding at fabs. Chou worked hard to make

[13] Brent Schlender, "Intel's $10 Billion Gamble," *Fortune,* November 11, 2002.

[14] Andy Bryant, "To Recovery and Beyond," Intel Spring Analysts' Meeting, Intel Corporation, April 25, 2002.

[15] All quotes from Pat Gelsinger are from the authors' interview on 16 October 2002. Subsequent quotes will not be cited.

[16] Mure Dickie, "Foundry Model Holds up Despite Slump in Demand," *Financial Times,* October 1, 2002.

[17] All quotes from Sunlin Chou are from the authors' interview on 13 November 2002, unless otherwise indicated. Subsequent quotes from this interview will not be cited.

sure TMG was closely integrated with the business units that developed and marketed Intel's products. Chou said, "We have to work with our business groups to do technology and capacity planning. We coordinate with product development teams to define technology features, and to make both the technologies and products ready for manufacturing at the same time. We work with business managers to forecast future production requirements. These take a tremendous amount of mindshare in TMG."

By 2002, many IDMs were reluctant to shoulder alone the burden of building new $2.5 billion 300 mm wafer fabs. Advanced Micro Devices (AMD) and Infineon both launched joint ventures with UMC. European chipmaker STMicroelectronics and Motorola increased their outsourced volume to TSMC.[18]

Fabs as a Weapon Intel raised the bar for the entire industry when it launched its 300 mm fab in 2002. Few other semiconductor companies could afford investments of this size. Intel's CTO Gelsinger explained his outlook on the impact that the escalating cost of manufacturing was having on the semiconductor industry: "The capitalization issue is driving three business models. You have to make a $10 billion investment every two years or so. The dotcom madness funded Intel's 300 mm conversion. This technology cost about $2–$3 billion, but gave us 2X chips per wafer, and gives a 30 percent reduction in cost per die." Gelsinger surmised, "Our 300 mm technology gives Intel a whole generation's lead over its competitors."

What effect would 300 mm manufacturing have on the industry? According to Gelsinger, three sustainable business models were emerging in semiconductors:

- Leaders: e.g., Intel, AMD, IBM, Texas Instruments (TI), and Motorola. Companies that can afford to maintain leadership in logic and the integration of process and logic products.
- Foundries: e.g., TSMC and UMC. Companies that amortize investment over many products for different companies.
- Low Cost Suppliers: e.g., Samsung, Micron, Infineon. Companies that become high volume suppliers of slightly differentiated chips for specific markets, such as mobile.

Gelsinger said, "We wonder if a company must be #1 or #2 in one of these business models or exit? As the costs

of R&D and production continue to increase, one wonders whether a company like TI will become a fabless semiconductor company" (Exhibits 5 to 9).

It was far from clear that TI would go gently. The company had a long and distinguished history in semiconductors in general and in communications in particular. They would likely prove a formidable competitor for even a refocused Intel. In September 2002, TI announced its plans to integrate several technologies, such as wireless networking and global positioning system locators, into one chip. Most observers agreed that TI already had the lead in integrating such technology. In 2002, TI accounted for about 50 percent of the cell phone semiconductor market. This was a sizeable market for chipmakers. Some estimated that silicon represented $40–$50 of the bill of materials for a mobile handset, resulting in a $20 billion market for silicon for mobile phones per year.[19] Some thought that the market for the next generation of cell phone semiconductors would be TI's to lose.[20] Chairman Andy Grove was cautious: "Intel's wireless strategy seems predicated on beating TI. But TI has honed its skills in this area; it has been a core competency of theirs for the past 15 years."[21]

Extending Moore's Law

Intel planned to compete against companies like TI by taking its proven skills into new areas. Intel's CTO Pat Gelsinger said, "Soon we'll be moving to the nano[22] region where we will encounter completely new physical challenges (Exhibit 10). We call this extending Moore's Law." Intel wanted to extend Moore's Law into the backyards of its competitors.

In a year or so, Intel would be manufacturing using 90 nm processes. The transistors manufactured in this process would be around 50 nm, roughly the size of a virus. Gelsinger noted, "Below 5 nm, entirely new processes will be needed." To paraphrase *Star Trek*'s William Shatner, who appeared at a recent Intel Developer Conference, Intel was planning to go where no company had gone before. To get there, Intel was reaching out beyond its own talent pool into universities. Intel was seeding the science with grants made directly to researchers at vari-

---

[18]Ibid.

[19]Estimate from Intel senior executive.
[20]Crayton Harrison, "Texas Instruments to Integrate Technologies into Single Chip for Cell Phones," *Dallas Morning News,* September 4, 2002.
[21]All quotes from Andy Grove are from the authors' interview on 25 October 2002, unless otherwise indicated. Subsequent quotes from this interview will not be cited.
[22]Nano refers to a one-billionth (10^{-19}) part; e.g., nanometer or nanosecond.

EXHIBIT 5 **Top 25 Semiconductor Companies by Sales and Market Share Worldwide, 2000 and 2001**

2001	2000	Company	Worldwide sales (millions) 2001	Market share 2001	Worldwide sales (millions) 2000	Market share 2000
1	1	Intel	$23,850	17.6%	$30,400	15.5%
2	2	Toshiba	$6,781	5.0%	$11,388	5.8%
3	6	STMicroelectronics	$6,359	4.7%	$7,910	4.0%
4	5	Texas Instruments	$6,100	4.5%	$9,200	4.7%
5	4	Samsung	$5,814	4.3%	$10,592	5.4%
6	3	NEC	$5,309	3.9%	$10,900	5.6%
7	8	Hitachi	$5,037	3.7%	$7,286	3.7%
8	7	Motorola	$4,828	3.6%	$7,875	4.0%
9	9	Infineon	$4,558	3.4%	$6,853	3.5%
10	12	Philips	$4,235	3.1%	$5,837	3.0%
11	17	IBM	$3,898	2.9%	$4,329	2.2%
12	15	AMD	$3,892	2.9%	$4,644	2.4%
13	14	Mitsubishi	$3,473	2.9%	$4,740	2.4%
14	18	Matsushita	$3,176	2.6%	$4,150	2.4%
15	16	Fujitsu	$3,084	2.3%	$4,470	2.1%
16	13	Agere (Lucent Tech.)	$3,051	2.3%	$4,875	2.3%
17	19	Sanyo	$2,675	2.3%	$3,260	2.5%
18	10	Hynix	$2,450	2.0%	$6,400	1.7%
19	11	Micron	$2,411	1.8%	$6,314	3.3%
20	20	Sony	$2,100	1.8%	$2,817	3.2%
21	21	Analog Devices	$1,897	1.6%	$2,710	1.4%
22	22	Sharp	$1,858	1.4%	$2,550	1.4%
23	24	Agilent	$1,671	1.4%	$2,414	1.3%
24	25	National Semi.	$1,626	1.2%	$2,301	1.2%
25	23	LSI Logic	$1,597	1.2%	$2,448	1.2%
			$111,729	1.2%	$166,663	1.2%
Total				82.6%		85.1%

Global chip sales in July 2002 totaled $11.7 billion, only 8 percent more than in July 2001, according to the Semiconductor Industry Association. Chip sales fell by one-third in 2001 from the year before, the worst annual decline ever. The association predicted that the industry would grow 20 percent in both 2003 and 2004, propelled mainly by digital consumer and wireless products.
Source: IN-STAT/MDR www.instat.com.

ous colleges around the country. Some of these grants, for example, for projects that might be as far away as 10 or more years from fruition, were for amounts as low as $50,000. For projects closer to realization, say five to ten years out, Intel sponsored "lablets," funding laboratories at selected universities. For nearer-term Strategic Research Projects (SRPs) that loomed about two to five years off, Intel used its own labs. Gelsinger said:

Intel's work here has two themes:

1. Recognition of the limits of traditional scaling in the way we think.
2. Necessity for Intel to start very advanced seeding.

Through this program, we are moving closer to the origins of science and technology. We engage with anybody who is of interest.

A metaphor describing our efforts at expanding Moore's Law is: For us, silicon is like a canvas. We have been using oil to paint on this canvas, but there are other mediums to use, such as watercolors and pastels. Our efforts in wireless, optical, etc., are like these different mediums. We are looking for domains of potential participation by Intel where silicon could become relevant.

Sales and Marketing: Reigniting Growth

In 2002, Intel's products were sold by a central sales organization, the Intel Sales and Marketing Group (SMG). Intel moved to a centralized sales group in its reorganizations in 2001 and 2002. The group was led by Michael Splinter, executive vice president and director of SMG. As Intel expanded into new areas beyond the microprocessors for PCs, its sales force faced new challenges. Splinter said:

Because we are trying to create products for the data center, we had to establish a reputation with IT managers who run data centers. A few years ago, the view was that Intel makes

EXHIBIT 6 Advanced Micro Devices (AMD) Selected Financial Information, 1997–2001

(In $ millions)

	30-Dec-2001	31-Dec-2000	26-Dec-1999	27-Dec-1998	28-Dec-1997
Sales—Core Business	3,891.8	4,644.2	2,857.6	2,542.1	2,356.4
Total Sales	**3,891.8**	**4,644.2**	**2,857.6**	**2,542.1**	**2,356.4**
Cost of Goods Sold	2,589.7	2,514.6	1,964.4	1,718.7	1,578.4
SG&A Expense	620.0	599.0	540.1	419.7	400.7
Research & Development	650.9	641.8	635.8	567.4	467.9
Unusual Inc./Exp.	89.3	0.0	38.2	0.0	0.0
Total Expenses	**3,950.0**	**3,755.5**	**3,178.5**	**2,705.8**	**2,447.0**
Interest Expense, Non-Oper.	−61.4	−60.0	−69.3	−66.5	−45.3
Other—Net	25.7	423.2	463.8	22.7	35.1
Pre-Tax Income	**−93.9**	**1,251.9**	**73.6**	**−207.4**	**−100.8**
Income Taxes	−14.5	256.9	167.4	−91.9	−55.2
Income After Taxes	**−79.5**	**995.0**	**−93.7**	**−115.6**	**−45.7**
Equity in Affiliates	18.9	11.0	4.8	11.6	24.6
Preferred Dividends	0.0	0.0	0.0	0.0	0.0
Net Income (Excluding Extraordinary Items and Depreciation)	**−60.6**	**1,006.1**	**−88.9**	**−104.0**	**−21.1**
Net Income (Including Extraordinary Items and Depreciation)	**−60.6**	**983.0**	**−88.9**	**−104.0**	**−21.1**

Source: OneSource.

microprocessors for the PC. They were concerned that we weren't reliable enough. We needed to establish credibility with end users . . . the CIOs (chief information officers) and IT decision makers. Most OEMs were conflicted and slow to drive Intel architecture in the data center. For example, HP had its own HPUX on their own Performance Architecture; IBM had its own version of AIX on their P series hardware. . . .[23]

Despite the success of its global brand, the company had to work to establish its credentials in new marketplaces (Exhibit 11). Splinter pointed out that Intel's thrust into the telecommunications industry required a different kind of "sell" than in the computer industry:

The network design win is more complicated and takes longer to achieve revenue than the computer design win. We sell to TEMs (Telecommunications Equipment Manufacturers), which in turn must sell to the telcos. Some products never get into production or at least not high volume production in the current environment. Because of the competitive nature of the telecommunications industry, the telecom part of the [Intel's] sales force works under very strict cost targets.

Splinter also observed that the microprocessor development cycle was quite long (up to four years), which

makes it difficult to incorporate short-term marketing input. Other products, such as telecom, chipsets, and graphic chips are developed on shorter cycles. One solution, he said, was to "use the end user market information in the peripheral chips, and then integrate it later into the microprocessor."

Intel thought its matrix organization was working well to meet the challenges associated with the convergence of computing and communications. Splinter said, "The beauty of the Intel matrix is that you can manage through this kind of change. You must be able to matrix the communications specialists with the computing specialists, have computing people working on account teams for communications customers."

Some of the ever-present challenges Splinter faced nevertheless included creating the right balance between centralization and decentralization in the company's sales and marketing activities. "This tension is especially acute during acquisitions, because the companies always want to keep their own models and sales forces," Splinter said. Acquisitions not withstanding, Intel had a history of evolving decentralized sales forces. "A renegade division would create its own sales force and one group's sales people would come across another's at a client. We work hard on eliminating that because of the ultimate inefficiencies and the confusion that it creates with the customers. They ask, 'Who is the account manager?'

---

[23] All quotes from Michael Splinter are from the authors' interview on 14 November 2002. Subsequent quotes will not be cited.

EXHIBIT 7 International Business Machines (IBM) Selected Financial Information, 1997–2001

(In $ millions)

	31-Dec-2001	31-Dec-2000	31-Dec-1999	31-Dec-1998	31-Dec-1997
Sales—Core Business	85,866.0	88,396.0	87,548.0	81,667.0	78,508.0
Total Sales	**85,866.0**	**88,396.0**	**87,548.0**	**81,667.0**	**78,508.0**
Cost of Goods Sold	54,084.0	56,342.0	55,994.0	50,795.0	47,899.0
SG&A Expense	17,197.0	17,535.0	16,294.0	16,662.0	16,634.0
Research & Development	5,290.0	5,374.0	5,505.0	5,046.0	4,877.0
Unusual Inc./Exp.	0.0	0.0	0.0	0.0	0.0
Total Expenses	**76,571.0**	**79,251.0**	**77,793.0**	**72,503.0**	**69,410.0**
Interest Expense, Non-Oper.	−238.0	−347.0	−352.0	−713.0	−728.0
Other—Net	1,896.0	2,736.0	2,354.0	589.0	657.0
Pre-Tax Income	**10,953.0**	**11,534.0**	**11,757.0**	**9,040.0**	**9,027.0**
Income Taxes	3,230.0	3,441.0	4,045.0	2,712.0	2,934.0
Income After Taxes	**7,723.0**	**8,093.0**	**7,712.0**	**6,328.0**	**6,093.0**
Preferred Dividends	−10.0	−20.0	−20.0	−20.0	−20.0
Net Income (Excluding Extraordinary Items and Depreciation)	**7,723.0**	**8,093.0**	**7,712.0**	**6,328.0**	**6,093.0**
Accounting Change	0.0	0.0	0.0	0.0	0.0
Net Income (Including Extraordinary Items and Depreciation)	**7,723.0**	**8,093.0**	**7,712.0**	**6,328.0**	**6,093.0**

Source: OneSource.

EXHIBIT 8 Texas Instruments (TI) Selected Financial Information, 1997–2001

(In $ millions)

	31-Dec-2001	31-Dec-2000	31-Dec-1999	31-Dec-1998	31-Dec-1997
Sales—Core Business	8,201.0	11,875.0	9,759.0	8,875.0	9,972.0
Total Sales	**8,201.0**	**11,875.0**	**9,759.0**	**8,875.0**	**9,972.0**
Cost of Goods Sold	5,824.0	6,120.0	5,069.0	5,605.0	6,179.0
SG&A Expense	1,361.0	1,669.0	1,556.0	1,549.0	1,571.0
Research & Development	1,598.0	1,747.0	1,379.0	1,265.0	1,556.0
Total Expenses	**8,783.0**	**9,536.0**	**8,004.0**	**8,419.0**	**9,306.0**
Interest Expense, Non-Oper.	−61.0	−75.0	−76.0	−76.0	−94.0
Other—Net	217.0	2,314.0	403.0	301.0	199.0
Pre-Tax Income	**−426.0**	**4,578.0**	**2,082.0**	**681.0**	**771.0**
Income Taxes	−225.0	1,491.0	631.0	229.0	432.0
Income After Taxes	**−201.0**	**3,087.0**	**1,451.0**	**452.0**	**339.0**
Preferred Dividends	0.0	0.0	0.0	0.0	0.0
Interest Adi. for Primary EPS	0.0	0.0	0.0	0.0	0.0
Net Income (Excluding Extraordinary Items and Depreciation)	**−201.0**	**3,087.0**	**1,451.0**	**452.0**	**339.0**
Discontinued Operations	0.0	0.0	0.0	0.0	1,525.0
Extraordinary Items	0.0	0.0	0.0	0.0	1,525.0
Accounting Change	0.0	−29.0	0.0	0.0	0.0
Net Income (Including Extraordinary Items and Depreciation)	**−201.0**	**3,058.0**	**1,451.0**	**452.0**	**1,842.0**

Source: OneSource.

EXHIBIT 9   Sun Microsystems Selected Financial Information, 1998–2002

(In $ millions)

	30-Jun-2002	30-Jun-2001	30-Jun-2000	30-Jun-1999	30-Jun-1998
Sales—Core Business	12,496.0	18,250.0	15,721.0	11,806.0	9,862.0
Total Sales	**12,496.0**	**18,250.0**	**15,721.0**	**11,806.0**	**9,862.0**
Cost of Goods sold	7,580.0	10,041.0	7,549.0	5,670.0	4,713.0
SG&A Expense	3,812.0	4,445.0	4,065.0	3,196.0	2,830.0
Depreciation	0.0	285.0	72.0	19.0	0.0
Research & Development	1,832.0	2,016.0	1,630.0	1,280.0	1,029.0
Unusual Inc./Exp.	520.0	152.0	12.0	121.0	176.0
Total Expenses	**13,744.0**	**16,939.0**	**13,328.0**	**10,286.0**	**8,748.0**
Interest Expense, Non-Oper.	−58.0	−100.0	−84.0	0.0	0.0
Other—Net	258.0	373.0	462.0	85.0	48.0
Pre-Tax Income	**−1,048.0**	**1,584.0**	**2,771.0**	**1,605.0**	**1,162.0**
Income Taxes	−461.0	603.0	917.0	575.0	407.0
Income After Taxes	**−587.0**	**981.0**	**1,854.0**	**1,030.0**	**755.0**
Net Income (Excluding Extraordinary Items and Depreciation)	**−587.0**	**981.0**	**1,854.0**	**1,030.0**	**755.0**
Accounting Change	0.0	−54.0	0.0	0.0	0.0
Net Income (Including Extraordinary Items and Depreciation)	**−587.0**	**927.0**	**1,854.0**	**1,030.0**	**755.0**

Source: OneSource.

EXHIBIT 10   Extending Moore's Law
Honey, I Shrank the Transistors

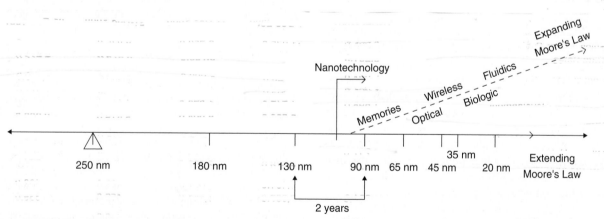

By following Moore's Law, Intel hopes to reduce the size of transistors to the point where they are smaller than viruses (< 100 nm). Intel hopes that silicon devices this small will exhibit a host of benefits including allowing new materials and device structures to be used, incrementally changing the silicon technology base, manipulating materials on an atomic scale in one or more dimensions, and increasing use of self-assembly, using chemical properties to form structures.
Source: Pat Gelsinger, Intel Corporation.

EXHIBIT 11   Top 10 Global Brands and Estimated Brand Value, 2001 and 2002

(Brand value in $ billions)

Rank	Company	2002 estimated brand value	2001 estimated brand value
1	Coca-Cola	$69.64	$68.95
2	Microsoft	$64.09	$65.07
3	IBM	$51.19	$52.75
4	GE	$41.31	$42.40
5	**Intel**	**$30.86**	**$34.67**
6	Nokia	$29.97	$35.04
7	Disney	$29.26	$32.59
8	McDonald's	$26.38	$22.05
9	Marlboro	$24.15	$22.05
10	Mercedes	$21.01	$21.73

NB: Interbrand Corp. attempts to estimate how much of a boost each brand delivers, how stable that boost is likely to be, and how much those future earnings are worth today. Interbrand uses analysis of cash flows rather than consumer perceptions to calculate brand values.
Sources: Interbrand Corp., JP Morgan Chase & Co; "The Best Global Brands," *BusinessWeek,* August 5, 2002.

Fortunately, all of the senior managers (e.g., Sean Maloney, Ron Smith) have a long history of working together. It is easy for us to get together to hammer out these issues."

In addition to competing in new product categories, Splinter also highlighted the importance of emerging markets to the company: "Emerging markets have become far more important to Intel. Our revenues would have shrunk more if not for our sales from the emerging markets (Exhibit 12). To be successful in these markets, we have to make sure our efforts are more than just sales. We have to take our brand there first; but also consider the right investments (e.g., R&D, design, and manufacturing), invest in education in the country, and work with governments on technology policies." Splinter also mentioned that he saw SMG's role, in part, as educating people at Intel on what was going on in the world. Splinter wanted Intel's executives and engineers to travel. He also has set up Corporate Strategic Discussion (CSD) meetings to focus on one major emerging market country at a time (e.g., China, India, Russia). "The CSD involves at least 70 percent of top management at any given time."

Asked what the top priorities were for SMG beyond 2002, Splinter said, "Number one is to reignite the corporate refresh cycle for computers; number two is to establish the mobile wireless computing experience. If we achieve these then we can grow again. My number three priority is to keep the emergent markets going."

Intel's Finance Group: Playing Devil's Advocate

A critically important asset for Intel was its financial strength. This resource was managed by Intel's CFO, Andy Bryant. For all of the reorganization and strategic refocusing Intel underwent during the past few years, the role of the finance group remained largely unchanged. Bryant said:

The finance group at the corporate level is much the same, even after the addition of the network group and wireless group [see sections on ICG and WCCG below]. We have always had a variety of businesses around microprocessors; some had lower margins [and thus similar financial challenges to those our new groups face today].

The biggest change to the finance group, given the $10 billion in acquisitions, is that the level of focus in the new areas has increased—as would be expected when the investment levels increase this much. We have created more tools to communicate with both management and the board of directors. The general management of our acquisitions has increased the level of financial scrutiny. They have to present and defend their data. The finance group still plays devil's advocate with management, making sure they have really thought about the businesses and their strategies, instead of just writing it down on paper.[24]

---

[24] All quotes from Andy D. Bryant are from the authors' interview on 1 October 2002, unless otherwise noted. Subsequent quotes from this interview will not be cited.

EXHIBIT 12 Selected Global Data for the Semiconductor Market

Total semiconductor market data by region in 2001

Region	Total semiconductor industry market share for region	Value ($ U.S.) of semiconductor market for region in 2001
Asia-Pacific	28%	$39.8 billion
Americas	26%	$35.8 billion
Japan	24%	$33.1 billion
Europe	22%	$30.2 billion

Source: Tom Foremski, "Hopes Dashed as Income Falls," *Financial Times,* September 23, 2002.

Intel top ten country markets

Rank in 2000	Country	Rank in 2005 (Intel est.)	Country
1	USA	1	USA
2	Japan	2	China
3	PRC/Hong Kong	3	Japan
4	Germany	4	Germany
5	UK	5	UK
6	France	6	India
7	India	7	Brazil
8	Canada	8	France
9	Brazil	9	Russia
10	Korea	10	Korea

Source: "Intel Executive Webcast," October 22, 2002.

Intel's financial resources gave the company many options. Intel's bank account and free cash flow gave it several options for growth. Bryant said:

There are three ways to broaden the company:

1. Acquire a business (this will usually be a company renewing its product cycle).
2. Develop our own technologies.
3. Develop technology plus acquire complementary technologies/assets.

We favor the third option. This gets the technologies just as they are becoming meaningful and getting ready to go to market. This has the best chance of success: Combining emerging technologies with Intel strategies. For example, we acquired an optical company in Fremont, California. They were ahead of us in their specific technology. After we acquired them, we were able to combine Intel's manufacturing process and technologies into the optical space.

Still, there was a limit to the depth of Intel's pockets and the downturn in the technology market had hit hard at Intel and other technology companies. Bryant considered some of the ways it would affect Intel:

How do you manage the company in a flat environment? If you think the recession will last for 12–18 months, you invest to take advantage. But if you think it will last for 18–36 months, that is a more difficult question.

An important question for Intel during a recession is: Will increased performance offer commensurate increased returns? Do you continue to widen performance gaps in an economic downturn? If you get too far ahead, you may not get a return on your investment.

Bryant offered the following illustration:

We have to ask, what does it cost to maintain products and capabilities one to two years ahead of your competitor? And do you earn enough to still get a reasonable return on investment?

Perhaps the Athlon architecture won't allow AMD to catch up to Intel, but perhaps if the Opteron architecture comes into the mainstream they can become a more credible threat [to Itanium in 64-bit processing][25] Or perhaps a merger between AMD and any number of other companies in the business would help them catch up. Our job it to anticipate and be prepared for various competitive strategies. The same sets of questions are relevant for networking. Can Intel over-invest for the lift off?

---

[25] Athlon is AMD's microprocessor that competes with Intel's Pentium line. Opteron is AMD's microprocessor that competes with Intel's Itanium line. Opteron can run both 32-bit and 64-bit applications.

Chairman Andy Grove also considered the fundamental strategic question facing the company. While Grove observed that "capacity is strategy," it was unclear whether the strategy of continuing investments in manufacturing was correct. Grove said, "Aggregate semiconductor sales volume has been flat since 1995, with the exception of 2000 when there was a blip upward. For every new fab we add, it gives us around five times the capacity of an individual old fab. Do we have too much fab capacity? Too little? What choice do we have?"

Intel Capital: Investing for the Future

Intel Capital was the investment arm of the company. Its charter was to "make and manage financially attractive investments in support of Intel's strategic objectives."

The program began in the early 1990s, and initially invested externally in PC and chip-related technologies that were needed by Intel to pursue its own business strategies. Les Vadasz, Intel Executive Vice President and President of Intel Capital, explained: "Working with leading-edge technologies often involves dependencies on the success of other, smaller companies. Intel needed to make investments and provide other support to assure timely delivery of these technologies for our needs."[26] Eventually the investment scope expanded to include investments into companies that complemented Intel's product lines. Vadasz said:

> We are an OEM supplier, and our customers need the availability of a number of other products and capabilities in addition to ours, to create new generations of products. By investing in companies that deliver these additional capabilities and aligning our mutual strategies, we are able to accelerate the development of market ecosystems. In a market segment like ours, where product cycles are relatively short, this can have huge financial benefits to all participants.

Intel Capital Investments The primary purpose for Intel Capital's investing was strategic. An investment opportunity needed to satisfy the requirement that its success would help Intel achieve its strategic goals. The investments were also evaluated for their potential for financial return. Vadasz said: "A company that has interesting technology, but fails to develop any commercial presence is not likely to help our strategies." This dual-test approach characterized Intel Capital's investment dis-

cipline. Intel Capital had not disclosed specific financial results from its strategic investments, but the program was said to have contributed billions in cash to Intel in its 10-year history.

The program typically made small investments for minority stakes, generally less than $10 million each, in private and some public companies. Additionally, Intel Capital had responsibility to oversee the acquisition of companies that helped Intel enter new business areas or that strengthened Intel's businesses.

In the late 1990s, Intel established a New Business Group to incubate various businesses. This activity was merged with Intel Capital in Q3 of 2002, and subsequent to this, Les Vadasz and John Miner (VP and GM of NBG, see below) were jointly managing Intel Capital. From this point on, Intel Capital's charter included not only external but also internal investments in areas that were potentially important for Intel's future businesses. These internal investments were done with a similar investment philosophy as that of venture-funded companies.

Intel Capital made different types of investments:

- *Building ecosystems:* A number of Intel Capital investments were made in technologies and supported the final products in which Intel's products were used. These companies' products complemented and helped drive demand for Intel products. For example, investments in enterprise software companies accelerated deployment of solutions optimized for the Intel Itanium processor family.
- *Developing international business:* Intel Capital invested in companies that helped accelerate the adoption of technology in emerging markets. For example, investments were often made in companies that provided local language content or services via the Internet or that helped improve or optimize the Internet infrastructure in a given region.
- *Working with the supply chain:* Investments were made in companies that sold products and technologies Intel needed to help market or produce its products. For example, Intel Capital invested in semiconductor equipment companies and process technology companies to fund next-generation technology development and/or accelerate product development. Those investments facilitated Intel's move to new manufacturing process generations every two to three years. Intel also invested in other suppliers, such as DRAM manufacturers Micron, Samsung, and Infineon, to help improve the availability of critical PC components to the PC market segment as a whole.

---

[26] All quotes from Les Vadasz are from the authors' interview on 9 October 2002. Subsequent quotes from this interview will not be cited.

- *Foster new silicon technologies:* Access to new companies and technologies provided a competitive advantage to Intel's Technology and Manufacturing Group. Intel made investments to insure availability of advanced materials, next-generation lithography tools, as well as new etching and deposition techniques. To address manufacturing quality issues, various investments were made in innovative defect diagnosis and location technologies that helped speed Intel's progress by accelerating equipment availability.
- *Scouting new technologies, being the "eyes and ears" for the Corporation:* Intel Capital made small investments in emerging technologies that might prove useful in the future, but were not necessarily related to a current Intel business. For example, Intel Capital had personnel looking at investments in MEMS,[27] nanotechnology, and robotics. Vadasz said: "We can often sniff out trends earlier than greater Intel can act on them. We get the company's technologists involved, and that creates a more open mind about important technologies."

Intel Capital portfolio companies enjoyed benefits beyond Intel's financial contribution. An investment by Intel Capital offered credibility to co-investors in the technology sector. Intel Capital also brought significant technological expertise from Intel Corporation and had the ability to work with other industry participants to help foster technology standards. Occasionally, Intel Capital facilitated the diffusion of Intel-developed technology to a portfolio company.

Intel Corporation had a worldwide marketing presence, and there was the opportunity for portfolio companies to network with a diverse range of companies whose technologies or business models may have been complementary. Intel Capital itself had a worldwide presence and had dramatically expanded its non-U.S. investing over the past few years. Vadasz said: "Developing international markets in emerging countries is important for Intel's continued growth. If the future of Intel's business is in the continued convergence of computing and communications, then the question arises what is the future of the Internet in China, India, Poland, and Brazil? Forty percent of our deals (by number) are outside the United States."

Intel Capital has physical presence in some 28 countries, and had investments in companies headquartered in more than 30 different countries, on five continents. In-

vestments were often made in companies that provide local language content or services via the Internet or that help improve or optimize the Internet infrastructure in a given region. Through these investments, Intel was able to support evolving computer and communications usage requirements and technology trends across many cultures and languages.

To provide investment focus on specific technologies critical to Intel's efforts, two specialized funds were developed within Intel Capital in 1999:

- The Intel 64 Fund was a $253 million equity fund created by Intel and other corporate investors to accelerate the development of solutions for the Intel Itanium processor family. The Intel 64 Fund included participation from computer makers and information technology companies.
- The $500 million Intel Communications Fund, which was funded solely by Intel, focused on accelerating Intel's voice and data communications and wireless networking initiatives. The Intel Communications Fund made more than 80 investments in 17 countries on five continents. In Q4 of 2002, Intel Capital committed $150 M of this Fund to be invested to accelerate the deployment of WiFi technologies and services around the world.

WiFi—an Illustrative Example For Vadasz and Intel, there were few adjacencies more compelling than wireless connectivity based on 802.11 protocols, commonly known as "WiFi" (wireless fidelity). WiFi was an emerging technology used to provide high-speed, wireless Internet access in many locations around the world, including airports, retail establishments, corporate offices, universities, factories, and homes.

According to Vadasz: "WiFi started as a wireless Ethernet technology for the home market, but now we find many enterprises are deploying it. It currently has warts; it is ugly in that in many cases it requires some new technical understanding to use. But WiFi enables ad hoc networks, and its adoption has been rapid when compared to other wireless data technologies such as 2.5G and 3G.[28] In fact, WiFi is happening in spite of the carriers: It's not elegant, but it's revolutionizing telecom."

Intel had high hopes for WiFi. Vadasz believed "eventually WiFi could lead to a restructuring of the wireless telecom industry." In October 2002, Intel Capital

---

[27] Micro-electromechanical systems (MEMS) is a technology that combines computers with tiny mechanical devices such as sensors, valves, and gears embedded in semiconductor chips.

[28] 2.5G and 3G refer to advanced ("third generation") mobile communications technologies.

Strategy for competitive advantage

announced that it planned to spend $150 million in companies developing WiFi technologies. Intel Capital had invested in many companies to round out a more robust WiFi ecosystem, including component suppliers, application development tools and management utilities, system level hardware and software, and even service providers.

In December 2002, Intel Capital, Apax Partners, and 3i announced the creation of a new company designed to meet the growing demand for wireless network access services. The company, Cometa Networks, will provide high-speed, nationwide wholesale wireless network access that will enable carriers, service providers, and national retail chains to offer WiFi services to their customers.

Cometa Networks will allow users to access the Internet wirelessly using 802.11a or 802.11b technology from thousands of hotspots, using the same sign-on procedure, email address, ID, password, and payment method that they now use with their current ISP providers and corporate VPN, DSL, or cable operators. IBM and AT&T were recruited to provide Cometa's network operating center and data center capabilities.

The idea for Cometa Networks was generated in Intel Capital based on a perceived need for such services.

In March 2003, Intel introduced its Centrino™ mobile technology. This technology promises connectivity for notebook uses, which should become more and more ubiquitous over time. By the time of this introduction, Intel Capital had made 15 investments in companies that can help make that happen.

New Business Incubation: Growing the Future

Companies and technologies that were too new to be easily placed within Intel were cared for in a corporate greenhouse where they could be nurtured and protected from the demands of the established groups. This itself was a new group called New Business Group (NBG) run by John Miner, former general manager of CPG. Miner said:

> After reorganizing the New Business Group, we completely refocused on activities that benefit from being part of Intel. All our ventures build products that can be done on a wafer. We have activities in handheld wireless, display and pixel processing technologies, wireless and non-wireless broadband, and photonic components. We focus on the early technology capture process to develop new business applications, and look for commercialization opportunities.[29]

---

[29] All quotes from John Miner are from the authors' interview on 9 October 2002. Subsequent quotes from this interview will not be cited.

Miner emphasized, "We always look for two-way linkages with other parts of Intel. Two business opportunities came directly from WCCG; they will go back there. On the other hand, we also have two for which it is not yet clear where they will go."

Miner also addressed some of the management issues associated with NBG activities:

> A key challenge is how to maintain corporate level interest. We continuously try to develop strategic value for the company and we want to pay our own way doing it. The biggest challenge is lateral, how to work with peers in other parts of the company and look farther out for strategic gaps they may need to fill without necessarily having agreement on the strategy. We think that doing new businesses internally and organically makes them easier to assimilate, and less costly. But sometimes we do it in parallel, both through incubation and through small acquisitions.

Miner said that Intel uses milestones as proxies for assessing the strategic value of new ventures. He concluded: "We need some successes. We already have some small successes. We need to prepare a fourth business for Intel."

Human Resource Management: Building Organizational Capability

Intel's new focus brought challenges to its organizational structure. The company needed to develop personnel capable of managing in this new, more interdependent environment. Barrett explained:

> We have to grow and develop general managers to be more encompassing in their abilities. We do this by burdening them with making decisions, giving them accountability and responsibility for product lines. We want to take the executive office out of every product decision. This is a work in progress. We are not doing enough to develop overseas talent. Of the 16 members of the executive staff, only one lives outside of the United States [in Israel]. We will also place development facilities in overseas locations, particularly emerging markets with good educational systems, such as Russia, China, and India.
>
> We used to say that Intel is the largest single cell organism in the world. Well, we were a $20 billion company with great market share and terrific margins [from its core business]. But that's not where we'll be 10 years from now.

That organism has changed its size, up and down, in the past. Patricia Murray, vice president and director of Human Resources, said, "Intel has a very effective system of redeployment that operated well to exit businesses and reduce teams, e.g., from one microprocessor to another, from one factory to another."[30] While the company faced layoffs in the past, including letting 3,000 people go in 1998, Murray said the recent retrenchment "has been an emotionally wrenching experience. We had to close down segments of businesses. We had to make sure we treated redundant people well in a declining environment."

Intel struggled with finding the right number of employees. Recently, Intel reduced headcount from 92,000 to 80,000 employees through a combination of business closures, attrition, and layoffs. Still, with 80,000 employees and declining sales, Wall Street suspiciously eyed the company's costs. Murray said:

> At 80,000 employees, we are still above our historical run rates for revenue per employee. But that is a gross measure that does not take into consideration a company's efforts to grow into new businesses. One could take a simple financial point of view and say that we have too much headcount for our revenue when compared to the past. In order to reduce our headcount further than we have already done, one has to balance the cost of the reduction against the possibility of future growth. Reducing headcount to meet some revenue per employee metric may have a short-term upside in Wall Street's eyes, but if you balance this against the cost in dollars, perhaps a charge of around $500 million, and the cost of being unprepared for the future, it is not as clear as it may have initially appeared. If you are unprepared for the future and you have to spend more money to rehire people six months later in a recovery, you made the wrong bet and you have lost great people at the same time. At our present level of headcount, we are making a bet on keeping our people.

A few years earlier, Intel was faced with a very different human resources challenge. Murray recalled, "We had to balance keeping compensation fair while dealing with the upward pressure on starting salaries. Sometimes the market had increased salaries by 300 percent, particularly in Intel Capital, and for senior management people. During the boom, our overall turnover never hit double digits. Some segments were higher, e.g., Intel Capital hit about 48 percent. But over 50 percent of our employees have been here less than five years. This is a function of the hiring we did in 1999 and 2000."

Intel believed that changes in technology, particularly the convergence between communications and computing, would force organizational and human resource changes at the company. Murray said, "We are still the world's biggest single cell organism." That single cell was governed from a nucleus located in Intel Architecture Group (IAG), which earned about 80 percent of the

company's annual revenue. To be successful in new technologies, this would have to change. Murray said:

> What is the right structure for the future? There is a lot of overlap with three of our businesses. They are closely aligned. But the skill sets that we have to attract and develop are different.
>
> We need general management skills. It is not true—at least not at Intel—that you have to run a P&L to be a good general manager. We have to develop virtual team skills, cross-organizational skills, and the ability to get results without direct line authority. If you are in the microprocessor group and you want to stay there and not interact with other groups, you won't be successful. Now, you have to work closely with WCCG, etc. Moreover, as a follow-on to our hiring, we are learning that we have too narrow a span of control and too many levels. Decision-making has become too difficult. At the moment, we are flattening the organization post-hiring spree.
>
> We also have to learn the language of our newer businesses to ensure effective communications across the company. For development, the challenge will be to manage cross-organizational opportunities. We have a few things working for us. . . . [W]e have a pretty honest culture. We are measurement based and analytical.

Murray believed that the culture of honesty and analytical rigor would help employees make the organizational adjustments that would be required to operate in a more interdependent company.

BEYOND 2002: INTEL'S BUSINESS GROUPS

Intel Architecture Group

The Intel Architecture Group (IAG) designed and produced microprocessors for PCs and servers, and other devices such as PC tablets. The group also designed and produced chipsets, which perform the essential logic functions surrounding the CPU, and motherboards, which combine Intel microprocessors and chipsets to form the key subsystem of a PC or server. This was the engine for Intel's cash machine, responsible for 81 percent of the company's revenue in 2001.

IAG had turned out to be an intermediate step. Intel combined its Intel Architecture Business Group and Microprocessor Products Group into a single organization to deliver platforms and solutions for the Internet economy. The group had been jointly run by senior vice president Albert Yu, a veteran Intel executive who retired in June 2002, and Paul Otellini. Under this reorganization, development of microprocessors, chipsets, motherboards, systems, and related software at the platform level was combined into platform-focused business operations

EXHIBIT 13   PC Industry Profit Pool 1990–2001, Vendors and Suppliers

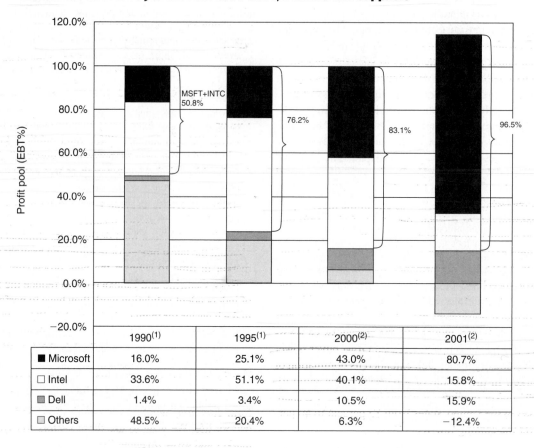

	1990[1]	1995[1]	2000[2]	2001[2]
■ Microsoft	16.0%	25.1%	43.0%	80.7%
□ Intel	33.6%	51.1%	40.1%	15.8%
▨ Dell	1.4%	3.4%	10.5%	15.9%
▤ Others	48.5%	20.4%	6.3%	−12.4%

Source: "Computer Hardware," Bear Stearns, July 2002.
[1] Data for "Others" category in 1990 and 1995 include total results for Apple Computer, Compaq Computer, and Gateway, Hewlett-Packard and IBM did not disclose data for PC operations.
[2] Data for "Others" category in 2000 and 2001 include total results for Apple Computer and Gateway, as well as the PC Operations of Compaq Computer, Hewlett-Packard, and IBM.

targeted at the enterprise (servers and workstations), desktop, and mobile market segments. In addition, the research and technology laboratory activities of the groups were combined.

Until recently, IAG had been run by Paul Otellini, who was promoted to president and COO. Under Otellini, the general manager of IAG oversaw all of Intel's computing business units, including the Enterprise Platforms Group, the Desktop Platforms Group, the Mobile Platforms Group, the Technology and Research Labs, Microprocessor Marketing, and Business Planning. When Otellini vacated the general manager position, IAG was split into three subgroups. These were the newly formed Enterprise Platform Group run by Mike Fister, the Desktop Platform Group run by Louis Burns, and the Mobile Platform Group run by David Perlmutter. Each of these

general managers reported to CEO Barrett and President and COO Otellini. This restructuring also created two new business groups; Intel Communications Group (ICG) and Wireless Communications and Computing Group (WCCG).

Desktop Platform Group: The New Millennium Opens with a Thud

Intel's core market—desktop microprocessors—was suffering from a recession that began around 2000 and lasted two years and counting. This slowdown had serious implications for Intel, since around 80 percent of IAG's revenue, and most of the company's profits, were derived from the sale of microprocessors for desktop PCs (Exhibit 13). In 2001, microprocessor unit demand fell and Intel earned lower average selling prices for microprocessors as competitors increased pricing pressure and raised their quality. Prices for Pentium 4 chips dropped between 50 percent and 60 percent in 2001. Prices for Intel's 1.7-gigahertz Pentium 4 dropped from $700 on its April 23, 2001, release date to $350 six days later. Intel wanted its 1.7-gHz chip to be at a mainstream price point before the company introduced its 2-gHz Pentium 4 later in 2001. Intel hoped to see computers with its Pentium 4 processors priced as low as $999 for a PC and monitor. Intel's moves may also have been designed to force AMD to reduce prices for its 1.2-gHz Athlon chip, which had outperformed Intel's 1.5-gHz Pentium 4 chip at equal clock speeds. AMD priced its chips according to their megahertz rating. Megahertz was one of the most important determinants to pricing, despite its being only one aspect of a chip's overall performance.[31]

In some desktop microprocessor categories, Intel dueled with AMD over performance specifications such as processor speed and processing power. Meanwhile, the recession in technology sectors forced the consolidation of the original equipment manufacturer (OEM) market for PCs. To a degree, moves like the merger of Hewlett-Packard (HP) and Compaq increased OEM buyer power while PC industry leader Dell extended its domination of the market. In the middle of a recession, that build-to-order PC maker predicted it would increase its PC share of market in the United States from 15 percent to 40 percent over the coming few years.[32]

Mobile Platforms Group

Intel's work in mobile computing technologies was led by its Mobile Platforms Group (MPG). This organization was based in Haifa, Israel, Santa Clara, California, and Portland, Oregon, in the United States. The group was run under the direction of vice president and general manager of MPG David Perlmutter and vice president and general manager of MPG Anand Chandrasekher.[33] In late 2002, this group was preparing to launch a project codenamed "Banias"[34]; a new mobile PC platform featuring an entirely new processor microarchitecture. The Banias project was designed to provide PC makers with ingredients to build mobile PCs with extended battery life, improved performance, reduced/varied form fac-

tors, and easier-to-use wireless connectivity. The Banias platforms would include single band (802.11b) or dual band (802.11a and 802.11b) WiFi capability through an mPCI communication device, codenamed "Calexico," which would contain the first 802.11 chips made by Intel. The company also planned to provide Calexico with its desktop processors and chipsets as well as a series of new "digital hubs" that would let consumers wire their TVs or other consumer electronics products to the Web via their PCs. In January 2003, Intel publicly launched Banias under the new brandname "Centrino," the first time Intel branded a combination of technologies under one name.[35]

Intel's efforts to provide Calexico with its Centrino notebook microprocessor recalled the company's earlier strategies in chipsets. Intel designed its chipsets to complement the latest processor features and brought them to market in time to support the new processors. For PC makers, Centrino and Calexico could reduce the amount of independent validation work they have to perform and make it easier for them to design mobile PCs with easier-to-use wireless capabilities and bring them to market more quickly. Perlmutter described the Mobile Platforms Group's strategy: "We want to expand what we do today to drive into what we are calling 'mobility.' We want to excel in all vectors of mobility: These are performance, form function, wireless communication, and extended battery life. We want to use these vectors to expand the market and grow revenues."[36]

The vectors of mobility that the Mobile Platforms Group sought were in conflict with the performance measures that had driven Intel's success in the past, particularly in desktop microprocessors. Perlmutter said:

There are some areas of divergence between us and the desktop group. The desktop microprocessor and chipset gives higher performance, but in the past this always led to increased power dissipation.

From a mobility perspective, these features require increased power consumption, expensive cooling systems, and a thicker box [increased form factor]. These contrast with mobility needs.

As recently as three years ago, we were reusing desktop microprocessors, and scaled voltages and frequencies to reduce power consumption, which reduced performance, until it fit into a reasonable form factor, with additional

[31] Robyn Weisman, "Intel to Slash Pentium 4 Prices," *NewsFactor Network,* April 16, 2001.
[32] Caroline Daniel, "Inside Dell," *Financial Times,* April 2, 2002.
[33] Several key positions at Intel were shared by two senior executives. In Intel parlance, Perlmutter and Chandrasekher were "two-in-a-box."
[34] Pronounced "Ban-yes."
[35] "Intel Announces Centrino™ Mobile Technology Brand Name," Intel Press Release, 8 January 2003.
[36] All quotes from David Perlmutter are from the authors' interview on 12 December 2002.

features to extend battery life. However, it started becoming clear back then that we would not be able to retrofit our desktop microprocessors into form factors much smaller than 1.2 inches of thickness.

To succeed in the mobile market, Perlmutter's group had to promote features in a way that amounted to apostasy for Intel. However, the toxins of the Intel "creosote bush" did not extend to the Middle East. Perlmutter explained:

> The development group in Israel, even before it was tasked as the mobility group, pushed ideas for mobility that went against the common wisdom at Intel.
>
> Being located in Israel both helped and hurt the effort to convince the company to pursue mobility. The Israeli team has a "renegade" culture, so we were very open to the idea of mobility in the first place. However, being in Israel, far apart from Intel's HQ, made it difficult to convince the company to move toward mobility. It took blood, sweat, and tears.
>
> We did this by creating alliances with the people who were influential and had a need for some of the mobility vectors that we were pushing. For example, at the time, I was heading a development team in Israel. We created alliances with a mobile team in the U.S. that was already finding that continuing on the path of using slightly modified desktop PC microprocessors for the mobile PC segment would create some issues discussed above. The effort was greatly helped by the fact that Craig [Barrett] and other Intel executives were on a vengeance that the microprocessor was starting to draw too much power, particularly in power-sensitive environments like mobile PCs. Craig found the idea of a low power microprocessor very appealing, although nobody had a clear idea of where it would lead.

The vectors of mobility seemed to apply equally to other devices in addition to computers. Perlmutter discussed the implications of the convergence of PCs and devices such as personal digital assistants (PDAs) and mobile phones.

> PDAs and mobiles phones are converging into what I like to call "smart phones." These will be devices that you can carry in your pocket. However, real computing requires a human interface: a keyboard or screen. Smart phones and mobile computers will have some similar capabilities; you will want both to be always "best connected." The user interface will decide which you use for what tasks.
>
> Intel is pursuing the smart phone market with its XScale technologies. We will sell our silicon into smart phones with XScale. But since we want to have the capabilities of a notebook, e.g., user interface, computing power, we are in the course of considering selectively adding some of the PDA and smart phone-like functions into notebook PCs to improve synergies among these devices.

Intel's success with this strategy relied upon certain dependencies. Perlmutter said:

We have dependencies on big manufacturers like Dell and IBM selling more; and on their and our abilities to promote new usage models using types of notebook PCs that excel in all four vectors of mobility. Also, Intel must help create the infrastructure for wireless (e.g., promote hot spot deployment) to help motivate consumers to use wireless-connected notebooks. In addition, there are technological dependencies, such as making sure we improve our performance along the vectors of mobility.

Enterprise Platform Group: Itanium Finally Inside

Before, during, and after the dotcom euphoria, indeed for most of the 1990s, Intel, in cooperation with Hewlett-Packard, worked to develop a new processor that would compete in the highest ends of the server market. In 2001, Intel released Itanium, a 64-bit microprocessor aimed at the server market. The Itanium processor family would likely compete with 64-bit architectures designed by Sun Microsystems and IBM. Itanium had a troubled history. Its development was slower than planned, four years late by some estimates. The project took a decade to complete. News reports speculated that Itanium cost around $5 billion to complete.[37] Intel did not release the figure, but said it was less than $5 billion. Itanium was also subject to litigation; Intel lost a court case in October 2002 when a United States Federal Judge ruled that the design of Intel's Itanium violated two patents held by Intergaph Corporation. Intel could be liable for up to $250 million in damages.

Mike Fister, senior vice president and general manager of Intel's Enterprise Platform Group, discussed some of the bumps Itanium experienced along the way.

> The problems were directly related to its complexity. The technological leap was probably underestimated on our part. Examples include defining the 64-bit instruction set, working in collaboration with HP, and engaging the software industry. We under-scoped in the beginning. The Itanium instruction set, VLIW (very long instruction words), was complex. Itanium involved creating a new overall architecture (think of this as "what the outside of the building looks like") and a new microarchitecture (analogous to optimizing the building for its intended use).[38]

Much of Itanium's early development had been shrouded in secrecy. Missed milestones led to rumors that Intel and HP were not working well together. When asked if having to collaborate outside of Intel presented

---

[37] John Markoff and Steve Lohr, "Intel's Bet Turns Iffy," *The New York Times,* September 29, 2002.

[38] All quotes from Mike Fister are from the authors' interview on 31 October 2002. Subsequent quotes from this interview will not be cited.

problems, Fister said, "Working with HP made things a bit more complicated, but the stories in the press were a bit overdone. Frankly we drove the process and we are used to collaborating on instruction set architectures. We do that all of the time, working with companies."

When the microprocessor did hit the market, customers had already slashed their IT budgets and Intel seemed to take an arms-length approach to its commercialization. Intel made the decision to leave it to original equipment manufacturers (OEMs) to work with solution providers to prime the channel for its 64-bit platform, at least at the outset. Paul Otellini, then executive vice president at Intel and general manager of the IAG, said, "From Intel's perspective, this is not a channel-enabled product the way we do with boxed processors and motherboards. At this point in its life, [Itanium] is strictly an OEM product, and the channel will get trained and served from the OEM customers."[39]

In July 2002, Intel began shipping its second-generation Itanium microprocessor, Itanium 2, and seemed to more heartily embrace this version. Twenty major computer systems makers, including HP, IBM, and NEC, planned to use the Itanium 2 chip. Several leading software makers, including Oracle, SAP, IBM, and Microsoft, were making commitments to tailor their programs to run on Itanium 2. Analysts thought that the Itanium 2 could gain 10 percent of the high-end market through 2007.[40]

Intel's domination of the lower-end server microprocessor market segment, with 85 percent share of segment,[41] resembled its position in the PC microprocessor market. However Intel's server market share resulted from sales of chips for less-expensive server computers, which handle tasks such as managing shared printers and distributing Web pages to desktop users. Half the revenue in the $49 billion-a-year computer server market was generated by more expensive higher-end server computers, selling for more than $50,000, that used non-Intel technology to perform crucial tasks such as automating the manufacturing, procurement, marketing, and financial operations of large companies. Intel aimed Itanium at that market, which used microprocessors with reduced instruction set computing (RISC) architectures and ran the UNIX operating system. In the fourth quarter of 2002, Advanced Micro Devices (AMD) planned to introduce its Opteron chip, which would offer both 32-bit and 64-bit processing, a capability that helps run large databases and solve scientific problems.[42] Opteron was part of a new AMD line, codenamed "Hammer," that was due out in 2003.

In a high-profile endorsement for AMD's Opteron, reports emerged in October 2002 that Sandia National Laboratories, which does research for the United States Department of Energy, and Cray Inc. planned to build a massive supercomputer using the chip. AMD said Hammer-based computers could run both 32-bit and 64-bit software at high speed. AMD released preliminary test results for Opteron that claimed to show the chip exceeded Intel's latest Itanium 2 model on one of two widely used speed measures. Meanwhile, Itanium 2 had enjoyed several important design wins since its release in the summer of 2002, including at least a half-dozen high-performance computing project installations.[43]

More worrying to Intel was the possibility that the market Itanium was designed to address, high-performance corporate computing, was fundamentally changing. At a conference at Stanford University in August 2002, Eric Schmidt, a computer scientist and CEO of the popular Internet search engine Google, discussed his vision for the industry. Schmidt spoke of small and inexpensive processors acting as Lego-style building blocks to execute powerful processing applications, displacing expensive server processors and the market that Itanium aimed to serve. Google cared less about raw processing power—the product of Moore's Law—and more about lower power consumption. Data centers, such as those used by Google, consumed as much electricity as cities. Google currently used servers with Intel's Xeon processors, which suited its requirements. Itanium was not aimed at search engines, which executed large volumes of processing power to execute fairly simple tasks, but the bigger and more complex problems of data warehousing and high performance technical computing. If Itanium failed to find success with companies in these markets, the ability of Itanium 2, or subsequent iterations, to pay back Intel's heavy investment with expected margins was less certain.

AMD also snapped at Intel's heels in other markets. Early in 2002, AMD expanded its Athlon processor family by introducing three high-end chips: the Athlon XP

[39] Edward F. Moltzen, "HP Plans Exit from PA-RISC Technology," *Computer Reseller News,* June 25, 2001, p. 36.

[40] Markoff and Lohr.

[41] Intel's share of segment revenue was estimated by the company at approximately 40 percent.

[42] Steve Lohr, "Intel to Begin Shipping a 64-Bit Microprocessor," *The New York Times,* July 8, 2002.

[43] Don Clark, "AMD Stages Supercomputer Coup—Hammer Chips Are Selected for U.S. Red Storm Project over Intel's Itanium Line," *Wall Street Journal,* October 21, 2002.

processor 2100+ for desktop PCs, the Athlon MP processor 2000+ for servers and workstations, and the mobile Athlon 4 processor 1600+ for notebook PCs, priced at $420, $415, and $380, respectively. At about this time Intel introduced the multiprocessor Xeon microprocessor at 1.4, 1.5, and 1.6GHz, priced from $1,177 to $3,692.[44] AMD also targeted its lower priced K7 line of microprocessors to compete against Intel's Xeon. AMD's Athlon chip line, mainly used in personal computers, had been falling behind the performance of comparable Intel chips.

INTEL COMMUNICATIONS GROUP

The Intel Communications Group (ICG) was formed in April 2001. Led by Sean Maloney, executive vice president and general manager, the group was involved in a variety of activities including designing and manufacturing microchips used in systems that transmit and direct traffic across the Internet and corporate networks; designing and manufacturing networking devices and equipment that provide access to the Internet, as well as local area networks and home networks; and designing and manufacturing hardware components for high-speed, high-capacity optical networks. Maloney said, "We will use Moore's Law to drive down the costs of chips, without threatening the business models of our customers. Internet traffic is approximately doubling every 12 to 18 months and I believe it will continue to do so through 2010."[45] To exploit this growth, ICG would look to double-down [bet heavily] on Ethernet and pull away as the world's largest supplier. In addition, ICG would provide three things:

1. Breakthrough cost/performance optical components,
2. Low cost, high performance processors to handle IP packets, and
3. World-leading Wi-Fi technology.

When the ICG was formed, Intel was extricating itself from its failed attempts in selling system products through CPG (see earlier). Maloney said: "There was fairly serious dissonance between Network Communications Group (NCG) and Communications Products Group (CPG). We needed to be either a components company or a systems company, but not both. We de-

cided to aim to be the world's largest communications components supplier."

John Miner, who had been general manager of CPG, recalled the reason for the group's founding and disbanding:

We met with Dell, Compaq, and IBM to convince them to go where Sun was. They were reluctant to join us in this space, except Compaq, who wanted to go it alone. We decided if they [the OEMs] didn't want to do it with us, we should go it alone. So we created CPG as a separate group because we didn't want to be perceived as competing with our customers. . . . We started in the middle of 1999. We wound down in 2001. We had over $1 billion in server sales in nine months. In the market place, the unbranded white box became equivalent to Intel. . . . Looking back, it was bad strategy to enter the market, but there had been some positive consequences. The OEMs did step in and participate when Intel showed them the way. However, it was not sustainable. Core microprocessor customers would eventually see that it was a good business, get into it themselves, and scream about competition from us. We have to listen to big microprocessor customers.

Sean Maloney also observed:

We manufactured around 80 percent of our communications chips in outside foundries. Our designers felt we couldn't (economically) make communications chips. I felt that Intel was essentially a building block company and the best manufacturer in the world. We know how to approach complex problems at the chip level and solve them. We should look to expand into adjacencies of approach or thought. After spending multiple hundreds of millions of dollars, we are now on track to make 90 percent of our communications chips in-house, with the world's best manufacturing technology.

In the reorganization that produced ICG, and the hard times the communications industry faced in the prolonged economic downturn, ICG reduced its headcount from 10,700 employees to 6,700. Maloney recalled, "It was a painful process getting here. We shut fifteen manufacturing and design sites. It was time consuming and expensive to do it right, to do it with dignity for the people." But now, Maloney was confident that Intel had the right tools, correctly aligned to compete in the telecommunications market. "We have been accumulating communication chip skills for some time. We now have more communication chip skills than any other company in the industry. In WiFi, Optical, etc. we have no excuses; we have the skills to be number one. We have our fate in our hands."

With the skills collected at ICG, Intel hoped to develop standardized chip-level products, or "building

[44] Robert Ristelhueber, "AMD, Intel Unveil Rival Processors at CeBIT Show," *EBN*, March 18, 2002. NB: Prices are for 1,000-unit purchases.
[45] All quotes from Sean Maloney are from the authors' interview on 24 October 2002. Subsequent quotes from this interview will not be cited.

blocks" that would serve the telecommunications industry. Currently, telecommunications suppliers such as Lucent and Cisco use specially designed, proprietary microprocessors and software in their products. In the absence of standard architectures for such systems, suppliers gained some advantage as customers tended to remain with their suppliers once such systems had been installed. Maloney hoped to use Moore's Law as a wedge to open—and perhaps standardize at the chip architecture level—the telecommunications supplier market. Maloney said, "The telecommunications industry had not benefited from Moore's Law because most of the processors used in their networks were not manufactured in volumes large enough to support leading-edge research or manufacturing technology. A standard 'building block' made with cutting-edge manufacturing technology, along with standard programming tools, could allow Intel to bring Moore's Law to the telecom industry."

Intel looked to key customers to help provide the volume necessary to get the benefits of Moore's Law to apply to this jurisdiction. Cisco, for example, would make a particularly valuable customer. Cisco was not immune to the technology downturn that affected the telecommunications and technology industries, but it fared better than most in those sectors. Its annual revenue in fiscal year 2002 exceeded $18 billion, with a gross profit margin of 68 percent. By the end of its fiscal year in July 2002, the company was sitting on a cash pile totaling $21 billion. Indeed, for the latter half of the 1990s, Cisco's revenues grew five-fold. But this growth decelerated by FY2001 and turned negative by FY2002. Some analysts estimated that the company's future annual growth rates would range between 7 and 8 percent, resembling those associated with more mature companies.

To boost its margins, and protect against declines in its core router business, Cisco was likely to move into new markets such as storage, security, and voice over Internet Protocol (VOIP) technologies. With a mountain of cash and a profitable but declining core market, Cisco resembled its would-be supplier, Intel.

Why would Cisco, mindful of how most of the margins from the PC market migrated to Microsoft and Intel, choose to work with Intel rather than going it alone in these new areas? "Because many communications customers feared another potential Wintel architecture, we had to overcome an attitude of 'ABI' (Anything but Intel)," Maloney explained, continuing:

A large problem we had to overcome with our customers was convincing them that we are not trying to commoditize their business. They suspected that we were trying to establish an-

other "Wintel" standard. It took up to 10 visits to convince them otherwise. It was a very complicated conversation.

Why do they not need to worry? Because there is no standard software and the rate of technology change is far higher than in the PC industry. It is a long way from commoditization with endless changes to differentiate in software and services.

We tell potential customers that the economics governing components at the chip level forces the industry into mass manufacturing and integration. You must embrace this trend and transformation. Intel helps you with this transformation. Our advice is: "Your intellectual property is above ASICs.[46] Customized components increase your inventory problem. Your value-add is in understanding and designing traffic networks, a far bigger challenge."

If entering the telecommunication supplier industry in the teeth of an extended telecom downturn did not seem like auspicious timing, according to Maloney, Intel had no alternative. He observed, "Our industry is already migrating to the communication space. PCs have been primarily about communications for almost 10 years (e.g., the popularity of email). We woke up to this fact. We want to lead it rather than be led by it." For Maloney, ICG's goal was to, "supply the underlying technologies that allow others to be creative." He held high hopes for WiFi and considered 802.11 directly analogous to the browser 10 years ago. Still, Maloney did not expect ICG to be profitable in the foreseeable future. He felt that in the mean time, appropriate performance measures would be the ability to get design wins in the right product-market spaces and to bring down the break-even level.

The communications market was both competitive and contracting. The market for communications systems (wired and wireless) semiconductors and optical components shrank by 38 percent in 2001. Analysts said a combination of demand-side issues, such as the worldwide economic slowdown, decreased spending for IT products, and decreased capital spending by telecommunications carriers, and an oversupply of components in the market at the beginning of 2001 led to the market decline. Looking at the broader telecommunications market, including optical components 2001, Intel ranked second, behind Agere Systems Inc., largely thanks to revenues Intel derived from sales of flash memory and because it gained share in the LAN adapter market. Agere Systems was an integrated design manufacturer specializing in optoelectronic components for communications networks. Agere had been spun-out from Lucent Technologies in March 2001. In June 2002, Lucent sold its remaining shares of

---

[46] ASIC is an acronym for Application-Specific Integrated Circuit.

Agere, which then became a fully separate company. Although Intel's communications revenue fell 22 percent to $2.7 billion, the decrease was relatively small enough to push it from fourth in 2000 to second place in 2001. Industry leader Agere earned sales of $2.8 billion. TI ranked third with communications revenues of $2.4 billion, a 33.1 percent decrease from 2000. Agere captured 5.8 percent share of the communications market, compared to Intel's 5.7 percent and TI's 5.1 percent.[47]

WIRELESS COMMUNICATIONS AND COMPUTING GROUP

Another group at Intel was interested in creating helpful and profitable building blocks. Intel's Wireless Communications and Computing Group (WCCG) designs and produces processors for data functions such as calendar and email programs, chipsets that enable voice communication functions for wireless handheld devices, and cellular phones and flash memories which retain data when a device's power is turned off.

This group is operated under the direction of Ron Smith, senior vice president and general manager. Smith described Intel's interest in wireless technologies:

> WCCG's goal is not to make the final product, but rather to provide the building blocks that make up the final product. These blocks must be standard, open and allow ease of programming. For example, they must allow for ease of migration of applications from PC to handheld devices.
>
> We want to be the building block supplier to the wireless data industry. We aim to construct an architecture that we call Personal Internet Client Architecture. This involves us in application processors, communications processors, and memory subsystems. We also provide core, low-level enabling software. We are evangelizing for increased performance, less power [energy consumption], and smaller size.[48]

For Smith, this did not entail a radical departure from Intel's core interests, at least as they have been aligned for the past few years:

> Intel was moving toward communications and computing convergence. For us, this convergence is embodied at the chip level. In 1996, Andy [Grove] told me we are a bit industry . . . moving bits, processing bits. If you consider a cell phone, a huge fraction of the bill of materials value is concerned with semiconductors. We thought there were op-

portunities to add value to integration. Now we are moving digital binary information units . . . done in silicon. Our currency is silicon, not our product. Our product is architecture, software support, etc.

Smith summed up his goals for WCCG and Intel in a formula that he described as a "figure of merit."

> We have created a new figure of merit: 2M/2m. That is MIPS $\times$ Mb/mW $\times$ mm^3.

- We want to increase MIPS, by keeping up with Moore's Law.
- We want to increase Mb (storage). We are already the world's leader in flash technology.
- We want to decrease power usage (mW). We are using low power architectures based on ARM[49] and Intel technologies. Intel acquired strong ARM from the Digital acquisition.
- We want to decrease size (mm^3). We have developed products such as "stacking package" and Intel StrataFlash™ to achieve this.[50]

Smith said, "Each component in this figure of merit is now a competency at Intel. We are leading in all the 'Ms' [each component of the figure of merit]."

In February 2003, some of these figures of merit translated into a new microprocessor, codenamed Manitoba, for the cell phone market. Manitoba offered cell phone manufacturers a low power consuming processor combined with flash and SRAM memories that will allow manufacturers to produce smaller phones with additional features. Intel looked to products like Manitoba, combining microprocessors and memories, to give the company—and a potential Intel platform—entrée into the growing cell phone market. Unlike its position in the PC microprocessor market, Intel was a relative newcomer to the wireless market, behind its well-established competitor TI. While some analysts estimated worldwide PC sales to increase from 136 million units in 2002 to 192 million units by 2006; more rapid growth was expected from the cell phone market, with increases expected from 400 million units sold worldwide in 2002 to 600 million units sold by 2006.[51]

---

[47] "Intel Nears Top of Shrinking Comms Market," *Electronic News,* May 27, 2002, p. 24.

[48] All quotes from Ron Smith are from the authors' interview on 24 October 2002. Subsequent quotes from this interview will not be cited.

[49] ARM (originally Advanced RISC Machines) technologies offer high performance with low power consumption, an important attribute for battery-powered devices.

[50] Stacking is a process whereby components that were formerly housed in separate chips are combined or stacked onto a single chip. For example, Intel integrates flash memory and RAM functionality into a single package for wireless OEMs. This stacking saves board space, an important attribute as devices become smaller.

[51] Cliff Edwards, Andy Reinhardt, Roger O. Crockett, "The Hulk Haunting Cell Phones," *Business Week,* March 3, 2003, p. 44.

BEYOND 2002: THE CORPORATE PERSPECTIVE

The Challenge of Making It Work Together

Much of the work that will govern the future of Intel involved formerly disparate groups working together. Barrett said, "If we have different architectures and want to simplify the software, we must set targets and reward employees on their ability to work across groups."

Asked how he gets employees to change longstanding habits, Barrett said:

> Communicate, communicate, communicate + organize, organize, organize + reward, reward, reward. That's how you turn the Queen Mary.
>
> We communicate directly to employees. For example we do a Webcast to all employees at the same time we do our presentations to analysts. Andy Bryant and Paul Otellini speak to Wall Street and I speak to employees. I don't want our employees to have to get their information from the street.

Barrett had to communicate closely with more than just his employees:

> Historically, microprocessors are cool, unique devices. The faster, the better. More recently, it's not about the microprocessor, but about the architecture of the device (e.g., PCs). Now the architecture of the platform is important. The lack of investment by PC OEMs forced us to pick up the slack (e.g., chipsets).
>
> More recently, it's about solution. We work with ISVs and operation system vendors. Processors are part of the solution. It's about much more than clock speed.
>
> I am spending more time working with Adobe, for example, making Photoshop run best on a Pentium 4.

Intel used to live by the performance of its microprocessors for PCs. Moore's Law governed the company, and its engineers devised sophisticated solutions to keep Intel pushing against Moore's Law curve. Now, Intel worried about new and different performance features, some of which had little to do with cramming more transistors onto integrated circuits. Barrett said, "We are looking at four aspects of performance: battery life, form function, wireless, and clock speed."

Barrett discussed the implications of these new performance measures.

> Now we have to do joint marketing with companies; our hardware and software engineers have to interact with their counterparts at other companies. There are also architecture implications: what's important in the next product? In the past we let desktop functionalities cascade to laptops. Now we design from the ground up, with segmentation and use in mind at the beginning.

Shift in how designs are done

Usage Models

The company now thinks about development in terms of usage models; evaluating at the outset how the architecture or platform will be used. Barrett said, "All customer expectations require individual design. We had to segment our products because the end users segmentation was growing. There are growing differences between desktops, mobiles, etc. The market segmentation drives our segmentation of development processes."

Paul Otellini explained:

> The usage model gets us away from diminishing returns on processor speeds. It gets away from the "who cares?" question. This changes the value proposition of what we offer.
>
> We want to start driving markets. We can do this because of the platforms. There are huge interdependencies, e.g., Microsoft, but our business models are more aligned. It used to be that Microsoft focused on installed base, while Intel focused on incremental units. Now, both care most about incremental units.
>
> Their business models work more like ours. More like what Apple does; developing software and hardware in harmony. This gives you vertical integration because of aligned set of business priorities.
>
> This interdependence goes across devices. We are aligned 80 percent of the time with Microsoft in what we do. Take telcos for example. Microsoft does less well in this space. We want to create reprogrammable silicon architectures based on Intel standards that people add value on top of. Sometimes with Microsoft, sometimes not. In this case, we use Linux and UNIX.
>
> There has not been much internal resistance to the change in focus. The biggest problem is getting people over the "brand barrier." It takes longer to create a brand than a product. We need to re-evaluate our brand. This will change the meaning of Intel Inside™. The brand change takes as much management encouragement as the planning issues.

Barrett compared this to where Intel has been. "In the past, we called Andy Grove the 'chief marketing officer.' In the 1990s, we were very vertical around desktop microprocessors. Every decision was make-or-break because we were a single-product company. Now we are migrating to a more horizontal structure."

LOOKING AHEAD

Otellini was specific about where he wanted Intel to go in the future. He said:

> We put stakes in the ground five years out. We have decided to focus on:

- Digital home
- Digital office/enterprise

- Mobile Internet clients
- Telco infrastructure

That's how people use computers. Our goal is to get Intel chips inside every one of those devices. Look at what we are doing for the next generation notebook. We are not just branding the chip, but branding the entire silicon platform. We will advertise the platform's usefulness, not its gigahertz. There may be a significant benefit to the consumer from an increase from 2.3 to 2.4 gHz, but it is increasingly difficult to make that case to consumers.

Barrett was confident about Intel's future and its bet on the convergence of communication and computing. He said:

It is happening at an interesting time. The convergence has been touted for a long time, but now we have the technical capability to create interesting mixed architecture solutions for communications and computing.

The telecom world is imploding from its historical structure. The same changes the PC industry underwent in a decade have happened to telecoms in 12 months. For example, Lucent, Nortel, Motorola, Ericsson, are all laying off large fractions of their development staffs. That means they'll have to add value by getting out of proprietary architectures and use standardized building blocks.

For the boldness of these bets, Intel was not betting the company on any of them, like it did with its decision to abandon memories in favor of microprocessors. Barrett continued:

I used to say that we're heading at 120 mph toward a brick wall . . . but it is worse to invest too late. Our strategy of maintaining cash has never wavered. We want a big bank account because the environment will be difficult, but we'll want to continue to invest. Our revenue is down 20 percent from 2000, but we're still profitable, generating cash and we have $10 billion in the bank. We are doing a $4 billion stock buy back. Use it or lose it? We chose to use it and replenish it. It's a prudent bet.

CONCLUSION

Due to the success of the company's "second act," dominating the market segment for PC microprocessors, Intel owned a cash-generating machine, a large bank account and a valuable global brand. The company would need these assets as it faced the simultaneous challenges of competitive pressure in its core and new market segments, a prolonged global technology recession, and the risk that its huge investments in manufacturing would not pay off as handsomely or strategically as it hoped. By late 2002, Intel had moved from letting chaos reign for a few years in order to explore new growth opportunities,

to reining in chaos to focus on exploiting the opportunities it had found in the convergence of communications and computing at the building block level. Yet, it was not proven that this convergence would be as profitable to Intel as the company hoped. Top management needed to address several key strategic questions. Is communications worth winning? What forms of communications? Does Intel have a clear strategic vision? How aggressively should the company pursue these market segments? Many interested outsiders as well as insiders were trying to determine what would have to happen for the company to replicate its past success and whether Intel would be able to find a comparable "third act."

Building a Learning Organization

David A. Garvin

Continuous improvement programs are sprouting up all over as organizations strive to better themselves and gain an edge. The topic list is long and varied, and sometimes it seems as though a program a month is needed just to keep up. Unfortunately, failed programs far outnumber successes, and improvement rates remain distressingly low. Why? Because most companies have failed to grasp a basic truth. Continuous improvement requires a commitment to learning.

How, after all, can an organization improve without first learning something new? Solving a problem, introducing a product, and reengineering a process all require seeing the world in a new light and acting accordingly. In the absence of learning, companies—and individuals—simply repeat old practices. Change remains cosmetic, and improvements are either fortuitous or short-lived.

A few farsighted executives—Ray Stata of Analog Devices, Gordon Forward of Chaparral Steel, Paul Allaire of Xerox—have recognized the link between learning and continuous improvement and have begun to refocus their companies around it. Scholars too have jumped on the bandwagon, beating the drum for "learning organizations" and "knowledge-creating companies." In rapidly changing businesses like semi-conductors and consumer electronics, these ideas are fast taking hold.

Source: Copyright © 1993 by The President and Fellows of Harvard College. All rights reserved. Reprinted with permission by *Harvard Business Review*, July–August 1993, pp. 78–91.

Yet despite the encouraging signs, the topic in large part remains murky, confused, and difficult to penetrate.

MEANING, MANAGEMENT, AND MEASUREMENT

Scholars are partly to blame. Their discussions of learning organizations have often been reverential and utopian, filled with near mystical terminology. Paradise, they would have you believe, is just around the corner. Peter Senge, who popularized learning organizations in his book *The Fifth Discipline,* described them as places

> where people continually expand their capacity to create the results they truly desire, where new and expansive patterns of thinking are nurtured, where collective aspiration is set free, and where people are continually learning how to learn together.[1]

To achieve these ends, Senge suggested the use of five "component technologies": systems thinking, personal mastery, mental models, shared vision, and team learning. In a similar spirit, Ikujiro Nonaka characterized knowledge-creating companies as places where "inventing new knowledge is not a specialized activity . . . it is a way of behaving, indeed, a way of being, in which everyone is a knowledge worker."[2] Nonaka suggested that companies use metaphors and organizational redundancy to focus thinking, encourage dialogue, and make tacit, instinctively understood ideas explicit.

Sound idyllic? Absolutely. Desirable? Without question. But does it provide a framework for action? Hardly. The recommendations are far too abstract, and too many questions remain unanswered. How, for example, will managers know when their companies have become learning organizations? What concrete changes in behavior are required? What policies and programs must be in place? How do you get from here to there?

Most discussions of learning organizations finesse these issues. Their focus is high philosophy and grand themes, sweeping metaphors rather than the gritty details of practice. Three critical issues are left unresolved, yet each is essential for effective implementation. First is the question of *meaning.* We need a plausible, well-grounded definition of learning organizations; it must be actionable and easy to apply. Second is the question of *management.* We need clearer guidelines for practice, filled with operational advice rather than high aspirations. And third is the question of *measurement.* We need better tools for assessing an organization's rate and level of learning to ensure that gains have in fact been made.

Once these "three Ms" are addressed, managers will have a firmer foundation for launching learning organi-

---

> **EXHIBIT 1   Definitions of Organizational Learning**
>
> Scholars have proposed a variety of definitions of organizational learning. Here is a small sample:
>
> *Organizational learning means the process of improving actions through better knowledge and understanding.* (C. Marlene Fiol and Marjorie A. Lyles, "Organizational Learning," *Academy of Management Review,* October 1985.)
>
> *An entity learns if, through its processing of information, the range of its potential behaviors is changed.* (George P. Huber, "Organizational Learning: The Contributing Processes and the Literatures," *Organization Science,* February 1991.)
>
> *Organizations are seen as learning by encoding inferences from history into routines that guide behavior.* (Barbara Levitt and James G. March, "Organizational Learning," *American Review of Sociology,* Vol. 14, 1988.)
>
> *Organizational learning is a process of detecting and correcting error.* (Chris Argyris, "Double Loop Learning in Organizations," *Harvard Business Review,* September–October 1977.)
>
> *Organizational learning occurs through shared insights, knowledge, and mental models. . . [and] builds on past knowledge and experience—that is, on memory.* (Ray Stata, "Organizational Learning—The Key to Management Innovation," *Sloan Management Review,* Spring 1989.)

zations. Without this groundwork, progress is unlikely, and for the simplest of reasons. For learning to become a meaningful corporate goal, it must first be understood.

WHAT IS A LEARNING ORGANIZATION?

Surprisingly, a clear definition of learning has proved to be elusive over the years. Organizational theorists have studied learning for a long time; the accompanying quotations suggest that there is still considerable disagreement (see Exhibit 1). Most scholars view organizational learning as a process that unfolds over time and link it with knowledge acquisition and improved performance. But they differ on other important matters.

Some, for example, believe that behavioral change is required for learning; others insist that new ways of thinking are enough. Some cite information processing as the mechanism through which learning takes place; others propose shared insights, organizational routines, even memory. And some think that organizational learning is common, while others believe that flawed, self-serving interpretations are the norm.

How can we discern among this cacophony of voices yet build on earlier insights? As a first step, consider the following definition:

A learning organization is an organization skilled at creating, acquiring, and transferring knowledge, and at modifying its behavior to reflect new knowledge and insights.

This definition begins with a simple truth: new ideas are essential if learning is to take place. Sometimes they are created de novo, through flashes of insight or creativity; at other times they arrive from outside the organization or are communicated by knowledgeable insiders. Whatever their source, these ideas are the trigger for organizational improvement. But they cannot by themselves create a learning organization. *Without accompanying changes in the way that work gets done, only the potential for improvement exists.*

This is a surprisingly stringent test for it rules out a number of obvious candidates for learning organizations. Many universities fail to qualify, as do many consulting firms. Even General Motors, despite its recent efforts to improve performance, is found wanting. All of these organizations have been effective at creating or acquiring new knowledge but notably less successful in applying that knowledge to their own activities. Total quality management, for example, is now taught at many business schools, yet the number using it to guide their own decision making is very small. Organizational consultants advise clients on social dynamics and small-group behavior but are notorious for their own infighting and factionalism. And GM, with a few exceptions, like Saturn and NUMMI (New United Motor Manufacturing Inc.), has had little success in revamping its manufacturing practices, even though its managers are experts on lean manufacturing, JIT production, and the requirements for improved quality of work life.

Organizations that do pass the definitional test—Honda, Corning, and General Electric come quickly to mind—have, by contrast, become adept at translating new knowledge into new ways of behaving. These companies actively manage the learning process to ensure that it occurs by design rather than by chance. Distinctive policies and practices are responsible for their success; they form the building blocks of learning organizations.

BUILDING BLOCKS

Learning organizations are skilled at five main activities: systematic problem solving, experimentation with new approaches, learning from their own experience and past history, learning from the experiences and best practices of others, and transferring knowledge quickly and efficiently throughout the organization. Each is accompanied by a distinctive mind-set, tool kit, and pattern of behavior. Many companies practice these activities to some degree. But few are consistently successful because they rely largely on happenstance and isolated examples. By creating systems and processes that support these activities and integrate them into the fabric of daily operations, companies can manage their learning more effectively.

1. Systematic Problem Solving

This first activity rests heavily on the philosophy and methods of the quality movement. Its underlying ideas, now widely accepted, include:

- Relying on the scientific method, rather than guess-work, for diagnosing problems (what Deming calls the Plan, Do, Check, Act cycle, and others refer to as hypothesis-generating, hypothesis-testing techniques).
- Insisting on data, rather than assumptions, as background for decision making (what quality practitioners call fact-based management).
- Using simple statistical tools (histograms, Pareto charts, correlations, cause-and-effect diagrams) to organize data and draw inferences.

Most training programs focus primarily on problem-solving techniques, using exercises and practical examples. These tools are relatively straightforward and easily communicated; the necessary mind-set, however, is more difficult to establish. Accuracy and precision are essential for learning. Employees must therefore become more disciplined in their thinking and more attentive to details. They must continually ask, "How do we know that's true?" recognizing that close enough is not good enough if real learning is to take place. They must push beyond obvious symptoms to assess underlying causes, often collecting evidence when conventional wisdom says it is unnecessary. Otherwise, the organization will remain a prisoner of "gut facts" and sloppy reasoning, and learning will be stifled.

Xerox has mastered this approach on a companywide scale. In 1983, senior managers launched the company's Leadership Through Quality initiative; since then, all employees have been trained in small-group activities and problem-solving techniques. Today a six-step process is used for virtually all decisions (see Exhibit 2). Employees are provided with tools in four areas: generating ideas and collecting information (brainstorming, interviewing, surveying); reaching consensus (list reduction, rating forms, weighted voting); analyzing and displaying data (cause-and-effect diagrams, force-field analysis); and planning actions (flow charts, Gantt charts). They then practice these tools during training

EXHIBIT 2   Xerox's Problem-Solving Process

Step	Question to be answered	Expansion/ divergence	Contraction/ convergence	What's needed to go to the next step
1. Identify and select problem	What do we want to change?	Lots of problems for consideration	One problem statement, one "desired state" agreed upon	Identification of the gap "Desired state" described in observable terms
2. Analyze problem	What's preventing us from reaching the "desired state"?	Lots of potential causes identified	Key cause(s) identified and verified	Key cause(s) documented and ranked
3. Generate potential solutions	How *could* we make the change?	Lots of ideas on how to solve the problem	Potential solutions clarified	Solution list
4. Select and plan the solution	What's the *best* way to do it?	Lots of criteria for evaluating potential solutions	Criteria to use for evaluating solution agreed upon	Plan for making and monitoring the change
		Lots of ideas on how to implement and evaluate the selected solution	Implementation and evaluation plans agreed upon	Measurement criteria to evaluate solution effectiveness
5. Implement the solution	Are we following the plan?		Implementation of agreed-on contingency plans (if necessary)	Solution in place
6. Evaluate the solution	How well did it work?		Effectiveness of solution agreed upon	Verification that the problem is solved, or
			Continuing problems (if any) identified	Agreement to address continuing problems

sessions that last several days. Training is presented in "family groups," members of the same department or business-unit team, and the tools are applied to real problems facing the group. The result of this process has been a common vocabulary and a consistent, companywide approach to problem solving. Once employees have been trained, they are expected to use the techniques at all meetings, and no topic is off-limits. When a high-level group was formed to review Xerox's organizational structure and suggest alternatives, it employed the very same process and tools.[3]

2. Experimentation

This activity involves the systematic searching for and testing of new knowledge. Using the scientific method is essential, and there are obvious parallels to systematic problem solving. But unlike problem solving, experimentation is usually motivated by opportunity and expanding horizons, not by current difficulties. It takes two main forms: ongoing programs and one-of-a-kind demonstration projects.

Ongoing programs normally involve a continuing series of small experiments, designed to produce incremental gains in knowledge. They are the mainstay of most continuous improvement programs and are especially common on the shop floor. Corning, for example, experiments continually with diverse raw materials and new formulations to increase yields and provide better grades of glass. Allegheny Ludlum, a specialty steelmaker, regularly examines new rolling methods and improved technologies to raise productivity and reduce costs.

Successful ongoing programs share several characteristics. First, they work hard to ensure a steady flow of new ideas, even if they must be imported from outside the organization. Chaparral Steel sends its first-line supervisors on sabbaticals around the globe, where they visit academic and industry leaders, develop an understanding of new work practices and technologies, then bring what they've learned back to the company and apply it to daily operations. In large part as a result of these initiatives, Chaparral is one of the five lowest cost steel plants in the world. GE's Impact Program originally sent manufacturing managers to Japan to study factory innovations, such as quality circles and kanban cards, and then apply them in their own organizations; today Europe is the destination, and productivity improvement practices the target. The program is one reason GE has recorded productivity gains averaging nearly 5 percent over the last four years.

Opportunity motivates experimentation. Corning, for example, continually strives to increase yields and provide better grades of glass.

Successful ongoing programs also require an incentive system that favors risk taking. Employees must feel that the benefits of experimentation exceed the costs; otherwise, they will not participate. This creates a difficult challenge for managers, who are trapped between two perilous extremes. They must maintain accountability and control over experiments without stifling creativity by unduly penalizing employees for failures. Allegheny Ludlum has perfected this juggling act: it keeps expensive, high-impact experiments off the scorecard used to evaluate managers but requires prior approvals from four senior vice presidents. The result has been a history of productivity improvements annually averaging 7 to 8 percent.

Finally, ongoing programs need managers and employees who are trained in the skills required to perform and evaluate experiments. These skills are seldom intuitive and must usually be learned. They cover a broad sweep: statistical methods, like design of experiments, that efficiently compare a large number of alternatives; graphical techniques, like process analysis, that are essential for redesigning work flows; and creativity techniques, like storyboarding and role playing, that keep novel ideas flowing. The most effective training programs are tightly focused and feature a small set of techniques tailored to employees' needs. Training in design of experiments, for example, is useful for manufacturing engineers, while creativity techniques are well suited to development groups.

Demonstration projects are usually larger and more complex than ongoing experiments. They involve holistic, systemwide changes, introduced at a single site, and are often undertaken with the goal of developing new organizational capabilities. Because these projects represent a sharp break from the past, they are usually designed from scratch, using a "clean slate" approach. General Foods's Topeka plant, one of the first high-commitment work systems in this country, was a pioneering demonstration project initiated to introduce the idea of self-managing teams and high levels of worker autonomy; a more recent example, designed to rethink small-car development, manufacturing, and sales, is GM's Saturn Division.

Demonstration projects share a number of distinctive characteristics:

• They are usually the first projects to embody principles and approaches that the organization hopes to adopt later on a larger scale. For this reason, they are more transitional efforts than endpoints and involve considerable "learning by doing." Mid-course corrections are common.

- They implicitly establish policy guidelines and decision rules for later projects. Managers must therefore be sensitive to the precedents they are setting and must send strong signals if they expect to establish new norms.
- They often encounter severe tests of commitment from employees who wish to see whether the rules have, in fact, changed.
- They are normally developed by strong multifunctional teams reporting directly to senior management. (For projects targeting employee involvement or quality of work life, teams should be multilevel as well.)
- They tend to have only limited impact on the rest of the organization if they are not accompanied by explicit strategies for transferring learning.

All of these characteristics appeared in a demonstration project launched by Copeland Corporation, a highly successful compressor manufacturer, in the mid-1970s. Matt Diggs, then the new CEO, wanted to transform the company's approach to manufacturing. Previously, Copeland had machined and assembled all products in a single facility. Costs were high, and quality was marginal. The problem, Diggs felt, was too much complexity.

At the outset, Diggs assigned a small, multifunctional team the task of designing a "focused factory" dedicated to a narrow, newly developed product line. The team reported directly to Diggs and took three years to complete its work. Initially, the project budget was $10 million to $12 million; that figure was repeatedly revised as the team found, through experience and with Diggs's prodding, that it could achieve dramatic improvements. The final investment, a total of $30 million, yielded unanticipated breakthroughs in reliability testing, automatic tool adjustment, and programmable control. All were achieved through learning by doing.

The team set additional precedents during the plant's start-up and early operations. To dramatize the importance of quality, for example, the quality manager was appointed second-in-command, a significant move upward. The same reporting relationship was used at all subsequent plants. In addition, Diggs urged the plant manager to ramp up slowly to full production and resist all efforts to proliferate products. These instructions were unusual at Copeland, where the marketing department normally ruled. Both directives were quickly tested; management held firm, and the implications were felt throughout the organization. Manufacturing's stature im-

proved, and the company as a whole recognized its competitive contribution. One observer commented, "Marketing had always run the company, so they couldn't believe it. The change was visible at the highest levels, and it went down hard."

Once the first focused factory was running smoothly—it seized 25 percent of the market in two years and held its edge in reliability for over a decade—Copeland built four more factories in quick succession. Diggs assigned members of the initial project to each factory's design team to ensure that early learnings were not lost; these people later rotated into operating assignments. Today focused factories remain the cornerstone of Copeland's manufacturing strategy and a continuing source of its cost and quality advantages.

Whether they are demonstration projects like Copeland's or ongoing programs like Allegheny Ludlum's, all forms of experimentation seek the same end: moving from superficial knowledge to deep understanding. At its simplest, the distinction is between knowing how things are done and knowing why they occur. Knowing how is partial knowledge; it is rooted in norms of behavior, standards of practice, and settings of equipment. Knowing why is more fundamental: it captures underlying cause-and-effect relationships and accommodates exceptions, adaptations, and unforeseen events. The ability to control temperatures and pressures to align grains of silicon and form silicon steel is an example of knowing how; understanding the chemical and physical process that produces the alignment is knowing why.

Further distinctions are possible, as Exhibit 3 suggests. Operating knowledge can be arrayed in a hierarchy, moving from limited understanding and the ability to make few distinctions to more complete understanding in which all contingencies are anticipated and controlled. In this context, experimentation and problem solving foster learning by pushing organizations up the hierarchy, from lower to higher stages of knowledge.

3. Learning from Past Experience

Companies must review their successes and failures, assess them systematically, and record the lessons in a form that employees find open and accessible. One expert has called this process the "Santayana Review," citing the famous philosopher George Santayana, who coined the phrase "Those who cannot remember the past are condemned to repeat it." Unfortunately, too many managers today are indifferent, even hostile, to the past, and by failing to reflect on it, they let valuable knowledge escape.

EXHIBIT 3   Stages of Knowledge

Scholars have suggested that production and operating knowledge can be classified systematically by level or stage of understanding. At the lowest levels of manufacturing knowledge, little is known other than the characteristics of a good product. Production remains an art, and there are few clearly articulated standards or rules. An example would be Stradivarius violins. Experts agree that they produce vastly superior sound, but no one can specify precisely how they were manufactured because skilled artisans were responsible. By contrast, at the highest levels of manufacturing knowledge, all aspects of production are known and understood. All materials and processing variations are articulated and accounted for, with rules and procedures for every contingency. Here an example would be a "lights out," fully automated factory that operates for many hours without any human intervention.

In total, this framework specifies eight stages of knowledge. From lowest to highest, they are:

1. Recognizing prototypes (what is a good product?).
2. Recognizing attributes within prototypes (ability to define some conditions under which process gives good output).
3. Discriminating among attributes (which attributes are important?—Experts may differ about relevance of patterns; new operators are often trained through apprenticeships).
4. Measuring attributes (some key attributes are measured; measures may be qualitative and relative).
5. Locally controlling attributes (repeatable performance; process designed by expert, but technicians can perform it).
6. Recognizing and discriminating between contingencies (production process can be mechanized and monitored manually).
7. Controlling contingencies (process can be automated).
8. Understanding procedures and controlling contingencies (process is completely understood).

Source: Adapted from Ramchandran Jaikumar and Roger Bohr, "The Development of Intelligent Systems for Industrial Use: A Conceptual Framework," *Research on Technological Innovation, Management and Policy,* Vol. 3 (1986), pp. 182–188.

A study of more than 150 new products concluded that "the knowledge gained from failures [is] often instrumental in achieving subsequent successes. . . . In the simplest terms, failure is the ultimate teacher."[4] IBM's 360 computer series, for example, one of the most popular and profitable ever built, was based on the technology of the failed Stretch computer that preceded it. In this case, as in many others, learning occurred by chance rather than by careful planning. A few companies, however, have established processes that require their managers to periodically think about the past and learn from their mistakes.

Boeing did so immediately after its difficulties with the 737 and 747 plane programs. Both planes were introduced with much fanfare and also with serious problems. To ensure that the problems were not repeated, senior managers commissioned a high-level employee group, called Project Homework, to compare the development processes of the 737 and 747 with those of the 707 and 727, two of the company's most profitable planes. The group was asked to develop a set of "lessons learned" that could be used on future projects. After working for three years, they produced hundreds of recommendations and an inch-thick booklet. Several members of the team were then transferred to the 757 and 767 start-ups, and guided by experience, they produced the most successful, error-free launches in Boeing's history.

Other companies have used a similar retrospective approach. Like Boeing, Xerox studied its product development process, examining three troubled products in an effort to understand why the company's new business initiatives failed so often. Arthur D. Little, the consulting company, focused on its past successes. Senior management invited ADL consultants from around the world to a two-day "jamboree," featuring booths and presentations documenting a wide range of the company's most successful practices, publications, and techniques. British Petroleum went even further and established the post-project appraisal unit to review major investment projects, write up case studies, and derive lessons for planners that were then incorporated into revisions of the company's planning guidelines. A five-person unit reported to the board of directors and reviewed six projects annually. The bulk of the time was spent in the field interviewing managers.[5] This type of review is now conducted regularly at the project level.

At the heart of this approach, one expert has observed, "is a mind-set that . . . enables companies to recognize the value of productive failure as contrasted with unproductive success. A productive failure is one that leads to insight, understanding, and thus an addition to the commonly held wisdom of the organization. An unproductive success occurs when something goes well, but nobody knows how or why."[6] IBM's legendary founder, Thomas Watson, Sr., apparently understood the distinction well. Company lore has it that a young manager, after losing $10 million in a risky venture, was called into Watson's office. The young man, thoroughly intimidated, began by saying, "I guess you want my resignation." Watson replied, "You can't be serious. We just spent $10 million educating you."

Fortunately, the learning process need not be so expensive. Case studies and postproject reviews like those

Boeing used lessons from earlier model development to help produce the 757 and 767—the most successful, error-free launches in its history.

of Xerox and British Petroleum can be performed with little cost other than managers' time. Companies can also enlist the help of faculty and students at local colleges or universities; they bring fresh perspectives and view internships and case studies as opportunities to gain experience and increase their own learning. A few companies have established computerized data banks to speed up the learning process. At Paul Revere Life Insurance, management requires all problem-solving teams to complete short registration forms describing their proposed projects if they hope to qualify for the company's award program. The company then enters the forms into its computer system and can immediately retrieve a listing of other groups of people who have worked or are working on the topic, along with a contact person. Relevant experience is then just a telephone call away.

4. Learning from Others

Of course, not all learning comes from reflection and self-analysis. Sometimes the most powerful insights come from looking outside one's immediate environment to gain a new perspective. Enlightened managers know that even companies in completely different businesses can be fertile sources of ideas and catalysts for creative thinking. At these organizations, enthusiastic borrowing is replacing the "not invented here" syndrome. Milliken calls the process SIS, for "Steal Ideas Shamelessly"; the broader term for it is benchmarking.

According to one expert, "Benchmarking is an ongoing investigation and learning experience that ensures that best industry practices are uncovered, analyzed, adopted, and implemented."[7] The greatest benefits come from studying *practices,* the way that work gets done, rather than results, and from involving line managers in

the process. Almost anything can be benchmarked. Xerox, the concept's creator, has applied it to billing, warehousing, and automated manufacturing. Milliken has been even more creative: in an inspired moment, it benchmarked Xerox's approach to benchmarking.

Unfortunately, there is still considerable confusion about the requirements for successful benchmarking. Benchmarking is not "industrial tourism," a series of ad hoc visits to companies that have received favorable publicity or won quality awards. Rather, it is a disciplined process that begins with a thorough search to identify best-practice organizations, continues with careful study of one's own practices and performance, progresses through systematic site visits and interviews, and concludes with an analysis of results, development of recommendations, and implementation. While time-consuming, the process need not be terribly expensive. AT&T's Benchmarking Group estimates that a moderate-sized project takes four to six months and incurs out-of-pocket costs of $20,000 (when personnel costs are included, the figure is three to four times higher).

Benchmarking is one way of gaining an outside perspective; another, equally fertile source of ideas is customers. Conversations with customers invariably stimulate learning; they are, after all, experts in what they do. Customers can provide up-to-date product information, competitive comparisons, insights into changing preferences, and immediate feedback about service and patterns of use. And companies need these insights at all levels, from the executive suite to the shop floor. At Motorola, members of the Operating and Policy Committee, including the CEO, meet personally and on a regular basis with customers. At Worthington Steel, all machine operators make periodic, unescorted trips to customers' factories to discuss their needs.

Customers can provide competitive comparisons and immediate feedback about service. And companies need these insights at all levels, from the executive suite to the shop floor.

Sometimes customers can't articulate their needs or remember even the most recent problems they have had with a product or service. If that's the case, managers must observe them in action. Xerox employs a number of anthropologists at its Palo Alto Research Center to observe users of new document products in their offices. Digital Equipment has developed an interactive process called "contextual inquiry" that is used by software engineers to observe users of new technologies as they go about their work. Milliken has created "first-delivery teams" that accompany the first shipment of all products; team members follow the product through the customer's production process to see how it is used and then develop ideas for further improvement.

Whatever the source of outside ideas, learning will only occur in a receptive environment. Managers can't be defensive and must be open to criticism or bad news. This is a difficult challenge, but it is essential for success. Companies that approach customers assuming that "we must be right, they have to be wrong" or visit other organizations certain that "they can't teach us anything" seldom learn very much. Learning organizations, by contrast, cultivate the art of open, attentive listening.

5. Transferring Knowledge

For learning to be more than a local affair, knowledge must spread quickly and efficiently throughout the organization. Ideas carry maximum impact when they are shared broadly rather than held in a few hands. A variety of mechanisms spur this process, including written, oral, and visual reports, site visits and tours, personnel rotation programs, education and training programs, and standardization programs. Each has distinctive strengths and weaknesses.

Reports and tours are by far the most popular mediums. Reports serve many purposes: they summarize findings, provide checklists of dos and don'ts, and describe important processes and events. They cover a multitude of topics, from benchmarking studies to accounting conventions to newly discovered marketing techniques. Today written reports are often supplemented by videotapes, which offer greater immediacy and fidelity.

Tours are an equally popular means of transferring knowledge, especially for large, multidivisional organizations with multiple sites. The most effective tours are tailored to different audiences and needs. To introduce its managers to the distinctive manufacturing practices of New United Motor Manufacturing Inc. (NUMMI), its joint venture with Toyota, General Motors developed a series of specialized tours. Some were geared to upper and middle managers, while others were aimed at lower ranks. Each tour described the policies, practices, and systems that were most relevant to that level of management.

Despite their popularity, reports and tours are relatively cumbersome ways of transferring knowledge. The gritty details that lie behind complex management concepts are difficult to communicate secondhand. Absorbing facts by reading them or seeing them demonstrated is one thing; experiencing them personally is quite another. As a leading cognitive scientist has observed, "It is very difficult to become knowledgeable in a passive way. Actively experiencing something is considerably more valuable than having it described." For this reason, personnel rotation programs are one of the most powerful methods of transferring knowledge.

In many organizations, expertise is held locally: in a particularly skilled computer technician, perhaps, a savvy global brand manager, or a division head with a track record of successful joint ventures. Those in daily contact with these experts benefit enormously from their skills, but their field of influence is relatively narrow. Transferring them to different parts of the organization helps share the wealth. Transfers may be from division to division, department to department, or facility to facility; they may involve senior-, middle-, or first-level managers. A supervisor experienced in just-in-time production, for example, might move to another factory to apply the methods there, or a successful division manager might transfer to a lagging division to invigorate it with already proven ideas. The CEO of Time Life used the latter approach when he shifted the president of the company's music division, who had orchestrated several years of rapid growth and high profits through innovative marketing, to the presidency of the book division, where profits were flat because of continued reliance on traditional marketing concepts.

Line to staff transfers are another option. These are most effective when they allow experienced managers to distill what they have learned and diffuse it across the company in the form of new standards, policies, or training programs. Consider how PPG used just such a transfer to advance its human resource practices around the concept of high-commitment work systems. In 1986, PPG constructed a new float-glass plant in Chehalis, Washington; it employed a radically new technology as well as innovations in human resource management that were developed by the plant manager and his staff. All workers were organized into small, self-managing teams with responsibility for work assignments, scheduling, problem solving and improvement, and peer review. After several years running the factory, the plant manager was promoted to director of human resources for the entire glass group. Drawing on his experiences at Chehalis, he developed a training program geared toward first-level supervisors that taught the behaviors needed to manage employees in a participative, self-managing environment.

As the PPG example suggests, education and training programs are powerful tools for transferring knowledge. But for maximum effectiveness, they must be linked explicitly to implementation. All too often, trainers assume that new knowledge will be applied without taking concrete steps to ensure that trainees actually follow through. Seldom do trainers provide opportunities for practice, and few programs consciously promote the application of their teachings after employees have returned to their jobs.

Xerox and GTE are exceptions. As noted earlier, when Xerox introduced problem-solving techniques to its employees in the 1980s, everyone, from the top to the bottom of the organization, was taught in small departmental or divisional groups led by their immediate superior. After an introduction to concepts and techniques, each group applied what they learned to a real-life work problem. In a similar spirit, GTE's Quality: The Competitive Edge program was offered to teams of business-unit presidents and the managers reporting to them. At the beginning of the 3-day course, each team received a request from a company officer to prepare a complete quality plan for their unit, based on the course concepts, within 60 days. Discussion periods of two to three hours were set aside during the program so that teams could begin working on their plans. After the teams submitted their reports, the company officers studied them, and then the teams implemented them. This GTE program produced dramatic improvements in quality, including a recent semifinalist spot in the Baldrige Awards.

The GTE example suggests another important guideline: knowledge is more likely to be transferred effectively when the right incentives are in place. If employees know that their plans will be evaluated and implemented—in other words, that their learning will be applied—progress is far more likely. At most companies, the status quo is well entrenched; only if managers and employees see new ideas as being in their own best interest will they accept them gracefully. AT&T has developed a creative approach that combines strong incentives with information sharing. Called the Chairman's Quality Award (CQA), it is an internal quality competition modeled on the Baldrige prize but with an important twist: awards are given not only for absolute performance (using the same 1,000-point scoring system as Baldrige) but also for improvements in scoring from the previous year. Gold, silver, and bronze Improvement Awards are given to units that have improved their scores 200, 150, and 100 points, respectively. These awards provide the incentive for change. An accompanying Pockets of Excellence program simplifies knowledge transfer. Every year, it identifies every unit within the company that has scored at least 60 percent of the possible points in each award category and then publicizes the names of these units using written reports and electronic mail.

MEASURING LEARNING

Managers have long known that "if you can't measure it, you can't manage it." This maxim is as true of learning as it is of any other corporate objective. Traditionally, the solution has been "learning curves" and "manufacturing progress functions." Both concepts date back to the

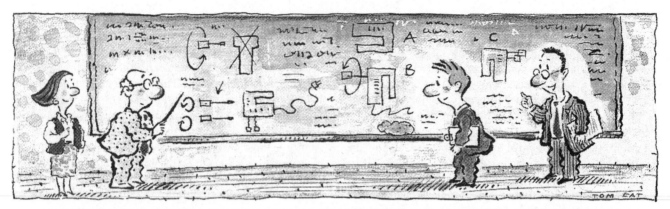

Progress is far more likely if employees know that their input is valued and will be put to good use.

discovery, during the 1920s and 1930s, that the costs of airframe manufacturing fell predictably with increases in cumulative volume. These increases were viewed as proxies for greater manufacturing knowledge, and most early studies examined their impact on the costs of direct labor. Later studies expanded the focus, looking at total manufacturing costs and the impact of experience in other industries, including shipbuilding, oil refining, and consumer electronics. Typically, learning rates were in the 80 to 85 percent range (meaning that with a doubling of cumulative production, costs fell to 80 to 85 percent of their previous level), although there was wide variation.

Firms like the Boston Consulting Group raised these ideas to a higher level in the 1970s. Drawing on the logic of learning curves, they argued that industries as a whole faced "experience curves," costs and prices that fell by predictable amounts as industries grew and their total production increased. With this observation, consultants suggested, came an iron law of competition. To enjoy the benefits of experience, companies would have to rapidly increase their production ahead of competitors to lower prices and gain market share.

Both learning and experience curves are still widely used, especially in the aerospace, defense, and electronics industries. Boeing, for instance, has established learning curves for every workstation in its assembly plant; they assist in monitoring productivity, determining work flows and staffing levels, and setting prices and profit margins on new airplanes. Experience curves are common in semiconductors and consumer electronics, where they are used to forecast industry costs and prices.

For companies hoping to become learning organizations, however, these measures are incomplete. They focus on only a single measure of output (cost or price) and ignore learning that affects other competitive variables, like quality, delivery, or new product introductions. They

suggest only one possible learning driver (total production volumes) and ignore both the possibility of learning in mature industries, where output is flat, and the possibility that learning might be driven by other sources, such as new technology or the challenge posed by competing products. Perhaps most important, they tell us little about the sources of learning or the levers of change.

Another measure has emerged in response to these concerns. Called the "half-life" curve, it was originally developed by Analog Devices, a leading semiconductor manufacturer, as a way of comparing internal improvement rates. A half-life curve measures the time it takes to achieve a 50 percent improvement in a specified performance measure. When represented graphically, the performance measure (defect rates, on-time delivery, time to market) is plotted on the vertical axis, using a logarithmic scale, and the time scale (days, months, years) is plotted horizontally. Steeper slopes then represent faster learning (see the Exhibit 4).

The logic is straightforward. Companies, divisions, or departments that take less time to improve must be learning faster than their peers. In the long run, their short learning cycles will translate into superior performance. The 50 percent target is a measure of convenience; it was derived empirically from studies of successful improvement processes at a wide range of companies. Half-life curves are also flexible. Unlike learning and experience curves, they work on any output measure, and they are not confined to costs or prices. In addition, they are easy to operationalize, they provide a simple measuring stick, and they allow for ready comparison among groups.

Yet even half-life curves have an important weakness: they focus solely on results. Some types of knowledge take years to digest, with few visible changes in performance for long periods. Creating a total quality culture, for instance, or developing new approaches to product

EXHIBIT 4   The Half-Life Curve

Analog Devices has used half-life curves to compare the performance of its divisions. Here monthly data on customer service are graphed for seven divisions. Division C is the clear winner: even though it started with a high proportion of late deliveries, its rapid learning rate led eventually to the best absolute performance. Divisions D, E, and G have been far less successful, with little or no improvement in on-time service over the period.

On-time customer service performance—monthly data (August 1987–July 1988)

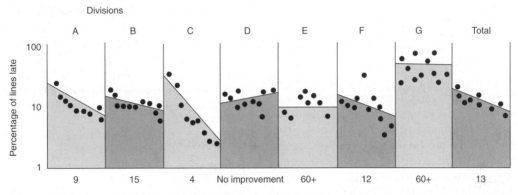

Source: Ray Stata, "Organizational Learning—The Key to Management Innovation," *Sloan Management Review,* Spring 1989, p. 72.

development are difficult systemic changes. Because of their long gestation periods, half-life curves or any other measures focused solely on results are unlikely to capture any short-run learning that has occurred. A more comprehensive framework is needed to track progress.

Organizational learning can usually be traced through three overlapping stages. The first step is cognitive. Members of the organization are exposed to new ideas, expand their knowledge, and begin to think differently. The second step is behavioral. Employees begin to internalize new insights and alter their behavior. And the third step is performance improvement, with changes in behavior leading to measurable improvements in results: superior quality, better delivery, increased market share, or other tangible gains. Because cognitive and behavioral changes typically precede improvements in performance, a complete learning audit must include all three.

Surveys, questionnaires, and interviews are useful for this purpose. At the cognitive level, they would focus on attitudes and depth of understanding. Have employees truly understood the meaning of self-direction and teamwork, or are the terms still unclear? At PPG, a team of human resource experts periodically audits every manufacturing plant, including extensive interviews with shop-floor employees, to ensure that the concepts are well understood. Have new approaches to customer service been fully accepted? At its 1989 Worldwide Marketing Managers' Meeting, Ford presented participants with a series of hypothetical situations in which customer complaints were in conflict with short-term dealer or company profit goals and asked how they would respond. Surveys like these are the first step toward identifying changed attitudes and new ways of thinking.

To assess behavioral changes, surveys and questionnaires must be supplemented by direct observation. Here the proof is in the doing, and there is no substitute for seeing employees in action. Domino's Pizza uses "mystery shoppers" to assess managers' commitment to customer service at its individual stores; L. L. Bean places telephone orders with its own operators to assess service levels. Other companies invite outside consultants to visit, attend meetings, observe employees in action, and then report what they have learned. In many ways, this approach mirrors that of examiners for the Baldrige Award, who make several-day site visits to semifinalists to see whether the companies' deeds match the words on their applications.

Finally, a comprehensive learning audit also measures performance. Half-life curves or other performance measures are essential for ensuring that cognitive and behavioral changes have actually produced results. Without them, companies would lack a rationale for investing in learning and the assurance that learning was serving the organization's ends.

FIRST STEPS

Learning organizations are not built overnight. Most successful examples are the products of carefully cultivated attitudes, commitments, and management processes that have accrued slowly and steadily over time. Still, some changes can be made immediately. Any company that wishes to become a learning organization can begin by taking a few simple steps.

The first step is to foster an environment that is conducive to learning. There must be time for reflection and analysis, to think about strategic plans, dissect customer needs, assess current work systems, and invent new products. Learning is difficult when employees are harried or rushed; it tends to be driven out by the pressures of the moment. Only if top management explicitly frees up employees' time for the purpose does learning occur with any frequency. That time will be doubly productive if employees possess the skills to use it wisely. Training in brainstorming, problem solving, evaluating experiments, and other core learning skills is therefore essential.

Another powerful lever is to open up boundaries and stimulate the exchange of ideas. Boundaries inhibit the flow of information; they keep individuals and groups isolated and reinforce preconceptions. Opening up boundaries, with conferences, meetings, and project teams, which either cross organizational levels or link the company and its customers and suppliers, ensures a fresh flow of ideas and the chance to consider competing perspectives. General Electric CEO Jack Welch considers this to be such a powerful stimulant of change that he has made "boundary-lessness" a cornerstone of the company's strategy for the 1990s.

Once managers have established a more supportive, open environment, they can create learning forums. These are programs or events designed with explicit learning goals in mind, and they can take a variety of forms: strategic reviews, which examine the changing competitive environment and the company's product portfolio, technology, and market positioning; systems audits, which review the health of large, cross-functional processes and delivery systems; internal benchmarking reports, which identify and compare best-in-class activities within the organization; study missions, which are dispatched to leading organizations around the world to better understand their performance and distinctive skills; and jamborees or symposiums, which bring together customers, suppliers, outside experts, or internal groups to share ideas and learn from one another. Each of these activities fosters learning by requiring employees to wrestle with new knowledge and consider its implications.

Each can also be tailored to business needs. A consumer goods company, for example, might sponsor a study mission to Europe to learn more about distribution methods within the newly unified Common Market, while a high-technology company might launch a systems audit to review its new product development process.

Together these efforts help to eliminate barriers that impede learning and begin to move learning higher on the organizational agenda. They also suggest a subtle shift in focus, away from continuous improvement and toward a commitment to learning. Coupled with a better understanding of the "three Ms," the meaning, management, and measurement of learning, this shift provides a solid foundation for building learning organizations.

REFERENCES

1. Peter M. Senge, *The Fifth Discipline* (New York: Doubleday, 1990), p. 1.
2. Ikujiro Nonaka, "The Knowledge-Creating Company," *Harvard Business Review,* November–December 1991, p. 97.
3. Robert Howard, "The CEO as Organizational Architect: An Interview with Xerox's Paul Allaire," *Harvard Business Review,* September–October 1992, p. 106.
4. Modesto A. Maidique and Billie Jo Zirger, "The New Product Learning Cycle," *Research Policy,* Vol. 14, No. 6 (1985), pp. 229, 309.
5. Frank R. Gulliver, "Post-Project Appraisals Pay," *Harvard Business Review,* March–April 1987, p. 128.
6. David Nadler, "Even Failures Can Be Productive," *The New York Times,* April 23, 1989, Sec. 3, p. 3.
7. Robert C. Camp, *Benchmarking: The Search for Industry Best Practices that Lead to Superior Performance* (Milwaukee: ASQC Quality Press, 1989), p. 12.
8. Roger Schank, with Peter Childers, *The Creative Attitude* (New York: Macmillan, 1988), p. 9.

READING V-2

The Power of Strategic Integration

Robert A. Burgelman and Yves L. Doz

All multibusiness corporations face the strategic imperative imposed by the stock market: maximizing the profitable growth of their businesses. Long-term success in meeting that imperative requires developing new strategy-making capabilities. During the early 1990s,

Source: MIT Sloan Management Review, Spring 2001.

many multibusiness companies focused on improving profitability through operational integration. They re-engineered, focusing on the capabilities that would improve speed, quality, and efficiency—and pruning business activities that no longer fit the value-creation logic of the corporate strategy. Then, starting in the late 1990s, senior managers began to focus on integrating strategies to add to revenue growth. Strategic integration involves more fully exploiting growth potential by combining resources and competencies from business units and directing those units toward new business opportunities that extend the existing corporate strategy.[1]

Today leaders of multibusiness corporations are learning to identify the *maximum-strategic-opportunity set*—those opportunities that can let companies take the fullest advantage of their capabilities and their potential to pursue new strategies. But to exploit those opportunities, managers need to become accomplished at what we call *complex strategic integration* (CSI). (See "About the Research.")

FIVE FORMS OF STRATEGIC INTEGRATION

Perceiving the maximum-strategic-opportunity set and tackling complex strategic integration are difficult responsibilities. Senior managers must be able to see potential business opportunities that do not yet exist—as well as the unarticulated strategies that are at the frontier of what a company is capable of doing. To help with those tasks, we propose a conceptual framework that features two dimensions (*scope* and *reach*) affecting the five forms of strategic integration (*overambitious, minimal, scope-driven, reach-driven,* and *complex*). (See "Strategic Integration in the Multibusiness Corporation.")

A location on the scope dimension indicates the extent to which pursuing a new business opportunity requires the collaboration of existing business units within the corporate strategy. Intel's chipset and motherboard businesses, for example, need to collaborate on developing demand for new products for the company's core microprocessor business.

A location on the reach dimension indicates the extent to which developing a new business opportunity does require changing the existing corporate strategy—perhaps by transforming a business unit or creating a new one. To cite Intel again, in 1999 the company extended its corporate strategy beyond its traditional focus on personal computers and pursued business opportunities in appliances by forming a Home Products Group within its Intel Architecture Business Group.[2]

About the Research

When the authors decided to start exploratory field research focused on complex strategic integration in multibusiness companies, systematic research on the subject was virtually nonexistent. They carried out some of the field research jointly during spring 1998, interviewing senior and top executives at several European companies. In parallel with those interviews, Yves Doz and his colleagues José Santos and Peter Williamson carried out detailed field studies at several European and Asian multinational companies, scrutinizing strategic integration among business units, geographic subunits, and partners. The research also explored how small entrepreneurial ventures (such as flat-screen developer PixTech) and new venture groups in established companies such as Nokia could mobilize competencies from longer, better-established partners, and achieve complex strategic integration (CSI) in multipartner value-creating webs.

Robert Burgelman's longitudinal research of Intel Corp.'s strategy-making process highlighted the difficulty of reach-driven strategic integration in a highly focused company. And his field study of Hewlett-Packard highlighted the difficulty of scope-driven strategic integration in a highly fragmented company. The study of the first nine months of Carly Fiorina's tenure as HP's new CEO (July 1999 to April 2000) focused on her efforts to create a CSI capability. The research involved interviews with all the members of HP's newly formed executive council and with several senior and midlevel general managers. Other parts of the research involved case writing about companies such as Intel, Disney, USA Networks, America Online, and Time Warner—companies trying to cope with the convergence of several industry segments in the information-processing industry and struggling to develop some CSI capability to capitalize on that convergence.

Among the five forms of strategic integration, overambitious strategic integration and minimal strategic integration are the two that value-minded companies should avoid. Overambitious strategic integration corresponds to the opportunity set defined by maximum scope and reach; it assumes that a company's available capabilities do not impose trade-offs between scope and reach. Jim Robinson's effort to turn American Express into a "financial supermarket" during the late 1980s and early 1990s is one example of that type of strategic integration.[3] Minimal strategic integration corresponds to the opportunity set defined by perceived limits on scope and reach. Traditional strategy-making approaches based on capital-investment and portfolio-planning decisions are typical. Two other forms, scope-driven strategic integration and

Strategic Integration in the Multibusiness Corporation

There are five forms of strategic integration: overambitious, minimal, scope-driven, reach-driven, and complex. Complex strategic integration (CSI) is the one that multibusiness corporations should seek. Although each form offers a set of opportunities, the maximum strategic opportunities flow from CSI. Complex strategic integration has the maximum scope and reach that is consistent with the realities of both external and internal constraints. Scope relates to the core strategy; reach refers to new strategies.

Overambitious strategic integration assumes that a company's available capabilities do not impose trade-offs between scope and reach. Companies that use minimal strategic integration have opportunities defined by the perceived limits on scope and reach. Scope-driven strategic integration corresponds to the opportunities defined by maximum scope and company perceptions about the limits of reach. Reach-driven strategic integration corresponds to the opportunity set defined by maximum reach and the perceived limit on scope.

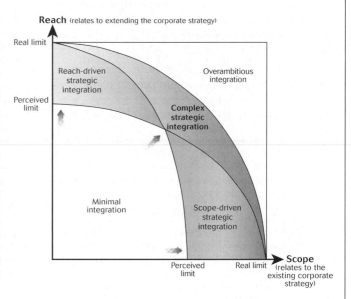

reach-driven strategic integration, are productive but fail to maximize the company's growth potential.

The fifth form, complex strategic integration, corresponds to the maximum-strategic-opportunity set. The maximum-strategic-opportunity set features as much scope and reach as is consistent with the trade-offs that the real world imposes. It is neither overambitious nor overly cautious. Companies achieving complex strategic integration take into account external constraints such as regulatory, technological, and market forces plus internal limitations on competencies, capabilities, and resources.[4] Complex strategic integration involves the discovery and creation of new business opportunities that combine resources from multiple units within the company (each with its particular perspective and vested interests) in order to extend the corporate strategy in new directions. It sometimes includes integrating contributions from external partners.[5]

Few multibusiness companies are currently proficient in exploiting the maximum-strategic-opportunity set, but some of the new high-technology giants—in particular Cisco Systems, Intel, Hewlett-Packard, and STMicroelectronics—are trying to develop the capability. (See "Hewlett-Packard's Transformation.") Cisco has pursued a corporate strategy that depends on the company's ability to achieve complex strategic integration. Cisco continues to be able to extend the frontier of the maximum-strategic-opportunity set. It does so by

quickly identifying, acquiring and integrating the winning companies in the technological-innovation races in newly emerging industry segments that are important for Cisco's strategy of serving corporate customers' networking needs. The stock market's perception that Cisco is succeeding in its efforts sustains the high share price that enables it to buy the winners in the first place, even at hefty premiums. STMicroelectronics offers another example of a company with a focus on improving complex strategic integration. (See "Complex Strategic Integration at STMicroelectronics.")

TWO COMPLEX-STRATEGIC-INTEGRATION CHALLENGES

Developing a complex-strategic-integration capability involves two important challenges for executives: first, managing the evolving tension between reinforcing the company's core business and redirecting strategy; second, managing the sharing and transferring of resources among business units.

The Tension Between Reinforcing the Core and Redirecting Strategy

Complex strategic integration depends on finding the right balance over time between reinforcing the core and redirecting strategy. Whereas reinforcement enables moving forcefully and rapidly along a given strategic tra-

Hewlett-Packard's Transformation

Hewlett-Packard is one of the world's most adaptive large, established companies. For decades, the HP Way provided guidance for transforming the company through organic growth and metamorphosis. Although occasionally succumbing to pressures to centralize, HP always reverted back to an organizational form containing distinct business units serving distinct markets with technology-based product-leadership strategies. By 1999, HP had 83 businesses, each with its own resources and profit-and-loss responsibility. However, as one top executive observed, "We weren't articulating a corporate strategy." Another said, "We talked about portfolio management, but we didn't do much."

Between 1996 and 1999, HP's profitable-growth performance disappointed the stock market. During that period, the company came to the conclusion that its measurement and instruments businesses no longer fit the corporate strategy and needed to be spun off. The current CEO was reaching retirement age, and HP's board of directors hired Carly Fiorina to replace him. The new CEO represented three firsts for HP: She was an outsider, she did not have a technical background, and she was a woman. Fiorina brought HP's senior executives together at an offsite meeting in August 1999 to, as she put it, "introduce them to their company. They had concentrated so much on their own businesses that they did not see that HP was unfocused and wide and shallow."

Fiorina went in search of what the founders had intended with the HP Way and reformulated the belief system, which she embodied in the "Rules of the Garage." The Rules of the Garage capture HP's traditional emphasis on inventiveness, product leadership, trust, collaboration, customer focus, abhorrence of bureaucracy, and the desire to make a contribution. The Rules of the Garage were designed to help change senior executives' attitudes and behavior, which Fiorina believed had become caricatures of what the founders had intended.

During the first nine months of her tenure, Fiorina made several changes to HP's structure to increase its strategic-integration capabilities. She quickly learned that customers found HP's fragmentation a hindrance to doing business. In early October 1999, she announced a new organizational structure. The new structure featured four worldwide regions cutting across 16 businesses in which the "back-end," or "product-facing," computer and printer groups would interact closely with the "front-end," or "customer-facing," organizations serving the business-to-business and business-to-consumer market segments. The purpose of the reorganization was to ensure a cohesive and coherent customer experience across all business units.

To increase interdependence at the top-management level, Fiorina also changed the way the executive council operated. And she altered the incentive structure, making top executives' variable compensation dependent on the overall performance of the corporation. One hundred top-level executives were placed on the scheme initially, with more targeted to join later.

Looking forward, HP's senior executives face three major strategic challenges. One is to continue to win in each of the core businesses against very strong competitors: Canon and Lexmark in printers, Sun Microsystems and IBM in high-end servers, Dell and Compaq in desktop system. The second challenge is to exploit existing synergies across HP's business units through scope-driven strategic integration. The third is to identify and exploit new business opportunities on the basis of HP's unique combination of assets: in short, complex strategic integration. It remains to be seen how Fiorina's efforts to increase CSI capability will work out over the next few years. But her efforts are on the frontier of multibusiness strategic leadership.

---

jectory, redirection helps a company shift its strategic trajectory, often in anticipation of or in response to major discontinuities. Finding a balance is hard for multibusiness companies used to pursuing more-limited forms of strategic integration. In practice, complex strategic integration may start as pure reinforcement or redirection and then evolve toward a more balanced approach.[6]

Scope-Driven Strategic Integration Reinforces the Core Strongly centralized companies that have emphasized the interdependencies among their various businesses tend to be scope-driven. Intel (during Andy Grove's tenure as CEO) and Disney (under Michael Eisner) are examples of companies that have been most comfortable finding opportunities by extending their scope.[7] Scope-driven strategic integration contributes to the reinforcement of the strategic thrust of the company's core

business. It strives to capitalize on deepening competence and capturing market share through the continuous concerted action of multiple business units. Reinforcing the core requires rapidly mobilizing resources across multiple business units, scaling up to selectively pursue major opportunities, and dropping opportunities that could stretch resources too thin.

If companies traditionally have emphasized scope and reinforcement, it may be hard for them to become comfortable with reach-driven strategic integration and redirection. Because redirection requires figuring out the strategic context for a new business, it is more risky and difficult than reinforcement. Only by increasing the quality of strategic decision making can companies improve the odds of making the right decisions in unfamiliar areas. That may require breaking major corporate decisions into sequences of learning and commitment, with

Complex Strategic Integration at STMicroelectronics

STMicroelectronics resulted from the merger of Italy's SGS Microelettronica and France's Thomson Semi-conducteurs. The merger brought together power, signal, analog, and digital capabilities in one company. ST developed its complex-strategic-integration capability while responding to the needs of a major customer, Seagate, which needed a smaller, simpler, highly reliable disk-drive controller (and read-write system). ST integrated the various required capabilities, which resided in different divisions and in locations as dispersed as Grenoble, Milan, Ireland, and Phoenix, Arizona. During the 1990s the approach pioneered for Seagate became a tried and tested CSI capability within ST, leading to the creation of new opportunities. The Seagate experience gave rise not only to a strategy but to a process that fostered lateral collaboration for creating and pursuing new opportunities.

ST's distinctive strategy is to develop "systems on a chip": to integrate into a single chip the functions normally performed by different integrated circuits assembled on a board. That strategy addresses a fast-growing market segment that lies between custom-made, application-specific integrated circuits (ASICs) and mass-produced general-purpose microprocessors. Often the system-on-a-chip strategy relies on customers who specify which capabilities they need to integrate from the various ST subunits. The customer becomes a strategic-integration hub for ST units.

Although seemingly random and often quite informal, complex strategic integration at ST is supported by managerial skills and increasingly well-honed tools (structure, control systems, incentives, and behavioral norms). In addition to the regular operating units, ST created a "headquarters region," which it uses deliberately to explore CSI opportunities. Following a period in the early 1990s when efforts to achieve complex strategic integration sometimes stumbled on transfer pricing and sales-credit issues, a see-through management control system was put in place to enable recognition of business-unit contributions to CSI projects. Measurement and reward systems encourage the pursuit of joint opportunities among business units.

Most ST managers have spent their whole career with the company, know one another well, and understand the perspectives and interests of others. ST is seen as a family in which individual motives are fairly transparent. Thus there is a high level of mutual understanding and trust. In addition, ST's managers come from more than a dozen countries, many of whom permanently reside in the United States but have maintained their ties to Europe. The pool of cosmopolitan managers has the necessary skills to integrate across national and cultural boundaries.

Customer needs are viewed as sources of CSI initiatives. At ST, a project requiring complex strategic integration becomes real as soon as it has a customer. Among the projects, some are considered of strategic importance for the company's future. Those are dubbed "Golden Projects," and top management gives them priority access to resources.

---

risks contained and reassessed at each stage and at each management level involved in the decision-making process.

Intel's networking venture provides an example of the difficulties of achieving redirection. Intel had entered the networking business in the late 1980s as a result of internal entrepreneurship, and it garnered several hundred million dollars in sales by the mid-1990s. Yet the general manager was not able to get Intel's highly focused top management to view the networking business as strategic. As result, it received only limited internal resources. In the face of the rapid growth of the networking industry during the mid-1990s, Intel remained a second-tier player. Only in 1997, when then-COO Craig Barrett raised concerns about Intel's ability to develop new businesses, was a new general manager able to get top management to view networking as strategic for the company.

Reach-Driven Strategic Integration Supports Redirection   Strongly decentralized companies that traditionally have emphasized corporate entrepreneurship and organic diversification around core competencies tend to be reach-driven. Johnson & Johnson, 3M, and

Hewlett-Packard (before the arrival of CEO Carly Fiorina) are classic examples. Reach-driven strategic integration helps companies achieve profitable growth through redirecting the strategy. Often discontinuities make previously peripheral competencies more central to the evolution of the company and lead to opportunities to leverage those competencies.

The technical or market signals associated with the discontinuities, however, are often difficult for corporate managers, who are removed from the front line, to detect. Redirection therefore requires the involvement of middle and senior managers. Dick Hackborn's successful effort to drive Hewlett-Packard toward a leading strategic position in digital printing during the early 1980s is illustrative.[8] Internal entrepreneurs also have redirected Johnson & Johnson's and 3M's evolution.

Becoming comfortable with scope-driven strategic integration and reinforcement is the key integration challenge for companies traditionally emphasizing reach and redirection. Pursuing scope-driven strategic integration often requires strong top-management intervention. That was the case at 3M and Johnson & Johnson during the early 1990s, when the CEOs sought to increase cross-business collaboration in their entrepreneurial, strategically fragmented companies.[9]

Johnson & Johnson's effort to create a Hospital Services Group (HSG) during the 1980s provides a prime example of the difficulties of achieving reinforcement in companies that traditionally emphasize reach and redirection.[10] HSG was a response to hospitals' demands for greater efficiency. HSG wanted to provide a unified interface with hospital customers for ordering, billing, and logistics. It took many years, however, for Johnson & Johnson to secure the collaboration of its fiercely independent product divisions for creating such a cross-business group.

Managing Resource Scarcity and Mobility

The second top-management challenge involves managing resource scarcity and mobility. Complex strategic integration requires sharing and transferring resources among business units. Tangible resources—such as money, capital equipment, raw materials, types of labor, and management time—must be allocated among different business units. The scarcity of such resources creates a zero-sum game: What one unit gets, the others cannot. By contrast, some intangible resources—such as corporate brands, patents, know-how, technology, and competencies (unless embodied in specific people)—are more like public goods: Their use in one part of the organization to pursue one set of opportunities does not prevent their use elsewhere. Although the sequence of specific projects may still occasionally pit managers against one another in competing for some resources, the availability of free resources creates a positive-sum game, in which self-interested but forthright cooperation pays off.[11]

Another important consideration is that some resources are more mobile than others. Corporate image, for example, is a resources that is highly mobile and applicable across multiple opportunities at no extra cost and without requiring managers to actively share. Some resources are less mobile because they require the sharing of information to create an information advantage (as the various business units of American Express did in trying to leverage data on consumers' spending patterns). Tapping other resources may require setting up and managing interdependent joint projects across units. That would be true for HP or Motorola to make automotive electronics. Again, top-level leadership can help. GE management, for example, helped overcome the inherent difficulties of moving resources when it established General Electric Credit Corp. to assist GE's industrial businesses in winning major customer contracts.

BUILDING A COMPLEX-STRATEGIC-INTEGRATION CAPABILITY

Like most other key corporate capabilities, building CSI capability is a task for the highest level of management. Only top management can create a corporate context that makes complex strategic integration an ongoing institutionalized process rather than an infrequent occurrence relying on ad hoc championing efforts of some highly dedicated managers. Top management needs to ensure that all high-level managers develop the skills necessary to effectively pursue CSI opportunities.[12]

CSI Context

To develop a corporate context that encourages complex strategic integration, top management should focus on organizational structure, managerial control systems, and managerial incentives. Each makes a distinct contribution to CSI, and each needs to reinforce the others.

Organizational Structure For effective collaboration, a company's organizational structure must be able to accommodate the real and evolving interdependencies among new and existing businesses. Companies need a framework for assessing the interdependencies that complex-strategic-integration initiatives create—and a repertoire of organizational-design options to augment the company's entrepreneurial capability.[13] Intel, Nokia, and Lucent, for instance, have created new-venture groups—a first step in using structure to facilitate CSI. As evolving CSI efforts generate new information, previous assessments must be re-evaluated and existing structural arrangements reconsidered.

Another structural approach might involve setting up integrators—senior executives or a corporate staff unit whose role is to stimulate operational units to pursue complex strategic integration. For instance, Bob Pittman played a key business-integrator role after the merger of Time Inc. and Warner Communications. Another structural approach is to redistribute the complex-strategic-integration task by giving senior executives dual responsibilities: being in charge of major functional or business activities while also being responsible for new-business development based on complex strategic integration. That is essentially the approach adopted by HP's Fiorina.[14]

Managerial Control Systems Managerial control systems can encourage CSI, too. One scholar has identified four types.[15] First are diagnostic control systems, which can foster cooperation if they register cross-unit contributions. However, most focus on individual business-unit performance and may deter business-unit managers from strategic-integration activities. For instance, ABB was initially successful in developing business-area strategies that required fairly intense cross-business collaboration.[16] However, ABB's Abacus diagnostic control system, which closely monitored the performance of the company's thousands of investment and profit centers, concentrated on individual unit performance and impeded strategic integration. By 1996, top management felt that ABB had become too fragmented. The result was "over-individualistic behaviors by the rulers of smaller kingdoms," as one observer noted. The problem is not uncommon. Collaboration requires a level of sophistication and self-confidence that may elude managers used to operating under control systems that emphasize individual unit performance.

Second are belief systems, which help define behavioral norms that support cooperation and reciprocity. Cooperation and reciprocity are probably easiest to develop in companies such as investment banks, which engage in multiple deals involving the same networks of people. In such companies, reciprocity norms govern repeated interactions. Cooperation and reciprocity are less easy to develop in situations involving the infrequent, large, one-time commitments that complex strategic integration may call for. They usually emerge gradually over time as part of a culture of trust and support among managers. For instance, at 3M, the business units own products, but not technologies. People really believe that technologies are freely available to anyone at 3M who wants to use them for new-business development.

Third are boundary-setting control systems. They are useful in identifying major risks, in particular those that lead companies to pursue overambitious strategic integration. Intel's New Business Group sets boundaries. It aims, as much as possible, to avoid entering new areas in direct competition with existing customers. However, boundaries need to be sufficiently dynamic that they can accommodate serendipity in complex strategic integration.

Finally, interactive control systems help top management signal the importance of CSI. With interactive control systems, complex strategic integration stays on the table in all high-level discussions about corporate strategy. Thus when Intel's Craig Barrett started involving several hundred senior executives in discussions about how to increase the company's new-business-development capability, he was able to spur the 1999 creation of the New Business Group.

Managerial Incentives   A major responsibility for the top management of multibusiness corporations is developing and maintaining incentives that encourage the most promising managers to pursue complex-strategic-integration initiatives—without losing their focus on the competitive reality their individual businesses face.[17] Incentives must be consistent with structural arrangements and control systems.[18] Unfortunately, business-unit managers often face conflicting incentives. And although managers of business units confronted by slowing growth may be motivated to seek cross-business cooperation, managers of profitable and growing businesses may not.

In addition, business-unit managers may perceive incentives for cooperation as blurring their accountability and diffusing responsibilities in dysfunctional ways. A senior executive at a European high-technology company observed that managers' ability to look beyond the borders of their own business and to think creatively always had been one of the most important criteria for ascending to higher levels in his company. He felt that job rotation and international assignments used for that purpose had led executives to focus on the scope dimension, which "in some cases perhaps led to weaker performance in terms of reach." The same executive added that the current preoccupation with single-business-unit performance was threatening to weaken the incentives for managers to focus on strategic integration.

CSI Skills

In addition to creating a corporate context that encourages complex strategic integration, top management needs to ensure that the corporation nurtures and develops three mutually supportive senior-executive skill sets. Cognitive, political, and entrepreneurial skills can be developed through education and job assignments.

Cognitive Skills   Part of the required CSI skill set is cognitive. Complex strategic integration requires senior executives to think up new strategies that bring together activities and projects located in different parts of the corporation. The challenge is one of imagination, intellectual grasp, and capacity for recognizing good strategies. Different managers undoubtedly have different aptitude. But executive development can play an important role by putting managers into positions where they can learn by doing. Sometimes, however, high-level managers try too hard, taking their dreams for reality until, as American Express did with its financial-supermarket strategy, they find themselves in the overambitious set. One of the skills needed is the ability to decide when to exit businesses and abandon dreams as Hewlett-Packard did when it divested its test-and-measurement businesses to focus more on its computer and printer businesses.

Political Skills Complex strategic integration involves reconfiguring the flow of company resources through cross-unit projects. Unit boundaries get redefined, and often individual business-unit charters do, too.[19] It is primarily top management that needs to build a consistent corporate context to foster and encourage cooperation among units.[20] But other high-level managers lobbying for changes in the structural and strategic contexts of the company play a key role. They need strong political skills to gain support from top management and peers for their complex-strategic-integration initiatives. They need to execute partnerships with peers, to create common ground and shared vision, and to manage conflicts between business units. They need to be able to define solutions that serve the interests of various business units (while serving the corporation) and to entice other business-unit managers and top management to cooperate. The skills match those of good politicians, successful coalition builders, and diplomats in complex alliances.

Entrepreneurial Skills Complex strategic integration also requires entrepreneurial skill: the ability to perceive profitable business opportunities and to attract the necessary corporate resources. CSI calls for transforming a project from a small venture to an opportunity for major corporate renewal. Senior executives must master such activities as strategic building and organizational championing so that they can determine the strategic context for major initiatives and convince top management to pour in resources.[21]

THE UNIQUE ROLE OF TOP MANAGEMENT

Top management's task is to develop a strategy-making process that can balance the challenges associated with exploiting existing and new opportunities simultaneously. In multibusiness corporations, that means developing a CSI capability. Corporate leaders must make an explicit commitment to articulating a corporate strategy that facilitates exploring and exploiting the maximum feasible strategic opportunities. Understanding the importance of both reach and scope, they must make sure that managers understand that their chances for increasingly senior positions depend on their demonstrated ability to bring complex-strategic-integration initiatives to successful completion. Promoting executives on the basis of their demonstrated CSI results speaks louder than statements about the need to create shareholder value. Top management will have to work on developing a CSI corporate context and CSI skills. Mistakes will be made,

but the key is to spot them quickly and correct them. The relative importance of CSI initiatives and individual businesses may vary over times as the company evolves through different life cycles and industry transitions. But the leaders of multibusiness corporations should never vacillate in their support for complex strategic integration and its critical role in the company's future.

ADDITIONAL RESOURCES

Little has been written about the management process involved in complex strategic integration. However, research on integration after acquisitions provides some insight on getting different organizational entities to work together. Interested readers will appreciate P. C. Haspeslagh and D. B. Jemison's 1991 Free Press book *Managing Acquisitions: Creating Value Through Corporate Renewal.* For research on strategic integration in companies operating in the global economy, we recommend Y. Doz, J. Santos, and P. Williamson's *From Global to Metanational: Competing in the Global Knowledge Economy,* which is scheduled for release this year.

REFERENCES

1. WPP, a holding company of independent marketing-services companies created by Martin Sorrell in 1985, is a good example. WPP seeks to create superior value for customers, employees, and shareholders by getting its highly independent business to collaborate. See J. L. Bower and S. Ellinson-Hout, "WPP: Integrating Icons," Harvard Business School case no. 9-396-249 (Boston: Harvard Business School Publishing Corp., 1996).

2. R. A. Burgelman, D. L. Carter, and R. S. Bamford, "Intel Corporation: The Evolution of an Adaptive Organization," Stanford Business School case no. SM-65 (Stanford, California: Stanford Business School, 1999).

3. D. A. Garvin, "Harvey Golub: Recharging American Express," Harvard Business School case no. 9-396-212 (Boston: Harvard Business School Publishing Corp., 1996).

4. The opportunities identified in the strategic-integration framework are different from the growth vectors in Ansoff's product-market framework. For instance, the scope-driven opportunity set could involve product development (new products developed by two or more business units together for their existing markets) or market development (new markets developed by two or more business units with their combined existing products) or both. Ansoff's framework also does not consider trade-offs among the various growth vectors as a result of resource constraints nor the strategic-integration issues across business units possibly involved in the various growth vectors. On the other hand, the business opportunities generated in the context of each form of strategic integration can be fruitfully interpreted in terms of

Ansoff's typology. The two frameworks are thus complementary. See H. T. Ansoff, *Corporate Strategy: An Analytic Approach to Business Policy for Growth and Expansion* (New York: McGraw-Hill, 1965). The assessments involved in establishing the different opportunity sets may vary across different parts of a company. A high degree of participation, negotiation, and flexibility will be necessary in the process of establishing the maximum strategic-opportunity set in order to get companywide support. And significant external and/or internal changes may affect the frontier over time. Sometimes, such changes force companies to disengage from a major profitable opportunity when it does not fit any more with the corporate value-creation logic. Hewlett-Packard's 1999 exit from test-and-measurement businesses is an example.

5. Y. L. Doz and G. Hamel, *Alliance Advantage* (Boston: Harvard Business School Press, 1998).

6. Robert Burgleman thanks Pekka Ala-Pietilla, president of Nokia Corp., for that insight (personal communication).

7. R. A. Burgelman, *Strategy is Destiny: How Strategy Making Shapes a Company's Future* (New York: The Free Press, 2002); J. Kolotouros, J. Maggioncalda, and R. A. Burgelman, "Disney in a Digital World," Stanford Business School, case no. SM-29 (Stanford, California: Stanford Business School, 1996); and J. K. Kolotouros and R. Burgelman, "Disney in a Digital World (B)," Stanford Business School case no. SM-29B (Stanford, California: Stanford Business School, 1998).

8. S. K. Yoder, "How HP Used Tactics of the Japanese to Beat Them at Their Game," *The Wall Street Journal,* Sept. 8. 1994, A1.

9. J. M. Hurstak and A. E. Pearson, "Johnson & Johnson in the 1990s," Harvard Business School case no. 9-393-001 (Boston: Harvard Business School Publishing Corp., 1993); and C. A. Bartlett and A. Mohammed, "3M: Profile of an Innovating Company, "Harvard Business School case no. 0-384-054 (Boston: Harvard Business School Publishing Corp., 1995).

10. F. Auilar, "Johnson & Johnson (B): Hospital Service, "Harvard Business Scholl case no. 9-384-054 (Boston: Harvard Business school Publishing Corp., 1983).

11. For early work on resource sharing among business units, see A. Gupta and V. Govindarajan, "Resource Sharing among SBU's Antecedents and Administrative Implications," *Academy of Management Journal* 29 (1986): 695–714. Also, top management can use various approaches to foster resource sharing. Bob Pittman, co-COO of AOL Time Warner, is renowned for his ability to get independent business-unit leaders to collaborate. He does so by convincing them that they'll win bigger by cooperating and also makes sure to given them the credit for successful cooperation. See C. Yang, R. Grover, and A. T. Palmer, "Shaw Time for AOL Time Warner," *Business Week,* Jan. 15, 2001, 56–64.

12. The contextual factors and skills proposed for building a company's CSI capability can be related to McKinsey &

Co.'s 7-S framework, which encompasses strategy, structure, systems, skills, style, staffing, and shared values. The 7-S framework also emphasizes the importance of configuration and the balancing of each in harmonious ways. The contextual factors we proposed touch on structure, systems, and shared values. The proposed cognitive, political, and entrepreneurial skills have obvious bearing on skills but also touch on style and staffing. Identifying the maximum strategic-opportunity set speaks directly to the strategy component in the 7-S framework. Examining what changes are needed in a company's existing 7-S configuration in order to build a company's CSI capability is an important task for top management.

13. R. A. Burgelman, "Designs for Corporate Entrepreneurship in Established firms," *California Management Review* 26 (spring 1984): 154–166.

14. R. A. Burgelman and P. Meza, "The New HP Way," Stanford Business School case no. SM-7 (Stanford, California: Stanford Business School, 2000).

15. R. Simons, *Levers of Control: How Managers Use Innovative Control Systems to Drive Strategic Renewal* (Boston: Harvard Business School Press, 1994).

16. C. A. Bartlett and S. Ghoshal, "Beyond the M-Form: Toward a Managerial Theory of the Firm:" *Strategic Management Journal* 14 (1993): 23–46.

17. The difficulties associated with aligning incentives in multibusiness companies lead economists to emphasize the benefits of narrow (single) business strategies. See J. J. Rotemberg and G. Saloner, "Benefits of Narrow Business Strategies," *American Economic Review* 84 (1994): 1330–1349.

18. For an analytical approach to designing the relationship among incentives and strategy and structure in complex corporations using multiple dimensions in their structure (for example, function product, geography), see D. P. Baron and D. Besanko, "Strategy, Organization and Incentives: Global Corporate Banking at Citibank," Research Paper Series no. 1488, Stanford University Graduate School of Business, Stanford, California, 1998.

19. D. C. Galunic, "Recreating Divisional Domains: Coevolution and the Multibusiness Firm," (Ph.D. diss., Department of Industrial Engineering and Engineering Management, Stanford University, 1994).

20. T. R. Eisenmann and J. L. Bower, "The Entrepreneurial M-Form: Strategic Integration in Global Media Firms," *Organization Science* (May–June 2003): 348–355.

21. For a discussion of the key entrepreneurial activities, see R. A. Burgelman, "Managing the Internal Corporate Venturing Process," *Sloan Management Review* 25 (winter 1984). On a smaller scale, "patching"—which involves adding, splitting, transferring, or combining chunks of businesses—is also a potentially useful entrepreneurial skill. See K. M. Eisenhardt and S. L. Brown, "Patching: Restitching Business Portfolios in Dynamic Markets," *Harvard Business Review* (May–June 1999): 72–85.

NAME INDEX

Abell, D., 4
Abernathy, William J., 34, 35, 140n, 143, 146, 147, 202, 285n, 443n, 444, 453, 489n, 659n, 691, 692, 717, 938n
Abrams, Robin, 234
Achi, P., 978n
Addison, Joseph, 987
Adner, Ron, 280, 282n, 283, 284
Adolph, Gerrry, 874
Agnew, H. M., 371n
Ahlstrand, B., 563
Akiyoshi, Hidenori, 635–641, 636
Ala-Pietilla, Pekka, 1182n
Alanis, A., 992
Albertson, Eric, 826, 828
Aldrich, Howard E., 142, 146, 511, 514, 516, 525, 563
Alexander, Robert, 763n
Alexander, Steve, 193, 200, 201
Allaire, Paul, 1162, 1174n
Allard, J., 588, 589, 590
Allen, T. J., 661, 717n, 719n, 720, 721
Allison, G., 563
Alsop, Stewart, 605n
Amelio, Gilbert, 929, 1110, 1116–1117
Ames, Charles, 140
Amit, Raphael, 32n
Ananthasubramanianium, G., 978n
Anastasi, Robert P., 1126n
Anderson, A., 8n
Anderson, J. R., 718
Anderson, Ken, 1079
Anderson, Philip, 146, 211, 247n, 248, 252, 441n, 444n, 489n, 691, 723, 938n
Andreessen, Marc, 589
Andrews, D. L., 645n
Andrews, Kenneth R., 142, 514, 550n
Angangco, R., 978n
Angelmar, R., 144
Angwin, Julia, 327n

Ansoff, H. Igor, 143, 550n, 659n, 987n, 1181n–1182n
Anthony, Scott D., 265, 801
Arai, Sakae, 632
Argyris, Chris, 447n, 1163
Arienzo, Maurizio, 265, 268, 271, 274, 275, 276, 278
Armstrong, C. Michael, 306
Armstrong, E., 282n
Arrow, Kenneth J., 445n, 725n, 983n
Arshi, Taymoor, 566
Arthur, W. Brian, 147, 368, 369n, 372n, 373, 374, 375n, 444n, 563, 570
Astley, W. Graham, 146, 511, 520, 525
Atherton, R. M., 664n
Atter, Frank, 748
Audia, James, 425
Audia, P. G., 564, 582
Auilar, F., 1182n
Auster, Ellen R., 525
Austin, Robert D., 877n
Ausube, J., 374n
Aymar, Michael A., 565, 577, 580, 823, 824, 827, 828, 834, 837, 838

Babbage, Charles, 957
Bacharach, S. B., 441n
Badger, C., 978n
Badger, Stephen, 1064, 1066, 1069
Baird, Bret, 869
Bakken, Earl, 1076, 1077
Baldwin, C. Y., 280, 283, 288n, 292, 693, 705, 708n
Ball, George W., 490n
Ball, Nigel, 234
Ballmer, Steven A., 588, 591
Bamford, Raymond S., 303n, 566, 576, 816, 1181n
Bandaru, Krish, 565, 828, 831, 835, 837

Bane, William, 321n
Banting, Frederick, 990
Baran, Andy, 577, 578
Barbieri, Lee, 272, 274, 277, 278
Barko, Randy, 503, 504, 508–509
Barksdale, James L., 591
Barnett, W. P., 147, 563, 564, 582
Barnevik, Percy, 935–936
Barney, J., 144
Barnfather, M., 139n
Baron, D. P., 1182n
Barrett, Craig R., 329, 493, 496, 500, 518, 563, 564, 565, 568, 572–573, 576, 578, 580, 583–584, 649, 824, 1128, 1137, 1140–1141, 1152, 1154, 1156, 1161, 1162, 1178, 1180
Barry, Hank, 389
Barry, P. J., 967
Bartenwerfer, David, 67
Bartkus, Joanne, 790
Bartlett, Christopher A., 902, 1182n
Bartlett, J., 140n, 987n, 989n
Basho, Eileen, 348, 354, 359, 360, 361
Bass, M. J., 282n, 289
Bau, Friedheim, 1047, 1049, 1051
Bayless, Jon, 190
Beard, D., 441n
Becker, David, 273n
Becker, Gary S., 280
Becker, R. H., 210
Becker, Selwyn W., 516
Bendor, J., 563
Beran, Andy, 565
Beresford, Charles, 433
Berger, D. G., 918n
Berman, Dennis K., 327n
Bernholt, Ned, 234
Bernstein, Sanford, 597
Besanko, D., 1182n

Besier, Klaus, 350, 358
Bessler, Joanne, 874
Best, Charles, 990
Bettis, R. A., 564, 582
Beyer, Janice M., 514
Bezos, Jeff, 610–629
Biddle, Jane, 359, 360
Biggadike, R., 917n
Billerbeck, B., 978n
Billington, C., 280
Bingham, A., 992
Bird, Larry, 74
Birdzell, L. E., Jr., 526
Birnbaum, Joel, 234
Blackman, Ross, 1009
Blake, Peter, 1008, 1009
Block, Zenas, 843
Boeker, Warren, 148, 514, 525
Bogler, Daniel, 610n
Bohr, Roger, 1168
Boies, David, 378
Bond, Bruce R., 342
Bono, Sonny, 407
Boomstein, David, 346
Bosack, Leonard, 745n
Botwinick, Stacy, 809n
Bourell, Beverly, 428, 429
Bourgeois, L. J., III, 511
Bowen, H. Kent, 629
Bower, G. H., 717
Bower, Joseph L., 148, 231, 232, 245, 246,
    258n, 259, 262, 282n, 286, 515, 516, 520,
    524, 570, 571, 1181n, 1182n
Boyd, Robert, 525
Bradley, Stephen P., 321n
Bradshaw, G. F., 718
Bradshaw, Thornton F., 132
Brault, Allen, 352
Braun, Artur, 1036, 1037, 1051
Braun, Erwin, 1036, 1037, 1051
Braun, Max, 1036, 1051
Brennan, Edward, 934
Bridges, W. P., 441n
Brinemeyer, J. R., 428
Brittain, Jack W., 514
Brock, G. W., 716
Broers, A. N., 450n
Brooker, Katrina, 613
Brooks, G., 938n
Brooks, Harvey, 32n
Brooks, Warren, 508
Brown, John Seely, 762, 765, 770, 773
Brown, S. L., 564, 581, 1182n
Brown, W. L., 450n
Browne, P. C., 132n
Bruce, L., 938n
Bruce, Richard, 762, 763, 765–766, 769–773
Bruck, Michael, 565
Bruegel, Tom, 565
Brunelleschi, Filippo, 399
Bruno, A. V., 981n
Brusoni, Stefano, 701, 705
Bryant, Andy D., 565, 1141n, 1142n, 1148–
    1149, 1161
Bucy, Fred, 139

Buffett, Warren, 801
Bunn, J., 377n
Burckhardt, Jacob, 434
Burgelman, Robert A., 3n, 4n, 6n, 8n, 13n,
    67, 83n, 99n, 139n, 141n, 142, 144, 146,
    147, 150, 157n, 179n, 189, 246, 256n,
    258n, 259, 260, 262, 263, 303n, 318, 325,
    330n, 378n, 398, 406n, 454, 478, 481,
    488n, 489n, 490, 511, 512, 513, 517, 520,
    524, 525, 553n, 562, 563, 564, 566, 567,
    571, 576, 579, 583, 592n, 610, 642n, 658n,
    659n, 661, 662, 663, 665, 666, 668, 682,
    816n, 915, 916n, 918n, 938n, 1127, 1128n,
    1140n, 1174, 1175, 1181n, 1182n
Burggraaf, P., 450n
Burns, I., 691, 719
Burns, Louis, 1154
Burns, T., 441n, 444n
Burrows, Peter, 568, 1126n, 1127n
Burstein, D., 577
Burton, R. L., 372n
Bushnell, Bob, 806, 812
Butterworth, Brad, 1009
Buzzell, Robert, 205

Cady, R. K., 413
Cameron, Kim, 522, 524
Caminiti, S., 938n
Campbell, Donald T., 146, 254n, 511, 513
Campi, Mike, 748
Cannon, Maria, 234
Cannon, R., 978n
Cannon, Walter, 434
Carlton, Jim, 1126n, 1127n
Carlton, Richard, 783
Carmine, B. D., 991
Carroll, Glenn R., 511, 525, 938n
Carroll, Lewis, 424
Carroll, Paul, 587
Carsten, Jack, 455, 467, 473, 497, 568
Carter, Dennis L., 455, 458, 462, 512, 565,
    566, 568, 569, 571, 572–573, 576, 823,
    1181n
Cary, Frank, 135
Case, Steven M., 590
Cassell, Steve, 565
Cha, Benjamin, 378
Chaddick, Steve, 190n, 193–194, 200
Chadha, Kanwar, 499
Chaffin, Janice, 234
Chakravarthy, Balaji S., 524
Chambers, John, 329, 746, 748, 749
Chamorro, German, 790
Chandler, Alfred D., 280, 283, 515
Chandler, M. K., 139n, 690n
Chandrasekher, Anand, 1155
Chang, I. H. P., 450n
Chapin, Chris, 32n
Chase, M., 133n
Chatman, J., 938n
Chen, M.-J., 564, 582
Chen, Reuben, 398n
Chesbrough, Henry W., 279, 280, 281, 291,
    296n, 298, 690n, 691, 699, 703, 705, 762,
    763n, 773

Chi, Charles, 194
Chiariglione, Leonardo, 397
Child, John, 511
Chinn, D., 978n
Chisum, Donald S., 399
Chou, Sun Lin, 455, 457, 458, 459, 464, 473,
    492, 497, 499n, 1142–1143
Christensen, Clayton M., 45n, 148, 208, 209,
    210, 213, 214, 218, 223, 227, 228, 231,
    232, 233n, 245, 248, 250, 252n, 254, 257n,
    258n, 263, 265, 278, 279, 280, 281, 282n,
    283, 284, 285n, 286, 288n, 289, 298, 300,
    302, 501n, 529n, 541, 544, 570, 674, 690n,
    691, 692, 693, 702, 708n, 775n, 801, 869,
    1062, 1076
Christensen, Mark, 565, 578
Christian, B., 978n
Christofanelli, Lynn, 234
Churchill, A., 1038
Churchill, Joan, 782, 786, 788, 789, 790,
    794n, 795, 796n, 798n
Cihra, Robert, 1117, 1126n, 1127n
Cioffi, John, 160, 162, 324
Clark, A. S., 991
Clark, Don, 1157n
Clark, James H., 589, 591
Clark, Jim, 1010
Clark, Kim B., 8n, 35, 143, 146, 147, 148,
    151, 210, 215, 223n, 224, 227, 233n, 247n,
    248, 252, 280, 283, 288n, 291, 292, 296,
    441, 442n, 443n, 444, 445n, 448n, 453,
    489n, 546, 658n, 691, 693, 694, 705, 707n,
    708n, 721, 938n, 940, 941, 942, 943, 944,
    947, 948, 949, 951, 954n, 998n, 1012,
    1017, 1023, 1051, 1060n, 1098
Clark, Larry, 1078
Clarke, Janet, 893, 898, 899, 900, 901
Clarke, Peter, 647n
Clausing, D., 281, 696, 954n
Clavenna, Scott, 188b
Clayman, M., 992
Clemenceau, Georges, 439
Coase, Ronald H., 280
Cobbley, Dave, 565
Cocke, John, 244
Cody, Bill, 965, 970
Cogan, George W., 454, 488n–489n, 490,
    512, 566
Cohen, Lawrence E., 511, 520
Cohen, S. D., 720n
Cohen, Wesley M., 150, 660, 716, 722n,
    724n, 725, 727n, 729, 730n, 731n
Cohn, Harry, 82
Colbeth, Douglas P., 590
Collins, J. C., 563
Collins, Michael, 801, 803, 805, 806, 809–
    810, 812–816
Colvin, C., 132n
Connelly, John, 148–149
Conner, Dennis, 1006
Connor, B., 978n
Constant, Edward W., 209, 210
Cooper, Arnold C., 8n, 147, 209, 246, 247,
    441n, 444n, 489n, 522, 659n, 937n, 981n
Cooper, R. C., 977n, 978

Cooper, R. G., 795n, 987n
Cooper, W., 377n
Coote, Jeremy, 348, 351, 353, 357, 358, 359, 360, 361
Coover, James, 404n
Copernicus, N., 34
Coppinger, Roy, 565, 828, 834, 835
Coppola, Francis Ford, 273
Cosier, Richard A., 490n
Cotteleer, Mark, 877
Court, Randolph, 1126n
Coutts, Russell, 1009
Cowan, M., 824
Cowan, Rory, 371n, 376, 892, 893, 894, 897, 898, 899, 900
Coyne, William, 786
Crabb, Tony, 754, 756
Crandall, Robert W., 319n, 321n
Crespi, Christopher J., 159n
Cristinziano, Michael, 166n
Crites, D. M., 664n
Crockett, Roger O., 1160n
Crowe, James, 313, 314
Cubell, Allen, 891
Cummings, L. L., 447n, 938n
Curran, R. P., 784
Curry, Bill, 628
Curtis, Pavel, 764, 768, 769
Cusumano, M. A., 143
Cyert, R. M., 444n

D'Arbeloff, Alexander, 137, 804
D'Arbeloff, George, 801, 803–806, 810, 813–814, 816
D'Aveni, Richard A., 521, 522, 524
D'Innocenzio, Anne D., 803n
Daft, Richard L., 441n, 444n, 516, 517
Dahlen, A., 978n
Daimler, Gottlieb, 1027
Daniel, Caroline, 1155n
Daniels, M. E., 991
Darling, Scott, 565
Darwall, Christina, 762
Darwin, Charles, 400
David, Paul A., 146, 147, 368n, 375n, 376, 377n
Davidow, Bill, 365, 648
Davidow, William H., 518
Davidson, Laurie, 1009
Davies, John, 565, 838
Davis, Jim, 233, 234, 235, 240, 242, 243, 1126n, 1127n
Dearborn, R., 720n
De Bendern, Paul, 277
DeCoudreaux, A., 992
Dell, John, 790
Dell, Michael, 959–961, 963, 965, 966–967, 1122
Demetrescu, S., 978n
Deming, W. Edwards, 1164
Demsetz, H., 280
Dere, William H., 1002
Derrick, Tim, 1067–1070, 1074, 1075
Descamps, Frederic, 83
Dess, G. G., 441n

Deutschman, A., 938n
Dewar, R. D., 441n
Deyo, Don, 1076, 1077, 1078, 1079, 1082, 1084, 1086
Dham, Vin, 565
Diaz, Manuel, 234
Dickens, Charles, 404
Dickie, Brian, 869, 870, 873, 874, 876–877
Dickie, Mure, 1142n
Diggs, Matt, 1167
Dilsaver, Evelyn, 605
DiMaggio, Paul J., 520
DiMarchi, Richard M., 426, 991, 992, 1002
DiMassi, J. A., 411n, 415n, 417, 993n
Disney, Walt, 235
Dittombee, Hans-Jürgen, 1038, 1044, 1050, 1051
Dixon, Christopher, 82
Dixon, Mike, 765, 768
Dodd, Rick, 194
Dodgson, Charles, 424
Dodson, Rick, 1009
Dolby, Ray, 56
Donaldson, Geoffrey, 147, 658n, 1064, 1066, 1069–1070
Donaldson, Gordon, 489n, 514, 526
Donaldson, Michael, 1063, 1064, 1066, 1067, 1068, 1070, 1074
Dosi, Giovanni, 146, 248, 249n, 260, 368n, 692, 707n
Douglass, Elizabeth, 199n
Dow, Ann, 814, 816
Doz, Yves L., 144, 150–151, 524, 1174, 1181, 1182n
Drennan, George, 533
Drew, Richard, 782, 783, 785
Drobenko, B., 978n
Drummond, Mike, 1009
DuBois, Kelly, 592
Dunlop, Sam, 789
Dunn, Debra, 234
Dunning, Peter, 359, 360
Dunwell, Stephen, 989
Dutton, Jane E., 441n, 447n, 522
Dvorak, John C., 648n
Dwight, Herb, 137
Dyck, B., 566
Dyer, D., 990n
Dyer, J., 296
Dyess, Kirby, 566, 823

Eads, Bill, 234
Eagle, M. L., 991
Eastham, Melville, 133
Eastman, George, 266
Eccles, R. G., 708n
Edding, Marilyn, 234
Eden, Scott, 629n
Edgecliffe-Johnson, Andrew, 610n, 620n
Edison, Thomas, 785
Edwards, Cliff, 1137n, 1160n
Egan, David, 1009, 1010, 1011
Eichler, Fritz, 1036
Eilers, Dan, 1113
Einspruch, N. G., 449n

Einstein, Albert, 400, 1124
Eisenhardt, Kathleen M., 489n, 526, 564, 581, 938n, 1182n
Eisenmann, T. R., 1182n
Eisner, Michael, 328, 1177
Eletr, Sam H., 664
Elio, Paul, 13, 14, 16, 17
Elizabeth I, 440
Ellenby, John, 672
Ellinson-Hout, S., 1181n
Ellis, Catherine, 823
Ellis, H. C., 717n, 718
Ellison, David, 1105n
Ellison, Larry, 577, 1116, 1117
Emerson, Ralph Waldo, 967
Engelmann, Frank, 368n
Enos, John, 203
Eppinger, Steven, 280, 705
Ermoliev, Y. M., 372n
Esrey, William, 209
Estes, W. K., 717
Estridge, Philip, 44
Ettlie, J. E., 441n
Evans, Bob, 989n
Evans, P., 4n, 142
Evans, Robley D., 436
Evans, Warren, 565
Everett, Carl, 827, 837

Faber, Bart, 897, 898, 899, 900, 901, 902
Faggin, Federico, 461
Fallon, Tom, 748
Fanning, Shawn, 325, 386, 396
Farmwald, Mike, 645
Farquhar, Norman, 40n
Farrell, F., 147
Farrell, J., 372, 375n, 376, 570
Farrell, R., 718
Farros, R., 978n
Fast, Norman D., 665n, 669, 915n
Fee, Elizabeth, 882, 885, 888
Ferguson, Charles H., 237n, 244n, 258n
Fife, Keith, 266, 268, 271
Fine, C., 281, 283
Fine, K. M., 566
Finger, H., 978n
Finkelstein, Sidney, 521
Finney, Laura, 566
Fiol, C. Marlene, 1163
Fiorina, Carly, 1175, 1177, 1178, 1179
Fisher, Jeff, 612n
Fisher, Ken, 134
Fiske, Bradley, 436
Fister, Mike, 1154, 1156–1157
Fixson, S., 280
Flaherty, Therese, 32n
Fleming, L., 280, 287
Fletcher, William, 368
Flynn, Laurie J., 1127n
Ford, D., 144
Ford, Henry, 204, 1023, 1026, 1142
Forward, Gordon, 1162
Foschi, Martha, 490n
Foster, John W., 303n

Foster, R. J., 209, 210, 214, 215, 223, 230, 231, 246, 249, 254n
Foster, R. N., 8n, 146, 490n, 660n, 690n
Foster, Richard, 926, 938n, 941
Fox, B. P., 991
Frankel, M., 369n
Frankel, Richard, 137
Freeman, Christopher, 368n, 441n, 447n, 980n
Freeman, John H., 147, 441n, 489n, 511, 514, 520, 522, 525, 526, 563, 564, 582
Freeze, Karen, 1035
Freud, Sigmund, 432
Friar, J., 4n
Friedland, Jonathan, 1126n
Friesen, Peter H., 489n, 514, 520, 525
Frohman, Dov, 455, 459, 516
Fu, Sai Wai, 499
Fujimoto, Takahiro, 280, 296, 721, 943, 948, 949, 1017, 1023, 1060n, 1098n
Fukatsu, Skihito, 635
Fuller, Brian, 404n
Fulton, Robert, 230
Fundakowski, Sally, 565
Fusfeld, Alan R., 6, 62

Gable, J. S., 983n, 984n
Gaddis, Tony, 234
Galante, S., 571
Galbraith, J. R., 445n, 915n
Galileo, 434, 787
Galunic, D. C., 1182n
Gardiner, J. P., 447n
Garman, Andy, 772, 773
Garrana, Henry, 401
Garrett, Sanford J., 671
Garud, R., 146, 147
Garvin, David A., 263, 348n, 889n, 1162, 1181n
Gasparino, Charles, 607n
Gates, Bill, 317, 587–592, 963n, 1110, 1114
Gatto, Andy, 803, 805, 809, 810
Gaut, Norman E., 342
Gazala, Michael E., 601n
Gear, C. W., 740, 742
Geiger, Marc, 388
Gelbach, Edward, 455, 457, 461, 463, 469, 568
Gelsinger, Patrick P., 333, 565, 577, 580, 824, 827, 1142, 1143, 1144, 1147
Geneen, Harold, 132
Gens, F., 45n
Georg, Denny, 234
Gersick, C. J. G., 564, 581
Gerstner, Louis V., Jr., 589, 699, 932, 934, 1123
Geyer, Hans, 565
Ghoshal, S., 564, 582, 1182n
Giancarlo, Charles, 749
Gibbons, M., 147, 716n
Gibeau, Frank, 94, 100
Gilbert, Richard, 32n
Gilder, George, 492n, 494n, 514, 563
Gill, Frank C., 565, 569, 572, 576, 577, 578, 580, 581, 824
Ginsburg, Ruth Bader, 408

Girault-Cuevas, L., 978n
Girishankar, Saroja, 606n
Glaser, Barney G., 513, 566
Glaser, Rob, 590
Glasgall, William, 600n, 601n
Glaspie, Bob, 14
Gluck, F. W., 690n, 941
Gobeli, David, 1080
Godden, C. E., 991
Godward, Choley, 389
Goes, J., 938n
Goldman, Jack, 673
Goldman, William, 82
Goldstein, Paul, 404n, 406n, 407
Gomes, Lee, 1126n
Goodman, Jim, 503
Gordon, Bernie, 137
Gordon, Bing, 72, 73, 75n, 81, 82
Gorman, Dan, 508
Goss, R. O., 991
Gould, S. I., 146
Gould, Stephen J., 525
Govindarajan, V., 1182n
Grabowsky, H., 411n, 415n
Graham, Bruce K., 489n
Graham, Margaret B. W., 172
Graham, Martha, 402n
Granadillo, P. P., 991
Grant, Mike, 1078
Greaves, Gilbert, 1035, 1038, 1040, 1043, 1045, 1050, 1051
Green, Stanley, 405n
Greenberg, Milt, 138
Greeve, Gerry, 343
Grein, T., 992
Greve, A., 986n
Greve, Gerry, 566
Griffin, Bob, 1078
Grosseteste, Robert, 434
Grosvenor, Jim, 234
Grove, Andrew S., 162, 190n, 283, 298, 303n, 333, 342, 454, 455, 467, 469, 474, 478, 485, 489n, 490n, 492, 500, 501, 512, 514, 515, 517, 520–521, 562–585, 592, 817, 824, 826, 834, 937, 938n, 1128, 1137n, 1140, 1142, 1143, 1150, 1160, 1161, 1177
Grover, R., 1182n
Gruen, Rhonda, 412
Guehler, Paul, 902–903, 907, 909, 910, 912, 914, 915
Guior, R., 978n
Gulliver, Frank R., 1174n
Gupta, A., 1182n
Gurr, Tim, 1009
Gutelius, Ted, 805
Gutterman, Donna, 413, 414
Guynn, Christine, 1064, 1066, 1067, 1070

Haas, C., 824
Hackborn, Dick, 531, 532, 533–534, 1178
Hage, J., 441n
Haggerty, Patrick E., 136, 514
Haken, R., 377n
Hall, G. W., 289
Halliday, Jean, 18n

Halliday, R. G., 412n, 421n
Halloway, Charles A., 745n
Hamberg, D., 716n
Hambrick, Donald C., 513, 514, 515, 520, 521, 522, 524
Hamburger, Daniel, 897, 899
Hamel, Gary, 4n, 102, 142, 144, 150–151, 488n, 489n, 524, 550, 1182n
Hamill, Mark, 80
Hamilton, Lyman, 132n
Hamilton, W. F., 150
Hammer, Michael, 874n
Hammond, T. H., 563
Hampson, K. D., 144
Hannan, Michael T., 147, 441n, 489n, 511, 520, 522, 525, 526, 563, 564, 582, 938n
Hansen, M. T., 563
Hansen, R., 415n
Hanson, W., 375
Haour, G., 209
Hardison, T., 978n
Harlow, H. F., 718
Harmon, Amy, 328n
Harmon, Gary, 642
Harper, James A., 991, 1002
Harris, J. M., 6, 7
Harris, Kendra, 194n
Harrison, Crayton, 1143n
Harstad, Chuck, 786
Haslanger, Martin, 416, 420, 427
Haspeslagh, Philippe, 515, 517, 1181
Hatch, Orrin, 378, 407
Hatzakis, M., 450n
Hauser, J. R., 954n
Haveman, Heather, 32n
Hawkins, D., 1038
Hawkins, Trip, 72–78
Hawley, George T., 323n, 324n
Hayek, Nicholas, 927
Hayes, Jim, 234
Hayes, Robert H., 130, 223, 233n, 941, 942
Hayes, T., 963n
Hays, L., 938n
Hazard, H., 441n
Heath, Bill, 426
Hedberg, Bo L. T., 524, 986n
Hedges, Brian, 828
Hefley, W., 731n
Heine, K., 416n, 422n
Henderson, B., 983n
Henderson, Rebecca M., 8n, 143, 146, 148, 209, 210, 215, 216, 224, 227, 232, 247n, 248, 252, 256n, 259, 263, 280, 291, 441, 451, 489n, 658n, 691, 694, 707n, 708n
Hennessy, John, 244
Henry, Jim, 18n
Henzler, H., 690n
Herbert, Tom, 880, 881, 882
Herman, R., 374n
Heron, S. D., 203
Hessedahl, Arik, 651n
Hewlett, William, 235, 538, 664
Hexner, Peter, 1038, 1049, 1051
Hiestand, Susan, 790, 793
Hilgard, E. R., 717
Hill, Heather, 805

Hill, R., 139n
Hillman, Michael R., 345
Hindery, Leo, 183n
Hodes, M. S., 289
Hofer, Charles W., 558n
Hoff, Ted, 243, 455, 461
Holland, Linc, 748
Hollander, Samuel, 203, 441n
Holliday, Mark, 965, 969
Hollings, Ernest F., 408
Holmstrom, B., 670n
Honda, Y., 978n
Hoole, Marc, 1064, 1066, 1067, 1070
Horowitz, Mark, 645
Horwitch, Mel, 4n, 32n
Houben, Huub, 417
Houndsfield, Godfrey, 33, 44
Hounshell, David A., 674n
Hout, T., 295n, 296
Howard, Robert, 1174n
Hrebniak, Lawrence G., 511
Huber, David, 190, 192, 198
Huber, George P., 1163
Hughes, Harold, 565, 569
Hulbert, David, 32n
Humer, Caroline, 652n
Hummer, John, 389
Hungate, Bob, 137
Hunt, Jack, 188b
Hunt, R. W., 439
Hurowich, M., 716n
Hurst, D., 938n
Hurstak, J. M., 1182n
Hutt, Michael D., 518

Iacocca, Lee, 561
Iansiti, Marco, 151, 286n, 300, 708n, 938n,
    1005n
Imai, K., 146, 150, 990
Isaacson, W., 563
Ishida, Kiyoji, 630
Itami, H., 144

Jackson, Charles L., 319n, 321n
Jackson, Peter, 1009
Jackson, S. E., 447n
Jackson, Tom, 600n
Jacobsen, Carl, 32n
Jacobson, Alan "Jake," 904, 907
Jacoby, Rebecca, 748
Jagadish, H., 978n
Jaikumar, Ramchandran, 1168
James, Renee, 565
Jander, Mary, 184n
Janis, Irving L., 490n
Janos, L., 144
Jantsch, E., 371n
Japp, S., 209
Jefferson, Thomas, 140n
Jemison, D. B., 1181
Jenkins, Reed, 1064, 1066
Jervis, V. I. P., 980n
Jestädt, Albrecht, 1035, 1038, 1044, 1046,
    1048, 1049, 1051
Jobs, Steve, 486, 659, 673, 688, 928, 929,
    1110, 1116, 1117, 1121, 1124, 1125, 1126

Johanson, Linda, 562n
John of Utynam, 399
Johnson, Jim, 333, 565
Johnson, Kris, 1078
Johnson, Lyndon B., 490n
Johnson, Mark, 788n, 790, 793
Johnston, R., 716n
Jones, Brian, 504, 506, 508
Jones, K., 964n
Jones, Murray, 1009
Jones, Reginald, 132n
Jones, Terry, 907
Jones, Tom, 133, 137
Jordan, Michael, 74
Jorgenson, Dale W., 319n
Jost, Kevin, 29n
Jover, J., 978n
Joyce, William J., 511
Judson, Ted, 99, 100
Jung, Carl G., 978, 986
Jungjohann, James, 180
Junnakar, Sandeep, 1127n

Kagono, Tadao, 511
Kahlcke, Hartwig, 1035, 1038, 1040, 1044,
    1046, 1049, 1051
Kahn, Joseph, 607n
Kahn, R. L., 720n
Kahneman, D., 447n
Kahng, Dawon, 737, 738, 739, 741–744, 745
Kaiser, Gary V., 1002
Kaitin, Kenneth I., 417
Kaldor, Stephen, 420, 422, 423, 426, 428,
    429
Kaniovski, Y. M., 373
Kanter, Rosabeth Moss, 516
Kantrow, Alan M., 146, 147, 489n, 659n,
    660, 663
Kaplan, R., 296
Karn, Richard, 1009
Kasper, Christine G., 745
Kato, Tsuneya, 737
Katrak, F. E., 967
Katz, D., 938n
Katz, M., 368n, 375–376
Katz, R., 720
Katzenberg, Jeffrey, 588
Kaufman, Stuart, 701
Kawamoto, Dawn, 571, 1126n, 1127n
Kawamoto, Nobuhiko, 1034
Kawanishi, Tsuyoshi, 631–632
Keay, Connie, 748
Kehoe, Louise, 1126n
Keighley, Geoff, 93n
Keller, David, 745, 748, 762
Keller, H. Cohen, 708
Kelly, P., 146
Kennedy, Robert D., 39n
Kennis, Jeffrey, 805
Kercher, Sherry, 195n
Kern, Susan, 812, 813
Kettering, Charles F., 134
Khanna, Tarun, 113n, 708n
Khosla, Vinod, 179, 183n
Kidd, Jason, 99
Kidder, Tracy, 516

Kilby, Jack S., 403, 1127n–1128n
Kim, L.-S., 231
Kimberly, John L., 525
King, Lord, 933
Kirkpatrick, David, 1127n
Kissinger, Henry A., 490n
Klausmeier, Dan, 194
Klein, B., 280
Klepper, S., 697
Klevorick, A. K., 34n, 727n
Kline, David, 399n, 401n, 577
Kloss, Henry, 49, 51, 54, 55–61
Knight, Kenneth, 203
Knight, Liz, 810, 812
Kobayashi, Kiichiro, 745
Kobayashi, Koji, 733, 735
Kober, Tim, 828
Kohli, P. S., 824
Kohn, Les, 499, 500, 517, 518, 521, 565
Kolotouros, J., 1182n
Koo, C., 978n
Korn, H., 938n
Kosnik, T. J., 8n
Kotter, J., 938n
Kozel, Ed, 746
Kozlov, Vladimir, 188b
Kramer, Bruce, 190n, 199, 200n
Kranzberg, M., 146
Krause, Jason, 329n
Kravacic, Bob, 765, 766, 768
Krebs, Michelle, 17n
Krishman, Vish V., 957
Kuemmerle, Walter, 745
Kuhn, R. L., 718n
Kuhn, Thomas, 34n, 140, 296
Kume, Yukata, 932
Kuneida, T., 978n
Kuraski, S., 978n
Kurian, Thomas, 489n
Kusiatin I., 918n
Kusunoki, Ken, 279, 280, 291, 296n, 690n,
    699, 705
Kuypers, Maurice, 788n, 790, 793
Kwak, Mary, 1110
Kwolek, Stephanie, 675, 677, 678

Lacayo, M., 978n
Laderman, Jeffrey, 603n
Laguzza, Ben, 426
Lamb, J. Douglas, 29
Lammers, David, 649n
Lampaya, D., 978n
Lampel, J., 563
Landau, R., 38n
Langley, P. W., 718
Langlois, Richard N., 280, 298, 702, 705
Langton, John, 525
Lankton, Gordon, 501–504, 506, 509, 510
Lao Tzu, 986n
Lappen, Alyssa A., 595n
Lardner, James, 406n
Larsen, Ralph, 935, 936, 937
Lasagna, L., 411n, 415n
Laseter, Timothy, 747n
Lawrence, B. S., 720n
Lawrence, P. R., 990n

Lawson, Linda, 234
Lazarus, Anthony, 1126n
Leahey, J., 938n
Learson, Vince, 138
Leazer, Annette, 234
Lechleider, Joseph W., 324
Lechleiter, J. C., 991
Ledakis, D., 978n
Lee, D. M. S., 721
Lee, Hae-Seung (Harry), 266, 268
Lee, John, 428, 429
Lee, Mark, 879, 882
Leemon, Daniel, 602–603
Leglise, Claude, 565
Le Grande, D., 986n
Lehr, Lewis, 139
Lei, L., 978n
Lennon, John, 1124
Leonard-Barton, Dorothy, 142, 489n, 542n, 564, 775n, 938n
Leonardo da Vinci, 434
Lepore, Dawn, 605
Lerner, Sandy, 745n
Levin, R. C., 34n, 724n, 726, 727n, 728
Levinthal, Daniel A., 150, 280, 282n, 283, 284, 563, 660, 716, 722n, 724n, 725, 729, 730n, 731n
Levitt, Barbara, 142, 489n, 521, 722n, 1163
Levitt, Theodore, 139n, 365
Lewent, Judy, 664n
Lewis, Eugene, 516
Lewis, Peter H., 325
Liggett, T., 377n
Lill, Jeffrey, 590
Lillie, Gordon, 966
Lilly, Eli, 417, 990
Linderholm, Owen, 650n
Lindsay, P. H., 717, 718
Ling, R., 978n
Link, A. N., 731
Lister, Benjamin, 785
Livermore, Ann, 234
Livis, A., 1038
Locke, Edwin A., 564, 582
Locoh-Donou, Francois, 189, 194n
Lohr, Steve, 960n, 963n, 970n, 1156n, 1157n
Longbaugh, Harry, 965, 968, 970
Lorange, P., 561n
Lorsch, Jay W., 147, 489n, 514, 526, 658n
Louis, M. R., 447n
Loutfy, Rafik, 763, 764
Lovas, B., 564, 582
Lucas, George, 82
Lucier, Chuck, 870–871
Lumley, C. E., 412n, 421n
Lyles, Marjorie A., 446n, 447n, 1163
Lyster, Michael, 1126n

MacCormack, Alan, 1005
Macdonald, Tom, 565
Machalek, Richard, 511, 520
Macher, J. T., 289
Machiavelli, Niccolò, 937, 938n
MacMillan, Ian C., 838, 843
Madden, John, 74, 99
Maggioncalda, Jeff, 592n, 1182n

Magleby, Matt, 872
Magretta, J., 960n, 966n
Mahan, Alfred Thayer, 437, 438
Mahle, Steve, 1076, 1078, 1085, 1087
Mahon, Stuart, 260
Mahoney, J. T., 280, 281, 283, 693, 697, 708n
Maidique, Modesto A., 8n, 130, 131n, 133n, 143, 150, 918n, 977, 980n, 983n, 984n, 1174n
Majestic, Jeff, 889n, 899
Majundar, B. A., 723n
Makin, C. E., 130
Makmuri, S., 978n
Makridakis, S., 8n
Malone, John C., 590
Maloney, Sean, 565, 1148, 1158, 1159
Mandl, Alex, 316
Mann, Charles C., 404n
Mann, Leon, 490n
Mansfield F., 716n, 721n
Mansfield, F., 444n
Mansfield, M., 441n
March, Artemis, 348, 889
March, James G., 142, 444n, 446n, 489n, 514, 519, 521, 522, 526, 562n, 563, 564, 584, 585, 716, 722n, 723, 1163
Marin, Michael V., 628n
Maritz, Paul A., 591
Markkula, A. C. "Mike," Jr., 1110, 1114
Markoff, John, 1127n, 1156n, 1157n
Marples, D. L., 442n
Marquardt, David F., 589
Marquis, D. G., 139n, 716n
Marshall, Lucia, 113n
Marshall, Sir Colin, 933
Marti, Eric, 303
Martin, Michael, 33n
Martin, Roger, 113n
Masaki, Ichiro, 266, 268
Matlock, P., 978n
Matsuda, Shiuchi, 838n
Matsumoto, Craig, 648n
Matt, Lauren, 873
Matteson, Fred, 606
Mauer, Jennifer Fron, 990n
Maynard, M., 297
Mayr, G., 991
McAvoy, Tom, 138
McCain, George, 609
McCarthy, Mike, 198, 200
McCarty, Henry, 965, 966, 968, 969
McClough, C. Peter, 671–672, 674
McCormick, Bruce, 565
McCoy, Charles, 1126n
McCoy, James, 16n
McCoy, John, 149, 674
McGahan, Anita, 113n
McGeady, Steve, 565
McGrath, Rita Gunther, 838
McHugh, Alexandra, 516
McKay, Kevin, 356, 358, 359
McKee, Stan, 94, 95n, 98, 100–101
McKelvey, Bill, 142, 514, 516, 520, 563
McKenna, Regis, 40n
McLaughlin, C., 372n

McNealy, Scott, 241, 499, 592
McReynolds, Rebecca, 592n
McWilliams, Gary, 1127n
Meadows, Lee, 795
Meer, E. V., 1038
Mehta, Stephanie N., 326n
Melby, Jeff, 907, 912
Melchiore, Paul, 357
Mentzer, Eric, 565, 578
Metcalfe, J. S., 147
Metzger, Tell, 601n
Meyer, A., 938n
Meyer, Christopher, 1022
Meyer, M. H., 989n
Meza, Philip F., 67, 83n, 99n, 189, 318, 325, 398, 406n, 610, 1127, 1182n
Middendorf, S., 907
Middlehoff, Thomas, 393
Miles, Robert H., 48, 522, 524, 525, 526
Milgrom, Paul, 122n
Miller, Avram, 565, 823, 825, 826, 827, 828
Miller, D., 564, 582, 938n
Miller, Danny, 489n, 514, 520, 525
Miller, Grant, 894
Miller, Marc, 907
Miller, R., 447n
Miner, John H. F., 565, 823, 824, 827, 828, 1150, 1152, 1158n
Mintzberg, Henry, 445n, 489n, 514, 515, 516, 520, 525, 563
Mitchell, Chris, 1009
Mitroff, I. I., 446n, 447n
Mitsch, Ron, 906, 908, 909
Miyano, Hideo, 1061
Moch, M., 441n
Mohammed, Afroze, 902, 1182n
Mohzen, Edward P., 649n
Molloy, B., 992
Moltzen, Edward F., 1157n
Monroe, Dan, 282n, 289
Monroe, H. K., 570
Monroe, J., 938n
Monteverde, K., 280, 281n, 701, 705
Montgomery, Curtis, 748
Moore, Geoffrey A., 362, 846
Moore, Gordon E., 48, 454, 455, 457, 458–459, 463, 466, 467, 469, 471, 474, 485, 516, 517, 521, 525, 563, 564, 565, 567, 568, 570, 571, 572, 817, 823, 824, 846, 1127–1128, 1140n
Moorthy, Ganesh, 565
Morgan, Paul, 675, 677
Morgenson, Gretchen, 602
Morgridge, John, 746, 747, 877, 881
Morison, Elting E., 431
Morris, Charles R., 237n, 244n, 258n
Morris, Sandra, 565
Morse, E. V., 441n
Morton, Douglas, 427
Morton, J. A., 135n
Mowery, D. C., 717n, 731n, 981
Mueller, W. F., 716n
Mungale, C., 978n
Munson, Robert, 18
Murphy, Kevin M., 280
Murray, Bill, 1076, 1083–1084

Murray, Patricia, 565, 1152–1153
Murthy, Vik, 642
Musgrove, Mike, 408n
Myers, Mark, 763, 765, 772
Myers, S., 136n, 716n
Myrum, Stan, 1078, 1082

Nacchio, Joe, 310
Nachtsheim, Stephen P., 823, 824, 828
Nadler, David, 938n, 1174n
Narayandas, D., 957n, 959n, 963n, 964
Narisetti, Raju, 1127n
Negroponte, Nicholas, 167n, 826
Nelson, Bob, 933
Nelson, David, 425
Nelson, Horatio, 437
Nelson, N., 34n
Nelson, R., 441n
Nelson, Richard R., 142, 368n, 377, 514, 525,
    716n, 720, 721, 725, 727n, 731
Nemeth, Charlan, 490n
Nettles, Patrick, 190
Newhouse, John, 686, 690n, 983n
Newman, W., 938n
Newton, Isaac, 436, 989
Ngongang, Yann, 189
Nichols, David, 765, 766
Nichols, N. A., 664n
Nicholson, G. C., 781n
Nightingale, Florence, 785
Nimgade, Ashok, 410, 415, 781, 786, 793
Noirjean, Rob, 907, 908–914
Nolan, Richard L., 877n
Nonaka, Ikujiro, 150, 990n, 1163, 1174n
Norcross, Robert P., 325n
Norman, David A., 38n, 377, 717, 718
Nourse, Robert, 205
Novak, Sharon, 705
Noyce, Robert, 403, 404, 455, 521, 567, 817,
    1127–1128
Nystrom, Paul C., 524

Oakley, Ann, 965, 970
Obermiller, Beth, 805
O'Brien, M. P., 210
Odlyzko, Andrew, 184n
O'Keefe, R. D., 441n
Olds, Ransom, 372
Oliver, Carrie C., 67
Oliver, Christine, 562n
Oliver, Keith, 873
Olsen, Roger, 790
Olson, Mark, 566
Olson, Peter, 40n
Opel, John, 135
Oppermann, Gunter, 1038, 1046, 1049,
    1051
O'Reilly, Charles A., III, 691, 925, 938n
Oritz, R., 978n
Orwell, George, 977, 1125
Otellini, Paul S., 565, 580, 823, 824, 1140,
    1141, 1153–1154, 1157, 1161
Ott, Alex, 350, 351–352, 353, 354, 355,
    359
Ouchi, William G., 130, 515
Overdorf, Michael, 541

Packard, David, 132, 235
Packard, Joy, 790
Padgett, John F., 524
Pake, George, 671
Palmer, A. T., 1182n
Paltridge, Sam, 322n
Pan, Edward, 428, 429
Panofsky, Erwin, 434
Parker, Gerard H., 493, 565, 572, 824
Parker, Robert, 965, 968, 969
Pascale, R., 130n
Pashley, Dick, 565
Pastore, Michael, 319n
Patch, P., 143
Patel, Marilyn Hall, 378, 389, 396
Patterson, David, 244
Patterson, John H., Jr., 149
Paul, S., 991, 992
Pavia, Michael, 423
Pavitt, Keith L. R., 144, 147, 690n
Payne, Robert, 652
Pearson, A. E., 1182n
Peck, Ashley, 429
Peck, M. J., 716
Peltz, James F., 598n
Penrose, Edith T., 147, 516, 664n
Perez, Antonio, 234
Perlmutter, David, 1154, 1155, 1156
Peters, Chris, 591
Peters, Thomas J., 130, 133n, 136n, 659n
Peterson, Cydney, 1070
Peterson, Doug, 1005, 1009, 1010, 1011
Peterson, Paul, 875
Peterson, R. A., 918n
Pettigrew, Andrew, 514
Petzold, Charles, 326n
Pfeffer, Jeffrey, 246, 259, 262, 514, 581
Phebus, Lee, 425
Phillips, Almarin, 204
Pilnik, R. D., 991
Pimentel, Clare, 429
Pine, B. J., 284
Pirolli, P. L., 718
Pisano, Gary, 32n, 142, 144, 702
Pittman, Bob, 1179, 1182n
Platt, Lew, 234, 531, 534, 538, 937
Plattner, Hasso, 350
Plug, Bryan, 358, 359
Plumb, Larry, 158–159
Pollack, A., 567
Pond, Randy, 748, 878–879, 881, 888
Pook, Jim, 907
Porter, James, 286n
Porter, Michael E., 4, 5, 7, 8, 32n, 113, 143,
    144, 147, 295n, 296, 480, 489n, 556n
Posada, Juan, 189
Pospisil, Paul, 415
Postlethwait, R. N., 991
Pottruck, Dave, 592, 601, 604, 605, 607,
    608–610
Pournoor, John, 788, 789, 790, 793
Powell, Michael K., 319, 328, 329–330
Powell, Walter W., 520
Prahalad, C. K., 4n, 102, 142, 144, 150–151,
    488n, 489n, 524, 550, 564, 582
Prencipe, Andrea, 701, 705

Pressman, Stan, 54, 56
Prestowitz, Clyde, 471n, 472n
Price, Tim, 209
Prigogine, I., 371n
Probst, Larry, 67, 73–74, 78, 80, 81, 82
Ptolemy, 34
Puffert, D., 377n
Pugh, E., 693
Punishill, Jaime, 601n

Qian, Yingyi, 122n
Quinn, James Brian, 514, 525
Quinn, Kathleen, 1062–1075

Rajgopal, Kausik, 378
Ramo, Simon, 130
Rams, Dieter, 1036, 1037, 1038, 1039, 1040,
    1043, 1044, 1046, 1049, 1051
Rangan, V. K., 957n, 959n, 963n, 964
Raschle, B., 978n
Rashtchy, S., 626n
Raynor, Michael, 690n, 708n
Redfield, Carl, 747, 748, 879, 880, 881
Reed, Bob, 455, 467, 469, 471, 496
Reich, Robert B., 722
Reid, T. R., 403n, 404n
Reingen, Peter H., 518
Reinhardt, Andy, 568, 1160n
Reis, R., 978n
Riccitiello, John, 83, 95, 98, 102
Rich, B. R., 144
Richardson, Eileen, 388, 389
Richerson, Peter J., 525
Rickover, Hyman, 371
Rigby, Pauline, 180, 187n
Riggs, H. E., 970n
Ringo, W. R., 991
Ristelhueber, Robert, 1158n
Rivette, Kevin G., 399n
Rivkin, Jan, 113n, 123n
Rizzo, Paul, 137–138
Roberts, E. B., 989n
Roberts, John, 122n
Robertson, Michael, 396
Robertson, P. L., 298
Robertson, Paul, 705
Robertson, Z. B., 980
Robinson, Jim, 1175
Robson, M. J., 144, 147
Rogers, Gregory C., 529
Rohlfs, Jeffrey H., 328n
Rolak, L. A., 424n
Rolling Stones, 1124
Romanelli, Elaine, 131n, 140n, 514, 522, 524,
    584, 938n
Ronchetto, John J., Jr., 518
Roosevelt, Theodore, 436, 437, 438
Rose, Norman, 490n
Rosenberg, Nathan, 38n, 146, 151, 368n,
    488n, 526, 662, 707n, 716n, 717, 724n,
    731n, 981n, 983
Rosenberg, S., 444n
Rosenbloom, Richard S., 49, 141n, 143, 144,
    147, 250, 263, 281n, 282n, 286, 659n, 660,
    663, 674n, 690n, 702, 704
Rosenkopf, L., 147, 938n

Rosenshein, Michele, 628n
Rotemberg, J. J., 583, 1182n
Roth, Daniel, 610n
Rothbard, N., 938n
Rothwell, R., 441n, 980n
Rouller, Sharon, 234
Roussel, P. A., 209, 210, 231
Roussel, Philip, 690n
Rowghani, Ali, 194n
Rowland, Pleasant, 801
Ruane, Vincent, 139
Rubino, Eric, 350, 355, 359
Rudelius, William, 1080
Rueff, Russell, 96–97
Rumelhart, D., 377
Rumelt, Richard P., 32n, 515, 520
Russ, B., 978n
Russell, Bill, 234
Russell, Scott, 899, 900, 901
Rutenberg, D., 144
Rutner, Ron, 18n
Ryan, C., 144

Sacks, Goldman, 499n
Saenger, E., 978n
Sager, Ira, 568, 1127n
Sahal, D., 209, 210, 444, 983, 988
Sakakibara, K., 716n, 721n
Salancik, G. R., 246, 259, 262, 581
Saloner, G., 147, 372, 375n, 376, 570, 583, 1182n
Salvucci, Robert, 351, 356, 357, 359, 361
Sanchez, R., 280, 281, 283, 693, 697, 708n
Sandelands, Lance E., 522
Sanghani, J., 978n
Sankara, Hari, 13, 14
Santayana, George, 1167
Santini, G., 991
Santos, José, 1175
Sanvido, V., 978n
Sarnoff, David, 132
Saronoff, Alex, 234
Sasselli, F., 978n
Sasser, W. Earl, Jr., 946, 1089
Sasson, Gideon, 600–601
Sauers, R., 718
Sayles, Leonard R., 139n, 147, 256n, 661, 662, 663, 682, 690n
Schank, Roger, 1174n
Schaus, John, 420, 425, 426, 428
Scheible, G., 1038
Scheirer, Eric, 379
Schendel, Dan E., 8n, 147, 209, 246, 247, 441n, 444n, 489n, 522, 558n, 567, 576, 659n
Schetter, Barbara, 889–902
Schlaifer, R. O., 203
Schlender, Brent, 1127n, 1142n
Schleussner, Hans, 685
Schmidt, Andreas, 393
Schmidt, Eric, 1157
Schmidt, Karen, 748
Schnackenberg, Tom, 1009
Schneider, Mary Lee, 889–902
Scholz, Matt, 788n, 790

Schön, D. A., 136n, 137n, 447n
Schon, Donald, 690n
Schonfeld, Eric, 603n
Schram, S. R., 139n
Schumpeter, Joseph A., 442, 670, 723
Schwab, Charles, 592, 593, 594, 597, 598, 599, 603
Schwartz, William, 355, 356, 359, 361
Schwenk, Charles R., 490n
Scott, Benjamin, 313
Scott, Sir Percy, 433–437, 440
Scott, W. Richard, 489n, 520
Sculley, John, 482, 561, 929, 1110, 1112–1114, 1115
Sedgwick, David, 16n
Sefton, Alan, 1009
Seiber, Chuck, 194n
Sekimoto, Tadahiro, 735, 737
Selznick, Philip, 142, 489n, 514
Senge, Peter M., 1163, 1174n
Servan-Schreiber, J. J., 130
Server, A., 959n, 961
Servi, I. S., 967
Seymour, Rick, 534, 535, 536, 537, 538, 540, 541
Shae, D. E., 612
Shakespeare, William, 968
Shamlin, Scott, 1016
Shankland, Stephen, 1127n
Shannon, Claude E., 323
Shapiro, C., 368n, 375–376
Sharma, Bianca, 427, 428, 429
Shatner, William, 1143n
Shaw, R. W., Jr., 6, 7
Sheff, David, 68n, 69n, 75n
Shepard, Steven, 144, 182n, 516
Sherman, S., 938n
Shih, Ben, 189
Shima, Toru, 629–630, 635–641
Shinoda, Daizaburo, 737, 738, 739, 741–744, 745
Shoch, John, 674
Shor, Rita, 781, 782, 785, 786, 789, 790, 792, 793, 799
Shott, Bill, 770, 772
Shuen, A., 142
Shulman, L. E., 4n, 142
Siegel, Rob, 565, 577, 580, 817, 824, 825, 826, 827, 828, 829, 830, 831, 832, 833, 834, 835, 836, 837, 838
Siegelman, Russell, 589, 590
Siggelkow, Nicolaj, 114n, 124n
Silverberg, Brad A., 589
Silverberg, Gerald, 368n
Simison, R. L., 297
Simon, H. A., 446n, 716, 718, 720, 723
Simon, R., 978n
Simone, Desi, 903, 904
Simons, John, 1126n
Simons, R., 1182n
Simonyi, Charles, 672–673
Sims, William S., 434–438
Singh, Jai, 938n, 1126n
Singh, Jitendra V., 511, 522, 524, 525, 526
Sinofsky, Steven, 588, 589

Skjefte, Paula, 1076, 1078, 1079, 1082–1083, 1085, 1086, 1087
Skoll, Jeffrey, 67, 489n
Slivka, Benjamin W., 589, 590, 591
Sloan, Alfred P., 134
Smelak, Ray, 531, 532, 533–534, 539, 540–541
Smith, Adam, 280
Smith, Barry, 828
Smith, C., 937n
Smith, Douglas, 763n
Smith, Gary, 189, 195, 199, 200, 202, 731n
Smith, K. G., 564, 582
Smith, Ron, 455, 463, 466, 565, 577, 578, 580–581, 1148, 1160
Smith, Wayne, 1009
Snow, Charles C., 44, 513, 514, 520, 521, 526
Sodini, Charles, 265–272, 277
Soete, Luc, 368n
Solow, Robert, 319
Solvic, P., 447n
Solvik, Pete, 877–883, 887–888
Somers, W. P., 6, 7
Sonnack, Mary, 781, 782, 785, 786, 788, 789, 790, 793n, 795
Sorenson, J. B., 564, 582
Sorenson, O., 287, 564
Sorrell, Martin, 1181n
Speltz, L. M., 210
Spence, M. A., 441n, 725n
Spencer, William, 674, 704
Spenner, Bruce, 531, 532, 534, 536, 538, 539, 541
Spiegel, Bob, 748
Spielberg, Steven, 82
Spindler, Michael, 929, 1110, 1114–1116
Staats, Elmer B., 140n
Staelin, Paul, 642
Stalk, George, 4n, 142, 144, 295n, 296
Stalker, George M., 441n, 444n, 691, 719
Stamats, P., 978n
Stanley, J. C., 254n
Starbuck, William H., 524, 986n
Starke, F. A., 566
Stata, Ray, 133n, 137, 140n, 272, 1162, 1163, 1173
Stauffer, R., 978n
Staw, Barry M., 447n, 522, 938n
Steck, Randy, 289
Steele, K., 215
Steere, Dan, 144, 489n, 566
Steinmueller, W. E., 716n, 724n
Sterling, Harry, 234
Stevens, Mike, 1076, 1078, 1080–1082, 1083, 1084, 1086
Stevens, Nicola, 790
Stevenson, Howard E., 515
Stewart, J. M., 143
Stigler, George, 206
Stigler, J., 283, 284
Stinchcombe, Arthur L., 520
Stock, David, 1070
Stoll, Peter, 471
Stone, Amy, 327n
Strack, W. C., 372n

Strauss, Anselm L., 513, 566
Streeter, D., 708
Streitfield, David, 628n
Strom, S., 938n
Stroth, Hartmut, 1035, 1038, 1051
Stuart, T., 564, 582
Stuckey, J., 283n
Studd, Susan, 566
Suarez, F., 708n
Sullivan, Arthur, 404
Sullivan, Jennifer, 388
Sun-tzu, 552
Sutherland, John, 566
Sutherland, Margot, 592
Sutton, R. I., 447n
Sutton, Willie, 213
Suzuki, Osamu, 330, 566
Swanger, C. C., 983n
Swank, Howard W., 674–675, 678
Swee, Dick, 745, 761
Sweeney, Dan, 565
Sweeney, Wilfred, 675
Sweezy, E. F., 136n
Sylvester, Dawn, 113n

Tabrizi, B., 938n
Taffel, Alan, 314
Taggart, Tom, 598n
Taguchi, G., 281, 696
Takashi, Dean, 273n
Takeuchi, H., 150, 990n
Tanners, Timna, 652n
Tate, Geoff, 642
Taurel, L., 978n
Taurel, S., 991
Taylor, Alva H., 303n, 489n
Taylor, Paul, 324n
Taylor, Pearl, 965, 968
Tedlow, R. S., 282n
Teece, David J., 32, 34n, 48n, 142, 144, 147,
    280, 281, 285, 298, 489n, 516, 658n, 691,
    703
Temin, P., 46n
Tempest, Nicole, 745
Termine, John D., 1002
Tesler, Lawrence, 673, 688
Thieu, Ann, 428
Thomas, Christopher, 179n, 180
Thomas, L. J., 210
Thomke, Stefan, 410, 415, 781, 786, 793,
    957
Thomsen, Thomas H., 1038, 1049, 1051
Thurston, William R., 133
Ticknor, Carolyn, 234
Tilton, John E., 203, 204, 717n
Tittert, C., 1038
Tobias, Randall I., 419, 420, 423, 991, 998
Tolbert, M., 359
Tong, Richard, 591
Toombs, Dean, 455, 464, 472, 473
Toplet, Mort, 965
Townsend, J. F., 144, 147, 980n
Toyota, Kiichiro, 1027
Trainer, T., 991
Transeth, Don, 98–99
Tredennick, N., 571

Treybig, Jimmy, 135n
Trujillo, Solomon, 310n
Tucker, David J., 525
Turner, James, 894, 895–896, 899
Tushman, Michael L., 8n, 131n, 140n, 146,
    147, 211, 247n, 248, 252, 441n, 444n,
    489n, 514, 522, 524, 584, 691, 719n, 720n,
    723, 925, 938n
Tversky, Amos, 447n
Twiss, B., 8n, 146, 215, 668n
Tylka, S., 983n, 984n
Tzuo, Tien, 157

Uenohara, Michiyuki, 735, 737, 745
Ulrich, K. T., 280, 281n, 283, 692, 702, 705
Utsch, Werner, 1039, 1046, 1049
Uttal, Bro, 659n, 671
Utterback, James M., 34, 35, 140n, 143, 147,
    202, 231, 260n, 285n, 444, 690n, 691, 692,
    707n, 708n, 720, 930, 938n

Vadasz, Leslie L., 455, 456, 457, 500, 501,
    514, 515, 518, 565, 572, 817, 822–823,
    824, 825, 826, 827, 828, 834, 838, 1150,
    1151
Valenti, Jack, 406
Valentine, Don, 877
Vancil, R. F., 132n, 561n
Van den Poel, M., 8n
Van de Ven, Andrew H., 146, 147, 511, 524,
    567
Van Voorhis, Lindsay, 67
Van Wyk, R. J., 209
Varasano, Frank, 869, 871, 872, 874, 875,
    876–877
Velanovich, Bob, 16
Velasquez, Amy, 427
Venkatesan, T., 450n
Verlinden, Matthew C., 233, 278, 288n, 690n,
    692, 693, 990
Vernon, Raymond, 32n
Vilchur, Edgar, 49
Virany, B., 938n
Voight, G., 1038, 1045
Von Hippel, Eric A., 147, 151, 259, 445n,
    716n, 720, 728, 782, 786, 793n, 795, 796n,
    797, 798n, 799n, 915n, 918n, 981
Voorheis, Rebecca, 501
Vyssotsky, V. A., 721

Waddington, C. H., 371n
Wade, J., 938n
Wagner, A., 450n
Wahl, Paul, 349, 350–351, 358, 359, 360
Waid, Dennis, 287n, 708n
Walker, S. R., 421n
Walpole, Horace, 434
Walsh, B., 978n
Walter, John, 891, 898, 899
Waltman, Lew, 898, 899
Watanabe, August M., 420, 990, 991, 992,
    998–999, 1005
Waterman, Robert H., Jr., 130, 133n, 136n,
    659n
Waters, James A., 489n, 514, 520

Watkins, Curt, 509
Watson, Thomas, Jr., 137, 138, 139
Watson, Thomas, Sr., 1168
Watson, Warren, 1077
Watts, Dick, 234
Watts, R. K., 449n
Waxlax, Lorne, 1036, 1037, 1038, 1039,
    1040, 1042, 1044, 1050
Wayman, Bob, 234
Webb, James E., 140n
Weber, J., 938n
Webster, Murray, 490n
Webster, Noah, 2
Wecker, John, 428, 429
Wegbreit, Ben, 672
Weick, Karl E., 146, 147, 444n, 447n, 489n,
    511, 514, 517, 526
Weinberg, A. M., 371n
Weinschenk, Bob, 273
Weisman, Robyn, 1155n
Welch, Jack, 563, 932, 1174
Werner, Steve, 827
West, Jonathan, 629, 690n
Westerman, George, 278
Westney, D. E., 716n, 721n
Wheeler, Jim, 234
Wheelwright, Steven C., 151, 223n, 233n,
    546, 690n, 745n, 940, 941, 942, 944, 946,
    947, 949, 954n, 998n, 1012, 1051, 1089,
    1098, 1105n
Whitaker, Todd, 828, 835, 837
White, D., 283n, 297n
White, George R., 172
White, H. C., 708n
White, Jeff, 534, 535, 536, 537, 540, 541
White, Jim, 426
Whiteside, Don, 565
Whittier, Ronald J., 455, 457, 464, 469, 471,
    472, 565, 823, 824, 833
Whyte, R. R., 983
Wigle, Lori, 565
Wilcox, Carolyn, 875
Wild, Bernard, 1038, 1039, 1047, 1051
Wilder, Gary, 745
Wilhelm, Randy, 565, 578
Wilkinson, Neil, 1009
Williams, David Alan, 565, 1009
Williams, Jeffrey, 489n
Williams, Romney, 272, 277, 278
Williamson, Oliver E., 280, 515, 520, 702,
    731n
Williamson, Peter, 1175, 1181
Willig, R., 724n
Willis, Tom, 565
Wilson, A. D., 450n
Wilson, D., 992
Wilson, Ron, 650n
Winkler, Scott, 588
Winkman, Harold, 13
Winter, Sidney G., 32n, 34n, 142, 377, 441n,
    514, 525, 720, 721, 725, 727n
Wirt, Richard, 565
Wise, I., 989n
Wise, T., 134n, 138
Woito, David, 534
Wong, Andy, 907, 908, 909, 912, 914

Woods, Tiger, 99
Woodward, 691
Wozniak, Steve, 659, 928, 1110
Wright, Frank Lloyd, 809
Wright, John, 67

Xuan Bul, 234

Yamajo, Keizo, 842
Yan, Tom, 565, 827, 828, 835, 837
Yang, C., 1182n
Yasso, Jim, 565

Yeats, William Butler, 318
Yetts, Katherine, 565
Yin, R. K., 247n, 254, 255, 261, 292, 564
Yoder, S. K., 1182n
Yoffie, David B., 489n, 1110
Young, John, 936
Yu, Albert Y. C., 455, 457, 459, 565, 823, 824, 1153

Zelikow, P., 563
Zemsky, P., 282n, 283
Zenger, T. R., 720n

Ziegel, Frederick D., 165n, 166n, 168n, 169n
Ziegler, Bart, 1127n
Zinman, David, 489n
Zipper, S., 139n
Zirger, Billie Jo, 131n, 133n, 150, 977, 978n, 980n, 1174n
Zitzner, Duane, 234
Zuckerman, Ezra W., 562n, 563
Zustak, F., 978n

SUBJECT INDEX

ABB (Asea Brown Boveri), 1180
   mastering change, 935–937
Abbott Laboratories, 418
Absolute elasticity of demand, 64
Absorptive capacity, 716–732
   cognitive structures, 717–719
   implications for innovative activity, 730–732
   individual to organizational, 719–722
   methods of study, 726–728
   path dependence, 722–724
   research and development investment, 724–726
   results, 728–730
ABTS mechanisms, 15–17
Access-based positioning, 118–119
Access network equipment manufacturers, 163–164
Access, 474
Acco, 910
Accord Video Telecommunications, 344–345
Acer, 1121
Acoustic Research, Inc., 49, 60
Acquisition cost, 64
Acquisitions, 657–659
   by Cisco Systems, 745–762
ACS, 1197
Active-matrix screen, 630
Activision, 85, 138
Activities, 3
Activity-system maps, 123
Actuator, 224
Adaptability, 133–134
Adaptation paradox, 520–522
Adaptive society, 440
Adjustment, 521–522
Admiral, 127
Adobe Systems, 770, 892, 1112, 1125
ADT Security Services, 276
Advanced development overlap, 710–711

Advanced Display, 633, 638
Advanced Micro Devices, 144, 403–404, 465, 469, 481, 496, 573, 574, 648, 777, 861, 926, 1122, 1123, 1143, 1149, 1157
   financial data, 1145
Advanced Radio Telecom Corporation, 310, 313
Advanced RISC Machines, 242, 243
Advent Corporation, 49–62
Advocate, 711
AEG, 1044
Agere Systems Inc., 187, 198, 1159–1160
Aggregate project matrix, 944
Aggregate project plan, 948, 1061–1062
Agilent Technologies, 775
Agreement on Trade-Related Aspects of Intellectual Property, 400
Airbus Industrie, 686
Alcatel Networks, 162, 163, 186–187, 195–198, 317, 342
Alcoa, 278
Aldus, 1112
Allegheny Ludlum, 1165–1166, 1167
Allegiance Telecom, 185
Alliances, 1055
Allied Signal, 932
Allocation process, 372–374
Amati Communications, 160, 161, 162, 163
Amazing Software, 72
Amazon.com, 610–629, 850
Amdahl, 557
American Airlines, 850
American Bell, 926
American Booksellers Association, 629
American Challenge (Servan-Schreiber), 130
American Express, 1175, 1180
American Home Products, 418
American Intellectual Property Lawyer's Association, 406
American Motors, 551

American National Standards Institute, 160
American Society of Composers, Authors, and Publishers, 385, 405–406
American Telecasting, 309n
America Online (AOL), 101, 325, 329, 389, 396, 587, 591, 592, 766, 768, 773, 1175
America's Cup race, 1005–1006
America's Technology Slip (Ramo), 130
Ameritech, 161, 163, 168, 304, 310, 317, 341, 343, 345
Ameritrade, 600
Amiga, 73, 74, 76
Amperex, 926
Ampex, 692
Ample Corporation, 183
Analog Devices, 132, 137, 162, 163, 272, 1162, 1172
Andersen Consulting, 357
Animal Farm (Orwell), 977
ANS Communications, 342
Antitrust legislation, 145
AOL-Time Warner, 327, 329, 379, 381, 388
   affiliates, 380
Apax Partners, 1152
Apollo Computer, 236, 245
Apple Computer, 33, 40, 44, 69, 71, 73, 136, 245, 333, 482, 487, 492n, 536, 538, 561, 574, 597, 633, 659, 670, 672, 688, 841, 893, 926, 931, 983, 984, 986, 1110–1126, 1119, 1154
   company history, 1110–1117
   company profile, 958
   growth and evolution, 928–930
   turnaround, 1124–1126
Application software, 1123
Applied Business Telecommunications, 346
Applied Magnetics, 224
Applied Materials, 296, 494, 932, 1197
Applied Micro Circuits, 182
Applied scientific research, 2

Appropriability, 726, 730
Appropriability regimes, 33–34, 144
 and industry structure, 46–47
 tight, 36–37, 43–44
 weak, 37–38
Aramid Industrial Fiber, 674–682
Arcadia Software, 74
Architectural change, 210–211
Architectural design, 213
Architectural efficiency, 286–287, 699–701
 calculation of, 300
Architectural innovation, 3, 692
 definition, 443
 different S-curve model, 229
 failure of firms, 441–454
 problems created by, 446–449
 reconfiguration of technology, 441–454
 underperformance, 228
Architectural knowledge, 442
 evolution of, 444–445
Architectural products, 691
Architectural technologies, 227–233
 framework for change, 230–232
Architectural technology S-curves, 218
Areal density, 211, 224–225
ARM Holdings, 242
Arthur D. Little, 9, 144, 1168
ArtistDirect, 388, 390
Art of Japanese Management (Pascale &
 Athos), 130
Ascend, 163, 166
Asset specificity, 283n
Associated Group, Inc., 316
AST, 831
Astra and Merck, 418
AstraCom, 194
Asuag, 927
Asymmetric digital subscriber line (ADSL),
 157–171
Atari Corporation, 67, 68
 company background, 79
@Home network, 171, 315
 problems for, 328–329
ATI Telecom International, 194
AT Kearney, 874, 875, 876
AT&T, 72, 135, 162, 169, 187, 192, 195, 196,
 199, 238, 303, 306, 309, 310, 312, 313–
 314, 315, 316, 317, 329, 334, 342, 343,
 345, 347, 396, 492n, 536, 721, 732, 760,
 892, 926, 1152, 1169, 1171
 recent history, 306–308
 in videoconferencing, 331–332
AT&T Broadband, 199
AT&T Business, 199
AT&T Consumer, 199
AT&T Paradyne, 160n
AT&T Wireless, 199, 327
Audio Home Recording Act, 385, 407
Automotive industry, 296–298
Automotive microprocessors, 178
Automotive seat manufacturers, 13–31
Automotive Systems Group, 20
Autonomous strategic action, 658–659
 business research interface, 661–662
 management challenge posed by, 664–666
 new directions, 660

Autonomous team structure, 951–954, 1015
Auto radios, 174–175, 176
Avid Technology, 543–544
Aware, 161, 162

Baan, 358
Baby Bells, 161
Baker & Taylor Corporation, 629
Baldrige Award, 1171, 1173
Banc One Corporation, 144, 149
Bancorp, 600
B&T, 623
Bandwagon effect, 327–328
Bandwidth roll-about systems, 332–333
Bank of America, 669
Bank One Corporation, 608–610
Barnes & Noble, 611, 624–626, 628–629
Barnesandnoble.com, 393
Barriers to entry, 28–29
Basic Fun, 803, 812, 813
Basic scientific research, 2
Battery technology, 966–970
Bayer AG, 418
BBN, 306
BCG, 873
Belief systems, 1180
Bell Atlantic, 158, 159, 161, 166, 168, 304,
 305, 306, 317, 343, 408
Bellcore, 158, 167
Bell Laboratories, 135, 237, 238, 282n, 323,
 477, 662, 674, 714, 716, 721, 735, 737,
 743
BellSouth, 163, 195, 196, 304
Benchmarking, 114, 116, 1169
Bendix Corporation, 178, 519, 659, 668
Berkeley Networks, 777
Berne Convention, 402
Bertelsmann AG, 378, 379, 381, 392, 393,
 396, 398
 affiliates, 380
Bertelsmann e-commerce group, 392, 393
Bertrand Faure, 19
Bessemer process, 439
Bessemer Trust Company, 118
Bic Corporation, 122
Big Flower Press, 115
Big Idea Group, 801–816
Big Six accounting firms, 879
BIIN Computer, 500n
Biogen, 135n
Biotronik, 1086
Bipolar, 474
Bipolar random-access memory, 455
Black & Decker, 64, 105, 109
Blockbuster, 72
BMG Entertainment, 378, 379, 392, 396
 affiliates, 380
 description, 381
BMW, 19, 22
Boca Research, 346, 347
Boeing Company, 33, 132, 177, 358, 675–
 676, 680, 790, 983, 1010, 1168
Book Industry Study Group, 629
Booksense.com, 629
BookSite.com, 629
Bootlegging, 918

Booz Allen Hamilton, 13, 14, 869–877
Borel function, 373n
Bose Corporation, 794, 830
Boston Consulting Group, 870, 983, 1172
Bostrom Seating, 13–31
Bottlenecks, 30
Boundary-setting control systems, 1180
Bounded innovation, 110
Bounding projects, 945–946
Bowling alley, 367
 definition, 848
Bowmar, 33
Branch office market, 169–171
Brand recognition, 575
Braun AG, 1035–1051
Breakthrough projects, 945–946, 1053
Bristol-Myers Squibb, 416, 418
British Airways, 932–933
British Navy, 433–434
British Petroleum, 1168–1169
British Telecom, 158, 166, 195, 308, 335,
 342, 343, 760
Broadband, 314–316, 318–330
 definition, 318
 digitalization of content, 325–326
 types of, 321–325
Broadcast Music, Inc., 385, 406
Broadcom Corporation, 182
Broadwing, 190, 195, 196, 198
Broderbund Software, 78
Brookings Institution, 319
Brooks Fiber, 308–309
Bucyrus-Erie, 554
Build phase, 1100
Bull, 103
Bullfrog Productions, 79
Bureau of Ordnance, 435–436
Burroughs, 252, 692, 694
Bus, 474
Busicom, 461
Business analysis phase, 1084
Business focus
 closely-related products, 132
 consistent priorities, 134
 focused research and development, 133–
 134
Business operations, financing, 173
Business portfolio, 7
 versus portfolio of competencies, 105–106
Business research interface, 661–662
Business Software Alliance, 408, 409
Business unit level audit, 9–10
Business Week, 40, 826

Cable modems, 312
Cable networks, 308
CableTel, 166
Cable television systems, 322–323
CAI Wireless, 309
Callternatives, 310
Cambria Steel Company, 439, 440
Campaign selling, 875–877
Canada, 319
Canon, 40, 104, 105, 108, 109, 110, 111, 113,
 116, 450–451, 452–453, 551, 553, 554,
 557, 562, 842

core competencies at, 112
Capabilities
    to cope with change, 546–549
    critical, 1061–1062
    definition, 142–143
    for innovation, 869–877
    migration of, 543–544
Capabilities-based organization, 142
Capabilities requirements, 30–31
Capacities, 542–543
Capacitor, 474
Capital Cities/ABC, 78
Cardiac pacemaker business, 1076–1088
CarMax, 118
Carmike Cinema, 119, 127
Carter-Hawley-Hale, 933
Casio, 104, 105, 106, 274
Category advantage, 859
Caterpillar Corporation, 552
CATV CyberLab, 169
Celestica, 296n
Cell-formation process, 633
Cell phones, 324
Cellular One, 306
CEO-driven strategy planning, 572–573
Cetus, 135n
Change; *see also* Innovation
    coping with, 546–549
    disruptive, 541–549
    management of, 925–937
    process of, 431–440
Channel strategy, 38–44
    analytic summary, 41–43
    contractual mode, 39–41
    integration mode, 41
    mixed modes, 43–44
Chaparral Steel, 232, 953–954, 1162, 1165
Charles Schwab & Company, 544, 592–610
Chartering projects, 945–946
Chasm, 367, 848
Chevron, 350
Chicago Controls, 538–539
Child World, 125
Chip, 474
Chrysler Corporation, 17, 20, 104, 107, 297n,
    546, 547, 552, 561, 1098
Ciba-Geigy, 418
CIENA Corporation, 189–202
Cipher Data Products, Inc., 40
Circuit City, 118, 611, 934, 1120
Circuit switched network, 165
Cisco Systems, 163–164, 188, 193n, 198–
    199, 317, 329, 549, 770, 779, 861, 1137,
    1159, 1178
    acquisitions, 745–762
    implementing ERP, 877–889
    mandatory manufacturing integration steps,
        757–759
    new product development, 749–753
Citibank, 118
Citicorp, 105, 109
Citigroup, 602
Citizen Watch Corporation, 538
City National Bank of Columbus, 149
Clarify, 770
Class 10 production facility, 474

Clevite, 926
CNN, 381, 385
Cobilt, 450
Coca-Cola Company, 33, 403, 552
Codified knowledge, 34
Coevolutionary lock-in, 562–585
    research method, 564–567
    and strategic inertia, 576–581
    of strategy and environment, 567–576
Cognitive skills, 1180–1181
Cognitive structure, 717–719
Coleco, 68
Collaborative Research, 135n
Collaborative revitalization, 558
Columbia Pictures, 80, 82
Combinatorial chemistry, 421–422, 423,
    425–427
Comcast, 306, 308, 315, 317, 329
Cometa Networks, 1152
Commercial development projects, 944
Commercialization, 35–36
Commitment review, 1084
Commodore, 73, 74, 245
Communication
    between engineering and production, 970–
        976
    within firms, 134–135
    in problem solving, 1101–1103
Communication channels, 445–446
CommunicationsWeek, 343
Compaq Computer, 239, 245, 257, 272, 288,
    295, 296n, 342, 343, 465, 544, 571, 573,
    574, 575, 633, 835, 861, 862, 958, 959,
    960, 963, 968, 1113, 1117, 1119, 1125,
    1126, 1137, 1154, 1155, 1157
    company profile, 1121–1122
    financial data, 1120
Compatibility, 64
Competence carriers, 113
Competency centers, 353
Competing technologies, 368–378
Competition
    and distinctive competence, 481–482
    in paradigmatic design phase, 34–35
    in tight appropriability regimes, 36–37
Competitive advantage, 121–126, 143–144,
    241–242, 480
    of architectural innovation, 448
    away from integrated firms, 284–285
    bowling alley stage, 855–856
    building, 550–562
    early market stage, 850–852
    main street stage, 864–865
    origins of, 1098–1099
    from rapid product development, 1105–
        1107
    roots of, 104–105
    and technology life cycle, 9
    tornado stage, 859–860
    from vertical integration, 279
Competitive convergence, 115
Competitive differentiation, 200
Competitive local exchange carriers
    (CLECs), 310–311, 315, 323, 326–327
Competitiveness, 550–552
    international, 47–48

Competitive position, 7
Competitive strategy, 5–6
    bases of, 116–120
Competitive strategy stance, 143–145
Complementary assets, 35–36, 41
Complementary MOS (CMOS), 466, 474–
    475
Complex instruction set computing (CISC),
    236n, 243–244, 498–499, 570–571
Complex strategic integration, 1176
    building, 1179–1181
    example, 1178
Component knowledge, 442
    evolution of, 444–445
Component manufacture, 294–295
Components, 143, 691
Component technologies
    change in, 213
    development of, 213–214, 232–233
    response to maturity in, 219–223
Compression Laboratories, Inc. (CLI), 332,
    333, 335
CompuAdd, 960
CompuCom Systems, 341
CompUSA, 1120
CompuServe Inc., 591, 766
Computer-aided design, 954
Computer aided manufacturing, 954
Computer Aided New Drug Approval, 366
Computer industry, 288
    profits, 295–296
    twenty largest companies, 631
ComputerLand, 1117
Computer Sciences Corporation (CSC), 366
Computer Systems Policy Project, 408–409
Concentric Network, 348
Concept generation, 799–800
Concept testing, 800
Concurrent engineering, 31
Conference room pilots, 883–888
Congruence, 931–932
Conner Peripherals, 224, 228, 252, 255, 257,
    260, 290n, 292, 533, 534, 540
Conservatives, 363–364
Conservative strategy, 847
Consistency, 122–123
Constructive confrontation, 487
Consultative selling, 901
Consulting firm, 850
Consumer Broadband and Digital Television
    Promotion Act, 408
Continental Airlines, 120
Continental Cable, 169
Continental Lite, 120, 121, 125
Contract book, 1018
Contractual channel strategy, 39–44
Control Data Corporation, 214, 216, 224,
    228, 254, 255, 256, 258, 261, 262, 692
    organizational units, 259–260
Convergent Technologies, 672
Coolidge Corporation, 1091–1098
Coordination, 123
Copeland Corporation, 1167
Copyright Act of 1790, 401–402
Copyright Act of 1831, 402
Copyright Act of 1909, 402

Copyright Act of 1976, 402
Copyright fights, 404–407
Copyright law, 385
Copyright protection, 401–402
  music industry, 392
Copyright royalty rates, 405
Cordis, 1079
Core competencies, 4
  and core products, 108–109
  definition, 105, 142
  of firms, 102–113
  identifying and losing, 106–108
  imprisoned in SBUs, 110
  redeploying to exploit, 111–113
  root of competitiveness, 104–105
  versus SBUs, 109–110
  strategic architecture for, 110–112
  and strategic fit, 121–126
  underinvestment in, 110
Core design concepts, 143
Core products, 103, 108–109
  strategic architecture for, 110–112
  underinvestment in, 110
Core technology, 145
Corning, 138, 660, 1164, 1165
Corporate culture, 487–488
Corporate development strategy, 920—921
Corporate entrepreneurship, 3
  administrative linkages, 667
  complete spin-off, 669
  design alternatives, 667–670
  framework for assessing, 666–667
  management of, 664–670
  new venture divisions, 665–666
  nurturing plus contracting, 669
  operational linkages, 667–669
  at 3M Corporation, 902–915
Corporate interests, 687–688
Corporate planning, 62–66
Corporate reorganizations, 139
Corporate reputation, 130n
Corporate research
  business environment, 661
  effective use of, 660–661
  functions of, 660
  linked to strategy, 662–664
  management levels, 663–664
  managing key interfaces, 661–662
  resource allocation, 664
  strategic management of, 659–664
Corporate strategy, 658–659
  development of, 7
  linked to corporate research, 662–664
  oscillations of, 919
Corporate value, 542–543
Corporate Venturing (Block & Macmillan),
  843
Corporations; *see* Firms
Corvis, 198, 201
Cospecialized assets, 35–36, 38
Costco, 1119
Cost leadership strategies, 5
Countrywide, 289
Covad Communications, 310, 315, 329
  financial data, 311
Cox Communications, 169, 315, 329

C-Phone, 335, 347
Cray Inc., 1010, 1157
Crayola, 507
Creative destruction, 442, 723–724
Creative Labs, 346
Credit Suisse First Boston, 603
Crescendo Communications, 750
Critical capabilities, 1061–1062
Crossing the Chasm, 366
Cross-licensing, 403–404
Crown Cork and Seal, 144, 148–149
Crystal Dynamics, 77
CSA press, 892–893
CTC Communications, 185
Cullinet, 132
Cultural inertia, 932
Cummins Engine, 554
Customer acquisition, 860
Customer power, 245–263
Customer satisfaction, 860
Customer segmentation, 118–119
Customer service, 864
Cyras Systems, 194, 195, 202
Cyrix, 648, 1122

Daewoo, 108, 560
DaimlerChrysler, 22, 547
Data access alternatives
  cable modems, 168–169
  high-speed digital subscriber line, 167
  high-speed POTS modems, 165–167
  hybrid fiber coax, 168–169
  ISDN, 165–167
  leased lines, 164–165
  satellite transmission, 169
  very high-speed DSL, 167–168
  wireless technologies, 169
Data General, 237, 245
Dataquest, 169, 331
Data Sources, 264
Data traffic, 314
Datek, 600, 698
Dayton Electronics Corporation, 536
Dayton Hudson Company, 541
Dean Witter, 601
Decentralization, 702
Defense General Corporation, 872, 875
De Haviland, 33, 37
Dell Computer Corporation, 239, 284n, 288,
  295, 401, 575, 642, 775, 850, 861, 862,
  1117, 1119, 1125, 1126, 1137, 1155,
  1157
  company profile, 1122
  financial data, 1120
  product development, 957–970
Dell Ventures, 775, 778–779
Delphi Corporation, 297
Delphi method, 8
Delta Air Lines, 119
Demand elasticities, 64
Demonstration phase, 1084
Demonstration projects, 1166–1167
Denial, 485
Dense wavelength division multiplexing
  (DWDM), 312–313
Derivative products, 1060

Derivative projects, 1053
Descriptive theory, 212
Design alternatives
  choosing, 668–669
  for corporate entrepreneurship, 667–670
  direct integration, 668
  implementing, 669–670
  new product department, 668
  special business units, 668
Design-build-test phase, 1098–1107
Design patents, 400
Design phase, 1099–1100
Designs, freezing, 971–972
Deutsche Telekom, 186, 195, 198, 342, 343
Development funnel, 942
Development strategy, 942–948
  leadership approach, 942–943
Development teams, 948–954, 1000
  types of, 1012–1015
Diamond Multimedia Systems, 338, 396
Diebold, Inc., 276
Dielectrics, 475
Differentiation, 200
  competitive strategy, 116–117
  disruption, disintegration, and dissipation
    of, 278–298
Differentiation strategies, 5
Diffusion of innovation, 846
Digital distribution, music industry, 378–398
Digital Equipment Corporation (DEC), 33,
  62, 216, 218, 237, 245, 283, 295, 333,
  692, 879, 958, 986, 1105, 1121, 1170
  dilemma, 545
Digitalization, 325–326
Digital Millennium Copyright Act, 385, 408
Digital Pixel System, 273
Digital rights management, 410
Digital satellite, 169
Digital subscriber lines, 167–168, 311–312,
  323–324
Digital subscriber technologies, 158–159
DirecPC, 169, 324
DirecTV, 169
Discontinuous innovators, 362
Discover Brokerage Direct, 600, 602
Discoveries, 2
Discovery-driven planning, 838–839
Diseconomies of scale, 145
Disintegration model, 285–289
Disk, 225
Disk drives, 263–264
Disk drive technologies, 691–699
Disk/Trend Report, 224, 262–263, 264,
  286n, 293, 301, 699, 701
  247–248
Disneyland Paris, 839–841
Display Technologies, Inc., 629–641
Disruptive technologies/innovation, 148, 250,
  541–549
  impact of, 250–252
  leaders in, 252–254
  and resource allocation, 254–259
  versus sustaining innovation, 544–546
Dissent, 483–485
Distinctive competence, 142, 480
  and competition, 481–482

Diversified corporations, 104
Diversion, 485
Divisional research and development interfaces, 661
DLJ Direct, 602
DMD, 537, 540
Documentum, 366
Dolby Laboratories, 53, 56, 57, 61
Dominant design, 444–445
Dominant design paradigm, 34–35
Domino's Pizza, 1173
Double metallization, 466, 475
Douglas Aircraft, 34, 37, 177
Downstream products, 29–30
Dream Works KG, 588
Drexel, Burnham, and Lambert, 211
Drive, 225
Driving investments, 775–776
Drug development, 410–414
    central nervous system diseases, 423–424
    glossary of terms, 430
    migraine project, 424–425
    phases of, 410–414
    strategy at Eli Lilly, 415–430
    U.S. summary, 417
Drugstore.com, 627
DSL; *see* Digital subscriber lines
DTI, 638
Du Pont, 33, 53, 55, 203, 245, 660, 663, 669
Du Pont Kevlar, 674–682
DVD-Audio, 394
Dynamic networks, 48
Dynamic random-access memory (DRAM)
    definition, 475
    industry, 643–645
    at Intel Corporation, 454–477
    producers, 492

Early adopters, 363
Early involvement mode, 1102–1103
Early majority, 363
Early market, 363, 364, 367
    competitive advantage, 850–852
    definition, 847–848
    stock market implications, 852–853
    value chain strategy, 849–850
    value disciplines, 852
Early start in the dark, 1102
EarthLink, 327
Ease-of-use characteristics, 64
eBay.com, 400, 850
eBroker, 600
Economic buyer, 850
Economies of scale, 145, 368
Economist, 958–959
Ecosystem of complementors, 575
EDS, 892
Eimac, 926
Electrically erasable programmable read-only memory, 475
Electrically programmable read-only memory (EPROM), 459–461, 463, 475, 494
Electrical Musical Industries (EMI), 33, 44, 379, 398, 660
    affiliates, 380
Electronic Arts, 67–102

Electronic Arts in 2002, 83–102
Electronic Business, 224, 248
Electronic level grooming, 198n
Electronic Media Management System, 395–397
Electronic News, 465
Electronics companies, twenty largest, 631
Eli Lilly & Company, 415–430, 546, 774, 1080, 1086
    Evista project, 990–1005
    organization chart, 420
Elio Engineering, Inc., 13–31
Elpida joint venture, 649
Embedded servo system, 225
EMI; *see* Electrical Musical Industries
Enabling investments, 776–777
End of life, 367
Engineering, communication with production, 970–976
Engineering changes
    cost-benefit trade-offs, 974–975
    new model *vs.* incremental, 975–976
    processing, 974
Engineering documentation
    effects on inventory control, 973–974
    level of detail, 973
Engineering resources, 976
Enron Corporation, 195
Enterprise Systems Group, 233, 236, 241, 242–243
Entertainment industry, 82
Entrant firms, 228
Entrepreneurial culture
    characteristics, 136
    outside projects, 137
    small divisions, 136
    tolerance of failure, 137
    variety of funding channels, 136–137
Entrepreneurial edge, 118
Entrepreneurial skills, 1181
Entrepreneurship, 3
    Schumpeterian, 670
Epson, 560
Ericsson, 92n, 1162
ERP implementation, 877–889
Escape, 485
ESPN, 98, 99
Ethernet, 673
Ethical values, 137–138
E*Trade Group Inc., 600, 601, 602, 603, 605, 607
Euro Disney, 839–841
European telecommunication carriers, 199
European Telecommunications Standards Institute, 160
European Union, 319
Evandale Corporation, 872, 875
Evolutionary innovation, 204–205
Evolutionary theory, 146
Excite, 850
Excite@Home, 329
Executive perks, 134
Executive sponsor, 1021
Experience curve, 1172
Experimentation, 1165–1167

External sourcing, 150–151
Exxon, 840

Fabco Automotive Corporation, 26
Failure
    of firms, 245–263
    tolerance of, 137
Fairchild Semiconductor, 204, 403–404, 455, 459, 926, 1127n–1128n
Farallon Communications, 338
Farm Journal, 892
Faurecia, 20
Feasibility studies, 710
Federal Communications Commission, 305, 306, 318, 328, 408
Federal Express, 838, 840, 898
Federal Motor Vehicle Safety Standard, 14n, 30
Federal Trade Commission, 727
Federated Department Stores, 933
Fellowes, 910, 911
Ferrite, 225
Fetzer-Woolley & Associates, 1070, 1074, 1075
Fiat, 22
Fidelity Investments, 597–598, 602
Field service, 151
Filmless printing technique, 892
Financial Times, 649
Financing, 173
Firms
    absorptive capacity, 716–732
    ambidextrous, 925–937
    autonomous strategy process, 516–519
    battle for global leadership, 109
    communication within, 134–135
    core competencies, 102–113
    corporate culture, 487–488
    in digital music, 391
    and disruptive change, 541–549
    diversified, 104
    dynamic forces in evolution of, 481
    entrepreneurial culture, 136–137
    executive perks, 134
    failure of, 245–263, 441–454
    individual strategy process, 514–516
    innovation challenges, 658–659, 1109–1110
    intraorganizational analysis, 562–563
    as money managers, 778
    multiple cultures, 936–937
    paradox of culture, 932–935
    in pharmaceutical industry, 418
    reorganization, 139
    rethinking, 103–104
    SBUs *vs.* core competencies, 109–110
    strategic architecture, 110–112
    strategic dissonance, 478–488
    technological character, 701–704
    transformation process, 484
First Amendment, 407–408
First-mover advantage, 850, 998
First-order fit, 122
Fit; *see* Organizational fit; Strategic fit
Fixed wireless technology, 313
Flagstar Bank, 345

Flag Telecom, 199
Flash memory, 494–496
Flat-panel displays, 630
Flextronics, 296n
Floating gate, 475
FNMA, 289
Food and Drug Administration, 47, 992, 993, 994, 998, 1003–1004
  review by, 414
Ford Motor Company, 17, 18, 19, 20, 22, 29, 34, 35, 109, 140, 204, 283, 296n, 297, 298, 482, 554, 558, 560, 931, 1032, 1089, 1098, 1173
  product management, 1033
Forecasting, 7–8
FORE Systems, 348
Forrester Research, 312, 379, 600
Fortune, 130, 241
Fortune 500, 877
Forward integration, 575
Foveon, 273
Fox Interactive, 100
Frame relay technology, 164n
France Telecom, 195, 342, 343
Fraunhoffer Institute, 388
Frontier, 312
FujiFilm, 272
Fujitsu Corporation, 211, 214, 215, 218, 237, 291, 292, 465, 471, 554, 557, 560, 638, 644, 652, 692, 697, 733–734, 831, 926, 1115, 1119, 1121
Fully allocated product cost, 293
Functional performance, 64
Functional team structure, 948–950, 1013–1014
Funding channels, 136–137

G. D. Searle, 33, 45, 46
Galazar, Inc., 182
Gallium arsenide, 475
Gap, Inc., 123
Gartner Group Inc., 166, 588, 879, 882–888
Gatekeeping, 918, 1070–1074
Gate oxide, 475
Gateway Computers, 288, 295, 826, 829, 959, 960, 1118, 1119, 1121, 1125, 1154
GCA, 453
GEC, 107
Gemini, 870, 876
Genentech, 132, 135n, 136, 664
General Agreement on Tariffs and Trade, 400
General Electric, 44, 59, 105, 107, 109, 145, 204, 388, 559, 561, 589, 686, 926, 932, 1164, 1165, 1174
General Electric Capital, 289
General Electric Credit Corporation, 1179
General Foods, 1166
General managers
  assessing innovative capabilities, 8–12
  relation to technology, 4
  tasks, 102
General Motors, 17, 20, 22, 29, 107, 109, 134, 278, 283, 296n, 297, 298, 558, 588, 679, 932, 1098, 1164
  Saturn Division, 1166–1167
  Toyota joint venture, 1164, 1170

General Motors Institute, 13
General Radio, 133, 931
Generic assets, 35–36
Generic strategies, 5–6, 119
Generic technologies, 65–66
Genetic engineering, 421
Genuity, 196
Gerald Klauer Mattison and Company, 71
Gillette Company, 865, 1037, 1038
Glaxo-Wellcome, 410–414, 418, 425
Global competition, 102, 550–562
  levels of, 109
Global Crossing, Ltd., 186, 196, 199
Globalization, and growth, 128
Global leadership, surrender of, 559
Globespan Technologies, 160, 161, 162, 163
GMAC, 289
Gnutella, 379, 389, 396
Goldman, Sachs and Company, 591
Goodyear, 678, 679
Google, 1157
Gould, Inc., 690
Government controls, 713
Graphics Communications Technologies, 335
Grid Systems, 672
Growth
  paths to, 779
  profitable, 127–128
Growth potential, 711
Growth trap, 127
Gruner + Jahr, 393
GTE, 102, 104, 107, 161, 162, 308, 317, 341, 345, 408, 1171
  description, 306
Guidant Corporation, 998, 1080, 1086
Guinness World Records, 270
Gunit Corporation, 26
Gunnery accuracy, 432–440

H. J. Heinz Company, 560
Half-life curve, 1172–1173
Half-life of knowledge, 134
Hambrecht & Quist, 331, 603
Hands-on top management, 138
Hard drives, 530
Hardwick Stove, 127
Harley-Davidson, 806
Harman, 830
Hartness International, 345
Harvard Business Review, 871
Harvard Business School, 224, 263, 302, 1062, 1063–1064
Harvard Graphics, 291
Hasbro, 803, 809, 810, 813
Hatch-Waxman Act of 1984, 998
Hattori-Seiko, 926
Head, 225
Heavyweight development teams, 1012–1023
  challenge of, 1016–1017
  contract book, 1018
  executive sponsor, 1021
  management challenges, 1017–1021
  member responsibilities, 1020–1021
  necessity of fundamental change, 1021–1023
  project charter, 1017–1018

  project leadership, 1019–1020
  staffing, 1018–1019
  structure, 1015–1016
Heavyweight project manager, 1019–1020, 1029–1032
  case for, 1023
Heavyweight team structure, 951–952, 1000, 1014–1015
Herd mentality, 853
Hewlett-Packard, 33, 62, 63–64, 130, 132, 135, 136, 137, 138, 139, 151, 216, 218, 219, 221, 223, 288, 295, 343, 488, 492n, 503, 536, 648, 664, 666, 670, 723, 770, 773, 861, 865, 931, 958, 959, 984, 1015, 1105, 1110, 1119, 1121, 1126, 1154, 1155, 1156, 1157, 1175, 1178, 1179, 1180–1181
  background, 234–236
  compared to IBM, 222
  corporate organization, 234
  Kittyhawk project, 529–541
  market and technology trajectories, 237–239
  mastering change, 935–937
  Merced decision, 233–245
  transformation, 1177
High-fiber coax systems, 322–323
High-speed digital subscriber line, 167
High-technology companies
  engineering documentation, 973–974
  inventory control, 973–974
  key test for, 973
High-technology industries, 130n
High-technology management, 130–140
  adaptability, 133–134
  business focus, 131–133
  central dilemma, 140
  continuity and chaos, 131
  entrepreneurial culture, 136–137
  hands-on top management, 138
  managing ambivalently, 140
  organizational cohesion, 134–136
  organizational flexibility, 134
  paradox of, 138–140
  sense of integrity, 137–138
  study of, 130–131
  winnowing old products, 140
High-throughput screening, 421–422, 423
Hill-Rom, 1058, 1197
Hitachi, 218, 241, 291, 292, 394, 465, 469, 471, 556, 633, 638, 644, 651, 692, 697, 861, 926
Hit rule, 82
HMOS, 475
Hoechst Celanese Corporation, 418
Hoffman-LaRoche, 312, 418
Hollow corporation, 40
Home Depot, 814, 934
Home office market, 171
Honda Motor Company, 104, 105, 106, 107, 108, 109, 110, 111, 121, 543, 551–552, 556–557, 559, 560, 945, 1053, 1061, 1098, 1164, 1197
  product integrity, 1023–1029
Honeywell Corporation, 103, 456, 692
Hoover, 127

Hoshiden, 633, 638
Hughes Electronics Corporation, 317, 733, 926
Hughes Network Systems, 169
Human capital specificity, 283n
Hummer Winblad Venture Partners, 389
Hyatt Hotels, 589
Hypercompetition, 114, 126
Hyundai Electronics, 107, 633, 642, 643, 644, 650, 652

IBM, 33, 34, 40, 43–44, 45, 47, 69, 71, 73, 74, 76, 130, 132, 133, 134, 137, 138, 139, 145, 150, 151, 204, 210, 211, 214, 216, 218, 219, 221, 223, 224, 225, 237, 241, 244, 245, 250, 252, 256, 257, 258n, 260, 271, 272, 279, 283, 284n, 288, 290, 291, 292, 294, 295, 298, 333, 342, 395, 401, 462, 472, 482, 492, 498, 536, 538, 545, 546, 547–549, 553, 554, 557, 560, 567, 573, 574, 575, 581, 588, 589, 593, 638, 648, 659, 660, 668, 669, 673, 674, 691–692, 693, 694, 695, 697, 698, 699, 704, 709, 710, 712, 732, 746, 775, 831, 832, 837, 840, 841, 855, 861, 862, 893, 931, 932, 934, 959, 960, 982, 983, 986, 987, 1090, 1105, 1112, 1113, 1114, 1115, 1117, 1119, 1121, 1123, 1152, 1156, 1157, 1168, 1177
    case study projects, 713–716
    company profile, 958, 1122
    compared to Hewlett-Packard, 222
    financial data, 1120, 1146
    joint venture with Toshiba, 630–632
IBM Global Network Services, 306
Idea generating, 918
Identification, 439
IDT Corporation, 272, 314
IKEA, 116–117, 119
Impetus process, 923–924
Implementation audit, 1074–1075
Improvement ethic, 1032–1034
Increasing returns to adoption, 368–369
Incremental change, 211, 975–976
Incremental innovation, 3, 441, 443
Incumbent local exchange carriers (ILECs), 303, 307, 308, 310, 315
Independent business units, 669
Individual absorptive capacity, 719–722
Individual entrepreneurship, 3
Individual strategic process, 514–516
Induced strategic action, 658–659
    divisional research and development interface, 661
    support of, 660
Industrial design, 1040–1042
Industrial innovation, 202–208
    consistency of management action, 206–208
    fostering, 206
    managing, 205–206
    radical or evolutionary, 204–205
    spectrum of innovators, 203–204
Industries
    emerging, 129
    unit of analysis, 208

Industry attractiveness, 7
Industry centers of expertise, 351
Industry consolidation, 115, 195
Industry context, 147, 148, 149
Industry-enabling technologies, 575
Industry maturity, 47
Industry structure
    and appropriability regimes, 46–47
    disintegration model, 285–289
    impact of technological change, 250–252
    reintegration studies, 289–292
    vertical integration *vs.* stratification, 281–292
Industry supply curve, 301–302
Industrywide differentiation, 5
Inertia, 520–521, 564, 576–581
Infineon, 643, 644, 650, 652, 1143, 1150
Inflection point, 479–480
Inflexibility, 370
Infogrames Entertainment, 89, 94
Informational increasing returns, 369
Information exchange, 123
Information filters, 445–446
Information superhighway speed bumps, 326–329
Information technology, 317
Information Week, 343
InfoSeek, 589
InfoWorld, 343
Ingram Micro, 341, 623
Injection molding, 1048
Innovation; *see also* Technological innovation
    appropriability regimes, 33–34
    in autonomous process, 659
    bounded, 110
    case study, 431–440
    challenges at Intel, 1127–1162
    channel strategy issues, 38–46
    complementary assets, 35–36
    context of, 173
    and corporate interests, 687–688
    cultivating capabilities, 869–877
    definition, 246
    demand for design paradigm, 34–35
    designer role in, 48
    determinants of success, 172–174
    discovery-driven planning, 838–839
    and financing, 173
    firm's capacity for, 2
    forecasting, 177–179
    framework for defining, 442–444
    historical examples, 174–177
    incremental, 2–3
    in induced process, 658–659
    industrial, 202–208
    and industry maturity, 47
    and industry structure, 46–47
    international competitiveness, 47–48
    from invention, 682–690
    management criteria, 172–179
    management of, 501–510
    marketing of, 173–174
    model comparisons, 687
    need-pull model, 685–687
    new perspectives on, 716–722

    in photolithographic equipment alignment, 448–453
    resource allocation for, 46, 246–247
    role in corporate advance, 207
    small-firm/large-firm comparisons, 46
    technical balance, 175
    technical constraints, 172–173
    technology-push model, 683–685
    at 3M Corporation, 781–794
    tight appropriability regimes, 36–37
    and trade barriers, 48
    unanticipated, 487
    weak appropriability regimes, 37–38
Innovation challenges
    at Apple Computer, 1110–1126
    in established firms, 658–659
    kinds of, 1109–1110
Innovation process, 2–3
    taxonomy of outcomes, 33
Innovation traps, 689–690
Innovative capabilities
    assessing, 8–12
    definition, 9
Innovative capabilities audit, 8
    business-level, 9–10
    corporate-level, 10–12
    frame of reference, 11
    responsibility for, 11
Innovators, 203–204, 362–363
    discontinuous, 362
Innovator's Dilemma (Christensen), 544, 851–852
In Search of Excellence (Peters & Waterman), 130
Inside the Tornado, 367
Integral Peripherals, 538, 870
Integrated circuit, 2
    invention of, 1127n–1128n
Integrated Communications Systems, 345
Integrated Information Technology, 332, 335
Integrated problem solving, 1103
Integrated services digital network, 165–167, 323, 338–339
Integration channel strategy, 41–43
Integration strategy, 298
Integrity, 137–138'
Intel Capital, 776, 1150–1152, 1153
Intel Corporation, 44, 48, 62, 132, 144, 162, 182, 235n, 238, 240, 241, 242, 243, 279, 296, 313, 329, 331, 333, 338, 347, 401, 403–404, 477, 544, 592, 642, 643, 648, 649, 653, 670, 705, 774, 777, 779, 860, 877, 926, 937, 1054, 1110, 1114, 1117, 1122, 1123, 1159, 1175, 1177, 1178, 1179, 1180
    attempts to regain leadership, 472–474
    coevolutionary lock-in, 562–585
    company history, 455–456
    DRAM decision, 454–477
    environmental forces, 469–471
    Epoch II, 564–585
    facility locations, 464
    field study, 512–514
    financial data, 1121
    financial highlights, 820–821
    future of, 1127–1162

Intel Corporation (*continued*)
  Hood River venture, 580
  intraorganizational ecology, 511–526
  loss of leadership position, 471–472
  manufacturing and process fungibility,
    467–469
  mission statement, 819
  networking business case, 581
  new microprocessor strategy, 496–500
  new technology drivers, 492–496
  PCI Chipset case, 580–581
  product line, 465–467
  Proshare venture, 579–580
  strategic dissonance, 478–488
  strategies, 342–343
  strategy for 1990s, 490–501
  strategy making, 511–526
  Systems Business, 500–501
  technology development groups, 465
Intellectual property rights, 43–44, 398–410
  Consumer Broadband and Digital Televi-
    sion Promotion Act, 408
  copyright, 401–402
  copyright fights, 404–406
  cross-licensing, 403–404
  Digital Millennium Copyright Act, 408
  music industry, 384–386
  patents, 398–401
  and regulation, 406–407
  trademarks, 403
  trade secrets, 403
  in wake of Internet, 407–408
InterAccess, 161
Interactive control systems, 1180
Interdependent interfaces, 281–282
Interfaces, 225, 280–281
  management of, 661–662
Intergraph Corporation, 1156
Intermedics Corporation, 1088
Intermountain Cardiology Clinic, 1087
Internal corporate venturing, 915–925
  assessment of, 821
  elaborating strategic context of, 920–921
  field study method of, 924–925
  indeterminate strategic context, 918–919
  major problems, 916–919
  managing core processes, 922–924
  managing corporate context, 919–922
  process models, 915–916
  recommendations for, 920
  stage models, 915
Internal selection, 519–520, 526
Internal selection environment, 480, 483
Internal sourcing, 150
International competitiveness, 47–48
International Data Corporation, 277
*International Directory of Company Histo-
  ries,* 783
International Harvester, 554
International Instruments, 982
International Standards Organization, 386,
  388
International Telecommunications Union,
  337
Internet, 318–330
  and copyright protection, 407–408

  and Microsoft, 587–592
  online access to music, 386–391
  online shopping, 610–629
  online trading, 592–610
  radio/streaming, 390
Internet access subscriptions/revenue, 320
Internet Protocol Technology, 303
Internet telephony, 313–314
InterTrust, 395, 396
Intraorganizational ecology, 511–526
Invention, 2
  transformed into innovation, 682–690
Investment; *see* Venture Capital
Investment barriers, 48
Investment companies, 592–610
Iridium, 316, 317
ISO Open System Interconnect model, 180–
  181
ITT, 132
IXC, 310, 312, 313

J. D. Power and Associates, 16n, 17
Japan
  disk drive firms, 697–698
  DRAM industry, 643
  DRAM production, 492
  operational effectiveness, 114–115
  portable radios, 174
JavaSoft, 768, 773
JC Penney, 120
JDS Uniphase, 186
Jenn-Air, 127
Jet aircraft industry, 446–447
Jiffy Lube International, 117
Job rotation, 135
Johnson & Johnson, 418, 1178, 1179
  mastering change, 935–937
Johnson Controls, 13, 14, 15–16, 18, 19, 28,
  31
  company profile, 20–22
Johnstown America Industries, Inc., 31
  company profile, 26–28
Joint Electronic Device Engineering Council
  (JEDEC), 645
Joint programs, 712
Joint venture
  IBM-Toshiba, 630–641
  Toyota-GM, 1164, 1170
Journal of Strategy and Business, 871
J-Phone, 277
Jupiter Communications, 165, 167, 312
Jupiter Research, 628
Just-in-time systems, 28
JVC, 106, 108, 394, 832

Kao Corporation, discovery-driven planning,
  841–846
Kasper Instruments, 450–453
Kevex Corporation, 137
Kia, 108
Kidder, Peabody, 82
Kid Galaxy, 801, 803
Kilobit, 475
Kirkham Instruments Corporation, 946
  product development, 1062–1075
Kleiner Perkins, 76, 768

KLH Corporation, 49, 56, 60, 61
Kmart, 99, 624–626, 801, 934
K'Nex, 809
Knowledge
  leveraging, 871–877
  stages of, 1168
Knowledge structures, 717–722
Knowledge transfer, 1170–1171
Kodak, 33, 57, 58, 110, 130, 132, 145, 557,
  560, 865, 945, 1060
Komag, 224, 291n, 294, 695, 697, 698
Komatsu, 104, 551–552
  competitive advantage at, 554
KPMG, 879, 882, 883, 888
Krups, 1043, 1044
Kulicke, 450

L. L. Bean, 1173
Laggards, 364
LANcity, 169
Lansdale, 926
Late majority, 363–364
Launch, 390
Leadership, role in strategy, 128–129
Lead user research, 785–792
  major activities/time allocation, 793
  methodology, 787, 795
  stages, 788–792
  study, 794–800
Lear Corporation, 19, 20, 28, 31
  company profile, 22–24
Learning
  across projects, 954–955
  cognitive structure, 717–719
  by doing, using, and failing, 983–985
  ease of, 726
  new perspectives on, 716–722
  and prior knowledge, 717–718
Learning by using, 368
Learning Curve, 803
Learning curve, 1172
Learning organization, 1162–1174
  building blocks, 1164–1171
  characteristics, 1163–1164
  experimentation, 1165–1167
  first steps, 1174
  knowledge transfer, 1170—1171
  learning from others, 1169–1170
  meaning, management, and measurement,
    1163
  measuring learning, 1171–1173
  past experience, 1167–1169
  systematic problem solving, 1164–1165
Leased lines, 164–165
Lego Interactive, 100
Level3, 195, 196, 310, 314
Lexus, 865
Libby Owens Ford, 111
Liberty Media Group, 316
Licensing, 144–145
Lightera, 193, 194
Lightweight team structure, 950–951, 1014
Likert scale, 727
Lincoln Laboratories, 714
Line coding, 160
Lionel Leisure, 125

Liquid Audio, 395
Liquid crystal displays, 630–641
Live365, 390
Lockheed Corporation, 177, 675–676, 680, 686
Lockheed Martin, 316, 317
Lockout, 722–723
Logitech, 273
Long-distance carriers, 306–310
Long-term employment, 135–136
Lotus Development, 161, 171, 291, 343
Lowe's, 814
LSI Logic, 332, 648
Lucent Technologies, 160n, 165, 188, 192, 198, 200, 201, 278, 312, 335, 341, 346, 396, 704, 746, 777, 779, 1159, 1162
  investment strategy, 778
Lucky Goldstar, 77, 108, 560, 633
Lycos, 850

Macy's Department Store, 933
Magic Chef, 127
Magna International, 15, 19, 31
  company profile, 24–26
Magnavox, 51, 67–68
Magnetic core, 475
Magneto-resistive technology, 698–699
Mainframes, 237
Mainstream market, 364
Main street, 367
  definition, 848
Management; see also High-technology management; Top management
  ambidextrous, 937
  career development vs. business know-how, 560–561
  challenge of disruptive change, 541–550
  of change, 925–937
  consistency of action, 206–208
  of corporate entrepreneurship, 664–670
  criteria for innovation, 172–179
  elitist view of, 561
  of internal corporate venturing, 915–925
  levels in corporate research, 663–664
  of resource scarcity and mobility, 1179
  of technological change, 205–206
  and technology S-curves, 209–210
  of technology strategy, 145–146
Management interface problems, 665–666
Managerial control systems, 1179–1180
Managerial incentives, 1180
Managers, success syndrome, 931–932
MAN Ethernet Service Providers, 185
Manufacturing, 970–973
  communication with engineering, 970–976
  international competitiveness, 47–48
  maximizing share in, 108–109
Manufacturing complexity, 30
Manufacturing resource planning software, 508
Marion Merrell Dow Inc., 418
Market evolution, interrelated streams of, 103
Market for innovation, 203
Marketing
  new technology, 173–174

in technology adoption life cycle, 362–364
Marketing High Technology (Davidow), 365
Market model vertigo, 849
Market segments, 65, 169–171, 333–335
  branch office, 171
  remote office, 171
  residential, 171
  small/home office, 171
Marks and Spencer, 144, 149
Martha Stewart Living Omnimedia, 625
Massachusetts High-Technology Council, 137
Massachusetts Institute of Technology, 786, 787, 792
Mass customization, 864–865
Matsushita, 33, 76, 107, 108, 394, 556, 557, 560, 633, 638, 829, 831, 832, 1197
Matsushita Kotobuki Electric, 290n
Mattel, 803, 812
Maximum strategic opportunity set, 1176
Maxtor, 252, 290, 292, 534, 695, 699
Mayer & Schweitzer, 592n, 598
Mayfield, 273
Maytag Corporation, 127, 128
Mazda, 35, 543, 554, 556, 558, 1023–1025
MBNA, 289
MCA, 76
McCaw Cellular, 306
McDonald's, 467
McDonnell Douglas, 686
MCI Communications, 334, 341, 345, 747, 760
MCI One, 171
MCI WorldCom, 306, 310, 312, 313–314
  recent history, 308–310
McKinsey & Company, 7, 82, 544, 685, 869–870, 873, 926
MediaOne, 308
Medtronic Corporation, 546, 946
  pacemaker business, 1076–1088
Megabit, 475
Memontec Communications, 348
Memorex, 216, 257
Memory chip makers, 642–655
Mercer Management Consulting, 321
Merck and Company, 47, 416, 418, 664, 774, 777, 779
Mergers; see Acquisitions
Meritor Automotive, Inc., 29
Merrill Lynch, 544, 545, 547, 592, 597, 601, 602, 608, 609, 610
Metal oxide semiconductor (MOS), 475–476
Metal-oxide semiconductor transistors, 455
Metro area networks, 184–188
MFS, 308
Microcomputer revolution, 958
Microcontrollers, 465
Microma, 1140
Micro new venture department, 669
Micron Technology, 492, 642, 643, 644, 650, 652, 1143, 1150
Micropolis Corporation, 218, 224, 228, 255, 256, 257, 258, 695
  management, 260–262
Microprocessor industry, 298
Microprocessors, 2, 237, 254, 1122–1123
  invention of, 461–463

new strategy for, 496–500
synergy with EPROMs, 463
Microsoft Corporation, 44, 72, 84, 89, 90, 91, 93, 94, 98, 102, 238, 241, 279, 291, 296, 317, 318, 325, 329, 333, 386, 388, 390, 395, 396, 398, 487, 498, 538–539, 571, 575, 576, 577, 591, 653, 673, 705, 735, 746, 747, 771, 774, 775, 776, 779, 817, 830–831, 837, 841, 850, 860, 861, 877, 892, 893, 926, 931, 963, 1110, 1112, 1114, 1116, 1117, 1118, 1122, 1123, 1125, 1128, 1157, 1159, 1161
  financial data, 1121
  and Internet, 587–592
Microsoft Network, 101, 325, 590
Middle managers, 923
Migraine project, 424–425
Millennium Pharmaceuticals, 774
Milliken Company, 1169
Minicomputers, 237
Minimal strategic integration, 1175
Miniscribe, 218, 224, 255, 257, 258
Minnesota Mining and Manufacturing; see 3M Corporation
Minolta, 560
MIPS, 237, 244, 499
MITS, 33
Mitsubishi, 107, 394, 465, 644, 652, 926
Mixed channel strategies, 43–44
Mobil Corporation, 345–346
Modem manufacturers, 163
Modems, 165
Modified frequency of modulation (MFM), 225
Modular innovation, 211, 443
Modular interface, 281–282
Modularity, 701–702
  advantages and disadvantages, 292–293
  cyclical character, 703–704
Module-assembly process, 635
Mohr Davidow Ventures, 273
Monitor and Company, 870
Monopoly, 374–375
  by copyright, 402
Monsanto, 659, 722
Montgomery Ward, 889
Moore Graphics, 892
Moore's law, 298, 846, 1128, 1157, 1158, 1159, 1161
  definition, 645n
  extending, 1143–1144, 1147
Morgan Stanley, 602
Morgan Stanley Dean Witter, 601
Mortgage banking, 288–289
Mosel-Vitelic, 644
MOSTEK, 458
Motion Picture Association of America, 406, 410
Motorola, 51, 69, 92n, 107, 108, 162, 163, 169, 176, 178, 272, 333, 335, 348, 458, 460, 461–462, 465, 466, 469, 499, 536, 571, 574, 636, 648, 926, 961, 1015, 1016, 1018, 1080, 1113, 1114, 1143, 1162, 1169, 1179
  and Iridium, 316

Moving Picture Experts Group, 326, 338, 386, 388, 396, 830
MP3, 386–390, 395–397
MSN Music, 398
MTV, 379, 385, 390
Multibusiness companies, 1176
MultiLink Corporation, 182, 330, 341
Multiplexing, 476
Multipoint control unit, 334–335
Multitasking, 462–463, 476
Multivariate regression analysis, 300
Museum of Modern Art, New York, 1037
Musical Copyright Act (UK), 404
Music industry
    companies in digital music, 391
    copyright protection, 392
    digital distribution, 378–398
    intellectual property rights, 384–386
    online access, 386–391
    record company policy principles, 409
    standards war, 394–397
    value chain, 379–384
Music licensing, 385
MusicMatch, 388
Music Publishers Association (UK), 404

Nakamichi, 56
Namco, 85
Napster, 325, 378–398, 401
    company background, 386–389
NASDAQ composite index, 611
National Aeronautics and Space Administration, 689–690
National Basketball Association, 84
National Cash Register (NCR), 149, 241, 498
National Football League, 84
National Highway Traffic Safety Administration, 15, 30
National Hockey League, 84
National Retail Hardware Association, 814
National Semiconductor, 273, 465, 926, 1116, 1122
National Telecommunications and Information Administration, 160n
National Video, 926
NEC, 76, 103, 104, 105, 106, 109, 110, 111, 163, 216, 471, 560, 633, 638, 644, 648, 652, 692, 697, 831, 832, 926, 1115, 1121, 1157
    new research and development site, 732–745
    organization chart, 735
NEC Corp. v. Intel Corp., 401
NEC Research Institute, Inc., 732–745
Need-pull innovation model, 685–687
Needs-based positioning, 117–118
NES, 76
Nested system of architecture, 213
NetPC, 837–838
Netscape Communications, 589, 591, 768, 769, 771, 773, 837
Network Computing Devices, 770
Network externalities, 368–369
Neutragena Corporation, 120, 122, 127
New business development, 658–659, 682–690

New business opportunities, 683
New Enterprise Associates, 273
New entrants, 47
New model changes, 975–976
New product development, 151, 202–208, 658–659, 939–955
    at Big Idea Group, 801–816
    at Braun AG, 1035–1051
    at Cisco, 749, 750
    at Dell Computer, 957–970
    design-build-test phase, 1098–1107
    development strategy, 942–948
    improving process, 1062–1075
    learning across projects, 954–955
    manufacturing phase, 970–973
    at Medtronic, Inc., 1076–1088
    pharmaceutical industry, 992–995
    pitfalls, 1089–1090
    preproject management, 942–948
    problem solving, 1099–1103
    project completion tools, 954
    project maps, 1053–1057
    project plans, 1051–1062
    skunk works, 972
    team structure, 948–954
New product development map, 1089–1098
New product evolution pattern, 988
New product learning cycle, 977–990
    lessons from, 985–990
    measuring success, 982–985
    product value, 980–982
    Stanford Innovation Project, 977–978
    study methodology, 978–980
    user needs, 980–982
NewsCorp, 770, 773
New United Motor Manufacturing Inc., 1164, 1170
New venture division, 665–666, 669
New-venture projects, 682–690
    classification scheme, 689
    comparison of models, 687
    conceptualization of opportunities, 683
    and corporate interests, 687–688
    effective conceptualization, 688–689
    innovation traps, 689–690
    need-pull model, 685–687
    technology-push model, 683–685
New York Times, 567, 686
Nextel Communications, 317
NeXT Software, 486, 1112, 1116
Niche market, 848, 854
Nielsen Media Research, 159
Nike, Inc., 98, 403, 932
Nikon, 453
Nintendo, 67, 70, 72, 75, 76, 78, 81, 84, 86–87, 89, 90, 91, 93, 535, 536, 540, 647
    company background, 68–69, 79–80
    financial data, 88
Nippon Denso, 296n
Nippon Telephone and Telegraph, 342, 343
Nissan, 543, 554, 932
Nixdorf, 237
NMB, 494
Nobody-knows-anything rule, 82
No Electronic Theft Law of 1997, 385
Nokia, Inc., 92n, 277, 932, 1179

Non-ergodic process, 370
Nordstrom, 932, 933–934
Normative view of strategy, 3–4
Nortel Networks, 163–164, 187, 188, 193n, 198, 200, 201, 746, 1162
NorthPoint Communications, 315, 328–329
    financial data, 311
Northrop Corporation, 133, 137
Northrup, 33
Notebooks (Leonardo da Vinci), 434
Not-invented-here syndrome, 720
Novell, 343, 1114
NTL, Inc., 317
NTT Human Interface Labs, 396
Nucor, 232
Nullsoft, 389, 396
Nullsoft-Winamp, 388
Nynex, 161, 166, 171, 304, 408
Nynex Cablecomms, 166
Nypro, Inc., 501–510
    new technologies, 506–508
    Novaplast roll-out, 509–510
    shifting basis of competition, 508–509
    structuring for innovation, 503–506
    worldwide locations, 505

OEM; *see* Original equipment manufacturers
Official corporate strategy, 480
Oki, 652
Olivetti, 561
Omnia, 194
Ongoing programs, 1165–1166
ONI, 194, 202
Online gaming, 92–94, 101
Online shopping, 610–629
Online trading, 592–610
Operating division interface problems, 665
Operating systems, 1123
Operational effectiveness
    in Japan, 114–115
    pursuit of, 126
    versus strategy, 113–116
Operational relatedness, assessing, 667–668
Optical Coating Laboratories, Inc., 910, 911
Optical components industry, 179–189
Optimization of effort, 123
Oracle, 241, 358, 366, 577, 837, 879–880, 880, 1116, 1117, 1157
Orange, 198
Oregon Scientific, 273
Organizational absorptive capacity, 719–722
Organizational adaptation, 520–522, 583–584
Organizational architecture, 935–936
Organizational championing, 919
Organizational cohesion, 134–136
    good communication, 134–135
    job rotation, 135
    long-term employment, 135–136
    role integration, 135
Organizational context, 147–148
Organizational control, 148, 149
Organizational ecology, 928
Organizational fit, 145–146
Organizational flexibility, 134

Organizational growth, 928–930
Organizational learning
  across projects, 954–955
  definition, 1163
  and strategy, 1173
Organizational structure, 1179
  and technological character, 701–704
Organization for Economic Cooperation and
  Development, 322
Organizations; *see also* Corporate *entries;*
  Firms
  ambidextrous, 925–937
  patterns of evolution, 925–931
Original equipment manufacturers, 17, 18–
  19, 29, 272, 697–698, 835–838
Outcomes, 3, 33
Outsourcing, 114, 186–187
Outsourcing strategy, 298
Overambitious strategic integration, 1175
Owens Corning Fiberglass, 346
Oxide, 225–226

Pacific Bell, 157, 162, 163, 164, 166, 338,
  341, 343
Pacific Telesis, 304
Packard Bell, 575, 831, 1119, 1121
Paine Webber, 601, 602, 671
PairGain, 167
Palo Alto Research Center; *see* Xerox Corpo-
  ration
Panasonic, 77, 108, 779
Paradigmatic design phase, 34–36, 37–38
Paradox of culture, 932–935
Paradyne, 162
Partnerships, 1055
Passive investments, 778–779
Past experience, 1167–1169
Patent protection, 29, 46–47, 399–401
  pharmaceutical industry, 996–998
Patents, 2, 34
  types of, 400
Path dependence, and absorptive capacity,
  722–724
Path-dependent process, 370
Path-dependent strong law of large numbers,
  372–374
Paul, Weiss, Rifkind, Wharton, and Garrison,
  389
Paul Revere Life Insurance, 1169
PC-based desktop systems, 444–458
PC Magazine, 343, 648
PC Week, 343
PC World, 343
Peer-to-peer architecture, 389
People'sChoice TV, 309n
PepsiCo, 33, 1112
Performance evaluation, 150
Perkin-Elmer, 450, 453
Personal computer industry
  Apple Computer, 1110–1126
  evolving, 1117–1124
  history of, 957–959
  Intel Corporation, 1127–1162
  Intel's Hood River program, 816–838
  manufacturers, 1125
  NetPC, 837–838

and Xerox PARC, 671–674
Personal computer software, 291–292
Personal Conference Work Group, 342–343
Pertec, 257
Pertinent action, 485
Peter Hart Research, 85n
Pfizer Inc., 418, 998
Pharmaceutical industry
  drug development and approval, 992–995
  Eli Lilly & Company, 415–430, 990–1015
  in mid-1990s, 415–417
  new drug development, 410–414
  patent protection, 996–998
  research and development in, 995–998
  top 20 firms, 418
  top 20 prescription drugs, 418
Philco, 204, 926
Philips Eindhoven laboratory, 714
Philips Electronics, 104, 106, 108, 110, 386,
  394, 557, 926, 1197
Photolithographic equipment alignment,
  448–453
Photolithography, 226
PictureTel Corporation, 166, 330, 332–333,
  335, 337, 346, 347, 348, 766
  strategies, 341–342
Pilkington Float Glass Process, 173
Pilkington Glass Ltd., 33, 668
Pilot project, 971
Pioneer, 394
Piper Jaffray, 600
Pixar Animation Studios, 1117
Pixim, 273
PixTech, 1175
PlaceWare, 762–773
Planning
  conventional, 839
  discovery-driven, 838–839
  platform-based, 839–841
Plant patents, 400
Plasma etching, 466, 476
Plastics injection molding industry, 501–510
Platform-based planning, 839–841
Platform projects, 945–946, 1053–1054
Platform strategy, 1057–1058
Playthings magazine, 812
Pleasant Company, 801
Plus Development Corporation, 260
PMC-Sierra Corporation, 182, 186
Pogo.com, 101
PointCast, 589
Pokemon Monsters Inc., 85
Polaroid, 62, 794, 838, 840, 911
Political skills, 1181
Polycrystalline silicon, 476
Polysilicon resistor, 476
Polysilicon resistor technology, 466
Portable radio, 174, 176
Portfolio planning techniques, 7
Positioning, 114
Positioning trade-offs, 120–121
Positive view of strategy, 3–4
Potential inefficiency, 370
POTS modems, 165
Power Computing, 1124
PPG, 1171, 1173

Pragmatists, 363
Pragmatist strategy, 847
Predictive theory, 212
Preliminary concept generation, 799
Preparadigmatic stage of design, 37
Preproject management, 942–948
Priam, 218, 228
Price Club, 246
Price Waterhouse, 357
Prime Computer, 134, 237
Printing industry, 889–902
Priorities, consistent, 134
PRML, 226
Problem framing, 1100
Problem solving
  communication in, 1101–1103
  integrated, 1103
  in new product development, 1099–1103
Process development, 151
Processes, 542
Process-related technology, 5
Procter & Gamble, 362, 1053
Product acceptability dimensions, 64
Product architecture, 143
Product champion, 686, 917, 923–924
Product change, 208
Product cost, 293
Product-customer centers, 139
Product description document, 1084
Product development, 151
  budget constraints, 184–185
  focus on, 1024
Product documentation, 1070–1074
Product families, 984
Product functionality, 282–285
Product integrity, 1023–1034
  heavyweight product manager, 1029–1032
  improvement ethic, 1032–1034
  organizing, 1026–1029
  power of product concept, 1025–1026
Production runs, 971
Productivity frontier, 114–115
Product leadership, 575
Product line complexity, 293, 302
Product managers, 1029–1032
Product map development, 1090–1091
Product-market strategy, 4
  and technology, 6–7
Product modification, 37
Product portfolio, 65–66
Product-related technology, 5
Products
  architectural, 691
  closely-related, 132
  components, 691
  power concept, 1025–1026
  processing engineering changes, 974
  as systems *vs.* set of components, 442
  winnowing out, 140
Product specification document, 1084
Product success, 982–985
Product-technology matrix, 6
Product value, 980–982
Profits
  component manufacture, 294–295
  computer industry, 295–296

Profits (*continued*)
  locus of, 292–298
Progressive Networks, 396
Project audit, 955
Project charter, 1017–1018, 1071
Project completion tools, 954
Project families, 946
Projection television tube, 58–62
Project leadership, 1019–1020
Project manager profile, 1019
Project maps, 1053–1057, 1089–1098
Project organization management options,
  948–954
Project planning, 796–798
Project plans, 1051–1062
Projects
  aggregate set of, 943–945
  chartering and bounding, 945–947
  developing and applying resources, 946–
    948
  single or multiple, 972–973
  types of, 944
Project sequencing, 1058–1060
Project teams, 539, 546
Property rights environment, 34; *see also* In-
  tellectual property rights
ProShare, 766
Prototype, 971
Prototyping, 954
Prudential, 602
PSA, 19
Psion PLC, 495
PTT Netherlands, 343

Qualcomm, 774, 860
Quality function deployment, 954
Quantum Corporation, 216, 218, 224, 228,
  255, 256, 257, 258, 262, 288, 290, 533,
  534, 540, 698, 1197
  disk drives, 260
Quark, 892
Quarterdeck, 771
Quebecor, 115
Questionnaires, 1173
Qwest Communications, 196, 198, 304, 306,
  314, 317
  recent history, 310

R. R. Donnelley & Sons, 115
  Digital Division, 889–902
Radical innovation, 3, 204–205, 211, 441,
  443
Rambus Inc., 642–655
Random-access memory, 476
Random House, 392
Rational drug discovery, 421
Rawland, 926
Raychem, 63
Raytheon, 925, 926
RCA, 48, 58, 106, 132, 204, 386, 388, 441–
  442, 559, 735, 925, 926, 927, 937
RC Cola, 33
Reach-driven strategic integration, 1176,
  1178–1179
Read-only memory, 476
Read-Rite, 224, 291n, 294, 695, 697

RealNetworks, 388, 390, 395, 396
Reciprocal responsibility, 555
Recontracting models, 376–377
Record companies, 380
Recording Industry Association of America,
  388, 408–409
Reduced instruction set computing (RISC),
  236n, 244–245, 498–499, 570–571
Reengineering, 874–875
Refresh, 476
Regional Bell operating companies (RBOCs),
  304–306, 323, 324, 326–327, 329
Regression analysis, 300
Regulatory issues, 30
Reintegration studies, 289–292
Relative elasticity of demand, 64
Relative inertia, 520–521
Relative technology position, 6
Reliability, 64
Remote office market, 169–171
Reorientation, 522
Research and advanced development, 944
Research and development, 150, 658, 659–
  662
  appropriating returns from, 690–705
  bias in, 63
  at Braun AG, 1038–1039
  business perspectives, 923
  definition, 1054–1055
  elements of, 682
  focused, 133–134
  managerial initiatives, 683
  at NEC, 732–745
  in pharmaceutical industry, 995–998
  resource allocation for, 46
  spillovers, 726
  technology push, 683–685
  transfer of technology from, 708–716
Research and development firms, 36–37
Research and development investment, 724–
  726
  conclusions on, 732
  study methods, 726–728
Research champion, 711
Research questions, 376–377
Residential market, 171
Resource allocation, 102, 976
  and disruptive change, 254–259
  factors influencing, 246–247
  link to resource dependence, 259–262
  for research and development, 46
  strategic architecture for, 111–112
  and types of innovation, 246
Resource-based strategy, 4
Resource commitment, 145
Resource dependence, 246
  and resource allocation, 259–262
Resources, 542
  developing and applying, 946–948
  imprisoned, 110
  leveraging, 551
  scarcity and mobility, 1179
Retention mechanisms, 514–515, 518–519
Retroactive rationalizing, 918
Return on assets managed, 174
Return on investment, 174

  at Cisco, 749–750
Revolutionizing Product Design (Wheel-
  wright & Clark), 546
Rhone-Poulenc, 418
Rhythms Net Connections, 310, 315, 329
  financial data, 311
Rigid disk drives, 530
Road Ahead (Gates), 588
Roadrunner, 315
Rockwell International, 165, 926, 1116
Rodime, 216
Role integration, 135
Roll-about systems, 332–333
RollingStone.com, 390
Rolm, 43, 47, 547–549
Rover, 932
Rowenta, 1043, 1044

Saab, 22
Saint Jude Medical, 1086
Sammina, 762
Samsung, 108, 560, 633, 643, 644, 649, 652,
  926, 932, 1143, 1150
Samsung Semiconductor, 492
Sandia National Laboratories, 1157
Sandoz, 418
Santayana review, 1167
Sanyo Company, 418, 556, 633
SAP AG, 241, 348–349, 350, 1157
SAP America, 348–361
  organization chart, 359
SAP Canada, 358
Satellite communications, 316–317, 324–
  325
Satellite data transmission, 169
Saturn Motors, 1166–1167
SBC Communications, 163, 186, 196, 304,
  317, 327
SBU; *see* Strategic business units
Scale economics, 301–302
Scale economies, 369
Scaling improvements, 476
Scenario development, 8
Schering-Plough, 418
Schumpeterian entrepreneur, 670
Scientific evolution, 34
Scientific research, 2
Scope-driven strategic integration, 1175–
  1176, 1177–1178
S-curves; *see* Technology S-curves
Seagate Technology, 138, 216, 218, 224, 254,
  255, 256, 257, 290, 292, 294, 534, 540,
  698, 1178
Sears, Roebuck, 120, 246, 934
Seat mechanism technologies, 15–17
Secondary wave planning, 1060–1061
Second-order fit, 122
Secure Digital Music Initiative, 396
Securities and Exchange Commission, 199
SEEQ, 471n
Sega Enterprises, 67, 69–70, 71, 72, 75–76,
  78, 81, 84, 86–87, 94, 98, 102, 116
  company profile, 79
  financial data, 88
Seiko, 33, 560, 925, 926–927
Selection mechanisms, 515–516, 517–518

Self-reinforcing behavior, 723
Self-understanding, 137
Semiconductor industry
    major companies, 926
    manufacturers, 163
    market, 1149
Semiconductor photolithographic equipment
    alignment, 448–453
Sendit, 317
Senior management, 942
Sequential freezing, 972
Sequoia Capital, 746, 877
Serial/batch mode of interaction, 1101–1102
Serial Copy Management System, 407
Serviceability, 64
SESAC Inc., 385
Sevin Rosen Funds, 190
Seybold Report on Professional Computing,
    673
SGS Microelettronica, 1178
Sharp, 245, 556, 638, 831, 832
Shift registers, 477
Shift resistors, 456
Shugart, 228
Siemens, 44, 342, 500n, 557, 560, 1044,
    1080, 1086
Siemens Building Technology, 276
Siemens-Nixdorf, 241
Silicon Graphics, 237, 238, 241, 288, 589,
    1010
Simple consistency, 122
Sir Speedy, 892
Skeptics, 364
Skeptic strategy, 847
Skil-Bosch Power Tool Company, 814, 815–
    816
Skunk works, 145, 972
SkyBridge LP, 317
SkyTel, 309
SMaL Camera Technologies, 265–278
Small-firm/large-firm comparisons, 46
SmithKline Beecham, 418
Soffa, 450
Software
    copyright protection, 402
    patent protection, 400
Software Publishers Association, 1123
Software Toolworks, 74, 78
Solectron, 288, 296n
Solow paradox, 319
Sonny Bono Copyright Term Extension Act,
    407–408
Sony Corporation, 59, 67, 84, 86, 89, 90, 91,
    93–94, 98, 104, 107, 108, 116, 274, 368,
    386, 394, 395, 396, 406, 410, 442, 560,
    647, 723, 829, 831, 832, 835, 945, 959,
    966, 969, 1058, 1089, 1123, 1197
    affiliates, 380
    company background, 80
Sony Music Entertainment, 379, 398
    affiliates, 380
    description, 381
Southern Bell, 345
Southern New England Telecommunications,
    304
South Korea, 319

Southwest Airlines, 116, 120, 121, 122
    activity system, 125
Southwestern Bell, 341
Spatial technological competition, 376–377
Special business units, 668
Specialized assets, 38
    control of, 144
Spectra Physics, 137
Spectrum Technologies, 1114
Sphinx Pharmaceutical, 416, 423, 426
Spindle, 226
Spin motor, 226
Spinner, 396
Spin-off, 669
Spinout organization, 546–547
Sports Illustrated, 98, 99
Sprague, 926
Sprint, 190, 195, 196, 199, 306, 310, 314,
    334, 345, 747, 760
    company history, 309–310
Spyglass Inc., 590
SSIH, 927, 937
Staffing, 1018–1019
Standard and Poor's, 603, 627
Standard Oil, 283
Standards, competing, 375–376
Stanford Innovation Project, 133, 977
Staples, 1119
StarBand, 324
Start-up organizations, 543–544
Stata Venture Partners, 272
Static random-access memory, 477
STC, 557
Steady stream sequencing, 1058–1060
Stepper alignment, 477
Stepper motors; *see* Actuator
STMicroelectronics, 1143, 1178
    strategic integration, 1178
Stochastic process, 987–989
Stock price implications
    bowling alley stage, 856–857
    early market stage, 852–853
    main street stage, 865–867
    tornado stage, 861–863
Storage Technology, 216, 692
StrataCom, 549, 753, 756, 762
Strategic action, 147, 148, 480, 482–483,
    486
Strategic architecture, 110–112
    at Vickers, 111
Strategic building, 918
Strategic business unit mindset, 105
Strategic business units
    bidding for core competencies, 112–113
    bounded innovation, 110
    imprisoned resources, 110
    overcommitment to, 560
    tyranny of, 109–110
    and underinvestment, 110
Strategic change, 870–871
Strategic context, 918–919
    determination, 585
Strategic dissonance, 478–488
    framework for analysis, 480–481
    managing, 483–488
    sources of, 481–483

and strategic implementation, 479–480
and strategic recognition, 480
Strategic fit, 121–126, 551
    and sustainability, 124–126
    types of, 122–125
Strategic forcing, 917–918
Strategic importance
    assessing, 666–667
    in choosing design alternatives, 668–669
    and corporate control, 667
    and operational relatedness, 667–668
Strategic inertia, 564, 576–581
Strategic inflection point, 479–480
Strategic integration, 1174–1181
    challenges, 1176–1178
    complex, 1179–1181
    forms of, 1175–1176
    in multibusiness companies, 1176
Strategic intent, 485–486, 550–562
Strategic investment, 245–263
Strategic long-range planning process, 572–
    573
Strategic management, 2
    of corporate research, 659–664
Strategic partnering, 40–41, 47
Strategic partner relationship, 864
Strategic positioning, 900–901
    access-based, 118–119
    characteristics of, 116–117
    entrepreneurial edge, 118
    needs-based, 117–118
    origins of, 117–120
    sustainable, 120–121
    trade-offs, 120–121
    variety-based, 117
Strategic process
    autonomous, 516–519
    induced, 514–516
Strategic recognition, 480, 485–486
Strategic renewal, 522
Strategic Simulations, 74
Strategic stagnation, 133
Strategic whitespace, 777
Strategy, 445–446
    alternative views, 126
    and capabilities, 4
    CEO-driven, 572–573
    coevolutionary lock-in, 567–576
    common threats to, 126–127
    definition, 126
    in emerging industries, 129
    and failure to choose, 126–127
    growth trap, 127
    integrated with technology, 3–7
    at Intel in 1990s, 490–501
    leadership role, 128–129
    and learning, 584–585
    versus operational effectiveness, 113–116
    place of technology in, 63
    positive *vs.* normative views, 3–4
    product-market *vs.* resource-based, 4
    profitable growth, 127–128
    reconnecting with, 128
    rediscovering, 126–129
    remaking, 551
    secondary wave planning, 1060–1061

Strategy (*continued*)
  and strategic action, 482–483
  unique activities, 116–120
  as vector, 562–585
Strategy formulation
  as elitist activity, 561–562
  at Intel Corporation, 511–526
  as internal selection, 519–520
  intraorganizational ecology, 511–526
  and organizational adaptation, 520–522
  propositions, 524–525
Strategy hierarchy, 561
Strategy vector, 567–571
Stratification, 281–292
Strong law of large numbers, 372–374
Structural Dynamics Research Corporation, 14
Structural inertia, 931
Success syndrome, 931–932
Sulzer Intermedics, 1080, 1086
Sumitomo Chemical, 914
Summa Four, Inc., 745, 760–762
Sunk cost rules, 82
Sun Microsystems, 235, 236n, 237, 238, 241, 243, 245, 288, 366, 492n, 499, 587, 589, 591, 592, 768, 773, 775, 837, 1105, 1116, 1123, 1156, 1177
  financial data, 1147
Super Audio CD, 394
Supersonic transport, 178–179
Supplier relationships, 863–864
Suppliers, 28–29
Supply chain, 162–164
Surveys, 1173
Sustainability, 121–126
Sustainable competitive advantage, 126
Sustaining projects, 944
Sustaining technologies, 249–250
  versus disruptive innovation, 544–546
  impact of, 250–252
  leaders in, 252–254
Swiss watch industry, 927
Sylvania, 102, 926
Synaptic Pharmaceutical Corporation, 425
Synaptics, 273
Synthetic chemistry, 420–421
System architecture, 213
Systematic problem solving, 1164–1165

T. Rowe Price, 597
Tacit knowledge, 34
Taiwan Semiconductor Manufacturing, 1142–1143
Tandem Computers, 132, 135, 1121
Tandon, 138, 228
Tandy Corporation, 245
Target market, 266–269, 900
Target Stores, 99, 803
TBWA Chiat/Day, 1125
TCI, 315, 317, 329
Team member responsibilities, 1020–1021
Team New Zealand, 1005–1012
Teams, 504–506, 546
Team structure, 1000
  autonomous, 951–954, 1015
  functional, 948–950, 1013–1014
  heavyweight, 950–951, 1014–1015

lightweight, 950, 1014
TechNet, 329
Technical buyers, 859
Technical constraints, 172–173
Technical Forums, 135
Technical modularity
  assessment of, 704–705
  cyclical character, 703–704
Technical support, 151
Technical understanding, 710
Technicare, 44
Technological barriers and risks, 30
Technological capability, 142–143
Technological change, 7–8
  disruptive, 250
  rapidity of, 137
  sustaining, 249–250
  types of, 442–444
  typologies of, 248–250
Technological character, 701–704
Technological competence, 142–143, 262
Technological entrepreneurship, 3
Technological evolution, 146–147, 148, 149
  and forecasting, 7–8
  interrelated streams of, 103
Technological innovation; *see also* Innovation
  definition, 2–3
  key concepts/relationships, 203
  management of, 205–206
  patterns of, 202–208
  profiting from, 32–48
  stages, 34–35
  uncertainties about, 662–663
Technological interdependence, 692–693, 702
  assessment of, 704–705
  cyclical character, 703–704
Technological interrelatedness, 369
Technological maturity, 210, 211–213
Technological monopoly, 374–375
Technological opportunities, 662–663, 728–730
  neglect of, 723–724
Technological progress functions, 8
Technology adoption life cycle, 362–368, 846–868
  bowling alley stage, 853
  chasm, 853
  constituencies, 362–364
  early market stage, 849
  evolution of market, 847–848
  landscape zones, 367–368
  main street stage, 866–867
  Moore's law, 846
  strategies, 847
  tornado stage, 857–863
Technology and record company policy principles, 408
Technology choice, 143
Technology cycle, 930–931
Technology enthusiast, 362–363, 847
Technology entry timing, 144
Technology forecasting, 7–8
Technology leadership, 143–144
Technology leadership trends, 253
Technology life cycle, 7–8
  and competitive advantage, 9

Technology markets, 690–705
Technology organization, 690–705
Technology phase shift, 291
Technology portfolio
  assessing, 65–66
  and business portfolio, 7
Technology provider, 850
Technology-push innovation model, 683–685
Technology risk, 944
Technology S-curves, 8, 146, 208–226
  ambiguity of, 223
  architectural, 218
  context of study, 210–211
  descriptive or predictive theory, 212
  and development of new technologies, 322–233
  examples of use, 214–219
  limits of, 227–233
  planning component technology change, 213
  prescribing new component technologies, 213–214
  propositions, 209–210
  resource methodology, 223–224
  response to component technology maturity, 219–223
  technical terms, 224–226
  and technological maturity, 211–213
  theory of, 209
  usefulness, 208–210
Technology sourcing
  external, 150–151
  internal, 150
Technology spinout, 762–773
Technology strategy
  competence and capability, 142–143
  competitive strategy stance, 143–145
  comprehensive, 152
  depth of, 145
  enactment of, 657–670, 939–955
  evolutionary basis, 146–149
  examples, 148–149
  experience through enactment, 150–152
  industry context, 147
  integrated, 152
  key tasks, 150
  learning framework, 141–142
  management stance, 145–146
  organizational context, 147–148
  organizational fit, 145–146
  product and process development, 151
  research on, 148
  resource commitment, 145
  scope of, 145
  strategic action, 147
  substance of, 143–146
  technical support, 151
  value chain, 145
Technology structure, 372–374
Technology/Technologies
  absorptive capacity, 716–732
  bottlenecks to commercialization, 30
  in business definition, 4
  competing, 368–378
  competing standards, 375–376
  and competitive strategy, 5–6
  in corporate planning, 62–66

definition, 2, 246
demand elasticities, 64
emerging, 129
foreign challenges, 130–131
fundamental units of, 63–64
importance, 6
integrated with strategy, 3–7
licensing, 144–145
and market change, 245
market segments for, 65
as organizational resource, 102
and product acceptability, 64
and product-market strategy, 6
reconfiguration of, 441–454
supporting, 30
and value chain, 7, 8
Technology transfer, 708–716
Technology Venture Investors, 589
Tekeda Chemical Industries, 418
Tekram Technology, 347
Tektronix, 931
Telecom bubble, 183–184
Telecom Italia, 342, 343
Telecommunications, 317
Telecommunications Act of 1996, 248, 303,
    310, 323
Tele-Communications Inc., 590
Telecommunications industry, 303–318
Telecon Incorporated, 185
Teledesic, 316–317
Telefonica, 343
Telefunken, 108, 557
Telephone industry, 318–330
Teleport Communications Group, 306
Teletechnology newsletter, 308
Television consoles, 175, 176
Telewest, 317
Telia, 162
Teligent, 315
Tellabs, 192
Tensilica, 289
Terabit, 194
Teradyne, 137, 804
Test phase, 1100–1101
Texas Instruments, 33, 133, 135, 136, 139,
    162, 163, 204, 335, 403–404, 455, 459,
    467, 469, 472, 492, 648, 926, 958, 1089,
    1127n–1128n, 1143, 1159–1160
    financial data, 1146
Textile fiber industry, 674–682
TheDJ.com, 396
Thin film, 226
Thin-film disks, 694–697
Thin-film transistor liquid crystal displays
    (TFT-LDC), 630–641
Thomson Electronics, 105, 108, 394, 557,
    829
Thomson Multimedia, 388
Thomson Semiconductors, 1178
Thorn Electrical Industries, 44, 107, 108
THQ, 85
3Com, 163–164, 317–318, 338, 770
3M Corporation, 62, 105, 109, 111, 133, 135,
    136, 139, 799, 1110, 1178, 1180
    innovation at, 781–794
    lead user research methodology, 787, 795
    milestones, 782

3M Optical Systems, 902–915
360 Networks, 196, 199
Threshold drift, 477
Threshold voltage, 456
Tier-one/-two/-three suppliers, 28–29
Tight appropriability regimes, 36–37
Time Inc., 381, 1179
Time Life, 1171
Timeliness, 712
Time Warner, 72, 76, 81, 308, 315, 327, 394,
    398, 589, 1175
Tobit analysis, 727
Tobuku Semiconductor Incorporated, 636
Tokyo Disneyland, 839
Toledo Motor, 872, 875
Top management, 138, 942
    new initiatives by, 486–487
    strategic intent, 485–486
    and strategy integration, 1181
Tornado stage, 367
    definition, 848
Torque motors; *see* Actuator
Toshiba, 218, 245, 291, 292, 335, 342, 394,
    471, 556, 557, 559, 560, 625, 636–638,
    644, 648, 649, 651, 652, 697, 829, 926,
    967, 1119, 1121
    joint venture, 630–632
Total quality management, 115
Toy industry, 801–816
Toyota Motor Corporation, 107, 121, 296n,
    543, 558, 954, 1098
    General Motors joint venture, 1164, 1170
Toys "R" Us, 125, 611, 803, 806, 809, 810,
    812, 813, 814
Trade barriers, 48
Trademark protection, 403
Trade-offs, 120–121
Trade secrets, 34, 403
Traditional senior management approach, 942
Transistor-array, 633
Transistors, 2, 455, 477
    effects of, 176
    uses, 174–177
Transitron, 926
Transwitch Corporation, 182, 188
Transworld Communications, 309n
Trench etched capacitor, 477
Trend extrapolation, 8
Trends/needs identification, 798
Trinova, 111
TRW, 18, 178
TS Tech, 19
Tupperware, 589
Turbine aircraft, 177–178
TV Guide, 892

U.S. Memories, Inc., 492
U.S. Robotics, 165
U.S. Robotics Access, 338
Umax Data Systems, 1124
Unanticipated innovation, 487
Underinvestment, 110
Underwriter's Laboratory, 676
Union Carbide, 39
Unisys, 241
United Airlines, 850
United Artists, 72

United Inventors Association, 809
United Microelectronics, 1142–1143
United Pan-Europe Communications, 317
United States, Internet access
    subscriptions/revenue, 320
United States Copyright Office, 401
United States National Library of Medicine,
    406
United States Navy, 432–440
United States Patent and Trademark Office,
    46–47, 399
United Technologies, 20, 687
Unit of analysis, 208
Unit volume, 302
Univac, 237, 692, 714
Universal Music Group, 379, 390, 396, 398
    affiliates, 380
    description, 382
Universal Oil Products, 36
Universal Studios, 406
UNIX operating system, 233–245
Upside magazine, 314
Upstream containment, 793
Upstream-downstream interaction, 1103–
    1105
Upstream products, 29–30
Uruguay Round, 400
USA Networks, 1175
User needs, 980–982
US West, 304, 310, 317, 345
Utility patents, 400
UUNet Technologies, 314, 590

Value added resellers, 338–340
Value chain
    music industry, 379–384
    and technology, 7, 8
    in technology strategy, 145
Value chain strategy
    bowling alley stage, 854–855
    early market stage, 849–850
    main street stage, 863–864
    tornado stage, 858–863
Value disciplines
    bowling alley stage, 856
    early market stage, 852
    main street stage, 865
    tornado stage, 860
Values, 542–543
Vanguard Cellular Systems, 306
Vanguard Group, 117, 119, 122
    activity system, 124
Variation, 516–517, 526
Variety-based positioning, 117
VCI HiTech, 346, 347
VCON, 347
VDOnet, 346, 347
Vectoring, 563
Vendor relationship, 863–864
Venture capital, 773–780
    driving investments, 775–776
    dual dimensions of, 774–775
    emergent investments, 777–778
    enabling investments, 776–777
    passive investments, 778–779
Venture Economics, 774–780
VeriFone, 236

Verizon Communications, 184, 186, 195, 196, 408
Vertical integration, 31, 278–298
  conclusions on, 279–280
  definitions, 280–281
  prior studies on, 280
  versus stratification, 281–292
Very high-speed DSL, 167–168
Very large scale integrated circuits, 332
Viacom, 101, 379
Vickers, 603
  strategic architecture, 111
Video compression technology, 335–338
Videoconferencing systems industry, 330–348
Video game industry, 67–102
Viewpoints, 875
Virgin Interactive, 100
Virtual memory addressing, 462–463, 477
Virtual Mortgage Network, 345
VisiCorp, 673
Visionaries, 363
Visionary strategy, 847
Visteon, 20, 29, 297
Vitesse Corporation, 182
Vivendi-Universal, 379
  affiliates, 380
Vivendi Universal Games, 89
Vivo Software, 347
Volkswagen, 19, 22
Volvo, 22, 589
VTEL, 335, 342, 347
  strategies, 343–345

Wafer, 477, 633
Wall Street Journal, 158, 162, 168, 471, 592

Wal-Mart Stores, 99, 127, 144, 611, 624–627, 803, 934, 1119
Walt Disney Company, 85, 100, 101, 328, 401, 838, 839–841, 1175, 1177
Wang Laboratories, 237, 746, 749
Warner Brothers, 381
Warner Communications, 67, 1179
Warner Music Group, 379, 396
  affiliates, 380
  description, 381
Warren Cable, 169
Waterloo Instruments Ltd., 1062
Weak appropriability regimes
  and manufacturing costs, 47–48
  paradigmatic stage, 37–38
  preparadigmatic phase, 37
Wedbush Morgan Securities, 86
West Bay Semiconductor, 182
Westell, 160, 161, 162
Western Digital, 288, 290, 292, 495–496, 533, 540, 699
Western Electric, 135, 733
Westinghouse, 109, 925, 926
Whirlpool, 346
White Pine Software, 346
Wide area networks, 182–183
Williams & Wilkins, 406
Williams Communications, 190, 195, 196, 198, 199, 310, 312, 313
Windows Magazine, 343
Wingspan Bank, 608–610
WinStar, 313, 315, 316
Wired, 388
Wireless broadband, 324–325
Wireless local loop, 313
Wireless One, 309

Wireless technologies, 169
Wireless telecommunication, 1160
WordPerfect, 291
Work-in-progress inventory, 947
Work teams, 504–506
World automotive industry, 296–298
World Color Press, 115
WorldCom, 190, 195, 196, 199
  recent history, 308–310
Worldwide Renaissance, 312
World Wide Web, 318
Worthington Steel, 1169

Xeikon, 894, 898
Xerox Corporation, 33, 104, 106, 110, 132, 145, 283, 441, 442, 552, 554, 557, 663, 692, 695, 704, 840, 900, 926, 1162, 1164, 1168, 1171
  Palo Alto Research Center, 659, 671–674, 688, 694, 762, 1170
  problem-solving process, 1165
  technology spinout, 762–773
Xerox Technology Ventures, 763
Xicor, 471n

Yacht design, 1006–1008, 1009–1111
Yahoo!, 101, 398, 589, 591, 850
Yahoo! Music, 390
Yamaha, 104, 558, 559, 830
Yipes Enterprise Services, 185, 199
Yokogawa Electric, 270
Yorktown Heights Research Center, 244

Zenith, 51, 169, 245, 312, 958
Zilog, 460, 461–462, 465